Merriam-Webster's French-English Dictionary

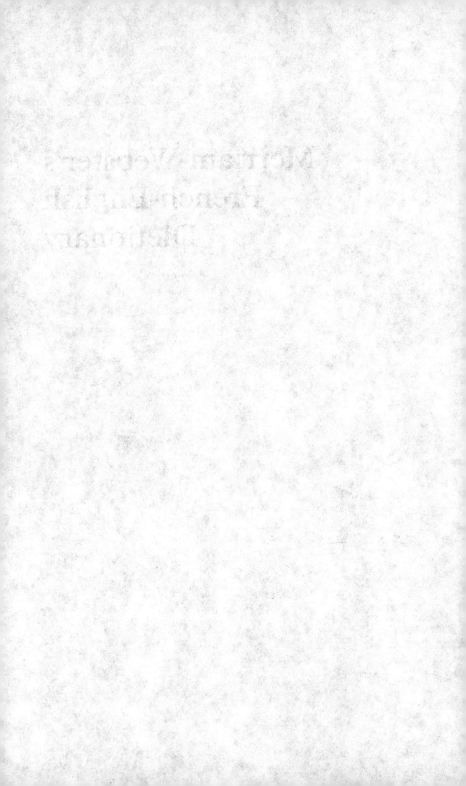

Merriam-Webster's French-English Dictionary

MERRIAM-WEBSTER, INCORPORATED
Springfield, Massachusetts, U.S.A.

A GENUINE MERRIAM-WEBSTER

The name *Webster* alone is no guarantee of excellence. It is used by a number of publishers and may serve mainly to mislead an unwary buyer.

Merriam-Webster™ is the name you should look for when you consider the purchase of dictionaries or other fine reference books. It carries the reputation of a company that has been publishing since 1831 and is your assurance of quality and authority.

Library of Congress Cataloging in Publication Data
Main entry under title:

Merriam-Webster's French-English dictionary.

p. cm.
ISBN 0-87779-166-X (hbk. : acid-free paper) —
ISBN 0-87779-917-2 (pbk. : acid-free paper)
1. French language—Dictionaries—English. 2. English language—Dictionaries—French. I. Merriam-Webster, Inc.

PC2640 .M48 2000
443′.21—dc21

00-028054

MADE IN THE UNITED STATES OF AMERICA

2345RRD020100

Contents

Preface

MERRIAM-WEBSTER'S FRENCH-ENGLISH DICTIONARY is a completely new dictionary designed to meet the needs of English and French speakers throughout the world. It is intended for language learners, teachers, office workers, tourists, business travelers—anyone who needs to communicate effectively in the French and English languages as they are spoken and written today.

This dictionary provides up-to-date coverage of French words and phrases as they are spoken in France and in other European countries, and special care has been taken to include the unique terminology of French-speaking Canada as well. The English vocabulary and spellings included here reflect North American usage and are primarily those of American English, but British terms and spellings commonly used in Canada are also included.

All of this material is presented in a format that is based firmly upon, and in many ways is similar to, the traditional styling found in other Merriam-Webster dictionaries. The reader who is familiar with Merriam-Webster dictionaries will immediately recognize the style, with its emphasis on clarity and concision of the information, precise discrimination of senses, and the frequent inclusion of example phrases to illustrate idiomatic usage. Also included are pronunciations (in the International Phonetic Alphabet) of the entered words in both languages, extensive coverage of French irregular verbs, a section on basic French grammar, a table of the most common French abbreviations, and a detailed Explanatory Notes section designed to assist readers in the use of this book.

Merriam-Webster's French-English Dictionary represents the combined efforts of many members of the Merriam-Webster Editorial Department, along with the help of consultants outside the company. The primary defining work was done by Anne Eason and Peter A. Sokolowski, with the assistance of Jocelyn Woods; early contributions to the text were also submitted by Jonathan Brook, Ronald Giguère, Lynn A. Prince, and Anna K. Sandström. Anne Eason, Seán O'Mannion-Espejo, and Peter A.

Sokolowski were responsible for preparing the front and back matter in the book. Joanne M. Despres, Ph.D. provided the pronunciations, assisted by Emily B. Arsenault, Deanna M. Chiasson, Kory L. Stamper, and Karen L. Wilkinson. The coordination of typesetting and other production steps was done by Thomas F. Pitoniak, Ph.D., who also offered many helpful suggestions regarding content and format. Proofreading was carried out by Joanne M. Despres, Anne Eason, Seán O'Mannion-Espejo, Thomas F. Pitoniak, Peter A. Sokolowski, Karen L. Wilkinson, and Jocelyn D. Woods. Georgette B. Boucher provided invaluable typing assistance. Madeline L. Novak provided guidance on typographic matters. John M. Morse was responsible for the conception of this book as well as for numerous ideas and continued support along the way.

Eileen M. Haraty
Editor

Explanatory Notes

Entries

1. Main Entries

A boldface letter, word, or phrase appearing flush with the left-hand margin of each column of type is a main entry or entry word. The main entry may consist of letters set solid, of letters joined by a punctuation mark (as a hyphen), or of letters separated by a space:

> **collant**[1], **-lante** . . . *adj* . . .
>
> **eye–opener** . . . *n* . . .
>
> **walk out** *vi* . . .

The main entry, together with the material that follows it on the same line and succeeding indented lines, constitutes a dictionary entry.

2. Order of Main Entries

The main entries follow one another in alphabetical order letter by letter without regard to intervening spaces or hyphens; for example, *shake-up* follows *shaker.*

Homographs (words with the same spelling) having different parts of speech are given separate dictionary entries. These entries are distinguished by superscript numerals following the entry word:

> **mauvais**[1] . . . *adv* . . .
>
> **mauvais**[2], **-vaise** *adj* . . .
>
> **salt**[1] . . . *vt* . . .
>
> **salt**[2] *adj* . . .
>
> **salt**[3] *n* . . .

Numbered homograph entries are listed in the following order: verb, adverb, adjective, noun, conjunction, preposition, pronoun, interjection, article.

Homographs having the same part of speech are normally included at the same dictionary entry, without regard to their different semantic origins. On the English-to-French side, however, separate entries are made if the homographs have distinct pronunciations or if homographic verbs have distinct inflected forms.

3. Guide Words

A pair of guide words is printed at the top of each page, indicating the first and last main entries that appear on that page:

velours • vérifiable

4. Variants

When a main entry is followed by the word *or* and another spelling, the two spellings are variants. Both are standard, and either one may be used according to personal inclination:

jailer *or* **jailor** . . . *n* . . .

lis *or* **lys** . . . *nms & pl* . . .

Occasionally, a variant spelling is used only for a particular sense of a word. In these cases, the variant spelling is listed after the sense number of the sense to which it pertains:

flier . . . *n* . . . **2** *or* **flyer** . . .

Sometimes the entry word is used interchangeably with a longer phrase containing the entry word. For the purposes of this dictionary, such phrases are considered variants of the headword:

bunk[2] *n* **1** *or* **bunk bed** . . .

risée . . . *nf or* **objet de risée** . . .

ward[1] . . . *vt or* **to ward off** . . .

Variant wordings of boldface phrases may also be shown:

table . . . *nf* . . . **4 table de chevet** *or* **table de nuit** . . .

abattre . . . *vt* . . . **5 abattre ses cartes** *or* **abattre son jeu** . . .

5. Run-On Entries

A main entry may be followed by a derivative word in a different part of speech. This is a run-on entry. It is introduced by a boldface dash and has a functional label. It is not defined, however, since its equivalent can be readily derived by adding the corresponding foreign-language suffix to the term or terms used to define the entry word:

illegal . . . *adj* : illégal **— illegally** *adv*

(the French adverb is *illégalement*)

bureaucratie . . . *nf* : bureaucracy **— bureaucratique** . . . *adj*

(the English adjective is *bureaucratic*)

On the French-to-English side of the book, reflexive verbs are sometimes run on undefined:

appauvrir . . . *vt* : to impoverish **— s'appauvrir** *vr*

The absence of a definition indicates that *s'appauvrir* has the simple reflexive meaning "to become impoverished" or "to impoverish oneself."

6. Bold Notes

A main entry may be followed by one or more phrases containing the entry word or an inflected form of it. These are bold notes. Each bold note is defined at its own numbered sense:

abeille . . . *nf* **1** : bee, honeybee **2 abeille mâle** : drone

hold[1] . . . *vi* . . . **3 to hold forth** : . . . **4 to hold to** : . . .

If the bold note consists only of the entry word and a single preposition, the entry word is represented by a boldface swung dash **~**.

> **pente** . . . *nf* **1** : slope **2 en ~** : sloping

The same bold note phrase may appear at two or more senses if it has more than one distinct meaning:

> **affaire** . . . *nf* . . . **5 affaires** *nfpl* : possessions, belongings **6 affaires** *nfpl* : business <homme d'affaires : businessman> . . .

Pronunciation

Pronunciation of Entry Words

The matter between a pair of brackets [ ] following the entry word indicates the pronunciation. The symbols used are from the International Phonetic Alphabet and are explained in the Pronunciation Symbols chart on page 60a.

The presence of variant pronunciations indicates that not all educated speakers pronounce words the same way. A second-place variant is not to be regarded as less acceptable than the pronunciation that is given first. It may, in fact, be used by as many educated speakers as the first variant, but the requirements of the printed page are such that one must precede the other:

> **often** ['ɔfən, 'ɔftən] . . .

When a compound word has less than a full pronunciation, the missing part is to be supplied from the pronunciation at the entry for the unpronounced element of the compound:

> **gamma ray** ['gæmə] . . .
>
> **ray** ['reɪ] . . .

In general, no pronunciation is indicated for open compounds consisting of two or more English words that are main entries at their own alphabetical place:

> **smoke detector** . . .
>
> **smoke**[1] ['smok] . . .
>
> **detector** [dɪ'tɛktər] . . .

Only the first entry in a series of numbered homographs is given a pronunciation if their pronunciations are the same:

dab[1] ['dæb] *vt* . . .

dab[2] *n* . . .

On the English-to-French side, no pronunciation is shown for principal parts of verbs that are formed by regular suffixation, nor for most derivative adverbs formed by the suffix *-ly*.

The aspirate pronunciation of the letter *h* in French is indicated by a symbol ['] preceding the pronunciation of the headword:

habile [abil]

hasard ['azar]

Functional Labels

An italic label indicating a part of speech or some other functional classification follows the pronunciation or, if no pronunciation is given, the main entry. The parts of speech are indicated as follows:

mendier . . . *v* . . .

maintenant . . . *adv* . . .

daily[2] *adj* . . .

jackal . . . *n* . . .

and . . . *conj* . . .

par . . . *prep* . . .

neither[3] *pron* . . .

allô . . . *interj* . . .

le . . . *art*

Verbs that are intransitive are labelled *vi;* verbs that are transitive are labelled *vt.* Entries for verbs that are both transitive and intransitive are labelled *v,* with the labels *vi* and *vt* serving to introduce any transitive and intransitive subdivisions:

necessitate . . . *vt* **-tated; -tating** : nécessiter, exiger

déborder . . . *vi* : to overflow

satisfy . . . *v* **-fied; -fying** *vt* . . . — *vi* . . .

Two other labels are used to indicate functional classifications of verbs: *v aux* (auxiliary verb) and *v impers* (impersonal verb).

> **may** . . . *v aux, past* **might** . . .
>
> **aller**[1] . . . *vi* . . . — *v aux* : to be going to, to be about to . . . — *v impers* **1** **en ~** : to happen, to go . . .

Gender Labels

In French-to-English noun entries, the gender of the entry word is indicated by an italic *m* (masculine), *f* (feminine), or *mf* (masculine or feminine), immediately following the functional label:

> **magnésium** . . . *nm* . . .
>
> **galaxie** . . . *nf* . . .
>
> **touriste** . . . *nmf* . . .

If both the masculine and feminine forms are shown for a noun referring to a person, the label is simply *n*:

> **directeur**[2], **-trice** *n* . . .

French noun equivalents of English entry words are also labeled for gender:

> **amnesia** . . . *n* : amnésie *f*
>
> **earache** . . . *n* : mal *m* d'oreille
>
> **gamekeeper** . . . *n* : garde-chasse *m*

Inflected Forms

1. Nouns

The plurals of nouns are shown in this dictionary when they are irregular, when plural suffixation brings about a change in the spelling of the root word, when an English noun ends in a consonant plus *-o* or in *-ey,* when an English noun ends in *-oo,* when an English noun is a compound that pluralizes any element but the last, when a French noun is a hyphenated compound, when a noun has variant plurals, or whenever the dictionary user might have reasonable doubts regarding the spelling of a plural:

> **tooth** . . . *n, pl* **teeth** . . .
>
> **madame** . . . *nf, pl* **mesdames** . . .

adieu . . . *nm, pl* **adieux** . . .

potato . . . *n, pl* **-toes** . . .

abbey . . . *n, pl* **-beys** . . .

cuckoo[2] *n, pl* **-oos** . . .

brother–in–law . . . *n, pl* **brothers–in–law** . . .

court–circuit . . . *nm, pl* **courts–circuits** . . .

quail[2] *n, pl* **quail** *or* **quails** . . .

récital . . . *nm, pl* **-tals** . . .

Cutback inflected forms are used for most multisyllabic nouns on the English-to-French side, regardless of the number of syllables. On the French-to-English side, cutback inflections are given for nouns that have three or more syllables; plurals for shorter words are written out in full:

shampoo[2] *n, pl* **-poos** . . .

calamity . . . *n, pl* **-ties** . . .

mouse . . . *n, pl* **mice** . . .

terminal[2] *nm, pl* **-naux** . . .

caillou . . . *nm, pl* **cailloux** . . .

If only the masculine gender form has a plural which is irregular, that plural form will be given with the appropriate label:

jumeau, -melle . . . *adj & n, mpl* **jumeaux** : twin

The plurals of nouns are usually not shown when the base word is unchanged by the addition of the regular *-s* plural or when the noun is unlikely to occur in the plural:

apple . . . *n* : pomme *f*

anglais[2] *nm* : English (language)

Nouns that are plural in form and that regularly occur in plural constructions are labeled *npl* (for English nouns), *nmpl* (for French masculine nouns), or *nfpl* (for French feminine nouns):

knickers . . . *npl* . . .

parages . . . *nmpl* . . .

tenailles . . . *nfpl* . . .

Entry words that are unchanged in the plural are labeled *ns & pl* (for English nouns), *nms & pl* (for French masculine nouns), *nfs & pl* (for French feminine nouns), and *nmfs & pl* (for French gender-variable nouns):

deer . . . *ns & pl* . . .

perdrix . . . *nfs & pl* . . .

débours . . . *nms & pl* . . .

après–midi . . . *nmfs & pl* . . .

2. Verbs

ENGLISH VERBS

The principal parts of verbs are shown in English-to-French entries when they are irregular, when suffixation brings about a change in spelling of the root word, when the verb ends in *-ey*, or when there are variant inflected forms:

break[1] . . . *v* **broke** . . . ; **broken** . . . ; **breaking** . . .

drag[1] . . . *v* **dragged; dragging** . . .

imagine . . . *vt* **-ined; -ining** . . .

monkey[1] . . . *vi* **-keyed; -keying** . . .

label[1] . . . *vt* **-beled** *or* **-belled; -beling** *or* **-belling** . . .

Cutback inflected forms are usually used when the verb has two or more syllables:

multiply . . . *v* **-plied; -plying** . . .

bevel[1] . . . *vt* **-eled** *or* **-elled; -eling** *or* **-elling** . . .

forgo *or* **forego** . . . *vt* **-went** . . . ; **-gone** . . . ; **-going** . . .

commit . . . *vt* **-mitted; -mitting** . . .

The principal parts of an English verb are usually not shown when they are regular and the root word is unchanged by suffixation.

delay[1] . . . *vt*

pack[1] . . . *vt*

FRENCH VERBS

The conjugations of French verbs are not shown at the entry but are included in the Conjugation of French Verbs section beginning on page 40a. Regular verbs ending in *-er* or *-ir* have no cross-reference number at their entries, and their conjugations are shown at the beginning of that section. Entries for irregular French verbs are cross-referenced by number to the model conjugations appearing in the Conjugation of French Verbs section:

arranger {17} *vt* . . .

joindre {50} *vt* . . .

Entries for frequently used irregular forms of French verbs are cross-referenced to the corresponding infinitive:

tenu[1] . . . *pp* → **tenir**

joigne . . . , *etc.* → **joindre**

Irregular composite verbs, such as *retenir* and *rejoindre*, do not have cross-referenced forms entered in the dictionary, since their conjugations are based upon the corresponding verbal root.

Adverbs and Adjectives

The comparative and superlative forms of English adjective and adverb main entries are shown when suffixation brings about a change in spelling of the root word, when the inflection is irregular, and when there are variant inflected forms:

fat . . . *adj* **fatter; fattest** . . .

well[2] *adv* **better** . . . ; **best** . . .

evil[1] . . . *adj* **eviler** *or* **eviller; evilest** *or* **evillest** . . .

The superlative forms of adjectives and adverbs of two or more syllables are usually cut back; the superlative is shown in full, however, when it is desirable to indicate the pronunciation of the inflected form:

gaudy . . . *adj* **gaudier; -est** . . .

early[1] . . . *adv* **earlier; -est** . . .

secure[1] . . . *adj* **securer; -est** . . .

but

young[1] . . . *adj* **younger** [ˈjəŋgər;]; **youngest** [ˈjəŋgəst] . . .

The absence of the comparative form at an adjective entry indicates that there is no evidence of its use:

mere . . . *adj, superlative* **merest** . . .

The comparative and superlative forms of adjectives and adverbs are usually not shown when the base word is unchanged by suffixation.

quiet[2] *adj* **1** . . .

Usage

1. Usage Labels

The two types of usage labels in this dictionary address a word's regional derivation and register. Words that are limited in use to France, French-speaking Canada, Belgium, Switzerland, or English-speaking Canada are given labels indicating the countries in which they are most commonly used:

bachoter . . . *vi France* : to cram . . .

cocotte . . . *nf* . . . **2** *Can* : pinecone . . .

auditoire . . . *nm* . . . **2** *Bel & Switz* : auditorium

furnace . . . *n* : fourneau *m*, fournaise *f Can*

bloke . . . *n Brit* : type *m*

The following regional labels are used in this book: *Bel* (Belgium), *Brit* (Great Britain and English-speaking Canada), *Can* (French-speaking Canada), *France, Switz* (Switzerland).

A number of French words are given a *fam* (familiar) label as well, indicating that these words are suitable for informal contexts but would not normally be used in formal writing or speaking. The stylistic labels *sometimes offensive* or *usu vulgar* are added for a word which is thought to be vulgar or offensive in many contexts but whose widespread use justifies its inclusion in this book. These labels are intended to warn the reader that the word in question may be inappropriate in polite conversation.

2. Usage Notes

Definitions are sometimes preceded by parenthetical usage notes that give supplementary semantic information:

not . . . *adv* **1** (*used to form a negative*) **:** . . .

when[2] *conj* **1** (*referring to a particular time*) **:** . . .

se . . . *pron* **1** (*used with reflexive verbs*) **:** . . . **2** (*used to indicate reciprocity*) **:** . . .

si[1] . . . *adv* . . . **2** (*used to contradict a negative statement or question*) **:** . . .

Additional semantic orientation is also occasionally given in the form of parenthetical notes appearing within the definition:

calibrate . . . *vt* . . . **:** calibrer (une arme, etc.), étalonner (une balance)

paille . . . *nf* . . . **2 :** (drinking) straw

Occasionally a usage note is used in place of a definition. This is usually done when the entry word has no single foreign-language equivalent. Usage notes of this type will be accompanied by an example or examples of common use:

shall . . . *v aux* . . . **1** (*used to express a command*) <you shall do as I say : vous ferez comme je vous dis> . . .

3. Illustrations of Usage

Definitions are sometimes followed by verbal illustrations that show a typical use of the word in context or a common idiomatic usage. These verbal illustrations include a translation and are enclosed in angle brackets:

ici . . . *adv* **1 :** here <ici et là : here and there> <par ici : this way> . . .

make[1] . . . *vt* . . . **8** EARN **:** gagner <to make a living : gagner sa vie> . . .

Sense Division

A boldface colon is used to introduce a definition:

failing[1] . . . *n* **:** défaut *m*

Boldface Arabic numerals separate the senses of a word that has more than one sense:

> **maîtriser** . . . *vt* **1** : to master **2** : to control, to restrain . . .

Whenever some information (such as a synonym, a boldface word or phrase, a usage note, a cross-reference, or a label) follows a sense number, it applies only to that specific numbered sense and not to any other boldface numbered senses:

> **abord** . . . *nm* **1** ACCÈS : . . .
>
> **pile**[1] . . . *vi* **1** *or* **to pile up** : . . .
>
> **caoutchouc** . . . *nm* . . . **2 caoutchoucs** *nmpl* : . . .
>
> **extension** . . . *n* . . . **5 extension cord** : . . .
>
> **myself** . . . *pron* **1** (*used reflexively*) : . . .
>
> **pike** . . . *n* . . . **3 → turnpike**
>
> **ambitionner** . . . *vt* . . . **2** *Can* : . . .

Cross-References

Three different kinds of cross-references are used in this dictionary: synonymous, cognate, and inflectional. In each instance the cross-reference is readily recognized by the boldface arrow following the entry word.

Synonymous and cognate cross-references indicate that a definition at the entry cross-referred to can be substituted for the entry word:

> **cable**[2] . . . **2 → cablegram**
>
> **sceptic** . . . **→ skeptic**

An inflectional cross-reference is used to identify the entry word as an inflected form of another word (as a noun or verb):

> **aura**[1] . . . , etc. **→ avoir**
>
> **mice → mouse**

Synonyms

At many entries or senses in this book, a synonym in small capital letters is provided before the boldface colon and the following defining text. These synonyms are all main entries or bold notes elsewhere in the book. They serve as a helpful guide to the meaning of the entry or sense and also give the reader an additional term that might be substituted in a similar context. On the English-to-French side synonyms are particularly abundant, since special care has been taken to guide the English speaker—by means of synonyms, verbal illustrations, or usage notes—to the meaning of the French terms at each sense of a multisense entry.

croiser . . . **3** RENCONTRER **:** . . .

demand[2] . . . **2** CLAIM **:** . . .

French Grammar

Accents and Diacritics

French makes use of accents and diacritics to indicate either the phonetic value of a given letter, or to distinguish one word from another which has the same pronunciation and would otherwise share the same spelling. There are three types of accents:

> ***The acute accent*** /´/ ordinarily indicates closed pronunciation.
>
> ***The grave accent*** /`/ ordinarily indicates open pronunciation.
>
> ***The circumflex*** /ˆ/ ordinarily indicates open pronunciation.

In addition to accents, French makes use of the ***diaeresis*** /¨/ which, as in English, indicates that the vowel preceding the marked letter is pronounced separately: *maïs* [mais] (corn) is thus pronounced differently from *mais* [mɛ] (but, however).

> The ***cedilla*** /¸/ indicates soft pronunciation of a *c* /s/ which precedes an *a, o,* or *u* (*ça, rançon, aperçu*).

Diacritics in the French language do not affect word stress.

Capitalization

In French, unlike English, the following words are usually not capitalized:

- Names of days, months, languages, and most religions (*jeudi, octobre, français, judaïsme*).
- Names of holidays composed of two or more words. Unlike English, in French only the distinguishing word and any preceding adjectives are capitalized (*la fête du Travail,* Labor Day; *mercredi des Cendres,* Ash Wednesday).

- French adjectives or nouns derived from proper nouns (*l'équipe sénégalaise, le marxisme*), except for nouns of geographic or national identity, which are usually capitalized (*les Antillais, une Vietnamienne*).

Articles

1. Definite Article

French has three forms of the definite article: *le* (masculine singular), *la* (feminine singular), and the plural article, *les,* which does not distinguish for gender. *Le* and *la* contract to *l'* when they precede a word beginning with a vowel sound (*l'arbre, l'heure*). In some instances an initial *h,* although mute, is considered to be aspirate, in which case the article does not contract (*le héros*). The definite article agrees in gender and number with the noun that follows it (*le bâtiment,* the building; *la rue,* the street; *les bâtiments,* the buildings; *les rues,* the streets).

Whenever the plural article *les* or the singular masculine article *le* immediately follows either *de* or *à,* the two combine to form the contractions *des, aux, du,* and *au* respectively (*les jouets des enfants,* the children's toys; *la maison aux fenêtres larges,* the house with the wide windows; *le cabinet du médecin,* the doctor's office; *elles sont allées au café,* they went to the café). However, if a singular article of either gender is preceded by *de* or *à* and followed by a word with an initial vowel sound, the article becomes *l'* (*le nom de l'église,* the name of the church; *arriver à l'heure,* to arrive on time). The use of *le, la,* and *les* in French corresponds largely to the use of *the* in English; some exceptions are noted below.

The definite article is used:

- With certain geographical regions, including countries and continents (*l'Afrique,* Africa; *le Canada,* Canada; *la Nouvelle-Écosse,* Nova Scotia).
- With languages, except when the language is preceded by *en* or *parler* (*Patti comprend le français,* Patti understands French; *Joseph parle hongrois,* Joseph speaks Hungarian; *c'est en japonais,* it's in Japanese).

- With abstract nouns (*il adore les chiens,* he loves dogs; *l'hiver est long,* winter is long; *le petit déjeuner est inclus,* breakfast is included).
- With body parts (*j'ai mal au bras,* my arm hurts; *elle se brosse les dents,* she's brushing her teeth).

2. Indefinite Article

French has three forms of the indefinite article: *un* (masculine singular), *une* (feminine singular), and the plural article *des,* which is used for both genders. The indefinite article agrees in number and gender with the noun it precedes (*une table,* a table; *un couteau,* a knife; *des verres,* some glasses).

- The use of *un, une,* and *des* in French corresponds largely to the use of *a, an,* and *some* in English (*un oiseau,* a bird; *une poupée,* a doll; *des oranges,* oranges, some oranges). The plural article *des* becomes *de* or *d'* when immediately followed by an adjective (*des amis,* friends; *de bons amis,* good friends). When the adjective begins with a vowel sound, then the article becomes *d'* (*d'énormes quantités,* enormous quantities).
- In a negative statement, the indefinite article is replaced with *de* or, when preceding a word with an initial vowel sound, *d'* (*Marc n'a pas de voiture,* Marc doesn't have a car; *il n'y a plus d'eau,* there is no more water). This rule does not apply to negative statements with the verb *être* (*ce livre n'est pas un roman,* this book is not a novel).

3. Partitive Article

French makes use of the partitive article to indicate that the following noun represents part of an implied, and uncountable, whole. The partitive is formed by *de* plus the definite article, contracting where applicable to *du, de la, de l',* or *des* (*elle écoute de la musique,* she listens to music; *pomper de l'essence,* to pump gas).

Nouns

1. Gender

Nouns in French are either masculine or feminine. Although a noun's gender can be arbitrary and must be learned as one acquires vocabulary, it can often be determined according to the following guidelines:

- Nouns ending in *-age, -èle, -exe, -isme, -oir, -phone,* and *-scope* are usually masculine (*un visage, un modèle, le sexe, le mysticisme, le miroir, un téléphone, un magnétoscope*).
- Nouns deriving from verbs will often signal masculine gender with the ending *-eur* or *-ant*, or feminine gender with the ending *-euse* or *-ante* (*un chanteur, la gagnante*).
- Nouns ending in *-ade, -ance, -ence, -esse, -ette, -ie, -ise, -sion, -té, -tion, -trice, -tude* or *-ure* are usually feminine (*une croisade, la chance, une essence, la jeunesse, une vedette, la patrie, une crise, une décision, l'université, une abstraction, l'empératrice, la similitude, une aventure*).

Most nouns referring to people or animals agree in gender with the subject (*un homme, une femme; le frère, la sœur; le cheval, la jument*). However, some nouns referring to people, including those ending in *-ique* and *-iste,* use the same form for both sexes (*un artiste, une artiste; un diabétique, une diabétique*).

Many names of animals exist in only one gender form (*la souris, le crapaud,* etc.). In these instances, the adjectives *mâle* and *femelle* are sometimes used to distinguish between males and females (*une souris mâle,* a male mouse).

2. Pluralization

Plurals of French nouns are formed as follows:

- As in English, most French nouns are pluralized by adding *-s* (*un médecin, des médecins; l'arbre, les arbres*).
- Nouns ending in *-au* or *-eu* are ordinarily pluralized by adding a final *-x* (*un tuyau, des tuyaux; le feu, les feux*).

- Nouns ending in *-al* are often pluralized by changing the ending to *-aux* (*un animal, des animaux*).
- Singular nouns which end in *-s, -x,* or *-z* do not change in the plural (*un matelas, deux matelas; la croix, les croix; un gaz, des gaz*).

Adjectives

1. Gender and Number

Most adjectives agree in gender and number with the nouns or pronouns they modify (*un poète espagnol, des poètes espagnols; elle est espagnole, elles sont espagnoles*). Many adjectives ending in *-e* (*riche*) and most of those ending in *-ble, -ique,* and *-iste* (*probable, fantastique, altruiste*) vary only for number.

Many masculine adjectives add a final *-e* to form the feminine (*petit* → *petite, français* → *française*). In some cases, the feminine is formed by modifying the final syllable, according to the following patterns:

-anc → *-anche* (*franc* → *franche*)

-el → *-elle* (*actuel* → *actuelle*)

-en → *-enne* (*moyen* → *moyenne*)

-er → *-ère* (*passager* → *passagère*)

-eur → *-euse* (*frondeur* → *frondeuse*)

-eux → *-euse* (*respectueux* → *respectueuse*)

-if → *-ive* (*tardif* → *tardive*)

-il → *-ille* (*gentil* → *gentille*)

Some masculine adjectives, including *beau, fou, nouveau,* and *vieux,* modify their ending when immediately followed by a word which begins with a vowel sound:

beau → *bel* (*un bel arbre,* a beautiful tree)

fou → *fol* (*un fol appétit,* a tremendous appetite)

nouveau → *nouvel* (*un nouvel album,* a new album)

vieux → *vieil* (*un vieil ami,* an old friend)

Adjectives of this type ordinarily form the feminine by adding *-le* to these modified masculine forms:

beau → *bel* → *belle*

vieux → *vieil* → *vieille*

2. Pluralization

Plurals of French adjectives are formed as follows:

- Most adjectives are pluralized by adding *-s* (*de bons livres,* some good books; *des yeux bleus,* blue eyes).
- Masculine adjectives ending in *-au* are ordinarily pluralized by adding a final *-x* (*les beaux arts,* the fine arts; *des mots nouveaux,* new words).
- Masculine adjectives ending in *-al* are often pluralized by changing the ending to *-aux* (*les moyens normaux,* the normal means).

3. Position

Unlike English, most descriptive adjectives in French follow the nouns they modify (*une chose utile, un écrivain célèbre*). Common exceptions include *autre, beau, bon, chaque, faux, gros, jeune, joli, nouveau, petit,* and *vieux,* which usually appear before the noun (*une belle maison, une vieille dame*).

Some adjectives change meaning depending on whether they occur before or after the noun: *un pauvre enfant,* a poor (pitiable) child, *un enfant pauvre,* a poor (not rich) child; *un grand homme,* a great man, *un homme grand,* a tall man; *mes chers amis,* my dear friends; *un ordinateur cher,* an expensive computer.

4. Comparative and Superlative Forms

The comparative of French adjectives is generally rendered as *plus . . . que* (more . . . than) or *moins . . . que* (less . . . than): *je suis plus grande que lui,* I'm taller than he; *ils sont moins intelligents que toi,* they're less intelligent than you.

The superlative of French adjectives usually follows the formula: (definite article + noun) + definite article + *plus/moins* + adjective (*elle est l'étudiante la plus travailleuse,* she is the hardest-working student; *il est le moins connu,* he's the least well-known; *les voitures les plus rapides,* the fastest cars).

Like their English counterparts *good* and *bad,* the adjectives *bon* and *mauvais* have irregular comparative and superlative forms:

Positive	Comparative	Superlative
c'est ***bon,*** it is good	*c'est* ***meilleur*** *que les autres,* it is better than the rest	*c'est* ***le meilleur*** *de tous,* it is the best (one) of all
c'est ***mauvais,*** it is bad	*c'est* ***pire*** *que les autres*, it is worse than the rest	*c'est* ***le pire*** *de tous,* it is the worst (one) of all

The absolute superlative is most often formed by placing *très,* or other adverbs such as *fort, extrêmement,* etc., before the adjective (*elle est très sympathique,* she is very nice; *c'est fort probable,* it is quite likely).

Adverbs

French adverbs are often formed by adding the adverbial suffix *-ment* to an adjective (*facile* → *facilement, prétendu* → *prétendument*). If the masculine form of an adjective ends with a consonant, the suffix is normally added to the feminine form (*ouvert* → *ouverte* → *ouvertement*). Adjectives whose masculine form ends in *-ant* or *-ent* will usually form the adverb by replacing this ending with *-amment* or *-emment* (*indépendant* → *indépendamment, prudent* → *prudemment*). A few adjectives add the acute accent to the final *e* to form the adverb (*énorme* → *énormément, expresse* → *expressément*).

As in English, there are many French adverbs that do not stem from an adjective (*assez,* enough; *bien,* well; *déjà,* already; *très,* very, etc.).

Pronouns

1. Personal (Subject) Pronouns

The personal pronouns in French are:

Person	Singular		Plural	
FIRST	**je**	I	**nous**	we
SECOND	**tu**	you (familiar)	**vous**	you[1]
	vous	you (formal)	**vous**	you[1]
THIRD	**il**	he	**ils,**	they
	elle	she	**elles**	
	on	one (*also* they, someone, you, we, people)		

[1] The pronoun *vous* acts as the plural for both the familiar *tu* and the formal *vous.*

FAMILIAR VS. FORMAL

The second person personal pronouns exist in both familiar and formal forms. The familiar forms are generally used when addressing relatives, friends, and children; the formal forms are ordinarily used to show courtesy, respect, or emotional distance.

USAGE OF *ON*

The third person pronoun *on* is an impersonal subject pronoun and is an approximate equivalent of the impersonal *you* or *they* in English (*comment dit-on ça en russe?,* how do you say it in Russian?; *on a fermé la pharmacie,* they've closed the drugstore).

2. Disjunctive Pronouns

The disjunctive pronouns in French are:

Singular		Plural	
moi	I, me	**nous**	us, we
toi	you	**vous**	you
vous	you (formal)	**vous**	you
lui	him	**eux**	them, they (masculine or mixed)
elle	her	**elles**	them, they (feminine)
soi[1]	oneself		

[1] Used in impersonal constructions (*travailler chez soi,* to work out of one's home)

Disjunctive pronouns are used:

- as the objects of prepositions (*est-ce pour moi?,* is it for me?; *il le leur a donné,* he gave it to them).
- after *c'est* or *ce sont* (*c'est moi,* it is I, it's me; *ce sont elles,* it is they, it's them).
- to add emphasis to, or merely to complement, the subject of a sentence (*c'est elle qui les a achetés,* she's the one who bought them; *il arrive toujours en retard, lui,* he always arrives late).
- in comparisons (*Danielle est plus sportive qu'eux,* Danielle is more athletic than they).
- in compound subjects (*Louis et moi, nous travaillons ensemble,* Louis and I work together).

3. Object Pronouns

DIRECT OBJECT PRONOUNS

Direct object pronouns represent the goal or result of the action of a verb (*Corinne va appeler Charlotte,* Corinne is going to call Charlotte → *Corinne va l'appeler,* Corinne is going to call her; *Jean-Luc a vu Michel et Isabelle,* Jean-Luc saw Michel and Isabelle → *Jean-Luc les a vus,* Jean-Luc saw them). The direct object pronouns in French are:

Singular		Plural	
me, m'[1]	me	**nous**	us
te, t'[1]	you (informal)	**vous**	you (informal and formal)
vous	you (formal)		
le, l'	him, it	**les**	them (masculine, feminine, or mixed)
la, l'	her, it		

[1]These become *moi* or *toi* in affirmative commands: *ne me regarde pas!,* don't look at me!; *regarde-moi!,* look at me!

INDIRECT OBJECT PRONOUNS

Indirect object pronouns represent the secondary goal of the action of a verb (*il m'a donné le cadeau,* he gave me the gift; *je leur ai dit non,* I told them no; *ils lui ont téléphoné hier,* they phoned her yesterday). The indirect object pronouns in French are:

Singular		Plural	
me, m'	(to, for, from) me	**nous**	(to, for, from) us
te, t'	(to, for, from) you	**vous**	(to, for, from) you
lui	(to, for, from) him, her	**leur**	(to, for, from) them

Position of Object Pronouns

The position of the object pronoun in French syntax differs from its English counterpart. The object pronoun can be found before the verb of which it is the object (*je ne peux pas la voir,* I can't see her; *Alice le lit,* Alice is reading it). In affirmative commands, the object pronoun follows the imperative and is linked to it by a hyphen (*écoutez-moi!,* listen to me!). In negative commands, the object pronoun precedes the verb (*ne les achète pas,* don't buy them).

Adverbial Pronouns *y* and *en*

The adverbial pronoun *y* is used to replace many prepositional phrases introduced by *à/dans/en* (+ article and/or adjective) + noun (but not the name of a person). *Y* is ordinarily placed immediately before the verb of which it is the object:

> *il faut répondre à leurs questions,* you have to answer their questions → *il faut y répondre,* you have to answer
>
> *je consens à l'examination,* I consent to the examination → *j'y consens,* I consent, I consent to it

In affirmative commands, *y* appears after the verb and is joined to it by a hyphen:

> *n'y pense pas!* don't think about it! → *penses-y!* think about it!

The pronoun *en* is frequently used to replace phrases consisting of *de* (+ article and/or adjective) + noun. Like *y, en* is placed immediately before the verb of which it is the object:

> *nous aurons besoin d'argent,* we'll need money → *nous en aurons besoin,* we'll need some
>
> *ils parlaient des impôts,* they were talking about taxes → *ils en parlaient,* they were talking about it
>
> *combien de pages as-tu lues?* how many pages have you read? → *j'en ai lu une centaine,* I've read about a hundred
>
> *Jean leur a donné de la nourriture,* Jean gave them some food → *Jean leur en a donné,* Jean gave them some

Word Order of Object Pronouns

When several object pronouns precede the verb, the following order applies:

me	→	*le*	→	*lui*	→	*y*	→	*en*	→	*verb*
te		*la*		*leur*						
nous		*les*								
vous										

For example:

ne le lui donne pas, don't give it to him

ne lui en donne pas, don't give any to him, don't give him any

je ne m'y fie plus, I no longer rely on it

When several object pronouns follow the verb (as in affirmative commands), the order is:

verb	→	*le*	→	*moi*	→	*y*	→	*en*
		la		*toi*				
		les		*lui*				
				nous				
				vous				
				leur				

For example:

donnez-leur en!, give them some!

envoie-le moi, send it to me

4. Reflexive Pronouns

Reflexive pronouns are used to refer back to the subject of the verb (*je m'habille,* I'm getting dressed, I'm dressing myself; *ils se préparent,* they're getting ready, they're preparing themselves). The reflexive pronouns in French are:

Singular		**Plural**	
me[1]	myself	**nous**	ourselves
te[1]	yourself	**vous**	yourselves
se[1]	yourself, himself, herself, itself	**se**[1]	yourselves, themselves

[1] These pronouns drop the final *e* when followed by words beginning with a vowel sound: *s'accoutumer, je m'y défends, ils s'habillent,* etc.

Reflexive pronouns normally appear before the verb (*ne t'en fais pas,* don't worry about it; *il faut que tu te dépêches,* you must hurry), but they are placed immediately after the verb in affirmative commands (*dépêchez-vous!* hurry!, hurry up!).

In the plural, reflexive pronouns can indicate reciprocal action (*nous nous voyons fréquemment,* we see each other frequently; *ils ne se parlent plus,* they no longer speak to each other).

It should be noted that many verbs which take reflexive pronouns in French have intransitive equivalents in English (*se coucher,* to lie down; *se réveiller,* to wake up; *s'en aller,* to leave, etc.).

5. Relative Pronouns

Relative pronouns introduce subordinate clauses or modifiers (*les fleurs que nous avons cueillies,* the flowers that we gathered; *les filles dont tu as fait la connaissance,* the girls whom you met). In French, the relative pronouns are:

que[1] (that, which, who, whom)

qui (that, which, who)

quoi (what)

où (where)

lequel, laquelle, lesquels, lesquelles (which)

dont (of which, of whom, whose)

[1]Contracts to *qu'* when followed by a word beginning with a vowel sound

The relative pronoun *qui* refers to the subject of the relative clause, regardless of whether it is a person or thing, while the pronoun *que* refers to its object:

le livre qui est sur le bureau	the book that/ which is on the desk	(*livre* is the subject)
le livre que j'aime	the book (that) I like	(*livre* is the object)

Quoi refers to things only and is used after prepositions:

on aura de quoi causer, people will have plenty to talk about

quelque chose sur quoi s'appuyer, something to lean on

Où also refers exclusively to things and can be used to refer to time as well as place:

le pays d'où tu viens, the country you come from

le jour où nous sommes partis, the day (on which) we left

The pronoun *lequel* varies for gender and number: *lequel* (masculine singular), *laquelle* (feminine singular), *lesquels* (masculine plural), *lesquelles* (feminine plural). Because the first component of this pronoun is the definite article *le,* it observes the same rules of contraction that apply to the masculine singular article *le* and the plural article *les* (see the section Definite Article on page 23a) and combines with the prepositions *à* and *de* to form the following:

à	+	*lequel*	→	*auquel*
à	+	*lesquels*	→	*auxquels*
à	+	*lesquelles*	→	*auxquelles*
de	+	*lequel*	→	*duquel*
de	+	*lesquels*	→	*desquels*
de	+	*lesquelles*	→	*desquelles*

des amis auxquels j'écris souvent, friends to whom I often write

un dîner au cours duquel un prix sera décerné, a dinner in the course of which a prize will be awarded

l'adresse à laquelle vous recevez votre courrier, the address at which you receive your mail

The relative pronoun *dont* can often be used in place of *de qui, de laquelle, duquel, desquels,* and *desquelles,* except after a preposition:

l'organisation dont il est le chef, the organization of which he is the head

tout ce dont elle a envie, all that she desires

les choses dont nous avons parlé, the things we talked about

Possessives

1. Possessive Adjectives

French possessive adjectives precede the nouns they modify. Unlike their English counterparts, they agree in both gender and number with the noun they precede, and not with their possessor (*il a mis sa chemise,* he put on his shirt; *mes chaussures,* my shoes; *notre voiture,* our car; *nos voitures,* our cars). Plural possessive adjectives do not vary for gender (*mes cousins, mes cousines*).

Singular Masculine	Singular Feminine	Plural	English Equivalent
mon	**ma**	**mes**	my
ton	**ta**	**tes**	your (informal)
son	**sa**	**ses**	his, her
notre	**notre**	**nos**	our
votre	**votre**	**vos**	your (formal and/or plural)
leur	**leur**	**leurs**	their

The feminine adjectives *ma, ta,* and *sa* change to the masculine forms *mon, ton,* and *son* when immediately followed by a word with an initial vowel sound (*mon amie, son histoire*).

2. Possessive Pronouns

French possessive pronouns are always preceded by the definite article, and they agree in number and gender with the nouns they replace (*mes clefs,* my keys → *les miennes,* mine; *nos gants,* our gloves → *les nôtres,* ours).

Sing. Masc.	Sing. Fem.	English Equivalent
le mien	**la mienne**	mine
le tien	**la tienne**	yours (informal)

continued

Sing. Masc.	Sing. Fem.	English Equivalent
le sien	**la sienne**	his, hers
le nôtre	**la nôtre**	ours
le vôtre	**la vôtre**	yours (formal and/or plural)
le leur	**la leur**	theirs

Plural Masc.	Plural Fem.	English Equivalent
les miens	**les miennes**	mine
les tiens	**les tiennes**	yours (informal)
les siens	**les siennes**	his, hers
les nôtres	**les nôtres**	ours
les vôtres	**les vôtres**	yours (formal)
les leurs	**les leurs**	theirs

Demonstratives

1. Demonstrative Adjectives

French demonstrative adjectives agree with the nouns they modify in gender and number, and precede them in a sentence. The demonstrative adjectives in French are:

ce masculine singular: *ce mur,* this wall

cet masculine singular, used when the following word begins with a vowel sound: *cet homme,* that man

cette feminine singular: *cette femme,* this woman

ces plural, does not vary for gender: *ces hommes,* these men; *ces femmes,* those women

When the difference between "this" and "that" or "these" and "those" cannot be ascertained from context, or if one wishes to stress the difference, the suffixes *-ci* and *-là* are added to the noun: *cet homme-ci,* this (particular) man; *ces hommes-là,* those (particular) men.

2. Demonstrative Pronouns

Demonstrative pronouns are used in place of a noun modified by *ce, cette,* or *ces* as outlined below:

CELUI AND VARIANTS

Pronouns belonging to the *celui* group always agree in gender and number with the noun which they replace. The pronouns are:

celui	masculine singular
ceux	masculine plural
celle	feminine singular
celles	feminine plural

j'ai reçu deux colis: le tien, et celui de ma sœur, I received two packages: yours, and my sister's

ceux qu'elle préfère sont plus chers, the ones she prefers are more costly

celles qui ont travaillé le plus sont Rose et Marie, the ones who worked the most are Rose and Marie

te souviens-tu de ce qu'elle t'a dit?, do you remember what she told you?

The suffixes *-ci* and *-là* are attached to the pronouns *celui, ceux, celle,* or *celles* for emphasis:

celui-ci est plus important que celui-là, this one is more important than that one

emporte-moi ceux-là, bring me those

CE

Ce does not change for gender and combines with *être* to form a rough equivalent of the English "it is" or "they are," but it differs somewhat in usage and application from its English counterpart. Note that *ce* contracts to *c'* when immediately followed by a vowel sound:

ce sont mes amis, they are my friends

ce sont eux qui me l'ont acheté, they're the ones who bought it for me

c'est chouette!, that's great!

c'est un médecin, he's a doctor, she's a doctor

est-ce vrai?, is it true?

ÇA, CECI, AND *CELA*

The demonstrative pronouns *ça, ceci,* and *cela* act as rough equivalents of the English "this" or "that," with some differences in usage and application:

ça m'est égal, it's all the same to me, it doesn't matter to me

oui, c'est ça!, yes, that's it!

ceci n'est qu'un test, this is only a test

ceci et cela, this and that

Although *cela* and *ça* are often interchangeable, *ça* tends to be used more frequently in spoken French.

Conjugation of French Verbs

Simple Tenses

Tense	Regular verbs ending in -ER PARLER	
PRESENT INDICATIVE	je parle tu parles il parle	nous parlons vous parlez ils parlent
PRESENT SUBJUNCTIVE	je parle tu parles il parle	nous parlions vous parliez ils parlent
PRETERIT INDICATIVE	je parlai tu parlas il parla	nous parlâmes vous parlâtes ils parlèrent
IMPERFECT INDICATIVE	je parlais tu parlais il parlait	nous parlions vous parliez ils parlaient
IMPERFECT SUBJUNCTIVE	je parlasse tu parlasses il parlât	nous parlassions vous parlassiez ils parlassent
FUTURE INDICATIVE	je parlerai tu parleras il parlera	nous parlerons vous parlerez ils parleront
CONDITIONAL	je parlerais tu parlerais il parlerait	nous parlerions vous parleriez ils parleraient
IMPERATIVE	 parle, parlez	parlons parlez
PRESENT PARTICIPLE (GERUND)	parlant	
PAST PARTICIPLE	parlé	

Tense	Regular verbs ending in -IR GRANDIR	
PRESENT INDICATIVE	je grandis tu grandis il grandit	nous grandissons vous grandissez ils grandissent
PRESENT SUBJUNCTIVE	je grandisse tu grandisses il grandisse	nous grandissions vous grandissiez ils grandissent
PRETERIT INDICATIVE	je grandis tu grandis il grandit	nous grandîmes vous grandîtes ils grandirent
IMPERFECT INDICATIVE	je grandissais tu grandissais il grandissait	nous grandissions vous grandissiez ils grandissaient
IMPERFECT SUBJUNCTIVE	je grandisse tu grandisses il grandît	nous grandissions vous grandissiez ils grandissent
FUTURE INDICATIVE	je grandirai tu grandiras il grandira	nous grandirons vous grandirez ils grandiront
CONDITIONAL	je grandirais tu grandirais il grandirait	nous grandirions vous grandiriez ils grandiraient
IMPERATIVE	grandis, grandissez	grandissons grandissez
PRESENT PARTICIPLE (GERUND)	grandissant	
PAST PARTICIPLE	grandi	

Perfect Tenses

The perfect tenses are formed with *avoir* and the past participle:

PRESENT PERFECT

j'ai parlé, nous avons parlé, etc. (*indicative*)
j'aie parlé, nous ayons parlé, etc. (*subjunctive*)

PAST PERFECT

j'avais parlé, nous avions parlé, etc. (*indicative*)
j'eusse parlé, nous eussions parlé, etc. (*subjunctive*)

PRETERIT PERFECT

j'eus parlé, nous eûmes parlé, etc.

FUTURE PERFECT

j'aurai parlé, nous aurons parlé, etc.

CONDITIONAL PERFECT

j'aurais parlé, nous aurions parlé, etc.
or
j'eusse parlé, nous eussions parlé, etc.

PAST IMPERATIVE

aie parlé, ayons parlé, ayez parlé

The perfect tenses of the following verbs are formed with *être*:

aller, arriver, décéder, devenir, échoir, éclore, entrer, mourir, naître, partir, repartir, rentrer, rester, retourner, sortir, tomber, venir, revenir, parvenir, survenir

For example, the present perfect of *arriver* would be as follows:

je suis arrivé, nous sommes arrivés, etc. (*indicative*)

Irregular Verbs

The *imperfect subjunctive*, the *conditional,* and the first and second person plural of the *imperative* are not included in the model conjugations list but can be derived from other verb forms:

The *imperfect subjunctive* is formed by using the second person singular of the preterit indicative, removing the final *s,* and adding the following suffixes: *-sse, -sses, -t* (and adding a circumflex accent on the preceding vowel), *-ssions, -ssiez, -ssent*. *Servir* is conjugated as follows:

PRETERIT INDICATIVE, SECOND PERSON SINGULAR	servis – *s* = servi
IMPERFECT SUBJUNCTIVE	je servisse, tu servisses, il servît, nous servissions, vous servissiez, ils servissent

The conditional is formed by using the stem of the future indicative and adding the following suffixes : *-ais, -ais, -ait, -ions, -iez,- aient*. *Prendre* is conjugated as follows:

FUTURE INDICATIVE	je prendrai – *ai* = prendr
CONDITIONAL	je prendrais, tu prendrais, il prendrait, nous prendrions, vous prendriez, ils prendraient

The first and second person plural of the *imperative* are the same as the corresponding forms of the present indicative.

Model Conjugations of Irregular Verbs

The model conjugations below include the following simple tenses : the *present indicative* (IND), the *present subjunctive* (SUBJ), the *preterit indicative* (PRET), the *imperfect indicative* (IMPF), the *future indicative* (FUT), the second person singular form of the *imperative* (IMPER), the *present participle* or *gerund* (PRP), and the *past participle* (PP). Each set of conjugations is preceded by the corresponding infinitive form of the verb, shown in bold type. Only tenses containing irregularities are listed, and the irregular verb forms within each tense are displayed in bold type.

Also note that some conjugated verbs are labeled *defective verb*. This refers to a verb lacking one or more of the usual forms of grammatical inflection (tense, mood, etc.), for example, in French, the verbs *bruire* and *ouïr*.

Each irregular verb entry in the French-English section of this dictionary is cross-referred by number to one of the following model conjugations. These cross-reference numbers are shown in curly braces { } immediately preceding the entry's functional label.

The three main categories of verbs are:

1) Verbs ending in -ER

2) Verbs ending in -IR

Present indicative endings for verbs in these categories are:

-is, -is, -it, -issons, -issez, -issent

For example, *j'arrondis, nous arrondissons,* etc. for infinitive *arrondir*

3) Verbs ending in -IR/-OIR/-RE

Present indicative endings for verbs in these categories are:

-e, -es, -e, -ons, -ez, -ent

For example, *j'accueille, nous accueillons,* etc. for infinitive *accueillir*

or

-s(x), -s(x), -t(d), -ons, -ez, -ent

For example, *je rends, nous rendons,* etc. for infinitive *rendre*

Note that in the third group there are two different sets of endings for both the present indicative and preterit indicative depending on the verb in question, as shown above for the present indicative. For clarity, these forms are included in the model conjugations in an attempt to prevent the reader from inadvertently choosing the wrong endings.

1 **absoudre :** *IND* **j'absous, tu absous, il absout, nous absolvons, vous absolvez, ils absolvent;** *SUBJ* **j'absolve, tu absolves, il absolve, nous absolvions, vous absolviez, ils absolvent;** *PRET* (*not used*); *IMPF* **j'absolvais, tu absolvais, il absolvait, nous absolvions, vous absolviez, ils absolvaient;** *IMPER* **absous;** *PRP* **absolvant;** *PP* **absous**

2 **accroire** (*defective verb*) *Used only in the infinitive*

3 **accueillir** : *IND* **j'accueille, tu accueilles, il accueille,** nous accueillons, vous accueillez, ils accueillent; *PRET* **j'accueillis, tu accueillis, il accueillit, nous accueillîmes, vous accueillîtes, ils accueillirent;** *FUT* **j'accueillerai, tu accueilleras, il accueillera, nous accueillerons, vous accueillerez, ils accueilleront;** *IMPER* **j'accueille**

4 **advenir** (*defective verb) Used only in the infinitive and in the following tenses* : *IND* **il advient;** *SUBJ* **il advienne;** *PRET* **il advint;** *IMPF* **il advenait;** *FUT* **il adviendra;** *PRP* **advenant;** *PP* **advenu**

5 **aller** : *IND* **je vais, tu vas, il va, nous allons, vous allez, ils vont;** *SUBJ* **j'aille, tu ailles, il aille, nous allions, vous alliez, ils aillent;** *FUT* **j'irai, tu iras, il ira, nous irons, vous irez, ils iront;** *IMPER* **va**

6 **annoncer** : *IND* j'annonce, tu annonces, il annonce, **nous annonçons,** vous annoncez, ils annoncent; *PRET* **j'annonçai, tu annonças, il annonça, nous annonçâmes, vous annonçâtes, ils annoncèrent;** *IMPF* **j'annonçais, tu annonçais, il annonçait,** nous annoncions, vous annonciez, **ils annonçaient;** *PRP* **annonçant**

7 **apparaître** : *IND* **j'apparais, tu apparais, il apparaît, nous apparaissons, vous apparaissez, ils apparaissent;** *SUBJ* **j'apparaisse, tu apparaisses, il apparaisse, nous apparaissions, vous appparaissiez, ils apparaissent;** *PRET* **j'apparus, tu apparus, il apparut, nous apparûmes, vous apparûtes, ils apparurent;** *IMPF* **j'apparaissais, tu apparaissais, il apparaissait, nous apparaissions, vous apparaissiez, ils apparaissaient;** *IMPER* **apparais;** *PRP* **apparaissant;** *PP* **apparu**

8 **appeler** : *IND* **j'appelle, tu appelles, il appelle,** nous appelons, vous appelez, **ils appellent;** *SUBJ* **j'appelle, tu appelles, il appelle,** nous appelions, vous appeliez, **ils appellent;** *FUT* **j'appellerai, tu appelleras, il appellera, nous appellerons, vous appellerez, ils appelleront;** *IMPER* **appelle**

9 **asseoir** : *IND* **j'assieds** *or* **j'assois, tu assieds** *or* **tu assois, il assied** *or* **il assoit, nous asseyons** *or* **nous assoyons, vous asseyez** *or* **vous assoyez, ils asseyent** *or* **ils assoient;** *SUBJ* **j'asseye** *or* **j'assoie, tu asseyes** *or* **tu assoies, il asseye** *or* **il assoie, nous asseyions** *or* **nous assoyions, vous asseyiez** *or*

vous assoyiez, ils asseyent *or* **ils assoient;** *PRET* **j'assis, tu assis, il assit, nous assîmes, vous assîtes, ils assirent;** *IMPF* **j'asseyais** *or* **j'assoyais, tu asseyais** *or* **tu assoyais, il asseyait** *or* **il assoyait, nous asseyions** *or* **nous assoyions, vous asseyiez** *or* **vous assoyiez, ils asseyaient** *or* **ils assoyaient;** *FUT* (*not used*); *IMPER* **assieds** *or* **assois;** *PRP* **asseyant** *or* **assoyant;** *PP* **assis**

10 **avoir :** *IND* **j'ai, tu as, il a, nous avons, vous avez, ils ont;** *SUBJ* **j'aie, tu aies, il ait, nous ayons, vous ayez, ils aient;** *PRET* **j'eus, tu eus, il eut, nous eûmes, vous eûtes, ils eurent;** *IMPF* **j'avais, tu avais, il avait, nous avions, vous aviez, ils avaient;** *FUT* **j'aurai, tu auras, il aura, nous aurons, vous aurez, ils auront;** *IMPER* **aie, ayons ayez;** *PRP* **ayant;** *PP* **eu**

11 **balayer :** *IND* **je balaie** *or* je balaye, **tu balaies** *or* tu balayes, **il balaie** *or* il balaye, nous balayons, vous balayez, **ils balaient** *or* ils balayent; *SUBJ* **je balaie** *or* je balaye, **tu balaies** *or* tu balayes, **il balaie** *or* il balaye, nous balayions, vous balayiez, **ils balaient** *or* ils balayent; *FUT* **je balaierai** *or* je balayerai, **tu balaieras** *or* tu balayeras, **il balaiera** *or* il balayera, **nous balaierons** *or* nous balayerons, **vous balaierez** *or* vous balayerez, **ils balaieront** *or* ils balayeront; *IMPER* **balaie** *or* balaye

12 **battre :** *IND* **je bats, tu bats, il bat,** nous battons, vous battez, ils battent; *PRET* **je battis, tu battis, il battit, nous battîmes, vous battîtes, ils battirent;** *IMPER* **bats;** *PP* **battu**

13 **boire :** *IND* je bois, tu bois, il boit, **nous buvons, vous buvez, ils boivent;** *SUBJ* **je boive, tu boives, il boive, nous buvions, vous buviez, ils boivent;** *PRET* **je bus, tu bus, il but, nous bûmes, vous bûtes, ils burent;** *IMPF* **je buvais, tu buvais, il buvait, nous buvions, vous buviez, ils buvaient;** *PRP* **buvant;** *PP* **bu**

14 **bouillir :** *IND* **je bous, tu bous, il bout,** nous bouillons, vous bouillez, ils bouillent; *PRET* **je bouillis, tu bouillis, il bouillit, nous bouillîmes, vous bouillîtes, ils bouillirent;** *IMPER* **bous**

15 **braire** (*defective verb*) *Used only in the infinitive and in the following tenses* : *IND* **il brait, ils braient;** *IMPF* **brayait, brayaient;** *FUT* **il braira, ils brairont**

16 **bruire** (*defective verb*) *Used only in the infinitive and in the following tenses* : *IND* **il bruit, ils bruissent;** *SUBJ* (*not used*); *PRET* (*not used*); *IMPF* **il bruissait, ils bruissaient;** *PRP* **bruissant;** *PP* **bruit**

17 **changer** : *IND* je change, tu changes, il change, **nous changeons,** vous changez, ils changent; *PRET* **je changeai, tu changeas, il changea, nous changeâmes, vous changeâtes, ils changèrent;** *IMPF* **je changeais, tu changeais, il changeait,** nous changions, vous changiez, **ils changeaient;** *PRP* **changeant**

18 **choir** (*defective verb*) *Used only in the following tenses* : *IND* **je chois, tu chois, il choit, ils choient;** *SUBJ* (*not used*); *PRET* **il chut;** *IMPF* (*not used*); *FUT* il choira; *IMPER* (*not used*); *PRP* (*not used*); *PP* **chu**

19 **clore** (*defective verb*) *Used only in the following tenses* : *IND* je clos, tu clos, **il clôt, ils closent;** *SUBJ* **je close, tu closes, il close, nous closions, vous closiez, ils closent;** *PRET* (*not used*); *IMPF* (*not used*); *FUT* (*used but regularly formed*); *PRP* **closant;** *PP* **clos**

20 **congeler** : *IND* **je congèle, tu congèles, il congèle,** nous congelons, vous congelez, **ils congèlent;** *SUBJ* **je congèle, tu congèles, il congèle,** nous congelions, vous congeliez, **ils congèlent;** *FUT* **je congèlerai, tu congèleras, il congèlera, nous congèlerons, vous congèlerez, ils congèleront;** *IMPER* **congèle**

21 **conquérir** : *IND* **je conquiers, tu conquiers, il conquiert,** nous conquérons, vous conquérez, **ils conquièrent;** *SUBJ* **je conquière, tu conquières, il conquière,** nous conquérions, vous conquériez, **ils conquièrent;** *PRET* **je conquis, tu conquis, il conquit, nous conquîmes, vous conquîtes, ils conquirent;** *FUT* **je conquerrai, tu conquerras, il conquerra, nous conquerrons, vous conquerrez, ils conquerront;** *IMPER* **conquiers;** *PP* **conquis**

22 **coudre** : *IND* je couds, tu couds, il coud, **nous cousons, vous cousez, ils cousent;** *SUBJ* **je couse, tu couses, il couse, nous cousions, vous cousiez, ils cousent;** *PRET* **je cousis, tu cousis, il cousit, nous cousîmes, vous cousîtes, ils cousirent;** *IMPF* **je cousais, tu cousais, il cousait, nous cousions, vous cousiez, ils cousaient;** *PRP* **cousant;** *PP* **cousu**

23 **courir** : *IND* **je cours, tu cours, il court**, nous courons, vous courez, ils courent; *PRET* **je courus, tu courus, il courut, nous courûmes, vous courûtes, ils coururent**; *FUT* **je courrai, tu courras, il courra, nous courrons, vous courrez, ils courront**; *IMPER* **cours**; *PP* **couru**

24 **croire** : *IND* je crois, tu crois, il croit, **nous croyons, vous croyez**, ils croient; *SUBJ* je croie, tu croies, il croie, **nous croyions, vous croyiez**, ils croient; *PRET* **je crus, tu crus, il crut, nous crûmes, vous crûtes, il crurent**; *IMPF* **je croyais, tu croyais, il croyait, nous croyions, vous croyiez, ils croyaient**; *PRP* **croyant**; *PP* **cru**

25 **croître** : *IND* **je croîs, tu croîs, il croît, nous croissons, vous croissez, ils croissent**; *SUBJ* **je croisse, tu croisses, il croisse, nous croissions, vous croissiez, ils croissent**; *PRET* **je crûs, tu crûs, il crût, nous crûmes, vous crûtes, ils crûrent**; *IMPF* **je croissais, tu croissais, il croissait, nous croissions, vous croissiez, ils croissaient**; *IMPER* **croîs**; *PRP* **croissant**; *PP* **crû**

26 **décevoir** : *IND* **je déçois, tu déçois, il déçoit**, nous décevons, vous décevez, **ils déçoivent**; *SUBJ* **je déçoive, tu déçoives, il déçoive**, nous décevions, vous déceviez, **ils déçoivent**; *PRET* **je déçus, tu déçus, il déçut, nous déçûmes, vous déçûtes, ils déçurent**; *IMPER* **déçois**; *PP* **déçu**

27 **déchoir** (*defective verb*) *Used only in the following tenses* : *IND* je déchois, tu déchois, il déchoit *or* **il déchet, nous déchoyons, vous déchoyez, ils déchoient**; *SUBJ* je déchoie, tu déchoies, il déchoie, **nous déchoyions, vous déchoyiez, ils déchoient**; *PRET* **je déchus, tu déchus, il déchut, nous déchûmes, vous déchûtes, ils déchurent**; *IMPF* (*not used*); *FUT* (*used but regularly formed*); *IMPER* (*not used*); *PRP* (*not used*); *PP* **déchu**

28 **devoir** : *IND* **je dois, tu dois, il doit**, nous devons, vous devez, **ils doivent**; *SUBJ* **je doive, tu doives, il doive**, nous devions, vous deviez, **ils doivent**; *PRET* **je dus, tu dus, il dut, nous dûmes, vous dûtes, ils durent**; *IMPER* **dois**; *PRP* **dû**

29 **dire** : *IND* je dis, tu dis, il dit, **nous disons, vous dites, ils disent**; *SUBJ* **je dise, tu dises, il dise, nous disions, vous disiez, ils disent**; *PRET* **je dis, tu dis, il dit, nous dîmes,**

vous dîtes, ils dirent; *IMPF* **je disais, tu disais, il disait, nous disions, vous disiez, ils disent;** *PRP* **disant;** *PP* **dit**

30 **dormir :** *IND* **je dors, tu dors, il dort**, nous dormons, vous dormez, ils dorment; *PRET* **je dormis, tu dormis, il dormit, nous dormîmes, vous dormîtes, ils dormirent;** *IMPER* **dors**

31 **échoir** (*defective verb*) *Used only in the following tenses* : *IND* **il échoit, ils échoient;** *SUBJ* **il échoie;** *PRET* **il échut, ils échurent;** *IMPF* (not used); *FUT* il échoira *or* **il écherra**; ils échoiront *or* **ils écherront;** *IMPER* (not used); *PRP* **échéant;** *PP* **échu**

32 **éclore** (*defective verb) Used only in the following tenses* : *IND* **il éclot;** *PP* **éclos**

33 **écrire :** *IND* j'écris, tu écris, il écrit, **nous écrivons, vous écrivez, ils écrivent;** *SUBJ* **j'écrive, tu écrives, il écrive, nous écrivions, vous écriviez, ils écrivent;** *PRET* **j'écrivis, tu écrivis, il écrivit, nous écrivîmes, vous écrivîtes, ils écrivirent;** *IMPF* **j'écrivais, tu écrivais, il écrivait, nous écrivions, vous écriviez, ils écrivaient;** *PRP* **écrivant;** *PP* **écrit**

34 **enclore** (*defective verb*) *Used only in the following tenses* : *IND* j'enclos, tu enclos, il enclot, **nous enclosons, vous enclosez, ils enclosent;** *SUBJ* **j'enclose, tu encloses, il enclose, nous enclosions, vous enclosiez, ils enclosent;** *PRET* (*not used*); *IMPF* (*not used*); *FUT* (*used but regularly formed*); *IMPER* enclos; *PRP* **enclosant;** *PP* **enclos**

35 **ensuivre (s')** (*defective verb*) *Used only in the following tenses* : *IND* **il s'ensuit;** *SUBJ* **il s'ensuive;** *PRET* **il s'ensuivit;** *IMPF* **il s'ensuivait;** *FUT* **il s'ensuivra;** *PP* **s'ensuivi**

36 **envoyer :** *IND* **j'envoie, tu envoies, il envoie**, nous envoyons, vous envoyez, **ils envoient;** *SUBJ* **j'envoie, tu envoies, il envoie**, nous envoyions, vous envoyiez, **ils envoient;** *FUT* **j'enverrai, tu enverras, il enverra, nous enverrons, vous enverrez, ils enverront;** *IMPER* **envoie**

37 **éteindre :** *IND* **j'éteins, tu éteins, il éteint, nous éteignons, vous éteignez, ils éteignent;** *SUBJ* **j'éteigne, tu éteignes, il éteigne, nous éteignions, vous éteigniez, ils éteignent;** *PRET* **j'éteignis, tu éteignis, il éteignit, nous éteignîmes, vous éteignîtes, ils éteignirent;** *IMPF* **j'éteignais, tu éteignais, il**

éteignait, nous éteignions, vous éteigniez, ils éteignaient; *IMPER* **j'éteins;** *PRP* **éteignant;** *PP* **éteint**

38 **être :** *IND* **je suis, tu es, il est, nous sommes, vous êtes, ils sont;** *SUBJ* **je sois, tu sois, il soit, nous soyons, vous soyez, ils soient;** *PRET* **je fus, tu fus, il fut, nous fûmes, vous fûtes, ils furent;** *IMPF* **j'étais, tu étais, il était, nous étions, vous étiez, ils étaient;** *FUT* **je serai, tu seras, il sera, nous serons, vous serez, ils seront;** *IMPER* **sois;** *PRP* **étant;** *PP* **été**

39 **exclure :** *IND* **j'exclus, tu exclus, il exclut, nous excluons, vous excluez, ils excluent;** *PRET* **j'exclus, tu exclus, il exclut, nous exclûmes, vous exclûtes, ils exclurent;** *IMPER* **exclus;** *PP* **exclu**

40 **extraire :** *IND* j'extrais, tu extrais, il extrait, **nous extrayons, vous extrayez**, ils extraient; *SUBJ* j'extraie, tu extraies, il extraie, **nous extrayions, vous extrayiez**, ils extraient; *PRET* (not used); *IMPF* **j'extrayais, tu extrayais, il extrayait, nous extrayions, vous extrayiez, ils extrayaient;** *PRP* **extrayant;** *PP* **extrait**

41 **faillir (***defective verb) Used only in the infinitve and as a* *PP* **failli**

42 **faire :** *IND* je fais, tu fais, ils fait, **nous faisons, vous faites, ils font;** *SUBJ* **je fasse, tu fasses, il fasse, nous fassions, vous fassiez, ils fassent;** *PRET* **je fis, tu fis, il fit, nous fîmes, vous fîtes, ils firent;** *IMPF* **je faisais, tu faisais, il faisait, nous faisions, vous faisiez, ils faisaient;** *FUT* **je ferai, tu feras, il fera, nous ferons, vous ferez, ils feront;** *PRP* **faisant;** *PP* **fait**

43 **falloir (***defective verb***)** *Used only in the following tenses* **:** *IND* **il faut;** *SUBJ* **il faille;** *PRET* **il fallut;** *IMPF* **il fallait;** *FUT* **il faudra;** *IMPER* (not used); *PRP* **(***not used***);** *PP* **fallu**

44 **forfaire (***defective verb) Used only in the infinitive and in the following tenses* **:** *IND* **il forfait;** *PP* **forfait**

45 **frire (***defective verb***)** *Used only in the following tenses* **:** *IND* **je fris, tu fris, il frit;** *FUT* je frirai, tu friras, il frira, nous frirons, vous frirez, ils friront; *IMPER* **fris;** *PP* **frit**

46 **fuir :** *IND* je fuis, tu fuis, il fuit, **nous fuyons, vous fuyez, ils fuient;** *SUBJ* je fuie, tu fuies, il fuie, **nous fuyions, vous**

fuyiez, ils fuient; *PRET* je fuis, tu fuis, il fuit, **nous fuîmes, vous fuîtes, ils fuirent;** *IMPF* **je fuyais, tu fuyais, il fuyait, nous fuyions, vous fuyiez, ils fuyaient;** *PRP* **fuyant;** *PP* **fui**

47 **gésir** (*defective verb*) *Used only in the following tenses* : *IND* **je gis, tu gis, il gît, nous gisons, vous gisez, ils gisent;** *IMPF* **je gisais, tu gisais, il gisait, nous gisions, vous gisiez, ils gisaient;** *PRP* **gisant**

48 **haïr** : *IND* **je hais, tu hais, il hait, nous haïssons, vous haïssez, ils haïssent;** *SUBJ* **je haïsse, tu haïsses, il haïsse, nous haïssions, vous haïssiez, ils haïssent;** *PRET* **je haïs, tu haïs, il haït, nous haïmes, vous haïtes, ils haïrent;** *IMPF* **je haïssais, tu haïssais, il haïssait, nous haïssions, vous haïsssiez, ils haïssaient;** *IMPER* **hais;** *PRP* **haïssant;** *PP* **haï**

49 **instruire** : *IND* j'instruis, tu instruis, il instruit, **nous instruisons, vous instruisez, ils instruisent;** *SUBJ* **j'instruise, tu instruises, il instruise, nous instruisions, vous instruisiez, ils instruisent;** *PRET* **j'instruisis, tu instruisis, il instruisit, nous instruisîmes, vous instruisîtes, ils instruisirent;** *IMPF* **j'instruisais, tu instruisais, il instruisait, nous instruisions, vous instruisiez, ils instruisaient;** *PRP* **instruisant;** *PP* **instruit**

50 **joindre** : *IND* **je joins, tu joins, il joint, nous joignons, vous joignez, ils joignent;** *SUBJ* **je joigne, tu joignes, il joigne, nous joignions, vous joigniez, ils joignent;** *PRET* **je joignis, tu joignis, il joignit, nous joignîmes, vous joignîtes, ils joignirent;** *IMPF* **je joignais, tu joignais, il joignait, nous joignions, vous joigniez, ils joignaient;** *IMPERF* **joins;** *PRP* **joignant;** *PP* **joint**

51 **lire** : *IND* je lis, tu lis, il lit, **nous lisons, vous lisez, ils lisent;** *SUBJ* **je lise, tu lises, il lise, nous lisions, vous lisiez, ils lisent;** *PRET* **je lus, tu lus, il lut, nous lûmes, vous lûtes, ils lurent;** *IMPF* **je lisais, tu lisais, il lisait, nous lisions, vous lisiez, ils lisaient;** *PRP* **lisant;** *PP* **lu**

52 **mener** : *IND* **je mène, tu mènes, il mène,** nous menons, vous menez, **ils mènent;** *SUBJ* **je mène, tu mènes, il mène,** nous menions, vous meniez, **ils mènent;** *FUT* **je mènerai, tu mèneras, il mènera, nous mènerons, vous mènerez, ils mèneront;** *IMPER* **mène**

53 **mettre :** *IND* **je mets, tu mets, il met,** nous mettons, vous mettez, ils mettent; *PRET* **je mis, tu mis, il mit, nous mîmes, vous mîtes, il mirent;** *IMPER* **mets;** *PP* **mis**

54 **moudre :** *IND* je mouds, tu mouds, il moud, **nous moulons, vous moulez, ils moulent;** *SUBJ* **je moule, tu moules, il moule, nous moulions, vous mouliez, ils moulent;** *PRET* **je moulus, tu moulus, il moulut, nous moulûmes, vous moulûtes, ils moulurent;** *IMPF* **je moulais, tu moulais, il moulait, nous moulions, vous mouliez, ils moulaient;** *PRP* **moulant;** *PP* **moulu**

55 **mourir :** *IND* **je meurs, tu meurs, il meurt,** nous mourons, vous mourez, **ils meurent;** *SUBJ* **je meure, tu meures, il meure,** nous mourions, vous mouriez, **ils meurent;** *PRET* **je mourus, tu mourus, il mourut, nous mourûmes, vous mourûtes, ils moururent;** *FUT* **je mourrai, tu mourras, il mourra, nous mourrons, vous mourrez, ils mourront;** *IMPER* **meurs;** *PRP* **mourant;** *PP* **mort**

56 **mouvoir :** *IND* **je meus, tu meus, il meut,** nous mouvons, vous mouvez, **ils meuvent;** *SUBJ* **je meuve, tu meuves, il meuve,** nous mouvions, vous mouviez, **ils meuvent;** *PRET* **je mus, tu mus, il mut, nous mûmes, vous mûtes, ils murent;** *IMPER* **meus;** *PP* **mû**

57 **naître :** *IND* **je nais, tu nais, il naît, nous naissons, vous naissez, ils naissent;** *SUBJ* **je naisse, tu naisses, il naisse, nous naissions, vous naissiez, ils naissent;** *PRET* **je naquis, tu naquis, il naquit, nous naquîmes, vous naquîtes, ils naquirent;** *IMPF* **je naissais, tu naissais, il naissait, nous naissions, vous naissiez, ils naissaient;** *IMPER* **nais;** *PRP* **naissant;** *PP* **né**

58 **nettoyer :** *IND* **je nettoie, tu nettoies, il nettoie,** nous nettoyons, vous nettoyez, **ils nettoient;** *SUBJ* **je nettoie, tu nettoies, il nettoie,** nous nettoyions, vous nettoyiez, **ils nettoient;** *FUT* **je nettoierai, tu nettoieras, il nettoiera, nous nettoierons, vous nettoierez, ils nettoieront;** *IMPER* **je nettoie**

59 **oindre** (*defective verb*) *Used only in the infinitive and as a* PP **oint**

60 **ouïr** (*defective verb*) *Used only in the infinitive and as a* PP **ouï**

61 **paître** (*defective verb*) *Used only in the following tenses* : *IND* **je pais, tu pais, il paît, nous paissons, vous paissez, ils paissent;** *SUBJ* **je paisse, tu paisses, il paisse, nous paissions, vous paissiez, ils paissent;** *PRET* (*not used*); *IMPF* **je paissais, tu paissais, il paissait, nous paissions, vous paissiez, ils paissaient;** *FUT* (*used but regular*); *IMPER* **pais;** *PRP* **paissant;** *PP* (*not used*)

62 **parfaire** (*defective verb*) *Used only in the infinitive and in the following tenses IND* **il parfait;** *PP* **parfait**

63 **perdre** : *IND* je perds, tu perds, **il perd**, nous perdons, vous perdez, ils perdent; *PRET* **je perdis, tu perdis, il perdit, nous perdîmes, vous perdîtes, ils perdirent;** *PP* **perdu**

64 **piéger** : *IND* **je piège, tu pièges, il piège, nous piégeons**, vous piégez, **ils piègent;** *SUBJ* **je piège, tu pièges, il piège**, nous piégions, vous piégiez, **ils piègent;** *PRET* **je piégeai, tu piégeas, il piégea, nous piégeâmes, vous piégeâtes, ils piégèrent;** *IMPF* **je piégeais, tu piégeais, il piégeait**, nous piégions, vous piégiez, **ils piégeaient;** *IMPER* **piège;** *PRP* **piégeant;** *PP* **piégé**

65 **plaindre** : *IND* je plains, tu plains, il plaint, **nous plaignons, vous plaignez, ils plaignent;** *SUBJ* **je plaigne, tu plaignes, il plaigne, nous plagnions, vous plagniez, ils plaignent;** *PRET* **je plaignis, tu plaignis, il plaignit, nous plaignîmes, vous plaignîtes, ils plaignirent;** *IMPF* **je plaignais, tu plaignais, il plaignait, nous plaignions, vous plaigniez, ils plaignaient;** *PRP* **plaignant;** *PP* **plaint**

66 **plaire** : *IND* je plais, tu plais, **il plaît, nous plaisons, vous plaisez, ils plaisent;** *SUBJ* **je plaise, tu plaises, il plaise, nous plaisions, vous plaisiez, ils plaisent;** *PRET* **je plus, tu plus, il plut, nous plûmes, vous plûtes, ils plurent;** *IMPF* **je plaisais, tu plaisais, il plaisait, nous plaisions, vous plaisiez, ils plaisaient;** *PRP* **plaisant;** *PP* **plu**

67 **pleuvoir** (*defective verb*) *Used in the infinitive and in the following tenses IND* **il pleut, ils pleuvent** (*only in the figurative*); *SUBJ* **il pleuve, ils pleuvent** (*only in the figurative*); *PRET* **il plut;** *IMPF* **il pleuvait, ils pleuvaient** (*only in the figurative*); *FUT* **il pleuvra;** *IMPER* (not used); *PRP* **pleuvant;** *PP* **plu**

68 **pourvoir** : *IND* **je pourvois, tu pourvois, il pourvoit, nous**

pourvoyons, vous pourvoyez, ils pourvoient; *SUBJ* **je pourvoie, tu pourvoies, il pourvoie, nous pourvoyions, vous pourvoyiez, ils pourvoient;** *PRET* **je pourvus, tu pourvus, il pourvut, nous pourvûmes, vous pourvûtes, ils pourvurent;** *IMPF* **je pourvoyais, tu pourvoyais, il pourvoyait, nous pourvoyions, vous pourvoyiez, ils pourvoyaient;** *FUT* **je pourvoirai, tu pourvoiras, il pourvoira, nous pourvoirons, vous pourvoirez, ils pourvoiront;** *IMPER* **pourvois;** *PRP* **pourvoyant;** *PP* **pourvu**

69 **pouvoir :** *IND* **je peux** *or* **je puis, tu peux, il peut,** nous pouvons, vous pouvez, **ils peuvent;** *SUBJ* **je puisse, tu puisses, il puisse, nous puissions, vous puissiez, ils puissent;** *PRET* **je pus, tu pus, il put, nous pûmes, vous pûtes, ils purent;** *FUT* **je pourrai, tu pourras, il pourra, nous pourrons, vous pourrez, ils pourront;** *IMPER* (*not used*); *PP* **pu**

70 **prendre :** *IND* je prends, tu prends, **il prend, nous prenons, vous prenez, ils prennent;** *SUBJ* **je prenne, tu prennes, il prenne, nous prenions, vous preniez, ils prennent;** *PRET* **je pris, tu pris, il prit, nous prîmes, vous prîtes, ils prirent;** *IMPF* **je prenais, tu prenais, il prenait, nous prenions, vous preniez, ils prenaient;** *PRP* **prenant;** *PP* **pris**

71 **prévaloir :** *IND* **je prévaux, tu prévaux, il prévaut,** nous prévalons, vous prévalez, ils prévalent; *PRET* **je prévalus, tu prévalus, il prévalut, nous prévalûmes, vous prévalûtes, ils prévalurent;** *FUT* **je prévaudrai, tu prévaudras, il prévaudra, nous prévaudrons, vous prévaudrez, ils prévaudront;** *IMPER* **prévaux;** *PP* **prévalu**

72 **rassir** (*defective verb*) *Used only in the infinitive and as a* *PP* **rassis**

73 **ravoir** (*defective verb*) *Used only in the infinitive*

74 **résoudre :** *INF* **je résous, tu résous, il résout, nous résolvons, vous résolvez, ils résolvent;** *SUBJ* **je résolve, tu résolves, il résolve, nous résolvions, vous résolviez, ils résolvent;** *PRET* **je résolus, tu résolus, il résolut, nous résolûmes, vous résolûtes, ils résolurent;** *IMPF* **je résolvais, tu résolvais, il résolvait, nous résolvions, vous résolviez, ils résolvaient;** *IMPER* **résous;** *PRP* **résolvant;** *PP* **résolu**

75 **résulter** (*defective verb) Used only in the infinitive and in the following tenses* : *IND* **il résulte;** *PRP* **résultant**

76 **rire** : *IND* **je ris, tu ris, il rit, nous rions, vous riez, ils rient;** *SUBJ* je rie, tu ries, il rie, **nous riions, vous riiez,** ils rient; *PRET* **je ris, tu ris, il rit, nous rîmes, vous rîtes, ils rirent;** *IMPER* **ris;** *PP* **ri**

77 **rompre** : *IND* je romps, tu romps, **il rompt**, nous rompons, vous rompez, ils rompent; *PRET* **je rompis, tu rompis, il rompit, nous rompîmes, vous rompîtes, ils rompirent;** *PP* **rompu**

78 **saillir** : *IND* **je saille, tu sailles, il saille,** nous saillons, vous saillez, ils saillent; *PRET* **je saillis, tu sallis, il saillit, nous saillîmes, vous saillîtes, ils saillirent;** *FUT* **je saillerai, tu sailleras, il saillera, nous saillerons, vous saillerez, ils sailleront;** *IMPER* **saille**

79 **savoir** : *IND* **je sais, tu sais, il sait,** nous savons, vous savez, ils savent; *SUBJ* **je sache, tu saches, il sache, nous sachions, vous sachiez, ils sachent;** *PRET* **je sus, tu sus, il sut, nous sûmes, vous sûtes, ils surent;** *FUT* **je saurai, tu sauras, il saura, nous saurons, vous saurez, ils sauront;** *IMPER* **sache, sachons, sachez;** *PRP* **sachant;** *PP* **su**

80 **seoir** (*defective verb*) *Used in the following tenses* : *IND* **il sied, il siéent;** *SUBJ* **il siée, ils siéent;** *PRET* (*not used*); *IMPF* **il seyait, ils seyaient;** *FUT* **il siéra, ils siéront;** *IMPER* (*not used*); *PRP* **séant** *or* **seyant;** *PP* (*not used*)

81 **servir** : *IND* **je sers, tu sers, il sert,** nous servons, vous servez, ils servent; *PRET* **je servis, tu servis, il servit, nous servîmes, vous servîtes, ils servirent;** *FUT* **je servirai, tu serviras, il servira, nous servirons, vous servirez, ils serviront;** *IMPER* **sers;** *PP* **servi**

82 **sortir** : *IND* **je sors, tu sors, il sort,** nous sortons, vous sortez, ils sortent; *PRET* **je sortis, tu sortis, il sortit, nous sortîmes, vous sortîtes, ils sortirent;** *FUT* **je sortirai, tu sortiras, il sortira, nous sortirons, vous sortirez, ils sortiront;** *IMPER* **sors;** *PRP* **sortant;** *PP* **sorti**

83 **souffrir** : *IND* **je souffre, tu souffres, il souffre,** nous souffrons, vous souffrez, ils souffrent; *PRET* **je souffris, tu souf-**

fris, il souffrit, nous souffrîmes, vous souffrîtes, ils souffrirent; *FUT* **je souffrirai, tu souffriras, il souffrira, nous souffrirons, vous souffrirez, ils souffriront;** *IMPER* **je souffre;** *PP* **souffert**

84 **sourdre** (*defective verb*) *Used only in the infinitive and in the following tenses* : *IND* **il sourd, ils sourdent;** *IMPF* **il sourdait, ils sourdaient**

85 **stupéfaire** (*defective verb*) *Used only in the following tense* *PP* **stupéfié**

86 **suffire** : *IND* je suffis, tu suffis, il suffit, **nous suffisons, vous suffisez, ils suffisent;** *SUBJ* **je suffise, tu suffises, il suffise, nous suffisions, vous suffisiez, ils suffisent;** *PRET* **je suffis, tu suffis, il suffit, nous suffîmes, vous suffîtes, ils suffirent;** *IMPF* **je suffisais, tu suffisais, il suffisait, nous suffisions, vous suffisiez, ils suffisaient;** *PRP* **suffisant;** *PP* **suffi**

87 **suggérer** : *IND* **je suggère, tu suggères, il suggère,** nous suggérons, vous suggérez, **ils suggèrent;** *SUBJ* **je suggère, tu suggères, il suggère,** nous suggérions, vous suggériez, **ils suggèrent;** *IMPER* **suggère**

88 **suivre** : *IND* **je suis, tu suis, il suit,** nous suivons, vous suivez, ils suivent; *PRET* **je suivis, tu suivis, il suivit, nous suivîmes, vous suivîtes, ils suivirent;** *IMPER* **suis;** *PP* **suivi**

89 **suppléer** : *IND* **je supplée, tu supplées, il supplée, nous suppléons, vous suppléez, ils suppléent;** *SUBJ* **je supplée, tu supplées, il supplée, nous suppléions, vous suppléiez, ils suppléent;** *PRET* **je suppléai, tu suppléas, il suppléa, nous suppléâmes, vous suppléâtes, ils suppléèrent;** *FUT* **je suppléerai, tu suppléeras, il suppléera, nous suppléerons, vous suppléerez, ils suppléeront;** *IMPER* **supplée;** *PP* **suppléé**

90 **surseoir** : *IND* **je sursois, tu sursois, il sursoit, nous sursoyons, vous sursoyez, ils sursoient;** *SUBJ* **je sursoie, tu sursoies, il sursoie, nous sursoyions, vous sursoyiez, ils sursoient;** *PRET* **je sursis, tu sursis, il sursit, nous sursîmes, vous sursîtes, ils sursirent;** *IMPF* **je sursoyais, tu sursoyais, il sursoyait, nous sursoyions, vous sursoyiez, ils sursoyaient;** *FUT* **je surseoirai, tu surseoiras, il surseoira, nous surseoirons, vous surseoirez, ils surseoiront;** *IMPER* **sursois;** *PRP* **sursoyant;** *PP* **sursis**

91 **taire** : *IND* je tais, tu tais, **il tait, nous taisons, vous taisez, ils taisent;** *SUBJ* **je taise, tu taises, il taise, nous taisions, vous taisiez, ils taisent;** *PRET* **je tus, tu tus, il tut, nous tûmes, vous tûtes, ils turent;** *IMPF* **je taisais, tu taisais, il taisait, nous taisions, vous taisiez, ils taisaient;** *PRP* **taisant;** *PP* **tu**

92 **tenir** : *IND* **je tiens, tu tiens, il tient,** nous tenons, vous tenez, **ils tiennent;** *SUBJ* **je tienne, tu tiennes, il tienne,** nous tenions, vous teniez, **ils tiennent;** *PRET* **je tins, tu tins, il tint, nous tînmes, vous tîntes, ils tinrent;** *FUT* **je tiendrai, tu tiendras, il tiendra, nous tiendrons, vous tiendrez, ils tiendront;** *IMPER* **tiens;** *PP* **tenu**

93 **tressaillir** : *IND* **je tressaille, tu tressailles, il tressaille,** nous tressaillons, vous tressaillez, ils tressaillent; *PRET* **je tressaillis, tu tressaillis, il tressaillit, nous tressaillîmes, vous tressaillîtes, ils tressaillirent;** *FUT* **je tressaillirai, tu tressailliras, il tressaillira, nous tressaillirons, vous tressaillirez, ils tressailliront;** *IMPF* **tressaille;** *PP* **tressailli**

94 **vaincre** : *IND* **je vaincs, tu vaincs, il vainc, nous vainquons, vous vainquez, ils vainquent;** *SUBJ* **je vainque, tu vainques, il vainque, nous vainquions, vous vainquiez, ils vainquent;** *PRET* **je vainquis, tu vainquis, il vainquit, nous vainquîmes, vous vainquîtes, ils vainquirent;** *IMPF* **je vainquais, tu vainquais, il vainquait, nous vainquions, vous vainquiez, ils vainquaient;** *IMPER* **vaincs;** *PRP* **vainquant;** *PP* **vaincu**

95 **valoir** : *IND* **je vaux, tu vaux, il vaut,** nous valons, vous valez, ils valent; *SUBJ* **je vaille, tu vailles, il vaille,** nous valions, vous valiez, **ils vaillent;** *PRET* **je valus, tu valus, il valut, nous valûmes, vous valûtes, ils valurent;** *FUT* **je vaudrai, tu vaudras, il vaudra, nous vaudrons, vous vaudrez, ils vaudront;** *IMPER* **vaux;** *PP* **valu**

96 **vérifier** : *SUBJ* je vérifie, tu vérifies, il vérifie, **nous vérifiions, vous vérifiiez,** ils vérifient; *IMPF* je vérifiais, tu vérifiais, il vérifiait, **nous vérifiions, vous vérifiiez,** ils vérifiaient

97 **vêtir** : *IND* **je vêts, tu vêts, il vêt,** nous vêtons, vous vêtez, ils vêtent; *PRET* **je vêtis, tu vêtis, il vêtit, nous vêtîmes, vous vêtîtes, ils vêtirent;** *FUT* **je vêtirai, tu vêtiras, il vêtira, nous vêtirons, vous vêtirez, ils vêtiront;** *IMPER* **vêts;** *PP* **vêtu**

98 **vivre :** *IND* **je vis, tu vis, il vit,** nous vivons, vous vivez, ils vivent; *PRET* **je vécus, tu vécus, il vécut, nous vécûmes, vous vécûtes, ils vécurent**; *IMPER* **vis;** *PP* **vécu**

99 **voir :** *IND* je vois, tu vois, il voit, **nous voyons, vous voyez,** ils voient; *SUBJ* je voie, tu voies, il voie, **nous voyions, vous voyiez,** ils voient; *PRET* **je vis, tu vis, il vit, nous vîmes, vous vîtes, ils virent;** *IMPF* **je voyais, tu voyais, il voyait, nous voyions, vous voyiez, ils voyaient;** *FUT* **je verrai, tu verras, il verra, nous verrons, vous verrez, ils verront;** *PRP* **voyant;** *PP* **vu**

100 **vouloir :** *IND* **je veux, tu veux, il veut,** nous voulons, vous voulez, **ils veulent;** *SUBJ* **je veuille, tu veuilles, il veuille,** nous voulions, vous vouliez; **ils veuillent;** *PRET* **je voulus, tu voulus, il voulut, nous voulûmes, vous voulûtes, ils voulurent;** *FUT* **je voudrai, tu voudras, il voudra, nous voudrons, vous voudrez, ils voudront;** *IMPER* **veux** *or* **veuille;** *PP* **voulu**

Notes explicatives

Entrées

1. Mots-vedettes

Le mot-vedette est une lettre, un mot ou une phrase en caractères gras qui apparaît en début de ligne à l'extrême gauche de chaque colonne. Il est composé de lettres continues, de lettres unies par un signe de ponctuation (tel qu'un trait d'union) ou de lettres séparées par une espace:

> **collant**[1], **-lante** . . . *adj*
> **eye–opener** . . . *n* . . .
> **walk out** *vi*

Le mot-vedette, ainsi que le texte qui suit sur la même ligne et les lignes suivantes en alinéa, constitue une entrée ou un article du dictionnaire.

2. Ordre des entrées

Les entrées se succèdent en ordre alphabétique, lettre par lettre, sans tenir compte des espaces intermédiaires ou des traits d'union; par exemple, *shake-up* suit *shaker.*

Les homographes (mots qui ont la même orthographe) ayant des parties du discours différentes ont des entrées distinctes. Chacune des entrées est suivie d'un exposant:

> **mauvais**[1] . . . *adv* . . .
> **mauvais**[2], **-vaise** *adj* . . .
> **salt**[1] . . . *vt* . . .
> **salt**[2] *adj* . . .
> **salt**[3] *n* . . .

Les entrées homographiques numérotées sont classées dans l'ordre suivant: verbe, adverbe, adjectif, nom, conjonction, préposition, pronom, interjection, article.

Les homographes ayant des parties du discours semblables font généralement partie du même article même si leurs origines sémantiques varient. Par contre, des entrées séparées sont nécessaires si les homographes ont des prononciations distinctes ou si les verbes homographiques ont des conjugaisons distinctes.

3. Mots guides

Dans la marge supérieure de chaque page on retrouve deux mots guides, qui indiquent la première et la dernière entrée à apparaître sur la page:

velours • vérifiable

4. Variantes

Quand une entrée est suivie du mot *or* et d'une variante orthographique, les deux formes sont des variantes et peuvent être utilisées selon les inclinations de chacun:

jailer *or* **jailor** . . . *n* . . .
lis *or* **lys** . . . *nms & pl* . . .

Parfois, la variante orthographique ne se rapporte qu'à un seul sens d'un mot et se trouve donc directement après celui-ci:

flier . . . *n* . . . **2** *or* **flyer** . . .

À l'occasion, le mot-vedette est utilisé de façon interchangeable avec une phrase plus longue qui comprend aussi le mot-vedette. À toutes fins pratiques, on considère ces phrases comme étant des variantes de l'entrée:

bunk^2 *n* **1** *or* **bunk bed** . . .
risée . . . *nf or* **objet de risée** . . .
ward^1 . . . *vt or* **to ward off** . . .

Les locutions peuvent, à leur tour, présenter des variantes:

table . . . *nf* . . . **4 table de chevet** *or* **table de nuit** . . .

abattre . . . *vt* . . . **5 abattre ses cartes** *or* **abattre son jeu** . . .

5. Entrées secondaires

Une entrée peut être suivie d'un mot dérivé ayant une partie du discours distincte. Il s'agit d'une entrée secondaire. Elle est précédée d'un tiret en caractères gras et suivie d'une abréviation qui désigne la partie du discours, mais elle n'est pas définie puisque chaque équivalent, dans sa langue étrangère respective, peut être dérivé en ajoutant le suffixe approprié au terme utilisé pour définir le mot-vedette:

> **illegal** . . . *adj* : illégal — **illegally** *adv*
> (l'adverbe français est *illégalement*)
>
> **bureaucratie** . . . *nf* : bureaucracy — **bureaucratique** . . . *adj*
> (l'adjectif anglais est *bureaucratic*)

Dans la partie français-anglais du dictionnaire, les verbes pronominaux sont parfois des entrées secondaires non définies:

> **appauvrir** . . . *vt* : to impoverish — **s'appauvrir** *vr*

L'absence d'une définition signale au lecteur que le verbe pronominal *s'appauvrir* a une fonction purement réfléchie, ce qui élimine le besoin d'ajouter une définition superflue, par exemple, "to become impoverished" ou "to impoverish oneself."

6. Locutions

Une entrée peut être suivie d'une ou de plusieurs locutions en gras qui incluent le mot-vedette ou une forme fléchie de celui-ci. Chaque locution est numérotée en chiffres arabes:

> **abeille** . . . *nf* **1** : bee, honeybee **2 abeille mâle** : drone
>
> **hold**[1] . . . *vi* . . . **3 to hold forth** : . . . **4 to hold to** : . . .

Si la locution est composée du mot-vedette et d'une seule préposition, le mot-vedette est remplacé par un tiret ondulé en caractères gras:

> **pente** . . . *nf* **1** : slope **2 en ~** : sloping

La même locution peut avoir plus d'un sens numéroté si chaque sens a une signification particulière:

> **affaire** . . . *nf* . . . **5 affaires** *nfpl* : possessions, belongings **6 affaires** *nfpl* : business <homme d'affaires : businessman> . . .

Prononciation

Prononciation des mots-vedettes

La transcription phonétique apparaît entre crochets [ ] immédiatement après le mot-vedette; les symbôles utilisés proviennent de l'Association internationale de phonétique. Pour une explication des symbôles, on peut consulter le tableau à la page 92a intitulé Pronunciation Symbols.

Certaines entrées comprennent plusieurs prononciations, signalant que tous les locuteurs ne prononcent pas le mot de la même façon. Une variante placée en deuxième n'est pas pour autant moins acceptable que la première. En fait, elle peut être utilisée par autant de locuteurs que la première, mais les exigences de la page imprimée sont telles que l'une doit précéder l'autre:

> **often** [ˈɔfən, ˈɔftən] . . .

Quand un mot composé n'a qu'une prononciation partielle, la notation faisant défaut peut être obtenue à l'entrée correspondante du mot dont la prononciation a été omise:

> **gamma ray** [ˈgæmə] . . .
> **ray** [ˈreɪ] . . .

En général, la prononciation n'est pas indiquée pour les mots non soudés comprenant deux ou plus de deux mots anglais qui ont leurs propres entrées, en ordre alphabétique respectif:

> **smoke detector** . . .
> **smoke**[1] [ˈsmok] . . .
> **detector** [dɪˈtɛktər] . . .

Lorsque les articles sont composés d'entrées homographiques numérotées, la transcription phonétique n'apparaît que pour la première entrée:

> **dab**[1] [ˈdæb] *vt* . . .
> **dab**[2] *n* . . .

Dans la partie anglais-français, il n'y a généralement pas de transcription phonétique pour les termes primitifs du verbe dérivés par suffixation ni pour la plupart des adverbes dérivés qui se terminent par le suffixe *-ly.*

Enfin, la prononciation du *h* aspiré en français est indiquée par le symbôle ['] et précède la prononciation du mot-vedette:

habile [abil]
hasard ['azar]

Parties du discours

Une abréviation en italique indique la partie du discours et suit la transcription phonétique ou, s'il n'y a pas de prononciation, le mot-vedette. Les parties du discours sont énumérées ci-dessous:

mendier . . . *v* . . .
maintenant . . . *adv* . . .
daily[2] *adj* . . .
jackal . . . *n* . . .
and . . . *conj* . . .
par . . . *prep* . . .
neither[3] *pron* . . .
allô . . . *interj* . . .
le . . . *art* . . .

Les verbes intransitifs et transitifs sont suivis des abréviations *vi* et *vt* respectivement; les verbes qui sont à la fois transitifs et intransitifs sont suivis de l'abréviation *v* et parfois des subdivisions *vi* et *vt,* s'il est nécessaire d'indiquer celles-ci:

necessitate . . . *vt* **-tated; -tating** : nécessiter, exiger

déborder . . . *vi* : to overflow

satisfy . . . *v* **-fied; -fying** *vt* . . . — *vi* . . .

Deux autres abréviations sont utilisées pour indiquer les catégories du verbe: *v aux* (verbe auxiliaire) et *v impers* (verbe impersonnel):

may . . . *v aux, past* **might** . . .

aller[1] . . . *vi* . . . — *v aux* : to be going to, to be about to . . . — *v impers* **1 en ~** : to happen, to go . . .

Genre

Dans la partie français-anglais du dictionnaire, le genre est indiqué pour chaque nom et suit directement la partie du discours, sans espaces, soit avec un *m* en italique pour le masculin soit avec un *f* en italique pour le féminin. Les mots à double genre sont suivis de l'abréviation *mf:*

magnésium . . . *nm* . . .
galaxie . . . *nf* . . .
touriste . . . *nmf* . . .

Si le nom varie au féminin, l'abréviation est simplement *n:*

directeur[2], **-trice** *n* . . .

De la même façon, les substantifs français qui définissent les mots-vedettes anglais sont suivis du genre du nom:

amnesia . . . *n* : amnésie *f*
earache . . . *n* : mal *m* d'oreille
gamekeeper . . . *n* : garde-chasse *m*

Flexions

1. Noms

Le pluriel des noms est indiqué dans les cas suivants: quand il est irrégulier, quand la suffixation du pluriel change le radical du mot, quand un nom anglais se termine par une consonne et *-o* ou par *-ey,* quand un nom anglais se termine par *-oo,* quand un nom anglais est un mot composé dont le dernier élément ne prend pas la marque du pluriel, quand un nom français est un mot composé avec trait d'union, quand le nom a plus d'une forme au pluriel et, finalement, quand le lecteur pourrait avoir un doute quant à l'orthographe du pluriel:

tooth . . . *n, pl* **teeth** . . .
madame . . . *nf, pl* **mesdames** . . .
adieu . . . *nm, pl* **adieux** . . .
potato . . . *n, pl* **-toes** . . .
abbey . . . *n, pl* **-beys** . . .
cuckoo[2] *n, pl* **-oos** . . .
brother-in-law . . . *n, pl* **brothers-in-law** . . .

court–circuit . . . *nm, pl* **courts–circuits** . . .

quail[2] *n, pl* **quail** *or* **quails** . . .

récital . . . *nm, pl* **-tals** . . .

La plupart des noms polysyllabiques dans la section anglais-français du dictionnaire ont des flexions réduites à la dernière syllabe du mot, et ce quel que soit le nombre de syllabes. Dans la section français-anglais du dictionnaire, on indique les flexions pour les noms ayant trois syllabes ou plus; le pluriel des mots plus courts est écrit au long:

shampoo[2] *n, pl* **-poos** . . . **calamity** . . . *n, pl* **-ties** . . .

mouse . . . *n, pl* **mice** . . .

terminal[2] *nm, pl* **-naux** . . .

caillou . . . *nm, pl* **cailloux** . . .

Si le masculin pluriel a une forme irrégulière, on indiquera celle-ci précédée de l'abréviation appropriée:

jumeau, -melle . . . *adj & n, mpl* **jumeaux** : twin

Le pluriel des noms n'est habituellement pas indiqué quand le radical du mot demeure inchangé par l'ajout du *-s* pluriel ou quand le nom est rarement utilisé au pluriel:

apple . . . *n* : pomme *f*

anglais[2] *nm* : English (language)

Les noms pluriels qui, par le fait même, sont suivis d'un verbe au pluriel, ont les abréviations suivantes: *npl* pour les noms anglais, *nmpl* pour les noms masculins français ou *nfpl* pour les noms féminins français:

knickers . . . *npl* . . .

parages . . . *nmpl* . . .

tenailles . . . *nfpl* . . .

Les mots-vedettes qui sont invariables au pluriel sont suivis de l'abréviation *ns & pl* pour les noms anglais, *nms & pl* pour les noms masculins français, *nfs & pl* pour les noms féminins français et *nmfs & pl* pour les noms français à double genre:

deer . . . *ns & pl* . . .

perdrix . . . *nfs & pl* . . .

débours . . . *nms & pl* . . .

après–midi . . . *nmfs & pl* . . .

2. Verbes

VERBES ANGLAIS

Dans la section anglais-français, les termes primitifs du verbe sont indiqués dans les cas suivants: quand le verbe est irrégulier, quand la suffixation change l'orthographe du radical, quand le verbe se termine en *-ey* ou, finalement, quand le verbe a des formes fléchies différentes:

break[1] . . . *v* **broke** . . . ; **broken** . . . ; **breaking** . . .

drag[1] . . . *v* **dragged; dragging** . . .

imagine . . . *vt* **-ined; -ining** . . .

monkey[1] . . . *vi* **-keyed; -keying** . . .

label[1] . . . *vt* **-beled** *or* **-belled; -beling** *or* **-belling** . . .

Des flexions sont habituellement indiquées quand le verbe est composé de deux syllabes ou plus:

multiply . . . *v* **-plied; -plying** . . .

bevel[1] . . . *vt* **-eled** *or* **-elled; -eling** *or* **-elling** . . .

forgo *or* **forego** . . . *vt* **-went** . . . ; **-gone** . . . ; **-going** . . .

commit . . . *vt* **-mitted; -mitting** . . .

Les termes primitifs du verbe anglais ne sont pas indiqués quand il s'agit d'un verbe régulier et quand le radical du mot demeure inchangé par la suffixation:

delay[1] . . . *vt*

pack[1] . . . *vt*

VERBES FRANÇAIS

Contrairement aux verbes anglais, la conjugaison des verbes français ne fait pas partie de l'entrée elle-même. La section intitulée Conjugation of French Verbs à la page 40a traite des particularités de la conjugaison française et comprend les conjugaisons modèles d'une centaine de verbes.

Les verbes réguliers qui ont des terminaisons en *-er* ou en *-ir* n'ont pas de renvois, mais leurs tableaux types figurent au début de la section. Les verbes irréguliers sont suivis d'un chiffre entre parenthèses qui renvoit le lecteur aux conjugaisons modèles:

arranger {17} *vt* . . .

joindre {50} *vt* . . .

Les entrées pour les formes irrégulières des verbes incluent un renvoi à l'infinitif correspondant:

tenu[1] . . . *pp* → **tenir**

joigne . . . , *etc.* → **joindre**

Les verbes irréguliers avec préfixes, par exemple **retenir** et **rejoindre,** n'ont pas de renvois puisque leurs conjugaisons modèles correspondent au radical du verbe.

Adverbes et adjectifs

Les formes comparatives et superlatives des adjectifs et des adverbes anglais sont indiquées après le mot-vedette dans les cas suivants: quand la forme fléchie est irrégulière, quand la suffixation change l'orthographe du radical, ou, enfin, quand l'entrée possède plus d'une forme fléchie:

fat . . . *adj* **fatter; fattest** . . .

well[2] *adv* **better** . . . ; **best** . . .

evil[1] . . . *adj* **eviler** *or* **eviller; evilest** *or* **evillest** . . .

Les formes superlatives des adjectifs et des adverbes polysyllabiques sont généralement fléchies. La forme superlative est écrite au long, cependant, quand il est souhaitable d'indiquer la prononciation de la flexion:

gaudy . . . *adj* **gaudier; -est** . . .

early[1] . . . *adv* **earlier; -est** . . .

secure[1] . . . *adj* **securer; -est** . . .
mais

young[1] . . . *adj* **younger** [ˈjəŋgər;]; **youngest** [ˈjəŋgəst] . . .

L'absence du comparatif à l'entrée adjectivale signale qu'il est inusité:

mere . . . *adj, superlative* **merest** . . .

Les formes comparatives et superlatives des adjectifs et des adverbes ne sont généralement pas indiquées quand le radical du mot demeure inchangé par la suffixation:

quiet[2] *adj* **1** . . .

Usage des mots

1. Régionalismes

L'usage des mots concernent à la fois le domaine géographique et le niveau de langue. Les mots dont le domaine géographique d'usage est limité à la France, au Canada français, à la Belgique, à la Suisse ou au Canada anglais, sont suivis d'une abréviation reflétant le ou les pays où ils sont le plus couramment employés:

bachoter . . . *vi France* : to cram . . .

cocotte . . . *nf* . . . **2** *Can* : pinecone

auditoire . . . *nm* . . . **2** *Bel & Switz* : auditorium

furnace . . . *n* : fourneau *m,* fournaise *f Can*

bloke . . . *n Brit* : type *m*

Les abréviations régionales suivantes sont utilisées: *Bel* (Belgique), *Brit* (Grande-Bretagne et Canada anglais), *Can* (Canada français), *France, Switz* (Suisse).

De nombreux mots français sont suivis de l'abréviation *fam* (emploi familier) et signalent au lecteur que le mot est surtout utilisé dans un contexte familier et ne serait pas normalement employé dans la langue parlée ou écrite soutenue. Les abréviations *sometimes offensive* ou *usu vulgar* indiquent qu'un mot a un usage grossier ou injurieux dans certains contextes, mais l'usage répandu du mot justifie son entrée dans notre dictionnaire. Les indicateurs de niveau de langue ont comme fonction de prévenir le lecteur que le mot en question pourrait être mal vu dans les conversations polies.

2. Indicateurs sémantiques

Les définitions sont parfois précédées d'un indicateur sémantique qui sert à fournir des renseignements sémantiques supplémentaires au lecteur:

not . . . *adv* **1** (*used to form a negative*) : . . .

when[2] *conj* **1** (*referring to a particular time*) : . . .

se . . . *pron* **1** (*used with reflexive verbs*) : . . . **2** (*used to indicate reciprocity*) : . . .

si[1] . . . *adv* . . . **2** (*used to contradict a negative statement or question*) **:** . . .

Des renseignements sémantiques supplémentaires peuvent aussi être placés entre parenthèses immédiatement après la définition d'un mot dans le but de préciser son sens:

calibrate . . . *vt* . . . **:** calibrer (une arme, etc.), étalonner (une balance)

paille . . . *nf* . . . **2 :** (drinking) straw

Il arrive à l'occasion qu'un indicateur sémantique remplace la définition au complet, surtout quand le mot-vedette n'a pas d'acception équivalente précise dans la langue cible. Il est alors suivi d'un ou de plusieurs exemples courants:

shall . . . *v aux* . . . **1** (*used to express a command*) <you shall do as I say : vous ferez comme je vous dis> . . .

3. Exemples

Les définitions comprennent parfois des exemples qui illustrent l'usage typique d'un mot en contexte ou d'une expression figée. Les exemples d'usage sont alors suivis d'une traduction et placés entre crochets:

ici . . . *adv* **1 :** here <ici et là : here and there> <par ici : this way> . . .

make[1] . . . *vt* . . . **8** EARN **:** gagner <to make a living : gagner sa vie> . . .

Catégories sémantiques

Les deux points en caractères gras précèdent la définition:

failing[1] . . . *n* **:** défaut *m*

Des chiffres arabes en gras séparent les catégories sémantiques ou les sens d'un mot quand ce dernier a plus d'un sens:

maîtriser . . . *vt* **1 :** to master **2 :** to control, to restrain . . .

Quand un synonyme, une locution, un exemple, un renvoi ou une abréviation précède la catégorie sémantique, chacune de ces parties se rapporte exclusivement au sens numéroté dont il est question et non aux autres sens:

abord . . . *nm* **1** ACCÈS **:** . . .
tone[1] . . . *vt* . . . *or* **to tone down :** . . .
caoutchouc . . . *nm* . . . **2 caoutchoucs** *nmpl* **:** . . .
extension . . . *n* . . . **5 extension cord :** . . .
myself . . . *pron* **1** (*used reflexively*) **:** . . .
pike . . . *n* . . . **3 → turnpike**
ambitionner . . . *vt* . . . **2** *Can* **:** . . .

Renvois

Les renvois ont trois fonctions particulières. On distingue le renvoi par une flèche en caractères gras placée après le mot-vedette ou parfois après le sens auquel il se rapporte.

D'une part, les renvois synonymiques indiquent que la définition à l'entrée auquelle on fait référence peut être substituée par le mot-vedette. D'autre part, les renvois peuvent illustrer les variantes orthographiques d'un mot:

cable[2] . . . **2 → cablegram**
sceptic . . . **→ skeptic**

Enfin, le renvoi identifie le mot-vedette comme étant une flexion d'un autre mot (souvent un verbe ou un nom):

aura[1] . . . , *etc.* **→ avoir**
mice → mouse

Synonymes

De nombreuses entrées, aussi bien que les sens qui s'y rapportent, comprennent des synonymes en petites capitales qui précèdent les deux-points en gras et les définitions. Tous les synonymes constituent un article ou une locution en caractères gras ailleurs dans le dictionnaire. Les synonymes servent à la fois à guider le lecteur en apportant des précisions sémantiques sur les différents sens du mot et à fournir un mot équivalent qui pourrait être utilisé dans le même contexte. La section anglais-français du dictionnaire est particulièrement riche en synonymes, en exemples et en indicateurs sémantiques dans le but de fournir autant d'information possible au lecteur qui apprend le français.

Grammaire anglaise

L'adjectif

L'adjectif anglais est invariable en nombre et en genre. Il précède généralement le nom qu'il modifie:

the black spider	l'araignée noire
the black spiders	les araignées noires
a white wall	un mur blanc
white walls	des murs blancs

1. Adjectifs positifs, comparatifs et superlatifs

Les formes comparatives et superlatives de l'adjectif anglais se construisent de trois façons. Lorsque l'adjectif positif consiste d'une seule syllabe, les suffixes *-er* ou *-est* s'ajoutent généralement au mot racine; si l'adjectif positif se compose de plus de deux syllabes, il est employé avec les adverbes *more*, *most*, *less* ou *least;* l'adjectif positif à deux syllabes peut être modifié suivant l'une de ces deux formules. Finalement, il existe des adjectifs irréguliers dont les formes comparatives et superlatives sont uniques:

Positif	Comparatif	Superlatif
clean (propre)	**cleaner** (plus propre)	**cleanest** (le plus propre)
narrow (étroit)	**narrower** (plus étroit)	**narrowest** (le plus étroit)
peaceful (paisible)	**more peaceful** (plus paisible)	**most peaceful** (le plus paisible)
	less peaceful (moins paisible)	**least peaceful** (le moins paisible)
good (bon)	**better** (meilleur)	**best** (le meilleur)
bad (mauvais)	**worse** (pire)	**worst** (le pire)

2. Adjectifs démonstratifs

L'adjectif démonstratif *this* ou *that* correspond généralement à l'adjectif français *ce;* son équivalent se traduit plus exactement en employant la particule *-ci* ou *-là* (*this time,* cette fois, cette fois-ci; *in those years,* dans ces années-là). Il est à noter que seul ce type d'adjectif varie au pluriel:

this	ce, cette, ce . . . -ci, cette . . . -ci	**these**	ces, ces . . . -ci
that	ce, cette, ce . . . -là, cette . . . -là	**those**	ces, ces . . . -là

3. Adjectifs descriptifs

Un adjectif descriptif décrit ou indique une qualité, une classe ou une condition (*a fascinating conversation,* une conversation fascinante; *a positive attitude,* une attitude positive; *a fast computer,* un ordinateur rapide).

4. Adjectifs indéfinis

Un adjectif indéfini s'emploie pour désigner des personnes ou des choses non identifiées (*some children,* des enfants *ou* quelques enfants; *other projects,* d'autres projets).

5. Adjectifs interrogatifs

L'adjectif interrogatif sert à formuler des questions:

Whose office is this?	***À qui*** est ce bureau?
Which book do you want?	***Quel*** livre voulez-vous?

6. Le substantif employé comme adjectif

Un substantif sert parfois à modifier un autre substantif et fonctionne alors comme adjectif (*the Vietnam War,* la guerre du Vietnam; *word processing,* traitement de texte).

7. Adjectifs possessifs

On appelle adjectif possessif la forme possessive du pronom personnel. Suivent une liste des adjectifs possessifs anglais et quelques exemples d'usage:

Singulier	Pluriel
my	our
your	your
his/her/its	their

Where's ***my*** watch?	Où est ***ma*** montre?
Your cab is here.	***Votre*** taxi est arrivé.
It was ***her*** idea.	C'était ***son*** idée.
They read ***his*** biography.	Ils ont lu ***sa*** biographie.
The box and ***its*** contents.	La boîte et ***son*** contenu.
She's ***our*** mother.	Elle est ***notre*** mère.
We paid for ***their*** ticket.	Nous avons payé ***leur*** billet.
Your tables are ready.	***Vos*** tables sont prêtes.

8. Adjectifs prédicatifs

Un adjectif prédicatif modifie le sujet d'un verbe copulatif (tel que *be, become, feel, taste, smell* ou *seem*):

She is ***happy*** with the outcome.	Elle est ***contente*** des résultats.
This coffee smells ***bad.***	Ce café sent ***mauvais***.
The student seems ***puzzled***.	L'étudiant a l'air ***perplexe***.

9. Adjectifs propres

Un adjectif propre dérive d'un nom propre et s'écrit généralement avec une majuscule:

Victorian furniture	mobilier ***victorien***
a ***Senegalese*** product	un produit ***sénégalais***

10. Adjectifs relatifs

Un adjectif relatif (tel que *which, that, who, whom, whose* ou *where*) sert à introduire une proposition adjectivale ou substantive:

toward late April, by ***which*** time the report should be finished	vers la fin avril, date avant laquelle le rapport devrait être terminé

not knowing ***whose*** advice she should follow	sans savoir qui elle devrait écouter

L'adverbe

La plupart des adverbes anglais se forment en ajoutant le suffixe *-ly* à l'adjectif:

mad***ly***	follement
wonderful***ly***	merveilleusement

Quand l'adjectif se termine en *-y*, l'adverbe est formé en changeant *-y* en *-i* et en ajoutant le suffixe *-ly:*

happ***ily***	heureusement
daint***ily***	délicatement

La forme adverbiale des adjectifs qui se terminent en *-ic* s'obtient en ajoutant le suffixe *-ally* à l'adjectif:

basic***ally***	fondamentalement
numeric***ally***	numériquement

Lorsqu'un adjectif se termine en *-ly*, l'adverbe demeure inchangé:

She called her mother ***daily.***	Elle appelait sa mère ***tous les jours.***
The show started ***early.***	Le spectacle a commencé ***tôt.***

Finalement, il existe des adverbes qui ne se terminent pas en *-ly*, par exemple:

again (de nouveau)	now (maintenant)
too (trop)	too (aussi)

1. Adverbes positifs, comparatifs et superlatifs

Comme les adjectifs, la plupart des adverbes anglais possèdent trois degrés de comparaison: positif, comparatif et superlatif. En règle générale, l'adverbe monosyllabique se termine en *-er* au comparatif et en *-est* au superlatif. Quant aux adverbes à trois syllabes ou plus, les formes comparatives et superlatives s'obtiennent en employant les adverbes *more/most* ou *less/least*. Le comparatif et le superlatif des adverbes à deux syllabes se forment ainsi:

Positif	Comparatif	Superlatif
fast	faster	fastest
easy	easier	easiest
madly	more madly	most madly
happily	more happily	most happily

Finalement, il existe des adverbes, tels que *quite* et *very*, qui n'ont pas de formes comparatives, et d'autres tels que *mere*, qui n'ont que la forme superlative.

2. Adverbes d'accentuation

Les adverbes d'accentuation tels que *just* et *only* ne s'emploient habituellement que pour accentuer d'autres mots. L'accent ainsi produit varie selon la place qu'occupe l'adverbe dans la phrase:

He ***just*** nodded to me as he passed. — Il m'a ***simplement*** salué de la tête en passant.

He nodded to me ***just*** as he passed. — Il m'a salué de la tête ***au moment même*** où il passait.

3. Adverbes relatifs

Les adverbes relatifs (comme *when*, *where* et *why*) s'emploient principalement pour introduire des questions:

When will he return? — ***Quand*** reviendra-t-il?

Where is the suitcase? — ***Où*** est la valise?

Why did you do it? — ***Pourquoi*** l'as-tu fait?

L'article

1. L'article défini

En anglais l'article défini n'a qu'une forme, *the*. Cet article est invariable en genre et en nombre:

The boys were expelled.	***Les*** garçons ont été expulsés.
The First Lady dined with ***the*** prince.	***La*** Première Dame a dîné avec ***le*** prince.

2. L'article indéfini

L'article indéfini *a* s'emploie avec tout substantif ou abréviation qui commence soit par une consonne, soit par un *son* consonantique:

a door	a union	a one
a B.A. degree	a hat	a U.S. Senator

L'article *a* s'emploie aussi avant un substantif dont la première syllabe commence par *h-* et n'est pas accentuée ou qui n'a qu'une accentuation modérée (a historian, a heroic attempt, a hilarious performance). Cependant dans l'anglais parlé, on utilise couramment l'article *an* dans ces cas-ci (an historian, an heroic attempt, an hilarious performance). Les deux formes sont parfaitement acceptables.

L'article indéfini *an* s'emploie avec tout substantif ou abréviation commençant par un *son* vocalique, sans tenir compte de la première lettre du substantif, voyelle ou consonne selon le cas (an icicle, an nth degree, an honor, an FBI investigation).

La conjonction

Il y a trois principaux types de conjonctions en anglais: les conjonctions de coordination, de correlation et de subordination.

1. Conjonctions de coordination

Les conjonctions de coordination, telles que *and, because, but, for, or, nor, since, so* et *yet,* s'emploient pour unir des éléments grammaticaux de même valeur. Ces éléments peuvent être des mots, des syntagmes, des propositions subordonnées, des propositions principales ou des phrases complètes. Les conjonctions de coordination s'emploient pour unir des éléments similaires, pour faire des exclusions ou des contrastes, pour indiquer une alternative, pour indiquer une raison ou pour préciser un résultat:

union d'éléments similaires:	She ordered pencils, pens, ***and*** erasers.
exclusion ou contraste:	He is a brilliant ***but*** arrogant man.
	They offered a promising plan, ***but*** it had not yet been tested.
alternative:	She can wait here ***or*** go on ahead.
raison:	The report is useless, ***for*** its information is no longer current.
résultat:	His diction is excellent, ***so*** every word is clear.

2. Conjonctions de correlation

Les conjonctions de correlation s'emploient en groupes de deux pour unir soit des choix soit des éléments de même valeur grammaticale:

Either you go ***or*** you stay.	***Ou*** tu restes ***ou*** tu t'en vas.
He had ***neither*** looks ***nor*** wit.	Il n'avait ***ni*** beauté ***ni*** intelligence.

3. Conjonctions de subordination

Les conjonctions de subordination servent à unir une proposition subordonnée à une proposition principale. Ces conjonctions expriment la cause, la condition ou la concession, la manière, le propos ou le résultat, le temps, le lieu ou la circonstance, ainsi qu'une condition ou une possibilité:

cause:	***Because*** she learns quickly, she is doing well in her new job.
condition ou concession:	Don't call ***unless*** you are coming.
manière:	We'll do it ***however*** you tell us to.
propos ou résultat:	He distributes the mail early ***so that*** they can read it.
temps:	She kept meetings to a minimum ***when*** she was president.

Le substantif

Par contraste avec le substantif français, le substantif anglais n'a généralement pas de genre. Quelques substantifs en *-ess* (empress, hostess) ont un genre féminin; d'autres ont un genre spécifique, par exemple: *husband, wife, father, mother, brother, sister,* ainsi que les noms de certains animaux: *bull, cow, stag, doe,* etc. La plupart des substantifs anglais cependant sont neutres. Quand il est nécessaire de spécifier le genre d'un substantif neutre, ce dernier s'emploie généralement avec des mots comme *male, female, man, woman,* etc., par exemple:

a ***male*** parrot	un perroquet ***mâle***
women painters	des ***femmes*** peintres

1. Usages de base

Le substantif anglais s'emploie en général comme sujet, objet direct, objet d'une préposition, objet indirect, prédicat nominal, complément d'objet, en apposition et en discours direct:

sujet:	The ***office*** was quiet.
objet direct:	He locked the ***office***.
objet d'une préposition:	The file is in the ***office***.
objet indirect:	He gave his ***client*** the papers.
prédicat nominal:	Mrs. Adams is the managing ***partner.***
complément d'objet:	They made Mrs. Adams managing ***partner.***
apposition:	Mrs. Adams, the managing ***partner,*** wrote that memo.
discours direct:	***Mrs. Adams,*** may I present Mr. Bonkowski.

2. Le substantif employé comme adjectif

Le substantif a un rôle adjectival quand il precède un autre substantif:

olive oil	huile d'olive
business management	gestion des affaires
emergency room	salle d'urgence

3. La formation du pluriel

Le pluriel des substantifs anglais est formé en ajoutant *-s* à la fin de la forme singulière (book, books; cat, cats; dog, dogs; tree, trees).

Lorsque le substantif singulier se termine en *-s, -x, -z, -ch* ou *-sh* la terminaison *-es* est ajoutée au singulier (cross, crosses; fox, foxes; witch, witches; wish, wishes). Pour les formes singulières en *-z,* la dernière lettre est doublée avant d'ajouter la terminaison (quiz, quizzes).

Si le substantif singulier se termine en *-y* précédé d'une consonne, le *-y* change en *-i* et la terminaison *-es* est ajoutée (fairy, fairies; pony, ponies; guppy, guppies).

Certains substantifs anglais ne se conforment pas à ces règles. Il y a quelques substantifs (généralement des noms d'animaux) qui ne changent pas toujours au pluriel (fish, fish ou parfois fishes; caribou, caribou ou parfois caribous). Finalement, il y a aussi des substantifs qui ont un pluriel unique (foot, feet; mouse, mice; knife, knives).

4. Le possessif

La forme possessive du substantif singulier s'obtient ordinairement en ajoutant un apostrophe et un *-s* à la fin du mot:

Jackie's passport	le passeport ***de Jackie***
this hat is ***Billy's***	ce chapeau est ***à Billy***

Lorsque le substantif se termine en *-s,* seul l'apostrophe est ajouté, ainsi:

the ***neighbors'*** dog	le chien ***des voisins***
Mr. ***Ross'*** briefcase	la serviette ***de M. Ross***

La préposition

La préposition anglaise s'unit généralement avec un substantif, un pronom ou l'équivalent d'un substantif (comme un syntagme ou une proposition) pour former une phrase à fonction adjectivale, adverbiale ou substantive. On distingue habituellement deux types de prépositions: la préposition simple, c'est-à-dire celle qui consiste d'un seul mot (par exemple, *against, from, near, of, on, out* ou *without*), et la préposition composée, qui consiste de plusieurs éléments (comme *according to, by means of* ou *in spite of*).

1. Usages de base

Tel qu'illustré précédemment, la préposition établit un lien avec le complément. Or, un syntagme prépositionnel s'emploie habituellement comme adverbe ou comme adjectif:

> She expected resistance ***on*** his part.
>
> He sat down ***beside*** her.

2. La conjonction vs la préposition

Les mots anglais *after, before, but, for* et *since* sont à la fois prépositions et conjonctions. Leur rôle se détermine d'après leur place dans la phrase. Les conjonctions servent ordinairement à unir deux éléments de même valeur grammaticale, tandis que les prépositions précèdent souvent un substantif, un pronom ou un syntagme nominal:

conjonction: I was a bit concerned ***but*** not panicky.
[***but*** lie deux adjectifs]

préposition: I was left with nothing ***but*** hope.
[***but*** précède un substantif]

conjonction: The device conserves fuel, ***for*** it is battery-powered.
[***for*** lie deux propositions]

préposition: The device conserves fuel ***for*** residual heating.
[***for*** précède un syntagme nominal]

3. Place dans la phrase

Une préposition se place devant le substantif ou le pronom (*below* the desk, *beside* them), après l'adjectif (antagonistic *to,* insufficient *in,* symbolic *of*) ou après le verbe pour former un verbe à particule (take *for,* put *on,* come *across*).

La préposition anglaise peut terminer une phrase, surtout si la préposition fait partie d'un verbe à particule:

After Rourke left, Joyce took ***over***.

What does this all add up ***to***?

Le pronom

Les pronoms possèdent les caractéristiques suivantes: cas (nominatif, possessif ou objectif); nombre (singulier ou pluriel); personne (première, deuxième ou troisième) et genre (masculin, féminin ou neutre). Les pronoms anglais se classent en sept catégories principales, chacune ayant un rôle spécifique.

1. Pronoms démonstratifs

Les mots *this, that, these* et *those* sont considérés comme pronoms lorsqu'ils fonctionnent comme substantifs. (Ils sont classés comme adjectifs démonstratifs lorsqu'ils modifient un substantif.) Le pronom démonstratif désigne une personne ou une chose afin de la distinguer d'une autre:

These are the best designs we've seen to date.

Those are strong words.

Le pronom démonstratif sert aussi à distinguer une personne ou une chose qui se trouve proche d'une autre plus lointaine (*this* is my desk; *that* is yours).

2. Pronoms indéfinis

Les pronoms indéfinis s'emploient pour désigner une personne ou une chose dont l'identité est inconnue ou n'est pas immédiatement évidente. Ils font habituellement allusion à la troisième personne, et n'ont pas de distinction de genre. Les pronoms indéfinis sont:

all	either	none
another	everybody	no one
any	everyone	one
anybody	everything	other(s)
anyone	few	several
anything	many	some
both	much	somebody
each	neither	someone
each one	nobody	something

Le pronom indéfini s'accorde en nombre avec le verbe qui suit. Les pronoms suivants s'emploient avec un verbe au singulier: *another, anything, each one, everything, much, nobody, no one, one, other, someone, something:*

Much *is* being done.

No one *wants* to go.

Les pronoms indéfinis *both, few, many* et *several* s'emploient avec des verbes au pluriel:

Many *were* called; ***few*** *were* chosen.

Certains pronoms, tels que *all, any, none* et *some,* posent parfois des difficultés puisqu'ils peuvent s'employer avec un verbe singulier ou pluriel. En règle générale, un pronom qui s'emploie avec un substantif non comptable nécessite un verbe au singulier, tandis qu'un pronom qui s'emploie avec un substantif comptable requiert un verbe au pluriel.

avec un substantif non comptable:

All of the ***property*** *is* affected.
None of the ***soup*** *was* spilled.
Some of the ***money*** *was* spent.

avec un substantif comptable:

All of my ***shoes*** *are* black.
None of the ***clerks*** *were* available.
Some of your ***friends*** *were* there.

3. Pronoms interrogatifs

Les pronoms interrogatifs *what, which, who, whom* et *whose,* ainsi que ceux qui sont soudés avec le suffixe *-ever* (*whatever, whichever,* etc.) servent à introduire une question:

Who is she?	He asked me ***who*** she was.
Whoever can that be?	We wondered ***whoever*** that could be.

4. Pronoms personnels

Le pronom personnel reflète la personne, le nombre et le genre de l'être ou de la chose qu'il représente. Chaque catégorie est constituée de pronoms personnels distincts:

Personne	Nominatif	Possessif	Objectif
PREMIÈRE			
singulier:	I	my, mine	me
pluriel:	we	our, ours	us
DEUXIÈME			
singulier:	you	your, yours	you
pluriel:	you	your, yours	you
TROISIÈME			
singulier:	he	his	him
	she	her, hers	her
	it	its	it
pluriel:	they	their, theirs	them

Il est important de noter que les pronoms possessifs ne prennent pas d'apostrophe et ne doivent pas être confondus avec les homophones *you're, they're, there's, it's.*

5. Pronoms réciproques

Les pronoms réciproques *each other* et *one another* indiquent une action ou une relation mutuelle:

They do not quarrel with ***one another.***	Ils ne se querellent pas (entre eux).
Lou and Andy saw ***each other*** at the party.	Lou et Andy se sont vus à la fête.

Le pronom réciproque s'emploie aussi avec le possessif:

They always borrowed ***one another's*** money.	Ils se prêtaient toujours de l'argent (l'un à l'autre).
The two companies depend on ***each other's*** success.	Chacune des deux sociétés dépend de la réussite de l'autre.

6. Pronoms réfléchis

Les pronoms réfléchis s'obtiennent à partir des pronoms personnels *him, her, it, my, our, them* et *your* auxquels la forme *-self* ou *-selves* est ajoutée. Le pronom réfléchi s'emploie habituellement pour exprimer une action réfléchie ou pour accentuer le sujet d'une phrase, d'une proposition ou d'un syntagme:

She dressed ***herself***.

He asked ***himself*** if it was worth it.

I ***myself*** am not concerned.

7. Pronoms relatifs

Les pronoms relatifs sont *that, what, which, who, whom* et *whose* ainsi que les formes obtenues en ajoutant la terminaison *-ever*. Ces pronoms servent à introduire des phrases subordonnées à fonction substantive ou adjectivale.

Le pronom relatif *who* s'emploie pour faire allusion aux personnes et parfois aux animaux, le pronom relatif *which* aux animaux et aux choses et le pronom relatif *that* aux personnes, aux animaux ou aux choses:

a man ***who*** sought success

a woman ***whom*** we trust

Kentucky Firebolt, ***who*** won yesterday's horse race

a movie ***which*** was a big hit

a dog ***which*** kept barking

a boy ***that*** behaves well

a movie ***that*** was a big hit

a lion ***that*** roared

Dans certains cas le pronom relatif peut être omis:

The man [***whom***] I was talking to is the senator.

Le verbe

Le verbe anglais typique possède les caractéristiques suivantes: flexion (par exemple, *help, helps, helping, helped*), personne (première, deuxième ou troisième), nombre (singulier ou pluriel), temps (présent, passé, futur), aspect (catégories temporelles autres que les temps simples du présent, du passé et du futur), voix (active ou passive) et mode (indicatif, subjonctif et impératif).

1. Flexion

Les verbes réguliers anglais ont quatre flexions différentes qui se forment en ajoutant les suffixes *-s* ou *-es, -ed* et *-ing*. La plupart des verbes irréguliers possèdent quatre ou cinq flexions (par exemple, *see, sees, seeing, saw, seen*); et le verbe *be* en a huit (*be, is, am, are, being, was, were, been*).

Les verbes qui se terminent en *-e* muet gardent en général le *-e* lorsqu'un suffixe consonantique (comme *-s*) est ajouté à la fin du mot, mais le *-e* disparaît si le suffixe commence par une voyelle (comme *-ed* ou *-ing*):

arrange; arranges; arranged; arranging
hope; hopes; hoped; hoping

Certains verbes conservent cependant le *-e* final dans le but de distinguer les verbes homographiques, par exemple:

dye; dyes; dyed; dyeing [vs ***dying***, du verbe ***die***]
singe; singes; singed; singeing [vs ***singing***, du verbe ***sing***]

Si un verbe monosyllabique se termine par une seule consonne précédée d'une seule voyelle, la consonne finale est souvent doublée:

brag; bragged; bragging
grip; gripped; gripping

Quand un verbe polysyllabique se termine de la même façon, et que la dernière syllabe est accentuée, la consonne finale est aussi doublée:

commit; committed; committing

occur; occurred; occurring

Il arrive fréquemment qu'un verbe qui se termine en *-y* précédé d'une consonne change *-y* en *-i* sauf lorsque le suffixe correspondant est *-ing:*

carry; carried; carrying

study; studied; studying

Quand un verbe se termine en *-c,* un *-k* est ajouté aux flexions si le suffixe commence en *-e* ou en *-i:*

mimic; mimics; mimicked; mimicking

traffic; traffics; trafficked; trafficking

2. Temps et aspect

Les conjugaisons des verbes anglais sont généralement formées d'un seul mot au présent et au prétérit:

I do, I did
we write, we wrote

Le futur se conjugue avec les verbes auxiliaires *shall* ou *will* et l'indicatif du présent ou le progressif:

I shall do it.	Je le ferai.
I shall be leaving shortly.	Je partirai bientôt.
We will come tomorrow.	Nous viendrons demain.

L'aspect concerne le temps du verbe autre que le présent, le prétérit ou le futur simple. L'aspect a quatre formes en anglais: le progressif, le passé composé, le plus-que-parfait et le futur antérieur.

Le progressif sert à exprimer une action qui se déroule dans le présent ou qui aura lieu dans l'avenir:

He ***is reading*** the paper at the moment.	Il ***lit (est en train de lire)*** le journal en ce moment.
I'm ***studying*** there next year.	Je ***vais*** y ***étudier*** l'année prochaine.

Le passé composé s'emploie pour exprimer une action commencée dans le passé mais qui continue dans le présent, ou bien pour exprimer une action qui a eu lieu à un moment indéfini du passé:

She ***has written*** many books.	Elle ***a écrit*** beaucoup de livres.

Le plus-que-parfait exprime une action accomplie qui s'est déroulée avant une autre action antérieure:

She ***had written*** several books previously.	Elle ***avait écrit*** plusieurs livres auparavant.

Le futur antérieur indique qu'une action future aura lieu avant une autre action ou un événement à venir:

We ***will have finished*** the project by then.	D'ici-là nous ***aurons terminé*** le projet.

3. Voix

La voix active indique que le sujet de la phrase remplit l'action du verbe, tandis que la voix passive indique qu'il en est l'objet:

Voix active:	He ***respected*** his colleagues.
	Il ***respectait*** ses collègues.
Voix passive:	He ***was respected*** by his colleagues.
	Il ***était respecté*** par ses collègues.

4. Mode

Il existe trois modes en anglais: l'indicatif, l'impératif et le subjonctif.

L'indicatif est employé soit pour indiquer un fait, soit pour poser une question:

He ***is*** here.	Il ***est*** ici.
Is he here?	***Est***-il ici?

L'impératif est employé pour exprimer une commande ou une demande:

Come here.	***Viens*** ici.
Please ***come*** here.	***Viens*** ici, s'il te plaît.

Le subjonctif exprime une condition contraire aux faits. Le subjonctif en anglais est tombé en désuétude, mais il apparaît parfois dans des propositions introduites par *if,* et après le verbe *wish:*

I wish he ***were*** here.	J'aurais voulu qu'il ***soit*** là.
If she ***were*** there, she could answer that.	Si elle ***était*** là, elle pourrait y répondre.

5. Verbes transitifs et intransitifs

Comme en français, le verbe anglais est soit transitif, soit intransitif. Le verbe transitif prend un objet direct:

She ***sold*** her car.	Elle ***a vendu*** sa voiture.

Le verbe intransitif n'a pas d'objet direct:

He ***talked*** all day.	Il ***a parlé*** toute la journée.

Abbreviations in this Work

adj	adjective
adv	adverb
Bel	Belgium
Brit	Great Britain
Can	Canada
conj	conjunction
esp	especially
f	feminine
fam	familiar or colloquial
fpl	feminine plural
France	France
interj	interjection
m	masculine
mf	masculine or feminine
mpl	masculine plural
n	noun
nf	feminine noun
nfpl	feminine plural noun
nfs & pl	invariable singular or plural feminine noun
nm	masculine noun
nmf	masculine or feminine noun
nmfpl	plural noun invariable for gender
nmfs & pl	noun invariable for both gender and number
nmpl	masculine plural noun
nms & pl	invariable singular or plural masculine noun
npl	plural noun
ns & pl	noun invariable for plural
pl	plural
pp	past participle
prep	preposition
pron	pronoun
s	singular
Switz	Switzerland
usu	usually
v	verb (transitive and intransitive)
v aux	auxiliary verb
vi	intransitive verb
vi impers	impersonal verb
vr	reflexive verb
vt	transitive verb

Abréviations utilisées dans cet ouvrage

Les abréviations utilisées dans cet ouvrage sont des formes raccourcies des mots anglais qui apparaissent entre parenthèses.

adj	adjectif (adjective)
adv	adverbe (adverb)
Bel	Belgique (Belgium)
Brit	Grande-Bretagne (Great Britain)
Can	Canada (Canada)
conj	conjonction (conjunction)
esp	surtout (especially)
f	féminin (feminine)
fam	familier ou populaire (familiar or colloquial)
fpl	féminin pluriel (feminine plural)
France	France
interj	interjection (interjection)
m	masculin (masculine)
mf	masculin ou féminin (masculine or feminine)
mpl	masculin pluriel (masculine plural)
n	nom (noun)
nf	nom féminin (feminine noun)
nfpl	nom pluriel féminin (feminine plural noun)
nfs & pl	nom féminin invariable en nombre (invariable singular or plural feminine noun)
nm	nom masculin (masculine noun)
nmf	nom masculin ou féminin (masculine or feminine noun)
nmfpl	nom pluriel invariable en genre (plural noun invariable for gender)
nmfs & pl	nom invariable en genre et en nombre (noun invariable for both gender and number)
nmpl	nom masculin pluriel (masculine plural noun)

nms & pl	nom masculin invariable en nombre (invariable singular or plural masculine noun)
npl	nom pluriel (plural noun)
ns & pl	nom pluriel invariable en nombre (noun invariable for plural)
pl	pluriel (plural)
pp	participe passé (past participle)
prep	préposition (preposition)
pron	pronom (pronoun)
s	singulier (singular)
Switz	Suisse (Switzerland)
usu	généralement (usually)
v	verbe transitif et intransitif (transitive and intransitive verb)
v aux	verbe auxiliaire (auxiliary verb)
vi	verbe intransitif (intransitive verb)
vi impers	verbe impersonnel (impersonal verb)
vr	verbe pronominal (reflexive verb)
vt	verbe transitif (transitive verb)

Pronunciation Symbols

VOWELS

æ **ask**, **ba**t, **gla**d
ɑ **co**t, **bo**mb
ɑ̃ *French* ch**an**t, **en**nui
a *New England* **au**nt, *British* **as**k, **gla**ss
ɛ **e**gg, **be**t, **fe**d
ɛ̃ *French* lap**in**, m**ain**
ə **a**bout, jav**e**lin, **A**l**a**bam**a**
ə when italicized as in əl, əm, ən, indicates a syllabic pronunciation of the consonant as in bot**tle**, pris**m**, butt**on**
i ver**y**, an**y**, thirt**y**
iː **ea**t, b**ea**d, b**ee**
ɪ **i**d, b**i**d, p**i**t
o **O**hio, yell**o**wer, potat**o**
oː **oa**ts, **ow**n, z**o**ne, bl**ow**
ɔ **aw**l, m**au**l, c**au**ght, p**aw**
ɔ̃ **om**bre, m**on**
ʊ s**u**re, sh**ou**ld, c**ou**ld
uː b**oo**t, tw**o**, c**oo**
ʌ **u**nder, p**u**tt, b**u**d
y *French* p**u**r, *German* f**ü**hlen
eɪ **ei**ght, w**a**de, b**ay**
aɪ **i**ce, b**i**te, t**ie**
aʊ **ou**t, g**ow**n, pl**ow**
ɔɪ **oy**ster, c**oi**l, b**oy**
ø *French* d**eu**x, *German* H**ö**he
œ *French* b**œu**f, *German* G**ö**tt
œ̃ *French* l**un**di, parf**um**

CONSONANTS

b **b**a**b**y, la**b**or, ca**b**
d **d**ay, rea**d**y, ki**d**
dʒ **j**ust, ba**dg**er, fu**dg**e
ð **th**en, ei**th**er, ba**th**e
f **f**oe, tou**gh**, bu**ff**
g **g**o, bi**gg**er, ba**g**
h **h**ot, a**h**a
j **y**es, vine**y**ard
k **c**at, **k**eep, la**cqu**er, flo**ck**
l **l**aw, ho**ll**ow, boi**l**
m **m**at, he**m**p, ha**mm**er, ri**m**
n **n**ew, te**n**t, te**n**or, ru**n**
ŋ ru**ng**, ha**ng**, swi**ng**er
ɲ *French* di**gn**e, a**gn**eau
p **p**ay, la**p**se, to**p**
r **r**ope, bu**r**n, ta**r**
s **s**ad, mi**s**t, ki**ss**
ʃ **sh**oe, mi**ss**ion, slu**sh**
t **t**oe, bu**tt**on, ma**t**
ţ indicates that some speakers of English pronounce this sound as a voiced alveolar flap, as in la**t**er, ca**tt**y, ba**tt**le
tʃ **ch**oose, ba**tch**
θ **th**in, e**th**er, ba**th**
v **v**at, ne**v**er, ca**v**e
w **w**et, soft**w**are
ɥ *French* c**u**ir, app**u**i
x *German* Ba**ch**, *Scottish* lo**ch**
z **z**oo, ea**s**y, bu**zz**
ʒ a**z**ure, bei**g**e
h, k, p, t when italicized indicate sounds which are present in the pronunciation of some speakers of English but absent in the pronunciation of others, so that *whence* [ˈ*h*wɛn*t*s] can be pronunced as [ˈhwɛns], [ˈhwɛnts], [ˈwɛnts], or [ˈwɛns].

OTHER SYMBOLS

ˈ high stress **pen**manship
ˌ low stress penman**ship**
ʼ aspiration; when used before French words in *h*-, indicates absence of liaison, as in *le héros* [lə ʼero]
( ) indicate sounds that are present in the pronunciation of some speakers of French but absent in that of others, as in *cenellier* [s(ə)nɛlje], *but* [by(t)]

French–English Dictionary

A

a [a] *nm* **:** a, the first letter of the alphabet

à [a] *prep* **1 :** to <je vais à Montréal : I am going to Montreal> <as-tu téléphoné à ton père? : did you call your dad?> <il a donné la clé à son frère : he gave the key to his brother> **2 :** at <à deux heures : at two o'clock> <nous sommes à l'aéroport : we are at the airport> **3 :** on <à pied : on foot, by foot> <à temps : on time> **4 :** with <la fille aux cheveux blonds : the girl with blond hair> **5** (*with infinitive*) **:** to <ils ont appris à lire : they learned how to read> <problèmes à résoudre : problems to be solved> **6 :** from <voler aux riches : to steal from the rich> **7 :** per <60 kilomètres à l'heure : 60 kilometers per hour> **8 :** in, according to <à leur avis : in their opinion>

abaissement [abɛsmɑ̃] *nm* **1 :** lowering **2** DIMINUTION **:** reduction, drop, fall **3 :** abasement, humbling

abaisser [abese] *vt* **1** BAISSER **:** to lower **2** DIMINUER **:** to reduce **3 :** to humble, to abase **— s'abaisser** *vr* **1 :** to go down, to slope (down) **2 :** to demean oneself, to grovel **3 ~ à :** to stoop to

abandon [abɑ̃dɔ̃] *nm* **1 :** state of neglect **2 :** desertion, abandonment **3 :** abandon, freedom **4 :** surrender, renunciation **5 :** withdrawal, retirement (in sports) **6 laisser à l'abandon :** to neglect, to abandon

abandonner [abɑ̃dɔne] *vt* **1 :** to abandon **2 :** to surrender, to renounce **—** *vi* **:** to give up **— s'abandonner** *vr* **1 :** to let oneself go, to neglect oneself **2 ~ à :** to give oneself up to (pleasures, etc.)

abaque [abak] *nm* **:** abacus

abasourdir [abazurdir] *vt* **1 :** to stun **2 :** to deafen

abâtardir [abatardir] *vt* **:** to debase, to degrade **— s'abâtardir** *vr* **:** to degenerate, to deteriorate

abat–jour [abaʒur] *nm* **:** lampshade

abats [aba] *nmpl* **1 :** entrails, offal **2 abats de volaille :** giblets

abattage [abataʒ] *nm* **1 :** felling (of trees) **2 :** slaughtering (of animals) **3 :** extraction (of metals) **4 avoir de l'abattage :** to be full of vim and vigor

abattant [abatɑ̃] *nm* **:** flap, leaf (of furniture)

abattement [abatmɑ̃] *nm* **1 :** reduction, allowance <abattement à la base : income-tax deduction> **2 :** despondency, sadness **3 :** weakness, exhaustion

abattis [abati] *nmpl* **:** giblets

abattoir [abatwar] *nm* **:** abattoir, slaughterhouse

abattre [abatr] {12} *vt* **1 :** to knock down, to cut down, to bring down **2** ÉPUISER **:** to wear out, to exhaust **3** DÉMORALISER **:** to demoralize <ne te laisse pas abattre : don't let things get you down> **4 :** to slaughter, to kill **5 abattre ses cartes** *or* **abattre son jeu :** to lay one's cards on the table **— s'abattre** *vr* **1 :** to come down, to fall, to crash **2 ~ sur :** to pounce on, to descend on

abattu, -tue [abaty] *adj* **:** despondent, downcast, dejected

abbaye [abei] *nf* **:** abbey

abbé [abe] *nm* **1 :** abbot **2** PRÊTRE **:** priest

abbesse [abɛs] *nf* **:** abbess

abcès [apsɛ] *nm* **:** abscess

abdication [abdikasjɔ̃] *nf* **:** abdication, renunciation

abdiquer [abdike] *vt* **1 :** to abdicate **2 :** to renounce **—** *vi* **1 :** to abdicate **2 :** to surrender, to give up

abdomen [abdɔmɛn] *nm* **:** abdomen

abdominal, -nale [abdɔminal] *adj, mpl* **-naux** [-no] **:** abdominal

abdominaux *nmpl* **les abdominaux :** stomach muscles, abs

abécédaire [abesedɛr] *nm* **:** speller, primer

abeille [abɛj] *nf* **1 :** bee, honeybee **2 abeille mâle :** drone

aberrant, -rante [abɛrɑ̃, -rɑ̃t] *adj* **1 :** aberrant, abnormal **2 :** absurd

aberration [abɛrasjɔ̃] *nf* **:** aberration

abêtir [abetir] *vt* **:** to make stupid **—** *vi* **:** to become stupid **— s'abêtir** *vr*

abhorrer [abɔre] *vt* **:** to abhor, to abominate

abîme [abim] *nm* **1 :** abyss, gulf **2 au bord de l'abîme :** on the brink of ruin **3 au fond de l'abîme :** in the depths of despair

abîmer [abime] *vt* DÉTÉRIORER **:** to damage, to spoil **— s'abîmer** *vr* **1 :** to spoil, to become damaged **2 :** to sink, to founder <s'abîmer dans la réflexion : to be lost in thought>

abject, -jecte [abʒɛkt] *adj* **1 :** despicable, contemptible **2 :** abject **— abjectement** [-ʒɛktəmɑ̃] *adv*

abjurer [abʒyre] *vt* **:** to abjure, to renounce

ablation [ablasjɔ̃] *nf* **:** removal, excision (in medicine)

ablution [ablysjɔ̃] *nf* **:** ablution

abnégation [abnegasjɔ̃] *nf* **:** selflessness, self-denial

aboie [abwa], **aboiera** [abwara], *etc.* → **aboyer**

aboiement [abwamɑ̃] *nm* **:** barking, baying

abois [abwa] *nmpl* **être aux abois :** to be at bay, to be desperate

abolir [abɔlir] *vt* **:** to abolish

abolition [abɔlisjɔ̃] *nf* **:** abolition

abominable [abɔminabl] *adj* : abominable — **abominablement** [-nabləmɑ̃] *adv*

abomination [abɔminasjɔ̃] *nf* : abomination

abominer [abɔmine] *vt* : to abominate, to loathe

abondamment [abɔ̃damɑ̃] *adv* : abundantly

abondance [abɔ̃dɑ̃s] *nf* **1** : abundance **2 en ~** : in plenty, galore

abondant, -dante [abɔ̃dɑ̃, -dɑ̃t] *adj* : abundant

abonder [abɔ̃de] *vi* **1** : to abound, to be plentiful <abonder en bonheur : to be full of happiness> **2 abonder dans le sens de** : to agree wholeheartedly with

abonné, -née [abɔne] *n* : subscriber

abonnement [abɔnmɑ̃] *nm* : subscription

abonner [abɔne] *vt* : to take out a subscription for — **s'abonner** *vr* : to subscribe

abord [abɔr] *nm* **1** ACCÈS : access, approach **2** : manner <il est d'un abord facile : he's very approachable> **3 abords** *nmpl* : surroundings **4 d' ~** : at first, firstly **5 de prime abord** *or* **au premier abord** : at first glance

abordable [abɔrdabl] *adj* **1** ACCESSIBLE : accessible **2** : affordable **3** : approachable

abordage [abɔrdaʒ] *nm* **1** : boarding (of a ship) **2** : collision

aborder [abɔrde] *vt* **1** : to approach **2** : to tackle, to deal with **3** : to board (an enemy ship) — *vi* : to land, to berth <aborder à port : to reach port>

aborigène[1] [abɔriʒɛn] *adj* : aboriginal, indigenous

aborigène[2] *nmf* : aborigine, native

abortif, -tive [abɔrtif, -tiv] *adj* : abortive

aboucher [abuʃe] *vt* : to join (things) end to end — **s'aboucher** *vr* : to get in touch

aboutir [abutir] *vi* **1** RÉUSSIR : to succeed **2 ~ à** *or* **~ dans** : to result in, to end up in

aboutissants [abutisɑ̃] *nmpl* → **tenant**

aboutissement [abutismɑ̃] *nm* : outcome, result

aboyer [abwaje] {58} *vi* : to bark, to bay — *vt* : to bark (out), to shout (an order, etc.)

aboyeur, -yeuse [abwajœr, -jøz] *adj* : barking

abraser [abraze] *vt* : to abrade

abrasif[1]**, -sive** [abrazif, -ziv] *adj* : abrasive

abrasif[2] *nm* : abrasive

abrasion [abrazjɔ̃] *nf* : abrasion

abrégé [abreʒe] *nm* : summary, abstract, abridgment <en abrégé : in summary, in brief>

abrègement [abrɛʒmɑ̃] *nm* : summarizing, abridgment

abréger [abreʒe] {64} *vt* : to shorten, to abridge, to abbreviate

abreuver [abrœve] *vt* **1** : to water (an animal) **2** : to soak, to irrigate **3** ACCABLER : to shower, to heap <abreuver qqn de : to overwhelm s.o. with> — **s'abreuver** *vr* : to drink

abreuvoir [abrœvwar] *nm* : watering place (in a river, etc.), drinking trough

abréviation [abrevjasjɔ̃] *nf* : abbreviation

abri [abri] *nm* **1** : shelter, shed <à l'abri : under cover> **2 les sans abri** : the homeless

abricot [abriko] *nm* : apricot

abrier [abrije] {96} *vt Can* : to cover (with a blanket, etc.)

abriter [abrite] *vt* **1** : to shelter, to protect **2** HÉBERGER : to house, to accommodate

abrogation [abrɔgasjɔ̃] *nf* : repeal, abrogation

abroger [abrɔʒe] {17} *vt* : to abrogate, to repeal, to annul

abrupt, -brupte [abrypt] *adj* **1** ESCARPÉ : sheer, steep **2** BRUSQUE : abrupt

abruti, -tie [abryti] *n fam* : fool, idiot

abrutir [abrytir] *vt* **1** ÉTOURDIR : to daze, to stupefy **2** : to wear out, to exhaust **3** ABÊTIR : to make stupid

abrutissant, -sante [abrytisɑ̃, -sɑ̃t] *adj* : exhausting, numbing, stupefying

absence [apsɑ̃s] *nf* : absence

absent[1]**, -sente** [apsɑ̃, -sɑ̃t] *adj* : absent

absent[2]**, -sente** *n* : absentee

absentéisme [apsɑ̃teism] *nm* : absenteeism

absenter [apsɑ̃te] *v* **s'absenter** *vr* : to leave, to stay away

absinthe [apsɛ̃t] *nf* **1** : absinthe **2** : wormwood

absolu[1]**, -lue** [apsɔly] *adj* : absolute — **absolument** [-lymɑ̃] *adv*

absolu[2] *nm* : absolute

absolution [apsɔlysjɔ̃] *nf* : absolution

absorbant, -bante [apsɔrbɑ̃, -bɑ̃t] *adj* **1** : absorbent **2** : absorbing, engrossing

absorber [apsɔrbe] *vt* **1** : to absorb, to engross **2** : to consume, to take up, to absorb — **s'absorber** *vr* **~ dans** : to become engrossed in

absorption [apsɔrpsjɔ̃] *nf* : absorption

absoudre [apsudr] {1} *vt* : to absolve

abstenir [apstənir] {92} *v* **s'abstenir** *vr* **1** : to abstain **2 s'abstenir de faire** : to refrain from doing

abstention [apstɑ̃sjɔ̃] *nf* : abstention

abstinence [apstinɑ̃s] *nf* : abstinence

abstraction [apstraksjɔ̃] *nf* **1** : abstraction **2 faire abstraction de** : to disregard, to set aside

abstraire [apstrɛr] {40} *vt* : to abstract — **s'abstraire** *vr* : to isolate oneself

abstrait[1]**, -traite** [apstrɛ, -trɛt] *adj* : abstract — **abstraitement** [-trɛtmɑ̃] *adv*

abstrait[2] *nm* : abstract <dans l'abstrait : in the abstract>

abstrus, -struse [apstry, -stryz] *adj* : abstruse

absurde [apsyrd] *adj* : absurd

absurdité [apsyrdite] *nf* : absurdity

abus [aby] *nm* : abuse, misuse <abus de confiance : breach of trust>

abuser [abyze] *vt* : to deceive, to mislead — *vi* **1 ~ de** : to misuse **2 ~ de** : to take advantage of, to exploit — **s'abuser** *vr* : to be mistaken

abuseur [abyzœr] *nm Can* : abuser

abusif, -sive [abyzif, -ziv] *adj* **1** EXAGÉRÉ : excessive <parents abusifs : overprotective parents> **2** IMPROPRE : incorrect, improper — **abusivement** [-zivmɑ̃] *adv*

abyssal, -sale [abisal] *adj, mpl* **-saux** [-so] : abyssal, unfathomable

acabit [akabi] *nm* : sort, type <de tout acabit : of every kind>

acacia [akasja] *nm* : acacia

académicien, -cienne [akademisjɛ̃, -sjɛn] *n* : academician

académie [akademi] *nf* **1** : academy **2** : school district **3** : learned society **4** : nude (in a work of art)

académique [akademik] *adj* : academic

acadien, -dienne [akadjɛ̃, -djɛn] *adj* **1** : Acadian **2** : Cajun

Acadien, -dienne *n* **1** : Acadian **2** : Cajun

acajou [akaʒu] *nm* : mahogany

acariâtre [akarjatr] *adj* : cantankerous

accablant, -blante [akablɑ̃, -blɑ̃t] *adj* : overwhelming, oppressive

accablement [akabləmɑ̃] *nm* : despondency, dejection

accabler [akable] *vt* **1** ÉCRASER : to overwhelm **2** : to condemn

accalmie [akalmi] *nf* : lull, respite

accaparement [akaparmɑ̃] *nm* : monopolizing, hoarding

accaparer [akapare] *vt* **1** MONOPOLISER : to monopolize **2** : to buy up, to hoard

accéder [aksede] {87} *vi* **1** : to gain access, to reach, to obtain **2** : to accede

accélérateur[1], -trice [akseleratœr, -tris] *adj* : accelerating

accélérateur[2] *nm* : accelerator

accélération [akselerasjɔ̃] *nf* : acceleration

accélérer [akselere] {87} *v* : to accelerate — **s'accélérer** *vr*

accent [aksɑ̃] *nm* **1** : accent <un accent allemand : a German accent> **2** : stress, emphasis **3** : accent mark <accent aigu : acute accent> **4** NUANCE : hint, tone <un accent plaintif : a plaintive tone>

accentuer [aksɑ̃tɥe] *vt* **1** : to mark with an accent **2** : to stress (a syllable) **3** : to emphasize, to highlight — **s'accentuer** *vr* : to become more pronounced

acceptabilité [akseptabilite] *nf* : acceptability

acceptable [akseptabl] *adj* : acceptable, passable

acceptation [akseptasjɔ̃] *nf* : acceptance

accepter [aksepte] *vt* : to accept, to agree to

acception [aksepsjɔ̃] *nf* **1** : sense, meaning **2 sans acception de** : regardless of

accès [aksɛ] *nm* **1** : access **2** : entry, entrance <accès interdit : no entry> **3** CRISE : fit, attack <accès de fièvre : bout of fever> <accès d'excitation : fit of excitement>

accessibilité [aksesibilite] *nf* : accessibility

accessible [aksesibl] *adj* ABORDABLE : accessible

accession [aksesjɔ̃] *nf* AVÈNEMENT : accession, attainment

accessoire[1] [akseswar] *adj* : accessory, incidental

accessoire[2] *nm* **1** : accessory **2 accessoires** *nmpl* : props

accessoirement [akseswarmɑ̃] *adv* **1** : secondarily, incidentally **2** : if necessary, if need be

accident [aksidɑ̃] *nm* : accident <par accident : by accident, accidentally>

accidenté[1], -tée [aksidɑ̃te] *adj* **1** BLESSÉ : injured **2** ENDOMMAGÉ : damaged **3** INÉGAL : uneven, broken <terrain accidenté : uneven ground>

accidenté[2], -tée *n* : victim (of an accident), injured person

accidentel, -telle [aksidɑ̃tɛl] *adj* : accidental — **accidentellement** [-tɛlmɑ̃] *adv*

accise [aksiz] *nf Bel, Can* : excise tax

acclamation [aklamasjɔ̃] *nf* : acclamation, cheering

acclamer [aklame] *vt* : to acclaim, to cheer

acclimatation [aklimatasjɔ̃] *nf* : acclimatization

acclimater [aklimate] *vt* : to acclimatize — **s'acclimater** *vr*

accolade [akɔlad] *nf* **1** : accolade **2** EMBRASSADE : embrace **3** : brace, bracket (in printing)

accoler [akɔle] *vt* **1** : to join side by side **2** : to bracket together (in printing)

accommodant, -dante [akɔmɔdɑ̃, -dɑ̃t] *adj* : accommodating, flexible

accommodation [akɔmɔdasjɔ̃] *nf* : accommodation, adaptation

accommodement [akɔmɔdmɑ̃] *nm* : arrangement, compromise, terms

accommoder [akɔmɔde] *vt* **1** ADAPTER : to accommodate, to adapt **2** PRÉPARER : to prepare (food) — *vi* : to focus — **s'accommoder** *vr* : to make do, to put up with

accompagnateur, -trice [akɔ̃paɲatœr, -tris] *n* **1** : accompanist **2** GUIDE : chaperone, guide

accompagnement [akɔ̃paɲmɑ̃] *nm* : accompaniment

accompagner [akɔ̃paɲe] *vt* : to accompany

accompli, -lie [akɔ̃pli] *adj* **1** ACHEVÉ : finished, accomplished **2** CONSOMMÉ : consummate, expert

accomplir [akɔ̃plir] *vt* : to accomplish, to perform, to realize — **s'accomplir** *vr* **1** : to take place **2** : to be fulfilled

accomplissement [akɔ̃plismɑ̃] *nm* : accomplishment, performance

accord [akɔr] *nm* **1** : agreement, understanding <d'accord : in agreement, agreed> <en accord avec : in harmony with> **2** PACTE : pact, agreement, accord (in politics, etc.) **3** : approval, consent **4** : chord (in music)

accordéon [akɔrdeɔ̃] *nm* : accordion

accorder [akɔrde] *vt* **1** : to make agree, to reconcile, to match **2** OCTROYER : to grant, to give **3** : to tune (a musical instrument) — **s'accorder** *vr* : to be in agreement

accordeur [akɔrdœr] *nm* : tuner (of musical instruments)

accoster [akɔste] *vt* **1** ABORDER : to approach, to accost **2** : to come alongside — *vi* : to dock, to land

accotement [akɔtmɑ̃] *nm* : shoulder (of a road)

accoter [akɔte] *vt* : to lean, to rest — **s'accoter** *vr* **~ à** *or* **~ contre** : to lean against

accouchement [akuʃmɑ̃] *nm* : childbirth

accoucher [akuʃe] *vt* : to deliver (a child) — *vi* **1** : to be in labor **2 ~ de** : to give birth to

accoucheur, -cheuse [akuʃœr, -ʃøz] *n* : obstetrician

accoucheuse *nf* SAGE-FEMME : midwife

accouder [akude] *v* **s'accouder** *vr* **1** : to lean on one's elbows **2 ~ à** *or* **~ sur** : to lean (one's elbows) on

accoudoir [akudwar] *nm* : armrest

accouplement [akupləmɑ̃] *nm* **1** : coupling **2** : mating

accoupler [akuple] *vt* **1** : to couple, to link **2** : to mate (of animals) **3** : to yoke (draft animals) — **s'accoupler** *vr* : to mate

accourir [akurir] {23} *vi* : to come running, to run up

accoutrement [akutrəmɑ̃] *nm* : outfit, getup

accoutumance [akutymɑ̃s] *nf* **1** ACCLIMATATION : acclimatization, habituation **2** DÉPENDANCE : dependency, addiction

accoutumé, -mée [akutyme] *adj* : usual, customary

accoutumer [akutyme] *vt* HABITUER : to accustom — **s'accoutumer** *vr* **~ à** : to get accustomed to, to get used to

accréditation [akreditasjɔ̃] *nf* : accreditation

accréditer [akredite] *vt* **1** : to accredit (a person) **2** : to substantiate (a rumor, etc.) —**s'accréditer** *vr* : to gain credibility

accroc [akro] *nm* **1** DÉCHIRURE : rip, tear **2** OBSTACLE : obstacle, hitch, snag

accrochage [akrɔʃaʒ] *nm* **1** : hanging (for display) **2** : hooking, hitching **3** : (military) skirmish **4** : clash, dispute **5** : minor collision (of an automobile)

accroche [akrɔʃ] *nf* : slogan, catch phrase

accrocher [akrɔʃe] *vt* **1** : to hang up **2** : to hook, to hitch **3** : to get hold of (a person), to catch <accrocher le regard : to catch the eye> <accrocher un client : to buttonhole a client> **4** : to bump into, to hit — *vi* **1** : to catch, to stick, to snag **2** : to attract attention, to catch on — **s'accrocher** *vr* **1** : to hang on, to persevere **2** SE DISPUTER : to quarrel **3 ~ à** : to hold on to, to cling to

accrocheur, -cheuse [akrɔʃœr, -ʃøz] *adj* **1** TENACE : tenacious **2** : catchy, eye-catching

accroire [akrwar] {2} *vt* **en faire accroire à** : to take in, to dupe

accroissement [akrwasmɑ̃] *nm* AUGMENTATION : growth, increase

accroître [akrwatr] {25} *vt* : to increase — **s'accroître** *vr*

accroupir [akrupir] *v* **s'accroupir** *vr* : to squat, to crouch

accueil [akœj] *nm* RÉCEPTION : welcome, reception <faire bon accueil à : to welcome>

accueillant, -lante [akœjɑ̃, -jɑ̃t] *adj* HOSPITALIER : welcoming, hospitable

accueillir [akœjir] {3} *vt* : to greet, to welcome

acculer [akyle] *vt* **1** : to drive, to force **2 ~ à** *or* **~ contre** : to drive (someone) back against **3 ~ dans** : to corner (someone) in

accumulateur [akymylatœr] *nm* : storage battery

accumulation [akymylasjɔ̃] *nf* : accumulation

accumuler [akymyle] *vt* : to accumulate, to amass — **s'accumuler** *vr*

accusateur[1], -trice [akyzatœr, -tris] *adj* : accusatory, incriminating

accusateur[2], -trice *n* : accuser

accusatif [akyzatif] *nm* : accusative (case)

accusation [akyzasjɔ̃] *nf* **1** : accusation **2 l'accusation** : the prosecution **3 mise en accusation** : indictment **4 mettre en accusation** : to indict

accusé[1], -sée [akyze] *adj* : marked, pronounced, prominent

accusé[2], -sée *n* : defendant, accused

accusé[3] *nm* **accusé de réception** : acknowledgment of receipt

accuser [akyze] *vt* **1** : to accuse, to blame **2** : to show (up), to emphasize, to accentuate **3 accuser réception de** : to acknowledge receipt of

acerbe [asɛrb] *adj* : acerbic, harsh

acéré, -rée [asere] *adj* : sharp

acétate[1] [asetat] *nm* : acetate

acétate[2] *nf Can* : transparency

acétylène [asetilɛn] *nm* : acetylene

achalandage [aʃalɑ̃daʒ] *nm* : clientele

achalandé, -dée [aʃalɑ̃de] *adj* **bien achalandé** : well-stocked

achaler [aʃale] *vt Can fam* : to annoy — **achalant, -lante** [aʃalɑ̃, -lɑ̃t] *adj*

acharné, -née [aʃarne] *adj* : fierce, unremitting, relentless

acharnement [aʃarnəmɑ] *nm* : determination, relentlessness

acharner [aʃarne] *v* **s'acharner** *vr* **1** : to persevere, to persist **2 ~ sur** : to persecute, to hound

achat [aʃa] *nm* **1** : purchasing, buying <faire des achats : to do some shopping> **2** EMPLETTE : purchase

acheminement [aʃminmɑ̃] *nm* : transporting, dispatch (of goods)

acheminer [aʃmine] *vt* : to transport, to convey — **s'acheminer** *vr* **~ vers** : to move toward, to head for

acheter [aʃte] {20} *vt* : to buy, to purchase

acheteur, -teuse [aʃtœr, -tøz] *n* ACQUÉREUR : buyer

achèvement [aʃɛvmɑ̃] *nm* : completion

achever [aʃve] {52} *vt* TERMINER : to complete, to finish — **s'achever** *vr* **1** : to reach completion, to end **2** : to draw to a close

achigan [aʃigɑ̃] *nm Can* : black bass

achoppement [aʃɔpmɑ̃] *nm* **pierre d'achoppement** : obstacle, stumbling block

achopper [aʃɔpe] *vi* : to stumble — **s'achopper** *vr*

acide[1] [asid] *adj* : acid, acidic

acide[2] *nm* : acid

acidité [asidite] *nf* : acidity, tartness, sourness

acidulé, -lée [asidyle] *adj* : somewhat acid, tangy

acier [asje] *nm* : steel <acier inoxydable : stainless steel>

aciérie [asjeri] *nf* : steelworks

acné [akne] *nf* : acne

acolyte [akɔlit] *nm* **1** : acolyte (in religion) **2** : accomplice, confederate

acompte [akɔ̃t] *nm* **1** : deposit, down payment **2** : installment

aconit [akɔnit] *nm* : monkshood

acoquiner [akɔkine] *v* **s'acoquiner** *vr* **~ avec** : to team up with, to gang up with

à–côté [akote] *nm, pl* **à–côtés 1** : side issue **2** : extra money, perk

à–coup [aku] *nm, pl* **à–coups** : jerk, jolt <par à-coups : in fits and starts>

acoustique[1] [akustik] *adj* : acoustic

acoustique[2] *nf* : acoustics

acquéreur, -reuse [akerœr, -røz] *n* ACHETEUR : buyer

acquérir [akerir] {21} *vt* **1** : to acquire, to obtain **2** : to purchase — **s'acquérir** *vr* : to gain, to win (approval, etc.)

acquière [akjɛr], **acquiert** [akjɛr], *etc.* → **acquérir**

acquiescement [akjɛsmɑ̃] *nm* : acquiescence

acquiescer [akjese] {6} *vi* : to aquiesce, to agree

acquis[1] [aki] *pp* → **acquérir**

acquis[2], **-quise** [aki, -kiz] *adj* **1** : acquired **2** : established, accepted <fait acquis : accepted fact> <tenir pour acquis : to take for granted>

acquis[3] *nms & pl* **1** : knowledge, experience **2** : benefit, gain

acquisition [akizisjɔ̃] *nf* **1** : acquisition **2** : purchase

acquit [aki] *nm* **1** : receipt <par acquit : received> **2 par acquit de conscience** : to put one's mind at ease

acquittement [akitmɑ̃] *nm* **1** : payment (of a debt), fulfillment (of a promise, etc.) **2** : acquittal

acquitter [akite] *vt* **1** : to acquit **2** PAYER : to settle, to pay (off) — **s'acquitter** *vr* **1** : to pay (a debt), to fulfill (an obligation, etc.)

acre [akr] *nf* : acre

âcre [akr] *adj* : acrid, bitter, pungent

âcreté [akrəte] *nf* : bitterness, pungency

acrimonie [akrimɔni] *nf* : acrimony

acrimonieux, -nieuse [akrimɔnjø, -njøz] *adj* : acrimonious — **acrimonieusement** [-njøzmɑ̃] *adv*

acrobate [akrɔbat] *nmf* : acrobat

acrobatie [akrɔbasi] *nf* : acrobatics

acrobatique [akrɔbatik] *adj* : acrobatic

acronyme [akrɔnim] *nm* : acronym

acrylique [akrilik] *adj & nm* : acrylic

acte [akt] *nm* **1** : action, deed <acte gratuit : gratuitous act> <faire acte de présence : to put in an appearance> **2** : act (in a play) **3** : certificate, document <acte de naissance : birth certificate> <acte de vente : bill of sale> **4 actes** *nmpl* : proceedings

acteur, -trice [aktœr, -tris] *n* COMÉDIEN : actor, actress *f*

actif[1], **-tive** [aktif, -tiv] *adj* **1** : active **2** : working <les mères actives : working mothers>

actif[2] *nm* **1** : assets *pl,* credits *pl* **2** : active voice (in grammar)

action [aksjɔ̃] *nf* **1** : action, act <une bonne action : a good deed> <passer à l'action : to go into action> **2** : effect <sous l'action de : due to the effect of, because of> **3** : share (of a security) **4** : lawsuit **5 action de grâce(s)** : thanksgiving (in religion)

actionnaire [aksjɔnɛr] *nmf* : stockholder, shareholder

actionner [aksjɔne] *vt* **1** : to engage, to put into motion, to turn on **2** : to sue

activement [aktivmɑ̃] *adv* : actively, busily

activer [aktive] *vt* **1** : to activate **2** : to speed up — **s'activer** *vr* **1** : to bustle

about, to be busy **2** *fam* : to get a move on
activisme [aktivism] *nm* : activism
activiste [aktivist] *adj & nmf* : activist
activité [aktivite] *nf* : activity <être en activité : to be active, to be in operation>
actrice → **acteur**
actuaire [aktɥɛr] *nmf* : actuary
actualisation [aktɥalizasjɔ̃] *nf* : updating, modernization
actualiser [aktɥalize] *vt* : to update, to modernize
actualité [aktɥalite] *nf* **1** : current events *pl* **2** : relevance **3 les actualités** *nfpl* : the news
actuel, -tuelle [aktɥɛl] *adj* : current, present — **actuellement** [-tɥɛlmɑ̃] *adv*
acuité [akɥite] *nf* : acuteness
acupuncture [akypɔ̃ktyr] *nf* : acupuncture
adage [adaʒ] *nm* MAXIME : adage
adaptabilité [adaptabilite] *nf* : adaptability
adaptable [adaptabl] *adj* : adaptable, adjustable
adaptateur [adaptatœr] *nm* : adapter
adaptation [adaptasjɔ̃] *nf* : adaptation
adapter [adapte] *vt* : to adapt, to fit — **s'adapter** *vr* **1** : to adapt **2** : to suit, to be appropriate
additif [aditif] *nm* : additive
addition [adisjɔ̃] *nf* **1** : addition **2** NOTE : bill, check (in a restaurant)
additionnel, -nelle [adisjɔnɛl] *adj* : additional
additionner [adisjɔne] *vt* : to add, to add up
adepte [adɛpt] *nmf* : follower, enthusiast
adéquat, -quate [adekwa, -kwat] *adj* **1** SUFFISANT : adequate **2** CONVENABLE : appropriate — **adéquatement** [-kwatmɑ̃] *adv*
adéquation [adekwasjɔ̃] *nf* : appropriateness, suitability
adhérence [aderɑ̃s] *nf* : adhesion
adhérent[1], -rente [aderɑ̃, -rɑ̃t] *adj* : adhering, sticking
adhérent[2], -rente *n* MEMBRE : member
adhérer [adere] {87} *vi* **1** : to adhere, to stick <adhérer à la route : to stick to the road> **2 ~ à** : to join
adhésif[1], -sive [adezif, -ziv] *adj* : adhesive
adhésif[2] *nm* : adhesive
adhésion [adezjɔ̃] *nf* **1** : adhesion, sticking **2** : adherence, support **3** : joining, membership
adieu [adjø] *nm, pl* **adieux** : farewell, good-bye <faire ses adieux à : to say good-bye to> <un discours d'adieu : a farewell address>
adjacent, -cente [adʒasɑ̃, -sɑ̃t] *adj* : adjacent
adjectif[1], -tive *adj* [adʒɛktif, -tiv] : adjectival
adjectif[2] *nm* : adjective
adjectival, -vale [adʒɛktival] *adj, mpl* **-vaux** [-vo] : adjectival
adjoindre [adʒwɛ̃dr] {50} *vt* **1** : to appoint (as an assistant) **2** : to add, to attach — **s'adjoindre** *vr* **s'adjoindre qqn** : to take s.o. on, to hire s.o.
adjoint, -jointe [adʒwɛ̃, -ʒwɛ̃t] *adj & n* : assistant
adjonction [adʒɔ̃ksjɔ̃] *nf* : addition
adjudant [adʒydɑ̃] *nm* : warrant officer, adjutant
adjudication [adʒydikasjɔ̃] *nf* **1** : auctioning, sale by auction **2** : awarding (of a contract)
adjuger [adʒyʒe] {17} *vt* **1** DÉCERNER : to award **2** : to auction — **s'adjuger** *vr* : to claim, to take for oneself
adjurer [adʒyre] *vt* SUPPLIER : to implore, to beseech
admettre [admɛtr] {53} *vt* **1** : to admit, to let in **2** : to acknowledge, to concede **3** : to permit, to accept
administrateur, -trice [administratœr, -tris] *n* : director, administrator
administratif, -tive [administratif, -tiv] *adj* : administrative — **administrativement** [-tivmɑ̃] *adv*
administration [administrasjɔ̃] *nf* : administration <administration commerciale : business administration>
administrer [administre] *vt* **1** GÉRER : to administer, to manage **2** : to dispense <administrer un médicament : to administer a drug>
admirable [admirabl] *adj* : admirable — **admirablement** [-rabləmɑ̃] *adv*
admirateur, -trice [admiratœr, -tris] *n* : admirer
admiratif, -tive [admiratif, -tiv] *adj* : admiring — **admirativement** [-tivmɑ̃] *adj*
admiration [admirasjɔ̃] *nf* : admiration
admirer [admire] *vt* : to admire
admissible [admisibl] *adj* : admissible, eligible
admission [admisjɔ̃] *nf* **1** : admission **2** : intake, induction
admonester [admɔnɛste] *vt* : to admonish
admonition [admɔnisjɔ̃] *nf* : admonition
ADN [adeɛn] *nm* : DNA
ado [ado] *nmf fam* : adolescent, teenager
adolescence [adɔlesɑ̃s] *nf* : adolescence — **adolescent, -cente** [-lesɑ̃, -sɑ̃t] *adj & n*
adon [adɔ̃] *nm Can* : lucky break
adonner [adɔne] *vi Can fam* : to be convenient <viens me voir si ça adonne : drop by if you get a chance> — **s'adonner** *vr* **1 ~ à** : to devote oneself to **2 ~ avec** *Can* : to get along well with
adopter [adɔpte] *vt* : to adopt
adoptif, -tive [adɔptif, -tiv] *adj* : adoptive, adopted

adoption [adɔpsjɔ̃] *nf* : adoption

adorable [adɔrabl] *adj* : adorable — **adorablement** [-rabləmɑ̃] *adv*

adoration [adɔrasjɔ̃] *nf* : adoration

adorer [adɔre] *vt* **1** : to adore, to worship **2** : to love

adosser [adose] *vt* **1** : to place back to back **2** **~ à** *or* **~ contre** : to lean against — **s'adosser** *vr*

adoucir [adusir] *vt* **1** : to soften, to tone down, to subdue **2** : to sweeten **3** : to alleviate, to ease — **s'adoucir** *vr*

adoucissement [adusismɑ̃] *nm* **1** : softening **2** : sweetening **3** : alleviation, easing, mitigation

adrénaline [adrenalin] *nf* : adrenalin

adresse [adrɛs] *nf* **1** : address **2** HABILETÉ : skill, dexterity <adresse au tir : marksmanship>

adresser [adrese] *vt* **1** : to address (correspondence) **2** : to direct, to aim (remarks, etc.) — **s'adresser** *vr*

adroit, -droite [adrwa, -drwat] *adj* **1** HABILE : skillful **2** : clever, shrewd — **adroitement** [-drwatmɑ̃] *adv*

aduler [adyle] *vt* : to adulate — **adulation** [adylasjɔ̃] *nf*

adulte [adylt] *adj & nmf* : adult, grown-up

adultère[1] [adyltɛr] *adj* : adulterous

adultère[2] *nm* : adultery

adultère[3] *nmf* : adulterer *m*, adulteress *f*

advenir [advənir] {4} *v impers* **1** : to occur, to happen <advienne que pourra : whatever happens, come what may> **2** **~ de** : to become of <qu'est-il advenu de Jeanne? : what(ever) became of Jeanne?>

adverbe [advɛrb] *nm* : adverb — **adverbial, -biale** [-vɛrbjal] *adj*

adversaire [advɛrsɛr] *nmf* : adversary, opponent

adverse [advɛrs] *adj* **1** : opposing **2** : adverse, unfavorable <circonstances adverses : adverse circumstances>

adversité [advɛrsite] *nf* : adversity

aération [aerasjɔ̃] *nf* **1** : ventilation **2** : aeration

aérer [aere] {87} *vt* **1** VENTILER : to ventilate, to air out **2** : to aerate (soil, etc.) **3** : to lighten, to thin out (a written text) — **s'aérer** *vr* : to get some fresh air

aérien, -rienne [aerjɛ̃, -rjɛn] *adj* **1** : aerial, air <transport aérien : air transport> **2** : overhead, aerial **3** : ethereal, airy

aérobic [aerɔbik] *nm* : aerobics

aérobie [aerɔbi] *adj* : aerobic

aérobique [aerɔbik] *adj Can* : aerobic <danse aérobique : aerobics>

aérodrome [aerɔdrom] *nm* : airfield

aérodynamique[1] [aerɔdinamik] *adj* : aerodynamic — **aérodynamiquement** [-mikmɑ̃] *adv*

aérodynamique[2] *nf* : aerodynamics

aérogare [aerɔgar] *nf* : air terminal

aéroglisseur [aerɔglisœr] *nm* : hovercraft

aérogramme [aerɔgram] *nm* : air letter, aerogram

aéronaute [aerɔnot] *nmf* : balloonist

aéronautique[1] [aerɔnotik] *adj* : aeronautical

aéronautique[2] *nf* : aeronautics

aéronaval, -vale [aerɔnaval] *adj, pl* **-vals** : air and sea

aéronef [aerɔnɛf] *nm* : aircraft

aéroport [aerɔpɔr] *nm* : airport

aéroporté, -tée [aerɔpɔrte] *adj* : airborne

aéropostal, -tale [aerɔpɔstal] *adj, mpl* **-taux** [-to] : airmail

aérosol [aerɔsɔl] *nm* : aerosol

aérospatial, -tiale [aerɔspasjal] *adj, mpl* **-tiaux** [-sjo] : aerospace

affabilité [afabilite] *nf* : affability

affable [afabl] *adj* : affable — **affablement** [afabləmɑ̃] *adv*

affadir [afadir] *vt* **1** : to make bland **2** : to cause to fade — **s'affadir** *vr*

affaiblir [afeblir] *vt* : to weaken — **s'affaiblir** *vr* **1** : to become weak **2** : to diminish, to fade

affaire [afɛr] *nf* **1** : affair, matter, business <ce n'est pas mon affaire : that's none of my business> <affaire de cœur : love affair> **2** : business, enterprise **3** : deal <une (bonne) affaire : a bargain, a good deal> **4** PROCÈS : case, lawsuit **5** **affaires** *nfpl* : possessions, belongings **6** **affaires** *nfpl* : business <homme d'affaires : businessman> **7** **avoir affaire à** : to be faced with, to be dealing with

affairé, -rée [afere] *adj* OCCUPÉ : busy

affairer [afere] *v* **s'affairer** *vr* : to be busy, to bustle about

affaissement [afɛsmɑ̃] *nm* **1** EFFONDREMENT : subsidence (of the earth), caving in **2** : sagging, sinking

affaisser [afese] *v* **s'affaisser** *vr* **1** : to collapse **2** : to sag, to sink, to subside

affaler [afale] *v* **s'affaler** *vr* : to collapse, to fall, to slump

affamé, -mée [afame] *adj* : famished, starving

affamer [afame] *vt* : to starve

affectation [afɛktasjɔ̃] *nf* **1** : assignment, appointment **2** : allocation, allotment <affectation des fonds : allocation of funds> **3** : affectation

affecté, -tée [afɛkte] *adj* : mannered, affected

affecter [afɛkte] *vt* **1** : to affect **2** : to assign **3** : to allocate, to allot **4** FEINDRE : to feign

affectif, -tive [afɛktif, -tiv] *adj* : affective, emotional

affection [afɛksjɔ̃] *nf* **1** : affection, caring **2** : ailment, condition <affection respiratoire : respiratory complaint>

affectionner [afɛksjɔne] *vt* AIMER : to like, to be fond of

affectueux, -tueuse [afɛktɥø, -tɥøz] *adj* : affectionate — **affectueusement** [-tɥøzmɑ̃] *adv*

afférent, -rente [aferɑ̃, -rɑ̃t] *adj* **~ à** : pertaining to, relating to

affermir [afɛrmir] *vt* **1** : to strengthen, to firm up (muscles, etc.) **2** : to reinforce, to consolidate

affermissement [afɛrmismɑ̃] *nm* : strengthening

affichage [afiʃaʒ] *nm* **1** : publicizing, posting **2** : display <affichage numérique : digital display> **3 panneau d'affichage** : bulletin board **4 tableau d'affichage** : scoreboard

affiche [afiʃ] *nf* **1** : poster, notice **2 tenir l'affiche** : to open (of a play, etc.)

afficher [afiʃe] *vt* **1** : to post <défense d'afficher : post no bills> **2** : to show, to display — **s'afficher** *vr*

affidavit [afidavit] *nm* : affidavit

affilé, -lée [afile] *adj* : sharp, keen

affilée [afile] *adv* **d'~** : in a row

affiler [afile] *vt* : to sharpen

affiliation [afiljasjɔ̃] *nf* : affiliation

affilier [afilje] {96} *vt* : to affiliate — **s'affilier** *vr* **~ à** : to become affiliated with, to join

affiner [afine] *vt* **1** : to refine **2** : to ripen (cheese) — **s'affiner** *vr*

affinité [afinite] *nf* : affinity

affirmatif, -tive [afirmatif, -tiv] *adj* : affirmative — **affirmativement** [-tivmɑ̃] *adv*

affirmative *nf* : affirmative <répondre par l'affirmative : to answer in the affirmative>

affirmation [afirmasjɔ̃] *nf* : affirmation, assertion

affirmative *nf* : affirmative

affirmer [afirme] *vt* **1** : to maintain, to contend, to affirm **2** : to assert (authority, etc.) — **s'affirmer** *vr* : to assert oneself

affleurement [aflœrmɑ̃] *nm* : outcrop

affleurer [aflœre] *vt* : to make even or flush — *vi* : to come to the surface

affliction [afliksjɔ̃] *nf* : affliction

affligeant, -geante [afliʒɑ̃, -ʒɑ̃t] *adj* : distressing, sorrowful

affliger [afliʒe] {17} *vt* : to afflict, to distress — **s'affliger** *vr*

affluence [aflyɑ̃s] *nf* **1** : crowd **2** ABONDANCE : abundance **3 heure d'affluence** : rush hour

affluent [aflyɑ̃] *nm* : tributary

affluer [aflye] *vi* **1** COULER : to flow, to roll in (of money) **2** : to flock, to surge

afflux [afly] *nm* : influx, rush

affolé, -lée [afɔle] *adj* : panicked, frightened

affolement [afɔlmɑ̃] *nm* : panic

affoler [afɔle] *vt* **1** : to drive crazy **2** EFFRAYER : to frighten — **s'affoler** *vr* : to panic

affranchir [afrɑ̃ʃir] *vt* **1** LIBÉRER : to liberate, to free **2** TIMBRER : to stamp, to postmark

affranchissement [afrɑ̃ʃismɑ̃] *nm* **1** LIBÉRATION : liberation, emancipation **2** : franking, stamping **3** : postage (of a letter, etc.)

affres [afr] *nfpl* : agony, pangs, throes

affrètement [afrɛtmɑ̃] *nm* : renting, chartering

affréter [afrete] {87} *vt* : to charter <vols affrétés : chartered flights>

affreux, -freuse [afrø, -frøz] *adj* : awful, dreadful — **affreusement** [afrøzmɑ̃] *adv*

affrioler [afrijɔle] *vt* : to tempt, to entice — **affriolant, -lante** [-jɔlɑ̃, -lɑ̃t] *adj*

affront [afrɔ̃] *nm* INSULTE : affront

affrontement [afrɔ̃tmɑ̃] *nm* : confrontation, clash

affronter [afrɔ̃te] *vt* : to confront, to brave, to face — **s'affronter** *vr*

affubler [afyble] *vt fam* : to dress up, to deck out — **s'affubler** *vr*

affût [afy] *nm* **1** : carriage (for heavy artillery) **2** : hiding place, blind <être à l'affût de : to lie in wait for, to be on the lookout for>

affûter [afyte] *vt* AIGUISER : to sharpen, to hone

afghan, -ghane [afgɑ̃, -gan] *adj* : Afghan

Afghan, -ghane *n* : Afghan

afin [afɛ̃] *adv* **1 ~ de** : in order to <afin de trouver une solution : in order to find a solution> **2 ~ que** : so that <afin que le public comprenne : so that the public understands>

africain, -caine [afrikɛ̃, -kɛn] *adj* : African

Africain, -caine *n* : African

agaçant, -çante [agasɑ̃, -sɑ̃t] *adj* : annoying, irritating

agacement [agasmɑ̃] *nm* IRRITATION : irritation, annoyance

agacer [agase] {6} *vt* ÉNERVER : to annoy, to irritate

agate [agat] *nf* : agate

âge [aʒ] *nm* **1** : age <quel âge avez-vous? : how old are you?> <les gens du troisième âge : senior citizens> **2** : age, era <le Moyen Âge : the Middle Ages>

âgé, -gée [aʒe] *adj* **1** : old, aged, of age <âgé de seize ans : sixteen years old> **2** VIEUX : elderly, old <les personnes âgées : elderly persons>

agence [aʒɑ̃s] *nf* BUREAU : agency, office <agence de voyage : travel agency> <agence immobilière : real estate agency>

agencement [aʒɑ̃smɑ̃] *nm* : layout, arrangement

agencer [aʒɑ̃se] {6} *vt* **1** : to arrange, to lay out **2** : to put together, to construct

agenda [aʒɛ̃da] *nm* **1** : agenda **2** CARNET : appointment book

agenouiller [aʒnuje] *v* **s'agenouiller** *vr* : to kneel

agent[1], **-gente** [aʒɑ̃, -ʒɑ̃t] *n* **1** : agent <agent d'assurances : insurance agent> <agent de change : stockbroker> **2** : officer <agent de police : police officer>

agent[2] *nm* **1** : agent, factor <agents économiques : economic factors> **2** : agent (in chemistry, medicine, etc.)

agglomération [aglɔmerasjɔ̃] *nf* **1** AMAS, ASSEMBLAGE : conglomeration, agglomeration **2** : city, town **3** : urban area

aggloméré [aglɔmere] *nm* **1** : particleboard, fiberboard **2** : briquette, charcoal

agglomérer [aglɔmere] {87} *vt* : to agglomerate, to pile up — **s'agglomérer** *vr* : to aggregate, to gather together

agglutiner [aglytine] *vt* : to stick together — **s'agglutiner** *vr* : to gather

aggravation [agravasjɔ̃] *nf* : aggravation, worsening

aggraver [agrave] *vt* : to aggravate, to make worse — **s'aggraver** *vr* EMPIRER : to worsen, to get worse

agile [aʒil] *adj* : agile — **agilement** [aʒilmɑ̃] *adv*

agilité [aʒilite] *nf* : agility

agir [aʒir] *vi* **1** : to act, to take action **2** : to behave <elle agit comme une sainte : she acts like a saint> **3** : to operate, to take effect <la drogue agira vite : the drug will take effect quickly> — **s'agir** *vr* **1 ~ de** : to concern, to be a question of <de quoi s'agit-il? : what is it about?> **2 ~ de** : to be necessary <pour vivre, il s'agit de manger : one must eat to live>

agissements [aʒismɑ̃] *nmpl* : dealings, schemes, machinations

agitation [aʒitasjɔ̃] *nf* **1** : agitation, restlessness **2** : hustle and bustle, activity **3** : (social) unrest **4** : choppiness (of the sea)

agité, -tée [aʒite] *adj* **1** : restless, agitated **2** : rough <eaux agités : rough waters>

agiter [aʒite] *vt* **1** SECOUER : to agitate, to shake **2** TROUBLER : to disturb **3** DÉBATTRE : to debate — **s'agiter** *vr* **1** : to bustle about **2** : to fidget **3** : to become agitated

agneau [aɲo] *nm, pl* **agneaux 1** : lamb **2** : lambskin

agnelle [aɲɛl] *nf* : young ewe

agnostique [agnɔstik] *adj & nmf* : agnostic

agonie [agɔni] *nf* : death throes *pl*

agoniser [agɔnize] *vi* : to be dying

agrafe [agraf] *nf* **1** : hook, fastener **2** : staple **3** : clamp, clip (in medicine)

agrafer [agrafe] *vt* **1** : to fasten **2** : staple **3** *fam* : to catch, to nab

agrafeuse [agraføz] *nf* : stapler

agraire [agrɛr] *adj* : agrarian <réforme agraire : land reform>

agrandir [agrɑ̃dir] *vt* : to enlarge, to expand — **s'agrandir** *vr* : to grow, to be enlarged

agrandissement [agrɑ̃dismɑ̃] *nm* : enlargement, expansion

agréable [agreabl] *adj* : pleasant, agreeable — **agréablement** [-abləmɑ̃] *adv*

agréé, agréée [agree] *adj* : accepted, certified <expert-comptable agréé : certified public accountant>

agréer [agree] *vt* {89} **1** ACCEPTER : to accept, to approve <veuillez agréer, l'expression de mes sentiments les meilleurs : yours sincerely> **2 ~ à** : to suit, to agree with

agrégat [agrega] *nm* : aggregate, mass

agrégation [agregasjɔ̃] *nf* **1** *France* : qualifying exam for a teacher or professor **2** : aggregation

agrégé, -gée [agreʒe] *n France* : certified teacher or professor

agréger [agreʒe] *vt* {64} **1** : to aggregate **2** INTÉGRER : to incorporate, to accept (into a group)

agrément [agremɑ̃] *nm* **1** CONSENTEMENT : consent, authorization **2** : pleasure <voyage d'agrément : pleasure trip> **3** : charm, attractiveness

agrémenter [agremɑ̃te] *vt* ORNER : to decorate, to trim, to embellish

agrès [agrɛ] *nmpl* : apparatus (for gymnastics)

agresser [agrese] *vt* ASSAILLIR : to attack, to assault

agresseur [agrɛsœr] *nm* : attacker, assailant, aggressor

agressif, -sive [agrɛsif, -siv] *adj* : aggressive — **agressivement** [-sivmɑ̃] *adv*

agression [agrɛsjɔ̃] *nf* **1** : attack, assault **2** : aggression

agressivité [agrɛsivite] *nf* : aggressiveness

agricole [agrikɔl] *adj* : agricultural

agriculteur, -trice [agrikyltœr, -tris] *n* : farmer

agriculture [agricyltyr] *nf* : agriculture, farming

agripper [agripe] *vt* : to clutch, to grab — **s'agripper** *vr* : to cling

agrumes [agrym] *nmpl* : citrus fruits

aguets [agɛ] *nmpl* **aux aguets** : on the lookout

aguicher [agiʃe] *vt* : to entice, to allure

ah [a] *interj* : oh <ah oui? : is that so?>

ahuri, -rie [ayri] *adj* **1** : amazed, dumbfounded **2** : dazed, stupefied

ahurir [ayrir] *vt* : to astound, to stun, to daze

ahurissant, -sante [ayrisɑ̃, -sɑ̃t] *adj* : astounding, amazing

ahurissement [ayrismɑ̃] *nm* STUPÉFACTION : amazement, stupefaction

aide[1] [ɛd] *nmf* : assistant

aide[2] *nf* **1** : help, aid <à l'aide! : help!> <à l'aide de : with the help of> **2** *Can* : assist (in sports)

aider [ede] *vt* ASSISTER : to help, to assist
aïe [aj] *interj* : ouch!
aïeul, aïeule [ajœl] *n* : grandfather *m,* grandmother *f*
aïeux [ajø] *nmpl* : ancestors, forefathers
aigle [ɛgl] *nm* **1** : eagle **2 aigle d'Amérique** *or* **aigle à tête blanche** : bald eagle
aiglefin [ɛgləfɛ̃] *nm* → **églefin**
aigre [ɛgr] *adj* **1** : sour, tart **2** : sharp, bitter <un vent aigre : a bitter wind>
aigre–doux, -douce [ɛgrədu, -dus] *adj* **1** : bittersweet **2** : sweet and sour
aigrette [ɛgrɛt] *nf* **1** : egret **2** : tuft, spray (of feathers)
aigreur [ɛgrœr] *nf* **1** : sourness, tartness **2** : bitterness
aigrir [egrir] *vt* **1** : to turn sour **2** : to embitter — *vi* : to sour, to become sour — **s'aigrir** *vr*
aigu, -guë [egy] *adj* **1** : sharp, keen **2** : acute, intense <une douleur aiguë : an acute pain> **3** STRIDENT : strident, high-pitched **4** → **accent**
aiguille [egɥij] *nf* **1** : needle **2** : hand (of a clock) <l'aiguille des minutes : the minute hand> **3** PIC : mountain peak **4 aiguille de glace** : icicle **5 travail à l'aiguille** : needlework
aiguiller [egɥije] *vt* **1** : to switch (in railroading) **2** : to steer, to direct
aiguilleur [egɥijœr] *nm* **1** : switchman **2 aiguilleur du ciel** : air traffic controller
aiguillon [egɥijɔ̃] *nm* **1** : goad **2** : stinger **3** : incentive, spur
aiguillonner [egɥijɔne] *vt* **1** : to goad, to prod **2** : to stimulate, to spur
aiguise–crayon [egizkrɛjɔ̃] *nm, pl* **aiguise–crayons** *Can* : pencil sharpener
aiguiser [egize] *vt* **1** AFFÛTER : to sharpen, to hone **2** : to stimulate, to whet
aiguisoir [egizwar] *nm* : (knife) sharpener
ail [aj] *nm, pl* **ails** *or* **aulx** [o] : garlic
aile [ɛl] *nf* **1** : wing **2** : fender (of an automobile) **3** : **voler de ses propres ailes** : to stand on one's own two feet
aileron [ɛlrɔ̃] *nm* **1** : flap, aileron **2** : fin (of a shark, etc.), wing tip (of a bird)
ailier [elje] *nm* : wing, winger (in sports)
aille [aj], *etc.* → **aller**
ailleurs [ajœr] *adv* **1** : elsewhere **2 d'~** : besides, moreover, by the way **3 par ~** : in addition, what's more
aimable [ɛmabl] *adj* GENTIL : kind, likeable — **aimablement** [ɛmabləmɑ̃] *adv*
aimant[1]**, -mante** [ɛmɑ̃, -mɑ̃t] *adj* : loving, caring
aimant[2] *nm* : magnet
aimanter [ɛmɑ̃te] *vt* : to magnetize
aimer [eme] *vt* **1** : to love **2** *or* **aimer bien** : to like **3 aimer mieux** : to prefer
aine [ɛn] *nf* : groin
aîné[1]**, -née** [ene] *adj* **1** : elder, older **2** : eldest, oldest **3** : senior
aîné[2]**, -née** *n* **1** : elder child, elder son *m,* elder daughter *f* **2** : eldest child, eldest son *m,* eldest daughter *f* **3** : older person, oldest person <il est mon aîné de cinq ans : he's five years older than me>
ainsi [ɛ̃si] *adv* **1** : thus, in this way, in that way <il m'a regardé ainsi : he looked at me like that> **2 ainsi que** : just as <elle l'a fait ainsi que tu disais : she did it just as you said she would> **3 ainsi que** : as well as <mes mains ainsi que mes pieds : my hands as well as my feet> **4 et ainsi de suite** : and so on **5 ainsi soit-il** : so be it, amen **6 pour ainsi dire** : so to speak
air [ɛr] *nm* **1** : air <en plein air : outside, in the open air> <courant d'air : draft> <air conditionné : air-conditioning> **2** MÉLODIE : tune, melody <air d'opéra : aria> **3** : appearance, look <avoir un air distingué : to look distinguished> **4** AMBIANCE : atmosphere, ambience **5 être en air** *Can* : to be ready and willing
aire [ɛr] *nf* **1** : area <aire de repos : rest area> **2** SURFACE : surface, area **3** DOMAINE : field, sphere <aire d'influence : sphere of influence> **4** : aerie
airelle [ɛrɛl] *nf* : blueberry
aisance [ezɑ̃s] *nf* **1** : ease, facility, fluency **2** : affluence, wealth <vivre dans l'aisance : to be well-off>
aise[1] [ɛz] *adj* : pleased
aise[2] *nf* **1** : ease <être mal à l'aise : to be ill at ease> **2** : pleasure **3 aises** *nfpl* : creature comforts
aisé, -sée [eze] *adj* **1** FACILE : easy **2** RICHE : wealthy, well-off **3** : graceful, fluent
aisément [ezemɑ̃] *adv* FACILEMENT : easily
aisselle [ɛsɛl] *nf* : armpit
ajouré, -rée [aʒure] *adj* : openworked, perforated
ajournement [aʒurnəmɑ̃] *nm* **1** : postponement **2** : adjournment, continuance (of a trial)
ajourner [aʒurne] *vt* **1** : to adjourn **2** : to postpone, to defer
ajout [aʒu] *nm* : addition (to a house, etc.)
ajouter [aʒute] *vt* ADDITIONNER : to add
ajustement [aʒystəmɑ̃] *nm* : adjustment
ajuster [aʒyste] *vt* **1** : to adjust, to adapt, to fit **2** : to arrange (hair, etc.) **3** VISER : to aim at <ajuster son tir : to aim, to adjust one's aim>
ajutage [aʒytaʒ] *nm* : nozzle (of a hose)
alambic [alɑ̃bik] *nm* : still
alambiqué, -quée [alɑ̃bike] *adj* : overcomplicated, convoluted
alangui, -guie [alɑ̃gi] *adj* : languid, listless
alanguir [alɑ̃gir] *vt* : to make languid

alarmant, -mante [alarmɑ̃, -mɑ̃t] *adj* : alarming

alarme [alarm] *nf* **1** ALERTE : alarm <donner l'alarme : to raise the alarm> **2** PEUR : alarm, fear <un état d'alarme : a state of alarm>

alarmer [alarme] *vt* : to alarm, to frighten — **s'alarmer** *vr*

albanais[1], -naise [albanɛ, -nɛz] *adj* : Albanian

albanais[2] *nm* : Albanian (language)

Albanais, -naise *n* : Albanian

albâtre [albatr] *nm* : alabaster

albatros [albatros] *nm* : albatross

albinos [albinos] *adj & nmfs & pl* : albino

album [albɔm] *nm* : album

albumen [albymɛn] *nm* : albumen

albumine [albymin] *nf* : albumin

alcali [alkali] *nm* **1** : alkali **2** AMMONIAQUE : ammonia

alcalin, -line [alkalɛ̃, -lin] *adj* : alkaline <pile alcaline : alkaline battery>

alchimie [alʃimi] *nf* : alchemy — **alchimiste** [-ʃimist] *nmf*

alcool [alkɔl] *nm* : alcohol

alcoolique [alkɔlik] *adj & nmf* : alcoholic — **alcoolisme** [-kɔlism] *nm*

alcoolisé, -sée [alkɔlize] *adj* : alcoholic <boisson non-alcoolisée : nonalcoholic beverage>

alcôve [alkov] *nf* **1** : alcove **2 secrets d'alcôve** : intimate secrets, pillow talk

alcyon [alsjɔ̃] *nm* : kingfisher

aléa [alea] *nm* : hazard, risk

aléatoire [aleatwar] *adj* **1** : uncertain, risky **2** : random

alêne [alɛn] *nf* : awl

alentour [alɑ̃tur] *adv* : around, about, surrounding <dans la forêt alentour : in the surrounding forest>

alentours [alɑ̃tur] *nmpl* **1** ENVIRONS : surrounding area, region **2 aux alentours de** : around, in the vicinity of

alerte[1] [alɛrt] *adj* **1** : alert **2** : lively, brisk — **alertement** [alɛrtəmɑ̃] *adv*

alerte[2] *nf* ALARME : alert, warning, alarm

alerter [alɛrte] *vt* PRÉVENIR : to alert, to warn

alésage [alezaʒ] *nm* : bore (of a pipe or tube)

aléser [aleze] {87} *vt* : to bore, to ream

alevin [alvɛ̃] *nm* : young fish, fry

alevinage [alvinaʒ] *nm* : fish farming <station d'alevinage : fish hatchery>

algarade [algarad] *nf* : altercation, quarrel

algèbre [alʒɛbr] *nf* : algebra

algébrique [alʒebrik] *adj* : algebraic — **algébriquement** [-brikmɑ̃] *adv*

algérien, -rienne [alʒerjɛ̃, -rjɛn] *adj* : Algerian

Algérien, -rienne *n* : Algerian

algue [alg] *nf* : alga, seaweed

alias [aljas] *adv* : alias

alibi [alibi] *nm* : alibi

aliénation [aljenasjɔ̃] *nf* **1** : alienation **2** *or* **aliénation mentale** : insanity

aliéné, -née [aljene] *n* : insane person <être reconnu aliéné : to be declared insane>

aliéner [aljene] {87} *vt* **1** : to transfer, to give over **2** : to alienate — **s'aliéner** *vr* : to lose support, esteem, etc.

alignement [aliɲmɑ̃] *nm* **1** : row, line <ne pas être à l'alignement : to be out of line> **2** : alignment

aligner [aliɲe] *vt* : to align, to line up — **s'aligner** *vr* : to fall into line

aliment [alimɑ̃] *nm* **1** : food **2 aliments** *nmpl* : alimony

alimentaire [alimɑ̃tɛr] *adj* **1** : alimentary, food <la chaîne alimentaire : the food chain> **2** : money-making <œuvre alimentaire : potboiler>

alimentation [alimɑ̃tasjɔ̃] *nf* **1** : feeding **2** : nourishment, diet **3** : food <magasin d'alimentation : grocery store, food store> **4** : provision, supply <l'alimentation en eau : the water supply>

alimenter [alimɑ̃te] *vt* **1** NOURRIR : to feed, to nourish **2** APPROVISIONNER : to supply

alinéa [alinea] *nm* **1** : indentation <à l'alinéa : indented> **2** : paragraph

alité, -tée [alite] *adj* : bedridden

alizé [alize] *nm* : trade wind

Allah [ala] *nm* : Allah

allaitement [alɛtmɑ̃] *nm* : feeding, nursing <allaitement maternel : breast-feeding>

allaiter [alete] *vt* : to nurse, to breastfeed

allant[1], -lante [alɑ̃, -lɑ̃t] *adj* : active

allant[2] *nm* : drive, spirit

alléchant, -chante [aleʃɑ̃, -ʃɑ̃t] *adj* : tempting, enticing

allécher [aleʃe] {87} *vt* : to allure, to tempt

allée [ale] *nf* **1** : path, passage **2** : road **3** : drive, driveway **4** : aisle **5** *or* **allée de quilles** *Can* : bowling alley **6 allées et venues** : comings and goings

allégation [alegasjɔ̃] *nf* : allegation

allégeance [aleʒɑ̃s] *nf* : allegiance

allègement [alɛʒmɑ̃] *nm* : lightening (up), easing

alléger [aleʒe] {64} *vt* **1** : to lighten **2** RÉDUIRE : to reduce **3** : to soothe, to relieve

allégorie [alegɔri] *nf* : allegory

allégorique [alegɔrik] *adj* : allegorical

allègre [alɛgr] *adj* : lively, cheerful — **allègrement** [alɛgrəmɑ̃] *adv*

allégresse [alegrɛs] *nf* : exuberance, joy

alléguer [alege] {87} *vt* **1** : to allege, to put forward **2** : to quote, to cite

alléluia [aleluja] *nm & interj* : hallelujah

allemand[1], -mande [almɑ̃, -mɑ̃d] *adj* : German

allemand[2] *nm* : German (language)

Allemand, -mande *n* : German

aller[1] [ale] {5} *vi* **1** : to go, to move, to travel <nous allons au cinéma : we're going to the movies> <aller à pied : to go by foot> <allons-y! : let's go!> **2** MARCHER : to work, to run <sa montre ne va pas : his watch isn't working> **3** : to proceed, to get along, to come along <ses études vont mal : her studies are going badly> <comment allez-vous? ça va : how are you? OK, fine> **4 ~ à** : to fit <cette robe me va bien : this dress fits me well> — *v aux* : to be going to, to be about to <il va terminer de bonne heure : he's going to finish early, he'll finish early> <nous allions partir : we were just leaving> — *v impers* **1 en ~** : to happen, to go <il en ira mieux demain : things will go better tomorrow> **2 y aller de** : to be a matter of <il y va de ton bonheur : you're risking your happiness> — **s'en aller** *vr* : to leave, to go <va-t'en! : go away!>

aller[2] *nm* **1** : outward journey **2** *or* **aller simple** : one-way, one-way ticket **3 aller–retour** : round-trip, round-trip ticket

allergène [alɛrʒɛn] *nm* : allergen

allergie [alɛrʒi] *nf* : allergy

allergique [alɛrʒik] *adj* : allergic

alliage [aljaʒ] *nm* : alloy

alliance [aljɑ̃s] *nf* **1** : alliance **2** : wedding ring **3** : marriage, union <tante par alliance : aunt by marriage> **4** : mixture, combination

allié[1], **-liée** [alje] *adj* : allied

allié[2], **-liée** *n* **1** : ally, supporter **2** : relative (by marriage)

allier [alje] {96} *vt* **1** : to mix, to combine **2** : to ally, to unite — **s'allier** *vr*

alligator [aligatɔr] *nm* : alligator

allitération [aliterasjɔ̃] *nf* : alliteration — **allitératif, -tive** [-ratif, -tiv] *adj*

allô [alo] *interj* : hello

allocation [alɔkasjɔ̃] *nf* **1** : allocation, allotment **2** : allowance, benefit <allocation de chômage : unemployment benefit>

allocution [alɔkysjɔ̃] *nf* : short speech, address

allongé, -gée [alɔ̃ʒe] *adj* **1** : elongated <un visage allongé : a long face> **2** : lying down

allongement [alɔ̃ʒmɑ̃] *nm* : lengthening, extension

allonger [alɔ̃ʒe] {17} *vt* **1** : to lengthen, to elongate **2** : to stretch (out) **3** : to thin (a sauce, etc.) **4** : to lay down **5** *fam* : to hand over, to fork over — *vi* : to get longer — **s'allonger** *vr* **1** : to lengthen **2** : to lie down

allouer [alwe] *vt* **1** : to allocate, to allot **2** : to allow, to grant

allumage [alymaʒ] *nm* **1** : lighting (of a fire), switching on (of a lamp, etc.) **2** : ignition (of a motor)

allumer [alyme] *vt* **1** : to light, to ignite **2** : to turn on, to switch on **3** : to excite — **s'allumer** *vr*

allumette [alymɛt] *nf* : match

allure [alyr] *nf* **1** : pace, speed <à toute allure : at full speed> **2** : look, appearance <avoir bonne allure : to look good> **3** : style <avoir de l'allure : to have style, to look stylish>

allusion [alyzjɔ̃] *nf* **1** : allusion **2 faire allusion à** : to allude to

almanach [almana] *nm* : almanac

aloès [alɔɛs] *nms & pl* : aloe

alors [alɔr] *adv* **1** : then, at that time **2** : then, in that case **3** : so, therefore <et alors? : so?, so what?> **4 alors même que** : even if, even though **5 alors que** : while, when, whereas **6 ou alors** : or else

alose [aloz] *nf* : shad

alouette [alwɛt] *nf* **1** : lark **2 alouette des champs** : skylark

alourdir [alurdir] *vt* **1** : to make heavy, to weigh down **2** : to increase — **s'alourdir** *vr* : to grow heavy

alourdissement [alurdismɑ̃] *nm* **1** : heaviness **2** : increase

aloyau [alwajo] *nm, pl* **aloyaux** : sirloin

alpaga [alpaga] *nm* : alpaca

alphabet [alfabɛ] *nm* : alphabet

alphabétique [alfabetik] *adj* : alphabetic, alphabetical — **alphabétiquement** [-tikmɑ̃] *adv*

alphabétisation [alfabetizasjɔ̃] *nf* **1** : alphabetizing **2** : literacy teaching

alphabétiser [alfabetize] *vt* **1** : to alphabetize **2** : to teach to read and write

alpin, -pine [alpɛ̃, -pin] *adj* : alpine

alpinisme [alpinism] *nm* : mountain climbing

alpiniste [alpinist] *nmf* : mountain climber, mountaineer

altération [alterasjɔ̃] *nf* **1** FALSIFICATION : falsification, distortion **2** DÉTÉRIORATION : deterioration **3** : extreme thirst

altercation [altɛrkasjɔ̃] *nf* : altercation, quarrel

altérer [altere] {87} *vt* **1** FALSIFIER : to falsify, to distort **2** CORROMPRE : to spoil, to impair **3** : to make thirsty — **s'altérer** *vr* : to deteriorate

alternance [altɛrnɑ̃s] *nf* **1** : alternation, rotation **2 en ~** : alternately

alternateur [altɛrnatœr] *nm* : alternator

alternatif, -tive [altɛrnatif, -tiv] *adj* **1** : alternative, alternate **2** : alternating

alternative [altɛrnativ] *nf* : alternative

alternativement [altɛrnativmɑ̃] *adv* : in turn, alternately

alterner [altɛrne] *v* : to alternate

altesse [altɛs] *nf* : highness <Son Altesse : His Highness, Her Highness>

altier, -tière [altje, -tjɛr] *adj* : haughty

altimètre [altimɛtr] *nm* : altimeter

altitude [altityd] *nf* : altitude <en altitude : at high altitude(s)> <à 2 000 mètres d'altitude : at a height of 2,000 meters>

alto [alto] *nm* **1** : viola **2** : alto (instrument)

altruisme [altrɥism] *nm* : altruism

altruiste[1] [altrɥist] *adj* : altruistic

altruiste[2] *nmf* : altruist

aluminium [alyminjɔm] *nm* : aluminum

alun [alœ̃] *nm* : alum

alunir [alynir] *vi* : to land on the moon

alvéole [alveɔl] *nmf* **1** : alveolus, cell <alvéole dentaire : tooth socket> **2** : pit, cavity (in geology)

alvéolé, -lée [alveɔle] *adj* : honeycombed

amabilité [amabilite] *nf* **1** : kindness <avoir l'amabilité de : to be so kind as to> **2** : politeness <avec amabilité : courteously> **3 amabilités** *nfpl* : civilities, polite remarks

amadou [amadu] *nm* : tinder

amadouer [amadwe] *vt* **1** : to coax, to cajole **2** : to mollify

amaigrir [amegrir] *vt* : to make thin

amaigrissement [amegrismɑ̃] *nm* **1** : reducing, slimming **2** : weight loss, emaciation

amalgame [amalgam] *nm* **1** : amalgam **2** MÉLANGE : mixture

amalgamer [amalgame] *vt* **1** : to amalgamate **2** : to mix, to combine — **s'amalgamer** *vr*

amande [amɑ̃d] *nf* **1** : almond **2** : kernel (of a fruit or nut)

amant, -mante [amɑ̃, -mɑ̃t] *n* : lover

amarrage [amaraʒ] *nm* : mooring <poste d'amarrage : anchorage, berth>

amarrer [amare] *vt* **1** : to moor **2** : to tie (up), to secure — **s'amarrer** *vr*

amaryllis [amarilis] *nf* : amaryllis

amas [ama] *nm* **1** : pile, heap **2** : cluster (in astronomy), mass (in mineralogy)

amasser [amase] *vt* ACCUMULER : to amass, to pile up — **s'amasser** *vr* : to build up

amateur[1] [amatœr] *adj* : amateur

amateur[2] *nm* **1** : connoisseur, enthusiast **2** : amateur

amazone [amazon] *nf* **1** : horsewoman **2 monter en amazone** : to ride sidesaddle

ambages [ɑ̃baʒ] *nfpl* **sans ~** : plainly, unambiguously

ambassade [ɑ̃basad] *nf* : embassy

ambassadeur, -drice [ɑ̃basadœr, -dris] *n* : ambassador

ambiance [ɑ̃bjɑ̃s] *nf* : ambience, atmosphere

ambiant, -biante [ɑ̃bjɑ̃, -bjɑ̃t] *adj* : ambient, surrounding

ambidextre [ɑ̃bidɛkstr] *adj* : ambidextrous

ambigu, -guë [ɑ̃bigy] *adj* : ambiguous — **ambiguïté** [ɑ̃bigɥite] *nf*

ambitieux, -tieuse [ɑ̃bisjø, -sjøz] *adj* : ambitious — **ambitieusement** [-sjøzmɑ̃] *adv*

ambition [ɑ̃bisjɔ̃] *nf* **1** : ambition **2** : claim, pretension

ambitionner [ɑ̃bisjɔne] *vt* **1** : to aim for, to aspire to **2** *Can* : to exaggerate, to go overboard

ambivalence [ɑ̃bivalɑ̃s] *nf* : ambivalence — **ambivalent, -lente** [-valɑ̃, -lɑ̃t] *adj*

ambler [ɑ̃ble] *vi* : to amble — **amble** [ɑ̃bl] *nm*

ambre [ɑ̃br] *nm* **1** : amber **2 ambre gris** : ambergris

ambroisie [ɑ̃brwazi] *nf* : ragweed

ambulance [ɑ̃bylɑ̃s] *nf* : ambulance

ambulancier, -cière [ɑ̃bylɑ̃sje, -sjɛr] *n* : ambulance driver

ambulant, -lante [ɑ̃bylɑ̃, -lɑ̃t] *adj* : traveling, itinerant <cirque ambulant : traveling circus>

ambulatoire [ɑ̃bylatwar] *adj* : ambulatory

âme [am] *nf* **1** : soul, spirit <rendre l'âme : to breathe one's last, to give up the ghost> <âme sœur : soul mate, kindred spirit> **2 état d'âme** : state of mind

amélioration [ameljɔrasjɔ̃] *nf* : amelioration, improvement

améliorer [ameljɔre] *vt* : to ameliorate, to improve — **s'ameliorer** *vr*

amen [amɛn] *interj* : amen

aménagement [amenaʒmɑ̃] *nm* **1** : development, planning <l'aménagement urbain : urban development> **2** : conversion (of rooms, buildings, etc.) **3** : equipping, fitting out <aménagements intérieurs : fittings, fixtures> **4** : adjustment (of taxes, schedules, etc.)

aménager [amenaʒe] {17} *vt* **1** : to plan, to lay out **2** : to convert <une grange aménagée : a converted barn> **3** : to equip, to fit out **4** : to adjust, to arrange

amende [amɑ̃d] *nf* **1** : fine, penalty **2 faire amende honorable** : to make amends

amendement [amɑ̃dmɑ̃] *nm* : amendment

amender [amɑ̃de] *vt* **1** : to amend **2** AMÉLIORER : to improve — **s'amender** *vr* : to mend one's ways

amener [amne] {52} *vt* **1** : to bring, to take **2** : to bring about, to cause **3** : to bring up — **s'amener** *vr fam* : to show up, to turn up

amenuiser [amənɥize] *vt* : to reduce — **s'amenuiser** *vr* : to diminish, to dwindle

amer, -mère [amɛr] *adj* : bitter — **amèrement** [amɛrmɑ̃] *adv*

américain, -caine [amerikɛ̃, -kɛn] *adj* : American

Américain, -caine *n* : American

américanisme [amerikanism] *nm* : Americanism

amertume [amɛrtym] *nf* : bitterness

améthyste [ametist] *nf* : amethyst

ameublement [amœbləmɑ̃] *nm* **1** : furnishing **2** MEUBLES : furniture

ameuter [amœte] *vt* : to stir up, to rouse — **s'ameuter** *vr* : to form a mob

ami[1], **-mie** [ami] *adj* : friendly

ami[2], **-mie** *n* **1** : friend <ami intime : close friend> <ami des bêtes : animal lover> <ami des arts : patron of the arts> **2** *or* **petit ami** : boyfriend **3** *or* **petite amie** : girlfriend

amiable [amjabl] *adj* **à l'amiable** : amicable, private <un accord à l'amiable : a settlement out of court>

amiante [amjɑ̃t] *nm* : asbestos

amibe [amib] *nf* : amoeba

amibien, -bienne [amibjɛ̃, -bjɛn] *adj* : amoebic

amical, -cale [amikal] *adj, mpl* **-caux** [-ko] : friendly

amicalement [amikalmɑ̃] *adv* **1** : amicably, in a friendly manner **2** (*used in correspondence*) : yours (truly), best wishes

amidon [amidɔ̃] *nm* : starch

amidonner [amidɔne] *vt* : to starch

amincir [amɛ̃sir] *vt* : to make thinner — **s'amincir** *vr*

aminé [amine] *adj* **acide aminé** : amino acid

amiral [amiral] *nm, pl* **-raux** [-ro] : admiral

amitié [amitje] *nf* **1** : friendship <prendre en amitié : to befriend, to take a liking to> **2** : kindness, favor **3 amitiés** *nfpl* : best wishes, best regards

ammoniac [amɔnjak] *nm* : ammonia (gas)

ammoniaque [amɔnjak] *nf* : ammonia, ammonia water

amnésie [amnezi] *nf* : amnesia

amnésique [amnezik] *adj & nmf* : amnesiac, amnesic

amnistie [amnisti] *nf* : amnesty

amocher [amɔʃe] *vt fam* : to bash

amoindrir [amwɛ̃drir] *vt* RÉDUIRE : to reduce, to diminish, to undermine — **s'amoindrir** *vr* : to lessen, to diminish

amoindrissement [amwɛ̃drismɑ̃] *nm* : reduction

amollir [amɔlir] *vt* : to soften — **s'amollir** *vr* **1** : to become soft **2** : to weaken

amonceler [amɔ̃sle] {8} *vt* : to pile up, to accumulate — **s'amonceler** *vr*

amoncellement [amɔ̃sɛlmɑ̃] *nm* : pile, heap, mass

amont [amɔ̃] *nm* **en ~** : upstream, uphill

amoral, -rale [amɔral] *adj, mpl* **-raux** [-ro] : amoral

amorce [amɔrs] *nf* **1** : beginning(s), start <l'amorce de récession : the beginnings of recession> **2** APPÂT : bait **3** : detonator, cap

amorcer [amɔrse] {6} *vt* **1** : to begin **2** APPÂTER : to bait, to entice **3** : to prime **4** : to boot (a computer)— **s'amorcer** *vr* : to begin

amorphe [amɔrf] *adj* **1** APATHIQUE : apathetic, passive **2** : amorphous

amorti [amɔrti] *nm Can* : bunt (in baseball) <amorti-sacrifice : sacrifice bunt>

amortir [amɔrtir] *vt* **1** : to absorb, to cushion (a blow, etc.), to deaden (sound) **2** : to make (something) pay for itself **3** : to pay off, to amortize

amortissement [amɔrtismɑ̃] *nm* **1** : absorption, cushioning **2** : amortization

amortisseur [amɔrtisœr] *nm* : shock absorber

amour [amur] *nm* **1** : love, affection, passion <l'amour du prochain : love of one's neighbor> <faire l'amour : to make love> **2** : romance, love affair

amoureusement [amurøzmɑ̃] *adv* : lovingly, amorously

amoureux[1], **-reuse** [amurø, -røz] *adj* **1** : in love, amorous **2** : loving

amoureux[2], **-reuse** *n* : lover

amour–propre [amurprɔpr] *nm* : self-esteem

amovible [amɔvibl] *adj* : removable, detachable

ampère [ɑ̃pɛr] *nm* : ampere

ampèremètre [ɑ̃pɛrmɛtr] *nm* : ammeter

amphétamine [ɑ̃fetamin] *nf* : amphetamine

amphibie [ɑ̃fibi] *adj* : amphibious

amphibien [ɑ̃fibjɛ̃] *nm* : amphibian

amphithéâtre [ɑ̃fiteatr] *nm* **1** : amphitheater **2** : lecture hall, auditorium

ample [ɑ̃pl] *adj* : ample, full, generous — **amplement** [ɑ̃pləmɑ̃] *adv*

ampleur [ɑ̃plœr] *nf* **1** : size, scale, extent **2** : fullness (of clothing)

amplificateur [ɑ̃plifikatœr] *nm* : amplifier

amplification [ɑ̃plifikasjɔ̃] *nf* **1** : amplification **2** : development, expansion

amplifier [ɑ̃plifje] {96} *vt* **1** : to amplify, to enlarge, to magnify **2** : to expand, to increase — **s'amplifier** *vr*

amplitude [ɑ̃plityd] *nf* : amplitude

ampoule [ɑ̃pul] *nf* **1** : lightbulb **2** : blister **3** : vial

ampoulé, -lée [ɑ̃pule] *adj* : pompous, bombastic

amputation [ɑ̃pytasjɔ̃] *nf* : amputation

amputer [ɑ̃pyte] *vt* **1** : to amputate **2** : to cut drastically

amulette [amylɛt] *nf* : amulet

amusant, -sante [amyzɑ̃, -zɑ̃t] *adj* : amusing

amuse–gueule [amyzgøl] *nms & pl* : appetizer, canapé

amusement [amyzmɑ̃] *nm* **1** : amusement **2** : diversion, pastime

amuser [amyze] *vt* DIVERTIR : to amuse — **s'amuser** *vr* **1** : to play **2** : to enjoy oneself, to have fun
amuseur, -seuse [amyzœr, -zøz] *n* : entertainer
amygdale [amidal] *nf* : tonsil
amygdalite [amidalit] *nf* : tonsilitis
an [ɑ̃] *nm* **1** : year <elle a treize ans : she is thirteen years old> <l'an prochain : next year> **2 bon an, mal an** : year in, year out **3 le Jour de l'an** *or* **le Nouvel An** : New Year's Day
anachronique [anakrɔnik] *adj* : anachronistic
anachronisme [anakrɔnism] *nm* : anachronism
anaconda [anakɔ̃da] *nm* : anaconda
anagramme [anagram] *nf* : anagram
anal, -nale [anal] *adj, mpl* **anaux** [ano] : anal
analgésique [analʒezik] *adj & nm* : analgesic
analogie [analɔʒi] *nf* : analogy
analogique [analɔʒik] *adj* : analog
analogue [analɔg] *adj* : analogous, similar
analphabète [analfabɛt] *adj & nmf* : illiterate
analphabétisme [analfabetism] *nm* : illiteracy
analyse [analiz] *nf* **1** : analysis **2** : test <analyse du sang : blood test>
analyser [analize] *vt* **1** : to analyze **2** : to test (in medicine)
analyste [analist] *nmf* : analyst
analytique [analitik] *adj* : analytic, analytical — **analytiquement** [-tikmɑ̃] *adv*
ananas [anana(s)] *nms & pl* : pineapple
anarchie [anarʃi] *nf* : anarchy — **anarchique** [anarʃik] *adj*
anarchiste[1] [anarʃist] *adj* : anarchist, anarchistic
anarchiste[2] *nmf* : anarchist
anathème [anatɛm] *nm* : anathema
anatife [anatif] *nm* : barnacle
anatomie [anatɔmi] *nf* : anatomy
anatomique [anatɔmik] *adj* : anatomic, anatomical — **anatomiquement** [-mikmɑ̃] *adv*
ancestral, -trale [ɑ̃sɛstral] *adj, mpl* **-traux** [-tro] : ancestral
ancêtre [ɑ̃sɛtr] *nmf* : ancestor
anche [ɑ̃ʃ] *nf* : reed (of a musical instrument)
anchois [ɑ̃ʃwa] *nms & pl* : anchovy
ancien[1], **-cienne** [ɑ̃sjɛ̃, -sjɛn] *adj* **1** : former <anciens combattants : veterans> **2** VIEUX : ancient, old **3 ancien elève, ancienne elève** : alumnus *m*, alumna *f*
ancien[2] *nm* **1** : elder, old man **2 l'ancien** : antiques *pl* **3 les anciens** *nmpl* : the ancients
anciennement [ɑ̃sjɛnmɑ̃] *adv* : formerly
ancienneté [ɑ̃sjɛnte] *nf* **1** : seniority **2** : antiquity **3** : oldness, age
ancrage [ɑ̃kraʒ] *nm* : anchorage
ancre [ɑ̃kr] *nf* : anchor <jeter l'ancre : to drop anchor>
ancrer [ɑ̃kre] *vt* **1** : to anchor **2** : to fix firmly, to root — **s'ancrer** *vr*
andorran, -rane [ɑ̃dɔrɑ̃, -ran] *adj* : Andorran
Andorran, -rane *n* : Andorran
andouille [ɑ̃duj] *nf* **1** : andouille (sausage made from chitterlings) **2** *fam* : fool
androgyne [ɑ̃drɔʒin] *adj* : androgynous
âne [an] *nm* **1** : ass, donkey **2** IMBÉCILE : fool, idiot
anéantir [aneɑ̃tir] *vt* **1** DÉTRUIRE : to destroy, to wipe out **2** : to overwhelm, to exhaust — **s'anéantir** *vr* : to be dashed, to be shattered
anéantissement [aneɑ̃tismɑ̃] *nm* : annihilation, destruction
anecdote [anɛkdɔt] *nf* : anecdote
anecdotique [anɛkdɔtik] *adj* : anecdotal
anémie [anemi] *nf* : anemia — **anémique** [anemik] *adj*
anémone [anemɔn] *nf* : anemone
ânerie [anri] *nf* **1** BÊTISE : blunder, stupid mistake **2** : stupidity **3** : stupid remark, nonsense
anesthésie [anɛstezi] *nf* : anesthesia
anesthésier [anɛstezje] {96} *vt* : to anesthetize
anesthésique [anɛstezik] *adj & nm* : anesthetic
anesthésiste [anɛstezist] *nmf* : anesthetist
anesthétique[1] [anɛstetik] *adj* : anesthetic
anesthétique[2] *nm* : anesthetic
aneth [anɛt] *nm* : dill
anfractuosité [ɑ̃fraktɥɔzite] *nf* : crevice
ange [ɑ̃ʒ] *nm* : angel <ange gardien : guardian angel>
angélique [ɑ̃ʒelik] *adj* : angelic, angelical — **angéliquement** [-likmɑ̃] *adv*
angelot [ɑ̃ʒlo] *nm* : cherub
angine [ɑ̃ʒin] *nf* **1** : sore throat, throat infection **2** *or* **angine rouge** : tonsillitis **3** *or* **angine de poitrine** : angina
anglais[1], **-glaise** [ɑ̃glɛ, -glɛz] *adj* : English
anglais[2] *nm* : English (language)
Anglais, -glaise *n* : Englishman *m*, Englishwoman *f*
angle [ɑ̃gl] *nm* **1** : angle <angle aigu : acute angle> **2** COIN : corner
anglicisme [ɑ̃glisism] *nm* : anglicism
anglophone[1] [ɑ̃glɔfɔn] *adj* : English-speaking
anglophone[2] *nmf* : English speaker
anglo-saxon[1], **-saxonne** [ɑ̃glɔsaksɔ̃, -saksɔn] *adj* : Anglo-Saxon
anglo-saxon[2] *nm* : Anglo-Saxon (language)
Anglo-Saxon, -Saxonne *n* : Anglo-Saxon
angoissant, -sante [ɑ̃gwasɑ̃, -sɑ̃t] *adj* : agonizing
angoisse [ɑ̃gwas] *nf* : anguish

angoisser [ɑ̃gwase] *vt* : to distress, to worry
angolais, -laise [ɑ̃gɔlɛ, -lɛz] *adj* : Angolan
Angolais, -laise *n* : Angolan
angora [ɑ̃gɔra] *nm* : angora
anguille [ɑ̃gij] *nf* **1** : eel **2 il y a anguille sous roche** : there's something fishy going on
angulaire [ɑ̃gylɛr] *adj* : angular
anguleux, -leuse [ɑ̃gylø, -løz] *adj* : angular, sharp
anicroche [anikrɔʃ] *nf* ACCROC : snag, small problem
animal[1]**, -male** [animal] *adj, mpl* **-maux** [-mo] : animal <le règne animal : the animal kingdom>
animal[2] *nm, pl* **-maux** : animal
animalier, -lière [animalje, -ljɛr] *adj* : animal <un peintre animalier : a wildlife painter>
animateur, -trice [animatœr, -tris] *n* **1** : leader, organizer **2** : host <animateur d'une émission de télévision : television show host> **3** : (cartoon) animator
animation [animasjɔ̃] *nf* **1** : organizing, coordinating **2** : liveliness, vivacity **3** : animation (in movies)
animé, -mée [anime] *adj* **1** : lively, animated **2** : living, animate
animer [anime] *vt* **1** : to enliven, to brighten up **2** : to drive, to impel **3** : to host, to present **4** : to animate, to bring to life — **s'animer** *vr* **1** : to become lively **2** : to come to life
animosité [animɔzite] *nf* : animosity
anis [ani(s)] *nm* : anise
ankyloser [ɑ̃kiloze] *v* **s'ankyloser** *vr* : to stiffen (up)
ankylostome [ɑ̃kilɔstɔm] *nm* : hookworm
annales [anal] *nfpl* : annals
anneau [ano] *nm, pl* **anneaux** : ring
année [ane] *nf* : year <année bissextile : leap year> <souhaiter la bonne année à qqn : to wish s.o. a happy New Year>
année–lumière [anelymjɛr] *nf, pl* **années–lumière** : light-year
annexe[1] [anɛks] *adj* **1** : related, associated **2** : appended, attached
annexe[2] *nf* **1** : annex (of a building) **2** : appendix, annex (of a document)
annexer [anɛkse] *vt* **1** : to annex **2** : to append
annexion [anɛksjɔ̃] *nf* : annexation
annihilation [aniilasjɔ̃] *nf* : destruction, annihilation
annihiler [aniile] *vt* : to destroy, to annihilate
anniversaire [anivɛrsɛr] *nm* **1** : anniversary **2** : birthday
annonce [anɔ̃s] *nf* **1** : announcement, notice **2** : advertisement <petite annonce : classified ad> <annonce publicitaire : commercial>
annoncer [anɔ̃se] {6} *vt* **1** DÉCLARER : to announce **2** PRÉDIRE : to predict — **s'annoncer** *vr* **1** : to be looming **2** : to look (to be) <les négociations s'annoncent difficiles : the negotiations promise to be difficult>
annonceur, -ceuse [anɔ̃sœr, -søz] *n* **1** : advertiser **2** *Can* : announcer (on radio, television, etc.)
annonciateur, -trice [anɔ̃sjatœr, -tris] *adj* : heralding, presaging
annoter [anɔte] *vt* : to annotate — **annotation** [anɔtasjɔ̃] *nf*
annuaire [anɥɛr] *nm* **1** : directory <annuaire téléphonique : telephone directory> **2** : yearbook
annuel, -nuelle [anɥɛl] *adj* : annual — **annuellement** [anɥɛlmɑ̃] *adv*
annulaire [anylɛr] *nm* : ring finger
annulation [anylasjɔ̃] *nf* **1** : cancellation **2** : annulment
annuler [anyle] *vt* **1** : to cancel, to call off **2** : to revoke, to annul
anode [anɔd] *nf* : anode
anodin, -dine [anɔdɛ̃, -din] *adj* **1** INSIGNIFIANT : insignificant **2** : harmless, innocuous
anomalie [anɔmali] *nf* : anomaly
ânonner [anɔne] *vt* : to stumble through (a speech) — *vi* : to hem and haw, to drone on
anonymat [anɔnima] *nm* : anonymity, obscurity
anonyme [anɔnim] *adj* : anonymous — **anonymement** [-nimmɑ̃] *adv*
anorexie [anɔrɛksi] *nf* : anorexia — **anorexique** [-rɛksik] *adj*
anormal, -male [anɔrmal] *adj, mpl* **-maux** [-mo] : abnormal — **anormalement** [-malmɑ̃] *adv*
anormalité [anɔrmalite] *nf* : abnormality
anse [ɑ̃s] *nf* **1** : handle **2** : cove
antagonisme [ɑ̃tagɔnism] *nm* : antagonism
antagoniste[1] [ɑ̃tagɔnist] *adj* : antagonistic
antagoniste[2] *nmf* : antagonist
antan [ɑ̃tɑ̃] *nm* **d'**~ : of old, of yesteryear
antarctique [ɑ̃tarktik] *adj* : antarctic
antécédent[1]**, -dente** [ɑ̃tesedɑ̃, -dɑ̃t] *adj* : previous
antécédent[2] *nm* **1** : antecedent **2** : history, record <antécédents médicaux : medical history>
antenne [ɑ̃tɛn] *nf* **1** : antenna <antenne parabolique : satellite dish> **2** : antenna, feeler (of an insect)
antérieur, -rieure [ɑ̃terjœr] *adj* **1** PRÉCÉDENT : prior, previous <engagements antérieurs : previous engagements> **2** : front
antérieurement [ɑ̃terjœrmɑ̃] *adv* : previously <antérieurement à : prior to>
anthère [ɑ̃tɛr] *nf* : anther
anthologie [ɑ̃tɔlɔʒi] *nf* FLORILÈGE : anthology

anthracite [ɑ̃trasit] *nm* : anthracite
anthropoïde[1] [ɑ̃trapɔid] *adj* : anthropoid
anthropoïde[2] *nm* : anthropoid, large ape
anthropologie [ɑ̃trɔpɔlɔʒi] *nf* : anthropology
anthropologique [ɑ̃trɔpɔlɔʒik] *adj* : anthropological
anthropologiste [ɑ̃trɔpɔlɔʒist] *or* **anthropologue** [-pɔlɔg] *nmf* : anthropologist
anthropophage[1] [ɑ̃trɔpɔfaʒ] *adj* : cannibalistic
anthropophage[2] *nmf* CANNIBALE : cannibal
anthropophagie [ɑ̃trɔpɔfaʒi] *nf* : cannibalism
antiadhésif, -sive [ɑ̃tiadesif, -siv] *adj* : antiadhesive, nonstick
antiaérien, -rienne [ɑ̃tiaerjɛn] *adj* : antiaircraft
antibiotique [antibiɔtik] *adj & nm* : antibiotic
antiblocage [ɑ̃tiblɔkaʒ] *adj* : antilock
antichambre [ɑ̃tiʃɑ̃br] *nf* : anteroom
anticipation [ɑ̃tisipasjɔ̃] *nf* **1** : anticipation **2 par ~** : in advance
anticiper [ɑ̃tisipe] *vt* **1** PRÉVOIR : to anticipate, to foresee **2** : to do or pay in advance — *vi* : to think ahead
anticlérical, -cale [ɑ̃tiklerikal] *adj, mpl* **-caux** [-ko] : anticlerical
anticommuniste [ɑ̃tikɔmynist] *adj & nmf* : anticommunist
anticonceptionnel, -nelle [ɑ̃tikɔ̃sɛpsjɔnɛl] *adj* CONTRACEPTIF : contraceptive
anticorps [ɑ̃tikɔr] *nms & pl* : antibody
antidater [ɑ̃tidate] *vt* : to antedate, to predate
antidémocratique [ɑ̃tidemɔkratik] *adj* : antidemocratic, undemocratic
antidépresseur [ɑ̃tidepresœr] *adj & nm* : antidepressant
antidérapant, -pante [ɑ̃tiderapɑ̃, -pɑ̃t] *adj* : nonskid
antidote [ɑ̃tidɔt] *nm* : antidote
antidrogue [ɑ̃tidrɔg] *adj* : antidrug
antifasciste [ɑ̃tifaʃist] *adj* : antifascist
antigel [ɑ̃tiʒɛl] *nm* : antifreeze
antihistaminique [ɑ̃tiistaminik] *nm* : antihistamine
anti–inflammatoire [ɑ̃tiɛ̃flamatwar] *adj* : anti-inflammatory
antillais, -laise [ɑ̃tijɛ, -jɛz] *adj* : West Indian
Antillais, -laise *n* : West Indian
antilope [ɑ̃tilɔp] *nf* : antelope
antimite [ɑ̃timit] *adj* **boules antimites** : mothballs
antimoine [ɑ̃timwan] *nm* : antimony
antinucléaire [ɑ̃tinykleɛr] *adj* : antinuclear
antioxydant [antiɔksidɑ̃] *nm* : antioxidant — **antioxydant, -dante** [-sidɑ̃, -dɑ̃t] *adj*
antipathie [ɑ̃tipati] *nf* AVERSION : antipathy
antipode [ɑ̃tipɔd] *nm* **1** : antipode **2 être aux antipodes de** : to be diametrically opposed to
antiquaire [ɑ̃tikɛr] *nmf* : antique dealer
antique [ɑ̃tik] *adj* **1** : ancient **2** : antique **3** : old-fashioned, antiquated
antiquité [ɑ̃tikite] *nf* **1** : antiquity **2** : antique
antirabique [ɑ̃tirabik] *adj* : rabies <vaccin antirabique : rabies vaccine>
antirévolutionnaire [ɑ̃tirevɔlysjɔnɛr] *adj* : antirevolutionary
antisémite [ɑ̃tisemit] *adj* : anti-Semitic
antisémitisme [ɑ̃tisemitism] *nm* : anti-Semitism
antiseptique [ɑ̃tisɛptik] *adj & nm* : antiseptic
antisocial, -ciale [ɑ̃tisɔsjal] *adj, mpl* **-ciaux** [-sjo] : antisocial
antitabac [ɑ̃titaba] *adj* : antismoking
antithèse [ɑ̃titɛz] *nf* : antithesis
antitoxine [ɑ̃titɔksin] *nf* : antitoxin
antitrust [ɑ̃titrœst] *adj* : antitrust
antitussif, -sive [ɑ̃titysif, -siv] *adj* : cough <sirop antitussif : cough syrup>
antivol [ɑ̃tivɔl] *adj* : antitheft
antonyme [ɑ̃tɔnim] *nm* : antonym
antre [ɑ̃tr] *nm* **1** : den, lair **2** : cave
anus [anys] *nms & pl* : anus
anxiété [ɑ̃ksjete] *nf* : anxiety
anxieux, anxieuse [ɑ̃ksjø, -sjøz] *adj* : anxious — **anxieusement** [-sjøzmɑ̃] *adv*
aorte [aɔrt] *nf* : aorta
août [u(t)] *nm* : August
apaisement [apɛzmɑ̃] *nm* **1** : calming (down), soothing **2** : appeasement (in politics) **3 apaisements** *nmpl* : reassurances
apaiser [apeze] *vt* **1** : to pacify, to appease **2** : to assuage (hunger, thirst, etc.) **3** : to soothe, to calm, to mollify — **s'apaiser** *vr* : to die down, to calm down, to abate
apanage [apanaʒ] *nm* : prerogative
aparté [aparte] *nm* **1** : aside (in theater) **2** : private conversation
apartheid [apartɛd] *nm* : apartheid
apathie [apati] *nf* : apathy
apathique [apatik] *adj* : apathetic
apercevoir [apɛrsəvwar] {26} *vt* : to perceive, to see — **s'apercevoir** *vr* **1** : to catch sight of each other **2 ~ de** : to notice, to become aware of **3 ~ que** : to notice that, to realize that
aperçu [apɛrsy] *nm* **1** : glimpse **2** : outline, general idea <avoir des aperçus sur : to have some insight into>
apéritif [aperitif] *nm* : aperitif
apesanteur [apəzɑ̃tœr] *nf* : weightlessness
à–peu–près [apøprɛ] *nms & pl* : approximation

apeuré, -rée [apœre] *adj* : frightened, scared

apex [apɛks] *nms & pl* : apex

aphorisme [afɔrism] *nm* : aphorism

aphrodisiaque [afrɔdizjak] *adj & nm* : aphrodisiac

apiculteur, -trice [apikyltœr, -tris] *n* : beekeeper

apitoiement [apitwamɑ̃] *nm* : pity, compassion

apitoyer [apitwaje] {58} *vt* : to move (someone) to pity — **s'apitoyer** *vr* **~ sur** : to feel sorry for

aplanir [aplanir] *vt* **1** : to plane, to level **2** : to iron out, to resolve (a problem) — **s'aplanir** *vr*

aplatir [aplatir] *vt* : to flatten — **s'aplatir** *vr*

aplomb [aplɔ̃] *nm* **1** : aplomb, composure <perdre son aplomb : to lose one's nerve> **2** : perpendicularity **3 d'aplomb** : steady, balanced, upright

apocalypse [apɔkalips] *nf* : apocalypse

apocalyptique [apɔkaliptik] *adj* : apocalyptic

apocryphe [apɔkrif] *nm* **les Apocryphes** : the Apocrypha

apogée [apɔʒe] *nm* **1** : peak, culmination **2** : apogee (in astronomy)

apolitique [apɔlitik] *adj* : apolitical

apologie [apɔlɔʒi] *nf* : defense, justification

apoplexie [apɔplɛksi] *nf* : apoplexy — **apoplectique** [-plɛktik] *adj*

apostolique [apɔstɔlik] *adj* : apostolic

apostrophe [apɔstrɔf] *nf* **1** : direct address (in grammar) **2** : invective, rude remark **3** : apostrophe (sign of punctuation)

apostropher [apɔstrɔfe] *vt* : to shout at, to address rudely

apothéose [apɔteoz] *nf* **1** : highlight, crowning moment, grand finale **2** : apotheosis

apôtre [apotr] *nm* : apostle

apparaître [aparɛtr] {7} *vi* : to appear — *v impers* : to appear, to seem <il apparaît que : it seems that>

apparat [apara] *nm* **1** CÉRÉMONIE : pomp **2 d'~** : ceremonial

appareil [aparɛj] *nm* **1** : apparatus, device, appliance <appareil de télévision : television set> <appareil photo : camera> <appareil auditif : hearing aid> <appareil de chauffage : heater> **2** : telephone **3** : system <appareil digestif : digestive system>

appareillage [aparɛjaʒ] *nm* **1** : outfitting, equipment **2** : casting off (of a ship)

appareiller [aparɛje] *vt* **1** : to fit out (a ship, etc.) **2** : to match up, to pair — *vi* : to get under way

apparemment [aparamɑ̃] *adv* : apparently

apparence [aparɑ̃s] *nf* **1** ASPECT : appearance, appearing, guise **2 en ~** : apparently

apparent, -rente [aparɑ̃, -rɑ̃t] *adj* : apparent

apparenté, -tée [aparɑ̃te] *adj* : related

apparier [aparje] {96} *vt* : to pair, to match (up)

apparition [aparisjɔ̃] *nf* **1** : appearance **2** : apparition, ghost

appartement [apartəmɑ̃] *nm* : apartment

appartenance [apartənɑ̃s] *nf* : membership, affiliation, belonging

appartenir [apartənir] {92} *vi* **1 ~ à** : to belong to <ça m'appartient : that belongs to me> **2 ~ à** : to be a member of — *v impers* : to be up to <il appartient à vous de le faire : it's up to you to do it>

appât [apa] *nm* : bait, lure <mordre à l'appât : to take the bait>

appâter [apate] *vt* **1** : to bait **2** : to lure, to entice

appauvrir [apovrir] *vt* : to impoverish — **s'appauvrir** *vr*

appauvrissement [apovrismɑ̃] *nm* : impoverishment

appeau [apo] *nm, pl* **appeaux** : decoy

appel [apɛl] *nm* **1** : call <un appel téléphonique : a telephone call> <cri d'appel : call for help> **2** : appeal

appelé [aple] *nm* : draftee

appeler [aple] {8} *vt* **1** : to call <appeler au secours : to call for help> <tu m'appelleras au téléphone ce soir? : you'll phone me tonight?> **2** : to summon <faire appeler le médecin : to send for the doctor> **3** EXIGER : to require, to call for **4** NOMMER : to name **5 en appeler à** : to appeal to **6 en appeler de** : to appeal against, to dispute — **s'appeler** *vr* : to be named, to be called <je m'appelle Isabelle : my name is Isabelle>

appellation [apɛlasjɔ̃] *nf* **1** : name, designation **2 appellation contrôlée** : guaranteed vintage (of wine)

appelle [apɛl], **appellera** [apɛləra], *etc.* → **appeler**

appendice [apɛ̃dis] *nm* **1** : appendix (of a book) **2** : appendix (in anatomy) **3** : appendage, annex

appendicectomie [apɛ̃disɛktɔmi] *nf* : appendectomy

appendicite [apɛ̃disit] *nf* : appendicitis

appentis [apɑ̃ti] *nm* : lean-to, shed

appesantir [apəzɑ̃tir] *vt* : to weigh down, to slow down, to dull <les sens appesantis par l'épuisement : senses dulled by fatigue> — **s'appesantir** *vr* **1** : to grow heavier **2 ~ sur** : to dwell upon

appétissant, -sante [apetisɑ̃, -sɑ̃t] *adj* : appetizing

appétit [apeti] *nm* : appetite <bon appétit! : enjoy your meal!> <ouvrir l'appétit de qqn : to whet s.o.'s appetite>

applaudir [aplodir] *vt* : to applaud <applaudir une décision : to applaud a

decision> — *vi* : to applaud, to clap — **s'applaudir** *vr* : to congratulate oneself

applaudissements [aplodismɑ̃] *nmpl* : applause

applicable [aplikabl] *adj* : applicable — **applicabilité** [-kabilite] *nf*

applicateur [aplikatœr] *nm* : applicator

application [aplikasjɔ̃] *nf* **1** : applying (of paint, etc.) **2** : application, practicing <mettre en application : to put into practice> **3** : care <avec application : diligently, industriously>

applique [aplik] *nf* : appliqué

appliqué, -quée [aplike] *adj* : careful, industrious, diligent

appliquer [aplike] *vt* : to apply — **s'appliquer** *vr* **1** : to apply oneself, to take pains **2 ~ à** : to apply to <la loi s'applique à tous : the law applies to all>

appoint [apwɛ̃] *nm* **1** : change <faire l'appoint : to make exact change> **2** : contribution, support **3 d'~** : supplementary, extra

appointements [apwɛ̃təmɑ̃] *nmpl* : salary

appointer [apwɛ̃te] *vt* **1** : to pay a salary to **2** : to sharpen

apport [apɔr] *nm* **1** : contribution **2** : intake, supply

apporter [apɔrte] *vt* **1** AMENER : to bring **2** : to provide, to supply

apposer [apoze] *vt* : to put, to affix <apposez votre signature ici : sign here>

appréciable [apresjabl] *adj* : appreciable, considerable

appréciatif, -tive [apresjatif, -tiv] *adj* : appreciative

appréciation [apresjasjɔ̃] *nf* **1** : assessment, judgment **2** : appraisal, estimate **3** : appreciation (in value)

apprécier [apresje] {96} *vt* **1** : to appreciate, to value **2** ESTIMER : to appraise, to estimate — **s'apprécier** *vr* : to appreciate in value

appréhender [apreɑ̃de] *vt* **1** ARRÊTER : to apprehend, to arrest **2** : to dread

appréhension [apreɑ̃sjɔ̃] *nf* **1** : arrest **2** : dread

apprenait [aprənɛ] *etc.* → **apprendre**

apprendre [aprɑ̃dr] {70} *vt* **1** : to learn <j'apprends à parler l'anglais : I am learning to speak English> **2** : to hear, to learn of **3** : to teach <il m'a appris à jouer : he taught me how to play> **4** : to inform of, to tell — *vi* : to apprehend — **s'apprendre** *vr* : to be learned

apprenne [aprɛn] *etc.* → **apprendre**

apprenti, -tie [aprɑ̃ti] *n* : apprentice

apprentissage [aprɑ̃tisaʒ] *nm* **1** : apprenticeship <mettre en apprentissage : to apprentice> **2** : learning <faire l'apprentissage de : to learn about>

apprêt [aprɛ] *nm* **1** : finish, sizing, primer **2** : affectation <sans apprêt : unaffectedly> **3 apprêts** *nmpl* : preparations

apprêté, -tée [aprɛte] *adj* : affected, mannered

apprêter [aprɛte] *vt* **1** : to finish, to size, to dress **2** PRÉPARER : to prepare — **s'apprêter** *vr* : to get ready

appris [apri] *pp* → **apprendre**

apprivoiser [aprivwaze] *vt* : to tame — **s'apprivoiser** *vr* : to become tame, to become more sociable

approbateur, -trice [aprɔbatœr, -tris] *adj* : approving

approbation [aprɔbasjɔ̃] *nf* : approbation, approval

approchant, -chante [aprɔʃɑ̃, -ʃɑ̃t] *adj* : similar <qqch d'approchant : sth like that>

approche [aprɔʃ] *nf* **1** : approach <à l'approche du printemps : at the coming of spring> **2 approches** *nfpl* : surrounding area, vicinity

approcher [aprɔʃe] *vt* : to approach, to draw near to — *vi* **1** : to come near, to get nearer **2 ~ de** : to approach, to near <nous approchons de la fin : we're nearing the end> — **s'approcher** *vr* : to approach <il s'est approché de moi : he came up to me, he approached me>

approfondi, -die [aprɔfɔ̃di] *adj* : thorough, detailed

approfondir [aprɔfɔ̃dir] *vt* **1** : to deepen **2** : to enter deeply into, to delve into

approfondissement [aprɔfɔ̃dismɑ̃] *nm* : deepening

appropriation [aprɔprijasjɔ̃] *nf* : appropriation (of property, etc.)

approprié, -priée [aprɔprije] *adj* : appropriate, suitable

approprier [aprɔprije] {96} *vt* : to adapt — **s'approprier** *vr* **1** : to appropriate **2** S'ADAPTER : to be appropriate, to be suited

approuver [apruve] *vt* **1** : to approve, to pass **2** : to approve of

approvisionnement [aprɔvizjɔnmɑ̃] *nm* : provision, supply

approvisionner [aprɔvizjɔne] *vt* **1** : to supply, to stock **2** : to pay money into (an account, etc.) — **s'approvisionner** *vr* : to stock up

approximatif, -tive [aprɔksimatif, -tiv] *adj* : approximate — **approximativement** [-tivmɑ̃] *adv*

approximation [aprɔksimasjɔ̃] *nf* : approximation

appui [apɥi] *nm* **1** SOUTIEN : support <à l'appui de : in support of> <prendre appui sur : to lean on> **2 appui de fenêtre** : windowsill

appui-bras [apɥibra] *nm, pl* **appuis-bras** : armrest

appuie [apɥi], **appuiera** [apɥira], *etc.* → **appuyer**

appui-livres [apɥilivr] *nm, pl* **appuis-livres** *Can* : bookend

appuyer [apɥije] {58} *vt* **1** : to rest, to lean **2** : to support, to back up — *vi* **1 ~ sur** : to push, to press **2 ~ sur** : to emphasize, to stress **3 ~ sur** : to bear <appuyer sur la droite : to bear right> — **s'appuyer** *vr* **1** : to lean **2 ~ à** *or* **~ contre** : to rest against **3 ~ sur** : to depend on, to rely on

âpre [apr] *adj* **1** : sour, acrid **2** : harsh, bitter <après un âpre débat : following a bitter debate> **3 âpre au gain** AVIDE : acquisitive, greedy

après[1] [aprɛ] *adv* **1** : afterwards, later **2** : after, farther on (in space) **3** : next <qui est après? : who's next?>

après[2] *prep* **1** : after <jour après jour : day after day> <tournez après le pont : turn after the bridge> **2** : at, with <crier après qqn : to shout at s.o.> <je suis furieux après toi : I'm angry with you> **3 après coup** : afterwards **4 après que** : after <après qu'il a parlé : after he spoke> **5 après tout** : after all **6 d'~** : according to, from <d'après lui : in his opinion>

après–demain [aprɛdmɛ̃] *adv* : the day after tomorrow

après–guerre [aprɛgɛr] *nm* : postwar period

après–midi [aprɛmidi] *nmfs & pl* : afternoon

âpreté [aprəte] *nf* **1** : bitterness, harshness **2** : tartness, pungency

à–propos [aprɔpo] *nm* : appropriateness, aptness <faire preuve d'à-propos : to show presence of mind> <avec à-propos : aptly, suitably>

apte [apt] *adj* : capable, fit

aptitude [aptityd] *nf* : aptitude

aquarelle [akwarɛl] *nf* : watercolor

aquarium [akwarjɔm] *nm* : aquarium

aquatique [akwatik] *adj* : aquatic <plantes aquatiques : aquatic plants>

aqueduc [akdyk] *nm* : aqueduct

aquilin [akilɛ̃] *adj m* : aquiline

ara [ara] *nm* : macaw

arabe[1] [arab] *adj* : Arab, Arabian, Arabic

arabe[2] *nm* : Arabic (language)

Arabe *nmf* : Arab, Arabian

arabesque [arabɛsk] *nf* : arabesque

arable [arabl] *adj* : arable

arachide [araʃid] *nf* : peanut

araignée [areɲe] *nf* **1** : spider **2 araignée de mer** : spider crab

arbalète [arbalɛt] *nf* : crossbow

arbitrage [arbitraʒ] *nm* **1** : arbitration **2** : refereeing, umpiring

arbitraire [arbitrɛr] *adj* : arbitrary — **arbitrairement** [-trɛrmɑ̃] *adv*

arbitre [arbitr] *nm* **1** : arbitrator **2** : umpire, referee **3** : arbiter <un arbitre du goût : an arbiter of taste> **4 libre arbitre** : free will

arbitrer [arbitre] *vt* **1** : to arbitrate **2** : to referee, to umpire — *vi* **~ entre** : to arbitrate between

arborer [arbɔre] *vt* **1** PORTER : to wear, to sport **2** : to bear, to display (a flag, etc.)

arboricole [arbɔrikɔl] *adj* : arboreal

arbre [arbr] *nm* **1** : tree <arbre de Noël : Christmas tree> <arbre généalogique : family tree> **2** : shaft

arbrisseau [arbriso] *nm* : shrub

arbuste [arbyst] *nm* : small shrub, bush

arc [ark] *nm* **1** : arc, curve **2** ARCHE : arch **3** : bow (in archery)

arcade [arkad] *nf* **1** : arch <arcade dentaire : dental arch> **2** : arcade

arcanes [arkan] *nmpl* : mysteries

arc–boutant [arkbutɑ̃] *nm, pl* **arcs–boutants** : flying buttress

arc–en–ciel [arkɑ̃sjɛl] *nm, pl* **arcs–en–ciel** : rainbow

archaïque [arkaik] *adj* : archaic

archange [arkɑ̃ʒ] *nm* : archangel

arche [arʃ] *nf* **1** : arch **2** : ark <l'arche de Noé : Noah's ark>

archéologie [arkeɔlɔʒi] *nf* : archaeology

archéologique [arkeɔlɔʒik] *adj* : archaeological

archéologue [arkeɔlɔg] *nmf* : archaeologist

archer [arʃe] *nm* : archer

archet [arʃɛ] *nm* : bow <archet de violon : violin bow>

archétype [arketip] *nm* : archetype

archevêque [arʃəvɛk] *nm* : archbishop

archidiocèse [arʃidjɔsɛz] *nm* : archdiocese

archipel [arʃipɛl] *nm* : archipelago

architecte [arʃitɛkt] *nmf* : architect

architecture [arʃitɛktyr] *nf* : architecture — **architectural, -rale** [-tyral] *adj, mpl* **-raux** [-ro]

archives [arʃiv] *nfpl* : archives

archiviste [arʃivist] *nmf* : archivist

arctique [arktik] *adj* : arctic <cercle arctique : arctic circle>

ardemment [ardamɑ̃] *adv* : ardently, passionately

ardent, -dente [ardɑ̃, -dɑ̃t] *adj* **1** : burning, glowing, blazing **2** : ardent, passionate

ardeur [ardœr] *nf* **1** : heat **2** : ardor, fervor

ardillon [ardijɔ̃] *nm* **1** : prong (of a buckle) **2** : barb (of a fishhook, etc.)

ardoise [ardwaz] *nf* : slate

ardu, -due [ardy] *adj* **1** : arduous, difficult **2** : steep

aréna [arena] *nm Can* : arena

arène [arɛn] *nf* **1** : arena **2 arènes** *nfpl* : amphitheater, bullring

arête [arɛt] *nf* **1** : fish bone **2** : edge, ridge **3 l'arête du nez** : the bridge of the nose

argent [arʒɑ̃] *nm* **1** : money <payer en argent comptant : to pay in cash> **2** : silver

argenté, -tée [arʒɑ̃te] *adj* **1** : silver-plated **2** : silvery **3** *fam* : loaded, well-heeled

argenterie [arʒɑ̃tri] *nf* : silverware

argentin, -tine [arʒɑ̃tɛ̃, -tin] *adj* **1** : silvery **2** : Argentine, Argentinean, Argentinian

Argentin, -tine *n* : Argentine, Argentinean, Argentinian

argile [arʒil] *nf* : clay

argileux, -leuse [arʒilø, -løz] *adj* : clayey

argon [argɔ̃] *nm* : argon

argot [argo] *nm* : argot, slang

argotique [argɔtik] *adj* : slang, slangy

arguer [argɥe] *vt* **1** : to deduce, to infer **2 ~ de** : to use as a pretext **3 ~ que** : to argue that, to protest that

argument [argymɑ̃] *nm* : argument

argumentation [argymɑ̃tasjɔ̃] *nf* : argumentation, rationale

argumenter [argymɑ̃te] *vi* : to argue, to debate

argutie [argysi] *nf* : quibble

aria [arja] *nf* : aria

aride [arid] *adj* **1** : arid, dry **2** : dull, uninteresting

aridité [aridite] *nf* : aridity

aristocrate [aristɔkrat] *nmf* : aristocrat — **aristocratique** [-kratik] *adj*

aristocratie [aristɔkrasi] *nf* : aristocracy

arithmétique[1] [aritmetik] *adj* : arithmetic, arithmetical

arithmétique[2] *nf* : arithmetic

arithmétiquement [aritmetikmɑ̃] *adv* : arithmetically

arlequin [arləkɛ̃] *nm* : harlequin

armada [armada] *nf* : armada

armature [armatyr] *nf* : frame, framework, reinforcement

arme [arm] *nf* **1** : weapon, arm <arme à feu : firearm> <prendre les armes : to take up arms> **2 armes** *nfpl* : coat of arms

armée [arme] *nf* : army

armement [arməmɑ̃] *nm* **1** : arming, equipping (of a military force) **2** : armament, weaponry, arms *pl* <la course aux armements : the arms race>

arménien[1], **-nienne** [armenjɛ̃, -njɛn] *adj* : Armenian

arménien[2] *nm* : Armenian (language)

Arménien, -nienne *n* : Armenian

armer [arme] *vt* **1** : to arm **2** : to cock (a gun) **3** : to reinforce

armistice [armistis] *nm* : armistice

armoire [armwar] *nf* : cupboard, cabinet, wardrobe <armoire à pharmacie : medicine cabinet>

armoiries [armwari] *nfpl* : coat of arms

armoise [armwaz] *nf* : sagebrush

armure [armyr] *nf* : armor

arnaque [arnak] *nf fam* : swindle, gyp

arnaquer [arnake] *vt fam* : to rip off, to swindle, to gyp

arnaqueur, -queuse [arnakœr, -køz] *n fam* : swindler

aromate [arɔmat] *nm* : spice, herb

aromatique [arɔmatik] *adj* : aromatic

aromatiser [arɔmatize] *vt* : to flavor

arôme [arom] *nm* **1** : aroma, fragrance **2** : flavor, flavoring

arpège [arpɛʒ] *nm* : arpeggio

arpentage [arpɑ̃taʒ] *nm* : surveying

arpenter [arpɑ̃te] *vt* **1** : to pace, to stride along **2** : to survey

arpenteur, -teuse [arpɑ̃tœr, -tøz] *n* : surveyor

arqué, -quée [arke] *adj* : arched, curved <jambes arquées : bandy legs>

arrache-pied [araʃpje] *adv* **d'arrache-pied** : nonstop, relentlessly

arracher [araʃe] *vt* **1** : to uproot, to tear out **2** : to extract, to pull out <arracher une dent : to extract a tooth> **3** : to snatch, to grab — *vi* **en ~** *Can* : to have difficulty, to have problems — **s'arracher** *vr* **1** : to pull out, to pluck <s'arracher les cheveux : to tear one's hair> **2** : to fight over **3 ~ de** : to tear oneself away from

arraisonner [arezɔne] *vt* : to board and inspect (a ship, plane, etc.)

arrangeant, -geante [arɑ̃ʒɑ̃, -ʒɑ̃t] *adj* : accommodating, obliging

arrangement [arɑ̃ʒmɑ̃] *nm* : arrangement

arranger [arɑ̃ʒe] {17} *vt* **1** : to arrange **2** RÉPARER : to repair, to fix **3** CONVENIR : to suit, to please <cette idée arrangera tout le monde : that idea will please everyone> **4** : to settle, to sort out — **s'arranger** *vr* **1** : to come to an agreement **2** : to get better, to improve <cela va s'arranger : things will turn out all right> **3 s'arranger pour faire** : to make sure something gets done

arrérages [areraʒ] *nmpl* : arrears

arrestation [arɛstasjɔ̃] *nf* : arrest

arrêt [arɛ] *nm* **1** : stopping, halt <sans arrêt : nonstop> **2** : stop <arrêt d'autobus : bus stop> **3** : ruling, decree **4** : save (in sports) **5 arrêts** *nmpl* : arrest (in the military) **6 arrêt du cœur** : heart failure, cardiac arrest

arrêt–court [arɛkur] *nm* : shortstop

arrêté[1], **-tée** [arete] *adj* : fixed, decided

arrêté[2] *nm* **1** : order, decree **2 arrêté de comptes** : settlement of accounts

arrêter [arete] *vt* **1** : to stop, to halt **2** : to switch off <arrêtez la radio : turn off the radio> **3** : to give up, to discontinue **4** : to arrest **5** : to decide upon, to fix — *vi* : to stop — **s'arrêter** *vr* **1** : to stop, to come to a halt **2 ~ à** : to dwell on **3 ~ de** : to give up <s'arrêter de fumer : to give up smoking>

arrhes [ar] *nfpl France* : deposit, down payment

arrière[1] [arjɛr] *adj* : back, rear <siège arrière : back seat>

arrière[2] *nm* **1** : back, rear <à l'arrière : in the back, at the rear, astern> <en arrière : backwards, back> <en arrière de : behind> **2** : fullback, back (in sports) **3 arrières** *nmpl* : rear (in the military) **4 prendre de l'arrière** *Can* : to be slow <ma montre prend de l'arrière : my watch is slow>

arriéré[1], **-rée** [arjere] *adj* **1** : late, overdue **2** : backward <être arriéré : to be behind the times> **3** : (mentally) retarded

arriéré[2] *nm* **1** : arrears *pl* **2** : backlog

arrière–cours [arjɛrkur] *nf* : backyard

arrière–garde [arjɛrgard] *nf* : rear guard

arrière–goût [arjɛrgu] *nm* : aftertaste

arrière–grand–mère [arjɛrgrɑ̃mɛr] *nf, pl* **arrière–grands–mères** : great-grandmother

arrière–grand–père [arjɛrgrɑ̃pɛr] *nm, pl* **arrière–grands–pères** : great-grandfather

arrière–grands–parents [arjɛrgrɑ̃parɑ̃] *nmpl* : great-grandparents

arrière–pays [arjɛrpei] *nms & pl* : hinterland

arrière–pensée [arjɛrpɑ̃se] *nf* : ulterior motive

arrière–petite–enfante *f* : great-granddaughter

arrière–petit–enfant *m* : great-grandson

arrière–plan [arjɛrplɑ̃] *nm* : background

arrière–saison [arjɛrsɛzɔ̃] *nf* : late autumn

arrière–train [arjɛrtrɛ̃] *nm* **1** : hindquarters **2** *fam* : buttocks, bottom

arrimer [arime] *vt* **1** : to stow **2** : to secure, to fix

arrivage [arivaʒ] *nm* **1** : delivery **2** : arrival, influx (of persons)

arrivant, -vante [arivɑ̃, -vɑ̃t] *n* : newcomer, new arrival

arrivée [arive] *nf* **1** : arrival **2** : finish <ligne d'arrivée : finish line> **3** : inlet, intake (for air, gas, etc.)

arriver [arive] *vi* **1** : to arrive, to come <j'arrive! : I'm coming!> <arriver en retard : to be late> **2** : to succeed <arriver à sa fin : to achieve one's goal> <arriver à faire : to succeed in doing> **3** : to happen, to occur <cela m'est arrivé : that happened to me> <il arrive que : it happens that> **4 ~ à** ATTEINDRE : to reach

arriviste[1] [arivist] *adj* : (overly) ambitious, pushy

arriviste[2] *nmf* : upstart, go-getter

arrogance [arɔgɑ̃s] *nf* : arrogance

arrogant, -gante [arɔgɑ̃, -gɑ̃t] *adj* : arrogant

arroger [arɔʒe] {17} *v* **s'arroger** *vr* : to assume, to take upon oneself

arrondi [arɔ̃di] *nm* **1** : roundness **2** : hemline

arrondir [arɔ̃dir] *vt* **1** : to round, to make round **2** : to round off **3** AUGMENTER : to increase — **s'arrondir** *vr*

arrondissement [arɔ̃dismɑ̃] *nm* : district, subdivision

arrosage [arozaʒ] *nm* : watering, spraying

arroser [aroze] *vt* **1** : to water, to sprinkle, to spray **2** : to wash down (with wine), to drink to (a success, etc.) **3** : to baste (in cooking)

arroseur [arozœr] *nm* : sprinkler

arrosoir [arozwar] *nm* : watering can

arsenal [arsənal] *nm, pl* **-naux** [-no] **1** : arsenal, armory **2** : (naval) shipyard **3** : gear, equipment

arsenic [arsənik] *nm* : arsenic

art [ar] *nm* **1** : art <musée des beaux arts : museum of fine arts> <un œuvre d'art : a work of art> **2** : technique, skill

artère [artɛr] *nf* **1** : artery <durcissement des artères : hardening of the arteries> **2** : main road, thoroughfare

artériel, -rielle [arterjɛl] *adj* : arterial

artériosclérose [arterjɔskleroz] *nf* : arteriosclerosis

arthrite [artrit] *nf* : arthritis

arthritique [artritik] *adj* : arthritic

arthropode [artrɔpɔd] *nm* : arthropod

artichaut [artiʃo] *nm* : artichoke

article [artikl] *nm* **1** : article (in a publication) <article de fond : feature (article)> **2** : clause, section, article **3** : item (in commerce) <articles de toilette : toiletries> **4** : dictionary entry **5** : article (in grammar) <l'article indéfini : the indefinite article>

articulation [artikylasjɔ̃] *nf* **1** : articulation **2** JOINTURE : joint (in anatomy)

articuler [artikyle] *vt* **1** PRONONCER : to articulate, to state, to pronounce **2** : to join, to hinge — **s'articuler** *vr* : to connect <s'articuler autour de : to be based on, to hinge on>

artifice [artifis] *nm* **1** : trick, ruse **2** : artifice, device

artificiel, -cielle [artifisjɛl] *adj* : artificial, false — **artificiellement** [-sjɛlmɑ̃] *adv*

artificieux, -cieuse [artifisjø, -sjøz] *adj* : deceitful, cunning

artillerie [artijri] *nf* : artillery, gunnery

artilleur [artijœr] *nm* **1** : artilleryman, gunner **2** *Can* : pitcher (in baseball)

artisan, -sane [artizɑ̃, -zan] *n* **1** : artisan, craftsman *m,* craftswoman *f* **2** : maker, architect <artisan de la paix : peacemaker>

artisanat [artizana] *nm* **1** : artisans **2** : craft industry

artiste [artist] *nmf* : artist

artistique [artistik] *adj* : artistic — **artistiquement** [-tikmɑ̃] *adv*

as [as] *nm* **1** : ace <l'as de pique : the ace of spades> **2** : champion, ace (in sports)

ascaride [askarid] *nm* : roundworm

ascendance [asɑ̃dɑ̃s] *nf* **1** : descent, ancestry <d'ascendance égyptienne : of Egyptian descent> **2** : ascent, rising (in astronomy)

ascendant[1], **-dante** [asɑ̃dɑ̃, -dɑ̃t] *adj* : rising, ascending
ascendant[2] *nm* **1** : ascendancy, influence **2** : ascendant (in astronomy) **3 ascendants** *nmpl* : ancestors
ascenseur [asɑ̃sœr] *nm* : elevator
ascension [asɑ̃sjɔ̃] *nf* **1** : ascent, climb **2 le jour de l'Ascension** : Ascension Day
ascensionnel, -nelle [asɑ̃sjɔnɛl] *adj* : upward
ascète [asɛt] *nmf* : ascetic
ascétique [asetik] *adj* : ascetic
ascétisme [asetism] *nm* : asceticism
aseptique [asɛptik] *adj* : aseptic
aseptiser [asɛptize] *vt* : to sterilize, to disinfect
asiatique [azjatik] *adj* : Asian
Asiatique *nmf* : Asian
asile [azil] *nm* **1** : asylum, refuge <asile politique : political asylum> **2** : retreat, shelter <un asile de paix : a peaceful retreat> <asile pour la nuit : shelter for the night>
aspect [aspɛ] *nm* **1** : aspect, side **2** APPARENCE : appearance, look
asperge [aspɛrʒ] *nf* : asparagus (spear)
asperger [aspɛrʒe] *vt* {17} : to spray, to sprinkle, to splash
aspérité [asperite] *nf* **1** : bump, protrusion **2** : harshness, asperity
asphalte [asfalt] *nm* : asphalt
asphyxie [asfiksi] *nf* : asphyxiation
asphyxier [asfiksje] {96} *vt* **1** : to asphyxiate, to suffocate **2** : to stifle — **s'asphyxier** *vr*
aspic [aspik] *nm* **1** : asp **2** : aspic
aspirant, -rante [aspirɑ̃, -rɑ̃t] *n* : aspirant
aspirateur [aspiratœr] *nm* **1** : vacuum cleaner **2 passer l'aspirateur** : to vacuum
aspiration [aspirasjɔ̃] *nf* **1** : aspiration, hope **2** : suction **3** : inhaling
aspirer [aspire] *vt* **1** : to aspirate, to suck up **2** : to inhale — *vi* : to aspire <aspirer à une carrière politique : to aspire to a political career>
aspirine [aspirin] *nf* : aspirin
assagir [asaʒir] *vt* **1** : to make wiser **2** : to calm, to quiet down — **s'assagir** *vr* : to settle down
assaillant, -lante [asajɑ̃, -jɑ̃t] *n* : assailant, attacker
assaillir [asajir] {93} *vt* ATTAQUER : to assail, to attack
assainir [asenir] *vt* **1** : to clean, to purify **2** : to stabilize (an economy, etc.) — **s'assainir** *vr*
assainissement [asenismɑ̃] *nm* **1** : cleaning up, purification **2** : stabilization
assaisonnement [ɑsɛzɔnmɑ̃] *nm* : seasoning
assaisonner [asɛzɔne] *vt* : to season
assassin[1], **-sine** [asasɛ̃, -sin] *adj* **1** : murderous **2** : provocative
assassin[2] *nm* : murderer, assassin
assassinat [asasina] *nm* : murder, assassination
assassiner [asasine] *vt* : to murder, to assassinate
assaut [aso] *nm* **1** : assault, attack <prendre d'assaut : to storm, to take by storm> **2** : match (in fencing)
assécher [aseʃe] {87} *vt* **1** : to drain **2** : to dry (up)
assemblage [asɑ̃blaʒ] *nm* **1** : assembling, combining **2** : assembly, collection **3** : joint
assemblée [asɑ̃ble] *nf* **1** RÉUNION : meeting **2** : gathering <assemblée des fidèles : congregation> **3** : assembly, parliament
assembler [asɑ̃ble] *vt* : to assemble, to bring together, to put together — **s'assembler** *vr* : to gather <s'assembler en troupeau : to herd together>
asséner [asene] {87} *vt* : to strike <asséner un coup : to deal a blow>
assentiment [asɑ̃timɑ̃] *nm* : assent, consent
asseoir [aswar] {9} *vt* **1** : to seat, to sit (someone) up, to sit (someone) down **2** : to set up, to establish — **s'asseoir** *vr* : to sit down
assermentation [asɛrmɑ̃tasjɔ̃] *nf Can* : swearing in
assermenté, -tée [asɛrmɑ̃te] *adj* : sworn
assertion [asɛrsjɔ̃] *nf* : assertion
asservir [asɛrvir] *vt* **1** : to enslave **2** : to control
asservissement [asɛrvismɑ̃] *nm* **1** : enslavement **2** : subservience
assez [ase] *adv* **1** SUFFISAMMENT : enough, sufficiently <il ne rit pas assez : he doesn't laugh enough> **2** : rather, quite <elle le fait assez bien : she does it fairly well> **3 ~ de** : enough of, sufficient
assidu, -due [asidy] *adj* **1** ZÉLÉ : diligent, zealous **2** FRÉQUENT : constant, regular — **assidûment** [-dymɑ̃] *adv*
assiduité [asidɥite] *nf* **1** APPLICATION : assiduousness, diligence **2** FRÉQUENTATION : regular attendance **3 assiduités** *nfpl* : attentions
assiéger [asjeʒe] {64} *vt* ASSAILLIR : to besiege, to assail
assiette [asjɛt] *nf* **1** : plate, dish **2** : seat (on a horse) **3** : tax base **4 ne pas être dans son assiette** : to feel unwell
assiettée [asjete] *nf* : plateful
assignation [asiɲasjɔ̃] *nf* **1** : assignment, allocation **2** : summons, subpoena
assigner [asiɲe] *vt* **1** : to assign, to allot **2** : to summon, to subpoena
assimilation [asimilasjɔ̃] *nf* : assimilation
assimiler [asimile] *vt* **1** INTÉGRER : to assimilate, to integrate **2** APPRENDRE : to learn **3** IDENTIFIER : to liken, to compare, to consider the equivalent of — **s'assimiler** *vr* : to become assimilated
assis [asi] *pp* → **asseoir**
assise[1] [asiz] *adj* : seated, sitting down

assise[2] *nf* **1** BASE : foundation, base **2** COUCHE : layer, stratum **3 assises** *nfpl* RÉUNION : meeting, conference **4 assises** *nfpl* : court <assises criminelles : criminal court>

assistance [asistɑ̃s] *nf* **1** AIDE : assistance, aid **2** : attendance **3** : audience

assistant, -tante [asistɑ̃, -tɑ̃t] *n* **1** ADJOINT : assistant <assistante sociale : social worker> **2** : spectator, audience member

assister [asiste] *vt* AIDER : to assist — *vi* **~ à** : to attend, to be present at

association [asɔsjasjɔ̃] *nf* **1** : association **2** : partnership

associé, -ciée [asɔsje] *n* : associate, partner

associer [asɔsje] {96} *vt* **1** : to associate, to bring together, to join <associer des idées : to associate ideas> **2 associer qqn à** : to include s.o. in — **s'associer** *vr* **1** : to join together, to be combined **2 ~ à** : to share in

assoie [aswa], **assoit** [aswa], *etc.* → **asseoir**

assoiffé, -fée [aswafe] *adj* : thirsty

assombrir [asɔ̃brir] *vt* **1** : to darken **2** : to cast a shadow over, to make gloomy — **s'assombrir** *vr*

assommant, -mante [asɔmɑ̃, -mɑ̃t] *adj* : boring, tiresome

assommer [asɔme] *vt* **1** : to stun, to knock out **2** *fam* : to bore stiff

assommoir [asɔmwar] *nm* : bludgeon, blackjack

assorti, -tie [asɔrti] *adj* : assorted

assortiment [asɔrtimɑ̃] *nm* **1** : assortment, collection, set **2** : matching, harmony (of colors, etc.) **3** : stock, inventory

assortir [asɔrtir] *vt* **1** : to match **2** APPROVISIONNER : to stock **3 ~ de** : to combine with, to add to — **s'assortir** *vr*

assoupir [asupir] *vt* **1** ENDORMIR : to make drowsy **2** ENGOURDIR : to dull, to numb — **s'assoupir** *vr* **1** : to doze off **2** : to wane, to die down

assoupissement [asupismɑ̃] *nm* : drowsiness

assouplir [asuplir] *vt* **1** : to make supple, to soften **2** : to ease, to relax, to limber up — **s'assouplir** *vr*

assouplisseur [asuplisœr] *nm* : fabric softener

assourdir [asurdir] *vt* **1** : to deafen **2** : to deaden, to muffle

assouvir [asuvir] *vt* : to appease, to satisfy, to satiate

assoyait [aswajɛ], *etc.* → **asseoir**

assujettir [asyʒetir] *vt* **1** : to subjugate **2** FIXER : to fix, to fasten **3** : **~ à** to subject to — **s'assujettir** *vr* : to submit

assujettissement [asyʒetismɑ̃] *nm* : subjugation

assumer [asyme] *vt* **1** : to assume, to take on **2** : to accept, to endure <le diagnostic était difficile à assumer : the diagnosis was difficult to accept>

assurance [asyrɑ̃s] *nf* **1** : insurance **2** PROMESSE : assurance, promise **3** CONFIANCE : confidence, self-confidence

assurance-vie *n, pl* **assurances-vie** [asyrɑ̃svi] *nf* : life insurance

assuré[1], **-rée** [asyre] *adj* **1** : certain, sure **2** : assured, self-confident

assuré[2], **-rée** *n* : insured person

assurément [asyremɑ̃] *adv* : certainly, definitely, assuredly

assurer [asyre] *vt* **1** GARANTIR : to assure, to guarantee **2** POURVOIR : to provide, to supply **3** : to insure **4** : to secure, to steady — **s'assurer** *vr* **1** : to make sure **2** : to secure, to get **3** : to steady

assureur [asyrœr] *nm* : insurance agent

aster [astɛr] *nm* : aster

astérisque [asterisk] *nm* : asterisk

astéroïde [asterɔid] *nm* : asteroid

asthmatique [asmatik] *adj & nmf* : asthmatic

asthme [asm] *nm* : asthma

asticot [astiko] *nm* : maggot

astigmate [astigmat] *adj* : astigmatic

astigmatisme [astigmatism] *nm* : astigmatism

astiquer [astike] *vt* : to polish

astral, -trale [astral] *adj, pl* **astraux** [astro] : astral

astre [astr] *nm* : star

astreignant, -gnante [astrɛɲɑ̃, -ɲɑ̃t] *adj* : demanding, exacting

astreindre [astrɛ̃dr] {37} *vt* : to oblige, to compel, to force — **s'astreindre** *vr*

astringent, -gente [astrɛ̃ʒɑ̃, -ʒɑ̃t] *adj* : astringent

astrologie [astrɔlɔʒi] *nf* : astrology

astrologique [astrɔlɔʒik] *adj* : astrological

astrologue [astrɔlɔg] *nmf* : astrologer

astronaute [astrɔnot] *nmf* : astronaut

astronautique [astrɔnotik] *nf* : astronautics

astronome [astrɔnɔm] *nmf* : astronomer

astronomie [astrɔnɔmi] *nf* : astronomy

astronomique [astrɔnɔmik] *adj* : astronomical — **astronomiquement** [-mikmɑ̃] *adv*

astuce [astys] *nf* **1** : astuteness, cleverness **2** TRUC : trick, maneuver **3** PLAISANTERIE : joke, pun

astucieux, -cieuse [astysjø, -sjøz] *adj* : astute, clever — **astucieusement** [-sjøzmɑ̃] *adv*

asymétrie [asimetri] *nf* : asymmetry

asymétrique [asimetrik] *adj* : asymmetrical, asymmetric

atavique [atavik] *adj* : atavistic

atavisme [atavism] *nm* : atavism

atelier [atəlje] *nm* **1** : studio **2** : workshop

atermoiements [atɛrmwamɑ̃] *nmpl* : procrastination

atermoyer [atɛrmwaje] {58} *vi* : to procrastinate

athée¹ [ate] *adj* : atheistic

athée² *nmf* : atheist

athéisme [ateism] *nm* : atheism

athlète [atlɛt] *nmf* : athlete

athlétique [atletik] *adj* : athletic

athlétisme [atletism] *nm* : athletics

atlantique [atlɑ̃tik] *adj* : Atlantic

atlas [atlas] *nm* : atlas

atmosphère [atmɔsfɛr] *nf* : atmosphere

atmosphérique [atmɔsferik] *adj* : atmospheric

atoca *or* **atocas** [atɔka] *nm Can* : cranberry

atoll [atɔl] *nm* : atoll

atome [atom] *nm* **1** : atom **2 avoir des atomes crochus avec qqn** : to hit it off with s.o.

atomique [atɔmik] *adj* : atomic

atomiseur [atɔmizœr] *nm* BOMBE : spray bottle, atomizer

atone [atɔn] *adj* **1** : dull, lifeless **2** : expressionless **3** : unaccented

atours [atur] *nmpl* : finery

atout [atu] *nm* **1** : trump (card) **2** AVANTAGE : advantage, asset

âtre [atr] *nm* : hearth

atroce [atrɔs] *adj* HORRIBLE : atrocious, horrible — **atrocement** [atrɔsmɑ̃] *adv*

atrocité [atrɔsite] *nf* : atrocity

atrophie [atrɔfi] *nf* : atrophy

atrophier [atrɔfje] {96} *vt* : to atrophy — **s'atrophier** *vr*

attabler [atable] *v* **s'attabler** *vr* : to sit down at the table

attachant, -chante [ataʃɑ̃, -ʃɑ̃t] *adj* : appealing, likeable

attache [ataʃ] *nf* **1** : fastener, string, strap **2** LIEN : tie, bond

attaché, -chée [ataʃe] *n* : attaché

attaché–case [ataʃekɛz] *nm, pl* **attachés–cases** : attaché case

attachement [ataʃmɑ̃] *nm* : attachment, close tie

attacher [ataʃe] *vt* **1** : to tie, to attach, to fasten **2** : to tie up — *vi* : to stick — **s'attacher** *vr* **1** : to fasten (up), to be buttoned **2** : to adhere, to cling **3 s'attacher à faire** : to apply oneself to doing

attaquant, -quante [atakɑ̃, -kɑ̃t] *n* **1** : attacker **2** : forward (in sports)

attaque [atak] *nf* **1** : attack **2** : stroke, fit, attack (in medicine)

attaquer [atake] *vt* **1** : to attack, to assault **2** : to tackle, to get started on — **s'attaquer** *vr* **~ à** : to attack

attardé [atarde] *adj* **1** : late **2** : retarded **3** ARRIÉRÉ : backward, old-fashioned

attarder [atarde] *vt* : to delay, to slow down — **s'attarder** : to linger

atteignait [ateɲɛ], **atteignions** [ateɲiɔ̃], *etc.* → **atteindre**

atteigne [ateɲə], *etc.* → **atteindre**

atteindre [atɛ̃dr] {37} *vt* **1** : to reach, to attain, to achieve **2** : to strike, to hit **3** : to affect **4** : to contact, to get in touch with

atteinte [atɛ̃t] *nf* **1** : attack <porter atteinte à : to undermine> **2 hors d'atteinte** : out of reach

attelage [atlaʒ] *nm* : team (of animals)

atteler [atle] {8} *vt* : to harness, to yoke — **s'atteler** *vr* **~ à** : to apply oneself to

attelle [atɛl] *nf* : splint

attenant, -nante [atnɑ̃, -nɑ̃t] *adj* : adjacent, adjoining

attendre [atɑ̃dr] {63} *vt* **1** : to wait for, to await <je l'attends : I'm waiting for him> <attendez voir : let's wait and see> **2** : to expect, to anticipate <attendre un bébé : to be expecting (a baby)> **3** : to be ready for <le dîner t'attend : your dinner's ready> **4** : to be in store for — *vi* **1** : to wait <faire attendre qqn : to keep s.o. waiting> **2 ~ après** : to be in a hurry for **3 en attendant** : in the meantime — **s'attendre** *vr* **~ à** : to expect

attendri, -drie [atɑ̃dri] *adj* : tender

attendrir [atɑ̃drir] *vt* **1** ÉMOUVOIR : to move, to touch **2** : to tenderize, to soften — **s'attendrir** *vr*

attendrissant, -sante [atɑ̃drisɑ̃, -sɑ̃t] *adj* ÉMOUVANT : moving, touching

attendrissement [atɑ̃drismɑ̃] *nm* **1** : compassion **2** : tenderness

attendu¹, -due [atɑ̃dy] *adj* **1** : expected **2** : long-awaited

attendu² *prep* **1** : considering, given <attendu sa pauvreté, il s'habille bien : considering his poverty, he dresses well> **2 attendu que** : considering that, seeing that

attentat [atɑ̃ta] *nm* **1** : attack, assault <attentat à la pudeur : indecent assault> **2** : murder attempt, assassination attempt

attente [atɑ̃t] *nf* **1** : wait, waiting <dix minutes d'attente : a ten-minute wait> **2** : expectation, hope

attenter [atɑ̃te] *vi* **~ à** : to make an attempt on (someone's life), to violate (rights, etc.)

attentif, -tive [atɑ̃tif, -tiv] *adj* **1** : attentive <être attentif à : to pay attention to> **2** : careful, scrupulous — **attentivement** [-tivmɑ̃] *adv*

attention [atɑ̃sjɔ̃] *nf* **1** : attention <faire attention : to pay attention> **2 attention!** : look out!, beware!

attentionné, -née [atɑ̃sjɔne] *adj* : considerate, attentive

atténuant, -nuante [atenɥɑ̃, -nɥɑ̃t] *adj* : extenuating, mitigating <circonstances atténuantes : extenuating circumstances>

atténuation [atenɥasjɔ̃] *nf* : reduction, easing, mitigation

atténuer [atenɥe] *vt* : to ease, to tone down, to reduce — **s'atténuer** *vr*

atterrer [atere] *vt* : to dismay, to appall

atterrir [aterir] *vi* : to land, to make a landing

atterrissage [aterisaʒ] *nm* : landing <atterrissage d'urgence : emergency landing>

attestation [atɛstasjɔ̃] *nf* **1** : affidavit, attestation **2** : certificate

attester [atɛste] *vt* : to attest, to vouch for, to testify to

attiédir [atjedir] *vt* : to make lukewarm, to cool down

attifer [atife] *vt fam* : to deck out, to doll up

attirail [atiraj] *nm* **1** : gear, equipment **2** *fam* : paraphernalia

attirance [atirɑ̃s] *nf* : attraction

attirant, -rante [atirɑ̃, -rɑ̃t] *adj* ATTRAYANT : attractive

attirer [atire] *vt* **1** : to attract **2** : to lure, to entice **3 attirer des ennuis à** : to make trouble for

attiser [atize] *vt* : to stir up, to fuel <attiser le feu : to fan the flames>

attitré, -trée [atitre] *adj* **1** OFFICIEL : official, authorized **2** HABITUEL : regular

attitude [atityd] *nf* **1** : attitude **2** : posture, bearing

attouchement [atuʃmɑ̃] *nm* : touching, fondling

attraction [atraksjɔ̃] *nf* **1** : attraction <l'attraction magnétique : magnetic force> **2 attractions** *nfpl* : attractions, amusements

attrait [atrɛ] *nm* **1** : appeal, attraction **2 attraits** *nmpl* : charms

attrape [atrap] *nm* : trick, joke, catch

attrape-nigaud [atrapnigo] *nm fam* : con, con game

attraper [atrape] *vt* : to capture, to catch <attraper un rhume : to catch a cold> — **s'attraper** *vr*

attrayant, -trayante [atrɛjɑ̃, -trɛjɑ̃t] *adj* ATTIRANT : attractive <peu attrayant : unappealing, unattractive>

attribuable [atribɥabl] *adj* : attributable, ascribable

attribuer [atribɥe] *vt* **1** : to attribute, to ascribe **2** : to assign — **s'attribuer** *vr* : to claim, to appropriate

attribut [atriby] *nm* : attribute

attribution [atribysjɔ̃] *nf* **1** : attribution **2** : awarding, allotment, allocation

attrister [atriste] *vt* : to sadden

attroupement [atrupmɑ̃] *nm* : crowd

attrouper [atrupe] *v* **s'attrouper** *vr* : to gather (together)

au [o] → **à, le**

aubaine [obɛn] *nf* **1** : godsend, windfall **2** : good deal, bargain

aube [ob] *nf* **1** AURORE : dawn **2** : paddle, blade <bateaux à aubes : paddle boat>

aubépine [obepin] *nf* : hawthorn

auberge [obɛrʒ] *nf* : inn <auberge de jeunesse : youth hostel>

aubergine [obɛrʒin] *nf* : eggplant

aubergiste [obɛrʒist] *nmf* : innkeeper

aucun[1], -cune [okœ̃, -kyn] *adj* **1** (*in negative constructions*) : no, none, not any <il n'y a aucun doute : there is no doubt> **2** : any <plus qu'aucun autre : more than any other>

aucun[2], -cune *pron* **1** : none, not any <aucune de ses idées n'est bonne : none of his ideas is good> **2** : any, anyone <il travaille plus qu'aucun de ses amis : he works more than any of his friends> **3 d'aucuns** : some, some people

aucunement [okynmɑ̃] *adv* NULLEMENT : not at all, in no way

audace [odas] *nf* **1** : audacity, nerve **2** COURAGE : boldness, daring

audacieux, -cieuse [odasjø, -jøz] *adj* **1** : audacious **2** HARDI : bold, daring — **audacieusement** [odasjøzmɑ̃] *adv*

au-dedans [odədɑ̃] *adv* **1** : inside **2 ~ de** : inside (of), within <au-dedans du bâtiment : inside the building>

au-dehors [odəɔr] *adv* **1** : outside **2 ~ de** : outside (of) <au-dehors de la ville : outside the city>

au-delà[1] [odəla] *adv* **1** : beyond **2 ~ de** : beyond <au-delà de l'horizon : beyond the horizon>

au-delà[2] *nm* **l'au-delà** : eternity, the afterlife

au-dessous [odsu] *adv* **1** : below **2 ~ de** : beneath, below, under <au-dessous de la table : under the table>

au-dessus [odsy] *adv* **1** : above **2 ~ de** : above, over <au-dessus de la terre : above ground>

au-devant [odvɑ̃] *adv* : ahead <aller au-devant de qqn : to go to meet s.o.> <aller au-devant des demandes : to anticipate requests> <aller au-devant du danger : to court danger>

audible [odibl] *adj* : audible — **audibilité** [-bilite] *nf*

audience [odjɑ̃s] *nf* **1** PUBLIC : audience **2** : hearing, session <audiences publiques : public hearings>

audio [odjo] *adj* : audio

audiovisuel, -suelle [odjɔvizɥɛl] *adj* : audiovisual

audit [odit] *nm* : audit

auditer [odite] *vt* : to audit

auditeur, -trice [oditœr, -tris] *n* **1** : listener <les auditeurs : the audience> **2** : auditor

auditif, -tive [oditif, -tiv] *adj* : auditory, hearing

audition [odisjɔ̃] *nf* **1** : hearing (sense) **2** : audition **3** : examination, (judicial) hearing

auditionner [odisjɔne] *v* : to audition

auditoire [oditwar] *nm* **1** PUBLIC : audience **2** *Bel & Switz* : auditorium

auditorium [oditɔrjɔm] *nm* : auditorium

auge [oʒ] *nf* : trough

augmentation [ogmɑ̃tasjɔ̃] *nf* **1** ACCROISSEMENT : augmentation, increase **2** : raise (in salary, prices, etc.)

augmenter [ogmɑ̃te] *vt* : to augment, to increase, to raise — *vi* : to increase, to rise

augure [ogyr] *nm* **1** : omen <c'est de bon augure : that's a good omen> **2** : oracle, soothsayer

augurer [ogyre] *vt* : to augur, to bode <cela augure mal pour lui : that doesn't bode well for him>

auguste [ogyst] *adj* : august, noble, majestic

aujourd'hui [oʒurdɥi] *adv & nm* : today <il y a aujourd'hui un mois : a month ago today>

aulne [on] *nm* : alder

aulx → **ail**

aumône [omon] *nf* : alms *pl* <faire l'aumône à : to give alms to>

aumônier [omonje] *nm* : chaplain

auparavant [oparavɑ̃] *adv* **1** AVANT : before, previously **2** : beforehand, first

auprès [oprɛ] *adv* **~ de 1** : beside, near, next to **2** : with, on, over <avoir de l'influence auprès de qqn : to have influence over s.o.> **3** : to <ambassadeur auprès des Nations Unies : ambassador to the United Nations> **4** : compared with **5** : in the opinion of

auquel [okɛl] → **lequel**

aura[1] [ɔra] *pp* → **avoir**

aura[2] [ora] *nf* : aura

auréole [oreɔl] *nf* **1** : halo **2** TACHE : spot, ring

auriculaire *nm* [orikylɛr] : little finger, pinkie

aurique [orik] *adj* : fore-and-aft

aurore [ɔrɔr] *nf* **1** : aurora <aurore boréale : aurora borealis, northern lights> **2** AUBE : dawn

ausculter [oskylte] *vt* : to examine (with a stethoscope), to sound

auspices [ospis] *nmpl* : auspices <sous les auspices de : under the auspices of>

aussi[1] [osi] *adv* **1** : too, also, as well **2** TELLEMENT : so <je ne savais pas qu'elle était aussi occupée : I didn't know she was so busy> **3** : as <il est aussi grand que moi : he is as tall as me> <aussi difficile qu'il soit : however difficult it may be> **4 aussi bien que** : as well as

aussi[2] *conj* **1** : so, therefore **2** D'AILLEURS : but, in any case

aussitôt [osito] *adv* **1** : immediately **2 aussitôt que** : as soon as

austère [ostɛr] *adj* : austere — **austèrement** [ostɛrmɑ̃] *adv*

austérité [osterite] *nf* : austerity

austral, -trale [ostral] *adj, mpl* **australs** : southern

australien, -lienne [ostraljɛ̃, -jɛn] *adj* : Australian

Australien, -lienne *n* : Australian

autant [otɑ̃] *adv* **1** : as much, as many, so much, so many <il n'en a jamais vu autant : he never saw so much of it> **2 ~ de** : as much, as many, so much, so many <autant d'enfants que d'adultes : as many children as adults> **3 ~ que** : as much as, as many as, as far as <j'en ai autant que vous : I have as much as you do> <(pour) autant que je sache : as far as I know> **4 autant comme autant** *Can* : time and time again **5 d'autant plus** : all the more **6 pour autant** : for all that **7 pour autant que** : insofar as, as far as

autel [otɛl] *nm* : altar

auteur [otœr] *nm* **1** : author, composer, artist <auteur dramatique : playwright> **2** : originator, inventor **3** : perpetrator

auteure [otœr] *nf Can* : author

authenticité [otɑ̃tisite] *nf* : authenticity

authentifier [otɑ̃tifje] {96} *vt* : to authenticate

authentique [otɑ̃tik] *adj* : authentic — **authentiquement** [-tikmɑ̃] *adv*

autisme [otism] *nm* : autism

autiste [otist] *or* **autistique** [otistik] *adj* : autistic

auto [oto] *nf* : car, automobile

autobiographie [otɔbjɔgrafi] *nf* : autobiography

autobiographique [otɔbjɔgrafik] *adj* : autobiographical

autobus [otɔbys] *nm* BUS : bus

autocar [otɔkar] *nm* : bus, coach

autochtone [otɔktɔn] *adj & nmf* : native

autocollant[1], **-lante** [otɔkɔlɑ̃, -lɑ̃t] *adj* : self-adhesive

autocollant[2] *nm* : sticker, bumper sticker

autocrate [otɔkrat] *nmf* : autocrat — **autocratique** [-kratik] *adj*

autocratie [otɔkrasi] *nf* : autocracy

autocritique [otɔkritik] *nf* : self-criticism

autocuiseur [otɔkɥizœr] *nm* : pressure cooker

autodéfense [otɔdefɑ̃s] *nf* : self-defense

autodestructeur, -trice [otɔdɛstryktœr, -tris] *adj* : self-destructive

autodétermination [otɔdeterminasjɔ̃] *nf* : self-determination

autodidacte[1] [otɔdidakt] *adj* : self-taught

autodidacte[2] *nmf* : autodidact, self-taught person

autodiscipline [otɔdisiplin] *nf* : self-discipline

autographe [otɔgraf] *nm* : autograph

auto-infligé, -gée [otɔɛ̃fliʒe] *adj* : self-inflicted

automate [otɔmat] *nm* : automaton

automation [otɔmasjɔ̃] *nf* : automation

automatique [otɔmatik] *adj* : automatic — **automatiquement** [-tikmɑ̃] *adv*

automatisation [otɔmatizasjɔ̃] *nf* : automation, automating

automatiser [otɔmatize] *vt* : to automate

automnal, -nale [otɔnal] *adj, mpl* **-naux** [-no] : autumnal

automne [otɔn] *nm* : autumn, fall

automobile[1] [otɔmɔbil] *adj* : automotive, motor <l'industrie automobile : the motor industry>

automobile[2] *nf* : automobile, car

automobiliste [otɔmɔbilist] *nmf* : motorist, driver

autonome [otɔnɔm] *adj* : autonomous

autonomie [otɔnɔmi] *nf* : autonomy

autoportrait [otɔpɔrtrɛ] *nm* : self-portrait

autopropulsé, -sée [otɔprɔpylsi] *adj* : self-propelled

autopsie [otɔpsi] *nf* : autopsy — **autopsier** [-sje] *vt*

autoradio [otɔradjo] *nm* : car radio

autorisation [otɔrizasjɔ̃] *nf* **1** : authorization, permission **2** : license, permit

autorisé, -sée [otɔrize] *adj* **1** : permitted, allowed **2** : authoritative

autoriser [otɔrize] *vt* : to authorize, to give permission for, to empower

autoritaire [otɔritɛr] *adj* : authoritative — **autoritairement** [-tɛrmɑ̃] *adv*

autorité [otɔrite] *nf* : authority <faire autorité : to be authoritative>

autoroute [otɔrut] *nf* : (interstate) highway, freeway <autoroute à péage : turnpike>

auto–stop [otɔstɔp] *nm* **1** : hitchhiking **2 faire de l'auto-stop** : to hitchhike

auto–stoppeur, -peuse [otɔstɔpœr, -pøz] *n* : hitchhiker

autosuffisance [otɔsyfizɑ̃s] *nf* : self-sufficiency, self-reliance

autosuffisant, -sante [otɔsyfizɑ̃, -zɑ̃t] *adj* : self-sufficient

autour [otur] *adv* **1** : around, about <tout autour : all around> **2 ~ de** : around, about <autour de la table : around the table> <autour de six heures : about six o'clock>

autre[1] [otr] *adj* **1** : other, different <l'autre jour : the other day> <un autre problème : another problem> <se sentir autre : to feel different> **2 autre chose** : something else, something different **3 autre part** : somewhere else

autre[2] *pron* : other, another <suivons les autres : let's follow the others> <prenez-en un autre : take another one>

autrefois [otrəfwa] *adv* **1** JADIS : formerly, in the past **2 d'~** : of old, of the past <ma vie d'autrefois : my past life>

autrement [otrəmɑ̃] *adv* **1** : otherwise, differently <elle ne pouvait pas faire autrement : she couldn't act differently> <autrement dit : in other words> **2** : otherwise, if not <autrement vous le regretterez : otherwise you will be sorry> **3** : far (more) <c'est autrement moins sérieux : it's much less serious> **4 pas autrement** : not especially

autrichien, -chienne [otriʃjɛ̃, -ʃjɛn] *adj* : Austrian

Autrichien, -chienne *n* : Austrian

autruche [otryʃ] *nf* : ostrich

autrui [otrɥi] *pron* : others, other people

auvent [ovɑ̃] *nm* : canopy, awning

aux [o] → **à, les**

auxiliaire[1] [oksiljɛr] *adj* : auxiliary

auxiliaire[2] *nmf* : auxiliary

auxiliaire[3] *nm* : auxiliary (verb)

auxquels, auxquelles [okɛl] → **lequel**

avachi, -chie [avaʃi] *adj* **1** : shapeless, misshapen **2** : limp, flabby

aval [aval] *nm* **1** : endorsement (in law and finance) **2** : SOUTIEN : support, backing **3** : **en ~** : downstream, lower down

avalanche [avalɑ̃ʃ] *nf* : avalanche

avaler [avale] *vt* **1** : to swallow **2** : to inhale

avaliser [avalize] *vt* : to endorse, to support

avance [avɑ̃s] *nf* **1** : advance **2** : lead **3 à l'avance** : in advance, ahead of schedule **4 d'avance** *or* **par ~** : in advance, already **5 en ~** : early **6 avances** *nfpl* : advances, overtures

avancé, -cée [avɑ̃se] *adj* **1** : advanced **2** : progressive

avancée *nf* : overhang, projection

avancement [avɑ̃smɑ̃] *nm* **1** : advancement, progress **2** : promotion

avancer [avɑ̃se] {6} *vt* **1** : to advance, to put forward **2** : to promote, to further — *vi* **1** : to advance, to go forward **2** : to be ahead of time <ma montre avance de trois minutes : my watch is three minutes fast> — **s'avancer** *vr* **1** : to advance, to move forward **2** : to progress, to get ahead **3** : to project, to protrude

avanie [avani] *nf* : snub

avant[1] [avɑ̃] *adv* **1** : before <quelques semaines avant : a few weeks before> <la page d'avant : the preceding page> **2** : first <tu devrais manger avant : you should eat first> **3** : far, deep <avant dans la forêt : deep within the forest> **4** : in front <elle marchait avant : she was walking in front> **5 ~ de** : before <avant de partir : before leaving> **6 avant que** : before, until <ne parlez pas avant qu'il ne le fasse : don't speak until he does>

avant[2] *adj* : front <la roue avant : the front wheel>

avant[3] *nm* **1** : front **2** : forward (in sports) **3 en ~** : forward, ahead **4 en avant de** : ahead of

avant[4] *prep* **1** : before, by <avant la fin : before the end> <avant huit heures : by eight o'clock> <avant peu : shortly> **2 avant tout** : first and foremost, above all

avantage [avɑ̃taʒ] *nm* **1** : advantage <tirer avantage de : to take advantage of> **2** : benefit <avantages sociaux : fringe benefits> **3 être à son avantage** : to look one's best

avantager [avɑ̃taʒe] {17} *vt* **1** FAVORISER : to favor, to give an advantage to **2** : to flatter, to show to advantage

avantageux, -geuse [avɑ̃taʒø, -ʒøz] *adj* **1** : advantageous, attractive <prix avantageux : attractive prices> **2** : flattering — **avantageusement** [-ʒøzmɑ̃] *adv*

avant-bras [avɑ̃bra] *nm* : forearm

avant-coureur [avɑ̃kurœr] *adj* : precursory, early

avant-dernier, -nière [avɑ̃dɛrnje, -njɛr] *adj* : next to last

avant-garde [avɑ̃gard] *nf* **1** : vanguard **2** : avant-garde

avant-goût [avɑ̃gu] *nm* : foretaste

avant-hier [avɑ̃tjɛr] *adv* : the day before yesterday

avant-midi [avɑ̃midi] *nf & pl Can nms & pl Belg* : morning

avant-poste [avɑ̃pɔst] *nm* : outpost

avant-première [avɑ̃prəmjɛr] *nf* : preview

avant-projet [avɑ̃prɔʒe] *nm* : (rough) draft

avant-propos [avɑ̃prɔpo] *nms & pl* : foreword

avant-toit [avɑ̃twa] *nm* : eaves *pl*

avare[1] [avar] *adj* : miserly, greedy

avare[2] *nmf* : miser

avarice [avaris] *nf* : avarice, miserliness

avaricieux, -cieuse [avarisjø, -sjøz] *adj* : miserly, stingy

avarie [avari] *nf* : damage (in shipping)

avatar [avatar] *nm* **1** : mishap **2** : metamorphosis, transformation **3** : avatar

avec[1] [avɛk] *adv fam* : with it, with that, with them <voulez-vous du vin avec? : would you like wine with that?>

avec[2] *prep* : with

aveline [avlin] *nf* : filbert (nut)

avenant[1], **-nante** [avnɑ̃, -nɑ̃t] *adj* : pleasant, attractive

avenant[2] *nm* **1** : endorsement **2** : codicil **3 à l'avenant** : in keeping, in conformity

avènement [avɛnmɑ̃] *nm* **1** : accession (to a throne) **2** : coming, advent

avenir [avnir] *nm* : future <à l'avenir : in the future>

avent [avɑ̃] *nm* **l'avent** : Advent

aventure [avɑ̃tyr] *nf* **1** : adventure **2** : venture **3** LIAISON : love affair **4 d'**~ : by chance

aventurer [avɑ̃tyre] *vt* : to risk — **s'aventurer** *vr* : to venture

aventureux, -reuse [avɑ̃tyrø, -røz] *adj* **1** : adventurous, venturesome **2** : risky

aventurier, -rière [avɑ̃tyrje, -rjɛr] *n* : adventurer

avenu, -nue [avny] *adj* **nul et non avenu** : null and void

avenue *nf* : avenue

avéré, -rée [avere] *adj* : acknowledged, recognized

avérer [avere] {87} *v* **s'avérer** *vr* : to prove to be, to turn out to be

averse [avɛrs] *nf* : shower, storm

aversion [avɛrsjɔ̃] *nf* : aversion, dislike

avertir [avɛrtir] *vt* **1** : to warn **2** AVISER : to advise, to inform

avertissement [avɛrtismɑ̃] *nm* **1** : warning **2** : official notice, reprimand **3** : foreword (of a book)

avertisseur [avɛrtisœr] *nm* **1** : (car) horn **2** : alarm <avertisseur de fumée : smoke alarm>

aveu [avø] *nm, pl* **aveux** : confession, admission <passer aux aveux : to confess>

aveuglant, -glante [avœglɑ̃, -glɑ̃t] *adj* : blinding, glaring

aveugle[1] [avœgl] *adj* : blind

aveugle[2] *nmf* : blind person

aveuglement [avœgləmɑ̃] *nm* : blindness

aveuglément [avœglemɑ̃] *adv* : blindly

aveugler [avœgle] *vt* **1** : to blind, to dazzle **2** : to block, to stop up — **s'aveugler** *vr* ~ **sur** : to turn a blind eye to

aveuglette [avœglɛt] *adv* **à l'aveuglette** : blindly <avancer à l'aveuglette : to grope one's way>

aviateur, -trice [avjatœr, -tris] *n* : aviator, pilot

aviation [avjasjɔ̃] *nf* : aviation

aviculture [avikyltyr] *nf* : poultry farming

avide [avid] *adj* **1** : greedy **2** : eager — **avidement** [avidmɑ̃] *adv*

avidité [avidite] *nf* **1** : greed **2** : eagerness

avilir [avilir] *vt* : to degrade, to debase — **s'avilir** *vr*

avilissement [avilismɑ̃] *nm* : degradation, debasement

aviné, -née [avine] *adj* : inebriated

avion [avjɔ̃] *nm* : airplane <avion à réaction : jet plane> <avion de ligne : airliner> <avion de chasse : fighter plane>

avion-cargo [avjɔ̃kargo] *nm, pl* **avions-cargos** : cargo plane, freighter

aviron [avirɔ̃] *nm* **1** RAME : oar **2 Can** : paddle **3** : rowing

avis [avis] *nm* **1** : opinion <à mon avis : in my opinion> <changer d'avis : to change one's mind> **2** ANNONCE : notice, notification **3** CONSEIL : advice

avisé, -sée [avize] *adj* : prudent, sensible

aviser [avize] *vt* INFORMER : to advise, to inform, to notify — *vi* RÉFLÉCHIR : to think things over, to decide — **s'aviser** *vr* : to realize, to take notice

aviver [avive] *vt* **1** : to revive, to stir up **2** : to brighten, to liven up

avocat[1], **-cate** [avɔka, -kat] *n* **1** : lawyer, attorney **2** : advocate

avocat[2] *nm* : avocado
avoine [avwan] *nf* : oats *pl*
avoir[1] [avwar] {10} *vt* **1** : to have <il a de l'argent : he has money> <elle va avoir un enfant : she's going to have a baby> **2** : to get <j'ai eu mes billets hier : I got my tickets yesterday> **3** : to be (a particular age) <j'ai seize ans : I'm sixteen years old> **4** : to suffer, to feel <qu'est-ce que tu as? : what's wrong?> <j'ai mal : I'm hurt> **5 ~ à** : to have to <j'ai à vous parler : I must speak to you> **6 se faire avoir** *fam* : to be had, to be conned — *v impers* **il y a** : there is, there are — *v aux* : to have <je l'ai écrit : I wrote it, I have written it, I did write it> <elle y avait été : she had been there> <ils auront fini demain : they will have finished tomorrow>
avoir[2] *nm* **1** : assets *pl*, property **2** : credit
avoirdupoids [avwardypwa] *nm* : avoirdupois
avoisiner [avwazine] *vt* : to neighbor, to be near
avortement [avɔrtəmɑ̃] *nm* **1** : abortion <avortement spontané : miscarriage> **2** : failure, collapse
avorter [avɔrte] *vi* **1** : to abort, to miscarry **2** : to fail, to abort
avorton [avɔrtɔ̃] *nm* : runt
avoué[1], **-vouée** [avwe] *adj* : avowed, declared
avoué[2] *nm* : attorney
avouer [avwe] *vt* : to admit, to confess to — *vi* : to own up — **s'avouer** *vr* : to admit <s'avouer coupable : to admit one's guilt>
avril [avril] *nm* : April
axe [aks] *nm* **1** : axis **2** : axle **3** : major road, highway **4** : main line, mainstream (in politics, etc.)
axer [akse] *vt* : to center, to focus
axiomatique [aksjɔmatik] *adj* : axiomatic
axiome [aksjom] *nm* : axiom
axis [aksis] *nms & pl* : axis
ayoye *or* **ayoille** [ajɔj] *interj Can* : ouch!
azalée [azale] *nf* : azalea
azimut [azimyt] *nm* **1** : azimuth **2 tous azimuts** : all out, total **3 dans tous les azimuts** : all over the place
azote [azɔt] *nm* : nitrogen
azur [azyr] *nm* : azure
azyme [azim] *adj* : unleavened

B

b [be] *nm* : b, the second letter of the alphabet
babeurre [babœr] *nm* : buttermilk
babiche [babiʃ] *nf Can* : leather lacing (for moccasins, snowshoes, etc.)
babillage [babijaʒ] *nm* : babbling, prattle
babillard [babijar] *nm Can* : bulletin board
babiller [babije] *vi* : to babble, to chatter
babines [babin] *nfpl* : chops <se lécher les babines : to lick one's chops>
babiole [babjɔl] *nf* : bauble, trinket
bâbord [babɔr] *nm* : port (side), larboard
babouin [babwɛ̃] *nm* : baboon
baboune [babun] *nf Can fam* **faire la baboune** : to sulk
baby-sitter [bebisitœr] *nmf, pl* **baby-sitters** *France* : baby-sitter
baby-sitting [bebisitiŋ] *nm France* : baby-sitting
bac [bak] *nm* **1** : ferry **2** : tub, vat <bac à glace : ice tray> **3** *fam* → **baccalauréat**
baccalauréat [bakalɔrea] *nm* **1** *France* : school-leaving certificate **2** *Can* : bachelor's degree
bâche [baʃ] *nf* : tarpaulin
bachelier, -lière [baʃəlje, -ljɛr] *n* : person who holds a *baccalauréat*
bachot [baʃo] *nm France fam* → **baccalauréat**
bachoter [baʃɔte] *vi France* : to cram (for an exam)
bacille [basil] *nm* : bacillus
bâcler [bakle] *vt* : to rush through, to dash off <travail bâclé : slapdash job, botched-up work>
bacon [bekɔn] *nm* : bacon
bactérie [bakteri] *nf* : bacterium
bactérien, -rienne [bakterjɛ̃, -rjɛn] *adj* : bacterial
bactériologie [bakterjɔlɔʒi] *nf* : bacteriology — **bactériologiste** [-lɔʒist] *nmf*
badaud, -daude [bado, -dod] *n* **1** : stroller, passerby **2** : (curious) onlooker
badge [badʒ] *nm* : badge
badigeonner [badiʒɔne] *vt* **1** : to daub, to smear **2** : to whitewash **3** : to paint (in medicine)
badin, -dine [badɛ̃, -din] *adj* : playful, jocular
badinage [badinaʒ] *nm* : banter, joking
badine [badin] *nf* : switch, cane
badiner [badine] *vi* **1** : to joke, to jest **2 ~ avec** : to trifle with, to toy with
badminton [badmintɔn] *nm* : badminton
bâdrer [badre] *vt Can fam* : to bother, to annoy

baffe [baf] *nf fam* : slap, smack

bafouer [bafwe] *vt* RIDICULISER : to ridicule, to scorn

bafouillage [bafujaʒ] *nm* **1** : mumbling, stammering **2** : gibberish

bafouiller [bafuje] *v* : to mumble, to stammer

bâfrer [bafre] *vt fam* : to gobble, to guzzle — *vi fam* : to stuff oneself

bagage [bagaʒ] *nm* **1** : baggage, luggage <bagages à main : hand luggage> <plier bagage : to pack up and leave> **2** : knowledge, background

bagarre [bagar] *nf* : fight, brawl

bagarrer [bagare] *vi* : to fight, to brawl — **se bagarrer** *vr*

bagarreur, -reuse [bagarœr, -røz] *n* : fighter, brawler

bagatelle [bagatɛl] *nf* **1** : trifle, trinket **2** : trifling sum

bagnard [baɲar] *nm* : convict

bagne [baɲ] *nm* **1** : penal colony **2** : hard labor

bagnole [baɲɔl] *nf fam* : jalopy, car

bague [bag] *nf* **1** : ring <bague de fiançailles : engagement ring> **2** : band, circlet

baguette [bagɛt] *nf* **1** : stick, rod, baton <baguette à fusil : ramrod> <baguette de tambour : drumstick> <baguette magique : magic wand> **2** : baguette (loaf of French bread) **3 baguettes** *nfpl* : chopsticks

bahreïni, -nie [barejni] *adj* : Bahraini

Bahreïni, -nie *n* : Bahraini

baie [bɛ] *nf* **1** : bay **2** : berry **3** *or* **baie vitrée** : picture window

baignade [bɛɲad] *nf* : swimming, bathing

baigner [beɲe] *vt* : to bathe, to wash — *vi* : to soak, to steep — **se baigner** *vr* **1** : to take a bath **2** : to go swimming

baigneur, -gneuse [bɛɲœr, -ɲøz] *n* : swimmer, bather

baignoire [beɲwar] *nf* : bathtub

bail [baj] *nm, pl* **baux** [bo] : lease

bâillement [bajmɑ̃] *nm* : yawn

bâiller [baje] *vi* **1** : to yawn **2** : to gape (open)

bailleur, -leresse [bajœr, -jrɛs] *n* **1** : lessor **2 bailleur de fonds** : financial backer

bâillon [bajɔ̃] *nm* : gag

bâillonner [bajɔne] *vt* **1** : to gag **2** : to silence

bain [bɛ̃] *nm* **1** : bath <bain de bouche : mouthwash> <bain de sang : bloodbath> <bain de soleil : sunbath> <prendre un bain : to take a bath> **2** : swim **3 se mettre dans le bain** : to get into the swing of things

bain-marie [bɛ̃mari] *nm, pl* **bains-marie** : double boiler

baïonnette [bajɔnɛt] *nf* : bayonet

baiser[1] [beze] *vt* : to kiss

baiser[2] *nm* : kiss

baisse [bɛs] *nf* **1** : fall, drop, decline **2 à la baisse** : downward

baisser [bese] *vt* **1** : to let down, to lower <baisser les yeux : to look down> <baisser les bras : to give up> **2** : to reduce (volume, light) — *vi* : to go down, to drop, to decline — **se baisser** : to bend down, to stoop, to duck

bajoues [baʒu] *nfpl* : chops, jowls

bal [bal] *nm* : ball, dance

balade [balad] *nf* PROMENADE : stroll, walk

balader [balade] *vt* : to take for a walk — *vi* : to stroll, to saunter — **se balader** *vr* : to go for a walk, to stroll about, to gallivant (around)

baladeur [baladœr] *nm* : portable radio–cassette player

balafre [balafr] *nf* **1** : gash, slash **2** CICATRICE : scar

balai [balɛ] *nm* **1** : broom, brush <passer le balai : to sweep the floor> **2** : windshield-wiper blade

balaie [bale], **balaiera** [balera], *etc.* → **balayer**

balance [balɑ̃s] *nf* **1** : scale, scales *pl* <faire pencher la balance : to tip the scales> **2** : balance <balance de commerce : balance of trade> **3** *Can* : difference, remainder <la balance de : the rest of>

Balance *nf* : Libra

balancement [balɑ̃smɑ̃] *nm* : swaying, swinging

balancer [balɑ̃se] {6} *vt* **1** : to sway, to swing, to rock **2** *fam* : to fling, to chuck, to junk — *vi* **1** : to sway **2** : to waver, to hesitate — **se balancer** *vr* : to rock, to swing, to sway

balancier [balɑ̃sje] *nm* : pendulum

balançoire [balɑ̃swar] *nf* **1** : swing **2** BASCULE : seesaw

balayage [balɛjaʒ] *nm* : sweeping

balayer [baleje] {11} *vt* **1** : to sweep, to sweep away **2** : to scan

balayeur, balayeuse [balɛjœr, balɛjøz] *n* : street sweeper

balayeuse [balɛjøz] *nf* **1** : street-cleaning truck **2** *Can* : vacuum cleaner

balbutiement [balbysimɑ̃] *nm* **1** : stammering, stuttering **2 balbutiements** *nmpl* : early stages, beginnings

balbutier [balbysje] {96} *v* : to stammer, to stutter

balbuzard [balbyzar] *nm or* **balbuzard pêcheur** : osprey

balcon [balkɔ̃] *nm* : balcony

baldaquin [baldakɛ̃] *nm* : canopy

baleine [balɛn] *nf* **1** : whale **2** : rib (of an umbrella)

baleinier [balenje] *nm* : whaler (ship or person)

baleinière [balenjɛr] *nf* : whaleboat

balise [baliz] *nf* **1** : buoy, beacon **2** : signpost, marker

baliser [balize] *vt* : to mark (with beacons or signs)

balistique[1] [balistik] *adj* : ballistic

balistique[2] *nf* : ballistics

balivernes [balivɛrn] *nfpl* SORNETTES : nonsense, humbug

ballade [balad] *nf* : ballad

ballant[1], **-lante** [balɑ̃, -lɑ̃t] *adj* : dangling

ballant[2] *nm* : slack, looseness

ballast [balast] *nm* : ballast

balle [bal] *nf* **1** : ball <balle de tennis : tennis ball> <renvoyer la balle : to pass the buck> **2** : bullet **3** : bale, bundle **4** : husk, chaff **5** *France fam* : franc

balle–molle [balmɔl] *nf Can* : softball

ballerine [balrin] *nf* : ballerina

ballet [balɛ] *nm* : ballet

ballon [balɔ̃] *nm* **1** : ball <ballon de football : football, soccer ball> **2** : balloon **3** : wine glass, brandy glass **4 ballon d'oxygène** : oxygen tank

ballonner [balɔne] *vt* : to bloat, to distend (the stomach)

ballon–panier [balɔ̃panje] *nm Can* : basketball (game)

ballot [balo] *nm* **1** BALUCHON : pack, bundle **2** *fam* : chump, fool

ballottage [balɔtaʒ] *nm* : second ballot

ballotter [balɔte] *vt* SECOUER : to shake, to toss about — *vi* : to toss, to roll around

balloune [balun] *nf Can* **1** : balloon **2** : bubble <gomme balloune : bubble gum>

balluchon [balyʃɔ̃] → **baluchon**

balnéaire [balneɛr] *adj* : seaside <station balnéaire : seaside resort>

balourd[1], **-lourde** [balur, -lurd] *adj* : awkward, clumsy, stupid

balourd[2], **-lourde** *n* : clumsy oaf, dolt

balourdise [balurdiz] *nf* **1** : awkwardness, clumsiness **2** : gaffe, blunder

balsa [balza] *nm* : balsa

balsamine [balzamin] *nf* : balsam fir

balte [balt] *adj* : Baltic

baluchon [balyʃɔ̃] *nm* BALLOT : pack, bundle <faire son baluchon : to pack one's bag>

balustrade [balystrad] *nf* **1** : balustrade **2** : railing, bannister

balustre [balystr] *nf* : baluster

bambin, -bine [bɑ̃bɛ̃, -bin] *n* : child, toddler

bambou [bɑ̃bu] *nm* : bamboo

ban [bɑ̃] *nm* **1** : round of applause **2 bans** *nmpl* : banns **3 mettre au ban** : to banish, to ostracize

banal, -nale [banal] *adj, mpl* **banaux 1** ORDINAIRE : commonplace, ordinary **2** : banal, trite

banaliser [banalize] *vt* **1** : to make commonplace **2 voiture banalisée** : unmarked car

banalité [banalite] *nf* **1** : banality, triteness **2** : platitude, cliché

banane [banan] *nf* : banana

bananier [bananje] *nm* : banana tree

banc [bɑ̃] *nm* **1** : bench <banc des accusés : dock (in court)> <banc d'église : pew> **2** : shoal, school (of fish) **3** : bank <banc de sable : sandbank> <banc de neige *Can* : snowbank>

bancaire [bɑ̃kɛr] *adj* : banking, bank <compte bancaire : bank account>

bancal, -cale [bɑ̃kal] *adj, mpl* **bancals** : shaky, wobbly

bandage [bɑ̃daʒ] *nm* **1** : bandaging **2** PANSEMENT : bandage, dressing

bande [bɑ̃d] *nf* **1** : gang, group, troop **2** : pack (of animals) **3** : band, strip <bande dessinée : comic strip> **4** : tape, (reel of) film <bande vidéo : videotape> <bande sonore : soundtrack> **5 donner de la bande** : to list (of a ship)

bandeau [bɑ̃do] *nm, pl* **bandeaux 1** : blindfold **2** : headband

bandelette [bɑ̃dlɛt] *nf* : narrow strip (of cloth, etc.)

bander [bɑ̃de] *vt* **1** : to bandage **2** : to bend (a bow) **3** : to flex, to tense **4 bander les yeux à** : to blindfold

banderole [bɑ̃drɔl] *nf* : banner, pennant

bandit [bɑ̃di] *nm* **1** VOLEUR : bandit, robber **2** : scoundrel **3** *or* **petit bandit** : rascal

banditisme [bɑ̃ditism] *nm* : banditry

bandoulière [bɑ̃duljɛr] *nf* : shoulder strap <en bandoulière : slung over one's shoulder>

bangladais, -daise [bɑ̃gladɛ, -dɛz] *adj* : Bangladeshi

Bangladais, -daise *n* : Bangladeshi

banjo [bɑ̃(d)ʒo] *nm* : banjo

banlieue [bɑ̃ljø] *nf* : suburb(s) <de banlieue : suburban>

banlieusard[1], **-sarde** [bɑ̃ljøzar, -zard] *adj* : suburban

banlieusard[2], **-sarde** *n* : suburbanite, suburban commuter

banni[1], **-nie** [bani] *adj* : exiled, banished

banni[2], **-nie** *n* : exile

bannière [banjɛr] *nf* : banner

bannir [banir] *vt* : to banish, to exile

bannissement [banismɑ̃] *nm* : banishment

banque [bɑ̃k] *nf* **1** : bank <banque commerciale : commercial bank> <banque du sang : blood bank> **2** : banking

banqueroute [bɑ̃krut] *nf* **1** : bankruptcy **2 faire banqueroute** : to go bankrupt

banquet [bɑ̃kɛ] *nm* FESTIN : banquet, feast

banquette [bɑ̃kɛt] *nf* : bench, seat (in a booth or vehicle) <banquette arrière : back seat>

banquier, -quière [bɑ̃kje, -kjɛr] *n* : banker

banquise [bɑ̃kiz] *nf* : ice floe

bans [bɑ̃] *nmpl* : banns (of marriage)

baptême [batɛm] *nm* : baptism, christening

baptiser [batize] *vt* : to baptize, to christen

baptismal, -male [batismal] *adj, mpl* **-maux** [-mo] : baptismal

baptistaire [batistɛr] *nm Can* : certificate of baptism

bar [bar] *nm* **1** : bar **2** : sea bass

baragouin [baragwɛ̃] *nm* : gibberish, gobbledegook

baragouiner [baragwine] *vi* : to talk gibberish — *vt* : to speak (a language) badly <baragouiner l'anglais : to speak broken English>

baraque [barak] *nf* **1** BICOQUE : hut, shack **2** : stall, stand (at a fair, etc.)

baraquement [barakmɑ̃] *nm* : group of shacks

baratin [baratɛ̃] *nm* : smooth talk, sales patter

baratte [barat] *nf* : churn

baratter [barate] *vt* : to churn

barauder [barode] *vt Can* : to move back and forth, to skid (on ice, etc.)

barbant, -bante [barbɑ̃, -bɑ̃t] *adj fam* RASANT : boring

barbare[1] [barbar] *adv* : barbarous, barbaric

barbare[2] *nmf* : barbarian

barbarie [barbari] *nf* : barbarity, barbarism

barbarisme [barbarism] *nm* : barbarism (in language, manners, etc.)

barbe [barb] *nf* **1** : beard **2** : barb (of a feather, of metal) **3** : tuft, awn (of a plant) **4** *fam* : bore <quelle barbe! : what a bore!>

barbecue [barbəkju] *nm* : barbecue

barbelé[1], **-lée** [barbəle] *adj* : barbed

barbelé[2] *nm* : barbed wire

barber [barbe] *vt fam* : to bore — **se barber** *vr*

barbiche [barbiʃ] *nf* **1** : goatee **2** : beard (of a goat)

barbier [barbje] *nm Can* : barber

barbiturique [barbityrik] *nm* : barbiturate

barboter [barbɔte] *vi* : to paddle, to splash around — *vt fam* : to filch

barboteuse [barbɔtøz] *nf Can* : wading pool

barbouillage [barbujaʒ] *nm* : daub, smear

barbouiller [barbuje] *vt* **1** : to smear, to daub **2** : to scribble **3** : to nauseate, to make sick <ça me barbouille le coeur : it turns my stomach>

barbu, -bue [barby] *adj* : bearded

barda [barda] *nm fam* : gear, stuff

bardane [bardan] *nf* : bur, burr (in botany)

barde [bard] *nm* : bard

bardeau [bardo] *nm, pl* **bardeaux 1** : shingle **2 manquer un bardeau** *Can fam* : to be a little crazy

barder [barde] *vt* : to bard (in cooking) — *v impers fam* **ça va barder!** : there's going to be trouble!, sparks will fly!

barème [barɛm] *nm* : scale, table <barème de salaires : salary scale>

baril [baril] *nm* TONNELET : barrel, keg

barillet [barijɛ] *nm* **1** : small barrel **2** : cylinder (of a revolver)

bariolé, -lée [barjɔle] *adj* MULTICOLORE : multicolored

barman [barman] *nm, pl* **barmans** *or* **barmen** : bartender

baromètre [barɔmɛtr] *nm* : barometer — **barométrique** [-metrik] *adj*

baron, -ronne [barɔ̃, -rɔn] *n* : baron *m*, baroness *f*

baroque [barɔk] *adj* **1** : baroque **2** BIZARRE : weird, odd

baroud [barud] *nm fam* : fight, set-to <baroud d'honneur : last stand>

barque [bark] *nf* : small boat

barracuda [barakyda] *nm* : barracuda

barrage [baraʒ] *nm* **1** : dam **2** : roadblock, barricade

barre [bar] *nf* **1** : bar, rod **2** : (written) line, stroke **3** : mark <sous la barre des deux pour cent : below the two percent mark> **4** : helm <prendre la barre : to take the helm, to take charge> **5** : bar (in law) **6** : sandbar

barreau [baro] *nm, pl* **barreaux 1** : bar <derrière les barreaux : behind bars> **2** : rung (of a ladder, etc.) **3 le barreau** : the bar, the legal profession

barrer [bare] *vt* **1** : to bar, to block **2** : to mark, to cross, to cross out **3** : to steer (a boat) **4** *Can* : to lock (a door) — **se barrer** *vr fam* : to clear out <barrez-vous! : get out of here!>

barrette [barɛt] *nf* **1** : barrette **2** : biretta

barricade [barikad] *nf* : barricade

barricader [barikade] *vt* : to barricade — **se barricader** *vr* : to barricade oneself, to shut oneself away

barrière [barjɛr] *nf* **1** OBSTACLE : barrier <barrières douanières : trade barriers> **2** : fence, gate

barrique [barik] *nf* TONNEAU : barrel, cask

barrir [barir] *vi* : to trumpet (of an elephant)

baryton [baritɔ̃] *nm* : baritone

baryum [barjɔm] *nm* : barium

bas[1] [ba] *adv* **1** : low <tomber bas : to sink low> **2** : softly, quietly

bas[2], **basse** [ba, baz (*before a vowel or mute h*), bas] *adj* **1** : low **2** : base, vile **3** : bass

bas[3] *nms & pl* **1** : bottom, lower part <de haut en bas : from top to bottom> <à bas : down with> <en bas : downstairs, below, at the bottom> <en bas de : at the bottom of, beneath> **2** : stocking **3** : bass (part)

basalte [bazalt] *nm* : basalt

basané, -née [bazane] *adj* **1** : tanned, sunburned **2** : swarthy

bascule [baskyl] *nf* **1** : balance, scales *pl* **2** : rocker <fauteuil à bascule : rocking chair> **3** BALANÇOIRE : seesaw

basculer [baskyle] *vi* **1** : to tip, to topple over **2** : to rock, to swing

base [baz] *nf* **1** : base <à la base de : at the root of> <base de lancement : launching site> **2** : basis **3 base de données** : database

baseball *or* **base–ball** [bɛzbol] *nm* : baseball

baseballeur, -leuse [bɛzbolœr, -løz] *n Can* : baseball player

baser [baze] *vt* FONDER : to base, to found

bas–fond [bafɔ̃] *nm* **1** : shallows *pl* **2** : lowland **3 bas–fonds** *nmpl* : dregs (of society), slums

basilic [bazilik] *nm* : basil

basilique [bazilik] *nf* : basilica

basique [bazik] *adj* : basic (in chemistry)

basket [baskɛt] *or* **basket-ball** *or* **basketball** [baskɛtbol] *nm* : basketball

basketteur, -teuse [baskɛtœr, -tøz] *n* : basketball player

basque[1] [bask] *adj* : Basque

basque[2] *nm* : Basque (language)

Basque *nmf* : Basque

bas–relief [barəljɛf] *nm, pl* **bas–reliefs** : bas-relief

basse [bas] *nf* **1** → **bas[2]** **2** : bass (in music)

basse–cour [baskur] *nf, pl* **basses–cours 1** : farmyard, barnyard **2** : poultry

bassesse [basɛs] *nf* : baseness, meanness

basset [basɛ] *nm* : basset hound

bassin [basɛ̃] *nm* **1** : basin (of a river) **2** : lake, pond, pool **3** : pelvis

bassine [basin] *nf* **1** : large bowl, basin **2** *Can* : bedpan **3** : bowlful

basson [basɔ̃] *nm* : bassoon

bastion [bastjɔ̃] *nm* : bastion

bas–ventre [bavɑ̃tr] *nm, pl* **bas–ventres** : lower abdomen

bât [ba] *nm* **1** : packsaddle **2 c'est là où le bât blesse** : that's where the shoe pinches

bataclan [bataklɑ̃] *nm fam* **1** : stuff, gear **2 tout le bataclan** : the whole kit and caboodle

bataille [bataj] *nf* **1** : battle, fight **2 en ~** : in disarray, disheveled

batailler [bataje] *vi* : to fight

batailleur[1], -leuse [batajœr, -jøz] *adj* : quarrelsome, belligerent

batailleur[2], -leuse *n* : fighter

bataillon [batajɔ̃] *nm* : battalion

bâtard[1], -tarde [batar, -tard] *adj* **1** : hybrid, crossbred **2** : bastard

bâtard[2], -tarde *n* : bastard

bâtard[3] *nm France* : small loaf of bread

bateau[1] [bato] *adj, s & pl* **bateau** : hackneyed

bateau[2] *nm, pl* **bateaux 1** : boat, ship <bateau de pêche : fishing boat> <bateau amiral : flagship> <bateau de guerre : warship> <bateau de plaisance : launch> <bateau à voile : sailboat> **2 faire du bateau** : to go sailing

bateau–mouche [batomuʃ] *nm, pl* **bateaux–mouches** : sightseeing boat

bateleur, -leuse [batlœr, -løz] *n* **1** : juggler, tumbler **2** : fool, buffoon

batelier, -lière [batəlje, -ljɛr] *n* : boatman

bâti [bati] *nm* **1** : framework, support **2** : tacking, basting (in sewing)

batifoler [batifɔle] *vi* : to frolic, to romp

bâtiment [batimɑ̃] *nm* **1** : building **2** : building trade **3** : ship <bâtiment de guerre : man-of-war>

bâtir [batir] *vt* **1** CONSTRUIRE : to build, to erect **2** : to build up, to develop **3** : to baste, to tack

bâtisseur, -seuse [batisœr, -søz] *n* : builder

bâton [batɔ̃] *nm* **1** : rod, pole <bâton de ski : ski pole> **2** : piece, stick <bâton de rouge (à lèvres) : lipstick> **3** : nightstick **4** : baton **5** *Can* : bat <bâton de baseball : baseball bat>

bâtonnet [batɔnɛ] *nm* : short stick, rod

battage [bataʒ] *nm* **1** : beating, threshing **2** : hype **3** : shuffle, shuffling (of playing cards)

battant[1], -tante [batɑ̃, -tɑ̃t] *adj* : beating, driving, banging <pluie battante : driving rain> <le cœur battant : with a pounding heart>

battant[2] *nm* **1** : flap, section (of a door, window, etc.) **2** : clapper (of a bell)

battant[3], -tante [batɑ̃, -tɑ̃t] *nmf* : fighter, go-getter

batte [bat] *nf* : bat (in sports)

battement [batmɑ̃] *nm* **1** : beating, fluttering, blinking **2** : clapping, tapping, banging **3** : interval, wait

batterie [batri] *nf* **1** : set, group, battery <une batterie de tests : a string of tests> **2** : battery (of artillery) **3** : drums, drum set **4** : battery (of a motor vehicle)

batteur [batœr, -tøz] *nm* **1** : (egg) whisk, eggbeater <batteur électrique : electric mixer> **2** : drummer **3** : batter (in sports)

batteuse [batøz] *nf* : thresher, threshing machine

battre [batr] {12} *vt* **1** FRAPPER : to hit, to strike, to beat **2** VAINCRE : to defeat <battre à plates coutures : to defeat soundly, to wallop> **3** : to shuffle (playing cards) — *vi* : to beat — **se battre** *vr* : to fight

batture [batyr] *nf Can* : sandbar

baudet [bodɛ] *nm fam* : jackass

baudrier [bodrije] *nm* BANDOULIÈRE : shoulder strap

bauge [boʒ] *nf* : wallow (for animals)

baume [bom] *nm* **1** : balm, balsam **2 mettre du baume au cœur** : to be of comfort

baux → **bail**

bavard[1], **-varde** [bavar, -vard] *adj* : talkative
bavard[2], **-varde** *n* : talkative person, chatterbox
bavardage [bavardaʒ] *nm* : idle talk, chatter
bavarder [bavarde] *vi* **1** : to chatter **2** : to gossip
bavarois, -roise [bavarwa, -rwaz] *adj* : Bavarian
Bavarois, -roise *n* : Bavarian
bave [bav] *nf* : dribble, drool, spittle
baver [bave] *vi* **1** : to dribble, to drool **2** : to run, to leak **3 ~ en** : to have a hard time of it **4 ~ sur** : to slander
bavette [bavɛt] *nf* **1** : bib **2** : flank (of beef) **3** : mudguard
baveux[1], **-veuse** [bavø, -vøz] *adj* **1** : dribbling, drooling **2** : runny (of an omelette, etc.)
baveux[2], **-veuse** *n Can fam* : pain in the neck, annoying person
bavoir [bavwar] *nm* : bib (for babies)
bavure [bavyr] *nf* **1** : smudge, blur **2** : error, blunder
bayer [baje] {11} *vi* **bayer aux corneilles** : to gape, to gaze into space
bayou [baju] *nm* : bayou
bazar [bazar] *nm* **1** : bazaar **2** : general store **3** : clutter, mess
bazou [bazu] *nm Can fam* : jalopy
beagle [bigœl] *nm* : beagle
béant, béante [beɑ̃, beɑ̃t] *adj* : gaping
béat, béate [bea, beat] *adj* **1** : blissful **2** : self-satisfied, smug
béatement [beatmɑ̃] *adv* : blissfully
béatitude [beatityd] *nf* **1** : bliss **2** : beatitude
beau[1] [bo] *adv* **1 avoir beau** : to do (something) in vain <j'ai beau essayer : it's useless for me to try> **2 faire beau** : to be fine, to be fair <il fait beau : it's nice outside>
beau[2] **(bel** [bɛl] *before vowel or mute h*), **belle** [bɛl] *adj, mpl* **beaux** [bo] **1** : beautiful, handsome **2** : good, noble **3** : fine, fair <beau temps : nice weather> **4** : excellent, desirable <belle santé : good health> **5** : considerable, great (in quantity) <un bel âge : a ripe old age> <une belle somme : a tidy sum> **6 bel et bien** : for sure, truly
beau[3] *nm* **1 le beau** : the beautiful, beauty **2 faire le beau** : to sit up and beg (of a dog)
beaucoup [boku] *adv* **1** : much, a lot <je t'aime beaucoup : I love you very much> **2 ~ de** : much, many, a lot of <beaucoup de livres : a lot of books> **3 de ~** : by far
beau-fils [bofis] *nm, pl* **beaux-fils 1** : son-in-law **2** : stepson
beau-frère [bofrɛr] *nm, pl* **beaux-frères 1** : brother-in-law **2** : stepbrother
beau-père [bopɛr] *nm, pl* **beaux-pères 1** : father-in-law **2** : stepfather
beauté [bote] *nf* : beauty
beaux-arts [bozar] *nmpl* : fine arts
beaux-parents [boparɑ̃] *nmpl* : in-laws
bébé [bebe] *nm* : baby, infant
bebelle [bəbɛl] *nf Can fam* **1** : gadget **2 bebelles** *nfpl* : things <tes bebelles puis dans ta cour : pack your things and go>
bébête [bebɛt] *adj* : silly, babyish
bébite [bebit] *nf Can fam* : bug, insect
bec [bɛk] *nm* **1** : beak, bill **2** *fam* : mouth, nose, face **3** EMBOUCHURE : mouthpiece **4** : burner <bec à gaz : gas burner> **5** : point, nib **6** : spout, lip (of a jug, etc.) **7** *Belg, Can, Switz fam* : kiss **8 bec fin** : gourmet **9 tomber sur un bec** : to run into a snag
bécane [bekan] *nf fam* : bike
bécasse [bekas] *nf* **1** : woodcock **2** *fam* : featherbrain, silly goose
bécasseau [bekaso] *nm* : sandpiper
bécassine [bekasiːn] *nf* : snipe
bec-de-lièvre [bɛkdəljɛvr] *nm, pl* **becs-de-lièvre** : harelip
bêche [bɛʃ] *nf* : spade
bêcher [beʃe] *vt* **1** : to dig (up) **2** : to criticize
bêcheur[1], **-cheuse** [bɛʃœr, -ʃøz] *adj* : stuck-up
bêcheur[2], **-cheuse** *n* : stuck-up person, snob
becqueter [bɛkte] {8} *vt* **1** : to peck at **2** *fam* : to eat
bedaine [bədɛn] *nf* : paunch, potbelly
bedonnant, -nante [bədɔnɑ̃, -nɑ̃t] *adj* : paunchy, portly, potbellied
bédouin, -douine [bedwɛ̃, -dwin] *n* : bedouin
bée [be] *adj* **bouche bée** : openmouthed <être bouche bée devant : to gape at>
beffroi [befrwa] *nm* : belfry
bégaie [bege], **bégaiera** [begera], *etc.* → **bégayer**
bégaiement [begɛmɑ̃] *nm* : stuttering, stammering
bégayer [begeje] {11} *v* : to stutter, to stammer
bégonia [begɔnja] *nm* : begonia
bégueule [begœl] *nmf* : prude
béguin [begɛ̃] *nm fam* : crush, infatuation
beige [bɛʒ] *adj & nm* : beige
beigne[1] [bɛɲ] *nf fam* : smack, sock, punch
beigne[2] *nm Can* : doughnut
beignet [bɛɲɛ] *nm* **1** : doughnut **2** : fritter
bel → **beau**
bêlement [bɛlmɑ̃] *nm* : bleat
bêler [bele] *vi* : to bleat
belette [bəlɛt] *nf* : weasel
belge [bɛlʒ] *adj* : Belgian
Belge *nmf* : Belgian
bélier [belje] *nm* **1** : ram **2** : battering ram
Bélier *nm* : Aries

bélizien, -zienne [belizjɛ̃] *adj* : Belizean

Bélizien, -zienne *n* : Belizean

belladone [beladɔn] *nf* : belladonna

belle[1] → **beau**

belle[2] *nf* : beauty, belle

belle–famille [bɛlfamij] *nf, pl* **belles–familles** : in-laws *pl*

belle–fille [bɛlfij] *nf, pl* **belles–filles 1** : daughter-in-law **2** : stepdaughter

belle–mère [bɛlmɛr] *nf, pl* **belles–mères 1** : mother-in-law **2** : stepmother

belle–sœur [bɛlsœr] *nf, pl* **belles–sœurs** : sister-in-law

bellicisme [bɛlisism] *nm* : bellicosity, warmongering

belliciste[1] [bɛlisist] *adj* : bellicose, warmongering

belliciste[2] *nmf* : warmonger

belligérant, -rante [beliʒerɑ̃, -rɑ̃t] *adj & n* : belligerent — **belligérance** [-ʒerɑ̃s] *nf*

belliqueux, -queuse [bɛlikø, -køz] *adj* GUERRIER : warlike

bémol [bemɔl] *adj & nm* : flat (in music)

bénédicité [benedisite] *nm* : grace <dire le bénédicité : to say grace>

bénédictin, -tine [benediktɛ̃, -tin] *adj & n* : Benedictine

bénédiction [benediksjɔ̃] *nf* **1** : blessing, benediction **2** AUBAINE : godsend

bénéfice [benefis] *nm* **1** AVANTAGE : benefit, advantage **2** : profit <faire du bénéfice : to make a profit>

bénéficiaire[1] [benefisjɛr] *adj* : profitable <marge bénéficiaire : profit margin>

bénéficiaire[2] *nmf* : beneficiary, payee

bénéficier [benefisje] {96} *vi* **∼ de** : to profit from, to receive the benefits of

bénéfique [benefik] *adj* : beneficial, advantageous

benêt[1] [bənɛ] *adj* : simpleminded, silly

benêt[2] *nm* : simpleton

bénévolat [benevɔla] *nm* : volunteer work

bénévole[1] [benevɔl] *adj* : voluntary, volunteer

bénévole[2] *nmf* : volunteer

bengali[1] [bɛ̃gali] *adj* : Bengali

bengali[2] *nm* : Bengali (language)

Bengali *nmf* : Bengali

bénin, -nigne [benɛ̃, beniɲ] *adj* **1** : slight, minor **2** : benign

béninois, -noise [beninwa, -nwaz] *adj* : Beninese

Béninois, -noise *n* : Beninese

bénir [benir] *vt* : to bless

bénit, -nite [beni, -nit] *adj* : blessed, consecrated <eau bénite : holy water>

bénitier [benitje] *nm* : holy water font

benjamin, -mine [bɛ̃ʒamɛ̃, -min] *n* CADET : youngest child

benzène [bɛ̃zɛn] *nm* : benzene

béotien, -tienne [beɔsjɛ̃, -sjɛn] *adj & n* : philistine

béquille [bekij] *nf* **1** : crutch **2** : kickstand

bercail [bɛrkaj] *nm* : fold <rentrer au bercail : to return to the fold>

berçante [bɛrsɑ̃t] *nf or* **chaise berçante** *Can* : rocking chair

berceau [bɛrso] *nm, pl* **berceaux** : cradle

bercer [bɛrse] {6} *vt* **1** : to rock (a baby) **2** : to soothe, to lull — **se bercer** *vr* **1** : to rock, to swing **2** : to delude oneself

berceuse [bɛrsøz] *nf* **1** : lullaby **2** : rocking chair

béret [berɛ] *nm* : beret

berge [bɛrʒ] *nf* RIVE : bank (of a river, etc.)

berger[1], **-gère** [bɛrʒe, -ʒɛr] *n* : shepherd, shepherdess *f*

berger[2] *nm* : sheepdog <berger allemand : German shepherd>

bergerie [bɛrʒəri] *nf* : sheepfold

berline [bɛrlin] *nf* : sedan

berlingot [bɛrlɛ̃go] *nm* **1** : carton (for milk, etc.) **2** : hard candy

berlue [bɛrly] *nf* **avoir la berlue** : to be seeing things, to delude oneself

berne [bɛrn] *nf* **en ∼** : at half mast

berner [bɛrne] *vt* : to fool, to deceive

besogne [bəzɔɲ] *nf* : task, job

besogner [bəzɔɲe] *vi* : to drudge, to slave away

besogneux, -gneuse [bəzɔɲø, -ɲøz] *adj* **1** : poor, needy **2** : plodding, hardworking

besoin [bəzwɛ̃] *nm* **1** : need, requirement <besoins essentiels : basic needs> **2** : neediness, want <enfants dans le besoin : needy children> **3 au ∼** *or* **si besoin est** : if necessary, if need be **4 avoir besoin de** : to need

bestial, -tiale [bɛstjal] *adj, mpl* **bestiaux** [bɛstjo] : brutish, bestial — **bestialement** [bɛstjalmɑ̃] *adv*

bestialité [bɛstjalite] *nf* : brutishness

bestiaux [bɛstjo] *nmpl* BÉTAIL : livestock, cattle

bestiole [bɛstjɔl] *nf* : bug, tiny creature

bétail [betaj] *nm* : livestock, cattle *pl*

bête[1] [bɛt] *adj* **1** STUPIDE : stupid, foolish **2** : simple <c'est tout bête! : there's nothing to it!> — **bêtement** [bɛtmɑ̃] *adv*

bête[2] *nf* **1** ANIMAL : animal <bête de somme : beast of burden> <bête sauvage : wild animal> **2** BESTIOLE : insect, creature <bête à bon Dieu : ladybug> **3** : fool, idiot **4 bête noire** : pet peeve **5 bête puante** *Can* : skunk

bêtise [betiz] *nf* **1** : stupidity, foolishness **2** : nonsense **3** : stupid mistake

béton [betɔ̃] *nm* : concrete

bétonnière [betɔnjɛr] *nf* : cement mixer

bette [bɛt] *nf* **1** : Swiss chard **2** *Can fam* : face <se montrer la bette : to show one's face>

betterave [bɛtrav] *nf* : beet

beuglement [bøgləmɑ̃] *nm* **1** : bellow **2** : blare (of a radio, etc.)

beugler [bøgle] *vi* : to low, to moo, to bellow — *vt* : to bellow out <beugler une chanson : to bellow out a song>

beurre [bœr] *nm* : butter

beurrée [bœre] *nf Can* : slice of bread and butter topped with jam or maple sugar

beurrer [bœre] *vt* : to butter

beurrier [bœrje] *nm* : butter dish

beuverie [bœvri] *nf* : drinking bout, binge

bévue [bevy] *nf* BOURDE : blunder

biais [bjɛ, bjɛz] *nm* **1** : means, way <par le biais de : by means of, via> **2** : bias, slant

biaiser [bjeze] *vi* : to hedge, to dodge the issue

bibelot [biblo] *nm* : trinket, curio

biberon [bibrɔ̃] *nm* : bottle (for a baby)

bible [bibl] *nf* **1** : bible **2 la Bible** : the Bible

bibliobus [biblijɔbys] *nm* : bookmobile

bibliographe [biblijɔgraf] *nmf* : bibliographer

bibliographie [biblijɔgrafi] *nf* : bibliography

bibliographique [biblijɔgrafik] *adj* : bibliographic

bibliothécaire [biblijɔtekɛr] *nmf* : librarian

bibliothèque [biblijɔtɛk] *nf* **1** : library **2** : bookcase

biblique [biblik] *adj* : biblical, scriptural

bicaméral, -rale [bikameral] *adj, mpl* **-raux** [-ro] : bicameral

bicarbonate [bikarbɔnat] *nm* : bicarbonate <bicarbonate de soude : baking soda>

bicentenaire [bisɑ̃tnɛr] *nm* : bicentennial

biceps [bisɛps] *nms & pl* : biceps

biche [biʃ] *nf* **1** : doe **2 ma biche** *fam* : my darling

bicher [biʃe] *vi France fam* : to get on well <ça biche? : how's it going?>

bichonner [biʃɔne] *vt* **1** : to pamper **2** : to spruce up, to doll up — **se bichonner** *vr* : to preen oneself

bicolore [bikɔlɔr] *adj* : two-colored, two-tone

bicoque [bikɔk] *nf* BARAQUE : shack, hut

bicorne [bikɔrn] *nm* : cocked hat

bicyclette [bisiklɛt] *nf* : bicycle <faire de la bicyclette : to ride a bicycle>

bidet [bidɛ] *nm* : bidet

bidon[1] [bidɔ̃] *adj fam* : bogus, phoney

bidon[2] *nm* **1** : can, (oil) drum **2** : flask, canteen **3** *fam* : belly, gut **4** *fam* : nonsense, hot air <c'est du bidon! : that's baloney!>

bidonner [bidɔne] *v* **se bidonner** *vr fam* : to laugh one's head off

bidonville [bidɔ̃vil] *nm* : shantytown

bidule [bidyl] *nm fam* MACHIN : thingamajig

bien[1] [bjɛ̃] *adv* **1** : well, satisfactorily **2** : very, quite <bien souvent : quite often> **3** : definitely, really **4** : readily, happily <j'aimerais bien un café : I could go for a coffee> **5** : at least <il y avait bien dix personnes : there were at least ten people> **6 ~ de** : a good many, many <bien des fois : many times> **7 bien que** : although <bien que malade, elle travaille : though ill, she is working> **8 bien sûr** : of course

bien[2] *adj* **1** : good, fine, satisfactory **2** : well, in good health <je me sens bien : I feel good> **3** : good-looking **4** : nice, decent, respectable <un voisinage bien : a nice neighborhood> **5** : comfortable

bien[3] *nm* **1** : good <faire le bien : to do good> **2 biens** *nmpl* : possessions, property <biens de consommation : consumer goods> <biens immobiliers : real estate>

bien[4] *interj* : OK, all right, good, very well <bien, allons-nous-en : OK, let's go> <bien! bien! j'entends : all right! all right! I understand> <bien, je le prendrai : good! I'll take it>

bien-aimé, -aimée [bjɛ̃neme] *adj & n* : beloved

bien-être [bjɛ̃nɛtr] *nm* **1** : well-being **2** : comfort **3 bien-être social** *Can* : (public) welfare

bienfaisance [bjɛ̃fəzɑ̃s] *nf* : charity, beneficence

bienfaisant, -sante [bjɛ̃fəzɑ̃, -zɑ̃t] *adj* **1** : charitable, beneficent **2** : beneficial

bienfait [bjɛ̃fɛ] *nm* **1** : act of kindness **2** AVANTAGE : benefit, advantage

bienfaiteur, -trice [bjɛ̃fɛtœr, -tris] *n* : benefactor, benefactress *f*

bien-fondé [bjɛ̃fɔ̃de] *nm* **1** : validity, soundness **2** LÉGITIMITÉ : legitimacy (in law)

bienheureux, -reuse [bjɛ̃nørø, -røz] *adj* **1** : happy, joyful **2** : blessed

biennal, -nale [bjenal] *adj, mpl* **-naux** [-no] : biennial — **biennalement** [-nalmɑ̃] *adv*

bien-pensant, -sante [bjɛ̃pɑ̃sɑ̃, -sɑ̃t] *adj* : right-minded, conformist

bienséance [bjɛ̃seɑ̃s] *nf* : propriety, decorum

bienséant, -séante [bjɛ̃seɑ̃, -seɑ̃t] *adj* : proper, seemly

bientôt [bjɛ̃to] *adv* **1** : soon <à bientôt! : see you soon!> **2** : nearly <il est bientôt trois heures : it's nearly three o'clock>

bienveillance [bjɛ̃vejɑ̃s] *nf* : kindness, benevolence

bienveillant, -lante [bjɛ̃vejɑ̃, -jɑ̃t] *adj* : kind, benevolent

bienvenu[1], **-nue** [bjɛ̃vny] *adj* : welcome, opportune
bienvenu[2], **-nue** *n* **être le bienvenu** : to be welcome
bienvenue *nf* **1** : welcome <souhaiter la bienvenue à : to welcome> **2 bienvenue** *Can fam* : you're welcome!
bière [bjɛr] *nf* **1** : beer <bière pression : draft beer> <bière blonde : lager> **2** : casket, coffin
biffer [bife] *vt* : to cross out
bifteck [biftɛk] *nm* : steak
bifurcation [bifyrkasjɔ̃] *nf* : fork, junction
bifurquer [bifyrke] *vi* : to fork, to branch off
bigame[1] [bigam] *adj* : bigamous — **bigamie** [-gami] *nf*
bigame[2] *nmf* : bigamist
bigarré [bigare] *adj* MULTICOLORE : multicolored, variegated
bigot[1], **-gote** [bigo, -gɔt] *adj* : overly devout, sanctimonious
bigot[2], **-gote** *n* : zealot, (religious) bigot
bigoterie [bigɔtri] *nf* : (religious) bigotry
bigoudi [bigudi] *nm* : hair curler, roller
bijou [biʒu] *nm, pl* **bijoux 1** : jewel, piece of jewelry **2** : gem, marvel
bijouterie [biʒutri] *nf* **1** BIJOUX : jewelry, jewels *pl* **2** : jewelry store
bijoutier, -tière [biʒutje, -tjɛr] *n* JOAILLIER : jeweler
bikini [bikini] *nm* : bikini
bilan [bilɑ̃] *nm* **1** : assessment, appraisal <faire le bilan de : to take stock of> **2** : balance sheet <déposer son bilan : to declare bankruptcy> **3** *or* **bilan de santé** : (medical) check-up
bilatéral, -rale [bilateral] *adj, mpl* **-raux** [-ro] : bilateral — **bilatéralement** [-ralmɑ̃] *adv*
bile [bil] *nf* **1** : bile **2 se faire de la bile** : to worry, to fret
biliaire [biljɛr] *adj* → **vésicule**
bilieux, -lieuse [biljø, -ljøz] *adj* : bilious, irritable
bilingue [bilɛ̃g] *adj* : bilingual
billard [bijar] *nm* : billiards *pl*
bille [bij] *nf* **1** : marble <jouer aux billes : to play marbles> **2** : billiard ball **3** : log **4** → **roulement**
billet [bijɛ] *nm* **1** : bill, banknote <un billet de vingt dollars : a twenty-dollar bill> **2** TICKET : ticket **3 billet doux** : love letter
billetterie [bijɛtri] *nf* **1** : ticket office, ticket agency **2** : automatic teller machine
billion [biljɔ̃] *nm* : trillion (United States), billion (Great Britain)
billot [bijo] *nm* **1** : block **2** *Can* : log
bimensuel, -suelle [bimɑ̃sɥɛl] *adj* : semimonthly, twice a month
binaire [binɛr] *adj* : binary
bine [bin] *nf Can* : white bean, broad bean
biner [bine] *vt* : to hoe, to harrow
binette [binɛt] *nf* : hoe
bingo [bingo] *nm Can* : bingo
binoculaire [binɔkylɛr] *adj* : binocular
biochimie [bjɔʃimi] *nf* : biochemistry — **biochimiste** [-ʃimist] *nmf*
biochimique [bjɔʃimik] *adj* : biochemical
biodégradable [bjɔdegradabl] *adj* : biodegradable
biographe [bjɔgraf] *nmf* : biographer
biographie [bjɔgrafi] *nf* : biography
biographique [bjɔgrafik] *adj* : biographical
biologie [bjɔlɔʒi] *nf* : biology — **biologiste** [-lɔʒist] *nmf*
biologique [bjɔlɔʒik] *adj* : biological
biophysicien, -cienne [bjɔfizisjɛ̃, -sjɛn] *n* : biophysicist
biophysique [bjɔfizik] *nf* : biophysics
biopsie [bjɔpsi] *nf* : biopsy
biosphère [bjɔsfɛr] *nf* : biosphere
biotechnologie [bjɔtɛknɔlɔʒi] *nf* : biotechnology
bip [bip] *nm* **1** : beep **2** *fam* : beeper
bipartite [bipartit] *adj* : bipartite, bipartisan
bipède [bipɛd] *adj & nm* : biped
bipolaire [bipɔlɛr] *adj* : bipolar
birman, -mane [birmɑ̃, -man] *adj* : Burmese
Birman, -mane *n* : Burmese
bis[1] [bis] *adv* **1** : twice, repeat (in music) **2** : A (in an address) <14 bis : 14A>
bis[2], **bise** [bi, biz] *adj* : grayish brown
bis[3] [bis] *nm & interj* : encore
bisannuel, -nuelle [bizanɥɛl] *adj & nf* : biannual, biennial — **bisannuellement** [-nɥɛlmɑ̃] *adv*
bisbille [bizbij] *nf fam* : squabble, tiff
biscornu, -nue [biskɔrny] *adj* **1** : misshapen, crooked **2** : quirky, bizarre
biscotte [biskɔt] *nf* : zwieback
biscuit [biskɥi] *nm* **1** : cookie **2** : sponge cake
bise [biz] *nf* **1** : north wind **2** *fam* : kiss, smack <faire la bise : to kiss on the cheeks>
biseau [bizo] *nm* **1** : bevel **2 en ~** : beveled
biseauter [bizote] *vt* : to bevel
bisexuel, -sexuelle [bisɛksɥɛl] *adj* : bisexual — **bisexualité** [-sɛksɥalite] *nf*
bismuth [bismyt] *nm* : bismuth
bison [bizɔ̃] *nm* : bison, buffalo
bisser [bise] *vt* : to encore
bissextile [bisɛkstil] *adj* **année bissextile** : leap year
bistouri [bisturi] *nm* : lancet
bistro *or* **bistrot** [bistro] *nm* : bistro, café
bit [bit] *nm* : bit (unit of information)
bitume [bitym] *nm* **1** : bitumen **2** : blacktop, asphalt
bitumineux, -neuse [bityminø, -nøz] *adj* : bituminous
bivalve [bivalv] *adj & nm* : bivalve

bivouac [bivwak] *nm* : bivouac
bivouaquer [bivwake] *vi* : to bivouac
bizarre [bizar] *adj* : bizarre, strange, odd — **bizarrement** [-zarmɑ̃] *adv*
bizarrerie [bizarri] *nf* **1** : strangeness **2** : eccentricity, peculiarity
blackbouler [blakbule] *vt* : to blackball
blafard, -farde [blafar, -fard] *adj* : pale, pallid
blague [blag] *nf* PLAISANTERIE : joke, trick, fib <sans blague! : no kidding!>
blaguer [blage] *vi* PLAISANTER : to joke, to kid, to fib
blagueur, -gueuse [blagœr, -gøz] *n fam* : joker, prankster
blaireau [blɛro] *nm, pl* **blaireaux** **1** : badger **2** : shaving brush
blairer [blɛre] *vt fam* : to stand, to stomach <personne ne peut la blairer : no one can stand her>
blamable [blamabl] *adj* : blameworthy
blâme [blam] *nm* **1** : blame, censure **2** : reprimand
blâmer [blame] *vt* **1** : to blame, to censure **2** : to reprimand
blanc[1], blanche [blɑ̃, blɑ̃ʃ] *adj* **1** : white **2** PÂLE : light-colored, pale **3** : blank **4** : pure, innocent
blanc[2] *nm* **1** : white **2** INTERVALLE : gap, blank space **3** **blanc d'œuf** : egg white
blanc–bec [blɑ̃bɛk] *nm, pl* **blancs–becs** : greenhorn
blanchâtre [blɑ̃ʃatr] *adj* : whitish, off-white
blancheur [blɑ̃ʃœr] *nf* : whiteness
blanchiment [blɑ̃ʃimɑ̃] *nm* **1** : whitening, bleaching **2** : money laundering
blanchir [blɑ̃ʃir] *vt* **1** : to whiten, to bleach **2** : to launder **3** : to blanch, to parboil (vegetables) **4** : to clear (someone's name) **5** *Can* : to shut out (in sports) — *vi* : to turn white — **se blanchir** *vr* : to clear one's name
blanchissage [blɑ̃ʃisaʒ] *nm* **1** : washing, laundering **2** : refining (of sugar, etc.) **3** *Can* : shutout (in sports)
blanchisserie [blɑ̃ʃisri] *nf* : laundry
blanchisseur, -seuse [blɑ̃ʃisœr, -søz] *n* : laundry worker
blasé, -sée [blaze] *adj* : blasé, jaded
blason [blazɔ̃] *nm* **1** : coat of arms **2** **redorer son blason** : to restore one's good name
blasphématoire [blasfematwar] *adj* : blasphemous
blasphème [blasfɛm] *nm* : blasphemy
blasphémer [blasfeme] {87} *v* : to blaspheme
blatte [blat] *nf France* : cockroach
blazer [blazɛr] *nm* : blazer (jacket)
blé [ble] *nm* **1** : wheat **2** **blé d'Inde** *Can* : Indian corn, maize **3** **blé noir** SARRASIN : buckwheat
bled [blɛd] *nm fam* : small village, boondocks *pl*
blême [blɛm] *adj* : pale, wan, pallid
blennorragie [blenɔraʒi] *nf* : gonorrhea
bléser [bleze] {87} *vi* : to lisp
blessé, -sée [blese] *n* : casualty, injured person
blesser [blese] *vt* : to injure, to wound, to hurt
blessure [blesyr] *nf* : injury, wound
bleu[1], bleue [blø] *adj* **1** : blue <des yeux bleus : blue eyes> **2** : very rare (of steak, etc.)
bleu[2] *nm* **1** : blue **2** : bruise <se faire un bleu : to bruise oneself> <couvert de bleus : black-and-blue> **3** *or* **fromage bleu** : blue cheese **4** : blueprint
bleuâtre [bløatr] *adj* : bluish
bleuet [bløɛ] *nm* **1** : cornflower **2** *Can* : blueberry
bleuir [bløir] *v* : to turn blue
bleuté, -tée [bløte] *adj* : bluish
blindage [blɛ̃daʒ] *nm* : armor (plating)
blindé[1], -dée [blɛ̃de] *adj* : armored
blindé[2] *nm* : armored vehicle
bloc [blɔk] *nm* **1** : block (of wood) **2** : bloc (in politics) **3** : pad (of paper) **4** *Can* : block <faire le tour du bloc en courant : to run around the block> **5** **en ~** : as a whole, outright
blocage [blɔkaʒ] *nm* **1** : locking, jamming (of mechanisms) **2** : mental block **3** : freezing (of prices, wages, etc.)
blocus [blɔkys] *nm* : blockade
blond, blonde [blɔ̃, blɔ̃d] *adj & n* : blond
blonde *nf Can fam* : girlfriend
blondeur [blɔ̃dœr] *nf* : blondness, fairness
bloquer [blɔke] *vt* **1** : to block **2** : to freeze (a bank account), to stop (a check) **3** : to jam, to lock — **se bloquer** *vr*
bloquiste [blɔkist] *nmf Can* : member of the Bloc québécois party
blottir [blɔtir] *v* **se blottir** *vr* : to nestle, to cuddle, to snuggle up
blouse [bluz] *nf* **1** CHEMISIER : blouse **2** SARRAU : smock **3** : pocket (in billiards)
blouson [bluzɔ̃] *nm* : jacket <blouson d'aviateur : bomber jacket>
blue–jean [bludʒin] *nm, pl* **blue–jeans** : jeans *pl*, blue jeans *pl*
bluff [blœf] *nm* : bluff <c'est du bluff : he's just bluffing>
bluffer [blœfe] *v* : to bluff
boa [bɔa] *nm* : boa
bob [bɔb] *nm* → **bobsleigh**
bobard [bɔbar] *nm fam* : fib, tall tale
bobine [bɔbin] *nf* **1** : spool, reel, bobbin <bobine de pellicule : roll of film> **2** : electric coil
bobo [bobo] *nm fam* : boo-boo, scratch
bobsleigh [bɔbslɛg] *nm* : bobsled
bocal [bɔkal] *nm, pl* **bocaux** [bɔko] : jar
bock [bɔk] *nm* **1** CHOPE : beer glass **2** : glass of beer
bœuf [bœf] *nm, pl* **bœufs** [bø] **1** : beef **2** : steer, ox

bohème [bɔɛm] *adj & nmf* : bohemian
bohémien, -mienne [bɔemjɛ̃, -mjɛn] *n* : Bohemian, gypsy
boire[1] [bwar] {13} *vt* **1** : to drink <boire un coup : to have a drink> **2** : to absorb, to soak up — *vi* **1** : to drink **2** ~ **à** : to toast
boire[2] *nm* : drink <le boire et le manger : food and drink>
bois [bwa] *nms & pl* **1** : wood <bois à brûler : firewood> <bois dur : hardwood> <petit bois : kindling> **2** FORÊT : woods *pl* **3** : woodcut **4 bois** *nmpl* : antlers **5 bois** *nmpl* : woodwinds
boisé[1], **-sée** [bwaze] *adj* : wooded
boisé[2] *nm Can* : woods *pl*, wooded area
boisement [bwazmɑ̃] *nm* : afforestation
boiserie [bwazri] *nf* **1** : woodwork **2 boiseries** *nfpl* : paneling
boisseau [bwaso] *nm* : bushel
boisson [bwasɔ̃] *nf* **1** : drink, beverage <boisson gazeuse : pop, soda> **2 en** ~ *Can* : drunk
boîte [bwat] *nf* **1** : (tin) can <mettre en boîte : to can> **2** : box <boîte à gantes : glove compartment> <boîte aux lettres : mailbox> **3** *fam* : nightclub **4 boîte de vitesses** : transmission (of a motor vehicle)
boiter [bwate] *vi* **1** : to limp **2** : to wobble
boiterie [bwatri] *nf* : limp
boiteux, -teuse [bwatø, -tøz] *adj* **1** : lame **2** : wobbly, shaky
boîtier [bwatje] *nm* : casing, housing
boitillement [bwatijmɑ̃] *nm* : hobble, (slight) limp
boitiller [bwatije] *vi* : to limp slightly
bol [bɔl] *nm* **1** : bowl **2** : bowlful <un bol d'air : a breath of fresh air> **3 coup de bol** : stroke of luck
boléro [bɔlero] *nm* : bolero
bolide [bɔlid] *nm* **1** : meteorite **2** : racing car
bolivien, -vienne [bɔlivjɛ̃, -vjɛn] *adj* : Bolivian
Bolivien, -vienne *n* : Bolivian
bombarde [bɔ̃bard] *nf* : Jew's harp
bombardement [bɔ̃bardəmɑ̃] *nm* : bombing, bombardment
bombarder [bɔ̃barde] *vt* **1** : to bomb **2** : to bombard, to pelt
bombardier [bɔ̃bardje] *nm* **1** : bomber **2** : bombardier
bombe [bɔ̃b] *nf* **1** : bomb **2** ATOMISEUR : aerosol spray, atomiser **3 faire la bombe** *fam* : to live it up, to go on a spree
bomber [bɔ̃be] *vt* **1** GONFLER : to puff up, to stick out <bomber le torse : to swell with pride> **2** : to spray (paint) — *vi* : to bulge out
bon[1] [bɔ̃, bɔn *before a vowel or mute h*] *adv* **1 faire bon** : to be nice, to be good, to be acceptable <il fait bon ici : it's nice here> <il ne ferait pas bon l'arrêter : it would be unwise to stop him> **2 tenir bon** : to hold firm, to stand fast
bon[2], **bonne** [bɔ̃ (bɔn *before a vowel or mute h*), bɔn] *adj* **1** : good, honest, upright **2** : sound, high-quality **3** : pleasant, desirable <bonne chance! : good luck!> <ça sent bon : that smells good> **4** : correct, proper **5** : capable, knowledgeable <bon en science : good at science> **6** : good, profitable <être bon à faire : to be worth doing> **7** : effective <bon contre la douleur : good for pain> **8** (*used as an intensive*) <un bon nombre : a good many> <trois bonnes heures : three solid hours> **9 bon enfant** : easygoing **10 bon marché** : cheap, inexpensive **11 bon mot** : witticism **12 bonne femme** *fam* : woman, old lady **13 bonne sœur** : nun **14 bon sens** : common sense **15 de bonne heure** : early **16 pour de bon** : really, for good <il est parti pour de bon : he's gone for good>
bon[3] *nm* **1** : good thing, good person <les bons : the good> <avoir du bon : to have (some) good points> **2** : voucher, coupon **3** : bond <bon du Trésor : treasury bond> <bon de commande : purchase order>
bon[4] *interj* **1** : right, OK, fine <bon, mangeons : OK, let's eat> **2** : so, now, well <bon, où en étions-nous? : now, where were we?>
bonasse [bɔnas] *adj* : meek
bonbon [bɔ̃bɔ̃] *nm* : candy
bonbonnière [bɔ̃bɔnjɛr] *nf* : candy box
bond [bɔ̃] *nm* **1** : bound, jump, leap <faire un bond : to leap> <bond en avant : leap forward, breakthrough> **2** : bounce
bondé, -dée [bɔ̃de] *adj* : crammed, jampacked
bondir [bɔ̃dir] *vi* **1** SAUTER : to jump, to leap **2** : to rush, to dash
bonheur [bɔnœr] *nm* **1** : happiness **2** : pleasure **3** : luck, good fortune <par bonheur : fortunately>
bonhomie [bɔnɔmi] *nf* : good-naturedness, cordiality
bonhomme[1] [bɔnɔm] *adj, pl* **bonshommes** : affable, good-natured
bonhomme[2] *nm, pl* **bonshommes 1** *fam* : fellow, guy **2 bonhomme de neige** : snowman
boni [bɔni] *nm* **1** : bonus **2** : surplus
bonification [bɔnifikasjɔ̃] *nf* **1** : improvement (of land, etc.) **2** : bonus points *pl* (in sports)
bonifier [bɔnifje] {96} *vt* : to improve — **se bonifier** *vr*
boniment [bɔnimɑ̃] *nm* **1** : sales pitch **2** *fam* : tall story **3** *Can* : short speech
bonimenteur [bɔnimɑ̃tœr] *nm* : barker (at a fair)

bonjour [bɔ̃ʒur] *nm* **1** : hello, good morning, good afternoon **2** *Can* : good-bye

bonne [bɔn] *nf* **1** DOMESTIQUE : maid **2 bonne d'enfants** : nanny

bonnement [bɔnmɑ̃] *adv* **tout bonnement** : quite simply

bonnet [bɔnɛ] *nm* **1** : cap, bonnet **2** : cup (of a brassiere) **3 c'est blanc bonnet et bonnet blanc** : it's six of one, half dozen of the other **4 gros bonnet** *fam* : bigwig, big shot

bonneterie [bɔnɛtri] *nf* : hosiery

bonsoir [bɔ̃swar] *nm* : good evening, good night

bonté [bɔ̃te] *nf* : goodness, kindness

bookmaker [bukmɛkœr] *nm* : bookmaker

boom [bum] *nm* : boom (in economics)

boomerang [bumrɑ̃g] *nm* : boomerang

bord [bɔr] *nm* **1** : edge **2** : bank, shore **3** : border (of fabric, etc.) **4** : rim, brim **5** CÔTÉ : side **6 à ~** : on board, aboard **7 au bord de** : on the verge of, on the brink of **8 par-dessus ~** : overboard

bordeaux [bɔrdo] *nm* **1** : Bordeaux (wine) **2** : maroon

bordée [bɔrde] *nf* **1** : broadside, volley <une bordée d'injures : a volley of abuse> **2** : tack (of a ship) <faire une bordée : to tack> **3 bordée de neige** *Can* : snowstorm

bordel [bɔrdɛl] *nm fam* **1** : brothel **2** : mess, shambles

bordelais, -laise [bɔrdəlɛ, -lɛz] *adj* : of or from Bordeaux

border [bɔrde] *vt* **1** : to border, to line, to ring **2** : to tuck in

bordereau [bɔrdəro] *nm, pl* **-reaux** [-ro] : statement (of an account), note, slip <bordereau de dépôt : deposit slip>

bordure [bɔrdyr] *nf* **1** BORD : border, edge **2** : side (of a road), curb

bore [bɔr] *nm* : boron

boréal, boréale [bɔreal] *adj, mpl* **boréaux** [bɔreo] **1** : boreal, northern **2 → aurore**

borgne [bɔrɲ] *adj* : one-eyed

borique [bɔrik] *adj* : **acide borique** : boric acid

borne [bɔrn] *nf* **1** : milestone, landmark **2** *France fam* : kilometer **3** : terminal (in electricity) **4 bornes** *nfpl* : limits, boundaries **5 borne d'incendie** : fire hydrant

borné, -née [bɔrne] *adj* : narrow-minded

borne–fontaine [bɔrnfɔ̃tɛn] *nf Can* : fire hydrant

borner [bɔrne] *vt* **1** : to mark out the boundaries of **2** LIMITER : to limit, to restrict — **se borner** *vr*

bosniaque [bɔsnjak] *adj* : Bosnian

Bosniaque *nmf* : Bosnian

bosquet [bɔske] *nm* : grove, copse

bosse [bɔs] *nf* **1** : hump (of a person or animal) **2** : lump, bump, dent **3 avoir la bosse de** : to have a flair for

bosseler [bɔsle] {8} *vt* **1** : to emboss **2** : to dent

bosser [bɔse] *vi France fam* : to work, to slave away

bossu[1], -sue [bɔsy] *adj* : hunchbacked

bossu[2], -sue *n* : hunchback (person)

botanique[1] [bɔtanik] *adj* : botanical

botanique[2] *nf* : botany — **botaniste** [-tanist] *nmf*

botte [bɔt] *nf* **1** : boot **2** : bunch, sheaf, bale **3** : thrust, lunge (in fencing)

botter [bɔte] *vt* **1** : to put boots on **2** : to kick (in sports)

botteur, -teuse [bɔtœr, -tøz] *n* : kicker (in sports)

bottillon [bɔtijɔ̃] *nm* : bootee

bottin [bɔtɛ̃] *nm* : telephone directory

bottine [bɔtin] *nf* : ankle boot

botulisme [bɔtylism] *nm* : botulism

bouc [buk] *nm* **1** : goat, billy goat **2** : goatee **3 bouc émissaire** : scapegoat

boucan [bukɑ̃] *nm fam* : din, racket

boucane [bukan] *nf Can* : smoke

boucanier [bukanje] *nm* : buccaneer

bouche [buʃ] *nf* **1** : mouth <de bouche à l'oreille : confidentially> **2** : opening, entrance <bouche d'égout : manhole> **3 le bouche à bouche** : mouth-to-mouth resuscitation **4 bouche d'incendie** : fire hydrant **5 faire la fine bouche** : to turn up one's nose **6 → bée**

bouchée [buʃe] *nf* : mouthful

boucher[1] [buʃe] *vt* : to stop up, to plug, to block — **se boucher** *vr* **1** : to get blocked **2 se boucher le nez** : to hold one's nose

boucher[2], -chère [buʃe, -ʃɛr] *n* : butcher

boucherie [buʃri] *nf* **1** : butcher's shop **2** MASSACRE : butchery, slaughter

bouche–trou [buʃtru] *nm, pl* **bouche–trous** : stand-in, stopgap

bouchon [buʃɔ̃] *nm* **1** : cork, stopper **2** : float (in fishing) **3** : traffic jam, gridlock

boucle [bukl] *nf* **1** : buckle, loop **2** : curl, loop **3 boucle d'oreille** : earring

boucler [bukle] *vt* **1** : to buckle, to fasten **2** : to complete, to finish off <boucler la boucle : to come full circle> **3** *fam* : to lock up, to imprison — *vi* : to curl

bouclier [buklije] *nm* : shield

bouddhisme [budism] *nm* : Buddhism — **bouddhiste** [budist] *adj & nmf*

bouder [bude] *vt* : to avoid, to be cool towards — *vi* : to sulk, to pout

bouderie [budri] *nf* : sulking, sulkiness

boudeur, -deuse [budœr, -døz] *adj* : sulky

boudin [budɛ̃] *nm* **1** : blood sausage **2** : flange (on a wheel)

boudiné, -née [budine] *adj* **1** : pudgy (of fingers, etc.) **2 ~ dans** : squeezed into, bulging out of
boue [bu] *nf* : mud
bouée [bwe] *nf* **1** : buoy **2 bouée de sauvetage** : life preserver
bouette [bwɛt] *nf Can fam* : mud
boueux, boueuse [buø, buøz] *adj* : muddy
bouffant, -fante [bufɑ̃, -fɑ̃t] *adj* **1** : puffed out, baggy **2** : bouffant
bouffe [buf] *nf fam* : grub, chow
bouffée [bufe] *nf* **1** : puff, gust **2** : surge, fit (of pride, etc.)
bouffer [bufe] *vt fam* : to eat, to gobble up
bouffi, -fie [bufi] *adj* : puffy, swollen
bouffir [bufir] *v* : to puff up
bouffisure [bufisyr] *nf* : puffiness (of the face, etc.)
bouffon[1], -fonne [bufɔ̃, bufɔn] *adj* : farcical, comical
bouffon[2] *nm* : clown, buffoon, jester
bouffonnerie [bufɔnri] *nf* : buffoonery, antics *pl*
bouge *nm* [buʒ] **1** : hovel, dump **2** : dive, seedy café
bougeoir [buʒwar] *nm* : candlestick
bougeotte [buʒɔt] *nf* : fidgets *pl* <avoir la bougeotte : to be fidgety>
bouger [buʒe] {17} *vt* : to move — *vi* : to budge, to stir — **se bouger** *vr*
bougie [buʒi] *nf* **1** : candle **2** : spark plug
bougonner [bugɔne] *vi* : to grumble, to complain
bougre [bugr] *nm fam* : guy, fellow
bougrement [bugrəmɑ̃] *adv fam* : awfully, damned
bouillabaisse [bujabɛs] *nf* : bouillabaisse, fish soup
bouillie [buji] *nf* : baby cereal, gruel
bouillir [bujir] {14} *vi* **1** : to boil **2** : to seethe (with anger, etc.)
bouilloire [bujwar] *nf* : kettle, teakettle
bouillon [bujɔ̃] *nm* **1** : broth, stock **2** : bubble
bouillonnant, -nante [bujɔnɑ̃, -nɑ̃t] *adj* **1** : bubbling, foaming **2** : lively
bouillonnement [bujɔnmɑ̃] *nm* **1** : bubbling, foaming **2** : agitation, ferment
bouillonner [bujɔne] *vi* **1** : to bubble, to foam **2** : to seethe
boulanger, -gère [bulɑ̃ʒe, -ʒɛr] *n* : baker
boulangerie [bulɑ̃ʒri] *nf* : bakery
boule [bul] *nf* **1** : ball <boule de neige : snowball> **2 se mettre en boule** *fam* : to blow one's top
bouleau [bulo] *nm, pl* **bouleaux** : birch
bouledogue [buldɔg] *nm* : bulldog
boulet [bulɛ] *nm* **1** : cannonball **2** : ball and chain **3** : fetlock (of a horse)
boulette [bulɛt] *nf* **1** : pellet **2** *fam* : blunder **3 boulette de pâte** : dumpling **4 boulette de viande** : meatball
boulevard [bulvar] *nm* : boulevard
bouleversant, -sante [bulvɛrsɑ̃, -sɑ̃t] *adj* : distressing, upsetting
bouleversement [bulvɛrsəmɑ̃] *nm* : upheaval, upset
bouleverser [bulvɛrse] *vt* **1** : to overwhelm, to upset **2** : to disrupt, to turn upside down
boulier [bulje] *nm* : abacus
boulimie [bulimi] *nf* : bulimia — **boulimique** [-limik] *adj*
boulon [bulɔ̃] *nm* : bolt
boulot[1], -lotte [bulo, -lɔt] *adj* : plump, chubby
boulot[2] *nm fam* **1** : work, task **2** : job <petit boulot : odd job>
boum[1] [bum] *nm* **1** : bang **2** : boom (of business, births, etc.)
boum[2] *nf France* : party
bouquet [bukɛ] *nm* **1** : bouquet, bunch (of flowers, etc.) **2** : clump (of trees) **3** : bouquet (of wine) **4** : crowning event <ça, c'est le bouquet! : that takes the cake!>
bouquetin [buktɛ̃] *nm* : ibex
bouquin [bukɛ̃] *nm fam* : book
bouquiner [bukine] *v fam* : to read
bouquiniste [bukinist] *nmf* : secondhand bookseller
bourbeux, -beuse [burbø, -bøz] *adj* : muddy, swampy
bourbier [burbje] *nm* : swamp, quagmire
bourbon [burbɔ̃] *nm* : bourbon
bourde [burd] *nf* BÉVUE : blunder
bourdon [burdɔ̃] *nm* **1** : bumblebee **2 avoir le bourdon** *fam* : to have the blues
bourdonnement [burdɔnmɑ̃] *nm* **1** : buzzing, droning **2 bourdonnement d'oreilles** : ringing in the ears
bourdonner [burdɔne] *vi* : to buzz, to hum, to drone
bourg [bur] *nm* : market town
bourgade [burgad] *nf* : small town, village
bourgeois, -geoise [burʒwa, -ʒwaz] *adj & n* : bourgeois
bourgeoisie [burʒwazi] *nf* : bourgeoisie, middle class
bourgeon [burʒɔ̃] *nm* : bud
bourgeonner [burʒɔne] *vi* : to bud
bourgogne [burgɔɲ] *nm* : Burgundy (wine)
bourguignon, -gnonne [burgiɲɔ̃, -ɲɔn] *adj* **1** : Burgundian **2 bœuf bourguignon** : beef bourguignon
bourrage [buraʒ] *nm* **1** : filling, stuffing **2** : cramming (for an exam) **3 bourrage de crâne** : brainwashing
bourrasque [burask] *nf* : squall, gust (of wind), flurry (of snow)
bourrasser [burase] *vt Can fam* : to be rough with, to push around
bourre [bur] *nf* : stuffing, padding, wad
bourreau [buro] *nm, pl* **bourreaux 1** : executioner, hangman **2** : torturer, tormentor **3 bourreau de travail** : workaholic

bourrée [bure] *nf Can* : spurt <travailler par bourrées : to work in spurts>

bourrelet [burlɛ] *nm* **1** : weather strip **2** : roll (of fat)

bourrer [bure] *vt* : to fill, to stuff, to cram — *vi* : to be filling — **se bourrer** *vr* : to stuff oneself

bourrique [burik] *nf* **1** ÂNE : ass, donkey **2** *fam* : stubborn fool

bourru, -rue [bury] *adj* : gruff

bourrure [buryr] *nf Can* : stuffing, padding

bourse [burs] *nf* **1** PORTE-MONNAIE : change purse **2** : scholarship, grant **3 la Bourse** : the stock market

boursier[1], -sière [bursje, -sjɛr] *adj* : stock, stock-market

boursier[2], -sière *n* **1** : scholarship holder, scholar **2** : stock-market trader

boursouflé, -flée [bursufle] *adj* **1** : puffy, bloated **2** : bombastic

boursoufler [bursufle] *vt* : to puff up, to cause to swell — **se boursoufler** *vr* **1** : to swell (up) **2** : to blister (of paint)

boursouflure [bursuflyr] *nf* **1** : swelling, puffiness **2** : pomposity **3** : blister (on paint, etc.)

bousculade [buskylad] *nf* **1** : crush, jostling **2** : rush, scramble

bousculer [buskyle] *vt* **1** : to bump into, to jostle, to shove **2** : to rush, to hurry — **se bousculer** *vr* : to bump into each other

bouse [buz] *nf* : cow dung, cowpat

bousiller [buzije] *vt fam* **1** : to bungle, to botch **2** : to wreck **3** : to bump off, to kill

bousilleur, -leuse [busijœr, -jøz] *n fam* : bungler

boussole [busɔl] *nf* : compass

bout[1] [bu], *etc.* → **bouillir**

bout[2] [bu] *nm* **1** EXTRÉMITÉ : end, tip <bout de doigt : fingertip> <bout de la table : head of the table> **2** : bit, piece **3 à bout portant** : point-blank **4 au bout de** : after <au bout de cinq minutes : after five minutes> **5 au bout du compte** : in the end, ultimately **6 être à bout** : to be exhausted <ma patience est à bout : my patience has run out>

boutade [butad] *nf* PLAISANTERIE : joke, witticism

bouteille [butɛj] *nf* : bottle

boutique [butik] *nf* : store, shop, boutique

boutiquier, -quière [butikje, -kjɛr] *n* : shopkeeper

bouton [butɔ̃] *nm* **1** : button **2** BOURGEON : bud **3** : pimple **4 bouton de porte** : doorknob

bouton–d'or [butɔ̃dɔr] *nm, pl* **boutons–d'or** : buttercup

boutonner [butɔne] *vt* : to button — **se boutonner** *vr* : to button up

boutonneux, -neuse [butɔnø, -nøz] *adj* : pimply

boutonnière [butɔnjɛr] *nf* : buttonhole

bouton–pression [butɔ̃presjɔ̃] *nm, pl* **boutons–pression** : snap (fastener)

bouture [butyr] *nf* : cutting (from a plant)

bouvier, -vière [buvje, -vjɛr] *n* : cowherd

bovin, -vine [bɔvɛ̃, -vin] *adj* : bovine

bovins [bɔvɛ̃] *nmpl* : cattle

bowling [buliŋ] *nm* **1** : bowling **2** : bowling alley

box [bɔks] *nm, pl* **boxes 1** : stall, alcove, cubicle **2 box des accusés** : dock (in court)

boxe [bɔks] *nf* : boxing

boxer[1] [bɔkse] *vi* : to box — *vt fam* : to strike, to punch

boxer[2] [bɔksɛr] *nm* : boxer (dog)

boxeur [bɔksœr] *nm* : boxer, fighter

box–office [bɔksɔfis] *nm, pl* **box–offices** : box office

boyau [bwajo] *nm, pl* **boyaux 1** TUYAU : hose, tube **2** INTESTIN : intestine, gut **3** : narrow passageway **4 boyau d'arrosage** *Can* : hose

boycott [bɔjkɔt] *or* **boycottage** [bɔjkɔtaʒ] *nm* : boycott

boycotter [bɔjkɔte] *vt* : to boycott

bozo [bozo] *nm Can fam* : idiot, fool

bracelet [braslɛ] *nm* **1** : bracelet **2** *or* **bracelet de montre** : watchband

bracelet–montre [braslɛmɔ̃tr] *nm, pl* **bracelets–montres** : wristwatch

braconner [brakɔne] *vi* : to poach

braconnier, -nière [brakɔnje, -njɛr] *n* : poacher

brader [brade] *vt* : to sell (off) cheaply

braderie [bradri] *nf* : clearance sale

braguette [bragɛt] *nf* : fly (of pants, etc.)

braille [braj] *nm* : braille

brailler [braje] *vi fam* : to bawl, to yell, to howl — *vt fam* : to bellow out

braiment [brɛmɑ̃] *nm* : bray, braying

braire [brɛr] {15} *vi* : to bray

braise [brɛz] *nf* : embers *pl,* coals *pl*

braiser [breze] *vt* : to braise

bran [brɑ̃] *nm* **1** : bran **2 bran de scie** : sawdust

brancard [brɑ̃kar] *nm* **1** CIVIÈRE : stretcher **2** : shaft (of a carriage, etc.)

branche [brɑ̃ʃ] *nf* **1** : branch, bough (of a tree) **2** : branch (of a family, a river, etc.) **3** : field (of activity) **4** : sidepiece (of eyeglasses)

branché, -chée [brɑ̃ʃe] *adj fam* : fashionable, trendy, in

brancher [brɑ̃ʃe] *vt* **1** : to connect up (a utility) **2** : to plug in **3** *fam* : to interest, to turn on <le rock, ça ne me branche pas : I'm not into rock music>

branchie [brɑ̃ʃi] *nf* : gill (of a fish, etc.)

brandir [brɑ̃dir] *vt* : to brandish, to wave about

branlant, -lante [brɑ̃lɑ̃, -lɑ̃t] *adj* : shaky, wobbly, unsteady
branle [brɑ̃l] *nm* **1** : oscillation, swing **2** : impetus, momentum <mettre en branle : to set in motion>
branle–bas [brɑ̃lba] *nms & pl* : commotion, bustle
branler [brɑ̃le] *vi* : to wobble, to be loose
branleux, -leuse [brɑ̃lø, -løz] *adj Can fam* **1** : lazy **2** : indecisive
braquer [brake] *vt* **1** : to aim, to point, to fix on **2** : to turn (a steering wheel) **3** : to antagonize — *vi* : to turn the steering wheel
bras [bra] *nms & pl* **1** : arm **2 bras** *nmpl* : workers, manpower **3 bras de mer** : inlet **4 bras droit** : right-hand man
brasero [brazero] *nm* : brazier
brasier [brazje] *nm* : blaze, inferno
bras–le–corps [bralkɔr] **à bras–le–corps** *adv* **1** : bodily **2** : head-on
brassage [brasaʒ] *nm* **1** : mixing, intermingling **2** : brewing
brasse [bras] *nf* **1** : breaststroke **2** : fathom
brassée [brase] *nf* **1** : armful **2** *Can* : load (of laundry)
brasser [brase] *vt* **1** : to mix, to toss, to shuffle **2** : to brew (beer)
brasserie [brasri] *nf* **1** : large café, restaurant **2** : brewery
brasseur, -seuse [brasœr, -søz] *n* **1** : brewer **2 brasseur d'affaires** : tycoon, financier
brassière [brasjɛr] *nf Can* : bra, brassiere
bravade [bravad] *nf* : bravado
brave[1] [brav] *adj* **1** GENTIL : good, decent, nice <c'est un brave homme : he's a good man> **2** : brave, courageous <c'est une femme brave : she's a brave woman>
brave[2] *nmf* : brave person, hero
bravement [bravmɑ̃] *adv* : bravely, boldly
braver [brave] *vt* : to defy, to challenge
bravo [bravo] *nm & interj* : bravo
bravoure [bravur] *nf* : bravery
break [brɛk] *nm* **1** *France* : station wagon **2** : break (in music, sports, etc.) **3 prendre un break** *Can* : to take a break
brebis [brəbi] *nf* **1** : ewe **2 brebis** *nfpl* : flock (in religion) **3 brebis galeuse** : black sheep
brèche [brɛʃ] *nf* **1** : hole, gap **2** : breach
bréchet [breʃɛ] *nm* : wishbone
bredouille [brəduj] *adj* : empty-handed
bredouiller [brəduje] *v* : to mumble, to mutter
bref[1] [brɛf] *adv or* **en bref** : briefly, in short
bref[2], **brève** [brɛf, brɛv] *adj* : brief, short
breloque [brəlɔk] *nf* : charm (on a bracelet)
brésilien, -lienne [breziljɛ̃, -ljɛn] *adj* : Brazilian
Brésilien, -lienne *n* : Brazilian
bretelle [brətɛl] *nf* **1** : strap, shoulder strap **2** : ramp <bretelle de sortie : exit ramp> **3 bretelles** *nfpl* : suspenders
breton, -tonne [brətɔ̃, brətɔn] *adj* : Breton
bretzel [brɛtzɛl] *nm* : pretzel
breuvage [brœvaʒ] *nm* : beverage, drink
brevet [brəvɛ] *nm* **1** : patent **2** : diploma, certificate **3** : commission (in the armed forces)
breveté, -tée [brəvte] *adj* **1** : patented **2** : qualified, certified
breveter [brəvte] {8} *vt* : to patent
bréviaire [brevjɛr] *nm* : breviary
bribes [brib] *nfpl* : bits, pieces <bribes de conversation : snatches of conversation>
bric–à–brac [brikabrak] *nms & pl* : bric-a-brac, odds and ends
brick [brik] *nm* : brig (ship)
bricolage [brikɔlaʒ] *nm* **1** : do-it-yourself work **2** : makeshift repairs
bricole [brikɔl] *nf* **1** : trifle, trinket **2 bricoles** *nfpl* : bits and pieces
bricoler [brikɔle] *vi* **1** : to fix things up **2** : to do odd jobs, to putter — *vt* **1** : to fix up, to mend **2** : to tinker with
bricoleur, -leuse [brikɔlœr, -løz] *n* **1** : handyman **2** : do-it-yourselfer
bride [brid] *nf* **1** : bridle <tenir en bride : to keep a tight rein on> **2** : flange (of a pipe, etc.)
brider [bride] *vt* **1** : to bridle (a horse) **2** : to keep in check
bridge [bridʒ] *nm* **1** : bridge (card game) **2** *or* **bridge dentaire** : denture, bridgework
brièvement [brijɛvmɑ̃] *adv* : briefly
brièveté [brijɛvte] *nf* : brevity
brigade [brigad] *nf* **1** : brigade **2** : squad, team
brigadier[1] [brigadje] *nm* **1** : corporal (in the military) **2** : police sergeant
brigadier[2], **-dière** [brigadje, -djɛr] *n Can* : crossing guard
brigand [brigɑ̃] *nm* : robber, thief
brigandage [brigɑ̃daʒ] *nm* : armed robbery
briguer [brige] *vt* **1** : to aspire to **2** : to solicit, to seek
brillamment [brijamɑ̃] *adv* : brilliantly
brillant, -lante [brijɑ̃, -jɑ̃t] *adj* **1** : brilliant, outstanding **2** : bright, sparkling, shiny
briller [brije] *vi* : to shine, to sparkle
brimade [brimad] *nf* : bullying, harassment, hazing
brimer [brime] *vt* : to bully, to haze
brin [brɛ̃] *nm* **1** : blade (of grass), sprig, twig **2** : touch, little bit <il est un brin ennuyeux : he's rather boring> **3** : iota **4** : strand (of wool, thread, etc.)
brindille [brɛ̃dij] *nf* : twig

bringue [brɛ̃g] *nf fam* : binge <faire la bringue : to go on a binge>
brio [brijo] *nm* **1** : brilliance, panache **2 avec ~** : brilliantly
brioche [brijɔʃ] *nf* **1** : brioche **2** *fam* : paunch
brique [brik] *nf* : brick
briquet [brikɛ] *nm* **1** : (cigarette) lighter **2** : beagle
bris [bri] *nms & pl* : breaking, breakage
brise [briz] *nf* : breeze
brise–glace [brizglas] *nms & pl* : icebreaker
brise–lames [brizlam] *nms & pl* : breakwater
briser [brize] *vt* **1** : to break, to smash **2** : to ruin, to wreck, to crush <des faux bruits ont brisé sa carrière : false rumors wrecked his career> — *vi* : to break <briser avec la tradition : to break with tradition> — **se briser** *vr* **1** : to shatter, to break up, to break down **2** : to break <son cœur se brisait : her heart was breaking>
briseur, -seuse [brizœr, -zøz] *n* **1** : wrecker **2 briseur de grève** : strikebreaker
brise–vent [brizvɑ̃] *nms & pl* : windbreak
brisure [brizyr] *nf* : break, crack
britannique [britanik] *adj* : British
Britannique *nmf* : British person, Briton
broc [bro] *nm* : jug, pitcher
brocante [brɔkɑ̃t] *nf* **1** : secondhand trade **2** : flea market
brocanteur, -teuse [brɔkɑ̃tœr, -tøz] *n* : secondhand dealer
brocart [brɔkar] *nm* : brocade
broche [brɔʃ] *nf* **1** : brooch **2** : spit, skewer **3** : spindle (on a spinning machine) **4** *Can* : wire <broche piquante : barbed wire>
broché, -chée [brɔʃe] *adj* : paperbound
brochet [brɔʃɛ] *nm* : pike (fish)
brochette [brɔʃɛt] *nf* **1** : skewer **2** : shish kebab
brochure [brɔʃyr] *nf* : brochure, pamphlet, booklet
brocoli [brɔkɔli] *nm* : broccoli
broder [brɔde] *vt* : to embroider — *vi* **~ sur** : to elaborate on, to embellish
broderie [brɔdri] *nf* : embroidery
broie [brwa], **broiera** [brwara], *etc.* → **broyer**
brome [brom] *nm* : bromine
broncher [brɔ̃ʃe] *vi* **1** : to flinch **2** : to stumble (of a horse)
bronches [brɔ̃ʃ] *nfpl* : bronchial tubes
bronchite [brɔ̃ʃit] *nf* : bronchitis
bronzage [brɔ̃zaʒ] *nm* : suntan
bronze [brɔ̃z] *nm* : bronze
bronzé, -zée [brɔ̃ze] *adj* : tanned, suntanned
bronzer [brɔ̃ze] *vt* **1** : to tan **2** : to bronze (metals) — *vi* : to get a suntan
brossage [brɔsaʒ] *nm* : brushing
brosse [brɔs] *nf* **1** : brush <brosse à cheveux : hairbrush> <brosse à dents : toothbrush>
brosser [brɔse] *vt* **1** : to brush **2** : to paint (a picture) — **se brosser** *vr* : to brush oneself <se brosser les cheveux : to brush one's hair>
broue [bru] *nf Can* **1** : froth **2 péter de la broue** *fam* : to show off
brouette [bruɛt] *nf* : wheelbarrow
brouhaha [bruaa] *nm* : brouhaha, hubbub
brouillard [brujar] *nm* **1** : fog, mist **2 être dans un brouillard** : to be in a fog
brouille [bruj] *nf* **1** : quarrel, misunderstanding **2** : discord
brouiller [bruje] *vt* **1** : to mix up, to shuffle (cards), to scramble (eggs, etc.) **2** : to blur, to cloud **3** : to interfere with (radio transmission, etc.) **4** : to turn against, to fall out with — **se brouiller** *vr* **1** : to quarrel, to fall out **2** : to become confused **3** : to cloud over
brouillon¹, -lonne [brujɔ̃, -jɔn] *adj* **1** DÉSORGANISÉ : disorganized **2** DÉSORDONNÉ : untidy
brouillon² *nm* : rough draft
broussaille [brusaj] *nf* : undergrowth
broussailleux, -leuse [brusajø, -jøz] *adj* : bushy, scrubby
brousse [brus] *nf* **1** : brush (vegetation) **2** *fam* : boondocks <en pleine brousse : in the middle of nowhere>
brouter [brute] *vt* : to graze on, to nibble on — *vi* : to graze
broutille [brutij] *nf* : trifle
broyer [brwaje] {58} *vt* **1** : to grind, to crush **2 broyer du noir** : to be in the doldrums, to brood, to mope
broyeur *nm* [brwajœr] **1** : grinder, crusher **2 broyeur à ordures** : garbage disposal unit
bru [bry] *nf* : daughter-in-law
bruant [bryɑ̃] *nm* : bunting, small finch
brucelles [brysɛl] *nfpl* : tweezers
brugnon *nm* [bryɲɔ̃] : nectarine
bruine [brɥin] *nf* : drizzle — **bruiner** [brɥine] *vi*
bruire [brɥir] {16} *vi* **1** : to rustle (of leaves, etc.) **2** : to murmur, to hum, to drone, to buzz
bruissement [brɥismɑ̃] *nm* : rustling, murmuring, humming
bruit [brɥi] *nm* **1** : noise, sound <faire du bruit : to make noise, to be noisy> <bruit de fond : background noise> **2** : commotion, fuss, uproar **3** : rumor, gossip
bruitage [brɥitaʒ] *nm* : sound effects *pl*
brûlant, -lante [brylɑ̃, -lɑ̃t] *adj* **1** : burning hot **2** : passionate, fervent **3** : urgent <un sujet brûlant : a burning issue>
brûlé, -lée [bryle] *adj Can fam* : worn-out, beat

brûler [bryle] *vt* **1** : to burn, to scald **2** : to run (a red light) — *vi* **1** : to burn (up), to be on fire **2 ~ de** : to long for, to be consumed with — **se bruler** *vr* : to burn oneself

brûleur [brylœr] *nm* : burner (of a stove)

brulôt [brylo] *nm Can* : gnat

brûlure [brylyr] *nf* **1** : burn **2** : burning <brûlures d'estomac : heartburn>

brume [brym] *nf* : mist, haze

brumeux, -meuse [brymø, -møz] *adj* : misty, foggy, hazy

brun[1], **brune** [brœ̃, bryn] *adj* : brown

brun[2], **brune** *n* : brown-haired person, brunet

brun[3] *nm* : brown

brunante [brynɑ̃t] *nf Can* : dusk

brunâtre [brynatr] *adj* : brownish

brunch [brœnʃ] *nm* : brunch

brunette [brynɛt] *nf* : brunette

brunir [brynir] *vt* **1** : to burnish **2** BRONZER : to tan — *vi* **1** : to get tan **2** : to darken, to brown

brusque [brysk] *adj* : brusque, abrupt, curt — **brusquement** [bryskəmɑ̃] *adv*

brusquer [bryske] *vt* **1** : to be brusque with **2** : to rush, to hurry

brusquerie [bryskəri] *nf* **1** : brusqueness **2** : suddenness

brut, brute [bryt] *adj* **1** : raw, crude, rough **2** : dry (of wine) **3** : total, gross <poids brut : gross weight>

brutal, -tale [brytal] *adj, mpl* **brutaux** [bryto] **1** : brutal, violent **2** : sudden, sharp **3** : blunt, stark — **brutalement** [-talmɑ̃] *adv*

brutaliser [brytalize] *vt* : to abuse, to mistreat

brutalité [brytalite] *nf* **1** : brutality **2** : suddenness

brute [bryt] *nf* : brute, beast

bruxellois, -loise [brysɛlwa, -lwaz] *adj* : of or from Brussels

Bruxellois, -loise *n* : person from Brussels

bruyamment [brɥijamɑ̃] *adv* : loudly, noisily

bruyant, bruyante [brɥijɑ̃, -jɑ̃t] *adj* : noisy

bruyère [bryjɛr] *nf* **1** : heather **2** : heath, moor

bu [by] *pp* → **boire**

buanderie [byɑ̃dri] *nf* **1** : laundry room **2** *Can* : self-service laundry

buandier, -dière [byɑ̃dje, -djɛr] *n Can* : laundry worker

buccal, -cale [bykal] *adj, mpl* **buccaux** [byko] : oral

buccin [byksɛ̃] *nm* : whelk

bûche [byʃ] *nf* : log

bûcher[1] [byʃe] *vt* **1** *fam* : to plod away at **2** *Can* : to chop down (trees) — *vi* **1** *fam* : to keep working, to slave away **2** *Can* : to fell trees

bûcher[2] *nm* **1** : stake, pyre **2** : woodshed

bûcheron, -ronne [byʃrɔ̃, -rɔn] *n* : logger, lumberjack

bûcheur[1], **-cheuse** [byʃœr, -ʃøz] *adj fam* : hardworking

bûcheur[2], **-cheuse** *n fam* : grind, hard worker

bucolique [bykɔlik] *adj* : bucolic

budget [bydʒɛ] *nm* : budget

budgétaire [bydʒetɛr] *adj* : budgetary

budgétiser [bydʒetize] *vt* : to budget

buée [bɥe] *nf* : steam, mist, condensation

buffet [byfɛ] *nm* **1** : sideboard **2** : buffet-style meal or restaurant

buffle [byfl] *nm* : Cape buffalo, water buffalo

buis [bɥi] *nm* : box (plant), boxwood

buisson [bɥisɔ̃] *nm* : bush, shrub

buissonnière [bɥisɔnjɛr] *adj* **faire l'école buissonnière** : to skip school

bulbe [bylb] *nm* : bulb (of a plant)

bulbeux, -beuse [bylbø, -bøz] *adj* : bulbous

bulgare[1] [bylgar] *adj* : Bulgarian

bulgare[2] *nm* : Bulgarian (language)

Bulgare *nmf* : Bulgarian

bulldozer [byldozɛr] *nm* : bulldozer

bulle [byl] *nf* **1** : bubble **2** : balloon (in a comic strip) **3** : papal bull

bulletin [byltɛ̃] *nm* **1** : report, bulletin, newsletter <bulletin météorologique : weather forecast> <bulletin scolaire : report card> **2** : certificate <bulletin de naissance : birth certificate> **3** : form, slip, ticket <bulletin de commande : order form> **4** *or* **bulletin de vote** : ballot (form)

bureau [byro] *nm, pl* **bureaux** **1** : office, study **2** : desk **3** : department, agency, bureau <bureau de poste : post office> <bureau de placement : employment agency> **4** : board, committee

bureaucrate [byrokrat] *nmf* : bureaucrat

bureaucratie [byrokrasi] *nf* : bureaucracy — **bureaucratique** [-kratik] *adj*

bureautique [byrotik] *nf* : office automation

burette [byrɛt] *nf* **1** : cruet **2** : oilcan

buriné, -née [byrine] *adj* : furrowed, deeply lined <un visage buriné : a craggy face>

burlesque[1] [byrlɛsk] *adj* : farcical, ludicrous

burlesque[2] *nm* : burlesque

burundais, -daise [burundɛ, -dɛz] *adj* : Burundian

Burundais, -daise *n* : Burundian

bus [bys] *nm* AUTOBUS : bus

buse [byz] *nf* : buzzard

buste [byst] *nm* **1** : chest **2** : bust (in sculpture) **3** : bust, bosom (of a woman)

but [by(t)] *nm* **1** : aim, objective <aller droit au but : to go straight to the point> <sans but : aimlessly> **2** : goal, target, touchdown **3** *Can* : base (in baseball) <but sur balles : base on balls, walk> **4 de but en blanc** : point-blank, bluntly

butane [bytan] *nm* : butane

buté, -tée [byte] *adj* : obstinate, stubborn

butée [byte] *nf* : abutment

buter [byte] *vi* **1 ~ contre** *or* **~ sur** : to stumble on, to trip over **2 ~ contre** : to rest on, to abut — *vt* **1** : to prop up **2** : to antagonize, to make (someone) stubborn **3** *fam* : to kill, to bump off

butin [bytɛ̃] *nm* : booty, loot, spoils *pl*

butiner [bytine] *vt* **1** : to gather (nectar) **2** : to glean, to pick up (ideas, information)

butoir [bytwar] *nm* **1** : buffer, stop <butoir de porte : doorstop> **2** *or* **date butoir** : deadline

butor [bytɔr] *nm* : bittern

butte [byt] *nf* **1** : small hill, mound **2 être en butte à** : to come up against

buvable [byvabl] *adj* POTABLE : drinkable, potable

buvard [byvar] *nm* : blotter

buveur, -veuse [byvœr, -vøz] *n* : drinker

buvons [byvɔ̃], *etc.* → **boire**

byzantin, -tine [bizɑ̃tɛ̃, -tin] *adj* : Byzantine

C

c [se] *nm* : c, the third letter of the alphabet

ça[1] [sa] *pron* **1** : that, this <je n'aime pas ça : I don't like that> <ça coûte combien? : how much does this cost?> **2** : it, that <ça va? : how's it going?> <c'est ça : that's it, that's right> **3 ça alors!** : well!, really! **4 ça y est** : there, that's it **5 et avec ça?** : anything else?

ça[2] *nm* **le ça** : the id

çà [sa] *adv* **çà et là** : here and there

cabale [kabal] *nf* : cabal

cabane [kaban] *nf* **1** HUTTE : cabin, hut **2** ABRI : shelter <cabane à lapins : rabbit hutch> **3** *or* **cabane à sucre** *Can* : sugarhouse **4 en ~** *fam* : in jail, in the clink

cabanon [kabanɔ̃] *nm* **1** ABRI : shed **2** : country cottage (in Provence)

cabaret [kabarɛ] *nm* : cabaret, nightclub

cabas [kaba] *nms & pl France* : shopping bag

cabestan [kabɛstɑ̃] *nm* : capstan

cabillaud [kabijo] *nm* : cod

cabine [kabin] *nf* : cabin, cubicle, cab (of a truck, etc.), booth <cabine téléphonique : telephone booth> <cabine de pilotage : cockpit>

cabinet [kabinɛ] *nm* **1** *or* **cabinet de travail** BUREAU : office **2** *or* **cabinet médical** : doctor's office **3** : cabinet (in government) **4 cabinet de toilette** *France* : toilet, bathroom

câblage [kablaʒ] *nm* : wiring

câble [kabl] *nm* **1** : cable, line, rope **2** : cable television **3** : cablegram

câbler [kable] *vt* : to cable

câblodistribution [kablɔdistribysjɔ̃] *nf* : cable television

câblogramme [kablɔgram] *nm* : cablegram

cabochard, -charde [kabɔʃar, -ʃard] *adj fam* : stubborn, pigheaded

caboche [kabɔʃ] *nf* **1** : hobnail **2** *fam* : head, nut

cabosser [kabɔse] *vt* : to dent <un chapeau cabossé : a battered hat>

cabotin, -tine [kabɔtɛ̃, -tin] *n* : ham actor, show-off

cabrer [kabre] *v* **se cabrer** *vr* **1** : to rear up (of a horse), to climb steeply (of a plane) **2** : to rebel, to protest

cabriole [kabrijɔl] *nf* : capering (about) **2 faire des cabrioles** : to caper, to gambol, to cavort, to prance

cabriolet [kabrijɔlɛ] *nm* DÉCAPOTABLE : convertible

caca [kaka] *nm fam* : excrement

cacahuète [kakaɥɛt] *nf* : peanut

cacao [kakao] *nm* **1** : cocoa **2** : cocoa bean

cacarder [kakarde] *vi* : to honk (of a goose)

cacatoès [kakatɔɛs] *nm* : cockatoo

cache [kaʃ] *nf* : hiding place, cache

cache–cache [kaʃkaʃ] *nms & pl* : hide-and-seek <jouer à cache-cache : to play hide-and-seek>

cache–col [kaʃkɔl] *nms & pl* : scarf

cachemire [kaʃmir] *nm* : cashmere

cache–nez [kaʃne] *nms & pl* : scarf, muffler

cache–pot [kaʃpo] *nm* : planter, container for a flowerpot

cacher [kaʃe] *vt* **1** : to hide, to conceal **2** : to cover up, to mask — **se cacher** *vr*

cachet [kaʃɛ] *nm* **1** COMPRIMÉ : tablet, pill **2** : seal, stamp <cachet de la poste : postmark> **3** : fee **4** : style, character, charm

cacheter [kaʃte] {8} *vt* SCELLER : to seal

cachette [kaʃɛt] *nf* **1** CACHE : hiding place, hide out **2** *Can* : hide-and-seek <jouer à la cachette : to play hide-and-seek> **3 en ~** : secretly

cachot [kaʃo] *nm* **1** : prison, dungeon **2** *Can* : penalty box (in hockey)

cachotterie [kaʃɔtri] *nf* : little secret

cachottier, -tière [kaʃotje, -tjɛr] *adj* : secretive

cacophonie [kakɔfɔni] *nf* : cacophony

cactus [kaktys] *nms & pl* : cactus

cadastre [kadastr] *nm* : land office

cadavérique [kadaverik] *adj* : deathly (pale)

cadavre [kadavr] *nm* : corpse, cadaver

caddie *or* **caddy** [kadi] *nm* : caddie, caddy

cadeau [kado] *nm, pl* **cadeaux** : gift, present <cadeau de Noël : Christmas present> <faire un cadeau à : to give a gift to>

cadenas [kadna] *nm* : padlock — **cadenasser** [-nase] *vt*

cadence [kadɑ̃s] *nf* **1** RYTHME : cadence, rhythm **2** : rate, pace

cadet[1], -dette [kadɛ, -dɛt] *adj* : younger, youngest

cadet[2], -dette *n* **1** : younger (son, daughter, child), youngest (son, daughter, child) **2** : junior <elle est son cadet de quatre ans : she is four years his junior> **3** : cadet **4 c'est le cadet de mes soucis** : that's the least of my worries

cadmium [kadmjɔm] *nm* : cadmium

cadran [kadrɑ̃] *nm* **1** : dial, face **2** *Can fam* : alarm clock **3 cadran solaire** : sundial

cadre [kadr] *nm* **1** : frame **2** : setting, surroundings *pl* **3** : framework, structure **4** : manager, executive

cadrer [kadre] *vt* : to center (an image, etc.) — *vi* : to fit, to correspond

caduc, -duque [kadyk] *adj* **1** : obsolete, outmoded **2** : null and void **3** : deciduous **4** : mute, silent <e caduc : silent e>

cafard[1] [kafar] *nm* **1** BLATTE : cockroach **2** : melancholy, blues <avoir le cafard : to be down in the dumps>

cafard[2], -farde [kafar, -fard] *n fam* : sneaky person, squealer

café [kafe] *nm* **1** : coffee <café en poudre : instant coffee> **2** : café, bar

caféine [kafein] *nf* : caffeine

cafétéria [kafeterja] *nf* : cafeteria

cafetière [kaftjɛr] *nf* **1** : coffeepot, coffeemaker **2 cafetière à pression** : percolator

cafouillage [kafujaʒ] *nm fam* : mess, confusion

cafouiller [kafuje] *vi fam* : to get into a mess, to flounder around

cage [kaʒ] *nf* **1** : cage <cage à oiseaux : birdcage> <cage thoracique : rib cage> **2 cage d'ascenseur** : elevator shaft **3 cage d'escalier** : stairwell

cageot [kaʒo] *nm* : crate

cagibi [kaʒibi] *nm* : storeroom

cagneux, -gneuse [kaɲø, -ɲøz] *adj* : knock-kneed

cagnotte [kaɲɔt] *nf* : pool, kitty

cagoulard, -larde [kagular, -lard] *n Can* : masked robber

cagoule [kagul] *nf* : hood, cowl

cahier [kaje] *nm* **1** : notebook **2** : section, supplement (of a periodical) **3 cahiers** *nmpl* : journal

cahin–caha [kaɛ̃kaa] *adv* **aller cahin–caha** : to struggle along

cahot [kao] *nm* SECOUSSE : bump, jolt

cahoter [kaɔte] *vi* : to bump around, to jolt along

cahoteux, -teuse [kaɔtø, -tøz] *adj* : rough, bumpy

cahute [kayt] *nf* : shack, hut

caïd [kaid] *nm fam* : ring leader, big shot

caille [kaj] *nf* : quail

caillé [kaje] *nm* : curds *pl*

cailler [kaje] *vt* : to curdle — *vi* **1** : to curdle, to congeal **2 ça caille** *fam* : it's freezing — **se cailler** *vr*

caillot [kajo] *nm* : clot

caillou [kaju] *nm, pl* **cailloux** : pebble, stone

caillouteux, -teuse [kajutø, -tøz] *adj* : pebbly, stony

cailloutis [kajuti] *nm* : gravel, crushed stone

caisse [kɛs] *nf* **1** BOÎTE : box, crate **2** : case, casing, body (of a vehicle) **3** *or* **caisse enregistreuse** : till, cash register **4** : fund, funding organization <caisse de retraite : pension fund> <caisse populaire *Can* : cooperative bank> **5** : drum <caisse claire : snare drum>

caissier, -sière [kesje, -sjɛr] *n* **1** : cashier, sales clerk **2** : (bank) teller

caisson [kɛsɔ̃] *nm* **1** : caisson **2 la maladie des caissons** : caisson disease, the bends

cajoler [kaʒɔle] *vt* **1** : to fuss over, to cuddle **2** : to cajole, to wheedle

cajolerie [kaʒɔlri] *nf* : cuddling

cajou [kaʒu] *nm* **noix de cajou** : cashew nut

cajun [kaʒœ̃] *adj* : Cajun

Cajun *nmf* : Cajun

cake [kɛk] *nm* : fruitcake

cal [kal] *nm, pl* **cals** : callus

calamine [kalamin] *nf* : calamine

calamité [kalamite] *nf* DÉSASTRE : calamity

calandre [kalɑ̃dr] *nf* : radiator grill (of an automobile)

calcaire[1] [kalkɛr] *adj* : chalky, hard (of water)

calcaire[2] *nm* : limestone

calciner [kalsine] *vt* : to char, to burn to a crisp

calcium [kalsjɔm] *nm* : calcium

calcul [kalkyl] *nm* **1** : calculation, sum (in mathematics) **2** : arithmetic **3** : calculus **4** : stone <calcul rénal : kidney stone> <calcul bilaire : gallstone>

calculateur, -trice [kalkylatœr, -tris] *adj* : calculating

calculatrice *nf* : calculator

calculer [kalkyle] *vt* : to calculate, to compute

cale [kal] *nf* **1** : wedge, chock **2** : hold (of a ship) **3 cale sèche** : dry dock

calé, -lée [kale] *adj fam* **1** : brainy, clever **2** : tough (of a problem, etc.)

calebasse [kalbas] *nf* : calabash

calèche [kalɛʃ] *nf* : (horse-drawn) carriage

caleçon [kalsɔ̃] *nm* **1** : boxer shorts *pl* **2** *or* **caleçons de bain** : swimming trunks **3** : leggings

calembour [kalɑ̃bur] *nm* : pun

calendes [kalɑ̃d] *nfpl* **renvoyer aux calendes grecques** : to put something off indefinitely

calendrier [kalɑ̃drije] *nm* : calendar

calepin [kalpɛ̃] *nm* : notebook

caler [kale] *vt* **1** : to wedge **2** : to prop up **3** *fam* : to fill up (one's stomach) **4** *Can fam* : to gulp down — *vi* **1** : to stall out **2** : to give up **3** *Can* : to sink (in snow, etc.)

calfeutrer [kalføtre] *vt* : to seal, to make draftproof — **se calfeutrer** *vr* : to make oneself snug

calibre [kalibr] *nm* **1** : caliber, bore **2** : grade, size **3** : class, stature

calibrer [kalibre] *vt* : to calibrate, to grade

calice [kalis] *nm* **1** : chalice **2** : calyx

calicot [kaliko] *nm* : calico

calife [kalif] *nm* : caliph

califourchon [kalifurʃɔ̃] **à califourchons** : astride, astraddle

câlin, -line [kalɛ̃, -lin] *adj* : tender, affectionate

câliner [kaline] *vt* : to cuddle — **se câliner** *vr*

calleux, -leuse [kalø, -løz] *adj* : calloused, hard

calligraphie [kaligrafi] *nf* : calligraphy — **calligraphique** [-grafik] *adj*

callosité [kalɔzite] *nf* : callus

calmant[1], -mante [kalmɑ̃, -mɑ̃t] *adj* : soothing

calmant[2] *nm* : sedative

calmar [kalmar] *nm* : squid, calamari

calme[1] [kalm] *adj* TRANQUILLE : calm — **calmement** [kalməmɑ̃] *adv*

calme[2] *nm* **1** : calm, peace <calme plat : dead calm> **2 garder son calme** : to keep one's head

calmer [kalme] *vt* **1** APAISER : to calm **2** : to ease, to soothe — **se calmer** *vr* : to calm down

calomnie [kalɔmni] *nf* DIFFAMATION : slander, libel

calomnier [kalɔmnje] {96} *vt* : to slander, to libel

calomnieux, -nieuse [kalɔmnjø, -njøz] *adj* : slanderous, libelous

calorie [kalɔri] *nf* : calorie

calorifère[1] [kalɔrifɛr] *adj* : heating, heat-carrying

calorifère[2] *nm* **1** : heater, stove **2** *Can* : room radiator

calorique [kalɔrik] *adj* : caloric

calotte [kalɔt] *nf* **1** : skullcap **2** *Can* : cap **3 calotte glaciaire** : ice cap

calque [kalk] *nm* **1** DESSIN : tracing <papier calque : tracing paper> **2** : exact copy, replica

calquer [kalke] *vt* **1** : to trace **2** IMITER : to copy exactly, to imitate

calumet [kalymɛ] *nm* : peace pipe

calvaire [kalvɛr] *nm* **1** : wayside cross **2** : ordeal, suffering

calvitie [kalvisi] *nf* : baldness

calypso [kalipso] *nm* : calypso

camarade [kamarad] *nmf* : comrade, friend <camarade de classe : classmate>

camaraderie [kamaradri] *nf* : camaraderie, friendship

cambiste [kɑ̃bist] *nm* : exchange broker, money changer

cambodgien[1], -dgienne [kɑ̃bɔdʒjɛ̃, -dʒjɛn] *adj* : Cambodian

cambodgien[2] *nm* : Cambodian (language)

Cambodgien, -dgienne *n* : Cambodian

cambrer [kɑ̃bre] *vt* : to bend, to arch <cambrer les reins : to arch one's back> — **se cambrer** *vr* : to arch one's back

cambriolage [kɑ̃brijɔlaʒ] *nm* : burglary

cambrioler [kɑ̃brjɔle] *vt* : to burglarize

cambrioleur, -leuse [kɑ̃brijɔlør, -løz] *n* : burglar

cambrure [kɑ̃bryr] *nf* **1** : arch, curve **2 cambrure des pieds** : instep

came [kam] *nf* : cam <arbre à cames : camshaft>

camée [kame] *nm* : cameo

caméléon [kameleɔ̃] *nm* : chameleon

camélia [kamelja] *nf* : camelia

camelot [kamlo] *nm* **1** : street vendor **2** *Can* : paperboy

camelote [kamlɔt] *nf fam* : trash, junk

camembert [kamɑ̃bɛr] *nm* : Camembert

caméra [kamera] *nf* : movie camera, television camera

camerounais, -naise [kamrunɛ, -nɛz] *adj* : Cameroonian

Camerounais, -naise *n* : Cameroonian

caméscope [kameskɔp] *nm* : camcorder

camion [kamjɔ̃] *nm* : truck

camionnage [kamjɔnaʒ] *nm* : trucking

camionner [kamjne] *vt* : to transport (by truck)

camionnette [kamjɔnɛt] *nf* : van, pickup truck

camionneur, -neuse [kamjɔnœr, -nøz] *n* ROUTIER : truck driver, trucker

camisole [kamizɔl] *nf* **1** : camisole **2 camisole de force** : straitjacket

camomille [kamɔmij] *nf* : camomile

camouflage [kamuflaʒ] *nm* : camouflage

camoufler [kamufle] *vt* : to camouflage

camp [kɑ̃] *nm* **1** CAMPEMENT : camp <lever le camp : to strike camp> <camp de concentration : concentra-

tion camp> **2** PARTI : side, team, faction

campagnard[1], **-gnarde** [kɑ̃paɲar, -ɲard] *adj* : country, rustic

campagnard[2], **-gnarde** *n* : countryman *m,* countrywoman *f*

campagne [kɑ̃paɲ] *nf* **1** : country, countryside **2** : campaign <faire campagne contre : to agitate against>

campagnol [kɑ̃paɲɔl] *nm* : vole

campement [kɑ̃pmɑ̃] *nm* : camp, encampment

camper [kɑ̃pe] *vt* **1** : to encamp **2** POSER : to place firmly **3** : to portray (a character) — *vi* : to camp — **se camper** *vr* : to stand firmly

campeur, -peuse [kɑ̃pœr, -pøz] *n* : camper

camphre [kɑ̃fr] *nm* : camphor

camping [kɑ̃piŋ] *nm* **1** : camping <faire du camping : to go camping> **2** : campground, campsite

campus [kɑ̃pys] *nm* : campus

camus, -muse [kamy, -myz] *adj* **nez camus** : pug nose

canadien, -dienne [kanadjɛ̃, -djɛn] *adj* : Canadian

Canadien, -dienne *n* : Canadian

canadien–français, canadienne–française *adj, pl* **canadiens–français, canadiennes–françaises** : French-Canadian

canaille [kanaj] *nf* **1** : rabble, riffraff **2** : scoundrel, rascal

canal [kanal] *nm, pl* **canaux** [kano] **1** : canal **2** : channel

canaliser [kanalize] *vt* : to channel

canapé [kanape] *nm* **1** : sofa, couch **2** : canapé

canapé–lit [kanapeli] *n, pl* **canapés–lits** : sofa bed

canard [kanar] *nm* **1** : duck **2** : false note (in music) **3** *fam* : rag, newspaper

canari [kanari] *nm* : canary

canasson [kanasɔ̃] *nm fam* : nag (horse)

cancan [kɑ̃kɑ̃] *nm* **1** : cancan **2** : rumor, gossip

cancaner [kɑ̃kane] *vi* **1** : to quack **2** : to spread gossip

cancanier, -nière [kɑ̃kanje, -njɛr] *n* : gossip

cancer [kɑ̃sɛr] *nm* : cancer

Cancer *nm* : Cancer

cancéreux[1], **-reuse** [kɑ̃serø, -røz] *adj* : cancerous

cancéreux[2], **-reuse** *n* : cancer patient

cancérigène [kɑ̃seriʒɛn] *adj* : carcinogenic

cancre [kɑ̃kr] *nm fam* : dunce

candélabre [kɑ̃delabr] *nm* : candelabrum

candeur [kɑ̃dœr] *nf* INGÉNUITÉ : ingenuousness

candidat, -date [kɑ̃dida, -dat] *n* : candidate

candidature [kɑ̃didatyr] *nf* : candidacy

candide [kɑ̃did] *adj* : ingenuous, naïve

cane [kan] *nf* : (female) duck

caneton [kantɔ̃] *nm* : duckling

canette [kanɛt] *nf* **1** BOUTEILLE : (small) bottle **2** BOÎTE : can (of a beverage) **3** : spool **4** : (female) duckling

canevas [kanva] *nms & pl* **1** : canvas **2** : framework

caniche [kaniʃ] *nm* : poodle

canicule [kanikyl] *nf* : heat wave

canidé [kanide] *nm* : canine

canif [kanif] *nm* : jackknife, pocketknife

canin, -nine [kanɛ̃, -nin] *adj* : canine

canine *nf* : canine (tooth)

caniveau [kanivo] *nm, pl* **-veaux** : (street) gutter

cannabis [kanabis] *nm* : cannabis

canne [kan] *nf* **1** : cane, walking stick **2** : cane (in botany) <canne à sucre : sugarcane> **3 canne à pêche** : fishing rod

canneberge [kanbɛrʒ] *nf* : cranberry

cannelé, -lée [kanle] *adj* : fluted, grooved

canneler [kanle] {8} *vt* : to groove

cannelle [kanɛl] *nf* : cinnamon

cannette [kanɛt] *nf* → **canette**

cannibale [kanibal] *nmf* : cannibal — **cannibalisme** [-balism] *nm*

cannonière [kanɔnjɛr] *nf* : gunboat

canoë [kanɔe] *nm* : canoe

canon [kanɔ̃] *nm* **1** : cannon **2** : barrel, muzzle (of a gun) **3** : canon, rule **4** : shank (of a horse)

canoniser [kanɔnize] *vt* : to canonize — **canonisation** [-nizasjɔ̃] *nf*

canot [kano] *nm* **1** *France* : boat, dinghy **2** *Can* : canoe **3 canot de sauvetage** : lifeboat

canotage [kanɔtaʒ] *nm* **1** *France* : boating **2** *Can* : canoeing

cantaloup [kɑ̃talu] *nm* : cantaloupe

cantate [kɑ̃tat] *nf* : cantata

cantatrice [kɑ̃tatris] *nf* : opera singer

cantilever [kɑ̃tilevœr] *adj & nm* : cantilever

cantine [kɑ̃tin] *nf* : canteen, cafeteria

cantique [kɑ̃tik] *nm* HYMNE : canticle, hymn

canton [kɑ̃tɔ̃] *nm* **1** *Can* : township <les cantons de l'Est : the Eastern Townships> **2** *France* : district

cantonnement [kantɔnmɑ̃] *nm* : billet, billeting

cantonner [kɑ̃tɔne] *v* **1** : to confine, to limit **2** : to station, to billet — **se cantonner** *vr* SE CONFINER : to confine oneself, to lock oneself away

cantonnière [kɑ̃tɔnjɛr] *nf* : valance

canular [kanylar] *nm* : hoax, practical joke

canyon [kaɲɔ̃] *nm* : canyon

caoutchouc [kautʃu] *nm* **1** : rubber **2 caoutchoucs** *nmpl* : galoshes

caoutchouteux, -teuse [kautʃutø, -tøz] *adj* : rubbery

cap [kap] *nm* **1** PROMONTOIRE : cape, headland **2** : mark, milestone **3** DIRECTION : course, direction
capable [kapabl] *adj* **1** : capable, able **2** : likely **3** *Can* : strong, robust
capacité [kapasite] *nf* **1** : capacity **2** APTITUDE : ability
cape [kap] *nf* : cape, cloak
capillaire[1] [kapilɛr] *adj* **1** : capillary **2** : hair <lotion capillaire : hair lotion>
capillaire[2] *nm* : capillary
capitaine [kapitɛn] *nm* **1** : captain **2** **capitaine de corvette** : lieutenant commander
capital[1], **-tale** [kapital] *adj, mpl* **-taux** [-to] **1** : major, crucial **2** : capital <peine capitale : capital punishment>
capital[2] *nm, pl* **-taux** : capital, assets *pl*
capitale *nf* : capital (city)
capitaliser [kapitalize] *vt* : to capitalize (in finance) — *vi* : to save
capitalisme [kapitalism] *nm* : capitalism
capitaliste[1] [kapitalist] *adj* : capitalist, capitalistic
capitaliste[2] *nmf* : capitalist
capiteux, -teuse [kapitø, -tøz] *adj* : heady, intoxicating
capitole [kapitɔl] *nm* : capitol
capitonner [kapitɔne] *vt* : to pad
capitulation [kapitylasjɔ̃] *nf* : capitulation, surrender
capituler [kapityle] *vi* : to capitulate, to surrender
caporal–chef [kapɔralʃɛf] *nm, pl* **caporaux–chefs** [-ro] : corporal
capot [kapo] *nm* **1** : cover, casing **2** : hood (of an automobile)
capote [kapɔt] *nf* **1** : greatcoat **2** : top (of a convertible)
capoter [kapɔte] *vi* **1** CHAVIRER : to capsize, to overturn **2** *fam* : to fall through, to come to nothing **3** *Can fam* : to lose one's head
câpre [kapr] *nf* : caper
caprice [kapris] *nm* **1** : caprice, whim **2** : tantrum <faire un caprice : to throw a tantrum>
capricieux, -cieuse [kaprisjø, -sjøz] *adj* : capricious, temperamental — **capricieusement** [-sjøzmɑ̃] *adv*
Capricorne [kaprikɔrn] *nm* : Capricorn
capsule [kapsyl] *nf* **1** : capsule <capsule spatiale : space capsule> **2** : top, cap **3** : capsule (in pharmacy)
capter [kapte] *vt* **1** RECEVOIR : to receive, to pick up (radio or television signals) **2** : to capture, to catch <capter l'attention de : to capture the attention of>
capteur [kaptœr] *nm* : sensor
captieux, -tieuse [kapsjø, -sjøz] *adj* FALLACIEUX : fallacious, misleading
captif, -tive [kaptif, -tiv] *adj & n* : captive
captivant, -vante [kaptivɑ̃, -vɑ̃t] *adj* FASCINANT : fascinating, captivating
captiver [kaptive] *vt* : to captivate, to fascinate
captivité [kaptivite] *nf* : captivity
capture [kaptyr] *nf* **1** : capture, seizure **2** PRISE : catch
capturer [kaptyre] *vt* : to capture, to catch
capuche [kapyʃ] *nf* : hood
capuchon [kapyʃɔ̃] *nm* **1** : hood **2** : cap, top (of a pen, etc.)
capucine [kapysin] *nf* : nasturtium
cap–verdien, -dienne [kapvɛrdjɛ̃, -djɛn] *adj* : Cape Verdean
Cap–verdien, -dienne *n* : Cape Verdean
caquet [kakɛ] *nm* **1** : cackle, cackling **2** BAVARDAGE : chatter, prattle
caqueter [kakte] {8} *vi* **1** : to cackle **2** BAVARDER : to chatter, to prattle
car[1] [kar] *nm* AUTOCAR : bus, coach
car[2] *conj* : for, because
carabine [karabin] *nf* : carbine, rifle
caractère [karaktɛr] *nm* **1** : letter, character, graphic sign <en gros caractères : in large print> **2** : character, nature, disposition <avoir mauvais caractère : to be ill-tempered> **3** : characteristic, feature
caracoler [karakɔle] *vt* **1** : to prance (of a horse) **2** : to gambol, to skip
caractériser [karakterize] *vt* : to characterize, to describe — **caractérisation** [-rizasjɔ̃] *nf*
caractéristique [karakteristik] *adj & nf* : characteristic
carafe [karaf] *nf* : carafe, decanter
caraïbe[1] [karaib] *adj* : Caribbean
caraïbe[2] *nm* : Carib (language)
carambolage [karɑ̃bɔlaʒ] *nm* **1** : pileup, multicar accident **2** : carom (in billiards, etc.)
caramboler [karɑ̃bɔle] *vi* : to carom (in billiards) — *vt* : to collide with, to crash into (an automobile)
caramel [karamɛl] *nm* : caramel
carapace [karapas] *nf* : shell
carat [kara] *nm* : carat
caravane [karavan] *nf* **1** : caravan **2** : trailer
carbone [karbɔn] *nm* **1** : carbon **2** *or* **papier carbone** : carbon paper
carbonique [karbɔnik] *adj* **1** **gaz carbonique** : carbon dioxide **2** **neige carbonique** : dry ice
carboniser [karbɔnize] *vt* : to char
carburant [karbyrɑ̃] *nm* : fuel
carburateur [karbyratœr] *nm* : carburetor
carcan [karkɑ̃] *nm* **1** : constraint, yoke **2** : iron collar
carcasse [karkas] *nf* **1** : carcass **2** : frame (of a building, vehicle, etc.)
carcéral, -rale [karseral] *adj, mpl* **-raux** [-ro] : prison
carcinogène [karsinɔʒɛn] *adj* : carcinogenic
carcinome [karsinom] *nm* : carcinoma
carder [karde] *vt* : to card (fibers)

cardiaque [kardjak] *adj* : cardiac

cardigan [kardigɑ̃] *nm* : cardigan

cardinal[1], **-nale** [kardinal] *adj, mpl* **-naux** [-no] : cardinal, chief

cardinal[2] *nm, pl* **-naux 1** : cardinal (in religion) **2** : cardinal number **3** : cardinal, redbird

cardiologie [kardjolɔʒi] *nf* : cardiology

cardiologue [kardjolɔg] *nmf* : cardiologist

cardio–vasculaire [kardjovaskylɛr] *adj* : cardiovascular

carême [karɛm] *nm* : Lent

carence [karɑ̃s] *nf* **1** ABSENCE : lack, deficiency **2** : shortcomings *pl* **3** : insolvency

carène [karɛn] *nf* : hull (of a ship)

caréner [karene] {87} *vt* **1** : to careen (a ship) **2** : to streamline

caressant, -sante [karɛsɑ̃, -sɑ̃t] *adj* : affectionate, tender

caresse [karɛs] *nf* : caress

caresser [karese] *vt* **1** : to caress **2** : to cherish, to entertain (hopes, etc.)

cargaison [kargɛzɔ̃] *nf* : cargo, freight

cargo [kargo] *nm* : freighter

cari [kari] *nm* → **curry**

caribou [karibu] *nm* : caribou

caricature [karikatyr] *nf* : caricature, cartoon

caricaturer [karikatyre] *vt* : to caricature — **caricaturiste** [-tyrist] *nmf*

carie [kari] *nf* **1** : blight (in botany) **2** *or* **carie dentaire** : caries, tooth decay <une carie : a cavity>

carier [karje] {96} *vt* : to rot, to decay — **se carier** *vr*

carillon [karijɔ̃] *nm* : bell, chime

carillonnement [karijɔnmɑ̃] *nm* : peal

carillonner [karijɔne] *v* : to chime, to peal

caritatif, -tive [karitatif, -tiv] *adj* : charitable

carlin [karlɛ̃] *nm* : pug (dog)

carlingue [karlɛ̃g] *nf* : cabin (of an airplane)

carmin [karmɛ̃] *adj & nm* : carmine (red)

carnage [karnaʒ] *nm* TUERIE : carnage, slaughter

carnassier[1], **-sière** [karnasje, -sjɛr] *adj* : carnivorous

carnassier[2] *nm* : carnivore

carnaval [karnaval] *nm, pl* **-vals** : carnival

carnet [karnɛ] *nm* **1** : notebook **2** : book (of stamps, tickets, etc.) <carnet de chèques : checkbook>

carnivore[1] [karnivɔr] *adj* : carnivorous

carnivore[2] *nm* : carnivore

carotte [karɔt] *nf* : carrot

carotter [karɔte] *vt fam* : to swindle, to chisel, to cheat

caroubier [karubje] *nm* : locust (tree)

carpe [karp] *nf* : carp

carpelle [karpɛl] *nm* : carpel

carpette [karpɛt] *nf* : rug

carquois [karkwa] *nm* : quiver

carré[1], **-rée** [kare] *adj* **1** : square **2** : straightforward, forthright

carré[2] *nm* **1** : square **2** : plot, patch (of land) **3** : (square) scarf **4** : four of a kind <un carré d'as : four aces>

carreau [karo] *nm, pl* **carreaux 1** : tile **2** VITRE : windowpane **3** : square, check <à carreaux : checkered> **4** : diamond (in playing cards)

carreauté, -tée [karote] *adj Can* : checkered, checked

carrefour [karfur] *nm* : intersection, crossroads

carrelage [karlaʒ] *nm* : tile, tiled floor

carreler [karle] {8} *vt* : to tile

carrément [karemɑ̃] *adv* **1** : squarely, firmly **2** : bluntly, straight out

carrer [kare] *v* **se carrer** *vr* : to settle oneself

carrière [karjɛr] *nf* **1** : career **2** : stone quarry

carriole [karjɔl] *nf* **1** : cart **2** *Can* : sleigh

carrossable [karɔsabl] *adj* : suitable for motor vehicles

carrosse [karɔs] *nm* **1** : carriage, coach **2** *Can* : baby carriage

carrosserie [karɔsri] *nf* **1** : body (of a car) **2** : (automobile) bodywork

carrousel [karuzɛl] *nm* : carousel

carrure [karyr] *nf* **1** : build, shoulder width **2** STATURE : stature, caliber

carry [kari] *nm* → **curry**

carte [kart] *nf* **1** : card <carte postale : postcard> <carte de crédit : credit card> <carte d'identité : identification card> **2** : map <carte routière : road map> **3** : menu <carte de vins : wine list> **4** *or* **carte à jouer** : playing card <jouer cartes sur table : to lay one's cards on the table>

cartel [kartɛl] *nm* : cartel

cartilage [kartilaʒ] *nm* : cartilage, gristle

cartilagineux, -neuse [kartilaʒinø, -nøz] *adj* : gristly, cartilaginous

cartographe [kartɔgraf] *nmf* : cartographer

cartographie [kartɔgrafi] *nf* : cartography

cartomancie [kartɔmɑ̃si] *nf* : fortune-telling (with cards)

cartomancien, -cienne [kartɔmɑ̃sjɛ̃, -sjɛn] *n* : fortune-teller (with cards)

carton [kartɔ̃] *nm* **1** : cardboard **2** : cardboard box, carton

carton–pâte [kartɔ̃pat] *nm* : pasteboard

cartouche [kartuʃ] *nf* **1** : cartridge <cartouche d'encre : fountain-pen refill> **2** : carton (of cigarettes, etc.)

carvi [karvi] *nm* : caraway

cas [ka] *nms & pl* **1** : case **2 en cas de** : in case of <en cas de bien : if need be> **3 en tout cas** : in any case **4** → **limite**

casanier, -nière [kazanje, -njɛr] *n* : homebody

cascade [kaskad] *nf* **1** : stream, cascade, torrent **2** CHUTE : waterfall **3** : stunt (in movies)

case [kaz] *nf* **1** : box (on a form or questionnaire) **2** : compartment **3** CABANE : hut **4** : square (in a board game) <retourner à la case départ : to go back to square one> **5 case postale** : post office box

caser [kaze] *vt* **1** PLACER : to put **2** *fam* : to put up, to lodge **3** *fam* : to marry off **4** *fam* : to find a job for

caserne [kazɛrn] *nf France* **1** : barracks *pl* **2 caserne de pompiers** : fire station

casher [kaʃɛr] → **kascher**

casier [kazje] *nm* **1** : compartment, pigeonhole **2** : rack (for bottles, etc.) **3 casier judiciaire** : police record

casino [kazino] *nm* : casino

casque [kask] *nm* **1** : helmet **2** : headphones *pl* **3** *Can* : fur cap

casquette [kaskɛt] *nf* : cap

cassable [kasabl] *adj* : breakable

cassant, -sante [kasɑ̃, -sɑ̃t] *adj* **1** : brittle **2** : abrupt, curt

casse [kas] *nf* **1** : breakage, damage **2** : scrap yard **3** : case (in printing) <haut de casse : uppercase>

cassé, -sée [kase] *adj fam* : out of money, broke

casse–cou [kasku] *nms & pl* **1** : danger spot **2** : daredevil

casse–croûte [kaskrut] *nms & pl* **1** : snack, lunch **2** *Can* : restaurant, snack bar

casse–noisettes [kasnwazɛt] *nms & pl* : nutcracker

casse–noix [kasnwa] *nms & pl* : nutcracker

casse–pieds [kaspje] *nmfs & pl fam* : pain in the neck, bore

casser [kase] *vt* **1** BRISER : to break **2** DÉGRADER : to demote **3** ANNULER : to quash, to annul — *vi* : to break — **se casser** *vr* **1** : to break <se casser le cou : to break one's neck> **2** *fam* : to go away <casse-toi! : get out of here!>

casserole [kasrɔl] *nf* : saucepan

casse–tête [kastɛt] *nms & pl* **1** : puzzle **2** : problem, headache

cassette [kasɛt] *nf* : cassette

cassonade [kasɔnad] *nf* : brown sugar

cassure [kasyr] *nf* **1** : break **2** : crack, fissure

castagnettes [kastaɲɛt] *nfpl* : castanets

caste [kast] *nf* : caste

castor [kastɔr] *nm* : beaver

castration [kastrasjɔ̃] *nf* : castration

castrer [kastre] *vt* : to castrate, to neuter

cataclysme [kataklism] *nm* : cataclysm

catacombes [katakɔ̃b] *nfpl* : catacombs

catafalque [katafalk] *nm* : bier (stand)

catalogue [katalɔg] *nm* : catalog

cataloguer [katalɔge] *vt* **1** : to catalog **2** : to categorize, to label (as)

catalyseur [katalizœr] *nm* : catalyst

catalytique [katalitik] *adj* : catalytic

catamaran [katamarɑ̃] *nm* : catamaran

cataplasme [kataplasm] *nm* : poultice

catapulte [katapylt] *nf* : catapult

catapulter [katapylte] *vt* : to catapult

cataracte [katarakt] *nf* **1** : cataract, falls **2** : cataract (in medicine)

catarrhe [katar] *nm* : catarrh

catastrophe [katastrɔf] *nf* : disaster, catastrophe

catastrophique [katastrɔfik] *adj* : disastrous, catastrophic

catch [katʃ] *nm* **1** : wrestling **2 faire du catch** : to wrestle

catéchisme [kateʃism] *nm* : catechism

catégorie [kategɔri] *nf* **1** : category **2** : grade, quality (of meat, etc.)

catégorique [kategɔrik] *adj* : categorical — **catégoriquement** [-rikmɑ̃] *adv*

catharsis [katarsis] *nf* : catharsis — **cathartique** [-tartik] *adj*

cathédrale [katedral] *nf* : cathedral

cathéter [katetɛr] *nm* : catheter

cathode [katɔd] *nf* : cathode

catholicisme [katɔlisism] *nm* : Catholicism

catholique[1] [katɔlik] *adj* **1** : Roman Catholic **2** : **pas (très) catholique** : dubious, questionable

catholique[2] *nmf* : Roman Catholic

catimini [katimini] **en ~** : stealthily, on the sly

caucasien, -sienne [kokazjɛ̃, -zjɛn] *adj* : Caucasian

cauchemar [kɔʃmar] *nm* : nightmare

cauchemardesque [kɔʃmardɛsk] *adj* : nightmarish

cause [koz] *nf* **1** : cause, reason <à cause de : because, on account of> <pour cause de : owing to> **2** AFFAIRE : case, lawsuit <être en cause : to be at issue, to be involved>

causer [koze] *vt* PROVOQUER : to cause — *vi* : to chat <causer de : to talk about>

causerie [kozri] *nf* : talk, chat

causette [kozɛt] *nf fam* : chat, chitchat <faire la causette à : to have a chat with>

causeur[1], **-seuse** [kozœr, -zøz] *adj* : talkative, chatty

causeur[2], **-seuse** *n* : conversationalist, talker

causeuse *nf* : love seat

caustique [kostik] *adj* : caustic

cauteleux, -leuse [kotlø, -løz] *adj* : sly, wily

cautériser [koterize] *vt* : to cauterize — **cautérisation** [-rizasjɔ̃] *nf*

caution [kosjɔ̃] *nf* **1** : security, guarantee **2 libérer sous caution** : to release on bail

cautionnement [kosjɔnmɑ̃] *nm* : bail, guarantee

cautionner [kosjɔne] *vt* **1** : to guarantee **2** : to support, to sanction

cavalcade [kavalkad] *nf* **1** : cavalcade **2** : stampede, rush

cavale [kaval] *nf fam* **en ~** : on the run

cavalerie [kavalri] *nf* : cavalry

cavalier[1], **-lière** [kavalje, -ljɛr] *adj* : cavalier, offhand

cavalier[2], **-lière** *n* **1** : rider, horseman *m,* horsewoman *f* **2** : dance partner, escort <faire cavalier seul : to go it alone>

cavalier[3] *nm* **1** : cavalryman **2** : knight (in chess)

cave[1] [kav] *adj* : hollow, sunken

cave[2] *nf* **1** : cellar **2 de la cave au grenier** : from top to bottom, high and low

caveau [kavo] *nm, pl* **caveaux 1** : small cellar **2** : burial vault

caverne [kavɛrn] *nf* GROTTE : cave, cavern

caverneux, -neuse [kavɛrnø, -nøz] *adj* : cavernous

caviar [kavjar] *nm* : caviar

cavité [kavite] *nf* : cavity

CD [sede] *nm* : CD (compact disc)

ce[1] [sə] (**cet** [sɛt] *before a vowel or mute h*), **cette** [sɛt] *adj, pl* **ces** [se] **1** : this, that, these, those <un de ces jours : one of these days> <cette fois-ci : this time> <cet homme-là : that man> <ces livres sur la table : those books on the table> **2** (*used for emphasis*) <cette idée! : what an idea!>

ce[2] (**c'** [s] *before a vowel*) *pron* **1** : it, that, these, those <c'est lui : it's him, that's him> <qui est-ce? : who is it?, who's that?> <ce sont mes amis : these are my friends, they are my friends> <c'est cela : that's right> **2 ce que, ce qui, ce dont** : what, which <il comprend ce que je lui dis : he understands what I'm telling him> <montrez-moi ce que vous avez fait : show me what you did> <ce dont on parle : what they're talking about> <il faut être patient, ce que je ne suis pas : you have to be patient, which I'm not> **3 ce faisant** : in so doing **4 pour ce faire** : to this end

ceci [səsi] *pron* **1** : this <écoutez ceci : listen to this> **2 à ceci près que** : except that

cécité [sesite] *nf* : blindness

céder [sede] {87} *vt* : to give up, to yield, to cede — *vi* : to give in

cédille [sedij] *nf* : cedilla

cédrat [sedra] *nm* : citron (fruit)

cèdre [sɛdr] *nm* : cedar

cégep [seʒɛp] **(collège d'enseignement général et professionnel)** *nm Can* : junior college

cégépien, -pienne [seʒepjɛ̃, -pjɛn] *n Can* : junior college student

ceindre [sɛ̃dr] {37} *vt* : to gird, to put on

ceinture [sɛ̃tyr] *nf* **1** : belt <ceinture de sauvetage : life belt> <ceinture de sécurité : safety belt> **2** : waist (in anatomy) **3** : waistband **4** : ring, belt, circle

ceinturer [sɛ̃tyre] *vt* ENTOURER : to surround

cela [səla] *pron* **1** : that <cela dit : that said> <malgré cela : in spite of that, nonetheless> **2** : it <cela ne fait rien : it doesn't matter>

célébration [selebrasjɔ̃] *nf* : celebration

célèbre [selɛbr] *adj* FAMEUX : famous

célébrer [selebre] {87} *vt* **1** : to celebrate **2** : to extol, to praise

célébrité [selebrite] *nf* **1** RENOMMÉE : fame, renown **2** : celebrity, famous person

celer [səle] {20} *vt* : to conceal

céleri [sɛlri] *nm* : celery

célérité [selerite] *nf* VITESSE : swiftness, speed

céleste [selɛst] *adj* : celestial, heavenly

célibat [seliba] *nm* **1** : unmarried life **2** : celibacy

célibataire[1] [selibatɛr] *adj* : single, unmarried

célibataire[2] *nmf* : single person, bachelor *m*, spinster *f*

celle, celles → **celui**

cellier [selje] *nm* : storeroom

cellophane [selɔfan] *nf* : cellophane

cellulaire [selylɛr] *adj* : cellular

cellule [selyl] *nf* : cell

cellulose [selyloz] *nf* : cellulose

Celsius [sɛlsjys] *adj s & pl* : Celsius

celte [sɛlt] *adj* : Celtic

Celte *nmf* : Celt

celtique [sɛltik] *adj* : Celtic

celui [səlɥi], **celle** [sɛl] *pron, pl* **ceux** [sø], **celles** [sɛl] **1** : the one(s), those <mon livre et celui de Jean : my book and John's> <les récipients en acier et ceux en plastique : steel containers and plastic ones> **2** : he, she, those <celui qui danse : he who dances> <ceux d'entre vous : those among you>

celui–ci [səlɥisi], **celle–ci** [sɛlsi] *pron, pl* **ceux–ci** [søsi], **celles–ci** [sɛlsi] **1** : this (one), these **2** : the latter **3** : one <celle-ci chante, celle-là joue de la guitare : one sings, another plays the guitar>

celui–là [səlɥila], **celle–là** [sɛlla] *pron, pl* **ceux–là** [søla], **celles–là** [sɛlla] **1** : that (one), those **2** : the former **3** : another <celui-ci fait la cuisine, celui-là fait la vaisselle : one cooks, another washes the dishes>

cénacle [senakl] *nm* : circle, (literary) club

cendre [sɑ̃dr] *nf* **1** : ashes *pl,* cinders *pl* **2 cendres** *nfpl* : ashes, remains (of the dead)

cendreux, -dreuse [sɑ̃drø, -drøz] *adj* **1** : ashen, pale **2** : ashy

cendrier [sɑ̃drije] *nm* : ashtray

cène [sɛn] *nf* **la Cène** : the Last Supper

cenellier [s(ə)nɛlje] *nm Can* : hawthorn (tree)
censé, -sée [sɑ̃se] *adj* : supposed <elle est censée arriver lundi : she is supposed to arrive on Monday>
censément [sɑ̃semɑ̃] *adv* : supposedly
censeur [sɑ̃sœr] *nm* **1** : censor **2** : critic
censure [sɑ̃syr] *nf* **1** : censorship **2** : censure
censurer [sɑ̃syre] *vt* **1** : to censor, to ban **2** : to censure
cent[1] [sɑ̃] *adj* : a hundred, one hundred <trois cents hommes : three hundred men>
cent[2] *nm* **1** : hundred <un cent de livres : one hundred books> **2** : cent, 1/100 of a dollar **3 pour ~** : percent
centaine [sɑ̃tɛn] *nf* : hundred <une centaine de chaises : about a hundred chairs> <des centaines de fleurs : hundreds of flowers>
centaure [sɑ̃tɔr] *nm* : centaur
centenaire[1] [sɑ̃tnɛr] *adj* : hundred-year-old
centenaire[2] *nm* : centennial
centenaire[3] *nmf* : centenarian
centième[1] [sɑ̃tjɛm] *adj & nmf & nm* : hundredth
centième[2] *nf* : hundredth performance
centigrade [sɑ̃tigrad] *adj* : centigrade, Celsius
centigramme [sɑ̃tigram] *nm* : centigram
centime [sɑ̃tim] *nm* : centime <il n'a pas un centime : he hasn't got a cent>
centimètre [sɑ̃timɛtr] *nm* **1** : centimeter **2** : tape measure
central[1], **-trale** [sɑ̃tral] *adj, mpl* **centraux** [sɑ̃tro] **1** : central **2** : main
central[2] *nm* **central téléphonique** : telephone exchange
centrale *nf* **1** : generating station <centrale électrique : electric power plant> **2** : confederation <centrales syndicales : labor unions>
centraliser [sɑ̃tralize] *vt* : to centralize — **centralisation** [-zasjɔ̃] *nf*
centraméricain, -caine [sɑ̃tramerikɛ̃, -kɛn] *adj* : Central American
Centraméricain, -caine *n* : Central American
centre [sɑ̃tr] *nm* **1** : center <centre de gravité : center of gravity> **2 centre commercial** : shopping center, shopping mall **3 centre communautaire** *Can* : community center **4 centre d'accueil** *Can* : nursing home **5 centres vitaux** : vital organs
centrer [sɑ̃tre] *vt* : to center
centre–ville [sɑ̃trəvil] *nm, pl* **centres–villes** : downtown
centrifuge [sɑ̃trifyʒ] *adj* : centrifugal
centripète [sɑ̃tripɛt] *adj* : centripetal
centuple [sɑ̃typl] *nm* **1 au ~** : a hundredfold **2 être le centuple de** : to be a hundred times (a number)
centupler [sɑ̃typle] *v* : to increase a hundredfold
cépage [sepaʒ] *nm* : vine
cependant [səpɑ̃dɑ̃] *conj* **1** : however, yet **2 cependant que** : while, whereas
céramique[1] [seramik] *adj* : ceramic
céramique[2] *nf* : ceramics
cerbère [sɛrbɛr] *nm* **1** : strict doorkeeper, watchdog **2** *Can* : goalkeeper, goalie
cerceau [sɛrso] *nm, pl* **cerceaux** : hoop
cercle [sɛrkl] *nm* **1** : circle <cercle vicieux : vicious circle> **2** : group, set (of friends, etc.) **3** : club **4** : range, scope **5** : hoop
cercueil [sɛrkœj] *nm* : coffin, casket
céréale [sereal] *nf* : cereal
céréalier, -lière [serealje, -ljɛr] *adj* : cereal
cérébral, -brale [serebral] *adj, mpl* **-braux** [-bro] : cerebral
cérémonial [seremɔnjal] *nm, pl* **-nials** : ceremonial
cérémonie [seremɔni] *nf* : ceremony
cérémoniel, -nielle [seremɔnjɛl] *adj* : ceremonial, ceremonious
cérémonieux, -nieuse [seremɔnjø, -njøz] *adj* : ceremonious, formal — **cérémonieusement** [-njøzmɑ̃] *adv*
cerf [sɛr] *nm* **1** : stag, red dear **2 cerf de Virginie** *Can* → **chevreuil**
cerf–volant [sɛrvɔlɑ̃] *nm* : kite <faire voler un cerf-volant : to fly a kite>
cerise[1] [səriz] *adj or* **rouge cerise** : cerise, cherry-colored
cerise[2] *nf* : cherry
cerisier [sərizje] *nm* : cherry tree
cerne [sɛrn] *nm* : ring <avoir des cernes : to have rings under one's eyes>
cerner [sɛrne] *vt* **1** : to surround **2** : to define, to determine
certain, -taine [sɛrtɛ̃, -tɛn] *adj* **1** : certain, sure, definite <c'est une chose certaine : there's no doubt about it> **2** : certain <une certaine aptitude : a certain aptitude, some aptitude> <dans un certain sens : in a way> <à certains moments : at certain times, sometimes>
certainement [sɛrtɛnmɑ̃] *adv* : certainly, surely
certains, certaines [sɛrtɛ̃, -tɛn] *pron pl* : some (people), certain (ones)
certes [sɛrt] *adv* : of course, indeed
certificat [sɛrtifika] *nm* : certificate <certificat de naissance : birth certificate>
certifier [sɛrtifje] {96} *vt* : to certify, to attest to, to notarize
certitude [sɛrtityd] *nf* : certainty, certitude
cérumen [serymɛn] *nm* : earwax
cerveau [sɛrvo] *nm, pl* **cerveaux 1** : brain, cerebrum **2** : mind, intellect
cervelet [sɛrvəlɛ] *nm* : cerebellum

cervelle [sɛrvɛl] *nf* **1** : brain (in anatomy) **2** : brains *pl* <se creuser la cervelle : to rack one's brains>

cervical, -cale [sɛrvikal] *adj, mpl* **-caux** [-ko] : cervical

ces → **ce**[1]

césarienne [sezarjɛn] *nf* : caesarean section

césium [sezjɔm] *nm* : cesium

cessation [sɛsasjɔ̃] *nf* : cessation, suspension

cesse [sɛs] *nf* **sans ~** : unceasingly, incessantly, constantly

cesser [sese] *v* : to cease, to stop

cessez-le-feu [seselfø] *nms & pl* : cease-fire

cession [sɛsjɔ̃] *nf* : transfer

c'est-à-dire [sɛtadir] *conj* **1** : that is (to say) **2 c'est-à-dire que** : which means (that) <il s'est endormi tard hier soir, c'est-à-dire qu'il sera fatigué aujourd'hui : he went to bed late last night, which means he'll be tired today>

cet, cette → **ce**

ceux → **celui**

ceux-ci → **celui-ci**

ceux-là → **celui-là**

chacal [ʃakal] *nm, pl* **chacals** : jackal

chacun, chacune [ʃakœ̃, -kyn] *pron* **1** : each (one) **2** : everybody, everyone <chacun pour soi : everybody for himself>

chagrin[1], **-grine** [ʃagrɛ̃, -grin] *adj* **1** : sorrowful, doleful **2** : peevish, ill-humored

chagrin[2] *nm* PEINE : grief, sorrow

chagriner [ʃagrine] *vt* **1** PEINER : to grieve, to distress **2** CONTRARIER : to annoy, to bother

chahut [ʃay] *nm* : uproar, racket, rumpus

chahuter [ʃayte] *vi* : to create an uproar — *vt* : to heckle

chaîne [ʃɛn] *nf* **1** : chain **2** : series, range <chaîne de montagnes : mountain range> <chaîne d'idées : train of thought> **3** : (television) channel **4** : audio system <chaîne hi-fi : hi-fi (system)> **5** : warp (in weaving)

chaînon [ʃɛnɔ̃] *nm* : link <chaînon manquant : missing link>

chair [ʃɛr] *nf* **1** : flesh **2** : meat **3 chair de poule** : goose bumps

chaire [ʃɛr] *nf* **1** : (university) chair **2** : pulpit

chaise [ʃɛz] *nf* **1** : chair, seat **2 chaise roulante** : wheelchair

chaland [ʃalɑ̃] *nm* : barge, scow

châle [ʃal] *nm* : shawl

chalet [ʃalɛ] *nm* **1** : chalet **2** *Can* : cottage

chaleur [ʃalœr] *nf* **1** : heat **2** : warmth, fervor

chaleureux, -reuse [ʃalœrø, -røz] *adj* : warm, cordial — **chaleureusement** [-røzmɑ̃] *adv*

challenge [ʃalɑ̃ʒ] *nm* **1** DÉFI : challenge **2** : tournament

chaloupe [ʃalup] *nf* **1** : launch <chaloupe de sauvetage : lifeboat> **2** : rowboat

chalumeau [ʃalymo] *nm, pl* **-meaux 1** : blowtorch **2** *Can* : tap (for collecting sap from a tree)

chalut [ʃaly] *nm* : trawl

chalutier [ʃalytje] *nm* : trawler

chamade [ʃamad] *nf* **battre la chamade** : to beat wildly, to pound

chamailler [ʃamaje] *v* **se chamailler** *vr* : to squabble, to bicker

chamarrer [ʃamare] *vt* : to adorn

chambardement [ʃɑ̃bardəmɑ̃] *nm fam* **1** : upheaval, shake-up **2** : mess

chambarder [ʃɑ̃barde] *vt fam* **1** : to mess up, to turn upside down **2** : to shake up

chambouler [ʃɑ̃bule] *vt fam* : to mess up, to turn upside down

chambranle [ʃɑ̃brɑ̃l] *nm* **1** : frame (of a door or window) **2** : mantelpiece

chambre [ʃɑ̃br] *nf* **1** : room, bedroom **2** : chamber (of a gun, etc.) **3** : (legislative) chamber, house **4 musique de chambre** : chamber music

chambrée [ʃɑ̃bre] *nf* : barracks

chambreur, -breuse [ʃɑ̃brœr, -brøz] *n Can* : roomer

chameau [ʃamo] *nm, pl* **chameaux** : camel

chamois[1] [ʃamwa] *adj s & pl* : buff(-colored)

chamois[2] *nms & pl* **1** : chamois (animal) **2** : buff (color)

champ [ʃɑ̃] *nm* **1** : field, land area <champ de maïs : cornfield> <champ de courses : racecourse, racetrack> <champ de bataille : battlefield> <petit champ : infield> **2** : area, domain <champ d'action : sphere of activity> **3** : field (in physics, physiology, mathematics) <champ magnétique : magnetic field> <champ visuel : visual field> **4 champs** *nmpl* : countryside, country **5** → **sur-le-champ**

champagne [ʃɑ̃paɲ] *nm* : champagne

champêtre [ʃɑ̃pɛtr] *adj* : rustic, rural

champignon [ʃɑ̃piɲɔ̃] *nm* : mushroom

champion[1], **-pionne** [ʃɑ̃pjɔ̃, -pjɔn] *adj fam* : great, terrific

champion[2], **-pionne** *n* : champion

championnat [ʃɑ̃pjɔna] *nm* : championship

champlure [ʃɑ̃plyr] *nf Can* : faucet

chance [ʃɑ̃s] *nf* **1** : luck, fortune <coup de chance : stroke of luck> <par chance : fortunately, luckily> **2** : chance, opportunity **3** : possibility, likelihood

chancelant, -lante [ʃɑ̃slɑ̃, -lɑ̃t] *adj* **1** : unsteady, groggy **2** : flagging, faltering

chanceler [ʃɑ̃sle] {8} *vi* **1** : to totter **2** : to waver, to falter

chancelier [ʃɑ̃səlje] *nm* : chancellor

chanceux, -ceuse [ʃɑ̃sø, -søz] *adj* : lucky, fortunate

chancre [ʃɑ̃kr] *nm* : chancre (in medicine)

chandail [ʃɑ̃daj] *nm* : sweater, pullover

chandelier [ʃɑ̃dəlje] *nm* **1** : candlestick **2** : candelabrum

chandelle [ʃɑ̃dɛl] *nf* : candle

change [ʃɑ̃ʒ] *nm* **1** : exchange, exchange rate **2 donner le change à qqn** : to throw s.o. off the trail

changeant, -geante [ʃɑ̃ʒɑ̃, -ʒɑ̃t] *adj* **1** : changing **2** : fickle, changeable

changement [ʃɑ̃ʒmɑ̃] *nm* **1** : change **2 changement de vitesse** : gears *pl* (of an automobile)

changer [ʃɑ̃ʒe] {17} *vt* **1** : to change, to exchange, to replace **2** : to alter, to transform — *vi* **1** : to undergo change **2 ~ de** : to change <changer d'avis : to change one's mind> <changer de vitesse : to change gears> — **se changer** *vr* **1** : to change (one's clothes) **2** : to be transformed

changeur, -geuse [ʃɑ̃ʒœr, -ʒøz] *n* : money changer

chanoine [ʃanwan] *nm* : canon (in religion)

chanson [ʃɑ̃sɔ̃] *nf* : song

chansonnette [ʃɑ̃sɔnɛt] *nf* : simple song, ditty

chansonnier, -nière [ʃɑ̃sɔnje, -njɛr] *n Can* : songwriter

chant [ʃɑ̃] *nm* **1** : song <chant de Noël : Christmas carol> **2** : singing **3** : canto, ode **4** : edge <de chant, sur chant : edgewise, on edge>

chantage [ʃɑ̃taʒ] *nm* : blackmail

chantant, -tante [ʃɑ̃tɑ̃, -tɑ̃t] *adj* **1** : singsong, lilting **2** : tuneful, catchy

chanter [ʃɑ̃te] *vt* **1** : to sing **2** : to relate, to tell of — *vi* **1** : to sing **2** : to chirp, to crow **3 ~ à** *fam* : to appeal to, to catch the fancy of **4 faire chanter** : to blackmail

chanteur, -teuse [ʃɑ̃tœr, -tøz] *n* : singer

chantier [ʃɑ̃tje] *nm* **1** : (construction) site **2** : depot, yard <chantier naval : shipyard> **3 mettre en chantier** : to start work on, to undertake

chantonner [ʃɑ̃tɔne] *v* : to croon, to hum

chantre [ʃɑ̃tr] *nm* : cantor

chanvre [ʃɑ̃vr] *nm* : hemp

chaos [kao] *nm* : chaos

chaotique [kaɔtik] *adj* : chaotic

chaparder [ʃaparde] *vt fam* PIQUER : to pilfer, to swipe

chapeau [ʃapo] *nm, pl* **chapeaux 1** : hat, cap <tirer son chapeau à : to take one's hat off to> **2 chapeau!** : well done!

chapeauter [ʃapote] *vt* : to head, to lead

chapelain [ʃaplɛ̃] *nm* : chaplain

chapelet [ʃaplɛ] *nm* **1** : rosary **2** : series, string <un chapelet d'îlots : a chain of small islands>

chapelier, -lière [ʃapəlje, -ljɛr] *n* : hatter

chapelle [ʃapɛl] *nf* : chapel

chapelure [ʃaplyr] *nf* : bread crumbs *pl*

chaperon [ʃaprɔ̃] *nm* : chaperon, chaperone

chaperonner [ʃaprɔne] *vt* : to chaperon

chapiteau [ʃapito] *nm, pl* **-teaux 1** : capital (of a column) **2** : big top, circus tent

chapitre [ʃapitr] *nm* **1** : chapter (of a book) **2** : topic, subject matter **3** : item, heading (in a budget)

chapon [ʃapɔ̃] *nm* : capon

chaque [ʃak] *adj* : each, every <chaque personne : each person, everyone> <cent dollars chaque : a hundred dollars each>

char [ʃar] *nm* **1** : cart, wagon **2** : chariot **3** *Can fam* : car **4** *or* **char d'assaut** : tank

charabia [ʃarabja] *nm fam* : gibberish, gobbledegook

charade [ʃarad] *nf* **1** : riddle **2** : charades (game)

charançon [ʃarɑ̃sɔ̃] *nm* : weevil

charbon [ʃarbɔ̃] *nm* **1** : coal **2** : smut (of grains) **3 charbon ardent** : ember **4 charbon de bois** : charcoal

charcuterie [ʃarkytri] *nf* **1** : delicatessen, pork butcher's shop **2** : cooked pork products

charcutier, -tière [ʃarkytje, -tjɛr] *n* : pork butcher

chardon [ʃardɔ̃] *nm* : thistle

chardonneret [ʃardɔnrɛ] *nm* : goldfinch

charge [ʃarʒ] *nf* **1** : load, weight <charge limite : maximum load> **2** : responsibility, job <à charge de : dependent on> <charge de travail : workload> **3** : office <charge élective : elective office> **4** : charge (of explosives or electricity) **5** : assault, (military) charge **6** : cost, expense <charges de l'état : government expenditures> **7** : accusation, indictment **8** : emotional burden **9** : caricature

chargé[1], -gée [ʃarʒe] *adj* **1** : full, loaded, heavy **2** : busy, full

chargé[2], -gée *n* **1 chargé d'affaires** : chargé d'affaires **2 chargé de cours** : (university) lecturer

chargement [ʃarʒəmɑ̃] *nm* **1** : loading **2** : load, cargo

charger [ʃarʒe] {17} *vt* **1** : to load, to fill (up), to overload **2** : to load (a gun, etc.), to charge (with electricity) **3** : to charge at, to attack **4 ~ de** : to put in charge of, to give responsibility for, to command — *vi* : to charge, to attack — **se charger** *vr* **~ de** : to take responsibility for

chargeur [ʃarʒœr] *nm* **1** : magazine, clip (of a firearm) **2** : shipper, shipping agent

chariot [ʃarjo] *nm* **1** : cart, wagon <chariot de supermarché : shopping cart> **2** : truck <chariot élévateur : forklift truck> **3** : carriage (of a typewriter)

charisme [karism] *nm* : charisma — **charismatique** [-rismatik] *adj*

charitable [ʃaritabl] *adj* : charitable — **charitablement** [-bləmɑ̃] *adv*

charité [ʃarite] *nf* : charity

charivari [ʃarivari] *nm* : racket, hullabaloo

charlatan [ʃarlatɑ̃] *nm* : charlatan, quack

charmant, -mante [ʃarmɑ̃, -mɑ̃t] *adj* : charming, delightful

charme [ʃarm] *nm* **1** : charm, attraction **2** : spell

charmer [ʃarme] *vt* : to charm

charmeur[1], **-meuse** [ʃarmœr, -møz] *adj* : charming

charmeur[2], **-meuse** *n* : charmer

charnel, -nelle [ʃarnɛl] *adj* : carnal

charnier [ʃarnje] *nm* : mass grave

charnière[1] [ʃarnjɛr] *adj* : transitional, pivotal

charnière[2] *nf* **1** : hinge **2** : turning point

charnu, -nue [ʃarny] *adj* : fleshy, plump

charognard [ʃarɔɲar] *nm* : scavenger (animal)

charogne [ʃarɔɲ] *nf* **1** : carrion **2** *fam* : bastard

charpente [ʃarpɑ̃t] *nf* **1** : framework, structure **2** : frame, build (of the body)

charpenté, -tée [ʃarpɑ̃te] *adj* : built, constructed

charpenterie [ʃarpɑ̃tri] *nf* : carpentry

charpentier [ʃarpɑ̃tje] *nm* : carpenter

charpie [ʃarpi] *nf* **1** : lint **2 en ∼** : in shreds

charrette [ʃarɛt] *nf* : cart <charrette à bras : pushcart>

charrier [ʃarje] {96} *vt* **1** : to cart, to carry along **2** *fam* : to poke fun at — *vi* : to exaggerate, to go too far

charrue [ʃary] *nf* : plow

charte [ʃart] *nf* : charter

charter [ʃarte] *nm* **1** : charter flight **2** : chartered plane

chas [ʃa] *nm* : eye (of a needle)

chasse [ʃas] *nf* **1** : hunting <aller à la chasse : to go hunting> **2** POURSUITE : chase <donner chasse à : to chase> <chasse à l'homme : manhunt> **3** *or* **chasse d'eau** : flush (of a toilet) <actionner la chasse d'eau : to flush the toilet>

chassé–croisé [ʃasekrwaze] *nm, pl* **chassés–croisés** : coming and going, moving back and forth

chasse–neige [ʃasnɛʒ] *nms & pl* : snowplow

chasser [ʃase] *vt* **1** : to hunt, to chase **2** : to chase away, to drive away **3** : to dispel — *vi* **1** : to go hunting, to hunt **2** : to skid

chasseur[1], **-seuse** [ʃasœr, -søz] *n* **1** : hunter **2 chasseur de têtes** : headhunter

chasseur[2] *nm* **1** : fighter <chasseur-bombardier : fighter-bomber> **2** : bellhop, bellboy

châssis [ʃasi] *nm* **1** : frame (of a window, etc.) **2** : chassis

chaste [ʃast] *adj* : chaste — **chastement** [ʃastmɑ̃] *adv*

chasteté [ʃastəte] *nf* : chastity

chasuble [ʃazybl] *nf or* **robe chasuble** : pinafore (dress)

chat, chatte [ʃa, ʃat] *n* **1** : cat **2 chat sauvage** : wildcat **3 chat sauvage** *Can* : raccoon

châtaigne [ʃatɛɲ] *nf* : chestnut

châtaignier [ʃateɲe] *nm* : chestnut tree

châtain [ʃatɛ̃] *adj* : chestnut brown

château [ʃato] *nm, pl* **châteaux 1** : castle **2 château fort** : fortified castle, stronghold

châtier [ʃatje] {96} *vt* **1** : to chastise, to punish **2** : to polish, to refine (style, etc.)

châtiment [ʃatimɑ̃] *nm* PUNITION : punishment

chaton [ʃatɔ̃] *nm* **1** : kitten **2** : catkin (in botany) **3** : setting (of a ring)

chatouillement [ʃatujmɑ̃] *nm* : tickle, tickling

chatouiller [ʃatuje] *vt* **1** : to tickle **2** : to titillate (the senses), to pique (curiosity, pride, etc.)

chatouilleux, -leuse [ʃatujø, -jøz] *adj* **1** : ticklish **2** : sensitive, touchy

chatoyant, -yante [ʃatwajɑ̃, -jɑ̃t] *adj* : iridescent, shimmering

chatoyer [ʃatwaje] {58} *vi* : to shimmer

châtrer [ʃatre] *vt* : to castrate, to neuter

chaud[1] [ʃo] *adv* **1 avoir chaud** : to feel warm, to feel hot **2 boire chaud** : to drink something hot **3 il fait chaud** : it's warm, it's hot **4 manger chaud** : to eat hot food

chaud[2], **chaude** [ʃo, ʃod] *adj* **1** : warm, hot **2** : enthusiastic, keen **3** : heated, tense

chaud[3] *nm* : heat, warmth

chaudement [ʃodmɑ̃] *adv* **1** : warmly **2** : heartily

chaudière [ʃodjɛr] *nf* : boiler

chaudron [ʃodrɔ̃] *nm* : cauldron

chauffage [ʃofaʒ] *nm* : heating <chauffage central : central heating>

chauffard [ʃofar] *nm* : reckless driver

chauffe–eau [ʃofo] *nms & pl* : water heater

chauffer [ʃofe] *vt* : to heat, to warm — *vi* : to become warm, to warm up — **se chauffer** *vr*

chaufferette [ʃofrɛt] *nf Can* **1** : space heater **2** : heater (in a car)

chaufferie [ʃofri] *nf* : boiler room

chauffeur [ʃofœr] *nm* **1** CONDUCTEUR : driver **2** : chauffeur **3** : stoker, fireman

chaume [ʃom] *nm* **1** : thatch **2** : stubble (of grain)

chaumière [ʃomjɛr] *nf* : (thatched) cottage

chaussée [ʃose] *nf* : roadway, causeway

chausser [ʃose] *vt* **1** : to put on (boots, skis, etc.) **2** : to put shoes on (s.o.) **3** : to fit (with shoes) — *vi* **~ de** : to take (a shoe size) — **se chausser** *vr* : to put on shoes

chausse–trape *or* **chausse–trappe** [ʃostrap] *nf* : trap, pitfall

chaussette [ʃosɛt] *nf* : sock

chausseur [ʃosœr] *nm* : shoemaker

chausson [ʃosɔ̃] *nm* **1** : slipper **2** : turnover <chausson aux pommes : apple turnover>

chaussure [ʃosyr] *nf* **1** : shoe **2** : footwear industry

chauve [ʃov] *adj* : bald

chauve–souris [ʃovsuri] *nf, pl* **chauves–souris** : bat (animal)

chauvin[1], -vine [ʃovɛ̃, -vin] *adj* : chauvinistic — **chauvinisme** [ʃovinism] *nm*

chauvin[2], -vine *n* : chauvinist

chaux [ʃo] *nf* **1** : lime **2 lait de chaux** : whitewash

chavirer [ʃavire] *vt* **1** CAPOTER : to capsize, to overturn, to keel over **2** ÉMOUVOIR : to upset, to overwhelm — *vi* : to capsize

cheddar [ʃedar] *nm* : cheddar

chef [ʃɛf] *nm* **1** : leader, boss, head **2** *or* **chef cuisinier** : chef **3 au premier chef** : above all, primarily **4 chef d'accusation** : charge, count (in law) **5 chef d'orchestre** : conductor **6 en chef** : chief, head

chef–d'oeuvre [ʃɛdœvr] *nm, pl* **chefs–d'oeuvre** : masterpiece

chefferie [ʃɛfri] *nf Can* : leadership (of a political party)

cheikh *or* **cheik** [ʃɛk] *nm* : sheikh

chemin [ʃəmɛ̃] *nm* **1** : way, road, path **2 chemin de fer** : railroad

cheminée [ʃəmine] *nf* **1** : fireplace **2** : chimney **3** : mantel, mantelpiece

cheminement [ʃəminmɑ̃] *nm* **1** AVANCE : advance, progress **2** : development

cheminer [ʃəmine] *vi* **1** : to walk along **2** : to advance, to progress

cheminot [ʃəmino] *nm* : railroad worker, railroader

chemise [ʃəmiz] *nf* **1** : shirt **2** : folder **3 chemise de nuit** : nightgown

chemisier [ʃəmizje] *nm* CORSAGE : blouse

chenal [ʃənal] *nm, pl* **chenaux** [ʃəno] : channel (in a river, harbor, etc.)

chêne [ʃɛn] *nm* : oak

chéneau [ʃeno] *nm, pl* **chéneaux** : gutter (of a roof)

chenet [ʃənɛ] *nm* : andiron

chenil [ʃənil] *nm* : kennel

chenille [ʃənij] *nf* **1** : caterpillar **2** : chenille (fabric)

chenu, -nue [ʃəny] *adj* : white-haired, hoary

cheptel [ʃɛptɛl] *nm* : livestock

chèque [ʃɛk] *nm* : check <chèque en blanc : blank check> <chèque de voyage : traveler's check>

chèque–cadeau [ʃɛkkado] *nm, pl* **chèques–cadeaux** : gift certificate

cher[1] [ʃɛr] *adv* **1 coûter cher** : to cost a lot **2 payer cher** : to pay dearly

cher[2], chère [ʃɛr] *adj* **1** : dear, beloved **2** COÛTEUX : expensive

cher[3], chère *n* : dear <ma chère : my dear>

chercher [ʃɛrʃe] *vt* **1** : to look for, to seek **2 chercher à faire** : to try to do **3 aller chercher** : to go and get

chercheur[1], -cheuse [ʃɛrʃœr, -ʃøz] *adj* : inquiring

chercheur[2], -cheuse *n* : researcher

chercheur[3] *nm* : finder (of a telescope, etc.)

chère [ʃɛr] *nf* : food, fare

chèrement *adv* [ʃɛrmɑ̃] : dearly, at great cost

chéri, -rie [ʃeri] *adj & n* : darling, dear

chérir [ʃerir] *vt* : to cherish

cherté [ʃɛrte] *nf* : expensiveness, high cost

chérubin [ʃerybɛ̃] *nm* : cherub

chétif, -tive [ʃetif, -tiv] *adj* **1** : sickly, weak **2** MALINGRE : puny

cheval [ʃəval] *nm, pl* **chevaux** [ʃəvo] **1** : horse <à cheval : on horseback> **2** *or* **cheval–vapeur** : horsepower

chevaleresque [ʃəvalrɛsk] *adj* : chivalrous, knightly

chevalerie [ʃəvalri] *nf* **1** : chivalry **2** : knighthood

chevalet [ʃəvalɛ] *nm* **1** : easel **2** : rack (instrument of torture) **3** : stand, trestle, sawhorse

chevalier [ʃəvalje] *nm* : knight

chevalin, -line [ʃəvalɛ̃, -lin] *adj* **1** : equine **2** : horsey

cheval–vapeur [ʃəvalvapœr] *nm, pl* **chevaux–vapeur** → **cheval**

chevauchée [ʃəvoʃe] *nf* : ride

chevauchement [ʃəvoʃmɑ̃] *nm* : overlap

chevaucher [ʃəvoʃe] *vt* **1** : to straddle **2** : to overlap — *vi* : to overlap

chevelu, -lue [ʃəvly] *adj* : hairy

chevelure [ʃəvlyr] *nf* CHEVEUX : hair

chevet [ʃəvɛ] *nm* : bedside, head (of a bed) <rester au chevet de qqn : to stay at s.o.'s bedside>

cheveu [ʃəvø] *nm, pl* **cheveux 1** POIL : hair <être à un cheveu de : to be within a hair's breadth of> **2 cheveux** *nmpl* : hair, head of hair

cheville [ʃəvij] *nf* **1** : ankle **2** : pin, peg **3 cheville ouvrière** : kingpin

chèvre [ʃɛvr] *nf* : goat

chevreau [ʃəvro] *nm, pl* **chevreaux** : kid, young goat (male)

chèvrefeuille [ʃɛvrəfœj] *nm* : honeysuckle

chevrette [ʃəvrɛt] *nf* : kid, young goat (female)
chevreuil [ʃəvrœj] *nm* **1** : roe deer **2** : venison **3** *Can* : white-tailed deer
chevron [ʃəvrɔ̃] *nm* **1** : rafter **2** : chevron
chevronné, -née [ʃəvrɔne] *adj* : seasoned, experienced
chevrotement [ʃəvrɔtmɑ̃] *nm* : quavering
chevroter [ʃəvrɔte] *vi* : to quaver
chevrotine [ʃəvrɔtin] *nf* : buckshot
chewing–gum [ʃwiŋgɔm] *nm France* : chewing gum
chez [ʃe] *prep* **1** : at the home, business, or practice of <chez elle : at her house> <chez le dentiste : at the dentist's office> **2** : among, in <chez les Suisses : among the Swiss> <chez les Québécois : in Quebec> **3** : in the works of <chez Victor Hugo : in Victor Hugo's writing> **4** : in (a person) <le meilleur trait chez lui, c'est sa gentillesse : his best trait is his kindness>
chez–soi [ʃeswa] *nm* : place of one's own, home
chialer [ʃiale] *vi* **1** *fam* : to blubber, to snivel **2** *Can fam* : to whine, to complain
chic[1] [ʃik] *adj s & pl* **1** : chic, stylish **2** : nice
chic[2] *nm* **1** : stylishness, elegance **2 avoir le chic pour** : to have a knack for
chicane [ʃikan] *nf* : bickering, squabble, quibble
chicaner [ʃikane] *vt* : to quibble with — *vi* : to bicker, to squabble <chicaner sur : to quibble over>
chiche [ʃiʃ] *adj* **1** AVARE : stingy, mean **2** : meager, scanty — **chichement** [ʃiʃmɑ̃] *adv*
chichi [ʃiʃi] *nm fam* **1** : affectation, airs **2 faire des chichis** : to make a fuss
chicorée [ʃikɔre] *nf* **1** : endive **2** : chicory (for coffee)
chicoter [ʃikɔte] *vt Can fam* : to worry, to bother
chien[1], **chienne** [ʃjɛ̃, -ʃjɛn] *n* **1** : dog, bitch *f* **2 chien d'arrêt** : bird dog, pointer, retriever **3 chien de berger** : sheepdog **4 chien de chasse** : retriever, hunting dog **5 chien courant** : hound **6 chien esquimau** : husky **7 chien de garde** : watchdog **8 chien de meute** : hound **9 chien de prairie** : prairie dog
chien[2] *nm* : hammer (of a firearm)
chien–loup [ʃjɛ̃lu] *nm, pl* **chiens–loups** : German shepherd
chiffe [ʃif] *nf* : spineless person
chiffon [ʃifɔ̃] *nm* : rag, dustcloth
chiffonner [ʃifɔne] *vt* **1** : to crease, to crumple **2** : to bother
chiffre [ʃifr] *nm* **1** : numeral <chiffre romain : Roman numeral> **2** : amount, sum <chiffre d'affaires : turnover> **3** : cipher, code **4** : monogram
chiffrer [ʃifre] *vt* **1** : to number (pages, etc.) **2** : to calculate, to assess **3** : to encode **4** : to mark, to monogram — *vi* **se chiffrer** *vr* ~ **à** : to amount to
chignon [ʃiɲɔ̃] *nm* : chignon, (hair) bun
chilien, -lienne [ʃiljɛ̃, -jɛn] *adj* : Chilean
Chilien, -lienne *n* : Chilean
chimère [ʃimɛr] *nf* **1** : Chimera (in mythology) **2** : illusion, pipe dream
chimérique [ʃimerik] *adj* : illusory, fanciful
chimie [ʃimi] *nf* : chemistry
chimique [ʃimik] *adj* : chemical — **chimiquement** [-mikmɑ̃] *adv*
chimiste [ʃimist] *nmf* : chemist
chimpanzé [ʃɛ̃pɑ̃ze] *nm* : chimpanzee
chinchilla [ʃɛ̃ʃila] *nm* : chinchilla
chine [ʃin] *nm* **1** : china, porcelain ware **2** : rice paper
chinois[1], **-noise** [ʃinwa, -nwaz] *adj* : Chinese
chinois[2] *nm* : Chinese (language)
Chinois, -noise *n* : Chinese
chinoiserie [ʃinwazri] *nf* **1** : chinoiserie, Chinese curio **2 chinoiseries administratives** : red tape
chintz [ʃints] *nm* : chintz
chiot [ʃjo] *nm* : puppy
chiper [ʃipe] *vt fam* : to pinch, to swipe
chipie [ʃipi] *nf* : shrew, vixen
chipoter [ʃipɔte] *vi* **1** : to haggle, to quibble **2** : to pick at one's food
chips [ʃips] *nfpl* : potato chips
chiquenaude [ʃiknod] *nf* : flick (with the finger)
chiquer [ʃike] *vt* : to chew (tobacco) — *vi* : to chew tobacco
chiropraticien, -cienne [kirɔpratisjɛ̃, -sjɛn] *n* : chiropractor
chiropratique [kiropratik] *nf Can* : chiropractic
chiropraxie *or* **chiropractie** *nf* : chiropractic
chirurgical, -cale [ʃiryrʒikal] *adj, mpl* **-caux** [-ko] : surgical
chirurgie [ʃiryrʒi] *nf* : surgery <chirurgie plastique *or* chirurgie esthétique : plastic surgery>
chirurgien, -gienne [ʃiryrʒjɛ̃, -ʒjɛn] *n* : surgeon
chirurgien–dentiste [ʃiryrʒjɛ̃dɑ̃tist] *nm, pl* **chirurgiens–dentistes** : oral surgeon
chlore [klɔr] *nm* : chlorine
chloroforme [klɔrɔfɔrm] *nm* : chloroform
chloroformer [klɔrɔfɔrme] *vt* : to chloroform
chlorophylle [klɔrɔfil] *nf* : chlorophyll
chlorure [klɔryr] *nm* : chloride
choc [ʃɔk] *nm* **1** : shock **2** : impact, crash **3** : clash (of opinions, etc.)
chocolat [ʃɔkɔla] *nm* : chocolate
chœur [kœr] *nm* **1** : choir **2** : chorus (song)

choir [ʃwar] {18} *vi* : to drop, to fall

choisi [ʃwazi] *adj* **1** : selected **2** : select, choice

choisir [ʃwazir] *vt* : to choose, to select

choix [ʃwa] *nm* **1** : choice, selection **2 de (premier) choix** : select, choice, first-rate

choléra [kɔlera] *nm* : cholera

cholestérol [kɔlɛsterɔl] *nm* : cholesterol

chômage [ʃomaʒ] *nm* : unemployment

chômer [ʃome] *vi* : to be unemployed, to be idle

chômeur, -meuse [ʃomœr, -møz] *n* : unemployed person

chope [ʃop] *nf* : (beer) mug, tankard

choquant, -quante [ʃɔkɑ̃, -kɑ̃t] *adj* : shocking

choquer [ʃɔke] *vt* **1** HEURTER : to knock, to bump **2** OFFUSQUER : to shock, to offend **3** : to shake up, to devastate — **se choquer** *vr* **1** : to be shocked **2** *Can* : to get angry

choral[1], -rale [kɔral] *adj, mpl* **chorals** or **choraux** [kɔro] : choral

choral[2] *nm, pl* **chorals** : chorale

chorale *nf* : choir

chorégraphe [kɔregraf] *nmf* : choreographer — **chorégraphique** [-grafik] *adj*

chorégraphie [kɔregrafi] *nf* : choreography — **chorégraphier** [-grafie] *vt*

choriste [kɔrist] *n* : choir member, chorus member

chose[1] [ʃoz] *adj fam* : peculiar, funny <se sentir tout chose : to feel out of sorts>

chose[2] *nf* **1** : thing <choses à faire : things to do> **2** : matter, affair <avant toute chose : above all, before all else>

chose[3] *nm fam* **1** : thingamajig **2** : what's-his-name, what's-her-name

chou[1] [ʃu] *adj fam* : sweet, nice, cute

chou[2], choute *n fam* : darling, dear

chou[3] *nm, pl* **choux 1** : cabbage **2 chou frisé** : kale

chouchou, -choute [ʃuʃu, -ʃut] *n fam* : pet, favorite <chouchou du prof : teacher's pet>

choucroute [ʃukrut] *nf* : sauerkraut

chouette[1] [ʃwɛt] *adj fam* : great, terrific, neat

chouette[2] *nf* **1** : owl **2** *fam* : goody, neat thing **3 ma chouette** *Can* : sweetheart, darling

chou–fleur [ʃuflœr] *nm, pl* **choux–fleurs** : cauliflower

chou–rave [ʃurav] *nm* : kohlrabi

chow–chow [ʃoʃo] *nm, pl* **chows–chows** : chow (dog)

choyer [ʃwaje] {58} *vt* : to pamper, to coddle

chrétien, -tienne [kretjɛ̃, -tjɛn] *adj & n* : Christian

chrétienté [kretjɛ̃te] *nf* : Christendom

christianisme [kristjanism] *nm* : Christianity

chromatique [krɔmatik] *adj* : chromatic

chrome [krom] *nm* **1** : chromium **2 chromes** *nmpl* : chrome (of an automobile)

chromé, -mée [krome] *adj* : chrome-plated

chromosome [krɔmɔzom] *nm* : chromosome

chronique[1] [krɔnik] *adj* : chronic

chronique[2] *nf* **1** : chronicle **2** : column (in a newspaper), report (in radio or television)

chroniqueur, -queuse [krɔnikœr, -køz] *n* **1** : chronicler **2** : columnist, commentator

chronologie [krɔnɔlɔʒi] *nf* : chronology

chronologique [krɔnɔlɔʒik] *adj* : chronological — **chronologiquement** [-ʒikmɑ̃] *adv*

chronomètre [krɔnɔmɛtr] *nm* **1** : chronometer **2** : stopwatch

chronométrer [krɔnɔmetre] {87} *vt* : to time

chronométreur, -treuse [krɔnɔmetrœr, -trøz] *n* : timekeeper

chrysalide [krizalid] *nf* : chrysalis

chrysanthème [krizɑ̃tɛm] *nm* : chrysanthemum

chu [ʃy] *pp* → **choir**

chuchotement [ʃyʃɔtmɑ̃] *nm* : whisper, murmur

chuchoter [ʃyʃɔte] *v* : to whisper, to murmur

chuintement [ʃɥɛ̃tmɑ̃] *nm* : hiss

chuinter [ʃɥɛ̃te] *vi* **1** : to hoot **2** : to hiss

chum[1] [tʃɔm] *nmf Can fam* : friend, pal

chum[2] *nm Can fam* : boyfriend

chut [ʃyt] *interj* : sh!, hush!

chute [ʃyt] *nf* **1** : fall <faire une chute : to take a fall> <chute de cheveux : hair loss> <chute du jour : nightfall> <chute de neige : snowfall> <chute de pluie : rainfall> **2** *or* **chute d'eau** CASCADE : waterfall **3 chute des reins** : small of the back

chuter [ʃyte] *vi fam* **1** : to fall down **2** : to fail, to flop

chypriote [ʃiprijɔt] *adj* : Cypriot

Chypriote *nmf* : Cypriot

ci[1] [si] *adv* **1** (*used with* **ce, cette, ces, celui, celle, ceux**) <ce livre-ci : this book> <ceux-ci : these ones> **2** : here <par-ci par-là : here and there>

ci[2] *pron* **1** : this <ci et ça : this and that> **2** → **comme**

ci–après [siaprɛ] *adv* : below, hereafter, herein

ci–bas [siba] *adv* : below

cible [sibl] *nf* : target, mark

cibler [sible] *vt* : to target

ciboule [sibul] *nf* : scallion

ciboulette [sibulɛt] *nf* : chive

cicatrice [sikatris] *nf* : scar

cicatriser [sikatrize] *v* : to heal, to scar over — **se cicatriser** *vr* : to scar

ci–contre [sikɔ̃tr] *adv* : opposite

ci–dessous [sidəsu] *adv* : below <voir ci-dessous : see below>
ci–dessus [sidəsy] *adv* : above <voir ci-dessus : see above>
ci–devant [sidəvɑ̃] *adv* : formerly, previously
cidre [sidr] *nm* : cider
cidrerie [sidrəri] *nf* **1** : cider house **2** : cidermaking
ciel [sjɛl] *nm* **1** *pl* **ciels** : sky (in meteorology) **2** *pl* **cieux** [sjø] : sky <à ciel ouvert : open-air> **3** *pl* **cieux** : heaven **4 en plein ciel** : midair
cierge [sjɛrʒ] *nm* : candle (in a church) **2 cierge magique** : sparkler
cigale [sigal] *nf* : cicada
cigare [sigar] *nm* : cigar
cigarette [sigarɛt] *nf* : cigarette
ci–gît [siʒi] *adv* : here lies
cigogne [sigɔɲ] *nf* : stork
ciguë [sigy] *nf* : hemlock (plant)
ci–inclus[1] [siɛ̃kly] *adv* : enclosed
ci–inclus[2], **-cluse** [siɛ̃kly, -klyz] *adj* : enclosed, included
ci–joint[1] [siʒwɛ̃] *adv* : enclosed, attached
ci–joint[2], **-jointe** [siʒwɛ̃, -ʒwɛ̃t] *adj* : enclosed, attached
cil [sil] *nm* : eyelash
ciller [sije] *vi* : to blink
cime [sim] *nf* SOMMET : summit, top, peak
ciment [simɑ̃] *nm* : cement
cimenter [simɑ̃te] *vt* : to cement
cimetière [simtjɛr] *nm* **1** : cemetery, graveyard **2** : churchyard
cinéaste [sineast] *nmf* : film director, filmmaker
cinéma [sinema] *nm* **1** : movie theater <aller au cinéma : to go to the movies> **2** : cinema, filmmaking
cinémathèque [sinematɛk] *nf* : film library
cinématographie [sinematɔgrafi] *nf* : cinematography
cinématographique [sinematɔgrafik] *adj* : film, movie, cinematic <œuvres cinématographiques : films, movies>
ciné–parc [sinepark] *nm Can, pl* **ciné–parcs** : drive-in theater
cinéphile [sinefil] *nmf* : movie buff
cinglant, -glante [sɛ̃glɑ̃, -glɑ̃t] *adj* : cutting, biting, scathing
cinglé, -glée [sɛ̃gle] *adj fam* : crazy, nuts
cingler [sɛ̃gle] *vt* : to whip, to lash — *vi* **~ vers** : to head for
cinq[1] [sɛ̃k] *adj* **1** : five **2** : fifth <le cinq juin : the fifth of June>
cinq[2] *nms & pl* : five
cinquantaine [sɛ̃kɑ̃tɛn] *nf* **une cinquantaine de** : about fifty
cinquante [sɛ̃kɑ̃t] *adj & nms & pl* : fifty
cinquantenaire [sɛ̃kɑ̃tnɛr] *nm* : fiftieth anniversary
cinquantième [sɛ̃kɑ̃tjɛm] *adj & nmf & nm* : fiftieth
cinquième[1] [sɛ̃kjɛm] *adj & nmf* : fifth
cinquième[2] *nm* **1** : fifth floor **2** : fifth (in mathematics)
cintre [sɛ̃tr] *nm* **1** : curve, bend **2** : arch <arc en plein cintre : semicircular arch> **3** : coat hanger
cintré, -trée [sɛ̃tre] *adj* **1** : arched, vaulted **2** : fitted, tailored
cirage [siraʒ] *nm* **1** : waxing, polishing **2** : shoe polish **3 être dans le cirage** *fam* : to be in a daze
circoncire [sirkɔ̃sir] {86} *vt* : to circumcise
circoncision [sirkɔ̃sizjɔ̃] *nf* : circumcision
circonférence [sirkɔ̃ferɑ̃s] *nf* : circumference
circonflexe [sirkɔ̃flɛks] *adj* **accent circonflexe** : circumflex (accent)
circonlocution [sirkɔ̃lɔkysjɔ̃] *nf* : circumlocution
circonscription [sirkɔ̃skripsjɔ̃] *nf* : district, ward <circonscription électorale : electoral district>
circonscrire [sirkɔ̃skrir] {33} *vt* **1** DÉLIMITER : to define, to mark out **2** : to contain (a fire, etc.)
circonspect, -specte [sirkɔ̃spɛ, -spɛkt] *adj* : circumspect, cautious, wary
circonspection [sirkɔ̃spɛksjɔ̃] *nf* : circumspection, caution
circonstance [sirkɔ̃stɑ̃s] *nf* : circumstance <circonstances atténuantes : mitigating circumstances> <être de circonstance : to be fitting>
circonstancié, -ciée [sirkɔ̃stɑ̃sje] *adj* : detailed
circonstanciel, -cielle [sirkɔ̃stɑ̃sjɛl] *adj* **complément circonstanciel** : adverbial phrase
circonvenir [sirkɔ̃vnir] {92} *vt* : to circumvent
circuit [sirkɥi] *nm* **1** : circuit <circuit intégré : integrated circuit> **2** : tour, trip **3** *or* **coup de circuit** *Can* : home run (in baseball)
circulaire [sirkylɛr] *adj & nf* : circular
circulation [sirkylasjɔ̃] *nf* **1** : circulation **2** : traffic
circulatoire [sirkylatwar] *adj* : circulatory
circuler [sirkyle] *vi* **1** : to circulate (of air, blood, etc.) **2** : to move along, to get around **3** : to run (of buses, etc.) **4 faire circuler** : to circulate, to spread (rumors, etc.)
cire [sir] *nf* **1** : wax **2 cire d'abeille** : beeswax
ciré [sire] *nm* : oilskin
cirer [sire] *vt* : to wax, to polish
cireux, -reuse [sirø, -røz] *adj* **1** : waxen, pale **2** : waxy
cirque [sirk] *nm* **1** : circus **2** *fam* : disorder, shambles
cirrhose [siroz] *nf* : cirrhosis
cirrus [sirys] *nms & pl* : cirrus
cisailler [sizaje] *vt* **1** : to cut, to snip **2** : to prune
cisailles [sizaj] *nfpl* : shears

ciseau [sizo] *nm, pl* **ciseaux 1** : chisel **2 ciseaux** *nmpl* : scissors
ciseler [sizle] {20} *vt* : to engrave, to carve
ciselure [sizlyr] *nf* **1** : engraving **2** : carving
citadelle [sitadɛl] *nf* : citadel, stronghold
citadin, -dine [sitadɛ̃, -din] *n* : city dweller
citation [sitasjɔ̃] *nf* **1** : citation, quotation **2** : summons (to court), subpoena **3** : (military) citation
cité [site] *nf* **1** : city **2 cité universitaire** *France* : college dormitories *pl* **3 cité universitaire** *Can* : college campus
citer [site] *vt* **1** : to quote **2** : to cite, to mention **3** : to summon, to subpoena
citerne [sitɛrn] *nf* : cistern, tank, reservoir
cithare [sitar] *nf* : zither
citoyen, citoyenne [sitwajɛ̃, -jɛn] *n* : citizen
citoyenneté [sitwajɛnte] *nf* : citizenship
citron[1] [sitrɔ̃] *adj* : lemon, lemon yellow
citron[2] *nm* **1** : lemon **2 citron vert** : lime
citronnade [sitrɔnad] *nf* : lemonade
citronné, -née [sitrɔne] *adj* : lemon-flavored, lemony
citronnier [sitrɔnje] *nm* : lemon tree
citrouille [sitruj] *nf* **1** : pumpkin **2** *fam* : head
cive [siv] *nf* : chive
civet [sivɛ] *nm* : stew <civet de lapin : rabbit stew>
civière [sivjɛr] *nf* : stretcher
civil[1], **-vile** [sivil] *adj* **1** : civil <droit civil : civil law> **2** : civilian, secular **3** : polite, civil
civil[2], **-vile** *n* : civilian
civilement [sivilmɑ̃] *adv* **1** : civilly, politely **2 se marier civilement** : to have a civil marriage
civilisation [sivilizasjɔ̃] *nf* : civilization
civiliser [sivilize] *vt* : to civilize
civilité [sivilite] *nf* : civility
civique [sivik] *adj* **1** : civic **2 instruction civique** *or* **éducation civique** : civics
civisme [sivism] *nm* : good citizenship
clair[1] [klɛr] *adv* **1** : clearly <voir clair : to see clearly> **2 il fait clair** : it's light, it's getting light (outside)
clair[2], **claire** [klɛr] *adj* **1** : clear **2** : light, bright **3** : light-colored
clair[3] *nm* **1** : light <clair de lune : moonlight> **2** : light color **3 mettre au clair** : to make clear, to shed light on
clairement [klɛrmɑ̃] *adv* : clearly
claire–voie [klɛrvwa] *nf, pl* **claires–voies** : openwork fence <à claire-voie : openwork, open-worked>
clairière [klɛrjɛr] *nf* : clearing, glade
clair–obscur [klɛropskyr] *nm, pl* **clairs–obscurs** : twilight
clairon [klɛrɔ̃] *nm* **1** : bugle **2** : bugler
claironnant [klɛrɔnɑ̃] *adj* : resonant, strident
claironner [klɛrɔne] *vt* : to trumpet, to broadcast (news, etc.)
clairsemé, -mée [klɛrsəme] *adj* : scattered, sparse
clairvoyant, -voyante [klɛrvwajɑ̃, -jɑ̃t] *adj* : clairvoyant — **clairvoyance** [-vwajɑ̃s] *nf*
clamer [klame] *vt* : to shout out, to proclaim
clameur [klamœr] *nf* : clamor, outcry
clan [klɑ̃] *nm* : clan, clique
clandestin[1], **-tine** [klɑ̃dɛstɛ̃, -tin] *adj* **1** : clandestine, covert, underground **2 passager clandestin** : stowaway
clandestin[2], **-tine** *n* : illegal alien
clapoter [klapɔte] *vi* : to lap (of waves)
clapotis [klapɔti] *nm* : lapping (of the waves)
claque [klak] *nf* **1** : slap, smack **2 claques** *nfpl Can* : rubbers, galoshes
claqué, -quée [klake] *adj fam* : dog-tired, exhausted
claquement [klakmɑ̃] *nm* : slamming, slapping, snapping, flapping
claquemurer [klakmyre] *v* **se claquemurer** *vr* : to shut oneself away
claquer [klake] *vt* **1** GIFLER : to slap **2** : to slam **3** *fam* : to spend, to squander **4** *fam* : to exhaust **5** : to strain (a muscle) — *vi* **1** : to make a clicking sound <ses dents claquent : his teeth are chattering> <faire claquer ses doigts : to snap one's fingers> **2** : to slam, to bang **3** *fam* : to wear out, to conk out, to fall through
claquettes [klakɛt] *nfpl* : tap dancing
clarifier [klarifje] {96} *vt* : to clarify — **clarification** [-rifikasjɔ̃] *nf*
clarinette [klarinɛt] *nf* : clarinet — **clarinettiste** [-nɛtist] *nf*
clarté [klarte] *nf* **1** : clearness **2** : clarity, lucidity **3** : brightness, light (of the moon, etc.)
classe [klas] *nf* **1** : class, category, rank <première classe : first class> <classe moyenne : middle class> **2** : class, classroom (in a school) <aller en classe : to go to school>
classement [klasmɑ̃] *nm* **1** : classification **2** : place, ranking
classer [klase] *vt* : to class, to classify, to rate — **se classer** *vr* : to be classified, to rank
classeur [klasœr] *nm* **1** : binder, looseleaf file **2** : filing cabinet
classicisme [klasisism] *nm* : classicism
classification [klasifikasjɔ̃] *nf* : classification
classifier [klasifje] {96} *vt* : to classify
classique[1] [klasik] *adj* : classic, classical
classique[2] *nm* **1** : classic **2** : classical author **3** : classical art, music, etc.
claudication [klodikasjɔ̃] *nf* : lameness
clause [kloz] *nf* : clause

claustrophobe [klostrɔfɔb] *adj* : claustrophobic
claustrophobie [klostrɔfɔbi] *nf* : claustrophobia
clavecin [klavsɛ̃] *nm* : harpsichord
clavicule [klavikyl] *nf* : collarbone, clavicle
clavier [klavje] *nm* **1** : keyboard **2** : range, gamut
clé[1] *or* **clef** [kle] *adj* : key, important
clé *or* **clef**[2] *nf* **1** : key <clé de contact : ignition key> <sous clé : under lock and key> **2** : clue, means, solution <la clé du bonheur : the key to happiness> <clé de sol : treble clef> **3** : clef **4 clé à molette** : monkey wrench **5 clé de voûte** : keystone
clémence [klemɑ̃s] *nf* : clemency, leniency
clément, -mente [klemɑ̃, -mɑ̃t] *adj* **1** : lenient **2** : mild, clement
clémentine [klemɑ̃tin] *nf* : tangerine
clenche [klɑ̃ʃ] *nf* : latch
clencher [klɑ̃ʃe] *vt Can* : to latch
cleptomanie [klɛptɔmani] *nf* → **kleptomanie**
clerc [klɛr] *nm* **1** : clerk **2** : cleric
clergé [klɛrʒe] *nm* : clergy
clérical, -cale [klerikal] *adj, mpl* **-caux** [-ko] : clerical
clic [klik] *nm* : click, clicking
cliché [kliʃe] *nm* **1** : negative (in photography) **2** : cliché
client, cliente [kliɑ̃, kliɑ̃t] *n* **1** : customer, client **2** : patient **3** : guest (in a hotel)
clientèle [kliɑ̃tɛl] *nf* **1** : clientele, customers *pl* **2** : practice (of a doctor)
cligner [kliɲe] *vi* **1** : to squint, to blink **2 cligner de l'œil** : to wink
clignotant *nm* [kliɲɔtɑ̃] : blinker, turn signal
clignoter [kliɲɔte] *vi* **1** : to flash, to twinkle, to flicker **2** : to blink
climat [klima] *nm* : climate
climatique [klimatik] *adj* : climatic
climatisation [klimatizasjɔ̃] *nf* : air-conditioning
climatisé, -sée [klimatize] *adj* : air-conditioned
climatiseur [klimatizœr] *nm* : air conditioner
clin [klɛ̃] *nm* **1 clin d'œil** : wink **2 en un clin d'œil** : in a flash
clinique[1] [klinik] *adj* : clinical — **cliniquement** [-nikmɑ̃] *adv*
clinique[2] *nf* : clinic, private hospital
clinquant[1], **-quante** [klɛ̃kɑ̃, -kɑ̃t] *adj* : flashy
clinquant[2] *nm* **1** : tinsel **2** : flashiness
clip [klip] *nm* **1** : (music) video **2** : brooch
clique [klik] *nf* **1** : clique **2** : (military) band **3 prendre ses cliques et ses claques** : to pack up and go
cliquer [klike] *vi* : to click (on a computer)
cliqueter [klikte] {8} *vi* : to clink, to clack, to rattle, to jingle
cliquetis [klikti] *nm* : clink, clack, rattle, jingle
clitoris [klitɔris] *nm* : clitoris
clivage [klivaʒ] *nm* **1** : cleaving, split **2** : cleavage
cloaque [klɔak] *nm* : cesspool
clochard, -charde [klɔʃar, -ʃard] *n* : tramp, hobo
cloche [klɔʃ] *nf* **1** : bell **2** *fam* : dope, idiot
cloche–pied [klɔʃpje] **sauter à cloche–pied** : to hop
clocher[1] [klɔʃe] *vi fam* : to go wrong
clocher[2] *nm* **1** : belfry, bell-tower **2 de ~** : parochial, small-town
clochette [klɔʃɛt] *nf* : small bell
cloison [klwazɔ̃] *nf* **1** : partition, divider <mur de cloison : dividing wall> **2** : bulkhead **3** : septum
cloisonner [klwazɔne] *vt* : to partition (off)
cloître [klwatr] *nm* : cloister — **cloîtrer** [klwatre] *vt*
clone [klon] *nm* : clone
cloner [klone] *vt* : to clone
clopin–clopant [klɔpɛ̃klɔpɑ̃] *adv* **aller clopin–clopant** *fam* : to hobble along
clopiner [klɔpine] *vi* : to hobble (along)
cloquer [klɔke] *vi* : to blister
clore [klor] {19} *vt* : to close, to conclude
clos[1], **close** [klo, -kloz] *adj* **1** : closed, shut **2** : concluded
clos[2] *nm* **1** : enclosure, enclosed field **2** *or* **clos de vigne** : vineyard
clôture [klotyr] *nf* **1** BARRIÈRE : enclosure, fence **2** : closure
clôturer [klotyre] *vt* **1** : to enclose **2** : to bring to a close
clou [klu] *nm, pl* **clous 1** : nail **2** : feature, attraction **3** FURONCLE : boil **4 clou de girofle** : clove **5 clous** *nmpl France fam* : crosswalk **6 au clou** *fam* : in hock **7 cogner des clous** *Can* : to nod off
clouer [klue] *vt* **1** : to nail **2** : to pin down <être cloué au lit : to be bedridden> **3 clouer le bec à qqn** *fam* : to shut s.o. up
clouté, -tée [klute] *adj* **1** : studded **2 passage clouté** *France* : crosswalk
clown [klun] *nm* : clown <faire le clown : to clown around, to play the fool>
club [klœb] *nm* : club
coaguler [kɔagyle] *vt* : to coagulate — **se coaguler** *vr* : to coagulate, to clot — **coagulation** [-gylasjɔ̃] *nf*
coaliser [kɔalize] *v* **se coaliser** *vr* : to unite, to form a coalition
coalition [kɔalisjɔ̃] *nf* : coalition
coassement [kɔasmɑ̃] *nm* : croaking
coasser [kɔase] *vi* : to croak
cobalt [kɔbalt] *nm* **1** : cobalt **2 bleu de cobalt** : cobalt blue
cobaye [kɔbaj] *nm* : guinea pig
cobra [kɔbra] *nm* : cobra

cocagne [kɔkaɲ] *nf* **pays de cocagne** : land of plenty

cocaïne [kɔkain] *nf* : cocaine

cocarde [kɔkard] *nf* : rosette

cocasse [kɔkas] *adj* : comical

coccinelle [kɔksinɛl] *nf* : ladybug

coche [kɔʃ] *nf* **1** : notch, mark **2 être à côté de la coche** *Can* : to be wrong, to be mistaken

cocher[1] [kɔʃe] *vt* **1** ENTAILLER : to notch **2** POINTER : to check (off)

cocher[2] *nm* : coachman

cochon[1], **-chonne** [kɔʃɔ̃, -ʃɔn] *adj fam* **1** : smutty, indecent **2** : dirty, messy

cochon[2], **-chonne** *n fam* : slob, dirty pig

cochon[3] *nm* **1** : pig **2 cochon d'Inde** : guinea pig **3 cochon de mer** : porpoise

cochonnerie [kɔʃɔnri] *nf* **1** : junk, trash **2** : filthiness, mess **3** : smut **4** : dirty trick

cockpit [kɔkpit] *nm* : cockpit

cocktail [kɔktɛl] *nm* : cocktail

coco [kɔkɔ] *nm or* **noix de coco** : coconut

cocon [kɔkɔ̃] *nm* : cocoon

cocotier [kɔkɔtje] *nm* : coconut palm

cocotte [kɔkɔt] *nf* **1** : casserole dish **2** *Can* : pinecone **3** *fam* : chicken (in baby talk) **4 ma cocotte** *fam* : my sweetie

code [kɔd] *nm* : code <code à barres : bar code> <code postal : zip code> <code d'honneur : code of honor>

codéine [kɔdein] *nf* : codeine

coder [kɔde] *vt* : to code, to encode

codicille [kɔdisil] *nm* : codicil

codifier [kɔdifje] {96} *vt* : to codify

coefficient [kɔefisjɑ̃] *nm* : coefficient <coefficient d'erreur : margin of error>

coéquipier, -pière [kɔekipje, -jɛr] *n* : teammate

coercitif, -tive [kɔɛrsitif, -tiv] *adj* : coercive

coercition [kɔɛrsisjɔ̃] *nf* : coercion

cœur [kœr] *nm* **1** : heart <maladie de cœur : heart disease> **2** : stomach <mal au cœur : upset stomach, nausea> **3** : spirit, courage <de bon cœur : with good spirits, willingly> **4** : heart, feelings *pl*, mind <avoir bon cœur : to be kindhearted> <à cœur joie : to one's heart's content> <apprendre par cœur : to learn by heart> **5** : center, middle <au cœur de la nuit : in the dead of night> <le cœur de l'été : the height of summer> **6** : core (of a fruit) **7** : hearts *pl* (in playing cards)

coexister [kɔɛgziste] *vi* : to coexist — **coexistence** [-zistɑ̃s] *nf*

coffre [kɔfr] *nm* **1** : chest, bin <coffre à jouets : toy chest> **2** : safe, strongbox **3** : trunk (of a car)

coffre–fort [kɔfrəfɔr] *nm, pl* **coffres–forts** : safe

coffrer [kɔfre] *vi Can* : to warp (of wood)

coffret [kɔfrɛ] *nm* : small box, case <coffret à bijoux : jewelry box>

cogiter [kɔʒite] *vi* RÉFLÉCHIR : to cogitate, to reflect

cognac [kɔɲak] *nm* : cognac

cogner [kɔɲe] *vt* : to knock, to bang — *vi* **cogner contre** : to bump against — **se cogner** *vr* : to bump oneself <se cogner la tête : to hit one's head>

cohabiter [kɔabite] *vi* : to live together

cohérent, -rente [kɔerɑ̃, -rɑ̃t] *adj* : coherent — **cohérence** [-erɑ̃s] *nf*

cohésion [kɔezjɔ̃] *nf* : cohesion, cohesiveness

cohorte [kɔɔrt] *nf fam* : band, troop

cohue [kɔy] *nf* **1** FOULE : crowd **2** BOUSCULADE : crush

coi, coite [kwa, kwat] *adj* SILENCIEUX : silent, speechless <se tenir coi : to keep quiet>

coiffe [kwaf] *nf* : headdress

coiffer [kwafe] *vt* **1** : to top, to cover **2** : to head **3 coiffer qqn** : to do s.o's hair — **se coiffer** *vr* : to do one's hair

coiffeur, -feuse [kwafœr, -føz] *n* : hairdresser, barber

coiffeuse [kwaføz] *nf* : vanity, dressing table

coiffure [kwafyr] *nf* **1** : hat, headdress **2** : hairdo **3** : hairdressing

coin [kwɛ̃] *nm* **1** : corner <au coin du feu : by the fireside> <regard en coin : sidelong glance> **2** : place, spot <un coin de ciel : a patch of sky> **3** : wedge

coincé, -cée [kwɛ̃se] *adj fam* : repressed, uptight

coincer [kwɛ̃se] {6} *vt* **1** : to wedge, to jam **2** : to catch (out), to get someone stuck — *vi* : to jam, to get stuck — **se coincer** *vr*

coïncidence [kɔɛ̃sidɑ̃s] *nf* : coincidence

coïncider [kɔɛ̃side] *vi* : to coincide, to tally

coin–coin [kwɛ̃kwɛ̃] *nm* : quack

coing [kwɛ̃] *nm* : quince

coït [kɔit] *nm* : coitus

coke [kɔk] *nm* : coke

col [kɔl] *nm* **1** : collar <col roulé : turtleneck> **2** : neck (of bottle) **3** : mountain pass, gap **4** *or* **col de l'utérus** : cervix

coléoptère [kɔleɔptɛr] *nm* : beetle

colère [kɔlɛr] *nf* **1** : anger **2 en ~** : angry <se mettre en colère : to get angry>

coléreux, -reuse [kɔlerø, -røz] *adj* : bad-tempered, irritable

colérique [kɔlerik] → **coléreux**

colibri [kɔlibri] *nm* : hummingbird

colifichet [kɔlifiʃɛ] *nm* : trinket

colimaçon [kɔlimasɔ̃] *nm* **1** : snail **2 en ~** : spiral

colin [kɔlɛ̃] *nm* : hake (for cooking)

colique [kɔlik] *nf* **1** : diarrhea **2** *or* **coliques** *nfpl* : colic, stomachache **3** *fam* : hassle, pain in the neck

colis [kɔli] *nm* PAQUET : parcel, package <colis postal : parcel post>

collaborateur, -trice [kɔlabɔratœr, -tris] *n* **1** COLLÈGUE : colleague, coworker **2** : contributor **3** : collaborator

collaborer [kɔlabɔre] *vi* : to collaborate — **collaboration** [-bɔrasjɔ̃] *nf*

collage [kɔlaʒ] *nm* : collage

collant[1], **-lante** [kɔlɑ̃, -lɑ̃t] *adj* **1** : sticky, tacky **2** : tight-fitting

collant[2] *nm* **1** : panty hose *pl* **2** *or* **collants** *mpl* : leotard, leggings *pl*, tights *pl* **3** *Can* : sticker

collation [kɔlasjɔ̃] *nf* : snack

collationner [kɔlasjɔne] *vt* : to collate

colle [kɔl] *nf* **1** : paste, glue **2 poser une colle** *fam* : to ask a trick question (on an exam)

collecte [kɔlɛkt] *nf* : collection

collecter [kɔlɛkte] *vt* : to collect

collecteur[1], **-trice** [kɔlɛktœr, -tris] *n* : collector

collecteur[2] *nm* **1** : main sewer **2** : manifold (of an automobile)

collectif, -tive [kɔlɛktif, -tiv] *adj* : collective, joint — **collectivement** [-tivmɑ̃] *adv*

collection [kɔlɛksjɔ̃] *nf* : collection

collectionner [kɔlɛksjɔne] *vt* : to collect <collectionner les timbres : to collect stamps>

collectionneur, -neuse [kɔlɛksjɔnœr, -nøz] *n* : collector

collectivité [kɔlɛktivite] *nf* : community

collège [kɔlɛʒ] *nm* **1** *France* : junior high school **2** *Can* : junior college, vocational college **3** : college <collège électoral : electoral college>

collégial, -giale [kɔleʒjal] *adj, mpl* **-giaux** [-ʒjo] : collegiate

collégien, -gienne [kɔleʒjɛ̃, -ʒjɛn] *n* **1** *France* : schoolboy *m*, schoolgirl *f* **2** *Can* CÉGÉPIEN : junior-college student

collègue [kɔlɛg] *nmf* : colleague

coller [kɔle] *vt* **1** : to stick, to glue **2** APPUYER : to press <coller son visage contre la fenêtre : to press one's face against the window> — *vi* **1** : to adhere, to cling **2 ~ à** : to stick close to — **se coller** *vr* **~ à** : to press oneself (up) against

collet [kɔlɛ] *nm* **1** : snare, noose **2** : collar, neck <être collet monté : to be prim, to be straight-laced>

colleter [kɔlte] {8} *vt* : to collar — **se colleter** *vr* **~ avec** : to fight with, to grapple with

colley [kɔlɛ] *nm* : collie

collier [kɔlje] *nm* **1** : necklace **2** : collar (of an animal, a machine, etc.) **3** *or* **collier de barbe** : short close beard

collimateur [kɔlimatœr] *nm* **avoir qqn dans le collimateur** : to have s.o. in one's sights

colline [kɔlin] *nf* : hill

collision [kɔlizjɔ̃] *nf* : collision <entrer en collision avec : to collide with>

colloque [kɔlɔk] *nm* : colloquium, symposium

collusion [kɔlyzjɔ̃] *nf* : collusion

collyre [kɔlir] *nm* : eye drops *pl*

colmater [kɔlmate] *vt* : to fill in, to seal up, to plug

colombe [kɔlɔ̃b] *nf* : dove

colombien, -bienne [kɔlɔ̃bjɛ̃, -bjɛn] *adj* : Colombian

Colombien, -bienne *n* : Colombian

colon [kɔlɔ̃] *nm* : colonist, settler

côlon [kolɔ̃] *nm* : colon

colonel [kɔlɔnɛl] *nm* : colonel

colonial[1], **-niale** [kɔlɔnjal] *adj, mpl* **-niaux** [-njo] : colonial — **colonialisme** [-njalism] *nm*

colonial[2], **-niale** *n, mpl* **-niaux** [-njo] : colonial (person)

colonie [kɔlɔni] *nf* : colony

colonisateur, -trice [kɔlɔnizatœr, -tris] *n* : colonist, settler

colonisation [kɔlɔnizasjɔ̃] *nf* : colonization

coloniser [kɔlɔnize] *vt* : to colonize, to settle

colonnade [kɔlɔnad] *nf* : colonnade

colonne [kɔlɔn] *nf* **1** : column <en colonne par quatre : four abreast> **2** : pillar, column (in architecture) **3 colonne vertébrale** : spinal column, backbone

colophane [kɔlɔfan] *nf* : rosin

colorant[1], **-rante** [kɔlɔrɑ̃, -rɑ̃t] *adj* : coloring

colorant[2] *nm* : dye, stain

coloration [cɔlɔrasjɔ̃] *nf* : coloring

coloré, -rée [kɔlɔre] *adj* **1** : colored **2** : colorful, lively

colorer [kɔlɔre] *vt* : to color, to tint — **se colorer** *vr* : to flush, to blush

colorier [kɔlɔrje] {96} *vt* : to color

coloris [kɔlɔri] *nm* **1** : color, shade **2** : colors *pl*, color scheme

colossal, -sale [kɔlɔsal] *adj, mpl* **-saux** [-so] ÉNORME : colossal, enormous

colosse [kɔlɔs] *nm* GÉANT : colossus, giant

colporter [kɔlpɔrte] *vt* : to hawk, to peddle

colporteur, -teuse [kɔlpɔrtœr, -tøz] *n* : peddler

coltiner [kɔltine] *vt* : to carry, to lug — **se coltiner** *vr* **1** : to lug around **2** : to get stuck with

colvert [kɔlvɛr] *nm* : mallard (duck)

colza [kɔlza] *nm* : rapeseed, rape (plant)

coma [kɔma] *nm* : coma

comateux, -teuse [kɔmatø, -tøz] *adj* : comatose

combat [kɔ̃ba] *nm* **1** : combat, fighting <combat de boxe : boxing match> **2** : conflict, struggle

combatif, -tive [kɔ̃batif, -tiv] *adj* : combative, aggressive

combattant, -tante [kɔ̃batɑ̃, -tɑ̃t] *n* : combatant, fighter

combattre [kɔ̃batr] {12} *v* : to fight

combien [kɔ̃bjɛ̃] *adv* **1** : how much, how many <combien coûte cela : how much does that cost?> <combien sont-ils? : how many (of them) are there?> **2 ~ de** : how much, how many <combien de temps : how long> <combien de livres : how many books>

combinaison [kɔ̃binɛzɔ̃] *nf* **1** : combination **2** : (full-length) slip **3** : suit, overalls <combinaison spatiale : space suit> **4** : plan, scheme

combine [kɔ̃bin] *nf fam* : scheme, trick

combiné [kɔ̃bine] *nm* : (telephone) receiver

combiner [kɔ̃bine] *vt* **1** : to combine **2** : to contrive, to work out (a plan, etc.) **— se combiner** *vr* : to combine

comble[1] [kɔ̃bl] *adj* : packed, filled up

comble[2] *nm* **1** : extreme point <le comble de la joie : the height of joy> <c'est le comble! : that takes the cake!> **2 combles** *nmpl* : attic **3 de fond en comble** : from top to bottom

combler [kɔ̃ble] *vt* **1** : to fill in, to fill up **2** : to fulfill, to satisfy

combustible[1] [kɔ̃bystibl] *adj* : combustible, inflammable

combustible[2] *nm* : fuel

combustion [kɔ̃bystjɔ̃] *nf* : combustion

comédie [kɔmedi] *nf* **1** : comedy <comédie musicale : musical> **2** : playacting, pretense

comédien, -dienne [kɔmedjɛ̃, -djɛn] *n* **1** ACTEUR : actor *m*, actress *f* **2** : comedian **3** HYPOCRITE : sham

comestible [kɔmɛstibl] *adj* : edible

comestibles *nmpl* : food

comète [kɔmɛt] *nf* : comet

comique[1] [kɔmik] *adj* **1** : comic **2** : comical, funny

comique[2] *nmf* : comedian, comic

comique[3] *nm* **1** : comedy **2** : funny thing, funny part

comité [kɔmite] *nm* : committee

commandant [kɔmɑ̃dɑ̃] *nm* **1** : commandant, commander **2** : major (in the army) **3 commandant de bord** : captain (in the navy or air force)

commande [kɔmɑ̃d] *nf* **1** : order <passer une commande : to place an order> **2 commande à distance** : remote control **3 fait sur commande** : made-to-order

commandement [kɔmɑ̃dmɑ̃] *nm* **1** ORDRE : command, order **2** AUTORITÉ : authority, control **3** : commandment (in religion)

commander [kɔmɑ̃de] *vt* **1** : to command **2** : to commission, to order (a meal, etc.) **—** *vi* : to be in command

commanditaire [kɔmɑ̃ditɛr] *nm* : sponsor, backer

commandite [kɔmɑ̃dit] *nf* : limited partnership

commanditer [kɔmɑ̃dite] *vt* : to finance, to back

commando [kɔmɑ̃do] *nm* : commando

comme[1] [kɔm] *adv* **1** : how <comme c'est beau! : how beautiful it is!> **2 comme de bonne** *Can* : naturally, as one might expect **3 comme du monde** *Can fam* : properly

comme[2] *conj* **1** : as, like <faites comme moi : do as I do> <blanc comme la neige : white as snow> **2** : since <comme elle se sentait malade, elle est partie : since she felt ill, she left> **3** : when, as <comme il disait au revoir, elle pleurait : as he said goodbye, she cried> **4 comme ci, comme ça** : so-so **5 comme il faut** : properly **6 comme si** : as if, as though

comme[3] *prep* **1** : like <un visage comme un masque : a face like a mask> **2** : as, in the capacity of <il travaille comme rédacteur : he works as an editor>

commémoration [kɔmemɔrasjɔ̃] *nf* : commemoration

commémorer [kɔmemɔre] *vt* : to commemorate **— commémoratif, -tive** [-mɔratif, -tiv] *adj*

commencement [kɔmɑ̃smɑ̃] *nm* **1** : beginning, start **2 au commencement** : in the beginning, at first

commencer [kɔmɑ̃se] {6} *v* : to begin, to start

comment[1] [kɔmɑ̃] *adv* **1** : how <comment ça va? : how is it going?> <je me demande comment elle va en finir : I wonder how she'll end up> **2** : what <comment! tu n'as pas d'argent? : what! you have no money?> **3** : sorry, who, what <Anne comment? : Anne who?> **4 comment donc** : of course, by all means

comment[2] *nm inv* **1 le comment** : the how **2 → pourquoi**

commentaire [kɔmɑ̃tɛr] *nm* **1** REMARQUE : comment, remark **2** : commentary

commentateur, -trice [kɔmɑ̃tatœr, -tris] *n* : commentator

commenter [kɔmɑ̃te] *vt* : to comment on

commérage [kɔmeraʒ] *nm fam* : gossip

commerçant[1], **-çante** [kɔmɛrsɑ̃, -sɑ̃t] *adj* : commercial, shopping

commerçant[2], **-çante** *n* : merchant, storekeeper

commerce [kɔmɛrs] *nm* : business, commerce, trade <faire du commerce : to be in business> <commerce en gros : wholesale trade>

commercer [kɔmɛrse] {6} *vi* : to trade, to deal

commercial [kɔmɛrsjal] *adj, mpl* **-ciaux** [-sjo] : commercial **— commercialement** [-sjalmɑ̃] *adv*

commercialisation [kɔmɛrsjalizasjɔ̃] *nf* : marketing

commercialiser [kɔmɛrsjalize] *vt* : to market
commère [kɔmɛr] *nf fam* : gossip (person)
commettre [kɔmɛtr] {53} *vt* **1** : to commit (a crime, etc.), to make (an error) **2** : to appoint, to nominate
commis [kɔmi] *nm* **1** : clerk **2** **commis voyageur** : traveling salesman
commisération [kɔmizerasjɔ̃] *nf* : commiseration
commissaire [kɔmisɛr] *nm* : superintendent, commissioner
commissaire–priseur [kɔmisɛrprizœr] *nm, pl* **commissaires–priseurs** : auctioneer
commissariat [kɔmisarja] *nm* **commissariat de police** : police station
commission [kɔmisjɔ̃] *nf* **1** : commission, committee **2** : commission, percentage **3** MESSAGE : message **4** COURSE : errand **5** **commissions** *nfpl* : shopping
commissionnaire [kɔmisjɔnɛr] *nm* **1** : agent, broker **2** : messenger
commissionner [kɔmisjɔne] *vt* : to commission
commode[1] [kɔmɔd] *adj* **1** : convenient, handy, useful **2** FACILE : easy <ce n'est pas commode! : it's not easy!> **3** AIMABLE : easy to get along with
commode[2] *nf* : chest of drawers
commodément [kɔmɔdemɑ̃] *adv* : comfortably, conveniently
commodité [kɔmɔdite] *nf* : comfort, convenience
commotion [kɔmɔsjɔ̃] *nf* **1** : shock **2** **commotion cérébrale** : concussion
commuer [kɔmɥe] *vt* : to commute, to reduce (a legal penalty)
commun[1], **-mune** [kɔmœ̃, -myn] *adj* **1** : common, joint **2** : mutual, shared **3** : usual, ordinary
commun[2] *nm* **1** : ordinary (one), average person or thing <le commun des lecteurs : the average reader> <hors du commun : out of the ordinary> **2** **en ~** : in common, jointly
communautaire [kɔmynotɛr] *adj* : community, communal
communauté [kɔmynote] *nf* **1** : community **2** : commune
commune [kɔmyn] *nf* **1** : village, town **2** *Can* : rural area used in common
communément [kɔmynemɑ̃] *adv* : commonly, generally
communicable [kɔmynikabl] *adj* : communicable
communicatif, -tive [kɔmynikatif, -tiv] *adj* **1** : communicative, talkative **2** CONTAGIEUX : contagious, infectious
communication [kɔmynikasjɔ̃] *nf* **1** : communication, report **2** : communication(s), communicating <la communication de masse : mass media> **3** **communication téléphonique** : telephone call
communier [kɔmynje] {96} *vi* **1** : to receive Communion **2** **~ avec** : to commune with
communion [kɔmynjɔ̃] *nf* **1** : Communion **2** **être en communion avec** : to be in communion with, to be of the same mind as
communiqué [kɔmynike] *nm* : communiqué, press release
communiquer [kɔmynike] *vt* : to communicate, to pass on, to transmit — *vi* **~ avec** : to communicate with
communisme [kɔmynism] *nm* : communism, Communism
communiste [kɔmynist] *adj & nmf* : communist, Communist
commutateur [kɔmytatœr] *nm* : switch
commutation [kɔmytasjɔ̃] *nf* **1** : commutation (in law) **2** : switching
compact[1], **-pacte** [kɔ̃pakt] *adj* : compact, dense
compact[2] *nm* : compact disc
compacte *nf* : compact (car)
compacter [kɔ̃pakte] *vt* : to compact
compagne [kɔ̃paɲ] *nf* : (female) companion, partner
compagnie [kɔ̃paɲi] *nf* **1** : company, companionship <tenir compagnie à qqn : to keep s.o. company> **2** : company, firm <compagnie d'assurances : insurance company> **3** : company (in the military, in theater) **4** **en compagnie de** : with, accompanied by
compagnon [kɔ̃paɲɔ̃] *nm* **1** CAMARADE : companion, comrade **2** : journeyman, apprentice
comparable [kɔ̃parabl] *adj* : comparable
comparaison [kɔ̃parɛzɔ̃] *nf* **1** : comparison **2** : simile
comparaître [kɔ̃parɛtr] {7} *vi* : to appear (before a court)
comparatif[1], **-tive** [kɔ̃paratif, -tiv] *adj* : comparative — **comparativement** [-tivmɑ̃] *adv*
comparatif[2] *nm* : comparative (case)
comparer [kɔ̃pare] *vt* : to compare
comparse [kɔ̃pars] *nmf* **1** : sidekick **2** FIGURANT : extra, bit player
compartiment [kɔ̃partimɑ̃] *nm* : compartment
compartimenter [kɔ̃partimɑ̃te] *vt* **1** : to partition **2** : to compartmentalize
comparution [kɔ̃parysjɔ̃] *nf* : appearance (in court)
compas [kɔ̃pa] *nms & pl* : compass
compassion [kɔ̃pasjɔ̃] *nf* : compassion
compatibilité [kɔ̃patibilite] *nf* : compatibility
compatible [kɔ̃patibl] *adj* : compatible
compatir [kɔ̃patir] *vi* **~ à** : to sympathize with
compatissant, -sante [kɔ̃patisɑ̃, -sɑ̃t] *adj* : compassionate, sympathetic
compatriote [kɔ̃patrijɔt] *nmf* : compatriot, fellow countryman, fellow countrywoman *f*

compensateur, -trice [kɔ̃pɑ̃satœr, -tris] *adj* : compensatory

compensation [kɔ̃pɑ̃sasjɔ̃] *nf* : compensation

compensatoire [kɔ̃pɑ̃satwar] *adj* : compensatory

compenser [kɔ̃pɑ̃se] *vt* : to compensate for, to make up for

compère [kɔ̃pɛr] *nm* : accomplice

compétent, -tente [kɔ̃petɑ̃, -tɑ̃t] *adj* : competent — **compétence** [-petɑ̃s] *nf*

compétiteur, -trice [kɔ̃petitœr, -tris] *n* : competitor, rival

compétitif, -tive [kɔ̃petitif, -tiv] *adj* : competitive

compétition [kɔ̃petisjɔ̃] *nf* **1** RIVALITÉ : rivalry **2** CONCOURS : competition, competitive event

compétitivité [kɔ̃petitivite] *nf* : competitiveness

compilateur, -trice [kɔ̃pilatœr] *n* : compiler

compilation [kɔ̃pilasjɔ̃] *nf* : compilation

compiler [kɔ̃pile] *vt* : to compile

complainte [kɔ̃plɛ̃t] *nf* : lament

complaire [kɔ̃plɛr] {66} *vi* **~ à** : to please — **se complaire** *vr* **1 ~ dans** : to delight in (something) **2 ~ à faire** : to delight in doing

complaisance [kɔ̃plɛzɑ̃s] *nf* **1** : obligingness, kindness **2** : complacency **3** : indulgence, leniency

complaisant, -sante [kɔ̃plɛzɑ̃, -zɑ̃t] *adj* **1** : obliging, kind **2** : complacent, smug **3** : indulgent — **complaisamment** [-zamɑ̃] *adv*

complément [kɔ̃plemɑ̃] *nm* : complement

complémentaire [kɔ̃plemɑ̃tɛr] *adj* **1** : complementary **2** ADDITIONNEL : supplementary

complet[1], -plète [kɔ̃plɛ, -plɛt] *adj* **1** : complete **2** PLEIN : full (of a hotel, theater, etc.)

complet[2] *nm* : suit

complètement [kɔ̃plɛtmɑ̃] *adv* **1** : completely, totally **2** : fully, thoroughly

compléter [kɔ̃plete] {87} *vt* **1** : to complete **2** : to complement, to supplement — **se compléter** *vr* : to complement one another

complexe [kɔ̃plɛks] *adj & nm* : complex

complexé, -plexée [kɔ̃plɛkse] *adj* : full of complexes, neurotic

complexité [kɔ̃plɛksite] *nf* : complexity, intricacy

complication [kɔ̃plikasjɔ̃] *nf* : complication

complice[1] [kɔ̃plis] *adj* **1** : knowing (of a look, etc.) **2** : accessory

complice[2] *nmf* : accomplice

complicité [kɔ̃plisite] *nf* : complicity

compliment [kɔ̃plimɑ̃] *nm* **1** : compliment **2 compliments** *nmpl* FÉLICITATIONS : compliments, congratulations

complimenter [kɔ̃plimɑ̃te] *vt* : to compliment, to congratulate

compliqué, -quée [kɔ̃plike] *adj* : complicated, complex

compliquer [kɔ̃plike] *vt* : to complicate — **se compliquer** *vr*

complot [kɔ̃plo] *nm* MACHINATION : plot, conspiracy

comploter [kɔ̃plɔte] *v* : to plot, to conspire

comploteur, -teuse [kɔ̃plɔtœr, -tøz] *n* : plotter, schemer

comportement [kɔ̃pɔrtəmɑ̃] *nm* **1** : behavior, conduct **2** : performance

comporter [kɔ̃pɔrte] *vt* **1** : to include **2** : to comprise, to consist of **3** : to entail (risks, etc.) — **se comporter** *vr* : to behave, to perform

composant[1], -sante [kɔ̃pozɑ̃, -zɑ̃t] *adj* : component, constituent

composant[2] *nm* ÉLÉMENT : component, constituent

composante *nf* : (mathematical) component, constituent

composé[1], -sée [kɔ̃poze] *adj* : compound

composé[2] *nm* : compound

composer [kɔ̃poze] *vt* **1** : to compose (music, writings, etc.) **2** : to constitute, to make up **3** : to dial (a number) **4** : to typeset — *vi* : to compromise — **se composer** *vr* : to be made up of

composite[1] [kɔ̃pozit] *adj* **1** : composite **2** : varied, heterogeneous

composite[2] *nm* : composite

compositeur, -trice [kɔ̃pozitœr, -tris] *n* **1** : composer **2** : typesetter

composition [kɔ̃pozisjɔ̃] *nf* **1** : composition **2** : typesetting **3 de bonne composition** : good-natured, accommodating

compost [kɔ̃pɔst] *nm* : compost

composter [kɔ̃pɔste] *vt* **1** : to compost **2** : to stamp, to validate (a ticket, etc.)

compote [kɔ̃pɔt] *nf* **1** : stewed fruit **2 compote de pommes** : apple sauce

compréhensible [kɔ̃preɑ̃sibl] *adj* : comprehensible

compréhensif, -sive [kɔ̃preɑ̃sif, -siv] *adj* **1** : comprehensive **2** : understanding

compréhension [kɔ̃preɑ̃sjɔ̃] *nf* : understanding

comprenait [kɔ̃prənɛ], *etc.* → **comprendre**

comprendre [kɔ̃prɑ̃dr] {70} *vt* **1** : to comprise, to consist of **2** : to include **3** : to understand <mal comprendre : to misunderstand> — **se comprendre** *vr* **1** : to understand each other **2** : to be understandable

comprenne [kɔ̃prɛn], *etc.* → **comprendre**

compresse [kɔ̃prɛs] *nf* : compress

compresseur [kɔ̃prɛsœr] *nm* : compressor
compression [kɔ̃prɛsjɔ̃] *nf* **1** : compression **2** : reduction
comprimé[1] [kɔ̃prime] *adj* : compressed <air comprimé : compressed air>
comprimé[2] *nm* : tablet, pill
comprimer [kɔ̃prime] *vt* **1** : to compress **2** : to reduce, to cut **3** : to repress
compris[1] [kɔ̃pri] *pp* → **comprendre**
compris[2], **-prise** [kɔ̃pri, -priz] *adj* **1** : understood **2** INCLUS : included <tout compris : inclusive, in total> <y compris : including>
compromettant, -tante [kɔ̃prɔmetɑ̃, -tɑ̃t] *adj* : compromising, incriminating
compromettre [kɔ̃prɔmɛtr] {53} *vt* **1** : to compromise, to implicate, to involve **2** : to endanger — **se compromettre** *vr* : to compromise oneself
compromis [kɔ̃prɔmi] *nm* : compromise
compromission [kɔ̃prɔmisjɔ̃] *nf* : compromising, (shady) deal
comptabiliser [kɔ̃tabilize] *vt* **1** : to count **2** : to enter into the books
comptabilité [kɔ̃tabilite] *nf* : accounting, bookkeeping
comptable[1] [kɔ̃tabl] *adj* **1** : accounting **2** : accountable
comptable[2] *nmf* : accountant, bookkeeper
comptant [kɔ̃tɑ̃] *adv & adj* **1** : cash <payer comptant : to pay cash> <500 francs comptant : 500 francs cash> **2** **au comptant** : in cash, for cash
compte [kɔ̃t] *nm* **1** : account <compte bancaire : bank account> **2** **à bon compte** : cheap, cheaply **3** **au bout de compte** : when all is said and done **4** **compte à rebours** : countdown **5** **compte rendu** : report, review **6** **en fin de compte** : all things considered **7** **se rendre compte de** : to notice, to realize **8** **tenir compte de** : to take into account, to allow for <sans tenir compte de : irrespective of>
compte–gouttes [kɔ̃tgut] *nms & pl* : dropper
compter [kɔ̃te] *vt* **1** : to count **2** : to allow (for) **3** INCLURE : to include, to count **4** : to have **5** : to charge (for) **6** : to intend **7** : to expect — *vi* **1** : to count **2** : to matter **3** **à compter de** : as from, as of **4** **compter sur** : to count on
compte–rendu [kɔ̃trɑ̃dy] *nm, pl* **comptes–rendus** → **compte**
compteur[1] [kɔ̃tœr] *nm* **1** : meter **2** **compteur de vitesse** : speedometer **3** **compteur Geiger** : Geiger counter
compteur[2], **-teuse** [kɔ̃tœr, -tøz] *n Can* : scorer
comptoir [kɔ̃twar] *nm* **1** : counter, bar **2** : trading post **3** SUCCURSALE : branch (of a bank)
compulsion [kɔ̃pylsjɔ̃] *nf* : compulsion — **compulsif, -sive** [-pylsif, -siv] *adj*
comte, -tesse [kɔ̃t, -tɛs] *n* : count *m*, countess *f*
comté [kɔ̃te] *nm* : county
con[1], **conne** [kɔ̃, kɔn] *adj, usu vulgar* : stupid, idiotic
con[2], **conne** *n, usu vulgar* : stupid idiot, fool
concasser [kɔ̃kase] *vt* : to crush, to grind
concave [kɔ̃kav] *adj* : concave
concéder [kɔ̃sede] {87} *vt* : to concede, to grant
concentration [kɔ̃sɑ̃trasjɔ̃] *nf* : concentration
concentré[1], **-trée** [kɔ̃sɑ̃tre] *adj* **1** : concentrated, condensed **2** ATTENTIF : concentrating
concentré[2] *nm* : concentrate <concentré de tomate : tomato paste>
concentrer [kɔ̃sɑ̃tre] *vt* : to concentrate — **se concentrer** *vr*
concentrique [kɔ̃sɑ̃trik] *adj* : concentric
concept [kɔ̃sɛpt] *nm* : concept
concepteur, -trice [kɔ̃sɛptœr, -tris] *n* : designer
conception [kɔ̃sɛpsjɔ̃] *nf* : conception
concernant [kɔ̃sɛrnɑ̃] *prep* : concerning, regarding
concerner [kɔ̃sɛrne] *vt* : to concern, to affect <en ce qui me concerne : as far as I'm concerned>
concert [kɔ̃sɛr] *nm* **1** : concert **2** **de ~** : together, jointly, in unison
concertation [kɔ̃sɛrtasjɔ̃] *nf* : dialogue, consultation
concerté, -tée [kɔ̃sɛrte] *adj* : concerted
concerter [kɔ̃sɛrte] *vt* : to devise, to plan (out) — **se concerter** *vr* : to consult (each other)
concerto [kɔ̃sɛrto] *nm* : concerto
concession [kɔ̃sesjɔ̃] *nf* **1** COMPROMIS : concession, compromise **2** : dealership **3** : plot (in a cemetery)
concessionnaire [kɔ̃sesjɔnɛr] *nmf* : dealer, agent
concevoir [kɔ̃səvwar] {26} *vt* **1** : to conceive (a child) **2** : to conceive of, to design, to imagine **3** : to understand — **se concevoir** *vr* **1** : to be imagined **2** : to be understandable
concierge [kɔ̃sjɛrʒ] *nmf* : concierge, superintendent
conciliant, -liante [kɔ̃siljɑ̃, -ljɑ̃t] *adj* : conciliatory
conciliateur, -trice [kɔ̃siljatœr, -tris] *adj* : conciliatory (of a person)
conciliation [kɔ̃siljasjɔ̃] *nf* **1** : conciliation **2** : reconciliation
concilier [kɔ̃silje] {96} *vt* : to reconcile — **se concilier** *vr* : to gain, to win (over)
concis, -cise [kɔ̃si, -siz] *adj* : concise
conclave [kɔ̃klav] *nm* : conclave
concluant, -cluante [kɔ̃klyɑ̃, -klyɑ̃t] *adj* : conclusive

conclure [kɔ̃klyr] {39} *vt* **1** : to conclude, to decide **2** : to conclude, to end **3** : to finish up, to settle <conclure un marché : to clinch a deal>
conclusion [kɔ̃klyzjɔ̃] *nf* : conclusion
concocter [kɔ̃kɔkte] *vt* : to concoct
conçoit [kɔ̃swa], **conçoive** [kɔ̃swav], *etc.* → **concevoir**
concombre [kɔ̃kɔ̃br] *nm* : cucumber
concomitant, -tante [kɔ̃kɔmitɑ̃, -tɑ̃t] *adj* : concomitant
concordance [kɔ̃kɔrdɑ̃s] *nf* **1** : similarity, agreement **2** : index, concordance
concordant, -dante [kɔ̃kɔrdɑ̃, -dɑ̃t] *adj* : conforming, corresponding
concorde [kɔ̃kɔrd] *nf* : concord, harmony
concorder [kɔ̃kɔrde] *vi* : to agree, to tally
concourir [kɔ̃kurir] {23} *vi* **1** : to compete **2** ~ **à** : to work toward
concours [kɔ̃kur] *nm* **1** COMPÉTITION : competition, contest **2** AIDE : assistance, aid **3 concours de circonstances** : combination of circumstances
concret, -crète [kɔ̃krɛ, -krɛt] *adj* : concrete
concrètement [kɔ̃krɛtmɑ̃] *adv* : in concrete terms
concrétiser [kɔ̃kretize] *vt* : to put in concrete form, to realize
conçu [kɔ̃sy] *pp* → **concevoir**
concubin, -bine [kɔ̃kybɛ̃, -bin] *n* : common-law spouse, partner
concupiscent, -cente [kɔ̃kypisɑ̃, -sɑ̃t] *adj* : lustful
concurremment [kɔ̃kyramɑ̃] *adv* : jointly, concurrently
concurrence [kɔ̃kyrɑ̃s] *nf* **1** RIVALITÉ : competition, rivalry <concurrence déloyale : unfair competition> <faire concurrence à : to compete with> **2 jusqu'à concurrence de** : up to, not exceeding
concurrencer [kɔ̃kyrɑ̃se] {6} *vt* : to rival, to compete with
concurrent¹, -rente [kɔ̃kyrɑ̃, -rɑ̃t] *adj* : competing, rival
concurrent², -rente *n* : competitor
concurrentiel, -tielle [kɔ̃kyrɑ̃sjɛl] *adj* : competitive
condamnable [kɔ̃danabl] *adj* RÉPRÉHENSIBLE : reprehensible
condamnation [kɔ̃danasjɔ̃] *nf* **1** : condemnation **2** PEINE : conviction, sentence
condamné, -née [kɔ̃dane] *n* : convict
condamner [kɔ̃dane] *vt* **1** : to condemn **2** : to sentence <condamner qqn à une amende : to fine s.o.> **3** : to block up, to seal off
condensation [kɔ̃dɑ̃sasjɔ̃] *nf* : condensation
condensé [kɔ̃dɑ̃se] *nm* : digest, summary
condenser [kɔ̃dɑ̃se] *vt* : to condense — **se condenser** *vr*
condescendance [kɔ̃desɑ̃dɑ̃s] *nf* : condescension
condescendant, -dante [kɔ̃desɑ̃dɑ̃, -dɑ̃t] *adj* : condescending
condescendre [kɔ̃desɑ̃dr] {63} *vi* ~ **à** : to condescend to
condiment [kɔ̃dimɑ̃] *nm* : condiment, seasoning
condisciple [kɔ̃disipl] *nmf* : schoolmate, fellow student
condition [kɔ̃disjɔ̃] *nf* **1** : condition, stipulation <sans conditions : unconditionally> <sous condition que : on the condition that> **2** FORME : condition, shape <se mettre en condition : to get in shape> **3** : social status, background, walk of life **4 conditions** *nfpl* : conditions, circumstances <conditions de vie : living conditions>
conditionné, -née [kɔ̃disjɔne] *adj* **1** : conditioned **2** : packaged <conditionné sous vide : vacuum-packed>
conditionnel, -nelle [kɔ̃disjɔnɛl] *adj* : conditional — **conditionnellement** [-nɛlmɑ̃] *adv*
conditionner [kɔ̃disjɔne] *vt* **1** : to condition **2** : to determine, to govern **3** EMBALLER : to package
condoléances [kɔ̃dɔleɑ̃s] *nfpl* : condolences
condom [kɔ̃dɔm] *nm* PRÉSERVATIF : condom
condominium [kɔ̃dɔminjɔm] *nm* : condominium
conducteur¹, -trice [kɔ̃dyktœr, -tris] *n* **1** : driver **2** : operator (of a machine, etc.)
conducteur² *nm* : conductor (of electricity)
conduction [kɔ̃dyksjɔ̃] *nf* : conduction
conductivité [kɔ̃dyktivite] *nf* : conductivity
conduire [kɔ̃dɥir] {49} *vt* **1** : to drive **2** MENER : to lead **3** DIRIGER : to run, to manage — **se conduire** *vr* : to behave
conduisait [kɔ̃dɥizɛ], **conduisions** [kɔ̃dɥizjɔ̃], *etc.* → **conduire**
conduise [kɔ̃dɥiz], *etc.* → **conduire**
conduit [kɔ̃dɥi] *nm* **1** : conduit, duct <conduit de fumée : flue> **2** : canal (in anatomy)
conduite [kɔ̃dɥit] *nf* **1** : conduct, behavior **2** : conducting, leading **3** : driving <conduite à droite : right-hand drive> **4** : pipe <conduite d'eau : water main>
cône [kon] *nm* : cone
confection [kɔ̃fɛksjɔ̃] *nf* **1** ÉLABORATION : making, preparation **2 la confection** : the clothing industry
confectionner [kɔ̃fɛksjɔne] *vt* : to make, to prepare
confédération [kɔ̃federasjɔ̃] *nf* : confederation, confederacy

confédérer [kɔ̃federe] {87} *vt* : to confederate — **se confédérer** *vr*

conférence [kɔ̃ferɑ̃s] *nf* **1** : conference <conférence de presse : press conference> **2** : lecture

conférencier, -cière [kɔ̃ferɑ̃sje, -sjɛr] *n* : lecturer

conférer [kɔ̃fere] {87} *v* : to confer

confesser [kɔ̃fese] *vt* : to confess

confession [kɔ̃fesjɔ̃] *nf* **1** : confession **2** : faith, denomination

confessionnal [kɔ̃fesjɔnal] *nm, pl* **-naux** [-no] : confessional

confessionnel, -nelle [kɔ̃fesjɔnɛl] *adj* : denominational

confetti [kɔ̃feti] *nm* : (piece of) confetti <des confettis : confetti>

confiance [kɔ̃fjɑ̃s] *nf* **1** : confidence, trust, faith <avoir confiance en : to have confidence in> <faire confiance à : to trust> **2 confiance en soi** : self-confidence **3 de confiance** : trustworthy, reliable

confiant, -fiante [kɔ̃nfjɑ̃, -fjɑ̃t] *adj* **1** : confident **2** : trusting, trustful **3** ASSURÉ : self-confident

confidence [kɔ̃fidɑ̃s] *nf* : confidence, secret <être dans la confidence : to be in the know> <faire des confidences à qqn : to confide in s.o.>

confident, -dente [kɔ̃fidɑ̃, -dɑ̃t] *n* : confidant, confidante *f*

confidentiel, -tielle [kɔ̃fidɑ̃sjɛl] *adj* SECRET : confidential, secret — **confidentiellement** [-sjɛlmɑ̃] *adv*

confier [kɔ̃fje] {96} *vt* **1 confier (qqch) à qqn** : to entrust (sth) to s.o. **2 confier à qqn** : to confide to s.o. — **se confier** *vr* **se confier à qqn** : to confide in s.o.

configuration [kɔ̃figyrasjɔ̃] *nf* : configuration

confiner [kɔ̃fine] *vt* **1** : to confine **2 confiner qqn à** : to restrict s.o. to — *vi* **∼ à** : to border on — **se confiner** *vr* **1** : to shut oneself away **2 ∼ à** *or* **dans** : to confine oneself to

confins [kɔ̃fɛ̃] *nmpl* : borders, confines

confire [kɔ̃fir] {86} *vt* : to preserve, to candy, to pickle

confirmation [kɔ̃firmasjɔ̃] *nf* : confirmation

confirmer [kɔ̃firme] *vt* : to confirm

confiscation [kɔ̃fiskasjɔ̃] *nf* : confiscation, seizure

confiserie [kɔ̃fizri] *nf* **1** : candy store **2** : candy, confection

confisquer [kɔ̃fiske] *vt* : to confiscate, to seize

confit, -fite [kɔ̃fi, -fit] *adj* : candied, crystallized

confiture [kɔ̃fityr] *nf* **1** : jam **2 confiture d'oranges** : (orange) marmalade

conflagration [kɔ̃flagrasjɔ̃] *nf* : conflagration

conflictuel, -tuelle [kɔ̃fliktɥɛl] *adj* : conflicting

conflit [kɔ̃fli] *nm* : conflict, struggle

confluence [kɔ̃flyɑ̃s] *nf* : confluence, convergence

confluer [kɔ̃flye] *vi* : to meet, to converge

confondre [kɔ̃fɔ̃dr] {63} *vt* **1** : to confuse **2** MÉLANGER : to merge, to intermingle **3** ÉTONNER : to astound **4** DÉMASQUER : to expose — **se confondre** *vr* **1** : to merge **2 se confondre en excuses** : to apologize profusely

conforme [kɔ̃fɔrm] *adj* **1 ∼ à** : corresponding to, in keeping with **2 ∼ à** : true to <une copie conforme à l'original : an exact copy>

conformé, -mée [kɔ̃fɔrme] *adj* : formed, shaped <bien conformé : well-formed> <mal conformé : misshapen>

conformément [kɔ̃fɔrmemɑ̃] *adv* **∼ à** : in accordance with, in compliance with

conformer [kɔ̃fɔrme] *vt* : to conform, to shape — **se conformer** *vr* **∼ à** : to conform to

conformiste [kɔ̃fɔrmist] *nmf* : conformist

conformité [kɔ̃fɔrmite] *nf* **1** : conformity, conventionality **2** RESSEMBLANCE : similarity

confort [kɔ̃fɔr] *nm* **1** : comfort **2 tout confort** : with all (modern) conveniences

confortable [kɔ̃fɔrtabl] *adj* : comfortable — **confortablement** [-tabləmɑ̃] *adv*

conforter [kɔ̃fɔrte] *vt* : to strengthen, to reinforce

confrère [kɔ̃frɛr] *nm* : colleague

confrérie [kɔ̃freri] *nf* : brotherhood, association

confrontation [kɔ̃frɔ̃tasjɔ̃] *nf* **1** : confrontation **2** : comparison

confronter [kɔ̃frɔ̃te] *vt* **1** : to confront **2** : to compare

confus [kɔ̃fy] *adj* **1** : confused **2** : embarrassed <je suis vraiment confus : I'm truly sorry>

confusément [kɔ̃fyzemɑ̃] *adv* **1** : indistinctly, vaguely **2** : confusedly

confusion [kɔ̃fyzjɔ̃] *nf* **1** DÉSORDRE : confusion, disarray **2** GÊNE : embarrassment **3** MÉPRISE: confusion, mix-up

congé [kɔ̃ʒe] *nm* **1** VACANCES : vacation **2** : leave <congé de maladie : sick leave> **3** : notice <donner son congé à : give (one's) notice to> **4 prendre congé de** : to take leave of

congédier [kɔ̃ʒedje] {96} *vt* : to dismiss, to give notice to

congélateur [kɔ̃ʒelatœr] *nm* : freezer

congeler [kɔ̃ʒle] {20} *vt* : to freeze — **se congeler** *vr*

congénère [kɔ̃ʒenɛr] *nmf* : fellow creature

congénital, -tale [kɔ̃ʒenital] *adj, mpl* **-taux** [-to] : congenital

congère [kɔ̃ʒɛr] *nf France* : snowdrift, snowbank
congestion [kɔ̃ʒɛstjɔ̃] *nf* : congestion
congestionner [kɔ̃ʒɛstjɔne] *vt* **1** : to congest **2** : to make (one's face) flushed — **se congestionner** *vr* : to flush
conglomérat [kɔ̃glɔmera] *nm* : conglomerate, conglomeration
congloméré, -rée [kɔ̃glɔmere] *adj* : conglomerate
congolais, -laise [kɔ̃gɔlɛ, -lɛz] *adj* : Congolese
Congolais, -laise *n* : Congolese
congratuler [kɔ̃gratyle] *vt* : to congratulate
congrès [kɔ̃grɛ] *nm* CONFÉRENCE : congress, conference, convention
congru, -grue [kɔ̃gry] *adj* : congruent (in mathematics)
conifère[1] [kɔnifɛr] *adj* : coniferous
conifère[2] *nm* : conifer
conique [kɔnik] *adj* : conic, conical
conjecture [kɔ̃ʒɛktyr] *nf* SUPPOSITION : conjecture, guess
conjecturer [kɔ̃ʒɛktyre] *vt* PRÉSUMER : to conjecture, to presume
conjoint[1], **-jointe** [kɔ̃ʒwɛ̃, -ʒwɛ̃t] *adj* : joint, conjoint — **conjointement** [-ʒwɛ̃tmɑ̃] *adv*
conjoint[2], **-jointe** *n* ÉPOUX : spouse
conjonctif, -tive [kɔ̃ʒɔ̃ktif, -tiv] *adj* **1** : conjunctive **2** → **tissu**
conjonction [kɔ̃ʒɔ̃ksjɔ̃] *nf* : conjunction
conjonctivite [kɔ̃ʒɔ̃ktivit] *nf or* **conjonctivite aiguë contagieuse** : pinkeye
conjoncture [kɔ̃ʒɔ̃ktyr] *nf* : circumstances *pl,* situation
conjugaison [kɔ̃ʒygɛzɔ̃] *nf* **1** : conjugation **2** : combination, uniting
conjugal, -gale [kɔ̃ʒygal] *adj, mpl* **-gaux** [-go] : conjugal, marital
conjuguer [kɔ̃ʒyge] *vt* **1** : to conjugate (a verb) **2** COMBINER, UNIR : to combine, to unite — **se conjuguer** *vr*
conjuration [kɔ̃ʒyrasjɔ̃] *nf* COMPLOT : conspiracy
conjuré, -rée [kɔ̃ʒyre] *n* : conspirator
conjurer [kɔ̃ʒyre] *vt* **1** : to avert, to ward off **2** IMPLORER : to beseech, to implore — **se conjurer** *vr* : to conspire
connaissable [kɔnɛsabl] *adj* : knowable
connaissait [kɔnɛsɛ], *etc.* → **connaître**
connaissance [kɔnɛsɑ̃s] *nf* **1** : knowledge, understanding <à ma connaissance : to the best of my knowledge> <connaissance anticipée : foreknowledge> **2** : acquaintance <faire connaissance avec qqn : to meet s.o.> **3** CONSCIENCE : consciousness <avoir connaissance de : to be aware of> **4 connaissances** *nfpl* : knowledge, learning
connaisse [kɔnɛs], *etc.* → **connaître**
connaisseur[1], **-seuse** [kɔnɛsœr, -søz] *adj* : knowledgeable, expert
connaisseur[2], **-seuse** *n* : connoisseur, expert
connaître [kɔnɛtr] {7} *vt* **1** : to know <il faut connaître la vérité : we need to know the truth> <faire connaître : to make known> **2** : to be acquainted with, to know <je connais bien cette ville : I know this city well> **3** : to experience (sensation, emotion), to enjoy (success), to have (problems) — **se connaître** *vr* **1** : to know each other **2** : to know oneself **3 s'y connaître en** : to know about, to be an expert in
connecter [kɔnɛkte] *vt* : to connect
connerie [kɔnri] *nf fam* : blunder, stupid remark
connexe [kɔnɛks] *adj* : connected, related
connivence [kɔnivɑ̃s] *nf* COMPLICITÉ : connivance, complicity
connu[1] [kɔny] *pp* → **connaître**
connu[2], **-nue** [kɔny] *adj* : well-known
conque [kɔ̃k] *nf* : conch
conquérant, -rante [kɔ̃kerɑ̃, -rɑ̃t] *n* : conqueror
conquérir [kɔ̃kerir] {21} *vt* **1** : to conquer, to capture **2** : to win, to win over
conquête [kɔ̃kɛt] *nf* : conquest
conquière [kɔ̃kjer], **conquiert** [kɔ̃kjer], *etc.* → **conquérir**
conquis [kɔ̃ki] *pp* → **conquérir**
consacrer [kɔ̃sakre] *vt* **1** : to consecrate **2** : to sanction **3 ~ à** : to devote to — **se consacrer** *vr* **~ à** : to dedicate oneself to
consciemment [kɔ̃sjamɑ̃] *adv* : consciously
conscience [kɔ̃sjɑ̃s] *nf* **1** : conscience **2** : consciousness, awareness <avoir conscience de : to become aware of>
consciencieux, -cieuse [kɔ̃sjɑ̃sjø, -sjøz] *adj* : conscientious — **consciencieusement** [-sjøzmɑ̃] *adv*
conscient, -ciente [kɔ̃sjɑ̃, -sjɑ̃t] *adj* : conscious, aware
conscrit [kɔ̃skri] *nm* : conscript, draftee
consécration [kɔ̃sekrasjɔ̃] *nf* **1** : sanctioning, recognition **2** : consecration (in religion)
consécutif, -tive [kɔ̃sekytif, -tiv] *adj* : consecutive — **consécutivement** [-tivmɑ̃] *adv*
conseil [kɔ̃sɛj] *nm* **1** : counsel, (piece of) advice <donner un conseil à qqn : to give s.o. advice> <des conseils : advice> **2** : council <conseil d'administration : board of directors>
conseiller[1] [kɔ̃seje] *vt* **1** : to counsel, to give advice to **2** : to recommend, to advise
conseiller[2], **-lère** [kɔ̃seje, -jɛr] *n* **1** : counselor, advisor **2** : councillor
consensus [kɔ̃sɛ̃sys] *nm* : consensus

consentant, -tante [kɔ̃sɑ̃tɑ̃, -tɑ̃t] *adj* : consenting, willing
consentement [kɔ̃sɑ̃tmɑ̃] *nm* : consent
consentir [kɔ̃sɑ̃tir] {82} *vi* : to consent, to agree — *vt* : to grant
conséquence [kɔ̃sekɑ̃s] *nf* **1** : consequence, outcome **2 agir en conséquence** : to act accordingly
conséquent[1], **-quente** [kɔ̃sekɑ̃, -kɑ̃t] *adj* **1** : consistent, logical **2** *fam* : substantial, important
conséquent[2] *nm* **par ~** : consequently, therefore
conservateur[1], **-trice** [kɔ̃sɛrvatœr, -tris] *adj* : conservative
conservateur[2], **-trice** *n* **1** : conservative **2** : curator
conservation [kɔ̃sɛrvasjɔ̃] *nf* PRÉSERVATION : preservation, conservation
conservatisme [kɔ̃sɛrvatism] *nm* : conservatism
conservatoire [kɔ̃sɛrvatwar] *nm* : academy, conservatory
conserve [kɔ̃sɛrv] *nf* **1** : canned food <en conserve : canned> **2 de ~** : in concert, together
conserver [kɔ̃sɛrve] *vt* **1** GARDER : to keep **2** : to preserve, to conserve (food) — **se conserver** *vr* : to keep, to store
conserverie [kɔ̃sɛrvəri] *nf* : cannery
considérable [kɔ̃siderabl] *adj* : considerable — **considérablement** [-rabləmɑ̃] *adv*
considération [kɔ̃siderasjɔ̃] *nf* **1** : consideration <en considération de : because of, in view of> **2** : respect, consideration
considérer [kɔ̃sidere] {87} *vt* **1** : to consider <tout bien considéré : all things considered> **2** : to think highly of, to regard
consigne [kɔ̃siɲ] *nf* **1** : instructions *pl*, orders *pl* **2** : checkroom **3** : deposit
consigner [kɔ̃siɲe] *vt* **1** : to record, to write down **2** : to check (luggage, etc.) **3** : to deposit
consistance [kɔ̃sistɑ̃s] *nf* **1** : consistency <prendre consistance : to thicken> **2** : substance, strength <sans consistance : unfounded, groundless>
consistant, -tante [kɔ̃sistɑ̃, -tɑ̃t] *adj* **1** : thick (of sauce, paint, etc.) **2** : substantial, nourishing **3** : solid, well-founded (of an argument, etc.)
consister [kɔ̃siste] *vi* **1 ~ dans** *or* **~ à** : to lie in, to consist in <le bonheur consiste dans la modération : happiness lies in moderation> <son devoir consiste à partir : it is her duty to leave> **2 ~ en** : to be composed of, to consist of
consolation [kɔ̃sɔlasjɔ̃] *nf* : consolation
console [kɔ̃sɔl] *nf* : console
consoler [kɔ̃sɔle] *vt* : to console, to comfort, to soothe — **se consoler** *vr*
consolidation [kɔ̃sɔlidasjɔ̃] *nf* : consolidation
consolider [kɔ̃sɔlide] *vt* : to consolidate, to strengthen — **se consolider** *vr* : to grow stronger
consommateur, -trice [kɔ̃sɔmatœr, -tris] *n* **1** : consumer **2** : customer (in a café, etc.)
consommation [kɔ̃sɔmasjɔ̃] *nf* **1** : consumption **2** BOISSON : drink **3** : consummation (of a marriage) **4** PERPÉTRATION : perpetration (of a crime)
consommé[1], **-mée** [kɔ̃sɔme] *adj* : consummate
consommé[2] *nm* : consommé, clear soup
consommer [kɔ̃sɔme] *vt* **1** : to consume **2** : to consummate — *vi* : to have a drink
consonance [kɔ̃sɔnɑ̃s] *nf* : consonance (in music or poetry)
consonne [kɔ̃sɔn] *nf* : consonant
corsortium [kɔ̃sɔrsjɔm] *nm* : consortium, syndicate
conspirateur, -trice [kɔ̃spiratœr, -tris] *n* : conspirator, plotter
conspiration [kɔ̃spirasjɔ̃] *nf* : conspiracy
conspirer [kɔ̃spire] *vi* : to conspire, to plot
constant, -tante [kɔ̃stɑ̃, -tɑ̃t] *adj* **1** : constant, unchanging **2** : continual **3** : firm, steadfast — **constamment** [kɔ̃stamɑ̃] *adv*
constante [kɔ̃stɑ̃t] *nf* : constant
constat [kɔ̃sta] *nm* **1** : affidavit, official report **2** : acknowledgment
constatation [kɔ̃statasjɔ̃] *nf* OBSERVATION : observation, noticing
constater [kɔ̃state] *v* **1** : to notice, to observe **2** : to certify, to state
constellation [kɔ̃stelasjɔ̃] *nf* : constellation
consternation [kɔ̃stɛrnasjɔ̃] *nf* : consternation, dismay
consterner [kɔ̃stɛrne] *vt* : to dismay, to distress
constiper [kɔ̃stipe] *vt* : to constipate — **constipation** [-stipasjɔ̃] *nf*
constituant, -tuante [kɔ̃stitɥɑ̃, -tɥɑ̃t] *adj* : constituent
constituer [kɔ̃stitɥe] *vt* **1** : to constitute, to make up, to impanel (a jury) **2** : to set up, to form **3** : to settle (in law)
constitutif, -tive [kɔ̃stitytif, -tiv] *adj* : constituent
constitution [kɔ̃stitysjɔ̃] *nf* **1** : establishment, setting up **2** : constitution (in politics or physiology) **3** : composition, makeup
constitutionnel, -nelle [kɔ̃stitysjɔnɛl] *adj* : constitutional
constructeur, -trice [kɔ̃stryktœr, -tris] *n* **1** : builder **2** : manufacturer (of automobiles, etc.)
constructif, -tive [kɔ̃stryktif, -tiv] *adj* : constructive
construction [kɔ̃stryksjɔ̃] *nf* : building, construction

construire [kɔ̃strɥir] {49} *vt* : to construct, to build — **se construire** *vr Can* : to build <il se construit à Québec : he's building in Quebec>

consul [kɔ̃syl] *nm* : consul

consulat [kɔ̃syla] *nm* : consulate

consultant, -tante [kɔ̃syltɑ̃, -tɑ̃t] *n* : consultant

consultatif, -tive [kɔ̃syltatif, -tiv] *adj* : advisory

consultation [kɔ̃syltasjɔ̃] *nf* **1** : consulting, checking **2** : consultation (with an expert, a doctor, etc.) <heures de consultation : office hours> <aller à la consultation : to go to the doctor's> <entrer en consultation avec : to consult with> **3 consultation électorale** : election, voting

consulter [kɔ̃sylte] *vt* **1** : to consult, to seek advice from **2** : to refer to — *vi France* : to see patients — **se consulter** *vr* : to confer

consumer [kɔ̃syme] *vt* **1** : to consume **2** : to burn, to destroy — **se consumer** *vr* **1** : to burn (up, out) **2** : to waste away

contact [kɔ̃takt] *nm* **1** : contact, touch <rester en contact : to keep in touch> **2** : electrical contact, switch <couper le contact : to switch off the ignition> **3** : contact, connection (person)

contacter [kɔ̃takte] *vt* : to contact <j'ai contacté ma sœur : I got in touch with my sister>

contagion [kɔ̃taʒjɔ̃] *nf* : contagion — **contagieux, -gieuse** [-taʒjœ, -ʒjøz] *adj*

contaminer [kɔ̃tamine] *vt* **1** POLLUER : to contaminate, to pollute **2** INFECTER : to infect — **contamination** [-minasjɔ̃] *nf*

conte [kɔ̃t] *nm* **1** HISTOIRE : tale, story **2 conte de fées** : fairy tale

contempler [kɔ̃tɑ̃ple] *vt* **1** : to contemplate, to gaze at **2** : to reflect upon — **contemplation** [-tɑ̃plasjɔ̃] *nf*

contemporain, -raine [kɔ̃tɑ̃pɔrɛ̃, -rɛn] *adj & n* : contemporary

contenance [kɔ̃tnɑ̃s] *nf* **1** CAPACITÉ : capacity (of a container) **2** AIR : bearing, attitude <perdre contenance : to lose (one's) composure>

contenant [kɔ̃tnɑ̃] *nm* RÉCIPIENT : container

contenir [kɔ̃tnir] {92} *vt* **1** : to contain, to hold **2** : to restrain — **se contenir** *vr* : to control oneself

content, -tente [kɔ̃tɑ̃, -tɑ̃t] *adj* HEUREUX : content, pleased, happy

contentable [kɔ̃tɑ̃tabl] *adj* **il n'est pas contentable** *Can* : he can't be satisfied

contentement [kɔ̃tɑ̃tmɑ̃] *nm* SATISFACTION : contentment, satisfaction

contenter [kɔ̃tɑ̃te] *vt* SATISFAIRE : to satisfy, to please — **se contenter** *vr* **~ de** : to be contented with

contentieux[1], -tieuse [kɔ̃tɑ̃sjø, -sjøz] *adj* : contentious

contentieux[2] *nm* **1** : dispute **2** : legal department **3** : litigation

contenu [kɔ̃tny] *nm* : contents *pl*

conter [kɔ̃te] *vt* **1** RELATER : to tell, to relate **2 s'en laisser conter** : to be fooled, to be taken in

contestable [kɔ̃tɛstabl] *adj* : contestable, debatable

contestation [kɔ̃tɛstasjɔ̃] *nf* **1** : challenging, questioning **2** DISPUTE : dispute **3** : (political) protest

contester [kɔ̃tɛste] *vt* : to contest, to dispute — *vi* : to protest

conteur, -teuse [kɔ̃tœr, -tøz] *n* : storyteller, narrator

contexte [kɔ̃tɛkst] *nm* : context

contigu, -gue [kɔ̃tigy] *adj* : adjacent

continence [kɔ̃tinɑ̃s] *nf* : self-restraint, continence — **continent, -nente** [-tinɑ̃, -nɑ̃t] *adj*

continent [kɔ̃tinɑ̃] *nm* **1** : continent **2 le continent** : the mainland — **continental, -tale** [-nɑ̃tal] *adj, mpl* **-taux** [-to]

contingence [kɔ̃tɛ̃ʒɑ̃s] *nf* : contingency

contingent [kɔ̃tɛ̃ʒɑ̃] *nm* : contingent

continu, -nue [kɔ̃tiny] *adj* : continuous, ongoing

continuation [kɔ̃tinɥasjɔ̃] *nf* **1** : continuation **2 bonne continuation!** : carry on!

continuel, -nuelle [kɔ̃tinɥɛl] *adj* **1** : continuous **2** : continual, constant — **continuellement** [kɔ̃tinɥɛlmɑ̃] *adv*

continuer [kɔ̃tinɥe] **1** : to continue, to keep up **2** PROLONGER : to extend — *vi* : to continue, to carry on — **se continuer** *vr*

continuité [kɔ̃tinɥite] *nf* : continuity

contorsion [kɔ̃tɔrsjɔ̃] *nf* : contortion, twisting

contorsionner [kɔ̃tɔrsjɔne] *v* **se contorsionner** *vr* : to contort oneself, to writhe

contour [kɔ̃tur] *nm* : contour, outline

contourner [kɔ̃turne] *vt* **1** : to skirt, to bypass **2** : to get around (a difficulty, a law, etc.)

contraceptif[1], -tive [kɔ̃trasɛptif, -tiv] *adj* : contraceptive

contraceptif[2] *nm* : contraceptive

contraception [kɔ̃trasɛpsjɔ̃] *nf* : contraception

contracter [kɔ̃trakte] *vt* **1** : to contract, to tense **2** : to incur (a debt) **3** : to contract, to catch (a cold, etc.) **4** : to shorten, to contract (a word)

contracteur, -teuse [kɔ̃traktœr, -tøz] *nm Can* : contractor

contraction [kɔ̃traksjɔ̃] *nf* **1** CRISPATION : contraction, tensing **2** : contraction, shortening (of a word) **3 contraction de texte** : summary, précis

contractuel, -tuelle [kɔ̃traktɥɛl] *adj* : contractual — **contractuellement** [-tɥɛlmɑ̃] *adv*
contradiction [kɔ̃tradiksjɔ̃] *nf* : contradiction
contradictoire [kɔ̃tradiktwar] *adj* : conflicting, contradictory
contraignait [kɔ̃trɛɲɛ], **contraignions** [kɔ̃trɛɲɔ̃], *etc.* → **contraindre**
contraigne, *etc.* → **contraindre**
contraindre [kɔ̃trɛ̃dr] {65} *vt* **1** : to compel, to constrain <elle l'a contraint à agir : she compelled him to act> <j'étais contraint de parler : I was forced to speak> **2** : to restrain — **se contraindre** *vr*
contraint, -trainte [kɔ̃trɛ̃, -trɛ̃t] *adj* **1** : strained, forced **2 contraint et forcé** : under duress
contrainte *nf* **1** : constraint, restraint <sans contrainte : freely> **2** : pressure, coercion
contraire [kɔ̃trɛr] *adj & nm* : contrary, opposite <au contraire : on the contrary>
contrairement [kɔ̃trɛrmɑ̃] *adv* **à** ~ : contrary to
contralto[1] [kɔ̃tralto] *nmf* : alto, contralto (singer)
contralto[2] *nm* : alto, contralto (voice)
contrariant, -riante [kɔ̃trarjɑ̃, -rjɑ̃t] *adj* **1** : contrary, balky **2** : annoying
contrarier [kɔ̃trarje] {96} *vt* **1** : to annoy, to vex **2** : to thwart
contrariété [kɔ̃trarjete] *nf* : annoyance, vexation
contraste [kɔ̃trast] *nm* : contrast
contraster [kɔ̃traste] *v* : to contrast
contrat [kɔ̃tra] *nm* **1** : contract, agreement **2 passer un contrat avec** : to enter into a contract with
contravention [kɔ̃travɑ̃sjɔ̃] *nf* **1** : infraction **2** : ticket, violation notice
contre[1] [kɔ̃tr] *adv* : being against <je m'appuyais contre : I was leaning against it> <parler contre : to speak in opposition>
contre[2] *nm* **1** : opposition <le pour et le contre : the pros and cons> **2** : counterattack (in sports) **3 par contre** : on the other hand
contre[3] *prep* **1** : against <contre le mur : against the wall> <contre la guerre : against the war> **2** : (in exchange) for <envoi contre remboursement : cash on delivery> **3** : (in proportion) to <trois contre un : three to one> **4** : from <se protéger contre le danger : to protect oneself from danger> **5** : in spite of
contre-amiral [kɔ̃tramiral] *nm, pl* **-raux** [-ro] : rear admiral
contre-attaque [kɔ̃tratak] *nf, pl* **-attaques** : counterattack — **contre-attaquer** [kɔ̃tratake] *vi*
contrebalancer [kɔ̃trəbalɑ̃se] {6} *vt* : to counterbalance, to offset — **se contrebalancer** *vr* **1** : to offset each other **2** *fam* : not to give a damn <je m'en contrebalance : I couldn't care less>
contrebande [kɔ̃trəbɑ̃d] *nf* **1** : smuggling **2** : contraband, smuggled goods
contrebandier, -dière [kɔ̃trəbɑ̃dje, -djɛr] *n* : smuggler
contrebas [kɔ̃trəba] **en contrebas** : (down) below
contrebasse [kɔ̃trəbas] *nf* : double bass
contrecarrer [kɔ̃trəkare] *vt* : to thwart
contrecœur [kɔ̃trəkœr] **à** ~ : unwillingly, grudgingly
contrecoup [kɔ̃trəku] *nm* : repercussion, consequence
contre-courant [kɔ̃trəkurɑ̃] *nm, pl* **-courants 1** : countercurrent **2 à** ~ : upstream, against the current
contredire [kɔ̃trədir] {29} *vt* : to contradict — **se contradire** *vr*
contredit [kɔ̃trədi] **sans** ~ : indisputably, without question
contrée [kɔ̃tre] *nf* : country, land, region
contre-espionnage [kɔ̃trɛspjɔnaʒ] *nm* : counterespionage
contrefaçon [kɔ̃trəfasɔ̃] *nf* **1** : counterfeiting **2** : forgery
contrefaire [kɔ̃trəfɛr] {42} *vt* **1** : to imitate, to mimic **2** : to counterfeit **3** : to disguise (one's voice, etc.)
contrefait, -faite [kɔ̃trəfɛ, -fɛt] *adj* **1** : counterfeit, forged **2** DIFFORME : deformed
contrefort [kɔ̃trəfɔr] *nm* **1** : buttress, abutment **2 contreforts** *nmpl* : foothills
contre-indiqué, -quée [kɔ̃trɛ̃dike] *adj* : inadvisable, unwise
contre-interrogatoire [kɔ̃trɛ̃terɔgatwar] *nm, pl* **-toires** : cross-examination
contremaître, -maîtresse [kɔ̃trəmɛtr, -mɛtrɛs] *n* : foreman *m*, forewoman *f*
contrepartie [kɔ̃trəparti] *nf* **1** : compensation <en contrepartie : in compensation, in return> **2** : opposing view
contre-performance [kɔ̃trəpɛrfɔrmɑ̃s] *nf, pl* **-mances** : poor performance
contre-pied [kɔ̃trəpje] *nm, pl* **-pieds 1** : opposite opinion **2 prendre qqn à contre-pied** : to catch s.o. off balance
contre-plaqué [kɔ̃trəplake] *nm, pl* **-plaqués** : plywood
contrepoids [kɔ̃trəpwa] *nm* : counterweight, counterbalance
contrepoint [kɔ̃trəpwɛ̃] *nm* : counterpoint
contrepoison [kɔ̃trəpwazɔ̃] *nm* : antidote
contrer [kɔ̃tre] *vt* : to counter, to block
contre-révolution [kɔ̃trərevɔlysjɔ̃] *nf* : counterrevolution — **contre-révolutionnaire** [-sjɔnɛr] *adj & nmf*
contresens [kɔ̃trəsɑ̃s] *nm* **1** : misinterpretation, mistranslation **2 à** ~ : the wrong way, in the opposite direction

contresigner [kɔ̃trəsiɲe] *vt* : to countersign
contretemps [kɔ̃trətɑ̃] *nm* **1** : mishap, hitch **2** : offbeat (in music) **3 à ~** : inopportunely
contre–torpilleur [kɔ̃trətɔrpijœr] *nm* : destroyer (ship)
contrevenant[1], -nante [kɔ̃trəvnɑ̃, -vnɑ̃t] *adj* : contravening, offending
contrevenant[2], -nante *n* : offender, lawbreaker
contrevenir [kɔ̃trəvnir] {92} *vi* **~ à** : to contravene, to infringe
contrevent [kɔ̃trəvɑ̃] *nm* : window shutter
contribuable [kɔ̃tribɥabl] *nmf* : taxpayer
contribuer [kɔ̃tribɥe] *vi* : to contribute
contribution [kɔ̃tribysjɔ̃] *nf* **1** : contribution **2 contributions** *nfpl* IMPÔTS : taxes, taxation
contrit, -trite [kɔ̃tri, -trit] *adj* : contrite
contrôle [kɔ̃trol] *nm* **1** : control <contrôle des naissances : birth control> <contrôle de soi-même : self-control> **2** : checking, monitoring, auditing <contrôle de sécurité : security check>
contrôler [kɔ̃trole] *vt* **1** : to control **2** : to check, to inspect **3** SUPERVISER : to supervise, to monitor
contrôleur, -leuse [kɔ̃trolœr, -løz] *n* **1** : inspector, assessor **2** : controller <contrôleur aérien : air-traffic controller>
controverse [kɔ̃trɔvɛrs] *nf* : controversy
controversé, -sée [kɔ̃trɔvɛrse] *adj* : controversial
contusion [kɔ̃tyzjɔ̃] *nf* : contusion, bruise
convaincant, -cante [kɔ̃vɛ̃kɑ̃, -kɑ̃t] *adj* : persuasive, convincing
convaincre [kɔ̃vɛ̃kr] {94} *vt* **1** PERSUADER : to convince, to persuade **2** : to convict
convalescence [kɔ̃valesɑ̃s] *nf* : convalescence
convalescent, -cente [kɔ̃valesɑ̃, -sɑ̃t] *adj & n* : convalescent
convenable [kɔ̃vnabl] *adj* **1** APPROPRIÉ : suitable, appropriate **2** ACCEPTABLE : acceptable, adequate **3** : proper, decent — **convenablement** [-vnabləmɑ̃] *adv*
convenance [kɔ̃vnɑ̃s] *nf* **1** : suitability **2 convenances** *nfpl* : conventions, proprieties
convenir [kɔ̃vnir] {92} *vt* : to agree, to admit <je conviens que j'ai eu tort : I admit that I was wrong> — *vi* **1 ~ à** : to suit, to fit **2 ~ de** : to acknowledge, to admit — *v impers* **il convient de** : it is advisable to <il convient de partir maintenant : we should leave now>
convention [kɔ̃vɑ̃sjɔ̃] *nf* **1** : convention, norm <de convention : conventional> **2** : agreement <convention collective : collective (labor) agreement> **3** : (political) convention
conventionnel, -nelle [kɔ̃vɑ̃sjɔnɛl] *adj* : conventional — **conventionnellement** [-nɛlmɑ̃] *adv*
convenu, -nue [kɔ̃vny] *adj* **1** : agreed **2** : conventional
converger [kɔ̃vɛrʒe] {17} *vi* **1** : to converge **2** : to meet, to agree <nos avis convergent : our opinions tend in the same direction>
conversation [kɔ̃vɛrsasjɔ̃] *nf* : conversation, talk
converser [kɔ̃vɛrse] *vi* : to converse, to talk
conversion [kɔ̃vɛrsjɔ̃] *nf* : conversion
convertible [kɔ̃vɛrtibl] *adj* : convertible
converti, -tie [kɔ̃vɛrti] *n* : convert (to a religion)
convertir [kɔ̃vɛrtir] *vt* **1** : to convert **2 ~ en** : to transform into — **se convertir** *vr*
convertisseur [kɔ̃vɛrtisœr] *nm* : converter
convexe [kɔ̃vɛks] *adj* : convex
conviction [kɔ̃viksjɔ̃] *nf* CERTITUDE : conviction
convier [kɔ̃vje] {96} *vt* **1** INVITER : to invite **2** : to urge
convive [kɔ̃viv] *nmf* : guest (at a meal)
convivial, -viale [kɔ̃vivjal] *adj, mpl* **-viaux** [-vjo] **1** : convivial **2** : user-friendly — **convivialité** [-vjalite] *nf*
convocation [kɔ̃vɔkasjɔ̃] *nf* **1** : inviting, summoning **2** : notification (to attend), summons
convoi [kɔ̃vwa] *nm* **1** : convoy **2** *or* **convoi funèbre** : funeral procession
convoiter [kɔ̃vwate] *vt* : to covet
convoitise [kɔ̃vwatiz] *nf* **1** : covetousness, greed **2** : lust
convoluté, -tée [kɔ̃vɔlyte] *adj* : coiled, convoluted
convoquer [kɔ̃vɔke] *vt* **1** : to convoke, to convene **2** : to summon
convoyer [kɔ̃vwaje] {58} *vt* : to escort
convoyeur [kɔ̃vwajœr] *nm* **1** : convoy, escort (ship) **2** : conveyor
convulser [kɔ̃vylse] *vt* : to convulse, to distort (one's face, etc.)
convulsif, -sive [kɔvylsif, -siv] *adj* : convulsive
convulsion [kɔ̃vylsjɔ̃] *nf* : convulsion
coopératif, -tive [kɔɔperatif, -tiv] *adj* : cooperative
coopérative *nf* : cooperative
coopérer [kɔɔpere] {87} *vi* : to cooperate — **coopération** [-perasjɔ̃] *nf*
coopter [kɔɔpte] *vt* : to co-opt
coordination [kɔɔrdinasjɔ̃] *nf* : coordination
coordonnateur[1], -trice [kɔɔrdɔnatœr, -tris] *adj* : coordinating
coordonnateur[2], -trice *n* : coordinator
coordonné, -née [kɔɔrdɔne] *adj* **1** : coordinated **2** : coordinate <prop-

osition coordonnée : coordinate clause>

coordonnées [koɔrdɔne] *nfpl* **1** : (mathematical) coordinates *pl* **2** *fam* : address and telephone number

coordonner [koɔrdɔne] *vt* : to coordinate

copain, -pine [kɔpɛ̃, -pin] *n* **1** : friend, pal, buddy **2** *or* **petit copain, petite copine** : boyfriend *m,* girlfriend *f*

copeau [kɔpo] *nm* : chip, flake (of wood, metal, etc.)

copie [kɔpi] *nf* **1** : copy, duplicate **2** IMITATION : imitation **3** : manuscript, printer's copy **4** : paper, schoolwork

copier [kɔpje] {96} *vt* **1** : to copy, to transcribe **2** REPRODUIRE : to reproduce **3** : to copy (s.o.'s schoolwork)

copieux, -pieuse [kɔpjø, -pjøz] *adj* : copious — **copieusement** [-pjøzmɑ̃] *adv*

copilote [kɔpilɔt] *nmf* : copilot

copine → **copain**

copiste [kɔpist] *nmf* : copyist

copropriété [kɔprɔprijete] *nf* : joint ownership

copuler [kɔpyle] *vi* : to copulate — **copulation** [-pylasjɔ̃] *nf*

copyright [kɔpirajt] *nm* : copyright

coq [kɔk] *nm* : rooster

coq–à–l'âne [kɔkalan] *nm, pl* **coqs–à–l'âne** : abrupt change of subject

coq–l'oeil[1] [kɔklœj] *adj Can* **1** : one-eyed **2** : cross-eyed

coq–l'oeil[2] *nmf Can* **1** : one-eyed person **2** : cross-eyed person

coque [kɔk] *nf* **1** : cockle **2** : shell (of a nut) **3** : bow, loop, curl (of hair) **4** : hull (of a boat) **5 œuf à la coque** : soft-boiled egg

coquelicot [kɔkliko] *nm* : poppy

coqueluche [kɔklyʃ] *nf* **1** : whooping cough **2** *fam* : idol (in entertainment, sports, etc.)

coquerelle [kɔkrɛl] *nf Can* : cockroach

coquet, -quette [kɔke, -kɛt] *adj* **1** : stylish **2** : charming, pretty **3** *fam* : considerable <une coquette somme : a substantial sum>

coquette *nf* : coquette, flirt

coquetterie [kɔkɛtri] *nf* **1** : affectation **2** : flirtatiousness **3** : clothes-consciousness, stylishness

coquillage [kɔkijaʒ] *nm* **1** : shellfish **2** COQUILLE : shell

coquille [kɔkij] *nf* **1** : shell <coquille de noix : nutshell> **2** FAUTE : misprint **3 coquille Saint–Jacques** : scallop

coquin[1], **-quine** [kɔkɛ̃, -kin] *adj* ESPIÈGLE : mischievous, naughty

coquin[2], **-quine** *n* : little rascal, scamp

cor [kɔr] *nm* **1** : horn <cor anglais : English horn> **2** : corn (on one's foot)

corail [kɔraj] *nm, pl* **coraux** [kɔro] : coral

Coran [kɔrɑ̃] *nm* **le Coran** : the Koran

corbeau [kɔrbo] *nm, pl* **corbeaux 1** : crow **2** *or* **grand corbeau** : raven

corbeille [kɔrbɛj] *nf* **1** : basket <corbeille à papier : wastepaper basket> **2 corbeille de mariage** : wedding presents *pl*

corbillard [kɔrbijar] *nm* : hearse

cordage [kɔrdaʒ] *nm* **1** : rope **2 cordages** *nmpl* : rigging

corde [kɔrd] *nf* **1** : rope, cord <corde raide : tightrope> **2** : string <instrument à cordes : stringed instrument> **3 corde dorsal** : spinal cord **4 cordes vocales** : vocal cords **5 usé jusqu'à la corde** : threadbare

cordée [kɔrde] *nf* **1** : cord (of wood) **2** : roped party (of climbers)

cordial[1], **-diale** [kɔrdjal] *adj, mpl* **-diaux** [-djo] : cordial — **cordialement** [-djalmɑ̃] *adv*

cordial[2] *nm, pl* **cordiaux** : cordial

cordialité [kɔrdjalite] *nf* : cordiality, geniality

cordon [kɔrdɔ̃] *nm* **1** : cord, string, lace <cordon ombilical : umbilical cord> <cordon de soulier : shoelace> **2** : cordon (of police, etc.)

cordon–bleu [kɔrdɔ̃blø] *nm, pl* **cordons–bleus** : cordon-bleu chef

cordonnerie [kɔrdɔnri] *nf* **1** : cobbler's shop **2** : shoemaking, shoe repair

cordonnier, -nière [kɔrdɔnje, -njɛr] *n* : shoemaker, cobbler

coréen[1], **-réenne** [kɔreɛ̃, -reɛn] *adj* : Korean

coréen[2] *nm* : Korean (language)

Coréen, -réenne *n* : Korean

coriace [kɔrjas] *adj* DUR : tough

coriandre [kɔrjɑ̃dr] *nf* : coriander

cormoran [kɔrmɔrɑ̃] *nm* : cormorant

corne [kɔrn] *nf* **1** : antler, horn **2** : horny substance, tortoiseshell **3** : callus **4** : horn (instrument) <corne de brume : foghorn> **5 corne d'abondance** : cornucopia, horn of plenty

corned–beef [kɔrnbif] *nms & pl* : corned beef

cornée [kɔrne] *nf* : cornea

corneille [kɔrnɛj] *nf* : crow, rook

cornemuse [kɔrnəmyz] *nf* : bagpipes *pl*

corner [kɔrne] *vt* : to turn down (the corner of a page) — *vi* KLAXONNER : to honk, to toot

cornet [kɔrnɛ] *nm* **1** : cone <cornet de crème glacée : ice-cream cone> **2 cornet à pistons** : cornet

corniche [kɔrniʃ] *nf* **1** : cornice **2** : ledge, cliff road

cornichon [kɔrniʃɔ̃] *nm* **1** : gherkin **2** *fam* : idiot, dope

cornouiller [kɔrnuje] *nm* : dogwood

cornu, -nue [kɔrny] *adj* : horned

corollaire [kɔrɔlɛr] *nm* : corollary

corolle [kɔrɔl] *nf* : corolla

coronaire [kɔrɔnɛr] *adj* : coronary <artère coronaire : coronary artery>

coroner [kɔrɔnɛr] *nm* : coroner

corporatif, -tive [kɔrpɔratif, -tiv] *adj* : corporate

corporation [kɔrpɔrasjɔ̃] *nf* : corporation

corporel, -relle [kɔrpɔrɛl] *adj* : bodily, corporeal

corps [kɔr] *nm* **1** : body <corps à corps : hand to hand> **2** : corps (in the army, etc.), professional body <corps médical : medical profession> **3** : substance, body <corps étranger : foreign body> <prendre corps : to take shape> **4** *Can* : undershirt **5 à corps perdu** : headlong, with all one's might **6 à son corps défendant** : unwillingly, despite oneself **7 corps à corps** : hand-to-hand combat, clinch (in boxing)

corpulence [kɔrpylɑ̃s] *nf* : corpulence, stoutness — **corpulent, -lente** [kɔrpylɑ̃, -lɑ̃t] *adj*

corpuscule [kɔrpyskyl] *nm* : corpuscle

correct, -recte [kɔrɛkt] *adj* : correct — **correctement** [-rɛktəmɑ̃] *adv*

correcteur[1], -trice [kɔrɛktœr, -tris] *adj* : corrective

correcteur[2], -trice *n* **1** : corrector, grader **2** : proofreader

correctif, -tive [kɔrɛktif, -tiv] *adj* : corrective

correction [kɔrɛksjɔ̃] *nf* **1** : correction **2** : grading, marking **3** : thrashing, punishment **4** : correctness **5** : proofreading

correctionnel, -nelle [kɔrɛksjɔnɛl] *adj* : correctional

corrélation [kɔrelasjɔ̃] *nf* **1** : correlation **2 mettre en corrélation** : to interrelate

correspondance [kɔrɛspɔ̃dɑ̃s] *nf* **1** : correspondence **2** : connection (of a plane, bus, etc.)

correspondant, -dante [kɔrɛspɔ̃dɑ̃, -dɑ̃t] *n* **1** : correspondent, letter writer **2** : person being called (on the telephone) **3** : press correspondent

correspondre [kɔrɛspɔ̃dr] {63} *vi* **1** : to correspond, to write <elle correspond avec lui : she writes to him> **2** : to communicate (by telephone, etc.) **3 ~ à** : to correspond to, to match

corrida [kɔrida] *nf* : bullfight

corridor [kɔridɔr] *nm* : corridor, passageway

corrigé [kɔriʒe] *nm* : correct version

corriger [kɔriʒe] {17} *vt* **1** : to correct, to mark, to proofread **2** : to alleviate, to remedy **3** : to thrash — **se corriger** *vr* **~ de** : to cure oneself of

corroborer [kɔrɔbɔre] *vt* : to corroborate — **corroboration** [-bɔrasjɔ̃] *nf*

corroder [kɔrɔde] *vt* : to corrode

corrompre [kɔrɔ̃pr] {77} *vt* **1** PERVERTIR : to corrupt **2** SOUDOYER : to bribe

corrompu, -pue [kɔrɔ̃py] *adj* : corrupt

corrosif, -sive [kɔrɔzif, -ziv] *adj* : corrosive

corrosion [kɔrɔzjɔ̃] *nf* : corrosion

corruption [kɔrypsjɔ̃] *nf* **1** : corruption **2** : bribery

corsage [kɔrsaʒ] *nm* **1** CHEMISIER : blouse **2** : bodice (of a dress)

corsaire [kɔrsɛr] *nm* : privateer

corse [kɔrs] *adj* : Corsican

Corse *nmf* : Corsican

corsé, -sée [kɔrse] *adj* **1** ÉPICÉ : spicy **2** DIFFICILE : tough, tricky **3** : full-bodied (of wine), strong (of coffee, etc.)

corser [kɔrse] *vt* **1** : to add spice to **2** : to aggravate <pour corser l'affaire : to complicate matters> **3** : to liven up **4** : to spike (a drink) — **se corser** *vr* : to get more complicated <l'affaire se corse : the plot thickens>

corset [kɔrsɛ] *nm* : corset

cortège [kɔrtɛʒ] *nm* : procession, cortege

cortex [kɔrtɛks] *nm* : cortex

cortisone [kɔrtizɔn] *nf* : cortisone

corvée [kɔrve] *nf* **1** : chore **2** : duty (in the military)

cosignataire [kɔsiɲatɛr] *nmf* : cosigner, cosignatory

cosigner [kɔsiɲe] *vt* : to cosign

cosmétique [kɔsmetik] *adj* : cosmetic

cosmétiques *nmpl* : cosmetics, beauty products

cosmique [kɔsmik] *adj* : cosmic

cosmonaute [kɔsmɔnot] *nmf* : cosmonaut

cosmopolite [kɔsmɔpɔlit] *adj* : cosmopolitan

cosmos [kɔsmos] *nm* : cosmos

cosse [kɔs] *nf* : pod, husk

cossins [kɔsɛ̃] *nmpl Can fam* : things, stuff <ramasse tes cossins : pick up your things>

cossu, -sue [kɔsy] *adj* **1** : well-to-do, affluent **2** : opulent, posh

costaricain, -caine [kɔstarikɛ̃, -kɛn] *adj* : Costa Rican

Costaricain, -caine *n* : Costa Rican

costaud, -taude [kɔsto, -tod] *adj fam* : strong, sturdy, robust

costume [kɔstym] *nm* **1** : suit **2** : costume, dress

costumer [kɔstyme] *vt* : to dress up — **se costumer** *vr* **~ en** : to get dressed up as

cotation [kɔtasjɔ̃] *nf* : quotation (in finance)

cote [kɔt] *nf* **1** : quotation, quoted value **2** : rating, standing <cote de popularité : popularity rating> **3** : odds **4** : dimension (in construction) **5** : height <cote d'alerte : flood level> **6** : call number (of a library book)

côte [kot] *nf* **1** : coast, shore **2** : rib **3** : side <côte à côte : side by side> **4** : chop, cutlet **5** : hill, slope

côté [kote] *nm* **1** : side <se coucher sur le côté : to lie on one's side> **2** ASPECT : aspect, point of view <d'un autre côté : on the other hand> <de mon côté : for my part> **3** : way, direction <de quel côté? : which way?> **4 à ~** : nearby **5 à côté de** : next to **6 de côté** : sideways, sidelong **7 de ~** : aside, to one side <mettre de côté : to put aside> **8 du côté de** : toward <allons du côté de la plage : let's head for the beach>

coteau [kɔto] *nm, pl* **coteaux** **1** PENTE, VERSANT : slope, hillside **2** COLLINE : hill

côtelé, -lée [kotle] *adj* **1** : ribbed **2 velours côtelé** : corduroy

côtelette [kotlɛt] *nf* : chop

coter [kɔte] *vt* **1** : to classify (books) **2** : to quote, to value (in finance)

coterie [kɔtri] *nf* : clique, set (of cronies)

côteux, -teuse [kotø, -tøz] *adj Can* : hilly

côtier, -tière [kotje, -tjɛr] *adj* : coastal

cotisation [kɔtizasjɔ̃] *nf* : dues *pl*, fee

cotiser [kɔtize] *vi* **1** : to subscribe, to pay one's dues **2** : to contribute (to a fund)

coton [kɔtɔ̃] *nm* : cotton

cotonnade [kɔtɔnad] *nf* : cotton fabric

cotonneux, -neuse [kɔtɔnø, -nøz] *adj* : fleecy, fluffy

côtoyer [kotwaye] {58} *vt* **1** : to skirt, to run alongside **2** : to be close to, to mix with

cotre [kɔtr] *nm* : cutter (boat)

cottage [kɔtaʒ] *nm* **1** *France* : cottage **2** → **fromage**

cotte [kɔt] *nf* **1** *France* : overalls *pl* **2 cotte de mailles** : coat of mail

cou [ku] *nm* : neck

couard[1], **couarde** [kwar, kward] *adj* POLTRON : cowardly

couard[2], **couarde** *n* : coward

couardise [kwardiz] *nf* : cowardice

couchage [kuʃaʒ] *nm* **1** : bed, sleeping arrangements **2** → **sac**

couchant[1], **-chante** [kuʃɑ̃, -ʃɑ̃t] *adj* : setting <le soleil couchant : the setting sun>

couchant[2] *nm* **1** : sunset **2** : west

couche [kuʃ] *nf* **1** : layer, stratum <couche d'ozone : ozone layer> <couche sociale : social stratum> **2** : coat (of paint) **3** : diaper **4 couches** *nfpl* : childbirth **5** → **faux**

coucher[1] [kuʃe] *vt* **1** : to put up, to provide a bed for **2** : to put to bed **3** : to lay down flat, to flatten **4** : to put in writing — *vi* **1** : to sleep, to spend the night **2 ~ avec** : to sleep with — **se coucher** *vr* : to lie down, to go to bed

coucher[2] *nm* **1** : bedtime **2 coucher du soleil** : sunset

couchette [kuʃɛt] *nf* **1** : cot (for a child) **2** : berth, bunk (in a train or ship)

coucou [kuku] *nm* **1** : cuckoo <coucou terrestre : roadrunner> **2** : cuckoo clock **3** : cowslip

coude [kud] *nm* **1** : elbow **2** : bend, angle **3 coude à coude** : side by side, shoulder to shoulder

coudée [kude] *nf* **avoir les coudées franches** : to have elbow room

cou–de–pied [kudpje] *nm, pl* **cous–de–pied** : instep

coudon [kudɔ̃] *interj Can fam* : come on! <coudon, que'est-ce qu'ils font? : what on earth are they doing?>

coudoyer [kudwaje] {58} *vt* : to rub shoulders with

coudre [kudr] {22} *v* : to sew

coudrier [kudrije] *nm* : hazel (tree)

couenne [kwan] *nf* **1** : pork rind **2 avoir la couenne dure** *Can* : to be resilient, to be hard-shelled

couette [kwɛt] *nf* **1** : comforter, duvet **2 couettes** *nfpl* : pigtails

couguar [kug(w)ar] *nm* PUMA : cougar, puma

couinement [kwinmɑ̃] *nm* : squeaking, squealing

couiner [kwine] *vt* : to squeak, to squeal

coulant[1], **-lante** [kulɑ̃, -lɑ̃t] *adj* **1** : flowing (of style, etc.) **2** : runny <fromage coulant : runny cheese> **3** : easygoing

coulant[2] *nm* : runner (of a plant)

coulée [kule] *nf* **1** : flow, slide <coulée de lave : lava flow> **2** : casting (of metal) **3** *Can* : ravine, gully

couler [kule] *vt* **1** : to sink (a ship) **2** : to pour, to cast **3** : to ruin, to cause to fail **4** : to spend, to pass (time) — *vi* **1** : to flow, to run **2** : to slide, to slip **3** : to leak **4** : to sink — **se couler** *vr* **1 ~ dans** : to slip into **2 se la couler douce** *fam* : to have an easy time of it

couleur [kulœr] *nf* **1** : color **2** : suit (of cards)

couleuvre [kulœvr] *nf* : grass snake

coulisse [kulis] *nf* **1** : groove, slot **2** : slide (of a trombone) **3** *Can* : trickle, drip (of paint, sap, water, etc.) **4 coulisses** *nfpl* : backstage, wings (in a theater)

coulisser [kulise] *vi* : to slide, to run (in a groove)

couloir [kulwar] *nm* **1** : corridor, passage **2** : lane (in sports or transportation) **3** : gully

coup [ku] *nm* **1** : knock, blow <coup de pied : kick> <coup de poing : punch> **2** : shock <ça lui a donné un coup : that gave him a shock> **3** : shot <coup de feu : gunshot> **4** : movement <un coup d'œil : a glance> **5** : stroke, shot (in sports) <coup droit : forehand (drive)> **6** : action, effect <coup de soleil : sunburn> <coup de téléphone : telephone call> <coup de foudre : love at first sight> **7** : (political) coup <coup d'État : coup d'état> **8 à coup sûr** : definitely, for sure **9 après coup** : afterwards **10 coups et blessures** : assault and battery **11 coup sûr** *Can* : base hit **12 coup sur coup** : one after another **13 du coup** : as a result **14 tout à coup** : suddenly

coupable[1] [kupabl] *adj* : guilty

coupable[2] *nmf* : culprit

coupant, -pante [kupɑ̃, -pɑ̃t] *adj* **1** : sharp **2** TRANCHANT : cutting, curt (of a remark, etc.)

coupe [kup] *nf* **1** : goblet, fruit dish **2** : cup (in sports) **3** : cut, cutting <coupe (de cheveux) : haircut> **4** : section (in biology)

coupé [kupe] *nm* : coupé, coupe

coupe–circuit [kupsirkɥi] *nms & pl* : circuit breaker

coupée [kupe] *nf* : gangway

coupe–feu [kupfø] *nms & pl* : firebreak

coupe–ongles [kupɔ̃gl] *nms & pl* : nail clippers

coupe–papier [kuppapje] *nms & pl* : letter opener

couper [kupe] *vt* **1** : to cut, to cut up, to cut down **2** : to cut off, to break off, to block off **3** : to cut across, to intersect **4** : to dilute (wine, etc.) — *vi* **1** : to cut **2** : to take a shortcut **3 couper à court** : to cut short, to curtail — **se couper** *vr* **1** : to cut oneself <il s'est coupé le doigt : he cut his finger> <se couper les cheveux : to cut one's hair> **2** : to intersect **3 ~ de** : to cut oneself off from

couperet [kuprɛ] *nm* **1** : cleaver **2** : blade (of a guillotine)

couperosé, -sée [kuproze] *adj* : blotchy

coupe–vent [kupvɑ̃] *nms & pl* : windbreaker

couplage [kuplaʒ] *nm* : (mechanical) coupling

couple [kupl] *nm* : couple, pair

coupler [kuple] *vt* : to couple, to pair (up)

couplet [kuplɛ] *nm* : verse

coupoir [kupwar] *nm* : cutter (tool)

coupole [kupɔl] *nf* : cupola, dome

coupon [kupɔ̃] *nm* **1** : coupon **2** : remnant (of cloth) **3** : ticket, pass

coupure [kupyr] *nf* **1** : cut <coupure profonde : deep cut> <coupure du salaire : salary cut> **2** : gap **3** : break <coupure publicitaire : commercial break> **4** BILLET : banknote **5 coupure de presse** : newspaper clipping

cour [kur] *nf* **1** : court <Cour suprême : Supreme Court> **2** : courtyard <cour de récréation : playground> **3** : courtship **4 cour martiale** : court-martial

courage [kuraʒ] *nm* **1** : courage **2** : will, spirit <bon courage! : stick to it!, good luck!>

courageux, -geuse [kuraʒø, -ʒøz] *adj* **1** : courageous, brave **2** : energetic — **courageusement** [-ʒøzmɑ̃] *adv*

courailler [kuraje] *vi Can fam* : to run around from one place to another

couramment [kuramɑ̃] *adv* **1** : fluently **2** : commonly

courant[1], **-rante** [kurɑ̃, -rɑ̃t] *adj* **1** : current **2** : common, frequent **3** COMMUN : usual, ordinary

courant[2] *nm* **1** : current <courant continu : direct current> <courant alternatif : alternating current> <courant d'air : draft> <contre le courant : against the tide> **2** : trend **3** : movement (of populations, etc.) **4** : course <dans le courant de l'année : in the course of the year> **5 au courant** : up-to-date, in the know

courbature [kurbatyr] *nf* : stiffness, ache, charley horse

courbaturé, -rée [kurbatyre] *adj* : aching

courbe[1] [kurb] *adj* : curved

courbe[2] *nf* **1** : (graphic) curve **2** : bend, curve

courber [kurbe] *vt* **1** : to bend, to curve **2** : to bow — *vi* : to bend (over), to bow — **se courber** *vr*

courbette [kurbɛt] *nf* : low bow <faire des courbettes à : to kowtow to>

courbure [kurbyr] *nf* : curvature

coureur[1], **-reuse** [kurœr, -røz] *n* **1** : runner **2** : racer <coureur cycliste : bicycle racer> <coureur automobile : race car driver>

coureur[2] *nm or* **oiseau coureur** : flightless bird

courge [kurʒ] *nf* : gourd, squash

courgette [kurʒɛt] *nf* : zucchini

courir [kurir] {23} *vt* **1** : to run <courir le risque : to run the risk> **2** : to go around, to roam **3** FRÉQUENTER : to frequent **4** POURSUIVRE : to run after, to pursue — *vi* **1** : to run **2** : to race **3** : to rush **4 le bruit court** : rumor has it **5 par les temps qui courent** : nowadays, at the present time

courlis [kurli] *nm* : curlew

couronne [kurɔn] *nf* **1** : crown **2** : wreath **3** : corona

couronnement [kurɔnmɑ̃] *nm* **1** : coronation, crowning **2** : crowning achievement

couronner [kurɔne] *vt* : to crown

courra [kura], *etc.* → **courir**

courriel [kurjɛl] *nm Can* : electronic mail, E-mail

courrier [kurje] *nm* : mail, correspondence <courrier des lecteurs : letters to the editor> <courrier électronique : electronic mail>

courroie [kurwa] *nf* **1** : strap **2** : belt <courroie de ventilateur : fan belt>

courroucé, -cée [kuruse] *adj* : wrathful, infuriated

courroux [kuru] *nm* COLÈRE : anger, wrath

cours [kur] *nm* **1** : course <au cours de : in the course of, during> **2** : course, class, lesson <suivre un cours : to take a class> **3** : school <cours du soir : night school> **4** MANUEL : textbook **5** : flow, current <cours d'eau : riv-

er, stream> **6** : rate, price <cours des devises : foreign exchange rate> <avoir cours : to be legal tender, to be current, to be used> **7 en ~** : current, in progress

course [kurs] *nf* **1** : run, running **2** : race <course cycliste : bicycle race> <course contre la montre : race against time> **3** : errand <faire des courses : to go shopping> **4** : course, path **5** : journey, ride (in a taxi)

coursier[1], -sière [kursje, -sjɛr] *n* : messenger

coursier[2] *nm* : steed

court[1] [kur] *adv* **1** : short <s'arrêter court : to stop short> **2 à court de** : short of **3 tout court** : simply

court[2], courte [kur, kurt] *adj* **1** : short (in height), narrow **2** : brief, quick

court[3] *nm* : court <court de tennis : tennis court> <tenir court : to hold court>

courtage [kurtaʒ] *nm* : brokerage

court–circuit [kursirkɥi] *nm, pl* **courts–circuits** : short circuit

court–circuiter [kursirkɥite] *vt* **1** : to short-circuit **2** : to bypass

courtepointe [kurtəpwɛ̃t] *nf* : duvet, quilt

courtesane [kurtizan] *nf* : courtesan

courtier, -tière [kurtje, -tjɛr] *n* : broker, agent

courtisan [kurtizɑ̃] *nm* **1** : sycophant, flatterer **2** : courtier

courtiser [kurtize] *vt* : to court, to woo

court–métrage [kurmetraʒ] *nm* : short (film)

courtois, -toise [kurtwa, -twaz] *adj* : courteous — **courtoisement** [-twazmɑ̃] *adv*

courtoisie [kurtwazi] *nf* : courtesy

cousait [kuzɛ], *etc.* → **coudre**

couse [kuz], *etc.* → **coudre**

cousin[1], -sine [kuzɛ̃, -zin] *n* : cousin <cousin germain : first cousin>

cousin[2] *nm* : mosquito

coussin [kusɛ̃] *nm* **1** : cushion **2** *Can* : base (in baseball)

cousu [kuzy] *pp* → **coudre**

coût [ku] *nm* : cost <le coût de la vie : the cost of living>

coûtant [kutɑ̃] *adj* **à prix coûtant** : at cost

couteau [kuto] *nm, pl* **couteaux** : knife <couteau de poche : pocketknife, jacknife>

coutelas [kutla] *nm* **1** : cutlass **2** : butcher knife

coutellerie [kutɛlri] *nf* **1** : cutlery, knives **2** *Can* : silverware (set)

coûter [kute] *vt* : to cost <coûter cher : to be expensive> <ça coûte combien? : how much is it?> — *vi* : to cost

coûteux, -teuse [kutø, -tøz] *adj* : costly

coutume [kutym] *nf* **1** : custom **2 de coutume** : usual, customary

coutumier, -mière [kutymje, -mjɛr] *adj* : customary

couture [kutyr] *nf* **1** : sewing, needlework **2** : dressmaking **3** : seam

couturier [kutyrje] *nm* : fashion designer

couturière [kutyrjɛr] *nf* : dressmaker

couvée [kuve] *nf* : brood

couvent [kuvɑ̃] *nm* : convent, monastery

couver [kuve] *vt* **1** : to brood, to hatch **2** : to overprotect — *vi* **1** : to smolder, to be brewing **2** : to brood

couvercle [kuvɛrkl] *nm* **1** : lid, cover **2** : top, cap (of a spray can, etc.)

couvert[1] [kuvɛr] *pp* → **couvrir**

couvert[2], -verte [kuvɛr, -vɛrt] *adj* **1** : covered, indoor <piscine couverte : indoor swimming pool> **2** : overcast, cloudy

couvert[3] *nm* **1** : place setting (at a table) <couverts : eating utensils, flatware> **2** ABRI : shelter, cover **3** : cover charge

couverture [kuvɛrtyr] *nf* **1** : cover (of a book, etc.) **2** : blanket **3** : news coverage **4** : roofing

couveuse [kuvøz] *nf* **1** : brood hen **2** : incubator

couvoir [kuvwar] *nm* : hatchery (for chickens, etc.)

couvre–chef [kuvrəʃɛf] *nm, pl* **couvre–chefs** : headgear

couvre–feu [kuvrəfø] *nm, pl* **couvre–feux** : curfew

couvre–lit [kuvrəli] *nm, pl* **couvre–lits** : bedspread

couvre–pieds [kuvrəpje] *nms & pl* : quilt, coverlet

couvre–plancher [kuvrəplɑ̃ʃe] *nm, pl* **couvre–planchers** *Can* : flooring

couvrir [kuvrir] {83} *vt* **1** : to cover **2** : to cover up for, to shield **3** : to drown out (sound) — **se couvrir** *vr* **1** : to wrap (oneself) up **2** : to cover oneself **3** : to cloud over **4 ~ de** : to be covered with

covoiturage [kovwatyraʒ] *nm Can* : car pool(ing)

cow–boy [kɔbɔj] *nm, pl* **cow–boys** : cowboy

coyote [kɔjɔt] *nm* : coyote

crabe [krab] *nm* : crab

crachat [kraʃa] *nm* : spittle

craché, -chée [kraʃe] *adj fam* **être (qqn) tout craché** : to be the spitting image (of s.o.)

cracher [kraʃe] *vt* **1** : to spit (out) **2** : to belch out (smoke, lava, etc.) **3** *fam* : to cough up (money, etc.) — *vi* : to spit

crachin [kraʃɛ̃] *nm* : drizzle — **crachiner** [kraʃine] *vi*

crachoir [kraʃwar] *nm* : spittoon

crack [krak] *nm* **1** : crack (cocaine) **2** *fam* : whiz, ace <c'est un crack aux échecs : he's a whiz at chess>

craie [krɛ] *nf* : chalk

craignait [krɛɲɛ], **craignions** [krɛɲiɔ̃], *etc.* → **craindre**

craigne [krɛɲ], *etc.* → **craindre**
craindre [krɛ̃dr] {65} *vt* **1** REDOUTER : to fear, to be afraid of **2 ~ que** : to regret that, to fear that **3** : to be susceptible to
crainte [krɛ̃t] *nf* : fear, dread <de crainte que : lest>
craintif, -tive [krɛ̃tif, -tiv] *adj* : fearful, timid — **craintivement** [-tivmɑ̃] *adv*
cramoisi [kramwazi] *nm* : crimson
crampe [krɑ̃p] *nf* : cramp, spasm
crampon [krɑ̃pɔ̃] *nm* **1** : clamp **2** : cleat
cramponner [krɑ̃pɔne] *vt* **1** : to clamp together **2** *fam* : to pester — **se cramponner** *vr* **~ à** : to hold on to, to cling to
cran [krɑ̃] *nm* **1** : notch, hole (in a belt) **2** *fam* : courage <avoir du cran : to have guts>
crâne [kran] *nm* **1** : cranium, skull **2 bourrer le crâne à qqn** *fam* : to brainwash s.o.
crâner [krane] *vi fam* : to show off
crâneur[1], -neuse [kranœr, -nøz] *adj fam* : boastful
crâneur[2], -neuse *n fam* : show-off
crânien, -nienne [kranjɛ̃, -njɛn] *adj* **1** : cranial **2 boîte crânienne** : cranium, skull
crapaud [krapo] *nm* : toad
crapule [krapyl] *nf* : scoundrel, crook
crapuleux, -leuse [krapylø, -løz] *adj* : crooked, villainous
craque [krak] *nf Can* : crack, crevasse
craquement [krakmɑ̃] *nm* : crack, crunch, creak
craquer [krake] *vi* **1** : to crack, to crunch, to creak **2** SE DÉCHIRER : to burst apart, to tear **3** *fam* : to collapse, to break down — *vt* **1** : to tear, to rip **2** : to strike (a match)
crasse[1] [kras] *adj* : crass, gross — **crassement** [krasmɑ̃] *adv*
crasse[2] *nf* **1** : filth, grime **2** : dross, slag **3 faire une crasse** : to play a dirty trick
crasseux, -seuse [krasø, -søz] *adj* : filthy, grimy
cratère [kratɛr] *nm* : crater
cravache [kravaʃ] *nf* : whip, crop
cravacher [kravaʃe] *vt* : to horsewhip
cravate [kravat] *nf* : necktie, cravat
crayeux, crayeuse [krɛjø, -jøz] *adj* : chalky (of the complexion)
crayon [krɛjɔ̃] *nm* **1** : pencil <crayon de couleur : colored pencil> **2 crayon à bille** : ballpoint pen **3 crayon de cire** : crayon
crayonner [krɛjɔne] *vt* **1** : to scribble, to jot down (in pencil) **2** : to sketch
créance [kreɑ̃s] *nf* **1** : debt **2** : letter of credit **3** : credence, credibility
créancier, -cière [kreɑ̃sje, -sjɛr] *n* : creditor
créateur[1], -trice [kreatœr, -tris] *adj* : creative
créateur[2], -trice *n* : creator, originator
création [kreasjɔ̃] *nf* : creation
créativité [kreativite] *nf* : creativity
créature [kreatyr] *nf* : creature
crécelle [kresɛl] *nf* : noisemaker
crèche [krɛʃ] *nf* **1** : crèche, Nativity scene **2** *France* : day-care center, nursery
crédible [kredibl] *adj* : credible — **crédibilité** [-dibilite] *nf*
crédit [kredi] *nm* **1** : credit <acheter à crédit : to buy on credit> **2** : credence, credibility **3 crédits** *nmpl* : funds
crédit–bail [kredibaj] *nm, pl* **crédits–bails** : leasing
créditer [kredite] *vt* : to credit
créditeur, -trice [kreditœr, -tris] *n* **1** : creditor **2 être crediteur** : to be in the black
crédo [kredo] *nm* : creed
crédule [kredyl] *adj* NAIF : credulous, gullible — **crédulité** [-dylite] *nf*
créer [kree] {89} *vt* **1** : to create **2** : to set up, to establish
crémage [krɛ(e)maʒ] *nm Can* : icing (on a cake)
crème [krɛm] *nf* **1** : cream <crème hydratante : moisturizer> **2 crème glacée** *Can* : ice cream
crémerie [krɛmri] *nf France* : dairy shop
crémeux, -meuse [kremø, -møz] *adj* : creamy
créneau [kreno] *nm, pl* **créneaux** **1** : slot, gap, window (of time) **2** : niche, share <créneau du marché : market share> **3** : crenellation, battlement **4 faire un créneau** : to back into a parking space
créole[1] [kreɔl] *adj* : creole
créole[2] *nm* : Creole (language)
Créole *nmf* : Creole
créosote [kreɔzɔt] *nf* : creosote
crêpe[1] [krɛp] *nf* : pancake, crepe
crêpe[2] *nm* : crepe (fabric)
crépitement [krepitmɑ̃] *nm* : crackling, clacking, patter (of rain)
crépiter [krepite] *vi* : to crackle, to splutter, to patter
crépuscule [krepyskyl] *nm* : twilight, dusk
crescendo [krɛʃɛndo, krɛʃɛ̃do] *nms & pl* : crescendo
cresson [krɛsɔ̃] *nm* : cress, watercress
crête [krɛt] *nf* **1** : crest, peak **2** : comb, crest
crétin, -tine [kretɛ̃, -tin] *n* IDIOT : idiot, moron
cretons [krətɔ̃] *nmpl Can* : pâté made with pork and veal
creusement [krøzmɑ̃] *nm* : digging, excavation
creuser [krøze] *vt* **1** : to dig, to hollow out, to furrow **2** : to study in depth **3** : to flex, to bend <creuser le dos : to arch one's back> **4 ça creuse!** *fam* : that gives one an appetite! — *vi* : to dig, to excavate — **se creuser**

vr **se creuser la tête** *fam* : to rack one's brains
creuset [krøzɛ] *nm* **1** : crucible **2** : melting pot
creux[1], creuse [krø, krøz] *adj* **1** VIDE : hollow, empty **2** CONCAVE : concave, sunken **3** : shallow, superficial
creux[2] *nm* : hollow, hole, cavity <le creux de l'estomac : the pit of the stomach>
crevaison [krəvɛzɔ̃] *nf* : flat tire, puncture
crevasse [krəvas] *nf* **1** : crevasse **2** : crack, crevice **3 avoir des crevasses aux mains** : to have chapped hands
crevé, -vée [krəve] *adj* **1** : punctured, flat (of a tire) **2** : dead **3** *fam* : exhausted, dead tired
crève–cœur [krɛvkœr] *nms & pl* : heartbreak
crever [krəve] {52} *vt* **1** : to burst, to puncture **2** *fam* : to wear out **3 crever de faim** : to be starving — *vi* **1** : to burst **2** *fam* : to die — **se crever** *vr fam* : to wear oneself out
crevette [krəvɛt] *nf* : shrimp, prawn
cri [kri] *nm* **1** : cry, shout <à grands cris : at the top of one's lungs> **2 le dernier cri** : the latest thing
criaillement [kriajmɑ̃] *nm* : squawking, screeching, honking
criailler [kriaje] *vi* **1** : to squawk, to screech, to honk **2** : to complain, to grumble
criant, criante [krijɑ̃, krijɑ̃t] *adj* : obvious, flagrant, striking
criard, criarde [krijar, krijard] *adj* **1** : shrill **2** : loud, garish
crible [kribl] *nm* **1** : sieve, screen **2 passer au crible** : to screen, to examine closely
cribler [krible] *vt* **1** : to sift, to screen **2** : to riddle, to fill with holes
cric [krik] *nm* VÉRIN : jack
cricket [krikɛt] *nm* : cricket (sport)
criée [krije] *nf* : auction
crier [krije] {96} *vi* **1** : to shout, to cry out **2** : to squeal, to squeak — *vt* **1** : to shout **2** : to proclaim, to protest
crieur, crieuse [krijœr, krijøz] *n* : hawker, peddler
crime [krim] *nm* **1** : crime **2** : murder
criminel[1], -nelle [kriminɛl] *adj* : criminal — **criminellement** [-nɛlmɑ̃] *adv*
criminel[2], -nelle *n* **1** : criminal **2** MEURTRIER : murderer
crin [krɛ̃] *nm* **1** : horsehair **2 à tout crin** : die-hard, fanatical
crinière [krinjɛr] *nf* : mane
crique[1] [krik] *nf* : cove, inlet
crique[2] *nm Can* : creek
criquet [krikɛ] *nm* **1** *or* **criquet migrateur** : locust (insect) **2** *Can* : cricket (insect)
crise [kriz] *nf* **1** : crisis **2** ACCÈS : fit, outburst <crise de désespoir : fit of despair> **3** ATTAQUE : attack (in medicine) <crise cardiaque : heart attack>
crispant, -pante [krispɑ̃, -pɑ̃t] *adj* AGAÇANT : aggravating, annoying
crispation [krispasjɔ̃] *nf* CONTRACTION : tension, contraction
crispé, -pée [krispe] *adj* : tense, strained, nervous
crisper [krispe] *vt* **1** CONTRACTER : to tense, to contract **2** *fam* : to irritate <sa voix me crispe : her voice gets on my nerves>
crissement [krismɑ̃] *nm* **1** : screeching, squealing **2** : grating, grinding **3** : crunching
crisser [krise] *vi* **1** : to screech, to squeal **2** : to grate, to grind **3** : to crunch
cristal [kristal] *nm, pl* **cristaux** [kristo] : crystal — **cristallin, -line** [-stalɛ̃, -lin] *adj*
cristallin [kristalɛ̃] *nm* : lens (of the eye)
cristalliser [kristalize] *v* : to crystallize — **se cristalliser** *vr*
critère [kritɛr] *nm* : criterion
critérium [kriterjɔm] *nm* : heat (in sports)
critiquable [kritikabl] *adj* : open to criticism, questionable
critique[1] [kritik] *adj* : critical
critique[2] *nmf* : critic
critique[3] *nf* **1** : criticism, reproach **2** : critique, review
critiquer [kritike] *vt* : to criticize
critiqueur, -queuse [kritikœr, -køz] *n* : faultfinder
croassement [krɔasmɑ̃] *nm* : caw, croak
croasser [krɔase] *vi* : to croak, to caw
croate [krɔat] *adj* : Croatian
Croate *nmf* : Croat, Croatian
croc [kro] *nm* **1** CROCHET : hook **2** : fang
croc–en–jambe [krɔkɑ̃ʒɑ̃b] *nm, pl* **crocs–en–jambe** : tripping <faire un croc-en-jambe à qqn : to trip s.o. up>
croche[1] [krɔʃ] *adj Can* **1** : bent, crooked **2** : dishonest
croche[2] *nf* : eighth note
croche–pied [krɔʃpje] *nm fam* → **croc–en–jambe**
crochet [krɔʃɛ] *nm* **1** : hook **2** : crochet, crocheting <faire du crochet : to crochet> **3** : crochet hook **4** : square bracket **5** : detour <faire un crochet : to make a detour> **6** : fang (of a snake) **7 vivre aux crochets de qqn** : to scrounge off s.o.
crocheter [krɔʃte] {20} *vt* **1** : to pick (a lock) **2** : to crochet
crochir [krɔʃir] *vt Can* : to bend (out of shape), to distort
crochu, -chue [krɔʃy] *adj* : hooked, bent, crooked
crocodile [krɔkɔdil] *nm* : crocodile
crocus [krɔkys] *nm* : crocus
croire [krwar] {24} *v* **1** : to believe, to trust **2** PENSER : to think <tu crois?

: do you think so?> — *vi* **1** : to believe (in religion) **2 ~ à** *or* **~ en** : to believe in, to have confidence in — **se croire** *vr* : to consider oneself

croisade [krwazad] *nf* : crusade

croisé[1], **-sée** [krwaze] *adj* **1** : crossed **2** : double-breasted

croisé[2] *nm* **1** : crusader **2** : twill

croisée *nf* **1** : crossroads, crossing **2** : casement (window)

croisement [krwazmɑ̃] *nm* **1** : crossing, intersection <croisement en trèfle : cloverleaf> **2** : crossbreeding

croiser [krwaze] *vt* **1** : to cross <croiser les bras : to fold one's arms> **2** : to intersect **3** RENCONTRER : to pass, to meet **4** : to crossbreed — *vi* : to cruise (of a ship) — **se croiser** *vr* **1** : to intersect **2** : to pass each other

croiseur [krwazœr] *nm* : cruiser (ship)

croisière [krwazjɛr] *nf* **1** : cruise **2 vitesse de croisière** : cruising speed

croissait [krwasɛ], *etc.* → **croître**

croissance [krwasɑ̃s] *nf* : growth

croissant[1], **-sante** [krwasɑ̃, -sɑ̃t] *adj* : growing, increasing

croissant[2] *nm* **1** : crescent **2** : croissant

croître [krwatr] {25} *vi* : to grow, to increase

croix [krwa] *nf* : cross

croquant, -quante [krɔkɑ̃, -kɑ̃t] *adj* : crisp, crunchy

croque–mitaine [krɔkmitɛn] *nm, pl* **croque–mitaines** : bogey, bogeyman

croque–monsieur [krɔkməsjø] *nms & pl* : grilled ham and cheese sandwich

croque–mort [krɔkmɔr] *nm, pl* **croque–morts** *fam* : undertaker

croquer [krɔke] *vt* **1** : to crunch, to munch **2** ESQUISSER : to sketch **3** *fam* : to squander — *vi* **1** : to be crunchy **2 ~ dans** : to bite into (an apple, etc.)

croquet [krɔkɛ] *nm* : croquet

croquette [krɔkɛt] *nf* : croquette

croquis [krɔki] *nm* ESQUISSE : sketch, drawing

cross [krɔs] *or* **cross–country** [krɔskuntri] *nm* : cross-country run, cross-country race

crosse [krɔs] *nf* **1** : butt, grip (of a gun) **2** : stick, lacrosse stick <crosse de hockey : hockey stick> **3** LACROSSE : lacrosse **4** : crosier, crook

crotale [krɔtal] *nm* : rattlesnake

crotte [krɔt] *nf* : droppings *pl,* dung

crotté, -tée [krɔte] *adj* : muddy

crottin [krɔtɛ̃] *nm* : (horse) manure

crouler [krule] *vi* : to collapse, to crumble

croupe [krup] *nf* **1** : rump (of a horse) **2** : crest, summit

croupir [krupir] *vi* **1** : to stagnate **2** : to wallow <croupir dans l'ignorance : to wallow in ignorance>

croustillant, -lante [krustijɑ̃, -jɑ̃t] *adj* **1** : crisp, crunchy **2** : spicy, bawdy

croustiller [krustije] *vi* : to crunch, to be crispy

croûte [krut] *nf* **1** : crust **2** : scab **3 casser la croûte** : to have a snack

croûteux, -teuse [krutø, -tøz] *adj* : scabby

croûton [krutɔ̃] *nm* **1** : crust, heel (of bread) **2** : crouton

croyable [krwajabl] *adj* : credible, believable

croyait [krwajɛ], *etc.* → **croire**

croyance [krwajɑ̃s] *nf* : belief

croyant[1], **croyante** [krwajɑ̃, -jɑ̃t] *adj* : believing <être croyant : to be a believer>

croyant[2], **croyante** *n* : believer

cru[1] [kry] *pp* → **croire**

cru[2], **crue** [kry] *adj* **1** : raw, uncooked **2** : crude, harsh **3 à ~** : bareback, barebacked

cru[3] *nm* **1** VIGNOBLE : vineyard **2** : vintage (of wine) **3 du ~** : local

crû [kry] *pp* → **croître**

cruauté [kryote] *nf* : cruelty

cruche [kryʃ] *nf* **1** : jug, pitcher **2** *fam* : nitwit, dumbell

crucial, -ciale [krysjal] *adj, pl* **-ciaux** [-sjo] : crucial

crucifier [krysifje] {96} *vt* : to crucify

crucifix [krysifi] *nms & pl* : crucifix

crucifixion [krysifiksjɔ̃] *nf* : crucifixion

crudité [krydite] *nf* **1** : crudeness **2 crudités** *nfpl* : raw vegetables (as hors d'oeuvres)

crue [kry] *nf* : rising (of waters), flood

cruel, cruelle [kryɛl] *adj* : cruel — **cruellement** [-ɛlmɑ̃] *adv*

crûment [krymɑ̃] *adv* **1** : crudely, coarsely **2** : bluntly

crustacé [krystase] *nm* **1** : crustacean **2 crustacés** *npl* : shellfish

crypte [kript] *nf* : crypt

cryptographie [kriptɔgrafi] *nf* : cryptography

cubain, -baine [kybɛ̃, -bɛn] *adj* : Cuban

Cubain, -baine *n* : Cuban

cube[1] [kyb] *adj* : cubic <mètre cube : cubic meter>

cube[2] *nm* : cube

cubique [kybik] *adj* : cubic

cubitus [kybitys] *nm* : ulna

cueillette [kœjɛt] *nf* : gathering, picking

cueillir [kœjir] {3} *vt* **1** : to pick, to gather **2** *fam* : to catch, to nab **3 être cueilli à froid** : to be caught off guard

cuillère *or* **cuiller** [kɥijɛr] *nf* **1** : spoon **2** : spoonful **3 cuillère à thé** *or* **cuillère à café** : teaspoon

cuillerée [kɥijere] *nf* **1** : spoonful **2 cuillerée à café** : teaspoonful

cuir [kɥir] *nm* **1** : leather **2** : hide <cuir brut : rawhide> **3 cuir chevelu** : scalp

cuirasse [kɥiras] *nf* **1** : breastplate **2** : armor (of a tank, etc.)

cuirassé [kɥirase] *nm* : battleship

cuirasser [kɥirase] *vt* **1** : to armor **2** : to harden — **se cuirasser** *vr* : to harden oneself

cuire [kɥir] {49} *vt* **1** : to cook, to bake **2** : to fire (pottery) — *vi* **1** : to cook **2** : to sting, to burn
cuisait [kɥizɛ], **cuisions** [kɥizjɔ̃], *etc.* → **cuire**
cuisant, -sante [kɥizɑ̃, -zɑ̃t] *adj* **1** : stinging, smarting **2** : bitter
cuise [kɥiz], *etc.* → **cuire**
cuisine [kɥizin] *nf* **1** : kitchen **2** : cooking, cuisine **3 faire la cuisine** : to cook
cuisiné, -née [kɥizine] *adj* **plat cuisiné** : prepared food
cuisiner [kɥizine] *vt* **1** : to cook **2** *fam* : to grill, to interrogate — *vi* : to cook
cuisinette [kɥizinɛt] *nf* : kitchenette
cuisinier, -nière [kɥizinje, -njɛr] *n* : chef, cook
cuisinière *nf* : stove
cuisse [kɥis] *nf* **1** : thigh **2** : leg <cuisses de grenouilles : frogs' legs>
cuisson [kɥisɔ̃] *nf* : cooking, baking
cuit, cuite [kɥi, kɥit] *adj* **1** : cooked <bien cuit : well-done> **2 être cuit** *fam* : to be done for, to have had it
cuite *nf* **prendre une cuite** *fam* : to get drunk
cuivre [kɥivr] *nm* **1** *or* **cuivre rouge** : copper **2** *or* **cuivre jaune** : brass **3 cuivres** *nmpl* : brass (musical instruments)
cuivré, -vrée [kɥivre] *adj* **1** : copper-colored, bronzed **2** : resonant
culbute [kylbyt] *nf* **1** : somersault **2** CHUTE : tumble, fall
culbuter [kylbyte] *vt* **1** : to knock over **2** : to overthrow — *vi* **1** : to somersault **2** TOMBER : to tumble, to fall
cul-de-sac [kydsak] *nm, pl* **culs-de-sac** : dead end, cul-de-sac
culinaire [kylinɛr] *adj* : culinary
culminant, -nante [kylminɑ̃, -nɑ̃t] *adj* **point culminant** : high point, peak
culminer [kylmine] *vi* **1** : to culminate, to peak **2** DOMINER : to dominate, to tower
culot [kylo] *nm fam* : impudence, cheek <avoire du culot : to have a lot of nerve>
culotte [kylɔt] *nf* **1** PANTALON : pants *pl,* trousers *pl* **2** : panties *pl*
culotté, -tée [kylɔte] *adj fam* : sassy, cheeky
culpabiliser [kylpabilize] *vt* **~ qqn** : to make someone feel guilty — *vi* : to feel guilty
culpabilité [kylpabilite] *nf* : guilt
culte [kylt] *nm* **1** : worship, cult <liberté de culte : freedom of worship> <le culte de personalité : the cult of personality> **2** : religion, creed **3** : (Protestant) service
cultivateur, -trice [kyltivatœr, -tris] *n* AGRICULTEUR : farmer
cultivé, -vée [kyltive] *adj* **1** : cultivated **2** : cultured
cultiver [kyltive] *vt* : to cultivate — **se cultiver** *vr*
culture [kyltyr] *nf* **1** : culture **2** : cultivation, growing **3 culture physique** : physical education
culturel, -relle [kyltyrɛl] *adj* : cultural — **culturellement** [-rɛlmɑ̃] *adv*
culturisme [kyltyrism] *nm* : bodybuilding
cumin [kymɛ̃] *nm* : cumin
cumul [kymyl] *nm* **1** : holding concurrently <cumul de fonctions : holding several offices at the same time> **2** : accumulation
cumulatif, -tive [kymylatif, -tiv] *adj* : cumulative
cumuler [kymyle] *vt* **1** : to hold concurrently **2** ACCUMULER : to accumulate, to pile up — **se cumuler** *vr* : to accrue
cumulus [kymylys] *nms & pl* : cumulus
cupide [kypid] *adj* : greedy
cupidité [kypidite] *nf* : greed
curatif, -tive [kyratif, -tiv] *adj* : curative
cure [kyr] *nf* **1** : treatment, cure **2** : parish, vicarage **3 n'avoir cure de** : to have little concern for <elle n'en a cure : she doesn't care about it>
curé [kyre] *nm* : pastor, parish priest
cure-dent *or* **cure-dents** [kyrdɑ̃] *nm, pl* **cure-dents** : toothpick
curer [kyre] *vt* : to clean out, to scrape out — **se curer** *vr* : to clean (one's nails, etc.)
curieusement [kyrjøzmɑ̃] *adv* : curiously, strangely
curieux[1], -rieuse [kyrjø, -rjøz] *adj* **1** : curious, inquisitive **2** : strange, odd
curieux[2], -rieuse *n* **1** : onlooker **2** : busybody
curieux[3] *nm* : curious thing, oddity <le curieux dans tout ça : the strange thing in all that>
curiosité [kyrjɔzite] *nf* : curiosity
curry [kyri] *nm* : curry
curseur [kyrsœr] *nm* : cursor
cuspide [kyspid] *nf* : cusp
cutané, -née [kytane] *adj* : cutaneous, skin
cuve [kyv] *nf* : tub, tank, vat
cuvée [kyve] *nf* : vintage
cuver [kyve] *vi* : to ferment
cuvette [kyvɛt] *nf* **1** : bowl, washbasin **2** : basin (in geology)
cyanure [sjanyr] *nm* : cyanide
cybernétique [sibɛrnetik] *nf* : cybernetics
cyclable [siklabl] *adj* **piste cyclable** : bicycle path
cycle [sikl] *nm* : cycle
cyclique [siklik] *adj* : cyclic, cyclical
cyclisme [siklism] *nm* : cycling, bicycling
cycliste[1] [siklist] *adj* : cycle, bicycle <course cycliste : bicycle race>
cycliste[2] *nmf* : cyclist, bicyclist
cyclomoteur [siklɔmɔtœr] *nm* : moped
cyclone [siklon] *nm* : cyclone
cygne [siɲ] *nm* : swan

cylindre [silɛ̃dr] *nm* : cylinder
cylindrée [silɛ̃dre] *nf* : capacity (of an engine)
cylindrique [silɛ̃drik] *adj* : cylindrical
cymbale [sɛ̃bal] *nf* : cymbal
cynique[1] [sinik] *adj* : cynical — **cyniquement** [-nikmɑ̃] *adv*
cynique[2] *nmf* : cynic
cynisme [sinism] *nm* : cynicism
cyprès [siprɛ] *nm* : cypress
cypriote [siprijɔt] *adj* : Cypriot
Cypriote *nmf* : Cypriot
cytoplasme [sitɔplasm] *nm* : cytoplasm

D

d [de] *nm* : d, the fourth letter of the alphabet
d'abord [dabɔr] → **abord**
d'accord [dakɔr] → **accord**
dactylo[1] [daktilo] *or* **dactylographe** [daktilɔgraf] *nmf* : typist
dactylo[2] *nf* **1** → **dactylographie 2** *Can* : typewriter
dactylographie [daktilɔgrafi] *nf* : typing
dactylographier [daktilɔgrafje] {96} *vt* : to type
dada [dada] *nm* **1** *fam* : hobbyhorse, pet subject **2** : Dada
dadais [dadɛ] *nms & pl* : silly fool, oaf
dague [dag] *nf* : dagger
dahlia [dalja] *nm* : dahlia
daigner [deɲe] *vt* : to deign, to condescend <il n'a pas daigné répondre : he didn't deign to reply>
daim [dɛ̃] *nm* **1** : fallow deer **2** : suede
dais [dɛ] *nms & pl* : canopy
dallage [dalaʒ] *nm* **1** : paving **2** : pavement
dalle [dal] *nf* **1** : paving stone, flagstone **2** : slab (of stone or concrete)
daller [dale] *vt* : to pave
dalmatien [dalmasjɛ̃] *nm* : dalmatian (dog)
daltonien, -nienne [daltɔnjɛ̃, -njɛn] *adj* : color-blind
dam [dam] *nm* **au grand dam de** : much to the detriment of, to the great displeasure of
damas [damɑ̊s] *nms & pl* : damask
dame [dam] *nf* **1** : lady **2** : queen (in chess or card games) **3 dames** *nfpl or* **jeu de dames** : checkers
damer [dame] *vt* **1** : to pack down **2** : to crown (in checkers) **3 damer le pion à** : to get the better of
damier [damje] *nm* : checkerboard
damnation [danasjɔ̃] *nf* : damnation
damné[1], **-née** [dane] *adj* : damned, cursed
damné[2], **-née** *n* : damned person
damner [dane] *vt* : to damn
dandinement [dɑ̃dinmɑ̃] *nm* : waddling, waddle
dandiner [dɑ̃dine] *v* **se dandiner** *vr* : to waddle
dandy [dɑ̃di] *nm* : dandy
danger [dɑ̃ʒe] *nm* : danger
dangereux, -reuse [dɑ̃ʒrø, -røz] *adj* : dangerous — **dangereusement** [-røzmɑ̃] *adv*
danois[1], **-noise** [danwa, -waz] *adj* : Danish
danois[2] *nm* **1** : Danish (language) **2** : Great Dane
Danois, -noise *n* : Dane
dans [dɑ̃] *prep* **1** : in <dans la boîte : in the box> <dans dix jours : in ten days> **2** : into <monter dans l'auto : to get into the car> **3** : from, out of <elle buvait dans une tasse : she was drinking from a cup>
dansant, -sante [dɑ̃sɑ̃, -sɑ̃t] *adj* : dancing <soirée dansante : dance (party)>
danse [dɑ̃s] *nf* : dance, dancing
danser [dɑ̃se] *v* : to dance
danseur, -seuse [dɑ̃sœr, -søz] *n* : dancer
dard [dar] *nm* **1** AIGUILLON : stinger **2** : spear, javelin **3** *Can* : dart <jouer aux darts : to play darts>
darder [darde] *vt* : to shoot forth, to hurl
date [dat] *nf* **1** : date <date de naissance : date of birth> **2** : time <de longue date : long-standing> **3** → **limite**
dater [date] *vt* : to date — *vi* **1** : to be dated, to be old-fashioned **2 ～ de** : to date from, to date back to
datte [dat] *nf* : date (fruit)
daube [dob] *nf* : casserole, stew
dauphin [dofɛ̃] *nm* **1** : dolphin **2** : dauphin, heir apparent
davantage [davɑ̃taʒ] *adv* **1** : more <elle ne se souvient pas davantage : she doesn't remember more> **2** : longer, any longer <je voudrais rester davantage : I'd like to stay longer>
DDT [dedete] *nm* : DDT
de [də] (**d'** *before vowels and mute h*) *prep* **1** : from <de Québec à Montréal : from Quebec to Montreal> **2** : by <de nuit : by night> <une comédie de Molière : a play by Molière> **3** : of <au bout du monde : at the ends of the earth> **4** : with <je tombe de fatigue : I'm completely worn out> **5** (*before infinitive*) : to, of <il craint d'être en retard : he's afraid of being late> **6 de la, du, des** : some, any <voulez-vous des haricots? : would you like some beans?>
dé [de] *nm* **1** : die, dice *pl* **2** *or* **dé à coudre** : thimble

déambuler [deɑ̃byle] *vi* : to stroll, to wander about
débâcle [debakl] *nf* : debacle, fiasco
déballer [debale] *vt* **1** : to unpack, to unwrap **2** : to display (merchandise)
débandade [debɑ̃dad] *nf* **1** : rout, stampede **2 à la débandade** : in disarray
débarbouiller [debarbuje] *v* **se débarbouiller** *vr* : to wash one's face
débarbouillette [debarbujɛt] *nf Can* : washcloth, facecloth
débarcadère [debarkadɛr] *nm* : wharf, dock
débardeur [debardœr] *nm* : longshoreman
débarquement [debarkəmɑ̃] *nm* **1** : unloading **2** : landing, disembarcation
débarquer [debarke] *vt* **1** : to unload (goods) **2** : to land (troops, etc.) — *vi* : to disembark
débarrasser [debarase] *vt* **1** : to clear **2 ~ de** : to relieve of, to free from — **se débarrasser** *vr* **~ de** : to get rid of
débarrer [debare] *vt Can* : to unlock
débat [deba] *nm* **1** : debate, discussion **2 débats** *nmpl* : proceedings
débattre [debatr] {12} *vt* : to debate, to discuss — *vi Can* : to pound, to race (of the heart) — **se débattre** *vr* : to struggle, to thrash about
débauche [deboʃ] *nf* : debauchery, vice
débauché[1], -chée [deboʃe] *adj* : debauched
débauché[2], -chée *n* : debauched person, libertine
débaucher [deboʃe] *vt* **1** CORROMPRE : to corrupt **2** LICENCIER : to lay off **3** : to cause to go on strike
débile [debil] *adj* **1** : weak, feeble **2** *fam* : stupid, idiotic
débilité [debilite] *nf* **1** : debility **2** *fam* : silliness, stupidity
débiliter [debilite] *vt* **1** : to debilitate **2** : to demoralize
débiner [debine] *vt Can fam* : to disconcert
débit [debi] *nm* **1** : debit **2** : turnover (of merchandise, etc.) **3** : (rate of) flow, discharge **4** ÉLOCUTION : delivery, speech **5** *France* : shop <débit de boissons : bar>
débiter [debite] *vt* **1** : to debit **2** : to sell, to retail **3** : to produce, to yield **4** : to cut up **5** : to discharge, to flow (out) **6** : to drone, to reel off
débiteur[1], -trice [debitœr, -tris] *adj* : debit <compte débiteur : debit account>
débiteur[2], -trice *n* : debtor
déblai [deblɛ] *nm* **1** : excavation **2 déblais** *nmpl* DÉCOMBRES : rubble, debris
déblaiement [deblɛmɑ̃] *nm* : clearing (of earth)
déblatérer [deblatere] {87} *vi* **~ contre** : to rant against
déblayer [debleje] {11} *vt* **1** : to clear (away) **2** : to prepare, to sort out
débloquer [debloke] *vt* **1** : to free, to release **2** : to unfreeze (funds), to release — *vi fam* **1** : to talk nonsense **2** : to be out of one's mind
déboguer [debɔge] *vt* : to debug
déboires [debwar] *nmpl* **1** DÉCEPTIONS : disappointments **2** ENNUIS : difficulties, tribulations
déboiser [debwaze] *vt* : to deforest
déboîtement [debwatmɑ̃] *nm* : dislocation
déboîter [debwate] *vt* **1** : to dislocate (in medicine) **2** : to disconnect, to unfasten — *vi* : to pull out, to change lanes (in an automobile) — **se déboîter** *vr* : to dislocate (one's shoulder, etc.)
débonnaire [debɔnɛr] *adj* : easygoing, good-natured
débordant, -dante [debɔrdɑ̃, -dɑ̃t] *adj* : overflowing, brimming <débordant d'énergie : bursting with energy>
débordé, -dée [debɔrde] *adj* : overwhelmed, overloaded (with work, etc.)
débordement [debɔrdəmɑ̃] *nm* : overflow, excess
déborder [debɔrde] *vi* : to overflow — *vt* **1** : to jut out from, to extend beyond **2** : to overwhelm **3** : to overflow
débouché [debuʃe] *nm* **1** : outlet, market **2** : opportunity, prospect
déboucher [debuʃe] *vt* **1** : to clear, to unblock **2** : to uncork, to open — *vi* **1 ~ de** : to emerge from, to come out of **2 ~ sur** : to open onto, to lead to — **se déboucher** : to become unblocked
déboucler [debukle] *vt* : to unbuckle, to undo
débouler [debule] *vi* **1** *fam* : to tumble down **2** : to bolt, to shoot out — *vt* : to charge down (a stairway, etc.)
débours [debur] *nms & pl* : expense, outlay
débourser [deburse] *vt* : to pay out, to spend <sans rien débourser : without paying a penny>
déboussolé, -lée [debusɔle] *adj fam* : disoriented, confused
debout [dəbu] *adv* **1** : standing up **2** : upright, on end **3** : up, out of bed **4 tenir debout** : to stand up to examination, to hold water
déboutonner [debutɔne] *vt* : to unbutton, to undo — **se déboutonner** *vr*
débraillé, -lée [debraje] *adj* : disheveled, slovenly
débrancher [debrɑ̃ʃe] *vt* : to unplug, to disconnect
débrayage [debrɛjaʒ] *nm* **1** : disengaging the clutch **2** : strike, walkout
débrayer [debreje] {11} *vi* **1** : to disengage the clutch **2** : to go on strike
débridé, -dée [debride] *adj* : unbridled, unrestrained

débris [debri] *nms & pl* **1** : fragment **2 débris** *nmpl* : rubbish, scraps, remains

débrouillard, -larde [debrujar, -jard] *adj fam* : resourceful

débrouillardise [debrujardiz] *nf fam* : resourcefulness

débrouiller [debruje] *vt* **1** DÉMÊLER : to disentangle **2** : to unravel, to solve — **se débrouiller** *vr* **1** : to manage <se débrouiller pour obtenir : to wangle, to finagle> **2** : to get by <il se débrouille bien : he's getting along all right>

débroussailler [debrusaje] *vt* **1** : to clear (land) **2** : to lay the groundwork for

débusquer [debyske] *vt* : to flush, to drive out (from hiding)

début [deby] *nm* **1** : beginning, start <au début : at the beginning> <dès le début : from the start> **2** (*used in expressions of time*) <début juin : in early June> **3 débuts** *nmpl* : debut, early stages <faire ses débuts : to make one's debut> **4 au début** : to begin with, at first

débutant, -tante [debytɑ̃, -tɑ̃t] *n* : beginner, novice, learner

débutante *nf* : debutante

débuter [debyte] *v* : to begin, to start

deçà [dəsa] *adv* **1 deçà, delà** : here and there **2 en deçà de** : on this side of **3 en deçà de** : short of, below

décacheter [dekaʃte] {8} *vt* : to unseal (an envelope)

décade [dekad] *nf* **1** : period of ten days **2** : decade

décadence [dekadɑ̃s] *nf* : decadence

décadent, -dente [dekadɑ̃, -dɑ̃t] *adj* : decadent

décaféiné, -née [dekafeine] *adj* : decaffeinated

décalage [dekalaʒ] *nm* **1** : discrepancy **2** : gap, space **3** : interval <décalage horaire : time difference>

décalcomanie [dekalkɔmani] *nf* : decal

décaler [dekale] *vt* **1** : to move forward or back (a time, a date) **2** : to move, to shift (an object)

décamper [dekɑ̃pe] *vi* : to clear out, to decamp

décanter [dekɑ̃te] *vt* **1** : to allow (a liquid) to settle **2** : to clarify (ideas, etc.) — **se décanter** *vr*

décapant[1], -pante [dekapɑ̃, -pɑ̃t] *adj* : caustic, abrasive

décapant[2] *nm* **1** : scouring agent **2** : paint stripper

décaper [dekape] *vt* **1** : to clean, to scour **2** : to strip (paint, etc.)

décapiter [dekapite] *vt* : to decapitate, to behead

décapotable [dekapɔtabl] *adj & nf* : convertible

décapsuleur [dekapsylœr] *nm* : bottle opener

décati, -tie [dekati] *adj* : decrepit

décédé, -dée [desede] *adj* : deceased

décéder [desede] {87} *vi* : to die, to pass away

déceler [desle] {20} *vt* **1** DÉCOUVRIR : to detect, to uncover **2** RÉVÉLER : to indicate, to reveal

décélération [deselerasjɔ̃] *nf* : deceleration

décembre [desɑ̃br] *nm* : December

décemment [desamɑ̃] *adv* : decently

décence [desɑ̃s] *nf* : decency

décennie [deseni] *nf* : decade

décent, -cente [desɑ̃, -sɑ̃t] *adj* : decent

décentraliser [desɑ̃tralize] *vt* : to decentralize — **décentralisation** [-lizasjɔ̃] *nf*

déception [desɛpsjɔ̃] *nf* : disappointment

décerner [desɛrne] *vt* **1** : to award **2** : to issue (a writ)

décès [desɛ] *nm* : death

décevant, -vante [desəvɑ̃, -vɑ̃t] *adj* : disappointing

décevoir [desəvwar] {26} *vt* : to disappoint

déchaîné, -née [deʃene] *adj* : raging, unbridled

déchaînement [deʃɛnmɑ̃] *nm* **1** : fury, raging (of the elements) **2** EXPLOSION : outburst (of emotion)

déchaîner [deʃene] *vt* : to unleash, to arouse — **se déchaîner** *vr* : to erupt, to burst out

déchanter [deʃɑ̃te] *vi* : to become disillusioned

décharge [deʃarʒ] *nf* **1** : discharge (of a firearm) **2** : garbage dump **3 décharge électrique** : electric shock

déchargement [deʃarʒəmɑ̃] *nm* : unloading

décharger [deʃarʒe] {17} *vt* **1** : to unload **2** : to discharge (a firearm, etc.) **3** : to relieve, to unburden **4** : to exonerate, to clear **5** : to give vent to

décharné, -née [deʃarne] *adj* : emaciated, bony

déchausser [deʃose] *v* **se déchausser** *vr* : to take off one's shoes

déchéance [deʃeɑ̃s] *nf* : decay, decline

déchet [deʃɛ] *nm* **1** : scrap **2** : waste, wastage **3 déchets** *nmpl* : refuse, waste (materials) <déchets toxiques : toxic waste>

déchiffrer [deʃifre] *vt* **1** : to decipher **2** : to sight-read (music)

déchiqueté, -tée [deʃikte] *adj* : jagged, ragged

déchiqueter [deʃikte] {8} *vt* : to tear into pieces

déchirant, -rante [deʃirɑ̃, -rɑ̃t] *adj* : heartbreaking, heartrending

déchirement [deʃirmɑ̃] *nm* **1** : tearing **2** : heartbreak **3** : rift, split

déchirer [deʃire] *vt* **1** : to tear up, to rip **2** : to tear apart, to split — **se déchirer** *vr*

déchirure [deʃiryr] *nf* : tear <déchirure ligamentaire : torn ligament>

déchoir [deʃwar] {27} *vi* **1** : to demean oneself **2** : to fall, to decline (in prestige)

déchu[1] [deʃy] *pp* → **décevoir**

déchu[2], **-chue** [deʃy] *adj* **1** : fallen (from grace or favor) **2** : deposed

décibel [desibɛl] *nm* : decibel

décidé, -dée [deside] *adj* **1** : decided, settled **2** DÉTERMINÉ : determined, resolved

décidément [desidemɑ̃] *adv* : definitely, really

décider [deside] *vt* **1** : to decide <j'ai décidé de partir : I decided to leave> **2** CONVAINCRE : to persuade **3 ~ de** : to decide on, to determine <nous avons décidé d'une date : we've set a date> **— se décider** *vr* : to make up one's mind

décimal, -male [desimal] *adj, mpl* **-maux** [-mo] : decimal

décimale *nf* : decimal

décimer [desime] *vt* : to decimate

décisif, -sive [desizif, -ziv] *adj* : decisive **— décisivement** [-zivmɑ̃] *adv*

décision [desizjɔ̃] *nf* **1** : decision <prendre une decision : to make a decision> **2** : decisiveness

déclamer [deklame] *vi* : to declaim

déclaratif, -tive [deklaratif, -tiv] *adj* : declarative

déclaration [deklarasjɔ̃] *nf* **1** : declaration, statement <déclaration de guerre : declaration of war> <faire sa déclaration : to declare one's love> **2** : (official) notification <déclaration d'impôts : income tax return> **3** : testimony, statement (in court)

déclarer [deklare] *vt* **1** : to declare, to announce **2** : to claim, to register (births, deaths, etc.) <déclarer qqch à la douane : to declare sth at customs> **— se déclarer** *vr* **1** : to declare oneself **2** : to declare one's love **3** : to break out, to show itself (of a disease, a fire, etc.)

déclassement [deklasmɑ̃] *nm* : downgrading, demotion

déclasser [deklase] *vt* **1** : to demote, to downgrade **2** : to get out of order, to disarrange **3** : to demean

déclenchement [deklɑ̃ʃmɑ̃] *nm* : start, launching

déclencher [deklɑ̃ʃe] *vt* **1** : to release, to set off **2** PROVOQUER : to trigger, to prompt **3** : to launch, to begin

déclencheur [deklɑ̃ʃœr] *nm* **1** : release mechanism **2** : trigger

déclic [deklik] *nm* **1** : trigger (mechanism) **2** : click

déclin [deklɛ̃] *nm* **1** : decline, waning **2** : close <le déclin du jour : the close of day>

déclinaison [deklinɛzɔ̃] *nf* : declension

décliner [dekline] *vi* : to decline, to wane **—** *vt* **1** : to refuse **2** : to decline (a noun) **3** : to state, to give (one's name, address, etc.)

déclivité [deklivite] *nf* : slope, incline

décloisonner [deklwazɔne] *vt* : to open up, to decompartmentalize

décocher [dekɔʃe] *vt* **1** : to shoot, to hurl **2** : to flash, to dart <il a décoché un sourire : he flashed a smile>

décoder [dekɔde] *vt* : to decode

décoiffer [dekwafe] *vt* **décoiffer qqn** : to mess up s.o.'s hair **—** *vi* **ça décoiffe** *fam* : it takes your breath away

décoincer [dekwɛ̃se] {6} *vt* **1** : to loosen, to unjam **2** *fam* : to loosen (someone) up **— se décoincer** *vr*

déçoit [deswa], **déçoive** [deswav], *etc.* → **décevoir**

décolérer [dekɔlere] {87} *vi* : to calm down, to cool off

décollage [dekɔltaʒ] *nm* : takeoff

décoller [dekɔle] *vt* : to unstick, to remove **—** *vi* : to take off (of an airplane, a project, etc.)

décolleté[1], **-tée** [dekɔlte] *adj* : low-cut

décolleté[2] *nm* **1** : low neckline **2** : cleavage

décolorant [dekɔlɔrɑ̃, -rɑ̃t] *nm* : bleach

décoloration [dekɔlɔrasjɔ̃] *nf* **1** : fading, discoloration **2** : bleaching

décolorer [dekɔlɔre] *vt* : to bleach, to cause to fade **— se décolorer** *vr* **1** : to fade **2** : to bleach one's hair

décombres [decɔ̃br] *nmpl* : rubble, debris

décommander [dekɔmɑ̃de] *vt* : to cancel **— se décommander** *vr* : to cancel one's appointment

décomposer [dekɔ̃poze] *vt* **1** : to break down, to break up **2** POURRIR : to rot, to cause to decompose **3** : to contort, to distort (one's face) **— se décomposer** *vr*

décomposition [dekɔ̃pozisjɔ̃] *nf* : decomposition, rotting

décompresser [dekɔ̃prese] *vt* : to decompress **—** *vi* : to relax, to unwind

décompte [dekɔ̃t] *nm* **1** : account, statement **2** : breakdown, count **3** : deduction, discount

décompter [dekɔ̃te] *vt* **1** : to deduct **2** : to calculate, to count **—** *vi* : to strike the wrong hour

déconcentration [dekɔ̃sɑ̃trasjɔ̃] *nf* **1** : decentralization **2** : distraction, loss of concentration

déconcentrer [dekɔ̃sɑ̃tre] *vt* **1** : to decentralize **2** : to distract **— se déconcentrer** *vr* : to lose one's concentration

déconcerter [dekɔ̃sɛrte] *vt* : to disconcert

déconfit, -fite [dekɔ̃fi, -fit] *adj* : downcast, crestfallen

déconfiture [dekɔ̃fityr] *nf* **1** : failure, collapse, defeat **2** : insolvency, bankruptcy

décongeler [dekɔ̃ʒle] {20} *v* : to thaw, to defrost

décongestif [dekɔ̃ʒɛstif, -tiv] *nm* : decongestant

décongestionnant[1], **-nante** [dekɔ̃ʒɛstjɔnɑ̃, -nɑ̃t] *adj* : decongestant
décongestionnant[2] *nm* : decongestant
décongestionner [dekɔ̃ʒɛstjɔne] *vt* : to relieve congestion in, to decongest
déconnecter [dekɔnɛkte] *vt* : to disconnect
déconner [dekɔne] *vi fam* **1** : to talk nonsense **2** : to mess around **3** : to be on the blink
déconseiller [dekɔ̃seje] *vt* : to dissuade, to advise against <elle m'a déconseillé d'y aller : she advised me not to go>
déconsidération [dekɔ̃siderasjɔ̃] *nf* : discredit
déconsidérer [dekɔ̃sidere] {87} *vt* : to discredit — **se déconsidérer** *vr*
décontaminer [dekɔ̃tamine] *vt* : to decontaminate
décontenancer [dekɔ̃tnɑ̃se] {6} *vt* : to disconcert — **se décontenancer** *vr* : to lose one's composure
décontracté, -tée [dekɔ̃trakte] *adj* **1** : relaxed **2** : casual, laid-back
décontracter [dekɔ̃trakte] *vt* : to relax — **se décontracter** *vr*
déconvenue [dekɔ̃vny] *nf* DÉCEPTION : disappointment
décor [dekɔr] *nm* **1** : decor **2** : scenery **3** : set, scenery (of movies or theater) **4 dans le décor** : off the road <il est rentré dans le décor : he drove off the road>
décorateur, -trice [dekɔratœr, -tris] *n* **1** : interior decorator **2** : set designer
décoratif, -tive [dekɔratif, -tiv] *adj* : decorative, ornamental
décorer [dekɔre] *vt* ORNER : to decorate — **décoration** [-kɔrasjɔ̃] *nf*
décortiquer [dekɔrtike] *vt* **1** : to shell, to hull **2** : to dissect, to analyze
décorum [dekɔrɔm] *nm* : decorum, propriety
découcher [dekuʃe] *vi* : to stay out all night
découdre [dekudr] {22} *vt* : to unstitch, to rip — *vi* **en** ∼ : to fight
découler [dekule] *vi* : to result, to follow, to ensue
découpage [dekupaʒ] *nm* **1** : cutting up, carving **2** : cutout **3** : shooting script (of a film) **4 découpage électoral** : districting
découper [dekupe] *vt* **1** : to cut up, to carve **2** : to cut out **3** : to indent (landforms, etc.) — **se découper** *vr* : to stand out
découplé, -plée [dekuple] *adj* **bien découplé** : well-built, well-proportioned
découpure [dekupyr] *nf* **1** : cutting **2** : indented outline
découragement [dekuraʒmɑ̃] *nm* : discouragement, despondency
décourager [dekuraʒe] {17} *vt* **1** : to discourage, to dishearten **2** : to deter, to put off
décousu, -sue [dekusy] *adj* **1** : unstitched **2** : disjointed, disconnected
découvert[1], **-verte** [dekuvɛr, -vɛrt] *adj* : bare, uncovered, exposed
découvert[2] *nm* : overdraft <être à découvert : to be overdrawn>
découverte *nf* : discovery, find
découvreur, -vreuse [dekuvrœr, -vrøz] *n* : discoverer, finder
découvrir [dekuvrir] {83} *vt* **1** : to discover **2** : to uncover **3** : to disclose, to reveal **4** : to catch sight of, to see — **se découvrir** *vr* **1** : to doff one's hat **2** : to undress, to uncover oneself **3** : to understand oneself **4** : to expose oneself to attack **5** : to clear up (of weather)
décrasser [dekrase] *vt* **1** : to clean, to scrub **2** : to polish, to remove the rough edges from (a person) — **se décrasser** *vr*
décrépit, -pite [dekrepi, -pit] *adj* : decrepit
décrépitude [dekrepityd] *nf* : decrepitude
décret [dekrɛ] *nm* : decree, edict
décréter [dekrete] {87} *vt* : to decree, to order
décrier [dekrije] {96} *vt* : to decry, to disparage
décrire [dekrir] {33} *vt* : to describe
décrocher [dekrɔʃe] *vt* **1** : to unhook, to take down, to undo <décrocher le téléphone : to pick up the telephone> **2** *fam* : to get, to land <décrocher une bonne situation : to land a good job> — *vi* **1** *fam* : to drop out, to give up **2** *fam* : to tune out, to stop paying attention **3** : to fall behind
décrocheur, -cheuse [dekrɔʃœr, -ʃøz] *n Can* : high school dropout
décroissance [dekrwasɑ̃s] *nf* : decrease, decline
décroître [dekrwatr] {25} *vi* : to decrease, to decline
décrotter [dekrɔte] *vt* : to scrape mud off
décrue [dekry] *nf* : drop in the water level
décrypter [dekripte] *vt* : to decipher
déçu[1] [desy] *pp* → **décevoir**
déçu[2], **-çue** [desy] *adj* : disappointed
décupler [dekyple] *v* : to increase tenfold
dédaigner [dedeɲe] *vt* : to disdain, to scorn
dédaigneux, -neuse [dedɛɲø, -ɲøz] *adj* : disdainful, scornful — **dédaigneusement** [-ɲøzmɑ̃] *adv*
dédain [dedɛ̃] *nm* MÉPRIS : disdain, scorn
dédale [dedal] *nm* : maze, labyrinth
dedans[1] [dədɑ̃] *adv* **1** : inside, in **2 de** ∼ : from within **3 en** ∼ : on the inside, inwardly, within
dedans[2] *nm* : inside, interior <du dehors vers le dedans : from the outside in>

dédicace [dedikas] *nf* : dedication, inscription (in a book, etc.)
dédicacer [dedikase] {6} *vt* : to inscribe, to autograph, to dedicate
dédier [dedje] {96} *vt* **1** : to dedicate (a work of art, etc.) **2** : to devote, to dedicate
dédire [dedir] {29} *v* **se dédire** *vr* **1** : to retract (a statement) **2 ~ de** : to go back on, to fail to honor
dédit [dedi] *nm* **1** : retraction **2** : penalty (for breach of contract)
dédommagement [dedɔmaʒmɑ̃] *nm* INDEMNITÉ : compensation
dédommager [dedɔmaʒe] {17} *vt* **1** : to compensate **2** : to repay, to make up for
dédouaner [dedwane] *vt* **1** : to clear through customs **2** : to clear (one's name), to rehabilitate
dédoubler [deduble] *vt* **1** : to divide, to split in two **2** : to remove the lining of (a garment) — **se dédoubler** *vr* **1** : to split (up), to come apart **2** : to be in two places at once
déductible [dedyktibl] *adj* : deductible
déduction [dedyksjɔ̃] *nf* **1** : deduction **2** : conclusion, inference
déduire [dedɥir] {49} *vt* **1** : to deduct **2** : to deduce, to infer
déesse [deɛs] *nf* : goddess
défaillance [defajɑ̃s] *nf* **1** : failure, fault **2** : failing, weakness **3** ÉVANOUISSEMENT : blackout, fainting fit
défaillant, -lante [defajɑ̃, -jɑ̃t] *adj* **1** : failing, unsteady **2** : weak, faint
défaillir [defajir] {93} *vi* **1** : to faint **2** : to weaken, to falter
défaire [defɛr] {42} *vt* **1** : to undo, to untie, to unravel **2** : to unpack **3** DÉMONTER : to dismantle, to take down, to break up **4 défaire le lit** : to strip the bed — **se défaire** *vr* **1** : to come undone, to come apart **2 ~ de** : to part with
défait, -faite [defɛ, -fɛt] *adj* **1** : undone **2** : defeated **3** : haggard
défaite *nf* : defeat
défaitisme [defetism] *nm* : defeatism — **défaitiste** [-fetist] *adj & nmf*
défalquer [defalke] *vt* : to deduct — **défalcation** [-falkasjɔ̃] *nf*
défausser [defose] *vt* : to straighten — **se défausser** *vr* : to discard (in card games)
défaut [defo] *nm* **1** IMPERFECTION : flaw, defect <défaut d'élocution : speech impediment> **2** FAIBLESSE : fault, shortcoming **3** MANQUE : lack, shortage <faire défaut : to be lacking> **4 à défaut de** : for lack of
défaveur [defavœr] *nf* : disfavor
défavorable [defavɔrabl] *adj* : unfavorable — **défavorablement** [-rabləmɑ̃] *adv*
défavoriser [defavɔrize] *vt* DÉSAVANTAGER : to put at a disadvantage
défection [defɛksjɔ̃] *nf* **1** : defection, desertion **2 faire défection** : to defect
défectueux, -tueuse [defɛktɥø, -tɥøz] *adj* : defective, faulty
défectuosité [defɛktɥozite] *nf* **1** : defectiveness **2** : defect, fault
défendable [defɑ̃dabl] *adj* : defensible, justifiable
défendeur, -deresse [defɑ̃dœr, -drɛs] *n* : defendant
défendre [defɑ̃dr] {63} *vt* **1** SOUTENIR : to defend, to champion **2** PROTÉGER : to protect, to safeguard **3** INTERDIRE : to forbid, to prohibit <il est défendu de fumer : smoking is prohibited> — **se défendre** *vr* **1** : to defend oneself **2** : to make sense <ses raisons se défendent : he's got a point> **3** *fam* : to get by, to manage **4 ~ de** : to refrain from **5 ~ de** : to deny
défense [defɑ̃s] *nf* **1** : defense **2** INTERDICTION : prohibition <défense d'entrer : no admittance> **3** : tusk
défenseur [defɑ̃sœr] *nm* **1** : defender, advocate **2** : defender (in sports) **3** : defense attorney
défensif, -sive [defɑ̃sif, -siv] *adj* : defensive — **défensivement** [-sivmɑ̃] *adv*
défensive *nf* : defensive <se tenir sur la défensive : to be on the defensive>
déféquer [defeke] {87} *vi* : to defecate
déférence [deferɑ̃s] *nf* : deference
déférent, -rente [deferɑ̃, -rɑ̃t] *adj* RESPECTUEUX : deferential, respectful
déférer [defere] {87} *vt* : to refer (a case) to a court — *vi* **~ à** : to defer to
déferlement [defɛrləmɑ̃] *nm* **1** : surge, breaking (of waves) **2** : surge, wave (of emotion)
déferler [defɛrle] *vt* : to unfurl — *vi* **1** : to break (of waves) **2** : to flood in <les spectateurs déferlent dans le théâtre : the audience is streaming into the theater>
défi [defi] *nm* **1** : challenge, dare **2** : (act of) defiance
défiance [defjɑ̃s] *nf* : distrust
défiant, -fiante [defjɑ̃, -fjɑ̃t] *adj* : distrustful
déficeler [defisle] {8} *vt* : to untie (a package) — **se déficeler** *vr*
déficience [defisjɑ̃s] *nf* : deficiency
déficient, -ciente [defisjɑ̃, -sjɑ̃t] *adj* : deficient
déficit [defisit] *nm* **1** : deficit **2** MANQUE : deficiency, lack
déficitaire [defisitɛr] *adj* **1** : in deficit **2** : meager, poor <une récolte déficitaire : a poor harvest>
défier [defje] {96} *vt* **1** : to challenge **2** : to defy — **se défier** *vr* **~ de** : to distrust
défigurement [defigyrmɑ̃] *n* : disfigurement

défigurer [defigyre] *vt* **1** : to disfigure **2** : to distort <défigurer les faits : to distort the facts>

défilé [defile] *nm* **1** : parade **2** : stream <défilé de pensées : stream of thoughts> **3** : gorge, pass

défiler [defile] *vi* **1** : to march, to parade **2** : to succeed one another <les heures défilent : the hours pass one after the other> **3** : to stream past **4** : to scroll (on a computer) — **se défiler** *vr* : to sneak off, to slip away

défini, -nie [defini] *adj* **1** : defined <bien défini : well-defined> **2** : definite <article défini : definite article>

définir [definir] *vt* : to define — **se définir** *vr*

définitif, -tive [definitif, -tiv] *adj* : definitive, final

définition [definisjɔ̃] *nf* **1** : definition **2** : clue (in a crossword puzzle) **3** : resolution (of a televised image)

définitive *nf* **en ~** : finally, in the final analysis

définitivement [definitivmɑ̃] *adv* **1** : definitively, permanently **2** : definitely

déflagration [deflagrasjɔ̃] *nf* : explosion, combustion

déflation [deflasjɔ̃] *nf* : deflation

déflorer [deflɔre] *vt* **1** : to deflower **2** : to spoil <la répétition a défloré la plaisanterie : repetition made the joke stale>

défoncer [defɔ̃se] {6} *vt* **1** : to smash, to demolish, to break **2** : to knock the bottom out of — **se défoncer** *vr fam* **1** : to give it one's all **2** : to get high (on drugs)

déforestation [defɔrɛstasjɔ̃] *nf* : deforestation

déformation [defɔrmasjɔ̃] *nf* **1** : deformation, distortion **2 déformation professionnelle** : conditioning by one's job, force of habit

déformer [defɔrme] *vt* **1** : to bend (out of shape) **2** : to deform, to distort — **se déformer** *vr* : to lose its shape

défoulement [defulmɑ̃] *nm* : release, letting off of steam

défouler [defule] *v* **se défouler** *vr* **1** : to unwind, to relax **2** : to vent (one's anger, etc.)

défraîchi, -chie [defreʃi] *adj* : faded, dingy, shopworn

défrayer [defreje] {11} *vt* **1** : to defray, to pay **2 défrayer la chronique** : to be in the news

défricher [defriʃe] *vt* **1** : to clear, to reclaim (land) **2** : to do the spadework for

défriser [defrize] *vt* **1** : to straighten (hair) **2** *fam* : to annoy, to bug

défroisser [defrwase] *vt* : to smooth out

défunt, -funte [defœ̃, -fœ̃t] *adj & n* : deceased

dégagé, -gée [degaʒe] *adj* **1** : clear, open, bare **2** LIBRE : casual, free and easy

dégager [degaʒe] {17} *vt* **1** DÉLIVRER : to release, to free **2** : to clear <dégagez la voie! : clear the way!> **3** : to make (funds) available <dégager des profits : to show a profit> **4** EXTRAIRE : to bring out, to extract **5** ÉMETTRE : to emit, to give off — **se dégager** *vr* **1** : to emanate **2** : to clear (up) **3 ~ de** : to get free of, to extricate oneself from

dégaine [degɛn] *nf* : odd gait, gawky appearance

dégainer [degene] *vt* : to draw (a weapon)

dégarnir [degarnir] *vt* **1** VIDER : to empty, to clear **2** : to withdraw (troops) — **se dégarnir** *vr* **1** : to empty, to be cleared out **2** : to go bald **3** : to lose its leaves

dégâts [dega] *nmpl* : damage <dégâts des eaux : flood damage>

dégel [deʒɛl] *nm* : thaw

dégeler [deʒle] {20} *vt* **1** : to thaw out, to defrost **2** : to unfreeze (assets) **3** *fam* : to relax, to loosen up — *vi* : to thaw

dégêner [deʒɛne] *vt Can* : to put at ease — **se dégêner** *vr* : to come out of one's shell

dégénéré, -rée [deʒenere] *adj* : degenerate

dégénérer [deʒenere] {87} *vi* : to degenerate

dégénérescence [deʒeneresɑ̃s] *nf* : degeneration

dégingandé, -dée [deʒɛ̃gɑ̃de] *adj* : lanky, gangling

dégivrer [deʒivre] *vt* : to defrost, to deice

dégivreur [deʒivrœr] *nm* : defroster, deicer

déglinguer [deglɛ̃ge] *vt fam* : to bust, to break — **se déglinguer** *vr fam* : to break down, to go on the blink

déglutir [deglytir] *vi* : to swallow

déglutition [deglytisjɔ̃] *nf* : swallowing

dégommer [degɔme] *vt fam* : to sack, to fire

dégonfler [degɔ̃fle] *vt* **1** : to deflate **2** : to reduce (swelling) **3** *fam* : to debunk — **se dégonfler** *vr* **1** : to deflate, to go flat **2** : to go down **3** *fam* : to chicken out, to lose one's nerve

dégonflement [degɔ̃fləmɑ̃] *nm* : deflation (of a tire, etc.)

dégorger [degɔrʒe] {17} *vt* **1** : to disgorge (liquid) **2** : to unblock, to clear **3** : to soak clean — *vi* **1** : to run (of fabric) **2 faire dégorger** : to soak

dégouliner [deguline] *vi* **1** : to trickle **2** : to drip

dégourdi, -die [degurdi] *adj* : smart, clever

dégourdir [degurdir] *vt* **1** : to warm up, to loosen up (one's legs, etc.) **2** *fam* : to bring (s.o.) out, to make less timid — **se dégourdir** *vr* **1** : to move about

<se dégourdir les jambes : to stretch one's legs> **2** *fam* : to wise up
dégoût [degu] *nm* **1** : disgust, repugnance **2 dégoût de la vie** : world-weariness
dégoûtant, -tante [degutɑ̃, -tɑ̃t] *adj* : disgusting, revolting
dégoûté, -tée [degute] *adj* **1** : disgusted **2** DIFFICILE : fastidious <il n'est pas dégoûté : he's not fussy>
dégoûter [degute] *vt* : to disgust — **se dégoûter** *vr* ~ **de** : to get sick of
dégoutter [degute] *vi* : to drip
dégradation [degradasjɔ̃] *nf* **1** : degradation, deterioration **2** : decline (of conditions, morals, etc.) **3** : damage **4 dégradation civique** : loss of civil rights
dégradé [degrade] *nm* : gradation, shading (of colors)
dégrader [degrade] *vt* **1** : to degrade **2** ABÎMER : to damage, to spoil — **se dégrader** *vr*
dégrafer [degrafe] *vt* : to unhook, to unclasp
dégraissage [degrɛsaʒ] *nm* **1** : downsizing, cutbacks *pl* **2** : removal of grease stains **3** : trimming (of meat)
dégraisser [degrese] *vt* **1** : to downsize **2** : to remove grease marks from **3** : to trim the fat from
degré [dəgre] *nm* **1** : degree <un angle de 90 degrés : a 90-degree angle> **2** : proof (of alcohol) **3** : level, extent <une brûlure du premier degré : a first-degree burn> <cousins au second degré : second cousins> **4** : step <les degrés de l'échelle sociale : the rungs of the social ladder> **5 par degrés** : gradually
dégressif, -sive [degrɛsif, -siv] *adj* : graduated (of taxes, etc.)
dégrèvement [degrɛvmɑ̃] *nm* : tax relief
dégringolade [degrɛ̃gɔlad] *nf fam* : tumble, collapse
dégringoler [degrɛ̃gɔle] *fam vt* : to tumble down, to rush down — *vi* : to fall, to tumble
déguerpir [degɛrpir] *vi* **1** : to clear out **2 faire déguerpir** : to drive away
dégueulasse [degœlas] *adj fam* : disgusting
déguisement [degizmɑ̃] *nm* : disguise
déguiser [degize] *vt* : to disguise — **se déguiser** *vr* ~ **en** : to dress up as, to masquerade as
dégustateur, -trice [degystatœr, -tris] *n* : taster
déguster [degyste] *vt* **1** : to taste, to sample **2** : to savor, to enjoy
dehors[1] [dəɔr] *adv* **1** : outside, outdoors **2** : out <allons dehors ce soir : let's go out tonight> **3 en** ~ : (toward the) outside **4 en dehors de** : outside of, apart from
dehors[2] *nms & pl* **1** : outside, exterior **2 les dehors** : appearances
déifier [deifje] {96} *vt* : to deify
déjà [deʒa] *adv* **1** : already **2** : before, previously **3** *fam* : again <tu viens quand, déjà? : tell me again when you're coming?> **4** (*used for reinforcement*) <ce n'est déjà pas si mal : it's not all that bad>
déjeté, -tée [deʒte] *adj* : warped, lopsided
déjeuner[1] [deʒœne] *vi* **1** : to have lunch **2** *Bel, Can, Switz* : to have breakfast
déjeuner[2] *nm* **1** : lunch **2** *Bel, Can, Switz* : breakfast
déjouer [deʒwe] *vt* : to thwart, to outsmart
delà [dəla] *adv* **1** → **deça 2** → **au–delà, par–delà**
délabré, -rée [delabre] *adj* : dilapidated
délabrement [delabrəmɑ̃] *nm* **1** : dilapidation, deterioration **2** : ruin (of reputation, health, etc.)
délabrer [delabre] *vt* : to ruin — **se délabrer** *vr* : to deteriorate
délai [delɛ] *nm* **1** : time limit, deadline **2** : extension (of time) **3** : waiting period <sans délai : immediately, without delay>
délaissement [delɛsmɑ̃] *nm* : abandonment, desertion, neglect
délaisser [delese] *vt* **1** ABANDONNER : to abandon, to desert **2** : to neglect
délassement [delasmɑ̃] *nm* : relaxation
délasser [delase] *vt* : to relax — **se délasser** *vr*
délateur, -trice [delatœr, -tris] *n* : informer
délation [delasjɔ̃] *nf* : informing, denunciation
délavé, -vée [delave] *adj* : faded
délayage [delɛjaʒ] *nm* **1** : mixing **2** : dragging out (of a speech, etc.)
délayer [deleje] {11} *vt* **1** : to dilute, to mix **2** : to pad out, to drag out (a speech, etc.)
délectable [delɛktabl] *adj* : delectable, delicious
délectation [delɛktasjɔ̃] *nf* : delight
délecter [delɛkte] *v* **se délecter** *vr* ~ **de** : to delight in
délégation [delegasjɔ̃] *nf* **1** : delegation, assignment **2** : group of delegates
délégué, -guée [delege] *n* : delegate, representative
déléguer [delege] {87} *vt* : to delegate
délester [delɛste] *vt* **1** : to remove ballast from, to unload **2** : to relieve, to unburden **3** : to divert traffic away from **4** *fam* : to rob
délibération [deliberasjɔ̃] *nf* : deliberation
délibéré, -rée [delibere] *adj* **1** INTENTIONNEL : deliberate **2** DÉCIDÉ : resolute, determined — **délibérément** [-remɑ̃] *adv*
délibérer [delibere] {87} *vi* : to deliberate
délicat, -cate [delika, -kat] *adj* **1** : delicate, sensitive, tender **2** : dainty, re-

fined, delicious **3** : considerate, tactful **4** : awkward, tricky **5** : scrupulous **6** : fussy, difficult

délicatement [delikatmɑ̃] *adv* **1** : delicately, gently, daintily **2** : thoughtfully, tactfully

délicatesse [delikatɛs] *nf* **1** : delicacy, tenderness **2** : fineness **3** : tactfulness **4** : awkwardness, difficulty **5** : scrupulousness

délice [delis] *nm* : delight

délicieux, -cieuse [delisjø, -sjøz] *adj* : delicious, delightful — **délicieusement** [-sjøzmɑ̃] *adv*

délictueux, -tueuse [deliktɥø, -tɥøz] *adj* : criminal

délié, -liée [delje] *adj* **1** : slender, fine **2** : nimble

délier [delje] {96} *vt* **1** : to untie **2** : to loosen (up) <l'alcool a délié sa langue : alcohol loosened his tongue> **3** ~ **de** : to release from — **se délier** *vr*

délimitation [delimitasjɔ̃] *nf* : delimitation, boundary

délimiter [delimite] *vt* **1** : to delimit, to demarcate **2** : to define, to determine

délinquance [delɛ̃kɑ̃s] *nf* : crime, delinquency <délinquance juvenile : juvenile delinquency>

délinquant, -quante [delɛ̃kɑ̃, -kɑ̃t] *adj & n* : delinquent, offender

délirant, -rante [delirɑ̃, -rɑ̃t] *adj* **1** : delirious **2** : frenzied, wild

délire [delir] *nm* **1** : delirium **2 en** ~ : delirious, frenzied

délirer [delire] *vi* **1** : to be delirious **2** : to rave, to be out of one's mind

délit [deli] *nm* : crime, offense

délivrance [delivrɑ̃s] *nf* **1** : freeing, release **2** : delivery, issue **3** : relief

délivrer [delivre] *vt* **1** : to set free **2** : to issue, to award, to hand over **3** : to relieve of — **se délivrer** *vr* ~ **de** : to rid oneself of

déloger [delɔʒe] {17} *vt* **1** : to evict, to throw out **2** : to remove, to dislodge — *vi* : to leave home, to move out

déloyal, déloyale [delwajal] *adj, mpl* **déloyaux** [-jo] **1** : disloyal **2** : unfair, dishonest — **déloyalement** [-mɑ̃] *adv*

déloyauté [delwajote] *nf* : disloyalty

delta [dɛlta] *nm* : delta

déluge [delyʒ] *nm* **1** : deluge, flood **2** : downpour

déluré, -rée [delyre] *adj* **1** : sharp, smart **2** : forward, brazen

démagogie [demagɔʒi] *nf* : demagogy — **démagogique** [-gɔʒik] *adj*

démagogue [demagɔg] *nmf* : demagogue

demain[1] [dəmɛ̃] *adv* **1** : tomorrow <demain soir : tomorrow evening> **2** : in the future

demain[2] *nm* **1** : tomorrow <à demain : see you tomorrow!> **2** : the future <le monde de demain : the world of the future, tomorrow's world>

démancher [demɑ̃ʃe] *vt Can* : to take apart, to dismantle

demande [dəmɑ̃d] *nf* **1** : request <demande en mariage : marriage proposal> **2** : application <demande d'emploi : job application> **3** : demand <l'offre et la demande : supply and demand> **4** : claim (in law)

demander [dəmɑ̃de] *vt* **1** : to ask for, to request **2** : to call for <on vous demande au téléphone : you are wanted on the telephone> **3** : to ask (about) <demander son chemin : to ask directions> **4** EXIGER : to demand, to ask <il m'en demande trop : he asks too much of me> **5** NÉCESSITER : to require, to need **6** : to send for (a doctor, etc.) — *vi* ~ **à** : to ask to — **se demander** *vr* : to wonder

demandeur[1], **-deuse** [dəmɑ̃dœr, -døz] *n* : applicant <demandeur d'emploi : job applicant>

demandeur[2], **-deresse** [dəmɑ̃dœr, -drɛs] *n* : plaintiff

démangeaison [demɑ̃ʒɛzɔ̃] *nf* **1** : itch, itching **2** : urge

démanger [demɑ̃ʒe] {17} *vt* : to itch, to make itchy

démanteler [demɑ̃tle] {20} *vt* **1** : to demolish **2** : to break up, to dismantle

démaquillant [demakijɑ̃, -jɑ̃t] *nm* : makeup remover, cleansing cream

démaquiller [demakije] *v* **se démaquiller** *vr* : to remove one's makeup

démarcation [demarkasjɔ̃] *nf* : demarcation

démarchage [demarʃaʒ] *nm* : door-to-door solicitation <démarchage électoral : canvassing>

démarche [demarʃ] *nf* **1** : gait, walk **2** : step, action <faire des démarches : to take steps> **3** : approach, thought process

démarquer [demarke] *vt* **1** : to mark down (merchandise) **2** : to plagiarize — **se démarquer** *vr* : to distance oneself

démarrage [demaraʒ] *nm* : starting up

démarrer [demare] *vt* **1** : to start up (an automobile) **2** : to start, to launch (a project) — *vi* **1** : to start up (of an automobile) **2** : to drive off (of a driver) **3** : to get under way

démarreur [demarœr] *nm* : starter (of an automobile)

démasquer [demaske] *vt* : to unmask — **se démasquer** *vr* : to drop one's mask

démêlé [demele] *nm* **1** : quarrel **2 démêlés** *nmpl* : problems <avoir des démêlés avec la justice : to get in trouble with the law>

démêler [demele] *vt* **1** : to disentangle, to untangle **2** : to clear up, to sort out — **se démêler** *vr* ~ **de** : to extricate oneself from (a problem, etc.)

démembrer [demɑ̃bre] *vt* **1** : to dismember, to cut up **2** : to divide up

déménagement [demenaʒmɑ̃] *nm* : moving, relocation

déménager [demenaʒe] {17} *v* : to move, to relocate

déménageur, -geuse [demenaʒœr, -ʒøz] *n* : (furniture) mover

démence [demɑ̃s] *nf* : madness, insanity

démener [demne] {52} *v* **se démener** *vr* **1** : to thrash about, to struggle **2** : to exert oneself

dément[1]**, -mente** [demɑ̃, -mɑ̃t] *adj* **1** : demented, insane **2** *fam* : incredible, fantastic

dément[2]**, -mente** *n* : demented person

démenti [demɑ̃ti] *nm* : denial

démentiel, -tielle [demɑ̃sjɛl] *adj* : insane

démentir [demɑ̃tir] {82} *vt* **1** : to deny **2** CONTREDIRE : to refute, to contradict

démérite [demerit] *nm* : demerit

démériter [demerite] *vi* **1** : to show oneself unworthy **2 démériter auprès de qqn** : to lose s.o.'s esteem

démesuré, -rée [deməzyre] *adj* : excessive, immoderate — **démesurément** [-remɑ̃] *adv*

démettre [demɛtr] {53} *vt* **1** DESTITUER : to dismiss, to fire **2** : to dislocate (in medicine) — **se démettre** *vr* **1** : to resign **2 se démettre l'épaule** : to dislocate one's shoulder

demeurant [dəmœrɑ̃] *adv* **au ~** : after all, for all that

demeure [dəmœr] *nf* **1** : residence, abode **2 à ~** : permanently **3 mettre en demeure** : to require **4 mise en demeure** : summons, demand

demeurer [dəmœre] *vi* **1** (*with auxiliary verb* **être**) : to remain **2** (*with auxiliary verb* **avoir**) : to reside **3 il n'en demeure pas moins** : the fact remains, nonetheless

demi[1] [dəmi] *adv* **1** : half <demi-cuit : half-cooked> **2 à ~** : halfway <faire les choses à demi : to do things by halves>

demi[2]**, -mie** *adj* **1** : half <un demi pain : half a loaf> **2 et ~** : and a half <sept litres et demi : seven and a half liters> <à cinq heures et demie : at five-thirty>

demi[3]**, -mie** *n* : half <voulez-vous une bouteille? non, une demie : do you want a bottle? no, (just) a half>

demi[4] *nm* **1** : half <trois demis : three halves> **2** *France* : half-pint (of beer) **2** : halfback

demi–bas [dəmiba] *nms & pl* : kneesock

demi–bouteille [dəmibutɛj] *nf, pl* **demi–bouteilles** : half-bottle

demi–cercle [dəmisɛrkl] *nm, pl* **demi–cercles** : semicircle — **demi–circulaire** [-sirkylɛr] *adj*

demi–dieu [dəmidjø] *nm, pl* **demi–dieux** : demigod

demi–douzaine [dəmiduzɛn] *nf, pl* **demi–douzaines** : half a dozen

demie *nf* : half hour <la cloche a sonné la demie : the bell rang the half hour> <à la demie : at half past>

demi–finale [dəmifinal] *nf, pl* **demi–finales** : semifinal — **demi–finaliste** [-nalist] *nmf*

demi–frère [dəmifrɛr] *nm, pl* **demi–frères** : half brother

demi–heure [dəmijœr] *nf, pl* **demi–heures** : half hour

demi–jour [dəmiʒur] *nm, pl* **demi–jours** : half-light

demi–journée [dəmiʒurne] *nf, pl* **demi–journées** : half a day, half day

demi–litre [dəmilitr] *nm, pl* **demi–litres** : half-liter

demi–lune [dəmilyn] *nf, pl* **demi–lunes** **1** : half-moon **2 en ~** : semicircular

demi–mal [dəmimal] *nm* **il n'y a que demi–mal** : things could be worse

demi–mesure [dəmiməzyr] *nf, pl* **demi–mesures** : half measure

demi–mot [dəmimo] **à ~** : without having to spell things out

demi–pension [dəmipɑ̃sjɔ̃] *nf, pl* **demi–pensions** : half board (one meal furnished daily)

demi–place [dəmiplas] *nf, pl* **demi–places** **1** : half-price seat (at the theater) **2** : half-price fare (on a train, etc.)

demi–saison [dəmisɛzɔ̃] *nf* **vêtements de demi–saison** : spring or fall clothing

demi–sel [dəmisɛl] *nms & pl* : slightly salted (cheese, butter, etc.)

demi–sœur [dəmisœr] *nf, pl* **demi–sœurs** : half sister

démission [demisjɔ̃] *nf* **1** : resignation **2** : abdication of responsibility

démissionnaire [demisjɔnɛr] *adj* : outgoing, resigning

démissionner [demisjɔne] *vi* **1** : to resign **2** : to give up <je démissionne après cet essai : I'm giving up after this try> — *vt fam* : to oust

demi–tarif [dəmitarif] *nm, pl* **demi–tarifs** : half-price ticket

demi–teinte [dəmitɛ̃t] *nf, pl* **demi–teintes** : halftone

demi–tour [dəmitur] *nm, pl* **demi–tours** **1** : half turn <faire un demi-tour : to turn back> **2** : about-face **3** : U-turn

demi–vie [dəmivi] *nf, pl* **demi–vies** : half-life

démobiliser [demɔbilize] *vt* : to demobilize — **démobilisation** [-lizasjɔ̃] *nf*

démocrate[1] [demɔkrat] *adj* : democratic

démocrate[2] *nmf* : democrat

démocratie [demɔkrasi] *nf* : democracy

démocratique [demɔkratik] *adj* : democratic — **démocratiquement** [-tikmɑ̃] *adv*
démodé, -dée [demɔde] *adj* : old-fashioned, out-of-date
démographie [demɔgrafi] *nf* : demography — **démographique** [-grafik] *adj*
demoiselle [demwazɛl] *nf* **1** : young lady **2 demoiselle d'honneur** : bridesmaid
démolir [demɔlir] *vt* **1** : to demolish, to tear down **2** : to destroy, to ruin
démolition [demɔlisjɔ̃] *nf* **1** : demolition **2** : destruction, ruin
démon [demɔ̃] *nm* **1 le démon** : the devil **2** : demon, evil spirit **3 être en démon** *Can fam* : to be furious
démoniaque [demɔnjak] *adj* : fiendish, diabolical
démonstrateur, -trice [demɔ̃stratœr, -tris] *n* : demonstrator
démonstratif, -tive [demɔ̃stratif, -tiv] *adj* : demonstrative
démonstration [demɔ̃strasjɔ̃] *nf* **1** MANIFESTATION : demonstration, show <une démonstration de force : a show of strength> **2** PREUVE : proof
démontable [demɔ̃tabl] *adj* : collapsible, able to be dismantled
démonter [demɔ̃te] *vt* **1** : to dismantle **2** : to remove, to take down **3** : to disconcert — **se démonter** *vr*
démontrer [demɔ̃tre] *vt* : to demonstrate, to show, to prove
démoralisant, -sante [demɔralizɑ̃, -zɑ̃t] *adj* : demoralizing
démoraliser [demɔralize] *vt* : to demoralize — **se démoraliser** *vr*
démordre [demɔrdr] {63} *vt* **ne pas démordre de** : to stick to, to refuse to give up
démuni, -nie [demyni] *adj* **1** : poor, impoverished **2** : powerless
démunir [demynir] *vt* : to deprive — **se démunir** *vr* **~ de** : to part with
démystifier [demistifje] {96} *vt* **1** : to demystify **2** : to disabuse
dénaturé, -rée [denatyre] *adj* **1** : denatured **2** : unnatural
dénaturer [denatyre] *vt* **1** : to distort, to misrepresent **2** : to denature, to alter completely
dénégation [denegasjɔ̃] *nf* : denial
déneigement [denɛʒmɑ̃] *nm* : snow removal
déneiger [deneʒe] {17} *vt* : to clear snow from
déni [deni] *nm* : denial
dénicher [deniʃe] *vt* **1** : to unearth, to discover **2** : to take (a bird) from the nest — *vi* : to leave the nest
denier [dənje] *nm* **deniers publics** : public funds
dénier [denje] {96} *vt* : to deny
dénigrement [denigrəmɑ̃] *nm* : disparagement
dénigrer [denigre] *vt* : to denigrate, to disparage
denim [dənim] *nm* : denim
dénivellation [denivɛlasjɔ̃] *nf* **1** : difference in altitude or level **2** : gradient, slope
dénivellement [denivɛlmɑ̃] *nm* → **dénivellation**
dénombrement [denɔ̃brəmɑ̃] *nm* : counting, count
dénombrer [denɔ̃bre] *vt* : to count
dénominateur [denɔminatœr] *nm* : denominator <dénominateur commun : common denominator>
dénomination [denɔminasjɔ̃] *nf* **1** : naming **2** : name, designation
dénommé, -mée [denɔme] *n* **un dénommé** : a person by the name of <une dénommée Marie : a certain Marie>
dénommer [denɔme] *vt* : to name, to call
dénoncer [denɔ̃se] {6} *vt* : to denounce, to inform on — **se dénoncer** *vr* : to give oneself up
dénonciation [denɔ̃sjasjɔ̃] *nf* : denunciation
dénoter [denɔte] *vt* : to denote, to indicate
dénouement [denumɑ̃] *nm* **1** : denouement (in theater) **2** : outcome
dénouer [denwe] *vt* **1** : to untie **2** : to unravel, to resolve — **se dénouer** *vr*
dénoyauter [denwajote] *vt* : to pit (a fruit)
denrée [dɑ̃re] *nf* : commodity <denrées alimentaires : foods> <une denrée rare : a rare commodity>
dense [dɑ̃s] *adj* : dense — **densément** [dɑ̃semɑ̃] *adv*
densité [dɑ̃site] *nf* : density, denseness
dent [dɑ̃] *nf* **1** : tooth <dents de sagesse : wisdom teeth> <dents de lait : baby teeth> **2** : cog (of a wheel, etc.) **3** : prong, tine (of a fork) **4 avoir une dent contre** : to hold a grudge against **5 en dents de scie** : serrated **6 faire ses dents** : to teethe
dentaire [dɑ̃tɛr] *adj* : dental
dent–de–lion [dɑ̃dəljɔ̃] *nf, pl* **dents–de–lion** : dandelion
denté, -tée [dɑ̃te] *adj* : toothed
dentelé, -lée [dɑ̃tle] *adj* : serrated, jagged, indented
dentelle [dɑ̃tɛl] *nf* : lace
dentier [dɑ̃tje] *nm* : dentures *pl*
dentifrice [dɑ̃tifris] *nm* : toothpaste
dentiste [dɑ̃tist] *nmf* : dentist
dentisterie [dɑ̃tistəri] *nf* : dentistry
dentition [dɑ̃tisjɔ̃] *nf* : teeth *pl*, dentition <avoir une belle dentition : to have nice teeth>
dénudé, -dée [denyde] *adj* **1** : bare **2** : bald
dénuder [denyde] *vt* **1** : to bare **2** : to strip (off) — **se dénuder** *vr* **1** : to strip **2** : to go bald
dénué, -nuée [denɥe] *adj* **~ de** : devoid of, lacking in

dénuement [denymɑ̃] *nm* : destitution
déodorant [deɔdɔrɑ̃] *adj & nm* : deodorant
dépanner [depane] *vt* **1** : to fix, to repair **2** : to help out
dépanneur[1], **-neuse** [depanœr, -nøz] *n* : repairman, repairwoman
dépanneur[2] *nm Can* : convenience store
dépanneuse *nf* : tow truck, wrecker
dépareillé, -lée [depareje] *adj* **1** : incomplete **2** : odd, unpaired
déparer [depare] *vt* : to spoil, to mar
déparler [deparle] *vi Can fam* : to rave, to talk nonsense
départ [depar] *nm* **1** : departure **2** : start (in sports) <ligne de départ : starting line> **3 au départ** : at first, initially **4 être sur le départ** : to be about to leave
départager [departaʒe] {17} *vt* : to decide between
département [departəmɑ̃] *nm* **1** : department **2** : territorial division in France — **départemental, -tale** [-mɑ̃tal] *adj*
départir [departir] {82} *vt* : to assign, to allot — **se départir** *vr* : to abandon, to give up
dépassé, -sée [depase] *adj* : outdated, outmoded
dépassement [depasmɑ̃] *nm* **1** : passing (with an automobile) **2** : excess, overrun
dépasser [depase] *vt* **1** : to pass, to go past **2** EXCÉDER : to exceed, to go beyond <l'addition a depassé la somme prévue : the bill exceeded the expected amount> **3** : to outshine, to surpass **4 cela me dépasse!** : that's beyond me! — *vi* : to show, to stick out <ton jupon dépasse : your slip is showing>
dépaysement [depeizmɑ̃] *nm* **1** : disorientation **2** : change of scenery
dépayser [depeize] *vt* **1** : to disorient **2** : to provide with a change of scenery
dépecer [depəse] {6} *and* {52} *vt* : to carve up, to cut up
dépêche [depɛʃ] *nf* **1** : dispatch **2** *or* **dépêche télégraphique** : telegram
dépêcher [depeʃe] *vt* : to dispatch — **se dépêcher** *vr* SE HÂTER : to hurry
dépeindre [depɛ̃dr] {37} *vt* : to depict, to describe
dépendamment [depɑ̃damɑ̃] *adv* **~ de** *Can* : depending on
dépendance [depɑ̃dɑ̃s] *nf* **1** : dependence **2** : dependency (on drugs, etc.) **3** : outbuilding
dépendant, -dante [depɑ̃dɑ̃, -dɑ̃t] *adj* : dependent
dépendre [depɑ̃dr] {63} *vi* **1 ~ de** : to depend on **2 ~ de** : to belong to — *vt* : to take down
dépens [depɑ̃] *nmpl* **aux dépens de** : at the expense of
dépense [depɑ̃s] *nf* **1** : spending, expenditure **2** : expense **3** : consumption
dépenser [depɑ̃se] *vt* **1** : to spend **2** : to use up, to expend <j'ai dépensé toute mon énergie : I've used up all my energy> — **se dépenser** *vr* : to exert oneself
dépensier[1], **-sière** [depɑ̃sje, -sjɛr] *adj* : extravagant, wasteful
dépensier[2], **-sière** *n* : spendthrift
déperdition [depɛrdisjɔ̃] *nf* : loss
dépérir [deperir] *vi* **1** : to wither (of a plant) **2** : to waste away (of persons) **3** : to be on the decline
dépêtrer [depetre] *v* **se dépêtrer** *vr* **~ de** : to extricate oneself from
dépeupler [depœple] *vt* : to depopulate
déphasé, -sée [defaze] *adj* : out of touch (with reality), out of it
dépilatoire [depilatwar] *adj* : depilatory
dépiler [depile] *vt* : to remove hair from
dépistage [depistaʒ] *nm* : screening, testing <dépistage précoce : early detection>
dépister [depiste] *vt* **1** : to detect (a disease) **2** : to track down
dépit [depi] *nm* **1** : pique, vexation **2 en dépit de** MALGRÉ : in spite of, despite <en dépit de sa bonne volonté : despite his good will>
déplacé, -cée [deplase] *adj* **1** MALVENU : out of place, uncalled-for **2** : displaced <personnes déplacées : displaced persons>
déplacement [deplasmɑ̃] *nm* **1** : displacement **2** : moving, shifting **3** : trip, traveling <frais de déplacement : travel expenses> <être en déplacement : to be away on business>
déplacer [deplase] {6} *vt* **1** : to move, to shift, to change **2** : to displace — **se déplacer** *vr*
déplaire [deplɛr] {66} *vi* **1** : to be disliked **2 ~ à** : to put off, to repel <cela me déplaît : I don't like it> **3 ~ à** : to annoy, to offend <ne t'en déplaise : whether you like it or not>
déplaisant, -sante [deplɛzɑ̃, -zɑ̃t] *adj* : unpleasant, disagreeable
déplaisir [deplezir] *nm* : annoyance, displeasure
déplantoir [deplɑ̃twar] *nm* : (garden) trowel
dépliant [deplijɑ̃, -jɑ̃t] *nm* : brochure, pamphlet
déplier [deplije] {96} *vt* : to unfold — **se déplier** *vr*
déplisser [deplise] *vt* : to smooth out, to remove the pleats from
déploiement [deplwamɑ̃] *nm* **1** : deployment **2** : unfolding, spreading **3** : display
déplorable [deplɔrabl] *adj* : deplorable — **déplorablement** [-rabləmɑ̃] *adv*
déplorer [deplɔre] *vt* : to deplore, to lament

déployer [deplwaje] {58} *vt* **1** : to deploy **2** : to unfold, to spread out **3** : to display, to exhibit

déplumer [deplyme] *vt* : to pluck (a bird) — **se déplumer** *vr* **1** : to molt **2** *fam* : to go bald

dépoli, -lie [depɔli] *adj* **verre dépoli** : frosted glass

déporter [depɔrte] *vt* **1** : to inter in a concentration camp **2** DÉVIER : to divert, to carry off course — **se déporter** *vr* : to swerve

déposant, -sante [depozɑ̃, -zɑ̃t] *n* **1** : depositor **2** : witness (in law)

déposé, -sée [depoze] *adj* : registered <marque déposée : registered trademark>

déposer [depoze] *vt* **1** : to lay down, to put down **2** : to deposit **3** : to drop off, to leave **4** : to register, to file **5** : to depose **6** : to remove, to take down — *vi* **1** : to settle, to form a sediment **2** : to give evidence (in court) — **se déposer** *vr* : to settle

dépositaire [depɔzitɛr] *nmf* **1** : agent, dealer **2** : trustee **3** : repository (of a secret, etc.)

déposition [depozisjɔ̃] *nf* : evidence, testimony (in court)

déposséder [depɔsede] {87} *vt* : to dispossess

dépôt [depo] *nm* **1** : deposit, depository <dépôt en coffre-fort : safe deposit> **2** ENTREPÔT : warehouse, depot **3** : (retail) outlet **4** : registration, filing (of documents) **5** : sediment, (geological) deposit

dépotoir [depɔtwar] *nm* : dump

dépouille [depuj] *nf* **1** : hide, skin **2** *or* **dépouille mortelle** : mortal remains *pl* **3 dépouilles** *nfpl* : spoils

dépouillement [depujmɑ̃] *nm* **1** : austerity, soberness **2** : counting, perusal <dépouillement du scrutin : tally of votes>

dépouiller [depuje] *vt* **1** : to strip (off) **2** : to dispossess, to despoil **3** : to peruse, to scrutinize <dépouiller le scrutin : to tally the votes> **4** : to skin — **se dépouiller** *vr* **~ de** : to divest oneself of

dépourvu, -vue [depurvy] *adj* **1 ~ de** : lacking in, devoid of, without **2 au ~** : by surprise

dépravation [depravasjɔ̃] *nf* : depravity

dépraver [deprave] *vt* : to deprave — **dépravé, -vée** [-ve] *adj*

dépréciation [depresjasjɔ̃] *nf* : depreciation

déprécier [depresje] {96} *vt* **1** : to depreciate **2** : to disparage, to belittle — **se déprécier** *vr* **1** : to depreciate **2** : to put oneself down

déprédations [depredasjɔ̃] *nfpl* : damage

dépresseur [depresœr] *nm* : depressant

dépressif, -sive [depresif, -siv] *adj & n* : depressive

dépression [depresjɔ̃] *nf* **1** : depression **2 dépression nerveuse** : nervous breakdown

déprimant, -mante [deprimɑ̃, -mɑ̃t] *adj* : depressing

déprimé, -mée [deprime] *adj* : depressed, dejected

déprimer [deprime] *vt* **1** : to depress, to demoralize **2** : to press in, to indent — *vi fam* : to be depressed

depuis[1] [dəpɥi] *adv* **1** : since (then) <nous ne les avons pas revus depuis : we've never seen them since> **2 depuis que** : (ever) since <depuis qu'ils sont partis : ever since they left>

depuis[2] *prep* **1** : since <depuis 1831 : since 1831> **2** : from <depuis le matin jusqu'au soir : from morning till night> <depuis Londres à New York : from London to New York> **3** : for <en fonction depuis deux ans : in office for two years>

députation [depytasjɔ̃] *nf* **1** : deputation **2** : position of deputy

député, -tée [depyte] *n* **1** : deputy, representative (in government) **2** : delegate

députer [depyte] *vt* : to delegate, to appoint as representative, to deputize

déraciner [derasine] *vt* **1** ARRACHER : to uproot **2** : to eradicate

déraillement [derajmɑ̃] *nm* : derailment

dérailler [deraje] *vi* : to derail

déraisonnable [derɛzɔnabl] *adj* : unreasonable — **déraisonnablement** [-nabləmɑ̃] *adv*

déraisonner [derɛzɔne] *vi* : to talk nonsense

dérangement [derɑ̃ʒmɑ̃] *nm* **1** : trouble **2** : disorder, breakdown <en dérangement : out of order>

déranger [derɑ̃ʒe] {17} *vt* **1** : to bother, to disturb <ne vous dérangez pas : don't bother> **2** : to disrupt, to upset — **se déranger** *vr* **1** : to get up, to go out **2** : to put oneself out

dérapage [derapaʒ] *nm* **1** : skid, slip **2** : blunder **3** : loss of control

déraper [derape] *vi* **1** : to skid, to slip **2** : to get out of hand

derby [dɛrbi] *nm*, *pl* **derbys** *or* **derbies** : derby (horse race)

déréglé, -lée [deregle] *adj* **1** : out of order **2** : dissolute

déréglementer [derɛgləmɑ̃te] *vt* : to deregulate — **déréglementation** [-mɑ̃tasjɔ̃] *nf*

dérégler [deregle] {87} *vt* **1** : to put out of order **2** : to upset, to disturb — **se dérégler** *vr* : to go wrong

dérhumer *v* **se dérhumer** *vr Can fam* : to clear one's throat

dérider [deride] *vt* : to cheer up

dérision [derizjɔ̃] *nf* MÉPRIS : derision

dérisoire [derizwar] *adj* **1** : ridiculous, laughable **2** : trivial, pathetic

dérivation [derivasjɔ̃] *nf* : derivation

dérivatif[1], -tive [derivatif, -tiv] *adj* : derivative

dérivatif[2] *nm* : distraction, diversion

dérive [deriv] *nf* **1** : drift **2 à la dérive** : adrift

dérivé [derive] *nm* **1** : derivation (of a word) **2** SOUS-PRODUIT : by-product

dériver [derive] *vt* **1** : to divert **2 ~ de** : to derive from — *vi* : to drift, to be adrift

dermatologie [dɛrmatɔlɔʒi] *nf* : dermatology

dermatologique [dɛrmatɔlɔʒik] *adj* : dermatologic, dermatological

dermatologue [dɛrmatɔlɔg] *nmf* : dermatologist

dernier[1], -nière [dɛrnje, -njɛr] *adj* **1** : last, previous <l'année dernière : last year> **2** : latest **3** : final, last **4** : highest <le dernier degré de : the height of> **5** : lowest <la dernière marche : the bottom step>

dernier[2], -nière *n* **1** : last (one) **2 ce dernier, cette dernière** : the latter

dernier[3] *nm* **en ~** : last <il est arrivé en dernier : he arrived last>

dernièrement [dɛrnjɛrmɑ̃] *adv* : recently, lately

dernier–né, dernière–née [dɛrnjene, dɛrnjɛrne] *n* : last-born child

dérobade [derɔbad] *nf* : evasion

dérobé, -bée [derɔbe] *adj* **1** : concealed, hidden **2 à la dérobée** : surreptitiously

dérober [derɔbe] *vt* **1** : to steal **2** MASQUER : to conceal, to hide — **se dérober** *vr* **1** : to shy away, to be evasive **2** : to give way, to collapse **3 ~ à** : to avoid, to shirk

dérogation [derɔgasjɔ̃] *nf* : dispensation, exemption

déroger [derɔʒe] {17} *vi* **~ à** : to depart from

dérougir [deruʒir] *vi Can fam* **ne pas dérougir** : to continue without interruption <le téléphone n'a pas dérougi : the phone rang off the hook>

dérouiller [deruje] *vt fam* : to beat up — *vi France fam* : to have a hard time — **se dérouiller** *vr* SE DÉGOURDIR : to limber up, to stretch (one's legs, etc.)

déroulement [derulmɑ̃] *nm* **1** : unwinding, unrolling **2** : development, progress

dérouler [derule] *vt* : to unwind, to unroll — **se dérouler** *vr* **1** : to take place **2** : to develop, to progress **3** : to unwind

déroute [derut] *nf* **1** : rout **2 en ~** : routed, in full flight

dérouter [derute] *vt* **1** : to reroute, to divert **2** : to disconcert, to confuse

derrière[1] [dɛrjɛr] *adv & prep* : behind

derrière[2] *nm* **1** : back, rear <le derrière de l'édifice : the back of the building> **2** : rump, haunches *pl* (of an animal) **3** *fam* : buttocks *pl,* bottom

des[1] [de]→ **de, le**

des[2] → **un**

dès [dɛ] *prep* **1** : from <dès le début : from the start> <dès Boston jusqu'à Portland : from Boston to Portland> <dès son arrivée : as soon as he arrived> **2 dès lors** : from then on **3 dès lors que** : from the moment that, since **4 dès que** : as soon as

désabusé, -sée [dezabyze] *adj* : disillusioned, disenchanted

désaccord [dezakɔr] *nm* **1** DIFFÉREND : disagreement **2** : discrepancy

désaccoutumer [dezakutyme] *vt* **désaccoutumer qqn de** : to cure s.o. of the habit of — **se désaccoutumer** *vr* **~ de** : to get out of the habit of

désaffecté, -tée [dezafɛkte] *adj* : disused

désaffection [dezafɛksjɔ̃] *nf* : disaffection

désagréable [dezagreabl] *adj* DÉPLAISANT : disagreeable, unpleasant — **désagréablement** [-abləmɑ̃] *adv*

désagrégation [dezagregasjɔ̃] *nf* : disintegration, breakup

désagréger [dezagreʒe] {64} *vt* : to break up — **se désagréger** *vr* : to disintegrate

désagrément [dezagremɑ̃] *nm* : inconvenience, annoyance

désaligné, -née [dezaliɲe] *adj* : out of alignment

désaltérant, -rante [dezalterɑ̃, -rɑ̃t] *adj* : thirst-quenching

désaltérer [dezaltere] {87} *vt* : to quench the thirst of — **se désaltérer** *vr* : to quench one's thirst

désamorcer [dezamɔrse] {6} *vt* : to defuse

désappointer [dezapwɛ̃te] *vt* : to disappoint — **désappointement** [-pwɛ̃tmɑ̃] *nm*

désapprobateur, -trice [dezaprɔbatœr, -tris] *adj* : disapproving

désapprobation [dezaprɔbasjɔ̃] *nf* : disapproval

désapprouver [dɛzapruve] *vt* : to disapprove of

désarçonner [dɛzarsɔne] *vt* **1** : to throw (a rider), to unseat **2** : to nonplus

désargenté, -tée [dezarʒɑ̃te] *adj fam* : short of cash, broke

désarmant, -mante [dezarmɑ̃, -mɑ̃t] *adj* : disarming

désarmement [dezarməmɑ̃] *nm* : disarmament

désarmer [dezarme] *vt* : to disarm — *vi* **1** : to disarm **2** : to relent, to abate

désarroi [dezarwa] *nm* : confusion, distress, dismay

désassembler [dezasɑ̃ble] *vt* : to disassemble

désastre [dezastr] *nm* : disaster

désastreux, -treuse [dezastrø, -trøz] *adj* : disastrous

désavantage [dezavɑ̃taʒ] *nm* : disadvantage, drawback

désavantager [dezavɑ̃taʒe] {17} *vt* : to put at a disadvantage

désavantageux, -geuse [dezavɑ̃taʒø, -ʒøz] *adj* : disadvantageous, unfavorable

désaveu [dezavø] *nm, pl* **-veux 1** : repudiation **2** : disavowal, denial

désavouer [dezavwe] *vt* **1** : to deny **2** : to disown

désaxé, désaxée [dezakse] *adj* : (mentally) unbalanced

descendance [desɑ̃dɑ̃s] *nf* **1** : lineage, descent <de descendance irlandaise : of Irish descent> **2** PROGÉNITURE : offspring, descendants *pl*

descendant[1], **-dante** [desɑ̃dɑ̃, -dɑ̃t] *adj* : descending, downward

descendant[2], **-dante** *n* : descendant

descendre [dəsɑ̃dr] {63} *vt* **1** : to descend, to go down **2** : to take down, to bring down **3** : to lower — *vi* **1** : to descend, to go down, to come down **2** : to get off, to get out, to disembark, to dismount **3 ~ à** : to stay at (a hotel, etc.) **4 ~ de** : to be descended from

descente [desɑ̃t] *nf* **1** : descent **2** : (police) raid **3** : slope

descriptif, -tive [dɛskriptif, -tiv] *adj* : descriptive

description [dɛskripsjɔ̃] *nf* : description

désemparé, -rée [dezɑ̃pare] *adj* **1** : distraught, at a loss **2** : disabled (of a plane, ship, etc.)

désemparer [dezɑ̃pare] *vi* **sans ~** : without interruption, continuously

désenchanter [dezɑ̃ʃɑ̃te] *vt* : to disenchant, to disillusion — **désenchantement** [-ʃɑ̃tmɑ̃] *nm*

désencombrer [dezɑ̃kɔ̃bre] *vt* : to unblock, to clear

désenfler [dezɛ̃fle] *vi* : to become less swollen, to go down

désengagement [dezɑ̃gaʒmɑ̃] *nm* : disengagement, withdrawal

désengager [dezɑ̃gaʒe] {17} *vt* : to disengage, to release — **se désengager** *vr* : to withdraw

désenivrer [dezɑ̃nivre] *vt* : to sober up — **se désenivrer** *vr*

déséquilibre [dezekilibr] *nm* **1** : lack of balance, instability **2** : imbalance

déséquilibrer [dezekilibre] *vt* : to unbalance — **déséquilibré, -brée** [dezekilibre] *adj*

désert[1], **-serte** [dezɛr, -zɛrt] *adj* : uninhabited, deserted <île déserte : desert island>

désert[2] *nm* : desert

déserter [dezɛrte] *v* : to desert

déserteur [dezɛrtœr] *nm* : deserter

désertion [dezɛrsjɔ̃] *nf* : desertion

désertique [dezɛrtik] *adj* **1** : desert **2** : barren

désespérance [dezɛsperɑ̃s] *nf* : despair

désespérant, -rante [dezɛsperɑ̃, -rɑ̃t] *adj* **1** : hopeless, despairing **2** : appalling, terrible

désespéré, -rée [dezɛspere] *adj* **1** : desperate **2** : hopeless

désespérément [dezɛsperemɑ̃] *adv* : desperately, hopelessly, helplessly

désespérer [dezɛspere] {87} *vi* : to despair <elle désespère d'une carrière : she has given up hope for a career> — *vt* : to drive to despair

désespoir [dezɛspwar] *nm* **1** : despair, desperation **2 en désespoir de cause** : as a last resort, in sheer desperation

déshabillé [dezabije] *nm* : negligee

déshabiller [dezabije] *vt* : to undress — **se déshabiller** *vr*

déshabituer [dezabitɥe] *vt* **déshabituer qqn de** : to break s.o. of the habit of — **se déshabituer** *vr* **~ de** : to get out of the habit of

désherber [dezɛrbe] *v* : to weed

déshérité[1], **-tée** [dezerite] *adj* **1** : disinherited **2** : deprived, underprivileged

déshérité[2], **-tée** *n* **les déshérités** : the underprivileged

déshériter [dezerite] *vt* : to disinherit

déshonneur [dezɔnœr] *nm* : dishonor, disgrace

déshonorant, -rante [dezɔnɔrɑ̃, -rɑ̃t] *adj* : dishonorable

déshonorer [dezɔnɔre] *vt* : to dishonor, to disgrace — **se déshonorer** *vr* : to disgrace oneself

déshumaniser [dezymanize] *vt* : to dehumanize

déshydratation [dezidratasjɔ̃] *nf* : dehydration

déshydrater [dezidrate] *vt* : to dehydrate — **se déshydrater** *vr*

design [dizajn] *nm* : design <design industriel : industrial design>

désignation [deziɲasjɔ̃] *nf* **1** : designation, name **2** NOMINATION : appointment, nomination

designer [dizajnœr] *nmf* : designer

désigner [deziɲe] *vt* **1** : to designate, to indicate **2** NOMMER : to name, to appoint

désillusion [dezilyzjɔ̃] *nf* : disillusionment

désillusionner [dezilyzjɔne] *vt* : to disillusion

désincarné, -née [dezɛ̃karne] *adj* : disembodied

désinfectant[1], **-tante** [dezɛ̃fɛktɑ̃, -tɑ̃t] *adj* : disinfectant

désinfectant[2] *nm* : disinfectant

désinfecter [dezɛ̃fɛkte] *vt* : to disinfect

désinformation [dezɛ̃fɔrmasjɔ̃] *nf* : disinformation

désintégrer [dezɛ̃tegre] {87} *vt* : to disintegrate, to break up — **se désintégrer** *vr* — **désintégration** [-tegrasjɔ̃] *nf*

désintéressé, -sée [dezɛ̃terese] *adj* : disinterested, impartial

désintéressement [dezẽterɛsmɑ̃] *nm* : disinterestedness
désintérêt [dezẽterɛ] *nm* : lack of interest
désinvolte [dezẽvɔlt] *adj* **1** : casual, unself-conscious **2** : offhand, flippant, glib
désinvolture [dezẽvɔltyr] *nf* **1** : casualness, nonchalance **2** : offhand manner, flippancy, glibness
désir [dezir] *nm* : desire
désirable [dezirabl] *adj* : desirable
désirer [dezire] *vt* **1** : to want, to wish for **2** : to desire (sexually) **3 laisser à désirer** : to leave something to be desired
désireux, -reuse [dezirø, -røz] *adj* : anxious, desirous
désistement [dezistəmɑ̃] *nm* : withdrawal
désister [deziste] *v* **se désister** *vr* : to withdraw
désobéir [dezɔbeir] *vi* : to disobey <désobéir à ses parents : to disobey one's parents>
désobéissance [dezɔbeisɑ̃s] *nf* : disobedience
désobéissant, -sante [dezɔbeisɑ̃, -sɑ̃t] *adj* : disobedient
désobligeant, -geante [dezɔbliʒɑ̃, -ʒɑ̃t] *adj* : disagreeable, unpleasant
désobliger [dezɔbliʒe] {17} *vt* : to offend
désodorisant [dezɔdɔrizɑ̃] *nm* : air freshener, deodorizer
désodoriser [dezɔdɔrize] *vt* : to deodorize
désœuvré, -vrée [dezœvre] *adj* : idle
désœuvrement [dezœvrəmɑ̃] *nm* : idleness
désolant, -lante [dezɔlɑ̃, -lɑ̃t] *adj* : distressing
désolation [dezɔlasjɔ̃] *nf* **1** : desolation, devastation **2** : distress, grief
désolé, -lée [dezɔle] *adj* **1** : bleak, desolate **2** : contrite <je suis désolé : I'm sorry>
désoler [dezɔle] *vt* : to upset, to distress — **se désoler** *vr*
désolidariser [desɔlidarize] *v* **se désolidariser** *vr* **~ de** : to dissociate oneself from
désopilant, -lante [dezɔpilɑ̃, -lɑ̃t] *adj* : hilarious
désordonné, -née [dezɔrdɔne] *adj* **1** : disorganized **2** : untidy
désordre [dezɔrdr] *nm* **1** : confusion, disorder **2** : untidiness <en désordre : in a mess>
désorganiser [dezɔrganize] *vt* : to disorganize — **désorganisation** [-nizasjɔ̃] *nf*
désorienter [dezɔrjɑ̃te] *vt* **1** : to disorient **2** : to bewilder, to confuse
désormais [dezɔrmɛ] *adv* : henceforth, from now on
désosser [dezɔse] *vt* : to bone (meat)
despote [dɛspɔt] *nm* : despot — **despotisme** [-pɔtism] *nm*
despotique [dɛspɔtik] *adj* : despotic
desquels, desquelles [dekɛl] → **lequel**
dessécher [deseʃe] {87} *vt* **1** : to dry up, to desiccate, to parch **2** : to harden (one's heart)
dessein [desẽ] *nm* **1** : design, plan, intention **2 à ~** : intentionally, on purpose
desserrer [desere] *vt* **1** : to loosen **2** : to release (a brake) **3** RELÂCHER : to relax, to unclench
dessert [desɛr] *nm* : dessert
desserte [desɛrt] *nf* **1** : (transportation) service <desserte par bus : bus service> **2** : sideboard, serving table
desservir [desɛrvir] {81} *vt* **1** : to serve **2** : to lead into <deux portes desservent la salle de bain : two doors lead into the bathroom> **3** : to clear (the table) **4** : to do a disservice to
dessin [desẽ] *nm* **1** : drawing **2** : design, pattern **3** : outline **4 dessin animé** : (animated) cartoon
dessinateur, -trice [desinatœr, -tris] *n* **1** : artist, draftsman **2** : designer **3 dessinateur humoristique** : cartoonist
dessiner [desine] *vt* **1** : to draw **2** : to design **3** : to outline — *vi* : to draw, to sketch— **se dessiner** *vr* **1** : to stand out **2** : to take shape
dessoûler [desule] *v* : to sober up
dessous[1] [dəsu] *adv* : underneath
dessous[2] *nms & pl* **1** : underneath, underside **2 dessous** *nmpl* : underwear, lingerie **3 de ~** : from underneath **4 en ~** : underneath, down below **5 en dessous de** : below, beneath **6** → **au–dessous, par–dessous**
dessous–de–verre [d(ə)sudvɛr] *nms & pl* : coaster
dessus[1] [dəsy] *adv* : on top, on
dessus[2] *nms & pl* **1** : top **2** : upper (of a shoe) **3** : upper floor, upstairs **4 de ~** : off, from **5 en ~** : on top, above **6 avoir le dessus** : to have the upper hand **7** → **au–dessus, par–dessus**
déstabiliser [destabilize] *vt* : to destabilize
destin [dɛstẽ] *nm* : fate, destiny
destinataire [dɛstinatɛr] *nmf* **1** : addressee **2** : payee, beneficiary
destination [dɛstinasjɔ̃] *nf* **1** : destination **2 à destination de** : bound for
destinée [dɛstine] *nf* : fate, destiny
destiner [dɛstine] *vt* **1** : to intend **2** : to destine — **se destiner** *vr* **~ à** : to intend to become
destituer [dɛstitɥe] *vt* **1** DÉMETTRE : to dismiss, to discharge **2** : to depose
destructeur[1], **-trice** [dɛstryktœr, -tris] *adj* : destructive
destructeur[2], **-trice** *n* : destroyer, wrecker
destructible [dɛstryktibl] *adj* : destructible

destructif, -tive [dɛstryktif, -tiv] *adj* : destructive

destruction [dɛstryksjɔ̃] *nf* : destruction

désuet, -suète [dezɥɛ, -zɥɛt] *adj* : outdated, obsolete

désuétude [dezɥetyd] *nf* : obsolescence <tomber en désuétude : to fall into disuse>

désuni, -nie [dezyni] *adj* : disunited, divided

désunion [dezynjɔ̃] *nf* : disunity, dissension

désunir [dezynir] *vt* : to separate, to divide

détaché, -chée [detaʃe] *adj* **1** : detached **2** : transferred

détachement [detaʃmɑ̃] *nm* : detachment

détacher [detaʃe] *vt* **1** : to detach, to tear off **2** : to untie, to unfasten **3** DÉTOURNER : to turn (one's eyes, attention, etc.) away from **4** : to transfer **5** : to make stand out — **se détacher** *vr* **1** : to come undone **2 ~ de** : to grow away from, to lose interest in **3 ~ sur** : to stand out against

détail [detaj] *nm* **1** : detail <entrer dans les détails : to go into detail> **2** : retail <ventes au détail : retail sales>

détaillant, -lante [detajɑ̃, -jɑ̃t] *n* : retailer

détaillé, -lée [detaje] *adj* : detailed

détailler [detaje] *vt* **1** : to retail **2** ÉNUMÉRER : to detail, to itemize **3** : to scrutinize

détecter [detɛkte] *vt* : to detect

détecteur [detɛktœr] *nm* : detector, sensor <détecteur de mensonges : lie detector>

détection [detɛksjɔ̃] *nf* : detection

détective [detɛktiv] *nm* : detective <détective privé : private detective>

déteindre [detɛ̃dr] {37} *vt* : to make fade — *vi* **1** : to fade **2** : to run (of colors) **3 ~ sur** : to rub off on

détendre [detɑ̃dr] {63} *vt* **1** : to slacken, to loosen **2** : to relax, to ease — **se détendre** *vr* : to relax, to ease up

détendu, -due [detɑ̃dy] *adj* : relaxed

détenir [detnir] {92} *vt* **1** POSSÉDER : to hold, to be in possession of <détenir un secret : to have a secret> **2** : to detain, to hold (a prisoner)

détente [detɑ̃t] *nf* **1** : relaxation **2** : détente **3** : trigger

détenteur, -trice [detɑ̃tœr, -tris] *n* : holder <détenteur du record : record holder>

détention [detɑ̃sjɔ̃] *nf* **1** : possession, holding <détention de stupéfiants : drug possession> **2** EMPRISONNEMENT : detention, imprisonment

détenu, -nue [detny] *n* : prisoner

détergent [detɛrʒɑ̃] *nm* : detergent

détérioration [deterjɔrasjɔ̃] *nf* : deterioration

détériorer [deterjɔre] *vt* : to damage, to harm — **se détériorer** *vr* : to deteriorate

déterminant, -nante [detɛrminɑ̃, -nɑ̃t] *adj* : decisive, determining <un facteur déterminant : a determining factor>

détermination [detɛrminasjɔ̃] *nf* **1** : determination, resoluteness **2** RÉSOLUTION : decision

déterminé, -née [detɛrmine] *adj* **1** : determined, resolute **2** : specified, definite

déterminer [detɛrmine] *vt* **1** : to determine, to specify **2** : to encourage, to incite **3** : to cause — **se déterminer** *vr* : to decide, to make up one's mind

déterrer [detere] *vt* : to dig up, to unearth

détersif [detɛrsif, -siv] *nm* DÉTERGENT : detergent

détestable [detɛstabl] *adj* : detestable, foul, hateful — **détestablement** [-bləmɑ̃] *adv*

détester [detɛste] *vt* : to detest, to hate — **se détester** *vr*

détonant, -nante [detɔnɑ̃, -nɑ̃t] *adj* : explosive

détonateur [detɔnatœr] *nm* : detonator

détonation [detɔnasjɔ̃] *nf* : detonation, explosion

détoner [detɔne] *vi* : to detonate, to explode

détonner [detɔne] *vi* **1** : to be out of tune **2** : to clash

détordre [detɔrdr] {63} *vt* : to untwist, to unbend

détour [detur] *nm* **1** : curve, bend **2** DÉVIATION : detour **3 sans ~** : directly, frankly

détourné, -née [deturne] *adj* : indirect, roundabout, circuitous

détournement [deturnəmɑ̃] *nm* **1** : diversion, rerouting **2** : hijacking **3 détournement de fonds** : embezzlement, misappropriation of funds **4 détournement de mineur** : corruption of a minor

détourner [deturne] *vt* **1** : to divert, to reroute **2** : to turn aside <détourner les soupçons : to avert suspicion> <détourner la conversation : to change the subject> **3** : to hijack **4** : to misappropriate, to embezzle **5** : to twist, to distort, to corrupt

détracteur, -trice [detraktœr, -tris] *n* : detractor, faultfinder

détraqué, -quée [detrake] *adj* **1** : broken-down, out of order **2** *fam* : deranged, crazy

détraquer [detrake] *vt* **1** : to put out of order, to make go wrong **2** *fam* : to upset (one's stomach, etc.), to unhinge (mentally) — **se détraquer** *vr* : to break down, to go wrong

détremper [detrɑ̃pe] *vt* **1** : to soak, to saturate **2** : to dilute

détresse [detrɛs] *nf* : distress

détriment [detrimɑ̃] *nm* **au détriment de** : to the detriment of

détritus [detrity̑s] *nmpl* : waste, garbage, litter

détroit [detrwa] *nm* : strait <le détroit de Gibraltar : the strait of Gibraltar>

détromper [detrɔ̃pe] *vt* : to set straight, to disabuse — **se détromper** *vr* : to set oneself straight <détrompez-vous! : think again!>

détrôner [detrɔne] *vt* **1** : to depose, to dethrone **2** : to oust

détruire [detrɥir] {49} *vt* : to destroy — **se détruire** *vr*

dette [dɛt] *nf* : debt

deuil [dœj] *nm* : bereavement, mourning <porter le deuil : to be in mourning>

deux[1] [dø] *adj* **1** : two <deux cents : two hundred> <les deux côtés : both sides> **2** : second <le deux mai : May second> **3 à deux pas** : nearby, close **4 deux fois** : twice **5 tous les deux jours** : every other day

deux[2] *nm* **1** : two <couper en deux : to cut in two> **2 tous les deux** : both (of them)

deuxième [døzjɛm] *adj & nmf* : second

deuxièmement [døzjɛmmɑ̃] *adv* : secondly, second

deux–pièces [døpjɛs] *nms & pl* **1** : two-piece suit, two-piece swimsuit **2** : two-room apartment

deux–points [døpwɛ̃] *nms & pl* : colon

deux–roues [døru] *nms & pl* : two-wheeled vehicle

dévaler [devale] *vt* : to hurtle down

dévaliser [devalize] *vt* : to rob

dévalorisation [devalɔrizasjɔ̃] *nf* : depreciation

dévaloriser [devalɔrize] *vt* **1** : to devalue **2** : to belittle

dévaluation [devalɥasjɔ̃] *nf* : devaluation

dévaluer [devalɥe] *vt* : to devalue

devancer [dəvɑ̃se] {6} *vt* **1** : to be ahead of <devancer ses rivaux : to be ahead of one's rivals> **2** PRÉCÉDER : to arrive before **3** : to anticipate

devant[1] [dəvɑ̃] *adv* : in front, ahead, before <il marche devant : he is walking ahead>

devant[2] *nm* **1** : front <le devant de la maison : the front of the house> **2 prendre les devants** : to take the initiative

devant[3] *prep* **1** : in front of <devant chez toi : in front of your house> <jurer devant témoins : to swear before witnesses> **2** : ahead of <avoir du temps devant soi : to have time to spare> **3** : in the face of <sans peur devant le danger : fearless in the face of danger>

devanture [dəvɑ̃tyr] *nf* **1** : storefront **2** : shopwindow **3 en ~** : on display

dévastateur, -trice [devastatœr, -tris] *adj* : devastating, destructive

dévastation [devastasjɔ̃] *nf* : devastation

dévaster [devaste] *vt* : to devastate, to ravage

développement [devlɔpmɑ̃] *nm* **1** : development **2** CROISSANCE : growth, expansion **3** : developing (of photographic film)

développer [devlɔpe] *vt* : to develop — **se développer** *vr*

devenir [dəvnir] {92} *vi* : to become <je deviens vieux : I'm growing old> <qu'est-il devenu? : what has become of him?> <qu'est-ce que tu deviens? : what are you up to?>

déverrouiller [deveruje] *vt* : to unbolt

déverser [devɛrse] *vt* : to pour (out), to dump — **se déverser** *vr* **~ dans** : to flow into

dévêtir [devetir] {97} *vt* : to undress — **se dévêtir** *vr*

déviation [devjasjɔ̃] *nf* **1** : deviation **2** DÉTOUR : detour

dévider [devide] *vt* : to unwind

dévier [devje] {96} *vi* **1** : to veer, to swerve **2 ~ de** : to deviate from — *vt* : to deflect, to divert <dévier la circulation : to divert traffic>

devin, -vineresse [dəvɛ̃,-vinrɛs] *n* : soothsayer, fortune-teller

deviner [dəvine] *vt* **1** : to guess **2** APERCEVOIR : to perceive, to sense **3** PRÉDIRE : to foretell

devinette [dəvinɛt] *nf* : riddle

devis [dəvi] *nms & pl* : estimate

dévisager [devizaʒe] {17} *vt* : to stare at

devise [dəviz] *nf* **1** : motto, slogan **2** : currency (money)

deviser [dəvize] *vi* : to converse

dévisser [devise] *vt* : to unscrew

dévoiler [devwale] *vt* : to unveil, to reveal

devoir[1] [dəvwar] {28} *vt* : to owe — *v aux* **1** : to have to, to be compelled to <il doit le faire : he must do it> **2** : to be advised to <tu dois lire les instructions : you should read the instructions> <elle doit répondre : she ought to reply> **3** : to be presumed to <il a dû payer : he must have paid> **4** : to be expected to <elles devaient se rencontrer plus tard : they were supposed to meet later> — **se devoir** *vr* **1** : to be obligated to each other **2 se devoir de faire** : to be duty bound to do (sth)> **3 comme il se doit** : as is proper, as might be expected

devoir[2] *nm* **1** : duty **2 devoirs** *nmpl* : homework

dévolu[1], **-lue** [devɔly] *adj* **~ à** : allotted to

dévolu[2] *nm* **jeter son dévolu sur** : to set one's sights on

dévorer [devɔre] *vt* **1** : to devour <être dévoré de : to be eaten up by> **2** CONSUMER : to consume

dévot, -vote [devo, -vɔt] *adj* : devout, pious

dévotion [devosjɔ̃] *nf* **1** : devotion <avec dévotion : devotedly> **2** : devoutness

dévoué, -vouée [devwe] *adj* : devoted

dévouement [devumɑ̃] *nm* : dedication, devotion

dévouer [devwe] *vt* : to devote — **se dévouer** *vr* **1** : to devote oneself **2** : to sacrifice oneself

dévoyé, -yée [devwaje] *adj & n* : delinquent

devra [dəvra], *etc.* → **devoir**

dextérité [dɛksterite] *nf* : dexterity, skill

diabète [djabɛt] *nm* : diabetes

diabétique [djabetik] *adj & nmf* : diabetic

diable [djabl] *nm* **1** : devil <avoir le diable au corps : to be the very devil> <ce n'est pas le diable : it's not all that bad> **2 à la diable** : any old way **3 au ~** : to hell with **4 en ~** : devilishly, terribly **5 mener le diable** *Can fam* : to make a racket **6 où (quand, qui, pourquoi) diable** : where (when, who, why) the devil

diablement [djabləmɑ̃] *adv fam* : very, extremely, awfully

diablerie [djabləri] *nf* : mischief

diablotin [djablɔtɛ̃] *nm* : little demon, imp

diabolique [djabɔlik] *adj* : diabolical, diabolic, devilish — **diaboliquement** [-likmɑ̃] *adv*

diachylon [djaʃilɔ̃] *nm Can* : adhesive bandage

diacre [djakr] *nm* : deacon

diadème [djadɛm] *nm* : diadem

diagnostic [djagnɔstik] *nm* : diagnosis — **diagnostique** [-nɔstik] *adj*

diagnostiquer [djagnɔstike] *vt* : to diagnose

diagonal, -nale [djagɔnal] *adj, mpl* **-naux** [-no] : diagonal

diagonale *nf* **1** : diagonal **2 en ~** : diagonally

diagramme [djagram] *nm* : graph, chart

dialecte [djalɛkt] *nm* : dialect

dialogue [djalɔg] *nm* : dialogue

dialoguer [djalɔge] *vi* **1** : to converse **2** : to engage in dialogue, to have talks

dialyse [djaliz] *nf* : dialysis

diamant [djamɑ̃] *nm* : diamond

diamétralement [djametralmɑ̃] *adv* : diametrically

diamètre [djamɛtr] *nm* : diameter

diapason [djapazɔ̃] *nm* **1** : tuning fork **2 être au même diapason** : to be on the same wavelength

diaphane [djafan] *adj* : diaphanous

diaphragme [djafragm] *nm* : diaphragm

diapositive [djapɔzitiv] *nf* : slide, transparency

diarrhée [djare] *nf* : diarrhea

diatribe [djatrib] *nf* : diatribe

dichotomie [dikɔtɔmi] *nf* : dichotomy

dictateur [diktatœr] *nm* : dictator

dictatorial, -riale [diktatɔrjal] *adj, mpl* **-riaux** [-rjo] : dictatorial

dictature [diktatyr] *nf* : dictatorship

dictée [dikte] *nf* : dictation

dicter [dikte] *vt* : to dictate

diction [diksjɔ̃] *nf* : diction

dictionnaire [diksjɔnɛr] *nm* : dictionary

dicton [diktɔ̃] *nm* : saying

didactique [didaktik] *adj* : didactic

dièse [djɛz] *adj & nm* : sharp (in music)

diesel [djezɛl] *adj & nm* : diesel

diète [djɛt] *nf* RÉGIME : diet — **diététique** [djɛtetik] *adj*

diététicien, -cienne [djetetisjɛ̃, -sjɛn] *n* : dietician

dieu [djø] *nm, pl* **dieux** : god

Dieu *nm* : God

diffamation [difamasjɔ̃] *nf* CALOMNIE : slander, libel

diffamatoire [difamatwar] *adj* : slanderous, defamatory

diffamer [difame] *vt* CALOMNIER : to defame, to slander, to libel

différé, -rée [difere] *adj* **1** : postponed, deferred **2 en ~** : prerecorded

différemment [diferamɑ̃] *adv* : differently

différence [diferɑ̃s] *nf* **1** : difference <faire la différence : to tell the difference> **2 à la différence de** : unlike

différencier [diferɑ̃sje] {96} *vt* DISTINGUER : to differentiate — **se différencier** *vr* **~ de** : to differ from

différend [diferɑ̃] *nm* : disagreement, difference (of opinion)

différent, -rente [diferɑ̃, -rɑ̃t] *adj* **1** : different, various **2 ~ de** : different from, unlike

différentiel, -tielle [diferɑ̃sjɛl] *adj* : differential

différer [difere] {87} *vt* : to defer, to postpone — *vi* **1** : to differ, to vary **2 ~ de** : to differ from

difficile [difisil] *adj* **1** : difficult, hard **2** : choosy, hard to please

difficilement [difisilmɑ̃] *adv* : with difficulty

difficulté [difikylte] *nf* **1** : difficulty **2** : problem <en difficulté : in trouble>

difforme [difɔrm] *adj* : deformed, misshapen

difformité [difɔrmite] *nf* : deformity

diffus, -fuse [dify, -fyz] *adj* : diffuse

diffuser [difyze] *vt* **1** : to broadcast **2** : to spread, to distribute **3** : to diffuse (light, etc.) — **se diffuser** *vr*

diffuseur [difyzœr] *nm* **1** : distributor **2** : broadcaster

diffusion [difyzjɔ̃] *nf* **1** : distribution **2** : diffusion **3** RADIODIFFUSION : broadcasting

digérer [diʒere] {87} *vt* **1** : to digest **2** : to assimilate **3** : to accept, to put up with

digeste [diʒɛst] *adj* : (easily) digestible

digestible [diʒɛstibl] *adj* : digestible

digestif, -tive [diʒɛstif, -tiv] *adj* : digestive

digestion [diʒɛstjɔ̃] *nf* : digestion

digital, -tale [diʒital] *adj, mpl* **-taux** [-to] **1** : digital **2** → **empreinte**

digitale [diʒital] *nf* **1** : digitalis **2** *or* **digitale pourprée** : foxglove

digne [diɲ] *adj* **1** : worthy <digne de foi : trustworthy> **2** : dignified

dignement [diɲmɑ̃] *adv* **1** : with dignity **2** : suitably, justly

dignitaire [diɲitɛr] *nm* : dignitary

dignité [diɲite] *nf* : dignity

digression [digresjɔ̃] *nf* : digression

digue [dig] *nf* **1** : dike, seawall **2** : barrier

dilapider [dilapide] *vt* : to squander, to waste

dilater [dilate] *vt* : to dilate, to expand — **se dilater** *vr*

dilatoire [dilatwar] *adj* : dilatory, delaying

dilemme [dilɛm] *nm* : dilemma

dilettante [diletɑ̃t] *nmf* : dilettante, amateur

diligence [diliʒɑ̃s] *nf* **1** : dispatch <faire diligence : to make haste> **2** : stagecoach

diligent, -gente [diliʒɑ̃, -ʒɑ̃t] *adj* : prompt, speedy

diluant [dilɥɑ̃] *nm* : thinner

diluer [dilɥe] *vt* : to dilute — **dilution** [dilysjɔ̃] *nf*

dimanche [dimɑ̃ʃ] *nm* : Sunday

dîme [dim] *nf* : tithe

dimension [dimɑ̃sjɔ̃] *nf* **1** : dimension, measurement **2** : aspect **3 dimensions** *nfpl* : dimensions, size

diminuer [diminɥe] *vt* RÉDUIRE : to lower, to reduce — *vi* : to diminish, to decrease, to drop

diminution [diminysjɔ̃] *nf* : reduction, decreasing

dinde [dɛ̃d] *nf* **1** : (female) turkey **2** : stupid woman

dindon [dɛ̃dɔ̃] *nm* **1** : (male) turkey **2 être le dindon de la farce** : to be made a fool of

dîner[1] [dine] *vi* **1** : to dine, to have dinner **2** *Bel, Can, Switz* : to have lunch

dîner[2] *nm* **1** : dinner **2** *Bel, Can, Switz* : lunch

dîneur, -neuse [dinœr, -nøz] *n* : diner (person)

dingue [dɛ̃g] *adj fam* **1** : crazy, nuts, goofy **2** : incredible

dinosaure [dinozɔr] *nm* : dinosaur

diocèse [djɔsɛz] *nm* : diocese

diphtérie [difteri] *nf* : diphtheria

diphtongue [diftɔ̃g] *nf* : diphthong

diplomate[1] [diplɔmat] *adj* : diplomatic

diplomate[2] *nmf* : diplomat

diplomatie [diplɔmasi] *nf* : diplomacy

diplomatique [diplɔmatik] *adj* : diplomatic — **diplomatiquement** [-tikmɑ̃] *adv*

diplôme [diplom] *nm* **1** : diploma, certificate, degree **2** : (qualifying) exam

diplômé[1], **-mée** [diplome] *adj* **1** : qualified, certified **2 être diplômé de** : to be a graduate of

diplômé[2], **-mée** *n* : graduate

dire[1] [dir] {29} *vt* **1** : to say <comme on dit : as they say> <cela va sans dire : that goes without saying> <sans dire mot : without saying a word> **2** : to tell <dire la vérité : to tell the truth> <c'est ce qu'on m'a dit : so I've been told> **3** : to think <qu'en dis-tu? : what do you think?> <on dirait qu'il est perdu : he seems lost> **4** : to show, to indicate <dire l'heure : to tell the time> **5** : to appeal to <cela vous dit d'aller dehors? : do you feel like going outside?> **6 pour ainsi dire** : so to speak **7 vouloir dire** : to mean <que veut dire ce mot? : what does this word mean?> — **se dire** *vr* **1** : to tell oneself **2** : to say to each other <se dire au revoir : to say good-bye (to each other)> **3** : to claim to be <elle se dit malade : she says she's sick> **4** : to say (in another language) <comment se dit *chien* en russe? : how do you say *dog* in Russian?> **5** : to be said <cela ne se dit pas : we shouldn't say that>

dire[2] *nm* **1 au dire de** : according to **2 avoir pour son dire** *Can* : to be in the habit of saying **3 dires** *nmpl* : statements

direct[1], **-recte** [dirɛkt] *adj* : direct — **directement** [-təmɑ̃] *adv*

direct[2] *nm* **1** : express train **2** : jab (in boxing) **3 en ~** : live, in person

directeur[1], **-trice** [dirɛktœr, -tris] *adj* **1** : directing, guiding <ligne directrice : guideline> **2** : main <idée directrice : main idea>

directeur[2], **-trice** *n* **1** : manager, director **2 directeur général** : general manager, chief executive officer **3 directeur d'école** : principal

direction [dirɛksjɔ̃] *nf* **1** : direction **2** GESTION : management, supervision, leadership <la direction du parti : party management> **3** : steering <direction assistée : power steering>

directive [dirɛktiv] *nf* ORDRE : order, directive

directorial, -riale [dirɛktɔrjal] *adj, pl* **-riaux** [-rjo] : managerial, directorial

dirigeable [diriʒabl] *nm* : airship, dirigible

dirigeant[1], **-geante** [diriʒɑ̃, -ʒɑ̃t] *adj* : ruling <la classe dirigeante : the ruling class>

dirigeant[2], **-geante** *n* **1** : leader (of a country, etc.) **2** : manager

diriger [diriʒe] {17} *vt* **1** : to direct, to manage <diriger une entreprise : to run a company> **2** : to aim, to direct (one's attention, efforts, etc.) **3** : to steer **4** : to conduct (an orchestra) — **se diriger** *vr* **1** : to find one's way **2** **~ vers** : to head toward

disait [dizɛ], **disions** [dizjɔ̃], *etc.* → **dire**

discernement [disɛrnəmɑ̃] *nm* : discernment, judgment

discerner [disɛrne] *vt* : to discern, to distinguish

disciple [disipl] *nm* : follower, disciple

disciplinaire [disiplinɛr] *adj* : disciplinary

discipline [disiplin] *nf* : discipline

discipliner [disipline] *vt* : to discipline — **se discipliner** *vr*

disc–jockey [diskʒɔkɛ] *nmf, pl* **disc–jockeys** : disc jockey

discontinu, -nue [diskɔ̃tiny] *adj* **1** : broken, dotted **2** : intermittent

discontinuer [diskɔ̃tinɥe] *vi* **sans ~** : without interruption

discordance [diskɔrdɑ̃s] *nf* **1** : clash, conflict **2** : dissonance

discordant, -dante [diskɔrdɑ̃, -dɑ̃t] *adj* **1** : conflicting, clashing **2** : dissonant

discorde [diskɔrd] *nf* **1** : discord, dissension **2** **pomme de discorde** : bone of contention

discothèque [diskɔtɛk] *nf* **1** : disco, nightclub **2** : record library

discourir [diskurir] {23} *vi* **1** : to discourse, to talk at length **2** **~ sur** : to hold forth on

discours [diskur] *nms & pl* **1** : speech, address **2** : discourse, speech (in grammar) <discours indirect : indirect discourse>

discourtois, -toise [diskurtwa, -twaz] *adj* : discourteous — **discourtoisement** [-twazmɑ̃] *adv*

discrédit [diskredi] *nm* : discredit

discréditer [diskredite] *vt* : to discredit, to disparage — **se discréditer** *vr*

discret, -crète [diskrɛ, -krɛt] *adj* **1** : discreet **2** : unassuming, unobtrusive

discrètement [diskrɛtmɑ̃] *adv* : discreetly

discrétion [diskresjɔ̃] *nf* **1** : discretion **2** **à ~** : unlimited, as much as one wants

discrétionnaire [diskresjɔnɛr] *adj* : discretionary

discrimination [diskriminasjɔ̃] *nf* **1** : discrimination **2** **sans ~** : indiscriminately

discriminatoire [diskriminatwar] *adj* : discriminatory

disculper [diskylpe] *vt* : to exonerate — **se disculper** *vr* : to vindicate oneself

discussion [diskysjɔ̃] *nf* **1** : discussion **2** : argument, debate

discutable [diskytabl] *adj* **1** : debatable, arguable **2** : questionable, doubtful

discuté, -tée [diskyte] *adj* : controversial

discuter [diskyte] *vt* **1** : to discuss, to debate **2** : to question — *vi* **1** : to talk **2** : to argue **3** **~ de** : to discuss

dise [diz], *etc.* → **dire**

disette [dizɛt] *nf* : shortage of food

diseur, -seuse [dizœr, -zøz] *n* **diseur de bonne aventure** : fortune-teller

disgrâce [disgras] *nf* **1** : disgrace, disfavor **2** : misfortune

disgracieux, -cieuse [disgrasjø, -sjøz] *adj* **1** : awkward, ungainly **2** : ugly

disjoindre [disʒwɛ̃dr] {50} *vt* **1** : to take apart **2** : to separate (out) — **se disjoindre** *vr* : to come apart

disjoncteur [disʒɔ̃ktœr] *nm* : circuit breaker

dislocation [dislɔkasjɔ̃] *nf* **1** : dislocation (in medicine) **2** : breaking up

disloquer [dislɔke] *vt* **1** LUXER : to dislocate (in medicine) **2** : to break up, to dismantle

disparaître [disparɛtr] {7} *vi* **1** : to disappear **2** MOURIR : to die (out) **3** **faire disparaître** : to get rid of

disparate [disparat] *adj* **1** : disparate, dissimilar **2** : clashing

disparité [diparite] *nf* : disparity

disparition [disparisjɔ̃] *nf* **1** : disappearance **2** : extinction, death

disparu[1], -rue [dispary] *adj* **1** : missing **2** : lost, vanished, extinct

disparu[2], -rue *n* **1** : missing person **2** : dead person <notre cher disparu : our dear departed>

dispendieux, -dieuse [dispɑ̃djø, -djøz] *adj* COÛTEUX : expensive, costly

dispensaire [dispɑ̃sɛr] *nm* : dispensary, free clinic

dispense [dispɑ̃s] *nf* : exemption, dispensation

dispenser [dispɑ̃se] *vt* **1** : to exempt, to excuse **2** : to dispense, to bestow — **se dispenser** *vr* **~ de** : to avoid, to get out of

disperser [dispɛrse] *vt* ÉPARPILLER : to disperse, to scatter — **se disperser** *vr*

dispersion [dispɛrsjɔ̃] *nf* : scattering, dispersal

disponibilité [dispɔnibilite] *nf* **1** : availability **2** **en ~** : on leave of absence **3** **disponibilités** *nfpl* : liquid assets

disponible [dispɔnibl] *adj* : available

dispos, -pose [dispo, -poz] *adj* **1** : refreshed **2** **frais et dispos** : as fresh as a daisy

disposé, -sée [dispoze] *adj* **1** : arranged **2** **~ à** : disposed to, willing to **3** **bien disposé envers** : well-disposed toward

disposer [dispoze] *vt* **1** PLACER : to arrange, to place **2** : to incline, to dispose — *vi* **1** : to leave <ils peuvent disposer : they may leave> **2** **~ de** : to have at one's disposal — **se disposer** *vr* **se disposer à faire** : to be about to do

dispositif [dispɔzitif] *nm* **1** : device, mechanism <dispositif de sûreté : safeguard> **2** : plan of action

disposition [dispozisjɔ̃] *nf* **1** : arrangement, layout **2** : aptitude **3** : tendency

4 **à la disposition de** : at the disposal of 5 **dispositions** *nfpl* : mood, state of mind 6 **dispositions** *nfpl* : steps, measures
disproportion [disprɔpɔrsjɔ̃] *nf* : disproportion
disproportionné, -née [disprɔpɔrsjɔne] *adj* : disproportionate
dispute [dispyt] *nf* : argument, quarrel
disputer [dispyte] *vt* **1** : to compete in, to play **2** : to contend with, to fight **3** *fam* : to tell off **4** *Can* : to scold, to chide — **se disputer** *vr* : to quarrel, to fight
disqualifier [diskalifje] {96} *vt* : to disqualify — **disqualification** [-lifikasjɔ̃] *nf*
disque [disk] *nm* **1** : record, disc <disque compact : compact disc> <disque vidéo : videodisc> **2** : disk (in anatomy, astronomy, etc.) **3** : discus
disquette [diskɛt] *nf* : diskette, floppy disk
dissection [disɛksjɔ̃] *nf* : dissection
dissemblable [disɑ̃babl] *adj* : dissimilar
dissemblance [disɑ̃blɑ̃s] *nf* : dissimilarity, difference
disséminer [disemine] *vt* **1** : to scatter **2** : to disseminate, to spread
dissémination [diseminasjɔ̃] *nf* **1** : scattering, dispersal **2** : dissemination, spread (of ideas, etc.)
dissension [disɑ̃sjɔ̃] *nf* : dissension, disagreement
dissentiment [disɑ̃timɑ̃] *nm* : dissent
disséquer [diseke] {87} *vt* : to dissect
dissertation [disɛrtasjɔ̃] *nf* : essay (in school)
dissident, -dente [disidɑ̃, -dɑ̃t] *adj & n* : dissident — **dissidence** [-sidɑ̃s] *nf*
dissimulation [disimylasjɔ̃] *nf* **1** : dissimulation, dissembling **2** : concealment
dissimulé, -lée [disimyle] *adj* **1** : hidden, concealed **2** : secretive
dissimuler [disimyle] *vt* CACHER : to conceal, to hide — **se dissimuler** *vr*
dissipation [disipasjɔ̃] *nf* **1** : dissipation **2** : squandering, wasting
dissipé, -pée [disipe] *adj* **1** : undisciplined, unruly **2** : dissipated, dissolute
dissiper [disipe] *vt* **1** : to disperse, to clear, to dispel **2** : to squander — **se dissiper** *vr* **1** : to clear (up), to vanish **2** : to become unruly
dissocier [disɔsje] {96} *vt* : to dissociate, to separate — **se dissocier** *vr*
dissolu, -lue [disɔly] *adj* : dissolute
dissolution [disɔlysjɔ̃] *nf* **1** : dissolution, breakup **2** : dissolving
dissolvant [disɔlvɑ̃] *nm* **1** : solvent **2** : nail polish remover
dissonant, -nante [disɔnɑ̃, -nɑ̃t] *adj* : dissonant, discordant — **dissonance** [-sɔnɑ̃s] *nf*
dissoudre [disudr] {1} *vt* : to dissolve — **se dissoudre** *vr*
dissuader [disɥade] *vt* : to dissuade
dissuasif, -sive [disɥazif, -ziv] *adj* : deterrent, dissuasive
dissuasion [disɥazjɔ̃] *nf* : dissuasion, deterrence
distance [distɑ̃s] *nf* **1** : distance <à distance : at a distance> <garder ses distances : to keep one's distance> **2** : gap, interval **3** **distance focale** : focal length
distancer [distɑ̃se] {6} *vt* : to outdistance, to outrun, to outstrip
distancier [distɑ̃sje] {96} *v* **se distancier** *vr* ~ **de** : to distance oneself from
distant, -tante [distɑ̃, -tɑt] *adj* **1** : distant <une ville distante de deux kilomètres : a town two kilometers away> **2** : distant, aloof
distendre [distɑ̃dr] {63} *vt* : to distend, to stretch, to strain — **se distendre** *vr* **1** : to distend **2** : to slacken
distillation [distilasjɔ̃] *nf* : distillation
distiller [distile] *vt* **1** : to distill **2** : to secrete, to exude
distillerie [distilri] *nf* : distillery
distinct, -tincte [distɛ̃, -tɛ̃kt] *adj* : distinct — **distinctement** [-tɛ̃ktəmɑ̃] *adv*
distinctif, -tive [distɛ̃ktif, -tiv] *adj* : distinctive, distinguishing
distinction [distɛ̃ksjɔ̃] *nf* **1** : distinction **2** **distinction honorifique** : award
distingué, -guée [distɛ̃ge] *adj* : distinguished
distinguer [distɛ̃ge] *vt* **1** : to distinguish, to differentiate **2** : to discern **3** : to set apart — *vi* : to distinguish, to make a distinction — **se distinguer** *vr* **1** : to stand out **2** : to distinguish oneself
distorsion [distɔrsjɔ̃] *nf* : distortion
distraction [distraksjɔ̃] *nf* **1** : distraction, absentmindedness **2** : recreation, amusement
distraire [distrɛr] {40} *vt* **1** : to distract **2** DIVERTIR : to amuse, to entertain — **se distraire** *vr* : to amuse oneself
distrait, -traite [distrɛ, -trɛt] *adj* : absentminded — **distraitement** [-trɛtmɑ̃] *adv*
distrayant, -trayante [distrɛjɑ̃, -trɛjɑ̃t] *adj* : entertainment
distribuer [distribɥe] *vt* **1** : to distribute, to deal out **2** : to assign, to allocate **3** : to supply (water, etc.)
distributeur[1], **-trice** [distribytœr, -tris] *n* : distributor
distributeur[2] *nm* **1** : distributor (of an automobile) **2** *or* **distributeur automatique** : dispenser, vending machine
distribution [distribysjɔ̃] *nf* **1** : distribution **2** : supplying (of utilities, etc.) **3** : casting (of a movie or play)
district [distrikt] *nm* : district
dit, dite [di, dit] *adj* **1** : agreed upon, stated <à l'heure dite : at the appointed time> **2** : called, known as
dites [dit] → **dire**

diurétique [djyretik] *adj & nm* : diuretic
diurne [djyrn] *adj* : diurnal, daytime
divagation [divagasjɔ̃] *nf* : rambling, raving
divaguer [divage] *vi* **1** : to ramble (on) **2** : to rave
divan [divɑ̃] *nm* : divan, couch
divergent, -gente [divɛrʒɑ̃, -ʒɑ̃t] *adj* : divergent — **divergence** [-vɛrʒɑ̃s] *nf*
diverger [divɛrʒe] {17} *vi* : to diverge
divers, -verse [divɛr, -vɛrs] *adj* **1** VARIÉ : diverse, varied **2** PLUSIEURS : various, sundry <en diverses occasions : on various occasions> **3** : miscellaneous
diversification [divɛrsifikasjɔ̃] *nf* : diversification
diversifier [divɛrsifje] {96} *vt* : to diversify, to vary — **se diversifier** *vr*
diversion [divɛrsjɔ̃] *nf* : diversion
diversité [divɛrsite] *nf* : diversity, variety
divertir [divɛrtir] *vt* : to amuse, to entertain — **se divertir** *vr*
divertissement [divɛrtismɑ̃] *nm* : entertainment, pastime
dividende [dividɑ̃d] *nm* : dividend
divine, -vine [divɛ̃, -vin] *adj* : divine — **divinement** [-vinmɑ̃] *adv*
divinité [divinite] *nf* : divinity
diviser [divize] *vt* **1** : to divide (in mathematics) <diviser 10 par 2 : to divide 10 by 2> **2** : to divide, to split up — **se diviser** *vr*
diviseur [divizœr] *nm* : divisor
divisible [divizibl] *adj* : divisible
division [divizjɔ̃] *nf* : division
divorce [divɔrs] *nm* : divorce
divorcé, -cée [divɔrse] *n* : divorced person, divorcé *m*, divorcée *f*
divorcer [divɔrse] {6} *vi* **1** : to get a divorce **2 ~ avec** *or* **~ d'avec** *or* **~ de** : to divorce (s.o.)
divulgation [divylgasjɔ̃] *nf* : disclosure
divulguer [divylge] *vt* : to divulge, to disclose
dix[1] [dis, *bef. consonant* di, *bef. vowel or mute h* diz] *adj* **1** : ten **2** : tenth <le dix avril : April tenth>
dix[2] *nms & pl* : ten
dix–huit[1] [dizɥit] *adj* **1** : eighteen **2** : eighteenth <le dix-huit juin : June eighteenth>
dix–huit[2] *nms & pl* : eighteen
dix–huitième [dizɥitjɛm] *adj & nmf & nm* : eighteenth
dixième [dizjɛm] *adj & nmf & nm* : tenth
dix–neuf[1] [diznœf] *adj* **1** : nineteen **2** : nineteenth <le dix-neuf mai : May nineteenth>
dix–neuf[2] *nms & pl* : nineteen
dix–neuvième [diznœvjɛm] *adj & nmf & nm* : nineteenth
dix–sept[1] [disɛt] *adj* **1** : seventeen **2** : seventeenth <le dix-sept avril : April seventeenth>
dix–sept[2] *nms & pl* : seventeen
dix–septième [disɛtjɛm] *adj & nmf & nm* : seventeenth
dizaine [dizɛn] *nf* **1** : ten **2** : about ten, ten or so
docile [dɔsil] *adj* : docile, obedient — **docilement** [-silmɑ̃] *adv*
dock [dɔk] *nm* : dock, berth (for a ship)
docker [dɔkɛr] *nm* : longshoreman, stevedore
docteur [dɔktœr] *nm* : doctor
doctorat [dɔktɔra] *nm* : doctorate
doctrine [dɔktrin] *nf* : doctrine
document [dɔkymɑ̃] *nm* : document
documentaire[1] [dɔkymɑ̃tɛr] *adj* **1** : documentary **2 à titre documentaire** : for your information
documentaire[2] *nm* : documentary (film)
documentation [dɔkymɑ̃tasjɔ̃] *nf* **1** : documentation, information **2** : research
documenter [dɔkymɑ̃te] *vt* : to inform, to provide with evidence — **se documenter** *vr* **~ sur** : to research
dodo [dodo] *nm* **1** : dodo (bird) **2 faire dodo** : to go to bed (in baby talk)
dodu, -due [dɔdy] *adj* : plump, chubby
dogmatique [dɔgmatik] *adj* : dogmatic
dogmatisme [dɔgmatism] *nm* : dogmatism
dogme [dɔgm] *nm* : dogma
dogue [dɔg] *nm* : mastiff
doigt [dwa] *nm* **1** : finger <bout du doigt : fingertip> **2 doigt du pied** : toe **3 montrer du doigt** : to point at **4 se mordre les doigts** : to regret
doigté [dwate] *nm* **1** TACT : diplomacy, tact **2** : fingering (in music)
doit [dwa], **doive** [dwav], *etc.* → **devoir**
doléance [dɔleɑ̃s] *nf* : grievance, complaint
dolent, -lente [dɔlɑ̃, -lɑ̃t] *adj* : doleful, plaintive
dollar [dɔlar] *nm* : dollar
domaine [dɔmɛn] *nm* **1** PROPRIÉTÉ : estate, property **2** SPÉCIALITÉ : field, domain **3 domaine public** : public domain
dôme [dom] *nm* : dome
domestique[1] [dɔmɛstik] *adj* **1** : domestic, home **2** : domesticated
domestique[2] *nmf* : domestic, servant
domestiquer [dɔmɛstike] *vt* **1** APPRIVOISER : to domesticate **2** : to harness (energy)
domicile [dɔmisil] *nm* : residence, home
domicilié, -liée [dɔmisilje] *adj* **être domicilié à** : to be a resident in
dominance [dɔminɑ̃s] *nf* : dominance
dominant, -nante [dɔminɑ̃, -nɑ̃t] *adj* **1** : dominant, ruling **2** : predominant
dominateur, -trice [dɔminatœr, -tris] *adj* : domineering, overbearing
domination [dɔminasjɔ̃] *nf* : domination

dominer [dɔmine] *vt* **1** : to dominate **2** MAÎTRISER : to master, to control **3** : to outclass, to surpass **4** : to tower over — *vi* **1** : to be in a dominant position **2** : to prevail — **se dominer** *vr* : to control oneself

dominicain, -caine [dɔminikɛ̃, -kɛn] *adj* : Dominican

Dominican, -caine *n* : Dominican

domino [dɔmino] *nm* : domino

dommage [dɔmaʒ] *nm* **1** PRÉJUDICE : harm, injury **2** DÉGÂTS : damage **3** **c'est dommage** : that's a pity, that's too bad

dommageable [dɔmaʒabl] *adj* : detrimental, harmful

dompter [dɔ̃te] *vt* : to tame, to subdue

dompteur, -teuse [dɔ̃tœr, -tøz] *n* : trainer, (wild-animal) tamer

don [dɔ̃] *nm* **1** CADEAU : gift **2** : donation **3** : talent **4** **don de soi** : self-sacrifice

donateur, -trice [dɔnatœr, -tris] *n* : donor, giver

donation [dɔnasjɔ̃] *nf* : donation

donc [dɔ̃k] *conj* **1** : so, therefore, consequently <je pense, donc je suis : I think, therefore I am> **2** : so, then <vous venez donc? : so you're coming?> **3** (*used for emphasis*) <écoute-moi donc! : would you listen to me!> <quoi donc? : what was that?>

donjon [dɔ̃ʒɔ̃] *nm* : keep (of a castle)

donne [dɔn] *nf* : deal (in card games)

donné, -née [dɔne] *adj* **1** : given <étant donné que : given that, considering that> **2** **c'est donné** : it's a bargain

donnée *nf* **1** : fact, piece of information **2** **données** *nfpl* : data <les données informatiques : computer data>

donner [dɔne] *vt* **1** : to give, to hand out, to donate **2** ATTRIBUER : to attribute to, to assign <quel âge lui donnez-vous? : how old would you say he is?> **3** : to provide, to transmit <donner un bon exemple : to set a good example> <donner un rhume à : to give a cold to> **4** CAUSER : to cause <donner du souci : to cause concern> <ça me donne froid : that makes me cold> **5** : to show, to put on (a film, play, etc.) **6** : to deal (cards) — *vi* **1** : to produce, to yield a crop **2** **~ contre** : to hit, to run into **3** **~ dans** : to lead toward (a place), to fall into (a trap), to tend toward (an opinion, etc.) — **se donner** *vr* **1** : to give to oneself, to have <se donner du bon temps : to have a good time> **2** **~ à** : to devote oneself to **3** **~ pour** : to pretend to be

donneur, -neuse [dɔnœr, -nøz] *n* **1** : donor **2** : dealer (in card games)

dont [dɔ̃] *pron* : of which, of whom, whose <la famille dont je sors : the family I come from> <ce dont il s'agit : what it's all about> <la fille dont la chevelure est bouclée : the girl whose hair is curly>

doper [dɔpe] *vt* : to dope

doré, -rée[1] [dɔre] *adj* **1** : gilded, gilt **2** : golden

dorénavant [dɔrenavɑ̃] *adv* : henceforth

dorer [dɔre] *vt* **1** : to gild **2** : to turn golden, to tan **3** : to glaze — *vi* : to brown (in cooking) — **se dorer** *vr* **se dorer au soleil** : to sunbathe, to tan

doris [dɔris] *nm* : dory (boat)

dorloter [dɔrlɔte] *vt* : to pamper, to baby

dormant, -mante [dɔrmɑ̃, -mɑ̃t] *adj* **1** : still, unmoving **2** : dormant (in botany)

dormeur, -meuse [dɔrmœr, -møz] *n* : sleeper

dormir [dɔrmir] {30} *vi* **1** : to sleep, to be asleep **2** : to be dormant, to be still, to lie idle

dorsal, -sale [dɔrsal, -sal] *adj, mpl* **dorsaux** [dɔrso] : dorsal

dort [dɔr], *etc.* → **dormir**

dortoir [dɔrtwar] *nm* : dormitory

dorure [dɔryr] *nf* **1** : gilt **2** : gilding

dos [do] *nms & pl* **1** : back <dos à dos : back to back> **2** : spine (of a book) **3** **de ~** : from behind

dos–d'âne [dodan] *nm* : speed bump

dose [doz] *nf* : dose

doser [doze] *vt* : to measure out (a dose of medicine, etc.), to apportion

doseur [dozœr] *nm* **1** : measure **2** *or* **bouchon doseur** : measuring cup

dossard [dosar] *nm* : number (worn by an athlete)

dossier [dosje] *nm* **1** : file, dossier <dossier criminel : criminal record> **2** : back (of a chair, etc.)

dot [dɔt] *nf* : dowry

dotation [dɔtasjɔ̃] *nf* : endowment

doter [dɔte] *vt* **1** : to endow **2** ÉQUIPER : to equip **3** : to allocate

douane [dwan] *nf* **1** : customs **2** : (import) duty

douanier[1], **-nière** [dwanje, -njɛr] *adj* : customs <tarif douanier : customs tariff>

douanier[2] *nm* : customs officer

doublage [dublaʒ] *nm* **1** : acting as an understudy **2** : lining **3** : dubbing

double[1] [dubl] *adv & adj* : double

double[2] *nm* **1** : double <le double de : twice as much as> <plus du double : more than double> **2** : copy, duplicate <un double de clés : a spare set of keys>

doublement[1] [dubləmɑ̃] *adv* : doubly

doublement[2] *nm* : doubling

doubler [duble] *vt* **1** : to double **2** : to line **3** : to dub (a film, etc.) **4** : to pass, to overtake **5** : *fam* : to double–cross — *vi* : to double, to increase twofold

doublure [dublyr] *nf* **1** : lining **2** : understudy, stand-in

doucement [dusmɑ̃] *adv* **1 :** gently, softly **2 :** slowly **3 :** meekly

doucereux, -reuse [dusrø, -røz] *adj* **1** MIELLEUX **:** smooth, unctuous **2 :** sugary, saccharine

douceur [dusœr] *nf* **1 :** softness, smoothness **2 :** gentleness, mildness, meekness **3 douceurs** *nmpl* **:** candy, sweets **4 en ~ :** gently, smoothly

douche [duʃ] *nf* **1 :** shower <prendre une douche : to take a shower> **2 :** douche (in medicine) **3 douche froide :** letdown

doucher [duʃe] *vt* **1 :** to give a shower to **2 :** to soak, to drench **— se doucher** *vr* **:** to take a shower

doué, douée [dwe] *adj* **1 :** gifted, talented **2 ~ de :** endowed with

douille [duj] *nf* **1 :** cartridge case **2 :** electric socket

douillet, -lette [dujɛ, -jɛt] *adj* **1 :** cozy **2 :** oversensitive

douillette *nf Can* **:** comforter (for a bed)

douleur [dulœr] *nf* **1 :** pain, ache **2** CHAGRIN **:** sorrow, grief

douloureusement [dulurøzmɑ̃] *adv* **1 :** grievously, terribly **2 :** painfully

douloureux, -reuse [dulurø, -røz] *adj* **1 :** painful, sore **2 :** distressing **3 :** sorrowful, sad

doute [dut] *nm* **:** doubt

douter [dute] *vt* **1 :** to doubt **2 ~ de :** to question <douter de l'honnêteté de : to question the honesty of> **— se douter** *vr* **:** to suspect <je ne me doutais de rien : I didn't suspect a thing>

douteux, -teuse [dutø, -tøz] *adj* **1** INCERTAIN **:** doubtful, uncertain **2 :** questionable, dubious **3 :** ambiguous

douve [duv] *nf* **1 :** moat **2 :** stave (of a barrel)

doux, douce [du, dus] *adj* **1 :** sweet **2 :** soft <une peau douce : soft skin> **3 :** mild, gentle <un hiver doux : a mild winter> **4 :** meek **5 en ~ :** quietly, secretly

douzaine [duzɛn] *nf* **1 :** dozen **2 une douzaine de :** about twelve

douze[1] [duz] *adj* **1 :** twelve **2 :** twelfth <le douze avril : April twelfth>

douze[2] *nms & pl* **:** twelve

douzième [duzjɛm] *adj & nmf & nm* **:** twelfth

doyen, doyenne [dwajɛ̃, -jɛn] *n* **1 :** dean **2 doyen d'âge :** oldest person

draconien, -nienne [drakɔnjɛ̃, -njɛn] *adj* **:** draconian, harsh

dragage [dragaʒ] *nm* **:** dredging

dragée [draʒe] *nf* **1** *France* **:** sugar-coated almond **2 :** pill

dragon [dragɔ̃] *nm* **:** dragon

drague [drag] *nf* **:** dredge

draguer [drage] *vt* **1 :** to dredge **2** *fam* **:** to cruise, to try to pick up <il drague les filles : he's trying to pick up girls>

drainage [drɛnaʒ] *nm* **:** drainage, draining

drainer [drene] *vt* **:** to drain

dramatique [dramatik] *adj* **1 :** dramatic **2 :** tragic

dramatiquement [dramatikmɑ̃] *adv* **:** tragically

dramatisation [dramatizasjɔ̃] *nf* **:** dramatization

dramatiser [dramatize] *v* **:** to dramatize

dramaturge [dramatyrʒ] *nmf* **:** playwright, dramatist

drame [dram] *nm* **1 :** drama **2 :** tragedy

drap [dra] *nm* **1 :** woolen fabric **2** *or* **drap de lit :** bed sheet **3 drap fin :** broadcloth **4 drap mortuaire :** pall

drapé [drape] *nm* **:** drape, hang (of fabric)

drapeau [drapo] *nm, pl* **drapeaux :** flag

draper [drape] *vt* **:** to drape **— se draper** *vr* **~ dans :** to drape oneself in

draperie [drapri] *nf* **1 :** drapery, wall hanging **2 :** cloth industry

drastique [drastik] *adj* **:** drastic

drave [drav] *nf Can* **:** drive (of logs)

draver [drave] *vt Can* **:** to drive (logs down a stream)

dressage [drɛsaʒ] *nm* **:** (animal) training

dresser [drese] *vt* **1** LEVER **:** to raise **2** ÉRIGER **:** to put up, to erect **3 :** to lay out, to set (up) **4 :** to draft, to draw up <dresser une liste : to draw up a list> **5 :** to train <dresser un chien : to train a dog> **6 dresser qqn contre :** to set s.o. against **— se dresser** *vr* **1 :** to stand up **2 :** to rise up, to tower **3 ~ contre :** to rebel against

dresseur, -seuse [drɛsœr, -søz] *n* **:** trainer, tamer <dresseur de lions : lion tamer>

dressoir [drɛswar] *nm* **:** cupboard, sideboard

dribble [dribl] *nm* **:** dribble (in basketball)

dribbler [drible] *vi* **:** to dribble (in basketball)

drille [drij] *nm* **un joyeux drille :** a cheerful fellow

drogue [drɔg] *nf* **:** drug

drogué, -guée [drɔge] *n* **:** drug addict

droguer [drɔge] *vt* **:** to drug **— se droguer** *vr* **:** to take drugs

droit[1] [drwa] *adv* **:** straight, directly <droit au but : straight to the point>

droit[2]**, droite** [drwa, drwat] *adj* **1 :** right, right-hand **2 :** straight, direct **3 :** upright, vertical **4 :** honest, upright

droit[3] *nm* **1 :** right <les droits de l'homme : human rights> <avoir droit à : to have the right to, to be eligible for> **2 :** fee <droit d'entrée : entrance fee> **3 :** law <droit pénal : criminal law> **4 droits d'auteur :** royalties **5 à qui de droit :** to whom it may concern

droite *nf* **1 :** right, right-hand side **2 la droite :** the right, the right wing

droitier[1], **-tière** [drwatje, -tjɛr] *adj* : right-handed
droitier[2], **-tière** *n* : right-handed person
droiture [drwatyr] *nf* : uprightness, integrity
drôle [drol] *adj* **1** COMIQUE : funny, droll **2** BIZARRE : strange, odd **3 ~ de** : funny, strange <un drôle de chapeau : a strange hat> <une drôle d'idée : a funny idea>
drôlement [drolmɑ̃] *adv* **1** : amusingly, comically **2** : strangely, oddly **3** *fam* : really, awfully <les prix sont drôlement élevés : prices are terribly high>
drôlerie [drolri] *nf* **1** : drollness **2** : funny remark
dromadaire [drɔmadɛr] *nm* : dromedary
dru[1] [dry] *adv* : thickly, heavily
dru[2], **drue** [dry] *adj* **1** : thick, dense, bushy <avoir la barbe drue : to have a thick beard> **2** : heavy <une pluie drue : heavy rain>
du [dy] → **de, le**
dû[1] [dy] *pp* → **devoir**
dû[2], **due** [dy] *adj* **1** : due, owing **2** : proper, appropriate **3 ~ à** : due to
dû[3] *nm* : due <réclamer son dû : to claim one's due>
dubitatif, -tive [dybitatif, -tiv] *adj* : dubious, skeptical
duc [dyk] *nm* : duke
duchesse [dyʃɛs] *nf* : duchess
duel [dɥɛl] *nm* : duel
dûment [dymɑ̃] *adv* : duly
dune [dyn] *nf* : dune
duo [dyo] *nm* **1** : duet **2** : duo, pair
dupe [dyp] *nf* : dupe
duper [dype] *vt* : to dupe, to deceive
duplex [dyplɛks] *nm* **1** : duplex apartment **2** : (radio or television) linkup
duplicata [dyplikata] *nms & pl* : duplicate
duplicité [dyplisite] *nf* : duplicity
duquel → **lequel**
dur[1] [dyr] *adv* : hard <travailler dur : to work hard>
dur[2], **dure** [dyr] *adj* **1** : hard, stiff **2** : difficult **3** : harsh
dur[3] *nm* **1** : solid structure <construire en dur : to build with permanent materials> **2** *fam* : toughie, roughneck
durabilité [dyrabilite] *nf* : durability
durable [dyrabl] *adj* : durable, lasting
durant [dyrɑ̃] *prep* **1** : for <durant dix jours : for ten days> **2** : during <durant la semaine : during the week>
durcir [dyrsir] *v* : to harden — **se durcir** *vr*
durcissement [dyrsismɑ̃] *nm* : hardening
dure *nf* **1 à la dure** : the hard way **2 coucher sur la dure** : to sleep on the ground
durée [dyre] *nf* **1** : duration, length **2 de longue durée** : long-term, long-lasting
durement [dyrmɑ̃] *adv* : harshly, severely
durer [dyre] *vi* : to last, to go on
dureté [dyrte] *nf* **1** : hardness, arduousness **2** : harshness
durillon [dyrijɔ̃] *nm* CAL : callus
duvet [dyvɛ] *nm* **1** : down (feathers) **2** : sleeping bag
duveteux, -teuse [dyvtø, -tøz] *adj* : downy, fluffy, fuzzy
dynamique[1] [dinamik] *adj* : dynamic — **dynamiquement** [-mikmɑ̃] *adv*
dynamique[2] *nf* : dynamics *pl*
dynamisme [dinamism] *nm* : dynamism
dynamite [dinamit] *nf* : dynamite
dynamiter [dinamite] *vt* : to dynamite, to blast
dynamo [dinamo] *nf* : dynamo
dynastie [dinasti] *nf* : dynasty — **dynastique** [-nastik] *adj*
dysenterie [disɑ̃tri] *nf* : dysentery
dyslexie [dislɛksi] *nf* : dyslexia — **dyslexique** [-lɛksik] *adj*
dyspepsie [dispɛpsi] *nf* : dyspepsia — **dyspepsique** [-pɛpsik] *or* **dyspeptique** [-pɛptik] *adj*
dystrophie [distrɔfi] *nf* **1** : dystrophy **2 dystrophie musculaire** : muscular dystrophy

E

e [ø] *nm* : e, fifth letter of the alphabet
eau [o] *nf, pl* **eaux 1** : water <eau douce : freshwater> <eau de pluie : rainwater> <eau bénite : holy water> <les eaux territoriales : territorial waters> **2 eau de Cologne** : cologne **3** → **Javel 4 eau oxygénée** : hydrogen peroxide **5 faire eau** : to leak **6 mettre l'eau à la bouche** : to make one's mouth water
eau–de–vie [odvi] *nf, pl* **eaux–de–vie** : brandy
eau–forte [ofɔrt] *nf, pl* **eaux–fortes** : etching
ébahi, -hie [ebai] *adj* : flabbergasted, dumbfounded
ébahir [ebair] *vt* ÉBERLUER : to astound, to dumbfound — **s'ébahir** *vr*
ébahissement [ebaismɑ̃] *nm* : astonishment

ébats [eba] *nmpl* GAMBADES : frolicking
ébattre [ebatr] {12} *v* **s'ébattre** *vr* : to frolic
ébauche [eboʃ] *nf* : outline, rough draft, sketch
ébaucher [eboʃe] *vt* : to sketch out, to outline — **s'ébaucher** *vr* : to form, to take shape
ébène [ebɛn] *nf* : ebony
ébéniste [ebenist] *nmf* : cabinetmaker
ébénisterie [ebenistəri] *nf* : cabinetmaking
éberluer [ebɛrlɥe] ÉBAHIR *vt* : to astonish, to astound
éblouir [ebluir] *vt* **1** : to dazzle **2** : to stun, to amaze — **éblouissant, -sante** [-isɑ̃, -sɑ̃t] *adj*
éblouissement [ebluismɑ̃] *nm* **1** ÉMERVEILLEMENT : amazement, wonder **2** VERTIGE : dizzy spell
éborgner [ebɔrɲe] *vt* **1** : to blind (in one eye) **2** *Can* : to chip (a glass, plate, etc.)
éboueur [ebwœr] *nm* : garbage collector, garbageman
ébouillanter [ebujɑ̃te] *vt* **1** : to scald, to burn (one's hands, etc.) **2** : to blanch (in cooking) — **s'ébouillanter** *vr*
éboulement [ebulmɑ̃] *nm* **1** : crumbling, collapse **2** : heap of fallen rocks or earth <éboulement de terre : landslide>
ébouler [ebule] *v* **s'ébouler** *vr* : to cave in, to collapse
éboulis [ebuli] *nms & pl* : heap of rocks or earth, debris
ébouriffer [eburife] *vt* **1** : to tousle, to ruffle **2** *fam* : to amaze, to stun
ébrancher [ebrɑ̃ʃe] *vt* ÉLAGUER : to prune
ébranlement [ebrɑ̃lmɑ̃] *nm* **1** : shaking, rattling **2** : shock
ébranler [ebrɑ̃le] *vt* **1** : to shake, to rattle **2** : to weaken, to undermine — **s'ébranler** *vr* : to move off
ébrécher [ebreʃe] {87} *vt* : to chip, to nick — **s'ébrécher** *vr*
ébréchure [ebreʃyr] *nf* : nick, chip, flaw
ébriété [ebrijete] *nf* : inebriation, drunkenness
ébrouer [ebrue] *v* **s'ébrouer** *vr* **1** : to snort **2** : to shake oneself
ébruiter [ebrɥite] *vt* : to spread, to divulge — **s'ébruiter** *vr* : to become known
ébullition [ebylisjɔ̃] *nf* **1** : boil, boiling <point d'ébullition : boiling point> **2** **en état d'ébullition** : in a fever of excitement, in turmoil
écaille [ekaj] *nf* **1** : scale (of fish, reptiles, etc.) **2** : oyster shell **3** : tortoiseshell **4** : flake, chip
écailler [ekaje] *vt* **1** : to scale (fish) **2** : to open (a shell) **3** : to chip (paint) — **s'écailler** *vr* : to flake off
écailleux, -leuse [ekajø, -jøz] *adj* : scaly, flaky
écale [ekal] *nf* : husk, hull
écaler [ekale] *vt* : to husk, to hull (nuts, etc.)
écarlate [ekarlat] *adj & nf* : scarlet
écarquiller [ekarkije] *vt* **écarquiller les yeux** : to open one's eyes wide
écart [ekar] *nm* **1** DISTANCE : distance, gap, interval **2** DIFFÉRENCE : difference, disparity, deviation **3** : lapse (in behavior, etc.) **4** : swerving <faire un écart : to swerve, to shy, to step aside> **5** **à l'écart** : apart, away <se tenir à l'écart : to stand apart, to keep to oneself> **6** **faire le grand écart** : to do the split (in gymnastics)
écarté, -tée [ekarte] *adj* **1** ISOLÉ : remote, secluded **2** : wide apart <avec les bras écartés : with arms outstretched>
écarteler [ekartəle] {20} *vt* **1** : to tear apart **2** **être écartelé entre** : to be torn between
écartement [ekartəmɑ̃] *nm* ESPACE : space, gap
écarter [ekarte] *vt* **1** : to spread, to open **2** ÉLOIGNER : to move aside, to push away **3** EXCLURE : to dismiss, to rule out **4** DÉTOURNER : to divert, to distract **5** *Can* : to lose **6** *France* : to discard (in card games) — **s'écarter** *vr* **1** : to move away, to deviate, to digress **2** : to part, to separate **3** **~ de** : to stray from
écartiller [ekartije] *vt Can fam* : to open, to spread <il a écartillé les bras pour les accueillir : he opened his arms to welcome them>
ecchymose [ekimoz] *nf* : bruise
ecclésiastique[1] [eklezjastik] *adj* : ecclesiastical
ecclésiastique[2] *nm* : clergyman
écervelé, -lée [esɛrvəle] *adj* ÉTOURDI : scatterbrained, empty-headed
échafaud [eʃafo] *nm* : scaffold
échafaudage [eʃafodaʒ] *nm* **1** : scaffolding **2** AMAS : heap, pile
échafauder [eʃafode] *vi* : to erect scaffolding — *vt* **1** : to stack, to pile up **2** : to construct, to build up (plans, theories, etc.)
échalier [eʃalje] *nm* **1** : gate **2** : stile
échalote [eʃalɔt] *nf* **1** : shallot **2** *Can* : scallion
échancré, -crée [eʃɑ̃kre] *adj* **1** : low-cut (of clothing) **2** : indented <un littoral échancré : a jagged coastline>
échancrure [eʃɑ̃kryr] *nf* **1** : low neckline **2** : indentation (of a coastline)
échange [eʃɑ̃ʒ] *nm* **1** : exchange <en échange de : in return for> **2** : trade <échange libre : free trade> <échanges internationaux : international trade>
échanger [eʃɑ̃ʒe] {17} *vt* : to exchange, to trade
échangeur [eʃɑ̃ʒœr] *nm* : interchange, junction (of highways)

échantillon [eʃɑ̃tijɔ̃] *nm* : sample, specimen

échantillonnage [eʃɑ̃tijɔnaʒ] *nm* **1** : sampling **2** : selection (of samples)

échappatoire [eʃapatwar] *nf* : way out, loophole

échappée [eʃape] *nf* **1** : breakaway (in sports) **2** VUE : vista, view **3** : brief period, break **4** : space, gap

échappement [eʃapmɑ̃] *nm* **1** : escapement (of a watch) **2** : exhaust (of an automobile) **3** → **pot**

échapper [eʃape] *vi* **1** **~ à** : to escape from (a person, a situation), to escape (danger, etc.) **2** **~ à** : to elude, to evade <rien ne lui échappe : nothing gets by him> **3** **échapper à qqn** : to slip out (of s.o.'s hands) <le stylo lui a échappé des mains : the pen slipped out of his hands> <son nom m'échappe : her name escapes me> **4** **laisser échapper** : to let out (a cry, a sigh, etc.) **5** **échapper belle** : to have a narrow escape — *vt Can* : to drop <échapper un colis : to drop a parcel> — **s'échapper** *vr* : to escape

écharde [eʃard] *nf* : splinter

écharpe [eʃarp] *nf* **1** : scarf **2** : sash (of office) **3** : sling **4** **prendre en écharpe** : to sideswipe

échasse [eʃas] *nf* : stilt

échassier [eʃasje] *nm* : wading

échauder [eʃode] *vt* **1** : to scald **2** : to teach a lesson, to make wary <échaudé par expérience : burned by experience>

échauffement [eʃofmɑ̃] *nm* **1** : heating up **2** : warm-up (in sports) **3** : overexcitement

échauffer [eʃofe] *vt* **1** : to make hot, to overheat **2** : to warm up (in sports) **3** EXCITER : to excite, to stimulate — **s'échauffer** *vr* : to warm up

échauffourée [eʃofure] *nf* **1** ESCARMOUCHE : skirmish **2** BAGARRE : brawl

échéance [eʃeɑ̃s] *nf* **1** : due date, expiration (date) <venir à échéance : to fall due> **2** : financial obligation, payment **3** : term <à longue échéance : in the long run>

échéancier [eʃeɑ̃sje] *nm* **1** : payment schedule **2** : schedule, calendar

échéant [eʃeɑ̃] *adv* **le cas échéant** : if need be

échec [eʃɛk] *nm* **1** : failure, setback **2** **échecs** *nmpl* : chess **3** **échec et mat** : checkmate **4** **mise en échec** *Can* : check (in hockey) **5** **tenir en échec** : to hold in check, to thwart

échelle [eʃɛl] *nf* **1** : ladder **2** : scale <carte à grande échelle : large-scale map> <échelle de salaires : pay scale> **3** GAMME : scale (in music) **4** : run, ladder (in stockings)

échelon [eʃlɔ̃] *nm* **1** : rung (of a ladder) **2** : step, grade, level **3** : echelon

échelonner [eʃlɔne] *vt* : to space out, to spread out — **s'échelonner** *vr*

écheveau [eʃvo] *nm, pl* **-veaux** **1** : skein, hank **2** ENCHEVÊTREMENT : tangle

échevelé, -lée [eʃəvle] *adj* **1** : disheveled **2** : wild, disorderly

échine [eʃin] *nf* : backbone, spine

échiner [eʃine] *v* **s'échiner** *vr* : to work oneself to the bone

échiquier [eʃikje] *nm* : chessboard

écho [eko] *nm* **1** : echo **2** : repeating <se faire l'écho de : to repeat, to spread> **3** : response <recevoir un écho : to get a response> **4** **échos** *nmpl* : gossip, rumors *pl*

échographie [ekɔgrafi] *nf* : ultrasound

échoir [eʃwar] {31} *vi* **1** : to expire **2** : to fall due **3** **~ à** : to fall to <le travail qui m'est échu : the task that fell to me>

échoppe [eʃɔp] *nf* : booth, stall

échouer [eʃwe] *vi* **1** : to run (a ship) aground **2** : to fail, to fall through — *vt* : to beach — **s'échouer** *vr* : to run aground

éclabousser [eklabuse] *vt* **1** : to splash, to spatter **2** : to stain, to smear (a reputation)

éclaboussure [eklabusyr] *nf* **1** : splash, spattering **2** : smear, blemish (on a reputation)

éclair [eklɛr] *nm* **1** : flash of lightning **2** : flash **3** : éclair

éclairage [eklɛraʒ] *nm* : lighting, illumination

éclaircie [eklɛrsi] *nf* **1** EMBELLIE : sunny spell **2** : clearing, glade

éclaircir [eklɛrsir] *vt* **1** : to lighten **2** CLARIFIER : to clarify, to shed light on **3** : to thin (in cooking) — **s'éclaircir** *vr* **1** : to clear <le temps s'éclaircit : the weather is clearing up> <s'éclaircir la gorge : to clear one's throat> **2** : to thin out **3** : to become clearer (of a situation, etc.)

éclaircissement [eklɛrsismɑ̃] *nm* : explanation, clarification

éclairer [eklere] *vt* **1** : to light, to light up **2** : to enlighten **3** CLARIFIER, EXPLIQUER : to shed light on, to clarify — *vi* : to give light — *v impers* **il éclaire** *Can* : it's thundering and lightening — **s'éclairer** *vr* **1** : to light up **2** : to become clearer

éclaireur[1], -reuse [eklɛrœr, -røz] *n* : boy scout *m*, girl scout *f*

éclaireur[2] *nm* : scout (in the military)

éclat [ekla] *nm* **1** : splinter, chip <voler en éclats : to fly into pieces> **2** : brilliance, radiance **3** : splendor, magnificence <coup d'éclat : remarkable feat> **4** : outburst, uproar <éclat de rire : burst of laughter> <éclats de voix : shouts, cries>

éclatant, -tante [eklatɑ̃, -tɑ̃t] *adj* **1** BRILLANT : bright, brilliant **2** RETENTISSANT : resounding <un succès écla-

tant : a resounding success> **3** : loud, piercing

éclatement [eklatmɑ̃] *nm* **1** EXPLOSION : explosion, bursting **2** : blowout (of a tire) **3** : rupture, split

éclater [eklate] *vi* **1** EXPLOSER : to burst, to explode **2** : to break up, to splinter **3** : to break out <la guerre a éclaté : war broke out> **— s'éclater** *vr fam* : to have a great time

éclectique [eklɛktik] *adj* : eclectic

éclipse [eklips] *nf* : eclipse

éclipser [eklipse] *vt* : to eclipse, to outshine **— s'éclipser** *vr* S'ESQUIVER : to slip away

éclopé, -pée [eklɔpe] *adj* : lame

éclore [eklɔr] {32} *vi* **1** : to hatch **2** : to open out, to blossom

éclosion [eklozjɔ̃] *nf* **1** : hatching **2** : blossoming

écluse [eklyz] *nf* : lock (of a canal)

écluser [eklyze] *vt* **1** : to provide with locks **2** *fam* : to swill down

écœurant, -rante [ekœrɑ̃, -rɑ̃t] *adj* **1** NAUSÉABOND : sickening, nauseating **2** : disgusting

écœuranterie [ekœrɑ̃tri] *nf Can fam* : dirty trick

écœurement [ekœrmɑ̃] *nm* **1** NAUSÉE : nausea **2** : disgust, distaste **3** DÉCOURAGEMENT : discouragement

écœurer [ekœre] *vt* **1** : to nauseate, to sicken **2** : to disgust **3** DÉCOURAGER : to discourage

école [ekɔl] *nf* **1** : school <école maternelle *France* : nursery school> <école maternelle *Can* : kindergarten> <école primaire : grade school> <école secondaire *Can* : high school> **2** : schooling, education **3** : training, experience <être à bonne école : to be in good hands> <être à rude école : to learn the hard way> **4** : movement, school (of artists, etc.)

écolier, -lière [ekɔlje, -ljɛr] *n* : schoolboy *m*, schoolgirl *f*

écologie [ekɔlɔʒi] *nf* : ecology

écologique [ekɔlɔʒik] *adj* : ecological **— écologiquement** [-ʒikmɑ̃] *adv*

écologiste [ekɔlɔʒist] *nmf* : ecologist, environmentalist

éconduire [ekɔ̃dɥir] {49} *vt* : to reject, to dismiss

économe[1] [ekɔnɔm] *adj* : thrifty, economical

économe[2] *nmf* : bursar

économie [ekɔnɔmi] *nf* **1** : economy **2** : economics **3** : saving, thrift <faire une économie de temps : to save time> **4 économies** *nfpl* : savings

économique [ekɔnɔmik] *adj* **1** : economic **2** : economical, inexpensive **— économiquement** [-mikmɑ̃] *adv*

économiser [ekɔnɔmize] *vt* : to economize, to save, to conserve **—** *vi* : to economize, to save money

économiste [ekɔnɔmist] *nmf* : economist

écoper [ekɔpe] *vt* : to bail out (a boat) **—** *vi fam* **~ de** : to get <écoper de trois ans de prison : to get a three-year sentence>

écorce [ekɔrs] *nf* **1** : bark **2** : peel, rind **3 l'écorce terrestre** : the earth's crust

écorcher [ekɔrʃe] *vt* **1** DÉPOUILLER : to skin **2** ÉRAFLER : to scratch, to graze, to chafe **3** : to mispronounce

écorchure [ekɔrʃyr] *nf* : graze, scratch, chafing

écorner [ekɔrne] *vt* **1** : to chip the corner off (furniture), to dog-ear (a page) **2** : to make a dent in (one's fortune, etc.) **— s'écorner** *vr*

écornifler [ekɔrnifle] *vt Can fam* : to spy on **—** *vi Can fam* : to snoop around

écossais[1], **-saise** [ekɔsɛ, -sɛz] *adj* **1** : Scottish **2 tissu écossais** : tartan, plaid **3 whisky écossais** : Scotch (whiskey)

écossais[2] *nm* **1** : Scots (language) **2** : tartan

Écossais, -saise *n* : Scot, Scottish person

écosser [ekɔse] *vt* : to shell

écosystème [ekɔsistɛm] *nm* : ecosystem

écot [eko] *nm* **payer son écot** : to pay one's share

écoulement [ekulmɑ̃] *nm* **1** : flowing, streaming **2** : discharge <écoulement sanguin : bleeding> **3** : dispersal (of a crowd) **4** : selling (of merchandise)

écouler [ekule] *vt* **1** : to sell **2** : to pass (into circulation) **— s'écouler** *vr* **1** : to flow (out) **2** : to drift away, to disperse **3** : to pass, to elapse <les minutes s'écoulent : the minutes pass by>

écourter [ekurte] *vt* : to cut short, to curtail

écoute [ekut] *nf* **1** : listening (in radio and television) <être aux écoutes : to be listening, to be tuned in> <les heures de grande écoute : prime time> **2** : listening (in) <écoutes téléphoniques : phone tapping> <poste d'écoute : listening post>

écouter [ekute] *vt* : to listen to **—** *vi* **1** : to listen **2 écouter aux portes** : to eavesdrop **— s'écouter** *vr*

écouteur [ekutœr] *nm* **1** : receiver (of a telephone) **2 écouteurs** *nmpl* : headphones, earphones

écoutille [ekutij] *nf* : hatchway

écrabouiller [ekrabuje] *vt fam* : to crush, to squash

écran [ekrɑ̃] *nm* : screen <le petit écran : television>

écrasant, -sante [ekrazɑ̃, -zɑ̃t] *adj* : crushing, overwhelming

écraser [ekraze] *vt* **1** : to crush, to squash, to mash **2** : to run over **3** ACCABLER : to overwhelm **— s'écraser** *vr* **1** : to get crushed **2** : to crash **3** *Can fam* : to collapse, to sink <elle s'est

écrasée sur le divan : she collapsed onto the sofa>

écrémer [ekreme] {87} *vt* : to skim (milk)

écrevisse [ekrəvis] *nf* : crayfish

écrier [ekrije] {96} *v* **s'écrier** *vr* : to exclaim

écrin [ekrɛ̃] *nm* : case, box

écrire [ekrir] {33} *vt* **1** : to write **2** ÉPELER : to spell <comment écrivez-vous ce mot? : how do you spell this word?> — *vi* : to write — **s'écrire** *vr* **1** : to be written, to be spelled **2** : to write to each other

écrit [ekri] *nm* **1** : writing, written work **2** : written exam **3** **écrits** *nmpl* : writings, works **4** **par ~** : in writing

écriteau [ekrito] *nm, pl* **-teaux** : notice, sign

écriture [ekrityr] *nf* **1** : handwriting, penmanship **2** : writing, script **3** **écritures** *nfpl* : accounts, books **4** **les Écritures** : the Scriptures

écrivaillon [ekrivajɔ̃] *nm fam* : hack (writer)

écrivain [ekrivɛ̃] *nm* : writer

écrivaine [ekrivɛn] *nf Can* : (female) writer

écrivait [ekrivɛ], **écrivions** [ekrivjɔ̃], *etc.* → **écrire**

écrive [ekriv], *etc.* → **écrire**

écrou [ekru] *nm* : nut <écrou à ailettes : wing nut>

écrouer [ekrue] *vt* : to imprison

écroulement [ekrulmɑ̃] *nm* : collapse

écrouler [ekrule] *v* **s'écrouler** *vr* : to collapse, to fail, to fold

écru, -crue [ekry] *adj* **1** : raw, unbleached, natural <soie écrue : raw silk> **2** : ecru (color)

écu [eky] *nm* **1** BOUCLIER : shield **2** : crown (monetary unit)

écueil [ekœj] *nm* **1** RÉCIF : reef **2** : pitfall

écuelle [ekɥɛl] *nf* **1** : bowl **2** : bowlful

éculé, -lée [ekyle] *adj* **1** : worn at the heel **2** : hackneyed

écume [ekym] *nf* **1** : foam, froth **2** : scum

écumer [ekyme] *vt* **1** : to skim **2** PILLER : to plunder **3** : to search through, to scour — *vi* : to foam, to froth

écumeur, -meuse [ekymœr, -møz] *adj* : foamy, frothy

écureuil [ekyrœj] *nm* : squirrel

écurie [ekyri] *nf* : stable

écusson [ekysɔ̃] *nm* : badge

écuyer, -yère [ekɥije, -jɛr] *n* : horseman *m*, horsewoman *f*, rider

eczéma [ɛgzema] *nm* : eczema

éden [edɛn] *nm* : Eden, paradise

édenté, -tée [edɑ̃te] *adj* : toothless

édicter [edikte] *vt* : to decree

édifiant, -fiante [edifjɑ̃, -fjɑ̃t] *adj* : edifying

édification [edifikasjɔ̃] *nf* **1** : edification **2** : construction, building

édifice [edifis] *nm* : edifice, building

édifier [edifje] {96} *vt* **1** CONSTRUIRE : to erect, to build **2** : to edify

édit [edi] *nm* : edict

éditer [edite] *vt* **1** : to publish **2** : to edit

éditeur[1], **-trice** [editœr, -tris] *n* **1** : publisher **2** : editor

éditeur[2] *nm* **éditeur de textes** : text editing program

édition [edisjɔ̃] *nf* **1** : publishing <maison d'édition : publishing house> **2** : edition <nouvelle édition : new edition> **3** : editing

éditorial[1], **-riale** [editɔrjal] *adj, mpl* **-riaux** [-rjo] : editorial

éditorial[2] *nm, pl* **-riaux** : editorial

éditorialiste [editɔrjalist] *nmf* : editorial writer

édredon [edrədɔ̃] *nm* : comforter, eiderdown

éducateur[1], **-trice** [edykatœr, -tris] *adj* : educational

éducateur[2], **-trice** *n* : teacher, educator

éducatif, -tive [edykatif, -tiv] *adj* : educational

éducation [edykasjɔ̃] *nf* **1** ENSEIGNEMENT : education **2** : upbringing, breeding <avoir de l'éducation : to have good manners> **3** : training

édulcorant [edylkɔrɑ̃] *nm* : sweetener

édulcorer [edylkɔre] *vt* **1** SUCRER : to sweeten **2** ATTÉNUER : to tone down

éduquer [edyke] *vt* **1** : to educate **2** ÉLEVER : to bring up, to raise **3** : to train

efface *nf Can* [efas] : eraser

effacé, -cée [efase] *adj* **1** : faded **2** : retiring, self-effacing

effacement [efasmɑ̃] *nm* : erasing, obliteration

effacer [efase] {6} *vt* **1** : to erase, to delete **2** : to wipe out, to obliterate **3** : to outshine — **s'effacer** *vr* **1** : to wear off **2** : to fade, to diminish **3** : to stand aside

effarant, -rante [efarɑ̃, -rɑ̃t] *adj* : startling, alarming

effarement [efarmɑ̃] *nm* : alarm

effarer [efare] *vt* : to alarm

effaroucher [efaruʃe] *vt* **1** : to frighten, to scare away **2** : to alarm — **s'effaroucher** *vr*

effectif[1], **-tive** [efɛktif, -tiv] *adj* : effective, real

effectif[2] *nm* : size, strength, total number <un effectif de 160 personnes : a total of 160 people>

effectivement [efɛktivmɑ̃] *adv* **1** RÉELLEMENT : actually, really **2** : indeed, in fact

effectuer [efɛktɥe] *vt* EXÉCUTER : to carry out, to make <effectuer une enquête : to carry out an investigation>

efféminé, -née [efemine] *adj* : effeminate

effervescence [efɛrvesɑ̃s] *nf* **1** : effervescence **2** : agitation, turmoil <être en effervescence : to be all excited>

effervescent, -cente [efɛrvesɑ, -sɑ̃t] *adj* : effervescent

effet [efɛ] *nm* **1** : effect, result <faire de l'effet : to have an effect, to be effective> **2** : impression <il fait bon effet : he makes a good impression> **3** : operation, action <mettre à effet : to put into action> **4 à cet effet** : for that purpose **5 en ~** : indeed, actually **6 effets** *nmpl* : things, belongings

efficace [efikas] *adj* **1** : efficient **2** : efficacious, effective — **efficacement** [-kasmɑ̃] *adv*

efficacité [efikasite] *nf* **1** : efficiency **2** : effectiveness

efficience [efisjɑ̃s] *nf* : efficiency

effigie [efiʒi] *nf* : effigy

effilé, -lée [efile] *adj* **1** : sharp **2** : slim, slender **3** : frayed

effiler [efile] *vt* **1** : to make pointed, to taper **2** : to fray, to unravel — **s'effiler** *vr* : to fray

effiloche [efilɔʃ] *nf* : fraying, ravel

effilocher [efilɔʃe] *vt* : to shred, to fray — **s'effilocher** *vr* : to fray, to unravel

efflanqué, -quée [eflɑ̃ke] *adj* : emaciated

effleurement [eflœrmɑ̃] *nm* : light touch, caress

effleurer [eflœre] *vt* **1** FRÔLER : to touch lightly, to brush against **2** : to touch on (an idea, etc.) <ça m'a effleuré l'esprit : it crossed my mind>

effluve [eflyv] *nm* ÉMANATION : emanation, odor

effondrement [efɔ̃drəmɑ̃] *nm* : collapse

effondrer [efɔ̃dre] *v* **s'effondrer** *vr* : to sink, to collapse

efforcer [efɔrse] {6} *v* **s'efforcer** *vr* : to strive, to endeavor

effort [efɔr] *nm* **1** : effort <sans effort : effortless> **2** : stress (in engineering)

effraction [efraksjɔ̃] *nf* : housebreaking, breaking and entering

effraie [efrɛ], **effraiera** [efrɛra], *etc.* → **effrayer**

effranger [efrɑ̃ʒe] {17} *vt* : to fray — **s'effranger** *vr*

effrayant, -yante [efrɛjɑ̃, -jɑ̃t] *adj* **1** : frightening, scary **2** *fam* : terrible, frightful

effrayer [efreje] {11} *vt* **1** : to frighten, to scare **2** REBUTER : to put off, to scare away — **s'effrayer** *vr*

effréné, -née [efrene] *adj* **1** DÉCHAÎNÉ : unbridled, unrestrained **2** : frantic

effritement [efritmɑ̃] *nm* : crumbling, disintegration

effriter [efrite] *vt* : to crumble — **s'effriter** *vr* : to crumble away, to disintegrate

effroi [efrwa] *nm* TERREUR : terror, dread

effronté, -tée [efrɔ̃te] *adj* INSOLENT : insolent, impudent — **effrontément** [-temɑ̃] *adv*

effronterie [efrɔ̃tri] *nf* INSOLENCE : insolence, impudence

effroyable [efrwajabl] *adj* AFFREUX : dreadful, appalling

effroyablement [efrwajabləmɑ̃] *adv* **1** : appallingly **2** : extremely, terribly

effusion [efyzjɔ̃] *nf* **1** : effusion **2 effusion de sang** : bloodshed

égailler [egaje] *v* **s'égailler** *vr* : to disperse, to scatter

égal[1], **-gale** [egal] *adj, mpl* **égaux** [ego] **1** : equal **2** RÉGULIER : steady, regular <un pouls égal : a steady heartbeat> **3** : level, even **4 ça m'est égal** : it makes no difference to me

égal[2], **-gale** *n* **1** : equal **2 sans égal** : unequaled, matchless

également [egalmɑ̃] *adv* **1** : equally **2** AUSSI : also, as well, too

égaler [egale] *vt* **1** : to equal, to be equal to <deux plus deux égalent quatre : two plus two equals four> **2** : to match, to rival <personne ne l'égale : no one can match him>

égalisateur, -trice [egalizatœr, -tris] *adj* **1** : equalizing **2** : tying <le but égalisateur : the tying goal>

égaliser [egalize] *vt* **1** : to equalize **2** : to level (out), to even up — *vi* : to tie (in sports)

égalitaire [egalitɛr] *adj* : egalitarian

égalitarisme [egalitarism] *nm* : egalitarianism

égalité [egalite] *nf* **1** : equality **2** : evenness **3 à ~** : tied (in sports)

égard [egar] *nm* **1** : regard, consideration <sans égard pour les autres : without considering others> <par égard pour : out of deference to> **2 à l'égard de** : toward, with regard to **3 à cet égard** : in this respect **4 eu égard à** : in view of **5 égards** *nmpl* : consideration, respect

égaré, -rée [egare] *adj* **1** : lost, stray **2** : distraught

égarement [egarmɑ̃] *nm* **1** : distraction **2** : derangement, folly

égarer [egare] *vt* **1** : to lead astray **2** : to lose, to misplace — **s'égarer** *vr* **1** : to lose one's way **2** : to be misplaced **3** : to ramble, to digress

égayer [egeje] {11} *vt* : to cheer up, to brighten — **s'égayer** *vr*

égide [eʒid] *nf* : aegis <sous l'égide de : under the aegis of>

églantier [eglɑ̃tje] *nm* : wild rose (bush)

églantine [eglɑ̃tin] *nf* : wild rose

églefin [egləfɛ̃] *nm* : haddock

église [egliz] *nf* : church

ego [ego] *nm* : ego

égocentrique [egɔsɑ̃trik] *adj* : egocentric, self-centered

égoïsme [egɔism] *nm* : selfishness, egoism

égoïste[1] [egɔist] *adj* : selfish, egoistic — **égoïstement** [-istəmɑ̃] *adv*

égoïste[2] *nmf* : selfish person, egoist

égorger [egɔrʒe] {17} *vt* : to cut the throat of

égosiller [egɔzije] *v* **s'égosiller** *vr* **1** : to shout oneself hoarse **2** : to sing at the top of one's lungs

égotisme [egɔtism] *nm* : egotism

égotiste[1] [egɔtist] *adj* : egotistic, egotistical

égotiste[2] *nmf* : egotist

égout [egu] *nm* **1** : sewer **2 eaux d'égout** : sewage

égoutter [egute] *vt* : to allow to drip, to drain — **s'égoutter** *vr*

égouttoir [egutwar] *nm* **1** : dish drainer **2** : strainer, colander

égratigner [egratiɲe] *vt* ÉRAFLER : to scratch, to graze — **s'égratigner** *vr*

égratignure [egratiɲyr] *nf* : scratch

égrener [egrəne] {52} *vt* **1** : to shell (peas, etc.), to seed (grains, fruit), to gin (cottton) **2 égrener son chapelet** : to say one's rosary **3 égrener les heures** : to mark the hours

égreneuse [egrənøz] *nf* : cotton gin

égrillard, -larde [egrijar, -jard] *adj* : ribald, bawdy

égyptien, -tienne [eʒipsjɛ̃, -sjɛn] *adj* : Egyptian

Égyptien, -tienne *n* : Egyptian

eh [e] *interj* **1** : hey! **2 eh bien** : well <eh bien, allons-y : well, let's go>

éhonté, -tée [eɔ̃te] *adj* : shameless, brazen

éjaculation [eʒakylasjɔ̃] *nf* : ejaculation

éjaculer [eʒakyle] *vt* : to ejaculate

éjecter [eʒɛkte] *vt* **1** : to eject **2** *fam* : to kick out

éjection [eʒɛksjɔ̃] *nf* : ejection

élaboration [elabɔrasjɔ̃] *nf* : development, making, drawing up

élaborer [elabɔre] *vt* : to develop, to put together

élagage [elagaʒ] *nm* : pruning

élaguer [elage] *vt* ÉMONDER : to prune, to lop

élan [elɑ̃] *nm* **1** : momentum **2** : burst, rush, surge <un élan de colère : a burst of anger> <avec élan : enthusiastically> **3** : (European) elk **4** *Can* : swing (in baseball) **5 élan d'Amérique** *Can* → **orignal**

élancé, -cée [elɑ̃se] *adj* : slender

élancement [elɑ̃smɑ̃] *nm* : shooting pain

élancer [elɑ̃se] {6} *vi* : to give shooting pains — **s'élancer** *vr* **1** SE PRÉCIPITER : to dash forward, to rush **2** : to soar **3** *Can* : to swing (in baseball)

élargir [elarʒir] *vt* **1** : to widen, to broaden, to extend **2** LIBÉRER : to release, to discharge — **s'élargir** *vr* : to broaden, to expand

élargissement [elarʒismɑ̃] *nm* **1** : widening, broadening **2** LIBÉRATION : release, discharge

élasticité [elastisite] *nf* **1** : elasticity **2** : flexibility

élastique[1] [elastik] *adj* FLEXIBLE : elastic, flexible

élastique[2] *nm* **1** : elastic **2** : rubber band **3** : bungee cord

électeur, -trice [elɛktœr, -tris] *n* : voter, elector

électif, -tive [elɛktif, -tiv] *adj* : elective

élection [elɛksjɔ̃] *nf* **1** : election **2** CHOIX : choice

électoral, -rale [elɛktɔral] *adj, mpl* **-raux** [-ro] : electoral, election

électorat [elɛktɔra] *nm* : electorate

électricien, -cienne [elɛktrisjɛ̃, -sjɛn] *n* : electrician

électricité [elɛktrisite] *nf* : electricity

électrifier [elɛktrifje] {96} *vt* : to electrify — **électrification** [-trifikasjɔ̃] *nf*

électrique [elɛktrik] *adj* : electric, electrical — **électriquement** [-trikmɑ̃] *adv*

électrisant, -sante [elɛktrizɑ̃, -zɑ̃t] *adj* : electrifying, thrilling

électriser [elɛktrize] *vt* : to electrify

électroaimant [elɛktrɔɛmɑ̃] *nm* : electromagnet

électrocardiogramme [elɛktrɔkardjɔgram] *nm* : electrocardiogram

électrocardiographe [elɛktrɔkardjɔgraf] *nm* : electrocardiograph

électrocuter [elɛktrɔkyte] *vt* : to electrocute — **électrocution** [-trɔkysjɔ̃] *nf*

électrode [elɛktrɔd] *nf* : electrode

électrolyse [elɛktrɔliz] *nf* : electrolysis

électrolyte [elɛktrɔlit] *nm* : electrolyte

électromagnétisme [elɛktrɔmaɲetism] *nm* : electromagnetism — **électromagnétique** [-ɲetik] *adj*

électroménager[1] [elɛktrɔmenaʒe] *adj* **appareil électroménager** : household (electrical) appliance

électroménager[2] *nm* **l'électroménager** : household (electrical) appliances

électron [elɛktrɔ̃] *nm* : electron

électronicien, -cienne [elɛktrɔnisjɛ̃, -sjɛn] *n* : electronics engineer

électronique[1] [elɛktrɔnik] *adj* : electronic — **électroniquement** [-nikmɑ̃] *adv*

électronique[2] *nf* : electronics

élégamment [elegamɑ̃] *adv* : elegantly

élégance [elegɑ̃s] *nf* : elegance

élégant, -gante [elegɑ̃, -gɑ̃t] *adj* : elegant

élégiaque [eleʒjak] *adj* : elegiac

élégie [eleʒi] *nf* : elegy

élément [elemɑ̃] *nm* **1** : element **2** COMPOSANT : component, ingredient, part **3** : cell (of a battery) **4 éléments** *nmpl* : rudiments, basics

élémentaire [elemɑ̃tɛr] *adj* : elementary, basic

éléphant [elefɑ̃] *nm* : elephant

éléphantesque [elefɑ̃tɛsk] *adj* : elephantine, gigantic
élevage [ɛlvaʒ] *nm* **1** : breeding, raising <l'élevage de chevaux : horse breeding> **2** : ranch, livestock farm
élévateur [elevatœr] *nm* : (grain) elevator
élévation [elevasjɔ̃] *nf* **1** : elevation **2** : rise, increase **3** : raising
élève [elɛv] *nmf* : pupil, student
élevé, -vée [elve] *adj* **1** : high **2** : elevated, noble **3 bien élevé** : well-mannered, well brought up
élever [elve] {52} *vt* **1** : to raise, to increase **2** ÉRIGER : to erect, to build **3** : to elevate (mind, spirit, etc.) **4** : to bring up, to raise <élever un enfant : to raise a child> — **s'élever** *vr* **1** : to rise, to go up **2** : to be built, to stand **3** : to arise, to come up **4 ~ à** : to amount to, to come to **5 ~ contre** : to rise (up) against, to protest
éleveur, -veuse [elvœr, -vøz] *n* : rancher, breeder
elfe [ɛlf] *nm* : elf
élider [elide] *vt* : to elide
éligibilité [eliʒibilite] *nf* : eligibility
éligible [eliʒibl] *adj* : eligible
élimé, -mée [elime] *adj* : threadbare, worn
élimination [eliminasjɔ̃] *nf* : elimination
éliminatoire[1] [eliminatwar] *adj* : qualifying
éliminatoire[2] *nf* : heat (in sports)
éliminer [elimine] *vt* : to eliminate
élire [elir] {51} *vt* **1** : to elect **2 élire domicile** : to take up residence
élision [elizjɔ̃] *nf* : elision
élite [elit] *nf* : elite
élixir [eliksir] *nm* : elixir
elle [ɛl] *pron* **1** : she, it <elle est heureuse : she's happy> <elle est toute neuve : it is brand new> **2** : her <c'était son idée à elle : it was her idea> **3 elles** *pron pl* : they, them <elles se trompent : they're mistaken> <selon elles : according to them>
elle-même [ɛlmɛm] *pron* **1** : herself, itself **2 elles-mêmes** *pron pl* : themselves
ellipse [elips] *nf* **1** OVALE : ellipse, oval **2** : ellipsis
elliptique [eliptik] *adj* : elliptical, elliptic
élocution [elɔkysjɔ̃] *nf* : elocution, diction
éloge [elɔʒ] *nm* **1** : eulogy **2** LOUANGE : praise
élogieux, -gieuse [elɔʒjø, -ʒjøz] *adj* : full of praise, laudatory
éloigné, -gnée [elwaɲe] *adj* : distant, remote
éloignement [elwaɲmɑ̃] *nm* **1** DISTANCE : remoteness, distance (in space or time) **2** : removal **3** : absence
éloigner [elwaɲe] *vt* **1** ÉCARTER : to push aside, to move away **2** DÉTOURNER : to divert, to turn away **3** : to postpone, to put off — **s'éloigner** *vr* : to move away, to go away
éloquence [elɔkɑ̃s] *nf* : eloquence
éloquent, -quente [elɔkɑ̃, -kɑ̃t] *adj* : eloquent — **éloquemment** [elɔkamɑ̃] *adv*
élu[1], **-lue** [ely] *adj* **1** : elect, future **2** : elected
élu[2], **-lue** *n* **1** : elected representative **2** : chosen one <l'élu de mon cœur : my beloved> <les élus : the elect>
élucider [elyside] *vt* CLARIFIER : to clarify, to elucidate — **élucidation** [-sidasjɔ̃] *nf*
élucubrations [elykybrasjɔ̃] *nfpl* : rantings, wild imaginings
éluder [elyde] *vt* : to elude, to evade
élusif, -sive [elyzif, -ziv] *adj* : elusive, evasive
émaciation [emasjasjɔ̃] *nf* : emaciation
émacié, -ciée [emasje] *adj* : emaciated
émail [emaj] *nm, pl* **émaux** [emo] **1** : enamel **2** *Can* : latex (paint)
émailler [emaje] *vt* **1** : to enamel **2** PARSEMER : to scatter, to sprinkle
émanation [emanasjɔ̃] *nf* **1** : emanation <émanations toxiques : toxic fumes> **2** : expression, manifestation
émancipation [emɑ̃sipasjɔ̃] *nf* : emancipation
émanciper [emɑ̃sipe] *vt* AFFRANCHIR : to emancipate, to liberate — **s'émanciper** *vr*
émaner [emane] *vi* **~ de** : to emanate from
émarger [emarʒe] {17} *vt* **1** : to sign, to initial **2** : to trim the margins of — *vi* **~ à** : to be paid from
émasculer [emaskyle] *vt* CASTRER : to emasculate
emballage [ɑ̃balaʒ] *nm* : packing, wrapping <papier d'emballage : wrapping paper>
emballement [ɑ̃balmɑ̃] *nm* **1** : surge, burst <un emballement d'enthousiasme : a burst of enthusiasm> **2** : racing (of an engine)
emballer [ɑ̃bale] *vt* **1** EMPAQUETER : to pack, to wrap **2** *fam* : to thrill <ça ne m'emballe pas : it doesn't thrill me> — **s'emballer** *vr* **1** : to surge **2** : to race (of an engine), to bolt (of a horse) **3** *fam* : to get carried away
embarcadère [ɑ̃barkadɛr] *nm* : wharf, pier
embarcation [ɑ̃barkasjɔ̃] *nf* BARQUE : small boat
embardée [ɑ̃barde] *nf* : swerve, lurch <faire une embardée : to swerve>
embargo [ɑ̃bargo] *nm* **1** : embargo **2 mettre l'embargo sur** : to embargo
embarquement [ɑ̃barkəmɑ̃] *nm* **1** : boarding, embarkation <carte d'embarquement : boarding pass> **2** CHARGEMENT : loading (on board)

embarquer [ɑ̃barke] *vt* **1** : to embark **2** : to load **3** *fam* : to start on, to get involved with — *vi* **1** : to board **2** **~ dans** *Can* : to get in, to climb in <embarque dans la voiture : get in the car> **3** **~ sur** *Can fam* : to climb (up) on — **s'embarquer** *vr* **1** : to board **2** **~ dans** *fam* : to get involved in, to launch into

embarras [ɑ̃bara] *nms & pl* **1** DIFFICULTÉ : difficulty, trouble <embarras financiers : financial problems> **2** GÊNE : embarrassment **3** : awkward situation, predicament <un embarras de choix : too much to choose from> **4** **embarras gastrique** : stomach upset

embarrassant, -sante [ɑ̃barasɑ̃, -sɑ̃t] *adj* **1** : embarrassing, awkward **2** ENCOMBRANT : cumbersome

embarrasser [ɑ̃barase] *vt* **1** ENCOMBRER : to clutter **2** : to hinder, to hamper **3** GÊNER : to embarrass — **s'embarrasser** *vr* **1** **~ dans** : to get tangled up in (lies, etc.) **2** **~ de** : to burden oneself with, to worry over

embarrer [ɑ̃bare] *vt Can* : to lock <ils l'ont embarré dans la chambre : they locked him in the room> — **s'embarrer** *vr Can* **~ dans** : to lock oneself in

embauche [ɑ̃boʃ] *nf* : hiring, employment

embaucher [ɑ̃boʃe] *vt* ENGAGER : to hire

embaumer [ɑ̃bome] *vt* **1** : to embalm **2** PARFUMER : to make fragrant, to scent — *vi* : to smell good

embellie [ɑ̃beli] *nf* **1** ÉCLAIRCIE : clear spell, bright spell **2** ACCALMIE : lull

embellir [ɑ̃belir] *vt* **1** ENJOLIVER : to make more attractive, to beautify **2** : to embellish (a story, etc.) — *vi* : to become more attractive

embellissement [ɑ̃bɛlismɑ̃] *nm* **1** : embellishment **2** : improvement

embêtant, -tante [ɑ̃bɛtɑ̃, -tɑ̃t] *adj* **1** : annoying **2** : awkward, tricky

embêtement [ɑ̃bɛtmɑ̃] *nm* : hassle, trouble, bother

embêter [ɑ̃bɛte] *vt* **1** : to annoy, to bother **2** : to bore — **s'embêter** *vr* : to be bored

emblée [ɑ̃ble] **d'~** : right away

emblématique [ɑ̃blemat'k] *adj* : emblematic

emblème [ɑ̃blɛm] *nm* : emblem

embobiner [ɑ̃bɔbine] *vt fam* : to bamboozle, to trick

emboîter [ɑ̃bwate] *vt* **1** : to fit together **2** **~ dans** : to fit into **3** **emboîter le pas à qqn** : to follow close behind s.o. — **s'emboîter** *vr*

embolie [ɑ̃bɔli] *nf* : embolism

embonpoint [ɑ̃bɔ̃pwɛ̃] *nm* CORPULENCE : stoutness, corpulence

embouchure [ɑ̃buʃyr] *nf* **1** : mouth (of a river) **2** : mouthpiece

embourber [ɑ̃burbe] *v* **s'embourber** *vr* **1** : to get stuck in the mud **2** S'EMPÊTRER : to get bogged down

embourgeoiser [ɑ̃burʒwaze] *v* **s'embourgeoiser** *vr* : to become middle-class

embouteillage [ɑ̃butɛjaʒ] *nm* **1** : bottling **2** : bottleneck, traffic jam

embouteiller [ɑ̃buteje] *vt* **1** : to bottle **2** : to block, to jam <la circulation est très embouteillée : traffic is very congested>

emboutir [ɑ̃butir] *vt* **1** : to stamp, to press (metal) **2** : to crash into, to ram

embranchement [ɑ̃brɑ̃ʃmɑ̃] *nm* **1** CARREFOUR : junction, fork <à l'embranchement des deux routes : at the fork in the road> **2** : branching **3** : branch (in botany and zoology) **4** : side street

embraser [ɑ̃braze] *vt* **1** : to set ablaze **2** ILLUMINER : to illuminate **3** : to inflame, to fire up (passion, enthusiasm, etc.) — **s'embraser** *vr* **1** : to catch fire **2** : to flare up

embrassade [ɑ̃brasad] *nf* : embrace, hugging and kissing

embrasser [ɑ̃brase] *vt* **1** : to kiss **2** ÉTREINDRE : to embrace, to hug **3** : to adopt, to take up (a cause, etc.) — **s'embrasser** *vr* : to kiss (each other)

embrasure [ɑ̃brazyr] *nf* OUVERTURE : opening <embrasure de la porte : doorway>

embrayage [ɑ̃brɛjaʒ] *nm* : clutch (of an automobile)

embrayer [ɑ̃breje] {11} *vi* **1** : to engage the clutch **2** **~ sur** *fam* : to get going on, to launch oneself into **3** **embraye** *Can fam* : get a move on!, hurry up!

embrigader [ɑ̃brigade] *vt* ENRÔLER : to recruit, to enlist

embrocher [ɑ̃brɔʃe] *vt* : to skewer, to put on a spit

embrouillamini [ɑ̃brujamini] *nm fam* : muddle, confusion

embrouillé, -lée [ɑ̃bruje] *adj* : confused, muddled

embrouiller [ɑ̃bruje] *vt* **1** : to tangle up **2** : to confuse, to mix up — **s'embrouiller** *vr*

embroussaillé, -lée [ɑ̃brusaje] *adj* **1** : overgrown (with plants) **2** : shaggy, bushy

embrumé, -mée [ɑ̃bryme] *adj* : misty

embruns [ɑ̃brœ̃] *nmpl* : sea spray

embryologie [ɑ̃brijɔlɔʒi] *nf* : embryology

embryon [ɑ̃brijɔ̃] *nm* : embryo

embryonnaire [ɑ̃brijɔnɛr] *adj* : embryonic

embûche [ɑ̃byʃ] *nf* : trap, pitfall

embuer [ɑ̃bɥe] *vt* : to mist up, to fog up <les yeux embués de larmes : eyes misty with tears> — **s'embuer** *vr*

embuscade [ɑ̃byskad] *nf* : ambush

embusquer [ɑ̃byske] *v* **s'embusquer** *vr* : to lie in ambush
éméché, -chée [emeʃe] *adj fam* : tipsy
émeraude[1] [emrod] *adj* : emerald green
émeraude[2] *nf* : emerald (stone)
émeraude[3] *nm* : emerald (color)
émergence [emɛrʒɑ̃s] *nf* : emergence
émerger [emɛrʒe] {17} *vi* **1** : to emerge **2** : to come to the fore, to stand out
émeri [emri] *nm* : emery
émérite [emerit] *adj* : eminent, outstanding
émerveillement [emɛrvɛjmɑ̃] *nm* ÉBLOUISSEMENT : amazement, wonder
émerveiller [emɛrveje] *vt* ÉBLOUIR : to amaze — **s'émerveiller** *vr* **~ de** : to marvel at, to be amazed at
émétique [emetik] *adj & nm* : emetic
émetteur[1], **-trice** [emetœr, -tris] *adj* **1** : transmitting **2** : issuing <banque émettrice : issuing bank>
émetteur[2], **-trice** *nm* **1** : transmitter **2** : issuer
émetteur[3] *n* : (radio or television) transmitter
émettre [emɛtr] {53} *vt* **1** PRODUIRE : to produce, to give off **2** DISTRIBUER : to issue **3** TRANSMETTRE : to transmit, to broadcast **4** EXPRIMER : to express
émeu [emø] *nm* : emu
émeute [emøt] *nf* : riot
émeutier, -tière [emøtje] *n* : rioter
émietter [emjete] *vt* **1** : to crumble, to flake **2** MORCELER : to break up, to disperse — **s'émietter** *vr*
émigrant, -grante [emigrɑ̃, -grɑ̃t] *n* : emigrant
émigration [emigrasjɔ̃] *nf* : emigration
émigré, -grée [emigre] *n* : emigrant, émigré
émigrer [emigre] *vi* **1** : to emigrate **2** : to migrate
éminemment [eminamɑ̃] *adv* : eminently
éminence [eminɑ̃s] *nf* **1** : eminence <Votre Éminence : Your Eminence> **2** COLLINE : hill **3** PROTUBÉRANCE : protuberance (in anatomy)
éminent, -nente [eminɑ̃, -nɑ̃t] *adj* : eminent, distinguished
émir [emir] *nm* : emir
émirat [emira] *nm* : emirate
émissaire [emisɛr] *nm* : emissary
émission [emisjɔ̃] *nf* **1** : emission **2** : transmission, broadcasting **3** : program, broadcast **4** : issue, issuing
emmagasinage [ɑ̃magazinaʒ] *nm* : storage
emmagasiner [ɑ̃magazine] *vt* **1** ENGRANGER : to store **2** ACCUMULER : to store up, to stockpile
emmailloter [ɑ̃majɔte] *vt* : to wrap up
emmêler [ɑ̃mele] *vt* **1** : to tangle up, to mat **2** : to muddle, to mix up — **s'emmêler** *vr*
emménager [ɑ̃menaʒe] {17} *vi* : to move in
emmener [ɑ̃mne] {52} *vt* **1** AMENER : to take <ils l'ont emmené au poste de police : they took him to the police station> **2** TRANSPORTER : to carry, to transport
emmitoufler [ɑ̃mitufle] *vt* : to wrap up, to bundle up — **s'emmitoufler** *vr*
emmurer [ɑ̃myre] *vt* : to wall in, to immure
émoi [emwa] *nm* **1** : agitation, strong emotion <en émoi : in a state, all agog> **2** : commotion, turmoil
émoluments [emɔlymɑ̃] *nmpl* : remuneration, salary
émonder [emɔ̃de] *vt* ÉLAGUER : to prune, to trim
émotif, -tive [emɔtif, -tiv] *adj* : emotional
émotion [emosjɔ̃] *nf* **1** : emotion, feeling **2 donner des émotions à qqn** *fam* : to give s.o. a fright
émotionnel, -nelle [emosjɔnɛl] *adj* : emotional
émousser [emuse] *vt* : to blunt, to dull — **s'émousser** *vr*
émoustiller [emustije] *vt* **1** : to exhilarate **2** : to titillate, to arouse
émouvant, -vante [emuvɑ̃, -vɑ̃t] *adj* TOUCHANT : moving, touching
émouvoir [emuvwar] {56} *vt* **1** TOUCHER : to move, to touch, to stir **2** TROUBLER : to disturb, to upset — **s'émouvoir** *vr*
empailler [ɑ̃paje] *vt* : to stuff
empaler [ɑ̃pale] *vt* : to impale
empaquetage [ɑ̃paktaʒ] *nm* EMBALLAGE : packaging, wrapping
empaqueter [ɑ̃pakte] {8} *vt* EMBALLER : to package, to wrap up
emparer [ɑ̃pare] *v* **s'emparer** *vr* **~ de** : to seize, to take hold of <s'emparer du pouvoir : to seize power>
empâté, -tée [ɑ̃pate] *adj Can* : spineless, weak
empâter [ɑ̃pate] *vt* **1** : to fatten out (the body) **2** : to thicken, to coat (the tongue) — **s'empâter** : to put on weight
empathie [ɑ̃pati] *nf* : empathy
empattement [ɑ̃patmɑ̃] *nm* **1** : footing, base (of a wall, etc.) **2** : wheelbase
empêchement [ɑ̃pɛʃmɑ̃] *nm* : unexpected obstacle, hitch, holdup
empêcher [ɑ̃peʃe] *vt* **1** : to prevent, to stop **2 il n'empêche que** : nevertheless, still — **s'empêcher** *vr* : to refrain, to stop oneself <il ne pouvait s'empêcher de rire : he couldn't keep from laughing>
empêcheur, -cheuse [ɑ̃pɛʃœr, -ʃøz] *n* **empêcheur de tourner en rond** : spoilsport, killjoy
empeigne [ɑ̃pɛɲ] *nf* : upper (of a shoe)
empereur [ɑ̃prœr] *nm* : emperor
empesé, -sée [ɑ̃pəze] *adj* **1** : starched **2** : stiff, affected
empeser [ɑ̃pəze] {52} *vt* AMIDONNER : to starch

empester [ɑ̃pɛste] *vt* **1** EMPUANTIR : to stink up **2** : to reek of — *vi* : to stink, to reek
empêtrer [ɑ̃petre] *vt* : to entangle, to involve — **s'empêtrer** *vr* **1** : to become entangled **2 ~ dans** : to get bogged down in
emphase [ɑ̃faz] *nf* GRANDILOQUENCE : pomposity, bombast
emphatique [ɑ̃fatik] *adj* **1** : pompous **2** : emphatic — **emphatiquement** [-tikmɑ̃] *adv*
empiècement [ɑ̃pjɛsmɑ̃] *nm* : yoke (of a garment)
empiéter [ɑ̃pjete] {87} *vi* **~ sur** : to encroach upon, to infringe on
empiffrer [ɑ̃pifre] *v* **s'empiffrer** *vr fam* : to stuff oneself
empilade [ɑ̃pilad] *nf Can* : pileup
empiler [ɑ̃pile] *vt* : to pile up, to stack — **s'empiler** *vr*
empire [ɑ̃pir] *nm* **1** : empire **2 sous l'empire de** : under the influence of
empirer [ɑ̃pire] *vt* AGGRAVER : to worsen, to make worse — *vi* : to worsen, to deteriorate
empirique [ɑ̃pirik] *adj* : empirical — **empiriquement** [-rikmɑ̃] *adv*
emplacement [ɑ̃plasmɑ̃] *nm* : site, location
emplâtre [ɑ̃platr] *nm* **1** : (medical) plaster **2** : patch (for a tire) **3** *fam* : clumsy oaf, clod
emplette [ɑ̃plɛt] *nf* **1** ACHAT : purchase **2 faire ses emplettes** : to go shopping
emplir [ɑ̃plir] *vt* **1** : REMPLIR : to fill **2 faire emplir** *Can* : to bamboozle, to trick — **s'emplir** *vr* : to fill up
emploi [ɑ̃plwa] *nm* **1** UTILISATION : use <mode d'emploi : instructions, directions> **2** TRAVAIL : employment, job **3** USAGE : usage (of language) **4 emploi du temps** : schedule, timetable
emploie [ɑ̃plwa], **emploiera** [ɑ̃plwara], *etc.* → **employer**
employé, -yée [ɑ̃plwaje] *n* : employee
employer [ɑ̃plwaje] {58} *vt* **1** UTILISER : to use **2** : to employ, to provide jobs for — **s'employer** *vr* **1** : to be used **2** : to apply oneself
employeur, -ployeuse [ɑ̃plwajœr, -plwajøz] *n* : employer
empocher [ɑ̃pɔʃe] *vt* : to pocket
empoignade [ɑ̃pwaɲad] *nf* : altercation, row
empoigner [ɑ̃pwaɲe] *vt* **1** SAISIR : to seize, to grasp **2** ÉMOUVOIR : to thrill, to grip — **s'empoigner** *vr* : to quarrel, to come to blows
empois [ɑ̃pwa] *nms & pl* : (laundry) starch
empoisonnement [ɑ̃pwazɔnmɑ̃] *nm* **1** : poisoning **2** *fam* : nuisance, trouble
empoisonner [ɑ̃pwazɔne] *vt* **1** : to poison **2** EMPUANTIR : to stink up **3** *fam* : to annoy, to bug — **s'empoisonner** *vr* **1** : to poison oneself **2** *fam* : to be bored stiff
emporté, -tée [ɑ̃pɔrte] *adj* : quick-tempered
emportement [ɑ̃pɔrtəmɑ̃] *nm* **1** : fit of anger, rage **2** : ardor, fervor
emporter [ɑ̃pɔrte] *vt* **1** : to take, to take away <plats à emporter : food to go> **2** : to carry away, to sweep away **3** : to carry off, to cause (a sick person) to die **4** : to carry, to win <l'emporter sur : to get the better of> — **s'emporter** *vr* : to lose one's temper
empoté, -tée [ɑ̃pɔte] *adj fam* : clumsy, awkward
empoter [ɑ̃pɔte] *vt* : to pot (a plant)
empourprer [ɑ̃purpre] *vt* : to turn crimson — **s'empourprer** *vr*
empreint, -preinte [ɑ̃prɛ̃, -prɛ̃t] *adj* **~ de** : marked with, stamped with <empreint de douleur : imbued with sadness>
empreinte *nf* **1** : print, track <empreinte de pied : footprint> <empreinte digitale : fingerprint> **2** IMPRESSION : impression, stamp, imprint
empressé, -sée [ɑ̃prese] *adj* : attentive, eager (to please)
empressement [ɑ̃prɛsmɑ̃] *nm* **1** : attentiveness **2** ENTHOUSIASME : eagerness, enthusiasm, haste
empresser [ɑ̃prese] *v* **s'empresser** *vr* **1 s'empresser auprès de** : to be attentive toward **2 ~ de** : to be in a hurry to <elle s'est empressée de partir : she hastened to leave>
emprise [ɑ̃priz] *nf* : influence, hold <sous l'emprise de : under the influence of>
emprisonnement [ɑ̃prizɔnmɑ̃] *nm* : imprisonment
emprisonner [ɑ̃prizɔne] *vt* **1** : to imprison **2** : to hold tightly, to grip
emprunt [ɑ̃prœ̃] *nm* **1** : loan **2** : borrowing **3** : word <un emprunt à l'allemand : a borrowing from the German> **4 d'~** : borrowed <nom d'emprunt : assumed name>
emprunté, -tée [ɑ̃prœ̃te] *adj* **1** : awkward, self-conscious **2** : sham, feigned
emprunter [ɑ̃prœ̃te] *vt* **1** : to borrow **2** PRENDRE : to take, to follow <empruntez la nouvelle route : take the new road> **3** : to assume, to take on <emprunter un nom : to assume a name>
empuantir [ɑ̃pɥɑ̃tir] *vt* : to stink up
ému, -mue [emy] *adj* : moved, touched
émulation [emylasjɔ̃] *nf* : competition, emulation
émule [emyl] *nmf* : imitator, emulator
émulsion [emylsjɔ̃] *nf* : emulsion
émulsionner [emylsjɔne] *vt* : to emulsify
en[1] [ɑ̃] *prep* **1** : in <j'habite en ville : I live in town> <en français : in

French> <en 1847 : in 1847> **2** : to <elle va en Belgique : she's going to Belgium> <de mal en pis : from bad to worse> **3** : by <elle va en voiture : she's going by car> **4** : of <fait en plastique : made of plastic> **5** : at <en guerre : at war> **6** : as <je te parle en ami : I'm speaking to you as a friend> <il est habillé en militaire : he is dressed as a soldier> **7** : into <traduit en français : translated into French>

en[2] *pron* **1** (*representing a noun governed by* de) <je m'en souviens : I remember it> <qu'est-ce que tu en sais? : what do you know about it?> **2** (*used with expressions of quantity*) <j'en ai plusieurs : I have several> **3** (*used to replace the possessive*) <j'en ai perdu la clef : I lost its key> **4** (*used to replace a phrase*) <il n'a pas joué mais il en est capable : he didn't play but he can> **5** (*used in partitive constructions*) <en avez-vous? : do you have some?> <j'en connais : I know a few>

enamourer [ɑ̃namure] *v* **s'enamourer** *vr* : to fall in love, to become enamored

encadrement [ɑ̃kadrəmɑ̃] *nm* **1** : frame **2** : staff <l'encadrement administratif : the administrative staff> **3** : supervision <les étudiants manquent d'encadrement : the students lack supervision> **4** : restriction, control (of prices, credit, etc.)

encadrer [ɑ̃kadre] *vt* **1** : to frame **2** : to surround, to flank **3** : to supervise, to train

encaisse [ɑ̃kɛs] *nf* : cash in hand

encaissé, -sée [ɑ̃kese] *adj* : steep-sided

encaisser [ɑ̃kese] *vt* **1** : to cash (a check), to collect (money) **2** *fam* : to take, to tolerate <encaisser un coup : to take a beating> <je ne peux pas l'encaisser! : I can't take it!>

encan [ɑ̃kɑ̃] *nm* : auction <vendre à l'encan : to auction off, to sell at auction>

encanailler [ɑ̃kanaje] *v* **s'encanailler** *vr* : to slum, to keep bad company

encanter [ɑ̃kɑ̃te] *vt Can* : to auction

encanteur, -teuse [ɑ̃kɑ̃tœr] *n Can* : auctioneer

encart [ɑ̃kar] *nm* : insert, pamphlet <encart publicitaire : advertising insert>

en–cas [ɑ̃ka] *nms & pl* : snack

encastré, -trée [ɑ̃kastre] *adj* : built-in <un four encastré : a built-in oven>

encastrer [ɑ̃kastre] *vt* : to fit, to embed, to build in — **s'encastrer** *vr*

encaustique [ɑ̃kostik] *nf* CIRE : polish, wax — **encaustiquer** [-stike] *vt*

enceinte[1] [ɑ̃sɛ̃t] *adj* : pregnant

enceinte[2] *nf* **1** : surrounding wall, fence **2** ESPACE : interior, enclosure <dans l'enceinte du tribunal : inside the courtroom> **3 enceinte acoustique** : speaker

encens [ɑ̃sɑ̃] *nm* : incense

encenser [ɑ̃sɑ̃se] *vt* **1** : to perfume (with incense) **2** FLATTER : to flatter

encensoir [ɑ̃sɑ̃swar] *nm* : censer

encercler [ɑ̃sɛrkle] *vt* ENTOURER : to surround, to encircle

enchaînement [ɑ̃ʃɛnmɑ̃] *nm* **1** SÉRIE : series, sequence **2** LIAISON : link, connection

enchaîner [ɑ̃ʃene] *vt* **1** : to chain (up) **2** LIER : to link, to connect — *vi* : to continue, to move on — **s'enchaîner** *vr* : to link up, to be connected

enchanté, -tée [ɑ̃ʃɑ̃te] *adj* **1** MAGIQUE : magic, enchanted **2** RAVI : delighted, pleased <enchanté de faire votre connaissance : pleased to meet you>

enchantement [ɑ̃ʃɑ̃tmɑ̃] *nm* **1** : enchantment **2** : delight

enchanter [ɑ̃ʃɑ̃te] *vt* **1** ENSORCELER : to enchant, to bewitch **2** RAVIR : to delight

enchanteur[1], **-teresse** [ɑʃɑ̃tœr, -trɛs] *adj* CHARMANT : enchanting, charming

enchanteur[2], **-teresse** *n* : enchanter *m*, enchantress *f*

enchâssement [ɑ̃ʃɑsmɑ̃] *nm* : setting, mounting (of gems)

enchâsser [ɑ̃ʃase] *vt* **1** : to mount, to set **2** INSÉRER : to insert (a word, etc.)

enchère [ɑ̃ʃɛr] *nf* **1** : bid, bidding **2 vente aux enchères** : auction

enchérisseur, -seuse [ɑ̃ʃerisœr, -søz] *n* : bidder

enchevêtrement [ɑ̃ʃəvɛtrəmɑ̃] *nm* **1** : tangle **2** : confusion

enchevêtrer [ɑ̃ʃəvɛtre] *vt* **1** : to tangle up **2** : to muddle, to confuse — **s'enchevêtrer** *vr*

enclave [ɑ̃klav] *nf* : enclave

enclaver [ɑ̃klave] *vt* **1** ENTOURER : to enclose, to surround **2** : to fit together, to interlock

enclencher [ɑ̃klɑ̃ʃe] *vt* **1** : to engage (a mechanism) **2** : to set in motion, to get under way — **s'enclencher** *vr*

enclin, -cline [ɑ̃klɛ̃, -klin] *adj* **~ à** : inclined to, prone to

enclore [ɑ̃klɔr] {34} *vt* : to enclose

enclos [ɑ̃klo] *nm* : enclosure

enclume [ɑ̃klym] *nf* : anvil

encoche [ɑ̃kɔʃ] *nf* : notch

encocher [ɑ̃kɔʃe] *vt* : to notch

encoder [ɑ̃kɔde] *vt* : to encode

encoignure [ɑ̃kwaɲyr] *nf* : corner (of a room)

encoller [ɑ̃kɔle] *vt* : to paste, to glue

encolure [ɑ̃kɔlyr] *nf* **1** COU : neck **2** : collar (size)

encombrant, -brante [ɑ̃kɔ̃brɑ̃, -brɑ̃t] *adj* : cumbersome

encombre [ɑ̃kɔ̃br] *adv* **sans ~** : without mishap, without a hitch

encombrement [ɑ̃kɔ̃brəmɑ̃] *nm* **1** : clutter **2** : overall size, bulk **3** : blocking, jamming **4** : traffic jam **5** : congestion (in medicine)

encombrer [ɑ̃kɔ̃bre] *vt* **1** : to clutter up, to congest **2** : to block, to jam **3** : to burden, to encumber — **s'encombrer** *vr* **~ de** : to burden oneself with

encontre [ɑ̃kɔ̃tr] **à l'encontre de** : against, counter to, contrary to

encore [ɑ̃kɔr] *adv* **1** TOUJOURS : still <je travaille encore ici : I'm still working here> **2** DAVANTAGE : more, again <encore une fois : once more, once again> <il m'a encore parlé : he spoke to me again> **3** : yet <pas encore : not yet> <encore mieux : better yet> **4** : another <pendant encore trois mois : for another three months> **5 encore que** : although **6 si encore** *or* **encore si** : if only

encorner [ɑ̃kɔrne] *vt* : to gore

encornet [ɑ̃kɔrnɛ] *nm* : squid

encouragement [ɑ̃kuraʒmɑ̃] *nm* : encouragement

encourager [ɑ̃kuraʒe] {17} *vt* : to encourage

encourir [ɑ̃kurir] {23} *vt* : to incur

encrasser [ɑ̃krase] *vt* **1** SALIR : to dirty **2** OBSTRUER : to clog up — **s'encrasser** *vr*

encre [ɑ̃kr] *nf* : ink

encrer [ɑ̃kre] *vt* : to ink

encrier [ɑ̃krije] *nm* : inkwell

encroûter [ɑ̃krute] *v* **s'encroûter** *vr* : to get in a rut <encroûté dans ses habitudes : set in one's ways>

encyclique [ɑ̃siklik] *nf* : encyclical

encyclopédie [ɑ̃siklɔpedi] *nf* : encyclopedia — **encyclopédique** [-pedik] *adj*

endémique [ɑ̃demik] *adj* : endemic

endetté, -tée [ɑ̃dete] *adj* : in debt

endettement [ɑ̃dɛtmɑ̃] *nm* : debt

endetter [ɑ̃dete] *v* **s'endetter** *vr* : to get into debt

endeuiller [ɑ̃dœje] *vt* **1** : to plunge into mourning **2** : to cast gloom over (an event, etc.)

endiablé, -blée [ɑ̃djable] *adj* **1** : wild, furious **2** : boisterous

endiguer [ɑ̃dige] *vt* **1** : to dam up **2** RETENIR : to check, to hold back, to contain

endimanché, -chée [ɑ̃dimɑ̃ʃe] *adj* : in one's Sunday best

endisquer [ɑ̃diske] *vt Can* : to record (a CD)

endive [ɑ̃div] *nf* : endive, chickory

endocrine [ɑ̃dɔkrin] *adj* : endocrine

endoctrinement [ɑ̃dɔktrinmɑ̃] *nm* : indoctrination

endoctriner [ɑ̃dɔktrine] *vt* : to indoctrinate

endolori, -rie [ɑ̃dɔlɔri] *adj* : painful, sore

endommager [ɑ̃dɔmaʒe] {17} *vt* : to damage

endormant, -mante [ɑ̃dɔrmɑ̃, -mɑ̃t] *adj* ENNUYEUX : boring

endormi, -mie [ɑ̃dɔrmi] *adj* **1** : asleep, sleeping **2** LÉTHARGIQUE : sluggish, lethargic

endormir [ɑ̃dɔrmir] {30} *vt* **1** : to put to sleep **2** ANESTHÉSIER : to anesthetize, to numb **3** : to allay, to calm — **s'endormir** *vr* **1** : to fall asleep **2** : to slack off **3** : to subside, to die down **4** : to pass away, to die

endossement [ɑ̃dɔsmɑ̃] *nm* : endorsement

endosser [ɑ̃dɔse] *vt* **1** : to take on, to shoulder **2** : to endorse, to sign **3** : to don, to put on (clothes)

endroit [ɑ̃drwa] *nm* **1** : place, spot, locale **2** : right side (of a garment, etc.) <à l'endroit : right side up> **3 à l'endroit de** : toward, with regard to **4 par endroits** : here and there, in places

enduire [ɑ̃dɥir] {49} *vt* : to coat, to cover — **s'enduire** *vr*

enduit [ɑ̃dɥi] *nm* : coating

endurance [ɑ̃dyrɑ̃s] *nf* : endurance

endurant, -rante [ɑ̃dyrɑ̃, -rɑ̃t] *adj* : hardy, tough

endurci, -cie [ɑ̃dyrsi] *adj* **1** DUR : hard **2** INVÉTÉRÉ : hardened, inveterate

endurcir [ɑ̃dyrsir] *vt* **1** : to toughen, to strengthen **2** : to harden — **s'endurcir** *vr*

endurer [ɑ̃dyre] *vt* SUPPORTER : to endure

énergétique [enɛrʒetik] *adj* **1** : energy <ressources énergétiques : energy resources> **2** : energizing

énergie [enɛrʒi] *nf* : energy

énergique [enɛrʒik] *adj* **1** : energetic **2** : vigorous, forceful, emphatic — **énergiquement** [-ʒikmɑ̃] *adv*

énervant, -vante [enɛrvɑ̃, -vɑ̃t] *adj* AGAÇANT : irritating, annoying

énervement [enɛrvəmɑ̃] *nm* **1** AGACEMENT : irritation **2** : agitation, edginess

énerver [enɛrve] *vt* AGACER : to irritate, to annoy — **s'énerver** *vr* **1** : to become annoyed **2** : to get worked up

enfance [ɑ̃fɑ̃s] *nf* **1** : childhood **2** DÉBUT : infancy, beginning **3** : children *pl*

enfant[1] [ɑ̃fɑ̃] *adj* : childish, childlike <il est resté très enfant : he's still very childlike>

enfant[2] *nmf* **1** : child <faire l'enfant : to act childishly> <enfant prodige : child prodigy> <enfant trouvé : foundling> **2** : offspring, child <un enfant unique : an only child> **3 bon enfant** : good-natured **4 enfant de chœur** : altar boy

enfantement [ɑ̃fɑ̃tmɑ̃] *nm* : childbirth

enfanter [ɑ̃fɑ̃te] *vt* : to give birth to

enfantillage [ɑ̃fɑ̃tijaʒ] *nm* : childishness

enfantin, -tine [ɑ̃fɑ̃tɛ̃, -tin] *adj* **1** : childlike **2** : simple <c'est enfantin : it's child's play> **3** PUÉRIL : childish

enfarger [ɑ̃farʒe] {17} *vt Can* : to make (someone) trip — **s'enfarger** *vr* : to trip, to stumble

enfer [ɑ̃fɛr] *nm* **1** : hell **2 d'~** : infernal, hellish

enfermer [ɑ̃fɛrme] *vt* **1** : to shut up, to lock up **2** ENTOURER : to enclose, to surround — **s'enfermer** *vr* **1** : to shut oneself away **2 ~ dans** : to retreat into

enferrer [ɑ̃fere] *v* **s'enferrer** *vr* **~ dans** : to get tangled up in

enfilade [ɑ̃filad] *nf* : row, succession

enfiler [ɑ̃file] *vt* **1** METTRE : to slip on, to put on <enfiler un chandail : to put on a sweater> **2** : to thread, to string **3** : to take, to go down (a street, corridor, etc.) — **s'enfiler** *vr* **1** *fam* : to guzzle, to devour **2 ~ dans** : to disappear into (a doorway, etc.)

enfin [ɑ̃fɛ̃] *adv* **1** : finally, at last <enfin seuls! : alone at last!> **2** : lastly <enfin et surtout : last but not least> **3** : in short, in a word **4** : well, at least <enfin, je crois : at least I think so> **5** : anyhow, after all **6** (*used to show impatience*) <mais enfin, donne-le-moi! : come on, give it to me!>

enflammé, -mée [ɑ̃flame] *adj* **1** BRÛLANT : burning **2** PASSIONNÉ : passionate **3** : inflamed (in medicine)

enflammer [ɑ̃flame] *vt* **1** ALLUMER : to ignite, to set fire to **2** : to inflame — **s'enflammer** *vr* : to catch fire

enfler [ɑ̃fle] *vt* **1** : to cause to swell **2** : to increase the volume of (a sound, one's voice) — *vi* : to swell (up) — **s'enfler** *vr*

enflure [ɑ̃flyr] *nf* : swelling

enfoncé, -cée [ɑ̃fɔ̃se] *adj* : sunken, deep-set

enfoncer [ɑ̃fɔ̃se] {6} *vt* **1** : to drive in (a nail, etc.) **2** : to push in, to insert <enfoncer ses mains dans ses poches : to thrust one's hands in one's pockets> **3** : to break open, to break down — *vi* : to sink — **s'enfoncer** *vr* **1** CÉDER : to yield, to give way **2** PÉNÉTRER : to penetrate, to sink in **3 ~ dans** : to disappear into

enfouir [ɑ̃fwir] *vt* **1** : to bury **2** CACHER : to hide, to tuck away — **s'enfouir** *vr* **~ dans** : to bury oneself in

enfouissement [ɑ̃fwismɑ̃] *nm* : burying

enfourcher [ɑ̃furʃe] *vt* : to mount, to get on, to straddle

enfourner [ɑ̃furne] *vt* **1** : to put in the oven **2** *fam* : to gobble up

enfreindre [ɑ̃frɛ̃dr] {37} *vt* : to infringe, to violate <enfreindre la loi : to break the law>

enfuir [ɑ̃fɥir] {46} *v* **s'enfuir** *vr* S'ÉCHAPPER : to run away, to escape, to flee

enfumer [ɑ̃fyme] *vt* : to fill with smoke

engagé, -gée [ɑ̃gaʒe] *adj* **1** : committed, involved **2** *Can fam* : busy <la ligne est engagée : the line is busy>

engageant, -geante [ɑ̃gaʒɑ̃, -ʒɑ̃t] *adj* : engaging, attractive

engagement [ɑ̃gaʒmɑ̃] *nm* **1** PROMESSE : commitment, promise **2** : engagement, contract, enlistment (in the military) **3** DÉBUT : start **4** : involvement, participation **5** : (military) engagement

engager [ɑ̃gaʒe] {17} *vt* **1** : to bind, to commit **2** RECRUTER : to hire, to take on **3** IMPLIQUER : to involve **4** : to invest, to lay out (capital, etc.) **5** EXHORTER : to urge **6** COMMENCER : to start, to begin **7** INTRODUIRE : to insert — **s'engager** *vr* **1** : to commit oneself, to undertake **2** : to enlist, to join up **3** : to begin, to start up **4 ~ dans** : to enter, to turn into (a street, etc.)

engelure [ɑ̃ʒlyr] *nf* : chilblain

engendrer [ɑ̃ʒɑ̃dre] *vt* **1** : to engender, to generate **2** : to father, to beget

engin [ɑ̃ʒɛ̃] *nm* **1** APPAREIL : machine, device <engin explosif : explosive device> **2** VÉHICULE : vehicle <engin blindé : armored vehicle> **3** MISSILE : missile **4** *fam* MACHIN : gadget, contraption

englober [ɑ̃glɔbe] *vt* : to include

engloutir [ɑ̃glutir] *vt* **1** : to gobble up, to devour **2** : to engulf, to swallow up **3** : to squander

engoncé, -cée [ɑ̃gɔ̃se] *adj* **~ dans** : squeezed into

engorgement [ɑ̃gɔrʒəmɑ̃] *nm* : blocking (up), congestion

engorger [ɑ̃gɔrʒe] {17} *vt* **1** : to block, to jam up **2** : to congest (in medicine)

engouement [ɑ̃gumɑ̃] *nm* : infatuation

engouer [ɑ̃gwe] *v* **s'engouer** *vr* **~ de** : to become infatuated with

engouffrer [ɑ̃gufre] *vt* **1** : to engulf, to swallow up **2** : to gobble up, to devour — **s'engouffrer** *vr* **~ dans** : to rush into

engourdi, -die [ɑ̃gurdi] *adj* **1** : numb **2** : dulled, lethargic

engourdir [ɑ̃gurdir] *vt* **1** : to numb **2** : to dull — **s'engourdir** *vr*

engourdissement [ɑ̃gurdismɑ̃] *nm* **1** : numbness **2** : dullness, torpor

engrais [ɑ̃grɛ] *nm* **1** : fertilizer, manure **2 mettre à l'engrais** : to fatten

engraisser [ɑ̃grese] *vt* **1** : to fatten **2** : to fertilize — *vi* GROSSIR : to get fat, to put on weight — **s'engraisser** *vr*

engranger [ɑ̃grɑ̃ʒe] {17} *vt* **1** : to garner, to gather **2** EMMAGASINER : to store

engrenage [ɑ̃grənaʒ] *nm* **1** : gears *pl* **2 être pris dans l'engrenage** : to be caught up in the system

engrener [ɑ̃grəne] {52} *vt* : to engage, to mesh (gears) — **s'engrener** *vr*

engueulade [ɑ̃gœlad] *nf fam* : argument, shouting match
engueuler [ɑ̃gœle] *vt fam* : to yell at, to bawl out — **s'engueuler** *vr*
enguirlander [ɑ̃girlɑ̃de] *vt* : to garland, to adorn with garlands
énième [enjɛm] *adj* : nth, umpteenth <pour l'énième fois : for the umpteenth time>
énigmatique [enigmatik] *adj* : enigmatic — **énigmatiquement** [-tikmɑ̃] *adv*
énigme [enigm] *nf* : enigma, riddle
enivrant, -vrante [ɑ̃nivrɑ̃, -vrɑ̃t] *adj* : intoxicating
enivrement [ɑ̃nivrəmɑ̃] *nm* : intoxication
enivrer [ɑ̃nivre] *vr* **1** : to intoxicate, to make drunk **2** : to elate, to exhilarate — **s'enivrer** *vr*
enjambée [ɑ̃ʒɑ̃be] *nf* : stride
enjamber [ɑ̃ʒɑ̃be] *vt* **1** : to step over **2** : to span, to straddle
enjeu [ɑ̃ʒø] *nm, pl* **enjeux** **1** : issue <les enjeux politiques : political issues> **2** : stake <son emploi est à l'enjeu : his job is at stake>
enjoindre [ɑ̃ʒwɛ̃dr] {50} *vt* : to enjoin, to order <enjoindre à qqn de faire qqch : to enjoin s.o. to do sth>
enjôler [ɑ̃ʒole] *vt* : to cajole, to wheedle
enjoliver [ɑ̃ʒɔlive] *vt* : to embellish
enjoliveur [ɑ̃ʒɔlivœr] *nm* : hubcap
enjoué, -jouée [ɑ̃ʒwe] *adj* : cheerful, light-hearted
enjouement [ɑ̃ʒumɑ̃] *nm* : playfulness, gaiety
enlacement [ɑ̃lasmɑ̃] *nm* **1** : embrace **2** : intertwining
enlacer [ɑ̃lase] {6} *vt* **1** ÉTREINDRE : to embrace, to hug **2** ENTRELACER : to entwine, to enlace — **s'enlacer** *vr*
enlaidir [ɑ̃ledir] *vt* : to make ugly — *vi* : to grow ugly — **s'enlaidir** *vr*
enlevant, -vante [ɑ̃lvɑ̃, -vɑ̃t] *adj Can* : lively, spirited
enlevé, -vée [ɑ̃lve] *adj* : lively, spirited
enlèvement [ɑ̃lɛvmɑ̃] *nm* **1** : kidnapping, abduction **2** : removal <enlèvement des ordures ménagères : garbage collection>
enlever [ɑ̃lve] {52} *vt* **1** : to remove, to take off, to take away **2** LEVER : to raise, to lift **3** KIDNAPPER : to abduct, to kidnap **4** GAGNER : to carry off, to win — **s'enlever** *vr* : to come off, to come out
enlisement [ɑ̃lizmɑ̃] *nm* : sinking, bogging down
enliser [ɑ̃lize] *v* **s'enliser** *vr* **1** : to sink, to get stuck **2** : to get bogged down
enneigé, -gée [ɑ̃neʒe] *adj* : snow-covered
enneigement [ɑ̃nɛʒmɑ̃] *nm* : snow accumulation, snow cover
ennemi[1], -mie [ɛnmi] *adj* : enemy, hostile <en pays ennemi : in enemy territory>
ennemi[2], -mie *n* : enemy
ennoblir [ɑ̃nɔblir] *vt* : to ennoble
ennui [ɑ̃nɥi] *nm* **1** PROBLÈME : trouble, problem <avoir des ennuis : to have problems> **2** : boredom, ennui
ennuie [ɑ̃nwi], **ennuiera** [ɑ̃nwira], *etc.* → **ennuyer**
ennuyant, ennuyante [ɑ̃nɥijɑ̃, ɑ̃nɥijɑ̃t] *adj Can* **1** : annoying, irritating **2** : boring
ennuyer [ɑ̃nɥije] {58} *vt* **1** AGACER : to annoy **2** : to bore — **s'ennuyer** *vr* : to be bored
ennuyeux, ennuyeuse [ɑ̃nɥijø, ɑ̃nɥijøz] *adj* **1** AGAÇANT : annoying, irritating **2** LASSANT : boring, tedious
énoncé [enɔ̃se] *nm* **1** : statement, declaration **2** : terms *pl*, wording **3** : utterance
énoncer [enɔ̃se] {6} *vt* : to express, to state — **s'énoncer** *vr*
énonciation [enɔ̃sjasjɔ̃] *nf* : stating, statement
enorgueillir [ɑ̃nɔrgœjir] *vt* : to make proud — **s'enorgueillir** *vr* : to pride oneself
énorme [enɔrm] *adj* : enormous, huge
énormément [enɔrmemɑ̃] *adv* **1** : enormously, tremendously **2** ~ **de** : a great number of
énormité [enɔrmite] *nf* **1** : enormity, hugeness **2** : outrageous remark
enquérir [ɑ̃kerir] {21} *v* **s'enquérir** *vr* ~ **de** : to inquire about
enquête [ɑ̃kɛt] *nf* **1** INVESTIGATION : investigation, inquiry, inquest **2** SONDAGE : poll, survey
enquêter [ɑ̃kete] *vi* : to investigate, to hold an inquiry
enquiquiner [ɑ̃kikine] *vt fam* : to irritate, to pester, to nag at
enraciner [ɑ̃rasine] *vt* **1** : to root **2** : to entrench, to establish — **s'enraciner** *vr* : to take root
enragé, -gée [ɑ̃raʒe] *adj* **1** : rabid **2** : furious
enrageant, -geante [ɑ̃raʒɑ̃, -ʒɑ̃t] *adj* : infuriating
enrager [ɑ̃raʒe] {17} *vi* **1** : to be furious, to be in a rage **2** **faire enrager** : to enrage
enrayer [ɑ̃reje] {11} *vt* **1** : to check, to stop, to curb <enrayer une maladie : to bring a disease under control> **2** BLOQUER : to jam — **s'enrayer** *vr*
enrégimenter [ɑ̃reʒimɑ̃te] *vt* : to regiment
enregistrement [ɑ̃rəʒistrəmɑ̃] *nm* **1** : registration **2** : recording <enregistrement magnétique : tape recording> **3** : checking in <enregistrement des bagages : luggage check-in>
enregistrer [ɑ̃rəʒistre] *vt* **1** INSCRIRE : to register **2** : to record, to tape **3** : to check in

enregistreur[1], **-treuse** [ɑ̃rəʒistrœr, -trøz] *adj* **1 :** recording **2 caisse enregistreuse :** cash register

enregistreur[2] *nm* **:** recorder <enregistreur de vol : flight recorder>

enrhumé, -mée [ɑ̃ryme] *adj* **être enrhumé :** to have a cold

enrhumer [ɑ̃ryme] *v* **s'enrhumer** *vr* **:** to catch a cold

enrichi, -chie [ɑ̃riʃi] *adj* **:** enriched, fortified <farine enrichie : enriched flour>

enrichir [ɑ̃riʃir] *vt* **1 :** to make rich **2 :** to enrich — **s'enrichir** *vr*

enrichissant, -sante [ɑ̃riʃisɑ̃, -sɑ̃t] *adj* **:** enriching, rewarding

enrichissement [ɑ̃riʃismɑ̃] *nm* **:** enrichment

enrobage [ɑ̃rɔbaʒ] *nm* **:** coating

enrober [ɑ̃rɔbe] *vt* **1** RECOUVRIR **:** to coat **2 :** to wrap up, to dress up (words, etc.)

enrôlement [ɑ̃rolmɑ̃] *nm* **:** enrollment, enlistment

enrôler [ɑ̃role] *vt* **:** to enroll, to enlist — **s'enrôler** *vr*

enroué, -rouée [ɑ̃rwe] *adj* **:** hoarse, husky

enrouer [ɑ̃rwe] *vt* **:** to make hoarse — **s'enrouer** *vr*

enrouler [ɑ̃rule] *vt* **:** to wind, to coil, to roll up — **s'enrouler** *vr* **1 ~ dans :** to wrap oneself up in **2 ~ sur :** to wind around

ensabler [ɑ̃sable] *v* **s'ensabler** *vr* **1 :** to get stuck in the sand **2 :** to silt up

ensacher [ɑ̃saʃe] *vt* **:** to bag (merchandise)

ensanglanté, -tée [ɑ̃sɑ̃glɑ̃te] *adj* **:** covered with blood, bloodstained

enseignant[1], **-gnante** [ɑ̃sɛɲɑ̃, -ɲɑ̃t] *adj* **:** teaching

enseignant[2], **-gnante** *n* **:** teacher

enseigne[1] [ɑ̃sɛɲ] *nf* **1 :** sign <enseigne lumineuse : neon sign> **2** DRAPEAU **:** flag, ensign **3 être logé à la même enseigne :** to be in the same boat

enseigne[2] *nm* **1 :** ensign **2 enseigne de vaisseau :** midshipman

enseignement [ɑ̃sɛɲmɑ̃] *nm* **1 :** teaching **2 :** education **3** LEÇON **:** lesson, lecture

enseigner [ɑ̃seɲe] *v* **:** to teach

ensemble[1] [ɑ̃sɑ̃bl] *adv* **:** together

ensemble[2] *nm* **1 :** group (of persons), set (of objects), series (of ideas, etc.) **2 :** whole <dans l'ensemble : on the whole> **3 :** unity <avec un ensemble parfait : simultaneously, in perfect unison> **4 :** ensemble (in music) **5 :** suit (of clothing), outfit **6 :** set (in mathematics) **7 d'~ :** overall, general **8 dans l'ensemble :** on the whole **9 grand ensemble :** housing development

ensemblier [ɑ̃sɑ̃blije] *nm* **:** interior decorator

ensemencer [ɑ̃səmɑ̃se] {6} *vt* **:** to sow, to seed

enserrer [ɑ̃sere] *vt* **1 :** to fit tightly around, to encircle **2** SERRER **:** to clasp, to grip

ensevelir [ɑ̃səvlir] *vt* ENTERRER **:** to bury

ensoleillé, -lée [ɑ̃sɔleje] *adj* **:** sunny

ensoleillement [ɑ̃sɔlɛjmɑ̃] *nm* **:** (amount of) sunshine

ensommeillé, -lée [ɑ̃sɔmeje] *adj* **:** sleepy, drowsy

ensorceler [ɑ̃sɔrsəle] {8} *vt* **:** to bewitch, to charm

ensorcellement [ɑ̃sɔrsɛlmɑ̃] *nm* **:** bewitchment, enchantment

ensuite [ɑ̃sɥit] *adv* **1 :** then, next **2 :** afterwards, later

ensuivre [ɑ̃sɥivr] {35} *v* **s'ensuivre** *vr* **:** to ensue, to follow <il s'ensuit que . . . : it follows that . . . >

entacher [ɑ̃taʃe] *vt* **1 :** to mar, to sully **2 entaché de nullité :** null and void

entaille [ɑ̃taj] *nf* **1 :** cut, gash **2** ENCOCHE **:** notch

entailler [ɑ̃taje] *vt* **:** to gash, to slash, to cut (into) — **s'entailler** *vr* **:** to get a gash in

entamer [ɑ̃tame] *vt* **1 :** to cut into, to make inroads into **2 :** to start, to initiate **3 :** to damage, to sully **4 :** to shake, to undermine

entassement [ɑ̃tasmɑ̃] *nm* **1 :** piling up **2 :** pile, heap

entasser [ɑ̃tase] *vt* **1 :** to pile up, to accumulate **2 :** to cram, to pack together — **s'entasser** *vr* **:** to pile up

entendement [ɑ̃tɑ̃dmɑ̃] *nm* **:** understanding

entendeur [ɑ̃tɑ̃dœr] *nm* **à bon entendeur, salut! :** a word to the wise!

entendre [ɑ̃tɑ̃dr] {63} *vt* **1 :** to hear **2** SIGNIFIER **:** to mean, to intend **3** COMPRENDRE **:** to understand <laisser entendre : to intimate> **4 entendre dire que :** to hear that **5 entendre parler de :** to hear of — *vi* **1 :** to hear **2 :** to understand — **s'entendre** *vr* **1 :** to get along, to understand one another **2 :** to agree **3 :** to be understood <cela s'entend : it goes without saying> **4 :** to be heard <cela s'entend à peine : it's barely audible> **5 ~ à :** to know about, to be good at

entendu, -due [ɑ̃tɑ̃dy] *adj* **1 :** agreed, understood <entendu! : OK!> **2 :** knowing, understanding <d'un air entendu : knowingly> **3 bien entendu :** of course

entente [ɑ̃tɑ̃t] *nf* **1 :** harmony **2 :** agreement, understanding **3 à double entente :** with a double meaning

entériner [ɑ̃terine] *vt* **:** to ratify, to confirm

enterrement [ɑ̃tɛrmɑ̃] *nm* **1** INHUMATION **:** burial, interment **2** FUNÉRAILLES **:** funeral **3 :** funeral procession **4 :** end, death <l'enterrement

de mon projet : the shelving of my project>
enterrer [ɑ̃tere] *vt* **1** : to bury, to inter **2** : to leave behind, to lay aside — **s'enterrer** *vr* : to bury oneself (away)
en–tête [ɑ̃tɛt] *nm, pl* **en–têtes 1** : letterhead **2** : heading
entêté[1], -tée [ɑ̃tete] *adj* : stubborn, obstinate
entêté[2], -tée *n* : stubborn person
entêtement [ɑ̃tɛtmɑ̃] *nm* : stubbornness, obstinacy
entêter [ɑ̃tete] *v* **s'entêter** *vr* : to persist
enthousiasmant, -mante [ɑ̃tuzjasmɑ̃, -mɑ̃t] *adj* : exciting
enthousiasme [ɑ̃tuzjasm] *nm* **1** : enthusiasm **2 avec ~** : enthusiastically
enthousiasmer [ɑ̃tuzjasme] *vt* : to fill with enthusiasm, to excite — **s'enthousiasmer** *vr* **~ pour** : to get enthusiastic about
enthousiaste[1] [ɑ̃tuzjast] *adj* : enthusiastic
enthousiaste[2] *nmf* : enthusiast
enticher [ɑ̃tiʃe] *v* **s'enticher** *vr* : to become infatuated <être entiché de : to be infatuated with>
entier[1], -tière [ɑ̃tje, -tjɛr] *adj* **1** : entire, whole <la ville entière : the whole town> <pendant des heures entières : for hours on end> **2** : complete, full <leur entière coopération : their full cooperation> **3** : intact, unaltered <rester entier : to remain unresolved> **4 tout entier** : completely, wholeheartedly <se donner tout entier : to devote oneself wholeheartedly>
entier[2] *nm* **1** : integer, whole number **2 en ~** : all of it, in its entirety
entièrement [ɑ̃tjɛrmɑ̃] *adv* : entirely, wholly, completely
entièreté [ɑ̃tjɛrte] *nf* : entirety, wholeness
entité [ɑ̃tite] *nf* : entity
entomologie [ɑ̃tɔmɔlɔʒi] *nf* : entomology — **entomologiste** [-lɔʒist] *nmf*
entomologique [ɑ̃tɔmɔlɔʒik] *adj* : entomological
entonner [ɑ̃tɔne] *vt* : to strike up (a song), to start singing
entonnoir [ɑ̃tɔnwar] *nm* **1** : funnel **2** : crater
entorse [ɑ̃tɔrs] *nf* **1** FOULURE : sprain <se faire une entorse à la cheville : to sprain one's ankle> **2** : infringement <faire une entorse à : to break (a law), to bend (a rule), to distort (the truth)>
entortiller [ɑ̃tɔrtije] *vt* **1** : to twist, to wind, to wrap (up) **2** : to tangle up, to complicate **3** *fam* : to hoodwink
entour [ɑ̃tur] *nm* **à l'entour** : in the vicinity, around
entourage [ɑ̃turaʒ] *nm* : circle, entourage
entouré, -rée [ɑ̃ture] *adj* **1** : popular **2 ~ de** : surrounded by
entourer [ɑ̃ture] *vt* **1** ENCERCLER : to surround, to encircle **2** : to rally around — **s'entourer** *vr* **~ de** : to surround oneself with <s'entourer de précautions : to take every possible precaution>
entourloupette [ɑ̃turlupɛt] *nf* : dirty trick
entournure [ɑ̃turnyr] *nf* **1** : armhole **2 être gêné aux entournures** : to be ill at ease, to be in awkward straits
entracte [ɑ̃trakt] *nm* : intermission
entraide [ɑ̃trɛd] *nf* : mutual aid
entraider [ɑ̃trede] *v* **s'entraider** *vr* : to help one another
entrailles [ɑ̃traj] *nfpl* **1** : entrails, guts **2** : womb **3** : depths, bowels, heart <les entrailles de la terre : the bowels of the earth> <sans entrailles : heartless>
entrain [ɑ̃trɛ̃] *nm* : liveliness, spirit
entraînant, -nante [ɑ̃trɛnɑ̃, -nɑ̃t] *adj* : lively
entraînement [ɑ̃trɛnmɑ̃] *nm* **1** : training <manquer d'entraînement : to be out of training> **2** : practice
entraîner [ɑ̃trene] *vt* **1** EMPORTER : to carry away <se laisser entraîner dans : to get carried away with> **2** PROVOQUER : to lead to, to provoke <cela pourrait entraîner des problèmes : that could lead to problems> **3** FORMER : to train, to coach — **s'entraîner** *vr* : to train, to practice
entraîneur, -neuse [ɑ̃trɛnœr, -nøz] *n* : trainer, coach
entrapercevoir *or* **entr'apercevoir** [ɑ̃trapɛrsəvwar] {26} *vt* : to catch a glimpse of
entrave [ɑ̃trav] *nf* **1** : hobble, shackle **2** : hindrance **3 sans entraves** : unfettered
entraver [ɑ̃trave] *vt* **1** : to shackle, to fetter **2** GÊNER : to hold up, to hinder
entre [ɑ̃tr] *prep* **1** : between <entre nous : between ourselves, between you and me> <entre les deux : in between> **2** PARMI : among <l'un d'entre eux : one of them> <entre autres : among others, among other things>
entrebâillement [ɑ̃trəbajmɑ̃] *nm* : gap, opening <par l'entrebâillement de la porte : through the half-open door>
entrebâiller [ɑ̃trəbaje] *vt* : to open halfway — **s'entrebâiller** *vr*
entrechoquer [ɑ̃trəʃɔke] *vt* : to bang together — **s'entrechoquer** *vr* **1** : to clink, to clatter, to chatter (of teeth) **2** : to clash (of ideas, etc.)
entrecôte [ɑ̃trəkot] *nf* : rib steak
entrecouper [ɑ̃trəkupe] *vt* **1** : to intersperse **2** : to interrupt — **s'entrecouper** *vr* : to intersect

entrecroiser [ɑ̃trəkrwaze] *vt* : to intertwine, to interlace — **s'entrecroiser** *vr* : to intersect

entre–deux [ɑ̃trədø] *nms & pl* : space, gap, interval

entrée [ɑ̃tre] *nf* **1** : entrance, entry **2** : admission, admittance <entrée libre : free admission> **3** PLACE : ticket, seat **4** : first course (of a meal) **5** VESTIBULE : hall, lobby **6** : entry (in a reference book), input (in a computer) **7** DÉBUT : beginning **8 d'~ (de jeu)** : from the start, right off

entrefaite [ɑ̃trəfɛt] *nf* **sur ces entrefaites** : at the moment

entrefilet [ɑ̃trəfilɛ] *nm* : paragraph, news item

entregent [ɑ̃trəʒɑ̃] *nm* : tact, diplomacy

entre–jambes *or* **entrejambes** [ɑ̃trəʒɑ̃b] *nms & pl* : crotch

entrelacer [ɑ̃trəlase] {6} *vt* : to intertwine, to interlace — **s'entrelacer** *vr*

entremêler [ɑ̃trəmele] *vt* : to mix together, to intermingle — **s'entremêler** *vr*

entremets [ɑ̃trəmɛ] *nms & pl* : dessert

entremetteur, -teuse [ɑ̃trəmɛtœr, -tøz] *n* **1** : go-between **2** : procurer, pimp

entremettre [ɑ̃trəmɛtr] {53} *v* **s'entremettre** *vr* : to intervene

entremise [ɑ̃trəmiz] *nf* : intervention <par l'entremise de son avocat : through his lawyer>

entreposage [ɑ̃trəpozaʒ] *nm* : storage

entreposer [ɑ̃trəpoze] *vt* **1** : to store **2** : to bond (in commerce)

entrepôt [ɑ̃trəpo] *nm* : warehouse

entreprenant, -nante [ɑ̃trəprənɑ̃, -nɑ̃t] *adj* **1** : enterprising **2** : forward, brash

entreprendre [ɑ̃trəprɑ̃dr] {70} *vt* : to undertake, to start, to embark on

entrepreneur, -neuse [ɑ̃trəprənœr, -nøz] *n* **1** : contractor **2** : entrepreneur **3 entrepreneur de pompes funèbres** : undertaker, funeral director

entreprise [ɑ̃trəpriz] *nf* **1** : enterprise, undertaking, venture **2** FIRME : business, firm **3** CONTRAT : contract

entrer [ɑ̃tre] *vt* **1** : to take in, to bring in <entrer les meubles : to bring in the furniture> **2** ENFONCER : to push in, to stick **3** : to enter (in a computer) — *vi* **1** : to enter, to go in, to come in <il est entré dans la pièce : he entered the room> <entrer à l'hôpital : to go into the hospital> <entrez! : come in!> **2** : to fit <cette clé n'entre pas dans la serrure : this key doesn't fit in the lock> **3** : to join, to go into <entrer dans l'armée : to join the army> **4 ~ en** : to begin <entrer en ébullition : to start boiling>

entresol [ɑ̃trəsɔl] *nm* : mezzanine

entre–temps [ɑ̃trətɑ̃] *adv* : meanwhile, in the meantime

entretenir [ɑ̃trətnir] {92} *vt* **1** MAINTENIR : to maintain, to keep up **2** : to keep alive, to cherish, to harbor <entretenir des doutes : to entertain doubts> **3** : to support, to look after **4** : to speak to, to address — **s'entretenir** *vr*

entretenu, -nue [ɑ̃trətny] *adj* : kept, maintained <mal entretenu : poorly maintained>

entretien [ɑ̃trətjɛ̃] *nm* **1** : maintenance, upkeep **2** : discussion, talk, interview <entretien d'embauche : job interview> **3** : support, (financial) maintenance

entrevoir [ɑ̃trəvwar] {99} *vt* **1** APERCEVOIR : to glimpse, to perceive **2** PRÉVOIR : to foresee, to anticipate

entrevue [ɑ̃trəvy] *nf* : meeting, interview

entrouvert, -verte [ɑ̃truvɛr, -vɛrt] *adj & adv* : half open, ajar

entrouvrir [ɑ̃truvrir] {83} *vt* : to open halfway — **s'entrouvrir** *vr* : to be half open

énumérer [enymere] {87} *vt* : to enumerate — **énumération** [-merasjɔ̃] *nf*

envahir [ɑ̃vair] *vt* **1** : to invade **2** : to overcome <envahi par le chagrin : overcome by grief>

envahissant, -sante [ɑ̃vaisɑ̃, -sɑ̃t] *adj* **1** : intrusive, invasive **2** : pervasive

envahissement [ɑ̃vaismɑ̃] *nm* : invasion

envahisseur, -seuse [ɑ̃vaisœr, -søz] *n* : invader

enveloppe [ɑ̃vlɔp] *nf* **1** : envelope **2** : cover, casing, shell, husk (of corn, etc.) **3** : exterior **4** : sum of money, budget

envelopper [ɑ̃vlɔpe] *vt* **1** : to envelop, to shroud **2** RECOUVRIR : to wrap up, to cover — **s'envelopper** *vr*

envenimer [ɑ̃vnime] *vt* **1** INFECTER : to infect **2** : to inflame, to aggravate

envergure [ɑ̃vɛrʒyr] *nf* **1** : wingspan **2** ÉTENDUE : breadth, scope, scale <de grande envergure : large-scale> **3** CALIBRE : caliber, stature

enverra [ɑ̃vera], *etc.* → **envoyer**

envers[1] [ɑ̃vɛr] *prep* **1** : toward, with regard to **2 envers et contre tout** : in spite of everything, against all opposition **3 être tout à l'envers** *Can* : to be very upset

envers[2] *nm* **1** REVERS : back, reverse **2 à l'envers** : inside out, upside down, backward

enviable [ɑ̃vjabl] *adj* : enviable

envie [ɑ̃vi] *nf* **1** JALOUSIE : envy, jealousy **2** DÉSIR : desire, wish, longing <avoir envie de : to feel like, to want> **3** : birthmark **4** : hangnail

envier [ɑ̃vje] {96} *vt* : to envy

envieux, -vieuse [ɑ̃vjø, -vjøz] *adj* : envious, jealous — **envieusement** [ɑ̃vjøzmɑ̃] *adv*

environ [ɑ̃virɔ̃] *adv* : about, around, approximately <viens dans environ une heure : come in an hour or so>

environnant, -nante [ɑ̃virɔnɑ̃, -nɑ̃t] *adj* : surrounding

environnement [ɑ̃virɔnmɑ̃] *nm* : environment

environnemental, -tale [ɑ̃virɔnmɑ̃tal] *adj, pl* **-taux** [-to] : environmental

environnementaliste [ɑ̃virɔnmɑ̃talist] *nmf* : environmentalist

environner [ɑ̃virɔne] *vt* : to surround

environs [ɑ̃virɔ̃] *nmpl* **1** : surroundings, vicinity **2 aux environs de** : around <aux environs de Pâques : around Easter>

envisager [ɑ̃vizaʒe] {17} *vt* **1** : to envisage, to contemplate **2 envisager de faire** : to plan to do, to consider doing

envoi [ɑ̃vwa] *nm* **1** : sending, dispatching <envoi contre remboursement : cash on delivery> **2** COLIS : parcel, package **3 coup d'envoi** : kickoff

envoie [ɑ̃vwa], *etc.* → **envoyer**

envol [ɑ̃vɔl] *nm* : takeoff

envolée [ɑ̃vɔle] *nf* **1** : takeoff, flight **2** *or* **envolée de l'imagination** : flight of fancy, inspired discourse **3** : rise, surge (in value, etc.)

envoler [ɑ̃vɔle] *v* **s'envoler** *vr* **1** : to take off **2** : to fly away **3** : to blow away **4** DISPARAÎTRE : to disappear, to vanish **5** : to surge (of prices, values, etc.)

envoûtement [ɑ̃vutmɑ̃] *nm* : spell, bewitchment

envoûter [ɑ̃vute] *vt* : to bewitch, to cast a spell over

envoyé, -voyée [ɑ̃vwaje] *n* **1** : messenger **2** : envoy **3 envoyé spécial** : special (press) correspondent

envoyer [ɑ̃vwaje] {36} *vt* **1** : to send, to send out <envoyer par la poste : to mail> **2** LANCER : to throw, to hurl **3 envoyer promener** *fam* : to send packing — **s'envoyer** *vr* **1** : to send to each other, to exchange **2** *fam* : to guzzle, to wolf down

envoyeur, -voyeuse [ɑ̃vwajœr, -vwajøz] *n* : sender

enzyme [ɑ̃zim] *nf* : enzyme

épagneul, -gneule [epaɲœl] *n* : spaniel

épais, épaisse [epɛ, -pɛs] *adj* : thick

épaisseur [epɛsœr] *nf* **1** : thickness **2** : layer

épaissir [epesir] *v* : to thicken — **s'épaissir** *vr* **1** : to thicken (up) **2** : to deepen <le mystère s'est épaissi : the mystery deepened>

épaississant [epesisɑ̃] *nm* : thickener

épaississement [epesismɑ̃] *nm* : thickening

épanchement [epɑ̃ʃmɑ̃] *nm* **1** : effusion, outpouring **2 épanchement de synovie** : water on the knee

épancher [epɑ̃ʃe] *vt* : to give vent to, to pour out (one's feelings, etc.) — **s'épancher** *vr* : to pour one's heart out

épandage [epɑ̃daʒ] *nm* : spreading

épandre [epɑ̃dr] {63} *vt* : to spread

épanoui, -nouie [epanwi] *adj* **1** : in full bloom **2** : radiant **3** : fully developed (of the body, etc.)

épanouir [epanwir] *vt* **1** : to make bloom **2** : to light up, to brighten — **s'épanouir** *vr* **1** : to bloom **2** : to light up **3** : to develop, to blossom, to flourish

épanouissement [epanwismɑ̃] *nm* **1** : blooming, flowering **2** : brightening, lighting up

épargnant, -gnante [eparɲɑ̃, -ɲɑ̃t] *n* : saver, investor

épargne [eparɲ] *nf* **1** ÉCONOMIE : saving, economy **2** : savings *pl*

épargner [eparɲe] *vt* **1** ÉCONOMISER : to save **2** : to spare — **s'épargner** *vr* : to spare oneself (trouble, etc.)

éparpillement [eparpijmɑ̃] *nm* : scattering, dispersal

éparpiller [eparpije] *vt* **1** : to scatter, to disperse **2** : to dissipate (efforts, etc.) — **s'éparpiller** *vr*

épars, éparse [epar, -pars] *adj* : scattered

épatant, -tante [epatɑ̃, -tɑ̃t] *adj fam* : great, fantastic

épater [epate] *vt fam* **1** ÉTONNER : to amaze **2** IMPRESSIONNER : to impress — **s'épater** *vr*

épaule [epol] *nf* : shoulder

épaulement [epolmɑ̃] *nm* **1** : retaining wall **2** : escarpment

épauler [epole] *vt* **1** AIDER : to back, to support **2** : to raise (a firearm), to take aim with — *vi* : to take aim

épaulette [epolɛt] *nf* **1** : epaulet **2** BRETELLE : shoulder strap **3** : shoulder pad

épave [epav] *nf* **1** : wreck (of a ship) **2 épave flottante** : flotsam

épée [epe] *nf* **1** : sword **2 coup d'épée dans l'eau** : wasted effort

épeler [eple] {8} *vt* : to spell — **s'épeler** *vr*

épelle [epɛl], **épellera** [epɛlra], *etc.* → **épeler**

épépiner [epepine] *vt* : to seed, to remove the seeds from

éperdu, -due [epɛrdy] *adj* **1** PASSIONNÉ : passionate, intense **2** : frantic, overwhelmed <éperdu de peur : overcome with fear>

éperdument [epɛrdymɑ̃] *adv* **1** : frantically, desperately <éperdument amoureux : madly in love> **2 je m'en moque éperdument** : I couldn't care less

éperlan [epɛrlɑ̃] *nm* : smelt

éperon [eprɔ̃] *nm* : spur

éperonner [eprɔne] *vt* : to spur (on)

épeurant, -rante [epørɑ̃, -rɑ̃t] *adj Can* : scary, frightening

éphémère[1] [efemɛr] *adj* : ephemeral, fleeting

éphémère[2] *nm* : mayfly

épi [epi] *nm* **1** : ear, cob <épi de maïs : corncob> **2** : tuft (of hair) **3 se garer en épi** : to park at an angle
épice [epis] *nf* : spice
épicé, -cée [epise] *adj* : highly spiced, spicy
épicéa [episea] *nm France* : spruce
épicentre [episɑ̃tr] *nm* : epicenter
épicer [epise] {6} *vt* : to spice
épicerie [episri] *nf* **1** : grocery store **2** : groceries *pl*
épicier, -cière [episje, -sjɛr] *n* : grocer
épicurien[1]**, -rienne** [epikyrjɛ̃, -rjɛn] *adj* : epicurean
épicurien[2]**, -rienne** *n* : epicure
épidémie [epidemi] *nf* : epidemic — **épidémique** [-demik] *adj*
épiderme [epidɛrm] *nm* : epidermis
épidermique [epidɛrmik] *adj* **1** : epidermal, skin **2 réaction épidermique** : automatic reaction, gut feeling
épier [epje] {96} *vt* **1** OBSERVER : to spy on, to watch closely **2** ATTENDRE : to watch out for
epigramme [epigram] *nf* : epigram
épilepsie [epilɛpsi] *nf* : epilepsy
épileptique [epilɛptik] *adj & nmf* : epileptic
épiler [epile] *vt* : to remove hair from, to pluck
épilogue [epilɔg] *nm* **1** : epilogue **2** : conclusion, outcome
épiloguer [epilɔge] *vt* **~ sur** : to hold forth on, to go on and on about
épinard [epinar] *nm* **1** : spinach (plant) **2 épinards** *nmpl* : spinach (for eating)
épine [epin] *nf* **1** : thorn, prickle **2 épine dorsale** : spine, backbone
épinette [epinɛt] *nf* **1** : spinet **2** *Can* : spruce
épineux, -neuse [epinø, -nøz] *adj* : thorny, prickly
épingle [epɛ̃gl] *nf* **1** : pin <épingle de sûreté : safety pin> <épingle à linge : clothespin> <épingle à cheveux : hairpin> **2 tiré à quatre épingles** : impeccably dressed **3 tirer son épingle du jeu** : to extricate oneself, to pull out in time
épingler [epɛ̃gle] *vt* **1** : to pin **2** *fam* : to nab
épinglette [epɛ̃glɛt] *nf Can* **1** : brooch **2** : pin, button, badge
épinière [epinjɛr] *adj* → **moelle**
épique [epik] *adj* : epic
episcopal, -pale [episkɔpal] *adj, mpl* **-paux** [-po] : episcopal
épisode [epizɔd] *nm* : episode
épisodique [epizɔdik] *adj* : episodic — **épisodiquement** [-dikmɑ̃] *adv*
épisser [epise] *vt* : to splice
épissure [episyr] *nf* : splice
épistolaire [epistɔlɛr] *adj* : epistolary <avoir des relations épistolaires avec : to correspond with>
épitaphe [epitaf] *nf* : epitaph
épithète [epitɛt] *nf* : epithet
épître [epitr] *nf* : epistle
éploré, -rée [eplɔre] *adj* : tearful, in tears
éplucher [eplyʃe] *vt* **1** PELER : to peel **2** DÉCORTIQUER : to analyze, to scrutinize, to plow through (a text, etc.)
épluchure [eplyʃyr] *nf* : peel, peelings (of potatoes, etc.)
épointer [epwɛ̃te] *vt* : to blunt
éponge [epɔ̃ʒ] *nf* **1** : sponge **2 jeter l'éponge** : to throw in the towel **3 passer l'éponge** : to forget about it, to let bygones be bygones
éponger [epɔ̃ʒe] {17} *vt* **1** : to sponge up, to mop up **2** : to soak up, to absorb **3 éponger ses dettes** : to pay off one's debts — **s'éponger** *vr* **s'éponger le front** : to mop one's brow
épopée [epɔpe] *nf* : epic
époque [epɔk] *nf* **1** : epoch, era, age **2** : time, period <à cette époque : at that time>
épouse [epuz] *nf* → **époux**
épouser [epuze] *vt* **1** : to marry, to wed **2** : to espouse (an idea, etc.) **3** MOULER : to take the shape of, to fit closely
époussetage [epustaʒ] *nm* : dusting
épousseter [epuste] {8} *vt* : to dust
époustouflant, -flante [epustuflɑ̃, -flɑ̃t] *adj fam* : amazing, mind-boggling
époustoufler [epustufle] *vt* : to amaze, to flabbergast
épouvantable [epuvɑ̃tabl] *adj* : dreadful, horrible — **épouvantablement** [-tabləmɑ̃] *adv*
épouvantail [epuvɑ̃taj] *nm* **1** : scarecrow **2** : bogey(man)
épouvante [epuvɑ̃t] *nf* : terror, horror <roman d'épouvante : horror story>
épouvanter [epuvɑ̃te] *vt* TERRIFIER : to terrify, to fill with dread — **s'épouvanter** *vr* : to get frightened
époux, épouse [epu, epuz] *n* : spouse, husband *m*, wife *f*
éprendre [eprɑ̃dr] {70} *v* **s'éprendre** *vr* **~ de** : to fall in love with, to be taken with
épreuve [eprœv] *nf* **1** : test <mettre à l'épreuve : to put to the test> <épreuve de force : test of strength, showdown> **2** : ordeal, trial **3** : examination, test <épreuve écrite : written exam> **4** : event (in sports) **5** : proof, print (in printing, photography, etc.) **6 à l'épreuve de** : proof against
épris, éprise [epri, epriz] *adj* **~ de** : in love with
éprouvant, -vante [epruvɑ̃, -vɑ̃t] *adj* : trying, difficult to endure
éprouver [epruve] *vt* **1** TESTER : to test, to try (out) **2** RESSENTIR : to feel, to experience **3** : to suffer, to endure (a loss) **4** : to distress **5** : to try, to make suffer
éprouvette [epruvɛt] *nf* : test tube

épuisant, -sante [epɥizɑ̃, -zɑ̃t] *adj* : exhausting
épuisé, -sée [epɥize] *adj* **1** : exhausted **2** : out of stock
épuisement [epɥizmɑ̃] *nm* **1** : exhaustion, fatigue **2** : depletion (of stock, etc.)
épuiser [epɥize] *vt* **1** FATIGUER : to tire out, to wear out, to fatigue **2** : to exhaust, to use up — **s'épuiser** *vr*
épuration [epyrasjɔ̃] *nf* **1** : purification (of substances) **2** : refinement (of style, morals, etc.) **3** : purge (in politics)
épurer [epyre] *vt* **1** : to purify, to filter **2** : to refine (language, etc.) **3** : to purge (in politics)
équanimité [ekwanimite] *nf* : equanimity
équarrir [ekarir] *vt* **1** : to quarter (an animal) **2** : to square off
équateur [ekwatœr] *nm* : equator
équation [ekwasjɔ̃] *nf* : equation
équatorial, -riale [ekwatɔrjal] *adj, mpl* **-riaux** [-rjo] : equatorial
équatorien, -rienne [ekwatɔrjɛ̃, -rjɛn] *adj* : Ecuadoran, Ecuadorean, Ecuadorian
Équatorien, -rienne *n* : Ecuadoran, Ecuadorean, Ecuadorian
équerre [ekɛr] *nf* **1** : square <équerre en T : T square> **2 d'～** : square, straight **3 en ～** : at right angles **4 mettre d'équerre** : to square, to true
équestre [ekɛstr] *adj* : equestrian
équilatéral, -rale [ekɥilateral] *adj, mpl* **-raux** [-ro] : equilateral
équilibre [ekilibr] *nm* : equilibrium, balance <en équilibre : balanced, stable> <perdre l'équilibre : to lose one's balance> <équilibre sur les mains : handstand>
équilibré, -brée [ekilibre] *adj* : well-balanced, levelheaded
équilibrer [ekilibre] *vt* : to balance — **s'équilibrer** *vr*
équilibriste [ekilibrist] *nmf* **1** ACROBATE : acrobat **2** FUNAMBULE : tightrope walker
équinoxe [ekinɔks] *nm* : equinox
équipage [ekipaʒ] *nm* : crew
équipe [ekip] *nf* **1** : team <esprit d'équipe : team spirit> <faire équipe avec : to team up with> **2** : crew, gang, squad <équipe de nuit : night crew, night shift> <équipe de secours : rescue squad>
équipement [ekipmɑ̃] *nm* **1** MATÉRIEL : equipment **2 équipements** *nmpl* : facilities, installations <équipements sportifs : sports facilities>
équipée [ekipe] *nf* **1** : escapade **2** : outing, jaunt
équiper [ekipe] *vt* : to equip, to outfit — **s'équiper** *vr*
équipier, -pière [ekipje, -pjɛr] *n* : team member
équitable [ekitabl] *adj* : fair, equitable — **équitablement** [-tabləmɑ̃] *adv*
équitation [ekitasjɔ̃] *nf* : horseback riding, horsemanship
équité [ekite] *nf* : equity
équivalence [ekivalɑ̃s] *nf* : equivalence
équivalent[1], -lente [ekivalɑ̃, -lɑ̃t] *adj* : equivalent
équivalent[2] *nm* : equivalent
équivaloir [ekivalwar] {95} *vi* **～ à** : to be equivalent to, to be tantamount to
équivoque[1] [ekivɔk] *adj* **1** AMBIGU : equivocal, ambiguous **2** DOUTEUX : questionable, doubtful
équivoque[2] *nf* **1** AMBIGUÏTÉ : ambiguity, uncertainty **2** MALENTENDU : misunderstanding **3 sans ～** : unequivocal, unequivocally
érable [erabl] *nm* : maple <sirop d'érable : maple syrup>
éradication [eradikasjɔ̃] *nf* : eradication
éradiquer [eradike] *vt* : to eradicate
érafler [erafle] *vt* **1** : to graze, to scratch (the skin) **2** : to scrape (a surface)
éraflure [eraflyr] *nf* : scratch, scrape
éraillé, -lée [eraje] *adj* **1** : hoarse, rasping **2** : frayed **3 avoir les yeux éraillés** : to have bloodshot eyes
ère [ɛr] *nf* : era
érection [erɛksjɔ̃] *nf* : erection
éreintant, -tante [erɛ̃tɑ̃, -tɑ̃t] *adj* : backbreaking, exhausting
éreinter [erɛ̃te] *vt* **1** ÉPUISER : to exhaust, to wear out **2** CRITIQUER : to criticize, to pan — **s'éreinter** *vr* : to wear oneself out
ergonomie [ɛrgɔnɔmi] *nf* : ergonomics
ergonomique [ɛrgɔnɔmik] *adj* : ergonomic
ergot [ɛrgo] *nm* **1** : spur (of a rooster) **2 se dresser sur ses ergots** : to get up on one's high horse
ergoter [ɛrgɔte] *vi* : to quibble
ergoteur, -teuse [ɛrgɔtœr, -tøz] *adj* : quibbling, argumentative
ergothérapeute [ɛrgɔterapøt] *nmf* : occupational therapist
ergothérapie [ɛrgɔterapi] *nf* : occupational therapy
ériger [eriʒe] {17} *vt* **1** : to erect **2** : to establish, to set up — **s'ériger** *vr* **～ en** : to set oneself up as
ermitage [ɛrmitaʒ] *nm* **1** : hermitage **2** : retreat
ermite [ɛrmit] *nm* : hermit
éroder [erɔde] *vt* : to erode, to eat away — **s'éroder** *vr*
érogène [erɔʒɛn] *adj* : erogenous
érosion [erozjɔ̃] *nf* : erosion
érotique [erɔtik] *adj* : erotic — **érotiquement** [-tikmɑ̃] *adv*
érotisme [erɔtism] *nm* : eroticism
errant, -rante [ɛrɑ̃, -rɑ̃t] *adj* : wandering <un chien errant : a stray dog>
errata [erata] *nms & pl* : errata

erratique [eratik] *adj* : erratic (in geology or medicine)

errements [ɛrmɑ̃] *nmpl* : transgressions, bad habits

errer [ɛre] *vi* **1** : to wander, to stray, to roam **2** : to err

erreur [ɛrœr] *nf* : error, mistake <être dans l'erreur : to be wrong, to be mistaken> <par erreur : by mistake>

erroné, -née [ɛrɔne] *adj* : erroneous, wrong — **erronément** [-nemɑ̃] *adv*

éructer [erykte] *vi* : to belch

érudit[1], -dite [erydi, -dit] *adj* : erudite, learned

érudit[2], -dite *n* : scholar

érudition [erydisjɔ̃] *nf* : erudition

éruption [erypsjɔ̃] *nf* **1** : eruption (of a volcano) **2** : eruption, rash **3** : outburst <une éruption de colère : a fit of anger>

erythréen, -thréenne [eritreɛ̃, -treɛn] *adj* : Eritrean

Erythréen, -thréenne *n* : Eritrean

ès [ɛs] *prep* **docteur ès lettres** : doctor of letters, Ph.D.

esbroufe [ɛzbruf] *nf fam* : showing off, swagger

escabeau [ɛskabo] *nm, pl* **-beaux 1** TABOURET : stool **2** : stepladder

escadre [ɛskadr] *nf* : squadron

escadrille [ɛskadrij] *nf* : squadron

escadron [ɛskadrɔ̃] *nm* **1** : squad, squadron <escadron de la mort : death squad> **2** : crowd, bunch

escalade [ɛskalad] *nf* **1** : climbing, scaling **2** : escalation

escalader [ɛskalade] *vt* : to climb, to scale

escalator [ɛskalatɔr] *nm* : escalator

escale [ɛskal] *nf* **1** : port of call **2** : stopover

escalier [ɛskalje] *nm* : stairs, steps <escalier en colimaçon : spiral staircase> <escalier mécanique : escalator> <escalier de secours : fire escape>

escalope [ɛskalɔp] *nf* : cutlet <escalope de veau : veal cutlet>

escamotable [ɛskamɔtabl] *adj* **1** : retractable **2** : foldaway, collapsible

escamoter [ɛskamɔte] *vt* **1** : to cause to disappear **2** : to retract, to fold away **3** VOLER : to snatch, to filch **4** SAUTER : to leave out, to skip **5** ÉLUDER : to dodge, to evade

escampette [ɛskɑ̃pɛt] *nf* **prendre la poudre d'escampette** *fam* : to take to one's heels

escapade [ɛskapad] *nf* : escapade, jaunt <faire une escapade : to run away>

escarbille [ɛskarbij] *nf* : cinder

escargot [ɛskargo] *nm* : snail

escarmouche [ɛskarmuʃ] *nf* : skirmish

escarpé, -pée [ɛskarpe] *adj* : steep

escarpement [ɛskarpəmɑ̃] *nm* : escarpment, steep slope

escarpin [ɛskarpɛ̃] *nm* : pump (shoe)

escient [ɛsjɑ̃] *nm* **1 à bon escient** : judiciously, advisedly **2 à mauvais escient** : injudiciously, unwisely

esclaffer [ɛsklafe] *v* **s'esclaffer** *vr* : to burst out laughing, to guffaw

esclandre [ɛsklɑ̃dr] *nm* : scene, fracas

esclavage [ɛsklavaʒ] *nm* : slavery

esclave [ɛsklav] *adj & nmf* : slave

escompte [ɛskɔ̃t] *nm* : discount

escompter [ɛskɔ̃te] *vt* **1** : to discount **2** ANTICIPER : to expect, to anticipate

escopette [ɛskɔpɛt] *nf* : blunderbuss

escorte [ɛskɔrt] *nf* : escort

escorter [ɛskɔrte] *vt* : to escort

escorteur [ɛskɔrtœr] *nm* : escort ship

escouade [ɛskwad] *nf* **1** ESCADRON : squad **2** GROUPE : gang, group

escrime [ɛskrim] *nf* : fencing <faire de l'escrime : to fence>

escrimer [ɛskrime] *v* **s'escrimer** *vr* **1 s'escrimer à faire** : to wear oneself out doing **2 ~ sur** : to struggle with, to work away at

escrimeur, -meuse [ɛskrimœr, -møz] *n* : fencer

escroc [ɛskro] *nm* : swindler, crook

escroquer [ɛskrɔke] *vt* : to swindle, to defraud, to gyp

escroquerie [ɛskrɔkri] *nf* : swindle, fraud, gyp

eskimo [ɛskimo] → **esquimau**

ésotérique [ezɔterik] *adj* : esoteric

espace[1] [ɛspas] *nm* **1** : space, outer space **2** PLACE : area, room, space **3** : interval, gap <laissez un espace entre les deux : leave a space between the two> <en l'espace de dix minutes : within the space of ten minutes> **4 espaces verts** : parks, gardens

espace[2] *nf* : space (in printing)

espacer [ɛspase] {6} *vt* : to space (out)

espadon [ɛspadɔ̃] *nm* : swordfish

espadrille [ɛspadrij] *nf* **1** : espadrille **2 espadrilles** *nfpl Can* : sneakers

espagnol[1], -gnole [ɛspaɲɔl] *adj* : Spanish

espagnol[2] *nm* : Spanish (language)

Espagnol, -gnole *n* **1** : Spaniard **2 les Espagnols** : the Spanish

espar [ɛspar] *nm* : spar

espèce [ɛspɛs] *nf* **1** : species **2** SORTE : sort, kind <de toute espèce : of every kind> <espèce d'idiot! : you idiot!> **3 espèces** *nfpl* : cash <payer en espèces : to pay in cash>

espérance [ɛsperɑ̃s] *nf* **1** : hope, expectation **2** : expectancy <espérance de vie : life expectancy>

espérer [ɛspere] {87} *vt* **1** : to hope, to hope for <je l'espère bien : I hope so> **2** : to expect — *vi* **1** : to hope **2 ~ en** : to trust in

esperluette [ɛspɛrlɥɛt] *nf* : ampersand

espiègle [ɛspjɛgl] *adj* : mischievous, impish

espièglerie [ɛspjɛgləri] *nf* **1** : mischievousness, impishness **2** : prank, mischief

espion, -pionne [ɛspjɔ̃, -pjɔn] *n* : spy
espionnage [ɛspjɔnaʒ] *nm* : espionage
espionner [ɛspjɔne] *vt* : to spy on
espoir [ɛspwar] *nm* : hope <avoir bon espoir : to be confident, to have high hopes> <un cas sans espoir : a hopeless case>
esprit [ɛspri] *nm* **1** CERVEAU : mind, intellect <venir à l'esprit : to come to mind> **2** CARACTÈRE : character, mentality <avoir l'esprit étroit : to be narrow-minded> **3** HUMOUR : wit <avoir de l'esprit : to be witty> **4** HUMEUR : mood, disposition **5** PERSONNE : person **6** FANTÔME : spirit, ghost <esprit frappeur : poltergeist>
esquif [ɛskif] *nm* : skiff
esquimau[1], -maude [ɛskimo, -mod] *adj, mpl* **-maux** [-mo] : Eskimo
esquimau[2] *nm* : Eskimo (language)
Esquimau, -maude *n, mpl* **-maux** : Eskimo
esquinter [ɛskɛ̃te] *vt fam* **1** : to ruin, to mess up **2** : to pan — **s'esquinter** *vr* **s'esquinter à faire qqch** : to knock oneself out doing sth
esquisse [ɛskis] *nf* : sketch, outline, summary
esquisser [ɛskise] *vt* **1** : to sketch, to outline **2** : to give a hint of <esquisser un sourire : to give a slight smile>
esquive [ɛskiv] *nf* **1** : dodge (in sports) **2** : evasion, sidestepping
esquiver [ɛskive] *vt* : to avoid, to dodge, to evade — **s'esquiver** *vr* : to slip away
essai [esɛ] *nm* **1** TENTATIVE : attempt, try **2** : trial, test <essai nucléaire : nuclear test> <mettre à l'essai : to put to the test> **3** : essay
essaie [esɛ], **essaiera** [esɛra], *etc.* → **essayer**
essaim [esɛ̃] *nm* : swarm
essaimer [eseme] *vt* **1** : to swarm **2** : to spread (out), to expand
essayage [esɛjaʒ] *nm* : fitting, trying on <cabine d'essayage : fitting room>
essayer [eseje] {11} *vt* **1** TENTER : to try, to attempt **2** : to test, to try out **3** : to try on **4** : to assay (metals) — *vi* : to try — **s'essayer** *vr* **∼ à** : to try one's hand at
essayeur, essayeuse [esɛjœr, esɛjøz] *n* : tester, fitter
essayiste [esejist] *nmf* : essayist
essence [ɛsɑ̃s] *nf* **1** : gasoline <essence sans plomb : unleaded gas> **2** : essence <par essence : in essence, essentially>
essentiel[1], -tielle [esɑ̃sjɛl] *adj* : essential — **essentiellement** [-sjɛlmɑ̃] *adv*
essentiel[2] *nm* **1** : main part, main thing, gist **2** : essentials *pl,* basics *pl*
esseulé, -lée [esœle] *adj* : forlorn
essieu [esjø] *nm, pl* **essieux** : axle
essor [esɔr] *nm* **1** : flight (of a bird) <prendre son essor : to take flight, to soar> **2** : expansion, growth, development <prendre son essor : to grow, to expand rapidly> <être en plein essor : to be booming>
essorer [esɔre] *vt* : to wring out, to spin dry
essoreuse [ɛsɔrøz] *nf* : wringer
essoufflement [esufləmɑ̃] *nm* : breathlessness
essouffler [esufle] *vt* : to make breathless, to wind — **s'essouffler** *vr* **1** : to get out of breath **2** : to become exhausted, to run out of steam
essuie [esɥi], **essuiera** [esɥira], *etc.* → **essuyer**
essuie–glace [esɥiglas] *nm, pl* **essuie–glaces** : windshield wiper
essuie–mains [esɥimɛ̃] *nms & pl* : hand towel
essuie–tout [esɥitu] *nms & pl* : paper towel
essuyer [esɥije] {58} *vt* **1** : to wipe, to dry **2** SUBIR : to suffer, to endure — **s'essuyer** *vr* : to dry oneself
est[1] [ɛ], *etc.* → **être**
est[2] [ɛst] *adj* : east, eastern
est[3] *nm* **1** : east <le vent d'est : the east wind> <vers l'est : eastward> **2 l'Est** : the East
estafilade [ɛstafilad] *nf* : gash, slash
estampe [ɛstɑ̃p] *nf* : engraving, print
estamper [ɛstɑ̃pe] *vt* **1** : to stamp **2** *fam* : to swindle, to rip off
estampille [ɛstɑ̃pij] *nf* **1** : stamp (on a document) **2** : trademark, label (on merchandise)
est–ce que [ɛskə] *adv* (*used to introduce questions*) <est-ce qu'elle aime le café? : does she like coffee?> <est-ce qu'il y était? : was he there?> <pourquoi est-ce que tu pleures? : why are you crying?>
ester [ɛste] *nm* : ester
esthète [ɛstɛt] *nmf* : aesthete
esthéticien, -cienne [ɛstetisjɛ̃, -sjɛn] *n* : beautician
esthétique[1] [ɛstetik] *adj* **1** : aesthetic **2** : aesthetically pleasing, attractive — **esthétiquement** [-tikmɑ̃] *adv*
esthétique[2] *nf* : aesthetics
estimable [ɛstimabl] *adj* **1** : estimable, respected **2** : decent, sound
estimation [ɛstimasjɔ̃] *nf* **1** ÉVALUATION : valuation, appraisal **2** : estimate, reckoning
estime [ɛstim] *nf* : esteem, respect
estimer [ɛstime] *vt* **1** ÉVALUER : to assess, to appraise **2** : to estimate, to reckon **3** RESPECTER : to esteem, to respect **4 estimer que** : to consider that, to judge that — **s'estimer** *vr* SE JUGER : to consider oneself <je m'estime heureux : I consider myself fortunate>
estival, -vale [ɛstival] *adj, mpl* **-vaux** [-vo] : summer <la saison estivale : the summer season>
estivant, -vante [ɛstivɑ̃, -vɑ̃t] *n* : summer vacationer

estocade [ɛstɔkad] *nf* : deathblow, final thrust

estomac [ɛstɔma] *nm* **1** : stomach <mal à l'estomac : stomachache> **2 avoir de l'estomac** *fam* : to have guts **3 avoir l'estomac dans les talons** *fam* : to be famished

estomaqué, -quée [ɛstɔmake] *adj fam* : astounded, flabbergasted

estomper [ɛstɔ̃pe] *vt* : to blur, to dim — **s'estomper** *vr* : to fade away, to diminish

estonien[1], -nienne [ɛstɔnjɛ̃, -njɛn] *adj* : Estonian

estonien[2] *nm* : Estonian (language)

Estonien, -nienne *n* : Estonian

estrade [ɛstrad] *nf* : platform, dais

estragon [ɛstragɔ̃] *nm* : tarragon

estrogène [ɛstrɔʒɛn] *nm* : estrogen

estropié[1], -piée [ɛstrɔpje] *adj* : crippled, maimed

estropié[2], -piée *n* : cripple, disabled person

estropier [ɛstrɔpje] {96} *vt* **1** : to cripple, to maim **2** : to mispronounce, to misspell, to misquote

estuaire [ɛstɥɛr] *nm* : estuary

estudiantin, -tine [ɛstydjɑ̃tɛ̃, -tin] *adj* : student

esturgeon [ɛstyrʒɔ̃] *nm* : sturgeon

et [e] *conj* **1** : and <mon père et moi : my father and me> <et moi? : what about me?> **2 et . . . et . . .** : both . . . and . . . **3** (*used in numbers and fractions*) <vingt et un : twenty-one> <trois heures et demie : three-thirty, half past three>

étable [etabl] *nf* : cowshed

établi[1], -blie [etabli] *adj* : established

établi[2] *nm* : workbench

établir [etablir] *vt* **1** INSTITUER : to set up, to establish **2** : to draw up, to make out **3** PROUVER : to prove (guilt, innocence) **4** : to set (a record) — **s'établir** *vr* **1** : to get established, to set oneself up **2** : to settle

établissement [etablismɑ̃] *nm* **1** : establishment, setting up **2** : institution, establishment <établissement industriel : factory> <établissement scolaire : school>

étage [etaʒ] *nm* **1** : story, floor **2** : stage (of a rocket) **3** : tier, level

étager [etaʒe] {17} *vt* **1** : to lay out in tiers **2** : to stagger, to alternate — **s'étager** *vr*

étagère [etaʒɛr] *nf* **1** : shelf **2** : shelves *pl*, shelving unit

étai [etɛ] *nm* : prop, support

étain [etɛ̃] *nm* **1** : tin **2** : pewter

était [etɛ], *etc.* → **être**

étal [etal] *nm, pl* **étals** [etal] *or* **étaux** [eto] **1** ÉVENTAIRE : stall (in a market) **2** : butcher's block

étalage [etalaʒ] *nm* **1** : display <faire étalage de : to show off, to flaunt> **2** DEVANTURE : window display

étaler [etale] *vt* **1** : to lay out, to spread out, to display **2** : to spread (on), to apply **3** ÉCHELONNER : to space out, to stagger **4** : to show off, to flaunt — **s'étaler** *vr* **1** : to spread <cette peinture s'étale mal : this paint doesn't spread well> **2** : to be spread, to extend (in time) **3** *fam* : to sprawl **4** *fam* : to fall on one's face

étalon [etalɔ̃] *nm* **1** : stallion **2** MODÈLE : standard, yardstick <l'étalon-or : the gold standard>

étalonner [etalɔne] *vt* **1** : to standardize **2** : to calibrate

étamine [etamin] *nf* **1** : stamen **2** : cheesecloth, muslin, bunting

étanche [etɑ̃ʃ] *adj* **1** : watertight, waterproof **2** *or* **étanche à l'air** : airtight

étancher [etɑ̃ʃe] *vt* **1** : to stem, to staunch **2** : to seal, to make watertight **3 étancher sa soif** : to quench one's thirst

étang [etɑ̃] *nm* : pond

étape [etap] *nf* **1** HALTE : stop, halt **2** : stage, leg (of a journey) **3** PHASE : step, stage, phase <les étapes de la vie : the stages of life>

état [eta] *nm* **1** : state, condition <en bon état : in good condition> <hors d'état : out of order> <état d'esprit : state of mind> <en état d'urgence : in a state of emergency> **2** : statement, inventory <états de comptes : financial statements> <faire état de : to give an account of> **3** : occupation, lot in life <de son état : by profession> **4 état civil** : civil status <bureau d'état civil : registry office>

État *nm* **1** : state, State <homme d'État : statesman> **2** : central government <monopole d'État : state monopoly>

étatique [etatik] *adj* : state, state-controlled

étatisation [etatizasjɔ̃] *nf* : state control, nationalization

étatiser [etatize] *vt* : to bring under state control

étatisme [etatism] *nm* : state control

état–major [etamaʒɔr] *nm, pl* **états–majors 1** : general staff (in the military) **2** : senior staff, management (in business, politics, etc.)

étau [eto] *nm, pl* **étaux** : vise

étayer [eteje] {11} *vt* **1** SOUTENIR : to prop up, to shore up **2** APPUYER : to support, to back up

et cætera *or* **et cetera** [ɛtsetera] : et cetera, and so on

été [ete] *nm* : summer

éteignait [etɛɲɛ], **éteignions** [etɛɲjɔ̃], *etc.* → **éteindre**

éteigne [etɛɲ], *etc.* → **éteindre**

éteindre [etɛ̃dr] {37} *vt* **1** : to extinguish, to put out **2** : to turn off, to switch off — **s'éteindre** *vr* **1** : to go out, to die out **2** S'AFFAIBLIR : to subside, to fade **3** MOURIR : to die

étendard [etɑ̃dar] *nm* : standard, flag
étendre [etɑ̃dr] {63} *vt* **1** ÉTALER : to spread, to spread out **2** PENDRE : to hang up (laundry, etc.) **3** ALLONGER : to stretch (out) **4** ÉLARGIR : to extend, to expand, to widen **5** DILUER : to dilute, to thin — **s'étendre** *vr* **1** : to stretch **2** : to lie down **3** : to spread **4 ~ sur** : to elaborate on
étendu, -due [etɑ̃dy] *adj* **1** VASTE : extensive, wide **2** ALLONGÉ : outstretched, spread
étendue *nf* **1** : area, expanse **2** : extent, range, scope
éternel, -nelle [etɛrnɛl] *adj* : eternal — **éternellement** [-nɛlmɑ̃] *adv*
éterniser [etɛrnize] *vt* **1** PERPÉTUER : to perpetuate **2** PROLONGER : to drag out, to prolong — **s'éterniser** *vr* : to go on and on
éternité [etɛrnite] *nf* : eternity <il y a une éternité que . . . : it's been ages since . . . > <de toute éternité : from time immemorial>
éternuement [etɛrnymɑ̃] *nm* : sneeze
éternuer [etɛrnɥe] *vi* : to sneeze
éthane [etan] *nm* : ethane
éther [etɛr] *nm* : ether
éthéré, -rée [etere] *adj* : ethereal
éthiopien, -pienne [etjɔpjɛ̃, -pjɛn] *adj* : Ethiopian
Éthiopien, -pienne *n* : Ethiopian
éthique[1] [etik] *adj* : ethical
éthique[2] *nf* : ethics
ethnie [ɛtni] *nf* : ethnic group
ethnique [ɛtnik] *adj* : ethnic
ethnologie [ɛtnɔlɔʒi] *nf* : ethnology
ethnologue [ɛtnɔlɔg] *nmf* : ethnologist
étincelant, -lante [etɛ̃slɑ, -lɑ̃t] *adj* : sparkling, glittering
étinceler [etɛ̃sle] {8} *vi* : to sparkle, to glitter
étincelle [etɛ̃sɛl] *nf* **1** : spark **2** : sparkle, flash
étioler [etjɔle] *v* **s'étioler** *vr* **1** : to wilt **2** : to weaken, to become sickly
étique [etik] *adj* : skinny, scrawny
étiqueter [etikte] {8} *vt* **1** : to label (merchandise) **2 ~ comme** : to label as, to classify as
étiquette [etikɛt] *nf* **1** : label **2** : etiquette
étirer [etire] *vt* : to stretch — **s'étirer** *vr*
étoffe [etɔf] *nf* **1** TISSU : material, fabric **2** : substance, stuff <l'étoffe d'un héros : the stuff heroes are made of> <avoir l'étoffe de : to have the makings of>
étoffer [etɔfe] *vt* : to flesh out, to give substance to — **s'étoffer** *vr* : to fill out
étoile [etwal] *nf* **1** : star (in astronomy) <étoile filante : shooting star> <étoile polaire : North Star> **2** : star (of movies, sports, etc.) **3** : starlike object <général à quatre étoiles : four-star general> <en étoile : star-shaped> **4 à la belle étoile** : outdoors, under the stars **5 étoile de mer** : starfish
étoilé, -lée [etwale] *adj* : starry
étole [etɔl] *nf* : stole
étonnant, -nante [etɔnɑ̃, -nɑ̃t] *adj* : surprising, astonishing, amazing — **étonnamment** [-namɑ̃] *adv*
étonné, -née [etɔne] *adj* : surprised, astonished, amazed
étonnement [etɔnmɑ̃] *nm* : surprise, astonishment
étonner [etɔne] *vt* : to surprise, to astonish, to amaze — **s'étonner** *vr*
étouffant, -fante [etufɑ̃, -fɑ̃t] *adj* : stifling
étouffée [etufe] *nf* **à l'étouffée** : braised, steamed
étouffement [etufmɑ̃] *nm* **1** RÉPRESSION : suppression **2** ASPHYXIE : suffocation, asphyxiation
étouffer [etufe] *vt* **1** RÉPRIMER : to stifle, to suppress **2** ASPHYXIER : to suffocate, to smother **3** : to muffle <étouffer ses pas : to muffle one's footsteps> **4** : to hush up — **s'étouffer** *vr* **1** : to choke **2** : to suffocate
étourderie [eturdəri] *nf* **1** : careless mistake **2** : carelessness, thoughtlessness
étourdi[1], **-die** [eturdi] *adj* : absent-minded, scatterbrained
étourdi[2], **-die** *n* : scatterbrain
étourdir [eturdir] *vt* **1** ASSOMMER : to stun, to daze **2** GRISER : to make dizzy, to overpower <les louanges l'étourdissaient : the praise was going to his head> — **s'étourdir** *vr* : to lose oneself <s'étourdir de paroles : to get drunk on words>
étourdissant, -sante [eturdisɑ̃, -sɑ̃t] *adj* **1** : deafening **2** : stunning, exhilarating
étourdissement [eturdismɑ̃] *nm* **1** VERTIGE : dizziness **2** GRISERIE : exhilaration
étourneau [eturno] *nm, pl* **-neaux** [-no] : starling
étrange [etrɑ̃ʒ] *adj* : strange — **étrangement** [etrɑ̃ʒmɑ̃] *adv*
étranger[1], **-gère** [etrɑ̃ʒe, -ʒɛr] *adj* **1** : foreign **2** : strange, unfamiliar
étranger[2], **-gère** *n* **1** : foreigner **2** : stranger **3 à l'étranger** : abroad
étrangeté [etrɑ̃ʒte] *nf* : strangeness, oddity
étranglement [etrɑ̃gləmɑ̃] *nm* **1** : strangulation **2** : narrowing, constriction
étrangler [etrɑ̃gle] *vt* **1** : to strangle **2** : to constrict — **s'étrangler** *vr* : to choke
étrangleur, -gleuse [etrɑ̃glœr, -gløz] *n* : strangler
être[1] [ɛtr] {38} *vi* **1** : to be <il est mon frère : he is my brother> <Denise est belle : Denise is pretty> <sois sage! : be good!> <nous sommes à Paris : we're in Paris> **2** : to exist, to live <être ou ne pas être : to be or not to

be> **3** (*used with expressions of time, date, season*) <nous sommes le 15 mai : it is May 15th> <il est 10 heures : it is 10 o'clock> **4** (*used in formal expressions*) <il est des moments pareils : there are such moments> <il était une fois : once upon a time> **5 ~ à** : to belong to <ce livre est à moi : this book is mine> **6** (*indicating a state of action*) <j'étais à travailler : I was working> <tu es toujours à apprendre qqch : you're always learning sth> **7 soit . . . soit** : either . . . or — *v aux* **1** (*used in composite constructions*) <je serais partie : I would have left> <merci d'être venus! : thanks for coming!> **2** (*used in passive constructions*) <je suis passé te voir : I stopped by to see you> <elle a été blessée : she was injured> <il est né en 1938 : he was born in 1938> **3** (*used with an infinitive to indicate obligation*) <c'est un film à voir : it's a film you must see> <ses avis sont à entendre : her opinions should be heard>

être[2] *nm* **1** : organism, being <être humain : human being> **2** : person <un être cher : a loved one> **3** : soul, heart, being <au fond de mon être : deep in my heart>

étreindre [etrɛ̃dr] {37} *vt* **1** : to embrace, to hug **2** : to grip, to seize — **s'étreindre** *vr* : to embrace each other

étreinte [etrɛ̃t] *nf* **1** : embrace, hug **2** : grip, grasp <sous l'étreinte de la misère : in the grip of poverty>

étrenner [etrene] *vt* : to use for the first time

étrennes [etrɛn] *nfpl* : Christmas or New Year's present

étrier [etrije] *nm* : stirrup

étriller [etrije] *vt* **1** : to curry, to brush **2** : to criticize harshly, to pan

étriper [etripe] *vt* **1** : to gut, to disembowel **2** *fam* : to slaughter, to tear into (a person) — **s'étriper** *vr fam* : to tear each other to pieces

étriqué, -quée [etrike] *adj* **1** : skimpy, tight **2** : narrow, petty

étroit, étroite [etrwa, etrwat] *adj* **1** : narrow **2** ÉTRIQUÉ : tight **3** RIGOUREUX : strict **4** INTIME : close <étroite collaboration : close collaboration> **5 à l'étroit** : cramped

étroitement [etrwatmɑ̃] *adv* **1** : tightly, closely **2** : strictly

étroitesse [etrwatɛs] *nf* **1** : narrowness **2 étroitesse d'esprit** : narrow-mindedness

étude [etyd] *nf* **1** : study, studying <l'étude de la médecine : the study of medicine> <faire des études : to study> **2** : study, (research) paper **3** BUREAU : office **4** CLIENTÈLE : (professional) practice **5** : consideration <mettre à l'étude : to take under consideration> **6** : étude (in music)

étudiant, -diante [etydjɑ̃, -djɑ̃t] *adj & n* : student

étudié, -diée [etydje] *adj* **1** : carefully designed **2** AFFECTÉ : studied, affected

étudier [etydje] {96} *vt* **1** : to study, to learn **2** : to consider **3** : to devise, to design — *vi* : to study

étui [etɥi] *nm* : case <étui à lunettes : glasses case> <étui de révolver : holster>

étuve [etyv] *nf* **1** : steam room **2** : sterilizer

étymologie [etimɔlɔʒi] *nf* : etymology

étymologique [etimɔlɔʒik] *adj* : etymological — **étymologiquement** [-ʒikmɑ̃] *adv*

eu [y] *pp* → **avoir**

eucalyptus [økaliptys] *nms & pl* : eucalyptus

Eucharistie [økaristi] *nf* : Eucharist

eunuque [ønyk] *nm* : eunuch

euphémique [øfemik] *adj* : euphemistic — **euphémiquement** [-mikmɑ̃] *adv*

euphémisme [øfemism] *nm* : euphemism

euphonie [øfɔni] *nf* : euphony

euphorie [øfɔri] *nf* : euphoria

euphorique [øfɔrik] *adj* : euphoric

eurasien, -sienne [ørazjɛ̃, -zjɛn] *adj* : Eurasian

Eurasien, -sienne *n* : Eurasian

euro [øro] *nm* : euro (monetary unit)

européen, -péenne [ørɔpeɛ̃, -peɛn] *adj* : European

Européen, -péenne *n* : European

eut [y], *etc.* → **avoir**

euthanasie [øtanazi] *nf* : euthanasia

eux [ø] *pron* : they, them <ce sont eux : they're the ones> <sans eux : without them> <eux deux : both of them>

eux-mêmes [ømɛm] *pron* : themselves

évacuation [evakɥasjɔ̃] *nf* **1** : evacuation **2** : draining, discharge

évacuer [evakɥe] *vt* **1** : to evacuate, to clear out **2** : to drain, to discharge

évadé, -dée [evade] *n* : fugitive, escapee

évader [evade] *v* **s'évader** *vr* : to escape

évaluateur, -trice [evalɥatœr, -tris] *n Can* : appraiser

évaluation [evalɥasjɔ̃] *nf* : evaluation, assessment, appraisal

évaluer [evalɥe] *vt* : to evaluate, to assess, to appraise

évangélique [evɑ̃ʒelik] *adj* : evangelical

évangéliste [evɑ̃ʒelist] *nm* **1** : Evangelist **2** : evangelist, preacher

évangile [evɑ̃ʒil] *nm* **1** : gospel **2 l'Évangile** : the Gospel

évanouir [evanwir] *v* **s'évanouir** *vr* **1** : to faint **2** DISPARAÎTRE : to vanish, to disappear

évanouissement [evanwismɑ̃] *nm* **1** : fainting, faint **2** DISPARITION : vanishing, disappearance

évaporation [evapɔrasjɔ̃] *nf* : evaporation
évaporé, -rée [evapɔre] *adj* : giddy, scatterbrained
évaporer [evapɔre] *v* **s'évaporer** *vr* **1** : to evaporate **2** *fam* : to vanish, to disappear
évasé, -sée [evaze] *adj* : flared, bell-shaped
évaser [evaze] *vt* : to widen, to flare — **s'évaser** *vr*
évasif, -sive [evazif,-ziv] *adj* : evasive — **évasivement** [-zivmɑ̃] *adv*
évasion [evazjɔ̃] *nf* **1** : escape **2 évasion fiscale** : tax evasion
évêché [eveʃe] *nm* : bishopric
éveil [evɛj] *nm* **1** : awakening **2 donner l'éveil** : to arouse suspicions **3 en ~** : on the alert
éveillé, -lée [eveje] *adj* **1** : awake **2** : bright, alert
éveiller [eveje] *vt* **1** RÉVEILLER : to awaken **2** STIMULER : to stimulate, to arouse (curiosity, suspicion, etc.) — **s'éveiller** *vr*
événement [evɛnmɑ̃] *nm* : event
éventail [evɑ̃taj] *nm* **1** : fan **2** : range, spread
éventaire [evɑ̃tɛr] *nm* : stall, stand
éventé, -tée [evɑ̃te] *adj* **1** : stale, flat **2** : exposed to the wind, breezy
éventer [evɑ̃te] *vt* **1** : to air (out) **2** : to fan **3** : to find out, to discover — **s'éventer** *vr* **1** : to fan oneself **2** : to go stale, to go flat
éventrer [evɑ̃tre] *vt* **1** : to disembowel **2** : to gore **3** : to tear open
éventualité [evɑ̃tɥalite] *nf* : eventuality, possibility
éventuel, -tuelle [evɑ̃tɥɛl] *adj* : possible — **éventuellement** [-tɥɛlmɑ̃] *adv*
évêque [evɛk] *nm* : bishop
évertuer [evɛrtɥe] *v* **s'évertuer** *vr* : to strive, to try one's best
éviction [eviksjɔ̃] *nf* **1** : eviction **2** : expulsion, ousting
évidemment [evidamɑ̃] *adv* : obviously, of course
évidence [evidɑ̃s] *nf* **1** : obviousness, clearness <de toute évidence : obviously> **2 mettre en évidence** : to display, to highlight **3 se mettre en évidence** : to come to the fore
évident, -dente [evidɑ̃, -dɑ̃t] *adj* : obvious, evident
évider [evide] *vt* : to hollow out, to scoop out
évier [evje] *nm* : (kitchen) sink
évincer [evɛ̃se] {6} *vt* **1** : to oust **2** : to evict
évitable [evitabl] *adj* : avoidable
éviter [evite] *vt* **1** : to avoid **2** : to dodge, to evade
évocateur, -trice [evɔkatœr, -tris] *adj* : evocative, suggestive
évocation [evɔkasjɔ̃] *nf* : evocation
évolué, -luée [evɔlɥe] *adj* : highly developed, advanced
évoluer [evɔlɥe] *vi* **1** : to evolve, to develop **2** : to maneuver, to move about
évolutif, -tive [evɔlytif, -tiv] *adj* : developing, progressive
évolution [evɔlysjɔ̃] *nf* **1** : evolution (in biology) **2** : development, advancement, change
évoquer [evɔke] *vt* **1** : to recall **2** : to mention **3** : to evoke, to conjure up
exacerber [ɛgzasɛrbe] *vt* : to exacerbate
exact, exacte [ɛgzakt] *adj* **1** PRÉCIS : exact, precise **2** JUSTE : accurate, correct <c'est exact : that's right> **3** PONCTUEL : punctual
exactement [ɛgzaktəmɑ̃] *adv* : exactly, precisely
exaction [ɛgzaksjɔ̃] *nf* : exaction, extortion
exactitude [ɛgzaktityd] *nf* **1** : exactness, accuracy **2** PONCTUALITÉ : punctuality
ex æquo [ɛgzeko] *adv* : equal, equally placed <ex æquo à la première place : tied for first place>
exagération [ɛgzaʒerasjɔ̃] *nf* : exaggeration
exagéré, -rée [ɛgzaʒere] *adj* : exaggerated, excessive — **exagérément** [-remɑ̃] *adv*
exagérer [ɛgzaʒere] {87} *vt* : to exaggerate — *vi* : to go too far, to overdo it
exaltant, -tante [ɛgzaltɑ̃, -tɑ̃t] *adj* : exciting, stirring
exaltation [ɛgzaltasjɔ̃] *nf* **1** GLORIFICATION : exalting, extolling **2** EXCITATION : excitement, enthusiasm
exalté, -tée [ɛgzalte] *adj* : excited, inflamed, hotheaded
exalter [ɛgzalte] *vt* **1** GLORIFIER : to exalt, to extol **2** EXCITER : to excite, to thrill — **s'exalter** *vr* : to get excited
examen [ɛgzamɛ̃] *nm* : examination <réussir à un examen : to pass an exam>
examinateur, -trice [ɛgzaminatœr, -tris] *n* : examiner
examiner [ɛgzamine] *vt* **1** : to examine **2** PESER : to consider — **s'examiner** *vr*
exaspération [ɛgzasperasjɔ̃] *nf* : exasperation
exaspérer [ɛgzaspere] {87} *vt* **1** IRRITER : to exasperate, to infuriate **2** AGGRAVER : to aggravate, to make worse — **s'exaspérer** *vr*
exaucer [ɛgzose] {6} *vt* : to fulfill, to grant
excavateur [ɛkskavatœr] *nm* : excavator, steam shovel
excavation [ɛkskavasjɔ̃] *nf* : excavation
excavatrice [ɛkskavatris] *nf* : excavator, steam shovel
excaver [ɛkskave] *vt* : to excavate
excédent [ɛksedɑ̃] *nm* : surplus, excess <excédent commercial : trade sur-

plus> <excédent de bagages : excess baggage>
excédentaire [ɛksedɑ̃tɛr] *adj* : surplus, excess
excéder [ɛksede] {87} *vt* **1** DÉPASSER : to exceed **2** EXASPÉRER : to exasperate, to infuriate
excellence [ɛkselɑ̃s] *nf* **1** : excellence **2** : excellency <Votre Excellence : Your Excellency>
excellent, -lente [ɛkselɑ̃, -lɑ̃t] *adj* : excellent
exceller [ɛksele] *vi* : to excel
excentricité [ɛksɑ̃trisite] *nf* **1** : eccentricity **2** : remoteness
excentrique[1] [ɛksɑ̃trik] *adj* **1** : eccentric, odd **2** : remote, outlying
excentrique[2] *nmf* : eccentric
excentriquement [ɛksɑ̃trikmɑ̃] *adv* : eccentrically
excepté [ɛksɛpte] *prep* SAUF : except, apart from
excepter [ɛksɛpte] *vt* : to except, to exclude
exception [ɛksɛpsjɔ̃] *nf* **1** : exception **2** **à l'exception de** : except for, with the exception of **3** **d'~** : exceptional, special
exceptionnel, -nelle [ɛksɛpsjɔnɛl] *adj* : exceptional, special
exceptionnellement [ɛksɛpsjɔnɛlmɑ̃] *adv* **1** : exceptionally, extremely **2** : by way of exception, in this instance
excès [ɛksɛ] *nm* **1** : excess <sans excès : in moderation> **2** **à l'excès** : to excess, excessively **3** **excès de vitesse** : speeding
excessif, -sive [ɛksɛsif, -siv] *adj* : excessive — **excessivement** [-sivmɑ̃] *adv*
exciser [ɛksize] *vt* : to excise, to cut out
excision [ɛksizjɔ̃] *nf* : excision
excitable [ɛksitabl] *adj* **1** : irritable, edgy **2** : excitable (in physiology)
excitant[1], **-tante** [ɛksitɑ̃, -tɑ̃t] *adj* : exciting, stimulating
excitant[2] *nm* : stimulant
excitation [ɛksitasjɔ̃] *nf* : excitement, arousal
excité[1], **-tée** [ɛksite] *adj* : excited
excité[2], **-tée** *n* : hothead
exciter [ɛksite] *vt* **1** ENTHOUSIASMER : to excite, to thrill **2** STIMULER : to stimulate, to arouse **3** INCITER : to incite, to stir up — **s'exciter** *vr* : to get excited
exclamatif, -tive [ɛksklamatif, -tiv] *adj* : exclamatory
exclamation [ɛksklamasjɔ̃] *nf* : exclamation
exclamer [ɛksklame] *v* **s'exclamer** *vr* : to exclaim
exclu, -clue [ɛkskly] *adj* **1** : excluded **2** **il n'est pas exclu que** : it is not impossible that
exclure [ɛksklyr] {39} *vt* **1** EXPULSER : to expel **2** EXCEPTER : to exclude, to rule out — **s'exclure** *vr*
exclusif, -sive [ɛksklyzif, -ziv] *adj* **1** : exclusive **2** : sole — **exclusivement** [-sivmɑ̃] *adv*
exclusion [ɛksklyzjɔ̃] *nf* **1** : expulsion **2** : exclusion **3** **à l'exclusion de** : with the exception of, except for
exclusivité [ɛksklyzivite] *nf* **1** : exclusive rights *pl* **2** : exclusive object, product, etc. **3** **en ~** : exclusively
excommunier [ɛkskɔmynje] {96} *vt* : to excommunicate
excréments [ɛkskremɑ̃] *nmpl* : excrement, feces
excréter [ɛkskrete] {87} *vt* : to excrete
excrétion [ɛkskresjɔ̃] *nf* : excretion
excroissance [ɛkskrwasɑ̃s] *nf* : outgrowth, excrescence
excursion [ɛkskyrsjɔ̃] *nf* : excursion, trip <faire une excursion : to go on a trip>
excursionniste [ɛkskyrsjɔnist] *nmf* : vacationer, tourist
excusable [ɛkskyzabl] *adj* : excusable
excuse [ɛkskyz] *nf* **1** : excuse **2** : apology <présenter des excuses : to apologize>
excuser [ɛkskyze] *vt* **1** PARDONNER : to forgive, to pardon <excusez-moi : I'm sorry, forgive me> **2** JUSTIFIER : to justify **3** : to excuse <se faire excuser : to ask to be excused> — **s'excuser** *vr* : to apologize <je m'excuse : I apologize>
exécrable [ɛgzekrabl] *adj* : atrocious, awful
exécrer [ɛgzekre] {87} *vt* : to abhor, to loathe
exécutant, -tante [ɛgzekytɑ̃, -tɑ̃t] *n* : performer
exécuter [ɛgzekyte] *vt* **1** : to execute, to carry out **2** : to perform (music, etc.) **3** : to execute, to put to death — **s'exécuter** *vr* : to comply
exécuteur[1], **-trice** [ɛgzekytœr, -tris] *n* **exécuteur testamentaire** : executor (of a will)
exécuteur[2] *nm* : executioner
exécutif[1], **-tive** [ɛgzekytif, -tiv] *adj* : executive
exécutif[2] *nm* **l'exécutif** : executive power (of government)
exécution [ɛgzekysjɔ̃] *nf* **1** : execution, performance <mettre à exécution : to carry out> **2** : execution, putting to death
exécutoire [ɛgzekytwar] *adj* : enforceable, binding
exemplaire[1] [ɛgzɑ̃plɛr] *adj* : exemplary
exemplaire[2] *nm* **1** : copy **2** : specimen, example
exemple [ɛgzɑ̃pl] *nm* **1** : example <pour l'exemple : as an example> <donner l'exemple : to set an example> **2** **par ~** : for example, for instance
exemplifier [ɛgzɑ̃plifje] {96} *vt* : to exemplify

exempt, exempte [ɛgzɑ̃, ɛgzɑ̃t] *adj* : exempt <exempt de taxes : tax-exempt>
exempter [ɛgzɑ̃te] *vt* : to exempt
exemption [ɛgzɑ̃psjɔ̃] *nf* : exemption
exercé, -cée [ɛgzɛrse] *adj* : trained, experienced
exercer [ɛgzɛrse] {6} *vt* **1** : to exercise, to train **2** : to exert (control, influence, etc.) **3** : to practice (a profession) — *vi* : to practice, to be in practice — **s'exercer** *vr*
exercice [ɛgzɛrsis] *nm* **1** : (physical or mental) exercise **2** : practice <en exercice : in office, in practice> **3** : exercising, carrying out **4 exercice budgétaire** : fiscal year
exerciseur [ɛgzɛrsizœr] *nm* : exercise machine
exergue [ɛgzɛrg] *nm* **1** : inscription, epigraph **2 mettre en exergue** : to highlight, to emphasize
exhalaison [ɛgzalɛzɔ̃] *nf* : odor, fume
exhaler [ɛgzale] *vt* **1** : to exhale (breath) **2** : to give off, to emit **3** : to utter, to give vent to
exhausser [ɛgzose] *vt* : to raise (up)
exhaustif, -tive [ɛgzostif, -tiv] *adj* : exhaustive
exhiber [ɛgzibe] *vt* **1** : to show, to exhibit **2** : to show off, to flaunt — **s'exhiber** *vr* : to make an exhibition of
exhibition [ɛgzibisjɔ̃] *nf* **1** : display, exhibition **2** : presentation **3** : flaunting
exhibitionnisme [ɛgzibisjɔnism] *nm* : exhibitionism
exhibitionniste [ɛgzibisjɔnist] *nmf* : exhibitionist
exhortation [ɛgzɔrtasjɔ̃] *nf* : exhortation
exhorter [ɛgzɔrte] *vt* : to exhort, to urge
exhumer [ɛgzyme] *vt* : to exhume, to dig up
exigeant, -geante [ɛgziʒɑ̃, -ʒɑ̃t] *adj* : demanding
exigence [ɛgziʒɑ̃s] *nf* : demand, requirement
exiger [ɛgziʒe] {17} *vt* : to demand, to require
exigu, -guë [ɛgzigy] *adj* : cramped, tiny
exiguïté [ɛgzigɥite] *nf* : smallness, narrowness
exil [ɛgzil] *nm* : exile <en exile : in exile>
exilé, -lée [ɛgzile] *n* : exile
exiler [ɛgzile] *vt* : to exile — **s'exiler** *vr* : to go into exile, to isolate oneself
existant, -tante [ɛgzistɑ̃, -tɑ̃t] *adj* : existing, extant
existence [ɛgzistɑ̃s] *nf* : existence
existentialisme [ɛgzistɑ̃sjalism] *nm* : existentialism
existentiel, -tielle [ɛgzistɑ̃sjɛl] *adj* : existential
exister [ɛgziste] *vi* : to exist
exode [ɛgzɔd] *nm* : exodus
exonération [ɛgzɔnerasjɔ̃] *nf* : exemption <exonération d'impôts : tax exemption>
exonérer [ɛgzɔnere] {87} *vt* EXEMPTER : to exempt
exorbitant, -tante [ɛgzɔrbitɑ̃, -tɑ̃t] *adj* : exorbitant
exorbité, -tée [ɛgzɔrbite] *adj* : bulging
exorciser [ɛgzɔrsize] *vt* : to exorcize — **exorcisme** [-zɔrsism] *nm*
exotique [ɛgzɔtik] *adj* : exotic
expansif, -sive [ɛkspɑ̃sif, -siv] *adj* : expansive, outgoing
expansion [ɛkspɑ̃sjɔ̃] *nf* : expansion
expansivité [ɛkspɑ̃sivite] *nf* : expansiveness
expatrié, -triée [ɛkspatrije] *adj & n* : expatriate
expatrier [ɛkspatrije] {96} *vt* : to expatriate, to deport — **s'expatrier** *vr* : to emigrate
expectative [ɛkspɛktativ] *nf* : expectation <être dans l'expectative : to be waiting to see>
expectorant[1], -rante [ɛkspɛktɔrɑ̃, -rɑ̃t] *adj* : expectorant <sirop expectorant : expectorant cough syrup>
expectorant[2] *nm* : expectorant
expédient[1], -diente [ɛkspedjɑ̃, -djɑ̃t] *adj* : expedient
expédient[2] *nm* : expedient <vivre d'expédients : to live by one's wits>
expédier [ɛkspedje] {96} *vt* **1** : to dispatch, to send **2** : to send (someone) off **3** : to deal with, to make short work of
expéditeur, -trice [ɛkspeditœr, -tris] *n* : sender, forwarder
expéditif, -tive [ɛkspeditif, -tiv] *adj* : expeditious, quick
expédition [ɛkspedisjɔ̃] *nf* **1** ENVOI : sending, dispatching **2** : shipment **3** : expedition
expérience [ɛksperjɑ̃s] *nf* **1** PRATIQUE : experience, practice **2** ESSAI : experiment
expérimental, -tale [ɛksperimɑ̃tal] *adj, mpl* **-taux** [-to] : experimental — **expérimentalement** [-talmɑ̃] *adv*
expérimentation [ɛksperimɑ̃tasjɔ̃] *nf* : experimentation
expérimenté, -tée [ɛksperimɑ̃te] *adj* : experienced
expérimenter [ɛksperimɑ̃te] *vt* **1** ESSAYER : to test **2** ÉPROUVER : to experience — *vi* : to experiment
expert, -perte [ɛkspɛr, -pɛrt] *adj & n* : expert — **expertement** [-pɛrtəmɑ̃] *adv*
expert-comptable [ɛkspɛrkɔ̃tabl] *nm, pl* **experts-comptables** : certified public accountant
expertise [ɛkspɛrtiz] *nf* **1** : expertise **2** : expert evaluation, appraisal
expertiser [ɛkspɛrtize] *vt* : to appraise, to assess
expiation [ɛkspjasjɔ̃] *nf* : atonement

expier [ɛkspje] {96} *vt* : to expiate, to atone for
expiration [ɛkspirasjɔ̃] *nf* **1** ÉCHÉANCE : expiration <venir à expiration : to expire> **2** : exhalation, breathing out
expirer [ɛkspire] *vi* **1** EXHALER : to exhale **2** : to expire <un bail qui expire le 30 juin : a lease which expires on June 30> — *vt* : to breathe out (air), to exhale
explicable [ɛksplikabl] *adj* : explicable
explicatif, -tive [ɛksplikatif, -tiv] *adj* : explanatory, illustrative
explication [ɛksplikasjɔ̃] *nf* **1** : explanation **2 explication de texte** : literary criticism
explicite [ɛksplisit] *adj* : explicit — **explicitement** [-sitmɑ̃] *adv*
expliciter [ɛksplisite] *vt* : to make explicit
expliquer [ɛksplike] *vt* : to explain — **s'expliquer** *vr* **1** : to explain oneself **2** : to understand <je m'explique mal sa réussite : I can't understand his success>
exploit [ɛksplwa] *nm* : exploit, feat
exploitable [ɛksplwatabl] *adj* : exploitable <exploitable par machine : machine-readable>
exploitant, -tante [ɛksplwatɑ̃, -tɑ̃t] *n* **1** : farmer **2** : manager of a movie theater
exploitation [ɛksplwatasjɔ̃] *nf* **1** : exploitation, utilizing **2** : running, operating, management **3 exploitation agricole** : farm
exploiter [ɛksplwate] *vt* **1** : to exploit **2** : to run, to operate, to manage
explorateur, -trice [ɛksplɔratœr, -tris] *n* : explorer
exploration [ɛksplɔrasjɔ̃] *nf* : exploration
exploratoire [ɛksplɔratwar] *adj* : exploratory
explorer [ɛksplɔre] *vt* : to explore
exploser [ɛksploze] *vi* **1** : to explode <faire exploser : to detonate, to blow up> **2** : to burst out, to flare up (with anger, etc.)
explosif[1], -sive [ɛksplozif, -ziv] *adj* : explosive
explosif[2] *nm* : explosive
explosion [ɛksplozjɔ̃] *nf* **1** : explosion **2** : outburst
exportateur[1], -trice [ɛkspɔrtatœr, -tris] *adj* : export, exporting
exportateur[2], -trice *n* : exporter
exportation [ɛkspɔrtasjɔ̃] *nf* : export, exportation
exporter [ɛkspɔrte] *vt* : to export
exposant[1], -sante [ɛkspozɑ̃, -zɑ̃t] *n* : exhibitor
exposant[2] *nm* : exponent
exposé[1], -sée [ɛkspoze] *adj* : exposed, oriented <exposé au nord : facing north>
exposé[2] *nm* **1** : lecture, talk **2** : account, report <un exposé des faits : an account of the facts>
exposer [ɛkspoze] *vt* **1** PRÉSENTER : to display, to exhibit **2** EXPLIQUER : to explain, to set out **3** ORIENTER : to orient, to set facing **4** : to endanger <exposer sa vie : to risk one's life> — **s'exposer** *vr* : to expose oneself (to the sun, to criticism, etc.)
exposition [ɛkspozisjɔ̃] *nf* **1** : display, exhibition <exposition d'art : art exhibition> **2** PRÉSENTATION : exposition, presentation (of facts, etc.) **3** : exposition (in literature or music) **4** : exposure **5** : orientation, aspect
exprès[1] [ɛksprɛ] *adv* **1** : on purpose, intentionally **2** SPÉCIALEMENT : specially, especially <une robe fabriquée exprès pour moi : a dress made specially for me>
exprès[2], -presse [ɛksprɛs] *adj* FORMEL : express, strict <défense expresse de nager : swimming strictly forbidden>
exprès[3] *adj* : special-delivery <lettre exprès : special-delivery letter> <envoyer en exprès : to send (as) special-delivery>
express[1] [ɛksprɛs] *adj* **1** : express <autobus express : express bus> **2** : espresso
express[2] *nms & pl* **1** : express **2** : espresso
expressément [ɛksprɛsemɑ̃] *adv* **1** : expressly, explicitly **2** : specially
expressif, -sive [ɛksprɛsif, -siv] *adj* : expressive
expression [ɛksprɛsjɔ̃] *nf* : expression <expression toute faite : set phrase, cliché> <sans expression : expressionless>
expressivité [ɛksprɛsivite] *nf* : expressiveness
exprimer [ɛksprime] *vt* **1** : to express **2** EXTRAIRE : to squeeze, to extract (juice, etc.) — **s'exprimer** *vr* : to express oneself
exproprier [ɛksprɔprije] {96} *vt* : to expropriate — **expropriation** [-prijasjɔ̃] *nf*
expulser [ɛkspylse] *vt* : to expel, to evict
expulsion [ɛkspylsjɔ̃] *nf* : expulsion, eviction, ouster
expurger [ɛkspyrʒe] {17} *vt* : to expurgate
exquis, -quise [ɛkski, -kiz] *adj* : exquisite, delightful
exsangue [ɛksɑ̃g] *adj* **1** : bloodless **2** : ashen, deathly pale
exsuder [ɛksyde] *v* : to exude
extase [ɛkstaz] *nf* : ecstasy
extasié, -siée [ɛkstazje] *nf* : rapturous, ecstatic
extasier [ɛkstazje] {96} *v* **s'extasier** *vr* : to be in ecstasy
extatique [ɛkstatik] *adj* : ecstatic, enraptured

extensible [ɛkstɑ̃sibl] *adj* : extendable, tensile
extensif, -sive [ɛkstɑ̃sif, -siv] *adj* **1** : extensive **2** : wider, extended <dans son sens extensif : in its extended sense>
extension [ɛkstɑ̃sjɔ̃] *nf* **1** : stretching (of a muscle, etc.) **2** : extension, expansion
exténuant, -ante [ɛkstenɥɑ, -ɥɑ̃t] *adj* : exhausting
exténuer [ɛkstenɥe] *vt* : to exhaust, to tire out
extérieur[1], **-rieure** [ɛksterjœr] *adj* **1** : exterior, external, outside <activités extérieures : outside activities> **2** : outward, apparent <signes extérieurs : outward signs> **3** : foreign <commerce extérieur : foreign trade>
extérieur[2] *nm* **1** : exterior, outside **2 à l'extérieur** : abroad **3 match à l'extérieur** : away game
extérieurement [ɛksterjœrmɑ̃] *adv* **1** : externally **2** : outwardly
extérioriser [ɛksterjɔrize] *vt* : to show, to express (one's feelings, etc.) — **s'extérioriser** *vr* : to express oneself
exterminateur, -trice [ɛkstɛrminatœr, -tris] *n* : exterminator
extermination [ɛkstɛrminasjɔ̃] *nf* : extermination
exterminer [ɛkstɛrmine] *vt* : to exterminate, to wipe out — **s'exterminer** *fam* : to knock oneself out (doing something)
externat [ɛkstɛrna] *nm* : day school
externe[1] [ɛkstɛrn] *adj* : external
externe[2] *nmf* : day student
extincteur [ɛkstɛ̃ktœr] *nm* : fire extinguisher
extinction [ɛkstɛ̃ksjɔ̃] *nf* **1** : extinction **2** : extinguishing **3 extinction de voix** : loss of voice
extirper [ɛkstirpe] *vt* **1** : to uproot (a plant) **2** : to root out, to eradicate
extorquer [ɛkstɔrke] *vt* : to extort
extorsion [ɛkstɔrsjɔ̃] *nf* : extortion
extra[1] [ɛkstra] *adj* **1** : first-rate, top-quality **2** *fam* : great, fantastic
extra[2] *nms & pl* **1** : extra person **2** : extra thing or amount **3 un petit extra** : a little extra, a treat
extraconjugal, -gale [ɛkstrakɔ̃ʒygal] *adj, pl* **-gaux** [-go] : extramarital
extraction [estraksjɔ̃] *nf* : extraction
extrader [ɛkstrade] *vt* : to extradite — **extradition** [-stradisjɔ̃] *nf*
extraire [ɛkstrɛr] {40} *vt* **1** : to extract **2** : to excerpt — **s'extraire** *vr* : to extricate oneself
extrait [ɛkstrɛ] *nm* **1** : extract **2** : excerpt **3** : certificate, certified copy <extrait de naissance : birth certificate>
extraordinaire [ɛkstraɔrdinɛr] *adj* **1** : extraordinary **2 par ~** : by some unlikely chance
extraordinairement [ɛkstraɔrdinɛrmɑ̃] *adv* : extraordinarily, amazingly
extrapoler [ɛkstrapɔle] *vt* : to extrapolate — **extrapolation** [-pɔlɑsjɔ̃] *nf*
extrasensoriel, -rielle [ɛkstrasɑ̃sɔrjɛl] *adj* : extrasensory
extraterrestre [ɛkstratɛrɛstr] *adj & nmf* : extraterrestrial
extravagant, -gante [ɛkstravagɑ̃, -gɑ̃t] *adj* : extravagant — **extravagance** [-vagɑ̃s] *nf*
extraverti[1], **-tie** [ɛkstravɛrti] *adj* : extroverted
extraverti[2], **-tie** *n* : extrovert
extrême[1] [ɛkstrɛm] *adj* : far, farthest, extreme <à l'extrême limite : to the farthest point> <l'extrême droite : the far right> **2** : extreme, great <avec extrême difficulté : with very great difficulty> **3** : extreme, excessive <il fait une chaleur extrême : it's extremely hot>
extrême[2] *nm* : extreme <pousser à l'extrême : to take to extremes> <passer d'un extrême à l'autre : to go from one extreme to the other>
extrêmement [ɛkstrɛmmɑ̃] *adv* : extremely
extrême-onction [ɛkstrɛmɔ̃ksjɔ̃] *nf, pl* **extrêmes-onctions** : extreme unction
Extrême-Orient [ɛkstrɛmɔrjɑ̃] *nm* : Far East
extrémisme [ɛkstremism] *nm* : extremism — **extrémiste** [-tremist] *adj & nmf*
extrémité [ɛkstremite] *nf* **1** : extremity, end **2** : extreme (act) <pousser à des extrémités : to drive to extremes> **3** : plight, straits *pl* <à la dernière extrémité : at the point of death> **4 extrémités** *nfpl* : extremities (in anatomy)
extruder [ɛkstryde] *vt* : extrude
exubérant, -rante [ɛgzyberɑ̃, -rɑ̃t] *adj* : exuberant — **exubérance** [-berɑ̃s] *nf*
exulter [ɛgzylte] *vi* : to exult — **exultation** [ɛgzyltasjɔ̃] *nf*
exutoire [ɛgzytwar] *nm* : outlet, release
ex-voto [ɛksvɔto] *nm* : commemorative plaque

F

f [ɛf] *nm* : f, the sixth letter of the alphabet

fable [fabl] *nf* **1** : fable **2** MENSONGE : story, lie

fabricant, -cante [fabrikɑ̃, -kɑ̃t] *n* : manufacturer

fabrication [fabrikasjɔ̃] *nf* : manufacture, making <de fabrication artisanale : handmade>

fabrique [fabrik] *nf* **1** USINE : factory, mill **2 marque de fabrique** : trademark

fabriquer [fabrike] *vt* **1** : to make, to manufacture **2** : to fabricate (a story), to forge (documents, money, etc.)

fabulation [fabylasjɔ̃] *nf* : fabrication, lie

fabuleusement [fabyløzmɑ̃] *adv* : fabulously

fabuleux, -leuse [fabylø, -løz] *adj* **1** EXTRAORDINAIRE : fabulous, extraordinary **2** : mythical

fac [fak] *nf France fam* : university

façade [fasad] *nf* **1** : facade, front **2** APPARENCE : appearance, pretense

face [fas] *nf* **1** VISAGE : face <face à face : face to face> **2** : side, facet <pile ou face : heads or tails> **3 de ∼** : from the front, head-on **4 d'en face** : facing, opposite **5 en ∼** : opposite, across the street, opposing **6 faire face à** : to face towards, to face up to **7 sauver la face** : to save face

facétie [fasesi] *nf* **1** : joke, witticism **2** FARCE : prank

facétieux, -tieuse [fasesjø, -sjøz] *adj* : mischievous, facetious — **facétieusement** [fasesjøzmɑ̃] *adv*

facette [fasɛt] *nf* : facet, aspect

fâché, -chée [faʃe] *adj* **1** : angry **2** DÉSOLÉ : sorry

fâcher [faʃe] *vt* : to anger — **se fâcher** *vr* : to get angry, to lose one's temper

fâcherie [faʃri] *nf* : quarrel, disagreement

fâcheux, -cheuse [faʃø, -ʃøz] *adj* **1** ENNUYEUX : annoying **2** REGRETTABLE : unfortunate — **fâcheusement** [-ʃøzmɑ̃] *adv*

facial, -ciale [fasjal] *adj, mpl* **faciaux** [fasjo] : facial

facile [fasil] *adj* **1** : easy **2** *or* **facile à vivre** : easygoing **3** : superficial, facile

facilement [fasilmɑ̃] *adv* : easily, readily

facilité [fasilite] *nf* **1** : easiness **2** MOYEN : means, opportunity **3** : aptitude **4 facilités de paiement** : easy terms (of payment)

faciliter [fasilite] *vt* : to facilitate, to make easier

façon [fasɔ̃] *nf* **1** : way, manner <de cette façon : in this way, thus> <façon de parler : manner of speaking> **2** : fashioning, making (of clothing, etc.) **3** : imitation <façon cuir : imitation leather> **4 façons** *nfpl* : behavior, manners <faire des façons : to put on airs> <sans façon : without a fuss, plain, simple> **5 de façon à** : so as to **6 de toute façon** : in any case **7 faire de la façon à qqn** *Can fam* : to be nice to s.o.

façonner [fasɔne] *vt* **1** : to shape, to fashion **2** FABRIQUER : to manufacture, to make

fac-similé [faksimile] *nm, pl* **fac-similés 1** REPRODUCTION : facsimile, copy **2** : fax

facteur[1], -trice [faktœr, -tris] *n* : letter carrier, mailman *m*

facteur[2] *nm* **1** : factor, element <le facteur chance : the element of chance> **2** : factor (in mathematics) **3** : builder, maker (of organs, pianos, etc.)

factice [faktis] *adj* : artificial, imitation, false

faction [faksjɔ̃] *nf* **1** : faction **2** : guard duty, watch

factionnaire [faksjɔnɛr] *nm* : sentry

factuel, -tuelle [faktɥɛl] *adj* : factual

facturation [faktyrasjɔ̃] *nf* : billing, invoicing

facture [faktyr] *nf* **1** : bill, invoice **2** : workmanship, technique

facturer [faktyre] *vt* : to bill, to invoice

facultatif, -tive [fakyltatif, -tiv] *adj* : optional

faculté [fakylte] *nf* **1** : faculty, ability **2** : right, option <la faculté de choisir : freedom of choice> **3** : faculty (of a college or university) **4** : department, school <faculté de droit : school of law>

fadaises [fadɛz] *nfpl* : drivel, nonsense

fade [fad] *adj* **1** : dull, drab **2** : tasteless, insipid

fadeur [fadœr] *nf* : blandness, dullness

fafiner [fafine] → **farfiner**

fagot [fago] *nm* : bundle of firewood

fagoté, -tée [fagɔte] *adj fam* : badly dressed, frumpy

Fahrenheit [farɛnajt] *adj* : Fahrenheit

faible[1] [fɛbl] *adj* **1** : weak, feeble <avoir la vue faible : to have weak eyes> <faible d'esprit : feebleminded> **2** : small, low <une faible quantité : a small quantity> <à faible revenu : low-income> **3** : faint, slight <un faible bruit : a faint sound> — **faiblement** [fɛbləmɑ̃] *adv*

faible[2] *nmf* : weak-willed person

faible[3] *nm* : weakness, partiality <avoir un faible pour : to have a soft spot for>

faiblesse [fɛblɛs] *nf* **1** : weakness, frailty **2** DÉFAUT : inadequacy, shortcoming **3** : faintness, dimness

faiblir [feblir] *vi* **1** : to weaken **2** DIMINUER : to diminish, to die down

faïence [fajɑ̃s] *nf* : earthenware

faille[1] [faj] → **falloir**

faille[2] [faj] *nf* **1** : fault (in geology) **2** : flaw, weakness

failli[1], **-lie** [faji] *adj* : bankrupt

failli[2], **-lie** *n* : bankrupt (person)

faillible [fajibl] *adj* : fallible

faillir [fajir] {41} *vi* : to fail <faillir à son devoir : to fail to do one's duty> — *vt* MANQUER : to barely escape, to narrowly miss <j'ai failli m'évanouir : I nearly fainted>

faillite [fajit] *nf* **1** ÉCHEC : failure **2** : bankruptcy <faire faillite : to go bankrupt>

faim [fɛ̃] *nf* : hunger <avoir faim : to be hungry> <mourir de faim : to be starving> <rester sur sa faim : to be disappointed>

fainéant[1], **fainéante** [feneɑ̃, -neɑ̃t] *adj* : lazy

fainéant[2], **fainéante** *n* : loafer, idler

fainéanter [feneɑ̃te] *vi* : to laze about, to bum around

faire [fɛr] {42} *vt* **1** : to do <que faites-vous comme métier? : what do you do for a living?> <elle fait ses études ici : she studies here> **2** : to make <tu fais une erreur : you're making a mistake> <faire savoir : to make known, to inform> **3** : to be <faire le difficile : to be fussy> <il fait soleil : it's sunny> **4** : to amount to, to measure <deux et deux font quatre : two plus two equals four> <la salle fait 7 mètres de long : the room is 7 meters long> **5** : to say <«eh bien,» fit-il : «well,» he said> **6 cela ne fait rien** : it doesn't matter **7 faire jeune** : to look young **8 faire mal à** : to hurt — **se faire** *vr* **1 ça ne se fait pas** : it's not done **2 s'en faire** : to worry, to be bothered **3 se faire à** : to get used to

faire–part [fɛrpar] *nms & pl* : announcement (of birth, death, marriage, etc.)

faire–valoir [fɛrvalwar] *nms & pl* : foil, straight man

faisable [fəzabl] *adj* : feasible — **faisabilité** [-zabilite] *nf*

faisait [fɛzɛ], **faisions** [fɛzjɔ̃], *etc.* → **faire**

faisan, -sane [fəzɑ̃] *n* : pheasant

faisandé, -dée [fəzɑ̃de] *adj* : gamy

faisceau [fɛso] *nm, pl* **faisceaux 1** : beam (of light) **2** : bundle

faiseur, -seuse [fɛzœr, -zøz] *n* : maker, doer <faiseur d'intrigues : schemer>

fait[1], **faite** [fɛ, fɛt] *adj* **1** : made, done <bien fait : well done> **2** : ripe (of cheese) **3** : mature <un homme fait : a grown man> **4 tout fait** : ready-made

fait[2] *nm* **1** : fact **2** ACTE : act, deed **3** EXPLOIT : exploit, feat **4** ÉVÉNEMENT : event **5 au fait** : by the way, incidentally **6 au fait de** : informed about **7 comme de fait** *Can* : indeed **8 en fait de** : as regards

faîte [fɛt] *nm* **1** SOMMET : summit, top **2** APOGÉE : pinnacle <le faîte de la gloire : the height of glory>

fakir [fakir] *nm* : fakir

falaise [falɛz] *nf* : cliff

fallacieux, -cieuse [falasjø, -sjøz] *adj* CAPTIEUX : fallacious, misleading

falloir [falwar] {43} *v impers* **1** (*indicating a need*) <il faut partir : we must go> <il faut que je le fasse : I need to do it> **2** (*indicating an obligation*) <il fallait le faire : we had to do it> <j'y vais, il le faut : I'm going, I have to> <il fallait me le dire! : you should have said so!> **3** (*indicating a probability*) <il faut avoir été fou : he must have been out of his mind> **4 comme il faut** : proper, properly — **s'en falloir** *vr* **1 il s'en faut de peu** *or* **peu s'en faut** : very nearly, only just **2 il s'en faut de beaucoup** : (very) far from it

falot[1], **-lote** [falo, -lɔt] *adj* : colorless, insipid

falot[2] *nm* : lantern

falsification [falsifikasjɔ̃] *nf* : falsification, forgery, faking

falsifier [falsifje] {96} *vt* **1** : to falsify **2** : to adulterate

famé, -mée [fame] *adj* **mal famé** : disreputable

famélique [famelik] *adj* : half-starved, scrawny

fameusement [famøzmɑ̃] *adv fam* : really <c'est fameusement bien fait : it's really well done>

fameux, -meuse [famø, -møz] *adj* **1** CÉLÈBRE : famous **2** : excellent, first-rate **3** : real, remarkable <c'est un fameux mensonge : it's a whopping lie> **4 pas fameux** *fam* : not very good

familial, -liale [familjal] *adj, mpl* **-liaux** [-ljo] : family <revenu familial : family income>

familiale *nf* : station wagon

familiariser [familjarize] *vt* : to familiarize — **se familiariser** *vr*

familiarité [familjarite] *nf* **1** : familiarity **2 familiarités** *nfpl* : liberties, forwardness

familier, -lière [familje, -ljɛr] *adj* **1** : familiar, known **2** : informal, (overly) friendly **3** : colloquial, informal (of language) **4 animal familier** : pet

famille [famij] *nf* : family <c'est de famille : it runs in the family> <en famille : at home, with one's family>

famine [famin] *nf* : famine

fan [fan] *nmf* : fan, enthusiast

fana [fana] *nmf fam* : fanatic, freak

fanal [fanal] *nm, pl* **fanaux** [fano] : lantern

fanatique[1] [fanatik] *adj* : fanatic, fanatical

fanatique[2] *nmf* : fanatic — **fanatisme** [-natism] *nm*

faner [fane] *vt* **1** : to fade **2** : to wither — *vi* **1** : to fade **2** : to make hay (in agriculture) — **se faner** *vr* **1** : to wilt, to wither **2** : to fade (away)

fanfare [fɑ̃far] *nf* **1** : fanfare **2** : brass band

fanfaron[1], **-ronne** [fɑ̃farɔ̃, -rɔn] *adj* : boastful

fanfaron[2], **-ronne** *n* : braggart

fanfaronnade [fɑ̃farɔnad] *nf* : bragging, boasting

fanfaronner [fɑ̃farɔne] *vi* : to brag, to boast

fange [fɑ̃ʒ] *nf* : mire <traîner dans la fange : to drag through the mire>

fanion [fanjɔ̃] *nm* : pennant

fanon [fanɔ̃] *nm* **1** : whalebone **2** : wattle, dewlap **3** : fetlock (of a horse)

fantaisie [fɑ̃tezi] *nf* **1** : fantasy, imagination **2** CAPRICE : fancy, whim **3** : fantasia (in music)

fantaisiste [fɑ̃tezist] *adj* **1** : far-fetched, fanciful **2** : eccentric

fantasme [fɑ̃tasm] *nm* : fantasy

fantasmer [fɑ̃tasme] *vi* : to fantasize

fantasque [fɑ̃task] *adj* **1** : whimsical, capricious **2** BIZARRE : strange, weird

fantassin [fɑ̃tasɛ̃] *nm* : infantryman

fantastique [fɑ̃tastik] *adj* : fantastic — **fantastiquement** [-tikmɑ̃] *adv*

fantoche[1] [fɑ̃tɔʃ] *adj* : puppet <gouvernement fantoche : puppet government>

fantoche[2] *nm* MARIONNETTE : puppet

fantomatique [fɑ̃tɔmatik] *adj* : ghostly

fantôme [fɑ̃tom] *nm* SPECTRE : ghost, phantom

faon [fɑ̃] *nm* : fawn

faramineux, -neuse [faraminø, -nøz] *adj fam* : incredible, fantastic <une somme faramineuse : a staggering sum>

farce [fars] *nf* **1** : farce (in theater) **2** BLAGUE : practical joke, prank **3** : stuffing (in cooking)

farceur, -ceuse [farsœr, -søz] *n* : practical joker, prankster

farcir [farsir] *vt* **1** : to stuff (in cooking) **2** ~ **de** *fam* : to cram with — **se farcir** *fam* : to have to put up with, to get stuck with

fard [far] *nm* **1** : makeup **2** **sans** ~ : plainly, openly

fardeau [fardo] *nm, pl* **fardeaux** **1** : load **2** : burden, responsibility

farder [farde] *vt* **1** : to put makeup on **2** : to disguise, to conceal — **se farder** *vr* : to put on makeup

fardoches [fardɔʃ] *nfpl Can* : undergrowth, brush

farfelu, -lue [farfəly] *adj fam* : harebrained, wacky

farfiner [farfine] *vi Can fam* : to dawdle, to dillydally

farfouiller [farfuje] *vi fam* : to rummage (around)

farine [farin] *nf* : flour <farine d'avoine : oatmeal> <farine de maïs : cornmeal>

fariner [farine] *vt* : to flour

farineur, -neuse [farinœr, -nøz] *adj* **1** : covered with flour **2** : starchy, mealy

farouche [faruʃ] *adj* **1** SAUVAGE : wild, savage **2** TIMIDE : shy, timid **3** : fierce, unyielding

farouchement [faruʃmɑ̃] *adv* : fiercely

fart [far(t)] *nm* : (ski) wax

fascicule [fasikyl] *nm* **1** : installment, fascicle **2** : booklet

fascinant, -nante [fasinɑ̃, -nɑ̃t] *adj* : fascinating

fascination [fasinasjɔ̃] *nf* : fascination

fasciner [fasine] *vt* CAPTIVER : to fascinate

fascisme [faʃism] *nm* : fascism — **fasciste** [faʃist] *adj & nmf*

fasse [fas], *etc.* → **faire**

faste[1] [fast] *adj* : auspicious, lucky

faste[2] *nm* : pomp, splendor

fastidieux, -dieuse [fastidjø, -djøz] *adj* : tedious — **fastidieusement** [-djøzmɑ̃] *adv*

fastueux, -tueuse [fastɥø, -tɥøz] *adj* : luxurious, sumptuous

fatal, -tale [fatal] *adj, mpl* **fatals** **1** MORTEL : fatal **2** INÉVITABLE : inevitable

fatalement [fatalmɑ̃] *adv* : inevitably

fatalisme [fatalism] *nm* : fatalism

fataliste[1] [fatalist] *adj* : fatalistic

fataliste[2] *nmf* : fatalist

fatalité [fatalite] *nf* **1** DESTIN : fate **2** : bad luck, misfortune **3** : inevitability

fatidique [fatidik] *adj* : fateful

fatigant, -gante [fatigɑ̃, -gɑ̃t] *adj* **1** : tiring **2** : tiresome

fatigue [fatig] *nf* : fatigue

fatigué, -guée [fatige] *adj* : tired, weary

fatiguer [fatige] *vt* **1** : to tire out **2** IMPORTUNER : to bother, to annoy **3** : to strain (an engine, a structure, etc.) — *vi* **1** : to labor (of an engine) **2** : to undergo strain — **se fatiguer** *vr* : to grow tired, to wear oneself out

fatras [fatra] *nm* : jumble

fatuité [fatɥite] *nf* : smugness, self-satisfaction

faubourg [fobur] *nm* BANLIEUE : suburb

fauché, -chée [foʃe] *adj fam* : broke <être complètement fauché : to be flat broke>

faucher [foʃe] *vt* **1** : to mow, to cut **2** : to mow down, to knock down **3** *fam* : to swipe, to pinch

faucheuse [foʃøz] *nf* : reaper, mowing machine

faucheux [foʃø] *nm* : harvestman, daddy longlegs

faucille [fosij] *nf* : sickle

faucon [fokɔ̃] *nm* : falcon, hawk

fauconnerie [fokɔnri] *nf* : falconry

faudra [fodra] → **falloir**
faufiler [fofile] *vt* : to baste (in sewing) — **se faufiler** *vr* : to thread one's way, to slip, to sneak
faune[1] [fon] *nf* : fauna, wildlife
faune[2] *nm* : faun
faunique [fonik] *adj* **réserve faunique** *Can* : wildlife reserve
faussaire [fosɛr] *nmf* : forger, counterfeiter
fausse → **faux**
faussement [fosmɑ̃] *adv* **1** : falsely **2** : wrongfully
fausser [fose] *vt* **1** : to falsify, to distort **2** DÉFORMER : to bend out of shape
fausset [fosɛ] *nm* **voix de fausset** : falsetto voice
fausseté [foste] *nf* **1** : falseness, falsity **2** : duplicity
faut [fo] → **falloir**
faute [fot] *nf* **1** : fault **2** : misdeed, transgression <faute professionnelle : malpractice> **3** ERREUR : mistake, error, foul (in sports) **4** MANQUE : lack, want <faute de mieux : for lack of anything better>
fauteuil [fotœj] *nm* **1** : armchair, easy chair **2** : seat (in a theater) **3** : chair, seat (in government or an organization) **4 fauteuil roulant** : wheelchair
fauteur, -trice [fotœr, -tris] *n* **fauteur de troubles** : troublemaker, agitator
fautif, -tive [fotif, -tiv] *adj* **1** : at fault **2** : faulty, inaccurate
fauve[1] [fov] *adj* : tawny, fawn
fauve[2] *nm* **1** : big cat **2** : fawn (color)
fauvette [fovɛt] *nf* : warbler
faux[1] [fo] *adv* **1** : out of tune **2** : false, wrong <ça sonne faux : that doesn't ring true>
faux[2], **fausse** [fo, fos] *adj* **1** : false, inaccurate **2** : wrong <faire un faux pas : to stumble> **3** : imitation, counterfeit, fake **4** : deceitful <un faux frère : a false friend> **5 fausse couche** : miscarriage **6 faux nom** : assumed name, alias **7 faux témoignage** : perjury
faux[3] *nm* **1** : forgery, fake **2 le faux** : the false, falsehood
faux[4] *nf* : scythe
faux–filet [fofilɛ] *nm, pl* **faux–filets** : sirloin
faux–fuyant [fofɥijɑ̃] *nm, pl* **faux–fuyants** : pretext, subterfuge
faux–monnayeur [fomɔnɛjœr] *nm, pl* **faux–monnayeurs** : counterfeiter, forger
faux–semblant [fosɑ̃blɑ̃] *nm, pl* **faux–semblants** : sham, pretense, pose
faux–sens [fosɑ̃s] *nms & pl* : mistranslation
faveur [favœr] *nf* **1** : favor **2 à la faveur de** : thanks to **3 en faveur de** : in favor of, on behalf of
favorable [favɔrabl] *adj* : favorable — **favorablement** [-rabləmɑ̃] *adv*
favori[1], **-rite** [favɔri, -rit] *adj* : favorite
favori[2], **-rite** *n* : favorite
favoris *nmpl* : sideburns
favoriser [favɔrize] *vt* **1** : to favor, to prefer **2** : to promote, to encourage
favoritisme [favɔritism] *nm* : favoritism
fax [faks] *nm* : fax
faxer [fakse] *vt* : to fax
fébrile [febril] *adj* : feverish, febrile — **fébrilement** [-brilmɑ̃] *adv*
fébrilité [febrilite] *nf* : feverishness
fécal, -cale [fekal] *adj, mpl* **fécaux** [-ko] : fecal
fèces [fɛs] *nfpl* : feces
fécond, -conde [fekɔ̃, -kɔ̃d] *adj* FERTILE : fecund, fertile — **fécondité** [fekɔ̃dite] *nf*
fécondation [fekɔ̃dasjɔ̃] *nf* **1** : fertilization **2 fécondation artificielle** : artificial insemination
féconder [fekɔ̃de] *vt* **1** : to fertilize **2** : to impregnate, to inseminate **3** : to pollinate
fécondité [fekɔ̃dite] *nf* FERTILITÉ : fecundity, fertility
fécule [fekyl] *nf* **1** : starch **2 fécule de maïs** : cornstarch
féculent[1], **-lente** [fekylɑ̃, -lɑ̃t] *adj* : starchy
féculent[2] *nm* : starchy food
fédéral, -rale [federal] *adj, mpl* **-raux** [-ro] : federal
fédéralisme [federalism] *nm* : federalism — **fédéraliste** [-ralist] *adj & nmf*
fédération [federasjɔ̃] *nf* : federation
fédérer [federe] {87} *vt* : to federate
fée [fe] *nf* : fairy
feed–back [fidbak] *nms & pl* : feedback
féerie [fe(e)ri] *nf* **1** : enchantment **2** : extravaganza, spectacular
féerique [fe(e)rik] *adj* : magical, enchanting
feignait [fɛɲɛ], **feignions** [fɛɲɔ̃], *etc.* → **feindre**
feigne [fɛɲ], *etc.* → **feindre**
feindre [fɛ̃dr] {37} *vt* : to feign — *vi* : to pretend, to dissemble
feinte [fɛ̃t] *nf* **1** : feint, fake (in sports) **2** PIÈGE : trick, ruse
feinter [fɛ̃te] *vt* : to fake, to feint at (in sports) — *vi* : to fake, to feint (in sports)
fêlé[1], **-lée** [fele] *adj* **1** : cracked **2 avoir la tête fêlée** *fam* : to be a little crazy
fêlé[2], **-lée** *n fam* : crackpot
fêler [fele] *vt* : to crack — **se fêler** *vr*
félicitations [felisitasjɔ̃] *nfpl* : congratulations
félicité [felisite] *nf* : bliss, happiness
féliciter [felisite] *vt* CONGRATULER : to congratulate — **se féliciter** *vr* **~ de** : to be very pleased about
félin[1], **-line** [felɛ̃, -lin] *adj* : feline
félin[2] *nm* : feline, cat
félon[1], **-lonne** [felɔ̃, -lɔn] *adj* : disloyal, treacherous
félon[2], **-lonne** *n* : traitor

félonie [felɔni] *nf* : treachery

fêlure [felyr] *nf* : crack

femelle [fəmɛl] *adj & nf* : female

féminin[1], **-nine** [feminɛ̃, -nin] *adj* : feminine

féminin[2] *nm* : feminine (in grammar)

féminisme [feminism] *nm* : feminism

féministe [feminist] *adj & nmf* : feminist

féminité [feminite] *nf* : femininity

femme [fam] *nf* **1** : woman **2** ÉPOUSE : wife **3 femme au foyer** : homemaker **4 femme d'affaires** : businesswoman **5 femme de chambre** : maid, chambermaid

fémoral, -rale [femɔral] *adj, mpl* **-raux** [-ro] : femoral

fémur [femyr] *nm* : femur, thighbone

fendant, -dante [fɑ̃dɑ̃, -dɑ̃t] *adj Can* : arrogant, pretentious

fendiller [fɑ̃dije] *vt* : to crack — **se fendiller** *vr* **1** SE GERCER : to chap **2** : to crack, to craze

fendre [fɑ̃dr] {63} *vt* **1** : to split <fendre le cœur : to break one's heart> **2** : to crack — **se fendre** *vr* : to crack, to split

fenêtre [fənɛtr] *nf* : window

fenouil [fənuj] *nm* : fennel

fente [fɑ̃t] *nf* **1** : slot, slit **2** : crack

féodal, -dale [feɔdal] *adj, mpl* **-daux** [-do] : feudal — **féodalisme** [-dalism] *nm*

fer [fɛr] *nm* **1** : iron <de fer : iron, strong> **2 fer à cheval** : horseshoe **3 fer à repasser** : iron (for pressing clothes) **4 fer de lance** : spearhead **5 fers** *nmpl* : irons, shackles

fera [fəra], *etc.* → **faire**

fer–blanc [fɛrblɑ̃] *nm, pl* **fers–blancs** : tinplate

férié, -riée [ferje] *adj* **jour férié** : holiday

ferme[1] [fɛrm] *adv* : firmly, hard <tiens ferme! : hold your ground!>

ferme[2] *adj* **1** : firm **2** : steady — **fermement** [fɛrməmɑ̃] *adv*

ferme[3] *nf* **1** : farm **2** *or* **maison de ferme** : farmhouse

fermé, -mée [fɛrme] *adj* **1** : closed **2** IMPÉNÉTRABLE : inscrutable, impassive **3** EXCLUSIF : exclusive

ferment [fɛrmɑ̃] *nm* : ferment

fermentation [fɛrmɑ̃tasjɔ̃] *nf* **1** : fermentation **2** AGITATION : agitation, ferment

fermenter [fɛrmɑ̃te] *vi* : to ferment

fermer [fɛrme] *vt* **1** : to close, to shut <fermer les rideaux : to draw the curtains> <fermer à clef : to lock up> <fermer au loquet : to latch> **2** : to close down, to shut down <fermer boutique : to close up shop> **3** : to close off, to block **4** ÉTEINDRE : to turn off, to switch off **5** CLORE : to conclude — *vi* : to close — **se fermer** *vr* **1** : to close up, to fasten **2 ~ à** : to be closed to

fermeté [fɛrməte] *nf* : firmness

fermeture [fɛrmətyr] *nf* **1** : closing, shutting **2** : latch, clasp, fastener **3 fermeture à glissière** : zipper

fermier[1], **-mière** [fɛrmje, -mjɛr] *adj* : farming, farm

fermier[2], **-mière** *n* : farmer

fermoir [fɛrmwar] *nm* : clasp

féroce [ferɔs] *adj* : ferocious — **férocement** [-rɔsmɑ̃] *adv*

férocité [ferɔsite] *nf* : ferocity, ferociousness

ferraille [fɛraj] *nf* **1** : scrap iron **2** : scrapheap, scrapyard **3** *fam* : small change

ferré, -rée [fɛre] *adj* **1** : ironclad, iron-tipped **2** : hobnailed **3** : shod (of a horse) **4 être ferré sur** *fam* : to be well up on, to be in the know about

ferrer [fɛre] *vt* **1** : to shoe (a horse) **2** : to tip with metal **3** : to catch (a fish on a hook)

ferreux, -reuse [fɛrø, -røz] *adj* : ferrous

ferrique [fɛrik] *adj* : ferric

ferronnerie [fɛrɔnri] *nf* **1** : ironworks **2** : metalwork, wrought iron

ferroviaire [fɛrɔvjɛr] *adj* : rail, railroad

ferry–boat [fɛribot] *nm, pl* **ferry–boats** : ferry

fertile [fɛrtil] *adj* **1** : fertile **2** : productive <fertile en événements : eventful>

fertilisant [fɛrtilizɑ̃] *nm* : fertilizer

fertiliser [fɛrtilize] *vt* : to fertilize — **fertilisation** [-lizasjɔ̃] *nf*

fertilité [fɛrtilite] *nf* : fertility

féru, -rue [fery] *adj* **être féru de** : to be passionately interested in

férule [feryl] *nf* **être sous la férule de qqn** : to be under s.o.'s authority

fervent[1], **-vente** [fɛrvɑ̃, -vɑ̃t] *adj* : fervent

fervent[2], **-vente** *n* : enthusiast, devotee

ferveur [fɛrvœr] *nf* : fervor

fesse [fɛs] *nf* **1** : buttock **2 fesses** *nfpl* : buttocks, bottom

fessée [fese] *nf* : spanking

fesser [fese] *vt* : to spank

festin [fɛstɛ̃] *nm* BANQUET : feast, banquet

festival [fɛstival] *nm, pl* **-vals** : festival

festivités [fɛstivite] *nfpl* : festivities

feston [fɛstɔ̃] *nm* : festoon

festonner [fɛstɔne] *vt* : to festoon

festoyer [fɛstwaje] {58} *vi* : to feast

fêtard, -tarde [fɛtar, -tard] *n fam* : merrymaker, reveler

fête [fɛt] *nf* **1** : party **2** : holiday <la fête des Mères : Mother's Day> **3** : festival <fête foraine : fair> **4 de ~** : festive **5 faire la fête** : to have a good time

fêter [fete] *vt* : to celebrate

fétiche [fetiʃ] *nm* : fetish

fétide [fetid] *adj* : foul, fetid

fétu [fety] *nm* **fétu de paille** : wisp of straw

feu[1], **feue** [fø] *adj* : late <feu la reine, la feue reine : the late queen>

feu[2] *nm, pl* **feux 1** : fire <prendre feu : to catch fire> <mettre le feu à : to set fire to> <feu de camp : campfire> <feu de joie : bonfire> **2** : light <feu de circulation : traffic light> <feux de la rampe : footlights> **3** : burner (of a stove) **4** : light (for a cigarette, etc.) <avez-vous du feu? : have you got a light?> **5** : fire, shooting <faire feu : to fire> <coup de feu : shot> **6** : passion, ardor <avec feu : passionately, heatedly> **7 feux d'artifice** : fireworks

feuillage [fœjaʒ] *nm* : foliage

feuille [fœj] *nf* **1** : leaf <feuille de nénuphar : lily pad> **2** : sheet (of paper or metal), foil **3** : form <feuille d'impôts : tax return>

feuillet [fœjɛ] *nm* : page, leaf

feuilleté[1], **-tée** [fœjte] *adj* **1** : laminated **2 pâte feuilletée** : puff pastry

feuilleté[2] *nm* : puff pastry

feuilleter [fœjte] {8} *vt* **1** : to leaf through (a book) **2** : to roll and fold (dough) **3** : to laminate (glass)

feuilleton [fœjtɔ̃] *nm* : series, serial

feuillu, -lue [fœjy] *adj* **1** : leafy **2** : broad-leaved

feutre [føtr] *nm* **1** : felt **2** → **stylo–feutre**

feutré, -trée [føtre] *adj* **1** : felt, feltlike **2** : muffled

fève [fɛv] *nf* : broad bean

février [fevrije] *nm* : February

fez [fɛz] *nm* : fez

fi [fi] *interj* **faire fi de** : to scorn, to turn up one's nose at

fiable [fjabl] *adj* : reliable — **fiabilité** [fjabilite] *nf*

fiacre [fjakr] *nm* : (horse-drawn) carriage, hackney

fiançailles [fijɑ̃saj] *nfpl* : engagement

fiancé, -cée [fijɑ̃se] *n* : fiancé *m,* fiancée *f*

fiancer [fijɑ̃se] {6} *v* **se fiancer** *vr* : to get engaged

fiasco [fjasko] *nm* : fiasco

fibre [fibr] *nf* **1** : fiber **2 fibre de verre** : fiberglass **3 fibres alimentaires** : roughage

fibreux, -breuse [fibrø, -brøz] *adj* : fibrous

ficeler [fisle] {8} *vt* : to tie up

ficelle [fisɛl] *nf* **1** : string, twine **2** : trick <les ficelles du métier : the tricks of the trade>

fiche [fiʃ] *nf* **1** : index card, slip (of paper) **2** FORMULAIRE : form **3** : (electric) plug

ficher [fiʃe] *vt* **1** ENFONCER : to drive in, to stick **2** : to put on file **3** *fam* : to do <qu'est-ce qu'elle fiche? : what's she doing?> **4** *fam* : to put, to push <fiche-le dehors! : kick him out!> **5** *fam* : to give <ficher une claque à qqn : to give s.o. a slap> — **se ficher** *vr* **1 ~ dans** : to stick into **2 ~ de** *fam* : to make fun of **3 je m'en fiche** *fam* : I don't give a damn

fichier [fiʃje] *nm* **1** : file, index **2** : index card box, filing cabinet

fichu[1] [fiʃy] *pp* → **ficher 3, 4, 5**

fichu[2], **-chue** *adj fam* **1** : rotten, awful <quelle fichue température! : what rotten weather!> **2** : done for, sunk **3 ~ de** : capable of

fichu[3] *nm* : scarf, shawl

fichument [fiʃymɑ̃] *adv Can fam* : really, extremely <fichument content : really pleased>

fictif, -tive [fiktif, -tiv] *adj* : fictional, fictitious — **fictivement** [-tivmɑ̃] *adv*

fiction [fiksjɔ̃] *nf* : fiction

fidèle[1] [fidɛl] *adj* **1** LOYAL : loyal **2** CONSTANT : faithful **3** : true, accurate — **fidèlement** [-dɛlmɑ̃] *adv*

fidèle[2] *nmf* **1** : believer <les fidèles : the faithful> **2** : supporter, follower **3** : regular (customer)

fidélité [fidelite] *nf* : fidelity, faithfulness

fidjien[1], **-jienne** [fidʒjɛ̃, -dʒjɛn] *adj* : Fijian

fidjien[2] *nm* : Fijian (language)

Fidjien, -jienne *n* : Fijian

fiduciaire[1] [fidysjɛr] *adj* : fiduciary

fiduciaire[2] *nmf* : trustee

fiducie [fidysi] *nf* : trust <société de fiducie : trust company>

fief [fjɛf] *nm* **1** : fief **2** : stronghold

fiel [fjɛl] *nm* **1** : gall, bile **2** : bitterness, acrimony

fier[1] [fje] *v* **se fier** *vr* **~ à** : to trust, to rely on

fier[2], **fière** [fjɛr] *adj* : proud — **fièrement** [fjɛrmɑ̃] *adv*

fierté [fjɛrte] *nf* : pride

fièvre [fjɛvr] *nf* : fever <avoir de la fièvre : to have a high fever> <fièvre jaune : yellow fever>

fiévreux, -vreuse [fjɛvrø, -vrøz] *adj* : feverish — **fiévreusement** [-vrøzmɑ̃] *adv*

fifre [fifr] *nm* : fife

figer [fiʒe] {17} *vt* **1** : to congeal, to coagulate **2** : to freeze, to paralyze <être figé sur place : to be rooted to the spot> — **se figer** *vr* **1** : to congeal **2** S'IMMOBILISER : to freeze <son sang se figea : his blood froze>

fignoler [fiɲɔle] *vt* : to refine, to put the finishing touch upon

figue [fig] *nf* : fig

figuier [figje] *nm* : fig tree

figurant, -rante [figyrɑ̃, -rɑ̃t] *n* COMPARSE : extra, bit player

figuratif, -tive [figyratif, -tiv] *adj* : figurative, representational

figuration [figyrasjɔ̃] *nf* **faire de la figuration** : to work as an extra

figurativement [figyrativmɑ̃] *adv* : figuratively

figure [figyr] *nf* **1** VISAGE : face **2** : appearance <faire bonne figure : to put

on a good show> **3** PERSONNAGE : figure, person **4** : illustration, figure (in a text) **5** : expression <figure de rhétorique : figure of speech>

figuré, -rée [figyre] *adj* : figurative

figurer [figyre] *vi* : to appear — *vt* REPRÉSENTER : to represent — **se figurer** *vr* : to imagine

figurine [figyrin] *nf* : figurine

fil [fil] *nm* **1** : thread, yarn <fil à coudre : sewing thread> <fil dentaire : dental floss> **2** : wire, cable <fil électrique : electric wire> <fil à pêche : fishing line> **3** : current, stream <le fil des événements : the chain of events> <au fil du temps : as time goes by> **4 coup de fil** *fam* : phone call

filament [filamɑ̃] *nm* : filament

filandreux, -dreuse [filɑ̃drø, -drøz] *adj* **1** : stringy **2** : rambling

filant, -lante [filɑ̃, -lɑ̃t] *adj* **1** : runny (in cooking) **2** → **étoile**

filature [filatyr] *nf* **1** FABRIQUE : mill **2** : spinning **3 prendre en filature** : to shadow, to tail

file [fil] *nf* **1** : line, file, row <prendre la file : to get in line> <file indienne : single file> **2** : lane (of a paved road) **3 en ~** *or* **à la file** : one after another

filée [file] *nf Can fam* : line, queue

filer [file] *vt* **1** : to spin (yarn) **2** : to shadow, to tail **3** *fam* : to give <je lui ai filé un billet de 100 francs : I slipped him a 100 franc note> — *vi* **1** : to trickle, to run **2** : to run (of stockings) **3** *fam* : to dash off, to rush away **4** *fam* : to fly by, to slip away <le temps filait : time was flying> **5 filer bien** *Can fam* : to be doing fine

filet [filɛ] *nm* **1** : net **2** : fillet **3** : trickle (of water)

filial, -liale [filjal] *adj, mpl* **-liaux** [-ljo] : filial

filiale *nf* : subsidiary (company)

filiation [filjasjɔ̃] *nf* **1** : line of descent **2** : relationship (of ideas, etc.)

filière [filjɛr] *nf* **1** : (official) channels *pl* **2** : field, line (of study or work) **3** : network, ring (of criminals)

filigrane [filigran] *nm* **1** : watermark **2** : filigree **3 lire en filigrane** : to read between the lines

fille [fij] *nf* **1** : girl **2** : daughter

fillette [fijɛt] *nf* : little girl

filleul, -leule [fijœl] *n* : godchild, godson *m*, goddaughter *f*

film [film] *nm* **1** : film, movie <film d'animation : cartoon> <film (pour projection) fixe : filmstrip> **2** PELLICULE : movie film **3** : film coating **4** : course, sequence (of events, etc.)

filmer [filme] *vt* : to film

filon [filɔ̃] *nm* **1** : vein, lode **2 trouver le filon** *fam* : to strike it rich

filou [filu] *nm* : crook, swindler

fils [fis] *nm* : son

filtrage [filtraʒ] *nm* **1** : filtering **2** : screening

filtration [filtrasjɔ̃] *nf* : filtration, filtering

filtre [filtr] *nm* : filter

filtrer [filtre] *vt* **1** : to filter **2** : to screen — *vi* : to filter through

fin[1], fine [fɛ̃, fin] *adv* **1** : finely, thinly, sharply **2 être fin prêt** : to be ready, to be all set

fin[2], fine *adj* **1** : fine, delicate <cheveux fins : fine hair> **2** : thin <tranches fines : thin slices> **3** : excellent, first-rate **4** : sharp, keen <avoir le nez fin : to have a keen sense of smell> **5** *Can* : nice **6** : ultimate, very <au fin fond : at the very bottom>

fin[3] *nf* **1** : end <mettre fin à : to put an end to> <prendre fin : to come to an end> <sans fin : endless, endlessly> **2** MORT : death, end <une fin prématurée : an untimely death> **3** BUT : aim, purpose, end **4 à la fin** : eventually, in the end **5 à toutes fins utiles** : for all practical purposes

final, -nale [final] *adj, mpl* **finals** *or* **finaux** [fino] : final, last

finale[1] *nm* : finale

finale[2] *nf* : final, finals *pl* (in sports)

finalement [finalmɑ̃] *adv* **1** : finally, at last **2** : after all, in fact

finaliser [finalize] *vt* : to finalize

finaliste [finalist] *nmf* : finalist

finance [finɑ̃s] *nf* **1** : finance **2 finances** *nfpl* : finances, resources

financement [finɑ̃smɑ̃] *nm* : financing

financer [finɑ̃se] {6} *vt* : to finance

financier[1], -cière [finɑ̃sje,-sjɛr] *adj* : financial — **financièrement** [-sjɛrmɑ̃] *adv*

financier[2] *nm* : financier

finasser [finase] *vi* : to scheme, to wheel and deal

finaud, -naude [fino, -nod] *adj* : cunning, crafty

finement [finmɑ̃] *adv* **1** : finely **2** : shrewdly, subtly **3** : precisely

finesse [finɛs] *nf* **1** : finesse, delicacy **2** : fineness, thinness **3** : subtlety, shrewdness

fini[1], -nie [fini] *adj* **1** : finished, ended, complete **2** : finite

fini[2] *nm Can* : finish (of a surface)

finir [finir] *vt* **1** : to finish, to end **2** : to use up — *vi* **1** : to finish, to come to an end **2 à n'en plus finir** : endless, never-ending **3 en finir avec** : to be done with **4 finir par faire** : to end up doing

finition [finisjɔ̃] *nf* : finish, finishing touches

finlandais[1], -daise [fɛ̃lɑ̃dɛ, -dɛz] *adj* : Finnish

finlandais[2] *nm* : Finnish (language)

Finlandais, -daise *n* : Finn

finnois[1], -noise [finwa, -nwaz] *adj* : Finnish

finnois[2] *nm* : Finnish (language)

fiole [fjɔl] *nf* : vial
fiord → **fjord**
fioriture [fjɔrityr] *nf* : ornament, embellishment
fioul [fjul] *nm* : fuel oil
firmament [firmamɑ̃] *nm* : firmament, heavens *pl*
firme [firm] *nf* : firm, company
fisc [fisk] *nm* : tax collection agency
fiscal, -cale [fiskal] *adj, mpl* **fiscaux** [fisko] : fiscal <fraude fiscale : tax evasion> — **fiscalement** [-kalmɑ̃] *adv*
fiscaliser [fiskalize] *vt* : to subject to tax
fiscalité [fiskalite] *nf* : tax system
fission [fisjɔ̃] *nf* : fission
fissure [fisyr] *nf* : fissure, crack
fiston [fistɔ̃] *nm fam* : son, youngster
fixatif [fiksatif] *nm* **1** : fixative **2** *Can* : hair spray
fixation [fiksasjɔ̃] *nf* **1** : fixing, fastening, attachment **2** : fixation (in psychology) **3** : ski binding
fixe [fiks] *adj* **1** IMMOBILE : fixed **2** : permanent, steady **3** : regular <à heure fixe : at a set time>
fixement [fikəmɑ̃] *adv* : fixedly
fixer [fikse] *vt* **1** : to fix, to fasten **2** DÉTERMINER : to determine, to set **3** ÉTABLIR : to establish **4** : to focus <fixer son regard sur : to fix one's gaze on> **5** : to stare at — **se fixer** *vr* **1** : to settle down **2** : to decide (on something), to set (for) oneself
fjord *or* **fiord** [fjɔrd] *nm* : fjord
flaccidité [flaksidite] *nf* : flaccidity, flabbiness
flacon [flakɔ̃] *nm* : flask, small bottle
flagellation [flaʒɛlasjɔ̃] *nf* : flogging, whipping
flageller [flaʒɛle] *vt* FOUETTER : to flog, to whip — **se flageller** *vr*
flageoler [flaʒɔle] *vi* : to feel unsteady, to tremble <flageoler sur ses jambes : to be quaking in one's boots>
flageolet [flaʒɔlɛ] *nm* : flageolet, dwarf kidney bean
flagorneur, -neuse [flagɔrnœr, -nøz] *n* : toady, flatterer
flagrant [flagrɑ̃] *adj* **1** : flagrant, blatant **2 en flagrant délit** : red-handed
flair [flɛr] *nm* **1** ODORAT : sense of smell, nose **2** INTUITION : intuition
flairer [flɛre] *vt* **1** : to sniff, to smell **2** : to sniff out, to detect
flamand¹, -mande [flamɑ̃, -mɑ̃d] *adj* : Flemish
flamand² *nm* : Flemish (language)
Flamand, -mande *n* **1** : Fleming **2 les Flamands** : the Flemish
flamant [flamɑ̃] *nm* : flamingo
flambant, -bante [flɑ̃bɑ̃, -bɑ̃t] *adj* **1** : flaming **2 flambant neuf** : brand-new
flambeau [flɑ̃bo] *nm, pl* **flambeaux 1** TORCHE : torch **2** CHANDELIER : candlestick
flambée [flɑ̃be] *nf* **1** : blaze, fire **2** : outburst, explosion (of anger, etc.) **3** : sudden increase <une flambée des prix : skyrocketing prices>
flamber [flɑ̃be] *vt* **1** : to singe, to char **2** : to sterilize — *vi* **1** : to flame, to burn **2** : to soar, to skyrocket
flamboiement [flɑ̃bwamɑ̃] *nm* : blaze, flash
flamboyant, -boyante [flɑ̃bwajɑ̃, -bwajɑ̃t] *adj* **1** : blazing **2** : flamboyant (in architecture)
flamboyer [flɑ̃bwaje] {58} *vi* : to blaze, to flash
flamme [flam] *nf* **1** : flame <en flammes : in flames> **2** : passion, fervor **3** : pennant (of a ship)
flammèche [flamɛʃ] *nf* : spark
flan [flɑ̃] *nm* : baked custard
flanc [flɑ̃] *nm* : side, flank
flancher [flɑ̃ʃe] *vi fam* **1** : to flinch, to waver **2** : to fail, to give out
flanelle [flanɛl] *nf* : flannel
flanellette [flanɛlɛt] *nf Can* : brushed cotton, cotton flannel
flâner [flane] *vi* **1** SE BALADER : to stroll **2** PARESSER : to loaf around, to idle
flâneur, -neuse [flanœr, -nøz] *n* : idler, loiterer
flanquer [flɑ̃ke] *vt* **1** : to flank **2** *fam* : to fling **3** *fam* : to give <flanquer la frousse à qqn : to give s.o. a fright> <flanquer un coup de poing : to land a blow>
flanqueur [flɑ̃kœr] *nm Can* : wing (in sports)
flaque [flak] *nf* : puddle, pool
flash [flaʃ] *nm, pl* **flashes 1** : flash (in photography) **2** : news flash
flasque¹ [flask] *adj* : flabby, limp
flasque² *nf* FLACON : flask
flatter [flate] *vt* **1** : to flatter <flatter bassement qqn : to pander to s.o.> **2** : to please, to delight **3** : to pat, to stroke (an animal) — **se flatter** *vr* : to pride oneself
flatterie [flatri] *nf* : flattery
flatteur¹, -teuse [flatœr, -tøz] *adj* : flattering
flatteur², -teuse *n* : flatterer
flatulence [flatylɑ̃s] *nf* : flatulence
flatulent, -lente [flatylɑ̃, -lɑ̃t] *adj* : flatulent
fléau [fleo] *nm, pl* **fléaux 1** : calamity, scourge **2** : flail (in agriculture)
flèche [flɛʃ] *nf* **1** : arrow <monter en flèche : to shoot up, to soar> **2** : spire
fléchette [fleʃɛt] *nf* **1** : dart **2 fléchettes** *nfpl* : darts (game)
fléchir [fleʃir] *vt* **1** COURBER : to bend, to flex **2** : to sway, to move — *vi* **1** : to bend, to give way **2** : to diminish, to fall off **3** : to yield, to relent
fléchissement [fleʃismɑ̃] *nm* **1** : weakening, fall, drop **2** : yielding, bending
flegmatique [flɛgmatik] *adj* : phlegmatic

flegme [flɛgm] *nm* : composure <avec flegme : coolly, phlegmatically>
flemme [flɛm] *nf France fam* : laziness
flet [flɛt] *nm* : flounder
flétan [fletɑ̃] *nm* : halibut
flétrir [fletrir] *vt* **1** : to wither, to fade **2** : to blacken (a reputation, etc.), to condemn — **se flétrir** *vr* : to wither, to fade
fleur [flœr] *nf* **1** : flower, blossom **2 fleur bleue** : sentimental **3 faire une fleur à qqn** : to do s.o. a favor **4 fleur de lis** *or* **fleur de lys** : fleur-de-lis
fleurdelisé[1] [flœrdəlize] *adj* : adorned with the fleur-de-lis
fleurdelisé[2] *nm* : the provincial flag of Quebec
fleurer [flœre] *vt* : to smell of
fleuret [flœrɛ] *nm* : foil (in fencing)
fleuri, -rie [flœri] *adj* **1** : flowered, flowery **2** : florid, ruddy **3** : ornate
fleurir [flœrir] *vt* : to decorate with flowers — *vi* **1** : to flower, to blossom **2** : to flourish
fleuriste [flœrist] *nmf* : florist
fleuron [flœrɔ̃] *nm* **1** : floret **2** : jewel <le fleuron de ma collection : the jewel of my collection>
fleuve [flœv] *nm* : river
flexibilité [flɛksibilite] *nf* : flexibility
flexible [flɛksibl] *adj* : flexible
flexion [flɛksjɔ̃] *nf* **1** : bending, flexing **2** : inflection (in grammar)
flic [flik] *nm fam* : cop
flirt [flœrt] *nm* : flirtation, fling
flirter [flœrte] *vi* : to flirt
flo [flo] → **flot**
flocon [flɔkɔ̃] *nm* : flake <flocon de neige : snowflake> <flocons de maïs : cornflakes>
flopée [flɔpe] *nf fam* **une flopée de** : a whole bunch of
floraison [flɔrɛzɔ̃] *nf* : flowering, blossoming
floral, -rale [flɔral] *adj, mpl* **floraux** [flɔro] : floral
flore [flɔr] *nf* : flora
florilège [flɔrilɛʒ] *nm* : anthology
florissant, -sante [flɔrisɑ̃, -sɑ̃t] *adj* : flourishing
flot [flo] *nm* **1** : tide **2** : flood, stream, torrent <entrer à flots : to stream in> **3 à ~** : afloat <être à flot : to be on an even keel> **4** *or* **flo** *Can* : young boy, kid **5 flots** *nmpl* : waves (in the ocean)
flottabilité [flɔtabilite] *nf* : buoyancy
flottable [flɔtabl] *adj* : buoyant
flottaison [flɔtɛzɔ̃] *nf* **1** : floating **2 ligne de flottaison** : waterline
flottant, -tante [flɔtɑ̃, -tɑ̃t] *adj* **1** : floating **2** : flowing, loose **3** : indecisive
flotte [flɔt] *nf* **1** : fleet **2** *fam* : water, rain
flottement [flɔtmɑ̃] *nm* **1** INDÉCISION : hesitation, indecision **2** : fluttering, flapping **3** : fluctuation (in finance)
flotter [flɔte] *vi* **1** : to float **2** : to fly, to flutter, to drift **3** : to fluctuate
flotteur [flɔtœr] *nm* : float
flottille [flɔtij] *nf* : flotilla
flou[1], **floue** [flu] *adj* **1** : blurred, fuzzy **2** : loose, soft **3** : vague, hazy (of ideas, etc.)
flou[2] *nm* **1** IMPRÉCISION : vagueness **2** : fuzziness (of focus, outline, etc.)
fluctuer [flyktɥe] *vi* : to fluctuate — **fluctuation** [flyktɥasjɔ̃] *nf*
fluet, fluette [flyɛ, flyɛt] *adj* GRÊLE : thin, slender
fluide[1] [flɥid] *adj* **1** : fluid **2** : smooth, flowing freely
fluide[2] *nm* **1** : fluid **2** : (occult) force, psychic powers *pl*
fluidité [flɥidite] *nf* **1** : fluidity, (free) flow **2** : flexibility
fluor [flyɔr] *nm* : fluorine
fluoration [flyɔrasjɔ̃] *nf* : fluoridation
fluoré, -rée [flyɔre] *adj* : fluoridated
fluorescent, -cente [flyɔresɑ̃, -sɑ̃t] *adj* : fluorescent — **fluorescence** [-sɑ̃s] *nf*
fluorure [flyɔryr] *nm* : fluoride
flûte[1] [flyt] *nf* **1** : flute <flûte à bec : recorder> <petite flûte : piccolo> **2** : baguette **3** : tall champagne glass
flûte[2] *interj* **flûte alors**! : fiddlesticks!, nonsense!
flûtiste [flytist] *nmf* : flutist
fluvial, -viale [flyvjal] *adj, mpl* **-viaux** [-vjo] : river <eau fluviale : river water>
flux [fly] *nm* **1** : flow **2** FLOT : flood, influx <un flux d'appels : a flood of calls> **3** : flood tide <le flux et reflux : the ebb and flow> **4** : flux (in medicine and physics)
foc [fɔk] *nm* : jib
focal, -cale [fɔkal] *adj* : focal
focaliser [fɔkalize] *vt* : to focus
fœtal, -tale [fetal] *adj, mpl* **fœtaux** [feto] : fetal
fœtus [fetys] *nms & pl* : fetus
foi [fwa] *nf* **1** : faith **2** : trust, confidence <digne de foi : reliable, trustworthy> **3 bonne foi** : sincerity, honesty **4 mauvaise foi** : dishonesty, insincerity **5 faire foi de** : to be proof of **6 ma foi !** : well! **7 sous la foi du serment** : under oath
foie [fwa] *nm* **1** : liver <crise de foie : indigestion> **2** : liver (in cooking) <foies de volaille : chicken livers>
foin [fwɛ̃] *nm* **1** : hay **2** *Can fam* : money <avoir du foin : to be well off> **3** → **rhume**
foire [fwar] *nf* : fair, market
fois [fwa] *nf* **1** : time <cette fois-ci : this time> <à chaque fois : each time> **2 il était une fois** : once upon a time **3 maintes et maintes fois** : time and time again **4 une fois pour toutes** : once and for all
foison [fwazɔ̃] **à ~** : in abundance, aplenty
foisonnant, -nante [fwazɔnɑ̃, -nɑ̃t] *adj* : abundant, plentiful

foisonnement [fwazɔnmɑ̃] *nm* **1** : profusion, abundance **2** : swelling, expansion

foisonner [fwazɔne] *vi* **1** ABONDER : to abound **2** : to expand

fol → **fou**

folâtre [fɔlatr] *adj* : playful, frolicsome

folâtrer [fɔlatre] *vi* : to frolic, to gambol

folichon, -chonne [fɔliʃɔ̃, -ʃɔn] *adj* **ça n'est pas folichon** : it's not much fun

folie [fɔli] *nf* **1** : craziness, madness <la folie des grandeurs : delusions of grandeur> **2** : folly **3 à la folie** : madly, passionately <aimer à la folie : to be madly in love with>

folio [fɔljo] *nm* : folio

folk [fɔlk] *or* **folksong** [fɔlksɔ̃g] *nm* : folk music

folklore [fɔlklɔr] *nm* : folklore

folklorique [fɔlklɔrik] *adj* **1** : folk <danse folklorique : folk dancing> **2** *fam* : bizarre, eccentric

folle → **fou**

follement [fɔlmɑ̃] *adv* : madly, wildly

follicule [fɔlikyl] *nm* : follicle

fomenter [fɔmɑ̃te] *vt* : to foment, to stir up

foncé, -cée [fɔ̃se] *adj* : dark <un bleu foncé : a dark blue>

foncer [fɔ̃se] {6} *vt* ASSOMBRIR : to darken — *vi* **1** : to rush, to charge **2** *fam* : to tear along **3** S'ASSOMBRIR : to darken

fonceur[1], -ceuse [fɔ̃sœr, -søz] *adj fam* : dynamic, driven

fonceur[2], -ceuse *n fam* : dynamic person, go-getter

foncier, -cière [fɔ̃sje, -sjɛr] *adj* **1** : land <propriétaire foncier : landowner> <impôt foncier : property tax> **2** INNÉ : innate, inherent

foncièrement [fɔ̃sjɛrmɑ̃] *adv* : fundamentally, inherently

fonction [fɔ̃ksjɔ̃] *nf* **1** : function **2** : job, duties *pl,* position <faire fonction de : to serve as> **3 en fonction de** : according to **4 fonction publique** : civil service

fonctionnaire [fɔ̃ksjɔnɛr] *nmf* : official, civil servant

fonctionnel, -nelle [fɔ̃ksjɔnɛl] *adj* : functional — **fonctionnellement** [-nɛlmɑ̃] *adv*

fonctionnement [fɔ̃ksjɔnmɑ̃] *nm* : functioning, working <bon fonctionnement : good working order>

fonctionner [fɔ̃ksjɔne] *vi* : to function, to work

fond [fɔ̃] *nm* **1** : bottom, back <au fond de : at the bottom of, at the back of, in the depths of> <sans fond : bottomless> **2** : root, heart, essence **3** : background <sur fond bleu : on a blue background> <fond sonore : background music> **4 à ~** : completely, deeply **5 au fond** : in fact, basically **6 de fond en comble** : from top to bottom, thoroughly **7 fond de teint** : foundation (makeup)

fondamental, -tale [fɔ̃damɑ̃tal] *adj, mpl* **-taux** [-to] : fundamental — **fondamentalement** [-talmɑ̃] *adv*

fondamentalisme [fɔ̃damɑ̃talism] *nm* : fundamentalism

fondateur, -trice [fɔ̃datœr, -tris] *n* : founder

fondation [fɔ̃dasjɔ̃] *nf* **1** : founding, establishment **2** : foundation, endowment **3 fondations** *nfpl* : foundation(s) (in construction)

fondé, -dée [fɔ̃de] *adj* : well-founded, justified <mal fondé : groundless>

fondement [fɔ̃dmɑ̃] *nm* **1** : foundation, basis <sans fondement : unfounded, groundless> **2** *fam* : bottom, buttocks

fonder [fɔ̃de] *vt* **1** : to found, to establish **2** : to base — **se fonder** *vr* **~ sur** : to be based on

fonderie [fɔ̃dri] *nf* : foundry

fondre [fɔ̃dr] {63} *vt* **1** : to melt, to smelt **2** : to dissolve <fondre en larmes : to dissolve into tears>**3** : to cast (a statue, etc.) **4** : to merge, to blend — *vi* **1** : to melt **2** : to dissolve **3 ~ sur** : to swoop down on — **se fondre** *vr* : to merge, to blend

fondrière [fɔ̃drijɛr] *nf* : pothole

fonds [fɔ̃] *nms & pl* **1** : collection (in a museum, etc.) **2** : fund <Fonds Monétaire International : International Monetary Fund> **3** *or* **fonds de commerce** : business **4 fonds** *nmpl* : funds, capital

fondue [fɔ̃dy] *nf* : fondue

fongicide[1] [fɔ̃ʒisid] *adj* : fungicidal

fongicide[2] *nm* : fungicide

fontaine [fɔ̃tɛn] *nf* **1** : fountain **2** SOURCE : spring

fonte [fɔ̃t] *nf* **1** : melting, smelting **2** : casting **3** : cast iron **4** : font (in printing)

fonts [fɔ̃] *nmpl* **fonts baptismaux** : baptismal font

foot [fut] *nm fam* : soccer

football [futbol] *nm* **1** : soccer **2** *Can* : football **3 football américain** : football

footballeur, -leuse [futbolœr, -løz] *n* : soccer player, football player

footing [futiŋ] *nm France* : jogging

for [fɔr] *nm* **en son for intérieur** : in one's heart of hearts, inwardly

forage [fɔraʒ] *nm* : drilling, boring

forain, -raine [fɔrɛ̃, -rɛn] *adj* : fairground <marchand forain : fairground merchant>

forban [fɔrbɑ̃] *nm* **1** PIRATE : pirate, freebooter **2** ESCROC : crook

forçat [fɔrsa] *nm* **1** : convict, galley slave **2 travail de forçat** : drudgery, hard work

force [fɔrs] *nf* **1** : strength <reprendre des forces : to regain one's strength> <force de caractère : strength of

character> <force d'âme : fortitude> <force vitale : lifeblood> **2** : force <entrer de force dans : to force one's way into> <la force d'habitude : the force of habit> **3** : force (in physics) <force électromagnétique : electromagnetic force> **4** : (military or security) force <les forces armées : the armed forces> <les forces de l'ordre : the police> **5 à force de** : as a result of, by dint of **6 à toute force** : at all costs **7 par la force des choses** : of necessity, inevitably

forcé, -cée [fɔrse] *adj* **1** : forced **2** : inevitable

forcément [fɔrsemɑ̃] *adv* : necessarily, inevitably

forcené[1], -née [fɔrsəne] *adj* : frantic, frenzied

forcené[2] *nm* : maniac

forceps [fɔrsɛps] *nms & pl* : forceps *pl*

forcer [fɔrse] {6} *vt* **1** : to force, to compel **2** : to force open, to force through **3** : to strain, to overtax — *vi* : to strain, to overdo it — **se forcer** *vr* : to force oneself, to make an effort

forclusion [fɔrklyzjɔ̃] *nf* : foreclosure

forer [fɔre] *vt* : to drill, to bore

foresterie [fɔrɛstəri] *nf* : forestry

forestier[1], -tière [fɔrɛstje, -tjɛr] *adj* : forest, forested

forestier[2], -tière *n* : forester

foret [fɔrɛ] *nm* : (manual) drill

forêt [fɔrɛ] *nf* : forest

foreuse [fɔrøz] *nf* : drill

forfaire [fɔrfɛr] {44} *vi* ~ **à** : to fail in, to be false to

forfait [fɔrfɛ] *nm* **1** : fixed price, package deal **2** : default <déclarer forfait : to withdraw, to give up> **3** : heinous crime

forfaitaire [fɔrfɛtɛr] *adj* : inclusive

forfanterie [fɔrfɑ̃tri] *nf* : bragging, boastfulness

forge [fɔrʒ] *nf* : forge

forgé, -gée [fɔrʒe] *adj* **1** : fabricated, made up **2 fer forgé** : wrought iron

forger [fɔrʒe] {16} *vt* **1** : to forge **2** : to form, to build (character, etc.) **3** : to concoct, to invent <c'est forgé de toutes pièces : it's a total fabrication>

forgeron [fɔrʒərɔ̃] *nm* : blacksmith

formaldéhyde [fɔrmaldeɪd] *nm* : formaldehyde

formaliser [fɔrmalize] *vt* : to formalize — **se formaliser** *vr* : to take offense

formalisme [fɔrmalism] *nm* : formalism

formalité [fɔrmalite] *nf* : formality

format [fɔrma] *nm* : format

formater [fɔrmate] *vt* : to format (a computer disk)

formateur[1], -trice [fɔrmatœr, -tris] *adj* : formative

formateur[2], -trice *n* : trainer

formation [fɔrmasjɔ̃] *nf* **1** : formation **2** : education, training <formation professionnelle : vocational training>

forme [fɔrm] *nf* **1** : form, shape <prendre forme : to take shape> <sans forme : formless, shapeless> **2** : method, way <forme de pensée : way of thinking> **3** : form, procedure <pour la forme : as a matter of form> **4** : form, fitness <être en pleine forme : to be in great shape> **5** : last (of shoes) **6 formes** *nfpl* : figure (of the human body), lines (of an object) **7 formes** *nfpl* : proprieties, conventions <y mettre les formes : to be tactful>

formel, -melle [fɔrmɛl] *adj* **1** : formal **2** CATÉGORIQUE : definitive, categorical, express — **formellement** [-mɛlmɑ̃] *adv*

former [fɔrme] *vt* **1** : to form, to shape **2** : to develop **3** : to constitute **4** : to train, to educate — **se former** *vr*

formidable [fɔrmidabl] *adj* **1** ÉNORME : tremendous <un formidable défi : a tremendous challenge> **2** *fam* : great, terrific **3** *fam* : incredible — **formidablement** [-dabləmɑ̃] *adv*

formulaire [fɔrmylɛr] *nm* : form, questionnaire

formulation [fɔrmylasjɔ̃] *nf* : formulation

formule [fɔrmyl] *nf* **1** : formula **2** : expression, phrase <formule de politesse : polite phrase, closing (of a letter)> **3** : method, way, option <formule de paiement : method of payment> **4** FORMULAIRE : (printed) form

formuler [fɔrmyle] *vt* **1** : to formulate, to express **2** : to draw up, to write out

fornication [fɔrnikasjɔ̃] *nf* : fornication

forniquer [fɔrnike] *vi* : to fornicate

fort[1] [fɔr] *adv* **1** TRÈS : very, extremely <vous savez fort bien : you know full well> **2** BEAUCOUP : greatly, very much <j'en doute fort : I doubt it very much> **3** : strongly, loudly, hard <frapper fort : to strike hard>

fort[2], forte [fɔr, fɔrt] *adj* **1** : strong, powerful <fort comme un bœuf : strong as an ox> <café fort : strong coffee> <c'est plus fort que moi : I can't help it> **2** : intense, loud, bright **3** : large, heavy, stout **4** : able, gifted <être fort de : to be good at> **5 c'est un peu fort!** *fam* : that's a bit much!

fort[3] *nm* **1** : strength, strong point **2** : strong person **3** : fort, fortress **4 au fort de** : at the height of, in the midst of, in the depths of

fortement [fɔrtəmɑ̃] *adv* : strongly, deeply, intensely

forteresse [fɔrtərɛs] *nf* : fortress

fortification [fɔrtifikasjɔ̃] *nf* : fortification

fortifier [fɔrtifje] {96} *vt* : to fortify, to strengthen — **se fortifier** *vr*

fortuit, -tuite [fɔrtɥi, -tɥit] *adj* : fortuitous, chance

fortuitement [fɔrtɥitmɑ̃] *adv* : fortuitously, by chance

fortune [fɔrtyn] *nf* **1** : fortune <faire fortune : to make one's fortune> **2** CHANCE : chance, luck **3 de ~** : makeshift

fortuné, -née [fɔrtyne] *adj* **1** : fortunate **2** RICHE : wealthy

forum [fɔrɔm] *nm* : forum

fosse [fos] *nf* **1** : pit <fosse septique : septic tank> <fosse d'aisances : cesspool> <fosse d'orchestre : orchestra pit> **2** TOMBE : grave

fossé [fose] *nm* **1** : ditch, trench **2** : gulf, gap <fossé de générations : generation gap>

fossette [fosɛt] *nf* : dimple

fossile[1] [fosil] *adj* : fossil, fossilized

fossile[2] *nm* : fossil

fossiliser [fosilize] *vt* : to fossilize **— se fossiliser** *vr*

fossoyeur [foswajœr] *nm* : gravedigger

fou[1] [fu] **(fol** [fɔl] *before a vowel or mute h*), **folle** [fɔl] *adj* **1** : crazy, insane <devenir fou : to go mad> <il est fou d'elle : he's crazy about her> **2** : silly, ridiculous **3** : tremendous, extreme <avoir un talent fou : to be extremely talented> **4 ~ de** : crazy with <fou de joie : jumping for joy> <fou de jalousie : green with envy>

fou[2], **folle** *n* **1** : crazy person, lunatic **2 comme un fou** *fam* : like crazy

fou[3] *nm* **1** : bishop (in chess) **2** : fool, jester **3 fou de Bassan** : gannet

foudre [fudr] *nf* **1** : lightning **2 foudres** *nfpl* : wrath

foudroyant, foudroyante [fudrwajɑ̃, fudrwajɑ̃t] *adj* **1** : overwhelming, crushing **2** : violent (of an illness) <une mort foudroyante : a sudden death>

foudroyer [fudrwaje] {58} *vt* : to strike down

fouet [fwɛ] *nm* **1** : whip **2** : whisk <fouet à œufs : egg whisk> **3 de plein fouet** : full-force, head-on

fouetter [fwete] *vt* **1** : to whip, to lash **2** : to whisk <crème fouettée : whipped cream>

fougère [fuʒɛr] *nf* : fern, bracken

fougue [fug] *nf* : ardor, spirit, passion

fougueusement [fugøzmɑ̃] *adv* : with spirit, ardently

fougueux, -geuse [fugø, -gøz] *adj* : ardent, spirited

fouille [fuj] *nf* **1** : digging **2** : search **3 fouilles** *nfpl* : excavations, (archaeological) dig

fouiller [fuje] *vt* **1** : to search, to go through (baggage, pockets, etc.) **2** : to excavate, to dig **—** *vi* **1** : to dig, to root (of a pig) **2 ~ dans** : to rummage through, to delve into

fouillis [fuji] *nm* : jumble, mess

fouiner [fwine] *vi fam* : to be nosy, to snoop around

fouineur[1], **-neuse** [fwinœr, -nøz] *adj* : inquisitive, nosy

fouineur[2], **-neuse** *n* **1** : busybody **2** : bargain hunter

fouir [fwir] *vt* : to burrow, to dig

foulard [fular] *nm* : scarf, neckerchief

foule [ful] *nf* **1** : crowd, mob **2 une foule de** : masses of, lots of

foulée [fule] *nf* **1** : stride **2 dans la foulée** : while I was (he was, etc.) at it **3 dans la foulée de** : on the heels of, in the wake of

fouler [fule] *vt* **1** : to press **2** : to tread, to set foot on <fouler aux pieds : to trample on> **3** : to sprain **—** *vi Can* : to shrink <mes pantalons ont foulé : my pants shrank> **— se fouler** *vr* **1** : to sprain **2** *fam* : to strain oneself

foulure [fulyr] *nf* ENTORSE : sprain

four [fur] *nm* **1** : oven <four à micro-ondes : microwave (oven)> **2** : kiln **3** *fam* : flop (in theater, etc.)

fourbe [furb] *adj* : deceitful

fourberie [furbəri] *nf* : deceit

fourbir [furbir] *vt* **1** : to polish up **2 fourbir ses armes** : to prepare for battle

fourbu, -bue [furby] *adj* : exhausted

fourche [furʃ] *nf* **1** : pitchfork **2** : fork, branching

fourcher [furʃe] *vi* **1** : to fork **2 ma (sa) langue a fourché** : it was a slip of the tongue **—** *vt* : to fork (in agriculture)

fourchette [furʃɛt] *nf* **1** : fork **2** : range, bracket

fourchu, -chue [furʃy] *adj* **1** : forked **2** : split

fourgon [furgɔ̃] *nm* **1** : van **2** : freight car, baggage car <fourgon de queue : caboose> **3** : poker (for a fireplace)

fourgonnette [furgɔnɛt] *nf* : minivan

fourmi [furmi] *nf* : ant

fourmilier [furmilje] *nm* : anteater

fourmilière [furmiljɛr] *nf* : anthill

fourmillement [furmijmɑ̃] *nm* **1** : swarming **2** : tingling, pins and needles *pl*

fourmiller [furmije] *vi* **1** : to swarm, to mill about **2** : to abound <fourmiller de : to be teeming with> **3** : to tingle, to have pins and needles

fournaise [furnɛz] *nf Can* : furnace

fourneau [furno] *nm, pl* **fourneaux** [furno] **1** : stove **2** : furnace

fournée [furne] *nf* : batch

fourni, -nie [furni] *adj* **1** : thick, bushy **2 bien fourni** : well-stocked

fournil [furnil] *nm* : bakery

fournir [furnir] *vt* **1** : to supply, to provide (with) **2** : to produce (wine, etc.) **3 fournir un effort** : to make an effort **—** *vi* **~ à** : to provide for **— se fournir** *vr* **~ chez** : to shop at

fournisseur, -seuse [furnisœr, -søz] *n* : supplier, dealer, purveyor

fourniture [furnityr] *nf* **1** : furnishing **2 fournitures** *nfpl* : equipment, supplies <fournitures de bureaux : office supplies>

fourrage [furaʒ] *nm* : feed, fodder

fourrager [furaʒe] {17} *vi* : to rummage, to forage

fourré[1], **-rée** [fure] *adj* **1** : fur-lined **2** : filled (of candies)

fourré[2] *nm* : thicket

fourreau [furo] *nm, pl* **fourreaux 1** : sheath, case, scabbard **2** *or* **robe fourreau** : sheath dress

fourrer [fure] *vt* **1** : to line with fur **2** : to stuff, to fill **3** *fam* : to thrust, to stick — **se fourrer** *vr* **1** *fam* : to get, to put oneself <se fourrer sous les couvertures : to crawl under the covers> **2** *Can fam* : to mess up

fourre–tout [furtu] *nms & pl* : tote bag, carryall

fourreur, -reuse [furœr, -røz] *n* : furrier

fourrière [furjɛr] *nf* : pound (for animals or vehicles)

fourrure [furyr] *nf* **1** : fur **2** : coat (of an animal)

fourvoyer [furvwaje] {58} *vt* : to lead astray — **se fourvoyer** *vr* **1** : to make an error, to go astray **2 ~ dans** : to stray into, to get involved in

foyer [fwaje] *nm* **1** : hearth, fireplace **2** RÉSIDENCE : home <femme au foyer : housewife> <sans foyer : homeless> **3** : home (for the elderly, etc.) **4** : focus <lunettes à double foyer : bifocals> **5** : center, seat, source

fracas [fraka] *nms & pl* : crash, din

fracassant, -sante [frakasɑ̃, -sɑ̃t] *adj* **1** : deafening, thunderous **2** : sensational <un succès fracassant : a stunning success>

fracasser [frakase] *vt* : to shatter, to smash — **se fracasser** *vr*

fraction [fraksjɔ̃] *nf* : fraction

fractionnaire [fraksjɔnɛr] *adj* : fractional

fractionner [fraksjɔne] *vt* : to divide, to split (up) — **se fractionner** *vr*

fracture [fraktyr] *nf* : fracture <fracture du crâne : fractured skull>

fracturer [fraktyre] *vt* **1** : to fracture, to break **2** : to break open

fragile [fraʒil] *adj* **1** CASSABLE : fragile, breakable **2** FAIBLE : sensitive, weak, frail

fragiliser [fraʒilize] *vt* : to weaken, to make fragile

fragilité [fraʒilite] *nf* **1** : fragility **2** : frailty

fragment [fragmɑ̃] *nm* **1** : fragment, bit **2** : passage (from a book), snatch (of a conversation)

fragmentaire [fragmɑ̃tɛr] *adj* : fragmentary, sketchy

fragmenter [fragmɑ̃te] *vt* : to fragment, to break up — **se fragmenter** *vr*

fragmentation [fragmɑ̃tasjɔ̃] *nf* : fragmentation, splitting up

frai [frɛ] *nm* **1** : fry **2** : fish eggs, spawn

fraîchement [frɛʃmɑ̃] *adv* **1** : freshly, newly <fraises fraîchement cueillies : freshly picked strawberries> **2** : coolly <fraîchement reçu : coolly received>

fraîcheur [frɛʃœr] *nf* **1** : freshness **2** : coolness

fraîchir [frɛʃir] *vi* **1** : to cool off **2** : to freshen

frais[1] [frɛ] *adv* **1** : freshly, recently **2 il fait frais** : it's cool outside

frais[2], **fraîche** [frɛ, frɛʃ] *adj* **1** : fresh <fruits frais : fresh fruit> **2** RÉCENT : new, recent <nouvelles fraîches : recent news> **3** : cool <températures plus fraîches : cooler temperatures> **4 peinture fraîche** : wet paint

frais[3] *nm* **1 mettre au frais** : to put in a cool place **2 prendre le frais** : to take a breath of fresh air **3 frais** *nmpl* : expenses, fees, charges

fraise [frɛz] *nf* **1** : strawberry **2** : (dentist's) drill

fraiser [frɛze] *vt* : to ream

framboise [frɑ̃bwaz] *nf* : raspberry

franc[1] [frɑ̃] *adv* **à parler franc** : frankly, to be quite frank

franc[2], **franche** [frɑ̃, frɑ̃ʃ] *adj* **1** : frank, straightforward **2** : pure (of colors, etc.) **3** : absolute, downright **4** : free, exempt <port franc : duty-free port>

franc[3] *nm* : franc

français[1], **-çaise** [frɑ̃sɛ, -sɛz] *adj* : French

français[2] *nm* : French (language)

Français, -çaise *n* : Frenchman *m*, Frenchwoman *f*

franchement [frɑ̃ʃmɑ̃] *adv* **1** : frankly, candidly **2** : clearly, definitely **3** : boldly, firmly **4** : downright <c'est franchement ridicule! : it's really silly!>

franchir [frɑ̃ʃir] *vt* **1** : to cross over, to surmount, to clear **2** : to cover (a distance) **3** : to last through (a period of time)

franchise [frɑ̃ʃiz] *nf* **1** : frankness **2** : exemption <en franchise douanière : duty-free> <franchise postale : postage paid> **3** : deductible **4** : franchise

franchissement [frɑ̃ʃismɑ̃] *nm* : crossing, clearing

franciscain, -caine [frɑ̃siskɛ̃, -kɛn] *adj & n* : Franciscan

franciser [frɑ̃size] *vt* : to frenchify

franc–jeu [frɑ̃ʒø] *nm* : fair play

franc–maçon [frɑ̃masɔ̃] *nm* : Freemason — **franc–maçonnerie** [frɑ̃masɔnri] *nf*

franco–canadien[1], **-dienne** [frɑ̃kokanadjɛ̃,-djɛn] *adj* : French-Canadian

franco–canadien[2], **-dienne** *n* : Canadian French

francophile [frɑ̃kɔfil] *adj & nmf* : francophile

francophone[1] [frɑ̃kɔfɔn] *adj* : French-speaking

francophone[2] *nmf* : French speaker

francophonie [frɑ̃kɔfɔni] *nf* : French-speaking community

franc–parler [frɑ̃parle] *nm, pl* **franc–parlers** : frankness <avoir son franc-parler : to speak one's mind>

franc–tireur [frɑ̃tirœr] *nm, pl* **francs–tireurs 1** : irregular (soldier), guerrilla **2** : maverick <agir en franc-tireur : to act independently>

frange [frɑ̃ʒ] *nf* **1** : fringe **2** : bangs (of hair)

franger [frɑ̃ʒe] {17} *vt* : to fringe

frangin, -gine [frɑ̃ʒɛ̃, -ʒin] *n France fam* : brother *m,* sister *f*

franquette [frɑ̃kɛt] *nf* **à la bonne franquette** : without ceremony, informally

frappant, -pante [frapɑ̃, -pɑ̃t] *adj* : striking <un contraste frappant : a striking contrast>

frappe [frap] *nf* **1** : impression, stamp **2** : typing

frapper [frape] *vt* **1** : to strike, to hit **2** : to strike, to impress, to astonish **3** : to mint **4** : to ice, to chill **5 frapper d'ostracisme** : to ostracize — *vi* **1** : to hit, to knock, to bang **2** : to clap <frapper dans ses mains : to clap one's hands> — **se frapper** *vr* : to get all worked up

frappeur, -peuse [frapœr, -pøz] *n Can* : hitter, batter <frappeur désigné : designated hitter>

frasque [frask] *nf* : prank, escapade <faire des frasques : to get into mischief>

fraternel, -nelle [fratɛrnɛl] *adj* : fraternal — **fraternellement** [-nɛlmɑ̃] *adv*

fraterniser [fratɛrnize] *vi* : to fraternize — **fraternisation** [-nizasjɔ̃] *nf*

fraternité [fratɛrnite] *nf* : fraternity, brotherhood

fratricide[1] [fratrisid] *adj* : fratricidal

fratricide[2] *nm* : fratricide

fraude [frod] *nf* **1** : fraud <fraude fiscale : tax evasion> **2 passer en fraude** : to smuggle in

frauder [frode] *v* : to cheat

fraudeur, -deuse [frodœr, -døz] *n* : cheat, swindler

frauduleux, -leuse [frodylø, -løz] *adj* : fraudulent — **frauduleusement** [-løzmɑ̃] *adv*

frayer [frɛje] {11} *vt* : to open up, to clear — *vi* **1** : to spawn **2 ~ avec** : to associate with — **se frayer** *vr* **se frayer un chemin** : to make one's way

frayeur [frɛjœr] *nf* : fright

fredaine [frədɛn] *nf* : prank, escapade

fredonner [frədɔne] *vt* : to hum

freezer [frizœr] *nm* : freezer (of a refrigerator)

frégate [fregat] *nf* : frigate

frein [frɛ̃] *nm* **1** : brake **2** : check, restraint <mettre un frein à : to curb, to block> <sans frein : unrestrained, unbridled>

freinage [frɛnaʒ] *nm* : braking

freiner [frene] *vt* : to slow down, to check — *vi* : to brake

frelaté, -tée [frəlate] *adj* **1** : adulterated **2** : unnatural, artificial, corrupt

frêle [frɛl] *adj* **1** : weak, flimsy **2** : frail

frelon [frəlɔ̃] *nm* : hornet

frémir [fremir] *vi* **1** FRISSONNER : to tremble, to shiver, to shudder **2** : to quiver, to flutter **3** : to start to boil, to simmer

frémissant, -sante [fremisɑ̃, -sɑ̃t] *adj* : quivering, trembling

frémissement [fremismɑ̃] *nm* : trembling, shivering, shuddering

frêne [frɛn] *nm* : ash (tree or wood)

frénésie [frenezi] *nf* : frenzy

frénétique [frenetik] *adj* : frantic, frenetic — **frénétiquement** [-tikmɑ̃] *adv*

fréquemment [frekamɑ̃] *adv* : frequently

fréquence [frekɑ̃s] *nf* : frequency

fréquent, -quente [frekɑ̃, -kɑ̃t] *adj* : frequent

fréquentation [frekɑ̃tasjɔ̃] *nf* **1** : frequenting **2** : attendance <taux de fréquentation : attendance rate> **3** RELATION : acquaintance <mauvaises fréquentations : bad company> **4 fréquentations** *nfpl Can* : dating, courting

fréquenter [frekɑ̃te] *vt* **1** : to frequent **2** : to attend **3** : to associate with, to consort with — **se fréquenter** *vr* **1** : to see each other **2** : to go out (with each other), to date

frère [frɛr] *nm* **1** : brother **2** : friar, brother (in religion)

fresque [frɛsk] *nf* : fresco

fret [frɛ(t)] *nm* : freight

fréter [frete] {87} *vt* : to charter

frétillement [fretijmɑ̃] *nm* : wagging, wag (of a tail)

frétiller [fretije] *vi* **1** : to wriggle, to quiver <frétillant de joie : quivering with delight> **2** : to wag <sa queue frétille : its tail is wagging>

fretin [frətɛ̃] *nm* **menu fretin** : small fry

freux [frø] *nm* CORBEAU : rook

friable [frijabl] *adj* : crumbly

friand, friande [frijɑ̃, -jɑ̃d] *adj* **~ de** : partial to, fond of

friandise [frijɑ̃diz] *nf* **1** BONBON : candy **2** : delicacy

fric [frik] *nm fam* : dough, cash

fricassée [frikase] *nf* : fricassee — **fricasser** [frikase] *vt*

friche [friʃ] *nf* : fallow land, wasteland <en friche : fallow>

friction [friksjɔ̃] *nf* **1** : friction **2** MASSAGE : massage, rubdown

frictionner [friksjɔne] *vt* : to rub (down), to massage — **se frictionner** *vr*

frigide [friʒid] *adj* : frigid — **frigidité** [-ʒidite] *nf*
frigo [frigo] *nm fam* : fridge
frigorifier [frigɔrifje] {96} *vt* **1** : to refrigerate **2 être frigorifié** *fam* : to be frozen stiff
frigorifique [frigɔrifik] *adj* : refrigerated (of a truck, etc.)
frileux, -leuse [frilø, -løz] *adj* **1** : sensitive to cold **2** : cautious, timid
frimas [frima] *nms & pl* : hoarfrost
frime [frim] *nf fam* : sham, pretense <c'est pour la frime : it's just for show>
frimer [frime] *vi fam* : to put on an act
frimousse [frimus] *nf fam* : pretty little face
fringale [frɛ̃gal] *nf fam* **1 avoir la fringale** : to be starving **2 avoir une fringale de** : to have a craving for
fringant, -gante [frɛ̃gɑ̃, -gɑ̃t] *adj* **1** : dashing **2** : spirited (of a horse)
fringillidé [frɛ̃ʒilide] *nm* : finch
fringues [frɛ̃g] *nfpl fam* : gear, duds
friper [fripe] *vt* : to wrinkle, to crumple — **se friper** *vr*
friperie [fripri] *nf France* **1** : secondhand clothes shop **2** : secondhand clothes
fripon[1], -ponne [fripɔ̃, -pɔn] *adj* COQUIN : mischievous
fripon[2], -ponne *n* : rascal
fripouille [fripuj] *nf fam* : scoundrel, crook
frire [frir] {45} *v* : to fry
frise [friz] *nf* : frieze
friser [frize] *vt* **1** : to curl **2** : to graze, to skim (a surface) **3** : to border on <elle doit friser la quarantaine : she must be close to forty> — *vi* : to curl — **se friser** *vr* **se faire friser** : to have one's hair curled
frisette [frizɛt] *nf* : ringlet
frisquet, -quette [friskɛ, -kɛt] *adj* : chilly, nippy
frisson [frisɔ̃] *nm* **1** : shiver, shudder **2** : ripple (of water, etc.), rustle (of leaves)
frissonnement [frisɔnmɑ̃] *nm* **1** : shiver, shudder **2** : rippling, rustling
frissonner [frisɔne] *vi* **1** : to shiver, to shudder **2** : to rustle, to ripple
frites [frit] *nfpl* : french fries
friture [frityr] *nf* **1** : frying **2** : deep fat, oil **3** : fried food
frivole [frivɔl] *adj* : frivolous, trivial — **frivolement** [-vɔlmɑ̃] *adv*
frivolité [frivɔlite] *nf* : frivolity
froc [frɔk] *nm* **1** : (religious) habit **2** *fam* : pants *pl*, trousers *pl*
froid[1] [frwa] *adv* **il fait froid** : it's cold (outside)
froid[2], froide [frwa, frwad] *adj* **1** : cold **2** : unfeeling, insensitive
froid[3] *nm* **1** : cold <un grand froid : intense cold> <avoir froid : to feel cold> <conservez au froid : keep in a cold place> **2** : cold (illness) <prendre froid : to catch cold> **3** : coolness, chill <être en froid avec : to be on bad terms with> **4 à ~** : calmly, cooly **5 à ~** : without preparation, spontaneous(ly)
froidement [frwadmɑ̃] *adv* : coldly, coolly
froideur [frwadœr] *nf* : coldness, coolness
froissement [frwasmɑ̃] *nm* **1** : crumpling, creasing **2** : rustle, rustling
froisser [frwase] *vt* **1** : to crumple, to crease, to muss up **2** BLESSER : to hurt, to offend, to upset — **se froisser** *vr* **1** : to crease, to crumple (up) **2 se froisser un muscle** : to strain a muscle
frôler [frole] *vt* EFFLEURER : to touch lightly, to brush, to graze
fromage [frɔmaʒ] *nm* **1** : cheese **2 fromage blanc** *or* **fromage cottage** : cottage cheese
fromager[1], -gère [frɔmaʒe, -ʒɛr] *adj* : cheese <l'industrie fromagère : the cheese industry>
fromager[2], -gère *n* : cheese maker, cheese merchant
fromagerie [frɔmaʒri] *nf* : cheese store
froment [frɔmɑ̃] *nm* : wheat
fronce [frɔ̃s] *nf* : gather (of fabric)
froncement [frɔ̃smɑ̃] *nm* **froncement de sourcils** : frown
froncer [frɔ̃se] {6} *vt* **1** : to gather (fabric) **2** : to wrinkle, to pucker <froncer les sourcils : to knit one's brow, to frown>
frondaison [frɔ̃dɛzɔ̃] *nf* : foliage
fronde [frɔ̃d] *nf* **1** : rebellion, revolt **2** : slingshot **3** : frond
frondeur, -deuse [frɔ̃dœr, -døz] *adj* : rebellious
front [frɔ̃] *nm* **1** : forehead, brow **2** : front (in meteorology, politics, war, etc.) **3** : audacity, effrontery <avoir le front de faire : to have the nerve to do> **4 de ~** : without hesitation, head-on **5 de ~** : abreast <à cinq de front : five abreast> **6 faire front à** : to confront, to face up to
frontal, -tale [frɔ̃tal] *adj, mpl* **frontaux** [frɔ̃to] : frontal
frontalier, -lière [frɔ̃talje, -ljɛr] *adj* : frontier, border
frontière [frɔ̃tjɛr] *nf* **1** : frontier, border **2** : boundary
frontispice [frɔ̃tispis] *nm* : frontispiece
fronton [frɔ̃tɔ̃] *nm* : pediment
frottement [frɔtmɑ̃] *nm* **1** : rubbing, scraping **2 frottements** *nmpl* : friction, disagreement
frotter [frɔte] *vt* **1** : to rub <frotter une allumette : to strike a match> **2** : to polish, to scrub — *vi* : to rub — **se frotter** *vr* **1** : to rub <ne te frotte pas les yeux : don't rub your eyes> **2** : to scrub oneself **3 ~ à** : to face up to, to take on

frou–frou *or* **froufrou** [frufru] *nm, pl* **frou–frous** *or* **froufrous** : rustle, swish
froufrouter [frufrute] *vi* : to rustle, to swish
frousse [frus] *nf fam* : scare, fright, jitters *pl*
fructifier [fryktifje] {96} *vi* **1** : to bear fruit **2** : to yield a profit
fructueux, -tueuse [fryktɥø, -tɥøz] *adj* **1** : fruitful, productive **2** RENTABLE : profitable
frugal, -gale [frygal] *adj, mpl* **frugaux** [frygo] : frugal — **frugalement** [-galmɑ̃] *adv*
frugalité [frygalite] *nf* : frugality
fruit [frɥi] *nm* **1** : fruit <jus de fruits : fruit juice> **2 fruits de mer** : seafood
fruité, -tée [frɥite] *adj* : fruity
fruitier[1], **-tière** [frɥitje, -tjɛr] *adj* : fruit <arbre fruitier : fruit tree>
fruitier[2], **-tière** *n* : fruit merchant
fruste [fryst] *adj* **1** : worn **2** GROSSIER : rough, uncouth
frustrant, -trante [frystrɑ̃, -trɑ̃t] *adj* : frustrating
frustration [frystrasjɔ̃] *nf* : frustration
frustrer [frystre] *vt* **1** DÉCEVOIR : to frustrate, to disappoint **2** PRIVER : to deprive
fuel [fjul] → **fioul**
fugace [fygas] *adj* ÉPHÉMÈRE : fleeting
fugitif[1], **-tive** [fyʒitif, -tiv] *adj* **1** : escaped, fugitive **2** : fleeting, elusive
fugitif[2], **-tive** *n* **1** : fugitive, escapee **2** : runaway
fugue [fyg] *nf* **1** : running away <faire une fugue : to run away (from home)> <fugue amoureuse : elopement> **2** : fugue
fuguer [fyge] *vi* : to run away
fugueur, -gueuse [fygœr, -gøz] *adj & n* : runaway
fuir [fɥir] {46} *vi* **1** : to flee **2** : to leak — *vt* **1** : to shun, to avoid **2** : to flee, to run away from
fuite [fɥit] *nf* **1** : flight, escape **2** : leak
fulgurant, -rante [fylgyrɑ̃, -rɑ̃t] *adj* **1** ÉBLOUISSANT : dazzling **2** : shooting, searing, intense
fulminant, -nante [fylminɑ̃, -nɑ̃t] *adj* : furious, enraged
fulminer [fylmine] *vt* : to bellow out (threats, etc.) — *vi* ENRAGER : to be enraged, to fulminate
fumé, -mée [fyme] *adj* **1** : smoked **2** : tinted
fumée *nf* **1** : smoke **2** : steam
fumer [fyme] *vt* **1** : to smoke **2** : to manure — *vi* **1** : to smoke **2** : to steam **3** : to fume (with anger)
fumet [fymɛ] *nm* : aroma (of food or wine)
fumier [fymje] *nm* : dung, manure
fumigation [fymigasjɔ̃] *nf* : fumigation
fumiste [fymist] *nmf fam* **1** : shirker **2** : phoney
fumisterie [fymistəri] *nf fam* **1** : joke, farce **2** : sham
fumoir [fymwar] *nm* **1** : smokehouse **2** : smoking room
fun [fœn] *nm Can fam* : fun <j'ai eu du fun : I had fun>
funambule [fynɑ̃byl] *nmf* ÉQUILIBRISTE : tightrope walker
funèbre [fynɛbr] *adj* **1** FUNÉRAIRE : funeral **2** LUGUBRE : funereal, gloomy
funérailles [fyneraj] *nfpl* : funeral
funéraire [fynerɛr] *adj* **1** : funeral, funerary **2 salon funéraire** *Can* : funeral home
funeste [fynɛst] *adj* **1** : fatal, deathly **2** CATASTROPHIQUE : disastrous, dire
fur [fyr] *nm* **au fur et à mesure** : little by little, as one goes along
furet [fyrɛ] *nm* : ferret
fureter [fyrte] {20} *vi* : to ferret around, to nose about
fureteur, -teuse [fyrtœr, -tøz] *adj* : inquisitive, prying
fureur [fyrœr] *nf* **1** RAGE : rage, fury **2 faire fureur** : to be all the rage
furibond, -bonde [fyribɔ̃, -bɔ̃d] *adj* : furious, livid
furie [fyri] *nf* **1** : fury, rage **2 avec ~** : furiously, violently
furieusement [fyrjøzmɑ̃] *adv* **1** : furiously **2** : extremely, tremendously
furieux, -rieuse [fyrjø, -jøz] *adj* **1** : furious, angry **2** : fierce, intense
furoncle [fyrɔ̃kl] *nm* : boil, carbuncle
furtif, -tive [fyrtif, -tiv] *adj* : furtive, sly — **furtivement** [-tivmɑ̃] *adv*
fusain [fyzɛ̃] *nm* **1** : spindle tree **2** : charcoal (for drawing) **3** : charcoal drawing
fuseau [fyzo] *nm, pl* **fuseaux 1** : spindle, bobbin **2 fuseau horaire** : time zone **3 pantalon fuseau** : ski pants
fusée [fyze] *nf* **1** : rocket **2 fusée éclairante** : flare
fuselage [fyzlaʒ] *nm* : fuselage
fuselé, -lée [fyzle] *adj* : slender, tapering
fuser [fyze] *vi* **1** : to stream out, to gush out **2** JAILLIR : to burst forth (of laughter, etc.)
fusible [fyzibl] *nm* : fuse <faire sauter un fusible : to blow a fuse>
fusil [fyzi] *nm* **1** : gun, rifle **2** : marksman
fusilier [fyzilje] *nm* **1** : rifleman **2 fusilier marin** : marine
fusillade [fyzijad] *nf* **1** : gunfire **2** : shooting
fusiller [fyzije] *vt* **1** : to shoot, to execute **2 fusiller du regard** : to look daggers at
fusil–mitrailleur [fyzimitrajœr] *nm, pl* **fusils–mitrailleurs** : automatic rifle, machine gun
fusion [fyzjɔ̃] *nf* **1** : fusion **2** : melting <roche en fusion : molten rock> **3** : merger
fusionner [fyzɔnje] *v* : to merge

fustiger [fystiʒe] {17} *vt* : to castigate, to censure
fut [fy], *etc.* → **être**
fût [fy] *nm* **1** TONNEAU : barrel, cask <bière en fût : draft beer> **2** : shaft (of a column) **3** : trunk (of a tree)
futaie [fytɛ] *nf* : forest (of tall trees)
futé, -tée [fyte] *adj* : cunning, crafty
futile [fytil] *adj* **1** : futile **2** FRIVOLE : trivial, frivolous
futilité [fytilite] *nf* : futility
futur[1], **-ture** [fytyr] *adj* : future
futur[2] *nm* **1** : future **2** : future tense
futuriste [fytyrist] *adj* : futuristic
fuyait [fɥijɛ], **fuyions** [fɥijɔ̃], *etc.* → **fuir**
fuyant, fuyante [fɥijɑ̃, fɥijɑ̃t] *adj* **1** INSAISISSABLE : elusive, shifty **2** : receding
fuyard, fuyarde [fɥijar, fɥijard] *n* **1** : runaway **2** : deserter (in the military)

G

g [ʒe] *nm* : g, the seventh letter of the alphabet
gabardine [gabardin] *nf* : gabardine
gabarit [gabari] *nm* **1** : template, gauge **2** : size, dimensions *pl* **3** *fam* : (physical) build **4** *fam* : caliber, sort <du même gabarit : of the same ilk>
gabonais, -naise [gabɔnɛ, -nɛz] *adj* : Gabonese
Gabonais, -naise *n* : Gabonese
gâcher [gaʃe] *vt* **1** : to spoil, to ruin **2** GASPILLER : to waste, to squander **3** : to mix (plaster, mortar, etc.)
gâchette [gaʃɛt] *nf* : trigger
gâchis [gaʃi] *nm* **1** DÉSORDRE : mess <faire du gâchis : to make a mess> **2** GASPILLAGE : waste
gadelle [gadɛl] *nf Can* : currant
gadget [gadʒɛt] *nm* **1** : gimmick, gadget **2 gadgets** *nmpl* : gadgetry
gadoue [gadu] *nf* **1** : mud, muck **2** *Can* : slush
gaélique[1] [gaelik] *adj* : Gaelic
gaélique[2] *nm* : Gaelic (language)
gaffe [gaf] *nf* **1** : boat hook **2** *fam* : blunder, stupidity, goof
gaffer [gafe] *vi fam* : to blunder, to goof (up)
gaffeur, -feuse [gafœr, -føz] *n fam* : blunderer
gag [gag] *nm* : gag, joke
gage [gaʒ] *nm* **1** : security <mettre en gage : to pawn> **2** : pledge, guarantee <en gage d'amitié : as a token of our friendship> **3** : forfeit (in games) **4 gages** *nmpl* : wages, pay
gager [gaʒe] {17} *vt* **1** : to bet, to wager **2** : to guarantee (a loan, etc.)
gageure [gaʒœr] *nf* **1** : challenge **2** *Can* : bet, wager
gagnant[1], **-gnante** [gaɲɑ̃, -ɲɑ̃t] *adj* : winning <billet gagnant : winning ticket>
gagnant[2], **-gnante** *n* : winner
gagne–pain [gaɲpɛ̃] *nms & pl* : job, livelihood
gagner [gaɲe] *vt* **1** : to win **2** : to earn <gagner sa vie : to earn one's living> **3** : to gain <gagner du terrain : to gain ground> <gagner de la vitesse : to pick up speed> **4** ÉCONOMISER : to save (time, space, etc.) **5** ATTEINDRE : to reach, to arrive at **6** : to win (someone) over **7** : to overcome — *vi* **1** : to win **2** : to gain, to advance, to encroach **3** : to increase <gagner en longueur : to grow longer> **4 ~ à** : to gain by <gagner à vieillir : to improve with age> **5 y gagner** : to be better off <ils y gagnent : it's to their advantage>
gai, gaie [gɛ] *adj* **1** JOYEUX : cheerful, happy, merry **2** HOMOSEXUEL : gay, homosexual
gaiement [gemɑ̃] *adv* : gaily, merrily
gaieté [gete] *nf* : cheerfulness, mirth
gaillard[1], **-larde** [gajar, -jard] *adj* **1** : lively, sprightly **2** GRIVOIS : ribald, bawdy
gaillard[2] , **-larde** *nmf* : sturdy fellow *m*, strapping individual
gaillard[3] *nm* **gaillard d'avant** : forecastle
gaillardement [gajardəmɑ̃] *adv* : cheerfully
gain [gɛ̃] *nm* **1** : earnings *pl* **2** : saving (of time, space, etc.) **3** : gain (in finance) **4** : winning <avoir gain de cause : to win the case>
gaine [gɛn] *nf* **1** : girdle, corset **2** : sheath
gainer [gene] *vt* : to cover, to sheathe
gala [gala] *nm* : gala, reception
galactique [galaktik] *adj* : galactic
galamment [galamɑ̃] *adv* : gallantly
galant[1], **-lante** [galɑ̃, -lɑ̃t] *adj* **1** : courteous, gallant **2 en galante compagnie** : with a person of the opposite sex **3 homme galant** : ladies' man
galant[2] *nm* : beau, suitor
galanterie [galɑ̃tri] *nf* : gallantry
galaxie [galaksi] *nf* : galaxy
galbe [galb] *nm* : curve, shapeliness
gale [gal] *nf* **1** : scabies **2** : mange **3** *Can* : scab
galéjade [galeʒad] *nf* : tall story
galère [galɛr] *nf* **1** : galley (ship) **2** *fam* : hard time, hassle
galerie [galri] *nf* **1** : gallery **2** : balcony (in a theater) **3** : roof rack (of an automobile) **4** *Can* : porch **5 galerie marchande** : shopping mall

galet [galɛ] *nm* CAILLOU : pebble
galette [galɛt] *nf* **1** : flat round cake **2** : pancake **3** *Can* : soft cookie <galette à la mélasse : molasses cookie> **4** *fam* : dough, cash
galeux, -leuse [galø, -løz] *adj* : mangy
galimatias [galimatja] *nm* : gibberish, nonsense
galion [galjɔ̃] *nm* : galleon
galipette [galipɛt] *nf fam* : somersault <faire des galipettes : to turn somersaults>
galipote [galipɔt] *nf* **courir la galipote** *Can* : to gallivant
galle [gal] *nf* : gall (in botany)
gallicisme [galisism] *nm* **1** : French idiom **2** : gallicism
gallium [galjɔm] *nm* : gallium
gallois[1], **-loise** [galwa, -lwaz] *adj* : Welsh
gallois[2] *nm* : Welsh (language)
Gallois, -loise *n* : Welshman *m*, Welshwoman *f*
gallon [galɔ̃] *nm* : gallon
galoche [galɔʃ] *nf* **1** SABOT : clog **2** : overshoe
galon [galɔ̃] *nm* **1** : braid (on fabric) **2** : stripe (in the military) <prendre du galon : to be promoted> **3** *Can* : measuring tape
galop [galo] *nm* : gallop <au galop : at a gallop>
galopant, -pante [galɔpɑ̃, -pɑ̃t] *adj* : runaway, galloping
galoper [galɔpe] *vi* **1** : to gallop **2** : to run about **3** : to run wild <son imagination galope : his imagination is running riot>
galopin [galɔpɛ̃] *nm* : rascal
galvaniser [galvanize] *vt* : to galvanize
galvauder [galvode] *vt* **1** : to tarnish, to sully **2** : to debase <une expression galvaudée : a hackneyed phrase> — **se galvauder** *vr*
gambade [gɑ̃bad] *nf* : leap, skip
gambader [gɑ̃bade] *vi* : to leap about, to gambol
gambien, -bienne [gɑ̃bjɛ̃, -bjɛn] *adj* : Gambian
Gambien, -bienne *n* : Gambian
gambit [gɑ̃bi] *nm* : gambit
gamelle [gamɛl] *nf* : mess kit
gamète *nm* [gamɛt]: gamete
gamin[1], **-mine** [gamɛ̃, -min] *adj* **1** ESPIÈGLE : mischievous, playful **2** PUÉRIL : childish
gamin[2], **-mine** *n fam* : kid, youngster
gaminerie [gaminri] *nf France* : childishness
gamme [gam] *nf* **1** : scale (in music) **2** SÉRIE : range (of colors, products, etc.), gamut (of emotions)
gang[1] [gɑ̃g] *nm France* : gang
gang[2] *nf Can fam* : gang, group <la gang du bureau : the gang in the office>
ganglion [gɑ̃glijɔ̃] *nm* **1** : ganglion **2** **avoir des ganglions** *fam* : to have swollen glands
gangrène [gɑ̃grɛn] *nf* **1** : gangrene **2** : scourge, corrupting influence
gangreneux, -neuse [gɑ̃grənø, -nøz] *adj* : gangrenous
gangster [gɑ̃gstɛr] *nm* : gangster
gannet [ganɛ] *nm* : gannet
ganse [gɑ̃s] *nf* : braid (in sewing)
gant [gɑ̃] *nm* **1** : glove <gant de boxe : boxing glove> **2** **gant de toilette** : washcloth **3** **jeter le gant** : to throw down the gauntlet **4** **prendre des gants pour** *or* **mettre des gants pour** : to handle with kid gloves
gantelet [gɑ̃tlɛ] *nm* : gauntlet
garage [garaʒ] *nm* **1** : garage <garage d'autobus : bus depot> <garage d'avions : hangar> **2** STATION-SERVICE : service station, repair shop
garagiste [garaʒist] *nmf* **1** : garage owner **2** : garage mechanic
garant[1], **-rante** [garɑ̃, -rɑ̃t] *n* **1** : guarantor, surety **2** **se porter garant de** : to be answerable for, to vouch for
garant[2] *nm* : guarantee, assurance
garantie [garɑ̃ti] *nf* : guarantee, warranty
garantir [garɑ̃tir] *vt* **1** ASSURER : to guarantee, to assure **2** **~ de** : to protect from
garçon [garsɔ̃] *nm* **1** : boy, young man **2** SERVEUR : waiter **3** CÉLIBATAIRE : bachelor **4** **garçon manqué** : tomboy
garçonnet [garsɔnɛ] *nm* : little boy
garde[1] [gard] *nm* **1** : guard, warden **2** **garde côtière** *Can* : coast guard **3** **garde du corps** : bodyguard **4** **garde de nuit** : night watchman **5** **garde forestier** : forest ranger
garde[2] *nf* **1** : nurse **2** : (military) guard, watch **3** : custody, care <avoir la garde des enfants : to have custody of the children> **4** : duty <être de garde : to be on duty> **5** **chien de garde** : watchdog **6** **mettre en garde** : to warn **7** **prendre garde** : to be careful
garde–à–vous [gardavu] *nms & pl* : standing at attention
garde–boue [gardəbu] *nms & pl* : mudguard
garde–chasse [gardəʃas] *nm, pl* **gardes–chasse(s)** : gamekeeper, game warden
garde–feu [gardəfø] *nms & pl* **1** : fire screen **2** *Can* : fire warden
garde–fou [gardəfu] *nm, pl* **garde–fous** PARAPET : railing, parapet
garde–malade [gardəmalad] *nmf* **gardes–malade(s)** INFIRMIER : nurse
garde–manger [gardəmɑ̃ʒe] *nms & pl* : pantry
gardénia [gardenja] *nm* : gardenia
garde–pêche [gardəpɛʃ] *nm, pl* **gardes–pêche** : fish warden

garder [garde] *vt* **1** CONSERVER : to keep **2** : to keep on (clothing) **3** : to keep (oneself) in <garder le lit : to stay in bed> **4** SURVEILLER : to guard, to watch over <garder des enfants : to look after children, to baby-sit> **5 ~ de** : to protect from — **se garder** *vr* **1** SE CONSERVER : to keep **2 ~ de** : to be careful not to <gardez-vous de parler : be careful not to talk>

garderie [gardəri] *nf Can* : day-care center, nursery

garde–robe[1] [gardərɔb] *nf, pl* **garde–robes** : wardrobe, clothes

garde–robe[2] *nmf Can* : wardrobe, closet

gardien[1], **-dienne** [gardjɛ̃, -djɛn] *n* **1** : caretaker, attendant, custodian **2** : guardian, keeper <gardien des droits humains : guardian of human rights>

gardien[2] *nm* **1 gardien de but** : goalkeeper **2 gardien de la paix** *France* : police officer, policeman **3 gardien de troupeau** : herdsman

gardienne *nf* **gardienne d'enfants** : day-care worker, baby-sitter

gare[1] [gar] *nf* **1** : railroad station **2 gare d'autobus** *Can or* **gare routière** *France* : bus station

gare[2] *interj* **1 gare à vous!** : watch out! **2 sans crier gare** : without warning

garenne [garɛn] *nf* : (rabbit) warren

garer [gare] *vt* STATIONNER : to park — **se garer** *vr* **1** : to park **2** SE RANGER : to pull over

gargantuesque [gargɑ̃tɥɛsk] *adj* : gargantuan

gargariser [gargarize] *v* **se gargariser** *vr* **1** : to gargle **2 ~ de** *fam* : to revel in

gargarisme [gargarism] *nm* **1** : gargling **2** : gargle (product)

gargote [gargɔt] *nf* : cheap restaurant

gargouille [garguj] *nf* : gargoyle

gargouillement [gargujmɑ̃] *nm* : rumble, rumbling

gargouiller [garguje] *vi* : to gurgle (of water), to rumble (of one's stomach)

garnement [garnəmɑ̃] *nm* : rascal

garni, -nie [garni] *adj* : garnished (in cooking) <plat garni : meal with vegetables> <hamburger garni : hamburger with all the trimmings>

garnir [garnir] *vt* **1** REMPLIR : to fill **2** : to cover **3** : to decorate, to trim **4** : to garnish (a dish) — **se garnir** *vr* : to fill up

garnison [garnizɔ̃] *nf* : garrison

garniture [garnityr] *nf* **1** : filling, garnish (in cooking) <sans garniture : without vegetables> **2** : trimming **3 garniture de frein** : brake lining

garrocher [garɔʃe] *vt Can fam* : to throw

garrot [garo] *nm* **1** : tourniquet **2** : garrote **3** : withers (of a horse)

garrotter [garɔte] *vt* **1** LIGOTER : to tie up, to bind **2** BÂILLONNER : to gag, to stifle

gars [ga] *nm fam* **1** : boy, lad **2** TYPE : guy, fellow

gascon, -conne [gaskɔ̃, -skɔn] *adj* : Gascon

Gascon, -conne *n* : Gascon

gaspillage [gaspijaʒ] *nm* : waste

gaspiller [gaspije] *vt* : to waste, to squander

gaspilleur, -leuse [gaspijœr, -jøz] *adj* : wasteful

gastrique [gastrik] *adj* : gastric

gastronome [gastrɔnɔm] *nmf* : gourmet

gastronomie [gastrɔnɔmi] *nf* : gastronomy

gastronomique [gastrɔnɔmik] *adj* : gastronomic, gourmet

gâteau [gato] *nm, pl* **gâteaux 1** : cake <gâteau d'anniversaire : birthday cake> **2 gâteau sec** *France* : cookie **3 c'est du gâteau** *fam* : it's a piece of cake

gâter [gate] *vt* **1** CHOYER : to spoil, to pamper **2** : to spoil, to ruin — **se gâter** *vr* **1** : to go bad **2** : to deteriorate, to change for the worse

gâterie [gatri] *nf* : little treat, delicacy

gâteux, -teuse [gatø, -tøz] *adj* : senile

gâtisme [gatism] *nm* : senility

gauche[1] [goʃ] *adj* **1** : left <tourner à gauche : to make a left turn> <du côté gauche : on the left-hand side> **2** MALADROIT : awkward, clumsy **3** : warped

gauche[2] *nf* **1** : left <à gauche de : to the left of> **2 la gauche** : the Left, the left wing

gauchement [goʃmɑ̃] *adv* : awkwardly, clumsily

gaucher[1], **-chère** [goʃe, -ʃɛr] *adj* : left-handed

gaucher[2], **-chère** *n* : left-handed person

gaucherie [goʃri] *nf* : awkwardness, clumsiness

gauchir [goʃir] *vt* **1** : to warp **2** : to distort (facts, etc.) — *vi* : to warp

gauchissement [goʃismɑ̃] *nm* **1** : warp, warping **2** : distortion

gauchiste [goʃist] *adj & nmf* : leftist — **gauchisme** [goʃism] *nm*

gaufre[1] [gofr] *nm Can* : gopher

gaufre[2] *nf* **1** : waffle **2** : honeycomb

gaufrer [gofre] *vt* **1** : to emboss **2** : to crinkle

gaufrette [gofrɛt] *nf* : wafer

gaufrier [gofrije] *nm* : waffle iron

gaulois, -loise [golwa, -lwaz] *adj* **1** : Gallic **2** GRIVOIS : bawdy

gauloiserie [galwazri] *nf* **1** : bawdy joke **2** : bawdiness

gaulthérie [golteri] *nf* : wintergreen

gausser [gose] *v* **se gausser** *vr* SE MOQUER : to deride, to make fun of

gaver [gave] *vt* **1** : to force-feed **2** : to fill up — **se gaver** *vr* SE BOURRER : to stuff oneself
gay [gɛ] → **gai**
gaz [gaz] *nms & pl* **1** : gas <gaz carbonique : carbon dioxide> <gaz lacrymogène : tear gas> <gaz naturel : natural gas> **2** *Can fam* : gasoline **3 mettre le gaz** *fam* : to step on the gas
gaze [gaz] *nf* : gauze
gazéifié, -fiée [gazeifje] *adj* : carbonated
gazelle [gazɛl] *nf* : gazelle
gazer [gaze] *vt* : to gas — *vi fam* : to be going well <ça gaze? : how are things going?>
gazette [gazɛt] *nf fam* : newspaper
gazeux, -zeuse [gazø, -zøz] *adj* **1** : gaseous **2 eau gazeuse** : sparkling water **3 boisson gazeuse** : soft drink
gazoduc [gazɔdyk] *nm* : gas pipeline
gazon [gazɔ̃] *nm* **1** : grass, turf, sod **2** PELOUSE : lawn
gazouillement [gazujmɑ̃] *nm* **1** : chirping, twittering **2** : babbling, gurgling
gazouiller [gazuje] *vi* **1** : to chirp **2** : to babble, to gurgle
gazouillis [gazuji] *nms & pl* **1** : chirp, twittering **2** : babbling
geai [ʒɛ] *nm* : jay
géant[1], **géante** [ʒeɑ̃, -ɑ̃t] *adj* : giant, gigantic
géant[2], **géante** *n* **1** : giant **2 à pas de géant** : with giant strides, rapidly
geignard, -narde [ʒeɲar, -ɲard] *adj fam* : whiny, whining
geignement [ʒɛɲəmɑ̃] *nm* : moaning, groaning
geindre [ʒɛ̃dr] {37} *vi* **1** : to groan, to moan **2** : to whine, to whimper
gel [ʒɛl] *nm* **1** : frost **2** : freeze, freezing **3** : gel <gel coiffant : hair gel>
gélatine [ʒelatin] *nf* : gelatine
gélatineux, -neuse [ʒelatinø, -nøz] *adj* : jelly-like, gelatinous
gelé, -lée [ʒəle] *adj* **1** : frozen **2** : frostbitten
gelée *nf* **1** : frost <gelée blanche : hoarfrost> **2** : jelly
geler [ʒəle] {20} *v* : to freeze — *v impers* : to freeze <il gèle! : it's freezing!> — **se geler** *vr*
gélifier [ʒelifje] {96} *vt* : to jell — **se gélifier** *vr* : to jell
gélule [ʒelyl] *nf* : capsule
gelure [ʒəlyr] *nf* : frostbite
Gémeaux [ʒemo] *nmpl* : Gemini
gémir [ʒemir] *vi* **1** : to groan, to moan **2** : to wail (of wind, etc.), to creak **3 ~ sur** : to bemoan
gémissement [ʒemismɑ̃] *nm* **1** : groan, moan **2** : creaking
gemme[1] [ʒɛm] *adj* **sel gemme** : rock salt
gemme[2] *nf* : gem, precious stone
gênant, -nante [ʒenɑ̃, -nɑ̃t] *adj* **1** EMBARRASSANT : embarrassing, awkward **2** ENCOMBRANT : cumbersome, in the way **3** ENNUYEUX : annoying, intrusive **4** *Can* : intimidating, imposing
gencives [ʒɑ̃siv] *nfpl* : gums
gendarme [ʒɑ̃darm] *nm* **1** *France* : gendarme, police officer **2** *Can* : federal police officer (member of the Royal Canadian Mounted Police)
gendarmerie [ʒɑ̃darməri] *nf* **1** *France* : police force **2** *France* : police station **3** *Can* : federal police force **3 gendarmerie maritime** *France* : coast guard
gendre [ʒɑ̃dr] *nm* : son-in-law
gène [ʒɛn] *nm* : gene
gêne [ʒɛn] *nf* **1** NUISANCE : inconvenience, bother **2** CONFUSION : embarrassment **3** : difficulty, (physical) discomfort **4** PAUVRETÉ : poverty
gêné, -née [ʒene] *adj* **1** : embarrassed **2** : short of money **3** : uncomfortable **4** *Can* : shy
généalogie [ʒenealɔʒi] *nf* : genealogy
généalogique [ʒenealɔʒik] *adj* : genealogical
gêner [ʒene] *vt* **1** : to embarrass, to make uncomfortable **2** DÉRANGER : to bother **3** : to hamper, to restrict, to disrupt — **se gêner** *vr* **1** : to get in each other's way **2** : to put oneself out <ne te gêne pas! : don't mind me!>
général[1], **-rale** [ʒeneral] *adj, mpl* **-raux** [-ro]: general <en général : in general, for the most part> — **généralement** [-ralmɑ̃] *adv*
général[2] *nm, pl* **-raux** : general <général de brigade : brigadier general>
générale *nf* **1** : general's wife **2** : dress rehearsal
généralisation [ʒeneralizasjɔ̃] *nf* **1** : general application, spreading **2** : generalization
généraliser [ʒeneralize] *vt* : to make general, to put to general use — *vi* : to generalize — **se généraliser** *vr* : to become widespread
généraliste[1] [ʒeneralist] *adj* : general, nonspecialist
généraliste[2] *nmf* : general practitioner
généralité [ʒeneralite] *nf* : generality
générateur[1], **-trice** [ʒeneratœr, -tris] *adj* : generating, generative
générateur[2] *nm* : generator, producer
génération [ʒenerasjɔ̃] *nf* : generation
génératrice *nf* : generator (of electricity)
générer [ʒenere] {87} *vt* : to generate
généreux, -reuse [ʒenerø, -røz] *adj* : generous — **généreusement** [-røzmɑ̃] *adv*
générique[1] [ʒenerik] *adj* : generic
générique[2] *nm* : credits *pl* (in movies)
générosité [ʒenerɔzite] *nf* : generosity
genèse [ʒənɛz] *nf* : genesis
genêt [ʒənɛ] *nm* : broom (plant)

généticien, -cienne [ʒenetisjɛ̃] *n* : geneticist

génétique[1] [ʒenetik] *adj* : genetic — **génétiquement** [-tikmɑ̃] *adv*

génétique[2] *nf* : genetics

genévrier [ʒənevrije] *nm* : juniper

génial, -niale [ʒenjal] *adj, mpl* **-niaux** [-njo] **1** : of genius, brilliant **2** *fam* : fantastic, great

génie [ʒeni] *nm* **1** : genius **2** : genie **3** : engineering <génie civil : civil engineering>

génisse [ʒenis] *nf* **1** : heifer **2** *Can* : female calf

génital, -tale [ʒenital] *adj, mpl* **-taux** [-to] : genital

génitif [ʒenitif] *nm* : genitive (in grammar)

génocide [ʒenɔsid] *nm* : genocide

genou [ʒənu] *nm, pl* **genoux 1** : knee **2 se mettre à genoux** : to kneel down

genre [ʒɑ̃r] *nm* **1** SORTE : kind, sort, type **2** : style, manner **3** : gender **4** : genre (in art, etc.) **5** : genus

gens [ʒɑ̃] *nmfpl* **1** : people <la plupart des gens : most people> <vieilles gens : old folk> <jeunes gens : young people, teenagers> **2 gens d'affaires** : businessmen *m,* businesswomen *f* **3 gens de lettres** : writers, scholars

gentil[1], **-tille** [ʒɑ̃ti, -tij] *adj* **1** AIMABLE : kind, nice **2** SAGE : good, well-behaved **3** AGRÉABLE : pleasant **4** : fair <une gentille somme : a tidy sum>

gentil[2] [ʒɑ̃ti] *nm* : gentile

gentilhomme [ʒɑ̃tijɔm] *nm, pl* **gentilshommes** : gentleman

gentillesse [ʒɑ̃tijɛs] *nf* AMABILITÉ : kindness, niceness

gentiment [ʒɑ̃timɑ̃] *adv* : nicely, kindly

gentleman [dʒɛntləman] *nm, pl* **gentlemen** [-tləmɛn] : gentleman

génuflexion [ʒenyflɛksjɔ̃] *nf* : genuflexion

géochimie [ʒeɔʃimi] *nf* : geochemistry

géodésique [ʒeɔdezik] *adj* : geodesic

géographe [ʒeɔgraf] *nmf* : geographer

géographie [ʒeɔgrafi] *nf* : geography

géographique [ʒeɔgrafik] *adj* : geographic, geographical — **géographiquement** [-fikmɑ̃] *adv*

geôlier, -lière [ʒolje, -ljɛr] *n* : jailer

géologie [ʒeɔlɔʒi] *nf* : geology

géologique [ʒeɔlɔʒik] *adj* : geologic, geological — **géologiquement** [-ʒikmɑ̃] *adv*

géologue [ʒeɔlɔg] *nmf* : geologist

géomagnétique [ʒeɔmaɲetik] *adj* : geomagnetic

géomètre [ʒeɔmɛtr] *nmf or* **arpenteur géomètre** : surveyor

géométrie [ʒeɔmetri] *nf* : geometry

géométrique [ʒeɔmetrik] *adj* : geometrical

gérance [ʒerɑ̃s] *nf* : management

géranium [ʒeranjɔm] *nm* : geranium

gérant, -rante [ʒerɑ̃, -rɑ̃t] *n* : manager

gerbe [ʒɛrb] *nf* **1** : sheaf (of wheat) **2** : bunch (of flowers, etc.) **3** : spray, burst (of water, sparks, etc.)

gerbille [ʒɛrbij] *nf* : gerbil

gercer [ʒɛrse] {6} *vt* : to chap, to crack — **se gercer** *vr*

gerçure [ʒɛrsyr] *nf* : chapping, crack (in the skin)

gérer [ʒere] {87} *vt* : to manage, to run, to handle

gériatrie [ʒerjatri] *nf* : geriatrics

gériatrique [ʒerjatrik] *adj* : geriatric

germain, -maine [ʒɛrmɛ̃, -mɛn] *adj* **cousin germain** : first cousin

germanium [ʒermanjɔm] *nm* : germanium

germe [ʒɛrm] *nm* **1** : germ **2** : sprout **3** : seed (of an idea, etc.)

germer [ʒɛrme] *vi* **1** : to sprout, to germinate **2** : to form (of ideas, hopes, etc.)

germination [ʒɛrminasjɔ̃] *nf* : germination

gérondif [ʒerɔ̃dif] *nm* : gerund

gérontologie [ʒerɔ̃tɔlɔʒi] *nf* : gerontology

gérontologue [ʒerɔ̃tɔlɔg] *nmf* : gerontologist

gésier [ʒezje] *nm* : gizzard

gésir [ʒezir] {47} *vi* : to lie, to be lying

gestation [ʒɛstasjɔ̃] *nf* : gestation

geste [ʒɛst] *nm* : gesture, movement <ne faites pas un geste : don't move>

gestion [ʒɛstjɔ̃] *nf* : management <gestion de fichiers : file management>

gestionnaire [ʒɛstjɔnɛr] *nmf* : administrator

geyser [ʒezɛr] *nm* : geyser

ghanéen, -néenne [ganeɛ̃, -neɛn] *adj* : Ghanaian

Ghanéen, -néenne *n* : Ghanaian

ghetto [gɛto] *nm* : ghetto

gibbon [ʒibɔ̃] *nm* : gibbon

gibecière [ʒibsjɛr] *nf* **1** : game bag **2** : shoulder bag

gibet [ʒibɛ] *nm* : gallows

gibier [ʒibje] *nm* **1** : game (animals) **2** : prey <un gibier facile : an easy target>

giboulée [ʒibule] *nf* : sudden shower <les giboulées de mars : April showers>

giclée [ʒikle] *nf* : spurt, squirt

gicler [ʒikle] *vi* : to spurt, to squirt, to spatter

gicleur [ʒiklœr] *nm Can* : sprinkler (for fire)

gifle [ʒifl] *nf* : slap (in the face)

gifler [ʒifle] *vt* : to slap

gigantesque [ʒigɑ̃tɛsk] *adj* : gigantic, huge

gigogne [ʒigɔɲ] *adj* **1 lit gigogne** : trundle bed **2 tables gigognes** : nest of tables

gigot [ʒigo] *nm* : leg of lamb

gigoter [ʒigɔte] *vi fam* : to wriggle, to fidget

gigue [ʒig] *nf* : jig

gilet [ʒilɛ] *nm* **1** : vest <gilet pare-balles : bulletproof vest> <gilet de sauvetage : life jacket> **2** : cardigan (sweater)

gin [dʒin] *nm* : gin

gingembre [ʒɛ̃ʒɑ̃br] *nm* : ginger

ginseng [ʒinsɑ̃g] *nm* : ginseng

girafe [ʒiraf] *nf* : giraffe

giratoire [ʒiratwar] *adj* **sens giratoire** : rotary, traffic circle

girofle [ʒirɔfl] *nm* **clou de girofle** : clove

giroflée [ʒirɔfle] *nf* : wallflower

giron [ʒirɔ̃] *nm* **1** : lap **2** : bosom <dans le giron familial : in the bosom of one's family>

girouette [ʒirwɛt] *nf* : weather vane

gisement [ʒizmɑ̃] *nm* : deposit, bed (in geology)

gitan, -tane [ʒitɑ̃, -tan] *n* : Gypsy

gîte[1] [ʒit] *nm* **1** : shelter, lodging <le gîte et le couvert : room and board> **2** : shank (of beef, etc.)

gîte[2] *nf* : list, listing (of a boat)

gîter [ʒite] *vi* : to heel, to list (of a ship)

givre [ʒivr] *nm* : frost

givrer [ʒivre] *vt* : to cover with frost — *vi* : to ice up — **se givrer** *vr*

glabre [glabr] *adj* **1** : hairless **2** : clean-shaven

glaçage [glasaʒ] *nm* **1** : glazing (of fabric, etc.) **2** : icing (on cake)

glace [glas] *nf* **1** : ice **2** *France* : ice cream **3** VITRE : glass **4** MIROIR : mirror **5 glaces** *nfpl* : ice sheets **6 rester de glace** : to remain unmoved

glacé, -cée [glase] *adj* **1** GLACIAL : icy **2** : iced <thé glacé : iced tea> **3** GELÉ : frozen **4** : glossy (of paper, etc.)

glacer [glase] {6} *vt* **1** : to freeze, to chill **2** : to frost (a cake) **3** : to glaze, to give a shiny finish to **4** INTIMIDER : to intimidate

glacial, -ciale [glasjal] *adj, mpl* **-cials** *or* **-ciaux** [-sjo] : icy, frigid — **glacialement** [-sjalmɑ̃] *adv*

glaciaire [glasjɛr] *adj* : glacial (in geology)

glacier [glasje] *nm* : glacier

glacière [glasjɛr] *nf* : cooler, ice chest

glaçon [glasɔ̃] *nm* **1** : icicle **2** : ice cube

gladiateur [gladjatœr] *nm* : gladiator

glaïeul [glajœl] *nm* : gladiolus

glaire [glɛr] *nf* **1** : white of an egg **2** : mucus

glaise [glɛz] *nf* : clay

glaive [glɛv] *nm* : sword

gland [glɑ̃] *nm* **1** : acorn **2** : tassel

glande [glɑ̃d] *nf* : gland — **glandulaire** [-dylɛr] *adj*

glaner [glane] *v* : to glean

glapir [glapir] *vi* : to yelp

glapissement [glapismɑ̃] *nm* : yelp

glas [gla] *nm* **1** : toll, knell **2 sonner le glas de** : to sound the death knell for

glaucome [glokom] *nm* : glaucoma

glauque [glok] *adj* **1** : dull blue-green **2** LUGUBRE : gloomy, dreary

glissade [glisad] *nf* **1** : slide, sliding **2** CHUTE : fall, slip

glissant, -sante [glisɑ̃, -sɑ̃t] *adj* : slippery

glissement [glismɑ̃] *nm* **1** : sliding, gliding **2** : shift <glissement politique vers la droite : political shift to the right> **3 glissement de terrain** : landslide

glisser [glise] *vi* **1** : to slide **2** : to slip **3** DÉRAPER : to skid — *vt* : to slip, to sneak <glissez la lettre sous la porte : slip the letter under the door> — **se glisser** *vr* : to slip, to creep

glissière [glisjɛr] *nf* **1** : slide, groove **2 porte à glissière** : sliding door

glissoire [gliswar] *nf* : slide

global, -bale [glɔbal] *adj, mpl* **globaux** [glɔbo] : overall, total

globalement [glɔbalmɑ̃] *adv* : as a whole

globe [glɔb] *nm* **1** : globe **2 globe oculaire** : eyeball **3 globe terrestre** : the earth

globe–trotter [glɔbtrɔtœr] *nm* : globetrotter

globulaire [glɔbylɛr] *adj* : globular

globule [glɔbyl] *nm* : corpuscle, blood cell <globules blancs : white blood cells>

globuleux, -leuse [glɔbylø, -løz] *adj* : protruding (of eyes)

gloire [glwar] *nf* **1** RENOMMÉE : glory, fame **2** MÉRITE : distinction, credit **3** HOMMAGE : praise, homage **4** : celebrity, star

glorieux, -rieuse [glɔrjø, -jøz] *adj* : glorious — **glorieusement** [-jøzmɑ̃] *adv*

glorification [glɔrifikasjɔ̃] *nm* : glorification

glorifier [glɔrifje] {96} *vt* : to glorify, to extol — **se glorifier** *vr* **~ de** : to glory in

gloriole [glɔrjɔl] *nf* : vainglory

glose [gloz] *nf* : gloss, annotation

gloser [gloze] *vt* : to annotate, to gloss — *vi* **~ sur** : to ramble on about

glossaire [glɔsɛr] *nm* : glossary

glouglou [gluglu] *nm* **1** *fam* : gurgling **2** : gobbling (of a turkey)

glouglouter [gluglute] *vi* **1** *fam* : to gurgle **2** : to gobble (of a turkey)

gloussement [glusmɑ̃] *nm* : **1** clucking **2** : chuckling, chortling

glousser [gluse] *vi* **1** : to cluck **2** : to chuckle, to chortle

glouton[1], **-tonne** [glutɔ̃, -tɔn] *adj* : gluttonous, greedy

glouton[2], **-tonne** *n* : glutton

glouton[3] *nm* : wolverine

gloutonnerie [glutɔnri] *nf* : gluttony

gluant, gluante [glyɑ̃, -ɑ̃t] *adj* COLLANT : sticky, gummy, glutinous

glucose [glykoz] *nm* : glucose

gluten [glytɛn] *nm* : gluten

glutineux, -neuse [glytinø, -nøz] *adj* : glutinous

glycérine [gliserin] *nf* : glycerine

glycine [glisin] *nf* : wisteria

gnôle [ɲol] *nf France fam* : booze

gnome [gnom] *nm* : gnome

gnou [gnu] *nm* : gnu

go [go] *adv France fam* **tout de go** : straightaway, at once

gobelet [gɔblɛ] *nm* : tumbler, beaker

gober [gɔbe] *vt* **1** : to swallow whole **2** *fam* : to swallow, to fall for

godasse [gɔdas] *nf fam* : shoe

godet [gɔdɛ] *nm* **1** : jar, small pitcher **2** : pucker (in clothing)

godille [gɔdij] *nf* : scull, paddle

godiller [gɔdije] *vi* : to scull

goéland [gɔelɑ̃] *nm* : gull

goélette [gɔelɛt] *nf* : schooner

goglu [gɔgly] *nm Can* : bobolink

gogo [gogo] *nm fam* **à ~** : galore

goguenard, -narde [gognar, -nard] *adj* MOQUEUR : mocking

goinfre [gwɛ̃fr] *nm fam* : pig, glutton

goitre [gwatr] *nm* : goiter

golf [gɔlf] *nm* : golf

golfe [gɔlf] *nm* : gulf, bay

golfeur, -feuse [gɔlfœr, -føz] *n* : golfer

gombo [gɔ̃bo] *nm* : gumbo

gomme [gɔm] *nf* **1** : gum, resin **2** : eraser **3 gomme à mâcher** : chewing gum

gommer [gɔme] *vt* **1** : to gum <papier gommé : gummed paper> **2** EFFACER : to erase

gond [gɔ̃] *nm* **1** : hinge **2 sortir de ses gonds** *fam* : to fly off the handle

gondole [gɔ̃dɔl] *nf* : gondola

gondoler [gɔ̃dɔle] *v* **se gondoler** *vr* **1** : to warp, to buckle **2** *fam* : to laugh, to be in stitches

gonflable [gɔ̃flabl] *adj* : inflatable

gonflé, -flée [gɔ̃fle] *adj* **1** : swollen, bloated **2 être gonflé** *fam* : to have a nerve

gonflement [gɔ̃fləmɑ̃] *nm* **1** : inflation **2** : swelling

gonfler [gɔ̃fle] *vt* **1** : to blow up, to inflate (a balloon, a tire, etc.) **2** : to swell <avoir les yeux gonflés : to have swollen eyes> **3** : to inflate, to exaggerate <prix gonflés : inflated prices> **—** *vi* : to swell, to rise **— se gonfler** *vr* **1** : to swell **2 ~ de** : to swell up with, to be filled with

gonfleur [gɔ̃flœr] *nm* : (air) pump

gong [gɔ̃g] *nm* : gong

goret [gɔrɛ] *nm* : piglet

gorge [gɔrʒ] *nf* **1** : throat <mal de gorge : sore throat> <avoir la gorge serrée : to have a lump in one's throat> **2** : bosom, chest **3** : gorge (in geography) **4** : groove, channel

gorgée [gɔrʒe] *nf* : mouthful, sip, gulp

gorger [gɔrʒe] {17} *vt* : to fill, to stuff **— se gorger** *vr* **1** : to fill up **2** SE BOURRER : to stuff oneself

gorille [gɔrij] *nm* **1** : gorilla **2** *fam* : bodyguard

gosier [gozje] *nm* : throat

gosse [gɔs] *nmf France fam* : kid, youngster

gosser [gɔse] *vt Can fam* : to whittle

gothique [gɔtik] *adj* : Gothic

gouache [gwaʃ] *nf* : poster paint

gouaille [gwaj] *nf* : cocky humor, cheek

goudron [gudrɔ̃] *nm* : tar

goudronner [gudrɔne] *vt* : to tar (a road)

gouffre [gufr] *nm* **1** : gulf, abyss **2 au bord du gouffre** : on the brink of despair

gouge [guʒ] *nf* : gouge, chisel

goujat [guʒa] *nm* : boor

goujon [guʒɔ̃] *nm* : dowel

goulasch *or* **goulache** [gulaʃ] *nmf* : goulash

goule [gul] *nf* : ghoul

goulet [gulɛ] *nm* **1** : gully **2** : narrows **3 goulet d'étranglement** : bottleneck

goulot [gulo] *nm* **1** : neck (of a bottle) <boire au goulot : to drink from the bottle> **2 goulot d'étranglement** : bottleneck, obstacle

goulu[1], -lue [guly] *adj* : greedy, gluttonous **— goulûment** [-lymɑ̃] *adv*

goulu[2], -lue *n* : glutton

goupille [gupij] *nf* : pin

gourbi [gurbi] *nm* : foxhole

gourd, gourde [gur, gurd] *adj* : numb (with cold)

gourde [gurd] *nf* **1** : canteen, flask **2** : gourd **3** *fam* : dope, blockhead

gourdin [gurdɛ̃] *nm* : cudgel, club

gourmand[1], -mande [gurmɑ̃, -mɑ̃d] *adj* **1** : greedy **2** : fond of eating

gourmand[2], -mande *n* **1** : glutton **2** : gourmet, epicure

gourmandise [gurmɑ̃diz] *nf* **1** : greed **2** : gluttony **3 gourmandises** *nfpl* : sweets, delicacies

gourmet [gurmɛ] *nm* GASTRONOME : gourmet

gourmette [gurmɛt] *nf* : chain bracelet

gourou [guru] *nm* : guru

gousse [gus] *nf* **1** : pod **2 gousse d'ail** : clove of garlic

gousset [gusɛ] *nm* : vest pocket, watch pocket

goût [gu] *nm* **1** : taste (sense) **2** SAVEUR : flavor **3** : taste, discernment <avoir du goût : to have good taste> <de mauvais goût : tasteless, in bad taste> **4** : liking, fondness <prendre goût à : to develop a liking for>

goûter[1] [gute] *vt* **1** : to taste **2** : to relish, to enjoy **—** *vi* **1** : to have an afternoon snack **2 ~ à** *or* **~ de** : to try out, to sample **3 ~ à** *or* **~ de** : to get a taste of

goûter[2] *nm* : afternoon snack

goutte [gut] *nf* **1** : drop <une goutte de sang : a drop of blood> <tomber goutte à goutte : to drip> **2** : gout **3 gouttes** *nfpl* : drops (in medicine)

gouttelette [gutlɛt] *nf* : droplet, globule

goutter [gute] *vi* : to drip

gouttière [gutjɛr] *nf* **1** : gutter (on a roof) **2** : downspout **3** : cast, splint

gouvernail [guvɛrnaj] *nm* **1** : rudder **2** BARRE : helm <tenir le gouvernail : to take the helm>

gouvernante [guvɛrnɑ̃t] *nf* **1** : governess **2** : housekeeper

gouverne [guvɛrn] *nf* **1 gouverne de direction** : rudder (of an airplane) **2 pour votre gouverne** : for your information

gouvernement [guvɛrnəmɑ̃] *nm* : government — **gouvernemental, -tale** [-mɑ̃tal] *adj*

gouverner [guvɛrne] *vt* **1** DIRIGER : to steer (a ship) **2** : to govern, to rule **3** MAÎTRISER : to control (one's emotions, etc.) — *vi* : to steer

gouverneur [guvɛrnœr] *nm* **1** : governor **2 gouverneur général** *Can* : governor-general

goyave [gɔjav] *nf* : guava (fruit)

grabat [graba] *nm* : pallet (bed)

grabataire[1] [grabatɛr] *adj* : bedridden

grabataire[2] *n* : (bedridden) invalid

grabuge [grabyʒ] *nm fam* BAGARRE : brawl, fighting

grâce [gras] *nf* **1** : gracefulness, charm <avec grâce : gracefully> **2** : willingness <de bonne grâce : with good grace, willingly> **3** : favor <accorder une grâce : to grant a favor> **4** : mercy, pardon **5 ~ à** : thanks to **6 grâces** *nfpl* : grace <dire les grâces : to say grace>

gracier [grasje] {96} *vt* : to pardon

gracieuseté [grasjøzte] *nf* **1** : kindliness **2** : free gift

gracieux, -cieuse [grasjø, -sjøz] *adj* **1** : graceful **2** AIMABLE : gracious, kind **3** GRATUIT : free — **gracieusement** [-sjøzmɑ̃] *adv*

gracile [grasil] *adj* ÉLANCÉ : slender

gradation [gradasjɔ̃] *nf* : gradation

grade [grad] *nm* **1** : rank <monter en grade : to be promoted> **2** : university degree, title **3** : grade (of oil)

gradin [gradɛ̃] *nm* **1** : tier **2 gradins** *nmpl* : bleachers, stands

graduel, -duelle [gradɥɛl] *adj* : gradual, progressive — **graduellement** [-dɥɛlmɑ̃] *adv*

graduer [gradɥe] *vt* **1** : to graduate (a measuring instrument) **2** : to increase gradually

graffiti [grafiti] *nmpl* : graffiti

grafigne [grafiɲ] *or* **grafignure** [grafiɲyr] *nf Can* : scratch, scrape

grafigner [grafiɲe] *vt Can* : to scratch, to scrape

grain [grɛ̃] *nm* **1** : (cereal) grain **2** : seed, berry <grain de café : coffee bean> <grain de poivre : peppercorn> <grain de raisin : grape> **3** : bead **4** : speck, particle <grain de sable : grain of sand> <un grain d'originalité : a touch of originality> **5 grain de beauté** : mole

graine [grɛn] *nf* **1** : seed <monter en graine : to go to seed> **2 être de la mauvaise graine** : to be incorrigible, to be a bad lot

graisse [grɛs] *nf* **1** : grease **2** : fat **3 graisse de baleine** : blubber

graisser [grɛse] *vt* **1** : to lubricate, to grease, to oil **2** : to stain with grease

graisseux, -seuse [grɛsø, -søz] *adj* **1** : greasy **2** : fatty (in medicine)

grammaire [gramɛr] *nf* : grammar

grammatical, -cale [gramatikal] *adj, mpl* **-caux** [-ko] : grammatical — **grammaticalement** [-kalmɑ̃] *adv*

gramme [gram] *nm* : gram

granade [granad] *nf* : pomegranate

grand[1] [grɑ̃] *adv* **1** : wide <ouvrir grand : to open wide> **2 voir grand** : to think big **3 en ~** : on a large scale, in a big way

grand[2], **grande** [grɑ̃, grɑ̃d] *adj* **1** : tall, long, wide **2** GROS : big, large **3** : abundant <un grand monde : many people> <au grand jour : in broad daylight> **4** : great <grandes distances : great distances> <c'est une grande travailleuse : she works very hard> **5** PRINCIPAL : main, principal **6** : important <un grand homme : a great man> **7** : elder, older, grown-up <ma grande sœur : my older sister> <les grandes personnes : grown-ups, adults> **8** : extreme, intense <avoir grand faim : to be very hungry> <il est grand temps que : it's high time that>

grand[3] *nm* : important person, leader, big power

grand–angle [grɑ̃tɑ̃gl] *or* **grand–angulaire** [-ɑ̃gylɛr] *nm, pl* **grands–angles** [grɑ̃zɑ̃gl] *or* **grands–angulaires** [grɑ̃zɑ̃gylɛr] : wide-angle lens

grand–chose [grɑ̃ʃoz] *adv* **pas grand–chose** : not much

grandement [grɑ̃dmɑ̃] *adv* **1** BEAUCOUP : greatly, a lot **2** : extremely

grandeur [grɑ̃dœr] *nf* **1** : size, scale, magnitude <grandeur nature : life-size> **2** NOBLESSE : greatness, nobility **3** SPLENDEUR : splendor, glory

grandiloquence [grɑ̃dilɔkɑ̃s] *nf* : pomposity, bombast

grandiloquent, -quente [grɑ̃dilɔkɑ̃, -kɑ̃t] *adj* : grandiloquent, pompous

grandiose [grɑ̃djoz] *adj* : grandiose

grandir [grɑ̃dir] *vt* **1** : to magnify, to make look taller **2** EXAGÉRER : to exaggerate **3** ENNOBLIR : to increase the stature of — *vi* **1** : to grow **2** AUGMENTER : to increase

grand–mère [grɑ̃mɛr] *nf, pl* **grands–mères** : grandmother

grand–oncle [grɑ̃tɔ̃kl] *nm, pl* **grands–oncles** [grɑ̃zɔ̃kl] : great-uncle

grand–peine [grɑ̃pɛn] *nf* **à ~** : with great difficulty

grand–père [grɑ̃pɛr] *nm, pl* **grands–pères** : grandfather

grands–parents [grɑ̃parɑ̃] *nmpl* : grandparents
grand–tante [grɑ̃tɑ̃t] *nf, pl* **grand(s)–tantes** : great-aunt
grand–voile [grɑ̃vwal] *nf, pl* **grand(s)–voiles** : mainsail
grange [grɑ̃ʒ] *nf* : barn
granit *or* **granite** [granit] *nm* : granite
granule [granyl] *nm* : small pill
granulé [granyle] *nm* : granule
granuleux, -leuse [granylø, -løz] *adj* : granular
graphique[1] [grafik] *adj* : graphic — **graphiquement** [-fikmɑ̃] *adv*
graphique[2] *nm* : graph
graphisme [grafism] *nm* **1** : writing, handwriting **2** : graphic arts *pl*
graphiste [grafist] *nmf* : graphic artist
graphite [grafit] *nm* : graphite
grappe [grap] *nf* : cluster <grappe de raisins : bunch of grapes>
grappiller [grapije] *vt* : to gather, to glean
grappin [grapɛ̃] *nm* **1** : grapnel **2 mettre le grappin sur** : to get one's hooks into
gras[1] [gra] *adv* **1 faire gras** : to eat meat (in religion) **2 manger gras** : to eat fatty foods **3 parler gras** : to talk coarsely
gras[2], **grasse** [gra, gras] *adj* **1** : fatty <matières grasses : fats> **2** GROS : fat (of persons) **3** HUILEUX : greasy, oily **4** : sticky, slimy **5** : throaty (of the voice), loose (of a cough) **6** VULGAIRE : crude, coarse **7** : lush, abundant **8** : bold (of type)
gras[3] *nm* **1** : fat **2** : grease **3** : fleshy part <gras de la jambe : calf>
grassement [grasmɑ̃] *adv* : highly, handsomely <grassement payé : well paid>
grassouillet, -lette [grasujɛ, -jɛt] *adj* POTELÉ : pudgy, plump
gratifiant, -fiante [gratifjɑ̃, -jɑ̃t] *adj* : gratifying, rewarding
gratification [gratifikasjɔ̃] *nf* **1** : bonus **2** : gratification
gratifier [gratifje] {96} *vt* **1** : to reward **2** : to gratify
gratin [gratɛ̃] *nm* **1** : dish baked with cheese or crumb topping **2** *fam* : upper crust (of society)
gratiné, -née [gratine] *adj* **1** : au gratin, browned **2** *fam* : extreme, difficult, weird
gratis [gratis] *adv* : free
gratitude [gratityd] *nf* : gratitude, gratefulness
gratte [grat] *nf Can* CHASSE-NEIGE : snowplow
gratte–ciel [gratsjɛl] *nms & pl* : skyscraper
grattement [gratmɑ̃] *n* : scratching (sound)
gratte–papier [gratpapje] *nms & pl* : pencil pusher, office drudge
gratte–pieds [gratpje] *nms & pl* : doormat
gratter [grate] *vt* **1** : to scratch **2** : to scrape (a surface) **3** *fam* : to scrape together **4** *fam* : to overtake **5 gratter (de) la guitare** : to strum a guitar — *vi* : to scratch — **se gratter** *vr* : to scratch oneself
gratteux, -teuse [gratø, -tøz] *adj Can fam* : stingy, cheap
grattoir [gratwar] *nm* : scraper
gratuit, -tuite [gratɥi, -tɥit] *adj* **1** : free **2** : gratuitous — **gratuitement** [-tɥitmɑ̃] *adv*
gratuité [gratɥite] *nf* **1** : exemption from payment **2** : gratuitousness
gravats [grava] *nmpl* : rubble
grave [grav] *adj* **1** SÉRIEUX : grave, serious **2** : solemn **3** : deep, low-pitched
graveleux, -leuse [gravlø, -løz] *adj* **1** : gravelly **2** : gritty **3** : indecent, smutty
gravelle [gravɛl] *nf Can* : fine gravel
gravement [gravmɑ̃] *adv* **1** : gravely, solemnly **2** : seriously
graver [grave] *vt* **1** : to engrave, to carve **2** : to fix, to etch <gravé dans ma mémoire : etched in my memory>
graveur, -veuse [gravœr, -vøz] *n* : engraver
gravier [gravje] *nm* : gravel, grit
gravillon [gravijɔ̃] *nm* : (fine) gravel
gravir [gravir] *vt* : to climb (up)
gravitation [gravitasjɔ̃] *nf* : gravitation
gravité [gravite] *nf* **1** : gravity **2** : seriousness, importance
graviter [gravite] *vi* : to gravitate, to revolve
gravure [gravyr] *nf* **1** : engraving <gravure sur bois : woodcutting> <gravure à l'eau forte : etching> **2** : print, plate
gré [gre] *nm* **1** VOLONTÉ : will <de plein gré : willingly> <contre son gré : unwillingly> **2** GOÛT : taste, liking <à votre gré : as you wish> **3 bon gré mal gré** : like it or not **4 savoir (bien) gré à** : to be grateful to
grèbe [grɛb] *nm* : grebe
grébiche [grebiʃ] *nf Can* : crone, hag
grec[1], **grecque** [grɛk] *adj* : Greek
grec[2] *nm* : Greek (language)
Grec, Grecque *n* : Greek
gréement [gremɑ̃] *nm* : rigging
gréer [gree] {89} *vt* : to rig (a ship)
greffe [grɛf] *nf* **1** : graft (in botany) **2** : graft, transplant (in medicine)
greffer [grɛfe] *vt* **1** : to graft **2** : to transplant (an organ) — **se greffer** *vr* : to come along, to arise
greffier, -fière [grɛfje, -fjɛr] *nm* : clerk of court
grégaire [gregɛr] *adj* : gregarious
grège [grɛʒ] *adj* : raw, unbleached
grêle[1] [grɛl] *adj* **1** : lanky, spindly **2** : high-pitched, shrill
grêle[2] *nf* : hail
grêlé, -lée [grele] *adj* : pockmarked

grêler [grele] *v impers* **il grêle** : it's hailing

grêlon [grɛlɔ̃] *nm* : hailstone

grelot [grəlo] *nm* : small bell, sleigh bell

grelotter [grəlɔte] *vi* **1** TREMBLER : to shiver **2** : to tinkle, to jingle

grenade [grənad] *nf* **1** : pomegranate **2** : grenade <grenade à main : hand grenade>

grenadin, -dine [grənadɛ̃, -din] *adj* : Grenadian

Grenadin, -dine *n* : Grenadian

grenadine [grənadin] *nf* : grenadine

grenat[1] [grəna] *adj* : dark red

grenat[2] *nm* : garnet

grenier [grənje] *nm* **1** : attic, loft <grenier à foin : hayloft> **2** *or* **grenier à blé** : breadbasket (region)

grenouille [grənuj] *nf* : frog

grès [grɛ] *nm* **1** : sandstone **2** : stoneware

grésil [grezil] *nm* : fine hail, sleet

grésillement [grezijmɑ̃] *nm* **1** : crackling (of a telephone, radio, etc.) **2** : sizzling

grésiller [grezije] *vi* : to crackle, to sizzle — *v impers* : to sleet, to hail

grève [grɛv] *nf* **1** PLAGE : shore **2** : strike <grève de la faim : hunger strike>

grever [grəve] {52} *vt* : to burden, to put a (financial) strain on

gréviste[1] [grevist] *adj* : striking

gréviste[2] *nmf* : striker

gribouillage [gribujaʒ] *nm* : scribble, scrawl

gribouiller [gribuje] *vt* : to scribble — *vi* : to doodle, to scribble

gricher [griʃe] *vt Can fam* : to grind (one's teeth)

grief [grijɛf] *nm* : grievance

grièvement [grijɛvmɑ̃] *adv* : seriously, severely

griffe [grif] *nf* **1** : claw <sortir ses griffes : to show one's claws> <les griffes de la mort : the jaws of death> **2** : signature, label (of a product)

griffer [grife] *vt* : to scratch — **se griffer** *vr*

griffonner [grifɔne] *vt* : to scribble, to jot down

griffure [grifyr] *nf* : scratch

grignoter [griɲɔte] *vt* **1** : to nibble **2** : to eat away at **3** : to gain, to acquire gradually — *vi* **1** : to gnaw **2** : to nibble

gril [gril] *nm* **1** : broiler **2** : grill (for cooking)

grill [gril] *nm* : grill (restaurant)

grillade [grijad] *nf* **1** : grilled meat, grill **2 faire des grillades** : to have a barbecue

grillage [grijaʒ] *nm* : wire fencing

grille [grij] *nf* **1** : metal fencing or gate **2** : bars *pl* **3** : grate **4** : grid, squares *pl* **5** : scale, table <grille des salaires : salary scale>

grille–pain [grijpɛ̃] *nms & pl* : toaster

griller [grije] *vt* **1** : to toast, to roast (nuts, etc.) **2** : to grill, to broil **3** : to burn out **4 griller un feu rouge** : to go through a red light — *vi* **1** : to broil **2 se faire griller** *Can fam* : to get a suntan

grillon [grijɔ̃] *nm* : cricket

grimace [grimas] *nf* : grimace, face <faire des grimaces : to make faces> <faire la grimace : to make a (long) face, to scowl>

grimacer [grimase] {6} *vi* : to grimace

grimper [grɛ̃pe] *vi* **1** : to climb **2** : to be steep **3** *fam* : to soar, to rocket — *vt* : to climb

grimpeur, -peuse [grɛ̃pœr, -pøz] *n* : climber

grinçant, -çante [grɛ̃sɑ̃, -sɑ̃t] *adj* **1** : creaking, grating **2** : caustic <humour grinçant : caustic wit>

grincement [grɛ̃smɑ̃] *nm* : creak, squeak

grincer [grɛ̃se] {6} *vi* **1** : to creak, to grate, to grind **2 grincer des dents** : to grind one's teeth

grincheux, -cheuse [grɛ̃ʃø, -ʃøz] *adj* GROGNON : grumpy

gringalet [grɛ̃galɛ] *nm* : puny person, weakling

grippe [grip] *nf* **1** : flu, influenza **2 prendre qqn en grippe** : to take a sudden dislike to s.o.

grippé, -pée [gripe] *adj* **être grippé** : to have the flu

gripper [gripe] *v* : to jam — **se gripper** *vr* : to seize up

grippe–sou [gripsu] *nm, pl* **grippe–sous** *fam* : tightwad, skinflint

gris[1], **grise** [gri, griz] *adj* **1** : gray **2** MORNE : dull, dreary <un temps gris : a gray day> **3** *fam* : tipsy

gris[2] *nm* : gray

grisaille [grizaj] *nf* **1** : grayness **2** MONOTONIE : dullness

grisant, -sante [grizɑ̃, -zɑ̃t] *adj* ENIVRANT : exhilarating, intoxicating

grisâtre [grizatr] *adj* : grayish

griser [grize] *vt* **1** ENIVRER : to intoxicate **2** : to exhilarate — **se griser** *vr*

griserie [grizri] *nf* : exhilaration

grisonnant [grizɔnɑ̃] *adj* : grizzled

grisonner [grizɔne] *vi* : to turn gray, to go gray

grive [griv] *nf* : thrush

grivois, -voise [grivwa, -waz] *adj* : bawdy, risqué

grizzli *or* **grizzly** [grizli] *nm* : grizzly bear

Groenlandais, -daise [grɔɛnlɑ̃dɛ, -dɛz] *n* : Greenlander

grog [grɔg] *nm* : grog

grogne [grɔɲ] *nf* : grumbling, discontent

grognement [grɔɲmɑ̃] *nm* **1** : growl, grunt **2** : grumble

grogner [grɔɲe] *vi* **1** : to growl, to grunt **2** : to grumble, to grouch

grognon, -gnonne [grɔɲɔ̃, -ɲɔn] *adj* : grumpy, grouchy

groin [grwɛ̃] *nm* : snout (of a pig)

grommeler [grɔmle] {8} *vt* : to mutter — *vi* **1** : to groan, to grumble **2** : to snort

grondement [grɔ̃dmɑ̃] *nm* **1** : rumble, roar **2** : growl

gronder [grɔ̃de] *vt* RÉPRIMANDER : to scold — *vi* **1** : to rumble, to roar **2** GROGNER : to growl **3** : to be brewing

gros[1] [gro] *adv* **1** BEAUCOUP : a great deal <coûter gros : to cost a lot> **2 écrire gros** : to write in big letters

gros[2]**, grosse** [gro, gros] *adj* **1** : big, large **2** : thick, bulky **3** : fat **4** : great, considerable <de gros dégâts : considerable damage> **5** : serious, major **6** : loud <une grosse voix : a booming voice> **7** : heavy <un gros fumeur : a heavy smoker> **8** : coarse, crude, rough **9 gros lot** : jackpot **10 gros plan** : close-up **11 gros titre** : headline **12 grosse caisse** : bass drum

gros[3]**, grosse** *n* **1** : fat person **2** : rich person

gros[4] *nm* **1** : bulk, main part <le gros des étudiants : most of the students> **2** : wholesale business **3 en ~** : roughly, in general

groseille [grozɛj] *nf* **1** : currant **2 groseille à maquereau** : gooseberry

gros–porteur [groportœr] *nm, pl* **gros–porteurs** : jumbo jet, liner

grosse [gros] *nf* : gross, twelve dozen

grossesse [grosɛs] *nf* : pregnancy

grosseur [grosœr] *nf* **1** : fatness, corpulence **2** : size **3** : lump, tumor

grossier, -sière [grosje, -sjɛr] *adj* **1** : coarse, rough **2** : crude, vulgar **3** : flagrant, glaring (of an error, etc.)

grossièrement [grosjɛrmɑ̃] *adv* **1** IMPOLIMENT : rudely **2** LOURDEMENT : grossly <se tromper grossièrement : to be grossly mistaken> **3** : roughly, crudely, coarsely **4** : approximately

grossièreté [grosjɛrte] *nf* **1** : rudeness **2** : crudeness **3** : coarseness, vulgarity

grossir [grosir] *vt* **1** AUGMENTER : to increase **2** EXAGÉRER : to exaggerate **3** AGRANDIR : to magnify, to enlarge **4** : to make appear fatter — *vi* **1** ENGRAISSER : to put on weight **2** : to grow larger

grossissant, -sante [grosisɑ̃, -sɑ̃t] *adj* **1** : magnifying <verre grossissant : magnifying glass> **2** : swelling, growing

grossissement [grosismɑ̃] *nm* **1** : enlargement **2** : magnification

grossiste [grosist] *nmf* : wholesaler, jobber

grosso modo [grosomodo] *adv* : more or less, roughly

grotesque [grɔtɛsk] *adj* **1** : grotesque **2** : ridiculous — **grotesquement** [-tɛskmɑ̃] *adv*

grotte [grɔt] *nf* : cave, grotto

grouiller [gruje] *vi* **~ de** : to swarm with, to teem with — **se grouiller** *vr fam* : to hurry, to get a move on

groupe [grup] *nm* **1** : group (of persons or objects) <groupe ethnique : ethnic group> <groupe de pression : pressure group, lobby> <groupe d'arbres : clump of trees> **2 groupe sanguin** : blood type

groupement [grupmɑ̃] *nm* **1** : grouping, group **2** : association

grouper [grupe] *vt* : to group, to pool (resources, etc.) — **se grouper** *vr* : to gather, to get together

groupuscule [grupyskyl] *nm* : faction, (political) clique

grouse [gruz] *nf* : grouse (bird)

gruau [gryo] *nm* **1** : (fine) wheat flour **2** : groats <gruau de maïs : grits> **3** *Can* : oatmeal, porridge

grue [gry] *nf* : crane

gruger [gryʒe] {17} *vt* **1** : to dupe, to swindle **2** *Can fam* : to eat away at

grumeau [grymo] *nm, pl* **grumeaux** : lump (in sauce, etc.)

grumeleux, -leuse [grymlø, -løz] *adj* : lumpy

gruyère [gryjɛr] *nm* : Gruyère (cheese)

guatémaltèque [gwatemaltɛk] *adj* : Guatemalan

Guatémaltèque *nmf* : Guatemalan

gué [ge] *nm* : ford, crossing <passer à gué : to ford>

guenille [gənij] *nf* **1** *Can* : rag **2 guenilles** *nfpl* : rags and tatters (clothing)

guenon [gənɔ̃] *nf* : female monkey

guépard [gepar] *nm* : cheetah

guêpe [gɛp] *nf* : wasp

guêpier [gepje] *nm* **1** : wasps' nest **2** : sticky situation, trap

guère [gɛr] *adv* **1 ne . . . guère** : hardly, scarcely <elle n'est guère aimable : she's not very kind> <il n'y a guère de voitures : there are hardly any cars> **2 ne . . . guère** : not for long, not often <il ne vient guère me voir : he rarely comes to see me>

guérilla [gerija] *nf* : guerrilla warfare, guerrillas *pl* (fighters)

guérillero [gerijero] *nm* : guerrilla

guérir [gerir] *vt* : to cure, to heal — *vi* **1** SE RÉTABLIR : to get better, to recover **2** : to heal — **se guérir** *vr* **1** : to be cured **2** : to break oneself of, to get over

guérison [gerizɔ̃] *nf* **1** : cure, healing **2** RÉTABLISSEMENT : recovery

guérissable [gerisabl] *adj* : curable

guérisseur, -seuse [gerisœr, -søz] *n* : healer

guérite [gerit] *nf* **1** : sentry box **2** *France* : workman's hut

guerre [gɛr] *nf* : war <faire la guerre à : to wage war against> <guerre chimique : chemical warfare>

guerrier[1], -rière [gɛrje, -jɛr] *adj* : warlike, martial

guerrier[2], -rière *n* : warrior

guerroyer [gerwaje] {58} *vi* : to wage war

guet [gɛ] *nm* : watch, lookout <faire le guet : to be on the lookout>

guet–apens [gɛtapɑ̃] *nm, pl* **guets–apens** : ambush

guetter [gete] *vt* **1** ÉPIER : to watch intently **2** ATTENDRE : to watch out for, to lie in wait for

guetteur [getœr] *nm* : lookout

gueule [gœl] *nf* **1** : mouth (of an animal, a tunnel, etc.) **2** *fam* : mouth, trap <(ferme) ta gueule! : shut up!> **3** *fam* : face <faire la gueule : to pull a face, to look sulky> **4 gueule de bois** : hangover

gueule–de–loup [gœldəlu] *nf, pl* **gueules–de–loup** : snapdragon

gueuler [gœle] *v fam* : to bawl, to bellow

gueuleton [gœltɔ̃] *nm fam* : feast, spread

gui [gi] *nm* **1** : mistletoe **2** : boom (of a ship)

guichet [giʃɛ] *nm* **1** : window, counter **2** : box office <jouer à guichets fermés : to play to a full house> **3 guichet automatique** : automatic teller machine

guichetier, -tière [giʃtje, -tjɛr] *n* : counter clerk

guide[1] [gid] *nmf* **1** : guide <guide de montagne : mountain guide> **2** CONSEILLER : counselor, advisor

guide[2] *nm* **1** : guide **2** : guidebook <guide touristique : tourist guide>

guide[3] *nf* **1** : girl scout **2 guides** *nfpl* : reins

guider [gide] *vt* : to guide

guidon [gidɔ̃] *nm* : handlebars *pl*

guigne [giɲ] *nf fam* : bad luck <avoir la guigne : to be jinxed>

guigner [giɲe] *vt* : to eye, to take a look at

guignol [giɲɔl] *nm* **1** : puppet show <c'est du guignol : it's a complete farce> **2** : silly person, clown, fool

guillemets [gijmɛ] *nmpl* : quotation marks

guilleret, -rette [gijrɛ, -rɛt] *adj* : sprightly, perky

guillotine [gijɔtin] *nf* : guillotine — **guillotiner** *vt*

guimauve [gimov] *nf* **1** : marshmallow **2** *fam* : sentimentality, mush

guimbarde [gɛ̃bard] *nf* **1** : Jew's harp **2** *fam* : jalopy

guindé, -dée [gɛ̃de] *adj* : stiff, affected, prim

guindeau [gɛ̃d] *nm* : windlass

guinéen, -néenne [gineɛ̃, -neɛn] *adj* : Guinean

Guinéen, -néenne *n* : Guinean

guingois [gɛ̃gwa] **de ~** : askew <être de guingois : to be lopsided>

guinguette [gɛ̃gɛt] *nf France* : café featuring music and dancing

guirlande [girlɑ̃d] *nf* **1** : garland **2 guirlandes de Noël** : tinsel

guise [giz] *nf* **1 à ta guise** : as you wish **2 en guise de** : by way of

guitare [gitar] *nf* : guitar

guitariste [gitarist] *nmf* : guitarist

guppy [gypi] *nm* : guppy

gustatif, -tive [gystatif, -tiv] *adj* : gustatory, of taste

guttural, -rale [gytyral] *adj, mpl* **-raux** [-ro] : guttural

guyanais, -naise [gɥijanɛ, -nɛz] *adj* : Guyanese

Guyanais, -naise *n* : Guyanese

gymnase [ʒimnaz] *nm* : gymnasium

gymnaste [ʒimnast] *nmf* : gymnast

gymnastique[1] [ʒimnastik] *adj* : gymnastic

gymnastique[2] *nf* : gymnastics

gynécologie [ʒinekɔlɔʒi] *nf* : gynecology

gynécologique [ʒinekɔlɔʒik] *adj* : gynecologic, gynecological

gynécologue [ʒinekɔlɔg] *nmf* : gynecologist

gypse [ʒips] *nm* : gypsum

gyrophare [ʒirɔfar] *nm* : revolving flashing light (on a vehicle)

gyroscope [ʒirɔskɔp] *nm* : gyroscope

H

h [aʃ] *nm* : h, the eighth letter of the alphabet

ha ['a] *interj* **ha ha** : ha-ha, very funny

habile [abil] *adj* **1** ADROIT : skillful **2** : clever — **habilement** [abilmɑ̃] *adv*

habileté [abilte] *nf* **1** : skill, skillfulness **2** : cleverness

habilité, -tée [abilite] *adj* **~ à** : entitled to, authorized to

habiliter [abilite] *vt* : to entitle, to empower

habillage [abijaʒ] *nm* **1** : dressing, getting dressed **2** : packaging, covering, casing

habillé, -lée [abije] *adj* **1** : dressed <tout habillé : fully clothed> **2** CHIC : smart, stylish

habillement [abijmɑ̃] *nm* **1** : clothes *pl*, clothing **2** : clothing industry

habiller [abije] *vt* **1** : to dress, to clothe **2** : to fit, to suit <cette robe vous habille bien : that dress really suits you> **3** REVÊTIR : to cover — **s'habiller** *vr* **1** : to get dressed <comment vais-je m'habiller? : what will I wear?> **2 ~ chez** : to buy one's clothes from **3 ~ en** : to dress up as
habit [abi] *nm* **1** : outfit, costume **2** : (religious) habit **3** *or* **habit de soirée** : evening dress, tails *pl* **4 habits** *nmpl* : clothes
habitable [abitabl] *adj* : habitable, inhabitable
habitacle [abitakl] *nm* : cockpit
habitant[1], **-tante** [abitɑ̃, -tɑ̃t] *n* **1** : inhabitant, resident **2** : occupant, dweller
habitant[2] *nm Can* : farmer
habitat [abita] *nm* **1** : housing **2** : habitat
habitation [abitasjɔ̃] *nf* **1** : living <conditions d'habitation : living conditions> **2** : house, dwelling **3** : residence, home
habiter [abite] *vt* **1** : to live in, to inhabit **2** : to dwell in (one's heart, etc.) — *vi* DEMEURER : to live, to reside <habiter à l'étranger : to live abroad>
habitude [abityd] *nf* **1** : habit <j'ai l'habitude de travailler dur : I'm used to working hard> **2** COUTUME : custom **3 comme d'habitude** : as usual **4 d'~** : usually **5 par habitude** : out of habit
habitué[1], **-tuée** [abitɥe] *adj* **~ à** : used to, accustomed to
habitué[2], **-tuée** *n* : regular (customer)
habituel, -tuelle [abitɥɛl] *adj* : usual, regular — **habituellement** [-tɥɛlmɑ̃] *adv*
habituer [abitɥe] *vt* ACCOUTUMER : to accustom — **s'habituer** *vr* **~ à** : to get used to
hableur[1], **-bleuse** ['ablœr, -bløz] *adj* : boastful
hableur[2], **-bleuse** *n* : braggart
hache ['aʃ] *nf* **1** : ax **2 hache d'armes** : battle-ax
haché, -chée ['aʃe] *adj* **1** : ground, chopped, minced <biftek haché : ground beef> **2** : jerky, disjointed
hacher ['aʃe] *vt* **1** : to chop, to mince **2** : to cut to pieces
hachette [aʃɛt] *nf* : hatchet
hache–viande ['aʃvjɑ̃d] *nms & pl* : meat grinder
hachis ['aʃi] *nms & pl* : ground or minced food, hash <hachis de viande : ground meat>
hachisch ['aʃiʃ]→ **haschish**
hachoir ['aʃwar] *nm* **1** : meat grinder **2** : chopper, cleaver **3** : cutting board
hachure ['aʃyr] *nf* : shading, hatching
hachurer [aʃyre] *vt* : to shade in
hagard, -garde ['agar, -gard] *adj* : distraught, wild, frantic
haie ['ɛ] *nf* **1** : hedge **2** : hurdle (in sports) **3** : row, line <haie d'honneur : honor guard>
haillons ['ajɔ̃] *nmpl* : rags, tatters
haine ['ɛn] *nf* : hatred, hate
haineux, -neuse ['ɛnø, -nøz] *adj* : full of hatred
haïr ['air] {48} *vt* : to hate — **se haïr** *vr*
haïssable ['aisabl] *adj* : hateful, detestable
haïtien, -tienne [aisjɛ̃, -sjɛn] *adj* : Haitian
Haïtien, -tienne *n* : Haitian
hâle ['al] *nm* : suntan
hâlé, -lée ['ale] *adj* : tanned, sunburned
haleine [alɛn] *nf* **1** : breath <avoir mauvaise haleine : to have bad breath> <hors d'haleine : out of breath> **2 de longue haleine** : long-term **3 tenir en haleine** : to hold spellbound
haler ['ale] *vt* : to haul (in), to tow
haletant, -tante ['altɑ̃, -tɑ̃t] *adj* : panting, breathless
halètement ['alɛtmɑ̃] *nm* : gasp
haleter ['alte] {20} *vi* **1** : to pant, to gasp for breath **2** : to puff, to chug (of an engine)
hall ['ol] *nm* : (entrance) hall, lobby
halle ['al] *nf France* : (covered) market
hallier ['alje] *nm* : thicket, brush
Halloween [alowin] *nf* : Halloween
hallucinant, -nante [alysinɑ̃, -nɑ̃t] *adj* : extraordinary, astounding
hallucination [alysinasjɔ̃] *nf* : hallucination <avoir des hallucinations : to hallucinate>
hallucinogène[1] [alysinɔʒɛn] *adj* : hallucinogenic
hallucinogène[2] *nm* : hallucinogen
halo ['alo] *nm* : halo
halogène [alɔʒɛn] *nm* : halogen <lampe (à) halogène : halogen lamp>
halte ['alt] *nf* **1** ARRÊT : stop, halt **2** : stopping place **3 halte routière** *Can* : rest stop (on a highway)
haltère [altɛr] *nm* : dumbbell, barbell
haltérophilie [alterɔfili] *nf* : weightlifting
hamac ['amak] *nm* : hammock
hamamélis [amamelis] *nm* : witch hazel
hamburger ['ɑ̃bœrgœr] *nm* : hamburger (cooked)
hameau ['amo] *nm, pl* **hameaux** : hamlet
hameçon [amsɔ̃] *nm* : fishhook
hampe ['ɑ̃p] *nf* **1** : pole (for a flag, etc.) **2** : shaft **3** : flank (of beef)
hamster ['amstɛr] *nm* : hamster
hanche ['ɑ̃ʃ] *nf* **1** : hip **2** : haunch (of a horse)
handball ['ɑ̃dbal] *nm* : handball
handicap ['ɑ̃dikap] *nm* : handicap
handicapé[1], **-pée** ['ɑ̃dikape] *adj* : handicapped, disabled

handicapé[2], **-pée** *n* : handicapped person, disabled person
handicaper ['ɑ̃dikape] *vt* : to handicap
hangar ['ɑ̃gar] *nm* **1** : (large) shed **2** : hangar
hanter ['ɑ̃te] *vt* : to haunt
hantise ['ɑ̃tiz] *nf* : obsessive fear, dread
happer ['ape] *vt* **1** : to seize, to snatch **2 être happé par** : to be hit by (a car, train, etc.)
harangue ['arɑ̃g] *nf* : harangue — **haranguer** ['arɑ̃ge] *vt*
harasser ['arase] *vt* EXTÉNUER : to exhaust, to tire out
harcèlement ['arsɛlmɑ̃] *nm* : harassment
harceler ['arsəle] {8 *and* 20} *vt* **1** : to harass, to harry **2** : to pester
hardes ['ard] *nfpl* : rags, old clothes
hardi, -die ['ardi] *adj* : bold, daring — **hardiment** [-dimɑ̃] *adv*
hardiesse ['ardjɛs] *nf* : boldness, audacity
harem ['arɛm] *nm* : harem
hareng ['arɑ̃] *nm* **1** : herring **2 hereng saur** : smoked herring, kipper
hargne ['arɲ] *nf* : aggressiveness, bad temper
hargneux, -neuse ['arɲø, -ɲøz] *adj* : quarrelsome, bad-tempered
haricot ['ariko] *nm* : bean <haricot de Lima : lima bean> <haricot rouge : kidney bean> <haricot vert : green bean, string bean>
harmonica [armɔnika] *nm* : harmonica
harmonie [armɔni] *nf* : harmony
harmonieux, -nieuse [armɔnjø, -njøz] *adj* : harmonious — **harmonieusement** [-njøzmɑ̃] *adv*
harmonique [armɔnik] *adj* : harmonic — **harmoniquement** [-nikmɑ̃] *adv*
harmoniser [armɔnize] *vt* **1** : to harmonize **2** : to bring into line, to reconcile — **s'harmoniser** *vr* : to coordinate, to go well together
harnachement ['arnaʃmɑ̃] *nm* **1** : harness, harnessing **2** *fam* : outfit, getup
harnacher ['arnaʃe] *vt* **1** : to harness (an animal) **2** *fam* : to rig out (a person)
harnais ['arnɛ] *nm* : harness
harpe ['arp] *nf* : harp — **harpiste** ['arpist] *nmf*
harpie ['arpi] *nf* : harpy
harpon ['arpɔ̃] *nm* : harpoon
harponner ['arpɔne] *vt* **1** : to harpoon **2** *fam* : to nab, to collar
hasard ['azar] *nm* **1** : chance, luck, coincidence <un heureux hasard : a stroke of luck> <à tout hasard : on the off chance, just in case> <au hasard : at random> **2** SORT : fate, destiny **3 hasards** *nmpl* : dangers, hazards
hasarder ['azarde] *vt* RISQUER : to risk, to venture — **se hasarder** *vr* **1 se hasarder à faire** : to risk doing **2 ~ dans** : to venture into
hasardeux, -deuse ['azardø, -døz] *adj* : hazardous, risky
haschisch ['aʃiʃ] *nm* : hashish
hâte ['at] *nf* **1** : haste, hurry **2 à la hâte** : hurriedly, hastily **3 avoir hâte de** : to be eager to
hâter ['ate] *vt* : to hasten, to hurry — **se hâter** *vr*
hâtif, -tive ['atif, -tiv] *adj* **1** : hurried **2** : hasty, rash **3** : early <une hâtive récolte : an early harvest>
hâtivement ['ativmɑ̃] *adv* : hurriedly, hastily
hausse ['os] *nf* **1** : rise, increase **2 à la hausse** *or* **en ~** : rising, up
haussement ['osmɑ̃] *nm* **1** : raising, increasing **2** : **haussement d'épaules** : shrug
hausser ['ose] *vt* : to raise <hausser la voix : to raise one's voice> <hausser les épaules : to shrug one's shoulders>
haut[1] ['o] *adv* **1** : high <voler haut : to fly high> <haut placé : in a high position, highly placed> **2** : loud, loudly <penser tout haut : to think out loud> **3 plus haut** : above, earlier (in a text)
haut[2], **haute** ['o, 'ot] *adj* **1** : high, tall <haut de cinq mètres : five meters high> <à mer haute : at high tide> **2** : high (up) <haut dans le ciel : high in the sky> <l'étagère la plus haute : the top shelf> **3** : high, advanced, increased <haute fréquence : high frequency> <haute pression : high blood pressure> <à haute voix : aloud, out loud> **4** : early <de la plus haute antiquité : from the earliest times> **5** : upper <le haut Nil : the Upper Nile>
haut[3] *nm* **1** HAUTEUR : height <un mètre de haut : one meter high> **2** : SOMMET : top <l'étage du haut : the top floor> <de haut en bas : from top to bottom> **3 avoir des hauts et des bas** : to have one's ups and downs **4 en ~** : upstairs **5 en ~** : on the top, atop
hautain, -taine ['otɛ̃, -tɛn] *adj* : haughty
hautbois ['obwa] *nms & pl* : oboe — **hautboïste** ['obɔist] *nmf*
haute–fidélité ['otfidelite] *nf, pl* **hautes–fidélités** : high fidelity
hautement ['otmɑ̃] *adv* **1** FORTEMENT : highly, extremely **2** OUVERTEMENT : openly
hauteur ['otœr] *nf* **1** : height <prendre de la hauteur : to take on height, to climb> <à la hauteur de : (on a) level with> **2** NOBLESSE : nobility, loftiness **3** : haughtiness **4** : hill, height (in geography)
haut–le–cœur ['olkœr] *nms & pl* : retching <avoir des haut-le-cœur : to retch, to gag>

haut–le–corps [ˈolkɔr] *nms & pl* : start, jump
haut–parleur [ˈoparlœr] *nm, pl* **haut–parleurs** : loudspeaker
hâve [ˈav] *adj* : gaunt
havre [ˈavr] *nm* : haven, refuge
hawaïen[1], **-waïenne** [awajɛ̃, -jɛn] *adj* : Hawaiian
hawaïen[2] *nm* : Hawaiian (language)
Hawaïen, -waïenne *n* : Hawaiian
hayon [ˈajɔ̃] *nm* : tailgate
hé [ˈe] *interj* **1** : hey **2 hé, hé!** : well! well!
hebdomadaire [ɛbdɔmadɛr] *adj & nm* : weekly
hébergement [ebɛrʒəmɑ̃] *nm* : accommodations *pl,* lodging
héberger [ebɛrʒe] {17} *vt* **1** : to accommodate, to put up **2** : to take in (a refugee, etc.)
hébété, -tée [ebete] *adj* AHURI : dazed, stupefied
hébéter [ebete] {87} *vt* : to daze, to stupefy
hébétude [ebetyd] *nf* : stupor
hébraïque [ebraik] *adj* : Hebrew, Hebraic
hébreu[1] (*masculine only*) [ebrø] *adj, pl* **hébreux** : Hebrew
hébreu[2] *nm* : Hebrew (language)
Hébreu *nm, pl* **Hébreux** : Hebrew
hédoniste [edɔnist] *adj* : hedonistic
hégémonie [eʒemɔni] *nf* : hegemony
hein [ˈɛ̃] *interj* : eh?, what?
hélas [ˈelas] *interj* : alas!
héler [ˈele] {87} *vt* : to hail, to summon
hélice [elis] *nf* **1** : helix **2** : propeller
hélicoptère [elikɔptɛr] *nm* : helicopter
héliotrope [eljɔtrɔp] *nm* : heliotrope
héliport [elipɔr] *nm* : heliport
hélium [eljɔm] *nm* : helium
hématologie [ematɔlɔʒi] *nf* : hematology
hémisphère [emisfɛr] *nm* : hemisphere
hémisphérique [emisferik] *adv* : hemispheric, hemispherical
hémoglobine [emɔglɔbin] *nf* : hemoglobin
hémophile [emɔfil] *adj & nmf* : hemophiliac
hémophilie [emɔfili] *nf* : hemophilia
hémorragie [emɔraʒi] *nf* : bleeding, hemorrhage <faire une hémorragie : to hemorrhage>
hémorroïdes [emɔrɔid] *nfpl* : hemorrhoids
henné [ˈene] *nm* : henna
hennir [ˈenir] *vi* : to neigh, to whinny
hennissement [ˈenismɑ̃] *nm* : neighing, whinny
hépatique [epatik] *adj* : hepatic, liver
hépatite [epatit] *nf* : hepatitis
héraldique[1] [eraldik] *adj* : heraldic
héraldique[2] *nf* : heraldry
héraut [ˈero] *nm* : herald, messenger
herbacé, -cée [ɛrbase] *adj* : herbaceous
herbage [ɛrbaʒ] *nm* : pasture
herbe [ɛrb] *nf* **1** : grass **2** : herb (in cooking) **3 en ~** : budding, in the making **4 herbe à (la) puce** *Can* : poison ivy, poison sumac **5 herbe aux chats** : catnip **6 mauvaise herbe** : weed
herbeux, -beuse [ɛrbø, -bøz] *adj* : grassy
herbicide [ɛrbisid] *nm* : herbicide, weed killer
herbivore[1] [ɛrbivɔr] *adj* : herbivorous
herbivore[2] *nm* : herbivore
herboriste [ɛrbɔrist] *nmf* : herbalist
herculéen, -léenne [ɛrkyleɛ̃, -ɛn] *adj* : herculean
hère [ˈɛr] *nm* **pauvre hère** : poor wretch
héréditaire [ereditɛr] *adj* : hereditary
hérédité [eredite] *nf* : heredity
hérésie [erezi] *nf* : heresy
hérétique[1] [eretik] *adj* : heretical
hérétique[2] *nmf* : heretic
hérissé, -sée [ˈerise] *adj* : standing on end, bristling
hérisser [ˈerise] *vt* **1** : to ruffle up (fur, feathers, etc.) **2 ~ de** : to spike with, to stud with <herissé de difficultés : fraught with problems> **3 hérisser qqn** *fam* : to ruffle s.o.'s feathers, to irritate s.o. — **se hérisser** *vr* **1** : to stand on end **2** *fam* : to bristle (with annoyance)
hérisson [ˈerisɔ̃] *nm* : hedgehog
héritage [eritaʒ] *nm* **1** : inheritance **2** : heritage, legacy
hériter [erite] *vi* **~ de** : to inherit <j'ai hérité de la maison : I inherited the house> — *vt* : to inherit
héritier, -tière [eritje, -tjɛr] *n* : heir, heiress *f*, inheritor
hermaphrodite [ɛrmafrɔdit] *nmf* : hermaphrodite
hermétique [ɛrmetik] *adj* **1** ÉTANCHE : airtight, watertight **2** OBSCUR : obscure, abstruse, hermetic
hermétiquement [ɛrmetikmɑ̃] *adv* : hermetically
hermine [ɛrmin] *nf* : ermine
herminette [ɛrminɛt] *nf* : adze
hernie [ˈɛrni] *nf* : hernia
héroïne [erɔin] *nf* **1** : heroine **2** : heroin
héroïque [erɔik] *adj* : heroic — **héroïquement** [-ikmɑ̃] *adv*
héroïsme [erɔism] *nm* : heroism
héron [ˈerɔ̃] *nm* : heron
héros [ˈerɔ] *nm* : hero
herpès [ɛrpɛs] *nms & pl* : herpes
herpétologie [ɛrpetɔlɔʒi] *nf* : herpetology
herse [ˈɛrs] *nf* : harrow
herser [ˈɛrse] *vt* : to harrow
hertz [ˈɛrts] *nms & pl* : hertz
hésitant, -tante [ezitɑ̃, -tɑ̃t] *adj* **1** : hesitant **2** : faltering, wavering
hésitation [ezitasjɔ̃] *nf* **1** : hesitation <avec hésitation : hesitantly> **2** : indecision, hesitancy

hésiter [ezite] *vi* **1** : to hesitate **2** : to vacillate, to waver
hétéroclite [eterɔklit] *adj* : disparate, sundry
hétérogène [eterɔʒɛn] *adj* : heterogeneous
hétérosexuel, -sexuelle [eterɔsɛksyɛl] *adj & n* : heterosexual — **hétérosexualité** [-sɛksɥalite] *nf*
hêtre ['ɛtr] *nm* : beech
heure [œr] *nf* **1** : time <quelle heure est-il? : what time is it?> <avez-vous l'heure? : do you have the time?> **2** : hour <une demi-heure : half an hour> <cent kilomètres à l'heure : sixty miles per hour> **3 à l'~** : on time **4 de bonne heure** : early **5 heure avancée** *Can* : daylight saving time **6 heure d'été** : daylight saving time **7 heure de pointe** : rush hour **8 heure normale** *Can* : standard time **9 heures supplémentaires** : overtime **10 tout à l'heure** : later on
heureusement [œrøzmɑ̃] *adv* : fortunately, luckily
heureux, -reuse [œrø, -røz] *adj* **1** : happy, cheerful <vivre heureux : to live happily> **2** : glad, pleased <heureux de te revoir : glad to see you again> **3** : fortunate, lucky <heureux en amour : lucky in love> **4** : apt, pleasing
heurt ['œr] *nm* **1** : collision, crash **2** CONFLIT : clash, conflict **3 sans heurts** : smoothly, smooth
heurter ['œrte] *vt* **1** : to strike, to hit, to collide with **2** : to conflict with, to go against **3** : to offend — *vi* : to hit, to collide <heurter contre : to strike> — **se heurter** *vr* **1** : to collide **2 ~ à** : to come up against
heurtoir ['œrtwar] *nm* : (door) knocker
hexagonal, -nale [ɛgzagɔnal] *adj, mpl* **-naux** [-no] : hexagonal
hexagone [ɛgzagɔn] *nm* **1** : hexagon **2 l'Hexagone** : France
hiatus [jatys] *nms & pl* : hiatus
hiberner [ibɛrne] *vi* : to hibernate — **hibernation** [ibɛrnasjɔ̃] *nf*
hibou ['ibu] *nm, pl* **hiboux** [ibu] : owl
hic ['ik] *nm fam* : snag <voilà le hic! : that's the trouble!>
hickory ['ikɔri] *nm* : hickory
hideux, -deuse ['idø, -døz] *adj* : hideous — **hideusement** [-døzmɑ̃] *adv*
hier [ijɛr] *adv* : yesterday <hier matin : yesterday morning> <comme si s'était hier : as if it were yesterday>
hiérarchie ['jerarʃi] *nf* : hierarchy
hiérarchique ['jerarʃik] *adj* : hierarchical
hiéroglyphe [jerɔglif] *nm* : hieroglyph, hieroglyphic
hilarant, -rante [ilarɑ̃, -rɑ̃t] *adj* : hilarious
hilare [ilar] *adj* : merry, mirthful
hilarité [ilarite] *nf* : hilarity, mirth
hindou, -doue [ɛ̃du] *adj* : Hindu
Hindou, -doue *n* : Hindu
hindouisme [ɛ̃duism] *nm* : Hinduism
hippie *or* **hippy** ['ipi] *nmf, pl* **hippies** : hippie
hippique [ipik] *adj* : equestrian, horse <course hippique : horse race
hippisme [ipism] *nm* : (horseback) riding
hippocampe [ipɔkɑ̃p] *nm* : sea horse
hippodrome [ipɔdrom] *nm* : racecourse
hippopotame [ipɔpɔtam] *nm* : hippopotamus
hirondelle [irɔ̃dɛl] *nf* **1** : swallow **2 hirondelle de mer** : STERNE : tern
hirsute [irsyt] *adj* **1** : tousled, disheveled **2** : hairy, shaggy
hispanique[1] [ispanik] *adj* : Hispanic
hispanique[2] *nmf* : Hispanic (person)
hispano–américain, -caine [ispanɔamerikɛ̃, -kɛn] *adj* : Spanish-American
Hispano–Américain, -caine *n* : Spanish American
hisser ['ise] *vt* : to hoist, to haul up — **se hisser** *vr* : to raise oneself up <se hisser sur la pointe des pieds : to stand on tiptoe>
histogramme [istɔgram] *nm* : bar graph
histoire [istwar] *nf* **1** : history **2** : story **3** : affair, matter <c'est toujours la même histoire : it's always the same old story> **4 histoires** *nfpl* ENNUIS : trouble, problems <s'attirer des histoires : to be asking for trouble> **5 ~ de** : just <histoire de voir : just to see> **6 histoire naturelle** : natural history
historien, -rienne [istɔrjɛ̃, -rjɛn] *n* : historian
historique[1] [istɔrik] *adj* **1** : historical **2** : historic <champs de batailles historiques : historic battlefields> — **historiquement** [-rikmɑ̃] *adv*
historique[2] *nm* : account, story, history
hiver [ivɛr] *nm* : winter
hivernal, -nale [ivɛrnal] *adj, mpl* **-naux** [-no] : winter, wintry
hiverner [ivɛrne] *vi* : to winter
hochement ['ɔʃmɑ̃] *nm* **hochement de tête** : shake of the head, nod
hocher ['ɔʃe] *vt* **hocher la tête** : to nod, to shake one's head
hochet ['ɔʃɛ] *nm* : rattle
hockey ['ɔkɛ] *nm* : hockey
holà ['ɔla] *interj* **1** : stop!, whoa! **2** : hey! **3 mettre le holà à** : to put a stop to
hold–up ['ɔldœp] *nms & pl* : holdup, robbery
holistique [ɔlistik] *adj* : holistic
hollandais[1], **-daise** ['ɔlɑ̃dɛ, -dɛz] *adj* : Dutch
hollandais[2] *nm* : Dutch (language)
Hollandais, -daise *n* **1** : Dutchman *m*, Dutchwoman *f* **2 les Hollondais** : the Dutch

holocauste [ɔlɔkost] *nm* : holocaust

hologramme [ɔlɔgram] *nm* : hologram

homard ['ɔmar] *nm* : lobster

homélie [ɔmeli] *nf* : homily, sermon

homéopathie [ɔmeɔpati] *nf* : homeopathy — **homéopathique** [ɔmeɔpatik] *adj*

homicide[1] [ɔmisid] *adj* : homicidal

homicide[2] *nm* **1** : homicide **2 homicide involontaire** : manslaughter

hommage [ɔmaʒ] *nm* : homage, tribute <rendre hommage à : to pay tribute to>

hommasse [ɔmas] *adj* : mannish

homme [ɔm] *nm* **1** : man **2 l'homme** : man, mankind **3 homme d'affaires** : businessman **4 homme à tout faire** : handyman

homme–grenouille [ɔmgrənuj] *nm, pl* **hommes–grenouilles** : frogman

homogène [ɔmɔʒɛn] *adj* : homogeneous

homogénéiser [ɔmɔʒeneize] *vt* : to homogenize — **homogénéisé, -sée** [-ize] *adj*

homogénéité [ɔmɔʒeneite] *nf* : homogeneity

homographe [ɔmɔgraf] *nm* : homograph

homologation [ɔmɔlɔgasjɔ̃] *nf* : probate, ratification

homologue [ɔmɔlɔg] *nmf* : counterpart, opposite number

homologuer [ɔmɔlɔge] *vt* **1** : to ratify, to approve **2** : to probate (a will)

homonyme [ɔmɔnim] *nm* **1** : homonym **2** : namesake

homophone [ɔmɔfɔn] *nm* : homophone

homosexualité [ɔmɔsɛksyalite] *nf* : homosexuality

homosexuel, -sexuelle [ɔmɔsɛksyɛl] *adj & n* : homosexual

hondurien, -rienne ['ɔ̃dyrjɛ̃, -rjɛn] *adj* : Honduran

Hondurien, -rienne *n* : Honduran

hongrois[1], **-groise** ['ɔ̃ngrwa, -grwaz] *adj* : Hungarian

hongrois[2] *nm* : Hungarian (language)

Hongrois, -groise *n* : Hungarian

honnête [ɔnɛt] *adj* **1** INTÈGRE : honest, honorable **2** JUSTE : reasonable, fair **3** RESPECTABLE : decent, respectable — **honnêtement** [ɔnɛtmɑ̃] *adv*

honnêteté [ɔnɛtte] *nf* : honesty

honneur [ɔnœr] *nm* : honor <avoir l'honneur de : to have the honor of> <en l'honneur de : in honor of> <se faire l'honneur de : to pride oneself on>

honorable [ɔnɔrabl] *adj* **1** : honorable **2** : decent, satisfactory <un salaire honorable : a decent salary> **3** : creditable, worthy — **honorablement** [-rabləmɑ̃] *adv*

honoraire [ɔnɔrɛr] *adj* : honorary

honoraires *nmpl* : fees

honorer [ɔnɔre] *vt* **1** : to honor **2** : to be a credit to **3** : to honor (a debt), to pay — **s'honorer** *vr* **1** : to gain distinction **2 ~ de** : to pride oneself on

honorifique [ɔnɔrifik] *adj* : honorary

honte ['ɔ̃t] *nf* : shame, disgrace <avoir honte : to be ashamed> <faire honte à : to put to shame>

honteux, -teuse ['ɔ̃tø, -tøz] *adj* **1** : ashamed **2** : shameful — **honteusement** ['ɔ̃tøzmɑ̃] *adv*

hôpital [ɔpital] *nm, pl* **-taux** [-to] : hospital

hoquet ['ɔkɛ] *nm* : hiccup <avoir le hocquet : to have the hiccups>

hoqueter ['ɔkte] {8} *vi* : to hiccup

horaire[1] [ɔrɛr] *adj* : hourly

horaire[2] *nm* : timetable, schedule

horde ['ɔrd] *nf* : horde

horizon [ɔrizɔ̃] *nm* **1** : horizon <à l'horizon : on the horizon> **2** PAYSAGE : view, landscape **3** : outlook, prospect <horizons économiques : economic prospects> **4** : field of activity <ouvrir ses horizons : to broaden one's horizons>

horizontal, -tale [ɔrizɔ̃tal] *adj, mpl* **-taux** [-to] : horizontal — **horizontalement** [-talmɑ̃] *adv*

horizontale *nf* **à l' horizontale** : in a horizontal position

horloge [ɔrlɔʒ] *nf* : clock

horloger, -gère [ɔrlɔrʒe, -ʒɛr] *n* : watchmaker

hormis ['ɔrmi] *prep* : except, save

hormonal, -nale [ɔrmɔnal] *adj, mpl* **-naux** [-no] : hormonal

hormone [ɔrmɔn] *nf* : hormone

horoscope [ɔrɔskɔp] *nm* : horoscope

horreur [ɔrœr] *nf* **1** ÉPOUVANTE : horror, fear **2** ATROCITÉ : horror, atrocity **3** AVERSION : loathing, repugnance <avoir horreur de : to loathe, to detest> <quelle horreur! : how sickening!>

horrible [ɔribl] *adj* : horrible — **horriblement** [ɔribləmɑ̃] *adv*

horrifiant, -fiante [ɔrifjɑ̃, -fjɑ̃t] *adj* : horrifying

horrifier [ɔrifje] {96} *vt* : to horrify

horripiler [ɔripile] *vt* : to exasperate

hors ['ɔr] *prep* **1** : except for, save **2** : outside, beyond <hors normes : nonstandard> <hors pair : outstanding, exceptional> <hors service : out of service> <hors tout : overall> **3 ~ de** : out of <hors d'atteinte : out of reach> <hors de doute : beyond doubt> <hors de question : out of the question> <hors de la ville : outside of town> **3 être hors de soi** : to be beside oneself

hors–bord ['ɔrbɔr] *nms & pl* **1** : outboard motor **2** : speedboat

hors–concours ['ɔrkɔ̃kur] *nms & pl* : disqualification

hors–d'œuvre ['ɔrdœvr] *nms & pl* : hors d'oeuvre

hors–la–loi ['ɔrlalwa] *nms & pl* : outlaw
hors–taxe ['ɔrtaks] *nms & pl* : duty-free articles
hors–texte ['ɔrtɛkst] *nms & pl* : plate (in a book)
horticole [ɔrtikɔl] *adj* : horticultural
horticulture [ɔrtikyltyr] *nf* : horticulture
hosanna [ozana] *nm & interj* : hosanna
hospice [ɔspis] *nm France* **1** : home (for the elderly, etc.) **2** : hospice
hospitalier, -lière [ɔspitalje, -jɛr] *adj* **1** : hospital <services hospitaliers : hospital services> **2** : hospitable
hospitalisation [ɔspitalizasjɔ̃] *nf* : hospitalization
hospitaliser [ɔspitalize] *vt* : to hospitalize
hospitalité [ɔspitalite] *nf* : hospitality
hostie [ɔsti] *nf* : host, eucharistic bread
hostile [ɔstil] *adj* : hostile — **hostilement** [ɔstilmɑ̃] *adv*
hostilité [ɔstilite] *nf* **1** : hostility **2 hostilités** *nfpl* : hostilities, war
hot–dog ['ɔtdɔg] *nm, pl* **hot–dogs** : hot dog
hôte[1], **hôtesse** [ot, otɛs] *n* : host, hostess *f*
hôte[2] *nmf* **1** INVITÉ : guest **2** : occupant, guest (in a hotel, etc.)
hôte[3] *nm* : host (in biology)
hôtel [otɛl] *nm* **1** : hotel **2 hôtel de ville** : town hall **3 hôtel particulier** : mansion, townhouse
hôtelier[1], **-lière** [otəlje, -jɛr] *adj* : hotel
hôtelier[2], **-lière** *n* : hotelier, hotel manager
hôtellerie [otɛlri] *nf* : hotel business
hôtesse [otɛs] *nf* **1** → **hôte**[1] **2** *or* **hôtesse de l'air** : stewardess, flight attendant **3** *or* **hôtesse d'accueil** : receptionist
hotte ['ɔt] *nf* **1** : basket (carried on the back) **2** : hood (of a chimney) **3** *or* **hotte aspirante** : range hood, ventilator
houblon ['ublɔ̃] *nm* **1** : hop (plant) **2** : hops *pl*
houe ['u] *nf* : hoe
houille ['uj] *nf* **1** : coal **2 houille blanche** : hydroelectric power
houiller, -lère ['uje, -jɛr] *adj* : coal, coal-mining
houillère *nf* : coal mine
houle ['ul] *nf* : swell, surge
houlette ['ulɛt] *nf* **1** : crook, staff (of a shepherd) **2 sous la houlette de** : under the guidance of
houleux, -leuse ['ulø, -løz] *adj* **1** : rough (of the sea) **2** : stormy, turbulent <débats houleux : stormy debates>
houppe ['up] *nf* **1** *or* **houppette** : powder puff **2** : tuft (of hair)
hourra ['ura] *nm & interj* : hurrah
houspiller ['uspije] *vt* RÉPRIMANDER : to scold
housse ['us] *nf* : cover, slipcover, dust cover
houx ['u] *nms & pl* : holly
huard *or* **huart** ['yar] *nm Can* : loon
hublot ['yblo] *nm* : porthole
huche ['yʃ] *nf* **1** COFFRE : chest **2 huche à pain** : bread box
huées ['ɥe] *nfpl* : boos
huer ['ɥe] *vt* : to boo — *vi* : to hoot
huile [ɥil] *nf* **1** : (cooking) oil <huile d'olive : olive oil> **2** : oil, lubricant <huile moteur : motor oil> <huile de coude : elbow grease> **3** : oil (in pharmacy) <huile solaire : suntan lotion> **4** : oil (painting) **5 mer d'huile** : calm sea, sea of glass
huiler [ɥile] *vt* : to oil
huileux, -leuse [ɥilø, -løz] *adj* : oily
huilier [ɥilje] *nm* : cruet
huis [ɥi] *nm* **à huis clos** : behind closed doors
huissier [ɥisje] *nm* **1** : usher (in a court of law) **2** : bailiff
huit[1] ['ɥit, *before consonant* 'ɥi] *adj* **1** : eight <huit jours : a week> **2** : eighth <le huit décembre : December eighth>
huit[2] *nms & pl* : eight
huitaine ['ɥitɛn] *nf* **1** : about a week **2** : about eight
huitième ['ɥitjɛm] *adj & nmf & nm* : eighth
huître [ɥitr] *nf* : oyster
hululement ['ylylmɑ̃] *nm* : hoot
hululer ['ylyle] *vi* : to hoot
humain[1], **-maine** [ymɛ̃, -mɛn] *adj* **1** : human <la nature humaine : human nature> **2** : humane — **humainement** [-mɛnmɑ̃] *adv*
humain[2] *nm* : human being
humaniser [ymanize] *vt* : to humanize
humanisme [ymanism] *nm* : humanism
humaniste[1] [ymanist] *adj* : humanist, humanistic
humaniste[2] *nmf* : humanist
humanitaire [ymanitɛr] *adj* : humanitarian
humanitarisme [ymanitarism] *nm* : humanitarianism
humanité [ymanite] *nf* : humanity
humanoïde [ymanɔid] *adj & nmf* : humanoid
humble [œ̃bl] *adj* : humble — **humblement** [œ̃bləmɑ̃] *adv*
humecter [ymɛkte] *vt* : to dampen, to moisten — **s'humecter** *vr*
humer ['yme] *vt* **1** : to breathe in, to inhale **2** : to smell
humérus [ymerys] *nms & pl* : humerus
humeur [ymœr] *nf* **1** : mood, humor <de bonne humeur : in a good mood> <sautes d'humeur : mood swings> **2** : temperament, temper <d'humeur égale : even-tempered> **3** : ill humor, bad temper <accès d'humeur : fit of bad temper>
humide [ymid] *adj* **1** : moist, damp **2** : humid, muggy
humidificateur [ymidifikatœr] *nm* : humidifier

humidifier [ymidifje] {96} *vt* : to humidify
humidité [ymidite] *nf* **1** : humidity **2** : dampness, moisture
humiliant, -liante [ymiljɑ̃, -jɑ̃t] *adj* : humiliating
humiliation [ymiljasjɔ̃] *nf* : humiliation
humilier [ymilje] {96} *vt* : to humiliate — **s'humilier** *vr* : to humble oneself
humilité [ymilite] *nf* : humility
humoriste [ymɔrist] *nmf* : humorist
humoristique [ymɔristik] *adj* : humorous
humour [ymur] *nm* : humor, wit <avoir de l'humour : to have a sense of humor>
humus [ymys] *nms & pl* : humus
huppé, -pée ['ype] *adj* **1** : tufted, crested **2** *fam* : posh, high-class
hurlement ['yrləmɑ̃] *nm* : howl, yell
hurler ['yrle] *vt* : to yell out — *vi* **1** : to howl, to roar **2** : to yell, to shout
hurluberlu, -lue [yrlybɛrly] *n* : oddball, crank
hurrah ['ura] → **hourra**
hutte ['yt] *nf* : hut
hyacinthe [jasɛ̃t] *nf* : hyacinth
hybride[1] [ibrid] *adj* : hybrid
hybride[2] *nm* : hybrid
hydratant[1], **-tante** [idratɑ̃, -tɑ̃t] *adj* : moisturizing
hydratant[2] *nm* : moisturizer
hydrate [idrat] *nm* **hydrate de carbon** : carbohydrate
hydraulique[1] [idrolik] *adj* : hydraulic
hydraulique[2] *nf* : hydraulics
hydravion [idravjɔ̃] *nm* : seaplane
hydrocarbure [idrɔkarbyr] *nm* : hydrocarbon
hydroélectrique *or* **hydro–électrique** [idrɔelɛktrik] *adj* : hydroelectric
hydrogène [idrɔʒɛn] *nm* : hydrogen
hydroglisseur [idrɔglisœr] *nm* : hydroplane (boat)
hydrophobie [idrɔfɔbi] *nf* : hydrophobia
hyène [jɛn] *nf* : hyena
hygiène [iʒjɛn] *nf* : hygiene <hygiène publique : public health>
hygiénique [iʒjenik] *adj* : hygienic
hygiéniste [iʒjenist] *nmf* : hygienist
hygromètre [igrɔmɛtr] *nm* : hygrometer
hymne [imn] *nm* **1** : hymn **2 hymne nationale** : national anthem
hyperactif, -tive *adj* : hyperactive
hyperbole [ipɛrbɔl] *nf* : hyberbole
hypermétrope [ipɛrmetrɔp] *adj* PRESBYTE : farsighted
hypermétropie [ipɛrmetrɔpi] *nf* PRESBYTIE : farsightedness
hypersensible [ipɛrsɑ̃sibl] *adj* : hypersensitive
hypertension [ipɛrtɑ̃sjɔ̃] *nf* : high blood pressure, hypertension
hypnose [ipnoz] *nf* : hypnosis
hypnotique [ipnɔtik] *adj* : hypnotic
hypnotiser [ipnɔtize] *vt* : to hypnotize
hypnotiseur [ipnɔtizœr] *nm* : hypnotist
hypnotisme [ipnɔtism] *nm* : hypnotism
hypocondriaque[1] [ipɔkɔ̃drijak] *adj* : hypochondriacal, hypochondriac
hypocondriaque[2] *nmf* : hypochondriac
hypocondrie [ipɔkɔ̃dri] *nf* : hypochondria
hypocrisie [ipɔkrizi] *nf* : hypocrisy
hypocrite[1] [ipɔkrit] *adj* : hypocritical — **hypocritement** [-kritmɑ̃] *adv*
hypocrite[2] *nmf* : hypocrite
hypodermique [ipɔdɛrmik] *adj* : hypodermic <seringue hypodermique : hypodermic needle>
hypotension [ipɔtɑ̃sjɔ̃] *nf* : low blood pressure, hypotension
hypoténuse [ipɔtenyz] *nf* : hypotenuse
hypothécaire [ipɔtekɛr] *adj* : mortgage <prêt hypothécaire : mortgage loan>
hypothèque [ipɔtɛk] *nf* : mortgage
hypothéquer [ipɔteke] {87} *vt* : to mortgage
hypothermie [ipɔtɛrmi] *nf* : hypothermia
hypothèse [ipɔtɛz] *nf* : hypothesis
hypothétique [ipɔtetik] *adj* : hypothetical — **hypothétiquement** [-tikmɑ̃] *adv*
hystérectomie [isterɛktɔmi] *nf* : hysterectomy
hystérie [isteri] *nf* : hysteria
hystérique [isterik] *adj* : hysterical — **hystériquement** [-rikmɑ̃] *adj*

I

i [i] *nm* : i, the ninth letter of the alphabet
ibis [ibis] *nms & pl* : ibis
iceberg [ajsbɛrg] *nm* : iceberg
ichtyologie [iktjɔlɔʒi] *nf* : ichthyology
ici [isi] *adv* **1** : here <ici et là : here and there> <par ici : this way> **2** : now <jusqu'ici : up until now> <d'ici là : by then> **3 d'ici** : hence, therefore <d'ici six ans : six years hence>
ici–bas [isiba] *adv* : here below, on earth
icône [ikon] *nf* : icon

iconoclasme [ikɔnɔklasm] *nm* : iconoclasm

iconoclaste[1] [ikɔnɔklast] *adj* : iconoclastic

iconoclaste[2] *nmf* : iconoclast

idéal[1], **idéale** [ideal] *adj, mpl* **idéals** *or* **idéaux** [ideo] : ideal — **idéalement** [-almɑ̃] *adv*

idéal[2] *nm* : ideal

idéaliser [idealize] *vt* : to idealize — **idéalisation** [-lizasjɔ̃] *nf*

idéalisme [idealism] *nm* : idealism

idéaliste[1] [idealist] *adj* : idealistic

idéaliste[2] *nmf* : idealist

idée [ide] *nf* **1** : idea <changer d'idée : to change one's mind> <se faire des idées : to imagine things> **2 idée de génie** : brainwave **3 idée fixe** : obsession **4 idée reçue** : accepted opinion, commonplace

idem [idɛm] *adv* : ditto, idem

identifiable [idɑ̃tifjabl] *adj* : identifiable

identification [idɑ̃tifikasjɔ̃] *nf* : identification

identifier [idɑ̃tifje] {96} *vt* **1** : to identify, to recognize **2** ASSIMILER : to liken, to consider equivalent — **s'identifier** *vr* **~ avec** : to identify with

identique [idɑ̃tik] *adj* : identical — **identiquement** [-tikmɑ̃] *adv*

identité [idɑ̃tite] *nf* : identity

idéologie [ideɔlɔʒi] *nf* : ideology

idéologique [ideɔlɔʒik] *adj* : ideological

idiomatique [idjɔmatik] *adj* : idiomatic

idiome [idjom] *nm* : idiom

idiosyncrasie [idjɔsɛ̃krazi] *nf* : idiosyncrasy

idiot[1], **-diote** [idjo, -djɔt] *adj* : idiotic — **idiotement** [idjɔtmɑ̃] *adv*

idiot[2], **-diote** *n* : idiot, fool

idiotie [idjɔsi] *nf* **1** : idiocy **2** : idiotic action or remark

idiotisme [idjɔtism] *nm* : idiom, idiomatic expression

idoine [idwan] *adj* : suitable, fitting

idolâtrer [idɔlatre] *vt* : to idolize

idolâtrie [idɔlatri] *nf* : idolatry

idole [idɔl] *nf* : idol

idylle [idil] *nf* **1** : romance, love affair **2** : idyll (poem)

idyllique [idilik] *adj* : idyllic

if [if] *nm* : yew

igloo [iglu] *nm* : igloo

igname [iɲam] *nf* : yam

ignare[1] [iɲar] *adj* : ignorant

ignare[2] *nmf* : ignoramus

ignifuge [iɲifyʒ] *adj* : fireproof

ignifuger [iɲifyʒe] {17} *vt* : to fireproof

ignoble [iɲɔbl] *adj* **1** INFÂME : base, vile **2** RÉPUGNANT : revolting, repugnant

ignominie [iɲɔmini] *nf* **1** : ignominy **2** : shameful act

ignominieux, -nieuse [iɲɔminjø, -njøz] *adj* : ignominious — **ignominieusement** [-njøzmɑ̃] *adv*

ignorance [iɲɔrɑ̃s] *nf* : ignorance

ignorant, -rante [iɲɔrɑ̃, -rɑ̃t] *adj* : ignorant

ignorer [iɲɔre] *vt* **1** : to be unaware of <je l'ignore : I don't know> **2** : to ignore

iguane [igwan] *nm* : iguana

il [il] *pron* **1** : he, it <il est en retard : he's late> <il se peut : it is possible> **2** (*as subject of an impersonal verb*) : it <il pleut : it's raining> **3 ils** *pron pl* : they **4 il y a** : there is, there are

île [il] *nf* : island, isle

illégal, -gale [ilegal] *adj, mpl* **-gaux** [-go] : illegal, unlawful — **illégalement** [-galmɑ̃] *adv*

illégalité [ilegalite] *nf* : illegality

illégitime [ileʒitim] *adj* **1** : illegitimate **2** : unwarranted, unjustified — **illégitimement** [-timmɑ̃] *adv*

illégitimité [ileʒitimite] *nf* : illegitimacy

illettré, -trée [iletre] *adj & n* ANALPHABÈTE : illiterate

illettrisme [iletrism] *nm* ANALPHABÉTISME : illiteracy

illicite [ilisit] *adj* : illicit — **illicitement** [-sitmɑ̃] *adv*

illico [iliko] *adv fam* : pronto, immediately

illimité, -tée [ilimite] *adj* **1** : unlimited, boundless **2** : indefinite

illisible [ilizibl] *adj* **1** : illegible **2** : unreadable

illisiblement [ilizibləmɑ̃] *adv* : illegibly

illogique [ilɔʒik] *adj* : illogical — **illogiquement** [-ʒikmɑ̃] *adv*

illumination [ilyminasjɔ̃] *nf* **1** : illumination, lighting **2** : inspiration **3 illuminations** *nfpl* : lights

illuminer [ilymine] *vt* ÉCLAIRER : to illuminate

illusion [ilyzjɔ̃] *nf* **1** : illusion <illusion d'optique : optical illusion> **2** : deception, delusion <se faire des illusions : to delude oneself>

illusionner [ilyzjɔne] *vt* : to delude, to deceive — **s'illusionner** *vr*

illusionniste [ilyzjɔnist] *nmf* : conjurer

illusoire [ilyzwar] *adj* : illusory

illustrateur, -trice [ilystratœr, -tris] *n* : illustrator

illustratif, -tive [ilystratif, -tiv] *adj* : illustrative

illustration [ilystrasjɔ̃] *nf* : illustration

illustre [ilystr] *adj* : illustrious, renowned

illustré[1], **-trée** [ilystre] *adj* : illustrated

illustré[2] *nm* : illustrated magazine

illustrer [ilystre] *vt* : to illustrate — **s'illustrer** *vr* : to distinguish oneself

îlot [ilo] *nm* **1** : small island **2** : block (of houses) **3** : pocket (of resistance, etc.)

ils [il] → **il**

image [imaʒ] *nf* **1** : image **2** DESSIN : picture **3 images** *nfpl* : imagery

imagé, -gée [imaʒe] *adj* : full of imagery, colorful

imagerie [imaʒri] *nf* **1** : images *pl* **2** : imaging

imaginable [imaʒinabl] *adj* : imaginable

imaginaire[1] [imaʒinɛr] *adj* : imaginary

imaginaire[2] *nm* : (world of the) imagination

imaginatif, -tive [imaʒinatif, -tiv] *adj* : imaginative

imagination [imaʒinasjɔ̃] *nf* : imagination

imaginer [imaʒine] *vt* **1** : to imagine, to suppose **2** : to devise, to think up — **s'imaginer** *vr* **1** : to imagine, to picture **2** : to picture oneself **3** : to believe, to delude oneself

imbattable [ɛ̃batabl] *adj* : invincible, unbeatable

imbécile[1] [ɛ̃besil] *adj* : stupid, idiotic

imbécile[2] *nmf* **1** : imbecile **2** : fool, idiot <faire l'imbécile : to goof off, to play the fool>

imbécillité [ɛ̃besilite] *nf* **1** : idiocy, stupidity **2** : stupid act or remark, nonsense

imbiber [ɛ̃bibe] *vt* TREMPER : to soak — **s'imbiber** *vr* **1** : to soak up, to get soaked **2** *fam* : to get drunk

imbrication [ɛ̃brikasjɔ̃] *nf* **1** : overlapping **2** : interweaving, interlocking

imbriquer [ɛ̃brike] *vt* **1** : to overlap **2** : to interweave — **s'imbriquer** *vr*

imbroglio [ɛ̃brɔljo] *nm* : imbroglio

imbu, -bue [ɛ̃by] *adj* **~ de** : imbued with, full of

imbuvable [ɛ̃byvabl] *adj* **1** : undrinkable **2** *fam* : insufferable

imitateur[1], **-trice** [imitatœr, -tris] *adj* : imitative

imitateur[2], **-trice** *n* **1** : imitator **2** : mimic, impersonator

imitatif, -tive [imitatif, -tiv] *adj* : imitative

imitation [imitasjɔ̃] *nf* **1** : imitation, copy <imitation cuir : simulated leather> **2** : impersonation, mimicry

imiter [imite] *vt* **1** : to imitate **2** : to mimic **3** : to copy, to forge

immaculé, -lée [imakyle] *adj* : immaculate

immanent, -nente [imanɑ̃, -nɑ̃t] *adj* : immanent

immangeable [ɛ̃mɑ̃ʒabl] *adj* : inedible

immanquable [ɛ̃mɑ̃kabl] *adj* **1** INÉVITABLE : inevitable **2** : impossible to miss

immanquablement [ɛ̃mɑ̃kabləmɑ̃] *adv* : without fail, inevitably

immatériel, -rielle [imaterjɛl] *adj* **1** : immaterial **2** : intangible

immatriculation [imatrikylasjɔ̃] *nf* **1** : registration **2 plaque d'immatriculation** : license plate

immatriculer [imatrikyle] *vt* : to register (a motor vehicle)

immature [imatyr] *adj* : immature

immaturité [imatyrite] *nf* : immaturity

immédiat[1], **-diate** [imedja, -djat] *adj* : immediate — **immédiatement** [-djatmɑ̃] *adv*

immédiat[2] *nm* **dans l'immédiat** : for the time being

immémorial, -riale [imemɔrjal] *adj, mpl* **-riaux** [-rjo] : immemorial, ancient

immense [imɑ̃s] *adj* : immense — **immensément** [imɑ̃semɑ̃] *adv*

immensité [imɑ̃site] *nf* : immensity

immerger [imɛrʒe] {17} *vt* : to submerge, to immerse — **s'immerger** *vr* : to dive, to submerge oneself

immérité, -tée [imerite] *adj* : undeserved

immersion [imɛrsjɔ̃] *nf* : immersion

immeuble[1] [imœbl] *adj* **biens immeubles** : real estate

immeuble[2] *nm* : building, apartment building, office building

immigrant, -grante [imigrɑ̃, -grɑ̃t] *adj & n* : immigrant

immigration [imigrasjɔ̃] *nf* : immigration

immigré, -grée [imigre] *n* : immigrant

immigrer [imigre] *vi* : to immigrate

imminence [iminɑ̃s] *nf* : imminence

imminent, -nente [iminɑ̃, -nɑ̃t] *adj* : impending, imminent

immiscer [imise] {6} *v* **s'immiscer** *vr* **~ dans** : to interfere with, to meddle in

immixtion [imiksjɔ̃] *nf* : interference

immobile [imɔbil] *adj* **1** : motionless, still **2** : fixed, unchanging

immobilier, -lière [imɔbilje, -jɛr] *adj* : real estate, property <agent immobilier : real estate agent>

immobilisation [imɔbilizasjɔ̃] *nf* **1** : immobilization **2 immobilisations** *nfpl* : fixed assets

immobiliser [imɔbilize] *vt* **1** : to immobilize **2** : to bring to a halt — **s'immobiliser** *vr* : to come to a halt

immobilisme [imɔbilism] *nm* : opposition to change, conservatism

immobilité [imɔbilite] *nf* : immobility, stillness

immodéré, -rée [imɔdere] *adj* : immoderate, excessive — **immodérément** [-remɑ̃] *adv*

immodeste [imɔdɛst] *adj* : immodest

immoler [imɔle] *vt* SACRIFIER : to immolate, to sacrifice

immonde [imɔ̃d] *adj* **1** : foul, filthy **2** : vile, sordid, revolting

immondices [imɔ̃dis] *nfpl* : waste, refuse

immoral, -rale [imɔral] *adj, mpl* **-raux** [-ro] : immoral — **immoralement** [-ralmɑ̃] *adv*

immoralité [imɔralite] *nf* : immorality

immortaliser [imɔrtalize] *vt* : to immortalize

immortalité [imɔrtalite] *nf* : immortality

immortel[1], **-telle** [imɔrtɛl] *adj* : immortal

immortel[2], **-telle** *n* : immortal
immuable [imɥabl] *adj* : immutable, unchanging — **immuablement** [imɥabləmɑ̃] *adv*
immuniser [imynize] *vt* : to immunize — **immunisation** [-nizasjɔ̃] *nf*
immunitaire [imynitɛr] *adj* : immune <système immunitaire : immune system>
immunité [imynite] *nf* : immunity
immunologie [imynɔlɔʒi] *nf* : immunology
impact [ɛ̃pakt] *nm* : impact
impair[1], **-paire** [ɛ̃pɛr] *adj* : odd <nombres impairs : odd numbers>
impair[2] *nm* : blunder, faux pas
impala [impala] *nm* : impala
imparable [ɛ̃parabl] *adj* : unstoppable
impardonnable [ɛ̃pardɔnabl] *adj* : unforgivable, unpardonable
imparfait[1], **-faite** [ɛ̃parfɛ, -fɛt] *adj* **1** : imperfect **2** : incomplete, unfinished — **imparfaitement** [-fɛtmɑ̃] *adv*
imparfait[2] *nm* : imperfect (tense)
impartial, -tiale [ɛ̃parsjal] *adj, mpl* **-tiaux** [-sjo] : unbiased, impartial — **impartialement** [-sjalmɑ̃] *adv*
impartialité [ɛ̃parsjalite] *nf* : impartiality
impartir [ɛ̃partir] *vt* : to grant, to bestow
impasse [ɛ̃pas] *nf* **1** : impasse, deadlock **2** CUL-DE-SAC : dead end
impassible [ɛ̃pasibl] *adj* : impassive — **impassiblement** [-sibləmɑ̃] *adv*
impatiemment [ɛ̃pasjamɑ̃] *adv* : impatiently
impatient, -tiente [ɛ̃pasjɑ̃, -sjɑ̃t] *adj* : impatient — **impatience** [-sjɑ̃s] *nf*
impatienter [ɛ̃pasjɑ̃te] *vt* : to irritate, to annoy — **s'impatienter** *vr* : to lose patience
impayable [ɛ̃pɛjabl] *adj fam* : priceless
impayé, -payée [ɛ̃pɛje] *adj* : unpaid, outstanding
impeccable [ɛ̃pekabl] *adj* : impeccable — **impeccablement** [-kabləmɑ̃] *adv*
impécunieux, -nieuse [ɛ̃pekynjø, -njøz] *adj* : impecunious
impénétrable [ɛ̃penetrabl] *adj* **1** : impenetrable **2** : inscrutable
impénitent, -tente [ɛ̃penitɑ̃, -tɑ̃t] *adj* : unrepentant
impensable [ɛ̃pɑ̃sabl] *adj* : unthinkable, inconceivable
imper [ɛ̃pɛr] *nm fam* → **imperméable**
impératif[1], **-tive** [ɛ̃peratif, -tiv] *adj* : imperative — **impérativement** [-tivmɑ̃] *adv*
impératif[2] *nm* **1** : requirement, necessity **2** : imperative (case)
impératrice [ɛ̃peratris] *nf* : empress
imperceptible [ɛ̃pɛ̃rsɛptibl] *adj* : imperceptible — **imperceptiblement** [-tibləmɑ̃] *adv*
imperfection [ɛ̃pɛrfɛksjɔ̃] *nf* : imperfection
impérial, -riale [ɛ̃perjal] *adj, mpl* **-riaux** [-rjo] : imperial
impérialisme [ɛ̃perjalism] *nm* : imperialism
impérialiste[1] [ɛ̃perjalist] *adj* : imperialist, imperialistic
impérialiste[2] *nmf* : imperialist
impérieusement [ɛ̃perjøzmɑ̃] *adv* **1** : imperiously **2** : urgently, absolutely
impérieux, -rieuse [ɛ̃perjø, -jøz] *adj* **1** : imperious **2** : pressing, urgent
impérissable [ɛ̃perisabl] *adj* : imperishable, undying
imperméabilisation [ɛ̃pɛrmeabilizasjɔ̃] *nf* : waterproofing
imperméabiliser [ɛ̃pɛrmeabilize] *vt* : to waterproof
imperméable[1] [ɛ̃pɛrmeabl] *adj* **1** : waterproof **2 ~ à** : impervious to
imperméable[2] *nm* : raincoat
impersonnel, -nelle [ɛ̃pɛrsɔnɛl] *adj* : impersonal — **impersonnellement** [-nɛlmɑ̃] *adv*
impertinent, -nente [ɛ̃pɛrtinɑ̃, -nɑ̃t] *adj* : impertinent — **impertinence** [-tinɑ̃s] *nf*
imperturbable [ɛ̃pɛrtyrbabl] *adj* : imperturbable, unflappable
impétueux, -tueuse, [ɛ̃petɥø, -tɥøz] *adj* **1** : impetuous, rash **2** : raging, wild — **impétueusement** [-tɥøzmɑ̃] *adv*
impétuosité [ɛ̃petɥozite] *nf* : impetuosity
impie [ɛ̃pi] *adj* : impious, godless
impiété [ɛ̃pjete] *nf* : impiety
impitoyable [ɛ̃pitwajabl] *adj* : merciless, pitiless — **impitoyablement** [-jabləmɑ̃] *adv*
implacable [ɛ̃plakabl] *adj* **1** : implacable **2** : relentless — **implacablement** [-kabləmɑ̃] *adv*
implant [ɛ̃plɑ̃] *nm* : implant (in medicine)
implantation [ɛ̃plɑ̃tasjɔ̃] *nf* **1** : establishment, installation, setting up **2** : implantation
implanter [ɛ̃plɑ̃te] *vt* **1** : to establish, to set up **2** : to implant — **s'implanter** *vr* **1** : to be set up **2** : to settle (of persons)
implication [ɛ̃plikasjɔ̃] *nf* : implication
implicite [ɛ̃plisit] *adj* : implicit — **implicitement** [-sitmɑ̃] *adv*
impliquer [ɛ̃plike] *vt* **1** : to implicate, to involve **2** : to imply, to mean — **s'impliquer** *vr* : to become involved
implorer [ɛ̃plɔre] *vt* : to implore
imploser [ɛ̃ploze] *vi* : to implode — **implosion** [ɛ̃plozjɔ̃] *nf*
impoli, -lie [ɛ̃pɔli] *adj* : impolite, rude — **impoliment** [-limɑ̃] *adv*
impolitesse [ɛ̃pɔlitɛs] *nf* : impoliteness, rudeness
impondérable [ɛ̃pɔ̃derabl] *adj* : imponderable
impopulaire [ɛ̃pɔpylɛr] *adj* : unpopular — **impopularité** [-pylarite] *nf*

importance [ɛ̃pɔrtɑ̃s] *nf* **1** : importance **2** : size, extent, amount **3 d'importance** : important, considerable

important[1], -tante [ɛ̃pɔrtɑ̃, -tɑ̃t] *adj* **1** : important, significant **2** LARGE : considerable, sizable

important[2] *nm* : important point, main thing

importateur, -trice [ɛ̃pɔrtatœr, -tris] *n* : importer

importation [ɛ̃pɔrtasjɔ̃] *nf* **1** : importation **2** : import

importer [ɛ̃pɔrte] *vt* : to import — *vi* **1** : to matter, to be important <peu importe : no matter> **2 n'importe** : I don't mind, it doesn't matter **3 n'importe où** : anywhere **4 n'importe quand** : anytime **5 n'importe qui** : anyone, anybody **6 n'importe quoi** : anything

import–export [ɛ̃pɔrɛkspɔr] *nms & pl* : import-export (business)

importun[1], -tune [ɛ̃pɔrtœ̃, -tyn] *adj* **1** : troublesome, bothersome **2** : inopportune, untimely

importun[2], -tune *n* : nuisance, pest

importuner [ɛ̃pɔrtyne] *vt* : to pester, to annoy

imposable [ɛ̃pɔzabl] *adj* : taxable

imposant, -sante [ɛ̃pɔzɑ̃, -zɑ̃t] *adj* : imposing

imposé, -sée [ɛ̃pɔze] *adj* **1** : prescribed, compulsory (in sports) **2** : fixed (of prices, etc.)

imposer [ɛ̃pɔze] *vt* **1** : to impose **2** : to command (respect, etc.) **3** : to tax — **s'imposer** *vr* **1** : to be essential **2** : to impose (something) on oneself, to make it a rule **3** : to become known, to stand out **4 ~ à** : to impose (oneself) on

imposition [ɛ̃pɔzisjɔ̃] *nf* : taxation, tax <taux d'imposition : tax rate>

impossibilité [ɛ̃pɔsibilite] *nf* : impossibility

impossible[1] [ɛ̃pɔsibl] *adj* : impossible

impossible[2] *nm* **l'impossible** : the impossible <faire l'impossible : to do one's utmost>

imposte [ɛ̃pɔst] *nf* : fanlight

imposteur [ɛ̃pɔstœr] *nm* : impostor

imposture [ɛ̃pɔstyr] *nf* : imposture, deception

impôt [ɛ̃po] *nm* : tax, duty <impôt sur le revenu : income tax>

impotence [ɛ̃pɔtɑ̃s] *nf* : infirmity, disability

impotent, -tente [ɛ̃pɔtɑ̃, -tɑ̃t] *adj* INFIRME : infirm, disabled

impraticable [ɛ̃pratikabl] *adj* **1** IRRÉALISABLE : impracticable, unworkable **2** : impassable

imprécis, -cise [ɛ̃presi, -siz] *adj* : imprecise, vague

imprécision [ɛ̃presizjɔ̃] *nf* : imprecision, vagueness

imprégner [ɛ̃preɲe] {87} *vt* **1** PÉNÉTRER : to impregnate, to soak **2** : to fill, to pervade — **s'imprégner** *vr* **~ de** : to immerse oneself in

imprenable [ɛ̃prənabl] *adj* : impregnable

imprégnation [ɛ̃preɲasjɔ̃] *nf* : impregnation, saturation

imprésario [ɛ̃presarjo] *nm* : impresario

impression [ɛ̃presjɔ̃] *nf* **1** : impression <faire bonne impression : to make a good impression> **2** : mark, imprint **3** : printing <envoyer à l'impression : to send to the press>

impressionnable [ɛ̃presjɔnabl] *adj* : impressionable

impressionnant, -nante [ɛ̃presjɔnɑ̃, -nɑ̃t] *adj* **1** : impressive, imposing **2** : disturbing, upsetting

impressionner [ɛ̃presjɔne] *vt* **1** : to impress **2** : to disturb, to upset **3** : to expose (film)

impressionnisme [ɛ̃presjɔnism] *nm* : impressionism

impressionniste[1] [ɛ̃presjɔnist] *adj* : impressionistic

impressionniste[2] *nmf* : impressionist

imprévisible [ɛ̃previzibl] *adj* : unforeseeable, unpredictable

imprévoyance [ɛ̃prevwajɑ̃s] *nf* : lack of foresight, improvidence

imprévoyant, -voyante [ɛ̃prevwajɑ̃, -vwajɑ̃t] *adj* : improvident

imprévu, -vue [ɛ̃prevy] *adj* : unforeseen, unexpected

imprimante [ɛ̃primɑ̃t] *nf* : printer <imprimante à laser : laser printer>

imprimé[1], -mée [ɛ̃prime] *adj* : printed

imprimé[2] *nm* **1** : print, printed fabric **2** FORMULAIRE : form **3** : printed matter

imprimer [ɛ̃prime] *vt* **1** : to print, to stamp **2** : to imprint **3** : to publish **4** : to impart, to transmit

imprimerie [ɛ̃primri] *nf* **1** : printing **2** : print shop, printer's

imprimeur, -meuse [ɛ̃primœr, -møz] *n* : printer

improbable [ɛ̃prɔbabl] *adj* : improbable — **improbabilité** [-babilite] *nf*

improductif, -tive [ɛ̃prɔdyktif, -tiv] *adj* : unproductive

impromptu, -tue [ɛ̃prɔ̃pty] *adj* : impromptu

impropre [ɛ̃prɔpr] *adj* **1** : inappropriate, incorrect (of words, etc.) **2 ~ à** : unsuited to, unfit for

improvisation [ɛ̃prɔvizasjɔ̃] *nf* : improvisation

improvisé, -sée [ɛ̃prɔvize] *adj* : improvised, makeshift

improviser [ɛ̃prɔvize] *v* : to improvise — **s'improviser** *vr* **1** : to be improvised **2** : to act as

improviste [ɛ̃prɔvist] **à l'improviste** : unexpectedly

imprudemment [ɛ̃prydamɑ̃] *adv* : carelessly, recklessly

imprudence [ɛ̃prydɑ̃s] *nf* : imprudence, carelessness

imprudent, -dente [ɛ̃prydɑ̃, -dɑ̃t] *adj* **1** : unwise, imprudent **2** : rash, foolhardy
impudence [ɛ̃pydɑ̃s] *nf* : impudence
impudent, -dente [ɛ̃pydɑ̃, -dɑ̃t] *adj* : impudent
impudeur [ɛ̃pydœr] *nf* : shamelessness, immodesty
impudique [ɛ̃pydik] *adj* : immodest, indecent — **impudiquement** [-dikmɑ̃] *adv*
impuissance [ɛ̃pɥisɑ̃s] *nf* **1** : helplessness, powerlessness **2** : (sexual) impotence
impuissant, -sante [ɛ̃pɥisɑ̃, -sɑ̃t] *adj* **1** : helpless, powerless **2** : impotent
impulsif, -sive [ɛ̃pylsif, -siv] *adj* : impulsive — **impulsivement** [-sivmɑ̃] *adv*
impulsion [ɛ̃pylsjɔ̃] *nf* **1** : impulse **2** : impetus
impulsivité [ɛ̃pylsivite] *nf* : impulsiveness
impunément [ɛ̃pynemɑ̃] *adv* : with impunity
impuni, -nie [ɛ̃pyni] *adj* : unpunished
impunité [ɛ̃pynite] *nf* : impunity
impur, -pure [ɛ̃pyr] *adj* : impure
impureté [ɛ̃pyrte] *nf* : impurity
imputable [ɛ̃pytabl] *adj* **1** : imputable, attributable **2 ~ sur** : chargeable to (an account, etc.)
imputer [ɛ̃pyte] *vt* **1** : to impute, to attribute **2** : to charge
inabordable [inabɔrdabl] *adj* **1** : unapproachable, inaccessible **2** : prohibitive (in price)
inacceptable [inaksɛptabl] *adj* : unacceptable
inaccessibilité [inaksesibilite] *nf* : inaccessibility
inaccessible [inaksesibl] *adj* **1** : inaccessible, unattainable **2 ~ à** : impervious to
inaccoutumé, -mée [inakutyme] *adj* : unaccustomed
inachevé, -vée [inaʃve] *adj* : unfinished
inactif, -tive [inaktif, -tiv] *adj* : inactive
inaction [inaksjɔ̃] *nf* : inaction, idleness
inactivité [inaktivite] *nf* : inactivity
inadaptation [inadaptasjɔ̃] *nf* **1** : maladjustment **2** : inappropriateness
inadapté[1], **-tée** [inadapte] *adj* **1** : maladjusted **2** INAPPROPRIÉ : unsuited, inappropriate
inadapté[2], **-tée** *n* : social misfit, maladjusted person
inadéquat, -quate [inadekwa, -kwat] *adj* : inadequate
inadéquation [inadekwasjɔ̃] *nf* : inadequacy
inadmissible [inadmisibl] *adj* : inadmissible, unacceptable
inadvertance [inadvɛrtɑ̃s] *nf* **par ~** : inadvertently
inaliénable [inaljenabl] *adj* : inalienable
inaltérable [inalterabl] *adj* **1** : stable, unchanging <inaltérable à : unaffected by> **2** : constant, unfailing
inamical, -cale [inamikal] *adj, mpl* **-caux** [-ko] : inimical, unfriendly
inamovible [inamɔvibl] *adj* : fixed, permanent
inanimé, -mée [inanime] *adj* **1** : inanimate **2** : unconscious, senseless
inanité [inanite] *nf* : futility, pointlessness
inanition [inanisjɔ̃] *nf* : starvation <tomber d'inanition : to faint with hunger>
inaperçu, -çue [inapɛrsy] *adj* : unseen, unnoticed <passer inaperçu : to go unnoticed>
inapplicable [inaplikabl] *adj* : inapplicable
inappliqué, -quée [inaplike] *adj* **1** : lacking in application **2** : not applied, unenforced
inappréciable [inapresjabl] *adj* **1** : invaluable **2** : inappreciable, imperceptible
inapproprié, -priée [inaprɔprije] *adj* : inappropriate
inapte [inapt] *adj* **1** : inept **2** : unfit, unsuited
inaptitude [inaptityd] *nf* : unfitness
inarticulé, -lée [inartikyle] *adj* : inarticulate
inassouvi, -vie [inasuvi] *adj* **1** : unsatisfied, unfulfilled **2** : insatiable
inattaquable [inatakabl] *adj* **1** IRRÉPROCHABLE : irreproachable **2** IRRÉFUTABLE : irrefutable **3** IMPRENABLE : impregnable
inattendu, -due [inatɑ̃dy] *adj* : unexpected
inattentif, -tive [inatɑ̃tif, -tiv] *adj* : inattentive, distracted <inattentif à l'avertissement : heedless of the warning>
inattention [inatɑ̃sjɔ̃] *nf* : inattention <faute d'inattention : careless mistake>
inaudible [inodibl] *adj* : inaudible
inaugural, -rale [inogyral] *adj, mpl* **-raux** [-ro] : inaugural <séance inaugurale : opening session>
inauguration [inogyrasjɔ̃] *nf* : inauguration
inaugurer [inogyre] *vt* **1** : to unveil, to open **2** : to inaugurate
inavouable [inavwabl] *adj* : shameful, unmentionable
inavoué, -vouée [inavwe] *adj* : unacknowledged, unavowed
incalculable [ɛ̃kalkylabl] *adj* : incalculable, countless
incandescent, -cente [ɛ̃kɑ̃desɑ̃, -sɑ̃t] *adj* : incandescent — **incandescence** [-desɑ̃s] *nf*
incantation [ɛ̃kɑ̃tasjɔ̃] *nf* : incantation
incapable [ɛ̃kapabl] *adj* : incapable, unable <incapable de chanter : unable to sing>

incapacité [ɛ̃kapasite] *nf* **1** : incapacity, inability <être dans l'incapacité de faire qqch : to be unable to do sth> **2** : incompetence **3** : (physical) disability

incarcérer [ɛ̃karsere] {87} *vt* : to incarcerate — **incarcération** [-serasjɔ̃] *nf*

incarnation [ɛ̃karnasjɔ̃] *nf* : incarnation

incarné, -née [ɛ̃karne] *adj* **1** : incarnate **2 ongle incarné** : ingrown toenail

incarner [ɛ̃karne] *vt* **1** : to incarnate, to embody **2** : to personify, to play

incartade [ɛ̃kartad] *nf* : escapade, prank

incassable [ɛ̃kasabl] *adj* : unbreakable

incendiaire[1] [ɛ̃sɑ̃djɛr] *adj* **1** : incendiary **2** : inflammatory

incendiaire[2] *nmf* : arsonist

incendie [ɛ̃sɑ̃di] *nm* **1** : fire **2 incendie criminel** : arson

incendier [ɛ̃sɑ̃dje] {96} *vt* **1** : to set on fire, to burn down **2** : to burn <ces piments incendient la gorge : these peppers burn my throat> **3** : to light up **4** : to stir up, to inflame

incertain, -taine [ɛ̃sɛrtɛ̃, -tɛn] *adj* **1** : uncertain, doubtful **2** : indistinct, blurred

incertitude [ɛ̃sɛrtityd] *nf* : uncertainty

incessant, -sante [ɛ̃sesɑ̃, -sɑ̃t] *adj* : incessant — **incessamment** [ɛ̃sesamɑ̃] *adv*

inceste [ɛ̃sɛst] *nm* : incest — **incestueux, -tueuse** [ɛ̃sɛstɥø, -tɥøz] *adj*

inchangé, -gée [ɛ̃ʃɑ̃ʒe] *adj* : unchanged

incidemment [ɛ̃sidamɑ̃] *adv* **1** : incidentally, in passing **2** : by chance

incidence [ɛ̃sidɑ̃s] *nf* **1** : effect, impact **2** : incidence (in physics)

incident[1], **-dente** [ɛ̃sidɑ̃, -dɑ̃t] *adj* : incidental

incident[2] *nm* **1** : incident, event **2** *or* **incident de parcours** : hitch, setback

incinérateur [ɛ̃sineratœr] *nm* : incinerator

incinération [ɛ̃sinerasjɔ̃] *nf* **1** : incineration **2** : cremation

incinérer [ɛ̃sinere] {87} *vt* **1** : to incinerate **2** : to cremate

inciser [ɛ̃size] *vt* **1** : to make an incision in, to incise **2** : to lance

incisif, -sive [ɛ̃sizif, -ziv] *adj* : incisive, cutting

incision [ɛ̃sizjɔ̃] *nf* : incision

incisive *nf* : incisor

incitatif, -tive [ɛ̃sitatif, -tiv] *adj* : motivating <mesure incitative : motivating factor, incentive>

incitation [ɛ̃sitasjɔ̃] *nf* **1** : incitement **2** : incentive

inciter [ɛ̃site] *vt* **1** : to incite (a riot, etc.) **2** : to encourage, to prompt

incivil, -vile [ɛ̃sivil] *adj* : uncivil, rude

inclassable [ɛ̃klasabl] *adj* : unclassifiable

inclinable [ɛ̃klinabl] *adj* : reclining, adjustable <fauteuil inclinable : recliner>

inclinaison [ɛ̃klinɛzɔ̃] *nf* : incline, slope, angle

inclination [ɛ̃klinasjɔ̃] *nf* **1** TENDANCE : inclination, tendency **2** : nod, bowing (of the head)

incliner [ɛ̃kline] *vt* **1** PENCHER : to tilt, to bend **2** : to incline, to prompt (s.o. to do sth) — *vi* **~ à** : to be inclined to, to tend toward — **s'incliner** *vr* **1** : to tilt, to lean **2 ~ devant** : to give in to **3 ~ devant** : to bow down before

inclure [ɛ̃klyr] {39} *vt* **1** : to include **2** : to enclose

inclus, -cluse [ɛ̃kly, -klyz] *adj* **1** COMPRIS : inclusive, including <de lundi à jeudi inclus : from Monday to Thursday inclusive> <samedi inclus : including Saturdays> **2** : impacted <dent incluse : impacted tooth> **3** → **ci–inclus**

inclusion [ɛ̃klyzjɔ̃] *nf* : inclusion

inclusivement [ɛ̃klyzivmɑ̃] *adv* : inclusive, inclusively

incognito [ɛ̃kɔɲito] *adv & adj* : incognito

incohérence [ɛ̃kɔerɑ̃s] *nf* **1** : incoherence **2** : inconsistency, discrepancy

incohérent, -rente [ɛ̃kɔerɑ̃, -rɑ̃t] *adj* **1** : incoherent **2** : inconsistent

incolore [ɛ̃kɔlɔr] *adj* : colorless

incomber [ɛ̃kɔ̃be] *vi* **~ à** : to be incumbent upon, to be the responsibility of

incombustible [ɛ̃kɔ̃bystibl] *adj* : incombustible

incommensurable [ɛ̃kɔmɑ̃syrabl] *adj* : immeasurable — **incommensurablement** [rabləmɑ̃] *adv*

incommodant, -dante [ɛ̃kɔmɔdɑ̃, -dɑ̃t] *adj* **1** : unpleasant **2** : annoying

incommode [ɛ̃kɔmɔd] *adj* **1** : inconvenient **2** : uncomfortable, awkward — **incommodément** [-demɑ̃] *adv*

incommoder [ɛ̃kɔmɔde] *vt* : to bother, to inconvenience

incommodité [ɛ̃kɔmɔdite] *nf* **1** : inconvenience **2** : discomfort

incomparable [ɛ̃kɔ̃parabl] *adj* : incomparable — **incomparablement** [-rabləmɑ̃] *adv*

incompatible [ɛ̃kɔ̃patibl] *adj* : incompatible — **incompatibilité** [-tibilite] *nf*

incompétence [ɛ̃kɔ̃petɑ̃s] *nf* **1** : incompetence **2** : lack of knowledge, ignorance

incompétent, -tente [ɛ̃kɔ̃petɑ̃, -tɑ̃t] *adj* **1** : incompetent **2** : ignorant

incomplet, -plète [ɛ̃kɔ̃plɛ, -plɛt] *adj* : incomplete — **incomplètement** [-plɛtmɑ̃] *adv*

incompréhensible [ɛ̃kɔ̃preɑ̃sibl] *adj* : incomprehensible

incompréhensif, -sive [ɛ̃kɔ̃preɑ̃sif, -siv] *adj* : unsympathetic
incompréhension [ɛ̃kɔ̃preɑ̃sjɔ̃] *nf* : lack of understanding
incompris, -prise [ɛ̃kɔ̃pri, -priz] *adj* : misunderstood
inconcevable [ɛ̃kɔ̃svabl] *adj* : inconceivable, unimaginable
inconciliable [ɛ̃kɔ̃siljabl] *adj* : irreconcilable
inconditionnel[1], -nelle [ɛ̃kɔ̃disjɔnɛl] *adj* : unconditional — **inconditionnellement** [-nɛlmɑ̃] *adv*
inconditionnel[2], -nelle *n* : enthusiast <un inconditionnel du jazz : a jazz enthusiast>
inconduite [ɛ̃kɔ̃dɥit] *nf* : misconduct
inconfort [ɛ̃kɔ̃fɔr] *nm* : discomfort
inconfortable [ɛ̃kɔ̃fɔrtabl] *adj* : uncomfortable — **inconfortablement** [-tabləmɑ̃] *adv*
incongru, -grue [ɛ̃kɔ̃gry] *adj* **1** : incongruous **2** : unseemly, inappropriate
incongruité [ɛ̃kɔ̃grɥite] *nf* **1** : incongruity **2** : unseemly remark
inconnu[1], -nue [ɛ̃kɔny] *adj* : unknown
inconnu[2], -nue *n* **1** : unknown (person) **2** : stranger
inconnue *nf* : unknown (in mathematics, etc.)
inconsciemment [ɛ̃kɔ̃sjamɑ̃] *adv* **1** : unconsciously **2** : thoughtlessly
inconscience [ɛ̃kɔ̃sjɑ̃s] *nf* **1** : unconsciousness **2** : thoughtlessness
inconscient[1], -ciente [ɛ̃kɔ̃sjɑ̃, -sjɑ̃t] *adj* **1** : unaware, oblivious **2** : unconscious
inconscient[2] *nm* **l'inconscient** : the unconscious
inconséquence [ɛ̃kɔ̃sekɑ̃s] *nf* **1** : inconsistency **2** : thoughtlessness
inconséquent, -quente [ɛ̃kɔ̃sekɑ̃, -kɑ̃t] *adj* **1** : inconsistent **2** : thoughtless
inconsidéré, -rée [ɛ̃kɔ̃sidere] *adj* : rash, thoughtless — **inconsidérément** [-remɑ̃] *adv*
inconsistant, -tante [ɛ̃kɔ̃sistɑ̃, -tɑ̃t] *adj* **1** : flimsy, weak **2** : watery, runny
inconsolable [ɛ̃kɔ̃sɔlabl] *adj* : inconsolable
inconstance [ɛ̃kɔ̃stɑ̃s] *nf* : inconstancy, fickleness
inconstant, -stante [ɛ̃kɔ̃stɑ̃, -stɑ̃t] *adj* : inconstant, fickle
inconstitutionnel, -nelle [ɛ̃kɔ̃stitysjɔnɛl] *adj* : unconstitutional
incontestable [ɛ̃kɔ̃tɛstabl] *adj* : unquestionable, indisputable — **incontestablement** [-stabləmɑ̃] *adv*
incontesté, -tée [ɛ̃kɔ̃tɛste] *adj* : uncontested, undisputed
incontinent, -nente [ɛ̃kɔ̃tinɑ̃, -nɑ̃t] *adj* : incontinent — **incontinence** [-tinɑ̃s] *nf*
incontournable [ɛ̃kɔ̃turnabl] *adj* : essential, that cannot be ignored
incontrôlable [ɛ̃kɔ̃trolabl] *adj* **1** : unverifiable **2** : uncontrollable
incontrôlé, -lée [ɛ̃kɔ̃trole] *adj* **1** : unchecked, unverified **2** : uncontrolled
inconvenance [ɛ̃kɔ̃vnɑ̃s] *nf* : impropriety, indecorousness
inconvenant, -nante [ɛ̃kɔ̃vnɑ̃, -nɑ̃t] *adj* INCONGRU : improper, indecorous, unseemly
inconvénient [ɛ̃kɔ̃venjɑ̃] *nm* : disadvantage, drawback
incorporation [ɛ̃kɔrpɔrasjɔ̃] *nf* **1** : incorporating, blending, mixing **2** : induction (into the military) **3** *Can* : incorporation (of a company)
incorporer [ɛ̃kɔrpɔre] *vt* **1** : to incorporate, to blend, to mix **2** : to induct (into the military) **3** *Can* : to incorporate (a company)
incorrect, -recte [ɛ̃kɔrɛkt] *adj* **1** IMPROPRE : incorrect **2** INCONVENANT : improper, unsuitable **3** DÉLOYAL : unfair, underhanded
incorrectement [ɛ̃kɔrɛktəmɑ̃] *adv* : incorrectly, wrongly
incorrigible [ɛ̃kɔriʒibl] *adj* : incorrigible
incorruptible [ɛ̃kɔryptibl] *adj* : incorruptible
incrédule [ɛ̃kredyl] *adj* : incredulous
incrédulité [ɛ̃kredylite] *nf* : incredulity
increvable [ɛ̃krəvabl] *adj* **1** : puncture-proof (of a tire) **2** *fam* : tireless
incriminer [ɛ̃krimine] *vt* : to incriminate — **incrimination** [ɛ̃kriminasjɔ̃] *nf*
incroyable [ɛ̃krwajabl] *adj* : unbelievable, incredible — **incroyablement** [-jabləmɑ̃] *adv*
incroyant, -croyante [ɛ̃krwajɑ̃, -jɑ̃t] *n* : unbeliever
incrustation [ɛ̃krystasjɔ̃] *nf* **1** : inlaying, inlay **2** : incrustation (in geology)
incruster [ɛ̃kryste] *vt* **1** : to encrust **2** : to inlay — **s'incruster** *vr* : to become embedded
incubateur [ɛ̃kybatœr] *nm* : incubator
incubation [ɛ̃kybasjɔ̃] *nf* : incubation
incuber [ɛ̃kybe] *vt* : to incubate
inculpation [ɛ̃kylpasjɔ̃] *nf* : indictment, charge
inculpé, -pée [ɛ̃kylpe] *n* : accused, defendant
inculper [ɛ̃kylpe] *vt* : to indict, to charge
inculquer [ɛ̃kylke] *vt* : to inculcate, to instill
inculte [ɛ̃kylt] *adj* **1** : uncultivated, wild **2** : unkempt **3** : uneducated, ignorant
inculture [ɛ̃kyltyr] *nf* : lack of culture
incurable [ɛ̃kyrabl] *adj* : incurable
incurie [ɛ̃kyri] *nf* NÉGLIGENCE : carelessness, negligence
incursion [ɛ̃kyrsjɔ̃] *nf* : foray, incursion, inroad
incurver [ɛ̃kyrve] *vt* : to bend, to curve — **s'incurver** *vr*
indécence [ɛ̃desɑ̃s] *nf* **1** : indecency **2** : indecent act or remark

indécent, -cente [ɛ̃desɑ̃, -sɑ̃t] *adj* : indecent — **indécemment** [-samɑ̃] *adv*

indéchiffrable [ɛ̃deʃifrabl] *adj* **1** : indecipherable **2** : incomprehensible

indécis, -cise [ɛ̃desi, -siz] *adj* **1** : indecisive **2** : undecided

indécision [ɛ̃desizjɔ̃] *nf* **1** : indecisiveness **2** : indecision

indécrottable [ɛ̃dekrɔtabl] *adj fam* : incorrigible

indéfectible [ɛ̃defɛktibl] *adj* : enduring, unfailing

indéfendable [ɛ̃defɑ̃dabl] *adj* : indefensible, untenable

indéfini, -nie [ɛ̃defini] *adj* **1** : indefinite **2** : undefined

indéfiniment [ɛ̃definimɑ̃] *adv* : indefinitely

indéfinissable [ɛ̃definisabl] *adj* : indefinable

indélébile [ɛ̃delebil] *adj* : indelible

indélicat, -cate [ɛ̃delika, -kat] *adj* **1** : coarse, indelicate **2** MALHONNÊTE : dishonest

indélicatesse [ɛ̃delikatɛs] *nf* : indelicacy

indemne [ɛ̃dɛmn] *adj* : undamaged, unharmed

indemnisation [ɛ̃dɛmnizasjɔ̃] *nf* : compensation, indemnity

indemniser [ɛ̃dɛmnize] *vt* **1** : to indemnify, to compensate **2** : to reimburse (for expenses)

indemnité [ɛ̃dɛmnite] *nf* **1** COMPENSATION : indemnity, compensation **2** ALLOCATION : allowance <indemnité de logement : housing allowance>

indéniable [ɛ̃denjabl] *adj* : undeniable — **indéniablement** [-njabləmɑ̃] *adv*

indépendamment [ɛ̃depɑ̃damɑ̃] *adv* **1** : independently **2** ~ **de** : regardless of, apart from **3** ~ **de** : in addition to

indépendant, -dante [ɛ̃depɑ̃dɑ̃, -dɑ̃t] *adj* : independent — **indépendance** [-pɑ̃dɑ̃s] *nf*

indescriptible [ɛ̃dɛskriptibl] *adj* : indescribable

indésirable [ɛ̃dezirabl] *adj* : undesirable

indestructible [ɛ̃dɛstryktibl] *adj* : indestructible — **indestructibilité** [-tibilite] *nf*

indéterminé, -née [ɛ̃detɛrmine] *adj* : indeterminate, unspecified

index [ɛ̃dɛks] *nm* **1** : index **2** : forefinger, index finger

indexation [ɛ̃dɛksasjɔ̃] *nf* **1** : indexing **2** : indexation (in economics)

indexer [ɛ̃dekse] *vt* : to index

indicateur[1], -trice [ɛ̃dikatœr, -tris] *adj* → **panneau, poteau**

indicateur[2] *nm* **1** INFORMATEUR : (police) informer **2** GUIDE : guide, directory **3** : gauge, meter <indicateur de vitesse : speedometer> **4** : economic indicator

indicatif[1], -tive [ɛ̃dikatif, -tiv] *adj* : indicative

indicatif[2] *nm* **1** : indicative (in grammar) **2** : theme (of a radio or television program) **3** **indicatif de zone** : area code

indication [ɛ̃dikasjɔ̃] *nf* **1** APERÇU, SIGNE : indication **2** RENSEIGNEMENT : information **3** **indications** *nfpl* : instructions, directions

indice [ɛ̃dis] *nm* **1** SIGNE : sign, indication **2** : clue, lead **3** : index <indice du coût de la vie : cost of living index> **4** : rating <indice d'écoute : audience ratings>

indicible [ɛ̃disibl] *adj* : unspeakable, inexpressible

indien, -dienne [ɛ̃djɛ̃, -djɛn] *adj* : Indian

Indien, -dienne *n* : Indian

indifféremment [ɛ̃diferamɑ̃] *adv* : indiscriminately, equally

indifférence [ɛ̃diferɑ̃s] *nf* : indifference

indifférent, -rente [ɛ̃diferɑ̃, -rɑ̃t] *adj* **1** : indifferent **2** : irrelevant, immaterial

indifférer [ɛ̃difere] {87} *vi* ~ **à** : to be of no importance to <cela m'indiffère : it's all the same to me>

indigence [ɛ̃diʒɑ̃s] *nf* : indigence

indigène[1] [ɛ̃diʒɛn] *adj* : indigenous, native

indigène[2] *nmf* : native (of a country or region)

indigent[1], -gente [ɛ̃diʒɑ̃, -ʒɑ̃t] *adj* : indigent, destitute

indigent[2], -gente *n* **1** : pauper **2** **les indigents** : the poor

indigeste [ɛ̃diʒɛst] *adj* : indigestible

indigestion [ɛ̃diʒɛstjɔ̃] *nf* : indigestion

indignation [ɛ̃diɲasjɔ̃] *nf* : indignation <avec indignation : indignantly>

indigne [ɛ̃diɲ] *adj* **1** : unworthy, undeserving **2** MÉPRISABLE : disgraceful

indigné, -gnée [ɛ̃diɲe] *adj* : indignant

indignement [ɛ̃diɲəmɑ̃] *adv* : disgracefully

indigner [ɛ̃diɲe] *vt* : to outrage — **s'indigner** *vr* : to be indignant

indignité [ɛ̃diɲite] *nf* **1** : unworthiness **2** : indignity, shameful act

indigo [ɛ̃digo] *adj & nm* : indigo

indiqué, -quée [ɛ̃dike] *adj* **1** : advisable, expedient **2** : appropriate

indiquer [ɛ̃dike] *vt* **1** : to indicate, to point out <ils m'ont indiqué le chemin : they showed me the way> **2** : to give, to name, to tell <indiquer l'heure : to give the time>

indirect, -recte [ɛ̃dirɛkt] *adj* : indirect — **indirectement** [-rɛktəmɑ̃] *adv*

indiscernable [ɛ̃disɛrnabl] *adj* : indiscernible

indiscipline [ɛ̃disiplin] *nf* : lack of discipline

indiscipliné, -née [ɛ̃disipline] *adj* : undisciplined, unruly

indiscret, -crète [ɛ̃diskrɛ, -krɛt] *adj* : indiscreet — **indiscrètement** [-krɛtmɑ̃] *adv*

indiscrétion [ɛ̃diskresjɔ̃] *nf* : indiscretion
indiscutable [ɛ̃diskytabl] *adj* : indisputable, unquestionable — **indiscutablement** [-tabləmɑ̃] *adv*
indispensable [ɛ̃dispɑ̃sabl] *adj* : indispensable, essential
indisponible [ɛ̃dispɔnibl] *adj* : unavailable
indisposé, -sée [ɛ̃dispoze] *adj* : unwell, indisposed
indisposer [ɛ̃dispoze] *vt* **1** : to annoy, to irritate **2** : to upset, to make ill
indisposition [ɛ̃dispozisjɔ̃] *nf* : indisposition, illness
indissociable [ɛ̃disɔsjabl] *adj* : inseparable
indistinct, -tincte [ɛ̃distɛ̃kt, -tɛ̃kt] *adj* : indistinct
indistinctement [ɛ̃distɛ̃ktəmɑ̃] *adv* **1** : indistinctly **2** : indiscriminately
individu [ɛ̃dividy] *nm* : individual
individualiser [ɛ̃dividɥalize] *vt* : to individualize
individualisme [ɛ̃dividɥalism] *nm* : individualism
individualiste[1] [ɛ̃dividɥalist] *adj* : individualistic
individualiste[2] *nmf* : individualist
individualité [ɛ̃dividɥalite] *nf* : individuality
individuel, -duelle [ɛ̃dividɥɛl] *adj* **1** : individual, particular **2** : personal, private
individuellement [ɛ̃dividɥɛlmɑ̃] *adv* : individually
indivis, -vise [ɛ̃divi, -viz] *adj* **1** : undivided **2 par ~** : jointly, in common
indivisible [ɛ̃divizibl] *adj* : indivisible
indolence [ɛ̃dɔlɑ̃s] *nf* **1** : indolence, laziness **2** : apathy
indolent, -lente [ɛ̃dɔlɑ̃, -lɑ̃t] *adj* **1** : indolent, lazy **2** : apathetic
indolore [ɛ̃dɔlɔr] *adj* : painless
indomptable [ɛ̃dɔ̃tabl] *adj* **1** : indomitable, invincible **2** : untamable
indonésien[1], **-sienne** [ɛ̃dɔnezjɛ̃, -zjɛn] *adj* : Indonesian
indonésien[2] *nm* : Indonesian (language)
Indonésien, -sienne *n* : Indonesian
indu, -due [ɛ̃dy] *adj* **1** : unseemly, ungodly <à des heures indues : at this ungodly hour> **2** : unwarranted, unjustified
indubitable [ɛ̃dybitabl] *adj* : indubitable — **indubitablement** [-tabləmɑ̃] *adv*
induction [ɛ̃dyksjɔ̃] *nf* : induction
inductif, -tive [ɛ̃dyktif, -tiv] *adj* : inductive
induire [ɛ̃dɥir] {49} *vt* **1** INCITER : to induce, to incite <induire en erreur : to mislead> **2** CONCLURE : to infer, to conclude
indulgence [ɛ̃dylʒɑ̃s] *nf* **1** : indulgence, leniency **2** : indulgence (in religion)
indulgent, -gente [ɛ̃dylʒɑ, -ʒɑ̃t] *adj* : indulgent, lenient
indûment [ɛ̃dymɑ̃] *adv* : unduly, unjustifiably
industrialiser [ɛ̃dystrijalize] *vt* : to industrialize — **industrialisation** [-lizasjɔ̃] *nf*
industrie [ɛ̃dystri] *nf* : industry
industriel[1], **-trielle** [ɛ̃dystrijɛl] *adj* : industrial
industriel[2], **-trielle** *n* : manufacturer, industrialist
industrieux, -trieuse [ɛ̃dystrijø, -trijøz] *adj* TRAVAILLEUR : industrious
inébranlable [inebrɑ̃labl] *adj* : unwavering, unshakeable
inédit, -dite [inedi, -dit] *adj* **1** : unpublished **2** ORIGINAL : novel, original
ineffable [inefabl] *adj* : ineffable, inexpressible — **ineffablement** [-fabləmɑ̃] *adv*
ineffaçable [inefasabl] *adj* : indelible
inefficace [inefikas] *adj* **1** : inefficient **2** : ineffective
inefficacité [inefikasite] *nf* **1** : inefficiency **2** : ineffectiveness
inégal, -gale [inegal] *adj, mpl* **-gaux** [-go] **1** : unequal **2** IRRÉGULIER : irregular, uneven — **inégalement** [-galmɑ̃] *adv*
inégalé, -lée [inegale] *adj* : unequaled
inégalité [inegalite] *nf* **1** : inequality **2** IRRÉGULARITÉ : unevenness, irregularity
inélégant, -gante [inelegɑ̃, -gɑ̃t] *adj* **1** : inelegant **2** : discourteous — **inélégance** [-gɑ̃s] *nf*
inéligible [inelizibl] *adj* : ineligible — **inéligibilité** [-ʒibilite] *nf*
inéluctable [inelyktabl] *adj* : inescapable — **inéluctablement** [-tabləmɑ̃] *adv*
inemployé, -ployée [inɑ̃plwaje] *adj* : unused
inénarrable [inenarabl] *adj* : hilarious, beyond words
inepte [inɛpt] *adj* : inept
ineptie [inɛpsi] *nf* **1** : ineptitude **2** : stupid action or remark
inépuisable [inepɥizabl] *adj* : inexhaustible
inéquitable [inekitabl] *adj* : inequitable
inerte [inɛrt] *adj* **1** : lifeless **2** : passive, apathetic **3** : inert
inertie [inɛrsi] *nf* : inertia
inespéré, -rée [inɛspere] *adj* : unhoped for, unexpected
inestimable [inɛstimabl] *adj* : inestimable, priceless
inévitable [inevitabl] *adj* : inevitable, unavoidable — **inévitablement** [-tabləmɑ̃] *adv*
inexact, inexacte [inɛgza(kt), -ɛgzakt] *adj* **1** : inaccurate **2** : unpunctual, late
inexactement [inɛgzaktəmɑ̃] *adv* : inaccurately, wrong
inexactitude [inɛgzaktityd] *nf* **1** : inaccuracy **2** : lateness, unpunctuality

inexcusable [inɛkskyzabl] *adj* : inexcusable

inexécutable [inɛgzekytabl] *adj* : impracticable, unworkable

inexercé, -cée [inɛgzɛrse] *adj* : untrained, inexperienced

inexistant, -tante [inɛgzistɑ̃, -tɑ̃t] *adj* : nonexistent — **inexistence** [-zistɑ̃s] *nf*

inexorable [inɛgzɔrabl] *adj* : inexorable — **inexorablement** [-rabləmɑ̃] *adv*

inexpérience [inɛksperjɑ̃s] *nf* : inexperience

inexpérimenté, -tée [inɛksperimɑ̃te] *adj* **1** : inexperienced **2** : untried, untested

inexplicable [inɛksplikabl] *adj* : inexplicable — **inexplicablement** [-kabləmɑ̃] *adv*

inexpliqué, -quée [inɛksplike] *adj* : unexplained

inexploité, -tée [inɛksplwate] *adj* : untapped, unexploited

inexpressif, -sive [inɛkspresif, -siv] *adj* : inexpressive, expressionless

inexprimable [inɛksprimabl] *adj* : inexpressible

inexprimé, -mée [inɛksprime] *adj* : unexpressed, unspoken

inextinguible [inɛkstɛ̃gibl] *adj* **1** : inextinguishable, unquenchable **2** : uncontrollable

in extremis [inɛkstremis] *adv* : at the last minute

inextricable [inɛkstrikabl] *adj* : inextricable — **inextricablement** [-kabləmɑ̃] *adv*

infaillibilité [ɛ̃fajibilite] *nf* : infallibility

infaillible [ɛ̃fajibl] *adj* **1** : infallible **2** : certain, reliable

infailliblement [ɛ̃fajibləmɑ̃] *adv* : without fail

infamant, -mante [ɛ̃famɑ̃, -mɑ̃t] *adj* **1** : defamatory **2** : dishonorable

infâme [ɛ̃fam] *adj* : vile, despicable

infamie [ɛ̃fami] *nf* **1** : infamy **2** CALOMNIE : calumny, slander

infanterie [ɛ̃fɑ̃tri] *nf* : infantry

infantile [ɛ̃fɑ̃til] *adj* : infantile, childish

infarctus [ɛ̃farktys] *nm or* **infarctus myocarde** : heart attack

infatigable [ɛ̃fatigabl] *adj* : indefatigable, tireless — **infatigablement** [-bləmɑ̃] *adv*

infatuation [ɛ̃fatɥasjɔ̃] *nf* : self-importance, conceit

infatué, -tuée [ɛ̃fatɥe] *adj* : conceited, self-important

infect, -fecte [ɛ̃fɛkt] *adj* **1** : foul, stinking **2** : horrible, vile

infecter [ɛ̃fɛkte] *vt* **1** : to infect **2** : to contaminate, to pollute, to poison — **s'infecter** *vr* : to become infected

infectieux, -tieuse [ɛ̃fɛksjø, -tjøz] *adj* : infectious

infection [ɛ̃fɛksjɔ̃] *nf* **1** : infection **2** PUANTEUR : stench

inférer [ɛ̃fere] {87} *vt* : to infer — **inférence** [ɛ̃ferɑ̃s] *nf*

inférieur[1], **-rieure** [ɛ̃ferjœr] *adj* **1** : inferior **2** : lower <lèvre inférieure : lower lip> **3 ~ à** : less than

inférieur[2], **-rieure** *n* : inferior

infériorité [ɛ̃ferjɔrite] *nf* : inferiority

infernal, -nale [ɛ̃fɛrnal] *adj, mpl* **-naux** [-no] **1** : infernal **2** : fiendish, diabolical

infertile [ɛ̃fɛrtil] *adj* : infertile — **infertilité** [-tilite] *nf*

infester [ɛ̃fɛste] *vt* : to infest

infidèle[1] [ɛ̃fidɛl] *adj* **1** : unfaithful, disloyal **2** : inaccurate

infidèle[2] *nmf* **1** : infidel, unbeliever **2** : unfaithful spouse or lover

infidélité [ɛ̃fidelite] *nf* **1** : infidelity **2** : unfaithfulness, inaccuracy

infiltration [ɛ̃filtrasjɔ̃] *nf* : infiltration

infiltrer [ɛ̃filtre] *vt* : to infiltrate — **s'infiltrer** *vr* **~ dans** : to penetrate, to seep into, to filter through

infime [ɛ̃fim] *adj* : minute, negligible

infini[1], **-nie** [ɛ̃fini] *adj* : infinite — **infiniment** [-nimɑ̃] *adv*

infini[2] *nm* **1** : infinity (in mathematics, etc.) **2 à l'infini** : endlessly, ad infinitum

infinité [ɛ̃finite] *nf* **1** : infinite number, lot **2** : infinity

infinitésimal, -male [ɛ̃finitezimal] *adj, mpl* **-maux** [-mo] : infinitesimal

infinitif [ɛ̃finitif] *nm* : infinitive

infirme[1] [ɛ̃firm] *adj* : disabled, infirm

infirme[2] *nmf* : disabled person, invalid

infirmer [ɛ̃firme] *vt* ANNULER : to invalidate, to annul

infirmerie [ɛ̃firməri] *nf* : infirmary

infirmier[1], **-mière** [ɛ̃firmje, -mjɛr] *adj* : nursing <personnel infirmier : nursing staff>

infirmier[2], **-mière** *n* GARDE-MALADE : nurse

infirmité [ɛ̃firmite] *nf* : disability, infirmity

inflammable [ɛ̃flamabl] *adj* : inflammable, flammable

inflammation [ɛ̃flamasjɔ̃] *nf* : inflammation

inflammatoire [ɛ̃flamatwar] *adj* : inflammatory

inflation [ɛ̃flasjɔ̃] *nf* : inflation

inflationniste [ɛ̃flasjɔnist] *adj* : inflationary

infléchir [ɛ̃fleʃir] *vt* **1** : to bend, to inflect **2** : to modify, to influence — **s'infléchir** *vr* **1** : to curve **2** : to deviate, to change course

inflexibilité [ɛ̃flɛksibilite] *nf* : inflexibility

inflexible [ɛ̃flɛksibl] *adj* : inflexible — **inflexiblement** [-sibləmɑ̃] *adv*

inflexion [ɛ̃flɛksjɔ̃] *nf* **1** CHANGEMENT : change, shift **2** COURBE : bend <inflexion de la tête : brief nod> **3** : inflection (of the voice)

infliger [ɛ̃fliʒe] {17} *vt* **1** : to inflict **2** : to impose (a penalty, etc.)
influence [ɛ̃flyɑ̃s] *nf* : influence
influencer [ɛ̃flyɑ̃se] {6} *vt* : to influence
influent, -fluente [ɛ̃flyɑ̃, -flyɑ̃t] *adj* : influential
influer [ɛ̃flye] *vi* ~ **sur** : to have an influence on, to affect
infographie [ɛ̃fografi] *nf* : computer graphics *pl*
informateur, -trice [ɛ̃fɔrmatœr, -tris] *n* INDICATEUR : informant, informer
informaticien, -cienne [ɛ̃fɔrmatisjɛ̃, -sjɛn] *n* : computer programmer
informatif, -tive [ɛ̃fɔrmatif, -tiv] *adj* : informative
information [ɛ̃fɔrmasjɔ̃] *nf* **1** : information **2** : news item **3** *France* : (judicial) inquiry
informatique[1] [ɛ̃fɔrmatik] *adj* : computer <analyste informatique : computer analyst>
informatique[2] *nf* **1** : computer science, information technology **2** : data processing
informatiser [ɛ̃fɔrmatize] *vt* : to computerize — **informatisation** [-tizasjɔ̃] *nf*
informe [ɛ̃fɔrm] *adj* : formless, shapeless
informel, -melle [ɛ̃fɔrmɛl] *adj* : informal
informer [ɛ̃fɔrme] *vt* : to inform — **s'informer** *vr* **1** : to inquire **2** : to inform oneself, to find out
infortune [ɛ̃fɔrtyn] *nf* : misfortune
infortuné, -née [ɛ̃fɔrtyne] *adj* : unfortunate, luckless
infraction [ɛ̃fraksjɔ̃] *nf* : infraction <infraction à la loi : breach of the law>
infranchissable [ɛ̃frɑ̃ʃisabl] *adj* **1** : insurmountable **2** : impassable
infrarouge [ɛ̃fraruʒ] *adj & nm* : infrared
infrastructure [ɛ̃frastryktyr] *nf* : infrastructure
infructueux, -tueuse [ɛ̃fryktɥø, -tɥøz] *adj* : fruitless
infus, -fuse [ɛ̃fy, -fyz] *adj* : innate <avoir la science infuse : to know a lot without studying>
infuser [ɛ̃fyze] *v* **1** : to infuse **2** : to brew, to steep
infusion [ɛ̃fyzjɔ̃] *nf* : infusion
ingénier [ɛ̃ʒenje] {96} *v* **s'ingénier** *vr* : to strive, to do one's utmost
ingénierie [ɛ̃ʒeniri] *nf* : engineering
ingénieur, -nieure [ɛ̃ʒenjœr] *n* : engineer
ingénieux, -nieuse [ɛ̃ʒenjø, -njøz] *adj* : ingenious — **ingénieusement** [-njøzmɑ̃] *adv*
ingéniosité [ɛ̃ʒenjɔzite] *nf* : ingenuity
ingénu, -nue [ɛ̃ʒeny] *adj* : ingenuous, naive — **ingénuement** *adv*
ingénue *nf* : ingenue
ingénuité [ɛ̃ʒenɥite] *nf* : ingenuousness, naïveté
ingérence [ɛ̃ʒerɑ̃s] *nf* : interference
ingérer [ɛ̃ʒere] {87} *vt* : to ingest — **s'ingérer** *vr* : to interfere, to meddle
ingouvernable [ɛ̃guvɛrnabl] *adj* : ungovernable
ingrat[1], **-grate** [ɛ̃gra, -grat] *adj* **1** : ungrateful **2** : thankless, unrewarding **3** : barren **4** : unattractive
ingrat[2], **-grate** *n* : ingrate
ingratitude [ɛ̃gratityd] *nf* : ingratitude
ingrédient [ɛ̃gredjɑ̃] *nm* : ingredient
inguérissable [ɛ̃gerisabl] *adj* : incurable
ingurgiter [ɛ̃gyrʒite] *vt* **1** ENGLOUTIR : to gulp down **2** : to take in, to absorb (knowledge, etc.)
inhabile [inabil] *adj* : inept, clumsy
inhabitable [inabitabl] *adj* : uninhabitable
inhabité, -tée [inabite] *adj* : uninhabited
inhabituel, -tuelle [inabitɥɛl] *adj* : unusual
inhalant [inalɑ̃] *nm* : inhalant
inhalateur [inalatœr] *nm* : inhaler
inhaler [inale] *vt* : to inhale — **inhalation** [-alasjɔ̃] *nf*
inhérent, -rente [inerɑ̃, -rɑ̃t] *adj* : inherent
inhiber [inibe] *vt* : to inhibit
inhibition [inibisjɔ̃] *nf* : inhibition
inhospitalier, -lière [inɔspitalje, -ljɛr] *adj* : inhospitable
inhumain, -maine [inymɛ̃, -mɛn] *adj* : inhuman
inhumanité [inymanite] *nf* : inhumanity
inhumation [inymasjɔ̃] *nf* : burial, interment
inhumer [inyme] *vt* : to bury, to inter
ininflammable [inɛ̃flamabl] *adj* : nonflammable
inimaginable [inimaʒinabl] *adj* : unimaginable, incredible
inimitable [inimitabl] *adj* : inimitable
inimitié [inimitje] *nf* HOSTILITÉ : enmity, hostility
inintelligent, -gente [inɛ̃tɛliʒɑ̃, -ʒɑ̃t] *adj* : unintelligent
inintelligible [inɛ̃teliʒibl] *adj* : unintelligible
inintéressant, -sante [inɛ̃terɛsɑ̃, -sɑ̃t] *adj* : uninteresting
ininterrompu, -pue [inɛ̃tɛrɔ̃py] *adj* **1** : uninterrupted, non-stop **2** : unbroken **3** : continuous, unremitting
inique [inik] *adj* : iniquitous
iniquité [inikite] *nf* : iniquity
initial, -tiale [inisjal] *adj, mpl* **-tiaux** [-sjo] : initial — **initialement** [-sjalmɑ̃] *adv*
initiale *nf* : initial
initiateur, -trice [inisjatœr, -tris] *n* **1** : initiator **2** NOVATEUR : innovator, pioneer
initiation [inisjasjɔ̃] *nf* : initiation
initiatique [inisjatik] *adj* : initiatory

initiative [inisjativ] *nf* : initiative <prendre l'initiative : to take the initiative>

initié, -tiée [inisje] *n* : initiate, insider

initier [inisje] {96} *vt* **1 ~ à** : to initiate, to start **2 ~ à** : to introduce to — **s'initier** *vr* **~ à** : to learn

injecté, -tée [ɛ̃ʒɛkte] *adj* **yeux injectés (de sang)** : bloodshot eyes

injecter [ɛ̃ʒɛkte] *vt* : to inject

injection [ɛ̃ʒɛksjɔ̃] *nf* : injection

injonction [ɛ̃ʒɔ̃ksjɔ̃] *nf* : order, injunction

injure [ɛ̃ʒyr] *nf* : insult, abuse <faire injure à qqn : to insult s.o.>

injurier [ɛ̃ʒyrje] {96} *vt* : to insult

injurieux, -rieuse [ɛ̃ʒyrjø, -rjøz] *adj* : insulting, abusive

injuste [ɛ̃ʒyst] *adj* : unjust, unfair — **injustement** [ɛ̃ʒystəmɑ̃] *adv*

injustice [ɛ̃ʒystis] *nf* : injustice

injustifiable [ɛ̃ʒystifjabl] *adj* : unjustifiable, indefensible

injustifié, -fiée [ɛ̃jystifje] *adj* : unjustified

inlassable [ɛ̃lasabl] *adj* : tireless — **inlassablement** [-sabləmɑ̃] *adv*

inné, -née [ine] *adj* : innate, inborn

innocemment [inɔsamɑ̃] *adv* : innocently

innocence [inɔsɑ̃s] *nf* : innocence

innocent, -cente [inɔsɑ̃, -sɑ̃t] *adj & n* : innocent

innocenter [inɔsɑ̃te] *vt* **1** DISCULPER : to exonerate, to clear **2** EXCUSER : to excuse, to justify

innocuité [inɔkɥite] *nf* : innocuousness

innombrable [inɔ̃brabl] *adj* : innumerable

innommable [inɔmabl] *adj* : unspeakable, foul

innovateur[1], -trice [inɔvatœr, -tris] *adj* : innovative

innovateur[2], -trice *n* : innovator

innover [inɔve] *v* : to innovate — **innovation** [inɔvasjɔ̃] *nf*

inoccupation [inɔkypasjɔ̃] *nf* : inactivity

inoccupé, -pée [inɔkype] *adj* **1** : idle **2** : unoccupied, vacant

inoculer [inɔkyle] *vt* : to inoculate — **inoculation** [-kylasjɔ̃] *nf*

inodore [inɔdɔr] *adj* : odorless

inoffensif, -sive [inɔfɑ̃sif, -siv] *adj* : inoffensive, harmless

inondation [inɔ̃dasjɔ̃] *nf* : flood, inundation

inonder [inɔ̃de] *vt* **1** : to flood **2** : to inundate, to overrun

inopérable [inɔperabl] *adj* : inoperable

inopérant, -rante [inɔperɑ̃, -rɑ̃t] *adj* : ineffective, inoperative

inopiné, -née [inɔpine] *adj* : unexpected — **inopinément** [-nemɑ̃] *adv*

inopportun, -tune [inɔpɔrtœ̃, -tyn] *adj* INTEMPESTIF : inopportune, untimely — **inopportunément** [-tynemɑ̃] *adv*

inorganique [inɔrganik] *adj* : inorganic

inorganisé, -sée [inɔrganize] *adj* **1** : disorganized **2** : unorganized

inoubliable [inublijabl] *adj* : unforgettable — **inoubliablement** [inublijabləmɑ̃]

inouï, inouïe [inwi] *adj* : incredible, unheard of

inoxydable[1] [inɔksidabl] *adj* **1** : rustproof **2 acier inoxydable** : stainless steel

inoxydable[2] *nm* : stainless steel

inqualifiable [ɛ̃kalifjabl] *adj* : unspeakable

inquiet, -quiète [ɛ̃kjɛ, -kjɛt] *adj* **1** ANXIEUX : worried, anxious **2** AGITÉ : restless

inquiétant, -tante [ɛ̃kjetɑ̃, -tɑ̃t] *adj* : worrisome, ominous

inquiéter [ɛ̃kjete] {87} *vt* **1** : to worry **2** : to bother, to disturb — **s'inquiéter** *vr* **1** : to be worried **2 ~ de** : to bother about, to inquire about

inquiétude [ɛ̃kjetyd] *nf* : worry, anxiety, concern

inquisiteur, -trice [ɛ̃kizitœr, -tris] *adj* : inquisitive

inquisition [ɛ̃kizisjɔ̃] *nf* : inquisition

insaisissable [ɛ̃sezisabl] *adj* **1** FUYANT : elusive **2** IMPERCEPTIBLE : imperceptible

insalubre [ɛ̃salybr] *adj* : unhealthy, insalubrious

insanité [ɛ̃sanite] *nf* **1** : insanity **2** : nonsense, rubbish

insatiable [ɛ̃sasjabl] *adj* : insatiable

insatisfaction [ɛ̃satisfaksjɔ̃] *nf* : dissatisfaction

insatisfait, -faite [ɛ̃satisfɛ, -fɛt] *adj* **1** : unsatisfied **2** MÉCONTENT : dissatisfied

inscription [ɛ̃skripsjɔ̃] *nf* **1** : inscription **2** : registration, enrollment

inscrire [ɛ̃skrir] {33} *vt* **1** : to inscribe **2** : to register, to enroll **3** : to write, to note down — **s'inscrire** *vr* **1** : to register, to enroll **2 s'inscrire en faux contre** : to deny strongly

inscrivait [ɛ̃skrivɛ], **inscrivions** [ɛ̃skrivjɔ̃], *etc.* → **inscrire**

inscrive [ɛ̃skriv] *etc.* → **inscrire**

insecte [ɛ̃sɛkt] *nm* : insect

insecticide [ɛ̃sɛktisid] *nm* : insecticide

insectifuge [ɛ̃sɛktifyʒ] *nm* : insect repellent

insécurité [ɛ̃sekyrite] *nf* : insecurity

insémination [ɛ̃seminasjɔ̃] *nf* : insemination <insémination artificielle : artificial insemination>

inséminer [ɛ̃semine] *vt* : to inseminate

insensé, -sée [ɛ̃sɑ̃se] *adj* **1** : crazy, foolish, nonsensical **2** : considerable, phenomenal

insensibiliser [ɛ̃sɑ̃sibilize] *vt* ANESTHÉSIER : to anesthetize

insensibilité [ɛ̃sɑ̃sibilite] *nf* **1** : insensibility, numbnesss **2** : insensitivity, indifference

insensible [ɛ̃sɑ̃sibl] *adj* **1** : insensible, numb **2** : insensitive **3** : imperceptible

insensiblement [ɛ̃sɑ̃sibləmɑ̃] *adv* : gradually, imperceptibly

inséparable [ɛ̃separabl] *adj* : inseparable

insérer [ɛ̃sere] {87} *vt* INTRODUIRE : to insert — **s'insérer** *vr* **1** ~ **dans** : to be part of, to be integrated into **2** ~ **sur** : to be attached to (in anatomy)

insertion [ɛ̃sɛrsjɔ̃] *nf* **1** INTRODUCTION : insertion **2** : integration

insidieux, -dieuse [ɛ̃sidjø, -djøz] *adj* : insidious — **insidieusement** [-djøzmɑ̃] *adv*

insigne[1] [ɛ̃siɲ] *adj* : great, distinguished <insigne honneur : great honor>

insigne[2] *nm* **1** : badge, emblem **2** *or* **insignes** *nmpl* : insignia

insignifiant, -fiante [ɛ̃siɲifjɑ̃, -fjɑ̃t] *adj* **1** : insignificant, trivial **2** : meager, trifling — **insignifiance** [-ɲifjɑ̃s] *nf*

insinuant, -nuante [ɛ̃sinɥwɑ̃] *adj* : ingratiating

insinuation [ɛ̃sinɥasjɔ̃] *nf* : insinuation, innuendo

insinuer [ɛ̃sinɥe] *vt* : to insinuate, to imply — **s'insinuer** *vr* **1** : to insinuate oneself **2 s'insinuer dans les bonnes grâces de** : to ingratiate oneself with

insipide [ɛ̃sipid] *adj* : insipid

insistant, -tante [ɛ̃sistɑ̃, -tɑ̃t] *adj* : insistent — **insistance** [ɛ̃sistɑ̃s] *nf*

insister [ɛ̃siste] *vi* **1** : to insist **2** ~ **sur** : to stress, to emphasize — *vt* : to insist

insociable [ɛ̃sɔsjabl] *adj* : unsociable

insolation [ɛ̃sɔlasjɔ̃] *nf* : sunstroke

insolence [ɛ̃sɔlɑ̃s] *nf* : insolence <avec insolence : insolently>

insolent, -lente [ɛ̃sɔlɑ̃, -lɑ̃t] *adj* **1** : insolent **2** : arrogant **3** : unabashed, outrageous

insolite [ɛ̃sɔlit] *adj* : unusual, bizarre

insoluble [ɛ̃sɔlybl] *adj* : insoluble

insolvabilité [ɛ̃sɔlvabilite] *nf* : insolvency

insolvable [ɛ̃sɔlvabl] *adj* : insolvent

insomniaque [ɛ̃sɔmnjak] *nmf* : insomniac

insomnie [ɛ̃sɔmni] *nf* : insomnia

insondable [ɛ̃sɔ̃dabl] *adj* : unfathomable

insonore [ɛ̃sɔnɔr] *adj* : soundproof

insonoriser [ɛ̃sɔnɔrize] *vt* : to soundproof

insouciance [ɛ̃susjɑ̃s] *nf* : insouciance, carefree attitude

insouciant, -ciante [ɛ̃susjɑ̃, -sjɑ̃t] *adj* **1** : carefree, happy-go-lucky **2** ~ **de** : unconcerned about, heedless of

insoumis[1], **-mise** [ɛ̃sumi, -miz] *adj* **1** : rebellious, unsubdued **2 soldat insoumis** : deserter, draft dodger

insoumis[2] *nm* : deserter, draft dodger

insoumission [ɛ̃sumisjɔ̃] *nf* **1** : rebelliousness **2** : desertion (of one's military post)

insoutenable [ɛ̃sutnabl] *adj* **1** INDÉFENDABLE : untenable **2** INSUPPORTABLE : unbearable

inspecter [ɛ̃spɛkte] *vt* : to inspect

inspecteur, -trice [ɛ̃spɛktœr, -tris] *n* : inspector

inspection [ɛ̃spɛksjɔ̃] *nf* : inspection

inspirant, -rante [ɛ̃spirɑ̃, -rɑ̃t] *adj* : inspirational

inspiration [ɛ̃spirasjɔ̃] *nf* **1** : inspiration **2** : inhalation

inspiré, -rée [ɛ̃spire] *adj* **1** : inspired **2 bien inspiré** : well-advised **3 mal inspiré** : ill-advised

inspirer [ɛ̃spire] *vt* **1** : to inspire **2** : to breathe in, to inhale — *vi* : to inhale — **s'inspirer** *vr* ~ **de** : to be inspired by

instabilité [ɛ̃stabilite] *nf* : instability

instable [ɛ̃stabl] *adj* **1** BRANLANT : unsteady, wobbly **2** : unsettled, unstable

installation [ɛ̃stalasjɔ̃] *nf* **1** : installation **2 installations** *nfpl* : installations, facilities, fittings <installations nucléaires : nuclear sites>

installer [ɛ̃stale] *vt* : to install, to put in, to set up — **s'installer** *vr* : to become established, to settle <ils se sont installés dans la maison : they have settled into the house>

instamment [ɛ̃stamɑ̃] *adv* : insistently

instance [ɛ̃stɑ̃s] *nf* **1** INSISTANCE : insistence, entreaty **2** AUTORITÉ : authority **3** : legal proceedings *pl*, lawsuit **4 en** ~ : pending

instant[1], **-tante** [ɛ̃stɑ̃, -tɑ̃t] *adj* : urgent, pressing

instant[2] *nm* : instant, moment <à l'instant : just this minute, a moment ago> <dans un instant : in a minute, soon> <en un instant : in no time at all> <par instants : at times>

instantané[1], **-née** [ɛ̃stɑ̃tane] *adj* **1** : instantaneous **2** : instant <café instantané : instant coffee> **3** : candid <photo instantané : candid photo> — **instantanément** [-nemɑ̃] *adv*

instantané[2] *nm* : snapshot

instar [ɛ̃star] **à l'instar de** : following the example of, like

instauration [ɛ̃storasjɔ̃] *nf* : institution, establishing

instaurer [ɛ̃store] *vt* **1** : to establish, to institute **2** : to instill

instigateur, -trice [ɛ̃stigatœr, -tris] *n* : instigator

instigation [ɛ̃stigasjɔ̃] *nf* : instigation

instiller [ɛ̃stile] *vt* **1** : to apply drop by drop (as eyedrops) **2** : to instill

instinct [ɛ̃stɛ̃] *nm* : instinct <d'instinct : instinctively>

instinctif, -tive [ɛ̃stɛ̃ktif, -tiv] *adj* : instinctive, instinctual — **instinctivement** [-tivmɑ̃] *adv*

instituer [ɛ̃stitɥe] *vt* **1** : to institute **2** : to appoint (in law)

institut [ɛ̃stity] *nm* **1** : institute **2 institut de beauté** : beauty salon

instituteur, -trice [ɛ̃stitytœr, -tris] *n* : schoolteacher

institution [ɛ̃stitysjɔ̃] *nf* **1** : instituting, establishment **2** : institution <institution dotée : endowment, foundation>

institutionnaliser [ɛ̃stitysjɔnalize] *vt* : to institutionalize

institutionnel, -nelle [ɛ̃stitysjɔnɛl] *adj* : institutional

instructeur, -trice [ɛ̃stryktœr, -tris] *n* : instructor

instructif, -tive [ɛ̃stryktif, -tiv] *adj* : instructive

instruction [ɛ̃stryksjɔ̃] *nf* **1** FORMATION : training, instruction **2** : education <sans instruction : uneducated> **3** DIRECTIVE : order, directive **4 instructions** *nfpl* : instructions, directions

instruire [ɛ̃strɥir] {49} *vt* **1** ÉDUQUER, FORMER : to teach, to train, to instruct **2** : to inform <ils m'ont instruit des règlements : they informed me of the rules> **3 instruire une affaire** *France* : to prepare a case (in law) — **s'instruire** *vr* **1** : to educate oneself, to learn **2 ~ de** : to find out about

instruisait [ɛ̃strɥizɛ], **instruisions** [ɛ̃strɥizjɔ̃], *etc.* → **instruire**

instruit, -truite [ɛ̃strɥi, -trɥit] *adj* : learned, educated

instrument [ɛ̃strymɑ̃] *nm* **1** : instrument, tool **2 instrument de musique** : musical instrument

instrumental, -tale [ɛ̃strymɑ̃tal] *adj, mpl* **-taux** [-to] : instrumental

instrumentation [ɛ̃strymɑ̃tasjɔ̃] *nf* : instrumentation

instrumentiste [ɛ̃strymɑ̃tist] *nmf* : instrumentalist

insu [ɛ̃sy] **à l'insu de** : without the knowledge of, unknown to

insubmersible [ɛ̃submɛrsibl] *adj* : unsinkable

insubordination [ɛ̃sybɔrdinasjɔ̃] *nf* : insubordination

insubordonné, -née [ɛ̃sybɔrdɔne] *adj* : insubordinate

insuccès [ɛ̃syksɛ] *nm* : failure

insuffisance [ɛ̃syfizɑ̃s] *nf* **1** : insufficiency, lack **2** : insufficiency (in medicine) **3 insuffisances** *nfpl* : shortcomings, weaknesses

insuffisant, -sante [ɛ̃syfizɑ̃, -zɑ̃t] *adj* **1** : insufficient **2** : inadequate, unsatisfactory — **insuffisamment** [-zamɑ̃] *adv*

insuffler [ɛ̃syfle] *vt* : to instill, to infuse <insuffler une nouvelle énergie à : to infuse new energy into>

insulaire[1] [ɛ̃sylɛr] *adj* **1** : island <la population insulaire : the island population> **2** : insular

insulaire[2] *nmf* : islander

insularité [ɛ̃sylarite] *nf* : insularity

insuline [ɛ̃sylin] *nf* : insulin

insultant, -tante [ɛ̃syltɑ̃, -tɑ̃t] *adj* : insulting

insulte [ɛ̃sylt] *nf* : insult

insulter [ɛ̃sylte] *vt* : to insult

insupportable [ɛ̃sypɔrtabl] *adj* : unbearable — **insupportablement** [-bləmɑ̃] *adv*

insurgé[1], **-gée** [ɛ̃syrʒe] *adj* : insurgent

insurgé[2], **-gée** *n* : insurgent, rebel

insurger [ɛ̃syrʒe] {17} *v* **s'insurger** *vr* : to rebel, to rise up

insurmontable [ɛ̃syrmɔ̃tabl] *adj* **1** : insurmountable **2** : invincible, unconquerable

insurrection [ɛ̃syrɛksjɔ̃] *nf* : insurrection

intact, -tacte [ɛ̃takt] *adj* : intact

intangible [ɛ̃tɑ̃ʒibl] *adj* **1** : intangible **2** : inviolable

intarissable [ɛ̃tarisabl] *adj* : inexhaustible

intégral, -grale [ɛ̃tegral] *adj, mpl* **-graux** [-gro] **1** : complete <remboursement intégral : repayment in full> **2** : uncut, unabridged

intégrale [ɛ̃tegral] *nf* **1** : integral **2** : complete works <l'intégrale des symphonies de Brahms : the complete symphonies of Brahms>

intégralement [ɛ̃tegralmɑ̃] *adv* : completely, in full

intégralité [ɛ̃tegralite] *nf* : entirety, whole

intégrant, -grante [ɛ̃tegrɑ̃, -grɑ̃t] *adj* **partie intégrante** : integral part

intégration [ɛ̃tegrasjɔ̃] *nf* : integration

intègre [ɛ̃tɛgr] *adj* HONNÊTE : honest

intégrer [ɛ̃tegre] {87} *vt* **1** : to insert, to include **2** : to integrate, to assimilate — **s'intégrer** *vr* **1** : to become integrated, to fit in **2** : to fit together

intégrisme [ɛ̃tegrism] *nm* : fundamentalism

intégriste [ɛ̃tegrist] *adj & nmf* : fundamentalist

intégrité [ɛ̃tegrite] *nf* : integrity

intellect [ɛ̃telɛkt] *nm* : intellect

intellectualisme [ɛ̃telɛktɥalism] *nm* : intellectualism

intellectuel, -tuelle [ɛ̃telɛktɥɛl] *adj & n* : intellectual — **intellectuellement** [-tɥɛlmɑ̃] *adv*

intelligemment [ɛ̃teliʒamɑ̃] *adv* : intelligently

intelligence [ɛ̃teliʒɑ̃s] *nf* **1** : intelligence **2** COMPRÉHENSION : understanding <avoir l'intelligence de : to have a (good) grasp of> **3** : (secret) agreement <agir d'intelligence avec : to have an understanding with> **4** : **intelligences** *nfpl* : collusion, (secret) dealings <elle a des intelligences dans l'industrie : she has contacts in industry>

intelligent, -gente [ɛ̃teliʒɑ̃, -ʒɑ̃t] *adj* : intelligent

intelligentsia [ɛ̃teliʒɑ̃sja] *nf* : intelligentsia
intelligibilité [ɛ̃teliʒibilite] *nf* : intelligibility
intelligible [ɛ̃teliʒibl] *adj* : intelligible — **intelligiblement** [-ʒibləmɑ̃] *adv*
intempérant, -rante [ɛ̃tɑ̃perɑ̃, -rɑ̃t] *adj* : intemperate — **intempérance** [-perɑ̃s] *nf*
intempéries [ɛtɑ̃peri] *nfpl* : bad weather
intempestif, -tive [ɛ̃tɑ̃pɛstif, -tiv] *adj* : untimely, inopportune
intemporel, -relle [ɛ̃tɑ̃pɔrɛl] *adj* : timeless
intenable [ɛ̃tənabl] *adj* **1** : unbearable **2** : untenable, indefensible
intendant, -dante [ɛ̃tɑ̃dɑ̃, -dɑ̃t] *n* **1** : steward **2** : quartermaster **3** : bursar
intense [ɛ̃tɑ̃s] *adj* : intense
intensément [ɛ̃tɑ̃semɑ̃] *adv* : intensely
intensif, -sive [ɛ̃tɑ̃sif, -siv] *adj* : intensive
intensification [ɛ̃tɑ̃sifikasjɔ̃] *nf* : intensification
intensifier [ɛ̃tɑ̃sifje] {96} *vt* : to intensify — **s'intensifier** *vr*
intensité [ɛ̃tɑ̃site] *nf* : intensity
intenter [ɛ̃tɑ̃te] *vt* : to initiate, to pursue (legal action) <intenter un procès contre : to sue>
intention [ɛ̃tɑ̃sjɔ̃] *nf* : intention, intent <avoir l'intention de : to intend to> <à l'intention de : aimed at, for> <sans intention : unintentionally>
intentionné, -née [ɛ̃tɑ̃sjɔne] *adj* **1 bien intentionné** : well-meaning **2 mal intentionné** : ill-disposed
intentionnel, -nelle [ɛ̃tɑ̃sjɔnɛl] *adj* : intentional, deliberate — **intentionnellement** [-nɛlmɑ̃] *adv*
interactif, -tive [ɛ̃tɛraktif, -tiv] *adj* : interactive
interaction [ɛ̃tɛraksjɔ̃] *nf* : interaction
intercalaire[1] [ɛ̃tɛrkalɛr] *adj* **1 feuillet intercalaire** : insert **2 fiche intercalaire** : divider
intercalaire[2] *nm* : insert, inset, divider
intercaler [ɛ̃tɛrkale] *vt* INSÉRER : to insert
intercéder [ɛ̃tɛrsede] {87} *vi* : to intercede
intercepter [ɛ̃tɛrsɛpte] *vt* : to intercept
interception [ɛ̃tɛrsɛpsjɔ̃] *nf* : interception
intercession [ɛ̃tɛrsesjɔ̃] *nf* : intercession
interchangeable [ɛ̃tɛrʃɑ̃ʒabl] *adj* : interchangeable
interconfessionnel, -nelle [ɛ̃tɛrkɔ̃fesjɔnɛl] *adj* : interdenominational
interconnexion [ɛ̃tɛrkɔnɛksjɔ̃] *nf* : (electronic) networking
intercontinental, -tale [ɛ̃tɛrkɔ̃tinɑ̃tal] *adj, mpl* **-taux** [-to] : intercontinental
interdépartemental, -tale [ɛ̃tɛrdepartəmɑ̃tal] *adj, mpl* **-taux** [-to] : interdepartmental
interdépendant, -dante [ɛ̃tɛrdepɑ̃dɑ̃, -dɑ̃t] *adj* : interdependent — **interdépendance** [-dɑ̃s] *nf*
interdiction [ɛ̃tɛrdiksjɔ̃] *nf* : ban, prohibition
interdire [ɛ̃tɛrdir] {29} *vt* **1** : to ban, to prohibit **2** : to prevent, to block — **s'interdire** *vr* : to refrain from <je m'interdis d'y penser : I don't let myself think about it>
interdisciplinaire [ɛ̃tɛrdisiplinɛr] *adj* : interdisciplinary
interdit, -dite [ɛ̃tɛrdi, -dit] *adj* **1** : forbidden, prohibited **2** STUPÉFAIT : taken aback, dumbfounded
intéressant[1]**, -sante** [ɛ̃terɛsɑ̃, -sɑ̃t] *adj* **1** : interesting **2** AVANTAGEUX : attractive, worthwhile
intéressant[2]**, -sante** *n* **faire l'intéressant** : to call attention to oneself, to show off
intéressé[1]**, -sée** *adj* **1** : interested, attentive **2** : concerned, involved **3** : self-interested, self-involved
intéressé[2]**, -sée** [ɛ̃terese] *n* : person involved <les intéressés : the interested parties>
intéresser [ɛ̃terese] *vt* **1** : to interest **2** CONCERNER : to concern, to affect **3 être intéressé dans** : to have a (financial) stake in — **s'intéresser** *vr* **~ à** : to take an interest in, to be interested in
intérêt [ɛ̃terɛ] *nm* **1** : interest <avoir de l'intérêt pour : to be interested in> <porter un intérêt à : to take an interest in> <elle a intérêt à refuser : she's well-advised to refuse> **2** : interest (in finance) <sans intérêt : interest-free> <intérêts composés : compound interest>
interface [ɛ̃tɛrfas] *nf* : interface (in computer science)
interférence [ɛ̃tɛrferɑ̃s] *nf* : interference
interférer [ɛ̃tɛrfere] {87} *vi* : to interfere
intergalactique [ɛ̃tɛrgalaktik] *adj* : intergalactic
intergouvernemental, -tale [ɛ̃tɛrguvɛrnəmɑ̃tal] *adj, mpl* **-taux** [-to] : intergovernmental
intérieur[1]**, -rieure** [ɛ̃terjœr] *adj* **1** : interior, inner, inside **2** : internal, domestic
intérieur[2] *nm* **1** : inside <à l'intérieur : inside, indoors, within> <d'intérieur : indoor> **2** : interior (of a country, etc.)
intérieurement [ɛ̃tɛrjœrmɑ̃] *adv* : inwardly, internally
intérim [ɛ̃terim] *nm* **1** : interim (period) **2** : temporary activity <faire des intérims : to work as a temp>

intérimaire[1] [ɛ̃terimɛr] *adj* : interim, temporary, acting
intérimaire[2] *nmf* : temporary employee, temp
interjection [ɛ̃tɛrʒɛksjɔ̃] *nf* : interjection
interjeter [ɛ̃tɛrʒəte] {8} *vt* **interjeter appel** : to file an appeal
interlocuteur, -trice [ɛ̃tɛrlɔkytœr, -tris] *n* **1** : speaker <mon interlocuteur : the person I am speaking to> **2** : representative, negotiator
interlope [ɛ̃tɛrlɔp] *adj* **1** LOUCHE : shady **2** ILLÉGAL : illegal
interloquer [ɛ̃tɛrlɔke] *vt* DÉCONTENANCER : to disconcert, to take aback
interlude [ɛ̃tɛrlyd] *nm* : (short) musical interlude
intermède [ɛ̃tɛrmɛd] *nm* : interlude
intermédiaire[1] [ɛ̃tɛrmedjɛr] *adj* : intermediate, intermediary
intermédiaire[2] *nmf* : intermediary, go-between, middleman
intermédiaire[3] *nm* : means, agency <sans intermédiaire : directly> <par l'intermédiaire de : by means of, through>
interminable [ɛ̃tɛrminabl] *adj* : interminable — **interminablement** [-nabləmɑ̃] *adv*
intermittence [ɛ̃tɛrmitɑ̃s] *nf* **par ~** : intermittently, off and on
intermittent, -tente [ɛ̃tɛrmitɑ̃, -tɑ̃t] *adj* : intermittent, sporadic
international, -nale [ɛ̃tɛrnasjɔnal] *adj, mpl* **-naux** [-no] : international — **internationalement** [-mɑ̃] *adv*
interne[1] [ɛ̃tɛrn] *adj* : internal, inner <enquête interne : internal investigation>
interne[2] *nmf* **1** : boarder (at a school) **2** : intern
interné, -née [ɛ̃tɛrne] *n* : internee
internement [ɛ̃tɛrnəmɑ̃] *nm* **1** : (political) internment **2** : confinement (to a mental hospital, etc.)
interner [ɛ̃tɛrne] *vt* **1** : to intern **2** : to confine (to an institution)
interniste [ɛ̃ternist] *nmf* : internist
interpellation [ɛ̃tɛrpelasjɔ̃] *nf* **1** : shouting out **2** : questioning
interpeller [ɛ̃tɛrpəle] *vt* **1** APOSTROPHER : to shout at, to call out to **2** INTERROGER : to question
interpersonnel, -nelle [ɛ̃tɛrpɛrsɔnɛl] *adj* : interpersonal
interphone [ɛ̃tɛrfɔn] *nm* : intercom
interplanétaire [ɛ̃tɛrplanetɛr] *adj* : interplanetary
interpoler [ɛ̃tɛrpɔle] *vt* : to interpolate
interposer [ɛ̃tɛrpoze] *vt* : to interpose — **s'interposer** *vr* : to intervene, to interpose
interprétation [ɛ̃tɛrpretasjɔ̃] *nf* : interpretation
interprète [ɛ̃tɛrprɛt] *nmf* **1** : interpreter **2** : spokesperson **3** : performer
interpréter [ɛ̃tɛrprete] {87} *vt* **1** : to interpret <mal interpreter : to misinterpret> **2** : to perform, to play (a role)
interprétif, -tive [ɛ̃tɛrpretif, -tiv] *adj* : interpretive, interpretative
interracial, -ciale [ɛ̃tɛrrasjal] *adj* : interracial
interrelation [ɛ̃terəlasjɔ̃] *nf* : interrelationship
interrogateur[1], **-trice** [ɛ̃terɔgatœr, -tris] *adj* : inquiring, questioning
interrogateur[2], **-trice** *n* : examiner, questioner
interrogatif[1], **-tive** [ɛ̃terɔgatif, -tiv] *adj* : interrogative
interrogatif[2] *nm* : interrogative (in grammar)
interrogation [ɛ̃terɔgasjɔ̃] *nf* **1** : questioning, interrogation **2** : test (in school) **3** : question <interrogation indirect : indirect question> **4** → **point**
interrogatoire [ɛ̃terɔgatwar] *nm* : interrogation, questioning, cross-examination
interroger [ɛ̃terɔʒe] {17} *vt* : to interrogate, to question — **s'interroger** *vr* **~ sur** : to wonder about
interrompre [ɛ̃tɛrɔ̃pr] {77} *v* : to interrupt — **s'interrompre** *vr* : to break off, to come to a halt
interrupteur [ɛ̃teryptœr] *nm* : switch
interruption [ɛ̃terypsjɔ̃] *nf* **1** : interruption **2** : break <sans interruption : continuously>
intersection [ɛ̃tɛrsɛksjɔ̃] *nf* : intersection (in geometry)
interstellaire [ɛ̃tɛrstelɛr] *adj* : interstellar
interstice [ɛ̃tɛrstis] *nm* : chink, crack
interuniversitaire [ɛ̃teryniversitɛr] *adj* : intercollegiate
interurbain[1], **-baine** [ɛ̃tɛryrbɛ̃, -bɛn] *adj* **1** : intercity **2** : long-distance
interurbain[2] *nm* **l'interurbain** : long-distance telephone service
intervalle [ɛ̃tɛrval] *nm* **1** : space, gap **2** : interval, period of time <dans l'intervalle : in the meantime>
intervenir [ɛ̃tɛrvənir] {92} *vi* **1** : to intervene **2** : to take place, to occur **3** OPÉRER : to operate (in medicine)
intervention [ɛ̃tɛrvɑ̃sjɔ̃] *nf* **1** : intervention **2** DISCOURS : speech **3** OPÉRATION : (medical) operation
interversion [ɛ̃tɛrverzjɔ̃] *nf* INVERSION : inversion
intervertir [ɛ̃tɛrvɛrtir] *vt* INVERSER : to invert, to reverse
interview [ɛ̃tɛrvju] *nf* : interview
interviewer [ɛ̃tɛrvjuve] *vt* : to interview
intervieweur, -vieweuse [ɛ̃tɛrvjuvœr, -vjuvøz] *n* : interviewer
intestat [ɛ̃tɛsta] *adj* : intestate
intestin [ɛ̃tɛstɛ̃] *nm* **1** : intestine <gros intestin : large intestine> <intestin

grêle : small intestine> **2 intestins** *nmpl* : intestines, bowels

intestinal, -nale [ɛ̃tɛstinal] *adj, mpl* **-naux** [-no] : intestinal

intime[1] [ɛ̃tim] *adj* **1** : intimate, close **2** : private **3** : personal <hygiène intime : personal hygiene> **4** : innermost, profound <ma conviction intime : my deep conviction>

intime[2] *nmf* : close friend

intimement [ɛ̃timmɑ̃] *adv* : intimately

intimer [ɛ̃time] *vt* **1** : to tell, to instruct <intimer l'ordre : to order> **2** : to summon (to court)

intimidant, -dante [ɛ̃timidɑ̃, -dɑ̃t] *adj* : intimidating

intimider [ɛ̃timide] *vt* : to intimidate — **intimidation** [-midasjɔ̃] *nf*

intimité [ɛ̃timite] *nf* **1** : intimacy **2** : privacy <dans l'intimité : in private> **3** : depths *pl* <dans l'intimité de son âme : in the depths of one's soul>

intitulé [ɛ̃tityle] *nm* : title, heading

intituler [ɛ̃tityle] *vt* : to call, to title — **s'intituler** *vr* **1** : to be called, to be titled **2** : to call oneself

intolérable [ɛ̃tɔlerabl] *adj* : intolerable — **intolérablement** [-rabləmɑ̃] *adv*

intolérant, -rante [ɛ̃tɔlerɑ̃, -rɑ̃t] *adj* : intolerant — **intolérance** [-rɑ̃s] *nf*

intonation [ɛ̃tɔnasjɔ̃] *nf* : intonation

intouchable [ɛ̃tuʃabl] *adj & nmf* : untouchable

intoxication [ɛ̃tɔksikasjɔ̃] *nf* **1** EMPOISONNEMENT : poisoning <intoxication alimentaire : food poisoning> **2** : brainwashing

intoxiquer [ɛ̃tɔksike] *vt* **1** EMPOISONNER : to poison **2** : to brainwash

intraduisable [ɛ̃tradɥizabl] *adj* **1** : untranslatable **2** : inexpressible

intraitable [ɛ̃trɛtabl] *adj* : uncompromising, inflexible, intractable

intransigeance [ɛ̃trɑ̃ziʒɑ̃s] *nf* : intransigence

intransigeant, -geante [ɛ̃trɑ̃ziʒɑ, -ʒɑ̃t] *adj* : intransigent, uncompromising

intransitif, -tive [ɛ̃trɑ̃zitif, -tiv] *adj* : intransitive

intraveineux, -neuse [ɛ̃travɛnø, -nøz] *adj* : intravenous

intrépide [ɛ̃trepid] *adj* : intrepid, fearless

intrépidité [ɛ̃trepidite] *nf* : fearlessness, boldness

intrigant[1], **-gante** [ɛ̃trigɑ̃, -gɑ̃t] *adj* : scheming, conniving

intrigant[2], **-gante** *n* : schemer

intrigue [ɛ̃trig] *nf* **1** : intrigue **2** : plot (of a story)

intriguer [ɛ̃trige] *vt* : to intrigue, to puzzle — *vi* : to plot, to scheme

intrinsèque [ɛ̃trɛ̃sɛk] *adj* : intrinsic — **intrinsèquement** [-sɛkmɑ̃] *adv*

introduction [ɛ̃trɔdyksjɔ̃] *nf* **1** : introduction <lettre d'introduction : letter of introduction> **2** : introduction, adoption (of customs, products, etc.) **3** INSERTION : insertion

introduire [ɛ̃trɔdɥir] {49} *vt* **1** : to introduce **2** : to show in, to usher into **3** INSÉRER : to insert **4** : to enter, to input (data in a computer) — **s'introduire** *vr* **1** : to be introduced **2** : to penetrate, to get in

introniser [ɛ̃trɔnize] *vt* **1** : to enthrone **2** : to establish, to set up

introspectif, -tive [ɛ̃trɔspɛktif, -tiv] *adj* : introspective — **introspectivement** [-tivmɑ̃] *adv*

introspection [ɛ̃trɔspɛksjɔ̃] *nf* : introspection

introuvable [ɛ̃truvabl] *adj* : unobtainable, nowhere to be found

introverti[1], **-tie** [ɛ̃trɔvɛrti] *adj* : introverted

introverti[2], **-tie** *n* : introvert

intrus, -truse [ɛ̃try, -tryz] *n* : intruder

intrusion [ɛ̃tryzjɔ̃] *nf* : intrusion

intuitif, -tive [ɛ̃tɥitif, -tiv] *adj* : intuitive — **intuitivement** [-tivmɑ̃] *adv*

intuition [ɛ̃tɥisjɔ̃] *nf* : intuition <avoir l'intuition de : to have a feeling about>

inuit, inuite [inɥi, inɥit] *adj* : Inuit

Inuit, Inuite *n* : Inuit

inusable [inyzabl] *adj* : durable

inusité, -tée [inyzite] *adj* INHABITUEL : unusual, uncommon

inutile [inytil] *adj* **1** : useless **2** : pointless, unnecessary

inutilement [inytilmɑ̃] *adv* : needlessly, unnecessarily

inutilisable [inytilizabl] *adj* : unusable

inutilisé, -sée [inytilize] *adj* : unused

inutilité [inytilite] *nf* : uselessness

invaincu, -cue [ɛ̃vɛ̃ky] *adj* **1** : unbeaten, undefeated **2** : unconquered

invalide[1] [ɛ̃valid] *adj* **1** : disabled **2** : invalid

invalide[2] *nmf* : disabled person <les invalides : the disabled>

invalider [ɛ̃valide] *vt* : to invalidate

invalidité [ɛ̃validite] *nf* **1** : invalidity **2** : disability

invariable [ɛ̃varjabl] *adj* : invariable — **invariablement** [-bləmɑ̃] *adv*

invasif, -sive [ɛ̃vazif, -ziv] *adj* : invasive

invasion [ɛ̃vazjɔ̃] *nf* : invasion

invective [ɛ̃vɛktiv] *nf* : invective

invectiver [ɛ̃vɛktive] *vt* : to abuse verbally — *vi* **~ contre** : to inveigh against

inventaire [ɛ̃vɑ̃tɛr] *nm* : inventory <faire l'inventaire de : to take an inventory of>

inventer [ɛ̃vɑ̃te] *vt* **1** : to invent **2** : to make up (excuses, etc.)

inventeur, -trice [ɛ̃vɑ̃tœr, -tris] *n* : inventor

inventif, -tive [ɛ̃vɑ̃tif, -tiv] *adj* : inventive

invention [ɛ̃vɑ̃sjɔ̃] *nf* **1** : invention **2** CRÉATIVITÉ : inventiveness **3** MENSONGE : fabrication, lie

inventivité [ɛ̃vɑ̃tivite] *nf* : inventiveness
inventorier [ɛ̃vɑ̃tɔrje] {96} *vt* : to inventory
inverse[1] [ɛ̃vɛrs] *adj* **1** : inverse <rapport inverse : inverse relationship> **2** : opposite, reverse <en sens inverse : in the opposite direction>
inverse[2] *nm* **1 l'inverse** : the reverse, the opposite **2 à l'inverse** : conversely
inversement [ɛ̃vɛrsəmɑ̃] *adv* **1** : conversely <et inversement : and vice versa> **2** : inversely (in mathematics)
inverser [ɛ̃vɛrse] *vt* : to reverse, to invert
inversion [ɛ̃vɛrsjɔ̃] *nf* : inversion, reversal
invertébré, -brée [ɛ̃vɛrtebre] *adj & nm* : invertebrate
investigateur, -trice [ɛ̃vɛstigatœr, -tris] *n* : investigator, inquirer
investigation [ɛ̃vɛstigasjɔ̃] *nf* : investigation, inquiry
investir [ɛ̃vɛstir] *vt* **1** : to invest **2** : to induct, to inaugurate — *vi* : to invest (in stocks, etc.) — **s'investir** *vr* **~ dans** : to become involved in
investissement [ɛ̃vɛstismɑ̃] *nm* : investment
investisseur, -seuse [ɛ̃vɛstisœr, -søz] *n* : investor
investiture [ɛ̃vɛstityr] *nf* **1** : investiture, inauguration **2** : nomination
invétéré, -rée [ɛ̃vetere] *adj* : inveterate
invincibilité [ɛ̃vɛ̃sibilite] *nf* : invincibility
invincible [ɛ̃vɛ̃sibl] *adj* **1** : invincible, unbeatable **2** : insurmountable **3** : irresistible
inviolé, -lée [ɛ̃vjɔle] *adj* : inviolate
invisibilité [ɛ̃vizibilite] *nf* : invisibility
invisible [ɛ̃vizibl] *adj* **1** : invisible **2** : unseen <rester invisible : to stay out of sight>
invisiblement [ɛ̃viziblǝmɑ̃] *adv* : invisibly
invitant, -tante [ɛ̃vitɑ̃, -tɑ̃t] *adj* : welcoming, hospitable
invitation [ɛ̃vitasjɔ̃] *nf* : invitation
invite [ɛ̃vit] *nf* : invitation, request
invité, -tée [ɛ̃vite] *n* : guest
inviter [ɛ̃vite] *vt* : to invite, to ask
invivable [ɛ̃vivabl] *adj* : unbearable
invocation [ɛ̃vɔkasjɔ̃] *nf* : invocation
involontaire [ɛ̃vɔlɔ̃tɛr] *adj* **1** : involuntary **2** : unintentional **3** : reluctant, unwilling
involontairement [ɛ̃vɔlɔ̃tɛrmɑ̃] *adv* : unintentionally, involuntarily
invoquer [ɛ̃vɔke] *vt* : to invoke
invraisemblable [ɛ̃vrɛsɑ̃blabl] *adj* **1** : improbable, unlikely **2** : incredible, fantastic, bizarre
invraisemblance [ɛ̃vrɛsɑ̃blɑ̃s] *nf* : improbability, unlikelihood
invulnérable [ɛ̃vylnerabl] *adj* : invulnerable
iode [jɔd] *nm* : iodine
iodé, -dée [jɔde] *adj* : iodized
iodler [jɔdle] *vi* : to yodel
iodure [jɔdyr] *nm* : iodide
ion [jɔ̃] *nm* : ion
ioniser [jɔnize] *vt* : to ionize
ionosphère [jɔnɔsfɛr] *nf* : ionosphere
iota [jɔta] *nm* : iota
ira [ira], *etc.* → **aller**
irakien, -kienne [irakjɛ̃, -kjɛn] *adj* : Iraqi
Irakien, -kienne *n* : Iraqi
iranien, -nienne [iranjɛ̃, -njɛn] *adj* : Iranian
Iranien, -nienne *n* : Iranian
iraquien, Iraquien [irakjɛ̃]→ **irakien, Irakien**
irascible [irasibl] *adj* : irascible
iris [iris] *nm* **1** : iris (of the eye) **2** : iris (plant)
irisation [irizasjɔ̃] *nf* : iridescence
irisé, -sée [irize] *adj* : iridescent
irlandais[1], **-daise** [irlɑ̃dɛ, -dɛz] *adj* : Irish
irlandais[2] *nm* : Irish (language)
Irlandais, -daise *n* : Irishman *m*, Irishwoman *f*
ironie [irɔni] *nf* : irony
ironique [irɔnik] *adj* : ironic, ironical — **ironiquement** [-mɑ̃] *adv*
ironiser [irɔnize] *vi* : to speak ironically, to be ironic
irradiation [iradjasjɔ̃] *nf* **1** : radiation **2** : irradiation
irradier [iradje] {96} *vt* : to irradiate — *vi* : to radiate
irraisonné, -née [irɛzɔne] *adj* : unreasoning
irrationalité [irasjɔnalite] *nf* : irrationality
irrationnel, -nelle [irasjɔnɛl] *adj* : irrational — **irrationnellement** [-nɛlmɑ̃] *adv*
irréalisable [irealizabl] *adj* IMPRATICABLE : impracticable, unworkable
irréaliste [irealist] *adj* : unrealistic
irréalité [irealite] *nf* : unreality
irrecevable [irəsəvabl] *adj* : inadmissible
irréconciliable [irekɔ̃siljabl] *adj* : irreconcilable
irrécupérable [irekyperabl] **1** : irretrievable **2** : beyond repair **3** : irredeemable, beyond hope
irréductible [iredyktibl] *adj* **1** : irreducible **2** INDOMPTABLE : indomitable
irréel, -réelle [ireɛl] *adj* : unreal
irréfléchi, -chie [irefleʃi] *adj* : thoughtless, rash
irréfutable [irefytabl] *adj* : irrefutable — **irréfutablement** [-tabləmɑ̃] *adv*
irrégularité [iregylarite] *nf* : irregularity
irrégulier, -lière [iregylje, -ljɛr] *adj* **1** : irregular, uneven **2** : erratic **3** : unauthorized, illegal
irrégulièrement [iregyljɛrmɑ̃] *adv* : irregularly

irréligieux, -gieuse [irelizjø, -zjøz] *adj* : irreligious

irrémédiable [iremedjabl] *adj* **1** : irreparable **2** : incurable — **irrémédiablement** [-djabləmɑ̃] *adv*

irremplaçable [irɑ̃plasabl] *adj* : irreplaceable

irréparable [ireparabl] *adj* : irreparable, beyond repair

irrépressible [irepresibl] *adj* : irrepressible

irréprochable [ireprɔʃabl] *adj* : irreproachable, beyond reproach

irrésistible [irezistibl] *adj* **1** : irresistible **2** : comical <elle est irrésistible : she's hilarious!>

irrésistiblement [irezistibləmɑ̃] *adv* : irresistibly

irrésolu, -lue [irezɔly] *adj* **1** : irresolute **2** : unresolved

irrespect [irɛspɛ] *nm* : disrespect

irrespectueux, -tueuse [irɛspɛktɥø, -tɥøz] *adj* : disrespectful

irrespirable [irɛspirabl] *adj* **1** : unbreathable **2** : stifling, oppressive

irresponsabilité [irɛspɔ̃sabilite] *nf* : irresponsibility

irresponsable [irɛspɔ̃sabl] *adj* : irresponsible

irrévérence [ireverɑ̃s] *nf* : irreverence

irrévérencieux, -cieuse [ireverɑ̃sjø, -sjøz] *adj* : irreverent

irréversible [ireversibl] *adj* : irreversible — **irréversibilité** [-sibilite] *nf*

irrévocabilité [irevɔkabilite] *nf* : irrevocability, finality

irrévocable [irevɔkabl] *adj* : irrevocable — **irrévocablement** [-kabləmɑ̃] *adv*

irrigation [irigasjɔ̃] *nf* : irrigation

irriguer [irige] *vt* : to irrigate

irritable [iritabl] *adj* : irritable — **irritabilité** [-tabilite] *nf*

irritant[1], **-tante** [iritɑ̃, -tɑ̃t] *adj* **1** : irritating, annoying **2** : irritant (in medicine)

irritant[2] *nm* : irritant (substance)

irritation [iritasjɔ̃] *nf* : irritation

irriter [irite] *vt* : to irritate — **s'irriter** *vr* : to get irritated

irruption [irypsjɔ̃] *nf* **1** : irruption **2** : inrush <faire irruption dans : to burst into>

islam [islam] *nm* : Islam

islamique [islamik] *adj* : Islamic

islandais[1], **-daise** [islɑ̃dɛ, -dɛz] *adj* : Icelandic

islandais[2] *nm* : Icelandic (language)

Islandais, -daise *n* : Icelander

isocèle [izɔsɛl] *adj* : isosceles

isolant[1], **-lante** [izɔlɑ̃, -lɑ̃t] *adj* : insulating

isolant[2] *nm* : insulating material, insulation

isolateur [izɔlatœr] *nm* : insulator

isolation [izɔlasjɔ̃] *nf* : insulation <isolation thermique : thermal insulation>

isolé, -lée [izɔle] *adj* **1** : isolated, separated **2** : remote, secluded

isolement [izɔlmɑ̃] *nm* **1** : isolation **2** ISOLATION : insulation

isolément [izɔlemɑ̃] *adv* : separately, individually

isoler [izɔle] *vt* **1** : to isolate **2** : to insulate — **s'isoler** *vr* : to isolate oneself, to withdraw

isoloir [izɔlwar] *nm* : voting booth

isométrique [izɔmetrik] *adj* : isometric

isotope [izɔtɔp] *nm* : isotope

israélien, -lienne [israeljɛ̃, -ljɛn] *adj* : Israeli

Israélien, -lienne *n* : Israeli

israélite [israelit] *adj* : Jewish

Israélite *nmf* **1** : Jew **2** : Israelite, Hebrew

issu, -sue [isy] *adj* **~ de 1** : descended from **2** : resulting from

issue *nf* **1** SORTIE : exit <rue sans issue : dead-end street> **2** SOLUTION : way out, solution **3** FIN : ending, outcome <à l'issue de : at the end of>

isthme [ism] *nm* : isthmus

italien[1], **-lienne** [italjɛ̃, -ljɛn] *adj* : Italian

italien[2] *nm* : Italian (language)

Italien, -lienne *n* : Italian

italique[1] [italik] *adj* : italic

italique[2] *nm* : italics *pl*

itinéraire [itinerɛr] *nm* : itinerary, route

itinérant[1], **-rante** [itinerɑ̃, -rɑ̃t] *adj* : itinerant, traveling

itinérant[2], **-rante** *n Can* : vagabond, tramp

ivoire [ivwar] *adj & nm* : ivory

ivoirien, -rienne [ivwarjɛ̃, -rjɛn] *adj* : of the Ivory Coast, Ivorian

Ivoirien, -rienne *n* : native or inhabitant of the Ivory Coast, Ivorian

ivre [ivr] *adj* **1** : drunk, intoxicated **2 ~ de** : drunk with <ivre de joie : delirious with joy>

ivresse [ivrɛs] *nf* : drunkenness, intoxication

ivrogne, ivrognesse [ivrɔɲ, -ɲɛs] *n* : drunkard

J

j [ʒi] *nm* : j, the 10th letter of the alphabet
jabot [ʒabo] *nm* **1** : crop (of a bird) **2** : jabot, ruffle
jacasser [ʒakase] *vi* BAVARDER : to chatter, to jabber
jachère [ʒaʃɛr] *nf* : fallow land <rester en jachère : to lie fallow>
jacinthe [ʒasɛ̃t] *nf* **1** : hyacinth **2 jacinthe des bois** : bluebell
jack [dʒak] *nm* : jack, (telephone) socket
jackpot *or* **jack pot** [dʒakpɔt] *nm* : jackpot
jade [ʒad] *nm* : jade
jadis[1] [ʒadis] *adv* AUTREFOIS : in times past, formerly
jadis[2] *adj* : former, olden <au temps jadis : in days of old>
jaguar [ʒagwar] *nm* : jaguar
jaillir [ʒajir] *vi* **1** : to spurt out, to gush (out) **2** : to spring up, to shoot out, to burst out **3** : to arise, to emerge
jaillissement [ʒajismɑ̃] *nm* JET : spurt, gush
jais [ʒɛ] *nms & pl* **1** : jet (stone) **2 de jet** *or* **d'un noir de jet** : jet-black
jalon [ʒalɔ̃] *nm* **1** : marker, milestone **2 poser les (premiers) jalons** : to pave the way
jalonner [ʒalɔne] *vt* **1** : to mark out (a route, etc.) **2** LONGER : to line, to border **3** MARQUER : to mark, to punctuate <une histoire jalonnée de tragédie : a story marked by tragedy>
jalouser [ʒaluze] *vt* : to be jealous of
jalousie [ʒaluzi] *nf* **1** : jealousy **2** : slatted blind, venetian blind
jaloux, -louse [ʒalu, -luz] *adj* : jealous — **jalousement** [-luzmɑ̃] *adv*
jamaïquain, -quaine [ʒamaikɛ̃, -kɛn] *adj* : Jamaican
Jamaïquain, -quaine *n* : Jamaican
jamais [ʒamɛ] *adv* **1** : never <il ne pense jamais aux autres : he never thinks of others> **2** : ever <c'est pire que jamais : it's worse than ever> **3 à (tout) jamais** *or* **pour ~** : forever
jambage [ʒɑ̃baʒ] *nm* **1** : downstroke (of a letter) **2** : jamb
jambe [ʒɑ̃b] *nf* **1** : leg **2 à toutes jambes** : as fast as one's legs can carry one **3 dans les jambes** *fam* : in the way, underfoot
jambon [ʒɑ̃bɔ̃] *nm* : ham
jamboree [ʒɑ̃bɔri] *nm* : jamboree
jante [ʒɑ̃t] *nf* : rim (of a wheel)
janvier [ʒɑ̃vje] *nm* : January
japonais[1], **-naise** [ʒapɔnɛ, -nɛz] *adj* : Japanese
japonais[2] *nm* : Japanese (language)
Japonais, -naise *n* : Japanese
jappement [ʒapmɑ̃] *nm* : yap, yelp
japper [ʒape] *vi* : to yap, to yelp
jaquette [ʒakɛt] *nf* **1** : dust jacket **2** : morning coat (for men), jacket (for women)
jardin [ʒardɛ̃] *nm* **1** : garden **2** : yard **3 jardin d'enfants** *France* : kindergarten **4 jardin zoologique** : zoo
jardinage [ʒardinaʒ] *nm* : gardening
jardiner [ʒardine] *vi* : to garden
jardinier[1], **-nière** [ʒardinje, -njɛr] *adj* : garden <plantes jardinières : garden plants>
jardinier[2], **-nière** *n* : gardener
jardinière *nf* **1** : window box **2** : mixed vegetables
jargon [ʒargɔ̃] *nm* **1** : jargon **2** : gibberish
jarre [ʒar] *nf* : (earthenware) jar
jarret [ʒarɛ] *nm* **1** : back of the knee, hamstring **2** : hock (of an animal) **3** : shank (in cooking)
jarretelle [ʒartɛl] *nf* : garter belt
jarretière [ʒartjɛr] *nf* : garter
jars [ʒar] *nms & pl* : gander (animal)
jaser [ʒaze] *vi* **1** BAVARDER : to chatter **2** MÉDIRE : to gossip
jasette [ʒazɛt] *or* **jase** [ʒaz] *nf* **avoir de la jasette** *Can fam* : to talk a mile a minute
jasmin [ʒasmɛ̃] *nm* : jasmine
jaspe [ʒasp] *nm* : jasper
jaspé, -pée [ʒaspe] *adj* : mottled, marbled
jatte [ʒat] *nf* : bowl, basin
jauge [ʒoʒ] *nf* **1** : capacity **2** : gauge <jauge d'essence : gas gauge> <jauge de niveau d'huile : dipstick>
jauger [ʒoʒe] {17} *vt* **1** : to gauge, to measure the capacity of **2** : to take the measure of, to size up
jaunâtre [ʒonatr] *adj* **1** : yellowish **2 teint jaunâtre** : sallow complexion
jaune[1] [ʒon] *adv* **rire jaune** : to force a laugh
jaune[2] *adj* : yellow
jaune[3] *nm* **1** : yellow **2** *or* **jaune d'œuf** : egg yolk
jaune[4] *nmf* : strikebreaker
jaunir [ʒonir] *v* : to turn yellow
jaunisse [ʒonis] *nf* : jaundice
javanais[1], **-naise** [ʒavanɛ, -nɛz] *adj* : Javanese
javanais[2], **-naise** *n* : Javanese (language)
Javanais, -naise *n* : Javanese
Javel [ʒavɛl] *nf* **eau de Javel** : bleach
javelliser [ʒavelize] *vt* : to chlorinate — **javellisation** [ʒavelizasjɔ̃] *nf*
javelot [ʒavlo] *nm* : javelin
jazz [dʒaz] *nm* : jazz
je [ʒə] (**j'** *before vowel or mute h*) *pron* : I
jean [dʒin] *nm* **1** : denim **2 jeans** *nmpl* : jeans, blue jeans
jeep [dʒip] *nf* : jeep
Jéhovah [ʒeɔva] *nm* : Jehovah

je-ne-sais-quoi [ʒənsekwa] *nms & pl* **un je-ne-sais-quoi** : a certain something

jérémiades [ʒeremjad] *nfpl fam* : whining, complaining

jersey [ʒɛrzɛ] *nm* : jersey (fabric)

je-sais-tout [ʒəsetu] *nmfs & pl* : know-it-all

Jésus [ʒezy] *nm* : Jesus

jet [ʒɛ] *nm* **1** : jet, spurt, flash (of light) <jet d'eau : fountain> **2** : throw, throwing <à un jet de pierre : a stone's throw away> **3** : jet (airplane) **4** : shoot (of a plant) **5 d'un seul jet** : in one try, at one go

jetable [ʒətabl] *adj* : disposable <rasoirs jetables : disposable razors>

jetée [ʒəte] *nm* **1** : pier, jetty **2** : breakwater

jeter [ʒəte] {8} *vt* **1** : to throw **2** : to throw away **3** ÉMETTRE : to cast, to give off, to let out <jeter un coup d'œil : to take a look at> **4 jeter l'éponge** : to throw in the towel **5 jeter un sort** : to cast a spell — **se jeter** *vr* **1** : to throw oneself <se jeter sur : to pounce on> **2** : to be disposable **3** : to be discarded, to be disposed of **4 ~ dans** : to flow into

jeton [ʒətɔ̃] *nm* : token, counter

jette [ʒɛt], **jettera** [ʒɛra], *etc.* → **jeter**

jeu [ʒø] *nm, pl* **jeux 1** : play, playing <jeu d'enfant : child's play> <le jeu : gambling> <jeux de mains : horseplay> **2** : game <jeu d'equipe : team sport> **3** : hand (of playing cards) **4** : set <jeu d'échecs : chess set> <jeu de cartes : deck of cards> **5 en ~** : at stake **6 jeu de jambes** : footwork (in sports) **7 jeu de mots** : pun **8** : jeu de société : board game

jeudi [ʒødi] *nm* : Thursday

jeun [ʒœ̃] *adv* **à ~** : on an empty stomach

jeune[1] [ʒœn] *adv* : youthfully <s'habiller jeune : to dress young>

jeune[2] *adj* **1** : young, youthful <jeune homme : young man> <jeunes gens : young people> <jeune fille : girl> **2** CADET : younger <ma jeune sœur : my younger sister> **3** : new, recent <jeunes mariés : newlyweds>

jeune[3] *nmf* : young person <les jeunes : young people>

jeûne [ʒøn] *nm* : fast <rompre le jeûne : to break one's fast>

jeûner [ʒøne] *vi* : to fast

jeunesse [ʒœnɛs] *nf* **1** : youth **2** : youthfulness **3** : young people

joaillerie [ʒɔajri] *nf* **1** : jewelry making, jewel trade **2** : jeweler's shop **3** : jewelry

joaillier, -lière [ʒɔaje, -jɛr] *n* BIJOUTIER : jeweler

job [dʒɔb] *nm fam* : job

jockey [ʒɔkɛ] *nm* : jockey

jodhpurs [ʒɔdpyr] *nmpl* : jodhpurs

jodler [jɔdle] → **iodler**

joggeur, -guese [dʒɔgœr, -gøz] *n* : jogger

jogging [dʒɔgiŋ] *nm* **1** : jogging **2** : sweatsuit

joie [ʒwa] *nf* **1** : joy <joie de vivre : joie de vivre, enjoyment of life> **2** PLAISIR : pleasure, delight <avec joie : with pleasure>

joignait [ʒwɛ̃ɲɛ], **joignions** [ʒwɛ̃ɲɔ̃], *etc.* → **joindre**

joigne [ʒwɛ̃ɲ], *etc.* → **joindre**

joindre [ʒwɛ̃dr] {50} *vt* **1** : to join, to link, to combine **2** : to enclose, to attach **3** : to reach, to get in touch with <joindre qqn par téléphone : to reach s.o. by phone> — **se joindre** *vr* **1** : to join together (of hands, etc.) **2 ~ à** : to join in with, to become a part of

joint[1], **jointe** [ʒwɛ̃, ʒwɛ̃t] *adj* **1** : joined <à mains jointes : with clasped hands> **2 ~ à** : attached to, enclosed with

joint[2] *nm* **1** : joint <joint universel : universal joint> **2** : seal, gasket <joint de robinet : washer (for a faucet)>

jointure [ʒwɛ̃tyr] *nf* : joint (in anatomy or technology)

joker [ʒɔkɛr] *nm* : joker (in playing cards)

joli, -lie [ʒɔli] *adj* **1** : pretty, attractive **2** : nice <une jolie somme d'argent : a nice sum of money>

joliment [ʒɔlimɑ̃] *adv* **1** : nicely, prettily **2** *fam* : really, awfully

jonc [ʒɔ̃] *nm* **1** : rush, bullrush **2** : plain band, ring <jonc de mariage : wedding band>

joncher [ʒɔ̃ʃe] *vt* : to strew, to litter

jonction [ʒɔ̃ksjɔ̃] *nf* : junction

jongler [ʒɔ̃gle] *vi* : to juggle

jongleur, -gleuse [ʒɔ̃glœr, -gløz] *n* : juggler

jonque [ʒɔ̃k] *nf* : junk (boat)

jonquille [ʒɔ̃kij] *nf* : daffodil, jonquil

jordanien, -nienne [ʒɔrdanjɛ̃, -njɛn] *adj* : Jordanian

Jordanien, -nienne *n* : Jordanian

jouable [ʒwabl] *adj* : playable

joue [ʒu] *nf* **1** : cheek **2 mettre en joue** : to take aim at

jouer [ʒwe] *vi* **1** S'AMUSER : to play <jouer avec des poupées : to play with dolls> <jouer aux cartes : to play cards> <jouer du piano : to play the piano> **2** : to play, to perform <elle a joué dans les plus grands théâtres : she played the leading theaters> **3** : to gamble, to speculate <il jouait aux courses : he was playing the horses> <jouer à la Bourse : to play the stock market> **4** : to come into play, to apply <la question d'argent ne joue pas entre nous : money is not an issue between us> **5 jouer sur les mots** : to play with words — *vt* **1** : to play (a card, etc.) **2** : to bet, to wager **3** : to perform <il jouera une sonate de

Mozart : he will play a Mozart sonata> <jouer la comédie : to put on an act> **4** : to feign, to affect <jouer les victimes : to play the victim> — **se jouer** *vr* **1** : to be played **2** : to be at stake **3 ~ de** : to make light work of **4 ~ de** : to defy

jouet [ʒwɛ] *nm* : toy, plaything

joueur, joueuse [ʒwœr, ʒwøz] *n* **1** : player <un beau joueur : a good sport> **2** : gambler

joufflu, -flue [ʒufly] *adj* : chubby-cheeked

joug [ʒu] *nm* : yoke

jouir [ʒwir] *vi* **1** : to have an orgasm **2 ~ de** : to enjoy, to make good use of, to benefit from

jouissance [ʒwisɑ̃s] *nf* **1** PLAISIR : pleasure, enjoyment **2** : orgasm, climax **3** : use, (legal) possession

jour [ʒur] *nm* **1** : day <tous les jours : every day> <huit jours : a week> <de nos jours : nowadays> <de jour en jour : day by day> <jour de l'An : New Year's Day> <jour férié : public holiday> **2** : daylight, daytime <il fait jour : it's (day)light> **3** : aspect <sous un jour favorable : in a favorable light> **4 donner le jour à** : to bring into the world, to give birth to **5 mettre à jour** : to bring up to date, to update

journal [ʒurnal] *nm, pl* **journaux 1** : diary, journal **2** : newspaper **3 journal télévisé** : television news

journalier¹, -lière [ʒurnalje, -ljɛr] *adj* : daily

journalier², -lière *n* : day worker, laborer

journalisme [ʒurnalism] *nm* : journalism

journaliste [ʒurnalist] *nmf* : journalist — **journalistique** [-listik] *adj*

journée [ʒurne] *nf* **1** : day <toute la journée : all day long> **2** : workday <journée de repos : day off>

joute [ʒut] *nf* **1** : joust **2** : sparring match, battle (of wits, etc.)

jouter [ʒute] *vi* : to joust

jovial, -viale [ʒɔvjal] *adj, mpl* **jovials** *or* **joviaux** [-vjo] : jovial, jolly — **jovialement** [-vjalmɑ̃] *adv*

jovialité [ʒɔvjalite] *nf* : cheerfulness, joviality

joyau [ʒwajo] *nm, pl* **joyaux** : jewel, gem

joyeux, joyeuse [ʒwajø, -jøz] *adj* : joyful, happy <Joyeux Noël! : Merry Christmas!> — **joyeusement** [-jøzmɑ̃] *adv*

jubilation [ʒybilasjɔ̃] *nf* : jubilation

jubilé [ʒybile] *nm* : jubilee

jubiler [ʒybile] *vi* : to rejoice, to exult

jucher [ʒyʃe] *vt* : to perch <elle a juché le bébé sur sa chaise : she perched the baby on his chair> — **se jucher** *vr* **~ sur** : to perch on

judaïque [ʒydaik] *adj* : Judaic

judaïsme [ʒydaism] *nm* : Judaism

judiciaire [ʒydisjɛr] *adj* : judicial — **judiciairement** [-sjɛrmɑ̃] *adv*

judicieux, -cieuse [ʒydisjø, -sjøz] *adj* : judicious — **judicieusement** [-sjøzmɑ̃] *adv*

judo [ʒydo] *nm* : judo

juge [ʒyʒ] *nm* **1** : judge <juge de paix : justice of the peace> <tu es seul juge : only you can judge> **2** *or* **juge–arbitre** : referee <juge de touche : linesman>

jugement [ʒyʒmɑ̃] *nm* **1** : decision, verdict, sentence **2** : judgment, opinion

jugeote [ʒyʒɔt] *nf fam* : common sense

juger [ʒyʒe] {17} *vt* **1** ÉVALUER : to judge, to form an opinion about **2** : to judge, to try **3** : to think, to consider **4 ~ de** : to assess, to judge <c'est vrai, autant que je puisse en juger : it's true, as far as I can tell> — **se juger** *vr* S'ESTIMER : to consider oneself

jugulaire [ʒygylɛr] *nf* : jugular vein

juguler [ʒygyle] *vt* **1** ENRAYER : to halt, to check, to curb **2** : to suppress, to put down

juif, juive [ʒɥif, ʒɥiv] *adj* : Jewish

Juif, Juive *n* : Jew

juillet [ʒɥijɛ] *nm* : July

juin [ʒɥɛ̃] *nm* : June

juke–box [dʒukbɔks] *nm, pl* **juke–box** *or* **juke–boxes** : jukebox

jumeau, -melle [ʒymo, -mɛl] *adj & n, mpl* **jumeaux** : twin

jumeler [ʒymle] {8} *vt* : to twin, to couple

jumelles [ʒymɛl] *nfpl* : binoculars, field glasses

jument [ʒymɑ̃] *nf* : mare

jungle [ʒœ̃gl] *nf* : jungle

junior [ʒynjɔr] *adj & nmf* : junior

junte [ʒœ̃t] *nf* : junta

jupe [ʒyp] *nf* : skirt

Jupiter [ʒypitɛr] *nf* : Jupiter (planet)

jupon [ʒypɔ̃] *nm* : slip, petticoat

juré, -rée [ʒyre] *n* : juror

jurer [ʒyre] *vt* : to swear, to vow — *vi* **1** SACRER : to swear, to curse **2 ~ avec** : to clash with **3 ~ de** : to swear to <j'en jurerais : I would swear to it, I'm sure of it>

juridiction [ʒyridiksjɔ̃] *nf* : jurisdiction — **juridictionel, -nelle** [-diksjɔnɛl] *adj*

juridique [ʒyridik] *adj* LÉGAL : legal — **juridiquement** [-dikmɑ̃] *adv*

jurisprudence [ʒyrisprydɑ̃s] *nf* **1** : jurisprudence **2 faire jurisprudence** : to set a precedent

juriste [ʒyrist] *nmf* : jurist, legal expert

juron [ʒyrɔ̃] *nm* : curse, oath, expletive

jury [ʒyri] *nm* : jury

jus [ʒy] *nms & pl* **1** : juice **2** : gravy **3** *fam* : juice, electricity

jusqu'au–boutiste [ʒyskobutist] *nmf fam, pl* **jusqu'au–boutistes** : hardliner, extremist

jusque [ʒyskə] (**jusqu'** [ʒysk] *before a vowel*) *prep* **1** *or* **jusqu'à** : up to, as far as <jusque chez moi : all the way to my house> <avoir de la boue jusqu'aux genoux : to be knee-deep in mud> <jusqu'à présent : up to now> **2** : even, as far as <des délits jusque dans les banlieues : crime even in the suburbs> **3 jusqu'à** : until, till <jusqu'à dix-sept heures : until five o'clock> **4 jusqu'à** : up to, as much as <jusqu'à 50 kilogrammes : not exceeding 50 kilograms> **5 jusqu'à** : up to, to the point of <méticuleux jusqu'au perfectionnisme : careful to the point of perfectionism> **6 jusqu'à ce que** *or* **jusqu'au moment où** : until

jusque-là [ʒyskəla] *adv* **1** : up to here, up to there **2** : up until then

justaucorps [ʒystokɔr] *nms & pl* : leotard

juste[1] [ʒyst] *adv* **1** : just, exactly <c'est juste le contraire : it's just the opposite> **2** : in tune, on key <chanter juste : to sing in tune> **3** : only, just <après juste un an : after only a year> **4** *or* **tout juste** : only just <arriver tout juste à temps : to arrive barely on time>

juste[2] *adj* **1** ÉQUITABLE : just, fair **2** EXACT : correct, accurate <l'heure juste : the exact time> **3** SERRÉ : tight **4 à juste titre** : justly, rightly **5 au juste** : exactly, precisely

justement [ʒystəmɑ̃] *adv* **1** EXACTEMENT : exactly, precisely **2** : correctly **3** : justifiably, justly **4** : just <il est justement parti : he just left>

justesse [ʒystɛs] *nf* **1** : accuracy **2** : aptness, soundness <avec justesse : aptly> **3 de ~** : just barely

justice [ʒystis] *nf* **1** : fairness, justice **2** : law, justice <être traduit en justice : to be brought before the courts> **3 se faire justice** : to take the law into one's own hands **4 se faire justice** : to commit suicide

justiciable [ʒystisjabl] *adj* **~ de** : subject to, answerable to

justifiable [ʒystifjabl] *adj* DÉFENDABLE : justifiable

justificatif[1], **-tive** [ʒystifikatif, -tiv] *adj* : supporting

justificatif[2] *nm* : supporting evidence

justification [ʒustifikasjɔ̃] *nf* **1** : justification, explanation **2** : proof

justifier [ʒystifje] {96} *vt* **1** : to justify **2** : to prove — *vi* **~ de** : to give proof of — **se justifier** *vr* : to justify oneself <se justifier d'une accusation : to clear one's name>

jute [ʒyt] *nm* : jute

juteux, -teuse [ʒytø, -tøz] *adj* : juicy

juvénile [ʒyvenil] *adj* : juvenile, youthful

juxtaposer [ʒykstapoze] *vt* : to juxtapose — **juxtaposition** [-pozisjɔ̃] *nf*

K

k [ka] *nm* : the 11th letter of the alphabet

kaki[1] [kaki] *adj* : khaki

kaki[2] *nm* **1** : khaki **2** : persimmon

kaléidoscope [kaleidɔskɔp] *nm* : kaleidoscope

kangourou [kɑ̃guru] *nm* : kangaroo

kaolin [kaɔlɛ̃] *nm* : kaolin

karaté [karate] *nm* : karate

kascher [kaʃɛr] *adj* : kosher

kayak *or* **kayac** [kajak] *nm* : kayak

kenyan, kenyane [kenjɑ̃, -jan] *adj* : Kenyan

Kenyan, Kenyane *n* : Kenyan

kermesse [kɛrmɛs] *nf* : fair, bazaar

kérosène [kerɔzɛn] *nm* : kerosene

ketchup [kɛtʃœp] *nm* : ketchup

khan [kɑ̃] *nm* : khan

kibboutz [kibuts] *nm* : kibbutz

kidnapper [kidnape] *vt* : to kidnap

kidnappeur, -peuse [kidnapœr, -pøz] *n* : kidnapper

kif-kif [kifkif] *adj fam* **c'est kif-kif** : it's all the same

kilo [kilo] *nm* : kilo

kilogramme [kilɔgram] *nm* : kilogram

kilohertz [kilɔɛrts] *nms & pl* : kilohertz

kilométrage [kilɔmetraʒ] *nm* : distance in kilometers, mileage

kilomètre [kilɔmɛtr] *nm* : kilometer

kilo-octet [kilɔɔktɛ] *nm, pl* **kilo-octets** : kilobyte

kilowatt [kilɔwat] *nm* : kilowatt

kilt [kilt] *nm* : kilt

kimono [kimɔno] *nm* : kimono

kinésithérapeute [kinesiterapœt] *nmf* : physiotherapist, physical therapist

kinésithérapie [kineziterapi] *nf* : physical therapy

kiosque [kjɔsk] *nm* **1** : (garden) pavilion **2** : kiosk, stall <kiosque à journaux : newsstand> **3 kiosque à musique** : bandstand

kipper [kipœr] *nm* : kipper

kirsch [kirʃ] *nm* : kirsch

kiwi [kiwi] *nm* : kiwi

klaxon [klaksɔn] *nm* : horn

klaxonner [klaksɔne] *vt* : to honk, to toot — *vi* : to honk one's horn

kleptomane [klɛptɔman] *nmf* : kleptomaniac

kleptomanie [klɛptɔmani] *nf* : kleptomania

knickers [knikərs] *nmpl* : knickers

koala [kɔala] *nm* **:** koala
koweïtien, -tienne *adj* [kɔwɛjtjɛ̃, -tjɛn] **:** Kuwaiti
Koweïtien, -tienne *n* **:** Kuwaiti
krach [krak] *nm* **:** crash <krach boursier : stock-market crash>
kraft [kraft] *nm or* **papier kraft** **:** brown (wrapping) paper
krypton [kriptɔ̃] *nm* **:** krypton
kumquat [kumkwat] *nm* **:** kumquat
kung-fu [kuŋfu] *nm* **:** kung fu
kurde[1] [kyrd] *adj* **:** Kurdish
kurde[2] *nm* **:** Kurdish (language)
Kurde *nmf* **:** Kurd
kyrielle [kirjɛl] *nf* **:** whole series, long list <une kyrielle de plaintes : a string of complaints>
kyste [kist] *nm* **:** cyst

L

l [ɛl] *nm* **:** l, the 12th letter of the alphabet
l' *pron & art* → **le**
la *pron & art* → **le**
là [la] *adv* **1** (*indicating a place*) **:** there, here <c'est là : there it is> <je suis là : I'm here> **2 :** then <à partir de là : after that, from then on> **3** (*indicating a situation or a certain point*) <c'est bien là où je voulais en venir : that's just it, that's the point> <c'est là que j'ai compris : that's when I understood> **4** (*referring to a specified person or thing*) <cette femme-là : that woman (over there)> **5 de ~ :** from there, hence **6 ~ où :** where **7 par ~ :** over here, this way **8 tout est là :** that's most important <la santé, tout est là : health is everything>
là-bas [laba] *adv* **:** over there
label [labɛl] *nm* **1 :** label, mark **2 :** seal, stamp <label de qualité : stamp of quality>
labeur [labœr] *nm* **:** toil, work
labial, -biale [labjal] *adj, mpl* **labiaux** [labjo] **:** labial
laboratoire [labɔratwar] *nm* **:** laboratory
laborieusement [labɔrjøzmɑ̃] *adv* **:** laboriously
laborieux, -rieuse [labɔrjø, -rjøz] *adj* **1** PÉNIBLE **:** laborious, arduous **2** TRAVAILLEUR **:** hardworking, industrious <les classes laborieuses : the working classes> **3 :** labored (in style)
labour [labur] *nm* **1 :** plowing **2 :** plowed field
labourage [laburaʒ] *nm* **:** plowing
labourer [labure] *vt* **1 :** to plow **2** CREUSER **:** to furrow, to churn up **3** LACÉRER **:** to dig into, to lacerate
labyrinthe [labirɛ̃t] *nm* DÉDALE **:** labyrinth, maze
lac [lak] *nm* **:** lake
lacer [lase] {6} *vt* **:** to lace up, to tie
lacération [laserasjɔ̃] *nf* **1 :** ripping, tearing up **2 :** laceration
lacérer [lasere] {87} *vt* **1** DÉCHIRER **:** to tear up **2 :** to lacerate
lacet [lasɛ] *nm* **1 :** shoelace **2 :** sharp bend, curve <une route en lacets : a winding road>
lâche[1] [laʃ] *adj* **1 :** loose, slack **2 :** lax, slipshod **3 :** cowardly
lâche[2] *nmf* POLTRON **:** coward
lâchement [laʃmɑ̃] *adv* **1 :** loosely **2 :** in a cowardly way
lâcher [laʃe] *vt* **1** RELÂCHER **:** to slacken, to loosen **2 :** to let go <lâche-moi! : let me go!> **3 :** to let out, to come out with **4** *fam* **:** to drop out of (school) **5** *fam* **:** to leave, to drop (someone) — *vi* **1 :** to give way **2 :** to fail (of brakes)
lâcheté [laʃte] *nf* **1** COUARDISE **:** cowardice **2** BASSESSE **:** baseness **3 :** cowardly act
lâcheur, -cheuse [laʃœr, -ʃøz] *n fam* **:** quitter, unreliable person
lacis [lasi] *nms & pl* **1 :** maze, tangle **2 :** network (of veins, etc.)
laconique [lakɔnik] *adj* **:** laconic, terse — **laconiquement** [-nikmɑ̃] *adv*
lacrymogène [lakrimɔʒɛn] *adj* **:** tear-inducing <gaz lacrymogène : tear gas>
lactation [laktasjɔ̃] *nf* **:** lactation
lacté, -tée [lakte] *adj* **1 :** milk, milky **2** → **voie**
lactique [laktik] *adj* **:** lactic
lacune [lakyn] *nf* **:** lacuna, gap
lacustre [lakystr] *adj* **:** lake, lakeside
là-dedans [laddɑ̃] *adv* **:** in here, in there
là-dessous [ladsu] *adv* **:** under here, under there
là-dessus [ladsy] *adv* **1 :** on here, on there **2 :** about it, on it <il n'y a aucun doute là-dessus : there's no doubt about it> **3 :** with that, at that point <il est parti là-dessus : with that, he left>
ladite [ladit] → **ledit**
ladre [ladr] *adj* **:** stingy, miserly
ladrerie [ladrəri] *nf* **:** miserliness, avarice
lagon [lagɔ̃] *nm* **:** (coral reef) lagoon
lagune [lagyn] *nf* **:** lagoon
là-haut [lao] *adv* **1 :** up there **2 :** upstairs
lai [lɛ] *nm* **:** lay, ballad
laïc [laik] *nm* **les laïcs :** the laity
laîche [lɛʃ] *nf* **:** sedge
laid, laide [lɛ, lɛd] *adj* **1 :** ugly **2 :** mean, rude

laideron [lɛdrɔ̃] *nm* : ugly girl
laideur [lɛdœr] *nf* **1** : ugliness **2** : meanness
lainage [lɛnaʒ] *nm* **1** : woolen fabric **2** : woolen garment
laine [lɛn] *nf* **1** : wool <laine peignée : worsted wool> **2 laine d'acier** *Can* : scouring pad, steel wool
laineux, -neuse [lɛnø, -nøz] *adj* : woolly
laïque¹ [laik] *adj* : lay, secular
laïque² *nmf* : layman, laywoman
laisse [lɛs] *nf* : lead, leash
laissé–pour–compte, laissée–pour–compte [lesepurkɔ̃t] *adj, pl* **laissés–pour–compte, laissées–pour–compte 1** : returned unsold **2** : rejected (of a person)
laisser [lese] *vt* **1** : to leave <laisser un pourboire : to leave a tip> <laissez la porte ouverte : leave the door open> **2** OUBLIER : to leave, to forget <j'ai laissé mes gants au bureau : I left my gloves at the office> **3** QUITTER : to leave, to abandon <elle a laissé son mari : she left her husband> **4** ACCORDER : to give <laisse-lui du temps : give him some time> — *v aux* **1** : to let, to allow <ne laissez rien voir : let nothing show> **2 laisse faire!** : never mind!, let it go! — **se laisser** *vr* **1** : to let oneself <il ne se laisse pas faire : he won't be pushed around> **2 se laisser aller** : to let oneself go
laisser–aller [lɛseale] *nms & pl* : carelessness, sloppiness
laisser–faire [lɛsefɛr] *nms & pl* : laissez-faire, noninterference
laissez–passer [lɛsepase] *nms & pl* : pass, permit
lait [lɛ] *nm* **1** : milk <lait concentré *or* lait condensé : condensed milk> <lait entier : whole milk> <lait écrémé : skim milk> <lait demi-écrémé : lowfat milk> **2 lait de poule** : eggnog
laiterie [lɛtri] *nf* **1** : dairy industry **2** : dairy
laiteux, -teuse [lɛtø, -tøz] *adj* : milky <peau laiteuse : milky skin>
laitier¹, -tière [lɛtje, -tjɛr] *adj* : dairy
laitier², -tière *n* **1** : milkman **2** : dairyman, dairymaid *f*
laiton [lɛtɔ̃] *nm* : brass
laitue [lety] *nf* : lettuce
laïus [lajys] *nms & pl fam* : spiel, speech
lama [lama] *nm* **1** : lama <le Grand Lama : the Dalai Lama> **2** : llama
lambeau [lɑ̃bo] *nm, pl* **lambeaux 1** GUENILLE : rag, scrap, shred <tomber en lambeaux : to fall to pieces> **2** : bit, fragment
lambiner [lɑ̃bine] *vi fam* : to dawdle
lambineux, -neuse [lɑ̃binœr, -nøz] *n Can fam* : slowpoke
lambrequin [lɑ̃brəkɛ̃] *nm* : valance (of a bed)
lambris [lɑ̃bri] *nms & pl* : paneling, wainscoting
lambrisser [lɑ̃brise] *vt* : to panel
lame [lam] *nf* **1** : strip, slat, lath **2** : blade <lame de rasoir : razor blade> **3** : sword **4** : wave <lame de fond : groundswell>
lamé [lame] *nm* : lamé
lamelle [lamɛl] *nf* **1** : small strip, sliver **2** : gill (of a mushroom) **3** : flake (of rock, etc.) **4** : slide (for a microscope)
lamentable [lamɑ̃tabl] *adj* **1** DÉPLORABLE : deplorable, lamentable **2** PITOYABLE : pitiful, pathetic — **lamentablement** [-tabləmɑ̃] *adv*
lamentation [lamɑ̃tasjɔ̃] *nf* **1** : lamentation, wailing **2** : whining, complaining
lamenter [lamɑ̃te] *v* **se lamenter** *vr* : to lament, to moan
laminer [lamine] *vt* **1** : to laminate **2** : to wipe out, to decimate
lampadaire [lɑ̃padɛr] *nm* **1** : floor lamp **2** : streetlight
lampe [lɑ̃p] *nf* **1** : lamp **2 lampe à souder** : blowtorch **3 lampe de poche** : flashlight
lampée [lɑ̃pe] *nf fam* : swig, gulp
lamper [lɑ̃pe] *vt* : to gulp down
lampion [lɑ̃pjɔ̃] *nm* : Chinese lantern
lamproie [lɑ̃prwa] *nf* : lamprey
lance [lɑ̃s] *nf* **1** : spear, lance **2** *or* **lance à eau** : hose <lance d'incendie : fire hose>
lancée [lɑ̃se] *nf* : momentum <continuer sur sa lancée : to keep on going, to forge ahead>
lance–flammes [lɑ̃sflam] *nms & pl* : flamethrower
lancement [lɑ̃smɑ̃] *nm* **1** : throwing **2** : launching, liftoff <base de lancement : launching site>
lance–missiles [lɑ̃smisil] *nms & pl* : missile launcher
lance–pierres [lɑ̃spjɛr] *nms & pl* : slingshot
lancer¹ [lɑ̃se] {6} *vt* **1** : to throw, to hurl **2** : to launch **3** : to issue, to put out <lancer un appel au calme : to issue an appeal for calm> **4** : to start up, to get going — **se lancer** *vr* **1** : to throw oneself, to jump **2** : to hurl at each other, to exchange (insults, etc.) **3 ~ dans** : to take up, to embark on
lancer² *nm* **1** : throw, toss <lancer de poids : shotput> **2** : casting, rod-and-reel fishing
lancette [lɑ̃sɛt] *nf* : lancet
lanceur, -ceuse [lɑ̃sœr, -søz] *n* **1** : thrower, pitcher (in baseball) **2** : promoter
lancinant, -nante [lɑ̃sinɑ̃, -nɑ̃t] *adj* **1** : shooting, throbbing **2** : haunting **3** : insistent, nagging
lanciner [lɑ̃sine] *vi* : to throb — *vt* **1** OBSÉDER : to haunt, to obsess **2** TOURMENTER : to torment
landau [lɑ̃do] *nm France* : baby carriage
lande [lɑ̃d] *nf* : moor

langage [lɑ̃gaʒ] *nm* : language <le langage des signes : sign language> <langage machine : machine language>

langagier, -gière [lɑ̃gaʒje, -ʒjɛr] *adj* LINGUISTIQUE : linguistic

lange [lɑ̃ʒ] *nm* **1** : baby blanket **2 être dans les langes** : to be in (its) infancy

langoureux, -reuse [lɑ̃gurø, -røz] *adj* : languorous — **langoureusement** [-røzmɑ̃] *adv*

langouste [lɑ̃gust] *nf* : crayfish, spiny lobster

langoustine [lɑ̃gustin] *nf* : langoustine, prawn

langue [lɑ̃g] *nf* **1** : tongue <tirer la langue : to stick out one's tongue> <donner sa langue au chat : to give up (guessing)> **2** : language <langue maternelle : native language, mother tongue> <de langue française : French-speaking> <langue vivante : modern language>

languette [lɑ̃gɛt] *nf* **1** : tongue (of a shoe) **2** : strip

langueur [lɑ̃gœr] *nf* : languor, languidness

languir [lɑ̃gir] *vi* **1** : to languish, to pine **2** : to flag, to wilt

languissant, -sante [lɑ̃gisɑ̃, -sɑ̃t] *adj* **1** : languid, listless **2** : dull, tiresome **3** : lovesick

lanière [lanjɛr] *nf* : strap, lash, thong

lanoline [lanɔlin] *nf* : lanolin

lanterne [lɑ̃tɛrn] *nf* **1** : lantern **2** : parking light **3 lanterne magique** : magic lantern

laotien, -tienne [laosjɛ̃, -sjɛn] *adj* : Laotian

Laotien, -tienne *n* : Laotian

laper [lape] *vt* : to lap up

lapidaire [lapidɛr] *adj* **1** : lapidary **2** : terse, pithy

lapider [lapide] *vt* : to stone

lapin, -pine [lapɛ̃, -pin] *n* **1** : rabbit **2 poser un lapin à qqn** : to stand s.o. up

lapon[1], **-pone** *or* **-ponne** [lapɔ̃, -pɔn] *adj* : Lappish

lapon[2] *nm* : Lapp, Lappish (language)

Lapon, -pone *or* **-ponne** *n* : Lapp

laps [laps] *nms & pl* : lapse (of time)

lapsus [lapsys] *nms & pl* : slip, error

laquais [lakɛ] *nms & pl* : lackey, footman

laque[1] [lak] *nm* : lacquer, lacquerware

laque[2] *nf* **1** VERNIS : lacquer, shellac **2** : hair spray

laquelle → **lequel**

laquer [lake] *vt* : to lacquer, to shellac

larbin [larbɛ̃] *nm fam* : flunkey, toady

larcin [larsɛ̃] *nm* **1** : petty theft **2** : booty, spoils *pl*

lard [lar] *nm* **1** : fat, lard **2** : bacon **3 faire du lard** *fam* : to put on weight

large[1] [larʒ] *adv* : on a large scale, generously <prévoir large : to allow a bit extra>

large[2] *adj* **1** : wide, broad **2** : considerable, extensive <dans une large mesure : to a large extent> **3** : loose-fitting **4** : generous **5 être large d'idées** : to be broad-minded

large[3] *nm* **1** LARGEUR : width, breadth <10 mètres de large : 10 meters wide> **2 le large** : the open sea

largement [larʒəmɑ̃] *adv* **1** : widely **2** : greatly, by far **3** : generously, lavishly **4** : easily, at least

largesse [larʒɛs] *nf* **1** GÉNÉROSITÉ : generosity **2 largesses** *nfpl* : gifts

largeur [larʒœr] *nf* **1** : width, breadth **2** OUVERTURE : openness <largeur d'esprit : broad-mindedness>

larguer [large] *vt* **1** : to release, to drop **2** *fam* PLAQUER : to ditch, to get rid of

larme [larm] *nf* **1** : tear <elle pleurait à chaudes larmes : she was crying her eyes out> **2** *fam* : small quantity, drop <une larme de vin : a drop of wine>

larmoyant, -moyante [larmwajɑ̃, -mwajɑ̃t] *adj* : tearful

larmoyer [larmwaje] {58} *vi* **1** : to water (of eyes) **2** : to whine, to whimper

larron [larɔ̃] *nm* : bandit, thief

larvaire [larvɛr] *adj* : larval

larve [larv] *nf* **1** : larva **2** *fam* : wimp, lazybones

larvé, -vée [larve] *adj* : latent

laryngite [larɛ̃ʒit] *nf* : laryngitis

larynx [larɛ̃ks] *nms & pl* : larynx

las, lasse [la, las] *adj* **1** FATIGUÉ : weary, tired **2 ~ de** : sick and tired of

lasagne [lazaɲ] *nf* : lasagna

lascif, -cive [lasif, -siv] *adj* : lascivious — **lascivement** [-sivmɑ̃] *adv*

lascivité [lasivite] *nf* : lasciviousness, lechery

laser [lazɛr] *nm* **1** : laser **2 disque laser** : laser disc, optical disc

lassant, -sante [lasɑ̃, -sɑ̃t] *adj* : wearisome, tiresome, tedious

lasser [lase] *vt* **1** : to weary, to tire out **2** ENNUYER : to bore, to try the patience of — **se lasser** *vr* **~ de** : to grow weary of

lassitude [lasityd] *nf* : weariness, lassitude

lasso [laso] *nm* : lasso, lariat

latence [latɑ̃s] *nf* : latency

latent, -tente [latɑ̃, -tɑ̃t] *adj* : latent

latéral, -rale [lateral] *adj, mpl* **-raux** [-ro] : side, lateral

latéralement [lateralmɑ̃] *adv* : laterally, sideways

latex [latɛks] *nms & pl* : latex

latin[1], **-tine** [latɛ̃, -tin] *adj* : Latin

latin[2] *nm* : Latin (language)

latino–américain, -caine [latinoamerikɛ̃, -kɛn] *adj* : Latin-American

Latino–Américain, -caine *n* : Latin American

latitude [latityd] *nf* **1** : latitude **2** : scope, freedom <je lui laissais toute latitude : I gave him all the room he needed>

latrines [latrin] *nfpl* : latrine

latte [lat] *nf* **1** : lath **2** : floorboard

lauréat, -réate [lɔrea, -reat] *n* : prizewinner

laurier [lɔrje] *nm* **1** : laurel <feuille de laurier : bay leaf> **2 lauriers** *nmpl* : laurels <reposer sur ses lauriers : to rest on one's laurels>

laurier–rose [lɔrjeroz] *nm, pl* **lauriers–roses** : oleander

lavable [lavabl] *adj* : washable

lavabo [lavabo] *nm* **1** : washbowl, (bathroom) sink **2 lavabos** *nmpl France* : toilets, washroom

lavage [lavaʒ] *nm* **1** : washing **2** : wash <mets tes chaussettes au lavage : put your socks in the wash> **3 lavage de cerveau** : brainwashing

lavande [lavɑ̃d] *nf* : lavender

lave [lav] *nf* : lava

lave–auto [lavɔto] *nm Can, pl* **lave–autos** : car wash

lave–glace [lavglas] *nm, pl* **lave–glaces** : windshield washer

lave–linge [lavlɛ̃ʒ] *nms & pl France* : washing machine

lavement [lavmɑ̃] *nm* : enema

laver [lave] *vt* **1** : to wash <laver la vaisselle : to do the dishes> <machine à laver : washing machine> **2** : to clear (one's conscience, someone's name, etc.) **— se laver** *vr* **1** : to wash oneself <se laver les mains : to wash one's hands> **2** SE DISCULPER : to vindicate oneself

laverie [lavri] *nf* : self-service laundry

lavette [lavɛt] *nf* **1** : dishcloth **2** *Can* : small mop or brush for washing dishes **3** *fam* : wimp, drip

laveur, -veuse [lavœr, -vøz] *n* : washer, cleaner <laveur de vitres : window washer>

laveuse *nf Can* : washing machine

lave–vaisselle [lavvesɛl] *nms & pl* : dishwasher

lavoir [lavwar] *nm Can* : self-service laundry

laxatif [laksatif] *nm* : laxative

laxisme [laksism] *nm* : laxity

le[1], la [lə, la] **(l'** [l] *before a vowel or mute h*) *pron, pl* **les** [le] **1** (*used as a direct object*) : him, her, it, them <je ne la connais pas : I don't know her> <il le mérite : he deserves it> <les voilà! : there they are!> **2** (*indicating a state or condition*) <elles le lui avaient bien dit : they told him so> <hier il n'était pas content, maintenant il l'est : he wasn't satisfied yesterday, (but) now he is>

le[2], la (l' *before a vowel or mute h*) *art, pl* **les 1** : the <le gateau est sur la table : the cake is on the table> <les enfants : the children> **2** (*used with abstract nouns and geographical names*) <la liberté : freedom> <le Canada : Canada> **3** (*used with parts of the body*) <avec un chapeau sur la tête : with a hat on his/her head> <se laver les dents : to brush one's teeth> **4** (*used with expressions of time*) <le 19 juin : June 19th> <je travaille le matin : I work mornings> **5** : a, an, per <trois fois la semaine : three times a week> <20 dollars l'once : 20 dollars an ounce> **6** (*used in exclamations*) <la belle fête! : (what) a lovely party!>

leader [lidœr] *nm* : leader

lécher [leʃe] {87} *vt* **1** : to lick **2** : to lap up **3** : to lick at, to wash up against **4** *fam* : to polish up (a text, etc.) **— se lécher** *vr* : to lick (one's fingers, etc.)

lèche–vitrines [lɛʃvitrin] *nms & pl* : window-shopping <faire du lèche-vitrines : to window-shop>

leçon [ləsɔ̃] *nf* **1** : schoolwork **2** COURS : lesson, class <prendre des leçons de piano : to take piano lessons> **3** ENSEIGNEMENT : lesson, lecture <il m'a fait la leçon : he gave me a lecture> <j'en ai tiré une leçon : I learned a lesson from it>

lecteur[1], -trice [lɛktœr, -tris] *n* : reader

lecteur[2] *nm* **1** : player <lecteur de cassettes : cassette player> **2** : drive <lecteur de disquettes : disk drive> **3** : reader <lecteur de microfiches : microfiche reader>

lectorat [lɛktɔra] *nm* : readership

lecture [lɛktyr] *nf* **1** : reading **2 lecture sur les lèvres** : lipreading

ledit, ladite [lədi, ladit] *adj, pl* **lesdits, lesdites** [ledi, ledit] : the aforementioned, the aforesaid

légal, -gale [legal] *adj, mpl* **légaux** [lego] : legal, lawful **— légalement** [-galmɑ̃] *adv*

légaliser [legalize] *vt* **1** : to legalize **2** : to authenticate **— légalisation** [-lizasjɔ̃] *nf*

légalité [legalite] *nf* : legality, lawfulness

légat [lega] *nm* : legate

légation [legasjɔ̃] *nf* : legation

légendaire [leʒɑ̃dɛr] *adj* : legendary

légende [leʒɑ̃d] *nf* **1** : legend, story **2** : caption (of an illustration) **3** : key, legend (of a map, etc.)

léger, -gère [leʒe, -ʒɛr] *adj* **1** : light <légère comme une plume : light as a feather> <d'un cœur léger : with a light heart> <un repas léger : a light meal> **2** : slight, faint, weak <une légère augmentation : a slight increase> **3** : flimsy, superficial, frivolous <parler à la légère : to speak thoughtlessly> **4** : loose, lax, flighty <une femme légère : a loose woman>

légèrement [leʒɛrmɑ̃] *adv* **1** : lightly **2** : slightly **3** : thoughtlessly, rashly

légèreté [leʒɛrte] *nf* **1** : lightness **2** DÉSINVOLTURE : thoughtlessness, casualness

légiférer [leʒifere] {87} *vi* : to legislate

légion [leʒjɔ̃] *nf* : legion

légionnaire [leʒjɔnɛr] *nm* : legionary, legionnaire

législateur, -trice [leʒislatœr, -tris] *n* : legislator, lawmaker

législatif[1], **-tive** [leʒislatif, -tiv] *adj* : legislative

législatif[2] *nm* : legislature, legislative body

législation [leʒislasjɔ̃] *nf* : legislation

législature [leʒislatyr] *nf* **1** : term (of office) **2** : legislature

légiste[1] [leʒist] *adj* → **médecin**

légiste[2] *nm* : jurist

légitime [leʒitim] *adj* **1** LÉGAL : lawful **2** : legitimate, justifiable **3** : just, fair **4 légitime défense** : self-defense

légitimement [leʒitimmɑ̃] *adv* : legitimately

légitimer [leʒitime] *vt* **1** : to legitimize **2** JUSTIFIER : to justify

légitimité [leʒitimite] *nf* **1** : legitimacy **2** : fairness

legs [lɛg] *nms & pl* : legacy, bequest

léguer [lege] {87} *vt* **1** : to bequeath **2** TRANSMETTRE : to pass on

légume[1] [legym] *nm* : vegetable <légumes verts : green vegetables>

légume[2] *nf fam* **grosse légume** : bigwig

légumier [legymje] *nm* : vegetable dish

légumineuse [legyminøz] *nf* : legume, leguminous plant

lemming [lɛmiŋ] *nm* : lemming

lendemain [lɑ̃dmɛ̃] *nm* **1** : next day <le lendemain matin : the next morning> **2 au lendemain de** : just after, following **3 du jour au lendemain** : in a very short time, overnight **4 le lendemain** : the future <des lendemains heureux : happy days ahead> <sans lendemain : short-lived> **5 lendemains** *nmpl* : consequences, outcome

lénifiant, -fiante [lenifjɑ̃, -fjɑ̃t] *adj* : soothing

lent, lente [lɑ̃, lɑ̃t] *adj* : slow — **lentement** [lɑ̃tmɑ̃] *adv*

lente [lɑ̃t] *nm* : nit

lenteur [lɑ̃tœr] *nf* : slowness <avec lenteur : slowly> <lenteurs bureaucratiques : bureaucratic delays>

lentille [lɑ̃tij] *nf* **1** : lentil **2** : lens <lentilles cornéennes : contact lenses>

léonin, -nine [leɔnɛ̃, -nin] *adj* **1** : leonine **2** : one-sided, unfair, inequitable

léopard [leɔpar] *nm* : leopard

lèpre [lɛpr] *nf* : leprosy

lépreux[1], **-preuse** [leprø, -prøz] *adj* **1** : leprous **2** : flaking, peeling

lépreux[2], **-preuse** *n* : leper

lequel, laquelle [ləkɛl, lakɛl] *pron, pl* **lesquels, lesquelles** [lekɛl] (*with* **à** *and* **de** *contracted to* **auquel, auxquels, auxquelles; duquel, desquels, desquelles**) **1** : which <la réunion à laquelle il était convié : the meeting to which he was invited > <le compromis auquel il est parvenu : the compromise he reached> **2** : which one <lequel préférez-vous? : which one do you prefer?> **3** : who, whom <un de ses amis avec lequel il joue au tennis : one of his friends with whom he plays tennis>

les → **le**

lesbianisme [lɛsbjanism] *nm* : lesbianism

lesbienne [lɛsbjɛn] *nf* : lesbian

lesdits, lesdites → **ledit**

léser [leze] {87} *vt* **1** : to wrong **2** BLESSER : to injure

lésiner [lezine] *vi* **~ sur** : to skimp on, to be stingy with

lésion [lezjɔ̃] *nf* : lesion

lesquels, lesquelles → **lequel**

lessivage [lɛsivaʒ] *nm* : washing

lessive [lɛsiv] *nf* **1** LAVAGE : washing, wash <faire la lessive : to do the wash> **2** DÉTERGENT : detergent **3** : lye

lessiver [lɛsive] *vt* **1** : to wash, to scrub **2** : to leach **3 être lessivé** *fam* : to be washed out, to be exhausted **4 se faire lessiver** *fam* : to be cleaned out (in a card game, etc.)

lest [lɛst] *nm* **1** : ballast **2 lâcher du lest** : to make concessions

leste [lɛst] *adj* **1** AGILE : nimble, agile **2** : coarse, risqué

lestement [lɛstəmɑ̃] *adv* : nimbly, agilely

lester [lɛste] *vt* **1** : to ballast, to weight **2** *fam* : to stuff, to cram

létal, -tale [letal] *adj, mpl* **létaux** [-to] : lethal

léthargie [letarʒi] *nf* : lethargy <tomber en léthargie : to become lethargic>

léthargique [letarʒik] *adj* : sluggish, lethargic

letton[1], **-tonne** [lɛtɔ̃, -tɔn] *adj* : Latvian

letton[2] *nm* : Latvian (language)

Letton, -tonne *n* : Latvian

lettre [lɛtr] *nf* **1** : letter (of the alphabet) <en toutes lettres : in words, written out> **2** : letter <lettre d'amour : love letter> **3 lettres** *nfpl* : arts, humanities **4 à la lettre** : to the letter, exactly

lettré, -trée [lɛtre] *adj* : well-read

leucémie [løsemi] *nf* : leukemia

leur[1] [lœr] *adj, pl* **leurs** : their <leur mère et leur père : their mother and father>

leur[2] *pron, pl* **leurs 1** : to them <nous leur donnerons le livre : we will give them the book> **2 le leur, la leur, les leurs** : theirs

leurre [lœr] *nm* **1** APPÂT : lure, bait **2** ILLUSION, TROMPERIE : deception, delusion

leurrer [lœre] *vt* TROMPER : to deceive, to delude — **se leurrer** *vr*

levain [ləvɛ̃] *nm* : leaven <sans levain : unleavened>

levant [ləvɑ̃] *adj m* **au soleil levant** : at sunrise
levé, -vée [ləve] *adj* **1** : up <voilà trois heures que je suis levé : I've been up for three hours> **2** : raised <voter à main levée : to vote by a show of hands>
levée [ləve] *nf* **1** : lifting, suspension **2** : collection <levée du courrier : mail pickup> **3** : levying (of troops or taxes) **4** : levee
lever[1] [ləve] {52} *vt* **1** : to raise <lever la main : to put up one's hand> **2** : to lift, to raise (an object) <lever les fenêtres : to raise the windows> <lever les filets : to haul up nets> **3** : to suspend, to end <lever une interdiction : to lift a ban> <elle a levé la séance : she closed the meeting> **4** : to levy (taxes), to raise (funds) **5** : to get (someone) out of bed **6** : to flush (game) **7** : to levy (troops) — *vi* **1** : to come up (of plants) **2** : to rise (in cooking) — **se lever** *vr* **1** : to get up <se lever tôt : to get up early> **2** : to stand up **3** : to rise (of the sun), to become light <le soleil se lève : the sun is rising> <le jour se lève : day is breaking> **4** : to clear up <l'orage s'est levé : the storm lifted>
lever[2] [ləve] *nm* **1** : rising, rise <le lever du jour : daybreak> <au lever du soleil : at sunrise> **2** (*referring to persons*) <au lever : on getting up (from bed)> **3 lever de rideau** : curtain, curtain-raising (in theater)
levier [ləvje] *nm* **1** : lever **2 levier de vitesse** : gearshift
lèvre [lɛvr] *nf* **1** : lip <du bout des lèvres : reluctantly, half-heartedly> <être suspendu aux lèvres de qqn : to hang on s.o.'s every word> **2** : edge, rim, lip (in geology)
lévrier [levrije] *nm* : greyhound
levure [ləvyr] *nf* **1** : yeast **2 levure chimique** : baking powder
lexicographe [lɛksikɔgraf] *nmf* : lexicographer
lexicographie [lɛksikɔgrafi] *nf* : lexicography — **lexicographique** [-grafik] *adj*
lexique [lɛksik] *nm* **1** : vocabulary, glossary **2** : lexicon
lézard [lezar] *nm* : lizard
lézarde [lezard] *nf* FISSURE : crack
lézarder [lezarde] *vt* : to crack — *vi fam* : to bask in the sun — **se lézarder** *vr* : to crack
liaison [ljɛzɔ̃] *nf* **1** : (logical) connection **2** : link <liaison satellite : satellite link> **3** : contact <établir une liaison : to establish contact> **4** AVENTURE : love affair **5** : liaison (in linguistics)
liant, liante [ljɑ̃, ljɑ̃t] *adj* AFFABLE : sociable
liard [ljar] *nm Can* : cottonwood (tree)
liasse [ljas] *nf* : bundle, wad <liasse d'argent : roll of bills>
libanais, -naise [libanɛ, -nɛz] *adj* : Lebanese
Libanais, -naise *n* : Lebanese
libelle [libɛl] *nm* : lampoon
libellé [libele] *nm* : wording (of a document)
libeller [libele] *vt* **1** : to word **2** : to draw up **3** : to make out (a check or money order)
libellule [libelyl] *nf* : dragonfly
libéral, -rale [liberal] *adj & n, mpl* **-raux** [-ro] : liberal — **libéralement** [-ralmɑ̃] *adv*
libéraliser [liberalize] *vt* : to liberalize — **libéralisation** [-lizasjɔ̃] *nf*
libéralisme [liberalism] *nm* : liberalism
libéralité [liberalite] *nf* : liberality, generosity
libérateur[1], **-trice** [liberatœr, -tris] *adj* : liberating
libérateur[2], **-trice** *n* : liberator
libération [liberasjɔ̃] *nf* **1** : freeing, releasing <libération conditionnelle : release on parole> **2** : liberation <libération de la femme : women's liberation>
libéré, -rée [libere] *adj* **1** : liberated **2 ~ de** : free from
libérer [libere] {87} *vt* **1** : to free, to release **2** : to liberate (a country, etc.) **3** : to relieve **4** : to deregulate
libérien, -rienne [liberjɛ̃, -rjɛn] *adj* : Liberian
Libérien, -rienne *n* : Liberian
liberté [libɛrte] *nf* **1** : freedom, liberty <liberté de la presse : freedom of the press> <en liberté conditionnelle : on probation> <mettre en liberté : to set free> **2 libertés** *nfpl* : liberties <prendre des libertés : to take liberties>
libertin[1], **-tine** [libɛrtɛ̃, -tin] *adj* : dissolute, licentious
libertin[2], **-tine** *n* : libertine
libidineux, -neuse [libidinø, -nøz] *adj* : lustful, lewd
libido [libido] *nf* : libido
libraire [librɛr] *nmf* : bookseller
librairie [librɛri] *nf* : bookstore
libre [libr] *adj* **1** : free <un pays libre : a free country> <libre de soucis : free from care> **2** : free (and easy), open <une manière libre : an easygoing manner> **3** DISPONIBLE : available, unoccupied <il y a deux chambres libres : there are two rooms available> <avoir du temps libre : to have some spare time> **4** DÉGAGÉ : clear, free <avoir les mains libres : to have one's hands free> <la voie est libre : the coast is clear> **5 libre arbitre** : free will
libre-échange [librеʃɑ̃ʒ] *nm, pl* **libres-échanges** [librəzeʃɑ̃ʒ] : free trade
librement [librəmɑ̃] *adv* : freely

libre–service [librəsɛrvis] *nm, pl* **libres–services 1** : self-service **2** : self-service store or restaurant
libyen, libyenne [libjɛ̃, libjɛn] *adj* : Libyan
Libyen, Libyenne *n* : Libyan
lice [lis] *nf* **entrer en lice** : to join in the fray, to be in the running
licence [lisɑ̃s] *nf* **1** : degree <licence ès lettres : bachelor of arts degree> **2** : license, permit **3** : license, freedom <licence poétique : poetic license>
licencié, -ciée [lisɑ̃sje] *n* **1** : (university) graduate <licencié de sciences : bachelor of science> **2** : permit holder, licensed vendor
licenciement [lisɑ̃simɑ̃] *nm* RENVOI : layoff, dismissal
licencier [lisɑ̃sje] {96} *vt* CONGÉDIER : to lay off, to dismiss
licencieux, -cieuse [lisɑ̃sjø, -sjøz] *adj* : licentious — **licencieusement** [-sjøzmɑ̃] *adv*
lichen [likɛn] *nm* : lichen
lichette [liʃɛt] *nf fam* : sliver, smidgin
licite [lisit] *adj* : lawful, licit
licorne [likɔrn] *nf* : unicorn
licou [liku] *nm* : halter (for an animal)
lie [li] *nf* **1** : sediment, lees *pl* **2 la lie de la société** : the dregs of society
lie–de–vin [lidvɛ̃] *adj s & pl* : wine-colored
liège [ljɛʒ] *nm* : cork (substance)
lien [ljɛ̃] *nm* **1** ATTACHE : bond, attachment **2** RAPPORT : link, connection **3** RELATION : tie, relationship <liens de parenté : family ties> <les liens d'amitié : the bonds of friendship>
lier [lje] {96} *vt* **1** : to bind, to tie up **2** RELIER : to link up, to join up **3** : to strike up (a friendship, etc.) **4** : to thicken (in cooking) — **se lier** *vr* **~ avec** : to become friends with
lierre [ljɛr] *nm* : ivy
liesse [ljɛs] *nf* : jubilation <être en liesse : to be jubilant>
lieu [ljø] *nm, pl* **lieux 1** ENDROIT : place <lieu de naissance : birthplace> **2 au lieu de** : instead of **3 avoir lieu** : to take place <le spectacle aura lieu ce soir : the show is tonight> **4 avoir lieu de** : to have grounds to, to have every reason to **5 en premier lieu** : in the first place **6 lieu commun** : commonplace **7 tenir lieu de** : to serve as **8 lieux** *nmpl* : premises
lieu–dit *or* **lieudit** [ljødi] *nm, pl* **lieux–dits** *or* **lieudits** : locality
lieue [ljø] *nf* : league (measure of distance)
lieutenant [ljøtnɑ̃] *nm* : lieutenant
lieutenant–colonel [ljøtnɑ̃kɔlɔnɛl] *nm, pl* **lieutenants–colonels** : lieutenant colonel
lièvre [ljɛvr] *nm* : hare
lift [lift] *nm Can fam* : lift, ride
lifting [liftiŋ] *nm* : face-lift
ligament [ligamɑ̃] *nm* : ligament
ligature [ligatyr] *nf* : ligature
ligne [liɲ] *nf* **1** : line <ligne pointillée : dotted line> <en ligne droite : in a straight line> **2** : line, route <ligne de métro : subway line> <ligne d'autobus : bus route> **3** : telephone line, electric line, cable <la ligne est occupée : the line is busy> **4** : range, row <se mettre en ligne : to get into line, to line up> **5** : figure, shape <elle surveille sa ligne : she watches her weight> **6** : line, orientation <ligne de conduite : line of conduct> <grandes lignes : broad outlines> **7** : line (of products) **8 en ~** : on-line (in computing) **9 lignes** *nfpl Can* : border (between the United States and Canada)
lignée [liɲe] *nf* **1** POSTÉRITÉ : descendants *pl* **2** : line, lineage **3** : tradition
ligneux, -neuse [liɲø, -ɲøz] *adj* : woody (of plants)
lignite [liɲit] *nm* : lignite
ligoter [ligɔte] *vt* GARROTTER : to tie up
ligue [lig] *nf* : league, alliance
liguer [lige] *v* **se liguer** *vr* **1** : to join forces **2 ~ contre** : to conspire against, to gang up on
lilas [lila] *nms & pl* : lilac
limace [limas] *nf* : slug (mollusk)
limbes [lɛ̃b] *nmpl* **1** : limbo **2** : uncertainty <tout était dans les limbes : everything was up in the air>
lime [lim] *nf* : file <lime à ongles : nail file>
limer [lime] *vt* : to file — **se limer** *vr* **se limer les ongles** : to file one's nails
limier [limje] *nm* **1** : bloodhound **2** *or* **fin limier** *fam* : sleuth
limitatif, -tive [limitatif, -tiv] *adj* : restrictive, limiting
limitation [limitasjɔ̃] *nf* : limitation, restriction <limitation de temps : time limit> <limitation des naissances : birth control>
limite[1] [limit] *adj* **1 cas limite** : borderline case **2 date limite** : deadline **3 vitesse limite** : speed limit
limite[2] *nf* **1** : border, boundary **2** : limit <limite d'âge : age limit> <sans limites : limitless, boundless> <à la limite de : on the verge of> <dans les limites de : within the limits of> **3 limites** *nfpl* : limitations
limité, -tée [limite] *adj* : limited
limiter [limite] *vt* **1** BORNER : to bound **2** RESTREINDRE : to limit, to restrict — **se limiter** *vr* **1** : to limit oneself **2 ~ à** : to be limited to, to be restricted to
limitrophe [limitrɔf] *adj* : bordering, adjoining
limogeage [limɔʒaʒ] *nm* : dismissal
limoger [limɔʒe] {17} *vt* : to dismiss
limon [limɔ̃] *nm* : silt
limonade [limɔnad] *nf* : lemonade
limousine [limuzin] *nf* : limousine
limpide [lɛ̃pid] *adj* **1** : limpid **2** : lucid, clear

limpidité [lɛ̃pidite] *nf* **1** : limpidity **2** : lucidity, clearness

lin [lɛ̃] *nm* **1** : flax <huile de lin : linseed oil> **2** : linen

linceul [lɛ̃sœl] *nm* : shroud

linéaire [lineɛr] *adj* : linear

linéaments [lineamɑ̃] *nmpl* : lineaments

linge [lɛ̃ʒ] *nm* **1** : linen <linge de maison : household linen(s)> **2** : wash, washing **3** : cloth <un linge doux : a soft cloth> <linge à vaisselle *Can* : dishcloth> **4** : underwear **5** *Can fam* : clothes *pl*, clothing

lingerie [lɛ̃ʒri] *nf* **1** : lingerie **2** *Can* : linen closet

lingot [lɛ̃go] *nm* : ingot

linguiste [lɛ̃gɥist] *nmf* : linguist

linguistique[1] [lɛ̃gɥistik] *adj* : linguistic

linguistique[2] *nf* : linguistics

liniment [linimɑ̃] *nm* : liniment

linoléum [linɔleɔm] *nm* : linoleum

linteau [lɛ̃to] *nm, pl* **linteaux** : lintel

lion, lionne [ljɔ̃, ljɔn] *n* : lion, lioness *f*

Lion *nm* : Leo

lionceau [ljɔ̃so] *nm, pl* **lionceaux** : lion cub

lippu, -pue [lipy] *adj* : thick-lipped

liquéfier [likefje] {96} *vt* : to liquefy — **se liquéfier** *vr*

liqueur [likœr] *nf* **1** : liqueur **2** *Can* : soft drink, soda

liquidation [likidasjɔ̃] *nf* **1** : liquidation **2** : clearance sale **3** : settlement, payment

liquide[1] [likid] *adj* : liquid

liquide[2] *nm* **1** : liquid **2** ESPÈCES : cash

liquider [likide] *vt* **1** : to liquidate, to settle **2** : to sell off, to clear (an inventory)

liquidité [likidite] *nf* **1** : liquidity **2 liquidités** *nfpl* : liquid assets

liquoreux, -reuse [likɔrø, -røz] *adj* : syrupy (of wine)

lire [lir] {51} *vt* **1** : to read <lire à haute voix : to read aloud> **2** : to discern, to see <elle lisait la peur dans mes yeux : she saw the fear in my eyes> **3 lire les lignes de la main** : to read one's palm

lis *or* **lys** [lis] *nms & pl* **1** : lily **2** → **fleur**

lisait [lizɛ], **lisions** [lizjɔ̃], *etc.* → **lire**

lise [liz], *etc.* → **lire**

lisible [lizibl] *adj* **1** : legible **2** : readable (of a novel, etc.) — **lisibilité** [-zibilite] *nf*

lisiblement [lizibləmɑ̃] *adv* : legibly

lisière [lizjɛr] *nf* **1** : selvage **2** : edge, outskirts *pl*

lisse [lis] *adj* : smooth, sleek

lisser [lise] *vt* **1** : to smooth out **2** : to preen (feathers)

liste [list] *nf* : list <liste d'attente : waiting list> <liste noire : blacklist> <liste électorale : electoral roll>

lit [li] *nm* **1** : bed <lit d'enfant : crib> <lit de mort : deathbed> <lits superposés : bunk (bed)> **2** : riverbed **3** : marriage <enfants du premier lit : children from the first marriage>

litanie [litani] *nf* : litany

literie [litri] *nf* : bedding

lithium [litjɔm] *nm* : lithium

lithographie [litɔgrafi] *nf* **1** : lithography **2** : lithograph

litière [litjɛr] *nf* **1** : litter, bedding (in a stable, etc.) **2 litière de chat** : kitty litter

litige [litiʒ] *nm* **1** : dispute <objet de litige : object of contention> **2** : litigation <parties en litige : litigants>

litigieux, -gieuse [litiʒjø, -ʒjøz] *adj* CONTENTIEUX : litigious, contentious

litote [litɔt] *nf* : understatement

litre [litr] *nm* : liter

littéraire [literɛr] *adj* : literary

littéral, -rale [literal] *adj, mpl* **-raux** [-ro] : literal — **littéralement** [-ralmɑ̃] *adv*

littérature [literatyr] *nf* : literature

littoral[1], **-rale** [litɔral] *adj, mpl* **-raux** [-ro] : littoral, coastal

littoral[2] *nm* : coast, coastline

lituanien[1], **-nienne** [litɥanjɛ̃, -njɛn] *adj* : Lithuanian

lituanien[2] *nm* : Lithuanian (language)

Lituanien, -nienne *n* : Lithuanian

liturgie [lityrʒi] *nf* : liturgy

liturgique [lityrʒik] *adj* : liturgical

livide [livid] *adj* **1** BLÊME : pallid, pale **2** BLEUÂTRE : livid, bluish

livraison [livrɛzɔ̃] *nf* : delivery <livraison à domicile : home delivery>

livre[1] [livr] *nm* **1** : book <livre de poche : paperback> <livre de recettes : cookbook> <grand livre : ledger> **2 le livre** : the book trade **3 livres de comptes** : accounts, (account) books

livre[2] *nf* **1** : pound <une livre de beurre : a pound of butter> **2** *or* **livre sterling** : pound (monetary unit)

livrée [livre] *nf* **1** : livery **2 en livrée** : liveried

livrer [livre] *vt* **1** : to deliver **2** : to hand over, to surrender **3 livré à soi-même** : left to one's own devices — **se livrer** *vr* **~ à 1** : to engage in, to devote oneself to **2** : to indulge in, to surrender to **3** : to confide in

livresque [livrɛsk] *adj* : derived from books <savoir livresque : book learning>

livret [livrɛ] *nm* **1** : booklet <livret de banque : bankbook> **2** : libretto

livreur, -vreuse [livrœr, -vrøz] *n* : deliveryman *m*, delivery woman *f*

lob [lɔb] *nm* : lob (in sports)

lobe [lɔb] *nm* : lobe <lobe de l'oreille : earlobe>

lober [lɔbe] *v* : to lob

lobotomie [lɔbɔtɔmi] *nf* : lobotomy

local[1], **-cale** [lɔkal] *adj, mpl* **locaux** [lɔko] : local — **localement** [-kalmɑ̃] *adv*

local[2] *nm, pl* **locaux** : place, premises *pl* <locaux commerciaux : office space>

localisation [lɔkalizasjɔ̃] *nf* **1** : localizing, confining **2** : location, locating

localiser [lɔkalize] *vt* **1** SITUER : to locate **2** CIRCONSCRIRE : to localize, to confine

localité [lɔkalite] *nf* **1** : locality **2** : village, small town

locataire [lɔkatɛr] *nmf* : tenant

location [lɔkasjɔ̃] *nf* **1** : renting, leasing **2** : rental <contrat de location : rental agreement>

lock–out [lɔkaut] *nms & pl* : lockout

locomoteur, -trice [lɔkɔmɔtœr, -tris] *adj* : locomotive

locomotion [lɔkɔmɔsjɔ̃] *nf* : locomotion

locomotive [lɔkɔmɔtiv] *nf* **1** : locomotive, engine **2** *fam* : driving force, pacesetter

locuteur, -trice [lɔkytœr, -tris] *n* : speaker <locuteur natif : native speaker>

locution [lɔkysjɔ̃] *nf* : phrase, locution <locution figée : set phrase>

logarithme [lɔgaritm] *nm* : logarithm

loge [lɔʒ] *nf* **1** : dressing room **2** : box (at the theater) <être aux premières loges : to have a ringside seat> **3** : lodge

logement [lɔʒmɑ̃] *nm* **1** APPARTEMENT : apartment, accommodations *pl* **2** : housing

loger [lɔʒe] {17} *vt* **1** : to put up, to house **2** : to accommodate <une salle qui loge 700 personnes : a room which accommodates 700 people> **3** : to put, to lodge — *vi* : to lodge, to stay (at a hotel) — **se loger** *vr* **1** : to find accommodations **2** : to lodge <la balle s'est logée dans son bras : the bullet lodged itself in his arm>

logiciel [lɔʒisjɛl] *nm* : software

logique[1] [lɔʒik] *adj* : logical — **logiquement** [-ʒikmɑ̃] *adv*

logique[2] *nf* : logic

logis [lɔʒi] *nms & pl* : dwelling, abode

logistique[1] [lɔʒistik] *adj* : logistic

logistique[2] *nf* : logistics

logo [logo] *nm* : logo

loi [lwa] *nf* **1** : law <voter une loi : to pass a law> <faire la loi : to lay down the law> <loi de la gravitation : law of gravity> **2** : rule, convention <les lois de la mode : the dictates of fashion> <loi du silence : code of silence>

loin[1] [lwɛ̃] *adv* **1** : far, a long way (off) **2** : a long time ago **3 ~ de** : far from, distant from **4 d'aussi loin que** : as far back as **5 plus loin** : farther, further

loin[2] *n* **1 au ~** : in the distance, afar **2 de ~** : from a distance **3 de ~** : by far, far and away **4 de loin en loin** : here and there, from time to time

lointain[1], **-taine** [lwɛ̃tɛ̃, -tɛn] *adj* **1** ÉLOIGNÉ : distant, far-off **2** : remote, distant (in time)

lointain[2] *nm* : distance (in space or time) <dans le lointain : in the distance>

loir [lwar] *nm* : dormouse

loisible [lwazibl] *adj* : permissible, allowable <il est loisible de nager ici : you're allowed to swim here>

loisir [lwazir] *nm* **1** : leisure <heures de loisir : leisure time, spare time> **2** : time, opportunity **3 loisirs** *nmpl* : leisure activities, recreation

lombago [lɔ̃bago] → **lumbago**

lombes [lɔ̃b] *nmpl* : loins

lombric [lɔ̃brik] *nm France* : earthworm

long[1] [lɔ̃] *adv* **1** BEAUCOUP : much, a lot <il en disait trop long : he revealed too much> **2 s'habiller long** : to wear long skirts

long[2], **longue** [lɔ̃, lɔ̃g] *adj* **1** : long (in space) <une jupe longue : a long skirt> <long de six mètres : six meters long> **2** : long (in time) <un long silence : a lengthy silence> <une longue amitié : a long-standing friendship> <être long à faire : to be slow to do> **3 de long en large** : up and down, to and fro

long[3] *nm* **1** : length (of space) <deux pouces de long : two inches long> <tomber de tout son long : to fall flat> **2** : length (of time) <tout au long de la nuit : throughout the night> **3 le long de** : along <le long de la route : along the road>

longanimité [lɔ̃ganimite] *nf* : forbearance

longe [lɔ̃ʒ] *nf* **1** : tether **2** : loin (in cooking)

longer [lɔ̃ʒe] {17} *vt* **1** : to go along, to follow **2** : to run alongside, to border

longévité [lɔ̃ʒevite] *nf* : longevity

longhorn [lɔ̃gɔrn] *nmf* : longhorn

longitude [lɔ̃ʒityd] *nf* : longitude

longitudinal, -nale [lɔ̃ʒitydinal] *adj, mpl* **-naux** [-no] : longitudinal — **longitudinalement** [-nalmɑ̃] *adv*

longtemps [lɔ̃tɑ̃] *adv* : a long time <il y a longtemps qu'il n'a pas joué : he hasn't gambled in a long time> <je n'en ai pas pour longtemps : I won't be long>

longue[1] → **long**[2]

longue[2] [lɔ̃g] *nf* **à la longue** : in the long run

longuement [lɔ̃gmɑ̃] *adv* **1** : for a long time **2** : at length, in detail

longueur [lɔ̃gœr] *nf* **1** : length <à longueur de journée : all day long> <sur une longueur de deux mètres : over two meters long> <longueur d'onde : wavelength> **2 longueurs** *nfpl* : tedious parts (of a film, etc.)

longue–vue [lɔ̃gvy] *nf, pl* **longues–vues** : telescope

look [luk] *nm* : look, image <un nouveau look : a new look>
lopin [lɔpɛ̃] *nm* **lopin de terre** : plot of land
loquace [lɔkas] *adj* BAVARD : talkative, loquacious
loquacité [lɔkasite] *nf* : loquacity, garrulousness
loque [lɔk] *nf* **1** : wreck (person) **2 loques** *nfpl* : rags
loquet [lɔkɛ] *nm* : latch
loqueteux, -teuse [lɔktø] *adj* : in rags, in tatters
lord [lɔr(d)] *nm* : lord (in Great Britain) <la Chambre de lords : the House of Lords>
lorgner [lɔrɲe] *vt* : to eye, to ogle, to leer at
lorgnette [lɔrɲɛt] *nf* : opera glasses *pl*
loriot [lɔrjo] *nm* : oriole
lors [lɔr] *adv* **1 ~ de** : at the time of **2 ~ de** : during **3 lors même que** : even though
lorsque [lɔrskə] **(lorsqu'** [lɔrsk] *before a vowel or mute h*) *conj* : when
losange [lɔzɑ̃ʒ] *nm* **1** : lozenge, diamond <en losange : diamond-shaped> **2** *Can* : baseball diamond
lot [lo] *nm* **1** SORT : fate, lot **2** : prize (in a lottery) **3** PART : share **4** : lot, plot (of land)
loterie [lɔtri] *nf* : lottery
loti, -tie [lɔti] *adj* **bien loti** : well-off
lotion [lɔsjɔ̃] *nf* : lotion
lotir [lɔtir] *vt* : to divide into plots
lotissement [lɔtismɑ̃] *nm* **1** : housing development **2** : division (into plots)
lotus [lɔtys] *nm* : lotus
louable [lwabl] *adj* **1** : praiseworthy, commendable **2** : rentable
louage [lwaʒ] *nm* : renting <voiture de louage : rental car>
louange [lwɑ̃ʒ] *nf* : praise <à la louange de : in praise of> <chanter ses louanges : to sing one's praises>
louche[1] [luʃ] *adj* SUSPECT : shady, suspicious
louche[2] *nf* : ladle
loucher [luʃe] *vi* : to squint, to be cross-eyed
louer [lwe] *vt* **1** : to praise <Dieu soit loué! : praise be to God!> **2** : to rent (a car, etc.) **3** *or* **louer à bail** : to rent out, to lease (property) — **se louer** *vr* **1** : to be for rent **2** : to congratulate oneself
loufoque [lufɔk] *adj fam* : crazy, zany
loup [lu] *nm* **1** : wolf **2** *or* **loup de mer** : sea bass **3** : (eye) mask, domino
loup–cervier [lusɛrvje] *nm, pl* **loups–cerviers** : lynx
loupe [lup] *nf* : magnifying glass
louper [lupe] *vt fam* **1** : to bungle, to mess up **2** : to miss (a train, etc.)
loup–garou [lugaru] *nm, pl* **loups–garous** : werewolf
loup–marin [lumarɛ̃] *nm Can, pl* **loups–marins** : seal (animal)
lourd[1] [lur] *adv* **1 peser lourd** : to carry a lot of weight, to count heavily **2 il fait lourd** : it's hot and sticky (outside)
lourd[2], **lourde** [lur, lurd] *adj* **1** : heavy **2** : sultry, oppressive (of the weather) **3** : clumsy, ungainly **4** : weighty, serious **5** : dull, heavy-handed **6 ~ de** : fraught with
lourdaud[1], **-daude** [lurdo, -dod] *adj* : oafish
lourdaud[2], **-daude** *n* : oaf, clod
lourdement [lurdəmɑ̃] *adv* **1** PESAMMENT : heavily **2** MALADROITEMENT : clumsily **3** : GROSSIÈREMENT : greatly, grossly
lourdeur [lurdœr] *nf* **1** : heaviness <avoir des lourdeurs d'estomac : to feel bloated> **2** : clumsiness
lousse [lus] *adj Can fam* : loose, slack
loutre [lutr] *nf* : otter
louve [luv] *nf* : she-wolf
louveteau [luvto] *nm, pl* **louveteaux 1** : wolf cub **2** : Cub Scout
louvoyer [luvwaje] {58} *vi* **1** : to tack (in navigation) **2** : to hedge, to beat around the bush
lover [lɔve] *v* **se lover** *vr* : to coil up
loyal, loyale [lwajal] *adj, mpl* **loyaux** [lwajo] **1** FIDÈLE : loyal, faithful **2** HONNÊTE : honest, fair — **loyalement** [-jalmɑ̃] *adv*
loyauté [lwajote] *nf* **1** FIDÉLITÉ : loyalty, faithfulness **2** HONNÊTETÉ : honesty, fairness
loyer [lwaje] *nm* **1** : rent **2 loyer de l'argent** : interest rate
LSD [ɛlɛsde] *nm* : LSD
lu [ly] *pp* → **lire**
lubie [lybi] *nf* CAPRICE : whim, craze
lubricité [lybrisite] *nf* : lechery, lewdness
lubrifiant[1], **-fiante** [lybrifjɑ̃, -fjɑ̃t] *adj* : lubricating
lubrifiant[2] *nm* : lubricant
lubrifier [lybrifje] {96} *vt* : to lubricate — **lubrification** [lybrifikasjɔ̃] *nf*
lubrique [lybrik] *adj* **1** : lustful, lecherous **2** : lewd
lucarne [lykarn] *nf* **1** : skylight **2** : dormer window
lucide [lysid] *adj* **1** : lucid, clear-sighted **2** CONSCIENT : conscious, aware
lucidement [lysidmɑ̃] *adv* : clearly, lucidly
lucidité [lysidite] *nf* : lucidity, clear-sightedness
luciole [lysjɔl] *nf* : firefly
lucratif, -tive [lykratif, -tiv] *adj* : lucrative, profitable <organisation à but non lucratif : nonprofit organization>
ludique [lydik] *adj* : play, playing
luette [lɥɛt] *nf* : uvula
lueur [lɥœr] *nf* **1** : faint light **2** : glimmer, gleam <une lueur de colère dans les yeux : a gleam of anger in one's eyes> **3** : glow (of a fire, etc.)

luge [lyʒ] *nf* : sled
lugubre [lygybr] *adj* : gloomy, dismal — **lugubrement** [-gybrəmɑ̃] *adv*
lui [lɥi] *pron* **1** (*used as indirect object*) : (to) him, (to) her, (to) it <je le lui ai remis : I gave it back to her> **2** (*used as subject or for emphasis*) : he <elle va au théâtre, lui reste ici : she's going to the theater, he's staying here> **3** (*used as object of a preposition*) : him, it <ils vont chez lui : they're going to his house> <cette plume est à lui : this pen belongs to him> **4** (*used as a reflexive pronoun*) : himself <il ne pense qu'à lui : he only thinks of himself> **5 c'est tout lui!** : that's just like him!
lui–même [lɥimɛm] *pron* : himself, itself <c'est lui-même qui l'a dit : he said it himself>
luire [lɥir] {49} *vi* **1** : to shine, to gleam, to glisten **2** : to glow, to glimmer <l'espoir luit : there's a glimmer of hope>
luisant[1], -sante [lɥizɑ̃, -zɑ̃t] *adj* : shining, gleaming
luisant[2] *nm* : sheen
lumbago [lɛ̃bago, lœ̃-, lɔ̃-] *nm* : lumbago
lumière [lymjɛr] *nf* **1** : light <lumière du jour : daylight> <lumière du soleil : sunlight> <lumière des étoiles : starlight> <allumer la lumière : to turn on the light> **2** ÉCLAIRCISSEMENT : light, clarification <à la lumière de : in (the) light of> <mettre en lumière : to bring to light, to shed light on> **3** GÉNIE : luminary, shining light <elle n'est pas une lumière : she's hardly a genius> **4 lumières** *nfpl* : insight, understanding
luminaire [lyminɛr] *nm* : lamp, light
luminescent, -cente [luminɛsɑ̃, -sɑ̃t] *adj* : luminescent — **luminescence** [-nɛsɑ̃s] *nf*
lumineusement [lyminøzmɑ̃] *adv* **1** : luminously **2** : clearly, lucidly
lumineux, -neuse [lyminø, -nøz] *adj* **1** : luminous, of light **2** : radiant <son sourire lumineux : her radiant smile> **3** : bright, intense <un jaune lumineux : bright yellow> **4** : clear, lucid <une idée lumineuse : a brilliant idea>
luminosité [lyminozite] *nf* : luminosity, radiance
lunaire [lynɛr] *adj* : lunar, moon
lunatique [lynatik] *adj* CAPRICIEUX : whimsical, temperamental
lunch [lœ̃ʃ] *nm, pl* **lunchs** *or* **lunches 1** BUFFET : buffet **2** *Can* : lunch
lundi [lœ̃di] *nm* : Monday
lune [lyn] *nf* **1** : moon <pleine lune : full moon> **2 être dans la lune** : to have one's head in the clouds **3 lune de miel** : honeymoon <passer la lune de miel : to honeymoon>
luné, -née [lyne] *adj* **être bien (mal) luné** : to be in a good (bad) mood
lunette [lynɛt] *nf* **1** : opening, (round) window <lunette arrière : rear window (of an automobile)> **2** : toilet seat **3** : telescope <lunette d'approche : astronomical telescope> **4 lunettes** *nfpl* : glasses, spectacles, goggles <lunettes de soleil : sunglasses> <lunettes de ski : ski goggles>
lurette [lyrɛt] *nf* **belle lurette** : ages, a long time <il y a belle lurette : a long time ago> <ça fait belle lurette que : it's been ages since>
lustre [lystr] *nm* **1** : chandelier **2** : lustre, sheen **3 lustres** *nmpl* : ages <il y a des lustres : ages ago>
lustré, -trée [lystre] *adj* : shiny, glossy
lustrer [lystre] *vt* : to polish, to make shiny
luth [lyt] *nm* : lute
lutin [lytɛ̃] *nm* : imp, goblin, pixie
lutjanidé [lytjanide] *nm* : snapper
lutrin [lytrɛ̃] *nm* : lectern
lutte [lyt] *nf* **1** : fight, conflict <une lutte armée : an armed conflict> **2** : struggle, fight <la lutte contre la drogue : the fight against drugs> <lutte pour la vie : struggle for life> **3** : wrestling
lutter [lyte] *vi* **1** SE BATTRE : to fight, to contend **2** : to struggle **3** : to wrestle
lutteur, -teuse [lytœr, -tøz] *n* **1** : fighter **2** : wrestler
luxation [lyksasjɔ̃] *nf* : dislocation (of a joint)
luxe [lyks] *nm* : luxury <hôtel de luxe : luxury hotel>
luxembourgeois, -geoise [lyksɑ̃burʒwa, -ʒwaz] *adj* : Luxembourgian
Luxembourgeois, -geoise *n* : Luxembourger
luxer [lykse] *vt* : to dislocate (a joint) — **se luxer** *vr* : to dislocate <je me suis luxé l'épaule : I dislocated my shoulder>
luxueux, -xueuse [lyksɥø, -sɥøz] *adj* : luxurious — **luxueusement** [lyksɥøzmɑ̃] *adv*
luxure [lyksyr] *nf* : lust
luxuriant, -riante [lyksyrjɑ̃, -rjɑ̃t] *adj* : luxuriant, lush
luxurieux, -rieuse [lyksyrjø, -rjøz] *adj* : lascivious, lewd
luzerne [lyzɛrn] *nf* : alfalfa
lycée [lise] *nm France* : high school
lycéen, -céenne [liseɛ̃, -seɛn] *n France* : high school student
lymphatique [lɛ̃fatik] *adj* **1** : lymphatic **2** : lethargic, sluggish
lymphe [lɛ̃f] *nf* : lymph
lyncher [lɛ̃ʃe] *vt* : to lynch
lynx [lɛ̃ks] *nm* : lynx
lyophilisé, -sée [ljɔfilize] *adj* : freeze-dried
lyophiliser [ljɔfilize] *vt* : to freeze-dry

lyre [lir] *nf* : lyre
lyrique [lirik] *adj* **1** : lyrical **2** : lyric <poésie lyrique : lyric poetry> **3** : operatic, opera <chanteur lyrique : opera singer> <comédie lyrique : comic opera>
lyrisme [lirism] *nm* : lyricism
lys → **lis**

M

m [ɛm] *nm* : m, the 13th letter of the alphabet
ma → **mon**
maboul, -boule [mabul] *adj fam* CINGLÉ : loony, crazy
macabre [makabr] *adj* : macabre, gruesome
macadam [makadam] *nm* **1** : macadam **2** : (macadam) road
macareux [makarø] *nms & pl* : puffin
macaron [makarɔ̃] *nm* **1** : macaroon **2** : coil (of hair) **3** : (round) badge, sticker
macaronis [makarɔni] *nmpl* : macaroni <macaronis au gratin : macaroni and cheese>
macédoine [masedwan] *nf* : mixture (of fruits or vegetables) <macédoine de fruits : fruit salad> <macédoine de légumes : mixed vegetables>
macédonien, -nienne [masedɔnjɛ̃, -njɛn] *adj* : Macedonian
Macédonien, -nienne *n* : Macedonian
macérer [masere] {87} *vt* : to steep, to soak — *vi* : to soak <macérer dans une marinade : to marinate>
mâchefer [maʃfɛr] *nm* : clinker, slag
mâcher [maʃe] *vt* **1** MASTIQUER : to chew **2 ne pas mâcher ses mots** : not to mince one's words
machette [maʃɛt] *nf* : machete
machin [maʃɛ̃] *nm fam* : thingamajig, thing
Machin, -chine [maʃɛ̃, -ʃin] *n fam* : what's-his-name *m*, what's-her-name *f*
machinal, -nale [maʃinal] *adj, mpl* **-naux** [-no] AUTOMATIQUE : mechanical, automatic <une réaction machinale : an automatic reaction> — **machinalement** [-nalmɑ̃] *adv*
machination [maʃinasjɔ̃] *nf* COMPLOT : machination, plot
machine [maʃin] *nf* **1** : machine <machine à coudre : sewing machine> <machine à écrire : typewriter> <machine à laver : washing machine> **2** : engine <machine à vapeur : steam engine> **3** SYSTÈME : system, process <la machine administrative : bureaucratic machinery>
machine–outil [maʃinuti] *nf, pl* **machines–outils** : machine tool
machinerie [maʃinri] *nf* **1** : machinery, physical plant **2** : engine room
machinisme [maʃinism] *nm* : mechanization
machisme [matʃism] *nm* : machismo, male chauvinism
macho [matʃo] *adj fam* : macho
mâchoire [maʃwar] *nf* **1** : jaw <mâchoire supérieure : upper jaw> **2 mâchoire de frein** : brake shoe
mâchonner [maʃɔne] *vt* **1** : to chew **2** MARMONNER : to mumble
mâchouiller [maʃuje] *vt* : to chew (on), to nibble (at)
macis [masi] *nm* : mace (spice)
maçon [masɔ̃] *nm* **1** : bricklayer, mason **2** : builder
maçonner [masɔne] *vt* **1** : to construct (with masonry) **2** : to face (with stone), to brick up
maçonnerie [masɔnri] *nf* **1** : building, bricklaying **2** : masonry, stonework **3** : Freemasonry
maçonnique [masɔnik] *adj* : masonic
macramé [makrame] *nm* : macramé
macrocosme [makrɔkɔsm] *nm* : macrocosm
maculer [makyle] *vt* : to stain
madame [madam] *nf, pl* **mesdames** [medam] **1** : Mrs., Ms., Madam <bonjour, madame Dupont : good morning, Mrs. Dupont> **2** (*used as a polite form of address*) : lady <bonjour, mesdames : good morning, ladies> **3** (*used as a salutation*) <Madame : Dear Madam> <Mesdames, Mesdemoiselles, Messieurs! : Ladies and Gentlemen!>
mademoiselle [madmwazɛl] *nf, pl* **mesdemoiselles** [medmwazɛl] **1** : Miss, Ms. <bonjour, mademoiselle Dupont : good morning, Miss Dupont> **2** (*used as a polite form of address*) : Miss, Madam <merci, mademoiselle : thank you, Miss> **3** (*used as a salutation*) <Mademoiselle : Dear Madam> <Mesdames, Mesdemoiselles, Messieurs! : Ladies and Gentlemen!>
madère [madɛr] *nm* : Madeira (wine)
madone [madɔn] *nf* : Madonna
madrier [madrije] *nm* : beam (of wood)
madrigal [madrigal] *nm, pl* **-gaux** [-go] : madrigal
maelström [maɛlstrɔm] *nm* : maelstrom
maestria [maɛstrija] *nf* : mastery, skill, brilliance
mafia *or* **maffia** [mafja] *nf* : Mafia

magané, -née [magane] *adj Can fam* **1** : run-down, shabby **2** : weakened, tired

maganer [magane] *vt Can fam* : to ruin, to damage **— se maganer** *vr Can fam* : to tire out

magasin [magazɛ̃] *nm* **1** : shop, store <en magasin : in stock> <grand magasin : department store> **2** ENTREPÔT : warehouse **3** : magazine (of a gun or camera)

magasinage [magazinaʒ] *nm Can* : shopping

magasiner [magazine] *vi Can* : to shop, to go shopping

magazine [magazin] *nm* **1** REVUE : magazine **2** : program <un magazine d'actualités quotidiennes : a daily news program>

magenta [maʒɛ̃ta] *nm* : magenta

magicien, -cienne [maʒisjɛ̃, -sjɛn] *n* : magician

magie [maʒi] *nf* : magic

magique [maʒik] *adj* : magic, magical **— magiquement** [-ʒikmɑ̃] *adv*

magistral, -trale [maʒistral] *adj, mpl* **-traux** [-tro] **1** : brilliant, masterly **2** : authoritative **3 cours magistral** : lecture

magistralement [maʒistralmɑ̃] *adv* : masterfully

magistrat [maʒistra] *nm* : magistrate

magistrature [maʒistratyr] *nf* : magistracy

magma [magma] *nm* **1** : magma **2** : jumble

magnanime [maɲanim] *adj* : magnanimous

magnanimité [maɲanimite] *nf* : magnanimity

magnat [maɲa] *nm* : magnate, tycoon

magnésie [maɲezi] *nf* : magnesia

magnésium [maɲezjɔm] *nm* : magnesium

magnétique [maɲetik] *adj* : magnetic **— magnétiquement** [-tikmɑ̃] *adv*

magnétiser [maɲetize] *vt* : to magnetize **— magnétisme** [maɲetism] *nm*

magnétite [maɲetit] *nf* : magnetite, lodestone

magnétophone [maɲetɔfɔn] *nm* : tape recorder

magnétoscope [maɲetɔskɔp] *nm* : videocassette recorder, VCR

magnétoscoper [maɲetɔskɔpe] *vt* : to videotape

magnificence [maɲifisɑ̃s] *nf* **1** SPLENDEUR : magnificence, splendor **2** PRODIGALITÉ : lavishness, extravagance

magnifier [maɲifje] {96} *nf* **1** : to idealize **2** : to glorify

magnifique [maɲifik] *adj* SPLENDIDE : magnificent **— magnifiquement** [-fikmɑ̃] *adv*

magnitude [maɲityd] *nf* : magnitude

magnolia [maɲɔlja] *nm* : magnolia

magot [mago] *nm fam* : stash (of money), nest egg

magouille [maguj] *nf fam* : scheming, skulduggery

magouiller [maguje] *vi fam* : to scheme, to intrigue

mai [mɛ] *nm* : May

maigre[1] [mɛgr] *adj* **1** : thin, skinny **2** : meager, scanty **3** : lean, low-fat

maigre[2] *nm* **1** : lean (meat) **2 faire maigre** : to abstain from meat

maigrement [mɛgrəmɑ̃] *adv* : meagerly, poorly

maigreur [mɛgrœr] *nf* **1** : thinness **2** : scantiness, meagerness

maigrichon, -chonne [mɛgriʃɔ̃, -ʃɔn] *adj* : skinny, scrawny

maigrir [megrir] *vt* : to thin, to make look thinner **—** *vi* : to lose weight, to reduce

mail [maj] *nm* : mall, promenade

maille [maj] *nf* **1** : stitch (in knitting) **2** : mesh **3** : link (in a chain) **4 → cotte**

maillet [majɛ] *nm* : mallet

maillon [majɔ̃] *nm* : link (in a chain)

maillot [majo] *nm* **1** : jersey, shirt (in sports) **2 maillot de bain** : bathing suit **3 maillot de corps** : undershirt

main [mɛ̃] *nf* **1** : hand <main droite : right hand> <la main dans la main : hand in hand> <serrer la main à : to shake hands with> <se tenir la main : to hold hands> **2** : skill <avoir la main : to have the knack> <se faire la main : to practice> **3** : style, touch <je reconnais la main d'un maître : I recognize the hand of a master> **4** : hand, deal (in card games) **5 de première main** : firsthand **6 de seconde main** : secondhand, used **7 donner un coup de main à** : to lend a helping hand to, to help **8 en mains propres** : in person **9 fait à la main** : handmade **10 main courante** : handrail **11 sous la main** : at hand, handy

main–d'œuvre [mɛ̃dœvr] *nf* : manpower, workforce

main–forte [mɛ̃fɔrt] *nf* : help, assistance <il m'a prêté main-forte : he came to my assistance>

mainmise [mɛ̃miz] *nf* : seizure, takeover

maint, mainte [mɛ̃, mɛ̃t] *adj* **1** : many a **2 maintes et maintes fois** : time and time again

maintenance [mɛ̃tnɑ̃s] *nf* : maintenance

maintenant [mɛ̃tnɑ̃] *adv* **1** : now <à partir de maintenant : from now on> **2** : nowadays

maintenir [mɛ̃tnir] {92} *vt* **1** ENTRETENIR : to maintain, to keep (up) **2** SOUTENIR : to hold up, to support **3** : to stand by (a decision, etc.) **— se maintenir** *vr* : to remain steady, to persist, to hold

maintien [mɛ̃tjɛ̃] *nm* **1** : maintaining, upholding <le maintien de l'ordre

: the maintenance of law and order> **2** : bearing, carriage

maire, mairesse [mɛr, merɛs] *n* : mayor

mairie [meri] *nf* **1** : town hall, city hall **2** : town or city council

mais[1] [mɛ] *adv* **1** (*used to reinforce an interjection*) <mais bien sûr! : but of course!, certainly!> <mais non! : of course not!> **2 n'en pouvoir mais** : to be able to do nothing, to be helpless

mais[2] *conj* **1** : but <elle est petite mais forte : she is small but strong> <mais ce n'est pas vrai : but that's not true> <non seulement délicieux mais encore salutaire : not only tasty but healthful>

maïs [mais] *nm* **1** : Indian corn, maize **2 maïs explosé** : popcorn

maison[1] [mɛzɔ̃] *adj* **1** : homemade <spécialité maison : specialty of the house> **2** : in-house **3** *fam* : first-rate

maison[2] *nf* **1** : house, home <maison de campagne : country house> <rester à la maison : to stay home> **2** : institution, home <maison de retraite : retirement home> **3** FIRME : firm, company <maison d'édition : publishing company> **4 maison close** : brothel **5 maison de correction** : reformatory **6 maison des jeunes** : youth center **7 maison mobile** *Can* : mobile home

maisonnée [mɛzɔne] *nf* : household

maisonnette [mɛzɔnɛt] *nf* : small house

maître[1], **-tresse** [mɛtr, -trɛs] *adj* **1** : main, key <l'idée maîtresse : the main idea> **2** : master, expert <maître boulanger : master baker>

maître[2], **-tresse** *n* **1** : master, mistress <maître de maison : host> <maîtresse de maison : lady of the house, hostess> **2** : owner (of a pet) **3 être maître de soi** : to have self-control <elle est maîtresse de soi : she's her own woman>

maître[3] *nm* **1** : expert, master <être maître passé de : to be a past master at> **2** : master (of a pet) **3** : master (in the arts, etc.) <les vieux maîtres : the old masters> **4** (*used as a title for attorneys and other professionals*) : Mr., Mrs., Ms. **5 maître d'équipage** : boatswain **6 maître d'hôtel** : maître d'hôtel, headwaiter, butler

maître–chanteur [mɛtrəʃɑ̃tœr] *nm, pl* **maîtres–chanteurs** : blackmailer

maîtresse *nf* AMANTE : mistress

maîtrisable [metrizabl] *adj* : controllable

maîtrise [metriz] *nf* **1** : skill, mastery **2** : control <maîtrise de soi : self-control> **3** : master's degree

maîtriser [metrize] *vt* **1** : to master **2** : to control, to restrain — **se maîtriser** *vr*

majesté [maʒɛste] *nf* : majesty

majestueux, -tueuse [maʒɛstɥø, -tɥøz] *adj* : majestic — **majestueusement** [-tɥøzmɑ̃] *adv*

majeur[1], **-jeure** [maʒœr] *adj* **1** IMPORTANT : major, main <en majeure partie : for the most part> **2** : of age **3** : major (in music)

majeur[2] *nm* : middle finger

majoration [maʒɔrasjɔ̃] *nf* : increase

majorer [maʒɔre] *vt* : to increase

majoritaire [maʒɔritɛr] *adj* : majority <le parti majoritaire : the majority party>

majorité [maʒɔrite] *nf* : majority <en majorité : in the majority>

majuscule[1] [maʒyskyl] *adj* : capital, uppercase

majuscule[2] *nf* : capital letter

mal[1] [mal] *adv* **1** : poorly, badly <j'ai mal dormi : I didn't sleep well> <mal tourner : to turn out badly> **2** : with difficulty <il respire mal : it's hard for him to breathe> **3** : in poor health <se porter mal : to be unwell> **4** : wrongly <mal comprendre : to misunderstand> **5 mal à l'aise** : ill at ease **6 pas mal** : not bad(ly) **7 pas mal de** : quite, quite a few <elle est pas mal sympathique : she's quite nice> <pas mal d'enfants : quite a lot of children>

mal[2] *adj* **1** : wrong <c'est mal de voler : it's wrong to steal> **2** : bad <pas mal du tout : not bad at all> **3** : sick, ill <se sentir mal : to feel sick>

mal[3] *nm, pl* **maux** [mo] **1** DOULEUR : pain <avoir mal à la gorge : to have a sore throat> **2** MALADIE : sickness <mal de mer : seasickness> **3** DOMMAGE : harm, hurt <le mal est fait : the damage is done> **4** : evil, ill <le bien et le mal : good and evil> **5** PEINE : trouble, difficulty <sans mal : easily>

malade[1] [malad] *adj* **1** : sick, ill <tomber malade : to get sick> <malade d'inquiétude : sick with worry> **2** : diseased (of an organ or a plant) **3** *fam* : crazy **4** : in a bad way <une économie malade : an ailing economy>

malade[2] *nmf* : sick person, patient

maladie [maladi] *nf* **1** : illness, disease <maladie mentale : mental illness> <maladie sexuellement transmissible : sexually transmitted disease> <maladie de Carré : distemper> **2** MANIE : mania, obsession

maladif, -dive [maladif, -div] *adj* **1** : sickly **2** MORBIDE : pathological <une jalousie maladive : pathological jealousy>

maladresse [maladrɛs] *nf* **1** : clumsiness, awkwardness **2** BÉVUE : blunder

maladroit, -droite [maladrwa, -drwat] *adj* MALHABILE : clumsy, awkward — **maladroitement** [-drwatmɑ̃] *adv*

malais[1], **-laise** [malɛ, -lɛz] *adj* : Malay, Malayan

malais[2] *nm* : Malay (language)

Malais, -laise *n* : Malay, Malayan

malaise [malɛz] *nm* **1** : faintness, dizziness <j'éprouvais un léger malaise : I was feeling faint> **2** : uneasiness, malaise

malaisé, -sée [maleze] *adj* PÉNIBLE : difficult

malaisément [malezemɑ̃] *adv* : with difficulty

malaisien, -sienne [malɛzjɛ̃, -zjɛn] *adj* : Malaysian

Malaisien, -sienne *n* : Malaysian

malard *or* **malart** [malar] *nm* **1** : drake **2** *Can* : mallard

malavenant, -nante [malavnɑ̃, -nɑ̃t] *adj Can* : disagreeable, unpleasant

malavisé, -sée [malvize] *adj* : ill-advised, unwise

malawien, -wienne [malawjɛ̃, -wjɛn] *adj* : Malawian

Malawien, -wienne *n* : Malawian

malaxer [malakse] *vt* : to blend, to mix

malaxeur [malaksœr] *nm* **1** : (cement) mixer **2** *Can* : (electric) beater, mixer **3** *Can* MÉLANGEUR : blender

malchance [malʃɑ̃s] *nf* : bad luck, misfortune

malchanceux, -ceuse [malʃɑ̃sø, -søz] *adj* : unlucky

malcommode [malkɔmɔd] *adj* **1** : impractical, uncomfortable, inconvenient **2** *Can* : ornery, cantankerous <un malade malcommode : a difficult patient>

mâle[1] [mal] *adj* **1** : male **2** : manly

mâle[2] *nm* : male

malédiction [malediksjɔ̃] *nf* : curse, malediction

maléfice [malefis] *nm* SORTILÈGE : evil spell

maléfique [malefik] *adj* : evil

malencontreusement [malɑ̃kɔ̃trøzmɑ̃] *adv* : inappropriately, ill-advisedly

malencontreux, -treuse [malɑ̃kɔ̃trø, -trøz] *adj* : unfortunate, untoward, inopportune

malendurant, -rante [malɑ̃dyrɑ̃, -rɑ̃t] *adj Can* : gruff, rough

malentendant[1], **-dante** [malɑ̃tɑ̃dɑ̃, -dɑ̃t] *adj* : hard of hearing

malentendant[2], **-dante** *n* **les malentendants** : the hearing impaired

malentendu [malɑ̃tɑ̃dy] *nm* : misunderstanding

mal–en–train [malɑ̃trɛ̃] *adj Can* : unwell, out of sorts

malfaçon [malfasɔ̃] *nf* DÉFAUT : fault, defect

malfaisant, -sante [malfəzɑ̃, -zɑ̃t] *adj* **1** NUISIBLE : harmful **2** : evil, wicked

malfaiteur [malfɛtœr] *nm* CRIMINEL : criminal, malefactor

malfamé, -mée [malfame] → **famé**

malformation [malfɔrmasjɔ̃] *nf* : malformation

malgache[1] [malgaʃ] *adj* : Madagascan, Malagasy

malgache[2] *nm* : Malagasy (language)

Malgache *nmf* : Madagascan, Malagasy

malgré [malgre] *prep* : in spite of, despite <malgré tout : in spite of everything, even so>

malhabile [malabil] *adj* MALADROIT : clumsy

malheur [malœr] *nm* **1** : misfortune, bad luck **2** CATASTROPHE : tragedy, calamity **3 faire un malheur** *fam* : to be very successful <le spectacle a fait un malheur : the show was a big hit>

malheureusement [malœrøzmɑ̃] *adv* : unfortunately

malheureux[1], **-reuse** [malœrø, -røz] *adj* **1** : unhappy, miserable **2** FÂCHEUX : unfortunate, regrettable <des suites malheureuses : unfortunate consequences> <c'est malheureux! : what a shame!>

malheureux[2], **-reuse** *n* **1** : unfortunate person, poor wretch **2** : poor person <les malheureux : the needy>

malhonnête [malɔnɛt] *adj* : dishonest — **malhonnêtement** [-nɛtmɑ̃] *adv*

malhonnêteté [malɔnɛtte] *nf* : dishonesty, uncleanliness

malice [malis] *nf* **1** : mischief, mischievousness <avec malice : mischievously> **2 sans ~** : innocent, guileless

malicieux, -cieuse [malisjø, -sjøz] *adj* ESPIÈGLE : mischievous — **malicieusement** [malisjøzmɑ̃] *adv*

malien, -lienne [maljɛ̃, -ljɛn] *adj* : Malian

Malien, -lienne *n* : Malian

malignité [maliɲite] *nf* **1** : malice, spite **2** : malignancy

malin, -ligne [malɛ̃, -liɲ] *adj* **1** FUTÉ : shrewd, clever **2** *fam* : tricky, difficult **3** : malicious **4** : malignant

malingre [malɛ̃gr] *adj* : puny

malintentionné, -née [malɛ̃tɑ̃sjɔne] *adj* : malicious, spiteful

malle [mal] *nf* **1** : trunk <faire ses malles : to pack one's bags> **2** *or* **malle arrière** : trunk (of a car)

malléable [maleabl] *adj* : malleable — **malléabilité** [-leabilite] *nf*

mallette [malɛt] *nf* **1** ATTACHÉ-CASE : attaché case, briefcase **2** : small suitcase, valise

malmener [malməne] {52} *vt* **1** MALTRAITER : to manhandle, to mistreat **2** : to give a rough time to

malnutrition [malnytrisjɔ̃] *nf* : malnutrition

malodorant, -rante [malɔdɔrɑ̃, -rɑ̃t] *adj* : foul-smelling, smelly

malotru, -true [malɔtry] *n* : boor

malpoli, -lie [malpɔli] *adj fam* : rude, impolite

malpropre [malprɔpr] *adj* **1** SALE : dirty, grubby **2** GROSSIER : vulgar,

smutty **3** MALHONNÊTE **:** dishonest, unsavory
malpropreté [malprɔprəte] *nf* **:** dirtiness
malsain, -saine [malsɛ̃, -sɛn] *adj* **:** unhealthy
malséant, -séante [malseɑ̃, -seɑ̃t] *adj* **:** unseemly, unbecoming
malsonnant, -nante [malsɔnɑ̃, -nɑ̃t] *adj* **:** offensive
malt [malt] *nm* **:** malt
maltais, -taise [maltɛ, -tɛz] *adj* **:** Maltese
Maltais, -taise *n* **:** Maltese
maltraiter [maltrete] *vt* **1 :** to mistreat **2 :** to criticize, to pan
malveillance [malvɛjɑ̃s] *nf* **:** spite, malevolence
malveillant, -lante [malvɛjɑ̃, -jɑ̃t] *adj* **:** spiteful, malicious
malvenu, -venue [malvəny] *adj* DÉPLACÉ **:** out of place <je suis malvenu de le critiquer **:** I'm in no position to criticize him>
malversation [malvɛrsasjɔ̃] *nf* **:** embezzlement
maman [mamɑ̃] *nf* **:** mom, mommy
mamelle [mamɛl] *nf* **1 :** teat **2** PIS **:** udder
mamelon [mamɛlɔ̃] *nm* **1 :** nipple **2 :** hillock
mamie [mami] *nf France fam* **:** grandma, granny
mammaire [mamɛr] *adj* **:** mammary
mammifère [mamifɛr] *nm* **:** mammal
mammographie [mamɔgrafi] *nf* **:** mammogram
mammouth [mamut] *nm* **:** mammoth
management [manaʒmɑ̃, manadʒmɛnt] *nm* **:** management
manager [manadʒœr] *nm* **:** manager
manant [manɑ̃] *nm* **:** yokel, boor
manche[1] [mɑ̃ʃ] *nf* **1 :** sleeve <sans manche **:** sleeveless> **2 :** round, game, set **3** *Can* **:** inning (in baseball) **4** channel, strait(s)
manche[2] *nm* **1 :** handle <manche à balai **:** broomstick> **2 :** neck (of a musical instrument)
manchette [mɑ̃ʃɛt] *nf* **1 :** cuff (of a shirt, etc.) **2 :** headline
manchon [mɑ̃ʃɔ̃] *nm* **:** muff
manchot[1], **-chote** [mɑ̃ʃo, -ʃɔt] *adj* **1 :** one-armed, one-handed **2 :** armless, handless
manchot[2] *nm* **:** penguin
mandarin [mɑ̃darɛ̃] *nm* **1 :** mandarin **2 :** Mandarin (language)
mandarine [mɑ̃darin] *nf* **:** tangerine, mandarin orange
mandat [mɑ̃da] *nm* **1 :** mandate **2 :** term of office **3 :** warrant <mandat d'arrêt **:** warrant for arrest> <mandat de perquisition **:** search warrant> **4** *or* **mandat postal** *or* **mandat-poste :** money order
mandataire [mɑ̃datɛr] *nmf* **1** REPRÉSENTANT **:** representative, agent **2 :** proxy
mandater [mɑ̃date] *vt* **:** to appoint, to commission
mandibule [mɑ̃dibyl] *nf* **:** mandible
mandoline [mɑ̃dɔlin] *nf* **:** mandolin
manège [manɛʒ] *nm* **1 :** riding school **2 :** game, scheme, ploy **3 :** merry-go-round, ride (in an amusement park)
manette [manɛt] *nf* **:** lever
manganèse [mɑ̃ganɛz] *nm* **:** manganese
mangeable [mɑ̃ʒabl] *adj* **:** edible
mangeoire [mɑ̃ʒwar] *nf* **:** feeding trough, manger
manger[1] [mɑ̃ʒe] {17} *vt* **1 :** to eat **2 :** to eat away, to devour **3 :** to fill up, to cover up, to hide **4 :** to consume, to use up **5 manger ses mots :** to mumble **—** *vi* **:** to eat
manger[2] *nm* **:** food <le boire et le manger **:** food and drink>
mange-tout [mɑ̃ʒtu] *nms & pl or* **pois mange-tout :** snow pea
mangeur, -geuse [mɑ̃ʒœr, -ʒøz] *n* **:** eater
manglier [mɑ̃glije] *nm* **:** mangrove
mangouste [mɑ̃gust] *nf* **:** mongoose
mangue [mɑ̃g] *nf* **:** mango
maniabilité [manjabilite] *nf* **:** maneuverability
maniable [manjabl] *adj* **1** COMMODE **:** handy **2 :** easy to handle, maneuverable **3 :** easily influenced
maniaque[1] [manjak] *adj* **1 :** fussy, finicky **2 :** maniacal
maniaque[2] *nmf* **1 :** crank, fanatic **2 :** maniac
manie [mani] *nf* **1 :** quirk, odd habit **2** OBSESSION **:** mania, obsession
maniement [manimɑ̃] *nm* **:** handling, use, operation <maniement d'une langue **:** command of a language>
manier [manje] {96} *vt* **1 :** to handle, to deal with **2 :** to use, to operate **— se manier** *vr fam* **:** to get a move on
manière [manjɛr] *nf* **1 :** manner, way <d'une certaine manière **:** in a way> <en aucune manière **:** in no way, under no circumstances> <de manière à **:** so as to> <de toute manière **:** in any case, anyway> **2 :** way, personal style <sa manière de parler **:** his way of speaking> **3 :** style <dans la manière romantique **:** in the romantic style> **4 manières** *nfpl* **:** manners
maniéré, -rée [manjere] *adj* **:** affected, mannered
manifestant, -tante [manifɛstɑ̃, -tɑ̃t] *n* **:** demonstrator, protestor
manifestation [manifɛstasjɔ̃] *nf* **1 :** (political) demonstration, protest **2 :** expression (of emotions) **3 :** event <une manifestation sportive **:** a sporting event> **4 :** symptom, sign
manifeste[1] [manifɛst] *adj* ÉVIDENT **:** manifest, obvious **— manifestement** [-fɛstmɑ̃] *adj*
manifeste[2] *nm* **:** manifesto

manifester [manifɛste] *vt* **1** : to express, to indicate **2** RÉVÉLER : to reveal, to show — *vi* : to demonstrate, to hold a demonstration — **se manifester** *vr* **1** : to manifest itself **2** : to appear

manigance [manigɑ̃s] *nf* : scheme, intrigue, trick

manigancer [manigɑ̃se] {6} *vt* : to plot, to scheme

manipulateur, -trice [manipylatœr, -tris] *n* **1** : technician **2** : conjurer **3** : manipulator

manipulation [manipylasjɔ̃] *n* **1** MANIEMENT : handling **2** : manipulation

manipuler [manipyle] *vt* **1** : to handle **2** : to manipulate

manivelle [manivɛl] *nf* : crank

manne [man] *nf* **1** : manna **2** : godsend

mannequin [mankɛ̃] *nm* **1** : dummy, mannequin **2** : model

manœuvrable [manœvrabl] *adj* : maneuverable

manœuvre [manœvr] *nf* **1** : maneuver **2 fausse manœuvre** : wrong move, error

manœuvrer [manœvre] *vt* **1** : to maneuver **2** : to work, to operate **3** MANIPULER : to manipulate — *vi* : to maneuver

manoir [manwar] *nm* : country estate, manor

manque [mɑ̃k] *nm* **1** INSUFFISANCE : lack, shortage <par manque d'imagination : for want of imagination> <manque de rapport : irrelevance> **2** LACUNE : gap <manque de crédit : credibility gap> **3 être en manque** : to be in withdrawal (from alcohol or drugs) **4 manque à gagner** : loss of earnings, shortfall

manqué, -quée [mɑ̃ke] *adj* **1** : failed <poète manqué : failed poet> **2** : missed <occasion manquée : missed opportunity **3** → **garçon**

manquement [mɑ̃kmɑ̃] *nm* : breach, lapse

manquer [mɑ̃ke] *vt* **1** : to miss <manquer une bonne occasion : to miss a good opportunity> **2** FAILLIR : to fall short of, to just miss <elle a manqué (de) tomber : she nearly fell> — *vi* **1** : to be lacking, to be missing <ce n'est pas l'envie qui me manque : it's not that I don't want to> <il manque deux tasses : two cups are missing> **2** ÉCHOUER : to fail <j'ai manqué à mon devoir : I failed to do my duty> **3** : to be absent <elle n'a jamais manqué : she's never been absent> **4 ~ de** : to be short of, to lack <il manque d'argent : he has no money>

mansarde [mɑ̃sard] *nf* : attic room, garret

mansuétude [mɑ̃sɥetyd] *nf* : leniency

mante [mɑ̃t] *nf or* **mante religieuse** : praying mantis

manteau [mɑ̃to] *nm, pl* **manteaux** [-to] **1** : coat **2** : blanket (of fog), mantle (of snow, etc.) **3 manteau de cheminée** : mantelpiece **4 sous le manteau** : undercover, clandestinely

manucure[1] [manykyr] *nmf* : manicurist

manucure[2] *nf* : manicure

manucurer [manykyre] *vt* : to manicure

manuel[1], **-elle** [manɥɛl] *adj* : manual — **manuellement** [-nɥɛlmɑ̃] *adv*

manuel[2] *nm* **1** : manual, handbook **2** *or* **manuel scolaire** : textbook

manuel[3], **-nuelle** *n* : manual worker

manufacture [manyfaktyr] *nf* **1** USINE : factory **2** : manufacture

manufacturer [manyfaktyre] *vt* : to manufacture

manufacturier, -rière [manyfaktyrje, -rjɛr] *n* : manufacturer, factory owner

manuscrit[1], **-scrite** [manyskri, -skrit] *adj* : handwritten

manuscrit[2] *nm* : manuscript

manutention [manytɑ̃sjɔ̃] *nf* **1** : handling <frais de manutention : handling charges> **2** ENTREPÔT : storehouse, warehouse

mappemonde [mapmɔ̃d] *nf* : map of the world

maquereau [makro] *nm, pl* **-reaux** [-ro] : mackerel

maquette [makɛt] *nf* : scale model

maquignon [makiɲɔ̃] *nm* **1** : horse dealer, cattle trader **2** *France* : shady operator

maquillage [makijaʒ] *nm* **1** : makeup **2** : doctoring, faking

maquiller [makije] *vt* **1** : to make up (one's face) **2** FALSIFIER : to falsify, to fake **3** DÉGUISER : to disguise, to hide <maquiller la vérité : to hide the truth> — **se maquiller** *vr* : to put on makeup

maquilleur, -leuse [makijœr, -jøz] *n* : makeup artist

maquis [maki] *nm* **1** *France* : scrubland, brush **2** : tangle, labyrinth

maraîcher[1], **-chère** [marɛʃe, -ʃɛr] *adj* : farming <culture maraîchère : truck farming>

maraîcher[2], **-chère** *n* : truck farmer

marais [marɛ] *nm* : marsh, swamp

marasme [marasm] *nm* **1** ACCABLEMENT : dejection, depression **2** : stagnation <marasme économique : economic stagnation>

marasquin [maraskɛ̃] *nm* : maraschino

marathon [maratɔ̃] *nm* : marathon

marâtre [maratr] *nf* : cruel mother

maraudage [marodaʒ] → **maraude**

maraude [marod] *nf* **1** : pilfering, thieving **2 en ~** : cruising <taxi en maraude : cruising taxi>

marauder [marode] *vi* **1** : to pilfer, to thieve **2** : to cruise (of a taxi), to prowl about

maraudeur, -deuse [marodœr, -døz] *n* **1** : prowler, pilferer **2** : marauder
marbre [marbr] *nm* **1** : marble **2** *Can* : home plate (in baseball) **3 rester de marbre** : to remain impassive, to be unmoved
marbrer [marbre] *vt* **1** : to marble <gateau marbré : marble cake> **2** : to mottle, to blotch
marbrure [marbryr] *nf* **1** : marbling (of paper, etc.) **2** : mottling, blotchiness
marc [mar] *nm* : (coffee) grounds
marchand[1], -chande [marʃɑ̃, -ʃɑ̃d] *adj* **1** : market, commercial <valeur marchande : market value> **2** → **marine**
marchand[2], -chande *n* **1** COMMERÇANT : storekeeper, merchant, dealer <marchand de vins : wine merchant> **2 marchand ambulant** : hawker, peddler **3 marchand en gros** GROSSISTE : wholesaler
marchandage [marʃɑ̃daʒ] *nm* : bargaining, haggling
marchander [marʃɑ̃de] *vt* **1** : to bargain over, to haggle over **2** : to spare <il n'a pas marchandé ses éloges : he wasn't sparing in his praise> — *vi* : to haggle, to bargain, to dicker
marchandeur, -deuse [marʃɑ̃dœr, -døz] *n* : haggler
marchandises [marʃɑ̃diz] *nfpl* : goods, merchandise
marche [marʃ] *nf* **1** : step, stair <attention à la marche : watch for the step!> **2** : walk, walking <faire une marche : to take a walk> **3** : moving, running <un véhicule en marche : a moving vehicle> <la marche du temps : the march of time> **4** : working, operating <en bon état de marche : in good working order> **5** : march, marching <marche de protestation : protest march> **6** : march (in music) <marche nuptiale : wedding march>
marché [marʃe] *nm* **1** : market <faire son marché : to do one's (grocery) shopping> <marché aux puces : flea market> **2** : market (in economics and finance) <le marché du travail : the labor market> <marché noir : black market> <étude de marché : market survey> **3** : deal <conclure un marché : to strike a deal> **4 bon marché** : cheap <à bon marché : at a good price, cheaply> **5 par–dessus le marché** : to top it all off
marchepied [marʃəpje] *nm* **1** : step, steps *pl* (of a vehicle) **2** : stepping-stone
marcher [marʃe] *vi* **1** : to walk **2** : to step, to tread **3** FONCTIONNER : to work, to go, to run <ma montre ne marche pas : my watch isn't running> <cette auto marche trop vite : that car's going too fast> **4** : to be working, to be going well <si ça marche : if it works out> **5 faire marcher qqn** *fam* : to pull s.o.'s leg **6 marcher au pas** : to march
marchette [marʃɛt] *nf Can* : walker (for babies)
marcheur, -cheuse [marʃœr, -ʃøz] *n* : walker
mardi [mardi] *nm* **1** : Tuesday **2 mardi gras** : Mardi Gras
mare [mar] *nf* **1** : pond **2** : pool <une mare de sang : a pool of blood>
marécage [marekaʒ] *nm* : marsh, swamp
marécageux, -geuse [marekaʒø, -ʒøz] *adj* : marshy, swampy
maréchal [mareʃal] *nm, pl* **-chaux** [-ʃo] : marshal
maréchal–ferrant [mareʃalferɑ̃] *nm, pl* **maréchaux–ferrants** [mareʃoferɑ̃] : blacksmith
marée [mare] *nf* **1** : tide <à marée haute : at high tide> <marée descendante : ebb tide> **2** : flood, surge (of emotions, etc.) **3 marée noire** : oil slick
marelle [marɛl] *nf* : hopscotch
marémoteur, -trice [maremɔtœr, -tris] *adj* : tidal
margarine [margarin] *nf* : margarine
marge [marʒ] *nf* **1** : margin **2** : leeway, room <marge de manœuvre : room to maneuver> **3** *or* **marge bénéficiaire** : profit margin, markup **4 en marge de** : on the fringes of, outside <vivre en marge de la société : to live on the fringes of society> <en marge de la loi : outside the law>
marginal[1], -nale [marʒinal] *adj, mpl* **-naux** [-no] : marginal — **marginalement** [-nalmɑ̃] *adv*
marginal[2], -nale *n, mpl* **-naux** : dropout
marguerite [margərit] *nf* : daisy
mari [mari] *nm* : husband
mariage [marjaʒ] *nm* **1** : marriage <mariage mixte : intermarriage, mixed marriage> **2** : wedding **3** : blend, merger, alliance
marié[1], -riée [marje] *adj* : married
marié[2], -riée *n* **1** : groom *m,* bride *f* **2 les mariés** : the newlyweds
marier [marje] {96} *vt* **1** : to marry, to unite in marriage <le curé les a mariés : the priest married them> **2** *Can* ÉPOUSER : to marry, to get married to <il voulait la marier : he wanted to marry her> **3** : to combine, to blend — **se marier** *vr* **1** : to get married <se marier avec : to get married to> **2** : to go well together
marieur, -rieuse [marjœr, -jøz] *n* : matchmaker
marijuana [marirwana] *nf* : marijuana
marin[1], -rine [marɛ̃, -rin] *adj* **1** : sea, marine <paysage marin : seascape> **2** : offshore
marin[2] *nm* : sailor, mariner
marina [marina] *nf* : marina
marine[1] [marin] *adj or* **bleu marine** : navy blue

marine[2] *nf* **1** : navy <officier de marine : naval officer> **2 marine marchande** : merchant marine

marine[3] *nm* : navy blue

mariner [marine] *v* : to marinate

maringouin [marɛ̃gwɛ̃] *nm Can* : mosquito

marinière [marinjɛr] *nf* : smock

marionnette [marjɔnɛt] *nf* **1** : puppet **2 marionnette à fils** : marionette

marionnettiste [marjɔnɛtist] *nmf* : puppeteer

marital, -tale [marital] *adj, mpl* **-taux** [-to] : marital

maritime [maritim] *adj* **1** : maritime, coastal, seaboard **2** : naval, nautical **3** : shipping

marjolaine [marʒɔlɛn] *nf* : marjoram

marketing [markɛtiŋ] *nm* : marketing

marmaille [marmaj] *nf fam* : brats *pl*, noisy kids *pl*

marmelade [marməlad] *nf* **1** COMPOTE : stewed fruit **2** : marmalade

marmite [marmit] *nf* : cooking pot

marmonnement [marmɔnmɑ̃] *nm* : mumble, mutter

marmonner [marmɔne] *v* : to mutter, to mumble

marmot [marmo] *nm fam* : kid, brat

marmotte [marmɔt] *nf* **1** : marmot **2 marmotte d'Amérique** : groundhog, woodchuck

marmotter [marmɔte] *v* MARMONNER : to mutter, to mumble

marocain, -caine [marɔkɛ̃, -kɛn] *adj* : Moroccan

Marocain, -caine *nmf* : Moroccan

marotte [marɔt] *nf* : craze, fad

marquant, -quante [markɑ̃, -kɑ̃t] *adj* MÉMORABLE : memorable, outstanding

marque [mark] *nf* **1** : mark, trace, sign <marques de doigts : finger marks> <marques d'usure : signs of wear> **2** : brand, make <marque déposée : registered trademark> **3** : eminence, prominence <personnalité de marque : prominent figure> **4** : hallmark, stamp **5** : proof, sign <une marque de confiance : a sign of confidence> **6** : score (in sports, in games) **7 à vos marques! prêts! partez!** : on your marks! get set! go!

marqué, -quée [marke] *adj* **1** : marked **2** NET : distinct, decided

marquer [marke] *vt* **1** : to mark **2** INDIQUER : to show, to indicate **3** : to brand **4** : to score (in sports) **5** : to write down, to note **6 marquer le pas** : to mark time — *vi* **1** : to leave a mark **2** : to be significant, to stand out

marqueur[1], **-queuse** [markœr, -køz] *n* : scorekeeper

marqueur[2] *nm* : marker (pen), highlighter

marquis, -quise [marki, -kiz] *n* : marquess *m*, marquis *m*, marchioness *f*, marquise *f*

marquise *nf* **1** : canopy, marquee **2** AUVENT : awning

marraine [marɛn] *nf* : godmother

marrant, -rante [marɑ̃, -rɑ̃t] *adj fam* : amusing, funny

marre [mar] *adv fam* : enough <j'en ai marre : I'm fed up>

marron[1], **-ronne** [marɔ̃, -rɔn] *adj* **1** MALHONNÊTE : crooked, bogus <médecin marron : quack> **2** : brown

marron[2] *nm* **1** : chestnut **2** : brown

marronnier [marɔnje] *nm* : chestnut tree

mars [mars] *nm* : March

Mars *nf* : Mars (planet)

marsouin [marswɛ̃] *nm* : porpoise

marsupial, -piale [marsypjal] *adj & nm, pl* **-piaux** [-pjo] : marsupial

marteau [marto] *nm, pl* **marteaux** [marto] **1** : hammer **2** : gavel **3** : knocker **4 marteau pneumatique** : pneumatic drill

marteau-piqueur [martopikœr] *nm, pl* **marteaux-piqueurs** : jackhammer

martèlement [martɛlmɑ̃] *nm* : hammering

marteler [martəle] {20} *vt* **1** : to hammer, to pound **2** : to hammer out (words)

martial, -tiale [marsjal] *adj, mpl* **-tiaux** [-sjo] : martial

martinet [martinɛ] *nm* **1** : small whip **2** : swift, martin

martin-pêcheur [martɛ̃pɛʃœr] *nm, pl* **martins-pêcheurs** : kingfisher

martre [martr] *nf* **1** : marten **2** : sable (fur)

martyr[1], **-tyre** [martir] *adj* **1** : martyred **2 enfant martyr** : battered child

martyr[2], **-tyre** *n* : martyr

martyre *nm* **1** : martyrdom **2** : agony, torture <souffrir le martyre : to be in agony>

martyriser [martirize] *vt* **1** : to martyr **2** : to torment, to maltreat

marxisme [marksism] *nm* : Marxism — **marxiste** [marksist] *adj & nmf*

mascara [maskara] *nm* : mascara

mascarade [maskarad] *nf* : masquerade

mascotte [maskɔt] *nf* : mascot

masculin[1], **-line** [maskylɛ̃, -lin] *adj* **1** : male **2** : men's **3** : masculine, manly

masculin[2] *nm* : masculine (in grammar)

masculinité [maskylinite] *nf* : masculinity

maskinongé [maskinɔ̃ʒe] *nm* : muskellunge

masochisme [mazɔʃism] *nm* : masochism

masochiste[1] [mazɔʃist] *adj* : masochistic

masochiste[2] *nmf* : masochist

masque [mask] *nm* **:** mask <masque à gaz : gas mask> <masque de plongée : diving mask>

masqué, -quée [maske] *adj* **1 :** masked **2 :** concealed, disguised

masquer [maske] *vt* DISSIMULER **:** to mask, to conceal, to block from view

massacrant, -crante [masakrɑ̃, -krɑ̃t] *adj* **humeur massacrante :** foul mood

massacre [masakr] *nm* **:** massacre

massacrer [masakre] *vt* **1 :** to massacre, to butcher **2** *fam* BOUSILLER **:** to botch

massage [masaʒ] *nm* **:** massage

masse [mas] *nf* **1 :** mass, body <masse d'air froide : mass of cold air> <masse d'eau : body of water> **2 :** great quantity <la (grande) masse : the majority> <une masse de renseignements : a mass of information> <en masse : en masse, in a body, in bulk> **3 :** common people <l'art de masse : popular art> <les masses : the masses, the people> **4 :** (electrical) ground <mettre à la masse : to ground> **5 :** sledgehammer **6 :** mass (in science) **7** *or* **masse d'armes :** mace

massepain [maspɛ̃] *nm* **:** marzipan

masser [mase] *vt* **1 :** to massage **2 :** to mass, to gather — **se masser** *vr* **:** to assemble, to gather together

massette [masɛt] *nf* **:** cattail

masseur, -seuse [masœr, -søz] *n* **:** massage therapist, masseur *m,* masseuse *f*

massif[1]**, -sive** [masif, -siv] *adj* **1 :** massive, solid, heavy <bois massif : solid wood> **2 :** mass <migrations massives : mass migrations>

massif[2] *nm* **1 :** clump, cluster <un massif d'arbres : a clump of trees> **2 :** massif

massivement [masivmɑ̃] *adv* **:** massively

mass media [masmedja] *nmpl* **:** mass media

massue [masy] *nf* **1 :** club, bludgeon **2 coup de massue :** staggering blow

mastic [mastik] *nm* **1 :** mastic **2 :** putty, caulk

mastication [mastikasjɔ̃] *nf* **:** chewing, mastication

mastiff [mastif] *nm* **:** mastiff

mastiquer [mastike] *vt* **1 :** to chew, to masticate **2 :** to fill in, to putty

mastoc [mastɔk] *adj* **:** hefty

mastodonte [mastɔdɔ̃t] *nm* **1 :** mastodon **2 :** huge person, hulk

mastoïde [mastɔid] *nf* **:** mastoid

masturbation [mastyrbasjɔ̃] *nf* **:** masturbation

masturber [mastyrbe] *v* **se masturber** *vr* **:** to masturbate

m'as–tu–vu [matyvy] *nmfs & pl* **:** show-off

masure [mazyr] *nf* **:** hovel

mat, mate [mat] *adj* **1 :** dull, unpolished, matte **2 :** checkmated

mât [ma] *nm* **1 :** mast **2** POTEAU **:** pole, post **3** *or* **mât de drapeau :** flagpole

matador [matadɔr] *nm* **:** matador, bullfighter

matamore [matamɔr] *nm* **:** braggart

match [matʃ] *nm* **1 :** match, game **2 match nul :** tie, draw

matelas [matla] *nm* **:** mattress <matelas pneumatique : air mattress> <matelas d'eau : waterbed>

matelasser [matlase] *vt* **1 :** to pad **2 :** to quilt

matelot [matlo] *nm* MARIN **:** sailor, seaman

mater [mate] *vt* **1** DOMPTER **:** to subdue, to curb **2 :** to checkmate

matérialiser [materjalize] *vt* CONCRÉTISER **:** to realize, to make happen — **se matérialiser** *vr* **:** to materialize

matérialisme [materjalism] *nm* **:** materialism

matérialiste[1] [materjalist] *adj* **:** materialistic, materialist

matérialiste[2] *nmf* **:** materialist

matériau [materjo] *nm, pl* **-riaux** [-rjo] **1 :** material, substance **2 matériaux** *nmpl* **:** materials (for construction, etc.) **3 matériaux** *nmpl* **:** material, documentation

matériel[1]**, -rielle** [materjɛl] *adj* **1 :** material, physical **2 :** materialistic — **matériellement** [-rjɛlmɑ̃] *adv*

matériel[2] *nm* **1 :** equipment, material(s) <matériel de pêche : fishing gear> **2 :** computer hardware

maternel, -nelle [matɛrnɛl] *adj* **1 :** maternal, motherly **2 langue maternelle :** mother tongue — **maternellement** [-nɛlmɑ̃] *adv*

maternelle *nf or* **école maternelle** [ekɔlmatɛrnɛl] **:** nursery school

materner [matɛrne] *vt* **:** to mother

maternité [matɛrnite] *nf* **1 :** maternity, motherhood **2** GROSSESSE **:** pregnancy **3 :** maternity hospital

mathématicien, -cienne [matematisjɛ̃, -sjɛn] *n* **:** mathematician

mathématique [matematik] *adj* **:** mathematical — **mathématiquement** [-tikmɑ̃] *adv*

mathématiques [matematik] *nfpl* **:** mathematics

maths *or* **math** [mat] *nfpl fam* **:** math

matière [matjɛr] *nf* **1 :** matter, substance <matière organique : organic matter> **2 :** subject, subject matter <ma meilleure matière : my best subject> <matière à discussion : matter for discussion> **3 :** material <matières premières : raw materials> **4 donner matière à :** to give cause for **5 en matière de :** as far as

matin[1] [matɛ̃] *adv* **:** early in the morning <elle déjeune très matin : she has breakfast very early>

matin[2] *nm* **:** morning <le matin : in the morning> <du matin au soir : from dawn to dusk>

matinal, -nale [matinal] *adj, mpl* **-naux** [-no] **1** : morning **2 être matinal** : to be up early, to be an early riser

matinée [matine] *nf* **1** : morning **2** : matinee

matois, -toise [matwa, -twaz] *adj* RUSÉ : sly, crafty

matou [matu] *nm* : tomcat

matraque [matrak] *nf* : (billy) club, nightstick

matraquer [matrake] *vt* **1** : to club, to bludgeon **2** : to plug (a product), to hype **3** *fam* : to rip off

matriarcal, -cale [matrijarkal] *adj, mpl* **-caux** [-ko] : matriarchal

matriarcat [matrijarka] *nm* : matriarchy

matrice [matris] *nf* **1** : womb **2** : matrix, mold

matricide [matrisid] *nm* : matricide

matricule[1] [matrikyl] *nm* : serial number

matricule[2] *nf* : register

matrimonial, -niale [matrimɔnjal] *adj, mpl* **-niaux** [-njo] : matrimonial, marriage

matrone [matrɔn] *nf* **1** : matron, matriarch **2** *Can* : female warden

maturation [matyrasjɔ̃] *nf* : maturing, maturation

mature [matyr] *adj* : mature

mâture [matyr] *nf* : masts *pl*

maturité [matyrite] *nf* : maturity

maudire [modir] *vt* : to curse, to damn

maudit, -dite [modi, -dit] *adj* : damned <cette maudite pluie! : this damned rain!>

maugréer [mogree] {89} *vi* GROGNER : to grumble

mauricien, -cienne [morisjɛ̃, -sjɛn] *adj* : Mauritian

Mauricien, -cienne *n* : Mauritian

mauritanien, -nienne [moritanjɛ̃, -njɛn] *adj* : Mauritanian

Mauritanien, -nienne *n* : Mauritanian

mausolée [mozɔle] *nm* : mausoleum

maussade [mosad] *adj* **1** MOROSE : sullen, morose **2** : dismal, gloomy

maussaderie [mosadri] *nf* : sullenness, moroseness

mauvais[1] [movɛ] *adv* : bad, poorly <il fait mauvais : the weather is bad>

mauvais[2], **-vaise** [movɛ, -vɛz] *adj* **1** : bad <ses mauvaises notes : his bad grades> **2** : wrong <un mauvais numéro : a wrong number> **3** : nasty, unpleasant **4** : rough <la mer est mauvaise : the sea is rough> **5** → **herbe 6 mauvaises rencontres** : bad company

mauve [mov] *adj & nm* : mauve

mauviette [movjɛt] *nf* : weakling

maxillaire [maksilɛr] *nm* : jawbone

maximal, -male [maksimal] *adj, mpl* **-maux** [-mo] : maximal, maximum

maxime [maksim] *nf* ADAGE : maxim, proverb

maximiser [maksimize] *vt* : to maximize

maximum[1] [maksimɔm] *adj, pl* **-mums** [-mɔm] *or* **-ma** [-ma] : maximum

maximum[2] *nm, pl* **-mums** *or* **-ma 1** : maximum **2 au ~** : as much as possible, at the very most

maya[1] [maja] *adj* : Mayan

maya[2] *nm* : Mayan (language)

Maya *nmf* : Maya

mayonnaise [majɔnɛz] *nf* : mayonnaise

mazout [mazut] *nm* : heating oil

me [mə] *pron* **1** (**m'** [m] *before a vowel or mute h*) : me, to me <elles m'ont aidé : they helped me> <il m'apparaît : it seems to me> **2** : myself, to myself <je me disais : I said to myself>

méandres [meɑ̃dr] *nmpl* : meandering, rambling

mec [mɛk] *nm fam* : guy

mécanicien, -cienne [mekanisjɛ̃, -sjɛn] *n* **1** : mechanic **2** : engineer (of a locomotive), flight engineer

mécanique[1] [mekanik] *adj* : mechanical — **mécaniquement** [-nikmɑ̃] *adv*

mécanique[2] *nf* **1** : mechanics **2** : mechanical engineering **3** : machine, mechanism

mécanisation [mekanizasjɔ̃] *nf* : mechanization

mécaniser [mekanize] *vt* : to mechanize

mécanisme [mekanism] *nm* : mechanism

mécano [mekano] *nm fam* : mechanic

mécénat [mesena] *nm* : patronage, sponsorship

mécène [mesɛn] *nm* : patron, sponsor

méchamment [meʃamɑ̃] *adv* : nastily, maliciously

méchanceté [meʃɑ̃ste] *nf* : nastiness, meanness, badness, malice

méchant[1], **-chante** [meʃɑ̃, -ʃɑ̃t] *adj* **1** : nasty, malicious **2** : naughty, bad **3** : vicious <attention chien méchant! : beware of the dog!> **4** : mediocre, second-rate **5** : bad, serious <ce n'est pas bien méchant : that's not too serious> **6** *fam* : remarkable, terrific <quelle méchante idée! : what a fantastic idea!>

méchant[2], **-chante** *n* : villain (in a book or film)

mèche [mɛʃ] *nf* **1** : wick **2** : fuse (of an explosive) **3** : lock (of hair) <mèche rebelle : cowlick> **4** : bit (of a drill)

mécompte [mekɔ̃t] *nm* DÉCEPTION : letdown, disappointment

méconnaissable [mekɔnɛsabl] *adj* : unrecognizable

méconnaissance [mekɔnɛsɑ̃s] *nf* : ignorance, lack of understanding

méconnaître [mekɔnɛtr] {7} *vt* **1** IGNORER : to be unaware of **2** MÉJUGER : to misjudge, to underestimate **3** : to disregard (rules, duties, etc.)

méconnu, -nue [mekɔny] *adj* : unrecognized

mécontent, -tente [mekɔ̃tɑ̃, -tɑ̃t] *adj* INSATISFAIT : discontented, dissatisfied

mécontentement [mekɔ̃tɑ̃tmɑ̃] *nm* INSATISFACTION : discontent, dissatisfaction

mécontenter [mekɔ̃tɑ̃te] *vt* : to annoy, to displease

mécréant[1], **-créante** [mekreɑ̃,-kreɑ̃t] *adj* : skeptical, unbelieving

mécréant[2], **-créante** *n* INFIDÈLE : unbeliever

médaille [medaj] *nf* : medal

médaillé, -lée [medaje] *n* : medalist

médaillon [medajɔ̃] *nm* **1** : medallion **2** : locket

médecin [medsɛ̃] *nm* : doctor, physician <médecin généraliste : general practitioner> <médecin légiste : medical examiner>

médecine [medsin] *nf* : medicine <médecine légale : forensic medicine>

média [medja] *nm* : medium <les médias : the (mass) media>

médian, -diane [medjɑ̃, -djan] *adj* : median

médiane *nf* : median (in mathematics)

médiateur, -trice [medjatœr, -tris] *n* : mediator, arbitrator, ombudsman

médiathèque [medjatɛk] *nf* : multimedia library

médiation [medjasjɔ̃] *nf* : mediation, arbitration

médiatique [medjatik] *adj* : media, newsworthy <geste médiatique : publicity stunt>

médiatisation [medjatizasjɔ̃] *nf* : media coverage

médiatiser [medjatize] *vt* : to cover in the media

médical, -cale [medikal] *adj, mpl* **-caux** [-ko] : medical — **médicalement** [-kalmɑ̃] *adv*

médicament [medikamɑ̃] *nm* : medicine, drug

médicamenteux, -teuse [medikamɑ̃tø, -tøz] *adj* : medicinal

médication [medikasjɔ̃] *nf* : medication, treatment

médicinal, -nale [medisinal] *adj, mpl* **-naux** [-no] : medicinal

médico–légal, -gale [medikɔlegal] *adj, mpl* **-gaux** [-go] : forensic

médiéval, -vale [medjeval] *adj, mpl* **-vaux** [-vo] : medieval

médiocre [medjɔkr] *adj* : mediocre, second-rate, ordinary

médiocrité [medjɔkrite] *nf* : mediocrity

médire [medir] {29} *vi* **∼ de** : to speak ill of

médisance [medizɑ̃s] *nf* : malicious gossip

médisant, -sante [medizɑ̃, -zɑ̃t] *adj* : slanderous, malicious

méditatif, -tive [meditatif, -tiv] *adj* PENSIF : meditative, thoughtful

méditation [meditasjɔ̃] *nf* : meditation

méditer [medite] *vt* **1** : to reflect on, to think over **2** : to have in mind <méditer un projet : to plan a project> — *vi* : to meditate

médium [medjɔm] *nm* : medium, psychic, spiritualist

méduse [medyz] *nf* : jellyfish

méduser [medyze] *vt* : to dumbfound

meeting [mitiŋ] *nm* **1** : meeting, rally **2** : meet (in sports)

méfait [mefɛ] *nm* **1** : misdeed, misdemeanour **2 méfaits** *nmpl* : ravages (of time, etc.)

méfiance [mefjɑ̃s] *nf* : distrust, suspicion

méfiant, -fiante [mefjɑ̃, -fjɑ̃t] *adj* : distrustful, suspicious

méfier [mefje] {96} *v* **se méfier** *vr* **1** : to be careful, to beware <méfiez-vous dans cette rue : be careful on this street> **2 ∼ de** : to distrust, to be wary of

mégahertz [megaɛrts] *nm* : megahertz

mégaoctet [megaɔktɛ] *nm* : megabyte

mégaphone [megafɔn] *nm* PORTE-VOIX : megaphone

mégarde [megard] *nf* **par ∼** : inadvertently

mégot [mego] *nm* : cigarette butt

meilleur[1] [mɛjœr] *adv* : better <il fait meilleur cet hiver : the weather is better this winter>

meilleur[2], **-leure** *adj* **1** (*comparative of* **bon**) : better <le meilleur des deux : the better of the two> **2** (*superlative of* **bon**) : best <le meilleur choix : the best choice> <meilleurs vœux : best wishes> **3 meilleur marché** : cheaper

meilleur[3], **-leure** *n* : best person <que le meilleur gagne : may the best man win>

meilleur[4] *nm* : better part, best bit <pour le meilleur et pour le pire : for better or for worse>

méjuger [meʒyʒe] {17} *vt* : to misjudge — *vi* **∼ de** : to underestimate — **se méjuger** *vr* : to underestimate oneself

mél [mel] *nm Bel, France* : electronic mail, E-mail

mélancolie [melɑ̃kɔli] *nf* : melancholy, gloom

mélancolique [melɑ̃kɔlik] *adj* : melancholy, gloomy

mélange [melɑ̃ʒ] *nm* **1** : mixing, blending **2** : mixture, blend

mélanger [melɑ̃ʒe] {17} *vt* **1** : to mix, to blend **2** : to mix up, to confuse — **se mélanger** *vr* : to mix, to intermingle

mélangeur [melɑ̃ʒœr] *nm Can* : blender

mélant, -lante [melɑ̃, -lɑ̃t] *adj Can* : complicated, difficult to understand

mélasse [melas] *nf* : molasses

melé, -lée [mele] *adj Can* **1** : mixed <des sentiments melés : mixed feelings> **2** *Can* : mixed-up, confused

mêlée [mele] *nf* **1** : battle, conflict, fray **2** : commotion, confusion <mêlée générale : free-for-all>

mêler [mele] *vt* : to mix — **se mêler** *vr* **1** : to mix, to mingle **2** : to meddle <mêlez-vous de vos affaires : mind your own business>

mélèze [melɛz] *nm* : larch

méli-mélo [melimelo] *nm, pl* **mélis-mélos** : hodgepodge, muddle

mélodie [melɔdi] *nf* : melody

mélodieux, -dieuse [melɔdjø, -djøz] *adj* : melodious — **mélodieusement** [-djøzmɑ̃] *adv*

mélodique [melɔdik] *adj* : melodic — **mélodiquement** [-dikmɑ̃] *adv*

mélodrame [melɔdram] *nm* : melodrama — **mélodramatique** [-dramatik] *adj*

mélomane [melɔman] *nmf* : music lover

melon [melɔ̃] *nm* **1** : melon <melon d'eau : watermelon> **2** *or* **chapeau melon** : derby (hat)

membrane [mɑ̃bran] *nf* : membrane

membre [mɑ̃br] *nm* **1** : limb, member **2** : member (of a group)

mémé [meme] *nf France fam* : grandma, granny

même[1] [mɛm] *adv* **1** : even <personne n'y va, pas même Robert : nobody's going, not even Robert> <même si : even if, even though> **2 à ~** : directly on, straight from, right against <à même la bouteille : straight from the bottle> **3 de ~** : likewise, the same **4 de même que** : just as **5 tout de même** : even so, nonetheless

même[2] *adj* **1** : same, identical <le même jour : the same day> <en même temps : at the same time> **2** (*used as an intensifier*) : very, actual <ce sont ses paroles mêmes : those were his very words> **3** → **elle-même, lui-même, eux-mêmes**

même[3] *pron* **le même, la même, les mêmes** : the same (one, ones)

mémérage [memeraʒ] *nm Can* : gossip

mémère [memɛr] *nf* **1** *fam* : grandma **2** *Can fam* : gossip

mémérer [memere] *vi Can fam* : to gossip

mémoire[1] [memwar] *nm* **1** : dissertation, thesis **2 mémoires** *nmpl* : memoirs

mémoire[2] *nf* **1** : memory <avoir de la mémoire : to have a good memory> <de mémoire : from memory> **2 mémoire vive** : random-access memory, RAM

mémorable [memɔrabl] *adj* : memorable — **mémorablement** [-rabləmɑ̃] *adv*

mémorandum [memɔrɑ̃dɔm] *nm* **1** : (diplomatic) memorandum **2** : note, memo

mémorial [memɔrjal] *nm, pl* **-riaux** [-rjo] : memorial

mémoriser [memɔrize] *vt* **1** : to memorize **2** : to store (data)

menaçant, -çante [mənasɑ̃, -sɑ̃t] *adj* : threatening, menacing, ominous

menace [mənas] *nf* : threat <menaces en l'air : idle threats>

menacer [mənase] {6} *vt* **1** : to threaten **2** : to pose a threat to <être menacé : to be at risk> — *vi* : to threaten <la pluie menace : it looks like rain>

ménage [menaʒ] *nm* **1** : household, family <un ménage de quatre personnes : a household of four people> **2** : married couple <heureux en ménage : happily married> **3** : housework, housekeeping <faire le ménage : to do the housework> **4 faire bon ménage avec** : to get along well with

ménagement [menaʒmɑ̃] *nm* : consideration, thoughtfulness <avec ménagement : gently, tactfully> <sans ménagement : bluntly>

ménager[1] [menaʒe] {17} *vt* **1** ÉPARGNER : to save <ménager son argent : to save one's money> **2** : to use carefully, to handle with care **3** : to treat considerately **4** : to arrange, to organize — **se ménager** *vr* : to take it easy

ménager[2], **-gère** [menaʒe, -ʒɛr] *adj* : household, domestic <travaux ménagers : housework>

ménagère [menaʒɛr] *nf* : housewife

ménagerie [menaʒri] *nf* : menagerie

mendiant, -diante [mɑ̃djɑ̃, -djɑ̃t] *n* : beggar, mendicant

mendicité [mɑ̃disite] *nf* : begging

mendier [mɑ̃dje] {96} *v* : to beg

mené [məne] *nm Can* : minnow

menées [məne] *nfpl* : scheming, intrigues

mener [məne] {52} *vt* **1** EMMENER : to take, to bring <mener promener un chien : to take a dog for a walk> **2** : to lead, to be at the head of **3** DIRIGER : to conduct, to run **4** : to carry out <mener à bien : to complete successfully, to see (something) through>

ménestrel [menɛstrɛl] *nm* : minstrel

meneur, -neuse [mənœr, -nøz] *n* **1** : leader <un meneur d'hommes : a born leader> **2** : ringleader **3 meneuse de claque** *Can* : cheerleader

méninges [menɛ̃ʒ] *nfpl fam* : brains <se creuser les méninges : to rack one's brains>

méningite [menɛ̃ʒit] *nf* : meningitis

ménopause [menɔpoz] *nf* : menopause

menotte [mənɔt] *nf* **1** : little hand **2 menottes** *nfpl* : handcuffs <passer les menottes à qqn : to handcuff s.o.>

mensonge [mɑ̃sɔ̃ʒ] *nm* **1** : lie **2 le mensonge** : lying

mensonger, -gère [mɑ̃sɔ̃ʒe, -ʒɛr] *adj* **1** FAUX : false **2** TROMPEUR : misleading

menstruation [mɑ̃stryasjɔ̃] *nf* RÈGLES : menstruation, period

menstruel, -struelle [mɑ̃stryɛl] *adj* : menstrual

mensualité [mɑ̃sɥalite] *nf* : monthly payment

mensuel[1], -suelle [mɑ̃sɥɛl] *adj* : monthly — **mensuellement** [-sɥɛlmɑ] *adv*

mensuel[2] *nm* : monthly (magazine)

mensurations [mɑ̃syrasjɔ̃] *nfpl* : measurements

mental, -tale [mɑ̃tal] *adj, mpl* **mentaux** [-to] : mental — **mentalement** [-talmɑ̃] *adv*

mentalité [mɑ̃talite] *nf* : mentality

menterie [mɑ̃tri] *nf Can fam* : lie, fib

menteur[1], -teuse [mɑ̃tœr, -tøz] *adj* : untruthful, false

menteur[2], -teuse *n* : liar

menthe [mɑ̃t] *nf* **1** : mint **2 menthe poivrée** : peppermint **3 menthe verte** : spearmint

menthol [mɑ̃tɔl] *nm* : menthol

mentholé, -lée [mɑ̃tɔle] *adj* : mentholated

mention [mɑ̃sjɔ̃] *nf* **1** : mention <faire mention de : to mention> **2** : note, comment <porter la mention «secret» : to be labeled "secret">

mentionner [mɑ̃sjɔne] *vt* : to mention

mentir [mɑ̃tir] {82} *vi* : to lie

menton [mɑ̃tɔ̃] *nm* : chin

menu[1] [məny] *adv* : finely, small <oignons coupés menu : finely chopped onions>

menu[2], -nue *adj* **1** PETIT : small, tiny, slender **2** : minor, trifling

menu[3] [məny] *nm* **1** : menu **2 par le menu** : in minute detail

menuet [mənɥɛ] *nm* : minuet

menuiserie [mənɥizri] *nf* : woodworking, carpentry

menuisier [mənɥizje] *nm* : woodworker, carpenter

méprendre [meprɑ̃dr] {70} *v* **se méprendre** *vr* **~ sur** : to be mistaken about

mépris [mepri] *nm* **1** DÉDAIN : contempt, scorn **2 au mépris de** : regardless of, in defiance of

méprisable [meprizabl] *adj* VIL : despicable, contemptible

méprisant, -sante [meprizɑ̃, -zɑ̃t] *adj* : contemptuous, scornful

méprise [mepriz] *nf* **1** ERREUR : mistake, error **2** MALENTENDU : misunderstanding

mépriser [meprize] *vt* : to despise, to scorn

mer [mɛr] *nf* **1** : sea <en mer : at sea> <niveau de la mer : sea level> <prendre la mer : to put to sea> **2** MARÉE : tide <mer haute : high tide> <mer basse : low tide>

mercantile [mɛrkɑ̃til] *adj* **1** : mercenary, greedy **2** : mercantile, commercial

mercenaire [mɛrsənɛr] *adj & nmf* : mercenary

mercerie [mɛrsəri] *nf* **1** : notions *pl* **2** : notions store

merci[1] [mɛrsi] *nm* : thank-you <mille mercis : thank you so much>

merci[2] *nf* **1** : mercy <à la merci de : at the mercy of> **2 sans ~** : merciless

merci[3] *interj* : thank you!, thanks! <merci beaucoup! *or* merci bien! : thank you very much!>

mercredi [mɛrkrədi] *nm* **1** : Wednesday **2 le mercredi des Cendres** : Ash Wednesday

mercure [mɛrkyr] *nm* : mercury

Mercure *nf* : Mercury (planet)

mère [mɛr] *nf* **1** : mother <mère célibataire : single mother> **2** : Mother (in religion)

méridien [meridjɛ̃] *nm* : meridian

méridional, -nale [meridjɔnal] *adj, mpl* **-naux** [-no] : southern

meringue [mərɛ̃g] *nf* : meringue

mérinos [merinos] *nm* : merino

merise [məriz] *nf* : wild cherry

méritant, -tante [meritɑ̃, -tɑ̃t] *adj* : deserving, meritorious

mérite [merit] *nm* **1** : merit, credit <le mérite lui revient : the credit goes to him> **2** VALEUR : merit, quality <ce film a ses mérites : this film has its merits>

mériter [merite] *vt* : to deserve, to merit

méritoire [meritwar] *adj* : commendable, praiseworthy

merlan [mɛrlɑ̃] *nm* : whiting

merle [mɛrl] *nm* : blackbird

merlu *or* **merlus** [mɛrly] *nm* : hake

mérou [meru] *nm* : grouper (fish)

merveille [mɛrvɛj] *nf* **1** : wonder, marvel **2 à ~** : wonderfully, excellently

merveilleux, -leuse [mɛrvɛjø, -jøz] *adj* : wonderful, marvelous — **merveilleusement** [-jøzmɑ̃] *adv*

mes → **mon**

mésange [mezɑ̃ʒ] *nf* : titmouse

mésaventure [mezavɑ̃tyr] *nf* : misfortune, mishap

mesdames → **madame**

mesdemoiselles → **mademoiselle**

mésentente [mezɑ̃tɑ̃t] *nf* DÉSACCORD : misunderstanding, disagreement

mésestimer [mezɛstime] *vt* SOUS-ESTIMER : to underestimate, to underrate

mesquin, -quine [mɛskɛ̃, -kin] *adj* **1** : mean, petty **2** : cheap, stingy — **mesquinement** [-kinmɑ̃] *adv*

mesquinerie [mɛskinri] *nf* **1** PETITESSE : pettiness **2** AVARICE : meanness, stinginess

mess [mɛs] *nm* : mess

message [mɛsaʒ] *nm* **1** : message **2 message publicitaire** : commercial

messager, -gère [mɛsaʒe, -ʒɛr] *n* : messenger

messagerie [mɛsaʒri] *nf* **1** : parcel delivery service **2 messagerie électronique** : electronic mail

messe [mɛs] *nf* : Mass (in religion)

messeigneurs [mesɛɲœr] → **monseigneur**

messie [mɛsi] *nm* **le Messie** : the Messiah

messieurs → **monsieur**

mesurable [məzyrabl] *adj* : measurable

mesurage [məzyraʒ] *nm* : measuring, measurement

mesure [məzyr] *nf* **1** : measurement, measuring **2** : measure <unité de mesure : unit of measure> <pour faire bonne mesure : for good measure> **3** : measure, step <mesures draconiennes : drastic measures> **4** RETENUE : moderation, restraint **5** : degree, limit <dans la mesure où : insofar as> **6 à la mesure de** : worthy of **7 à mesure que** : as **8 outre ~** : excessively **9 sur ~** : made-to-order

mesuré, -rée [məzyre] *adj* : measured, restrained

mesurer [məzyre] *vt* **1** : to measure, to take measurements of **2** : to weigh, to assess <mesurer ses paroles : to measure one's words> **3** : to limit <le temps lui est mesuré : his time is limited> **4** : to adapt, to gear — **se mesurer** *vr* **1** : to be measurable **2 ~ avec** : to pit oneself against

métabolique [metabɔlik] *adj* : metabolic

métaboliser [metabɔlize] *vt* : to metabolize

métabolisme [metabɔlism] *nm* : metabolism

métal [metal] *nm, pl* **métaux** [meto] : metal

métallique [metalik] *adj* : metallic

métallurgie [metalyrʒi] *nf* : metallurgy

métallurgique [metalyrʒik] *adj* : metallurgical

métallurgiste [metalyrʒist] *nm* : metallurgist, metalworker

métamorphose [metamɔrfoz] *nf* : metamorphosis

métaphore [metafɔr] *nf* : metaphor

métaphorique [metafɔrik] *adj* : metaphoric, metaphorical — **métaphoriquement** [-rikmɑ̃] *adv*

métaphysique[1] [metafizik] *adj* : metaphysical

métaphysique[2] *nf* : metaphysics

métayer, -tayère [meteje, -tejɛr] *n* : sharecropper

météo [meteo] *nf* : weather forecast

météore [meteɔr] *nm* : meteor

météorique [meteɔrik] *adj* : meteoric

météorite [meteɔrit] *nmf* : meteorite

météorologie [meteɔrɔlɔʒi] *nf* : meteorology

météorologique [meteɔrɔlɔʒik] *adj* : meteorological, weather <prévisions météorologiques : weather forecast>

météorologiste [meteɔrɔlɔʒist] *nmf* : meteorologist

méthane [metan] *nm* : methane

méthode [metɔd] *nf* **1** : method, system, way <avec méthode : methodically> **2** : manual, primer

méthodique [metɔdik] *adj* : methodical — **méthodiquement** [-dikmɑ̃] *adv*

méticuleux, -leuse [metikylø, -løz] *adj* : meticulous — **méticuleusement** [-løzmɑ̃] *adv*

métier [metje] *nm* **1** : job, profession, occupation <gens du métier : professionals, experts> **2** : experience, skill <manquer de métier : to lack experience> **3** *or* **métier à tisser** : loom

métis, -tisse [metis] *adj & n* : half-breed, half-caste

métrage [metraʒ] *nm* **1** : length (of an object) **2** : footage, length (of a film) <court métrage : short film> <long métrage : feature film>

mètre [mɛtr] *nm* **1** : meter <mètre carré : square meter> **2** : metric ruler <mètre ruban : tape measure>

métrer [metre] {87} *vt* : to measure (in meters)

métrique [metrik] *adj* : metric

métro [metro] *nm* : subway, metro

métronome [metrɔnɔm] *nm* : metronome

métropole [metrɔpɔl] *nf* : city, metropolis

métropolitain, -taine [metrɔpɔlitɛ̃, -tɛn] *adj* : metropolitan

mets [mɛ] *nm* PLAT : dish <c'est mon mets préféré : it's my favorite dish>

mettable [mɛtabl] *adj* PORTABLE : wearable

metteur [mɛtœr] *nm* **metteur en scène** : producer, director

mettre [mɛtr] {53} *vt* **1** PLACER : to put, to place <mets la plante par terre : put the plant on the floor> **2** : to put on, to wear <mets tes chaussures : put your shoes on> <elle met des jupes longues : she wears long skirts> **3** AJOUTER : to add (in), to put in **4** ÉCRIRE : to put down, to put in writing **5** INSTALLER : to put in, to install **6** : to prepare, to arrange <mettre la table : to set the table> **7** : to take (time) <elle a mis trois heures à le considérer : she took three hours to consider it> **8** : to turn on, to switch on **9** *fam* : to suppose <mettons qu'il n'était pas content : let's say he wasn't very happy> **10 mettre à la poste** : to mail **11 mettre au monde** : to give birth to **12 mettre au point** : to develop — **se mettre** *vr* **1** : to become, to get <il s'est mis en colère : he got angry> **2** : to put on, to wear <je n'ai

rien à me mettre : I have nothing to wear> **3 ∼ à** : to start (doing something) <se mettre au travail : to get to work> **4 se mettre à table** : to sit down at the table

meuble[1] [mœbl] *adj* **1** : easily worked, friable **2 biens meubles** : movable goods, personal assets

meuble[2] *nm* **1** : piece of furniture **2 meubles** *nmpl* : furniture <meubles de bureau : office furniture>

meublé, -blée [mœble] *adj* : furnished

meubler [mœble] *vt* **1** : to furnish **2** REMPLIR : to occupy, to fill up <il meuble bien son temps : he fills up his time well> — **se meubler** *vr* : to acquire furniture, to furnish one's home

meuglement [møgləmɑ̃] *nm* : mooing, lowing

meugler [møgle] *vi* : to moo, to low

meule [møl] *nf* **1** : millstone, grindstone **2** : round (of cheese) **3 meule de foin** : haystack

meuler [møle] *vt* : to grind down

meunier, -nière [mønje, -njɛr] *n* : miller

meure [mør], **meurt** [mœr], *etc.* → **mourir**

meurtre [mœrtr] *nm* : murder

meurtrier[1], **-trière** [mœrtrije, -trijɛr] *adj* **1** : deadly, lethal **2** : murderous, dangerous

meurtrier[2], **-trière** *n* ASSASSIN : murderer, murderess *f*

meurtrir [mœrtrir] *vt* **1** : to bruise **2** BLESSER : to wound, to hurt (one's feelings, etc.)

meurtrissure [mœrtrisyr] *nf* : bruise

meut [mœ], **meuve** [møv], *etc.* → **mouvoir**

meute [møt] *nf* **1** : pack (of hounds) **2** : horde, crowd

mévente [mevɑ̃t] *nf* : slump, drop (in sales)

mexicain, -caine [meksikɛ̃, -kɛn] *adj* : Mexican

Mexicain, -caine *n* : Mexican

mezzanine [mɛdzanin] *nf* : mezzanine

miaou [mjau] *nm* : meow

miasme [mjasm] *nm* : miasma

miauler [mjole] *vi* : to meow

mi–bas [miba] *nms & pl* : kneesock

mica [mika] *nm* : mica

miche [miʃ] *nf* : round loaf of bread

mi–chemin [miʃmɛ̃] *adv* **à ∼** : halfway, midway

mi–clos, -close [miklo, -kloz] *adj* : half-closed

mi–côte [mikot] *adv* **à ∼** : halfway up (or down)

micro [mikro] *nm* : mike, microphone

microbe [mikrɔb] *nm* : germ, microbe

microbiologie [mikrɔbjɔlɔʒi] *nf* : microbiology

microcosme [mikrɔkɔsm] *nm* : microcosm

microfiche [mikrɔfiʃ] *nf* : microfiche

microfilm [mikrɔfilm] *nm* : microfilm

micromètre [mikrɔmɛtr] *nm* : micrometer

micro–onde [mikrɔɔ̃d] *nf* : microwave

micro–ondes [mikrɔɔ̃d] *nms & pl* : microwave oven

micro–ordinateur [mikrɔɔrdinatœr] *nm* : microcomputer

micro–organisme [mikrɔɔrganism] *nm* : microorganism

microphone [mikrɔfɔn] *nm* : microphone

microprocesseur [mikrɔprɔsesœr] *nm* : microprocessor

microscope [mikrɔskɔp] *nm* : microscope

microscopie [mikrɔskɔpi] *nf* : microscopy

microscopique [mikrɔskɔpik] *adj* : microscopic

microsillon [mikrɔsijɔ̃] *nm* : long-playing record, LP

midi [midi] *nm* **1** : midday, noon **2** : lunchtime **3** : south

mie [mi] *nf* : inside, soft part (of a loaf of bread)

miel [mjɛl] *nm* : honey

mielleux, -leuse [mjɛlø, -løz] *adj* DOUCEREUX : sugary, saccharine

mien,[1] **mienne** [mjɛ̃, mjɛn] *adj* : mine, my own <cette devise, que j'ai faite mienne : this motto that I have adopted> <une mienne amie : a friend of mine>

mien,[2] **mienne** *pron* **1 le mien, la mienne, les miens, les miennes** : mine <ce n'est pas le mien : it's not mine> **2 les miens** : my family

miette [mjɛt] *nf* **1** : crumb **2** : bit, scrap <en miettes : in pieces>

mieux[1] [mjø] *adv* **1** (*comparative of* **bien**) : better <il va mieux : he's feeling better> **2 le mieux, la mieux, les mieux** (*superlative of* **bien**) : the best <le mieux payé : the best paid> <c'est ici que je travaille le mieux : here's where I work best> **3 être mieux de** *Can* : to be better off to <vous seriez mieux de partir : it would be in your best interest to leave>

mieux[2] *adj* **1** (*comparative of* **bien**) : better <ses notes sont mieux cette année : her grades are better this year> **2 le mieux, la mieux, les mieux** (*superlative of* **bien**) : the best <le mieux de la ville : the best in town>

mieux[3] *nm* **1** : best <faire de son mieux : to do one's best> <pour le mieux : for the best> **2** : improvement <il y a du mieux : there's some improvement>

mieux–être [mjøzɛtr] *nm* : improved state, better quality of life

mièvre [mjɛvr] *adj* **1** : insipid **2** : mawkish, soppy

mièvrerie [mjɛvrəri] *nf* : sentimentality, mush

mignon, -gnonne [miɲɔ̃, -ɲɔn] *adj* **1** : sweet, cute **2** GENTIL : nice, kind

migraine [migrɛn] *nf* : headache, migraine

migrant, -grante [migrɑ̃, -grɑ̃t] *adj & n* : migrant

migrateur, -trice [migratœr, -tris] *adj* : migratory <oiseaux migrateurs : migratory birds>

migration [migrasjɔ̃] *nf* : migration

migrer [migre] *vi* : to migrate

mijoter [miʒɔte] *vt* **1** : to simmer **2** MANIGANCER : to plot, to cook up — *vi* : to simmer, to stew

mil [mil] → **mille**

milan [milɑ̃] *nm* : kite (bird)

mildiou [mildju] *nm* : mildew

mile [majl] *nm* MILLE : mile

milice [milis] *nf* : militia

milicien, -cienne [milisjɛ̃, -sjɛn] *n* : militiaman *m*, member of a militia

milieu [miljø] *nm, pl* **milieux 1** : middle <au beau milieu de la table : right in the middle of the table> <le milieu du jour : midday, noon> **2** : middle ground <un juste milieu : a happy medium> **3** : milieu, environment **4 au milieu de** : among, in the midst of **5 le milieu** : the underworld

militaire[1] [militɛr] *adj* : military — **militairement** [-tɛrmɑ̃] *adv*

militaire[2] *nm* SOLDAT : soldier, serviceman

militant,[1] **-tante** [militɑ̃, -tɑ̃t] *adj* : militant

militant,[2] **-tante** *n* : militant, activist

militarisme [militarism] *nm* : militarism

militariste [militarist] *adj* : militaristic

millage [milaʒ] *nm Can* : mileage (of a motor vehicle)

mille[1] [mil] *adj* : a thousand, one thousand <mille lumières : a thousand lights>

mille[2] *nm* **1** : mile **2 mille marin** : (nautical) knot

mille[3] *nms & pl* **1** : a thousand, one thousand **2** : bull's eye <taper dans le mille : to hit the bull's eye>

millénaire[1] [milenɛr] *adj* **1** : thousand-year-old **2** : age-old, ancient

millénaire[2] *nm* : millennium

mille–pattes [milpat] *nms & pl* **1** : centipede **2** : millipede

millésime [milezim] *nm* **1** : year of manufacture **2** : vintage year

millésimé, -mée [milezime] *adj* : vintage

millet [mijɛ] *nm* : millet

milliard [miljar] *nm* : billion

milliardaire [miljardɛr] *nmf* : billionaire

millième [miljɛm] *adj & nmf & nm* : thousandth

millier [milje] *nm* : thousand <par milliers : by the thousands>

milligramme [miligram] *nm* : milligram

millilitre [mililitr] *nm* : milliliter

millimètre [milimɛtr] *nm* : millimeter

million [miljɔ̃] *nm* : million

millionième [miljɔnjɛm] *adj & nmf & nm* : millionth

millionnaire [miljɔnɛr] *nmf* : millionaire

mime[1] [mim] *nmf* : mime (performer)

mime[2] *nm* : mime, miming

mimer [mime] *vt* **1** : to mime **2** : to mimic

mimétisme [mimetism] *nm* : mimicry (in biology)

mimique [mimik] *nf* **1** GRIMACE : facial expression, (funny) face **2** : gesticulations *pl*, sign language

minable [minabl] *adj* **1** MISÉRABLE : shabby, miserable **2** *fam* : pitiful, pathetic, measly <un film minable : a third-rate movie>

minaret [minarɛ] *nm* : minaret

minauder [minode] *vi* : to simper, to mince

mince [mɛ̃s] *adj* **1** : thin **2** : slim, slender **3** NÉGLIGEABLE : meager, scanty

minceur [mɛ̃sœr] *nf* : thinness, slenderness

mine [min] *nf* **1** : expression, appearance, demeanor <il avait bonne mine : he looked well> <je faisais mine de rien : I was acting as if nothing had happened> **2** : mine <mine de houille : coal mine> **3** : lead, graphite

miner [mine] *vt* **1** : to mine, to set mines in **2** : to erode, to eat away at **3** : to undermine

minerai [minrɛ] *nm* : ore

minéral[1], **-rale** [mineral] *adj, mpl* **-raux** [-ro] : mineral

minéral[2] *nm* : mineral

minéralogie [mineralɔʒi] *nf* : mineralogy — **minéralogiste** [-lɔʒist] *nmf*

minéralogique [mineralɔʒik] *adj* : mineralogical

minet, -nette [minɛ, -nɛt] *n* : kitty, pussy

mineur[1], **-neure** [minœr] *adj* : minor

mineur[2], **-neure** *nmf* : minor, underage person

mineur[3] *nm* : miner

miniature [minjatyr] *adj & nf* : miniature

minibus [minibys] *nm* : minibus

minier, -nière [minje, -njɛr] *adj* : mining

minijupe [miniʒyp] *nf* : miniskirt

minimal, -male [minimal] *adj, mpl* **-maux** [-mo] : minimal, minimum

minime [minim] *adj* : minimal, negligible, trifling

minimiser [minimize] *vt* : to minimize, to play down

minimum[1] [minimɔm] *adj, pl* **-mums** [-mɔm] *or* **-ma** [-ma] : minimum

minimum[2] *nm, pl* **-mums** *or* **-ma 1** : minimum <au minimum : at the least> **2 minimum vital** : living wage

mini–ordinateur [miniɔrdinatœr] *nm* : minicomputer

ministère [ministɛr] *nm* **1** : ministry, department (of government) <ministère des Relations extérieures : State Department> **2** : government, cabinet

ministériel, -rielle [ministerjɛl] *adj* : ministerial, governmental

ministre [ministr] *nm* : minister, secretary <premier ministre : prime minister> <le ministre du Commerce : the Secretary of Commerce>

minois [minwa] *nms & pl* : sweet little face

minoritaire [minɔritɛr] *adj* : minority

minorité [minɔrite] *nf* : minority

minoterie [minɔtri] *nf* : flour mill

minotier [minɔtje] *nm* MEUNIER : miller

minou [minu] *nm fam* **1** : kitty, pussy **2** : honey, sweetie

minoucher [minuʃe] *vt Can fam* : to caress, to pat

minoune [minun] *nf Can fam* **1** : (female) kitty **2** : honey, sweetie

minuit [minɥi] *nm* : midnight

minuscule[1] [minyskyl] *adj* : minute, tiny

minuscule[2] *nf* : small (lowercase) letter

minutage [minytaʒ] *nm* : timing

minute [minyt] *nf* **1** : minute **2 minute!** *fam* : just a minute!, hang on!

minuter [minyte] *vt* : to time

minuteur [minytœr] *nm* : timer

minuterie [minytri] *nf* : timer

minutie [minysi] *nf* : meticulousness <avec minutie : meticulously>

minutieux, -tieuse [minysjø, -sjøz] *adj* **1** MÉTICULEUX : meticulous **2** : detailed <travail minutieux : detailed work> — **minutieusement** [-sjøzmɑ̃] *adv*

miracle [mirakl] *nm* : miracle <par miracle : miraculously>

miraculeux, -leuse [mirakylø, -løz] *adj* : miraculous — **miraculeusement** [-løzmɑ̃] *adv*

mirador [miradɔr] *nm* : watchtower

mirage [miraʒ] *nm* : mirage

mire [mir] *nf* **1** : sight <ligne de mire : line of sight> **2 point de mire** : target, focal point <être le point de mire : to be the focus of attention>

mirifique [mirifik] *adj* : amazing, fabulous

mirobolant, -lante [mirɔbɔlɑ̃, -lɑ̃t] *adj fam* : fabulous, fantastic

miroir [mirwar] *nm* : mirror

miroitement [mirwatmɑ̃] *nm* : sparkling, shimmering

miroiter [mirwate] *vi* **1** BRILLER : to sparkle, to shimmer, to glint **2 faire miroiter** : to paint in glowing colors

mis[1] [mi] *pp* → **mettre**

mis[2], **mise** [mi, miz] *adj* : clad <bien mis : well dressed>

misanthrope[1] [mizɑ̃trɔp] *adj* : misanthropic

misanthrope[2] *nmf* : misanthrope

misanthropie [mizɑ̃trɔpi] *nf* : misanthropy

mise [miz] *nf* **1** : putting, placing <mise en marche : starting up> <mise en scène : production (in theater)> <mise à jour : updating> **2** : stake (in games of chance) **3** : dress, attire **4 mise de fonds** : investment

miser [mize] *vt* : to bet — *vi* **1 ~ sur** : to bet on **2 ~ sur** : to count on

misérable[1] [mizerabl] *adj* **1** PITOYABLE : wretched, pitiful **2** INSIGNIFIANT : meager, paltry **3** PAUVRE : poverty-stricken

misérable[2] *nmf* **1** : wretch, pauper **2** : scoundrel

misérablement [mizerabləmɑ̃] *adv* **1** : miserably, wretchedly **2** : in poverty

misère [mizɛr] *nf* **1** : poverty, destitution **2** : misery, misfortune **3** : pittance, paltry sum

miséreux, -reuse [mizerø, -røz] *adj* : destitute, poverty-stricken

miséricorde [mizerikɔrd] *nf* : mercy, forgiveness

miséricordieux, -dieuse [mizerikɔrdjø, -djøz] *adj* : merciful, forgiving

misogyne [mizɔʒin] *nmf* : misogynist

missel [misɛl] *nm* : missal

missile [misil] *nm* : missile

mission [misjɔ̃] *nf* : mission

missionnaire [misjɔnɛr] *adj & nmf* : missionary

missive [misiv] *nf* : missive, letter

mitaine [mitɛn] *nf Can, Swiss* : mitten

mite [mit] *nf* : clothes moth

mi–temps[1] [mitɑ̃] *nms & pl* : part-time job <travailler à mi-temps : to work part-time>

mi–temps[2] *nfs & pl* : halftime (in sports)

miteux, -teuse [mitø, -tøz] *adj* : seedy, dingy, shabby

mitigation [mitigasjɔ̃] *nf* : mitigation

mitigé, -gée [mitiʒe] *adj* **1** : lukewarm, reserved **2** : mixed <sentiments mitigés : mixed feelings>

mitonner [mitɔne] *vt* **1** : to cook slowly, to simmer **2** : to prepare lovingly — **se mitonner** *vr* : to cook up for oneself

mitose [mitoz] *nf* : mitosis

mitoyen, mitoyenne [mitwajɛ̃, -jɛn] *adj* : common, dividing <mur mitoyen : dividing wall>

mitraille [mitraj] *nf* : hail of bullets

mitrailler [mitraje] *vt* : to machine-gun

mitraillette [mitrajɛt] *nf* : submachine gun

mitrailleuse [mitrajøz] *nf* : machine gun

mitre [mitr] *nf* : miter

mi–voix [mivwa] *nf* **à ~** : in a low voice

mixage [miksaʒ] *nm* : sound mixing

mixer [miksɛr] *or* **mixeur** [miksœr] *nm* : (food) mixer

mixette [miksɛt] *nf Can* : (small) mixer
mixité [miksite] *nf* : coeducation
mixte [mikst] *adj* **1** : mixed, joint **2** : coeducational
mixture [mikstyr] *nf* **1** : mixture **2** : concoction
mnémotechnique [mnemɔtɛknik] *adj* : mnemonic
mobile[1] [mɔbil] *adj* **1** : movable, removable <feuilles mobiles : loose-leaf paper> **2** : changeable <échelle mobile : sliding scale> **3** : mobile, moving (of populations, etc.) **4** : mobile, changing <un visage mobile : mobile features>
mobile[2] *n* : mobile
mobilier[1], **-lière** [mɔbilje, -ljɛr] *adj* **1** : movable <biens mobiliers : movable property> **2 valeurs mobilières** : securities, stocks and bonds
mobilier[2] *nm* MEUBLES : furniture
mobilisation [mɔbilizasjɔ̃] *nf* : mobilization
mobiliser [mɔbilize] *vt* : to mobilize
mobilité [mɔbilite] *nf* : mobility
mocassin [mɔkasɛ̃] *nm* : moccasin
moche [mɔʃ] *adj fam* **1** : ugly, awful **2** : rotten, despicable
modalité [mɔdalite] *nf* : form, mode <modalités de paiement : terms of payment>
mode[1] [mɔd] *nm* **1** : way, mode, method <mode de vie : way of life> <mode d'emploi : directions for use> **2** : mood (in grammar) **3** : mode (in computer science, music, philosophy)
mode[2] [mɔd] *nf* **1** : fashion <jupe à la mode : fashionable skirt> **2** : fashion industry
modèle[1] [mɔdɛl] *adj* : model, exemplary
modèle[2] *nm* **1** : model, pattern, example <prendre modèle sur : to take as a model> <servir de modèle : to serve as an example> <un modèle du bon élève : a model student> **2** : model, prototype <modèle réduit : small-scale model> **3** : (artist's) model, subject, sitter **4** : model, mannequin (in fashion) **5** : model (in commerce) <le dernier modèle : the latest model>
modeler [mɔdle] {20} *vt* **1** : to mold **2** : to model, to shape — **se modeler** *vr* **~ sur** : to model oneself on
modéliste [mɔdelist] *nmf* **1** : (clothing) designer **2** : model maker
modem [mɔdɛm] *nm* : modem
modérateur[1], **-trice** [mɔderatœr, -tris] *adj* : moderating, restraining
modérateur[2], **-trice** *n* : moderator, mediator
modération [mɔderasjɔ̃] *nf* MESURE : moderation, restraint
modéré, -rée [mɔdere] *adj* : moderate — **modérément** [-remɑ̃] *adv*
modérer [mɔdere] {87} *vt* : to moderate, to restrain, to curb — **se modérer** *vr* : to restrain oneself
moderne[1] [mɔdɛrn] *adj* : modern
moderne[2] *nm* : modern style
moderniser [mɔdɛrnize] *vt* : to modernize — **modernisation** [-nizasjɔ̃] *nf*
modernité [mɔdɛrnite] *nf* : modernity
modeste [mɔdɛst] *adj* **1** HUMBLE : modest, humble, simple <d'origine modeste : of humble origin> **2** MODIQUE : modest, small <un modeste salaire : a modest salary> **3** : modest, unpretentious, unassuming — **modestement** [-dɛstəmɑ̃] *adv*
modestie [mɔdɛsti] *nf* : modesty
modificateur [mɔdifikatœr, -tris] *nm* : modifier
modification [mɔdifikasjɔ̃] *nf* : modification
modifier [mɔdifje] {96} *vt* **1** : to modify, to alter **2** : to modify (in grammar) — **se modifier** *vr* : to change
modique [mɔdik] *adj* : modest <une somme modique : a modest sum> — **modiquement** [-dikmɑ̃] *adv*
modiste [mɔdist] *nmf* : milliner
modulaire [mɔdylɛr] *adj* : modular
modulation [mɔdylasjɔ̃] *nf* : modulation <modulation de fréquence : frequency modulation, FM>
module [mɔdyl] *nm* : module
moduler [mɔdyle] *vt* : to modulate
moelle [mwal] *nf* **1** : marrow (of bone), pith (of plants) **2 jusqu'à la moelle** : to the core **3 moelle épinière** : spinal cord
moelleux[1], **-leuse** [mwalø, -løz] *adj* **1** DOUX : soft <coussins moelleux : soft cushions> **2** : moist <gateau moelleux : moist cake> **3** : mellow, smooth
moelleux[2] *nm* : softness, mellowness
mœurs [mœr(s)] *nfpl* **1** CONDUITE : manners, morals **2** USAGES : customs, habits <c'est entré dans les mœurs : it's common practice> **3** : behavior (in zoology)
mohair [mɔɛr] *nm* : mohair
moi[1] [mwa] *nm* **le moi** : the self, the ego
moi[2] *pron* **1** : I <elle a depensé plus que moi : she spent more than I did> **2** : me <aide-moi : help me> <plus jeune que moi : younger than me> <moi, j'aime les chats : as for me, I like cats> **3 à ~** : mine <c'est à moi : it's mine> <c'est à moi de jouer : it's my turn to play>
moignon [mwaɲɔ̃] *nm* : stump (of a limb)
moi–même [mwamɛm] *pron* : myself
moindre [mwɛ̃dr] *adj* **1** : lesser, smaller, lower <à un moindre degré : to a lesser degree> **2 le moindre, la moindre** : the lesser, the least, the slightest <le moindre de deux maux : the lesser of two evils> <sans la moindre

hésitation : without a moment's hesitation>
moindrement [mwɛ̃drəmɑ̃] *adv Can* : <s'ils sont le moindrement intéressés : if they are the least bit interested>
moine [mwan] *nm* : monk
moineau [mwano] *nm, pl* **moineaux** : sparrow
moins[1] [mwɛ̃] *adv* **1** : less <moins grand que son frère : less tall than his brother> <moins je travaille, moins j'ai envie de travailler : the less I work, the less I feel like working> <de moins en moins : less and less> **2 le moins** : least, the least <le moins souvent : least often> <il est le moins fort : he's the least strong, he's the weakest (one)> **3 ~ de** : less than, fewer <moins de gens : fewer people> <pas moins de : no less than> **4 à moins de** : short of, barring **5 à moins que** : unless **6 en ~** : missing <une dent en moins : a missing tooth>
moins[2] *nm* **1** : minus (sign) **2 au ~** *or* **du ~** : at (the) least **3 pour le moins** *or* **tout le moins** : at (the very) least
moins[3] *prep* **1** : minus <sept moins deux font cinq : seven minus two equals five> **2** (*in expressions of time*) : to, of <il est cinq heures moins dix : it's ten to five> **3** (*in expressions of temperature*) : below <il fait moins cinq : it's five below zero, it's minus five>
mois [mwa] *nm* **1** : month **2** *France* : monthly salary **3** *Can* : monthly payment
moisi[1], **-sie** [mwazi] *adj* : moldy
moisi[2] *nm* : mold, mildew
moisir [mwazir] *vi* **1** : to become moldy, to mildew **2** *fam* : to stagnate, to rot <moisir en prison : to rot in jail>
moisissure [mwazisyr] *nf* : mold, mildew
moisson [mwasɔ̃] *nf* **1** : harvest, crop **2** : abundance <une moisson de renseignements : a wealth of information>
moissonner [mwasɔne] *vt* : to harvest, to reap
moissonneuse [mwasɔnøz] *nf* : harvester (machine)
moissonneuse–batteuse [mwasɔnøzbatøz] *nf, pl* **moissonneuses–batteuses** : combine (harvester)
moite [mwat] *adj* **1** : sweaty, sticky **2** : muggy
moitié [mwatje] *nf* **1** : half <la moitié du temps : half the time> <réduire de moitié : to reduce by half> **2 à ~** : half <à moitié rempli : half full> <faire à moitié : to do half-heartedly>
moitié–moitié *adv* : fifty-fifty
moka [moka] *nm* : mocha
molaire [mɔlɛr] *nf* : molar
moldave [mɔldav] *adj* : Moldavian
Moldave *nmf* : Moldavian
moléculaire [mɔlekylɛr] *adj* : molecular
molécule [mɔlekyl] *nf* : molecule
molester [mɔlɛste] *vt* : to maul, to manhandle
mollasse [mɔlas] *adj* **1** APATHIQUE : apathetic, lethargic **2** FLASQUE : soft, flabby
mollasson [mɔlasɔ̃] *adj fam* : sluggish
molle → **mou**
mollement [mɔlmɑ̃] *adv* **1** DOUCEMENT : softly, gently **2** : weakly, feebly **3** : halfheartedly
mollesse [mɔlɛs] *adj* **1** : softness **2** : limpness, flabbiness **3** INDOLENCE : indolence, apathy
mollet [mɔlɛ] *nm* : calf (of the leg)
molleton [mɔltɔ̃] *nm* : fleece, flannel
mollir [mɔlir] *vi* **1** : to soften, to go soft **2** : to die down, to abate (of wind, etc.) **3** : to weaken, to give way **4** : to flag, to wane
mollusque [mɔlysk] *nm* : mollusk
môme [mom] *nmf France fam* GOSSE : kid, youngster
moment [mɔmɑ̃] *nm* **1** : moment, while <prendre un moment : to take (quite) a while> <pour un bon moment : for a good while> **2** INSTANT : minute, instant <attends un moment! : just wait a minute!> **3** : moment, time, occasion <à tout moment : at any time> <au moment de sortir : just as she was leaving> <à ce moment : at this moment, now> **4** : present (time) <sujets du moment : issues of the day> **5 du moment que** PUISQUE : since **6 par moments** : at times, now and again
momentané, -née [mɔmɑ̃tane] *adj* : momentary, temporary — **momentanément** [-nemɑ̃] *adv*
momie [mɔmi] *nf* : mummy
mon [mɔ̃] , **ma** [ma] **(mon** *before feminine nouns or adjectives beginning with a vowel or mute h*) *adj, pl* **mes** [mɛ] : my
monarchie [mɔnarʃi] *nf* : monarchy — **monarchiste** [mɔnarʃist] *nmf*
monarque [mɔnark] *nm* : monarch
monastère [mɔnastɛr] *nm* : monastery
monastique [mɔnastik] *adj* : monastic
monceau [mɔ̃so] *nm, pl* **monceaux** [mɔ̃so] : heap, pile
mondain, -daine [mɔ̃dɛ̃, -dɛn] *adj* **1** : society, social <soirées mondaines : social gatherings> **2** : fashionable, refined **3** : wordly, mundane
mondanités [mɔ̃danite] *nfpl* **1** : social events **2** : small talk
monde [mɔ̃d] *nm* **1** TERRE : world, earth <au monde : in the world, on earth> **2** SOCIÉTÉ : world, society <le monde est petit : it's a small world> <le tiers monde : the third world> **3** COMMUNAUTÉ, DOMAINE : world, community <le monde des affaires : the business world> <le monde

végétal : the vegetable kingdom> **4** GENS : people *pl* <il y avait du monde partout : there were people everywhere> **5 comme du monde** *Can* : properly **6 tout le monde** : everyone **7 venir au monde** NAÎTRE : to be born

mondial, -diale [mɔ̃djal] *adj, mpl* **-diaux** [-djo] **1** : world <record mondial : world record> **2** : worldwide, global

mondialement [mɔ̃djalmɑ̃] *adv* : throughout the world, globally

monétaire [mɔnetɛr] *adj* : monetary

mongol[1], -gole [mɔ̃gɔl] *adj* : Mongolian, Mongol

mongol[2] *nm* : Mongolian (language)

Mongol, -gole *n* : Mongolian

moniteur[1], -trice [mɔnitœr, -tris] *n* **1** : instructor, coach **2** : counselor (in a camp)

moniteur[2] *nm* : monitor, screen

monitorat [mɔnitɔra] *nm* : instructorship

monnaie [mɔnɛ] *nf* **1** : money, currency <fausse monnaie : counterfeit money> **2** APPOINT : change <petite monnaie : small change> **3** PIÈCE : coin <monnaies d'or : gold coins> **4 monnaie courante** : commonplace

monnayer [mɔneje] {11} *vt* **1** : to convert into cash **2** : to capitalize on (experience, etc.)

monnayeur [mɔnɛjœr] *nm* → **faux monnayeur**

monochrome [mɔnɔkrom] *adj & nm* : monochrome

monocle [mɔnɔkl] *nm* : monocle

monocorde [mɔnɔkɔrd] *adj* : droning, monotonous

monogame [mɔnɔgam] *adj* : monogamous

monogamie [mɔnɔgami] *nf* : monogamy

monogramme [mɔnɔgram] *nm* : monogram

monographie [mɔnɔgrafi] *nf* : monograph

monolingue [mɔnɔlɛ̃g] *adj* : monolingual

monolithe[1] [mɔnɔlit] *adj* : monolithic

monolithe[2] *nm* : monolith

monolithique [mɔnɔlitik] *adj* : monolithic

monologue [mɔnɔlɔg] *nm* : monologue, soliloquy

monopole [mɔnɔpɔl] *nm* : monopoly

monopoliser [mɔnɔpɔlize] *vt* : to monopolize — **monopolisation** [-lizasjɔ̃] *nf*

monopolistique [mɔnɔpɔlistik] *adj* : monopolistic

monosyllabe [mɔnɔsilab] *nm* : monosyllable

monosyllabique [mɔnɔsilabik] *adj* : monosyllabic

monothéisme [mɔnɔteism] *nm* : monotheism

monothéiste [mɔnɔteist] *adj* : monotheistic

monotone [mɔnɔtɔn] *adj* : monotonous, dull

monotonie [mɔnɔtɔni] *nf* : monotony, dullness

monseigneur [mɔ̃sɛɲœr] *nm, pl* **messeigneurs** [mesɛɲœr] **1** (*form of address*) : Your Royal Highness (for a prince), Your Eminence (for a cardinal) **2** (*title*) : His Grace (for a duke, an archbishop, etc.)

monsieur [məsjø] *nm, pl* **messieurs** [mɛsjø] **1** (*form of address*) : Mr., Sir <bonjour, monsieur : good morning, Sir; good morning, Mr. X> **2** (*used in corrrespondence*) <Monsieur : Dear Sir> **3** : man, gentleman <c'est un grand monsieur : he's a great man>

monstre[1] [mɔ̃str] *adj* : huge, colossal

monstre[2] *nm* : monster

monstrueusement [mɔ̃stryøzmɑ̃] *adv* : monstruously, hideously

monstrueux, -trueuse [mɔ̃stryø, -tryøz] *adj* **1** : monstrous **2** : hideous, ugly **3** : terrible <une monstrueuse erreur : an awful mistake>

monstruosité [mɔ̃stryozite] *nf* : monstrosity

mont [mɔ̃] *nm* : mount, mountain

montage [mɔ̃taʒ] *nm* **1** : assembly <chaîne de montage : assembly line> **2** : mounting, setting (of jewelry) **3** : editing (of a film)

montagnard[1], -narde [mɔ̃taɲar, -ɲard] *adj* : mountain

montagnard[2], -narde *n* : mountain dweller

montagne [mɔ̃taɲ] *nf* **1** : mountain **2 la montagne** : the mountains **3 montagnes russes** : roller coaster

montagneux, -neuse [mɔ̃taɲø, -ɲøz] *adj* : mountainous, hilly

montant[1], -tante [mɔ̃tɑ̃, -tɑ̃t] *adj* : uphill, rising <chemin montant : uphill road>

montant[2] *nm* **1** : upright, post **2** SOMME : total, sum

mont-de-piété [mɔ̃dpjete] *nm, pl* **monts-de-piété** *France* : pawnshop

monte-charge [mɔ̃tʃarʒ] *nms & pl* : freight elevator

montée [mɔ̃te] *nf* **1** : rise, rising **2** : ascent, climb **3** PENTE : slope, upgrade

monter [mɔ̃te] *vi* **1** : to go up, to come up, to climb up <elle est montée : she went upstairs> **2** : to go uphill, to slope upward **3** : to rise (of rivers, temperature, prices, etc.) **4** : to well up <les larmes lui sont montées aux yeux : his eyes filled with tears> **5 ~ à** : to ride <monter à bicyclette : to ride a bicycle> **6 ~ dans** : to get into (a car or train), to board (a ship or plane) **7 ~ sur** : to get on (a horse) — *vt* (*with auxiliary verb* **avoir**) **1** : to take up, to bring up **2** : to put up, to raise (a curtain, etc.) **3** : to go up, to climb (up) **4** : to raise, to turn up (volume, etc.) **5** : to ride (a horse) **6** : to put together, to assemble (a machine, etc.), to edit (a film) **7** : to mount (an attack), to set up (a scheme, etc.), to put on (a show) — **se monter** *vr* **1 ~ à** : to amount to **2 ~ en** : to equip oneself with

monteur, -teuse [mɔ̃tœr, -tøz] *n* : film editor

montgolfière [mɔ̃gɔlfjɛr] *nf* : hot-air balloon

monticule [mɔ̃tikyl] *nm* **1** : hillock, mound **2** *Can* : pitcher's mound (in baseball)

montre [mɔ̃tr] *nf* **1** : watch <montre à quartz : quartz watch> **2** : show, display <en montre : on display> <faire montre de : to show, to display>

montréalais, -laise [mɔrealɛ, -lɛz] *adj* : of or from Montreal

Montréalais, -laise *n* : Montrealer

montre–bracelet [mɔ̃trəbraslɛ] *nf, pl* **montres–bracelets** : wristwatch

montrer [mɔ̃tre] *vt* **1** : to show **2** : to reveal, to display **3** : to point at, to point out <montrer qqn du doigt : to point the finger at s.o.> — **se montrer** *vr* **1** : to show oneself, to be seen **2** : to prove to be **3** : to appear, to come out

monture [mɔ̃tyr] *nf* **1** : mount (animal) **2** : setting (for jewelry) **3** : frames *pl* (for eyeglasses)

monument [mɔnymɑ̃] *nm* **1** : monument, memorial <monument aux morts : war memorial> **2** : (historic) building

monumental, -tale [mɔnymɑ̃tal] *adj, mpl* **-taux** [-to] : monumental

moquer [mɔke] *v* **se moquer** *vr* **1** : to make fun, to mock <on se moque de toi : people are laughing at you> **2** : to be indifferent <je m'en moque : I couldn't care less>

moquerie [mɔkri] *nf* : mockery

moquette [mɔkɛt] *nf* : wall-to-wall carpeting

moqueur[1], -queuse [mɔkœr, -køz] *adj* : mocking — **moqueusement** [-køzmɑ̃] *adv*

moqueur[2] *nm* : mockingbird

moraillon [mɔrɑjɔ̃] *nm* : hasp (for a door)

moraine [mɔrɛn] *nf* : moraine

moral[1], -rale [mɔral] *adj, mpl* **moraux** [mɔro] **1** : moral, ethical <sens moral : sense of right and wrong> **2** : mental <une victoire morale : a moral victory>

moral[2] *nm* : morale, spirits *pl* <je lui ai remonté le moral : I cheered him up>

morale *nf* **1** ÉTHIQUE : morals *pl*, ethics *pl* **2** : moral (of a story) **3 faire la morale à** SERMONNER : to lecture

moralement [mɔralmɑ̃] *adv* : morally, ethically

moralisateur, -trice [mɔralizatœr, -tris] *adj* : moralizing, sanctimonious

moraliser [mɔralize] *vi* : to moralize — *vt* SERMONNER : to lecture, to preach to

moraliste[1] [mɔralist] *adj* : moralistic

moraliste[2] *nmf* : moralist

moralité [mɔralite] *nf* **1** : morals *pl* **2** : morality **3** : moral, lesson

moratoire [mɔratwar] *nm* : moratorium

morbide [mɔrbid] *adj* : morbid — **morbidité** [-bidite] *nf*

morceau [mɔrso] *nm, pl* **morceaux** **1** : piece, bit <couper en morceaux : to cut into pieces> <manger un morceau : to have a bite to eat> **2** : extract, passage (of a text) **3** : piece (of music)

morceler [mɔrsəle] {8} *vt* : to break up, to divide

mordant[1], -dante [mɔrdɑ̃, -dɑ̃t] *adj* : biting, cutting, scathing

mordant[2] *nm* : keenness, bite, punch

mordicus [mɔrdikys] *adv fam* : obstinately, stubbornly

mordillement [mɔrdijmɑ̃] *nm* : nibbling

mordiller [mɔrdije] *vt* : to nibble at, to chew at

mordoré, -rée [mɔrdɔre] *adj* : bronze-colored

mordre [mɔrdr] {63} *vt* **1** : to bite **2** : to eat into (of acid, etc.) — *vi* **1** : to bite <ça mord : the fish are biting> **2 ~ dans** : to bite into, to take a bite out of **3 ~ sur** : to cross over (a line) — **se mordre** *vr* **1 se mordre la langue** : to bite one's tongue **2 se mordre les doigts** : to have bitter regrets

mordu[1] [mɔrdy] *pp* → **mordre**

mordu[2], -due *adj* : smitten (with love)

mordu[3], -due *n fam* : fan, buff <un mordu de sport : a sports buff>

morelle [mɔrɛl] *nf* : nightshade

morfondre [mɔrfɔ̃dr] {63} *v* **se morfondre** *vr* : to hang around, to mope <se morfondre à attendre : to wait around dejectedly> **2** *Can* : to exhaust oneself, to wear oneself out

morgue [mɔrg] *nf* **1** : morgue, mortuary **2** ARROGANCE : haughtiness, arrogance

moribond[1], -bonde [mɔribɔ̃, -bɔ̃d] *adj* : moribund, dying

moribond[2], -bonde *n* : dying person

morille [mɔrij] *nf* : morel

morne [mɔrn] *adj* **1** SOMBRE : dismal, gloomy **2** : glum, sullen

morose [mɔroz] *adj* : morose, sullen

morosité [mɔrozite] *nf* : moroseness, sullenness

morphine [mɔrfin] *nf* : morphine

mors [mɔr] *nm* : bit (of a horse)

morse [mɔrs] *nm* **1** : walrus **2** : Morse code

morsure [mɔrsyr] *nf* : bite (of a dog, etc.)

mort[1] [mɔr] *pp* → **mourir**

mort[2], **morte** [mɔr, mɔrt] *adj* **1** : dead **2** : dying <être mort de faim : to be starving, to be dying of hunger> **3** : lifeless, stagnant <un temps mort : a slack period>

mort[3] *nf* **1** : death <mettre à mort : to put to death> <peine de mort : death penalty> <jusqu'à la mort : to the death, to the bitter end> **2** : great sorrow, agony <avoir la mort dans l'âme : to have a heavy heart>

mort[4], **morte** *n* **1** : dead person, corpse **2** VICTIME : fatality, casualty

mortalité [mɔrtalite] *nf* : mortality <taux de mortalité : death rate>

mortel[1], **-telle** [mɔrtɛl] *adj* **1** : mortal **2** FATAL : fatal, deadly, lethal <maladie mortelle : fatal disease>

mortel[2], **-telle** *n* : mortal

mortellement [mɔrtɛlmɑ̃] *adv* **1** : mortally, fatally **2** : deadly <mortellement ennuyeux : deadly boring>

mortier [mɔrtje] *nm* : mortar

mortifier [mɔrtifje] {96} *vt* : to mortify — **mortification** [-tifikasjɔ̃] *nf*

mort–né, -née [mɔrne] *adj, pl* **mort–nés, mort–nées** : stillborn

mortuaire [mɔrtɥɛr] *adj* **1** FUNÈBRE : funeral **2 salon mortuaire** *Can* : funeral home

morue [mɔry] *nf* : cod

morve [mɔrv] *nf* : nasal mucus

morveux, -veuse [mɔrvø, -vøz] *adj* : runny-nosed

mosaïque [mɔzaik] *adj & nf* : mosaic

mosquée [mɔske] *nf* : mosque

mot [mo] *nm* **1** : word (in language) <mot à mot : word for word> <peser ses mots : to weigh one's words> **2** PAROLE : word <avoir le dernier mot : to have the last word> <sans mot dire : without saying a word> **3** : note, line <écrire un mot à qqn : to drop a line to s.o.> **4 mot de passe** : password **5 mot d'ordre** : watchword, catchword **6 mots croisés** : crossword puzzle

motard [mɔtar] *nm* : motorcycle policeman

motel [mɔtɛl] *nm* : motel

moteur[1], **-trice** [mɔtœr, -tris] *adj* **1** : motor **2** : driving <force motrice : driving force> **3 à quatre roues motrices** : four-wheel drive

moteur[2] *nm* **1** : engine, motor **2 moteur à vapeur** : steam engine **3 moteur à combustion interne** *or* **moteur à explosion** : internal combustion engine **4 moteur à réaction** : jet engine

motif [mɔtif] *nm* **1** RAISON : motive, reason, grounds *pl* **2** DESSIN : pattern, design <nappe à motifs floraux : floral-design tablecloth> **3** : motif (in music)

motion [mosjɔ̃] *nf* **1** : motion <voter une motion : to pass a motion> **2 motion de censure** : vote of no confidence

motivant, -vante [mɔtivɑ̃, -vɑ̃t] *adj* : motivating

motivation [mɔtivasjɔ̃] *nf* : motivation

motivé, -vée [mɔtive] *adj* **1** : motivated <être peu motivé : to lack motivation> **2** : reasoned, justified

motiver [mɔtive] *vt* **1** : to motivate, to impel **2** : to justify, to explain

moto [mɔto] *nf* : motorbike

motocyclette [mɔtɔsiklɛt] *nf* : motorcycle

motocycliste [mɔtɔsiklist] *nmf* : motorcyclist

motoneige [mɔtɔnɛʒ] *nf* : snowmobile

motoriser [mɔtɔrize] *vt* : to motorize, to mechanize

motte [mɔt] *nf* : clod, lump (of earth, etc.), slab (of butter)

motton [mɔtɔ̃] *nm Can* : lump (of earth, of ice, etc.)

mou[1] [mu] **(mol** [mɔl] *before vowel or mute h*), **molle** [mɔl] *adj* **1** : soft **2** : weak, feeble <avoir les jambes molles : to be weak in the knees> **3** : limp, lifeless <une poignée de main molle : a limp handshake> **4** : sluggish, listless **5** : indulgent, lax

mou[2] *nm* : looseness, slack <donner du mou à : to loosen, to give some leeway to>

mouchard, -charde [muʃar, -ʃard] *n fam* : informer, stool pigeon

moucharder [muʃarde] *vt fam* : to spy on, to squeal on

mouche [muʃ] *nf* **1** : fly <mouche domestique : housefly> <mouche à miel : honeybee> **2** *or* **mouche artificielle** : fly (in fishing) **3** : beauty spot **4 faire mouche** : to hit the bull's eye

moucher [muʃe] *vt* **1** : to wipe the nose of (a child, etc.) **2** : to snuff out (a candle) — **se moucher** *vr* : to blow one's nose

moucheron [muʃrɔ̃] *nm* : gnat, midge

moucheter [muʃte] {8} *vt* TACHETER : to fleck, to speckle, to mottle

moucheture [muʃtyr] *nf* : spot, speck, speckle

mouchoir [muʃwar] *nm* **1** : handkerchief **2 mouchoir en papier** : tissue

moudre [mudr] {54} *vt* : to grind

moue [mu] *nf* **1** : pout **2 faire la moue** : to pout

mouette [mwɛt] *nf* : gull, seagull

mouffette *or* **moufette** [mufɛt] *nf* : skunk

moufle [mufl] *nf* : mitten

mouillage [mujaʒ] *nm* **1** : anchoring **2** : anchorage, moorings *pl*

mouillé, -lée [muje] *adj* : wet

mouiller [muje] *vt* **1** : to wet, to moisten **2** : to add liquid to, to dilute **3 mouiller l'ancre** : to drop anchor — **se mouiller** *vr* **1** : to get wet **2** *fam* : to become involved

moulage [mulaʒ] *nm* **1** : molding, casting **2** : cast

moulait [mulɛ], **moulions** [muljɔ̃], *etc.* → **moudre**

moulant, -lante [mulɑ̃, -lɑ̃t] *adj* : tight-fitting

moule[1] [mul], *etc.* → **moudre**

moule[2] [mul] *nm* **1** MATRICE : mold, matrix **2** : mold (in cooking) <moule à gâteau : cake pan>

moule[3] [mul] *nf* : mussel

mouler [mule] *vt* **1** : to mold **2** : to cast <moulé en bronze : cast in bronze> **3** : to hug (the body), to fit tightly

moulin [mulɛ̃] *nm* **1** : mill **2 moulin à café** : coffee grinder **3 moulin à paroles** *fam* : chatterbox **4 moulin à vent** : windmill

moulinet [mulinɛ] *nm* **1** : reel, winch **2** : waving (about)

moulu[1] [muly] *pp* → **moudre**

moulu[2], **-lue** *adj* **1** : ground <café moulu : ground coffee> **2** *fam* : worn-out, all in

moulure [mulyr] *nf* : molding

moumoute [mumut] *nf fam* : wig, toupee

mourant[1], **-rante** [murɑ̃, -rɑ̃t] *adj* : dying

mourant[2], **-rante** *n* : dying person

mourir [murir] {55} *vi* **1** : to die **2** : to die out, to die away **3 ~ de** : to be dying of <mourir d'ennui : to be bored to death> <mourir de faim : to be dying of hunger> <il l'aimait à en mourir : he was desperately in love with her>

mourra [mura], *etc.* → **mourir**

mousquet [muskɛ] *nm* : musket

mousquetaire [muskətɛr] *nm* : musketeer

mousqueton [muskətɔ̃] *nm* : carbine

moussant, -sante [musɑ̃, -sɑ̃t] *adj* **1** : foaming, lathering **2 bain moussant** : bubble bath

mousse [mus] *nf* **1** : moss **2** : froth, foam, lather **3** : mousse <mousse au chocolat : chocolate mousse> **4** *or* **caoutchouc mousse** : foam rubber

mousseline [muslin] *nf* **1** : muslin, chiffon **2 pommes mousseline** : pureed potatoes

mousser [muse] *vi* **1** : to foam, to froth, to lather **2 faire mousser** *fam* : to sing the praises of

mousseux[1], **-seuse** [musø, -søz] *adj* **1** : foaming, frothy **2 vin mousseux** : sparkling wine

mousseux[2] *nm* : sparkling wine

mousson [musɔ̃] *nf* : monsoon

moussu, -sue [musy] *adj* : mossy

moustache [mustaʃ] *nf* **1** : mustache **2 moustaches** *nfpl* : whiskers (of an animal)

moustachu, -chue [mustaʃy] *adj* : wearing a mustache

moustiquaire [mustikɛr] *nf* **1** : mosquito net **2** : screen (on windows and doors)

moustique [mustik] *nm* : mosquito

moutarde [mutard] *nf* : mustard

mouton [mutɔ̃] *nm* **1** : sheep, sheepskin **2** : mutton **3 moutons** *nmpl* : small fluffy clouds **4 moutons** *nmpl* : whitecaps

mouvement [muvmɑ̃] *nm* **1** : bodily movement, gesture **2** : movement, motion <mouvement perpétuel : perpetual motion> **3** : impulse, reaction **4** : activity, bustle **5** : trend, evolution <mouvement en hausse : upward trend> **6** : movement (in politics, etc.)

mouvementé, -tée [muvmɑ̃te] *adj* **1** VIVANT : animated, lively, hectic **2** ACCIDENTÉ : rough, uneven <terrain mouvementé : rough terrain>

mouvoir [muvwar] {56} *vt* **1** POUSSER : to move, to prompt **2** ACTIONNER : to drive <machine mue par l'électricité : electric-powered machine> — **se mouvoir** *vr* : to move

moyac [mɔjak] *nm Can* : eider (duck)

moyen[1], **-yenne** [mwajɛ̃, -jɛn] *adj* **1** : medium, medium-sized **2** : average, mean **3 la classe moyenne** : the middle class

moyen[2] *nm* **1** : way, means *pl* <par quel moyen? : how?> **2** : possibility <y a-t-il moyen de le voir? : is it possible to see him?> **3 moyens** *nmpl* : means, resources **4 au moyen de** : with, by means of

Moyen Âge [mwajɛnaʒ] *nm* : Middle Ages

moyennant [mwajɛnɑ̃] *prep* : for, in return for

moyenne [mwajɛn] *nf* : average <en moyenne : on an average>

moyennement [mwajɛnmɑ̃] *adv* MODÉRÉMENT : fairly, moderately

moyeu [mwajø] *nm, pl* **moyeux** : hub

mozambicain, -caine [mɔzɑ̃bikɛ̃, -kɛn] *adj* : Mozambican

Mozambicain, -caine *n* : Mozambican

mû [my] *pp* → **mouvoir**

mucilage [mysilaʒ] *nm* : mucilage

mucosité [mykozite] *nf* : mucus

mucus [mykys] *nm* : mucus

mue [my] *nf* : molting, shedding, sloughing

muer [mɥe] *vi* **1** : to molt, to shed, to slough **2** : to change, to break <sa voix mue : his voice is changing> — **se muer** *vr* : to transform oneself

muet[1], **muette** [mɥɛ, mɥɛt] *adj* **1** : dumb <sourd et muet : deaf and dumb> **2** : speechless, dumbfounded **3** SILENCIEUX : silent

muet[2], **-ette** *n* : mute, dumb person

muffin [mɔfœn] *nm Can* : muffin

mufle [myfl] *nm* **1** : muzzle **2** *fam* : boor, lout

muge [myʒ] *nm* : gray mullet

mugir [myʒir] *vi* **1** BEUGLER : to low, to moo, to bellow **2** : to howl, to wail, to roar

mugissement [myʒismɑ̃] *nm* **1** : lowing, bellowing, mooing **2** : howling (of the wind), roar (of the sea)

muguet [mygɛ] *nm* : lily of the valley

mulâtre, -tresse [mylatr, -trɛs] *n* : mulatto

mule [myl] *nf* **1** : female mule **2** PANTOUFLE : mule

mulet [mylɛ] *nm* **1** : male mule **2** : gray mullet

mulot [mylo] *nm* : field mouse

multicolore [myltikɔlɔr] *adj* : multicolored

multiculturel, -relle [myltikyltyrɛl] *adj* : multicultural

multiforme [myltifɔrm] *adj* : multiform, many-sided

multilatéral, -rale [myltilateral] *adj, mpl* **-raux** [-ro] : multilateral

multilingue [myltilɛ̃g] *adj* : multilingual — **multilinguisme** [-lɛ̃gɥism] *nm*

multimédia [myltimedja] *adj* : multimedia

multimillionnaire [myltimiljɔnɛr] *nmf* : multimillionaire

multinational, -nale [myltinasjɔnal] *adj, mpl* **-naux** [-no] : multinational

multiple[1] [myltipl] *adj* **1** NOMBREUX : multiple, numerous **2** DIVERS : many, various, diverse

multiple[2] *nm* : multiple

multiplication [myltiplikasjɔ̃] *nf* : multiplication

multiplicité [myltiplisite] *nf* : multiplicity

multiplier [myltiplije] {96} *vt* **1** ACCROÎTRE : to multiply, to increase **2** : to multiply (in mathematics) — **se multiplier** *vr* PROLIFÉRER : to increase, to proliferate

multitude [myltityd] *nf* : multitude, mass <une multitude de gens : a vast number of people>

municipal, -pale [mynisipal] *adj, mpl* **-paux** [-po] : municipal, local, town

municipalité [mynisipalite] *nf* **1** : municipality, town **2** : town council

munificent, -cente [mynifisɑ̃, -sɑ̃t] *adj* : munificent — **munificence** [-fisɑ̃s] *adj*

munir [mynir] *vt* : to equip, to provide <munir d'armes : to supply with arms> — **se munir** *vr* **~ de** : to equip oneself with

munitions [mynisjɔ̃] *nfpl* : ammunition, munitions

muqueuse *nf* : mucous membrane

muqueux, -queuse [mykø, -køz] *adj* : mucous

mur [myr] *nm* **1** : wall **2** OBSTACLE : obstacle, brick wall **3 mur du son** : sound barrier

mûr, mûre [myr] *adj* **1** : ripe **2** : mature <l'âge mûr : middle age> **3** : ready, prepared <mûr pour des responsabilités accrues : ready for increased responsibility>

muraille [myraj] *nf* : (high) wall

mural, -rale [myral] *adj, mpl* **muraux** [myro] : wall, mural

murale [myral] *nf* : mural

mûre [myr] *nf* **1** : blackberry **2** : mulberry

mûrement [myrmɑ̃] *adv* : carefully, with thought <ayant mûrement réfléchi : after much thought>

murène [myrɛn] *nf* : moray eel

murer [myre] *vt* : to wall in, to wall up — **se murer** *vr* : to shut oneself away

mûrier [myrje] *nm* : mulberry (tree)

mûrir [myrir] *vi* **1** : to ripen **2** : to mature, to develop — *vt* **1** : to ripen **2** : to develop, to nurture (a project, etc.)

murmure [myrmyr] *nm* **1** CHUCHOTEMENT : murmur **2 murmures** *nmpl* : mutterings, murmurings

murmurer [myrmyre] *vi* **1** CHUCHOTER : to murmur **2** SE PLAINDRE : to mutter, to complain — *vt* : to murmur

musaraigne [myzarɛɲ] *nf* : shrew

musarder [myzarde] *vi* FLÂNER : to idle around, to dawdle about

musc [mysk] *nm* : musk

muscade [myskad] *nf or* **noix muscade** : nutmeg

muscat [myska] *nm* : muscatel

muscle [myskl] *nm* : muscle

musclé, -clée [myskle] *adj* **1** : muscular **2** *fam* : powerful, strong <une politique musclée : a forceful stand>

musculaire [myskylɛr] *adj* : muscular

musculation [myskylasjɔ̃] *nf* : bodybuilding

musculature [mysklatyr] *nf* : musculature, muscles *pl*

muse [myz] *nf* : muse

museau [myzo] *nm, pl* **museaux** : muzzle, snout

musée [myze] *nm* : museum

museler [myzle] {8} *vt* : to muzzle

muselière [myzəljɛr] *nf* : muzzle (for a dog, etc.)

musette [myzɛt] *nf* : satchel, haversack

muséum [myzeɔm] *nm* : museum of natural history

musical, -cale [myzikal] *adj* **-caux** [-ko] : musical — **musicalement** [-kalmɑ̃] *adv*

musicien[1], **-cienne** [myzisjɛ̃, -sjɛn] *adj* : musical

musicien[2], **-cienne** *n* : musician

musique [myzik] *nf* **1** : music <musique d'ambiance : background music> <musique de chambre : chamber music> **2** : piece of music **3** : band <musique militaire : military band>

musqué, -quée [myske] *adj* **1** : musky **2 bœuf musqué** : musk ox **3 rat musqué** ONDATRA : muskrat

musulman, -mane [myzylmɑ̃, -man] *adj & n* : Muslim

mutable [mytabl] *adj* : mutable, changeable — **mutabilité** [-tabilite] *nf*

mutant[1], **-tante** [mytɑ̃, -tɑ̃t] *adj* : mutant
mutant[2], **-tante** *n* : mutant
mutation [mytasjɔ̃] *nf* **1** : transformation, change **2** : transfer (of an employee) **3** : mutation
muter [myte] *vt* : to transfer, to move — *vi* : to mutate
mutilation [mytilasjɔ̃] *nf* : mutilation
mutiler [mytile] *vt* : to mutilate, to maim
mutin[1], **-tine** [mytɛ̃, -tin] *adj* ESPIÈGLE : mischievous
mutin[2] *nm* : mutineer
mutiné[1], **-née** [mytine] *adj* : mutinous, rebellious
mutiné[2], **-née** *n* : mutineer
mutiner [mytine] *v* **se mutiner** *vr* : to mutiny, to rebel
mutinerie [mytinri] *nf* RÉBELLION : mutiny, rebellion
mutisme [mytism] *nm* **1** : dumbness, muteness **2** : silence
mutuel, -elle [mytɥɛl] *adj* : mutual — **mutuellement** [-tɥɛlmɑ̃] *adv*
myope [mjɔp] *adj* : shortsighted, nearsighted
myopie [mjɔpi] *nf* : myopia, shortsightedness, nearsightedness
myosotis [mjozɔtis] *nm* : forget-me-not
myriade [mirjad] *nf* : myriad
myrrhe [mir] *nf* : myrrh
myrte [mirt] *nf* : myrtle
myrtille [mirtil] *nf France* : blueberry
mystère [mistɛr] *nm* : mystery
mystérieux, -rieuse [misterjø, -rjøz] *adj* : mysterious — **mystérieusement** [-rjøzmɑ̃] *adv*
mysticisme [mistisism] *nm* : mysticism
mystification [mistifikasjɔ̃] *nf* **1** : hoax, practical joke **2** : myth, unfounded idea
mystifier [mistifje] {96} *vt* DUPER : to deceive, to dupe
mystique[1] [mistik] *adj* : mystical, mystic
mystique[2] *nmf* : mystic
mystique[3] *nf* **1** : mysticism **2** : mystique
mythe [mit] *nm* : myth
mythique [mitik] *adj* : mythical
mythologie [mitɔlɔʒi] *nf* : mythology
mythologique [mitɔlɔʒik] *adj* : mythological

N

n [ɛn] *nm* : n, the 14th letter of the alphabet
nacre [nakr] *nf* : mother-of-pearl
nacré, -crée [nakre] *adj* : pearly
nadir [nadir] *nm* : nadir
nage [naʒ] *nf* **1** : swimming **2** : stroke (in swimming) <nage libre : freestyle> **3 en ~** : dripping with sweat
nageoire [naʒwar] *nf* **1** : fin (of a fish) **2** : flipper
nager [naʒe] {17} *vi* **1** : to swim **2 ~ dans** : to be filled with <il nageait dans l'amour : he was brimming with love> — *vt* : to swim
nageur, -geuse [naʒœr, -ʒøz] *n* : swimmer
naguère [nagɛr] *adv* **1** RÉCEMMENT : recently, a short time ago **2** AUTREFOIS : formerly
naïade [najad] *nf* : naiad
naïf, naïve [naif, -iv] *adj* **1** INGÉNU : ingenuous, naive **2** CRÉDULE : credulous, gullible — **naïvement** [naivmɑ̃] *adv*
nain[1], **naine** [nɛ̃, nɛn] *adj* : dwarf, miniature <rosier nain : miniature rosebush>
nain[2], **naine** *n* : dwarf, midget
naissait [nɛsɛ], **naissions** [nɛsjɔ̃], *etc.* → **naître**
naissance [nɛsɑ̃s] *nf* **1** : birth **2** DÉBUT : origin, beginning <prendre naissance : to arise, to originate>
naissant, -sante [nɛsɑ̃, -sɑ̃t] *adj* : incipient
naisse [nɛs], *etc.* → **naisse**
naître [nɛtr] {57} *vi* **1** : to be born <il est né en 1970 : he was born in 1970> **2** : to rise, to originate <faire naître : to give rise to>
naïveté [naivte] *nf* : naïveté
namibien, -bienne [namibjɛ̃, -bjɛn] *adj* : Namibian
Namibien, -bienne *n* : Namibian
nanti, -tie [nɑ̃ti] *adj* : affluent, well-to-do
nantir [nɑ̃tir] *vt* **~ de** : to provide with
nantissement [nɑ̃tismɑ̃] *nm* : collateral
naphtaline [naftalin] *nf or* **boules de naphtaline** : mothballs *pl*
naphte [naft] *nm* : naphtha
nappe [nap] *nf* **1** : tablecloth **2** : layer, sheet <nappe de brouillard : blanket of fog> <nappe d'eau : sheet of water> <nappe de mazout : oil slick>
napper [nape] *vt* : to coat, to cover <napper de sauce : to cover with sauce>
napperon [naprɔ̃] *nm* : mat, doily
narcisse [narsis] *nm* **1** : narcissus **2** : narcissist
narcissique [narsisik] *adj* : narcissistic — **narcissisme** [-sisism] *nm*
narcotique [narkɔtik] *adj & nm* : narcotic
narguer [narge] *vt* **1** : to mock, to taunt **2** : to flout (danger, etc.)
narine [narin] *nf* : nostril
narquois, -quoise [narkwa, -kwaz] *adj* RAILLEUR : sneering, derisive

narrateur, -trice [naratœr, -tris] *n* : narrator

narratif, -tive [naratif, -tiv] *adj* : narrative

narration [narasjɔ̃] *nf* : narration, narrative

narrer [nare] *vt* : to tell (a story), to relate (events, etc.)

narval [narval] *nm* : narwhal

nasal, -sale [nazal] *adj, mpl* **nasaux** [nazo] : nasal

naseau [nazo] *nm, pl* **naseaux** : nostril (of an animal)

nasillard, -larde [nazijar, -jard] *adj* : nasal <voix nasillarde : nasal voice>

nasiller [nazije] *vi* : to speak through one's nose, to have a nasal twang

natal, -tale [natal] *adj, mpl* **natals** : native, natal

natalité [natalite] *nf* : birthrate

natation [natasjɔ̃] *nf* : swimming

natif[1], -tive [natif, -tiv] *adj* : native

natif[2], -tive *n* : native

nation [nasjɔ̃] *nf* : nation

national, -nale [nasjɔnal] *adj, mpl* **-naux** [-no] : national — **nationalement** [-nalmɑ̃] *adv*

nationale *nf France* : highway

nationaliser [nasjɔnalize] *vt* : to nationalize — **nationalisation** [-lizasjɔ̃] *nf*

nationalisme [nasjɔnalism] *nm* : nationalism — **nationaliste** [-nalist] *adj & nmf*

nationalité [nasjɔnalite] *nf* : nationality

nativité [nativite] *nf* : nativity

natte [nat] *nf* **1** : mat **2** : braid, plait, pigtail

natter [nate] *vt* : to braid, to plait

naturaliser [natyralize] *vt* : to naturalize — **naturalisation** [-lizasjɔ̃] *nf*

naturalisme [natyralism] *nm* : naturalism

naturaliste[1] [natyralist] *adj* : naturalistic

naturaliste[2] *nmf* : naturalist

nature [natyr] *nf* **1** : nature <les beautés de la nature : the beauties of nature> **2** CARACTÈRE : character, nature <une nature passive : a passive nature> **3** : plain <yaourt nature : plain yogurt> **4 nature humaine** : human nature **5 nature morte** : still life

naturel[1], -relle [natyrɛl] *adj* : natural

naturel[2] *nm* **1** : nature, disposition **2** : naturalness **3 au naturel** : plain, unprocessed **4 au naturel** : in reality, in real life

naturellement [natyrɛlmɑ̃] *adv* **1** : naturally, by nature **2** : naturally, of course

naturisme [natyrism] *nm* : nudism — **naturiste** [-tyrist] *adj & nmf*

naufrage [nofraʒ] *nm* : shipwreck

naufragé, -gée [nofraʒe] *adj & n* : castaway

nauséabond, -bonde [nozeabɔ̃, -bɔnd] *adj* **1** : nauseating, revolting **2** : foul-smelling

nausée [noze] *nf* **1** : nausea **2 avoir la nausée** *or* **avoir des nausées** : to get sick to one's stomach

nautile [notil] *nm* : nautilus

nautique [notik] *adj* : nautical <ski nautique : water skiing>

nautisme [notism] *nm* : water sports

naval, -vale [naval] *adj, mpl* **navals** : naval

navet [navɛ] *nm* **1** : turnip **2** *fam* : third-rate film, novel, etc.

navette [navɛt] *nf* **1** : shuttle <navette spatiale : space shuttle> **2 faire la navette** : to commute

navigable [navigabl] *adj* : navigable — **navigabilité** [-gabilite] *nf*

navigant, -gante [navigɑ̃, -gɑ̃t] *adj* **1** : flying <personnel navigant : flight personnel, crew> **2** : seafaring

navigateur, -trice [navigatœr, -tris] *n* **1** : navigator **2** : sailor, seafarer

navigation [navigasjɔ̃] *nf* **1** : navigation **2** : shipping

naviguer [navige] *vi* **1** : to sail **2** : to navigate **3** *fam* : to travel

navire [navir] *nm* **1** : ship, vessel **2 navire de guerre** : warship, man-of-war

navire–citerne [navirsitɛrn] *nm, pl* **navires–citernes** : tanker

navrant, -vrante [navrɑ̃, -vrɑ̃t] *adj* **1** : upsetting, distressing **2** : annoying

navrer [navre] *vt* **1** : to upset, to distress **2 être navré de** : to be sorry about

nazi, -zie [nazi] *adj & nmf* : Nazi — **nazisme** [nazism] *nm*

ne [nə] (**n'** *before a vowel or mute h*) *adv* **1** (*used with a negative word*) <il n'y a plus aucun espoir : there's no longer any hope> <elle ne sait pas : she doesn't know> <je ne lui parle guère : I almost never speak to him> **2** (*used with que*) : only, all that, not just <il n'y a pas que vous : you're not the only one> <il ne fait que se plaindre : all (that) he does is complain> **3** (*used alone*) <j'ai peur qu'elle n'oublie : I'm afraid she'll forget> <à moins qu'on ne t'appelle : unless they call you> <n'ayez crainte : don't worry, never fear>

né[1] [ne] *pp* → **naître**

né[2], née *adj* : born <un chanteur né : a born singer>

néanmoins [neɑ̃mwɛ̃] *adv* : nevertheless, yet

néant [neɑ̃] *nm* **1** : worthlessness, emptiness **2 le néant** : nothingness

nébuleuse [nebyløz] *nf* : nebula

nébuleux, -leuse [nebylø, -løz] *adj* **1** : cloudy <ciel nébuleux : cloudy sky> **2** : nebulous

nécessaire[1] [nesesɛr] *adj* : necessary <nécessaire à la vie : necessary for life>

nécessaire[2] *nm* **1** : necessity <le strict nécessaire : the bare essentials> **2**

: need <je ferai le nécessaire : I'll do what's needed> **3** : bag, kit <nécessaire de toilette : toilet kit>

nécessairement [nesesɛrmɑ̃] *adv* **1** : necessarily **2** INÉVITABLEMENT : inevitably

nécessité [nesesite] *nf* **1** : necessity **2** : need <être dans la nécessité : to be in need>

nécessiter [nesesite] *vt* EXIGER : to require, to call for

nécessiteux, -teuse [nesesitø, -tøz] *adj* : needy

nécrologie [nekrɔlɔʒi] *nf* : obituary

nécromancie [nekrɔmɑ̃si] *nf* : necromancy

nectar [nɛktar] *nm* : nectar

nectarine [nɛktarin] *nf* : nectarine

néerlandais[1], **-daise** [neɛrlɑ̃dɛ, -dɛz] *adj* : Dutch

néerlandais[2] *nm* : Dutch (language)

Néerlandais, -daise *n* **1** : Dutch person, Dutchman *m* **2 les Néerlandais** : the Dutch

nef [nɛf] *nf* : nave

néfaste [nefast] *adj* **1** NUISIBLE : harmful **2** : ill-fated, unlucky

négatif[1], **-tive** [negatif, -tiv] *adj* : negative — **négativement** [-tivmɑ̃] *adv*

négatif[2] *nm* : negative (of a photograph)

négation [negasjɔ̃] *nf* **1** : denial, negation **2** : negative (in grammar)

négative *nf* : negative <répondre par la négative : to reply in the negative>

négativement [negativmɑ̃] *adv* : negatively

négligé[1], **-gée** [negliʒe] *adj* **1** : neglected **2** : slovenly, untidy

négligé[2] *nm* **1** LAISSER-ALLER : slovenliness **2** DÉSHABILLÉ : negligee

négligeable [negliʒabl] *adj* INSIGNIFIANT : negligible, insignificant

négligemment [negliʒamɑ̃] *adv* : negligently, carelessly

négligence [negliʒɑ̃s] *nf* : negligence, carelessness

négligent, -gente [negliʒɑ̃, -ʒɑ̃t] *adj* : negligent, neglectful

négliger [negliʒe] {17} *vt* **1** : to neglect **2** : to disregard, to ignore **3** OMETTRE : to omit, to forget <il a négligé de m'avertir : he forgot to let me know> — **se négliger** *vr* : to neglect oneself

négoce [negɔs] *nm* : business, trade

négociable [negɔsjabl] *adj* : negotiable

négociant, -ciante [negɔsjɑ̃, -sjɑ̃t] *n* : merchant

négociateur, -trice [negɔsjatœr, -tris] *n* : negotiator

négociation [negɔsjasjɔ̃] *nf* : negotiation

négocier [negɔsje] {96} *v* : to negotiate — **négociable** [negɔsjabl] *adj*

nègre, négresse [nɛgr, negrɛs] *adj & n sometimes offensive* : Negro

neige [nɛʒ] *nf* **1** : snow **2 neige carbonique** : dry ice **3 neige fondue** : slush

neiger [neʒe] {17} *v impers* : to snow <il neige : it's snowing>

neigeux, -geuse [nɛʒø, -ʒøz] *adj* : snowy

nénuphar [nenyfar] *nm* : water lily

néologisme [neɔlɔʒism] *nm* : neologism

néon [neɔ̃] *nm* : neon <éclairage au néon : neon lighting>

néophyte [neɔfit] *nmf* : neophyte, beginner

Néo-Zéalandais, -daise [neɔelɑ̃dɛ, -dɛz] *n* : New Zealander

népalais[1], **-laise** [nepalɛ, -lɛz] *adj* : Nepali

népalais[2] *nm* : Nepali (language)

Népalais, -laise *n* : Nepali

népotisme [nepɔtism] *nm* : nepotism

Neptune [nɛptyn] *nf* : Neptune (planet)

nerf [nɛr] *nm* **1** : nerve **2** VIGUEUR : vigor, spirit **3 nerfs** *nmpl* : nerves <avoir les nerfs à vif : to be a bundle of nerves>

nerveux, -veuse [nɛrvø, -vøz] *adj* : nervous, tense — **nerveusement** [-vøzmɑ̃] *adv*

nervosité [nɛrvozite] *nf* : nervousness

nervure [nɛrvyr] *nf* **1** : vein (of a leaf, an insect's wing, etc.) **2** : rib (in architecture)

n'est-ce pas [nɛspa] *adv* : no?, isn't that right?, isn't it?, aren't you? <c'est bien ça, n'est-ce pas? : that's right, isn't it?> <tu viens, n'est-ce pas? : you're coming, aren't you?>

net[1], **nette** [nɛt] *adv* : plainly, flatly <j'ai refusé net : I flatly refused>

net[2], **nette** *adj* **1** PROPRE : clean, tidy **2** : net <salaire net : net earnings> **3** : clear <une nette amélioration : a clear improvement> **4** MARQUÉ : marked, distinct

nettement [nɛtmɑ̃] *adv* **1** : flatly, bluntly **2** DISTINCTEMENT : clearly, distinctly **3** : definitely

netteté [nɛtte] *nf* **1** : cleanness **2** : clearness, sharpness

nettoie [nɛtwa], **nettoiera** [nɛtwara], *etc.* → **nettoyer**

nettoyage [netwajaʒ] *nm* : cleaning

nettoyant [netwajɑ̃] *nm* : cleaning agent

nettoyer [nɛtwaje] {58} *vt* **1** : to clean, to clean off, to clean up **2** *fam* : to clean out, to rob

neuf[1] [nœf] *adj* **1** : nine **2** : ninth <le neuf juin : June ninth>

neuf[2] *nms & pl* : nine

neuf[3], **neuve** [nœf, nœv] *adj* : new <tout neuf : brand new>

neuf[4] *nm* : new thing <quoi de neuf? : what's new?>

neurologie [nørɔlɔʒi] *nf* : neurology

neurologique [nørɔlɔʒik] *adj* : neurological, neurologic

neurologue [nøʀɔlɔg] *nmf* : neurologist
neutraliser [nøtʀalize] *vt* : to neutralize — **neutralisation** [-lizasjɔ̃] *nf*
neutralité [nøtʀalite] *nf* : neutrality
neutre[1] [nøtʀ] *adj* **1** : neuter **2** : neutral
neutre[2] *nm* **1** : neuter (in grammar) **2** *Can* : neutral (gear position)
neutron [nøtʀɔ̃] *nm* : neutron
neuvième [nœvjɛm] *adj & nmf & nm* : ninth
neveu [nəvø] *nm* : nephew
névralgie [nevʀalʒi] *nf* : neuralgia
névralgique [nevʀalʒik] *adj* **1** : neuralgic **2 point névralgique** : sensitive area, key point
névrite [nevʀit] *nf* : neuritis
névrose [nevʀoz] *nf* : neurosis
névrosé, -sée [nevʀoze] *adj & n* : neurotic
névrotique [nevʀɔtik] *adj* : neurotic
nez [ne] *nm* **1** : nose **2** : flair, good judgement **3 nez à nez** : face to face
ni [ni] *conj* **1 ni . . . ni** : neither . . . nor <ni l'un ni l'autre : neither one nor the other> **2 ni plus ni moins** : no more, no less
niais[1], **niaise** [njɛ, njɛz] *adj* : simple, foolish — **niaisement** [njɛzmɑ̃] *adv*
niais[2], **niaise** *n* : fool, simpleton
niaiser [njeze] *vi Can fam* **1** : to dilly-dally, to waste time **2 faire niaiser qqn** : to make s.o. wait — *vt Can fam* : to make (someone) look stupid
niaiserie [njɛzʀi] *nf* SOTTISE : silliness, foolishness, stupid remark <dire des niaiseries : to talk nonsense>
niaiseux, -seuse [njezø, -zøz] *n Can fam* : silly person, fool
nicaraguayen, -guayenne [nikaʀagwɛjɛ̃, -jɛn] *adj* : Nicaraguan
Nicaraguayen, -guayenne *n* : Nicaraguan
niche [niʃ] *nf* **1** : niche, recess **2** : kennel, doghouse
nicher [niʃe] *vi* : to nest, to brood — **se nicher** *vr* **1** : to nest **2** : to nestle **3** : to hide away
nickel [nikɛl] *nm* : nickel
nicotine [nikɔtin] *nf* : nicotine
nid [ni] *nm* **1** : nest **2** : den, lair <nid de brigands : den of thieves>
nid–de–poule *nm, pl* **nids–de–poule** : pothole
nièce [njɛs] *nf* : niece
nier [nje] {96} *vt* : to deny
nigaud, -gaude [nigo, nigod] *n* : simpleton, fool
nigérian, -rianne [niʒeʀjɑ̃, -ʀjan] *adj* : Nigerian
Nigérian, -rianne *n* : Nigerian
n'importe → **importer**
nirvana [niʀvana] *nm* : nirvana
nitrate [nitʀat] *nm* : nitrate
nitrique [nitʀik] *adj* **acide nitrique** : nitric acid
nitrite [nitʀik] *nm* : nitrite
nitroglycérine [nitʀɔglisəʀin] *nf* : nitroglycerin, nitroglycerine
niveau [nivo] *nm, pl* **niveaux** [nivo] **1** : level <niveau de la mer : sea level> **2** : story <un bâtiment à trois niveaux : a three-story building> **3** : level, standard <niveau de vie : standard of living> **4** : stage, level, degree <négociations au plus haut niveau : top-level negotiations>
niveler [nivle] {8} *vt* : to level (off), to even out
nivellement [nivɛlmɑ̃] *nm* : leveling
noble[1] [nɔbl] *adj* **1** : noble **2 métaux nobles** : precious metals
noble[2] *nmf* : noble, nobleman *m*, noblewoman *f*
noblesse [nɔblɛs] *nf* : nobility
noce [nɔs] *nf* **1** : wedding, wedding party **2 noces** *nfpl* : wedding <noces d'or : golden wedding anniversary>
nocif, -cive [nɔsif, -siv] *adj* : noxious, harmful
noctambule [nɔktɑ̃byl] *nmf* : night owl
nocturne[1] [nɔktyʀn] *adj* : nocturnal, night
nocturne[2] *nm* **1** : nocturne **2** : night hunter (bird)
nodule [nɔdyl] *nm* : nodule
Noël [nɔɛl] *nm* **1** : Christmas <joyeux Noël : Merry Christmas> **2 père Noël** : Santa Claus
noeud [nø] *nm* **1** : knot <noeud coulant : noose> **2** : bow <noeud papillon : bow tie> **3** : crux **4** : node **5** : knot (nautical speed)
noie [nwa], **noiera** [nwaʀa], *etc.* → **noyer**
noir[1], **noire** [nwaʀ] *adj* **1** : black **2** SALE : dirty, grimy **3** : dark <il fait noir : it's dark>
noir[2] *nm* **1** : black (color) **2** : darkness <peur du noir : fear of the dark> **3 au noir** : on the black market, on the side <travailler au noir : to moonlight> **4 noir à chaussures** *Can* : (black) shoe polish
Noir, Noire *n* : black man, black woman
noirâtre [nwaʀatʀ] *adj* : blackish
noirceur [nwaʀsœʀ] *nf* **1** : blackness **2** *Can* : darkness
noircir [nwaʀsiʀ] *vi* : to darken, to turn black — *vt* : to black, to blacken <une réputation noircie : a tarnished reputation>
noircissure [nwaʀsisyʀ] *nf* : black mark
noise [nwaz] *nf* **chercher noise à qqn** : to pick a fight with s.o.
noisetier [nwaztje] *nm* : hazel (tree)
noisette [nwazɛt] *nf* **1** : hazelnut **2** : hazel (color)
noix [nwa] *nfs & pl* **1** : nut, walnut **2** : piece, lump <noix de beurre : round lump of butter> **3** → **cajou, coco, muscade**
noliser [nɔlize] *vt* : to charter, to rent out
nom [nɔ̃] *nm* **1** : name <nom de plume : pen name> <nom de famille : sur-

name> <nom de jeune fille : maiden name> **2** : noun **3 au nom de** : in the name of, on behalf of
nomade[1] [nɔmad] *adj* : nomadic
nomade[2] *nmf* : nomad
nombre [nɔ̃br] *nm* **1** : number <nombre entier : whole number, integer> <nombre impair : odd number> **2** QUANTITÉ : quantity, number <un grand nombre de : a lot of, many> <sans nombre : countless> **3** MASSE : numbers *pl* <la loi du nombre : the sheer weight of numbers> **4 au nombre de** : among
nombreux, -breuse [nɔ̃brø, -brøz] *adj* **1** : large <une famille nombreuse : a large family> **2** : many, numerous
nombril [nɔ̃bril] *nm* : navel
nombrilisme [nɔ̃brilism] *nm fam* : self-centeredness
nomenclature [nɔmɑ̃klatyr] *nf* **1** : nomenclature **2** : word list
nominal, -nale [nɔminal] *adj, mpl* **-naux** [-no] : nominal <valeur nominale : face value> — **nominalement** [-nalmɑ̃] *adv*
nominatif [nɔminatif] *nm* : nominative
nomination [nɔminasjɔ̃] *nf* : appointment, nomination
nommément [nɔmemɑ̃] *adv* : by name, namely
nommer [nɔme] *vt* **1** PRÉNOMMER : to name, to call **2** : to appoint, to nominate **3** CITER : to name, to mention — **se nommer** *vr* **1** S'APPELER : to be named <elle se nomme Julie : her name is Julie> **2** : to introduce oneself
non [nɔ̃] *adv* **1** : no <mais non! : no!, of course not!> **2** (*used to replace a clause*) <je pense que non : I don't think so> <c'est à ton goût, non? : you like it, don't you?> <moi non plus : me neither, neither do I, neither am I> **3** (*used to modify an adjective or adverb*) <non loin d'ici : not far from here> <non moins : no less> **4 non seulement . . . mais (encore)** : not only . . . but (also)
non-aligné, -née [nɔnaliɲe] *adj* : nonaligned
nonante[1] [nɔnɑ̃t] *adj* : *Belg, Switz* : ninety
nonante[2] *n* : *Belg, Switz* : ninety
nonchalamment [nɔ̃ʃalamɑ̃] *adv* : nonchalantly
nonchalance [nɔ̃ʃalɑ̃s] *nf* : nonchalance, casualness
nonchalant, -lante [nɔ̃ʃalɑ̃, -lɑ̃t] *adj* : nonchalant, casual
non-combattant, -tante [nɔ̃kɔ̃batɑ̃, -tɑ̃t] *n* : noncombatant
non-conformité [nɔ̃kɔ̃fɔrmite] *nf* : nonconformity — **non-conformiste** [-fɔrmist] *nmf*
non-croyant, -croyante [nɔ̃krwajɑ̃, -jɑ̃t] *n* : nonbeliever
non-existence [nɔnɛgzistɑ̃s] *nf* : nonexistence — **non-existent** [nɔnɛgzistɑ̃] *adj*
non-fumeur, -meuse [nɔ̃fymœr, -møz] *n* : nonsmoker
non-intervention [nɔnɛ̃tɛrvɑ̃sjɔ̃] *nf* : nonintervention
nono, nonote [nɔno] *n Can fam* : fool, idiot
nonobstant [nɔnɔpstɑ̃] *adv & prep* : notwithstanding
nonoune [nɔnun] *adj Can fam* : stupid, thick
non-paiement [nɔ̃pɛmɑ̃] *nm* : nonpayment
non-prolifération [nɔ̃prɔliferasjɔ̃] *nf* : nonproliferation
non-sens [nɔsɑ̃s] *nms & pl* **1** ABSURDITÉ : absurdity, nonsense **2** : meaningless word or phrase
non-violence [nɔ̃vjɔlɑ̃s] *nf* : nonviolence
non-violent, -lente [nɔ̃vjɔlɑ̃, -lɑ̃t] *adj* : nonviolent
non-voyant, -voyante [nɔ̃vwajɑ̃, -jɑ̃t] *n* : blind person
nord[1] [nɔr] *adj* : north, northern
nord[2] *nm* **1** : north <exposé au nord : with a northerly aspect> <vent du nord : north wind> **2 le Nord** : the North **3 perdre le nord** *fam* : to become disoriented
nord-américain, -caine [nɔramerikɛ̃, -kɛn] *adj* : North American
Nord-Américain, -caine *n* : North American
nord-coréen, -réenne [nɔrkɔreɛ̃, -ɛn] *adj* : North Korean
Nord-Coréen, -réenne *n* : North Korean
nord-est[1] [nɔrɛst] *adj s & pl* **1** : northeast, northeastern **2** : northeasterly
nord-est[2] *nm* : northeast
nordique[1] [nɔrdik] *adj* : Nordic, Scandinavian
nordique[2] *nm* : Norse (language)
Nordique *nmf* : Scandinavian
nord-ouest[1] [nɔrwɛst] *adj s & pl* **1** : northwest, northwestern **2** : northwesterly
nord-ouest[2] *nm* : northwest
normal, -male [nɔrmal] *adj, mpl* **normaux** [nɔrmo] **1** : normal, standard, usual **2** : normal, natural <c'est bien normal : it's only natural>
normale *nf* **1** : average, normal <audessous de la normale : below normal> **2** NORME : norm, standard
normalement [nɔrmalmɑ̃] *adv* : normally, usually
normaliser [nɔrmalize] *vt* : to normalize, to standardize — **normalisation** [-lizasjɔ̃] *nf*
norme [nɔrm] *nf* : norm, standard
norvégien[1], **-gienne** [nɔrveʒjɛ̃, -ʒjɛn] *adj* : Norwegian
norvégien[2] *nm* : Norwegian (language)

Norvégien, -gienne *n* : Norwegian
nos → **notre**
nostalgie [nɔstalʒi] *nf* : nostalgia — **nostalgique** [nɔstalʒik] *adj*
notable[1] [nɔtabl] *adj* : notable, noteworthy
notable[2] *nm* : notable
notablement [nɔtabləmɑ̃] *adv* : notably, considerably
notaire [nɔtɛr] *nm* : notary public
notamment [nɔtamɑ̃] *adv* PARTICULIÈREMENT : especially, particularly
notation [nɔtasjɔ̃] *nf* : notation
note [nɔt] *nf* **1** : note <prendre des notes : to take notes> **2** ADDITION : bill, check **3** : mark, grade (in school) **4** : note (in music) **5** : touch, hint <une note de tristesse : a note of sadness> **6 note de service** : memorandum **7 note en bas de la page** : footnote
noter [nɔte] *vt* **1** REMARQUER : to note, to take notice of **2** MARQUER : to mark <noter un passage important : to mark an important passage> **3** : to mark, to grade **4** INSCRIRE : to write, to note down
notice [nɔtis] *nf* **1** : note <notice bibliographique : bibliographical note> **2** : instructions *pl*
notifier [nɔtifje] {96} *vt* : to notify — **notification** [-tifikasjɔ̃] *nf*
notion [nɔsjɔ̃] *nf* **1** : notion, idea **2 notions** *nfpl* : rudiments, basic knowledge
notoire [nɔtwar] *adj* **1** CONNU : well-known **2** : notorious
notoirement [nɔtwarmɑ̃] *adv* : notoriously
notoriété [nɔtɔrjete] *nf* **1** : fame, renown **2** : celebrity (person) **3 de notoriété publique** : common knowledge
notre [nɔtr] *adj, pl* **nos** [no] : our
nôtre[1] [notr] *adj* : our own <nous avons fait nôtres ces idées : we have made these ideas ours>
nôtre[2] *pron* **le nôtre, la nôtre, les nôtres** : ours <nous avons les nôtres : we have ours>
nouer [nwe] *vt* **1** : to tie, to knot, to fasten **2** : to start up, to establish <nouer des relations avec : to begin a relationship with> **3 avoir la gorge nouée** : to have a lump in one's throat
noueux, noueuse [nwø, -øz] *adj* : knotty, knobby, gnarled
nougat [nuga] *nm* : nougat
nouille [nuj] *nf* **1** *fam* : nitwit, idiot **2 nouilles** *nfpl* : noodles, pasta
nourri, -rie [nuri] *adj* **1** : heavy (of gunfire) **2** : sustained, prolonged
nourrice [nuris] *nf* : wet nurse
nourrir [nurir] *vt* **1** ALIMENTER : to feed, to nourish **2** ALLAITER : to breast-feed **3** : to provide for (a family, etc.) **4** : to nurse, to harbor <nourrir des doutes : to entertain doubts> **— se nourrir** *vr* **1** : to eat **2 ~ de** : to feed on
nourrissant, -sante [nurisɑ̃, -sɑ̃t] *adj* : nourishing, nutritious
nourrisson [nurisɔ̃] *nm* : infant
nourriture [nurityr] *nf* **1** : food **2** : diet **3** : (intellectual) nourishment
nous [nu] *pron* **1** : we **2** : us <il nous a dit de partir : he told us to go> **3** : ourselves <nous nous amusons : we're enjoying ourselves> **4 nous autres** *Can fam* : we <ils ne travaillent pas comme nous autres : they don't work as hard as we do>
nous–mêmes [numɛm] *pron* : ourselves
nouveau[1] [nuvo] **(-vel** [-vɛl] *before a vowel or mute h*), **-velle** [-vɛl] *adj, mpl* **nouveaux 1** : new **2** : novel, fresh <une nouvelle idée : an original idea> **3 de ~** *or* **à ~** : again, once again **4 nouveau venu** : newcomer
nouveau[2] *nm* **1 du nouveau** : something new **2 le nouveau** : the new
nouveau–né, -née [nuvone] *adj & n, mpl* **nouveau–nés** : newborn
nouveauté [nuvote] *nf* **1** : newness, novelty **2** : innovation
nouvelle [nuvɛl] *nf* **1** : piece of news <c'est une bonne nouvelle : that's good news> **2** : short story **3 nouvelles** *nfpl* : news <les nouvelles vont vite : news travels fast> <regarder les nouvelles : to watch the news>
nouvellement [nuvɛlmɑ̃] *adv* : newly, recently
novateur[1], **-trice** [nɔvatœr, -tris] *adj* : innovative
novateur[2], **-trice** *n* : innovator
novembre [nɔvɑ̃br] *nm* : November
novice[1] [nɔvis] *adj* : inexperienced
novice[2] *nmf* : novice, beginner
noviciat [nɔvisja] *nm* : novitiate
noyade [nwajad] *nf* : drowning
noyau [nwajo] *nm, pl* **noyaux 1** : pit, stone (of a fruit) **2** : nucleus, core (in science) **3** : group, core <un noyau de résistance : a pocket of resistance>
noyautage [nwajotaʒ] *nm* : infiltration
noyauter [nwajote] *vt* : to infiltrate
noyé[1], **noyée** [nwaje] *adj* **1** PERDU : lost, out of one's depth **2** : flooded <des yeux noyés de larmes : eyes brimming with tears>
noyé[2], **noyée** *n* : drowning victim
noyer[1] [nwaje] {58} *vt* **1** : to drown **2** : to flood <noyer le moteur : to flood the engine> **3** : to shroud, to blur, to drown out **— se noyer** *vr* **1** : to drown **2** : to be swamped, to be drowned (out) **3 ~ dans** : to get bogged down in
noyer[2] *nm* **1** : walnut tree **2 noyer blanc d'Amérique** : hickory (tree)
nu[1], **nue** [ny] *adj* **1** : naked, nude **2** : uncovered <être pieds nus : to be barefoot(ed)> <à main nue : bare-handed> **3** : bare, plain, unadorned

nu[2] *nm* **1** : nude (in art) **2 à ~** : bare, exposed <mettre à nu : to expose, to lay bare>
nuage [nɥaʒ] *nm* **1** : cloud <sans nuages : cloudless, unclouded> <être dans les nuages : to have one's head in the clouds> **2** : cloud, mass (of dust, smoke, etc.) <un nuage de lait : a dash of milk>
nuageux, -geuse [nɥaʒø, -ʒøz] *adj* **1** COUVERT : cloudy, overcast **2** : hazy, obscure
nuance [nɥɑ̃s] *nf* **1** TON : hue, shade <nuance de vert : shade of green> **2** : subtlety, nuance **3 une nuance de** : a touch of, a trace of
nuancer [nɥɑ̃se] {6} *vt* : to qualify (thoughts, opinions, etc.)
nubile [nybil] *adj* : nubile
nucléaire[1] [nykleɛr] *adj* : nuclear
nucléaire[2] *nm* : nuclear energy
nudisme [nydism] *nm* : nudism — **nudiste** [nydist] *adj & nmf*
nudité [nydite] *nf* **1** : nudity, nakedness **2** : bareness
nuée [nɥe] *nf* : cloud, swarm
nues [ny] *nfpl* **1 porter qqn aux nues** : to praise s.o. to the skies **2 tomber des nues** : to be taken aback
nuire [nɥir] {49} *vi* **~ à** : to harm, to injure — **se nuire** *vr*
nuisait [nɥizɛ], **nuisions** [nɥizjɔ̃], *etc.* → **nuire**
nuisance [nɥizɑ̃s] *nf* : pollution <nuisance sonore : noise pollution>
nuise [nɥiz], *etc.* → **nuire**
nuisible [nɥizibl] *adj* : harmful, injurious
nuit [nɥi] *nf* **1** : night, nighttime **2** : darkness <il fait nuit : it's dark out> **3 de ~** : nocturnal, at night, by night
nul[1], **nulle** [nyl] *adj* **1** : no <je n'ai nul besoin de sortir : I have no need to go out> <sans nul doute : without a doubt, undoubtedly> <nulle part : nowhere> **2** : nil, nonexistent **3** : invalid, null and void **4** : hopeless, useless, worthless <il est nulle en biologie : he is hopeless in biology>
nul[2] *pron* : no one, nobody
nullement [nylmɑ̃] *adv* : by no means
nullité [nylite] *nf* **1** : incompetence, worthlessness **2** : nonentity **3** : nullity (of a contract, etc.)
numéraire [nymerɛr] *nm* : cash
numéral[1], **-rale** [nymeral] *adj, mpl* **-raux** : numeral
numéral[2] *nm, pl* **-raux** : numeral
numérateur [nymeratœr] *nm* : numerator
numération [nymerasjɔ̃] *nf* **1** : notation <numération décimale : decimal notation> **2 numération globulaire** : blood count
numérique [nymerik] *adj* **1** : numerical **2** : digital — **numériquement** *adv*
numéro [nymero] *nm* **1** : number <le numéro deux : number two> <numéro de téléphone : telephone number> **2** : issue (of a periodical) **3 quel numéro!** *fam* : what a character!
numéroter [nymerɔte] *vt* : to number
numismate [nymismat] *nmf* : numismatist, coin collector
numismatique [nymismatik] *nf* : numismatics
nu–pieds [nypje] *adj* : barefoot(ed)
nuptial, -tiale [nypsjal] *adj, mpl* **-tiaux** [-sjo] : nuptial, wedding
nuque [nyk] *nf* : nape of the neck
nutritif, -tive [nytritif, -tiv] *adj* **1** : nourishing, nutritious **2** : nutritional
nutrition [nytrisjɔ̃] *nf* : nutrition — **nutritionnel, -nelle** [-sjɔnɛl] *adj*
nylon [nilɔ̃] *nm* **1** : nylon **2 bas de nylon** : nylon stockings, panty hose
nymphe [nɛ̃f] *nf* : nymph

O

o [o] *nm* : o, the 15th letter of the alphabet
oasis [ɔazis] *nf* : oasis
obédience [ɔbedjɑ̃s] *nf* : allegiance, persuasion <pays d'obédience communiste : Communist countries>
obéir [ɔbeir] *vi* **~ à 1** : to obey **2** SE CONFORMER : to follow, to comply with **3** : to respond to <les freins obéissent à la pression : the brakes respond to pressure>
obéissance [ɔbeisɑ̃s] *nf* : obedience
obéissant, -sante [ɔbeisɑ̃, -sɑ̃t] *adj* : obedient
obélisque [ɔbelisk] *nm* : obelisk
obèse [ɔbɛz] *adj* : obese
obésité [ɔbezite] *nf* : obesity
objecter [ɔbʒɛkte] *vt* **1** : to raise as an objection <il m'objecta que . . . : he objected (to me) that . . .> **2** PRÉTEXTER : to plead <objecter la fatigue : to plead tiredness>
objecteur [ɔbʒɛktœr] *nm* : objector <objecteur de conscience : conscientious objector>
objectif[1], **-tive** [ɔbʒɛktif, -tiv] *adj* : objective — **objectivement** [-tivmɑ̃] *adv*
objectif[2] *nm* **1** BUT : objective, goal **2** : lens (of an optical instrument)
objection [ɔbʒɛksjɔ̃] *nf* : objection
objectivité [ɔbʒɛktivite] *nf* : objectivity
objet [ɔbʒɛ] *nm* **1** : object, thing **2** : subject, topic **3** BUT : goal, purpose <sans objet : pointless, aimless> **4** : object (in grammar) **5 bureau des objets**

trouvés : lost-and-found department **6 objet de famille** : heirloom

obligation [ɔbligasjɔ̃] *nf* **1** : obligation, duty **2** : bond, debenture

obligatoire [ɔbligatwar] *adj* **1** : compulsory, obligatory, mandatory **2** *fam* : inevitable

obligatoirement [ɔbligatwarmɑ̃] *adv* **1** : necessarily, imperatively **2** *fam* : inevitably

obligé, -gée [ɔbliʒe] *adj* **1 être obligé à** : to be indebted to **2 c'est obligé** *fam* : it's bound to happen, it's inevitable

obligeamment [ɔbliʒamɑ̃] *adv* : obligingly

obligeance [ɔbliʒɑ̃s] *nf* AMABILITÉ : kindness, helpfulness

obligeant, -geante [ɔbliʒɑ̃, -ʒɑ̃t] *adj* COMPLAISANT : obliging, kind

obliger [ɔbliʒe] {17} *vt* **1** CONTRAINDRE : to force, to compel **2** : to oblige <vous m'obligez beaucoup : I am much obliged to you>

oblique [ɔblik] *adj* **1** : oblique **2 en ~** : crosswise, diagonally — **obliquement** [ɔblikmɑ̃] *adv*

obliquer [ɔblike] *vi* : to bear, to turn (off) <obliquer à droite : to turn right>

oblitérer [ɔblitere] {87} *vt* : to cancel (a stamp) — **oblitération** [-terasjɔ̃] *nf*

oblong, oblongue [ɔblɔ̃, ɔblɔ̃g] *adj* : oblong

obnubiler [ɔbnybile] *vt* **1** OBSCURCIR : to cloud, to obscure **2** OBSÉDER : to obsess

obole [ɔbɔl] *nf* : small contribution

obscène [ɔpsɛn] *adj* : obscene

obscénité [ɔpsenite] *nf* : obscenity

obscur, -cure [ɔpskyr] *adj* **1** SOMBRE : dark **2** : obscure, vague **3** : abstruse, recondite — **obscurément** [-skyremɑ̃] *adv*

obscurcir [ɔpskyrsir] *vt* **1** ASSOMBRIR : to darken **2** : to obscure, to blur **3** : to make obscure, to confuse — **s'obscurcir** *vr* **1** : to become dark **2** : to become confused

obscurité [ɔpskyrite] *nf* **1** : darkness **2** ANONYMAT : obscurity

obsédant, -dante [ɔpsedɑ̃, -dɑ̃t] *adj* : obsessive, haunting

obsédé, -dée [ɔpsede] *n* : obsessive, fanatic

obséder [ɔpsede] {87} *vt* : to obsess, to haunt

obsèques [ɔpsɛk] *nfpl* : funeral

obséquieux, -quieuse [ɔpsekjø, -kjøz] *adj* : obsequious — **obséquieusement** [-kjøzmɑ̃] *adv*

obséquiosité [ɔpsekjozite] *nf* : obsequiousness

observance [ɔpsɛrvɑ̃s] *nf* : observance

observateur[1], **-trice** [ɔpsɛrvatœr, -tris] *adj* : observant, perceptive

observateur[2], **-trice** *n* : observer

observation [ɔpsɛrvasjɔ̃] *nf* **1** : observance **2** : observing, observation **3** REMARQUE : observation, remark

observatoire [ɔpsɛrvatwar] *nm* **1** : observatory **2** : observation post, vantage point

observer [ɔpsɛrve] *vt* **1** : to observe, to watch **2** : to note, to notice **3** : to keep, to maintain <observer sa position : to maintain one's position> <observer le silence : to keep quiet> — **s'observer** *vr*

obsession [ɔpsesjɔ̃] *nf* : obsession

obsessionnel, -nelle [ɔpsesjɔnɛl] *adj* : obsessive

obsolescent, -cente [ɔpsɔlɛsɑ̃, -sɑ̃t] *adj* : obsolescent — **obsolescence** [-lɛsɑ̃s] *nf*

obsolète [ɔpsɔlɛt] *adj* : obsolete

obstacle [ɔpstakl] *nm* **1** : obstacle <faire obstacle : to obstruct> **2** : fence, hurdle (in horseback riding)

obstétrical, -cale [ɔpstetrikal] *adj, mpl* **-caux** [-ko] : obstetric, obstetrical

obstétricien, -cienne [ɔpstetrisjɛ̃, -sjɛn] *n* : obstetrician

obstétrique [ɔpstetrik] *nf* : obstetrics

obstination [ɔpstinasjɔ̃] *nf* : obstinacy, stubbornness

obstiné, -née [ɔpstine] *adj* ENTÊTÉ : obstinate, stubborn — **obstinément** [-nemɑ̃] *adv*

obstiner [ɔpstine] *v* **s'obstiner** *vr* **1 s'obstiner à faire** : to insist on doing **2 ~ dans** : to persist in, to cling to

obstruction [ɔpstryksjɔ̃] *nf* **1** : obstruction, blockage <faire de l'obstruction : to obstruct, to be obstructive> **2** : filibuster <faire de l'obstruction parlementaire : to filibuster>

obstructionniste [ɔpstryksjɔnist] *adj* : obstructive

obstruer [ɔpstrye] *vt* : to obstruct, to block — **s'obstruer** *vr*

obtempérer [ɔptɑ̃pere] {87} *vi* **~ à** : to obey, to comply with

obtenir [ɔptənir] {92} *vt* : to obtain, to get, to secure — **s'obtenir** *vr*

obtention [ɔptɑ̃sjɔ̃] *nf* : obtaining

obtient [ɔptjɛ̃] *pp* → **obtenir**

obturateur [ɔptyratœr] *nm* : shutter (of a camera)

obturation [ɔptyrasjɔ̃] *nf* **1** : closing up, sealing **2** *or* **obturation dentaire** : filling

obturer [ɔptyre] *vt* **1** : to seal, to stop up **2** : to fill (a tooth)

obtus, -tuse [ɔpty, -tyz] *adj* **1** : obtuse (of an angle) **2** : slow-witted, dull

obus [ɔby] *nm* **1** : shell <obus de mortier : mortar shell> **2 éclats d'obus** : shrapnel

obusier [ɔbyzje] *nm* : howitzer

obvier [ɔbvje] {96} *vi* **~ à** : to guard against, to obviate

occasion [ɔkazjɔ̃] *nf* **1** : opportunity, chance **2** : occasion <les grandes occasions : special occasions> **3** : bargain **4 d'~** : secondhand <vêtements d'occasion : secondhand clothing>

occasionnel[1], -nelle [ɔkazjɔnɛl] *adj* **1** : occasional **2** FORTUIT : chance, fortuitous

occasionnel[2], -nelle *n Can* : temp, temporary employee

occasionnellement [ɔkazjɔnɛlmɑ̃] *adv* : occasionally

occasionner [ɔkazjɔne] *vt* CAUSER : to cause, to bring about

occident [ɔksidɑ̃] *nm* **1** : west **2 l'Occident** : the West

occidental, -tale [ɔksidɑ̃tal] *adj, mpl* **-taux** [-to] : western, Western

Occidental, -tale *n, mpl* **-taux** [-to] : Westerner

occidentaliser [ɔsidɑ̃talize] *vt* : to westernize

occulte [ɔkylt] *adj* : supernatural, occult

occulter [ɔkylte] *vt* **1** : to overshadow **2** : to cover up, to conceal

occupant[1], -pante [ɔkypɑ̃,-pɑ̃t] *adj* : occupying

occupant[2], -pante *n* : occupant, occupier

occupation [ɔkypasjɔ̃] *nf* **1** : occupation, job **2** : occupancy **3** : (military) occupation

occupé, -pée [ɔkype] *adj* **1** : busy **2** : taken, in use <cette place est occupée : this seat is taken> <la ligne est occupée : the line is busy> **3** : occupied <zone occupée : occupied zone>

occuper [ɔkype] *vt* **1** : to occupy, to hold **2** : to employ, to keep busy **3** REMPLIR : to take up, to fill **4** : to inhabit **— s'occuper** *vr* **1** : to keep busy **2 ~ de** : to handle, to deal with, to take care of

occurrence [ɔkyrɑ̃s] *nf* : instance, case <en l'occurrence : in this case>

océan [ɔseɑ̃] *nm* : ocean

océanien, -nienne [ɔseanjɛ̃, -njɛn] *adj* : Oceanian

Océanien, -nienne *n* : Oceanian

océanique [ɔseanik] *adj* : oceanic, ocean

océanographie [ɔseanɔgrafi] *nf* : oceanography **— océanographique** [-grafik] *adj*

ocelot [ɔslo] *nm* : ocelot

ocre [ɔkr] *nmf* : ocher

octave [ɔktav] *nf* : octave

octet [ɔktɛ] *nm* : byte

octobre [ɔktɔbr] *nm* : October

octogone [ɔktɔgɔn] *nm* : octagon **— octogonal, -nale** [-gɔnal] *adj*

octroi [ɔktrwa] *nm* : granting

octroyer [ɔktrwaje] {58} *vt* : to grant, to bestow

oculaire[1] [ɔkylɛr] *adj* : ocular, eye

oculaire[2] *nm* : eyepiece

oculiste [ɔkylist] *nmf* : oculist

ode [ɔd] *nf* : ode

odeur [ɔdœr] *nf* : odor, smell, scent

odieux, -dieuse [ɔdjø, -djøz] *adj* EXÉCRABLE : odious, hateful **— odieusement** [-djøzmɑ̃] *adv*

odorant, -rante [ɔdɔrɑ̃, -rɑ̃t] *adj* PARFUMÉ : fragrant, sweet-smelling, odorous

odorat [ɔdɔra] *nm* : sense of smell

odoriférant, -rante [ɔdɔriferɑ̃, -rɑ̃t] *adj* : fragrant

odyssée [ɔdise] *nf* : odyssey

œcuménique [ekymenik] *adj* : ecumenical, nondenominational

œdème [edɛm] *nm* : edema

œil [œj] *nm, pl* **yeux** [jø] **1** : eye <yeux verts : green eyes> <avoir à l'œil : to keep an eye on> <coup d'œil : glance> **2** : look, view <jeter un œil à : to have a quick look at> <d'un œil jaloux : jealously> <voir d'un mauvais œil : to take a dim view of> **3** : eye (of a needle, potato, storm, etc.) **4** → **clin**

œillade [œjad] *nf* **1** : wink, glance **2 faire des œillades à** : to make eyes at

œillères [œjɛr] *nfpl* **1** : blinders, blinkers **2 avoir des œillères** : to be narrow-minded

œillet [œjɛ] *nm* **1** : eyelet, grommet **2** : carnation, pink

œsophage [ezɔfaʒ] *nm* : esophagus

œstrogène [ɛstrɔʒɛn] *nm* : estrogen

œuf [œf] *nm, pl* **œufs** [ø] **1** : egg <œufs pochés : poached eggs> **2 étouffer dans l'œuf** : to nip in the bud

œuvre[1] [œvr] *nm* : body of work <l'œuvre peint de Monet : Monet's paintings>

œuvre[2] *nf* **1** : work <œuvre d'art : work of art> **2** : undertaking, task, work <se mettre à l'œuvre : to get down to work> <mise en œuvre : implementation> **3** : effect, work <le médicament a fait son œuvre : the medicine has done its work> **4** *or* **œuvre de bienfaisance** : charitable organization

œuvrer [œvre] *vi* : to work

offensant, -sante [ɔfɑ̃sɑ̃, -sɑ̃t] *adj* INJURIEUX : offensive, insulting

offense [ɔfɑ̃s] *nf* **1** : offense, insult **2** : trespass, sin

offenser [ɔfɑ̃se] *vt* : to offend, to hurt **— s'offenser** *vr* : to take offense

offensif, -sive [ɔfɑ̃sif, -siv] *adj* : offensive, attacking **— offensivement** [-sivmɑ̃] *adv*

offensive *nf* **1** : offensive <passer à l'offensive : to go on the offensive> **2** : onset, onslaught

offert [ɔfɛr] *pp* → **offrir**

offertoire [ɔfɛrtwar] *nm* : offertory

office [ɔfis] *nm* **1** : bureau, agency **2** : office, service (in religion) **3** : office, function <faire office de : to act as> **4 d'~** : automatically, as a matter of course <rejeter d'office : to dismiss out of hand>

officialiser [ɔfisjalize] *vt* : to make official

officiel[1], -cielle [ɔfisjɛl] *adj* : official — **officiellement** [-sjɛlmɑ̃] *adv*

officiel[2], -cielle *n* : official

officier[1] [ɔfisje] {96} *vi* : to officiate

officier[2] *nm* : officer

officieux, -cieuse [ɔfisjø, -sjøz] *adj* : unofficial, informal — **officieusement** [-sjøzmɑ̃] *adv*

officinal, -nale [ɔfisinal] *adj, mpl* **-naux** [-no] : medicinal <plantes officinales : medicinal plants>

officine [ɔfisin] *nf* **1** : pharmacy **2** : group, den (of conspirators, etc.)

offrande [ɔfrɑ̃d] *nf* : offering

offrant [ɔfrɑ̃] *nm* **vendre au plus offrant** : to sell to the highest bidder

offre [ɔfr] *nf* **1** : offer, bid <offre d'emploi : job opening> **2 l'offre et la demande** : supply and demand

offrir [ɔfrir] {83} *vt* : to give, to offer — **s'offrir** *vr* **1** : to offer oneself, to volunteer **2** : to treat oneself to <je me suis offerte des vacances : I gave myself a vacation> **3** SE PRÉSENTER : to present itself

offusquer [ɔfyske] *vt* : to offend — **s'offusquer** *vr* : to take offense

ogive [ɔʒiv] *nf* **1** : rib (in architecture) **2** : warhead <ogive nucléaire : nuclear warhead>

ogre, ogresse [ɔgr, ɔgrɛs] *n* **1** : ogre **2 manger comme un ogre** : to eat like a horse

oh[1] [o] *nm* **pousser des oh et des ah** : to ooh and ah

oh[2] *interj* : oh!

ohé [ɔe] *interj* **1** : hey there! **2 ohé du navire!** : ship ahoy!

ohm [om] *nm* : ohm

oie [wa] *nf* : goose

oignon [ɔɲɔ̃] *nm* **1** : onion **2** : bulb (of a flower) **3** : bunion **4 occupe-toi de tes oignons** *fam* : mind your own business

oindre [wɛ̃dr] {59} *vt* : to anoint

oiseau [wazo] *nm, pl* **oiseaux 1** : bird <oiseau chanteur : songbird> <oiseau de proie : bird of prey> <oiseau marin : seabird> **2** : hod (for bricks, etc.) **3** *fam* : character, oddball

oiseau-mouche [wazomuʃ] *nm, pl* **oiseaux-mouches** : hummingbird

oiseux, -seuse [wazø, -zøz] *adj* INUTILE : pointless, idle

oisif[1], -sive [wazif, -ziv] *adj* : idle — **oisivement** [-zivmɑ̃] *adv*

oisif[2], -sive *n* : idler

oisillon [wazijɔ̃] *nm* : fledgling

oisiveté [wazivte] *nf* : idleness

oison [wazɔ̃] *nm* : gosling

oléoduc [ɔleɔdyk] *nm* : (oil) pipeline

olfactif, -tive [ɔlfaktif, -tiv] *adj* : olfactory

oligarchie [ɔligarʃi] *nf* : oligarchy

olive[1] [ɔliv] *adj* : olive green

olive[2] *nf* : olive

olivier [ɔlivje] *nm* **1** : olive tree **2** : olive wood

olympiade [ɔlɛ̃pjad] *nf or* **olympiades** [-pjad] *nfpl* : Olympic Games, Olympics

olympique [ɔlɛ̃pik] *adj* : Olympic <les Jeux olympiques : the Olympic Games>

omanais, -naise [ɔmanɛ, -nɛz] *adj* : Omani

Omanais, -naise *n* : Omani

ombilical, -cale [ɔ̃bilikal] *adj, mpl* **-caux** [-ko] : umbilical

ombrage [ɔ̃braʒ] *nm* **1** : shade **2 porter ombrage de** : to offend **3 prendre ombrage de** : to take umbrage at

ombragé, -gée [ɔ̃braʒe] *adj* : shady, shaded

ombrager [ɔ̃braʒe] {17} *vt* : to shade, to darken

ombrageux, -geuse [ɔ̃braʒø, -ʒøz] *adj* **1** : skittish (of a horse) **2** : touchy, easily offended

ombre [ɔ̃br] *nf* **1** : shade <20 degrés à l'ombre : 20 degrees in the shade> **2** : shadow **3** : obscurity <sortir de l'ombre : to come out into the open> **4** : hint, trace <sans l'ombre d'un doute : without a shadow of a doubt> **5 ombre à paupières** : eyeshadow

ombrelle [ɔ̃brɛl] *nf* : parasol, sunshade

ombrer [ɔ̃bre] *vt* : to shade

omelette [ɔmlɛt] *nf* : omelet

omettre [ɔmɛtr] {53} *vt* : to omit, to leave out

omission [ɔmisjɔ̃] *nf* : omission

omnibus [ɔmnibys] *nm* : local train

omnipotent, -tente [ɔmnipɔtɑ̃, -tɑ̃t] *adj* : omnipotent — **omnipotence** [-tɑ̃s] *nf*

omniprésent, -sente [ɔmniprezɑ̃, -zɑ̃t] *adj* : omnipresent, ubiquitous

omniscient, -ciente [ɔmnisjɑ̃, -sjɑ̃t] *adj* : omniscient

omnivore [ɔmnivɔr] *adj* : omnivorous

omoplate [ɔmɔplat] *nf* : shoulder blade, scapula

on [ɔ̃] *pron* **1** : one, they, someone, you, we, people <on ne sait jamais : one never knows, you never know> <mon frère et moi, on va à Québec : my brother and I are going to Quebec> <on vous a appelé : someone called you> <comme on dit : as they say> <on jasait : people were talking> <ici on parle français : French is spoken here> **2** *fam* : we, you <alors, on est prêt? : well, are you (finally) ready?> <assez! on s'en va! : that's enough! we're leaving!>

once [ɔ̃s] *nf* : ounce

oncle [ɔ̃kl] *nm* : uncle

onction [ɔ̃ksjɔ̃] → **extrême-onction**

onctueux, -tueuse [ɔ̃ktɥø, -tɥøz] *adj* **1** : smooth, creamy **2** : unctuous

ondatra [ɔ̃datra] *nm* : muskrat

onde [ɔ̃d] *nf* **1** : wave <onde sonore : sound wave> <onde de choc : shock wave> <ondes courtes : shortwave> **2 sur les ondes** : on the radio, on the air
ondée [ɔ̃de] *nf* : (rain) shower
on–dit [ɔ̃di] *nms & pl* : rumor <ce ne sont que des on-dit : that's just hearsay>
ondoyer [ɔ̃dwaje] {58} *vi* : to ripple, to wave
ondulation [ɔ̃dylasjɔ̃] *nf* : undulation, wave
ondulé, -lée [ɔ̃dyle] *adj* **1** : wavy <cheveux ondulés : wavy hair> **2** : corrugated
onduler [ɔ̃dyle] *vi* **1** : to undulate, to wave **2 se faire onduler les cheveux** : to have one's hair waved, to get a permanent
onduleux, -leuse [ɔ̃dylø, -løz] *adj* : undulating, wavy
onéreux, -reuse [ɔnerø, -røz] *adj* COÛTEUX : costly — **onéreusement** [-røzmɑ̃] *adv*
ongle [ɔ̃gl] *nm* **1** : nail <ongles des mains : fingernails> <ongles des pieds : toenails> **2** : claw, talon
onglet [ɔ̃glɛ] *nm* **1** : thumbnail groove (on a knife, etc.) <assemblage à onglet : miter joint> **2** : thumb index
onguent [ɔ̃gɑ̃] *nm* : ointment
onirique [ɔnirik] *adj* : dreamlike, dreamy
onyx [ɔniks] *nm* : onyx
onze[1] [ɔ̃z] *adj* **1** : eleven **2** : eleventh <le onze mai : May eleventh>
onze[2] *nms & pl* : eleven
onzième [ɔ̃zjɛm] *adj & nmf & nm* : eleventh
opacité [ɔpasite] *nf* : opacity
opale [ɔpal] *nf* : opal
opaque [ɔpak] *adj* : opaque
opéra [ɔpera] *nm* **1** : opera <opéra bouffe : comic opera> **2** : opera house
opéra–comique [ɔperakɔmik] *nm, pl* **opéras–comiques** [-kɔmik] : light opera
opérateur, -trice [ɔperatœr, -tris] *n* **1** : operator (of a machine) **2 opérateur de saisie** : computer operator, keyboarder
opération [ɔperasjɔ̃] *nf* **1** : operation, process **2** : operation, surgery <salle d'opération : operating room> **3** CALCUL : calculation, (mathematical) operation **4** : transaction, dealing <opérations de bourse : stock transactions>
opérationnel, -nelle [ɔperasjɔnɛl] *adj* : operational
opératoire [ɔperatwar] *adj* **1** : operating, surgical **2** : operative
opérer [ɔpere] {87} *vt* **1** : to produce, to bring about **2** : to operate on **3** : to carry out, to implement — *vi* **1** : to take effect, to work **2** : to proceed, to operate — **s'opérer** *vr* SE PRODUIRE : to occur, to take place
opérette [ɔperɛt] *nf* : operetta, light opera
ophtalmologie [ɔftalmɔlɔgi] *nf* : ophthalmology — **ophtalmologiste** [-lɔʒist] *or* **ophtalmologue** [-lɔg] *nmf*
opiacé [ɔpjase] *nm* : opiate
opiner [ɔpine] *vi* **1 ~ à** : to consent to **2 opiner du bonnet** : to nod in agreement
opiniâtre [ɔpinjatr] *adj* **1** OBSTINÉ : obstinate, stubborn **2** : dogged, persistent — **opiniâtrement** [-jatrəmɑ̃] *adv*
opiniâtreté [ɔpinjatrəte] *nf* **1** OBSTINATION : obstinacy, stubbornness **2** : doggedness, tenacity
opinion [ɔpinjɔ̃] *nf* : opinion, belief
opium [ɔpjɔm] *nm* : opium
opossum [ɔpɔsɔm] *nm* : opossum
opportun, -tune [ɔpɔrtœ̃, -tyn] *adj* : opportune, timely
opportunément [ɔpɔrtynemɑ̃] *adv* : at the right time, opportunely
opportunisme [ɔpɔrtynism] *nm* : opportunism
opportuniste[1] [ɔpɔrtynist] *adj* : opportunist, opportunistic
opportuniste[2] *nmf* : opportunist
opportunité [ɔpɔrtynite] *nf* : timeliness, appropriateness
opposant[1], **-sante** [ɔpozɑ̃, -zɑ̃t] *adj* : opposing
opposant[2], **-sante** *n* ADVERSAIRE : opponent
opposé[1], **-sée** [ɔpoze] *adj* **1** : opposing, conflicting <points de vues opposés : opposing views> **2** : opposite <le côté opposé : the opposite side> **3 ~ à** : opposed to
opposé[2] *nm* **1** : opposite **2 à l'opposé** : on the other hand **3 à l'opposé de** : contrary to
opposer [ɔpoze] *vt* **1** : to put forth (an objection, etc.) <il n'y a rien à opposer à celà : there's nothing to object to in that> **2** : to put up against <opposer nos troupes à l'ennemi : to pit our forces against the enemy> **3** : to set in opposition, to contrast (ideas, etc.) **4** : to divide, to bring into conflict — **s'opposer** *vr* **1** : to clash, to conflict, to be the opposite **2 ~ à** : to be opposed to
opposition [ɔpozisjɔ̃] *nf* **1** : opposition <en opposition avec : contrary to, against> <par opposition à : in contrast to> **2** : objection (in law, etc.) <faire opposition à un chèque : to stop a check>
oppressant, -sante [ɔpresɑ̃, -sɑ̃t] *adj* : oppressive
oppresser [ɔprese] *vt* : to oppress, to burden
oppresseur [ɔpresœr] *nm* : oppressor
oppressif, -sive [ɔpresif, -siv] *adj* : oppressive

oppression [ɔpresjɔ̃] *nf* **1** : oppression **2** : feeling of suffocation

opprimé, -mée [ɔprime] *n* : oppressed person, underdog

opprimer [ɔprime] *vt* **1** : to oppress **2** : to suppress, to stifle

opprobre [ɔprɔbr] *nm* : opprobrium, disgrace

opter [ɔpte] *vi* **~ pour** : to opt for, to choose

opticien, -cienne [ɔptisjɛ̃, -sjɛn] *n* : optician

optimal, -male [ɔptimal] *adj, mpl* **-maux** [-mo] : optimal, optimum

optimisme [ɔptimism] *nm* : optimism

optimiste[1] [ɔptimist] *adj* : optimistic

optimiste[2] *nmf* : optimist

optimum [ɔptimɔm] *adj & nm* : optimum

option [ɔpsjɔ̃] *nf* : option, choice

optionnel, -nelle [ɔpsjɔnɛl] *adj* FACULTATIF : optional

optique[1] [ɔptik] *adj* : optic, optical

optique[2] *nf* **1** : optics **2** : perspective, viewpoint

optométrie [ɔptɔmetri] *nf* : optometry — **optométriste** [-metrist] *nmf*

opulent, -lente [ɔpylɑ̃, -lɑ̃t] *adj* : opulent — **opulence** [-lɑ̃s] *nf*

opus [ɔpys] *nm* : opus

or[1] [ɔr] *nm* : gold

or[2] *conj* **1** : but, yet **2** : now

oracle [ɔrakl] *nm* : oracle

orage [ɔraʒ] *nm* **1** : storm, thunderstorm **2** : turmoil

orageux, -geuse [ɔraʒø, -ʒøz] *adj* : stormy

oraison [ɔrɛzɔ̃] *nf* **1** PRIÈRE : prayer **2 oraison funèbre** : funeral oration

oral, -rale [ɔral] *adj, mpl* **oraux** [ɔro] : oral — **oralement** [ɔralmɑ̃] *adv*

orange[1] [ɔrɑ̃ʒ] *adj* : orange

orange[2] *nf* : orange (fruit)

orange[3] *nm* : orange (color)

orangeade [ɔrɑ̃ʒad] *nf* : orangeade

oranger [ɔrɑ̃ʒe] *nm* : orange tree

orang-outan [ɔrɑ̃utɑ̃] *nm, pl* **orangs-outans** [-utɑ̃] : orangutan

orateur, -trice [ɔratœr, -tris] *n* : orator, speaker

oratoire[1] [ɔratwar] *adj* **1** : oratorical **2 l'art oratoire** : oratory, eloquence

oratoire[2] *nm* : chapel, oratory

oratorio [ɔratɔrjo] *nm* : oratorio

orbe [ɔrb] *nm* : orb

orbital, -tale [ɔrbital] *adj* **1** : orbital **2** : orbiting <station orbitale : space station>

orbite [ɔrbit] *nf* **1** : orbit <graviter une orbite de : to orbit> **2** : eye socket

orchestre [ɔrkɛstr] *nm* : orchestra — **orchestral, -trale** [-kɛstral] *adj*

orchestrer [ɔrkɛstre] *vt* : to orchestrate — **orchestration** [-kɛstrasjɔ̃] *nf*

orchidée [ɔrkide] *nf* : orchid

ordinaire[1] [ɔrdinɛr] *adj* **1** : ordinary, common, standard **2** HABITUEL : habitual, usual — **ordinairement** [-nɛrmɑ̃] *adv*

ordinaire[2] *nm* **1** : ordinary <hors de l'ordinaire : out of the ordinary> **2** : regular (gas) **3 comme à l'ordinaire** : as usual **4 d'ordinaire** : usually, as a rule

ordinal[1], **-nale** [ɔrdinal] *adj, mpl* **-naux** [-no] : ordinal

ordinal[2] *nm* : ordinal number

ordinateur [ɔrdinatœr] *nm* **1** : computer **2 ordinateur personnel** *or* **ordinateur individuel** : personal computer, PC

ordination [ɔrdinasjɔ̃] *nf* : ordination

ordonnance [ɔrdɔnɑ̃s] *nf* **1** : order, organization **2** : ordinance, ruling **3** : (medical) prescription

ordonnateur, -trice [ɔrdɔnatœr, -tris] *n* **1** : organizer **2 ordonnateur des pompes funèbres** : funeral director

ordonné, -née [ɔrdɔne] *adj* : tidy, orderly

ordonner [ɔrdɔne] *vt* **1** ARRANGER : to put in order, to arrange **2** COMMANDER : to order, to decree **3** : to ordain (in religion)

ordre [ɔrdr] *nm* **1** : order <ordre alphabétique : alphabetical order> **2** : orderliness, tidiness **3** : order, command <à l'ordre de : payable to> **4** NATURE : nature, sort <d'ordre personnel : of a personal nature> **5** : order (in biology and architecture) **6** : order, society <l'ordre jésuite : the Jesuit order> **7** : (social) order <l'ordre publique : law and order> **8 ordre du jour** : agenda

ordure [ɔrdyr] *nf* **1** : filth **2 ordures** *nfpl* : trash, garbage

ordurier [ɔrdyrje] *adj* OBSCÈNE : obscene, filthy

oreille [ɔrɛj] *nf* **1** : ear <l'oreille interne : inner ear> <prêter l'oreille : to lend an ear, to listen> **2** OUÏE : hearing <avoir l'oreille fine : to have a keen sense of hearing> <dur d'oreille : hard of hearing> **3** : handle (of a bowl, etc.), wing (of furniture)

oreiller [ɔrɛje] *nm* : pillow

oreillette [ɔrɛjɛt] *nf* : auricle (of the heart)

oreillons [ɔrɛjɔ̃] *nmpl* : mumps

ores [ɔr] *adv* **d'ores et déjà** : already

orfèvre [ɔrfɛvr] *nm* : goldsmith

organe [ɔrgan] *nm* **1** : organ <organes génitaux : genitals> <organes des sens : sense organs> **2** : vehicle, instrument **3** VOIX : voice

organigramme [ɔrganigram] *nm* **1** : organizational chart **2** : diagram, flowchart

organique [ɔrganik] *adj* : organic — **organiquement** [-nikmɑ̃] *adv*

organisateur, -trice [ɔrganizatœr, -tris] *n* : organizer

organisation [ɔrganizasjɔ̃] *nf* : organization, organizing

organisationnel, -nelle [ɔrganizasjɔnɛl] *adj* : organizational

organisé, -sée [ɔrganize] *adj* : orderly, organized

organiser [ɔrganize] *vt* : to organize, to arrange, to structure — **s'organiser** *vr* : to get organized

organisme [ɔrganism] *nm* **1** : organism **2** : organization, body

organiste [ɔrganist] *nmf* : organist

orgasme [ɔrgasm] *nm* : orgasm, climax

orge[1] [ɔrʒ] *nm* : barley (grain)

orge[2] *nf* : barley (plant)

orgelet [ɔrʒəlɛ] *nm* : sty, stye (in the eye)

orgie [ɔrʒi] *nf* : orgy

orgue [ɔrg] *nm* : organ (musical instrument)

orgueil [ɔrgœj] *nm* : pride

orgueilleux, -leuse [ɔrgœjø, -jøz] *adj* : proud, haughty — **orgueilleusement** [-jøzmɑ̃] *adv*

orient [ɔrjɑ̃] *nm* **1** : east **2 l'Orient** : the Orient, the East

oriental, -tale [ɔrjɑ̃tal] *adj, mpl* **-taux** [-to] **1** : eastern **2** : oriental

Oriental, -tale *n, mpl* **-taux** : Oriental

orientation [ɔrjɑ̃tasjɔ̃] *nf* **1** POSITION : positioning, aspect (of a house, etc.) **2** : leanings *pl,* tendencies *pl* <orientation sexuelle : sexual orientation> **3** : guidance, counseling **4** : orientation, direction <sens de l'orientation : sense of direction>

orienter [ɔrjɑ̃te] *vt* **1** : to position, to orient **2** GUIDER : to guide, to direct — **s'orienter** *vr* : to find one's bearings

orifice [ɔrifis] *nm* : opening, orifice

oriflamme [ɔriflam] *nf* : banner

origan [ɔrigɑ̃] *nm* : oregano

originaire [ɔriʒinɛr] *adj* **être originaire de** : to be a native of

original[1], **-nale** [ɔriʒinal, -nal] *adj, mpl* **-naux** [-no] **1** : original **2** : eccentric

original[2], **-nale** *n, mpl* **-naux** : character, eccentric

original[3] *nm, pl* **-naux** : original (of a document, painting, etc.)

originalité [ɔriʒinalite] *nf* **1** : originality **2** : eccentricity

origine [ɔriʒin] *nf* **1** : origin **2 à l'origine** : originally

originel, -nelle [ɔriʒinɛl] *adj* : original <péché originel : original sin>

originellement [ɔriʒinɛlmɑ̃] *adv* **1** : originally **2** : from the beginning

orignal [ɔriɲal] *nm, pl* **-naux** [-ɲo] : moose

oripeaux [ɔripo] *nmpl* GUENILLES : rags, cheap finery

orme [ɔrm] *nm* : elm

ormeau [ɔrmo] *nm, pl* **ormeaux** [-mo] : abalone

orné, -née [ɔrne] *adj* : ornate, flowery

ornement [ɔrnəmɑ̃] *nm* **1** : ornament, adornment **2 ornements sacerdotaux** : (liturgical) vestments

ornemental, -tale [ɔrnəmɑ̃tal] *adj, mpl* **-taux** [-to] : ornamental

ornementation [ɔrnəmɑ̃tasjɔ̃] *nf* : ornamentation

orner [ɔrne] *vt* **1** DÉCORER : to decorate, to adorn **2** EMBELLIR : to embellish

ornière [ɔrnjɛr] *nf* **1** : rut (in a road) **2 sortir de l'ornière** : to get out of a rut, to get out of trouble

ornithologie [ɔrnitɔlɔʒi] *nf* : ornithology

ornithologiste [ɔrnitɔlɔʒist] *or* **ornithologue** [-tɔlɔg] *nmf* : ornithologist

ornithorynque [ɔrnitɔrɛ̃k] *nm* : platypus

orphelin, -line [ɔrfəlɛ̃, -lin] *n* : orphan

orphelinat [ɔrfəlina] *nm* : orphanage

orteil [ɔrtɛj] *nm* : toe <gros orteil : big toe>

orthodontie [ɔrtɔdɔ̃si] *nf* : orthodontics — **orthodondiste** [-dɔ̃tist] *nmf*

orthodoxe [ɔrtɔdɔks] *adj* : orthodox

orthodoxie [ɔrtɔdɔksi] *nf* : orthodoxy

orthographe [ɔrtɔgraf] *nf* : spelling, orthography

orthographier [ɔrtɔgrafje] {96} *vt* **1** : to spell **2 mal orthographier** : to misspell

orthographique [ɔrtɔgrafik] *adj* : orthographic

orthopédie [ɔrtɔpedi] *nf* : orthopedics — **orthopédiste** [-pedist] *nmf*

orthopédique [ɔrtɔpedi] *adj* : orthopedic

orthophonie [ɔrtɔfɔni] *nf* : speech therapy — **orthophoniste** [-fɔnist] *nmf*

ortie [ɔrti] *nf* : nettle

oryctérope [ɔrikterɔp] *nm* : aardvark

os [ɔs] *nm* **1** : bone **2 en chair et en os** : in the flesh, in person **3 jusqu'à l'os** *or* **jusqu'aux os** : to the core, completely <il était mouillé jusqu'aux os : he was soaked to the bone>

oscillation [ɔsilasjɔ̃] *nf* **1** : oscillation **2** VARIATION : fluctuation, variation **3** : rocking, swaying

osciller [ɔsile] *vi* **1** : to oscillate **2** HÉSITER : to vacillate, to waver **3** : to rock, to sway

osé, -sée [oze, -ze] *adj* **1** : daring, bold **2** : risqué

oseille [ozɛj] *nf* : sorrel (plant)

oser [oze] *vt* **1** : to dare **2 si j'ose dire** : if I may say so

osier [ozje] *nm* **1** : willow **2** : wicker <chaise en osier : wickerwork chair>

osmose [ɔsmɔz] *nf* : osmosis

ossature [ɔsatyr] *nf* **1** : skeleton, bone structure **2** : framework

osselets [ɔslɛ] *nmpl* : jacks (game)

ossements [ɔsmɑ̃] *nmpl* : remains, bones

osseux, -seuse [ɔsø, -søz] *adj* : bony <tissu osseux : bone tissue>

ostensible [ɔstɑ̃sibl] *adj* : conspicuous, open — **ostensiblement** [-sibləmɑ̃] *adv*

ostentation [ɔstɑ̃tasjɔ̃] *nf* : ostentation, display
ostentatoire [ɔstɑ̃tatwar] *adj* : ostentatious, showy
ostéopathie [ɔsteɔpati] *nf* : osteopathy — **ostéopathe** [-pat] *nmf*
ostéoporose [ɔsteɔpɔroz] *nf* : osteoporosis
ostracisme [ɔstrasism] *nm* : ostracism
otage [ɔtaʒ] *nm* : hostage
otarie [ɔtari] *nf* : sea lion
ôter [ote] *vt* **1** RETIRER : to remove, to take away **2** : to take off <ôte tes bottes : take off your boots> **3** SOUSTRAIRE : to subtract <3 ôté de 10 égale 7 : 3 (subtracted) from 10 equals 7> — **s'ôter** *vr fam* **ôte-toi de là!** : get out of the way!
otite [ɔtit] *nf* : ear infection
oto-rhino-laryngologiste [ɔtɔrinɔlarɛ̃ʒɔlɔʒist] *nmf* : ear, nose, and throat specialist
ottomane [ɔtɔman] *nf* CANAPÉ : ottoman, sofa
ou [u] *conj* **1** : or **2 ou . . . ou . . .** : either . . . or . . . <ou bien en Grèce ou bien en Inde : either in Greece or India>
où[1] [u] *adv* **1** : where, wherever <où étiez-vous? : where were you?> <où que tu ailles : wherever you go> <par où passer? : which way should we go?> **2 d'∼** : from which, from where, therefore
où[2] *pron* : where, that, in which, on which, to which <la ville où je suis né : the town where I was born> <le jour où il est parti : the day that he left>
ouailles [waj] *nfpl* : flock (in religion)
ouais [wɛ] *interj fam* : yeah!, oh sure!
ouate [wat] *nf* **1** : absorbent cotton **2** BOURRE : padding, wadding
ouaté, -tée [wate] *adj* : padded, quilted
oubli [ubli] *nm* **1** : forgetfulness **2** : omission, oversight **3 tomber dans l'oubli** : to sink into oblivion
oublier [ublije] {96} *vt* **1** : to forget, to forget about **2** OMETTRE : to leave out, to omit **3** NÉGLIGER : to forget, to neglect — **s'oublier** *vr* **1** : to be forgotten **2** : to forget oneself
oubliettes [ublijɛt] *nfpl* **1** : dungeon **2 jeter aux oubliettes** : to put completely out of mind
oublieux, -lieuse [ublijø, -jøz] *adj* : forgetful
ouest[1] [wɛst] *adj* : west, western
ouest[2] *nm* **1** : west <un vent d'ouest : west wind> <vers l'ouest : westward> **2 l'Ouest** : the West
ougandais, -daise [ugɑ̃dɛ, -dɛz] *adj* : Ugandan
Ougandais, -daise *n* : Ugandan
oui[1] [wi] *adv* : yes <mais oui! : yes!> <je pense que oui : I think so> <faut-il le prévenir, oui ou non? : do we have to warn him or not?> <tu viens, oui? : are you (really) coming?>
oui[2] *nms & pl* **1** : yes **2 pour un oui ou pour un non** : at the drop of a hat, for no apparent reason
ouï-dire [widir] *nms & pl* : hearsay
ouïe [wi] *nf* **1** : sense of hearing **2 ouïes** *nfpl* : gills (of a fish)
ouïr [wir] {60} *vt* : to hear
ouistiti [wistiti] *nm* : marmoset
ouragan [uragɑ̃] *nm* **1** : hurricane **2** : storm, tumult
ourdir [urdir] *vt* : to hatch (a plot, etc.)
ourler [urle] *vt* : to hem
ourlet [urlɛ] *nm* : hem
ours [urs] *nm* **1** : bear **2 ours polaire** : polar bear
ourse [urs] *nf* **1** : she-bear **2 la Grande Ourse** : the Big Dipper, Ursa Major **3 la Petite Ourse** : the Little Dipper, Ursa Minor
oursin [ursɛ̃] *nm* : sea urchin
ourson [ursɔ̃] *nm* : bear cub
ouste *or* **oust** [ust] *interj fam* : out!
outarde [utard] *nf Can* : Canada goose
outil [uti] *nm* : tool
outillage [utijaʒ] *nm* **1** : set of tools **2** : equipment <outillage agricole : agricultural equipment>
outiller [utije] *vt* ÉQUIPER : to equip — **s'outiller** *vr*
outrage [utraʒ] *nm* **1** : insult **2 outrage à la pudeur** : indecent behavior **3 outrage à magistrat** *France* : contempt of court **4 outrage au tribunal** *Can* : contempt of court
outragé, -gée [utraʒe] *adj* : gravely offended, outraged
outrageant, -geante [utraʒɑ̃, -ʒɑ̃t] *adj* INJURIEUX : insulting, abusive
outrager [utraʒe] {17} *vt* INSULTER : to offend, to insult
outrageusement [utraʒøzmɑ̃] *adv* : outrageously, excessively
outrance [utrɑ̃s] *nf* : excess <boire à outrance : to drink to excess>
outrancier, -cière [utrɑ̃sje, -sjɛr] *adj* : excessive, extreme
outre[1] [utr] *adv* **1 en ∼** : in addition, besides **2 outre mesure** : overly, unduly **3 passer outre à** : to pay no heed to, to disregard
outre[2] *prep* : besides, in addition to <outre cela : in addition to that, furthermore>
outré, -trée [utre] *adj* **1** EXAGÉRÉ : exaggerated, excessive **2** INDIGNÉ : indignant, outraged
outre-Atlantique [utratlɑ̃tik] *adv* : across the Atlantic
outrecuidance [utrəkɥidɑ̃s] *nf* : presumptuousness
outrecuidant, -dante [utrəkɥidɑ̃, -dɑ̃t] *adj* : presumptuous, arrogant
outre-mer [utrəmɛr] *adv* : overseas
outrepasser [utrəpase] *vt* : to exceed, to overstep

outrer [utre] *vt* **1** EXAGÉRER : to exaggerate **2** INDIGNER : to outrage
ouvert[1] [uvɛr] *pp* → **ouvrir**
ouvert[2], **-verte** [uvɛr, -vɛrt] *adj* **1** : open <ouvert au public : open to the public> <grand ouvert : wide open> <à bras ouverts : with open arms> **2** : frank, open **3** : on, running <laissez la lumière ouverte : leave the light on>
ouvertement [uvɛrtəmɑ̃] *adv* : openly
ouverture [uvɛrtyr] *nf* **1** : opening, aperture **2** : openness <ouverture d'esprit : open-mindedness> **3** : overture (in music)
ouvrable [uvrabl] *adj* **1 jour ouvrable** : weekday, working day **2 heures ouvrables** : business hours
ouvrage [uvraʒ] *nm* **1** : work, working <se mettre à l'ouvrage : to get down to work> **2** : book **3** : piece of work <ouvrage d'art : construction work>
ouvragé, -gée [uvraʒe] *adj* : finely worked, elaborate
ouvrant, -vrante [uvrɑ̃, -vrɑ̃t] *adj* **toit ouvrant** : sunroof
ouvré, -vrée [uvre] *adj* : elaborate, finely worked
ouvre–boîtes [uvrəbwat] *nms & pl* : can opener
ouvre–bouteilles [uvrəbutɛj] *nms & pl* : bottle opener
ouvreur, -vreuse [uvrœr, -vrøz] *n* **1** : usher, usherette *f* (in a theater) **2** : opener (in games)
ouvrier[1], **-vrière** [uvrije, -vrijɛr] *adj* : working-class <la class ouvrière : the working class>
ouvrier[2], **-vrière** *n* : worker
ouvrir [uvrir] {83} *vt* **1** : to open **2** : to unlock, to undo **3** : to turn on (a light, radio, etc.) **4** : to start up, to begin <ouvrir le feu : to open fire> — *vi* : to open — **s'ouvrir** *vr* **1** : to open, to come open **2** : to open up, to confide **3** : to cut <s'ouvrir la main : to cut one's hand> **4 ~ à** : to become open to (opportunities, etc.)
ouzbek [uzbɛk] *adj* : Uzbek
Ouzbek *nmf* : Uzbek
ovaire [ɔvɛr] *nm* : ovary — **ovarien, -rienne** [ɔvarjɛ̃, -rjɛn] *adj*
ovale [ɔval] *adj & nm* : oval
ovation [ɔvasjɔ̃] *nf* : ovation
ovationner [ɔvasjɔne] *vt* : to applaud, to give an ovation to
overdose [ɔvœrdoz] *nf* SURDOSE : overdose
ovuler [ɔvyle] *vi* : to ovulate
ovulation [ɔvylasjɔ̃] *nf* : ovulation
ovule [ɔvyl] *nm* : ovum
oxydable [ɔksidabl] *adj* : liable to rust
oxyde [ɔksid] *nm* **1** : oxide **2 oxyde de carbone** : carbon monoxide
oxyder [ɔkside] *vt* : to oxidize — **oxydation** [-sidasjɔ̃] *nf*
oxygène [ɔksiʒɛn] *nm* : oxygen
oxyure [ɔksyr] *nm* : pinworm
ozone [ozɔn] *nm* : ozone <couche d'ozone : ozone layer>

P

p [pe] *nm* : p, the 16th letter of the alphabet
pacage [pakaʒ] *nm* **1** : grazing **2** : pasture
pacane [pakan] *nf Can or* **noix de pacane** : pecan
pacemaker [pɛsmekœr] *nm* : pacemaker
pachyderme [paʃidɛrm] *nm* : pachyderm, elephant
pacificateur[1], **-trice** [pasifikatœr, -tris] *adj* : pacifying, peacemaking
pacificateur[2], **-trice** *n* : peacemaker
pacification [pasifikasjɔ̃] *nf* : pacification
pacifier [pasifje] {96} *vt* APAISER : to pacify, to calm
pacifique [pasifik] *adj* **1** PAISIBLE : peaceful, pacific **2 l'océan Pacifique** : the Pacific Ocean — **pacifiquement** [-fikmɑ̃] *adv*
pacifisme [pasifism] *nm* : pacificism
pacifiste[1] [pasifist] *adj* : pacifist, pacifistic
pacifiste[2] *nmf* : pacifist
pack [pak] *nm* : pack
pacotille [pakɔtij] *nf* : shoddy goods <bijoux de pacotille : cheap jewelry>
pacte [pakt] *nm* ACCORD : pact, agreement
pactiser [paktize] *vi* : to come to an agreement, to come to terms
pactole [paktɔl] *nm* : gold mine, bonanza
paddock [padɔk] *nm* : paddock
pagaie [pagɛ] *nf* : paddle
pagaille *or* **pagaïe** [pagaj] *nf fam* **1** : mess, chaos **2 il y en a en pagaille** : there are loads of them
paganisme [paganism] *nm* : paganism
pagayer [pagaje] {11} *vi* : to paddle
page [paʒ] *nf* **1** : page <page blanche : blank page> **2** : passage (in a book or piece of music)
pagination [paʒinasjɔ̃] *nf* : pagination
paginer [paʒine] *vt* : to paginate
pagne [paɲ] *nm* : loincloth
pagode [pagɔd] *nf* : pagoda
paie[1] [pɛ], **paiera** [pɛra], *etc.* → **payer**
paie[2] [pɛ] *nf* : pay, wages *pl*
paiement [pɛmɑ̃] *nm* : payment
païen, païenne [pajɛ̃, -jɛn] *adj & n* : pagan, heathen

paillard, -larde [pajar, -jard] *adj* : bawdy

paillardise [pajardiz] *nf* : bawdiness

paillasse[1] [pajas] *nf* : straw mattress

paillasse[2] *nm* : clown

paillasson [pajasɔ̃] *nm* : doormat

paille [paj] *nf* **1** : straw, piece of straw <être sur la paille : to be penniless> **2** : (drinking) straw **3 paille de fer** : steel wool

pailler [paje] *vt* : to mulch

paillette [pajɛt] *nf* **1** : sequin <robe à paillettes : sequined dress> **2** : speck, flake <savon en paillettes : soap flakes>

paillis [paji] *nms & pl* : mulch

pain [pɛ̃] *nm* **1** : bread <pain grillé : toast> <pain d'épice : gingerbread> <pain doré *Can* : French toast> **2** : loaf **3** : cake, bar <pain de savon : bar of soap>

pair[1], **paire** [pɛr] *adj* : even <nombre pair : even number>

pair[2] *nm* **1** NOBLE : peer **2** ÉGAL : peer, equal <aller de pair : to go hand in hand> <hors pair : without equal, unrivaled> **3** : par (in finance) **4 travailler au pair** : to work as an au pair

paire [pɛr] *nf* : pair

paisible [pezibl] *adj* : peaceful, quiet — **paisiblement** [-zibləmɑ̃] *adv*

paître [pɛtr] {61} *vi* : to graze

paix [pɛ] *nf* **1** : peace <la paix mondiale : world peace> **2** CALME, TRANQUILLITÉ : peace, calm, tranquility

pakistanais, -naise [pakistanɛ, -nɛz] *adj* : Pakistani

Pakistanais, -naise *n* : Pakistani

palabrer [palabre] *vi* : to discuss endlessly

palabres [palabr] *nfpl* : endless discussions, palaver

palace [palas] *nm* : luxury hotel

palais [palɛ] *nms & pl* **1** : palace **2** : palate **3 palais de justice** : courthouse, courts of law

palan [palɑ̃] *nm* : hoist

pale [pal] *nf* **1** : blade (of a propeller, etc.) **2** : paddle

pâle [pal] *adj* **1** BLÊME : pale, pallid **2** CLAIR : light, pale <jaune pâle : pale yellow>

palefrenier, -nière [palfrənje] *n* : groom (in a stable)

paléontologie [paleɔ̃tɔlɔʒi] *nf* : paleontology — **paléontologiste** [-lɔʒist] *nmf*

paleron [palrɔ̃] *nm* : chuck (steak)

palestinien, -nienne [palestinjɛ̃, -njɛn] *adj* : Palestinian

Palestinien, -nienne *n* : Palestinian

palet [palɛ] *nm* : puck (in ice hockey)

paletot [palto] *nm* : short coat

palette [palɛt] *nf* **1** *Can* : wooden spatula (used in making maple products) **2** : palette **3** : shoulder <palette de porc : shoulder of pork> **4** : pallet, loading platform **5** : range (of colors, ideas, etc.)

palétuvier [paletyvje] *nm* : mangrove

pâleur [palœr] *nf* : paleness, pallor

palier [palje] *nm* **1** : landing (of a staircase), floor **2** NIVEAU : level, stage <par paliers : by stages>

pâlir [palir] *vi* **1** : to turn pale **2** : to fade, to dim

palissade [palisad] *nf* : fence, palisade

palissandre [palisɑ̃dr] *nm* : rosewood

palliatif[1], **-tive** [paljatif, -tiv] *adj* : palliative

palliatif[2] [paljatif] *nm* **1** : palliative **2** : stopgap, expedient

pallier [palje] {96} *vt* : to compensate for, to mitigate

palmarès [palmarɛs] *nms & pl* **1** : list of winners **2** : record of achievements

palme [palm] *nf* **1** : palm leaf **2** : palm, distinction <remporter la palme : to be victorious> **3** : flipper

palmé, -mée [palme] *adj* : webbed <patte palmée : webbed foot>

palmier [palmje] *nm* : palm tree

palmure [palmyr] *nf* : web (of a bird's foot)

pâlot, -lotte [palo, -lɔt] *adj* : pale, peaked

palourde [palurd] *nf* : clam

palpable [palpabl] *adj* : palpable, tangible

palper [palpe] *vt* **1** : to palpate (in medicine) **2** : to feel, to finger

palpitant, -tante [palpitɑ̃, -tɑ̃t] *adj* : thrilling, exciting

palpitation [palpitasjɔ̃] *nf* : palpitation

palpiter [palpite] *vi* **1** : to palpitate, to throb **2** : to quiver, to flutter

paludisme [palydism] *nm* : malaria

pâmer [pame] *v* **se pâmer** *vr* **1** : to be ecstatic, to swoon **2 ~ de** : to be overcome with

pâmoison [pamwazɔ̃] *nf* **tomber en pâmoison** : to swoon

pampa [pɑ̃pa] *nf* : pampas *pl*

pamphlet [pɑ̃flɛ] *nm* : lampoon

pamplemousse [pɑ̃pləmus] *nmf* : grapefruit

pan [pɑ̃] *nm* **1** : section, piece **2** : side, face **3** : tail (of a garment) <pan de chemise : shirttail>

panacée [panase] *nf* : panacea, nostrum

panache [panaʃ] *nm* **1** : plume <panache de fumée : trail of smoke> **2** : panache, verve

panaché, -chée [panaʃe] *adj* **1** : variegated, multicolored **2** : mixed <salade panachée : mixed salad>

panais [panɛ] *nms & pl* : parsnip

panaméen, -méenne [panameɛ̃, -meɛn] *adj* : Panamanian

Panaméen, -méenne *n* : Panamanian

pancarte [pɑ̃kart] *nf* **1** : sign, notice **2** : placard

pancréas [pɑ̃kreas] *nm* : pancreas — **pancréatique** [-kreatik] *adj*

panda [pɑ̃da] *nm* : panda

panégyrique [paneʒirik] *nm* : panegyric

paner [pane] *vt* : to coat with breadcrumbs, to bread

panier [panje] *nm* **1** : basket <panier à provisions : shopping basket> <panier de pêche : creel> **2 panier à salade** : lettuce spinner **3 panier percé** *fam* : spendthrift

panique[1] [panik] *adj* : panic <peur panique : terror>

panique[2] *nf* : panic <pris de panique : panic-stricken>

paniquer [panike] *vi fam* : to panic — *vt fam* : to throw into a panic

panne [pan] *nf* **1** : breakdown, failure <panne d'électricité : power failure, blackout> **2 en panne de** : out of <en panne d'essence : out of gas>

panneau [pano] *nm, pl* **panneaux 1** : panel **2** : sign, notice **3 panneau de signalisation** : road sign **4 panneau fibreux** : fiberboard **5 panneau indicateur** : signpost **6 panneau publicitaire** : billboard

panonceau [panɔ̃so] *nm, pl* **-ceaux 1** : plaque (at a professional office, etc.) **2** PANCARTE : sign

panoplie [panɔpli] *nf* **1** : display of arms **2** : array, range **3** : outfit, costume (for children)

panorama [panɔrama] *nm* **1** : panorama **2** : overview

panoramique [panɔramik] *adj* : panoramic

panse [pɑ̃s] *nf fam* : paunch, belly

pansement [pɑ̃smɑ̃] *nm* : dressing, bandage

panser [pɑ̃se] *vt* **1** : to groom (a horse) **2** : to dress, to bandage

pansu, -sue [pɑ̃sy] *adj* : potbellied

pantalon [pɑ̃talɔ̃] *nm* : pants *pl*, trousers *pl*

pantelant, -lante [pɑ̃tlɑ̃, -lɑ̃t] *adj* : panting, gasping for breath

panthère [pɑ̃tɛr] *nf* : panther

pantin [pɑ̃tɛ̃] *nm* **1** : jumping jack (toy) **2** FANTOCHE : puppet (person)

pantois, -toise [pɑ̃twa, -twaz] *adj* : flabbergasted

pantomime [pɑ̃tɔmim] *nf* **1** : mime **2** : pantomime show **3** : scene, fuss

pantouflard, -flarde [pɑ̃tuflar, -flard] *n fam* : homebody

pantoufle [pɑ̃tufl] *nf* : slipper

pantoute [pɑ̃tut] *adv Can fam* : no, not at all

panure [panyr] *nf* CHAPELURE : bread crumbs *pl*

paon [pɑ̃] *nm* : peacock

papa [papa] *nm fam* : dad, daddy

papal, -pale [papal] *adj, mpl* **papaux** [papo] : papal

papauté [papote] *nf* : papacy

papaye [papaj] *nf* : papaya

pape [pap] *nm* : pope

paperasserie [paprasri] *nf* : paperwork, red tape

papeterie [papɛtri] *nf* : stationery

papier [papje] *nm* **1** : paper **2** : document, paper **3** : article, review **4 papier d'aluminium** : aluminum foil, tinfoil **5 papier de verre** *France* : sandpaper **6 papier hygiénique** : toilet paper **7 papier journal** : newsprint **8 papier mouchoir** *Can* : tissue **9 papier peint** : wallpaper **10 papier sablé** *Can* : sandpaper **11 papier tue–mouches** : flypaper **12 papiers** *nmpl* : (identification) papers

papier–monnaie [papjemɔnɛ] *nm, pl* **papiers–monnaies** : paper money

papille [papij] *nf* **papilles gustatives** : taste buds

papillon [papijɔ̃] *nm* **1** : butterfly **2 papillon de nuit** : moth

papillonner [papijɔne] *vi* : to flit about, to flutter around

papillote [papijɔt] *nf* : aluminum foil, foil wrapping

papilloter [papijɔte] *vi* **1** : to flicker, to twinkle **2** : to blink, to flutter (of eyelids)

papotage [papɔtaʒ] *nm* : gabbing, chattering

papoter [papɔte] *vi* : to gab, to chatter

paprika [paprika] *nm* : paprika

papyrus [papirys] *nm* : papyrus

Pâque [pak] *nf* : Passover

paquebot [pakbo] *nm* : liner, ship

pâquerette [pakrɛt] *nf* : daisy

Pâques[1] [pak] *nm* : Easter <la semaine de Pâques : Easter week>

Pâques[2] *nfpl* : Easter <joyeuses Pâques! : Happy Easter!>

paquet [pakɛ] *nm* **1** : package, bundle **2** : packet, pack (of cigarettes, etc.) **3** : heap, pile, mass **4 mettre le paquet** *fam* : to go all out

paqueter [pakte] *vt Can fam* **1** : to pack (a suitcase) **2** : to pack, to fill to capacity

par [par] *prep* **1** : through <par la porte : through the door> **2** : by, by means of <par avion : by airmail> **3** : as, for <par exemple : for example> **4** : per <dix dollars par personne : ten dollars per person> **5** : around, near <il habite par ici : he lives around here> **6** : at, during <par moments : at times> **7** : from, out of, for the sake of <par amour : out of love> **8** : according to, by <classé par âge : ranked by age> **9 de ~** : throughout <de par le monde : all over the world> **10 de ~** : by virtue of **11** : **par–ci par–là** : here and there **12** : **par trop** : excessively

parabole [parabɔl] *nf* **1** : parable **2** : parabola

parabolique [parabɔlik] *adj* : parabolic

parachever [paraʃve] {52} *vt* PARFAIRE : to complete, to perfect

parachute [paraʃyt] *nm* : parachute — **parachuter** [-ʃyte] *vt*

parachutiste [paraʃytist] *nmf* **1** : parachutist **2** : paratrooper

parade [parad] *nf* **1** DÉFILÉ : parade **2** : parry (in sports) **3 de ~** : outward, superficial **4 faire parade de** : to display, to make a show of

parader [parade] *vi* : to strut about, to show off

paradigme [paradim] *nm* : paradigm

paradis [paradi] *nm* : paradise, heaven

paradisiaque [paradizjak] *adj* : heavenly

paradoxal, -xale [paradɔksal] *adj, mpl* **-xaux** [-kso] : paradoxical — **paradoxalement** [-ksalmɑ̃] *adv*

paradoxe [paradɔks] *nm* : paradox

parafe, parafer [paraf, parafe] → **paraphe, parapher**

paraffine [parafin] *nf* : paraffin

parafoudre [parafudr] *nm* : lightning rod

parages [paraʒ] *nmpl* **1** : waters <parages étrangers : foreign waters> **2 dans les parages** : in the vicinity, around

paragraphe [paragraf] *nm* : paragraph

paraguayen, -guayenne [paragwejɛ̃, -gwejɛn] *adj* : Paraguayan

Paraguayen, -guayenne *n* : Paraguayan

paraissait [parɛsɛ], *etc.* → **paraître**

paraisse [parɛs], *etc.* → **paraître**

paraître [parɛtr] {7} *vi* **1** : to appear <paraître en public : to appear in public> **2** : to be published <à paraître : forthcoming> **3** : to show, to be visible **4** SEMBLER : to seem, to look — *v impers* **1** : to seem, to appear <il paraît que tout s'est arrangé : everything seems to be all right> **2 paraît-il** *or* **à ce qu'il paraît** : apparently

parallèle[1] [paralɛl] *adj* **1** : parallel **2** SEMBLABLE : similar **3** : unofficial, alternative

parallèle[2] *nm* **1** : parallel **2** : comparison <mettre en parallèle : to compare>

parallèle[3] *nf* : parallel line

parallèlement [paralɛlmɑ̃] *adv* : at the same time, concurrently

parallélogramme [paralelɔgram] *nm* : parallelogram

paralyser [paralyze] *vt* **1** : to paralyze **2** : to bring to a standstill

paralysie [paralizi] *nf* **1** : paralysis **2 paralysie cérébrale** : cerebral palsy

paralytique [paralitik] *adj* : paralytic

paramètre [paramɛtr] *nm* : parameter

parangon [parɑ̃gɔ̃] *nm* MODÈLE : paragon

paranoïa [paranɔja] *nf* : paranoia

paranoïaque [paranɔjak] *adj & nmf* : paranoiac, paranoid

paranormal, -male [paranɔrmal] *adj, mpl* **-maux** [-mo] : paranormal

parapet [parapɛ] *nm* : parapet

paraphe [paraf] *nm* **1** : initials *pl* **2** : signature **3** : flourish, ornamental stroke (on a signature)

parapher [parafe] *vt* **1** : to initial **2** : to sign **3** : to add a flourish to (a signature)

paraphrase [parafraz] *nf* : paraphrase

paraphraser [parafraze] *vt* : to paraphrase

paraplégique [parapleʒik] *adj & nmf* : paraplegic

parapluie [paraplɥi] *nm* : umbrella

parascolaire [paraskɔlɛr] *adj* : extracurricular

parasitaire [parazitɛr] *adj* : parasitic

parasite[1] [parazit] *adj* : parasitic

parasite[2] *nm* **1** : parasite **2 parasites** *nmpl* : interference, static

parasol [parasɔl] *nm* : parasol, sunshade

paratonnerre [paratɔnɛr] *nm* : lightning rod

paravent [paravɑ̃] *nm* : screen, partition

parc [park] *nm* **1** : park <parc d'attractions : amusement park> <parc zoologique : zoological gardens> **2** : grounds *pl* **3** ENCLOS : playpen, pen, enclosure <parc à huîtres : oyster bed> <parc à moutons : sheepfold> <parc de stationnement : parking lot> **4** : total number, stock <parc de voitures : fleet of automobiles>

parcelle [parsɛl] *nf* **1** : fragment **2** : plot, parcel <parcelle de terre : plot of land>

parcelliser [parselize] *vt* : to divide, to split up

parce que [parskə] *conj* : because

parchemin [parʃəmɛ̃] *nm* : parchment

parcimonie [parsimɔni] *nf* : parsimony <avec parcimonie : sparingly>

parcimonieux, -nieuse [parsimɔnjø, -njøz] *adj* : parsimonious, sparing — **parcimonieusement** [-njøzmɑ̃] *adv*

par-ci, par-là [parsiparla] → **par**

parcmètre [parkmɛtr] *nm France* : parking meter

parcomètre [parkɔmɛtr] *nm Can* : parking meter

parcourir [parkurir] {23} *vt* **1** : to cover (a distance), to travel through **2** : to leaf through, to skim (a text)

parcours [parkur] *nm* **1** : course (of a river), route (of a bus, etc.) **2** : course (in sports) **3** : career, (professional) development

par-delà *or* **par delà** [pardəla] *prep* : beyond, across <par-delà les mers : beyond the seas> <par-delà les siècles : across the centuries>

par-dessous [pardəsu] *adv & prep* : underneath

pardessus [pardəsy] *nm* **1** : overcoat **2** *Can* CLAQUES : rubbers *pl*

par-dessus[1] [pardəsy] *adv* : over, above, on top <sauter par-dessus : to

jump over (it)> <mets-le par-dessus : put it up top>

par–dessus[2] *prep* **1** : over, above <par-dessus le mur : above the wall> <jeter qqch par-dessus bord : to throw sth overboard> **2 par–dessus tout** : above all

par–devant[1] [pardəvɑ̃] *adv* : in front, at the front

par–devant[2] *prep* : in front of, in the presence of

pardon [pardɔ̃] *nm* **1** : forgiveness, pardon **2 pardon?** : pardon?, what did you say? **3 pardon!** : pardon me!, sorry!

pardonnable [pardɔnabl] *adj* : forgivable, pardonable, excusable

pardonner [pardɔne] *vt* **1** : to forgive, to pardon **2 pardonnez–moi!** : excuse me! — *vi* **ne pas pardonner** : to be fatal <une maladie qui ne pardonne pas : a fatal illness>

paré, -rée [pare] *adj* : ready, prepared <vous voilà paré! : you're all set!>

pare–balles [parbal] *adj s & pl* : bulletproof

pare–brise [parbriz] *nms & pl* : windshield

pare–chocs [parʃɔk] *nms & pl* : bumper

pare–feu [parfø] *nms & pl* : firebreak

parégorique [paregɔrik] *nm or* **élixir parégorique** : paregoric

pareil[1] [parɛj] *adv fam* **1** : the same, in the same way <faire pareil : to do the same (thing)> **2** *Can fam* : all the same, anyhow <viens nous voir pareil : come see us anyway>

pareil[2], **-reille** [parɛj] *adj* **1** SEMBLABLE : similar, alike **2** TEL : such <une pareille maison : such a house, a house like this>

pareil[3], **-reille** *n* **1** : equal <il n'a pas son pareil : he's second to none> <son talent est sans pareil : her talent is unequaled> <une vue sans pareille : a view beyond compare> **2 ses pareils** : one's peers, one's fellows

pareil[4] *nm fam* **c'est du pareil au même** : it's all the same, six of one and a half dozen of the other

pareillement [parɛjmɑ̃] *adv* **1** ÉGALEMENT : in the same way <s'habiller pareillement : to dress alike> **2** AUSSI : also, too <et à vous pareillement : to you, too>

parement [parmɑ̃] *nm* : facing

parent[1], **-rente** [parɑ̃, -rɑ̃t] *adj* **1** : similar, related **2 ~ à** *or* **~ avec** : related to, kin to

parent[2], **-rente** *n* **1** : relative, relation **2 parent par alliance** : in-law

parental, -tale [parɑ̃tal] *adj, mpl* **-taux** [-to] : parental

parenté [parɑ̃te] *nf* **1** : relationship, kinship **2** : family, relations *pl*

parenthèse [parɑ̃tɛz] *nf* **1** : parenthesis, bracket **2** : digression <entre parenthèses *or* par parenthèse : incidentally, by the way>

parents [parɑ̃] *nmpl* **1** : parents **2** ANCÊTRES : ancestors, forebears

parer [pare] *vt* **1** : to adorn **2** : to dress, to trim (in cooking) **3** : to ward off, to parry — *vi* **~ à** : to guard against, to be prepared for, to deal with — **se parer** *vr* **1** : to dress oneself up **2 ~ contre** : to prepare oneself for

pare–soleil [parsɔlɛj] *nms & pl* : sun visor

paresse [parɛs] *nf* : laziness, idleness

paresser [parɛse] *vi* FAINÉANTER : to laze around

paresseux[1], **-seuse** [parɛsø, -søz] *adj* : lazy — **paresseusement** [-søzmɑ̃] *adv*

paresseux[2] *nm* : sloth (animal)

parfaire [parfɛr] {62} *vt* PEAUFINER : to perfect, to complete, to refine (style, etc.)

parfait[1], **-faite** [parfɛ, -fɛt] *adj* **1** : perfect **2** : absolute, complete — **parfaitement** [-fɛtmɑ̃] *adv*

parfait[2] *nm* **1** : perfect (tense) **2** : parfait (dessert)

parfois [parfwa] *adv* QUELQUEFOIS : sometimes

parfum [parfœ̃] *nm* **1** : scent, fragrance **2** : flavor (of ice cream, tea, etc.) **3** : perfume

parfumé, -mée [parfyme] *adj* **1** ODORANT : fragrant, scented, sweet-smelling **2** : flavored <parfumé au citron : lemon-flavored>

parfumer [parfyme] *vt* **1** : to scent, to perfume **2** : to flavor — **se parfumer** *vr* : to wear perfume

parfumerie [parfymri] *nf* **1** : perfume shop **2** : perfume industry **3** : perfumes *pl*

pari [pari] *nm* : bet, wager

paria [parja] *nm* : pariah, outcast

parier [parje] {96} *vt* : to bet, to wager

parieur, -rieuse [parjœr, -rjøz] *n* : bettor, better

parisien, -sienne [parizjɛ̃, -zjɛn] *adj* : Parisian

Parisien, -sienne *n* : Parisian

paritaire [paritɛr] *adj* : joint <commission paritaire : joint commission>

parité [parite] *nf* : parity, equality

parjure[1] [parʒyr] *adj* : disloyal, faithless

parjure[2] *nm* : betrayal

parjure[3] *nmf* : traitor

parjurer [parʒyre] *v* **se parjurer** *vr* : to perjure oneself

parka [parka] *nm* : parka

parking [parkiŋ] *nm* **1** STATIONNEMENT : parking **2** : parking lot

parlant, -lante [parlɑ̃, -lɑ̃t] *adj* **1** : talking (of movies, etc.) **2** : vivid, eloquent, graphic **3** : talkative

parlement [parləmɑ̃] *nm* : parliament

parlementaire[1] [parləmɑ̃tɛr] *adj* : parliamentary

parlementaire[2] *nmf* : parliamentarian

parlementer [parləmɑ̃te] *vi* NÉGOCIER : to negotiate, to parley

parler[1] [parle] *vt* : to talk, to speak <parler (le) français : to speak French> <parler affaires : to talk business> — *vi* **1** : to talk, to speak **2 ~ à** : to talk to (someone) **3 ~ de** : to mention, to refer to <sans parler de son accent : not to mention his accent> **4 n'en parlons plus** : let's forget about it — **se parler** *vr* **1** : to speak to each other **2** : to be on speaking terms **3** : to be spoken

parler[2] *nm* **1** : speech, way of speaking **2** : dialect

parleur, -leuse [parlœr, -løz] *n* : talker, speaker <beau parleur : smooth talker>

parloir [parlwar] *nm* : parlor

parlote *or* **parlotte** [parlɔt] *nf fam* CAUSETTE : chat, chitchat

parmesan [parməzɑ̃] *nm* : Parmesan

parmi [parmi] *prep* **1** : among <une possibilité parmi d'autres : one possibility among others> **2** : in the midst of, with

parodie [parɔdi] *nf* : parody

parodier [parɔdje] {96} *vt* : to parody, to mimic

paroi [parwa] *nf* **1** CLOISON : partition **2** : wall (in anatomy and biology) **3** : inner surface, face <paroi rocheuse : rock face>

paroisse [parwas] *nf* : parish

paroissial, -siale [parwasjal] *adj, mpl* **-siaux** [-sjo] : parish, parochial

paroissien, -sienne [parwasjɛ̃, -sjɛn] *n* : parishioner

parole [parɔl] *nf* **1** : (spoken) word <prendre la parole : to speak> **2** PROMESSE : word, promise <parole d'honneur : word of honor> **3** : speech <elle a retrouvé la parole : she regained the power of speech> **4 paroles** *nfpl* : lyrics

paroxysme [parɔksism] *nm* : height, climax (of pain, enthusiasm, etc.)

parquer [parke] *vt* **1** : to pen <bétail parqué : penned cattle> **2** ENTASSER : to herd together **3** GARER : to park

parquet [parkɛ] *nm* **1** : parquet (floor) **2** *France* : public prosecutor's office **3 parquet de la bourse** : floor of the stock exchange

parrain [parɛ̃] *nm* **1** : godfather **2** : sponsor, patron

parrainage [parɛnaʒ] *nm* : sponsorship

parrainer [parɛne] *vt* : to sponsor

parsemer [parsəme] {52} *vt* **1** : to sprinkle **2 ~ de** : to scatter with, to strew with, to intersperse with

part [par] *nf* **1** : portion, share, piece **2** : proportion, element <une part de chance : an element of chance> **3** : part, share <faire sa part : to do one's share> <prendre part à : to take part in> **4** : side, position <de toutes parts : from all sides> <d'une part . . . : on (the) one hand . . .> <de la part de : on behalf of> **5 à ~** : apart from <à part ça : besides that> **6 à ~** : to one side, separate(ly) **7 à ~** : apart, unique <un cas à part : a special case> **8 → autre, nul, quelque**

partage [partaʒ] *nm* **1** : sharing, dividing <sans partage : total, undivided> **2** : share, lot

partagé, -gée [partaʒe] *adj* **1** : divided <opinions partagées : divided opinions> **2** : shared, mutual

partager [partaʒe] {17} *vt* **1** DIVISER : to divide up **2** : to share — **se partager** *vr*

partance [partɑ̃s] *nf* **1 en ~** : outbound, ready to depart **2 en partance pour** : bound for

partant[1] [partɑ̃] *adj* **être partant pour** : to be ready for, to be up to

partant[2], **-tante** [partɑ̃, -tɑ̃t] *n* : runner, starter (in sports)

partenaire [partənɛr] *nmf* : partner

partenariat [partənarja] *nm* : partnership

parterre [partɛr] *nm* **1** : flower bed **2** : orchestra section (in a theater)

parti[1], **-tie** [parti] *adj fam* : intoxicated, high

parti[2] *nm* **1** : group, camp, side **2** : political party **3** : course of action, option <prendre parti : to take a stand> <prendre son parti : to make up one's mind, to come to terms> **4** : advantage, profit <tirer parti de : to take advantage of> **5 parti pris** : bias

partial, -tiale [parsjal] *adj, mpl* **-tiaux** [-sjo] : biased, partial

partialement [parsjalmɑ̃] *adv* : in a biased manner

partialité [parsjalite] *nf* : bias, partiality

participant, -pante [partisipɑ̃, -pɑ̃t] *n* **1** : participant **2** : entrant (in a competition)

participation [partisipasjɔ̃] *nf* **1** : participation **2** : contribution **3** : share, interest (in a company, etc.)

participe [partisip] *nm* : participle

participer [partisipe] *vi* **~ à 1** : to participate in, to take part in **2** : to contribute to **3** : to share in

particulariser [partikylarize] *vt* : to distinguish, to characterize — **se particulariser** *vr*

particularité [partikylarite] *nf* : distinctive feature, characteristic, idiosyncrasy

particule [partikyl] *nf* : particle

particulier[1], **-lière** [partikylje, -ljɛr] *adj* **1** : particular, specific **2** : special, unique, idiosyncratic **3** SINGULIER : unusual **4** : private, personal <cours particuliers : private lessons> **5 en ~** : especially, in particular

particulier[2] *nm* : individual, private person

particulièrement [partikyljɛrmɑ̃] *adv* SPÉCIALEMENT : especially, particularly

partie [parti] *nf* **1** : part (of a whole) **2** : game, match **3** : party, participant **4** SORTIE : party, outing <partie de pêche : fishing party> **5** : field, line (of work) **6 en ~** : partly, in part **7 faire partie de** : to be a part of, to belong to

partiel, -tielle [parsjɛl] *adj* : partial — **partiellement** [-sjɛlmɑ̃] *adv*

partir [partir] {82} *vi* **1** : to leave, to depart **2** : to start up, to take off **3** COMMENCER : to start, to begin **4** S'ENLEVER : to come off, to come out (of a stain, etc.) **5 à partir de** : from <à partir de maintenant : from now on>

partisan[1], -sane [partizɑ̃, -zan] *adj* : partisan

partisan[2], -sane *n* : supporter, partisan

partition [partisjɔ̃] *nf* : score <partition de piano : piano score>

partout [partu] *adv* **1** : everywhere **2** : all (in sports) <trois partout : three all>

paru [pary] *pp* → **paraître**

parure [paryr] *nf* **1** : finery **2** ENSEMBLE : set (of jewelry, linens, etc.)

parution [parysjɔ̃] *nf* : publication, launch

parvenir [parvənir] {92} *vi* **1 ~ à** : to reach, to arrive at <elle est parvenue à une résolution : she arrived at a solution> **2 ~ à** : to manage to, to succeed in, to achieve

parvenu, -nue [parvəny] *n* : parvenu, upstart

parvis [parvi] *nm* : square (in front of a church)

party [parti] *nm Can fam* : party, gathering

pas[1] [pa] → **ne**

pas[2] *adv* (*without* **ne**) **1** : not <pas du tout : not at all> <pas vraiment : not really> <pas mal de : quite a lot of> <pas croyable! : incredible!> **2 pas un, pas une** : no one, none <il le fait comme pas un : he does it like nobody else>

pas[3] *nms & pl* **1** : step, footstep **2** : footprint **3** : pace, gait **4** : move, progression <un pas en avant : a step forward> <faire le premier pas : to make the first move> **5** : step (in dancing) **6 de ce pas** : right away

pascal, -cale [paskal] *adj, mpl* **pascaux** [pasko] : Easter <congé pascal : Easter holiday>

passable [pasabl] *adj* **1** : passable, fair **2** *Can* : passable, negotiable <chemins passables : passable roads>

passablement [pasabləmɑ̃] *adv* **1** : quite, rather **2** : reasonably well

passade [pasad] *nf* : passing fancy

passage [pasaʒ] *nm* **1** : passing (by), crossing (through), traffic <être de passage : to be passing through> <au passage : in passing> **2** TARIF : fare, ticket **3** : transition, passage **4** CHEMIN : route, way **5** CORRIDOR : corridor, passageway <passage pour piétons : pedestrian crossing> **6** : entry <passage interdit : do not enter> **7** : passage (in a text)

passager[1], -gère [pasaʒe, -ʒɛr] *adj* **1** : passing, temporary **2** : busy <rue passagère : busy street>

passager[2], -gère *n* **1** : passenger **2 passager clandestin** : stowaway

passagèrement [pasaʒɛrmɑ̃] *adv* : temporarily

passant[1], -sante [pasɑ̃, -sɑ̃t] *adj* : busy <rue passante : busy street>

passant[2], -sante *n* : passerby

passe [pas] *nf* **1** : pass (in sports) **2** : period, time <j'ai traversé une mauvaise passe : I went through a difficult time> **3** : channel (in navigation)

passé[1], -sée [pase] *adj* **1** : last, past <l'an passé : last year> **2** : after, past <il est midi passé : it's after twelve> **3** : faded

passé[2] *nm* **1** : past <par le passé : in the past> **2** : past tense <passé composé : perfect tense>

passé[3] *prep* : after, beyond <passé l'église il y a un parc : beyond the church is a park> <passé minuit : after midnight>

passe–droit [pasdrwa] *nm, pl* **passe–droits** : privilege, special treatment

passementerie [pasmɑ̃tri] *nf* : trimmings *pl* (for clothing, etc.)

passe–partout [paspartu] *nms & pl* : master key

passe–passe [paspas] *nms & pl* **tour de passe–passe** : conjuring trick, sleight of hand

passepoil [paspwal] *nm* : piping (in sewing)

passeport [paspɔr] *nm* : passport

passer [pase] *vt* **1** : to cross, to go over **2** : to pass, to go past **3** : to pass, to run <passer la main sur une surface : to pass one's hand over a surface> **4** : to pass, to hand over, to give <passer un ballon : to pass a ball> <passez-moi le poivre : pass me the pepper> <passer un rhume à qqn : to give s.o. a cold> **5** : to put through to (on the telephone) **6** : to take (an exam, etc.), to take on **7** : to spend (time) **8** : to excuse, to forgive **9** : to skip, to pass over **10** : to go over <passer l'aspirateur : to vacuum> **11** ENFILER : to slip on **12** : to show (a film), to play (a cassette, etc.) **13** : to shift into (a gear) — *vi* **1** : to pass, to go past, to run <le chemin passe devant ma maison : the road runs in front of my house> **2** : to drop by **3** : to go <où est-il passé? : where did he go?> **4** : to get through <laissez-moi passer : let me through> **5** : to be over, to pass, to go by **6** : to pass down, to be handed down **7 ∼ par** : to go through <en passant par : including> **8 ∼ pour** : to pass for, to appear to be **9 ∼ sur** : to pass over, to overlook, to forget about **10 en passant** : incidentally **11 y passer** *fam* : to die — **se passer** *vr* **1** : to take place, to happen **2** : to go, to turn out **3** : to pass, to go by (of time) **4 ∼ de** : to do without, to dispense with **5 se faire passer** : to masquerade, to disguise oneself

passereau [pasro] *nm, pl* **-reaux** : sparrow

passerelle [pasrɛl] *nf* **1** : footbridge **2** : gangplank, ramp (of an airplane) **3** : bridge (of a ship)

passe–temps [pastɑ̃] *nms & pl* : hobby, pastime

passeur, -seuse [pasœr, -søz] *n* : smuggler

passible [pasibl] *adj* **∼ de** : liable to, punishable by <passible d'une amende : liable to a fine>

passif[1], **-sive** [pasif, -siv] *adj* : passive — **passivement** [-sivmɑ̃] *adv*

passif[2] *nm* **1** : passive case **2** : liabilities *pl*

passion [pasjɔ̃] *nf* : passion

passionnant, -nante [pasjɔnɑ̃, -nɑ̃t] *adj* CAPTIVANT : exciting, fascinating

passionné[1], **-née** [pasjɔne] *adj* : passionate, enthusiastic — **passionnément** [-nemɑ̃] *adv*

passionné[2], **-née** *n* : enthusiast

passionnel, -nelle [pasjɔnɛl] *adj* : passionate <crime passionnel : crime of passion>

passionner [pasjɔne] *vt* **1** CAPTIVER : to fascinate **2** : to impassion, to inflame — **se passionner** *vr* **∼ pour** : to have a passion for

passivement [pasivmɑ̃] *adv* : passively

passivité [pasivite] *nf* : passivity

passoire [paswar] *nf* : sieve, strainer, colander

pastel [pastɛl] *adj & nm* : pastel

pastèque [pastɛk] *nf* : watermelon

pasteur [pastœr] *nm* : minister, pastor

pasteuriser [pastœrize] *vt* : to pasteurize — **pasteurisation** [-rizasjɔ̃] *nf*

pastiche [pastiʃ] *nm* : pastiche

pastille [pastij] *nf* : lozenge <pastilles contre la toux : cough drops>

pastoral, -rale [pastɔral] *adj, mpl* **-raux** [-ro] : pastoral

pastorat [pastɔra] *nm* : pastorate, (Protestant) ministry

pat [pat] *nm* : stalemate

patate [patat] *nf* **1** *fam* : potato **2** *fam* : blockhead **3** *or* **patate douce** : sweet potato

pataud, -taude [pato, -tod] *adj* : clumsy, lumbering

patauger [patoʒe] {17} *vi* **1** : to splash about, to paddle **2** S'EMBROUILLER : to flounder about, to get confused

patchwork [patʃwœrk] *nm* : patchwork

pâte [pat] *nf* **1** : dough, pastry, batter **2** : paste <pâte dentifrice : toothpaste> <pâte à modeler : modeling clay> **3** : pulp <pâte à papier : paper pulp> **4 être bonne pâte** : to be easygoing **5 pâtes** *nfpl* : pasta

pâté [pate] *nm* **1** : pâté **2** : inkblot **3** *or* **pâté de maisons** : block (of houses)

pâtée [pate] *nf* : mash, feed, slop

patelin [patlɛ̃] *nm fam* : little village

patent, -tente [patɑ̃, -tɑ̃t] *adj* : obvious, patent

patente [patɑ̃t] *nf Can fam* **1** : thing, thingamajig **2** : gadget, gizmo

patenté, -tée [patɑ̃te] *adj fam* : established, out-and-out

patère [patɛr] *nf* : peg, hook (for coats, etc.)

paternel, -nelle [patɛrnɛl] *adj* : fatherly, paternal — **paternellement** [-nɛlmɑ̃] *adv*

paternité [patɛrnite] *nf* **1** : fatherhood, paternity **2** : authorship

pâteux, -teuse [patø, -tøz] *adj* **1** : pasty, doughy **2** : thick <avoir la langue pâteuse : to have a coated tongue>

pathétique [patetik] *adj* : pathetic, moving — **pathétiquement** [-tikmɑ̃] *adv*

pathologie [patɔlɔʒi] *nf* : pathology

pathologique [patɔlɔʒik] *adj* : pathological

pathologiste [patɔlɔʒist] *nmf* : pathologist

pathos [patos] *nms & pl* : pathos

patibulaire [patibylɛr] *adj* : sinister-looking

patiemment [pasjamɑ̃] *adv* : patiently

patience [pasjɑ̃s] *nf* **1** : patience <j'ai perdu patience : I lost my patience> **2 jeu de patience** : solitaire

patient, -tiente [pasjɑ̃, -sjɑ̃t] *adj & n* : patient

patienter [pasjɑ̃te] *vi* : to wait

patin [patɛ̃] *nm* : skate <patins à glace : ice skates> <patins à roulettes : roller skates>

patinage [patinaʒ] *nm* : skating <patinage artistique : figure skating>

patine [patin] *nf* : patina

patiner [patine] *vi* **1** : to skate **2** : to spin, to slip (of wheels) **3** *Can* : to hedge, to shilly-shally

patinette [patinɛt] *nf* TROTTINETTE : scooter

patineur, -neuse [patinœr, -nøz] *n* : skater

patinoire [patinwar] *nf* : skating rink

patio [patjo, pasjo] *nm* : patio

pâtir [patir] *vi* **∼ de** : to suffer because of

pâtisserie [patisri] *nf* **1** : cake, pastry **2** : pastry shop, bakery

pâtissier, -sière [patisje, -sjɛr] *n* : pastry chef

patois [patwa] *nms & pl* **1** : patois **2** *Can* : swearword, oath

patraque [patrak] *adj fam* : out of sorts

patriarcat [patrijarka] *nm* : patriarchy

patriarche [patrijarʃ] *nm* : patriarch — **patriarcal, -cale** [-jarkal] *adj*

patrie [patri] *nf* : mother country, homeland, fatherland

patrimoine [patrimwan] *nm* **1** : patrimony, legacy **2** HÉRITAGE : heritage

patriote[1] [patrijɔt] *adj* : patriotic

patriote[2] *nmf* : patriot — **patriotique** [patrijɔtik] *adj*

patriotisme [patrijɔtism] *nm* : patriotism

patron[1], **-tronne** [patrɔ̃, -trɔn] *n* **1** : patron saint **2** : owner **3** : boss, manager, employer

patron[2] *nm* : pattern (in sewing)

patronage [patrɔnaʒ] *nm* : patronage

patronal, -nale [patrɔnal] *adj, mpl* **-naux** [-no] : of employers <syndicat patronal : employers' union>

patronat [patrɔna] *nm* : management

patronner [patrɔne] *vt* : to support, to sponsor

patrouille [patruj] *nf* : patrol

patrouiller [patruje] *vi* : to patrol

patrouilleur[1], **-leuse** [patrujœr, -jøz] *n* **1** : soldier on patrol **2** *Can* : police officer (in a patrol car)

patrouilleur[2] *nm* : patrol boat, patrol plane

patte [pat] *nf* **1** : paw, hoof, foot (of a bird), leg (of an insect) <patte de devant : foreleg> **2** *fam* : leg, foot, hand <traîner la patte : to drag one's feet, to fall behind> **3** : tab, flap

pattes–d'oie [patdwa] *nfpl* : crow's feet

pâturage [patyraʒ] *nm* : pasture

pâture [patyr] *nf* **1** : feed, fodder **2** : pasture

paume [pom] *nf* : palm (of the hand)

paumer [pome] *v fam* : to lose — **se paumer** *vr fam* : to get lost

paupière [popjɛr] *nf* : eyelid

pause [poz] *nf* **1** : break <faire une pause : to pause, to take a break> **2** : pause **3** : rest (in music)

pauvre[1] [povr] *adj* **1** : poor, impoverished **2** : unfortunate **3** : poor, sparse

pauvre[2] *nm* : poor man, pauper <les pauvres : the poor>

pauvrement [povrəmɑ̃] *adv* : poorly

pauvreté [povrəte] *nf* : poverty

pavage [pavaʒ] *nm* : paving, cobblestones *pl*

pavaner [pavane] *v* **se pavaner** *vr* : to strut about

pavé [pave] *nm* **1** : pavement **2** : cobblestone, paving stone

paver [pave] *vt* : to pave

pavillon [pavijɔ̃] *nm* **1** : pavilion **2** *France* : (detached) house **3** : ward (in a hospital), (university) building **4** : auricle (of the ear) **5** : bell (of a wind instrument) **6** : flag (on a ship)

pavoiser [pavwaze] *vt* : to deck with flags — *vi* : to rejoice

pavot [pavo] *nm* : poppy

payable [pɛjabl] *adj* : payable

payant, payante [pɛjɑ̃, -jɑ̃t] *adj* **1** : paying **2** : for which one pays <télé payante : pay-TV>

paye [pɛj] → **paie**

payement [pɛmɑ̃] → **paiement**

payer [peje] {11} *vt* **1** : to pay, to pay for **2** *fam* : to buy <je lui ai payé un verre : I bought him a drink> **3** : to pay for, to suffer the consequences of **4** : to cover (one's expenses, etc.) — *vi* : to pay <un métier qui paie bien : a well-paying job> — **se payer** *vr* **1** : to have to be paid for **2** : to treat oneself

pays [pei] *nm* **1** : country **2** : region, area <du pays : local> **3** : village **4** : people (of a country) <s'adresser au pays : to address the nation>

paysage [peizaʒ] *nm* : scenery, landscape

paysagiste [peizaʒist] *nm* **1** : landscape painter **2** : landscape gardener

paysan[1], **-sanne** [peizɑ̃, -zan] *adj* **1** : agricultural, farming **2** : rural, rustic

paysan[2], **-sanne** *n* **1** : small farmer **2** : peasant

péage [peaʒ] *nm* **1** : toll **2** : tollbooth

peau [po] *nf, pl* **peaux** **1** : (human) skin <être bien dans sa peau : to be at peace with oneself> **2** : hide, pelt <peau de mouton : sheepskin> <peau de daim : buckskin> <gants de peau : leather gloves> **3** : peel, rind, skin (of fruits or vegetables)

peaufiner [pofine] *vt* : to put the finishing touches on, to perfect

pécan *or* **pecan** [pekɑ̃] *nm France or* **noix de pécan** : pecan

peccadille [pɛkadij] *nf* : peccadillo

pêche [pɛʃ] *nf* **1** : peach **2** : fishing **3** : catch <une bonne pêche : a good catch of fish>

péché [peʃe] *nm* : sin

pécher [peʃe] {87} *vi* : to sin

pêcher[1] [pɛʃe] *vt* **1** : to fish for **2** *fam* : to get, to unearth — *vi* : to fish <pêcher à la ligne : to angle>

pêcher[2] [pɛʃœr] *nm* : peach tree

pêcherie [pɛʃri] *nf* **1** : fishery, fishing ground **2** : fish processing factory

pécheur, -cheresse [peʃœr, -ʃrɛs] *n* : sinner

pêcheur, -cheuse [pɛʃœr, -ʃøz] *n* **1** : fisherman **2** **pêcheur à la ligne** : angler

pectine [pɛktin] *nf* : pectin

pectoral[1], **-rale** [pɛktɔral] *adj, mpl* **-raux** [-ro] **1** : pectoral **2** : cough <sirop pectoral : cough syrup>

pectoraux [pɛktɔro] *nmpl* : pectoral muscles

pécule [pekyl] *nm* ÉCONOMIES : savings *pl*

pécuniaire [pekynjɛr] *adj* FINANCIER : financial — **pécuniairement** [-njɛrmɑ̃] *adv*

pédagogie [pedagɔʒi] *nf* **1** : education, pedagogy **2** : teaching skill

pédagogique [pedagɔʒik] *adj* : educational, teaching <formation pédagogique : teacher training>
pédagogue [pedagɔg] *nmf* : educator, teacher
pédale [pedal] *nf* : pedal
pédaler [pedale] *vi* : to pedal
pédalier [pedalje] *nm* **1** : drive mechanism (of a bicycle) **2** : pedals *pl* (of an organ)
pédalo [pedalo] *nm* : pedal boat
pédant[1], **-dante** [pedɑ̃, -dɑ̃t] *adj* : pedantic
pédant[2], **-dante** *n* : pedant
pédantisme [pedɑ̃tism] *nm* : pedantry
pédestre [pedɛstr] *adj* : on foot <randonnée pédestre : hike>
pédiatre [pedjatr] *nmf* : pediatrician
pédiatrie [pedjatri] *nf* : pediatrics
pédiatrique [pedjatrik] *adj* : pediatric
pédicure [pedikyr] *nmf* : chiropodist
pedigree [pedigre] *nm* : pedigree
pègre [pɛgr] *nf* : (criminal) underworld
peignait [pɛɲɛ], **peignions** [pɛɲɔ̃], *etc.* → **peindre**
peigne[1] [pɛɲ], *etc.* → **peindre**
peigne[2] [pɛɲ] *nm* : comb
peigner [peɲe] *vt* **1** : to comb **2** : to card (fibers) — **se peigner** *vr* : to comb one's hair
peignoir [pɛɲwar] *nm* : bathrobe, dressing gown
peignure [pɛɲyr] *nf Can fam* : hairdo, hairstyle
peindre [pɛ̃dr] {37} *vt* **1** : to paint **2** : to depict, to portray — *vi* : to paint — **se peindre** *vr* : to show, to manifest itself
peine [pɛn] *nf* **1** : sorrow, sadness **2** : trouble, effort <se donner la peine de : to take the trouble to> <ce n'est pas la peine : it's not worth the effort, never mind, forget it> **3** : difficulty <sans peine : easily> **4** : punishment, penalty <peine capitale : capital punishment> **5 à ~** : hardly, just, barely
peiner [pene] *vt* ATTRISTER : to distress, to sadden — *vi* **1** : to have trouble, to struggle **2** : to strain, to labor (of an engine, etc.)
peintre [pɛ̃tr] *nm* : painter
peinture [pɛ̃tyr] *nf* **1** : paint **2** : painting, picture **3** : painting <elle fait de la peinture à l'huile : she paints in oil>
peinturer [pɛ̃tyre] *vt Can* : to paint <peinturer la maison : to paint the house>
peinturlurer [pɛ̃tyrlure] *vt* : to daub (with paint)
péjoratif, -tive [peʒɔratif, -tiv] *adj* : pejorative, derogatory — **péjorativement** [-tivmɑ̃] *adv*
pelage [pəlaʒ] *nm* : coat, fur (of an animal)
pelé, -lée [pəle] *adj* **1** : hairless, bald **2** : bare, barren
pêle-mêle [pɛlmɛl] *adv* : every which way, pell-mell
peler [pəle] {20} *v* : to peel
pèlerin, -rine [pɛlrɛ̃] *n* : pilgrim
pèlerinage [pɛlrinaʒ] *nm* : pilgrimage
pèlerine [pɛlrin] *nf* : cape
pélican [pelikɑ̃] *nm* : pelican
pellagre [pɛlagr] *nf* : pellagra
pelle [pɛl] *nf* **1** : shovel **2 pelle à poussière** : dustpan
pelletée [pɛlte] *nf* : shovelful
pelleter [pɛlte] {8} *vt* : to shovel
pelleteuse [pɛltøz] *nf* : power shovel, excavator
pellicule [pelikyl] *nf* **1** : (photographic) film **2** : thin layer, film **3 pellicules** *nfpl* : dandruff
pelote [pələt] *nf* **1** : ball (of string, thread, yarn, etc.) **2** : pincushion **3 pelote de neige** *Can* : snowball
peloter [pələte] *vt fam* : to grope, to paw, to fondle — *vi fam* : to neck
peloton [plɔtɔ̃] *nm* **1** : group <peloton de tête : front runners, leaders of the pack> **2** : squad, platoon <peloton d'exécution : firing squad>
pelotonner [pələtɔne] *v* **se pelotonner** *vr* : to curl up (into a ball), to snuggle
pelouse [pəluz] *nf* **1** : lawn, grass **2** : field (in sports)
peluche [pəlyʃ] *nf* **1** : plush **2** : (piece of) fluff, lint **3** *or* **animal en peluche** : stuffed animal, soft toy
pelucheux, -cheuse [pəlyʃø, -ʃøz] *adj* : fluffy
pelure [pəlyr] *nf* : peel, skin (of an apple, etc.)
pelvien, -vienne [pɛlvjɛ̃, -vjɛn] *adj* : pelvic
pelvis [pɛlvis] *nm* : pelvis
pénal, -nale [penal] *adj, mpl* **pénaux** [peno] : penal
pénalisation [penalizasjɔ̃] *nf* : penalty (in sports)
pénaliser [penalize] *vt* : to penalize
pénalité [penalite] *nf* : penalty (in sports)
penaud, -naude [pəno, -nod] *adj* : sheepish
penchant [pɑ̃ʃɑ̃] *nm* : tendency, inclination
pencher [pɑ̃ʃe] *vt* INCLINER : to tilt, to tip — *vi* **1** : to slant, to lean **2 ~ pour** : to incline towards, to favor — **se pencher** *vr* **1** : to hunch over, to bend (down) **2 ~ sur** : to look into, to examine
pendaison [pɑ̃dɛzɔ̃] *nf* **1** : hanging **2 pendaison de crémaillère** : housewarming
pendant[1], **-dante** [pɑ̃dɑ̃, -dɑ̃t] *adj* **1** : hanging, dangling **2** : pending
pendant[2] *nm* **1** *or* **pendant d'oreille** : drop earring **2** : counterpart, matching piece
pendant[3] *prep* **1** : during, for <pendant l'été : during the summer> <tra-

vailler pendant des heures : to work for hours> **2 pendant que** : while <pendant que vous y êtes : while you're at it>
pendentif [pɑ̃dɑ̃tif] *nm* : pendant
penderie [pɑ̃dri] *nf* : closet, wardrobe
pendre [pɑ̃dr] {63} *vt* **1** SUSPENDRE : to hang, to suspend **2** : to hang (someone) — *vi* **1** : to hang **2** : to hang down, to sag — **se pendre** *vr* : to hang oneself
pendule[1] [pɑ̃dyl] *nm* : pendulum
pendule[2] *nf* : clock
pêne [pɛn] *nm* : bolt (of a lock)
pénétrant, -trante [penetrɑ̃, -trɑ̃t] *adj* **1** : penetrating, piercing **2** : shrewd, perceptive
pénétration [penetrasjɔ̃] *nf* **1** : penetration **2** : perception, insight
pénétré, -trée [penetre] *adj* : earnest, intense <être pénétré de son importance : to be full of one's own importance>
pénétrer [penetre] {87} *vt* **1** IMPRÉGNER : to penetrate, to soak into **2** COMPRENDRE : to fathom, to understand — *vi* **1** S'ENFONCER : to penetrate, to sink in **2** S'INTRODUIRE : to enter, to penetrate
pénible [penibl] *adj* **1** : painful, distressing **2** ARDU : difficult, arduous
péniblement [peniblәmɑ̃] *adv* **1** : with difficulty, laboriously **2** : barely, just about
péniche [peniʃ] *nf* **1** : barge **2 péniche aménagée** : houseboat
pénicilline [penisilin] *nf* : penicillin
péninsule [penɛ̃syl] *nf* : peninsula — **péninsulaire** [-sylɛr] *adj*
pénis [penis] *nm* : penis
pénitence [penitɑ̃s] *nf* **1** : penitence, repentance **2** : punishment
pénitencier [penitɑ̃sje] *nm* : penitentiary
pénitent[1], **-tente** [penitɑ̃, -tɑ̃t] *adj* : penitent, repentant
pénitent[2], **-tente** *n* : penitent
pénitentiaire [penitɑ̃sjɛr] *adj* : penal
penne [pɛn] *nf* : quill, quill pen
pénombre [penɔ̃br] *nf* : half-light
pense-bête [pɑ̃sbɛt] *nm, pl* **pense-bêtes** [-bɛt] : reminder
pensée [pɑ̃se] *nf* **1** : thought **2** : mind <en pensée : in one's mind> **3** : thinking <pensée claire : clear thinking> **4** : pansy
penser [pɑ̃se] *vt* **1** : to think <penser du bien de : to think well of> <qu'en pensez-vous? : what do you think about it?> **2** : to believe, to suppose <penser que oui : to think so> <je pense qu'elle a raison : I think she's right> **3** : to intend, to plan on <il pense sortir : he intends to go out> — *vi* **1** : to think **2 ~ à** : to think about <penser au passé : to think about the past>
penseur, -seuse [pɑ̃sœr, -søz] *n* : thinker
pensif, -sive [pɑ̃sif, -siv] *adj* MÉDITATIF : pensive, thoughtful
pension [pɑ̃sjɔ̃] *nf* **1** : pension <pension alimentaire : alimony> **2** : boardinghouse **3** : room and board
pensionnaire [pɑ̃sjɔnɛr] *nmf* : boarder, roomer
pensionnat [pɑ̃sjɔna] *nm* : boarding school
pensivement [pɑ̃sivmɑ̃] *adv* : pensively, thoughtfully
pentagone [pɛ̃tagɔn] *nm* : pentagon — **pentagonal** [-gɔnal] *adj*
pente [pɑ̃t] *nf* **1** : slope **2 en ~** : sloping
Pentecôte [pɑ̃tkot] *nf* : Pentecost
pénurie [penyri] *nf* : shortage, scarcity
péon [peɔ̃] *nm* : peon
pépé [pepe] *nm France fam* : grandpa
pépère[1] [pepɛr] *adj fam* : quiet, easy
pépère[2] *nm fam* **1** : chubby boy **2** : old-timer **3** : grandpa
pépiement [pepimɑ̃] *nm* : peep, peeping
pépier [pepje] {96} *vi* : to chirp, to tweet, to peep
pépin [pepɛ̃] *nm* **1** : pip, seed **2** *fam* : snag, hitch
pépinière [pepinjɛr] *nf* **1** : (tree) nursery **2** : breeding ground
pépite [pepit] *nf* : nugget
péquenaud, -naude [pekno, -nod] *n France fam* : yokel, bumpkin
percale [pɛrkal] *nf* : percale
perçant, -çante [pɛrsɑ̃, -sɑ̃t] *adj* **1** : piercing, shrill **2** : sharp, keen <vue perçante : keen eyesight>
percée [pɛrse] *nf* **1** : opening, gap **2** : breakthrough, discovery
perce-neige [pɛrsәnɛʒ] *nmfs & pl* : snowdrop
perce-oreille [pɛrsɔrɛj] *nm, pl* **perce-oreilles** [-ɔrɛj] : earwig
percepteur [pɛrsɛptœr] *nm* : tax collector
perceptible [pɛrsɛptibl] *adj* : perceptible, noticeable
perception [pɛrsɛpsjɔ̃] *nf* **1** : perception **2** RECOUVREMENT : collection (of taxes)
percer [pɛrse] {6} *vt* **1** : to pierce **2** : to open up, to build (a road, etc.) **3** PÉNÉTRER : to fathom, to penetrate **4 percer ses dents** : to be teething — *vi* **1** : to break through (of the sun) **2** : to come through (of a tooth)
perceuse [pɛrsøz] *nf* : drill
percevable [pɛrsәvabl] *adj* : collectable, payable
percevoir [pɛrsәvwar] {26} *vt* **1** : to perceive, to sense **2** RECOUVRER : to receive (money, etc.), to collect (taxes)
perche [pɛrʃ] *nf* **1** : pole **2** : perch, bass (fish)
percher [pɛrʃe] *vi* : to perch — **se percher** *vr* : to roost

perchoir [pɛrʃwar] *nm* : perch, roost
perclus, -cluse [pɛrkly, -klyz] *adj* **~ de** : crippled with
perçoit [pɛrswa], **perçoive** [pɛrswav], *etc.* → **percevoir**
percolateur [pɛrkɔlatœr] *nm* : percolator
perçu [pɛrsy] *pp* → **percevoir**
percussion [pɛrkysjɔ̃] *nf* : percussion — **percussionniste** [-kysjɔnist] *nmf*
percutant, -tante [pɛrkytɑ̃, -tɑ̃t] *adj* : forceful, striking
percuter [pɛrkyte] *vt* : to strike, to crash into — *vi* **1** : to explode **2 ~ contre** : to crash into
perdant[1], -dante [pɛrdɑ̃, -dɑ̃t] *adj* : losing
perdant[2], -dante *n* : loser
perdition [pɛrdisjɔ̃] *nf* **1** : perdition **2 en ~** : in distress
perdre [pɛrdr] {63} *vt* **1** : to lose **2** : to waste <perdre son temps : to waste one's time> **3** MANQUER : to miss **4** : to ruin (one's reputation, etc.) — *vi* : to lose — **se perdre** *vr* **1** : to get lost, to disappear **2** : to get lost, to lose one's way
perdreau [pɛrdro] *nm, pl* **perdreaux** : (young) partridge
perdrix [pɛrdri] *nfs & pl* : partridge
perdu, -due [pɛrdy] *adj* **1** : lost **2** : wasted **3** : ruined **4** : spare, free <à mes moments perdus : in my spare time> **5** : isolated, remote
père [pɛr] *nm* **1** : father **2 pères** *nmpl* : ancestors, forefathers
pérégrinations [peregrinasjɔ̃] *nfpl* : travels
péremptoire [perɑ̃ptwar] *adj* : peremptory
péréquation [perekwasjɔ̃] *nf* : equalization, adjustment (in finance)
perfectible [pɛrfɛktibl] *adj* : perfectible
perfection [pɛrfɛksjɔ̃] *nf* **1** : perfection **2 à la perfection** : to perfection, perfectly
perfectionné, -née [pɛrfɛksjɔne] *adj* : advanced, sophisticated
perfectionnement [pɛrfɛksjɔnmɑ̃] *nm* : perfecting, improvement
perfectionner [pɛrfɛksjɔne] *vt* : to perfect, to improve — **se perfectionner** *vr*
perfectionnisme [pɛrfɛksjɔnism] *nm* : perfectionism
perfectionniste[1] [pɛrfɛksjɔnist] *adj* : perfectionist, perfectionistic
perfectionniste[2] *nmf* : perfectionist
perfide [pɛrfid] *adj* : treacherous, perfidious — **perfidement** [-fidmɑ̃] *adv*
perfidie [pɛrfidi] *nf* : treachery
perforation [pɛrfɔrasjɔ̃] *nf* : perforation
perforer [pɛrfɔre] *vt* PERCER : to perforate, to pierce
performance [pɛrfɔrmɑ̃s] *nf* **1** : performance **2** : achievement
performant, -mante [pɛrfɔrmɑ̃, -mɑ̃t] *adj* **1** : high-performance (of machines, etc.) **2** : high-return (of investments)
péricliter [periklite] *vi* : to decline sharply
péril [peril] *nm* : peril, danger <au péril de sa vie : at the risk of one's life>
périlleux, -leuse [perijø, -jøz] *adj* : perilous — **périlleusement** [-jøzmɑ̃] *adv*
périmé, -mée [perime] *adj* **1** : outdated **2** : out-of-date, expired
périmètre [perimɛtr] *nm* : perimeter
période [perjɔd] *nf* **1** : period, time **2 par périodes** : periodically, from time to time
périodique[1] [perjɔdik] *adj* **1** : periodic (in science) **2** : periodical **3** : recurring
périodique[2] *nm* : periodical
périodiquement [perjɔdikmɑ̃] *adv* : periodically
péripétie [peripesi] *nf* : incident, event
périphérie [periferi] *nf* **1** : periphery, circumference **2** : outskirts *pl*
périphérique[1] [periferik] *adj* **1** : peripheral **2** : outlying
périphérique[2] *nm* : peripheral (in computer science)
périple [peripl] *nm* : journey
périr [perir] *vi* : to perish
périscope [periskɔp] *nm* : periscope
périssable [perisabl] *adj* : perishable
perle [pɛrl] *nf* **1** : pearl, bead **2** : gem, treasure, paragon **3** : drop <perle de sang : drop of blood> **4** *fam* : howler, blunder
perlé, -lée [pɛrle] *adj* **1** : pearly **2** : beaded
perler [pɛrle] *vi* : to form in droplets
permanence [pɛrmanɑ̃s] *nf* **1** : permanence **2 en ~** : permanently, without interruption **3 être de permanence** : to be on duty
permanent[1], -nente [pɛrmanɑ̃, -nɑ̃t] *adj* **1** : permanent **2** : constant
permanent[2], -nente *n* : permanent employee or member
permanente *nf* : permanent, perm
perméable [pɛrmeabl] *adj* **1** : permeable **2 ~ à** : receptive to
permettre [pɛrmɛtr] {53} *vt* **1** : to allow, to permit **2** : to enable, to make possible — **se permettre** *vr* **1** : to allow oneself **2 ~ de** : to take the liberty of
permis [pɛrmi] *nm* LICENCE : license, permit <permis de conduire : driver's license>
permissif, -sive [pɛrmisif, -siv] *adj* : permissive
permission [pɛrmisjɔ̃] *nf* **1** : permission **2** : leave (in the military)
permissivité [pɛrmisivite] *nf* : permissiveness
permutation [pɛrmytasjɔ̃] *nf* **1** : permutation **2** : exchange (of jobs)
permuter [pɛrmyte] *vt* : to exchange, to switch around — *vi* : to switch places

pernicieux, -cieuse [pɛrnisjø, -sjøz] *adj* : pernicious — **pernicieusement** [-sjøzmɑ̃] *adv*
péroné [perɔne] *nm* : fibula
pérorer [perɔre] *vi* : to declaim, to hold forth
peroxyde [pɛrɔksid] *nm* : peroxide <peroxyde d'hydrogène : hydrogen peroxide>
perpendiculaire [pɛrpɑ̃dikylɛr] *adj* : perpendicular — **perpendiculairement** [-lɛrmɑ̃] *adv*
perpétration [pɛrpetrasjɔ̃] *nf* : perpetration (of a crime, etc.)
perpétrer [pɛrpetre] {87} *vt* : to perpetrate
perpétuel, -tuelle [pɛrpetɥɛl] *adj* **1** : perpetual **2** : permanent, for life
perpétuellement [pɛrpetɥɛlmɑ̃] *adv* : constantly, perpetually
perpétuer [pɛrpetɥe] *vt* ÉTERNISER : to perpetuate
perpétuité [pɛrpetɥite] *nf* **à ~** : for life
perplexe [pɛrplɛks] *adj* : perplexed, puzzled
perplexité [pɛrplɛksite] *nf* : perplexity, bafflement
perquisition [pɛrkizisjɔ̃] *nf* : (police) search
perquisitionner [pɛrkizisjɔne] *vi* : to carry out a search
perron [perɔ̃] *nm* **1** : (front) steps **2** *Can* GALERIE : porch
perroquet [perɔkɛ] *nm* : parrot
perruche [peryʃ] *nf* : parakeet
perruque [peryk] *nf* : wig
pers [pɛr] *adj* : bluish green
persan[1], -sane [pɛrsɑ̃, -san] *adj* : Persian
persan[2] *nm* : Persian (language)
Persan, -sane *n* : Persian
persécuter [pɛrsekyte] *vt* **1** MARTYRISER : to persecute, to torment **2** HARCELER : to harass
persécuteur, -trice [pɛrsekytœr, -tris] *n* : persecutor, tormentor
persécution [pɛrsekysjɔ̃] *nf* : persecution
persévérance [pɛrseverɑ̃s] *nf* : perseverance
persévérant, -rante [pɛrseverɑ̃, -rɑ̃t] *adj* : persevering, persistent
persévérer [pɛrsevere] {87} *vi* : to persevere, to persist
persienne [pɛrsjɛn] *nf* : shutter
persiflage [pɛrsiflaʒ] *nm* : mockery
persil [pɛrsi] *nm* : parsley
persistance [pɛrsistɑ̃s] *nf* : persistence
persistant, -tante [pɛrsistɑ̃, -tɑ̃t] *adj* : persistent — **persistance** [-tɑ̃s] *nf*
persister [pɛrsiste] *vi* **1** PERSÉVÉRER : to persist, to persevere **2** : to continue, to last
personnage [pɛrsɔnaʒ] *nm* **1** : (fictional) character **2** : character, individual **3** : influential person, celebrity
personnaliser [pɛrsɔnalize] *vt* : to personalize
personnalité [pɛrsɔnalite] *nf* **1** : personality <une personnalité forte : a strong personality> **2** : celebrity
personne[1] [pɛrsɔn] *nf* **1** : person <quelques personnes : a few people> <la personne : the individual> **2** : self, (bodily) person <être bien de sa personne : to be good-looking> <content de sa (petite) personne : pleased with oneself> <en personne : in person> **3** : person (in grammar)
personne[2] *pron* **1** (*in negative constructions*) : no one, nobody <je n'ai vu personne : I didn't see anyone> <personne ne dit ça : nobody says that> **2** : anyone, anybody <mieux que personne : better than anybody> <presque personne : hardly anyone>
personnel[1], -nelle [pɛrsɔnɛl] *adj* **1** : personal, private **2** : selfish, self-centered **3** : personal (in grammar)
personnel[2] *nm* : personnel, staff
personnellement [pɛrsɔnɛlmɑ̃] *adv* : personally, in person
personne–ressource [pɛrsɔnrəsurs] *nf Can, pl* **personnes–ressources** : specialist, expert
personnifier [pɛrsɔnifje] {96} *vt* : to personify — **personnification** [-nifikasjɔ̃] *nf*
perspective [pɛrspɛktiv] *nf* **1** : perspective (in art) **2** : view **3** : point of view, viewpoint **4** : outlook, prospect <en perspective : in prospect, in the offing>
perspicace [pɛrspikas] *adj* : perspicacious, insightful, perceptive
perspicacité [pɛrspikasite] *nf* : insight, perspicacity
persuader [pɛrsɥade] *vt* CONVAINCRE : to persuade, to convince — **se persuader** *vr*
persuasif, -sive [pɛrswazif, -ziv] *adj* : persuasive
persuasion [pɛrsɥazjɔ̃] *nf* : persuasion
perte [pɛrt] *nf* **1** : loss **2** : waste **3** : disaster, ruin **4 à perte de vue** : as far as the eye can see **5 pertes** *nfpl* : losses
pertinemment [pɛrtinamɑ̃] *adv* : to the point <savoir pertinemment : to know full well>
pertinence [pɛrtinɑ̃s] *nf* : pertinence, relevance
pertinent, -nente [pɛrtinɑ̃, -nɑ̃t] *adj* : pertinent, relevant
perturbateur[1], -trice [pɛrtyrbatœr, -tris] *adj* : disruptive
perturbateur[2], -trice *n* : troublemaker
perturber [pɛrtyrbe] *vt* **1** : to disrupt **2** DÉRANGER : to disturb, to upset
péruvien, -vienne [peryvjɛ̃, -vjɛn] *adj* : Peruvian
Péruvien, -vienne *n* : Peruvian
pervenche [pɛrvɑ̃ʃ] *nf* : periwinkle (plant)

pervers[1], **-verse** [pɛrvɛr, -vɛrs] *adj* : perverted, depraved

pervers[2], **-verse** *n* : pervert

perversion [pɛrvɛrsjɔ̃] *nf* : perversion

perversité [pɛrvɛrsite] *nf* : perversity

pervertir [pɛrvɛrtir] *vt* CORROMPRE : to pervert, to corrupt

pesage [pəzaʒ] *nm* : weighing

pesamment [pəzamɑ̃] *adv* LOURDEMENT : heavily

pesant, -sante [pəzɑ̃, -zɑ̃t] *adj* **1** : heavy **2** : burdensome, oppressive **3** : unwieldy, ungainly

pesanteur [pəzɑ̃tœr] *nf* **1** : gravity **2** : heaviness, weight

pesée [pəze] *nf* **1** : weighing **2** : weight **3** : force

pèse–personne [pɛzpɛrsɔn] *nm, pl* **pèse–personnes** : (bathroom) scales *pl*

peser [pəze] {52} *vt* **1** : to weigh **2** EXAMINER : to consider — *vi* **1** : to weigh <combien pèses-tu? : how much do you weigh?> <peser lourd : to be heavy> **2** INFLUER : to carry weight, to have bearing **3 ∼ sur** : to press, to pressure, to weigh on

pessimisme [pesimism] *nm* : pessimism

pessimiste[1] [pesimist] *adj* : pessimistic

pessimiste[2] *nmf* : pessimist

peso [pezo, peso] *nm* : peso

peste [pɛst] *nf* **1** : plague, pestilence **2** : pest, nuisance

pester [pɛste] *vi* **∼ contre** : to curse

pesticide [pɛstisid] *nm* : pesticide

pestilence [pɛstilɑ̃s] *nf* : stench

pestilentiel, -tielle [pɛstilɑ̃sjɛl] *adj* FÉTIDE : foul, fetid

pétale [petal] *nm* : petal

pétanque [petɑ̃k] *nf* : petanque (game of bowls)

pétant, -tante [petɑ̃, -tɑ̃t] *adj fam* : sharp, on the dot <à neuf heures pétantes : at nine o'clock sharp>

pétarade [petarad] *nf* : backfiring

pétarader [petarade] *vi* : to backfire

pétard [petar] *nm* **1** : firecracker **2 être en pétard** *fam* : to be fuming

péter [pete] {87} *vi fam* **1** : to go off, to explode **2** : to bust, to break — *vt fam* **1** : to bust, to break **2 péter le feu** : to be full of energy

pétillant, -lante [petijɑ̃, -jɑ̃t] *adj* **1** : sparkling **2** : bubbly

pétillement [petijmɑ̃] *nm* **1** : fizziness, fizz **2** : crackling **3** : sparkle (of the eyes, etc.)

pétiller [petije] *vi* **1** : to sparkle **2** : to bubble, to fizz **3** : to crackle (of fire)

petit[1] [p(ə)ti] *adv* **1 tailler petit** : to run small **2 voir petit** : to underestimate **3 petit à petit** : gradually, little by little

petit[2], **-tite** [p(ə)ti, -tit] *adj* **1** : small, little **2** COURT : short **3** : young <ma petite sœur : my little sister> **4** (*used in terms of affection*) <mon petit chéri : my sweetie> **5** : minor, insignificant, slight **6 petit ami, petite amie** : boyfriend, girlfriend **7 petit déjeuner** : breakfast **8 petit doigt** : little finger **9 petite monnaie** : small change **10 petit pois** : (green) pea **11 petite vérole** : smallpox

petit[3], **-tite** *n* : child, little boy *m,* little girl *f*

petit[4] *nm* : cub (of an animal)

petitement [p(ə)titmɑ̃] *adv* **1** : poorly, humbly <petitement logé : living in cramped quarters> **2** : pettily

petitesse [p(ə)titɛs] *nf* **1** : smallness **2** MESQUINERIE : pettiness

petit–fils, petite–fille [p(ə)tifis, p(ə)titfij] *n* : grandson *m,* granddaughter *f*

pétition [petisjɔ̃] *nf* : petition

pétitionnaire [petisjɔnɛr] *nmf* : petitioner

pétitionner [petisjɔne] *vi* : to petition

petit–lait [p(ə)tilɛ] *nm, pl* **petits–laits** : whey

petits–enfants [p(ə)tizɑ̃fɑ̃] *nmpl* : grandchildren

pétrification [petrifikasjɔ̃] *nf* : petrification

pétrifier [petrifje] {96} *vt* : to petrify

pétrin [petrɛ̃] *nm fam* : fix, jam

pétrir [petrir] *vt* : to knead

pétrole [petrɔl] *nm* **1** : oil, petroleum **2** *or* **pétrole lampant** : kerosene

pétrolier[1], **-lière** [petrɔlje, -ljɛr] *adj* : oil, petroleum <industrie pétrolière : oil industry>

pétrolier[2] *nm* **1** : oil tanker **2** : oilman

pétulance [petylɑ̃s] *nf* EXUBÉRANCE : vivacity, exuberance

pétulant, -lante [petylɑ̃, -lɑ̃t] *adj* EXUBÉRANT : vivacious, exuberant

pétunia [petynja] *nm* : petunia

peu[1] [pø] *adv* **1** : little, not much <elle a dormi peu : she slept little> **2** : not very <peu connu : little known> **3** : shortly <peu après : not long after>

peu[2] *n* **1** : lack <peu d'appétit : lack of appetite> **2** : little, bit <attends un peu : wait a little (longer)> <un peu moins de gens : somewhat fewer people> **3 le peu de** : the few, the little <le peu d'argent que j'ai mis de côté : the little money I've saved up> **4 peu à peu** : little by little **5 pour un peu** : almost, very nearly

peu[3] *pron* **1** : few (people) <peu lui font confiance : few trust him> **2 ∼ de** : few, little <peu de mots : few words> <c'est peu de chose : it's just a little, it's not much>

peuplade [pøplad] *nf* : (small) tribe

peuple [pøpl] *nm* **1** : people *pl,* nation <le peuple anglais : the English people> **2** : common people *pl,* masses *pl* <un homme du peuple : a man of the people> **3** FOULE : crowd, multitude

peuplé, -lée [pœple] *adj* : populated

peuplement [pœpləmɑ̃] *nm* **1** : populating **2** : population

peupler [pœple] *vt* **1** : to populate, to stock, to plant **2** HABITER : to inhabit **3** : to occupy, to fill — **se peupler** *vr* : to fill up with
peuplier [pøplije] *nm* : poplar
peur [pœr] *nf* **1** : fear **2 de peur que** : lest **3 faire peur à** : to frighten
peureusement [pœrøzmɑ̃] *adv* : fearfully
peureux, -reuse [pœrø, -røz] *adj* CRAINTIF : fearful, afraid
peut [pø], *etc.* → **pouvoir**
peut–être [pøtɛtr] *adv* : perhaps, maybe
phalange [falɑ̃ʒ] *nf* : phalanx
phallique [falik] *adj* : phallic
phallus [falys] *nms & pl* : phallus
pharaon [faraɔ̃] *nm* : pharaoh
phare [far] *nm* **1** : lighthouse **2** : headlight **3** : beacon
pharmaceutique [farmasøtik] *adj* : pharmaceutical
pharmacie [farmasi] *nf* : pharmacy, drugstore
pharmacien, -cienne [farmasjɛ̃, -sjɛn] *n* : pharmacist
pharmacologie [farmakɔlɔʒi] *nf* : pharmacology
pharynx [farɛ̃ks] *nm* : pharynx
phase [faz] *nf* : phase, stage
phénix [feniks] *nm* **1** : phoenix **2** : paragon
phénoménal, -nale [fenɔmenal] *adj, mpl* **-naux** [-no] : phenomenal — **phénoménalement** [-nalmɑ̃] *adv*
phénomène [fenɔmɛn] *nm* **1** : phenomenon **2** : freak (in a circus, etc.)
philanthrope [filɑ̃trɔp] *nmf* : philanthropist
philanthropie [filɑ̃trɔpi] *nf* : philanthropy — **philanthropique** [-trɔpik] *adj*
philatélie [filateli] *nf* : stamp collecting, philately
philippin, -pine [filipɛ̃, -pin] *adj* : Filipino, Philippine
Philippin, -pine *n* : Filipino
philistin[1], **-tine** [filistɛ̃, -tin] *adj* : philistine
philistin[2] *nm* : philistine
philodendron [filɔdɛ̃drɔ̃] *nm* : philodendron
philosophe[1] [filɔzɔf] *adj* : philosophical
philosophe[2] *nmf* : philosopher
philosopher [filɔzɔfe] *vi* : to philosophize
philosophie [filɔzɔfi] *nf* : philosophy
philosophique [filɔzɔfik] *adj* : philosophical — **philosophiquement** [-fikmɑ̃] *adv*
phlébite [flebit] *nf* : phlebitis
phlox [flɔks] *nms & pl* : phlox
phobie [fɔbi] *nf* : phobia
phonème [fɔnɛm] *nm* : phoneme
phonétique[1] [fɔnetik] *adj* : phonetic
phonétique[2] *nf* : phonetics
phonograph [fɔnɔgraf] *nm* : phonograph
phoque [fɔk] *nm* **1** : seal **2** : sealskin
phosphate [fɔsfat] *nm* : phosphate
phosphore [fɔsfɔr] *nm* : phosphorous
phosphorescence [fɔsfɔresɑ̃s] *nf* : phosphorescence — **phosphorescent, -cente** [-resɑ̃, -sɑ̃t] *adj*
photo [fɔto] *nf* : photo <photo d'identité : passport photo>
photocopie [fɔtɔkɔpi] *nf* **1** : photocopy **2** : photocopying
photocopier [fɔtɔkɔpje] {96} *vt* : to photocopy
photocopieur [fɔtɔkɔpjœr] *nm* : photocopier
photocopieuse [fɔtɔkɔpjøz] *nf* → **photocopieur**
photoélectrique [fɔtɔelɛktrik] *adj* : photoelectric
photogénique [fɔtɔʒenik] *adj* : photogenic
photographe [fɔtɔgraf] *nmf* : photographer
photographie [fɔtɔgrafi] *nf* **1** : photography **2** : photograph
photographier [fɔtɔgrafje] {96} *vt* : to photograph
photographique [fɔtɔgrafik] *adj* : photographic — **photographiquement** [-fikmɑ̃] *adv*
photosynthèse [fɔtɔsɛ̃tɛz] *nf* : photosynthesis
phrase [fraz] *nf* **1** : sentence **2** : phrase
phraséologie [frazeɔlɔʒi] *nf* **1** : phraseology **2** : verbiage, verbosity
phylum [filɔm] *nm* : phylum
physicien, -cienne [fizisjɛ̃, -sjɛn] *n* : physicist
physiologie [fizjɔlɔʒi] *nf* : physiology
physiologique [fizjɔlɔʒik] *adj* : physiological, physiologic
physiologiste [fizjɔlɔʒist] *nmf* : physiologist
physionomie [fizjɔnɔmi] *nf* : physiognomy
physiothérapie [fizjɔterapi] *nf* : physiotherapy, physical therapy
physique[1] [fizik] *adj* : physical — **physiquement** [-zikmɑ̃] *adv*
physique[2] *nm* : physique
physique[3] *nf* : physics
pi [pi] *nm* : pi
piaffer [pjafe] *vi* : to stamp one's feet, to tap one's foot
piailler [pjaje] *vi* : to squawk, to chirp
pianiste [pjanist] *nmf* : pianist
piano [pjano] *nm* : piano <piano à queue : grand piano>
pianoter [pjanɔte] *vi* **1** : to tinkle away (at the piano) **2** : to tap, to drum (one's fingers)
piastre [pjastr] *nf Can fam* : dollar, buck
piaule [pjol] *nf fam* : room, pad
piaulement [pjolmɑ̃] *nm* : cheep, peep
piauler [pjole] *vi* **1** : to cheep, to peep **2** *fam* : to whimper, to whine

pic [pik] *nm* **1** : woodpecker **2** CIME : peak <à pic : straight down, vertically> **3** : pick, pickax <pic à glace : ice pick>

pic–bois [pikbwa] *nm Can, pl* **pic–bois** : woodpecker

piccolo *or* **picolo** [pikɔlo] *nm* : piccolo

pichet [piʃɛ] *nm* **1** : pitcher **2** : pitcherful

pichou [piʃu] *nm Can fam* : slipper, (baby's) bootee

pickpocket [pikpɔkɛt] *nm* : pickpocket

pick–up [pikœp] *nm* : pickup (truck)

picoler [pikɔle] *vi fam* : to tipple, to drink

picorer [pikɔre] *v* : to peck

picot [piko] *nm Can* : polka dot

picotement [pikɔtmɑ̃] *nm* : prickling, stinging, tingling

picoter [pikɔte] *vt* **1** PICORER : to peck **2** : to sting — *vi* : to prickle, to sting

picotin [pikɔtɛ̃] *nm* : peck

pictural, -rale [piktyral] *adj, mpl* **-raux** [-ro] : pictorial

pick–up [pikœp] *nm* : pickup (truck)

pie[1] [pi] *adj* : piebald, pied

pie[2] [pi] *nf* **1** : magpie **2** *fam* : chatterbox

pièce [pjɛs] *nf* **1** : piece, bit <mettre en pièces : to smash to pieces> **2** : piece, item <la pièce : apiece> <pièce de collection : collector's item> <pièce à conviction : exhibit (in a court of law)> **3** : room, bedroom **4** : paper, document <pièce jointe : enclosure> **5** : piece (in music or theater) <pièce de théâtre : play> **6** *or* **pièce de monnaie** : coin

pied [pje] *nm* **1** : foot <coup de pied : kick> <à pied : on foot> <pied à pied : inch by inch> **2** : base, bottom, leg (of a table, etc.) **3** : foot (in measurement) **4** : stalk, bunch, head <pied de salade : head of lettuce> **5 mettre sur pied** : to set up, to get off the ground

piédestal [pjedɛstal] *nm, pl* **-taux** [-to] : pedestal

piège [pjɛʒ] *nm* **1** : trap, snare **2** : snag, pitfall **3 prendre au piège** : to entrap

piéger [pjeʒe] {64} *vt* **1** : to trap **2** : to booby-trap

pie–grièche [pigrijɛʃ] *nf, pl* **pies–grièches** : shrike

pierre [pjɛr] *nf* **1** : stone **2 pierre à aiguiser** : whetstone **3 pierre angulaire** : cornerstone **4 pierre tombale** : tombstone, gravestone, headstone

pierreries [pjɛrri] *nfpl* : precious stones, gems

pierreux, -reuse [pjɛrø, -røz] *adj* : stony

piété [pjete] *nf* : piety

piétiner [pjetine] *vt* : to trample on, to crush underfoot — *vi* **1** : to stamp one's feet (with impatience, etc.) **2** STAGNER : to make no headway

piéton, -tonne [pjetɔ̃, -tɔn] *n* : pedestrian

piétonnier, -nière [pjetɔnje, -njɛr] *adj* : pedestrian

piètre [pjɛtr] *adj* : very poor, sorry <piètre consolation : cold comfort> <une piètre figure : a sorry figure>

pieu [pjø] *nm, pl* **pieux** : post, stake

pieuvre [pjøvr] *nf* POULPE : octopus

pieux, pieuse [pjø, pjøz] *adj* : pious — **pieusement** [pjøzmɑ̃] *adv*

pige [piʒ] *nf* **travailler à la pige** *or* **faire des piges** : to work freelance

pigeon [piʒɔ̃] *nm* : pigeon

pigeonneau [piʒɔno] *nm* : squab

pigeonnier [piʒɔnje] *nm* : pigeon house, dovecote

piger [piʒe] {17} *vt* **1** *fam* : to understand, to catch on to <tu piges? : get it?> **2** *Can* : to pick (a card, a number, etc.)

pigiste [piʒist] *nmf* : freelancer

pigment [pigmɑ̃] *nm* : pigment — **pigmentation** [-mɑ̃tasjɔ̃] *nf*

pignon [piɲɔ̃] *nm* **1** : gable **2** : cogwheel

pilaf [pilaf] *nm* : pilaf

pile[1] [pil] *adv fam* **1** : abruptly <arrêter pile : to stop dead> **2** : exactly <à dix heures pile : at ten o'clock sharp>

pile[2] *nf* **1** : pile, heap **2** : (storage) battery **3** : pier (of a bridge) **4** : reverse (of a coin) <pile ou face? : heads or tails?>

piler [pile] *vt* **1** BROYER : to crush, to pound **2** *fam* : to clobber, to defeat **3** *Can* : to mash (potatoes, etc.) — *vi* **1** *Can fam* : to walk, to step <j'ai pilé dans une flaque d'eau : I walked into a puddle> **2** *France fam* : to slam on the brakes

pilier [pilje] *nm* **1** : pillar, column **2** SOUTIEN : prop, mainstay

pillage [pijaʒ] *nm* : looting, pillaging

pillard, -larde [pijar, -jard] *n* : looter

piller [pije] *vt* : to loot, to pillage, to plunder

pilleur, -leuse [pilœr, -løz] *n* : pillager, looter

pilon [pilɔ̃] *nm* **1** : pestle **2** : wooden leg **3** : (chicken) drumstick

pilonner [pilɔne] *vt* **1** : to crush **2** : to bombard, to shell

pilori [pilɔri] *nm* : stocks *pl,* pillory

pilosité [pilozite] *nf* : hairiness

pilotage [pilɔtaʒ] *nm* : piloting, flying

pilote[1] [pilɔt] *adj* : pilot, test <projet pilote : pilot project>

pilote[2] *nm* **1** : pilot <pilote de ligne : airline pilot> **2** GUIDE : guide **3 pilote de course** : racing-car driver

piloter [pilɔte] *vt* **1** : to pilot, to fly, to drive **2** : to guide, to direct

pilotis [pilɔti] *nm* : stilts *pl,* piling

pilule [pilyl] *nf* : pill

piment [pimɑ̃] *nm* **1** : pepper <piment rouge : chili pepper> <piment de la Jamaïque : allspice> <piment doux : pimiento> **2** : piquancy, spice

pimenter [pimɑ̃te] *vt* **1** : to season with red pepper **2** : to spice up

pimpant, -pante [pɛ̃pɑ̃] *adj* : spruce, dapper
pin [pɛ̃] *nm* : pine (tree or wood)
pinacle [pinakl] *nm* **1** : pinnacle, summit **2 porter qqn au pinacle** : to praise s.o. to the skies
pinailler [pinaje] *vi fam* : to split hairs, to quibble
pinard [pinar] *nm fam* : (cheap) wine
pince [pɛ̃s] *nf* **1** : pliers *pl* **2** : tongs *pl* **3** : pincer, claw **4** : pleat, fold **5 pince à cheveux** : bobby pin **6 pince à épiler** : tweezers *pl* **7 pince à linge** : clothespin
pincé, -cée [pɛ̃se] *adj* : forced, stiff
pinceau [pɛ̃so] *nm, pl* **pinceaux** : paintbrush
pincée [pɛ̃se] *nf* : pinch <une pincée de sel : a pinch of salt>
pincement [pɛ̃smɑ̃] *nm* **1** : pinch **2** : twinge, pang
pince–monseigneur [pɛ̃smɔ̃sɛɲœr] *nf, pl* **pinces–monseigneur** : crowbar, jimmy
pincer [pɛ̃se] {6} *vt* **1** : to pinch **2** : to nip at, to sting (of wind, cold, etc.) **3** : to purse (one's lips) **4** : to pluck (a stringed instrument) **5** *fam* : to nab — *vi* : to be nippy (of weather) — **se pincer** *vr* **1** : to pinch oneself <se pincer le nez : to hold one's nose> **2** : to get caught, to be pinched <je me suis pincé le doigt dans la porte : I caught my finger in the door>
pince–sans–rire [pɛ̃ssɑ̃rir] *adj s & pl* : deadpan
pincettes [pɛ̃sɛt] *nfpl* **1** : small tweezers **2** : (fire) tongs
pinçon [pɛ̃sɔ̃] *nm* : pinch mark
pinède [pinɛd] *nf* : pine forest
pingouin [pɛ̃gwɛ̃] *nm* : auk
pingre [pɛ̃gr] *adj* AVARE : niggardly, stingy
pingrerie [pɛ̃grəri] *nf* : meanness, stinginess
pinotte [pinɔt] *nf Can fam* : peanut
pintade [pɛ̃tad] *nf* : guinea fowl
pinte [pɛ̃t] *nf* : pint
pioche [pjɔʃ] *nf* : pickax, pick
piocher [pjɔʃe] *vt* **1** CREUSER : to dig (up) **2** : to draw (a card) **3** *fam* : to cram for (an exam)
piolet [pjɔlɛ] *nm* : ice ax
pion[1], pionne [pjɔ̃, pjɔn] *n France fam* : student monitor
pion[2] *nm* **1** : pawn (in chess) **2** : piece (in checkers)
pionnier, -nière [pjɔnje, -njɛr] *n* : pioneer
pipe [pip] *nf* : pipe <fumer la pipe : to smoke a pipe>
pipeau [pipo] *nm, pl* **pipeaux** : (reed) pipe, flute
pipeline [pajplajn] *nm* : pipeline
piper [pipe] *vi* **ne pas piper (mot)** : to keep mum
piquant[1], -quante [pikɑ̃, -kɑ̃t] *adj* **1** : prickly, bristly **2** ÉPICÉ : hot, spicy **3** : sharp, biting **4** : racy, spicy
piquant[2] *nm* **1** : spiciness, piquancy **2** : prickle, thorn, barb **3** : spine, quill (of a porcupine, etc.)
pique[1] [pik] *nm* : spade (in playing cards)
pique[2] *nf* **1** : pike (weapon) **2** POINTE : cutting remark
piqué[1], -quée [pike] *adj* **1** : quilted **2** : sour, mildewed **3** : staccato (in music)
piqué[2] *nm* **1** : piqué (fabric) **2** : nosedive
pique–assiette [pikasjɛt] *nmfs & pl* : freeloader, sponger
pique–feu [pikfø] *nms & pl* TISONNIER : poker
pique–nique [piknik] *nm, pl* **pique–niques** : picnic
pique–niquer [piknike] *vi* : to have a picnic
piquer [pike] *vt* **1** : to prick, to puncture **2** : to give an injection to, to vaccinate **3** : to sting, to bite **4** : to stick (on), to pin (up) **5** : to make holes in **6** : to stitch **7** : to prickle, to tickle **8** : to needle, to irritate **9** ÉVEILLER : to arouse, to stimulate (interest, etc.) **10** *fam* : to pinch, to swipe **11** *fam* : to nab, to catch **12 piquer un somme** : to take a nap — *vi* **1** : to be prickly **2** : to sting, to burn **3** : to dive, to swoop down — **se piquer** *vr* **1** : to prick oneself, to inject oneself **2** : to get mildewed, to turn sour **3 ~ de** : to pride oneself on
piquet [pikɛ] *nm* **1** : post, stake **2** : peg **3 piquet de grève** : picket line
piqueter [pikte] {8} *vt* **1** : to stake out **2** : to mark, to dot — *vi Can* : to picket
piqueteur, -teuse [piktœr, -tøz] *n Can* : picketer, striker
piquette [pikɛt] *nf* : (cheap) wine
piqûre [pikyr] *nf* **1** : prick **2** : sting, bite **3** : injection, shot **4** : small hole, pitting **5** : stitch (in sewing)
piranha [pirana] *nm* : piranha
piratage [piratаʒ] *nm* : piracy (of software, etc.)
pirate [pirat] *nm* **1** : pirate **2** : crook, swindler **3 pirate de l'air** : hijacker
pirater [pirate] *vt* : to pirate
piraterie [piratri] *nf* **1** : piracy **2 piraterie aérienne** : hijacking
pire[1] [pir] *adj* **1** : worse <pire que jamais : worse than ever> **2 le pire, la pire, les pires** : the worst <le pire jour de ma vie : the worst day of my life> **3 pas tant pire** *Can* : not too bad, OK
pire[2] *nm* **1 le pire** : the worst **2 au pire** : at the worst
pirogue [pirɔg] *nf* : dugout (canoe)
pirouette [pirwɛt] *nf* : pirouette
pis[1] [pi] *adv* **1** : worse <de mal en pis : from bad to worse> **2 au pis aller**

: if worst comes to worst **3 tant pis** : too bad
pis[2] *adj* : worse
pis[3] *nms & pl* **1** : udder **2 le pis** : the worst
pis–aller [pizale] *nms & pl* : last resort, stopgap
piscine [pisin] *nf* : swimming pool
pissenlit [pisɑ̃li] *nm* : dandelion
pistache [pistaʃ] *nf* : pistachio
piste [pist] *nf* **1** TRACE : track, trail <sur la bonne piste : on the right track> **2** : trail, slope <piste de ski : ski slope> **3** : racetrack **4** INDICE : lead, clue **5** : path, route, course <piste cyclable : bike path> **6** *or* **piste d'atterrissage** : runway, airstrip **7 piste sonore** : soundtrack
pistil [pistil] *nm* : pistil
pistolet [pistɔlɛ] *nm* **1** : pistol, handgun **2** : spray gun
piston [pistɔ̃] *nm* **1** : piston **2** : valve (in a musical instrument)
pistonner [pistɔne] *vt fam* : to pull strings for
pitance [pitɑ̃s] *nf* : ration, sustenance
piteusement [pitøzmɑ̃] *adv* : pathetically, pitifully
piteux, -teuse [pitø, -tøz] *adj* : pitiful, miserable <un état piteux : a sorry state>
pitié [pitje] *nf* COMPASSION : pity, mercy
piton [pitɔ̃] *nm* **1** : hook **2** : piton **3** : peak (of a mountain) **4** *Can fam* : button, switch
pitonner [pitɔne] *vi Can fam* : to push a button, to flip a switch, to zap (with a remote control)
pitoyable [pitwajabl] *adj* : pitiful, pathetic — **pitoyablement** [-jabləmɑ̃] *adv*
pitre [pitr] *nm* CLOWN : clown, buffoon
pittoresque [pitɔrɛsk] *adj* : picturesque
pituitaire [pitɥitɛr] *adj* : pituitary <glande pituitaire : pituitary gland>
pivoine [pivwan] *nf* : peony
pivot [pivo] *nm* : pivot
pivoter [pivɔte] *vi* : to pivot, to revolve, to swivel
pizza [pidza] *nf* : pizza
pizzeria [pidzerja] *nf* : pizzeria
placage [plakaʒ] *nm* **1** : veneer **2** : (metal) plating **3** : tackle (in football)
placard [plakar] *nm* **1** : cupboard, closet **2** AFFICHE : poster, placard
placarder [plakarde] *vt* : to post, to put up (posters, notices, etc.)
place [plas] *nf* **1** : place, spot <chaque chose à sa place : everything in its place> <mets-les à leur place : put them where they belong> **2** : room, space <prendre de la place : to take up space> <il n'y a pas de place : there's no room> **3** : seat <louer des places au théâtre : to book seats at the theater> **4** : rank, position <prendre la première place : to take first place> **5** : placing, position, situation <à la place de : instead of, in place of> <se mettre en place : to be set up, to position oneself> **6** : (public) square **7** : job, position **8** : (financial) market **9 de place en place** : here and there
placebo [plasebo] *nm* : placebo
placement [plasmɑ̃] *nm* **1** : investment **2** : placement <bureau de placement : placement agency> **3** : field goal
placenta [plasɛ̃ta] *nm* : placenta
placer [plase] {6} *vt* **1** : to place, to set, to put **2** : to put in, to slip in, to interject <je n'ai pas pu placer un seul mot : I couldn't get a word in edgewise> **3** : to seat (someone) **4** : to sell, to place (a product) **5** : to invest **6** : to place, to find a job for — **se placer** *vr* **1** : to position oneself **2** : to rank **3** : to get a job
placeur, -ceuse [plasœr, -søz] *n* : usher (in a theater)
placide [plasid] *adj* : placid, calm — **placidement** [-sidmɑ̃] *adv*
placier, -cière [plasje, -sjɛr] *n* : traveling salesman
placoter [plakɔte] *vi Can fam* : to chat, to chitchat — *vt Can fam* : to divulge, to disclose
plafond [plafɔ̃] *nm* : ceiling
plafonner [plafɔne] *vt* : to put a ceiling in — *vi* : to reach a maximum
plafonnier [plafɔnje] *nm* : ceiling light
plage [plaʒ] *nf* **1** : beach, shore **2** : seaside resort **3 plage horaire** : time slot
plagiaire [plaʒjɛr] *nmf* : plagiarist
plagiat [plaʒja] *nm* : plagiarism
plagier [plaʒje] {96} *vt* : to plagiarize
plaider [plede] *vi* : to plead, to litigate — *vt* : to plead (a case)
plaideur, -deuse [plɛdœr, -døz] *n* : litigant
plaie [plɛ] *nf* **1** BLESSURE : wound, cut, sore **2** : scourge, plague **3** *fam* : pest
plaignait [plɛɲɛ], *etc.* → **plaindre**
plaignard, -gnarde [plɛɲar, -ɲard] *n Can* : complainer, grouch
plaignant, -gnante [plɛɲɑ̃, -ɲɑ̃t] *n* : plaintiff
plaigne [plɛɲ], *etc.* → **plaindre**
plain [plɛ̃] *nm* : high tide
plaindre [plɛ̃dr] {65} *vt* : to pity, to feel sorry for — **se plaindre** *vr* **1** : to complain, to moan **2** : to protest
plaine [plɛn] *nf* : plain, lowland
plain–pied [plɛ̃pje] *adj* **1 de ~** : on the same level <une maison de plain-pied : a single-story house> **2 être de plain–pied avec** : to be at ease with, to be on an equal footing with
plainte [plɛ̃t] *nf* **1** : complaint **2** : moan, groan
plaintif, -tive [plɛ̃tif, -tiv] *adj* : plaintive — **plaintivement** [-tivmɑ̃] *adv*
plaire [plɛr] {66} *vi* **1** : to be attractive, to be pleasing **2 ~ à** : to please, to suit — *v impers* : to please <ce qu'il

vous plaît : whatever you like> <s'il vous plaît : please> — **se plaire** *vr* **1** : to like oneself **2** : to like each other **3** ~ **à** : to enjoy

plaisait [plɛzɛ], **plaisions** [plɛzjɔ̃], *etc.* → **plaire**

plaisamment [plɛzamɑ̃] *adv* **1** : pleasantly **2** DRÔLEMENT : amusingly

plaisance [plɛzɑ̃s] *nf or* **navigation de plaisance** : sailing, boating

plaisancier, -cière [plɛzɑ̃sje, -sjɛr] *n* : amateur sailor, boating enthusiast

plaisant[1], -sante [plɛzɑ̃, -zɑ̃t] *adj* **1** AGRÉABLE : pleasant **2** AMUSANT : amusing, funny

plaisant[2] *nm* **mauvais plaisant** : practical joker

plaisanter [plɛzɑ̃te] *vi* : to joke, to jest — *vt* : to tease, to make fun of

plaisanterie [plɛzɑ̃tri] *nf* **1** BLAGUE : joke, jest **2** FARCE : prank

plaisantin [plɛzɑ̃tɛ̃] *nm* FARCEUR : practical joker

plaise [plɛz], *etc.* → **plaire**

plaisir [plezir] *nm* **1** : pleasure <avec plaisir! : with pleasure> <faire plaisir à : to please> **2** **au plaisir** : see you soon **3** **avec plaisir!** : of course!

plan[1], plane [plɑ̃, plan] *adj* PLAT : flat, level, plane

plan[2] *nm* **1** : plane **2** : plan, strategy, program **3** : map, diagram, blueprint **4** : outline, synopsis **5** **laisser en plan** : to leave in the lurch **6** **premier plan** : foreground

planche[1] [plɑ̃ʃ] *adj Can* : flat, even

planche[2] *nf* **1** : board, plank <planche à repasser : ironing board> **2** : plate (in engraving) **3** : plate, illustration (in a book) **4** **planche à roulettes** : skateboard **5** **les planches** : the stage

plancher [plɑ̃ʃe] *nm* **1** : floor **2** : minimum, lower limit

plancton [plɑ̃ktɔ̃] *nm* : plankton

planer [plane] *vi* **1** : to glide, to soar, to hover **2** ~ **sur** : to hang over, to hover over **3** **avoir l'air de planer** : to be above it all, to appear distracted

planétaire [planetɛr] *adj* **1** : planetary **2** MONDIAL : global, worldwide

planétarium [planetarjɔm] *nm* : planetarium

planète [planɛt] *nf* : planet

planification [planifikasjɔ̃] *nf* : planning

planifier [planifje] {96} *vt* : to plan

planning [planiŋ] *nm* : planning <planning familial : family planning>

planque [plɑ̃k] *nf fam* **1** : hideout **2** : easy job

planquer [plɑ̃ke] *vt fam* : to hide away, to stash

plant [plɑ̃] *nm* **1** : patch, bed **2** : seedling, young plant

plantain [plɑ̃tɛ̃] *nm* : plantain

plantation [plɑ̃tasjɔ̃] *nf* **1** : planting **2** : plantation

plante [plɑ̃t] *nf* **1** : sole (of the foot) **2** : plant <plante grimpante : climbing plant>

planté, -tée [plɑ̃te] *adj* **1** : positioned, placed <dents mal plantées : uneven teeth> **2** *fam* : standing, rooted (to the spot) **3** **bien planté** : sturdy, robust (of a child)

planter [plɑ̃te] *vt* **1** : to plant **2** : to stick in, to drive in **3** : to set, to set up **4** *fam* : to ditch, to drop — **se planter** *vr* **1** : to become embedded **2** *fam* : to stand, to plant oneself **3** *fam* : to crash, to smash **4** *fam* : to get it wrong, to mess up

planteur, -teuse [plɑ̃tœr, -tøz] *n* : planter

planton [plɑ̃tɔ̃] *nm* : orderly (in the military)

plantureux, -reuse [plɑ̃tyrø, -røz] *adj* **1** : copious, lavish <un repas plantureux : a lavish repast> **2** : buxom

plaque [plak] *nf* **1** : plate, sheet <plaques de glace : patches of ice> **2** : plaque, nameplate, badge (of a policeman) **3** : patch (of ice, etc.) **4** **plaque chauffante** : hotplate, griddle **5** **plaque d'immatriculation** : license plate **6** **plaque dentaire** : dental plaque

plaqué, -quée [plake] *adj* : plated <plaqué or : gold-plated>

plaquer [plake] *vt* **1** : to veneer, to plate **2** : to stick, to plaster, to pin down **3** : to tackle (in football) **4** *fam* : to ditch, to get rid of

plaquette [plakɛt] *nf* **1** : small sheet <plaquette de beurre : pat of butter> **2** : booklet

plasma [plasma] *nm* : plasma

plastique[1] [plastik] *adj* **1** : plastic, malleable **2** **chirurgie plastique** : plastic surgery

plastique[2] *nm* : plastic

plastique[3] *nf* **1** : plastic arts *pl*, modeling, sculpture **2** : beauty of form

plat[1], plate [pla, plat] *adj* **1** : flat, level **2** : shallow **3** : dull, bland, insipid **4** : obsequious **5** : lank <cheveux plats : lank hair> **6** *Can* : boring, dull

plat[2] *nm* **1** : plate **2** : dish <un plat méditerranéen : a Mediterranean dish> **3** : course <plat de résistance : main course, entrée> **4** : flat (part) <plat de la main : flat of the hand> **5** **à** ~ : flat (down) <tomber à plat : to fall flat> **6** **à** ~ : dead (of a battery)

platane [platan] *nm* : plane tree

plat–bord [plabɔr] *nm, pl* **plats–bords** : gunwale

plateau [plato] *nm, pl* **plateaux** **1** : tray, platter **2** : plateau <plateau continental : continental shelf> **3** : stage, set (in theater) **4** : pan (of a scale)

plate–bande [platbɑ̃d] *nf, pl* **plates–bandes** : flower bed

plate–forme [platfɔrm] *nf, pl* **plates–formes** : platform

platement [platmɑ̃] *adv* **1** : dully, uninterestingly **2** : abjectly

platine[1] [platin] *nm* : platinum

platine[2] *nf* **1** : turntable **2 platine cassette** : cassette deck **3 platine laser** : CD player

platitude [platityd] *nf* **1** BANALITÉ : banality, triteness **2** : platitude

platonique [platɔnik] *adj* : platonic

plâtre [platr] *nm* **1** : plaster **2** : plaster cast

plâtrer [platre] *vt* **1** : to plaster **2** : to put in a (plaster) cast

plâtrier [platrije] *nm* : plasterer

plausibilité [plozibilite] *nf* : plausibility

plausible [plozibl] *adj* VRAISEMBLABLE : plausible, likely

plèbe [plɛb] *nf* : common people *pl*, masses *pl*

plébéien, -béienne [plebejɛ̃, -bejɛn] *adj* : plebeian

plébiscite [plebisit] *nm* : plebiscite

plein[1], **pleine** [plɛ̃, plɛn] *adj* **1** REMPLI : full <une tasse pleine : a full cup> **2** : filled (up) <une salle pleine de monde : a roomful of people, a crowded room> <saisir à pleines mains : to grasp with both hands, to take a firm hold> <une journée pleine : a busy day> **3** : solid, rounded, full <la pleine lune : the full moon> **4** : pregnant (of an animal) **5** (*used as an intensifier*) <en pleine rue : in the middle of the street> <en plein jour : in broad daylight> **6 la pleine mer** : the open sea **7 le plein air** : the outdoors **8 plein d'entrain** : high-spirited **9 plein de soi–même** : conceited, self-centered

plein[2] *nm* **1** : fullest point, maximum <faire le plein de : to fill up on, to stock up with> <donner son plein : to give one's all> **2 à ~** *or* **en ~** : fully, totally, at full capacity

pleinement [plɛnmɑ̃] *adv* ENTIÈREMENT : fully, entirely

plénier, -nière [plenje, -njɛr] *adj* : plenary

plénipotentiaire [plenipɔtɑ̃sjɛr] *nmf* : plenipotentiary

plénitude [plenityd] *nf* **1** AMPLEUR : scale, extent **2** : fullness, peak

pléthore [pletɔr] *nf* : plethora, overabundance

pleumer [plə(œ)me] *vi Can fam* : to peel (of skin)

pleurer [plœre] *vt* **1** : to weep for, to lament **2** : to cry <pleurer des larmes de joie : to cry tears of joy> — *vi* **1** : to cry, to weep **2** : to water <il a les yeux qui pleurent : his eyes are watering> **3 ~ sur** : to shed tears over, to bemoan

pleurésie [plœrezi] *nf* : pleurisy

pleurnicher [plœrniʃe] *vi fam* : to whine, to snivel

pleurs [plœr] *nmpl* **être en pleurs** : to be in tears

pleut [plø] → **pleuvoir**

pleuvoir [pløvwar] {67} *v impers* : to rain <il pleut à verse : it's pouring> — *vi* : to rain down, to pour down <les invitations pleuvaient sur nous : invitations were pouring in on us>

pli [pli] *nm* **1** : fold, pleat **2** : crease **3** HABITUDE : habit <prendre un mauvais pli : to get into a bad habit> **4** : envelope, letter <sous ce pli : enclosed> **5** : trick (in card games)

pliable [plijabl] *adj* : pliable, flexible

pliant, pliante [plijɑ̃, plijɑ̃t] *adj* : folding <chaise pliante : folding chair>

plier [plije] {96} *vt* **1** : to fold, to fold up **2** : to bend **3 plié en deux** *fam* : doubled up with laughter — *vi* **1** : to bend, to sag **2** : to yield, to give in — **se plier** *vr* **1** : to bend over, to fold **2 ~ à** : to submit to

plinthe [plɛ̃t] *nf* **1** : plinth **2** : baseboard

plissé[1], **-sée** [plise] *adj* : pleated

plissé[2] *nm* : pleating, pleats *pl*

plisser [plise] *vt* **1** : to pleat, to fold **2** : to crease, to wrinkle (clothing) **3** FRONCER : to wrinkle (one's brow), to pucker (one's lips), to screw up (one's eyes) — **se plisser 1** : to get wrinkled **2** : to pucker up

pliure [plijyr] *nf* : fold, bend (of the arm or leg)

plomb [plɔ̃] *nm* **1** : lead <essence sans plomb : unleaded gas> **2** : shot, (lead) pellet **3** FUSIBLE : (electrical) fuse **4** : sinker (in fishing)

plombage [plɔ̃baʒ] *nm* : filling (of a tooth)

plomber [plɔ̃be] *vt* **1** : to weight with lead **2** : to fill (a tooth) **3** : to plumb

plomberie [plɔ̃bri] *nf* : plumbing

plombier [plɔ̃bje] *nm* : plumber

plonge [plɔ̃ʒ] *nf* **1** : dishwashing <faire la plonge : to wash dishes> **2 prendre une plonge** *Can fam* : to tumble down, to crash down

plongeant, -geante [plɔ̃ʒɑ̃, -ʒɑ̃t] *adj* **1** : plunging **2** : from above <vue plongeante : bird's-eye view>

plongée [plɔ̃ʒe] *nf* **1** : diving **2 plongée sous–marine** : skin diving, deep-sea diving

plongeoir [plɔ̃ʒwar] *nm* : diving board

plongeon [plɔ̃ʒɔ̃] *nm* **1** : dive **2** : loon (bird)

plonger [plɔ̃ʒe] {17} *vt* : to thrust, to plunge — *vi* **1** : to dive **2 ~ dans** : to plunge into — **se plonger** *vr* **~ dans** : to immerse oneself in, to sink into

plongeur, -geuse [plɔ̃ʒœr, -ʒøz] *n* **1** : diver **2** : dishwasher (person)

plot [plo] *nm* : (electrical) contact

plouc [pluk] *nm France fam* : bumpkin

plouf [pluf] *nm* : splash

ploutocratie [plutɔkrasi] *nf* : plutocracy

ployer [plwaje] {58} *vt* : to bow, to bend — *vi* **1** : to bend, to sag **2** CÉDER : to give in, to yield

plu[1] [ply] *pp* → **plaire**

plu[2] [ply] *pp* → **pleuvoir**

pluie [plɥi] *nf* **1** : rain, rainfall **2** : shower, hail, stream <une pluie de compliments : a shower of compliments>

plumage [plymaʒ] *nm* : plumage, feathers *pl*

plume [plym] *nf* **1** : feather **2** : quill pen, pen nib

plumeau [plymo] *nm, pl* **plumeaux** [plymo] : feather duster

plumer [plyme] *vt* : to pluck

plumet [plymɛ] *nm* : plume

plumitif [plymitif] *nm* : pencil pusher, hack writer

plupart [plypar] *nf* **1 la plupart des** : most, the majority of <dans la plupart des cas : in most cases> **2 pour la plupart** : mostly, for the most part

pluralité [plyralite] *nf* : plurality

pluriel[1], **-rielle** [plyrjɛl] *adj* : plural

pluriel[2] *nm* : plural

plus[1] [ply(s)] *adv* **1** : more <peux-tu aller plus vite? : can you go faster?> <plus je dors, plus j'ai envie de dormir : the more I sleep, the more I want to sleep> <plus que tout : more than anything> **2** (*used in negation*) : no more, no longer <il ne les voit plus : he doesn't see them anymore> <je n'ai plus soif : I'm no longer thirsty> **3 ~ de** : more, more than <plus de café : more coffee> <avoir plus de 50 ans : to be over 50> **4 le plus** : most, the most <le plus souvent : most often, most of the time> <le plus d'argent : the most money> <au plus : at the most> **5 de ~** : in addition, furthermore **6 en ~** : as well, extra **7 non plus** : neither, either <moi non plus : me neither> **8 plus ou moins** : more or less, approximately

plus[2] *nm* **1** : plus (sign) **2** *fam* : plus, advantage <son expérience est un vrai plus : his experience is a real plus>

plus[3] *conj* : plus <deux plus cinq font sept : two plus five equals seven>

plusieurs [plyzjœr] *adj & pron* : several

plutocracy [plytɔkrasi] *nf* : plutocracy

Pluton [plytɔ̃] *nf* : Pluto (planet)

plutonium [plytɔnjɔm] *nm* : plutonium

plutôt [plyto] *adv* : rather, instead <plutôt moins que trop : rather too little than too much> <plutôt du beurre que de l'huile : butter instead of oil> <plutôt que de les convaincre : rather than convincing them>

pluvial, -viale [plyvjal] *adj, mpl* **pluviaux** [plyvjo] : rain <eau pluviale : rainwater>

pluvier [plyvje] *nm* : plover

pluvieux, -vieuse [plyvjø, -vjøz] *adj* : rainy, wet

pneu [pnø] *nm, pl* **pneus** : tire

pneumatique [pnømatik] *adj* **1** : pneumatic **2** : inflatable <matelas pneumatique : inflatable mattress>

pneumonie [pnømɔni] *nf* : pneumonia

poche [pɔʃ] *nf* **1** : pocket (in clothing) **2** : pocket, cavity <une poche d'eau : a pocket of water> **3** SAC : bag, pouch **4 poches** *nfpl* CERNES : bags, circles <il a des poches sous les yeux : he has bags under his eyes>

pocher [pɔʃe] *vt* **1** : to poach (in cooking) **2 pocher l'œil à qqn** : to give s.o. a black eye — *vi* : to get baggy

pochette [pɔʃɛt] *nf* **1** : folder, case, (record) sleeve <pochette d'allumettes : book of matches> **2** : pocket handkerchief **3** : pouch, clutch bag

pochoir [pɔʃwar] *nm* : stencil

podium [pɔdjɔm] *nm* : podium

podologie [pɔdɔlɔʒi] *nf* : chiropody, podiatry

podologue [pɔdɔlɔg] *nmf* : podiatrist

poêle[1] [pwal] *nm* **1** FOURNEAU : stove <poêle à bois : wood-burning stove> **2** : pall, coffin cloth

poêle[2] *nf or* **poêle à frire** : frying pan

poêlon [pwalɔ̃] *nm* **1** : casserole dish **2** *Can* : frying pan

poème [pɔɛm] *nm* : poem

poésie [pɔezi] *nf* **1** : poetry **2** : poem

poète [pɔɛt] *nmf* : poet

poétique [pɔetik] *adj* : poetic

pogné, -gnée [pɔɲe] *adj Can fam* : uptight, tense

pogner [pɔɲe] *vt Can fam* **1** : to get, to catch <il l'a pognée à voler : he caught her stealing> **2 pogner les nerfs** : to have a fit — *vi Can fam* **1** : to be inhibited, to be hung up **2** : to be successful <artiste qui pogne : successful artist> — **se pogner** *vr Can fam* **~ avec** : to get into a fight with

pognon [pɔɲɔ̃] *nm France fam* : dough, money

pogrom [pɔgrɔm] *nm* : pogrom

poids [pwa] *nms & pl* **1** : weight, heaviness **2** FARDEAU : burden, responsibility **3** : weight <les poids et mesures : weights and mesures> <poids et haltères : weight lifting> **4** : meaning, importance <avoir du poids : to carry weight> **5 poids lourd** : heavyweight (in sports)

poignant, -gnante [pwaɲɑ̃, -ɲɑ̃t] *adj* ÉMOUVANT : moving, poignant

poignard [pwaɲar] *nm* : dagger

poignarder [pwaɲarde] *vt* : to stab

poigne [pwaɲ] *nf* **1** : grip, grasp **2 à ~** : firm, forceful

poignée [pwaɲe] *nf* **1** : handful **2** : handle **3 poignée de main** : handshake

poignet [pwaɲɛ] *nm* **1** : wrist **2** : cuff

poil [pwal] *nm* **1** : hair **2** : fur, coat <chat à poil long : long-haired cat> **3** : bristle (of a brush) **4** : nap (of fabric) **5 à ~** *fam* : stark naked

poilu, -lue [pwaly] *adj* : hairy

poinçon [pwɛ̃sɔ̃] *nm* **1** : awl, punch **2** MARQUE : hallmark, stamp

poinçonner [pwɛ̃sɔne] *vt* **1** : to hallmark, to stamp **2** : to punch, to perforate

poinçonneuse [pwɛ̃sɔnøz] *nf* : punch

poing [pwɛ̃] *nm* **1** : fist **2 coup de poing** : punch

point[1] [pwɛ̃] *adv* : not <je ne l'aime point : I do not like him> <point du tout : not at all>

point[2] *nm* **1** : point, position <point de départ : point of departure> <aller d'un point à un autre : to go from one place to the next> **2** DEGRÉ : degree, extent <à tel point que : to such an extent that, so much so that> **3** : period, dot (in punctuation) <point décimal : decimal point> <point d'exclamation : exclamation point> <point d'interrogation : question mark> <points de suspension : ellipsis> **4** QUESTION : question, matter, point <sur ce point, ils n'étaient pas d'accord : they couldn't agree on this matter> **5** : point (in sports) **6** : stitch (in sewing) **7 à ~** : just right <arriver à point : to arrive just in time> <faire cuire à point : to cook medium rare> **8 au point** : well designed, well done <mettre au point : to adjust, to perfect> **9 point culminant** : highlight **10 point de fusion** : melting point **11 point de vue** : point of view **12 point du jour** : daybreak **13 point mort** : blind spot (of an automobile) **14 point noir** : blackhead **15 points cardinaux** : points of the compass **16** → **deux–points**

pointage [pwɛ̃taʒ] *nm* **1** : checking off, marking off (on a list) **2** : aiming (of a firearm) **3** *Can* : points *pl*, score (in sports)

pointe [pwɛ̃t] *nf* **1** : point, tip <en pointe : pointed> <sur la pointe des pieds : on tiptoe> **2** : point, headland **3** : high (level), peak <vitesse de pointe : top speed> <heures de pointe : rush hour> <technologie de pointe : state-of-the-art technology> **4** SOUPÇON : touch, hint **5** PIQUE : cutting remark, dig **6** CLOU : nail **7 pointes** *nfpl* : spiked shoes (in sports)

pointer [pwɛ̃te] *vt* **1** COCHER : to check, to mark off **2** : to aim, to point <pointer un doigt sur : to point a finger at> <pointer un fusil vers : to aim a rifle at> — *vi* **1** : to clock in **2** : to stick out, to rise up **3** : to break, to dawn, to come up — **se pointer** *vr fam* : to show up

pointeur, -teuse [pwɛ̃tœr, -tøz] *n* **1** : timekeeper **2** *Can* : scorekeeper

pointillé[1], **-lée** [pwɛ̃tije] *adj* : dotted, stippled

pointillé[2] *nm* : dotted line

pointilleux, -leuse [pwɛ̃tijø, -jøz] *adj* : finicky, fussy

pointu, -tue [pwɛ̃ty] *adj* **1** : pointed, sharp **2** : sharp, querulous **3** : shrill **4** : precise, specialized

pointure [pwɛ̃tyr] *nf* : size (of clothing)

point–virgule [pwɛ̃virgyl] *nm, pl* **points–virgules** : semicolon

poire [pwar] *nf* : pear

poireau [pwaro] *nm, pl* **poireaux** : leek

poireauter [pwarote] *vi fam* : to hang around

poirier [pwarje] *nm* : pear tree

pois [pwa] *nms & pl* **1** : pea <petit pois : green peas> <pois chiche : chickpea> **2** : dot <à pois : spotted, polka-dot>

poison [pwazɔ̃] *nm* : poison

poisse [pwas] *nf fam* : bad luck

poisser [pwase] *vt* : to make sticky — *vi* : to be sticky

poisseux, -seuse [pwasø, -søz] *adj* GLUANT : sticky

poisson [pwasɔ̃] *nm* **1** : fish <poisson rouge : goldfish> <poisson plat : flatfish> **2 poisson d'avril!** : April fool!

poisson–chat [pwasɔ̃ʃa] *nm, pl* **poissons–chats** : catfish

poissonnerie [pwasɔnri] *nf* : fish market

poissonnier, -nière [pwasɔnje, -njɛr] *n* : fish merchant, fishmonger

Poissons [pwasɔ̃] *nmpl* : Pisces

poitrine [pwatrin] *nf* **1** : chest **2** : breasts *pl*, bust, bosom **3** : breast (in cooking)

poivre [pwavr] *nm* **1** : pepper **2 poivre de cayenne** : cayenne pepper

poivré, -vrée [pwavre] *adj* : peppery

poivrer [pwavre] *vt* : to pepper

poivrier [pwavrije] *nm* **1** : pepper plant **2** : pepper shaker

poivrière [pwavrijɛr] *nf* : pepper shaker

poivron [pwavrɔ̃] *nm* : pepper <poivron vert : green pepper>

poix [pwa] *nm* : pitch, tar

poker [pɔkɛr] *nm* : poker <partie de poker : game of poker>

polaire [pɔlɛr] *adj* : polar

polarisation [pɔlarizasjɔ̃] *nf* : polarization

polariser [pɔlarize] *vt* **1** : to polarize **2** : to concentrate, to focus **3** ATTIRER : to attract — **se polariser** *vr*

pôle [pol] *nm* : pole <le pôle Nord : the North Pole>

polémique[1] [pɔlemik] *adj* : controversial, polemical

polémique[2] *nf* : debate, controversy, polemics

poli[1], **-lie** [pɔli] *adj* **1** COURTOIS : polite **2** LISSE : polished, smooth

poli[2] *nm* : polish, shine

police [pɔlis] *nf* **1** : police, police force **2** : law enforcement, policing **3** : font (in printing) **4 police d'assurance** : insurance policy

policier[1], **-cière** [pɔlisje, -sjɛr] *adj* **1** : police **2** : detective <roman policier : detective novel>
policier[2], **-cière** *n* : police officer
policlinique [pɔliklinik] *nf* : outpatient clinic
poliment [pɔlimɑ̃] *adv* : politely
poliomyélite [pɔljɔmjelit] *nf* : poliomyelitis
polir [pɔlir] *vt* **1** : to polish, to shine **2** PARFAIRE : to refine, to perfect (style, etc.)
polisson, -sonne [pɔlisɔ̃, -sɔn] *n* : scamp, naughty child, brat
politesse [pɔlitɛs] *nf* **1** COURTOISIE : politeness, courtesy **2** : polite remark, pleasantry <échanger des politesses : to exchange courtesies>
politicien, -cienne [pɔlitisjɛ̃, -sjɛn] *n* : politician
politique[1] [pɔlitik] *adj* : political — **politiquement** [-tikmɑ̃] *adv*
politique[2] *nf* **1** : politics **2** TACTIQUE : policy, procedure
politique[3] *nm* : politician
polka [pɔlka] *nf* : polka
pollen [pɔlɛn] *nm* : pollen
pollinisation [pɔlinizasjɔ̃] *nf* : pollination
polliniser [pɔlinize] *vt* : to pollinate
polluant[1], **-luante** [pɔlɥɑ̃, -lɥɑ̃t] *adj* : polluting
polluant[2] *nm* : pollutant
polluer [pɔlɥe] *vt* : to pollute — **pollution** [pɔlysjɔ̃] *nf*
polo [pɔlo] *nm* **1** : polo **2** : polo shirt
polonais[1], **-naise** [pɔlɔnɛ, -nɛz] *adj* : Polish
polonais[2] *nm* : Polish (language)
Polonais, -naise *n* : Pole
poltron,[1] **-tronne** [pɔltrɔ̃, -trɔn] *adj* : cowardly
poltron,[2] **-tronne** *n* : coward
polycopie [pɔlikɔpi] *nf* : mimeograph
polyester [pɔliɛstɛr] *nm* : polyester
polygame[1] [pɔligam] *adj* : polygamous
polygame[2] *nmf* : polygamist
polygamie [pɔligami] *nf* : polygamy
polygone [pɔligɔn] *nm* **1** : polygon **2** *or* **polygone de tir** : firing range
polymère [pɔlimɛr] *nm* : polymer
polynésien[1], **-sienne** [pɔlinezjɛ̃, -zjɛn] *adj* : Polynesian
polynésien[2] *nm* : Polynesian (language)
Polynésien, -sienne *n* : Polynesian
polype [pɔlip] *nm* : polyp
polythéisme [pɔliteism] *nm* : polytheism
polythéiste [pɔliteist] *adj* : polytheist, polytheistic
polyvalent, -lente [pɔlivalɑ̃, -lɑ̃t] *adj* **1** : polyvalent **2** : versatile, multipurpose, all-around
polyvalente [pɔlivalɑ̃, -lɑ̃t] *nf or* **école polyvalente** *Can* : general and vocational high school
pommade [pɔmad] *nf* : ointment
pomme [pɔm] *nf* **1** : apple **2** **pomme d'Adam** : Adam's apple **3** **pomme de discorde** : bone of contention **4** **pomme de pin** : pinecone **5** **pomme de terre** : potato **6** **pommes frites** : French fries
pommeau [pɔmo] *nm* : knob, pommel
pommelé, -lée [pɔmle] *adj* : dappled, mottled
pommette [pɔmɛt] *nf* : cheekbone
pommier [pɔmje] *nm* : apple tree
pompe [pɔ̃p] *nf* **1** : pump <pompe à essence : gas pump> **2** : pomp, ceremony **3** **pompes funèbres** : funeral home, funeral parlor
pomper [pɔ̃pe] *vt* **1** : to pump **2** : to soak up
pompette [pɔ̃pɛt] *adj fam* : tipsy
pompeux, -peuse [pɔ̃pø, -pøz] *adj* : pompous — **pompeusement** [-pøzmɑ̃] *adv*
pompier[1], **-pière** [pɔ̃pje, -pjɛr] *adj* : pompous, pretentious
pompier[2] *nm* : firefighter, fireman
pompiste [pɔ̃pist] *nmf* : service station attendant
pompon [pɔ̃pɔ̃] *nm* : pompom
pomponner [pɔ̃pɔne] *vt* : to dress up — **se pomponner** *vr* : to get all dressed up, to preen oneself, to primp (up)
ponce [pɔ̃s] *nf* **pierre ponce** : pumice stone
ponceau [pɔ̃so] *nm, pl* **ponceaux** : small bridge
poncer [pɔ̃se] {6} *vt* : to sand (down)
poncho [pɔ̃tʃo] *nm* : poncho
poncif [pɔ̃sif] *nm* BANALITÉ : cliché, platitude
ponction [pɔ̃ksjɔ̃] *nf* : puncture (in medicine)
ponctualité [pɔ̃ktɥalite] *nf* : punctuality
ponctuation [pɔ̃ktɥasjɔ̃] *nf* : punctuation
ponctuel, -elle [pɔ̃ktɥɛl] *adj* **1** : prompt, punctual **2** : limited, selective
ponctuellement [pɔ̃ktɥɛlmɑ̃] *adv* : punctually
ponctuer [pɔ̃ktɥe] *vt* : to punctuate
pondération [pɔ̃derasjɔ̃] *nf* **1** : balancing **2** MESURE : levelheadedness
pondéré, -rée [pɔ̃dere] *adj* : levelheaded, sensible
pondérer [pɔ̃dere] {87} *vt* : to balance
pondeuse [pɔ̃døz] *nf* : laying hen, layer
pondre [pɔ̃dr] {63} *vt* **1** : to lay (eggs) **2** *fam* : to crank out, to produce
poney [pɔnɛ] *nm* : pony
pont [pɔ̃] *nm* **1** : bridge <pont suspendu : suspension bridge> **2** : deck (of a ship) **3** : axle (of an automobile) **4** **pont aérien** : airlift
ponte [pɔ̃t] *nf* : laying (of eggs)
pontife [pɔ̃tif] *nm* : pontiff
pontifical, -cale [pɔ̃tifikal] *adj* : pontifical

pontifier [pɔ̃tifje] {96} *vi* : to pontificate

pont–levis [pɔ̃ləvi] *nm, pl* **ponts–levis** : drawbridge

ponton [pɔ̃tɔ̃] *nm* : pontoon

pop [pɔp] *adj s & pl* **pop** : pop <musique pop : pop music>

pop–corn [pɔpkɔrn] *nms & pl* : popcorn

popeline [pɔplin] *nf* : poplin

popote [pɔpɔt] *nf* **1** : mess (in the military) **2 faire la popote** *fam* : to do the cooking

populace [pɔpylas] *nf* : rabble

populaire [pɔpylɛr] *adj* **1** : popular **2** : working-class **3** : colloquial, vernacular

populariser [pɔpylarize] *vt* : to popularize

popularité [pɔpylarite] *nf* : popularity

population [pɔpylasjɔ̃] *nf* : population

populeux, -leuse [pɔpylø, -løz] *adj* : densely populated

populiste [pɔpylist] *adj & nmf* : populist — **populisme** [-pylism] *nm*

poque [pɔk] *nf Can fam* : bump, bruise

poquer [pɔke] *vt Can fam* : to dent (a car)

porc [pɔr] *nm* **1** : pig, hog **2** : pork **3** : pigskin

porcelaine [pɔrsəlɛn] *nf* **1** : porcelain **2** : china, chinaware

porcelet [pɔrsəlɛ] *nm* : piglet

porc–épic [pɔrkepik] *nm, pl* **porcs–épics** : porcupine

porche [pɔrʃ] *nm* : porch

porcherie [pɔrʃəri] *nf* : pigpen, pigsty

porcin, -cine [pɔrsɛ̃, -sin] *adj* **1** : pig, porcine **2** : piglike, piggy

pore [pɔr] *nm* : pore

poreux, -reuse [pɔrø, -røz] *adj* : porous

pornographie [pɔrnɔgrafi] *nf* : pornography — **pornographique** [-grafik] *adj*

porridge [pɔridʒ] *nm* : porridge

port [pɔr] *nm* **1** : port, harbor **2** : port city **3** HAVRE : haven, refuge **4** : wearing, carrying (a weapon, etc.) **5** MAINTIEN : carriage, bearing **6** : postage <port payé : postpaid>

portable [pɔrtabl] *adj* **1** METTABLE : wearable **2** PORTATIF : portable, laptop

portage [pɔrtaʒ] *nm* **1** : carrying, porterage **2** : portage

portail [pɔrtaj] *nm* : portal, gate

portant, -tante [pɔrtɑ̃, -tɑ̃t] *adj* **1 bien portant** : in good health **2 mal portant** : in poor health, ailing

portatif, -tive [pɔrtatif, -tiv] *adj* **1** : portable **2 ordinateur portatif** : laptop computer

porte [pɔrt] *nf* **1** : door, doorway <porte d'entrée : front door> <porte de sortie : exit, way out> <de porte à porte : door-to-door> **2** : gate <porte d'embarquement : departure gate> **3** : gateway, opening <ouvrir la porte à : to pave the way for>

porte–à–faux [pɔrtafo] *nms & pl* **1** : overhang, cantilever **2 être en porte à faux** : to be in an awkward position

porte–avions [pɔrtavjɔ̃] *nms & pl* : aircraft carrier

porte–bagages [pɔrtbagaʒ] *nms & pl* : luggage rack, roof rack

porte–bébé [pɔrtbebe] *nm, pl* **porte–bébés** : baby carrier

porte–bonheur [pɔrtbɔnœr] *nms & pl* : lucky charm

porte–clés *or* **porte–clefs** [pɔrtəkle] *nms & pl* : key ring

porte–documents [pɔrtdɔkymɑ̃] *nms & pl* ATTACHÉ-CASE : attaché case, briefcase

porte–drapeau [pɔrtdrapo] *nm, pl* **porte–drapeaux** : standard-bearer

portée [pɔrte] *nf* **1** : range <à longue portée : long-range> <portée de voix : earshot> <d'une grande portée : far-reaching> <à la portée de la main : within arm's reach, handy> **2** : impact, significance **3** : litter (of kittens) **4** : staff (in music)

portefeuille [pɔrtəfœj] *nm* **1** : wallet, billfold **2** : portfolio (in politics or finance)

porte–jarretelles [pɔrtʒartɛl] *nms & pl* : garter belt

portemanteau [pɔrtmɑ̃to] *nm, pl* **-teaux** [-to] : coat rack

porte–monnaie [pɔrtmɔnɛ] *nms & pl* : change purse

porte–parole [pɔrtparɔl] *nms & pl* : spokesperson, spokesman *m*, spokeswoman *f*

porte–poussière [pɔrt(ə)pusjɛr] *nms & pl Can* : dustpan

porter [pɔrte] *vt* **1** TRANSPORTER : to carry, to bear **2** : to wear **3** APPORTER : to bring **4** : to hold, to keep, to use <elle porte son nom de fille : she uses her maiden name> **5 être porté à** : to be inclined to — *vi* **1** : to carry <une voix qui porte : a voice that carries> **2 ~ sur** : to be about — **se porter** *vr* **1** : to be worn **2** : to be (in a certain state) <il se porte bien : he is doing well> **3 ~ à** : to carry out, to indulge in **4 se porter garant de** : to vouch for **5 ~ sur** : to turn to, to spread to

porte–savon [pɔrtsavɔ̃] *nms & pl* : soap dish

porte–serviettes [pɔrtsɛrvjɛt] *nms & pl* : towel rack

porteur[1], **-teuse** [pɔrtœr, -tøz] *adj* **1** : load-bearing, carrier (in technology) **2** : flourishing, booming (in commerce) **3 ~ de** : bringing, expressing <être porteur de : to be the bearer of> <être porteur de sens : to have meaning>

porteur[2], **-teuse** *n* **1** : porter **2** : holder, bearer **3** : carrier (of disease)

porte–voix [pɔrtəvwa] *nms & pl* : megaphone
portier, -tière [pɔrtje, -tjɛr] *n* : doorman *m,* attendant (at an entrance)
portière *nf* : door (of an automobile)
portillon [pɔrtijɔ̃] *nm* : gate
portion [pɔrsjɔ̃] *nf* **1** : portion, share **2** : helping (of food) **3** : part, section (of a road, etc.)
portique [pɔrtik] *nm* **1** : portico **2** *Can fam* : hall, lobby
porto [pɔrto] *nm* : port wine
portoricain, -caine [pɔrtɔrikɛ̃, -kɛn] *adj* : Puerto Rican
Portoricain, -caine *n* : Puerto Rican
portrait [pɔrtrɛ] *nm* **1** : portrait **2** : picture, description **3** : image, likeness <il est le portrait de son père : he looks just like his father>
portraitiste [pɔrtretist] *nmf* : portrait painter
portuaire [pɔrtɥɛr] *adj* : harbor, port
portugais[1], **-gaise** [pɔrtygɛ, -gɛz] *adj* : Portuguese
portugais[2] *nm* : Portuguese (language)
Portugais, -gaise *n* : Portuguese
pose [poz] *nf* **1** : installing, putting in, laying **2** : pose, posture <prendre la pose : to pose> **3** : pose, affectation **4** : exposure <film de 24 poses : 24-exposure film>
posé, -sée [poze] *adj* **1** : composed, calm **2** : steady, even
posément [pozemɑ̃] *adv* : calmly, coolly, thoughtfully
poser [poze] *vt* **1** : to put (down), to place **2** INSTALLER : to put up, to install **3** : to state, to assert **4** : to ask (a question) **5 poser sa candidature** : to apply for a job — *vi* **1** : to pose, to sit **2** : to put on airs — **se poser** *vr* **1** : to be installed <cette fenêtre se pose facilement : this window is easy to install> **2** : to land, to touch down, to alight **3** : to arise, to come up <la question ne se pose pas : it goes without saying> **4 ~ en** : to pose as, to claim to be
positif, -tive [pɔzitif, -tiv] *adj* : positive
position [pozisjɔ] *nf* **1** : position, place **2** : position, stance <prendre position : to take a stand> **3** SITUATION : position, situation <une position délicate : a difficult situation>
positionner [pozisjɔne] *vt* : to position, to place
positivement [pozitivmɑ̃] *adv* : positively
posologie [pozɔlɔʒi] *nf* : dosage
possédé, -dée [pɔsede] *adj* : possessed
posséder [pɔsede] {87} *vt* **1** AVOIR : to possess, to have **2** MAÎTRISER : to know thoroughly, to have mastered — **se posséder** *vr* : to control oneself
possesseur [pɔsesœr] *nm* : owner, possessor
possessif, -sive [pɔsesif, -siv] *adj* : possessive
possession [pɔsesjɔ̃] *nf* : possession, ownership
possibilité [pɔsibilite] *nf* **1** ÉVENTUALITÉ : possibility **2** OCCASION : opportunity, option **3 possibilités** *nfpl* : means, resources
possible[1] [pɔsibl] *adj* **1** : possible, feasible <dès que possible : as soon as possible> **2** PROBABLE : possible, probable <il est possible qu'il pleuve : it's likely to rain>
possible[2] *nm* **1 dans la mesure du possible** : as far as possible **2 faire son possible** : to do one's utmost
possiblement [pɔsibləmɑ̃] *adv Can* : possibly, perhaps
postal, -tale [pɔstal] *adj, mpl* **postaux** [pɔsto] : postal, mail
postdater [pɔstdate] *vt* : to postdate
poste[1] [pɔst] *nm* **1** : job, position **2** : post, station <poste d'essence : gas station, service station> <poste de travail : workstation> <poste de pilotage : cockpit> **3** : set <poste de télévision : television set> **4** : extension (of a phone system) **5 poste de pompiers** *Can* : fire station
poste[2] *nf* **1** : mail service <mettre à la poste : to put in the mail> **2** : post office
poster[1] [pɔste] *vt* **1** : to post, to station **2** : to mail
poster[2] [pɔstɛr] *nm* : poster
postérieur[1], **-rieure** [pɔsterjœr] *adj* **1** : later **2** : posterior, rear, back
postérieur[2] *nm fam* : bottom, buttocks *pl*
postérieurement [pɔsterjœrmɑ̃] *adv* : subsequently, later
postérité [pɔsterite] *nf* **1** : posterity **2** LIGNÉE : descendants *pl*
posthume [pɔstym] *adj* : posthumous
postiche[1] [pɔstiʃ] *adj* : false, fake
postiche[2] *nm* : hairpiece, toupee
postier, -tière [pɔstje, -tjɛr] *n* : postal worker
postnatal, -tale [pɔstnatal] *adj, mpl* **-tals** *or* **-taux** [-to] : postnatal
postopératoire [pɔstɔperatwar] *adj* : postoperative
postscolaire [pɔstskɔlɛr] *adj* **l'enseignement postscolaire** : continuing education
post–scriptum [pɔstskriptɔm] *nms & pl* : postscript
postulant, -lante [pɔstylɑ̃, -lɑ̃t] *n* **1** CANDIDAT : candidate, contestant **2** : postulant (in religion)
postulat [pɔstyla] *nm* : postulate
postuler [pɔstyle] *vt* **1** : to apply for **2** : to postulate
posture [pɔstyr] *nf* **1** POSITION : posture, position **2** SITUATION : situation
pot [po] *nm* **1** : pot, jar, container <pot de fleurs : flowerpot> **2** : potful **3** *fam* : drink, glass **4 pot d'échappement** : muffler (of an automobile)

potable [pɔtabl] *adj* **1** BUVABLE : drinkable <eau potable : drinking water> **2** *fam* : fair, passable

potage [pɔtaʒ] *nm* : soup

potager[1], **-gère** [pɔtaʒe, -ʒɛr] *adj* : edible <plantes potagères : edible plants>

potager[2] *nm or* **jardin potager** : vegetable garden

potasse [pɔtas] *nf* : potash

potassium [pɔtasjɔm] *nm* : potassium

pot–au–feu [pɔtofø] *nms & pl* : beef stew

pot–de–vin [podvɛ̃] *nm, pl* **pots–de–vin** : bribe

pote [pot] *nm fam* : pal, buddy

poteau [pɔto] *nm, pl* **poteaux 1** : post, stake, pole <poteau de téléphone : telephone pole> **2** : goalpost **3 poteau indicateur** : signpost, guidepost

potelé, -lée [pɔtle] *adj* GRASSOUILLET : chubby, plump

potence [pɔtɑ̃s] *nf* : gallows

potentat [pɔtɑ̃ta] *nm* : potentate, ruler

potentiel[1], **-tielle** [pɔtɑ̃sjɛl] *adj* : potential — **potentiellement** [-sjɛlmɑ̃] *adv*

potentiel[2] *nm* : potential

poterie [pɔtri] *nf* : pottery

potiche [pɔtiʃ] *nf* **1** : large vase **2** : figurehead, puppet

potier, -tière [pɔtje, -tjɛr] *n* : potter

potin [pɔtɛ̃] *nm fam* **1** *France* : noise, racket **2 potins** *nmpl* : gossip

potion [pɔsjɔ̃] *nf* : potion

potiron [pɔtirɔ̃] *nm* : variety of large pumpkin

pot–pourri [popuri] *nm, pl* **pots–pourris** : potpourri

pou [pu] *nm, pl* **poux** : louse

poubelle [pubɛl] *nf* : garbage can, trash barrel

pouce [pus] *nm* **1** : thumb <se tourner les pouces : to twiddle one's thumbs> **2** : big toe **3** : inch **4 faire du pouce** *Can* : to hitchhike

pouding → **pudding**

poudre [pudr] *nf* **1** : powder <lait en poudre : powdered milk> **2** *or* **poudre à canon** : gunpowder **3** : face powder **4 poudre à pâte** *Can* : baking powder

poudrer [pudre] *vt* : to powder — *v impers Can* : to drift (of snow) — **se poudrer** *vr*

poudrerie [pudrəri] *nf Can* : (snow) flurries *pl*

poudreux, -dreuse [pudrø, -drøz] *adj* : powdery

poudrier [pudrije] *nm* : (face powder) compact

pouf [puf] *nm* : hassock

pouffer [pufe] *vi* **pouffer de rire** : to burst out laughing

pouilleux, -leuse [pujø, -jøz] *adj* **1** : lousy, flea-ridden **2** : seedy, shabby

pouillot [pujo] *nm* : warbler

poulailler [pulaje] *nm* : henhouse, chicken coop

poulain [pulɛ̃] *nm* **1** : colt, foal **2** PROTÉGÉ : protégé

poule [pul] *nf* **1** : hen **2** : (stewing) chicken **3 poule mouillée** *fam* : chicken, wimp

poulet [pulɛ] *nm* : chicken

poulette [pulɛt] *nf* : pullet, young hen

pouliche [puliʃ] *nf* : filly

poulie [puli] *nf* : pulley

pouliner [puline] *vi* : to foal

poulpe [pulp] *nm* PIEUVRE : octopus

pouls [pu] *nms & pl* : pulse

poumon [pumɔ̃] *nm* : lung

poupe [pup] *nf* : stern <en poupe : astern>

poupée [pupe] *nf* **1** : doll **2** : finger bandage

poupin, -pine [pupɛ̃, -pin] *adj* : chubby <visage poupin : baby face>

poupon [pupɔ̃] *nm* **1** : tiny baby **2** : baby doll

pouponner [pupɔne] *vi* : to dote (over a baby), to play mother

pouponnière [pupɔnjɛr] *nf* : nursery (for babies)

pour[1] [pur] *prep* **1** : for <en avance pour son âge : advanced for his age> <partir pour Québec : to leave for Quebec> **2** : to, in order to <on doit travailler dur pour réussir : you have to work hard to succeed> **3 pour cent** : percent **4 pour que** : in order that, so that

pour[2] *nm* **le pour et le contre** : the pros and cons

pourboire [purbwar] *nm* : tip

pourcentage [pursɑ̃taʒ] *nm* : percentage

pourchasser [purʃase] *vt* POURSUIVRE : to pursue, to hunt down

pourlécher [purleʃe] {87} *v* **se pourlécher** *vr* : to lick one's lips

pourparlers [purparle] *nmpl* : talks, negotiations, parley

pourpre[1] [purpr] *adj & nm* : crimson, reddish purple

pourpre[2] *nf* : purple (dye)

pourquoi[1] [purkwa] *adv & conj* : why

pourquoi[2] *nm* **1** : reason, cause **2 le pourquoi et le comment** : the whys and wherefores

pourra [pura], *etc.* → **pouvoir**

pourri, -rie [puri] *adj* **1** : rotten, decayed **2** : coddled, spoiled **3** CORROMPU : corrupt, rotten **4** *fam* DÉGUEULASSE : lousy, abominable (of weather, etc.)

pourrir [purir] *vi* **1** SE DÉCOMPOSER : to rot **2** : to spoil, to go bad **3** SE DÉTÉRIORER : to deteriorate — *vt* **1** : to rot, to decay **2** GÂTER : to spoil, to pamper

pourrissement [purismɑ̃] *nm* : deterioration

pourriture [purityr] *nf* **1** : rot, rottenness **2** : corruption, (moral) decay **3** *fam* : rotten person, swine

poursuite [pursɥit] *nf* **1** : pursuit, chase **2 poursuites** *nfpl* : legal proceedings, lawsuit

poursuivant, -vante [pursɥivɑ̃, -vɑ̃t] *n* **1** : pursuer **2** : plaintiff

poursuivre [pursɥivr] {88} *vt* **1** : to pursue, to chase **2** : to carry on with, to continue **3** : to sue, to prosecute **4** HARCELER : to pester, to hound — *vi* : to continue, to go on

pourtant [purtɑ̃] *adv* : however, yet, nevertheless

pourtour [purtur] *nm* **1** CIRCONFÉRENCE : perimeter, circumference **2** : periphery, surrounding area

pourvoi [purvwa] *nm* : appeal (in law)

pourvoir [purvwar] {68} *vt* **1** : to fill (a position, etc.) **2 ~ de** : to provide with, to equip with **3 ~ de** : to endow with <pourvu d'un remarquable talent : gifted with an extraordinary talent> — *vi* **~ à** : to provide for — **se pourvoir** *vr* **1** : to appeal (in law) **2 ~ de** : to provide oneself with

pourvoyeur, -voyeuse [purvwajœr, -vwajøz] *n* : provider, supplier, purveyor

pourvu [purvy] *conj* **~ que 1** : provided that **2** : let's hope (that) <pourvu qu'il fasse beau! : let's hope the weather is good!>

pousse [pus] *nf* **1** : growth, sprouting **2** : shoot, sprout

poussé, -sée [puse] *adj* : elaborate, extensive, exhaustive <un argument poussé : an elaborate argument> <études poussées : advanced studies>

poussée [puse] *nf* **1** : pressure **2** : push, shove **3** : rise, upsurge **4** ACCÈS : fit, attack (in medicine)

pousse–pousse [puspus] *nms & pl* : rickshaw

pousser [puse] *vt* **1** : to push, to shove **2** INCITER : to encourage, to urge **3** POURSUIVRE : to pursue, to continue **4** : to let out, to emit <il a poussé un cri : he let out a scream> <pousser un soupir : to heave a sigh> — *vi* **1** : to push **2** CROÎTRE : to grow — **se pousser** *vr* **1** : to move along, to get out of the way **2** *fam* : to push ahead, to make one's way

poussette [pusɛt] *nf* : stroller

poussière [pusjɛr] *nf* : dust

poussiéreux, -reuse [pusjerø, -røz] *adj* : dusty

poussif, -sive [pusif, -siv] *adj* : wheezing, wheezy

poussin [pusɛ̃] *nm* : chick

poussoir [puswar] *nm* : push button

poutine [putin] *nf Can* : French fries served with cheese and gravy

poutre [putr] *nf* : beam, girder

pouvoir[1] [puvwar] {69} *v aux* **1** : to be able to, to have the capacity to <peux-tu m'aider? : can you help me?> <elle pourrait vous surprendre : she might surprise you> **2** : to be permitted to <est-ce que je peux m'en aller maintenant? : can I go now?> — *v impers* : to be possible <il pourrait y avoir un changement à l'horaire : there might be a change of plans> — *vt* **1** : to do something about, to cope with **2 je n'en peux plus!** : I can't take anymore! — **se pouvoir** *vr impers* : to be possible <ça ne se peut pas! : it can't be!>

pouvoir[2] *nm* **1** FACULTÉ : faculty, ability **2** : power, control **3** : authority

pragmatique [pragmatik] *adj* : pragmatic — **pragmatisme** [-matism] *nm*

praire [prɛr] *nf* : clam

prairie [preri] *nf* **1** PRÉ : meadow **2** *or* **prairies** *nfpl* : prairie, grassland, meadowland

praticable [pratikabl] *adj* **1** FAISABLE : practicable, feasible **2** ACCESSIBLE : accessible, passable (of roads, etc.)

praticien, -cienne [pratisjɛ̃, -sjɛn] *n* : practitioner

pratiquant[1], **-quante** [pratikɑ̃, -kɑ̃t] *adj* : practicing

pratiquant[2], **-quante** *n* : churchgoer, follower (of a religion)

pratique[1] [pratik] *adj* **1** : practical, useful **2** COMMODE : convenient, handy

pratique[2] *nf* **1** : practice <mettre en pratique : to put into practice> **2** : practicing, observance

pratiquer [pratike] *vt* **1** : to practice **2** : to play (a sport) **3** : to use, to apply **4** : to carry out, to execute — *vi* : to attend church regularly — **se pratiquer** *vr* : to be done, to be practiced

pré [pre] *nm* : meadow

préalable[1] [prealabl] *adj* **1** : preliminary **2** : previous, prior <sans avis préalable : without prior notice> **3 ~ à** : preceding

préalable[2] *nm* **1** : prerequisite, precondition **2 au préalable** : beforehand, in advance

préalablement [prealabləmɑ̃] *adv* **1** AUPARAVANT : beforehand **2 ~ à** : prior to

préambule [preɑ̃byl] *nm* **1** : preamble, prelude **2 sans ~** : without warning

préau [preo] *nm, pl* **préaux** [preo] : courtyard

préavis [preavi] *nm* : (prior) notice

précaire [prekɛr] *adj* : precarious, fragile, insecure

précarité [prekarite] *nf* : precariousness

précaution [prekosjɔ̃] *nf* **1** : precaution **2** PRUDENCE : caution, care <avec précaution : cautiously> <prends des précautions : be careful>

précautionneux, -neuse [prekosjɔnø, -nøz] *adj* : cautious, careful —

précautionneusement [-sjɔnøzmɑ̃] *adv*
précédemment [presedamɑ̃] *adv* : previously, before
précédent[1], **-dente** [presedɑ̃, -dɑ̃t] *adj* ANTÉRIEUR : previous, prior
précédent[2] *nm* : precedent
précéder [presede] {87} *vt* **1** : to precede **2** : to get ahead of
précepte [presɛpt] *nm* : precept
précepteur, -trice [presɛptœr, -tris] *n* : (private) tutor
préchauffer [preʃofe] *vt* : to preheat
prêcher [preʃe] *v* : to preach
prêcheur[1], **-cheuse** [prɛʃœr, -ʃøz] *adj* : preachy, moralizing
prêcheur[2], **-cheuse** *n* : preacher
précieusement [presjøzmɑ̃] *adv* SOIGNEUSEMENT : carefully
précieux, -cieuse [presjø, -sjøz] *adj* **1** : precious, valuable **2** : valued, invaluable, useful **3** : affected
préciosité [presjozite] *nf* : affectation, preciosity
précipice [presipis] *nm* **1** GOUFFRE : abyss, chasm **2 au bord du précipice** : on the brink of collapse
précipitamment [presipitamɑ̃] *adv* : hurriedly, hastily
précipitation [presipitasjɔ̃] *nf* **1** : hurry, haste **2 précipitations** *nfpl* : precipitation, rain, snow
précipité, -tée [presipite] *adj* **1** : hurried, rapid **2** : hasty, rash
précipiter [presipite] *vt* **1** : to hurl, to throw **2** : to hasten, to speed up — **se précipiter** *vr* **1** : to rush **2** : to act rashly **3** : to throw oneself <je me suis précipitée dans ses bras : I threw myself into his arms>
précis[1], **-cise** [presi, -siz] *adj* **1** EXACT : precise, exact, accurate **2** : clear, specific **3** : particular, very <à ce moment précis : at that very moment>
précis[2] *nms & pl* **1** ABRÉGÉ : abstract, summary **2** : handbook
précisément [presizemɑ̃] *adv* EXACTEMENT : precisely, exactly
préciser [presize] *vt* **1** DÉTERMINER : to specify, to state exactly **2** : to clarify — **se préciser** *vr* : to take shape, to become clearer
précision [presizjɔ̃] *nf* **1** EXACTITUDE : precision, accuracy **2** CLARTÉ : clarity
précoce [prekɔs] *adj* **1** : early <dépistage précoce : early detection> **2** : precocious <enfant précoce : precocious child>
précocement [prekɔsmɑ̃] *adv* : precociously
précocité [prekɔsite] *nf* : precocity
préconçu, -çue [prekɔ̃sy] *adj* : preconceived
préconiser [prekɔnize] *vt* PRÔNER : to recommend, to advocate
précurseur[1] [prekyrsœr] *adj* : precursory
précurseur[2] *nm* : forerunner, precursor
prédateur[1], **-trice** [predatœr, -tris] *adj* : predatory
prédateur[2] *nm* : predator
prédécesseur [predesesœr] *nm* : predecessor
prédestiner [predɛstine] *vt* : to predestine — **prédestination** [-stinasjɔ̃] *nf*
prédéterminer [predetɛrmine] *vt* : to predetermine
prédicateur, -trice [predikatœr, -tris] *n* : preacher
prédiction [prediksjɔ̃] *nf* : prediction
prédilection [predilɛksjɔ̃] *nf* **1** : predilection, partiality **2 de ~** : favorite <c'est mon lieu de prédilection : it's my favorite place>
prédire [predir] {29} *vt* : to foretell, to predict
prédisposer [predispoze] *vt* : to predispose — **prédisposition** [-pozisjɔ̃] *nf*
prédominance [predɔminɑ̃s] *nf* : predominance, prevalence
prédominer [predɔmine] *vi* : to predominate, to prevail
prééminence [preeminɑ̃s] *nf* : preeminence — **prééminent, -nente** [-minɑ̃, -nɑ̃t] *adj*
préexister [preɛgziste] *vi* : to preexist
préfabriqué, -quée [prefabrike] *adj* : prefabricated
préface [prefas] *nf* : preface — **préfacer** [-fase] *vt*
préfecture [prefɛktyr] *nf* **préfecture de police** *France* : police headquarters
préférable [preferabl] *adj* : preferable — **préférablement** [-rabləmɑ̃] *adv*
préféré[1], **-rée** [prefere] *adj* : favorite
préféré[2], **-rée** *n* : favorite (personal thing)
préférence [preferɑ̃s] *nf* **1** : preference **2 de ~** : preferably
préférentiel, -tielle [preferɑ̃sjɛl] *adj* : preferential
préférer [prefere] {87} *vt* : to prefer
préfet [prefɛ] *nm* **préfet de police** *France* : police commissioner
préfigurer [prefigyre] *vt* : to prefigure
préfixe [prefiks] *nm* : prefix
préhensile [preɑ̃sil] *adj* : prehensile
préhistorique [preistɔrik] *adj* : prehistoric
préjudice [preʒydis] *nm* : harm, damage <porter préjudice à : to harm, to cause harm to> <au préjudice de : to the detriment of>
préjudiciable [preʒydisjabl] *adj* **~ à** : detrimental to, harmful to
préjugé [preʒyʒe] *nm* : prejudice, bias
préjuger [preʒyʒe] {17} *vt* : to prejudge
prélart [prelar] *nm Can* : linoleum
prélasser [prelase] *v* **se prélasser** *vr* : to lounge (around)
prélat [prela] *nm* : prelate
prélèvement [prelɛvmɑ̃] *nm* **1** : withdrawal, deduction **2** : sample

<prélèvement de sang : blood sample>

prélever [prelәve] {52} *vt* **1** : to withdraw, to deduct, to debit **2** : to take (a sample of), to remove (an organ)

préliminaire [preliminɛr] *adj* : preliminary

préliminaires [preliminɛr] *nmpl* : preliminaries

prélude [prelyd] *nm* : prelude

prématuré, -rée [prematyre] *adj* : premature — **prématurément** [-tyremɑ̃] *adv*

préméditation [premeditasjɔ̃] *nf* **1** : premeditation **2 avec préméditation** : with malice aforethought

préméditer [premedite] *vt* : to premeditate

prémenstruel, -struelle [premɑ̃stryɛl] *adj* : premenstrual

premier[1], **-mière** [prәmje, -mjɛr] *adj* **1** : first <à première vue : at first sight> **2** : top, leading **3** : primary, principal **4** : initial, original **5 premier ministre** : prime minister

premier[2], **-mière** *n* : first (person or thing)

premier[3] *nm* **1** (*used in dates*) : first <le premier avril : the first of April> **2 en ~** : first of all, in the first place

première *nf* **1** : first class <billet de première : first-class ticket> **2** : premiere **3** : first gear, low gear

premièrement [prәmjɛrmɑ̃] *adv* : in the first place, firstly

prémisse [premis] *nf* : premise

prémolaire [premɔlɛr] *nf* : premolar, bicuspid

prémonition [premɔnisjɔ̃] *nf* : premonition

prémunir [premynir] *vt* **~ contre** : to protect (someone) against — **se prémunir** *vr* **~ contre** : to protect oneself against

prenait [prәnɛ], *etc.* → **prendre**

prendre [prɑ̃dr] {70} *vt* **1** : to take <prendre en main : to take in hand> **2** : to bring (along) <prends ton chapeau : take your hat> **3** : to get, to take out, to pick up **4** : to have (food or drink), to take (medicine) **5** : to take (a break, holiday, etc.) **6** : to take up (space or time) **7** : to take on (an employee, etc.) **8** : to catch (a thief, etc.) <se faire prendre : to get caught> **9** : to get (a warning, etc.), to catch (a cold) **10** : to take (a train, a road, etc.) **11** : to take on (responsibility), to tackle (a problem) **12** : to take down (notes, etc.) **13** : to assume, to take over (control) **14** : to seize, to capture — *vi* **1** : to set, to thicken (of cement, gelatin, etc.) **2** : to take hold, to catch on **3** : to break out (of fire) **4** : to go, to turn, to follow <prendre à droite : to bear right> **5 prendre sur soi** : to take upon oneself, to take responsibility — **se prendre** *vr* **1** : to be taken <ce médicament se prend avant les repas : this medicine is taken before meals> **2** : to get caught **3** : to catch <se prendre les doigts dans la porte : to catch one's fingers in the door> **4 ~ à** : to get caught up in **5 ~ pour** : to consider oneself <il se prend pour un autre : he thinks he's better than anyone else> **6 s'y prendre** : to go about it, to act <il faut s'y prendre à l'avance : it must be done in advance>

preneur, -neuse [prәnœr, -nøz] *n* : buyer, taker <je suis preneur : I'll take it>

prenne [prɛn], *etc.* → **prendre**

prénom [prenɔ̃] *nm* : given name, first name

prénommer [prenɔme] *vt* : to name — **se prénommer** *vr* : to be called <elle se prénomme Anne : her first name is Anne>

prénuptial, -tiale [prenypsjal] *adj, mpl* **-tiaux** [-sjo] : prenuptial

préoccupant, -pante [preɔkypɑ̃, -pɑ̃t] *adj* INQUIÉTANT : worrisome

préoccupation [preɔkypasjɔ̃] *nf* INQUIÉTUDE : worry, concern

préoccuper [preɔkype] *vt* **1** INQUIÉTER : to worry, to concern **2** : to preoccupy — **se préoccuper** *vr*

préparateur, -trice [preparatœr, -tris] *n* : (laboratory) assistant

préparatifs [preparatif] *nmpl* : preparations

préparation [preparasjɔ̃] *nf* : preparation

préparatoire [preparatwar] *adj* : preparatory

préparer [prepare] *vt* **1** : to prepare, to make ready <préparer un repas : to prepare a meal> <préparer une prescription : to dispense a prescription> **2** : to prepare for (an exam, etc.) **3** : to prepare, to train — **se préparer** *vr* **1** : to prepare, to get ready **2** : to be in the offing

prépondérance [prepɔ̃derɑ̃s] *nf* : predominance

prépondérant, -rante [prepɔ̃derɑ̃, -rɑ̃t] *adj* : predominant, dominating

préposé, -sée [prepoze] *n* **1** : official, clerk, attendant **2** *France* : mailman

préposer [prepoze] *vt* : to appoint <être préposé à : to be (put) in charge of>

préposition [prepɔzisjɔ̃] *nf* : preposition — **prépositionnel, -nelle** [prepɔzisjɔnɛl] *adj*

prérequis [prereki] *nms & pl Can* : prerequisite (in college)

prérogative [prerɔgativ] *nf* : prerogative

près [prɛ] *adv* **1** : close, near <c'est tout près : it's close by> **2** : near, soon <lundi, c'est trop près : Monday's too soon> <les vacances sont tout près maintenant : it's almost time for vacation> **3 à . . . près** : more or less, close enough to, within about <à un centimètre près : within about a centimeter> <à cela près : except for that> **4 à peu près** PRESQUE : almost, just about, approximately **5 de ~** : closely <regarder de près : to take a close look at> **6 ~ de** : near, close to <près de partir : about to leave> <près d'ici : nearby>

présage [prezaʒ] *nm* : omen, sign, augur

présager [prezaʒe] {17} *vt* **1** PRÉVOIR : to foresee, to predict **2** : to portend, to bode

presbyte [prɛsbit] *adj* HYPERMÉTROPE : farsighted

presbytère [prɛsbitɛr] *nm* : rectory

presbytie [prɛsbisi] *nf* HYPERMÉTROPIE : farsightedness

prescience [presjɑ̃s] *nf* : foresight, prescience

préscolaire [preskɔlɛr] *adj* : preschool

prescription [prɛskripsjɔ̃] *nf* **1** : prescription **2** : limitation (in law)

prescrire [prɛskrir] {33} *vt* **1** : to prescribe **2** : to stipulate, to lay down

prescrivait [prɛskrivɛ], **prescrivions** [prɛskrivjɔ̃], *etc.* → **prescrire**

prescrive [prɛskriv], *etc.* → **prescrire**

préséance [preseɑ̃s] *nf* : precedence

présence [prezɑ̃s] *nf* **1** : presence, attendance **2 en ~** : face to face **3 en présence de** : in the presence of, in front of **4 présence d'esprit** : presence of mind

présent[1], -sente [prezɑ̃, -zɑ̃t] *adj* **1** : present, in attendance **2** : existing, actual, current <le souvenir toujours présent : the ever-present memory> **3** : present, at hand <la présente lettre : the present letter, this letter>

présent[2] *nm* : present (time) <jusqu'à présent : until now>

présentateur, -trice [prezɑ̃tatœr, -tris] *n* : newscaster, anchor

présentation [prezɑ̃tasjɔ̃] *nf* **1** : presentation **2** ALLURE : appearance, look **3** : introduction <il a fait les présentations : he introduced us>

présente [prezɑ̃t] *nf* **1 par la présente** : hereby **2 des présentes** : hereof

présentement [prezɑ̃tmɑ̃] *adv* ACTUELLEMENT : at the moment, now

présenter [prezɑ̃te] *vt* **1** MONTRER : to present, to show, to display **2** : to introduce **3** : to offer, to give <présenter ses condoléances : to offer one's condolences> <présenter des excuses : to apologize> **4** : to submit (a proposal, etc.) **5** : to anchor (a television news program) **—** *vi* **présenter bien** : to have a pleasing appearance, to look well **— se présenter** *vr* **1** : to go, to come, to appear **2** : to introduce oneself **3 ~ à** : to run for (an office), to apply for (a job)

présentoir [prezɑ̃twar] *nm* : display shelf

préservatif [prezɛrvatif] *nm* CONDOM : condom

préservation [prezɛrvasjɔ̃] *nf* **1** : protection **2** CONSERVATION : preservation, conservation

préserver [prezɛrve] *vt* **1** : to protect **2** CONSERVER : to preserve, to conserve

présidence [prezidɑ̃s] *nf* **1** : presidency **2** : chairmanship

président, -dente [prezidɑ̃, -dɑ̃t] *n* **1** : president **2** : chair, chairperson **3 président de jury** : foreman (of a jury)

présidentiel, -tielle [prezidɑ̃sjɛl] *adj* : presidential

présidentielles [prezidɑ̃sjɛl] *nfpl France* : presidential election

présider [prezide] *vt* : to preside over, to chair **—** *vi* **~ à** : to rule over, to govern

présomption [prezɔ̃psjɔ̃] *nf* **1** : presumption, supposition **2** PRÉTENTION : pretentiousness

présomptueux, -tueuse [prezɔ̃ptɥø, -tɥøz] *adj* : presumptuous

presque [prɛsk] *adv* : almost, hardly, scarcely <presque jamais : hardly ever> <presque rien : next to nothing>

presqu'île [prɛskil] *nf* : peninsula

pressant, -sante [prɛsɑ̃, -sɑ̃t] *adj* : urgent, pressing

presse [prɛs] *nf* **1** : press (newspapers, magazines, etc.) <agence de presse : news agency> **2** : printing press **3 il n'y a pas de presse** *Can* : there's no hurry

pressé, -sée [prese] *adj* **1** : hurried **2** : urgent **3** : squeezed, pressed

presse–fruits [prɛsfrɥi] *nms & pl* : juicer

pressentiment [presɑ̃timɑ̃] *nm* : premonition, hunch

pressentir [presɑ̃tir] {82} *vt* **1** : to sense, to have a premonition about **2** : to contact, to approach

presse–papiers [prɛspapje] *nms & pl* : paperweight

presser [prese] *vt* **1** : to press, to squeeze **2** : to push **3** : to urge **4** : to hurry, to rush <presser le pas : to hurry up> **5 presser de questions** : to ply with questions **—** *vi* : to be pressing, to be urgent <le temps presse : time is running out> **— se presser** *vr* **1** : to crowd, to throng **2** SE HÂTER : to hurry up **3 ~ contre** *or* **~ sur** : to snuggle up against

pression [prɛsjɔ̃] *nf* **1** : pressure <pression artérielle : blood pressure> <faire pression sur : to put pressure on> **2** BOUTON-PRESSION : snap (fastener)

pressurer [presyre] *vt* : to press, to squeeze

pressuriser [presyrize] *vt* : to pressurize

prestance [prɛstɑ̃s] *nf* : (imposing) presence, bearing

prestataire [prɛstatɛr] *nm* **1** : recipient **2 prestataire de bien–être social** *Can* : welfare recipient

prestation [prɛstasjɔ̃] *nf* **1** : benefit, allowance **2** : performance **3 prestations d'assurance–chômage** *Can* : unemployment insurance benefits

preste [prɛst] *adj* : nimble — **prestement** [prɛstəmɑ̃] *adv*

prestidigitateur, -trice [prɛstidiʒitatœr, -tris] *n* : magician, conjurer

prestidigitation [prɛstidiʒitasjɔ̃] *nf* : sleight of hand, conjuring

prestige [prɛstiʒ] *nm* : prestige

prestigieux, -gieuse [prɛstiʒjø, -ʒjøz] *adj* : prestigious

presto [prɛsto] *interj* : presto!

présumément [prezymemɑ̃] *adv Can* : presumably, supposedly

présumer [prezyme] *vt* : to presume, to suppose — *vi* ~ **de** : to overestimate, to overrate

présupposer [presypoze] *vt* : to presuppose — **présupposition** [-pozisjɔ̃] *nf*

prêt[1], prête [prɛ, prɛt] *adj* **1** PRÉPARÉ : ready, prepared <tout est prêt : everything's ready> **2** DISPOSÉ : willing <être tout prêt à : to be ready and willing to>

prêt[2] *nm* EMPRUNT : loan

prêt–à–porter [prɛtapɔrte] *nm, pl* **prêts–à–porter** : ready-to-wear (clothing)

prétendant[1], -dante [pretɑ̃dɑ̃, -dɑ̃t] *n* : pretender (to a throne)

prétendant[2] *nm* : suitor

prétendre [pretɑ̃dr] {63} *vt* **1** AFFIRMER : to claim, to maintain **2** : to expect <il ne prétend pas être récompensé : he doesn't expect to be rewarded> — *vi* ~ **à** : to lay claim to, to aspire to

prétendu, -due [pretɑ̃dy] *adj* SOI-DISANT : so-called, alleged

prétendument [pretɑ̃dymɑ̃] *adv* : allegedly, supposedly

prétentieux, -tieuse [pretɑ̃sjø, -sjøz] *adj* : pretentious — **prétentieusement** [-sjøzmɑ̃] *adv*

prétention [pretɑ̃sjɔ̃] *nf* **1** : pretentiousness **2** AMBITION : claim, pretension, pretense

prêter [prete] *vt* **1** : to lend **2** ATTRIBUER : to attribute, to ascribe <prêter de l'importance à : to attach importance to> **3** ACCORDER : to offer, to give <prêter l'oreille : to listen, to lend an ear> <prêter attention : to pay attention> <prêter une main : to lend a hand> — *vi* ~ **à** : to cause, to give rise to — **se prêter** *vr* **1** ~ **à** : to lend oneself to **2** ~ **à** : to be suitable for

prêteur, -teuse [prɛtœr, -tøz] *n* **1** : lender, moneylender **2 prêteur sur gages** : pawnbroker

prétexte [pretɛkst] *nm* : pretext, excuse

prétexter [pretɛkste] *vt* : to give as a pretext, to plead

prêtre [prɛtr] *nm* : priest

prêtresse [prɛtrɛs] *nf* : priestess

prêtrise [prɛtriz] *nf* : priesthood

preuve [prœv] *nf* **1** : proof, evidence **2 faire preuve de** : to show

prévale [preval], *etc.* → **prévaloir**

prévaloir [prevalwar] {71} *vi* PRÉDOMINER : to prevail — **se prévaloir** *vr* **1** ~ **de** : to take advantage of **2** ~ **de** : to claim, to boast of

prévaudra [prevodra], *etc.* → **prévaloir**

prévaut [prevo], *etc.* → **prévaloir**

prévenance [prevnɑ̃s] *nf* : consideration, thoughtfulness

prévenant, -nante [prevnɑ̃, -nɑ̃t] *adj* ATTENTIONNÉ : considerate, thoughtful

prévenir [prevnir] {92} *vt* **1** ÉVITER : to prevent, to avoid **2** AVISER, INFORMER : to inform **3** AVERTIR : to warn **4** ANTICIPER : to anticipate **5** ~ **contre** : to prejudice (someone) against

préventif, -tive [prevɑ̃tif, -tiv] *adj* : preventive

prévention [prevɑ̃sjɔ̃] *nf* **1** : prevention <prévention routière : road safety> **2** : prejudice, bias

prévenu, -nue [prevny] *n* : defendant, accused

prévisible [previzibl] *adj* : predictable, foreseeable

prévision [previzjɔ̃] *nf* **1** : prediction, expectation **2 prévisions** *nfpl* : forecast <prévisions météorologiques : weather forecast>

prévoir [prevwar] {99} *vt* **1** : to predict, to anticipate, to forecast **2** : to plan (on), to schedule **3** : to provide for, to allow (for)

prévoyance [prevwajɑ̃s] *nf* : foresight

prévoyant, -voyante [prevwajɑ̃, -vwajɑ̃t] *adj* : provident, farsighted

prier [prije] {96} *vi* : to pray — *vt* **1** : to beg, to implore **2** : to ask, to request <vous êtes prié d'assister : you are requested to attend> **3 je vous en prie** : please, don't mention it, you're welcome

prière [prijɛr] *nf* **1** : prayer **2** : request, entreaty, plea

primaire [primɛr] *adj* **1** : primary, elementary **2** : limited, simplistic

primate [primat] *nm* : primate (in zoology)

prime[1] [prim] *adj* **1** : first <de prime abord : at first> <prime enfance : early childhood> **2** : prime (in mathematics) **3** *Can* : temperamental, irascible

prime[2] *nf* **1** INDEMNITÉ : premium, allowance **2** : bonus, gift

primer [prime] *vt* **1** : to take precedence over, to prevail over **2** : to award a prize to — *vi* : to dominate, to be of primary importance

primesautier, -tière [primsotje, -tjɛr] *adj* : impulsive

primeur [primœr] *nf* **1 avoir la primeur de** : to be the first with, to be the first to hear **2 primeurs** *nfpl* : early fruit and vegetables

primevère [primvɛr] *nf* : primrose

primitif, -tive [primitif, -tiv] *adj* **1** : primitive **2** INITIAL : original, initial

primo [primo] *adv* : firstly, first (of all)

primordial, -diale [primɔrdjal] *adj, mpl* **-diaux** [-djo] **1** : essential, vital **2** : primordial

prince [prɛ̃s] *nm* : prince

princesse [prɛ̃sɛs] *nf* : princess

princier, -cière [prɛ̃sje, -sjɛr] *adj* : princely

principal[1], **-pale** [prɛ̃sipal] *adj, mpl* **-paux** [-po] : main, principal <plat principal : main course> <un rôle principal : a leading role>

principal[2] *nm* **1** ESSENTIEL : main thing **2** CAPITAL : principal (in finance)

principalement [prɛ̃sipalmɑ̃] *adv* : primarily, mainly

principauté [prɛ̃sipote] *nf* : principality

principe [prɛ̃sip] *nm* **1** : principle, rule <en principe : in principle, as a rule> **2** : assumption <partir du principe que : to work on the assumption that> **3** : concept, guiding principle **4** : origin, prime mover

printanier, -nière [prɛ̃tanje, -njɛr] *adj* : spring, springlike

printemps [prɛ̃tɑ̃] *nms & pl* : spring

priorité [prijɔrite] *nf* **1** : priority <en priorité : first> **2** : right-of-way

pris[1] [pri] *pp* → **prendre**

pris[2], **prise** [pri, priz] *adj* **1** : taken, full, sold (out) **2** : stricken, afflicted <pris de peur : panic-stricken> **3** : occupied, busy

prise [priz] *nf* **1** : taking, capture, catch **2** : hold, grip **3** *Can* : strike (in baseball) **4** *or* **prise de médicament** : dose (of medicine) **5 prise de bec** : squabble, spat **6 prise de courant** : (electrical) outlet **7 prise de sang** : blood specimen **8 prise d'eau** : hydrant **9 prise directe** : high gear

priser [prize] *vt* **1** : to take, to snort (drugs, snuff) **2** : to prize, to value

prisme [prism] *nm* : prism

prison [prizɔ̃] *nf* **1** : prison **2** : imprisonment <faire de la prison : to serve time>

prisonnier[1], **-nière** [prizɔnje, -njɛr] *adj* : captive, imprisoned

prisonnier[2], **-nière** *n* : prisoner

privation [privasjɔ̃] *nf* **1** : deprivation, loss **2** : privation, want <une vie de privations : a life of hardships>

privatisation [privatizasjɔ̃] *nf* : privatization — **privatiser** [-tize] *vt*

privautés [privote] *nfpl* : liberties <se permettre des privautés avec : to take liberties with>

privé[1], **-vée** [prive] *adj* : private

privé[2] *nm* **1** : private life <en privé : in private> **2** : private sector

priver [prive] *vt* : to deprive — **se priver** *vr* **1** ~ **de** : to go without, to do without **2 ne pas se priver de** : not to hesitate to

privilège [privilɛʒ] *nm* : privilege

privilégier [privileʒje] {96} *vt* FAVORISER : to privilege, to favor — **privilégié, -giée** [-leʒje] *adj*

prix [pri] *nms & pl* **1** : price, cost <hors de prix : exorbitantly expensive> <à tout prix : at all costs> <à prix coûtant : at cost> **2** : prize

probabilité [prɔbabilite] *nf* : probability, likelihood

probable [prɔbabl] *adj* : probable, likely <peu probable : unlikely>

probablement [prɔbabləmɑ̃] *adv* : probably

probant, -bante [prɔbɑ̃, -bɑ̃t] *adj* : convincing, conclusive

probité [prɔbite] *nf* : probity, integrity

problématique [prɔblematik] *adj* : problematic

problème [prɔblɛm] *nm* : problem

procédé [prɔsede] *nm* **1** : process, procedure **2** COMPORTEMENT : conduct, behavior

procéder [prɔsede] {87} *vi* **1** AVANCER : to proceed **2** : to act, to behave **3** ~ **à** : to carry out, to proceed with

procédure [prɔsedyr] *nf* **1** : procedure **2** : (legal) proceedings *pl*

procès [prɔsɛ] *nms & pl* **1** : lawsuit **2** : trial

procession [prɔsesjɔ̃] *nf* : procession

processus [prɔsesys] *nms & pl* : process, system

procès–verbal [prɔsɛvɛrbal] *nm, pl* **procès–verbaux** [-vɛrbo] **1** : minutes *pl* (of a meeting) **2** : (judicial) record, (police) report **3** *France* : (parking) ticket

prochain[1], **-chaine** [prɔʃɛ̃, -ʃɛn] *adj* **1** SUIVANT : next, following **2** : imminent, forthcoming **3 à la prochaine!** *fam* : see you!, until next time!

prochain[2] *nm* : fellowman

prochainement [prɔʃɛnmɑ̃] *adv* BIENTÔT : soon, shortly

proche [prɔʃ] *adj* **1** : near, nearby <proche de : close to, neighboring on> **2** : near, imminent <l'avenir proche : the near future> **3** : closely related <le plus proche parent : the next of kin> **4 de proche en proche** : step by step, gradually

proches [prɔʃ] *nmpl* : close relatives

proclamation [prɔklamasjɔ̃] *nf* : proclamation

proclamer [prɔklame] *vt* **1** : to proclaim **2** : to announce, to declare

procréer [prɔkree] {89} *vt* : to procreate — **procréation** [-kreasjɔ̃] *nf*

procuration [prɔkyrasjɔ̃] *nf* **1** : proxy (in an election) **2** : power of attorney

procurer [prɔkyre] *vt* **1** : to provide, to give <procurer un emploi à qqn : to give s.o. a job> **2** OCCASIONNER : to provide, to cause <le plaisir procuré par la musique : the pleasure provided by music> — **se procurer** *vr* : to get, to obtain

procureur [prɔkyrœr] *nm* **1** *or* **procureur général** : prosecutor **2 procureur de la République** *France* : attorney general **3 procureur de la Couronne** *Can* : Crown attorney (attorney general)

prodigalité [prɔdigalite] *nf* : lavishness, extravagance

prodige [prɔdiʒ] *nm* **1** : prodigy **2** : marvel, wonder

prodigieux, -gieuse [prɔdiʒjø, -ʒjøz] *adj* EXTRAORDINAIRE : prodigious, extraordinary — **prodigieusement** [-ʒjøzmɑ̃] *adv*

prodigue [prɔdig] *adj* **1** DÉPENSIER : prodigal, extravagant **2** GÉNÉREUX : generous, lavish

prodiguer [prɔdige] *vt* : to lavish

producteur[1], **-trice** [prɔdyktœr, -tris] *adj* : producing

producteur[2] *nm* : producer

productif, -tive [prɔdyktif, -tiv] *adj* **1** : productive **2** RENTABLE : profitable

production [prɔdyksjɔ̃] *nf* **1** : production, output **2** : produce, products *pl*

productivité [prɔdyktivite] *nf* : productivity

produire [prɔdɥir] {49} *vt* **1** : to produce, to generate, to yield **2** : to cause, to bring about — **se produire** *vr* **1** : to occur, to happen **2** : to perform, to appear (on stage)

produisait [prɔdɥizɛ], **produisions** [prɔdɥizjɔ̃], *etc.* → **produire**

produise [prɔdɥiz], *etc.* → **produire**

produit [prɔdɥi] *nm* **1** : product **2** : proceeds *pl*, yield

proéminence [prɔeminɑ̃s] *nf* : prominence, protuberance — **proéminent, -nente** [prɔeminɑ̃, -nɑ̃t] *adj*

profanation [prɔfanasjɔ̃] *nf* : desecration, defilement

profane[1] [prɔfan] *adj* **1** : secular **2** : ignorant, uninitiated

profane[2] *nmf* **1** : layperson **2** : beginner, tyro

profaner [prɔfane] *vt* : to defile, to desecrate

proférer [prɔfere] {87} *vt* : to utter <proférer des menaces : to make threats>

professer [prɔfese] *vt* : to profess, to declare

professeur [prɔfesœr] *nm* **1** : teacher, schoolteacher **2** : professor

profession [prɔfesjɔ̃] *nf* **1** OCCUPATION : occupation, trade **2** : profession, declaration

professionnel, -nelle [prɔfɛsjɔnɛl] *adj & n* : professional — **professionnellement** [-nɛlmɑ̃] *adv*

professoral, -rale [prɔfɛsɔral] *adj, mpl* **-raux** [-ro] : professorial

professorat [prɔfɛsɔra] *nm* : teaching

profil [prɔfil] *nm* **1** : profile **2 de ~** : in profile, from the side

profiler [prɔfile] *vt* : to profile, to outline — **se profiler** *vr* **1** : to emerge, to take shape **2** : to stand out

profit [prɔfi] *nm* **1** : profit **2** : benefit, advantage <tirer profit de : to benefit from, to take advantage of>

profitable [prɔfitabl] *adj* : profitable — **profitablement** [-tabləmɑ̃] *adv*

profiter [prɔfite] *vi* **1 ~ à** : to be of benefit to **2 ~ de** : to take advantage of

profiteur, -teuse [prɔfitœr, -tøz] *n* : profiteer

profond[1] [prɔfɔ̃] *adv* : deeply

profond[2], **-fonde** [prɔfɔ̃, -fɔ̃d] *adj* **1** : deep <profond de deux mètres : two meters deep> <une voix profonde : a deep voice> <au plus profond de : in the depths of> **2** : deep-seated, underlying **3** : profound, penetrating

profondément [prɔfɔ̃demɑ̃] *adv* : deeply, profoundly

profondeur [prɔfɔ̃dœr] *nf* : depth, profundity

profusion [prɔfyzjɔ̃] *nf* : profusion <à profusion : in abundance>

profusément [prɔfyzemɑ̃] *adv* : profusely

progéniture [prɔʒenityr] *nf* : offspring, progeny

programmable [prɔgramabl] *adj* : programmable

programmation [prɔgramasjɔ̃] *nf* : programming

programme [prɔgram] *nm* **1** : program **2** : plan, schedule **3** : curriculum, syllabus

programmer [prɔgrame] *vt* **1** : to program (a computer) **2** : to plan, to schedule

programmeur, -meuse [prɔgramœr, -møz] *n* : (computer) programmer

progrès [prɔgrɛ] *nm* : progress <faire des progrès : to make progress>

progresser [prɔgrese] *vi* **1** : to progress, to advance **2** : to make progress, to improve

progressif, -sive [prɔgresif, -siv] *adj* : progressive — **progressivement** [-sivmɑ̃] *adv*

progression [prɔgrɛsjɔ̃] *nf* **1** : progress, advance **2** : progression, spread, increase

prohiber [prɔibe] *vt* : to prohibit, to ban

prohibitif, -tive [prɔibitif, -tiv] *adj* : prohibitive

prohibition [prɔibisjɔ] *nf* : prohibition

proie [prwa] *nf* **1** : prey **2 en proie à** : prey to, beset with, suffering from

projecteur [prɔʒɛktœr] *nm* **1** : projector **2** : spotlight, floodlight

projectile [prɔʒɛktil] *nm* : missile, projectile

projection [prɔʒɛksjɔ̃] *nf* **1** : projection, showing <salle de projection : screening room> **2** : throwing (off), discharge, spattering **3** : projection (in mathematics or psychology)

projet [prɔʒɛ] *nm* **1** : plan, project **2** ÉBAUCHE : draft, outline

projeter [prɔʃte] {8} *vt* **1** LANCER : to throw **2** : to project, to show (a film, etc.) **3** : to cast, to project (light) **4** : to plan

prolétaire [prɔletɛr] *adj & nmf* : proletarian

prolétariat [prɔletarjat] *nm* : proletariat

prolétarien, -rienne [prɔletarjɛ̃, -rjɛn] *adj* : proletarian

proliférer [prɔlifere] {87} *vi* SE MULTIPLIER : to proliferate — **prolifération** [-ferasjɔ̃] *nf*

prolifique [prɔlifik] *adj* : prolific

prolixe [prɔliks] *adj* : verbose, wordy

prologue [prɔlɔg] *nm* : prologue

prolongation [prɔlɔ̃gasjɔ̃] *nf* **1** ALLONGEMENT : extension, prolongation **2** *or* **prolongations** *nfpl* : overtime (in sports)

prolongement [prɔlɔ̃ʒmɑ̃] *nm* **1** : extension (of a road, railway, etc.) **2** : outcome, consequence

prolonger [prɔlɔ̃ʒe] {17} *vt* : to prolong, to extend — **se prolonger** *vr* : to continue, to persist, to go on

promenade [prɔmnad] *nf* **1** : walk, stroll **2** : ride, trip **3** : walkway, promenade

promener [prɔmne] {52} *vt* **1** : to take (out) for a walk <promener son chien : to walk one's dog> **2** : to run over, to move across <promener son regard sur une foule : to cast one's eyes over a crowd> — **se promener** *vr* **1** SE BALADER : to go for a walk **2 ~ sur** : to wander over, to roam across (with one's eyes, fingers, etc.)

promeneur, -neuse [prɔmnœr, -nøz] *n* : walker, stroller

promesse [prɔmɛs] *nf* **1** : promise <manquer à sa promesse : to break one's word> **2** : (legal) commitment <promesse d'achat : commitment to buy> **3 être plein de promesses** : to be full of promise

prometteur, -teuse [prɔmɛtœr, -tøz] *adj* : promising

promettre [prɔmɛtr] {53} *vt* : to promise — *vi* : to promise, to show promise — **se promettre** *vr* **~ de** : to resolve to

promis, -mise [prɔmi, -miz] *adj* **1** : promised **2 ~ à** : destined for

promiscuité [prɔmiskɥite] *nf* : overcrowding, lack of privacy

promontoire [prɔmɔ̃twar] *nm* : promontory, headland

promoteur, -trice [prɔmɔtœr, -tris] *n* : promoter

promotion [prɔmɔsjɔ̃] *nf* **1** : promotion, advancement **2** : promotion, (special) offer (in advertising)

promotionnel, -nelle [prɔmɔsjɔnɛl] *adj* : promotional

promouvoir [prɔmuvwar] {56} *vt* : to promote

prompt, prompte [prɔ̃, prɔ̃t] *adj* : prompt, swift, rapid <être prompt à réagir : to be quick to react>

promptement [prɔ̃tmɑ̃] *adv* : promptly, swiftly

promptitude [prɔ̃tityd] *nf* : swiftness, rapidity

promulgation [prɔmylgasjɔ̃] *nf* : promulgation, enactment

promulguer [prɔmylge] *vt* : to promulgate

prôner [prone] *vt* : to extol, to advocate, to commend

pronom [prɔnɔ̃] *nm* : pronoun

pronominal, -nale [prɔnɔminal] *adj, mpl* **-naux** [-no] **1** : pronominal **2** : reflexive <verbe pronominal : reflexive verb>

prononcé, -cée [prɔnɔ̃se] *adj* : pronounced, marked

prononcer [prɔnɔ̃se] {6} *vt* **1** : to pronounce **2** : to state, to declare — *vi* : to hand down a decision (in law) — **se prononcer** *vr* **1** : to be pronounced **2** : to give one's opinion, to declare oneself

prononciation [prɔnɔ̃sjasjɔ̃] *nf* : pronunciation

pronostic [prɔnɔstik] *nm* **1** : prognosis **2** PRÉDICTION : forecast, prediction

pronostiquer [prɔnɔstike] *vt* : to forecast

propagande [prɔpagɑ̃d] *nf* : propaganda

propagation [prɔpagasjɔ̃] *nf* **1** : propagation **2** : spreading

propager [prɔpaʒe] {17} *vt* **1** : to propagate **2** : to spread — **se propager** *vr*

propane [prɔpan] *nm* : propane

propension [prɔpɑ̃sjɔ̃] *nf* TENDANCE : propensity

propergol [prɔpɛrgɔl] *nm* : (rocket) propellant

prophète, prophétesse [prɔfɛt, prɔfetɛs] *n* : prophet, prophetess *f*

prophétie [prɔfesi] *nf* : prophecy

prophétique [prɔfetik] *adj* : prophetic — **prophétiquement** [-tikmɑ̃] *adv*

prophétiser [prɔfetize] *vt* : to prophesy

propice [prɔpis] *adj* : favorable, propitious

proportion [prɔpɔrsjɔ̃] *nf* **1** : proportion, ratio, relation <hors de proportion : out of proportion> <une proportion de dix contre un : a ratio of ten to one> <à proportion de : proportional to> <en proportion

: proportionately> **2 proportions** *nfpl* : dimensions, size

proportionné, -née [prɔpɔrsjɔne] *adj* **1** : proportioned <bien proportionné : well-proportioned> **2 ~ à** : proportionate to

proportionnel, -nelle [prɔpɔrsjɔnɛl] *adj* : proportional — **proportionnellement** [-nɛlmɑ̃] *adv*

proportionner [prɔpɔrsjɔne] *vt* : to proportion

propos [prɔpo] *nms & pl* **1** : subject **2** : intention, point **3 propos** *nmpl* : comments, talk **4 à ~** : appropriate, apropos **5 à propos de** : regarding, about

proposer [prɔpoze] *vt* **1** : to suggest, to propose **2** : to offer **3** : to nominate — **se proposer** *vr* **~ de** : to intend to

proposition [prɔpozisjɔ̃] *nf* **1** : suggestion **2** : proposal, offer **3** : proposition (in logic) **4** : clause <proposition subordonnée : subordinate clause>

propre[1] [prɔpr] *adj* **1** NET : clean, neat **2** : toilet trained, housebroken **3** : own <par sa propre faute : through his own fault> **4** : correct, proper <le mot propre : the correct word> **5 ~ à** : likely to <propre à lui faire plaisir : likely to please her> **6 ~ à** : characteristic of **7 ~ à** : suitable for

propre[2] *nm* **1** : cleanliness, neatness <cette maison sent le propre : this house smells clean> **2** : distinctive feature <être le propre de : to be peculiar to> **3 au propre** : literally

proprement [prɔprəmɑ̃] *adv* **1** : cleanly, neatly **2** : properly, correctly **3** : strictly, precisely <à proprement parler : strictly speaking> **4 proprement dit** : actual, as such <le débat proprement dit : the debate itself>

propret, -prette [prɔprɛ, -prɛt] *adj* : clean and neat

propreté [prɔprəte] *nf* : cleanliness, neatness

propriétaire [prɔprijetɛr] *nmf* **1** : owner, proprietor **2** : landlord, landlady *f*

propriété [prɔprijete] *nf* **1** : property <propriété privée : private property> **2** : ownership **3** CARACTÉRISTIQUE : property, characteristic **4** : appropriateness, suitability

propulser [prɔpylse] *vt* **1** : to propel **2** : to hurl, to fling

propulsif, -sive [prɔpylsif, -siv] *adj* : propellant, propulsive

propulsion [prɔpylsjɔ̃] *nf* : propulsion

prorata [prɔrata] *nms & pl* **au prorata de** : in proportion to

prorogation [prɔrɔgasjɔ̃] *nf* **1** : extension, deferment **2** : adjournment

proroger [prɔrɔʒe] {17} *vt* **1** : to extend, to defer **2** : to adjourn

prosaïque [prɔzaik] *adj* : prosaic, mundane

proscription [prɔskripsjɔ̃] *nf* **1** : ban, prohibition **2** : banishment

proscrire [prɔskrir] {33} *vt* **1** INTERDIRE : to ban, to prohibit **2** BANNIR : to banish

proscrit, -scrite [prɔskri, -skrit] *n* : outcast

prose [proz] *nf* : prose

prospecter [prɔspɛkte] *vt* **1** : to prospect (for oil, etc.) **2** : to canvass

prospecteur, -trice [prɔspɛktœr, -tris] *n* **1** : prospector **2** : canvasser

prospectus [prɔspɛktys] *nms & pl* : prospectus, leaflet

prospère [prɔspɛr] *adj* **1** : prosperous **2** : thriving, flourishing

prospérer [prɔspere] {87} *vi* : to flourish, to thrive

prospérité [prɔsperite] *nf* : prosperity

prostate [prɔstat] *nf* : prostate (gland)

prosterner [prɔstɛrne] *v* **se prosterner** *vr* : to bow down, to prostrate oneself

prostituée [prɔstitɥe] *nf* : prostitute

prostituer [prɔstitɥe] *vi* : to prostitute — **se prostituer** *vr* : to prostitute oneself

prostitution [prɔstitysjɔ̃] *nf* : prostitution

prostration [prɔstrasjɔ̃] *nf* : prostration

prostré, -trée [prɔstre] *adj* : prostrate

protagoniste [prɔtagɔnist] *nmf* : protagonist

protecteur[1], **-trice** [prɔtɛktœr, -tris] *adj* : protective

protecteur[2], **-trice** *n* **1** : protector, guardian **2** : patron **3 protecteur du citoyen** *Can* : ombudsman

protection [prɔtɛksjɔ̃] *nf* **1** : protection **2** : patronage, support

protectorat [prɔtɛktɔra] *nm* : protectorate

protégé, -gée [prɔteʒe] *n* : protégé

protéger [prɔteʒe] {64} *vt* **1** : to protect, to defend **2** PATRONNER : to support, to encourage — **se protéger** *vr* **~ de** : to protect oneself from

protéine [prɔtein] *nf* : protein

protestant, -tante [prɔtɛstɑ̃, -tɑ̃t] *adj & n* : Protestant — **protestantisme** [-tɑ̃tism] *nm*

protestataire [prɔtɛstatɛr] *nmf* : protester

protestation [prɔtɛstasjɔ̃] *nf* **1** : protest **2** : protestation, declaration

protester [prɔtɛste] *vi* **1** : to protest **2 ~ de** : to declare, to profess

prothèse [prɔtɛz] *nf* **1** : prosthesis **2 prothèse dentaire** : denture

protocolaire [prɔtɔkɔlɛr] *adj* : formal, conforming to protocol

protocole [prɔtɔkɔl] *nm* : protocol

proton [prɔtɔ̃] *nm* : proton

protoplasme [prɔtɔplasm] *nm* : protoplasm

prototype [prɔtɔtip] *nm* : prototype

protozoaire [prɔtɔzɔɛr] *nm* : protozoan

protubérance [prɔtyberɑ̃s] *nf* : protuberance
protubérant, -rante [prɔtyberɑ̃, -rɑ̃t] *adj* : protuberant, bulging, protruding
proue [pru] *nf* : prow, bow (of a ship)
prouesse [pruɛs] *nf* EXPLOIT : feat, exploit
prouver [pruve] *vt* **1** ÉTABLIR : to prove **2** MONTRER : to show, to demonstrate
provenance [prɔvnɑ̃s] *nf* **1** : source, origin **2 en provenance de** : from <train en provenance de Paris : train (arriving) from Paris>
provençal, -çale [prɔvɑ̃sal] *adj, mpl* **-çaux** [-so] : Provençal
Provençal, -çale *n* : Provençal
provenir [prɔvnir] {92} *vi* **1 ∼ de** : to come from (a place) **2 ∼ de** : to result from, to stem from
proverbe [prɔvɛrb] *nm* : proverb
proverbial, -biale [prɔvɛrbjal] *adj, mpl* **-biaux** [-bjo] : proverbial — **proverbialement** [-bjalmɑ̃] *adv*
providence [prɔvidɑ̃s] *nf* : providence — **providentiel, -tielle** [-dɑ̃sjɛl] *adj*
province [prɔvɛ̃s] *nf* : province — **provincial, -ciale** [-vɛ̃sjal] *adj, mpl* **-ciaux** [-sjo]
proviseur [prɔvizœr] *nm France* : principal (of a school)
provision [prɔvizjɔ̃] *nf* **1** : stock, supply <faire provision de : to stock up on> **2** : advance, retainer **3** : funds *pl* (in a bank) <un chèque sans provision : a bad check> **4 provisions** *nfpl* : provisions, food
provisoire [prɔvizwar] *adj* : provisional, temporary, interim — **provisoirement** [-zwarmɑ̃] *adv*
provocant, -cante [prɔvɔkɑ̃, -kɑ̃t] *adj* : provocative
provocateur¹, -trice [prɔvɔkatœr, -tris] *adj* : provocative, challenging
provocateur² *nm* : agitator, troublemaker
provocation [prɔvɔkasjɔ̃] *nf* : provocation
provoquer [prɔvɔke] *vt* **1** : to cause, to give rise to <provoquer des rires : to provoke laughter> **2** : to provoke, to stir up, to trigger
proximité [prɔksimite] *nf* : proximity, nearness, closeness
pruche [pryʃ] *nf Can* : hemlock (tree)
prude¹ [pryd] *adj* : prudish
prude² *nf* : prude
prudemment [prydamɑ̃] *adv* : carefully, cautiously
prudence [prydɑ̃s] *nf* **1** : care, caution **2 avec ∼** : cautiously
prudent, -dente [prydɑ̃, -dɑ̃t] *adj* **1** AVISÉ : prudent, sensible **2** : careful, cautious <soyez prudents : be careful>
prune¹ [pryn] *adj* : plum-colored
prune² *nf* **1** : plum **2** *Can* : bruise
pruneau [pryno] *nm, pl* **pruneaux 1** : prune **2** *Can* : plum
prunelle [prynɛl] *nf* : pupil (of the eye)
prunier [prynje] *nm* : plum tree
psalmodie [psalmɔdi] *nf* : chanting, droning
psalmodier [psalmɔdje] {96} *v* **1** : to chant **2** : to drone
psaume [psom] *nm* : psalm
pseudonyme [psødɔnim] *nm* : pseudonym
psoriasis [psɔrjazis] *nm* : psoriasis
psychanalyse [psikanaliz] *nf* : psychoanalysis — **psychanalyste** [-list] *nmf*
psychanalyser [psikanalize] *vt* : to psychoanalyse
psychanalytique [psikanalitik] *adj* : psychoanalytic
psyché [psiʃe] *nf* : psyche
psychédélique [psikedelik] *adj* : psychedelic
psychiatre [psikjatr] *nmf* : psychiatrist
psychiatrie [psikjatri] *nf* : psychiatry
psychiatrique [psikjatrik] *adj* : psychiatric
psychique [psiʃik] *adj* : psychic, mental
psychisme [psiʃism] *nm* : psyche, mind
psychologie [psikɔlɔʒi] *nf* : psychology
psychologique [psikɔlɔʒik] *adj* : psychological — **psychologiquement** [-ʒikmɑ̃] *adv*
psychologue [psikɔlɔg] *nmf* : psychologist
psychopathe¹ [psikɔpat] *adj* : psychopathic
psychopathe² *nmf* : psychopath
psychose [psikoz] *nf* : psychosis
psychosomatique [psikɔsɔmatik] *adj* : psychosomatic
psychothérapeute [psikɔterapøt] *nmf* : psychotherapist
psychothérapie [psikɔterapi] *nf* : psychotherapy
psychotique [psikɔtik] *adj & nmf* : psychotic
pseudonyme¹ [psødɔnim] *adj* : pseudonymous
pseudonyme² *nm* : pseudonym
pu [py] *pp* → **pouvoir**
puant, puante [pɥɑ̃, -ɑ̃t] *adj* **1** : foul-smelling, stinking **2** *fam* : conceited, obnoxious
puanteur [pɥɑ̃tœr] *nf* : stink, stench
puberté [pybɛrte] *nf* : puberty
pubien, -bienne [pybjɛ̃, -bjɛn] *adj* : pubic
public¹, -blique [pyblik] *adj* : public
public² *nm* **1** : public <le grand public : the general public> **2** : audience, spectators *pl*
publication [pyblikasjɔ̃] *nf* : publication
publiciste [pyblisist] *nmf* : publicist, advertising executive
publicitaire [pyblisitɛr] *adj* : advertising, promotional

publicité [pyblisite] *nf* **1** : publicity **2** : advertisement, commercial
publier [pyblije] {96} *vt* : to publish
publiquement [pyblikmɑ̃] *adv* : publicly
puce [pys] *nf* **1** : flea **2** : computer chip
puceron [pysrɔ̃] *nm* : aphid
pudding *or* **pouding** [pudiŋ] *nm* : pudding
pudeur [pydœr] *nf* **1** : modesty, decency **2** : sense of propriety, tact
pudibond, -bonde [pydibɔ̃, -bɔ̃d] *adj* : prudish, prim
pudibonderie [pydibɔ̃dri] *nf* : prudishness
pudique [pydik] *adj* **1** : modest, decent **2** : restrained, discreet
pudiquement [pydikmɑ̃] *adv* **1** : modestly **2** : discreetly
puer [pɥe] *vi* : to smell, to stink — *vt* : to reek of
puéril, -rile [pɥeril] *adj* : childish, puerile
puérilité [pɥerilite] *nf* : childishness
pugilat [pyʒila] *nm* : fistfight
pugnace [pygnas] *adj* : pugnacious
puis [pɥi] *adv* **1** ENSUITE : then, afterwards, next **2 et puis** : and besides **3 et puis après?** *or* **et puis quoi?** *fam* : so?, so what?
puisard [pɥizar] *nm* : cesspool
puiser [pɥize] *vt* **~ dans** : to draw from, to dip into
puisque [pɥiskə] *conj* **1** : since, as, because <puisque vous insistez : since you insist> **2** (*used as an intensifier*) <puisque je te le dis! : because I'm telling you so!>
puissance [pɥisɑ̃s] *nf* : power
puissant, -sante [pɥisɑ̃, -sɑ̃t] *adj* : powerful
puisse [pɥis], *etc.* → **pouvoir**
puits [pɥi] *nms & pl* **1** : well <puits artésien : artesian well> <puits de pétrole : oil well> **2** : shaft <puits de mine : mine shaft> **3 puits de science** : font of knowledge, learned person
pull *or* **pull–over** [pyl, pylɔvɛr] *nm France* : pullover sweater
pullulement [pylylmɑ̃] *nm* : proliferation
pulluler [pylyle] *vi* **1** SE MULTIPLIER : to proliferate **2** GROUILLER : to swarm, to teem
pulmonaire [pylmɔnɛr] *adj* : pulmonary, lung
pulpe [pylp] *nf* : pulp
pulpeux, -peuse [pylpø, -pøz] *adj* : pulpy
pulsation [pylsasjɔ̃] *nf* **1** : beat, pulsation **2** POULS : pulse
pulsion [pylsjɔ̃] *nf* : drive, urge
pulvérisateur [pylverizatœr] *nm* VAPORISATEUR : spray, atomizer
pulvériser [pylverize] *vt* **1** : to pulverize **2** : to spray **3** : to demolish (an argument, etc.)
puma [pyma] *nm* : puma, cougar
punaise [pynɛz] *nf* **1** : bug <punaise de lit : bedbug> **2** : thumbtack
punch [pɔ̃ʃ] *nm* **1** : punch (drink) **2** [pœnʃ] : punch, blow (of a boxer, etc.) **3** : drive, energy
punir [pynir] *vt* **1** : to punish **2** *Can* : to penalize (in sports)
punissable [pynisabl] *adj* : punishable
punitif, -tive [pynitif, -tiv] *adj* : punitive
punition [pynisjɔ̃] *nf* **1** : punishment **2** *Can* : penalty (in sports)
pupe [pyp] *nf* : pupa
pupille[1] [pypij] *nmf* : ward (of the court), orphan
pupille[2] *nf* : pupil (of the eye)
pupitre [pypitr] *nm* **1** BUREAU : desk **2** LUTRIN : lectern **3** : console, keyboard, control panel **4** : music stand
pur, pure [pyr] *adj* : pure — **purement** [pyrmɑ̃] *adv*
purée [pyre] *nf* **1** : puree <purée de pommes de terre : mashed potatoes> **2 purée de pois** : thick fog, pea soup
pureté [pyrte] *nf* : purity
purgatif[1], **-tive** [pyrgatif, -tiv] *adj* : purgative
purgatif[2] *nm* : purgative, laxative
purgatoire [pyrgatwar] *nm* : purgatory
purge [pyrʒ] *nf* : purge, purging
purger [pyrʒe] {17} *vt* **1** : to drain (a radiator, etc.), to bleed (brakes) **2** : to rid of, to purge **3** : to purge, to give a laxative to **4** : to serve (a jail sentence)
purificateur [pyrifikatœr] *nm* : purifier <purificateur d'air : air purifier>
purification [pyrifikasjɔ̃] *nf* : purification
purifier [pyrifje] {96} *vt* : to purify — **se purifier** *vr*
purin [pyrɛ̃] *nm* : liquid manure
puritain[1], **-taine** [pyritɛ̃, -tɛn] *adj* : puritanical
puritain[2], **-taine** *n* : puritan
pur–sang [pyrsɑ̃] *nms & pl* : Thoroughbred
pus [py] *nm* : pus
pusillanime [pyzilanim] *adj* : pusillanimous
pustule [pystyl] *nf* : pustule
putain [pytɛ̃] *nf usu vulgar* : whore
putois [pytwa] *nms & pl* : polecat
putréfier [pytrefje] {96} *vt* : to putrefy — **se putréfier** *vr* : to putrefy, to rot
putride [pytrid] *adj* : putrid, rotten
puzzle [pœzl] *nm* : jigsaw puzzle
Pygmée [pigme] *nmf* : Pygmy
pyjama [piʒama] *nm* : pajamas *pl*
pylône [pilon] *nm* : pylon
pyramide [piramid] *nf* : pyramid
pyromane [pirɔman] *nmf* : pyromaniac
pyromanie [pirɔmani] *nf* : pyromania
pyrotechnie [pirɔtɛkni] *nf* : fireworks *pl*, pyrotechnics *pl*
python [pitɔ̃] *nm* : python

Q

q [ky] *nm* : q, the 17th letter of the alphabet
quadrant [kwadrɑ̃] *nm* : quadrant
quadrilatère [kwadrilatɛr] *nm* : quadrilateral, quadrangle (in geometry)
quadrillage [kadrijaʒ] *nm* : crisscross pattern, grid
quadrillé, -lée [kadrije] *adj* : squared <papier quadrillé : graph paper>
quadriller [kadrije] *vt* **1** : to mark into squares **2** : to surround, to control (an area)
quadrupède [k̃w̃adrypɛd] *nm* : quadruped
quadruple [k(w)adrypl] *adj* : quadruple
quadrupler [k(w)adryple] *v* : to quadruple
quadruplés, -plées [k(w)adryple] *npl* : quadruplets
quai [kɛ] *nm* **1** : quay, wharf **2** : platform (at a railway station)
qualification [kalifikasjɔ̃] *nf* : qualification
qualifié, -fiée [kalifje] *adj* : qualified, skilled
qualifier [kalifje] {96} *vt* **1** : to qualify **2** CARACTÉRISER : to describe, to call — **se qualifier** *vr*
qualité [kalite] *nf* **1** : quality, excellence **2** : quality, property, attribute **3** : capacity, role <en qualité d'observateur : in his role as an observer>
quand[1] [kɑ̃] *adv* : when <quand partez-vous? : when are you leaving?> <je sais quand ils arriveront : I know when they will arrive>
quand[2] *conj* **1** : when <quand je la verrai : when I see her> **2** (*used for emphasis*) <quand je vous le disais! : I told you so!> **3 quand même** : still, even so
quant [kɑ̃] **~ à** : as for, as to, regarding
quant–à–soi [kɑ̃taswa] *nm* : reserve, aloofness <rester sur son quant-à-soi : to keep one's distance>
quantifier [kɑ̃tifje] {96}*vt* : to quantify — **quantifiable** [-tifjabl] *adj*
quantitatif, -tive [kɑ̃titatif, -tiv] *adj* : quantitative — **quantitativement** [-tivmɑ̃] *adv*
quantité [kɑ̃tite] *nf* : quantity, amount, number <une quantité de : a lot of>
quantum [kwɑ̃tɔm] *nm, pl* **quanta** : quantum <théorie des quanta : quantum theory>
quarantaine [karɑ̃tɛn] *nf* **1** : quarantine **2 avoir la quarantaine** : to be in one's forties **3 une quarantaine de** : about forty
quarante [karɑ̃t] *adj & nms & pl* : forty
quarantième [karɑ̃tjɛm] *adj & nmf & nm* : fortieth
quart [kar] *nm* **1** : quarter, forth <un kilo et quart : a kilo and a quarter> **2** (*in expressions of time*) : quarter <deux heures et quart : a quarter after two> <un quart d'heure : fifteen minutes>
quarte–arrière [kartarjɛr] *nm Can* : quarterback (in football)
quartier [kartje] *nm* **1** : piece, segment, quarter <un quartier de pomme : a piece of apple> <quartier de devant : forequarter> **2** : area, district **3 quartier général** : headquarters (in the army, etc.)
quartz [kwarts] *nm* : quartz
quasi [kazi] *adv* : nearly, almost <quasi impossible : practically impossible>
quasiment [kazimɑ̃] *adv* : nearly, almost
quatorze[1] [katɔrz] *adj* **1** : fourteen **2** : fourteenth <le quatorze février : the fourteenth of February>
quatorze[2] *nms & pl* : fourteen
quatorzième [katɔrzjɛm] *adj & nmf & nm* : fourteenth
quatre[1] [katr] *adj* **1** : four **2** : fourth <le quatre avril : the fourth of April>
quatre[2] *nms & pl* **1** : four **2 à quatre pattes** : on all fours
quatre–vingt–dix [katrəvɛ̃dis] *adj & nms & pl* : ninety
quatre–vingt–dixième [katrəvɛ̃dizjɛm] *adj & nmf & nm* : ninetieth
quatre–vingtième [katrəvɛ̃tjɛm] *adj & nmf & nm* : eightieth
quatre–vingts [katrəvɛ̃] (**quatre-vingt** *with another numeral adjective*) *adj & nms & pl* : eighty <quatre-vingt-un : eighty-one> <quatre-vingts personnes : eighty people>
quatrième[1] [katrijɛm] *adj & nmf* **1** : fourth **2 en quatrième vitesse** : in a hurry
quatrième[2] *nmf* : fourth (in a series)
quatuor [kwatɥɔr] *nm* : quartet
que[1] [kə] *adv* **1** : how <que c'est beau! : how beautiful!> **2** : why <que n'est-il venu? : why didn't he come?>
que[2] *conj* **1** : that <il a avoué qu'il avait tort : he admitted that he was wrong> **2** : than <travailler plus que nécessaire : to work harder than necessary> **3** (*used in a subjunctive clause expressing an order or desire*) <qu'elle vienne! : tell her to come!> **4** : whether <qu'il fasse soleil ou non : whether it's sunny or not> **5** → **ne**
que[3] *pron* **1** : who, whom, that <l'homme que vous aimez : the man that you love> **2** : that, which <c'était la seule chose qu'il pouvait faire : it was the only thing that he could do> **3** : what <que faire? : what should we do?> <qu'est-ce que tu as? : what's wrong?> <qu'est-ce que c'est que ça? : what's that?>
québécois, -coise [kebekwa, -kwaz] *adj* : Quebec, from or of Quebec

Québécois, -coise *n* : Quebecer, person from Quebec
quel[1], **quelle** [kɛl] *adj* **1** : what, which <quelle heure est-il? : what time is it?> **2** (*used as an intensifier*) <quel dommage! : what a pity!> **3** : whatever, whichever, whoever <quelle que soit la raison : whatever the reason may be>
quel[2], **quelle** *pron* : who, which, one <de quel s'agit-il? : which one are you talking about?>
quelconque [kɛlkɔ̃k] *adj* **1** : some sort of, any <une quelconque mesure : some sort of action> **2** : ordinary <un être quelconque : an ordinary person>
quelque[1] [kɛlkə] *adv* **1** : about, approximately <quelque 200 personnes : about 200 people> **2** : however <quelque important qu'il soit : however important he may be>
quelque[2] *adj* **1** : a few, several, some <il a dit quelques mots : he said a few words> **2 quelque chose** : something **3 quelque part** : somewhere **4 quelque peu** : somewhat <quelque peu déçu : somewhat disappointed>
quelquefois [kɛlkəfwa] *adv* : sometimes
quelques–uns, quelques–unes [kɛlkəzœ̃, kɛlkəzyn] *pron* : some, a few
quelqu'un [kɛlkœ̃] *pron* **1** : someone, somebody <quelqu'un d'autre : someone else> **2** : anyone, anybody <y a-t-il quelqu'un? : is anyone there?>
quémander [kemɑ̃de] *vt* : to beg for
qu'en–dira–t–on [kɑ̃diratɔ̃] *nms & pl* : gossip
quenouille [kənuj] *nf Can* : cattail (plant)
querelle [kərɛl] *nf* : quarrel
quereller [kərele] *v* **se quereller** *vr* : to quarrel
querelleur, -leuse [kərɛlœr, -løz] *adj* : quarrelsome
question [kɛstjɔ̃] *nf* **1** : question <poser une question : to ask a question> **2** : matter, issue
questionnaire [kɛstjɔnɛr] *nm* : questionnaire
questionner [kɛstjɔne] *vt* : to question — **se questionner** *vr*
quétaine [ketɛn] *adj Can fam* : hokey, corny
quête [kɛt] *nf* **1** : quest, search **2** : collection (of money)
quêter [kete] *vt* : to seek, to solicit (favors, money, etc.) — *vi* : to take a collection
quêteur, -teuse [kɛtœr, -tøz] *n* : collector
quêteux, -teuse [kɛtœ, -tøz] *n Can* : beggar
queue [kø] *nf* **1** : tail **2** : tail end, rear, bottom **3** : stem, stalk **4** : handle (of a pot) **5** : cue (in billiards) **6** : line <faire la queue : to stand in line> **7 queue d'aronde** : dovetail **8 queue de cheval** : ponytail
qui [ki] *pron* **1** : who, whom <qui est-ce? : who is it?> <à qui de droit : to whom it may concern> **2** : which, that <un livre qui est sur la table : a book which is on the table> **3 qui que** : whoever, whomever
quiconque [kikɔ̃k] *pron* **1** : whoever, whomever **2** : anyone, anybody
quiétude [kjetyd] *nf* : quiet, tranquility
quignon [kiɲɔ̃] *nm* : hunk, heel (of a loaf of bread)
quille [kij] *nf* **1** : keel **2 quilles** *nfpl or* **jeu de quilles** : ninepins
quincaillerie [kɛ̃kajri] *nf* **1** : hardware **2** : hardware store
quincaillier, -lière [kɛ̃kaje, -jɛr] *n* : hardware dealer
quinine [kinin] *nf* : quinine
quinquagénaire [kɛ̃kaʒenɛr] *nmf* : person in his or her fifties
quinquennal, -nale [kɛ̃kenal] *adj, mpl* **-naux** [-no] : five-year <plan quinquennal : five-year plan>
quintal [kɛ̃tal] *nm, pl* **quintaux** [kɛ̃to] : quintal
quinte [kɛ̃t] *nf or* **quinte de toux** : coughing fit
quintessence [kɛ̃tesɑ̃s] *nf* : quintessence — **quintessentiel, -tielle** [-sɑ̃sjɛl] *adv*
quintette [kɛ̃tɛt] *nm* : quintet
quintuple [kɛ̃typl] *adj* : quintuple, fivefold
quintupler [kɛ̃typle] *vt* : to quintuple
quintuplés, -plées [kɛ̃typle] *npl* : quintuplets
quinzaine [kɛ̃zɛn] *nf* **1 une quinzaine de** : about fifteen **2 une quinzaine de jours** : two weeks, a fortnight
quinze[1] [kɛ̃z] *adj* **1** : fifteen **2** : fifteenth <le quinze juin : June fifteenth>
quinze[2] *nms & pl* : fifteen
quinzième [kɛ̃zjɛm] *adj & nmf & nm* : fifteenth
quiproquo [kiprɔko] *nm* **1** : mistake, mistaken identity **2** MALENTENDU : misunderstanding
quiscale [kɥiskal] *nm* : grackle
quittance [kitɑ̃s] *nf* : receipt
quitte [kit] *adj* **1** : released from debt <être quitte envers : to be squared away with, to be quits with> <en être quitte pour : to get away with> **2 ~ à** : even if, at the risk of
quitter [kite] *vt* **1** : to leave, to abandon, to separate from **2** : to leave, to depart **3 ne quittez pas** : hold the (telephone) line — **se quitter** *vr* : to part, to separate
qui–vive [kiviv] *nms & pl* **être sur le qui–vive** : to be on the alert
quoi [kwa] *pron* **1** : what <à quoi bon? : what's the point?> <je sais à quoi tu penses : I know what you're thinking

about> **2** (*used as an interjection or interrogative)* : what!, what? **3 quoi que** : whatever <quoi qu'il arrive : whatever happens>
quoique [kwakə] *conj* : although, though, notwithstanding
quolibet [kɔlibɛ] *nm* : gibe, jeer
quorum [k(w)orɔm] *nm* : quorum
quota [kɔta] *nm* **1** : quota **2** : **avoir son quota** *Can fam* : to have had enough
quote–part [kɔtpar] *nf, pl* **quotes–parts** : share <payer sa quote-part : to pay one's share>
quotidien[1], -dienne [kɔtidjɛ̃, -djɛn] *adj* **1** : daily, every day **2** : everyday, routine
quotidien[2] *nm* **1** : daily (newspaper) <quotidien populaire : tabloid> **2 le quotidien** : everyday life
quotidiennement [kɔtidjɛnmɑ̃] *adv* : daily
quotient [kɔsjɑ̃] *nm* : quotient

R

r [ɛr] *nm* : r, the 18th letter of the alphabet
rabâcher [rabaʃe] *vt* : to repeat endlessly, to keep harping on — *vi* : to keep repeating oneself
rabais [rabɛ] *nms & pl* **1** RÉDUCTION : reduction, discount **2 au ~** : at a discount, cut-rate
rabaisser [rabɛse] *vt* **1** : to reduce, to lower, to lessen **2** DÉPRÉCIER : to belittle
rabat [raba] *nm* : flap
rabat–joie [rabaʒwa] *nmfs & pl* : killjoy, spoilsport
rabattre [rabatr] {12} *vt* **1** : to reduce, to diminish **2** : to bring down, to pull down **3** : to fold back — **se rabattre** *vr* **1** : to fold up, to go back (by itself) **2 ~ sur** : to fall back on, to make do with
rabbin [rabɛ̃] *nm* : rabbi
râblé, -blée [rable] *adj* : heavyset, stocky
rabot [rabo] *nm* : plane (tool)
raboter [rabɔte] *vt* : to plane (down)
raboteux, -teuse [rabɔtø, -tøz] *adj* INÉGAL : rough, uneven
rabougri, -grie [rabugri] *adj* **1** : stunted, puny **2** : wizened, shriveled (up)
rabrouer [rabrue] *vt* : to snub, to slight
racaille [rakaj] *nf* : riffraff, rabble
raccommoder [rakɔmɔde] *vt* RAPIÉCER : to mend, to patch up — **se raccommoder** *vr fam* : to make up (with someone)
raccompagner [rakɔ̃paɲe] *vt* : to take (someone) back, to see home
raccord [rakɔr] *nm* **1** : linkage, connection **2** : touch-up (in painting)
raccordement [rakɔrdəmɑ̃] *nm* : linking, connecting, joining (up)
raccorder [rakɔrde] *vt* : to connect, to link up — **se raccorder** *vr*
raccourci [rakursi] *nm* **1** : shortcut **2 en ~** : in short, briefly
raccourcir [rakursir] *vt* : to shorten — *vi* : to become shorter, to shrink
raccrocher [rakrɔʃe] *vt* **1** : to hang back up **2** : to rescue, to save at the last minute — *vi* : to hang up — **se raccrocher** *vr* : to hang on, to grab hold
race [ras] *nf* **1** : race <la race humaine : the human race> **2** : breed (of animals) **3** : line, descent **4 de ~** : Thoroughbred
racé, -cée [rase] *adj* **1** : Thoroughbred **2** DISTINGUÉ : distinguished
rachat [raʃa] *nm* **1** : repurchase **2** : atonement
racheter [raʃte] {20} *vt* **1** : to buy back **2** : to buy more of **3** : to redeem **4** : to atone for — **se racheter** *vr* : to redeem oneself
rachitisme [raʃitism] *nm* : rickets
racial, -ciale [rasjal] *adj, mpl* **raciaux** [rasjo] : racial, race — **racialement** [-sjalmɑ̃] *adv*
racine [rasin] *nf* **1** : root **2** : origin, source **3 racine carrée** : square root
racisme [rasism] *nm* : racism
raciste [rasist] *adj & nmf* : racist
racket [rakɛt] *nm* : racket, racketeering
racketteur [rakɛtœr] *nm* : racketeer
raclée [rakle] *nf fam* : beating, thrashing
racler [rakle] *vt* : to scrape (off), to scrape against
racloir [raklwar] *nm* GRATTOIR : scraper
racolage [rakɔlaʒ] *nm* : canvassing (in politics)
racoler [rakɔle] *vt* : to solicit (support, etc.), to canvass
racoleur, -leuse [rakɔlœr, -løz] *adj* : enticing, eye-catching
racontars [rakɔ̃tar] *nmpl* : gossip
raconter [rakɔ̃te] *vt* **1** CONTER : to tell, to relate **2** : to say, to talk about <qu'est-ce que tu racontes? : what are you talking about?>
raconteur, -teuse [rakɔ̃tœr, -tøz] *n* : raconteur, storyteller
racornir [rakɔrnir] *vt* : to toughen, to harden — **se racornir** *vr* **1** : to become hardened **2** SE RATATINER : to shrivel up
radar [radar] *nm* : radar

rade [rad] *nf* **1** : harbor **2 laisser en rade** : to leave stranded

radeau [rado] *nm, pl* **radeaux** : raft

radial, -diale [radjal] *adj, mpl* **radiaux** [radjo] : radial

radiant, -diante [radjɑ̃, -djɑ̃t] *adj* : radiant

radiateur [radjatœr] *nm* **1** : radiator **2** : heater <radiateur électrique : electric heater>

radiation [radjasjɔ̃] *nf* **1** : radiation **2** : crossing off (from a list)

radical[1], **-cale** [radikal] *adj, mpl* **-caux** [-ko] : radical — **radicalement** [-kalmɑ̃] *adv*

radical[2], **-cale** *n* : radical

radier [radje] {96} *vt* **1** : to radiate **2** RAYER : to cross off <radier un avocat : to disbar a lawyer>

radieux, -dieuse [radjø, -djøz] *adj* **1** : radiant, glowing (with joy, etc.) **2** : glorious, dazzling — **radieusement** [-djøzmɑ̃] *adv*

radin[1], **-dine** [radɛ̃, -din] *adj fam* : stingy

radin[2], **-dine** *n fam* : skinflint, cheapskate

radio[1] [radjo] *nf* **1** : radio **2** RADIOGRAPHIE : X ray

radio[2] *nm* : radio operator

radioactif, -tive [radjɔaktif, -tiv] *adj* : radioactive — **radioactivité** [-tivite] *nf*

radioamateur [radjɔamatœr] *nm* : ham (radio operator)

radiodiffuser [radjɔdifyze] *vt* : to broadcast

radiodiffusion [radjɔdifyzjɔ̃] *nf* : broadcasting

radiographie [radjɔgrafi] *nf* : radiography, X ray

radiographier [radjɔgrafje] {96} *vt* : to X-ray

radiologie [radjɔlɔʒi] *nf* : radiology

radiologique [radjɔlɔʒik] *adj* : radiological, radiologic

radiologiste [radjɔlɔʒist] *or* **radiologue** [radjɔlɔg] *nmf* : radiologist

radis [radi] *nm* : radish

radium [radjɔm] *nm* : radium

radja [radʒa] → **rajah**

radon [radɔ̃] *nm* : radon

radoter [radɔte] *vi* : to ramble on

radoucir [radusir] *vt* : to soften (up) — **se radoucir** *vr* **1** : to grow milder **2** : to calm down

rafale [rafal] *nf* **1** BOURRASQUE : gust (of wind, etc.) **2** : burst (of gunfire)

raffermir [rafɛrmir] *vt* **1** TONIFIER : to firm up, to tone up **2** : to strengthen, to reinforce

raffinage [rafinaʒ] *nm* : refining

raffiné, -née [rafine] *adj* : refined, sophisticated

raffinement [rafinmɑ̃] *nm* : refinement

raffiner [rafine] *vt* : to refine — *vi* ~ **sur** : to be meticulous about

raffinerie [rafinri] *nf* : refinery

raffoler [rafɔle] *vi* ~ **de** : to adore, to be crazy about

raffut [rafy] *nm fam* : din, racket

rafiot [rafjo] *nm fam* : old vessel, tub

rafistoler [rafistɔle] *vt fam* : to patch up, to fix up

rafle [rafl] *nf* DESCENTE : (police) raid

rafler [rafle] *vt fam* **1** : to swipe **2** : to walk off with <elle a raflé tous les prix : she walked off with all the prizes>

rafraîchir [rafrɛʃir] *vt* : to refresh, to cool, to chill — **se rafraîchir** *vr* **1** : to get cooler **2** : to freshen up **3 se rafraîchir la mémoire** : to refresh one's memory

rafraîchissant, -sante [rafrɛʃisɑ̃, -sɑ̃t] *adj* : refreshing

rafraîchissement [rafrɛʃismɑ̃] *nm* **1** : cooling **2 rafraîchissements** *nmpl* : cool drinks, refreshments

ragaillardir [ragajardir] *vt* REVIGORER : to perk up, to invigorate — **se ragaillardir** *vr* : to perk up

rage [raʒ] *nf* **1** : rage, fury <mettre en rage : to enrage> **2** : rabies **3 avoir la rage de** : to have a passion for **4 faire rage** : to rage (of storms, etc.)

rager [raʒe] {17} *vi* : to rage, to fume

rageur, -geuse [raʒœr, -ʒøz] *adj* **1** FURIEUX : furious **2** COLÉREUX : bad-tempered

rageusement [raʒøzmɑ̃] *adv* : furiously

ragot [rago] *nm fam* COMMÉRAGE : gossip, malicious rumor

ragoût [ragu] *nm* : ragout, stew

ragoûtant, -tante [ragutɑ̃, -tɑ̃t] *adj* **peu ragoûtant** : unappetizing, not very pleasant

ragtime [ragtajm] *nm* : ragtime

rai [rɛ] *nm* : ray, shaft (of light)

raid [rɛd] *nm* : raid <raid aérien : air raid>

raide[1] [rɛd] *adv* **1** : steeply **2 tomber raide** : to drop dead

raide[2] *adj* **1** : stiff, rigid **2** : taut, tight **3** : steep **4** : straight

raideur [rɛdœr] *nf* **1** : stiffness <avec raideur : stiffly> **2** : steepness

raidir [rɛdir] *vt* : to stiffen, to tighten, to tense (up) — **se raidir** *vr*

raie [rɛ] *nf* **1** : stripe **2** : part (in hair) **3** : ray, skate (fish)

raifort [rɛfɔr] *nm* : horseradish

rail [raj] *nm* **1** : rail, track **2 remettre sur les rails** : to put back on track

railler [raje] *vt* : to make fun of, to jeer at — **se railler** *vr* : to scoff

raillerie [rajri] *nf* : mockery

railleur, -leuse [rajœr, -jøz] *adj* MOQUEUR : mocking, derisive

rainer [rene] *vt* : to groove, to cut a groove in

rainure [rɛnyr] *nf* : groove, slot

raisin [rɛzɛ̃] *nm* **1** : grape **2 raisin sec** : raisin **3 raisin de Corinthe** : currant

raison [rɛzɔ̃] *nf* **1** : reason, rationality, good sense <as-tu perdu la raison? : are you out of your mind?> <comme de raison : as one might expect> <à juste raison : justifiably> **2** MOTIF : reason, motive, grounds *pl* **3** : rate, ratio <à raison de deux par semaine : at the rate of two a week> **4 avoir raison** : to be right **5 en raison de** : due to, because of

raisonnable [rɛzɔnabl] *adj* **1** SENSÉ : sensible, reasonable **2** : moderate, fair <à des prix raisonnables : moderately priced>

raisonnablement [rɛzɔnabləmɑ̃] *adv* **1** : reasonably **2** : moderately, fairly

raisonné, -née [rɛzɔne] *adj* : well thought-out, reasoned

raisonnement [rɛzɔnmɑ̃] *nm* **1** : reasoning **2** ARGUMENTATION : argument, rationale

raisonner [rɛzɔne] *vi* **1** PENSER : to reason, to think **2** : to argue, to reason <raisonner sur : to argue about> — *vt* : to reason with — **se raisonner** *vr* : to try to be reasonable, to reason with oneself

raja *or* **rajah** [raʒa] *nm* : rajah

rajeunir [raʒœnir] *vt* **1** : to rejuvenate, to make (someone) look younger **2** : to modernize, to update — *vi* : to look younger — **se rajeunir** *vr*

rajeunissement [raʒœnismɑ̃] *nm* : rejuvenation

rajout [raʒu] *nm* : addition

rajouter [raʒute] *vt* **1** : to add **2 en ～** : to exaggerate

rajuster [raʒyste] *vt* **1** : to adjust, to straighten (clothing, etc.) **2** RÉAJUSTER : to readjust

râle [ral] *nm* **1** : groan **2 râle de la mort** : death rattle

ralenti[1], -tie [ralɑ̃ti] *adj* : slow, idling

ralenti[2] *nm* **1** : slow motion **2** : idling speed (of an automobile)

ralentir [ralɑ̃tir] *v* : to slow down, to decelerate

ralentissement [ralɑ̃tismɑ̃] *nm* : slowing down, slowdown

râler [rale] *vi* **1** : to groan **2** *fam* : to moan, to grumble

ralliement [ralimɑ̃] *nm* : rallying

rallier [ralje] {96} *vt* **1** : to rally (troops, etc.) **2** : to win over **3** : to rejoin — **se rallier** *vr* **～ à** : to rally to, to join up with

rallonge [ralɔ̃ʒ] *nf* **1** : extension **2** : extension cord **3** : leaf (of a table)

rallonger [ralɔ̃ʒe] {17} *vt* : to lengthen, to extend — *vi fam* : to get longer

rallumer [ralyme] *vt* **1** : to relight, to turn back on **2** : to rekindle, to revive

ramage [ramaʒ] *nm* **1** : song (of a bird) **2 ramages** *nmpl* : floral pattern (on cloth, etc.)

ramassage [ramasaʒ] *nm* **1** : collection **2** : picking, gathering **3 ramassage scolaire** *France* : school bus service

ramassé, -sée [ramase] *adj* **1** : squat, stocky **2** : compact (of style, etc.)

ramasser [ramase] *vt* **1** : to pick up, to collect **2** CUEILLIR : to pick, to gather <ramasser des framboises : to pick raspberries> — **se ramasser** *vr* SE PELOTONNER : to huddle up, to crouch

ramassis [ramasi] *nm* : bunch, pile, jumble

rambarde [rɑ̃bard] *nf* : guardrail

rame [ram] *nf* **1** AVIRON : oar **2** : train <rame de métro : subway train> **3** : ream (of paper)

rameau [ramo] *nm, pl* **rameaux 1** : branch, bough **2 dimanche des Rameaux** : Palm Sunday

ramener [ramne] {52} *vt* **1** : to bring back, to take back **2** : to restore <ramener la semaine de travail à 32 heures : to restore the work week to 32 hours> **3** RÉDUIRE : to reduce **4** : to draw up, to pull back — **se ramener** *vr* **～ à** : to come down to, to be nothing more than

ramer [rame] *vi* : to row

rameur, -meuse [ramœr, -møz] *n* : rower

rami [rami] *nm* : rummy (card game)

ramification [ramifikasjɔ̃] *nf* : ramification

ramifier [ramifje] {96} *v* **se ramifier** *vr* : to branch out, to ramify

ramolli, -lie [ramɔli] *adj* **1** : soft, softened **2** *fam* : soft in the head

ramollir [ramɔlir] *vt* : to soften — **se ramollir** *vr*

ramoner [ramɔne] *vt* : to sweep (a chimney), to clean out (pipes, etc.)

ramoneur [ramɔnœr] *nm* : chimney sweep

rampe [rɑ̃p] *nf* **1** : ramp **2** : banister, handrail **3** : footlights *pl* **4 rampe de lancement** : launching pad

ramper [rɑ̃pe] *vi* **1** : to crawl **2** : to creep (of a plant) **3** S'ABAISSER : to grovel, to lower oneself

ramure [ramyr] *nf* **1** : branches *pl* (of a tree) **2** : antlers *pl*

rancard [rɑ̃kar] *nm France fam* **1** : rendezvous, date **2** : lowdown, tip

rancart [rɑ̃kar] *nm* **mettre au rancart** *fam* : to discard, to scrap

rance [rɑ̃s] *adj* : rancid

ranch [rɑ̃tʃ] *nm* : ranch

rancir [rɑ̃sir] *vi* : to turn rancid

rancoeur [rɑ̃kœr] *nf* RESSENTIMENT : rancor, resentment

rançon [rɑ̃sɔ̃] *nf* : ransom

rançonner [rɑ̃sɔne] *vt* : to ransom

rancune [rɑ̃kyn] *nf* **1** : rancor, resentment **2** : grudge <garder rancune à : to hold a grudge against>

rancunier, -nière [rɑ̃kynje, -njɛr] *adj* : vindictive, spiteful

randonnée [rɑ̃dɔne] *nf* **1** : ride, trip **2** : walk, hike <faire de la randonnée : to backpack>

randonneur, -neuse [rɑ̃dɔnœr, -nøz] *n* : hiker, walker

rang [rɑ̃] *nm* **1** RANGÉE : row, line **2** : rank <de haut rang : high-ranking> **3** : standing, position (in society, etc.) **4** : ranks *pl* (in the military) <sortir du rang : to come up through the ranks>

rangé, -gée [rɑ̃ʒe] *adj* **1** : orderly, tidy **2** : well-behaved

rangée *nf* : row, line <une rangée d'arbres : a row of trees>

rangement [rɑ̃ʒmɑ̃] *nm* **1** : tidying up, putting away **2** AGENCEMENT : arrangement, layout **3** : storage space

ranger [rɑ̃ʒe] {17} *vt* **1** : to tidy up **2** : to put away, to store **3** CLASSER : to put in order — **se ranger** *vr* **1** : to line up **2** SE GARER : to pull over, to move aside **3** : to go along with, to side with **4** S'ASSAGIR : to settle down

ranimer [ranime] *vt* **1** : to revive, to resuscitate **2** : to renew, to rekindle — **se ranimer** *vr* **1** : to revive, to come to **2** : to flare up, to be rekindled

rapace[1] [rapas] *adj* : rapacious

rapace[2] *nm* : bird of prey

rapatriement [rapatrimɑ̃] *nm* : repatriation

rapatrier [rapatrije] {96} *vt* : to repatriate

râpe [rap] *nf* **1** : grater **2** : rasp

râpé, -pée [rape] *adj* **1** : grated **2** : threadbare

râper [rape] *vt* **1** : to grate **2** : to file down (with a rasp)

rapetasser [raptase] *vt fam* : to patch up

rapetisser [raptise] *vt* **1** : to shorten, to make smaller **2** : to belittle — *vi* **1** : to get shorter **2** : to shrink — **se rapetisser** *vr* : to get smaller, to shrink

râpeux, -peuse [rapø, -pøz] *adj* **1** : rough, harsh, grating **2** ÂPRE : bitter, harsh (of wine, etc.)

rapide[1] [rapid] *adj* **1** : quick, rapid **2** : steep

rapide[2] *nm* **1** : rapid **2** : express train

rapidement [rapidmɑ̃] *adv* : rapidly, quickly

rapidité [rapidite] *nf* : rapidity, speed

rapiécer [rapjese] {6} *vt* : to patch (up), to mend

rapière [rapjɛr] *nf* : rapier

rappel [rapɛl] *nm* **1** : reminder **2** : recall, return **3** : curtain call **4** ÉVOCATION : recall, remembrance **5** : repeat, repetition **6** : booster shot **7 rappel à l'ordre** : call to order

rappeler [raple] {8} *vt* **1** : to remind **2** : to call back — **se rappeler** *vr* : to remember, to recall

rapport [rapɔr] *nm* **1** : report **2** : connection, association <sans rapport : irrelevant> **3** RENDEMENT : return, yield **4** : contact <en rapport avec : in touch with> **5** : ratio **6 rapports** *nmpl* : dealings, affairs, relations <avoir de bons rapports avec : to have good relations with> <rapports avec l'étranger : foreign affairs> **7 rapports** *nmpl* : sexual intercourse

rapporter [rapɔrte] *vt* **1** : to bring back, to take back **2** : to yield (in finance) **3** RELATER : to tell, to report **4** : to add, to insert **5** : to relate to — *vi* **1** : to yield a profit **2** *fam* : to tell tales — **se rapporter** *vr* ~ **à** : to relate to

rapporteur[1], **-teuse** [rapɔrtœr, -tøz] *n* : tattletale

rapporteur[2] *nm* : protractor

rapproché, -chée [raprɔʃe] *adj* **1** : close, nearby **2** frequent, at close intervals

rapprochement [raprɔʃmɑ̃] *nm* **1** : bringing together, coming together **2** : reconciliation **3** LIEN : link, connection

rapprocher [raprɔʃe] *vt* **1** : to bring closer, to move closer **2** COMPARER : to compare — **se rapprocher** *vr* **1** : to come closer **2** ~ **de** : to get closer to, to approximate **3** ~ **de** : to resemble

rapsodie [rapsɔdi] *nf* → **rhapsodie**

rapt [rapt] *nm* : abduction, kidnapping

raquette [rakɛt] *nf* **1** : racket <raquette de tennis : tennis racket> **2** : snowshoe

rare [rar] *adj* **1** : rare, uncommon, unusual **2** : rare, infrequent **3** : few, sparse, thin

raréfaction [rarefaksjɔ̃] *nf* **1** : rarefaction **2** : scarcity

raréfier [rarefje] {96} *vt* **1** : to rarefy **2** : to make scarce — **se raréfier** *vr*

rarement [rarmɑ̃] *adv* : seldom, rarely

rareté [rarte] *nf* : rarity, scarcity

ras[1] [ra] *adv* : short <couper ras : to cut short>

ras[2], **rase** [ra, raz] *adj* **1** : close-cropped <à poil ras : short-haired> <pelouse rase : closely-mown grass> **2** : level <cuillerée rase : level spoonful> <à ras bord : to the brim> **3 en rase campagne** : in open country

rasage [razaʒ] *nm* : shaving

rasant, -sante [razɑ̃, -zɑ̃t] *adj fam* : boring

raser [raze] {87} *vt* **1** : to shave **2** : to raze **3** FRÔLER : to graze, to skim — **se raser** *vr* : to shave

raseur, -seuse [razœr, -zøz] *n fam* : bore <quelle raseuse! : what a bore she is!>

rasoir [razwar] *nm* : razor <rasoir électrique : electric razor>

rassasier [rasazje] {96} *vt* : to satisfy, to satiate — **se rassasier** *vr*

rassemblement [rasɑ̃bləmɑ̃] *nm* : gathering, assembly

rassembler [rasɑ̃ble] *vt* **1** RÉUNIR : to gather, to collect **2 rassembler en**

troupeau : to herd — **se rassembler** *vr* : to gather together, to assemble

rasseoir [raswar] {9} *v* **se rasseoir** *vr* : to sit down again

rasséréner [raserene] {87} *vt* CALMER : to calm, to make serene — **se rasséréner** *vr* : to calm down

rassir [rasir] {72} *vi* : to go stale — **se rassir** *vr*

rassis, -sise [rasi, -siz] *adj* : stale

rassurant, -rante [rasyrɑ̃, -rɑ̃t] *adj* : reassuring

rassurer [rasyre] *vt* : to reassure

rat [ra] *nm* **1** : rat **2 rat musqué** : muskrat

ratatiner [ratatine] *v* **se ratatiner** *vr* **1** : to dry up, to shrivel **2** : to become wizened

rate [rat] *nf* : spleen

raté[1], -tée [rate] *n* : failure

raté[2] *nm* : backfiring

râteau [rato] *nm, pl* **râteaux** : rake

râteler [ratle] {8} *vt* : to rake up

râtelier [ratəlje] *nm* **1** : hayrack **2 manger à tous les râteliers** : to have a finger in every pie

rater [rate] *vt* **1** MANQUER : to miss (a chance, a train, etc.) **2** : to fail at — *vi* **1** ÉCHOUER : to fail, to miss **2** : to misfire

ratifier [ratifje] {96} *vt* : to ratify — **ratification** [-tifikasjɔ̃] *nf*

ratine [ratin] *nf Can* : terry cloth

ratio [rasjo] *nm* : ratio

ration [rasjɔ̃] *nf* **1** PORTION : share, ration **2** : rations *pl* (in the military)

rationaliser [rasjɔnalize] *vt* : to rationalize — **rationalisation** [-lizasjɔ̃] *nf*

rationnel, -nelle [rasjɔnɛl] *adj* : rational — **rationnellement** [-nɛlmɑ̃] *adv*

rationner [rasjɔne] *vt* : to ration

ratisser [ratise] *vt* **1** : to rake **2** : to search, to comb

raton [ratɔ̃] *nm* **raton laveur** : raccoon

ratoureur[1], -reuse [raturœr, -røz] *adj Can* : crafty, sly

ratoureur[2], -reuse *n* : crafty person

rattacher [rataʃe] *vt* **1** : to tie up again **2** RELIER : to link, to connect — **se rattacher** *vr* **~ à** : to be connected with, to relate to

rattrapage [ratrapaʒ] *nm* **1** : adjustment (of salaries, etc.) **2 cours de rattrapage** : remedial class(es)

rattraper [ratrape] *vt* **1** : to recapture **2** : to catch up with **3** : to make up for

raturer [ratyre] *vt* BIFFER : to cross out

rauque [rok] *adj* **1** : hoarse **2** : raucous

ravager [ravaʒe] {17} *vt* : to ravage, to devastate

ravages [ravaʒ] *nmpl* **1** : ravages, devastation **2 faire des ravages** : to wreak havoc

ravalement [ravalmɑ̃] *nm* : refacing (of a building), restoration

ravaler [ravale] *vt* **1** : to clean, to restore (a building, etc.) **2** : to choke back, to stifle, to swallow <ravaler ses larmes : to hold back tears>

ravauder [ravode] *vt Can* : to make a racket

ravi, -vie [ravi] *adj* ENCHANTÉ : delighted

ravigoter [ravigɔte] *vt fam* : to perk up, to invigorate

ravin [ravɛ̃] *nm* : ravine, gulch

raviner [ravine] *vt* : to furrow

ravir [ravir] *vt* **1** ENCHANTER : to delight **2 ~ à** : to rob of (a loved one, etc.) **3 à ~** : delightfully, beautifully

raviser [ravise] *v* **se raviser** *vr* : to change one's mind

ravissant, -sante [ravisɑ̃, -sɑ̃t] *adj* : delightful, beautiful

ravissement [ravismɑ̃] *nm* : rapture

ravisseur, -seuse [ravisœr, -søz] *n* KIDNAPPEUR : kidnapper, abductor

ravitaillement [ravitajmɑ̃] *nm* **1** : provision, supplying **2** : refueling

ravitailler [ravitaje] *vt* **1** : to supply (with food, etc.) **2** : to refuel

raviver [ravive] *vt* **1** RANIMER : to rekindle **2** : to brighten up

ravoir [ravwar] {73} *vt* : to get back

rayé, -yée [rɛje] *adj* **1** : striped, lined **2** : scratched

rayer [rɛje] {11} *vt* **1** ÉRAFLER : to scratch **2** : to cross out, to delete, to erase

rayon [rɛjɔ̃] *nm* **1** : ray, beam <rayon de soleil : sunbeam> <rayon de lune : moonbeam> **2** : radius **3** : range, scope **4** ÉTAGÈRE : shelf, bookshelf **5** : department (in a store) **6** : domain, concern **7 rayon de miel** : honeycomb **8 rayons** *nmpl* : rays, radiation <rayons gamma : gamma rays> <rayons X : X rays>

rayonnant, -nante [rɛjɔnɑ̃, -nɑ̃t] *adj* RADIEUX : radiant

rayonne [rɛjɔn] *nf* : rayon

rayonnement [rɛjɔnmɑ̃] *nm* **1** : radiation **2** : radiance **3** : influence (of art, culture, etc.)

rayonner [rɛjɔne] *vi* **1** : to radiate **2** : to shine, to glow **3** : to exert influence **4** : to tour around

rayure [rɛjyr] *nf* **1** : stripe <chemise à rayures : striped shirt> **2** ÉRAFLURE : scratch

raz-de-marée [radmare] *nms & pl* : tidal wave

razzia [razja] *nf* : raid, foray

réabonner [reabɔne] *v* **se réabonner** *vr* : to renew one's subscription

réaccoutumer [reakutyme] *v* **se réaccoutumer** *vr* SE RÉHABITUER : to get reaccustomed to

réacteur [reaktœr] *nm* **1** : jet engine **2** : reactor <réacteur nucléaire : nuclear reactor>

réaction [reaksjɔ̃] *nf* **1** : reaction <réaction en chaîne : chain reaction> **2 à ~** : jet-propelled **3** → **avion, moteur**

réactionnaire [reaksjɔnɛr] *adj & nmf* : reactionary
réactiver [reaktive] *vt* : to reactivate
réadaptation [readaptasjɔ̃] *nf* **1** : readjustment **2** : (physical) rehabilitation
réadapter [readapte] *v* **se réadapter** *vr* : to readjust
réaffirmer [reafirme] *vt* : to reaffirm
réagir [reaʒir] *vi* : to react
réajuster [reaʒyste] *vt* : to readjust, to adjust — **réajustement** [-ʒystəmɑ̃] *nm*
réalisable [realizabl] *adj* FAISABLE : feasible
réalisateur, -trice [realizatœr, -tris] *n* : director (in movies, television, theater)
réalisation [realizasjɔ̃] *nf* **1** EXÉCUTION : execution, carrying out **2** : directory, production (of a film) **3** : achievement, accomplishment
réaliser [realize] *vt* **1** : to carry out, to execute **2** : to produce, to direct (a film) **3** : to achieve, to accomplish **4** : to realize (a profit) — **se réaliser** *vr* **1** : to materialize, to come true **2** : to fulfill oneself
réalisme [realism] *nm* : realism
réaliste[1] [realist] *adj* : realistic
réaliste[2] *nmf* : realist
réalité [realite] *nf* **1** : reality **2 en ~** : in fact, actually
réaménager [reamenaʒe] {17} *vt* : to refurbish
réanimer [reanime] *vt* : to resuscitate — **réanimation** [-nimasjɔ̃] *nf*
réapparaître [reaparɛtr] {7} *vi* : to reappear, to come back, to recur
réapparition [reaparisjɔ̃] *nf* : reappearance
réarranger [rearɑ̃ʒe] {17} *vt* : to rearrange
rebaptiser [rəbatize] *vt* : to rename
rébarbatif, -tive [rebarbatif, -tiv] *adj* **1** : forbidding, grim-looking **2** : daunting
rebattu, -tue [rəbaty] *adj* : hackneyed
rebelle[1] [rəbɛl] *adj* **1** : rebellious, unruly **2** : rebel <le camp rebelle : the rebel camp>
rebelle[2] *nmf* : rebel
rebeller [rəbɛle] *v* **se rebeller** *vr* : to rebel
rébellion [rebɛljɔ̃] *nf* : rebellion
rebiffer [rəbife] *v* **se rebiffer** *vr fam* : to rebel against, to strike back at
rebond [rəbɔ̃] *nm* : bounce, rebound
rebondi, -die [rəbɔ̃di] *adj* **1** : rounded **2** : plump, chubby
rebondir [rəbɔ̃dir] *vi* **1** : to bounce, to rebound **2** : to start (up) again
rebondissement [rəbɔ̃dismɑ̃] *nm* : new development
rebord [rəbɔr] *nm* : rim, edge, sill (of a window)
reboucher [rəbuʃe] *vt* **1** : to put the cork back in **2** : to plug, to stop up
rebours [rəbur] *nm* **1 à ~** : the wrong way **2** → **compte**
rebrousse–poil [rəbruspwal] **à rebrousse–poil** : the wrong way, against the grain
rebrousser [rəbruse] *vt* **1** : to brush back **2 rebrousser chemin** : to turn back
rebuffade [rəbyfad] *nf* : rebuff, snub
rébus [rebys] *nm* : rebus, riddle
rebut [rəby] *nm* **1** : trash, waste, scrap **2 de ~** : rejected, unwanted **3 mettre au rebut** : to discard, to throw away
rebutant, -tante [rəbytɑ̃, -tɑ̃t] *adj* : repellent, disagreeable
rebuter [rəbyte] *vt* **1** DÉCOURAGER : to dishearten, to discourage, to put off **2** : to disgust, to repel
récalcitrant, -trante [rekalsitrɑ̃, -trɑ̃t] *adj* : recalcitrant
recaler [rəkale] *vt France fam* : to fail (a student)
récapitulatif, -tive [rekapitylatif, -tiv] *adj* : summary
récapituler [rekapityle] *vt* RÉSUMER : to recapitulate, to sum up — **récapitulation** [-tylasjɔ̃] *nf*
recel [rəsɛl] *nm* : possession of stolen goods
receler [rəsəle] {20} *vt* : to receive (stolen goods), to conceal (a criminal)
récemment [resamɑ̃] *adv* DERNIÈREMENT : recently
recensement [rəsɑ̃smɑ̃] *nm* **1** : census (of populations) **2** : inventory
recenser [rəsɑ̃se] *vt* **1** : to take a census of **2** : to list, to inventory
récent, -cente [resɑ̃, -sɑ̃t] *adj* : recent
récépissé [resepise] *nm* : receipt
réceptacle [resɛptakl] *nm* : container, receptacle
récepteur[1], **-trice** [resɛptœr, -tris] *adj* : receiving
récepteur[2] *nm* : receiver <récepteur de téléphone : telephone receiver> <récepteur de radiomessagerie : beeper>
réceptif, -tive [resɛptif, -tiv] *adj* : receptive — **réceptivité** [-tivite] *nf*
réception [resɛpsjɔ̃] *nf* **1** : receiving, receipt **2** ACCUEIL : reception, welcome **3** : admission (into an organization, etc.) **4** FÊTE : reception, party **5** : registration desk **6** : reception (of radio, television, etc.)
réceptionner [resɛpsjɔne] *vt* : to receive, to take delivery of
réceptionniste [resɛpsjɔnist] *nmf* : receptionist
récession [resesjɔ̃] *nf* : recession
recette [rəsɛt] *nf* **1** : recipe **2** : formula, prescription **3** : take, receipts *pl*
recevable [rəsəvabl] *adj* : admissible, acceptable
recevant, -vante [rəsəvɑ̃, -vɑ̃t] *adj Can* : welcoming, hospitable
receveur, -veuse [rəsəvœr, -vøz] *n* **1** : recipient (of blood, transplants, etc.) **2** *Can* : catcher (in sports) **3 receveur**

des contributions : tax collector **4 receveur des postes** : postmaster
recevoir [rəsəvwar] {26} *vt* **1** : to receive, to get **2** ACCUEILLIR : to welcome, to be host to **3** : to see, to receive (patients, etc.) **4** ADMETTRE : to admit, to accept (into a society, school, etc.) <être reçu à l'université : to be accepted at the university> **5** : to accommodate, to hold **6** : to receive (radio or television signals) — **se recevoir** *vr* : to land (in sports, dance, etc.)
rechange [rəʃɑ̃ʒ] *nm* **1 de ~** : spare, extra <vêtements de rechange : change of clothes> **2 de ~** : alternative
réchapper [reʃape] *vi* **~ de** : to come through, to pull through
recharge [rəʃarʒ] *nf* **1** : refill, reload(ing) **2** : recharging (of a battery, etc.)
rechargeable [rəʃarʒabl] *adj* : rechargeable, refillable
recharger [rəʃarʒe] {17} *vt* **1** : to refill, to reload **2** : to recharge
réchaud [reʃo] *nm* **1** : (portable) stove **2 réchaud de table** : chafing dish
réchauffer [reʃofe] *vt* : to reheat, to warm up — **se réchauffer** *vr* **1** : to warm up, to get warmer **2** : to warm oneself up
rêche [rɛʃ] *adj* : rough, prickly, scratchy
recherche [rəʃɛrʃ] *nf* **1** : search <à la recherche de : in search of> **2** : research **3** : meticulousness, refinement **4** : affectation, pretentiousness **5 recherches** *nfpl* : investigations
recherché, -chée [rəʃɛrʃe] *adj* **1** : sought-after, in demand **2** : refined, studied, meticulous **3** : affected, pretentious
rechercher [rəʃɛrʃe] *vt* **1** : to search for, to seek **2** : to look into, to investigate
rechigner [rəʃiɲe] *vi* **1** : to grumble **2 ~ à** : to balk at
rechute [rəʃyt] *nf* : relapse <faire une rechute : to have a relapse>
rechuter [rəʃyte] *vi* : to relapse
récidive [residiv] *nf* **1** : second (or subsequent) offense **2** : recurrence (of an illness)
récidiver [residive] *vi* **1** : to relapse into crime **2** : to recur (of an illness)
récif [resif] *nm* : reef
récipiendaire [resipjɑ̃dɛr] *nmf* : recipient (of a diploma, a nomination, etc.)
récipient [resipjɑ̃] *nm* : container
réciprocité [resiprɔsite] *nf* : reciprocity
réciproque [resiprɔk] *adj* : reciprocal, mutual — **réciproquement** [-prɔkmɑ̃] *adv*
récit [resi] *nm* : account, story
récital [resital] *nm, pl* **-tals** : recital
récitation [resitasjɔ̃] *nf* **1** : recitation **2 apprendre une récitation** : to learn a text by heart
réciter [resite] *vt* : to recite
réclamation [reklamasjɔ̃] *nf* **1** PLAINTE : complaint **2** : claim (in law)
réclame [reklam] *nf* **1** : advertisement **2** : advertising, publicity **3 en ~** : on special (offer), on sale
réclamer [reklame] *vt* **1** : to ask for, to claim **2** : to demand, to call for — *vi* : to complain — **se réclamer** *vr* **~ de** : to claim an association with (a person or an organization)
reclasser [rəklase] *vt* : to reclassify
reclus, -cluse [rəkly, -klyz] *n* : recluse
réclusion [reklyzjɔ̃] *nf* DÉTENTION : imprisonment
recoin [rəkwɛ̃] *nm* : nook, corner <tous les coins et les recoins : every nook and cranny>
reçoit [rəswa], **reçoive** [rəswav], *etc.* → **recevoir**
recoller [rəkɔle] *vt* : to stick back together
récolte [rekɔlt] *nf* **1** : harvesting, gathering **2** : harvest, crop
récolter [rekɔlte] *vt* **1** : to harvest **2** : to gather, to collect
recommandable [rəkɔmɑ̃dabl] *adj* : commendable
recommandation [rəkɔmɑ̃dasjɔ̃] *nf* : recommendation
recommander [rəkɔmɑ̃de] *vt* **1** : to recommend **2** : to advise **3** : to register (a letter, etc.)
recommencement [rəkɔmɑ̃smɑ̃] *nm* : new beginning
recommencer [rəkɔmɑ̃se] {6} *v* : to begin again, to start anew
récompense [rekɔ̃pɑ̃s] *nf* : reward
récompenser [rekɔ̃pɑ̃se] *vt* : to reward
réconciliation [rekɔ̃siljasjɔ̃] *nf* : reconciliation
réconcilier [rekɔ̃silje] {96} *vt* : to reconcile — **se réconcilier** *vr*
reconduction [rəkɔ̃dyksjɔ̃] *nf* : renewal (of a budget, contract, etc.)
reconduire [rəkɔ̃dɥir] {49} *vt* **1** RACCOMPAGNER : to take home **2** : to show to the door **3** : to renew, to extend <reconduire qqn dans ses fonctions : to reelect s.o.>
réconfort [rekɔ̃fɔr] *nm* : comfort
réconfortant, -tante [rekɔ̃fɔrtɑ̃, -tɑ̃t] *adj* **1** : comforting **2** : fortifying, invigorating
réconforter [rəkɔ̃fɔrte] *vt* **1** CONSOLER : to comfort **2** REVIGORER : to fortify, to invigorate
reconnaissable [rəkɔnɛsabl] *adj* : recognizable
reconnaissance [rɛkɔnɛsɑ̃s] *nf* **1** : recognition **2** GRATITUDE : gratitude **3** : admission, acknowledgment (of wrongs, debts, etc.) **4** : reconnaissance (in the military)

reconnaissant, -sante [rəkɔnɛsɑ̃, -sɑ̃t] *adj* : grateful
reconnaître [rəkɔnɛtr] {7} *vt* **1** : to recognize **2** : to admit, to acknowledge **3** : to reconnoiter — **se reconnaître** *vr* **1** : to see oneself (in someone) **2** : to recognize each other **3** : to be recognizable **4** : to orient oneself, to find one's way **5** S'AVOUER : to admit (to being), to own up
reconnu, -nue [rəkɔny] *adj* : recognized, well-known
reconquérir [rəkɔ̃kerir] {21} *vt* **1** : to reconquer **2** : to regain, to win back
reconsidérer [rəkɔ̃sidere] {87} *vt* : to reconsider
reconstituer [rəkɔ̃stitɥe] *vt* **1** : to piece together, to recreate, to rebuild **2** : to reconstruct (a crime)
reconstruction [rəkɔ̃stryksjɔ̃] *nf* : reconstruction, rebuilding
reconstruire [rəkɔ̃strɥir] {49} *vt* : to reconstruct, to rebuild
reconvertir [rəkɔ̃vɛrtir] *vt* **1** : to redeploy **2** : to convert, to restructure
recopier [rəkɔpje] {96} *vt* : to copy out (again), to transcribe
record [rəkɔr] *nm* : record
recoudre [rəkudr] {22} *vt* **1** : to sew back on **2** : to stitch up (in surgery)
recouper [rəkupe] *vt* **1** : to cut again **2** : to tally with — **se recouper** *vr* **1** : to tally, to add up **2** : to intersect
recourbé, -bée [rəkurbe] *adj* : curved, hooked <un nez recourbé : a hooked nose>
recourir [rəkurir] {23} *vi* **1** : to run again **2** : to appeal **3 ~ à** : to resort to
recours [rəkur] *nm* **1** : recourse, resort <en dernier recours : as a last resort> <avoir recours à : to have recourse to, to fall back on> **2** : appeal (in law)
recouvert, -verte [rkuvɛr, -vɛrt] *adj* : overgrown
recouvrement [rəkuvrəmɑ̃] *nm* **1** : collection **2** : recovery **3** : covering, cover
recouvrer [rəkuvre] *vt* **1** : to recover, to regain **2** : to collect (taxes, etc.)
recouvrir [rəkuvrir] {83} *vt* **1** : to cover, to re-cover **2** MASQUER : to conceal, to hide — **se recouvrir** *vr* : to overlap
récréatif, -tive [rekreatif, -tiv] *adj* : recreational, entertaining
récréation [rekreasjɔ̃] *nf* **1** : recreation, entertainment **2** : recess, break
recréer [rəkree] {89} *vt* : to re-create
récrier [rekrije] {96} *v* **se récrier** *vr* : to exclaim
récrimination [rekriminasjɔ̃] *nf* : recrimination, reproach
récriminer [rekrimine] *vi* **~ contre** : to recriminate against, to reproach
récrire [rekrir] {33} *vt* : to rewrite
recroqueviller [rəkrɔkvije] *v* **se recroqueviller** *vr* **1** : to huddle up, to curl up **2** : to shrivel up
recru, -crue [rəkry] *adj or* **recru de fatigue** : exhausted
recrudescence [rəkrydesɑ̃s] *nf* : new outbreak
recrue [rəkry] *nf* : recruit
recrutement [rəkrytmɑ̃] *nm* : recruitment
recruter [rəkryte] *vt* : to recruit, to appoint, to take on
rectal, -tale [rɛktal] *adj, mpl* **-taux** [-to] : rectal
rectangle [rɛktɑ̃gl] *nm* : rectangle — **rectangulaire** [-tɑ̃gylɛr] *adj*
recteur, -trice [rɛktœr, -tris] *nm* **1** *France* : superintendent (of schools) **2** : rector, administrator (of a university) **3** : rector (in religion)
rectificatif [rɛktifikatif] *nm* : correction <publier un rectificatif : to publish a correction>
rectification [rɛktifikasjɔ̃] *nf* : correcting, correction
rectifier [rɛktifje] {96} *vt* : to rectify, to correct
rectitude [rɛktityd] *nf* **1** : straightness (of a line) **2** DROITURE : uprightness, rectitude
recto [rɛkto] *nm* : recto
rectum [rɛktɔm] *nm* : rectum
reçu[1] [rəsy] *pp* → **recevoir**
reçu[2], **-cue** [rəsy] *adj* : accepted, approved
reçu[3] *nm* : receipt
recueil [rəkœj] *nm* : collection, compilation
recueillement [rəkœjmɑ̃] *nm* MÉDITATION : meditation, contemplation
recueillir [rəkœjir] {3} *vt* **1** : to collect, to gather **2** : to get, to obtain, to win **3** : to take in (a stray, etc.) — **se recueillir** *vr* **1** : to collect one's thoughts, to reflect **2** : to meditate
recuire [rəkɥir] {49} *vt* : to anneal
recul [rəkyl] *nm* **1** : recoil (of a firearm) **2** : retreat, backward movement <prendre du recul : to stand back> **3** : detachment <avec le recul : in retrospect, with hindsight> **4** : decline, drop (in production, prices, etc.)
reculer [rəkyle] *vt* **1** REPOUSSER : to move back, to push back **2** : to defer, to postpone — *vi* **1** : to move back **2** : to back up **3** : to be on the decline **4 ~ devant** : to shrink from, to balk at
reculons [rəkylɔ̃] **à ~** : backwards
récupérable [rekyperabl] *adj* **1** : recoverable **2** : salvageable, reusable
récupération [rekyperasjɔ̃] *nf* **1** : recovery, recuperation **2** : salvage, recycling
récupérer [rekypere] {87} *vt* **1** : to recover, to get back **2** : to salvage, to recycle **3** : to make up <récupérer des heures de travail : to make up the hours (at work)> **4** : to take over, to appropriate — *vi* SE RÉTABLIR : to recover, to recuperate

récurer [rekyre] *vt* : to scour <poudre à récurer : scouring powder>
récurrent, -rente [rekyrɑ̃, -rɑ̃t] *adj* : recurrent, recurring
récuser [rekyze] *vt* : to challenge, to object to (in law)
recyclable [rəsiklabl] *adj* : recyclable
recyclage [rəsiklaʒ] *nm* **1** : retraining **2** : recycling
recycler [rəsikle] *vt* **1** : to retrain **2** : to recycle — **se recycler** *vr* **1** : to update one's skills, to retrain **2** : to change jobs
rédacteur, -trice [redaktœr, -tris] *n* : editor
rédaction [redaksjɔ̃] *nf* **1** : writing, editing **2** : editorial staff
rédactionnel, -nelle [redaksjɔnɛl] *adj* : editorial
reddition [redisjɔ̃] *nf* : surrender
redécouvrir [rədekuvrir] *vt* : to rediscover
redéfinir [rədefinir] *vt* : to redefine
rédempteur[1], **-trice** [redɑ̃ptœr, -tris] *adj* : redeeming
rédempteur[2] *nm* : redeemer
rédemption [redɑ̃psjɔ̃] *nf* : redemption
redescendre [rədesɑ̃dr] {63} *vt* **1** : to take down again **2** : to go down (stairs, a hill, etc.) again — *vi* : to go down again
redevable [rədəvabl] *adj* **être redevable à** : to be indebted to
redevance [rədəvɑ̃s] *nf* : payments *pl,* fees *pl* (for services)
rediffusion [rədifyzjɔ̃] *nf* : rerun, rebroadcast, repeat
rédiger [rediʒe] {17} *vt* : to write, to draft
redire [rədir] {29} *vt* RÉPÉTER : to say again, to repeat
redistribuer [rədistribɥe] *vt* : to redistribute
redite [rədit] *nf* : (needless) repetition
redondant, -dante [rədɔ̃dɑ̃, -dɑ̃t] *adj* SUPERFLU : redundant — **redondance** [-dɔ̃dɑ̃s] *nf*
redonner [rədɔne] *vt* **1** RENDRE : to give back, to return **2** RÉTABLIR : to restore (confidence, etc.) **3** : to give again
redoubler [rəduble] *vt* **1** DOUBLER : to double **2** : to repeat (a class, etc.) **3** : to intensify <redoubler ses efforts : to redouble one's efforts> — *vi* **1** : to intensify **2 ~ de** : to increase in, to step up <redoubler de larmes : to cry even harder>
redoutable [rədutabl] *adj* : formidable, fearsome
redouter [rədute] *vt* : to fear, to dread
redressement [rədrɛsmɑ̃] *nm* **1** : recovery, upturn (of the economy) **2 maison de redressement** : reformatory
redresser [rədrɛse] *vt* **1** : to set upright, to straighten up, to straighten out **2** : to turn around, to set back on its feet **3** : to rectify, to redress (errors, wrongs, etc.) — **se redresser** *vr* **1** : to stand up, to sit up (straight) **2** : to recover, to pick up again
réduction [redyksjɔ̃] *nf* **1** : discount, rebate **2** : decrease, cut, reduction
réduire [redɥir] {49} *vt* **1** DIMINUER : to reduce, to decrease **2** : to scale down, to boil down **3** : to subdue (an enemy) **4 ~ à** : to reduce to, to constrain to <réduit au silence : reduced to silence> **5 ~ en** : to crush into <réduit en cendres : reduced to ashes>
réduit[1], **-duite** [redɥi, -dɥit] *adj* **1** : reduced, smaller, lower **2** : small, limited
réduit[2] *nm* : recess, nook
réédition [reedisjɔ̃] *nf* : new edition
rééducation [reedykasjɔ̃] *nf* **1** : rehabilitation (of criminals, etc.) **2** : physical therapy, (medical) rehabilitation
rééduquer [reedyke] *vt* : to rehabilitate (in law or medicine)
réel[1], **-elle** [reɛl] *adj* **1** : real **2** VÉRITABLE : true
réel[2] *nm* : reality
réélire [reelir] {51} *vt* : to reelect — **réélection** [-elɛksjɔ̃] *nf*
réellement [reɛlmɑ̃] *adv* : really, in fact
réemployer [reɑ̃plwaje] {58} *vt* **1** : to reuse **2** : to reinvest **3** : to reemploy, to take on again
rééquilibrer [reekilibre] *vt* : to readjust, to balance
réévaluer [reevalɥe] *vt* **1** : to revalue **2** : to reappraise, to reevaluate
réexamen [reɛgzamɛ̃] *nm* : reassessment, reconsideration
réexaminer [reɛgzamine] *vt* : to reexamine, to reassess
refaire [rəfɛr] {42} *vt* **1** : to do again **2** : to redo, to redecorate **3** : to change completely, to start all over again — **se refaire** *vr* **1** : to recoup one's losses **2** : to change (oneself) **3 se refaire une santé** : to regain one's health, to recuperate
réfection [refɛksjɔ̃] *nf* : repairing
référence [referɑ̃s] *nf* **1** : reference **2 faire référence à** : to refer to
référendum [referɛ̃dɔm] *nm* : referendum
référer [refere] {87} *vi* **en référer à** : to consult, to refer (a matter) to — **se référer** *vr* **~ à** : to refer to
refermer [rəfɛrme] *vt* : to close again
refiler [rəfile] *vt fam* : to palm off, to foist
réfléchi, -chie [refleʃi] *adj* **1** : reflective, thoughtful **2** : reflexive <verbe réfléchi : reflexive verb>
réfléchir [refleʃir] *vt* : to reflect — *vi* **1** PENSER : to reflect, to think things over **2 ~ à** : to think about, to reflect on
réfléchissant, -sante [refleʃisɑ̃, -sɑ̃t] *adj* : reflective (in physics)
réflecteur [reflɛktœr] *nm* : reflector

reflet [rəflɛ] *nm* **1** : reflection, image **2** : sheen, highlight

refléter [rəflete] {87} *vt* : to reflect — **se refléter** *vr*

réflexe [reflɛks] *adj & nm* : reflex

réflexion [reflɛksjɔ̃] *nf* **1** : reflection (of light, waves, etc.) **2** : reflection, thought **3** : comment, remark

refluer [rəflye] *vi* **1** : to ebb, to flow back **2** : to surge back (of crowds, etc.)

reflux [rəflys] *nm* **1** : ebb, flowing back **2** : backward surge

refondre [rəfɔ̃dr] {63} *vt* **1** : to recast **2** : to rewrite, to rework (a text)

réformateur[1], **-trice** [refɔrmatœr, -tris] *adj* : reforming

réformateur[2], **-trice** *n* : reformer

réforme [refɔrm] *nf* **1** : reform **2 la Réforme** : the Reformation

reformer [rəfɔrme] *vt* : re-form, to form again — **se reformer** *vr*

réformer [refɔrme] *vt* **1** AMÉLIORER : to reform, to improve <réformer les écoles : to reform the school system> **2** : to declare unfit for service, to discharge (a soldier) — **se réformer** *vr* : to reform, to turn over a new leaf

refoulement [rəfulmɑ̃] *nm* **1** : pushing back, holding back **2** : repression (in psychology)

refouler [rəfule] *vt* **1** : to drive back **2** : to hold back, to suppress **3** : to repress (in psychology)

réfractaire [refraktɛr] *adj* **1** : refractory **2 ∼ à** : resistant to

réfracter [refrakte] *vt* : to refract — **réfraction** [-fraksjɔ̃] *nf*

refrain [rəfrɛ̃] *nm* : refrain, chorus

refréner [rəfrene] *or* **réfréner** [refrene] {87} *vt* : to curb, to check

réfrigérant, -rante [refriʒerɑ̃, -rɑ̃t] *adj* : cooling, refrigerating

réfrigérateur [refriʒeratœr] *nm* : refrigerator

réfrigérer [refriʒere] {87} *vt* : to refrigerate — **réfrigération** [-ʒerasjɔ̃] *nf*

refroidir [rəfrwadir] *vt* **1** : to cool, to chill **2** : to cool down, to dampen — *vi* : to cool down, to get cold — **se refroidir** *vr*

refroidissement [rəfrwadismɑ̃] *nm* **1** : cooling **2** RHUME : cold, chill <prendre un refroidissement : to catch a cold>

refuge [rəfyʒ] *nm* : refuge, shelter, haven

réfugié, -giée [refyʒje] *n* : refugee

réfugier [rəfyʒje] {96} *v* **se réfugier** *vr* : to take refuge

refus [rəfy] *nm* : refusal

refuser [rəfyze] *vt* **1** : to refuse, to turn down **2** : to deny (access, etc.) **3** : to reject, to turn away — **se refuser** *vr* **1** : to deny oneself **2 ∼ à** : to refuse to

réfuter [refyte] *vt* : to refute — **réfutation** [-fytasjɔ̃] *nf*

regagner [rəgaɲe] *vt* **1** : to win back, to regain **2** : to return to

regain [rəgɛ̃] *nm* **1** : renewal, resurgence **2** : second crop (in agriculture)

régal [regal] *nm, pl* **régals** DÉLICE : delight, treat

régaler [regale] *vt* : to treat to a delicious meal — **se régaler** *vr* **1** : to eat something delicious **2** : to enjoy oneself thoroughly

regard [rəgar] *nm* **1** : look, glance, gaze **2** : look, expression **3 au regard de** : in regard to, concerning **4 en regard de** : in comparison with

regardant, -dante [rəgardɑ̃, -dɑ̃t] *adj* **1** : fussy, particular **2** AVARE : stingy

regarder [rəgarde] *vt* **1** : to look at, to watch **2** : to consider, to regard **3** : to concern, to involve <ça ne vous regarde pas : it's none of your business> — *vi* **1** : to look <regarder par la fenêtre : to look out the window> **2 ∼ à** : to think about, to take into account — **se regarder** *vr* : to look at oneself

régate [regat] *nf* : regatta

régénération [reʒenerasjɔ̃] *nf* : regeneration

régénérer [reʒenere] {87} *vt* : to regenerate — **se régénérer** *vr*

régent, -gente [reʒɑ̃, -ʒɑ̃t] *n* : regent

régenter [reʒɑ̃te] *vt* : to dictate, to rule over

régie [reʒi] *nf* **1** *France or* **régie d'État** : state-owned corporation **2** *Can* : provincially controlled public-service agency

régime [reʒim] *nm* **1** : regime, government **2** : scheme, system, regulations *pl* <régime pénitentiaire : prison system> **3** : diet, regimen <être au régime : to be on a diet> **4** : cluster, bunch <régime de bananes : bunch of bananas>

régiment [reʒimɑ̃] *nm* : regiment

région [reʒjɔ̃] *nf* : region, area

régional, -nale [reʒjɔnal] *adj, mpl* **-naux** [-no] : regional — **régionalement** [-nalmɑ̃] *adv*

régir [reʒir] *vt* : to control, to govern

régisseur [reʒisœr] *nm* **1** : steward, manager **2** : stage manager

registre [rəʒistr] *nm* **1** : register, record **2** : range (of a voice or instrument) **3** : damper (in a chimney)

réglable [reglabl] *adj* **1** : adjustable **2** : payable

réglage [reglaʒ] *nm* **1** : regulating, setting, tuning (of a motor) **2** : adjustment

règle [rɛgl] *nf* **1** : ruler **2** : rule, regulation **3 règles** *nfpl* : menstrual period <avoir ses règles : to menstruate> **4 en ∼** : in order, valid **5 en règle générale** : generally, as a rule

réglé, -glée [regle] *adj* **1** ORGANISÉ : orderly, organized **2** : settled, decided

<tout est réglé : everything has been taken care of> **3** : ruled, lined

règlement [rɛgləmɑ̃] *nm* **1** : rules *pl,* regulations *pl* **2** : settlement, resolution **3** : payment

réglementaire [rɛgləmɑ̃tɛr] *adj* **1** : prescribed, regulation **2** : regulatory

réglementation [rɛgləmɑ̃tasjɔ̃] *nf* **1** : regulation, control **2** : rules *pl*

réglementer [rɛgləmɑ̃te] *vt* : to regulate, to control

régler [regle] {87} *vt* **1** : to regulate, to adjust **2** : to resolve, to settle **3** : to rule (a page)

réglisse [reglis] *nf* : licorice

règne [rɛɲ] *nm* **1** : reign, rule **2** : kingdom <le règne animal : the animal kingdom>

régner [reɲe] {87} *vi* : to reign, to rule, to prevail

regorger [rəgɔrʒe] {17} *vi* **~ de** : to overflow with, to abound with

régresser [regrese] *vi* **1** : to diminish, to recede, to decline **2** : to regress

régressif, -sive [regresif, -siv] *adj* : regressive

régression [regresjɔ̃] *nf* **1** : decline **2** : regression

regret [rəgrɛ] *nm* : regret <avec regret : regretfully> — **regrettable** [-grɛtabl] *adj*

regretter [rəgrɛte] *vt* **1** : to regret, to be sorry about <je regrette de ne pas t'avoir écrit : I'm sorry I haven't written to you> **2** : to miss <nous la regrettons beaucoup : we miss her very much>

regroupement [rəgrupmɑ̃] *nm* **1** : grouping together **2** : merger **3** : rallying, rounding up

regrouper [rəgrupe] *vt* **1** : to group together, to pool **2** : to reassemble, to regroup

régulariser [regylarize] *vt* **1** : to put in order, to sort out **2** : to regulate

régularité [regylarite] *nf* : regularity

régulateur[1], **-trice** [regylatœr, -tris] *adj* : regulating

régulateur[2] *nm* : regulator, governor (of a machine)

régulation [regylasjɔ̃] *nf* : regulation

régulier, -lière [regylje, -ljɛr] *adj* **1** : regular, fixed, established <un programme régulier : a regular schedule> **2** : even, symmetrical <visage régulier : regular features> **3** : steady, consistent <à intervalles réguliers : with regularity, at regular intervals> **4** : legitimate, in order

régulièrement [regyljɛrmɑ̃] *adv* **1** : regularly **2** : evenly **3** : steadily

régurgiter [regyrʒite] *vt* : to regurgitate

réhabilitation [reabilitasjɔ̃] *nf* : rehabilitation

réhabiliter [reabilite] *vt* **1** : to rehabilitate **2** : to restore to favor **3** RÉNOVER : to renovate — **se réhabiliter** *vr* : to redeem oneself

réhabituer [reabitɥe] *vt* : to reaccustom — **se réhabituer** *vr* : to get reaccustomed to

rehausser [rəose] *vt* **1** SURÉLEVER : to heighten **2** : to set off, to enhance

réimpression [reɛ̃prɛsjɔ̃] *nf* **1** : reprinting **2** : reprint

réimprimer [reɛ̃prime] *vt* : to reprint

rein [rɛ̃] *nm* **1** : kidney **2 reins** *nmpl* : back <avoir mal aux reins : to have a backache>

réincarnation [reɛ̃karnasjɔ̃] *nf* : reincarnation

réincarner [reɛ̃karne] *vt* : to reincarnate

reine [rɛn] *nf* : queen

réinsérer [reɛ̃sere] {87} *vt* **1** : to reinsert **2** : to rehabilitate, to reintegrate (into society, etc.) — **réinsertion** [reɛ̃sɛrsjɔ̃] *nf*

réintégrer [reɛ̃tegre] {87} *vt* **1** : to return to (a place) **2** : to reinstate

réitérer [reitere] {87} *vt* : to reiterate, to repeat — **réitération** [-terasjɔ̃] *nf*

rejaillir [rəʒajir] *vi* **1** : to splash up **2 ~ sur** : to reflect on, to fall upon (someone)

rejet [rəʒɛ] *nm* **1** : rejection **2** : discharge, disposal **3** : shoot (from a tree stump)

rejeter [rəʒte] {8} *vt* **1** RELANCER : to throw back **2** : to reject (in medicine), to throw up **3** : to discharge, to eject **4** REFUSER : to decline, to turn down **5 rejeter la faute** : to shift the blame

rejeton [rəʒtɔ̃] *nm* : offshoot (in botany)

rejoindre [rəʒwɛ̃dr] {50} *vt* **1** RENCONTRER : to meet, to join **2** RATTRAPER : to catch up with **3** REGAGNER : to return to, to get back to **4** : to agree with — **se rejoindre** *vr* **1** SE RENCONTRER : to meet **2** : to be in agreement

réjouir [reʒwir] *vt* : to gladden, to delight — **se réjouir** *vr* : to be delighted, to exult, to rejoice

réjouissance [reʒwisɑ̃s] *nf* **1** : rejoicing **2 réjouissances** *nfpl* : festivities, merrymaking

réjouissant, -sante [reʒwisɑ̃, -sɑ̃t] *adj* : cheering, delightful

relâche [rəlaʃ] *nf* **1** RÉPIT : break, respite **2** : closure <le lundi est notre jour de relâche : we're closed on Mondays>

relâché, -chée [rəlaʃe] *adj* : loose, lax

relâcher [rəlaʃe] *vt* **1** DESSERRER : to relax, to loosen up (restraints, muscles, etc.) **2** LIBÉRER : to release, to let go **3** : to relax, to slacken (efforts, discipline, etc.) — **se relâcher** *vr* **1** : to loosen, to go slack **2** : to become lax

relais [rəlɛ] *nm* **1** : relay (in sports and telecommunications) <course de relais : relay race> <relais de télévision : television relay station> **2** : shift

<travailler par relais : to work shifts> **3 prendre le relais** : to take over

relance [rəlɑ̃s] *nf* : boost, revival, upsurge

relancer [rəlɑ̃se] {6} *vt* **1** REJETER : to throw back **2** : to restart (an engine) **3** : to revive, to boost

relater [rəlate] *vt* : to recount, to relate

relatif, -tive [rəlatif, -tiv] *adj* : relative — **relativement** [-tivmɑ̃] *adv*

relation [rəlasjɔ̃] *nf* **1** RAPPORT : relation, connection **2** : relationship <relations professionnelles : professional relationships> **3** CONNAISSANCE : acquaintance <avoir des relations : to have (personal) connections> **4 relations** *nfpl* : relations <relations extérieures : foreign relations> <relations sexuelles : sexual relations>

relativité [rəlativite] *nf* : relativity

relax, -laxe [rəlaks] *adj fam* : relaxed, easygoing

relaxation [rəlaksasjɔ̃] *nf* : relaxation

relaxer [rəlakse] *vt* : to relax — **se relaxer** *vr*

relayer [rəlɛje] {11} *vt* **1** : to take over from, to relieve **2** : to relay (in telecommunications) — **se relayer** *vr* : to take turns

reléguer [rəlege] {87} *vt* : to relegate — **relégation** [-legasjɔ̃] *nf*

relent [rəlɑ̃] *nm* **1** : foul smell, stench **2** TRACE : hint, trace

relève [rəlɛv] *nf* **1** : relief, replacement **2 prendre la relève** : to take over

relevé[1], -vée [rəlɛve] *adj* **1** RETROUSSÉ : turned up, rolled up **2** : elevated, refined **3** : spicy, pungent

relevé[2] *nm* **1** : statement <relevé de compte : bank statement> **2** : reading (of electricity, gas, etc.)

relèvement [rəlɛvmɑ̃] *nm* **1** : rise, increase **2** : rebuilding, recovery (of the economy, etc.)

relever [rəlve] {52} *vt* **1** : to stand up again, to raise (up) **2** : to turn up, to roll up **3** AUGMENTER : to raise, to increase **4** : to rebuild **5** RAMASSER : to collect, to pick up **6** ASSAISONNER : to season, to spice up **7** : to relieve, to take over from **8** NOTER : to take notice of **9** : to enhance, to elevate — *vi* **1 ~ de** : to be a matter for, to concern **2 ~ de** : to recover from (an illness) — **se relever** *vr* **1** : to get up again **2 ~ de** : to get over (an illness)

relief [rəljɛf] *nm* **1** : relief (in art, geography, etc.) **2 mettre en relief** : to accentuate, to highlight

relier [rəlje] {96} *vt* **1** : to link, to join **2** : to bind (a book)

relieur, -lieuse [rəljœr, -ljøz] *n* : binder, bookbinder

religieusement [rəliʒjøzmɑ̃] *adv* : religiously, faithfully

religieux[1], -gieuse [rəliʒjø, -ʒjøz] *adj* **1** : religious **2** : reverent, conscientious

religieux[2], -gieuse *n* : monk *m,* friar *m,* nun *f*

religion [rəliʒjɔ̃] *nf* : religion

reliquat [rəlika] *nm* : remainder, balance

relique [rəlik] *nf* : relic

relire [rəlir] {51} *vt* : to reread

relish [rəliʃ] *nf Can* : relish (condiment)

reliure [rəljyr] *nf* : binding

reluire [rəlɥir] {49} *vi* BRILLER : to glisten, to gleam, to shine

reluisant, -sante [rəlɥizɑ̃, -zɑ̃t] *adj* **1** : gleaming **2 peu reluisant** : unpromising, far from brilliant

reluquer [rəlyke] *vt fam* : to ogle, to eye

remâcher [rəmaʃe] *vt* : to stew over, to brood about

remaniement [rəmanimɑ̃] *nm* : revision, modification

remanier [rəmanje] {96} *vt* : to revise, to redraft, to modify

remarier [rəmarje]{96} *v* **se remarier** *vr* : to remarry

remarquable [rəmarkabl] *adj* : remarkable — **remarquablement** [-kabləmɑ̃] *adv*

remarque [rəmark] *nf* : remark, comment

remarquer [rəmarke] *vt* **1** : to remark, to observe <faire remarquer : to point out> **2** : to notice **3 se faire remarquer** : to attract attention, to come to the fore

remballer [rɑ̃bale] *vt* : to repack, to pack up (again)

rembarrer [rɑ̃bare] *vt fam* : to rebuff, to put someone in his or her place

remblai [rɑ̃blɛ] *nm* : embankment

remblayer [rɑ̃bleje] {11} *vt* : to fill in, to bank up

rembobiner [rɑ̃bɔbine] *vt* : to rewind

rembourrage [rɑ̃buraʒ] *nm* : stuffing, padding

rembourrer [rɑ̃bure] *vt* : to stuff, to pad

remboursable [rɑ̃bursabl] *adj* : refundable

remboursement [rɑ̃bursəmɑ̃] *nm* : repayment, reimbursement

rembourser [rɑ̃burse] *vt* **1** : to repay **2** : to refund, to reimburse

rembrunir [rɑ̃brynir] *v* **se rembrunir** *vr* : to cloud over, to become gloomy

remède [rəmɛd] *nm* : remedy, cure

remédier [rəmedje] {96} *vt* **~ à** : to remedy, to cure, to put right

remémorer [rəmemɔre] *v* **se remémorer** *vr* SE RAPPELER : to remember, to recall

remerciement [rəmɛrsimɑ̃] *nm* **1** : thanking <lettre de remerciement : thank-you letter> **2 remerciements** *nmpl* : thanks

remercier [rəmɛrsje] {96} *vt* **1** : to thank **2** CONGÉDIER : to dismiss, to fire

remettre [rəmɛtr] {53} *vt* **1** REPLACER : to put back **2** : to put back on, to switch back on, to restart **3** RA-

JOUTER : to add, to put more in **4** REMPLACER : to replace (a button, etc.) **5** DONNER : to deliver, to hand over **6** REPORTER : to postpone, to put off **7** RECONNAÎTRE : to recognize, to place **8 : remettre à neuf** : to restore, to refurbish — **se remettre** *vr* **1** : to return, to get back **2** : to put on again **3** : to recover, to get better **4 ~ à** : to begin again <elle s'est remise à parler : she started to talk again> **5 ~ à** : to rely on **6 s'en remettre à** : to leave it up to, to defer to

réminiscence [reminisɑ̃s] *nf* : reminiscence

remise [rəmiz] *nf* **1** : putting off, postponement **2** LIVRAISON : handing over, delivery <remise des diplômes : commencement, graduation> **3** : remission (of a debt, etc.) **4** RABAIS : discount **5** : shed

remiser [rəmize] *vt* : to put away, to store

rémission [remisjɔ̃] *nf* : remission

remodeler [rəmɔdle] {20} *vt* **1** : to remodel **2** : to reorganize, to restructure

remontant [rəmɔ̃tɑ̃] *nm* TONIQUE : tonic

remontée [rəmɔ̃te] *nf* **1** : climb, ascent **2 remontée mécanique** : ski lift

remonte–pente [rəmɔ̃tpɑ̃t] *nm, pl* **remonte–pentes** : ski lift

remonter [rəmɔ̃te] *vt* **1** : to take back up, to bring back up, to raise up (again) **2** : to go back up **3** : to cheer up, to invigorate — *vi* **1** : to rise (again) **2 ~ à** : to date back to **3 remonter dans le temps** : to go back in time

remontrance [rəmɔ̃trɑ̃s] *nf* REPROCHE : reproach, reprimand

remords [rəmɔr] *nm* : remorse

remorquage [rəmɔrkaʒ] *nm* : towing, tow

remorque [rəmɔrk] *nf* **1** : trailer **2 être en remorque** : to be in tow

remorquer [rəmɔrke] *vt* : to tow

remorqueur [rəmɔrkœr] *nm* : tugboat

remorqueuse [rəmɔrkøz] *nf Can* : tow truck

remous [rəmu] *nm* **1** : eddy **2** : backwash

rempart [rɑ̃par] *nm* : rampart

rempirer [rɑ̃pire] *vi Can fam* : to worsen, to become worse

remplaçable [rɑ̃plasabl] *adj* : replaceable

remplaçant, -çante [rɑ̃plasɑ̃, -sɑ̃t] *n* SUPPLÉANT : substitute, stand-in, alternate

remplacement [rɑ̃plasmɑ̃] *nm* : replacement

remplacer [rɑ̃plase] {6} *vt* **1** : to replace **2** : to substitute for, to stand in for

remplir [rɑ̃plir] *vt* **1** : to fill (up) **2** : to fill out (a form, etc.) **3** : to carry out, to fulfill

remplissage [rɑ̃plisaʒ] *nm* : filling, filler

remporter [rɑ̃pɔrte] *vt* **1** REPRENDRE : to take back, to take away (again) **2** : to win, to achieve

remuant, -ante [rəmɥɑ̃, -ɑ̃t] *adj* : restless, fidgety

remue–ménage [rəmymenaʒ] *nms & pl* : commotion, upheaval

remue–méninges [rəmymenɛ̃ʒ] *nms & pl* : brainstorming

remuer [rəmɥe] *vt* **1** : to move <remuer les lèvres : to move one's lips> <remuer la queue : to wag its tail> **2** : to stir, to mix **3** ÉMOUVOIR : to stir, to touch, to move — *vi* **1** : to move **2** : to fidget, to squirm — **se remuer** *vr* **1** : to move (about) **2** *fam* : to get a move on

rémunérateur, -trice [remyneratœr, -tris] *adj* LUCRATIF : lucrative

rémunération [remynerasjɔ̃] *nf* : remuneration

rémunérer [remynere] {87} *vt* : to remunerate

renâcler [rənakle] *vi* **1** : to snort (of an animal) **2 ~ à** : to be reluctant to, to grumble about

renaissance [rənɛsɑ̃s] *nf* **1** : rebirth, revival **2 la Renaissance** : the Renaissance

renaître [rənɛtr] {57} *vi* **1** : to be reborn, to come back to life **2** : to revive, to return

rénal, -nale [renal] *adj, mpl* **rénaux** [reno] : renal

renard [rənar] *nm* : fox

renarde [rənard] *nf* : vixen

renchérir [rɑ̃ʃerir] *vi* **1** : to become more expensive **2 ~ sur** : to go (one step) further than

renchérissement [rɑ̃ʃerismɑ̃] *nm* : rise, increase (in price)

rencontre [rɑ̃kɔ̃tr] *nf* **1** : meeting <rencontre au sommet : summit meeting> **2** : encounter **3** : junction, intersection **4** : (military) engagement **5** : match, game, meet (in sports)

rencontrer [rɑ̃kɔ̃tre] *vt* **1** : to meet **2** : to come across, to encounter **3** : to join, to intersect **4** HEURTER : to strike **5** : to oppose, to play against (in sports) — **se rencontrer** *vr* **1** : to meet, to come together **2** : to be found

rendement [rɑ̃dmɑ̃] *nm* **1** : output, production **2** : yield, return

rendez–vous [rɑ̃devu] *nms & pl* **1** : appointment, meeting **2** : meeting place, rendezvous

rendre [rɑ̃dr] {63} *vt* **1** : to give back, to return **2** : to give, to render <rendre grâce : to give thanks> <rendre service : to render aid> **3** : to yield **4** : to pronounce (a verdict or decree) **5** : to express, to convey **6 rendre les larmes** : to give up **7 rendre la monnaie** : to make change — **se rendre** *vr* **1** : to surrender, to give in **2 ~ à**

: to go to, to travel to **3 se rendre compte de** : to realize, to be aware of

rêne [rɛn] *nf* : rein

renégat, -gate [rənega, -gat] *n* : renegade, turncoat

renégocier [rənegɔsje] {96} *vt* : to renegotiate

renfermé[1], **-mée** [rɑ̃fɛrme] *adj* : withdrawn

renfermé[2] *nm* : mustiness <sentir le renfermé : to smell musty>

renfermer [rɑ̃fɛrme] *vt* **1** : to contain, to hold **2** : to hold in, to hide — **se renfermer** *vr* : to withdraw (into oneself)

renflé, -flée [rɑ̃fle] *adj* : bulging, bulbous

renflement [rɑ̃fləmɑ̃] *nm* : bulge

renflouer [rɑ̃flue] *vt* **1** : to refloat **2** : to bail out (a person, business, etc.)

renfoncement [rɑ̃fɔ̃smɑ̃] *nm* : recess

renfoncer [rɑ̃fɔ̃se] {6} *vt* : to push further in

renforcement [rɑ̃fɔrsəmɑ̃] *nm* : reinforcement

renforcer [rɑ̃fɔrse] {6} *vt* : to reinforce, to strengthen — **se renforcer** *vr* : to increase, to become stronger

renfort [rɑ̃fɔr] *nm* **1** : reinforcement **2 à grand renfort de** : with a great deal of

renfrogné, -gnée [rɑ̃frɔɲe] *adj* : sullen, scowling

renfrogner [rɑ̃frɔɲe] *v* **se renfrogner** *vr* : to scowl

rengager [rɑ̃gaʒe] {17} *vt* : to rehire, to take on again — **se rengager** *vr* : to reenlist

rengaine [rɑ̃gɛn] *nf* : cliché, old story <c'est toujours la même rengaine : it's always the same old story>

rengainer [rɑ̃gene] *vt* : to sheathe, to put back in its holster

reniement [rɛnimɑ̃] *nm* : denial, disavowal

renier [rənje] {96} *vt* **1** : to deny, to disavow **2** : to renounce, to repudiate

reniflement [rənifləmɑ̃] *nm* : sniffing, sniffling, snorting

renifler [rənifle] *v* : to sniff, to sniffle, to snort

renne [rɛn] *nm* : reindeer

renom [rənɔ̃] *nm* **1** : renown, fame **2** : reputation

renommé, -mée [rənɔme] *adj* : famous, renowned

renommée *nf* : fame, renown

renoncement [rənɔ̃smɑ̃] *nm* : renouncing, renunciation

renoncer [rənɔ̃se] {6} *vi* **～ à** : to renounce, to give up

renonciation [rənɔ̃sjasjɔ̃] *nf* : renunciation

renouer [rənwe] *vt* **1** : to retie **2** : to renew, to revive — **se renouer** *vr* : to get together again

renouveau [rənuvo] *nm, pl* **-veaux** : revival

renouvelable [rənuvlabl] *adj* : renewable

renouveler [rənuvle] {8} *vt* **1** : to renew, to revive **2** : to repeat — **se renouveler** *vr* : to recur, to be repeated

renouvellement [rənuvɛlmɑ̃] *nm* **1** : renewal **2** : recurrence, repetition

rénovation [renɔvasjɔ̃] *nf* : renovation

rénover [renɔve] *vt* **1** : to renovate, to restore **2** : to reform

renseignement [rɑ̃sɛɲəmɑ̃] *nm* **1** : information <bureau des renseignements : information center> **2** : intelligence <agent de renseignements : intelligence agent>

renseigner [rɑ̃seɲe] *vt* : to inform <mal renseigner : to misinform> <bien renseigné : well-informed> — **se renseigner** *vr* **1** : to ask, to make inquiries <renseignez-vous auprès de la réceptionniste : please ask the receptionist> **2 ～ sur** : to inquire about

rentable [rɑ̃tabl] *adj* : profitable — **rentabilité** [-tabilite] *nf*

rente [rɑ̃t] *nf* **1** : annuity **2** : (private) income

rentrée [rɑ̃tre] *nf* **1** : start, beginning <la rentrée des classes : the start of the new school year> **2** : return **3** : comeback (in entertainment, politics, etc.) **4** : income, revenue

rentrer [rɑ̃tre] *vi* **1** : to go in, to get in **2** : to go back in **3** : to return <rentrer chez soi : to return home> **4** : to start (up) again, to reopen **5** : to come in <faire rentrer l'argent : to bring in money> **6** : to fit <rentrer dans la serrure : to fit into the lock> **7 ～ dans** : to be a part of, to be included in — *vt* **1** : to bring in, to take in **2** : to put in **3** : to hold back, to suppress

renversant, -sante [rɑ̃vɛrsɑ̃, -sɑ̃t] *adj* AHURISSANT : astounding, amazing

renverse [rɑ̃vɛrs] *nf* **tomber à la renverse** : to fall over backward

renversement [rɑ̃vɛrsəmɑ̃] *nm* **1** INVERSION : reversal, inversion **2** : shift, change (of direction) **3** : overthrow **4** : spilling, spillage

renverser [rɑ̃vɛrse] *vt* **1** : to knock down, to overturn **2** : to spill **3** : to turn over, to invert **4** : to reverse (sides, roles, etc.) **5** : to tilt (back) **6** : to overthrow **7** : to astound, to astonish — **se renverser** *vr* **1** : to fall over **2** : to bend over backwards

renvoi [rɑ̃vwa] *nm* **1** : return, sending back **2** : dismissal, discharge **3** : cross-reference **4** : postponement **5** : burp, belch <avoir des renvois : to burp>

renvoie [rɑ̃vwa], *etc.* → **renvoyer**

renvoyer [rɑ̃vwaje] {36} *vt* **1** : to send back, to throw back **2** CONGÉDIER : to dismiss, to expel **3** REMETTRE : to put back, to postpone **4 ～ à** : to refer to, to relate back to **5** *Can fam* : to throw up

réorganiser [reɔrganize] *vt* : to reorganize — **réorganisation** [-nizasjɔ̃] *nf*

repaire [rəpɛr] *nm* : den, lair

répandre [repɑ̃dr] {63} *vt* **1** : to spread, to scatter, to spill **2** : to shed (blood, tears) **3** : to spread, to propagate (rumors, terror, etc.) **4** : to give off, to emit — **se répandre** *vr*

répandu, -due [repɑ̃dy] *adj* : widespread

réparable [reparabl] *adj* : reparable

reparaître [rəparɛtr] → **réapparaître**

réparation [reparasjɔ̃] *nf* **1** : repair, repairing **2** : **réparations** *nfpl* : reparations, damages

réparer [repare] *vt* **1** : to repair, to fix, to mend **2** : to make up for **3** : to restore (health, strength, etc.)

repartie [rəparti] *nf* : repartee, rejoinder

repartir [rəpartir] {82} *vt* : to retort — *vi* **1** : to leave again **2** : to start again <repartir à zero : to rebound>

répartir [repartir] *vt* **1** : to divide up, to distribute **2** : to spread (out) — **se répartir** *vr* : to divide, to split

répartition [repartisjɔ̃] *nf* : distribution, dividing up

repas [rəpa] *nm* **1** : meal **2 l'heure du repas** : mealtime

repassage [rəpasaʒ] *nm* : ironing

repasser [rəpase] *vt* **1** : to pass again, to take again, to show again **2** : to iron, to press **3** : to go (back) over <repasser ses leçons : to go over one's lessons> **4** : to hand over — *vi* : to pass by again, to come again

repentant, -tante [rəpɑ̃tɑ̃, -tɑ̃t] *adj* : repentant, penitent

repentir[1] [rəpɑ̃tir] {82} *v* **se repentir** *vr* **1** : to repent **2** : to regret

repentir[2] *nm* : repentance

répercussion [repɛrkysjɔ̃] *nf* : repercussion

répercuter [repɛrkyte] *vt* **1** : to reverberate, to echo **2** TRANSMETTRE : to reflect, to pass on — **se répercuter** *vr* **1** : to echo **2 ~ sur** : to affect, to have an effect on

repère [rəpɛr] *nm* **1** : line, mark **2** : point of reference, landmark (in space or time)

repérer [rəpere] {87} *vt* **1** : to mark **2** : to locate, to pinpoint **3** : to spot, to catch sight of — **se repérer** *vr fam* : to get one's bearings, to find one's way

répertoire [repɛrtwar] *nm* **1** : list, index **2** : notebook, directory <répertoire d'adresses : address book> **3** : repertory, repertoire

répertorier [repɛrtɔrje] {96} *vt* : to index, to list

répéter [repete] {87} *vt* **1** : to repeat **2** : to tell, to relate **3** : to go over, to rehearse — **se répéter** *vr* **1** : to repeat oneself **2** : to recur

répétitif, -tive [repetitif, -tiv] *adj* : repetitive

répétition [repetisjɔ̃] *nf* **1** : repetition **2** : rehearsal

répit [repi] *nm* : respite, break

replacer [rəplase] {6} *vt* **1** : to replace, to put back **2** : to reassign (to a new job) — **se replacer** *vr* : to find a new job

replanter [rəplɑ̃te] *vt* **1** : to transplant **2** : to replant

replâtrer [rəplatre] *vt* **1** : to replaster **2** *fam* : to patch up, to paper over

replet, -plète [rəplɛ, -plɛt] *adj* GRASSOUILLET : plump, chubby

repli [rəpli] *nm* **1** : fold, crease **2** : withdrawal (of troops, etc.) **3 replis** *nmpl* : inner recesses <les replis de l'âme : the depths of the soul>

replier [rəplije] {96} *vt* **1** : to fold up, to fold over **2** : to withdraw, to pull back — **se replier** *vr* **1** : to fold up **2** : to withdraw **3 se replier sur soi–même** : to withdraw into oneself

réplique [replik] *nf* **1** RIPOSTE : retort, reply **2** : line (in a play) **3** : replica

répliquer [replike] *vt* RÉPONDRE : to reply, to retort — *vi* **1** : to respond, to answer back <répliquer à la critique : to respond to criticism> **2** : to retaliate

répondant, -dante [repɔ̃dɑ̃, -dɑ̃t] *n* : guarantor

répondeur [repɔ̃dœr] *nm* : answering machine

répondre [repɔ̃dr] {63} *vt* : to answer, to reply — *vi* **1** : to answer, to reply, to respond **2** : to meet, to fulfill <répondre aux critères : to meet the criteria> **3** RÉPLIQUER : to answer back **4 ~ de** : to answer for, to vouch for

réponse [repɔ̃s] *nf* : answer, reply

report [rəpɔr] *nm* RENVOI : postponement

reportage [rəpɔrtaʒ] *nm* **1** : report **2** : reporting

reporter[1] [rəpɔrte] *vt* **1** : to take back **2** REMETTRE : to postpone, to put off **3** : to carry forward (a calculation, etc.), to transfer, to copy out **4** : to transfer, to shift <reporter ses affections : to shift one's affections>

reporter[2] [rəpɔrtɛr] *nm* : reporter

repos [rəpo] *nm* **1** : rest <jour de repos : day of rest> **2** TRANQUILLITÉ : peace, tranquillity <avoir l'esprit en repos : to put one's mind at rest> **3 à repos!** : at ease! **4 de tout repos** : safe, secure

reposant, -sante [rəpozɑ̃, -zɑ̃t] *nm* : restful, relaxing

reposé, -sée [rəpoze] *adj* : rested, refreshed

repose–pied [rəpozpje] *nm, pl* **repose–pieds** : footrest

reposer [rəpoze] *vt* **1** : to put (back) down, to put down again **2** : to ask again **3** : to rest (one's body or mind) — *vi* **1** : to rest, to lie **2** : to sleep, to be at rest <qu'il repose en paix : may he rest in peace> **3 ~ sur** : to be based on, to rest upon — **se reposer** *vr* **1** : to rest **2 ~ sur** : to rely on

repoussant, -sante [rəpusɑ̃, -sɑ̃t] *adj* DÉGOÛTANT : repulsive

repousser [rəpuse] *vi* : to grow back — *vt* **1** : to push back **2** : to disgust, to repel **3** REJETER : to refuse, to turn down **4** REPORTER : to put off, to postpone

repoussoir [rəpuswar] *nm* : foil, complement <servir de repoussoir : to act as a foil>

répréhensible [repreɑ̃sibl] *adj* : reprehensible

reprendre [rəprɑ̃dr] {70} *vt* **1** : to take (up) again **2** : to take back, to regain, to recapture **3** : to take over (a business, etc.) **4** : to take back (merchandise) <ça ne peut être ni repris ni échangé : it can't be returned or exchanged> **5** : to begin again, to continue <reprendre la parole : to resume speaking> **6** : to repair, to touch up, to correct — *vi* **1** : to pick up, to improve **2** RECOMMENCER : to start again — **se reprendre** *vr* **1** : to correct oneself **2** : to pull oneself together

représailles [rəprezaj] *nfpl* : reprisals, retaliation

représentant, -tante [rəprezɑ̃tɑ̃, -tɑ̃t] *n* **1** : representative **2** : salesman <représentant de commerce : traveling salesman>

représentatif, -tive [rəprezɑ̃tatif, -tiv] *adj* : representative

représentation [rəprezɑ̃tasjɔ̃] *nf* **1** : representation **2** : performance (in theater)

représenter [rəprezɑ̃te] *vt* **1** : to represent, to act for **2** JOUER : to perform **3** : to depict, to show **4** : to symbolize, to stand for **5** : to signify, to mean — **se représenter** *vr* **1** : to imagine, to picture **2** : to come up again

répressif, -sive [represif, -siv] *adj* : repressive

répression [represjɔ̃] *nf* : repression, suppression

réprimande [reprimɑ̃d] *nf* : reprimand

réprimander [reprimɑ̃de] *vt* : to reprimand, to scold

réprimé, -mée [reprime] *adj* : suppressed, held in

réprimer [reprime] *vt* : to repress, to suppress

reprise [rəpriz] *nf* **1** : recapture **2** : resumption **3** : rerun, repeat, revival (in movies, television, etc.) **4** : recovery <reprise économique : economic recovery> **5** : trade-in (of goods) **6** : round (in sports) **7** : acceleration (of an automobile) **8** : mend, darn (in sewing) **9 à maintes reprises** : on numerous occasions, repeatedly

repriser [rəprize] *vt* : to darn, to mend

réprobateur, -trice [reprɔbatœr, -tris] *adj* : reproving, reproachful

réprobation [reprɔbasjɔ̃] *nf* : disapproval

reproche [rəprɔʃ] *nm* : reproach <faire des reproches à : to reproach, to blame> <sans reproche : beyond reproach>

reprocher [rəprɔʃe] *vt* **~ à** : to reproach, to rebuke

reproducteur, -trice [rəprɔdyktœr, -tris] *adj* : reproductive

reproduction [rəprɔdyksjɔ̃] *nf* : reproduction

reproduire [rəprɔdɥir] {49} *vt* **1** : to reproduce **2** : to make a copy of **3** : to breed — **se reproduire** *vr* **1** : to reproduce, to breed **2** SE RÉPÉTER : to recur

réprouver [repruve] *vt* : to reprove, to condemn

reptile [rɛptil] *nm* : reptile

reptilien, -lienne [rɛptiljɛ̃, -ljɛn] *adj* : reptilian

repu, -pue [rəpy] *adj* : satiated, full

républicain, -caine [repyblikɛ̃, -kɛn] *adj & n* : republican

république [repyblik] *nf* : republic

répudier [repydje] {96} *vt* : to repudiate — **répudiation** [repydjasjɔ̃] *nf*

répugnance [repyɲɑ̃s] *nf* **1** : repugnance, aversion **2** : reluctance

répugnant, -nante [repyɲɑ̃, -ɲɑ̃t] *adj* : repugnant, disgusting

répugner [repyɲe] *vt* : to disgust, to be repugnant to — *vi* **~ à** : to be averse to <je ne répugne pas au travail : I'm not averse to work>

répulsion [repylsjɔ̃] *nf* : repulsion, repugnance

réputation [repytasjɔ̃] *nf* : reputation

réputé, -tée [repyte] *adj* : renowned, famous

requérir [rəkerir] {21} *vt* **1** NÉCESSITER : to call for, to require **2** : to request, to summon

requête [rəkɛt] *nf* **1** : request **2** : petition (in law)

requiem [rekɥijɛm] *nms & pl* : requiem

requière [rəkjɛr], **requiert** [rəkjɛr], *etc.* → **requérir**

requin [rəkɛ̃] *nm* : shark

requinquer [rəkɛ̃ke] *vt fam* : to pep up

requis[1] [rəki] *pp* → **requérir**

requis[2], **-quise** [rəki, -kiz] *adj* : requisite, required

réquisition [rekizisjɔ̃] *nf* : requisition

réquisitionner [rekizisjɔne] *vt* : to requisition

réquisitoire [rekizitwar] *nm* : indictment <un réquisitoire contre les moeurs contemporaines : an indictment against contemporary mores>

rescapé, -pée [rɛskape] *n* : survivor

rescousse [rɛskus] *nf* : rescue, aid <aller à la rescousse : to go to the rescue>
réseau [rezo] *nm, pl* **réseaux** : network
réservation [rezɛrvasjɔ̃] *nf* : reservation
réserve [rezɛrv] *nf* **1** : reserve, stock **2** RETENUE : reserve, restraint **3** : reservation <réserve indienne : Indian reservation> **4** : preserve, sanctuary **5** : storeroom **6** : reservation, hesitation <sous réserve de : subject to>
réservé, -vée [rezɛrve] *adj* **1** : private, reserved **2** : reserved, reticent
réserver [rezɛrve] *vt* **1** : to reserve, to book **2** : to reserve, to set aside — **se réserver** *vr* **1** : to save oneself **2** : to set aside for oneself
réservoir [rezɛrvwar] *nm* **1** : tank, cistern **2** : reservoir **3** : bulb (of a thermometer)
résidence [rezidɑ̃s] *nf* **1** : residence **2** **résidence universitaire** : dormitory
résident, -dente [rezidɑ̃, -dɑ̃t] *adj & n* : resident
résidentiel, -tielle [rezidɑ̃sjɛl] *adj* : residential
résider [rezide] *vi* **1** : to reside, to dwell **2** ~ **en** : to lie in, to consist of
résidu [rezidy] *nm* **1** : residue **2** RESTE : remainder **3** **résidus** *nmpl* : waste <résidus industriels : industrial waste>
résiduel, -duelle [rezidɥɛl] *adj* : residual
résignation [reziɲasjɔ̃] *nf* : resignation
résigner [reziɲe] *vt* : to relinquish, to resign — **se résigner** *vr* ~ **à** : to resign oneself to
résilier [rezilje] {96} *vt* : to terminate (a contract, etc.)
résille [rezij] *nf* : hair net
résine [rezin] *nf* : resin
résineux[1], **-neuse** [rezinø, -nøz] *adj* : resinous
résineux[2] *nmpl* : coniferous trees
résistance [rezistɑ̃s] *nf* **1** : resistance, opposition **2** : strength, endurance
résistant, -tante [rezistɑ̃, -tɑ̃t] *adj* **1** : resistant **2** : tough, hardy, durable
résister [reziste] *vi* **1** ~ **à** : to resist, to oppose **2** ~ **à** : to stand up to, to withstand **3** ~ **à** : to bear, to tolerate
résolu[1] [rezɔly] *pp* → **résoudre**
résolu[2], **-lue** [rezɔly] *adj* : resolute, determined
résolument [rezɔlymɑ̃] *adj* : resolutely, firmly, adamantly
résolution [rezɔlysjɔ̃] *nf* **1** : resolution, decision **2** : determination, resolve **3** : solution
résonance [rezɔnɑ̃s] *nf* **1** : resonance **2** : echo, overtone
résonnant, -nante [rezɔnɑ̃, -nɑ̃t] *adj* : resonant
résonner [rezɔne] *vi* : to resound, to ring out
résorber [rezɔrbe] *vt* : to absorb, to reduce — **se résorber** *vr*
résoudre [rezudr] {74} *vt* : to solve, to resolve — **se résoudre** *vr* **1** ~ **à** : to decide to **2** ~ **à** : to reconcile oneself to
respect [rɛspɛ] *nm* **1** : respect, consideration **2** **respects** *nmpl* : respects, regards
respectabilité [rɛspɛktabilite] *nf* : respectability
respectable [rɛspɛktabl] *adj* : respectable
respecter [rɛspɛkte] *vt* **1** : to respect **2** **faire respecter** : to enforce
respectif, -tive [rɛspɛktif, -tiv] *adj* : respective — **respectivement** [-tivmɑ̃] *adv*
respectueux, -euse [rɛspɛktɥø, -øz] *adj* : respectful — **respectueusement** [-tɥøzmɑ̃] *adv*
respirateur [rɛspiratœr] *nm* : respirator
respiration [rɛspirasjɔ̃] *nf* : breathing, respiration
respiratoire [rɛspiratwar] *adj* : respiratory
respirer [rɛspire] *vi* : to breathe — *vt* **1** : to breathe in, to inhale **2** : to exude
resplendir [rɛsplɑ̃dir] *vi* **1** : to shine **2** ~ **de** : to be radiant with (joy, etc.)
resplendissant, -sante [rɛsplɑ̃disɑ̃, -sɑ̃t] *adj* : radiant, resplendent
responsabilité [rɛspɔ̃sabilite] *nf* **1** : responsibility **2** : liability
responsable [rɛspɔ̃sabl] *adj* : responsible, answerable
resquiller [rɛskije] *vi fam* **1** : to sneak in without paying **2** : to cut in line
ressac [rəsak] *nm* : undertow, backwash
ressaisir [rəsezir] *v* **se ressaisir** *vr* : to pull oneself together, to rally
ressasser [rəsase] *vt* **1** RABÂCHER : to keep repeating **2** RUMINER : to brood over, to dwell on
ressemblance [rəsɑ̃blɑ̃s] *nf* **1** : resemblance, likeness <avoir une ressemblance avec qqn : to resemble s.o.> **2** : similarity
ressemblant, -blante [rəsɑ̃blɑ̃, -blɑ̃t] *adj* : lifelike
ressembler [rəsɑ̃ble] *vi* ~ **à** : to look like, to resemble — **se ressembler** *vr* **1** : to look alike **2** : to be alike
ressentiment [rəsɑ̃timɑ̃] *nm* : resentment
ressentir [rəsɑ̃tir] {82} *vt* : to feel — **se ressentir** *vr* ~ **de** : to feel the effects of
resserre [rəsɛr] *nf* REMISE : shed
resserrement [rəsɛrmɑ̃] *nm* **1** : tightening (up) **2** : narrowing, narrow part
resserrer [rəsere] *vt* **1** : to tighten **2** : to close up, to constrict — **se resserrer** *vr*
ressort [rəsɔr] *nm* **1** : spring (of a watch, mattress, etc.) **2** : impulse, drive, mo-

tivation **3** : recourse, appeal <en dernier ressort : as a last resort>

ressortir [rəsɔrtir] {82} *vt* **1** : to take out again, to bring out again **2** : to release again, to rerun — *vi* **1** : to go out again **2** : to stand out — *v impers* : to emerge, to be evident <il en ressort des faits intéressants : interesting facts are coming to light>

ressortissant, -sante [rəsɔrtisɑ̃, -sɑ̃t] *n* : national <ressortissants étrangers : foreign nationals>

ressource [rəsurs] *nf* **1** : recourse, option **2** : resourcefulness <avoir de la ressource : to be resourceful> **3 ressources** *nfpl* : resources, funds, reserves <ressources énergétiques : energy reserves> **4 ressources** *nfpl* : resources, possibilities <ressources de l'imaginaire : powers of the imagination>

ressusciter [resysite] *vt* **1** : to resuscitate, to bring back to life **2** : to revive, to rekindle — *vi* : to revive, to come back to life

restant[1], **-tante** [rɛstɑ̃, -tɑ̃t] *adj* : remaining

restant[2] *nm* : remainder, rest

restaurant [rɛstɔrɑ̃] *nm* : restaurant

restaurateur, -trice [rɛstɔratœr, -tris] *n* **1** : restaurant owner **2** : restorer (of artwork, etc.)

restauration [rɛstɔrasjɔ̃] *nf* **1** : restoration **2** : catering, food service <la restauration rapide : the fast-food industry>

restaurer [rɛstɔre] *vt* : to restore — **se restaurer** *vr* : to have something to eat

reste [rɛst] *nm* **1** : remainder, rest **2 au ~** *or* **du ~** : besides, moreover **3 restes** *nmpl* : leftovers, leavings **4 restes** *nmpl* : (last) remains

rester [rɛste] *vi* **1** DEMEURER : to stay, to remain <rester éveillé : to stay awake> <il ne peut pas rester en place : he can't sit still> **2** : to be left, to remain <il ne nous reste plus d'argent : we have no money left> **3** DURER : to last, to live on — *v impers* : to remain <il reste à savoir : it remains to be seen>

restituer [rɛstitɥe] *vt* **1** : to restore, to return **2** : to reconstruct **3** : to reproduce (sound, etc.) **4** *Can fam* : to throw up

restitution [rɛstitysjɔ̃] *nf* **1** : restitution, restoration **2** : reproduction

restreindre [rɛstrɛ̃dr] {37} *vt* : to restrict, to limit, to constrain — **se restreindre** *vr* **1** : to cut back **2** : to narrow, to become more limited

restreint, -treinte [rɛstrɛ̃, -trɛ̃t] *adj* : restricted, limited

restrictif, -tive [rɛstriktif, -tiv] *adj* : restrictive

restriction [rɛstriksjɔ̃] *nf* : restriction, limitation

restructuration [rəstryktyrasjɔ̃] *nf* : restructuring

restructurer [rəstryktyre] *vt* : to restructure

résultant, -tante [rezyltɑ̃, -tɑ̃t] *adj* : resultant

résultat [rezylta] *nm* **1** : result, outcome **2 résultats** *nmpl* : results (of an election, etc.), grades (of an exam) **3 résultats** *nmpl* : findings, results

résulter [rezylte] {75} *vi* **~ de** : to result from — *v impers* : to follow

résumé [rezyme] *nm* **1** : summary **2 en ~** : in short

résumer [rezyme] *vt* : to summarize, to sum up — **se résumer** *vr* **1** : to sum up **2 ~ à** : to come down to

résurgence [rezyrʒɑ̃s] *nf* : resurgence

résurrection [rezyrɛksjɔ̃] *nf* **1** : resurrection **2** : revival, rebirth

rétablir [retablir] *vt* **1** : to reestablish, to restore **2** : to reinstate (in a job, etc.) — **se rétablir** *vr* **1** : to get better, to recover **2** : to be restored, to return

rétablissement [retablismɑ̃] *nm* **1** : reestablishment, restoration **2** GUÉRISON : recovery

retaper [rətape] *vt* **1** : to retype **2** : to renovate **3** *fam* : to pep up — **se retaper** *vr fam* : to recover, to get back on one's feet

retard [rətar] *nm* **1** : lateness, delay <avoir du retard : to be late> <sans retard : without delay> <être en retard : to be behind schedule> <prendre du retard : to fall behind> **2** : backwardness <être en retard pour son âge : to be backward for one's age> <en retard sur son temps : behind the times>

retardataire[1] [rətardatɛr] *adj* **1** : late, delayed **2** : outdated

retardataire[2] *nmf* : latecomer

retardé, -dée [rətarde] *adj* : backward

retardement [rətardəmɑ̃] *nm* **1 à ~** : delayed-action **2 bombe à retardement** : time bomb

retarder [rətarde] *vt* **1** : to delay **2** : to put off, to postpone **3** : to set back (a clock, etc.) — *vi* **1** : to be slow, to lose time **2** : to be behind the times **3** *fam* : to be out of touch

retenir [rətənir] {92} *vt* **1** : to hold back, to stop, to check **2** : to keep, to detain **3** : to retain, to absorb **4** : to reserve, to book **5** : to remember **6** : to carry (in mathematics) — **se retenir** *vr* **1** : to restrain oneself **2 ~ à** : to hold onto, to grip

rétention [retɑ̃sjɔ̃] *nf* : retention, withholding

retentir [rətɑ̃tir] *vi* **1** : to ring, to resound, to boom **2 ~ sur** : to have an effect on

retentissant, -sante [rətɑ̃tisɑ̃, -sɑ̃t] *adj* : resounding <succès retentissant : resounding success>

retentissement [rətɑ̃tismɑ̃] *nm* **1** : resounding, ringing, booming **2** : effect, impact, repercussions *pl*
retenue [rətəny] *nf* **1** : deduction **2** : detention (in school) **3** RÉSERVE : reserve, self-restraint
réticent, -cente [retisɑ̃, -sɑ̃t] *adj* : reticent, reluctant — **réticence** [-tisɑ̃s] *nf*
rétif, -tive [retif, -tiv] *adj* **1** : restive **2** : rebellious
rétine [retin] *nf* : retina
retiré, -rée [rətire] *adj* **1** : remote, secluded **2** : isolated, withdrawn **3** : retired
retirer [rətire] *adj* **1** : to take off (clothing, etc.), to remove **2** : to withdraw, to move away **3** : to withdraw, to take back **4** : to collect (baggage, etc.), to withdraw (funds), to extract (minerals, etc.) **5** RECUEILLIR : to derive, to obtain <retirer un bénéfice : to make a profit> **6** *Can* : to retire, to put out (in baseball) — **se retirer** *vr* **1** : to withdraw, to retreat **2** : to retire
retombées [rətɔ̃be] *nfpl* **1** : repercussions, consequences **2 retombées radioactives** : radioactive fallout
retomber [rətɔ̃be] *vi* **1** : to come down, to land **2** : to fall again **3** : to subside, to die away **4** : to fall back, to relapse **5** : to fall, to go down (of temperature, value, etc.) **6 ~ sur** : to fall on <la responsabilité retombe toujours sur nous : the responsibility always falls on us>
rétorquer [retɔrke] *vt* : to retort
retors, -torse [rətɔr, -tɔrs] *adj* : wily, sly
rétorsion [retɔrsjɔ̃] *nf* : retaliation
retouche [rətuʃ] *nf* **1** : touching up **2** : alteration
retoucher [rətuʃe] *vt* **1** : to touch up **2** : to alter, to make alterations
retour [rətur] *nm* **1** : return <à mon retour : on my return> <être sur le chemin de retour : to be on the way back> <billet de retour : return ticket> **2 de ~** : back <de retour de la campagne : back (home) from the country> **3 retour de flamme** : backfire **4 retour en arrière** : flashback **5 sans ~** : irrevocably, forever
retournement [rəturnəmɑ̃] *nm* : reversal
retourner [rəturne] *vt* **1** : to turn over, to turn upside down, to turn around <retourner la situation : to reverse the situation> **2** : to turn inside out **3** : to return (a compliment, etc.) **4** : to return, to send back **5** *fam* : to shake up, to upset — *vi* REVENIR : to return, to go back — **se retourner** *vr* **1** : to turn around **2** : to turn over, to overturn **3** : to sort things out, to turn things around **4 ~ contre** : to turn against **5 s'en retourner** : to go back
retracer [rətrase] {6} *vt* **1** : to redraw, to trace over **2** : to recount (an event)
rétracter [retrakte] *v* **se rétracter** *vr* : to retract — **rétractable** [-traktabl] *adj* — **rétraction** [-traksjɔ̃] *nf*
retrait [rətrɛ] *nm* **1** : withdrawal (of funds, permission, etc.) **2 en ~** : set back <rester en retrait : to stand back, to stay in the background> **3** *Can* : out (in baseball) **4 retrait au bâton** : strikeout
retraite [rətrɛt] *nf* **1** : retreat (in religion, the military, etc.) **2** : pension <mettre à la retraite : to pension off> **3** : retirement <prendre sa retraite : to retire>
retraité[1], -tée [rətrɛte] *adj* : retired
retraité[2], -tée *n* : retiree
retrancher [rətrɑ̃ʃe] *vt* **1** ENLEVER : to take out, to remove **2** : to deduct **3** FORTIFIER : to entrench — **se retrancher** *vr* : to entrench oneself, to take refuge
retransmettre [rətrɑ̃smɛtr] {53} *vt* : to broadcast, to relay
retransmission [rətrɑ̃smisjɔ̃] *nf* : broadcast
rétrécir [retresir] *vt* **1** : to shrink **2** : to take in, to shorten (clothing) — *vi* : to shrink — **se rétrécir** *vr* **1** : to become narrower **2** : to contract, to shrink
rétrécissement [retresismɑ̃] *nm* **1** : narrowing (of a road, etc.) **2** : shrinkage (of clothing, etc.)
rétribuer [retribɥe] *vt* RÉMUNÉRER : to pay, to remunerate
rétribution [retribysjɔ̃] *nf* RÉMUNÉRATION : payment, remuneration
rétroactif, -tive [retrɔaktif, -tiv] *adj* : retroactive — **rétroactivement** [-tivmɑ̃] *adv*
rétrograde [retrɔgrad] *adj* **1** RÉACTIONNAIRE : reactionary, retrograde **2** : backward <a backward movement : un mouvement rétrograde>
rétrograder [retrɔgrade] *vt* : to demote — *vi* **1** : to regress **2** : to downshift
rétrospective [retrɔspɛktiv] *nf* : retrospective — **rétrospectif, -tive** [-tif, -tiv] *adj*
rétrospectivement [retrɔspɛktivmɑ̃] *adv* : retrospectively, in retrospect
retrousser [rətruse] *vt* : to turn up, to roll up <retrousser ses manches : to roll up one's sleeves>
retrouvailles [rətruvaj] *nfpl* : reunion
retrouver [rətruve] *vt* **1** : to find (again) **2** REDÉCOUVRIR : to rediscover **3** REVOIR : to see again, to be reunited with **4** SE RAPPELER : to recall, to remember **5** RECONNAÎTRE : to recognize — **se retrouver** *vr* **1** : to find oneself **2** : to meet again **3** : to find one's way
rétroviseur [retrɔvizœr] *nm* : rearview mirror
réunion [reynjɔ̃] *nf* **1** : meeting **2** : gathering, reunion **3** : uniting, merging
réunir [reynir] *vt* RASSEMBLER : to gather, to collect, to bring together

— **se réunir** *vr* : to meet, to get together
réussi, -sie [reysi] *adj* : successful
réussir [reysir] *vi* : to succeed — *vt* **1** : to make a success of, to bring off **2** : to pass (an exam)
réussite [reysit] *nf* : success
réutiliser [reytilize] *vt* : to reuse
revaloir [rəvalwar] {95} *vt* : to pay back <je te revaudrai cela! : I'll get even with you for that!>
revalorisation [rəvalɔrizasjɔ̃] *nf* : revaluation, raising (of salaries, fees, etc.)
revaloriser [rəvalɔrize] *vt* **1** : to revalue, to raise (salaries, etc.) **2** : to reassess, to upgrade
revanche [rəvɑ̃ʃ] *nf* **1** : revenge **2** : return match (in sports) **3 en ~** : on the other hand
rêvasser [rɛvase] *vi* : to daydream
rêve [rɛv] *nm* **1** : dream **2 de ~** *or* **de ses rêves** : ideal, of one's dreams <la maison de ses rêves : the house of his dreams> **3 rêve éveillé** : daydream
rêvé, -vée [rɛve] *adj* : ideal
revêche [rəvɛʃ] *adj* ACARIÂTRE : surly, crabby
réveil [revɛj] *nm* **1** : waking up **2** : awakening <un réveil brutal : a rude awakening> **3** : reawakening, recurrence **4** : alarm clock
réveille-matin [revɛjmatɛ̃] *nms & pl* : alarm clock
réveiller [reveje] *vt* **1** : to wake up **2** : to awaken, to revive, to arouse — **se réveiller** *vr*
réveillon [revɛjɔ̃] *nm* **1** : Christmas Eve supper or party **2** : New Year's Eve supper or party
réveillonner [revɛjɔne] *vi* : to celebrate Christmas Eve or New Year's Eve
révélateur, -trice [revelatœr, -tris] *adj* : revealing
révélation [revelasjɔ̃] *nf* : revelation
révéler [revele] {87} *vt* **1** DÉVOILER : to reveal, to disclose **2** INDIQUER : to show **3** : to develop (photographic film) — **se révéler** *vr* **1** : to show oneself as **2** : to turn out to be **3** : to be revealed
revenant, -nante [rəvnɑ̃, -nɑ̃t] *n* SPECTRE : ghost
revendeur, -deuse [rəvɑ̃dœr, -døz] *n* **1** DÉTAILLANT : retailer **2** : secondhand dealer
revendication [rəvɑ̃dikasjɔ̃] *nf* : claim, demand
revendiquer [rəvɑ̃dike] *vt* **1** : to claim **2** EXIGER : to demand
revendre [rəvɑ̃dr] {63} *vt* **1** : to sell (one's car, house, etc.) **2 à ~** : in abundance, to spare
revenir [rəvnir] {92} *vi* **1** : to come back, to return <je reviens tout de suite : I'll be right back> **2** : to recur, to reappear <un problème qui revient : a problem that comes up again> **3 ~ à** : to return to, to go back to <revenir à la barbarie : to revert to savagery> **4 ~ à** : to hark back to <ça me revient! : now it comes back to me!, now I remember!> **5 ~ à** : to come down to, to amount to **6 ~ de** : to get over (an illness, etc.), to abandon (ideas) **7 ~ sur** : to go back over, to review **8 faire revenir** : to brown (in cooking) **9 revenir à la vie** : to come back to life, to revive **10 revenir à soi** : to come to, to regain consciousness
revente [rəvɑ̃t] *nf* : resale
revenu [rəvəny] *nm* : revenue, income
rêver [rɛve] *vt* **1** : to dream **2** : to dream of, to imagine — *vi* **1** : to dream **2 ~ de** : to dream of, to aspire to
réverbération [revɛrberasjɔ̃] *nf* **1** : reflection **2** : reverberation
réverbère [revɛrbɛr] *nm* LAMPADAIRE : streetlight, streetlamp
réverbérer [revɛrbere] {87} *vt* : to reflect (light, heat, etc.) — **se réverbérer** *vr* **1** : to be reflected **2** : to reverberate
révérence [reverɑ̃s] *nf* **1** : reverence **2** : bow, curtsy <faire une révérence : to curtsy>
révérencieux, -cieuse [reverɑ̃sjø, -sjøz] *adj* : reverent
révérend, -rende [reverɑ̃, -rɑ̃d] *adj* : reverend <le Révérend Père Michel : Reverend Father Michel>
révérer [revere] {87} *vt* : to revere, to venerate
rêverie [rɛvri] *nf* : daydreaming, reverie
revers [rəvɛr] *nm* **1** ENVERS : back, reverse (side) **2** : lapel, cuff **3** : backhand (in tennis) **4** ÉCHEC : setback
réversible [revɛrsibl] *adj* : reversible
revêtement [rəvɛtmɑ̃] *nm* **1** : coating, covering, facing (in construction) **2** : surface (of a road)
revêtir [rəvɛtir] {97} *vt* **1** : to put on, to don **2** : to assume, to take on (an appearance, etc.) **3** : to coat, to cover, to surface — **se revêtir** *vr* **1 ~ de** : to dress up in **2 ~ de** : to be covered with
rêveur[1], -veuse [rɛvœr, -vøz] *adj* : dreamy
rêveur[2], -veuse *n* : dreamer
revigorant, -rante [rəvigɔrɑ̃, -rɑ̃t] *adj* : invigorating
revigoration [rəvigɔrasjɔ̃] *nf* : invigoration
revigorer [rəvigɔre] *vt* : to invigorate, to revive
revirement [rəvirmɑ̃] *nm* : reversal, turnabout
revirer [rəvire] *vi Can fam* **revirer à l'envers** : to turn upside down and inside out — **se revirer** *vr Can fam* : to turn one's back
réviser [revize] *vt* **1** : to review, to reexamine **2** : to overhaul (a vehicle, etc.) **3** : to revise

révision [revizjɔ̃] *nf* **1** : review, reappraisal **2** : checkup, service (of a vehicle) **3** : revision (of a text)
revitaliser [rəvitalize] *vt* : to revitalize
revivre [rəvivr] {98} *vt* : to relive — *vi* : to come to life again
révocation [revɔkasjɔ̃] *nf* **1** : dismissal **2** : revocation, repeal
revoir[1] [rəvwar] {99} *vt* **1** : to see again **2** : to review, to reexamine — **se revoir** *vr* : to meet (each other) again
revoir[2] *nm* **1** : meeting again **2 au revoir** : goodbye
revoler [rəvɔle] *vi Can fam* **1** : to be flung into the air **2** : to spurt, to squirt
révoltant, -tante [revɔltɑ̃, -tɑ̃t] *adj* : revolting, appalling
révolte [revɔlt] *nf* **1** : revolt, rebellion **2** : outrage
révolter [revɔlte] *vt* : to outrage, to revolt — **se révolter** *vr* : to rebel
révolu, -lue [revɔly] *adj* : past, completed, over <en des temps révolus : in days gone by>
révolution [revɔlysjɔ̃] *nf* : revolution
révolutionnaire [revɔlysjɔnɛr] *adj & nmf* : revolutionary
révolutionner [revɔlysjɔne] *vt* **1** : to revolutionize **2** : to agitate, to stir up
revolver [revɔlvɛr] *nm* : revolver
révoquer [revɔke] *vt* **1** : to dismiss **2** : to revoke, to rescind
revue [rəvy] *nf* **1** : magazine, journal **2** : review, inspection (of troops) **3** : review, examination <passer en revue : to have a look at, to go over> **4** : revue
révulser [revylse] *vt* **1** : to revolt, to appall **2** : to contort — **se révulser** *vr* **1** : to be contorted **2** : to roll upward (of eyes)
révulsion [revylsjɔ̃] *nf* : revulsion
rez-de-chaussée [redʃose] *nms & pl* : first floor, ground floor
rhabiller [rabije] *vt* : to dress again — **se rhabiller** *vr*
rhapsodie [rapsɔdi] *nf* : rhapsody
rhéostat [reɔsta] *nm* : dimmer (for lights)
rhétorique[1] [retɔrik] *adj* : rhetorical
rhétorique[2] *nf* : rhetoric
rhinocéros [rinɔserɔs] *nm* : rhinoceros
rhododendron [rɔdɔdɛ̃drɔ̃] *nm* : rhododendron
rhombe [rɔ̃b] *nm* : rhombus
rhubarbe [rybarb] *nf* : rhubarb
rhum [rɔm] *nm* : rum
rhumatismal, -male [rymatismal] *adj, mpl* **-maux** [-mo] : rheumatic
rhumatisme [rymatism] *nm* : rheumatism
rhume [rym] *nm* **1** : cold <rhume de cerveau : head cold> **2 rhume des foins** : hay fever
riant, riante [rijɑ̃, -jɑ̃t] *adj* **1** : smiling **2** : cheerful, pleasant
ribambelle [ribɑ̃bɛl] *nf* : flock, swarm, multitude
riboflavine [riboflavin] *nf* : riboflavin
ricanement [rikanmɑ̃] *nm* : snickering, sneering, giggling
ricaner [rikane] *vi* : to snicker, to giggle, to sneer
riche [riʃ] *adj* **1** : rich, wealthy **2** : sumptuous, luxurious **3** : fertile (of soil), nutritious, rich (of foods) **4 ~ en** : rich in, full of
richement [riʃmɑ̃] *adv* : richly
richesse [riʃɛs] *nf* **1** : wealth **2** : richness, luxuriousness **3** : **richesses** *nfpl* : riches, wealth
ricin [risɛ̃] *nf* **huile de ricin** : castor oil
ricocher [rikɔʃe] *vi* : to ricochet, to rebound
ricochet [rikɔʃɛ] *nm* : ricochet, rebound
ride [rid] *nf* **1** : wrinkle **2** : ripple (on water)
rideau [rido] *nm, pl* **rideaux** : curtain <rideau de douche : shower curtain>
rider [ride] *vt* **1** : to wrinkle **2** : to ripple (water) — **se rider** *vr*
ridicule[1] [ridikyl] *adj* : ridiculous — **ridiculement** [-kylmɑ̃] *adv*
ridicule[2] *nm* **1** : ridicule **2** : ridiculousness, absurdity
ridiculiser [ridikylize] *vt* : to ridicule — **se ridiculiser** *vr* : to make a fool of oneself
rien[1] [rjɛ̃] *nm* : trifle, little thing <perdre son temps à des riens : to waste one's time on trivia> <en un rien de temps : in no time at all>
rien[2] *pron* **1** : nothing <rien de nouveau : nothing new> <il n'y a plus rien : there's nothing left> <ça ne fait rien : it doesn't matter> **2** : anything <avant de ne rien faire : before doing anything> <rien d'autre : nothing else> **3 de ~** : don't mention it, you're welcome **4 rien que** : only, just <rien que pour elle : only for her>
rieur, rieuse [rijœr, -jøz] *adj* : cheerful
rigide [riʒid] *adj* **1** : rigid **2** : strict — **rigidement** [-ʒidmɑ̃] *adv*
rigidité [riʒidite] *nf* : rigidity, stiffness
rigolade [rigɔlad] *nf fam* **1** : fun <quelle rigolade! : what fun!, what a laugh!> **2** : joke, farce <la vie n'est qu'une rigolade : life is just a joke>
rigole [rigɔl] *nf* : trench, ditch, channel
rigoler [rigɔle] *vi fam* **1** : to have fun **2** : to laugh, to joke
rigolo[1], **-lote** [rigɔlɔ, -lɔt] *adj fam* : funny, comical
rigolo[2], **-lote** *n fam* : joker, card
rigoureux, -reuse [rigurø, -røz] *adj* **1** : rigorous, strict **2** : harsh, severe — **rigoureusement** [-røzmɑ̃] *adv*
rigueur [rigœr] *nf* **1** : rigor, harshness **2** : precision, meticulousness **3 à la rigueur** : if absolutely necessary **4 à la rigueur** : at the most **5 de ~** : essential, obligatory **6 rigueurs** *nfpl* : rigors, hardships

rime [rim] *nf* : rhyme

rimer [rime] *vi* : to rhyme

rinçage [rɛ̃saʒ] *nm* : rinsing, rinse

rince–doigts [rɛ̃sdwa] *nms & pl* : finger bowl

rincer [rɛ̃se] {6} *vt* : to rinse — **se rincer** *vr*

ring [riŋ] *nm* : boxing ring

ringard, -garde [rɛ̃gar, -gard] *adj France fam* : old-fashioned, corny

ripaille [ripaj] *nf fam* **faire ripaille** : to have a feast

riposte [ripɔst] *nf* **1** RÉPLIQUE : retort **2** CONTRE-ATTAQUE : counterattack, reprisal

riposter [ripɔste] *v* : to retort

rire[1] [rir] {76} *vi* **1** : to laugh **2** : to joke around, to have fun **3 ~ de** : to mock, to make fun of

rire[2] *nm* : laugh, laughter

risée [rize] *nf or* **objet de risée** : laughingstock

risible [rizibl] *adj* : ridiculous, laughable

risque [risk] *nm* **1** : risk **2 à vos risques et périls** : at your own risk

risqué, -quée [riske] *adj* **1** : risky **2** : risqué

risquer [riske] *vt* **1** : to risk **2 ~ de** : to be liable to, to have a chance of <il risque de s'ennuyer : he might be bored> <ça risque d'arriver : it may very well happen> — **se risquer** *vr* : to venture, to take a chance

rissoler [risɔle] *v* : to brown (in cooking)

ristourne [risturn] *nf* REMISE : discount, rebate

rite [rit] *nm* : rite, ritual

rituel[1], **-tuelle** [ritɥɛl] *adj* : ritual

rituel[2] *nm* : rite, ritual

rituellement [ritɥɛlmɑ̃] *adj* **1** : ritually **2** : religiously, unfailingly

rivage [rivaʒ] *nm* : shore

rival, -vale [rival] *adj & n, mpl* **rivaux** [rivo] : rival

rivaliser [rivalize] *vi* **~ avec** : to compete with, to rival

rivalité [rivalite] *nf* : rivalry

rive [riv] *nf* : bank (of a river)

river [rive] *vt* **1** : to rivet, to fasten **2** : to clinch (a nail)

riverain[1], **-raine** [rivrɛ̃, -rɛn] *adj* **1** : riverside, lakeside **2** : bordering the street, roadside

riverain[2], **-raine** *n* **1** : riverside or lakeside resident **2** : resident (along a street)

rivet [rivɛ] *nm* : rivet

riveter [rivte] {8} *vt* : to rivet

rivière [rivjɛr] *nf* : river

rixe [riks] *nf* BAGARRE : brawl, fight

riz [ri] *nm* : rice

rizière [rizjɛr] *nf* : (rice) paddy

robe [rɔb] *nf* **1** : dress, robe <robe de chambre : bathrobe> <robe d'intérieur : housecoat> <robe de mariée : wedding gown> **2** : gown (of a judge, etc.) **3** PELAGE : coat (of an animal) **4 robe de nuit** *Can* : nightgown

robinet [rɔbinɛ] *nm* : faucet

robot [rɔbo] *nm* **1** : robot **2 robot de cuisine** : food processor

robotique [rɔbɔtik] *nf* : robotics

robuste [rɔbyst] *adj* : robust, sturdy

robustesse [rɔbystɛs] *nf* : robustness, sturdiness

roc [rɔk] *nm* : rock

rocaille [rɔkaj] *nf* **1** : loose stones *pl* **2** : rock garden

rocailleux, -leuse [rɔkajø, -jøz] *adj* **1** : stony, rocky **2** : harsh, gravelly (of a voice)

rocambolesque [rɔkɑ̃bɔlɛsk] *adj* : incredible, extraordinary

roche [rɔʃ] *nf* : rock

rocher [rɔʃe] *nm* : rock

rochet [rɔʃɛ] *nm* : ratchet

rocheux, -cheuse [rɔʃø, -ʃøz] *adj* : rocky

rock [rɔk] *nm* : rock (music)

rodéo [rɔdeo] *nm* : rodeo

roder [rɔde] *vt* **1** : to break in (a vehicle) **2** *fam* : to polish up (a performance, etc.)

rôder [rode] *vi* **1** : to prowl **2** ERRER : to wander around, to roam about

rôdeur, -deuse [rodœr, -døz] *n* : prowler

rodomontades [rɔdɔmɔ̃tad] *nfpl* : bragging, boasting

rogne [rɔɲ] *nf fam* : anger, bad temper <être en rogne : to get mad, to see red>

rogner [rɔɲe] *vt* **1** : to trim, to clip **2** : to cut back on, to reduce (expenses, etc.)

rognon [rɔɲɔ̃] *nm* : kidney (in cooking)

rognures [rɔɲyr] *nfpl* **1** : trimmings, clippings **2** : scraps

rogue [rɔg] *adj* : arrogant, haughty

roi [rwa] *nm* : king

roitelet [rwatlɛ] *nm* : wren

rôle [rol] *nm* **1** : role, part **2** : list, roll **3 à tour de rôle** : one after the other, in turn

romain, -maine [rɔmɛ̃, -mɛn] *adj* : Roman

Romain, -maine *n* : Roman

romaine *nf* : romaine (lettuce)

roman[1], **-mane** [rɔmɑ̃, -man] *adj* **1** : Romance (in linguistics) **2** : Romanesque

roman[2] *nm* **1** : romance, chivalric tale **2** : novel

romance [rɔmɑ̃s] *nf* : ballad, love song

romancer [rɔmɑ̃se] {6} *vt* : to romanticize

romancier, -cière [rɔmɑ̃sje, -sjɛr] *n* : novelist

romanesque [rɔmanɛsk] *adj* **1** : fabulous, fantastic **2** : romantic **3** : fictional, novelistic

roman–feuilleton [rɔmɑ̃fœjtɔ̃] *nm, pl* **romans–feuilletons** → **feuilleton**

roman–savon [rɔmɑ̃savɔ̃] *nm Can, pl* **romans–savons** : soap opera

romantique [rɔmɑ̃tik] *adj* : romantic

romantisme [rɔmɑ̃tism] *nm* : romanticism

romarin [rɔmarɛ̃] *nm* : rosemary

rompre [rɔ̃pr] {77} *vt* **1** : to break (off) **2** : to break, to burst, to shatter **3** : to break (someone) in — *vi* : to break up

rompt [rɔ̃] → **rompre**

rompu, -pue [rɔ̃py] *adj* **1** FOURBU : worn-out, exhausted **2 ~ à** : well accustomed to

romsteck [rɔmstɛk] *nm* : rump steak

ronce [rɔ̃s] *nf* : bramble (bush)

ronchonnement [rɔ̃ʃɔnmɑ̃] *nm fam* : griping, grousing

ronchonner [rɔ̃ʃɔne] *vi fam* ROUSPÉTER : to grumble, to grouse

rond[1] [rɔ̃] *adv* **tourner rond** : to run smoothly, to go well <ça ne tourne pas rond : something's not quite right>

rond[2], **ronde** [rɔ̃, rɔ̃d] *adj* : round

rond[3] *nm* **1** : circle <en rond : in a circle> **2** : ring <rond de serviette : napkin ring> **3** : round slice **4** *Can* : burner (of a stove)

ronde *nf* **1** : rounds *pl,* patrol <faire sa ronde : to be on patrol> **2** : round dance **3** : whole note **4 à la ronde** : around <à des milles à la ronde : for miles around>

rondelet, -lette [rɔ̃dlɛ, -lɛt] *adj fam* **1** : plump **2 une somme rondelette** : a tidy sum

rondelle [rɔ̃dɛl] *nf* **1** : washer **2** : (round) slice **3** *Can* : (hockey) puck

rondement [rɔ̃dmɑ̃] *adv* **1** : briskly, promptly **2** : frankly, straight out

rondeur [rɔ̃dœr] *nf* **1** : roundness, curve (of the body) **2** : frankness

rondin [rɔ̃dɛ̃] *nm* : log <cabane en rondins : log cabin>

rond–point [rɔ̃pwɛ̃] *nm, pl* **ronds–points** : traffic circle, rotary

ronéo [rɔneɔ] *nf* : mimeograph

ronflement [rɔ̃fləmɑ̃] *nm* **1** : snore, snoring **2** : humming, drone, roar (of a fire, etc.)

ronfler [rɔ̃fle] *vi* **1** : to snore **2** : to hum, to drone, to roar

ronger [rɔ̃ʒe] {17} *vt* **1** : to gnaw, to nibble **2** : to corrode **3** : to eat away at, to wear down <rongé par le chagrin : grief-stricken> — **se ronger** *vr* **se ronger les ongles** : to bite one's nails

rongeur [rɔ̃ʒœr] *nm* : rodent

ronronnement [rɔ̃rɔnmɑ̃] *nm* : purring, humming

ronronner [rɔ̃rɔne] *vi* **1** : to purr **2** : to hum (of an engine, etc.)

roquette [rɔkɛt] *nf* : rocket

rosaire [rozɛr] *nm* : rosary

rosbif [rɔzbif] *nm* : roast beef

rose[1] [roz] *adj & nm* : rose, pink (color)

rose[2] *nf* **1** : rose (flower) **2 rose trémière** : hollyhock

rosé, -sée [roze] *adj* : rose, pinkish

roseau [rozo] *nm, pl* **roseaux** : reed

rosée [roze] *nf* : dew <goutte de rosée : dewdrop>

rosette [rozɛt] *nf* : rosette

rosier [rozje] *nm* : rosebush

rosir [rozir] *v* : to turn pink

rosse[1] [rɔs] *adj fam* : nasty, horrid, mean

rosse[2] *nf fam* : nasty person, beast

rosser [rɔse] *vt* : to beat, to thrash

rossignol [rɔsiɲɔl] *nm* : nightingale

rostre [rɔstr] *nm* : rostrum

rot [ro] *nm fam* : belch, burp

rotatif, -tive [rɔtatif, -tiv] *adj* : rotary

rotation [rɔtasjɔ̃] *nf* : rotation

roter [rote] *vi fam* : to burp, to belch

rôti [roti] *nm* : roast (meat)

rôtie [roti] *nf* : toasted bread, toast

rotin [rɔtɛ̃] *nm* : rattan

rôtir [rotir] *v* : to roast

rôtissoire [rotiswar] *nf* : rotisserie, spit

rotonde [rɔtɔ̃d] *nf* : rotunda

rotondité [rɔtɔ̃dite] *nf* : roundness

rotor [rɔtɔr] *nm* : rotor

rotule [rɔtyl] *nf* : kneecap, patella

roturier, -rière [rɔtyrje, -rjɛr] *n* : commoner

rouage [rwaʒ] *nm* **1** : cogwheel <les rouages d'une montre : the movement of a watch> **2 rouages** *nmpl* : workings <les rouages de l'État : the wheels of state>

rouan[1], **rouanne** [rwɑ̃, rwan] *adj* : roan

rouan[2], **rouanne** *n* : roan (horse)

roublard, -blarde [rublar, -blard] *adj fam* : crafty, sly

rouble [rubl] *nm* : ruble

roucoulement [rukulmɑ̃] *nm* **1** : cooing **2** *fam* : billing and cooing

roucouler [rukule] *vi* : to coo

roue [ru] *nf* **1** : wheel (of a vehicle) <roue de secours : spare tire> **2** : (mechanical) wheel <roue dentée : cogwheel> <grande roue : Ferris wheel> **3** : cartwheel (in gymnastics)

roué, rouée [rwe] *adj* FUTÉ : slick, cunning

rouer [rwe] *vt* **rouer de coups** : to thrash, to beat

rouerie [ruri] *nf* : slyness, cunning

rouet [ruɛ] *nm* : spinning wheel

rouge[1] [ruʒ] *adj* : red

rouge[2] *n* : red <rouge à lèvres : lipstick> <être dans le rouge : to be in the red>

rougeâtre [ruʒatr] *adj* : reddish

rougeaud, -geaude [ruʒo, -ʒod] *adj* : red-faced, ruddy, florid

rouge–gorge [ruʒgɔrʒ] *nm, pl* **rouges–gorges** : robin

rougeoiement [ruʒwamɑ̃] *nm* : reddish glow

rougeole [ruʒɔl] *nf* : measles

rougeoyant, -geoyante [ruʒwajɑ̃, -ʒwajɑ̃t] *adj* : red, glowing

rougeoyer [ruʒwaje] {58} *vi* : to turn red, to glow
rouget [ruʒɛ] *nm* : red mullet
rougeur [ruʒœr] *nf* **1** : redness **2** : flushing **3** : red blotch, eruption (in medicine)
rougir [ruʒir] *vt* **1** : to make red **2** : to make red-hot — *vi* **1** : to redden, to turn red **2** : to blush **3** : to glow red
rouille [ruj] *nf* : rust
rouillé, -lée [ruje] *adj* : rusty
rouiller [ruje] *v* : to rust — **se rouiller** *vr*
roulant, -lante [rulɑ̃, -lɑ̃t] *adj* **1** : rolling **2** : on wheels
rouleau [rulo] *nm, pl* **rouleaux 1** : roller <rouleau à pâtisserie : rolling pin> <rouleau compresseur : steamroller> **2** : roll, scroll <rouleau de papier : roll of paper> **3** : roller, curler **4** : breaker (wave)
roulement [rulmɑ̃] *nm* **1** : rolling <avoir un roulement d'yeux : to roll one's eyes> **2** : rumble, roll <roulement de tonnerre : rumble of thunder> <roulement de tambour : drum roll> **3** : circulation, turnover (in finance) **4** : rotation, shift(s) <travailler par roulement : to work (in) shifts> **5 roulement à billes** : ball bearing
rouler [rule] *vt* **1** : to roll, to move along, to wheel **2** : to roll up **3** : to roll, to sway, to swing <rouler les yeux : to roll one's eyes> <rouler les hanches : to swing one's hips> — *vi* **1** : to roll <rouler en bas de la colline : to roll down the hill> **2** : to go, to run, to drive <roule moins vite! : slow down!> <ça roule bien : traffic is moving along well> **3** : to take turns, to rotate **4** : to circulate (of funds) **5** : to rumble, to roll **6 ~ sur** : to turn on, to be centered upon
roulette [rulɛt] *nf* **1** : caster (on furniture, etc.) **2** : roulette **3** : (dentist's) drill
roulis [ruli] *nm* : rolling (of a ship)
roulotte [rulɔt] *nf Can* : trailer, camper
roumain[1], **-maine** [rumɛ̃, -mɛn] *adj* : Romanian
roumain[2] *nm* : Romanian (language)
Roumain, -maine *n* : Romanian
roupie [rupi] *nf* : roupee
roupiller [rupije] *vi fam* : to snooze, to sleep
rouquin[1], **-quine** [rukɛ̃, -kin] *adj fam* : red-haired
rouquin,[2] **-quine** *n fam* : redhead
rouspétance [ruspetɑ̃s] *nf fam* : complaint, gripe
rouspéter [ruspete] {87} *vi fam* RONCHONNER : to fuss, to grumble
rouspéteur, -teuse [ruspetœr, -tøz] *n fam* : grumbler, grouch, nag
roussâtre [rusatr] *adj* **1** : reddish **2** : reddish brown, russet
rousseler [rusle] *vt Can* : to freckle
rousseur [rusœr] *nf* **1** : redness, russet color **2** → **tache**
roussir [rusir] *vt* **1** : to turn brown **2** : to scorch, to singe — *vi* **1** : to become brown **2 faire roussir** : to brown (in cooking)
route [rut] *nf* **1** : road <route de montagne : mountain road> <tenir la route : to hold the road> <par (la) route : by road> **2** : route, way, course <route aérienne : air route> <se mettre en route : to set out, to get going> <perdre sa route : to lose one's way> **3** : trip, journey <il y a deux heures de route : it's a two-hour journey> <bonne route! : have a good trip!>
routier[1], **-tière** [rutje, -tjɛr] *adj* : road <transport routier : road transportation>
routier[2] *nm* **1** : truck driver **2** : cyclist (in bicycle racing) **3** : truck stop
routine [rutin] *nf* : routine
routinier, -nière [rutinje, -njɛr] *adj* **1** : routine, humdrum **2** : set in one's ways
rouvrir [ruvrir] {83} *v* : to reopen, to open again — **se rouvrir** *vr*
roux[1], **rousse** [ru, rus] *adj* **1** : russet, red **2** : redheaded
roux[2], **rousse** *n* : redhead
royal, royale [rwajal] *adj, mpl* **royaux** [rwajo] : royal, regal — **royalement** [-jalmɑ̃] *adv*
royaume [rwajom] *nm* : kingdom, realm
royauté [rwajɔte] *nf* : royalty
ruade [ryad] *nf* : kick, bucking (of a horse)
ruban [rybɑ̃] *nm* **1** : ribbon **2 ruban adhésif** : adhesive tape
rubéole [rybeɔl] *nf* : German measles
rubicond, -conde [rybikɔ̃, -kɔ̃d] *adj* : ruddy, rosy-cheeked
rubis [rybi] *nms & pl* **1** : ruby **2** : jewel (of a watch)
rubrique [rybrik] *nf* **1** : column (in a newspaper) **2** : heading
ruche [ryʃ] *nf* : beehive
rucher [ryʃe] *nm* : apiary
rude [ryd] *adj* **1** : rough (to the touch) **2** PÉNIBLE : hard, tough, difficult **3** : harsh, severe <un rude hiver : a harsh winter>
rudement [rydmɑ̃] *adv* **1** : roughly, harshly **2** *fam* DRÔLEMENT : awfully, terribly
rudesse [rydɛs] *nf* **1** RUGOSITÉ : roughness **2** SÉVÉRITÉ : harshness, severity
rudimentaire [rydimɑ̃tɛr] *adj* ÉLÉMENTAIRE : rudimentary, basic
rudiments [rydimɑ̃] *nmpl* : rudiments
rudoyer [rydwaje] {58} *vt* : to treat harshly
rue [ry] *nf* : street <rue à sens unique : one-way street>
ruée [rɥe] *nf* : rush
ruelle [rɥɛl] *nf* : alley(way)

ruer [rɥe] *v* **se ruer** *vr* **1 ~ sur** : to fling oneself at **2 ~ vers** : to rush toward
rugir [ryʒir] *vt* : to bellow out — *vi* **1** : to roar (of lions, etc.) **2** : to howl
rugissement [ryʒismɑ̃] *nm* **1** : roar **2** : howling <rugissement du vent : howling of the wind>
rugosité [rygozite] *nf* : roughness
rugueux, -gueuse [rygø, -gøz] *adj* : rough, rugged
ruine [rɥin] *nf* **1** : ruin **2** : destruction, collapse **3 ruines** *nfpl* : ruins
ruiner [rɥine] *vt* **1** : to ruin **2** : to destroy, to wreck — **se ruiner** *vr*
ruineux, -neuse [rɥinø, -nøz] *adj* : extravagantly expensive, exorbitant
ruisseau [rɥiso] *nm, pl* **ruisseaux 1** : stream, brook **2** : flood, stream (of tears, etc.) **3** : gutter
ruisseler [rɥisle] {8} *vi* **1** : to stream, to flood
ruisselet [rɥislɛ] *nm* : small brook, stream
ruissellement [rɥisɛlmɑ̃] *nm* : streaming <le ruissellement de l'eau sur la rue : water streaming down the street>
rumeur [rymœr] *nf* **1** : rumor **2** : murmur, hum, rumble
ruminant[1], -nante [ryminɑ̃, -nɑ̃t] *adj* : ruminant
ruminant[2] *nm* : ruminant
ruminer [rymine] *vt* : to ruminate over — *vi* **1** : to ruminate, to chew the cud **2** : to brood
rupture [ryptyr] *nf* **1** : break, breaking **2** : breakup (of a relationship) **3** : breach (of contract)
rural, -rale [ryral] *adj, mpl* **ruraux** [ryro] : rural, country
ruse [ryz] *nf* **1** : ruse, trick **2** : cunning, cleverness
rusé, -sée [ryze] *adj* FUTÉ, MALIN : cunning, sly
russe[1] [rys] *adj* : Russian
russe[2] *nm* : Russian (language)
Russe *nmf* : Russian
rustaud, -taude [rysto, -tod] *n* : bumpkin, hick
rustique [rystik] *adj* : rural, rustic
rustre [rystr] *nmf* : boor, oaf, clod, bumpkin
rut [ryt] **être en rut** : to be in rut, to be in heat
rutilant, -lante [rytilɑ̃, -lɑ̃t] *adj* : gleaming
rutiler [rytile] *vi* BRILLER : to gleam, to shine
rwandais, -daise [rwɑ̃dɛ, -dɛz] *adj* : Rwandan
Rwandais, -daise *n* : Rwandan
rythme [ritm] *nm* **1** : rhythm, beat **2** : rate, pace, tempo
rythmé, -mée [ritme] *adj* : rhythmic, rhythmical
rythmer [ritme] *vt* : to give rhythm to
rythmique [ritmik] *adj* : rhythmic, rhythmical — **rythmiquement** [-mikmɑ̃] *adv*

S

s [ɛs] *nm* : s, the 19th letter of the alphabet
sabbat [saba] *nm* : Sabbath
sabbatique [sabatik] *adj* **congé sabbatique** : sabbatical
sable [sabl] *nm* **1** : sand **2 sables mouvants** : quicksand
sablé[1], -blée [sable] *adj* **1** : sandy **2** → **papier**
sablé[2] *nm* : shortbread (cookie)
sabler [sable] *vt* **1** : to sand **2 sabler le champagne** : to celebrate with champagne
sableux, -bleuse [sablø, -bløz] *adj* : sandy
sablier [sablije] *nm* : hourglass
sablonneux, -neuse [sablɔnø, -nøz] *adj* : sandy
saborder [sabɔrde] *vt* **1** : to scuttle (a ship) **2** : to put an end to, to scrap (a project, etc.)
sabot [sabo] *nm* **1** : clog, wooden shoe **2** : hoof **3 sabot de frein** : brake shoe **4 sabot de la Vierge** *or* **sabot de Vénus** : lady's slipper
sabotage [sabɔtaʒ] *nm* **1** : sabotage **2** : sabotaging, botching up
saboter [sabɔte] *vt* **1** : to sabotage **2** BÂCLER : to spoil, to botch up
saboteur, -teuse [sabɔtœr, -tøz] *n* : saboteur
sabre [sabr] *nm* : saber
sabrer [sabre] *vt* **1** : to cut down (an enemy) **2** : to cut, to slash <sabrer les dépenses : to cut spending> **3** *fam* : to tear to shreds, to pan
sac [sak] *nm* **1** : sack, bag <sac à dos : backpack, knapsack> <sac de couchage : sleeping bag> <sac à main : handbag, purse> <sac de voyage : traveling bag, valise> **2** : sac (in anatomy and botany) **3 mettre à sac** : to sack, to ransack
saccade [sakad] *nf* : jerk, jolt
saccadé, -dée [sakade] *adj* : jerky, abrupt
saccage [sakaʒ] *nm* : destruction, havoc
saccager [sakaʒe] {17} *vt* **1** PILLER : to sack, to pillage **2** DÉVASTER : to ravage, to vandalize, to wreck

saccharine [sakarin] *nf* : saccharin

saccharose [sakaroz] *nm* : sucrose

sacerdoce [sasɛrdɔs] *nm* **1** PRÊTRISE : priesthood **2** VOCATION : vocation

sacerdotal, -tale [sasɛrdɔtal] *adj, pl* **-taux** [-to] : sacerdotal, priestly

sache [saʃ], *etc.* → **savoir**

sachet [saʃɛ] *nm* **1** : packet, small bag <sachet de thé : tea bag> **2** : sachet

sacoche [sakɔʃ] *nf* **1** : bag, satchel **2** : saddlebag **3** *Bel, Can* : purse, pocketbook

sacramentel, -telle [sakramɑ̃tɛl] *adj* : sacramental

sacre [sakr] *nm* **1** COURONNEMENT : coronation **2** CONSÉCRATION : consecration

sacré, -crée [sakre] *adj* **1** : sacred, holy **2** *fam* : damned, hell of a <un sacré spectacle : a damned good show>

sacrement [sakrəmɑ̃] *nm* : sacrament

sacrer [sakre] *vt* **1** COURONNER : to crown **2** CONSACRER : to consecrate — *vi* : to swear

sacrifice [sakrifis] *nm* : sacrifice — **sacrificiel, -cielle** [-fisjɛl] *adj*

sacrifier [sakrifje] {96} *vt* : to sacrifice — *vi* **~ à** : to conform to — **se sacrifier** *vr* : to sacrifice oneself

sacrilège[1] [sakrilɛʒ] *adj* : sacrilegious

sacrilège[2] *nm* : sacrilege

sacristain [sakristɛ̃] *nm* : sexton

sacristie [sakristi] *nf* : sacristy, vestry

sacro–saint, -sainte [sakrɔsɛ̃, sakrɔsɛ̃t] *adj* : sacrosanct

sadique[1] [sadik] *adj* : sadistic — **sadiquement** [-dikmɑ̃] *adv*

sadique[2] *nmf* : sadist

sadisme [sadism] *nm* : sadism

safari [safari] *nm* : safari

safran [safrɑ̃] *nm* : saffron

saga [saga] *nf* : saga

sagace [sagas] *adj* : shrewd, sagacious

sagacité [sagasite] *nf* : shrewdness, sagacity

sage[1] [saʒ] *adj* **1** SENSÉ : wise, sensible, sage **2** DOCILE : well-behaved, obedient **3** MODÉRÉ : moderate, restrained, sober

sage[2] *nm* : sage, wise person

sage–femme [saʒfam] *nf, pl* **sages–femmes** : midwife

sagement [saʒmɑ̃] *adv* **1** : wisely, sensibly **2** : quietly, properly

sagesse [saʒɛs] *nf* **1** : wisdom, good sense **2** : good behavior **3** MODÉRATION : moderation, restraint

Sagittaire [saʒitɛr] *nm* : Sagittarius

saignant, -gnante [sɛɲɑ̃, -ɲɑ̃t] *adj* **1** : bleeding **2** : rare, undercooked

saignée [seɲe] *nf* **1** : bleeding, bloodletting **2** *or* **saignée du bras** : bend of the arm **3** : drain (on finances) **4** : cut, groove, channel

saignement [seɲmɑ̃] *nm* **1** : bleeding **2** **saignement de nez** : nosebleed

saigner [seɲe] *v* : to bleed

saillant, -lante [sajɑ̃, -jɑ̃t] *adj* **1** : prominent, projecting **2** : salient, notable

saillie [saji] *nf* **1** : projection, protuberance, ledge <en saillie : projecting> **2** : sally, witticism

saillir [sajir] {78} *vi* : to jut out, to project

sain, saine [sɛ̃, sɛn] *adj* **1** : healthy, sound <sain et sauf : safe and sound> <sain d'esprit : sane> **2** : wholesome, salutary

saindoux [sɛ̃du] *nm* : lard

sainement [sɛnmɑ̃] *adv* : healthily, soundly

saint[1], **sainte** [sɛ̃, sɛ̃t] *adj* **1** : holy <la Sainte Bible : the Holy Bible> **2** : godly, saintly **3** **la Sainte Vierge** : the Blessed Virgin

saint[2], **sainte** *n* : saint

Saint–Esprit [sɛ̃tɛspri] *nm* : Holy Spirit

sainteté [sɛ̃tte] *nf* : holiness, sanctity, saintliness

saisie [sezi] *nf* **1** : seizure (of property) **2** **saisie de données** : data entry

saisir [sezir] *vt* **1** : to seize, to grab, to impound **2** COMPRENDRE : to grasp, to understand **3** IMPRESSIONNER : to strike, to impress **4** : to keyboard, to enter (data) — **se saisir** *vr* **~ de** : to take possession of, to capture

saisissant, -sante [sezisɑ̃, -sɑ̃t] *adj* **1** FRAPPANT : striking, gripping **2** : biting, piercing (of cold)

saison [sɛzɔ̃] *nf* : season

saisonnier, -nière [sɛzɔnje, -njɛr] *adj* : seasonal

salace [salas] *adj* : salacious

salade [salad] *nf* **1** : salad **2** LAITUE : lettuce **3** *fam* : muddle, mess **4** **salades** *nfpl fam* : stories, tall tales

saladier [saladje] *nm* : salad bowl

salaire [salɛr] *nm* **1** : salary, wages **2** : reward

salamandre [salamɑ̃dr] *nf* : salamander

salami [salami] *nm* : salami

salarial, -riale [salarjal] *adj, mpl* **-riaux** [-rjo] : wage, pay <hausse salariale : wage increase>

salarié, -riée [salarje] *n* : salaried employee, wage earner

salaud [salo] *nm usu vulgar* : bastard

sale [sal] *adj* **1** : dirty, dingy, grimy **2** : nasty, foul <un sale tour : a dirty trick> <sale temps : nasty weather>

salé, -lée [sale] *adj* **1** : salty **2** : salted **3** *fam* : steep, stiff <condamnation salée : stiff sentence> **4** *fam* : risqué, spicy

saler [sale] *vt* : to salt

saleté [salte] *nf* **1** : dirt, filth **2** : dirtiness, filthiness, mess **3** OBSCÉNITÉ : obscenity **4** *fam* : dirty trick

salière [saljɛr] *nf* : saltshaker

salin, -line [salɛ̃, -lin] *adj* : saline

salir [salir] *vt* : to soil, to dirty — **se salir** *vr* : to get dirty

salissant, -sante [salisɑ̃, -sɑ̃t] *adj* **1** : easily soiled **2** : dirty, messy <travail salissant : dirty work>

salivaire [salivɛr] *adj* : salivary

saliver [salive] *vi* : to salivate

salive [saliv] *nf* : saliva

salle [sal] *nf* **1** : room <salle d'attente : waiting room> <salle de bains : bathroom> <salle à manger : dining room> <salle de séjour : living room> **2** : auditorium, hall <salle de concert : concert hall> <salles obscures : movie theaters> **3** : audience, house <faire salle comble : to play to a full house>

salmigondis [salmigɔ̃di] *nms & pl* : hodgepodge

salon [salɔ̃] *nm* **1** : living room, parlor, lounge **2** : salon <salon de beauté : beauty salon, beauty parlor> **3** EXPOSITION : exhibition, show **4 salon de thé** : tearoom **5 salon funéraire** *or* **salon mortuaire** *Can* : funeral parlor

salopette [salɔpɛt] *nf* : overalls *pl*

salsepareille [salsəparɛj] *nf* : sarsaparilla

saltimbanque [saltɛ̃bɑ̃k] *nmf* : acrobat

salubre [salybr] *adj* : salubrious, healthy

salubrité [salybrite] *nf* **1** : healthiness **2 salubrité publique** : public health

saluer [salɥe] *vt* **1** : to greet **2** : to say goodbye to **3** : to salute

salut [saly] *nm* **1** : greeting, wave, nod <salut! : hello!, hi!, good-bye!> **2** : salute **3** SAUVEGARDE : safety, security **4** : salvation (in religion)

salutaire [salytɛr] *adj* : salutary, beneficial

salutation [salytasjɔ̃] *nf* **1** : salutation, greeting **2 veuillez agréer mes salutations distinguées** : yours truly, yours sincerely

salvadorien, -rienne [salvadɔrjɛ̃, -rjɛn] *adj* : El Salvadoran

Salvadorien, -rienne *n* : El Salvadoran

salve [salv] *nf* : salvo, volley

samedi [samdi] *nm* : Saturday

samoan, -moane [samɔɑ̃, -mɔan] *adj* : Samoan

Samoan, -moane *n* : Samoan

sanatorium [sanatɔrjɔm] *nm* : sanitarium

sanctifier [sɑ̃ktifje] {96} *vt* : to sanctify

sanction [sɑ̃ksjɔ̃] *nf* **1** APPROBATION : sanction, approval **2** : sanction, penalty <prendre des sanctions contre : to take sanctions against>

sanctionner [sɑ̃ksjɔne] *vt* **1** CONSACRER : to sanction, to approve **2** PUNIR : to penalize

sanctuaire [sɑ̃ktɥɛr] *nm* **1** : sanctuary (in a church) **2** : shrine

sandale [sɑ̃dal] *nf* : sandal

sandwich [sɑ̃dwitʃ] *nm, pl* **sandwiches** *or* **sandwichs** [-witʃ] : sandwich

sang [sɑ̃] *nm* : blood

sang–froid [sɑ̃frwa] *nms & pl* **1** : composure, calm **2 de ~** : in cold blood

sanglant, -glante [sɑ̃glɑ̃, -glɑ̃t] *adj* **1** ENSANGLANTÉ : bloody **2** : cruel, savage <critique sanglante : scathing criticism>

sangle [sɑ̃gl] *nf* : strap, cinch

sangler [sɑ̃gle] *vt* : to girth, to cinch (a horse)

sanglier [sɑ̃glije] *nm* : wild boar

sanglot [sɑ̃glo] *nm* : sob

sangloter [sɑ̃glɔte] *vi* : to sob

sangsue [sɑ̃sy] *nf* : leech, bloodsucker

sanguin, -guine [sɑ̃gɛ̃, -gin] *adj* **1** : blood <groupe sanguin : blood type> **2** : sanguine

sanguinaire [sɑ̃ginɛr] *adj* **1** : bloodthirsty **2** : bloody

sanguinolent, -lente [sɑ̃ginɔlɑ̃, -lɑ̃t] *adj* : bloodstained

sanitaire [sanitɛr] *adj* **1** : sanitary **2** : health, medical <risques sanitaires : health risks> **3 appareils sanitaires** : bathroom plumbing fixtures

sans[1] [sɑ̃] *adv* : without <je ferai sans : I'll do without>

sans[2] *prep* **1** : without <sans doute : doubtless, no doubt> <sans plus tarder : without further ado> **2 sans que** : without <sans que vous le sachiez : without your knowing it>

sans–abri [sɑ̃zabri] *nmfs & pl* : homeless person

sans–emploi [sɑ̃zɑ̃plwa] *nmfs & pl* : unemployed person

sans–gêne[1] [sɑ̃ʒɛn] *adj* : inconsiderate

sans–gêne[2] *nm* : lack of consideration

santal [sɑ̃tal] *nm* : sandalwood

santé [sɑ̃te] *nf* **1** : health **2 à votre santé!** : to your health!, cheers!

saoudien, -dienne [saudjɛ̃, -djɛn] *adj* : Saudi, Saudi Arabian

Saoudien, -dienne *n* : Saudi, Saudi Arabian

saoul, saoule [su, sul] → **soûl**

saouler [sule] → **soûler**

saper [sape] *vt* MINER : to undermine

sapeur–pompier [sapœrpɔ̃pje] *nm, pl* **sapeurs–pompiers** *France* : firefighter

saphir [safir] *nm* **1** : sapphire **2** : needle (of a record player)

sapin [sapɛ̃] *nm* **1** : fir **2 sapin baumier** : balsam fir **3 sapin de Noël** : Christmas tree

sapinette [sapinɛt] *nf* : spruce

sarcasme [sarkasm] *nm* : sarcasm

sarcastique [sarkastik] *adj* : sarcastic — **sarcastiquement** [-tikmɑ̃] *adv*

sarcelle [sarsɛl] *nf* : teal (duck)

sarcler [sarkle] *vt* : to weed, to hoe

sarcophage [sarkɔfaʒ] *nm* : sarcophagus

sardine [sardin] *nf* : sardine

sardonique [sardɔnik] *adj* : sardonic — **sardoniquement** [-nikmɑ̃] *adv*

sari [sari] *nm* : sari

sarrasin [sarazɛ̃] *nm* : buckwheat

sarrau [saro] *nm, pl* **sarraus** : smock

sas [sas] *nm* **1** CRIBLE : sieve **2** : enclosure (in a canal lock) **3** : airlock

sassafras [sasafra] *nm* : sassafras

Satan [satɑ̃] *nm* : Satan

satanique [satanik] *adj* : satanic

satellite [satelit] *nm* : satellite

satiété [sasjete] *nf* : satiation, satiety <manger à satiété : to eat one's fill>

satin [satɛ̃] *nm* : satin

satire [satir] *nf* : satire

satirique [satirik] *adj* : satiric, satirical

satiriser [satirize] *vt* : to satirize

satisfaction [satisfaksjɔ̃] *nf* : satisfaction, gratification

satisfaire [satisfɛr] {42} *vt* CONTENTER : to satisfy — *vi* ~ **à** : to satisfy, to fulfill, to meet — **se satisfaire** *vr* ~ **de** : to be content with

satisfaisant, -sante [satisfəzɑ̃, -zɑ̃t] *adj* **1** : satisfactory, acceptable **2** : satisfying, pleasing

satisfait, -faite [satisfɛ, -fɛt] *adj* : satisfied, pleased

saturer [satyre] *vt* : to saturate — **saturation** [-tyrasjɔ̃] *nf*

Saturne [satyrn] *nf* : Saturn (planet)

satyre [satir] *nm* **1** : satyr **2** : lecher

sauce [sos] *nf* : sauce

saucisse [sosis] *nf* **1** : sausage (meat) **2** **saucisse de Francfort** *or* **saucisse à hot-dog** *Can* : frankfurter, hot dog

saucisson [sosisɔ̃] *nm* : sausage, bologna, cold cut

sauf[1]**, sauve** [sof, sov] *adj* **1** : safe, unharmed **2** : intact, saved

sauf[2] *prep* **1** : except (for), apart from **2** **sauf si** : unless <sauf s'il neige : unless it snows>

sauge [soʒ] *nf* : sage (herb)

saugrenu, -nue [sogrəny] *adj* ABSURDE : preposterous, absurd

saule [sol] *nm* : willow <saule pleureur : weeping willow>

saumâtre [somatr] *adj* : brackish, briny

saumon[1] [somɔ̃] *adj* : salmon pink

saumon[2] *nm* : salmon

saumure [somyr] *nf* : brine

sauna [sona] *nm* : sauna

saupoudrer [sopudre] *vt* : to sprinkle

saura [sɔra], *etc.* → **savoir**

saut [so] *nm* **1** BOND : jump <saut en hauteur : high jump> <saut de main : handspring> <saut périlleux : somersault> <saut à skis : ski jump> **2** : leap, drop <faire le saut : to take the plunge> **3** **faire faire un saut à qqn** *Can* : to scare s.o., to make s.o. jump **4** **faire un saut chez qqn** : to drop in on s.o.

saute-mouton [sotmutɔ̃] *nms & pl* : leapfrog

sauter [sote] *vt* **1** FRANCHIR : to jump over, to clear **2** OMETTRE : to skip, to leave out — *vi* **1** BONDIR : to jump, to leap <sauter à cloche-pied : to hop> <sauter à la corde : to jump rope> **2** : to leap up, to jump <sauter aux yeux : to be glaringly obvious> **3** : to come off, to slip (of a gear, etc.) **4** EXPLOSER : to go off, to blow up **5** **faire sauter** : to sauté

sauterelle [sotrɛl] *nf* : grasshopper

sauteur, -teuse [sotœr, -tøz] *n* : jumper (in sports)

sautillement [sotijmɑ̃] *nm* : hop, skip

sautiller [sotije] *vi* **1** : to hop, to skip **2** : to flit about

sautoir [sotwar] *nm* : long necklace, chain

sauvage[1] [sovaʒ] *adj* **1** : savage **2** : wild **3** FAROUCHE : unsociable, shy

sauvage[2] *nmf* **1** : savage **2** : unsociable person

sauvagerie [sovaʒri] *nf* **1** : savagery **2** : shyness, unsociability

sauvagine [sovaʒin] *nf* : waterfowl

sauve → **sauf**[1]

sauvegarde [sovgard] *nf* **1** : safeguard **2** : safety, security **3** : backup (of a computer file)

sauvegarder [sovgarde] *vt* **1** : to safeguard **2** : to save (a computer file)

sauve-qui-peut [sovkipø] *nms & pl* : stampede, panic

sauver [sove] *vt* **1** : to save, to rescue **2** : to salvage **3** : to redeem — **se sauver** *vr* **1** : to escape **2** *fam* FILER : to leave, to split, to rush off

sauvetage [sovtaʒ] *nm* **1** : rescue, lifesaving **2** : salvage

sauveteur [sovtœr] *nm* : rescuer, lifesaver

sauvette [sovɛt] **à la sauvette** **1** : hastily, in a rush **2** : illegally, on the sly

sauveur [sovœr] *nm* : savior

savamment [savamɑ̃] *adv* **1** : learnedly **2** HABILEMENT : skillfully

savane [savan] *nf* **1** : savanna **2** *Can* : swamp

savant[1]**, -vante** [savɑ̃, -vɑ̃t] *adj* **1** ÉRUDIT : learned, scholarly **2** HABILE : skillful, clever

savant[2]**, -vante** *n* **1** ÉRUDIT : savant, scholar **2** SCIENTIFIQUE : scientist

saveur [savœr] *nf* GOÛT : flavor, savor

savoir[1] [savwar] {79} *vt* **1** : to know <savoir par coeur : to know by heart> <je le sais loyal : I know he's loyal> <en savoir long de : to know a great deal about> <sans le savoir : unknowingly> **2** POUVOIR : to know how to, to be able to <elle sait jouer du piano : she can play the piano> <je ne sais pas mentir : I cannot tell a lie> **3** **à** ~ : that is to say, namely — **se savoir** *vr* : to become known

savoir[2] *nm* : learning, knowledge

savoir-faire [savwarfɛr] *nms & pl* : know-how, expertise

savoir-vivre [savwarvivr] *nms & pl* : good manners *pl,* tact

savon [savɔ̃] *nm* **1** : soap **2** *fam* **passer un savon à** : to reprimand

savonner [savɔne] *vt* : to soap (up), to lather

savonnette [savɔnɛt] *nf* : bar of soap

savonneux, -neuse [savɔnø, -nøz] *adj* : soapy

savourer [savure] *vt* : to savor

savoureux, -reuse [savurø, -røz] *adj* **1** DÉLECTABLE : savory, tasty **2** PIQUANT : racy, juicy <anecdote savoureuse : racy anecdote>

saxophone [saksɔfɔn] *nm* : saxophone — **saxophoniste** [-fɔnist] *nmf*

scabreux, -breuse [skabrø, -brøz] *adj* **1** INDÉCENT : indecent, risqué **2** : risky, tricky

scalpel [skalpɛl] *nm* : scalpel

scalper [skalpe] *vt* : to scalp

scandale [skɑ̃dal] *nf* **1** : scandal <faire scandale : to cause a scandal> **2** ÉCLAT : scene, uproar

scandaleux, -leuse [skɑ̃dalø, -løz] *adj* : scandalous, disgraceful — **scandaleusement** [-løzmɑ̃] *adv*

scandaliser [skɑ̃dalize] *vt* : to scandalize

scander [skɑ̃de] *vt* **1** : to scan (poetry) **2** : to chant **3** : to accentuate, to stress

scandinave [skɑ̃dinav] *adj* : Scandinavian

Scandinave *nmf* : Scandinavian

scanner [skanɛr] *nm* : scanner

scansion [skɑ̃sjɔ̃] *nf* : scan, scanning (in literature)

scaphandre [skafɑ̃dr] *nm* **1** : diving suit **2** : space suit

scaphandrier [skafɑ̃drije] *nm* : deep-sea diver

scarabée [skarabe] *nm* **1** : beetle **2** : scarab

scarlatine [skarlatin] *nf* : scarlet fever

scarole [skarɔl] *nf* : endive, escarole

sceau [so] *nm* **1** : seal **2** : hallmark, stamp

scélérat[1], -rate [selera, -rat] *adj* : villainous

scélérat[2], -rate *n* : villain, rogue

scellé [sele] *nm* : seal

sceller [sele] *vt* **1** : to seal **2** : to attach securely, to fix

scénario [senarjo] *nm* **1** : scenario **2** : screenplay

scène [sɛn] *nf* **1** : scene (in theater) **2** : stage <être en scène : to be on stage> **3** : scene, row <faire une scène : to make a scene> **4** → **metteur, mise**

scénique [senik] *adj* : theatrical

scepticisme [sɛptisism] *nm* : skepticism

sceptique[1] [sɛptik] *adj* : skeptical

sceptique[2] *nmf* : skeptic

sceptre [sɛptr] *nm* : scepter

scheik [ʃɛk] *nm* → **cheik**

schéma [ʃema] *nm* **1** : diagram **2** ESQUISSE : sketch, outline

schématique [ʃematik] *adj* **1** : schematic **2** : (over)simplified

schisme [ʃism] *nm* : schism

schiste [ʃist] *nm* **schiste argileux** : shale

schizophrène [skizɔfrɛn] *adj & nmf* : schizophrenic

schizophrénie [skizɔfreni] *nf* : schizophrenia

schooner [ʃunœr] *nm* GOÉLETTE : schooner

scie [si] *nf* **1** : saw <scie à métaux : hacksaw> <scie sauteuse : jigsaw> <scie à chaîne : chainsaw> **2** : catchphrase **3** *fam* : drag, bore

sciemment [sjamɑ̃] *adv* : knowingly

science [sjɑ̃s] *nf* **1** : science **2** SAVOIR : knowledge, learning

science-fiction [sjɑ̃sfiksjɔ̃] *nf* : science fiction

scientifique[1] [sjɑ̃tifik] *adj* : scientific — **scientifiquement** [-fikmɑ̃] *adv*

scientifique[2] *nmf* : scientist

scier [sje] {96} *vt* : to saw

scierie [siri] *nf* : sawmill

scinder [sɛ̃de] *vt* DIVISER : to split, to divide — **se scinder** *vr* : to be divided, to split up

scintillant, -lante [sɛ̃tijɑ̃, -jɑ̃t] *adj* : sparkling, twinkling

scintillement [sɛ̃tijmɑ̃] *nm* : sparkling, twinkling

scintiller [sɛ̃tije] *vi* : to scintillate, to twinkle, to sparkle

scission [sisjɔ̃] *nf* **1** : schism, split <faire scission : to secede, to break away> **2** : fission (in biology and physics)

sciure [sjyr] *nf* : sawdust

scolaire [skɔlɛr] *adj* : school, scholastic <l'année scolaire : the school year>

scolarité [skɔlarite] *nf* : schooling

scooter [skutœr] *nm* : motor scooter

scorbut [skɔrbyt] *nm* : scurvy

score [skɔr] *nm* : score

scorie [skɔri] *nf* **1** : slag **2** : dross, dregs

scorpion [skɔrpjɔ̃] *nm* : scorpion

Scorpion *nm* : Scorpio

scotch [skɔtʃ] *nm* : Scotch whiskey

scout[1], scoute [skut] *adj* : scout <camp scout : scout camp>

scout[2], scoute *n* : Boy Scout *m*, Girl Scout *f*

scribe [skrib] *nm* : scribe

script [skript] *nm* **1** : printing, lettering **2** : script (in movies, television, etc.)

scrotum [skrɔtɔm] *nm* : scrotum

scrupule [skrypyl] *nm* : scruple, qualm, compunction

scrupuleux, -leuse [skrypylø, -løz] *adj* : scrupulous — **scrupuleusement** [-løzmɑ̃] *adv*

scruter [skryte] *vt* : to scrutinize

scrutin [skrytɛ̃] *nm* **1** : ballot, voting **2** : polling, polls *pl*

sculpter [skylte] *vt* : to sculpt, to sculpture, to carve

sculpteur [skyltœr] *nm* : sculptor <elle est sculpteur : she's a sculptor>

sculpture [skyltyr] *nf* : sculpture — **sculptural, -rale** [-tyral] *adj*

se [sə] (**s'** *before a vowel or mute h*) *pron* **1** (*used with reflexive verbs*) : oneself, himself, herself, themselves, itself <elle se regarde : she looks at herself> **2** (*used to indicate reciprocity*) : each other, one another <ils se sont parlés : they spoke to each other> **3** (*used in passive constructions*) <ça ne se fait pas : that is not done> **4** (*used when referring to parts of the body*) <il se lave les dents : he brushes his teeth> **5** (*used with impersonal verbs*) <il se peut qu'elle arrive demain : she may arrive tomorrow>

séance [seɑ̃s] *nf* **1** : session, meeting **2** : showing, performance **3 séance de spiritisme** : séance **4 séance tenante** : immediately, without delay

seau [so] *nm, pl* **seaux** : bucket, pail

sec[1] [sɛk] *adv* **1** : hard <frapper sec : to strike hard> **2** BRUSQUEMENT : abruptly, sharply

sec[2], **sèche** [sɛk, sɛʃ] *adj* **1** : dry **2** : dried <abricots secs : dried apricots> **3** MAIGRE : lean, gaunt **4** DUR : hard, harsh, sharp <une voix sèche : a harsh voice> <avec un bruit sec : with a snap>

sec[3] *nm* **1** : dryness **2 être à sec** *fam* : to be dried up, to go broke

sécateur [sekatœr] *nm* : clippers *pl*, (garden) shears

sécession [sesesjɔ̃] *nf* : secession <faire sécession : to secede>

sèche–cheveux [sɛʃʃəvø] *nms & pl* : hairdryer

sèchement [sɛʃmɑ̃] *adv* : dryly, curtly

sécher [seʃe] {87} *vt* **1** : to dry **2** *France fam* : to skip, to cut (a class, etc.) — *vi* **1** : to dry, to dry up, to dry out **2** *fam* : to be stumped, to draw a blank

sécheresse [sɛʃrɛs] *nf* **1** : drought **2** : dryness **3** : curtness

séchoir [seʃwar] *nm* : dryer

second[1], **-conde** [səgɔ̃, -gɔ̃d] *adj & nmf* : second

second[2] *nm* **1** : assistant, helper **2** : first mate **3** : second floor

secondaire [səgɔ̃dɛr] *adj* **1** : secondary **2** → **école**

seconde [səgɔ̃d] *nf* **1** : second <attends une seconde! : wait a second!> **2** : second class <voyager en seconde : to travel second class> **3 de seconde main** : secondhand

seconder [səgɔ̃de] *vt* : to assist, to back up

secouer [səkwe] *vt* **1** : to shake <secouer la tête : to shake one's head> **2** : to shake off **3** *fam* : to shake up, to rouse — **se secouer** *vr* : to pull oneself together, to get going

secourable [səkurabl] *adj* : helpful

secourir [səkurir] {23} *vt* **1** AIDER : to help, to aid **2** : to rescue

secourisme [səkurism] *nm* : first aid

secouriste [səkurist] *nmf* : first aid worker

secours [səkur] *nms & pl* **1** : help, aid <au secours! : help!> **2 de ~** : for emergency <pneu de secours : spare tire> <sortie de secours : emergency exit> **3 secours** *nmpl* : rescuers, reinforcements

secousse [səkus] *nf* **1** CAHOT : jolt, jerk **2** CHOC : shock, upset **3** *Can* : period of time **4** *or* **secousse sismique** : tremor

secret[1], **-crète** [səkrɛ, -krɛt] *adj* **1** : secret **2** : secretive, reserved

secret[2] *nm* **1** : secret **2** : secrecy

secrétaire[1] [səkretɛr] *nmf* : secretary

secrétaire[2] *nm* : secretary (desk)

secrétariat [səkretarjat] *nm* **1** : secretariat **2** : secretarial work

secrètement [səkrɛtmɑ̃] *adv* : secretly

sécréter [sekrete] {87} *vt* : to secrete <sécréter du lait : to lactate> — **sécrétion** [-resjɔ̃] *nf*

sectaire [sɛktɛr] *adj* : sectarian

secte [sɛkt] *nm* : sect

secteur [sɛktœr] *nm* : sector, area, zone <le secteur privé : the private sector>

section [sɛksjɔ̃] *nf* **1** : section **2** : department, branch

sectionner [sɛksjɔne] *vt* **1** DIVISER : to section, to divide **2** TRANCHER : to sever

séculaire [sekylɛr] *adj* **1** : ancient, age-old, a hundred years old **2** : secular

séculier, -lière [sekylje, -ljɛr] *adj* LAÏQUE : secular

secundo [səgɔ̃do] *adv* : second, secondly

sécuriser [sekyrize] *vt* **1** RASSURER : to reassure **2** : to make (someone) feel secure

sécurité [sekyrite] *nf* **1** : security <sentiment de sécurité : sense of security> **2** : safely <sécurité publique : public safety>

sédatif, -tive [sedatif, -tiv] *adj & nm* : sedative

sédation [sedasjɔ̃] *nf* : sedation

sédentaire [sedɑ̃tɛr] *adj* : sedentary

sédiment [sedimɑ̃] *nm* : sediment — **sédimentaire** [-mɑ̃tɛr] *adj*

séditieux, -tieuse [sedisjø, -sjøz] *adj* : seditious

sédition [sedisjɔ̃] *nf* : insurrection, revolt

séducteur[1], **-trice** [sedyktœr, -tris] *adj* : seductive

séducteur[2], **-trice** *n* : seducer

séduction [sedyksjɔ̃] *nf* **1** : seduction **2** : charm, appeal

séduire [sedɥir] {49} *vt* **1** : to seduce **2** : to charm **3** : to appeal to

séduisant, -sante [sedɥizɑ̃, -zɑ̃t] *adj* : seductive, attractive

segment [sɛgmɑ̃] *nm* **1** : segment **2 segment de piston** : piston ring

segmentaire [sɛgmɑ̃tɛr] *adj* : segmented

ségrégation [segregasjɔ̃] *nf* : segregation

seiche [sɛʃ] *nf* : cuttlefish

seigle [sɛgl] *nm* : rye

seigneur [sɛɲœr] *nm* **1** : lord **2 le Seigneur** : the Lord
sein [sɛ̃] *nm* **1** : breast, bosom <donner le sein à : to breast-feed> **2** VENTRE : womb **3 au sein de** : within
séisme [seism] *nm* : earthquake
seize[1] [sɛz] *adj* **1** : sixteen **2** : sixteenth <le seize octobre : October sixteenth>
seize[2] *nms & pl* : sixteen
seizième [sɛzjɛm] *adj & nmf & nm* : sixteenth
séjour [seʒur] *nm* **1** : stay, sojourn **2** → **salle**
séjourner [seʒurne] *vi* **1** : to stay (at a hotel, etc.) **2** RESTER : to lie, to remain (of water, fog, etc.)
sel [sɛl] *nm* **1** : salt <sel gemme : rock salt> **2** : piquancy, wit
sélect, -lecte [selɛkt] *adj fam* : select, exclusive, posh
sélectif, -tive [selɛktif, -tiv] *adj* : selective
sélection [selɛksjɔ̃] *nf* **1** : selection **2 sélection naturelle** : natural selection
sélectionner [selɛksjɔne] *vt* : to select, to choose
self-made-man [sɛlfmedman] *nm* : self-made man
self-service [sɛlfsɛrvis] *nm, pl* **self-services** : self-service store or restaurant
selle [sɛl] *nf* **1** : saddle **2 aller à la selle** : to have a bowel movement
seller [sele] *vt* : to saddle
sellette [sɛlɛt] *nf* **être sur la sellette** : to be in the hot seat
selon [səlɔ̃] *prep* **1** : according to **2 ~ que** : depending on whether
semailles [səmaj] *nfpl* : sowing, seeding
semaine [səmɛn] *nf* **1** : week <une semaine de quarante heures : a forty-hour week> **2 vivre à la petite semaine** : to live day by day
sémantique[1] [semɑ̃tik] *adj* : semantic
sémantique[2] *nf* : semantics
sémaphore [semafɔr] *nm* : semaphore
semblable[1] [sɑ̃blabl] *adj* **1** : similar, like **2** TEL : such <il faut de semblables mesures : such measures are necessary>
semblable[2] *nmf* : fellow creature, like <vous et vos semblables : you and your kind>
semblant [sɑ̃blɑ̃] *nm* **1** : semblance, appearance **2 faire semblant** : to pretend
sembler [sɑ̃ble] *vi* : to seem <elle semble contente : she seems (to be) happy> — *v impers* **il semble que** : it seems that
semelle [səmɛl] *nf* **1** : sole **2** *or* **semelle intérieure** : insole
semence [səmɑ̃s] *nf* **1** GRAINE : seed **2** : tack, brad
semer [səme] {52} *vt* **1** : to sow, to seed **2** RÉPANDRE : to strew, to scatter **3** *fam* : to lose, to shake off (pursuers, etc.)
semestre [səmɛstr] *nm* : semester
semestriel, -trielle [səmɛstrijɛl] *adj* : biannual — **semestriellement** *adv*
semeur, -meuse [səmœr, -møz] *n* : sower
semi-circulaire [səmisirkylɛr] *adj* DEMI-CIRCULAIRE : semicircular
semi-conducteur [sɛmikɔ̃dyktœr] *nm, pl* **semi-conducteurs** : semiconductor
sémillant, -lante [semijɑ̃, -jɑ̃t] *adj* VIF : lively, spirited
séminaire [seminɛr] *nm* **1** : seminary **2** : seminar
séminal, -nale [seminal] *adj, mpl* **-naux** [-no] : seminal
semi-remorque [səmirəmɔrk] *nm, pl* **semi-remorques** : semitrailer
semis [səmi] *nm* **1** : seedling **2** : sowing **3** : seedbed **4** : small repeated pattern
semoir [səmwar] *nm* : drill (in agriculture)
semonce [səmɔ̃s] *nf* **1** RÉPRIMANDE : reprimand **2 coup de semonce** : warning shot
semoule [səmul] *nf* : semolina <semoule de maïs : cornflour>
sempiternel, -nelle [sɑ̃pitɛrnɛl] *adj* ÉTERNEL : eternal
sénat [sena] *nm* : senate
sénateur [senatœr] *nm* : senator
sénatrice [senatris] *nf Can* : (female) senator
sénégalais, -laise [senegalɛ, -lɛz] *adj* : Senegalese
Sénégalais, -laise *n* : Senegalese
sénile [senil] *adj* : senile
sénilité [senilite] *nf* : senility
sens [sɑ̃s] *nms & pl* **1** : sense (in physiology) <sens du toucher : sense of touch> **2** SIGNIFICATION : sense, meaning <dépourvu de sens : meaningless> **3** INSTINCT : sense, feeling <sens du rythme : sense of rhythm> **4** RAISON : sense <cela n'a pas de sens : that doesn't make any sense> **5** DIRECTION : direction, way <sens unique : one-way> **6** OPINION : opinion <à mon sens : in my opinion> **7 sens dessus dessous** : upside down
sensation [sɑ̃sasjɔ̃] *nf* **1** : sensation, feeling **2 faire sensation** : to cause a sensation
sensationnel, -nelle [sɑ̃sasjɔnɛl] *adj* : sensational
sensé, -sée [sɑ̃se] *adj* : sensible
sensibiliser [sɑ̃sibilize] *vt* : to sensitize
sensibilité [sɑ̃sibilite] *nf* : sensitivity, sensibility
sensible [sɑ̃sibl] *adj* **1** : sensitive **2** APPRÉCIABLE : appreciable, considerable **3** PERCEPTIBLE : perceptible

sensiblement [sɑ̃sibləmɑ̃] *adv* **1** : appreciably, noticeably **2** : roughly, approximately
sensiblerie [sɑ̃sibləri] *nf* : sentimentality
sensitif, -tive [sɑ̃sitif, -tiv] *adj* **1** : oversensitive **2** : sensory
sensoriel, -rielle [sɑ̃sɔrjɛl] *adj* : sensory
sensualité [sɑ̃sɥalite] *nf* : sensuality, sensuousness
sensuel, -suelle [sɑ̃sɥɛl] *adj* : sensual, sensuous — **sensuellement** [-sɥɛlmɑ̃] *adv*
sentence [sɑ̃tɑ̃s] *nf* **1** JUGEMENT : sentence **2** MAXIME : maxim, proverb
sentencieux, -cieuse [sɑ̃tɑ̃sjø, -sjøz] *adj* : sententious
senteur [sɑ̃tœr] *nf* : scent
senti, -tie [sɑ̃ti] *adj* **bien senti** : blunt, forthright <mots bien sentis : well-chosen words>
sentier [sɑ̃tje] *nm* : path <hors des sentiers battus : off the beaten track>
sentiment [sɑ̃timɑ̃] *nm* **1** : sentiment, feeling <avoir le sentiment de : to be aware of> <faire du sentiment : to be sentimental> **2** AVIS : opinion, feeling <c'est mon sentiment : that's my feeling, that's what I think> **3 recevez l'expression de mes sentiments respectueux** : yours truly
sentimental, -tale [sɑ̃timɑ̃tal] *adj, mpl* **-taux** [-to] : sentimental — **sentimentalité** [-talite] *nf*
sentinelle [sɑ̃tinɛl] *nf* : sentinel, sentry
sentir [sɑ̃tir] {82} *vt* **1** : to smell, to taste **2** : to smell like, to smell of <ça sent la rose : it smells like a rose> **3** : to feel <il n'a rien senti : he felt nothing> **4** : to have a feeling (for), to appreciate <je sens que c'est important : I have a feeling that it's important> <elle sent l'art moderne : she appreciates modern art> **5** : to smack of, to be indicative of — *vi* : to smell — **se sentir** *vr* **1** : to feel <il se sent malade : he feels sick> **2** : to be felt, to show
seoir [swar] {80} *vi* **~ à** : to suit, to be appropriate to — *v impers* **il sied** : it is fitting, it is appropriate
séparation [separasjɔ̃] *nf* : separation
séparé, -rée [separe] *adj* **1** : separate **2** : separated (from one's spouse)
séparément [separemɑ̃] *adv* : separately, apart
séparer [separe] *vt* **1** DÉTACHER : to separate, to detach **2** DISTINGUER : to distinguish (between) **3** : to divide — **se séparer** *vr* **1** : to separate, to part, to split up **2** : to divide **3 ~ de** : to part with, to be without
sépia [sepja] *nf* : sepia
sept[1] [sɛt] *adj* **1** : seven **2** : seventh <le sept mai : May seventh>
sept[2] *nms & pl* : seven
septante[1] [sɛptɑ̃t] *adj Bel, Switz* **1** : seventy **2** : seventieth
septante[2] *nms & pl Bel, Switz* : seventy
septembre [sɛptɑ̃br] *nm* : September
septentrional, -nale [sɛptɑ̃trijɔnal] *adj, mpl* **-naux** [-no] : northern
septième [sɛtjɛm] *adj & nmf & nm* : seventh
septique [sɛptik] *adj* **1** : septic **2** → **fosse**
sépulcre [sepylkr] *nm* : sepulchre, tomb
sépulture [sepyltyr] *nf* **1** TOMBE : grave **2** ENTERREMENT : burial
séquelle [sekɛl] *nf* **1** CONSÉQUENCE : consequence **2 séquelles** *nfpl* : aftereffects
séquence [sekɑ̃s] *nf* SUITE : sequence
séquentiel, -tielle [sekɑ̃sjɛl] *adj* : sequential
séquestre [sekɛstr] *nm* : escrow <en séquestre : in escrow>
séquestrer [sekɛstre] *vt* : to sequester
séquoia [sekɔja] *nm* : sequoia
sera [səra], *etc.* → **être**
sérail [seraj] *nm* : seraglio
séraphine, -phine [serafɛ̃, -fin] *adj Can fam* : stingy, miserly
serbe[1] [sɛrb] *adj* : Serb, Serbian
serbe[2] *nm* : Serbian (language)
Serbe *nmf* : Serb, Serbian
serein, -reine [sərɛ̃, -rɛn] *adj* **1** : clear, tranquil (of the sky, weather, etc.) **2** CALME : calm, serene — **sereinement** [-rɛnmɑ̃] *adv*
sérénade [serenad] *nf* : serenade
sérénité [serenite] *nf* : serenity
serf, serve [sɛrf, sɛrv] *n* : serf
serge [sɛrʒ] *nf* : serge
sergé [sɛrʒe] *nm* : twill
sergent [sɛrʒɑ̃] *nm* : sergeant
série [seri] *nf* **1** : series **2** : set, range, line **3 de ~** : mass-produced, standard, stock **4 fabrication en série** : mass production
sériel, -rielle [serjɛl] *adj* : serial
sérieusement [serjøzmɑ̃] *adv* : seriously
sérieux[1], **-rieuse** [serjø, -rjøz] *adj* **1** : serious, solemn **2** : important <une sérieuse argumentation : a weighty argument> **3** : reliable, dependable **4** : responsible, conscientious
sérieux[2] *nm* : seriousness, earnestness <se prendre au sérieux : to take oneself seriously>
serin [sərɛ̃, -rin] *nm* : canary
seringue [sərɛ̃g] *nf* : syringe
serment [sɛrmɑ̃] *nm* **1** : oath <prêter serment : to take the oath> **2** : vow, promise
sermon [sɛrmɔ̃] *nm* **1** : sermon **2** : lecture, talking-to
sermonner [sɛrmɔne] *vt* : to lecture
serpent [sɛrpɑ̃] *nm* **1** : snake, serpent **2 serpent à sonnettes** CROTALE : rattlesnake
serpenter [sɛrpɑ̃te] *vi* : to wind, to meander

serpentin [sɛrpɑ̃tɛ̃] *nm* : streamer

séquestre [sekɛstr] *nm* : escrow <en séquestre : in escrow>

serrage [sɛraʒ] *nm* : tightening

serre [sɛr] *nf* **1** : greenhouse, hothouse <l'effet de serre : greenhouse effect> **2 serres** *nfpl* : claws, talons

serré, -rée [sere] *adj* **1** : tight **2** : thick, cramped, dense **3** : strict, tight, close <surveillance serrée : close supervision>

serre–livres [sɛrlivr] *nms & pl* : bookend

serrement [sɛrmɑ̃] *nm* : pressing, squeezing, constriction <serrement de main : handshake> <serrement de coeur : pang (of sorrow)>

serrer [sere] *vt* **1** : to press, to squeeze, to grip <serrer les poings : to clench one's fists> **2** : to tighten **3** : to squeeze tightly <ces chaussures me serrent : these shoes are too tight> **4** : to stay close to <serrer le trottoir : to hug the curb> **5** : to push (close) together, to pack together **6** : to cut (expenses, etc.) — **se serrer** *vr* **1** : to huddle up (together) **2** : to tighten up **3 se serrer la main** : to shake hands

serre–tête [sɛrtɛt] *nm, pl* **serre–têtes** : headband

serrure [sɛryr] *nf* : lock

serrurier [sɛryrje] *nm* : locksmith

sert [sɛr], *etc.* → **servir**

sertir [sɛrtir] *vt* : to set, to mount (gems)

sérum [serɔm] *nm* : serum

serveur[1], -veuse [sɛrvœr, -vøz] *n* : waiter *m*, waitress *f*

serveur[2] *nm* **1** : server (in sports) **2** : dealer (in card games) **3** : (computer) server

serviable [sɛrvjabl] *adj* OBLIGEANT : obliging

service [sɛrvis] *nm* **1** : service <mettre en service : to put in service, to set up> <hors service : out of order> <service de bus : bus service> **2** FAVEUR : favor <rendre un service à : to do a favor for> **3** : serving, course <repas à trois services : three-course meal> **4** : service, serving <être au service se son pays : to serve one's country> <à votre service! : not at all!, don't mention it!> <service militaire : military service> <faire le service : to serve a meal, to wait tables> **5** : department <service du personnel : personnel department> <services sociaux : social services> **6** : set <service de café : coffee service> **7** : service, serve (in sports)

serviette [sɛrvjɛt] *nf* **1** : napkin **2** : towel **3** : briefcase, portfolio **4 serviette hygiénique** : sanitary napkin

servile [sɛrvil] *adj* : servile — **servilité** [sɛrvilite] *nf*

servir [sɛrvir] {81} *vt* **1** : to serve **2** AIDER : to help, to assist **3** : to deal (cards) — *vi* **1** : to be useful <ça ne sert à rien : that is of no use> **2** : to serve (in the military) **3** : to deal (in card games) **4 ~ de** : to serve as — **se servir** *vr* **1** : to serve oneself, to help oneself **2 ~ de** : to make use of

serviteur [sɛrvitœr] *nm* : servant

servitude [sɛrvityd] *nf* **1** : servitude **2** : obligation, constraint

sésame [sezam] *nm* : sesame (plant and seed)

session [sesjɔ̃] *nf* : session

set [sɛt] *nm* **1** : set (in tennis, etc.) **2** *or* **set de table** : placemat

seuil [sœj] *nm* **1** : threshold, doorstep **2 au seuil de** : on the threshold, on the brink of

seul[1], seule [sœl] *adv* **1** : alone, only <seule Marie répondit : only Marie replied> **2** : by oneself, singlehandedly <tout seul : all by oneself>

seul[2], seule *adj* **1** : alone <j'ai besoin d'être seul : I need to be alone> **2** : only, unique <le seul problème : the only problem> **3** SOLITAIRE : lonely, solitary

seul[3], seule *pron* : only one, single one <c'est le seul qui reste : it's the only one left>

seulement[1] [sœlmɑ̃] *adv* **1** : only <seulement trois fois : only three times> <pas seulement . . . , mais encore : not only . . . , but also> **2** MÊME : even <sans seulement dire un mot : without even saying a word>

seulement[2] *conj* CEPENDANT : however, but, only <je l'achèterais, seulement je n'ai pas d'argent : I'd buy it, only I don't have any money>

sève [sɛv] *nf* **1** : sap **2** VIGUEUR : vim, vigor

sévère [sevɛr] *adj* **1** : strict, severe, stern **2** : austere — **sévèrement** [-vɛrmɑ̃] *adv*

sévérité [severite] *nf* : severity

serviable [sɛrvjabl] *adj* : helpful, obliging

sévices [sevis] *nmpl* : cruelty, brutality, abuse

sévir [sevir] *vi* **1** : to clamp down, to impose restrictions **2** : to be rampant, to rage

sevrage [səvraʒ] *nm* : weaning

sevrer [səvre] *vt* : to wean

sexe [sɛks] *nm* **1** : sex **2** : sex organs, genitals

sexisme [sɛksism] *nm* : sexism

sexiste [sɛksist] *adj & nmf* : sexist

sextant [sɛkstɑ̃] *nm* : sextant

sextuor [sɛkstɥɔr] *nm* : sextet

sexualité [sɛksɥalite] *nf* : sexuality

sexuel, sexuelle [sɛksɥɛl] *adj* : sexual — **sexuellement** [-sɥɛlmɑ̃] *adv*

sexy [sɛksi] *adj* : sexy

seyant, seyante [sɛjɑ̃, -jɑ̃t] *adj* : becoming, flattering

shampooing [ʃɑ̃pwɛ̃] *nm* : shampoo

shampouiner *or* **shampooiner** [ʃɑ̃pwine] *vt* : to shampoo
shérif [ʃerif] *nm* : sheriff
shopping [ʃɔpiŋ] *nm* : shopping <faire le shopping : to go shopping>
short [ʃɔrt] *nm* : shorts *pl*
si[1] [si] *adv* **1** TELLEMENT : so, such, as <elle est si intelligente : she is so intelligent> <un si grand pays : such a big country> <il n'est pas si célèbre que ça : he's not as famous as all that> **2** (*used to contradict a negative statement or question*) : yes <il n'est pas arrivé à l'heure? si : he didn't arrive on time? yes, he did> **3 si bien que** : with the result that, so **4 si . . . que** : however <si riche qu'elle soit : however wealthy she is>
si[2] *conj* : if, whether <si vous voulez : if you please> <je ne sais pas si elle vient ou pas : I don't know whether she's coming or not>
siamois, -moise [sjamwa, -waz] *adj* : Siamese
Siamois, -moise *n* : Siamese
sida [sida] *nm* : AIDS
sidérer [sidere] {87} *vt fam* : to stagger, to amaze
sidérurgie [sideryrʒi] *nf* : steel industry
sidérurgique [sideryrʒik] *adj* : steel <usine sidérurgique : ironworks, steelworks>
siècle [sjɛkl] *nm* : century
siège [sjɛʒ] *nm* **1** : seat <siège arrière : back seat (of an automobile)> **2** *or* **siège social** : headquarters **3** : siege
siéger [sjeʒe] {64} *vi* **1** : to sit, to serve <siéger à un comité : to sit on a committee> **2** : to be in session **3** : to be located, to have its headquarters
sien[1], **sienne** [sjɛ̃, sjɛn] *adj* : his, hers, its, one's
sien[2], **sienne** *pron* **le sien, la sienne, les siens, les siennes** : his, hers, its, one's, theirs
sieste [sjɛst] *nf* : siesta, nap
sifflement [sifləmɑ̃] *nm* **1** : whistle, whistling, hoot (of a train) **2** : hiss, hissing
siffler [sifle] *vt* **1** : to whistle **2** : to whistle for, to whistle at **3** : to boo **4** *fam* : to swill down, to swig — *vi* **1** : to whistle, to blow a whistle, to hoot (of a train) **2** : to hiss **3** : to wheeze
sifflet [siflɛ] *nm* **1** : whistle **2 sifflets** *nmpl* : boos, catcalls
siffloter [siflɔte] *v* : to whistle
sigle [sigl] *nm* : acronym
signal [siɲal] *nm, pl* **signaux** [siɲo] **1** : sign, signal (gesture) <donner le signal : to give the signal> **2** : signal <signal d'alarme : alarm (signal)>
signalement [siɲalmɑ̃] *nm* : description
signaler [siɲale] *vt* **1** : to signal **2** : to point out, to indicate **3** : to report — **se signaler** *vr* : to distinguish oneself, to stand out
signalisation [siɲalizasjɔ̃] *nf* : signals *pl*, signs *pl* <signalisation routière : road signs>
signataire [siɲatɛr] *nmf* : signatory
signature [siɲatyr] *nf* **1** : signature **2** : signing
signe [siɲ] *nm* **1** : sign, gesture <en signe d'estime : as a sign of respect> <faire signe que oui : to nod in agreement> **2** : sign, indication <signes de vie : signs of life> **3** : mark, symbol <signe de ponctuation : punctuation mark> <signe du zodiaque : sign of the zodiac> **4 signe avant–coureur** : herald, precursor
signer [siɲe] *vt* : to sign (one's name) — **se signer** *vr* : to cross oneself
signet [siɲɛ] *nm* : bookmark
significatif, -tive [siɲifikatif, -tiv] *adj* : significant
signification [siɲifikasjɔ̃] *nf* : significance, meaning
signifier [siɲifje] {96} *vt* : to signify, to mean
silence [silɑ̃s] *nm* **1** : silence <silence absolu : dead silence> <garder le silence : to keep quiet> **2** : rest (in music)
silencieux[1], **-cieuse** [silɑ̃sjø, -sjøz] *adj* : silent, quiet — **silencieusement** [-sjøzmɑ̃] *adv*
silencieux[2] *nm* **1** : silencer (of a firearm) **2** : muffler
silex [silɛks] *nm* : flint
silhouette [silwɛt] *nf* : silhouette, outline
silice [silis] *nf* : silica
silicium [silisjɔm] *nm* : silicon
sillage [sijaʒ] *nm* : wake (of a ship)
sillon [sijɔ̃] *nm* **1** : furrow **2** : groove (of a disc, etc.)
sillonner [sijɔne] *vt* **1** CREUSER : to furrow **2** PARCOURIR : to go all over, to crisscross
silo [silo] *nm* : silo
simagrée [simagre] *nf* **faire des simagrées** : to put on airs
similaire [similɛr] *adj* : similar — **similarité** [similarite] *nf*
simili [simili] *nm* : imitation (of leather, gems, etc.)
similitude [similityd] *nf* : similarity, resemblance
simple[1] [sɛ̃pl] *adj* **1** : simple, straightforward <directions simples : easy instructions> **2** : mere <une simple formalité : a mere formality> **3** : simple, plain, unaffected **4** *or* **simple d'esprit** : simpleminded **5** : single <lit simple : single bed> <un aller simple : a one-way ticket>
simple[2] *nm* **1** : singles (in tennis) **2** *Can* : single (in baseball)
simplement [sɛ̃pləmɑ̃] *adv* **1** : simply, merely, just **2** : simply, plainly **3** : easily
simplet, -plette [sɛ̃plɛ, -plɛt] *adj* **1** : simpleminded **2** SIMPLISTE : simplistic

simplicité [sɛ̃plisite] *nf* **1** : simplicity, informality **2** : simpleness

simplifier [sɛ̃plifje] {96} *vt* : to simplify — **simplification** [sɛ̃plifikasjɔ̃] *nf*

simpliste [sɛ̃plist] *adj* : simplistic, oversimplified

simulacre [simylakr] *nm* : sham, pretense

simuler [simyle] *vt* : to simulate — **simulation** [simylasjɔ̃] *nf*

simultané, -née [simyltane] *adj* : simultaneous — **simultanément** [-nemɑ̃] *adv*

sincère [sɛ̃sɛr] *adj* : sincere — **sincèrement** [-sɛrmɑ̃] *adv*

sincérité [sɛ̃serite] *nf* : sincerity

singapourien, -rienne [sɛ̃gapurjɛ̃, -rjɛn] *adj* : Singaporean

Singapourien, -rienne *n* : Singaporean

singe [sɛ̃ʒ] *nm* **1** : monkey <les grands singes : the great apes> **2 faire le singe** : to monkey about, to clown around

singer [sɛ̃ʒe] {17} *vt* **1** IMITER : to ape, to mimic **2** : to feign

singeries [sɛ̃ʒri] *nfpl* : antics

singulariser [sɛ̃gylarize] *vt* : to draw attention to (someone) — **se singulariser** *vr* : to call attention to oneself

singularité [sɛ̃gylarite] *nf* **1** : peculiarity, strangeness **2** : uniqueness

singulier[1], -lière [sɛ̃gylje, -ljɛr] *adj* **1** : uncommon, strange, remarkable **2** : singular (in grammar)

singulier[2] *nm* : singular (in grammar)

singulièrement [sɛ̃gyljɛrmɑ̃] *nm* **1** BEAUCOUP : very much, extremely **2** BIZARREMENT : oddly, strangely **3** PARTICULIÈREMENT : particularly

sinistre[1] [sinistr] *adj* **1** : sinister, eerie **2** : dismal, gloomy

sinistre[2] *nm* **1** DÉSASTRE : disaster **2** DOMMAGE : damage

sinistré[1], -trée [sinistre] *adj* : damaged, stricken

sinistré[2], -trée *n* : disaster victim

sinon [sinɔ̃] *conj* **1** : except that **2** : or else **3** : if not (for the fact) that

sinueux, -nueuse [sinɥø, -nɥøz] *adj* **1** : sinuous **2** : winding, meandering

sinus [sinys] *nms & pl* **1** : sinus **2** : sine (in mathematics)

sionisme [sjɔnism] *nm* : Zionism

sioniste [sjɔnist] *adj & nmf* : Zionist

siphon [sifɔ̃] *nm* **1** : siphon **2** : trap (in plumbing)

siphonner [sifɔne] *vt* : to siphon

sire [sir] *nm* **1** SEIGNEUR : lord **2 triste sire** : unsavory individual

sirène [sirɛn] *nf* **1** : siren, mermaid (in mythology) **2** : siren, alarm

sirop [siro] *nm* : syrup <sirop d'érable : maple syrup> <sirop contre la toux : cough syrup>

siroter [sirɔte] *vt fam* : to sip

sirupeux, -peuse [sirypø, -pøz] *adj* : syrupy

sis, sise [si, siz] *adj* : located (in law)

sisal [sizal] *nm* : sisal

sismique [sismik] *adj* : seismic

site [sit] *nm* **1** : site <site historique : historic site> **2** : setting, locale

sitôt [sito] *adv* **1** (*used with a participle*) <sitôt arrivé : as soon as he arrives, immediately upon his arrival> <sitôt dit, sitôt fait : no sooner said than done> **2 sitôt après** : immediately after **3 sitôt que** : as soon as

sittelle [sitɛl] *nf* : nuthatch

situation [sitɥasjɔ̃] *nf* **1** : situation **2 situation de famille** : marital status

situer [sitɥe] *vt* : to situate, to locate — **se situer** *vr*

six[1] [sis, *before consonant* si, *before vowel* siz] *adj* **1** : six **2** : sixth <le six décembre : December sixth>

six[2] *nms & pl* : six

sixième [sizjɛm] *adj & nmf & nm* : sixth

ski [ski] *nm* **1** : ski **2** : skiing **3 ski nautique** : waterskiing

skier [skje] {96} *vi* : to ski

skieur, skieuse [skjœr, skjøz] *n* : skier

slave [slav] *adj* : Slavic

Slave *nmf* : Slav

slip [slip] *nm* **1** : briefs *pl*, men's underpants *pl* **2** : panties *pl*

slogan [slɔgɑ̃] *nm* : slogan

slovaque[1] [slɔvak] *adj* : Slovak, Slovakian

slovaque[2] *nm* : Slovakian (language)

Slovaque *nmf* : Slovak

slovène[1] [slɔvɛn] *adj* : Slovene, Slovenian

slovène[2] *nm* : Slovene (language)

Slovène *nmf* : Slovene, Slovenian

smoking [smɔkiŋ] *nm* : tuxedo

snob[1] [snɔb] *adj* : snobbish

snob[2] *nmf* : snob

snober [snɔbe] *vt* : to snub

snobisme [snɔbism] *nm* : snobbery, snobbishness

sobre [sɔbr] *adj* **1** : sober, abstemious **2** : restrained — **sobrement** [-brəmɑ̃] *adv*

sobriété [sɔbrijete] *nf* : sobriety

sobriquet [sɔbrikɛ] *nm* : nickname

soc [sɔk] *nm* : plowshare

soccer [sɔkɛr] *nm Can* : soccer

sociable [sɔsjabl] *adj* : sociable — **sociabilité** [sɔsjabilite] *nf*

social, -ciale [sɔsjal] *adj, mpl* **-ciaux** [-sjo] : social — **socialement** [-sjalmɑ̃] *adv*

socialiser [sksjalize] *vt* : to socialize

socialisme [sɔsjalism] *nm* : socialism — **socialiste** [-sjalist] *adj & nmf*

sociétaire [sɔsjetɛr] *nmf* : member

société [sɔsjete] *nf* **1** : society <la haute société : high society> <la société de ses semblables : the society of one's peers> **2** : colony (of bees, etc.) **3** COMPAGNIE : company, firm **4**

ASSOCIATION : society, association, club

sociologie [sɔsjɔlɔʒi] *nf* : sociology

sociologique [sɔsjɔlɔʒik] *adj* : sociological

sociologue [sɔsjɔlɔg] *nmf* : sociologist

socle [sɔkl] *nm* BASE : base, pedestal

socque [sɔk] *nm* SABOT : clog, wooden shoe

soda [sɔda] *nm* **1** : soda, soft drink **2** : soda water

sodium [sɔdjɔm] *nm* : sodium

soeur [sœr] *nf* **1** : sister **2** : nun, sister

sofa [sɔfa] *nm* : sofa

soi [swa] *pron* : oneself, himself, herself, itself <chacun pour soi : every man for himself> <en soi : in itself> <cela va de soi : it goes without saying>

soi–disant[1] [swadizɑ̃] *adv* : supposedly

soi–disant[2] *adj* : so-called

soie [swa] *nf* **1** : silk **2** : bristle

soif [swaf] *nf* : thirst <avoir soif : to be thirsty>

soigné, -gnée [swaɲe] *adj* **1** : carefully done, meticulous **2** : well-groomed, neat

soigner [swaɲe] *vt* **1** : to treat, to nurse **2** : to look after, to take care of **3** : to do with care, to take trouble over — **se soigner** *vr* **1** : to treat oneself (for an illness, etc.) **2** : to be treatable

soigneux, -gneuse [swaɲø, -ɲøz] *adj* **1** : careful, meticulous **2** : neat, tidy — **soigneusement** [swaɲøzmɑ̃] *adv*

soi–même [swamɛm] *pron* : oneself <par soi-même : (all) by oneself>

soin [swɛ̃] *nm* **1** ATTENTION : care, attention <prendre soin de : to take care of, to look after> **2** SOUCI : concern **3 soins** *nmpl* : (medical) attention, treatment <premiers soins : first aid> **4 soins** *nmpl* : care <confier aux bons soins de : to leave in the care of>

soir [swar] *nm* : evening, night <demain soir : tomorrow night>

soirée [sware] *nf* **1** : evening <pendant la soirée : during the evening> **2** FÊTE : party **3** : evening performance (of a show)

soit[1] [swa], *etc.* → **être**

soit[2] *adv* : so be it, very well

soit[3] *conj* **1** : that is, in other words, or <48 heures soit deux jours : 48 hours, that is, two days> **2** (*introducing an hypothesis*) <soit un triangle XYZ : let XYZ be a triangle> **3 soit . . . soit . . .** : either . . . or . . . <soit ceci soit cela : either this or that>

soixante[1] [swasɑ̃t] *adj* : sixty <les années soixantes : the sixties>

soixante[2] *nms & pl* : sixty

soixante–dix[1] [swasɑ̃tdis] *adj* : seventy

soixante–dix[2] *nms & pl* : seventy

soixante–dixième [swasɑ̃tdizjɛm] *adj & nmf & nm* : seventieth

soixantième [swasɑ̃tjɛm] *adj & nmf & nm* : sixtieth

soja [sɔʒa] *nm* : soybean <sauce de soja : soy sauce>

sol [sɔl] *nm* **1** : ground, floor, surface **2** PLANCHER : flooring **3** TERRE : soil (in agriculture, etc.) **4** TERRITOIRE : territory, soil <sol canadien : Canadian soil>

solage [sɔlaʒ] *nm Can* : foundation (of a house)

solaire [sɔlɛr] *adj* **1** : solar **2** : sun <crème solaire : suntan lotion>

soldat [sɔlda] *nm* : soldier

solde[1] [sɔld] *nf* : pay

solde[2] *nm* **1** : balance (in finance) **2** : sale <en solde : on sale> **3 soldes** *nmpl* : sale, bargains

solder [sɔlde] *vt* **1** : to settle (an account, etc.) **2** BRADER : to sell off, to put on sale — **se solder** *vr* **1 ~ par** : to end in **2 ~ par** : to show <se solder par un excédent : to show a surplus>

sole [sɔl] *nf* : sole (fish)

soleil [sɔlɛj] *nm* **1** : sun **2** : sunshine, sunlight **3** : sunflower

solennel, -nelle [sɔlanɛl] *adj* **1** : solemn **2** : formal — **solennellement** *adv*

solennité [sɔlanite] *nf* : solemnity

solfège [sɔlfɛʒ] *nm* : music theory

solidaire [sɔlidɛr] *adj* **1** : united, in solidarity <être solidaire de : to stand by, to back> **2** INTERDÉPENDANT : interdependent

solidariser [sɔlidarize] *v* **se solidariser avec** *vr* : to show solidarity with

solidarité [sɔlidarite] *nf* : solidarity

solide[1] [sɔlid] *adj & nm* **1** : solid **2** : sturdy, strong

solide[2] *nm* : solid

solidement [sɔlidmɑ̃] *adv* **1** : solidly **2** : firmly, securely

solidité [sɔlidite] *nf* : solidity

solidifier [sɔlidifje] {96} *vt* : to solidify — **se solidifier** *vr*

soliloque [sɔlilɔk] *nm* : soliloquy

soliste [sɔlist] *nmf* : soloist

solitaire[1] [sɔlitɛr] *adj* **1** SEUL : solitary, lonely **2** ISOLÉ : isolated

solitaire[2] *nmf* : loner, recluse

solitaire[3] *nm* : solitaire

solitude [sɔlityd] *nf* **1** : solitude **2** : loneliness

solive [sɔliv] *nf* : joist

sollicitation [sɔlisitasjɔ̃] *nf* : appeal, entreaty

solliciter [sɔlisite] *vt* **1** : to solicit, to seek (a favor, etc.) **2** : to appeal to, to approach

solliciteur, -teuse [sɔlisitœr] *nm* **1** : supplicant **2 solliciteur général** *Can* : attorney general

sollicitude [sɔlisityd] *nf* : solicitude, concern

solo[1] [sɔlo] *adj* : solo

solo[2] [sɔlo] *nm, pl* **solos** *or* **soli** : solo

solstice [sɔlstis] *nm* : solstice <solstice d'été : summer solstice>

soluble [sɔlybl] *adj* **1** : soluble **2** : solvable

solution [sɔlysjɔ̃] *nf* : solution

solutionner [sɔlysjɔne] *vt* : to solve

solvabilité [sɔlvabilite] *nf* : solvency

solvable [sɔlvabl] *adj* : solvent

solvant [sɔlvɑ̃] *nm* : solvent

somali, -lie [sɔmali] *adj* : somali

Somali, -lie *n* : Somali

somalien, -lienne [sɔmaljɛ̃, -ljɛn] *adj* : Somalian

Somalien, -lienne *n* : Somalian, Somali

sombre [sɔ̃br] *adj* **1** OBSCUR : dark **2** TRISTE : somber, gloomy — **sombrement** [sɔ̃brəmɑ̃] *adv*

sombrer [sɔ̃bre] *vi* **1** COULER : to sink **2** : to decline, to collapse, to fail

sommaire[1] [sɔmɛr] *adj* **1** COURT : brief **2** EXPÉDITIF : summary **3** RUDIMENTAIRE : rudimentary, superficial

sommaire[2] *nm* : summary

sommation [sɔmasjɔ̃] *nf* **1** : notice, summons (in law) **2** : warning <tirer sans sommation : to shoot without warning>

somme[1] [sɔm] *nf* **1** : sum **2 en somme** : on the whole, all in all

somme[2] *nm* : short nap, catnap

sommeil [sɔmɛj] *nm* : sleep <avoir sommeil : to be sleepy>

sommeiller [sɔmeje] *vi* **1** SOMNOLER : to doze **2** : to lie dormant

sommelier, -lière [sɔməlje, -ljɛr] *n* : wine steward

sommer [sɔme] *vt* **1** : to summon **2** ENJOINDRE : to enjoin, to order <il m'a sommé de répondre : he commanded me to answer>

sommet [sɔmɛ] *nm* **1** CIME : summit, top, apex **2** : vertex (in geometry)

sommier [sɔmje] *nm* **1** : bed springs *pl*, box spring **2** : lintel, crossbar **3** *France* : register, (police) records *pl*

sommité [sɔmite] *nf* : leading figure, authority

somnambule [sɔmnɑ̃byl] *nmf* : sleepwalker

somnambulisme [sɔmnɑ̃bylism] *nm* : sleepwalking

somnifère [sɔmnifɛr] *nm* : sleeping pill

somnolence [sɔmnɔlɑ̃s] *nf* **1** : somnolence, drowsiness **2** LÉTHARGIE : lethargy

somnolent, -lente [sɔmnɔlɑ̃, -lɑ̃t] *adj* **1** : drowsy **2** LÉTHARGIQUE : lethargic

somnoler [sɔmnɔle] *vi* : to doze

somptueux, -tueuse [sɔ̃ptɥø, -tɥøz] *adj* : sumptuous, lavish

son[1], **sa** [sɔ̃, sa] *adj, pl* **ses** [se] : his, her, its, one's

son[2] *nm* **1** : sound <au son de : to the sound of> **2** : volume <monter le son : to turn up the volume> **3** : bran

sonar [sɔnar] *nm* : sonar

sonate [sɔnat] *nf* : sonata

sondage [sɔ̃daʒ] *nm* **1** ENQUÊTE : poll, survey **2** : probing, sounding

sonde [sɔ̃d] *nf* **1** : probe <sonde spatiale : space probe> **2** : sounding line **3** : catheter, probe (in medicine) **4** : drill (in geology, etc.)

sonder [sɔ̃de] *vt* **1** : to sound out, to survey, to poll **2** : to sound, to probe **3** : to drill (in geology)

songe [sɔ̃ʒ] *nm* RÊVE : dream

songer [sɔ̃ʒe] {17} *vt* : to consider, to imagine <avez-vous songé aux frais? : have you considered the costs?> — *vi* **1** : to dream **2 ~ à** : to think about, to contemplate, to consider

songeur, -geuse [sɔ̃ʒœr, -ʒøz] *adj* PENSIF : pensive

sonique [sɔnik] *adj* : sonic, sound

sonnant, -nante [sɔnɑ̃, -nɑ̃t] *adj* **à dix heures sonnantes** : at the stroke of ten

sonné, -née [sɔne] *adj* **1** : past <deux heures sonnées : past two o'clock> **2** *fam* : groggy **3** *fam* : crazy, nuts

sonner *v* **1** : to ring **2** : to strike, to sound

sonnerie [sɔnri] *nf* **1** : ringing, ring **2** : alarm (bell), chimes *pl* **3** : sounding, blare (of a trumpet, etc.)

sonnet [sɔnɛ] *nm* : sonnet

sonnette [sɔnɛt] *nf* : bell, doorbell, buzzer

sonore [sɔnɔr] *adj* **1** : sonorous, resonant **2** : sound <bande sonore : soundtrack> <effets sonores : sound effects> **3** : voiced (in linguistics)

sonorisation [sɔnɔrizasjɔ̃] *nf* : sound system, public address system

sonoriser [sɔnɔrize] *vt* **1** : to add sound to **2** : to install a sound system

sonorité [sɔnɔrite] *nf* **1** : sonority, tone **2** : resonance, acoustics

sophistication [sɔfistikasjɔ̃] *nf* : sophistication

sophistiqué, -quée [sɔfistike] *adj* : sophisticated

soporifique [sɔpɔrifik] *adj* : soporific

soprano [sɔprano] *nmf* : soprano

sorbet [sɔrbɛ] *nm* : sorbet, sherbet

sorcellerie [sɔrsɛlri] *nf* : sorcery, witchcraft

sorcier, -cière [sɔrsje, -sjɛr] *n* : sorcerer, wizard, witch

sordide [sɔrdid] *adj* **1** RÉPUGNANT : sordid **2** MISÉRABLE : squalid — **sordidement** [-didmɑ̃] *adv*

sorgho [sɔrgo] *nm* : sorghum

sornettes [sɔrnɛt] *nfpl* : nonsense

sort [sɔr] *nm* **1** : fate, lot, destiny **2** SORTILÈGE : spell, hex <jeter un sort à : to hex>

sortant, -tante [sɔrtɑ̃, -tɑ̃t] *adj* : outgoing, resigning <le président sortant : the outgoing president>

sorte [sɔrt] *nf* **1** ESPÈCE : sort, kind **2 de sorte à** : in order to **3 en aucune sorte** : not in the least **4 en quelque sorte** : somewhat, in a way

sortie [sɔrti] *nf* **1** : exit <sortie de secours : emergency exit> **2** DÉPART

: departure **3** : launch, release (of a film, book, etc.) **4** EXCURSION : outing **5** : sortie (of troops, etc.) **6** *fam* : quip, sally

sortilège [sɔrtilɛʒ] *nm* : spell, hex, enchantment

sortir[1] [sɔrtir] {82} *vt* **1** : to take out, to bring out **2** : to launch, to release, to issue — *vi* **1** : to go out, to come out, to open (of a film, etc.) **2** PARTIR : to leave, to exit **3 ~ de** : to come from, to come out of — **se sortir** *vr* **1 ~ de** : to get out of **2 s'en sortir** : to manage, to get by, to pull through (of an illness)

sortir[2] *nm* **au sortir de** : at the end of

sosie [sɔzi] *nm* : double

sot, sotte[1] [so, sɔt] *adj* RIDICULE : foolish, silly — **sottement** [sɔtmɑ̃] *adv*

sot, sotte[2] *n* : fool

sottise [sɔtiz] *nf* **1** : foolishness, stupidity **2** : foolish act or remark

sou [su] *nm* **1 sans le sou** : penniless **2 un sou de** : the least bit of <ils n'ont pas un sou de bon sens : they haven't an ounce of common sense>

soubassement [subasmɑ̃] *nm* : bedrock

soubresaut [subrəso] *nm* : jolt, start

souche [suʃ] *nf* **1** : stump (of a tree) **2** : stock, descent **3** : stub (of a check, etc.)

souci [susi] *nm* **1** INQUIÉTUDE : worry, care, concern **2** : marigold

soucier [susje] {96} *v* **se soucier** *vr* : to worry, to care

soucieux, -cieuse [susjø, -sjøz] *adj* : worried, concerned

soucoupe [sukup] *nf* **1** : saucer **2 soucoupe volante** : flying saucer

soudain[1] [sudɛ̃] *adv* SOUDAINEMENT : suddenly

soudain[2], **-daine** [sudɛ̃, -dɛn] *adj* : sudden — **soudainement** [-dɛnmɑ̃] *adv*

soudaineté [sudɛnte] *nf* : suddenness

soudanais, -naise [sudanɛ, -nɛz] *adj* : Sudanese

Soudanais, -naise *n* : Sudanese

soude [sud] *nf* : soda (in chemistry)

souder [sude] *vt* **1** : to weld, to solder **2** UNIR : to join, to bind

soudeur, -deuse [sudœr, -døz] *n* : welder

soudoyer [sudwaje] {58} *vt* : to bribe

soudure [sudyr] *nf* **1** : solder **2** : soldering, welding **3** : weld, joint

soue [su] *nf Can or* **soue à cochon** : sty, pigpen

souffert [sufɛr] *pp* → **souffrir**

souffle [sufl] *nm* **1** : breath <être à bout de souffle : to be out of breath> <second souffle : second wind> **2** RESPIRATION : breathing **3** : puff, gust, breath (of air) **4** INSPIRATION : inspiration

soufflé [sufle] *nm* : soufflé

souffler [sufle] *vt* **1** : to blow **2** : to blow out **3** CHUCHOTER : to whisper **4** : to blast, to blow down **5** *fam* : to take, to pinch **6 souffler son rôle à** : to prompt, to cue — *vi* **1** : to blow **2** : to pant, to puff

soufflet [suflɛ] *nm* **1** : bellows **2** GIFLE : slap **3** AFFRONT : insult, affront

souffleur, -fleuse [suflœr, -fløz] *n* **1** : glassblower **2** : prompter (in theater)

souffleuse *nf Can or* **souffleuse à neige** : snowblower

souffrance [sufrɑ̃s] *nf* **1** : suffering **2 en ~** : pending, awaiting

souffrant, -frante [sufrɑ̃, -frɑ̃t] *adj* **1** INDISPOSÉ : unwell **2** : suffering, miserable

souffreteux, -teuse [sufrətø, -tøz] *adj* : sickly

souffrir [sufrir] {83} *vt* **1** SUPPORTER : to tolerate, to stand, to put up with **2** PERMETTRE : to allow, to permit — *vi* : to suffer

soufre [sufr] *nm* : sulfur, brimstone

souhait [swɛ] *nm* **1** VOEU : wish **2 à vos souhaits!** : bless you!

souhaitable [swɛtabl] *adj* : desirable

souhaiter [swete] *vt* : to wish, to wish for, to hope for <souhaiter la bonne année à qqn : to wish s.o. Happy New Year>

souiller [suje] *vt* **1** SALIR : to soil **2** : to sully, to defile

souillure [sujyr] *nf* : stain, taint, blemish

soûl, soûle [su, sul] *adj fam* : drunk

soulagement [sulaʒmɑ̃] *nm* : relief

soulager [sulaʒe] {17} *vt* : to relieve — **se soulager** *vr*

soûler [sule] *vt* ENIVRER : to make drunk, to intoxicate — **se soûler** *vr* **1** : to get drunk **2 ~ de** : to be intoxicated with

soulèvement [sulɛvmɑ̃] *nm* **1** : uprising, upheaval (of the earth, etc.) **2** : insurrection, uprising

soulever [sulve] {52} *vt* **1** LEVER : to lift, to raise **2** PROVOQUER : to stir up, to arouse — **se soulever** *vr* **1** : to rise up **2** : to lift oneself up

soulier [sulje] *nm* : shoe

soulignement [suliɲmɑ̃] *nm* : underlining

souligner [suliɲe] *vt* **1** : to underline **2** : to emphasize

soumettre [sumɛtr] {53} *vt* **1** SUBJUGUER : to subjugate, to subdue **2** PRÉSENTER : to submit **3 ~ à** : to subject to — **se soumettre** *vr* : to submit, to give in

soumis, -mise [sumi, -miz] *adj* : submissive

soumission [sumisjɔ̃] *nf* **1** : submission, subjection **2** : bid

soumissionner [sumisjɔne] *vt* : to bid for

soupape [supap] *nf* : valve

soupçon [supsɔ̃] *nm* **1** : suspicion <au dessus de tout soupçon : above sus-

picion> **2** : drop, touch <un soupçon d'ironie : a hint of irony>
soupçonner [supsɔne] *vt* : to suspect
soupçonneux, -neuse [supsɔnø, -nøz] *adj* : suspicious — **soupçonneusement** [supsɔnøzmɑ̃] *adv*
soupe [sup] *nf* : soup <soupe à l'oignon : onion soup>
soupente [supɑ̃t] *nf* **1** : attic, garret **2** : closet (under the stairs)
souper[1] [supe] *vi Bel, Switz, Can* : to have supper
souper[2] *nm Bel, Switz, Can* : supper
soupeser [supəze] {52} *vt* **1** : to feel the weight of, to heft **2** PESER : to weigh, to consider
soupière [supjɛr] *nf* : tureen
soupir [supir] *nm* **1** : sigh **2** : quarter rest (in music)
soupirant [supirɑ̃] *nm* : suitor
soupirer [supire] *vi* **1** : to sigh **2 ~ après** *or* **~ pour** : to yearn for, to pine for
souple [supl] *adj* **1** : supple, flexible **2** : smooth, flowing — **souplement** [supləmɑ̃] *adv*
souplesse [suplɛs] *nf* : suppleness, flexibility
source [surs] *nf* **1** : source <tenir de bonne source : to have on good authority> **2** : spring, source (of waters) **3 sources** *nfpl* : headwaters
sourcil [sursi] *nm* **1** : eyebrow **2 froncer les sourcils** : to frown
sourciller [sursije] *vi* : to raise one's eyebrows, to react <sans sourciller : without batting an eye>
sourcilleux, -leuse [sursijø, -jøz] *adj* **1** HAUTAIN : haughty, supercilious **2** POINTILLEUX : finicky, fussy
sourd[1], **sourde** [sur, surd] *adj* **1** : deaf **2** : dull, muffled **3** : secret, clandestine **4** : voiceless <consonnes sourdes : voiceless consonants>
sourd[2], **sourde** *n* : deaf person
sourdine [surdin] *nf* **1** : mute (in music) <en sourdine : muted, quietly> **2 mettre une sourdine à** : to tone down
sourd–muet, sourde–muette [surmɥɛ, surdmɥɛt] *n* : deaf-mute
sourdre [surdr] {84} *vi* **1** : to rise, to seep up **2** MONTER : to well up
souriant, -riante [surjɑ̃, -rjɑ̃t] *adj* : smiling, cheerful
souricière [surisjɛr] *nf* : mousetrap
sourire[1] [surir] {76} *vi* **1** : to smile **2 ~ à** : to smile on, to be favorable to **3 ~ à** : to appeal to
sourire[2] *nm* : smile
souris [suri] *nf* : mouse
sournois[1], **-noise** [surnwa, -nwaz] *adj* **1** : sly, shifty **2** : underhanded, backhanded
sournois[2], **-noise** *n* : sly person, sneaky person
sournoisement [surnwazmɑ̃] *adv* : slyly, in an underhanded manner
sous [su] *prep* **1** : under, beneath **2** : within <sous huit jours : within a week> <sous peu : shortly> **3** : during <sous le règne de : during the reign of> **4** : under the effect of <sous anesthésie : under anesthesia> <sous la pression : under pressure>
sous–alimentation [suzalimɑ̃tasjɔ̃] *nf* : malnutrition
sous–alimenté, -tée [suzalimɑ̃te] *adj* : malnourished, undernourished
sous–bois [subwa] *nms & pl* : undergrowth, underbrush
sous–comité [sukɔmite] *nm, pl* **sous–comités** : subcommittee
souscripteur, -trice [suskriptœr] *n* : subscriber
souscription [suskripsjɔ̃] *nf* : subscription
souscrire [suskrir] {33} *vi* **~ à** : to subscribe to
sous–développé, -pée [sudevlɔpe] *adj* : underdeveloped
sous–développement [sudevlɔpmɑ̃] *nm, pl* **sous–développements** : underdevelopment
sous–entendre [suzɑ̃tɑ̃dr] {63} *vt* : to imply, to infer
sous–entendu [suzɑ̃tɑ̃dy] *nm, pl* **sous–entendus** : insinuation, innuendo
sous–estimer [suzɛstime] *vt* : to underestimate
sous–évaluer [suzevalɥe] *vt* : undervalue
sous–exposer [suzɛkspoze] *vt* : to underexpose (a photograph)
sous–jacent, -cente [suʒasɑ̃, -sɑ̃t] *adj* : underlying
sous–lieutenant [suljøtnɑ̃] *nm, pl* **sous–lieutenants** : second lieutenant
sous–louer [sulwe] *vt* : to sublet
sous–marin[1], **-rine** [sumarɛ̃, -rin] *adj* : underwater, submarine
sous–marin[2] *nm, pl* **sous–marins** : submarine
sous–officier [suzɔfisje] *nm, pl* **sous–officiers** : noncommissioned officer
sous–produit [suprɔdɥi] *nm, pl* **sous–produits** : by-product
sous–secrétaire [susəkretɛr] *nmf* : undersecretary
sous–sol [susɔl] *nm, pl* **sous–sols** : basement, cellar
sous–titre [sutitr] *nm, pl* **sous–titres** : subtitle
soustraction [sustraksjɔ̃] *nf* : subtraction
soustraire [sustrɛr] {40} *vt* **1** : to subtract **2** : to remove, to take away, to steal **3** : to shield, to hide (a person) — **se soustraire** *vr* **~ à** : to escape from, to evade
sous–traîter [sutrete] *vt* : to subcontract
sous–verre [suvɛr] *nms & pl Can* : coaster

sous–vêtement [suvɛtmɑ̃] *nm* **1** : undergarment **2 sous–vêtements** *nmpl* : underwear, underclothes
soutane [sutan] *nf* : cassock
soute [sut] *nf* : hold (of a ship)
soutenable [sutnabl] *adj* **1** DÉFENDABLE : defensible, supportable (of an argument, etc.) **2** SUPPORTABLE : bearable
soutènement [sutɛnmɑ̃] *nm* **mur de soutènement** : retaining wall
souteneur [sutnœr] *nm* : pimp
soutenir [sutnir] {92} *vt* **1** MAINTENIR : to support, to hold up **2** : to support, to back, to stand by **3** : to defend, to uphold <soutenir que : to maintain that> **4** : to sustain, to keep up **5** : to withstand, to bear — **se soutenir** *vr* **1** : to support each other **2** : to be defensible **3** : to hold oneself up
soutenu, -nue [sutny] *adj* **1** ÉLEVÉ : elevated, formal **2** : sustained, steady **3** VIF : bold, vivid (of colors)
souterrain[1], **-raine** [sutɛrɛ̃, -rɛn] *adj* **1** : underground, subterranean **2** : secret, hidden
souterrain[2] *nm* : underground passage
soutien [sutjɛ̃] *nm* **1** : support **2 soutien de famille** : breadwinner
soutien–gorge [sutjɛ̃gɔrʒ] *nm, pl* **soutiens–gorge** : bra, brassiere
soutirer [sutire] *vt* **∼ à** : to extract from, to squeeze out of
souvenir[1] [suvnir] {92} *v* **se souvenir** *vr* **1 ∼ de** : to remember **2 ∼ que** : to remember that — *v impers* **il me (lui, etc.) souvient** : I remember (he remembers, etc.)
souvenir[2] *nm* **1** : memory **2** : souvenir, memento **3** : regards, (good) wishes <mes meilleurs souvenirs à : my best regards to>
souvent [suvɑ̃] *adv* : often
souverain[1], **-raine** [suvrɛ̃, -rɛn] *adj* **1** SUPRÊME : supreme, superior <un remède souverain : an excellent remedy> **2** : sovereign <territoire souverain : sovereign territory>
souverain[2], **-raine** *n* : sovereign, monarch
souveraineté [suvrɛnte] *nf* : sovereignty
soviétique [sɔvjetik] *adj* : Soviet
soya [sɔja] → **soja**
soyeux, soyeuse [swajø, -jøz] *adj* : silky
spacieux, -cieuse [spasjø, -sjøz] *adj* : spacious
spaghetti [spagɛti] *nmpl* : spaghetti <boîte de spaghettis : box of spaghetti>
sparadrap [sparadra] *nm* : adhesive tape, adhesive bandage
spasme [spasm] *nm* : spasm — **spasmodique** [spasmɔdik] *adj*
spatial, -tiale [spasjal] *adj, mpl* **spatiaux 1** : spatial **2** : space <vaisseau spatial : spaceship>
spatule [spatyl] *nf* **1** : spatula **2** : tip (of a ski)
speaker[1], **-kerine** [spikœr, -krin] *n France* : announcer (on radio, TV, etc.)
speaker[2] *nm* **le Speaker** : the Speaker (of a legislative body)
spécial, -ciale [spesjal] *adj, mpl* **spéciaux** [-sjo] **1** : special **2** BIZARRE : odd, peculiar
spécialement [spesjalmɑ̃] *adv* **1** EXPRÈS : specially **2** TRÈS : especially, particularly
spécialiser [spesjalize] *v* **se spécialiser** *vr* : to specialize — **spécialisation** [-lizasjɔ̃] *nf*
spécialiste [spesjalist] *nmf* : specialist
spécialité [spesjalite] *nf* : specialty, field
spécieux, -cieuse [spesjø, -sjøz] *adj* : specious — **spécieusement** [-sjøzmɑ̃] *adv*
spécifier [spesifje] {96} *vt* : to specify — **spécification** [spesifikasjɔ̃] *nf*
spécifique [spesifik] *adj* : specific — **spécifiquement** [-fikmɑ̃] *adv*
spécimen [spesimɛn] *nm* **1** : specimen, example **2** : sample
spectacle [spɛktakl] *nm* **1** : spectacle, sight <se donner en spectacle : to make a spectacle of oneself> **2** REPRÉSENTATION : show, performance <spectacle somptueux : extravaganza> **3** : show businesss
spectaculaire [spɛktakylɛr] *adj* : spectacular
spectateur, -trice [spɛktatœr, -tris] *n* **1** : spectator, audience member **2** : observer, onlooker, bystander
spectre [spɛktr] *nm* **1** : specter, ghost **2** : spectrum
spéculateur, -trice [spekylatœr, -tris] *n* : speculator
spéculatif, -tive [spekylatif, -tiv] *adj* : speculative
spéculer [spekyle] *vi* : to speculate — **spéculation** [spekylasjɔ̃] *nf*
sperme [spɛrm] *nm* : sperm, semen
sphère [sfɛr] *nf* : sphere
sphérique [sferik] *adj* : spherical
spinal, -nale [spinal] *adj, mpl* **spinaux** [-no] : spinal
spiral, -rale [spiral] *adj, mpl* **spiraux** [-ro] : spiral
spirale *nf* : spiral
spire [spir] *nf* : whorl (of a shell)
spiritisme [spiritism] *nm* : spiritualism
spiritualité [spiritɥalite] *nf* : spirituality
spirituel, -tuelle [spiritɥɛl] *adj* **1** : spiritual **2** : witty — **spirituellement** [-tɥɛlmɑ̃] *adv*
spiritueux [spiritɥø] *nms & pl* : spirit <vins et spiritueux : wines and spirits>
spleen [splin] *nm* : spleen, melancholy
splendeur [splɑ̃dœr] *nf* MAGNIFICENCE : splendor, magnificence, glory

splendide [splɑ̃did] *adj* MAGNIFIQUE : splendid, magnificent — **splendidement** [-didmɑ̃] *adv*

spolier [spɔlje] {96} *vt* : to despoil

spongieux, -gieuse [spɔ̃ʒjø, -ʒjøz] *adj* : spongy

sponsor [spɔ̃sɔr] *nm* : sponsor

sponsoriser [spɔ̃sɔrize] *vt* : to sponsor

spontané, -née [spɔ̃tane] *adj* : spontaneous — **spontanément** [-nemɑ̃] *adv*

spontanéité [spɔ̃taneite] *nf* : spontaneity

sporadique [spɔradik] *adj* : sporadic — **sporadiquement** [-dikmɑ̃] *adv*

spore [spɔr] *nf* : spore

sport[1] [spɔr] *adj* **1** : sport, sports <vêtements sport : sport clothes> **2** SPORTIF : sporting

sport[2] *nm* : sport <sports d'équipe : team sports>

sportif[1], **-tive** [spɔrtif, -tiv] *adj* **1** : sport, sports <chroniqueur sportif : sportscaster> **2** : sporting, sportsmanlike **3** : athletic, sporty

sportif[2], **-tive** *n* : sportsman *m*, sportswoman *f*

sportivité [spɔrtivite] *nf* : sportsmanship

spot [spɔt] *nm* **1** : spotlight **2** PUBLICITÉ : spot, commercial

sprint [sprint] *nm* : sprint

sprinter [sprinte] *vi* : to sprint

square [skwar] *nm France* : small public garden

squash [skwaʃ] *nm* : squash (sport)

squatter[1] [skwate] *vt* : to squat in (land, a property, etc.)

squatter[2] [skwatœr] *nm* : squatter

squelette [skəlɛt] *nm* **1** : skeleton **2** : outline **3** : framework, skeleton (of a ship, etc.)

squelettique [skəletik] *adj* **1** : skeletal, scrawny **2** : sketchy, skimpy

sri lankais, -kaise [srilɑ̃kɛ, -kɛz] *adj* : Sri Lankan

Sri Lankais, -kaise *n* : Sri Lankan

stabilisateur[1], **-trice** [stabilizatœr, -tris] *adj* : stabilizing

stabilisateur[2] *nm* : stabilizer

stabiliser [stabilize] *vt* : to stabilize — **se stabiliser** *vr* **1** : to become stable **2** : to settle down

stabilité [stabilite] *nf* : stability

stable [stabl] *adj* : stable, steady

stade [stad] *nm* **1** : stadium **2** ÉTAPE : stage, phase

stage [staʒ] *nm* : training period, internship <faire un stage : to intern>

stagiaire [staʒjɛr] *nmf* : trainee, intern

stagnant, -nante [stagnɑ̃, -nɑ̃t] *adj* : stagnant

stagner [stagne] *vi* : to stagnate — **stagnation** [-gnasjɔ̃] *nf*

stalactite [stalaktit] *nf* : stalactite

stalagmite [stalagmit] *nf* : stalagmite

stalle [stal] *nf* : stall

stand [stɑ̃d] *nm* **1** : stand, stall **2 stand de tir** : shooting range

standard[1] [stɑ̃dar] *adj* : standard

standard[2] *nm* **1** : norm, standard **2** : (telephone) switchboard

standardiser [stɑ̃dardize] *vt* : to standardize

standardiste [stɑ̃dardist] *nmf* : switchboard operator, telephone operator

standing [stɑ̃diŋ] *nm* **1** : standing, status **2 de grand standing** : luxury

star [star] *nf* VEDETTE : star <star de cinéma : movie star>

starter [startɛr] *nm* **1** : choke (of an automobile) **2** : starter (in a race)

station [stasjɔ̃] *nf* **1** : station **2** : resort <station balnéaire : seaside resort> **3** : posture, position **4** : stop, pause

stationnaire [stasjɔnɛr] *adj* **1** : stationary **2** : stable (in medicine)

stationnement [stasjɔnmɑ̃] *nm* : parking <stationnement interdit : no parking>

stationner [stasjɔne] *vi* : to park

station–service [stasjɔ̃sɛrvis] *nf, pl* **stations–service** : gas station, service station

statique [statik] *adj* : static

statisticien, -cienne [statistisjɛ̃, -sjɛn] *n* : statistician

statistique[1] [statistik] *adj* : statistical

statistique[2] *nf* **1** : statistic **2** : statistics (field)

statue [staty] *nf* : statue

statuer [statɥe] *vi* : to decree, to ordain

statuette [statɥɛt] *nf* : statuette

statu quo [statykwo] *nm* : status quo

stature [statyr] *nf* : stature

statut [staty] *nm* **1** : statute **2** : status

statutaire [statytɛr] *adj* : statutory

steak [stɛk] *nm* : steak <steak haché : ground beef>

stellaire [stelɛr] *adj* : stellar

sténographe [stenɔgraf] *nmf* : stenographer

sténographie [stenɔgrafi] *nf* : stenography

steppe [stɛp] *nf* : steppe

stéréo [stereo] *adj & nf* : stereo

stéréophonique [stereɔfɔnik] *adj* : stereophonic

stéréotype [stereɔtip] *nm* **1** : stereotype **2** : cliché

stéréotypé, -pée [stereɔtipe] *adj* : stereotyped, stereotypical

stérile [steril] *adj* : sterile

stériliser [sterilize] *vt* : to sterilize — **stérilisation** [-lizasjɔ̃] *nf*

stérilité [sterilite] *nf* : sterility

sterne [stɛrn] *nf* : tern

sternum [stɛrnɔm] *nm* : sternum, breastbone

stéthoscope [stetɔskɔp] *nm* : stethoscope

stigmate [stigmat] *nm* : stigma

stigmatiser [stigmatize] *vt* : to stigmatize — **stigmatisation** [-tizasjɔ̃] *nf*

stimulant[1], **-lante** [stimylɑ̃, -lɑ̃t] *adj* : stimulating

stimulant[2] *nm* **1** : stimulant **2** : stimulus
stimulateur [stimylatœr] *nm* : stimulator (in medicine) <stimulateur cardiaque : pacemaker>
stimuler [stimyle] *vt* : to stimulate — **stimulation** [-mylasjɔ̃] *nf*
stipuler [stipyle] *vt* : to stipulate — **stipulation** [-pylasjɔ̃] *nf*
stock [stɔk] *nm* : stock (of merchandise) <en stock : in stock>
stocker [stɔke] *vt* : to stock, to store
stoïcisme [stɔisizm] *nm* : stoicism
stoïque[1] [stɔik] *adj* : stoic, stoical — **stoïquement** [-ikmɑ̃] *adv*
stoïque[2] *nmf* : stoic
stolon [stɔlɔ̃] *nm* : runner (of a plant)
stop[1] [stɔp] *nm* **1** : stop sign **2** : brake light
stop[2] *interj* : stop
stopper [stɔpe] *vt* **1** ARRÊTER : to stop, to halt **2** RÉPARER : to mend — *vi* : to stop
store [stɔr] *nm* **1** : awning **2** : blind, window shade <store vénitien : venetian blind>
strabisme [strabism] *nm* : squint
strangulation [strɑ̃gylasjɔ̃] *nf* : strangulation
strapontin [strapɔ̃tɛ̃] *nm* : folding seat, jump seat
stratagème [stratazɛm] *nm* : stratagem
strate [strat] *nf* : stratum
stratégie [strateʒi] *nf* : strategy
stratégique [strateʒik] *adj* : strategic — **stratégiquement** [-ʒikmɑ̃] *adv*
stratifié, -fiée [stratifje] *adj* : laminated, stratified
stratosphère [stratɔsfɛr] *nf* : stratosphere
stress [strɛs] *nms & pl* : stress
stressant, -sante [strɛsɑ̃, -sɑ̃t] *adj* : stressful
stresser [strɛse] *vt* : to put under stress
strict, stricte [strikt] *adj* **1** : strict **2** : austere, severe, plain — **strictement** [striktəmɑ̃] *adv*
strident, -dente [stridɑ̃, -dɑ̃t] *adj* : strident, shrill
strier [strije] {96} *vt* **1** : to streak **2** : to groove
strophe [strɔf] *nf* : stanza
structural, -rale [stryktyral] *adj, mpl* **-raux** [-ro] : structural — **structuralement** [-ralmɑ̃] *adv*
structure [stryktyr] *nf* : structure, framework
structurer [stryktyre] *vt* : to structure, to organize — **se structurer** *vr* : to be structured, to take shape
stuc [styk] *nm* : stucco
studieux, -dieuse [stydjø, -djøz] *adj* : studious — **studieusement** [-djøzmɑ̃] *adv*
studio [stydjo] *nm* **1** : studio **2** : studio apartment
stupéfaction [stypefaksjɔ̃] *nf* ÉTONNEMENT : stupefaction, astonishment
stupéfaire [stypefɛr] {85} *vt* : to amaze, to astonish
stupéfait, -faite [stypefɛ, -fɛt] *adj* ÉTONNÉ : amazed, astounded
stupéfiant[1], **-fiante** [stypefjɑ̃, -fjɑ̃t] *adj* ÉTONNANT : amazing, astounding
stupéfiant[2] *nm* : drug, narcotic
stupéfié [stypefje] *pp* → **stupéfaire**
stupéfier [stypefje] {96} *vt* **1** : to astonish, to stun **2** : to stupefy (in medicine)
stupeur [stypœr] *nf* **1** ÉTONNEMENT : astonishment, amazement **2** HÉBÉTUDE : stupor
stupide [stypid] *adj* : stupid — **stupidement** [-pidmɑ̃] *adv*
stupidité [stypidite] *nf* : stupidity
style [stil] *nm* **1** : style <style de vie : lifestyle> <style gothique : Gothic style> **2** : speech form <style direct : direct speech> **3** : stylus
stylet [stilɛ] *nm* : stiletto
styliser [stilize] *vt* : to stylize
stylo [stilo] *nm* : pen <stylo à bille : ballpoint pen>
stylo–feutre [stiloføtr] *nm, pl* **stylos–feutres** : felt-tip pen, marker
su [sy] *pp* → **savoir**
suave [sɥav] *adj* **1** : sweet (of odors) **2** : smooth, mellow **3** : suave, sophisticated
suavement [sɥavmɑ̃] *adv* : sweetly
suavité [sɥavite] *nf* **1** : sweetness **2** : smoothness
subalterne [sybaltɛrn] *adj & nmf* : subordinate
subconscient[1], **-ciente** [sybkɔ̃sjɑ̃, -sjɑ̃t] *adj* : subconscious
subconscient[2] *nm* : subconscious
subdiviser [sybdivize] *vt* : to subdivide — **subdivision** [-vizjɔ̃] *nf*
subir [sybir] *vt* **1** : to undergo **2** : to suffer, to sustain <subir des pertes : to suffer losses> **3** : to be under, to come under <subir l'influence de : to come under the influence of> **4 faire subir à** : to inflict on
subit, -bite [sybi, -bit] *adj* : sudden — **subitement** [-bitmɑ̃] *adv*
subjectif, -tive [sybʒɛktif, -tiv] *adj* : subjective
subjectivité [sybʒɛktivite] *nf* : subjectivity
subjonctif [sybʒɔ̃ktif] *nm* : subjunctive
subjuguer [sybʒuge] *vt* **1** : to captivate **2** : to subjugate
sublime [syblim] *adj* : sublime
sublimer [syblime] *v* : to sublimate
submerger [sybmɛrʒe] {17} *vt* **1** : to submerge **2** : to overwhelm, to engulf, to swamp
submersible [sybmɛrsibl] *adj & nm* : submersible
submersion [sybmɛrsjɔ̃] *nf* : submersion

subordination [sybɔrdinasjɔ̃] *nf* **:** subordination
subordonné, -née [sybɔrdɔne] *adj & n* **:** subordinate
subordonner [sybɔrdɔne] *vt* **:** to subordinate
suborner [syborne] *vt* **:** to bribe (a witness)
subreptice [sybrɛptis] *adj* **:** surreptitious **— subrepticement** [-tismɑ̃] *adv*
subséquent, -quente [sybsekɑ̃, -kɑ̃t] *adj* **:** subsequent
subside [sypsid] *nm* **:** grant, subsidy
subsidiaire [sybzidjɛr] *adj* **:** subsidiary
subsistance [sybzistɑ̃s] *nf* **:** subsistence
subsister [sybziste] *vi* **1** SURVIVRE **:** to subsist, to survive (on) **2** RESTER **:** to remain
substance [sypstɑ̃s] *nf* **:** substance
substantiel, -tielle [sypstɑ̃sjɛl] *adj* **:** substantial
substantif [sypstɑ̃tif] *nm* **:** substantive, noun
substituer [sypstitɥe] *vt* **:** to substitute **— se substituer** *vr* **~ à :** to substitute for
substitut [sypstity] *nm* **:** substitute
substitution [sypstitysjɔ̃] *nf* **:** substitution
subterfuge [syptɛrfyʒ] *nm* **:** subterfuge, ploy
subtil, -tile [syptil] *adj* **:** subtle **— subtilement** [-tilmɑ̃] *adv*
subtiliser [syptilize] *vt fam* **:** to steal, to pinch
subtilité [syptilite] *nf* **:** subtlety
subvenir [sybvənir] {92} *vi* **~ à :** to provide for (a family), to meet (expenses, etc.)
subvention [sybvɑ̃sjɔ̃] *nf* SUBSIDE **:** subsidy
subventionner [sybvɑ̃sjɔne] *vt* **:** to subsidize
subversif, -sive [sybvɛrsif, -siv] *adj* **:** subversive
subversion [sybvɛrsjɔ̃] *nf* **:** subversion
suc [syk] *nm* **1** JUS **:** juice **2** SÈVE **:** sap **3 :** pith, substance
succédané [syksedane] *nm* **:** substitute (for a medication, food product, etc.) <succédané de sucre : sugar substitute>
succéder [syksede] {87} *vi* **~ à :** to succeed, to follow **— se succéder** *vr*
succès [syksɛ] *nm* **:** success <avoir du succès : to be successful>
successeur [syksesœr] *nm* **:** successor
successif, -sive [syksesif, -siv] *adj* **:** successive **— successivement** [-sivmɑ̃] *adv*
succession [syksesjɔ̃] *nf* **:** succession
succinct, -cincte [syksɛ̃, -sɛ̃t] *adj* **:** succinct **— succinctement** [-sɛ̃tmɑ̃] *adv*
succion [syksjɔ̃, sysjɔ̃] *nf* **:** suction, sucking
succomber [sykɔ̃be] *vi* **1 :** to die **2 :** to collapse, to give way **3 ~ à :** to succumb to
succulent, -lente [sykylɑ̃, -lɑ̃t] *adj* **:** succulent
succursale [sykyrsal] *nf* **:** branch (of a bank, store, etc.)
sucer [syse] {6} *vt* **:** to suck
sucette [sysɛt] *nf* **1 :** lollipop **2 :** pacifier
suçon [sysɔ̃] *nm Can* **:** lollipop
sucre [sykr] *nm* **:** sugar <sucre en poudre : powdered sugar> <sucre d'érable : maple sugar>
sucré, -crée [sykre] *adj* **1 :** sweet, sweetened **2 :** sugary, honeyed (of speech, etc.)
sucrer [sykre] *vt* **:** to sweeten, to add sugar to
sucrerie [sykrəri] *nf* **1 :** sugar refinery **2** *Can* **:** sugar-maple forest **3 sucreries** *nfpl* **:** sweets, candy
sucrier[1], -crière [sykrije, -krijɛr] *adj* **:** sugar <la production sucrière : sugar production>
sucrier[2] *nm* **:** sugar bowl
sud[1] [syd] *adj* **:** south, southern, southerly
sud[2] *nm* **1 :** south <au sud de Montréal : south of Montreal> <exposé au sud : with a southerly aspect> <vent du sud : south wind> **2 le Sud :** the South
sud–africain, -caine [sydafrikɛ̃, -kɛn] *adj* **:** South African
Sud–Africain, -caine *n* **:** South African
sud–américain, -caine [sydamerikɛ̃, -kɛn] *adj* **:** South American
Sud–Américain, -caine *n* **:** South American
sud–est[1] [sydɛst] *adj s & pl* **:** southeast, southeastern
sud–est[2] *nm* **:** southeast
sud–ouest[1] [sydwɛst] *adj s & pl* **:** southwest, southwestern
sud–ouest[2] *nm* **:** southwest
suède [sɥɛd] *nm* **:** suede
suédois[1], -doise [sɥedwa, -dwaz] *adj* **:** Swedish
suédois[2] *nm* **:** Swedish (language)
Suédois, -doise *n* **:** Swede
suer [sɥe] *vi* **:** to sweat **—** *vt* **1 :** to sweat, to ooze **2 :** to exude
sueur [sɥœr] *nf* **:** sweat
suffire [syfir] {86} *vi* **:** to suffice, to be enough <ça suffit! : that's enough!> **— se suffire** *vr or* **se suffire à soi–même :** to be self-sufficient
suffisais [syfizɛ], **suffisions** [syfizjɔ̃], *etc.* → **suffire**
suffisamment [syfizamɑ̃] *adv* **:** sufficiently, enough
suffisance [syfizɑ̃s] *nf* **1 :** self-importance, conceit **2 en ~ :** sufficient
suffisant, -sante [syfizɑ̃, -zɑ̃t] *adj* **1** ADÉQUAT **:** sufficient, adequate **2** VANITEUX **:** self-important, conceited
suffise [syfiz], *etc.* → **suffire**
suffixe [syfiks] *nm* **:** suffix

suffocant, -cante [syfɔkɑ̃, -kɑ̃t] *adj* : suffocating

suffocation [syfɔkasjɔ̃] *nf* : suffocation

suffoquer [syfɔke] *vt* **1** ÉTOUFFER : to suffocate, to choke **2** : to stagger, to stun — *vi* S'ÉTOUFFER : to suffocate

suffrage [syfraʒ] *nm* : suffrage, vote

suggérer [sygʒere] {86} *vt* : to suggest

suggestible [sygʒɛstibl] *adj* : suggestible

suggestif, -tive [sygʒɛstif, -tiv] *adj* : suggestive

suggestion [sygʒɛstjɔ̃] *nf* : suggestion <faire une suggestion : to suggest>

suicidaire [sɥisidɛr] *adj* : suicidal

suicide [sɥisid] *nm* : suicide

suicidé, -dée [sɥiside] *n* : suicide

suicider *v* **se suicider** *vr* : to commit suicide

suie [sɥi] *nf* : soot

suif [sɥif] *nm* **1** : tallow **2** : suet

suintement [sɥɛ̃tma] *nm* : seepage

suinter [sɥɛ̃te] *vi* : to ooze, to seep

suisse[1] [sɥis] *adj* : Swiss

suisse[2] *nm Can* : chipmunk

Suisse *nmf* : Swiss

suit [sɥi], *etc.* → **suivre**

suite [sɥit] *nf* **1** : suite **2** CONTINUATION : continuation, rest <sans suite : disconnected, discontinuous> **3** SÉRIE : series, sequence <à la suite : one after another> **4** CONSÉQUENCE : consequence, result <donner suite à : to follow up> **5 par la suite** : later, afterwards **6 par ~** : therefore, consequently **7 par suite de** : due to, as a result of

suivant[1], **-vante** [sɥivɑ̃, -vɑ̃t] *adj* : following, next

suivant[2], **-vante** *n* : next one, following one <au suite! : next!>

suivant[3] *prep* **1** SELON : according to **2** : along, in the direction of **3** : depending on

suivi[1], **-vie** [sɥivi] *adj* **1** RÉGULIER : regular, steady **2** COHÉRENT : coherent

suivi[2] *nm* : follow-up

suivre [sɥivr] {88} *vt* **1** : to follow **2** : to take (a course) **3** : to keep up with — *vi* **1** : to follow **2** : to pay attention, to keep up **3 faire suivre** : to forward (mail) — **se suivre** *vr* **1** : to follow one another **2** : to be in (the right) order **3** : to be coherent

sujet[1], **-jette** [syʒɛ, -ʒɛt] *adj* **~ à** : subject to, prone to

sujet[2], **-jette** *n* : subject (of a state or country)

sujet[3] *nm* **1** : subject, topic **2** RAISON : cause

sujétion [syʒesjɔ̃] *nf* **1** SOUMISSION : subjection **2** CONTRAINTE : constraint

sulfureux, -reuse [sylfyrø, -røz] *adj* : sulfurous

sulfurique [sylfyrik] *adj* **acide sulfurique** : sulfuric acid

sultan [syltɑ̃] *nm* : sultan

sumac [symak] *nm* **1** : sumac **2 sumac vénéneux** : poison ivy

summum [sɔmɔm] *nm* : height, peak, acme

sundae [sɔnde] *nm Can* : sundae

super [sypɛr] *adj s & pl fam* EXTRA : super, great

superbe[1] [sypɛrb] *adj* : superb — **superbement** [-pɛrbəmɑ̃] *adv*

superbe[2] *nm* : arrogance, pride

supercherie [sypɛrʃəri] *nf* : deception, fraud

superficialité [sypɛrfisjalite] *nf* : superficiality

superficie [sypɛrfisi] *nf* : area, surface

superficiel, -cielle [sypɛrfisjɛl] *adj* : superficial

superflu[1], **-flue** [sypɛrfly] *adj* : superfluous

superflu[2] *nm* : superfluity

supérieur[1], **-rieure** [syperjœr] *adj* **1** : superior **2** : upper <coin gauche supérieur : upper left-hand corner> **3** : higher <à un taux supérieur : at a higher rate>

supérieur[2], **-rieure** *n* : superior

supérieurement [syperjœrmɑ̃] *adv* : exceptionally

supériorité [sypɛrjɔrite] *nf* : superiority

superlatif[1], **-tive** [sypɛrlatif, -tiv] *adj* : superlative

superlatif[2] *nm* : superlative

supermarché [sypɛrmarʃe] *nm* : supermarket

superposer [sypɛrpoze] *vt* **1** : to stack **2** : to superimpose

superpuissance [sypɛrpɥisɑ̃s] *nf* : superpower

supersonique [sypɛrsɔnik] *adj* : supersonic

superstitieux, -tieuse [sypɛrstisjø, -sjøz] *adj* : superstitious — **superstitieusement** [-sjøzmɑ̃] *adv*

superstition [sypɛrstisjɔ̃] *nf* : superstition

superstructure [sypɛrstryktyr] *nf* : superstructure

superviser [sypɛrvize] *vt* : to supervise — **supervision** [-vizjɔ̃] *nf*

superviseur [sypɛrvizœr] *nm* : supervisor

supplanter [syplɑ̃te] *vt* : to supplant

suppléant, -pléante [sypleɑ̃, -pleɑ̃t] *adj & n* : substitute, replacement, alternate

suppléer [syplee] {89} *vt* **1** REMPLACER : to replace, to fill in for **2** COMPENSER : to make up for, to compensate for — *vi* **~ à** : to make up for, to compensate for

supplément [syplemɑ̃] *nm* **1** : supplement **2** : extra charge, extra amount

supplémentaire [syplemɑ̃tɛr] *adj* **1** : additional, extra, supplementary **2** → **heure**

supplication [syplikasjɔ̃] *nf* : supplication, entreaty

supplice [syplis] *nm* **1** TORTURE : torture **2 être au supplice** : to be in agony
supplicier [syplisje] {96} *vt* TORTURER : to torture
supplier [syplije] {96} *vt* : to supplicate, to implore, to beg
support [sypɔr] *nm* **1** ÉTAI : support, stay, prop **2** : medium <support publicitaire : advertising medium>
supportable [sypɔrtabl] *adj* : bearable, tolerable
supporter[1] [sypɔrte] *vt* **1** SOUTENIR : to support, to hold up **2** ENDURER : to tolerate, to bear, to endure **3** : to stand up to, to withstand — **se supporter** *vr* **1** : to be bearable **2** : to stand each other
supporter[2] [sypɔrtɛr] *nm* : supporter, fan (in sports, etc.)
supposer [sypoze] *vt* **1** IMAGINER : to suppose, to assume **2** IMPLIQUER : to imply, to presuppose
supposition [sypozisjɔ̃] *nf* : supposition, assumption
suppositoire [sypozitwar] *nm* : suppository
suppôt [sypo] *nm* : henchman <suppôt de Satan : fiend>
suppression [syprɛsjɔ̃] *nf* **1** : abolition, elimination, suppression **2** : deletion (from a text)
supprimer [syprime] *vt* **1** : to abolish, to eliminate, to suppress **2** : to take out, to delete
suppurer [sypyre] *vi* : to suppurate, to fester
supputer [sypyte] *vt* : to compute, to calculate — **supputation** [-pytasjɔ̃] *nf*
suprématie [sypremasi] *nf* : supremacy
suprême [syprɛm] *adj* : supreme — **suprêmement** [-prɛmmɑ̃] *adv*
sur[1] [syr] *prep* **1** : on, upon, in <sur la table : on the table> <sur la photo : in the photo> **2** : over, above <sur les montagnes : over the mountains> **3** : about, on <un essai sur l'histoire : an essay about history> **4** VERS : towards <sur mon quatre-vingtième an : towards my eightieth year> **5** PARMI : out of <quatre sur cinq : four out of five> **6** : by <cinq mètres sur trois : five by three meters> **7 sur ce** : whereupon, upon which, hereon
sur[2], **sure** [syr] *adj* : sour
sûr, sûre [syr] *adj* **1** CERTAIN : sure, certain **2** FIABLE : reliable, trustworthy **3** : safe, secure **4** : sound <jugement sûr : sound judgment> — **sûrement** [syrmɑ̃] *adv*
surabondant, -dante [syrabɔ̃dɑ̃, -dɑ̃t] *adj* : overabundant — **surabondance** [-bɔ̃dɑ̃s] *nf*
suralimenter [syralimɑ̃te] *vt* : to overfeed
suranné, -née [syrane] *adj* : outdated, old-fashioned
surcharge [syrʃarʒ] *nf* **1** : extra load, overload **2** : correction, alteration **3** : surcharge
surcharger [syrʃarʒe] {17} *vt* **1** : to overload, to overburden **2** : to correct, to alter **3** : to impose a surcharge
surchauffer [syrʃofe] *vt* : to overheat
surclasser [syrklase] *vt* : to outclass
surcroît [syrkrwa] *nm* **1** : increase <un surcroît de travail : extra work> **2 de ~** *or* **par ~** : in addition, moreover **3 en ~** : in addition
surdité [syrdite] *nf* : deafness
surdose [syrdoz] *nf* : overdose
surdoué, -douée [syrdwe] *adj* : extremely intelligent, gifted
sureau [syro] *nm, pl* **sureaux** : elder (tree)
surélever [syrelve] {52} *vt* : to raise, to heighten
surenchère [syrɑ̃ʃɛr] *nf* **1** : higher bid **2** : exaggeration, overstatement
surenchérir [syrɑ̃ʃerir] *vi* **1** : to bid higher **2 ~ sur** : to outbid, to go one better than
surestimer [syrɛstime] *vt* : to overestimate, to overrate
sûreté [syrte] *nf* **1** SÉCURITÉ : safety, security **2** : soundness, steadiness, reliability **3** : surety, guarantee (in law) **4** : safety catch, safety lock
surexcité, -tée [syrɛksite] *adj* : overexcited
surexposer [syrɛkspoze] *vt* : to overexpose
surf [sœrf] *nm* : surfing, surfboarding
surface [syrfas] *nf* **1** : surface <faire surface : to surface> <en surface : on the surface, aboveground> **2 de ~** : superficial
surfait, -faite [syrfɛ, -fɛt] *adj* : overrated
surgelé [syrʒəle] *nm* : frozen food
surgeler [syrʒəle] {20} *vt* : to quick-freeze
surgir [syrʒir] *vi* **1** : to appear suddenly, to loom up **2** : to come up, to arise
surhumain, -maine [syrymɛ̃, -mɛn] *adj* : superhuman
surinamien, -mienne [syrinamjɛ̃, -mjɛn] *adj* : Surinamese
Surinamien, -mienne *n* : Surinamese
sur-le-champ [syrləʃɑ̃] *adv* : immediately, at once
surlendemain [syrlɑ̃dmɛ̃] *nm* **le surlendemain** : two days later
surmener [syrməne] {52} *vt* : to overwork — **se surmener** *vr* : to overwork, to work too hard
surmonter [syrmɔ̃te] *vt* **1** : to overcome, to surmount **2** : to top, to crown (a building, etc.)
surnager [syrnaʒe] {17} *vi* **1** FLOTTER : to float **2** PERSISTER : to persist, to linger on
surnaturel[1], **-relle** [syrnatyrɛl] *adj* : supernatural

surnaturel[2] *nm* **le surnaturel** : the supernatural
surnom [syrnɔ̃] *nm* SOBRIQUET : nickname
surnombre [syrnɔ̃br] *nm* **en ~** : excess, surplus <trois copies en surnombre : three too many copies>
surnommer [syrnɔme] *vt* : to nickname, to call
surpasser [syrpase] *vt* : to surpass, to outdo — **se surpasser** *vr*
surpeuplé, -plée [syrpœple] *adj* : overpopulated
surpeuplement [syrpœpləmɑ̃] *nm* : overpopulation
surplis [syrpli] *nm* : surplice
surplomb [syrplɔ̃] *nm* : overhang <en surplomb : overhanging>
surplomber [syrplɔ̃be] *v* : to overhang
surplus [syrply] *nm* **1** : surplus **2 au surplus** : moreover
surpopulation [syrpɔpylasjɔ̃] *nf* : overpopulation
surprenant, -nante [syrprənɑ̃, -nɑ̃t] *adj* : surprising, amazing
surprendre [syrprɑ̃dr] {70} *vt* **1** ÉTONNER : to surprise, to amaze **2** : to take by surprise, to catch in the act **3** : to overhear, to intercept
surprise [syrpriz] *nf* : surprise <avoir la bonne surprise : to be pleasantly surprised> <par surprise : by surprise>
surproduction [syrprɔdyksjɔ̃] *nf* : overproduction
surréalisme [syrrealism] *nm* : surrealism — **surréaliste** [-alist] *adj & nmf*
sursaut [syrso] *nm* **1** : start, jump <en sursaut : with a start> **2** : burst <un sursaut d'énergie : a burst of energy>
sursauter [syrsote] *vi* : to start, to jump
surseoir [syrswar] {90} *vi* **~ à** : to postpone, to defer
sursis[1] [syrsi] *pp* → **surseoir**
sursis[2] [syrsi] *nm* **1** : reprieve <condamné avec sursis : given a suspended sentence> **2** : respite, deferment, extension **3 être un mort en sursis** : to live on borrowed time
surtaxe [syrtaks] *nf* : surcharge
surtension [syrtɑ̃sjɔ̃] *nf* : surge (of electricity)
surtout[1] [syrtu] *adv* **1** : above all <surtout, pas de peur : above all, don't be afraid> **2** : especially, particularly <j'aime surtout la poésie : I especially like poetry>
surtout[2] *nm* : centerpiece
surveillance [syrvɛjɑ̃s] *nf* : surveillance, supervision <en surveillance médicale : under medical supervision>
surveillant, -lante [syrvɛjɑ̃, -jɑ̃t] *n* **1** : supervisor, overseer **2 surveillant de baignade** : lifeguard **3 surveillant de prison** : prison warden
surveiller [syrvɛje] *vt* **1** : to watch (over), to keep an eye on **2** : to supervise, to oversee
survenir [syrvənir] {92} *vi* **1** : to occur, to take place **2** : to arrive (unexpectedly)
survie [syrvi] *nf* **1** : survival (of a person) **2** : afterlife
survivance [syrvivɑ̃s] *nf* : survival
survivant, -vante [syrvivɑ̃, -vɑ̃t] *n* : survivor
survivre [syrvivr] {98} *vi* **1** : to survive **2 ~ à** : to survive, to outlive, to outlast
survol [syrvɔl] *nm* **1** : flying over **2** : quick look, overview
survoler [syrvɔle] *vi* **1** : to fly over **2** : to skim through
survolté, -tée [syrvɔlte] *adj* **1** : boosted (of an electronic circuit) **2** : overexcited
sus [sy(s)] *adv* **1 en ~** : extra **2 en sus de** : in addition to, on top of
susceptibilité [sysɛptibilite] *nf* : sensitivity, touchiness
susceptible [sysɛptibl] *adj* **1** : sensitive, touchy **2 ~ de** : likely to, capable of
susciter [sysite] *vt* **1** ÉVEILLER : to arouse (interest, feeling, etc.) **2** CRÉER : to create, to give rise to (problems, obstacles, etc.)
susmentionné, -née [sysmɑ̃sjɔne] *adj* : aforesaid, aforementioned
suspect[1], **-pecte** [syspɛ, -pɛkt] *adj* : suspicious, suspect
suspect[2], **-pecte** *n* : suspect
suspecter [syspɛkte] *vt* : to suspect
suspendre [syspɑ̃dr] {63} *vt* **1** : to suspend, to break off **2** PENDRE : to hang, to hang up — **se suspendre** *vr* **~ à** : to hang from
suspens [syspɑ̃] *nm* **1 en ~** : unresolved, uncertain **2 tenir en suspens** : to keep in suspense
suspense [syspɑ̃s] *nm* : suspense
suspension [syspɑ̃sjɔ̃] *nf* **1** : suspension **2 en ~** : suspended, hanging
suspicieux, -cieuse [syspisjø, -sjøz] *adj* : suspicious
suspicion [syspisjɔ̃] *nf* : suspicion
susurrer [sysyre] *v* CHUCHOTER : whisper
suture [sytyr] *nf* **1** : suture **2 point de suture** : stitch
suturer [sytyre] *vt* : to suture, to stitch
suzerein [syzrɛ̃] *nm* : liege, (feudal) lord
svelte [zvɛlt] *adj* : slender, svelte
sycomore [sikɔmɔr] *nm* : sycamore
syllabe [silab] *nf* : syllable — **syllabique** [-labik] *adj*
sylvestre [silvɛstr] *adj* : sylvan, forest
sylviculture [silvikyltyr] *nf* : forestry
symbole [sɛ̃bɔl] *nm* **1** : symbol **2** : creed <le Symbole des Apôtres : the Apostle's Creed>
symbolique [sɛ̃bɔlik] *adj* : symbolic — **symboliquement** [-likmɑ̃] *adv*
symboliser [sɛ̃bɔlize] *vt* : to symbolize
symbolisme [sɛ̃bɔlism] *nm* : symbolism

symétrie [simetri] *nf* : symmetry
symétrique [simetrik] *adj* : symmetrical, symmetric — **symétriquement** [-trikmɑ̃] *adv*
sympa [sɛ̃pa] *adj fam* : friendly, nice
sympathie [sɛ̃pati] *nf* **1** : liking, affection, fellow feeling **2** CONDOLÉANCES : condolences, sympathy
sympathique [sɛ̃patik] *adj* **1** AIMABLE : nice, likeable, pleasant **2** : sympathetic (in medicine)
sympathisant, -sante [sɛ̃patizɑ̃, -zɑ̃t] *n* : sympathizer
sympathiser [sɛ̃patize] *vi* : to get along <sympathiser avec qqn : to get on well with s.o.>
symphonie [sɛ̃fɔni] *nf* : symphony
symphonique [sɛ̃fɔnik] *adj* : symphonic
symptomatique [sɛ̃ptɔmatik] *adj* : symptomatic
symptôme [sɛ̃ptom] *nm* : symptom
synagogue [sinagɔg] *nf* : synagogue
synchroniser [sɛ̃krɔnize] *vt* : to synchronize
syncope [sɛ̃kɔp] *nf* **1** : faint, blackout **2** : syncopation
syncopé, -pée [sɛ̃kɔpe] *adj* : syncopated
syndicaliser [sɛ̃dikalize] *vt* : to unionize — **se syndicaliser** *vr*
syndicat [sɛ̃dika] *nm* : union, labor union
syndiquer [sɛ̃dike] *vt* : to unionize — **se syndiquer** *vr* : to join a union
syndrome [sɛ̃drom] *nm* : syndrome
synonyme[1] [sinɔnim] *adj* : synonymous
synonyme[2] *nm* : synonym
synopsis [sinɔpsis] *nf* : synopsis
syntaxe [sɛ̃taks] *nf* : syntax
synthèse [sɛ̃tɛz] *nf* : synthesis
synthétique [sɛ̃tetik] *adj* : synthetic — **synthétiquement** [-tikmɑ̃] *adv*
synthétiser [sɛ̃tetize] *vt* : to synthesize
syphilis [sifilis] *nf* : syphilis
syrien, -rienne [sirjɛ̃, -rjɛn] *adj* : Syrian
Syrien, -rienne *n* : Syrian
systématique [sistematik] *adj* : systematic — **systématiquement** [-tikmɑ̃] *adv*
systématiser [sistematize] *vt* : to systematize
système [sistɛm] *nm* : system <système métrique : metric system> <système solaire : solar system>
systémique [sistemik] *adj* : systemic

T

t [te] *nm* : t, the 20th letter of the alphabet
tabac [taba] *nm* **1** : tobacco **2 tabac à priser** : snuff **3** *France* : tobacco shop **4 c'est toujours le même tabac** *fam* : it's always the same old thing
tabagie [tabaʒi] *nf* **1** smoke-filled place **2** : *Can* : tobacco shop
tabasser [tabase] *vt fam* : to beat up, to clobber
tabatière [tabatjɛr] *nf* **1** : snuffbox **2** : skylight
tabernacle [tabɛrnakl] *nm* : tabernacle
table [tabl] *nf* **1** : table <mettre la table : to set the table> <se mettre à table : to sit down to eat> **2** : table, list <table des matières : table of contents> <table de multiplication : multiplication table> **3 table basse** : coffee table **4 table de chevet** *or* **table de nuit** : bedside table, night table **5 table ronde** : round table, roundtable
tableau [tablo] *nm, pl* **tableaux 1** PEINTURE : painting **2** : picture, scene **3** : table, chart **4 tableau d'affichage** : bulletin board **5 tableau de bord** : dashboard **6** *or* **tableau noir** : blackboard
tabler [table] *vt* **~ sur** : to count on, to rely on
tablette [tablɛt] *nf* **1** : shelf **2** : bar (of candy), stick (of gum) **3** : tablet (in pharmacy) **4** *Can* : notepad
tableur [tablœr] *nm* : spreadsheet
tablier [tablije] *nm* **1** : apron **2** : roadway, deck (on a bridge)
tabloïde *or* **tabloïd** [tablɔid] *nm* : tabloid
tabou[1], **-boue** [tabu] *adj* : taboo
tabou[2] *nm* : taboo
tabouret [taburɛ] *nm* : stool, footstool
tabulaire [tabylɛr] *adj* : tabular
tabulateur [tabylatœr] *nm* : tab, tabulator
tac [tak] *nm* **1** : tap, click **2 du tac au tac** : tit for tat
tache [taʃ] *nf* **1** : stain, spot **2 taches de rousseur** : freckles
tâche [taʃ] *nf* : task, job
tacher [taʃe] *vt* SALIR : to stain, to spot — **se tacher** *vr*
tâcher [taʃe] *vt* **tâcher que** : to try and be sure that <tâchez que ce soit correct : make sure that it's correct> — *vi* **~ de** : to try to <tâcher de réussir : to try to succeed>
tâcheron [taʃrɔ̃] *nm* **1** : hard worker, drudge **2** : jobber
tacheter [taʃte] {8} *vt* : to spot, to speckle
tacite [tasit] *adj* : tacit — **tacitement** [tasitmɑ̃] *adv*

taciturne [tasityrn] *adj* **:** taciturn
tacot [tako] *nm fam* **:** jalopy
tact [takt] *nm* DÉLICATESSE **:** tact <avec tact : tactfully>
tactile [taktil] *adj* **:** tactile
tactique[1] [taktik] *adj* **:** tactical **— tactiquement** [-tikmɑ̃] *adv*
tactique[2] *nf* STRATÉGIE **:** tactics *pl,* strategy, procedure
taffetas [tafta] *nms & pl* **:** taffeta
tahitien[1], **-tienne** [taisjɛ̃, -sjɛn] *adj* **:** Tahitian
tahitien[2] *nm* **:** Tahitian (language)
Tahitien, -tienne *n* **:** Tahitian
taie [tɛ] *nf or* **taie d'oreiller :** pillowcase
taillader [tajade] *vt* **:** to slash, to gash, to hack
taille [taj] *nf* **1 :** cutting, pruning **2 :** size <de taille moyenne : medium-sized> <de taille : sizable> **3 :** height <une femme de haute taille : a tall woman> **4 :** waist, waistline
taille–crayon [tajkrɛjɔ̃] *nm, pl* **taille–crayons :** pencil sharpener
tailler [taje] *vt* **1 :** to cut, to prune, to trim **2 :** to sharpen (a pencil) **—** *vi* **1 ~ dans :** to cut into **2 tailler grand/petit :** to run large/small (of clothes) **— se tailler** *vr* **:** to carve out (a way, a success, etc.) for oneself
tailleur [tajœr] *nm* **1 :** woman's suit **2 :** tailor
taillis [taji] *nms & pl* **:** coppice, copse
taire [tɛr] {91} *vt* **:** to hush up, to keep secret **— se taire** *vr* **1 :** to be quiet <tais-toi! : be quiet!> **2 :** to fall silent
taisait [tɛzɛ], **taisions** [tɛzjɔ̃], *etc.* → **taire**
taise [tɛz], *etc.* → **taire**
taiwanais, -naise [tajwanɛ, -nɛz] *adj* **:** Taiwanese
Taiwanais, -naise *n* **:** Taiwanese
talc [talk] *nm* **:** talc, talcum powder
talent [talɑ̃] *nm* **:** talent, gift <avoir du talent : to be talented>
talentueux, -tueuse [talɑ̃tɥø, -tɥøz] *adj* **:** talented
taler [tale] *vt* **:** to bruise (fruit)
talion [taljɔ̃] *nm* **la loi du talion :** an eye for an eye
talisman [talismɑ̃] *nm* **:** talisman
taloche [talɔʃ] *nf fam* **:** slap, blow
talon [talɔ̃] *nm* **1 :** heel **2 :** stub (of a check)
talonner [talɔne] *vt* **1 :** to follow closely **2 :** to hound, to harass
talus [taly] *nms & pl* **:** embankment, slope
tambour [tɑ̃bur] *nm* **1 :** drum **2 :** drummer **3 sans tambour ni trompette :** without fanfare **4 tambour battant :** briskly
tambourin [tɑ̃burɛ̃] *nm* **:** tambourine
tambouriner [tɑ̃burine] *vt* **:** to drum, to tap (one's fingers, one's feet, etc.)
tamia [tamja] *nm* **:** chipmunk
tamis [tami] *nms & pl* **:** sieve, sifter
tamiser [tamize] *vt* **1 :** to sift **2 :** to filter <lumière tamisée : subdued lighting>
tampon [tɑ̃pɔ̃] *nm* **1** BOUCHON **:** plug, stopper **2 :** pad <tampon à récurer : scouring pad> <tampon encreur : stamp pad, ink pad> **3 :** buffer **4 :** rubber stamp **5 tampon hygiénique :** tampon
tamponner [tɑ̃pɔne] *vt* **1 :** to dab, to swab **2** HEURTER **:** to crash into, to collide with **3 :** to stamp, to validate
tam–tam [tamtam] *nm, pl* **tam–tams :** tom-tom
tancer [tɑ̃se] {6} *vt* **:** to reprimand
tandem [tɑ̃dɛm] *nm* **1 :** tandem (bicycle) **2 travailler en tandem :** to work in tandem
tandis [tɑ̃di] **tandis que 1 :** while **2 :** whereas
tangent, -gente [tɑ̃ʒɑ̃, -ʒɑ̃t] *adj* **:** tangential
tangente [tɑ̃ʒɑ̃t] *nf* **:** tangent
tangible [tɑ̃ʒibl] *adj* **:** tangible **— tangiblement** [-ʒibləmɑ̃] *adv*
tango [tɑ̃go] *nm* **:** tango
tanguer [tɑ̃ge] *vi* **:** to pitch, to toss about
tanière [tanjɛr] *nf* **:** lair, den
tanin [tanɛ̃] *nm* **:** tannin
tank [tɑ̃k] *nm* **:** tank
tanker [tɑ̃kœr] *nm* **:** tanker
tanné, -née [tane] *adj* **:** weathered, leathery (of skin)
tanner [tane] *vt* **1 :** to tan (leather, skin) **2** *fam* **:** to pester, to annoy
tannerie [tanri] *nf* **:** tannery
tanneur, -neuse [tanœr, -nøz] *n* **:** tanner
tant [tɑ̃] *adv* **1 :** so much, so many <tant de bruit : so much noise> <comme tant d'autres : like so many others> <il y a tant à faire : there's so much to do> **2 :** so <tant il est déterminé : (since) he is so determined> **3 en tant que :** as, in so far as **4 en tant que tel :** as such **5 tant mieux! :** so much the better! **6 tant pis! :** too bad! **7 tant que :** as much as, so much as **8 tant que :** as long as
tante [tɑ̃t] *nf* **:** aunt
tantinet [tɑ̃tinɛ] *nm* **:** little bit
tantôt [tɑ̃to] *adv* **1 :** sometimes <tantôt à bicyclette, tantôt à pied : sometimes by bicycle, sometimes on foot> **2** *Can* **:** later **3** *France* **:** this afternoon
tanzanien, -nienne [tɑ̃zanjɛ̃, -njɛn] *adj* **:** Tanzanian
Tanzanien, -nienne *n* **:** Tanzanian
taon [tɑ̃] *nm* **:** horsefly
tapage [tapaʒ] *nm* **1** VACARME **:** racket, uproar, din **2** SCANDALE **:** furor, scandal
tapageur, -geuse [tapaʒœr, -ʒøz] *adj* **1 :** noisy, rowdy **2** VOYANT **:** flashy, ostentatious, garish

tapant, -pante [tapɑ̃, -pɑ̃t] *adj* : sharp, on the dot <à midi tapant : at twelve o'clock sharp>
tape [tap] *nf* : slap, tap, pat
tape–à–l'oeil[1] [tapalœj] *adj* : flashy, showy, gaudy
tape–à–l'oeil[2] *nms & pl* : flashiness, show
taper [tape] *vt* **1** : to hit, to slap, to beat **2** : to type **3 taper qqn de qqch** : to bum sth from s.o. — *vi* **1** : to hit, to knock, to bang <taper sur un clou : to hit (on) a nail> <taper à la porte : to knock on the door> **2** : to beat down (of the sun) **3** *or* **taper à la machine** : to type **4 taper des mains** : to clap one's hands **5 taper des pieds** : to stamp one's feet — **se taper** *vr* **1** *fam* : to knock each other down **2** *fam* : to put away, to eat, to drink **3** *fam* : to get stuck with (a chore)
tapette [tapɛt] *nf* **1** : light tap, pat **2 tapette à mouches** : flyswatter
tapinois [tapɛnwa] **en ~** : furtively
tapioca [tapjɔka] *nm* : tapioca
tapir [tapir] *v* **se tapir** *vr* **1** : to crouch (down) **2** : to hide away, to retreat
tapis [tapi] *nms & pl* **1** : carpet **2 tapis roulant** : moving walkway, (baggage) carousel, conveyor belt
tapisser [tapise] *vt* **1** : to wallpaper **2** : to upholster **3** : to cover, to carpet
tapisserie [tapisri] *nf* **1** : tapestry **2** : wallpaper **3 faire tapisserie** : to be a wallflower
taponner [tapɔne] *vt Can fam* : to touch, to handle <arrête de taponner mes choses : stop playing with my things>
tapotement [tapɔtmɑ̃] *nm* : tap, pat
tapoter [tapɔte] *vt* : to tap, to pat
taquin[1], **-quine** [takɛ̃, -kin] *adj* : teasing
taquin[2], **-quine** *n* : tease
taquiner [takine] *vt* : to tease
taquinerie [takinri] *nf* : teasing
tarabiscoté, -cotée [tarabiskɔte] *adj* : fussy, overelaborate
tarabuster [tarabyste] *vt* **1** : to pester **2** : to worry, to bother <ça me tarabuste : that's getting me down>
tard [tar] *adv* : late <plus tard : later> <au plus tard : at the latest>
tarder [tarde] *vi* **1** : to delay, to be a long time coming <ça ne devrait pas tarder : it shouldn't take long> **2 sans ~** : without delay
tardif, -dive [tardif, -div] *adj* : late <repas tardif : late meal>
tardivement [tardivmɑ̃] *adv* : late, belatedly
tare [tar] *nf* DÉFAUT : defect, flaw
tarentule [tarɑ̃tyl] *nf* : tarantula
targette [tarʒɛt] *nf* : bolt (on a door, etc.)
targuer [targe] *v* **se targuer** *vr* **~ de** : to boast about
tarif [tarif] *nm* **1** : rate, fare <payer plein tarif : to pay full fare> **2** : price, schedule of prices <tarif horaire : price per hour> **3 tarif douanier** : tariff, customs duty
tarir [tarir] *vt* : to dry up — *vi* **1** : to run dry, to dry up **2 ne pas tarir d'éloges** : to be full of praise
tartan [tartɛ̃] *nm* : tartan
tarte[1] [tart] *adj fam* : stupid, ridiculous
tarte[2] *nf* : pie
tartelette [tartəlɛt] *nf* : tart
tartine [tartin] *nf or* **tartine beurrée** : slice of bread and butter
tartiner [tartine] *vt* : to spread (with butter, etc.) <fromage à tartiner : cheese spread>
tartre [tartr] *nm* : tartar
tas [ta] *nms & pl* **1** : heap, pile **2 des tas de** : a lot of, piles of **3 formation sur le tas** : on-the-job training
tasse [tas] *nf* : cup <tasse à thé : teacup>
tasseau [taso] *nm, pl* **tasseaux** : brace, bracket
tasser [tase] *vt* **1** : to pack down **2** ENTASSER : to pack together, to cram **3** *Can* : to move over, to move aside — **se tasser** *vr* **1** : to shrink **2** : to squeeze together, to cram <elles sont tassées dans la voiture : they are crammed into the car>
tâter [tate] *vt* **1** PALPER : to feel **2** : to sound out <tâter le terrain : to check out the lay of the land> — *vi* **~ de** : to try one's hand at
tatillon[1], **-lonne** [tatijɔ̃, -jɔn] *adj* POINTILLEUX : fussy, finicky
tatillon[2], **-lonne** *n* : fussy person, fussbudget
tâtonner [tatɔne] *vi* : to grope one's way, to feel around
tâtons [tatɔ̃] **avancer à tâtons** : to feel one's way (along)
tatou [tatu] *nm* : armadillo
tatouage [tatwaʒ] *nm* **1** : tattoo **2** : tattooing
tatouer [tatwe] *vt* : to tattoo
taudis [todi] *nms & pl* : hovel, slum
taule [tol] *nf fam* : prison <faire de la taule : to do time>
taupe [top] *nf* **1** : mole **2 myope comme une taupe** : blind as a bat
taupinière [topinjɛr] *nf* : molehill
taureau [tɔro] *nm, pl* **taureaux** : bull
Taureau *nm* : Taurus
tauromachie [tɔrɔmaʃi] *nf* : bullfighting
taux [to] *nms & pl* **1** : rate <taux de change : exchange rate> <taux de natalité : birthrate> **2** : level <taux de cholestérol : cholesterol level>
tavelé, -lée [tavle] *adj* : marked, spotted
taverne [tavɛrn] *nf* : inn, tavern
taxe [taks] *nf* : tax — **taxation** [taksasjɔ̃] *nf*

taxer [takse] *vt* **1** IMPOSER : to tax **2** ACCUSER : to accuse <il m'a taxé de paresse : he accused me of laziness>
taxi [taksi] *nm* : taxi, taxicab
taxidermie [taksidɛrmi] *nf* : taxidermy — **taxidermiste** [-dɛrmist] *nmf*
tchadien, -dienne [tʃadjɛ̃, -djɛn] *adj* : Chadian
Tchadien, -dienne *n* : Chadian
tchécoslovaque [tʃekɔslɔvak] *adj* : Czechoslovak, Czechoslovakian
Tchécoslovaque *nmf* : Czechoslovak, Czechoslovakian
tchèque[1] [tʃɛk] *adj* : Czech
tchèque[2] *nm* : Czech (language)
Tchèque *nmf* : Czech
te [tə] (**t'** *before a vowel or mute h*) *pron* **1** : you, to you <je t'aime : I love you> <je te le donne : I'm giving it to you> **2** : yourself <tu vas te couper : you're going to cut yourself>
technicien, -cienne [tɛknisjɛ̃, -sjɛn] *n* : technician
technique[1] [tɛknik] *adj* : technical — **techniquement** [-nikmɑ̃] *adv*
technique[2] *nf* : technique
technologie [tɛknɔlɔʒi] *nf* : technology
technologique [tɛknɔlɔʒik] *adj* : technological
technologue [tɛknɔlɔg] *nmf* : technologist
teck [tɛk] *nm* : teak
teckel [tekɛl] *nm* : dachshund
tee–shirt [tiʃœrt] *nm, pl* **tee–shirts** : T-shirt
teigne [tɛɲ] *nf* **1** : ringworm **2** : moth **3** *fam* : nasty person, louse
teindre [tɛ̃dr] {37} *vt* : to dye — **se teindre** *vr* **se teindre les cheveux** : to dye one's hair
teint [tɛ̃] *nm* **1** : complexion, coloring **2 grand teint** *or* **bon teint** : colorfast
teinte [tɛ̃t] *nf* **1** TON : shade, hue **2** : tinge, hint
teinter [tɛ̃te] *vt* **1** : to tint, to stain **2 ~ de** : to tinge with <tristesse teintée de soulagement : sorrow tinged with relief>
teinture [tɛ̃tyr] *nf* **1** : dye **2** : dyeing **3** : tincture <teinture d'iode : tincture of iodine>
teinturerie [tɛ̃tyrri] *nf* : dry cleaner (shop)
teinturier, -rière [tɛ̃tyrje, -rjɛ] *n* : dry cleaner
tel[1], **telle** [tɛl] *adj* **1** : such <une telle femme : such a woman, a woman like that> <un tel bonheur! : such happiness!> <de telle manière que : in such a way that> **2** : such and such, a certain <je viens tel jour : I'm coming on such and such a day> **3 tel que** : such as, like <des livres tels que les dictionnaires : books such as dictionaries> **4 tel quel** : as (it) is <laissez-les tels quels : leave them as they are>
tel[2], **telle** *pron* **1** : a certain one, someone **2 un tel, une telle** : so-and-so, what's-his-name, what's-her-name
télé [tele] *nf fam* : TV
téléavertisseur [teleavɛrtisœr] *nm Can* : beeper
télécharger [teleʃarʒe] {17} *vt* : to download (a computer file)
télécommande [telekɔmɑ̃d] *nf* : remote control
télécommunication [telekɔmynikasjɔ̃] *nf* : telecommunication
télécopie [telekɔpi] *nf* : fax, facsimile
télécopieur [telekɔpjœr] *nm* : fax machine
télédiffuser [teledifyze] *vt* : to broadcast (on television), to televise
téléfilm [telefilm] *nm* : film made for TV
télégramme [telegram] *nm* : telegram
télégraphe [telegraf] *nm* : telegraph — **télégraphique** [-grafik] *adj*
télégraphier [telegrafje] {96} *v* : to telegraph
télépathie [telepati] *nf* : telepathy
télépathique [telepatik] *adj* : telepathic
téléphone [telefɔn] *nm* : telephone, phone <donner un coup de téléphone : to make a phone call> <être au téléphone : to be (talking) on the telephone>
téléphoner [telefɔne] *vt* **1** : to telephone, to call **2 téléphoner en PVC** *France* : to call collect **3 téléphoner à frais virés** *Can* : to call collect
téléphonique [telefɔnik] *adj* : telephone <cabine téléphonique : telephone booth>
téléphoniste [telefɔnist] *nmf* : telephone operator
télescope [teleskɔp] *nm* : telescope
télescoper [teleskɔpe] *vt* : to crash into, to collide with (a vehicle) — **se télescoper** *vr* **1** : to collide with each other **2** : to overlap, to intermingle (of ideas, etc.)
télescopique [teleskɔpik] *adj* : telescopic
télésiège [telesjɛʒ] *nm* : chairlift
téléski [teleski] *nm* : ski lift
téléspectateur, -trice [telespɛktatœr, -tris] *n* : television viewer
téléviser [televize] *vt* : to televise
téléviseur [televizœr] *nm* : television set
télévision [televizjɔ̃] *nf* **1** : television <à la télévision : on television> **2** TÉLÉVISEUR : television set
tellement [tɛlmɑ̃] *adv* **1** : so, so much <tellement vite : so fast> <c'est tellement mieux : it's so much better> **2 ~ de** : so many, so much <tellement de travail : so much work> **3 pas tellement** : not much, not really <il n'a pas tellement changé : he hasn't really changed>
téméraire [temerɛr] *adj* : rash, reckless

témérité [temerite] *nf* : rashness, recklessness

témoignage [temwaɲaʒ] *nm* **1** RÉCIT : account, story **2** : testimony (in court) **3** PREUVE : evidence, sign <témoignage d'affection : token of affection>

témoigner [temwaɲe] *vt* **1** : to testify, to attest **2** MONTRER : to show, to evince — *vi* **1** : to testify, to give evidence **2** ~ **de** : to show, to give evidence of

témoin [temwɛ̃] *nm* **1** : witness <témoin oculaire : eyewitness> **2** PREUVE : evidence, mark **3** : baton (in a relay race)

tempe [tɑ̃p] *nf* : temple <tempes grisonnantes : graying temples>

tempérament [tɑ̃peramɑ̃] *nm* CARACTÈRE : temperament, disposition

tempérance [tɑ̃perɑ̃s] *nf* : temperance

tempérant, -rante [tɑ̃perɑ̃, -rɑ̃t] *adj* : temperate, sober

température [tɑ̃peratyr] *nf* : temperature

tempéré, -rée [tɑ̃pere] *adj* : temperate <climat tempéré : temperate climate>

tempérer [tɑ̃pere] {87} *vt* : to temper, to ease, to moderate

tempête [tɑ̃pɛt] *nf* : storm <tempête de neige : snowstorm, blizzard>

tempêter [tɑ̃pete] *vi* FULMINER : to rage, to rant

temple [tɑ̃pl] *nm* **1** : temple **2** : (protestant) church, meetinghouse

tempo [tɛmpo] *nm* : tempo

temporaire [tɑ̃pɔrɛr] *adj* : temporary — **temporairement** [-rɛrmɑ̃] *adv*

temporel, -relle [tɑ̃pɔrɛl] *adj* : temporal

temporiser [tɑ̃pɔrize] *vi* : to stall, to play for time

temps [tɑ̃] *nms & pl* **1** : time <à temps : in time, on time> <de temps à autre : from time to time> <pendant ce temps : meanwhile, in the meantime> <travailler à plein temps : to work full-time> <les temps ont changé : times have changed> **2** : weather <un temps pluvieux : rainy weather> <quel temps fait-il? : what's the weather like?, what's it like outside?> **3** : tense (in grammar)

tenable [tənabl] *adj* SUPPORTABLE : bearable <ce n'était pas tenable : it was unbearable>

tenace [tənas] *adj* : tenacious, persistent

tenacité [tənasite] *nf* : tenacity

tenailler [tenaje] *vt* TOURMENTER : to torture, to torment

tenailles [tənaj] *nfpl* **1** : pincers, nippers **2** : tongs

tenancier, -cière [tənɑ̃sje, -sjɛr] *n* : manager (of a hotel, etc.)

tenant, -nante [tənɑ̃, -nɑ̃t] *n* **1** PARTISAN : supporter **2 tenant d'un titre** : titleholder (in sports) **3 les tenants et les aboutissants** : the ins and outs

tendance [tɑ̃dɑ̃s] *nf* **1** : tendency **2** COURANT : trend

tendineux, -neuse [tɑ̃dinø, -nøz] *adj* **1** : tendinous, sinewy **2** : stringy (of meat)

tendon [tɑ̃dɔ̃] *nm* : tendon, sinew, hamstring

tendre[1] [tɑ̃dr] {63} *vt* **1** : to tense, to stretch (out), to draw tight **2** : to put up, to set up <tendre un piège à : to set a trap for> **3** : to spread out (cloth, etc.) **4** : to hold out, to extend <tendre la main : to hold out one's hand> <tendre le cou : to crane one's neck> <tendre l'oreille : to prick up one's ears> — *vi* **1** ~ **à** : to tend to **2** ~ **vers** : to strive for — **se tendre** *vr* **1** : to tighten, to become taut **2** : to become strained

tendre[2] *adj* **1** : tender, soft **2** : loving <un regard tendre : a tender glance>

tendrement [tɑ̃drəmɑ̃] *adv* : lovingly, tenderly

tendresse [tɑ̃drɛs] *nf* : tenderness, affection

tendu, -due [tɑ̃dy] *adj* **1** : tight, taut **2** : tense, strained

ténèbres [tenɛbr] *nfpl* : darkness

ténébreux, -breuse [tenebrø, -brøz] *adj* **1** OBSCUR : dark, gloomy **2** MYSTÉRIEUX : mysterious, obscure

teneur [tənœr] *nf* : content <teneur en gras : fat content>

ténia [tenja] *nm* : tapeworm

tenir [tənir] {92} *vt* **1** : to hold, to keep <tenir en position : to hold in place> <tenez la porte fermée : keep the door shut> **2** : to have, to catch <je te tiens! : I've got you!> <tenir les voleurs : to catch the thieves> **3** : to take hold of, to control <tenir les enfants : to keep the children under control> **4** : to run, to manage (a hotel, store, etc.) **5** : to hold down, to hold up, to keep up **6** : to hold (a quantity), to take up (a space) **7** : to regard, to consider <il me tient responsable : he holds me responsible> — *vi* **1** : to hold, to stay in place **2** : to hold up, to last **3** : to fit (into a space) **4** *or* **tenir bon** : to hang on, to hold out **5** ~ **à** : to be fond of, to like **6** ~ **à** : to be due to **7** ~ **à** : to want to, to be anxious to **8** ~ **de** : to be like (someone), to take after **9** ~ **de** : to border on — *v impers* : to depend <il ne tient qu'à toi : it's up to you> — **se tenir** *vr* **1** : to hold, to hold up, to hold onto <se tenir par la main : to hold hands> **2** : to remain, to stay <se tenir prêt : to be ready> <se tenir debout : to stand still> **3** : to behave (oneself) **4** : to hold up, to make sense **5** : to consider oneself **6** : to hold to, to stand by <s'en tenir à : to confine oneself to>

tennis [tenis] *nm* **1** : tennis <tennis de table : table tennis> **2 tennis** *nmpl France* : sneakers

ténor [tenɔr] *nm* : tenor

tension [tɑ̃sjɔ̃] *nf* **1** : tension **2** *or* **tension artérielle** : blood pressure

tentacule [tɑ̃takyl] *nm* : tentacle

tentant, -tante [tɑ̃tɑ̃, -tɑ̃t] *adj* : tempting, tantalizing

tentateur, -trice [tɑ̃tatœr, -tris] *n* : tempter

tentation [tɑ̃tasjɔ̃] *nf* : temptation

tentative [tɑ̃tativ] *nf* : attempt <tentative d'homicide : attempted murder>

tente [tɑ̃t] *nf* : tent

tenter [tɑ̃te] *vt* **1** : to tempt <tenter le diable : to tempt fate> **2** ESSAYER : to attempt, to try <tenter la chance : to try one's luck>

tenture [tɑ̃tyr] *nf* : hanging, wall covering

tenu[1] [təny] *pp* → **tenir**

tenu[2], **-nue** [təny] *adj* **1** : obliged, bound **2** : controlled, kept in check **3 bien tenu** : well kept, tidy

ténu, -nue [teny] *adj* **1** : fine, slender **2** : thin (of voices, air, etc.) **3** : tenuous, subtle

tenue *nf* **1** : holding, running (of a meeting, etc.) **2** : organizing, keeping <tenue de livres : bookkeeping> **3** : conduct, manners *pl* **4** MAINTIEN : bearing, posture **5** : clothes *pl*, dress, outfit <tenue d'hiver : winter clothing> <tenue militaire : military dress, uniform> <tenue de soirée : formal dress>

térébenthine [terebɑ̃tin] *nf* : turpentine

tergiverser [tɛrʒivɛrse] *vi* : to shilly-shally, to beat around the bush

terme [tɛrm] *nm* **1** : term, word <en d'autres termes : in other words> **2** : end, termination <mettre un terme à : to put an end to> **3** ÉCHÉANCE : due date, deadline (for payment) **4 termes** *nmpl* : terms (of a contract) **5 termes** *nmpl* : relations <être en bons termes avec : to be on good terms with>

terminaison [tɛrminɛzɔ̃] *nf* : termination, ending

terminal[1], **-nale** [tɛrminal] *adj, mpl* **-naux** [-no] **1** : final, last **2** : terminal (in medicine)

terminal[2] *nm, pl* **-naux 1** : station, terminal **2** : computer terminal

terminer [tɛrmine] *v* FINIR : to end, to finish — **se terminer** *vr* : to end, to finish up

terminologie [tɛrminɔlɔʒi] *nf* : terminology

terminus [tɛrminys] *nms & pl* : terminus, end of the line (of a train, bus, etc.)

termite [tɛrmit] *nm* : termite

terne [tɛrn] *adj* **1** FADE : colorless, drab **2** ENNUYEUX : dull, dreary

ternir [tɛrnir] *vt* **1** : to tarnish, to dull **2** : to stain, to tarnish (one's reputation, etc.)

ternissure [tɛrnisyr] *nf* : tarnish

terrain [tɛrɛ̃] *nm* **1** : ground, soil **2** PARCELLE : plot (of land) **3** : land, terrain **4** : field <terrain de football : football field> <terrain de jeu : playground> <terrain de camping : campsite> <terrain d'aviation : airfield> **5** : field, sphere (of activity) <le terrain juridique : the field of law> **6** : area, ground, territory <perdre du terrain : to lose ground> <terrain d'entente : common ground> <être en terrain connu : to be on familiar territory>

terrasse [tɛras] *nf* : terrace

terrassement [tɛrasmɑ̃] *nm* : excavation

terrasser [tɛrase] *vt* **1** : to knock down, to floor **2** : to strike down <terrassé par une maladie : struck down by sickness>

terre [tɛr] *nf* **1** : ground <par terre : on the ground, on the floor> <sous terre : underground> **2** TERRAIN : land <basse terre : lowland> **3** : (dry) land <aller à terre : to go ashore> **4** : dirt, soil <chemin de terre : dirt road> **5** : earth, world <sur la terre : on earth, in the world> **6** : clay (for pottery), earthenware **7 terre à terre** : down-to-earth, matter-of-fact **8 terre cuite** : terra-cotta

Terre *nf* : Earth (planet)

terreau [tɛro] *nm, pl* **terreaux** : loam, compost

terre–plein [tɛrplɛ̃] *nm, pl* **terre–pleins** : median strip

terrer [tɛre] *v* **se terrer** *vr* : to hide, to go underground

terrestre [tɛrɛstr] *adj* **1** : earth, terrestrial **2** : earthly, worldly

terreur [tɛrœr] *nf* : terror

terreux, -reuse [tɛrø, -røz] *adj* **1** : muddy **2** BLAFARD : sallow, pallid **3** : earthy

terrible [tɛribl] *adj* **1** : terrible, dreadful **2** : intense, excessive **3** *fam* FORMIDABLE : terrific, great

terrien, -rienne [tɛrjɛ̃, -rjɛn] *adj* **propriétaire terrien** : landowner

terrier [tɛrje] *nm* **1** : hole, burrow **2** : terrier

terrifiant, -fiante [tɛrifjɑ̃, -fjɑ̃t] *adj* : terrifying

terrifier [tɛrifje] {96} *vt* ÉPOUVANTER : to terrify

territoire [tɛritwar] *nm* : territory

territorial, -riale [tɛritɔrjal] *adj, mpl* **-riaux** [-rjo] : territorial

terroir [tɛrwar] *nm* **1** : region, locality **2** : country, rural region

terroriser [tɛrɔrize] *vt* : to terrorize

terrorisme [tɛrɔrism] *nm* : terrorism — **terroriste** [-rɔrist] *adj & nmf*

tertiaire [tɛrsjɛr] *adj* : tertiary

tertre [tɛrtr] *nm* MONTICULE : hillock, mound

tes → ton[1]

tesson [tɛsɔ̃] *nm* : piece, fragment, shard <tesson de bouteille : piece of broken glass>

test [tɛst] *nm* : test

testament [tɛstamɑ̃] *nm* **1** : will, last will and testament **2** : legacy **3 Testament** *m* : Testament <Ancien Testament : Old Testament> <Nouveau Testament : New Testament>

tester [tɛste] *vt* : to test — *vi* : to make a will

testicule [tɛstikyl] *nm* : testicle

tétanos [tetanos] *nms & pl* : tetanus, lockjaw

têtard [tɛtar] *nm* : tadpole

tête [tɛt] *nf* **1** : head <être tête nue : to be bareheaded> <la tête haute : with head held high> **2** : (head of) hair <se laver la tête : to wash one's hair> **3** : face <faire la tête : to make a face, to sulk> **4** : mind, head <passer par la tête : to cross one's mind> <garder sa tête : to keep one's head> **5** : neck, life <risquer sa tête : to risk one's neck> **6** : head, leader **7** : head (of cattle, etc.) **8** : top, lead, head <tête d'un arbre : treetop> <à la tête de la classe : at the head of the class> **9** : header (in soccer) **10 tenir tête à** : to stand up to **11 tête brulée** : hothead **12 tête de mort** : skull **13 tête de pont** : beachhead

tête–à–queue [tɛtakø] *nms & pl* : spin (of an automobile)

tête–à–tête [tɛtatɛt] *nms & pl* **1** : tête-à-tête **2 être en tête–à–tête** : to be alone together

tétée [tete] *nf* : nursing, feeding (at the breast)

téter [tete] {87} *vt* : to suck at (the breast) — *vi* : to suckle, to nurse

tétine [tetin] *nf* **1** : teat **2** : nipple (of a baby bottle) **3** : pacifier

téton [tetɔ̃] *nm fam* : breast

têtu, -tue [tety] *adj* : stubborn

texte [tɛkst] *nm* : text

textile [tɛkstil] *nm* : textile

textuel, -elle [tɛkstɥɛl] *adj* : literal, word for word

textuellement [tɛkstɥɛlmɑ̃] *adv* : literally, verbatim

texture [tɛkstyr] *nf* : texture

thaï [taj] *nm* : Thai (language)

thaïlandais, -daise [tajlɑ̃dɛ, -dɛz] *adj* : Thai

Thaïlandais, -daise *n* : Thai

thé [te] *nm* : tea

théâtral, -trale [teatral] *adj, mpl* **-traux** [-tro] : theatrical

théâtre [teatr] *nm* **1** : theater (building, area) **2** : drama, theater **3 faire du théâtre** : to be an actor

théière [tejɛr] *nf* : teapot

théisme [teism] *nm* : theism

thème [tɛm] *nm* : theme

théologie [teɔlɔʒi] *nf* : theology

théologique [teɔlɔʒik] *adj* : theological

théologien, -gienne [teɔlɔʒjɛ̃, -ʒjɛn] *n* : theologian

théorème [teɔrɛm] *nm* : theorem

théorie [teɔri] *nf* : theory

théorique [teɔrik] *adj* : theoretical — **théoriquement** [-rikmɑ̃] *adv*

théoriser [teɔrize] *vi* : to theorize

thérapeute [terapøt] *nmf* : therapist

thérapeutique[1] [terapøtik] *adj* : therapeutic

thérapeutique[2] *nf* : therapy, treatment

thérapie [terapi] *nf* : therapy

thermal, -male [tɛrmal] *adj, mpl* **thermaux** [tɛrmo] : thermal <station thermale : spa>

thermique [tɛrmik] *adj* : thermal <centrale thermique : thermal power station>

thermodynamique [tɛrmɔdinamik] *nf* : thermodynamics

thermomètre [tɛrmɔmɛtr] *nm* : thermometer

thermos [tɛrmos] *nmfs & pl* : thermos

thermostat [tɛrmɔsta] *nm* : thermostat

thésauriser [tezɔrize] *vt* : to hoard — *vi* : to hoard money

thèse [tɛz] *nf* : thesis

thiamine [tjamin] *nf* : thiamine

thon [tɔ̃] *nm* : tuna

thorax [tɔraks] *nm* : thorax

thym [tɛ̃] *nm* : thyme

thyroïde [tirɔid] *nf* : thyroid (gland)

tiare [tjar] *nf* : tiara

tibétain[1], **-taine** [tibetɛ̃, -tɛn] *adj* : Tibetan

tibétain[2] *nm* : Tibetan (language)

Tibétain, -taine *n* : Tibetan

tibia [tibja] *nm* **1** : tibia, shinbone **2** : shin

tic [tik] *nm* **1** : tic, twitch **2** : mannerism

ticket [tikɛ] *nm* BILLET : ticket

tic–tac [tiktak] *nms & pl* : tick, ticking

tiède [tjɛd] *adj* **1** : lukewarm, tepid **2** : warm, mild (of weather, etc.)

tièdement [tjɛdmɑ̃] *adv* : halfheartedly

tiédir [tjedir] *vi* : to warm up, to cool down

tien[1], **tienne** [tjɛ̃, tjɛn] *adj* : yours, of yours <une tienne amie : a friend of yours> <je suis tien : I'm yours>

tien[2], **tienne** *pron* **le tien, la tienne, les tiens, les tiennes** : yours <le tien est plus joli : yours is prettier>

tiendra [tjɛ̃dra], *etc.* → **tenir**

tienne [tjɛn], *etc.* → **tenir**

tient [tjɛ̃], *etc.* → **tenir**

tiers[1], **tierce** [tjɛr, tjɛrs] *adj* : third <tierce personne : third person>

tiers[2] *nm* **1** : third <un tiers du livre : a third of the book> **2** : third party

tiers–monde [tjɛrmɔ̃d] *nm, pl* **tiers–mondes** : Third World

tige [tiʒ] *nf* **1** : stem, stalk **2** : (metal) rod

tignasse [tiɲas] *nf* : mop, shock (of hair)

tigre [tigr] *nm* : tiger

tigré, -grée [tigre] *adj* : striped

tigresse [tigrɛs] *nf* : tigress

tilleul [tijœl] *nm* : linden (tree)

timbale [tɛ̃bal] *nf* **1** : kettledrum **2 timbales** *nfpl* : timpani

timbre [tɛ̃br] *nm* **1** : (postage) stamp **2** : official stamp, postmark **3** SONNETTE : bell **4** TON : timbre, tone

timbré, -brée [tɛ̃bre] *adj* **1** : rich, mellow (of the voice) **2** *fam* : crazy, nuts

timbre-poste [tɛ̃brəpɔst] *nm, pl* **timbres-poste** : (postage) stamp

timbrer [tɛ̃bre] *vt* : to stamp, to postmark

timide [timid] *adj* : timid, shy — **timidement** [-midmɑ̃] *adv*

timidité [timidite] *nf* : timidity, shyness

timoré, -rée [timɔre] *adj* : timorous

tintamarre [tɛ̃tamar] *nm* : din, racket

tintement [tɛ̃tmɑ̃] *nm* : ringing, chiming, tinkling, clinking

tinter [tɛ̃te] *vt* : to ring, to toll — *vi* **1** : to ring, to chime **2** : to tinkle, to jingle, to clink **3** : to ring, to buzz (of ears)

tipi [tipi] *nm* : tepee

tique [tik] *nf* : tick (insect)

tiquer [tike] *vi* : to wince, to flinch

tir [tir] *nm* **1** : shooting, gunnery **2** : firing <déclencher le tir : to open fire> **3 tir à l'arc** : archery **4 tir antiaérien** : flak

tirade [tirad] *nf* : tirade

tirage [tiraʒ] *nm* **1** IMPRESSION : printing **2** : impression, run <second tirage : second printing> **3** : circulation (of a newspaper, etc.) **4** : (computer) printout **5** *or* **tirage au sort** : drawing (in a lottery) **6** : draft (of a chimney, etc.) **7** : pulling, hauling

tiraillement [tirajmɑ̃] *nm* **1** : tugging, pulling **2** : cramp, pang **3** : conflict <tiraillements internes : internal conflicts>

tirailler [tiraje] *vt* : to pull at, to tug at <être tiraillé entre le bien et le mal : to be torn between right and wrong>

tirant [tirɑ̃] *nm* **tirant d'eau** : draft (of a ship)

tire [tir] *nf Can* **1** : taffy **2** *or* **tire d'érable** : maple-sugar candy

tiré, -rée [tire] *adj* : drawn, haggard

tire-bouchon [tirbuʃɔ̃] *nm, pl* **tire-bouchons** : corkscrew

tire-d'aile [tirdɛl] **à ~** : in a flurry, hurriedly

tirelire [tirlir] *nf* : piggy bank

tirer [tire] *vt* **1** : to pull, to pull up, to pull back **2** : to draw (a curtain), to pull down (a blind, etc.) **3** : to fire, to shoot **4** : to take (in sports) <tirer un coup franc : to take a free kick> **5** : to draw (a card, a ticket, etc.) **6** : to withdraw **7** : to draw away, to pull out **8** : to derive (information) — *vi* **1** : to pull **2** : to fire, to shoot **3** : to take a shot (in sports) **4** *or* **tirer au sort** : to draw lots **5** : to draw (of a chimney) **6 ~ sur** : to draw from (an account, etc.) — **se tirer** *vr* **1 ~ de** : to get through, to extricate oneself from **2 se tirer une balle** : to shoot oneself **3 s'en tirer** *fam* : to cope, to pull through

tiret [tirɛ] *nm* **1** : dash **2** : hyphen

tireur, -reuse [tirœr, -røz] *n* **1** : gunman, marksman, markswoman *f* <tireur d'élite : sharpshooter> **2 tireur de cartes** : fortune-teller>

tiroir [tirwar] *nm* : drawer

tiroir-caisse [tirwarkɛs] *nm, pl* **tiroirs-caisses** : cash register, till

tisane [tizan] *nf* : herbal tea

tisonnier [tizɔnje] *nm* : poker

tissage [tisaʒ] *nm* **1** : weaving **2** : weave

tisser [tise] *vt* : to weave

tisserand, -rande [tisrɑ̃, -rɑ̃d] *n* : weaver

tissu [tisy] *nm* **1** : material, fabric **2** : tissue <tissu conjonctif : connective tissue> **3** : web, string (of lies, etc.) **4** : makeup, fabric <tissu social : social fabric>

titane [titan] *nm* : titanium

titanesque [titanɛsk] *adj* GIGANTESQUE : titanic, gigantic

titiller [titije] *vt* **1** : to titillate **2** : to tickle

titre [titr] *nm* **1** : title (of a book, song, etc.) **2** : title, rank, qualification <titre mondial : world title> **3** *or* **gros titre** : headline **4** : basis, respect, capacity <à titre d'exemple : as an example, for example> <à titre d'information : for your information> **5** : security (in the stock market) **6** : deed, title

titrer [titre] *vt* **1** : to run as a headline **2** : to subtitle (in movies) **3** : to titrate, to assay (in chemistry)

titubant, -bante [titybɑ̃, -bɑ̃t] *adj* : reeling, unsteady

tituber [titybe] *vi* : to reel, to stagger

titulaire[1] [titylɛr] *adj* : tenured, permanent

titulaire[2] *nmf* : officeholder, incumbent

titularisation [titylarizasjɔ̃] *nf* : tenure

toast [tost] *nm* **1** : toast <un toast aux nouveaux mariés : a toast to the newlyweds> **2** : (slice of) toast

toaster [toste] *vt Can* : to toast (bread)

toboggan [tɔbɔgɑ̃] *nm* : toboggan

toc[1] [tɔk] *adj fam* : trashy, tacky

toc[2] *nm* **en ~** : imitation, fake

tocsin [tɔksɛ̃] *nm* : alarm <sonner le tocsin : to sound the alarm>

toge [tɔʒ] *nf* **1** : gown, robe (of a judge, etc.) **2** : toga

togolais, -laise [tɔgɔlɛ, -lɛz] *adj* : Togolese

Togolais, -laise *n* : Togolese

tohu-bohu [tɔybɔy] *nms & pl* : noisy confusion, hubbub

toi [twa] *pron* **1** : you <je crois en toi : I believe in you> <occupe-toi! : keep

busy!> <toi, tu t'imagines des choses : you're imagining things> **2** TOI-MÊME : yourself <prends soin de toi : take care of yourself>

toile [twal] *nf* **1** : cloth, fabric <de la grosse toile : canvas> <toile à sac : burlap> <toile cirée : oilcloth> <toile goudronnée : tarpaulin> **2** TABLEAU : canvas, painting **3 toile d'araignée** : spider's web **4 toile de fond** : backdrop

toilette [twalɛt] *nf* **1** : washing up, grooming <faire sa toilette : to get washed up> <produits de toilette : toiletries> **2** : grooming (of animals) **3** TENUE : clothing, outfit **4** *Can* : toilet, bathroom **5 toilettes** *nfpl* : toilet, bathroom <aller aux toilettes : to go to the bathroom>

toi–même [twamɛm] *pron* : yourself <tu l'as fait toi-même : you did it yourself>

toiser [twaze] *vt* : to look (a person) up and down

toison [twazɔ̃] *nf* **1** : fleece **2** : mane, mop (of hair)

toit [twa] *nm* : roof

toiture [twatyr] *nf* : roofing

tôle [tol] *nf* **1** : sheet metal **2 tôle ondulée** : corrugated iron

tolérable [tɔlerabl] *adj* : tolerable

tolérance [tɔlerɑ̃s] *nf* : tolerance — **tolérant, -rante** [tɔlerɑ̃, -rɑ̃t] *adj*

tolérer [tɔlere] {87} *vt* : to tolerate

tolet [tɔlɛ] *nm* : oarlock

tollé [tɔle] *nm* : outcry

tomate [tɔmat] *nf* : tomato

tombant, -bante [tɔ̃bɑ̃, -bɑ̃t] *adj* : sloping, drooping

tombe [tɔ̃b] *nf* **1** SÉPULTURE : grave, tomb **2** : gravestone, tombstone

tombeau [tɔ̃bo] *nm, pl* **tombeaux** : tomb, mausoleum

tombée [tɔ̃be] *nf* **à la tombée du jour** *or* **à la tombée de la nuit** : at nightfall, at the close of day

tomber [tɔ̃be] *vi* **1** : to fall (down), to fall off, to drop **2** : to come down, to fall <la pluie tombait : rain was falling> **3** : to go down (of prices, etc.), to die down, to subside **4** : to droop, to sag, to slope **5** : to hang, to fall (of hair, clothing, etc.) **6** : to come, to fall <tomber dans la désuétude : to fall into disuse> <tomber aux mains de : to fall into the hands of> **7** : to become <tomber amoureux : to fall in love> <elle est tombée malade : she fell ill> **8 ~ sur** : to run into, to come across **9 faire tomber** : to bring down, to break down **10 laisser tomber** : to give up, to drop (plans, etc.)

tombola [tɔ̃bɔla] *nf* : raffle

tome [tɔm] *nm* : volume (of a book)

ton[1] [tɔ̃[tɔn] *before a vowel or mute h*)], **ta** [ta] *adj, pl* **tes** [te] : your

ton[2] *nm* **1** : tone, pitch **2** : hue, shade **3 de bon ton** : in good taste, appropriate

tonalité [tɔnalite] *nf* **1** : tone (of voice, etc.) **2** : tonality, key (in music) **3** : dial tone

tondeuse [tɔ̃døz] *nf* **1** *or* **tondeuse à gazon** : lawn mower **2** : clippers *pl*, shears *pl*

tondre [tɔ̃dr] {63} *vt* **1** : to mow **2** : to clip, to shear

tongane, -ganne [tɔ̃gan] *adj* : Tongan

Tongane, -ganne *n* : Tongan

tonifiant, -fiante [tɔnifjɑ̃, -fjɑ̃t] *adj* : invigorating, bracing

tonifier [tɔnifje] {96} *vt* **1** REVIGORER : to invigorate **2** RAFFERMIR : to tone <muscles bien tonifiés : well-toned muscles>

tonique[1] [tɔnik] *adj* : fortifying, stimulating

tonique[2] *nm* : tonic (in medicine)

tonique[3] *nf* : tonic (in music)

tonitruant, -truante [tɔnitryɑ̃, -tryɑ̃t] *adj* : thundering, booming

tonnage [tɔnaʒ] *nm* : tonnage

tonne [tɔn] *nf* : ton

tonneau [tɔno] *nm, pl* **tonneaux 1** BARRIQUE : barrel, cask **2** : rollover (of a motor vehicle)

tonnelet [tɔnlɛ] *nm* : keg

tonnelle [tɔnɛl] *nf* : arbor

tonner [tɔne] *vi* : to thunder

tonnerre [tɔnɛr] *nm* **1** : thunder <coup de tonnerre : thunderbolt> **2** : tumult, thundering <un tonnerre d'applaudissements : thundering applause> **3 du tonnerre** *fam* : great, terrific

tonte [tɔ̃t] *nf* : shearing

tonton [tɔ̃tɔ̃] *nm fam* : uncle

tonus [tɔnys] *nms & pl* **1** : tone <tonus musculaire : muscular tone> **2** : energy, vigor

topaze [tɔpaz] *nf* : topaz

topo [tɔpo] *nm fam* : spiel, story <c'est toujours le même topo : it's always the same old story>

topographie [tɔpɔgrafi] *nf* : topography

topographique [tɔpɔgrafik] *adj* : topographical, topographic

toquade [tɔkad] *nf fam* **1** : craze, fad **2** : crush, infatuation

toque [tɔk] *nf* : brimless hat <toque de fourrure : fur hat> <toque de cuisinier : toque, chef's hat>

toqué, -quée [tɔke] *adj fam* : crazy, touched

toquer [tɔke] *vi fam* : to rap, to knock <toquer à la porte : to knock on the door>

torche [tɔrʃ] *nf* : torch

torcher [tɔrʃe] *vt fam* : to wipe

torchon [tɔrʃɔ̃] *nm* CHIFFON : piece of cloth, rag

tordant, -dante [tɔrdɑ̃, -dɑ̃t] *adj fam* MARRANT : very funny, hilarious

tordre [tɔrdr] {63} *vt* : to twist, to wring **— se tordre** *vr* **1** : to twist <se tordre la cheville : to twist one's ankle> **2** : to writhe, to double up (with pain, laughter, etc.)
tordu, -due [tɔrdy] *adj* : twisted, warped
torero [tɔrero] *nm* : bullfighter, matador
tornade [tɔrnad] *nf* : tornado
toron [tɔrɔ̃] *nm* : strand (of rope)
torpeur [tɔrpœr] *nf* : torpor
torpide [tɔrpid] *adj* : torpid
torpille [tɔrpij] *nf* : torpedo
torréfier [tɔrefje] {96} *vt* : to roast (coffee, etc.)
torrent [tɔrɑ̃] *nm* **1** : torrent <pleuvoir à torrents : to be pouring> **2 un torrent de** : a flood of
torrentiel, -tielle [tɔrɑ̃sjɛl] *adj* : torrential
torride [tɔrid] *adj* : torrid, scorching hot
tors, torse [tɔr, tɔrs] *adj* **1** : twisted **2** : crooked, bent
torsade [tɔrsad] *nf* : twist, coil
torsader [tɔrsade] *vt* : to twist
torse [tɔrs] *nm* : torso, chest
torsion [tɔrsjɔ̃] *nf* **1** : twisting **2** : torsion
tort [tɔr] *nm* **1** : fault <reconnaître ses torts : to admit one's faults> **2** DÉFAUT : error, mistake **3** DOMMAGE : wrong, harm <faire du tort à qqn : to do harm to s.o.> **4 avoir tort** : to be wrong **5 à ~** : wrongly, unjustly **6 à tort et à travers** : senselessly
torticolis [tɔrtikɔli] *nms & pl* : stiff neck, crick in the neck
tortillement [tɔrtijmɑ̃] *nm* : wiggling, twisting
tortiller [tɔrtije] *vt* : to twist **—** *vi* : to wriggle **— se tortiller** *vr* : to squirm
tortillon [tɔrtijɔ̃] *nm* : twist
tortionnaire [tɔrsjɔnɛr] *nmf* : torturer
tortue [tɔrty] *nf* : turtle, tortoise
tortueux, -euse [tɔrtɥø, -øz] *adj* **1** : winding **2** : convoluted, tortuous
torture [tɔrtyr] *nf* : torture
torturer [tɔrtyre] *vt* : to torture
tôt [to] *adv* **1** : soon <le plus tôt possible : as soon as possible> **2** : early <se coucher tôt : to go to bed early> **3 tôt ou tard** : sooner or later
total[1], -tale [tɔtal] *adj, mpl* **totaux** [tɔto] : total **— totalement** [tɔtalmɑ̃] *adv*
total[2] *nm, mpl* **totaux** [tɔto] : total
totaliser [tɔtalize] *vt* : to total
totalitaire [tɔtalitɛr] *adj* : totalitarian
totalitarisme [tɔtalitarism] *nm* : totalitarianism
totalité [tɔtalite] *nf* **1** : total amount, totality **2 en ~** : completely, entirely
totem [tɔtɛm] *nm* : totem
touchant, -chante [tuʃɑ̃, -ʃɑ̃t] *adj* ÉMOUVANT : touching, moving
touche [tuʃ] *nf* **1** : key (on a keyboard), button **2** : stroke, touch (in art) **3** : trace, hint, touch **4** : touchline (in sports) **5** : bite (in fishing)
touché [tuʃe] *nm* : touchdown (in football)
toucher[1] [tuʃe] *vt* **1** : to touch, to handle **2** : to be in contact with, to hit **3** : to touch (in sports) **4** : to affect, to concern **5** ÉMOUVOIR : to move, to touch <toucher son coeur : to touch one's heart> **6** : to receive, to earn <toucher un bon salaire : to earn a good salary> **7** : to touch on, to be adjacent to **—** *vi* **1 ~ à** : to touch upon, to get into, to bring up **2 ~ à** : to relate to, to concern **3 ~ à** : to infringe on **— se toucher** *vr* : to touch, to be in contact
toucher[2] *nm* **1** : sense of touch **2** : feel
touffe [tuf] *nf* : tuft, clump
touffu, -fue [tufy] *adj* **1** : thick, dense, bushy <forêt touffue : dense forest> **2** : complex, dense (of style)
toujours [tuʒur] *adv* **1** : always, forever **2** ENCORE : still **3** : anyway, in any case
toundra [tundra] *nf* : tundra
toupet [tupɛ] *nm* **1** : forelock **2** *fam* : nerve, cheek
toupie [tupi] *nf* : top (toy)
tour[1] [tur] *nm* **1** : tour, circuit <faire le tour du monde : to go around the world> **2** : walk, ride <faire un tour : to go for a stroll> **3** : turn, revolution, rotation **4** : circumference, measurement (around) <tour de faille : girth (of a person)> **5** : turn, move <attendre son tour : to wait one's turn> **6** : trick <jouer un tour à qqn : to play a trick on s.o.> **7** : direction, aspect <prendre un mauvais tour : to take a bad turn, to go wrong> **8** : lathe **9 avoir le tour** *Can* : to be clever, to be skillful **10 tour de scrutin** : ballot, round of voting
tour[2] *nf* **1** : tower **2** : high-rise building **3** : castle (in chess)
tourbe [turb] *nf* : peat
tourbière [turbjɛr] *nf* : peat bog, peat marsh
tourbillon [turbijɔ̃] *nm* **1** : whirlwind, whirlpool **2** : whirl, bustle
tourbillonner [turbijɔne] *vi* : to whirl, to swirl (around)
tourelle [turɛl] *nf* : turret
tourisme [turism] *nm* : tourism
touriste [turist] *nmf* : tourist
touristique [turistik] *adj* : tourist <la saison touristique : the tourist season>
tourment [turmɑ̃] *nm* : torment
tourmente [turmɑ̃t] *nf* **1** : tempest, storm **2** : turmoil
tourmenter [turmɑ̃te] *vt* : to torment **— se tourmenter** *vr* S'INQUIÉTER : to worry
tournant[1], -nante [turnɑ̃, -nɑ̃t] *adj* : turning, revolving

tournant[2] *nm* **1** : bend (in a road, etc.) **2** : turning point

tourne–disque [turnədisk] *nm, pl* **tourne–disques** : record player

tournée [turne] *nf* **1** : tour **2** *fam* : round (of drinks)

tourner [turne] *vt* **1** : to turn, to rotate **2** : to stir, to toss **3** : to shoot (a film, scene, etc.) **4** : to get around, to circumvent **5** : to phrase, to present <une lettre bien tournée : a nicely phrased letter> **6 tourner en dérision** : to ridicule — *vi* **1** : to turn, to revolve, to spin <tourner autour de : to revolve around> <tourner en rond : to go around in circles> **2** : to turn, to change direction <tournez à droite : turn right> **3** : to run (of an engine, etc.) <tourner rond : to run smoothly> **4** : to turn out <bien tourner : to turn out well, to go well> **5** : to film, to make a film **6** : to go bad, to sour — **se tourner** *vr* : to turn around

tournesol [turnəsɔl] *nm* **1** : sunflower **2** : litmus <papier de tournesol : litmus paper>

tournevis [turnəvis] *nms & pl* : screwdriver

tourniquet [turnikɛ] *nm* **1** : turnstile **2** : tourniquet **3** : sprinkler

tournoi [turnwa] *nm* : tournament

tournoiement [turnwamɑ̃] *nm* : spinning, whirling

tournoyer [turnwaje] {58} *vi* **1** : to whirl, to spin, to gyrate **2** : to swirl around

tournure [turnyr] *nf* **1** : turn <tournure des événements : turn of events> **2** : turn of phrase, expression

tourte [turt] *nf France* : (meat or fish) pie

tourtereaux [turtəro] *nmpl* : lovebirds

tourterelle [turtərɛl] *nf* : turtledove

tourtière [turtjɛr] *nf* **1** *France* : pie pan **2** *Can* : meat pie

tousser [tuse] *vi* : to cough

tout[1] [tu] **(toute(s)** [tut] *before feminine adjectives beginning with a consonant or an aspirate h*) *adv* **1** COMPLÈTEMENT : completely <tout neuf : completely new> **2** : quite, very, all <tout dernièrement : very recently> <elle sont toutes seules : they are all alone> **3** : while <tout en travaillant : while working> **4** : already <tout prêt : ready-made> **5 tout à coup** : suddenly **6 tout à fait** : completely, entirely **7 tout de suite** : immediately, right away

tout[2], **toute** *adj, pl* **tous, toutes 1** : all <tout le monde : everyone, everybody> <tous les dix : all ten of them> <en toute franchise : in all honesty> **2** : each, every <toutes les fois : every time> <tous les jours : every day> <tous les trois ans : every three years> **3** : any <toute autre solution : any other solution> <à tout âge : at any age> **4** : utmost, full <à toute vitesse : at full speed>

tout[3] *nm* **1 le tout** : the main thing, the whole **2 du tout au tout** : completely, entirely **3 du tout** *or* **pas du tout** : not at all

tout[4] *pron, pl* **tous, toutes 1** : all, everything <tout change : everything changes> <nous sommes tous coupables : we are all guilty> **2** : anyone, everyone <oublié de tous : forgotten by everyone> **3 tout compte fait** : all in all

toutefois [tutfwa] *adv* : however

toute–puissance [tutpɥisɑ̃s] *nf, pl* **toutes–puissances** : omnipotence

tout–puissant, toute–puissante [tutpwisɑ̃,-sɑ̃t] *adj, pl* **tout–puissants, toutes–puissantes** : all-powerful

toutou [tutu] *nm* **1** *fam* : doggie **2** *Can fam* : stuffed animal

toux [tu] *nfs & pl* : cough

toxicité [tɔksisite] *nf* : toxicity

toxicomane [tɔksikɔman] *nmf* : drug addict

toxicomanie [tɔksikɔmani] *nf* : drug addiction

toxine [tɔksin] *nf* : toxin

toxique [tɔksik] *adj* : toxic, poisonous

trac [trak] *nm* : stage fright, jitters *pl*

tracas [traka] *nms & pl* **1** : worry **2 tracas** *nmpl* ENNUIS : troubles, problems

tracasser [trakase] *vt* : to worry, to bother — **se tracasser** *vr*

trace [tras] *nf* **1** : track, trail <traces d'ours : bear tracks> <traces de pas : footprints> <suivre les traces de qqn : to follow in s.o.'s footsteps> **2** : mark <traces de doigts : finger marks> **3** : trace, vestige, sign <traces d'une ville disparue : traces of a lost city>

tracé [trase] *nm* **1** PLAN : plan, layout **2** : course (of a river, road, etc.) **3** : line, contour

tracer [trase] {6} *vt* **1** : to trace, to lay out **2** DESSINER : to draw <tracer une ligne : to draw a line> **3** : to map out, to plot <tracer le chemin : to pave the way>

trachée [traʃe] *nf* : trachea, windpipe

tract [trakt] *nm* : leaflet

tractations [traktasjɔ̃] *nfpl* : negotiations

tracter [trakte] *vt* : to tow

tracteur [traktœr] *nm* : tractor

traction [traksjɔ̃] *nf* **1** : traction **2** : pulling, haulage **3** : push-up, chin-up **4 traction avant** : front-wheel drive

tradition [tradisjɔ̃] *nf* : tradition

traditionnel, -nelle [tradisjɔnɛl] *adj* : traditional — **traditionnellement** [-nɛlmɑ̃] *adv*

traducteur, -trice [tradyktœr, -tris] *n* : translator

traduction [tradyksjɔ̃] *nf* : translation

traduire [tradɥir] {49} *vt* **1** : to translate **2 traduire en justice** : to arraign — **se traduire** *vr* **1** : to be translated **2 ∼ par** : to result in

traduisait [tradɥizɛ], **traduisions** [tradɥizjɔ̃], *etc.* → **traduire**

traduise [tradɥiz], *etc.* → **traduire**

trafic [trafik] *nm* **1** : traffic **2** : trafficking <trafic de drogue : drug trafficking>

trafiquant, -quante [trafikɑ̃, -kɑ̃t] *n* : dealer, trafficker <trafiquant de drogue : drug dealer>

trafiquer [trafike] *vt* : to doctor, to tamper with — *vi* : to traffic, to trade (in the black market)

tragédie [traʒedi] *nf* : tragedy

tragique [traʒik] *adj* : tragic — **tragiquement** [-ʒikmɑ̃] *adv*

trahir [trair] *vt* **1** : to betray **2** RÉVÉLER : to reveal, to divulge **3** : to go against, to break <trahir sa promesse : to break one's word>

trahison [traizɔ̃] *nf* : betrayal

train [trɛ̃] *nm* **1** : train <train de voyageurs : passenger train> **2** : pace, rate <au train où vont les choses : at the rate things are going> **3** : series, set <train de réformes : series of reforms> **4 en train de** : in the process of **5 train de vie** : lifestyle

traînant, -nante [trɛnɑ̃, -nɑ̃t] *adj* : drawling <parler d'une voix traînante : to drawl>

traînard, -narde [trɛnar, -nard] *n* : slowpoke, laggard, straggler

traîne [trɛn] *nf* **1** : train (of a dress) **2** : dragnet, seine **3** *Can* : toboggan, sled **4 rester à la traîne** : to lag behind

traîneau [trɛno] *nm, pl* **traîneaux 1** : sled, sleigh **2** : dragnet

traînée [trene] *nf* **1** : streak (of blood, paint, etc.) **2** : trail (of light, of a comet, etc.) **3** : drag (of an airplane, etc.)

traîner [trene] *vt* **1** : to pull, to drag **2 traîner les pieds** : to drag one's feet — *vi* **1** : to drag along, to trail (on the ground) **2** : to dawdle, to lag behind **3** : to linger, to drag on **4** : to be lying around <elle laisse traîner son linge : she doesn't pick up after herself> **5** : to speak slowly, to drawl **6** : to wander about <traîner dans les rues : to roam the streets> — **se traîner** *vr* **1** : to drag oneself, to crawl (along) **2** : to drag on

train–train [trɛ̃trɛ̃] *nms & pl* ROUTINE : routine

traire [trɛr] {40} *vt* : to milk (an animal)

trait [trɛ] *nm* **1** : trait <trait de caractère : character trait> **2** : stroke <d'un trait de plume : with a stroke of the pen> **3 avoir trait à** : to relate to, to concern **4 tout d'un trait** : in one breath, in one gulp **5 trait d'esprit** : witticism, quip **6 trait d'union** : hyphen **7 traits** *nmpl* : features <traits fins : delicate features>

traitant, -tante [trɛtɑ̃, -tɑ̃t] *adj* **médecin traitant** : family doctor

traite [trɛt] *nf* **1** : trade (in human beings) <la traite des Noirs : the slave trade> **2** : milking **3 d'une traite** : in one go, without stopping **4 traite bancaire** : bank draft

traité [trete] *nm* **1** : treaty **2** : treatise

traitement [trɛtmɑ̃] *nm* **1** : treatment **2** : stipend, salary **3 traitement des données** *or* **traitement de l'information** : data processing **4 traitement de texte** : word processing

traiter [trete] *vt* **1** : to treat **2** : to process (data) **3** : to characterize as, to call <je l'ai traité d'imbécile : I called him a fool> **4** : to deal with, to handle — *vi* **∼ de** : to deal with, to be concerned with

traiteur [trɛtœr] *nm* : caterer

traître[1], **-tresse** [trɛtr, -trɛs] *adj* **1** : treacherous, betraying **2 pas un traître mot** : not a single word

traître[2], **-tresse** *n* **1** : traitor **2 en ∼** : in an underhanded way, treacherously

traîtreusement [trɛtrøzmɑ̃] *adv* : treacherously

traîtrise [trɛtriz] *nf* : treachery, betrayal

trajectoire [traʒɛktwar] *nf* : path, trajectory

trajet [traʒɛ] *nm* **1** CHEMIN : path, way, route <le trajet le plus direct : the quickest route> **2** : journey, trip

tralala [tralala] *nm fam* : fuss

trame [tram] *nf* **1** : weft (of fabric) **2** : framework

tramer [trame] *vt* **1** : to plot **2** : to weave

trampoline [trampɔlin] *nm* : trampoline

tramway [tramwɛ] *nm* : streetcar, trolley

tranchant[1], **-chante** [trɑ̃ʃɑ̃, -ʃɑ̃t] *adj* **1** : sharp, keen-edged **2** COUPANT : curt, sharp <une remarque tranchante : a cutting remark>

tranchant[2] *nm* **1** : cutting edge, sharpness **2 à double tranchant** : double-edged

tranche [trɑ̃ʃ] *nf* **1** : slice **2** : period, phase, stage <tranche horaire : time slot> <tranche d'âge : age bracket> **3** : edge (of a book, coin, etc.)

tranché, -chée [trɑ̃ʃe] *adj* **1** : sliced **2** : distinct, contrasting **3** : clear-cut, marked

tranchée *nf* : trench

trancher [trɑ̃ʃe] *vt* **1** COUPER : to cut (through), to slice, to sever **2** : to settle, to resolve **3** : to cut short — *vi* **1** : to contrast, to stand out **2** : to come to a decision

tranquille [trɑ̃kil] *adj* **1** : calm, quiet <tiens-toi tranquille! : sit still!> **2** : untroubled, assured <avoir la con-

science tranquille : to have a clear conscience> <soyez tranquille! : don't worry!>

tranquillement [trɑ̃kilmɑ̃] *adv* **1** CALMEMENT : quietly, calmly **2** LENTEMENT : unhurriedly, at a leisurely pace

tranquillisant[1], **-sante** [trɑ̃kilizɑ̃, -zɑ̃t] *adj* RASSURANT : reassuring

tranquillisant[2] *nm* : tranquilizer

tranquilliser [trɑ̃kilize] *vt* RASSURER : to reassure

tranquillité [trɑ̃kilite] *nf* **1** CALME : peacefulness, tranquillity **2 tranquillité d'esprit** : peace of mind

transaction [trɑ̃zaksjɔ̃] *nf* : transaction <transactions financières : financial transactions>

transatlantique [trɑ̃zatlɑ̃tik] *adj* : transatlantic

transcendant, -dante [trɑ̃sɑ̃dɑ̃, -dɑ̃t] *adj* **1** SUBLIME : sublime, transcendent **2** : transcendental

transcender [trɑ̃sɑ̃de] *vt* : to transcend — **se transcender** *vr* : to surpass oneself

transcontinental, -tale [trɑ̃skɔ̃tinɑ̃tal] *adj, mpl* **-taux** [-to] : transcontinental

transcription [trɑ̃skripsjɔ̃] *nf* : transcription, transcript

transcrire [trɑ̃skrir] {33} *vt* : to transcribe

transe [trɑ̃s] *nf* **1** : trance <entrer en transe : to go into a trance> **2 transes** *nfpl* : anxiety, upset <être dans les transes : to get all worked up>

transférer [trɑ̃sfere] *vt* : to transfer — **transférable** [trɑ̃sferabl] *adj*

transfert [trɑ̃sfɛr] *nm* : transfer <transfert de fonds : transfer of funds>

transfigurer [trɑ̃sfigyre] *vt* : to transfigure — **transfiguration** [-gyrasjɔ̃] *nf*

transformateur [trɑ̃sfɔrmatœr] *nm* : transformer

transformation [trɑ̃sfɔrmasjɔ̃] *nf* **1** : transformation **2** : conversion (in sports)

transformer [trɑ̃sfɔrme] *vt* **1** : to transform, to change, to alter **2** : to convert (in sports) **3** ~ **en** : to convert (a building, etc.) into — **se transformer** *vr* **1** : to change, to be transformed **2** ~ **en** : to turn into

transfuge [trɑ̃sfyʒ] *nmf* **1** : renegade, defector **2** : deserter (in the military)

transfuser [trɑ̃sfyze] *vt* : to transfuse

transfusion [trɑ̃sfyzjɔ̃] *nf* : transfusion

transgresser [trɑ̃sgrese] *vt* ENFREINDRE : to infringe, to violate, to disobey

transgression [trɑ̃sgrɛsjɔ̃] *nf* : infringement, transgression

transi, -sie [trɑ̃zi] *adj* **1** : numb (with cold) **2** : paralyzed (with fear)

transiger [trɑ̃ziʒe] {17} *vi* : to compromise

transir [trɑ̃zir] *vt* : to numb (with cold)

transistor [trɑ̃zistɔr] *nm* : transistor

transit [trɑ̃zit] *nm* : transit <en transit : in transit>

transitif, -tive [trɑ̃zitif, -tiv] *adj* : transitive

transition [trɑ̃zisjɔ̃] *nf* : transition

transitoire [trɑ̃zitwar] *adj* **1** : transitory, transient **2** : transitional

translucide [trɑ̃slysid] *adj* : translucent

transmetteur [trɑ̃smɛtœr] *nm* : transmitter

transmettre [trɑ̃smɛtr] {53} *vt* **1** : to transmit (signals, data, etc.) **2** : to pass on, to convey **3** : to broadcast **4** : to transfer (power, etc.) **5** : to transmit (a disease)

transmissible [trɑ̃smisibl] *adj* : transmittable, communicable

transmission [trɑ̃smisjɔ̃] *nf* : transmission

transparaître [trɑ̃sparɛtr] {7} *vi* **1** : to show through **2 laisser transparaître** : to manifest, to let show (of emotions, etc.)

transparence [trɑ̃sparɑ̃s] *nf* : transparency

transparent, -rente [trɑ̃sparɑ̃, -rɑ̃t] *adj* : transparent

transpercer [trɑ̃spɛrse] {6} *vt* : to go through, to pierce <la douleur me transperçait le dos : pain was shooting through my back>

transpiration [trɑ̃spirasjɔ̃] *nf* **1** SUEUR : perspiration, sweat **2** : transpiration (in botany)

transpirer [trɑ̃spire] *vt* **1** SUER : to perspire, to sweat **2** : to transpire (in botany) **3** : to come to light

transplantation [trɑ̃splɑ̃tasjɔ̃] *nm* : transplant

transplanter [trɑ̃splɑ̃te] *vt* : to transplant

transport [trɑ̃spɔr] *nm* **1** : transport (of goods, etc.) <transport aérien : air transport> **2 transports** *nmpl* : (system of) transportation <transports en commun : public transportation> **3 transports** *nmpl* : transports, strong emotions

transporter [trɑ̃spɔrte] *vt* **1** : to carry, to bear **2** : to transport, to convey (goods, etc.) **3** : to transport, to carry away <être transporté de joie : to be overjoyed>

transporteur [trɑ̃spɔrtœr] *nm* **1** : carrier, transporter (company) **2** : conveyor (machine)

transposer [trɑ̃spoze] *vt* : to transpose — **transposition** [-pozisjɔ̃] *nf*

transvaser [trɑ̃svaze] *vt* : to decant (a liquid)

transversal, -sale [trɑ̃svɛrsal] *adj, mpl* **-saux** [-so] : transverse, cross(ing) <coupe transversale : cross section> <rues transversales : cross streets>

transversalement [trɑ̃svɛrsalmɑ̃] *adv* : crosswise

trapèze [trapɛz] *nm* **1** : trapezoid **2** : trapeze

trappe [trap] *nf* **1** PIÈGE : trap, snare **2** : trapdoor

trappeur [trapœr] *nm* : trapper

trapu, -pue [trapy] *adj* : stocky, squat

traquenard [traknar] *nm* : trap

traquer [trake] *vt* POURSUIVRE : to pursue, to chase, to track down

traumatisant, -sante [tromatizɑ̃, -zɑ̃t] *adj* : traumatic

traumatiser [tromatize] *vt* : to traumatize

traumatisme [tromatism] *nm* : trauma

travail [travaj] *nm, pl* **travaux** [travo] **1** : work <travail scolaire : schoolwork> <se mettre au travail : to get down to work> **2** TÂCHE : task, job, work <avoir du travail : to have work to do> **3** EMPLOI : work, employment <travail à plein temps : full-time work> <sans travail : unemployed> <vivre de son travail : to work for one's living> **4** : labor <division de travail : division of labor> **5** : working, fashioning <travail du bois : woodworking> **6** : work (of art, literature, etc.) **7** : labor (in giving birth) **8** **travaux** *nmpl* : works <travaux publics : public works> **9** **travaux** *nmpl* : work, operations <travaux d'aiguille : needlework> <travaux de la ferme : farmwork>

travaillant, -lante [travajɑ̃, -jɑt] *adj Can* : hardworking, industrious

travaillé, -lée [travaje] *adj* : elaborate, finely made

travailler [travaje] *vt* **1** : to work, to treat <travailler la terre : to work the land> **2** : to mix together (in cooking) **3** : to work on, to practice, to polish up **4** : to bother, to worry <ça me travaille : it's preying on my mind> — *vi* **1** : to work <travailler beaucoup trop : to work too hard> **2** : to work (at a job) <travailler en indépendent : to be self-employed> <travailler au noir : to moonlight> **3** : to train, to work out **4** **~ à** : to work toward, to endeavor to

travailleur[1], -leuse [travajœr, -jøz] *adj* : hardworking, industrious

travailleur[2], -leuse *n* : worker

travée [trave] *nf* **1** : row (of seats) **2** : span (of a bridge)

travers [travɛr] *nms & pl* **1** : fault, failing **2** **à ~** : across, through <à travers la chambre : across the room> <à travers les siècles : down through the centuries> **3** **au travers** : through <passer au travers : to escape> **4** **au travers de** : by means of **5** **de ~** : askew, crooked, wrongly <comprendre de travers : to misunderstand> **6** **en ~** : crosswise, sideways

traverse [travɛrs] *nf* **1** : railroad tie **2** : transom

traversée [travɛrse] *nf* : crossing

traverser [travɛrse] *vt* **1** : to cross <traverser la rue : to cross the road> **2** : to run through, to pass through, to flow through **3** : to penetrate, to soak through **4** : to go through, to experience (a crisis, etc.) **5** **traverser l'esprit de qqn** : to cross s.o.'s mind

traversier [travɛrsje] *nm Can* : ferryboat

traversin [travɛrsɛ̃] *nm* : bolster

trayait [trɛjɛ], **trayions** [trɛjɔ̃], *etc.* → **traire**

trébuchement [trebyʃmɑ̃] *nm* : stumble, stumbling

trébucher [trebyʃe] *vi* : to stumble

trèfle [trɛfl] *nm* **1** : clover, shamrock **2** : clubs *pl* (in playing cards)

treillage [trɛjaʒ] *nm* : trellis, lattice

treille [trɛj] *nf* : climbing vine

treillis [trɛji] *nms & pl* : trellis, lattice

treize[1] [trɛz] *adj* **1** : thirteen **2** : thirteenth <le treize janvier : January thirteenth>

treize[2] *nms & pl* : thirteen

treizième [trɛzjɛm] *adj & nmf & nm* : thirteenth

tremblant, -blante [trɑ̃blɑ̃, -blɑ̃t] *adj* : shaking, trembling

tremble [trɑ̃bl] *nm* : aspen

tremblement [trɑ̃bləmɑ̃] *nm* **1** : shaking, trembling **2** : quavering, shakiness (of the voice, etc.) **3** : fluttering, flickering **4** **tremblement de terre** : earthquake

trembler [trɑ̃ble] *vi* **1** : to shake, to tremble **2** : to quiver, to quaver **3** : to flutter, to flicker

trembloter [trɑ̃blɔte] *vi* : to tremble, to quiver, to shiver

trémie [tremi] *nf* : hopper

trémousser [tremuse] *v* **se trémousser** *vr* : to wriggle around

trempage [trɑ̃paʒ] *nm* : soak, soaking

trempe [trɑ̃p] *nf* **1** : temper (of metals) **2** : caliber, quality <un homme de sa trempe : a man of his caliber>

trempé, -pée [trɑ̃pe] *adj* **1** : soaked, drenched **2** **acier trempé** : tempered steel

tremper [trɑ̃pe] *vt* **1** : to soak **2** : to dip, to dunk **3** : to temper (steel, etc.)

trempette [trɑ̃pɛt] *nf* **1** : dip (in swimming) <faire trempette : to take a quick dip> **2** *Can* : dip <trempette aux légumes : vegetable dip>

tremplin [trɑ̃plɛ̃] *nm* **1** : springboard **2** : stepping stone (in a career, etc.) **3** *or* **tremplin à ski** : ski jump

trémulation [tremylasjɔ̃] *nf* : tremor

trente[1] [trɑ̃t] *adj* **1** : thirty **2** : thirtieth <le trente septembre : September thirtieth>

trente[2] *nms & pl* : thirty

trente–sous [trɑ̃tsu] *nms & pl Can fam* : quarter (unit of currency)

trentième [trɑ̃tjɛm] *adj & nmf & nm* : thirtieth

trépasser [trepase] *vi* DÉCÉDER : to pass away

trépidant, -dante [trepidɑ̃, -dɑ̃t] *adj* **1** : vibrating **2** : hectic, frantic

trépidation [trepidasjɔ̃] *nf* **1** : vibration **2** : flurry, bustle

trépider [trepide] *vi* : to vibrate

trépied [trepje] *nm* : tripod

trépigner [trepiɲe] *vi* : to stamp one's feet

très [trɛ] *adv* : very <très heureux : very happy> <très bien : very well> <très à la mode : very fashionable> <elle a très soif : she's very thirsty>

trésor [trezɔr] *nm* **1** : treasure **2 le Trésor (public)** : public revenue **3 mon trésor** : my darling

trésorerie [trezɔrri] *nf* **1** : funds *pl,* accounts *pl* **2** : public revenue office

trésorier, -rière [trezɔrje, -rjɛr] *n* : treasurer

tressaillement [tresajmɑ̃] *nm* : wincing, flinching

tressaillir [trɛsajir] {93}*vi* **1** : to start, to flinch, to wince **2** : to quiver, to vibrate

tressauter [trɛsote] *vi* SURSAUTER : to start, to jump

tresse [trɛs] *nf* : braid, plait

tresser [trɛse] *vt* **1** : to braid, to plait **2** : to weave (a basket, etc.)

tréteau [treto] *nm, pl* **tréteaux** : trestle

treuil [trœj] *nm* : winch, windlass

trêve [trɛv] *nf* **1** : truce **2** : respite

tri [tri] *nm* : sorting (out)

triade [triad] *nf* : triad

triangle [trijɑ̃gl] *nm* : triangle

triangulaire [trijɑ̃gylɛr] *adj* : triangular

tribal, -bale [tribal] *adj, mpl* **tribaux** [tribo] : tribal

tribord [tribɔr] *nm* : starboard

tribu [triby] *nf* : tribe

tribulations [tribylasjɔ̃] *nfpl* : tribulations

tribunal [tribynal] *nm, pl* **-naux** [-no] **1** : courthouse, court <porter une affaire devant le tribunal : to take a matter to court> **2** : judgment, justice <le tribunal de l'histoire : the judgment of history>

tribune [tribyn] *nf* **1** : gallery, grandstand **2** : rostrum, platform **3** DÉBAT : forum

tribut [triby] *nm* : tribute

tributaire [tribytɛr] *adj* **être tributaire de** : to be dependent on

tricher [triʃe] *vi* **1** : to cheat **2 ~ sur** : to lie about

tricherie [triʃri] *nf* : cheating

tricheur, -cheuse [triʃœr, -ʃøz] *n* : cheat

tricolore [trikɔlɔr] *adj* : tricolor

tricot [triko] *nm* **1** : knitting **2** : knitted fabric **3** CHANDAIL : sweater, jersey

tricoter [trikɔte] *v* : to knit

tricoteur, -teuse [trikɔtœr, -tøz] *n* : knitter

trictrac [triktrak] *nm France* : backgammon

tricycle [trisikl] *nm* : tricycle

trident [tridɑ̃] *nm* : trident

tridimensionnel, -nelle [tridimɑ̃sjɔnɛl] *adj* : three-dimensional

triennal, -nale [trijenal] *adj, mpl* **-naux** [-no] : triennial

trier [trije] {96} *vt* **1** CLASSER : to sort (out) **2** : to pick out, to select

trigonométrie [trigɔnɔmetri] *nf* : trigonometry

trille [trij] *nf* : trill

triller [trije] *v* : to trill

trilogie [trilɔʒi] *nf* : trilogy

trimbaler *or* **trimballer** [trɛ̃bale] *vt fam* : to cart around, to drag along

trimer [trime] *vi fam* : to slave away

trimestre [trimɛstr] *nm* **1** : quarter (in economics, etc.) **2** : term (in school)

trimestriel, -trielle [trimɛstrijɛl] *adj* : quarterly

trimestriellement [trimɛstrijɛlmɑ̃] *adv* : quarterly

tringle [trɛ̃gl] *nf* : rod

trinidadien, -dienne [trinidadjɛ̃, -djɛn] *adj* : Trinidadian

Trinidadien, -dienne *n* : Trinidadian

trinité [trinite] *nf* **1** : trinity **2 la Trinité** : the (Holy) Trinity

trinquer [trɛ̃ke] *vi* **1** : to clink glasses, to toast **2** *fam* : to pay the price, to take the rap

trio [trijo] *nm* : trio

triomphal, -phale [trijɔ̃fal] *adj, mpl* **triomphaux** [-fo] : triumphal, triumphant

triomphalement [trijɔ̃falmɑ̃] *adv* : triumphantly

triomphant, -phante [trijɔ̃fɑ̃, -fɑ̃t] *adj* : triumphant

triomphateur, -trice [trijɔ̃fatœr, -tris] *n* : victor

triomphe [trijɔ̃f] *nm* : triumph, success

triompher [trijɔ̃fe] *vi* : to triumph, to prevail

tripartite [tripartit] *adj* : tripartite

tripe [trip] *nf* **1 tripes** *nfpl* : tripe **2 tripes** *nfpl fam* : guts <rendre tripes et boyaux : to vomit, to be sick as a dog>

triple [tripl] *adj & nm* : triple, treble

triplement [tripləmɑ̃] *adv* : triply, three times over

tripler [triple] *v* : to triple

triplés, -plées [triple] *npl* : triplets

tripoter [tripɔte] *vt* **1** : to fiddle with, to play around with **2** : to handle, to paw — *vi* **1** : to rummage about **2** : to dabble (in shady activities)

trique [trik] *nf* : cudgel

trisannuel, -nuelle [trizanɥɛl] *adj* : triennial

triste [trist] *adj* **1** : sad, sorrowful **2** : dismal, dreary <un paysage triste : a bleak landscape> **3** LAMENTABLE : deplorable, sorry <en un triste état : in a sorry state>

tristement [tristəmɑ̃] *adv* **1** : sadly, sorrowfully **2** : regrettably <c'est tristement vrai : it's all too true>

tristesse [tristɛs] *nf* : sadness, sorrow

triton [tritɔ̃] *nm* : newt

triturer [trityre] *vt* **1** BROYER : to grind **2** PÉTRIR : to knead **3** MANIPULER : to manipulate

trivial, -viale [trivjal] *adj, mpl* **triviaux** [-vjo] **1** GROSSIER : coarse, crude **2** BANAL : mundane, trivial

trivialité [trivjalite] *nf* **1** : coarseness, crudeness **2** : banality, triteness

troc [trɔk] *nm* **1** ÉCHANGE : exchange, swap **2** : barter

troène [trɔɛn] *nm* : privet (hedge)

trognon [trɔɲɔ̃] *nm* : core (of an apple, etc.), stalk (of cabbage, etc.)

trois[1] [trwa] *adj* **1** : three **2** : third <le trois juin : June third>

trois[2] *nms & pl* : three

troisième[1] [trwazjɛm] *adj & nmf* : third

troisième[2] *nm* : third floor

troisièmement [trwazjɛmmɑ̃] *adv* : thirdly

trolley [trɔlɛ] *nm* : trolley

trombe [trɔ̃b] *nf* **1** : waterspout **2** : whirlwind <en trombe : in a flurry> **3 trombes d'eau** : downpour, cloudburst

tromblon [trɔ̃blɔ̃] *nm* : blunderbuss

trombone [trɔ̃bɔn] *nm* **1** : trombone **2** : paper clip

tromboniste [trɔ̃bɔnist] *nmf* : trombonist

trompe [trɔ̃p] *nf* **1** : horn **2** : trunk, proboscis

trompe–l'oeil [trɔ̃plœj] *nms & pl* : trompe l'oeil

tromper [trɔ̃pe] *vt* **1** DUPER : to deceive, to mislead **2** : to be unfaithful to **3** : to elude, to outwit **4** : to fool, to trick <c'est ce qui m'a trompé : that's what fooled me> **5** : to stave off — **se tromper** *vr* : to make a mistake <se tromper de route : to take the wrong road>

tromperie [trɔ̃pri] *nf* : deception, deceit

trompette [trɔ̃pɛt] *nf* : trumpet

trompettiste [trɔ̃petist] *nmf* : trumpet player

trompeur[1], -peuse [trɔ̃pœr, -pøz] *adj* **1** : deceitful **2** : deceptive, misleading

trompeur[2], -peuse *n* : deceiver

trompeusement [trɔ̃pøzmɑ̃] *adv* : deceitfully, deceptively

tronc [trɔ̃] *nm* **1** : trunk (of a tree) **2** : collection box (in a church) **3** TORSE : torso **4 tronc commun** : common origin

tronçon [trɔ̃sɔ̃] *nm* : section

tronçonner [trɔ̃sɔne] *vt* : to cut into sections, to saw up

tronçonneuse [trɔ̃sɔnøz] *nf* : chain saw

trône [tron] *nm* : throne

trôner [trone] *vi* : to have the place of honor

tronquer [trɔ̃ke] *vt* **1** : to truncate **2** : to curtail, to shorten

trop [tro] *adv* **1** : too <trop difficile : too hard> <j'ai beaucoup trop dit : I've said far too much> **2 ~ de** : too many, too much <trop de livres : too many books> <il a bu trop de café : he's had too much coffee> **3 de ~** *or* **en ~** : too many, extra <une personne de trop : one person too many>

trophée [trɔfe] *nm* : trophy

tropical, -cale [trɔpikal] *adj, mpl* **-caux** [-ko] : tropical

tropique [trɔpik] *nm* **1** : tropic <tropique du Cancer : tropic of Cancer> **2 tropiques** *nmpl* : tropics

trop–plein [trɔplɛ̃] *nm, pl* **trop–pleins** **1** : overflow **2** SURPLUS : excess, surplus

troquer [trɔke] *vt* : to swap, to trade

trot [tro] *nm* : trot

trotte [trɔt] *nf fam* : good distance <ça fait une trotte : it's a good walk>

trotter [trɔte] *vi* **1** : to trot **2** : to scamper, to run along **3 trotter dans la tête** : to keep running through one's mind

trotteuse [trɔtøz] *nf* : second hand (of a watch)

trottiner [trɔtine] *vi* : to scurry along

trottinette [trɔtinɛt] *nf* PATINETTE : scooter

trottoir [trɔtwar] *nm* **1** : sidewalk **2 trottoir roulant** : moving walkway

trou [tru] *nm* **1** : hole **2** TERRIER : burrow **3** : eye (of a needle) **4** DÉCHIRURE : tear, rip, hole **5** : gap (of time) <avoir une heure de trou : to have an hour's free time> <trou de mémoire : blank, memory lapse> **6** *fam* : little place, hole-in-the-wall **7 trou d'homme** : manhole **8 trou noir** : black hole **9 trou de serrure** : keyhole

troubadour [trubadur] *nm* : troubadour

troublant, -blante [trublɑ̃, -blɑ̃t] *adj* : disturbing, unsettling

trouble[1] [trubl] *adj* **1** : cloudy, dim **2** FLOU : blurred **3** : confused, unclear

trouble[2] *nm* **1** : distress, confusion, embarrassment **2** : trouble, discord <semer le trouble : to sow discord> **3** : disorder (in medicine) <trouble respiratoire : respiratory disorder> **4 troubles** *nmpl* : unrest <troubles politiques : political unrest>

troubler [truble] *vt* **1** : to disturb, to trouble **2** : to disrupt **3** BROUILLER : to blur, to cloud **4** : to confuse, to disconcert — **se troubler** *vr* **1** : to become cloudy **2** : to get confused

trouée [true] *nf* : gap, breach

trouer [true] *vt* : to make a hole in, to pierce

trouillard, -larde [trujar, -jard] *n fam* : chicken, coward

trouille [truj] *nf fam* : fear, fright <avoir la trouille : to be scared stiff>

troupe [trup] *nf* **1** : troop **2** : troupe **3** : herd (of horses, elephants, etc.) **4 la troupe** : the army

troupeau [trupo] *nm, pl* **troupeaux** : herd, flock

trousse [trus] *nf* **1** : kit, case <trousse de secours : first-aid kit> **2 aux trousses de** : on the heels of <la police est à mes trousses : the police are after me>

trousseau [truso] *nm, pl* **trousseaux 1** : trousseau **2 trousseau de clefs** : bunch of keys

trousser [truse] *vt* : to truss (a fowl)

trouvaille [truvaj] *nf* **1** DÉCOUVERTE : find **2** : inspiration, brainstorm

trouver [truve] *vt* **1** DÉCOUVRIR : to find, to discover **2** SE PROCURER : to find, to obtain, to get **3** IMAGINER : to find, to think up **4** ESTIMER : to think, to consider <je trouve que c'est incroyable : I think it's incredible> — **se trouver** *vr* **1** : to be (found) <ça se trouve un peu partout : it's found almost anywhere> **2** : to find oneself <je me suis trouvé incapable de répondre : I found myself unable to answer> **3** : to feel <il se trouve mieux : he feels better> — *v impers* **il se trouve que** : it turns out that

truand [tryɑ̃] *nm* : gangster, crook

truc [tryk] *nm* **1** ASTUCE : trick <trucs du métier : tricks of the trade> **2** *fam* MACHIN : thingamajig, contraption

trucage [trykaʒ] *nm* : special effect (in movies)

truchement [tryʃmɑ̃] *nm* **par le truchement de** : through, with the help of, by means of

truculent, -lente [trykylɑ̃, -lɑ̃t] *adj* : earthy, racy, colorful

truelle [tryɛl] *nf* : trowel

truffe [tryf] *nf* **1** : truffle **2** : nose (of a dog)

truffer [tryfe] *vt* : to fill with, to pepper with, to riddle with

truie [trɥi] *nf* : sow (pig)

truisme [tryism] *nm* : truism

truite [trɥit] *nf* : trout

truquage [trykaʒ] *nm* → **trucage**

truquer [tryke] *vt* **1** : to fix, to rig (an election, etc.) **2** : to use special effects in

trust [trœst] *nm* : trust, cartel

tsar [tsar, dzar] *nm* : czar

tsarine [tsarin, dzarin] *nf* : czarina

t–shirt [tiʃœrt] *nm* → **tee–shirt**

tu[1] [ty] *pp* → **taire**

tu[2] [ty] *pron* : you

tuant, tuante [tɥɑ̃, tɥɑ̃t] *adj fam* **1** : exhausting **2** : exasperating

tuba [tyba] *nm* **1** : tuba **2** : snorkel

tube [tyb] *nm* **1** : tube, pipe **2** : tube (of toothpaste, lipstick, etc.) **3 tube digestif** : digestive tract, alimentary canal

tubercule [tybɛrkyl] *nm* : tuber

tuberculeux, -leuse [tybɛrkylø, -løz] *adj* : tubercular, tuberculous

tuberculose [tybɛrkyloz] *nf* : tuberculosis

tubulaire [tybylɛr] *adj* : tubular

tubulure [tybylyr] *nf* : manifold (of an automobile)

tue–mouches[1] [tymuʃ] *adj* **papier tue–mouches** : flypaper

tue–mouches[2] *nms & pl Can* : flyswatter

tuer [tɥe] *vt* **1** : to kill **2** ÉPUISER : to wear out, to exhaust **3 tuer le temps** : to kill time — **se tuer** *vr* **1** : to be killed, to die **2** : to kill oneself

tuerie [tyri] *nf* CARNAGE : slaughter, carnage

tue–tête [tytɛt] **à ~** : at the top of one's lungs

tueur, tueuse [tɥœr, tɥøz] *n* MEURTRIER : killer, murderer

tuile [tɥil] *nf* **1** : tile **2** *fam* : bad luck

tulipe [tylip] *nf* : tulip

tuméfié, -fiée [tymefje] *adj* : swollen, puffed-up

tumeur [tymœr] *nf* : tumor, growth

tumulte [tymylt] *nm* **1** BROUHAHA : tumult, commotion, hubbub **2** : (emotional) turmoil

tumultueux, -tueuse [tymyltɥø, -tɥøz] *adj* : stormy, turbulent — **tumultueusement** [-tɥøzmɑ̃] *adv*

tungstène [tœ̃kstɛn] *nm* : tungsten

tunique [tynik] *nf* : tunic

tunisien, -sienne [tynizjɛ̃, -zjɛn] *adj* : Tunisian

Tunisien, -sienne *n* : Tunisian

tunnel [tynɛl] *nm* : tunnel

tuque [tyk] *nf Can* : stocking cap, tuque

turban [tyrbɑ̃] *nm* : turban

turbide [tyrbid] *adj* : turbid

turbine [tyrbin] *nf* : turbine

turbopropulseur [tyrbɔpropylsœr] *nm* : turboprop

turboréacteur [tyrbɔreaktœr] *nm* : turbojet

turbulence [tyrbylɑ̃s] *nf* : turbulence

turbulent, -lente [tyrbylɑ̃, -lɑ̃t] *adj* **1** : boisterous, unruly **2** : turbulent

turc[1], **turque** [tyrk] *adj* : Turkish

turc[2] *nm* : Turkish (language)

Turc, Turque *n* : Turk

turf [tœrf] *nm* **1** : racetrack **2** : horse racing

turquoise[1] [tyrkwaz] *adj* : turquoise

turquoise[2] *nf* : turquoise (stone)

turquoise[3] *nm* : turquoise (color)

tutelle [tytɛl] *nf* **1** : guardianship **2** : trusteeship **3** : care, protection (of the law, etc.)

tuteur[1], **-trice** [tytœr, -tris] *n* **1** : guardian **2** : tutor

tuteur[2] *nm* : stake, prop (for plants)

tutoiement [tytwamɑ̃] *nm* : use of the familiar "tu" form

tutoyer [tytwaje] {58} *vt* : to address someone as "tu"
tuyau [tɥijo] *nm, pl* **tuyaux 1** : pipe, tube, conduit <tuyau d'échappement : exhaust pipe> <tuyau d'arrosage : garden hose> **2** : quill **3** *fam* : tip, inside information
tuyauter [tɥijote] *vt* **1** : to flute, to pleat **2** *fam* : to give someone a tip
tuyauterie [tɥijotri] *nf* : piping, pipes *pl*, plumbing
tuyère [tyjɛr] *nf* : nozzle
TV [teve] *nf* : TV
tweed [twid] *nm* : tweed
tympan [tɛ̃pɑ̃] *nm* : eardrum
type [tip] *nm* **1** : type, kind **2** : example, model **3** : (physical) type **4** *fam* : guy, fellow
typé, -pée [tipe] *adj* : typical, distinctive (of features)
typhoïde [tifɔid] *adj & nf* : typhoid
typhon [tifɔ̃] *nm* : typhoon
typhus [tifys] *nms & pl* : typhus
typique [tipik] *adj* : typical — **typiquement** [-pikmɑ̃] *adv*
typographie [tipɔgrafi] *nf* : typography
typographique [tipɔgrafik] *adj* : typographic, typographical — **typographiquement** [-fikmɑ̃] *adv*
tyran [tirɑ̃] *nm* : tyrant
tyrannie [tirani] *nf* : tyranny
tyrannique [tiranik] *adj* : tyrannical — **tyranniquement** [-nikmɑ̃] *adv*
tyranniser [tiranize] *vt* : to tyrannize
tzar [tsar, dzar] → **tsar**
tzigane [dzigan] *adj & nmf* : gypsy

U

u [y] *nm* : u, the 21st letter of the alphabet
ubiquité [ybikɥite] *nf* : ubiquity
ukrainien[1], -nienne [ykrɛnjɛ̃, -njɛn] *adj* : Ukrainian
ukrainien[2] *nm* : Ukrainian (language)
Ukrainien, -nienne *n* : Ukrainian
ulcération [ylserasjɔ̃] *nf* : ulceration
ulcère [ylsɛr] *nm* : ulcer <ulcère à l'estomac : stomach ulcer>
ulcérer [ylsere] {87} *vt* **1** : to ulcerate **2** RÉVOLTER : to revolt, to appall
ulcéreux, -reuse [ylserø, -røz] *adj* **1** : ulcerous **2** : ulcerated
ultérieur, -rieure [ylterjœr] *adj* : later, subsequent
ultérieurement [ylterjœrmɑ̃] *adv* : at a later time, subsequently
ultimatum [yltimatɔm] *nm* : ultimatum
ultime [yltim] *adj* : ultimate, final
ultraviolet, -lette [yltravjolɛ, -lɛt] *adj* : ultraviolet
ululement, uluer [ylylmɑ̃] → **hululement, hululer**
un[1], une [œ̃ (œn *before a vowel or mute h*), yn] *adj* : a, an, one <rester une semaine : to stay a week, to stay one week> <il y a un seul problème : there's just one problem>
un[2], une *n* : one <les filles marchent une par une : the girls are walking one by one> <la page une : page one>
un[3] *nm* : (number) one <huit et un font neuf : eight and one are nine>
un[4], une *pron, pl* **uns, unes** : one <un de ces jours : one of these days> <l'une de mes amies : one of my friends>
un[5], une *art, pl* **des 1** (*used in the singular*) : a, an <un exemple : an example> <une nouvelle maison : a new house> **2** (*used in the plural*) : some <voici des bonbons : here are some candies> <des gens sont déjà arrivés : some people have already arrived> **3** (*used for emphasis*) <il a attendu des heures : he waited for hours> <il y a une pluie! : there's so much rain!>
unanime [ynanim] *adj* : unanimous — **unanimement** [-nimmɑ̃] *adv*
unanimité [ynanimite] *nf* : unanimity
une [yn] *nf* **faire la une** : to be on the front page
uni, -nie [yni] *adj* **1** : united <les États-Unis : the United States> **2** LISSE : smooth, even **3** : plain-colored, solid **4** : close-knit
unième [ynjɛm] *adj* : first <trente et unième : thirty-first>
unificateur, -trice [ynifikatœr, -tris] *adj* : unifying
unification [ynifikasjɔ̃] *nf* : unification
unifier [ynifje] {96} *vt* **1** UNIR : to unite, to unify **2** NORMALISER : to standardize — **s'unifier** *vr* : to unite
uniforme[1] [ynifɔrm] *adj* **1** RÉGULIER : uniform, even **2** : unchanging
uniforme[2] *nm* : uniform
uniformément [ynifɔrmemɑ̃] *adv* : uniformly
uniformiser *vt* **1** : to make uniform **2** STANDARDISER : to standardize
uniformité [ynifɔrmite] *nf* : uniformity, evenness
unilatéral, -rale [ynilateral] *adj, pl* **-raux** [-ro] : unilateral — **unilatéralement** [-ralmɑ̃] *adv*
unilingue [ynilɛ̃g] *adj* : monolingual
union [ynjɔ̃] *nf* **1** : union <union conjugale : marriage> <Union soviétique : Soviet Union> **2** ASSOCIATION : association
unique [ynik] *adj* **1** SEUL : only <mon unique espoir : my only hope> **2** EXCEPTIONNEL : unique, exceptional **3** → **enfant**

uniquement [ynikmɑ̃] **1** EXCLUSIVEMENT : exclusively **2** SEULEMENT : only, solely

unir [ynir] *vt* **1** : to unite, to bring together **2** : to combine — **s'unir** *vr* **1** : to unite **2** : to be joined in marriage

unisson [ynisɔ̃] *nm* : unison

unitaire [ynitɛr] *adj* **1** : unitary **2 prix unitaire** : unit price

unité [ynite] *nf* **1** : unity **2** : unit

univers [ynivɛr] *nm* : universe

universel, -selle [ynivɛrsɛl] *vt* : universal — **universellement** [-sɛlmɑ̃] *adv*

universitaire[1] [ynivɛrsitɛr] *adj* : university, academic

universitaire[2] *nmf* : academic

université [ynivɛrsite] *nf* : university

univoque [ynivɔk] *adj* : unambiguous, certain

uranium [yranjɔm] *nm* : uranium

Uranus [yranys] *nm* : Uranus

urbain, -baine [yrbɛ̃, -bɛn] *adj* : urban, city

urbanisme [yrbanism] *nm* : city planning

urbanité [yrbanite] *nf* : urbanity

urètre [yrɛtr] *nm* : urethra

urgence [yrʒɑ̃s] *nf* **1** : urgency **2** : emergency **3 d'urgence** : immediately, without delay

urgent, -gente [yrʒɑ̃, -ʒɑ̃t] *adj* : urgent

urinaire [yrinɛr] *adj* : urinary

urinal [yrinal] *nm, pl* **-naux** [-no] : urinal, bedpan

urine [yrin] *nf* : urine

uriner [yrine] *vi* : to urinate — **urination** [yrinasjɔ̃] *nf*

urinoir [yrinwar] *nm* : (public) urinal

urne [yrn] *nf* **1** : urn **2** : ballot box

urticaire [yrtikɛr] *nf* : hives

uruguayen, -guayenne [yrygwejɛ̃, -jɛn] *adj* : Uruguayan

Uruguayen, -guayenne *n* : Uruguayan

us [ys] *nmpl* **les us et coutumes** : habits and customs

usage [yzaʒ] *nm* **1** : use <à usage thérapeutique : for therapeutic use> <perdre l'usage d'un bras : to lose the use of an arm> **2** : usage (of a word or expression) **3** COUTUME : usage, custom <c'est l'usage : it's customary> **4** POLITESSE : (good) manners

usagé, -gée [yzaʒe] *adj* **1** : worn **2** : used, secondhand

usager [yzaʒe] *nm* : user

usé, -sée [yze] *adj* **1** : worn (down), worn-out **2** : hackneyed, trite

user [yze] *vt* **1** CONSOMMER : to use, to consume **2** : to wear out, to use up — *vi* **1 ~ de** : to exercise (one's rights) **2 ~ de** : to make use of — **s'user** *vr* **1** : to wear out, to get used up **2** : to wear oneself out

usine [yzin] *nf* : factory

usiner [yzine] *vt* **1** : to machine **2** : to manufacture

usité, -tée [yzite] *adj* : common, commonly used <prénom peu usité : uncommon name>

ustensile [ystɑ̃sil] *nm* : utensil, implement

usuel, -suelle [yzɥɛl] *adj* **1** : common, everyday **2** : usual <dans l'ordre usuel : in the usual order>

usuellement [yzɥɛlmɑ̃] *adv* : usually, ordinarily

usure [yzyr] *nm* **1** : wear (and tear) **2** : wearing down, erosion **3** : usury

usurpateur, -trice [yzyrpatœr, -tris] *n* : usurper

usurper [yzyrpe] *vt* : to usurp

utérin, -rine [yterɛ̃, -rin] *adj* : uterine

utérus [yterys] *nms & pl* : uterus

utile [ytil] *adj* : useful — **utilement** [ytilmɑ̃] *adv*

utilisable [ytilizabl] *adj* : usable

utilisateur, -trice [ytilizatœr, -tris] *n* : user

utilisation [ytilizasjɔ̃] *nf* : utilization, use

utiliser [ytilize] *vt* : to utilize, to use

utilitaire [ytilitɛr] *adj* : utilitarian

utilité [ytilite] *nf* : utility, usefulness

utopie [ytɔpi] *nf* : utopia

utopique [ytɔpik] *adj* : utopian

V

v [ve] *nm* : v, the 22d letter of the alphabet

va [va], *etc.* → **aller**

vacance [vakɑ̃s] *nf* **1** : vacancy, opening **2 vacances** *nfpl* : vacation, holiday *Brit* <en vacances : on vacation>

vacancier, -cière [vakɑ̃sje, -sjɛr] *n* : vacationer

vacant, -cante [vakɑ̃, -kɑ̃t] *adj* : vacant <poste vacant : vacant position>

vacarme [vakarm] *nm* : racket, din

vacataire [vakatɛr] *nmf France* : temporary worker, substitute

vaccin [vaksɛ̃] *nm* : vaccine

vacciner [vaksine] *vt* : to vaccinate — **vaccination** [vaksinasjɔ̃] *nf*

vache[1] [vaʃ] *adj fam* : mean, nasty

vache[2] *nf* **1** : cow <vache laitière : dairy cow> **2** : cowhide **3** *fam* : nasty person, swine

vachement [vaʃmɑ̃] *adv fam* JOLIMENT : really, very <cela m'aide vachement! : that's a big help!>

vacher, -chère [vaʃe, -ʃɛr] *n* : cowherd, cowboy *m*, cowgirl *f*

vacherie [vaʃri] *nf fam* **1** : nastiness, meanness **2** : dirty trick

vacillant, -lante [vasijɑ̃, -jɑ̃t] *adj* **1** : unsteady, shaky **2** : flickering **3** : failing, faltering (of memory, etc.)

vacillement [vasijmɑ̃] *nm* **1** : flickering **2** : wavering, faltering

vaciller [vasije] *vi* **1** : to stagger, to totter **2** : to flicker, to wobble, to sway **3** : to waver, to falter, to be failing

vacuité [vakɥite] *nf* : vacuity, emptiness

vadrouille [vadruj] *nf* **1** *Can* : long-handled mop for cleaning or dusting floors **2 en ~** *fam* : wandering

vadrouiller [vadruje] *vi fam* : to wander about, to ramble

va–et–vient [vaevjɛ̃] *nms & pl* **1** : comings and goings **2** : to-and-fro motion **3** : two-way switch

vagabond[1]**, -bonde** [vagabɔ̃, -bɔ̃d] *adj* : wandering, roving

vagabond[2]**, -bonde** *n* : vagrant, tramp, vagabond

vagabondage [vagabɔ̃daʒ] *nm* **1** : vagrancy **2** : wandering <vagabondage de l'esprit : wandering(s) of the mind>

vagabonder [vagabɔ̃de] *vi* **1** : to wander **2** : to stray (of thoughts, etc.)

vagin [vaʒɛ̃] *nm* : vagina

vaginal, -nale [vaʒinal] *adj, mpl* **-naux** [-no] : vaginal

vague[1] [vag] *adj* **1** IMPRÉCIS : vague **2** : vacant, abstracted **3** : loose-fitting, ample

vague[2] *nf* : wave

vague[3] *nm* **1** : vagueness <rester dans le vague : to remain vague> **2 regarder dans le vague** : to stare into space

vaguement [vagmɑ̃] *adv* : vaguely

vaillamment [vajamɑ̃] *adv* : bravely, courageously

vaillance [vajɑ̃s] *nf* : valor, courage

vaillant, -lante [vajɑ̃, -jɑ̃t] *adj* **1** COURAGEUX : valiant, courageous **2** : strong, robust

vaille [vaj], *etc.* → **valoir**

vain, vaine [vɛ̃, vɛn] *adj* **1** FUTILE : vain, futile <en vain : in vain> **2** VANITEUX : vain — **vainement** [vɛnmɑ̃] *adv*

vaincre [vɛ̃kr] {94} *vt* **1** BATTRE : to defeat **2** SURMONTER : to overcome, to master

vaincu[1]**, -cue** [vɛ̃ky] *adj* : defeated

vaincu[2]**, -cue** *n* : loser

vainquais [vɛ̃kɛ], **vainquions** [vɛ̃kjɔ̃], *etc.* → **vaincre**

vainque [vɛ̃k], *etc.* → **vaincre**

vainqueur [vɛ̃kœr] *nm* : victor, winner

vairon [vɛrɔ̃] *nm* : minnow

vaisseau [vɛso] *nm, pl* **vaisseaux** **1** : vessel <vaisseau sanguin : blood vessel> **2** : vessel, ship <vaisseau spatial : spaceship> **3** : nave

vaisselle [vɛsɛl] *nf* : crockery, dishes *pl*

val [val] *nm, pl* **vals** *or* **vaux** : valley

valable [valabl] *adj* **1** VALIDE : valid **2** BON : good, worthwhile

valablement [valabləmɑ̃] *adv* : validly, legitimately

valentin [valɑ̃tɛ̃] *nm Can* : valentine

valet [valɛ] *nm* **1** : valet, manservant <valet de pied : footman> **2** : jack (in playing cards)

valeur [valœr] *nf* **1** : value, worth, merit <objets de valeur : valuables> <valeur nominale : face value> **2** VALIDITÉ : validity **3** : (moral) value <valeurs familiales : family values> **4 valeurs** *nfpl* : stocks, securities **5 c'est de valeur** *Can fam* : that's a pity, that's too bad **6 mettre en valeur** : to develop (land)

valeureux, -reuse [valœrø, -røz] *adj* : courageous, valiant

valide [valid] *adj* **1** : valid **2** : fit, able-bodied

valider [valide] *vt* : to validate

validité [validite] *nf* : validity

valise [valiz] *nf* : suitcase <faire ses valises : to pack one's bags>

vallée [vale] *nf* : valley

vallon [valɔ̃] *nm* : small valley, dale

vallonné, -née [valɔne] *adj* : undulating, hilly

valoir [valwar] {95} *vi* **1** : to have a (certain) cost <valoir très cher : to be very expensive> **2** : to have value <il sait ce qu'il vaut : he knows what he's worth> <valoir rien : to be worthless> **3** : to apply, to be valid <cela vaut pour tous les employés : that holds for all employees> **4 faire valoir** : to put forth, to point out, to assert <faire valoir ses droits : to assert one's rights> — *vt* **1** PROCURER : to provide, to bring (to) **2** : to be equivalent to <un dollar vaut 100 cents : one dollar equals 100 cents> **3** : to be worth <valoir la peine : to be worth the trouble> — *v impers* **valoir mieux** : to be better <il vaut mieux rester ici : it would be better to stay here> — **se valoir** *vr* : to be the same (thing)

valoriser [valɔrize] *vt* : to increase the value of, to develop, to enhance

valse [vals] *nf* : waltz

valser [valse] *vi* : to waltz

valve [valv] *nf* : valve

vampire [vɑ̃pir] *nm* : vampire

vandale [vɑ̃dal] *nmf* : vandal

vandalisme [vɑ̃dalism] *nm* : vandalism

vanille [vanij] *nf* : vanilla

vanité [vanite] *nf* : vanity

vaniteux, -teuse [vanitø, -tøz] *adj* : vain, conceited — **vaniteusement** [-tøzmɑ̃] *adv*

vanne [van] *nf* **1** : sluice, sluiceway **2** *fam* : dig, gibe

vanner [vane] *vt* : to winnow, to husk

vannerie [vanri] *nf* : wickerwork
vantail [vɑ̃taj] *nm, pl* **-taux** [-to] : leaf, casement <portes à deux vantaux : double doors>
vantard[1], **-tarde** [vɑ̃tar, -tard] *adj* : boastful, bragging
vantard[2], **-tarde** *n* : braggart
vantardise [vɑ̃tardiz] *nf* **1** : boastfulness **2** : boast, brag
vanter [vɑ̃te] *vt* : to vaunt — **se vanter** *vr* **1** : to boast, to brag **2 ~ de** : to pride oneself on
va–nu–pieds [vanypje] *nmfs & pl* : beggar, tramp, ragamuffin
vapeur[1] [vapœr] *nf* **1** : steam **2** : vapor, fume <vapeurs d'essence : gas fumes>
vapeur[2] *nm* : steamship, steamboat
vaporeux, -reuse [vapɔrø, -røz] *adj* **1** : misty, hazy **2** : filmy, diaphanous
vaporisateur [vapɔrizatœr] *nm* ATOMISEUR : spray, atomizer
vaporiser [vapɔrize] *vt* **1** : to spray **2** : to vaporize
vaquer [vake] *vi* **~ à** : to attend to, to see to
varappe [varap] *nf* : rock climbing
varech [varɛk] *nm* : kelp, seaweed
vareuse [varøz] *nf* **1** : loose-fitting jacket, tunic **2** : pea jacket
variable[1] [varjabl] *adj* CHANGEANT : variable, changeable
variable[2] *nf* : variable
variante [varjɑ̃t] *nf* : variant
variation [varjasjɔ̃] *nf* : variation
varice [varis] *nf* : varicose vein
varicelle [varisɛl] *nf* : chicken pox
varié, -riée [varje] *adj* **1** : varied, varying **2** : various
varier [varje] {96} *v* : to vary
variété [varjete] *nf* : variety
variole [varjol] *nf* : smallpox
vasculaire [vaskylɛr] *adj* : vascular
vase[1] [vaz] *nf* BOUE : mud, silt
vase[2] *nm* **1** : vase (for flowers) **2** : vessel, container <vase à bec : beaker>
vaseux, -seuse [vazø, -zøz] *adj* **1** BOUEUX : muddy **2** *fam* : sickly, under the weather **3** : hazy, woolly (of thinking, etc.)
vasistas [vazistas] *nms & pl* : fanlight, transom
vasque [vask] *nf* **1** : basin (of a fountain) **2** : bowl **3 vasque pour les oiseaux** : birdbath
vaste [vast] *adj* **1** IMMENSE : huge, immense **2** ÉTENDU : extensive, wide
va–tout [vatu] *nms & pl* **jouer son va–tout** : to risk one's all
vaudeville [vodvil] *nm* : vaudeville
vaudou [vodu] *nm* : voodoo
vaudra [vodra], *etc.* → **valoir**
vau–l'eau [volo] *adv* **aller à vau–l'eau** : to be ruined, to be going down the drain
vaurien, -rienne [vorjɛ̃, -rjɛn] *n* : good-for-nothing, scoundrel, rogue
vaut [vo], *etc.* → **valoir**
vautour [votur] *nm* : vulture
vautrer [votre] *v* **se vautrer** *vr* **1** : to sprawl **2** : to wallow
va–vite [vavit] **à la va–vite** : quickly, hurriedly
veau [vo] *nm, pl* **veaux 1** : calf **2** : veal **3** : calfskin
vecteur [vɛktœr] *nm* **1** : vector **2** : carrier (of disease)
vécu[1] [veky] *pp* → **vivre**
vécu[2], **-cue** [veky] *adj* : real, real-life
vedette [vədɛt] *nf* **1** STAR : star (in movies, etc.), celebrity <avoir la vedette : to be in the limelight> <mettre en vedette : to put the spotlight on> **2** : patrol boat, launch
végétal[1], **-tale** [veʒetal] *adj, mpl* **-taux** : vegetable, plant <le règne végétal : the plant kingdom>
végétal[2] *nm* : vegetable, plant
végétarien, -rienne [veʒetarjɛ̃, -rjɛn] *adj & n* : vegetarian
végétarisme [veʒetarism] *nm* : vegetarianism
végétatif, -tive [veʒetatif, -tiv] *adj* : vegetative
végétation [veʒetasjɔ̃] *nf* **1** : vegetation **2 végétations** *nfpl* : adenoids
végéter [veʒete] {87} *vi* : to vegetate
véhémence [veemɑ̃s] *nf* : vehemence <avec véhémence : vehemently>
véhément, -mente [veemɑ̃, -mɑ̃t] *adj* : vehement
véhicule [veikyl] *nm* **1** : vehicle **2 véhicule utilitaire sport** *Can* : sport-utility vehicle
véhiculer [veikyle] *vt* : to convey
veille [vɛj] *nf* **1** : day before, eve <la veille de Noël : Christmas Eve> **2** : watch, vigil **3** : wakefulness
veillée [veje] *nf* **1** SOIRÉE : evening **2 veillée funèbre** : wake
veiller [veje] *vt* : to sit up with, to watch over — *vi* **1** : to stay awake **2** : to keep watch **3** : to be vigilant **4 ~ à** : to watch over, to look after
veilleur, -leuse [vejœr, -jøz] *n* **1** : lookout, sentry **2 veilleur de nuit** : night watchman
veilleuse *nf* **1** : night-light **2** : pilot light **3 mettre en veilleuse** : to put on hold, to set aside **4 mettre en veilleuse** : to dim (a light)
veine [vɛn] *nf* **1** : vein (in anatomy and botany) **2** : vein, lode (of a mineral) **3** : (artistic) inspiration **4** *fam* : luck <coup de veine : fluke> **5 en veine de** : in the mood for
veiné, -née [vene] *adj* : veined, grained
velléitaire [veleitɛr] *adj* : indecisive
velléité [veleite] *nf* : vague impulse, whim
vélo [velo] *nm* : bike, bicycle <faire du vélo : to ride a bike>
véloce [velɔs] *adj* : swift
vélocité [velɔsite] *nf* **1** : swiftness **2** : velocity

velours [vəlur] *nm* **1 :** velvet, velour **2 velours côtelé :** corduroy
velouté[1], **-tée** [vəlute] *adj* **:** velvety, smooth
velouté[2] *nm* **:** softness, smoothness
velu, -lue [vəly] *adj* POILU **:** hairy
venaison [vənɛzɔ̃] *nf* **:** venison
vénal, -nale [venal] *adj* **:** venal
vendable [vɑ̃dabl] *adj* **:** marketable
vendange [vɑ̃dɑ̃ʒ] *nf* **:** grape harvest
vendanger [vɑ̃dɑ̃ʒe] {17} *vi* **:** to harvest (the) grapes — *vt* **:** to harvest (grapes)
vendetta [vɑ̃deta] *nf* **:** vendetta
vendeur, -deuse [vɑ̃dœr, -døz] *n* **1 :** salesperson, salesman *m*, saleswoman *f* **2 :** seller, vendor
vendre [vɑ̃dr] {63} *vt* **1 :** to sell **2 à ~ :** for sale — **se vendre** *vr* **1 :** to be sold **2 :** to sell <ça se vend bien : it's selling well>
vendredi [vɑ̃drədi] *nm* **:** Friday <vendredi saint : Good Friday>
vénéneux, -neuse [venenø, -nøz] *adj* **:** poisonous
vénérable [venerabl] *adj* **:** venerable, revered
vénérer [venere] {87} *vt* RÉVÉRER **:** to venerate — **vénération** [-rasjɔ̃] *nf*
vénérien, -rienne [venerjɛ̃, -rjɛn] *adj* **:** venereal <maladie vénérienne : venereal disease>
vénézuélien, -lienne [venezɥeljɛ̃, -ljɛn] *adj* **:** Venezuelan
Vénézuélien, -lienne *n* **:** Venezuelan
vengeance [vɑ̃ʒɑ̃s] *nf* **:** vengeance, revenge
venger [vɑ̃ʒe] {17} *vt* **:** to avenge — **se venger** *vr* **:** to take revenge, to avenge oneself
vengeur[1], **-geresse** [vɑ̃ʒœr, -ʒrɛs] *adj* **:** vengeful
vengeur[2], **-geresse** *n* **:** avenger
véniel, -nielle [venjɛl] *adj* **:** venial
venimeux, -meuse [vənimø, -møz] *adj* **1 :** venomous, poisonous **2 :** spiteful
venin [vənɛ̃] *nm* **1 :** venom, poison **2 :** ill will, malice
venir [vənir] {92} *vi* **1 :** to come **2 en venir à :** to come to <en venir aux coups : to come to blows> <j'en suis venu à une conclusion : I've reached a conclusion> **3 faire venir :** to send for **4 ~ de :** to come from — *v aux* **1 :** to come and, to come to <viens la voir : come and see her> **2 :** to have just <je viens de nager : I've just been swimming>
vent [vɑ̃] *nm* **1 :** wind <il y a du vent : it's windy> <le vent du changement : the winds of change> **2 avoir vent de :** to get wind of
vente [vɑ̃t] *nf* **:** sale, selling <en vente : for sale>
venteux, -teuse [vɑ̃tø, -tøz] *adj* **:** windy
ventilateur [vɑ̃tilatœr] *nm* **:** (electric) fan, ventilator
ventilation [vɑ̃tilasjɔ̃] *nf* **1 :** ventilation **2 :** breakdown (in finance)
ventiler [vɑ̃tile] *vt* **1** AÉRER **:** to ventilate **2 :** to break down <ventiler les dépenses : to break down expenses>
ventouse [vɑ̃tuz] *nf* **1 :** suction cup **2 :** plunger **3 :** sucker (in zoology)
ventre [vɑ̃tr] *nm* **1 :** stomach, belly <avoir mal au ventre : to have a stomachache> **2 :** womb **3 avoir qqch dans le ventre** *fam* **:** to have guts
ventricule [vɑ̃trikyl] *nm* **:** ventricle
ventriloque [vɑ̃trilɔk] *nmf* **:** ventriloquist
ventriloquie [vɑ̃trilɔki] *nf* **:** ventriloquism
ventru, -true [vɑ̃try] *adj* **1** PANSU **:** potbellied **2** RENFLÉ **:** bulging, swelling
venu[1] [vəny] *pp* → **venir**
venu[2], **-nue** [vəny] *adj* **1 bien venu :** timely, welcome **2 mal venu :** ill-advised, unwelcome **3 nouveau venu :** newcomer **4 premier venu :** just anyone
venue *nf* AVÈNEMENT **:** coming, advent
Vénus [venys] *nf* **:** Venus (planet)
vêpres [vɛpr] *nfpl* **:** vespers
ver [vɛr] *nm* **:** worm <vers blanc : grub> <ver luisant : glowworm> <ver à soie : silkworm> <ver de terre : earthworm> <ver solitaire : tapeworm>
véracité [verasite] *nf* **:** veracity, truthfulness
véranda [verɑ̃da] *nf* **:** veranda, porch
verbal, -bale [vɛrbal] *adj, mpl* **verbaux** [-bo] **:** verbal — **verbalement** [-balmɑ̃] *adv*
verbaliser [vɛrbalize] *vt* **:** to verbalize
verbe [vɛrb] *nm* **1 :** verb <verbe pronominal : reflexive verb> **2 :** language, words <la magie du verbe : the magic of words> **3 :** tone of voice
verbeux, -beuse [vɛrbø, -bøz] *adj* **:** wordy, verbose
verbiage [vɛrbjaʒ] *nm* **:** verbiage
verdâtre [vɛrdatr] *adj* **:** greenish
verdeur [vɛrdœr] *nf* **1** ACIDITÉ **:** tartness, acidity **2** VIGUEUR **:** vigor, vitality **3** GROSSIÈRETÉ **:** crudeness
verdict [vɛrdikt] *nm* **:** verdict
verdir [vɛrdir] *v* **:** to turn green
verdoyant, verdoyante [vɛrdwajɑ̃, -jɑ̃t] *adj* **:** green, verdant
véreux, -reuse [verø, -røz] *adj* **1 :** wormy **2** LOUCHE **:** shady, suspect
verge [vɛrʒ] *nf* **1** BAGUETTE **:** rod, stick **2** *Can* **:** yard (measure) **3** PÉNIS **:** penis **4 verge d'or :** goldenrod
verger [vɛrʒe] *nm* **:** orchard
verglacé, -cée [vɛrglase] *adj* **:** icy
verglas [vɛrgla] *nm* **:** black ice
vergogne [vɛrgɔɲ] *nf* **sans ~ :** shamelessly
vergue [vɛrg] *nf* **:** yard (of a ship)
véridique [veridik] *adj* **:** truthful
vérifiable [verifjabl] *adj* **:** verifiable

vérificateur, -trice [verifikatœr, -tris] *n* **1** : controller, inspector **2 vérificateur de comptes** : (financial) auditor
vérification [verifikasjɔ̃] *nf* : check, verification
vérifier [verifje] {96} *vt* CONFIRMER : to verify, to check
vérin [verɛ̃] *nm* : jack <vérin hydraulique : hydraulic jack>
véritable [veritabl] *adj* **1** RÉEL : true, actual, real <mon véritable nom : my real name> **2** AUTHENTIQUE : genuine, authentic **3** (*used as an intensive*) : real <c'est un véritable cauchemar! : it's a real nightmare!>
véritablement [-tabləmɑ̃] *adv* **1** : actually, really **2** (*used as an intensive*) : absolutely
vérité [verite] *nf* **1** : truth <dire la vérité : to tell the truth> **2** : fact, truth <une vérité éternelle : an eternal truth> **3** : sincerity, truthfulness
vermeil, -meille [vɛrmɛj] *adj* : vermilion
vermicelle [vɛrmisɛl] *nm* : vermicelli
vermine [vɛrmin] *nf* : vermin
vermoulu, -lue [vɛrmuly] *adj* : worm-eaten, dilapidated
vermouth *or* **vermout** [vɛrmut] *nm* : vermouth
vernir [vɛrnir] *vt* : to varnish
vernis [vɛrni] *nms & pl* **1** LAQUE : varnish, lacquer **2** APPARENCE : veneer, facade **3 vernis à ongles** : nail polish
vernissage [vɛrnisaʒ] *nm* **1** : varnishing **2** : opening (of an art exhibition)
vernisser [vɛrnise] *vt* : to glaze
vérole [verɔl] *nf* **1** *fam* : syphilis **2** → **petit**[2]
verra [vera], *etc.* → **voir**
verrat [vera] *nm* : male pig, boar
verre [vɛr] *nm* **1** : glass **2** : (drinking) glass <verre à vin : wineglass> <verre à pied : goblet> **3** : glassful <prendre un verre : to have a drink> **4 verres** *nmpl* : eyeglasses, lenses <verres de contact : contact lenses> <verres à double foyer : bifocals>
verrerie [vɛrri] *nf* **1** : glassware **2** : glassmaking **3** : glass factory
verrière [vɛrjɛr] *nf* **1** : glass roof **2** : stained-glass window
verrou [vɛru] *nm* : bolt <sous les verrous : locked up>
verrouiller [vɛruje] *vt* : to bolt, to lock
verrue [vɛry] *nf* : wart
vers[1] [vɛr] *nms & pl* **1** : line, verse (of poetry) **2** : verse <vers libre : free verse>
vers[2] *prep* **1** : toward, towards <vers le nord : toward the north> **2** : about, around, near <vers treize heures : around one o'clock>
versant [vɛrsɑ̃] *nm* : slope, side (of a hill, etc.)
versatile [vɛrsatil] *adj* : fickle
verse [vɛrs] *nf* **pleuvoir à verse** : to pour (rain)
versé, -sée [vɛrse] *adj* **~ dans** : (well) versed in
Verseau [vɛrso] *nm* : Aquarius
versement [vɛrsəmɑ̃] *nm* **1** : payment **2** : installing, installment
verser [vɛrse] *vt* **1** : to pour **2** PAYER : to pay **3** RÉPANDRE : to shed (tears, blood etc.) — *vi* **1** : to overturn **2 ~ dans** : to lapse into
verset [vɛrsɛ] *nm* : verse (of the Bible, etc.)
version [vɛrsjɔ̃] *nf* **1** : version **2** : translation (into one's native language)
verso [vɛrso] *nm* : verso, back (of a page)
vert[1], **verte** [vɛr, vɛrt] *adj* **1** : green **2** : unripe, sour **3** GAILLARD : vigorous, sprightly **4** CRU : crude, forthright **5** SÉVÈRE : harsh, severe
vert[2] *nm* : green
vertébral, -brale [vɛrtebral] *adj, mpl* **-braux** [-bro] : vertebral, back
vertèbre [vɛrtɛbr] *nf* : vertebra
vertébré[1], **-brée** [vɛrtebre] *adj* : vertebrate
vertébré[2] *nm* : vertebrate
vertement [vɛrtəmɑ̃] *adv* : sharply, severely
vertical, -cale [vɛrtikal] *adj, mpl* **-caux** [-ko] : vertical — **verticalement** [-kalmɑ̃] *adv*
verticale *nf* : vertical
verticille [vɛrtisil] *nf* : whorl (of petals, leaves etc.)
vertige [vɛrtiʒ] *nm* : vertigo, dizziness
vertigineux, -neuse [vɛrtiʒinø, -nøz] *adj* **1** : dizzy, giddy <hauteurs vertigineuses : dizzying heights> **2** : breathtaking
vertu [vɛrty] *nf* **1** : virtue **2** : power, property **3 en vertu de** : by virtue of, according to
vertueux, -tueuse [vɛrtɥø, -tɥøz] *adj* : virtuous — **vertueusement** [-tɥøzmɑ̃] *adv*
verve [vɛrv] *nf* BRIO : verve, panache
vésicule [vezikyl] *nf* **1** : vesicle **2 vésicule biliaire** : gallbladder
vessie [vesi] *nf* : bladder
veste [vɛst] *nf* **1** : jacket **2** *Can* : vest
vestiaire [vɛstjɛr] *nm* **1** : cloakroom **2** : locker room **3** : locker
vestibule [vɛstibyl] *nm* : vestibule, hall
vestige [vɛstiʒ] *nm* **1** RESTE : vestige, trace **2** : relic, remains *pl*
vestimentaire [vɛstimɑ̃tɛr] *adj* : clothing, sartorial
veston [vɛstɔ̃] *nm* : (man's) jacket
vêtement [vɛtmɑ̃] *nm* **1** : garment, article of clothing **2 vêtements** *nmpl* : clothes, clothing **3 vêtement sacerdotal** : vestment (in religion)
vétéran [veterɑ̃] *nm* : veteran
vétérinaire[1] [veterinɛr] *adj* : veterinary
vétérinaire[2] *nmf* : veterinarian
vétille [vetij] *nf* BAGATELLE : trifle

vêtir [vetir] {97} *vt* HABILLER : to dress **— se vêtir** *vr*
veto [veto] *nms & pl* : veto
vêtu, -tue [vɛty] *adj* : dressed <bien vêtu : well-dressed>
vétuste [vetyst] *adj* : dilapidated
veuf[1], veuve [vœf, vœv] *adj* : widowed
veuf[2], veuve *n* : widower *m,* widow *f*
veuille [vœj], *etc.* → **vouloir**
veule [vœl] *adj* : weak, spineless
veut [vœ], *etc.* → **vouloir**
veuvage [vœvaʒ] *nm* : widowhood
veuve → **veuf**
vexant, vexante [vɛksɑ̃, -ksɑ̃t] *adj* **1** : hurtful (of a remark, etc.) **2** : vexing, annoying
vexation [vɛksasjɔ̃] *nf* : humiliation
vexer [vɛkse] *vt* : to vex, to upset **— se vexer** *vr* : to be upset, to take offense
via [vja] *prep* : via
viabilité [vjabilite] *nf* **1** : viability **2** : practicality
viable [vjabl] *adj* **1** : viable **2** : practical, feasible
viaduc [vjadyk] *nm* : viaduct
viager, -gère [vjaʒe, -ʒɛr] *adj* or **rente viagère** : life annuity
viande [vjɑ̃d] *nf* : meat <viande de bœuf : beef> <viande hachée : hamburger>
vibrant, -brante [vibrɑ̃, -brɑ̃t] *adj* **1** : vibrating **2** : vibrant, stirring
vibration [vibrɑsjɔ̃] *nf* : vibration
vibrer [vibre] *vi* **1** : to vibrate **2** : to stir, to thrill
vicaire [vikɛr] *nm* : vicar, curate
vice [vis] *nm* **1** DÉBAUCHE : vice **2** DÉFAUT : defect, fault, flaw
vice–amiral [visamiral] *nm, pl* **-raux** [-ro] : vice admiral
vice–président, -dente [visprezidɑ̃, -dɑ̃t] *n, pl* **-dents, -dentes** : vice president
vice–roi [visrwa] *nm, pl* **vice–rois** : viceroy
vice versa *or* **vice–versa** [vis(e)vɛrsa] *adv* : vice versa
vichy [viʃi] *nm* **1** : gingham **2** : Vichy water
vicier [visje] {96} *vt* **1** : to pollute, to taint **2** : to invalidate (in law)
vicieusement [visjøzmɑ̃] *nm* : viciously
vicieux, -cieuse [visjø, -sjøz] *adj* **1** : vicious (of an animal) **2** : devious, sly **3** PERVERS : perverse, depraved **4** FAUTIF : incorrect, faulty **5 cercle vicieux** : vicious circle
vicissitudes [visisityd] *nfpl* : vicissitudes, trials and tribulations
vicomte [vikɔ̃t] *nm* : viscount
vicomtesse [vikɔ̃tɛs] *nf* : viscountess
victime [viktim] *nf* : victim
victoire [viktwar] *nf* : victory
victorien, -rienne [viktɔrjɛ̃, -rjɛn] *adj* : Victorian
victorieux, -rieuse [viktɔrjø, -rjøz] *adj* : victorious <l'équipe victorieuse : the winning team> **— victorieusement** [-rjøzmɑ̃] *adv*
victuailles [viktɥaj] *nfpl* : victuals, provisions
vidange [vidɑ̃ʒ] *nf* **1** : emptying, draining **2** : oil change <faire la vidange : to change the oil> **3 vidanges** *nfpl* : sewage **4 vidanges** *nfpl Can* : garbage collection
vidanger [vidɑ̃ʒe] {17} *vt* : to empty, to drain
vide[1] [vid] *adj* **1** : empty <les mains vides : empty-handed> **2** : blank
vide[2] *nm* **1** : emptiness, void, space **2** : vacuum **3** : gap <combler le vide : to fill the gap>
vidéo[1] [video] *adj s & pl* : video
vidéo[2] *nf* : video
vidéocassette [videɔkasɛt] *nf* : videocassette, videotape
vider [vide] *vt* **1** : to empty **2** : to empty out (a place) **3** VIDANGER : to drain **4** : to core (fruit), to clean (a fowl), to gut (a fish) **5** *fam* : to kick out, to throw out
vie [vi] *nf* **1** : life <être en vie : to be alive> **2** : lifetime, life <à vie : for life> <jamais de la vie! : never!> **3** : living, livelihood
vieil → **vieux**
vieillard [vjɛjar] *nm* : old man
vieille → **vieux**
vieillesse [vjɛjɛs] *nf* : old age
vieilli, -lie [vjeji] *adj* **1** : aged, old-looking **2** DÉMODÉ : old-fashioned, dated
vieillir [vjejir] *vt* : to make (someone) look older **—** *vi* **1** : to grow old, to age **2** : to become outdated **— se vieillir** *vr* : to make oneself seem older
vieillissant, -sante [vjejisɑ̃, -sɑ̃t] *adj* : aging, ageing
vieillissement [vjejismɑ̃] *nm* : aging, growing old
vieillot, -lotte [vjejo, -jɔt] *adj* : quaint, antiquated
viendra [vjɛ̃dra], *etc.* → **venir**
vienne [vjɛn], *etc.* → **venir**
vient [vjɛ̃], *etc.* → **venir**
vierge[1] [vjɛrʒ] *adj* **1** : virgin **2** : blank, empty <cassette vierge : blank tape> **3** : fresh, unspoiled
vierge[2] *nf* : virgin <la Sainte Vierge : the Blessed Virgin>
Vierge *nf* : Virgo
vietnamien[1], -mienne [vjɛtnamjɛ̃, -mjɛn] *adj* : Vietnamese
vietnamien[2] *nm* : Vietnamese (language)
Vietnamien, -mienne *n* : Vietnamese
vieux[1] [vjø] (**vieil** [vjɛj] *before a vowel or mute h*), **vieille** [vjɛj] *adj, mpl* **vieux** **1** : old **2 vieille fille** : old maid **3 vieux jeu** : old-fashioned, old hat
vieux[2], vieille *n* : old man *m,* old woman *f*
vif[1], vive [vif, viv] *adj* **1** VIVANT : living, live <de vive voix : in person> **2**

ANIMÉ : lively, vivacious **3** AIGU : sharp, keen **4** EMPORTÉ : brusque, quick-tempered **5** : bright, vivid **6** : brisk, bracing **7** → **mémoire**
vif[2] *nm* **1 à ~** : open, raw, exposed **2 entrer dans le vif du sujet** : to get to the heart of the matter **3 piqué au vif** : cut to the quick **4 sur le vif** : on the spot, live
vif–argent [vifarʒɑ̃] *nm, pl* **vifs–argents** : quicksilver
vigie [viʒi] *nf* **1** : lookout **2** : crow's nest, lookout (post)
vigilant, -lante [viʒilɑ̃, -lɑ̃t] *adj* : vigilant — **vigilance** [viʒilɑ̃s] *nf*
vigile[1] [viʒil] *nf* : vigil (in religion)
vigile[2] *nm* : security guard, night watchman
vigne [viɲ] *nf* **1** : grapevine **2** VIGNOBLE : vineyard
vigneron, -ronne [viɲrɔ̃, -rɔn] *n* : winegrower
vignette [viɲɛt] *nf* **1** : label **2** : vignette
vignoble [viɲɔbl] *nm* : vineyard
vigoureux, -reuse [vigurø, -røz] *adj* **1** : vigorous, sturdy **2** : lively, energetic — **vigoureusement** [-røzmɑ̃] *adv*
vigueur [vigœr] *nf* **1** : vigor **2 en ~** : in force, in effect
VIH [veiaʃ] *nm* : HIV
Viking [vikiŋ] *nmf* : Viking
vil, vile [vil] *adj* **1** MÉPRISABLE : vile, despicable **2 à vil prix** : very cheap
vilain, -laine [vilɛ̃, -lɛn] *adj* **1** MÉCHANT : naughty **2** LAID : ugly **3** : nasty, disagreeable
vilebrequin [vilbrəkɛ̃] *nm* **1** : brace (for a bit) **2** : crankshaft
vilement [vilmɑ̃] *adv* : vilely, basely
vilenie [vileni] *nf* **1** : vileness, baseness **2** : base deed
vilipender [vilipɑ̃de] *vt* : to revile
villa [vila] *nf* : villa
village [vilaʒ] *nm* : village
villageois, -geoise [vilaʒwa, -ʒwaz] *n* : villager
ville [vil] *nf* : city, town <aller en ville : to go into town, to go downtown>
villégiature [vileʒjatyr] *nf* **1** : vacation **2** *or* **lieu de villégiature** : resort
vin [vɛ̃] *nm* : wine
vinaigre [vinɛgr] *nm* : vinegar
vinaigrette [vinɛgrɛt] *nf* : vinaigrette
vinaigrier [vinɛgrije] *nm* : vinegar cruet
vindicatif, -tive [vɛ̃dikatif, -tiv] *adj* : vindictive
vingt[1] [vɛ̃ (vɛ̃t *before a vowel, mute h, and the numbers 22-29*)] *adj* **1** : twenty **2** : twentieth <le vingt avril : April twentieth>
vingt[2] *nms & pl* : twenty
vingtaine [vɛ̃tɛn] *nf* : about twenty, group of twenty
vingtième [vɛ̃tjɛm] *adj & nmf & nm* : twentieth
vinicole [vinikɔl] *adj* VITICOLE : wine, wine-growing
vinyle [vinil] *nm* : vinyl
viol [vjɔl] *nm* **1** : rape **2** PROFANATION : violation, desecration
violacé, -cée [vjɔlase] *adj* : purplish
violateur, -trice [vjɔlatœr] *n* : violator
violation [vjɔlasjɔ̃] *nf* : violation
violemment [vjɔlamɑ̃] *adv* : violently
violent, -lente [vjɔlɑ̃, -lɑ̃t] *adj* : violent — **violence** [vjɔlɑ̃s] *nf*
violenter [vjɔlɑ̃te] *vt* **1** : to do violence to **2** VIOLER : to rape
violer [vjɔle] *vt* **1** : to rape **2** : to desecrate **3** : to violate, to break (a law, promise, etc.)
violet[1], **-lette** [vjɔlɛ, -lɛt] *adj* : purple, violet
violet[2] *nm* : purple, violet
violette *nf* : violet (flower)
violeur [vjɔlœr] *nm* : rapist
violon [vjɔlɔ̃] *nm* : violin, fiddle
violoncelle [vjɔlɔ̃sɛl] *nm* : cello
violoncelliste [vjɔlɔ̃selist] *nmf* : cellist
violoniste [vjɔlɔnist] *nmf* : violinist, fiddler
vipère [vipɛr] *nf* : adder, viper
virage [viraʒ] *nm* **1** COURBE : bend, turn, curve **2** : change, shift (in orientation) **3** : change in color
viral, -rale [viral] *adj, mpl* **viraux** [viro] : viral <infection virale : viral infection>
virée [vire] *nf fam* : outing, trip <faire une virée : to go for a spin>
virement [virmɑ̃] *nm* : transfer (in finance) <virement bancaire : bank transfer>
virer [vire] *vt* **1** : to transfer (funds) **2** : to tone (a photograph) **3** *fam* : to fire, to expel, to throw out — *vi* **1** : to veer, to turn **2** : to change color **3 ~ à** : to turn (to), to change to <virer au vert : to turn green>
virevolte [virvɔlt] *nf* **1** : twirl **2** VOLTE-FACE : about-face
virevolter [virvɔlte] *vi* : to twirl
virginité [virʒinite] *nf* : virginity
virgule [virgyl] *nf* **1** : comma **2** : point, decimal point <5 virgule 7 milliards : 5 point 7 billion>
viril, -rile [viril] *adj* : virile, manly
virilité [virilite] *nf* : virility, manliness
virtuel, -tuelle [virtɥɛl] *adj* **1** : virtual (in science) **2** POTENTIEL : potential
virtuose [virtɥoz] *nmf* : virtuoso
virtuosité [virtɥozite] *nf* : virtuosity
virulent, -lente [virylɑ̃, -lɑ̃t] *adj* : virulent — **virulence** [virylɑ̃s] *nf*
virus [virys] *nms & pl* : virus
vis [vi] *nfs & pl* : screw
visa [viza] *nm* **1** : visa **2** : stamp, seal
visage [vizaʒ] *nm* **1** : face <un visage familier : a familiar face> <à visage découvert : openly> **2** : aspect, nature
visagiste [vizaʒist] *nmf* ESTHÉTICIEN : beautician

vis–à–vis[1] [vizavi] *adv* **1 ~ de** : opposite, facing **2 ~ de** : towards, with respect to

vis–à–vis[2] *nms & pl* **1** : person opposite **2** : building opposite

viscéral, -rale [viseral] *adj, mpl* **-raux** [-ro] : visceral

viscères [visɛr] *nmpl* : viscera, innards

viscosité [viskozite] *nf* : viscosity

visée [vize] *nf* **1** : aim, design **2** : sighting, aiming

viser [vize] *vt* **1** : to aim for, to aim at **2** : to stamp (a document) — *vi* **1** : to aim, to take aim **2 ~ à** : to aim at, to intend

viseur [vizœr] *nm* **1** : viewfinder **2** : sight (of a firearm)

visibilité [vizibilite] *nf* : visibility

visible [vizibl] *adj* **1** : visible **2** : obvious — **visiblement** [-ziblәmɑ̃] *adv*

visière [vizjɛr] *nf* : visor (of a cap, etc.)

vision [vizjɔ̃] *nf* **1** : vision, eyesight **2** : view, outlook **3** : vision, apparition

visionnaire [vizjɔnɛr] *adj & nmf* : visionary

visionner [vizjɔne] *vt* : to view

visionneuse [vizjɔnøz] *nf* : viewer (for slides)

visite [vizit] *nf* **1** : visit <rendre visite à : to visit> <heures de visite : visiting hours> **2** VISITEUR : visitor <avoir une visite : to have a visitor> **3** : examination, inspection <visite de douane : customs inspection>

visiter [vizite] *vt* **1** : to visit **2** EXAMINER : to inspect, to examine

visiteur, -teuse [vizitœr, -tøz] *n* **1** : visitor **2** : inspector

vison [vizɔ̃] *nm* : mink

visqueux, -queuse [viskø, -køz] *adj* **1** : viscous **2** : slimy, gooey

visser [vise] *vt* : to screw, to screw on — **se visser** *vr* : to screw together

visualiser [vizɥalize] *vt* : to visualize — **visualisation** [-zɥalizasjɔ̃] *nf*

visuel, -suelle [vizɥɛl] *adj* : visual — **visuellement** [-zɥɛlmɑ̃] *adv*

vital, -tale [vital] *adj, mpl* **vitaux** [vito] : vital

vitalité [vitalite] *nf* : vitality

vitamine [vitamin] *nf* : vitamin

vite [vit] *adv* **1** RAPIDEMENT : fast, quickly <fais vite! : hurry up!> **2** TÔT : soon <au plus vite : as soon as possible>

vitesse [vitɛs] *nf* **1** : speed <à toute vitesse : at full speed> **2** : gear <en première vitesse : in first gear> **3 boîte de vitesses** : transmission **4** → **limite**

viticole [vitikɔl] *adj* VINICOLE : wine, wine-growing

viticulture [vitikyltyr] *nf* : wine growing

vitrail [vitraj] *nm, pl* **vitraux** [vitro] : stained-glass window

vitre [vitr] *nf* **1** : pane, windowpane **2** : window (of a car, train, etc.) <vitre arrière : rear window>

vitré, -trée [vitre] *adj* **1** : glass, glazed **2** → **baie**

vitreux, -treuse [vitrø, -trøz] *adj* **1** : vitreous **2** : glassy <les yeux vitreux : glassy eyes>

vitrier [vitrije] *nm* : glazier

vitrine [vitrin] *nf* **1** : shop window **2** : showcase, display case

vitupération [vityperasjɔ̃] *nf* : vituperation

vitupérer [vitypere] {87} *vt* : to vituperate, to berate — *vi* **~ contre** : to rant and rave against

vivable [vivabl] *adj* SUPPORTABLE : bearable

vivace [vivas] *adj* **1** : hardy <plante vivace : perennial plant> **2** DURABLE : enduring

vivacité [vivasite] *nf* **1** : vivacity, liveliness **2** : brusqueness, quickness **3** : vividness, intensity

vivant[1]**, -vante** [vivɑ̃, -vɑ̃t] *adj* **1** VIF : living, live **2** ANIMÉ : lively, vivacious, peppy **3** → **langue**

vivant[2] *nm* **1** : living being **2 du vivant de** : during the lifetime of

vivats [viva] *nmpl* : cheers

vive [viva] *interj* : long live, three cheers for <vive le roi! : long live the king!>

vivement [vivmɑ̃] *adv* **1** RAPIDEMENT : quickly **2** FORTEMENT : strongly, sharply, hotly

vivier [vivje] *nm* **1** : fishpond, fish tank **2** : breeding ground

vivifiant, -fiante [vivifjɑ̃, -fjɑ̃t] *adj* : bracing, invigorating

vivifier [vivifje] {96} *vt* REVIGORER : to invigorate

vivisection [viviseksjɔ̃] *nf* : vivisection

vivoter [vivɔte] *vi* : to get by, to subsist

vivre [vivr] {98} *vt* : to live through, to experience — *vi* **1** : to live **2 faire vivre** : to support **3 ~ de** : to live on, to live by

vivres [vivr] *nmpl* PROVISIONS : food, provisions

vocable [vɔkabl] *nm* MOT : term, word

vocabulaire [vɔkabylɛr] *nm* : vocabulary

vocal, -cale [vɔkal] *adj, mpl* **vocaux** [vɔko] : vocal — **vocalement** [-kalmɑ̃] *adv*

vocaliser [vɔkalize] *v* : to vocalize

vocation [vɔkasjɔ̃] *nf* : vocation, calling

vociférer [vɔsifere] {87} *v* : to shout, to scream

vodka [vɔdka] *nf* : vodka

vœu [vø] *nm, pl* **vœux 1** SOUHAIT : wish <faire un vœu : to make a wish> <mes meilleurs vœux : my best wishes> **2** SERMENT : vow

vogue [vɔg] *nf* : vogue, fashion

voguer [vɔge] *vi* : to sail, to navigate

voici [vwasi] *prep* **1** : here is, here are <me voici : here I am> <la voici qui vient : here she comes> **2** : this is, these are <voici pourquoi : this is why> **3** (*indicating a period of time*) <il est parti voici trois jours : he left three days ago> <voici un mois que je ne les vois plus : it's a month since I've seen them>

voie [vwa] *nf* **1** : road, route, way <voie express : expressway> <voie à sens unique : one-way street> <voie navigable : waterway> **2** : lane <route à deux voies : two-lane road> **3** *or* **voie ferrée** : railroad track **4** : way, course <montrer la voie : to show the way> <une voie médiane : a middle course> **5** : means *pl,* channels *pl* **6** : passage, duct (in physiology) **7 en voie de** : on the way to, in the process of **8 voie d'eau** : leak (of a boat) **9 la Voie lactée** : the Milky Way

voilà [vwala] *prep* **1** : there is, there are <les voilà! : there they are!> **2** : that is, those are <voilà tout! : that's all!> **3** VOICI : here is, here are **4** (*indicating a period of time*) <voilà un an : a year ago> <voilà quatre jours qu'il neige : it's been snowing for four days>

voile[1] [vwal] *nf* **1** : sail **2** : sailing

voile[2] *nm* **1** : veil **2** : voile (fabric) **3** : veil, covering <lever le voile : to reveal, to bring to the open> **4** : mist (of tears, fog, etc.)

voiler [vwale] *vt* **1** : to veil, to cover **2** : to conceal **3** : to mist (up), to cloud **4** : to warp — **se voiler** *vr*

voilier [vwalje] *nm* : sailboat

voilure [vwalyr] *nf* : sails *pl*

voir [vwar] {99} *v* **1** : to see **2** : to view, to imagine **3** : to look at, to consider **4** : to discover <c'est à voir : that remains to be seen> **5** : to visit, to call on **6 faire voir** *or* **laisser voir** : to show **7 n'avoir rien à voir avec** : to have nothing to do with — *vi* **1** : to see <voir double : to see double> **2** : to find out, to understand <il faut voir : we must wait and see> **3** : to take a look <voyons : well, let's see> **4 ~ à** : to see to, to make sure that <voyez à la prévenir : be sure to warn her> — **se voir** *vr* **1** : to see oneself **2** : to see each other **3** : to be visible, to show <ça se voit : that's obvious, it shows>

voire [vwar] *adv* : indeed, or even

voirie [vwari] *nf* **1** : highway department **2** *France* : garbage collection

voisin[1], **-sine** [vwazɛ̃, -zin] *adj* **1** : adjoining, neighboring **2** : similar, closely related <voisin de : akin to, resembling>

voisin[2], **-sine** *n* : neighbor

voisinage [vwazinaʒ] *nm* **1** : neighborhood **2** : proximity, closeness **3** : neighbors *pl*

voisiner [vwazine] *vi* **1** : to visit one's neighbors **2 ~ avec** : to be side by side with

voiture [vwatyr] *nf* **1** AUTOMOBILE : car, automobile <voiture de course : racing car> **2** WAGON : (railroad) car, coach **3** : carriage, cart <voiture d'enfant : baby carriage>

voix [vwa] *nfs & pl* **1** : voice <à haute voix : out loud, aloud> <voix traînante : drawl> **2** : voice, counsel <la voix de la raison : the voice of reason> **3** VOTE : vote <mettre aux voix : to put to the vote>

vol [vɔl] *nm* **1** : flight <prendre son vol : to take flight> <vols internationaux : international flights> **2** : theft, robbery <vol à main armée : armed robbery> <vol à la tire : pickpocketing> **3** VOLÉE : flock **4 au vol** : in midair

volage [vɔlaʒ] *adj* INCONSTANT : fickle, flighty

volaille [vɔlaj] *nf* **1** : poultry **2** : fowl, bird

volant[1], **-lante** [vɔlɑ̃, -lɑ̃t] *adj* : flying

volant[2] *nm* **1** : steering wheel **2** : shuttlecock **3** : flounce (of a skirt, etc.)

volatil, -tile [vɔlatil] *adj* : volatile

volatile *nm* : fowl, chicken, bird

volatiliser [vɔlatilize] *v* **se volatiliser** *vr* **1** : to volatilize **2** : to disappear, to vanish into thin air

volcan [vɔlkɑ̃] *nm* **1** : volcano **2** : hothead

volcanique [vɔlkanik] *adj* : volcanic

volée [vɔle] *nf* **1** : volley **2** VOL : flock, flight

voler [vɔle] *vt* **1** : to steal **2** : to rob, to cheat **3 voler à l'étalage** : to shoplift — *vi* **1** : to fly **2 voler en éclats** : to smash to bits, to shatter

volet [vɔlɛ] *nm* **1** : shutter **2** : flap (of an airplane, etc.) **3** : section (of a document) **4** : constituent, part, facet

voleter [vɔlte] {8} *vi* : to flutter, to flit

voleur[1], **-leuse** [vɔlœr, -løz] *adj* : thieving, dishonest

voleur[2], **-leuse** *n* **1** : thief, robber **2 voleur à la tire** : pickpocket **3 voleur à l'étalage** : shoplifter

volière [vɔljɛr] *nf* : aviary

volley [vɔlɛ] *or* **volley–ball** [vɔlɛbol] *nm* : volleyball

volontaire[1] [vɔlɔ̃tɛr] *adj* **1** : voluntary **2** : willful, deliberate **3** : headstrong

volontaire[2] *nmf* : volunteer

volontairement [vɔlɔ̃tɛrmɑ̃] *adv* : voluntarily, deliberately

volonté [vɔlɔ̃te] *nf* **1** : will <bonne volonté : willingness, goodwill> **2** : willpower **3 à ~** : at will

volontiers [vɔlɔ̃tje] *adv* : willingly, gladly

volt [vɔlt] *nm* : volt

voltage [vɔltaʒ] *nm* : voltage

volte–face [vɔltəfas] *nfs & pl* : about-face

voltige [vɔltiʒ] *nf* : acrobatics

voltiger [vɔltiʒe] {17} *vi* **1** : to do acrobatics **2** : to flutter about, to flit

voltigeur, -geuse [vɔltiʒœr, -ʒøz] *n Can* : outfielder

volubile [vɔlybil] *adj* : voluble

volume [vɔlym] *nm* : volume

volumineux, -neuse [vɔlyminø, -nøz] *adj* : voluminous

volupté [vɔlypte] *nf* : sensual pleasure, voluptuousness

voluptueux, -tueuse [vɔlyptɥø, -tɥøz] *adj* : voluptuous — **voluptueusement** [-tɥøzmɑ̃] *adv*

volute [vɔlyt] *nf* : curl, coil (of smoke, etc.)

vomi [vɔmi] *nm* : vomit

vomir [vɔmir] *vt* **1** : to vomit, to bring up **2** : to spew out — *vi* : to vomit

vomissement [vɔmismɑ̃] *nm* : vomiting

vorace [vɔras] *adj* : voracious — **voracement** [-rasmɑ̃] *adv*

voracité [vɔrasite] *nf* : voracity

votant, -tante [vɔtɑ̃, -tɑ̃t] *n* : voter

vote [vɔt] *nm* : vote

voter [vɔte] *vi* : to vote — *vt* : to vote for

votre [vɔtr] *adj, pl* **vos** [vo] : your

vôtre[1] [votr] *adj* : yours <ce livre est vôtre : this book is yours>

vôtre[2] *pron* **le vôtre, la vôtre, les vôtres** : yours, your own <c'est le vôtre : it's yours> <mes amitiés à vous et les vôtres : my regards to you and yours>

voudra [vudra], *etc.* → **vouloir**

vouer [vwe] *vt* **1** PROMETTRE : to vow, to pledge **2** CONSACRER : to dedicate, to consecrate <vouer sa vie : to devote one's life> **3** DESTINER : to destine, to doom <voué à l'échec : doomed to failure>

voulait [vulɛ], **voulions** [vuljɔ̃], *etc.* → **vouloir**

vouloir[1] [vulwar] {100} *vt* **1** : to want, to wish for <veux-tu du vin? : do you want some wine?> <je voudrais y aller : I would like to go> **2** ACCEPTER : to agree to, to be willing to <veuillez patienter : please wait> <voudriez-vous ouvrir la porte? : would you mind opening the door?> **3** : to expect, to intend <je ne leur veux aucun mal : I mean them no harm> <sans le vouloir : unintentionally> **4 en vouloir à** : to bear a grudge against **5 vouloir dire** : to mean <qu'est-ce que ça veut dire? : what does that mean?> — **se vouloir** *vr* **1** : to think of oneself as **2** : to try to be **3 s'en vouloir** : to be annoyed with oneself

vouloir[2] *nm* : will <bon vouloir : goodwill>

voulu, -lue [vuly] *adj* **1** DÉLIBÉRÉ : intentional, deliberate **2** REQUIS : required

vous [vu] *pron* **1** (*as subject or direct object*) : you <vous êtes mon ami : you're my friend> <elle vous aime : she loves you> **2** (*as indirect object*) : you, to you <il vous a écrit une lettre : he wrote you a letter> **3** : yourself <servez-vous : help yourself> <pensez à vous : think about yourselves> **4 à ~** : yours <est-ce que cette maison est à vous? : is this house yours?, is this your house?>

vous–même [vumɛm], *pl* **vous–mêmes** *pron* : yourself

voûte [vut] *nf* **1** : vault, arch **2 voûte du palais** : roof of the mouth

voûter [vute] *vt* : to vault, to arch — **se voûter** *vr* : to become stooped

vouvoyer [vuvwaje] {58} *vt* : to address as *vous*

voyage [vwajaʒ] *nm* **1** : voyage, trip **2 avoir son voyage** *Can fam* : to be fed up

voyager [vwajaʒe] {17} *vi* : to travel

voyageur, -geuse [vwajaʒœr, -ʒøz] *n* **1** : traveler **2** PASSAGER : passenger

voyait [vwajɛ], **voyions** [vwajɔ̃], *etc.* → **voir**

voyance [vwajɑ̃s] *nf* : clairvoyance

voyant[1], **voyante** [vwajɑ̃, -jɑ̃t] *adj* : loud, gaudy, garish

voyant[2], **voyante** *n* : seer, clairvoyant

voyant[3] *nm* : warning light, indicator light

voyelle [vwajɛl] *nf* : vowel

voyeur, voyeuse [vwajœr, -jøz] *n* : voyeur

voyou [vwaju] *nm* : thug, hoodlum

vrac [vrak] *adv* **1 en ~** : loose, in bulk **2 en ~** : jumbled, disorganized

vrai[1], **vraie** [vrɛ] *adj* **1** : true **2** : real

vrai[2] *nm* : truth <à vrai dire : to tell the truth>

vraiment [vrɛmɑ̃] *adv* : really

vraisemblable [vrɛzɑ̃blabl] *adj* : likely, probable — **vraisemblablement** [-blabləmɑ̃] *adv*

vraisemblance [vrɛzɑ̃blɑ̃s] *nf* **1** : likelihood, probability **2** : verisimilitude

vrille [vrij] *nf* **1** : gimlet (tool), auger **2** : spiral, tailspin **3** : tendril

vriller [vrije] *vt* : to bore into, to pierce

vrombir [vrɔ̃bir] *vi* **1** : to hum, to buzz **2** : to roar (of an engine)

vrombissement [vrɔ̃bismɑ̃] *nm* : humming, buzzing, roaring

vu[1] [vy] *pp* → **voir**

vu[2], **vue** [vy] *adj* : seen, regarded <bien vu : well thought of>

vu[3] *prep* : in view of, considering <vu sa timidité, c'est un homme brave : considering his timidity, he's a brave man>

vue *nf* **1** : sight <à première vue : at first sight> **2** : eyesight **3** : view, vista <vue d'ensemble : overall view> **4** : opinion, view **5 vues** *nfpl* : plans, designs **6 vues** *nfpl Can* : <aller aux vues : to go to the movies>

vulcaniser [vylkanize] *vt* : to vulcanize
vulgaire [vylgɛr] *adj* **1** GROSSIER : vulgar, coarse **2** ORDINAIRE : common, ordinary
vulgairement [vylgɛrmɑ̃] *adv* : vulgarly
vulgariser [vylgarize] *vt* : to popularize — **vulgarisation** [vylgarizasjɔ̃] *nf*
vulgarité [vylgarite] *nf* : vulgarity
vulnérabilité [vylnerabilite] *nf* : vulnerability
vulnérable [vylnerabl] *adj* : vulnerable
vulve [vylv] *nf* : vulva

W

w [dubləve] *nm* : w, the 23rd letter of the alphabet
wagon [vagɔ̃] *nm* **1** : car (of a train) **2** : carload, truckload, wagonload
wagon–citerne [vagɔ̃sitɛrn] *nm, pl* **wagons–citernes** : tanker
wagon–lit [vagɔ̃li] *nm, pl* **wagons–lits** : sleeping car, Pullman
wagonnet [vagɔnɛ] *nm* : small transport car (on a train)
wagon–restaurant [vagɔ̃rɛstɔrɑ̃] *nm, pl* **wagons–restaurants** : dining car
wallaby [walabi] *nm, pl* **wallabies** : wallaby
wallon[1], **-lonne** [walɔ̃, -lɔn] *adj* : Walloon
wallon[2] *nm* : Walloon (language)
Wallon, -lonne *n* : Walloon
wampum [wampum] *nm* : wampum
wapiti [wapiti] *nm* : wapiti
water–polo [watɛrpɔlo] *nm* : water polo
watt [wat] *nm* : watt
week–end [wikɛnd] *nm, pl* **week–ends** : weekend
western [wɛstɛrn] *nm* : western (movie)
wharf [warf] *nm* : wharf
whippet [wɪpɛt] *nm* : whippet
whisky [wiski] *nm, pl* **whiskies** : whiskey
wigwam [wigwam] *nm* : wigwam
wolfram [vɔlfram] *nm* : wolfram

X

x [iks] *nm* : x, the 24th letter of the alphabet
X [iks] *nm* (*used to designate an unknown*) <monsieur X : Mr. X>
xénon [gzenɔ̃] *nm* : xenon
xénophile [gzenɔfil] *adj & nmf* : xenophile
xénophobe[1] [gzenɔfɔb] *adj* : xenophobic
xénophobe[2] *nmf* : xenophobe
xénophobie [gzenɔfɔbi] *nf* : xenophobia
xérès [gzerɛs, kserɛs] *nm* : sherry
xylophone [ksilɔfɔn] *nm* : xylophone

Y

y [igrɛk] *nm* : y, the 25th letter of the alphabet
y[1] [i] *adv* **1** : there <il n'y était pas : he was not there> **2 ça y est !** : finally!, there you have it!
y[2] *pron* : it, for it, about it <nous n'y pouvons rien : we can't do anything about it> <pensons-y : let's think about it> <j'y suis! : I've got it!>
yacht [jot] *nm* : yacht
yachting [jotiŋ] *nm* : yachting
yack *or* **yak** [jak] *nm* : yak
yankee[1] [jɑ̃ki] *adj* : yankee
Yankee[2] *nmf* : Yankee
yaourt [jaurt] *nm* : yogurt
yéménite [jemenit] *adj* : Yemeni
Yéménite *nmf* : Yemeni
yeux [jø] → **œil**
yoga [jɔga] *nm* : yoga
yogourt *or* **yoghourt** [jɔgurt] → **yaourt**
Yom Kippour [jɔmkipur] *nm* : Yom Kippur
yo–yo *or* **yoyo** [jojo] *nm* : yo-yo
yucca [juka] *nm* : yucca
yougoslave [jugɔslav] *adj* : Yugoslav, Yugoslavian
Yougoslave *nmf* : Yugoslav, Yugoslavian

Z

z [zɛd] *nm* **:** z, the 26th letter of the alphabet
zaïrois, -roise [zairwa, -rwaz] *adj* **:** Zairian
Zaïrois, -roise *n* **:** Zairian
zambien, -bienne [zɑ̃bjɛ̃, -bjɛn] *adj* **:** Zambian
Zambien, -bienne *n* **:** Zambian
zèbre [zɛbr] *nm* **:** zebra
zébré, -brée [zebre] *adj* RAYÉ **:** striped, streaked
zébrure [zebryr] *nf* **1** RAYURE **:** stripe **2 :** wheal, welt (on the skin) **3 :** streak (of lightning)
zélateur, -trice [zelatœr, -tris] *n* **:** zealot, partisan
zèle [zɛl] *nm* **:** zeal
zélé, -lée [zele] *adj* **:** zealous
zénith [zenit] *nm* **:** zenith
zéphyr [zefir] *nm* **:** zephyr
zeppelin [zɛplɛ̃] *nm* **:** zeppelin
zéro[1] [zero] *adj* **1 :** zero **2 :** nil, worthless
zéro[2] *nm* **:** zero, nought
zeste [zɛst] *nm* **:** zest, peel (of a lemon, etc.)
zézaiement [zezɛmɑ̃] *nm* **:** lisp
zézayer [zezeje] {11} *vi* **:** to lisp
zibeline [ziblin] *nf* **:** sable
zieuter [zjøte] *vt fam* RELUQUER **:** to ogle, to eye
zig *or* **zigue** [zig] *nm fam* **:** guy, fellow
zigzag [zigzag] *nm* **:** zigzag
zigzaguer [zigzage] *vi* **:** to zigzag
zimbabwéen, -wéenne [zimbabweɛ̃, -weɛn] *adj* **:** Zimbabwean
Zimbabwéen, -wéenne *n* **:** Zimbabwean
zinc [zɛ̃g] *nm* **:** zinc
zinnia [zinja] *nm* **:** zinnia
zip [zip] *nm* **:** zipper
zipper [zipe] *vt* **:** to zip (up)
zircon [zirkɔ̃] *nm* **:** zircon
zirconium [zirkɔnjɔm] *nm* **:** zirconium
zizanie [zizani] *nf* DISCORDE **:** discord, conflict
zodiaque [zɔdjak] *nm* **:** zodiac
zombie [zɔ̃bi] *nm* **:** zombie
zona [zona] *nm* **:** shingles
zonage [zonaʒ] *nm* **:** zoning
zone [zon] *nf* **:** zone, area
zoo [zo(o)] *nm* **:** zoo
zoologie [zɔɔlɔʒi] *nf* **:** zoology
zoologique [zɔɔlɔʒik] *adj* **:** zoological
zoologiste [zɔɔlɔʒist] *nmf* **:** zoologist
zoom [zum] *nm* **1 :** zoom lens **2 faire un zoom :** to zoom in (in photography)
zozo [zozo] *nm fam* **:** nitwit
zozoter [zɔzɔte] *vi* **:** to lisp
zut [zyt] *interj fam* **:** darn!, damn it!
zygote [zigɔt] *nm* **:** zygote

English–French Dictionary

A

a[1] ['eɪ] *n, pl* **a's** or **as** ['eɪz] : a *m,* première lettre de l'alphabet

a[2] [ə, 'eɪ] *art* **(an** [ən, 'æn] *before a vowel or silent h)* **1** : un *m,* une *f* <a book : un livre> <half an hour : une demi-heure> **2** PER : par <twice a month : deux fois par mois>

aardvark ['ɑrd͵vɑrk] *n* : oryctérope *m*

aback [ə'bæk] *adv* **taken aback** : déconcerté, décontenancé

abacus ['æbəkəs] *n, pl* **abaci** ['æbə͵saɪ, -kiː] or **abacuses** : boulier *m*

abaft [ə'bæft] *adv* : en poupe, sur l'arrière

abalone [͵æbə'loːni] *n* : ormeau *m*

abandon[1] [ə'bændən] *vt* **1** DESERT, FORSAKE : abandonner, délaisser **2** LEAVE : abandonner, quitter (un lieu) <abandon ship! : abandonnez le navire!> **3** GIVE UP, SUSPEND : renoncer à, laisser tomber <she abandoned her studies : elle a laissé tomber ses études> **4 to abandon oneself to** : se livrer à, s'abandonner à

abandon[2] *n* : abandon *m,* désinvolture *m*

abandoned [ə'bændənd] *adj* **1** DESERTED : abandonné, délaissé **2** UNRESTRAINED : sans retenue

abandonment [ə'bændənmənt] *n* : abandon *m*

abase [ə'beɪs] *vt* **abased; abasing** : abaisser, humilier

abasement [ə'beɪsmənt] *n* : abaissement *f,* humiliation *f*

abash [ə'bæʃ] *vt* : décontenancer, confondre

abashed [ə'bæʃt] *adj* : décontenancé, confondu

abate [ə'beɪt] *v* **abated; abating** *vt* REDUCE : baisser, réduire, diminuer — *vi* DECREASE : s'apaiser, se calmer, diminuer <the fever abated : la fièvre s'est calmée>

abatement [ə'beɪtmənt] *n* : apaisement *m,* diminution *f*

abattoir ['æbə͵twɑr] *n* : abattoir *m*

abbess ['æbɪs, -͵bɛs, -bəs] *n* : abbesse *f*

abbey ['æbi] *n, pl* **-beys** : abbaye *f*

abbot ['æbət] *n* : abbé *m*

abbreviate [ə'briːvi͵eɪt] *vt* **-ated; -ating** : abréger

abbreviation [ə͵briːvi'eɪʃən] *n* : abréviation *f*

abdicate ['æbdɪ͵keɪt] *v* **-cated; -cating** : abdiquer

abdication [͵æbdɪ'keɪʃən] *n* : abdication *f*

abdomen ['æbdəmən, æb'doːmən] *n* : abdomen *m*

abdominal [æb'dɑmənəl] *adj* : abdominal

abduct [æb'dʌkt] *vt* : enlever

abduction [æb'dʌkʃən] *n* : enlèvement *m*

abductor [æb'dʌktər] *n* : ravisseur *m,* -seuse *f*

abed [ə'bɛd] *adv & adj* : au lit, dans le lit

aberrant [æ'bɛrənt, 'æbərənt] *adj* : aberrant

aberration [͵æbə'reɪʃən] *n* : aberration *f*

abet [ə'bɛt] *vt* **abetted; abetting 1** ENCOURAGE : encourager, soutenir **2 to aid and abet** : être complice de

abettor *or* **abetter** [ə'bɛtər] *n* : complice *mf*

abeyance [ə'beɪənts] *n* **1** SUSPENSION : suspension *f,* interruption *f* **2 in ~** : en suspens

abhor [əb'hɔr, æb-] *vt* **-horred; -horring** : abhorrer, détester

abhorrence [əb'hɔrənts, æb-] *n* : horreur *f*

abhorrent [əb'hɔrənt, æb-] *adj* : odieux, détestable

abide [ə'baɪd] *v* **abode** [ə'boːd] *or* **abided; abiding** *vt* STAND, TOLERATE : endurer, supporter — *vi* **1** LAST : continuer, durer **2** RESIDE : demeurer, habiter **3 to abide by** : respecter, se conformer à

ability [ə'bɪləṭi] *n, pl* **-ties 1** CAPABILITY : capacité *f,* aptitude *f* **2** SKILL : habileté *f,* talent *m*

abject ['æb͵dʒɛkt, æb'-] *adj* **1** WRETCHED : abject, misérable **2** SERVILE : servile, obséquieux — **abjectly** *adv*

ablaze [ə'bleɪz] *adj* **1** BURNING : en flammes, en feu **2** RADIANT : brillant, resplendissant

able ['eɪbəl] *adj* **abler; ablest 1** CAPABLE : capable **2** SKILLED : compétent, habile

able–bodied [͵eɪbəl'bɑdid] *n* : robuste, vigoureux

ably ['eɪbəli] *adv* : habilement

abnormal [æb'nɔrmel] *adj* : anormal — **abnormally** *adv*

abnormality [͵æbnər'mæləṭi, -nɔr-] *n, pl* **-ties** : anormalité *f* (état), anomalie *f* (trait)

aboard[1] [ə'bord] *adv* : à bord

aboard[2] *prep* : à bord de, dans <aboard the train : dans le train>

abode [ə'boːd] *n* : demeure *f,* domicile *m*

abolish [ə'bɑlɪʃ] *vt* : supprimer, abolir

abolition [͵æbə'lɪʃən] *n* : abolition *f,* suppression *f*

abominable [ə'bɑmənəbəl] *adj* : abominable

abominate [ə͵bɑmə'neɪʃən] *vt* **-nated; -nating** : abhorrer, abominer

abomination [ə'bɑməneɪt] *n* : abomination *f*

aboriginal [͵æbə'rɪdʒənəl] *adj* : aborigène, indigène

aborigine [͵æbə'rɪdʒəni] *n* : aborigène *mf*

abort [ə'bɔrt] *vt* **1** TERMINATE : faire avorter **2** SUSPEND : abandonner, interrompre — *vi* : avorter

abortion [ə'bɔrʃən] *n* : avortement *m*

abortive [ə'bɔrṭɪv] *adj* **1** : avorté, manqué <abortive efforts : efforts avortés> **2** : abortif <abortive agent : agent abortif>

abound [ə'baʊnd] *vi* : abonder

about[1] [ə'baʊt] *adv* **1** APPROXIMATELY : vers, environ, à peu près **2** AROUND : autour, à la ronde <he looked all about : il regardait tout autour> **3** NEARBY : près, par ici, par là **4** : de tous côtés, ça et là, ici et là <books lying all about : des livres de tous côtés> **5** ALMOST : tout juste, à peu près, presque **6 to be about to** : être sur le point de

about[2] *prep* **1** AROUND : autour de, par, dans <to walk about the city : se promener dans la ville> **2** CONCERNING : sur, de, concernant <a book about jazz : un livre sur le jazz> <he's talking about me : il parle de moi> <what's it about? : de quoi s'agit-il?>

above[1] [ə'bʌv] *adv* **1** OVERHEAD : au-dessus, en haut **2** : ci-dessus, plus haut <as mentioned above : comme cité ci-dessus>

above[2] *prep* **1** OVER : au-dessus de, en haut de **2** EXCEEDING : plus de, au-dessus de <above one hundred applicants : plus de cent candidats> **3** BEYOND : au-delà de <above the call of duty : au-delà du strict devoir>

aboveboard[1] [ə'bʌv'bord, -ˌbord] *adv* : ouvertement, franchement

aboveboard[2] *adj* : ouvert, franc

abrade [ə'breɪd] *vt* **abraded; abrading** **1** SCRAPE : érafler (la peau), user en frottant **2** IRRITATE : agacer, irriter

abrasion [ə'breɪʒən] *n* **1** ABRADING : abrasion *f* **2** SCRATCH : écorchure *f*, éraflure *f*

abrasive[1] [ə'breɪsɪv] *adj* : abrasif

abrasive[2] *n* : abrasif *m*

abreast [ə'brɛst] *adv* **1** : de front, côte à côte <two abreast : à deux de front> **2 to keep abreast of** : se tenir au courant de

abridge [ə'brɪdʒ] *vt* **abridged; abridging** : abréger

abridgment *or* **abridgement** [ə'brɪdʒmənt] *n* **1** ABRIDGING : abrégement *m* **2** SUMMARY : abrégé *m*, résumé *m*

abroad [ə'brɔd] *adv* **1** WIDELY : au loin, de tous côtés <to spread abroad : circuler de tous côtés> **2** OVERSEAS : à l'étranger

abrupt [ə'brʌpt] *adj* **1** SUDDEN : soudain, précipité **2** CURT : abrupt, brusque **3** STEEP : escarpé, abrupt

abruptly [ə'brʌptli] *adv* : brusquement, tout d'un coup

abscess ['æbˌsɛs] *n* : abcès *m*

abscond [æb'skɑnd] *vi* : s'enfuir

absence ['æbsənts] *n* **1** : absence *f* (d'une personne) **2** LACK : manque *m*

absent[1] [æb'sɛnt] *vt* **to absent oneself** : s'absenter

absent[2] ['æbsənt] *adj* : absent

absentee [ˌæbsən'tiː] *n* : absent *m*, -sente *f*

absentminded [ˌæbsənt'maɪndəd] *adj* : distrait, préoccupé

absentmindedly [ˌæbsənt'maɪndədli] *adv* : d'un air distrait, distraitement

absentmindedness [ˌæbsənt'maɪndədnəs] *n* : distraction *f*

absolute ['æbsəˌluːt, ˌæbsə'luːt] *adj* **1** COMPLETE, PERFECT : absolu, total, parfait **2** UNCONDITIONAL : absolu, inconditionnel **3** DEFINITE : formel, définitif

absolutely ['æbsəˌluːtli, ˌæbsə'luːtli] *adv* **1** : absolument, tout à fait **2 absolutely not** : pas du tout

absolution [ˌæbsə'luːʃən] *n* : absolution *f*

absolve [əb'zɑlv, æb-, -'sɑlv] *vt* **-solved; -solving** : absoudre

absorb [əb'zɔrb, æb-, -'sɔrb] *vt* **1** : absorber (des liquides), amortir (des chocs, des sons, etc.), assimiler (personnes) **2 to become absorbed in** : s'absorber dans

absorbency [əb'zɔrbəntsi, æb-, -'sɔr-] *n, pl* **-cies** : pouvoir *m* absorbant

absorbent [əb'zɔrbənt, æb-, -'sɔr-] *adj* : absorbant

absorbing [əb'zɔrbɪŋ, æb-, -'sɔr-] *adj* : absorbant, fascinant

absorption [əb'zɔrpʃən, æb-, -'sɔrp-] *n* **1** : absorption *f* (des liquides), amortissement *m* (d'un choc, etc.) **2** CONCENTRATION : concentration *f* (d'esprit)

abstain [əb'steɪn, æb-] *vi* : s'abstenir

abstemious [æb'stiːmiəs] *adj* : sobre, frugal — **abstemiously** *adv*

abstemiousness [æb'stiːmiəsnəs] *n* : sobriété *f*, tempérence *f*

abstention [əb'stɛntʃən, æb-] *n* : abstention *f*

abstinence ['æbstənənts] *n* : abstinence *f*

abstinent ['æbstənənt] *adj* : sobre, frugal, modéré

abstract[1] [æb'strækt, 'æbˌ-] *vt* **1** REMOVE : extraire, retirer **2** SUMMARIZE : résumer

abstract[2] *adj* : abstrait — **abstractly** [æb'stræktli, 'æbˌ-] *adv*

abstract[3] ['æbˌstrækt] *n* **1** SUMMARY : résumé *m* **2** : abstrait *m* <in the abstract : dans l'abstrait>

abstraction [æb'strækʃən] *n* **1** : abstraction *f*, idée *f* abstraite **2** REMOVAL : extraction *f* **3** PREOCCUPATION : préoccupation *f*, distraction *f*

abstruse [əb'struːs, æb-] *adj* : abstrus

absurd [əb'sərd, -'zərd] *adj* : absurde, ridicule, insensé

absurdity [əb'sərdət̬i, -'zər-] *n, pl* **-ties** : absurdité *f,* ridicule *m*
absurdly [əb'sərdli, -'zərd-] *adv* : ridiculement, de manière insensée
abundance [ə'bʌndənts] *n* : abondance *f,* profusion *f*
abundant [ə'bʌndənt] *adj* : abondant
abundantly [ə'bʌndəntli] *adv* : abondamment, en profusion
abuse[1] [ə'bju:z] *vt* **abused; abusing 1** MISUSE : abuser de **2** MISTREAT : maltraiter **3** INSULT : injurier, insulter
abuse[2] [ə'bju:s] *n* **1** MISUSE : abus *m* **2** MISTREATMENT : abus *m,* mauvais traitement *m* **3** INSULTS : insultes *fpl,* injures *fpl*
abusive [ə'bju:sɪv] *adj* **1** IMPROPER : abusif **2** HURTFUL : injurieux, brutal **3** OFFENSIVE : grossier — **abusively** *adv*
abut [ə'bʌt] *v* **abutted; abutting** *vt* : juxtaposer — *vi* **to abut on** : être contigu à
abutment [ə'bʌtmənt] *n* : contrefort *m,* butée *f*
abysmal [ə'bɪzməl] *adj* **1** DEEP : abyssal, insondable **2** WRETCHED : épouvantable
abysmally [ə'bɪzməli] *adv* : atrocement, abominablement
abyss [ə'bɪs, 'æbɪs] *n* : abîme *m,* gouffre *m*
acacia [ə'keɪʃə] *n* : acacia *m*
academic[1] [ˌækə'dɛmɪk] *adj* **1** SCHOLASTIC : académique, scolaire <the academic year : l'année scolaire> **2** THEORETICAL : théorique
academic[2] *n* : universitaire *mf*
academically [ˌækə'dɛmɪkli] *adv* : sur le plan intellectuel, intellectuellement
academy [ə'kædəmi] *n, pl* **-mies 1** SCHOOL : école *f,* collège *m* **2** SOCIETY : académie *f,* société *f* <the French Academy : l'Académie française>
acanthus [ə'kæntθəs] *ns & pl* : acanthe *f*
accede [æk'si:d] *vi* **-ceded; -ceding 1** : monter <to accede to the throne : monter sur le trône> **2 to accede to** : agréer, accepter <she acceded to his request : elle a agréé sa demande>
accelerate [ɪk'sɛləˌreɪt, æk-] *v* **-ated; -ating** : accélérer
acceleration [ɪkˌsɛlə'reɪʃən, æk-] *n* : accélération *f*
accelerator [ɪk'sɛləˌreɪt̬ər, æk-] *n* : accélérateur *m*
accent[1] ['ækˌsɛnt, æk'sɛnt] *vt* : accentuer
accent[2] ['ækˌsɛnt, -sənt] *n* : accent *m* <a Russian accent : un accent russe> <to put the accent on : mettre l'accent sur>
accentuate [ɪk'sɛntʃʊˌeɪt, æk-] *vt* **-ated; -ating** : accentuer, souligner
accept [ɪk'sɛpt, æk-] *vt* **1** : accepter <to accept a present : accepter un cadeau> **2** ACKNOWLEDGE : accepter, admettre
acceptability [ɪkˌsɛptə'bɪlət̬i, æk-] *n* : acceptabilité *f*
acceptable [ɪk'sɛptəbəl, æk-] *adj* : acceptable
acceptably [ɪk'sɛptəbli] *adv* : passablement, suffisamment
acceptance [ɪk'sɛptənts, æk-] *n* **1** ACCEPTING : acceptation *f* **2** APPROVAL : approbation *f*
access[1] ['ækˌsɛs] *vt* : accéder à
access[2] *n* : accès *m* <no access : accès interdit>
accessibility [ɪkˌsɛsə'bɪlət̬i] *n* : accessibilité *f*
accessible [ɪk'sɛsəbəl, æk-] *adj* : accessible
accession [ɪk'sɛʃən, æk-] *n* **1** : accession *f* <accession to the throne : accession au trône> **2** INCREASE : augmentation *f* **3** ACQUISITION : acquisition *f*
accessory[1] [ɪk'sɛsəri, æk-] *adj* : accessoire, auxiliaire
accessory[2] *n, pl* **-ries 1** ACCOMPLICE : complice *mf* **2** ADJUNCT : accessoire *m*
accident ['æksədənt] *n* **1** MISHAP : accident *m* **2** CHANCE : hasard *m,* chance *f* <by accident : par hasard>
accidental [ˌæksə'dɛntəl] *adj* : accidentel, fortuit
accidentally [ˌæksə'dɛntəli, -'dɛntli] *adv* : accidentellement, par hasard
acclaim[1] [ə'kleɪm] *vt* **1** PRAISE : acclamer **2** DECLARE, PROCLAIM : proclamer
acclaim[2] *n* : acclamation *f,* louange *f*
acclamation [ˌæklə'meɪʃən] *n* : acclamation *f* <elected by acclamation : élu par acclamation>
acclimate ['ækləˌmeɪt, ə'klaɪmət] → **acclimatize**
acclimatize [ə'klaɪməˌtaɪz] *vt* **-tized; -tizing 1** : acclimater **2 to acclimatize oneself** : s'acclimater
accolade ['ækəˌleɪd, -ˌlɑd] *n* : acclamation *f,* accolade *f*
accommodate [ə'kɑməˌdeɪt] *vt* **-dated; -dating 1** ADAPT : accommoder, adapter **2** RECONCILE : concilier **3** SATISFY : satisfaire, répondre aux besoins de **4** HOLD : contenir, avoir une capacité de
accommodation [əˌkɑmə'deɪʃən] *n* **1** ADJUSTMENT : accommodation *f,* adaptation *f* **2 accomodations** *npl* LODGING : logement *m,* hébergement *m*
accompaniment [ə'kʌmpənəmənt, -'kɑm-] *n* : accompagnement *m*
accompanist [ə'kʌmpənɪst, -'kɑm-] *n* : accompagnateur *m,* -trice *f*
accompany [ə'kʌmpəni, -'kɑm-] *vt* **-nied; -nying** : accompagner
accomplice [ə'kɑmpləs, -'kʌm-] *n* : complice *mf*

accomplish [əˈkɑmplɪʃ, -ˈkʌm-] *vt* : accomplir, réaliser

accomplished [əˈkɑmplɪʃt, -ˈkʌm-] *adj* : accompli <an accomplished pianist : un pianiste accompli>

accomplishment [əˈkɑmplɪʃmənt, -ˈkʌm-] *n* **1** COMPLETION : réalisation *f,* accomplissement *m* **2** ACHIEVEMENT : œuvre *f* accomplie, réussite *f* **3** SKILL : talent *m*

accord[1] [əˈkɔrd] *vt* CONCEDE, GRANT : accorder, concéder — *vi* AGREE : s'accorder, concorder

accord[2] *n* **1** AGREEMENT : accord *m* **2 of one's own accord** : de son plein gré, de soi-même

accordance [əˈkɔrdənts] *n* **1** ACCORD : accord *m,* conformité *f* **2 in accordance with** : conformément à, suivant

accordingly [əˈkɔrdɪŋli] *adv* **1** CORRESPONDINGLY : en conséquence <to act accordingly : agir en conséquence> **2** CONSEQUENTLY, THEREFORE : donc, par conséquent

according to [əˈkɔrdɪŋ] *prep* **1** : conformément à, selon, suivant <according to plan : conformément au plan prévu> **2** : selon, d'après <according to them : d'après eux>

accordion [əˈkɔrdiən] *n* : accordéon *m*

accordionist [əˈkɔrdiənɪst] *n* : accordéoniste *mf*

accost [əˈkɔst] *vt* : accoster, aborder

account[1] [əˈkaʊnt] *vt* CONSIDER : estimer, juger — *vi* **1 to account for** EXPLAIN : justifier, expliquer **2 to account for** REPRESENT : représenter

account[2] *n* **1** : compte *m* <bank account : compte bancaire> **2** REPORT : compte *m* rendu, exposé *m* **3** WORTH : importance *f* <to be of little account : avoir peu d'importance> **4 on account of** BECAUSE OF : à cause de **5 on no account** : en aucun cas, sous aucun prétexte **6 on one's account** : à cause de soi, à son sujet <don't worry on my account : ne t'inquiète pas à mon sujet> **7 to take into account** : tenir compte de

accountability [əˌkaʊntəˈbɪlət̬i] *n* : responsabilité *f*

accountable [əˈkaʊntəbəl] *adj* : responsable

accountant [əˈkaʊntənt] *n* : comptable *mf*

accounting [əˈkaʊntɪŋ] *n* : comptabilité *f*

accoutrements *or* **accouterments** [əˈkuːtrəmənts, -ˈkuːt̬ər-] *npl* **1** EQUIPMENT : équipement *m* **2** ACCESSORIES : accessoires *mpl* **3** TRAPPINGS : attributs *mpl* (du pouvoir, etc.)

accredit [əˈkrɛdət] *vt* : accréditer

accreditation [əˌkrɛdəˈteɪʃən] *n* : accréditation *f*

accrual [əˈkruːəl] *n* : accumulation *f*

accrue [əˈkruː] *vi* **-crued; -cruing 1** : s'accumuler **2 to accrue to** : revenir à

accumulate [əˈkjuːmjəˌleɪt] *v* **-lated; -lating** *vt* : accumuler — *vi* s'accumuler

accumulation [əˌkjuːmjəˈleɪʃən] *n* : accumulation *f*

accuracy [ˈækjərəsi] *n, pl* **-cies** : exactitude *f,* précision *f*

accurate [ˈækjərət] *adj* : exact, précis, juste — **accurately** *adv*

accuse [əˈkjuːz] *vt* **-cused; -cusing** : accuser

accused [əˈkjuːzd] *ns & pl* : accusé *m,* -sée *f;* inculpé *m,* -pée *f*

accuser [əˈkjuːzər] *n* : accusateur *m,* -trice *f*

accustom [əˈkʌstəm] *vt* **1** : habituer, accoutumer **2 to get accustomed to** : s'habituer à, s'accoutumer à

accustomed [əˈkʌstəmd] *adj* **1** USED : habitué, accoutumé **2** USUAL : habituel, familier

ace [ˈeɪs] *n* : as *m*

acerbic [əˈsərbɪk, æ-] *adj* : acerbe

acetate [ˈæsəˌteɪt] *n* : acétate *m*

acetylene [əˈsɛt̬ələn, -t̬əˌliːn] *n* : acétylène *m*

ache[1] [eɪk] *vi* **ached; aching 1** HURT : avoir mal, faire mal <he aches all over : il a mal partout> <my leg aches : ma jambe me fait mal> **2 to ache for** : avoir très envie de

ache[2] *n* : douleur *f,* mal *m*

achieve [əˈtʃiːv] *vt* **achieved; achieving** : accomplir, atteindre

achievement [əˈtʃiːvmənt] *n* : accomplissement *m,* réussite *f*

acid[1] [ˈæsəd] *adj* : acide

acid[2] *n* : acide *m*

acidic [əˈsɪdɪk, æ-] *adj* : acide

acidity [əˈsɪdət̬i, æ-] *n, pl* **-ties** : acidité *f*

acknowledge [ɪkˈnɑlɪdʒ, æk-] *vt* **-edged; -edging 1** ADMIT : admettre, reconnaître **2** RECOGNIZE : reconnaître **3** : remercier de, manifester sa gratitude pour <she acknowledged his help : elle l'a remercié de son assistance> **4 to acknowledge receipt of** : accuser réception de

acknowledgment [ɪkˈnɑlɪdʒmənt, æk-] *n* **1** RECOGNITION : reconnaissance *f* **2** THANKS : remerciement *m* **3 acknowledgment of receipt** : accusé *m* de réception

acme [ˈækmi] *n* : point *m* culminant, apogée *m*

acne [ˈækni] *n* : acné *f*

acorn [ˈeɪˌkɔrn, -kərn] *n* : gland *m*

acoustic [əˈkuːstɪk] *or* **acoustical** [əˈkuːstɪkəl] *adj* : acoustique — **acoustically** *adv*

acoustics [əˈkuːstɪks] *ns & pl* : acoustique *f*

acquaint [əˈkweɪnt] *vt* **1** INFORM : informer, aviser, renseigner **2 to be ac-**

quainted with : connaître (une personne, un lieu, etc.), être au courant de (un fait, une situation, etc.)
acquaintance [ə'kweɪntənts] *n* **1** KNOWLEDGE : connaissance *f* **2** : relation *f,* connaissance *f* <friends and acquaintances : amis et relations>
acquiesce [ˌækwi'ɛs] *vi* **-esced; -escing** : acquiescer
acquiescence [ˌækwi'ɛsənts] *n* : acquiescement *m*
acquire [ə'kwaɪr] *vt* **-quired; -quiring** : acquérir
acquisition [ˌækwə'zɪʃən] *n* : acquisition *f*
acquisitive [ə'kwɪzət̬ɪv] *adj* : âpre au gain, avide
acquit [ə'kwɪt] *vt* **-quitted; -quitting 1** : acquitter <to be acquitted of a crime : être disculpé d'un délit> **2 to acquit oneself** : se conduire, s'en tirer
acquittal [ə'kwɪt̬əl] *n* : acquittement *m*
acre ['eɪkər] *n* : acre *m*
acreage ['eɪkərɪdʒ] *n* : superficie *f*
acrid ['ækrəd] *adj* **1** PUNGENT : âcre **2** CAUSTIC : caustique, acerbe
acrimonious [ˌækrə'moːniəs] *adj* : acrimonieux — **acrimoniously** *adv*
acrimony ['ækrəˌmoːni] *n, pl* **-nies** : acrimonie *f*
acrobat ['ækrəˌbæt] *n* : acrobate *mf* — **acrobatic** [ˌækrə'bæt̬ɪk] *adj*
acrobatics [ˌækrə'bæt̬ɪks] *ns & pl* : acrobatie *f*
across[1] [ə'krɔs] *adv* **1** : de large <40 feet across : 40 pieds de large> **2 ~ from** : en face de **3 to get one's point across** : se faire comprendre
across[2] *prep* **1** : de l'autre côté de <the house across the street : la maison de l'autre côté de la rue> <to go across the mountain : traverser la montagne> **2** : en travers de <a tree (lying) across the stream : un arbre en travers du ruisseau>
acrylic [ə'krɪlɪk] *n* : acrylique *m*
act[1] ['ækt] *vt* PERFORM : jouer (un rôle) — *vi* **1** : agir <we must act quickly : il faut agir rapidement> **2** PERFORM : jouer, faire du théâtre **3** BEHAVE : agir, se comporter **4** : agir (en médecine) **5 to act as** : servir de, faire office de **6 to act on** : suivre (de l'avis, etc.)
act[2] *n* **1** DEED : action *f,* acte *m* **2** DECREE : loi *f* **3** : acte *m* <a three-act play : une pièce en trois actes> **4** PRETENSE : comédie *f* <to put on an act : jouer la comédie>
action ['ækʃən] *n* **1** ACT, DEED : action *f,* acte *m,* fait *m* **2** LAWSUIT : procès *m,* action *f* <to take legal action : poursuivre en justice> **3** COMBAT : combat *m* **4** PLOT : intrigue *f* **5** MOVEMENT : mouvement *m* **6** MECHANISM : mécanisme *m* **7 actions** *npl* CONDUCT : conduite *f,* actes *mpl*
activate ['æktəˌveɪt] *vt* **-vated; -vating** : activer
active ['æktɪv] *adj* : actif
actively ['æktɪvli] *adv* : activement
activity [æk'tɪvət̬i] *n, pl* **-ties** : activité *f*
actor ['æktər] *n* : acteur *m,* -trice *f;* comédien *m,* -dienne *f*
actress ['æktrəs] *n* : actrice *f,* comédienne *f*
actual ['æktʃuəl] *adj* **1** REAL : réel, véritable **2** VERY : même <the actual house where he was born : la maison même où il est né>
actuality [ˌæktʃu'æləti] *n, pl* **-ties** : réalité *f*
actually ['æktʃuəli, -ʃəli] *adv* : vraiment, en fait, en réalité
actuary ['æktʃuˌeri] *n, pl* **-aries** : actuaire *mf*
acumen [ə'kjuːmən] *n* : perspicacité *f,* finesse *f* <business acumen : sens des affaires>
acupuncture ['ækjuˌpʌŋktʃər] *n* : acupuncture *f*
acute [ə'kjuːt] *adj* **acuter; acutest 1** KEEN : fin <an acute sense of hearing : une ouïe fine> **2** PERCEPTIVE : perspicace, pénétrant **3** SEVERE : aigu, grave <an acute illness : une maladie grave> **4 acute accent** : accent *m* aigu **5 acute angle** : angle *m* aigu
acuteness [ə'kjuːtnəs] *n* **1** SEVERITY : violence *f* (d'une maladie) **2** : finesse *f* (d'un sens) **3** PERSPICACITY : perspicacité *f,* finesse *f*
ad ['æd] *n* **1** → **advertisement 2 classified ad** *or* **want ad** : petite annonce *f*
adage ['ædɪdʒ] *n* : adage *m*
adamant ['ædəmənt, -ˌmænt] *adj* : inflexible, résolu — **adamantly** *adv*
adapt [ə'dæpt] *vt* : adapter — *vi* : s'adapter
adaptability [əˌdæptə'bɪlət̬i] *n* : adaptabilité *f*
adaptable [əˌdæptəbəl] *adj* : adaptable
adaptation [ˌæˌdæp'teɪʃən, -dəp-] *n* : adaptation *f*
adapter [ə'dæptər] *n* : adapteur *m*
add ['æd] *vt* **1** : ajouter <I have nothing to add : je n'ai rien à ajouter> **2 to add up** TOTAL : additionner, totaliser — *vi* **1** : faire des additions **2 that doesn't add up** : cela ne s'accorde pas
adder ['ædər] *n* : vipère *f*
addict[1] [ə'dɪkt] *vt* **to be addicted to** : s'adonner à, avoir une dépendance à
addict[2] ['ædɪkt] *n* **1** DEVOTEE : fanatique *mf* **2** *or* **drug addict** : toxicomane *mf;* drogué *m,* -guée *f*
addiction [ə'dɪkʃən] *n* **1** : dépendance *f* **2 drug addiction** : toxicomanie *f*
addictive [ə'dɪktɪv] *adj* : qui crée une dépendance
addition [ə'dɪʃən] *n* **1** : ajout *m,* adjonction *f* (à une maison, une liste,

etc.) 2 : addition *f* (en mathématiques) 3 **in ~** : en plus

additional [ə'dɪʃənəl] *adj* : additionnel, supplémentaire

additionally [ə'dɪʃənəli] *adv* : en plus, en outre

additive ['ædət̬ɪv] *n* : additif *m*

addle ['ædəl] *vt* **-dled; -dling** : embrouiller

address[1] [ə'drɛs] *vt* **1** : adresser, mettre l'adresse sur (une lettre, etc.) **2** : s'adresser à <to address the chair : s'adresser au président> **3** TACKLE : aborder (un problème, etc.)

address[2] [ə'drɛs, 'æˌdrɛs] *n* **1** : adresse *f* <change of address : changement d'adresse> **2** SPEECH : discours *m*

addressee [ˌæˌdrɛ'si, əˌdrɛ'si] *n* : destinataire *mf*

adduce [ə'du:s, -'dju:s] *vt* **-duced; -ducing** : citer, alléguer

adenoids ['ædˌnɔɪdz, -dənˌɔɪdz] *npl* : végétations *fpl* (adénoïdes)

adept [ə'dɛpt] *adj* : expert, adroit, habile — **adeptly** *adv*

adequate ['ædɪkwət] *adj* : adéquat, suffisant

adequately ['ædɪkwətli] *adv* : suffisamment

adhere [æd'hir, əd-] *vi* **-hered; -hering 1** STICK : adhérer, coller **2 to adhere to** : adhérer à (un conviction, etc.), observer (une règle, etc.)

adherence [æd'hɪrənts, əd-] *n* : adhésion *f*

adherent [æd'hɪrənt, əd-] *n* FOLLOWER : partisan *m*, -sane *f*; adhérent *m*, -rente *f*

adhesion [æd'hiʒən, əd-] *n* : adhésion *f*, adhérence *f*

adhesive[1] [æd'hi:sɪv, əd-, -zɪv] *adj* : adhésif

adhesive[2] *n* : adhésif *m*

adjacent [ə'dʒeɪsənt] *adj* : contigu, voisin, adjacent

adjectival [ˌædʒɪk'taɪvəl] *adj* : adjectif, adjectival

adjective ['ædʒɪktɪv] *n* : adjectif *m*

adjoin [ə'dʒɔɪn] *vt* : avoisiner, être contigu à, toucher à — *vi* : être contigu, se toucher

adjoining [ə'dʒɔɪnɪŋ] *adj* : attenant, contigu

adjourn [ə'dʒərn] *vt* SUSPEND : ajourner, lever <to adjourn the meeting : lever la séance> — *vi* **1** : suspendre la séance, lever la séance **2** : se retirer, passer <they adjourned to another room : ils sont passés dans une autre pièce>

adjournment [ə'dʒərnmənt] *n* : ajournement *m*, suspension *f*

adjudicate [ə'dʒu:dɪˌkeɪt] *vt* **-cated; -cating** : juger, décider, régler

adjunct ['æˌdʒʌŋkt] *n* **1** ASSISTANT : adjoint *m*, -jointe *f* **2** ACCESSORY : accessoire *m*

adjust [ə'dʒʌst] *vt* : régler, ajuster — *vi* ADAPT : s'adapter

adjustable [ə'dʒʌstəbəl] *adj* : réglable, ajustable

adjustment [ə'dʒʌstmənt] *n* : ajustement *m*, réglage *m*

adjutant ['ædʒətənt] *n* : adjudant *m* (dans les forces armées)

ad–lib[1] ['æd'lɪb] *vt* **ad–libbed; ad–libbing** : improviser

ad–lib[2] *adj* : improvisé, spontané

ad–lib[3] *n* : improvisation *f*

administer [æd'mɪnəstər, əd-] *vt* : administrer, diriger, gérer

administration [ædˌmɪnə'streɪʃən, əd-] *n* **1** MANAGING : administration *f*, gestion *f* **2** GOVERNMENT, MANAGEMENT : gouvernement *m*, direction *f*

administrative [æd'mɪnəˌstreɪt̬ɪv, əd-] *adj* : administratif — **administratively** *adv*

administrator [æd'mɪnəˌstreɪt̬ər, əd-] *n* : administrateur *m*, -trice *f*

admirable ['ædmərəbəl] *adj* : admirable — **admirably** *adv*

admiral ['ædmərəl] *n* : amiral *m*

admiration [ˌædmə'reɪʃən] *n* : admiration *f*

admire [æd'maɪr] *vt* **-mired; -miring** : admirer

admirer [æd'maɪrər] *n* : admirateur *m*, -trice *f*

admiring [æd'maɪrɪŋ] *adj* : admiratif

admiringly [æd'maɪrɪŋli] *adv* : avec admiration, admirativement

admissible [æd'mɪsəbəl] *adj* : admissible

admission [æd'mɪʃən] *n* **1** ADMITTANCE : admission *f*, entrée *f*, accès *m* <no admission : accès interdit> <admission is free : l'entrée est gratuite> **2** CONFESSION : aveu *m* <by her own admission : de son propre aveu>

admit [æd'mɪt, əd-] *vt* **-mitted; -mitting 1** ACKNOWLEDGE : admettre, reconnaître, avouer <he admits his guilt : il reconnaît sa culpabilité> **2** : laisser entrer, laisser passer, admettre <to admit light : laisser entrer la lumière> <admitted to the hospital : admis à l'hôpital> <the ticket admits one : le billet est valable pour une personne>

admittance [æd'mɪtənts, əd-] *n* : entrée *f*, admission *f*, accès *m*

admittedly [æd'mɪt̬ədli, əd-] *adv* : il faut en convenir, c'est vrai

admonish [æd'mɑnɪʃ, əd-] *vt* **1** REPRIMAND : admonester, réprimander **2** ADVISE, EXHORT : conseiller, exhorter

admonition [ˌædmə'nɪʃən] *n* **1** REPROOF : réprimande *f*, admonition *f* **2** WARNING : avertissement *m*

ado [ə'du:] *n* **1** FUSS : agitation *f* **2 without further ado** : sans plus de cérémonie

adobe [ə'do:bi] *n* : adobe *m*

adolescence [ˌædəlˈɛsənts] *n* : adolescence *f*
adolescent[1] [ˌædəlˈɛsənt] *adj* : adolescent, de l'adolescence
adolescent[2] *n* : adolescent *m,* -cente *f*
adopt [əˈdɑpt] *vt* : adopter
adoption [əˈdɑpʃən] *n* : adoption *f*
adorable [əˈdorəbəl] *adj* : adorable — **adorably** [-rəbli] *adv*
adoration [ˌædəˈreɪʃən] *n* : adoration *f*
adore [əˈdor] *vt* **adored; adoring** : adorer
adorn [əˈdɔrn] *vt* **1** DECORATE : orner, parer **2 to adorn oneself** : se parer
adornment [əˈdɔrnmənt] *n* : ornement *m,* décoration *f*
adrift [əˈdrɪft] *adv & adj* : à la dérive
adroit [əˈdrɔɪt] *adj* : adroit, habile — **adroitly** *adv*
adroitness [əˈdrɔɪtnəs] *n* : adresse *f,* habileté *f*
adult[1] [əˈdʌlt, ˈæˌdʌlt] *adj* : adulte
adult[2] *n* : adulte *mf*
adulterate [əˈdʌltəˌreɪt] *vt* **-ated; -ating** : frelater, falsifier
adulterer [əˈdʌltərər] *n* : adultère *m*
adulteress [əˈdʌltərəs] *n* : adultère *f*
adulterous [əˈdʌltərəs] *adj* : adultère
adultery [əˈdʌltəri] *n, pl* **-teries** : adultère *m*
adulthood [əˈdʌltˌhʊd] *n* : âge *m* adulte
advance[1] [ædˈvænts, əd-] *v* **-vanced; -vancing** *vt* **1** : avancer, faire avancer <to advance the troops : avancer les troupes> **2** PROMOTE : promouvoir, servir (une cause, etc.) **3** PROPOSE : avancer (une théorie, etc.) **4** : avancer, faire une avance de (une somme d'argent) — *vi* **1** PROCEED : avancer **2** PROGRESS : progresser
advance[2] *adj* : fait à l'avance
advance[3] *n* **1** PROGRESSION : avance *f* **2** PROGRESS : progrès *m* <advances in medicine : des progrès en médecine> **3** INCREASE : hausse *f,* augmentation *f* **4 in ~** : à l'avance, d'avance **5 in advance of** : avant, en avance sur
advanced [ædˈvæntst, əd-] *adj* **1** : avancé <the advanced stages : les étapes avancées> **2** SUPERIOR : supérieur, avancé <advanced technology : technologie de pointe>
advancement [ædˈvæntsmənt, əd-] *n* : avancement *m*
advantage [ədˈvæntɪdʒ, æd-] *n* **1** : avantage *m* **2 to take advantage of** : profiter de
advantageous [ˌædˌvænˈteɪdʒəs, -vən-] *adj* : avantageux — **advantageously** *adv*
advent [ˈædˌvɛnt] *n* **1** : avènement *m,* venue *f,* arrivée *f* <the advent of spring : la venue du printemps> **2 Advent** : l'avent *m*
adventure [ædˈvɛntʃər, əd-] *n* : aventure *f*
adventurer [ædˈvɛntʃərər, əd-] *n* : aventurier *m,* -rière *f*
adventuresome [ædˈvɛntʃərsəm, əd-] *adj* : téméraire, aventureux
adventurous [ædˈvɛntʃərəs, əd-] *adj* **1** : aventureux <adventurous explorers : explorateurs aventureux> **2** RISKY : hasardeux, dangereux <an adventurous voyage : un voyage hasardeux>
adverb [ˈædˌvərb] *n* : adverbe *m* — **adverbial** [ædˈvɛrbiəl] *adj*
adversary [ˈædvərˌsɛri] *n, pl* **-saries** : adversaire *mf*
adverse [ædˈvɛrs, ˈædˌ-] *adj* : adverse, défavorable <in adverse circumstances : dans l'adversité>
adversity [ædˈvərsəṭi, əd-] *n, pl* **-ties** : adversité *f*
advertise [ˈædvərˌtaɪz] *v* **-tised; -tising** *vt* **1** : faire de la publicité pour (un produit) **2** : mettre une annonce pour (un poste, etc.) **3** PUBLICIZE : afficher, signaler — *vi* **1** : faire de la publicité (en commerce) **2** : passer une annonce <to advertise on television : passer une annonce à la télévision>
advertisement [ˈædvərˌtaɪzmənt; ædˈvərtəzmənt] *n* **1** : publicité *f,* annonce *f* (publicitaire), réclame *f* **2** → **ad**
advertiser [ˈædvərˌtaɪzɛr] *n* : annonceur *m* (publicitaire)
advertising [ˈædvərˌtaɪzɪŋ] *n* : publicité *f,* réclame *f*
advice [ædˈvaɪs] *n* **1** COUNSEL : conseils *mpl,* avis *m* **2** NOTICE : avis *m,* annonce *f*
advisability [ædˌvaɪzəˈbɪləṭi, əd-] *n* : opportunité *f*
advisable [ædˈvaɪzəbəl, əd-] *adj* : recommandé, prudent
advise [ædˈvaɪz, əd-] *v* **-vised; -vising** *vt* **1** COUNSEL : conseiller, donner des conseils à **2** RECOMMEND : recommander <they advised caution : ils ont recommandé la prudence> **3** INFORM : aviser — *vi* **to advise on** : conseiller sur
adviser [ædˈvaɪzər, əd-] *or* **advisor** *n* : conseiller *m,* -lère *f*
advisory [ædˈvaɪzəri, əd-] *adj* : consultatif <in an advisory capacity : à titre consultatif>
advocate[1] [ˈædvəˌkeɪt] *vt* **-cated; -cating** : recommander, préconiser
advocate[2] [ˈædvəkət] *n* **1** SUPPORTER : défenseur *m;* avocat *m,* -cate *f;* partisan *m,* -sane *f* **2** ATTORNEY : avocat *m,* -cate *f*
adze [ˈædz] *n* : herminette *f*
aegis [ˈiːdʒəs] *n* : égide *f*
aeon [ˈiːən, ˈiːˌɑn] *n* : éternité *f*
aerate [ˈærˌeɪt] *vt* **-ated; -ating** : aérer
aeration [ˌærˈeɪʃən] *n* : aération *f*
aerial[1] [ˈæriəl] *adj* : aérien
aerial[2] *n* : antenne *f*
aerie [ˈæri, ˈɪri, ˈeɪəri] *n* : aire *f* (d'aigle)

aerobic [ˌær'oːbɪk] *adj* : aérobie, aérobique *Can*
aerobics [ˌær'oːbɪks] *ns & pl* : aérobic *m*
aerodynamic [ˌæroːdaɪ'næmɪk] *adj* : aérodynamique — **aerodynamically** *adv*
aerodynamics [ˌæroːdaɪ'næmɪks] *ns & pl* : aérodynamique *f*
aeronautical [ˌærə'nɔţɪkəl] *adj* : aéronautique
aeronautics [ˌærə'nɔţɪks] *n* : aéronautique *f*
aerosol ['ærəˌsɔl] *n* : aérosol *m*
aerospace ['æroˌspeɪs] *adj* : aérospatial <the aerospace industry : l'industrie aérospatiale>
aesthetic [ɛs'θɛţɪk] *adj* : esthétique — **aesthetically** [-ţɪkli] *adv*
aesthetics [ɛs'θɛţɪks] *ns & pl* : esthétique *f*
afar [ə'fɑr] *adv* **1** : au loin, à distance **2 from ~** : de loin
affability [ˌæfə'bɪləţi] *n* : affabilité *f*
affable ['æfəbəl] *adj* : affable — **affably** *adv*
affair [ə'fær] *n* **1** : affaire *f* <their affairs are in order : leurs affaires sont réglées> <a grand affair : une affaire prestigieuse> **2** *or* **love affair** : liaison *f*, affaire *f* de cœur
affect [ə'fɛkt, æ-] *vt* **1** INFLUENCE : affecter, influencer **2** FEIGN : affecter, feindre **3** MOVE : émouvoir, toucher
affectation [ˌæˌfɛk'teɪʃən] *n* : affectation *f*
affected [ə'fɛktəd, æ-] *adj* **1** MANNERED : affecté, maniéré **2** MOVED : ému, touché
affectedly [ə'fɛktədli] *adv* : avec affectation
affecting [ə'fɛktɪŋ, æ-] *adj* MOVING : touchant, émouvant
affection [ə'fɛkʃən] *n* : affection *f*
affectionate [ə'fɛkʃənət] *adj* : affectueux — **affectionately** *adv*
affidavit [ˌæfə'deɪvət, 'æfəˌ-] *n* : déclaration *f* (écrite) sous serment
affiliate[1] [ə'fɪliˌeɪt] *vt* **-ated; -ating** : affilier
affiliate[2] [ə'fɪliət] *n* : filiale *f* (organisation); affilié *m*, -liée *f* (personne)
affiliation [əˌfɪli'eɪʃən] *n* : affiliation *f*
affinity [ə'fɪnəţi] *n, pl* **-ties** : affinité *f*
affirm [ə'fərm] *vt* : affirmer, soutenir
affirmation [ˌæfər'meɪʃən] *n* : affirmation *f*
affirmative[1] [ə'fərməţɪv] *adj* : affirmatif — **affirmatively** *adv*
affirmative[2] *n* **1** : affirmatif *m* (en grammaire) **2** : affirmative *f* <to answer in the affirmative : répondre par l'affirmative, répondre affirmativement>
affix [ə'fɪks] *vt* : apposer (une signature), coller (un timbre)
afflict [ə'flɪkt] *vt* **1** : affliger **2 to be afflicted with** : souffrir de, être touché de
affliction [ə'flɪkʃən] *n* : affliction *f*
affluence ['æˌfluːənts; æ'fluː-, ə-] *n* **1** WEALTH : richesse *f* **2** PROFUSION : abondance *f*
affluent ['æˌfluːənt; æ'fluː-, ə-] *adj* **1** WEALTHY : riche, aisé **2** ABUNDANT, PROFUSE : abondant
afford [ə'ford] *vt* **1** : avoir les moyens de <he can't afford to buy a car : il n'a pas les moyens d'acheter une voiture> **2** PROVIDE : fournir, offrir **3** : se permettre <I can't afford to wait : je ne peux pas me permettre d'attendre>
affront[1] [ə'frʌnt] *vt* : offenser, insulter
affront[2] *n* : affront *m*, insulte *f*
afghan ['æfˌgæn, -gən] *n* : couverture *f* en lainage
Afghan[1] *adj* : afghan
Afghan[2] *n* : Afghan *m*, -ghane *f*
afire[1] [ə'faɪr] *adv* **1** : en feu **2 to set afire** : mettre le feu à, embraser
afire[2] *adj* : en feu, embrasé
aflame [ə'fleɪm] *adj & adv* : en flammes
afloat [ə'floːt] *adj & adv* : à flot
afoot [ə'fʊt] *adv & adj* **1** WALKING : à pied **2** UNDER WAY : en train
aforesaid [ə'forˌsɛd] *adj* : susmentionné
afraid [ə'freɪd] *adj* **1 to be afraid of** FEAR : avoir peur de, craindre <he's afraid of falling : il a peur de tomber> **2** (*indicating regret*) <I'm afraid I can't come : je regrette de ne pas pouvoir venir> <I'm afraid not : hélas, non>
afresh [ə'frɛʃ] *adv* **1** ANEW : de nouveau **2 to start afresh** : recommencer
African[1] ['æfrɪkən] *adj* : africain
African[2] *n* : Africain *m*, -caine *f*
aft ['æft] **adv** : l'arrière
after[1] ['æftər] *adv* **1** AFTERWARD : après, ensuite **2** BEHIND : en arrière
after[2] *adj* (*indicating a later time*) <in after years : plus tard dans la vie>
after[3] *conj* : après que <after he leaves : après qu'il part>
after[4] *prep* **1** FOLLOWING : après <after lunch : après le déjeuner> <day after day : tous les jours> <after four o'clock : après quatre heures> **2** BEHIND : derrière, après <close the door after me : fermez la porte derrière moi> **3** (*indicating pursuit*) <he was running after the cat : il courait après le chat> <the police are after me : je suis recherché par la police> **4 after all** : après tout
aftereffect ['æftərɪˌfɛkt] *n* : répercussion *f*, séquelle *f* (en médecine)
afterlife ['æftərˌlaɪf] *n* : vie *f* future, vie *f* après la mort
aftermath ['æftərˌmæθ] *n* CONSEQUENCES : suites *fpl*

afternoon [ˌæftərˈnuːn] *n* : après-midi *mf*

afterthought [ˈæftərˌθɔt] *n* : pensée *f* après coup

afterward [ˈæftərwərd] *or* **afterwards** [-wərdz] *adv* : après, ensuite <soon afterward : peu après>

again [əˈgɛn, -gɪn] *adv* **1** : encore (une fois), de nouveau <say it again : dites-le encore> <again and again : maintes et maintes fois> **2** BESIDES : en plus, d'ailleurs **3 then again** : d'autre part

against [əˈgɛntst, -ˈgɪntst] *prep* **1** : contre <against the wall : contre le mur> <a war against drugs : une guerre contre les drogues> **2** : sur <red flowers against the blue sky : des fleurs rouges sur un ciel bleu> **3 to go against** : aller à l'encontre

agape [əˈgeɪp] *adj* : bouche bée

agate [ˈægət] *n* : agate *f*

age[1] [ˈeɪdʒ] *v* : vieillir

age[2] *n* **1** : âge *m* <what age is she? : quel âge a-t-elle?> <she's 16 years of age : elle a 16 ans> **2** ERA : ère *f*, époque *f* **3 for ages** : depuis longtemps **4 to come of age** : atteindre la majorité **5 old age** : vieillesse *f*

aged [ˈeɪdʒəd, ˈeɪdʒd] *adj* **1** : âgé de <a man aged 40 years : un homme âgé de 40 ans> **2** : âgé, vieux (se dit du vin, du fromage, etc.) **3** [ˈeɪdʒd] OLD : vieux, âgé <my aged mother : ma vieille mère>

ageless [ˈeɪdʒləs] *adj* **1** : sans âge, toujours jeune **2** TIMELESS : éternel

agency [ˈeɪdʒəntsi] *n, pl* **-cies 1** : agence *f*, bureau *m* <travel agency : agence de voyages> **2 through the agency of** : par l'entremise de

agenda [əˈdʒɛndə] *n* : ordre *m* du jour, programme *m*

agent [ˈeɪdʒənt] *n* : agent *m*

aggravate [ˈægrəˌveɪt] *vt* **-vated; -vating 1** WORSEN : aggraver, empirer **2** IRRITATE : agacer, énerver

aggravation [ˌægrəˈveɪʃən] *n* **1** WORSENING : aggravation *f* **2** IRRITATION : agacement *m*, irritation *f*

aggregate[1] [ˈægrɪˌgeɪt] *vt* **-gated; -gating** : agréger, rassembler — *vi* : s'agréger

aggregate[2] [ˈægrɪgət] *adj* : total, global

aggregate[3] [ˈægrɪgət] *n* **1** TOTAL : ensemble *m*, total *m* **2** MASS : agrégat *m* (en géologie, etc.)

aggression [əˈgrɛʃən] *n* : agression *f*

aggressive [əˈgrɛsɪv] *adj* : agressif — **aggressively** *adv*

aggressiveness [əˈgrɛsɪvnəs] *n* : agressivité *f*

aggressor [əˈgrɛsər] *n* : agresseur *m*

aggrieved [əˈgriːvd] *adj* **1** DISTRESSED : affligé, peiné **2 the aggrieved party** : la partie lésée

aghast [əˈgæst] *adj* : horrifié, atterré

agile [ˈædʒəl] *adj* : agile, leste

agility [əˈdʒɪləṭi] *n, pl* **-ties** : agilité *f*

agitate [ˈædʒəˌteɪt] *v* **-tated; -tating** *vt* **1** SHAKE : agiter, secouer **2** TROUBLE : agiter, troubler — *vi* **to agitate against** : faire campagne contre

agitation [ˌædʒəˈteɪʃən] *n* : agitation *f*

agnostic[1] [ægˈnɑstɪk] *adj* : agnostique

agnostic[2] *n* : agnostique *mf*

ago [əˈgoː] *adv* : il y a <a week ago : il y a une semaine> <not long ago : il y a peu de temps>

agog [əˈgɑg] *adj* : en émoi

agonize [ˈægəˌnaɪz] *vi* **-nized; -nizing** : se tourmenter

agonizing [ˈægəˌnaɪzɪŋ] *adj* PAINFUL : douloureux, déchirant

agony [ˈægəni] *n, pl* **-nies 1** : angoisse *f*, douleur *f* atroce **2 death agony** : agonie *f*

agrarian [əˈgrɛriən] *adj* : agraire

agree [əˈgriː] *v* **agreed; agreeing** *vt* **1** ACKNOWLEDGE, ADMIT : convenir, reconnaître <I agree that you should go : je reconnais que vous devriez y aller> **2** CONSENT : accepter, consentir — *vi* **1** CONCUR : être d'accord **2** CONSENT : consentir **3** CORRESPOND, TALLY : correspondre, concorder **4 to agree with** : réussir à, convenir (bien) à <spicy food doesn't agree with me : la nourriture épicée ne me réussit pas>

agreeable [əˈgriːəbəl] *adj* **1** PLEASING : agréable **2** WILLING : consentant <to be agreeable to : être d'accord pour> **3** ACCEPTABLE : acceptable, satisfaisant

agreeably [əˈgriːəbli] *adv* : agréablement

agreement [əˈgriːmənt] *n* : accord *m* <to be in agreement : être d'accord> <international agreement : accord international>

agricultural [ˌægrɪˈkʌltʃərəl] *adj* : agricole

agriculture [ˈægrɪˌkʌltʃər] *n* : agriculture *f*

aground[1] [əˈgraʊnd] *adv* **to run aground** : s'échouer

aground[2] *adj* : échoué

ahead [əˈhɛd] *adv* **1** FORWARD : en avant, devant <he walked ahead : il marchait en avant> **2** BEFOREHAND : à l'avance **3** LEADING : de tête, en avance **4 go ahead!** : allez-y! **5 to get ahead** : prendre de l'avance

ahead of *prep* **1** : devant, d'avance sur <go ahead of me : mettez-vous devant moi> **2** : avant, en avance sur <to be ahead of one's time : être en avance sur son temps>

ahoy [əˈhɔɪ] *interj* **ship ahoy!** : ohé du navire!

aid[1] [ˈeɪd] *vt* **1** HELP : aider **2 to aid and abet** : être complice de

aid[2] *n* **1** HELP : aide *f*, secours *m* **2** ASSISTANT : aide *mf*; assistant *m*, -tante *f* **3** DEVICE : appareil *m* <hearing aid : appareil auditif>

aide ['eɪd] *n* : aide *mf;* assistant *m,* -tante *f*
AIDS ['eɪdz] *n* : sida *m,* SIDA *m*
ail ['eɪl] *vt* TROUBLE : affliger <what ails you? : qu'avez-vous?> — *vi* : être souffrant
aileron ['eɪləˌrɑn] *n* : aileron *m*
ailment ['eɪlmənt] *n* : maladie *f,* affection *f*
aim[1] ['eɪm] *vt* **1** : braquer (une arme à feu), diriger (une remarque, etc.) **2** INTEND : avoir l'intention de — *vi* **to aim at** *or* **to aim for** : viser
aim[2] *n* **1** GOAL : but *m,* objectif *m* **2 to take aim at** : viser
aimless ['eɪmləs] *adj* : sans but, sans objet
aimlessly ['eɪmləsli] *adv* : sans but
air[1] ['ær] *vt* **1** VENTILATE : aérer, ventiler **2** EXPRESS : exprimer, faire connaître **3** BROADCAST : diffuser
air[2] *n* **1** : air *m* **2** MELODY : air *m* **3** APPEARANCE : air *m,* aspect *m* <an air of mystery : un air mystérieux> **4 to be on the air** : être à l'antenne **5 to go by air** : voyager par avion **6 to put on airs** : se donner de grands airs
airborne ['ærˌborn] *adj* **1** : aéroporté (se dit des troupes, etc.) **2 to become airborne** : décoller
air–conditioned [ˌærkən'dɪʃənd] *adj* : climatisé
air conditioner [ˌærkən'dɪʃənər] *n* : climatiseur *m*
air–conditioning [ˌærkən'dɪʃənɪŋ] *n* : climatisation *f*
aircraft ['ærˌkræft] *ns & pl* : avion *m,* aéronef *m*
aircraft carrier *n* : porte-avions *m*
airfield ['ærˌfiːld] *n* : aérodrome *m,* terrain *m* d'aviation
air force *n* : armée *f* de l'air
airlift ['ærˌlɪft] *n* : pont *m* aérien
airline ['ærˌlaɪn] *n* : ligne *f* (aérienne), compagnie *f* d'aviation
airliner ['ærˌlaɪnər] *n* : avion *m* de ligne
airmail ['ærˌmeɪl] *n* **1** : poste *f* aérienne **2 by ~** : par avion
airman ['ærmən] *n, pl* **-men** [-mən, -ˌmɛn] **1** AVIATOR : aviateur *m* **2** : soldat *m* de l'armée de l'air
airplane ['ærˌpleɪn] *n* : avion *m*
airport ['ærˌport] *n* : aéroport *m*
airship ['ærˌʃɪp] *n* : dirigeable *m*
airstrip ['ærˌʃtrɪp] *n* : piste *f* (d'atterrissage)
airtight ['ær'taɪt] *adj* : hermétique, étanche (à l'air)
airwaves ['ærˌweɪvz] *npl* : ondes *fpl*
airy ['æri] *adj* **airier; -est 1** VENTILATED : aéré **2** DELICATE, LIGHT : léger **3** LOFTY : en l'air
aisle ['aɪl] *n* : nef *f* latérale (d'une église), allée *f* (d'un théâtre ou d'un magasin), couloir *m* (d'un avion, d'un train, etc.)
ajar [ə'dʒɑr] *adj & adv* : entrouvert
akimbo [ə'kɪmbo] *adj & adv* **with arms akimbo** : les poings sur les hanches
akin [ə'kɪn] *adj* **1** RELATED : apparenté **2 ~ to** : semblable à, qui ressemble à
alabaster ['æləˌbæstər] *n* : albâtre *m*
alacrity [ə'lækrəṭi] *n* : empressement *m*
alarm[1] [ə'lɑrm] *vt* **1** WARN : alerter **2** FRIGHTEN : alarmer, faire peur à
alarm[2] *n* **1** WARNING : alarme *f,* alerte *f* **2** FEAR : inquiétude *f,* alarme *f*
alarm clock *n* : réveil *m,* réveille-matin *m,* cadran *m Can fam*
alas [ə'læs] *interj* : hélas!
Albanian[1] [æl'beɪniən] *adj* : albanais
Albanian[2] *n* **1** : Albanais *m,* -naise *f*
albatross ['ælbəˌtrɔs] *n, pl* **-tross** *or* **-trosses** : albatros *m*
albeit [ɔl'biːət, æl-] *conj* : bien que, quoique
albino [æl'baɪno] *n, pl* **-nos** : albinos *mf*
album ['ælbəm] *n* : album *m*
albumen [æl'bjuːmən] *n* **1** : albumen *m,* blanc *m* d'œuf **2** → **albumin**
albumin [æl'bjuːmən] *n* : albumine *f*
alchemy ['ælkəmi] *n* : alchimie *f*
alcohol ['ælkəˌhɔl] *n* **1** : alcool *m* **2** DRINK : boisson *f* alcoolisée, verre *m*
alcoholic[1] [ˌælkə'hɔlɪk] *adj* : alcoolisé, alcoolique
alcoholic[2] *n* : alcoolique *mf*
alcoholism ['ælkəhɔˌlɪzəm] *n* : alcoolisme *m*
alcove ['ælˌkoːv] *n* **1** : alcôve *f* (d'une salle) **2** RECESS : renfoncement *m,* niche *f*
alderman ['ɔldərmən] *n, pl* **-men** [-mən, -ˌmɛn] : conseiller *m* municipal, conseillère *f* municipale
ale ['eɪl] *n* : bière *f*
alert[1] [ə'lərt] *vt* : alerter, donner l'alerte à
alert[2] *adj* **1** WATCHFUL : vigilant **2** LIVELY : alerte, vif, éveillé
alert[3] *n* : alerte *f* <on the alert : en état d'alerte>
alertness [ə'lərtnəs] *n* **1** VIGILANCE : vigilance *f* **2** LIVELINESS : vivacité *f*
alfalfa [æl'fælfə] *n* : luzerne *f*
alga ['ælgə] *n, pl* **-gae** ['ælˌdʒiː] : algue *f*
algebra ['ældʒəbrə] *n* : algèbre *f*
algebraic [ˌældʒə'breɪɪk] *adj* : algébrique — **algebraically** *adv*
Algerian[1] [æl'dʒɪriən] *adj* : algérien
Algerian[2] *n* : Algérien *m,* -rienne *f*
alias[1] ['eɪliəs] *adv* : alias
alias[2] *n* : nom *m* d'emprunt, faux nom *m*
alibi ['æləˌbaɪ] *n* : alibi *m*
alien[1] ['eɪliən] *adj* **1** FOREIGN : étranger **2** EXTRATERRESTRIAL : extraterrestre
alien[2] *n* **1** FOREIGNER : étranger *m,* -gère *f* **2** EXTRATERRESTRIAL : extraterrestre *mf*
alienate ['eɪliəˌneɪt] *vt* **-ated; -ating** : aliéner
alienation [ˌeɪliə'neɪʃən] *n* : aliénation *f*

alight [ə'laɪt] *vi* **1** : descendre (se dit des personnes), se poser (se dit des oiseaux)

align [ə'laɪn] *vt* : aligner

alignment [ə'laɪnmənt] *n* **1** : alignement *m* <to be out of alignment : être désaligné> **2** *or* **wheel alignment** : parallélisme *m* des roues

alike[1] [ə'laɪk] *adv* : de la même façon

alike[2] *adj* **1** : semblable, pareil **2 to be alike** : se ressembler

alimentary [ˌælə'mɛntəri] *adj* **1** : alimentaire **2 alimentary canal** : tube *m* digestif

alimony ['æləˌmoːni] *n, pl* **-nies** : pension *f* alimentaire

alive [ə'laɪv] *adj* **1** LIVING : vivant, en vie **2** LIVELY : vif, animé **3** AWARE : conscient, sensible <they are alive to the danger : ils sont conscients du danger>

alkali ['ælkəlaɪ] *n, pl* **-lies** *or* **-lis** : alcali *m*

alkaline ['ælkələn, -ˌlaɪn] *adj* : alcalin

all[1] ['ɔl] *adv* **1** COMPLETELY : tout, complètement <all alone : tout seul> **2** : partout <the score is six all : le score est de six partout> **3 all at once** : tout d'un coup **4 all the better** : tant mieux

all[2] *adj* : tout <in all probability : en toute probabilité> <all those people : tous ces gens>

all[3] *pron* **1** EVERYTHING : tout <is that all? : c'est tout?> **2** EVERYONE : tous, toutes <all have left the premises : tous sont partis des lieux> <they've all left : elles sont toutes parties> **3 all in all** : tout compte fait

Allah ['ɑlɑ, ɑ'lɑ] *n* : Allah *m*

all–around [ˌɔlə'raʊnd] *adj* **1** GENERAL : général **2** VERSATILE : complet, polyvalent <an all-around athlete : un athlète polyvalent>

allay [ə'leɪ] *vt* : soulager, apaiser

allegation [ˌælɪ'geɪʃən] *n* : allégation *f*

allege [ə'lɛdʒ] *vt* **-leged; -leging** : alléguer, prétendre

alleged [ə'lɛdʒd, ə'lɛdʒəd] *adj* : présumé, prétendu, allégué

allegedly [ə'lɛdʒədli] *adv* : prétendument

allegiance [ə'liːdʒənts] *n* : allégeance *f*

allegorical [ˌælə'gɔrɪkəl] *adj* : allégorique

allegory ['æləˌgori] *n, pl* **-ries** : allégorie *f*

alleluia [ˌɑlə'luːjə, ˌæ-] → **hallelujah**

allergic [ə'lərdʒɪk] *adj* : allergique

allergy ['ælərdʒi] *n, pl* **-gies** : allergie *f*

alleviate [ə'liːviˌeɪt] *vt* **-ated; -ating** : soulager, alléger, apaiser

alleviation [əˌliːvi'eɪʃən] *n* : soulagement *m*, allègement *m*

alley ['æli] *n, pl* **-leys 1** : ruelle *f*, allée *f* (dans un jardin, etc.) **2 bowling alley** : bowling *m*

alliance [ə'laɪənts] *n* : alliance *f*

alligator ['æləˌgeɪtər] *n* : alligator *m*

alliteration [əˌlɪtə'reɪʃən] *n* : allitération *f*

allocate ['æləˌkeɪt] *vt* **-cated; -cating** : allouer, assigner

allocation ['ælə'keɪʃən] *n* : allocation *f*, affectation *f*

allot [ə'lɑt] *vt* **allotted; allotting 1** ASSIGN : attribuer, assigner **2** DISTRIBUTE : répartir, distribuer

allotment [ə'lɑtmənt] *n* : répartition *f*, allocation *f*

allow [ə'laʊ] *vt* **1** PERMIT : permettre **2** CONCEDE : admettre, reconnaître **3** GRANT : accorder, allouer — *vi* **to allow for** : tenir compte de

allowable [ə'laʊəbəl] *adj* **1** PERMISSIBLE : permis, admissible **2** DEDUCTIBLE : déductible

allowance [ə'laʊənts] *n* **1** : allocation *f* (pour les dépenses), argent *m* de poche (pour les enfants) **2 to make allowances for** : tenir compte de

alloy ['æˌlɔɪ] *n* : alliage *m*

all right[1] *adv* **1** YES : d'accord **2** WELL : bien <she's doing all right : elle va bien> **3** CERTAINLY : bien, sans doute <it's hot all right : il fait bien chaud>

all right[2] *adj* : pas mal, bien <I'm all right, thanks : je vais bien, merci>

all–round [ˌɔl'raʊnd] → **all–around**

allspice ['ɔlspaɪs] *n* : piment *m* de la Jamaïque

allude [ə'luːd] *vi* **-luded; -luding** : faire allusion (à)

allure[1] [ə'lʊr] *vt* **-lured; -luring** : séduire, attirer

allure[2] *n* : attrait *m*, charme *m*

allusion [ə'luːʒən] *n* : allusion *f*

ally[1] [ə'laɪ, 'æˌlaɪ] *vt* **-lied; -lying 1** : allier **2 to ally oneself with** : s'allier avec

ally[2] ['æˌlaɪ, ə'laɪ] *n, pl* **allies** : allié *m*, -liée *f*

almanac ['ɔlməˌnæk, 'æl-] *n* : almanach *m*

almighty [ɔl'maɪti] *adj* : tout puissant, formidable

almond ['ɑmənd, 'ɑl-, 'æ-, 'æl-] *n* : amande *f*

almost ['ɔlˌmoːst, ɔl'moːst] *adv* : presque <almost everyone : presque tout le monde> <she almost died : elle a failli mourir>

alms ['ɑmz, 'ɑlmz, 'ælmz] *ns & pl* : aumône *f*

aloft [ə'lɔft] *adv* : en haut, en l'air

alone[1] [ə'loːn] *adv* **1** : seul <il travaille seul : he works alone> <she alone can do it : elle seule peut le faire> **2 to leave alone** : laisser tranquille, laisser en paix

alone[2] *adj* : seul <I'm all alone : je suis tout seul>

along[1] [ə'lɔŋ] *adv* **1** FORWARD : en avant <to step along : faire un pas en avant, avancer> <further along : plus avancé> **2** (*often not translated*) <to

bring along : apporter> <to run along : courir> <to pull along : tirer avec soi> **3 ~ with** : avec, accompagné de
along[2] *prep* **1** : le long de <along the coast : le long de la côte> **2** ON : sur <along the way : sur le chemin>
alongside[1] [ə͵lɔŋ'saɪd] *adv* **1** : à côté **2 to come alongside** : accoster
alongside[2] *or* **alongside of** *prep* BESIDE : à côté de
aloof [ə'lu:f] *adj* : distant <to stand aloof from : se tenir à l'écart de>
aloofness [ə'lu:fnəs] *n* : réserve *f*
aloud [ə'laʊd] *adv* : à haute voix
alpaca [æl'pækə] *n* : alpaga *m*
alphabet ['ælfə͵bɛt] *n* : alphabet *m*
alphabetic [͵ælfə'bɛtɪk] *or* **alphabetical** [-tɪkəl] *adj* : alphabétique — **alphabetically** [-tɪkli] *adv*
alphabetize ['ælfəbə͵taɪz] *vt* **-ized; -izing** : alphabétiser, classer par ordre alphabétique
already [ɔl'rɛdi] *adv* : déjà
also ['ɔl͵so:] *adv* **1** TOO : aussi, également **2** FURTHERMORE : de plus, en outre
altar ['ɔltər] *n* : autel *m*
alter ['ɔltər] *vt* **1** CHANGE : changer, modifier **2** : retoucher (un vêtement)
alteration [͵ɔltə'reɪʃən] *n* **1** : changement *m*, modification *f* **2 alterations** *npl* : retouches *fpl*
altercation [͵ɔltər'keɪʃən] *n* : altercation *f*
alternate[1] ['ɔltər͵neɪt] *v* **-nated; -nating** *vt* : faire alterner — *vi* : alterner, se relayer
alternate[2] ['ɔltərnət] *adj* : alternatif — **alternately** *adv*
alternate[3] ['ɔltərnət] *n* : remplaçant *m*, -çante *f*
alternating current ['ɔltər͵neɪt̬ɪŋ] *n* : courant *m* alternatif
alternation [͵ɔltər'neɪʃən] *n* : alternance *f*
alternative[1] [ɔl'tərnət̬ɪv] *adj* : alternatif
alternative[2] *n* **1** : alternative *f* **2 to have no alternative** : ne pas avoir le choix
alternator ['ɔltər͵neɪt̬ər] *n* : alternateur *m*
although [ɔl'ðo:] *conj* : bien que, quoique
altitude ['æltə͵tu:d, -͵tju:d] *n* : altitude *f*
alto ['æl͵to:] *n, pl* **-tos** : contralto *m* (voix), alto *m* (instrument)
altogether [͵ɔltə'gɛðər] *adv* **1** COMPLETELY : complètement, tout à fait **2** ON THE WHOLE : dans l'ensemble **3** : en tout <how much altogether? : combien en tout?>
altruism ['æltrʊ͵ɪzəm] *n* : altruisme *m*
altruist ['æltrʊɪst] *n* : altruiste *mf*
altruistic [͵æltrʊ'ɪstɪk] *adj* : altruiste
alum ['æləm] *n* : alun *m*
aluminum [ə'lu:mənəm] *n* : aluminium *m*
alumna [ə'lʌmnə] *n, pl* **-nae** [-͵ni:] : ancienne élève *f*
alumnus [ə'lʌmnəs] *n, pl* **-ni** [-͵naɪ] : ancien élève *m*
always ['ɔlwiz, -͵weɪz] *adv* **1** INVARIABLY : toujours **2** FOREVER : pour toujours
am → **be**
amalgam [ə'mælgəm] *n* : amalgame *m*
amalgamate [ə'mælgə͵meɪt] *v* **-ated; -ating** *vt* : amalgamer, fusionner — *vi* : s'amalgamer, fusionner
amalgamation [ə͵mælgə'meɪʃən] *n* : fusion *f*, amalgamation *f*
amaryllis [͵æmə'rɪləs] *n* : amaryllis *f*
amass [ə'mæs] *vt* : amasser, accumuler
amateur[1] ['æmətʃər, -tər, -͵tʊr, -͵tjʊr] *adj* : amateur
amateur[2] *n* : amateur *m*
amateurish ['æmə͵tʃərɪʃ, -͵tər-, -͵tʊr-, -͵tjʊr-] *adj* : d'amateur
amaze [ə'meɪz] *vt* **amazed; amazing** : étonner, stupéfier
amazement [ə'meɪzmənt] *n* : stupéfaction *f*, étonnement *m*
amazing [ə'meɪzɪŋ] *adj* : étonnant, stupéfiant
amazingly [ə'meɪzɪŋli] *adv* : étonnamment, incroyablement
ambassador [æm'bæsə͵dər] *n* : ambassadeur *m*, -drice *f*
amber ['æmbər] *n* : ambre *m*
ambergris ['æmbər͵grɪs, -gri:s] *n* : ambre *m* gris
ambidextrous [͵æmbɪ'dɛkstrəs] *adj* : ambidextre
ambience *or* **ambiance** ['æmbiən*t*s, 'ɑmbi͵ɑn*t*s] *n* : ambiance *f*
ambiguity [͵æmbə'gju:ət̬i] *n, pl* **-ties** : ambiguïté *f*
ambiguous [æm'bɪgjʊəs] *adj* : ambigu
ambition [æm'bɪʃən] *n* : ambition *f*
ambitious [æm'bɪʃəs] *adj* : ambitieux — **ambitiously** *adv*
ambivalence [æm'bɪvələn*t*s] *n* : ambivalence *f*
ambivalent [æm'bɪvələnt] *adj* : ambivalent
amble[1] ['æmbəl] *vi* **-bled; -bling** : marcher d'un pas tranquille, aller l'amble (se dit d'un cheval)
amble[2] *n* : pas *m* tranquille, amble *m* (de cheval)
ambulance ['æmbjələn*t*s] *n* : ambulance *f*
ambulatory ['æmbjələ͵to:ri] *adj* : ambulatoire
ambush[1] ['æmbʊʃ] *vt* **1** : tendre une embuscade à **2** WAYLAY : attirer dans une embuscade
ambush[2] *n* : embuscade *f*
ameba, amebic → **amoeba, amoebic**
ameliorate [ə'mi:ljə͵reɪt] *v* **-rated; -rating** *vt* : améliorer — *vi* : s'améliorer
amelioration [ə͵mi:ljə'reɪʃən] *n* : amélioration *f*
amen ['eɪ'mɛn, 'ɑ-] *interj* : amen, ainsi soit-il

amenable [ə'mi:nəbəl, -'mɛ-] *adj* : accommodant <to be amenable to : être disposé à>
amend [ə'mɛnd] *vt* : amender
amendment [ə'mɛndmənt] *n* : amendement *m*
amends [ə'mɛndz] *ns & pl* **1 to make amends** : se racheter, réparer ses torts **2 to make amends for** : dédommager de, réparer
amenity [ə'mɛnəti, -'mi:-] *n, pl* **-ties 1** PLEASANTNESS : agrément *m* **2 amenities** *npl* : équipements *mpl,* aménagements *mpl*
American[1] [ə'mɛrɪkən] *adj* : américain
American[2] *n* : Américain *m,* -caine *f*
American Indian *n* : indien *m,* -dienne *f* d'Amérique
amethyst ['æməθəst] *n* : améthyste *f*
amiability [,eɪmi:ə'bɪləti] *n* : amabilité *f*
amiable ['eɪmi:əbəl] *adj* : aimable — **amiably** *adv*
amicable ['æmɪkəbəl] *adj* : amical — **amicably** *adv*
amid [ə'mɪd] *or* **amidst** [ə'mɪdst] *prep* : au milieu de, parmi
amino acid [ə'mi:no] *n* : acide *m* aminé
amiss[1] [ə'mɪs] *adv* **1** WRONGLY : incorrectement, mal **2 to take sth amiss** : prendre qqch de travers
amiss[2] *adj* **1** WRONG : incorrect, mal à propos **2 something is amiss** : quelque chose ne va pas
ammeter ['æ,mi:tər] *n* : ampèremètre *m*
ammonia [ə'mo:njə] *n* **1** : ammoniac *m* (gaz) **2** : ammoniaque *f* (liquide)
ammunition [,æmjə'nɪʃən] *n* : munitions *fpl*
amnesia [æm'ni:ʒə] *n* : amnésie *f*
amnesiac[1] [æm'ni:ʒi,æk, -zi-] *or* **amnesic** [æm'ni:ʒɪk, -sɪk] *adj* : amnésique
amnesiac[2] *or* **amnesic** *n* : amnésique *mf*
amnesty ['æmnəsti] *n, pl* **-ties** : amnistie *f*
amoeba [ə'mi:bə] *n, pl* **-bas** *or* **-bae** [-bi:] : amibe *f*
amoebic [ə'mi:bɪk] *adj* : amibien
amok [ə'mʌk, -'mɑk] *adv* **to run amok** : être pris d'un accès de folie furieuse
among [e'mʌŋ] *prep* : parmi, entre <among others : entre autres> <among young people : chez les jeunes>
amoral [eɪ'mɔrəl] *adj* : amoral
amorous ['æmərəs] *adj* : amoureux — **amorously** *adv*
amorphous [ə'mɔrfəs] *adj* : informe, amorphe (en science)
amortize ['æmər,taɪz, ə'mɔr-] *vt* **-tized; -tizing** : amortir
amount[1] [ə'maʊnt] *vi* **to amount to 1** TOTAL : se monter à, s'élever à **2** : équivaloir à, revenir à <that amounts to the same thing : cela revient au même>
amount[2] *n* **1** QUANTITY : quantité *f* **2** SUM : somme *f,* montant *m*
ampere ['æm,pɪr] *n* : ampère *m*
ampersand ['æmpər,sænd] *n* : esperluette *f*
amphibian [æm'fɪbiən] *n* : amphibien *m*
amphibious [æm'fɪbiəs] *adj* : amphibie
amphitheater ['æmfə,θi:ətər] *n* : amphithéâtre *m*
ample ['æmpəl] *adj* **-pler; -plest 1** LARGE, SPACIOUS : ample, grand, vaste **2** PLENTIFUL : largement suffisant, abondant
amplification [,æmpləfə'keɪʃən] *n* : amplification *f*
amplifier ['æmplə,faɪər] *n* : amplificateur *m*
amplify ['æmplə,faɪ] *vt* **-fied; -fying** : amplifier
amply ['æmpli] *adv* : largement, amplement
amputate ['æmpjə,teɪt] *v* **-tated; -tating** : amputer
amputation [,æmpjə'teɪʃən] *n* : amputation *f*
amuck [ə'mʌk] → **amok**
amulet ['æmjələt] *n* : amulette *f*
amuse [ə'mju:z] *vt* **amused; amusing 1** ENTERTAIN : distraire, divertir **2** : amuser, faire rire <the joke amused me : la plaisanterie m'a fait rire>
amusement [ə'mju:zmənt] *n* **1** ENTERTAINMENT : distraction *f,* divertissement *m* **2** ENJOYMENT, MIRTH : amusement *m*
an → **a[2]**
anachronism [ə'nækrə,nɪzəm] *n* : anachronisme *m*
anachronistic [ə,nækrə'nɪstɪk] *adj* : anachronique
anaconda [,ænə'kɑndə] *n* : anaconda *m*
anagram ['ænə,græm] *n* : anagramme *f*
anal ['eɪnəl] *adj* : anal
analgesic[1] [,ænəl'dʒi:zɪk, -sɪk] *adj* : analgésique
analgesic[2] *n* : analgésique *m*
analog ['ænə,lɔg, -,lɑg] *adj* : analogique
analogous [ə'næləgəs] *adj* : analogue
analogy [ə'nælədʒi] *n, pl* **-gies** : analogie *f*
analyse *Brit* → **analyze**
analysis [ə'næləsəs] *n, pl* **-yses** [-,si:z] **1** : analyse *f* **2** → **psychoanalysis**
analyst ['ænəlɪst] *n* **1** : analyste *mf* **2** → **psychoanalyst**
analytic [,ænə'lɪtɪk] *or* **analytical** [-tɪkəl] *adj* : analytique — **analytically** [-tɪkli] *adv*
analyze *or Brit* **analyse** ['ænə,laɪz] *vt* **-lyzed** *or Brit* **-lysed; -lyzing** *or Brit* **-lysing** : analyser
anarchist ['ænərkɪst, -,nɑr-] *n* : anarchiste *mf*
anarchy ['ænərki, -,nɑr-] *n* : anarchie *f*
anathema [ə'næθəmə] *n* : anathème *m*
anatomic [,ænə'tɑmɪk] *or* **anatomical** [-mɪkəl] *adj* : anatomique — **anatomically** [-mɪkli] *adv*

anatomy [ə'næţəmi] *n, pl* **-mies** : anatomie *f*
ancestor ['æn,sɛstər] *n* : ancêtre *mf*
ancestral [æn'sɛstrəl] *adj* : ancestral
ancestry ['æn,sɛstri] *n* **1** LINEAGE : ascendance *f* **2** ANCESTORS : ancêtres *mpl*
anchor[1] ['æŋkər] *vt* **1** MOOR : ancrer, mettre à l'ancre **2** SECURE : fixer, ancrer **3** : présenter (un programme de télévision) — *vi* : jeter l'ancre, mouiller l'ancre
anchor[2] *n* **1** : ancre *f* **2** : présentateur *m*, -trice *f* (à la télévision)
anchorage ['æŋkərɪdʒ] *n* : mouillage *m*
anchovy ['æn,tʃo:vi, æn'tʃo:-] *n, pl* **-vies** *or* **-vy** : anchois *m*
ancient ['eɪntʃənt] *adj* **1** : ancien <ancient history : histoire ancienne> **2** OLD : très vieux
ancients ['eɪntʃənts] *npl* : les anciens
and [ænd] *conj* **1** : et **2** (*used with numbers*) <three hundred and two : trois cent deux> **3** (*used between two verbs*) <come and see : venez voir> **4** (*used between two adjectives*) <better and better : de mieux en mieux> <more and more : de plus en plus>
andiron ['æn,deɪərn] *n* : chenet *m*
Andorran[1] [æn'dɔrən] *adj* : andorran
Andorran[2] *n* : Andorran *m*, -rane *f*
androgynous [æn'drɑdʒənəs] *adj* : androgyne
anecdotal [,ænɪk'do:ţəl] *adj* : anecdotique
anecdote ['ænɪk,do:t] *n* : anecdote *f*
anemia [ə'ni:miə] *n* : anémie *f*
anemic [ə'ni:mɪk] *adj* **1** : anémique **2** INSIPID : fade
anemone [ə'nɛməni] *n* : anémone *f*
anesthesia [,ænəs'θi:ʒə] *n* : anesthésie *f*
anesthetic[1] ['ænəs'θɛţɪk] *adj* : anesthésique
anesthetic[2] *n* : anesthésique *m*
anesthetist [ə'nɛsθətɪst] *n* : anesthésiste *mf*
anesthetize [ə'nɛsθətaɪz] *vt* **-tized; -tizing** : anesthésier
anew [ə'nu:, -'nju:] *adv* : encore, de nouveau
angel ['eɪndʒəl] *n* : ange *m*
angelic [æn'dʒɛlɪk] *or* **angelical** [-lɪkəl] *adj* : angélique — **angelically** [-lɪkli] *adv*
anger[1] ['æŋgər] *vt* : fâcher, mettre en colère — *vi* : se fâcher, se mettre en colère
anger[2] *n* : colère *f*
angina [æn'dʒaɪnə] *n or* **angina pectoris** : angine *f* de poitrine
angle[1] ['æŋgəl] *v* **-gled; -gling** *vt* : orienter, incliner — *vi* FISH : pêcher à la ligne
angle[2] *n* **1** : angle *m* <at an angle : de biais> **2** POINT OF VIEW : point *m* de vue
angler ['æŋglər] *n* : pêcheur *m*, -cheuse *f* à la ligne
angling ['æŋglɪŋ] *n* : pêche *f* (à la ligne)
Anglo–Saxon[1] [,aŋglo'sæksən] *adj* : anglo-saxon
Anglo–Saxon[2] *n* **1** : Anglo-Saxon *m*, -Saxonne *f* (personne) **2** : anglo-saxon *m* (langue)
Angolan[1] [æŋ'go:lən, æn-] *adj* : angolais
Angolan[2] *n* : Angolais *m*, -laise *f*
angora [æŋ'gorə, æn-] *n* : angora *m*
angrily ['æŋgrəlɪ] *adv* : avec colère
angry ['æŋgri] *adj* **-grier; -est** : fâché, en colère, furieux
anguish ['æŋgwɪʃ] *n* : angoisse *f*, douleur *f*
anguished ['æŋgwɪʃt] *adj* : angoissé, tourmenté
angular ['æŋgjələr] *adj* : anguleux (se dit du visage), angulaire (se dit des objets)
animal ['ænəməl] *n* : animal *m*
animate[1] ['ænə,meɪt] *vt* **-mated; -mating** : animer, stimuler
animate[2] ['ænəmət] *adj* **1** ALIVE : vivant **2** ANIMATED : animé
animated ['ænə,meɪţəd] *adj* **1** LIVELY : animé **2 animated cartoon** : dessin *m* animé
animation [,ænə'meɪʃən] *n* : animation *f*
animosity [,ænə'mɑsəţi] *n, pl* **-ties** : animosité *f*
anise ['ænəs] *n* : anis *m*
ankle ['æŋkəl] *n* : cheville *f*
annals ['ænəlz] *npl* : annales *fpl*
anneal [ə'ni:l] *vt* : recuire
annex[1] [ə'nɛks, 'æ,nɛks] *vt* : annexer
annex[2] ['æ,nɛks, -nɪks] *n* : annexe *f*
annexation [,æ,nɛk'seɪʃən] *n* : annexion *f*
annihilate [ə'naɪə,leɪt] *vt* **-lated; -lating** : anéantir, annihiler
annihilation [ə,naɪə'leɪʃən] *n* : anéantissement *m*
anniversary [,ænə'vərsəri] *n, pl* **-ries** : anniversaire *m*
annotate ['ænə,teɪt] *vt* **-tated; -tating** : annoter
annotation [,ænə'teɪʃən] *n* : annotation *f*
announce [ə'naʊnts] *vt* **-nounced; -nouncing** : annoncer
announcement [ə'naʊntsmənt] *n* **1** DECLARATION : annonce *f* **2** NOTIFICATION : avis *m*, faire-part *m*
announcer [ə'naʊntsər] *n* : présentateur *m*, -trice *f*; annonceur *m*, -ceuse *f*; speaker *m*, -kerine *f France*
annoy [ə'nɔɪ] *vt* : agacer, gêner, ennuyer, achaler *Can fam*
annoyance [ə'nɔɪənts] *n* : agacement *m*, contrariété *f*
annoying [ə'nɔɪɪŋ] *adj* : agaçant, gênant, ennuyant *Can*
annual[1] ['ænjʊəl] *adj* : annuel — **annually** *adv*

annual[2] *n* **1** YEARBOOK : annuaire *m* **2** *or* **annual plant** : plante *f* annuelle
annuity [ə'nuːəṭi] *n, pl* **-ties** : rente *f*
annul [ə'nʌl] *vt* **anulled; anulling** : annuler
annulment [ə'nʌlmənt] *n* : annulation *f*
anode ['æˌnoːd] *n* : anode *f*
anoint [ə'nɔɪnt] *vt* : oindre
anomalous [ə'nɑmələs] *adj* ABNORMAL : anormal
anomaly [ə'nɑməli] *n, pl* **-lies** : anomalie *f*
anonymity [ˌænə'nɪməṭi] *n* : anonymat *m*
anonymous [ə'nɑnəməs] *adj* : anonyme — **anonymously** *adv*
anorexia [ˌænə'rɛksiə] *n* : anorexie *f* — **anorexic** *adj*
another[1] [ə'nʌðər] *adj* : un autre, encore un <another girl : une autre fille> <another beer : encore une bière> <without another word : sans rien dire de plus> <in another three years : dans trois ans>
another[2] *pron* **1** : un autre *m*, une autre *f* **2 many another** : beaucoup d'autres **3 one after another** : l'un après l'autre
answer[1] ['æn*t*sər] *vt* **1** : répondre à **2 to answer the door** : aller ouvrir la porte — *vi* **1** : répondre, donner une réponse **2 to answer for** : répondre de
answer[2] *n* **1** REPLY : réponse *f* <in answer to : en réponse à> **2** SOLUTION : solution *f*
answerable ['æn*t*sərəbəl] *adj* : responsable
ant ['ænt] *n* : fourmi *f*
antagonism [æn'tægəˌnɪzəm] *n* : antagonisme *m*
antagonist [æn'tægəˌnɪst] *n* : antagoniste *mf*
antagonistic [ænˌtægə'nɪstɪk] *adj* : antagoniste
antagonize [æn'tægəˌnɑɪz] *vt* **-nized; -nizing** : éveiller l'hostilité de, contrarier
antarctic [ænt'ɑrktɪk, -'ɑrṭɪk] *adj* : antarctique <antarctic circle : cercle polaire antarctique>
anteater ['æntˌiṭər] *n* : fourmilier *m*
antecedent[1] [ˌæntə'siːdənt] *adj* : antérieur, précédent
antecedent[2] *n* : antécédent *m*
antelope ['æntəlˌoːp] *n, pl* **-lope** *or* **-lopes** : antilope *f*
antenna [æn'tɛnə] *n, pl* **-nae** *or* **-nas** : antenne *f*
anterior [æn'tɪriər] *adj* : antérieur
anteroom ['æntiˌruːm] *n* : antichambre *f*
anthem ['ænθəm] *n* : hymne *m* <national anthem : hymne national>
anther ['ænθər] *n* : anthère *f*
anthill ['æntˌhɪl] *n* : fourmilière *f*
anthology [æn'θɑlədʒi] *n, pl* **-gies** : anthologie *f*
anthracite ['ænθrəˌsaɪt] *n* : anthracite *m*
anthropoid[1] ['ænθrəˌpɔɪd] *adj* : anthropoïde
anthropoid[2] *n* : anthropoïde *m*
anthropological [ˌænθrəpə'lɑdʒɪkəl] *adj* : anthropologique
anthropologist [ˌænθrə'pɑlədʒɪst] *n* : anthropologue *mf*, anthropologiste *mf*
anthropology [ˌænθrə'pɑlədʒi] *n* : anthropologie *f*
antiaircraft [ˌænti'ærˌkræft, ˌænˌtaɪ-] *adj* : antiaérien
antibiotic[1] [ˌæntibaɪ'ɑṭɪk, ˌænˌtaɪ-, -bi-] *adj* : antibiotique
antibiotic[2] *n* : antibiotique *m*
antibody ['æntiˌbɑdi] *n, pl* **-bodies** : anticorps *m*
anticipate [æn'tɪsəˌpeɪt] *vt* **-pated; -pating 1** FORESEE : anticiper, prévoir **2** EXPECT : s'attendre à **3** FORESTALL : devancer
anticipation [ænˌtɪsə'peɪʃən] *n* : anticipation *f*
anticipatory [æn'tɪsəpəˌtori] *adj* : d'anticipation
anticlerical [ˌænti'klɛrɪkəl, ˌænˌtaɪ-] *adj* : anticlérical
anticlimax [ˌænti'klaɪˌmæks] *n* : déception *f*
anticommunist[1] [ˌænti'kɑmjənɪst, ˌænˌtaɪ-] *adj* : anticommuniste
anticommunist[2] *n* : anticommuniste *mf*
antics ['æntɪks] *npl* : bouffonnerie *f*
anticyclone [ˌænti'saɪˌklon] *n* : anticyclone *m*
antidemocratic [ˌænti'dɛmə'kræṭɪk, ˌænˌtaɪ-] *adj* : antidémocratique
antidepressant[1] [ˌæntɪdɪ'prɛsənt, ˌænˌtaɪ] *adj* : antidépresseur
antidepressant[2] *n* : antidépresseur *m*
antidote ['æntɪˌdoːt] *n* : antidote *m*
antifreeze ['æntɪˌfriːz] *n* : antigel *m*
antihistamine [ˌæntɪ'hɪstəˌmin, ˌænˌtaɪ-, -mən] *n* : antihistaminique *m*
anti–inflammatory [ˌæntɪn'flæməˌtori] *adj* : anti-inflammatoire
antilock ['æntiˌlɑk, 'ænˌtaɪ-] *adj* **antilock brakes** : freins *mpl* antiblocage
antimony ['æntəˌmoːni] *n* : antimoine *m*
antioxidant[1] [ˌænti'ɑksədənt, ˌænˌtaɪ-] *adj* : antioxydant
antioxidant[2] *n* : antioxydant *m*
antipathy [æn'tɪpəθi] *n, pl* **-thies** : antipathie *f*
antiperspirant [ˌænti'pərspərənt, ˌænˌtaɪ-] *n* : déodorant *m*
antiquated ['æntəˌkweɪṭəd] *adj* **1** OUTMODED : vieillot, dépassé **2** ANCIENT : très vieux
antique[1] [æn'tiːk] *adj* : ancien, antique
antique[2] *n* : objet *m* ancien, antiquité *f*
antiquity [æn'tɪkwəṭi] *n, pl* **-ties** : antiquité *f*
anti–Semitic [ˌæntisə'mɪṭɪk, ˌænˌtaɪ-] *adj* : antisémite
anti–Semitism [ˌænti'sɛməˌtɪzəm, ˌænˌtaɪ-] *n* : antisémitisme *m*

antiseptic[1] [ˌæntəˈsɛptɪk] *adj* : antiseptique

antiseptic[2] *n* : antiseptique *m*

antismoking [ˌæntiˈsmoːkɪŋ, ˌænˌtaɪ-] *n* : antitabac

antisocial [ˌæntiˈsoːʃəl, ˌænˌtaɪ-] *adj* **1** : antisocial <antisocial behavior : comportement antisocial> **2** UNSOCIABLE : peu sociable

antitheft [ˌæntiˈθɛft, ˌænˌtaɪ-] *adj* : antivol

antithesis [ænˈtɪθəsɪs] *n, pl* **-eses** [-ˌsiːz] : antithèse *f*

antitoxin [ˌæntiˈtɑksən, ˌænˌtaɪ-] *n* : antitoxine *f*

antitrust [ˌæntiˈtrʌst, ˌænˌtaɪ-] *adj* : antitrust

antlers [ˈæntlərz] *npl* : bois *mpl,* ramure *f*

antonym [ˈæntəˌnɪm] *n* : antonyme *m*

anus [ˈeɪnəs] *n* : anus *m*

anvil [ˈænvəl, -vɪl] *n* : enclume *f*

anxiety [æŋkˈzaɪət̬i] *n, pl* **-ties 1** APPREHENSION, UNEASINESS : anxiété *f,* appréhension *f* **2** CONCERN : souci *m* <he's a great anxiety to me : il me donne énormément de soucis> **3** EAGERNESS : désir *m* ardent

anxious [ˈæŋkʃəs] *adj* **1** WORRIED : inquiet, anxieux **2** EAGER : impatient, anxieux

anxiously [ˈæŋkʃəsli] *adv* **1** UNEASILY : avec inquiétude, anxieusement **2** EAGERLY : avec impatience

any[1] [ˈɛni] *adv* **1** (*used in questions and conditional clauses*) : un peu <can they work any faster? : peuvent-ils travailler un peu plus vite?> <do you want any more coffee? : voulez-vous encore du café?> **2** (*used in negative constructions*) <I don't smoke any longer : je ne fume plus> <she doesn't know any more than that : c'est tout ce qu'elle sait> **3** AT ALL : du tout <that didn't help any : cela n'a pas aidé du tout>

any[2] *adj* **1** (*used in questions*) : de, de la, du, des <do you have any advice? : avez-vous des conseils?> **2** (*used in negative constructions*) <we don't have any money : nous n'avons pas d'argent> <without any problem : sans le moindre problème> <he hasn't any idea : il n'a aucune idée> **3** WHICHEVER : quelconque, n'importe quel, tout <take any book : prenez n'importe quel livre> <at any moment : à tout moment>

any[3] *pron* **1** : en <if you have any : si tu en as> <I don't like any of them : je n'en aime aucun d'entre eux> **2** : n'importe lequel <take any you want : prenez n'importe lequel>

anybody [ˈɛniˌbʌdi, -ˌbɑ-] → **anyone**

anyhow [ˈɛniˌhaʊ] *adv* **1** IN ANY CASE : de toute façon, en tout cas **2** HAPHAZARDLY : n'importe comment

anymore [ˌɛniˈmor] *adv* : plus <I don't dance anymore : je ne danse plus>

anyone [ˈɛniˌwʌn] *pron* **1** (*in questions or conditional clauses*) : quelqu'un <is anyone home? : est-ce qu'il y a quelqu'un à la maison?> **2** (*in negative constructions*) : personne <you didn't see anyone? : tu n'as vu personne?> **3** : tout le monde <anyone can play : tout le monde peut jouer>

anyplace [ˈɛniˌpleɪs] → **anywhere**

anything [ˈɛniˌθɪŋ] *pron* **1** : tout, n'importe quoi <he eats anything : il mange n'importe quoi> **2** SOMETHING : quelque chose <can anything be done? : peut-on faire quelque chose?> **3** : rien <hardly anything : presque rien> **4 anything but** : tout sauf

anytime [ˈɛniˌtaɪm] *adv* : n'importe quand <call me anytime : appelez-moi n'importe quand>

anyway [ˈɛniˌweɪ] → **anyhow**

anywhere [ˈɛniˌhwɛr] *adv* **1** : n'importe où, partout <sit down anywhere : asseyez-vous n'importe où> <anywhere else : partout ailleurs> **2** (*in questions*) : quelque part <do you have some glue anywhere? : avez-vous de la colle quelque part?> **3** (*in negative constructions*) : nulle part <she doesn't go anywhere : elle ne va nulle part>

aorta [eɪˈɔrt̬ə] *n, pl* **-tas** *or* **-tae** : aorte *f*

apart [əˈpɑrt] *adv* **1** : l'un de l'autre, d'intervalle <far apart : éloigné l'un de l'autre> <shots five minutes apart : des coups de feu à cinq minutes d'intervalle> **2** ASIDE : à part, à l'écart <apart from : en dehors de> **3** SEPARATELY : séparément **4 to fall apart** : s'en aller en morceaux, se défaire **5 to take apart** : démonter **6 to tell apart** : distinguer

apartheid [əˈpɑrˌteɪt, -ˌtaɪt] *n* : apartheid *m*

apartment [əˈpɑrtmənt] *n* **1** : appartement *m* **2** *or* **apartment house** : immeuble *m*

apathetic [ˌæpəˈθɛt̬ɪk] *adj* : apathique

apathetically [ˌæpəˈθɛt̬ɪkli] *adv* : avec apathie

apathy [ˈæpəθi] *n* : apathie *f*

ape[1] [ˈeɪp] *vt* **aped; aping** : singer

ape[2] *n* : grand singe *m*

aperture [ˈæpərtʃər, -ˌtʃʊr] *n* : ouverture *f*

apex [ˈeɪˌpɛks] *n, pl* **apexes** *or* **apices** [ˈeɪpəˌsiːz, ˈæ-] : sommet *m,* point *m* culminant

aphid [ˈeɪfɪd, ˈæ-] *n* : puceron *m*

aphorism [ˈæfəˌrɪzəm] *n* : aphorisme *m*

aphrodisiac [ˈæfrəˈdiːziˌæk, -ˈdɪ-] *n* : aphrodisiaque *m*

apiary [ˈeɪpiˌɛri] *n, pl* **-aries** : rucher *m*

apiece [əˈpiːs] *adv* **1** : par personne, chacun <two candies apiece : deux bon-

bons par personne> **2** : la pièce, chacun <they cost two dollars apiece : ils coûtent deux dollars la pièce>

aplenty [ə'plɛnti] *adv* : en abondance

aplomb [ə'plɑm, -'plʌm] *n* : aplomb *m*

apocalypse [ə'pɑkə,lɪps] *n* : apocalypse *f*

apocalyptic [ə,pɑkə'lɪptɪk] *adj* : apocalyptique

apocrypha [ə'pɑkrəfə] *n* **the Apocrypha** : les Apocryphes

apologetic [ə'pɑlə'dʒɛt̬ɪk] *adj* **1** : d'excuse <in an apologetic tone : d'un ton contrit> **2 to be apologetic** : s'excuser

apologetically [ə'pɑlə'dʒɛt̬ɪkli] *adv* : en s'excusant, d'un air contrit

apologize [ə'pɑlə,dʒaɪz] *vi* **-gized; -gizing** : s'excuser, faire des excuses

apology [ə'pɑlədʒi] *n, pl* **-gies** : excuses *fpl*

apoplectic [,æpə'plɛktɪk] *adj* : apoplectique

apoplexy ['æpə,plɛksi] *n* : apoplexie *f*

apostle [ə'pɑsəl] *n* : apôtre *m*

apostolic [,æpə'stɑlɪk] *adj* : apostolique

apostrophe [ə'pɑstrə,fi:] *n* : apostrophe *f*

apothecary [ə'pɑθə,kɛri] *n, pl* **-caries** : pharmacien *m*, -cienne *f*

appall *or Brit* **appal** [ə'pɔl] *vt* **-palled; -palling** : épouvanter, horrifier

appalling [ə'pɔlɪŋ] *adj* : épouvantable, effroyable <appalling ignorance : ignorance consternante>

apparatus [,æpə'ræt̬əs, -'reɪ-] *n, pl* **-tuses** *or* **-tus** : appareil *m*, équipement *m*, agrès *mpl* (de gymnastique)

apparel [ə'pærəl] *n* : habillement *m*, vêtements *mpl*

apparent [ə'pærənt] *adj* **1** VISIBLE : visible **2** OBVIOUS : évident **3** SEEMING : apparent

apparently [ə'pærəntli] *adv* : apparemment

apparition [,æpə'rɪʃən] *n* : apparition *f*

appeal[1] [ə'pi:l] *vt* : faire appel contre, en appeler de (un jugement) — *vi* **1** : interjeter appel (en droit) **2 to appeal for** : lancer un appel à **3 to appeal to** ATTRACT : attirer, plaire **4 to appeal to** INVOKE : faire appel à

appeal[2] *n* **1** CALL : appel *m* **2** ENTREATY : supplication *f* **3** ATTRACTION : attrait *m*

appear [ə'pɪr] *vi* **1** : apparaître, arriver <to appear on the scene : arriver sur place> **2** SEEM : sembler, paraître **3** COME OUT : sortir, paraître, être publié **4 to appear in court** : comparaître (devant le tribunal)

appearance [ə'pɪrənts] *n* **1** APPEARING : apparition *f*, arrivée *f*, comparution *f* (devant le tribunal) **2** LOOK : apparence *f*, semblant *m* **3 appearances** *npl* : apparences *fpl* <to keep up appearances : sauver les apparences>

appease [ə'pi:z] *vt* **-peased; -peasing** : apaiser

appeasement [ə'pi:zmənt] *n* : apaisement *m*

append [ə'pɛnd] *vt* : ajouter

appendage [ə'pɛndɪdʒ] *n* : appendice *m*

appendectomy [,æpən'dɛktəmi] *n, pl* **-mies** : appendicectomie *f*

appendicitis [ə,pɛndə'saɪt̬əs] *n* : appendicite *f*

appendix [ə'pɛndɪks] *n, pl* **-dixes** *or* **-dices** [-də,si:z] : appendice *m*

appetite ['æpə,taɪt] *n* : appétit *m*

appetizer ['æpə,taɪzər] *n* : amuse-gueule *m*

appetizing ['æpə,taɪzɪŋ] *adj* : appétissant

applaud [ə'plɔd] *v* : applaudir

applause [ə'plɔz] *n* : applaudissements *mpl*

apple ['æpəl] *n* : pomme *f*

appliance [ə'plaɪənts] *n* : appareil *m*

applicable ['æplɪkəbəl, ə'plɪkə-] *adj* : applicable

applicant ['æplɪkənt] *n* : candidat *m*, -date *f*

application [,æplə'keɪʃən] *n* **1** USE : application *f* **2** REQUEST : demande *f* <application form : formulaire de demande> **3** DILIGENCE : assiduité *f*, zèle *m*

applicator ['æplə,keɪt̬ər] *n* : applicateur *m*

appliqué[1] [,æplə'keɪ] *vt* **-quéd; -quéing** : orner d'appliques

appliqué[2] *n* : applique *f*

apply [ə'plaɪ] *v* **-plied; -plying** *vt* **1** : appliquer, mettre <to apply varnish : appliquer du vernis> **2** EXERT : exercer <apply pressure : exercez une pression> **3 to apply oneself** : s'appliquer — *vi* **1** : s'appliquer <the law applies to everyone : la loi s'applique à tous> **2 to apply for** : poser sa candidature pour, faire une demande de

appoint [ə'pɔɪnt] *vt* **1** DESIGNATE, SET : désigner, fixer **2** NAME : nommer **3** EQUIP : équiper <a well-appointed office : un bureau bien aménagé>

appointee [ə,pɔɪn'ti:, ,æ-] *n* : candidat *m* retenu, candidate *f* retenue

appointment [ə'pɔɪntmənt] *n* **1** NOMINATION : nomination *f*, désignation *f* **2** MEETING : rendez-vous *m* **3** POSITION : poste *m*

apportion [ə'porʃən] *vt* ALLOT : répartir, distribuer

apportionment [ə'porʃənmənt] *n* : répartition *f*

apposite ['æpəzət] *adj* PERTINENT : pertinent, juste

appraisal [ə'preɪzəl] *n* : évaluation *f*, appréciation *f*

appraise [ə'preɪz] *vt* **-praised; -praising** : évaluer, estimer, apprécier

appreciable [ə'pri:ʃəbəl, -'prɪʃiə-] *adj* : appréciable, sensible

appreciably [ə'pri:ʃəbli, -'prɪʃiə-] *adv* : sensiblement

appreciate [ə'pri:ʃi,eɪt, -'prɪ-] *v* **-ated; -ating** *vt* **1** VALUE : apprécier **2** REALIZE, UNDERSTAND : comprendre, se rendre compte de **3** : être sensible à, être reconnaissant de <I appreciate your kindness : je vous suis reconnaissant de votre gentillesse> — *vi* : s'apprécier

appreciation [ə,pri:ʃi'eɪʃən, -,prɪ-] *n* **1** EVALUATION : appréciation *f*, estimation *f* **2** GRATITUDE : reconnaissance *f* **3** UNDERSTANDING : compréhension *f* **4** INCREASE : hausse *f* (de valeur)

appreciative [ə'pri:ʃət̬ɪv, -'prɪ-; ə'pri:ʃi ,eɪ-] *adj* **1** GRATEFUL : reconnaissant **2** ADMIRING : admiratif, élogieux

apprehend [,æprɪ'hɛnd] *vt* **1** ARREST : arrêter, appréhender **2** UNDERSTAND : comprendre **3** DREAD : appréhender, redouter

apprehensive [,æprɪ'hɛntsɪv] *adj* : inquiet

apprehensively [,æprɪ'hɛntsɪvli] *adv* : avec inquiétude

apprentice[1] [ə'prɛntɪs] *vt* **-ticed; -ticing** : mettre en apprentissage

apprentice[2] *n* : apprenti *m*, -tie *f*

apprenticeship [ə'prɛntɪs,ʃɪp] *n* : apprentissage *m*

apprise [ə'praɪz] *vt* **-prised; -prising** : informer, prévenir

approach[1] [ə'pro:tʃ] *vt* **1** NEAR : s'approcher de, s'avancer vers **2** : s'adresser à, aborder <he approached me : il m'a abordé> **3** CONSIDER : aborder (un problème, etc.) — *vi* NEAR : s'approcher

approach[2] *n* **1** NEARING : approche *f*, arrivée *f* <the approach of winter : la venue de l'hiver> **2** HANDLING : façon *f* (de faire), approche *f* **3** ACCESS : accès *m*, voie *f* d'accès

approachable [ə'pro:tʃəbəl] *adj* : abordable, d'un abord facile, accessible

approbation [,æprə'beɪʃən] *n* : approbation *f*

appropriate[1] [ə'pro:pri,eɪt] *vt* **-ated; -ating 1** SEIZE, TAKE : s'approprier **2** ALLOCATE, ASSIGN : affecter, consacrer

appropriate[2] [ə'pro:priət] *adj* : approprié, convenable, qui convient

appropriately [ə'pro:priətli] *adv* : convenablement, avec à-propos

appropriateness [ə'pro:priətnəs] *n* : convenance *f*, à-propos *m*

appropriation [ə,pro:pri'eɪʃən] *n* **1** SEIZURE : appropriation *f* **2** ALLOCATION : affectation *f*, allocation *f*

approval [ə'pru:vəl] *n* **1** : approbation *f* **2 on ~** : à l'essai

approve [ə'pru:v] *v* **-proved; -proving** *vt* : approuver — *vi* **to approve of** : apprécier, être d'accord avec

approximate[1] [ə'prɑksə,meɪt] *vt* **-mated; -mating** : se rapprocher de

approximate[2] [ə'prɑksəmət] *adj* : approximatif

approximately [ə'prɑksəmətli] *adv* : à peu près, environ

approximation [ə,prɑksə'meɪʃən] *n* : approximation *f*

appurtenance [ə'pərtənənts] *n* : accessoire *m*

apricot ['æprə,kɑt, 'eɪ-] *n* : abricot *m*

April ['eɪprəl] *n* : avril *m*

apron ['eɪprən] *n* : tablier *m*

apropos[1] [,æprə'po:, 'æprə,po:] *adv* : à propos

apropos[2] *adj* : opportun, à propos

apropos of *prep* CONCERNING : quant à, à propos de

apt ['æpt] *adj* **1** SUITABLE : convenable, approprié **2** CLEVER : doué **3 to be apt to** : avoir tendance à <she's apt to forget : elle oublie facilement>

aptitude ['æptə,tu:d, -,tju:d] *n* : aptitude *f*

aptly ['æptli] *adv* : avec justesse, bien <aptly chosen : bien choisi>

aqua ['ækwə, 'ɑ-] *adj* : bleu-vert

aquarium [ə'kwæriəm] *n, pl* **-iums** *or* **-ia** [-iə] : aquarium *m*

Aquarius [ə'kwæriəm] *n* : Verseau *m*

aquatic [ə'kwɑt̬ɪk, -'kwæ-] *adj* : aquatique (se dit des plantes et des animaux), nautique (se dit des sports)

aqueduct ['ækwə,dʌkt] *n* : aqueduc *m*

aquiline ['ækwə,laɪn, -lən] *adj* : aquilin

Arab[1] ['ærəb] *adj* : arabe

Arab[2] *n* : Arabe *mf*

arabesque [,ærə'bɛsk] *n* : arabesque *f*

Arabian[1] [ə'reɪbiən] *adj* : arabe

Arabian[2] *n* → **Arab**[2]

Arabic[1] ['ærəbɪk] *adj* : arabe

Arabic[2] *n* : arabe *m* (langue)

arable ['ærəbəl] *adj* : arable

arbiter ['ɑrbət̬ər] *n* : arbitre *m*

arbitrary ['ɑrbə,trɛri] *adj* : arbitraire — **arbitrarily** [,ɑrbə'trɛrəli] *adv*

arbitrate ['ɑrbə,treɪt] *v* **-trated; -trating** *vt* : arbitrer, juger — *vi* : arbitrer

arbitration [,ɑrbə'treɪʃən] *n* : arbitrage *m*

arbitrator ['ɑrbə,treɪt̬ər] *n* : médiateur *m*, -trice *f*; arbitre *m*

arbor *or Brit* **arbour** ['ɑrbər] *n* : tonnelle *f*

arboreal [ɑr'boriəl] *adj* : arboricole

arbour *Brit* → **arbor**

arc[1] ['ɑrk] *vi* **arced; arcing** : décrire un arc

arc[2] *n* : arc *m*

arcade [ɑr'keɪd] *n* **1** ARCHES : arcade *f* **2 shopping arcade** : galerie *f* marchande

arcane [ɑr'keɪn] *adj* : mystérieux, obscur

arch[1] ['ɑrtʃ] *vt* **1** BEND : arquer, courber **2** VAULT : voûter — *vi* : former une voûte

arch[2] *adj* **1** CHIEF : principal <your arch opponent : ton principal adversaire> **2** MISCHIEVOUS : espiègle, malicieux

arch[3] *n* **1** : voûte *f,* arc *m,* arche *f* **2** ARCHING : courbe *f* (des sourcils, etc.)

archaeological [ˌɑrkiəˈlɑdʒɪkəl] *adj* : archéologique

archaeologist [ˌɑrkiˈɑlədʒɪst] *n* : archéologue *mf*

archaeology *or* **archeology** [ˌɑrkiˈɑlədʒi] *n* : archéologie *f*

archaic [ɑrˈkeɪɪk] *adj* : archaïque

archangel [ˈɑrkˌeɪndʒəl] *n* : archange *m*

archbishop [ɑrtʃˈbɪʃəp] *n* : archevêque *m*

archdiocese [ɑrtʃˈdaɪəsəs, -ˌsiːz, -ˌsiːs] *n* : archidiocèse *m*

archer [ˈɑrtʃər] *n* : archer *m*

archery [ˈɑrtʃəri] *n* : tir *m* à l'arc

archetype [ˈɑrkɪˌtaɪp] *n* : archétype *m*

archipelago [ˌɑrkəˈpɛləˌgoː, ˌɑrtʃə-] *n, pl* **-goes** *or* **-gos** [-goːz] : archipel *m*

architect [ˈɑrkəˌtɛkt] *n* : architecte *mf*

architectural [ˌɑrkəˈtɛktʃərəl] *adj* : architectural

architecturally [ˌɑrkəˈtɛktʃərəli] *adv* : du point de vue architectural

architecture [ˈɑrkəˌtɛktʃər] *n* : architecture *f*

archives [ˈɑrˌkaɪvz] *npl* : archives *fpl*

archivist [ˈɑrkəvɪst, -ˌkaɪ-] *n* : archiviste *mf*

archway [ˈɑrtʃˌweɪ] *n* : voûte *f,* arcade *f*

arctic [ˈɑrktɪk, ˈɑrt̬-] *adj* **1** : arctique **2** FRIGID : glacial

arctic circle *n* : cercle *m* polaire arctique

ardent [ˈɑrdənt] *adj* : ardent

ardently [ˈɑrdəntli] *adv* : ardemment, passionnément

ardor *or Brit* **ardour** [ˈɑrdər] *n* : ardeur *f*

arduous [ˈɑrdʒʊəs] *adj* : ardu, pénible

arduously [ˈɑrdʒʊəsli] *adv* : péniblement

arduousness [ˈɑrdʒʊəsnəs] *n* : difficulté *f,* dureté *f*

area [ˈæriə] *n* **1** REGION : région *f,* zone *f,* quartier *m* **2** SURFACE : aire *f,* superficie *f* <the area of a circle : l'aire d'un cercle> **3** FIELD : domaine *m* <area of expertise : domaine d'expertise>

area code *n* : indicatif *m* de zone, indicatif *m* régional *Can*

arena [əˈriːnə] *n* : arène *f,* aréna *m Can*

aren't [ˈɑrnt, ˈɑrənt] (*contraction of* **are** *and* **not**) → **be**

Aries [ˈɛriːz, -iˌiːz] *n* : Bélier *m*

Argentine[1] [ˈɑrdʒənˌtaɪn, -ˌtiːn] *or* **Argentinean** *or* **Argentinian** [ˌɑrdʒənˈtɪniən] *adj* : argentin

Argentine[2] *or* **Argentinean** *or* **Argentinian** *n* : Argentin *m,* -tine *f*

argon [ˈɑrˌgɑn] *n* : argon *m*

argot [ˈɑrgət, -ˌgoː] *n* : argot *m*

arguable [ˈɑrgjʊəbəl] *adj* : discutable

argue [ˈɑrˌgjuː] *v* **-gued; -guing** *vt* **1** DEBATE, DISCUSS : discuter **2** PLEAD : plaider <to argue a case : plaider une cause> **3** MAINTAIN : soutenir **4** PERSUADE : persuader — *vi* **1** QUARREL : se disputer **2** DEBATE : argumenter

argument [ˈɑrgjəmənt] *n* **1** QUARREL : dispute *f* **2** DEBATE : discussion *f,* débat *m* **3** REASONING : argument *m,* raisonnement *m* <his argument is that : il soutient que>

argumentative [ˌɑrgjəˈmɛntət̬ɪv] *adj* : querelleur, ergoteur

argyle [ˈɑrˌgaɪl] *adj* : à motifs de losanges

aria [ˈɑriə] *n* : aria *f*

arid [ˈærəd] *adj* : aride

aridity [əˈrɪdət̬i, æ-] *n* : aridité *f*

arise [əˈraɪz] *vi* **arose** [əˈroːz]; **arisen** [əˈrɪzən]; **arising 1** RISE : se lever **2** APPEAR, OCCUR : se présenter, survenir <if the occasion arises : si l'occasion se présente> **3 to arise from** : provenir de, résulter de

aristocracy [ˌærəˈstɑkrəsi] *n, pl* **-cies** : aristocratie *f*

aristocrat [əˈrɪstəˌkræt] *n* : aristocrate *mf*

aristocratic [əˌrɪstəˈkræt̬ɪk] *adj* : aristocratique

arithmetic[1] [ˌærɪθˈmɛt̬ɪk] *or* **arithmetical** [-t̬ɪkəl] *adj* : arithmétique

arithmetic[2] [əˈrɪθməˌtɪk] *n* : arithmétique *f*

ark [ˈɑrk] *n* : arche *f*

arm[1] [ˈɑrm] *vt* : armer

arm[2] *n* **1** : bras *m* (du corps ou d'une machine), accoudoir *m* (d'une chaise), manche *f* (d'un vêtement) **2** WEAPON : arme *f* <to take up arms : prendre les armes> **3** BRANCH : branche *f,* section *f* **4** → **coat of arms**

armada [ɑrˈmɑdə, -ˈmeɪ-] *n* : armada *f*

armadillo [ˌɑrməˈdɪlo] *n, pl* **-los** : tatou *m*

armament [ˈɑrməmənt] *n* : armement *m*

armchair [ˈɑrmˌtʃɛr] *n* : fauteuil *m*

armed [ˈɑrmd] *adj* : armé <armed robbery : vol à main armée>

armed forces *npl* : forces *fpl* armées

Armenian[1] [ɑrˈmiːniən] *adj* : arménien

Armenian[2] *n* **1** : Arménien *m,* -nienne *f* **2** : arménien *m* (langue)

armistice [ˈɑrməstɪs] *n* : armistice *m*

armor *or Brit* **armour** [ˈɑrmər] *n* **1** : armure *f* <a suit of armor : une armure complète> **2** *or* **armor plating** : blindage *m*

armored *or Brit* **armoured** [ˈɑrmərd] *adj* : blindé

armory *or Brit* **armoury** [ˈɑrməri] *n, pl* **-mories** *or Brit* **-mouries** : arsenal *m* (dépôt d'armes), fabrique *f* d'armes

armpit [ˈɑrmˌpɪt] *n* : aisselle *f*

army ['ɑrmi] *n, pl* **-mies** : armée *f*
aroma [ə'ro:mə] *n* : arôme *m*
aromatic [ˌærə'mæt̬ɪk] *adj* : aromatique
around[1] [ə'raʊnd] *adv* **1** : de circonférence <a tree two meters around : un arbre deux mètres de circonférence> **2** : autour, de tous côtés <all around : tout autour> <for miles around : sur un rayon de plusieurs milles> **3** NEARBY : pas loin, là, dans les parages <will he be around tonight? : il sera là ce soir?> **4** APPROXIMATELY : environ, à peu près <it costs around five dollars : ça coûte environ cinq dollars>
around[2] *prep* **1** SURROUNDING : autour de <the trees around the house : les arbres autour de la maison> **2** THROUGHOUT : à travers de <she traveled around the country : elle a voyagé partout dans le pays> <somewhere around the house : quelque part dans la maison> **3** AT : vers <come around noon : viens vers midi> **4 around here** : par ici **5 to go around the corner** : tourner le coin
arousal [ə'raʊzəl] *n* : excitation *f*
arouse [ə'raʊz] *vt* **aroused; arousing 1** AWAKEN : réveiller **2** STIMULATE : exciter, éveiller
arraign [ə'reɪn] *vt* : accuser, traduire en justice
arraignment [ə'reɪnmənt] *n* : lecture *f* de l'acte d'accusation
arrange [ə'reɪndʒ] *v* **-ranged; -ranging** *vt* : arranger — *vi* **to arrange for** : s'arranger pour, prendre des dispositions pour
arrangement [ə'reɪndʒmənt] *n* **1** LAYOUT : arrangement *m,* disposition *f* **2** AGREEMENT : arrangement *m,* accord *m* <under the present arrangement : selon l'accord actuel> **3 arrangements** *npl* PLANS : mesures *fpl,* dispositions *fpl*
array[1] [ə'reɪ] *vt* **1** ARRANGE : arranger, disposer, déployer (des troupes) **2** ADORN : parer <to array oneself : se parer>
array[2] *n* **1** ARRANGEMENT : arrangement *m,* ordre *m,* déploiement *m* (de troupes) **2** FINERY : parure *f,* habits *mpl* d'apparat **3** RANGE, SELECTION : panoplie *f,* sélection *f*
arrears [ə'rɪrz] *npl* **1** : arriéré *m* <rent arrears : arriéré de loyer> **2 to be in arrears** : avoir du retard
arrest[1] [ə'rɛst] *vt* : arrêter
arrest[2] *n* **1** : arrêt *m* <cardiac arrest : arrêt du cœur> **2** : arrestation *f* <under arrest : en état d'arrestation>
arrival [ə'raɪvəl] *n* : arrivée *f* (de personnes, d'avions, etc.), arrivage *m* (de marchandises)
arrive [ə'raɪv] *vi* **-rived; -riving 1** : arriver **2 to arrive at** : parvenir à (une résolution, etc.), atteindre (un état)
arrogance ['ærəgənts] *n* : arrogance *f*
arrogant ['ærəgənt] *adj* : arrogant, insolent
arrogantly ['ærəgəntli] *adv* : avec arrogance
arrow ['æro] *n* : flèche *f*
arrowhead ['æroˌhɛd] *n* : pointe *f* de flèche
arsenal ['ɑrsənəl] *n* : arsenal *m*
arsenic ['ɑrsənɪk] *n* : arsenic *m*
arson ['ɑrsən] *n* : incendie *m* criminel
arsonist ['ɑrsənɪst] *n* : incendiaire *mf*
art ['ɑrt] *n* **1** : art *m* **2** SKILL : art *m,* habileté *f*
artefact *Brit* → **artifact**
arterial [ɑr'tɪriəl] *adj* : artériel
arteriosclerosis [ɑrˌtɪriosklə'ro:sɪs] *n* : artériosclérose *f*
artery ['ɑrt̬əri] *n, pl* **-teries** : artère *f*
artful ['ɑrtfəl] *adj* **1** CLEVER, INGENIOUS : astucieux, ingénieux **2** CRAFTY : rusé, malin
arthritic [ɑr'θrɪt̬ɪk] *adj* : arthritique
arthritis [ɑr'θraɪt̬əs] *n, pl* **-thritides** [-'θrɪt̬əˌdi:z] : arthrite *f*
arthropod ['ɑrθrəˌpɑd] *n* : arthropode *m*
artichoke ['ɑrt̬əˌtʃo:k] *n* : artichaut *m*
article ['ɑrtɪkəl] *n* **1** THING : objet *m* <articles of clothing : vêtements> **2** : article *m* (dans une publication ou dans un acte judiciaire) **3** : article *m* <definite article : article défini>
articulate[1] [ɑr'tɪkjəˌleɪt] *vt* **-lated; -lating** : articuler
articulate[2] [ɑr'tɪkjələt] *adj* **1** INTELLIGIBLE : distinct, intelligible **2** WELL-SPOKEN : qui s'exprime bien **3** JOINTED : articulé
articulately [ɑr'tɪkjələtli] *adv* : clairement, distinctement
articulation [ɑrˌtɪkjə'leɪʃən] *n* : articulation *f*
artifact *or Brit* **artefact** ['ɑrt̬əˌfækt] *n* : objet *m* fabriqué
artifice ['ɑrt̬əfəs] *n* : artifice *m*
artificial [ˌɑrt̬ə'fɪʃəl] *adj* : artificiel — **artificially** *adv*
artificial respiration *n* : respiration *f* artificielle
artillery [ɑr'tɪləri] *n, pl* **-leries** : artillerie *f*
artisan ['ɑrt̬əzən, -sən] *n* : artisan *m,* -sane *f*
artist ['ɑrt̬ɪst] *n* : artiste *mf*
artistic [ɑr'tɪstɪk] *adj* : artistique — **artistically** [-tɪkli] *adv*
artistry ['ɑrt̬əstri] *n* : art *m*
artless ['ɑrtləs] *adj* **1** NATURAL : naturel **2** NAIVE : naïf, ingénu — **artlessly** *adv*
arty ['ɑrt̬i] *adj* **artier; -est** : prétentieusement artistique
as[1] ['æz] *adv* **1** EQUALLY : aussi <as green as grass : aussi vert que l'herbe> **2** : par exemple <some trees, as oak or pine : des arbres, par exemple le chêne ou le pin>
as[2] *conj* **1** LIKE : comme <white as snow : blanc comme la neige> **2**

WHEN, WHILE : tandis que, alors que, comme <he spoke to me as I was leaving : il m'a parlé tandis que je partais> **3** SINCE : puisque, comme <she stayed home as she has no car : elle est restée chez elle puisqu'elle n'a pas de voiture> **4** : que <so guilty as to leave no doubt : si coupable qu'il n'y a aucun doute> **5 as is** : tel quel
as[3] *prep* **1** LIKE : comme <to behave as a child : se comporter comme un enfant> **2** : en tant que <she works as an editor : elle travaille en tant qu'éditeur> **3** : en <he dressed as a clown : il s'est habillé en clown>
as[4] *pron* **1** : que <the same price as before : le même prix qu'avant> **2** : comme <she's rich, as you know : elle est riche, comme vous savez>
asbestos [æz'bɛstəs, æs-] *n* : amiante *m*
ascend [ə'sɛnd] *vt* : monter, monter à, gravir <to ascend the staircase : monter l'escalier> <to ascend to the throne : monter sur le trône> — *vi* : monter
ascendancy [ə'sɛndəntsi] *n* : ascendant *m*
ascendant[1] [ə'sɛndənt] *adj* : dominant
ascendant[2] *n* **to be in the ascendant** : être à l'ascendant
ascension [ə'sɛntʃən] *n* : ascension *f*
ascent [ə'sɛnt] *n* **1** RISING : ascension *f* **2** INCLINE : montée *f,* pente *f*
ascertain [ˌæsər'teɪn] *vt* : vérifier, établir, constater
ascertainable [ˌæsər'teɪnəbəl] *adj* : vérifiable
ascetic[1] [ə'sɛt̬ɪk] *adj* : ascétique
ascetic[2] *n* : ascète *mf*
asceticism [ə'sɛt̬əˌsɪzəm] *n* : ascétisme *m*
ascribable [ə'skraɪbəbəl] *adj* : attribuable
ascribe [ə'skraɪb] *vt* **-cribed; -cribing** : attribuer
aseptic [eɪ'sɛptɪk] *adj* : aseptique
as for *prep* CONCERNING : quant à
ash ['æʃ] *n* **1** : cendre *f* <to reduce to ashes : réduire en cendres> **2** : frêne *m* (arbre)
ashamed [ə'ʃeɪmd] *adj* **1** : honteux **2 to be ashamed** : avoir honte
ashen ['æʃən] *adj* : cendreux, blême
ashore [ə'ʃor] *adv* **1** : à terre **2 to go ashore** : débarquer
ashtray ['æʃˌtreɪ] *n* : cendrier *m*
Asian[1] ['eɪʒən, -ʃən] *adj* : asiatique
Asian[2] *n* : Asiatique *mf*
aside[1] [ə'saɪd] *adv* **1** : de côté <let's put it aside : mettons-le de côté> **2** APART : à part, à l'écart
aside[2] *n* : aparté *m*
aside from *prep* **1** BESIDES : à part, en plus de **2** EXCEPT : sauf
as if *conj* : comme si
asinine ['æsənˌaɪn] *adj* : sot
ask ['æsk] *vt* **1** : poser, demander <to ask a question : poser une question> <to ask directions : demander son chemin> **2** REQUEST : demander <that's asking a lot! : c'est beaucoup en demander!> **3** INVITE : inviter <to ask s.o. in : inviter qqn à entrer> **4 to ask oneself** : se demander — *vi* : demander
askance [ə'skænts] *adv* **to look askance at** : regarder de travers, regarder d'un air méfiant
askew [ə'skjuː] *adv & adj* : de travers
asleep [ə'sliːp] *adj* **1** : endormi **2 to fall asleep** : s'endormir
as of *prep* : dès, à partir de
asparagus [ə'spærəgəs] *ns & pl* : asperge *f* <do you have any asparagus? : avez-vous des asperges?>
aspect ['æˌspɛkt] *n* **1** SIDE : aspect *m* <to study the question from every aspect : étudier la question sous tous ses aspects> **2** ORIENTATION : orientation *f,* exposition *f* **3** APPEARANCE : aspect *m,* air *m,* mine *f*
aspen ['æspən] *n* : tremble *m*
asperity [æ'spɛrət̬i, ə-] *n, pl* **-ties** : aspérité *f*
aspersion [ə'spərʒən] *n* **1** : calomnie *f* **2 to cast aspersions on** : dénigrer
asphalt ['æsˌfɔlt] *n* : asphalte *m*
asphyxiate [æ'sfɪksiˌeɪt] *vt* **-ated; -ating** : asphyxier
asphyxiation [æˌsfɪksi'eɪʃən] *n* : asphyxie *f*
aspic ['æspɪk] *n* : aspic *m*
aspirant ['æspərənt, ə'spaɪrənt] *n* : aspirant *m,* -rante *f*
aspiration [ˌæspə'reɪʃən] *n* : aspiration *f*
aspire [ə'spaɪr] *vi* **-pired; -piring** : aspirer
aspirin ['æsprən, 'æspə-] *n, pl* **aspirin** *or* **aspirins** : aspirine *f*
ass ['æs] *n* **1** : âne *m* **2** FOOL : idiot *m,* -diote *f*
assail [ə'seɪl] *vt* : assaillir, attaquer
assailant [ə'seɪlənt] *n* : agresseur *m;* assaillant *m,* -lante *f*
assassin [ə'sæsən] *n* : assassin *m*
assassinate [ə'sæsənˌeɪt] *vt* **-nated; -nating** : assassiner
assassination [əˌsæsən'eɪʃən] *n* : assassinat *m*
assault[1] [ə'sɔlt] *vt* : agresser, attaquer
assault[2] *n* : agression *f,* assaut *m* (militaire) <sexual assault : agression sexuelle> <assault and battery : coups et blessures>
assay[1] [æ'seɪ, 'æˌseɪ] *vt* : essayer
assay[2] ['æˌseɪ, æ'seɪ] *n* ANALYSIS : analyse *f*
assemble [ə'sɛmbəl] *v* **-bled; -bling** *vt* **1** CONSTRUCT : assembler **2** GATHER : rassembler — *vi* CONVENE : se rassembler, se réunir
assembly [ə'sɛmbli] *n, pl* **-blies 1** MEETING : assemblée *f,* réunion *f* **2** ASSEMBLING : assemblage *m,* montage *m* <assembly line : chaîne de montage>

assent[1] [ə'sɛnt] *vi* : consentir, donner son assentiment
assent[2] *n* : assentiment *m*
assert [ə'sərt] *vt* **1** DECLARE : affirmer, déclarer **2** DEMAND : revendiquer (ses droits, etc.) **3 to assert oneself** : s'affirmer, s'imposer
assertion [ə'sərʃən] *n* **1** DECLARATION : affirmation *f,* assertion *f* **2** CLAIM : revendication *f*
assertive [ə'sərt̬ɪv] *adj* : assuré
assertiveness [ə'sərt̬ɪvnəs] *n* : manière *f* assurée
assess [ə'sɛs] *vt* **1** EVALUATE : évaluer, estimer **2** IMPOSE : imposer (un impôt, etc.)
assessment [ə'sɛsmənt] *n* : évaluation *f,* estimation *f*
assessor [ə'sɛsər] *n* : expert *m;* contrôleur *m,* -leuse *f* (des impôts)
asset ['æˌsɛt] *n* **1** ADVANTAGE : avantage *m,* atout *m* **2 assets** *npl* : biens *mpl,* actif *m,* capital *m* <assets and liabilities : l'actif et le passif>
assiduity [ˌæsə'du:əti, -'dju:-] *n, pl* **-ities** : assiduité *f*
assiduous [ə'sɪdʒʊəs] *adj* : assidu
assiduously [ə'sɪdʒʊəsli] *adv* : assidûment
assign [ə'saɪn] *vt* **1** ALLOT : assigner **2** FIX, SPECIFY : fixer **3** APPOINT : nommer **4** ATTRIBUTE : attribuer
assignment [ə'saɪnmənt] *n* **1** TASK : tâche *f,* mission *f* **2** HOMEWORK : devoir *m* **3** ALLOCATION : allocation *f,* affectation *f*
assimilate [ə'sɪməˌleɪt] *v* **-lated; -lating** *vt* : assimiler — *vi* : s'assimiler
assimilation [əˌsɪmə'leɪʃən] *n* : assimilation *f*
assist [ə'sɪst] *vt* : aider, assister
assistance [ə'sɪstənts] *n* : aide *f,* assistance *f*
assistant [ə'sɪstənt] *n* : assistant *m,* -tante *f;* adjoint *m,* -jointe *f*
associate[1] [ə'so:ʃiˌeɪt, -si-] *v* **-ated; -ating** *vt* **1** : associer **2 to be associated with** : être associé à, faire partie de — *vi* **to associate with** : fréquenter
associate[2] [ə'so:ʃiət, -siət] *n* : associé *m,* -ciée *f*
association [əˌso:ʃi'eɪʃən, -si-] *n* : association *f*
as soon as *conj* : aussitôt que
assorted [ə'sɔrt̬əd] *adj* : assorti
assortment [ə'sɔrtmənt] *n* : assortiment *m*
assuage [ə'sweɪdʒ] *vt* **-suaged; -suaging** **1** CALM, EASE : apaiser, calmer **2** SATISFY : assouvir (la faim, etc.)
assume [ə'su:m] *vt* **-sumed; -suming** **1** TAKE ON : prendre, assumer **2** ADOPT, FEIGN : adopter, affecter **3** SUPPOSE : supposer, présumer
assumption [ə'sʌmpʃən] *n* **1** SUPPOSITION : supposition *f* **2** APPROPRIATION : appropriation *f,* prise *f* (de pouvoir, etc.)
assurance [ə'ʃʊrənts] *n* : assurance *f*
assure [ə'ʃʊr] *vt* **-sured; -suring** : assurer
assured [ə'ʃʊrd] *adj* **1** CERTAIN : assuré **2** CONFIDENT : assuré, plein d'assurance
assuredly [ə'ʃʊrədli] *adv* : assurément
aster ['æstər] *n* : aster *m*
asterisk ['æstəˌrɪsk] *n* : astérisque *m*
astern [ə'stərn] *adv* : à l'arrière
asteroid ['æstəˌrɔɪd] *n* : astéroïde *m*
asthma ['æzmə] *n* : asthme *m*
asthmatic [æz'mæt̬ɪk] *adj* : asthmatique
as though → **as if**
astigmatism [ə'stɪgməˌtɪzəm] *n* : astigmatisme *m*
astir [ə'stər] *adj* **1** UP : debout **2** ACTIVE, MOVING : en mouvement, animé
as to *prep* **1** ABOUT : sur, concernant **2** → **according to**
astonish [ə'stɑnɪʃ] *vt* : étonner, ahurir
astonishing [ə'stɑnɪʃɪŋ] *adj* : étonnant, ahurissant
astonishingly [ə'stɑnɪʃɪŋli] *adv* : incroyablement
astonishment [ə'stɑnɪʃmənt] *n* : étonnement *m,* stupéfaction *f*
astound [ə'staʊnd] *vt* : stupéfier
astounding [ə'staʊndɪŋ] *adj* : stupéfiant, ahurissant
astraddle [ə'strædəl] → **astride**
astral ['æstrəl] *adj* : astral
astray [ə'streɪ] *adv* **1 to go astray** : s'égarer **2 to lead s.o. astray** : égarer qqn, détourner qqn du droit chemin
astride [ə'straɪd] *adv* : à califourchon
astringent [ə'strɪndʒənt] *adj* : astringent
astrologer [ə'strɑlədʒər] *n* : astrologue *mf*
astrological [ˌæstrə'lɑdʒɪkəl] *adj* : astrologique
astrology [ə'strɑlədʒi] *n* : astrologie *f*
astronaut ['æstrəˌnɔt] *n* : astronaute *mf*
astronautics [ˌæstrə'nɔt̬ɪks] *ns & pl* : astronautique *f*
astronomer [ə'strɑnəmər] *n* : astronome *mf*
astronomical [ˌæstrə'nɑmɪkəl] *adj* : astronomique
astronomy [ə'strɑnəmi] *n, pl* **-mies** : astronomie *f*
astute [ə'stu:t, -'stju:t] *adj* : astucieux — **astutely** *adv*
astuteness [ə'stu:tnəs, -'stju:t-] *n* : astuce *f*
asunder [ə'sʌndər] *adv* **1** : en morceaux **2 to tear asunder** : déchirer
as well as[1] *conj* AND : en plus de
as well as[2] *prep* : ainsi que, à part
asylum [ə'saɪləm] *n* : asile *m*
asymmetrical [ˌeɪsə'mɛtrɪkəl] *or* **asymmetric** [ˌeɪsə'mɛtrɪk] *adj* : asymétrique
asymmetry [ˌeɪ'sɪmətri] *n* : asymétrie *f*
at ['æt] *prep* **1** : à <at the end : à la fin> <be here at 3 o'clock : soyez là à trois

heures> <at his age : à son âge> **2** : chez <at the dentist's : chez le dentiste> **3** : en <at war : en guerre> <to be good at : être bon en> **4** : de <to laugh at : rire de> **5** : sur <to shoot at : tirer sur> **6** : contre <to be angry at : être fâché contre>

at all *adv* : du tout

ate ['eɪt] → **eat**

atheism ['eɪθiˌɪzəm] *n* : athéisme *m*

atheist ['eɪθiɪst] *n* : athée *mf*

atheistic [ˌeɪθi'ɪstɪk] *adj* : athée

athlete ['æθˌliːt] *n* : athlète *mf*

athletic [æθ'lɛt̬ɪk] *adj* : athlétique

athletics [æθ'lɛt̬ɪks] *ns & pl* : athlétisme *m*

atlas ['ætləs] *n* : atlas *m*

atmosphere ['ætməˌsfɪr] *n* : atmosphère *f*

atmospheric [ˌætmə'sfɪrɪk, -'sfɛr-] *adj* : atmosphérique

atoll ['æˌtɔl, 'eɪ-, -ˌtɑl] *n* : atoll *m*

atom ['æt̬əm] *n* : atome *m*

atomic [ə'tɑmɪk] *adj* : atomique

atomic bomb *n* : bombe *f* atomique

atomizer ['æt̬əˌmaɪzər] *n* : atomiseur *m*

atone [ə'toːn] *v* **atoned; atoning** *vt* EXPIATE : expier — *vi* **to atone for** : expier

atonement [ə'toːnmənt] *n* : expiation *f*

atop[1] [ə'tɑp] *adv & adj* : en haut

atop[2] *prep* : sur, en haut de

atrocious [ə'troːʃəs] *adj* : atroce — **atrociously** *adv*

atrocity [ə'trɑsət̬i] *n, pl* **-ties** : atrocité *f*

atrophy[1] ['ætrəfi] *v* **-phied; phying** *vt* : atrophier — *vi* : s'atrophier

atrophy[2] *n, pl* **-phies** : atrophie *f*

attach [ə'tætʃ] *vt* **1** FASTEN, JOIN : attacher, fixer, joindre **2** ATTRIBUTE : attribuer, attacher <she attached little importance to the message : elle a attaché peu d'importance au message> **3** SEIZE : saisir (des biens) **4 to become attached to** : s'attacher à — *vi* ADHERE : s'attacher

attaché [ˌæt̬ə'ʃeɪ, ˌæˌtæ-, əˌtæ-] *n* : attaché *m*, -chée *f*

attaché case *n* : attaché-case *m*

attachment [ə'tætʃmənt] *n* **1** AFFECTION, CLOSENESS : attachement *m*, affection *f* **2** ACCESSORY : accessoire *m* **3** SEIZURE : saisie *f* (de biens) **4** FASTENING : fixation *f*

attack[1] [ə'tæk] *vt* **1** ASSAULT : attaquer, agresser **2** TACKLE : s'attaquer à <he attacked the problem aggressively : il s'est attaqué au problème agressivement>

attack[2] *n* **1** ASSAULT : attaque *f*, assaut *m* **2** : crise *f*, accès *m* <heart attack : crise cardiaque> <an attack of fever : un accès de fièvre>

attain [ə'teɪn] *vt* : atteindre

attainable [ə'teɪnəbəl] *adj* : réalisable

attainment [ə'teɪnmənt] *n* **1** ACHIEVING : réalisation *f* **2** ACCOMPLISHMENT : réussite *f*, résultat *m* obtenu

attempt[1] [ə'tɛmpt] *vt* : tenter

attempt[2] *n* : tentative *f*, effort *m*, essai *m*

attend [ə'tɛnd] *vt* **1** : assister à (une réunion, etc.), aller à (l'église, etc.) **2** LOOK AFTER : soigner, servir **3** ACCOMPANY : accompagner — *vi* **1 to attend to** : s'occuper de (affaires, etc.), s'appliquer à (travaux) **2 to attend to** HEED : prêter attention à

attendance [ə'tɛndənts] *n* **1** PRESENCE : présence *f* **2** TURNOUT : assistance *f*

attendant[1] [ə'tɛndənt] *adj* : concomitant

attendant[2] *n* **1** : gardien *m*, -dienne *f* (à un musée, etc.) **2 service station attendant** : pompiste *mf*

attention [ə'tɛntʃən] *n* **1** : attention *f* **2 to stand at attention** : se mettre au garde-à-vous **3** → **pay**

attentive [ə'tɛntɪv] *adj* : attentif — **attentively** *adv*

attentiveness [ə'tɛntɪvnəs] *n* **1** CONCENTRATION : attention *f* **2** SOLICITUDE : prévenance *f*, égard *m*

attenuate [ə'tɛnjəˌweɪt] *vt* **-ated; -ating** : atténuer

attest [ə'tɛst] *vt* **1** AFFIRM : attester **2** PROVE, SHOW : démontrer, témoigner de — *vi* TESTIFY : témoigner

attestation [ˌæˌtɛs'teɪʃən] *n* : attestation *f*

attic ['ætɪk] *n* : grenier *m*

attire[1] [ə'taɪr] *vt* **-tired; -tiring** : vêtir

attire[2] *n* : vêtements *mpl*

attitude ['æt̬əˌtuːd, -ˌtjuːd] *n* **1** : attitude *f* <a negative attitude : une attitude négative> **2** POSTURE : position *f*, attitude *f* <to strike an attitude : prendre une pose affectée>

attorney [ə'tərni] *n, pl* **-neys** : avocat *m*, -cate *f*

attract [ə'trækt] *vt* : attirer

attraction [ə'trækʃən] *n* : attraction *f*

attractive [ə'træktɪv] *adj* : séduisant, attrayant, attirant

attractively [ə'træktɪvli] *adv* : de manière attrayante

attractiveness [ə'træktɪvnəs] *n* : attrait *m*, charme *m*

attributable [ə'trɪbjut̬əbəl] *adj* : attribuable

attribute[1] [ə'trɪˌbjuːt] *vt* **-uted; -uting** : attribuer

attribute[2] ['ætrəˌbjuːt] *n* : attribut *m*

attribution [ˌætrə'bjuːʃən] *n* : attribution *f*

attune [ə'tuːn, -'tjuːn] *vt* : accorder <to be attuned to : être en accord avec>

auburn ['ɔbərn] *adj* : auburn

auction[1] ['ɔkʃən] *vt* : vendre aux enchères, encanter *Can*

auction[2] *n* : vente *f* aux enchères

auctioneer [ˌɔkʃə'nɪr] *n* : commissaire-priseur *m,* encanteur *m Can*

audacious [ɔ'deɪʃəs] *adj* : audacieux — **audaciously** *adv*

audacity [ɔ'dæsəṯi] *n, pl* **-ties** : audace *f*

audible ['ɔdəbəl] *adj* : audible

audibly ['ɔdəbli] *adv* : distinctement

audience ['ɔdiənts] *n* **1** PUBLIC : assistance *f,* public *m* **2** HEARING, INTERVIEW : audience *f*

audio[1] ['ɔdiˌoː] *adj* : audio

audio[2] *n* : son *m,* acoustique *f*

audiovisual [ˌɔdio'vɪʒuəl] *adj* : audiovisuel

audit[1] ['ɔdət] *vt* **1** : vérifier (des comptes, etc.) **2 to audit a course** : suivre un cours en auditeur libre

audit[2] *n* : audit *m*

audition[1] [ɔ'dɪʃən] *v* : auditionner

audition[2] *n* : audition *f*

auditor ['ɔdəṯər] *n* **1** : vérificateur *m,* -trice *f* (de comptes) **2** : auditeur *m,* -trice *f* (d'un cours)

auditorium [ˌɔdə'toriəm] *n, pl* **-riums** *or* **-ria** [-riə] : salle *f,* amphithéâtre *m*

auditory ['ɔdəˌtori] *adj* : auditif

auger ['ɔgər] *n* : vrille *f*

augment [ɔg'mɛnt] *vt* : augmenter

augmentation [ˌɔgmən'teɪʃən] *n* : augmentation *f*

augur[1] ['ɔgər] *vt* : présager — *vi* **to augur well** : être de bon augure

augur[2] *n* : augure *m*

augury ['ɔgjʊri, -gər-] *n, pl* **-ries** : augure *m,* présage *m*

august [ɔ'gʌst] *adj* : auguste

August ['ɔgəst] *n* : août *m*

auk ['ɔk] *n* **great auk** : grand pingouin *m*

aunt ['ænt, 'ant] *n* : tante *f*

aura ['ɔrə] *n* : aura *f,* atmosphère *f*

aural ['ɔrəl] *adj* : auditif

auricle ['ɔrɪkəl] *n* : oreillette *f* (du cœur)

aurora borealis [ə'rorəˌbori'æləs] *n* : aurore *f* boréale

auspices ['ɔspəsəz, -ˌsiːz] *npl* : auspices *mpl*

auspicious [ɔ'spɪʃəs] *adj* : favorable, propice, prometteur

austere [ɔ'stɪr] *adj* : austère — **austerely** *adv*

austerity [ɔ'stɛrəṯi] *n, pl* **-ties** : austérité *f*

Australian[1] [ɔ'streɪljən] *adj* : australien

Australian[2] *n* : Australien *m,* -lienne *f*

Austrian[1] ['ɔstriən] *adj* : autrichien

Austrian[2] *n* : Autrichien *m,* -chienne *f*

authentic [ə'θɛntɪk, ɔ-] *adj* : authentique — **authentically** [-tɪkli] *adv*

authenticate [ə'θɛntɪˌkeɪt, ɔ-] *vt* **-cated; -cating** : authentifier

authenticity [ɔˌθɛn'tɪsəṯi] *n* : authenticité *f*

author ['ɔθər] *n* : auteur *m,* auteure *f Can*

authoritarian [ɔˌθɔrə'tɛriən, ə-] *adj* : autoritaire

authoritative [ə'θɔrəˌteɪṯɪv, ɔ-] *adj* **1** DICTATORIAL : autoritaire **2** DEFINITIVE : qui fait autorité

authoritatively [ə'θɔrəˌteɪṯɪvli, ɔ-] *adv* : de manière autoritaire, avec autorité

authority [ə'θɔrəṯi, ɔ-] *n, pl* **-ties 1** AUTHORIZATION : autorisation *f,* droit *m* **2** POWER : autorité *f,* pouvoir *m* **3** FORCEFULNESS : autorité *f,* assurance *f* <to speak with authority : parler avec autorité> **4 authorities** *npl* : autorités *fpl,* administration *f*

authorization [ˌɔθərə'zeɪʃən] *n* : autorisation *f*

authorize ['ɔθəˌraɪz] *vt* **-rized; -rizing** : autoriser

authorship ['ɔθərˌʃɪp] *n* : paternité *f*

auto ['ɔto] *n, pl* **autos** : auto *f,* voiture *f*

autobiographical [ˌɔṯobaɪə'græfɪkəl] *adj* : autobiographique

autobiography [ˌɔṯoˌbaɪ'ɑgrəfi] *n, pl* **-phies** : autobiographie *f*

autocracy [ɔ'tɑkrəsi] *n, pl* **-cies** : autocratie *f*

autocrat ['ɔtoˌkræt] *n* : autocrate *mf*

autocratic [ˌɔtə'kræṯɪk] *adj* : autocratique

autograph[1] ['ɔtəˌgræf] *vt* : dédicacer (un livre, etc.), signer

autograph[2] *n* : autographe *m*

automate ['ɔtəˌmeɪt] *v* **-mated; -mating** : automatiser

automatic [ˌɔtə'mæṯɪk] *adj* : automatique — **automatically** [-ṯɪkli] *adv*

automation [ˌɔṯə'meɪʃən] *n* : automatisation *f*

automaton [ɔ'tɑməˌtɑn] *n, pl* **-atons** *or* **-ata** [-ṯə, -tɑ] : automate *m*

automobile [ˌɔṯəmo'biːl, -'moːˌbiːl] *n* : automobile *f,* voiture *f*

automotive [ˌɔṯə'moːṯɪv] *adj* : automobile

autonomous [ɔ'tɑnəməs] *adj* : autonome

autonomy [ɔ'tɑnəmi] *n, pl* **-mies** : autonomie *f*

autopsy ['ɔˌtɑpsi, -təp-] *n, pl* **-sies** : autopsie *f*

autumn ['ɔṯəm] *n* : automne *m*

autumnal [ɔ'tʌmnəl] *adj* : automnal, d'automne

auxiliary[1] [ɔg'zɪljəri, -'zɪləri] *adj* : auxiliaire

auxiliary[2] *n, pl* **-ries 1** : auxiliaire *mf* **2** *or* **auxiliary verb** : auxiliaire *m*

avail[1] [ə'veɪl] *vt* **to avail oneself of** : profiter de, se servir de

avail[2] *n* **1 to be of no avail** : être inutile, n'avoir aucun effet **2 to no avail** : en vain, sans résultat

availability [əˌveɪlə'bɪləṯi] *n, pl* **-ties** : disponibilité *f*

available [ə'veɪləbəl] *adj* : disponible

avalanche ['ævəˌlæntʃ] *n* : avalanche *f*

avarice ['ævərəs] *n* : avarice *f,* avidité *f,* cupidité *f*

avaricious [ˌævə'rɪʃəs] *adj* : avare, cupide, pingre

avenge [ə'vɛndʒ] *vt* **avenged; avenging** : venger

avenger [ə'vɛndʒər] *n* : vengeur *m,* -geresse *f*

avenue ['ævəˌnuː, -ˌnjuː] *n* **1** STREET : avenue *f* **2** MEANS, WAY : voie *f,* route *f*

average[1] ['ævrɪdʒ, 'ævə-] *vt* **-aged; -aging 1** : faire en moyenne <she averaged two goals per game : elle a fait en moyenne deux buts par jeu> **2** : faire la moyenne de (en mathématiques)

average[2] *adj* : moyen

average[3] *n* : moyenne *f*

averse [ə'vərs] *adj* **1** : opposé **2 to be averse to** : répugner à

aversion [ə'vərʒən] *n* : aversion *f*

avert [ə'vərt] *vt* **1** : détourner <to avert one's eyes : détourner les yeux> **2** AVOID : éviter, prévenir

aviary ['eɪviˌɛri] *n, pl* **-aries** : volière *f*

aviation [ˌeɪvi'eɪʃən] *n* : aviation *f*

aviator ['eɪviˌeɪt̬ər] *n* : aviateur *m,* -trice *f*

avid ['ævɪd] *adj* **1** GREEDY : avide <to be avid for : être avide de> **2** ENTHUSIASTIC : passionné, fervent

avidly ['ævɪdli] *adv* : avidement, avec ferveur

avocado [ˌævə'kɑdo, ˌɑvə-] *n, pl* **-dos** : avocat *m*

avocation [ˌævə'keɪʃən] *n* HOBBY : passe-temps *m*

avoid [ə'vɔɪd] *vt* : éviter, prévenir

avoidable [ə'vɔɪdəbəl] *adj* : évitable

avoidance [ə'vɔɪdənts] *n* : action *f* d'éviter

avoirdupois [ˌævərdə'pɔɪz] *n* : avoirdupois *m*

avow [ə'vaʊ] *vt* **1** DECLARE : affirmer, déclarer **2** ADMIT : avouer, reconnaître

avowal [ə'vaʊəl] *n* **1** DECLARATION : affirmation *f* **2** ADMISSION : aveu *m*

await [ə'weɪt] *vt* : attendre

awake[1] [ə'weɪk] *v* **awoke** [ə'woːk]; **awoken** [ə'woːkən] *or* **awaked** [ə'weɪkt]; **awaking** *vt* AROUSE : réveiller, éveiller — *vi* WAKE UP : se réveiller, s'éveiller

awake[2] *adj* : éveillé, réveillé

awaken [ə'weɪkən] **awakened; awakening → awake**[1]

award[1] [ə'wɔrd] *vt* **1** GRANT : accorder **2** CONFER : décerner

award[2] *n* **1** PRIZE : prix *m,* distinction *f* honorifique **2** GRANT : bourse *f*

aware [ə'wær] *adj* **1** CONSCIOUS : conscient **2** INFORMED : au courant

awareness [ə'wærnəs] *n* : conscience *f*

awash [ə'wɔʃ] *adj* : inondé

away[1] [ə'weɪ] *adv* **1** (*indicating movement*) <to get away early : partir en avance> <go away! : hors d'ici!, allez-vous en!> **2** (*indicating the opposite direction*) <to look away : détourner les yeux> **3** (*indicating an ending*) <the wind died away : le vent s'est arrêté> **4** (*indicating the end of possession*) <she gave away her money : elle a donné son argent> **5** NONSTOP : sans arrêt <to chatter away : bavarder sans arrêt> **6** (*indicating distance in space or time*) <away back in 1850 : en 1850>

away[2] *adj* **1** ABSENT : absent **2** : de distance <10 kilometers away : à 10 kilomètres de distance> **3** : à l'extérieur (aux sports) <an away game : un match à l'extérieur>

awe[1] ['ɔ] *vt* **awed; awing** : impressionner, intimider

awe[2] *n* : crainte *f* mêlée de respect, crainte *f* révérentielle

awesome ['ɔsəm] *adj* : impressionnant, imposant

awestruck ['ɔˌstrʌk] *adj* : impressionné

awful ['ɔfəl] *adj* **1** TERRIBLE : affreux, terrible **2 an awful lot of** : énormément de

awfully ['ɔfəli] *adv* EXTREMELY : extrémement, terriblement, très

awhile [ə'*h*waɪl] *adv* : un moment

awkward ['ɔkwərd] *adj* **1** CLUMSY : gauche, maladroit **2** EMBARRASSING : embarrassant, gênant **3** DIFFICULT : difficile, incommode

awkwardly ['ɔkwərdli] *adv* **1** CLUMSILY : maladroitement, avec maladresse **2** EMBARRASSEDLY : d'un ton embarrassé **3** INCONVENIENTLY : de façon malcommode

awkwardness ['ɔkwərdnəs] *n* **1** CLUMSINESS : gaucherie *f,* maladresse *f* **2** EMBARRASSMENT : embarras *m,* gêne *f*

awl ['ɔl] *n* : poinçon *m,* alène *f* (pour le cuir)

awning ['ɔnɪŋ] *n* : auvent *m*

awoke, awoken → awake[1]

awry [ə'raɪ] *adv & adj* **1** : de travers **2 to go awry** : mal tourner

ax *or* **axe** ['æks] *n* : hache *f*

axiom ['æksiəm] *n* : axiome *m*

axiomatic ['æksiəmæt̬ɪk] *adj* : axiomatique

axis ['æksɪs] *n, pl* **axes** [-siːz] : axe *m*

axle ['æksəl] *n* : essieu *m*

aye[1] ['aɪ] *adv* : oui <to vote aye : voter oui>

aye[2] *n* : oui *m*

azalea [ə'zeɪljə] *n* : azalée *f*

azimuth ['æzəməθ] *n* : azimut *m*

azure[1] ['æʒər] *adj* : d'azur

azure[2] *n* : azur *m*

B

b ['biː] *n, pl* **b's** *or* **bs** biːz] : b *m,* deuxième lettre de l'alphabet

babble[1] ['bæbəl] *v* **-bled; -bling** *vt* : bafouiller <babbling an excuse : bafouillant une excuse> — *vi* **1** PRATTLE : babiller **2** CHATTER : bavarder **3** : gazouiller <a babbling brook : un ruisseau gazouillant>

babble[2] *n* : babillage *m* (d'un enfant), bavardage *m* (d'un adulte), rumeur *f* (de voix), gazouillement *m* (d'un ruisseau, etc.)

babe ['beɪb] → **baby**[2]

babel ['beɪbəl, 'bæ-] *n* HUBBUB : brouhaha *m*

baboon [bæ'buːn] *n* : babouin *m*

baby[1] ['beɪbi] *vt* **-bied; -bying** : dorloter

baby[2] *n, pl* **-bies** : bébé *m*

baby carriage *n* : voiture *f* d'enfant, landau *m France*

babyhood ['beɪbi,hʊd] *n* : petite enfance *f*

babyish ['beɪbiɪʃ] *adj* : enfantin, puéril

baby–sit ['beɪbi,sɪt] *vi* **-sat** [-,sæt]; **-sitting** : garder des enfants, faire du baby-sitting *France*

baby–sitter ['beɪbi,sɪt̬ər] *n* : gardienne *f* d'enfants, baby-sitter *mf France*

baccalaureate ['bækə'lɔriət] *n* : licence *f*

bachelor ['bætʃələr] *n* **1** : célibataire *m* **2** GRADUATE : licencié *m,* -ciée *f* <bachelor of science : licencié de sciences>

bacillus [bə'sɪləs] *n, pl* **-li** [-,laɪ] : bacille *m*

back[1] ['bæk] *vt* **1** *or* **to back up** SUPPORT : soutenir, appuyer **2** FINANCE : financer **3** *or* **to back up** : reculer (un véhicule), mettre en marche arrière — *vi* **1 to back up** : reculer, faire marche arrière **2 to back out of** : se soustraire à, se dégager de **3 to back down** : céder, se résigner

back[2] *adv* **1** BACKWARD : en arrière, vers l'arrière **2** AGO : antérieurement **3 to come back** : être de retour **4 to give back** : rendre **5 to go back** : retourner **6 to walk back and forth** : marcher de long en large

back[3] *adj* **1** REAR : arrière, de derrière <the back door : la porte arrière> **2** OVERDUE : arriéré, impayé <back pay : rappel de salaire> **3 back street** : petite rue *f*

back[4] *n* **1** : dos *m* (du corps) <back to back : dos à dos> **2** REAR : derrière *m,* arrière *m,* fond *m* **3** : dossier *m* (d'un siège) **4** : arrière *m* (aux sports)

backache ['bæk,eɪk] *n* : mal *m* de dos

backbite ['bæk,baɪt] *vt* **-bit** [-,bɪt]; **-bitten** [-,bɪtən]; **-biting** : médire de, dénigrer

backbone ['bæk,boːn] *n* **1** : colonne *f* vertébrale **2** FORTITUDE : fermeté *f,* caractère *m*

backdrop ['bæk,drɑp] *n* : toile *f* de fond

backer ['bækər] *n* SUPPORTER : partisan *m,* -sane *f;* allié *m,* -liée *f*

backfire[1] ['bæk,faɪr] *vi* **-fired; -firing 1** : pétarader (se dit d'une voiture) **2** FAIL : échouer, tourner mal

backfire[2] *n* : pétarade *f* (d'une voiture)

background ['bæk,graʊnd] *n* **1** : arrière-plan *m,* fond *m* (d'un tableau) **2** EXPERIENCE, EDUCATION : expérience *f,* formation *f*

backhand[1] ['bæk,hænd] *adj & adv* : en revers

backhand[2] *n* : revers *m* (au tennis)

backhanded ['bæk,hændəd] *adj* **1** : en revers, de revers **2** INDIRECT, DEVIOUS : équivoque, sournois

backing ['bækɪŋ] *n* **1** SUPPORT : soutien *m,* appui *m* **2** REINFORCEMENT : renfort *m,* renforcement *m*

backlash ['bæk,læʃ] *n* : contrecoup *m,* répercussion *f*

backlog ['bæk,lɔg] *n* : arriéré *m,* accumulation *f*

backpack[1] ['bæk,pæk] *vi* : faire de la randonnée

backpack[2] *n* : sac *m* à dos

backrest ['bæk,rɛst] *n* : dossier *m*

backslide ['bæk,slaɪd] *vi* **-slid** [-,slɪd]; **-slid** *or* **-slidden** [-,slɪdən]; **-sliding** : retomber, récidiver

backstage [,bæk'steɪdʒ, 'bæk,-] *adv* : dans les coulisses, derrière la scène

backtrack ['bæk,træk] *vi* **1** : revenir sur ses pas **2** : faire marche arrière, revenir <she backtracked on her commitment : elle est revenue sur son engagement>

backup ['bæk,ʌp] *n* **1** SUPPORT : soutien *m,* appui *m* **2** SUBSTITUTE : réserve *f,* remplaçant *m* **3** : sauvegarde *f* (en informatique)

backward[1] ['bækwərd] *or* **backwards** [-wərdz] *adv* **1** BACK : en arrière **2** : à la renverse <to fall over backward : tomber à la renverse> **3** : à l'envers <say it backwards : dis-le à l'envers>

backward[2] *adj* **1** : en arrière, rétrograde <a backward glance : un regard en arrière> <backward motion : mouvement rétrograde> **2** RETARDED, SLOW : arriéré, peu avancé **3** UNDERDEVELOPED : sous-développé, arriéré <backward countries : pays arriérés> **4** BASHFUL, HESITANT : timide, peu disposé

backwardness ['bækwərdnəs] *n* **1** : retard *m* mental (d'une personne), sous-développement *m* (d'un pays) **2** BASHFULNESS : timidité *f*

backwoods [,bæk'wʊdz] *ns & pl* : région *f* forestière peu peuplée, forêts *fpl* de l'intérieur

bacon [beɪkən] *n* : lard *m,* bacon *m*
bacterial [bæk'tɪriəl] *adj* : bactérien
bacteriologist [bæk,tɪri'ɑlədʒɪst] *n* : bactériologiste *mf*
bacteriology [bæk,tɪri'ɑlədʒi] *n* : bactériologie *f*
bacterium [bæk'tɪriəm] *n, pl* **-ria** [-riə] : bactérie *f*
bad[1] ['bæd] *adv* → **badly**
bad[2] *adj* **worse; worst 1** POOR : mauvais <bad weather : mauvais temps> <bad breath : mauvaise haleine> **2** ROTTEN : pourri **3** SERIOUS, SEVERE : grave (se dit d'un accident, etc.), aigu (se dit d'une douleur) **4** DEFECTIVE : défectueux, de mauvaise qualité **5** WICKED : méchant, mauvais **6** UNWELL : malade, mal <to feel bad : se sentir mal> **7** HARMFUL : néfaste, nuisible **8** : sans provision <a bad check : un chèque sans provision> **9** NAUGHTY : méchant **10 from bad to worse** : de mal en pis
bad[3] *n* : mauvais *m* <to take the good with the bad : prendre le bon avec le mauvais>
bade → **bid**
badge ['bædʒ] *n* : insigne *m,* plaque *f* (d'un agent de police)
badger[1] ['bædʒər] *vt* : harceler, importuner
badger[2] *n* : blaireau *m*
badly ['bædli] *adv* **1** : mal <badly dressed : mal habillé> **2** SEVERELY : gravement, grièvement <badly injured : grièvement blessé> **3** URGENTLY : énormément, avec grand besoin <to want sth badly : avoir très envie de qqch>
badminton ['bæd,mɪntən, -,mɪt-] *n* : badminton *m*
badness [bædnəs] *n* : méchanceté *f*
baffle ['bæfəl] *vt* **-fled; -fling** : déconcerter, confondre
bafflement ['bæfəlmənt] *n* : confusion *f,* perplexité *f*
bag[1] ['bæg] *v* **bagged; bagging** *vt* **1** : mettre en sac, ensacher (des marchandises) **2** KILL : tuer (du gibier) — *vi* SAG : pocher, faire des poches
bag[2] *n* **1** : sac *m* <plastic bag : sac en plastique> **2** POCKETBOOK : sac *m* à main **3** SUITCASE : valise *f,* mallette *f*
bagatelle [,bægə'tɛl] *n* : bagatelle *f*
bagel ['beɪgəl] *n* : petit pain *m* en couronne, bagel *m Can*
baggage ['bægɪdʒ] *n* : bagages *mpl*
baggy ['bægi] *adj* **baggier; -est** : ample, qui fait des poches
bagpipes ['bæg,paɪps] *npl* : cornemuse *f*
Bahamian[1] [bə'heɪmiən, -'hɔ-] *adj* : des Bahamas
Bahamian[2] *n* : habitant *m,* -tante *f* des Bahamas
Bahraini[1] [bɑ'reɪni] *adj* : bahreïni
Bahraini[2] *n* : Bahreïni *m,* -nie *f*
bail[1] [,beɪl] *vt* **1** : vider (l'eau d'un bateau), écoper (un bateau) **2 to bail out** RELEASE : mettre en liberté sous caution **3 to bail out** EXTRICATE : tirer d'affaire — *vi* **to bail out** : sauter en parachute
bail[2] *n* **1** SECURITY : caution *f* **2 to release on bail** : mettre en liberté sous caution
bailiff ['beɪlif] *n* : huissier *m*
bailiwick ['beɪli,wɪk] *n* : domaine *m*
bait[1] ['beɪt] *vt* **1** : appâter, amorcer (un hameçon, etc.) **2** HARASS : harceler, tourmenter
bait[2] *n* : appât *m,* amorce *f*
bake ['beɪk] *v* **baked; baking** *vt* : faire cuire au four — *vi* : cuire au four
baker ['beɪkər] *n* : boulanger *m,* -gère *f*
bakery ['beɪkəri] *n, pl* **-ries** : boulangerie *f*
bakeshop ['beɪk,ʃɑp] → **bakery**
baking powder *n* : levure *f* chimique, poudre *f* à pâte *Can*
baking soda *n* : bicarbonate *m* de soude
balance[1] ['bælən*t*s] *v* **-anced; -ancing** *vt* **1** ADJUST : équilibrer (un budget, des roues, etc.) **2** WEIGH : peser <to balance the pros and cons : peser le pour et le contre> **3** : mettre en équilibre, poser en équilibre <he balanced the book on his head : il a posé le livre en équilibre sur sa tête> **4** OFFSET : compenser, contrebalancer — *vi* : être en équilibre, s'équilibrer
balance[2] *n* **1** SCALES : balance *f* <to hang in the balance : être en jeu> **2** EQUILIBRIUM : équilibre *m* **3** REMAINDER : solde *m* (en finances), restant *m* **4** COUNTERBALANCE, WEIGHT : contrepoids *m*
balcony ['bælkəni] *n, pl* **-nies** : balcon *m*
bald ['bɔld] *adj* **1** HAIRLESS : chauve **2** BARREN : pelé <a bald mountain : une montagne pelée> **3** PLAIN : pur, simple <the bald truth : la vérité pure et simple>
bald eagle *n* : aigle *m* d'Amérique, aigle *m* à tête blanche
balding ['bɔldɪŋ] *adj* : qui devient chauve
baldly ['bɔldli] *adv* : franchement, sans détours
baldness ['bɔldnəs] *n* : calvitie *f*
bale[1] ['beɪl] *vt* **baled; baling** : mettre en balles, emballer
bale[2] *n* : balle *f*
baleful ['beɪlfəl] *adj* OMINOUS : menaçant, sinistre
balk[1] ['bɔk] *vt* THWART : contrecarrer, frustrer — *vi* **to balk at** : reculer devant, rechigner à
balk[2] *n* HINDRANCE : obstacle *m*
balky ['bɔki] **balkier; -est** *adj* : contrariant, entêté

ball[1] ['bɔl] *vt* : mettre en boule, pelotonner — *vi or* **to ball up** : s'agglomérer

ball[2] *n* **1** : balle *f,* ballon *m,* boule *f* <to play ball : jouer au ballon> **2** : pelote *f* (de ficelle, etc.) **3** DANCE : bal *m* **4** **ball of the foot** : plante *f* du pied

ballad ['bæləd] *n* **1** : ballade *f* (poème) **2** : romance *f* (chanson populaire)

ballast[1] ['bæləst] *vt* : lester

ballast[2] *n* : lest *m,* ballast *m*

ball bearing *n* : roulement *m* à billes

ballerina [ˌbælə'riːnə] *n* : ballerine *f*

ballet [bæ'leɪ, 'bæˌleɪ] *n* : ballet *m*

ballistic [bə'lɪstɪk] *adj* : balistique <ballistic missile : engin balistique>

ballistics [bə'lɪstɪks] *ns & pl* : balistique *f*

balloon[1] [bə'luːn] *vi* **1** : faire une ascension en ballon **2** SWELL : gonfler **3** INCREASE : augmenter (rapidement)

balloon[2] *n* **1** : ballon *m,* balloune *f Can* **2** *or* **hot–air balloon** : montgolfière *f*

balloonist [bə'luːnɪst] *n* : aéronaute *mf*

ballot[1] ['bælət] *vt* : sonder par vote — *vi* : voter au scrutin

ballot[2] *n* **1** VOTE : vote *m* **2** VOTING : scrutin *m*

ballroom ['bɔlˌruːm, -ˌrʊm] *n* : salle *f* de danse, salle *f* de bal

balm ['bɑm, 'bɑlm] *n* : baume *m*

balmy ['bɑmi, 'bɑl-] *adj* **balmier; -est** **1** MILD : doux <a balmy climate : un climat doux> **2** CRAZY : toqué *fam,* timbré *fam*

baloney [bə'loːni] *n* NONSENSE : balivernes *fpl*

balsa ['bɔlsə] *n* : balsa *m*

balsam ['bɔlsəm] *n* **1** : baume *m* **2** *or* **balsam fir** : balsamine *f*

baluster ['bæləstər] *n* : balustre *m*

balustrade ['bæləˌstreɪd] *n* : balustrade *f*

bamboo [bæm'buː] *n, pl* **-boos** : bambou *m*

bamboozle [bæm'buːzəl] *vt* **-zled; -zling** : embobiner *fam,* faire emplir *Can*

ban[1] ['bæn] *vt* **banned; banning** : interdire, défendre

ban[2] *n* : interdiction *f*

banal [bə'nɑl, -'næl, 'beɪnəl] *adj* : banal

banality [bə'næləṭi] *n* : banalité *f*

banana [bə'nænə] *n* : banane *f*

band[1] ['bænd] *vt* **1** BIND : lier, attacher **2** *or* **to band together** UNITE : unir, réunir — *vi* **to band together** : se réunir, se grouper

band[2] *n* **1** STRIP : bande *f,* bandelette *f* **2** GROUP : groupe *m,* troupe *f* **3** : ruban *m* (d'un chapeau) **4** : bande *f* (de transmission) **5** → **rubber band**

bandage[1] ['bændɪdʒ] *vt* : bander, mettre un pansement sur

bandage[2] *n* : pansement *m,* bandage *m*

bandanna *or* **bandana** [bæn'dænə] *n* : foulard *m*

bandit ['bændət] *n* : bandit *m*

banditry ['bændətri] *n* : banditisme *m*

bandstand ['bændˌstænd] *n* : kiosque *m* à musique

bandwagon ['bændˌwægən] *n* **to jump on the bandwagon** : suivre le mouvement, prendre le train en marche

bandy[1] ['bændi] *vt* **-died; -dying** **1** EXCHANGE : échanger **2** **to bandy about** : faire circuler, avancer (des idées)

bandy[2] *adj* : arqué <bandy legs : jambes arquées>

bane ['beɪn] *n* **1** POISON : poison *m* **2** : fléau *m* <the bane of one's existence : le fléau de son existence>

bang[1] ['bæŋ] *vt* **1** SLAM : claquer **2** HIT, STRIKE : se cogner, se frapper <to bang one's head : se cogner la tête> <he banged his fists on the table : il a frappé ses poings sur la table>

bang[2] *adv* : exactement, en plein <bang in the middle : en plein milieu>

bang[3] *n* **1** : claquement *m* (d'une porte, etc.) **2** : détonation *f* (d'un fusil) **3** BLOW : coup *m* **4** **bangs** *npl* : frange *f* (de cheveux)

Bangladeshi[1] [ˌbɑŋglə'dɛʃi, ˌbæŋ-, ˌbʌŋ-, -deɪ-] *adj* : bangladais

Bangladeshi[2] *n* : Bangladais *m,* -daise *f*

bangle ['bæŋgəl] *n* : bracelet *m*

banish ['bænɪʃ] *vt* **1** EXILE : exiler, bannir **2** EXPEL : expulser

banishment ['bænɪʃmənt] *n* **1** EXILE : exile *m,* bannissement *m* **2** EXPULSION : expulsion *f*

banister ['bænəstər] *n* **1** BALUSTER : balustre *m* **2** HANDRAIL : rampe *f* (d'escalier)

banjo ['bænˌdʒoː] *n, pl* **-jos** : banjo *m*

bank[1] ['bæŋk] *vt* **1** : déposer (de l'argent, des chèques) à la banque **2** *or* **to bank up** : relever (un virage) **3** : couvrir (un feu) — *vi* **1** : avoir un compte en banque **2** PILE UP : s'entasser, s'amonceler **3** TILT : s'incliner sur l'aile (se dit d'un avion) **4** **to bank on** : compter sur

bank[2] *n* **1** EMBANKMENT : talus *m* **2** : bord *m,* rive *f* <left bank : rive gauche> <the bank of a road : le bord d'une rue> **3** SHOAL : banc *m* <sand bank : banc de sable> **4** : banque *f,* institution *f* bancaire **5** **data bank** : banque *f* de données

bankbook ['bæŋkˌbʊk] *n* : carnet *m* de banque, livret *m* bancaire

banker ['bæŋkər] *n* : banquier *m*

banking ['bæŋkɪŋ] *n* **1** : opérations *fpl* bancaires **2** : profession *f* de banquier

banknote ['bæŋkˌnoːt] *n* : billet *m* (de banque)

bankrupt[1] ['bæŋˌkrʌpt] *vt* : mettre en faillite, ruiner

bankrupt[2] *adj* **1** : failli **2** LACKING : dépourvu, dénué <bankrupt of ideas : dénué d'idées>
bankrupt[3] *n* : failli *m*, -lie *f*
bankruptcy ['bæŋ,krʌptsi] *n, pl* **-cies** : faillite *f*
banner[1] ['bænər] *adj* : record, excellent <a banner year : une année record>
banner[2] *n* : bannière *f*, étendard *m*
banns ['bænz] *npl* : bans *mpl* (de mariage)
banquet ['bæŋkwət] *adj* : banquet *m*, festin *m*
bantam ['bæntəm] *n* : coq *m* nain, poule *f* naine
banter[1] ['bæntər] *vi* : badiner, plaisanter
banter[2] *n* : badinage *m*, plaisanterie *f*
baptism ['bæp,tɪzəm] *n* : baptême *m*
baptismal [bæp'tɪzməl] *adj* : de baptême, baptismal
baptize [bæp'taɪz, 'bæp,taɪz] *vt* **-tized; -tizing** : baptiser
bar[1] ['bɑr] *vt* **barred; barring 1** OBSTRUCT : barrer, bloquer **2** EXCLUDE : exclure **3** BAN, PROHIBIT : défendre, interdire **4** : mettre la barre à (une porte, etc.)
bar[2] *n* **1** ROD, STRIP : barre *f* (de métal), barreau *m* (d'une fenêtre) **2** : barre *f*, tablette *f* (de chocolat, etc.) **3** OBSTRUCTION : obstacle *m*, barrière *f* **4** : barreau *m* <to be admitted to the bar : s'inscrire au barreau> **5** BAND, STREAK : raie *f* (de lumière), bande *f* (de couleur) **6** COUNTER : comptoir *m* **7** CAFÉ, TAVERN : bar *m*, café *m* **8 behind bars** : sous les verrous
bar[3] *prep* **1** : excepté, sauf **2 bar none** : sans exception
barb ['bɑrb] *n* **1** POINT : ardillon *m* (d'hameçon), barbe *f* (d'une plume) **2** GIBE : moquerie *f*, raillerie *f*
barbarian[1] [bɑr'bæriən] *adj* : barbare, de barbare
barbarian[2] *n* : barbare *mf*
barbaric [bɑr'bærɪk] *adj* : barbare
barbarism ['bɑrbə,rɪzəm] *n* : barbarie *f*
barbarity [bɑr'bærəṭi] *n, pl* **-ties** : barbarie *f*, cruauté *f*
barbarous ['bɑrbərəs] *adj* : barbare, cruel
barbarously ['bɑrbərəsli] *adv* : d'une façon barbare, cruellement
barbecue[1] ['bɑrbɪ,kjuː] *vt* **-cued; -cuing** : griller au charbon de bois
barbecue[2] *n* : barbecue *m*
barbed [bɑrbd] *adj* : barbelé <a barbed-wire fence : une haie barbelée>
barber ['bɑrbər] *n* : coiffeur *m*, -feuse *f*; barbier *m*
barbiturate [bɑr'bɪtʃərət] *n* : barbiturique *m*
bard ['bɑrd] *n* : barde *m*, poète *m*
bare[1] ['bær] *vt* **bared; baring 1** UNCOVER : mettre à nu, se découvrir (la tête) **2 to bare one's teeth** : montrer les dents
bare[2] *adj* **barer; barest 1** NAKED : nu **2** EXPOSED : découvert, nu **3** EMPTY : vide <the cupboard was bare : l'armoire était vide> **4** PLAIN, STRICT : strict <the bare minimum : le strict minimum> **5** MERE : simple <the bare statement of facts : le simple énoncé des faits>
bareback ['bær,bæk] *or* **barebacked** [-,bækt] *adv & adj* : à cru
barefaced ['bær,feɪst] *adj* : éhonté <barefaced lie : mensonge éhonté>
barefoot[1] ['bær,fʊt] *or* **barefooted** [-,fʊtəd] *adv* : nu-pieds, pieds nus
barefoot[2] *or* **barefooted** *adj* : aux pieds nus, nu-pieds
bareheaded[1] ['bær,hɛdəd] *adv* : nu-tête, (la) tête nue
bareheaded[2] *adj* : à la tête nue
barely ['bærli] *adv* : à peine, tout juste
bareness ['bærnəs] *n* **1** NUDITY : nudité *f* **2** AUSTERITY : dépouillement *m*
bargain[1] ['bɑrgən] *vi* **1** NEGOTIATE *m* : négocier **2** HAGGLE : marchander
bargain[2] *n* **1** : occasion *f*, (bonne) affaire *f* <that's a real bargain : c'est une véritable occasion> **2** AGREEMENT : marché *m* <to strike a bargain : conclure un marché>
barge[1] ['bɑrdʒ] *vi* **barged; barging 1** : se bousculer <they were barging through the crowd : ils se bousculaient à travers la foule> **2 to barge into** : faire irruption dans (une pièce, etc.), interrompre (une conversation)
barge[2] *n* : chaland *m*, péniche *f*
bar graph *n* : histogramme *m*
baritone ['bærə,toːn] *n* : baryton *m*
barium ['bæriəm] *n* : baryum *m*
bark[1] ['bɑrk] *vi* **1** : aboyer (se dit d'un chien) **2** SHOUT : crier, gueuler *fam* — *vt or* **to bark out** : aboyer
bark[2] *n* **1** : écorce *f* (d'un arbre) **2** : aboiement *m* (d'un chien) **3** BOAT : barque *f*
barker ['bɑrkər] *n* : bonimenteur *m* (à une foire)
barley ['bɑrli] *n* : orge *f* (plante), orge *m* (grain)
barn ['bɑrn] *n* : grange *f*, écurie *f* (de chevaux), étable *f* (de bovins)
barnacle ['bɑrnɪkəl] *n* : anatife *m*
barnyard ['bɑrn,jɑrd] *n* : basse-cour *f*
barometer [bə'rɑməṭər] *n* : baromètre *m*
barometric ['bærə'mɛtrɪk] *adj* : barométrique
baron ['bærən] *n* : baron *m*
baroness ['bærənɪs, -nəs, -'nɛs] *n* : baronne *f*
baronet [,bærə'nɛt, 'bærənət] *n* : baronnet *m*
baronial [bə'roːniəl] *adj* **1** : de baron **2** STATELY : imposant

baroque [bə'ro:k, -'rɑk] *adj* : baroque

barracks ['bærəks] *ns & pl* : caserne *f*

barracuda [ˌbærə'ku:də] *n, pl* **-da** *or* **-das** : barracuda *m*

barrage [bə'rɑʒ, -'rɑdʒ] *n* **1** : tir *m* de barrage (en artillerie) **2** DELUGE : pluie *f,* déluge *m* (de questions, etc.)

barrel[1] ['bærəl] *v* **-reled** *or* **-relled; -reling** *or* **-relling** *vt* : mettre en tonneau — *vi or* **to barrel along** : foncer *fam*

barrel[2] *n* **1** : tonneau *m,* fût *m,* baril *m* **2** : canon *m* (d'une arme à feu)

barren ['bærən] *adj* **1** STERILE : stérile, infertile <barren plants : plantes stériles> **2** BARE, DESOLATE : désertique, aride **3** UNPRODUCTIVE : aride, stérile

barrenness ['bærənnəs] *n* : aridité *f,* stérilité *f*

barrette [bɑ'rɛt, bə-] *n* : barrette *f*

barricade[1] *vt* ['bærəˌkeɪd, ˌbærə'-] **-caded; -cading** : barricader

barricade[2] *n* : barricade *f*

barrier ['bæriər] *n* : barrière *f*

barring ['bɑrɪŋ] *prep* : excepté, sauf, à moins de

barroom ['bɑrˌru:m, -rʊm] *n* : bar *m*

barrow ['bærˌo:] → **wheelbarrow**

bartender ['bɑrˌtɛndər] *n* : barman *m*

barter[1] ['bɑrṭər] *vt* : échanger, troquer — *vi* : faire un échange, faire un troc

barter[2] *n* : échange *m,* troc *m*

basalt [bə'sɔlt, 'beɪˌ-] *n* : basalte *m*

base[1] ['beɪs] *vt* **based; basing 1** FOUND : baser, fonder (une opinion, un calcul, etc.) **2** LOCATE : baser

base[2] *adj* **baser; basest 1** CONTEMPTIBLE : bas, vil **2 base metal** : métal *m* non précieux

base[3] *n, pl* **bases 1** BOTTOM : base *f,* pied *m* **2** BASIS : fondement *m,* base *f,* point *m* de départ **3** *or* **army base** : base *f* militaire **4** : but *m Can* (au baseball)

baseness ['beɪsnəs] *n* : bassesse *f,* vilenie *f*

baseball ['beɪsˌbɔl] *n* : baseball *m,* baseball *m*

baseless ['beɪsləs] *adj* : sans fondement

basely ['beɪsli] *adv* : bassement, vilement

basement ['beɪsmənt] *n* : sous-sol *m*

bash[1] ['bæʃ] *vt* **1** HIT : cogner, frapper **2 to bash in** SMASH : enfoncer, défoncer

bash[2] *n* **1** BLOW : coup *m* **2** PARTY : fête *f*

bashful ['bæʃfəl] *adj* SHY : timide, gêné *Can*

bashfulness ['bæʃfəlnəs] *n* : timidité *f*

basic ['beɪsɪk] *adj* **1** : fondamental, de base <basic principle : principe fondamental> **2** : basique <basic salt : sel basique>

basically ['beɪsɪkli] *adv* : au fond, fondamentalement

basil ['beɪzəl, 'bæzəl] *n* : basilic *m*

basilica [bə'sɪlɪkə] *n* : basilique *f*

basin ['beɪsən] *n* **1** WASHBOWL : cuvette *f,* lavabo *m* **2** : bassin *m* (d'un fleuve)

basis ['beɪsəs] *n, pl* **bases 1** BASE : base *f,* fondement *m* **2** PRINCIPLE : condition *f,* terme *m* <on that basis : dans ces conditions> **3 on a weekly basis** : à la semaine

bask ['bæsk] *vi* **1** : se prélasser (au soleil, etc.) **2** REVEL : se délecter

basket ['bæskət] *n* : corbeille *f,* panier *m*

basketball ['bæskətˌbɔl] *n* **1** : basket *m,* basket-ball *m,* basketball *m,* ballon-panier *m Can* (jeu) **2** : ballon *m* de basket <lancer un ballon de basket : to throw a basketball>

bas–relief [ˌbɑrɪ'li:f] *n* : bas-relief *m*

bass[1] ['bæs] *n, pl* **bass** *or* **basses 1** : perche *f,* bar *m* (pêche) **2** *or* **black bass** : achigan *m Can*

bass[2] ['beɪs] *n* : basse *f* (voix, instrument)

basset hound ['bæsətˌhaʊnd] *n* : basset *m*

bassinet [ˌbæsə'nɛt] *n* : berceau *m,* bercelonnette *f*

bassoon [bə'su:n, bæ-] *n* : basson *m*

bastard[1] ['bæstərd] *adj* : bâtard

bastard[2] *n* : bâtard *m,* -tarde *f*

bastardize ['bæstərˌdaɪz] *vt* **-ized; -izing** DEBASE : corrompre, abâtardir

baste ['beɪst] *vt* **basted; basting 1** : faufiler, bâtir (en couture) **2** : arroser (un rôti, etc.)

bastion ['bæstʃən] *n* : bastion *m*

bat[1] ['bæt] *v* **batted; batting** *vt* **1** HIT : frapper (une balle) **2 without batting an eye** : sans sourciller — *vi* : manier la batte (au cricket)

bat[2] *n* **1** : batte *f,* bâton *m Can* <baseball bat : batte de baseball> **2** STROKE : coup *m* (au cricket) **3** : chauve-souris *f* (animal)

batch ['bætʃ] *n* **1** : fournée *f* <a batch of bread : une fournée de pain> **2** QUANTITY : liasse *f* (de papiers, etc.), lot *m* (de marchandises)

bate ['beɪt] *vt* **bated; bating 1** REDUCE : réduire, diminuer **2 with bated breath** : en retenant son souffle

bath ['bæθ, 'bɑθ] *n, pl* **baths 1** : bain *m* <to take a bath : prendre un bain> **2** BATHROOM : salle *f* de bains **3** LOSS : perte *f* <he took a bath in the market : il a subi des pertes sur le marché>

bathe ['beɪð] *v* **bathed; bathing** *vt* : baigner, laver — *vi* : se baigner, prendre un bain

bather ['beɪðər] *n* : baigneur *m,* -gneuse *f*

bathrobe ['bæθˌro:b] *n* : peignoir *m* (de bain), robe *f* de chambre

bathroom ['bæθˌruːm, -ˌrʊm] *n* **1** : salle *f* de bains **2 to go to the bathroom** : aller aux toilettes

bathtub ['bæθˌtʌb] *n* : baignoire *f*

batiste [bə'tiːst] *n* : batiste *f*

baton [bə'tɑn] *n* : bâton *m*

battalion [bə'tæljən] *n* : bataillon *m*

batten ['bætən] *vt* **to batten down the hatches** : fermer les écoutilles

batter[1] ['bæt̬ər] *vt* BEAT : battre, frapper

batter[2] *n* **1** : pâte *f* <pancake batter : pâte à crêpes> **2** : batteur *m* (au baseball)

battered ['bæt̬ərd] *adj* : cabossé <a battered old hat : un vieux chapeau cabossé>

battering ram *n* : bélier *m*

battery ['bæt̬əri] *n, pl* **-teries 1** : pile *f* (d'une radio, etc.), batterie *f* (d'un véhicule) **2** : batterie *f* (d'artillerie) **3** SERIES : série *f,* batterie *f* <a battery of tests : une batterie d'examens> **4** → **assault**

batting ['bæt̬ɪŋ] *n* **1** *or* **cotton batting** : ouate *f,* bourre *f* **2** : maniement *m* de la batte (aux sports)

battle[1] ['bæt̬əl] *v* **-tled; -tling** *vi* : lutter, se battre — *vt* : lutter contre

battle[2] *n* **1** FIGHT : bataille *f,* combat *m* **2** STRUGGLE : lutte *f*

battle-ax ['bæt̬əlˌæks] *n* : hache *f* d'armes

battlefield ['bæt̬əlˌfiːld] *n* : champ *m* de bataille

battlement ['bæt̬əlmənt] *n* : rempart *m,* créneau *m*

battleship ['bæt̬əlˌʃɪp] *n* : cuirassé *m*

batty ['bæt̬i] *adj* **battier; battiest** : toqué *fam,* fou

bauble ['bɔbəl] *n* : babiole *f*

bawdiness ['bɔdinəs] *n* : paillardise *f*

bawdy ['bɔdi] *adj* **bawdier; -est** : paillard, grivois

bawl ['bɔl] *vi* : brailler *fam*

bawl out *vt* : engueuler *fam*

bay[1] ['beɪ] *vi* : aboyer

bay[2] *adj* : bai (se dit d'un cheval)

bay[3] *n* **1** INLET : baie *f,* golfe *m* **2** *or* **bay horse** : cheval *m* bai **3** LAUREL : laurier *m* **4** BAYING : aboiement *m* (d'un chien, etc.) **5** AREA : aire *f* <cargo bay : aire de chargement> **6 to be at bay** : être aux abois

bayberry ['beɪˌbɛri] *n, pl* **-ries** : baie *f* de laurier

bayonet[1] [ˌbeɪə'nɛt, 'beɪəˌnɛt] *vt* **-neted; -neting** : passer à la baïonnette

bayonet[2] *n* : baïonnette *f*

bayou ['baɪˌuː, -ˌo] *n* : bayou *m*

bay window *n* : fenêtre *m* en saillie

bazaar [bə'zɑr] *n* **1** : bazar *m* **2** SALE : vente *f* (de charité)

bazooka [bə'zuːkə] *n* : bazooka *m*

BB ['biːbiː] *n* **1** : plomb *m* **2 BB gun** : carabine *f* à air comprimé

be ['biː] *v* **was** ['wəz, 'wɑz], **were** ['wər]; **been** ['bɪn]; **being; am** ['æm], **is** ['ɪz], **are** ['ɑr] *vi* **1** (*expressing an attribute*) : être <the sky is blue : le ciel est bleu> **2** (*expressing a state*) : être, avoir <he is healthy : il est en bonne santé> <I'm hot : j'ai chaud> **3** (*expressing age*) : avoir <how old is he? : quel âge a-t-il?> **4** (*expressing origin*) : être <she is from Canada : elle est canadienne> **5** LIVE : être, exister <I think, therefore I am : je pense, donc je suis> **6** (*expressing location*) : être, se trouver <the cottage is on a lake : la villa se trouve au bord d'un lac> **7** (*expressing equality*) : faire, égaler <two and two are four : deux et deux font quatre> **8** (*expressing health or well-being*) : aller, se porter <how are you? : comment allez-vous?> **9** (*expressing cost*) : coûter <meat is very expensive : la viande coûte très cher> — *v aux* **1** : être en train de <he is reading : il lit, il est en train de lire> **2** (*indicating obligation*) : devoir <you are to come when called : tu dois venir quand on t'appelle> **3** (*used in passive constructions*) : être <the doors had been locked : les portes avaient été barrées> — *v impers* **1** (*indicating weather*) : faire <it's nice out : il fait beau> **2** (*indicating time*) : être <it's ten o'clock : il est dix heures> <it's late : il est tard>

beach[1] ['biːtʃ] *vt* : échouer (un bateau)

beach[2] *n* : plage *f,* grève *f*

beachhead ['biːtʃˌhɛd] *n* : tête *f* de pont

beacon ['biːkən] *n* : phare *m,* signal *m* lumineux

bead[1] ['biːd] *vt* STRING : enfiler — *vi* : perler (se dit d'un liquide)

bead[2] *n* **1** : perle *f,* grain *m* <rosary beads : grains d'un chapelet> **2** DROP : goutte *f,* perle *f* **3 beads** *npl* NECKLACE : collier *m*

beady ['biːdi] *adj* **beadier; -est** : perçant, brillant

beagle ['biːgəl] *n* : beagle *m*

beak ['biːk] *n* : bec *m*

beaker ['biːkər] *n* **1** CUP : gobelet *m* **2** : vase *f* à bec (en chimie)

beam[1] ['biːm] *vt* : transmettre, diffuser (une émission) — *vi* **1** SHINE : rayonner **2** SMILE : sourire d'un air radieux

beam[2] *n* **1** : poutre *f* (de bois) **2** RAY : rayon *m* **3** *or* **radio beam** : faisceau *m* de guidage **4** SMILE : grand sourire *m*

bean ['biːn] *n* **1** : haricot *m* <green bean : haricot vert> **2** : grain *m* (de café) **3** → **broad bean**

bear[1] ['bær] *v* **bore** ['bor]; **borne** ['bɔrn]; **bearing** *vt* **1** CARRY : porter, transporter **2** PRODUCE : produire, porter <a fruit-bearing tree : un arbre qui

produit des fruits> **3** : donner naissance *f* à (un enfant) **4** ENDURE : supporter, tolérer <he doesn't bear pain well : il ne supporte pas bien la douleur> — *vi* **1** : diriger, prendre <bear right : prenez à droite> **2 to bear down on** : exercer une pression sur **3 to bear with** : patienter **4 to bear in mind** : ne pas oublier

bear[2] *n, pl* **bears** *or* **bear** : ours *m,* ourse *f*

bearable ['bærəbəl] *adj* : supportable, tolérable

beard[1] ['bɪrd] *vt* DEFY : affronter, braver

beard[2] *n* **1** : barbe *f* (d'un homme), barbiche *f* (d'une chèvre) **2** TUFT : barbe *f* (d'une plante)

bearded ['bɪrdəd] *adj* : barbu, à barbe

bearer ['bærər] *n* **1** : porteur *m,* -teuse *f* **2** : titulaire *mf* (d'un passeport)

bearing ['bærɪŋ] *n* **1** MANNER : allure *f,* maintien *m* **2** SIGNIFICANCE : relation *f,* rapport *m* <to have no bearing : n'avoir aucun rapport> **3** COURSE, DIRECTION : orientation *f,* direction *f* <I've lost my bearings : je suis désorienté> **4** → **ball bearing**

bearish ['bærɪʃ] *adj* : rude, bourru

beast ['bi:st] *n* **1** : bête *f,* animal *m* **2** BRUTE : brute *f* (personne)

beastly ['bi:stli] *adj* **beastlier; -est 1** BRUTAL : bestial, brutal **2** NASTY : sale <what beastly weather! : quel sale temps!>

beat[1] ['bi:t] *v* **beat; beaten** ['bi:tən] *or* **beat; beating** *vt* **1** STRIKE : battre, frapper **2** DEFEAT : vaincre, battre <to beat one's competitors : devancer la compétition> <to beat s.o. up the hill : arriver au sommet avant qqn> <it beats me! : ça me dépasse!> **3** AVOID : éviter <to beat the crowds : éviter la foule> **4** MASH, WHIP : battre (des œufs, des pommes de terre, etc.) — *vi* THROB : battre, palpiter <with beating heart : le cœur battant>

beat[2] *adj* EXHAUSTED : éreinté, crevé *fam*

beat[3] *n* **1** BEATING : battement *m* <the beat of a drum : le battement d'un tambour> **2** RHYTHM : rythme *m,* temps *m*

beater ['bi:t̬ər] → **eggbeater**

beatific [ˌbi:ə'tɪfɪk] *adj* : béatifique

beating ['bitɪŋ] *n* **1** : battement *m* (de cœur, d'un tambour, etc.) **2** THRASHING : correction *f,* raclée *f fam* **3** DEFEAT : défaite *f*

beatitude [bi'æt̬əˌtu:d] *n* **1** : béatitude *f* **2 the Beatitudes** : les béatitudes

beau ['bo] *n, pl* **beaux** *or* **beaus** : galant *m*

beauteous ['bju:t̬iəs] → **beautiful**

beautician [bju:'tɪʃən] *n* : esthéticien *m,* -cienne *f*

beautiful ['bju:t̬ɪfəl] *adj* **1** : beau <a beautiful woman : une belle femme> **2** SPLENDID : magnifique, merveilleux

beautifully ['bju:t̬ɪfəli] *adv* **1** ATTRACTIVELY : admirablement, à la perfection **2** SPLENDIDLY : parfaitement, merveilleusement <that will do beautifully : cela convient parfaitement>

beautify ['bju:t̬ɪˌfaɪ] *vt* **-fied; -fying** : embellir, orner

beauty ['bju:t̬i] *n, pl* **-ties** : beauté *f*

beauty shop *n or* **beauty salon** : salon *m* de beauté

beaver ['bi:vər] *n* : castor *m*

because [bi'kʌz, -'kɔz] *conj* : parce que

because of *prep* : à cause de

beck ['bɛk] *n* **to be at the beck and call of** : obéir au doigt et à l'œil à

beckon ['bɛkən] *vt* : faire signe à, attirer — *vi* : faire signe

become [bi'kʌm] *v* **-came** [-'keɪm]; **-come; -coming** *vt* SUIT : aller à, convenir à <the moustache doesn't become him : la moustache ne lui va pas> — *vi* : devenir <what's become of him? : qu'est-ce qu'il est devenu?> <they became friends : elles sont devenues amies>

becoming [bi'kʌmɪŋ] *adj* **1** SUITABLE : convenable, correct <becoming modesty : modestie convenable> **2** FLATTERING : seyant <a becoming hat : un chapeau seyant>

bed[1] ['bɛd] *vt* **bedded; bedding 1** : coucher **2** *or* **to bed out** : repiquer (des plantes)

bed[2] *n* **1** : lit *m* <to go to bed : se coucher, se mettre au lit> <to get out of bed : se lever> **2** LAYER : couche *f,* gisement *m* **3** BOTTOM : fond *m* (de la mer), lit *m* (d'un fleuve)

bedbug ['bɛdˌbʌg] *n* : punaise *f* de lit

bedclothes ['bɛdˌklo:ðz, -ˌklo:z] *npl* : draps *mpl* et couvertures *fpl*

bedding ['bɛdɪŋ] *n* **1** → **bedclothes 2** : litière *f* (pour les animaux)

bedeck [bɪ'dɛk] *vt* : parer, orner

bedevil [bɪ'dɛvəl] *vt* **-iled** *or* **-illed; -iling** *or* **-illing 1** PLAGUE : tourmenter, harceler **2** BEWILDER : déconcerter, embrouiller

bedlam ['bɛdləm] *n* UPROAR : chahut *m,* charivari *m*

bedraggled [bɪ'drægəld] *adj* : débraillé, désordonné

bedridden ['bɛdˌrɪdən] *adj* : alité, cloué au lit

bedrock ['bɛdˌrɑk] *n* **1** : soubassement *m* (en géologie) **2** BASIS : base *f,* fondation *f*

bedroom ['bɛdˌru:m, -ˌrʊm] *n* : chambre *f* (à coucher)

bedsheet → **sheet**

bedspread ['bɛdˌsprɛd] *n* : couvre-lit *m*

bee ['bi:] *n* **1** : abeille *f* **2** GATHERING : groupe *m,* club *m* <sewing bee : groupe de couture>

beech [ˈbiːtʃ] *n, pl* **beeches** *or* **beech** : hêtre *m*
beechnut [ˈbiːtʃˌnʌt] *n* : faine *f*
beef[1] [ˈbiːf] *vt or* **to beef up** : renforcer, étoffer (un discours, etc.) — *vi* COMPLAIN : se plaindre, rouspéter *fam*
beef[2] *n* **1** : bœuf *m* <roast beef : rôti de bœuf> **2** *pl* **beefs** [ˈbiːfs] *or* **beeves** [ˈbiːvz] STEER : bœuf *m*
beefsteak [ˈbifˌsteɪk] *n* : bifteck *m*
beehive [ˈbiːˌhaɪv] *n* : ruche *f*
beekeeper [ˈbiːˌkiːpər] *n* : apiculteur *m*, -trice *f*
beeline [ˈbiːˌlaɪn] *n* : ligne *f* droite <to make a beeline for : se diriger tout droit vers>
been → **be**
beep[1] [ˈbiːp] *vi* : klaxonner (se dit d'une voiture), faire bip (se dit d'un appareil électronique)
beep[2] *n* : coup *m* de klaxon, bip *m*
beeper [ˈbiːpər] *n* : récepteur *m* de radiomessagerie *f*, téléavertisseur *m Can*
beer [ˈbɪr] *n* : bière *f*
beeswax [ˈbiːzˌwæks] *n* : cire *f* d'abeille
beet [ˈbiːt] *n* : betterave *f*
beetle [ˈbiːṭəl] *n* : scarabée *m*
befall [bɪˈfɔl] *v* **-fell** [-ˈfɛl] ; **-fallen** [-ˈfɔlən] *vt* : arriver à <a misfortune befell her : il lui arriva un malheur> — *vi* HAPPEN : arriver, advenir
befit [bɪˈfɪt] *vt* **-fitted; -fitting** : convenir à
before[1] [bɪˈfor] *adv* **1** AHEAD : devant, en avant <marching on before : marchant devant> **2** PREVIOUSLY : avant <before and after : avant et après> <long before : bien avant> **3** EARLIER : en avance, avant <come at six o'clock, not before : viens à six heures, pas avant>
before[2] *prep* **1** : devant, en présence de <before the court : devant le tribunal> **2** : avant <before long : avant longtemps> **3** ABOVE : avant, plutôt que <he puts quantity before quality : il préfère la quantité plutôt que la qualité> **4 before my eyes** : sous mes yeux
before[3] *conj* **1** : avant de, avant que <before going : avant de partir> <before you go : avant que tu partes> **2** : plutôt que de <he would die before surrendering : il mourrait plutôt que de se rendre>
beforehand [bɪˈforˌhænd] *adv* : d'avance, à l'avance, au préalable
befriend [bɪˈfrɛnd] *vt* : se lier d'amitié avec
befuddle [bɪˈfʌdəl] *vt* **-dled; -dling** : brouiller les idées de, embrouiller
beg [ˈbɛg] *v* **begged; begging** *vt* **1** : mendier (la charité, la nourriture) **2** REQUEST, SOLICIT : demander, solliciter **3** ENTREAT : supplier, prier <I beg your mercy : je vous prie grâce> — *vi* **1** : mendier **2** : faire le beau (se dit d'un chien)
beget [bɪˈgɛt] *vt* **-got** [-gɑt]; **-gotten** [-gɑtən] *or* **-got; -getting** : engendrer
beggar [ˈbɛgər] *n* : mendiant *m*, -diante *f;* quêteux *m*, -teuse *f*
begin [bɪˈgɪn] *v* **-gan** [-ˈgæn]; **-gun** [-ˈgʌn]; **-ginning** *vt* **1** START : commencer, débuter **2** FOUND : inaugurer, fonder — *vi* **1** START : commencer **2** ORIGINATE : débuter, être fondé **3 to begin with** FIRST : d'abord
beginner [bɪˈgɪnər] *n* : débutant *m*, -tante *f*
beginning [bɪˈgɪnɪŋ] *n* : début *m*, commencement *m*
begone [biˈgɔn] *interj* : va-t-en!
begonia [bɪˈgoːnjə] *n* : bégonia *m*
begrudge [bɪˈgrʌdʒ] *vt* **-grudged; -grudging 1** : en vouloir à, accorder à regret **2** ENVY : envier
beguile [bɪˈgaɪl] *vt* **-guiled; -guiling 1** DECEIVE : tromper, duper **2** CHARM : séduire **3 to beguile (away) the time** : faire passer le temps agréablement
behalf [bɪˈhæf, -haf] *n* **1** INTEREST : défense *f*, sujet *m* <he argued in our behalf : il a argumenté pour notre défense> <in my behalf : à mon sujet> **2 on behalf of** : de la part de, au nom de
behave [bɪˈheɪv] *vi* **-haved; -having** : se conduire, se comporter
behavior *or Brit* **behaviour** [bɪˈheɪvjər] *n* : conduite *f*, comportement *m*
behead [bɪˈhɛd] *vt* : décapiter
behest [bɪˈhɛst] *n* **1** : demande *f*, instance *f* **2 at the behest of** : sur l'ordre de
behind[1] [bɪˈhaɪnd] *adv* **1** BACK : derrière, en arrière <I looked behind : j'ai regardé en arrière> <from behind : par derrière> **2** LATE : en retard <she's behind in her work : elle est en retard dans son travail>
behind[2] *prep* **1** : derrière, en arrière de <behind the building : derrière l'édifice> **2** : en retard sur <behind the times : en retard sur son temps> **3** SUPPORTING : soutenant <to be behind s.o. : soutenir qqn>
behold [bɪˈhoːld] *vt* **-held; -holding** : voir, apercevoir
beholder [bɪˈhoːldər] *n* : spectateur *m*, -trice *f*
behoove [bɪˈhuːv] *vt* **-hooved; -hooving** : incomber à, être de l'intérêt de
beige[1] [ˈbeɪʒ] *adj* : beige
beige[2] *n* : beige *m*
being [ˈbiːɪŋ] *n* **1** : être *m*, créature *f* **2** EXISTENCE : existence *f*
belabor *or Brit* **belabour** [bɪˈleɪbər] *vt* **to belabor the point** : insister sur le point
belated [bɪˈleɪṭəd] *adj* : tardif
belch[1] [ˈbɛltʃ] *vi* BURP : faire un renvoi, roter *fam* — *vt* : vomir, cracher <to

belch (out) smoke : cracher de la fumée>

belch[2] *n* : renvoi *m,* rot *m fam*

beleaguer [bɪ'li:gər] *vt* **1** BESIEGE : assiéger **2** HARASS : harceler, assaillir

belfry ['bɛlfri] *n, pl* **-fries** : beffroi *m,* clocher *m*

Belgian[1] ['bɛldʒən] *adj* : belge

Belgian[2] *n* : Belge *mf*

belie [bɪ'laɪ] *vt* **-lied; -lying 1** MISREPRESENT : donner une fausse idée de **2** CONTRADICT : démentir, contredire

belief [bə'li:f] *n* **1** OPINION : croyance *f,* conviction *f* **2** TRUST : confiance *f* **3** FAITH : foi *f,* confession *f*

believe [bə'li:v] *v* **-lieved; -lieving** *vt* **1** : croire <she believes the reports : elle croit les reportages> **2** SUPPOSE : croire, estimer, penser <I believe it will rain : je crois qu'il va pleuvoir> — *vi* : croire <he believes in God : il croit en Dieu>

believable [bə'li:vəbəl] *adj* : croyable, crédible

believer [bə'li:vər] *n* **1** : croyant *m,* croyante *f* (en religion) **2** SUPPORTER : partisan *m,* -sane *f;* adepte *mf*

belittle [bɪ'lɪtəl] *vt* **-littled; -littling** : déprécier, rabaisser

Belizean[1] [bə'li:ziən] *adj* : bélizien

Belizean[2] *n* : Bélizien *m,* -zienne *f*

bell ['bɛl] *n* **1** : cloche *f,* clochette *f* **2** : sonnette *f* (d'une porte, etc.)

belladonna [ˌbɛlə'dɑnə] *n* : belladone *f*

belle ['bɛl] *n* : beauté *f,* belle *f* <the belle of the ball : la reine du bal>

bellhop ['bɛlˌhɑp] *n* : chasseur *m*

bellicose ['bɛlɪˌko:s] *adj* : belliqueux, guerrier

belligerence [bə'lɪdʒərənts] *or* **belligerency** [bə'lɪdʒərəntsi] *n* : belligérance *f*

belligerent [bə'lɪdʒərənt] *adj* : belligérant

bellow[1] ['bɛˌlo:] *vt* : brailler *fam* — *vi* **1** : beugler, mugir **2** HOWL, SHOUT : brailler *fam,* hurler

bellow[2] *n* **1** : beuglement *m,* mugissement *m* **2** HOWL : hurlement *m*

bellows ['bɛˌlo:z] *ns & pl* : soufflet *m*

bellwether ['bɛlˌwɛðər] *n* LEADER : dirigeant *m,* -geante *f;* chef *m*

belly[1] ['bɛli] *vi* **-lied; -lying** SWELL, BULGE : se gonfler, bomber

belly[2] *n, pl* **-lies** : ventre *m*

belong [bɪ'lɔŋ] *vi* **1 to belong to** : appartenir à, être à <it belongs to me : c'est à moi> **2** : être à sa place, aller <put it back where it belongs : remets-le à sa place> <where does it belong? : où va-t-il?> **3** : être membre, faire partie <he belongs to the athletic club : il fait partie du cercle sportif>

belongings [bɪ'lɔŋɪŋz] *npl* : affaires *fpl,* possessions *fpl,* effets *mpl* <personal belongings : effets personnels>

beloved[1] [bɪ'lʌvəd, -'lʌvd] *adj* : bien-aimé, chéri

beloved[2] *n* : bien-aimé *m,* -mée *f;* chéri *m,* -rie *f*

below[1] [bɪ'lo:] *adv* : en dessous, en bas, plus bas

below[2] *prep* **1** : sous, au-dessous de, en dessous de <below the surface : sous la surface> <below average : au-dessous de la moyenne **2** : au-dessous de, inférieur à <temperatures below normal : températures inférieures à la normale>

belt[1] ['bɛlt] *vt* **1** : mettre une ceinture à (des pantalons, etc.) **2** THRASH : donner un coup à

belt[2] *n* **1** : ceinture *f* <safety belt : ceinture de sécurité> **2** : courroie *f* (d'une machine) <courroie de ventilateur : fan belt> **3** AREA : zone *f,* région *f*

bemoan [bɪ'mo:n] *vt* : déplorer, se lamenter sur

bemuse [bɪ'mju:z] *vt* **-mused; -musing 1** BEWILDER : déconcerter, rendre perplexe **2** ENGROSS : absorber

bench ['bɛntʃ] *n* **1** : banc *m,* banquette *f* **2** : cour *f,* tribunal *m* <to appear before the bench : comparaître devant le tribunal> **3** → **workbench**

bend[1] ['bɛnd] *v* **bent** ['bɛnt]; **bending** *vt* **1** : plier, courber, fléchir <to bend one's arm : plier le bras> <bend your head : baissez ta tête> **2** DIRECT : diriger <to bend one's step toward : se diriger vers> **3** DISTORT, TWIST : tordre, crochir *Can,* travestir (la vérité) <to bend the rules : contourner les règlements> — *vi* **1** : se courber, se pencher, plier **2** TURN : tourner, faire un coude

bend[2] *n* **1** BENDING : pli *m,* flexion *f* **2** CURVE, TURN : tournant *m,* virage *m,* coude *m* **3 bends** *npl* : maladie *f* des caissons

beneath[1] [bɪ'ni:θ] *adv* : au-dessous, dessous, en bas

beneath[2] *prep* **1** UNDER : sous, en dessous de <beneath the bed : sous le lit> **2** : indigne de <the work is beneath him : le travail est indigne de lui>

benediction [ˌbɛnə'dɪkʃən] *n* : bénédiction *f*

benefactor ['bɛnəˌfæktər] *n* : bienfaiteur *m,* -trice *f*

beneficence [bə'nɛfəsənts] *n* : bienfaisance *f*

beneficent [bə'nɛfəsənt] *adj* : bienfaisant, généreux

beneficial [ˌbɛnə'fɪʃəl] *adj* : avantageux, salutaire, favorable

beneficially [ˌbɛnə'fɪʃəli] *adv* : avantageusement

beneficiary [ˌbɛnə'fɪʃiˌɛri, -'fɪʃəri] *n, pl* **-ries** : bénéficiaire *mf*

benefit[1] ['bɛnəfɪt] *vt* : faire du bien à, profiter à, être avantageux pour — *vi* : profiter, faire du bien, tirer avantage

benefit[2] *n* **1 :** avantage *m* <it's to your benefit : c'est à votre avantage> <fringe benefits : avantages sociaux> **2 :** allocation *f* <unemployment benefit : allocation de chômage>
benevolence [bəˈnɛvələnts] *n* **:** bienveillance *f,* charité *f*
benevolent [bəˈnɛvələnt] *adj* **:** bienveillant
benevolently [bəˈnɛvələntli] *adv* **:** avec bienveillance
Bengali[1] [bɛnˈgɔli, bɛŋ-] *adj* **:** bengali
Bengali[2] *n* **1 :** bengali *m* (langue) **2 :** Bengali *mf*
benign [bɪˈnaɪn] *adj* **1** KINDLY **:** bienveillant, affable, gentil **2 :** bénin (en médecine) **3** MILD **:** doux
Beninese[1] [bəˌnɪˈniːz, -ˌniː-, -ˈniːs; ˌbɛnɪˈ-] *adj* **:** béninois
Beninese[2] *n* **:** Béninois *m,* -noise *f*
bent[1] [ˈbɛnt] *adj* **1** CURVED **:** tordu, courbé **2 to be bent on doing :** être décidé à faire
bent[2] *n* **:** aptitude *f,* dispositions *fpl,* penchant *m*
benumb [bɪˈnʌm] *vt* **:** engourdir, endormir
benzene [ˈbɛnˌziːn] *n* **:** benzène *m*
bequeath [bɪˈkwiːθ, -kwiːð] *vt* **:** léguer
bequest [bɪˈkwɛst] *n* **:** legs *m*
berate [bɪˈreɪt] *vt* **-rated; -rating :** réprimander
bereaved[1] [bɪˈriːvd] *adj* **:** endeuillé, attristé
bereaved[2] *ns & pl* **the bereaved :** la famille du défunt
bereavement [bɪˈriːvmənt] *n* **:** deuil *m*
bereft [bɪˈrɛft] *adj* **:** privé, dénué <bereft of hope : désespérée>
beret [bəˈreɪ] *n* **:** béret *m*
beriberi [ˌbɛriˈbɛri] *n* **:** béribéri *m*
berry [ˈbɛri] *n, pl* **-ries :** baie *f*
berserk [bərˈsərk, -ˈzərk] *adj* **1 :** fou, enragé **2 to go berserk :** être pris de folie furieuse
berth[1] [ˈbɛrθ] *vt* **:** amarrer, donner un poste d'amarrage à **—** *vi* **:** mouiller l'ancre, s'amarrer
berth[2] *n* **1** ANCHORAGE **:** mouillage *m,* poste *m* d'amarrage **2** BUNK **:** couchette *f* **3 to give s.o. a wide berth :** éviter qqn
beryl [ˈbɛrəl] *n* **:** béryl *m*
beseech [bɪˈsiːtʃ] *vt* **-seeched** *or* **-sought** [-ˈsɔt]; **-seeching :** supplier, implorer
beset [bɪˈsɛt] *vt* **-set; -setting 1** ASSAIL, HARASS **:** assaillir, harceler <beset with doubts : assailli de doutes> **2** SURROUND **:** encercler
beside [bɪˈsaɪd] *prep* **1 :** à côté de, près de **2 to be beside oneself :** être hors de soi
besides[1] [bɪˈsaɪdz] *adv* **1 :** de plus, en outre <nothing besides : rien de plus> **2** MOREOVER **:** d'ailleurs, du reste <besides, I like him : d'ailleurs, je l'aime>
besides[2] *prep* **1 :** en plus de, outre <besides being rich, he's handsome : outre qu'il est riche, il est beau> **2** EXCEPT **:** sauf, hormis <no one besides me : personne hormis moi>
besiege [bɪˈsiːdʒ] *vt* **-sieged; -sieging :** assiéger, encercler
besmirch [bɪˈsmərtʃ] *vt* **:** souiller, entacher
besought → beseech
best[1] [ˈbɛst] *vt* OUTDO **:** l'emporter sur, vaincre
best[2] *adv* (*superlative of* **well**) **:** le mieux, le plus <the best dressed man : l'homme le mieux habillé> <the best known actress : l'actrice la plus connue>
best[3] *adj* (*superlative of* **good**) **1 :** meilleur <the best student : le meilleur élève> **2 :** plus beau <her best dress : sa plus belle robe>
best[4] *n* **1 :** meilleur *m,* -leure *f* <she's the best : elle est la meilleure> **2 :** mieux *m* <all for the best : tout pour le mieux> **3 to do one's best :** faire tout son possible
bestial [ˈbɛstʃəl, ˈbiːs-] *adj* **:** bestial
bestir [biˈstər] *vt* **-stirred; -stirring 1 :** activer, pousser à agir **2 to bestir oneself :** s'activer, s'agiter
best man *n* **:** garçon *m* d'honneur, témoin *m*
bestow [bɪˈstoː] *vt* **:** accorder, conférer
bet[1] [ˈbɛt] *v* **bet; betting** *vt* **:** parier, miser, gager *Can* **—** *vi* **to bet on :** parier sur
bet[2] *n* **:** pari *m,* gageure *f Can*
betoken [bɪˈtoːkən] *vt* **:** présager, annoncer, être l'indice de
betray [bɪˈtreɪ] *vt* **1** DECEIVE **:** trahir, tromper **2** REVEAL **:** révéler, laisser voir, divulguer (un secret, etc.)
betrayal [bɪˈtreɪəl] *n* **1 :** trahison *f* **2 betrayal of trust :** abus *m* de confiance
betrothal [bɪˈtroːðəl, -ˈtrɔ-] *n* **:** fiançailles *fpl*
betrothed [bɪˈtroːðd, -trɔθt] *n* **:** fiancé *m,* -cée *f*
better[1] [ˈbɛt̬ər] *vt* **1** IMPROVE **:** améliorer <to better oneself : améliorer sa condition> **2** SURPASS **:** dépasser, surpasser
better[2] *adv* (*comparative of* **well**) **1 :** mieux <he plays better than you : il joue mieux que toi> **2 all the better :** tant mieux
better[3] *adj* (*comparative of* **good**) **1 :** meilleur <this store is better than that one : ce magasin est meilleur que celui-là> **2** MORE **:** plus <better than nine miles : plus de neuf milles> **3 to get better :** s'améliorer, se remettre
better[4] *n* **1 :** meilleur *m* <the better of the two : le meilleur des deux> **2 change for the better :** amélioration *f,* changement *m* en mieux **3 to get the better of :** l'emporter sur

betterment ['bɛt̬ərmənt] *n* : amélioration *f*

bettor *or* **better** ['bɛt̬ər] *n* : parieur *m*, -rieuse *f*

between[1] [bɪ'twiːn] *adv* **1** : au milieu, dans l'intervalle **2 in ~** : entre les deux

between[2] *prep* : entre <between five and ten : entre cinq et dix> <between you and me : entre nous>

bevel[1] ['bɛvəl] *vt* **-eled** *or* **-elled; -eling** *or* **-elling** : biseauter, tailler en biseau

bevel[2] *n* **1** : surface *f* oblique **2** *or* **bevel edge** : biseau *m*

beverage ['bɛvrɪdʒ, 'bɛvə-] *n* : boisson *f*

bevy ['bɛvi] *n, pl* **bevies** : groupe *m* (de personnes), volée *f* (d'oiseaux)

bewail [bɪ'weɪl] *vt* : se lamenter sur, pleurer

beware [bɪ'wær] *vi* **to beware of** : se méfier de, prendre garde à

bewilder [bɪ'wɪldər] *vt* : dérouter, rendre perplexe, déconcerter

bewilderment [bɪ'wɪldərmənt] *n* : perplexité *f*, confusion *f*

bewitch [bɪ'wɪtʃ] *vt* **1** : ensorceler **2** CHARM : enchanter, captiver

beyond[1] [bi'jɑnd] *adv* : au-delà, plus loin, au loin <the mountains beyond : les montagnes au loin> <2000 and beyond : 2000 et au-delà>

beyond[2] *prep* **1** : au-delà de <beyond the sea : au-delà de la mer> **2** : au-dessus de, hors de <beyond doubt : hors de doute> **3** : plus de <he won't stay beyond a week : il ne restera pas plus d'une semaine> **4 it's beyond me** : ça me dépasse

biannual [ˌbaɪ'ænjuəl] *adj* : bisannuel, semestriel — **biannually** *adv*

bias[1] ['baɪəs] *vt* **-ased** *or* **-assed; -asing** *or* **-assing** : influencer, prévenir (contre)

bias[2] *n* **1** : biais *m* <cut on the bias : coupé en biais> **2** PREJUDICE : préjugé *m*, parti *m* pris **3** TENDENCY : penchant *m*, tendance *f*

biased ['baɪəst] *adj* : partial

bib ['bɪb] *n* : bavoir *m* (d'un bébé), bavette *f* (sur un vêtement)

Bible ['baɪbəl] *n* : Bible *f*

biblical ['bɪblɪkəl] *adj* : biblique

bibliographer [ˌbɪbli'ɑgrəfər] *n* : bibliographe *mf*

bibliography [ˌbɪbli'ɑgrəfi] *n, pl* **-phies** : bibliographie *f* — **bibliographic** [-bliə'græfɪk] *adj*

bicameral [ˌbaɪ'kæmərəl] *adj* : bicaméral

bicarbonate [ˌbaɪ'kɑrbənət, -ˌneɪt] *n* : bicarbonate *m*

bicentennial [ˌbaɪsɛn'tɛniəl] *n* : bicentenaire *m*

biceps ['baɪˌsɛps] *ns & pl* : biceps *m*

bicker ['bɪkər] *vi* : se chamailler

bicuspid [baɪ'kʌspɪd] *n* : prémolaire *f*

bicycle[1] ['baɪsɪkəl, -ˌsɪ-] *vi* **-cled; -cling** : faire de la bicyclette, faire du vélo

bicycle[2] *n* : bicyclette *f*, vélo *m*

bicyclist ['baɪsɪkəlɪst] *n* : cycliste *mf*

bid[1] ['bɪd] *v* **bade** ['bæd, 'beɪd] *or* **bid** ['bɪd]; **bidden** ['bɪdən] *or* **bid; bidding** *vt* **1** ORDER : demander, ordonner **2** SAY : dire, souhaiter <to bid s.o. goodbye : dire au revoir à qqn> **3** INVITE : inviter <I bid him to come in : je l'ai invité à rentrer> **4** OFFER : offrir, faire une offre de <she bid five dollars : elle a fait une offre de cinq dollars> — *vi* : offrir, faire une offre

bid[2] *n* **1** OFFER : offre *f*, enchère *f* **2** INVITATION : invitation *f* **3** ATTEMPT : essai *m*, tentative *f*

bidder ['bɪdər] *n* : offrant *m*; enchérisseur *m*, -seuse *f* <to the highest bidder : au plus offrant>

bide ['baɪd] *vt* **bode** ['boːd] *or* **bided; bided; biding** : attendre <to bide one's time : attendre le bon moment>

biennial [baɪ'ɛniəl] *adj* : biennal — **biennially** *adv*

bier ['bɪr] *n* **1** STAND : catafalque *m* **2** COFFIN : bière *f*

bifocals [baɪˌfoːkəlz] *npl* : lunettes *fpl* bifocales, verres *mpl* à double foyer

big ['bɪg] *adj* **bigger; biggest 1** LARGE : grand, gros **2** OLDER : grand, aîné <his big brother : son frère aîné> **3** IMPORTANT : important, grand <a big difference : une grande différence> <a big mistake : une grave erreur> **4** POPULAR : à la mode **5 to have a big heart** : avoir grand cœur

bigamist ['bɪgəmɪst] *n* : bigame *mf*

bigamous ['bɪgəməs] *adj* : bigame

bigamy ['bɪgəmi] *n* : bigamie *f*

Big Dipper → **dipper**

bighorn sheep ['bɪgˌhɔrn] *n* : mouton *m* sauvage à grandes cornes

bight ['baɪt] *n* **1** COIL, LOOP : boucle *f* **2** BAY : baie *f*, anse *f*

bigot ['bɪgət] *n* : fanatique *mf*; bigot *m*, -gote *f* (en religion)

bigoted ['bɪgət̬əd] *adj* : fanatique, intolérant

bigotry ['bɪgətri] *n, pl* **-tries** : fanatisme *m*, intolérance *f*

big shot *n* : grosse légume *f fam*, gros bonnet *m fam*

bigwig ['bɪgˌwɪg] → **big shot**

bike ['baɪk] *n* **1** : vélo *m* **2** MOTORBIKE, MOTORCYCLE : moto *f*, motocyclette *f*

bikini [bə'kiːni] *n* : bikini *m*

bilateral [baɪ'læt̬ərəl] *adj* : bilatéral — **bilaterally** *adv*

bile ['baɪl] *n* **1** : bile *f* **2** IRRITABILITY : mauvaise humeur *f*

bilingual [baɪ'lɪŋgwəl] *adj* : bilingue

bilious ['bɪliəs] *adj* : bilieux

bilk ['bɪlk] *vt* : escroquer, frauder

bill[1] ['bɪl] *vt* **1** : facturer, envoyer la facture à **2** ADVERTISE : annoncer, mettre à l'affiche — *vi* **to bill and coo** : roucouler

bill[2] *n* **1 :** bec *m* (d'un oiseau) **2** INVOICE **:** facture *f,* note *f,* addition *f* (au restaurant) **3 :** projet *m* de loi <to pass a bill : voter un projet de loi> **4** POSTER **:** affiche *f* **5** BANKNOTE **:** billet *m* (de banque)
billboard ['bɪl,bɔrd] *n* **:** panneau *m* publicitaire
billet[1] ['bɪlət] *vt* **:** cantonner, loger
billet[2] *n* **:** cantonnement *m*
billfold ['bɪl,fo:ld] *n* **:** portefeuille *m*
billiards ['bɪljərdz] *n* **:** billard *m*
billion ['bɪljən] *n* **:** milliard *m*
billow[1] ['bɪlo] *vi* **1** RISE, ROLL **:** se soulever (se dit de la mer) **2** SWELL **:** se gonfler (se dit d'une voile), onduler (se dit d'un drapeau)
billow[2] *n* **1** WAVE **:** vague *f* **2** CLOUD **:** nuage *m* <a billow of smoke : un nuage de fumée>
billowy ['bɪlowi] *adj* **:** houleux (se dit de la mer), ondoyant (se dit des nuages, de la fumée, etc.)
billy goat ['bɪli,go:t] *n* **:** bouc *m*
bin ['bɪn] *n* **:** coffre *m,* boîte *f*
binary ['baɪnəri, -,nɛri] *adj* **:** binaire
bind ['baɪnd] *vt* **bound** ['baʊnd]; **binding 1** TIE **:** lier, attacher, ligoter **2** OBLIGATE **:** obliger, contraindre **3** ENCIRCLE, GIRD **:** entourer, ceindre **4** BANDAGE **:** bander, panser (une blessure) **5 :** relier (un livre)
binder ['baɪndər] *n* **1 :** relieur *m,* -lieuse *f* (de livres) **2** FOLDER **:** classeur *m*
binding ['baɪndɪŋ] *n* **:** reliure *f* (d'un livre)
binge ['bɪndʒ] *n* **:** bringue *f fam* <to go on a binge : faire la bringue>
bingo ['bɪŋ,go:] *n, pl* **-gos :** bingo *m*
binocular [baɪ'nɑkjələr, bə-] *adj* **:** binoculaire
binoculars [bə'nɑkjələrz, baɪ-] *npl* **:** jumelles *fpl*
biochemical [baɪo'kɛmɪkəl] *adj* **:** biochimique
biochemist [,baɪo'kɛmɪst] *n* **:** biochimiste *mf*
biochemistry [,baɪo'kɛməstri] *n* **:** biochimie *f*
biodegradable [,baɪodɪ'greɪdəbəl] *adj* **:** biodégradable
biographer [baɪ'ɑgrəfər] *n* **:** biographe *mf*
biographical [,baɪə'græfɪkəl] *adj* **:** biographique
biography [baɪ'ɑgrəfi, bi:-] *n, pl* **-phies :** biographie *f*
biological [-dʒɪkəl] *adj* **:** biologique
biologist [baɪ'ɑlədʒɪst] *n* **:** biologiste *mf*
biology [baɪ'ɑlədʒi] *n* **:** biologie *f*
biophysicist [,baɪo'fɪzəsɪst] *n* **:** biophysicien *m,* -cienne *f*
biophysics [,baɪo'fɪzɪks] *ns & pl* **:** biophysique *f*
biopsy ['baɪ,ɑpsi] *n, pl* **-sies :** biopsie *f*
biotechnology [,baɪotɛk'nɑlədʒi] *n* **:** biotechnologie *f*
bipartisan [baɪ'pɑrṱəzən, -sən] *adj* **:** bipartite
biped ['baɪ,pɛd] *n* **:** bipède *m*
birch ['bərtʃ] *n* **:** bouleau *m*
bird ['bərd] *n* **1 :** oiseau *m* **2** FOWL **:** volaille *f*
birdbath ['bərd,bæθ, -baθ] *n* **:** vasque *f* pour les oiseaux
bird dog *n* **:** chien *m* d'arrêt
birdhouse ['bərd,haʊs] *n* **:** volière *f*
bird of prey *n* **:** oiseau *m* de proie, rapace *m*
birdseed ['bərd,si:d] *n* **:** graines *fpl* pour les oiseaux
bird's–eye view ['bərdz,aɪ] *n* **:** vue *f* panoramique, vue *f* d'ensemble
birth ['bərθ] *n* **1 :** naissance *f,* accouchement *m* <to give birth : accoucher> **2** ORIGIN **:** naissance *f,* début *m* **3** LINEAGE **:** descendance *f,* lignée *f*
birthday ['bərθ,deɪ] *n* **:** anniversaire *m* <happy birthday! : joyeux anniversaire!>
birthmark ['bərθ,mɑrk] *n* **:** tache *f* de vin
birthplace ['bərθ,pleɪs] *n* **:** lieu *m* de naissance
birthrate ['bərθ,reɪt] *n* **:** natalité *f*
birthright ['bərθ,raɪt] *n* **:** droit *m* (acquis à la naissance)
biscuit ['bɪskət] *n* **:** petit pain *m* au lait
bisect ['baɪ,sɛkt, ,baɪ'-] *vt* **:** couper en deux, diviser — *vi* INTERSECT **:** se couper, se croiser
bisexual [,baɪ'sɛkʃəwəl, -'sɛkʃəl] *adj* **:** bisexuel
bishop ['bɪʃəp] *n* **1 :** évêque *m* **2 :** fou *m* (aux échecs)
bishopric ['bɪʃə,prɪk] *n* **:** évêché *m*
bismuth ['bɪzməθ] *n* **:** bismuth *m*
bison [baɪzən, -sən] *ns & pl* **-son :** bison *m*
bistro ['bi:stro, 'bɪs-] *n, pl* **-tros :** bistro *m,* bistrot *m*
bit ['bɪt] *n* **1 :** mors *m* (d'un cheval) **2** PIECE **:** morceau *m,* bout *m,* petit peu *m* <a bit of paper : un bout de papier> **3 :** bit *m* (en informatique) **4 a bit** RATHER, SOMEWHAT **:** un peu *m,* un petit peu *m*
bitch[1] ['bɪtʃ] *vi* COMPLAIN **:** râler *fam,* rouspéter *fam*
bitch[2] *n* **:** chienne *f*
bite[1] ['baɪt] *v* **bit** ['bɪt]; **bitten** ['bɪtən]; **biting** *vt* **1 :** mordre **2** STING **:** piquer — *vi* **:** mordre
bite[2] *n* **1 :** morsure *f* (de chien, etc.) **2** STING **:** piqûre *f* **3** MOUTHFUL **:** bouchée *f* **4** SNACK **:** morceau *m* <let's grab a bite : mangeons un morceau> **5 :** touche *f* (de pêche)
biting *adj* **1** PENETRATING **:** pénétrant, cinglant **2** CAUSTIC **:** mordant, caustique
bitter ['bɪṱər] *adj* **1** ACRID **:** amer, âpre <a bitter taste : un goût amer> **2** PENETRATING **:** pénétrant, cinglant <bitter cold : froid glacial> **3** HARSH **:** acerbe, dur <to the bitter end

: jusqu'au bout> **4** FIERCE, RELENTLESS : acharné, féroce, violent <a bitter hatred : une haine profonde>

bitterly ['bɪt̬ərli] *adv* : amèrement

bittern ['bɪt̬ərn] *n* : butor *m*

bitterness ['bɪt̬ərnəs] *n* : amertume *f*, âpreté *f*

bituminous [bə'tu:mənəs, -'tju:-] *adj* **1** : bitumineux **2 bituminous coal** : huile *f* grasse

bivalve ['baɪ,vælv] *n* : bivalve *m*

bivouac[1] ['bɪvə,wæk, 'bɪv,wæk] *vi* **-ouacked; -ouacking** : bivouaquer

bivouac[2] *n* : bivouac *m*

bizarre [bə'zɑr] *adj* : bizarre — **bizarrely** *adv*

blab ['blæb] *vi* **blabbed; blabbing** CHATTER : jaser, jacasser, babiller

black[1] ['blæk] *vt* : noircir

black[2] *adj* **1** : noir (se dit de la couleur ou de la race) **2** DARK : obscur, sans lumière **3** WICKED : noir, mauvais **4** DIRTY : sale, noir **5** GLOOMY : noir, sombre

black[3] *n* **1** : noir *m* (couleur) **2** : Noir *m*, Noire *f* (personne) **3** DARKNESS : obscurité *f*, ténèbres *fpl* **4 to be in the black** : être créditeur

black-and-blue [,blækən'blu:] *adj* : couvert de bleus

blackball[1] ['blæk,bɔl] *vt* : blackbouler *fam*

blackball[2] *n* : vote *m* contraire

blackberry ['blæk,bɛri] *n, pl* **-ries** : mûre *f*

blackbird ['blæk,bərd] *n* : merle *m*

blackboard ['blæk,bɔrd] *n* : tableau *m* (noir)

blacken ['blækən] *vt* **1** BLACK : noircir **2** DEFAME : ternir, souiller, noircir

blackhead ['blæk,hɛd] *n* : point *m* noir

black hole *n* : trou *m* noir

blackish [blækɪʃ] *adj* : noirâtre

blackjack ['blæk,jæk] *n* **1** : assommoir *m* (arme) **2** : vingt-et-un *m* (jeu de cartes)

blacklist[1] ['blæk,lɪst] *vt* : mettre sur la liste noire

blacklist[2] *n* : liste *f* noire

blackmail[1] ['blæk,meɪl] *vi* : faire chanter

blackmail[2] *n* : chantage *m*

blackmailer ['blæk,meɪlər] *n* : maître-chanteur *m*

blackness ['blæk,nəs] *n* **1** : noirceur *f* **2** DARKNESS : obscurité *f*

blackout ['blæk,aʊt] *n* **1** : panne *f* d'électricité **2** FAINT : évanouissement *m*

black out *vi* **1** : avoir une panne d'électricité **2** FAINT : s'évanouir

blacksmith ['blæk,smɪθ] *n* : forgeron *m*

blacktop ['blæk,tɑp] *n* : asphalte *m*

bladder ['blædər] *n* : vessie *f*

blade ['bleɪd] *n* **1** : brin *m* (d'herbe) **2** : lame *f* (de couteau) **3** : pale *f* (d'hélice, de rame, etc.)

blame[1] ['bleɪm] *vt* **blamed; blaming** : blâmer, reprocher

blame[2] *n* **1** CONDEMNATION : blâme *m*, reproches *mpl* **2** RESPONSIBILITY : faute *f*, responsabilité *f*

blameless ['bleɪmləs] *adj* : irréprochable

blameworthy ['bleɪm,wərði] *adj* : blâmable, coupable

blanch ['blæntʃ] *vt* WHITEN : blanchir — *vi* PALE : pâlir

bland ['blænd] *adj* **1** SUAVE : affable, aimable **2** SOOTHING : apaisant, calmant **3** DULL, INSIPID : fade, insipide

blandly ['blændli] *adv* : avec affabilité, affablement

blandness ['blændnəs] *n* **1** SUAVENESS : affabilité *f* **2** TASTELESSNESS : fadeur *f*

blandishment ['blændɪʃmənt] *n* : flatterie *f*, cajoleries *fpl*

blank[1] ['blæŋk] *adj* **1** EXPRESSIONLESS : sans expression **2** DAZED, DISCONCERTED : déconcerté, dérouté **3** : blanc, vierge <a blank sheet : une feuille blanche> **4** EMPTY : vide <a blank wall : un mur vide> **5** DOWNRIGHT : catégorique, absolu <a blank refusal : un refus catégorique>

blank[2] *n* **1** GAP, SPACE : blanc *m*, vide *m*, trou *m* (de mémoire, etc.) **2** FORM : formulaire *m* à remplir, fiche *f* vierge **3** CARTRIDGE : cartouche *f* à blanc

blanket[1] ['blæŋkət] *vt* : couvrir, recouvrir

blanket[2] *adj* : général, global <blanket agreement : accord général>

blanket[3] *n* **1** : couverture *f* (d'un lit) **2** : couche *f*, manteau *f* <a blanket of snow : une couche de neige>

blankly ['blænkli] *adv* : sans expression, d'un air ébahi

blare[1] ['blær] *vi* **blared; blaring** : beugler, jouer à plein volume

blare[2] *n* : beuglement *m* (d'une radio, etc.), sonnerie *f* (d'une trompette)

blarney ['blɑrni] *n* : boniment *m*, baratin *m*

blasé [blɑ'zeɪ] *adj* : blasé

blaspheme [blæs'fi:m, 'blæs,-] *v* **-phemed; -pheming** : blasphémer

blasphemous ['blæsfəməs] *adj* : blasphématoire

blasphemy ['blæsfəmi] *n, pl* **-mies** : blasphème *m*

blast[1] ['blæst] *vt* **1** BLOW UP : faire sauter, dynamiter **2** ATTACK, CRITICIZE : attaquer violemment **3** BLIGHT : flétrir, détruire (des cultures) — *vi* **1** BLARE : beugler, retentir **2 to blast off** : décoller

blast[2] *n* **1** GUST : coup *m* de vent, rafale *f* **2** EXPLOSION : explosion *f* **3 at full blast** : à plein volume

blatant ['bleɪtənt] *adj* : flagrant, criant

blatantly ['bleɪtəntli] *adv* : d'une manière flagrante

blaze[1] [ˈbleɪz] *v* **blazed**; **blazing** *vt* MARK : griffer, marquer (un arbre), frayer <to blaze a trail : frayer un chemin> — *vi* **1** BURN, FLAME : flamber **2** SHINE : flamboyer, resplendir <the blazing sun : le soleil flamboyant>

blaze[2] *n* **1** : marque *f,* encoche *f* (sur un arbre) **2** FLAME : flamme *f,* feu *m* **3** BURST : éclat *m* (de couleur), torrent *m* (de lumière), explosion *f* (de colère)

blazer [ˈbleɪzər] *n* : blazer *m*

bleach[1] [ˈbliːtʃ] *vt* : blanchir, décolorer

bleach[2] *n* : décolorant *m,* eau *f* de Javel

bleachers [ˈbliːtʃərz] *npl* : gradins *mpl*

bleak [ˈbliːk] *adj* **1** GLOOMY : sombre, morne, lugubre <bleak thoughts : de sombres réflections> **2** DESOLATE : désolé <a bleak landscape : un terrain désolé>

bleakly [ˈbliːkli] *adv* : sombrement, lugubrement

bleakness [ˈbliːknəs] *n* **1** GLOOMINESS : caractère *m* sombre, monotonie *f* **2** BARRENNESS : désolation *f* (d'un paysage)

bleary [ˈblɪri] *adj* : trouble, voilé <bleary-eyed : aux yeux troubles>

bleat[1] [ˈbliːt] *vi* : bêler

bleat[2] *n* : bêlement *m*

bleed [ˈbliːd] *v* **bled** [ˈblɛd]; **bleeding** *vt* **1** : saigner **2** DRAIN : purger (des freins, etc.) **3 to bleed s.o. dry** : tirer de l'argent à qqn — *vi* **1** : saigner, perdre du sang **2 my heart bleeds for you** : tu me fends le cœur

blemish[1] [ˈblɛmɪʃ] *vt* : tacher, ternir

blemish[2] *n* : tache *f,* défaut *m,* imperfection *f*

blend[1] [ˈblɛnd] *vt* : mélanger, mêler, marier (des couleurs) — *vi* : se mélanger, se mêler

blend[2] *n* : mélange *m,* alliance *f*

blender [ˈblɛndər] *n* : mixer *m,* mélangeur *m Can*

bless [ˈblɛs] *vt* **blessed** [ˈblɛst]; **blessing** **1** GLORIFY : bénir, glorifier <bless the Lord : béni soit le Seigneur> **2** CONSECRATE : bénir, sanctifier **3** ENDOW : doter <to be blessed with : avoir le bonheur de, être doué de> **4 bless you!** : à vos souhaits! (lorsqu'on éternue) **5 to bless oneself** : se signer

blessed [ˈblɛsəd] *or* **blest** [ˈblɛst] *adj* **1** HOLY : bénit, saint **2** HAPPY : bienheureux, heureux

blessing [ˈblɛsɪŋ] *n* **1** : bénédiction *f* (en religion) **2** BENEFIT : avantage *m,* bienfait *m* <a blessing in disguise : un bienfait inattendu> **3** APPROVAL : bénédiction *f,* approbation *f*

blew → **blow**

blight[1] [ˈblaɪt] *vt* : détruire, flétrir

blight[2] *n* **1** : rouille *f* (des plantes) **2** SCOURGE : fléau *m* <urban blight : dégradation urbaine>

blimp [ˈblɪmp] *n* : dirigeable *m*

blind[1] [ˈblaɪnd] *adv* : sans visibilité <to fly blind : voler aux instruments>

blind[2] *vt* **1** : aveugler, rendre aveugle **2** DAZZLE : éblouir

blind[3] *adj* **1** SIGHTLESS : aveugle **2** UNQUESTIONING : aveugle, absolu, ignorant <blind faith : foi absolue> **3** CLOSED : sans issue <a blind alley : une voie sans issue>

blind[4] *n* **1** : store *m* <venetian blind : store vénitien> **2** COVER : affût *m* (en chasse) **3 the blind** : les non-voyants

blindfold[1] [ˈblaɪnd,foːld] *vt* : bander les yeux à

blindfold[2] *n* : bandeau *m*

blindly [ˈblaɪndli] *adv* : aveuglément, à l'aveuglette

blindness [ˈblaɪndnəs] *n* **1** : cécité *f* <snow blindness : cécité des neiges> **2** : aveuglement *m* <blindness to the truth : aveuglement devant la verité>

blink[1] [ˈblɪŋk] *vt* : cligner (des yeux) — *vi* **1** : cligner des yeux **2** FLICKER : clignoter, vaciller

blink[2] *n* : battement *m* des paupières

blinker [ˈblɪŋkər] *n* : clignotant *m*

bliss [ˈblɪs] *n* **1** HAPPINESS : félicité *f,* bonheur *m* absolu **2** HEAVEN : paradis *m*

blissful [ˈblɪsfəl] *adj* : heureux, bienheureux — **blissfully** *adv*

blister[1] [ˈblɪstər] *vi* **1** : se couvrir d'ampoules, cloquer (se dit de la peau) **2** : se boursoufler (se dit de la peinture, etc.)

blister[2] *n* **1** : ampoule *f,* cloque *f* (sur la peau) **2** : boursouflure *f* (sur une surface peinte)

blithe [ˈblaɪθ, ˈblaɪð] *adj* **blither**; **blithest** CHEERFUL : joyeux, gai — **blithely** *adv*

blitz[1] [ˈblɪts] *vt* : bombarder

blitz[2] *n* : bombardement *m,* raid *m* aérien

blizzard [ˈblɪzərd] *n* : tempête *f* de neige

bloat [ˈbloːt] *vi* SWELL : se gonfler, enfler

bloated [ˈbloːtəd] *adj* : boursouflé, gonflé

blob [ˈblɑb] *n* : tache *f,* (grosse) goutte *f*

bloc [ˈblɑk] *n* : bloc *m*

block[1] [ˈblɑk] *vt* **1** OBSTRUCT : bloquer, barrer **2** IMPEDE : bloquer, gêner, faire opposition à (un adversaire, un projet de loi, etc.) **3 to block out** HIDE : cacher, empêcher d'entrer **4 to block out** OUTLINE : ébaucher

block[2] *n* **1** : bloc *m,* billot *m* <a block of ice : un bloc de glace> <butcher's block : billot de boucherie> **2** OBSTRUCTION : obstacle *m,* obstruction *f* **3** : pâté *m* de maisons, bloc *m Can* <to walk around the block : faire le tour du pâté de maisons> <two blocks away : à deux rues d'ici> **4**

BUILDING : immeuble *m* <office block : immeuble de bureaux> **5** GROUP : groupe *m,* série *f* (de billets, etc.) **6 block and tackle** HOIST : palan *m*

blockade[1] [blɑˈkeɪd] *vt* **-aded; -ading 1** OBSTRUCT : bloquer **2** : faire le blocus de (un port)

blockade[2] *n* : blocus *m*

blockage [ˈblɑkɪdʒ] *n* : obstruction *f,* blocage *m*

blockhead [ˈblɑkˌhɛd] *n* : imbécile *mf fam*

bloke [ˈbloːk] *n Brit* : type *m*

blond[1] *or* **blonde** [ˈblɑnd] *adj* : blond

blond[2] *or* **blonde** *n* : blond *m,* blonde *f*

blood [ˈblʌd] *n* **1** : sang *m* **2** LINEAGE : lignée *f,* descendance *f*

blood bank *n* : banque *f* du sang

bloodcurdling [ˈblʌdˌkərdəlɪŋ] *adj* : à vous figer le sang

bloodhound [ˈblʌdˌhaʊnd] *n* : limier *m*

bloodless [ˈblʌdləs] *adj* **1** : sans effusion de sang **2** SPIRITLESS : apathique, sans vie

bloodmobile [ˈblʌdmoˌbiːl] *n* : centre *m* mobile de collecte du sang

blood pressure *n* : tension *f* artérielle

bloodshed [ˈblʌdˌʃɛd] *n* : effusion *f* de sang, carnage *m*

bloodshot [ˈblʌdˌʃɑt] *adj* : injecté de sang

bloodstain [ˈblʌdˌsteɪn] *n* : tache *f* de sang

bloodstream [ˈblʌdˌstriːm] *n* : sang *m,* système *m* sanguin

bloodsucker [ˈblʌdˌsʌkər] *n* : sangsue *f*

bloodthirsty [ˈblʌdˌθərsti] *adj* : sanguinaire, assoiffé de sang

blood vessel *n* : vaisseau *m* sanguin

bloody [ˈblʌdi] *adj* **bloodier; -est 1** : sanglant <a bloody battle : un combat sanglant> **2** : ensanglanté <bloody hands : mains ensanglantées>

bloom[1] [ˈbluːm] *vi* **1** FLOWER : s'épanouir, éclore **2** FLOURISH : être épanoui, être florissant

bloom[2] *n* **1** FLOWER : fleur *f* **2** BLOOMING : floraison *f,* épanouissement *m* **3 in bloom** *or* **in full bloom** : en fleurs, en pleine floraison

blooper [ˈbluːpər] *n* : gaffe *f fam*

blossom[1] [ˈblɑsəm] *vi* **1** : fleurir, être en fleurs **2** MATURE : s'épanouir, se développer **3 to blossom into** : devenir

blossom[2] *n* : fleur *f*

blot[1] [ˈblɑt] *vt* **blotted; blotting 1** STAIN : tacher, souiller **2** DRY : sécher (encre, etc.) **3 to blot out** : rayer, effacer

blot[2] *n* **1** SPOT : tache *f* **2** *or* **inkblot** : pâté *m* **3** BLEMISH : souillure *f,* tare *f*

blotch[1] [ˈblɑtʃ] *vt* : tacher, marbrer

blotch[2] *n* : tache *f,* marbrure *f* (sur la peau)

blotchy [ˈblɑtʃi] *adj* **blotchier; -est 1** : couvert de taches, marbré <blotchy complexion : teint marbré> **2** SMEARED : barbouillé <blotchy drawing : dessin barbouillé>

blotter [ˈblɑt̬ər] *n* : buvard *m*

blouse [ˈblaʊs, ˈblaʊz] *n* : chemisier *m,* corsage *m*

blow[1] [bloː] *v* **blew** [ˈbluː]; **blown** [ˈbloːn]; **blowing** *vt* **1** : souffler, pousser (un navire), chasser (des feuilles, etc.) <to blow sth away : faire voler qqch> <to blow one's nose : se moucher> **2** SOUND : jouer de (une trompette, etc.), donner (un coup de sifflet) **3** SHAPE : souffler, donner une forme à (le verre) **4** BUNGLE : rater, manquer <I blew it! : j'ai tout raté!> **5 to blow out** : souffler sur (une chandelle, etc.) — *vi* **1** : souffler **2** *or* **to blow away** : s'envoler **3** SOUND : sonner (se dit d'une trompette, etc.) **4 to blow down** FALL : se renverser, tomber **5 to blow out** : éclater (se dit d'un pneu), s'éteindre (se dit d'une bougie)

blow[2] *n* **1** GALE : coup *m* de vent **2** HIT, STROKE : coup *m,* coup *m* de poing **3** MISFORTUNE : coup *m,* malheur *m* **4 to come to blows** : en venir aux mains

blowout [ˈbloːˌaʊt] *n* : éclatement *m* (d'un pneu)

blowtorch [ˈbloˌtɔrtʃ] *n* : lampe *f* à souder, chalumeau *m*

blow up *vt* **1** EXPLODE : faire sauter, faire exploser **2** INFLATE : gonfler — *vi* : exploser, sauter

blubber[1] [ˈblʌbər] *vi* : pleurer (comme un veau)

blubber[2] *n* : graisse *f* de baleine

bludgeon[1] [ˈblʌdʒən] *vt* : matraquer

bludgeon[2] *n* : gourdin *m,* matraque *f*

blue[1] [ˈbluː] *adj* **bluer; bluest 1** : bleu <blue with cold : bleu de froid> **2** MELANCHOLY : triste

blue[2] *n* **1** : bleu *m,* azur *m* **2 out of the blue** : de façon imprévue

bluebell [ˈbluːˌbɛl] *n* : jacinthe *f* des bois

blueberry [ˈbluːˌbɛri] *n, pl* **-ries** : myrtille *f France,* bleuet *m Can*

bluebird [ˈbluːˌbərd] *n* : oiseau *m* bleu

blue cheese *n* : (fromage *m*) bleu *m*

bluefish [ˈbluːˌfɪʃ] *n, pl* **-fish** *or* **-fishes** : poisson *m* bleu de la côte atlantique

blue jay *n* : geai *m* bleu

blueprint [ˈbluːˌprɪnt] *n* **1** : bleu *m* **2** PROGRAM : plan *m* (de travail), projet *m*

blues [ˈbluːz] *npl* **1** DEPRESSION : cafard *m,* mélancolie *f* **2** : blues *m* (en musique)

bluff[1] [ˈblʌf] *v* : bluffer

bluff[2] *adj* **1** STEEP : escarpé, à pic **2** FRANK : carré, direct

bluff[3] *n* **1** CLIFF : falaise *f,* escarpement *m* **2** DECEPTION, RUSE : bluff *m*

bluing *or* **blueing** [ˈbluːɪŋ] *n* : produit *m* blanchissant

blunder[1] [ˈblʌndər] *vi* **1** *or* **to blunder along** : avancer à l'aveuglette, avancer à tâtons **2** ERR : faire une bévue, faire une gaffe
blunder[2] *n* MISTAKE : bévue *f,* gaffe *f fam,* impair *m*
blunderbuss [ˈblʌndərˌbʌs] *n* : tromblon *m*
blunt[1] [ˈblʌnt] *vt* : émousser (des couteaux, des ciseaux, etc.), épointer (des crayons), couper (l'appétit)
blunt[2] *adj* **1** DULL : émoussé, épointé **2** ABRUPT, DIRECT : brusque, abrupt, carré
bluntly [ˈblʌntli] *adv* : franchement, carrément
bluntness *n* **1** DULLNESS : manque *m* de tranchant **2** ABRUPTNESS, FRANKNESS : brusquerie *f,* franc-parler *m*
blur[1] [ˈblər] *v* **blurred; blurring** *vt* : troubler, brouiller, rendre flou <eyes blurred with tears : yeux brouillés de larmes> — *vi* : se brouiller
blur[2] *n* **1** : image *f* floue, contour *m* imprécis **2** SMEAR : tache *f*
blurb [ˈblərb] *n* : notice *f* publicitaire
blurry [ˈbləri] *adj* **blurrier; -est** : flou, troublé <blurry vision : vision troublée>
blurt [ˈblərt] *vt or* **to blurt out** : laisser échapper
blush[1] [ˈblʌʃ] *vi* : rougir
blush[2] *n* : rougeur *f*
bluster[1] [ˈblʌstər] *vi* **1** BLOW, STORM : souffler violemment **2** BOAST : fanfaronner
bluster[2] *n* **1** : hurlement *m* (du vent) **2** BOASTING : fanfaronnade *f*
blustery [ˈblʌstəri] *adj* : violent, orageux
boa [ˈboːə] *n* : boa *m*
boar [ˈbor] *n* **1** PIG : verrat *m* **2** → **wild boar**
board[1] [ˈbord] *vt* **1** : monter à bord de (un avion, un navire), monter dans (un train) **2** LODGE : prendre en pension **3 to board up** : couvrir de planches
board[2] *n* **1** PLANK : planche *f* **2** : pension *f* <room and board : pension complète> **3** COMMITTEE, COUNCIL : conseil *m,* commission *f* <board meeting : réunion du conseil> **4** : tableau *m* (d'un jeu) **5 to go on board** : monter à bord
boarder [ˈbordər] *n* : pensionnaire *mf*
boardinghouse [ˈbordɪŋˌhaʊs] *n* : pension *f*
boarding school *n* : pensionnat *m*
boardwalk [ˈbordˌwɔk] *n* : promenade *f* (en planches)
boast[1] [ˈboːst] *vt* : se glorifier de, être fier de posséder <the town boasts five churches : la ville est fière de posséder cinq églises> — *vi* : se vanter, fanfaronner
boast[2] *n* : vantardise *f,* fanfaronnade *f*
boaster [ˈboːstər] *n* : vantard *m,* -tarde *f;* fanfaron *m,* -ronne *f*
boastful [ˈboːstfəl] *adj* : vantard, fanfaron
boastfully [ˈboːstfəli] *adv* : en se vantant, en fanfaronnant
boat[1] [ˈboːt] *vt* : transporter en bateau — *vi* : aller en bateau
boat[2] *n* **1** : bateau *m* <to go by boat : prendre le bateau> <to be in the same boat : être tous dans la même galère> **2** → **rowboat, ship, sailboat**
boatswain [ˈboːsən] *n* : maître *m* d'équipage
bob[1] [ˈbɑb] *v* **bobbed; bobbing** *vt* : couper court (les cheveux) — *vi* **1** : monter et descendre <to bob in the water : danser sur l'eau> **2 to bob up** APPEAR : apparaître, surgir
bob[2] *n* **1** : coupe *f* au carré (des cheveux) **2** FLOAT : bouchon *m* (de pêche) **3** NOD : hochement *m* de tête
bobbin [ˈbɑbən] *n* : bobine *f*
bobby pin [ˈbɑbiˌpɪn] *n* : pince *f* à cheveux
bobcat [ˈbɑbˌkæt] *n* : lynx *m* (roux)
bobolink [ˈbɑbəˌlɪŋk] *n* : oiseau *m* chanteur de l'Amérique du Nord, goglu *m Can*
bobsled [ˈbɑbˌslɛd] *n* : bob *m,* bobsleigh *m*
bobwhite [ˈbɑbˈhwaɪt] *n* : caille *f* de l'Amérique du Nord
bode[1] [ˈboːd] *vt* **boded; boding** : présager, augurer <to bode well for : être de bon augure pour>
bode[2] → **bide**
bodice [ˈbɑdəs] *n* : corsage *m* (d'une robe)
bodily[1] [ˈbɑdəli] *adv* **1** PHYSICALLY : physiquement, à bras-le-corps **2** ENTIRELY : tout entier
bodily[2] *adj* PHYSICAL : physique, corporel <bodily contact : contact physique>
body [ˈbɑdi] *n, pl* **bodies 1** : corps *m* **2** CORPSE : cadavre *m* **3** PERSON : personne *f,* être *m* humain **4** COLLECTION, MASS : masse *f,* ensemble *m* <in a body : en masse> <a body of evidence : un ensemble de preuves> **5** SUBSTANCE : corps *m,* fond *m* <the body of a letter : le corps d'une lettre> **6** : carrosserie *f* (d'une voiture), fuselage *m* (d'un avion)
bodyguard [ˈbɑdiˌgɑrd] *n* : garde *m* du corps
bog[1] [ˈbɑg, ˈbɔg] *vi* **bogged; bogging** *or* **to bog down** : s'embourber, s'enliser, s'empêtrer (dans un discours)
bog[2] *n* **1** MARSH : marais *m,* marécage *m* **2** *or* **peat bog** : tourbière *f*
bogey [ˌbʊgi, ˈboː-] *n, pl* **-geys 1** GHOST : fantôme *m,* spectre *m* **2** *or* **bogeyman** : croque-mitaine *m,* épouvantail *m*
boggle [ˈbɑgəl] *v* **-gled; -gling** *vt* **to boggle the mind** : dépasser l'imagination

— *vi* **the mind boggles :** ça laisse perplexe, on a du mal à imaginer ça

boggy ['bɑgi, 'bɔ-] *adj* **boggier; -est** : marécageux

bogus ['bo:gəs] *adj* SHAM : faux, bidon *fam*

bohemian[1] [bo:'hi:miən] *adj* : bohème

bohemian[2] *n* : bohème *mf*

boil[1] ['bɔɪl] *vt* : faire bouillir — *vi* **1** : bouillir **2** SEETHE : bouillir, bouillonner

boil[2] *n* **1** : ébullition *f* <to bring to a boil : amener à ébullition> **2** : furoncle *m* (en médecine)

boiler ['bɔɪlər] *n* : chaudière *f*

boisterous ['bɔɪstərəs] *adj* **1** NOISY, ROWDY : bruyant, tapageur **2** STORMY : houleux, tumultueux

boisterously ['bɔɪstərəsli] *adv* : bruyamment, tumultueusement

bold ['bo:ld] *adj* **1** COURAGEOUS, DARING : hardi, audacieux **2** IMPUDENT : insolent, effronté — **boldly** *adv*

boldface ['bo:ld,feɪs] *n or* **boldface type** : caractères *mpl* gras

boldness ['bo:ldnəs] *n* : hardiesse *f,* audace *f*

bolero [bə'lɛro] *n, pl* **-ros** : boléro *m*

Bolivian[1] [bə'lɪviən] *adj* : bolivien

Bolivian[2] *n* : Bolivien *m,* -vienne *f*

boll weevil ['bo:l,wi:vəl] *n* : charançon *m* (du cotonnier)

bologna [bə'lo:ni] *n* : gros saucisson *m*

bolster[1] ['bo:lstər] *vt* **-stered; -stering** : soutenir, renforcer <to bolster morale : remonter le moral>

bolster[2] *n* : traversin *m*

bolt[1] ['bo:lt] *vt* **1** LOCK : verrouiller, fermer au verrou **2** *or* **to bolt down** : engloutir (de la nourriture) — *vi* **1** : s'emballer (se dit d'un cheval) **2** DASH : se précipiter, se lancer

bolt[2] *n* **1** THUNDERBOLT : éclair *m,* coup *m* de foudre **2** LOCK : verrou *m* **3** : rouleau *m* (de tissu) **4** : boulon *m* <nuts and bolts : écrous et boulons>

bomb[1] ['bɑm] *vt* : bombarder

bomb[2] *n* : bombe *f*

bombard [bɑm'bɑrd, bəm-] *vt* : bombarder

bombardier [,bɑmbə'dɪr] *n* : bombardier *m*

bombardment [bɑm,bɑrdmənt] *n* : bombardement *m*

bombast ['bɑm,bæst] *n* : grandiloquence *f*

bombastic [bɑm'bæstɪk] *adj* : grandiloquent, ampoulé

bomber ['bɑmər] *n* : bombardier *m* (avion)

bombshell ['bɑm,ʃɛl] *n* : bombe *f*

bona fide ['bo:nə,faɪd, 'bɑ-; ,bo:nə'faɪdi] *adj* **1** : de bonne foi **2** GENUINE : authentique, véritable

bonanza [bə'nænzə] *n* : filon *m,* aubaine *f*

bonbon ['bɑn,bɑn] *n* : bonbon *m*

bond[1] ['bɑnd] *vt* **1** : entreposer (des marchandises) **2** *or* **to bond together** STICK : coller, faire adhérer — *vi* **1** STICK : adhérer **2 to bond with** : s'attacher à

bond[2] *n* **1** TIE : lien *m,* attache *f* <the bonds of marriage : les liens conjugaux> **2** AGREEMENT : contrat *m,* engagement *m,* caution *f* (en droit) **3** ADHESION : adhérence *f* **4** SECURITY : bon *m* <savings bond : bon d'épargne> **5 bonds** *npl* FETTERS : fers *mpl,* chaînes *fpl*

bondage ['bɑndɪdʒ] *n* : esclavage *m*

bondholder ['bɑnd,ho:ldər] *n* : porteur *m* de bons

bondsman ['bɑndzmən] *n* **1** SLAVE : esclave *m,* serf *m* **2** SURETY : garant *m,* -rante *f*

bone[1] ['bo:n] *vt* **boned; boning** : désosser (de la viande), ôter les arêtes de (un poisson)

bone[2] *n* : os *m,* arête *f* (de poisson)

boneless ['bo:nləs] *adj* : sans os, sans arêtes

boner ['bo:nər] *n* BLUNDER : gaffe *f,* bourde *f*

bonfire ['bɑn,faɪr] *n* : feu *m* de joie

bonito [bə'ni:t̬o] *n, pl* **-tos** *or* **-to** : bonite *f*

bonnet ['bɑnət] *n* : bonnet *m,* chapeau *m*

bonny [bɑni] *adj* **bonnier; -est** *Brit* : joli, beau

bonus ['bo:nəs] *n* : gratification *f,* prime *f*

boo[1] ['bu:] *vt* : huer, siffler

boo[2] *n, pl* **boos** : huée *f*

booby ['bu:bi] *n, pl* **-bies** DOPE : nigaud *m,* -gaude *f*

book[1] ['bʊk] *vt* : réserver, retenir <to book a room : réserver une chambre>

book[2] *n* **1** : livre *m,* bouquin *m fam* **2** : carnet *m,* pochette *f* <a book of stamps : un carnet de timbres> <a book of matches : une pochette d'allumettes> **3** STANDARD : règlement *m* <to go by the book : suivre le règlement> **4** LIBRETTO : livret *m* **5 books** *npl* RECORDS : registre *m* **6 books** *npl* ACCOUNTS : comptes *mpl*

bookcase ['bʊk,keɪs] *n* : bibliothèque *f*

bookend ['bʊk,ɛnd] *n* : serre-livres *m,* appui-livres *m Can*

bookie ['bʊki] → **bookmaker**

bookish ['bʊkɪʃ] *adj* : studieux

bookkeeper ['bʊk,ki:pər] *n* : comptable *mf*

bookkeeping ['bʊk,ki:pɪŋ] *n* : comptabilité *f*

booklet ['bʊklət] *n* : brochure *f*

bookmaker ['bʊk,meɪkər] *n* : bookmaker *m*

bookmark ['bʊk,mɑrk] *n* : signet *m*

bookseller ['bʊk,sɛlər] *n* : libraire *mf*

bookshelf ['bʊk,ʃɛlf] *n, pl* **-shelves** : rayon *m,* étagère *f*

bookstore ['bʊk,stor] *n* : librairie *f*

bookworm ['bʊk,wərm] *n* : rat *m* de bibliothèque

boom[1] ['bu:m] *vi* **1** RESOUND : gronder, mugir (se dit de la mer), retentir (se dit de la voix) **2** FLOURISH, PROSPER : être en expansion, être en plein essor

boom[2] *n* **1** BOOMING : grondement *m,* mugissement *m,* retentissement *m* **2** : gui *m* (d'un bateau) **3** FLOURISHING : essor *m,* boom *m* (en commerce)

boomerang ['bu:mə,ræŋ] *n* : boomerang *m*

boon[1] ['bu:n] *adj* **boon companion** : gai compagnon *m,* bon compère *m*

boon[2] *n* : bienfait *m,* bénédiction *f,* aubaine *f*

boondocks ['bu:n,dɑks] *npl* : bled *m fam*

boor ['bʊr] *n* : rustre *m;* malotru *m,* -true *f*

boorish ['bʊrɪʃ] *adj* : rustre, grossier

boost[1] ['bu:st] *vt* **1** : soulever (une personne) **2** INCREASE, RAISE : augmenter, faire monter (des prix, etc.) <to boost morale : remonter le moral> **3** : survolter (un circuit électrique)

boost[2] *n* **1** INCREASE : hausse *f,* augmentation *f* **2** STIMULATION : encouragement *m,* stimulation *f* **3 to give s.o. a boost** : soulever qqn

booster ['bu:stər] *n* **1** SUPPORTER : partisan *m,* -sane *f;* supporter *m* **2** : survolteur *m* (en électricité) **3** *or* **booster rocket** : fusée *f* d'appoint **4** *or* **booster shot** : vaccin *m* de rappel

boot[1] ['bu:t] *vt* **1** KICK : donner un coup de pied à **2** : amorcer (en informatique) **3 to boot out** FIRE : mettre à la porte, congédier

boot[2] *n* **1** : botte *f,* bottine *f* **2** KICK : coup *m* de pied

bootee *or* **bootie** ['bu:ţi] *n* : petit chausson *m* (de bébé), pichou *m Can fam*

booth ['bu:θ] *n, pl* **booths** ['bu:ðz, 'bu:θs] : baraque *f* (d'un marché), cabine *f* (téléphonique), guichet *m* (pour acheter des billets)

booty ['bu:ţi] *n, pl* **-ties** : butin *m*

booze ['bu:z] *n* : alcool *m,* boissons *fpl* alcoolisées

borax ['bɔr,æks] *n* : borax *m*

border[1] ['bɔr,dər] *vt* **1** EDGE, SURROUND : border, entourer <bordered with flowers : entouré de fleurs> **2** BOUND : toucher, avoir une frontière commune avec — *vi* **to border on** : friser, frôler <it borders on insanity : cela frôle la folie>

border[2] *n* **1** EDGE : bord *m,* lisière *f* <the border of a lake : le bord d'un lac> **2** BOUNDARY : frontière *f* (d'un pays, etc.) **3** EDGING, STRIP : bordure *f* <a cement border : une bordure en ciment>

bore[1] ['bor] *vt* **bored; boring 1** DRILL, PIERCE : percer, creuser (un trou), forer (un puits) **2** TIRE : ennuyer, embêter

bore[2] *n* **1** DIAMETER : calibre *m* (d'un fusil) **2** : barbe *f fam,* corvée *f* <what a bore! : quelle barbe!> **3** : raseur *m,* -seuse *f fam;* casse-pieds *mf fam* (personne)

bore[3] → **bear**[1]

boredom ['bordəm] *n* : ennui *m*

boring ['borɪŋ] *adj* : ennuyeux, sans intérêt, ennuyant *Can,* plat *Can*

born ['bɔrn] *adj* **1** : né <born in Paris : né à Paris> **2** INNATE : né, parfait <he's a born dancer : il est né danseur> <a born fool : un parfait idiot>

borne → **bear**[1]

boron ['bor,ɑn] *n* : bore *m*

borough ['bəro] *n* : arrondissement *m* urbain

borrow ['bɑro] *vt* : emprunter, s'approprier <I borrowed his pen : j'ai emprunté son stylo> <to borrow an idea : s'approprier une idée>

Bosnian[1] ['bɑzniən, bɔz-] *adj* : bosniaque

Bosnian[2] *n* : Bosniaque *mf*

bosom[1] ['bʊzəm, 'bu:-] *adj* : intime <bosom friend : ami intime>

bosom[2] *n* **1** CHEST : poitrine *f* **2** BREASTS : seins *mpl,* poitrine *f* <a big bosom : une grosse poitrine> **3** : sein *m,* milieu *m* <in the bosom of her family : au sein de sa famille>

boss[1] ['bɔs] *vt* **1** SUPERVISE : diriger **2 to boss around** : mener à la baguette

boss[2] *n* : patron *m,* -tronne *f;* chef *m*

bossy ['bɔsi] *adj* **bossier; -est** : autoritaire, dictatorial

botanical [bə'tænɪkəl] *adj* : botanique

botanist ['bɑtənɪst] *n* : botaniste *mf*

botany ['bɑtəni] *n* : botanique *f*

botch ['bɑtʃ] *vt* : bousiller *fam,* saboter, estropier

both[1] ['bo:θ] *adj* : les deux <I like both dresses : j'aime les deux robes>

both[2] *conj* : et . . . et, à la fois <both his brother and his sister : et son frère et sa sœur> <she's both beautiful and intelligent : elle est à la fois belle et intelligente>

both[3] *pron* : tous les deux, l'un et l'autre <they were both there : elles étaient là toutes les deux>

bother[1] ['bɑðər] *vt* **1** ANNOY, IRK : agacer, ennuyer, embêter **2** PESTER : harceler **3** WORRY : inquiéter, préoccuper — *vi* : s'en faire, se déranger <don't bother : ne te dérange pas>

bother[2] *n* **1** ANNOYANCE : ennui *m* <what a bother! : quel ennui!> **2** TROUBLE : peine *f* <it's not worth the bother : ça ne vaut pas la peine>

bothersome ['bɑðərsəm] *adj* : ennuyeux, gênant

bottle[1] ['bɑtəl] *vt* **bottled; bottling** : mettre en bouteille

bottle[2] *n* **1** : bouteille *f* **2** : biberon *m* (d'un bébé) **3** FLASK : flacon *m* <a bottle of perfume : un flacon de parfum> **4 bottle opener** : ouvre-bouteilles *m*
bottleneck ['bɑtəl,nɛk] *n* **1** NARROWING : rétrécissement *m* (de la chaussée) **2** CONGESTION : embouteillage *m* (de la circulation) **3** HOLDUP : goulot *m* d'étranglement
bottom[1] ['bɑṱəm] *adj* **1** : du bas, inférieur <bottom lip : lèvre inférieure> **2** : premier <the bottom step : la première marche>
bottom[2] *n* **1** : bas *m,* pied *m* (d'un escalier, d'une page, etc.), fond *m* (de la mer) **2** : dernière place *f;* bas *m* <at the bottom of her class : dernière de classe> **3** ORIGIN, ROOT : origine *f,* fond *m* <to get to the bottom of sth : découvrir le fin fond de qqch> **4** BUTTOCKS : fesses *fpl,* derrière *m fam*
bottomless ['bɑṱəmləs] *adj* : sans fond, insondable
botulism ['bɑtʃə,lɪzəm] *n* : botulisme *m*
bough ['baʊ] *n* : branche *f,* rameau *m*
bought → **buy**[1]
bouillon ['bu:,jɑn; 'bʊl,jɑn, -jən] *n* : bouillon *m*
boulder ['bo:ldər] *n* : rocher *m*
boulevard ['bʊlə,vɑrd, 'bu:-] *n* : boulevard *m*
bounce[1] ['baʊnts] *v* **bounced; bouncing** *vt* : faire rebondir (une balle) — *vi* **1** : rebondir, faire des bonds <the ball bounced into the air : la balle a rebondi dans l'espace> **2** : être sans provision (se dit d'un chèque)
bounce[2] *n* **1** : bond *m* (d'une balle) **2** LIVELINESS : vitalité *f*
bound[1] ['baʊnd] *vt* CONFINE : limiter, borner — *vi* LEAP : bondir, sauter
bound[2] *adj* **1** TIED : lié, attaché <bound hand and foot : pieds et poings liés> **2** OBLIGED : obligé, tenu **3** CERTAIN : sûr, certain <it's bound to rain : il est sûr de pleuvoir> **4** : relié (se dit d'un livre) **5 bound for** : à destination de, en route pour
bound[3] *n* **1** LEAP : bond *m,* saut *m* **2 bounds** *npl* LIMIT : limite *f,* bornes *fpl*
boundary ['baʊndri, -dəri] *n, pl* **-aries 1** : limite *f,* frontière *f* **2** *or* **boundary line** : limites *fpl* du terrain
boundless ['baʊndləs] *adj* : sans limites, sans bornes
bounteous ['baʊntiəs] *adj* **1** GENEROUS : généreux **2** ABUNDANT : abondant <a bounteous harvest : une bonne récolte>
bountiful ['baʊntɪfəl] *adj* **1** GENEROUS : généreux, libéral **2** PLENTIFUL : abondant, copieux
bounty ['baʊnti] *n, pl* **-ties 1** : générosité *f,* libéralité *f* **2** REWARD : prime *f*
bouquet [bo:'keɪ, bu:-] *n* **1** : bouquet *m* (de fleurs) **2** : arôme *m,* bouquet *m* (de vin, etc.)
bourbon ['bərbən, 'bʊr-] *n* : bourbon *m*
bourgeois[1] ['bʊrʒ,wɑ, bʊrʒ'wɑ] *adj* : bourgeois
bourgeois[2] *n* : bourgeois *m,* -geoise *f*
bourgeoisie [,bʊrʒ,wɑ'zi] *n* : bourgeoisie *f*
bout ['baʊt] *n* **1** CONTEST : combat *m,* match *m* **2** ATTACK : accès *m,* crise *f* <a bout of fever : un accès de fièvre> **3** PERIOD : période *f* (de travail, etc.) <a drinking bout : une beuverie>
boutique [bu:'ti:k] *n* : boutique *f*
bovine ['bo:,vaɪn, -,vi:n] *adj* : bovin
bow[1] ['baʊ] *vi* **1** : s'incliner, saluer de la tête <to bow to the audience : saluer le public> **2** BEND : se courber **3** YIELD : s'incliner, se soumettre — *vt* : incliner, courber <to bow one's head : baisser la tête>
bow[2] ['baʊ:] *n* **1** BOWING : révérence *f,* salut *m* **2** : proue *f,* avant *m* (d'un navire)
bow[3] ['bo:] *n* **1** ARCH, BEND : arche *f,* arc *m,* courbe *f* **2** : arc *m* <bows and arrows : des arcs et des flèches> **3** : nœud *m* <bow tie : nœud papillon> **4** : archet *m* (de violon)
bowels ['baʊəlz] *npl* **1** INTESTINES : intestins *mpl* **2** DEPTHS : entrailles *fpl,* profondeurs *fpl* <the bowels of the earth : les entrailles de la terre>
bower ['baʊər] *n* : tonnelle *f,* berceau *m* de verdure
bowl[1] ['bo:l] *vt* **1** : faire rouler (une boule) **2 to bowl over** OVERWHELM : bouleverser, renverser — *vi* : jouer au bowling
bowl[2] *n* : bol *m,* bassin *m,* cuvette *f*
bowling ['bo:lɪŋ] *n* : bowling *m*
bowling alley *n* : bowling *m,* allée *f* de quilles *Can*
box[1] ['bɑks] *vt* **1** : mettre en boîte **2** SLAP : gifler, claquer (les oreilles, etc.) — *vi* : boxer, faire de la boxe
box[2] *n* **1** : boîte *f,* caisse *f,* coffre *m* <a box of chocolates : une boîte de chocolats> **2** : loge *f* (de théâtre), barre *f* (de témoin) **3** SLAP : gifle *f,* claque *f* **4** *pl* **box** *or* **boxes** : buis *m* (plante)
boxcar ['bɑks,kɑr] *n* : wagon *m* de marchandises
boxer ['bɑksər] *n* **1** FIGHTER : boxeur *m* **2** : boxer *m* (chien)
boxing ['bɑksɪŋ] *n* : boxe *f*
box office *n* : guichet *m,* billetterie *f*
boxwood ['bɑks,wʊd] *n* : buis *m*
boy ['bɔɪ] *n* : garçon *m*
boycott[1] ['bɔɪ,kɑt] *vt* : boycotter
boycott[2] *n* : boycott *m,* boycottage *m*
boyfriend ['bɔɪ,frɛnd] *n* : petit ami *m,* chum *m Can fam*
boyhood ['bɔɪ,hʊd] *n* : enfance *f*
boyish ['bɔɪɪʃ] *adj* : de garçon, d'enfant
bra ['brɑ] → **brassiere**
brace[1] ['breɪs] *vt* **braced; bracing 1** STRENGTHEN : soutenir, renforcer **2**

INVIGORATE : revigorer **3 to brace oneself** : rassembler ses forces

brace[2] *n* **1** PAIR : paire *f* <a brace of quail : une paire de cailles> **2** SUPPORT : attache *f*, support *m* **3** *or* **brace and bit** : vilbrequin *m* **4** : appareil *m* orthopédique, appareil *m* orthodontique (en médecine) **5** BRACKET : accolade *f*

bracelet ['breɪslət] *n* : bracelet *m*

bracken ['brækən] *n* : fougère *f*

bracket[1] ['brækət] *vt* **1** : mettre entre parenthèses, mettre entre crochets **2** GROUP : regrouper, mettre dans le même groupe

bracket[2] *n* **1** SUPPORT : support *m*, tasseau *m* **2** : parenthèse *f*, crochet *m* <in square brackets : entre crochets> **3** CATEGORY : catégorie *f*, tranche *f* <the lower income bracket : la tranche des petits revenus>

brackish ['brækɪʃ] *adj* : saumâtre

brad ['bræd] *n* : semence *f*, clou *m* (sans tête)

brag[1] ['bræg] *vi* **bragged; bragging** : se vanter

brag[2] *n* : vantardise *f*, fanfaronnades *fpl*

braggart ['brægərt] *n* : vantard *m*, -tarde *f*

braid[1] ['breɪd] *vt* **1** INTERWEAVE : entrelacer **2** : tresser (les cheveux)

braid[2] *n* **1** TRIMMING : galon *m*, ganse *f* **2** : tresse *f*, natte *f* (de cheveux)

braille ['breɪl] *n* : braille *m*

brain[1] ['breɪn] *vt* KNOCK OUT : assommer

brain[2] *n* **1** : cerveau *m*, cervelle *f* **2** : intelligence *f* <to have brains : être intelligent>

brainless ['breɪnləs] *adj* : stupide, idiot

brainstorm ['breɪn,stɔrm] *n* : idée *f* de génie, inspiration *f*

brainy ['breɪni] *adj* **brainier; -est** : intelligent, calé *fam*

braise ['breɪz] *vt* **braised; braising** : braiser

brake[1] ['breɪk] *vi* **braked; braking** : freiner

brake[2] *n* : frein *m*

bramble ['bræmbəl] *n* : ronce *f*

bran ['bræn] *n* : son *m*

branch[1] ['bræntʃ] *vi* **1** : se ramifier (se dit d'une plante) **2** *or* **to branch off** DIVERGE : bifurquer

branch[2] *n* **1** : branche *f* (d'une plante) **2** : embranchement *m* (d'une route) **3** DIVISION : succursale *f*, agence *f*, section *f* <branch manager : directeur de succursale>

brand[1] ['brænd] *vt* **1** : marquer (au fer rouge) **2** LABEL, STIGMATIZE : flétrir, étiqueter, stigmatiser

brand[2] *n* **1** : marque *f* (sur des animaux) **2** STIGMA : marque *f*, stigmate *m* **3** MAKE : marque *f* (de fabrique)

brandish ['brændɪʃ] *vt* : brandir

brand–new ['brænd'nuː, -'njuː] *adj* : tout neuf

brandy ['brændi] *n, pl* **-dies** : cognac *m*, eau-de-vie *f*

brash ['bræʃ] *adj* **1** IMPULSIVE, RASH : impétueux, irréfléchi **2** IMPUDENT : impertinent, effronté

brass ['bræs] *n* **1** : cuivre *m* (jaune), laiton *m* **2** : cuivres *mpl* (d'un orchestre) **3** GALL, NERVE : impudence *f*, toupet *m fam* **4** OFFICERS : officiers *mpl* (militaires)

brassiere [brə'zɪr, brɑ-] *n* : soutien-gorge *m*, brassière *f Can*

brassy ['bræsi] *adj* **brassier; -est 1** : cuivré **2** IMPUDENT : effronté, impertinent

brat ['bræt] *n* : môme *mf France fam;* gosse *mf France fam;* polisson *m*, -sonne *f*

bravado [brə'vɑdo] *n, pl* **-does** *or* **-dos** : bravade *f*

brave[1] ['breɪv] *vt* **braved; braving** : braver, défier

brave[2] *adj* **braver; bravest** : courageux, brave — **bravely** *adv*

brave[3] *n* : guerrier *m* indien

bravery ['breɪvəri] *n, pl* **-eries** : courage *m*, bravoure *f*

bravo ['brɑ,voː] *n, pl* **-vos** : bravo *m*

brawl[1] ['brɔl] *vi* : se bagarrer

brawl[2] *n* : bagarre *f*, rixe *f*

brawn ['brɔn] *n* : muscles *mpl*

brawny ['brɔni] *adj* **brawnier; -est** : musclé

bray[1] ['breɪ] *vi* : braire

bray[2] *n* : braiment *m*

brazen ['breɪzən] *adj* **1** COPPER : de cuivre **2** IMPUDENT : effronté, impudent <a brazen lie : un mensonge effronté>

brazenly ['breɪzənli] *adv* : effrontément

brazier ['breɪʒər] *n* : brasero *m*

Brazilian[1] [brə'zɪljən] *adj* : brésilien

Brazilian[2] *n* : Brésilien *m*, -lienne *f*

breach[1] [briːtʃ] *vt* **1** BREAK, VIOLATE : enfreindre, transgresser **2** PENETRATE : ouvrir une brèche dans (un mur, etc.)

breach[2] *n* **1** VIOLATION : infraction *f*, violation *f* **2** : abus *m* <breach of faith : abus de confiance> **3** : rupture *f*, annulation *f* <breach of contract : rupture de contrat> **4** GAP : brèche *f*, ouverture *f*

bread[1] ['brɛd] *vt* : paner, couvrir de chapelure

bread[2] *n* : pain *m*

breadth ['brɛtθ] *n* : largeur *f*

breadwinner ['brɛd,wɪnər] *n* : soutien *m* de famille

break[1] ['breɪk] *v* **broke** ['broːk]; **broken** ['broːkən]; **breaking** *vt* **1** : casser, briser **2** VIOLATE : violer, transgresser **3** TELL : annoncer, faire part de <to break the news : annoncer la nouvelle> **4** SOFTEN : amortir, adoucir (une chute) **5** INTERRUPT : interrompre <to break the silence : percer le silence> **6** SURPASS : battre (un record, etc.) **7 to break down** : abattre, enfoncer <she broke down the door : elle a enfoncé la porte> — *vi* **1** : se casser, se briser **2** : se lever, se montrer <day is breaking : le jour se lève> **3** *or* **to break out** ESCAPE : s'évader, se libérer **4** HALT : prendre une pause, arrêter **5 to break down** FAIL : tomber en panne **6 to break down** COLLAPSE : s'effondrer, s'écrouler **7 to break in** : entrer par effraction (dans une maison) **8 to break up** SEPARATE : rompre, se quitter

break[2] *n* **1** : cassure *f,* rupture *f* **2** GAP : trouée *f,* brèche *f* **3** REST : pause *f,* récréation *f,* break *m Can* <to take a break : faire une pause> **4** CHANCE : chance *f,* veine *f fam* <I had a lucky break : j'ai eu de la chance> **5** : interruption *f* (d'une émission)

breakage ['breɪkɪdʒ] *n* : casse *f,* bris *m*

breakdown ['breɪk,daʊn] *n* **1** : rupture *f* <breakdown in negotiations : rupture des négociations> **2** FAILURE : panne *f* (d'une machine) **3** *or* **nervous breakdown** : dépression *f* nerveuse

breaker [breɪkər] *n* **1** WAVE : brisant *m* **2** → **circuit breaker**

breakfast ['brɛkfəst] *n* : petit déjeuner *m France*, déjeuner *m Can*

breakwater ['brek,wɔt̬ər, -,wɑ-] *n* : jetée *f,* brise-lames *m*

breast ['brɛst] *n* **1** : sein *m* (d'une femme) **2** CHEST : poitrine *f*

breastbone ['brɛst,bo:n] *n* : sternum *m*

breast–feed ['brɛst,fi:d] *vt* **-fed** [-,fɛd]; **-feeding** : allaiter

breath ['brɛθ] *n* **1** : souffle *m,* haleine *f* <out of breath : à bout de souffle> <bad breath : mauvaise haleine> **2** GUST : souffle *m* <a breath of air : un souffle d'air>

breathe ['bri:ð] *v* **breathed; breathing** *vt* **1** : respirer **2** : pousser, laisser échapper <I breathed a sigh of relief : j'ai poussé un soupir de soulagement> **3** UTTER : souffler <don't breathe a word about it : n'en souffle pas mot> — *vi* **1** : respirer **2** LIVE : vivre, être en vie

breathless ['brɛθləs] *adj* : à bout de souffle, haletant

breathlessly ['brɛθləsli] *adv* : en haletant

breathtaking ['brɛθ,teɪkɪŋ] *adj* : à vous couper le souffle, stupéfiant

breeches ['brɪtʃəz, bri:-] *npl* PANTS : culotte *f,* pantalon *m*

breed[1] ['bri:d] *v* **bred** ['brɛd]; **breeding** *vt* **1** RAISE : élever, faire l'élevage de **2** CAUSE, PRODUCE : faire naître, engendrer — *vi* : se reproduire, se multiplier

breed[2] *n* **1** : race *f,* espèce *f* **2** KIND : espèce *f,* sorte *f*

breeze[1] ['bri:z] *vi* **breezed; breezing 1** : aller vite <to breeze in : entrer en coup de vent> **2 to breeze through** : réussir facilement (un examen, etc.)

breeze[2] *n* **1** : brise *f* **2 it's a breeze!** : c'est du gâteau!, c'est facile comme tout!

breezy ['bri:zi] *adj* **breezier; -est 1** AIRY, WINDY : venteux, éventé **2** NONCHALANT : désinvolte, léger

brevity ['brɛvət̬i] *n, pl* **-ties** : brièveté *f*

brew[1] ['bru:] *vt* **1** : brasser (de la bière) **2** : préparer, faire infuser (du thé) — *vi* **1** : fermenter (se dit de la bière), infuser (se dit du thé, etc.) **2** : se préparer <there's a storm brewing : un orage se prépare, il y a de l'orage dans l'air>

brew[2] *n* **1** BEER : bière *f* **2** INFUSION : infusion *f* (de thé, etc.)

brewery ['bru:əri, 'brʊri] *n, pl* **-ries** : brasserie *f*

briar → **brier**

bribe[1] ['braɪb] *vt* **bribed; bribing** : soudoyer, acheter, suborner (un témoin)

bribe[2] *n* : pot-de-vin *m*

bribery ['braɪbəri] *n, pl* **-eries** : corruption *f*

bric–a–brac ['brɪkə,bræk] *ns & pl* : bric-à-brac *m*

brick[1] ['brɪk] *vt* **to brick up** : murer

brick[2] *n* : brique *f*

bricklayer ['brɪk,leɪər] *n* : maçon *m*

bricklaying ['brɪk,leɪɪŋ] *n* : maçonnerie *f*

bridal ['braɪdəl] *adj* : nuptial, de mariée, de noce

bride ['braɪd] *n* : mariée *f*

bridegroom ['braɪd,gru:m] *n* : marié *m*

bridesmaid ['braɪdz,meɪd] *n* : demoiselle *f* d'honneur

bridge[1] ['brɪdʒ] *vt* **1** : construire un pont sur **2 to bridge a gap** : combler une lacune, établir un rapprochement

bridge[2] *n* **1** : pont *m* **2** : arête *f* (du nez) **3** : passerelle *f* (d'un navire) **4** DENTURE : bridge *m* (dentaire) **5** : bridge *m* (jeu de cartes)

bridle[1] ['braɪdəl] *v* **-dled; -dling** *vt* **1** : brider (un cheval) **2** RESTRAIN : refréner, brider <to bridle one's tongue : tenir sa langue> — *vi* **to bridle at** : se cabrer contre

bridle[2] *n* : bride *f* (d'un cheval)

brief[1] ['bri:f] *vt* : donner des instructions à, mettre au courant

brief[2] *adj* : bref, court, concis

brief[3] *n* **1** SYNOPSIS : résumé *m* **2** : cause *f* à plaider, dossier *m* (en droit) **3 briefs** *npl* UNDERPANTS : slip *m*

briefcase ['bri:f,keɪs] *n* : serviette *f,* porte-documents *m*

briefly ['bri:fli] *adv* **1** CONCISELY : brièvement, de façon concise **2** IN SHORT : en bref

brier ['braɪər] *n* **1** BRAMBLE : ronce *f* **2** HEATH : bruyère *f*

brig ['brɪg] *n* **1** : brick *m* (navire) **2** : cellule *f* à bord d'un navire
brigade [brɪ'geɪd] *n* : brigade *f*
brigadier general [ˌbrɪgə'dɪr] *n* : général *m* de brigade
brigand ['brɪgənd] *n* : brigand *m*, bandit *m*
bright ['braɪt] *adj* **1** BRILLIANT, SHINING : brillant, éclatant **2** CLEVER : intelligent **3** VIVID : vif <bright colors : couleurs vives> **4** CHEERFUL : joyeux, animé, gai
brighten ['braɪtən] *vt* **1** : faire briller **2** ENLIVEN : égayer, animer — *vi* : s'éclaircir (se dit du temps)
brightly ['braɪtli] *adv* **1** INTENSELY : brillamment, intensément **2** CHEERFULLY : joyeusement, gaiement
brilliance ['brɪljən*t*s] *n* **1** RADIANCE : éclat *m* (d'une lumière) **2** SPLENDOR : splendeur *f*, éclat *m* **3** : grande intelligence *f*
brilliant ['brɪljənt] *adj* **1** BRIGHT : éclatant **2** SPLENDID : brillant, génial <a brilliant idea : une idée géniale> **3** GIFTED : très intelligent, doué
brilliantly ['brɪljəntli] *adv* **1** RADIANTLY : avec éclat **2** EXCELLENTLY : brillamment **3** PARTICULARLY : extrêmement
brim[1] ['brɪm] *vi* **brimmed; brimming 1** *or* **to brim over** : être plein jusqu'à déborder **2 to brim with tears** : se remplir de larmes
brim[2] *n* : bord *m* <full to the brim : plein à ras bord>
brimful ['brɪm'fʊl] *adj* : plein à déborder
brimstone ['brɪm,sto:n] *n* : soufre *m*
brindled ['brɪndəld] *adj* : moucheté, tacheté
brine ['braɪn] *n* **1** : eau *f* salée, saumure *f* **2** OCEAN : mer *f*, océan *m*
bring ['brɪŋ] *vt* **brought** ['brɔt]; **bringing 1** CARRY, CONVEY : amener (une personne ou un animal), apporter (une chose) **2** *or* **to bring about** PRODUCE : provoquer, causer, entraîner **3** INDUCE, PERSUADE : amener, pousser, persuader **4** LEAD : amener, mener, conduire **5** YIELD : rapporter (en finance) **6 to bring to light** : mettre en lumière **7 to bring sth to an end** : mettre fin à qqch
bring around *vt* **1** PERSUADE : convaincre, convertir **2** → **bring to**
bring out *vt* : sortir (un produit, un livre, etc.)
bring to *vt* REVIVE : ranimer
bring up *vt* **1** REAR : élever **2** MENTION : mentionner, signaler, aborder
brink ['brɪŋk] *n* : bord *m* <on the brink of war : au bord de la guerre> <on the brink of doing : sur le point de faire>
briny ['braɪni] *adj* **brinier; -est** : saumâtre, salé
brisk ['brɪsk] *adj* **1** LIVELY : vif, animé **2** INVIGORATING : vivifiant, frais **3** QUICK : vif, rapide
bristle[1] ['brɪsəl] *vi* **-tled; -tling 1** : se hérisser (se dit des cheveux, etc.) **2** : s'irriter, se hérisser <she's bristling with anger : elle se hérisse de colère>
bristle[2] *n* **1** : soie *f* (d'un animal) **2** : poil *m* (d'une brosse)
bristly ['brɪsəli] *adj* **bristlier; -est 1** PRICKLY : qui pique **2** : hérissé (se dit des cheveux, etc.)
British[1] ['brɪtɪʃ] *adj* : britannique
British[2] *npl* **the British** : les Britanniques
brittle ['brɪtəl] *adj* **-tler; -tlest** : fragile, cassant
broach ['bro:tʃ] *vt* BRING UP : aborder, entamer <to broach a subject : aborder un sujet>
broad ['brɔd] *adj* **1** WIDE : large **2** SPACIOUS : vaste, immense **3** GENERAL : grand, général <broad outlines : grandes lignes> **4** OBVIOUS : transparent <a broad hint : une allusion transparente> **5** LIBERAL : large, libéral <broad ideas : idées larges> **6** CRUDE : gros, vulgaire **7 in broad daylight** : en plein jour
broad bean *n* : fève *f*
broadcast[1] ['brɔd,kæst] *v* **-cast; -casting** *vt* **1** SCATTER : semer (des graines, etc.) **2** TRANSMIT : diffuser, téléviser **3** SPREAD : répandre — *vi* : émettre, faire des émissions
broadcast[2] *n* **1** BROADCASTING : transmission *f*, diffusion *f* **2** PROGRAM : émission *f* <news broadcast : bulletin d'informations>
broadcaster ['brɔd,kæstər] *n* : personnalité *f*, journaliste *mf* (de la radio, de la télévision)
broadcloth ['brɔdklɔθ] *n* : drap *m* fin
broaden ['brɔdən] *vt* : élargir <to broaden one's outlook : élargir ses horizons> — *vi* EXPAND, WIDEN : s'élargir
broadloom ['brɔd,lu:m] *adj* : en grande largeur
broadly ['brɔdli] *adv* **1** WIDELY : largement **2** GENERALLY : en gros, en général
broad–minded ['brɔd'maɪndəd] *adj* : tolérant, large d'esprit
broad–mindedness [brɔd'maɪndədnəs] *n* : largeur *f* d'esprit
broadside[1] ['brɔd,saɪd] *adv* : par le travers
broadside[2] *n* **1** VOLLEY : bordée *f* **2** TIRADE : invective *f*, attaque *f* cinglante
brocade [bro'keɪd] *n* : brocart *m*
broccoli ['brɑkəli] *n* : brocoli *m*
brochure [bro'ʃʊr] *n* : brochure *f*, dépliant *m*
brogue ['bro:g] *n* : accent *m* irlandais
broil ['brɔɪl] *v* : griller
broiler ['brɔɪlər] *n* **1** GRILL : gril *m* **2** : poulet *m* à rôtir

broke[1] ['bro:k] → **break**[1]
broke[2] *adj* : fauché *fam,* à sec *fam,* cassé *Can fam* <to go broke : faire faillite>
broken ['bro:kən] *adj* **1** DAMAGED, SHATTERED : cassé, brisé **2** IRREGULAR, UNEVEN : brisé, découpé, accidenté <a broken line : une ligne brisée> <broken coastlines : littoraux découpés> **3** VIOLATED : rompu, manqué <a broken promise : une promesse manquée> **4** IMPERFECT : mauvais, imparfait <in broken French : en mauvais français> **5** CRUSHED : brisé, abattu <he's a broken man : il a le cœur brisé>
brokenhearted [ˌbro:kən'hɑrṭəd] *adj* : au cœur brisé
broker ['bro:kər] *n* **1** : courtier *m,* -tière *f;* agent *m* **2** → **stockbroker**
brokerage ['bro:kərɪdʒ] *n* : courtage *m*
bromine ['bro:ˌmi:n] *n* : brome *m*
bronchial tubes ['brɑnkiəl] *npl* : bronches *fpl*
bronchitis [brɑŋ'kaɪṭəs, brɑn-] *n* : bronchite *f*
bronze[1] ['brɑnz] *vt* **bronzed; bronzing** : bronzer
bronze[2] *n* : bronze *m*
brooch ['bro:tʃ, 'bru:tʃ] *n* : broche *f,* épinglette *f Can*
brood[1] ['bru:d] *vi* **1** : couver (se dit d'un oiseau) **2** PONDER : broyer du noir, ruminer
brood[2] *n* : couvée *f,* nichée *f*
brook[1] ['brʊk] *vt* TOLERATE : accepter, tolérer
brook[2] *n* : ruisseau *m*
broom ['bru:m, 'brʊm] *n* **1** : genêt *m* (plante) **2** : balai *m* (pour balayer)
broomstick ['bru:mˌstɪk, 'brʊm-] *n* : manche *m* à balai
broth ['brɔθ] *n, pl* **broths** ['brɔθs, 'brɔðz] : bouillon *m*
brothel ['brɑθəl, 'brɔ-] *n* : maison *f* close, bordel *m fam*
brother ['brʌðər] *n* : frère *m*
brotherhood ['brʌðərˌhʊd] *n* **1** : fraternité *f* **2** ASSOCIATION : confrérie *f*
brother–in–law ['brʌðərɪnˌlɔ] *n, pl* **brothers–in–law** : beau-frère *m*
brotherly ['brʌðərli] *adj* : fraternel <brotherly love : amour fraternel>
brought → **bring**
brow ['braʊ] *n* **1** EYEBROW : sourcil *m* **2** FOREHEAD : front *m* **3** : sommet *m* <the brow of a hill : le sommet d'une colline>
browbeat ['braʊˌbi:t] *vt* **-beat; -beaten** [-ˌbi:ṭən] *or* **-beat; -beating** : intimider
brown[1] [ˌbraʊn] *vt* **1** : faire dorer (en cuisine) **2** TAN : bronzer, brunir — *vi* : dorer (en cuisine)
brown[2] *adj* **1** : brun, marron **2** TANNED : bronzé, bruni
brown[3] *n* : brun *m,* marron *m*
brownish [ˌbraʊnɪʃ] *adj* : brunâtre
browse ['braʊz] *vi* **browsed; browsing** **1** GRAZE : brouter, paître **2** LOOK : regarder
bruin ['bru:ɪn] *n* BEAR : ours *m*
bruise[1] ['bru:z] *v* **bruised; bruising** *vt* **1** : faire un bleu à, contusionner **2** : taler (un fruit) — *vi* : se faire des bleus (se dit d'une personne), se taler (se dit d'un fruit)
bruise[2] *n* : bleu *m,* contusion *f,* meurtrissure *f,* prune *f Can*
brunch ['brʌntʃ] *n* : brunch *m*
brunet[1] [bru:'nɛt] *or* **brunette** *adj* : châtain, brun (se dit des cheveux)
brunet[2] *or* **brunette** *n* : brun *m,* brune *f*
brunt ['brʌnt] *n* BURDEN : poids *m* <to bear the brunt of : subir tout le poids de, porter le plus gros de>
brush[1] ['brʌʃ] *vt* **1** : brosser, se brosser <I brushed my hair : je me suis brossé les cheveux> **2** GRAZE : frôler, effleurer **3** *or* **to brush up** SWEEP : balayer, ramasser **4 to brush off** DISMISS : écarter, repousser — *vi* **to brush up on** : se remettre à, réviser
brush[2] *n* **1** : brosse *f* (à cheveux), pinceau *m* (de peintre) **2** SCRUB, UNDERBRUSH : brousse *f,* broussailles *fpl,* fardoches *fpl Can* **3** TOUCH : effleurement *m* **4** SKIRMISH : accrochage *m,* escarmouche *f* <to have a brush with the law : avoir des démêlés avec la justice>
brush–off ['brʌʃˌɔf] *n* **to give s.o. the brush–off** : envoyer promener qqn
brusque ['brʌsk] *adj* : brusque
brusquely ['brʌskli] *adv* : brusquement, avec brusquerie
brutal ['bru:ṭəl] *adj* : brutal, cruel — **brutally** *adv*
brutality [bru:'tæləṭi] *n, pl* **-ties** : brutalité *f*
brutalize ['bru:ṭəlˌaɪz] *vt* **-ized; -izing** : brutaliser
brute[1] ['bru:t] *adj* **1** : bestial, animal **2** SHEER : brutal, vif, simple <brute force : force brutale>
brute[2] *n* **1** BEAST : brute *f,* bête *f* **2** : brute *f* (personne)
brutish ['bru:ṭɪʃ] *adj* **1** : de brute, bestial **2** CRUEL : brutal, cruel **3** STUPID : bête, stupide
bubble[1] ['bʌbəl] *vi* **-bled; -bling** **1** : bouillonner (se dit de l'eau), pétiller (se dit du champagne) **2 to bubble over** : déborder
bubble[2] *n* : bulle *f*
bubbly ['bʌbəli] *adj* **bubblier; -est** **1** BUBBLING : plein de bulles, pétillant **2** LIVELY : plein d'entrain
bubonic plague [bu:'bɑnɪk, 'bju:-] *n* : peste *f* bubonique
buccaneer [ˌbʌkə'nɪr] *n* : boucanier *m*
buck[1] ['bʌk] *vi* **1** : lancer une ruade (se dit d'un cheval) **2 to buck up** : se secouer — *vt* OPPOSE : résister, s'op-

poser à <to buck the system : lutter contre le système>

buck[2] *n, pl* **bucks 1** *or pl* **buck** : mâle *m* (d'un animal) **2** DOLLAR : dollar *m,* piastre *f Can fam* **3** MONEY : fric *m fam* <to make a buck : se faire du fric> **4 to pass the buck** : refiler la responsabilité aux autres

bucket ['bʌkət] *n* : seau *m*

buckle[1] ['bʌkəl] *v* **-led; -ling** *vt* **1** FASTEN : boucler **2** DISTORT, WARP : gauchir, déformer — *vi* **1** BEND, WARP : se courber, se voiler **2 to buckle down** : s'atteler, s'appliquer

buckle[2] *n* **1** CLASP : boucle *f* **2** WARPING : gauchissement *m*

buckshot ['bʌk,ʃɑt] *n* : chevrotine *f*

buckskin ['bʌk,skɪn] *n* : peau *f* de daim

bucktooth ['bʌk,tu:θ] *n, pl* **-teeth** : dent *f* saillante <to have buckteeth : avoir des dents de lapin>

buckwheat ['bʌk,*h*wi:t] *n* : sarrasin *m,* blé *m* noir

bucolic [bju:'kɑlɪk] *adj* : bucolique

bud[1] ['bʌd] *vi* **budded; budding** : bourgeonner, former des boutons

bud[2] *n* : bourgeon *m* (d'une feuille), bouton *m* (d'une fleur)

Buddhism ['bu:,dɪzəm, 'bʊ-] *n* : bouddhisme *m*

Buddhist[1] ['bu:,dɪst, 'bʊ-] *adj* : bouddhiste

Buddhist[2] *n* : bouddhiste *mf*

buddy ['bʌdi] *n, pl* **-dies** : copain *m,* -pine *f*

budge ['bʌdʒ] *vi* **budged; budging 1** MOVE : bouger, se déplacer **2** YIELD : changer d'avis, céder

budget[1] ['bʌdʒət] *vt* : budgétiser — *vi* : dresser un budget

budget[2] *n* : budget *m*

budgetary ['bʌdʒə,tɛri] *adj* : budgétaire

buff[1] ['bʌf] *vt* POLISH : polir, lustrer

buff[2] *adj* : chamois, beige

buff[3] *n* **1** : chamois *m* (couleur) **2** ENTHUSIAST : mordu *m,* -due *f fam;* fanatique *mf*

buffalo ['bʌfə,lo:] *n, pl* **-lo** *or* **-loes** : buffle *m,* bison *m* (d'Amérique)

buffer ['bʌfər] *n* **1** : tampon *m* <buffer zone : région tampon> **2 nail buffer** : polissoir à ongles

buffet[1] ['bʌfət] *vt* BATTER : frapper, battre

buffet[2] *n* BLOW : coup *m*

buffet[3] [,bʌ'feɪ, ,bu:-] *n* **1** : buffet *m* (repas) **2** SIDEBOARD : buffet *m*

buffoon [,bʌ'fu:n] *n* : bouffon *m,* clown *m*

buffoonery [,bʌ'fu:nəri] *n, pl* **-eries** : bouffonnerie *f*

bug[1] ['bʌg] *vt* **bugged; bugging 1** : installer un microphone dans **2** BOTHER : embêter

bug[2] *n* **1** INSECT : insecte *m,* bestiole *f,* bébite *f Can fam* **2** FLAW : défaut *m,* erreur *f* (en informatique, etc.) **3** GERM : microbe *m,* virus *m* **4** MICROPHONE : microphone *m*

bugaboo ['bʌgə,bu:] *n, pl* **-boos** → **bugbear**

bugbear ['bʌg,bær] *n* BOGEY : épouvantail *m,* croque-mitaine *m*

buggy ['bʌgi] *n, pl* **-gies 1** CARRIAGE : buggy *m,* boghei *m,* calèche *f* **2** BABY CARRIAGE : voiture *f* d'enfant, landau *m France*

bugle ['bju:gəl] *n* : clairon *m*

bugler ['bju:gələr] *n* : clairon *m*

build[1] ['bɪld] *v* **built** ['bɪlt]; **building** *vt* **1** CONSTRUCT : construire, bâtir **2** DEVELOP, ESTABLISH : bâtir, établir, fonder **3** INCREASE : augmenter — *vi* INTENSIFY : augmenter

build[2] *n* PHYSIQUE : carrure *f,* charpente *f*

building ['bɪldɪŋ] *n* **1** EDIFICE : bâtiment *m,* immeuble *m* **2** CONSTRUCTION : construction *f*

built–in ['bɪlt'ɪn] *adj* : encastré

bulb ['bʌlb] *n* **1** : bulbe *m* (d'une plante), réservoir *m* (d'un thermomètre) **2** LIGHTBULB : ampoule *f*

bulbous ['bʌlbəs] *adj* : bulbeux

Bulgarian[1] [bʌl'gæriən, bʊl-] *adj* : bulgare

Bulgarian[2] *n* **1** : Bulgare *mf* **2** : bulgare *m* (langue)

bulge[1] ['bʌldʒ] *vi* **bulged; bulging 1** SWELL : bomber, être gonflé **2** : sortir de la tête (se dit des yeux)

bulge[2] *n* : renflement *m*

bulk ['bʌlk] *n* **1** MAGNITUDE : masse *f,* volume *m* **2** FIBER : fibre *m* (alimentaire) **3 in ~** : en gros **4 the bulk of** : la majeure partie de, le plus gros de

bulkhead ['bʌlk,hɛd] *n* : cloison *f*

bulky ['bʌlki] *adj* **bulkier; -est** : volumineux, encombrant

bull ['bʊl] *n* **1** : taureau *m* **2** MALE : mâle *m* (de l'orignal, de la baleine, etc.) **3** *or* **papal bull** : bulle *f* (papale) **4** DECREE : décret *m,* règlement *m*

bulldog ['bʊl,dɔg] *n* : bouledogue *m*

bulldoze ['bʊl,do:z] *vt* **-dozed; -dozing 1** : démolir au bulldozer, raser au bulldozer **2** FORCE : forcer <to bulldoze one's way : se frayer un chemin>

bulldozer ['bʊl,do:zər] *n* : bulldozer *m*

bullet ['bʊlət] *n* : balle *f* (d'un fusil)

bulletin ['bʊlətən, -lət̬ən] *n* **1** NOTICE : bulletin *m,* communiqué *m* <news bulletin : bulletin d'informations> **2** NEWSLETTER : bulletin *m*

bulletin board *n* : tableau *m* d'affichage, babillard *m Can*

bulletproof ['bʊlət,pru:f] *adj* : pareballes (se dit des vêtements), blindé (se dit d'une voiture)

bullfight ['bʊl,faɪt] *n* : corrida *f*

bullfighter ['bʊl,faɪt̬ər] *n* : matador *m,* torero *m*

bullfrog ['bʊl,frɔg] *n* : grenouille *f* taureau

bullheaded [ˈbʊlˌhɛdəd] *adj* : entêté, têtu
bullion [ˈbʊljən] *n* : or *m* en lingots, argent *m* en lingots
bullock [ˈbʊlək] *n* **1** : bouvillon *m* **2** STEER : bœuf *m*
bull's–eye [ˈbʊlzˌaɪ] *n, pl* **bull's–eyes** : centre *m* (de la cible), mille *m*
bully[1] [ˈbʊli] *vt* **-lied; -lying** : intimider, malmener, tyranniser
bully[2] *n, pl* **-lies** : tyran *m*, petite brute *f*
bulrush [ˈbʊlˌrʌʃ] *n* : jonc *m*
bulwark [ˈbʊlˌwərk, -ˌwɔrk; ˈbʌlˌwərk] *n* : rempart *m*, fortification *f*
bum[1] [ˈbʌm] *v* **bummed; bumming** *vt* : taper qqn de *fam*, quémander <to bum money : quémander de l'argent> — *vi* **to bum around** LOAF : fainéanter, paresser
bum[2] *adj* BAD : minable, faux, mauvais <a bum rap : une accusation mensongère>
bum[3] *n* **1** HOBO, TRAMP : clochard *m*, -charde *f* **2** LOAFER : fainéant *m*, fainéante *f*
bumblebee [ˈbʌmbəlˌbiː] *n* : bourdon *m*
bump[1] [ˈbʌmp] *vt* HIT : heurter, cogner <to bump one's head : se cogner la tête> — *vi* **to bump into** MEET : tomber sur, rencontrer par hasard
bump[2] *n* **1** JOLT : secousse *f* **2** COLLISION, IMPACT : choc *m*, heurt *m* **3** LUMP : bosse *f*, poque *f Can fam*
bumper[1] [ˈbʌmpər] *adj* : exceptionnel, record
bumper[2] *n* : pare-chocs *m*
bumpkin [ˈbʌmpkən] *n* : péquenaud *m*, -naude *f France fam;* rustre *mf*
bumpy [ˈbʌmpi] *adj* **bumpier; -est 1** ROUGH, UNEVEN : cahoteux, bosselé **2** : agité <a bumpy crossing : une traversée agitée>
bun [ˈbʌn] *n* : petit pain *m* (au lait)
bunch[1] [ˈbʌntʃ] *vt* : mettre ensemble, mettre en bottes — *vi* **to bunch up** : se serrer (se dit des personnes), être retroussé (se dit des vêtements)
bunch[2] *n* **1** : bouquet *m* (de fleurs), grappe *f* (de raisins), botte *f* (de légumes, etc.) **2** GROUP : groupe *m*
bundle[1] [ˈbʌndəl] *v* **-dled; -dling** *vt* **1** PACKAGE : mettre en paquet, empaqueter **2 to bundle up** : emmitoufler (un enfant, etc.) — *vi* **to bundle up** : s'emmitoufler
bundle[2] *n* **1** PACKAGE : paquet *m*, ballot *m* **2** : liasse *f* (de papiers, etc.), botte *f* (de foin, de légumes) **3** LOT : grande quantité *f*, tas *m* (d'argent, etc.)
bungalow [ˈbʌŋgəˌloː] *n* : maison *f* sans étage
bungle [ˈbʌŋgəl] *vt* **-gled; -gling** BOTCH : gâcher, bousiller *fam*
bungler [ˈbʌŋgələr] *n* : bousilleur *m*, -leuse *f*
bunion [ˈbʌnjən] *n* : oignon *m*
bunk[1] [ˈbʌŋk] *vi* : coucher
bunk[2] *n* **1** BERTH : couchette *f* **2** NONSENSE : balivernes *fpl*, sottises *fpl* **3** *or* **bunk bed** : lits *mpl* superposés
bunker [ˈbʌŋkər] *n* **1** : coffre *m*, soute *f* (d'un navire) <coal bunker : soute à charbon> **2** : blockhaus *m* (militaire)
bunny [ˈbʌni] *n, pl* **-nies** → **rabbit**
bunt [ˈbʌnt] *n* : amorti *m Can* (au baseball)
bunting [ˈbʌntɪŋ] *n* **1** : bruant *m* (oiseau) **2** : étamine *f*, étoffe *f* (pour les drapeaux)
buoy[1] [ˈbuːi, ˈbɔɪ] *vt* **1** : faire flotter **2** *or* **to buoy up** CHEER, HEARTEN : revigorer, soutenir
buoy[2] *n* : bouée *f*, balise *f* (flottante)
buoyancy [ˈbɔɪəntsi, ˈbuːjən-] *n* : flottabilité *f*
buoyant [ˈbɔɪənt, ˈbuːjənt] *adj* **1** : flottable **2** LIGHTHEARTED : gai, enjoué
bur *or* **burr** [ˈbər] *n* : bardane *f*
burden[1] [ˈbərdən] *vt* : charger, accabler
burden[2] *n* : charge *f*, fardeau *m*
burdensome [ˈbərdənsəm] *adj* : lourd, pesant
burdock [ˈbərˌdɑk] *n* : bardane *f*
bureau [ˈbjʊro] *n* **1** CHEST OF DRAWERS : commode *f* **2** DEPARTMENT : service *m* (gouvernemental) **3** AGENCY : agence *f*, bureau *m* <credit bureau : agence de recouvrement>
bureaucracy [bjʊˈrɑkrəsi] *n, pl* **-cies** : bureaucratie *f*
bureaucrat [ˈbjʊrəˌkræt] *n* : bureaucrate *mf* — **bureaucratic** [ˌbjʊrəˈkræṭɪk] *adj*
burgeon [ˈbərdʒən] *vi* **1** BLOOM : éclore, bourgeonner **2** FLOURISH : fleurir, croître
burglar [ˈbərglər] *n* : cambrioleur *m*, -leuse *f*
burglarize [ˈbərgləˌraɪz] *vt* **-ized; -izing** : cambrioler, dévaliser
burglary [ˈbərgləri] *n, pl* **-glaries** : cambriolage *m*
burgundy [ˈbərgəndi] *n, pl* **-dies** : bourgogne *m* (vin)
burial [ˈbɛriəl] *n* : enterrement *m*, inhumation *f*
burlap [ˈbərˌlæp] *n* : toile *f* à sac
burlesque[1] [bərˈlɛsk] *vt* **-lesqued; -lesquing** : tourner en ridicule, parodier
burlesque[2] *n* **1** PARODY : burlesque *m*, parodie *f* **2** *or* **burlesqe show** : revue *f* déshabillée
burly [ˈbərli] *adj* **burlier; -est** : de forte carrure, costaud *fam*
burn[1] [ˈbərn] *v* **burned** [ˈbərnd, ˈbərnt] *or* **burnt** [ˈbərnt]; **burning** *vi* **1** : brûler <to burn down : brûler complètement> <burning with desire : brûlant de désir> <she burns easily : elle brûle facilement> **2** : être allumé (se dit d'une lumière) — *vt* **1** : brûler, incendier **2** CONSUME : consommer, brûler (de l'essence, des calories, etc.)

burn[2] *n* : brûlure *f*

burner ['bərnər] *n* : brûleur *m* (d'une cuisinière), rond *m Can*

burnish ['bərnɪʃ] *vt* : brunir, polir

burp[1] ['bərp] *vi* : avoir des renvois, roter *fam*

burp[2] *n* : renvoi *m,* rot *m fam*

burro ['bəro, 'bʊr-] *n, pl* **burros** : (petit) âne *m*

burrow[1] ['bəro] *vt* : creuser — *vi* **1** : creuser un terrier **2 to burrow into** SEARCH : fouiller dans

burrow[2] *n* : terrier *m*

bursar ['bərsər] *n* : économe *mf*

burst[1] ['bərst] *v* **burst** *or* **bursted; bursting** *vt* : crever, faire éclater — *vi* **1** : crever, éclater (se dit d'un obus, d'une bombe, etc.) **2** OVERFLOW : déborder, être rempli <bursting with energy : débordant d'énergie> **3 to burst in** : entrer en coup de vent **4 to burst into tears** : fondre en larmes **5 to burst out laughing** : éclater de rire

burst[2] *n* **1** EXPLOSION : éclatement *m,* explosion *f* **2** OUTBURST : élan *m* (d'enthousiasme), éclat *m* (de rire)

Burundian[1] [bʊ'ru:ndiən, -'rʊn-] *adj* : burundais

Burundian[2] *n* : Burundais *m,* -daise *f*

bury ['bɛri] *vt* **buried; burying 1** INTER : enterrer, ensevelir **2** CONCEAL : enfouir, cacher **3** IMMERSE : plonger, immerger

bus[1] ['bʌs] *v* **bused** *or* **bussed** ['bʌst]; **busing** *or* **bussing** ['bʌsɪŋ] *vt* : transporter en autobus — *vi* : voyager en autobus

bus[2] *n, pl* **buses** *or* **busses** : bus *m,* autobus *m*

bush ['bʊʃ] *n* **1** SHRUB : buisson *m,* arbuste *m* **2** THICKET : fourré *m* **3 the bush** WILDERNESS : la brousse

bushel ['bʊʃəl] *n* : boisseau *m*

bushy ['bʊʃi] *adj* **bushier; -est** : touffu, broussailleux

busily ['bɪzəli] *adv* : activement

business ['bɪznəs, -nəz] *n* **1** OCCUPATION : occupation *f,* profession *f* <he's in the restaurant business : il est restaurateur de profession> **2** COMMERCE, TRADE : affaires *fpl,* commerce *m* **3** FIRM : entreprise *f,* firme *f,* affaire *f* **4** AFFAIR, CONCERN : affaire *f,* question *f* <that's none of your business : ce n'est pas de vos affaires>

businessman ['bɪznəs,mæn, -nəz-] *n, pl* **-men** : homme *m* d'affaires

businesswoman ['bɪznəs,wʊmən, -nəz-] *n, pl* **-women** : femme *f* d'affaires

bust[1] ['bʌst] *vt* **1** BREAK, SMASH : casser, briser **2** TAME : dresser (un cheval sauvage, etc.)

bust[2] *n* **1** : buste *m* (en sculpture) **2** BREASTS : seins *mpl,* poitrine *f*

bustle[1] ['bʌsəl] *vi* **-tled; -tling** : s'affairer, s'agiter

bustle[2] *n or* **hustle and bustle** : agitation *f,* activité *f*

busy[1] ['bɪzi] *vt* **busied; busying 1** : occuper **2 to busy oneself** : s'occuper

busy[2] *adj* **busier; -est 1** : occupé, affairé <to look busy : avoir l'air occupé> **2** : occupé, engagé *Can fam* (se dit d'une ligne téléphonique) **3** BUSTLING : animé, actif (se dit d'une rue, d'une ville, etc.)

busybody ['bɪzi,bɑdi] *n* **to be a busybody** : faire la mouche du coche

but[1] ['bʌt] *conj* **1** EXCEPT : mais <I would like to stay but I can't : j'aimerais rester mais je ne peux pas> **2** THAT : que <there is no doubt but he will win : il n'y a pas de doute qu'il gagnera> **3** YET : mais <poor but proud : pauvre mais fière>

but[2] *prep* EXCEPT : sauf, excepté <everyone but Anne : tout le monde sauf Anne> <it's nothing but an insult : ça n'est qu'une insulte>

butcher[1] ['bʊtʃər] *vt* **1** SLAUGHTER : abattre, tuer (un animal) **2** KILL : massacrer (une personne) **3** BOTCH : bousiller *fam*

butcher[2] *n* : boucher *m,* -chère *f*

butler ['bʌtlər] *n* : maître *m* d'hôtel

butt[1] ['bʌt] *vt* **1** : donner un coup de tête à, donner un coup de corne à **2** ABUT : être contigu à — *vi* **to butt in** : interrompre, se mêler

butt[2] *n* **1** BUTTING : coup *m* de tête, coup *m* de corne **2** TARGET : cible *f,* victime *f* <the butt of a practical joke : la victime d'une farce> **3** END : crosse *f* (d'un rifle), mégot *m fam* (de cigarette)

butte ['bju:t] *n* : butte *f,* tertre *m*

butter[1] ['bʌt̬ər] *vt* : beurrer

butter[2] *n* : beurre *m*

buttercup ['bʌt̬ər,kʌp] *n* : bouton-d'or *m*

butterfat ['bʌt̬ər,fæt] *n* : matière *f* grasse

butterfly ['bʌt̬ər,flaɪ] *n, pl* **-flies** : papillon *m*

buttermilk ['bʌt̬ər,mɪlk] *n* : babeurre *m*

butterscotch ['bʌt̬ər,skɑtʃ] *n* : caramel *m* dur au beurre

buttocks ['bʌt̬əks, -,tɑks] *npl* : fesses *fpl*

button[1] ['bʌt̬ən] *vt* : boutonner (une blouse, etc.) — *vi* : se boutonner

button[2] *n* **1** : bouton *m* (de vêtements) **2** SWITCH : bouton *m,* piton *m Can fam*

buttonhole[1] ['bʌtən,ho:l] *vt* **-holed; -holing** : accrocher, retenir (une personne)

buttonhole[2] *n* : boutonnière *f*

buttress[1] ['bʌtrəs] *vt* : étayer

buttress[2] *n* **1** : contrefort *m* (en architecture) **2** SUPPORT : pilier *m,* soutien *m*

buxom ['bʌksəm] *adj* : plantureux, bien en chair

buy[1] ['baɪ] *vt* **bought** ['bɔt]; **buying** : acheter

buy[2] *n* **1** BARGAIN : affaire *f* <a good buy : une bonne affaire> **2** PURCHASE : acquisition *f*
buyer ['baɪər] *n* : acheteur *m,* -teuse *f*
buzz[1] ['bʌz] *vi* : bourdonner, vrombrir
buzz[2] *n* **1** : bourdonnement *m* (des insectes) **2** MURMUR : brouhaha *m* (de voix), murmure *m* **3** : coup *m* de fil *fam* <I gave him a buzz : je lui ai passé un coup de fil>
buzzard ['bʌzərd] *n* : buse *f*
buzzer ['bʌzər] *n* : sonnette *f*
buzzword ['bʌzˌwərd] *n* : mot *m* à la mode
by[1] ['baɪ] *adv* **1** NEAR : près <close by : tout près> **2 to go by** : passer <he walked straight by : il est passé tout droit> <in times gone by : il y a bien longtemps> **3 to stop by** : s'arrêter en passant
by[2] *prep* **1** NEAR : près de, à côté de <he's sitting by the window : il est assis près de la fenêtre> **2** VIA : par, en <by car : en voiture> <by airmail : par avion> **3** PAST : devant, à côté de <she went by the house : elle est passée devant la maison> **4** DURING : pendant <he studied by night : il étudiait pendant la nuit> **5** BEFORE : avant, pas plus tard que <he'll be home by ten : il sera rentré avant dix heures> **6** ACCORDING TO : d'après, selon <by what she says : d'après ce qu'elle dit> **7** (*indicating cause or agent*) : par <she was sent by me : elle était envoyée par moi> <to divide by 4 : diviser par 4>
by and by *adv* : bientôt
by and large *adv* : en général
bygone[1] ['baɪˌgɔn] *adj* : passé, d'autrefois <in bygone days : jadis>
bygone[2] *n* **let bygones be bygones** : oublions le passé
bylaw *or* **byelaw** ['baɪˌlɔ] *n* : statut *m* (d'une organisation), arrêté *m* (municipal)
by–line ['baɪˌlaɪn] *n* : signature *f* de journaliste
bypass[1] ['baɪˌpæs] *vt* CIRCUMVENT : contourner, éviter
bypass[2] *n* **1** : route *f* de contournement, déviation *f* **2** : pontage *m* (en médecine)
by–product ['baɪˌprɑdəkt] *n* : sous-produit *m,* dérivé *m*
bystander ['baɪˌstændər] *n* : spectateur *m,* -trice *f*
byway ['baɪˌweɪ] *n* : route *f* secondaire
byword ['baɪˌwərd] *n* : proverbe *m*

C

c ['siː] *n, pl* **c's** *or* **cs** : c *m,* troisième lettre de l'alphabet
cab ['kæb] *n* **1** TAXICAB : taxi *m* **2** : cabine *f* (d'un camion, d'une locomotive, etc.) **3** CARRIAGE : fiacre *m*
cabal [kə'bɑl, -'bæl] *n* : cabale *f*
cabana [kə'bænjə, -'bænə] *n* : cabine *f* de plage, tente *f* de plage
cabaret [ˌkæbə'reɪ] *n* : cabaret *m*
cabbage ['kæbɪdʒ] *n* : chou *m*
cabdriver ['kæbˌdraɪvər] *n* : chauffeur *m* de taxi
cabin ['kæbən] *n* **1** : cabine *f* (d'un navire, d'un avion, etc.) **2** HUT : cabane *f*
cabinet ['kæbnət, 'kæbə-] *n* **1** : meuble *m* de rangement, vitrine *f* **2** : cabinet *m* (du gouvernement) **3** *or* **filing cabinet** : classeur *m* **4** *or* **medicine cabinet** : armoire *f* à pharmacie
cabinetmaker ['kæbnətˌmeɪkər 'kæbə-] *n* : ébéniste *mf*
cabinetmaking ['kæbnətˌmeɪkɪŋ 'kæbə-] *n* : ébénisterie *f*
cable[1] ['keɪbəl] *vt* **-bled; -bling** : câbler
cable[2] *n* **1** ROPE, WIRE : câble *m* **2** → **cablegram**
cablegram ['keɪbəlˌgræm] *n* : câblogramme *m,* câble *m*
caboose [kəˌbuːs] *n* : fourgon *m* de queue
cabstand ['kæbˌstænd] *n* : station *f* de taxis
cacao [kə'kaʊ, -'keɪo] *n, pl* **cacaos** : cacao *m*
cache ['kæʃ] *n* : cache *f* (de provisions), cachette *f*
cachet [kæ'ʃeɪ] *n* : cachet *m*
cackle[1] ['kækəl] *vi* **-led; -ling** : caqueter, glousser
cackle[2] *n* : caquet *m,* gloussement *m*
cacophony [kə'kɑfəni, -kɔ-] *n, pl* **-nies** : cacophonie *f*
cactus ['kæktəs] *n, pl* **cacti** [-ˌtaɪ] *or* **-tuses** : cactus *m*
cadaver [kə'dævər] *n* : cadavre *m*
caddie *or* **caddy** ['kædi] *n, pl* **-dies** : caddie *m*
caddy ['kædi] *n, pl* **-dies** : boîte *f* à thé
cadence ['keɪdənts] *n* : cadence *f,* rythme *m*
cadet [kə'dɛt] *n* : élève *mf* officier, élève *mf* agent de police
cadge ['kædʒ] *vt* **cadged; cadging** : quémander, se procurer en quémandant
cadmium ['kædmiəm] *n* : cadmium *m*
cadre ['kæˌdreɪ, 'kɑ-, -driː] *n* : cadre *m*
caesarean [sɪ'zæriən, -zɛr-] → **cesarean**
caesium *Brit* → **cesium**
café [kæ'feɪ] *n* : café *m*
cafeteria [ˌkæfə'tɪriə] *n* : cafétéria *f,* restaurant *m* libre-service, cantine *f* (dans une école)
caffeine [kæ'fiːn, kə-] *n* : caféine *f*
cage[1] ['keɪdʒ] *vt* **caged; caging** : mettre en cage

cage[2] *n* : cage *f*
cagey ['keɪdʒi] *adj* **cagier; -est 1** CAUTIOUS : prudent, réticent **2** SHREWD : perspicace, astucieux
caisson ['keɪˌsɑn, -sən] *n* : caisson *m*
cajole [kə'dʒoːl] *vt* **-joled; -joling** : cajoler, enjôler
Cajun[1] ['keɪdʒən] *adj* : acadien, cajun
Cajun[2] *n* : Acadien *m,* -dienne *f;* Cajun *mf*
cake[1] ['keɪk] *v* **caked; caking** *vt* ENCRUST : former une croûte sur <caked with mud : couvert de boue séchée> — *vi* HARDEN : durcir, faire croûte
cake[2] *n* **1** : gâteau *m* **2** BAR : pain *m* (de savon)
calabash ['kæləˌbæʃ] *n* : calebasse *f*
calamine ['kæləˌmaɪn] *n* : calamine *f*
calamitous [kə'læmət̬əs] *adj* : catastrophique, désastreux — **calamitously** *adv*
calamity [kə'læmət̬i] *n, pl* **-ties** : calamité *f*
calcium ['kælsiəm] *n* : calcium *m*
calculate ['kælkjəˌleɪt] *v* **-lated; -lating** *vt* **1** COMPUTE : calculer **2** ESTIMATE : calculer, évaluer, estimer — *vi* **1** : calculer, faire des calculs **2** COUNT, RELY : compter <he had calculated on winning : il avait compté sur une victoire>
calculating ['kælkjəˌleɪt̬ɪŋ] *adj* : calculateur, astucieux
calculation [ˌkælkjə'leɪʃən] *n* : calcul *m*
calculator ['kælkjəˌleɪt̬ər] *n* : calculatrice *f*
calculus ['kælkjələs] *n, pl* **-li** [-ˌlaɪ] : calcul *m*
caldron ['kɔldrən] → **cauldron**
calendar ['kæləndər] *n* **1** : calendrier *m* **2** SCHEDULE : programme *m,* agenda *f*
calf ['kæf, 'kaf] *n, pl* **calves** ['kævz, 'kavz] **1** : veau *m* (de bovin) **2** : mollet *m* (de la jambe)
calfskin ['kæfskɪn] *n* : veau *m*
caliber *or* **calibre** ['kæləbər] *n* **1** : calibre *m* <a .38 caliber revolver : un revolver de calibre 38> **2** QUALITY, STATURE : qualité *f,* calibre *m*
calibrate ['kæləbreɪt] *vt* **-brated; -brating** : calibrer (une arme, etc.), étalonner (une balance)
calibration ['kæləˌbreɪʃən] *n* : calibrage *m,* étalonnage *m*
calico ['kælɪˌkoː] *n, pl* **-coes** *or* **-cos 1** : calicot *m* **2** *or* **calico cat** : chat *m* tigré
calipers *or Brit* **callipers** ['kæləpərz] *n* : compas *m* (à calibrer)
caliph *or* **calif** ['keɪləf, 'kæ-] *n* : calife *m*
calisthenics [ˌkæləs'θɛnɪks] *ns & pl* : gymnastique *f* suédoise
calk ['kɔk] → **caulk**
call[1] ['kɔl] *vi* **1** CRY, SHOUT : crier **2 to call for** REQUIRE : exiger, demander **3** VISIT : rendre visite, passer — *vt* **1** *or* **to call out** : appeler (un nom, etc.), crier (un ordre), annoncer (des résultats) **2** SUMMON : appeler, faire venir, convoquer **3** TELEPHONE : téléphoner à, appeler (au téléphone) **4** NAME : appeler, nommer **5** WAKEN : réveiller **6 to call back** : rappeler **7 to call off** CANCEL : annuler
call[2] *n* **1** CRY, SHOUT : appel *m,* cri *m* (d'un animal) **2** *or* **telephone call** : appel *m* <to give a call to : appeler, téléphoner à> **3** SUMMONS : appel *m* **4** DEMAND, NEED : demande *f* <a call for improvement : une demande d'amélioration> <there's no call to worry : il n'y a aucune raison de s'inquiéter> **5** VISIT : visite *f* <to pay a call : rendre visite>
caller ['kɔlər] *n* **1** VISITOR : visiteur *m,* -teuse *f* **2** : personne *f* qui appelle (au téléphone)
calling ['kɔlɪŋ] *n* : vocation *f,* profession *f*
calliope [kə'laɪəˌpiː, 'kæliˌoːp] *n* : orgue *m* à vapeur
callipers *Brit* → **calipers**
callous[1] ['kæləs] *vt* : rendre calleux
callous[2] *adj* **1** : calleux <callous skin : peau calleuse> **2** UNFEELING : insensible, sans cœur
callously ['kæləsli] *adv* : insensiblement, impitoyablement
callousness ['kæləsnəs] *n* : insensibilité *f,* dureté *f*
callow ['kælo] *adj* : sans expérience, gauche
callus ['kæləs] *n* : cal *m*
calm[1] ['kɑm, 'kɑlm] *v* **calmed; calming** *vt* : calmer, apaiser — *vi* : se calmer <calm down! : calmez-vous!>
calm[2] *adj* : calme, tranquille — **calmly** *adv*
calm[3] *n* **1** QUIETNESS : calme *m,* tranquillité *f* **2** COMPOSURE : sang-froid *m*
caloric [kə'lɔrɪk] *adj* : calorique
calorie ['kæləri] *n* : calorie *f*
calve ['kæv, 'kav] *vi* **calved; calving** : vêler (se dit de la vache)
calves → **calf**
calypso [kə'lɪpˌsoː] *n, pl* **-sos** : calypso *m*
calyx ['keɪlɪks, 'kæ-] *n, pl* **-lyxes** *or* **-lyces** [-ləˌsiːz] : calice *m*
cam ['kæm] *n* : came *f*
camaraderie [ˌkɑm'rɑdəri, ˌkæm-; ˌkɑmə'rɑ-] *n* : camaraderie *f*
Cambodian[1] [kæm'boːdiən] *adj* : cambodgien
Cambodian[2] *n* : Cambodgien *m,* -gienne *f*
came → **come**
camel ['kæməl] *n* : chameau *m*
camellia [kə'miːljə] *n* : camélia *f*
cameo ['kæmiˌoː] *n, pl* **-eos** : camée
camera ['kæmrə, 'kæmərə] *n* : appareil *m* photo, caméra *f*

Cameroonian[1] [ˌkæməˈruːniən] *adj* : camerounais
Cameroonian[2] *n* : Camerounais *m*, -naise *f*
camouflage[1] [ˈkæməˌflɑʒ, -ˌflɑdʒ] *vt* **-flaged; -flaging** : camoufler
camouflage[2] *n* : camouflage *m*
camp[1] [ˈkæmp] *vi* : camper, faire du camping
camp[2] *n* **1** : camp *m* <to pitch camp : planter son camp> **2** FACTION, GROUP : camp *m*, parti *m* <in the same camp : du même côté>
campaign[1] [kæmˈpeɪn] *vi* : faire campagne
campaign[2] *n* : campagne *f*
campground [ˈkæmpˌgraʊnd] *n* : camping *m*, terrain *m* de camping
camphor [ˈkæmpfər] *n* : camphre *m*
campus [ˈkæmpəs] *n* : campus *m*, cité *f* universitaire *Can*
can[1] [ˈkæn] *v aux, past* **could** [ˈkʊd]; *present s & pl* **can 1** (*expressing possibility*) : pouvoir <he couldn't go : il ne pouvait pas aller> <how can we know? : comment peut-on savoir?> **2** (*expressing knowledge or ability*) : savoir <I can speak three languages : je sais parler trois langues> <her son can't drive : son fils ne sait pas conduire> **3** (*expressing permission*) <can they stay? : peuvent-ils rester?> <you can't smoke here : vous n'avez pas le droit de fumer ici> **4** (*with verbs of sense perception*) <he can see the mountain : il voit la montagne> <I can taste garlic : je goûte l'ail> **5** (*in emphatic expressions*) <that cannot be! : cela n'est pas possible!>
can[2] *vt* **canned; canning** : mettre en boîte, conserver, canner *Can*
can[3] *n* : boîte *f* (d'aliments), canette *f* (de boissons), bidon *m* (d'essence, etc.)
Canada goose *n* : outarde *f Can*
Canadian[1] [kəˈneɪdiən] *adj* : canadien
Canadian[2] *n* : Canadien *m*, -dienne *f*
canal [kəˈnæl] *n* **1** : canal *m* <Panama Canal : Canal de Panama> **2** : conduit *m*, canal *m* (en anatomie)
canapé [ˈkænəpi, -ˌpeɪ] *n* : canapé *m*
canary [kəˈnɛri] *n, pl* **-naries** : canari *m*, serin *m*
cancel [ˈkæntsəl] *vt* **-celed** *or* **-celled; -celing** *or* **-celling** : annuler
cancellation [ˌkæntsəˈleɪʃən] *n* : annulation *f*
cancer [ˈkæntsər] *n* : cancer *m* — **cancerous** *adj*
Cancer *n* : Cancer *m*
cancerous [ˈkæntsərəs] *adj* : cancéreux
candelabra [ˌkændəˈlɑbrə, -læ-] *n* : candélabre *m*
candelabrum [ˌkændəˈlɑbrəm, -læ-] *n, pl* **-bra** → **candelabra**
candid [ˈkændɪd] *adj* **1** : franc, sincère **2** : instantané (se dit d'une photo)
candidacy [ˈkændədəsi] *n, pl* **-cies** : candidature *f*
candidate [ˈkændəˌdeɪt, -dət] *n* : candidat *m*, -date *f*
candidly [ˈkændɪdli] *adv* : franchement, sincèrement
candidness [ˈkændɪdnəs] *n* : franchise *f*
candle [ˈkændəl] *n* : bougie *f*, chandelle *f*, cierge *m* (à l'église)
candlestick [ˈkændəlˌstɪk] *n* : chandelier *m*, bougeoir *m*
candor *or Brit* **candour** [ˈkændər] *n* : franchise *f*
candy[1] [ˈkændi] *vt* **-died; -dying** : confire
candy[2] *n, pl* **-dies 1** : bonbon *m* **2 candies** *pl* : confiserie *f*
cane[1] [ˈkeɪn] *vt* **caned; caning 1** FLOG : donner des coups de badine à (un élève, etc.) **2** : canner (une chaise, etc.)
cane[2] *n* **1** : canne *f* (d'une plante) **2** STICK : canne *f* (pour marcher), badine *f* (pour punir) **3** RATTAN, RUSH : rotin *m*, jonc *m*
canine[1] [ˈkeɪˌnaɪn] *adj* : canin
canine[2] *n* **1** *or* **canine tooth** : canine *f* **2** DOG : canidé *m*
canister [ˈkænəstər] *n* : boîte *f* (métallique)
canker [ˈkæŋkər] *n* : ulcère *f* buccale
cannery [ˈkænəri] *n, pl* **-ries** : conserverie *f*
cannibal [ˈkænəbəl] *n* : cannibale *mf*, anthropophage *mf*
cannibalism [ˈkænəbəˌlɪzəm] *n* : cannibalisme *m*, anthropophagie *f*
cannon [ˈkænən] *n, pl* **-nons** *or* **-non** : canon *m*
cannonball [ˈkænənˌbɔl] *n* : boulet *m* de canon
cannot (can not) [ˈkænˌɑt, kəˈnɑt] → **can**[1]
canny [ˈkæni] *adj* **cannier; -est** SHREWD : prudent, astucieux
canoe [kəˈnuː] *n* : canoë *m*, canot *m Can*
canon [ˈkænən] *n* **1** : canon *m* <canon law : droit canon> **2** WORKS : œuvres *fpl* (littéraires) **3** RULE : canon *m*, règle *f* <the canons of good taste : les règles du bon goût> **4** : chanoine *m* (ecclésiastique)
canonize [ˈkænəˌnaɪz] *vt* **-ized; -izing** : canoniser
canopy [ˈkænəpi] *n, pl* **-pies** : auvent *m*, baldaquin *m*
cant[1] [ˈkænt] *v* **canted; canting** *vt* TILT : incliner, pencher — *vi* LEAN, TIP : s'incliner, se pencher
cant[2] *n* **1** SLANT : pente *f*, inclinaison *f* **2** JARGON : jargon *m* **3** : paroles *fpl* hypocrites
can't [ˈkænt, ˈkɑnt] (*contraction of* **can not**) → **can**[1]
cantaloupe [ˈkæntəlˌoːp] *n* : cantaloup *m*
cantankerous [kænˈtæŋkərəs] *adj* : acariâtre, grincheux, malcommode *Can*

cantata [kən'tɑt̬ə] *n* : cantate *f*
canteen [kæn'ti:n] *n* **1** CAFETERIA : cantine *f* **2** FLASK : flasque *f,* gourde *f*
canter[1] ['kæntər] *vi* : aller au petit galop
canter[2] *n* : petit galop *m*
cantilever[1] ['kæntə,li:vər, -lɛvər] *adj* : cantilever <cantilever bridge : pont cantilever>
cantilever[2] *n* : cantilever *m*
canto ['kæn,to:] *n, pl* **-tos** : chant *m* (d'un poème)
cantor ['kæntər] *n* : chantre *m*
canvas ['kænvəs] *n* **1** : toile *f,* canevas *m* **2** SAIL : voile *f* **3** PAINTING : toile *f*
canvass[1] ['kænvəs] *vt* **-vassed; -vassing** **1** POLL : sonder (des opinions) **2** SOLICIT : faire du démarchage électoral auprès
canvass[2] *n* **1** SURVEY : sondage *m* **2** : démarchage *m* électoral
canyon ['kænjən] *n* : canyon *m*
cap[1] ['kæp] *vt* **capped; capping** **1** COVER : couvrir **2** CROWN : couronner (une dent) **3** OUTDO : surpasser **4** LIMIT : restreindre, limiter
cap[2] *n* **1** : casquette *f,* bonnet *m,* calotte *f Can* <baseball cap : casquette de baseball> **2** COVER, TOP : capsule *f* (d'une bouteille), capuchon *m* (d'un stylo), couronne *f* (d'une dent) **3** LIMIT : plafond *m,* limite *f*
capability [,keɪpə'bɪlət̬i] *n, pl* **-ties** : aptitude *f,* capacité *f*
capable ['keɪpəbəl] *adj* : compétent, capable
capably ['keɪpəbli] *adv* : avec compétence
capacious [kə'peɪʃəs] *adj* : de grande capacité
capacity[1] [kə'pæsət̬i] *adj* FILLED, PACKED : comble
capacity[2] *n, pl* **-ties** **1** ROOM, SPACE : capacité *f,* contenance *f* **2** ABILITY : aptitude *f,* capacité *f* **3** FUNCTION, ROLE : qualité *f,* fonction *f* <in his capacity as supervisor : en qualité de superviseur>
cape ['keɪp] *n* **1** CLOAK : cape *f,* pèlerine *f* **2** : cap *m* <Cape of Good Hope : le cap de Bonne Espérance>
caper[1] ['keɪpər] *vi* GAMBOL : gambader, cabrioler
caper[2] *n* **1** : câpre *f* (assaisonnement) **2** LEAP : gambade *f,* cabriole *f* **3** PRANK : farce *f*
Cape Verdean[1] ['keɪp'vərdiən] *adj* : capverdien
Cape Verdean[2] *n* : Cap-Verdien *m,* -dienne *f*
capillary[1] ['kæpə,lɛri] *adj* : capillaire
capillary[2] *n, pl* **-laries** : capillaire *m*
capital[1] ['kæpət̬əl] *adj* **1** : capital <capital punishment : peine capitale> **2** UPPERCASE : majuscule <capital A : A majuscule> **3** : de capital, des capitaux <capital gain : revenu des capitaux> **4** FIRST-RATE : excellent <a capital idea : une idée excellente>
capital[2] *n* **1** *or* **capital letter** : majuscule *f* **2** *or* **capital city** : capitale *f* **3** WEALTH : capital *m,* fonds *mpl* **4** : chapiteau *m* (d'une colonne)
capitalism ['kæpət̬əl,ɪzəm] *n* : capitalisme *m*
capitalist[1] ['kæpət̬əlɪst] *or* **capitalistic** ['kæpət̬əl,ɪstɪk] *adj* : capitaliste
capitalist[2] *n* : capitaliste *mf*
capitalization [,kæpət̬ələ'zeɪʃən] *n* **1** : capitalisation *f* (en finance) **2** : emploi *m* de lettres majuscules
capitalize ['kæpət̬əl,aɪz] *v* **-ized; -izing** *vt* **1** : capitaliser (en finance) **2** : écrire en majuscules — *vi* **to capitalize on** : tirer profit de, tirer parti de
capitol ['kæpət̬əl] *n* : capitole *m*
capitulate [kə'pɪtʃə,leɪt] *vi* **-lated; -lating** : capituler
capitulation [kə,pɪtʃə'leɪʃən] *n* : capitulation *f*
capon ['keɪ,pɑn, -pən] *n* : chapon *m*
caprice [kə'pri:s] *n* : caprice *m*
capricious [kə'prɪʃəs, -'pri:-] *adj* : capricieux — **capriciously** *adv*
Capricorn ['kæprɪ,kɔrn] *n* : Capricorne *m*
capsize ['kæp,saɪz, kæp'saɪz] *v* **-sized; -sizing** *vt* : faire chavirer — *vi* : chavirer
capstan ['kæpstən, -,stæn] *n* : cabestan *m*
capsule ['kæpsəl, -,su:l] *n* : capsule *f*
captain[1] ['kæptən] *vt* : être le capitaine de
captain[2] *n* : capitaine *m*
caption[1] ['kæpʃən] *vt* : mettre une légende à (une illustration), sous-titrer (un film)
caption[2] *n* **1** HEADING, TITLE : titre *m* **2** : légende *f* (d'une illustration) **3** SUBTITLE : sous-titre *m*
captivate ['kæptə,veɪt] *vt* **-vated; -vating** : captiver, fasciner
captive[1] ['kæptɪv] *adj* : captif
captive[2] *n* : captif *m,* -tive *f*
captivity [kæp'tɪvət̬i] *n* : captivité *f*
captor ['kæptər] *n* : personne *f* qui capture
capture[1] ['kæpʃər] *vt* **-tured; -turing** **1** SEIZE : capturer, prendre **2** : rendre (une ressemblance), gagner (l'intérêt), captiver (l'imagination)
capture[2] *n* : capture *f,* prise *f*
car ['kɑr] *n* **1** AUTOMOBILE : voiture *f,* automobile *f* **2** *or* **railroad car** : wagon *m* **3** *or* **elevator car** : cabine *f* (d'ascenseur)
carafe [kə'ræf, -'rɑf] *n* : carafe *f*
caramel ['kɑrməl; 'kærəməl, -,mɛl] *n* : caramel *m*
carat ['kærət] *n* : carat *m*
caravan ['kærə,væn] *n* : caravane *f*
caraway ['kærə,weɪ] *n* : carvi *m*
carbine ['kɑr,baɪn, -,bi:n] *n* : carabine *f*

carbohydrate [ˌkɑrboˈhaɪˌdreɪt, -drət] *n* : hydrate *m* de carbone
carbon [ˈkɑrbən] *n* : carbone *m*
carbonated [ˈkɑrbəˌneɪtəd] *adj* : gazéifié
carbon copy *n* **1** : copie *f* carbone **2** REPLICA : réplique *f*
carbon paper *n* : carbone *m*, papier *m* carbone
carbuncle [ˈkɑrˌbʌŋkəl] *n* : furoncle *m*
carburetor [ˈkɑrbəˌreɪtər, -bjə-] *n* : carburateur *m*
carcass [ˈkɑrkəs] *n* : carcasse *f*
carcinogen [kɑrˈsɪnədʒən, ˈkɑrsənəˌdʒɛn] *n* : carcinogène *m*, cancérogène *m*
carcinogenic [ˌkɑrsənoˈdʒɛnɪk] *adj* : carcinogène, cancérogène
card[1] [ˈkɑrd] *vt* **carded; carding** : carder (des fibres textiles)
card[2] *n* **1** : carte *f* <library card : carte de bibliothèque> <Christmas card : carte de Noël> **2** : carde *f* (pour carder fibres) **3** → **playing card**
cardboard [ˈkɑrdˌbord] *n* : carton *m*
cardiac [ˈkɑrdiˌæk] *adj* : cardiaque
cardigan [ˈkɑrdɪgən] *n* : cardigan *m*
cardinal[1] [ˈkɑrdənəl] *adj* CHIEF : cardinal
cardinal[2] *n* : cardinal *m*
cardinal number *n* : nombre *m* cardinal
cardinal point *n* : point *m* cardinal
cardiologist [ˌkɑrdiˈɑlədʒɪst] *n* : cardiologue *mf*
cardiology [ˌkɑrdiˈɑlədʒi] *n* : cardiologie *f*
cardiovascular [ˌkɑrdioˈvæskjələr] *adj* : cardio-vasculaire
care[1] [ˈkær] *v* **cared; caring** *vi* **1** : se soucier, s'intéresser <she cares about the poor : elle se soucie des pauvres> <I don't care : ça m'est égal> **2 to care for** LIKE : aimer **3 to care for** LOOK AFTER : s'occuper de, soigner <to care for the sick : soigner les malades> — *vt* WISH : vouloir, désirer <would you care to come in? : voulez-vous entrer?>
care[2] *n* **1** ANXIETY : souci *m*, ennui *m* **2** TREATMENT : soins *mpl*, traitement *m* <medical care : soins médicaux> **3** MAINTENANCE, UPKEEP : entretien *m* **4** ATTENTION : soin *m*, attention *f* <take care not to fall : faites attention de ne pas tomber>
careen [kəˈriːn] *vi* **-reened; -reening 1** LURCH : tanguer **2** → **career**[1]
career[1] [kəˈrɪr] *vi* : aller à toute vitesse
career[2] *n* : carrière *f*, profession *f*
carefree [ˈkærˌfriː, ˌkærˈ-] *adj* : insouciant
careful [ˈkærfəl] *adj* **1** CAUTIOUS : prudent <be careful! : soyez prudent!> <be careful of the ice : fais attention à la glace> **2** THOROUGH : soigneux, approfondi
carefully [ˈkærfəli] *adv* : prudemment, avec soin
careless [ˈkærləs] *adj* : négligent
carelessly [ˈkærləsli] *adv* : négligemment, sans faire attention
carelessness [ˈkærləsnəs] *n* : négligence *f*, étourderie *f*, inattention *f*
caress[1] [kəˈrɛs] *vt* : caresser, minoucher *Can fam*
caress[2] *n* : caresse *f*
caret [ˈkærət] *n* : signe *m* d'insertion
caretaker [ˈkɛrˌteɪkər] *n* : gardien *m*, -dienne *f*; concierge *mf* (d'un immeuble, etc.)
cargo [ˈkɑrˌgoː] *n, pl* **-goes** *or* **-gos** : chargement *m*, cargaison *f*
caribou [ˈkærəˌbuː] *n, pl* **-bou** *or* **-bous** : caribou *m*
caricature[1] [ˈkærɪkəˌtʃʊr] *vt* **-tured; -turing** : caricaturer
caricature[2] *n* : caricature *f*
caricaturist [ˈkærɪkəˌtʃʊrɪst] *n* : caricaturiste *mf*
caries [ˈkærˌiːz] *ns & pl* : carie *f*
carillon [ˈkærəˌlɑn] *n* : carillon *m*
carmine [ˈkɑrmən, -ˌmaɪn] *n* : carmin *m*
carnage [ˈkɑrnɪdʒ] *n* : carnage *m*, boucherie *f*
carnal [ˈkɑrnəl] *adj* : charnel
carnation [kɑrˈneɪʃən] *n* : œillet *m*
carnival [ˈkɑrnəvəl] *n* : carnaval *m*, fête *f* foraine
carnivore [ˈkɑrnəˌvor] *n* : carnivore *m*, carnassier *m*
carnivorous [kɑrˈnɪvərəs] *adj* : carnivore, carnassier
carol[1] [ˈkærəl] *vi* **-oled** *or* **-olled; -oling** *or* **-olling** : chanter des chants de Noël
carol[2] *n* : chant *m* de Noël
carom[1] [ˈkærəm] *vi* **1** : caramboler (au billiard) **2** REBOUND : rebondir
carom[2] *n* : carambolage *m*
carouse [kəˈraʊz] *vi* **-roused; -rousing** : faire la bombe *fam*
carousel [ˌkærəˈsɛl, ˈkærəˌ-] *n* **1** MERRY-GO-ROUND : manège *m* **2** : carrousel *m* (pour les bagages, les diapositives, etc.)
carp[1] [ˈkɑrp] *vi* **1** COMPLAIN : se plaindre **2 to carp at** : critiquer
carp[2] *n, pl* **carp** *or* **carps** : carpe *f*
carpel [ˈkɑrpəl] *n* : carpelle *m*
carpenter [ˈkɑrpəntər] *n* : charpentier *m*, menuisier *m*
carpentry [ˈkɑrpəntri] *n* : charpenterie *f*, menuiserie *f*
carpet[1] [ˈkɑrpət] *vt* **1** : recouvrir d'un tapis, recouvrir d'une moquette **2** COVER : tapisser <carpeted with leaves : tapissé de feuilles>
carpet[2] *n* : tapis *m*, moquette *f*
carpeting [ˈkɑrpətɪŋ] *n* : moquette *f*
carport [ˈkɑrˌpɔrt] *n* : abri *m* d'auto, auvent *m* pour voiture
carriage [ˈkærɪdʒ] *n* **1** TRANSPORT : transport *m* **2** BEARING : maintien *m*, port *m* **3** *or* **horse–drawn carriage** : calèche *f*, fiacre *m*, carrosse *m* **4** → **baby carriage**

carrier ['kæriər] *n* **1** TRANSPORTER : transporteur *m* **2** : porteur *m*, -teuse *f* (d'une maladie) **3** → **aircraft carrier**

carrion ['kærien] *n* : charogne *f*

carrot ['kærət] *n* : carotte *f*

carrousel → **carousel**

carry ['kæri] *v* **-ried; -rying** *vt* **1** TRANSPORT : transporter, porter, emporter **2** BEAR : porter, supporter **3** STOCK : vendre, tenir en magasin **4** WIN : remporter, emporter, gagner <the motion was carried by 10 votes : la motion l'a emporté par 10 votes> **5** ENTAIL : comporter, entraîner **6 to carry oneself** : se présenter, se comporter — *vi* : porter <her voice carries well : sa voix porte bien>

carryall ['kæri,ɔl] *n* : fourre-tout *m*

carry away *vt* **to get carried away** : se laisser emporter, s'emballer

carry on *vt* CONDUCT : conduire (des affaires), entretenir (une correspondence, etc.) — *vi* **1** : se conduire, faire des histoires <he's always carrying on over nothing : il fait toujours des histoires pour des riens> **2** CONTINUE : continuer

carry out *vt* ACCOMPLISH, EXECUTE : réaliser, effectuer, accomplir, mettre à l'exécution

cart[1] ['kɑrt] *vt* **1** CONVEY : charrier **2** HAUL : trimbaler *fam*

cart[2] *n* : charette *f* (de foin, etc.), chariot *m* <shopping cart : chariot de supermarché>

cartel [kɑr'tɛl] *n* : cartel *m*

cartilage ['kɑrṭəlɪdʒ] *n* : cartilage *m*

cartilaginous [,kɑrṭəl'ædʒənəs] *adj* : cartilagineux

cartographer [kɑr'tɑgrəfər] *n* : cartographe *mf*

cartography [kɑr'tɑgrəfi] *n* : cartographie *f*

carton ['kɑrtən] *n* **1** : carton *m*, boîte *f* de carton **2** : cartouche *f* (de cigarettes)

cartoon [kɑr'tu:n] *n* **1** : dessin *m* humoristique, caricature *f* **2** COMIC STRIP : bande *f* dessinée **3** *or* **animated cartoon** : dessin *m* animé

cartoonist [kɑr'tu:nɪst] *n* : dessinateur *m*, -trice *f* (humoristique); caricaturiste *mf*

cartridge ['kɑrtrɪdʒ] *n* : cartouche *f*

carve ['kɑrv] *vt* **carved; carving 1** : tailler (la pierre, le bois, etc.) **2** INSCRIBE : graver **3** SLICE : couper <to carve a turkey : couper une dinde>

cascade[1] [kæs'keɪd] *vi* **-caded; -cading** : tomber en cascade

cascade[2] *n* : cascade *f*

case[1] ['keɪs] *vt* **cased; casing 1** BOX, PACK : emballer, empaqueter **2** INSPECT : surveiller (un lieu)

case[2] *n* **1** BOX, CRATE : boite *f*, caisse *f* **2** CONTAINER : étui *m* (à lunettes, etc.), écrin *m*, coffre *m*, boîte *f* <a display case : une vitrine> **3** INSTANCE : cas *m*, exemple *m* <a case of the flu : un cas de grippe> **4** : cas *m* (en grammaire) **5** : affaire *f*, procès *m* (en droit) **6 in any case** : en tout cas **7 in case** : au cas où **8 in case of** : en cas de

casement ['keɪsmənt] *n or* **casement window** : fenêtre *f* à battants

cash[1] ['kæʃ] *vt* **1** : encaisser (un chèque) **2 to cash in** : se faire rembourser, réaliser (un bon, etc.)

cash[2] *n* : espèces *fpl*, argent *m* liquide

cash register *n* : caisse *f* (enregistreuse)

cashew ['kæ,ʃu:, kə'ʃu:] *n or* **cashew nut** : noix *f* de cajou

cashier[1] [kæ'ʃɪr] *vt* DISMISS : renvoyer, congédier

cashier[2] *n* : caissier *m*, -sière *f*

cashmere ['kæʒ,mɪr, 'kæʃ-] *n* : cachemire *m*

casino [kə'si:,no:] *n, pl* **-nos** : casino *m*

cask ['kæsk] *n* : fût *m*, tonneau *f*

casket *n* ['kæskət] : cercueil *m*

casserole ['kæsə,ro:l] *n* **1** *or* **casserole dish** : cocotte *f*, marmite *f* **2** : ragoût *m* (cuit au four)

cassette [kə'sɛt, kæ-] *n* : cassette *f*

cassock ['kæsək] *n* : soutane *f*

cast[1] ['kæst] *vt* **cast; casting 1** THROW : jeter, lancer <to cast dice : jeter les dés> <to cast an eye on : jeter un coup d'œil sur> <to cast aside : mettre de côté> **2** : déposer (un vote) <to cast a vote for : voter pour> **3** : distribuer les rôles de (une pièce de théâtre, un film, etc.) <he was cast in the leading role : on lui a donné le rôle principal> **4** MOLD : mouler, couler, fondre <to cast metal : faire fondre du métal>

cast[2] *n* **1** : lancer *m* (d'une ligne de pêche) **2** : distribution *f* (d'acteurs) **3** MOLD : moulage *m* **4** *or* **plaster cast** : plâtre *m* **5** APPEARANCE : aspect *f*, forme *f* <the delicate cast of her features : la finesse de ses traits>

castanets [,kæstə'nɛts] *npl* : castagnettes *fpl*

castaway[1] ['kæstə,weɪ] *adj* : naufragé

castaway[2] *n* : naufragé *m*, -gée *f*

caste ['kæst] *n* : caste *f*

caster ['kæstər] *n* : roulette *f* (d'un meuble)

castigate ['kæstə,geɪt] *vt* **-gated; -gating 1** PUNISH : punir, châtier **2** CRITICIZE : critiquer sévèrement

castigation ['kæstə,geɪʃən] *n* **1** PUNISHMENT : punition *f*, châtiment *m* **2** CRITICISM : critique *f* sévère, condamnation *f*

cast iron *n* : fonte *f*

castle ['kæsəl] *n* **1** : château *m* **2** : tour *f* (aux échecs)

cast–off ['kæst,ɔf] *adj* : dont on ne veut, mis au rebut

castoff ['kæst,ɔf] *n, pl* **castoffs** : vêtement *m* dont on ne veut

castrate ['kæs,treɪt] *vt* **-trated; -trating** : castrer, châtrer

castration [kæ'streɪʃən] *n* : castration *f*

casual ['kæʒuəl] *adj* **1** CHANCE : fortuit, de hasard **2** OCCASIONAL : intermittent, de passage **3** NONCHALANT : désinvolte, nonchalant **4** INFORMAL : simple, détendu <casual clothes : vêtements sport>

casually ['kæʒuəli, 'kæʒəli] *adv* **1** FORTUITOUSLY : par hasard, accidentellement **2** NONCHALANTLY : nonchalamment **3** INFORMALLY : simplement

casualty ['kæʒuəlti, 'kæʒəl-] *n, pl* **-ties 1** ACCIDENT : accident *m* grave, désastre *m* **2** VICTIM : blessé *m*, -sée *f*; accidenté *m*, -tée *f*; mort *m*, morte *f* <casualties of battle : pertes de bataille>

cat ['kæt] *n* **1** : chat *m*, chatte *f* **2** FELINE : félin *m* <the big cats : les grands félins>

cataclysm ['kæṭə,klɪzəm] *n* : cataclysme *m*

catacombs ['kæṭə,ko:mz] *npl* : catacombes *fpl*

catalog[1] *or* **catalogue** ['kæṭə,lɔg] *vt* **-loged** *or* **-logued; -loging** *or* **-loguing** : cataloguer, dresser un catalogue de

catalog[2] *or* **catalogue** *n* : catalogue *m*

catalpa [kə'tælpə, -'tɔl-] *n* : catalpa *m*

catalyst ['kætəl̩əst] *n* : catalyseur *m*

catalytic [,kæṭəl'ɪtɪk] *adj* : catalytique

catamaran [,kæṭəmə'ræn, 'kæṭəmə,ræn] *n* : catamaran *m*

catapult[1] ['kæṭə,pʌlt, -,pʊlt] *vt* : catapulter

catapult[2] *n* : catapulte *f*

cataract ['kæṭə,rækt] *n* : cataracte *f*

catarrh [kə'tɑr] *n* : catarrhe *m*

catastrophe [kə'tæstrə,fi:] *n* : catastrophe *f* — **catastrophic** [,kæṭə'strɑfɪk] *adj* : catastrophique

catcalls ['kæt,kɔlz] *npl* : huées *fpl*, sifflets *mpl*

catch[1] ['kætʃ, 'kɛtʃ] *v* **caught** ['kɔt]; **catching** *vt* **1** CAPTURE, TRAP : attraper, piéger **2** CONTRACT : attraper, prendre <to catch a cold : attraper un rhume> **3** SURPRISE : surprendre, prendre <I caught him red-handed : je l'ai pris en flagrant délit> **4** GRASP, SEIZE : attraper, saisir **5** SNAG : accrocher **6** PERCEIVE : discerner, remarquer (une expression, une odeur, etc.) <to catch sight of : apercevoir> **7** : attraper, prendre (un train, etc.) **8 to catch one's breath** : reprendre son souffle — *vi* **1** START : démarrer (se dit d'un moteur), prendre (se dit du feu) **2** HOOK, SNAG : s'accrocher, se prendre <her fingers caught in a drawer : ses doigts se sont pris dans un tiroir>

catch[2] *n* **1** CATCHING : prise *f* **2** : prise *f*, pêche *f* (de poissons) **3** LATCH : loquet *m* **4** PITFALL, SNAG : piège *f*

catcher ['kætʃər, 'kɛ-] *n* : receveur *m Can* (au baseball)

catching ['kætʃɪŋ, 'kɛ-] *adj* : contagieux

catch on *vi* **1** UNDERSTAND : comprendre, saisir **2** : devenir populaire, devenir célèbre <the song caught on : la chanson est devenue populaire>

catchup ['kætʃəp, 'kɛ-] → **ketchup**

catch up *vi* **to catch up with** : rattraper

catchword ['kætʃ,wərd, 'kɛtʃ-] *n* : slogan *m*, mot *m* d'ordre

catchy ['kætʃi, 'kɛ-] *adj* **catchier; -est** : entraînant <a catchy tune : un air entraînant>

catechism ['kæṭə,kɪzəm] *n* : catéchisme *m*

categorical [,kæṭə'gɔrɪkəl] *adj* : catégorique, absolu, indiscutable — **categorically** [-rəkli] *adv*

categorize ['kæṭɪgəraɪz] *vt* **-ized; -izing** : classer (par catégories)

category ['kæṭə,gori] *n, pl* **-ries** : catégorie *f*, classe *f*

cater ['keɪṭər] *vi* **1** : fournir des repas (pour les fêtes, les noces, etc.) **2 to cater to** : pourvoir à <she caters to his every need : elle pourvoit à tous ses besoins>

catercorner[1] ['kæṭi,kɔrnər, 'kæṭə-, 'kɪṭi-] *adv* : diagonalement

catercorner[2] *adj* : diagonal

caterer ['keɪṭərər] *n* : traiteur *m*

caterpillar ['kæṭər,pɪlər] *n* : chenille *f*

catfish ['kæt,fɪʃ] *n* : poisson-chat *m*

catgut ['kæt,gʌt] *n* : boyau *m* (de chat)

catharsis [kə'θɑrsɪs] *n, pl* **catharses** [-,si:z] : catharsis *f*

cathartic [kə'θɑrṭɪk] *adj* : cathartique

cathedral [kə'θi:drəl] *n* : cathédrale *f*

catheter ['kæθəṭər] *n* : cathéter *m*, sonde *f*

cathode ['kæ,θo:d] *n* : cathode *f*

catholic ['kæθəlɪk] *adj* UNIVERSAL : universel

Catholic[1] *adj* : catholique <the Catholic Church : l'Église catholique>

Catholic[2] *n* : catholique *mf*

Catholicism [kə'θɑlə,sɪzəm] *n* : catholicisme *m*

catkin ['kætkɪn] *n* : chaton *m*

catnap[1] ['kæt,næp] *vi* **-napped; -napping** : faire un somme

catnap[2] *n* : somme *m*

catnip ['kæt,nɪp] *n* : herbe *f* aux chats

catsup ['kɛtʃəp, 'kætsəp] → **ketchup**

cattail ['kæt,teɪl] *n* : massette *f*, quenouille *f Can*

cattiness ['kæṭinəs] *n* : méchanceté *f*, malveillance *f*

cattle ['kæṭəl] *npl* : bétail *m*, bovins *mpl*

cattleman ['kæṭəlmən, -,mæn] *n* : bouvier *m*, -vière *f*; vacher *m*, -chère *f*

catty ['kæṭi] *adj* **cattier; -est** : méchant, malveillant

catwalk ['kæt,wɔk] *n* : passerelle *f*

Caucasian[1] [kɔ'keɪʒən] *adj* : caucasien

Caucasian[2] *n* : Caucasien *m*, -sienne *f*

caucus ['kɔkəs] *n* : comité *m* électoral

caught → **catch**[1]

cauldron ['kɔldrən] *n* : chaudron *m*

cauliflower ['kɑlɪˌflaʊər, 'kɔ-] *n* : chou-fleur *m*

caulk[1] ['kɔk] *vt* : calfater (un bateau), mastiquer (une fenêtre, etc.)

caulk[2] *n* : mastic *m*

causal ['kɔzəl] *adj* : causal

cause[1] ['kɔz] *vt* **caused; causing** : causer, occasionner

cause[2] *n* **1** ORIGIN : cause *f* **2** MOTIVE, REASON : raison *f*, motif *m* <with good cause : à juste titre> **3** GROUNDS : cause *f* (en droit) **4** MOUVEMENT : cause *f*, mouvement *m*

causeway ['kɔzˌweɪ] *n* : chaussée *f*

caustic ['kɔstɪk] *adj* **1** CORROSIVE : caustique, corrosif **2** BITING : mordant, sarcastique

cauterize ['kɔt̬əˌraɪz] *vt* **-ized; -izing** : cautériser

caution[1] ['kɔʃən] *vt* WARN : avertir, mettre en garde

caution[2] *n* **1** WARNING : avertissement *m* **2** CARE : prudence *f*, précaution *f*

cautious ['kɔʃəs] *adj* : prudent, avisé, circonspect

cautiously ['kɔʃəsli] *adv* : prudemment, avec prudence

cavalcade [ˌkævəl'keɪd, 'kævəl-] *n* **1** : cavalcade *f* **2** SERIES : série *f*

cavalier[1] [ˌkævə'lɪr] *adj* OFFHAND : cavalier, désinvolte

cavalier[2] *n* : cavalier *m*

cavalierly [ˌkævə'lɪrli] *adv* : de façon cavalière

cavalry ['kævəlri] *n, pl* **-ries** : cavalerie *f*

cavalryman ['kævəlrimən] *n, pl* **-men** [-mən, -ˌmɛn] : cavalier *m*

cave[1] ['keɪv] *vi* **caved; caving** *or* **to cave in** : s'affaisser, s'effondrer

cave[2] *n* : grotte *f*, caverne *f*

cavern ['kævərn] *n* : caverne *f*

cavernous ['kævərnəs] *adj* : caverneux

caviar *or* **caviare** ['kæviˌɑr, 'kɑ-] *n* : caviar *m*

cavity ['kævət̬i] *n, pl* **-ties 1** HOLE : cavité *f* **2** CARIES : carie *f* (dentaire), cavité *f*

cavort [kə'vɔrt] *vi* CAPER : gambader, faire des cabrioles

caw[1] ['kɔ] *vi* : croasser

caw[2] *n* : croassement *m*

cayenne pepper [ˌkaɪ'ɛn, ˌkeɪ-] *n* : poivre *m* de cayenne

CD [ˌsiː'diː] *n* : CD *m*, disque *m* compact

cease ['siːs] *v* **ceased; ceasing** : cesser

ceaseless ['siːsləs] *adj* : incessant, continuel

cedar ['siːdər] *n* : cèdre *m*

cede ['siːd] *vt* **ceded; ceding** : céder

cedilla [sɪ'dɪlə] *n* : cédille *nf*

ceiling ['siːlɪŋ] *n* **1** : plafond *m* **2** LIMIT : plafond *m*, limite *f*

celebrate ['sɛləˌbreɪt] *v* **-brated; -brating** *vt* **1** FETE : fêter, célébrer <to celebrate Christmas : fêter la Noël> **2** : célébrer <to celebrate Mass : célébrer la messe> **3** EXTOL : louer, glorifier

celebration [ˌsɛlə'breɪʃən] *n* **1** : célébration *f*, fête *f* **2** PRAISE : louange *f*

celebrated ['sɛləˌbreɪt̬əd] *adj* FAMOUS : célèbre, réputé

celebrity [sə'lɛbrət̬i] *n, pl* **-ties 1** FAME : célébrité *f*, renommée *f* **2** PERSONALITY : célébrité *f*, vedette *f*

celery ['sɛləri] *n, pl* **-eries** : céleri *m*

celestial [sə'lɛstʃəl, -'lɛstiəl] *adj* : céleste

celibacy ['sɛləbəsi] *n* : célibat *m*

celibate[1] ['sɛləbət] *adj* **1** CHASTE : chaste **2** UNMARRIED : célibataire

celibate[2] *n* : célibataire *mf*

cell ['sɛl] *n* **1** : cellule *f* (d'un organisme, d'une prison, etc.) **2** : élément *m* (d'une pile)

cellar ['sɛlər] *n* : cave *f* <wine cellar : cave à vin>

cellist ['tʃɛlɪst] *n* : violoncelliste *mf*

cello ['tʃɛˌloː] *n, pl* **-los** : violoncelle *m*

cellophane ['sɛləˌfeɪn] *n* : cellophane *f*

cellular ['sɛljələr] *adj* : cellulaire

cellulose ['sɛljəˌloːs] *n* : cellulose *f*

Celsius ['sɛlsiəs] *adj* : Celsius, centigrade

Celt ['kɛlt, 'sɛlt] *n* : Celte *mf*

Celtic ['kɛltɪk, 'sɛl-] *adj* : celte, celtique

cement[1] [sɪ'mɛnt] *vt* : cimenter

cement[2] *n* **1** : ciment *m* **2** GLUE : colle *f*

cemetery ['sɛməˌtɛri] *n, pl* **-teries** : cimetière *m*

censer ['sɛn*t*sər] *n* : encensoir *m*

censor[1] ['sɛn*t*sər] *vt* : censurer

censor[2] *n* : censeur *m*

censorship ['sɛn*t*sərˌʃɪp] *n* : censure *f*

censure[1] ['sɛntʃər] *vt* **-sured; -suring** : critiquer, blâmer

censure[2] *n* : censure *f*

census ['sɛn*t*səs] *n* : recensement *m*

cent ['sɛnt] *n* : cent *m*

centaur ['sɛnˌtɔr] *n* : centaure *m*

centennial [sɛn'tɛniəl] *n* : centenaire *m*

center[1] *or Brit* **centre** ['sɛntər] *vt* **centered** *or Brit* **centred; centering** *or Brit* **centring 1** : centrer **2** CONCENTRATE, FOCUS : concentrer, fixer — *vi* **to center around** : se concentrer sur, tourner autour de

center[2] *or Brit* **centre** *n* **1** : centre *m* <center of attention : centre d'attention> **2** SEAT : siège (du gouvernement, etc.) **3** : centre *m* (aux sports)

centigrade ['sɛntəˌgreɪd, 'sɑn-] *adj* : centigrade

centigram ['sɛntəˌgræm, 'sɑn-] *n* : centigramme *m*

centimeter ['sɛntəˌmiːt̬ər, 'sɑn-] *n* : centimètre *m*

centipede ['sɛntəˌpiːd] *n* : mille-pattes *m*

central ['sɛntrəl] *adj* **1** : central <in a central location : au centre-ville> **2**

MAIN, PRINCIPAL : fundamental, principal
Central American[1] *adj* : centraméricain
Central American[2] *n* : Centraméricain *m,* -caine *f*
centralization [ˌsɛntrələ'zeɪʃən] *n* : centralisation *f*
centralize ['sɛntrəˌlaɪz] *vt* **-ized; -izing** : centraliser
central nervous system *n* : système *m* nerveux central
centre ['sɛntər] *Brit* → **center**
centrifugal force [sɛn'trɪfjəgəl, -'trɪfɪgəl] *n* : force *f* centrifuge
century ['sɛntʃəri] *n, pl* **-ries** : siècle *m*
ceramic [sə'ræmɪk] *adj* : céramique <ceramic tiles : carreaux en céramique>
ceramics [sə'ræmɪks] *npl* : céramique *f*
cereal[1] ['sɪriəl] *adj* : céréalier
cereal[2] *n* : céréale *f*
cerebellum [ˌsɛrə'bɛləm] *n, pl* **-bellums** *or* **-bella** [-'bɛlə] : cervelet *m*
cerebral [sə'ri:brəl, 'sɛrə-] *adj* : cérébral
cerebral palsy *n* : paralysie *f* cérébrale
cerebrum [sə'ri:brəm, 'sɛrə-] *n, pl* **-brums** *or* **-bra** [-brə] : cerveau *m*
ceremonial[1] [ˌsɛrə'mo:niəl] *adj* : cérémoniel, de cérémonie
ceremonial[2] *n* : cérémonial *m*
ceremonious [ˌsɛrə'mo:niəs] *adj* **1** FORMAL : cérémonieux **2** CEREMONIAL : cérémonial
ceremony ['sɛrəˌmo:ni] *n, pl* **-nies** : cérémonie *f*
cerise [sə'ri:s] *n* : cerise *f*
certain[1] ['sərtən] *adj* **1** FIXED : certain, déterminé <a certain percentage : un pourcentage déterminé> **2** SURE : certain, convaincu <I'm certain that he got lost : je suis convaincu qu'il s'est perdu> **3** : certain, quelconque <a certain charm : un certain charme> **4** : sûr, assuré <she is certain to win : elle est assurée de gagner> **5** INEVITABLE : certain <a certain death : une mort certaine>
certain[2] *pron* : certains, certaines *pl* <certain of my friends : certains de mes amis>
certainly ['sərtənli] *adv* **1** DEFINITELY : certainement, assurément **2** OF COURSE : bien sûr
certainty ['sərtənti] *n, pl* **-ties** : certitude *f*
certificate [sər'tɪfɪkət] *n* : certificat *m,* acte *m,* extrait *m* <birth certificate : extrait de naissance>
certification [ˌsərt̬əfə'keɪʃən] *n* : certification *f,* attestation *f*
certify ['sərt̬əˌfaɪ] *vt* **-fied; -fying 1** CONFIRM : certifier **2** GUARANTEE : certifier (un chèque), garantir (des marchandises, etc.)
certitude ['sərt̬əˌtu:d, -ˌtju:d] *n* : certitude *f*
cervical ['sərvɪkəl] *adj* : cervical
cervix ['sərvɪks] *n, pl* **-vices** [-vəˌsi:z] *or* **-vixes** : col *m* de l'utérus
cesarean section [sɪ'zæriən] *n* : césarienne *f*
cesium *or Brit* **caesium** ['si:ziəm] *n* : césium *m*
cessation [sɛ'seɪʃən] *n* : cessation *f*
cesspool ['sɛsˌpu:l] *n* : fosse *f* d'aisances
Chadian[1] ['tʃædiən] *adj* : tchadien
Chadian[2] *n* : Tchadien *m,* -dienne *f*
chafe ['tʃeɪf] *v* **chafed; chafing** *vt* IRRITATE : irriter — *vi* **1** RUB : frotter **2** : s'irriter, s'impatienter <to chafe at : s'irriter de>
chaff ['tʃæf] *n* : balle *f* (en agriculture)
chafing dish ['tʃeɪfɪŋˌdɪʃ] *n* : réchaud *m* de table
chagrin[1] [ʃə'grɪn] *vt* VEX : contrarier, décevoir
chagrin[2] *n* : dépit *m,* déception *f*
chain[1] ['tʃeɪn] *vt* : enchaîner
chain[2] *n* **1** : chaîne *f* **2** SEQUENCE, SERIES : série *f,* suite *f* <a chain of events : une série d'événements> **3 chains** *npl* FETTERS : entraves *fpl*
chair[1] ['tʃɛr] *vt* : présider
chair[2] *n* **1** : chaise *f* **2** : chaire *f* (dans une université) **3** CHAIRMAN, CHAIRWOMAN : président *m,* -dente *f*
chairman ['tʃɛrmən] *n, pl* **-men** [-mən, -ˌmɛn] : président *m*
chairmanship ['tʃɛrmənˌʃɪp] : présidence *f*
chairwoman ['tʃɛrˌwʊmən] *n, pl* **-women** [-ˌwɪmən] : présidente *f*
chaise longue ['ʃeɪz'lɔŋ] *n, pl* **chaise longues** [-'lɔŋ, -'lɔŋz] : chaise *f* longue
chalet [ʃæ'leɪ] *n* : chalet *m*
chalice ['tʃælɪs] *n* : calice *m*
chalk[1] ['tʃɔk] *vt* **1** : écrire avec de la craie **2 to chalk up** CREDIT : attribuer, mettre <chalk it up to experience : mets-le au compte de l'expérience> **3 to chalk up** ACHIEVE, ATTAIN : marquer (des points), remporter (une victoire)
chalk[2] *n* **1** LIMESTONE : calcaire *m* **2** : craie *f* (pour écrire)
chalkboard ['tʃɔkˌbɔrd] → **blackboard**
chalky ['tʃɔki] *adj* **chalkier; -est** : calcaire (se dit de l'eau, du sol, etc.), couvert de craie (se dit des mains), crayeux (se dit du teint)
challenge[1] ['tʃælɪndʒ] *vt* **-lenged; -lenging 1** DISPUTE : contester, remettre en question **2** DARE, DEFY : défier
challenge[2] *n* : défi *m* <to meet the challenge : relever le défi>
challenger ['tʃælɪndʒər] *n* : challenger *m* (aux sports, en politique)
challenging ['tʃælɪndʒɪŋ] *adj* : stimulant, provocateur
chamber ['tʃeɪmbər] *n* **1** ROOM : chambre *f,* salle *f* **2** BODY : chambre *f* <chamber of commerce : chambre de commerce> **3** : chambre *f* (d'une

arme à feu) **4** CAVITY : cavité *f* (du cœur) **5 chambers** *npl* : cabinet *m* (d'un juge)

chambermaid ['tʃeɪmbər,meɪd] *n* : femme *f* de chambre

chamber music *n* : musique *f* de chambre

chameleon [kə'mi:ljən, -liən] *n* : caméléon *m*

chamois ['ʃæmi] *n, pl* **chamois** [-mi, -miz] : chamois *m*

champ[1] ['tʃæmp, 'tʃɑmp] *vi* **1** CHEW : mâchonner **2 to champ at the bit** : ronger son frein

champ[2] ['tʃæmp] → **champion**[1]

champagne [ʃæm'peɪn] *n* : champagne *m*

champion[1] ['tʃæmpiən] *vt* : défendre, soutenir <to champion a cause : se faire le champion d'un mouvement>

champion[2] *n* : champion *m*, -pionne *f*

championship ['tʃæmpiən,ʃɪp] *n* : championnat *m*

chance[1] ['tʃænts] *v* **chanced; chancing** *vi* **1** HAPPEN : arriver (par hasard) **2 to chance upon** : rencontrer par hasard — *vt* RISK : hasarder, courir le risque de

chance[2] *adj* : fortuit, accidentel

chance[3] *n* **1** LUCK : hasard *m* **2** OPPORTUNITY : occasion *f* **3** PROBABILITY : chances *fpl* **4** RISK : risque *m* **5** : billet *m* (de loterie) **6 by chance** : par hasard

chancellor ['tʃæntsələr] *n* **1** : chancelier *m* **2** : président *m*, -dente *f* (d'une université)

chancre ['ʃæŋkər] *n* : chancre *m*

chandelier [,ʃændə'lɪr] *n* : lustre *m*

change[1] ['tʃeɪndʒ] *v* **changed; changing** *vt* **1** ALTER : changer, modifier **2** EXCHANGE : changer de <to change places : changer de place> — *vi* **1** : changer <times change : les temps changent> **2** *or* **to change clothes** : se changer **3** : muer (se dit de la voix)

change[2] *n* **1** : changement *m*, modification *f* **2** COINS : monnaie *f*

changeable ['tʃeɪndʒəbəl] *adj* : changeant, variable

changeless ['tʃeɪndʒləs] *adj* UNCHANGING : inaltérable, immuable

channel[1] ['tʃænəl] *vt* **-neled** *or* **-nelled; -neling** *or* **-nelling** : canaliser, creuser

channel[2] *n* **1** PASSAGE : voie *f*, canal *m* **2** : chenal *m* (dans un fleuve, un port, etc.) **3** STRAIT : détroit *m* **4** : chaîne *f* (de télévision)

chant[1] ['tʃænt] *vt* **1** : psalmodier, chanter **2** : scander (un slogan, etc.) — *vi* : psalmodier

chant[2] *n* : chant *m*, psalmodie *f* (en religion), chant *m* scandé (d'un slogan, etc.)

chantey *or* **chanty** ['ʃænti, 'tʃæn-] *n, pl* **-teys** *or* **-ties** : chanson *f* de marin

Chanukah ['xɑnəkə, 'hɑ-] → **Hanukkah**

chaos ['keɪ,ɑs] *n* : chaos *m*

chaotic [keɪ'ɑt̬ɪk] *adj* : chaotique

chap[1] ['tʃæp] *v* **chapped; chapping** *vt* : gercer — *vi* : se gercer

chap[2] *n* : type *m fam*, bonhomme *m fam*

chapel ['tʃæpəl] *n* : chapelle *f*

chaperon[1] *or* **chaperone** ['ʃæpə,ro:n] *vt* **-oned; -oning** : chaperonner

chaperon[2] *or* **chaperone** *n* : chaperon *m*

chaplain ['tʃæplɪn] *n* : aumônier *m*

chapter ['tʃæptər] *n* **1** : châpitre *m* (d'un livre, etc.) **2** BRANCH : section *f*, division *f* (d'un groupe)

char ['tʃɑr] *vt* **charred; charring 1** BURN : carboniser, réduire en charbon **2** SCORCH : brûler légèrement

character ['kærɪktər] *n* **1** LETTER, SYMBOL : caractère *m* **2** CHARACTERISTIC : caractère *m* **3** NATURE, PERSONALITY : caractère *m*, personnalité *f* **4** PERSON : individu *m* <he's quite a character : c'est un drôle de type> **5** : personnage *m* (d'un roman, d'un film, etc.)

characteristic[1] [,kærɪktə'rɪstɪk] *adj* : caractéristique, distinctif

characteristic[2] *n* : caractéristique *f*

characteristically [,kærɪktə'rɪstɪkli] *adv* : typiquement, comme d'habitude

characterization [,kærɪktərə'zeɪʃən] *n* : caractérisation *f*

characterize ['kærɪktə,raɪz] *vt* : caractériser

charade [ʃə'reɪd] *n* **1** PRETENSE : feinte *f*, comédie **2 charades** *npl* : charades *fpl* (jeu)

charcoal ['tʃɑr,ko:l] *n* **1** : charbon *m* de bois **2** : fusain *m* <charcoal drawing : portrait au fusain>

chard ['tʃɑrd] → **Swiss chard**

charge[1] ['tʃɑrdʒ] *v* **charged; charging** *vt* **1** : charger <to charge a battery : charger une batterie> **2** ENTRUST : charger, confier **3** COMMAND : ordonner **4** ACCUSE : inculper **5** ATTACK : donner l'assaut à, charger **6** : porter à un compte, payer par carte de crédit — *vi* **1** ATTACK : charger, donner l'assaut **2** RUSH : se précipiter, foncer, se précipiter **3** ASK : demander, faire payer <they charge too much : ils font payer de trop>

charge[2] *n* **1** : charge *f* (éléctrique) **2** RESPONSIBILITY : charge *f*, responsabilité *f* <to be in charge : être responsable> **3** COST : frais *mpl*, charge *f* <free of charge : gratuit> **4** ACCUSATION : inculpation *f*, accusation *f* **5** ATTACK : charge *f*, attaque *f* <charge! : à l'assaut!>

charge card → **credit card**

charger ['tʃɑrdʒər] *n* : cheval *m* de bataille

chariot ['tʃæriət] *n* : char *m*

charisma [kə'rɪzmə] *n* : charisme *m*

charismatic [,kærəz'mæt̬ɪk] *adj* : charismatique

charitable ['tʃærət̬əbəl] *adj* : charitable, caritatif <a charitable organization : une organisation caritative>
charitably ['tʃærət̬əbli] *adv* : charitablement
charity ['tʃærət̬i] *n, pl* **-ties 1** GOODWILL : charité *f* **2** GENEROSITY : charité *f,* générosité *f* **3** ALMS : aumônes *fpl* **4** : organisation *f* caritative
charlatan ['ʃɑrlətən] *n* : charlatan *m*
charley horse ['tʃɑrli,hɔrs] *n* : courbature *f* (de jambe)
charm[1] ['tʃɑrm] *vt* : charmer, enchanter
charm[2] *n* **1** SPELL : charme *m,* sortilège *m* **2** AMULET : amulette *f* <a lucky charm : un porte-bonheur> **3** APPEAL : charme *m* **4** : breloque *f* <a charm bracelet : un bracelet à breloques>
charming ['tʃɑrmɪŋ] *adj* : charmant, engageant
charmingly ['tʃɑrmɪŋli] *adv* : de façon charmante
chart[1] ['tʃɑrt] *vt* **1** MAP : porter (une route) sur la carte **2** GRAPH : faire la courbe de **3** *or* **to chart out** : tracer (un plan, etc.)
chart[2] *n* **1** MAP : carte *f* (marine) **2** GRAPH, DIAGRAM : courbe *f,* graphique *m,* tableau *m*
charter[1] ['tʃɑrt̬ər] *vt* **1** : accorder une charte à (une organisation) **2** HIRE : affréter, noliser <chartered flights : vols affrétés>
charter[2] *n* **1** STATUTES : charte *f,* statuts *mpl* **2** LEASE : affrètement *m*
chartreuse [ʃɑr'tru:z, -'tru:s] *n* : couleur *f* vert-jaune intense
chary ['tʃæri] *adj* **charier; -est** : prudent, méfiant, circonspect
chase[1] ['tʃeɪs] *v* **chased; chasing** *vt* **1** PURSUE : poursuivre, courir après **2** *or* **to chase away** : chasser <he chased the dog from the garden : il a chassé le chien du jardin> **3** : ciseler (des métaux)
chase[2] *n* **1** PURSUIT : poursuite *f* **2 the chase** HUNTING : la chasse
chasm ['kæzəm] *n* : gouffre *m,* abîme *m*
chassis ['tʃæsi, 'ʃæsi] *ns & pl* : châssis *m*
chaste ['tʃeɪst] *adj* **chaster; chastest 1** MODEST : chaste, pure **2** AUSTERE : austère, sévère
chastely ['tʃeɪstli] *adv* : chastement
chasten ['tʃeɪsən] *vt* DISCIPLINE : châtier
chastise ['tʃæs,taɪz, tʃæs'-] *vt* **-tised; -tising 1** PUNISH : châtier, punir **2** CASTIGATE : fustiger, critiquer
chastisement ['tʃæs,taɪzmənt, tʃæs'taɪz-, 'tʃæstəz-] *n* : châtiment *m,* admonition *f*
chastity ['tʃæstət̬i] *n* : chasteté *f*
chat[1] ['tʃæt] *vi* **chatted; chatting** : bavarder, causer, placoter *Can fam*
chat[2] *n* : causerie *f,* causette *f fam*
château [ʃæ'to:] *n, pl* **-teaus** [-'to:z] *or* **-teaux** [-'to:, -'to:z] : château *m*
chattel ['tʃæt̬əl] *n* : bien *m* meuble <goods and chattels : biens et effets>
chatter[1] ['tʃæt̬ər] *vi* **1** : claquer (se dit des dents) **2** GAB : bavarder, papoter, jacasser
chatter[2] *n* **1** : claquement *m* (de dents) **2** GABBING : bavardage *m,* papotage *m*
chatterbox ['tʃæt̬ər,bɑks] *n* : moulin *m* à paroles *fam*
chatterer ['tʃæt̬ərər] *n* : bavard *m,* -varde *f*
chatty ['tʃæt̬i] *adj* **chattier; -est** : bavard
chauffeur[1] ['ʃo:fər, ʃo'fər] *vi* : travailler comme chauffeur — *vt* : conduire
chauffeur[2] *n* : chauffeur *m*
chauvinism ['ʃo:və,nɪzəm] *n* : chauvinisme *m*
chauvinist[1] ['ʃo:vənɪst] *or* **chauvinistic** [,ʃo:və'nɪstɪk] *adj* : chauvin
chauvinist[2] *n* : chauvin *m,* -vine *f*
cheap[1] ['tʃi:p] *adv* : à bon marché, au rabais
cheap[2] *adj* **1** INEXPENSIVE : bon marché **2** SHODDY : de mauvaise qualité **3** STINGY : mesquin
cheapen ['tʃi:pən] *vt* **1** : baisser le prix de **2** DEGRADE, LOWER : rabaisser, abaisser
cheaply ['tʃi:pli] *adv* : à bon marché, à bon compte
cheapskate ['tʃi:p,skeɪt] *n* : radin *m,* -dine *f fam*
cheat[1] ['tʃi:t] *vt* : frauder, tromper, duper — *vi* **to cheat on** : tricher à (un examen, etc.), tromper (un époux)
cheat[2] *n* **1** DECEPTION : déception *f,* fraude *f* **2** → **cheater**
cheater ['tʃi:t̬ər] *n* : tricheur *m,* -cheuse *f;* fraudeur *m,* -deuse *f*
check[1] ['tʃɛk] *vt* **1** HALT : freiner, arrêter **2** RESTRAIN : retenir, contenir **3** VERIFY : vérifier **4** INSPECT : inspecter, contrôler **5** MARK : cocher **6** : enregistrer (ses bagages), mettre au vestiaire (un manteau, un chapeau) **7** CHECKER : faire des carreaux — *vi* **1** STOP : s'arrêter **2** CONFIRM : vérifier
check[2] *n* **1** HALT : arrêt *m,* pause *f* **2** RESTRAINT : limite *f,* frein *m* **3** INSPECTION : contrôle *m,* vérification *f* **4** *or Brit* **cheque** : chèque *m* <to pay by check : payer par chèque> **5** : ticket *m* <baggage check : ticket de bagages> **6** BILL : addition *f,* note *f* **7** SQUARE : carreau *m* **8** MARK, TICK : croix *f* **9** : échec *m* au roi (aux échecs)
checker[1] ['tʃɛkər] *vt* : marquer avec des carreaux
checker[2] *n* **1** : pièce *f* (de jeu de dames) **2** CASHIER : caissier *m,* -sière *f* **3** SQUARE : carreau *m* **4** : personne *f* qui vérifie qqch

checkerboard ['tʃɛkər,bɔrd] *n* : damier *m*
checkers ['tʃɛkərz] *n* : jeu *m* de dames
check in *vi* : s'inscrire (à l'hôtel), enregistrer
checkmate[1] ['tʃɛk,meɪt] *vt* **1** THWART : contrecarrer **2** : faire échec et mat à (aux échecs)
checkmate[2] *n* : échec *m* et mat
check out *vt* INVESTIGATE : enquêter sur, vérifier — *vi* : régler sa note (à l'hôtel)
checkpoint ['tʃɛk,pɔɪnt] *n* : poste *m* de contrôle
checkup ['tʃɛk,ʌp] *n* : examen *m* médical, bilan *m* de santé
cheddar ['tʃɛdər] *n* : cheddar *m*
cheek ['tʃik] *n* **1** : joue *f* **2** IMPUDENCE : culot *m fam,* toupet *m fam*
cheeky ['tʃi:ki] *adj* **cheekier; -est** : effronté, culotté *fam*
cheep[1] ['tʃi:p] *vi* : piauler
cheep[2] *n* : piaulement *m*
cheer[1] ['tʃɪr] *vt* **1** COMFORT : encourager, réconforter <his card cheered me up : sa carte m'a remonté le moral> **2** GLADDEN : réjouir **3** ACCLAIM : applaudir, acclamer
cheer[2] *n* **1** GLADNESS : bonne humeur *f,* gaieté *f* **2** APPLAUSE : acclamation *f,* bravos *mpl* **3 cheers!** : à votre santé!, à la vôtre!
cheerful ['tʃɪrfəl] *adj* : de bonne humeur, joyeux, gaie
cheerfully ['tʃɪrfəli] *adv* : joyeusement, gaiement
cheerfulness ['tʃɪrfəlnəs] *n* : gaieté *f*
cheerily ['tʃɪrəli] *adv* : joyeusement
cheerleader ['tʃɪr,li:dər] *n* : meneuse *f* de claque *Can*
cheerless ['tʃɪrləs] *adj* : sombre, triste, morne
cheery ['tʃɪri] *adj* **cheerier; -est** : gai, joyeux
cheese ['tʃi:z] *n* : fromage *m*
cheesecloth ['tʃi:z,klɔθ] *n* : étamine *f*
cheesy ['tʃi:zi] *adj* **cheesier; -est 1** : qui a le goût de fromage, qui sent le fromage **2** CHEAP, TACKY : de mauvaise qualité, minable
cheetah ['tʃi:ţə] *n* : guépard *m*
chef ['ʃɛf] *n* : cuisinier *m,* -nière *f;* chef *m* cuisinier
chemical[1] ['kɛmɪkəl] *adj* : chimique — **chemically** [-mɪkli] *adv*
chemical[2] *n* : produit *m* chimique
chemise [ʃə'mi:z] *n* **1** : chemise *f* (de femme) **2** *or* **chemise dress** : robe-chemisier *f*
chemist ['kɛmɪst] *n* : chimiste *mf*
chemistry ['kɛmɪstri] *n, pl* **-tries** : chimie *f*
chemotherapy [,ki:mo'θɛrəpi, ,kɛmo-] *n, pl* **-pies** : chimiothérapie *f*
chenille [ʃə'ni:l] *n* : chenille *f*
cheque *Brit* → **check**[2] **4**
cherish ['tʃɛrɪʃ] *vt* **1** LOVE : chérir, aimer **2** HARBOR, ENTERTAIN : caresser, tenir à (des espoirs, etc.)
cherry ['tʃɛri] *n, pl* **cherries** : cerise *f* (fruit), cerisier *m* (arbre)
cherub ['tʃɛrəb] *n* **1** *pl* **cherubim** ['tʃɛrə,bɪm, 'tʃɛrjə-] ANGEL : chérubin *m,* ange *m* **2** *pl* **cherubs** : angelot *m,* enfant *m* au visage angélique
cherubic [tʃɛ'ru:bɪk] *adj* : de chérubin, angélique
chess ['tʃɛs] *n* : échecs *mpl*
chest ['tʃɛst] *n* **1** BOX : coffre *m,* caisse *f* **2** : poitrine *f* <chest pain : douleur à la poitrine>
chestnut[1] ['tʃɛsţ,nʌt] *adj* : châtain (couleur)
chestnut[2] *n* **1** : marron *m,* châtaigne *f* (fruit) **2** : marronier *m,* châtaignier *m* (arbre)
chest of drawers *n* : commode *f*
chevron ['ʃɛvrən] *n* : chevron *m*
chew[1] ['tʃu:] *vt* **1** : mâcher, mastiquer **2** : chiquer (du tabac)
chew[2] *n* : chique *f* (de tabac)
chewing gum *n* : chewing-gum *m France,* gomme *f* à mâcher
chic[1] ['ʃi:k] *adj* : chic, élégant, à la mode
chic[2] *n* : chic *m,* élégance *f*
chick ['tʃɪk] *n* **1** : poussin *m* (de poulet) **2** FLEDGLING : oisillon *m*
chickadee ['tʃɪkədi] *n* : mésange *f* à tête noire
chicken ['tʃɪkən] *n* **1** : poulet *m* **2** COWARD : poltron *m,* -tronne *f;* poule *f* mouillée *fam*
chickenhearted ['tʃɪkən,hɑrţəd] *adj* : poltron, peureux
chicken pox *n* : varicelle *f*
chicle ['tʃɪkəl] *n* : chiclé *m*
chicory ['tʃɪkəri] *n, pl* **-ries 1** : endive *f* (pour les salades) **2** : chicorée *f* (additif de café)
chide ['tʃaɪd] *vt* **chid** ['tʃɪd] *or* **chided; chid** *or* **chidden** ['tʃɪdən] *or* **chided; chiding** ['tʃaɪdɪŋ] : gronder, réprimander
chief[1] ['tʃi:f] *adj* : principal, en chef <chief editor : rédacteur en chef>
chief[2] *n* : chef *m*
chiefly ['tʃi:fli] *adv* : principalement, surtout
chieftain ['tʃi:ftən] *n* : chef *m* (d'une tribu)
chiffon [ʃɪ'fɑn, 'ʃɪ,-] *n* : mousseline *f* (de soie)
chigger ['tʃɪgər] *n* : aoûtat *m*
chignon ['ʃi:n,jɑn, -jɔn] *n* : chignon *m*
chilblain ['tʃɪl,bleɪn] *n* : engelure *f*
child ['tʃaɪld] *n, pl* **children** ['tʃɪldrən] **1** YOUNGSTER : enfant *mf* **2** OFFSPRING : fils *m,* fille *f*
childbirth ['tʃaɪld,bərθ] *n* : accouchement *m*
childhood ['tʃaɪld,hʊd] *n* : enfance *f*
childish ['tʃaɪldɪʃ] *adj* : puéril, enfantin
childishly ['tʃaɪldɪʃli] *adv* : puérilement

childishness ['tʃaɪldɪʃnəs] *n* : puérilité *f*, enfantillage *m*

childless ['tʃaɪldləs] *adj* : sans enfants

childlike ['tʃaɪld,laɪk] *adj* : enfantin, d'enfant <a childlike voice : une voix d'enfant>

childproof ['tʃaɪld,pru:f] *adj* : de sécurité pour enfants

Chilean[1] ['tʃɪliən, tʃɪ'leɪən] *adj* : chilien

Chilean[2] *n* : Chilien *m*, -lienne *f*

chili *or* **chile** *or* **chilli** ['tʃɪli] *n, pl* **chilies** *or* **chiles** *or* **chillies 1** *or* **chili pepper** : piment *m* fort **2** : chili *m* con carne

chill[1] ['tʃɪl] *vt* : refroidir, réfrigérer, mettre au frais — *vi* : se refroidir

chill[2] *adj* : frais <a chill wind : un vent frais>

chill[3] *n* **1** CHILLINESS : fraîcheur *f*, froideur *f* **2** SHIVER : frisson *m* <it sent a chill down my spine : ça m'a donné des frissons> **3 to catch a chill** : attraper un coup de froid

chilliness ['tʃɪlinəs] *n* : fraîcheur *f*, froideur *f*

chilly ['tʃɪli] *adj* **chillier; -est** : frais, froid

chime[1] ['tʃaɪm] *v* **chimed; chiming** *vt* : sonner <to chime the hour : sonner l'heure> — *vi* : carillonner, sonner

chime[2] *n* : carillon *m*

chime in *vi* : interrompre

chimera *or* **chimaera** [kaɪ'mɪrə, kə-] *n* : chimère *f*

chimney ['tʃɪmni] *n, pl* **-neys 1** : cheminée *f* **2** : verre *m* (d'une lampe)

chimney sweep *n* : ramoneur *m*

chimp ['tʃɪmp, 'ʃɪmp] → **chimpanzee**

chimpanzee [,tʃɪm,pæn'zi:, ,ʃɪm-; tʃɪm'pænzi, ʃɪm-] *n* : chimpanzé *m*

chin *n* : menton *m*

china ['tʃaɪnə] *n* **1** PORCELAIN : porcelaine *f* **2** TABLEWARE : vaisselle *f*

chinchilla [tʃɪn'tʃɪlə] *n* : chinchilla *m*

Chinese[1] [tʃaɪ'ni:z, -ni:s] *adj* : chinois

Chinese[2] *n* **1** : Chinois *m*, -noise *f* **2** : chinois *m* (langue)

chink ['tʃɪŋk] *n* : fente *f*, fissure *f*

chintz ['tʃɪnts] *n* : chintz *m*

chip[1] ['tʃɪp] *v* **chipped; chipping** *vt* : ébrécher, éborgner *Can* (de la vaisselle, etc.), écorner (des meubles), écailler (de la peinture) — *vi* **1** : s'ébrécher, s'écorner, s'écailler **2 to chip in** CONTRIBUTE : contribuer

chip[2] *n* **1** PIECE : éclat *m* (de verre, etc.), copeau *m* (de bois ou de métal), fragment *m* <he's a chip off the old block : il est bien le fils de son père> **2** COUNTER : jeton *m* (de poker, etc.) **3** NICK : ébréchure *f* **4** *or* **computer chip** : puce *f* **5** → **potato chips**

chipmunk ['tʃɪp,mʌŋk] *n* : tamia *m*, suisse *m Can*

chipper ['tʃɪpər] *adj* : vif, en pleine forme

chiropodist [kə'rɑpədɪst, ʃə-] PODIATRIST : pédicure *mf*, podologue *mf*

chiropody [kə'rɑpədi, ʃe-] PODIATRY : podologie *f*

chiropractic ['kaɪrə,præktɪk] *n* : chiropraxie *f*, chiropractie *f*, chiropractique *f Can*

chiropractor ['kaɪrə,præktər] *n* : chiropraticien *m*, -cienne *f*

chirp[1] ['tʃərp] *vi* : pépier (se dit des oiseaux), chanter (se dit des insectes)

chirp[2] *n* : pépiement *m*, chant *m*

chisel[1] ['tʃɪzəl] *vt* **-eled** *or* **-elled; -eling** *or* **-elling 1** : ciseler, tailler au ciseau **2** CHEAT : carotter *fam*

chisel[2] *n* : ciseau *m*

chit ['tʃɪt] *n* VOUCHER : bon *m*, note *f*

chitchat ['tʃɪt,tʃæt] *n* : bavardage *m*

chivalric [ʃə'vælrɪk] → **chivalrous**

chivalrous ['ʃɪvəlrəs] *adj* **1** KNIGHTLY : chevaleresque **2** GENTLEMANLY : galant, courtois

chivalry ['ʃɪvəlri] *n, pl* **-ries 1** : chevalerie *f* **2** COURTESY : courtoisie *f*, galanterie *f*

chive ['tʃaɪv] *n* : ciboulette *f*

chloride ['klo,raɪd] *n* : chlorure *m*

chlorinate ['klorə,neɪt] *vt* **-nated; -nating** : javelliser

chlorination [,klorə'neɪʃən] *n* : javellisation *f*

chlorine ['klor,i:n] *n* : chlore *m*

chloroform[1] ['klorə,fɔrm] *vt* : chloroformer

chloroform[2] *n* : chloroforme *m*

chlorophyll ['klorə,fɪl] *n* : chlorophylle *f*

chock–full ['tʃɑk'fʊl, 'tʃʌk-] *adj* : bondé, plein à craquer

chocolate ['tʃɑkələt, 'tʃɔk-] *n* : chocolat *m*

choice[1] ['tʃɔɪs] *adj* **choicer; choicest** EXCELLENT, SELECT : de choix, de première qualité

choice[2] *n* : choix *m*

choir ['kwaɪr] *n* : chœur *m*

choke[1] ['tʃo:k] *v* **choked; choking** *vt* **1** STRANGLE : étrangler, asphyxier, étouffer **2** BLOCK : boucher, embouteiller, obstruer — *vi* : s'étouffer, s'étrangler <to choke to death : mourir étouffé>

choke[2] *n* **1** CHOKING : étouffement *m* **2** : starter *m* (d'une voiture)

choker ['tʃo:kər] *n* : collier *m* court

cholera ['kɑlərə] *n* : choléra *m*

cholesterol [kə'lɛstə,rɔl] *n* : cholestérol *m*

choose ['tʃu:z] *v* **chose** ['tʃo:z]; **chosen** ['tʃo:zən]; **choosing** *vt* **1** SELECT : choisir, élire <to choose sides : choisir son camp> **2** DECIDE : décider **3** PREFER : préférer, aimer mieux — *vi* : choisir

choosy *or* **choosey** ['tʃu:zi] *adj* **choosier; -est** : difficile, exigeant

chop[1] ['tʃɑp] *vt* **chopped; chopping 1** : couper <to chop wood : couper du bois> **2** MINCE : hacher (des légumes, etc.) **3 to chop down** : abattre **4 to chop off** : trancher, couper

chop[2] *n* **1** BLOW, CUT : coup *m* **2** : côtelette *f* <pork chops : côtelettes de porc> **3 chops** *npl* : joue *f* (d'une personne), bajoues *fpl* (d'un animal) <to lick one's chops : se lécher les babines>

chopper ['tʃɑpər] → **helicopter**

choppy ['tʃɑpi] *adj* **choppier; -est 1** : agité <a choppy sea : une mer agitée> **2** DISCONNECTED, JERKY : saccadé, discontinu, irrégulier

chopsticks ['tʃɑp,stɪks] *npl* : baguettes *fpl*

choral ['korəl] *adj* : choral

chorale [kə'ræl, -'rɑl] *n* **1** : choral *m*, chant *m* religieux **2** CHOIR, CHORUS : chorale *f*

chord ['kɔrd] *n* **1** : accord *m* (en musique) **2** : corde *f* (géométrique)

chore ['tʃor] *n* **1** TASK : besogne *f*, travail *m* de routine <household chores : travaux ménagers> **2** BURDEN : corvée *f*

choreograph ['koriə,græf] *vt* : chorégraphier

choreographer [,kori'ɑgrəfər] *n* : chorégraphe *mf*

choreography [,kori'ɑgrəfi] *n, pl* **-phies** : chorégraphie *f* — **choreographic** [-ə'græfɪk] *adj*

chorister ['korɪstər] *n* : choriste *mf*

chortle[1] ['tʃɔrt̬əl] *vi* **-tled; -tling** : glousser

chortle[2] *n* : gloussement *m*, petit rire *m*

chorus[1] ['korəs] *vt* : chanter en chœur

chorus[2] *n* **1** : chœur *m* (de chanteurs), troupe *f* (de danseurs) **2** REFRAIN : refrain *m* **3** SONG : chœur *m*, choral *m* **4** : concert *m* <a chorus of cries : un concert de cris>

chose → **choose**

chosen ['tʃo:zən] *adj* : choisi, privilégié <the chosen few : les privilégiés>

chow ['tʃaʊ] *n* **1** FOOD, GRUB : bouffe *f fam* **2** → **chow chow**

chow chow ['tʃaʊ,tʃaʊ] *n* : chow-chow *m* (chien)

chowder ['tʃaʊdər] *n* : soupe *f* au poisson, soupe *f* aux fruits de mer

christen ['krɪsən] *vt* **1** BAPTIZE : baptiser **2** NAME : appeler, nommer

Christendom ['krɪsəndəm] *n* : chrétienté *f*

christening ['krɪsənɪŋ] *n* : baptême *m*

Christian[1] ['krɪstʃən] *adj* : chrétien

Christian[2] *n* : chrétien *m*, -tienne *f*

Christianity [,krɪstʃi'ænət̬i, ,krɪs'tʃæ-] *n* : christianisme *m*

Christian name *n* : nom *m* de baptême, prénom *m*

Christmas ['krɪsməs] *n* : Noël *m* <the Christmas season : la période de Noël>

chromatic [kro:'mæt̬ɪk] *adj* : chromatique

chrome ['kro:m] *n* : chrome *m*

chromium ['kro:miəm] *n* : chrome *m*

chromosome ['kro:mə,so:m, -,zo:m] *n* : chromosome *m*

chronic ['krɑnɪk] *adj* : chronique — **chronically** [-nɪkli] *adv*

chronicle[1] ['krɑnɪkəl] *vt* **-cled; -cling** : faire la chronique de, écrire une chronique de

chronicle[2] *n* : chronique *f*

chronicler ['krɑnɪklər] *n* : chroniqueur *m*, -queuse *f*

chronological [,krɑnəl'ɑdʒɪkəl] *adj* : chronologique — **chronologically** [-kli] *adv*

chronology [krə'nɑlədʒi] *n, pl* **-gies** : chronologie *f*

chronometer [krə'nɑmət̬ər] *n* : chronomètre *m*

chrysalis ['krɪsələs] *n, pl* **chrysalides** [krɪ'sælə,di:z] *or* **chrysalises**: chrysalide *f*

chrysanthemum [krɪ'sæn*t*θəməm] *n* : chrysanthème *m*

chubby ['tʃʌbi] *adj* **chubbier; -est** : dodu, potelé, grassouillet

chuck[1] ['tʃʌk] *vt* **1** PAT, TAP : tapoter <to chuck s.o. under the chin : tapoter le menton de qqn> **2** TOSS : tirer, lancer **3** GIVE UP : renoncer à, laisser tomber (une activité)

chuck[2] *n* **1** PAT, TAP : tapotement *m* **2** TOSS : lancer *m* **3** *or* **chuck steak** : paleron *m* de bœuf

chuckle[1] ['tʃʌkəl] *vi* **-led; -ling** : glousser, rire tout bas

chuckle[2] *n* : gloussement *m*, petit rire *m*

chug ['tʃʌg] *vi* **chugged; chugging** PUFF : haleter (se dit d'un moteur)

chum[1] ['tʃʌm] *vi* **chummed; chumming** : être copain, être copine <to chum around with : être copain avec>

chum[2] *n* : copain *m*, -pine *f;* camarade *mf*

chummy ['tʃʌmi] **chummier; -est** : familier, amical, sociable

chump ['tʃʌmp] *n* : gourde *f fam;* idiot *m*, -diote *f*

chunk ['tʃʌŋk] *n* **1** PIECE : morceau *m* **2** : grande quantité *f* (d'argent, etc.)

chunky ['tʃʌŋki] *adj* **chunkier; -est 1** STOCKY : trapu **2** : qui contient des morceaux

church ['tʃərtʃ] *n* **1** : église *f* **2** : Église *f* <Church and State : l'Église et l'État> **3** DENOMINATION : culte *m*, confession *f* **4** CONGREGATION : assemblée *f* de fidèles

churchgoer ['tʃərtʃ,go:ər] *n* : pratiquant *m*, -quante *f*

churchyard ['tʃərtʃ,jɑrd] *n* : cimetière *m* (autour d'une église)

churn[1] ['tʃərn] *vt* **1** : battre (du beurre), baratter (de la crème) **2** STIR : agiter, remuer — *vi* : bouillonner

churn[2] *n* : baratte *f*

chute ['ʃuːt] *n* **1** : glissière *f* (de paquets, etc.) **2** : piste *f* de toboggan (aux sports) **3** → **parachute**
chutney ['tʃʌtni] *n, pl* **-neys** : chutney *m*
chutzpah ['hʊtspə, 'xʊt-, -ˌspɑ] *n* GALL, NERVE : culot *m fam,* toupet *m fam*
cicada [sə'keɪdə, -'kɑ-] *n* : cigale *f*
cider ['saɪdər] *n* : cidre *m*
cigar [sɪ'gɑr] *n* : cigare *m*
cigarette [ˌsɪgə'rɛt, 'sɪgəˌrɛt] *n* : cigarette *f*
cinch[1] ['sɪntʃ] *vt* **1** : sangler (un cheval) **2** : attacher (une selle) par une sangle
cinch[2] *n* **1** : sangle *f* (de selle) **2** : quelque chose facile ou sûr <it's a cinch : c'est du gateau>
cincture ['sɪŋktʃər] *n* : ceinture *f* (d'un religieux)
cinder ['sɪndər] *n* **1** EMBER : morceau *m* de braise **2 cinders** *npl* ASHES : cendres *fpl*
cinema ['sɪnəmə] *n* : cinéma *m*
cinematic [ˌsɪnə'mæt̬ɪk] *adj* : cinématographique
cinnamon ['sɪnəmən] *n* : cannelle *f*
cipher ['saɪfər] *n* **1** ZERO : zéro *m* **2** CODE : chiffre *m,* code *m* secret
circa ['sərkə] *prep* : environ, vers <born circa 1700 : né au début du 18e siècle>
circle[1] ['sərkəl] *v* **-cled; -cling** *vt* **1** SURROUND : entourer, encercler **2** : tourner autour de, faire le tour de <the earth circles the sun : la terre tourne autour du soleil> — *vi* : faire des cercles
circle[2] *n* **1** : cercle *m* **2** CYCLE : cycle *m* <to come full circle : boucler la boucle> **3** GROUP : cercle *m,* milieu *m* (social)
circuit ['sərkət] *n* **1** BOUNDARY : limite *f,* frontière *f* **2** TOUR : circuit *m,* tour *m* **3** : circuit *m* (électrique)
circuit breaker *n* : disjoncteur *m*
circuitous [ˌsər'kjuːət̬əs] *adj* **1** : détourné, indirect <a circuitous route : un chemin détourné> **2** : contourné, compliqué <circuitous reasoning : raisonnement contourné>
circuitry ['sərkətri] *n, pl* **-ries** : système *m* de circuits
circular[1] ['sərkjələr] *adj* ROUND : circulaire, rond
circular[2] *n* **1** LEAFLET : circulaire *f* **2** ADVERTISEMENT : prospectus *m*
circulate ['sərkjəˌleɪt] *v* **-lated; -lating** *vt* : faire circuler, propager <to circulate a rumor : propager une rumeur> — *vi* : circuler
circulation [ˌsərkjə'leɪʃən] *n* **1** FLOW : circulation *f* **2** : tirage *m* (d'un journal)
circulatory ['sərkjələˌtori] *adj* : circulatoire
circumcise ['sərkəmˌsaɪz] *vt* **-cised; -cising** : circoncire
circumcision [ˌsərkəm'sɪʒən, 'sərkəmˌ-] *n* : circoncision *f*
circumference [sər'kʌmpfrənts] *n* : circonférence *f*
circumflex ['sərkəmˌflɛks] *n* : accent *m* circonflexe
circumlocution [ˌsərkəmlo'kjuːʃən] *n* : circonlocution *f*
circumnavigate [ˌsərkəm'nævəˌgeɪt] *vt* **-gated; -gating** : faire le tour de, contourner
circumscribe ['sərkəmˌskraɪb] *vt* **1** : circonscrire (en géométrie) **2** LIMIT : circonscrire, limiter
circumspect ['sərkəmˌspɛkt] *adj* : circonspect, prudent
circumspection [ˌsərkəm'spɛkʃən] *n* : circonspection *f,* prudence *f*
circumstance ['sərkəmˌstænts] *n* **1** EVENT, FACT : circonstance *f,* événement *m* **2 circonstances** *npl* CONDITIONS : circonstances *fpl,* situation *f* <financial circumstances : situation financière> <under no circumstances : en aucun cas>
circumstantial [ˌsərkəm'stæntʃəl] *adj* **1** INCIDENTAL : accidentel, fortuit <circumstantial evidence : preuves indirectes> **2** DETAILED : détaillé, circonstancié
circumvent [ˌsərkəm'vɛnt] *vt* : contourner, circonvenir <to circumvent the law : contourner la loi>
circus ['sərkəs] *n* : cirque *m*
cirrhosis [sə'roːsɪs] *n, pl* **-rhoses** [-ˌsiːz] : cirrhose *f*
cirrus ['sɪrəs] *n, pl* **-ri** ['sɪrˌaɪ] : cirrus *m*
cistern ['sɪstərn] *n* TANK : citerne *f*
citadel ['sɪt̬ədəl, -ˌdɛl] *n* : citadelle *f*
citation [saɪ'teɪʃən] *n* : citation *f*
cite ['saɪt] *vt* **cited; citing 1** SUMMON : citer, appeler (en justice) **2** QUOTE : citer **3** COMMEND : citer
citizen ['sɪt̬əzən] *n* : citoyen *m,* -toyenne *f*
citizenry ['sɪtəzənri] *n, pl* **-ries** : ensemble *m* des citoyens
citizenship ['sɪt̬əzənˌʃɪp] *n* : citoyenneté *f*
citron ['sɪtrən] *n* : cédrat *m*
citrus ['sɪtrəs] *n, pl* **citrus** *or* **citruses** *or* **citrus fruit** : agrume *m*
city ['sɪt̬i] *n, pl* **cities** : ville *f*
city hall *n* : hôtel *m* de ville
civic ['sɪvɪk] *adj* : civique
civics ['sɪvɪks] *ns & pl* : instruction *f* civique
civil ['sɪvəl] *adj* **1** : civil <civil engineering : génie civil> **2** POLITE : courtois, civil
civilian [sə'vɪljən] *n* : civil *m,* -vile *f*
civility [sə'vɪlət̬i] *n, pl* **-ties** POLITENESS : civilité *f,* courtoisie *f*
civilization [ˌsɪvələ'zeɪʃən] *n* : civilisation *f*
civilize ['sɪvəˌlaɪz] *vt* **-lized; -lizing** : civiliser

civilly [ˈsɪvəli] *adj* : poliment
civil rights *npl* : droits *mpl* civiques, droits *mpl* civils
civil service *n* : fonction *f* publique
civil war *n* : guerre *f* civile
clack[1] [ˈklæk] *vi* : cliqueter
clack[2] *n* : cliquetis *m*
clad [ˈklæd] *adj* **1** CLOTHED : vêtu, habillé **2** COVERED : couvert
claim[1] [ˈkleɪm] *vt* **1** DEMAND : revendiquer, réclamer <to claim one's rights : réclamer ses droits> **2** MAINTAIN : déclarer, prétendre <he claims to know you : il prétend vous connaître> **3 to claim a life** : faire un mort, faire une victime
claim[2] *n* **1** DEMAND : revendication *f*, demande *f* **2** ASSERTION : déclaration *f*, affirmation *f* **3** *or* **land claim** : concession *f* (de terrain)
clairvoyance [klærˈvɔɪənts] *n* : voyance *f*, don *m* de seconde vue
clairvoyant[1] [klærˈvɔɪənt] *adj* : doué de seconde vue
clairvoyant[2] *n* : voyant *m*, -voyante *f*
clam [ˈklæm] *n* : palourde *f*
clamber [ˈklæmbər] *vi* : grimper, se hisser (avec difficulté)
clammy [ˈklæmi] *adj* **clammier; -est** : moite, humide et froid
clamor[1] *or Brit* **clamour** [ˈklæmər] *vi* **1** : vociférer, crier **2 to clamor for** : demander, réclamer
clamor[2] *or Brit* **clamour** *n* **1** UPROAR : clameur *f*, vociférations *fpl* **2** DEMAND : réclamations *fpl* **3** PROTEST : protestation *f*
clamorous [ˈklæmərəs] *adj* : bruyant, vociférant
clamour *Brit* → **clamor**
clamp[1] [ˈklæmp] *vt* **1** CLENCH : serrer <she clamped her mouth shut : elle serrait les mâchoires> **2** ATTACH : cramponner, fixer
clamp[2] *n* : crampon *m*, pince *f*
clan [ˈklæn] *n* : clan *m*
clandestine [klænˈdɛstɪn] *adj* : clandestin, secret
clang[1] [ˈklæŋ] *vi* : résonner, retentir
clang[2] *n* : bruit *m* métallique
clangor *or Brit* **clangour** [ˈklæŋər, -gər] *n* : suite *f* de bruits métalliques
clank[1] [ˈklæŋk] *vi* : résonner, cliqueter
clank[2] *n* : cliquetis *m*
clannish [ˈklænɪʃ] *adj* : exclusif, fermé
clap[1] [ˈklæp] *vt* **clapped; clapping 1** STRIKE : frapper bruyamment **2** APPLAUD : applaudir — *vi* APPLAUD : applaudir
clap[2] *n* **1** NOISE : retentissement *m*, coup *m* <a clap of thunder : un grondement de tonnerre> **2** PAT, SLAP : claque *f*, petite tape *f* **3** APPLAUDING : applaudissement *m*
clapboard [ˈklæbərd, ˈklæpˌbord] *n* : bardeau *m* (en bois)
clapper [ˈklæpər] *n* : battant *m* (d'une cloche)
claret [ˈklærət] *n* : bordeaux *m* (vin)
clarification [ˌklærəfəˈkeɪʃən] *n* : clarification *f*
clarify [ˈklærəˌfaɪ] *vt* **-fied; -fying** : clarifier, éclaircir
clarinet [ˌklærəˈnɛt] *n* : clarinette *f*
clarinetist *or* **clarinettist** [ˌklærəˈnɛt̬ɪst] *n* : clarinettiste *mf*
clarion [ˈklæriən] *adj* : claironnant, sonore
clarity [ˈklærət̬i] *n* : clarté *f*
clash[1] [ˈklæʃ] *vi* **1** : produire un bruit métallique, résonner **2** CONFLICT, COLLIDE : s'opposer, se heurter
clash[2] *n* **1** : bruit *m* métallique, retentissement *m* **2** CONFLICT : conflit *m*, incompatibilité *f* **3** : discordance *f* (se dit des couleurs)
clasp[1] [ˈklæsp] *vt* **1** FASTEN : attacher **2** EMBRACE, GRASP : étreindre, embrasser, serrer
clasp[2] *n* **1** FASTENER : attache *f*, fermoir *m* **2** EMBRACE, HOLD : étreinte *f*, prise *f*
class[1] [ˈklæs] *vt* : classer, classifier
class[2] *n* **1** TYPE, KIND : classe *f*, division *f*, catégorie *f* **2** *or* **social class** : classe *f*, rang *m* social **3** COURSE : cours *m* <night classes : cours du soir> **4** : classe *f* (d'élèves)
classic[1] [ˈklæsɪk] *adj* : classique
classic[2] *n* : classique *m*
classical [ˈklæsɪkəl] *adj* : classique
classically [ˈklæsɪkli] *adv* : de façon classique, dans un style classique
classicism [ˈklæsəˌsɪzəm] *n* : classicisme *m*
classification [ˌklæsəfəˈkeɪʃən] *n* : classification *f*
classified [ˈklæsəˌfaɪd] *adj* **1** : classifié <classified ads : des petites annonces> **2** SECRET : secret, confidentiel
classify [ˈklæsəˌfaɪ] *vt* **-fied; -fying** : classer, classifier
classmate [ˈklæsˌmeɪt] *n* : compagnon *m* de classe, compagne *f* de classe
classroom [ˈklæsˌruːm] *n* : salle *f* de classe
clatter[1] [ˈklæt̬ər] *vi* : faire du bruit, s'entrechoquer
clatter[2] *n* : bruit *m*, cliquetis *m*
clause [ˈklɔz] *n* **1** : clause *f* (dans les actes judiciares, etc.) **2** : proposition *f* (en grammaire)
claustrophobia [ˌklɔstrəˈfoːbiə] *n* : claustrophobie *f* — **claustrophobic** [-ˈfoːbɪk] *adj*
clavicle [ˈklævɪkəl] *n* : clavicule *f*
claw[1] [ˈklɔ] *vt* : griffer
claw[2] *n* : griffe *f* (d'un chat, etc.), pince *f* (des crustacés)
clay [ˈkleɪ] *n* : argile *m*
clayey [ˈkleɪi] *adj* : argileux
clean[1] [ˈkliːn] *vt* : nettoyer, laver
clean[2] *adv* **1** FAIRLY, PROPERLY : de façon propre, sans faute (en sports) **2** COMPLETELY : complètement **3 to**

come clean about : tout dire sur, révéler
clean[3] *adj* **1** : propre **2** UNADULTERATED : pur **3** DECENT, UNSULLIED : honorable, sans tache **4** COMPLETE : définitif
cleanliness ['klɛnlinəs] *n* : propreté *f*
cleanly[1] ['kli:nli] *adv* : proprement, nettement
cleanly[2] ['klɛnli] *adj* **cleanlier; -est** : propre
cleanness ['kli:nnəs] *n* : propreté *f*
cleanse ['klɛnz] *vt* **cleansed; cleansing** : nettoyer, purifier
clear[1] ['kli:r] *vt* **1** CLARIFY : clarifier **2** *or* **to clear away** : débarrasser, déblayer, déboucher (un tuyau, etc.), dégager (une voie) <to clear the table : débarrasser la table> **3** VINDICATE : innocenter, disculper <to clear one's name : blanchir son nom, se disculper> **4** LIQUIDATE : liquider (un compte, etc.) **5** NET : réaliser, rapporter <to clear a profit : réaliser un profit> **6** : franchir, éviter <to clear a hurdle : franchir une haie> **7 to clear up** RESOLVE : résoudre (un problème) — *vi* **1** *or* **to clear up** : s'éclaircir, se lever (se dit du temps) **2** *or* **to clear up** VANISH : disparaître <the symptoms cleared up : les symptômes ont disparu> **3** : être compensé (se dit d'un chèque)
clear[2] *adv* **1** DISTINCTLY : distinctement, nettement **2** COMPLETELY : complètement **3 to get clear of** : se débarrasser de
clear[3] *adj* **1** BRIGHT : éclatant, lumineux **2** FAIR : clair, beau (se dit du temps) <a clear sky : un ciel sans nuages> **3** TRANSPARENT : transparent, clair, limpide **4** EXPLICIT, STRAIGHTFORWARD : clair, explicite, intelligible **5** FREE, UNBLOCKED : libre, dégagé
clear[4] *n* **in the clear** : libre de tout soupçon
clearance ['klırənts] *n* **1** : déblaiement *m*, dégagement *m* **2** SPACE : espace *m* libre **3** AUTHORIZATION : autorisation *f* (d'une chèque)
clearing ['klırıŋ] *n* : clairière *f* (dans un bois)
clearly ['klırli] *adv* **1** DISTINCTLY : clairement, distinctement **2** EVIDENTLY : évidemment, manifestement
cleat ['kli:t] *n* **1** : taquet *m* (d'un navire) **2 cleats** *mpl* : chaussures *fpl* à crampons
cleavage ['kli:vıdʒ] *n* **1** CLEAVING, SPLIT : clivage *m* **2** : décolleté *m* <a dress showing cleavage : une robe décolletée>
cleave[1] ['kli:v] *vi* **cleaved** ['kli:vd] *or* **clove** ['klo:v]; **cleaving** CLING : adhérer, coller
cleave[2] *vt* **cleaved; cleaving** SPLIT : diviser, fendre
cleaver ['kli:vər] *n* : couperet *m*
clef ['klɛf] *n* : clé *f*, clef *f* (en musique)
cleft ['klɛft] *n* : crevasse *f*, fissure *f*
clemency ['klɛməntsi] *n, pl* **-cies** : clémence *f*
clement ['klɛmənt] *adj* **1** LENIENT, MERCIFUL : clément, indulgent **2** MILD : doux, clément (se dit de la température)
clench ['klɛntʃ] *vt* : serrer <to clench one's fist : serrer le poing> <to clench one's teeth : serrer les dents>
clergy ['klərdʒi] *n, pl* **-gies** : clergé *m*
clergyman ['klərdʒimən] *n, pl* **-men** [-mən, -ˌmɛn] : ecclésiastique *m*
cleric ['klɛrık] *n* : ecclésiastique *m*
clerical ['klɛrıkəl] *adj* **1** : clérical, du clergé **2** : de bureau <clerical work : travail de bureau>
clerk ['klərk, *Brit* 'klɑrk] *n* **1** : commis *mf* (de bureau); employé *m*, -ployée *f* de bureau **2** SALESPERSON : vendeur *m*, -deuse *f*
clever ['klɛvər] *adj* **1** SKILLFUL : habile, adroit **2** WITTY : ingénieux, astucieux
cleverly ['klɛvərli] *adv* **1** SKILLFULLY : habilement **2** INTELLIGENTLY : astucieusement, intelligemment
cleverness ['klɛvərnəs] *n* **1** SKILL : habileté *f* **2** INTELLIGENCE : intelligence *f*
clew ['klu:] → **clue**
cliché [kli'ʃeı] *n* : cliché *m*
click[1] ['klık] *vt* : faire claquer — *vi* **1** : faire un déclic **2** AGREE, GET ALONG : bien fonctionner ensemble, bien s'entendre **3** SUCCEED : bien marcher **4** : cliquer (en informatique)
click[2] *n* : clic *m*, déclic *m*
client ['klaıənt] *n* : client *m*, cliente *f*
clientele [ˌklaıən'tɛl, ˌkli:-] *n* : clientèle *f*
cliff ['klıf] *n* : falaise *f*, escarpement *m*
climate ['klaımət] *n* : climat *m*
climax[1] ['klaıˌmæks] *vi* : atteindre un point culminant
climax[2] *n* : point *m* culminant, apogée *m*
climb[1] ['klaım] *vt* : monter, gravir, escalader <to climb a mountain : gravir une montagne> — *vi* RISE, ASCEND : monter, augmenter <prices are climbing : les prix augmentent>
climb[2] *n* : montée *f*, ascension *f*
clinch[1] ['klıntʃ] *vt* **1** FASTEN, SECURE : river (un clou), attacher **2** SETTLE : résoudre, conclure <to clinch the deal : conclure l'affaire>
clinch[2] *n* EMBRACE : étreinte *f*, corps à corps *m* (en boxe)
cling ['klıŋ] *vi* **clung** ['klʌŋ]; **clinging 1** STICK : adhérer, coller **2** : se cramponner, s'agripper <he was clinging to the railing : il se cramponnait à la balustrade>

clinic ['klɪnɪk] *n* : clinique *f*

clinical ['klɪnɪkəl] *adj* : clinique — **clinically** [-kli] *adv*

clink[1] ['klɪŋk] *vi* : tinter

clink[2] *n* : tintement *m*

clinker ['klɪŋkər] *n* : mâchefer *m,* scories *fpl*

clip[1] ['klɪp] *vt* **clipped; clipping 1** CUT : couper, tailler **2** HIT : frapper, donner un coup de poing à **3** FASTEN : attacher (avec un trombone)

clip[2] *n* **1** → **clippers 2** BLOW : coup *m,* taloche *f fam* **3** PACE : pas *m* rapide <at a good clip : à vive allure> **4** FASTENER : attache *f,* pince *f* **5** → **paper clip**

clipper ['klɪpər] *n* **1** *or* **clipper ship** : clipper *m* **2 clippers** *npl or* **nail clippers** : coupe-ongles *m* **3 clippers** *npl* SHEARS : tondeuse *f*

clique ['kli:k, 'klɪk] *n* : clique *m,* coterie *f*

clitoris ['klɪṭərəs, klɪ'tɔrəs] *n, pl* **clitorides** [-'tɔrəˌdi:z] : clitoris *m*

cloak[1] ['klo:k] *vt* : cacher, camoufler <cloaked in secrecy : empreint de secret>

cloak[2] *n* **1** CAPE : cape *f* **2** PRETENSE, DISGUISE : masque *m,* voile *m*

clobber ['klɑbər] *vt* : tabasser *fam*

clock[1] ['klɑk] *vi* : chronométrer (un coureur, etc.)

clock[2] *n* **1** : horloge *f,* chronomètre *m* (aux sports) **2 to work around the clock** : travailler 24 heures d'affilée

clockwise ['klɑkwaɪz] *adv & adj* : dans le sens des aiguilles d'une montre

clod ['klɑd] *n* **1** : motte *f* (de terre) **2** OAF : rustre *m;* lourdaud *m,* -daude *f*

clog[1] ['klɑg] *v* **clogged; clogging** *vt* **1** HINDER : entraver, gêner **2** OBSTRUCT : boucher, bloquer, obstruer — *vi or* **to clog up** : se boucher

clog[2] *n* **1** HINDRANCE : entrave *f* **2** : sabot *m* (chaussure)

cloister[1] ['klɔɪstər] *vt* : cloîtrer

cloister[2] *n* : cloître *m*

clone ['klo:n] *n* : clone *m*

close[1] ['klo:z] *v* **closed; closing** *vt* **1** SHUT : fermer **2** STOP, END : terminer, clore, conclure **3** REDUCE : réduire, diminuer <to close a gap : réduire un espace> — *vi* **1** : fermer, se fermer **2** TERMINATE : prendre fin, se terminer **3 to close in** APPROACH : se rapprocher

close[2] ['klo:s] *adv* **1** NEARBY : tout près **2** SOON : dans peu de temps **3 to hold s.o. close** : serrer qqn dans ses bras

close[3] *adj* **closer; closest 1** CONFINING : étroit, limité <to live in close quarters : vivre à l'étroit> **2** SECRETIVE : peu communicatif, réservé **3** STRICT : rigoureux, étroit <a close watch : une surveillance étroite> **4** STUFFY : mal aéré (se dit d'une salle, etc.), lourd (se dit du temps) **5** TIGHT : serré <it's a close fit : il est très serré> **6** INTIMATE : intime, proche <close friends : amies intimes> **7** ACCURATE : précis, exact <a close translation : une traduction très exacte> **8** : serré (se dit d'une concurrence) <a close contest : une lutte serrée>

close[4] ['klo:z] *n* CONCLUSION, END : fin *f,* conclusion *f*

closely ['klo:sli] *adv* **1** NEAR : de près **2** ATTENTIVELY : attentivement

closeness ['klo:snəs] *n* : proximité *f*

closet[1] ['klɑzət] *vt* : enfermer <to be closeted with s.o. : être tête à tête avec qqn>

closet[2] *n* : placard *m,* garde-robe *f,* penderie *f*

closure ['klo:ʒər] *n* : fermeture *f,* clôture *f*

clot[1] ['klɑt] *vi* **clotted; clotting** : former des caillots, se coaguler

clot[2] *n* : caillot *m*

cloth ['klɔθ] *n, pl* **cloths** ['klɔðz, 'klɔθs] **1** FABRIC : tissu *m,* étoffe *f* **2** RAG : chiffon *m* **3** TABLECLOTH : nappe *f*

clothe ['klo:ð] *vt* **clothed** *or* **clad** ['klæd]; **clothing** : habiller, vêtir

clothes ['klo:z, 'klo:ðz] *npl* **1** → **clothing 2** → **bedclothes**

clothespin ['klo:zˌpɪn, 'klo:ðz-] *n*: pince *f* (à linge)

clothier ['klo:ðjər, 'klo:ðiər] *n* : marchand *m* de vêtements

clothing ['klo:ðɪŋ] *n* : vêtements *mpl*

cloud[1] ['klaʊd] *vt* : embuer, obscurcir — *vi or* **to cloud over** : se couvrir de nuages

cloud[2] *n* **1** : nuage *m* **2** SWARM : essaim *m,* nuée *f* (d'insectes)

cloudburst ['klaʊdˌbərst] *n* : trombes *fpl* d'eau, grosse averse *f*

cloudy ['klaʊdi] *adj* **cloudier; -est** : nuageux, couvert

clout[1] ['klaʊt] *vt* : donner un coup (de poing) à

clout[2] *n* **1** BLOW : coup *m,* taloche *f fam* **2** INFLUENCE, PULL : influence *m,* pouvoir *m*

clove[1] ['klo:v] *n* **1** : clou *m* de girofle **2** *or* **garlic clove** : gousse *f* d'ail

clove[2] → **cleave**

clover ['klo:vər] *n* : trèfle *m*

cloverleaf ['klo:vərˌli:f] *n, pl* **-leafs** *or* **-leaves** [-ˌli:vz] : croisement *m* en trèfle

clown[1] ['klaʊn] *vi or* **to clown around** : faire le clown

clown[2] *n* : clown *m*

cloying ['klɔɪɪŋ] *adj* **1** DISGUSTING : écœurant **2** MAWKISH : mièvre

club[1] ['klʌb] *vt* **clubbed; clubbing** : frapper

club[2] *n* **1** BLUDGEON : massue *f,* matraque *f* **2** : club *m* (aux sports) **3** : trèfle *m* (aux cartes) **4** ASSOCIATION : club *m,* groupe *m,* association *f*

clubfoot ['klʌbˌfʊt] *n, pl* **-feet** : pied *m* bot

clubhouse ['klʌb,haʊs] *n* : club *m,* maison *f* de club

cluck[1] ['klʌk] *vi* : glousser

cluck[2] *n* : gloussement *m*

clue[1] ['klu:] *vt* **clued; clueing** *or* **cluing** INFORM : mettre au courant, informer

clue[2] *n* : indice *m,* indication *f* <I haven't got a clue : je n'ai aucune idée>

clump[1] ['klʌmp] *vi* : marcher lourdement

clump[2] *n* **1** : massif *f* (d'arbres), touffe (d'herbe) **2** : pas *m* lourd

clumsiness ['klʌmzinəs] *n* **1** AWKWARDNESS : gaucherie *f* **2** TACTLESSNESS : manque *m* de tact

clumsy ['klʌmzi] *adj* **clumsier; -est 1** AWKWARD : maladroit, gauche **2** TACTLESS : sans tact, malhabile, gauche — **clumsily** *adv*

clung → **cling**

cluster[1] ['klʌstər] *vt* : rassembler — *vi* : se rassembler, se grouper

cluster[2] *n* : groupe *m* (de personnes), grappe *f* (de raisins, etc.), ensemble *m* (de maisons, d'idées, etc.)

clutch[1] ['klʌtʃ] *vt* GRASP : saisir, étreindre — *vi* **to clutch at** : s'agripper à, se cramponner à

clutch[2] *n* **1** GRASP, GRIP : prise *f,* étreinte *f* <to fall into s.o.'s clutches : tomber dans les griffes de qqn> **2** : embrayage *m* (d'une voiture) **3** *or* **clutch pedal** : pédale *f* d'embrayage

clutter[1] ['klʌt̬ər] *vt* : encombrer, mettre en désordre

clutter[2] *n* : désordre *m,* fouillis *m*

coach[1] ['ko:tʃ] *vt* **1** : entraîner (une équipe sportive) **2** TUTOR : donner des leçons à

coach[2] *n* **1** CARRIAGE : carrosse *m* **2** : voiture *f,* wagon *m* (d'un train) **3** BUS : autocar *m,* autobus *m* **4** : deuxième classe *f* (en avion) **5** TRAINER : entraîneur *m,* -neuse *f*

coagulate [ko'ægjə,leɪt] *v* **-lated; -lating** CLOT *vt* : coaguler — *vi* : se coaguler

coagulation [ko,ægjə'leɪʃən] *n* : coagulation *f*

coal ['ko:l] *n* **1** : charbon *m,* houille *f* **2** **coals** *npl* : EMBERS : braise *f*

coalesce [,ko:ə'lɛs] *vi* **-alesced; -alescing** : s'unir

coalition [,ko:ə'lɪʃən] *n* : coalition *f*

coarse [,kors] *adj* **coarser; coarsest 1** : gros (se dit du sable, du sel, etc.), grossier (se dit des textiles), épais (se dit des cheveux, etc.) **2** CRUDE : grossier, vulgaire

coarsely [,korsli] *adv* : grossièrement

coarsen ['korsən] *vt* : rendre rude, rendre grossier — *vi* : devenir rude, devenir grossier

coarseness ['korsnəs] *n* **1** ROUGHNESS : rudesse *f* **2** CRUDENESS : grossièreté *f,* vulgarité *f*

coast[1] ['ko:st] *vi* : avancer en roue libre

coast[2] *n* : côte *f,* littoral *m*

coastal ['ko:stəl] *adj* : côtier, littoral

coaster ['ko:stər] *n* : dessous-de-verre *m,* sous-verre *m Can*

coast guard *n* : gendarmerie *f* maritime *France,* garde *f* côtière *Can*

coastline ['ko:st,laɪn] *n* : littoral *m*

coat[1] ['ko:t] *vt* : couvrir (d'une couche), enduire

coat[2] *n* **1** : manteau *m* (vêtement) **2** FUR : fourrure *f,* pelage *m,* poil *m* **3** LAYER : couche *f* <a coat of paint : une couche de peinture>

coat hanger → **hanger**

coating ['ko:t̬ɪŋ] *n* : couche *f,* revêtement *m*

coat of arms *n* : blason *m,* armoires *fpl*

coatrack ['ko:t,ræk] *n* : portemanteau *m*

coax ['ko:ks] *vt* : amadouer, cajoler, enjoler

cob ['kɑb] → **corncob**

cobalt ['ko:,bɔlt] *n* : cobalt *m*

cobble ['kɑbəl] *vt* **-bled; -bling** *or* **to cobble together** : concocter (à la hâte), bricoler

cobbled ['kɑbəld] *adj* : pavé

cobbler ['kɑblər] *n* **1** SHOEMAKER : cordonnier *m,* -nière *f* **2** *or* **fruit cobbler** : tarte *f* aux fruits

cobblestone ['kɑbəl,sto:n] *n* : pavé *m*

cobra ['ko:brə] *n* : cobra *m*

cobweb ['kɑb,wɛb] *n* : toile *f* d'araignée

cocaine [ko'keɪn, 'ko:,keɪn] *n* : cocaïne *f*

cock[1] ['kɑk] *vt* **1** : armer (un fusil) **2** TILT : pencher (la tête, etc.) **3** **to cock one's ears** : dresser les oreilles

cock[2] *n* **1** ROOSTER : coq *m* **2** FAUCET : robinet *m* **3** : chien *m* (de fusil)

cockatoo ['kɑkə,tu:] *n, pl* **-toos** : cacatoès *m*

cockeyed ['kɑk,aɪd] *adj* **1** ASKEW : de travers **2** ABSURD : absurde, insensé

cockiness ['kɑkinəs] *n* : impertinence *f,* impudence *f*

cockle ['kɑkəl] *n* : coque *f*

cockpit ['kɑk,pɪt] *n* : cockpit *m,* poste *m* de pilotage

cockroach ['kɑk,ro:tʃ] *n* : cafard *m,* blatte *f France,* coquerelle *f Can*

cocktail ['kɑk,teɪl] *n* : cocktail *m*

cocky ['kɑki] *adj* **cockier; -est** : impudent, suffisant

cocoa ['ko:,ko:] *n* : cacao *m*

coconut ['ko:kə,nʌt] *n* : noix *f* de coco

coconut palm *n* : cocotier *m*

cocoon [kə'ku:n] *n* : cocon *m*

cod ['kɑd] *ns & pl* : morue *f*

coddle ['kɑdəl] *vt* **-dled; -dling** : dorloter

code ['ko:d] *n* **1** CIPHER : code *m,* chiffre *m* **2** RULES : code *m,* règlement *m* <penal code : code pénal>

codeine ['ko:,di:n] *n* : codéine *f*

codger ['kɑdʒər] *n* : vieux bonhomme *m,* vieillard *m*

codicil ['kɑdəsəl, -ˌsɪl] *n* : codicille *m*
codify ['kɑdəˌfaɪ, 'koː-] *vt* **-fied; -fying** : codifier
coeducation [ˌkoːˌɛdʒə'keɪʃən] *n* : éducation *f* mixte
coeducational [ˌkoːˌɛdʒə'keɪʃənəl] *adj* : mixte
coefficient [ˌkoːə'fɪʃənt] *n* : coefficient *m*
coerce [ko'ərs] *vt* **-erced; -ercing** : obliger, contraindre
coercion [ko'ərʒən, -ʃən] *n* : contrainte *f*, coercition *f*
coercive [ko'ərsɪv] *adj* : coercitif
coexist [ˌkoːɪg'zɪst] *vi* : coexister
coexistence [ˌkoːɪg'zɪstən*t*s] *n* : coexistence *f*
coffee ['kɔfi] *n* : café *m*
coffeepot ['kɔfiˌpɑt] *n* : cafetière *f*
coffer ['kɔfər] *n* : coffre *m*, caisse *f*
coffin ['kɔfən] *n* : cercueil *m*, bière *f*
cog ['kɑg] *n* : dent *f* (d'une roue)
cogent ['koːdʒənt] *adj* : convaincant, persuasif
cogitate ['kɑdʒəˌteɪt] *vi* **-tated; -tating** : réfléchir, méditer
cogitation [ˌkɑdʒə'teɪʃən] *n* : réflexion *f*, méditation *f*
cognac ['koːnˌjæk] *n* : cognac *m*
cognate[1] ['kɑgˌneɪt] *adj* : apparenté
cognate[2] *n* : mot *m* apparenté
cognizant ['kɑgnəzənt] *adj* : conscient
cogwheel ['kɑgˌ*h*wiːl] *n* : roue *f* dentée, pignon *m*
cohabit [ˌkoː'hæbət] *vi* : cohabiter
cohere [ko'hɪr] *vi* **-hered; -hering 1** ADHERE : adhérer **2** : être cohérent, être logique
coherence [ko'hɪrən*t*s] *n* : cohérence *f*
coherent [ko'hɪrənt] *adj* : cohérent, logique — **coherently** *adv*
cohesion [ko'hiːʒən] *n* : cohésion *f*
cohort *n* ['koːˌhɔrt] **1** : cohorte *f* (militaire) **2** COMPANION : compagnon *m*, compagne *f*, collègue *mf*
coiffure [kwɑ'fjʊr] *n* : coiffure *f*
coil[1] ['kɔɪl] *vt* : enrouler — *vi* : s'enrouler
coil[2] *n* : rouleau *m*, bobine *f*, boucle *f* (de cheveux), volute *f* (de fumée)
coin[1] ['kɔɪn] *vt* **1** MINT : frapper (de la monnaie) **2** INVENT : forger, inventer (un mot, un terme) <to coin a phrase : comme on dit>
coin[2] *n* : pièce *f* de monnaie
coincide [ˌkoːɪn'saɪd, 'koːɪnˌsaɪd] *vi* **-cided; -ciding** : coïncider
coincidence [ko'ɪn*t*sədən*t*s] *n* : coïncidence *f*
coincidental [koˌɪn*t*sə'dɛntəl] *adj* : fortuit, de coïncidence
coincidentally [koˌɪn*t*sə'dɛntəli] *adv* : par hasard
coitus ['koːət̬əs] *n* : coït *m*
coke ['koːk] *n* : coke *m* <coke stove : four à coke>
colander ['kɑləndər, 'kʌ-] *n* : passoire *f*
cold[1] ['koːld] *adj* : froid <it's cold out : il fait froid> <my feet are cold : j'ai froid aux pieds> <to be cold toward s.o. : être froid avec qqn> <a cold heart : un cœur de pierre>
cold[2] *n* **1** : froid *m* **2** : rhume *m* (en médecine) <to have a cold : être enrhumé>
cold–blooded ['koːld'blʌdəd] *adj* **1** : à sang froid (se dit des animaux) **2** CRUEL : cruel, sans pitié
coldly ['koːldli] *adv* : avec froideur, froidement
coldness ['koːldnəs] *n* : froideur *f*
coleslaw ['koːlˌslɔ] *n* : salade *f* de chou cru
colic ['kɑlik] *n* : coliques *fpl*
coliseum [ˌkɑlə'siːəm] *n* : stade *m*, arène *f*
collaborate [kə'læbəˌreɪt] *vi* **-rated; -rating** : collaborer, coopérer
collaboration [kəˌlæbə'reɪʃən] *n* : collaboration *f*
collaborator [kə'læbəˌreɪt̬ər] *n* : collaborateur *m*, -trice *f*
collapse[1] [kə'læps] *vi* **-lapsed; -lapsing 1** : s'effondrer, s'écrouler **2** FOLD : se plier
collapse[2] *n* : effondrement *m*, écroulement *m*
collapsible [kə'læpsəbəl] *adj* : pliant <collapsible chair : chaise pliante>
collar[1] ['kɑlər] *vt* : saisir au collet, arrêter (un criminel)
collar[2] *n* : col *m*
collarbone ['kɑlərˌboːn] *n* : clavicule *f*
collate [kə'leɪt; 'kɑˌleɪt; 'koː-] *vt* **-lated; -lating 1** COMPARE : comparer **2** ASSEMBLE : collationner (les feuilles d'un livre)
collateral[1] [kə'læt̬ərəl] *adj* **1** SECONDARY : secondaire, subsidiaire **2** PARALLEL : parallèle, concomitant
collateral[2] *n* : nantissement *m*
colleague ['kɑˌliːg] *n* : confrère *m*, consœur *f*, collègue *mf*
collect[1] [kə'lɛkt] *vt* **1** GATHER : ramasser, recueillir **2** : percevoir, encaisser (une somme d'argent) **3** : collectionner (des objets) — *vi* **1** CONGREGATE : se regrouper, se rejoindre **2** ACCUMULATE : accumuler
collect[2] *adv* **to call collect** : téléphoner en PCV *France*, téléphoner à frais virés *Can*
collection [kə'lɛkʃən] *n* **1** COLLECTING : ramassage *m* (d'objets), recouvrement *m* (de dettes, etc.), rassemblement *m* (d'information), accumulation *f* (de richesses) **2** : collection *f* <book collection : collection de livres>
collective[1] [kə'lɛktɪv] *adj* : collectif
collective[2] *n* : coopérative *f*, entreprise *f* collective
college ['kɑlɪdʒ] *n* **1** : établissement *m* d'enseignement supérieur **2** GROUP

: association *f* (de professionels, etc.), collège *m* (électoral)

collegiate [kəˈliːdʒət] *adj* : universitaire

collide [kəˈlaɪd] *vi* **-lided; -liding** : se heurter, entrer en collision

collie [ˈkɑli] *n* : colley *m*

collision [kəˈlɪʒən] *n* : collision *f*

colloquial [kəˈloːkwiəl] *adj* : familier

colloquialism [kəˈloːkwiəˌlɪzəm] *n* : expression *f* familière

collusion [kəˈluːʒən] *n* : collusion *f*

cologne [kəˈloːn] *n* : eau *f* de Cologne

Colombian[1] [kəˈlʌmbiən] *adj* : colombien

Colombian[2] *n* : Colombien *m,* -bienne *f*

colon[1] [ˈkoːlən] *n, pl* **colons** *or* **cola** [-lə] : côlon *m* (en anatomie)

colon[2] *n, pl* **colons** : deux-points *m* (signe orthographique)

colonel [ˈkərnəl] *n* : colonel *m*

colonial[1] [kəˈloːniəl] *adj* : colonial

colonial[2] *n* : colonial *m,* -niale *f*

colonist [ˈkɑlənɪst] *n* : colon *m*

colonization [ˌkɑlənəˈzeɪʃən] *n* : colonisation *f*

colonize [ˈkɑləˌnaɪz] *vt* **-nized; -nizing** : établir une colonie en, coloniser

colonnade [ˌkɑləˈneɪd] *n* : colonnade *f*

colony [ˈkɑləni] *n, pl* **-nies** : colonie *f*

color[1] *or Brit* **colour** [ˈkʌlər] *vt* **1** : colorer **2** INFLUENCE : influer sur, influencer — *vi* BLUSH : rougir

color[2] *or Brit* **colour** *n* **1** : couleur *f* <bright colors : couleurs vives> **2** INTEREST, VIVIDNESS : couleur *f* <local color : couleur locale> **3 colors** *npl* FLAG : couleurs *fpl*

color–blind *or Brit* **colour–blind** [ˈkʌlərˌblaɪnd] *adj* : daltonien

colored *or Brit* **coloured** [ˈkʌlərd] *adj* **1** : coloré **2** : de couleur (se dit des personnes)

colorfast *or Brit* **colourfast** [ˈkʌlərˌfæst] *adj* : grand teint, bon teint

colorful *or Brit* **colourful** [ˈkʌlərfəl] *adj* **1** : coloré **2** PICTURESQUE, STRIKING : pittoresque, frappant, original

colorless *or Brit* **colourless** [ˈkʌlərləs] *adj* **1** : incolore **2** DULL : terne, fade

colossal [kəˈlɑsəl] *adj* : colossal

colossus [kəˈlɑsəs] *n, pl* **-si** [-ˌsaɪ] : colosse *m*

colour *Brit* → **color**

colt [ˈkoːlt] *n* : poulain *m*

column [ˈkɑləm] *n* **1** : colonne *f* (en architecture) **2** : colonne *f* (en imprimerie), rubrique *f* (dans la presse), chronique *f* (dans un journal)

columnist [ˈkɑləmnɪst, -ləmɪst] *n* : chroniqueur *m,* -queuse *f*

coma [ˈkoːmə] *n* : coma *m*

comatose [ˈkoːməˌtoːs, ˈkɑ-] *adj* : comateux, dans le coma

comb[1] [ˈkoːm] *vt* **1** : peigner <to comb one's hair : se peigner> **2** *or* **to comb out** : démêler (les cheveux) **3** SEARCH : ratisser, passer (un lieu) au peigne fin

comb[2] *n* **1** : peigne *m* **2** : crête *f* (d'un coq)

combat[1] [kəmˈbæt, ˈkɑmˌbæt] *vt* **-bated** *or* **-batted; -bating** *or* **-batting** : combattre, lutter contre

combat[2] [ˈkɑmˌbæt] *n* : combat *m*

combatant [kəmˈbætənt] *n* : combattant *m,* -tante *f*

combative [kəmˈbæt̬ɪv] *adj* : combatif, belliqueux

combination [ˌkɑmbəˈneɪʃən] *n* : combinaison *f*

combine[1] [kəmˈbaɪn] *v* **-bined; -bining** *vt* : combiner, joindre, unir — *vi* : se combiner, s'associer, s'unir

combine[2] [ˈkɑmˌbaɪn] *n* **1** ASSOCIATION : association *f,* cartel *m* (en finances) **2** HARVESTER : moisonneuse-batteuse *f*

combustible [kəmˈbʌstəbəl] *adj* : combustible, inflammable

combustion [kəmˈbʌstʃən] *n* : combustion *f*

come [ˈkʌm] *vi* **came; come; coming 1** APPROACH : venir, s'approcher <come here! : viens ici!> <he came running : il est venu en courant> **2** ARRIVE : arriver <they came last night : ils sont arrivés hier soir> **3** ORIGINATE : venir, provenir <this cheese comes from Provence : ce fromage provient de Provence> **4** AMOUNT : monter, s'élever <the charge comes to $200 : les frais s'élèvent à $200> **5 to come clean** : décharger sa conscience **6 to come into** GAIN : acquérir, gagner <to come into a fortune : hériter d'une fortune> **7 to come off** SUCCEED : réussir **8 to come out** : paraître, sortir (se dit d'une publication, d'un produit commercial, etc.) **9 to come to** REVIVE : revenir à soi, reprendre conscience **10 to come to pass** HAPPEN : arriver, se produire <how come? : comment ça se fait?> **11 to come to terms** : parvenir à une entente

comeback [ˈkʌmˌbæk] *n* **1** RETORT : réplique *f* **2** RETURN : retour *f,* rentrée *f* <to make a comeback : faire une rentrée>

come back *vi* **1** RETORT : répliquer, rétorquer **2** RETURN : revenir <I came back with him : je suis revenu avec lui> <this hairdo is coming back : cette coiffure revient à la mode>

comedian [kəˈmiːdiən] *n* : comédien *m,* -dienne *f;* comique *mf*

comedienne [kəˌmiːdiˈɛn] *n* : comédienne *f*

comedy [ˈkɑmədi] *n, pl* **-dies** : comédie *f*

comely [ˈkʌmli] *adj* **comelier; -est** : beau, gracieux

comet [ˈkɑmət] *n* : comète *f*

comfort[1] ['kʌmpfərt] *vt* **1** CONSOLE : consoler **2** CHEER : encourager, réconforter

comfort[2] *n* **1** SOLACE : consolation *f* **2** WELL-BEING : confort *m,* bien-être *m* **3** CONVENIENCE : commodité *f,* confort *m* <the comforts of home : le confort du foyer>

comfortable ['kʌmpfərṭəbəl, 'kʌmpftə-] *adj* : confortable, agréable — **comfortably** *adv*

comforter ['kʌmpfərṭər] *n* **1** : consolateur *m,* -trice *f* **2** QUILT : édredon *m,* douillette *f Can*

comic[1] ['kɑmɪk] *adj* **1** : comique, qui appartient à la comédie **2** COMICAL : drôle, amusant

comic[2] *n* **1** COMEDIAN : comédien *m,* -dienne *f;* comique *mf* **2** *or* **comic book** : magazine *m* de bandes dessinées

comical ['kɑmɪkəl] *adj* : drôle, amusant

comic strip *n* : bande *f* dessinée

coming ['kʌmɪŋ] *adj* : suivante <during the coming week : pendant la semaine suivante>

comma ['kɑmə] *n* : virgule *f*

command[1] [kə'mænd] *vt* **1** ORDER : ordonner, mandater **2** CONTROL : diriger, commander **3** DEMAND : demander, exiger <he commands a high price : il exige un prix élevé> — *vi* **1** ORDER : donner des ordres **2** GOVERN : diriger, gouverner

command[2] *n* **1** ORDER : ordre *m,* commande *f* (en informatique) **2** : commandement *m* (dans les forces armées) **3** MASTERY : maîtrise *f*

commandant ['kɑmən,dɑnt, -,dænt] *n* : commandant *m*

commandeer [,kɑmən'dɪr] *vt* : réquisitionner

commander [kə'mændər] *n* : commandant *m*

commandment [kə'mændmənt] *n* : commandement *m* <the Ten Commandments : les dix commandements>

commemorate [kə'mɛmə,reɪt] *vt* **-rated; -rating** : commémorer

commemoration [kə,mɛmə'reɪʃən] *n* : commémoration *f*

commemorative [kə'mɛmrəṭɪv, -'mɛmə,reɪṭɪv] *adj* : commémoratif

commence [kə'mɛnts] *v* **-menced; -mencing** *vt* : commencer <to commence working : commencer à travailler> — *vi* : commencer

commencement [kə'mɛntsmənt] *n* **1** BEGINNING : commencement *m,* début *m* **2** : remise *f* des diplômes

commend [kə'mɛnd] *vt* **1** ENTRUST : confier **2** RECOMMEND : recommander, préconiser **3** PRAISE : louer

commendable [kə'mɛndəbəl] *adj* : louable

commendation [,kɑmən'deɪʃən] *n* : louange *f,* éloge *m*

commensurate [kə'mɛntsərət, -'mɛntʃʊrət] *adj* **to be commensurate with** : être proportionné à

comment[1] ['kɑ,mɛnt] *vi* : faire des commentaires, faire une remarque

comment[2] *n* : commentaire *m,* remarque *f*

commentary ['kɑmən,tɛri] *n, pl* **-taries** : commentaire *m*

commentator ['kɑmən,teɪṭər] *n* : commentateur *m,* -trice *f*

commerce ['kɑmərs] *n* : commerce *m*

commercial[1] [kə'mɛrʃəl] *adj* : commercial

commercial[2] *n* : annonce *f* publicitaire

commercialize [kə'mərʃə,laɪz] *vt* **-ized; -izing** : commercialiser

commiserate [kə'mɪzə,reɪt] *vi* **-ated; -ating** : éprouver de la sympathie, compatir

commiseration [kə,mɪzə'reɪʃən] *n* : commisération *f*

commission[1] [kə'mɪʃən] *vt* **1** APPOINT : nommer (un officier) **2** : commander <to commission a portrait : commander un portrait>

commission[2] *n* **1** : brevet *m* (militaire) **2** COMMITTEE : commission *f,* comité *m* **3** COMMITTING : perpétration *f,* commission *f* **4** FEE, PERCENTAGE : commission *f*

commissioned officer *n* : officier *m*

commissioner [kə'mɪʃənər] *n* : commissaire *m*

commit [kə'mɪt] *vt* **committed; committing** **1** ENTRUST : confier **2** CONFINE : interner (dans un hôpital) **3** PERPETRATE : commettre <to commit a crime : commettre un crime> **4 to commit oneself** : s'engager

commitment [kə'mɪtmənt] *n* **1** ENGAGEMENT, PROMISE : engagement *m* **2** OBLIGATION : obligation *f,* responsabilité *f*

committee [kə'mɪṭi] *n* : comité *m*

commodious [kə'mo:diəs] *adj* : spacieux, ample, vaste

commodity [kə'mɑdəṭi] *n, pl* **-ties** : produit *m,* denrée *f* (alimentaire), marchandise *f*

commodore ['kɑmə,dor] *n* : commodore *m*

common[1] ['kɑmən] *adj* **1** PUBLIC : commun, public <for the common good : pour le bien commun> **2** GENERAL : universel, général, public <it's common knowledge : c'est de notoriété publique> **3** ORDINARY : commun, ordinaire <the common man : l'homme du peuple> **4** SHARED : commun, semblable <common tastes : goûts semblables>

common[2] *n* **1** : terre *f* commune **2 in common** : en commun

common cold *n* : rhume *m*

common denominator *n* : dénominateur *m* commun

commoner ['kɑmənər] *n* : roturier *m,* -rière *f*
commonly ['kɑmənli] *adv* : communément, généralement
commonplace[1] ['kɑmənˌpleɪs] *adj* : commun, banal, ordinaire
commonplace[2] *n* : lieu *m* commun, banalité *f*
common sense *n* : bon sens *m,* sens *m* commun
commonwealth ['kɑmənˌwɛlθ] *n* : corps *m* politique <the British Commonwealth : le Commonwealth>
commotion [kə'mo:ʃən] *n* **1** AGITATION : agitation *f,* émoi *m* **2** RUCKUS, TUMULT : vacarme *m,* brouhaha *m*
communal [kə'mju:nəl] *adj* : communautaire
commune[1] [kə'mju:n] *vi* **-muned; -muning** : communier <to commune with nature : communier avec la nature>
commune[2] ['kɑˌmju:n, kə'mju:n] *n* : communauté *f*
communicable [kə'mju:nɪkəbəl] *adj* CONTAGIOUS : contagieux, transmissible
communicate [kə'mju:nəˌkeɪt] *v* **-cated; -cating** *vt* **1** CONVEY : communiquer, transmettre **2** TRANSMIT : transmettre (une maladie) — *vi* : communiquer
communication [kəˌmju:nə'keɪʃən] *n* : communication *f*
communicative [kə'mju:nɪˌkeɪt̬ɪv, -kət̬ɪv] *adj* : communicatif
communion [kə'mju:njən] *n* **1** SHARING : communion *f* **2 Communion** : Communion *f*
communiqué [kə'mju:nəˌkeɪ, -ˌmju:nə'keɪ] *n* : communiqué *m*
communism *or* **Communism** ['kɑmjəˌnɪzəm] *n* : communisme *m*
communist[1] *or* **Communist** ['kɑmjəˌnɪst] *adj* : communiste
communist[2] *or* **Communist** *n* : Communiste *mf*
communistic *or* **Communistic** *adj* : communiste
community [kə'mju:nət̬i] *n, pl* **-ties** : communauté *f*
commute[1] [kə'mju:t] *v* **-muted; -muting** *vt* REDUCE : commuer (une peine) — *vi* : faire la navette, faire un trajet journalier (à son travail)
commute[2] *n* : trajet *m* journalier
compact[1] [kəm'pækt, 'kɑmˌpækt] *vt* PACK : comprimer, tasser
compact[2] [kəm'pækt, 'kɑmˌpækt] *adj* **1** DENSE, SOLID : compact, dense **2** CONCISE : concis, bref
compact[3] ['kɑmˌpækt] *n* **1** AGREEMENT : entente *f,* accord *m* **2** *or* **powder compact** : poudrier *m* **3** *or* **compact car** : voiture *f* compacte
compact disc ['kɑmˌpækt'dɪsk] *n* : disque *m* compact, compact *m*
companion [kəm'pænjən] *n* **1** FRIEND : compagnon *m,* compagne *f* **2** COUNTERPART : pendant *m*
companionable [kəm'pænjənəbəl] *adj* : sociable
companionship [kəm'pænjənˌʃɪp] *n* : compagnie *f*
company ['kʌmpəni] *n, pl* **-nies 1** FIRM : compagnie *f,* société *f* **2** GROUPE : compagnie *f* (militaire), troupe *f* (de théâtre) **3** VISITORS : invités *mpl*
comparable ['kɑmpərəbəl] *adj* : comparable
comparative[1] [kəm'pærət̬ɪv] *adj* : comparatif — **comparatively** *adv*
comparative[2] *n* : comparatif *m*
compare [kəm'pær] *v* **-pared; -paring** *vt* : comparer — *vi* : être comparable
comparison [kəm'pærəsən] *n* : comparaison *f*
compartment [kəm'pɑrtmənt] *n* : compartiment *m*
compass ['kʌmpəs, 'kɑm-] *n* **1** : boussole *f* <the points of the compass : les points cardinaux> **2** : compas *m* (en géométrie) **3** RANGE, SCOPE : étendue *f,* portée *f*
compassion [kəm'pæʃən] *n* : compassion *f,* sympathie *f*
compassionate [kəm'pæʃənət] *adj* : compatissant
compatibility [kəmˌpæt̬ə'bɪlət̬i] *n* : compatibilité *f*
compatible [kəm'pæt̬əbəl] *adj* : compatible
compatriot [kəm'peɪtriət, -'pæ-] *n* : compatriote *mf*
compel [kəm'pɛl] *vt* **-pelled; -pelling** : contraindre, obliger
compelling [kəm'pɛlɪŋ] *adj* : irrésistible, convaincant
compendium [kəm'pendiəm] *n, pl* **-diums** *or* **-dia** [-diə] : abrégé *m*
compensate ['kɑmpənˌseɪt] *v* **-sated; -sating** *vt* : compenser, indemniser — *vi* **to compensate for** : compenser
compensation [ˌkɑmpən'seɪʃən] *n* : compensation *f,* indemnisation *f*
compensatory [kəm'pɛn*t*səˌtori] *adj* : compensatoire
compete [kəm'pi:t] *vi* **-peted; -peting** : faire concurrence, rivaliser
competence ['kɑmpətən*t*s] *n* : compétence *f,* capacité *f,* aptitude *f*
competency ['kɑmpətən*t*si] *n, pl* **-cies** → **competence**
competent ['kɑmpətənt] *adj* : compétent, qualifié, capable
competition [ˌkɑmpə'tɪʃən] *n* : compétition *f,* concurrence *f*
competitive [kəm'pɛt̬ət̬ɪv] *adj* : compétitif, concurrentiel
competitiveness [kəm'pɛt̬ət̬ɪvnəs] *n* : compétitivité *f*
competitor [kəm'pɛt̬ət̬ər] *n* : concurrent *m,* -rente *f*
compilation ['kɑmpɪ'leɪʃən] *n* : compilation *f*

compile [kəm'paɪl] *vt* **-piled; -piling** : compiler, dresser (une liste, etc.)
compiler [kəm'paɪlər] *n* : compilateur *m,* -trice *f*
complacency [kəm'pleɪsəntsi] *n, pl* **-cies** : satisfaction *f* de soi, suffisance *f*
complacent [kəm'pleɪsənt] *adj* : satisfait de soi, suffisant
complain [kəm'pleɪn] *vi* **1** GRIPE, GRUMBLE : se plaindre **2** PROTEST : faire une réclamation, se plaindre
complaint [kəm'pleɪnt] *n* **1** GRIPE : plainte *f* **2** AILMENT : maladie *f,* affection *f* **3** ACCUSATION, PROTEST : réclamation *f* <to lodge a complaint : se plaindre>
complement[1] ['kɑmplə,mɛnt] *vt* : compléter
complement[2] ['kɑmpləmənt] *n* **1** : complément *m* (en mathématiques, en grammaire, etc.) **2** QUOTA : effectif *m* (complet)
complementary [,kɑmplə'mɛntəri] *adj* : complémentaire
complete[1] [kəm'pliːt] *vt* **-pleted; -pleting** **1** FINISH : terminer, achever **2** : compléter <this piece completes the puzzle : cette pièce complète le puzzle>
complete[2] *adj* **-pleter; -est** **1** WHOLE : complet, intégral <a complete set : un jeu complet> **2** FINISHED : terminé, achevé **3** THOROUGH : complet, total, absolu
completely [kəm'pliːtli] *adv* : complètement, totalement
completion [kəm'pliːʃən] *n* : achèvement *m*
complex[1] [kɑm'plɛks, kəm-; 'kɑm,plɛks] *adj* INTRICATE : complexe
complex[2] ['kɑm,plɛks] *n* **1** : complexe *m* (psychologique) **2** GROUP : complexe *m*, ensemble *m* <housing complex : complexe résidentiel
complexion [kəm'plɛkʃən] *n* : teint *m* <a fair complexion : un teint clair>
complexity [kəm'plɛksəṭi, kɑm-] *n, pl* **-ties** : complexité *f*
compliance [kəm'plaɪənts] *n* **1** : conformité *f* **2 in compliance with** : conformément
compliant [kəm'plaɪənt] *n* : docile, accommodant
complicate ['kɑmplə,keɪt] *vt* **-cated; -cating** : compliquer
complicated ['kɑmplə,keɪṭəd] *adj* : compliqué, complexe
complication [,kɑmplə'keɪʃən] *n* : complication *f,* difficulté *f*
complicity [kəm'plɪsəṭi] *n, pl* **-ties** : complicité *f*
compliment[1] ['kɑmplə,mɛnt] *vt* : complimenter
compliment[2] ['kɑmpləmənt] *n* **1** : compliment *m* **2 compliments** *npl* : compliments *mpl*, respects *mpl* <to pay one's compliments to s.o. : faire ses compliments à qqn>
complimentary [,kɑmplə'mɛntəri] *adj* **1** FLATTERING : flatteur **2** FREE : gratuit, (à titre) gracieux <complimentary ticket : billet de faveur>
comply [kəm'plaɪ] *vi* **-plied; -plying** **1** : se soumettre, obéir **2 to comply with** : respecter, observer
component[1] [kəm'poːnənt, 'kɑm,poː-] *adj* : composant, constituant
component[2] *n* : composant *m,* composante *f* (en mathématiques), pièce *f*
compose [kəm'poːz] *vt* **-posed; -posing** **1** FORM : former, composer **2** : composer (un texte, une chanson, etc.) **3 to compose oneself** : retrouver son calme
composer [kəm'poːzər] *n* : compositeur *m,* -trice *f*
composite[1] [kɑm'pɑzət, kəm-; 'kɑmpəzət] *adj* : composite
composite[2] *n* : composite *m*
composition [,kɑmpə'zɪʃən] *n* **1** CREATION : composition *f,* création *f* **2** WORK : œuvre *m,* composition *f,* dissertation *f* (à l'école)
compost ['kɑm,poːst] *n* : compost *m*
composure [kəm'poːʒər] *n* : calme *m,* sang-froid *m,* sérénité *f*
compound[1] [kɑm'paʊnd, kəm-; 'kɑm,paʊnd] *vt* **1** COMBINE : combiner, mélanger **2** AUGMENT : augmenter, aggraver <to compound a problem : aggraver un problème>
compound[2] ['kɑm,paʊnd; kɑm'paʊnd, kəm-] *adj* : composé <compound interest : intérêt composé>
compound[3] ['kɑm,paʊnd] *n* **1** *or* **compound word** : mot *m* composé **2** ENCLOSURE : enceinte *f,* enclos *m* **3** : composé *m* (en chimie)
comprehend [,kɑmprɪ'hɛnd] *vt* **1** UNDERSTAND : comprendre, saisir **2** INCLUDE : comprendre, comporter
comprehensible [,kɑmprɪ'hɛntsɪbəl] *adj* : compréhensible, clair
comprehension [,kɑmprɪ'hɛntʃən] *n* : compréhension *f*
comprehensive [,kɑmprɪ'hɛntsɪv] *adj* : compréhensif, complet, détaillé
compress[1] [kəm'prɛs] *vt* : comprimer
compress[2] ['kɑm,prɛs] *n* : compresse *f*
compression [kəm'prɛʃən] *n* : compression *f*
comprise [kəm'praɪz] *vt* **-prised; -prising** **1** INCLUDE : comprendre, inclure, consister en **2** MAKE UP : constituer, composer <girls comprise half of the students : les filles constituent une moitié des étudiants>
compromise[1] ['kɑmprə,maɪz] *v* **-mised; -mising** *vi* : faire un compromis — *vt* JEOPARDIZE : compromettre, mettre en péril
compromise[2] *n* : compromis *m*
comptroller [kən'troːlər, 'kɑmp,troː-] *n* : contrôleur *m,* -leuse *f* (de finances)

compulsion [kəm'pʌlʃən] *n* **1** COERCION : coercition *f,* contrainte *f* **2** IMPULSE : compulsion *f* (en psychologie)

compulsive [kəm'pʌlsɪv] *adj* : compulsif

compulsory [kəm'pʌlsəri] *adj* : obligatoire

compunction [kəm'pʌŋkʃən] *n* **1** QUALM : scruple *m* **2** REMORSE : remords *m*

computation [kɑmpjʊ'teɪʃən] *n* : calcul *m*

compute [kəm'pju:t] *vt* **-puted; -puting** : calculer

computer [kəm'pju:t̬ər] *n* : ordinateur *m*

computerize [kəm'pju:t̬ə,raɪz] *vt* **-ized; -izing** : informatiser, mettre sur ordinateur

comrade ['kɑm,ræd] *n* : camarade *mf,* compagnon *m,* compagne *f*

comradeship ['kɑmræd,ʃɪp] *n* : camaraderie *f*

con[1] ['kɑn] *vt* **conned; conning** SWINDLE : duper, escroquer

con[2] *adv* : contre

con[3] *n* **1** DISADVANTAGE : désavantage *m,* inconvénient *m* <the pros and cons : le pour et le contre> **2** SWINDLE : escroquerie *f*

concave [kɑn'keɪv, 'kɑn,keɪv] *adj* : concave

conceal [kən'si:l] *vt* : dissimuler, cacher

concealment [kən'si:lmənt] *n* : dissimulation *f*

concede [kən'si:d] *v* **-ceded; -ceding** *vt* GRANT : accorder, concéder — *vi* YIELD : céder

conceit [kən'si:t] *n* : suffisance *f,* vanité *f*

conceited [kən'si:təd] *adj* : suffisant, vaniteux

conceive [kən'si:v] *v* **-ceived; -ceiving** *vt* **1** : concevoir (un enfant) **2** IMAGINE : imaginer, concevoir — *vi* **1** : devenir enceinte **2 to conceive of** : concevoir

concentrate[1] ['kɑntsən,treɪt] *v* **-trated; -trating** *vt* : concentrer — *vi* : se concentrer

concentrate[2] *n* : concentré *m* <orange juice concentrate : concentré du jus d'orange>

concentration [,kɑntsən'treɪʃən] *n* : concentration *f*

concentric [kən'sɛntrɪk] *adj* : concentrique

concept ['kɑn,sɛpt] *n* : concept *m*

conception [kən'sɛpʃən] *n* **1** : conception *f* (en médecine) **2** IDEA : idée *f,* concept *m*

concern[1] [kən'sərn] *vt* **1** AFFECT : concerner, intéresser **2** INVOLVE : concerner <as far as I'm concerned : en ce qui me concerne> **3** : traiter de, parler de <the novel concerns the war : le roman traite de la guerre> **4** WORRY : inquiéter <that concerns me very much : ça m'inquiète beaucoup>

concern[2] *n* **1** AFFAIR : affaire *f* <it's not my concern : ce n'est pas de mes affaires> **2** WORRY : inquiétude *f* **3** BUSINESS : firme *f,* société *f* <a banking concern : une firme bancaire>

concerned [kən'sərnd] *adj* **1** ANXIOUS : préoccupé, inquiet **2** INTERESTED : intéressé **3** IMPLICATED : impliqué

concerning [kən'sərnɪŋ] *prep* REGARDING : concernant, touchant

concert ['kɑn,sərt] *n* **1** : concert *m,* récital *m* (musical) **2** AGREEMENT, UNISON : concert *m* <to work in concert : travailler de concert>

concerted [kən'sərt̬əd] *adj* : concerté

concertina [,kɑntsər'ti:nə] *n* : concertina *m*

concerto [kən'tʃɛrt̬o:] *n, pl* **-ti** [-t̬i, -,ti:] *or* **-tos** : concerto *m* <piano concerto : concerto pour piano>

concession [kən'sɛʃən] *n* : concession *f*

conch ['kɑŋk, 'kɑntʃ] *n, pl* **conchs** ['kɑŋks] *or* **conches** ['kɑntʃəz] : conque *f*

conciliatory [kən'sɪliə,tori] *adj* : conciliateur, conciliant

concise [kən'saɪs] *adj* : concis, bref, succinct

concisely [kən'saɪsli] *adv* : avec concision

conciseness [kən'saɪsnəs] *n* : concision *f*

conclave ['kɑn,kleɪv] *n* : conclave *m*

conclude [kən'klu:d] *v* **-cluded; -cluding** *vt* **1** END : terminer, conclure **2** DECIDE : décider **3** INFER : inférer, déduire — *vi* END : s'achever, se terminer

conclusion [kən'klu:ʒən] *n* : conclusion *f*

conclusive [kən'klu:sɪv] *adj* : concluant, définitif

conclusively [kən'klu:sɪvli] *adv* : définitivement, de façon concluant

concoct [kən'kɑkt, kɑn-] *vt* **1** PREPARE : préparer, confectionner **2** DEVISE : fabriquer, concocter (une excuse, etc.)

concoction [kən'kɑkʃən] *n* **1** PREPARATION : élaboration *f* **2** MIXTURE : mélange *m*

concord ['kɑn,kɔrd, 'kɑŋ-] *n* : concorde *f,* harmonie *f*

concordance [kən'kɔrdənts] *n* **1** AGREEMENT : accord *m* **2** INDEX : concordance *f,* index *f*

concourse ['kɔn,kors] *n* **1** GATHERING : rassemblement *m,* assemblée *f* **2** HALL : hall *m,* lieu *m* de rassemblement

concrete[1] [kɑn'kri:t, 'kɑn,kri:t] *adj* **1** REAL : concret, réel **2** : de béton <concrete walls : murs de béton>

concrete[2] ['kɑn,kri:t, kɑn'kri:t] *n* : béton *m*

concur [kən'kər] *vi* **-curred, -curring 1** AGREE : être d'accord **2** TALLY : coïncider, concorder

concurrent [kən'kərənt] *adj* : simultané, concomitant

concussion [kən'kʌʃən] *n* **:** commotion *f* cérébrale
condemn [kən'dɛm] *vt* **1** CENSURE **:** condamner, censurer **2** CONVICT **:** condamner <condemned to death : condamné à mort> **3 :** déclarer inhabitable (se dit d'un bâtiment)
condemnation [ˌkɑnˌdɛm'neɪʃən] *n* **:** condamnation *f*
condensation [ˌkɑnˌdɛn'seɪʃən] *n* **:** condensation *f*
condense [kən'dɛnts] *vt* **-densed; -densing 1** COMPRESS **:** condenser, comprimer **2** ABRIDGE **:** abréger, condenser
condescend [ˌkɑndɪ'sɛnd] *vt* **1 to condescend to do :** daigner faire, condescendre à faire **2 to condescend to s.o. :** condescendre envers qqn
condescension [ˌkɑndɪ'sɛntʃən] *n* **:** condescendance *f*
condiment ['kɑndəmənt] *n* **:** condiment *m*
condition[1] [kən'dɪʃən] *vt* **1** TRAIN **:** conditionner **2 :** mettre en forme (le corps, etc.), traiter (les cheveux)
condition[2] *n* **1** STIPULATION **:** condition *f,* stipulation *f* <on the condition that : à condition que> **2** STATE **:** état *m,* condition *f* **3 conditions** *npl* **:** circonstances *fpl,* conditions *fpl* <living conditions : conditions de vie>
conditional [kən'dɪʃənəl] *adj* **:** conditionnel — **conditionally** *adv*
condolence [kən'do:lənts] *n* **:** condoléance *f*
condom ['kɑndəm] *n* **:** condom *m,* préservatif *m*
condominium [ˌkɑndə'mɪniəm] *n, pl* **-ums :** condominium *m*
condone [kən'do:n] *vt* **-doned; -doning :** fermer les yeux sur, pardonner
condor ['kɑndər, -ˌdɔr] *n* **:** condor *m*
conducive [kən'du:sɪv, -'dju:-] *adj* **:** favorable
conduct[1] [kən'dʌkt] *vt* **1** GUIDE **:** conduire, guider <a conducted tour : une visite guidée> **2** DIRECT **:** diriger (un orchestre) **3** CARRY ON **:** mener, conduire <to conduct an investigation : conduire une enquête> **4** TRANSMIT **:** conduire (l'électricité, etc.) **5 to conduct oneself :** se comporter
conduct[2] ['kɑnˌdʌkt] *n* **1** BEHAVIOR **:** comportement *m,* conduite *f* **2** MANAGEMENT **:** conduite *f* (des affaires, etc.)
conduction [kən'dʌkʃən] *n* **:** conduction *f*
conductivity [ˌkɑnˌdʌk'tɪvəṭi] *n, pl* **-ties :** conductivité *f*
conductor [kən'dʌktər] *n* **1 :** conducteur *m* (d'électricité) **2 :** chef *m* d'orchestre **3 :** contrôleur *m* (de train)
conduit ['kɑnˌdu:ət, -dju:-] *n* **:** conduit *m,* tuyau *m*
cone ['ko:n] *n* **1 :** cône *m* (fruit du pin) **2 :** cône *m* (en géométrie) **3** *or* **ice-cream cone :** cornet *m* (de crème glacée)
confection [kən'fɛkʃən] *n* **:** confiserie *f,* friandise *f,* bonbon *m*
confectioner [kən'fɛkʃənər] *n* **:** confiseur *m,* -seuse *f*
confederacy [kən'fɛdərəsi] *n, pl* **-cies :** confédération *f*
confederate[1] [kən'fɛdəˌreɪt] *v* **-ated; -ating** *vt* **:** confédérer — *vi* **:** se confédérer
confederate[2] [kən'fɛdəˌrət] *adj* **:** confédéré
confederate[3] *n* **:** allié *m,* -liée *f;* complice *mf*
confederation [kənˌfɛdə'reɪʃən] *n* **:** confédération *f*
confer [kən'fər] *v* **-ferred; -ferring** *vt* BESTOW **:** conférer, accorder — *vi* CONSULT **:** conférer, parler
conference ['kɑnfrənts, -fərənts] *n* **:** conférence *f*
confess [kən'fɛs] *vt* **:** confesser, avouer — *vi* **1 :** avouer, faire des aveux <the prisoner confessed : le prisonnier a fait des aveux> **2 :** se confesser (en religion)
confession [kən'fɛʃən] *n* **:** confession *f*
confessional [kən'fɛʃənəl] *n* **:** confessionnal *m*
confetti [kən'fɛṭi] *n* **:** confettis *mpl*
confidant ['kɑnfəˌdɑnt, -ˌdænt] *n* **:** confident *m*
confidante ['kɑnfəˌdɑnt, -ˌdænt] *n* **:** confidente *f*
confide [kən'faɪd] *v* **-fided; -fiding** *vt* ENTRUST **:** confier — *vi* **:** se confier <to confide in s.o. : se confier en qqn>
confidence ['kɑnfədənts] *n* **1** TRUST **:** confiance *f* **2** SELF-CONFIDENCE **:** confiance *f,* assurance *f* **3** SECRET **:** confidence *f*
confident ['kɑnfədənt] *adj* **1** TRUSTFUL **:** confiant, ouvert **2** SELF-CONFIDENT **:** confiant, sûr de soi
confidential [ˌkɑnfə'dɛntʃəl] *adj* **:** confidentiel — **confidentially** *adv*
configuration [kənˌfɪgjə'reɪʃən] *n* **:** configuration *f*
confine [kən'faɪn] *vt* **-fined; -fining 1** LIMIT **:** confiner, limiter **2** IMPRISON **:** emprisonner, enfermer
confines ['kɑnˌfaɪnz] *npl* BOUNDS **:** confins *mpl,* limites *fpl*
confirm [kən'fərm] *vt* **1 :** confirmer, fortifier <to confirm one's faith : confirmer sa foi> **2** RATIFY **:** approuver, sanctionner **3** VERIFY **:** démontrer, corroborer **4 :** confirmer (en religion)
confirmation [ˌkɑnfər'meɪʃən] *n* **:** confirmation *f*
confiscate ['kɑnfəˌskeɪt] *vt* **-cated; -cating :** confisquer
confiscation [ˌkɑnfə'skeɪʃən] *n* **:** confiscation *f*

conflagration [ˌkɑnflə'greɪʃən] *n* : conflagration *f,* incendie *f*

conflict[1] [kən'flɪkt] *vi* : être en conflit, s'opposer

conflict[2] ['kɑnˌflɪkt] *n* : conflit *m*

conform [kən'fɔrm] *vi* **to conform with** : se conformer à, être conforme à

conformity [kən'fɔrməṭi] *n, pl* **-ties** : conformité *f*

confound [kən'faʊnd, kɑn-] *vt* : confondre, déconcerter

confront [kən'frʌnt] *vt* : confronter, affronter, faire face à

confrontation [ˌkɑnfrən'teɪʃən] *n* : confrontation *f*

confuse [kən'fju:z] *vt* **-fused; -fusing 1** PERPLEX : confondre, déconcerter **2** JUMBLE : embrouiller, brouiller

confusing [kən'fju:zɪŋ] *adj* : dévoutant, embrouillé, mêlant *Can*

confusion [kən'fju:ʒən] *n* **1** PERPLEXITY : confusion *f,* embarras *m* **2** MESS, TURMOIL : désordre *m,* confusion *f*

congeal [kən'dʒi:l] *vt* **1** FREEZE : congeler **2** COAGULATE : figer, coaguler — *vi* : se figer, se coaguler

congenial [kən'dʒi:niəl] *adj* : agréable, sympathique

congenital [kən'dʒɛnəṭəl] *adj* : congénital

congest [kən'dʒɛst] *vt* **1** : congestionner (en médecine) **2** CLOG, OBSTRUCT : embouteiller, encombrer

congestion [kən'dʒɛstʃən] *n* : congestion *f*

conglomerate[1] [kən'glɑmərət] *adj* : congloméré

conglomerate[2] *n* : conglomérat *m*

conglomeration [kənˌglɑmə'reɪʃən] *n* : conglomérat *m,* agglomération *f*

Congolese[1] [ˌkɑŋgə'li:z, -'li:s] *adj* : congolais

Congolese[2] *n* : Congolais *m,* -laise *f*

congratulate [kən'grædʒəˌleɪt, -'grætʃə-] *vt* **-lated; -lating** : féliciter

congratulations [kənˌgrædʒə'leɪʃənz, -ˌgrætʃə-] *npl* : félicitations *fpl*

congregate ['kɑŋgrɪˌgeɪt] *v* **-gated; -gating** *vt* ASSEMBLE : rassembler, réunir — *vi* GATHER : se réunir

congregation [ˌkɑŋgrɪ'geɪʃən] *n* **1** GATHERING : assemblée *f,* rassemblement *m* **2** CHURCHGOERS : assemblée *f* des fidèles

congress ['kɑŋgrəs] *n* : congrès *m*

congressional [kən'grɛʃənəl, kɑn-] *adj* : d'un congrès

congressman ['kɑŋgrəsmən] *n, pl* **-men** [-mən, -mɛn] : membre *m* du Congrès

congresswoman ['kɑŋgrəsˌwʊmən] *n, pl* **-women** [-ˌwɪmən] : membre *m* du Congrès

congruent [kən'gru:ənt, 'kɑngrʊənt] *adj* : congru <congruent triangles : triangles congrus>

conic ['kɑnɪk] → **conical**

conical ['kɑnɪkəl] *adj* : conique

conifer ['kɑnəfər, 'ko:-] *n* : conifère *m*

coniferous [ko:'nɪfərəs, kə-] *adj* : conifère

conjecture[1] [kən'dʒɛktʃər] *vt* : conjecturer, présumer

conjecture[2] *n* : conjecture *f,* supposition *f*

conjugal ['kɑndʒɪgəl, kən'dʒu:-] *adj* : conjugal

conjugate ['kɑndʒəˌgeɪt] *vt* **-gated; -gating** : conjuguer

conjugation [ˌkɑndʒə'geɪʃən] *n* : conjugaison *f*

conjunction [kən'dʒʌŋkʃən] *n* **1** UNION : conjonction *f,* union *f* **2** : conjonction *f* (en astronomie, en grammaire) **3 in conjunction with** : conjointement avec

conjure ['kɑndʒər, 'kʌn-] *v* **-jured; -juring** *vt* **1** ENTREAT : implorer, supplier **2 to conjure up** : invoquer (des esprits), évoquer (une image) — *vi* : faire des tours de magie

connect [kə'nɛkt] *vt* **1** JOIN, LINK : joindre, relier **2** ASSOCIATE : associer, lier — *vi* : assurer la correspondance (se dit des trains, des avions, etc.)

connection [kə'nɛkʃən] *n* **1** LINK : lien *m,* rapport *m* **2** RELATIONSHIP : lien *m,* relation *f* <business connections : relations d'affaires> **3** : correspondance *f* <train connection : correspondance de train>

connective [kə'nɛktɪv] *adj* : conjonctif <connective tissue : tissu conjonctif>

connivance [kə'naɪvənts] *n* : connivence *f,* complicité *f*

connive [kə'naɪv] *vi* **-nived; -niving** : être de connivence

connoisseur [ˌkɑnə'sər] *n* : connaisseur *m,* -seuse *f*

connotation [ˌkɑnə'teɪʃən] *n* : connotation *f*

connote [kə'no:t] *vt* **-noted; -noting 1** CONVEY : évoquer **2** IMPLY : indiquer

conquer ['kɑŋkər] *vt* : conquérir, vaincre

conqueror ['kɑŋkərər] *n* : conquérant *m,* -rante *f*

conquest ['kɑnˌkwɛst, 'kɑŋ-] *n* : conquête *f*

conscience ['kɑntʃənts] *n* : conscience *f* <to have a clear conscience : avoir la conscience tranquille>

conscientious [ˌkɑntʃi'ɛntʃəs] *adj* : consciencieux — **conscientiously** *adv*

conscious ['kɑntʃəs] *adj* **1** AWARE : conscient <to become conscious of : prendre conscience de> **2** ALERT, AWAKE : conscient, lucide **3** INTENTIONAL : délibéré, intentionnel

consciously ['kɑntʃəsli] *adv* : consciemment

consciousness ['kɑntʃəsnəs] *n* **1** AWARENESS : conscience *f* **2** : connaissance *f* <to lose consciousness : perdre connaissance>

conscription [kən'skrɪpʃən] *n* : conscription *f*

consecrate ['kantsə,kreɪt] *vt* **-crated; -crating** : consacrer

consecration [,kantsə'kreɪʃən] *n* : consécration *f*

consecutive [kən'sɛkjəṭɪv] *adj* : consécutif — **consecutively** *adv*

consensus [kən'sɛntsəs] *n* : consensus *m*

consent[1] [kən'sɛnt] *vi* : consentir

consent[2] *n* : consentement *m,* accord *m*

consequence ['kantsə,kwɛnts, -kwənts] *n* **1** RESULT : conséquence *f,* effet *m,* suite *f* **2** IMPORTANCE : importance *f,* conséquence *f* <a person of consequence : une personne importante>

consequential [,kantsə'kwɛntʃəl] *adj* : important, conséquent

consequently ['kantsəkwəntli, -,kwɛnt-] *adv* : par conséquent

conservation [,kantsər'veɪʃən] *n* : conservation *f,* préservation *f*

conservatism [kən'sɛrvə,tɪzəm] *n* : conservatisme *m*

conservative[1] [kən'sərvəṭɪv] *adj* **1** : conservateur **2** CAUTIOUS : prudent, modéré <a conservative estimate : une estimation prudente>

conservative[2] *n* : conservateur *m,* -trice *f*

conservatory [kən'sərvə,tori] *n, pl* **-ries** : conservatoire *m*

conserve[1] [kən'sərv] *vt* **-served; -serving** : conserver, préserver

conserve[2] *n* PRESERVE : confiture *f*

consider [kən'sɪdər] *vt* **1** STUDY, WEIGH : considérer, étudier **2** REGARD : tenir compte de <he doesn't consider my feelings : il ne tient pas compte de mes sentiments> **3** BELIEVE : croire, penser, considérer <he considers this essential : il considère que c'est essentiel>

considerable [kən'sɪdərəbəl] *adj* : considérable — **considerably** *adv*

considerate [kən'sɪdərət] *adj* THOUGHTFUL : attentionné, prévenant

consideration [kən,sɪdə'reɪʃən] *n* **1** DELIBERATION : considération *f,* réflexion *f* **2** THOUGHTFULNESS : attention *f,* considération *f* **3** PAYMENT : rémunération *f,* paiement *m*

considering [kən'sɪdərɪŋ] *prep* : étant donné, vu <considering the circumstances, it's better to stay here : vu les circonstances, il vaut mieux rester ici>

consign [kən'saɪn] *vt* **1** ENTRUST : confier **2** SEND : expédier, envoyer (des marchandises)

consignment [kən'saɪnmənt] *n* : expédition *f,* envoi *m*

consist [kən'sɪst] *vi* **1** LIE, RESIDE : consister <charity consists in good deeds : la charité consiste en bonnes actions> **2 to consist of** : se composer de, consister en

consistency [kən'sɪstəntsi] *n, pl* **-cies 1** TEXTURE : consistance *f* **2** UNIFORMITY : cohérence *f,* uniformité *f*

consistent [kən'sɪstənt] *adj* **1** REGULAR, STEADY : constant, régulier <consistent behavior : comportement constant> **2 consistent with** : selon <consistent with our records : selon nos dossiers>

consistently [kən'sɪstəntli] *adv* : constamment, régulièrement

consolation [,kantsə'leɪʃən] *n* : consolation *f*

console[1] [kən'so:l] *vt* **-soled; -soling** : consoler, réconforter

console[2] ['kan,so:l] *n* : console *f*

consolidate [kən'salə,deɪt] *vt* **-dated; -dating** : consolider

consolidation [kən,salə'deɪʃən] *n* : consolidation *f*

consommé [,kantsə'meɪ] *n* : consommé *m*

consonant ['kantsənənt] *n* : consonne *f*

consort[1] [kən'sɔrt] *vi* **to consort with** : fréquenter

consort[2] ['kan,sɔrt] *n* : époux *m,* épouse *f* (d'un roi ou d'une reine)

conspicuous [kən'spɪkjʊəs] *adj* **1** OBVIOUS : évident, visible **2** STRIKING : remarquable, voyant

conspicuously [kən'spɪkjʊəsli] *adv* **1** NOTICEABLY : bien en évidence **2** STRIKINGLY : de façon voyante, remarquablement

conspiracy [kən'spɪrəsi] *n, pl* **-cies** : conspiration *f,* complot *m*

conspirator [kən'spɪrəṭər] *n* : conspirateur *m,* -trice *f*

conspire [kən'spaɪr] *vi* **-spired; -spiring** : conspirer, comploter — **conspiratorial** [kən,spɪrə'toriel] *adj*

constable ['kantstəbəl] *n* : gendarme *m,* agent *m* de police

constancy ['kantstəntsi] *n, pl* **-cies 1** STEADFASTNESS : constance *f* **2** LOYALTY : fidélité *f,* loyauté *f*

constant[1] ['kantstənt] *adj* **1** STEADFAST : constant **2** UNCHANGING : constant, régulier **3** CONTINUAL : continuel, constant

constant[2] *n* : constante *f*

constantly ['kantstəntli] *adv* : constamment, continuellement

constellation [,kantstə'leɪʃən] *n* : constellation *f*

consternation [,kantstər'neɪʃən] *n* : consternation *f*

constipate ['kantstə,peɪt] *vt* **-pated; -pating** : constiper

constipation [,kantstə'peɪʃən] *n* : constipation *f*

constituent[1] [kən'stɪtʃʊənt] *adj* **1** COMPONENT : composant, constituant **2** : constituant, constitutif <constituent assembly : assemblée constituante>

constituent[2] *n* **1** ELEMENT : élément *m* constitutif, composant *m* **2** VOTER : électeur *m* , -trice *f*

constitute ['kɑntstəˌtu:t, -tju:t] *vt* **-tuted; -tuting** **1** ESTABLISH : constituer, créer **2** FORM : composer, former

constitution [ˌkɑntstə'tu:ʃən, -'tju:-] *n* **1** COMPOSITION : constitution *f,* composition *f* **2** : constitution *f* (d'un pays)

constitutional[1] [ˌkɑntstə'tu:ʃənəl, -'tju:-] *adj* : constitutionnel

constitutional[2] *n* WALK : promenade *f,* petit tour *m*

constrain [kən'streɪn] *vt* **1** COMPEL, FORCE : contraindre, obliger **2** CONFINE : restreindre, limiter

constraint [kən'streɪnt] *n* : contrainte *f*

constrict [kən'strɪkt] *vt* : resserrer, serrer

constriction [kən'strɪkʃən] *n* : constriction *f,* resserrement *m*

construct [kən'strʌkt] *vt* : construire, bâtir

construction [kən'strʌkʃən] *n* : construction *f*

constructive [kən'strʌktɪv] *adj* : constructif

construe [kən'stru:] *vt* **-strued; -struing** : interpréter, expliquer

consul ['kɑntsəl] *n* : consul *m* — **consular** ['kɑntsələr] *adj*

consulate ['kɑntsələt] *n* : consulat *m*

consult [kən'sʌlt] *vt* : consulter — *vi* : se consulter <to consult with : entrer en consultation avec>

consultant [kən'sʌltənt] *n* : consultant *m,* -tante *f*

consultation [ˌkɑntsəl'teɪʃən] *n* : consultation *f*

consume [kən'su:m] *vt* **-sumed; -suming** **1** DESTROY : détruire <consumed by fire : détruit par le feu> **2** USE UP : utiliser, consommer **3** INGEST : consommer (de la nourriture ou de la boisson)

consumer [kən'su:mər] *n* : consommateur *m,* -trice *f*

consummate[1] ['kɑntsəˌmeɪt] *vt* **-mated; -mating** : consommer (un mariage, etc.)

consummate[2] [kən'sʌmət, 'kɑntsəmət] *adj* : consommé, accompli, parfait <a consummate liar : un menteur accompli>

consummation [ˌkɑntsə'meɪʃən] *n* : consommation *f*

consumption [kən'sʌmpʃən] *n* **1** : consommation *f* <oil consumption : consommation d'huile> **2** TUBERCULOSIS : tuberculose *f*

contact[1] ['kɑnˌtækt, kən'-] *vt* : contacter, se mettre en contact avec

contact[2] ['kɑnˌtækt] *n* **1** TOUCHING : contact *m* **2** CONNECTION : contact *m* <business contacts : contacts professionnels> **3** COMMUNICATION : contact *m,* communication *f* <to be in contact with : être en rapport avec>

contact lens ['kɑnˌtækt'lɛnz] *n* : verre *m* de contact, lentille *f* de contact

contagion [kən'teɪdʒən] *n* : contagion *f*

contagious [kən'teɪdʒəs] *adj* : contagieux

contain [kən'teɪn] *vt* **1** HOLD : contenir, renfermer **2** INCLUDE : contenir, inclure **3** RESTRAIN : contenir, maîtriser <to contain oneself : se contenir>

container [kən'teɪnər] *n* : récipient *m,* conteneur *m* (de transport)

contaminate [kən'tæməˌneɪt] *vt* **-nated; -nating** : contaminer

contamination [kənˌtæmə'neɪʃən] *n* : contamination *f*

contemplate ['kɑntəmˌpleɪt] *vt* **-plated; -plating** **1** VIEW : contempler **2** PONDER : réfléchir sur **3** CONSIDER, PLAN : envisager, considérer

contemplation [ˌkɑntəm'pleɪʃən] *n* : contemplation *f,* réflexion *f*

contemplative [kən'tɛmplətɪv, 'kɑntəmˌpleɪṭɪv] *adj* : contemplatif

contemporaneous [kənˌtɛmpə'reɪniəs] *adj* → **contemporary**[1]

contemporary[1] [kən'tɛmpəˌrɛri] *adj* : contemporain, moderne

contemporary[2] *n* : contemporain *m,* -raine *f*

contempt [kən'tɛmpt] *n* **1** SCORN : mépris, dédain **2** *or* **contempt of court** : outrage *m* à magistrat *France,* outrage *m* au tribunal *Can*

contemptible [kən'tɛmptəbəl] *adj* DESPICABLE : méprisable

contemptuous [kən'tɛmptʃʊəs] *adj* : méprisant — **contemptuously** *adv*

contend [kən'tɛnd] *vt* ARGUE, MAINTAIN : soutenir, maintenir — *vi* **1** COMPETE : rivaliser <to contend for first prize : rivaliser pour le premier prix> **2** **to contend with** : affronter, faire face à <problems to contend with : problèmes à affronter>

contender [kən'tɛndər] *n* : concurrent *m,* -rente *f* (aux sports); candidat *m,* -date *f* (en politique)

content[1] [kən'tɛnt] *vt* : contenter, satisfaire

content[2] *adj* : content, satisfait

content[3] *n* → **contentment**

content[4] ['kɑnˌtənt] *n* **1** GIST : contenu *m,* signification *f* **2** : teneur *f* <high fiber content : haute teneur en fibres> **3** **contents** *npl* : contenu *m* **4** **table of contents** : table *f* des matières

contented [kən'tɛntəd] *adj* : satisfait, content

contention [kən'tɛntʃən] *n* **1** ARGUMENT : dispute *f,* discussion *f* **2** RIVALRY : compétition *f,* rivalité *f* **3** OPINION : assertion *f,* affirmation *f*

contentious [kən'tɛntʃəs] *adj* **1** : litigieux **2** BELLIGERENT : bel-

liqueux, combatif — **contentiously** *adv*
contentment [kən'tɛntmənt] *n* : contentement *m,* satisfaction *f*
contest[1] [kən'tɛst] *vt* : contester, disputer
contest[2] ['kɑn,tɛst] *n* **1** STRUGGLE : lutte *f* **2** GAME : concours *m,* compétition *f*
contestant [kən'tɛstənt] *n* : concurrent *m,* -rente *f;* adversaire *mf*
context ['kɑn,tɛkst] *n* : contexte *m*
contiguous [kən'tɪgjʊəs] *adj* : contigu
continence ['kɑntənənts] *n* : continence *f*
continent[1] ['kɑntənənt] *adj* : continent
continent[2] *n* : continent *m* — **continental** [,kɑntən'ɛntəl] *adj*
contingency [kən'tɪndʒəntsi] *n, pl* **-cies** : éventualité *f,* contingence *f*
contingent[1] [kən'tɪndʒənt] *adj* **1** : contingent **2 to be contingent on** : dépendre de
contingent[2] *n* : contingent *m*
continual [kə'tɪnjʊəl] *adj* : continuel — **continually** [-'tɪnjʊəli, -'tɪnjəli] *adv*
continuance [kə'tɪnjʊənts] *n* **1** CONTINUATION : continuation *f* **2** DURATION : durée *f* **3** : ajournement *m* (d'un procès)
continuation [kən,tɪnjʊ'eɪʃən] *n* : continuation *f*
continue [kən'tɪnjuː] *v* **-tinued; -tinuing** *vt* **1** KEEP UP : continuer <to continue writing : continuer à écrire> **2** RESUME : continuer, reprendre **3** EXTEND : continuer, prolonger — *vi* **1** CARRY ON : continuer **2** LAST : durer, se perpétuer <his good luck seems to continue : sa bonne fortune semble durer>
continuity [,kɑntən'uːəṭi, -'juː-] *n, pl* **-ties** : continuité *f*
continuous [kən'tɪnjʊəs] *adj* : continu
continuously [kən'tɪnjʊəsli] *adv* : continuellement, constamment
contort [kən'tɔrt] *vt* : tordre
contortion [kən'tɔrʃən] *n* : contorsion *f*
contour ['kɑn,tʊr] *n* **1** OUTLINE : contour *m* **2 contours** *npl* SHAPE : contours *fpl,* forme *f*
contraband ['kɑntrə,bænd] *n* : contrebande *f*
contraception [,kɑntrə'sɛpʃən] *n* : contraception *f*
contraceptive[1] [,kɑntrə'sɛptɪv] *adj* : contraceptif
contraceptive[2] *n* : contraceptif *m*
contract[1] [kən'trækt, *vt* _ *and vi usu* 'kɑn,trækt] *vt* **1** INCUR : contracter (des dettes, etc.) **2** ARRANGE : contracter (un mariage, etc.) **3** CATCH : contracter, attraper (un virus) **4** TIGHTEN : contracter (un muscle) **5** SHORTEN : contracter (un mot) — *vi* : se contracter
contract[2] ['kɑn,trækt] *n* AGREEMENT : contrat *m*
contraction [kən'trækʃən] *n* : contraction *f*
contractor ['kɑn,træktər, kən'træk-] *n* : entrepreneur *m,* -neuse *f;* contracteur *n,* -teuse *f Can*
contractual [kən'træktʃʊəl] *adj* : contractuel — **contractually** *adv*
contradict [,kɑntrə'dɪkt] *vt* : contredire
contradiction [,kɑntrə'dɪkʃən] *n* : contradiction *f*
contradictory [,kɑntrə'dɪktəri] *adj* : contradictoire
contralto [kən'træl,toː] *n, pl* **-tos** : contralto *m* (voix), contralto *mf* (chanteur)
contraption [kən'træpʃən] *n* : truc *m fam*, machin *m fam*
contrary[1] ['kɑn,trɛri *often* kən'trɛri] *adj* **1** OPPOSITE : contraire **2** CONFLICTING : contradictoire <contrary evidence : preuves contradictoires> **3** BALKY, STUBBORN : têtu, opiniâtre **4 contrary to** : contrairement à
contrary[2] *n, pl* **-traries** : contraire *m* <on the contrary : au contraire>
contrast[1] [kən'træst] *vt* : mettre en contraste — *vi* : contraster
contrast[2] *n* : contraste *m*
contribute [kən'trɪbjət] *v* **-uted; -uting** *vi* : contribuer — *vt* GIVE, SUPPLY : donner, apporter
contribution [,kɑntrə'bjuːʃən] *n* : contribution *f*
contrite ['kɑn,traɪt, kən'traɪt] *adj* : contrit, pénitent
contrition [kən'trɪʃən] *n* : contrition *f,* pénitence *f*
contrivance [kən'traɪvənts] *n* **1** DEVICE : appareil *m,* dispositif *m* **2** SCHEME : machination *f,* manigance *f*
contrive [kən'traɪv] *v* **-trived; -triving** *vt* DEVISE : concevoir, inventer — *vi* **to contrive to** : parvenir à, réussir à, trouver le moyen de <she contrived to extricate herself from the situation : elle a trouvé le moyen de s'en sortir>
control[1] [kən'troːl] *vt* **-trolled; -trolling** **1** REGULATE : contrôler **2** RULE : diriger, dominer **3** RESTRAIN : maîtriser (des émotions, etc.)
control[2] *n* **1** AUTHORITY : contrôle *m,* autorité *f* **2** RESTRAINT : maîtrise *f* **3** REGULATION : régulation *f,* contrôle *m* <price control : régulation des prix> **4** DEVICE : bouton *m,* commande *f* <remote control : commande à distance>
controller [kən'troːlər, 'kɑn,-] *n* : contrôleur *m,* -leuse *f* <air traffic controller : contrôleur du trafic aérien>
controversial [,kɑntrə'vərʃəl, -siəl] *adj* : controversé, contesté
controversy ['kɑntrə,vərsi] *n, pl* **-sies** : controverse *f*
contusion [kən'tuːʒən, -tjuː-] *n* : contusion *f,* ecchymose *f*

conundrum [kə'nʌndrəm] *n* : énigme *f*
convalesce [ˌkɑnvə'lɛs] *vi* **-lesced; -lescing** : se remettre, être en convalescence
convalescence [ˌkɑnvə'lɛsənts] *n* : convalescence *f*
convalescent[1] [ˌkɑnvə'lɛsənt] *adj* : convalescent
convalescent[2] *n* : convalescent *m*, -cente *f*
convection [kən'vɛkʃən] *n* : convection *f*
convene [kən'vi:n] *v* **-vened; -vening** *vt* : convoquer — *vi* MEET : se réunir, s'assembler
convenience [kən'vi:njənts] *n* **1** AMENITY : commodité *f*, confort *m* <modern conveniences : commodités modernes> **2 at your convenience** : quand cela vous conviendra **3 at your earliest convenience** : dans les meilleurs délais, dès que cela vous sera possible
convenient [kən'vi:njənt] *adj* : commode, qui convient
conveniently [kən'vi:njəntli] *adv* : commodément
convent ['kɑnvənt, -ˌvɛnt] *n* : couvent *m*
convention [kən'vɛntʃən] *n* **1** AGREEMENT : convention *f* **2** ASSEMBLY, MEETING : conférence *f*, congrès *m* **3** CUSTOM : convention *f*, usage *m*
conventional [kən'vɛntʃənəl] *adj* : conventionnel — **conventionally** *adv*
converge [kən'vərdʒ] *vi* **-verged; -verging** : converger
conversant [kən'vərsənt] *adj* **to be conversant with** : connaître, être versé dans
conversation [ˌkɑnvər'seɪʃən] *n* : conversation *f*
conversational [ˌkɑnvər'seɪʃənəl] *adj* : familier <conversational style : style familier>
converse[1] [kən'vɛrs] *vi* **-versed; -versing** : converser
converse[2] [kən'vərs, 'kɑnˌvɛrs] *adj* : contraire, inverse (en mathématiques, etc.)
conversely [kən'vərsli, 'kɑnˌvɛrs-] *adv* : inversement
conversion [kən'vərʒən] *n* **1** : conversion *f* (en religion) **2** CHANGE : transformation *f*, changement *m*
convert[1] [kən'vɛrt] *vt* **1** : convertir (en religion) **2** CHANGE : transformer, changer — *vi* : se convertir
convert[2] ['kɑnˌvərt] *n* : converti *m*, -tie *f*
converter *or* **convertor** [kən'vərt̬ər] *n* : convertisseur *m*
convertible[1] [kən'vərt̬əbəl] *adj* : convertible
convertible[2] *n* : décapotable *f* (voiture)
convex [kɑn'vɛks, 'kɑnˌ-, kən'-] *adj* : convexe
convey [kən'veɪ] *vt* **-veyed; -veying 1** TRANSPORT : transporter **2** COMMUNICATE, TRANSMIT : transmettre, exprimer, communiquer
conveyance [kən'veɪənts] *n* **1** TRANSPORT : transport *m* **2** COMMUNICATION : transmission *f*, communication *f*
convict[1] [kən'vɪkt] *vt* : déclarer coupable, condamner
convict[2] ['kɑnˌvɪkt] *n* : détenu *m*, -nue *f*
conviction [kən'vɪkʃən] *n* **1** : condamnation *f* (en droit) **2** BELIEF : conviction *f*, certitude *f* <personal convictions : convictions personnelles>
convince [kən'vɪnts] *vt* **-vinced; -vincing** : convaincre, persuader
convincing [kən'vɪntsɪŋ] *adj* : convaincant, persuasif
convivial [kən'vɪvjəl, -'vɪviəl] *adj* : convivial, jovial
conviviality [kənˌvɪvi'ælət̬i] *n, pl* **-ties** : convivialité *f*, gaieté *f*
convocation [ˌkɑnvə'keɪʃən] *n* : convocation *f*
convoke [kən'vo:k] *vt* **-voked; -voking** : convoquer
convoluted ['kɑnvəˌlu:t̬əd] *adj* **1** TWISTED : convoluté **2** INTRICATE : alambiqué, compliqué <convoluted reasoning : raisonnement alambiqué>
convoy ['kɑnˌvɔɪ] *n* : convoi *m*
convulse [kən'vʌls] *v* **-vulsed; -vulsing** *vt* : convulser <convulsed with pain : convulsé par la douleur> <to be convulsed with laughter : se tordre de rire> — *vi* : se convulser, souffrir de convulsions
convulsion [kən'vʌlʃən] *n* : convulsion *f*
convulsive [kən'vʌlsɪv] *adj* : convulsif
coo[1] ['ku:] *vi* : roucouler
coo[2] *n* : roucoulement *m*
cook[1] ['kʊk] *vi* **1** : cuire (se dit des aliments) **2**: cuisiner, faire la cuisine (se dit d'une personne) — *vt* **1** : cuisiner, cuire **2** *or* **to cook up** CONCOCT : inventer, mijoter
cook[2] *n* : cuisinier *m*, -nière *f*
cookbook ['kʊkˌbʊk] *n* : livre *m* de recettes, livre *m* de cuisine
cookery ['kʊkəri] *n, pl* **-eries** : cuisine *f*
cookie *or* **cooky** ['kʊki] *n, pl* **-ies** : biscuit *m*, gâteau *m* sec
cool[1] ['ku:l] *vt* : refroidir — *vi* **1** *or* **to cool down** : se refroidir **2** : se dissiper <his anger cooled : sa colère s'est dissipée>
cool[2] *adj* **1** : frais <a cool breeze : une brise fraîche> **2** CALM : calme **3** UNFRIENDLY : indifférent, froid
cool[3] *n* **1** COOLNESS : fraîcheur *m* **2** COMPOSURE : calme *m*, sang-froid *m* <to lose one's cool : perdre son sang-froid>
coolant ['ku:lənt] *n* : liquide *m* de refroidissement
cooler ['ku:lər] *n* : glacière *f*
coolie ['ku:li] *n* : coolie *m*

coolly ['ku:li] *adv* : froidement

coolness ['ku:lnəs] *n* **1** : fraîcheur *m* <the coolness of the evening : la fraîcheur du soir> **2** COLDNESS, INDIFFERENCE : froideur *m,* indifférence *f* **3** COMPOSURE : calme *m,* sang-froid *m*

coop[1] ['ku:p, 'kʊp] *vt or* **to coop up** : enfermer <cooped up in his apartment : enfermé dans son appartement>

coop[2] *n* : poulailler *m*

co–op ['ko:ˌɑp] → **cooperative**[2]

cooperate [ko'ɑpəˌreɪt] *vi* **-ated; -ating** : coopérer, collaborer

cooperation [koˌɑpə'reɪʃən] *n* : coopération *f,* collaboration *f*

cooperative[1] [ko'ɑpərət̬ɪv] *adj* : coopératif

cooperative[2] *n* : coopérative *f*

co–opt [ko'ɑpt] *vt* : coopter

coordinate[1] [ko'ɔrdənˌeɪt] *v* **-nated; -nating** *vt* : coordonner **—** *vi* : agir en coordination

coordinate[2] [ko'ɔrdənət] *adj* : coordonné <coordinate clause : proposition coordonnée>

coordinate[3] [ko'ɔrdənət] *n* : coordonnée *f*

coordination [koˌɔrdən'eɪʃən] *n* : coordination *f*

coordinator [ko'ɔrdənˌeɪt̬ər] *n* : coordinateur *m,* -trice *f*

cop ['kɑp] *n* : flic *m fam*

cope ['ko:p] *vi* **coped; coping 1** MANAGE : se débrouiller, s'en sortir **2 to cope with** DEAL, FACE : faire face à, affronter <I can't cope with all that : je ne peux pas supporter tout cela>

copier ['kɑpiər] *n* **1** : copieur *m,* -pieuse *f* (personne) **2** PHOTOCOPIER : photocopieur *m,* machine à photocopier

copilot ['ko:ˌpaɪlət] : copilote *mf*

copious ['ko:piəs] *adj* : copieux, abondant

copiously ['ko:piəsli] *adv* : copieusement, abondamment

copper ['kɑpər] *n* : cuivre *m*

copperhead ['kɑpərˌhɛd] *n* : vipère *f* cuivrée

coppery ['kɑpəri] *adj* : cuivré

coppice ['kɑpəs] *n* THICKET : taillis *m*

copra ['ko:prə, 'kɑ-] *n* : copra *m*

copse ['kɑps] → **coppice**

copulate ['kɑpjəˌleɪt] *vi* **-lated; -lating** : copuler

copulation [ˌkɑpjə'leɪʃən] *n* : copulation *f*

copy[1] ['kɑpi] *v* **copied; copying** : copier

copy[2] *n, pl* **copies 1** IMITATION, REPRODUCTION : copie *f,* reproduction *f* **2** : exemplaire *m* (d'un livre, etc.), numéro *m* (d'une revue)

copyright[1] ['kɑpiˌraɪt] *vt* : protéger les droits d'auteur de

copyright[2] *n* : droits *mpl* d'auteur, copyright *m*

coquette [ko:'kɛt] *n* : coquette *f*

coral ['kɔrəl] *n* **1** : corail *m* <coral reef : récif de corail> **2** : couleur *f* de corail

coral snake *n* : serpent *m* corail

cord ['kɔrd] *n* **1** ROPE, STRING : corde *f,* cordon *m* **2** : cordon *m* (anatomique) <umbilical cord : cordon ombilical> **3** *or* **electrical cord** : fil *m* (électrique) **4** : corde *f* (de bois)

cordial[1] ['kɔrdʒəl] *adj* : cordial, amical **— cordially** *adv*

cordial[2] *n* LIQUEUR : cordial *m*

cordon ['kɔrdən] *n* : cordon *m* (d'agents de police)

corduroy ['kɔrdəˌrɔɪ] *n* **1** : velours *m* côtelé **2 corduroys** *npl* : pantalon *m* en velours côtelé

core[1] ['kor] *vt* **cored; coring** : enlever le cœur de (un fruit)

core[2] *n* **1** : cœur *m,* trognon *m* (d'un fruit) **2** CENTER : cœur *m,* noyau *m* <the core of the problem : le cœur du problème> **3 to the core** : jusqu'à l'os <honest to the core : honnête jusqu'à l'os>

cork[1] ['kɔrk] *vt* : boucher (avec un bouchon)

cork[2] *n* **1** : liège *m* **2** : bouchon *m* (d'une bouteille)

corkscrew ['kɔrkˌskru:] *n* : tire-bouchon *m*

cormorant ['kɔrmərənt, -ˌrænt] *n* : cormoran *m*

corn ['kɔrn] *n* **1** GRAIN : grain *m* (de blé, etc.) **2** → **Indian corn 3** : cor *f* (sur le pied)

corncob ['kɔrnˌkɑb] *n* : épi *m* de maïs

cornea ['kɔrniə] *n* : cornée *f*

corned beef *n* : corned-beef *m*

corner[1] ['kɔrnər] *vt* **1** TRAP : acculer (un animal, etc.) **2** MONOPOLIZE : accaparer <to corner the market : accaparer le marché> **—** *vi* TURN : prendre un virage (se dit d'une voiture)

corner[2] *n* **1** : coin *m,* angle *m,* encoignure *f* <the corner of a room : le coin d'une chambre> **2** INTERSECTION : coin *m,* intersection *f* <to turn the corner : tourner au coin de la rue> <around the corner : à deux pas d'ici> **3** PLACE : coin *m,* endroit *m* <a quiet corner : un endroit tranquille> **4** MONOPOLY : monopole *m*

cornerstone ['kɔrnərˌsto:n] *n* : pierre *f* angulaire

cornet [kɔr'nɛt] *n* : cornet *m* à pistons

cornice ['kɔrnɪs] *n* : corniche *f*

cornmeal ['kɔrnˌmi:l] *n* : farine *f* de maïs

cornstalk ['kɔrnˌstɔk] *n* : tige *f* de maïs

cornstarch ['kɔrnˌstɑrtʃ] *n* : fécule *f* de maïs

cornucopia [ˌkɔrnə'ko:piə, -njə-] *n* : corne *f* d'abondance

corny ['kɔrni] *adj* **cornier; -est** : bateau, banal, quétaine *Can fam*

corolla [kə'rɑlə] *n* : corolle *f*

corollary [ˈkɔrəˌlɛri] *n, pl* **-laries** : corollaire *m*
corona [kəˈroːnə] *n* : couronne *f* (en astronomie)
coronary[1] [ˈkɔrəˌnɛri] *adj* : coronaire
coronary[2] *n, pl* **-naries** HEART ATTACK : infarctus *m* myocarde, crise *f* cardiaque
coronation [ˌkɔrəˈneɪʃən] *n pl* **-naries** : couronnement *m*
coroner [ˈkɔrənər] *n* : coroner *m*
corporal[1] [ˈkɔrpərəl] *adj* : corporel <corporal punishment : châtiment corporel>
corporal[2] *n* : caporal-chef *m*
corporate [ˈkɔrpərət] *adj* **1** : de la société, d'entreprise **2** COLLECTIVE : collectif, commun
corporation [ˌkɔrpəˈreɪʃən] *n* : compagnie *f* commerciale, société *f*
corporeal [kɔrˈporiəl] *adj* **1** PHYSICAL : physique, corporel **2** MATERIAL : matériel
corps [ˈkor] *n, pl* **corps 1** : corps *m* (militaire) **2** BODY, GROUP : corps *m* <diplomatic corps : corps diplomatique>
corpse [ˈkɔrps] *n* : cadavre *m*
corpulence [ˈkɔrpjələnts] *n* : corpulence *f,* embonpoint *m*
corpulent [ˈkɔrpjələnt] *adj* : corpulent, gras
corpus [ˈkɔrpəs] *n, pl* **-pora** [-pərə] : recueil *m* (d'œuvres écrits)
corpuscle [ˈkɔrˌpʌsəl] *n* **1** : corpuscule *m* (en physiologie) **2 red blood corpuscles** : globules *m* rouges
corral[1] [kəˈræl] *vt* **-ralled; -ralling** : enfermer dans un corral (se dit du bétail)
corral[2] *n* : corral *m*
correct[1] [kəˈrɛkt] *vt* **1** RECTIFY : corriger (un texte, etc.), rectifier (une situation, etc.) **2** : corriger (un examen, une erreur), reprendre (à une personne) <to correct s.o.'s French : corriger le français de qqn>
correct[2] *adj* **1** RIGHT : exact, correct, juste <that's correct : c'est exact> **2** APPROPRIATE : correct, convenable
correction [kəˈrɛkʃən] *n* : correction *f*
corrective [kəˈrɛktɪv] *adj* : correctif
correctly [kəˈrɛktli] *adv* : correctement
correlate [ˈkɔrəˌleɪt] *vt* **-lated; -lating** : mettre en corrélation
correlation [ˌkɔrəˈleɪʃən] *n* : corrélation *f*
correspond [ˌkɔrəˈspɑnd] *vi* **1** MATCH, TALLY : correspondre, concorder **2** WRITE : correspondre, s'écrire
correspondence [ˌkɔrəˈspɑndənts] *n* : correspondance *f*
correspondent [ˌkɔrəˈspɑndənt] *n* **1** : correspondant *m,* -dante *f* **2** REPORTER : journaliste *mf;* correspondant *m,* -dante *f*
corridor [ˈkɔrədər, -ˌdɔr] *n* : corridor *m,* passage *m,* couloir *m*
corroborate [kəˈrɑbəˌreɪt] *vt* **-rated; -rating** : corroborer, confirmer
corroboration [kəˌrɑbəˈreɪʃən] *n* : confirmation *f,* corroboration *f*
corrode [kəˈroːd] *v* **-roded; -roding** *vt* : corroder — *vi* : se corroder
corrosion [kəˈroːʒən] *n* : corrosion *f*
corrosive [kəˈroːsɪv] *adj* : corrosif
corrugated [ˈkɔrəˌgeɪt̬əd] *adj* : ondulé <corrugated cardboard : carton ondulé>
corrupt[1] [kəˈrʌpt] *vt* **1** DEBASE, PERVERT : corrompre, pervertir **2** BRIBE : corrompre, soudoyer **3** ALTER : altérer (un texte)
corrupt[2] *adj* **1** IMMORAL : corrumpu, dépravé **2** ALTERED : altéré
corruption [kəˈrʌpʃən] *n* : corruption *f*
corsage [kɔrˈsɑʒ, -ˈsɑdʒ] *n* : petit bouquet *m* de fleurs (porté au corsage d'une robe, etc.)
corset [ˈkɔrsət] *n* : corset *m*
Corsican[1] [ˈkɔrsɪkən] *adj* : corse
Corsican[2] *n* : Corse *mf*
cortege [kɔrˈtɛʒ] *n* : cortège *m*
cortex [ˈkɔrˌtɛks] *n, pl* **-tices** [ˈkɔrt̬əˌsiːz] *or* **-texes** : cortex *m*
cortisone [ˈkɔrt̬əˌsoːn, -zoːn] *n* : cortisone *f*
cosmetic[1] [kɑzˈmɛt̬ɪk] *adj* : cosmétique, esthétique <cosmetic surgery : chirurgie esthétique>
cosmetic[2] *n* : cosmétique *f*
cosmic [ˈkɑzmɪk] *adj* **1** : cosmique <cosmic ray : rayon cosmique> **2** VAST : vaste, gigantesque
cosmonaut [ˈkɑzməˌnɔt] *n* : cosmonaute *mf*
cosmopolitan [ˌkɑzməˈpɑlətən] *adj* : cosmopolite
cosmos [ˈkɑzməs, -ˌmoːs, -ˌmɑs] *n* : cosmos *m,* univers *m*
cost[1] [ˈkɔst] *v* **cost; costing** *vt* : coûter <how much does it cost? : combien ça coûte?> <it cost him his job : ça lui a coûté son emploi> — *vi* : coûter <this one costs less : celui-ci coûte moins cher>
cost[2] *n* **1** PRICE : coût *m,* prix *m* <the cost of living : le coût de la vie> <victory at any cost : la victoire à tout prix> <at cost : à prix coûtant> **2 costs** *npl* : frais *mpl,* dépenses *fpl* <traveling costs : frais de voyagement>
Costa Rican[1] [ˌkɔstəˈriːkən] *adj* : costaricain
Costa Rican[2] *n* : Costaricain *m,* -caine *f*
costly [ˈkɔstli] *adj* **costlier; -est** : coûteux, cher
costume [ˈkɑsˌtuːm, -ˌtjuːm] *n* **1** : costume *f* <national costume : costume national> <Halloween costume : costume d'Halloween> **2** OUTFIT : costume *f* (d'une femme)
cosy [ˈkoːzi] → **cozy**
cot [ˈkɑt] *n* : lit *m* de camp

cottage ['kɑṭɪdʒ] *n* : petite maison *f*, chalet *m Can*
cottage cheese *n* : fromage *m* blanc, fromage *m* cottage
cotton ['kɑtən] *n* : coton *m*
cottonwood ['kɑtən,wʊd] *n* : liard *m Can*
couch[1] ['kaʊtʃ] *vt* : formuler, exprimer <couched in diplomatic language : formulé en langage diplomatique>
couch[2] *n* SOFA : canapé *m*, sofa *m*, divan *m*
cougar ['ku:gər] *n* : puma *m*, couguar *m*
cough[1] ['kɔf] *vi* : tousser
cough[2] *n* : toux *m*
could ['kʊd] → **can**
council ['kaʊntsəl] *n* : conseil *m*, assemblée *f* <city council : conseil municipal>
councillor *or* **councilor** ['kaʊntsələr] *n* : conseiller *m*, -lère *f*
counsel[1] ['kaʊntsəl] *v* **-seled** *or* **-selled; -seling** *or* **-selling** *vt* ADVISE : conseiller, guider — *vi* CONSULT : consulter
counsel[2] *n* **1** ADVICE : conseil *m* **2** CONSULTATION : consultation *f*, délibération *f* **3** LAWYER : avocat *m*, -cate *f*
counselor *or* **counsellor** ['kaʊntsələr] *n* **1** : conseiller *m*, -lère *f* <guidance counselor : conseiller d'orientation> **2** LAWYER : avocat *m*, -cate *f* **3** *or* **camp counselor** : moniteur *m*, -trice *f*
count[1] ['kaʊnt] *vt* ENUMERATE : dénombrer, compter — *vi* **1** : compter <to count to ten : compter jusqu'à dix> **2** MATTER : compter, importer **3 to count on** : compter sur
count[2] *n* **1** COMPUTATION : compte *m*, décompte *m* **2** CHARGE : chef *m* d'accusation <convicted on two counts : condamné pour deux chefs d'accusation> **3** : comte *m* (noble)
countable ['kaʊntəbəl] *adj* : nombrable, dénombrable
countenance[1] ['kaʊntənənts] *vt* **-nanced; -nancing** : approuver, sanctionner
countenance[2] *n* FACE : visage *m*, expression *f*
counter[1] ['kaʊntər] *vt* OPPOSE : s'opposer à, contrecarrer — *vi* RETALIATE : contre-attaquer, riposter
counter[2] *adv* **counter to** : à l'encontre de <to act counter to his advice : agir à l'encontre de ses conseils>
counter[3] *adj* : contraire, opposé
counter[4] *n* **1** PIECE : jeton *m* (d'un jeu de société) **2** : comptoir *m*, guichet *m* <post office counter : guichet de la poste> **3** : compteur *m* (dispositif) <Geiger counter : compteur Geiger>
counteract [,kaʊntər'ækt] *vt* : contrebalancer, neutraliser
counterattack[1] ['kaʊntərə,tæk] *vi* : contre-attaquer
counterattack[2] *n* : contre-attaque *f*
counterbalance[1] [,kaʊntər'bælənts] *vt* : contrebalancer, faire contrepoids à
counterbalance[2] *n* : contrepoids *m*
counterclockwise [,kaʊntər'klɑk,waɪz] *adv & adj* : dans le sens contraire des aiguilles d'une montre
counterfeit[1] ['kaʊntər,fɪt] *vt* **1** : contrefaire, falsifier (une monnaie, etc.) **2** FEIGN : feindre (une émotion)
counterfeit[2] *adj* : faux <counterfeit money : fausse monnaie>
counterfeit[3] *n* : contrefaçon *f*, faux *m*
counterfeiter ['kaʊntər,fɪṭər] *n* : faussaire *mf*, faux-monnayeur *m*
countermand ['kaʊntər,mænd] *vt* : annuler (un ordre)
counterpart ['kaʊntər,pɑrt] *n* : homologue *mf* (d'une personne), équivalent *m* (d'une chose)
counterpoint ['kaʊntər,pɔɪnt] *n* : contrepoint *m*
counterrevolution [,kaʊntər,rɛvə'lu:ʃən] *n* : contre-révolution *f*
counterrevolutionary[1] [,kaʊntər,rɛvə'lu:ʃən,ɛri] *adj* : contre-révolutionnaire
counterrevolutionary[2] *n, pl* **-aries** : contre-révolutionnaire *mf*
countersign ['kaʊntər,saɪn] *vt* : contresigner
countess ['kaʊntɪs] *n* : comtesse *f*
countless ['kaʊntləs] *adj* : innombrable, incalculable
country[1] ['kʌntri] *adj* RURAL : champêtre, rural
country[2] *n, pl* **-tries 1** NATION : pays *m*, patrie *f*, nation *f* <neighboring countries : pays voisins> <love of one's country : amour de la patrie> **2** : campagne *f* <she lives in the country : elle demeure à la campagne>
countryman ['kʌntrimən] *n, pl* **-men** [-mən, -,mɛn] **1** COMPATRIOT : compatriote *mf* **2** RUSTIC : campagnard *m*, -gnarde *f*; habitant *m*, -tante *f* de la campagne
countryside ['kʌntri,saɪd] *n* : campagne *f*
county ['kaʊnti] *n, pl* **-ties** : comté *m*
coup ['ku:] *n, pl* **coups 1** ACT, FEAT : (beau) coup *m* **2** *or* **coup d'état** : coup *m* d'état
coupé [ku:'peɪ] *or* **coupe** ['ku:p] *n* : coupé *m*
couple[1] ['kʌpəl] *v* **-pled; -pling** *vt* : accoupler — *vi* : s'accoupler
couple[2] *n* **1** : couple *m* <a happy couple : un couple heureux> **2 a couple of** : deux <a couple of days ago : il y a deux ou trois jours>
coupling ['kʌplɪŋ] *n* : couplage *m* (en électricité, etc.)
coupon ['ku:,pɑn, 'kju:-] *n* : coupon *m*
courage ['kərɪdʒ] *n* : courage *m*
courageous [kə'reɪdʒəs] *adj* : courageux — **courageously** *adv*
courier ['kʊriər, 'kəriər] *n* MESSENGER : messager *m*, -gère *f*

course[1] ['kors] *vi* **coursed; coursing** FLOW : couler, ruisseler <blood was coursing through his veins : le sang coulait dans ses veines>

course[2] *n* **1** PROGRESS : cours *m* <in the course of : au cours de> **2** DIRECTION, PATH : cours *m* (d'un fleuve, etc.), direction *f,* ligne *f* <to change course : changer de direction> <course of action : ligne de conduite> **3** : parcours *m,* terrain *m* (aux sports) <golf course : terrain de golf> **4** : service *m,* plat *m* <seven-course meal : repas de sept services> **5** : cours *m* (universitaire) **6 of course** : évidemment, bien sûr

court[1] ['kort] *vt* : courtiser, faire la cour à

court[2] *n* **1** : cour *f* (d'un souverain) **2** COURTYARD : cour *f* **3** : court *m,* terrain *m* (aux sports) **4** TRIBUNAL : cour *f,* tribunal *m* <to appear in court : comparaître au tribunal>

courteous ['kərt̬iəs] *adj* : courtois, poli — **courteously** *adv*

courtesan ['kort̬əzən, 'kər-] *n* : courtisane *f*

courtesy ['kərt̬əsi] *n, pl* **-sies** : courtoisie *f*

courthouse ['kort,haʊs] *n* : palais *m* de justice

courtier ['kort̬iər, 'kortjər] *n* : courtisan *m*

courtly ['kortli] *adj* **courtlier; -est** : poli, élégant

court–martial ['kort,mɑrʃəl] *n, pl* **courts–martial** ['korts,mɑrʃəl] : cour *f* martiale

courtroom ['kort,ru:m] *n* : salle *f* d'audience

courtship ['kort,ʃɪp] *n* : cour *f*

courtyard ['kort,jɑrd] *n* : cour *f,* patio *m*

cousin ['kʌzən] *n* : cousin *m,* -sine *f*

cove ['ko:v] *n* : anse *f,* crique *f*

coven ['kəvən, 'ko:-] *n* : groupe *m* de sorcières

covenant ['kʌvənənt] *n* : contrat *m,* pacte *m*

cover[1] ['kʌvər] *vt* **1** : couvrir, recouvrir **2** PROTECT : couvrir, protéger **3** HIDE : cacher, dissimuler **4** INCLUDE, TREAT : inclure, comprendre **5** : faire un reportage sur <she covered the story : elle a fait un reportage sur l'affaire> **6** INSURE : assurer, couvrir

cover[2] *n* **1** SHELTER : abri *m,* refuge *m* <to take cover : se mettre à l'abri> **2** LID : couvercle *m* **3** : couverture *f* (d'un livre), pochette *f* (d'un disque) **4** → **slipcover 5 covers** *npl* BEDCLOTHES : couvertures *fpl*

coverage ['kʌvərɪdʒ] *n* **1** COVERING : couverture *f* **2** REPORTING : reportage *m,* couverture *f* **3** *or* **insurance coverage** : couverture *f* d'assurance

coverlet ['kʌvərlət] *n* BEDSPREAD : couvre-lit *m*

covert[1] ['ko:,vərt, 'kʌvərt] *adj* : voilé, secret

covert[2] ['kʌvərt, 'ko:-] *n* THICKET : fourré *m*

cover-up ['kʌvər,ʌp] *n* : opération *f* de camouflage

covet ['kʌvət] *vt* : convoiter

covetous ['kʌvət̬əs] *adj* : avide, cupide

covey ['kʌvi] *n, pl* **-eys 1** : compagnie *f* (d'oiseaux) **2** GROUP : groupe *m*

cow[1] ['kaʊ] *vt* : intimider, effrayer

cow[2] *n* : vache *f*

coward ['kaʊərd] *n* : lâche *mf;* poltron *m,* -tronne *f*

cowardice ['kaʊərdɪs] *n* : lâcheté *f*

cowardly ['kaʊərdli] *adj* : lâche

cowboy ['kaʊ,bɔɪ] *n* : cow-boy *m,* vacher *m*

cower ['kaʊər] *vi* : se tapir (se dit d'un animal), trembler (de peur)

cowgirl ['kaʊ,gərl] *n* : vachère *f*

cowhide ['kaʊ,haɪd] *n* : peau *f* de vache

cowl ['kaʊl] *n* : capuchon *m*

cowlick ['kaʊ,lɪk] *n* : mèche *f* rebelle

cowpuncher ['kaʊ,pʌntʃər] → **cowboy**

cowslip ['kaʊ,slɪp] *n* : primevère *f* sauvage, coucou *m*

coxswain ['kɑksən, -,sweɪn] *n* : patron *m* (d'un bateau)

coy ['kɔɪ] *adj* **1** SHY : (faussement) timide **2** COQUETTISH : coquet

coyote [kaɪ'o:t̬i, 'kaɪ,o:t] *n, pl* **coyotes** *or* **coyote** : coyote *m*

cozen ['kʌzən] *vt* : décevoir

cozy ['ko:zi] *adj* **cozier; -est** : douillet, confortable

crab ['kræb] *n* : crabe *m*

crabby ['kræbi] *adj* **crabbier; -est** : revêche, acariâtre, grognon

crack[1] ['kræk] *vt* **1** SPLIT : fêler, fendre **2** BREAK : casser (un œuf, etc.) **3** : faire claquer (un fouet), faire craquer (les jointures) **4 to crack jokes** : faire des blagues — *vi* **1** SPLIT : se fêler, se fendre **2** : craquer, claquer <the whip cracked : le fouet a claqué> **3** BREAK : se casser, muer (se dit de la voix) **4** : craquer, s'effondrer <he cracked under the strain : il s'est effondré faute d'un trop grand effort>

crack[2] *adj* FIRST-RATE : de première classe, d'élite

crack[3] *n* **1** SNAP : craquement *m,* bruit *m* sec **2** SPLIT : crevasse *f,* fissure *f,* craque *f Can* **3** JOKE : plaisanterie *f,* blague *f* **4** ATTEMPT : essai *m,* tentative *f* <to have a crack at : essayer (un coup)>

crackdown ['kræk,daʊn] *n* : mesures *fpl* énergiques

crack down *vi* : prendre des mesures énergiques

cracker ['krækər] *n* : biscuit *m* salé

crackle[1] ['krækəl] *vi* **-led; -ling** : crépiter, pétiller <a crackling fire : un feu qui crépite>

crackle[2] *n* : crépitement *m*

crackpot ['kræk,pɑt] *n* : excentrique *mf,* personne *f* originale

crack–up ['kræk,ʌp] *n* **1** CRASH : accident *m,* collision *f* **2** BREAKDOWN : dépression *f* nerveuse

crack up *vi* **1** CRASH : s'écraser **2** LAUGH : rire **3** BREAK DOWN : s'effondrer

cradle[1] ['kreɪdəl] *vt* **-dled; -dling** : tenir délicatement, bercer (un enfant)

cradle[2] *n* : berceau *m*

craft ['kræft] *n* **1** SKILL, TRADE : métier *m,* art *m* **2** CRAFTINESS : astuce *f,* ruse *f* **3** *pl usu* **craft** BOAT : bateau *m,* embarcation *f* **4** *pl usu* **craft** AIRCRAFT : avion *m,* aéronef *m*

craftiness ['kræftinəs] *n* : astuce *f,* ruse *f*

craftsman ['kræftsmən] *n, pl* **-men** [-mən, -,mɛn] : artisan *m,* -sane *f*

crafty ['kræfti] *adj* **craftier; -est** : astucieux, rusé, ratourneur *Can*

crag ['kræg] *n* : rocher *m* escarpé

craggy ['krægi] *adj* **craggier; -est** : escarpé et rocheux

cram ['kræm] *v* **crammed; cramming** *vt* JAM, PACK : fourrer, bourrer, entasser — *vi* : étudier (à la dernière minute)

cramp[1] ['kræmp] *vt* HAMPER : entraver, gêner <to cramp s.o.'s style : priver qqn de ses moyens> — *vi* : avoir une crampe

cramp[2] *n* : crampe *f* (musculaire)

cranberry ['kræn,bɛri] *n, pl* **-berries** : canneberge *f,* atoca(s) *m Can*

crane[1] ['kreɪn] *vt* **craned; craning** STRETCH : tendre <to crane one's neck : tendre le cou>

crane[2] *n* : grue *f* (oiseau ou machine)

cranial ['kreɪniəl] *adj* : crânien

cranium ['kreɪniem] *n, pl* **-niums** *or* **-nia** : crâne *m,* boîte *f* crânienne

crank[1] ['kræŋk] *vt or* **to crank up** : démarrer (un moteur) à la manivelle

crank[2] *n* **1** : manivelle *f* **2** ECCENTRIC : excentrique *mf*

cranky ['kræŋki] *adj* **crankier; -est** : de mauvaise humeur, irritable

cranny ['kræni] *n, pl* **-nies** **1** CREVICE : (petite) fente *f* **2** NOOK : coin *m,* recoin *m* <every nook and cranny : tous les coins et recoins>

crash[1] ['kræʃ] *vt* **to crash one's car** : avoir un accident de voiture — *vi* **1** SMASH : se fracasser, s'écraser <to crash to the ground : s'écraser au sol> **2** RESOUND : retentir **3** : faire faillite (se dit des banques, etc.), s'effondrer (se dit des prix à la Bourse)

crash[2] *n* **1** DIN : fracas *m,* bruit *m* sourd <a crash of thunder : un coup de tonnerre> **2** COLLISION : accident *m,* collision *f* **3** FAILURE : effondrement *m,* krach *m* (boursier)

crass ['kræs] *adj* : crasse, grossier

crate[1] ['kreɪt] *vt* **crated; crating** : mettre en cageot, mettre en caisse

crate[2] *n* : cageot *m,* caisse *f*

crater ['kreɪt̬ər] *n* : cratère *m*

cravat [krə'væt] *n* **1** SCARF : foulard *m* **2** NECKTIE : cravate *f*

crave ['kreɪv] *vt* **craved; craving** : désirer, avoir très envie de

craven ['kreɪvən] *adj* : lâche, poltron

craving ['kreɪvɪŋ] *n* : envie *f* (incontrôlable), soif *f*

crawfish ['krɔ,fɪʃ] → **crayfish**

crawl[1] ['krɔl] *vi* **1** : ramper, se traîner, marcher à quatre pattes (se dit d'un bébé) **2** SWARM : fourmiller, grouiller <to be crawling with : grouiller de>

crawl[2] *n* **1** : pas *m* de tortue <to move at a crawl : avancer à un pas de tortue> **2** : crawl *m* (en natation)

crayfish ['kreɪ,fɪʃ] *n* **1** : écrevisse *f* (d'eau douce) **2** : langouste *f* (de mer)

crayon ['kreɪ,ɑn, -ən] *n* : crayon *m* de cire

craze ['kreɪz] *n* FAD : mode *f,* vogue *f*

crazily ['kreɪzəli] *adv* : comme un fou, d'une manière insensée

craziness ['kreɪzinəs] *n* : folie *f*

crazy ['kreɪzi] *adj* **crazier; -est** **1** INSANE : fou, dément **2** FOOLISH : fou, insensé **3** **to be crazy about** : être fou de

creak[1] ['kri:k] *vi* : grincer, craquer

creak[2] *n* : grincement *m,* craquement *m*

creaky ['kri:ki] *adj* **creakier; -est** : grinçant, qui craque

cream[1] ['kri:m] *vt* **1** BEAT, BLEND : battre en crème, travailler <to cream butter and sugar together : travailler le beurre et le sucre> **2** : préparer (des légumes, etc.) à la béchamel

cream[2] *n* **1** : crème *f* (de lait) **2** LOTION : crème *f,* lotion *f* **3** ELITE : crème *f,* élite *f* <the cream of society : la crème de la société>

creamery ['kri:məri] *n, pl* **-eries** DAIRY : laiterie *f*

creamy ['kri:mi] *adj* **creamier; -est** **1** : crémeux **2** : laiteux <creamy skin : peau laiteuse>

crease[1] ['kri:s] *v* **creased; creasing** *vt* **1** : faire les plis de (pantalons, etc.) **2** CRUMPLE : froisser — *vi* : se froisser

crease[2] *n* : pli *m,* faux pli *m*

create [kri'eɪt] *vt* **-ated; -ating** **1** MAKE : créer, faire **2** CAUSE : créer, provoquer

creation [kri'eɪʃən] *n* : création *f*

creative [kri'eɪt̬ɪv] *adj* : créatif, créateur

creatively [kri'eɪt̬ɪvli] *adv* : de manière créative

creativity [,kri:eɪ'tɪvət̬i] *n* : créativité *f*

creator [kri'eɪt̬ər] *n* **1** : créateur *m,* -trice *f* **2** **the Creator** : le Créateur

creature ['kri:tʃər] *n* **1** : créature *f* **2** ANIMAL : animal *m,* bête *f*

credence ['kri:dənts] *n* : crédit *m*

credentials [krɪ'dɛntʃəlz] *n* : références *fpl,* lettres *fpl* de créance

credibility [ˌkrɛdəˈbɪləṭi] *n* : crédibilité *f*

credible [ˈkrɛdəbəl] *adj* : credible

credit[1] [ˈkrɛdɪt] *vt* **1** BELIEVE : croire, ajouter foi à (une histoire, etc.) **2** ATTRIBUTE : attribuer <they credit him with the new idea : on lui attribue la nouvelle idée> **3** : créditer (un compte de banque)

credit[2] *n* **1** *or* **credit balance** : solde *m* créditeur (d'un compte) **2** : crédit *m* <to buy on credit : acheter à crédit> **3** CREDENCE : crédit *m,* croyance *f* <to lose credit in s.o.'s eyes : perdre de son crédit aux yeux de qqn> **4** HONOR : honneur *m,* mérite *m* <it's to his credit : c'est à son honneur> <to be a credit to : faire honneur à>

creditable [ˈkrɛdɪṭəbəl] *adj* : honorable <a creditable attempt : une tentative honorable> — **creditably** [-bli] *adv*

credit card *n* : carte *f* de crédit

creditor [ˈkrɛdɪṭər] *n* : créancier *m,* -cière *f*

credulity [krɪˈduːləṭi, -ˈdjuː-] *n* : crédulité *f*

credulous [ˈkrɛdʒələs] *adj* : crédule

creed [ˈkriːd] *n* : crédo *m,* croyance *f*

creek [ˈkriːk, ˈkrɪk] *n* **1** STREAM : ruisseau *m,* crique *m Can* **2** *Brit* COVE, INLET : crique *f,* anse *f*

creel [ˈkriːl] *n* : panier *m* de pêche

creep[1] [ˈkriːp] *vi* **crept; creeping 1** CRAWL : ramper, se glisser, marcher à quatre pattes (se dit des enfants) **2** : avancer lentement, marcher sans bruit <to creep out of the house : partir de la maison sans aucun bruit> **3** SPREAD : ramper, grimper (se dit des plantes) **4 to creep up on** : s'approcher furtivement

creep[2] *n* **1** CRAWL : pas *m* de tortue, ralenti *m* <traffic's moving at a creep : la circulation avance au ralenti> **2 creeps** *npl* : frissons *mpl* <to give s.o. the creeps : donner froid dans le dos à qqn>

cremate [ˈkriːˌmeɪt] *vt* **-mated; -mating** : incinérer

cremation [krɪˈmeɪʃən] *n* : incinération *f*

creole [ˈkriːˌoːl] *adj* : créole

Creole *n* **1** : créole *m* (langue) **2** : Créole *mf* (personne)

creosote [ˈkriːəˌsoːt] *n* : créosote *f*

crepe *or* **crêpe** [ˈkreɪp] *n* **1** : crêpe *m* (tissu) **2** PANCAKE : crêpe *f*

crescendo [krɪˈʃɛnˌdoː] *n, pl* **-dos** *or* **-does** : crescendo *m*

crescent [ˈkrɛsənt] *n* : croissant *m*

cress [ˈkrɛs] *n* : cresson *m*

crest [ˈkrɛst] *n* **1** : crête *f* (d'un oiseau) **2** PEAK : crête *f,* sommet *m* (d'une montagne) **3** COAT OF ARMS : armoiries *fpl* **4** : timbre *m* (au-dessus des armoiries)

crestfallen [ˈkrɛstˌfɔlən] *adj* : déconfit, abattu

cretin [ˈkriːtən] *n* : crétin *m,* -tine *f*

crevasse [krɪˈvæs] *n* : crevasse *f*

crevice [ˈkrɛvəs] *n* : fissure *f,* fente *f*

crew[1] *Brit* → **crow**[1]

crew[2] [ˈkruː] *n* **1** : équipage *m* (d'un navire) **2** TEAM : équipe *f* (d'ouvriers ou d'athlètes)

crib [ˈkrɪb] *n* **1** MANGER : mangeoire *f* **2** : lit *m* d'enfant

crick [ˈkrɪk] *n* SPASM : crampe *f* <to have a crick in one's neck : avoir un torticolis>

cricket [ˈkrɪkət] *n* **1** : grillon *m* (insecte), criquet *m Can* **2** : cricket *m* (jeu)

crier [ˈkraɪər] *n* : crieur *m* <the town crier : le crieur public>

crime [ˈkraɪm] *n* : crime *m,* délit *m*

criminal[1] [ˈkrɪmənəl] *adj* : criminel

criminal[2] *n* : criminel *m,* -nelle *f*

crimp [ˈkrɪmp] *vt* : onduler, friser <to crimp one's hair : friser ses cheveux>

crimson [ˈkrɪmzən] *n* : cramoisi *m*

cringe [ˈkrɪndʒ] *vi* **cringed; cringing** : avoir un mouvement de recul

crinkle [ˈkrɪŋkəl] *v* **-kled; -kling** *vt* : froisser, gaufrer, chiffonner — *vi* : se froisser, se chiffonner

crinkly [ˈkrɪŋkəli] *adj* **crinklier; -est** : gaufré

cripple[1] [ˈkrɪpəl] *vt* **-pled; -pling 1** DISABLE : estropier **2** INCAPACITATE : mettre hors d'usage, paralyser <crippled by fear : paralysé par la peur>

cripple[2] *n, sometimes taken to be offensive* : infirme *mf;* handicapé *m,* -pée *f*

crisis [ˈkraɪsɪs] *n, pl* **crises** [-ˌsiːz] : crise *f*

crisp [ˈkrɪsp] *adj* **1** CRUNCHY : croustillant, croquant <crisp cereal : céréale croustillante> <crisp celery : céleri croquant> **2** SHARP : sec, brusque <a crisp comment : un commentaire sec> **3** INVIGORATING : frais, rafraîchissant <the air was crisp : l'air était rafraîchissant> **4** CLEAR : net, clair <a crisp illustration : une illustration nette>

crisply [ˈkrɪspli] *adv* SHARPLY : d'un ton acerbe, brusquement

crispy [ˈkrɪspi] *adj* **crispier; -est** : croustillant, croquant

crisscross [ˈkrɪsˌkrɔs] *vt* : entrecroiser

criterion [kraɪˈtɪriən] *n, pl* **-ria** [-riə] : critère *m*

critic [ˈkrɪṭɪk] *n* **1** : critique *mf* <movie critic : critique de cinéma> **2** FAULTFINDER : critiqueur *m,* -queuse *f;* détracteur *m,* -trice *f*

critical [ˈkrɪṭɪkəl] *adj* **1** DISAPPROVING : critique **2** ANALYTICAL : critique <critical analysis : analyse critique> **3** CRUCIAL : critique, décisif <critical stage : étape critique>

criticism [ˈkrɪṭəˌsɪzəm] *n* : critique *f*

criticize [ˈkrɪṭəˌsaɪz] *vt* **-cized; -cizing** : critiquer

critique [krɪ'ti:k] *n* : critique *f*
croak[1] ['kro:k] *vi* : coasser (se dit d'une grenouille)
croak[2] *n* : coassement *m*
Croatian[1] [kro'eɪʃən] *adj* : croate
Croatian[2] *n or* **Croat** ['kro,æt] : Croate *mf*
crochet[1] [kro:'ʃeɪ] *vt* : faire (qqch) au crochet — *vi* : faire du crochet
crochet[2] *n* : crochet *m*
crock ['krɑk] *n* : pot *m* (en terre cuite)
crockery ['krɑkəri] *n* EARTHENWARE : faïence *f*
crocodile ['krɑkə,daɪl] *n* : crocodile *m*
crocus ['kro:kəs] *n, pl* **-cuses** : crocus *m*
crone ['kro:n] *n* : vieille *f* bique, vieille *f* taupe
crony ['kro:ni] *n, pl* **-nies** : copain *m*, -pine *f*
crook[1] ['krʊk] *vt* : recourber (le doigt), plier (le coude)
crook[2] *n* **1** : houlette *f* (d'un berger), crosse *f* (d'un évêque) **2** CRIMINEL : escroc *m* **3** BEND, CURVE : courbe *f*, coude *m*
crooked ['krʊkəd] *adj* **1** BENT : crochu, croche *Can* <nez crochu : crooked nose> **2** DISHONEST : malhonnête
croon ['kru:n] *v* : chantonner, chanter doucement
crop[1] ['krɑp] *v* **cropped; cropping** *vt* TRIM : tailler, couper court — *vi* **to crop up** : surgir, se présenter
crop[2] *n* **1** : jabot *m* (d'un oiseau) **2** WHIP : cravache *f* **3** PRODUCE : culture *f* <food crops : cultures vivières> **4** : HARVEST : récolte *f*, moisson *f*
croquet [,kro:'keɪ] *n* : croquet *m*
croquette [,kro:'kɛt] *n* : croquette *f*
crosier ['kro:ʒər] *n* : crosse *f* (d'évêque)
cross[1] ['krɔs] *vt* **1** TRAVERSE : traverser <to cross the road : traverser la rue> **2** *or* **to cross out** CANCEL : rayer, biffer <to cross out a word : rayer un mot> **3** CROSSBREED : croiser (deux espèces) **4** OPPOSE : aller à l'encontre de **5** : se croiser (les bras, les jambes, etc.) — *vi* INTERSECT : se croiser
cross[2] *adj* **1** : transversal <cross street : rue transversale> **2** CONTRARY : contraire, opposé <at cross purposes : ayant des buts contraires> **3** ANGRY : fâché, contrarié
cross[3] *n* **1** : croix *f* **2** HYBRID : croisement *m*, hybride *m*
crossbones ['krɔs,bo:nz] *npl* **1** : os *mpl* en croix **2** → **skull**
crossbow ['krɔs,bo:] *n* : arbalète *f*
crossbreed ['krɔs,bri:d] *vt* **-bred** [-,brɛd, -'brɛd]; **-breeding** : croiser (deux espèces)
cross–examination [,krɔsɪg,zæmə'neɪʃən] *nm* : contre-interrogatoire *m*
cross–examine [,krɔsɪg'zæmən] *vt* **-ined; -ining** : faire subir un contre-interrogatoire à, interroger
cross–eyed ['krɔs,aɪd] *adj* : qui louche, coq-d'œil *Can*
crossing ['krɔsɪŋ] *n* **1** INTERSECTION : croisement *m* **2** VOYAGE : traversée *f* (de la mer) **3** → **crosswalk**
cross–reference [,krɔs'rɛfrənts, -'rɛfərənts] *n* : renvoi *m*
crossroads ['krɔs,ro:dz] *ns & pl* : carrefour *m*
cross section *n* **1** SECTION : coupe *f* transversale **2** SAMPLE : échantillon *m* <a cross section of the population : un échantillon de la population>
crosswalk ['krɔs,wɔk] *n* : passage *m* pour piétons
crossways ['krɔs,weɪz] → **crosswise**
crosswise[1] ['krɔs,waɪz] *adv* : transversalement
crosswise[2] *adj* : en travers
crossword puzzle ['krɔs,wərd] *n* : mots *mpl* croisés
crotch ['krɑtʃ] *n* : entre-jambes *m* (d'un vêtement), fourche *f* (d'un arbre)
crotchety ['krɑtʃət̬i] *adj* : grincheux, grognon
crouch ['kraʊtʃ] *vi* : s'accroupir
croup ['kru:p] *n* : croup *m*
crouton ['kru:,tɑn] *n* : croûton *m*
crow[1] ['kro:] *vi* **crowed** *or in sense 1 Brit* **crew; crowing 1** : chanter (se dit du coq) **2** EXULT : exulter **3** BOAST : se vanter
crow[2] *n* **1** : corbeau *m* (oiseau) **2** : chant *m* (du coq)
crowbar ['kro:,bɑr] *n* : (pince à) levier *m*
crowd[1] ['kraʊd] *vt* CRAM, PACK : entasser, serrer — *vi* : se presser, s'entasser
crowd[2] *n* **1** THRONG : foule *f* **2** GROUP : bande *f* <to stand out from the crowd : se distinguer de la masse>
crown[1] ['kraʊn] *vt* : couronner
crown[2] *n* **1** : couronne *f* **2** SUMMIT : sommet *m*, cime *f* **3** : fond *m* (d'une casquette)
crow's nest *n* : nid *m* de pie
crucial ['kru:ʃəl] *adj* : crucial
crucible ['kru:səbəl] *n* : creuset *m*
crucifix ['kru:sə,fɪks] *n* : crucifix *m*
crucifixion [,kru:sə'fɪkʃən] *n* : crucifixion *f*
crucify ['kru:sə,faɪ] *vt* **-fied; -fying** : crucifier
crude ['kru:d] *adj* **cruder; -est 1** RAW, UNREFINED : brut <crude sugar : sucre brut> **2** VULGAR : grossier, fruste **3** ROUGH : grossier, rudimentaire <a crude shelter : un abri rudimentaire>
crudely ['kru:dli] *adv* : grossièrement
cruel ['kru:əl] *adj* **-eler** *or* **-eller; -elest** *or* **-ellest** : cruel — **cruelly** *adv*
cruelty ['kru:əlti] *n, pl* **-ties** : cruauté *f*
cruet ['kru:ɪt] *n* **1** : burette *f* (en religion) **2** : huilier *m*, vinaigrier *m* (pour la table)
cruise[1] ['kru:z] *vi* **cruised; cruising 1** : faire une croisière, croiser (se dit

d'un bateau) **2** : rouler à sa vitesse de croisière (se dit d'une voiture), voler à sa vitesse de croisière (se dit d'un avion)
cruise² *n* : croisière *f*
cruiser ['kru:zər] *n* **1** WARSHIP : croiseur *m* **2** *or* **police cruiser** : véhicule *m* de police
crumb ['krʌm] *n* : miette *f*
crumble ['krʌmbəl] *v* **-bled; -bling** *vt* : émietter — *vi* : s'émietter, s'effriter
crumbly ['krʌmbli] *adj* **crumblier; -est** : friable
crumple ['krʌmpəl] *v* **-pled; -pling** *vt* : froisser, chiffonner — *vi* **1** *or* **to crumple up** : se froisser **2** COLLAPSE : s'effondrer
crunch¹ ['krʌntʃ] *vt* **1** CHEW : croquer **2** CRUSH : faire crisser — *vi* : craquer, crisser <the snow was crunching underfoot : la neige craquait sous nos pas>
crunch² *n* : craquement *m,* crissement *m*
crunchy ['krʌntʃi] *adj* **crunchier; -est** : croquant
crusade [kru:'seɪd] *n* **1** CAMPAIGN : croisade *f,* campagne *f* **2** **the Crusades** : les croisades *f*
crusader [kru:'seɪdər] *n* **1** : croisé *m* (militaire) **2** ACTIVIST : militant *m,* -tante *f*
crush¹ ['krʌʃ] *vt* **1** SQUASH : écraser, aplatir, écrapoutir *Can* **2** GRIND : broyer, concasser **3** OVERWHELM : écraser
crush² *n* **1** CROWD, MOB : bousculade *f,* cohue *f* **2** INFATUATION : tocade *f fam,* béguin *m*
crust ['krʌst] *n* **1** : croûte *f* (de pain) **2** LAYER : couche *f* <a crust of snow : une couche de neige>
crustacean [ˌkrʌs'teɪʃən] *n* : crustacé *m*
crusty ['krʌsti] *adj* **crustier; -est** **1** : croustillant **2** CROSS, GRUMPY : grincheux, hargneux <a crusty reply : une brusque réplique>
crutch ['krʌtʃ] *n* : béquille *f*
crux ['krʌks, krʊks] *n, pl* **cruxes** : point *m* crucial, cœur *m,* noyau *m* <the crux of the matter : le cœur de l'affaire>
cry¹ ['kraɪ] *v* **cried; crying** *vi* **1** SHOUT : crier, pousser un cri **2** WEEP : pleurer — *vt* SHOUT : crier
cry² *n, pl* **cries** : cri *m*
crypt ['krɪpt] *n* : crypte *f*
cryptic ['krɪptɪk] *adj* : énigmatique, secret
crystal ['krɪstəl] *n* : cristal *m*
crystalline ['krɪstəlɪn] *adj* : cristallin
crystallize ['krɪstəˌlaɪz] *v* **-lized; -lizing** *vt* : cristalliser — *vi* : se cristalliser
cub ['kʌb] *n* : petit *m* (d'un animal)
Cuban¹ ['kju:bən] *adj* : cubain
Cuban² *n* : Cubain *m,* -baine *f*
cubbyhole ['kʌbiˌho:l] *n* : réduit *m*
cube¹ ['kju:b] *vt* **cubed; cubing** **1** : élever (un nombre) au cube **2** DICE : couper en cubes
cube² *n* : cube *m*
cubic ['kju:bɪk] *adj* : cubique
cubicle ['kju:bɪkəl] *n* : box *m*
Cub Scout *n* : louveteau *m*
cuckoo¹ ['ku:ˌku:, 'kʊ-] *adj* : toqué *fam,* cinglé *fam*
cuckoo² *n, pl* **-oos** : coucou *m* (oiseau)
cucumber ['kju:ˌkʌmbər] *n* : concombre *m*
cud ['kʌd] *n* **to chew the cud** : ruminer
cuddle ['kʌdəl] *v* **-dled; -dling** *vt* : caresser, câliner — *vi* : se câliner
cudgel¹ ['kʌdʒəl] *vt* **-geled** *or* **-gelled; -geling** *or* **-gelling** : battre (à coups de gourdin), matraquer
cudgel² *n* : gourdin *m,* trique *f*
cue ['kju:] *n* **1** SIGNAL : signal *m,* réplique *f* (au théâtre) **2** *or* **cue stick** : queue *f* de billard
cuff¹ ['kʌf] *vt* SLAP : gifler, claquer
cuff² *n* **1** : poignet *m* (de chemise), revers *m* (de pantalon) **2** SLAP : gifle *f,* claque *f* **3** **cuffs** *npl* → **handcuffs**
cuisine [kwɪ'zi:n] *n* : cuisine *f*
culinary ['kʌləˌnɛri, 'kju:lə-] *adj* : culinaire
cull ['kʌl] *vt* CHOOSE : choisir, sélectionner
culminate ['kʌlməˌneɪt] *vi* **-nated; -nating** : culminer, plafonner
culmination [ˌkʌlmə'neɪʃən] *n* : point *m* culminant
culpable ['kʌlpəbəl] *adj* BLAMEWORTHY : répréhensible, condamnable
culprit ['kʌlprɪt] *n* : coupable *mf*
cult ['kʌlt] *n* : culte *m*
cultivate ['kʌltəˌveɪt] *vt* **-vated; -vating** **1** : cultiver (la terre) **2** FOSTER : promouvoir, encourager **3** IMPROVE, REFINE : cultiver, perfectionner <to cultivate one's mind : se cultiver l'esprit>
cultivation [ˌkʌltə'veɪʃən] *n* **1** : culture *f* <under cultivation : en culture> **2** REFINEMENT : raffinement *m,* perfectionnement *m*
cultural ['kʌltʃərəl] *adj* : culturel — **culturally** *adv*
culture ['kʌltʃər] *n* **1** CULTIVATION : culture *f* **2** REFINEMENT : culture *f,* savoir *m* **3** CIVILIZATION : culture *f,* civilisation *f*
culvert ['kʌlvərt] *n* : passage *m* hydraulique
cumbersome ['kʌmbərsəm] *adj* : encombrant, embarrassant, lourd
cumulative ['kju:mjələṭɪv, -ˌleɪṭɪv] *adj* : cumulatif
cumulus ['kju:mjələs] *n, pl* **-li** [-laɪ, -li:] : cumulus
cunning¹ ['kʌnɪŋ] *adj* **1** CRAFTY : astucieux **2** CLEVER : ingénieux, habile **3**

CUTE : joli, mignon <a cunning baby : un joli petit bébé>

cunning[2] *n* **1** CRAFTINESS : astuce *f,* ruse *f* **2** SKILL : ingéniosité *f,* habileté *f*

cup[1] ['kʌp] *vt* **cupped; cupping** : faire prendre la forme d'une tasse <to cup one's hands around sth : mettre les mains autour de qqch>

cup[2] *n* **1** : tasse *f* <a cup of tea : une tasse de thé> <a cup of flour : une tasse *f* de farine> **2** TROPHY : coupe *f*

cupboard ['kʌbərd] *n* : placard *m,* armoire *f*

cupcake ['kʌp,keɪk] *n* : petit gateau *m*

cupful ['kʌp,fʊl] *n* : tasse *f*

cupidity [kju:'pɪdəti] *n, pl* **-ties** GREED : cupidité *f*

cupola ['kju:pələ, -,lo:] *n* : coupole *f*

cur ['kər] *n* : chien *m* métis, sale chien *m*

curate ['kjʊrət] *n* : vicaire *m*

curator ['kjʊr,eɪt̬ər, kjʊ'reɪt̬ər] *n* : conservateur *m,* -trice *f* (d'un musée)

curb[1] ['kərb] *vt* : refréner, mettre un frein à

curb[2] *n* **1** CHECK : contrainte *f,* frein *m* **2** : bord *m* du trottoir <to step off the curb : descendre du trottoir>

curdle ['kərdəl] *v* **-dled; -dling** *vt* : cailler — *vi* : se cailler, se figer

curds ['kərdz] *npl* : lait *m* caillé

cure[1] ['kjʊr] *vt* **cured; curing 1** HEAL, REMEDY : guérir **2** : fumer, saler <to cure meat : fumer de la viande>

cure[2] *n* **1** RECOVERY : rétablissement *m,* guérison *f* **2** REMEDY : remède *m*

curfew ['kər,fju:] *n* : couvre-feu *m*

curio ['kjʊri,o:] *n, pl* **-rios** : curiosité *f,* babiole *f*

curiosity [,kjʊri'ɑsət̬i] *n, pl* **-ties 1** INQUISITIVENESS : curiosité *f* **2** → **curio**

curious ['kjʊriəs] *adj* **1** INQUISITIVE : curieux **2** ODD : étrange, curieux

curl[1] ['kərl] *vt* **1** : friser (les cheveux) **2** COIL : enrouler **3 to curl one's lip** : faire une moue (de mépris) — *vi* : se friser, boucler

curl[2] *n* **1** RINGLET : boucle *m* (de cheveux) **2** SPIRAL : spirale *f* <curl of smoke : spirale de fumée>

curler ['kərlər] *n* : bigoudi *m,* rouleau *m*

curlew ['kər,lu:, 'kərl,ju:] *n, pl* **-lews** *or* **-lew** : courlis *m*

curly ['kərli] *adj* **curlier; -est** : frisé

currant ['kərənt] *n* **1** : groseille *f,* gadelle *f Can* **2** RAISIN : raisin *m* de Corinthe

currency ['kərəntsi] *n, pl* **-cies 1** MONEY : monnaie *m,* devise *f* <foreign currency : devises étrangères> **2** PREVALENCE : cours *m,* acceptation *f*

current[1] ['kərənt] *adj* **1** PRESENT : actuel, en cours <the current week : la semaine en cours> **2** PREVALENT : courant, commun <current customs : coutumes usuelles>

current[2] *n* **1** FLOW : courant *m,* cours *m* <the current of a river : le cours d'un fleuve> **2** TREND : tendance *f,* penchant *m* **3** : courant *m* (électrique)

curriculum [kə'rɪkjələm] *n, pl* **-la** [-lə] : programme *m* (scolaire)

curry[1] ['kəri] *vt* **-ried; -rying 1** : étriller (un cheval) **2** : faire un curry de (en cuisine) **3 to curry favor with** : chercher à gagner la faveur de

curry[2] *n, pl* **-ries** : curry *m*

curse[1] ['kərs] *v* **cursed; cursing** *vt* **1** : maudire <the gods cursed him : les dieux l'ont maudit> **2** AFFLICT : affliger — *vi* SWEAR : sacrer, jurer

curse[2] *n* **1** : malédiction *f* <to put a curse on : appeler une malédiction sur> **2** CALAMITY : fléau *m,* calamité *f* **3** OATH, SWEARWORD : juron *m*

cursor ['kərsər] *n* : curseur *m* (en informatique)

cursory ['kərsəri] *adj* : superficiel, hâtif

curt ['kərt] *adj* : brusque, sec

curtail [kər'teɪl] *vt* : réduire, diminuer <to curtail expenses : réduire les dépenses>

curtailment [kər'teɪlmənt] *n* : réduction *f,* diminution *f*

curtain ['kərtən] *n* : rideau *m*

curtly ['kərtli] *adv* : brusquement, sèchement

curtsy[1] *or* **curtsey** ['kərtsi] *vi* **-sied** *or* **-seyed; -sying** *or* **-seying** : faire une révérence

curtsy[2] *or* **curtsey** *n, pl* **-sies** *or* **-seys** : révérence *f*

curvature ['kərvə,tʃʊr] *n* : courbure *f*

curve[1] ['kərv] *v* **curved; curving** *vt* : courber — *vi* : se courber

curve[2] *n* : courbe *f*

cushion[1] ['kʊʃən] *vt* **1** : mettre des coussins à **2** LESSEN : amortir, réduire <to cushion the blow : amortir le choc>

cushion[2] *n* : coussin *m*

cusp ['kʌsp] *n* : cuspide *f* (d'une dent, etc.)

cuspid ['kʌspɪd] *n* : canine *f* (dent)

custard ['kʌstərd] *n* : flan *m*

custody ['kʌstədi] *n, pl* **-dies 1** CARE : garde *f* <in the custody of : sous la garde de> **2** DETENTION : détention *f,* emprisonnement *m*

custom[1] ['kʌstəm] *adj* : fait sur commande

custom[2] *n* **1** CONVENTION, TRADITION : coutume *f,* tradition *f,* usage *m* **2 customs** *npl* : douane *f*

customarily [,kʌstə'mɛrəli] *adv* : habituellement, normalement

customary ['kʌstə,mɛri] *adj* : habituel, coutumier

customer ['kʌstəmər] *n* : client *m,* cliente *f*

cut[1] ['kʌt] *v* **cut; cutting** *vt* **1** : couper <to cut paper : couper du papier> **2** SLICE : découper (du gâteau, des viandes, etc.) **3** SLASH : se couper <I cut my finger : je me suis coupé le doigt> **4** TRIM : couper (les ongles), tailler (une barbe, des cheveux, etc.) **5** INTERSECT : croiser **6** SHORTEN : couper (un texte, etc.) **7** REDUCE : réduire, diminuer <to cut costs : réduire les coûts> **8 to cut a tooth** : faire une dent — *vi* **1** : couper **2 to cut in** : interrompre, s'interposer, s'immiscer

cut[2] *n* **1** : coupure *f* **2** REDUCTION : réduction *f,* diminution *f* <a cut in pay : une réduction de salaire>

cute ['kju:t] *adj* **cuter; -est** : mignon, joli

cuticle ['kju:tɪkəl] *n* : petites peaux *fpl* (d'ongle)

cutlass ['kʌtləs] *n* : coutelas *m*

cutlery ['kʌtləri] *n* **1** KNIVES : coutellerie *f* **2** FLATWARE : couverts *mpl*

cutlet ['kʌtlət] *n* : escalope *f*

cutter ['kʌṭər] *n* **1** : coupoir *m* (outil) **2** : cotre *m* (bateau)

cutthroat[1] ['kʌtˌθro:t] *adj* : acharné, féroce <cutthroat competition : compétition acharnée>

cutthroat[2] *n* : meurtrier *m,* -trière *f;* assassin *m*

cutting ['kʌṭɪŋ] *adj* **1** SHARP : aigu, cinglant <a cutting wind : un vent cinglant> **2** CURT, SCATHING : mordant, tranchant

cyanide ['saɪəˌnaɪd, -nɪd] *n* : cyanure *m*

cycle[1] ['saɪkəl] *vi* **-cled; -cling** : faire de la bicyclette

cycle[2] *n* **1** : cycle *m* <life cycle : cycle de vie> **2** BICYCLE : bicyclette *f,* vélo *m* **3** MOTORCYCLE : motocyclette *f*

cyclic ['saɪklɪk, sɪ-] *or* **cyclical** [-klɪkəl] *adj* : cyclique, périodique

cyclist ['saɪklɪst] *n* : cycliste *mf*

cyclone ['saɪˌklo:n] *n* **1** : cyclône *m* **2** TORNADO : tornade *f*

cyclopedia *or* **cyclopaedia** [ˌsaɪklə'pi:diə] → **encyclopedia**

cylinder ['sɪləndər] *n* : cylindre *m*

cylindrical [sə'lɪndrɪkəl] *adj* : cylindrique

cymbal ['sɪmbəl] *n* : cymbale *f*

cynic ['sɪnɪk] *n* : cynique *mf*

cynical ['sɪnɪkəl] *adj* : cynique

cynicism ['sɪnəsɪzəm] *n* : cynisme *m*

cypress ['saɪprəs] *n* : cyprès *m*

Cypriot[1] *or* **Cypriote** ['sɪpriət, -ˌɑt] *adj* : chypriote, cypriote

Cypriot[2] *or* **Cypriote** *n* : Chypriote *mf,* Cypriote *mf*

cyst ['sɪst] *n* : kyste *m*

cytoplasm ['saɪṭoˌplæzəm] *n* : cytoplasme *m*

czar ['zɑr, 'sɑr] *n* : tsar *m*

czarina [zɑ'ri:nə, sɑ-] *n* : tsarine *f*

Czech[1] ['tʃɛk] *adj* : tchèque

Czech[2] *n* **1** : Tchèque *mf* **2** : tchèque *m* (langue)

Czechoslovak[1] [ˌtʃɛko'slo:ˌvɑk, -ˌvæk] *or* **Czechoslovakian** [-slo'vɑkiən, -'væ-] *adj* : tchécoslovaque

Czechoslovak[2] *or* **Czechoslovakian** *n* : Tchécoslovaque *mf*

D

d ['di:] *n, pl* **d's** *or* **ds** ['di:z] : d *m,* quatrième lettre de l'alphabet

dab[1] ['dæb] *vt* **dabbed; dabbing 1** PAT : tamponner **2** APPLY : appliquer (par petites touches)

dab[2] *n* BIT, TOUCH : touche *f,* petite quantité *f*

dabble ['dæbəl] *v* **-bled; -bling** *vt* SPATTER : éclabousser — *vi* **1** SPLASH : faire des éclaboussures (dans l'eau) **2** : s'intéresser brièvement <to dabble in art : faire un peu d'art>

dabbler ['dæbələr] *n* : dilettante *mf,* amateur *m*

dachshund ['dɑksˌhʊnt, -hʊnd; 'dɑksənt, -sənd] *n* : teckel *m*

dad ['dæd] *n* : papa *m fam*

daddy ['dædi] *n, pl* **-dies** : papa *m fam*

daffodil ['dæfəˌdɪl] *n* : jonquille *f*

daft ['dæft] *adj* : idiot, bête

dagger ['dægər] *n* : dague *f,* poignard *m*

dahlia ['dæljə, 'dɑl-, 'deɪl-] *n* : dahlia *m*

daily[1] ['deɪli] *adv* : quotidiennement

daily[2] *adj* : quotidien, journalier

daily[3] *n, pl* **-lies** *or* **daily newspaper** : quotidien *m*

daintily ['deɪntəli] *adv* : délicatement

daintiness ['deɪntinəs] *n* : délicatesse *f*

dainty[1] ['deɪnti] *adj* **daintier; -est 1** DELICATE : délicat, mignon **2** TASTY : de choix <dainty food : nourriture de choix> **3** FINICKY : difficile (sur la nourriture)

dainty[2] *n, pl* **-ties** DELICACY : mets *m* délicat

dairy ['dæri] *n, pl* **-ies** : laiterie *f,* crémerie *f France*

dairymaid ['dæriˌmeɪd] *n* : fille *f* de laiterie

dairyman ['dærimən, -mæn] *n, pl* **-men** [-mən, -ˌmɛn] : employé *m* de laiterie

dais ['deɪəs] *n* : estrade *f*

daisy ['deɪzi] *n, pl* **-sies** : marguerite *f*

dale ['deɪl] *n* : vallée *f,* val *m*

dally ['dæli] *vi* **-lied; -lying 1** TRIFLE : jouer, badiner **2** DAWDLE : traîner, lambiner *fam*

dalmatian [dælˈmeɪʃən, dɔl-] *n* : dalmatien *m*

dam[1] [ˈdæm] *vt* **dammed; damming** : construire un barrage sur

dam[2] *n* **1** : barrage *m* **2** : mère *f* (d'un animal domestique)

damage[1] [ˈdæmɪdʒ] *vt* **-aged; -aging** : endommager (des objets), abîmer (sa santé), nuire à (une réputation, etc.)

damage[2] *n* **1** : dégâts *mpl* **2 damages** *npl* : dommages *mpl* et intérêts *mpl*

damask [ˈdæməsk] *n* : damas *m*

dame [ˈdeɪm] *n* LADY : dame *f*

damn[1] [ˈdæm] *vt* **1** CONDEMN : condamner **2** CURSE : maudire

damn[2] *n* **1 not to give a damn** : s'en ficher *fam* **2 it's not worth a damn** : ça ne vaut pas un clou

damnable [ˈdæmnəbəl] *adj* **1** REPREHENSIBLE : condamnable **2** DETESTABLE : fichu *fam* <this damnable weather! : ce fichu temps!>

damnation [dæmˈneɪʃən] *n* : damnation *f*

damned [ˈdæmd] *adj* DAMNABLE : sacré *fam,* fichu *fam*

damp[1] [ˈdæmp] → **dampen**

damp[2] *adj* : humide, moite

damp[3] *n* : humidité *f*

dampen [ˈdæmpən] *vt* **1** MOISTEN : humecter **2** COOL, DEADEN : refroidir <to dampen s.o.'s spirits : décourager qqn>

damper [ˈdæmpər] *n* **1** : registre *m* (d'une cheminée) **2 to put a damper on** : jeter un froid sur, décourager

dampness [ˈdæmpnəs] *n* : humidité *f*

damsel [ˈdæmzəl] *n* : demoiselle *f*

dance[1] [ˈdænts] *v* **danced; dancing** : danser

dance[2] *n* **1** : danse *f* **2** : soirée *f* dansante

dancer [ˈdæntsər] *n* : danseur *m,* -seuse *f*

dandelion [ˈdændəˌlaɪən] *n* : pissenlit *m*

dander [ˈdændər] *n* TEMPER : colère *f,* rogne *f* <don't get your dander up : ne te mets pas en colère>

dandruff [ˈdændrəf] *n* : pellicules *fpl*

dandy[1] [ˈdændi] *adj* **dandier; -est** : chouette *fam,* épatant *fam*

dandy[2] *n, pl* **-dies** : dandy *m*

Dane [ˈdeɪn] *n* : danois *n,* -noise *f*

danger [ˈdeɪndʒər] *n* : danger *m*

dangerous [ˈdeɪndʒərəs] *adj* : dangereux

dangle [ˈdæŋgəl] *v* **-gled; -gling** *vi* HANG : se balancer, pendre — *vt* **1** SWING : balancer, laisser pendre **2** : faire miroiter <they dangled the prospect of a promotion before him : on lui a fait miroiter une promotion>

Danish[1] [ˈdeɪnɪʃ] *adj* : danois

Danish[2] *nm* **1** : danois *m* (langue) **2 the Danish** : les Danois *mpl*

Danish[3] *n* **the Danish** : les Danois

dank [ˈdæŋk] *adj* : froid et humide

dapper [ˈdæpər] *adj* : soigné

dappled [ˈdæpəld] *adj* : tacheté, pommelé

dare[1] [ˈdær] *v* **dared; daring** *vt* CHALLENGE : lancer un défi à, défier — *vi* VENTURE : oser

dare[2] *n* CHALLENGE : défi *m*

daredevil [ˈdærˌdɛvəl] *n* : casse-cou *mf*

daring[1] [ˈdeɪrɪŋ] *adj* BOLD : audacieux, hardi

daring[2] *n* : audace *f,* hardiesse *f*

dark[1] [ˈdɑrk] *adj* **1** : noir, sombre, foncé <dark clothes : vêtements foncés> <to get dark : faire nuit> **2** GLOOMY : lugubre, sombre

dark[2] *n* **1** NIGHT : tombée *f* du jour **2** DARKNESS : noir *m,* obscurité *f*

darken [ˈdɑrkən] *vt* : obscurcir, assombrir — *vi* : s'obscurcir, s'assombrir

darkly [ˈdɑrkli] *adv* **1** DIMLY : sombrement **2** GLOOMILY : d'un air lugubre **3** MYSTERIOUSLY : énigmatiquement, mystérieusement

darkness [ˈdɑrknəs] *n* : obscurité *f,* ténèbres *fpl,* noirceur *f Can*

darling[1] [ˈdɑrlɪŋ] *adj* **1** BELOVED : bien-aimé, chéri **2** CHARMING : adorable <a darling puppy : un chiot adorable>

darling[2] *n* **1** BELOVED : chéri *m,* -rie *f* **2** FAVORITE : chouchou *m,* -choute *f fam;* coqueluche *f fam*

darn[1] [ˈdɑrn] *vt* : repriser (en couture)

darn[2] *n* **1** : reprise *f* **2** → **damn**[2]

dart[1] [ˈdɑrt] *vi* : se précipiter, s'élancer <he darted out : il est sorti comme une flèche>

dart[2] *n* **1** : flèche *f* (courte), fléchette *f,* dard *m Can* **2 darts** *npl* : fléchettes *fpl* (jeu) **3** : pince *f* (en couture)

dash[1] [ˈdæʃ] *vt* **1** SMASH : briser, fracasser **2** HURL : lancer violemment **3** SPLASH : éclabousser **4** RUIN : détruire, anéantir <to dash s.o.'s hopes : anéantir les espoirs de qqn> **5** *or* **to dash off** : terminer à la hâte — *vi* : se précipiter, se ruer

dash[2] *n* **1** BURST, SPLASH : éclat *m,* plouf *m* **2** : tiret *m* (signe de ponctuation) **3** DROP, PINCH : pincée *f,* soupçon *m* <a dash of pepper : une pincée de poivre> **4** VERVE : brio *m,* panache *m* **5** RUSH : mouvement *m* précipité, course *f* folle **6** : sprint *m* (aux sports) **7** → **dashboard**

dashboard [ˈdæʃˌbord] *n* : tableau *m* de bord

dashing [ˈdæʃɪŋ] *adj* : fringant, élégant

data [ˈdeɪtə, ˈdæ-, ˈdɑ-] *ns & pl* : données *fpl*

database [ˈdeɪt̬əˌbeɪs, ˈdæ-, ˈdɑ-] *n* : base *f* de données

date[1] [ˈdeɪt] *v* **dated; dating** *vt* **1** : dater (un chèque, un objet, etc.) **2** : sortir avec — *vi* **1** : sortir avec quelqu'un, se fréquenter **2** ORIGINATE : remonter <a friendship dating from high school : une amitié qui remonte au lycée>

date[2] *n* **1** : date *f* <date of birth : date de naissance> **2** PERIOD : date *f,* période *f* (historique) **3** APPOINTMENT : rendez-vous *m* **4** : datte *f* (fruit) **5 to ~** : à ce jour, jusqu'à maintenant
dated ['deɪt̬əd] *adj* OLD-FASHIONED : vieilli, démodé
datum ['deɪt̬əm, 'dæ-, 'dɑ-] *n, pl* **-ta** [-tə] *or* **-tums** : donnée *f*
daub[1] ['dɔb] *vt* **1** COVER : couvrir <daubed with mud : couvert de boue> **2** SMEAR : barbouiller
daub[2] *n* : barbouillage *m*
daughter ['dɔt̬ər] *n* : fille *f*
daughter–in–law ['dɔt̬ərɪn,lɔ] *n, pl* **daughters–in–law** : belle-fille *f,* bru *f*
daunt ['dɔnt] *vt* : décourager, intimider
dauntless ['dɔntləs] *adj* : intrépide, hardi
davenport ['dævən,port] *n* : canapé *m*
dawdle ['dɔdəl] *vi* **-dled; -dling 1** DALLY : traîner, lambiner *fam,* farfiner *Can fam* **2** LOITER : flâner
dawn[1] ['dɔn] *vi* **1** : se lever (se dit du jour) **2 to dawn on** : venir à <it dawned on him that it was late : il s'est aperçu qu'il était tard>
dawn[2] *n* **1** : aube *f* **2** BEGINNING : aube *f,* début *m* <the dawn of the space age : le début de l'ère spatiale>
day ['deɪ] *n* **1** : jour *m* <every day : tous les jours> <day by day : jour après jour> **2** : journée *f* <have a good day! : bonne journée!> <an eight-hour day : une journée de huit heures> **3** AGE, TIME : époque *f,* temps *m* <in my day : à mon époque> <in this day and age : par les temps qui courent> **4** → **weekday, workday**
daybreak ['deɪ,breɪk] *n* : aube *f,* point *m* du jour, lever *m* du jour
day care *n* : service *m* de garderie
daydream[1] ['deɪ,dri:m] *vi* : rêver, rêvasser
daydream[2] *n* : rêve *m,* rêverie *f*
daylight ['deɪ,laɪt] *n* **1** : lumière *f* du jour <in broad daylight : en plein jour> **2** → **daybreak 3** → **daytime**
daylight saving time *n* : heure *f* d'été, heure *f* avancée (de l'Est) *Can*
daytime ['deɪ,taɪm] *n* : jour *m,* journée *f* <in the daytime : pendant le jour>
daze[1] ['deɪz] *vt* **dazed; dazing 1** STUN : étourdir, abasourdir **2** DAZZLE : éblouir
daze[2] *n* : ahurissement *m,* étourdissement *m*
dazzle ['dæzəl] *vt* **-zled; -zling 1** BLIND : éblouir, aveugler **2** IMPRESS : impressionner, épater *fam*
DDT [,di:,di:'ti:] *n* : DDT *m*
deacon ['di:kən] *n* : diacre *m*
dead[1] ['dɛd] *adv* **1** ABSOLUTELY : absolument <dead certain : absolument sûr> **2** SUDDENLY : soudainement <to stop dead : s'arrêter net> **3** DIRECTLY : directement, droit <dead ahead : droit devant, tout droit>
dead[2] *adj* **1** LIFELESS : mort **2** NUMB : engourdi **3** EXTINCT, INACTIVE : inactif, éteint, mort **4** : coupé (se dit d'une ligne téléphonique), à plat (se dit d'une batterie) **5** EXHAUSTED : éreinté, crevé *fam* **6** OBSOLETE : mort, désuet <dead language : langue morte> **7** EXACT : exact, précis <at the dead center : exactement au centre> **8** COMPLETE : absolu, total <dead silence : silence absolu>
dead[3] *ns & pl* **1** DEPTHS : milieu *m,* profondeur *f* <in the dead of night : au plus profond de la nuit> <in the dead of winter : en plein hiver> **2 the dead** : les morts
deadbeat ['dɛd,bi:t] *n* : bon à rien *m,* bonne à rien *f*
deaden ['dɛdən] *vt* **1** ALLAY : calmer, endormir (des douleurs) **2** CUSHION, SOFTEN : assourdir (des sons), amortir (un coup, etc.)
dead–end ['dɛd'ɛnd] *adj* : sans issue (se dit d'une rue), sans perspectives (se dit d'un travail)
dead end *n* : cul-de-sac *m,* impasse *f*
dead heat *n* TIE : match *m* nul
deadline *n* ['dɛd,laɪn] : date *f* limite, délai *m*
deadlock[1] ['dɛd,lɑk] *vt* : mettre dans une impasse
deadlock[2] *n* : impasse *f*
deadly[1] ['dɛdli] *adv* : extrêmement, très <deadly serious : très sérieux>
deadly[2] *adj* **deadlier; -est 1** LETHAL : mortel **2** ACCURATE : précis, juste <deadly accuracy : une extrême précision> **3** : capital <the seven deadly sins : les sept péchés capitaux> **4** EXTREME : extrême, absolu
deadpan ['dɛd,pæn] *adj* : impassible, pince-sans-rire
deaf ['dɛf] *adj* : sourd
deafen ['dɛfən] *vt* : assourdir
deaf–mute ['dɛf'mju:t] *n* : sourd-muet *m,* sourde-muette *f*
deafness ['dɛfnəs] *n* : surdité *f*
deal[1] ['di:l] *v* **dealt; dealing** *vt* **1** APPORTION : rendre <to deal (out) justice : rendre la justice> **2** DISTRIBUTE : donner, distribuer (des cartes à jouer) **3** DELIVER : administrer, assener (un coup) **4** SELL : revendre (des drogues) — *vi* **1** : distribuer les cartes **2 to deal in** SELL : être dans le commerce de **3 to deal with** CONCERN, TREAT : traiter de **4 to deal with** FACE : accepter, faire face à
deal[2] *n* **1** : donne *f* (aux cartes) **2** AGREEMENT, TRANSACTION : accord *m,* affaire *f,* marché *m* **3** TREATMENT : traitement *m* <to get a bad deal : être mal traité> **4** BARGAIN : bonne affaire *f* **5 a good deal** LOTS : beaucoup

dealer ['diːlər] *n* : marchand *m,* -chande *f;* négociant *m,* -ciante *f*

dealings ['diːlɪŋz] *npl* **1** : relations *fpl* (personnelles) **2** TRANSACTIONS : transactions *fpl,* affaires *fpl*

dean ['diːn] *n* : doyen *m,* doyenne *f*

dear[1] ['dɪr] *adj* **1** ESTEEMED, LOVED : cher <a dear friend : un ami très cher> **2** (*used in correspondence*) : cher <Dear Anne : Chère Anne> **3** COSTLY : cher, coûteux **4** EARNEST : cher, sincère <my dearest wish : mon vœu le plus cher>

dear[2] *n* : chéri *m,* -rie *f*

dearly ['dɪrli] *adv* **1 to love dearly** : aimer tendrement, aimer beaucoup **2 to pay dearly** : payer cher

dearness ['dɪrnəs] *n* **1** FONDNESS : affection *f,* amitié *f* **2** COSTLINESS : cherté *f*

dearth ['dərθ] *n* : pénurie *f,* manque *m*

death ['dɛθ] *n* **1** : mort *f,* décès *m* **2** DESTRUCTION, END : disparition *f* <the death of all hope : la disparition de tout espoir> <he'll be the death of me : il me fera mourir>

deathless ['dɛθləs] *adj* : immortel

deathly[1] ['dɛθli] *adv* : de mort, comme la mort <deathly pale : pâle comme la mort>

deathly[2] *adj* **1** FATAL : mortel **2** : cadavérique <deathly pallor : pâleur cadavérique>

debacle [dɪ'bɑkəl, -'bæ-] *n* : débâcle *f,* désastre *m,* fiasco *m*

debar [di'bɑr] *vt* **-barred; -barring** : exclure, interdire à

debark [di'bɑrk] → **disembark**

debase [di'beɪs] *vt* **-based; -basing** : avilir, abaisser, dégrader

debasement [di'beɪsmənt] *n* : avilissement *m,* abaissement *m,* dégradation *f*

debatable [dɪ'beɪt̬əbəl] *adj* : discutable

debate[1] [dɪ'beɪt] *v* **-bated; -bating** *vt* : débattre, discuter — *vi* : discuter

debate[2] *n* : débat *m,* discussion *f*

debauch [dɪ'bɔtʃ] *vt* : débaucher

debauchery [dɪ'bɔtʃəri] *n, pl* **-eries** : débauche *f*

debilitate [dɪ'bɪləˌteɪt] *vt* **-tated; -tating** : débiliter, affaiblir

debility [dɪ'bɪlət̬i] *n, pl* **-ties** : débilité *f*

debit[1] ['dɛbɪt] *vt* : débiter (un compte bancaire, etc.)

debit[2] *n* : débit

debonair [ˌdɛbə'nær] *adj* : élégant, raffiné

debris [də'briː, deɪ-; 'deɪˌbriː] *n, pl* **-bris** [-'briːz, -ˌbriːz] **1** RUBBLE : décombres *mpl,* débris *mpl* **2** RUBBISH : déchets *mpl*

debt ['dɛt] *n* : dette *f,* créance *f*

debtor ['dɛt̬ər] *n* : débiteur *m,* -trice *f*

debug [di'bʌg] *vt* **-bugged; -bugging** : déboguer

debunk [di'bʌŋk] *vt* : discréditer, démentir

debut[1] [deɪ'bjuː, 'deɪˌbjuː] *vi* : débuter

debut[2] *n* **1** : débuts *mpl* <my acting debut : mes débuts sur la scène> **2** : entrée *f* dans le monde

debutante ['dɛbjʊˌtɑnt] *n* : débutante *f*

decade ['dɛˌkeɪd, dɛ'keɪd] *n* : décennie *f*

decadence ['dɛkədənts] *n* : décadence *f*

decadent ['dɛkədənt] *adj* : décadent

decal ['diːˌkæl, di'kæl] *n* : décalcomanie *f*

decamp [di'kæmp] *vi* : décamper, déguerpir

decant [di'kænt] *vt* : transvaser (un liquide), décanter (du vin)

decanter [di'kæntər] *n* : carafe *f*

decapitate [di'kæpəˌteɪt] *vt* **-tated; -tating** : décapiter

decay[1] [di'keɪ] *vi* **1** DETERIORATE : se détériorer, se délabrer (se dit d'un édifice) **2** DECOMPOSE, ROT : se décomposer, se putréfier **3** : se carier (se dit d'une dent)

decay[2] *n* **1** DETERIORATION : délabrement *f,* pourrissement *m* **2** DECOMPOSITION, ROTTING : décomposition *f* **3** *or* **tooth decay** : carie *f* (dentaire)

decease[1] [di'siːs] *vi* **-ceased; -ceasing** : décéder

decease[2] *n* DEATH : décès *m*

deceit [dɪ'siːt] *n* **1** DUPLICITY : duplicité *f,* fausseté *f* **2** TRICK : tromperie *f*

deceitful [dɪ'siːtfəl] *adj* **1** MISLEADING : trompeur **2** DISHONEST : malhonnête

deceitfully [dɪ'siːtfəli] *adv* : de façon malhonnête, trompeusement

deceive [dɪ'siːv] *v* **-ceived; -ceiving** *vt* : tromper, leurrer — *vi* : donner une fausse impression

deceiver [dɪ'siːvər] *n* : trompeur *m,* -peuse *f*

decelerate [di'sɛləˌreɪt] *v* **-ated; -ating** : ralentir

December [di'sɛmbər] *n* : décembre *m*

decency ['disəntsi] *n, pl* **-cies** : décence *f,* bienséance f

decent ['diːsənt] *adj* **1** PROPER, SUITABLE : décent, convenable, approprié **2** CLOTHED : habillé **3** ADEQUATE : acceptable, suffisant **4** KIND : gentil, sympathique

decently ['diːsəntli] *adv* **1** PROPERLY : décemment, convenablement **2** ADEQUATELY : acceptablement

deception [dɪ'sɛpʃən] *n* **1** : tromperie *f,* duperie *f* **2** FRAUD : fraude *f*

deceptive [dɪ'sɛptɪv] *adj* : trompeur

deceptively [di'sɛptɪvli] *adv* : trompeusement <it's deceptively small : c'est plus grand qu'il n'y paraît>

decibel ['dɛsəbəl, -ˌbɛl] *n* : décibel *m*

decide [dɪ'saɪd] *v* **-cided; -ciding** *vt* **1** : décider <I decided to buy a hat : j'ai décidé d'acheter un chapeau> **2** DETERMINE, SETTLE : décider de, trancher **3** PERSUADE : décider — *vi* : se décider

decided [dɪ'saɪdəd] *adj* **1** RESOLUTE : décidé, ferme **2** UNQUESTIONABLE : incontestable, certain
decidedly [dɪ'saɪdədli] *adv* **1** RESOLUTELY : résolument **2** UNQUESTIONABLY : vraiment, décidément
deciduous [dɪ'sɪdʒʊəs] *adj* : caduc <deciduous tree : arbre à feuilles caduques>
decimal[1] ['dɛsəməl] *adj* : décimal
decimal[2] *n* : décimale *f*
decimal point *n* : virgule *f*
decipher [di'saɪfər] *vt* : déchiffrer
decision [dɪ'sɪʒən] *n* : décision *f*
decisive [dɪ'saɪsɪv] *adj* **1** DECIDING : décisif <the decisive vote : le vote décisif> **2** RESOLUTE : résolu, déterminé **3** CONCLUSIVE : définitif, décisif
deck[1] ['dɛk] *vt* **1** FLOOR : envoyer par terre **2 to deck out** : orner, décorer, parer (une personne)
deck[2] *n* **1** : pont *m* (d'un navire) **2** *or* **deck of cards** : jeu *m* de cartes **3** TERRACE : terrasse *f* (d'une maison, etc.)
declaim [di'kleɪm] *v* : déclamer
declaration [ˌdɛklə'reɪʃən] *n* : déclaration *f*
declarative [dɪ'klærət̬ɪv, -klɛr-] *adj* : déclaratif
declare [dɪ'klær] *vt* **-clared; -claring 1** ANNOUNCE : déclarer, annoncer <to declare war : déclarer la guerre> **2** AFFIRM : déclarer, maintenir
declension [dɪ'klɛntʃən] *n* : déclinaison *f* (en grammaire)
decline[1] [dɪ'klaɪn] *v* **-clined; -clining** *vt* **1** REFUSE : décliner, refuser **2** : décliner (un nom) — *vi* **1** DESCEND, DROP : descendre, baisser **2** WANE : être sur le déclin **3** DETERIORATE, WEAKEN : s'affaiblir, dépérir **4** REFUSE : refuser
decline[2] *n* **1** DETERIORATION : déclin *m* **2** LOWERING : baisse *f*, chute *f* (des prix) **3** SLOPE : pente *f*, descente *f*
decode [di'ko:d] *vt* **-coded; -coding** : décoder, déchiffrer
decompose [ˌdi:kəm'po:z] *vt* **-posed; -posing** : décomposer — *vi* : se décomposer
decomposition [ˌdi:ˌkɑmpə'zɪʃən] *n* : décomposition *f*
decongestant [ˌdi:kən'dʒɛstənt] *n* : décongestif *m*, décongestionnant *m*
decor *or* **décor** [deɪ'kɔr, 'deɪˌkɔr] *n* : décor *m*
decorate ['dɛkəˌreɪt] *vt* **-rated; -rating 1** ADORN : décorer, embellir **2** : décorer <decorated for bravery : décoré pour son courage>
decoration [ˌdɛkə'reɪʃən] *n* : décoration *f*
decorative ['dɛkərət̬ɪv, -ˌreɪ-] *adj* : décoratif, ornemental
decorator ['dɛkəˌreɪt̬ər] *n* : décorateur *m*, -trice *f*
decorum [dɪ'ko:rəm, -kɔr-] *n* : bienséance *f*, décorum *m*
decoy[1] ['diˌkɔɪ] *vt* : attirer avec un appeau
decoy[2] *n* : appeau *m*, leurre *m*
decrease[1] [di'kri:s] *v* **-creased; -creasing** *vi* : diminuer, décroître — *vt* REDUCE : diminuer, réduire
decrease[2] ['diˌkris, di'-] *n* : diminution *f*, baisse *f*
decree[1] [di'kri:] *vt* **-creed; -creeing** : décréter
decree[2] *n* : décret *m*
decrepit [dɪ'krɛpɪt] *adj* **1** FEEBLE : décrépit **2** DILAPIDATED : délabré, en ruine
decry [dɪ'krɑɪ] *vt* **-cried; -crying** : décrier, dénigrer
dedicate ['dɛdɪˌkeɪt] *vt* **-cated; -cating 1** DEVOTE : dédier, consacrer **2** : dédier <she dedicated the book to her daughter : elle a dédié le livre à sa fille>
dedication [dɛdɪ'keɪʃən] *n* **1** DEVOTION : dévouement *m* **2** INSCRIPTION : dédicace *f* **3** CONSECRATION : consécration *f* (d'une église, etc.)
deduce [dɪ'du:s, -'dju:s] *vt* **-duced; -ducing** : déduire, inférer
deduct [dɪ'dʌkt] *vt* : déduire, prélever
deductible [dɪ'dʌktəbəl] *adj* : déductible
deduction [dɪ'dʌkʃən] *n* **1** SUBTRACTION : déduction *f* **2** CONCLUSION : déduction *f*, raisonnement *m* déductif
deed[1] ['di:d] *vt* : transférer (par acte notarié)
deed[2] *n* **1** ACT : action *f* **2** FEAT : exploit *m* **3** : acte *m* notarié, titre *m* de propriété
deem ['di:m] *vt* CONSIDER : juger, estimer, considérer
deep[1] ['di:p] *adj* **1** : profond <a deep well : un puits profond> **2** WIDE : large, profond **3** ENGROSSED : préoccupé, absorbé <deep in thought : préoccupé par ses pensées> **4** LOW : grave, profond <a deep voice : une voix profonde> **5** DARK : intense <a deep blue : un bleu intense> **6** INTENSE, PROFOUND : profond <a deep insight : un aperçu profond>
deep[2] *n* **1** : cœur *m*, profondeur *f* <in the deep of winter : au plus profond de l'hiver, au cœur de l'hiver> **2 the deep** : l'océan *m*
deepen ['di:pən] *vt* **1** : approfondir **2** INTENSIFY : intensifier, augmenter — *vi* **1** : devenir plus profond **2** INTENSIFY : augmenter, s'intensifier
deeply ['di:pli] *adv* : profondément
deep–seated ['dip'sit̬əd] *adj* : fermement établi, profondément enraciné
deer ['dɪr] *ns & pl* : cerf *m*, chevreuil *m*, biche *f*
deerskin ['dɪrˌskɪn] *n* : peau *f* de daim
deface [dɪ'feɪs] *vt* **-faced; -facing** : abîmer, dégrader, défigurer

defamation [ˌdɛfəˈmeɪʃən] *n* : diffamation *f*
defamatory [dɪˈfæməˌtori] *adj* : diffamatoire
defame [dɪˈfeɪm] *vt* **-famed; -faming** : diffamer
default[1] [dɪˈfɔlt, ˈdiːˌfɔlt] *vi* **1** : ne pas s'acquitter (se dit d'une dette), ne pas régler (se dit d'un compte) **2** : manquer de comparaître (devant le tribunal)
default[2] *n* **1** : non-paiement *m* (d'une dette) **2** : non-comparution *f* (en cour) **3 by ~** : par forfait
defeat[1] [dɪˈfiːt] *vt* **1** BEAT : battre, vaincre **2** FRUSTRATE : faire échouer, mettre fin à (un plan, une ambition)
defeat[2] *n* : défaite *f,* échec *m*
defecate [ˈdɛfɪˌkeɪt] *vi* **-cated; -cating** : déféquer
defect[1] [dɪˈfɛkt] *vi* : faire défection, s'enfuir
defect[2] [ˈdiːˌfɛkt, diˈfɛkt] *n* : défaut *m*
defection [dɪˈfɛkʃən] *n* : défection *f*
defective [dɪˈfɛktɪv] *adj* **1** FAULTY : défectueux **2** DEFICIENT : déficient <defective eyesight : yeux déficients>
defector [dɪˈfɛktər] *n* : transfuge *mf*
defence *Brit* → **defense**
defend [dɪˈfɛnd] *vt* : défendre
defendant [dɪˈfɛndənt] *n* : défendeur *m,* -deresse *f;* intimé *m,* -mée *f* (en appel)
defender [dɪˈfɛndər] *n* **1** ADVOCATE : défenseur *m,* avocat *m* **2** : défenseur *m* (aux sports)
defense *or Brit* **defence** [dɪˈfɛnts, ˈdiːˌfɛnts] *n* : défense *f*
defenseless *or Brit* **defenceless** [dɪˈfɛntsləs] *adj* : sans défense
defensive[1] [dɪˈfɛntsɪv] *adj* : défensif
defensive[2] *n* : défensive *f* <to be on the defensive : se tenir sur la défensive>
defer [dɪˈfər] *v* **-ferred; -ferring** *vt* POSTPONE : remettre, reporter — *vi* **to defer to** : s'en remettre à, déférer à
deference [ˈdɛfərənts] *n* : déférence *f,* égard *m* <in deference to his family : par égard pour sa famille>
deferential [ˌdɛfəˈrɛntʃəl] *adj* : déférent, respectueux
deferment [dɪˈfərmənt] *n* : report *m,* renvoi *m*
defiance [dɪˈfaɪənts] *n* **1** : défi *m* **2 in defiance of** : au mépris de
defiant [dɪˈfaɪənt] *adj* : provocant, de défi
deficiency [dɪˈfɪʃəntsi] *n, pl* **-cies 1** INADEQUACY : manque *m,* insuffisance *f* **2** FLAW : faille *f,* faiblesse *f*
deficient [dɪˈfɪʃənt] *adj* **1** INADEQUATE : insuffisant **2** FAULTY : défectueux
deficit [ˈdɛfəsɪt] *n* : déficit *m*
defile [dɪˈfaɪl] *vt* **-filed; -filing 1** SULLY : souiller **2** PROFANE : profaner, déshonorer
defilement [dɪˈfaɪlmənt] *n* **1** DEBASEMENT : souillure *f* **2** DESECRATION : profanation *f*
define [dɪˈfaɪn] *vt* **-fined; -fining 1** BOUND : définir, délimiter **2** CLARIFY : clarifier, définir <the issues are not well defined : les problèmes ne sont pas clairs> **3** : définir (un mot)
definite [ˈdɛfənɪt] *adj* **1** CLEAR, DISTINCT : précis, déterminé, net **2** CERTAIN : certain, sûr <is that definite? : c'est sûr?> **3** : défini (en grammaire) <definite article : article défini>
definitely [ˈdɛfənɪtli] *adv* **1** CERTAINLY : certainement, sans aucun doute **2** APPRECIABLY : sensiblement, nettement **3** CATEGORICALLY : absolument, catégoriquement <definitely! : bien sûr!>
definition [ˌdɛfəˈnɪʃən] *n* : définition *f*
definitive [dəˈfɪnət̬ɪv] *adj* **1** CONCLUSIVE : définitif, décisif **2** AUTHORITATIVE : qui fait autorité
deflate [dɪˈfleɪt] *v* **-flated; -flating** *vt* **1** : dégonfler (un ballon, etc.) **2** REDUCE : saper, miner (l'égo, la confiance) — *vi* : se dégonfler
deflation [dɪˈfleɪʃən] *n* **1** : dégonflement *m* (d'un ballon, etc.) **2** : déflation *f* (économique)
deflect [dɪˈflɛkt] *vt* : faire dévier, détourner — *vi* DEVIATE : dévier
deforest [diˈfɔrəst] *vt* : déboiser
deform [diˈfɔrm] *vt* : déformer
deformity [diˈfɔrmət̬i] *n, pl* **-ties** : difformité *f*
defraud [diˈfrɔd] *vt* : frauder, escroquer
defray [diˈfreɪ] *vt* : rembourser, couvrir (des coûts)
defrost [diˈfrɔst] *vt* **1** THAW : décongeler (des aliments) **2** : dégivrer (un réfrigérateur, etc.)
deft [ˈdɛft] *adj* : adroit, habile — **deftly** *adv*
defunct [dɪˈfʌŋkt] *adj* : défunt
defy [dɪˈfaɪ] *vt* **-fied; -fying 1** CHALLENGE : défier, braver **2** RESIST : résister à, s'opposer à <to defy all one's efforts : résister à tous les efforts>
degenerate[1] [dɪˈdʒɛnəˌreɪt] *vi* **-ated; -ating** : dégénérer, s'abâtardir
degenerate[2] [dɪˈdʒɛnərət] *adj* : dégénéré
degeneration [didʒɛnəˈreɪʃən] *n* : dégénérescence *f*
degradation [ˌdɛgrəˈdeɪʃən] *n* : dégradation *f*
degrade [dɪˈgreɪd] *vt* **-graded; -grading 1** : dégrader **2 to degrade oneself** : s'abaisser
degree [dɪˈgriː] *n* **1** AMOUNT, EXTENT : degré *m,* point *m,* mesure *f* <to a certain degree : à un certain degré, jusqu'à un certain point> **2** : diplôme *m* <college degree : diplôme universitaire> **3** : degré *m* (en physique, en mathématiques, etc.) **4 by degrees** : par degrés, petit à petit

dehydrate [di'haɪˌdreɪt] *v* **-drated; -drating** *vt* : déshydrater — *vi* : se déshydrater

dehydration [ˌdiːhaɪ'dreɪʃən] *n* : déshydratation *f*

deice [ˌdiː'aɪs] *vt* **-iced; -icing** : dégivrer

deify ['diːəˌfaɪ, 'deɪ-] *vt* **-fied; -fying** : déifier

deign ['deɪn] *vt* : daigner, condescendre à

deity ['diːəṭi, 'deɪ-] *n, pl* **-ties 1** GOD, GODDESS : dieu *m,* déesse *f* **2 the Deity** : Dieu *m*

dejected [dɪ'dʒɛktəd] *adj* : découragé, abattu

dejection [dɪ'dʒɛkʃən] *n* : découragement *m,* abattement *m*

delay[1] [dɪ'leɪ] *vt* **1** POSTPONE : reporter, différer **2** HOLD UP : retarder, retenir <he delayed me for no reason : il m'a retenu sans raison>

delay[2] *n* **1** POSTPONEMENT : report *m* **2** HOLDUP : délai *m* <without further delay : sans plus tarder>

delectable [dɪ'lɛktəbəl] *adj* : délicieux

delegate[1] ['dɛlɪˌgeɪt] *vt* **-gated; -gating** : déléguer

delegate[2] ['dɛlɪgət, -ˌgeɪt] *n* : délégué *m,* -guée *f*

delegation [ˌdɛlə'geɪʃən] *n* : délégation *f*

delete [dɪ'liːt] *vt* **-leted; -leting** : supprimer, effacer

deletion [dɪ'liːʃən] *n* : suppression *f*

deliberate[1] [dɪ'lɪbəˌreɪt] *v* **-ated; -ating** *vt* : délibérer sur, réfléchir sur — *vi* : délibérer, considérer

deliberate[2] [dɪ'lɪbərət] *adj* **1** CONSIDERED : délibéré, réfléchi **2** INTENTIONAL : délibéré, intentionnel **3** UNHURRIED : mesuré, posé

deliberately [dɪ'lɪbərətli] *adv* **1** INTENTIONALLY : délibérément, à dessein, exprès **2** STEADILY : de façon mesurée

deliberation [dɪˌlɪbə'reɪʃən] *n* **1** CONSIDERATION : délibération *f,* réflexion *f* **2** DISCUSSION : délibérations *fpl,* débats *mpl* **3** RESTRAINT : mesure *f,* manière *f* posée

delicacy ['dɛlɪkəsi] *n, pl* **-cies 1** : mets *m* délicat **2** FINENESS : délicatesse *f,* finesse *f* **3** FRAILTY : délicatesse *f,* fragilité *f*

delicate ['dɛlɪkət] *adj* **1** SUBTLE : délicat <a delicate fragrance : un parfum délicat> **2** DAINTY, FINE : délicat, fin **3** FRAGILE : fragile **4** SENSITIVE : délicat, sensible <a delicate situation : une question délicate>

delicately ['dɛlɪkətli] *adv* : délicatement, avec délicatesse

delicatessen [ˌdɛlɪkə'tɛsən] *n* : charcuterie *f*

delicious [dɪ'lɪʃəs] *adj* : délicieux

delight[1] [dɪ'laɪt] *vt* : réjouir, enchanter — *vi* **to delight in** : prendre plaisir à

delight[2] *n* **1** PLEASURE : plaisir *m,* joie *f* **2** : délice *m,* merveille *f* <my new car is a delight : ma nouvelle voiture est une merveille>

delightful [dɪ'laɪtfəl] *adj* : charmant, merveilleux, ravissant

delightfully [dɪ'laɪtfəli] *adv* : de façon charmante, merveilleusement

delineate [dɪ'lɪniˌeɪt] *vt* **-eated; -eating 1** SKETCH : tracer **2** PORTRAY : décrire, dépeindre

delinquency [dɪ'lɪŋkwən*t*si] *n, pl* **-cies** : délinquance *f*

delinquent[1] [dɪ'lɪŋkwənt] *adj* **1** : délinquant <delinquent children : enfants délinquants> **2** OVERDUE : arriéré

delinquent[2] *n* : délinquant *m,* -quante *f*

delirious [dɪ'lɪriəs] *adj* : délirant, en délire

delirium [dɪ'lɪriəm] *n* : délire *m*

deliver [dɪ'lɪvər] *vt* **1** FREE : délivrer <deliver us from evil : délivre-nous de tout mal> **2** DISTRIBUTE : livrer **3** : mettre au monde (un enfant) **4** : faire, prononcer <to deliver a speech : prononcer un discours> **5** DEAL : porter, asséner <to deliver a blow : porter un coup>

deliverance [dɪ'lɪvərən*t*s] *n* : délivrance *f*

delivery [dɪ'lɪvəri] *n, pl* **-eries 1** LIBERATION : délivrance *f* **2** DISTRIBUTION : livraison *f,* distribution *f* **3** CHILDBIRTH : accouchement *m* **4** SPEECH : élocution *f,* débit *m*

dell ['dɛl] *n* : vallon *m* (boisé)

delta ['dɛltə] *n* : delta *m*

delude [dɪ'luːd] *vt* **-luded; -luding 1** : tromper, duper **2 to delude oneself** : se leurrer, se faire des illusions

deluge[1] ['dɛlˌjuːdʒ, -juːʒ] *vt* **-uged; -uging 1** FLOOD : inonder **2** SWAMP : inonder, submerger <deluged with calls : inondé d'appels>

deluge[2] *n* : inondation *f,* déluge *m*

delusion [dɪ'luːʒən] *n* **1** : illusion *f* **2 delusions of grandeur** : la folie des grandeurs

deluxe [dɪ'lʌks, -lʊks] *adj* : de luxe, luxueux

delve ['dɛlv] *vi* **delved; delving 1** DIG : creuser **2 to delve into** : fouiller dans

demand[1] [dɪ'mænd] *vt* : exiger, réclamer

demand[2] *n* **1** REQUIREMENT : exigence *f* **2** CLAIM : réclamation *f,* revendication *f* **3** : demande *f* (en commerce) **4** → **supply**

demarcation [ˌdiːˌmɑr'keɪʃən] *n* : démarcation *f*

demean [dɪ'miːn] *vt* **1** : abaisser, rabaisser **2 to demean oneself** : s'abaisser

demeanor *or Brit* **demeanour** [dɪ'miːnər] *n* **1** BEHAVIOR : comportement *m* **2** MANNER : air *m,* allure *f,* mine *f*

demented [dɪ'mɛntəd] *adj* : dément, fou
demerit [dɪ'mɛrət] *n* : démérite *m*
demigod ['dɛmi,gɑd, -,gɔd] *n* : demi-dieu *m*
demise [dɪ'maɪz] *n* **1** DEATH : mort *f,* décès *m* **2** END : fin *f,* mort *f* (d'une institution, etc.)
demitasse ['dɛmi,tæs, -,tɑs] *n* : tasse *f* de café noir
demobilize [di'mo:bə,laɪz-] *vt* **-lized; -lizing** : démobiliser
democracy [dɪ'mɑkrəsi] *n, pl* **-cies** : démocratie *f*
democrat ['dɛmə,kræt] *n* : démocrate *mf*
democratic [,dɛmə'kræṱɪk] *adj* : démocratique — **democratically** *adv*
demolish [di'mɑlɪʃ] *vt* **1** RAZE : démolir, raser **2** DESTROY : détruire, démolir (une théorie, etc.)
demolition [,dɛmə'lɪʃən, ,di:-] *n* : démolition *f*
demon ['di:mən] *n* : démon *m*
demonic [dɪ'mɑnɪk, di-] *adj* : diabolique
demonstrably [də'mɑn*t*strəbli] *adv* : manifestement
demonstrate ['dɛmən,streɪt] *v* **-strated; -strating** *vt* **1** SHOW : manifester, démontrer **2** EXPLAIN, PROVE : démontrer, établir **3** : faire une démonstration de — *vi* **1** : faire une démonstration **2** PROTEST : manifester, protester
demonstration [dɛmən'streɪʃən] *n* **1** : démonstration *f* **2** PROTEST : manifestation *f*
demonstrative [dɪ'mɑn*t*strəṱɪv] *adj* : démonstratif
demonstrator ['dɛmən,streɪṱər] *n* **1** : démonstrateur *m,* -trice *f* **2** PROTESTOR : manifestant *m,* -tante *f*
demoralize [dɪ'mɔrə,laɪz] *vt* **-ized; -izing** : démoraliser
demote [di'mo:t] *vt* **-moted; -moting** : rétrograder
demur [dɪ'mər] *vi* **-murred; -murring** : élever des objections, s'opposer
demure [dɪ'mjʊr] *adj* : modeste, réservé
den ['dɛn] *n* **1** LAIR : antre *m,* tanière *f* **2** HIDEOUT : repaire *m* <a den of iniquity : un lieu de perdition> **3** STUDY : petit salon *m,* petit bureau *m* de travail
denature [di'neɪtʃər] *vt* **-tured; -turing** : dénaturer
denial [di'naɪəl] *n* **1** DENYING : démenti *m,* dénégation *f* **2** REFUSAL : refus *m,* rejet *m* **3** DISAVOWAL : reniement *m*
denigrate ['dɛnɪ,greɪt] *vt* **-grated; -grating** : dénigrer
denim ['dɛnəm] *n* **1** : jean *m* **2 denims** *npl* JEANS : jean *m,* blue-jean *m*
denizen ['dɛnəzən] *n* : habitant *m,* -tante *f*
denomination [dɪ,nɑmə'neɪʃən] *n* **1** : confession *f* (religieuse) **2** DESIGNATION : dénomination *f* **3** VALUE : valeur *f* (de monnaie)
denominator [dɪ'nɑmə,neɪṱər] *n* : dénominateur *m*
denote [di'no:t] *vt* **-noted; -noting 1** INDICATE : dénoter **2** MEAN : signifier
denouement [,deɪ,nu:'mɑ:] *n* : dénouement *m*
denounce [dɪ'naʊn*t*s] *vt* **-nounced; -nouncing 1** CENSURE : dénoncer **2** ACCUSE : accuser
dense ['dɛn*t*s] *adj* **denser; -est 1** THICK : dense **2** STUPID : bête, obtus
densely ['dɛn*t*sli] *adv* : densément
density ['dɛn*t*səṱi] *n, pl* **-ties** : densité *f*
dent[1] ['dɛnt] *vt* : bosseler, poquer *Can fam* (une voiture), cabosser (un chapeau, etc.)
dent[2] *n* : bosse *f* (en métal), creux *m*
dental ['dɛntəl] *adj* : dentaire
dental floss *n* : fil *m* dentaire
dentifrice ['dɛntəfrɪs] *n* : dentifrice *m,* pâte *f* dentifrice
dentist ['dɛntɪst] *n* : dentiste *mf*
dentistry ['dɛntɪstri] *n* : dentisterie *f*
dentures ['dɛntʃərz] *npl* : dentier *m*
denude [di'nu:d, -'nju:d] *vt* **-nuded; -nuding** : dénuder
denunciation [dɪ,nʌn*t*si'eɪʃən] *n* : dénonciation *f*
deny [dɪ'naɪ] *vt* **-nied; -nying 1** REFUTE : démentir, nier <he denied the charges : il a démenti les accusations> **2** REPUDIATE : renier <to deny one's religion : renier sa religion> **3** REFUSE : refuser **4 to deny oneself** : se priver
deodorant [di'o:dərənt] *n* **1** : déodorant *m* **2** *or* **room deodorant** : désodorisant *m*
deodorize [di'o:də,raɪz] *vt* **-ized; -izing** : désodoriser
depart [dɪ'pɑrt] *vt* : quitter <to depart this life : quitter ce monde> — *vi* LEAVE : partir
department [dɪ'pɑrtmənt] *n* **1** DIVISION : ministère *m* (gouvernemental), service *m* (d'un hôpital, etc.), rayon *m* (d'un magasin) **2** FIELD : champ *m,* domaine *m* <it's not my department : ce n'est pas mon champ d'expertise>
departmental [dɪ,pɑrt'mɛntəl, ,di:-] *adj* : de service, de département
department store *n* : grand magasin *m*
departure [dɪ'pɑrtʃər] *n* **1** LEAVING : départ *m* **2** DEVIATION : écart *m,* déviation *f,* entorse *f* <a departure from procedure : un écart à la procédure>
depend [dɪ'pɛnd] *vi* **1** RELY : compter, se fier <depend on me! : comptez sur moi!> **2 to depend on** : dépendre de <success depends on hard work : le succès est le résultat d'un travail acharné> **3 depending on** : selon, dépendamment de *Can* <depending

on what happens : selon ce qui se passera>

dependable [dɪˈpɛndəbəl] *adj* : fiable, sûr

dependent[1] [dɪˈpɛndənt] *adj* : dépendant

dependent[2] *n* : personne *f* à charge

depict [dɪˈpɪkt] *vt* : dépeindre, décrire

deplete [dɪˈpliːt] *vt* **-pleted; -pleting** : épuiser, réduire

depletion [dɪˈpliːʃən] *n* : diminution *f*, réduction *f*

deplorable [dɪˈplorəbəl] *adj* : déplorable, lamentable

deplore [dɪˈplor] *vt* **-plored; -ploring** : déplorer, regretter

deploy [dɪˈplɔɪ] *vt* : déployer

deployment [dɪˈplɔɪmənt] *n* : déploiement *m*

deport [dɪˈport] *vt* **1** EXPEL : déporter, expulser (d'un pays) **2 to deport oneself** BEHAVE : se comporter

deportment [dɪˈportmənt] *n* BEHAVIOR : comportement *m*

depose [dɪˈpoːz] *vt* **-posed; -posing** : déposer (un souverain, etc.)

deposit[1] [dɪˈpɑzət] *vt* **-ited; -iting** : déposer

deposit[2] *n* **1** : dépôt *m* <a $500 deposit : un dépôt de 500$> **2** DOWN PAYMENT : acompte *m*, arrhes *fpl France* **3** : dépôt *m* (en géologie)

depositor [dɪˈpɑzət̬ər] *n* : déposant *m*, -sante *f*

depository [dɪˈpɑzəˌtori] *n, pl* **-ries** : dépôt *m*, lieu *m* sûr

depot [*1 usu* ˈdɛˌpoː, *2 usu* ˈdiː-] *n* **1** WAREHOUSE : dépôt *m*, entrepôt *m* **2** STATION : gare *f* (ferroviaire), gare *f* d'autobus

deprave [dɪˈpreɪv] *vt* **-praved; -praving** : dépraver, corrompre

depravity [dɪˈprævət̬i] *n, pl* **-ties** : dépravation *f*

depreciate [dɪˈpriːʃiˌeɪt] *v* **-ated; -ating** *vt* **1** DEVALUE : dévaluer **2** DISPARAGE : déprécier, dénigrer — *vi* : se déprécier (se dit d'une valeur)

depreciation [dɪˌpriʃiˈeɪʃən] *n* : dépréciation *f*

depress [dɪˈprɛs] *vt* **1** PRESS : appuyer sur **2** REDUCE : réduire, faire baisser (les ventes, les prix, etc.) **3** DISCOURAGE, SADDEN : déprimer, attrister **4** DEVALUE : dévaluer

depressant [dɪˈprɛsənt] *n* : dépresseur *m*

depressed [dɪˈprɛst] *adj* : déprimé, abattu

depressing [dɪˈprɛsɪŋ] *adj* : déprimant, décourageant

depression [dɪˈprɛʃən] *n* **1** : dépression *f* (en médecine) **2** : récession *f*, crise *f* <economic depression : crise économique> **3** HOLLOW : creux *m*, dépression *f*

deprivation [ˌdɛprəˈveɪʃən] *n* : privation *f*

deprive [dɪˈpraɪv] *vt* **-prived; -priving** : priver

depth [ˈdɛpθ] *n, pl* **depths 1** : profondeur *f* <the depth of a cupboard : la profondeur d'une armoire> **2** EXTENT : étendue *f* <the depth of his knowledge : l'étendue de ses connaissances> **3** INTENSITY : intensité *f* (de couleurs) **4 in the depths of** : au milieu de, au cœur de

deputize [ˈdɛpjʊˌtaɪz] *vt* **-tized; -tizing** : députer

deputy [ˈdɛpjʊt̬i] *n, pl* **-ties** : député *m*, -tée *f*

derail [diˈreɪl] *vt* : faire dérailler — *vi* : dérailler

derailment [diˈreɪlmənt] *n* : déraillement *m*

derange [dɪˈreɪndʒ] *vt* **-ranged; -ranging 1** DISARRANGE : déranger, déplacer **2** CRAZE : rendre fou

derangement [dɪˈreɪndʒmənt] *n* **1** DISARRAY : confusion *f*, désordre *m* **2** INSANITY : aliénation *f* mentale

derby [ˈdərbi] *n, pl* **-bies 1** : derby *m* (course de chevaux) **2** *or* **derby hat** : chapeau *m* melon

deregulate [diˈrɛgjʊˌleɪt] *vt* **-lated; -lating** : déréglementer

deregulation [diˌrɛgjʊˈleɪʃən] *n* : déréglementation *f*

derelict[1] [ˈdɛrəˌlɪkt] *adj* **1** ABANDONED : abandonné **2** NEGLIGENT : négligent, insouciant

derelict[2] *n* **1** : propriété *f* abandonnée, navire *m* abandonné **2** VAGRANT : vagabond *m*, -bonde *f*; clochard *m*, -charde *f*

deride [dɪˈraɪd] *vt* **-rided; -riding** : railler, tourner en dérision

derision [dɪˈrɪʒən] *n* : dérision *f*

derisive [dɪˈraɪsɪv] *adj* : moqueur, railleur

derivation [ˌdɛrəˈveɪʃən] *n* : dérivation *f*

derivative[1] [dɪˈrɪvət̬ɪv] *adj* : dérivé

derivative[2] *n* : dérivé *m*

derive [dɪˈraɪv] *v* **-rived; -riving** *vt* **1** OBTAIN : tirer, trouver **2** DEDUCE : déduire, dériver de — *vi* **to derive from** : découler de, provenir de

dermatologist [ˌdərməˈtɑlədʒɪst] *n* : dermatologue *mf*

dermatology [ˌdərməˈtɑlədʒi] *n* : dermatologie *f*

derogatory [dɪˈrɑgəˌtori] *adj* : désobligeant

derrick [ˈdɛrɪk] *n* **1** CRANE : grue *f* **2** : tour *f* de forage (pour le pétrole)

descend [dɪˈsɛnd] *vt* : descendre — *vi* **1** : descendre <she descended from the train : elle est descendue du train> **2** DERIVE : dériver, provenir <to be descended from : descendre de> **3** INCLINE : descendre **4** STOOP : s'abaisser, descendre (au niveau de qqn) **5 to descend upon** : se précipiter sur, s'élancer vers

descendant[1] *or* **descendent** [dɪ'sɛndənt] *adj* : descendant
descendant[2] *or* **descendent** *n* : descendant *m,* -dante *f*
descent [dɪ'sɛnt] *n* **1** : descente *f* <the descent of the airplane : la descente de l'avion> **2** LINEAGE : origine *f,* descendance *f* **3** DECLINE, SLOPE : descente *f* **4** ATTACK, INRUSH : descente *f,* irruption *f*
describe [dɪ'skraɪb] *vt* **-scribed; -scribing** : décrire
description [dɪ'skrɪpʃən] *n* : description *f*
descriptive [dɪ'skrɪptɪv] *adj* : descriptif
desecrate ['dɛsɪ,kreɪt] *vt* **-crated; -crating** : profaner
desecration [,dɛsɪ'kreɪʃən] *n* : profanation *f*
desegregate [di'sɛgrə,geɪt] *vt* **-gated; -gating** : éliminer la ségrégation raciale dans
desegregation [di,sɛgrə'geɪʃən] *n* : déségrégation *f*
desert[1] [dɪ'zərt] *vt* : abandonner (une personne ou un lieu), déserter (une cause) — *vi* : déserter
desert[2] ['dɛzərt] *adj* : désert <a desert isle : une île déserte>
desert[3] *n* **1** ['dɛzərt] : désert *m* **2** [di'zərt] → **deserts**
deserter [dɪ'zərţər] *n* : déserteur *m*
desertion [dɪ'zərʃən] *n* : désertion *f*
deserts [dɪ'zərts] *npl* **to get one's just deserts** : avoir ce que l'on mérite
deserve [dɪ'zərv] *vt* **-served; -serving** : mériter
desiccate ['dɛsɪ,keɪt] *vt* **-cated; -cating** : sécher, dessécher
design[1] [dɪ'zaɪn] *vt* **1** DEVISE : concevoir, élaborer **2** DRAW, SKETCH : dessiner **3** INTEND : concevoir, destiner <a book designed for students : un livre destiné pour les étudiants>
design[2] *n* **1** CONCEPTION : conception *f,* élaboration *f* **2** PLAN : plan *m,* projet *m* **3** PURPOSE : dessein *m,* intention *f* <by design : à dessein, exprès> **4** SKETCH : dessin *m,* croquis *m* **5** PATTERN : motif *m*
designate ['dɛzɪg,neɪt] *vt* **-nated; -nating 1** INDICATE : indiquer, montrer **2** APPOINT : nommer, désigner
designation [,dɛzɪg'neɪʃən] *n* **1** APPOINTMENT : nomination *f,* désignation *f* **2** NAME : désignation *f,* dénomination *f*
designer [də'zaɪnər] *n* **1** : concepteur *m,* -trice *f;* dessinateur *m,* -trice *f* **2** *or* **fashion designer** : designer *m,* couturier *m*
desirable [dɪ'zaɪrəbəl] *adj* **1** ATTRACTIVE : désirable, enviable **2** ADVISABLE : désirable, souhaitable
desire[1] [dɪ'zaɪr] *vt* **-sired; -siring 1** WANT : désirer, avoir envie de **2** REQUEST : demander
desire[2] *n* **1** LONGING : désir *m,* envie *f* **2** REQUEST : demande *f,* requête *f*
desist [dɪ'sɪst] *vi* : cesser, s'arrêter
desk ['dɛsk] *n* : bureau *m,* pupitre *m* (d'un élève)
desolate[1] ['dɛsə,leɪt, -zə-] *vt* **-lated; -lating** RAVAGE : dévaster, ravager
desolate[2] ['dɛsələt, -zə-] *adj* **1** BARREN : désolé, désert <a desolate landscape : un paysage désert> **2** GLOOMY : morne, sombre
desolation ['dɛsə'leɪʃən, -zə-] *n* **1** BARRENNESS : désolation *f* **2** GRIEF : affliction *f,* chagrin *m*
despair[1] [dɪ'spær] *vi* : désespérer, perdre espoir
despair[2] *n* : désespoir *m*
desperate ['dɛspərət] *adj* : désespéré — **desperately** *adv*
desperation [,dɛspə'reɪʃən] *n* : désespoir *m*
despicable [dɪ'spɪkəbəl, 'dɛspɪ-] *adj* : ignoble, méprisable
despise [dɪ'spaɪz] *vt* **-spised; -spising** : mépriser, détester
despite [də'spaɪt] *prep* : malgré, en dépit de
despoil [də'spɔɪl] *vt* : dépouiller, spolier
despondency [dɪ'spɑndəntsi] *n* : abattement *m,* découragement *m*
despondent [dɪ'spɑndənt] *adj* : abattu, découragé
despot ['dɛspət, -,pɑt] *n* : despote *m*
despotic [dəs'pɑţɪk] *adj* : despotique, tyrannique
despotism ['dɛspə'tɪzəm] *n* : despotisme *m*
dessert [dɪ'zərt] *n* : dessert *m*
destination [,dɛstɪ'neɪʃən] *n* : destination *f*
destined ['dɛstənd] *adj* **1** FATED : prédestiné **2** BOUND : destiné, en route <destined for Quebec : à destination de Québec>
destiny ['dɛstəni] *n, pl* **-nies** : destin *m,* destinée *f*
destitute ['dɛstə,tuːt] *adj* **1** LACKING : dépourvu, dénué <a lake destitute of fish : un lac dépourvu de poissons> **2** POOR : sans ressources, indigent
destitution ['dɛstə'tuːʃən, -'tjuː-] *n* : misère *f,* indigence *f*
destroy [dɪ'strɔɪ] *vt* **1** RUIN : détruire **2** KILL : détruire, anéantir
destroyer [dɪ'strɔɪər] *n* **1** : destructeur *m,* -trice *f* **2** WARSHIP : contre-torpilleur *m*
destructible [dɪ'strʌktəbəl] *adj* : destructible
destruction [dɪ'strʌkʃən] *n* : destruction *f*
destructive [dɪ'strʌktɪv] *adj* : destructeur, destructif
desultory ['dɛsəl,tori] *adj* : décousu, sans suite

detach [dɪ'tætʃ] *vt* **1** SEPARATE : détacher, séparer **2 to detach oneself** : se détacher

detached [dɪ'tætʃt] *adj* **1** SEPARATE : détaché, séparé **2** ALOOF : distant, indifférent **3** IMPARTIAL : objectif, désintéressé

detachment [dɪ'tætʃmənt] *n* **1** SEPARATION : séparation *f* **2** ALOOFNESS : détachement *m,* indifférence *f* **3** IMPARTIALITY : impartialité *f* **4** : détachement *m* (militaire)

detail[1] [dɪ'teɪl, 'diːˌteɪl] *vt* : détailler, énumérer

detail[2] *n* **1** : détail *m* <to go into details : rentrer dans les détails> **2** : détachement *m* (militaire)

detain [dɪ'teɪn] *vt* **1** : détenir (un prisonnier) **2** DELAY : retenir, retarder

detect [dɪ'tɛkt] *vt* : détecter, déceler, découvrir

detection [dɪ'tɛkʃən] *n* : détection *f,* découverte *f*

detective [dɪ'tɛktɪv] *n* : détective *mf* <private detective : détective privé>

detector [dɪ'tɛktər] *n* : détecteur *m*

detention [dɪ'tɛntʃən] *n* : détention *f*

deter [dɪ'tər] *vt* **-terred; -terring** : dissuader, décourager

detergent [dɪ'tərdʒənt] *n* : détergent *m*

deteriorate [dɪ'tɪriəˌreɪt] *vi* **-rated; -rating** : se détériorer, se dégrader

deterioration [dɪˌtɪriə'reɪʃən] *n* : détérioration *f*

determination [dɪˌtərmə'neɪʃən] *n* **1** DECISION : décision *f,* jugement *m* **2** RESOLVE : détermination *f,* résolution *f*

determine [dɪ'tərmən] *vt* **-mined; -mining 1** FIND OUT : déterminer, découvrir **2** FIX, SETTLE : fixer, déterminer **3** RESOLVE : décider **4** CAUSE, GOVERN : décider de, déterminer

determined [di'tərmənd] *adj* RESOLUTE : déterminé, résolu

deterrence [dɪ'tərənts, -'tɛr-] *n* : dissuasion *f*

deterrent[1] [dɪ'tərənt] *adj* : dissuasif

deterrent[2] *n* : moyen *m* de dissuasion

detest [dɪ'tɛst] *vt* : détester, haïr

detestable [dɪ'tɛstəbəl] *adj* : détestable

dethrone [di'θroːn] *vt* **-throned; -throning** : détrôner

detonate ['dɛtənˌeɪt] *v* **-nated; -nating** *vt* : faire détoner — *vi* EXPLODE : détoner

detonation [ˌdɛtən'eɪʃən, 'dɛtən-] *n* : détonation *f,* explosion *f*

detour[1] ['diːˌtʊr, di'tʊr] *vt* DIVERT : détourner, dévier — *vi* : faire un détour

detour[2] *n* : détour *m*

detract [dɪ'trækt] *vt* : détourner <to detract attention : détourner l'attention> — *vi* **to detract from** : diminuer, porter atteinte à

detriment ['dɛtrəmənt] *n* : détriment *m,* préjudice *m*

detrimental [ˌdɛtrə'mɛntəl] *adj* : nuisible, préjudiciable

devaluation [diˌvæljʊ'eɪʃən] *n* : dévaluation *f*

devalue [di'vælˌjuː] *vt* : dévaluer

devastate ['dɛvəˌsteɪt] *vt* **-tated; -tating** : dévaster, ravager

devastation [ˌdɛvə'steɪʃən] *n* : dévastation *f*

develop [dɪ'vɛləp] *vt* **1** FOSTER, PERFECT : mettre au point, développer, cultiver **2** EXPLOIT : développer, exploiter, mettre en valeur (des terres, etc.) **3** : développer (un film) **4** CONTRACT : contracter (une maladie) **5** ACQUIRE : développer, acquérir <he acquired a taste for olives : il a développé un goût pour les olives> — *vi* **1** GROW : se développer, grandir **2** HAPPEN : se produire, se manifester **3** UNFOLD : se développer, se dérouler

developing [dɪ'vɛləpɪŋ] *adj* : en expansion <developing countries : pays en expansion>

development [dɪ'vɛləpmənt] *n* **1** FORMATION, GROWTH : développement *m,* formation *f,* expansion *f* **2** : exploitation *f,* mise *f* en valeur (de ressources) **3** INCIDENT : événement *m,* fait *m* nouveau **4** *or* **housing development** : ensemble *m* résidentiel

deviant ['diːviənt] *adj* : déviant

deviate ['diːviˌeɪt] *vi* **-ated; -ating** : dévier, s'écarter

deviation [ˌdiːvi'eɪʃən] *n* : déviation *f*

device [dɪ'vaɪs] *n* **1** MECHANISM : appareil *m,* dispositif *m,* mécanisme *m* **2** SCHEME : ruse *f,* stratagème *m* **3 to leave s.o. to their own devices** : laisser qqn se débrouiller tout seul

devil[1] ['dɛvəl] *vt* **-iled** *or* **-illed; -iling** *or* **-illing 1** : assaisonner avec des épices fortes <deviled eggs : œufs à la diable> **2** PESTER : ennuyer, agacer

devil[2] *n* **1** DEMON : diable *m,* démon *m* **2 the Devil** : le Démon *m,* Satan *m* **3** : monstre *m,* démon *m* <what a little devil! : quel petit monstre!>

devilish ['dɛvəlɪʃ] *adj* : diabolique

devious ['diːviəs] *adj* **1** CUNNING : sournois, astucieux **2** WINDING : tortueux, sinueux

devise [dɪ'vaɪz] *vt* **-vised; -vising 1** INVENT : inventer, concevoir **2** PLOT : manigancer

devoid [dɪ'vɔɪd] *adj* **~ of** : dépourvu de, dénué de

devote [dɪ'voːt] *vt* **-voted; -voting 1** DEDICATE : consacrer, vouer **2 to devote oneself to** : se consacrer à

devoted [dɪ'voːtəd] *adj* **1** FAITHFUL : dévoué, fidèle **2 to be devoted to** : être très attaché à

devotee [ˌdɛvə'tiː, -'teɪ] *n* **1** ENTHUSIAST : passionné *m,* -née *f* (d'un sport, etc.) **2** FOLLOWER : adepte *mf;* partisan *m,* -sane *f*

devotion [dɪ'vo:ʃən] *n* **1** DEDICATION : dévouement *m* **2** PIETY : dévotion *f,* piété *f* **3 devotions** *npl* PRAYER : dévotions *fpl,* prières *fpl*

devour [dɪ'vaʊər] *vt* : dévorer

devout [dɪ'vaʊt] *adj* **1** PIOUS : dévot, pieux **2** EARNEST : fervent, ardent

devoutness [dɪ'vaʊtnəs] *n* : dévotion *f,* piété *f*

dew ['du:, 'dju:] *n* : rosée *f*

dewdrop ['du:ˌdrɑp, 'dju:-] *n* : goutte *f* de rosée

dewlap ['duˌlæp, 'dju-] *n* : fanon *m*

dexterity [dɛk'stɛrət̬i] *n, pl* **-ties** : dextérité *f,* adresse *f*

dexterous ['dɛkstrəs] *adj* : adroit, habile, agile

dextrose ['dɛkˌstro:s] *n* : dextrose *m*

diabetes [ˌdaɪə'bi:t̬iz] *n* : diabète *m*

diabetic[1] [ˌdaɪə'bɛt̬ɪk] *adj* : diabétique

diabetic[2] *n* : diabétique *mf*

diabolic [ˌdaɪə'bɑlɪk] *or* **diabolical** [-lɪkəl] *adj* : diabolique

diacritic [ˌdaɪə'krɪt̬ɪk] *n or* **diacritical mark** [ˌdaɪə'krɪt̬ɪkəl] : signe *m* diacritique

diadem ['daɪəˌdɛm, -dəm] *n* : diadème *m*

diagnose ['daɪɪgˌno:s, ˌdaɪɪg'no:s] *vt* **-nosed; -nosing** : diagnostiquer

diagnosis [ˌdaɪɪg'no:sɪs] *n, pl* **-noses** [-'no:ˌsi:z] : diagnostic *m*

diagnostic [ˌdaɪɪg'nɑstɪk] *adj* : diagnostique

diagonal[1] [daɪ'ægənəl] *adj* : diagonal

diagonal[2] *n* : diagonale *f*

diagram[1] ['daɪəˌgræm] *vt* **-grammed** *or* **-gramed; -gramming** *or* **-graming** : donner une représentation graphique de

diagram[2] *n* : diagramme *m,* schéma *m*

dial[1] ['daɪl] *vt* **-aled** *or* **-alled; -aling** *or* **-alling** : faire, composer (un numéro de téléphone)

dial[2] *n* : cadran *m* (d'une horloge, d'un téléphone), bouton *m* (d'une radio, etc.)

dialect ['daɪəˌlɛkt] *n* : dialecte *m*

dialogue ['daɪəˌlɔg] *n* : dialogue *m*

diameter [daɪ'æmət̬ər] *n* : diamètre *m*

diametric [ˌdaɪə'mɛtrɪk] *or* **diametrical** [-trɪkəl] *adj* : diamétral — **diametrically** [-trɪkəli] *adv*

diamond ['daɪmənd, 'daɪə-] *n* **1** : diamant *m* (pierre précieuse) **2** : losange *m* (forme géométrique) **3** : carreau *m* (aux cartes) **4** INFIELD : terrain *m* de baseball, losange *m Can*

diaper ['daɪpər, 'daɪə-] *n* : couche *f* (de bébé)

diaphragm ['daɪəˌfræm] *n* : diaphragme *m*

diarrhea *or Brit* **diarrhoea** [ˌdaɪə'ri:ə] *n* : diarrhée *f*

diary ['daɪəri:] *n, pl* **-ries** : journal *m* intime

diatribe ['daɪəˌtraɪb] *n* : diatribe *f*

dice[1] ['daɪs] *vt* **diced; dicing** CUBE : couper en dés

dice[2] *ns & pl* **1** → **die**[2] **2** : dé *m* (jeu) <to play dice : jouer aux dés>

dicker ['dɪkər] *vi* : marchander

dictate[1] ['dɪkˌteɪt] *vt* **-tated; -tating** : dicter

dictate[2] *n* : précepte *m,* ordre *m* <the dictates of conscience : la voix de la conscience>

dictation [dɪk'teɪʃən] *n* : dictée *f*

dictator ['dɪkˌteɪt̬ər] *n* : dictateur *m*

dictatorship [dɪk'teɪt̬ərˌʃɪp, 'dɪkˌ-] *n* : dictature *f*

diction ['dɪkʃən] *n* **1** WORDING : langage *m,* style *m* **2** ENUNCIATION : diction *f,* élocution *f*

dictionary ['dɪkʃəˌnɛri] *n, pl* **-naries** : dictionnaire *m*

did → **do**

didactic [daɪ'dæktɪk] *adj* : didactique

die[1] ['daɪ] *vi* **died** ['daɪd]; **dying** ['daɪɪŋ] **1** : mourir, décéder **2** *or* **to die down** SUBSIDE : tomber (se dit du vent, de la colère, etc.) **3** STOP : s'arrêter <the motor died : le moteur s'est arrêté> **4** LONG : mourir d'envie <I'm dying to go : je meurs d'envie d'y aller>

die[2] ['daɪ] *n, pl* **dice** ['daɪs] : dé *m* (à jouer)

die[3] *n, pl* **dies** ['daɪz] MOLD, STAMP : étampe *f,* matrice *f*

diesel ['di:zəl, -səl] *n* : diesel *m*

diet[1] ['daɪət] *vt* : suivre un régime

diet[2] *n* **1** NOURISHMENT : alimentation *f,* nourriture *f* <a balanced diet : une alimentation équilibrée> **2** : régime *m* <to be on a diet : être au régime>

dietary ['daɪəˌtɛri] *adj* : alimentaire, diététique

dietitian *or* **dietician** [daɪə'tɪʃən] *n* : diététicien *m,* -cienne *f*

differ ['dɪfər] *vi* **1** : différer, être différent **2** VARY : varier **3** DISAGREE : être en désaccord

difference ['dɪfrənts, 'dɪfərənts] *n* : différence *f*

different ['dɪfrənt, 'dɪfərənt] *adj* **1** DISSIMILAR : différent **2** OTHER : autre <that's different : c'est autre chose> **3** VARIOUS : divers, différent, plusieurs

differentiate [dɪfə'rɛntʃiˌeɪt] *v* **-ated; -ating** *vt* : différencier, distinguer — *vi* **to differentiate between** : faire la différence entre

differently ['dɪfrəntli, 'dɪfərəntli] *adv* : différemment, autrement

difficult ['dɪfɪˌkʌlt] *adj* : difficile

difficulty ['dɪfɪˌkʌlti] *n, pl* **-ties** : difficulté *f*

diffidence ['dɪfədənts] *n* **1** SHYNESS : timidité *f,* manque *m* d'assurance **2** RETICENCE : réserve *f,* réticence *f*

diffident ['dɪfədənt] *adj* **1** SHY : qui manque d'assurance, timide **2** RESERVED : réservé

diffuse[1] [dɪ'fju:z] *v* **-fused; -fusing** *vt* : diffuser — *vi* : se diffuser

diffuse[2] [dɪ'fju:s] *adj* **1** WORDY : verbeux, diffus **2** : diffus, non concentré (se dit de la lumière, etc.)
diffusion [dɪ'fju:ʒən] *n* : diffusion *f*
dig[1] ['dɪg] *v* **dug** ['dʌg]; **digging** *vt* **1** : creuser (un trou), bêcher (la terre) **2** *or* **to dig up** EXTRACT : arracher, extraire **3** POKE, THRUST : enfoncer <to dig s.o. in the ribs : donner un coup de coude dans les côtes de qqn> **4 to dig up** UNEARTH : déterrer — *vi* **1** EXCAVATE : creuser **2 to dig in** : se retrancher
dig[2] *n* **1** POKE : coup *m* de coude **2** GIBE : pointe *f,* remarque *f* blessante
digest[1] ['daɪˌdʒɛst, dɪ-] *vt* **1** : digérer (de la nourriture) **2** ASSIMILATE : assimiler, digérer **3** SUMMARIZE : résumer
digest[2] ['daɪˌdʒɛst] *n* : résumé *m*
digestible [daɪ'dʒɛstəbəl, dɪ-] *adj* : digestible
digestion [daɪ'dʒɛstʃən] *n* : digestion *f*
digestive [daɪ'dʒɛstʃən, dɪ-] *adj* : digestif <the digestive system : l'appareil digestif>
digit ['dɪdʒət] *n* **1** NUMERAL : chiffre *m* **2** FINGER : doigt *m* **3** TOE : orteil *m*
digital ['dɪdʒətəl] *adj* : digital
dignified ['dɪgnəˌfaɪd] *adj* : digne, plein de dignité
dignify ['dɪgnəˌfaɪ] *vt* **-fied; -fying** : donner de la dignité à
dignitary ['dɪgnə'tɛri] *n, pl* **-taries** : dignitaire *m*
dignity ['dɪgnəti] *n, pl* **-ties** : dignité *f*
digress [daɪ'grɛs, də-] *vi* : faire une digression, s'écarter
digression [daɪ'grɛʃən, də-] *n* : digression *f*
dike ['daɪk] *n* : digue *f*
dilapidated [də'læpəˌdeɪtəd] *adj* : délabré
dilapidation [dəˌlæpə'deɪʃən] *n* : délabrement *m*
dilate [daɪ'leɪt, 'daɪˌleɪt] *v* **-lated; -lating** *vt* : dilater — *vi* : se dilater
dilemma [dɪ'lɛmə] *n* : dilemme *m*
dilettante ['dɪləˌtɑnt, -ˌtænt] *n, pl* **-tantes** *or* **-tanti** [-tɑnts, -tænts] : dilettante *mf*
diligence ['dɪlədʒənts] *n* : assiduité *f,* application *f*
diligent ['dɪlədʒənt] *adj* : assidu, appliqué
diligently ['dɪlədʒəntli] *adv* : assidûment, avec zèle
dill ['dɪl] *n* : aneth *m*
dillydally ['dɪliˌdæli] *vi* **-lied; -lying** : traîner, lambiner *fam,* farfiner *Can fam,* niaiser *Can fam*
dilute [daɪ'lu:t, də-] *vt* **-luted; -luting** : diluer
dilution [daɪ'lu:ʃən, də-] *n* : dilution *f*
dim[1] ['dɪm] *v* **dimmed; dimming** *vt* : baisser (les lumières), ternir (des couleurs, etc.), affaiblir (des sons), effacer (des souvenirs) — *vi* : baisser, se ternir, s'effacer, s'affaiblir
dim[2] *adj* **dimmer; dimmest 1** DARK : sombre **2** FAINT : faible (se dit de la lumière), terne (se dit des couleurs, etc.), vague (se dit des sons, des formes, de la mémoire)
dime ['daɪm] *n* : pièce *f* de dix cents
dimension [də'mɛntʃən, daɪ-] *n* **1** : dimension *f* **2 dimensions** *npl* SCOPE : étendue *f,* ampleur *f*
diminish [də'mɪnɪʃ] *vt* REDUCE : diminuer, réduire, amoindrir — *vi* DWINDLE : diminuer, se réduire
diminutive [də'mɪnjʊtɪv] *adj* : minuscule
dimly ['dɪmli] *adv* **1** : sombrement <dimly lit : sombrement éclairé> **2** FAINTLY : vaguement, indistinctement
dimmer ['dɪmər] *n* : rhéostat *m* (d'une lumière)
dimple ['dɪmpəl] *n* : fossette *f*
din ['dɪn] *n* : vacarme *m,* tapage *m*
dine ['daɪn] *vi* **dined; dining** : dîner
diner ['daɪnər] *n* **1** : dîneur *m,* -neuse *f* **2** : wagon-restaurant *m* (d'un train) **3** : petit restaurant *m*
dinghy ['dɪŋi, 'dɪŋgi, 'dɪŋki] *n, pl* **-ghies** : petit canot *m*
dingy ['dɪndʒi] *adj* **dingier; -est 1** DIRTY : malpropre, sale **2** SHABBY : minable, miteux
dinner ['dɪnər] *n* : dîner *m*
dinosaur ['daɪnəˌsɔr] *n* : dinosaure *m*
dint ['dɪnt] *n* **by dint of** : à force de
diocese ['daɪəsəs, -ˌsi:z, -ˌsi:s] *n, pl* **-ceses** ['daɪəsəzəz] : diocèse *m*
dip[1] ['dɪp] *v* **dipped; dipping** *vt* **1** PLUNGE : plonger, tremper **2** LADLE : servir avec une louche — *vi* **1** DESCEND, DROP : baisser, diminuer <prices dipped : les prix ont baissé> <to dip below the horizon : disparaître derrière l'horizon> **2** INCLINE : descendre, s'incliner
dip[2] *n* **1** SWIM : petite baignade *f* <to go for a dip : aller faire trempette> **2** DROP : baisse *f,* diminution *f* **3** INCLINE : inclinaison *f,* pente *f* **4** SAUCE : trempette *f Can,* sauce *f*
diphtheria [dɪf'θɪriə] *n* : diphtérie *f*
diphthong ['dɪfˌθɔŋ] *n* : diphtongue *f*
diploma [də'plo:mə] *n* : diplôme *m*
diplomacy [də'plo:məsi] *n* : diplomatie *f*
diplomat ['dɪpləˌmæt] *n* : diplomate *mf*
diplomatic [ˌdɪplə'mætɪk] *adj* **1** : diplomatique <diplomatic relations : relations diplomatiques> **2** TACTFUL : diplomate, plein de tact
dipper ['dɪpər] *n* **1** LADLE : louche *f* **2 Big Dipper** : Grande Ourse *f* **3 Little Dipper** : Petite Ourse *f*
dire ['daɪr] *adj* **direr; -est 1** HORRIBLE : affreux, terrible **2** EXTREME : extrême, absolu <dire poverty : misère noire> <dire necessity : nécessité absolue>

direct[1] [də'rɛkt, daɪ-] *vt* **1** ADDRESS : adresser, diriger **2** AIM : destiner <directed to the public : destiné au grand public> **3** GUIDE : diriger, indiquer le chemin à **4** CONTROL : diriger, gérer, être en charge de **5** ORDER : ordonner
direct[2] *adv* : directement
direct[3] *adj* **1** : direct <a direct flight : un vol direct> **2** FRANK : direct, franc
direct current *n* : courant *m* continu
direction [də'rɛkʃən, daɪ-] *n* **1** SUPERVISION : direction *f* **2** ORDER : instruction *f*, ordre *m* **3** COURSE : direction *f*, sens *m* <in the right direction : dans le bon sens> **4** TENDENCY, TREND : direction *f*, tendence *f* **5 directions** *npl* INSTRUCTIONS : indications *fpl*
directly [də'rɛktli, daɪ-] *adv* **1** STRAIGHT : directement **2** FRANKLY : franchement **3** EXACTLY : juste, exactement <directly opposite my house : juste en face de ma maison> **4** IMMEDIATELY : immédiatement, tout de suite
directness [də'rɛktnəs, daɪ-] *n* FRANKNESS : franchise *f*
director [də'rɛktər, daɪ-] *n* **1** HEAD, MANAGER : directeur *m*, -trice *f* **2** : réalisateur *m*, -trice *f* (d'un film ou d'une pièce de théatre); metteur *m* en scène (d'une pièce de théâtre)
directory [də'rɛktəri, daɪ-] *n, pl* **-ries** : répertoire *m* (d'adresses), annuaire *m* (téléphonique)
dirge ['dərdʒ] *n* : hymne *m* funèbre
dirigible ['dɪrədʒəbəl, də'rɪdʒə-] *n* : dirigeable *m*
dirt ['dərt] *n* **1** FILTH : saleté *f*, crasse *f* **2** SOIL : terre *f*
dirtiness ['dərt̬inəs] *n* : saleté *f*
dirty[1] ['dərt̬i] *vt* **dirtied; dirtying** : salir
dirty[2] *adj* **dirtier; -est 1** SOILED : sale, malpropre **2** DISHONEST, UNFAIR : sale, malhonnête <a dirty trick : un sale tour> **3** INDECENT : obscène, cochon *fam*
disability [ˌdɪsə'bɪlət̬i] *n, pl* **-ties** : infirmité *f*, incapacité *f*, handicap *m*
disable [dɪs'eɪbəl] *vt* **-abled; -abling 1** : rendre infirme, handicaper (une personne) **2** : immobiliser (une machine), mettre hors d'action (un navire, etc.)
disabled [dɪs'eɪbəld] *adj* : handicapé
disabuse [ˌdɪsə'bjuːz] *vt* **-bused; -busing** : détromper
disadvantage [ˌdɪsəd'væntɪdʒ] *n* : désavantage *m*
disadvantageous [ˌdɪsˌædˌvæn'teɪdʒəs] *adj* : défavorable, désavantageux
disagree [ˌdɪsə'griː] *vi* **1** DIFFER : ne pas concorder, différer **2** DISSENT : être en désaccord, s'opposer **3** : ne pas convenir <fried foods disagree with me : les aliments frits ne me conviennent pas>
disagreeable [ˌdɪsə'griːəbəl] *adj* : désagréable, déplaisant, malavenant *Can*
disagreement [ˌdɪsə'griːmənt] *n* **1** DISAGREEING : désaccord *m* **2** DISCREPANCY : différence *f* **3** ARGUMENT : différend *m*
disappear [ˌdɪsə'pɪr] *vi* : disparaître
disappearance [ˌdɪsə'piːrənts] *n* : disparition *f*
disappoint [ˌdɪsə'pɔɪnt] *vt* : désappointer, décevoir
disappointment [ˌdɪsə'pɔɪntmənt] *n* : désappointement *m*, déception *f*
disapproval [ˌdɪsə'pruːvəl] *n* : désapprobation *f*
disapprove [ˌdɪsə'pruːv] *vi* **-proved; -proving 1** : ne pas être d'accord **2 to disapprove of** : désapprouver
disarm [dɪs'ɑrm] *v* : désarmer
disarmament [dɪs'ɑrməmənt] *n* : désarmement *m*
disarming [dɪs'ɑrmɪŋ] *adj* : désarmant
disarrange [ˌdɪsə'reɪndʒ] *vt* **-ranged; -ranging** : mettre en désordre, déranger
disarray [dɪsə'reɪ] *n* **1** DISORDER, MESS : désordre *m* **2** CONFUSION : désarroi *m*, confusion *f*
disassemble [dɪsə'sɛmbəl] *vt* **-bled; -bling** : démonter
disaster [dɪ'zæstər] *n* : désastre *m*, catastrophe *f*
disastrous [dɪ'zæstrəs] *adj* : désastreux
disband [dɪs'bænd] *vi* DISPERSE : se disperser — *vt* DISSOLVE : dissoudre
disbar [dɪs'bɑr] *vt* **-barred; -barring** : radier (un avocat)
disbelief [ˌdɪsbɪ'liːf] *n* : incrédulité *f*
disbelieve [ˌdɪsbɪ'liːv] *vt* **-lieved; -lieving** : ne pas croire
disburse [dɪs'bərs] *vt* **-bursed; -bursing** : débourser
disbursement [dɪsˌbərsmənt] *n* : débours *m*
disc ['dɪsk] → **disk**
discard [dɪs'kɑrd, 'dɪsˌkɑrd] *vt* **1** THROW AWAY : se débarrasser de, jeter **2** : se défausser de (une carte à jouer)
discern [dɪ'sərn, -'zərn] *vt* : discerner, percevoir
discernible [dɪ'sərnəbəl, -'zərn-] *adj* : perceptible, visible
discernment [dɪ'sərnmənt, -zərn-] *n* : discernement *m*
discharge[1] [dɪs'tʃɑrdʒ, 'dɪs-] *vt* **-charged; -charging 1** UNLOAD : décharger (un chargement), débarquer (des passagers) **2** SHOOT : décharger (un fusil) **3** DISMISS : renvoyer (un salarié) **4** RELEASE : décharger, libérer (un soldat) **5** EMIT : émettre (un gaz, un courant d'électricité) **6** PERFORM : remplir, s'acquitter de (un devoir)
discharge[2] ['dɪsˌtʃɑrdʒ, dɪs'-] *n* **1** FIRING : décharge *f* (d'un fusil) **2** FLOW : écoulement *m* <discharge of blood : écoulement de sang> **3** DISMISSAL

: renvoi *m* 4 RELEASE : libération *f* (d'un soldat)

disciple [dɪ'saɪpəl] *n* : disciple *mf*

disciplinary ['dɪsəpə,nɛri] *adj* : disciplinaire

discipline[1] ['dɪsəplən] *vt* **-plined; -plining 1** PUNISH : punir **2** CONTROL, TRAIN : discipliner, former **3 to discipline oneself** : se discipliner

discipline[2] *n* **1** FIELD : discipline *f*, matière *f* **2** TRAINING : discipline *f* **3** PUNISHMENT : punition *f* **4** CONTROL : discipline *f*, maîtrise *f*

disc jockey *n* : disc-jockey *mf*

disclaim [dɪs'kleɪm] *vt* DENY : démentir, nier

disclose [dɪs'klo:z] *vt* **-closed; -closing** : divulguer, révéler

disclosure [dɪs'klo:ʒər] *n* : divulgation *f*, révélation *f*

discolor [dɪs'kʌlər] *vt* **1** FADE : décolorer **2** YELLOW : jaunir — *vi* : se décolorer

discoloration [dɪs'kʌlə'reɪʃən] *n* : décoloration *f*

discomfit [dɪs'kəmpfət] *vt* : déconcerter

discomfort [dɪs'kʌmfərt] *n* : malaise *m*

disconcert [,dɪskən'sərt] *vt* : déconcerter, dérouter

disconnect [,dɪskə'nɛkt] *vt* : débrancher (un appareil électrique), couper (l'électricité, etc.)

disconsolate [dɪs'kɑntsələt] *adj* : inconsolable, triste

discontent [,dɪskən'tɛnt] *n* : mécontentement *m*

discontented [,dɪskən'tɛntəd] *adj* : mécontent

discontinue [,dɪskən'tɪn,ju:] *vt* **-tinued; -tinuing** : cesser, interrompre

discord ['dɪs,kɔrd] *n* **1** STRIFE : discorde *m*, dissensions *fpl* **2** : dissonance *f* (en musique)

discordant [dɪs'kɔrdənt] *adj* : discordant

discount[1] ['dɪs,kaʊnt, dɪs'-] *vt* **1** : faire une remise de, escompter (de l'argent) **2** DISREGARD : ne pas tenir compte de

discount[2] ['dɪs,kaʊnt] *n* : rabais *m*, remise *f*

discourage [dɪs'kərɪdʒ] *vt* **-aged; -aging 1** DISHEARTEN : décourager, abattre **2** DISSUADE : décourager, détourner, dissuader

discouragement [dɪs'kərɪdʒmənt] *n* : découragement *m*

discourse[1] [dɪs'kors] *vi* **-coursed; -coursing** : discourir

discourse[2] ['dɪs,kors] *n* **1** CONVERSATION : conversation *f* **2** SPEECH : discours *m*

discourteous [dɪs'kərtiəs] *adj* : impoli, peu courtois

discourtesy [dɪs'kərtəsi] *n, pl* **-sies** : manque *m* de courtoisie

discover [dɪs'kʌvər] *vt* : découvrir

discoverer *n* [dɪs'kʌvərər] : découvreur *m* (d'une terre), personne *f* qui a découvert qqch

discovery [dɪs'kʌvəri] *n, pl* **-eries** : découverte *f*

discredit[1] [dɪs'krɛdət] *vt* **1** DISBELIEVE : ne pas croire **2** QUESTION : discréditer, mettre en doute

discredit[2] *n* : discrédit *m*

discreet [dɪ'skri:t] *adj* : discret

discreetly [dɪs'kri:tli] *adv* : discrètement

discrepancy [dɪs'krɛpəntsi] *n, pl* **-cies** : divergence *f*, désaccord *m*

discrete [dɪs'kri:t] *adj* : distinct

discretion [dɪs'krɛʃən] *n* : discrétion *f*

discriminate [dɪs'krɪmə,neɪt] *v* **-nated; -nating** *vt* DIFFERENTIATE : distinguer, différencier — *vi* **1** DISTINGUISH : distinguer, faire une distinction **2 to discriminate against** : établir une discrimination contre

discrimination [dɪs,krɪmə'neɪʃən] *n* **1** DISCERNMENT : discernement *m* **2** PREJUDICE : discrimination *f*, préjugés *mpl*

discriminatory [dɪs'krɪmənə,tori] *adj* : discriminatoire

discus ['dɪskəs] *n, pl* **-cuses** [-kəsəz] : disque *m* <discus thrower : lanceur de disque>

discuss [dɪs'kʌs] *vt* : discuter de, parler de

discussion [dɪs'kʌʃən] *n* : discussion *f*, conversation *f*, débat *m*

disdain[1] [dɪs'deɪn] *vt* : dédaigner <he disdained to answer : il a dédaigné de répondre>

disdain[2] *n* : dédain *m*

disdainful [dɪs'deɪnfəl] *adj* : dédaigneux — **disdainfully** *adv*

disease [dɪ'zi:z] *n* : maladie *f*

diseased [dɪ'zi:zd] *adj* : malade

disembark [,dɪsɪm'bɑrk] *v* : débarquer

disembarkation [dɪs,ɛm,bɑr'keɪʃən] *n* : débarquement *m*

disembodied [,dɪsɪm'bɑdid] *adj* : désincarné

disenchant [,dɪsɪn'tʃænt] *vt* : désenchanter

disenchantment [,dɪsɪn'tʃæntmənt] *n* : désenchantement *m*

disengage [,dɪsɪn'geɪdʒ] *vt* **-gaged; -gaging 1** RELEASE : dégager **2 to disengage the clutch** : débrayer

disentangle [,dɪsɪn'tæŋgəl] *vt* **-gled; -gling** : démêler

disfavor [dɪs'feɪvər] *n* : défaveur *f*, désapprobation *f*

disfigure [dɪs'fɪgjər] *vt* **-ured; -uring** : défigurer

disfigurement [dɪs'fɪgjərmənt] *n* : défigurement *m*

disfranchise [dɪs'fræn,tʃaɪz] *vt* **-chised; -chising** : priver du droit électoral

disgrace[1] [dɪ'skreɪs] *vt* **-graced; -gracing** : déshonorer, faire honte à

disgrace[2] *n* **1** DISFAVOR : disgrâce *f,* défaveur *f* <fallen into disgrace : tombé en disgrâce> **2** SHAME : honte *f,* déshonneur *f*
disgraceful [dɪ'skreɪsfəl] *adj* : honteux, scandaleux — **disgracefully** *adv*
disgruntled [dɪs'grʌntəld] *adj* : mécontent
disguise[1] [dɪ'skaɪz] *vt* **-guised; -guising 1** : déguiser <to be disguised as : être déguisé en> **2** CONCEAL : camoufler, dissimuler
disguise[2] *n* : déguisement *m*
disgust[1] [dɪ'skʌst] *vt* : dégoûter, écœurer
disgust[2] *n* : dégoût *m,* aversion *f,* répugnance *f*
disgusting [dɪ'skʌstɪŋ] *adj* : dégoûtant
dish[1] ['dɪʃ] *vt or* **to dish up** : servir (de la nourriture)
dish[2] *n* **1** PLATE : assiette *f* **2** : mets *m,* plat *m* <a Mexican dish : un mets mexicain> **3** SERVING : plat *m* <a dish of strawberries : un plat de fraises> **4 dishes** *npl* : vaisselle *f* <to wash the dishes : faire la vaisselle>
dishcloth ['dɪʃˌklɔθ] *n* : torchon *m* (à vaisselle), linge à vaisselle
dishearten [dɪs'hɑrtən] *vt* : décourager, abattre
disheveled *or* **dishevelled** [dɪ'ʃɛvəld] *adj* : en désordre (se dit des vêtements, etc.), échevelé (se dit des cheveux)
dishonest [dɪ'sɑnəst] *adj* : malhonnête — **dishonestly** *adv*
dishonesty [dɪ'sɑnəsti] *n* : malhonnêteté *f*
dishonor[1] [dɪ'sɑnər] *vt* : déshonorer
dishonor[2] *n* : déshonneur *m*
dishonorable [dɪ'sɑnərəbəl] *adj* : déshonorant
dishonorably [dɪ'sɑnərəbli] *adv* : de façon déshonorante
dishrag ['dɪʃˌræg] → **dishcloth**
dishwasher ['dɪʃˌwɔʃər] *n* : lave-vaisselle *m*
disillusion [dɪsə'luːʒən] *vt* : désillusionner
disillusionment [ˌdɪsə'luːʒənmənt] *n* : désillusion *f*
disinclination [dɪsˌɪnklə'neɪʃən, -ɪŋ-] *n* : manque *m* d'enthousiasme
disinclined [ˌdɪsɪn'klaɪnd] *adj* : peu disposé
disinfect [ˌdɪsɪn'fɛkt] *vt* : désinfecter
disinfectant[1] [ˌdɪsɪn'fɛktənt] *adj* : désinfectant
disinfectant[2] *n* : désinfectant *m*
disinherit [ˌdɪsɪn'hɛrət] *vt* : déshériter
disintegrate [dɪs'ɪntəˌgreɪt] *v* **-grated; -grating** *vt* : désintégrer, désagréger — *vi* : se désintégrer, se désagréger
disintegration [dɪs'ɪntə'greɪʃən] *n* : désintégration *f,* désagrégation *f*
disinterested [dɪs'ɪntərəstəd, -ˌrɛs-] *adj* **1** INDIFFERENT : indifférent **2** UNBIASED : désintéressé
disjointed [dɪs'dʒɔɪntəd] *adj* : décousu, incohérent <disjointed speech : discours décousu>
disk *or* **disc** ['dɪsk] *n* : disque *m*
diskette [ˌdɪs'kɛt] → **floppy disk**
dislike[1] [dɪs'laɪk] *vt* **-liked; -liking** : ne pas aimer
dislike[2] *n* : aversion *f,* antipathie *f*
dislocate ['dɪsloˌkeɪt, dɪs'loː-] *vt* **-cated; -cating** : luxer, déboîter, démettre <to dislocate one's knee : se luxer le genou>
dislocation [ˌdɪslo'keɪʃən] *n* : luxation *f,* déboîtement *m*
dislodge [dɪs'lɑdʒ] *vt* **-lodged; -lodging** : déplacer, dégager, déloger
disloyal [dɪs'lɔɪəl] *adj* : déloyal
disloyalty [dɪs'lɔɪəlti] *n* : déloyauté *f*
dismal ['dɪzməl] *adj* : sombre, lugubre, triste
dismantle [dɪs'mæntəl] *vt* **-tled; -tling** : démanteler, démonter
dismay[1] [dɪs'meɪ] *vt* : consterner
dismay[2] *n* : consternation *f,* désarroi *m*
dismember [dɪs'mɛmbər] *vt* : démembrer
dismiss [dɪs'mɪs] *vt* **1** : laisser sortir <class dismissed! : vous pouvez sortir!> **2** DISCHARGE : démettre (de ses fonctions), renvoyer, congédier **3** REJECT : ne pas tenir compte de, écarter
dismissal [dɪs'mɪsəl] *n* **1** : permission *f* de salir **2** DISCHARGE, LAYOFF : licenciement *m,* renvoi *m* **3** : rejet *m* (devant les tribunaux)
dismount [dɪs'maʊnt] *vt* DISASSEMBLE : démonter — *vi* **to dismount from** : descendre de
disobedience [ˌdɪsə'biːdiənts] *n* : désobéissance *f*
disobedient [dɪsə'biːdiənt] *adj* : désobéissant
disobey [ˌdɪsə'beɪ] *vt* : désobéir à — *vi* : désobéir
disorder[1] [dɪs'ɔrdər] *vt* : mettre en désordre
disorder[2] *n* **1** UNTIDINESS : désordre *m,* fouillis *m* **2** CONFUSION : désordre *m,* confusion *f* **3** RIOTING, UNREST : troubles *mpl,* émeutes *fpl* **4** AILMENT : troubles *mpl,* maladie *f* <digestive disorder : troubles digestifs>
disorderly [dɪs'ɔrdərli] *adj* **1** UNTIDY : désordonné **2** UNRULY : turbulent, incontrôlé, désordonné <disorderly conduct : conduite désordonnée>
disorganization [dɪsˌɔrgənə'zeɪʃən] *n* : désorganisation *f*
disorganize [dɪs'ɔrgəˌnaɪz] *vt* **-nized; -nizing** : désorganiser
disown [dɪs'oːn] *vt* : désavouer, renier
disparage [dɪs'pærɪdʒ] *vt* **-aged; -aging** : dénigrer, déprécier
disparagement [dɪs'pærɪdʒmənt] *n* : dénigrement *m*

disparate ['dɪspərət, dɪs'pærət] *adj* : disparate
disparity [dɪs'pærət̬i] *n, pl* **-ties** : disparité *f*
dispassionate [dɪs'pæʃənət] *adj* : impartial, objectif
dispatch[1] [dɪs'pætʃ] *vt* **1** SEND : envoyer, expédier **2** KILL : tuer **3** HANDLE : expédier (une tâche, etc.)
dispatch[2] *n* **1** SHIPMENT : envoi *m,* expédition *f* **2** PROMPTNESS : promptitude *f* **3** *or* **news dispatch** : dépêche *f*
dispel [dɪs'pɛl] *vt* **-pelled; -pelling** : chasser, dissiper
dispensation [ˌdɪspɛn'seɪʃən] *n* : dispense *f*
dispense [dɪs'pɛn*t*s] *v* **-pensed; -pensing** *vt* **1** DISTRIBUTE : dispenser, distribuer **2** ADMINISTER : exercer, administrer (la justice, etc.) **3** : préparer (une prescription) — *vi* **to dispense with** : se passer de
dispenser [dɪs'pɛn*t*sər] *n* : distributeur *m*
dispersal [dɪs'pərsəl] *n* : dispersion *f*
disperse [dɪs'pərs] *v* **-persed; -persing** *vt* **1** SCATTER : disperser, disséminer **2** DISSIPATE : disperser, dissiper — *vi* : se disperser
displace [dɪs'pleɪs] *vt* **-placed; -placing** **1** EXPEL : expulser, déplacer <displaced persons : personnes déplacées> **2** REPLACE : supplanter, remplacer **3** : déplacer (un liquide, etc.)
displacement [dɪs'pleɪsmənt] *n* : déplacement *m,* remplacement *m*
display[1] [dɪs'pleɪ] *vt* **1** PRESENT : exposer, étaler **2** SHOW : faire preuve de, montrer <he displayed great talent : il a montré beaucoup de talent>
display[2] *n* **1** PRESENTATION : exposition *f,* étalage *m* **2** MANIFESTATION : démonstration *f,* manifestation *f*
displease [dɪs'pli:z] *vt* **-pleased; -pleasing** : déplaire à, mécontenter
displeasure [dis'plɛʒər] *n* : déplaisir *m,* mécontentement *m*
disposable [dɪs'po:zəbəl] *adj* **1** : jetable <disposable diapers : couches jetables> **2** AVAILABLE : disponible <disposable income : revenu disponible>
disposal [dɪs'po:zəl] *n* **1** ARRANGEMENT : disposition *f,* ordre *m* **2** AVAILABILITY : disposition *f* <to have at one's disposal : avoir à sa disposition> **3** : élimination *f* (des déchets)
dispose [dɪs'po:z] *v* **-posed; -posing** *vt* **1** ARRANGE : disposer, arranger **2** INCLINE : disposer <disposed to help : prêt à aider> — *vi* **1 to dispose of** HANDLE : expédier **2 to dispose of** DISCARD : se débarrasser de
disposition [ˌdɪspə'zɪʃən] *n* **1** ARRANGEMENT : disposition *f,* arrangement *m* **2** TEMPERAMENT : tempérament *m,* caractère *m* **3** TENDENCY : inclination *f,* penchant *m*
dispossess [ˌdɪspə'zɛs] *vt* : déposséder, dépouiller
disproportion [ˌdɪsprə'porʃən] *n* : disproportion *f*
disproportionate [ˌdɪsprə'porʃənət] *adj* : disproportionné
disprove [dɪs'pru:v] *vt* **-proved; -proving** : réfuter
disputable [dɪs'pju:t̬əbəl, 'dɪspjʊt̬əbəl] *adj* : discutable, contestable
dispute[1] [dɪs'pju:t] *v* **-puted; -puting** *vt* **1** QUESTION : contester, mettre en doute **2** CONTEST : disputer — *vi* ARGUE, DEBATE : se disputer, débattre
dispute[2] *n* **1** DEBATE : débat *m* <beyond dispute : incontestable> **2** QUARREL : dispute *f,* conflit *m*
disqualification [dɪsˌkwɑləfə'keɪʃən] *n* : exclusion *f,* disqualification *f*
disqualify [dɪs'kwɑləˌfaɪ] *vt* **-fied; -fying** : disqualifier
disquiet[1] [dɪs'kwaɪət̬] *vt* : inquiéter, troubler
disquiet[2] *n* ANXIETY : inquiétude *f*
disregard[1] [ˌdɪsrɪ'gɑrd] *vt* : ne tenir aucun compte de, ne pas s'occuper de
disregard[2] *n* : indifférence *f,* négligence *f,* mépris *m* (du danger)
disrepair [ˌdɪsrɪ'pær] *n* : délabrement *m*
disreputable [dɪs'rɛpjʊt̬əbəl] *adj* : peu recommandable, mal famé
disrepute [ˌdɪsrɪ'pju:t] *n* : discrédit *m,* déconsidération *f*
disrespect [ˌdɪsrɪ'spɛkt] *n* : irrespect *m,* manque *m* de respect
disrespectful [ˌdɪsrɪ'spɛktfəl] *adj* : irrespectueux
disrobe [dɪs'ro:b] *vi* **-robed; -robing** UNDRESS : se déshabiller
disrupt [dɪs'rʌpt] *vt* : perturber, déranger
disruption [dɪs'rʌpʃən] *n* : perturbation *f,* bouleversement *m*
disruptive [dɪs'rʌptɪv] *adj* : perturbateur
dissatisfaction [dɪsˌsæt̬əs'fækʃən] *n* : insatisfaction *f,* mécontentement *m*
dissatisfied [dɪs'sæt̬əsˌfaɪd] *adj* : mécontent
dissatisfy [dɪs'sæt̬əsˌfaɪ] *vt* **-fied; -fying** : ne pas satisfaire
dissect [dɪ'sɛkt] *vt* : disséquer
dissection [dɪ'sɛkʃən] *n* : dissection *f*
dissemble [dɪ'sɛmbəl] *v* **-bled; -bling** : dissimuler
disseminate [dɪ'sɛməˌneɪt] *vt* **-nated; -nating** : disséminer, propager
dissemination [dɪˌsɛmə'neɪʃən] *n* : dissémination *f*
dissension [dɪ'sɛntʃən] *n* : dissension *f*
dissent[1] [dɪ'sɛnt] *vi* : différer, être en désaccord
dissent[2] *n* : dissentiment *m*
dissertation [ˌdɪsər'teɪʃən] *n* **1** TREATISE : traité *m* **2** THESIS : thèse *f*

disservice [dɪs'sərvɪs] *n* : mauvais service *m*
dissident[1] ['dɪsədənt] *adj* : dissident
dissident[2] *n* : dissident *m*, -dente *f*
dissimilar [dɪ'sɪmələr] *adj* : dissemblable, différent
dissimilarity [dɪˌsɪmə'lærəṭi] *n, pl* **-ties** : dissemblance *f*
dissipate ['dɪsəˌpeɪt] *v* **-pated; -pating** *vt* **1** DISPERSE : dissiper, disperser **2** SQUANDER : gaspiller — *vi* : se dissiper
dissipation [ˌdɪsə'peɪʃən] *n* : dissipation *f*
dissolute ['dɪsəˌlu:t] *adj* : dissolu, corrompu
dissolution [ˌdɪsə'lu:ʃən] *n* : dissolution *f*
dissolve [dɪ'zɑlv] *v* **-solved; -solving** *vt* : dissoudre — *vi* : se dissoudre <to dissolve into tears : fondre en larmes>
dissonance ['dɪsənənts] *n* : dissonance *f*
dissonant ['dɪsənənt] *adj* : dissonant
dissuade [dɪ'sweɪd] *vt* **-suaded; -suading** : dissuader
distance ['dɪstənts] *n* **1** : distance *f* <at a distance of nine miles : à une distance de neuf milles> <in the distance : au loin> **2** RESERVE : distance *f*, réserve *f* <to keep one's distance : garder ses distances>
distant ['dɪstənt] *adj* **1** (*indicating separation*) <five miles distant from here : à cinq milles d'ici> **2** FARAWAY, REMOTE : lointain, éloigné **3** COLD : distant, réservé
distantly ['dɪstəntli] *adv* **1** : vaguement, un peu <distantly related : d'une parenté éloignée> **2** COLDLY : froidement, d'un air distant
distaste [dɪs'teɪst] *n* : aversion *f*, répugnance *f*
distasteful [dɪs'teɪstfəl] *adj* : déplaisant, répugnant
distemper [dɪs'tɛmpər] *n* : maladie *f* de Carré
distend [dɪs'tɛnd] *vt* : gonfler — *vi* : se gonfler, se distendre
distill *or Brit* **distil** [dɪ'stɪl] *vt* **-tilled; -tilling** : distiller
distillation [ˌdɪstə'leɪʃən] *n* : distillation *f*
distillery [dɪ'stɪləri, -'stɪlri] *n, pl* **-ries** : distillerie *f*
distinct [dɪ'stɪŋkt] *adj* **1** DIFFERENT : distinct, différent **2** CLEAR : distinct, net <a distinct impression : une nette impression>
distinction [dɪ'stɪŋkʃən] *n* : distinction *f*
distinctive [dɪ'stɪŋktɪv] *adj* : distinctif
distinctively [dɪ'stɪŋktɪvli] *adv* : de manière distinctive
distinctly [dɪ'stɪŋktli] *adv* : distinctement, clairement
distinguish [dɪ'stɪŋgwɪʃ] *vt* **1** DIFFERENTIATE : distinguer, différencier **2** DISCERN : distinguer, discerner **3 to distinguish oneself** : se distinguer, s'illustrer — *vi* DISCRIMINATE : faire une distinction
distinguished [dɪ'stɪŋgwɪʃt] *adj* : distingué <distinguished-looking : à l'allure distinguée>
distort [dɪ'stɔrt] *vt* **1** DEFORM : déformer, distordre <a face distorted by pain : un visage déformé par la douleur> **2** MISREPRESENT : déformer, dénaturer
distortion [dɪ'stɔrʃən] *n* : déformation *f*
distract [dɪ'strækt] *vt* : distraire <to distract s.o.'s attention : détourner l'attention de qqn>
distraction [dɪ'strækʃən] *n* **1** INTERRUPTION : distraction *f*, interruption *f* **2** INATTENTION : inattention *f* **3** CONFUSION, MADNESS : folie *f* <to drive to distraction : rendre fou> **4** AMUSEMENT : distraction *f*, divertissement *m*
distraught [dɪ'strɔt] *adj* : bouleversé, éperdu
distress[1] [dɪ'strɛs] *vt* : affliger, peiner
distress[2] *n* **1** SUFFERING : douleur *f*, souffrance *f*, affliction *f* **2** MISFORTUNE : détresse *f*, adversité *f* **3** DANGER : détresse *f* <a ship in distress : un navire en détresse>
distressful [dɪ'strɛsfəl] *adj* : pénible, affligeant
distribute [dɪ'strɪˌbju:t, -bjʊt] *vt* **-uted; -uting** : distribuer, répartir
distribution [ˌdɪstrə'bju:ʃən] *n* : distribution *f*, répartition *f*
distributor [dɪ'strɪbjʊṭər] *n* **1** : distributeur *m*, -trice *f* (personne) **2** : distributeur *m* (d'une voiture)
district ['dɪsˌtrɪkt] *n* **1** AREA : région *f* **2** : quartier *m* <residential district : quartier résidentiel> **3** : district *m* (administratif), circonscription *f* (électorale)
distrust[1] [dɪs'trʌst] *vt* : se méfier de
distrust[2] *n* : méfiance *f*
distrustful [dɪs'trʌstfəl] *adj* : méfiant
disturb [dɪ'stərb] *vt* **1** BOTHER : déranger, interrompre **2** DISARRANGE : déplacer, déranger **3** WORRY : troubler, inquiéter **4 to disturb the peace** : troubler l'ordre public
disturbance [dɪ'stərbənts] *n* **1** INTERRUPTION : dérangement *m*, interruption *f* **2** COMMOTION : troubles *mpl*, émeute *f*, tapage *m* <to cause a disturbance : faire du tapage>
disuse [dɪs'ju:s] *n* : désuétude *f*
ditch[1] ['dɪtʃ] *vt* **1** : creuser un fossé dans **2** DISCARD : se débarrasser de
ditch[2] *n* : fossé *m*
dither ['dɪðər] *n* **to be in a dither** : être dans tous ses états
ditto ['dɪṭo:] *adv* : idem
ditty ['dɪṭi] *n, pl* **-ties** : chansonnette *f*

diurnal [daɪ'ərnəl] *adj* **1** DAILY : quotidien **2** : diurne (se dit des animaux et des plantes)
divan ['daɪˌvæn, dɪ'-] *n* : divan *m*
dive[1] ['daɪv] *vi* **dived** *or* **dove** ['do:v]; **dived; diving 1** : plonger <to dive into the water : plonger dans l'eau> **2** SUBMERGE : s'immerger **3** DESCEND : descendre en piqué, piquer (se dit d'un avion, etc.)
dive[2] *n* **1** : plongeon *m* (dans l'eau) **2** DESCENT, NOSEDIVE : piqué *m*
diver ['daɪvər] *n* : plongeur *m*, -geuse *f*
diverge [də'vərdʒ, daɪ-] *vi* **-verged; -verging 1** SEPARATE : diverger, s'écarter **2** DIFFER : diverger, différer
divergence [də'vərdʒənts, daɪ-] *n* : divergence *f* — **divergent** [-dʒənt] *adj*
diverse [daɪ'vərs, də-, 'daɪˌvərs] *adj* : divers, varié
diversification [dəˌvərsəfə'keɪʃən] *n* : diversification *f*
diversify [daɪ'vərsəˌfaɪ, də-] *v* **-fied; -fying** *vt* : diversifier — *vi* : se diversifier
diversion [daɪ'vərʒən, də-] *n* **1** DEVIATION : déviation *f* **2** AMUSEMENT : distraction *f*, divertissement *m*
diversity [daɪ'vərsəti, də-] *n, pl* **-ties** : diversité *f*
divert [də'vərt, daɪ-] *vt* **1** DEFLECT : détourner, dévier **2** DISTRACT : distraire **3** AMUSE : divertir
divest [daɪ'vɛst, də-] *vt* **1** DISPOSSESS : dépouiller **2 to divest oneself of** : se débarrasser de, se défaire de
divide [də'vaɪd] *v* **-vided; -viding** *vt* **1** SEPARATE : diviser, séparer, désunir **2** SHARE : diviser, partager **3** : diviser <twelve divided by three is four : douze divisé par trois égale quatre> — *vi* : se diviser, se séparer
dividend ['dɪvɪˌdɛnd, -dənd] *n* **1** : dividende *m* (en finance et en mathématiques) **2** BONUS : prime *f*
divider [dɪ'vaɪdər] *n* **1** *or* **file divider** : intercalaire *m*, fiche *f* intercalaire **2** *or* **room divider** : cloison *f*, meuble *m* de séparation
divine[1] [də'vaɪn] *adj* **diviner; -est 1** : divin **2** SUPERB : divin, sublime
divine[2] *n* CLERGYMAN : ecclésiastique *m*
divinely [də'vaɪnli] *adv* : divinement
divinity [də'vɪnəti] *n, pl* **-ties** : divinité *f*
divisible [dɪ'vɪzəbəl] *adj* : divisible
division [dɪ'vɪʒən] *n* : division *f*
divisor [dɪ'vaɪzər] *n* : diviseur *m*
divorce[1] [də'vors] *v* **-vorced; -vorcing** *vi* : divorcer — *vt* : divorcer de, divorcer avec
divorce[2] *n* : divorce *m*
divorcé [dɪˌvor'seɪ, -si:; -'vorˌ-] *n* : divorcé *m*
divorcée [dɪˌvor'seɪ, -si:; -'vorˌ-] *n* : divorcée *f*
divulge [də'vʌldʒ, daɪ-] *vt* **-vulged; -vulging** : divulguer, révéler, placoter *Can fam*
dizziness *n* ['dɪzinəs] : vertige *m*, étourdissement *m*
dizzy ['dɪzi] *adj* **dizzier; -est 1** GIDDY, UNSTEADY : pris de vertiges **2** : vertigineux <dizzy heights : des hauteurs vertigineuses>
DNA [ˌdi:ˌɛn'eɪ] *n* : ADN *m*
do ['du:]; **did** ['dɪd]; **done** ['dʌn]; **doing; does** ['dʌz] *vt* **1** CARRY OUT, PERFORM : faire, accomplir (une action, une tâche) <do your best : fais de ton mieux> **2** PRACTICE : faire, entreprendre <what does he do for a living? : que fait-il comme métier?> **3** ARRANGE : arranger <to do one's hair : se coiffer> **4** PREPARE : faire, préparer <do your homework : fais tes devoirs> — *vi* **1** ACT, BEHAVE : faire <do as I say : faites ce que je dis> **2** FARE : réussir <he does well in school : il réussit bien à l'école> **3** SUFFICE : suffire, faire l'affaire <that will do : ça suffit> **4 to do away with** DESTROY, KILL : tuer, détruire **5 to do away with** ELIMINATE : éliminer, abolir — *v aux* **1** (*in interrogative sentences*) <does he work? : travaille-t-il?> **2** (*in negative sentences*) <I don't know : je ne sais pas> <don't go : n'y va pas> **3** (*for emphasis*) <do be careful : fais attention, je t'en prie> **4** (*as a substitute for a preceding predicate*) <he succeeds better than I do : il réussit mieux que moi>
docile ['dɑsəl] *adj* : docile
dock[1] ['dɑk] *vt* **1** SHORTEN : couper la queue à (un chien) **2** DEDUCT : faire une retenue sur <they docked $10 from his paycheck : ils ont retenu 10 $ sur son chèque de paie> — *vi* : se mettre à quai (se dit d'un bateau)
dock[2] *n* **1** BERTH : dock *m* **2** WHARF : embarcadère *m*, quai *m* **3** : banc *m* des accusés (dans un tribunal)
doctor[1] ['dɑktər] *vt* **1** TREAT : soigner (un patient) **2** ALTER : altérer, falsifier
doctor[2] *n* **1** : docteur *m* <Doctor of Law : docteur en droit> **2** PHYSICIAN : médecin *m;* docteur *m*
doctrine ['dɑktrɪn] *n* : doctrine *f*
document[1] ['dɑkjʊˌmɛnt] *vt* : documenter
document[2] ['dɑkjʊmənt] *n* : document *m*
documentary[1] [ˌdɑkjʊ'mɛntəri] *adj* : documentaire
documentary[2] *n, pl* **-ries** : documentaire *m*
documentation [ˌdɑkjʊmən'teɪʃən] *n* : documentation *f*
dodge[1] ['dɑdʒ] *v* **dodged; dodging** *vt* : esquiver, éviter, échapper à — *vi* : faire un saut de côté, faire une esquive

dodge[2] *n* **1** : mouvement *m* de côté, esquive *f* (aux sports) **2** RUSE, TRICK : ruse *f,* truc *m*

dodo ['dːˌdoː] *n, pl* **-does** *or* **-dos** : dodo *m*

doe ['doː] *n, pl* **does** *or* **doe** : biche *f*

doer ['duːər] *n* : personne *f* qui préfère l'action, personne *f* efficace

does → **do**

doff ['dɑf, 'dɔf] *vt* : ôter, enlever (son chapeau, etc.)

dog[1] ['dɔg, 'dɑg] *vt* **dogged; dogging 1** FOLLOW : talonner, suivre de près <he's dogging my footsteps : il marche sur mes talons> **2** HOUND : poursuivre, être en proie à <dogged by financial worries : en proie à des difficultés financières>

dog[2] *n* : chien *m*

dog–eared ['dɔgˌɪrd] *adj* : écorné

dogged ['dɔgəd] *adj* : tenace, persévérant

doghouse ['dɔgˌhaʊs] *n* : niche *f* (à chien)

dogma ['dɔgmə] *n* : dogme *m*

dogmatic [dɔg'mæt̬ɪk] *adj* : dogmatique

dogmatism ['dɔgmə'tɪzəm] *n* : dogmatisme *m*

dogwood ['dɔgˌwʊd] *n* : cornouiller *m*

doily ['dɔɪli] *n, pl* **-lies** : napperon *m*

doings ['duːɪŋz] *npl* GOINGS-ON : événements *mpl,* faits *mpl* et gestes *mpl*

doldrums ['doːldrəmz, 'dɑl-] *npl* **1** : zone *f* des calmes (équatoriaux) **2** BLUES : cafard *m,* mélancolie *f* **3** STAGNATION : marasme *m* <economic doldrums : marasme économique>

dole ['doːl] *n* : allocation *f* de chômage, indemnité *f* de chômage

doleful ['doːlfəl] *adj* : dolent, triste

dolefully ['doːlfəli] *adv* : d'un air triste

dole out *vt* **doled out; doling out** : distribuer, donner

doll ['dɑl, 'dɔl] *n* : poupée *f*

dollar ['dɑlər] *n* : dollar *m,* piastre *f Can fam*

dolly ['dɑli] *n, pl* **-lies 1** → **doll 2** CART, PLATFORM : chariot *m,* plate-forme *f*

dolphin ['dɑlfən, 'dɔl-] *n* : dauphin *m*

dolt ['doːlt] *n* : balourd *m,* -lourde *f*

domain [do'meɪn, də-] *n* **1** TERRITORY : domaine *m,* territoire *m* **2** SPHERE : domaine *m* <the domain of art : le domaine de l'art>

dome ['doːm] *n* : dôme *m,* coupole *f*

domestic[1] [də'mɛstɪk] *adj* **1** HOUSEHOLD : domestique **2** : intérieur, national <domestic affairs : affaires intérieures> **3** TAME : domestique

domestic[2] *n* SERVANT : domestique *mf*

domesticate [də'mɛstɪˌkeɪt] *vt* **-cated; -cating** : domestiquer, apprivoiser

domicile ['dɑməˌsaɪl, 'doː-; 'dɑməsɪl] *n* : domicile *m*

dominance ['dɑmənənts] *n* : dominance *f,* prédominance *f*

dominant ['dɑmənənt] *adj* : dominant

dominate ['dɑməˌneɪt] *v* **-nated; -nating** : dominer

domination [ˌdɑmə'neɪʃən] *n* : domination *f*

domineer [ˌdɑmə'nɪr] *vi* : agir en maître, se montrer autoritaire

Dominican[1] [də'mɪnɪkən] *adj* : dominicain

Dominican[2] *n* : Dominicain *m,* -caine *f*

dominion [də'mɪnjən] *n* **1** SUPREMACY : domination *f* **2** TERRITORY : territoire *m,* domaine *m*

domino ['dɑməˌnoː] *n, pl* **-noes** *or* **-nos** : domino *m*

don ['dɑn] *vt* **donned; donning** : mettre (des vêtements)

donate ['doːˌneɪt, doː'-] *v* **-nated; -nating** *vt* : faire (un) don de — *vi* : faire un don

donation [doː'neɪʃən] *n* : don *m,* donation *f*

done[1] ['dʌn] → **do**

done[2] *adj* **1** FINISHED : fini, terminé **2** WELL-DONE : bien cuit

donkey ['dɑŋki, 'dʌŋ] *n, pl* **-keys** : âne *m*

donor ['doːnər] *n* : donateur *m,* -trice *f;* donneur *m,* -neuse *f* <blood donor : donneur de sang>

doodle[1] ['duːdəl] *v* **-dled; -dling** : gribouiller

doodle[2] *n* : gribouillage *m*

doom[1] ['duːm] *vt* **1** CONDEMN : condamner **2** DESTINE : vouer <doomed to failure : voué à l'échec>

doom[2] *n* **1** JUDGMENT : jugement *m,* sentence *f* **2** DESTINY : destin *m,* sort *m* **3** RUIN : perte *f,* ruine *f*

door ['dor] *n* **1** : porte *f,* portière *f* (d'une voiture) **2** ENTRANCE : entrée *f* <pay at the door : payez à l'entrée>

doorbell ['dorˌbɛl] *n* : sonnette *f*

doorknob ['dorˌnɑb] *n* : poignée *f* de porte, bouton *m* de porte

doorman ['dormən] *n, pl* **-men** : portier *m*

doormat ['dorˌmæt] *n* : paillasson *m*

doorstep ['dorˌstɛp] *n* : seuil *m* (de porte), pas *m* de la porte

doorway ['dorˌweɪ] *n* : embrasure *f* (de la porte)

dope[1] ['doːp] *vt* **doped; doping** : droguer (une personne), doper (un animal, un athlète)

dope[2] *n* **1** DRUG : narcotique *m,* stupéfiant *m* **2** IDIOT : cornichon *m fam,* imbécile *mf* **3** INFORMATION, TIP : tuyau *m fam,* renseignement *m*

dormant ['dormənt] *adj* : qui sommeille, latent, dormant (en botanique)

dormer ['dɔrmər] *n* : lucarne *f*

dormitory ['dɔrməˌtori] *n, pl* **-ries** : dortoir *m,* résidence *f* universitaire

dormouse ['dɔrˌmaʊs] *n, pl* **-mice** : loir *m*

dorsal ['dɔrsəl] *adj* : dorsal
dory ['dori] *n, pl* **-ries** : doris *m*
dosage ['do:sɪdʒ] *n* : posologie *f*
dose[1] ['do:s] *vt* **dosed; dosing** : doser, administrer un médicament à
dose[2] *n* : dose *f*
dot[1] ['dɑt] *vt* **dotted; dotting** : mettre un point sur (un *i,* etc.)
dot[2] *n* **1** POINT, SPECK : point *m* **2 on the dot** : à l'heure pile *fam*
dote ['do:t] *vi* **doted; doting** : raffoler, adorer <to dote on s.o. : aimer qqn à la folie, raffoler de qqn>
double[1] ['dʌbəl] *v* **-bled; -bling** *vt* **1** : doubler (une quantité) **2** BEND, FOLD : plier (en deux) **3 to double one's fists** : serrer les poings — *vi* **1** : doubler **2 to double up in pain** : se plier en deux par la douleur
double[2] *adv* **1** TWICE : deux fois <she's double your age : elle est deux fois plus âgé que toi> **2** : double <to see double : voir double>
double[3] *adj* : double
double[4] *n* : double *m*
double bass *n* : contrebasse *f*
double–cross [ˌdʌbəl'krɔs] *vt* : trahir, doubler *fam*
double–jointed [ˌdʌbəl'dʒɔɪntəd] *adj* : désarticulé
double–talk ['dʌbəlˌtɔk] *n* : paroles *fpl* trompeuses, paroles *fpl* ambiguës
doubly ['dʌbli] *adv* : doublement, deux fois plus
doubt[1] ['daʊt] *vt* **1** : douter <I doubt that he'll accept : je doute qu'il accepte> **2** DISTRUST : douter de <I doubt it very much : j'en doute beaucoup>
doubt[2] *n* **1** UNCERTAINTY : doute *m,* incertitude *f* **2** DISTRUST : doute *m,* méfiance *f* **3** SKEPTICISM : doute *m,* scepticisme *m*
doubtful ['daʊtfəl] *adj* **1** UNCERTAIN : douteux, incertain **2** QUESTIONABLE : douteux, discutable
doubtless ['daʊtləs] *adv* : sans aucun doute, sûrement
douche ['du:ʃ] *n* : douche *f* (en médecine)
dough ['do:] *n* : pâte *f* (en cuisine)
doughnut ['do:ˌnʌt] *n* : beignet *m,* beigne *m Can*
doughty ['daʊṭi] *adj* **doughtier; -est** : vaillant
dour ['daʊər, 'dʊr] *adj* **1** STERN : austère, dur **2** SULLEN : maussade, renfrogné
douse ['daʊs, 'daʊz] *vt* **doused; dousing 1** DRENCH : inonder, tremper **2** EXTINGUISH : éteindre
dove[1] ['do:v] → **dive[1]**
dove[2] ['dʌv] *n* : colombe *f*
dovetail ['dʌvˌteɪl] *vt* **1** : assembler à queue d'aronde (en charpenterie) **2** : faire concorder (des plans, etc.) — *vi* AGREE : concorder, bien cadrer
dowdy ['daʊdi] *adj* **dowdier; -est** : sans chic
dowel ['daʊəl] *n* : goujon *m*
down[1] ['daʊn] *vt* **1** KNOCK DOWN : terrasser, abattre **2** DEFEAT : vaincre
down[2] *adv* **1** DOWNWARD : en bas, vers le bas **2 down to** : jusqu'à <down to the present : jusqu'à nos jours> **3 to lie down** : se coucher, s'allonger **4 to put down** PAY : payer, verser **5 to put down** WRITE : écrire **6 to sit down** : s'asseoir
down[3] *adj* **1** : qui descend <the down escalator : l'escalier mécanique qui descend> **2** LOWER : qui diminue, qui baisse <sales were down : les ventes avaient diminué> **3** DOWNCAST : déprimé, abattu
down[4] *n* : duvet *m*
down[5] *prep* **1** : en bas, de, dans <he fell down the stairs : il est tombé en bas dans l'escalier> **2** ALONG : le long de <to walk down the road : marcher le long de la rue> **3** THROUGH : au cours de, à travers de <down through the ages : à travers les siècles>
downcast ['daʊnˌkæst] *adj* **1** SAD : abattu, découragé **2** LOWERED : baissé <with a downcast glance : avec les yeux baissés>
downfall ['daʊnˌfɔl] *n* : chute *f,* renversement *m*
downgrade[1] ['daʊnˌgreɪd] *vt* **-graded; -grading** : déclasser (un poste, etc.), rétrograder (une personne)
downgrade[2] *n* : descente *f,* pente *f*
downhearted ['daʊnˌhɑrṭəd] *adj* : abattu, découragé
downhill[1] ['daʊn'hɪl] *adv* **to go downhill** : descendre
downhill[2] *adj* : en pente, qui descend
download ['daʊnˌlo:d] *vt* : télécharger (en informatique)
down payment *n* : acompte *m,* arrhes *fpl France*
downpour ['daʊnˌpor] *n* : déluge *m,* averse *f*
downright[1] ['daʊnˌraɪt] *adv* THOROUGHLY : carrément, tout à fait
downright[2] *adj* ABSOLUTE : véritable, catégorique
downstairs[1] [*adv* 'daʊn'stærz, *adj* 'daʊnˌstærz] *adv & adj* : en bas
downstairs[2] ['daʊn'stærz, -ˌstærz] *n* : rez-de-chaussé *m*
downstream ['daʊn'stri:m] *adv* : en aval
down–to–earth [ˌdaʊntu'ərθ] *adj* : terre à terre, avec les pieds sur terre
downtown[1] [ˌdaʊn'taʊn] *adv* : en ville
downtown[2] *adj* : du centre-ville
downtown[3] [ˌdaʊn'taʊn, 'daʊnˌtaʊn] *n* : centre-ville *m*
downtrodden ['daʊnˌtrɑdən] *adj* : opprimé
downward[1] ['daʊnwərd] *or* **downwards** [-wərdz] *adv* : en bas, vers le bas <to look downward : regarder en bas> <the prophets from Elijah downward : les prophètes depuis Élie>

downward[2] *adj* : vers le bas <a downward movement : un mouvement vers le bas> <a downward trend : une tendence à la baisse>
downwind ['daʊn'wɪnd] *adv & adj* : dans le sens du vent
downy ['daʊni] *adj* **downier; -est** : duveteux
dowry ['daʊri] *n, pl* **-ries** : dot *f*
doze[1] ['do:z] *vi* **dozed; dozing** : sommeiller, somnoler
doze[2] *n* : somme *m,* sieste *f*
dozen ['dʌzən] *n, pl* **-ens** *or* **-en** : douzaine *f*
drab ['dræb] *adj* **drabber; drabbest** : terne, fade
draft[1] ['dræft, 'drɑft] *vt* **1** : appeler (des soldats) sous les drapeaux **2** OUTLINE : faire le brouillon de **3** COMPOSE : rédiger
draft[2] *adj* : en fût, à la pression <draft beer : bière en fût>
draft[3] *n* **1** HAULAGE : tirage *m,* traction *f* **2** DRINK, GULP : trait *m,* gorgée *f* **3** OUTLINE : brouillon *m,* avant-projet *m* **4** CONSCRIPTION : service *m* militaire, conscription *f* **5** : courant *m* d'air **6** *or* **bank draft** : traite *f* bancaire
draftsman ['dræftsmən] *n, pl* **-men** [-mən, -ˌmɛn] : dessinateur *m,* -trice *f*
drafty ['dræfti] *adj* **draftier; -est** : plein de courants d'air
drag[1] ['dræg] *v* **dragged; dragging** *vt* **1** HAUL : tirer, traîner **2** TRAIL : traîner <to drag one's feet : traîner les pieds> **3** DREDGE : draguer — *vi* TRAIL : traîner
drag[2] *n* **1** RESISTANCE : résistance *f,* traînée *f* **2** DREDGE : drague *f* **3** SLEDGE : traîneau *m* **4** : barbe *f fam* <what a drag! : quelle barbe!> **5** PUFF : bouffée *f* (de cigarette)
dragnet ['drægˌnɛt] *n* **1** TRAWL : drège *f* **2** : rafle *f,* descente *f* (policière)
dragon ['drægən] *n* : dragon *m*
dragonfly ['drægənˌflaɪ] *n, pl* **-flies** : libellule *f*
drain[1] ['dreɪn] *vt* **1** EMPTY : vider, drainer **2** DEPLETE, EXHAUST : fatiguer, épuiser — *vi* : s'écouler (se dit d'un cours d'eau), s'égoutter (se dit de la vaisselle)
drain[2] *n* **1** : tuyau *m* d'écoulement **2** SEWER : égout *m* **3** DEPLETION : épuisement *m,* perte *f*
drainage ['dreɪnɪdʒ] *n* : drainage *m*
drainpipe ['dreɪnˌpaɪp] *n* : tuyau *m* d'évacuation, drain *m*
drake ['dreɪk] *n* : canard *m* (mâle)
drama ['drɑmə, 'dræ-] *n* **1** : art *m* dramatique, théâtre *m* **2** PLAY : drame *m,* pièce *f* de théâtre
dramatic [drə'mætɪk] *adj* : dramatique
dramatically [drə'mæt̬ɪkli] *adv* : d'une manière dramatique
dramatist ['dræmət̬ɪst, 'drɑ-] *n* : dramaturge *mf*
dramatization [ˌdræmət̬ə'zeɪʃən] *n* **1** : adaptation *f* pour la scène **2** DRAMATIZING : dramatisation *f*
dramatize ['dræməˌtaɪz, 'drɑ-] *vt* **-tized; -tizing** : dramatiser
drank → **drink**[1]
drape[1] ['dreɪp] *v* **draped; draping** *vt* : draper — *vi* : tomber <silk drapes beautifully : la soie tombe à merveille>
drape[2] *nm* **1** HANG : drapé *m* (d'une étoffe) **2 drapes** *npl* CURTAINS : rideaux *mpl*
drapery ['dreɪpəri] *n, pl* **-eries 1** HANGINGS : tentures *fpl* **2** CURTAINS : rideaux *mpl*
drastic ['dræstɪk] *adj* **1** : drastique <a drastic purgative : un purgatif drastique> **2** SEVERE : rigoureux, énergique <drastic measures : mesures énergiques>
draught ['dræft, 'draft] → **draft**[3]
draughty ['drafti] → **drafty**
draw[1] ['drɔ] *v* **drew** ['dru:]; **drawn** ['draʊn]; **drawing** ['drɔɪŋ] *vt* **1** PULL : tirer **2** ATTRACT : attirer **3** PROVOKE : provoquer, susciter **4** INHALE : aspirer, respirer **5** EXTRACT : extraire, retirer **6** TAKE : prendre <to draw a number : prendre un numéro> **7** COLLECT : toucher (un salaire) **8** BEND : bander <to draw a bow : bander un arc> **9** TIE : faire match de (aux sports) **10** SKETCH : dessiner, tracer **11** MAKE : faire (une distinction, une comparaison, etc.) **12** *or* **to draw up** DRAFT, FORMULATE : dresser (une liste, etc.), rédiger (un plan) — *vi* **1** SKETCH : dessiner **2** (*indicating movement*) <to draw near : approcher> <to draw to an end : tirer à sa fin> **3** : tirer (se dit d'une cheminée, d'une pipe, etc.)
draw[2] *n* **1** DRAWING : tirage *m* (au sort) **2** TIE : match *m* nul (aux sports) **3** ATTRACTION : attraction *f* **4** PUFF : bouffée *f* (de cigarette, etc.)
drawback ['drɔˌbæk] *n* : désavantage *m,* inconvénient *m*
drawbridge ['drɔˌbrɪdʒ] *n* : pont-levis *m*
drawer ['drɔr, 'drɔər] *n* **1** ILLUSTRATOR : dessinateur *m,* -trice *f* **2** : tiroir *m* (d'un meuble) **3 drawers** *npl* UNDERPANTS : caleçon *m* (d'homme), culotte *f* (de femme)
drawing ['drɔɪŋ] *n* **1** LOTTERY : tirage *m* (au sort), loterie *f* **2** SKETCH : dessin *m*
drawl[1] ['drɔl] *vt* : dire d'une voix traînante — *vi* : parler d'une voix traînante
drawl[2] *n* : voix *f* traînante
draw out *vt* : faire parler (une personne)
draw up *vt* **1** FORMULATE : dresser, rédiger **2** APPROACH : approcher **3** *or* **to draw oneself up** : se redresser — *vi* STOP : s'arrêter

dread[1] ['drɛd] *vt* : redouter, craindre

dread[2] *adj* : redoutable, terrible

dread[3] *n* : crainte *f,* terreur *f*

dreadful ['drɛdfəl] *adj* **1** HORRIBLE : affreux, épouvantable **2** TERRIBLE, UNPLEASANT : terrible <a dreadful cold : un rhume terrible>

dream[1] ['dri:m] *v* **dreamed** ['drɛm*p*t, 'dri:md] *or* **dreamt** ['drɛm*p*t]; **dreaming** *vi* **1** : rêver <to dream about : rêver de> **2** DAYDREAM : rêvasser, songer — *vt* **1** : rêver <to dream a dream : faire un rêve> **2** IMAGINE : imaginer, penser, songer

dream[2] *n* **1** : rêve *m* **2** DAYDREAM : rêverie *f* **3** : merveille *f,* bijou *m* <my new car is a dream : ma nouvelle voiture est une merveille> **4** IDEAL : idéal *m*

dreamer ['dri:mər] **1** : rêveur *m,* -veuse *f* **2** IDEALIST : idéaliste *mf*

dreamless ['dri:mləs] *adj* : sans rêves

dreamlike ['dri:m,laɪk] *adj* : irréel

dreamy ['dri:mi] *adj* **dreamier; -est 1** : rêveur <a dreamy child : un enfant rêveur> **2** SOOTHING : apaisant, reposant **3** DELIGHTFUL : ravissant, superbe

drearily ['drɪrəli] *adv* : tristement, sombrement

dreary ['drɪri] *adj* **drearier; -est** : morne, sombre

dredge[1] ['drɛdʒ] *vt* **dredged; dredging 1** : draguer **2** COAT : saupoudrer, paner (en cuisine)

dredge[2] *n* : drague *f*

dregs ['drɛgz] *npl* : lie *f* <the dregs of society : la lie de la société>

drench ['drentʃ] *vt* : tremper, mouiller

dress[1] ['drɛs] *vt* **1** CLOTHE : habiller, vêtir **2** DECORATE : décorer <to dress a shop window : faire une vitrine> **3** : préparer, parer (une dinde, etc.), assaisonner (une salade) **4** BANDAGE : panser (une blessure) **5** FERTILIZE : fertiliser (la terre) — *vi* **1** : s'habiller **2** *or* **to dress up** : se mettre en grande toilette

dress[2] *n* **1** CLOTHING : habillement *m,* tenue *f* **2** : robe *f* (de femme) <a silk dress : une robe de soie>

dresser ['drɛsər] *n* : commode *f* à miroir

dressing ['drɛsɪŋ] *n* **1** CLOTHING : habillement *m* **2** SAUCE : sauce *f,* vinaigrette *f* **3** BANDAGE : pansement *m* **4** FERTILIZER : engrais *m*

dressmaker ['drɛs,meɪkər] *n* : couturière *f*

dressmaking ['drɛs,meɪkɪŋ] *n* : couture *f*

dressy ['drɛsi] *adj* **dressier; -est** : habillé, élégant

drew → **draw**[1]

dribble[1] ['drɪbəl] *vi* **-bled; -bling 1** TRICKLE : dégoutter, tomber goutte à goutte **2** DROOL : baver **3** : dribbler (au basketball)

dribble[2] *n* **1** TRICKLE : filet *m* (d'eau) **2** DROOL : bave *f* **3** : dribble *m* (au basketball)

drier, driest → **dry**[2]

drift[1] ['drɪft] *vi* **1** : dériver (sur l'eau), être emporté (par le vent) **2** ACCUMULATE : s'amonceler, former des bancs *Can,* poudrer *Can* (se dit de la neige) **3 to drift along** : flâner, errer <she drifted through life : elle a passé sa vie à errer> **4 to drift away** : s'éloigner

drift[2] *n* **1** COURSE : mouvement *m,* courant *m* **2** HEAP, MASS : amoncellement *m,* entassement *m,* banc *m* (de neige) *Can* **3** MEANING : sens *m,* portée *f*

drill[1] ['drɪl] *vt* **1** BORE : percer, forer **2** TRAIN : faire faire des exercices à, entraîner — *vi* **1** BORE : forer, percer un trou **2** PRACTICE, TRAIN : faire de l'exercice

drill[2] *n* **1** : perceuse *f* (outil) **2** EXERCISE, PRACTICE : exercice *m* **3** : semoir *m* (en agriculture)

drily → **dryly**

drink[1] ['drɪŋk] *v* **drank** ['dræŋk]; **drunk** ['drʌŋk] *or* **drank; drinking** *vt* **1** : boire **2 to drink up** ABSORB : boire, s'imbiber — *vi* : boire

drink[2] *n* **1** BEVERAGE : boisson *f* **2** : boisson *f* alcoolisée

drip[1] ['drɪp] *v* **dripped; dripping** *vt* : laisser tomber goutte à goutte — *vi* : tomber goutte à goutte, dégoutter

drip[2] *n* **1** DROP : goutte *f* **2** : bruit *m* de goutte

drive[1] ['draɪv] *v* **drove** ['dro:v]; **driven** ['drɪvən]; **driving** *vt* **1** : mener, conduire (un troupeau) **2** : conduire, piloter (un véhicule) **3** COMPEL : inciter **4** PUSH : conduire, amener <hunger drove him to steal : la faim l'a amené à voler> **5** PROPEL : envoyer (une balle) — *vi* : conduire, rouler <I was driving at 65 mph : je roulais à 65 milles à l'heure>

drive[2] *n* **1** : promenade *f* (en voiture) **2** CAMPAIGN : campagne *f* **3** VIGOR : énergie *f,* initiative *f* **4** NEED : besoin *m* fondamental

drivel ['drɪvəl] *n* : bêtises *fpl*

driver ['draɪvər] *n* **1** : conducteur *m,* -trice *f* **2** CHAUFFEUR : chauffeur *m*

driveway ['draɪv,weɪ] *n* : allée *f,* entrée *f* (de garage)

drizzle[1] ['drɪzəl] *vi* **-zled; -zling** : bruiner, crachiner

drizzle[2] *n* : bruine *f,* crachin *m*

droll ['dro:l] *adj* **1** COMICAL : drôle, comique **2** ODD : curieux, bizarre

dromedary ['drɑmə,dɛri] *n, pl* **-daries** : dromadaire *m*

drone[1] ['dro:n] *vi* **droned; droning 1** BUZZ, HUM : bourdonner (se dit d'un insecte), ronronner (se dit d'un moteur) **2** *or* **to drone on** : parler d'un ton monotone

drone[2] *n* **1** BEE : abeille *f* mâle **2** HUM : bourdonnement *m* (d'un insecte), ronronnement *m* (d'un moteur)
drool[1] ['dru:l] *vi* : baver
drool[2] *n* : bave *f*
droop[1] ['dru:p] *vi* **1** HANG, SAG : pencher (se dit de la tête), tomber (se dit des épaules ou des paupières), se faner (se dit des fleurs) **2** FLAG : baisser <her spirits were drooping : elle était démoralisée>
droop[2] *n* : abaissement *m*, affaissement *m*, attitude *f* penchée
drop[1] ['drɑp] *v* **dropped; dropping** *vt* **1** : laisser tomber <he dropped the book : il a laissé tomber le livre> **2** LOWER : baisser <to drop one's voice : baisser la voix> **3** SEND : envoyer <drop me a line : écris-moi un mot> **4** ABANDON : abandonner (une conversation, une matière, etc.) **5** OMIT : omettre, supprimer **6 to drop a hint about** : faire allusion à, suggérer **7 to drop off** LEAVE : déposer, laisser — *vi* **1** DRIP : tomber goutte à goutte **2** FALL : tomber **3** DECREASE : se calmer (se dit du vent), baisser (se dit des prix) **4 to drop back** *or* **to drop behind** : rester en arrière, prendre du retard **5 to drop by** VISIT : passer, entrer en passant
drop[2] *n* **1** : goutte *f* (de liquide) **2** DECLINE, FALL : réduction *f*, diminution *f* **3** DESCENT : hauteur *f* de chute, descente *f* <a 10-foot drop : une hauteur de 10 pieds> **4** : pastille *f*, bonbon *f* <cough drops : pastilles contre la toux>
droplet ['drɑplət] *n* : gouttelette *f*
dropper ['drɑpər] *n* : compte-gouttes *m*
dross ['drɑs, 'drɔs] *n* **1** : crasse *f*, scories *fpl* (de métaux) **2** WASTE : déchets *mpl*
drought ['draʊt] *n* : sécheresse *f*
drove[1] ['dro:v] → **drive**[1]
drove[2] *n* **1** HERD : troupeau *m* **2** CROWD : foule *f* <people came in droves : il y avait une foule de gens>
drown ['draʊn] *vt* **1** : noyer **2** *or* **to drown out** : noyer, couvrir (un son, une voix) — *vi* : se noyer
drowse[1] ['draʊz] *vi* **drowsed; drowsing** : somnoler, sommeiller
drowse[2] *n* DOZE : somme *m*, sieste *f*
drowsiness ['draʊzinəs] *n* : somnolence *f*
drowsy ['draʊzi] *adj* **drowsier; -est** : somnolent, qui a envie de dormir
drub ['drʌb] *vt* **drubbed; drubbing 1** BEAT : battre, maltraiter **2** DEFEAT : vaincre
drudge[1] ['drʌdʒ] *vi* **drudged; drudging** : besogner, trimer *fam*
drudge[2] *n* : bête *f* de somme, gratte-papier *m*
drudgery ['drʌdʒəri] *n, pl* **-eries** : corvée *f*, (grosse) besogne *f*
drug[1] ['drʌg] *vt* **drugged; drugging** : droguer
drug[2] *n* **1** MEDICATION : médicament *m* **2** NARCOTIC : drogue *f*, stupéfiant *m*
druggist ['drʌgɪst] *n* : pharmacien *m*, -cienne *f*
drugstore ['drʌg,stor] *n* : pharmacie *f*
drum[1] ['drʌm] *v* **drummed; drumming** *vi* : jouer du tambour — *vt* **1** TAP : tambouriner (les doigts, les pieds, etc.) **2** DRIVE, PUSH : enfoncer, fourrer <he drummed it into my head : il me l'a enfoncé dans la tête>
drum[2] *n* **1** : tambour *m* **2** *or* **oil drum** : bidon *m*
drumbeat ['drʌm,bi:t] *n* : roulement *m* de tambour
drumstick ['drʌm,stɪk] *n* **1** : baguette *f* de tambour **2** : cuisse *f* (de poulet)
drunk[1] → **drink**[1]
drunk[2] ['drʌŋk] *adj* : ivre, soûl *fam*, en boisson *Can* <drunk driving : conduite en état d'ébriété>
drunk[3] *n* : ivrogne *m*, ivrognesse *f*
drunkard ['drʌŋkərd] *n* : ivrogne *m*, ivrognesse *f*
drunken ['drʌŋkən] *adj* : ivre, en état d'ébriété
drunkenly ['drʌŋkənli] *adv* : comme un ivrogne
drunkenness ['drʌŋkənli] *n* : ivresse *f*, ébriété
dry[1] ['draɪ] *v* **dried; drying** *vt* **1** : sécher **2** WIPE : essuyer — *vi* : sécher
dry[2] *adj* **drier; driest 1** : sec <a dry climate : un climat sec> **2** THIRSTY : assoiffé **3** : qui interdit la vente d'alcool <a dry town : une ville où on ne vend pas d'alcool> **4** UNINTERESTING : plate, aride **5** BITING, KEEN : mordant, caustique <to have a dry wit : être pince-sans-rire> **6** : sec (se dit du vin), brut (se dit du champagne) **7 on dry land** : sur la terre ferme
dry–clean ['draɪ,kli:n] *vt* : nettoyer à sec
dry cleaner *n* : teinturerie *f* (service)
dry cleaning *n* : nettoyage *m* à sec
dryer ['draɪər] *n* : séchoir *m*
dry goods *npl* : tissus *mpl*, étoffes *fpl*
dry ice *n* : neige *f* carbonique
dryly ['draɪli] *adv* : sèchement
dryness ['draɪnəs] *n* : sécheresse *f*
dual ['du:əl, 'dju:-] *adj* : double
dub ['dʌb] *vt* **dubbed; dubbing 1** NAME, NICKNAME : surnommer **2** : doubler (un film, etc.)
dubious ['du:biəs, 'dju:-] *adj* **1** DOUBTFUL : dubitatif **2** QUESTIONABLE : louche, suspect
dubiously ['du:biəsli, 'dju:-] *adv* : d'un air incertain, avec doute
duchess ['dʌtʃəs] *n* : duchesse *f*
duck[1] ['dʌk] *vt* **1** PLUNGE : plonger (dans l'eau) **2** LOWER : baisser <to duck one's head : baisser la tête> **3** AVOID, DODGE : éviter, esquiver — *vi* : se baisser vivement, esquiver un coup (en boxe)
duck[2] *n, pl* **ducks** *or* **duck** : canard *m**

duckling ['dʌklɪŋ] *n* : caneton *m*, canette *f*

duct ['dʌkt] *n* **1** PIPE : conduite *f* (d'eau, etc.) **2** CHANNEL, TUBE : conduit *m*, canal *m* <tear duct : canal lacrymal>

dude ['du:d, 'dju:d] *n* **1** DANDY : dandy *m* **2** GUY : gars *m fam*, mec *m fam*

due[1] ['du:, 'dju:] *adv* DIRECTLY : plein, droit vers <due north : plein nord>

due[2] *adj* **1** OWING : dû, payable **2** APPROPRIATE : qui convient, dû <after due consideration : après mûre réflexion> **3** EXPECTED : attendu <the plane is due at midnight : l'avion doit arriver à minuit>

due[3] *n* **1 to give s.o. his (her) due** : rendre justice à qqn **2 dues** *npl* FEE : cotisation *f*

duel[1] ['du:əl, 'dju:-] *vi* **duelled; duelling** : se battre en duel

duel[2] *n* : duel *m*

duet [du'ɛt, dju:-] *n* : duo *m*

due to *prep* : en raison de, à cause de

dug → **dig**[1]

dugout ['dʌg,aʊt] *n* **1** CANOE : pirogue *f* **2** SHELTER : tranchée-abri *f*

duke ['du:k, 'dju:k] *n* : duc *m*

dull[1] ['dʌl] *vt* **1** BLUNT : émousser, épointer **2** DIM, TARNISH : ternir (des couleurs, des métaux, etc.)

dull[2] *adj* **1** STUPID : stupide, lent **2** BLUNT : émoussé <a dull knife : un couteau émoussé> **3** BORING : ennuyeux, ennuyant *Can* **4** LACKLUSTER : terne, fade <a dull red : un rouge fade>

dullness ['dʌlnəs] *n* **1** STUPIDITY : stupidité *f*, lenteur *f* **2** BLUNTNESS : manque *m* de tranchant **3** TEDIUM : monotonie *f*

duly ['du:li] *adv* **1** PROPERLY : dûment, de façon convenable <duly recorded : dûment enregistré> **2** EXPECTEDLY : comme prévu

dumb ['dʌm] *adj* **1** MUTE : muet **2** STUPID : bête

dumbbell ['dʌm,bɛl] *n* **1** WEIGHT : haltère *m* **2** DOPE : idiot *m*, -diote *f*; gourde *f fam*

dumbfound *or* **dumfound** [,dʌm'faʊnd] *vt* AMAZE : abasourdir, sidérer *fam*

dummy ['dʌmi] *n, pl* **-mies 1** DOPE, FOOL : imbécile *mf*, ballot *m fam* **2** MANNEQUIN : mannequin *m*

dump[1] ['dʌmp] *vt* : déposer, jeter, déverser

dump[2] *n* **1** : tas *m* d'ordures **2 to be down in the dumps** : avoir le cafard

dumpling ['dʌmplɪŋ] *n* : boulette *f* de pâte

dumpy ['dʌmpi] *adj* **dumpier; -est** CHUBBY : boulot, rondelet *fam*

dun[1] ['dʌn] *vt* **dunned; dunning** : harceler (afin d'obtenir un paiement)

dun[2] *adj* : brun gris

dunce [dʌnts] *n* : cancre *m fam*

dune ['du:n, 'dju:n] *n* : dune *f*

dung ['dʌŋ] *n* : excréments *mpl*, fumier *m*, bouse *f* (de vache), crottin *m* (de cheval)

dungaree [,dʌŋgə'ri:] *n* **1** DENIM : jean *m* **2 dungarees** *npl* JEANS : jean *m*, blue-jean *m*

dungeon ['dʌndʒən] *n* : cachot *m* (souterrain)

dunghill ['dʌŋ,hɪl] *n* : tas *m* de fumier

dunk ['dʌŋk] *vt* : tremper

duo ['du:o:, 'dju:-] *n, pl* **duos** : duo *m*

dupe[1] ['du:p, 'dju:p] *vt* **duped; duping** : duper, tromper

dupe[2] *n* : dupe *f*

duplex[1] ['du:,plɛks, 'dju:-] *adj* : double

duplex[2] *n* : duplex *m*, maison *f* jumelée

duplicate[1] ['du:plɪ,keɪt, 'dju:-] *vt* **-cated; -cating 1** COPY : faire un double de, copier **2** REPEAT : répéter, refaire

duplicate[2] ['du:plɪkət, 'dju:-] *adj* : en double

duplicate[3] ['du:plɪkət, 'dju:-] *n* : double *m*, copie *f* exacte

duplication [,du:plɪ'keɪʃən, ,dju:-] *n* **1** DUPLICATING : action *f* de copier, reproduction *f* **2** REPETITION : répétition *f*

duplicity [dʊ'plɪsəṭi, ,dju:-] *n, pl* **-ties** : duplicité *f*

durability [,dʊrə'bɪləṭi, ,djʊr-] *n* : durabilité *f*, résistance *f*

durable ['dʊrəbəl, 'djʊr-] *adj* : durable, résistant

duration [dʊ'reɪʃən, djʊ-] *n* : durée *f*

duress [dʊ'rɛs, djʊ-] *n* : contrainte *f*

during ['dʊrɪŋ, 'djʊr-] *prep* : durant, pendant

dusk ['dʌsk] *n* : crépuscule *m*, nuit *f* tombante, brunante *f Can*

dusky ['dʌski] *adj* **duskier; -est** : sombre, obscur (se dit des couleurs)

dust[1] ['dʌst] *vt* **1** : épousseter **2** SPRINKLE : saupoudrer

dust[2] *n* : poussière *f*

duster ['dʌstər] *n* **1** *or* **dust cloth** : chiffon *m* à poussière **2** *or* **feather duster** : plumeau *m* **3** HOUSECOAT : blouse *f*, sarrau *m*

dustpan ['dʌst,pæn] *n* : pelle *f* à poussière, porte-poussière *m Can*

dusty ['dʌsti] *adj* **dustier; -est** : poussiéreux

Dutch[1] ['dʌtʃ] *adj* : néerlandais, hollandais

Dutch[2] *n* **1** : néerlandais *m*, hollandais *m* (langue) **2 the Dutch** *npl* : les Néerlandais, les Hollandais

Dutch treat *n* : sortie *f* où chacun paie sa part

dutiful ['du:ṭɪfəl, 'dju:-] *adj* : obéissant, respectueux, consciencieux

duty ['du:ṭi, 'dju:-] *n, pl* **-ties 1** TASK : fonction *f* <to perform one's duties : remplir ses fonctions> **2** OBLIGATION : devoir *m* **3** TAX : taxe *f*, droit *m* **4 to be on duty** : être de garde

dwarf[1] ['dwɔrf] *vt* **1** STUNT : rabougrir (un arbre) **2** : faire paraître tout petit

dwarf[2] *n* : nain *m*, naine *f*
dwell ['dwɛl] *vi* **dwelled** *or* **dwelt** ['dwɛlt]; **dwelling 1** RESIDE : résider, demeurer **2 to dwell on** : penser sans cesse à, ruminer
dweller ['dwɛlər] *n* : habitant *m*, -tante *f*
dwelling ['dwɛlɪŋ] *n* : demeure *f*, résidence *f*
dwindle ['dwɪndəl] *vi* **-dled; -dling** : diminuer
dye[1] ['daɪ] *vt* **dyed; dyeing** : teindre <to dye one's hair : se teindre les cheveux>
dye[2] *n* : teinture *f*
dying → **die**[1]
dyke → **dike**
dynamic [daɪ'næmɪk] *adj* : dynamique
dynamite[1] ['daɪnə,maɪt] *vt* **-mited; -miting** : dynamiter
dynamite[2] *n* : dynamite *f*
dynamo ['daɪnə,moː] *n, pl* **-mos** : dynamo *f*
dynasty ['daɪnəsti, -næs-] *n, pl* **-ties** : dynastie *f*
dysentery ['dɪsən,tɛri] *n, pl* **-teries** : dysenterie *f*
dyslexia [dɪs'lɛksiə] *n* : dyslexie *f* — **dyslexic** [-'lɛksik] *adj*
dystrophy ['dɪstrəfi] *n, pl* **-phies 1** : dystrophie *f* **2** → **muscular dystrophy**

E

e ['iː] *n, pl* **e's** *or* **es** ['iːz] : e *m*, cinquième lettre de l'alphabet
each[1] ['iːtʃ] *adv* APIECE : chacun, la pièce <one dollar each : un dollar la pièce>
each[2] *adj* : chaque <each week : chaque semaine>
each[3] *pron* **1** : chacun *m*, -cune *f* <each of the girls : chacune des filles> <each and every one : chacun sans exception> **2 each other** : l'un l'autre <they love each other : ils s'aiment (l'un l'autre)> **3 to each his own** : chacun son goût
eager ['iːgər] *adj* **1** ENTHUSIASTIC : désireux, avide **2** ANXIOUS, IMPATIENT : impatient, pressé
eagerly ['iːgərli] *adv* : avidement, avec empressement
eagerness ['iːgərnəs] *n* : avidité *f*, empressement *m*
eagle ['iːgəl] *n* : aigle *m*
ear ['ɪr] *n* **1** : oreille *f* (en anatomie) **2** : épi *m* (de maïs, etc.)
earache ['ɪr,eɪk] *n* : mal *m* d'oreille
eardrum ['ɪr,drʌm] *n* : tympan *m*
earl ['ərl] *n* : comte *m*
earlobe ['ɪr,loːb] *n* : lobe *m* de l'oreille
early[1] ['ərli] *adv* **earlier; -est 1** : tôt, de bonne heure <to go to bed early : se coucher de bonne heure> <as early as possible : le plus tôt possible> **2** : en avance <five minutes early : en avance de cinq minutes>
early[2] *adj* **earlier; -est 1** FIRST : premier <his early novels : ses premiers romans> **2** (*referring to a designated time*) <to be early : arriver de bonne heure> <early fruits : fruits précoces> <an early death : une mort prématurée> **3** (*referring to a beginning*) <in the early afternoon : au commencement de l'après-midi> <in early December : début décembre> **4** ANCIENT : ancien, primitif <early man : l'homme primitif>
earmark ['ɪr,mɑrk] *vt* : réserver, désigner
earn ['ərn] *vt* **1** : gagner <to earn one's living : gagner sa vie> **2** DESERVE : mériter
earnest[1] ['ərnəst] *adj* **1** SERIOUS : sérieux **2** SINCERE : sincère — **earnestly** *adv*
earnest[2] *n* **in ~** : sérieusement
earnestness ['ərnəstnəs] *n* : sérieux *m*, gravité *f*
earnings ['ərnɪŋz] *npl* **1** WAGES : salaire *m* **2** PROFITS : bénéfices *mpl*, profits *mpl*
earphone ['ɪr,foːn] *n* : écouteur *m*
earring ['ɪr,rɪŋ] *n* : boucle *f* d'oreille
earshot ['ɪr,ʃɑt] *n* : portée *f* de voix
earth ['ərθ] *n* **1** GROUND, SOIL : terre *f*, sol *m* **2 the Earth** : la Terre
earthen ['ərθən, -ðən] *adj* : en terre
earthenware ['ərθən,wær, -ðən-] *n* : faïence *f*
earthly ['ərθli] *adj* **1** : terrestre <earthly pleasures : joies terrestres> **2** (*indicating possibility*) <of no earthly use : d'aucune utilité>
earthquake ['ərθ,kweɪk] *n* : tremblement *m* de terre
earthworm ['ərθ,wərm] *n* : ver *m* de terre, lombric *m France*
earthy ['ərθi] *adj* **earthier; -est 1** : terreux <earthy colors : couleurs de terre> **2** DOWN-TO-EARTH : pratique, terre à terre **3** COARSE, CRUDE : truculent, grossier
earwax ['ɪr,wæks] *n* : cérumen *m*
earwig ['ɪr,wɪg] *n* : perce-oreille *m*
ease[1] ['iːz] *v* **eased; easing** *vt* **1** FACILITATE : faciliter **2** ALLEVIATE, LESSEN : soulager, atténuer, calmer (l'inquiétude) **3 to ease oneself into** : se laisser glisser dans — *vi or* **to ease up** : s'atténuer, se détendre
ease[2] *n* **1** : aise *f* <to put s.o. at ease : mettre qqn à son aise> **2** FACILITY : facilité *f* **3** COMFORT : bien-être *m*,

tranquillité *f* **4** AFFLUENCE : aisance *f* **5 at ease!** : repos! **6 with ~** : aisément, facilement

easel ['i:zəl] *n* : chevalet *m*

easily ['i:zəli] *adv* **1** : facilement, aisément **2** UNQUESTIONABLY : sans doute, de loin

easiness ['i:zinəs] *n* : facilité *f*

east[1] ['i:st] *adv* : vers l'est, à l'est

east[2] *adj* : est <the east coast : la côte est> <the east wind : le vent d'est>

east[3] *n* **1** : est *m* **2 the East** : l'Est *m*, l'Orient *m*

Easter ['i:stər] *n* : Pâques *m*, Pâques *fpl*

easterly[1] ['i:stərli] *adv* : vers l'est

easterly[2] *adj* : d'est, de l'est <in an easterly direction : en direction de l'est>

eastern ['i:stərn] *adj* **1** : est, de l'est **2 Eastern** : de l'Est, d'Orient

easy[1] ['i:zi] *adv* **easier; -est** : doucement <to go easy on : aller doucement avec> <easy does it! : doucement!>

easy[2] *adj* **easier; -est 1** : facile, aisé **2** RELAXED : décontracté <an easy manner : une attitude pleine d'aisance> **3** LENIENT : indulgent, clément

easygoing [ˌi:zi'go:ɪŋ] *adj* : accommodant, complaisant

eat ['i:t] *v* **ate** ['eɪt]; **eaten** ['i:tən]; **eating** *vt* **1** : manger, prendre (un repas) **2** CONSUME : manger, consommer (des ressources, des bénéfices, etc.) **3** CORRODE : ronger, corroder — *vi* : manger

eatable ['i:ṭəbəl] *adj* : mangeable, bon à manger

eaves ['i:vz] *npl* : avant-toit *m*

eavesdrop ['i:vzˌdrɑp] *vi* **-dropped; -dropping** : écouter aux portes

ebb[1] ['ɛb] *vi* **1** : refluer, descendre (se dit de la mer) **2** DECLINE : décliner, baisser

ebb[2] *n* **1** : reflux *m* (de la mer) **2** DECLIN : déclin *m*, baisse *f*

ebony[1] ['ɛbəni] *adj* **1** : d'ébène **2** BLACK : d'un noir d'ébène

ebony[2] *n, pl* **-nies** : ébène *f*

ebullience [ɪ'bʊljənts, -'bʌl-] *n* : exubérance *f*

ebullient [ɪ'bʊljənt, -'bʌl-] *adj* : exubérant

eccentric[1] [ɪk'sɛntrɪk] *adj* : excentrique — **eccentrically** [-trɪkli] *adv*

eccentric[2] *n* : excentrique *mf*

eccentricity [ˌɛkˌsɛn'trɪsəṭi] *n, pl* **-ties** : excentricité *f*

ecclesiastic [ɪˌkli:zi'æstɪk] *n* : ecclésiastique *mf*

ecclesiastical [ɪˌkli:zi'æstɪkəl] *or* **ecclesiastic** *adj* : ecclésiastique

echelon ['ɛʃəˌlɑn] *n* : échelon *m*

echo[1] ['ɛˌko:] *v* **echoed; echoing** *vt* : répercuter (un son), répéter (des mots) — *vi* : se répercuter, résonner

echo[2] *n, pl* **echoes** : écho *m*

éclair [eɪ'klær, i-] *n* : éclair *m*

eclectic [ɛ'klɛktɪk, ɪ-] *adj* : éclectique

eclipse[1] [ɪ'klɪps] *vt* **eclipsed; eclipsing** : éclipser

eclipse[2] *n* : éclipse *f*

ecological [ˌi:kə'lɑdʒɪkəl, ˌɛkə-] *adj* : écologique — **ecologically** *adv*

ecologist [i'kɑlədʒɪst, ɛ-] *n* : écologiste *mf*

ecology [i'kɑlədʒi, ɛ-] *n, pl* **-gies** : écologie *f*

economic [ˌi:kə'nɑmɪk, ˌɛkə-] *adj* : économique

economical [ˌi:kə'nɑmɪkəl, ˌɛkə-] *adj* THRIFTY : économe

economically [ˌi:kə'nɑmɪkli, ˌɛkə-] *adv* : économiquement, de façon économique

economics [ˌi:kə'nɑmɪks, ˌɛkə-] *ns & pl* : sciences *fpl* économiques, économie *f*

economist [i'kɑnəmɪst] *n* : économiste *mf*

economize [i'kɑnəˌmaɪz] *v* **-mized; -mizing** : économiser

economy [i'kɑnəmi] *n, pl* **-mies** : économie *f*

ecosystem ['i:koˌsɪstəm] *n* : écosystème *m*

ecru ['ɛˌkru:, 'eɪ-] *n* : écru *m*

ecstasy ['ɛkstəsi] *n, pl* **-sies** : extase *f*

ecstatic [ɛk'stæṭɪk, ɪk-] *adj* : extatique, ravi, en extase

ecstatically [ɛk'stæṭɪkli, ɪk-] *adv* : avec extase

Ecuadoran[1] [ˌɛkwə'dorən] *or* **Ecuadorean** *or* **Ecuadorian** [-'doriən] *adj* : équatorien

Ecuadoran[2] *or* **Ecuadorean** *or* **Ecuadorian** *n* : Équatorien *m*, -rienne *f*

ecumenical [ˌɛkjʊ'mɛnɪkəl] *adj* : œcuménique

eczema [ɪg'zi:mə, 'ɛgzəmə, 'ɛksə-] *n* : eczéma *m*

eddy[1] ['ɛdi] *vi* **eddied; eddying** : tourbillonner

eddy[2] *n, pl* **-dies** : tourbillon *m*

edema [ɪ'di:mə] *n* : œdème *m*

edge[1] ['ɛdʒ] *vt* **edged; edging 1** BORDER : border **2** SHARPEN : aiguiser, affiler **3 to edge one's way** : avancer lentement **4 to edge out** : pousser (qqn) doucement vers la sortie, évincer en douceur — *vi* ADVANCE : avancer (doucement)

edge[2] *n* **1** BORDER, MARGIN : bord *m* **2** : tranchant *m*, fil *m* (d'un couteau, etc.) **3** ADVANTAGE : avantage *m*

edgewise ['ɛdʒˌwaɪz] *adv* **1** → **sideways 2 to get a word in edgewise** : placer un mot

edginess ['ɛdʒinəs] *n* : nervosité *f*

edging ['ɛdʒɪŋ] *n* : bordure *f*

edgy ['ɛdʒi] *adj* **edgier; -est** : énervé

edible ['ɛdəbəl] *adj* : comestible

edict ['i:ˌdɪkt] *n* : édit *m*, décret *m*

edification [ˌɛdəfə'keɪʃən] *n* : édification *f*

edifice ['ɛdəfɪs] *n* : édifice *m*

edify ['ɛdəˌfaɪ] *vt* **-fied; -fying** : édifier

edit ['ɛdɪt] *vt* **1** : réviser, corriger, diriger la rédaction de **2 to edit out** : couper, supprimer

edition [ɪ'dɪʃən] *n* : édition *f* <limited edition : édition à tirage limité>

editor ['ɛdɪt̬ər] *n* : rédacteur *m*, -trice *f* (d'un journal); éditeur *m*, -trice *f* (d'un livre); monteur *m*, -teuse *f* (d'un film)

editorial[1] [ˌɛdɪ'toriəl] *adj* **1** : de la rédaction <editorial staff : personnel de rédaction> **2** : éditorial <an editorial comment : un commentaire éditorial>

editorial[2] *n* : éditorial *m*

educate ['ɛdʒəˌkeɪt] *vt* **-cated; -cating 1** INSTRUCT, TEACH : instruire, donner l'instruction à (des élèves) **2** DEVELOP, REFINE : éduquer <to educate s.o.'s taste : éduquer le goût de qqn>

education [ˌɛdʒə'keɪʃən] *n* **1** : éducation *f*, études *fpl* <university education : études supérieures> **2** TEACHING : enseignement *m*, instruction *f*

educational [ˌɛdʒə'keɪʃənəl] *adj* **1** INSTRUCTIVE : éducatif **2** TEACHING : d'enseignement, pédagogique

educator ['ɛdʒəˌkeɪt̬ər] *n* : éducateur *m*, -trice *f*

eel ['iːl] *n* : anguille *f*

eerie ['ɪri] *adj* **eerier; -est** : sinistre, étrange

eerily ['ɪrəli] *adv* : d'une manière sinistre

efface [ɪ'feɪs, ɛ-] *vt* **-faced; -facing** : effacer

effect[1] [ɪ'fɛkt] *vt* : effectuer, réaliser

effect[2] *n* **1** RESULT : effet *m*, conséquence *f* **2** MEANING : sens *m* <something to that effect : quelque chose dans ce sens> **3** EFFECTIVENESS : efficacité *f* <to little effect : sans grand résultat> **4 effects** *npl* BELONGINGS : effets *mpl* (personnels) **5 to go into effect** : entrer en vigueur **6 in ~** REALLY : en fait, en réalité

effective [ɪ'fɛktɪv] *adj* **1** EFFECTUAL : efficace **2** ACTUAL : effectif **3** OPERATIVE : en vigueur

effectively [ɪ'fɛktɪvli] *adv* **1** EFFICIENTLY : efficacement **2** ACTUALLY, REALLY : effectivement

effectiveness [ɪ'fɛktɪvnəs] *n* : efficacité *f*

effectual [ɪ'fɛktʃʊəl] *adj* : efficace — **effectually** *adv*

effeminate [ə'fɛmənət] *adj* : efféminé

effervesce [ˌɛfər'vɛs] *vi* **-vesced; -vescing 1** FIZZ : pétiller **2** : être exubérant (se dit des personnes)

effervescence [ˌɛfər'vɛsənts] *n* : effervescence *f*

effervescent [ˌɛfər'vɛsənt] *adj* : effervescent

effete [ɛ'fiːt, ɪ-] *adj* **1** DECADENT, WEAKENED : veule, affaibli, décadent **2** EFFEMINATE : efféminé

efficacious [ˌɛfə'keɪʃəs] *adj* : efficace

efficacy ['ɛfɪkəsi] *n, pl* **-cies** : efficacité *f*

efficiency [ɪ'fɪʃəntsi] *n pl* **-cies** : efficacité *f*, efficience *f*

efficient [ɪ'fɪʃənt] *adj* : efficace, efficient

efficiently [ɪ'fɪʃəntli] *adv* : efficacement <to work efficiently : fonctionner à bon rendement>

effigy ['ɛfədʒi] *n, pl* **-gies** : effigie *f*

effort ['ɛfərt] *n* **1** EXERTION : effort *m* <to be worth the effort : en valoir la peine> **2** ATTEMPT : essai *m*, tentative *f*

effortless ['ɛfərtləs] *adj* : facile, aisé — **effortlessly** *adv*

effrontery [ɪ'frʌntəri] *n, pl* **-teries** : effronterie *f*

effusion [ɪ'fjuːʒən, ɛ-] *n* : effusion *f*

effusive [ɪ'fjuːsɪv, ɛ-] *adj* : expansif, démonstratif <an effusive welcome : un accueil chaleureux>

effusively [ɪ'fjuːsɪvli, ɛ-] *adv* : avec effusion

egg[1] ['ɛg] *vt* **to egg on** : inciter, pousser

egg[2] *n* : œuf *m*

eggbeater ['ɛgˌbiːt̬ər] *n* : batteur *m* (à œufs)

eggnog ['ɛgˌnɑg] *n* : lait *m* de poule

eggplant ['ɛgˌplænt] *n* : aubergine *f*

eggshell ['ɛgˌʃɛl] *n* : coquille *f* d'œuf

ego ['iːˌgoː] *n, pl* **egos 1** SELF : ego *m*, moi *m* **2** SELF-ESTEEM : amour-propre *m*

egocentric [iːgo'sɛntrɪk] *adj* : égocentrique

egoism ['iːgoˌwɪzəm] *m* : égoïsme *m*

egoist ['iːgowɪst] *n* : égoïste *mf*

egoistic [ˌiːgo'wɪstɪk] *adj* : égoïste

egotism ['iːgəˌtɪzəm] *n* : égotisme *m*

egotist ['iːgətɪst] *n* : égotiste *mf*

egotistic [ˌiːgə'tɪstɪk] *or* **egotistical** [-'tɪstɪkəl] *adj* : égotiste

egregious [ɪ'griːdʒəs] *adj* : flagrant <an egregious error : une erreur énorme>

egress ['iːˌgrɛs] *n* : sortie *f*, issue *f*

egret ['iːgrət, -ˌgrɛt] *n* : aigrette *f*

Egyptian[1] [i'dʒɪpʃən] *adj* : égyptien

Egyptian[2] *n* : Égyptien *m*, -tienne *f*

eider ['aɪdər] *n* : eider *m*, moyac *m* Can

eiderdown ['aɪdərˌdaʊn] *n* **1** DOWN : duvet *m* **2** COMFORTER : édredon *m*

eight[1] ['eɪt] *adj* : huit

eight[2] *n* : huit *m*

eighteen[1] [eɪt'tiːn] *adj* : dix-huit

eighteen[2] *n* : dix-huit *m*

eighteenth[1] [eɪt'tiːnθ] *adj* : dix-huitième

eighteenth[2] *n* **1** : dix-huitième *mf* (dans une série) **2** : dix-huitième *m* (en mathématiques) **3** (*used for dates*) <the eighteenth of May : le dix-huit mai>

eighth[1] ['eɪtθ] *adj* : huitième
eighth[2] *n* **1** : huitième *mf* (dans une série) **2** : huitième *m* (en mathématiques) **3** (*used in dates*) <the eighth of June : le huit juin>
eightieth[1] [eɪt̬iəθ] *adj* : quatre-vingtième
eightieth[2] *n* **1** : quatre-vingtième *mf* (dans une série) **2** : quatre-vingtième *m* (en mathématiques)
eighty[1] [eɪt̬i] *adj* : quatre-vingts
eighty[2] *n, pl* **eighties** : quatre-vingts *m* <in the late eighties : vers la fin des années quatre-vingts>
either[1] ['iːðər, 'aɪ-] *adj* **1** EACH : chaque <there are trees on either side : il y a des arbres de chaque côté> **2** (*referring to one or the other*) <take either road : prenez l'une ou l'autre des deux routes> <he doesn't like either restaurant : il n'aime ni l'un ni l'autre de ces restaurants> <give me either book : donnez-moi n'importe quel livre>
either[2] *pron* : l'un ou l'autre, n'importe lequel <take either one : prenez l'un ou l'autre> <I don't believe either of them : je ne les crois ni l'un ni l'autre>
either[3] *conj* **either . . . or** : ou . . . ou, ou bien . . . ou bien, soit . . . soit <you either love him or hate him : soit on l'adore, soit on le déteste>
ejaculate [i'dʒækjəˌleɪt] *vi* **-lated; -lating 1** : éjaculer (en physiologie) **2** EXCLAIM : s'exclamer, s'écrier
ejaculation [iˌdʒækjə'leɪʃən] *n* **1** : éjaculation *f* (en physiologie) **2** EXCLAMATION : exclamation *f*, cri *m*
eject [i'dʒɛkt] *vt* : éjecter, expulser
ejection [i'dʒɛkʃən] *n* : éjection *f*, expulsion *f*
eke [iːk] *vt* **eked; eking** *or* **to eke out 1** SUPPLEMENT : augmenter **2** : gagner difficilement <she eked out a living : elle a gagné tout juste sa vie>
elaborate[1] [i'læbəˌreɪt] *v* **-rated; -rating** *vt* : élaborer (un plan, etc.) — *vi* **to elaborate on** : donner des détails sur, développer
elaborate[2] [i'læbərət] *adj* **1** DETAILED : minutieux **2** ORNATE : orné, travaillé **3** COMPLEX : compliqué, complexe
elapse [i'læps] *vi* **elapsed; elapsing** : s'écouler, passer
elastic[1] [i'læstɪk] *adj* : élastique
elastic[2] *n* : élastique *m*
elasticity [iˌlæs'tɪsət̬i, ˌiːˌlæs-] *n, pl* **-ties** : élasticité *f*
elate [i'leɪt] *vt* **elated; elating** : ravir, transporter de joie
elation [i'leɪʃən] *n* : exultation *f*, joie *f*
elbow[1] ['ɛlˌboː] *vt* : donner un coup de coude à
elbow[2] *n* : coude *m* <to be at s.o.'s elbow : être à portée de main>
elder[1] ['ɛldər] *adj* : aîné, plus âgé <an elder sister : une sœur aînée>
elder[2] *n* **1** : aîné *m*, aînée *f* **2** : ancien *m* (d'une église ou d'un village)
elderberry ['ɛldərˌbɛri] *n, pl* **-ries 1** : sureau *m* (arbre) **2** : baie *f* de sureau (fruit)
elderly ['ɛldərli] *adj* : âgé
eldest ['ɛldəst] *adj* : aîné <his eldest son : son fils aîné>
elect[1] [i'lɛkt] *vt* : élire, choisir
elect[2] *adj* : élu, futur <the president elect : le futur president>
elect[3] *npl* **the elect** : les élus
election [i'lɛkʃən] *n* : élection *f*
elective[1] [i'lɛktɪv] *adj* **1** : électif **2** OPTIONAL : facultatif
elective[2] *n* : cours *m* facultatif
electoral [i'lɛktərəl] *adj* : électoral
electorate [i'lɛktərət] *n* : électorat *m*
electric [i'lɛktrɪk] *or* **electrical** [-trɪkəl] *adj* : électrique — **electrically** [-trɪkəli] *adv*
electrician [iˌlɛk'trɪʃən] *n* : électricien *m*, -cienne *f*
electricity [iˌlɛk'trɪsət̬i] *n, pl* **-ties 1** : électricité *f* **2** CURRENT : courant *m* électrique
electrification [iˌlɛktrəfə'keɪʃən] *n* : électrification *f*
electrify [i'lɛktrəˌfaɪ] *vt* **-fied; -fying 1** : électrifier, électriser **2** THRILL : électriser
electrocardiogram [iˌlɛktro'kɑrdiəˌgræm] *n* : électrocardiogramme *m*
electrocardiograph [iˌlɛktro'kɑrdiəˌgræf] *n* : électrocardiographe *m*
electrocute [i'lɛktrəˌkjuːt] *vt* **-cuted; -cuting** : électrocuter
electrocution [iˌlɛktrə'kjuːʃən] *n* : électrocution *f*
electrode [i'lɛkˌtroːd] *n* : électrode *f*
electrolysis [iˌlɛk'trɑləsɪs] *n* : électrolyse *f*
electrolyte [i'lɛktrəˌlaɪt] *n* : électrolyte *m*
electromagnet [iˌlɛktro'mægnət] *n* : électroaimant *m*
electromagnetic [iˌlɛktromæg'nɛt̬ɪk] *adj* : électromagnétique
electromagnetism [iˌlɛktro'mægnətɪzəm] *n* : électromagnétisme *m*
electron [i'lɛkˌtrɑn] *n* : électron *m*
electronic [iˌlɛk'trɑnɪk] *adj* : électronique — **electronically** [-nɪkli] *adv*
electronic mail *n* : courrier *m* électronique, courriel *m Can*, mél *m Bel, France*
electronics [iˌlɛk'trɑnɪks] *n* : électronique *f*
elegance ['ɛlɪgənts] *n* : élégance *f*
elegant ['ɛlɪgənt] *adj* : élégant
elegantly ['ɛlɪgəntli] *adv* : élégamment
elegiac [ˌɛlə'dʒaɪək] *adj* : élégiaque
elegy ['ɛlədʒi] *n, pl* **-gies** : élégie *f*
element ['ɛləmənt] *n* **1** : élément *m* (en science) **2** COMPONENT : élément *m*, part *f*, facteur *m* <an element of truth : une part de vérité> <the element of

chance : le facteur chance> **3 elements** *npl* RUDIMENTS : éléments *mpl*, rudiments *mpl* **4 the elements** WEATHER : les éléments

elemental [ˌɛləˈmɛntəl] *adj* : élémentaire

elementary [ˌɛləˈmɛntri] *adj* **1** SIMPLE : élémentaire **2** : de l'enseignement primaire

elementary school *n* : école *f* primaire

elephant [ˈɛləfənt] *n* : éléphant *m*

elevate [ˈɛləˌveɪt] *vt* **-vated; -vating** : élever

elevation [ˌɛləˈveɪʃən] *n* **1** ELEVATING : élévation *f* **2** ALTITUDE : altitude *f*, hauteur *f*

elevator [ˈɛləˌveɪt̬ər] *n* **1** : ascenseur *m* (dans un bâtiment) **2** *or* **grain elevator** : élévateur *m*

eleven[1] [ɪˈlɛvən] *adj* : onze

eleven[2] *n* : onze *m*

eleventh[1] [ɪˈlɛvənθ] *adj* : onzième

eleventh[2] *n* **1** : onzième *mf* (dans une série) **2** : onzième *m* (en mathématiques) **3** (*used in dates*) <the eleventh of February : le onze février>

elf [ˈɛlf] *n, pl* **elves** [ˈɛlvz] : elfe *m*, lutin *m*

elfin [ˈɛlfən] *adj* **1** : d'elfe, de lutin **2** ENCHANTING, MAGICAL : féerique

elicit [ɪˈlɪsət] *vt* : tirer, arracher, provoquer

eligibility [ˌɛlədʒəˈbɪlət̬i] *n, pl* **-ties** : éligibilité *f*, admissibilité *f*

eligible [ˈɛlədʒəbəl]*adj* : éligible, admissible <eligible for a job : admissible à un poste> <to be eligible for a pension : avoir droit à une retraite>

eliminate [ɪˈlɪməˌneɪt] *vt* **-nated; -nating** : éliminer

elimination [ɪˌlɪməˈneɪʃən] *n* : élimination *f* <by process of elimination : en procédant par élimination>

elite [eɪˈliːt, i-] *n* : élite *f*

elixir [iˈlɪksər] *n* : élixir *m*

elk [ˈɛlk] *n* : élan *m* (d'Europe), wapiti *m* (d'Amérique)

ellipse [ɪˈlɪps, ɛ-] *n* : ellipse *f*

ellipsis [ɪˈlɪpsəs, ɛ-] *n, pl* **-lipses 1** : ellipse *f* **2** : points *mpl* de suspension (en ponctuation)

elliptical [ɪˈlɪptɪkəl, ɛ-] *or* **elliptic** [-tɪk] *adj* : elliptique

elm [ˈɛlm] *n* : orme *m*

elocution [ˌɛləˈkjuːʃən] *n* : élocution *f*

elongate [iˈlɔŋˌgeɪt] *vt* **-gated; -gating** : allonger

elongation [ˌiːˌlɔŋˈgeɪʃən] *n* : allongement *m*

elope [iˈloːp] *vi* **eloped; eloping** : s'enfuir (pour se marier)

elopement [iˈloːpmənt] *n* : fugue *f* amoureuse

eloquence [ˈɛləkwənts] *n* : éloquence *f*

eloquent [ˈɛləˌkwənt] *adj* : éloquent

eloquently [ˈɛləˌkwəntli] *adv* : éloquemment

El Salvadoran[1] [ɛlˌsælvəˈdɔrən] *adj* : salvadorien

El Salvadoran[2] *n* : Salvadorien *m*, -rienne *f*

else[1] [ˈɛls] *adv* **1** DIFFERENTLY : d'autre, de plus <what else could I do? : que pouvais-je faire d'autre?> **2** ELSEWHERE : ailleurs, autre part <everywhere else : partout ailleurs> **3 or else** : autrement, sinon, ou bien <leave now or else you'll be late : partez vite, autrement vous serez en retard>

else[2] *adj* **1** OTHER : d'autre <somebody else : quelqu'un d'autre> **2** MORE : de plus, d'autre <nothing else : rien d'autre> <what else did he say? : que disait-il de plus?>

elsewhere [ˈɛlsˌhwɛr] *adv* : ailleurs, autre part <my thoughts were elsewhere : j'avais l'esprit ailleurs>

elucidate [iˈluːsəˌdeɪt] *vt* **-dated; -dating** : élucider, expliquer

elucidation [iˌluːsəˈdeɪʃən] *n* : élucidation *f*, explication *f*

elude [iˈluːd] *vt* **eluded; eluding** : éluder, échapper à

elusive [iˈluːsɪv] *adj* : élusif, évasif, insaisissable

elusively [iˈluːsɪvli] *adv* : de façon élusive

elves → **elf**

emaciated [iˈmeɪʃiˌeɪt̬əd] *adj* : émacié, décharné

emaciation [iˈmeɪsiˌeɪʃən, -ʃi-] *n* : émaciation *f*, amaigrissement *m*

E–mail [ˈiːˌmeɪl] → **electronic mail**

emanate [ˈɛməˌneɪt] *v* **-nated; -nating** *vi* : émaner — *vt* : exsuder, rayonner de

emanation [ˌɛməˈneɪʃən] *n* : émanation *f*

emancipate [iˈmæntsəˌpeɪt] *vt* **-pated; -pating** : émanciper, affranchir (un esclave)

emancipation [iˌmæntsəˈpeɪʃən] *n* : émancipation *f*, affranchissement *m* (d'un esclave)

emasculate [iˌmæskjəˈleɪt] *vt* **-lated; -lating** : émasculer

embalm [ɪmˈbɑm, ɛm-, -bɑlm] *vt* : embaumer

embankment [ɪmˈbæŋkmənt, ɛm-] *n* **1** : digue *f* (d'une rivière) **2** : remblai *m*, talus *m* (d'une route)

embargo[1] [ɪmˈbɑrgo, ɛm-] *vt* **-goed; -going** : mettre l'embargo sur

embargo[2] *n, pl* **-goes** : embargo *m*

embark [ɪmˈbɑrk, ɛm-] *vt* : embarquer — *vi* **1** : s'embarquer **2 to embark upon** : entreprendre, s'embarquer dans

embarkation [ˌɛmˌbɑrˈkeɪʃən] *n* : embarquement *m*

embarrass [ɪmˈbærəs, ɛm-] *vt* : gêner, embarrasser

embarrassment [ɪmˈbærəsmənt, ɛm-] *n* : gêne *f*, embarras *m*

embassy ['ɛmbəsi] *n, pl* **-sies** : ambassade *f*
embed [ɪm'bɛd, ɛm-] *vt* **-bedded; -bedding** : enfoncer, enchâsser <embedded in one's memory : gravé dans sa mémoire>
embellish [ɪm'bɛlɪʃ, ɛm-] *vt* : embellir, orner, décorer
embellishment [ɪm'bɛlɪʃmənt, ɛm-] *n* : embellissement *m*, ornement *m*
ember ['ɛmbər] *n* **1** : charbon *m* ardent, morceau *m* de braise **2 embers** *npl* : braise *f*
embezzle [ɪm'bɛzəl, ɛm-] *vt* **-zled; -zling** : détourner
embezzlement [ɪm'bɛzəlmənt, ɛm-] *n* : détournement *m* de fonds
embitter [ɪm'bɪt̬ər, ɛm-] *vt* : aigrir, remplir d'amertume
emblem ['ɛmbləm] *n* : emblème *m*
emblematic [ˌɛmblə'mæt̬ɪk] *adj* : emblématique
embodiment [ɪm'bɑdɪmənt, ɛm-] *n* : incarnation *f*, personnification *f*
embody [ɪm'bɑdi, ɛm-] *vt* **-bodied; -bodying 1** INCARNATE : incarner, personnifier **2** INCLUDE : incorporer, inclure
emboss [ɪm'bɑs, ɛm-, -'bɔs] *vt* : emboutir, estamper (un métal), gaufrer (des étoffes, du cuir, du papier)
embrace[1] [ɪm'breɪs, ɛm-] *vt* **-braced; -bracing 1** HUG : embrasser, étreindre **2** ADOPT, TAKE ON : embrasser, adopter, épouser **3** INCLUDE : comprendre, inclure
embrace[2] *n* : étreinte *f*, enlacement *m*
embroider [ɪm'brɔɪdər, ɛm-] *vt* : broder
embroidery [ɪm'brɔɪdəri, ɛm-] *n, pl* **-deries** : broderie *f*
embroil [ɪm'brɔɪl, ɛm-] *vt* : entraîner, mêler <to become embroiled in : se laisser entraîner dans>
embryo ['ɛmbriˌoː] *n* : embryon *m*
embryonic [ˌɛmbri'ɑnɪk] *adj* : embryonnaire
emend [i'mɛnd] *vt* : corriger
emendation [ˌiːmɛn'deɪʃən] *n* : correction *f*
emerald[1] ['ɛmrəld, 'ɛmə-] *adj* : émeraude, en émeraude
emerald[2] *n* : émeraude *f* (pierre précieuse), émeraude *m* (couleur)
emerge [i'mərdʒ] *vi* **emerged; emerging 1** APPEAR : apparaître, surgir **2 to emerge from** : émerger de
emergence [i'mərdʒən*t*s] *n* : apparition *f*, émergence *f*
emergency [i'mərdʒən*t*si] *n, pl* **-cies 1** : cas *m* d'urgence *f* <in case of emergency : en cas d'urgence> **2 emergency exit** : sortie *f* de secours **3 emergency room** : salle *f* des urgences **4 state of emergency** : état *m* d'urgence
emergent [i'mərdʒənt] *adj* : qui émerge, naissant <emergent nations : pays en voie de développement>
emery ['ɛməri] *n, pl* **-eries** : émeri *m*
emery board *n* : lime *f* à ongles
emetic[1] [i'mɛt̬ɪk] *adj* : émétique
emetic[2] *n* : émétique *m*
emigrant ['ɛmɪgrənt] *n* : émigrant *m*, -grante *f*
emigrate ['ɛməˌgreɪt] *vi* **-grated; -grating** : émigrer
emigration [ˌɛmə'greɪʃən] *n* : émigration *f*
eminence ['ɛmənən*t*s] *n* **1** DISTINCTION, PROMINENCE : distinction *f*, rang *m* éminent **2** ELEVATION : éminence *f*, hauteur *f* **3 Your Eminence** : Votre Éminence
eminent ['ɛmənənt] *adj* : éminent
eminently ['ɛmənəntli] *adv* : éminemment, hautement
emissary ['ɛməˌsɛri] *n, pl* **-saries** : émissaire *m*
emission [i'mɪʃən] *n* : émission *f*
emit [i'mɪt] *vt* **emitted; emitting** : émettre, dégager
emote [i'moːt] *vi* **emoted; emoting** : donner dans les émotions (exalté)
emotion [i'moːʃən] *n* : émotion *f*
emotional [i'moːʃənəl] *adj* **1** : émotionnel, émotif <emotional reactions : réactions émotives> **2** MOVING : émouvant
emotionally [i'moːʃənəli] *adv* : avec émotion <to be emotionally disturbed : avoir des troubles émotifs>
emperor ['ɛmpərər] *n* : empereur *m*
emphasis ['ɛmfəsɪs] *n, pl* **-phases** [-ˌsiːz] : accent *m*
emphasize ['ɛmfəˌsaɪz] *vt* **-sized; -sizing** : insister sur, mettre l'accent sur
emphatic [ɪm'fætɪk, ɛm-] *adj* : énergique, catégorique <an emphatic refusal : un refus catégorique> — **emphatically** [-ɪkli] *adv*
empire ['ɛmˌpaɪr] *n* : empire *m*
empirical [ɪm'pɪrɪkəl, ɛm-] *adj* : empirique — **empirically** [-ɪkli] *adv*
employ[1] [ɪm'plɔɪ, ɛm-] *vt* : employer
employ[2] [ɪm'plɔɪ, ɛm-; 'ɪmˌ-, 'ɛmˌ-] *n* **to be in the employ of** : être employé par
employee *or* **employe** [ɪmˌplɔɪ'iː, ɛm-, -'plɔɪˌiː] *n* : employé *m*, -ployée *f*; salarié *m*, -riée *f*
employer [ɪm'plɔiər, ɛm-] *n* : employeur *m*, -ployeuse *f*
employment [ɪm'plɔɪmənt, ɛm-] *n* : emploi *m*, travail *m*
empower [ɪm'paʊər, ɛm-] *vt* : autoriser, habiliter
empowerment [ɪm'paʊərmənt, ɛm-] *n* : autorisation *f*
empress ['ɛmprəs] *n* : impératrice *f*
emptiness ['ɛmptinəs] *n* : vide *m*
empty[1] ['ɛmpti] *v* **-tied; -tying** *vt* : vider — *vi* **1** : se vider **2** : se jeter <the river empties into the ocean : la rivière se jette dans l'océan>
empty[2] *adj* **emptier; -est 1** : vide **2** VACANT : inocupé, vacant, désert **3**

MEANINGLESS : creux (se dit d'un discours), vain (se dit d'une menace, d'une promesse, etc.)

empty–handed [ˌɛmptiˈhændəd] *adj* : les mains vides

empty–headed [ˌɛmptiˈhɛdəd] *adj* : écervelé

emu [ˈiːˌmjuː] *n* : émeu *m*

emulate [ˈɛmjəˌleɪt] *vt* **-lated; -lating** : imiter

emulation [ˌɛmjəˈleɪʃən] *n* : émulation *f*, imitation *f*

emulsify [ɪˈmʌlsəˌfaɪ] *vt* **-fied; -fying** : émulsionner

emulsion [ɪˈmʌlʃən] *n* : émulsion *f*

enable [ɪˈneɪbəl, ɛ-] *vt* **-abled; -abling 1** EMPOWER : habiliter **2** PERMIT : permettre <it enabled him to swim : ça lui permettait de nager>

enact [ɪˈnækt, ɛ-] *vt* **1** : promulguer (une loi, etc.) **2** PERFORM : jouer, représenter (une scène, un rôle, etc.)

enactment [ɪˈnæktmənt, ɛ-] *n* **1** : promulgation *f* (d'une loi) **2** PERFORMANCE : représentation *f*

enamel[1] [ɪˈnæməl] *vt* **-eled** *or* **-elled; -eling** *or* **-elling** : émailler

enamel[2] *n* : émail *m*

enamor *or Brit* **enamour** [ɪˈnæmər] *vt* **to be enamored of** : être épris de (une personne), être enchanté de (une chose)

encamp [ɪnˈkæmp, ɛn-] *vi* : camper

encampment [ɪnˈkæmpmənt, ɛn-] *n* : campement *m*

encase [ɪnˈkeɪs, ɛn-] *vt* **-cased; -casing 1** CONTAIN : enfermer **2** COVER : recouvrir, entourer

enchant [ɪnˈtʃænt, ɛn-] *vt* : enchanter

enchanting [ɪnˈtʃæntɪŋ, ɛn-] *adj* : charmant, enchanteur, ravissant

enchantment [ɪnˈtʃæntmənt, ɛn-] *n* : enchantement *m*

enchantress [ɪnˈtʃæntrəs, ɛn-] *n* : enchanteresse *f*

encircle [ɪnˈsərkəl, ɛn-] *vt* **-cled; -cling** : entourer, encercler

enclose [ɪnˈkloːz, ɛn-] *vt* **-closed; -closing 1** SURROUND : entourer, clôturer **2** INCLUDE : joindre (à une lettre) <enclosed please find : veuillez trouver ci-joint>

enclosure [ɪnˈkloːʒər, ɛn-] *n* **1** ENCLOSING : clôture *f* **2** AREA, SPACE : enclos *m*, enceinte *f* **3** : pièce *f* jointe (à une lettre)

encompass [ɪnˈkʌmpəs, ɛn-, -ˈkɑm-] *vt* **1** ENCIRCLE : entourer **2** INCLUDE : inclure, comprendre

encore [ˈɑnˌkor] *n* **1** : bis *m* **2 to call for an encore** : bisser

encounter[1] [ɪnˈkaʊntər, ɛn-] *vt* : rencontrer

encounter[2] *n* : rencontre *f*

encourage [ɪnˈkərɪdʒ, ɛn-] *vt* **-aged; -aging 1** HEARTEN : encourager **2** FOSTER, STIMULATE : stimuler, favoriser

encouragement [ɪnˈkərɪdʒmənt, ɛn-] *n* : encouragement *m*

encroach [ɪnˈkroːtʃ, ɛn-] *vi* **to encroach upon** : empiéter sur

encrust [ɪnˈkrʌst, ɛn-] *vt* : incruster

encumber [ɪnˈkʌmbər, ɛn-] *vt* : encombrer, grever <encumbered by debts : grevé de dettes>

encumbrance [ɪnˈkʌmbrənts, ɛn-] *n* **1** BURDEN : charge *f*, fardeau *m* **2** HINDRANCE : gêne *f*, entrave *f*, handicap *m*

encyclopedia [ɪnˌsaɪkləˈpiːdiə, ɛn-] *n* : encyclopédie *f* — **encyclopedic** [-dɪk] *adj*

end[1] [ˈɛnd] *vt* **1** STOP : finir, achever, terminer **2** CONCLUDE : conclure — *vi* **1** : finir, s'achever, se terminer **2 to end up with** : finir par

end[2] *n* **1** : fin *f* **2** EXTREMITY : bout *m*, extrémité *f* **3** PURPOSE : but *m*, fin *f*, dessein *m* <to this end : dans ce but>

endanger [ɪnˈdeɪndʒər, ɛn-] *vt* : mettre en danger

endear [ɪnˈdɪr, ɛn-] *vt* : faire aimer <to endear oneself to s.o. : se faire aimer de qqn>

endearment [ɪnˈdɪrmənt, ɛn-] *n* : tendresse *f* <terms of endearment : mots tendres>

endeavor[1] *or Brit* **endeavour** [ɪnˈdɛvər, ɛn-] *vt* : s'efforcer, essayer <to endeavor to understand : s'efforcer de comprendre>

endeavor[2] *or Brit* **endeavour** *n* : effort *m*, tentative *f*

ending [ˈɛndɪŋ] *n* **1** CONCLUSION : fin *f*, dénouement *m* <a happy ending : un dénouement heureux> **2** SUFFIX : terminaison *f*

endive [ˈɛnˌdaɪv, ˌɑnˈdiːv] *n* : endive *f*

endless [ˈɛndləs] *adj* **1** INTERMINABLE : sans fin, interminable **2** INNUMERABLE : innombrable, sans nombre **3** INEXHAUSTIBLE : inépuisable, infini

endlessly [ˈɛndləsli] *adv* : interminablement, continuellement, sans fin

endocrine [ˈɛndəkrən, -ˌkraɪn, -ˌkriːn] *adj* : endocrine

endorse [ɪnˈdɔrs, ɛn-] *vt* **-dorsed; -dorsing 1** SIGN : endosser **2** SUPPORT : avaliser **3** APPROVE : approuver

endorsement [ɪnˈdɔrsmənt, ɛn-] *n* **1** SIGNATURE : endossement *m* **2** SUPPORT : aval *m* **3** APPROVAL : approbation *f*

endow [ɪnˈdaʊ, ɛn-] *vt* : doter

endowment [ɪnˈdaʊmənt, ɛn-] *n* : dotation *f*

endurable [ɪnˈdʊrəbəl, ɛn-, -ˈdjʊr-] *adj* : supportable, endurable

endurance [ɪnˈdʊrənts, ɛn-, -ˈdjʊr-] *n* : endurance *f*

endure [ɪnˈdʊr, ɛn-, -ˈdjʊr-] *v* **-dured; -during** *vt* BEAR, TOLERATE : supporter, endurer — *vi* LAST : durer

enema [ˈɛnəmə] *n* : lavement *m*

enemy [ˈɛnəmi] *n, pl* **-mies** : ennemi *m*, -mie *f*

energetic [ˌɛnərˈdʒɛṭɪk] *adj* : énergique — **energetically** [-ṭɪkli] *adv*

energize [ˈɛnərˌdʒaɪz] *vt* **-gized; -gizing** : donner de l'énergie à, stimuler

energy [ˈɛnərdʒi] *n, pl* **-gies** : énergie *f*

enervate [ˈɛnərˌveɪt] *vt* **-vated; -vating** : affaiblir, débiliter

enfold [ɪnˈfoːld, ɛn-] *vt* : envelopper, étreindre

enforce [ɪnˈfors, ɛn-] *vt* **-forced; -forcing** : appliquer, imposer (la discipline, etc.), faire respecter (une loi) <to enforce obedience : se faire obéir>

enforcement [ɪnˈforsmənt, ɛn-] *n* : exécution *f*, application *f*

enfranchise [ɪnˈfrænˌtʃaɪz, ɛn-] *vt* **-chised; -chising** : accorder le droit de vote à

enfranchisement [ɪnˈfrænˌtʃaɪzmənt, ɛn-] *n* : admission *f* au suffrage

engage [ɪnˈgeɪdʒ, ɛn-] *v* **-gaged; -gaging** *vt* **1** INVOLVE : engager <to engage s.o. in conversation : engager la conversation avec qqn> **2** EMPLOY : embaucher, engager **3** ATTRACT, DRAW : attirer, éveiller <to engage s.o.'s attention : éveiller l'attention de qqn> **4 to engage the clutch** : embrayer — *vi* **1 to engage in** : se lancer dans, prendre part à **2 to engage in combat** : engager l'ennemi

engaged [ɪnˈgeɪdʒd, ɛn-] *adj* : fiancé <to get engaged to : se fiancer à>

engagement [ɪnˈgeɪdʒmənt, ɛn-] *n* **1** APPOINTMENT : rendez-vous *m* **2** : engagement *m* (d'un acteur, etc.) **3** BETROTHAL : fiançailles *fpl*

engaging [ɪnˈgeɪdʒɪŋ, ɛn-] *adj* : engageant, attirant

engender [ɪnˈdʒɛndər, ɛn-] *vt* **-dered; -dering** : engendrer

engine [ˈɛndʒən] *n* **1** MOTOR : moteur *m* (d'une voiture) **2** LOCOMOTIVE : locomotive *f*

engineer[1] [ˌɛndʒəˈnɪr] *vt* **1** CONSTRUCT : construire **2** CONTRIVE, PLOT : manigancer

engineer[2] *n* **1** : ingénieur *m*, -nieure *f* <civil engineer : ingénieur civil> **2** : mécanicien *m*, -cienne *f* (d'une locomotive)

engineering [ˌɛndʒəˈnɪrɪŋ] *n* : ingénierie *f*, génie *m* <chemical engineering : génie chimique>

English[1] [ˈɪŋglɪʃ, ˈɪŋlɪʃ] *adj* : anglais

English[2] *n* **1** : anglais *m* (langue) **2 the English** : les Anglais

Englishman [ˈɪŋglɪʃmən, ˈɪŋlɪʃ-] *n* : Anglais *m*

Englishwoman [ˈɪŋglɪʃˌwʊmən, ˈɪŋlɪʃ-] *n* : Anglaise *f*

engrave [ɪnˈgreɪv, ɛn-] *vt* **-graved; -graving** : graver

engraver [ɪnˈgreɪvər, ɛn-] *n* : graveur *m*, -veuse *f*

engraving [ɪnˈgreɪvɪŋ, ɛn-] *n* : gravure *f*

engross [ɪnˈgroːs, ɛn-] *vt* : absorber, occuper

engulf [ɪnˈgʌlf, ɛn-] *vt* : engouffrer, engloutir

enhance [ɪnˈhænts, ɛn-] *vt* **-hanced; -hancing** : améliorer, augmenter, rehausser

enhancement [ɪnˈhæntsmənt, ɛn-] *n* : amélioration *f*, augmentation *f*, majoration *f*

enigma [ɪˈnɪgmə] *n* : énigme *f*

enigmatic [ˌɛnɪgˈmæṭɪk, ˌiːnɪg-] *adj* : énigmatique — **enigmatically** [-ṭɪkli] *adv*

enjoin [ɪnˈdʒɔɪn, ɛn-] *vt* **1** COMMAND : enjoindre, ordonner **2** FORBID : interdire

enjoy [ɪnˈdʒɔɪ, ɛn-] *vt* **1** : aimer, prendre plaisir à <I enjoy reading : je prends plaisir à lire> **2** : jouir de <she enjoys good health : elle jouit d'une bonne santé> **3 to enjoy oneself** : s'amuser

enjoyable [ɪnˈdʒɔɪəbəl, ɛn-] *adj* : agréable

enjoyment [ɪnˈdʒɔɪmənt, ɛn-] *n* : plaisir *m*, jouissance *f*

enlarge [ɪnˈlɑrdʒ, ɛn-] *v* **-larged; -larging** *vt* : agrandir, élargir — *vi* **1** : s'agrandir **2 to enlarge upon** : s'étendre sur, développer

enlargement [ɪnˈlɑrdʒmənt, ɛn-] *n* : agrandissement *m*, élargissement *m*

enlighten [ɪnˈlaɪtən, ɛn-] *vt* : éclairer

enlightenment [ɪnˈlaɪtənmənt, ɛn-] *n* **1** CLARIFICATION : éclaircissements *mpl* **2** EDIFICATION : édification *f*, instruction *f* **3 the Enlightenment** : le Siècle des lumières

enlist [ɪnˈlɪst, ɛn-] *vt* **1** ENROLL : enrôler, recruter **2** OBTAIN : obtenir, mobiliser (du soutien, etc.) — *vi* : s'engager, s'enrôler <he enlisted in the army : il s'est engagé dans l'armée>

enlistment [ɪnˈlɪstmənt, ɛn-] *n* : engagement *m*, recrutement *m*, enrôlement *m*

enliven [ɪnˈlaɪvən, ɛn-] *vt* : animer, égayer

enmity [ˈɛnməṭi] *n, pl* **-ties** : inimitié *f*, hostilité *f*

ennoble [ɪˈnoːbəl, ɛ-] *vt* **-bled; -bling** : ennoblir, élever

ennui [ˌɑnˈwiː] *n* : ennui *m*

enormity [ɪˈnɔrməṭi] *n, pl* **-ties 1** ATROCITY : atrocité *f* **2** IMMENSITY : énormité *f*

enormous [ɪˈnɔrməs] *adj* : énorme, immense

enormously [ɪˈnɔrməsli] *adv* EXTREMELY : énormément, extrêmement

enough[1] [iˈnʌf] *adv* : assez, suffisamment <he's old enough : il est suffisamment grand> <she writes well enough : elle écrit assez bien>

enough[2] *adj* **1** : assez de, suffisant **2 more than enough** : plus qu'il n'en faut

enough[3] *pron* (*representing a sufficient number, quantity, or amount*) <to have eaten enough : avoir assez mangé> <I've had enough of his foolishness : j'en ai assez de ses bêtises>

enquire [ɪn'kwaɪr, ɛn-], **enquiry** ['ɪnˌkwaɪri, 'ɛn-, -kwəri; ɪn'kwaɪri, ɛn-] → **inquire, inquiry**

enrage [ɪn'reɪdʒ, ɛn-] *vt* **-raged; -raging** : rendre furieux, mettre en rage

enrich [ɪn'rɪtʃ, ɛn-] *vt* : enrichir

enrichment [ɪn'rɪtʃmənt, ɛn-] *n* : enrichissement *m*

enroll *or* **enrol** [ɪn'ro:l, ɛn-] *v* **-rolled; -rolling** *vt* **1** : inscrire (à l'école, etc.) **2** ENLIST : enrôler — *vi* : s'inscrire, s'enrôler

enrollment [ɪn'ro:lmənt, ɛn-] *n* **1** REGISTRATION : inscription *f* **2** ENLISTMENT : enrôlement *m*

en route [ɑn'ru:t, ɛn'raʊt] *adv* : en route

ensconce [ɪn'skɑnts, ɛn-] *vt* **-sconced; -sconcing 1** INSTALL, SETTLE : installer, placer **2 to ensconce oneself** : bien s'installer

ensemble [ɑn'sɑmbəl] *n* : ensemble *m*

enshrine [ɪn'ʃraɪn, ɛn-] *vt* **-shrined; -shrining** : conserver pieusement

ensign ['ɛntsən, 'ɛnˌsaɪn] *n* **1** FLAG : drapeau *m*, pavillon *m* **2** : enseigne *m* (de vaisseau)

enslave [ɪn'sleɪv, ɛn-] *vt* **-slaved; -slaving** : asservir

ensnare [ɪn'snær, ɛn-] *vt* **-snared; -snaring** : prendre au piège, attraper

ensue [ɪn'su:, ɛn-] *vi* **-sued; -suing** : s'ensuivre

ensure [ɪn'ʃʊr, ɛn-] *vt* **-sured; -suring** : assurer, garantir

entail [ɪn'teɪl, ɛn-] *vt* : entraîner, occasionner

entangle [ɪn'tæŋgəl, ɛn-] *vt* **-gled; -gling** : emmêler, enchevêtrer

entanglement [ɪn'tæŋgəlmənt, ɛn-] *n* : enchevêtrement *m*

enter ['ɛntər] *vt* **1** : entrer dans, entrer à **2** RECORD : inscrire, noter **3** INSERT : entrer des données (en informatique) **4** BEGIN : entrer dans, entamer **5 to enter one's mind** : venir à l'esprit — *vi* **1** : entrer **2 to enter into** : entamer, entrer en

enterprise ['ɛntərˌpraɪz] *n* **1** UNDERTAKING : entreprise *f* **2** BUSINESS : affaire *f* commerciale **3** INITIATIVE : initiative *f*

enterprising ['ɛntərˌpraɪzɪŋ] *adj* : entreprenant

entertain [ˌɛntər'teɪn] *vt* **1** AMUSE : amuser, divertir **2** : recevoir <to entertain guests : recevoir des invités> **3** CONSIDER : penser à, considérer (une idée, etc.)

entertainment [ˌɛntər'teɪnmənt] *n* **1** AMUSEMENT : amusement *m*, divertissement *m* **2** PERFORMANCE : spectacle *m*

enthrall *or* **enthral** [ɪn'θrɔl, ɛn-] *vt* **-thralled; -thralling** : captiver, passionner

enthusiasm [ɪn'θu:ziˌæzəm, ɛn-, -'θju:-] *n* : enthousiasme *m*

enthusiast [ɪn'θu:ziˌæst, ɛn-, -'θju:-, -əst] *n* : enthousiaste *mf;* passionné *m*, -née *f* <a soccer enthusiast : un passionné de football>

enthusiastic [ɪnˌθu:zi'æstɪk, ɛn-, -'θju:-] *adj* : enthousiaste

enthusiastically [ɪnˌθu:zi'æstɪkli, ɛn-, -'θju:-] *adv* : avec enthousiasme

entice [ɪn'taɪs, ɛn-] *vt* **-ticed; -ticing** : attirer, allécher <to entice s.o. away from : entraîner qqn à l'écart de>

enticement [ɪn'taɪsmənt, ɛn-] *n* : attrait *m*

entire [ɪn'taɪr, ɛn-] *adj* : entier, complet <my entire life : toute ma vie>

entirely [ɪn'taɪrli, ɛn-] *adv* : entièrement, totalement

entirety [ɪn'taɪrt̬i, ɛn-, -taɪrət̬i] *n, pl* **-ties 1** : totalité *f* **2 in its entirety** : en son entier, dans son ensemble

entitle [ɪn'taɪt̬əl, ɛn-] *vt* **-tled; -tling 1** NAME : intituler **2** AUTHORIZE : autoriser, donner droit à **3 to be entitled to** : avoir le droit de

entitlement [ɪn'taɪt̬əlmənt, ɛn-] *n* : droit *m*

entity ['ɛntət̬i] *n, pl* **-ties** : entité *f*

entomologist [ˌɛntə'mɑlədʒɪst] *n* : entomologiste *mf*

entomology [ˌɛntə'mɑlədʒi] *n* : entomologie *f*

entourage [ˌɑntʊ'rɑʒ] *n* : entourage *m*

entrails ['ɛnˌtreɪlz, -trəlz] *npl* : entrailles *fpl*

entrance[1] [ɪn'træn*t*s, ɛn-] *vt* **-tranced; -trancing** : transporter, ravir

entrance[2] ['ɛntrən*t*s] *n* : entrée *f* <main entrance : entrée principale> <to make an entrance : faire son entrée>

entrant ['ɛntrənt] *n* : concurrent *m*, -rente *f* (dans une course); candidat *m*, -date *f;* participant *m*, -pante *f*

entrap [ɪn'træp, ɛn-] *vt* **-trapped; -trapping** : prendre au piège

entreat [ɪn'tri:t, ɛn-] *vt* : implorer, supplier

entreaty [ɪn'tri:t̬i, ɛn-] *n, pl* **-ties** : supplication *f*, prière *f*

entrée *or* **entree** ['ɑnˌtreɪ, ˌɑn'-] *n* : entrée *f*, plat *m* principal

entrench [ɪn'trɛntʃ, ɛn-] *vt* : retrancher

entrenched [ɪn'trɛntʃt, ɛn-] *adj* **1** UNWAVERING : inébranlable, ferme **2** ESTABLISHED : implanté, bien établi

entrepreneur [ˌɑntrəprə'nər, -'njʊr] *n* : entrepreneur *m*, -neuse *f*

entrust [ɪn'trʌst, ɛn-] *vt* : confier <to entrust s.o. with a mission : confier une mission à qqn>

entry ['ɛntri] *n, pl* **-tries 1** ENTRANCE : entrée *f* **2** : inscription *f* (sur une liste), entrée *f*

entwine [ɪn'twaɪn, ɛn-] *vt* **-twined; -twining** : entrelacer, enlacer
enumerate [ɪ'nu:mə,reɪt, ɛ-, -'nju:-] *vt* **-ated; -ating 1** LIST : énumérer **2** COUNT : dénombrer
enumeration [ɪ,nu:mə'reɪʃən, ɛ-, -,nju:-] *n* : énumération *f,* dénombrement *m*
enunciate [i'nʌntsi,eɪt, ɛ-] *vt* **-ated; -ating 1** STATE : énoncer, exprimer **2** PRONOUNCE : articuler, prononcer
enunciation [i,nʌntsi'eɪʃən, ɛ-] *n* **1** STATEMENT : énonciation *f,* exposition *f* **2** PRONUNCIATION : articulation *f*
envelop [ɪn'vɛləp, ɛn-] *vt* : envelopper
envelope ['ɛnvə,lo:p, 'ɑn-] *n* : enveloppe *f*
enviable ['ɛnviəbəl] *adj* : enviable
envious ['ɛnviəs] *adj* : envieux, jaloux
enviously ['ɛnviəsli] *adv* : avec envie
environment [ɪn'vaɪrənmənt, ɛn-, -vaɪərn-] *n* : environnement *m,* milieu *m*
environmental [ɪn,vaɪrən'mɛntəl, ɛn-, -,vaɪərn-] *adj* : du milieu, écologique <environmental studies : études de l'environnement>
environmentalist [ɪn,vaɪrən'məntəlɪst, ɛn-, -,vaɪərn] *n* : écologiste *mf*
environs [ɪn'vaɪrənz, ɛn-, -'vaɪərnz] *npl* : environs *mpl,* alentours *mpl*
envisage [ɪn'vɪzɪdʒ, ɛn-] *vt* **-aged; -aging 1** IMAGINE : envisager **2** FORESEE : prévoir
envision [ɪn'vɪʒən, ɛn-] *vt* : envisager
envoy ['ɛn,vɔɪ, 'ɑn-] *n* : envoyé *m,* -voyée *f*
envy[1] ['ɛnvi] *vt* **-vied; -vying** : envier
envy[2] *n* : envie *f,* jalousie *f*
enzyme ['ɛn,zaɪm] *n* : enzyme *f*
eon ['i:ən, i:,ɑn] → **aeon**
epaulet [,ɛpə'lɛt] *n* : épaulette *f*
ephemeral [ɪ'fɛmərəl, -'fi:-] *adj* : éphémère
epic[1] ['ɛpɪk] *adj* : épique
epic[2] *n* : épopée *f*
epicure ['ɛpɪ,kjʊr] *n* : gourmet *m,* gastronome *mf*
epicurean [,ɛpɪkjʊ'ri:ən, -'kjʊriən] *adj* : épicurien
epidemic[1] [,ɛpə'dɛmɪk] *adj* : épidémique
epidemic[2] *n* : épidémie *f*
epidermis [,ɛpə'dərməs] *n* : épiderme *m*
epigram ['ɛpə,græm] *n* : épigramme *f*
epilepsy ['ɛpə,lɛpsi] *n, pl* **-sies** : épilepsie *f*
epileptic[1] [,ɛpə'lɛptɪk] *adj* : épileptique <epileptic fit : crise d'épilepsie>
epileptic[2] *n* : épileptique *mf*
episcopal [ɪ'pɪskəpəl] *adj* : épiscopal <the Episcopal Church : l'Église épiscopale>
episode ['ɛpə,so:d] *n* : épisode *m*
episodic [,ɛpə'sɑdɪk] *adj* : épisodique
epistle [ɪ'pɪsəl] *n* : épître *f*
epitaph ['ɛpə,tæf] *n* : épitaphe *f*
epithet ['ɛpə,θɛt, -θət] *n* : épithète *f*
epitome [ɪ'pɪt̬əmi] *n* **1** SUMMARY : abrégé *m,* résumé *m* **2** EMBODIMENT : exemple *m* même, modèle *m*
epitomize [ɪ'pɪt̬ə,maɪz] *vt* **-mized; -mizing 1** SUMMARIZE : abréger **2** EMBODY : incarner, personnifier
epoch ['ɛpək, 'ɛ,pɑk, 'i:,pɑk] *n* : époque *f*
equable ['ɛkwəbəl, 'i:-] *adj* : égal, constant (se dit du climat), placide (se dit des personnes)
equal[1] ['i:kwəl] *vt* **equaled** *or* **equalled; equaling** *or* **equalling** : égaler
equal[2] *adj* **1** SAME : égal, même <equal pay : salaire égal> <of equal value : de même valeur> **2 to be equal to** : être à la hauteur de <I didn't feel equal to going : je ne me sentais pas capable de sortir>
equal[3] *n* : égal *m,* -gale *f*
equality [ɪ'kwɑlət̬i] *n, pl* **-ties** : égalité *f*
equalize ['i:kwə,laɪz] *vt* **-ized; -izing** : égaliser
equally ['i:kwəli] *adv* : également <to divide sth equally : diviser qqch en parts égales>
equanimity [,i:kwə'nɪmət̬i, ,ɛ-] *n, pl* **-ties** : égalité *f* d'humeur, sérénité *f,* équanimité *f*
equate [ɪ'kweɪt] *vt* **equated; equating 1** LIKEN, COMPARE : mettre sur le même pied, assimiler **2** EQUALIZE : égaliser **3 to equate with** : mettre en équation avec (en mathématiques)
equation [ɪ'kweɪʒən] *n* : équation *f*
equator [ɪ'kweɪt̬ər] *n* : équateur *m*
equatorial [,i:kwə'toriəl, ,ɛ-] *adj* : équatorial
equestrian[1] [ɪ'kwɛstriən, ɛ-] *adj* : équestre
equestrian[2] *n* : cavalier *m,* -lière *f*
equilateral [,i:kwə'læt̬ərəl, ,ɛ-] *adj* : équilatéral
equilibrium [,i:kwə'lɪbriəm, ,ɛ-] *n, pl* **-riums** *or* **-ria** : équilibre *m*
equine ['i:,kwaɪn, 'ɛ-] *adj* : chevalin
equinox ['i:kwə,nɑks, 'ɛ-] *n* : équinoxe *m*
equip [ɪ'kwɪp] *vt* **equipped; equipping 1** FURNISH, SUPPLY : équiper, outiller, munir **2** PREPARE : préparer
equipment [ɪ'kwɪpmənt] *n* : équipement *m,* matériel *m*
equitable ['ɛkwət̬əbəl] *adj* : équitable, juste
equity ['ɛkwət̬i] *n, pl* **-ties 1** FAIRNESS : équité *f* **2 equities** *npl* SECURITIES : actions *fpl* ordinaires
equivalence [ɪ'kwɪvələnts] *n* : équivalence *f*
equivalent[1] [ɪ'kwɪvələnt] *adj* : équivalent
equivalent[2] *n* : équivalent *m*
equivocal [ɪ'kwɪvəkəl] *adj* : équivoque
equivocate [ɪ'kwɪvə,keɪt] *vi* **-cated; -cating** : user d'équivoques
equivocation [ɪ,kwɪvə'keɪʃən] *n* : paroles *fpl* équivoques

era ['ɪrə, 'ɛrə, 'i:rə] *n* : ère *f,* époque *f*
eradicate [ɪ'rædə,keɪt] *vt* **-cated; -cating** : éradiquer
erase [ɪ'reɪs] *vt* **erased; erasing** : effacer, gommer
eraser [ɪ'reɪsər] *n* : gomme *f,* efface *f Can*
erasure [ɪ'reɪʃər] *n* : effacement *m*
ere[1] ['ɛr] *conj* : avant que <ere I can leave : avant que je puisse partir>
ere[2] *prep* **1** BEFORE : avant **2 ere long** : sous peu, bientôt
erect[1] [ɪ'rɛkt] *vt* **1** BUILD : bâtir, construire **2** RAISE : ériger, élever (une statue, un édifice, etc.) **3** ESTABLISH : ériger, établir
erect[2] *adj* : droit <to stand erect : se tenir droit>
erection [ɪ'rɛkʃən]*n* **1** CONSTRUCTION : construction *f* **2** : érection *f* (en physiologie)
Eritrean[1] [,ɛrə'tri:ən, -'treɪən] *adj* : erythréen
Eritrean[2] *n* : Erythréen *m,* -thréenne *f*
ermine ['ərmən] *n* : hermine *f*
erode [ɪ'ro:d] *v* **eroded; eroding** *vt* : éroder, ronger — *vi* : s'éroder
erosion [ɪ'ro:ʒən] *n* : érosion *f*
erotic [ɪ'rɑṭɪk] *adj* : érotique — **erotically** [-ṭɪkli] *adv*
eroticism [ɪ'rɑṭə,sɪzəm] *n* : érotisme *m*
err ['ɛr, 'ər] *vi* : se tromper <to err on the side of caution : pécher par excès de prudence>
errand ['ɛrənd] *n* : course *f,* commission *f* <to run errands : faire des commissions>
errant ['ɛrənt] *adj* **1** WANDERING : errant **2** MISBEHAVING : dévoyé
erratic [ɪ'ræṭɪk] *adj* **1** IRREGULAR, UNPREDICTABLE : irrégulier, imprévisible **2** : erratique (en géologie, en médecine)
erratically [ɪ'ræṭɪkli] *adv* : irregulièrement, de manière capricieuse
erroneous [ɪ'ro:niəs, ɛ-] *adj* : erroné, faux
erroneously [ɪ'ro:niəsli, ɛ-] *adv* : à tort, erronément
error ['ɛrər] *n* : erreur *f,* faute *f* <to see the error of one's ways : revenir de ses erreurs>
erstwhile ['ərst,*h*waɪl] *adj* FORMER : d'autrefois, ancien
erudite ['ɛrə,daɪt, 'ɛrjʊ-] *adj* : érudit, savant
erudition [,ɛrə'dɪʃən, ,ɛrjʊ-] *n* : érudition *f*
erupt [ɪ'rʌpt] *vi* **1** : entrer en éruption (se dit d'un volcan) **2** : éclater (se dit de la guerre, d'un rire, etc.)
eruption [ɪ'rʌpʃən] *n* : éruption *f*
escalate ['ɛskə,leɪt] *v* **-lated; -lating** *vt* **1** INTENSIFY : intensifier, aggraver **2** INCREASE : augmenter — *vi* **1** INTENSIFY : s'intensifier, s'aggraver **2** INCREASE : monter en flèche (se dit des prix, etc.)
escalation [,ɛskə'leɪʃən] *n* **1** INTENSIFICATION : intensification *f* **2** INCREASE : montée *f* en flèche
escalator ['ɛskə,leɪtər] *n* : escalier *m* mécanique
escapade ['ɛskə,peɪd] *n* : équipée *f,* frasque *f*
escape[1] [ɪ'skeɪp, ɛ-] *v* **-caped; -caping** *vt* **1** AVOID : échapper à, éviter **2** ELUDE : échapper à <his name escapes me : son nom m'échappe> **3 to escape notice** : passer inaperçu — *vi* **1** : s'échapper, s'évader **2 to escape from reality** : fuir la réalité
escape[2] *n* **1** FLIGHT : fuite *f,* évasion *f* **2** LEAKAGE : fuite *f* (d'un liquide ou d'un gaz), échappement *m* (de vapeurs)
escapee [ɪ,skeɪ'pi:, ,ɛ-] *n* : évadé *m,* -dée *f*
escarole ['ɛskə,ro:l] *n* : scarole *f*
escarpment [ɪs'kɑrpmənt, ɛs-] *n* : escarpement *m*
eschew [ɛ'ʃu:, ɪs'tʃu:] *vt* : éviter, s'abstenir de
escort[1] [ɪ'skɔrt, ɛ-] *vt* : escorter, accompagner
escort[2] ['ɛs,kɔrt] *n* **1** : escorte *f* <under police escort : sous escorte policière> **2** COMPANION : compagnon *m,* compagne *f*
escrow ['ɛs,kro:] *n* : séquestre *m* <in escrow : en séquestre>
esophagus [ɪ'sɑfəgəs, i:-] *n, pl* **-gi** [-,gaɪ, -,dʒaɪ] : œsophage *m*
esoteric [,ɛsə'tɛrɪk] *adj* : ésotérique
especially [ɪ'spɛʃəli] *adv* **1** PARTICULARLY : particulièrement, surtout **2** EXPRESSLY : exprès <he came especially to see you : il est venu exprès pour vous voir> **3 especially as** : d'autant plus que
espionage ['ɛspiə,nɑʒ, -,nɑdʒ] *n* : espionnage *m*
espouse [ɪ'spaʊz, ɛ-] *vt* **espoused; espousing** : épouser
espresso [ɛ'sprɛ,so:] *n, pl* **-sos** : express *m,* café *m* express
essay[1] [ɛ'seɪ, 'ɛ,seɪ] *vt* ATTEMPT : essayer, tenter
essay[2] ['ɛ,seɪ] *n* **1** ATTEMPT : essai *m,* tentative *f* **2** COMPOSITION : essai *m* (littéraire), dissertation *f* (à l'école)
essayist ['ɛ,seɪɪst] *n* : essayiste *mf*
essence ['ɛsən*t*s] *n* **1** CORE : essence *f* <in essence : par essence, essentiellement> **2** EXTRACT : essence *f,* extrait *m* <essence of violets : essence de violette> <essence of vanilla : extrait de vanille>
essential[1] [ɪ'sɛntʃəl] *adj* : essentiel — **essentially** *adv*
essential[2] *n* **1** : objet *m* essentiel **2 the essentials** : l'essentiel *m*
establish [ɪ'stæblɪʃ, ɛ-] *vt* **1** PROVE : établir, démontrer **2** FOUND : établir, fonder, créer

establishment [ɪ'stæblɪʃmənt, ɛ-] *n* **1** ESTABLISHING : fondation *f,* création *f,* établissement *m* **2** INSTITUTION : établissement *m* **3 the Establishment** : les pouvoirs établis

estate [ɪ'steɪt, ɛ-] *n* **1** POSSESSIONS : biens *mpl,* fortune *f* **2** LAND, PROPERTY : propriété *f,* domaine *m*

esteem[1] [ɪ'sti:m, ɛ-] *vt* : estimer

esteem[2] *n* : estime *f* <in high esteem : en haute estime>

ester ['ɛstər] *n* : ester *m*

esthetic [ɛs'θɛt̬ɪk] → **aesthetic**

estimable ['ɛstəməbəl] *adj* : estimable

estimate[1] ['ɛstəˌmeɪt] *vt* **-mated; -mating** : estimer, évaluer

estimate[2] ['ɛstəmət] *n* : estimation *f,* évaluation *f,* devis *m*

estimation [ˌɛstə'meɪʃən] *n* **1** JUDGMENT : jugement *m* <in my estimation : à mon avis> **2** ESTIMATE : estimation *f* **3** ESTEEM : estime *f,* considération *f*

Estonian[1] [ɛ'sto:niən] *adj* : estonien

Estonian[2] *n* **1** : Estonien *m,* -nienne *f* **2** : estonien *m* (langue)

estrange [ɪ'streɪndʒ, ɛ-] *vt* **-tranged; -tranging** : brouiller, éloigner

estrangement [ɪ'streɪndʒmənt, ɛ-] *n* : éloignement *m,* brouille *f* (avec un ami), séparation *f* (d'un époux)

estrogen ['ɛstrədʒən] *n* : estrogène *m*

estuary ['ɛstʃʊˌwɛri] *n, pl* **-aries** : estuaire *m*

et cetera [ɛt'sɛt̬ərə, -'sɛtrə] : et cætera, et cetera

etch ['ɛtʃ] *vt* : graver à l'eau-forte <etched in her memory : gravé dans sa mémoire>

etching ['ɛtʃɪŋ] *n* : eau-forte *f* (dessin), gravure *f* à l'eau-forte (technique)

eternal [ɪ'tərnəl, i:-] *adj* : éternel — **eternally** *adv*

eternity [ɪ'tərnət̬i, i:-] *n, pl* **-ties** : éternité *f*

ethane ['ɛˌθeɪn] *n* : éthane *m*

ether ['i:θər] *n* : éther *m*

ethereal [ɪ'θɪriəl, i:-] *adj* : éthéré

ethical ['ɛθɪkəl] *adj* : éthique, moral

ethically ['ɛθɪkəli] *adv* : moralement

ethics ['ɛθɪks] *ns & pl* : éthique *f,* morale *f*

Ethiopian[1] [ˌi:θi'o:piən] *adj* : éthiopien

Ethiopian[2] *n* : Éthiopien *m,* -pienne *f*

ethnic ['ɛθnɪk] *adj* : ethnique

ethnologist [ɛθ'nɑlədʒɪst] *n* : ethnologue *mf*

ethnology [ɛθ'nɑlədʒi] *n* : ethnologie *f*

etiquette ['ɛt̬ɪkət, -ˌkɛt] *n* : étiquette *f,* convenances *fpl,* bienséance *f*

etymological [ˌɛt̬əmə'lɑdʒɪkəl] *adj* : étymologique

etymology [ˌɛt̬ə'mɑlədʒi] *n, pl* **-gies** : étymologie *f*

eucalyptus [ˌju:kə'lɪptəs] *n, pl* **-ti** [-ˌtaɪ] *or* **-tuses** [-təsəz] : eucalyptus *m*

Eucharist ['ju:kərɪst] *n* : Eucharistie *f*

eulogize ['ju:ləˌdʒaɪz] *vt* **-gized; -gizing** : faire l'éloge de, faire le panégyrique de

eulogy ['ju:lədʒi] *n, pl* **-gies** : éloge *m,* panégyrique *m*

eunuch ['ju:nək] *n* : eunuque *m*

euphemism ['ju:fəˌmɪzəm] *n* : euphémisme *m*

euphemistic [ˌju:fə'mɪstɪk] *adj* : euphémique

euphony ['ju:fəni] *n, pl* **-nies** : euphonie *f*

euphoria [jʊ'foriə] *n* : euphorie *f*

euphoric [jʊ'forɪk] *adj* : euphorique

European[1] [ˌju:rə'pi:ən, -pi:n] *adj* : européen

European[2] *n* : Européen *m,* -péenne *f*

euthanasia [ju:θə'neɪʒə, -ʒiə] *n* : euthanasie *f*

evacuate [ɪ'vækjʊˌeɪt] *vt* **-ated; -ating** : évacuer

evacuation [ɪˌvækjʊ'eɪʃən] *n* : évacuation *f*

evade [ɪ'veɪd] *vt* **evaded; evading** : éviter, esquiver, échapper à

evaluate [ɪ'væljʊˌeɪt] *vt* **-ated; -ating** : évaluer

evaluation [ɪ'væljʊ'eɪʃən] *n* : évaluation *f*

evangelical [ˌi:ˌvæn'dʒɛlɪkəl, ˌɛvən-] *adj* : évangélique

evangelist [ɪ'vændʒəlɪst] *n* : évangéliste *m*

evaporate [ɪ'væpəˌreɪt] *v* **-rated; -rating** *vi* **1** VAPORIZE : s'évaporer **2** DISAPPEAR : s'envoler, s'évaporer *fam* — *vt* : faire évaporer

evaporation [ɪˌvæpə'reɪʃən] *n* : évaporation *f*

evasion [ɪ'veɪʒən] *n* : évasion *f*

evasive [ɪ'veɪsɪv] *adj* : évasif

eve ['i:v] *n* : veille *f* <Christmas Eve : la veille de Noël>

even[1] ['i:vən] *vt* : égaliser — *vi or* **to even out** : s'égaliser

even[2] *adv* **1** : même <even a child can do it : même un enfant peut le faire> <he didn't even try : il n'a même pas essayé> **2** (*in comparisons*) : encore <even better : encore mieux> **3 even as** : au moment même où **4 even if** : même si **5 even so** : quand même **6 even then** : même alors

even[3] *adj* **1** REGULAR, STEADY : régulier, égal, constant <an even temperature : une température constante> **2** FLAT, SMOOTH : uni, plat **3** EQUAL : égal, équitable <an even trade : un échange équitable> <to get even : se venger> <we're even! : nous sommes quittes!> **4** : pair <an even number : un nombre pair>

evening ['i:vnɪŋ] *n* **1** : soir *m* <he's going out this evening : il sort ce soir> <good evening! : bon soir!> <every evening : tous les soirs> **2** (*emphasizing duration*) : soirée *f* <the whole

evening : toute la soirée> <have a nice evening! : bonne soirée!>

event [ɪ'vɛnt] *n* **1** OCCURRENCE : événement *m* **2** CONTINGENCY : cas *m* <in any event : en tout cas> <in the event that : au cas où> **3** : épreuve *f* (aux sports)

eventful [ɪ'vɛntfəl] *adj* **1** : mouvementé <an eventful week : une semaine mouvementée> **2** MOMENTOUS : mémorable

eventual [ɪ'vɛntʃʊəl] *adj* : final, qui s'ensuit <his eventual ruin : sa ruine finale>

eventuality [ɪ,vɛntʃʊ'ælət̬i] *n, pl* **-ties** : éventualité *f*

eventually [ɪ'vɛntʃʊəli] *adv* : finalement

ever ['ɛvər] *adv* **1** ALWAYS : toujours <he's the same as ever : il est toujours le même> **2** : jamais <more beautiful than ever : plus belle que jamais> <nothing ever happens : il ne se passe jamais rien> **3 ever since** : depuis (lors)

evergreen[1] ['ɛvər,gri:n] *adj* : à feuilles persistantes

evergreen[2] *n* : plante *f* à feuilles persistantes

everlasting [,ɛvər'læstɪŋ] *adj* : éternel

every ['ɛvri] *adj* **1** EACH : chaque, tout, tous les <every morning : chaque matin> <every moment : à tout moment> <every store in town : tous les magasins de la ville> **2** ALL : tous <every kind of : toutes sortes de> **3** COMPLETE : plein, entier <to have every confidence in : avoir pleine confiance en> **4 every other** : tous les deux <every other day : tous les deux jours>

everybody ['ɛvri,bʌdi, -'bɑ-] *pron* : tout le monde, chacun

everyday [,ɛvri'deɪ, 'ɛvri,-] *adj* : quotidien, de tous les jours <everyday clothes : vêtements de tous les jours> <in everyday use : d'usage courant>

everyone ['ɛvri,wʌn] → **everybody**

everything ['ɛvri,θɪŋ] *pron* : tout

everywhere ['ɛvri,*h*wɛr] *adv* : partout <everywhere in the world : partout dans le monde>

evict [ɪ'vɪkt] *vt* : expulser

eviction [ɪ'vɪkʃən] *n* : expulsion *f*

evidence ['ɛvədən*t*s] *n* **1** INDICATION : signe *m,* marque *f* <to be in evidence : être (très) en vue> **2** PROOF : témoignage *m,* évidence *f* **3** TESTIMONY : témoignage *m,* déposition *f* <to give evidence : témoigner>

evident ['ɛvɪdənt] *adj* : évident, manifeste

evidently ['ɛvɪdəntli, ,ɛvɪ'dɛntli] *adv* **1** OBVIOUSLY : évidemment, manifestement **2** APPARENTLY : apparemment

evil[1] ['i:vəl, -vɪl] *adj* **eviler** *or* **eviller; evilest** *or* **evillest** : mauvais, méchant

evil[2] *n* : mal *m* <good and evil : le bien et le mal>

evildoer [,i:vəl'du:ər, ,i:vɪl-] *n* : malfaiteur *m;* scélérat *m,* -rate *f*

evince [ɪ'vɪn*t*s] *vt* **evinced; evincing** : manifester, faire preuve de

eviscerate [ɪ'vɪsə,reɪt] *vt* **-ated; -ating** : éventrer, étriper

evocation [,i:vo'keɪʃən, ,ɛ-] *n* : évocation *f*

evocative [i'vɑkət̬ɪv] *adj* : évocateur

evoke [i'vo:k] *vt* **evoked; evoking** : évoquer

evolution [,ɛvə'lu:ʃən, ,i:-] *n* : évolution *f*

evolve [i'vɑlv] *v* **evolved; evolving** *vt* : développer, élaborer — *vi* : évoluer

ewe ['ju:] *n* : brebis *f*

exact[1] [ɪg'zækt, ɛ-] *vt* : exiger

exact[2] *adj* : exact, précis, juste <to have the exact time : avoir l'heure juste> <can you be more exact? : pouvez-vous préciser un peu?>

exacting [ɪ'zæktɪŋ, ɛg-] *adj* : exigeant, astreignant

exactitude [ɪg'zæktə,tu:d, ɛg-, -,tju:d] *n* : exactitude *f*

exactly [ɪg'zæktli, ɛg-] *adv* : exactement, juste <that's exactly what I thought : c'est exactement ce que je pensais> <it's exactly four o'clock : il est quatre heures juste>

exaggerate [ɪg'zædʒə,reɪt, ɛg-] *v* **-ated; -ating** : exagérer

exaggeration [ɪg'zædʒə'reɪʃən, ɛg-] *n* : exagération *f*

exalt [ɪg'zɔlt, ɛg-] *vt* : exalter, glorifier

exaltation [,ɛg,zɔl'teɪʃən, ɛk,sɔl-] *n* : exaltation *f*

exam [ɪg'zæm, ɛg-] → **examination**

examination [ɪg,zæmə'neɪʃən, ɛg-] *n* **1** TEST : examen *m* **2** INSPECTION : inspection *f,* examen *m* **3** INTERROGATION : interrogatoire *m*

examine [ɪg'zæmən, ɛg-] *vt* **-ined; -ining 1** TEST : examiner **2** INSPECT : examiner, inspecter, étudier **3** QUESTION : interroger <to examine a witness : interroger un témoin>

example [ɪg'zæmpəl, ɛg-] *n* : exemple *m* <for example : par exemple> <to set an example : donner l'exemple>

exasperate [ɪg'zæspə,reɪt, ɛg-] *vt* **-ated; -ating 1** : exaspérer **2 to become exasperated** : s'exaspérer

exasperation [ɪg,zæspə'reɪʃən, ɛg-] *n* : exaspération *f*

excavate ['ɛkskə,veɪt] *v* **-vated; -vating** *vt* **1** DIG : creuser, excaver **2** UNEARTH : fouiller, déterrer — *vi* : faire des fouilles (en archéologie)

excavation [,ɛkskə'veɪʃən] *n* **1** DIGGING : excavation *f,* creusement *m* **2** : fouilles *nfpl* (en archéologie)

exceed [ɪk'si:d, ɛk-] *vt* **1** SURPASS : excéder, dépasser **2** OVERSTEP : excéder, outrepasser <to exceed one's authority : outrepasser ses pouvoirs>

exceedingly [ɪk'si:dɪŋli, ɛk-] *adv* : extrêmement

excel [ɪk'sɛl, ɛk-] *v* **-celled; -celling** *vt* : surpasser — *vi* : exceller

excellence ['ɛksəˌlənts] *n* : excellence *f*

excellency ['ɛksələntsi] *n, pl* **-cies** : excellence *f* <Your Excellency : Votre Excellence>

excellent ['ɛksəˌlənt] *adj* : excellent

excellently *adv* : admirablement, de façon excellente

except[1] [ɪk'sɛpt] *vt* : excepter, exclure

except[2] *conj* : sauf que, mais <I'd go except it's too far : j'irais mais c'est trop loin>

except[3] *prep* **1** : sauf, excepté <everyone except me : tout le monde sauf moi> **2** (*in questions and negative constructions*) : sinon, sauf <what can one do except wait? : que peut-on faire sinon attendre?> **3 except for** : à part, à l'exception de

exception [ɪk'sɛpʃən] *n* **1** : exception *f* <to make an exception for : faire une exception pour> **2 to take exception to** : s'offenser de

exceptional [ɪk'sɛpʃənəl] *adj* : exceptionnel — **exceptionally** *adv*

excerpt[1] [ɛk'sərpt, ɛg'zərpt, 'ɛkˌ-, 'ɛgˌ-] *vt* : extraire

excerpt[2] [ɛk'sərpt, 'ɛgˌzərpt] *n* : extrait *m*

excess[1] ['ɛkˌsɛs, ɪk'sɛs] *adj* : excédentaire, en trop <excess baggage : un excédent de bagages>

excess[2] [ɪk'sɛs, 'ɛkˌsɛs] *n* **1** : excès *m* <to drink to excess : boire à l'excès> **2** SURPLUS : surplus *m*, excédent *m* **3 in excess of** : en plus de, dépassant

excessive [ɪk'sɛsɪv, ɛk-] *adj* : excessif — **excessively** *adv*

exchange[1] [ɪks'tʃeɪndʒ, ɛks-; 'ɛksˌtʃeɪndʒ] *vt* **-changed; -changing** : échanger

exchange[2] *n* **1** : échange *m* <in exchange for : en échange de> <exchange of ideas : échange d'idées> **2** : change *m* (en finances) <rate of exchange : taux de change>

excise[1] [ɪk'saɪz, ɛk-] *vt* **-cised; -cising** : exciser

excise[2] ['ɛkˌsaɪz] *n or* **excise tax** : taxe *f*

excision [ɪk'sɪʒən, ɛk-] *n* : excision *f*

excitable [ɪk'saɪt̬əbəl, ɛk-] *adj* : excitable, nerveux (se dit d'une personne)

excite [ɪk'saɪt, ɛk-] *vt* **-cited; -citing 1** STIMULATE : exciter <to excite enthusiasm : enthousiasmer> **2** AROUSE : exciter, éveiller, piquer (l'intérêt, la curiosité, etc.)

excited [ɪk'saɪt̬əd, ɛk-] *adj* **1** : excité, énervé, agité **2 to get excited** : s'exciter

excitedly [ɪk'saɪt̬ədli, ɛk-] *adv* : avec agitation <to speak excitedly : parler sur un ton animé>

excitement [ɪk'saɪtmənt, ɛk-] *n* : excitation *f*, agitation *f*

exciting [ɪk'saɪtɪŋ, ɛk-] *adj* : passionnant, excitant

exclaim [ɪks'kleɪm, ɛk-] *vt* : s'écrier — *vi* : s'exclamer

exclamation [ˌɛksklə'meɪʃən] *n* : exclamation *f*

exclamation point *n* : point *m* d'exclamation

exclamatory [ɪks'klæməˌtori, ɛks-] *adj* : exclamatif

exclude [ɪks'klu:d, ɛks-] *vt* **-cluded; -cluding** : exclure

excluding [ɪks'klu:dɪŋ, ɛks-] *prep* : à part, à l'exclusion de

exclusion [ɪks'klu:ʒən, ɛks-] *n* : exclusion *f*

exclusive [ɪks'klu:sɪv, ɛks-] *adj* : exclusif — **exclusively** *adv*

excommunicate [ˌɛkskə'mju:nəˌkeɪt] *vt* **-cated; -cating** : excommunier

excommunication [ˌɛkskəˌmju:nə'keɪʃən] *n* : excommunication *f*

excrement ['ɛkskrəmənt] *n* : excréments *mpl*

excrete [ɪk'skri:t, ɛk-] *vt* **-creted; -creting** : excréter

excretion [ɪk'skri:ʃən, ɛk-] *n* : excrétion *f*

excruciating [ɪk'skru:ʃiˌeɪt̬ɪŋ, ɛk-] *adj* : atroce, insupportable — **excruciatingly** *adv*

exculpate ['ɛkskəlˌpeɪt] *vt* **-pated; -pating** : disculper

excursion [ɪk'skərʒən, ɛk-] *n* **1** OUTING : excursion *f*, sortie *f* **2** DIGRESSION : digression *f*

excuse[1] [ɪk'skju:z, ɛk-] *vt* **-cused; -cusing 1** PARDON : excuser, pardonner **2** EXEMPT : exempter, dispenser **3** JUSTIFY : excuser, justifier **4 to excuse oneself** : s'excuser (de la table, etc.)

excuse[2] [ɪk'skju:s, ɛk-] *n* **1** JUSTIFICATION : excuse *f* **2** PRETEXT : prétexte *m*, excuse *f* **3 to make one's excuses** : présenter ses excuses

execute ['ɛksɪˌkju:t] *vt* **-cuted; -cuting** : exécuter

execution [ˌɛksɪ'kju:ʃən] *n* : exécution *f*

executioner [ˌɛksɪ'kju:ʃənər] *n* : bourreau *m*

executive[1] [ɪg'zɛkjət̬ɪv, ɛg-] *adj* : exécutif

executive[2] *n* **1** MANAGER : cadre *m*; dirigeant *m*, -geante *f* **2** *or* **executive branch** : pouvoir *m* exécutif

executor [ɪg'zɛkjət̬ər, ɛg-] *n* : exécuteur *m* testamentaire

executrix [ɪg'zɛkjəˌtrɪks, ɛg-] *n, pl* **executrices** [-zɛkjə'traɪˌsi:z] *or* **executrixes** [-'zɛkjəˌtrɪksəz] : exécutrice *f* testamentaire

exemplary [ɪg'zɛmpləri, ɛg-] *adj* : exemplaire

exemplify [ɪg'zɛmpləˌfaɪ, ɛg-] *vt* **-fied; -fying** : exemplifier, illustrer

exempt[1] [ɪg'zɛmpt, ɛg-] *vt* : exempter, dispenser
exempt[2] *adj* : exempt
exemption [ɪg'zɛmpʃən, ɛg-] *n* : exemption *f*
exercise[1] ['ɛksər,saɪz] *v* **-cised; -cising** *vt* **1** : exercer (le corps) **2** APPLY : exercer, user de, faire valoir — *vi* : faire de l'exercise
exercise[2] *n* **1** : exercice *m* **2 exercises** *npl* CEREMONY : cérémonie *f*
exert [ɪg'zərt, ɛg-] *vt* **1** APPLY, WIELD : exercer, employer **2 to exert oneself** : se dépenser, s'appliquer, se donner de la peine
exertion [ɪg'zərʃən, ɛg-] *n* **1** EFFORT : effort *m* **2** USE : exercice *m*, emploi *m* (de la force, etc.)
exhalation [,ɛksə'leɪʃən, ,ɛkshə-] *n* : expiration *f*, exhalation *f*
exhale [ɛks'heɪl] *v* **-haled; -haling** *vt* **1** : expirer, exhaler **2** EMIT : exhaler (une odeur) — *vi* : expirer
exhaust[1] [ɪg'zɔst, ɛg-] *vt* **1** : épuiser **2 to exhaust oneself** : s'épuiser, se morfondre *Can*
exhaust[2] *n* **1** *or* **exhaust fumes** : gaz *m* d'échappement **2** *or* **exhaust pipe** : tuyau *m* d'échappement
exhaustion [ɪg'zɔstʃən, ɛg-] *n* : épuisement *m*
exhaustive [ɪg'zɔstɪv, ɛg-] *adj* : exhaustif
exhibit[1] [ɪg'zɪbət, ɛg-] *vt* **1** DISPLAY : exposer (des œuvres d'art, etc.), étaler (des marchandises) **2** PRESENT : montrer, présenter (un document, etc.) **3** MANIFEST : manifester, montrer
exhibit[2] *n* **1** : objet *m* exposé, œuvre *f* exposée **2** EXHIBITION : exposition *f* **3** : pièce *f* à conviction (dans les poursuites judiciaires)
exhibition [,ɛksə'bɪʃən] *n* **1** EXHIBIT : exposition *f* **2 to make an exhibition of oneself** : se donner en spectacle
exhibitor [ɪg'zɪbət̬ər] *n* : exposant *m*, -sante *f*
exhilarate [ɪg'zɪlə,reɪt, ɛg-] *vt* **-rated; -rating** : griser, vivifier
exhilaration [ɪg,zɪlə'reɪʃən, ɛg-] *n* : joie *f*, griserie *f*
exhort [ɪg'zɔrt, ɛg-] *vt* : exhorter
exhortation [,ɛk,sɔr'teɪʃən, -sər-; ,ɛg,zɔr-] *n* : exhortation *f*
exhume [ɪg'zu:m, -'zju:m; ɪks'ju:m, -'hju:m] *vt* **-humed; -huming** : exhumer
exigencies ['ɛksɪdʒəntsiz, ɪg'zɪdʒənt,si:z] *npl* : exigences *fpl*
exile[1] ['ɛg,zaɪl, 'ɛk,saɪl] *vt* **exiled; exiling** : exiler
exile[2] *n* **1** BANISHMENT : exil *m* **2** OUTCAST : exilé *m*, -lée *f*
exist [ɪg'zɪst, ɛg-] *vi* **1** BE : exister **2** LIVE, SURVIVE : vivre, survivre
existence [ɪg'zɪstənts, ɛg-] *n* : existence *f*
exit[1] ['ɛgzət, 'ɛksət] *vi* : sortir — *vt* LEAVE : sortir de, quitter
exit[2] *n* : sortie *f*
exodus ['ɛksədəs] *n* : exode *m*
exonerate [ɪg'zɑnə,reɪt, ɛg-] *vt* **-ated; -ating** : disculper, innocenter
exoneration [ɪg,zɑnə'reɪʃən, ɛg-] *n* : disculpation *f*
exorbitant [ɪg'zɔrbətənt, ɛg-] *adj* : exorbitant, excessif
exorcise ['ɛk,sɔr,saɪz, -sər-] *vt* **-cised; -cising** : exorciser
exorcism ['ɛksər,sɪzəm] *n* : exorcisme *m*
exotic [ɪg'zɑtɪk, ɛg-] *adj* : exotique
expand [ɪk'spænd, ɛk-] *vt* **1** ENLARGE, EXTEND : étendre, élargir **2** DEVELOP : développer — *vi* **1** GROW, SPREAD : s'étendre, s'agrandir, se dilater (se dit des métaux) **2** DEVELOP : se développer
expanse [ɪk'spænts, ɛk-] *n* : étendue *f*
expansion [ɪk'spæntʃən, ɛk-] *n* : expansion *f*, élargissement *m*, développement *m*
expansive [ɪk'spæntsɪv, ɛk-] *adj* **1** OUTGOING : expansif, démonstratif **2** AMPLE : large, vaste
expansively [ɪk'spæntsɪvli, ɛk-] *adv* : de manière expansive
expansiveness [ɪk'spæntsɪvnəs, ɛk-] *n* : expansivité *f*
expatriate[1] [,ɛks'peɪtri,eɪt] *vt* **-ated; -ating** : expatrier
expatriate[2] [ɛks'peɪtriət, -,eɪt] *adj* : expatrié
expatriate[3] [ɛks'peɪtriət, -,eɪt] *n* : expatrié *m*, -triée *f*
expect [ɪk'spɛkt, ɛk-] *vt* **1** ANTICIPATE : s'attendre à <expect the worst : attendez-vous au pire> **2** AWAIT : attendre **3** REQUIRE : exiger, demander — *vi* **to be expecting** : attendre un bébé, être enceinte
expectancy [ɪk'spɛktəntsi, ɛk-] *n, pl* **-cies** : attente *f*, espérance *f* <life expectancy : espérance de vie>
expectant [ɪk'spɛktənt, ɛk-] *adj* **1** ANTICIPATING : qui attend **2** EXPECTING : futur <an expectant mother : une future mère>
expectation [,ɛk,spɛk'teɪʃən] *n* : attente *f*
expedient[1] [ɪk'spi:diənt] *adj* : opportun, indiqué, convenable
expedient[2] *n* : expédient *m*
expedite ['ɛkspə,daɪt] *vt* **-dited; -diting** : expédier, accélerer, hâter
expedition [,ɛkspə'dɪʃən] *n* : expédition *f*
expeditious [,ɛkspə'dɪʃəs] *adj* : expéditif, rapide
expel [ɪk'spɛl, ɛk-] *vt* **-pelled; -pelling** : expulser, renvoyer (un élève)
expend [ɪk'spɛnd, ɛk-] *vt* **1** SPEND : dépenser (de l'argent) **2** UTILIZE : utiliser, employer, consacrer (de l'énergie, du temps, etc.) **3** EXHAUST : épuiser

expendable [ɪk'spɛndəbəl, ɛk-] *adj* : remplaçable

expenditure [ɪk'spɛndɪtʃər, ɛk-, -ˌtʃʊr] *n* : dépense *f*

expense [ɪk'spɛnts, ɛk-] *n* **1** COST : coût *m,* dépense *f* **2 expenses** *npl* : frais *mpl* **3 at the expense of** : aux dépens de

expensive [ɪk'spɛntsɪv, ɛk-] *adj* : cher, coûteux

expensively [ɪk'spɛntsɪvli, ɛk-] *adv* : à grands frais

experience[1] [ɪk'spɪriənts, ɛk-] *vt* **-enced; -encing** : éprouver, faire l'expérience de, connaître <to experience difficulties : rencontrer des difficultés>

experience[2] *n* : expérience *f*

experienced [ɪk'spɪriəntst, ɛk-] *adj* : expérimenté

experiment[1] [ɪk'spɛrəmənt, ɛk-, -'spɪr-] *vi* : expérimenter, faire des expériences

experiment[2] *n* : expérience *f*

experimental [ɪkˌspɛrə'mɛntəl, ɛk-, -ˌspɪr-] *adj* : expérimental

experimentation [ɪkˌspɛrəmən'teɪʃən, ɛk-, -ˌspɪr-] *n* : expérimentation *f*

expert[1] ['ɛkˌspərt, ɪk'spərt] *adj* : expert <expert testimony : témoignage d'expert>

expert[2] ['ɛkˌspərt] *n* : expert *m,* -perte *f;* spécialiste *mf*

expertise [ˌɛkspər'tiːz] *n* : compétence *f,* expertise *f*

expertly ['ɛkˌspərtli] *adv* : de manière experte

expiate ['ɛkspiˌeɪt] *vt* **-ated; -ating** : expier

expiation [ˌɛkspi'eɪʃən] *n* : expiation *f*

expiration [ˌɛkspə'reɪʃən] *n* : expiration *f*

expire [ɪk'spaɪr, ɛk-] *vi* **-pired; -piring 1** EXHALE : expirer **2** END : expirer, arriver à terme **3** DIE : mourir

explain [ɪk'spleɪn, ɛk-] *vt* **1** : expliquer **2 to explain oneself** : s'expliquer

explanation [ˌɛksplə'neɪʃən] *n* : explication *f*

explanatory [ɪk'splænəˌtori, ɛk-] *adj* : explicatif

expletive ['ɛksplətɪv] *n* SWEARWORD : juron *m*

explicable [ɛk'splɪkəbəl, 'ɛksplɪ-] *adj* : explicable

explicit [ɪk'splɪsət, ɛk-] *adj* : explicite — **explicitly** *adv*

explode [ɪk'sploːd, ɛk-] *v* **-ploded; -ploding** *vt* **1** BURST : faire exploser **2** DISCREDIT : discréditer — *vi* **1** : exploser **2 to explode with laughter** : éclater de rire

exploit[1] [ɪk'splɔɪt, ɛk-] *vt* : exploiter

exploit[2] ['ɛkˌsplɔɪt] *n* : exploit *m*

exploitation [ˌɛkˌsplɔɪ'teɪʃən] *n* : exploitation *f*

exploration [ˌɛksplə'reɪʃən] *n* : exploration *f*

exploratory [ɪk'splorəˌtori, ɛk-] *adj* : exploratoire

explore [ɪk'splor, ɛk-] *v* **-plored; -ploring** : explorer

explorer [ɪk'splorər, ɛk-] *n* : explorateur *m,* -trice *f*

explosion [ɪk'sploːʒən, ɛk-] *n* : explosion *f*

explosive[1] [ɪk'sploːsɪv, ɛk-] *adj* : explosif

explosive[2] *n* : explosif *m*

exponent [ɪk'spoːnənt, 'ɛkˌspoː-] *n* **1** : exposant *m* (en mathématiques) **2** ADVOCATE : partisan *m,* -sane *f;* avocat *m,* -cate *f*

export[1] [ɛk'sport, 'ɛkˌsport] *v* : exporter

export[2] ['ɛkˌsport] *n* : exportation *f*

expose [ɪk'spoːz, ɛk-] *vt* **-posed; -posing 1** DISPLAY : exposer **2** DISCLOSE : révéler, démasquer **3 to expose oneself to** : s'exposer à

exposé [ˌɛkspo'zeɪ] *n* : exposé *m,* révélation *f*

exposition [ˌɛkspə'zɪʃən] *n* : exposition *f*

exposure [ɪk'spoːʒər, ɛk-] *n* **1** : exposition *f* (au danger, etc.) <to die of exposure : mourir de froid> **2** DISCLOSURE : révélation *f,* divulgation *f* **3** : pose *f* (en photographie) **4** ORIENTATION : exposition *f* <to have a southern exposure : être exposé au sud>

expound [ɪk'spaʊnd, ɛk-] *vt* : exposer, expliquer — *vi* **to expound on** : disserter sur

express[1] [ɪk'sprɛs, ɛk-] *vt* **1** CONVEY : exprimer, énoncer **2** SQUEEZE : exprimer, extraire (du jus, etc.)

express[2] *adv* : en exprès <to send express : envoyer en exprès>

express[3] *adj* **1** EXPLICIT, SPECIFIC : exprès, explicite, formel <with the express purpose of : dans le seul but de> **2** FAST : rapide, express <an express bus : un autobus express>

express[4] *n* **1** *or* **express train** : rapide *m,* express *m* **2 to send by express** : envoyer par transport rapide

expression [ɪk'sprɛʃən, ɛk-] *n* : expression *f*

expressionless [ɪk'sprɛʃənləs, ɛk-] *adj* : inexpressif, sans expression

expressive [ɪk'sprɛsɪv, ɛk-] *adj* : expressif

expressiveness [ɪk'sprɛsɪvnəs, ɛk-] *n* : expressivité *f*

expressly [ɪk'sprɛsli, ɛk-] *adv* : expressément

expressway [ɪk'sprɛsˌweɪ, ɛk-] *n* : autoroute *f*

expulsion [ɪk'spʌlʃən, ɛk-] *n* : expulsion *f,* renvoi *m* (d'un élève)

expurgate ['ɛkspərˌgeɪt] *vt* **-gated; -gating** : expurger

exquisite [ɛk'skwɪzət, 'ɛkˌskwɪ-] *adj* **1** FINE : exquis, raffiné **2** INTENSE : vif (se dit des plaisirs, etc.), aigu (se dit d'une douleur)

extant ['ɛkstənt, ɛk'stænt] *adj* : existant

extemporaneous [ɛkˌstɛmpəˈreɪniəs] *adj* : improvisé, impromptu

extend [ɪkˈstɛnd, ɛk-] *vt* **1** STRETCH : étendre **2** PROLONG : prolonger **3** ENLARGE : agrandir **4 to extend one's hand** : tendre la main — *vi* **1** STRETCH : s'étendre **2** LAST : se prolonger

extension [ɪkˈstɛntʃən, ɛk-] *n* **1** EXTENDING : extension *f* **2** PROLONGATION : prolongation *f,* délai *m* **3** ADDITION, ANNEX : agrandissement *m* (d'une maison), prolongement *m* (d'une route, etc.) **4** : poste *m* (de téléphone) **5 extension cord** : rallonge *f*

extensive [ɪkˈstɛn*t*sɪv, ɛk-] *adj* : étendu, vaste

extensively [ɪkˈstɛn*t*sɪvli, ɛk-] *adv* : considérablement, abondamment

extent [ɪkˈstɛnt, ɛk-] *n* **1** SIZE : étendue *f* **2** SCOPE : importance *f,* ampleur *f* **3** DEGREE : mesure *f,* degré *m* <to a certain extent : dans une certaine mesure, jusqu'à un certain point>

extenuating [ɪkˈstɛnjəˌweɪtɪŋ, ɛk-] *n* : atténuant

exterior[1] [ɛkˈstɪriər] *adj* : extérieur

exterior[2] *n* : extérieur *m*

exterminate [ɪkˈstərməˌneɪt, ɛk-] *vt* **-nated; -nating** : exterminer

extermination [ɪkˌstərməˈneɪʃən, ɛk-] *n* : extermination *f*

external [ɪkˈstərnəl, ɛk-] *adj* : externe <for external use only : à usage externe>

externally [ɪkˈstərnəli, ɛk-] *adv* : extérieurement

extinct [ɪkˈstɪŋkt, ɛk-] *adj* : éteint (se dit d'un volcan, d'un feu, etc.), disparu (se dit d'une espèce)

extinction [ɪkˈstɪŋkʃən, ɛk-] *n* : extinction *f,* disparition *f*

extinguish [ɪkˈstɪŋgwɪʃ, ɛk-] *vt* : éteindre

extinguisher [ɪkˈstɪŋgwɪʃər, ɛk-] *n* : extincteur *m*

extirpate [ˈɛkstərˌpeɪt] *vt* **-pated; -pating** : extirper

extol [ɪkˈstoːl, ɛk-] *vt* **-tolled; -tolling** : louer

extort [ɪkˈstɔrt, ɛk-] *vt* : extorquer

extortion [ɪkˈstɔrʃən, ɛk-] *n* : extorsion *f*

extra[1] [ˈɛkstrə] *adv* **1** ESPECIALLY : plus que d'habitude, particulièrement <extra nice : plus gentil que d'habitude> **2 to pay extra** : payer un supplément **3 to cost extra** : coûter plus cher

extra[2] *adj* **1** ADDITIONAL : supplémentaire, en supplément <extra hours : heures supplémentaires> <the wine is extra : le vin est en plus> **2** SPARE : en trop, de trop <an extra chair : une chaise en trop> **3** SUPERIOR : supérieur <extra quality : de qualité supérieure>

extra[3] *n* **1** ADDITION : supplément *m* **2** : édition *f* spéciale (d'un journal) **3** : figurant *m,* -rante *f* (au cinéma)

extract[1] [ɪkˈstrækt, ɛk-] *vt* : extraire, arracher (une dent, un aveu, etc.)

extract[2] [ˈɛkˌstrækt] *n* : extrait *m*

extraction [ɪkˈstrækʃən, ɛk-] *n* **1** REMOVAL : extraction *f* **2** ORIGIN : origine *f* <of French extraction : d'origine française>

extracurricular [ˌɛkstrəkəˈrɪkjələr] *adj* : parascolaire

extradite [ˈɛkstrəˌdaɪt] *vt* **-dited; -diting** : extrader

extradition [ˌɛkstrəˈdɪʃən] *n* : extradition *f*

extramarital [ˌɛkstrəˈmærəṭəl] *adj* : extraconjugal

extraneous [ɛkˈstreɪniəs] *adj* **1** OUTSIDE : extérieur, étranger **2** SUPERFLUOUS : superflu

extraordinary [ɪkˈstrɔrdənˌɛri, ˌɛkstrəˈɔrd-] *adj* : extraordinaire — **extraordinarily** [ɪkˌstrɔrdənˈɛrəli, ˌɛkstrəˌɔrd-] *adv*

extrasensory [ˌɛkstrəˈsɛn*t*səri] *adj* : extrasensoriel

extraterrestrial[1] [ˌɛkstrətəˈrɛstriəl] *adj* : extraterrestre

extraterrestrial[2] *n* : extraterrestre *mf*

extravagance [ɪkˈstrævɪgən*t*s, ɛk-] *n* **1** EXCESS : extravagance *f* **2** WASTEFULNESS : prodigalité *f* **3** LUXURY : luxe *m*

extravagant [ɪkˈstrævɪgənt, ɛk-] *adj* **1** EXCESSIVE : extravagant, excessif **2** WASTEFUL : prodigue **3** LUXURIOUS : luxueux

extravagantly [ɪkˈstrævɪgəntli, ɛk-] *adv* **1** LAVISHLY : avec prodigalité, luxueusement **2** EXCESSIVELY : d'une manière extravagante, à outrance

extravaganza [ɪkˌstrævəˈgænzə, ɛk-] *n* : œuvre *f* à grand spectacle, spectacle *m* somptueux

extreme[1] [ɪkˈstriːm, ɛk-] *adj* : extrême — **extremely** *adv*

extreme[2] *n* **1** : extrême *m* **2 to go to extremes** : pousser (les choses) à l'extrême

extremity [ɪkˈstrɛməṭi, ɛk-] *n, pl* **-ties** : extrémité *f*

extricate [ˈɛkstrəˌkeɪt] *vt* **-cated; -cating** **1** : dégager, extirper **2 to extricate oneself from** : se dégager de, se sortir de

extrovert [ˈɛkstrəˌvərt] *n* : extraverti *m,* -tie *f*

extroverted [ˈɛkstrəˌvərṭəd] *adj* : extraverti

extrude [ɪkˈstruːd, ɛk-] *vt* **-truded; -truding** : extruder, faire sortir

exuberance [ɪgˈzuːbərən*t*s, ɛg-] *n* : exubérance *f*

exuberant [ɪgˈzuːbərənt, ɛg-] *adj* : exubérant

exuberantly [ɪgˈzuːbərəntli, ɛg-] *adv* : avec exubérance

exude [ɪg'zu:d, ɛg-] *v* **-uded; -uding** *vt* **1** : exsuder (un liquide) **2 to exude confidence** : respirer la confiance en soi — *vi* : exsuder
exult [ɪg'zʌlt, ɛg-] *vi* : exulter, se réjouir
exultant [ɪg'zʌltənt, ɛg-] *adj* : triomphant, jubilant
exultation [,ɛksəl'teɪʃən, ,ɛgzəl-] *n* : exultation *f*
eye[1] ['aɪ] *vt* **eyed; eyeing** *or* **eying** : regarder, lorgner
eye[2] *n* **1** : œil *m* <to have brown eyes : avoir les yeux bruns> <the eye of the storm : l'œil de la tempête> **2** VISION : vision *f* **3** GLANCE : regard *m* <her eyes fell on the letter : son regard est tombé sur la lettre> **4** POINT OF VIEW : point *m* de vue <in the eyes of the law : selon la loi> **5 eye of a needle** : chas *m*
eyeball ['aɪ,bɔl] *n* : globe *m* oculaire
eyebrow ['aɪ,braʊ] *n* : sourcil *m*
eyedropper ['aɪ,drɑpər] → **dropper**
eyeglasses ['aɪ,glæsəz] *npl* : lunettes *fpl*
eyelash ['aɪ,læʃ] *n* : cil *m*
eyelet ['aɪlət] *n* : œillet *m*
eyelid [aɪ,lɪd] *n* : paupière *f*
eye–opener ['aɪ,o:pənər] *n* : révélation *f*
eyepiece ['aɪ,pi:s] *n* : oculaire *m*
eyesight ['aɪ,saɪt] *n* : vue *f,* vision *f* <to lose one's eyesight : perdre la vue>
eyesore ['aɪ,sor] *n* : horreur *f* <to be an eyesore : choquer la vue>
eyestrain ['aɪ,streɪn] *n* : fatigue *f* des yeux
eyetooth ['aɪ,tu:θ] *n, pl* **-teeth** [-,ti:θ] : dent *f* canine
eyewitness ['aɪ'wɪtnəs] *n* : témoin *m* oculaire
eyrie ['aɪri] → **aerie**

F

f ['ɛf] *n, pl* **f's** *or* **fs** ['ɛfs] : f *m,* sixième lettre de l'alphabet
fable ['feɪbəl] *n* : fable *f,* légende *f*
fabled ['feɪbəld] *adj* : légendaire, fabuleux
fabric ['fæbrɪk] *n* **1** CLOTH : tissu *m,* étoffe *f* **2** STRUCTURE : structure *f* <the fabric of society : la structure de la société>
fabricate ['fæbrɪ,keɪt] *vt* **-cated; -cating 1** CONSTRUCT : fabriquer (un objet) **2** INVENT : fabriquer, inventer (une histoire, etc.)
fabrication [,fæbrɪ'keɪʃən] *n* **1** CONSTRUCTION : fabrication *f* **2** FALSEHOOD : mensonge *m*
fabulous ['fæbjələs] *adj* **1** LEGENDARY : fabuleux, légendaire **2** INCREDIBLE : incroyable **3** MARVELOUS : fabuleux, formidable
fabulously ['fæbjələsli] *adv* : fabuleusement
facade [fə'sɑd] *n* : façade *f*
face[1] ['feɪs] *vt* **faced; facing 1** CONFRONT : faire face à, affronter <to be faced with : se trouver confronté à> **2** COVER : revêtir (un mur, etc.) **3** : faire face à <to face the sun : faire face au soleil> **4** FRONT, OVERLOOK : être en face de, donner sur
face[2] *n* **1** : visage *m,* figure *f* **2** EXPRESSION : mine *f,* air *m* <he put on a sad face : il faisait triste mine> **3** : grimace *f* <to make a face : faire la grimace> **4** APPEARANCE : aspect *m,* visage *m,* apparence *f* (de la société, etc.) **5** PRESENCE : présence *f* <in the face of the enemy : face à l'ennemi> **6** SURFACE : face *f* (d'une monnaie), façade *f* (d'un bâtiment) **7** DIGNITY : face *f* <to lose face : perdre la face> **8 in the face of** DESPITE : en dépit de
facedown ['feɪs,daʊn] *adv* : face contre terre <to lie facedown : être étendu à plat ventre>
faceless ['feɪsləs] *adj* ANONYMOUS : anonyme
face–lift ['feɪs,lɪft] *n* **1** : lifting *m* **2** RENOVATION : ravalement *m* (d'une façade), restauration *f*
facet ['fæsət] *n* **1** : facette *f* (d'une pierre précieuse) **2** ASPECT : aspect *m,* facette *f*
facetious [fə'si:ʃəs] *adj* : facétieux — **facetiously** *adv*
facetiousness [fə'si:ʃəsnəs] *n* : caractère *m* facétieux
face–to–face *adv* : face à face, en personne
faceup ['feɪs'ʌp] *adv* : face en dessus <to lie faceup : être étendu sur le dos>
face value *n* : valeur *f* nominale
facial[1] ['feɪʃəl] *adj* : facial, du visage
facial[2] *n* : soin *m* du visage
facile ['fæsəl] *adj* **1** EASY : facile **2** SUPERFICIAL : superficiel, creux **3** FLUENT : coulant, aisé
facilitate [fə'sɪlə,teɪt] *vt* **-tated; -tating** : faciliter
facility [fə'sɪləṭi] *n, pl* **-ties 1** EASE : facilité *f,* aisance *f* **2** APTITUDE : facilité *f,* aptitude *f* **3** CENTER, COMPLEX : complexe *m* <hospital facility : complexe hospitalier> **4 facilities** *npl* : installations *fpl,* équipements *mpl* <sports facilities : équipements sportifs>
facing ['feɪsɪŋ] *n* **1** : revers *m* (en couture) **2** : revêtement *m* (d'un bâtiment)
facsimile [fæk'sɪməli] *n* **1** REPRODUCTION : fac-similé *m* **2** FAX : fac-similé *m,* télécopie *f*

fact ['fækt] *n* **1** DATA, INFORMATION : fait *m* **2** REALITY : faits *mpl,* réalité *f* **3 in ~** : en fait, effectivement
faction ['fækʃən] *n* : faction *f*
factitious [fæk'tɪʃəs] *adj* : factice, artificiel
factor ['fæktər] *n* : facteur *m*
factory ['fæktəri] *n, pl* **-ries** : usine *f,* fabrique *f*
factual ['fæktʃʊəl] *adj* : factuel, basé sur les faits
factually ['fæktʃʊəli] *adv* : en se tenant aux faits
faculty ['fækəlti] *n, pl* **-ties 1** : faculté *f* <the faculty of hearing : la faculté de l'ouïe> **2** APTITUDE : aptitude *f,* faculté *f* **3** TEACHERS : faculté *f* (dans une université), corps *m* enseignant
fad ['fæd] *n* : mode *f* passagère, marotte *f*
fade ['feɪd] *v* **faded; fading** *vt* : décolorer — *vi* **1** WITHER : se flétrir, se faner **2** DISCOLOR : se décolorer **3** DIM : s'affaiblir, diminuer (se dit de la lumière) **4** VANISH : disparaître <to fade from sight : disparaître aux regards>
faded ['feɪdəd] *adj* : décoloré, délavé
fag ['fæg] *vt* **fagged; fagging** EXHAUST : épuiser, fatiguer
fagot *or* **faggot** ['fægət] *n* : fagot *m*
Fahrenheit ['færən,haɪt] *adj* : Fahrenheit
fail[1] ['feɪl] *vi* **1** WEAKEN : faiblir, baisser <my eyes are failing : ma vue faiblit> **2** BREAK DOWN : tomber en panne, lâcher (se dit des freins) <her heart failed : son cœur s'est arrêté> **3** (*indicating a lack of success*) : échouer, ne pas réussir, faire faillite <the business is failing : l'entreprise fait faillite> **4 to fail in** : manquer à, faire défaut à <I failed in my duty : j'ai manqué à mon devoir> — *vt* **1** DISAPPOINT, LET DOWN : décevoir, laisser tomber, faire défaut **2** NEGLECT : manquer à, négliger <to fail to keep one's word : manquer à sa parole> **3** : échouer à, ne pas réussir à <to fail an exam : échouer à un examen>
fail[2] *n* **1** FAILURE : échec *m* **2 without ~** : à coup sûr, sans faute
failing[1] ['feɪlɪŋ] *n* : défaut *m*
failing[2] *prep* : à défaut de
failure ['feɪljər] *n* **1** : échec *m,* insuccès *m,* faillite *f* (en finances) <a complete failure : un échec total> **2** LACK, OMISSION : manque *m,* manquement *m,* défaut *m* **3** BREAKDOWN, LOSS : panne *f,* défaillance *f* (en médecine) <power failure : panne de courant> <crop failure : perte des récoltes> **4 to be a failure** : être nul, ne pas être doué
faint[1] ['feɪnt] *vi* : s'évanouir
faint[2] *adj* **1** COWARDLY : lâche, peureux **2** WEAK : défaillant, faible <to feel faint : se sentir mal> **3** FEEBLE, SLIGHT : faible, léger **4** INDISTINCT : vague, flou
faint[3] *n* : évanouissement *m*
fainthearted ['feɪnt'hɑrṭəd] *adj* : timide, timoré
faintly ['feɪntli] *adv* **1** SLIGHTLY : faiblement **2** INDISTINCTLY : vaguement
faintness ['feɪntnəs] *n* **1** INDISTINCTNESS : faiblesse *f,* légèreté *f* **2** DIZZINESS : vertige *m*
fair[1] ['fær] *adv* → **fairly**
fair[2] *adj* **1** BEAUTIFUL : beau **2** FINE : beau (se dit du temps), favorable (se dit du vent) **3** HONEST, JUST : juste, équitable <it's not fair : ce n'est pas juste> <fair play : franc jeu> **4** BLOND, LIGHT : blond (se dit des cheveux), clair (se dit de la peau) **5** ADEQUATE : assez bon, passable **6** LARGE : considérable, important
fair[3] *n* : foire *f,* fête *f* foraine
fairground ['fær,graʊnd] *n* : champ *m* de foire
fairly ['færli] *adv* **1** HONESTLY, JUSTLY : équitablement, impartialement, honnêtement **2** QUITE, RATHER : assez, passablement **3** POSITIVELY : vraiment <fairly bursting with pride : vraiment fier de soi>
fairness ['færnəs] *n* **1** IMPARTIALITY : équité *f,* impartialité *f,* justice *f* <in all fairness : en toute justice> **2** LIGHTNESS : blondeur *f* (des cheveux), blancheur *f* (de la peau)
fairy ['færi] *n, pl* **fairies** : fée *f*
fairyland ['færi,lænd] *n* : royaume *m* des fées, féerie *f*
fairy tale *n* : conte *m* de fées
faith ['feɪθ] *n, pl* **faiths** ['feɪθs, 'feɪðz] **1** LOYALTY : loyauté *f,* foi *f* **2** BELIEF : foi *f,* croyance *f* (en Dieu) **3** CONFIDENCE, TRUST : confiance *f,* foi *f* <to have faith in : avoir confiance en> <in good faith : en toute bonne foi> **4** RELIGION : foi *f,* religion *f*
faithful ['feɪθfəl] *adj* **1** RELIABLE : fidèle, loyal **2** ACCURATE : fidèle, exact — **faithfully** *adv*
faithfulness ['feɪθfəlnəs] *n* : fidélité *f*
faithless ['feɪθləs] *adj* : déloyal, infidèle — **faithlessly** *adv*
faithlessness ['feɪθləsnəs] *n* : déloyauté *f,* infidélité *f*
fake[1] ['feɪk] *v* **faked; faking** *vt* **1** COUNTERFEIT, FALSIFY : falsifier, contrefaire **2** FEIGN : simuler, feindre — *vi* **1** PRETEND : faire semblant **2** : feinter (aux sports)
fake[2] *adj* : faux, falsifié
fake[3] *n* **1** : article *m* truqué, faux *m* (œuvre d'art) **2** : imposteur *m* (personne) **3** : feinte *f* (aux sports)
fakir [fə'kɪr, 'feɪkər] *n* : fakir *m*
falcon ['fælkən, 'fɔl-] *n* : faucon *m*
falconry ['fælkənri, 'fɔl-] *n* : fauconnerie *f*

fall[1] [ˈfɔl] *vi* **fell** [ˈfɛl]; **fallen** [ˈfɔlən]; **falling** **1** : tomber <to fall off a roof : tomber d'un toit> <the snow was falling : la neige tombait> **2** DROP : baisser, tomber, diminuer **3** HANG : tomber (se dit des cheveux), descendre (se dit des rideaux, etc.) **4** : tomber, être renversé <the government has fallen : le gouvernement a été renversé> **5** SIN : tomber, pécher **6** OCCUR : tomber, arriver <Christmas falls on a Wednesday : Noël tombe un mercredi> **7 to fall asleep** : s'endormir **8 to fall behind** : prendre du retard **9 to fall in love** : tomber amoureux

fall[2] *n* **1** : chute *f* <to have a fall : faire une chute, tomber> <a heavy fall of snow : une forte chute de neige> **2** DECREASE : baisse *f,* chute *f* (des prix, de la température, etc.), dépréciation *f* (de la monnaie) **3** COLLAPSE : effondrement *m* (d'un édifice), chute *f,* renversement *m* (d'un régime, etc.) **4** AUTUMN : automne *m* **5 falls** → **waterfall**

fallacious [fəˈleɪʃəs] *adj* : fallacieux

fallacy [ˈfæləsi] *n, pl* **-cies** : erreur *f,* faux raisonnement *m*

fall back *vi* **1** RETREAT : reculer, se retirer **2 to fall back on** : avoir recours à

fallible [ˈfæləbəl] *adj* : faillible

fallout [ˈfɔlˌaʊt] *n* **1** : retombées *fpl* (radioactives) **2** CONSEQUENCES : répercussions *fpl*

fall out *vi* QUARREL : se disputer, se quereller

fallow[1] [ˈfælo] *vt* : labourer une terre en vue des récoltes à venir

fallow[2] *adj* **1** : en jachère (se dit d'une terre) **2** DORMANT : inactif

false [ˈfɔls] *adj* **falser; falsest** **1** UNTRUE : faux, erroné **2** FAKE : faux, artificiel **3** DECEPTIVE : faux, mensonger **4** DISLOYAL : faux, déloyal

falsehood [ˈfɔlsˌhʊd] *n* **1** LIE : mensonge *m* **2** LYING : fausseté *f*

falsely [ˈfɔlsli] *adv* : faussement

falseness [ˈfɔlsnəs] *n* : fausseté *f*

falsetto [fɔlˈsɛt̬oː] *n, pl* **-tos** : fausset *m*

falsification [ˌfɔlsəfəˈkeɪʃən] *n* : falsification *f*

falsify [ˈfɔlsəˌfaɪ] *vt* **-fied; -fying** : falsifier

falsity [ˈfɔlsət̬i] *n, pl* **-ties** : fausseté *f*

falter [ˈfɔltər] *vi* **1** STUMBLE : chanceler, trébucher **2** STAMMER : bredouiller **3** WAVER : hésiter, vaciller, chanceler

fame [ˈfeɪm] *n* : célébrité *f,* renommée *f*

famed [ˈfeɪmd] *adj* : célèbre, renommé

familial [fəˈmɪljəl, -liəl] *adj* : familial

familiar [fəˈmɪljər] *adj* **1** KNOWN : familier, (bien) connu <to be on familiar ground : être en terrain connu> <to be familiar with sth : bien connaître qqch> **2** INFORMAL, INTIMATE : familier, intime **3** FORWARD : entreprenant, effronté

familiarity [fəˌmɪliˈærət̬i, -ˌmɪlˈjær-] *n, pl* **-ties** **1** ACQUAINTANCE, KNOWLEDGE : connaissance *f,* caractère *m* familier **2** INFORMALITY, INTIMACY : familiarité *f,* intimité *f* **3** FORWARDNESS : familiarités *fpl,* privautés *fpl*

familiarize [fəˈmɪljəˌraɪz] *vt* **-ized; -izing** **1** : familiariser **2 to familiarize oneself with** : se familiariser avec

family [ˈfæmli, ˈfæmə-] *n, pl* **-lies** : famille *f*

family name → **surname**

family tree *n* : arbre *m* généalogique

famine [ˈfæmən] *n* : famine *f*

famished [ˈfæmɪʃt] *adj* : affamé <I'm famished! : je meurs de faim!>

famous [ˈfeɪməs] *adj* : célèbre, renommé

famously [ˈfeɪməsli] *adv* : à merveille, rudement bien *fam*

fan[1] [ˈfæn] *vt* **fanned; fanning** **1** : éventer (le visage, etc.), attiser (un feu) **2** STIMULATE : attiser, aviver

fan[2] *n* **1** : éventail *m,* ventilateur *m* (électrique) **2** ADMIRER, ENTHUSIAST : admirateur *m,* -trice *f;* enthousiaste *mf;* fan *mf* (d'une vedette)

fanatic[1] [fəˈnæt̬ɪk] *or* **fanatical** [-t̬ɪkəl] *adj* : fanatique

fanatic[2] *n* : fanatique *mf*

fanaticism [fəˈnæt̬əˌsɪzəm] *n* : fanatisme *m*

fanciful [ˈfæntsɪfəl] *adj* **1** IMAGINATIVE : imaginatif **2** CAPRICIOUS, WHIMSICAL : fantasque, bizarre, capricieux

fancy[1] [ˈfæntsi] *vt* **-cied; -cying** **1** IMAGINE : s'imaginer, se figurer, croire **2** LIKE, WANT : avoir envie de, aimer

fancy[2] *adj* **fancier; -est** **1** ELABORATE : élaboré, extravagant **2** LUXURIOUS : de luxe

fancy[3] *n, pl* **-cies** **1** LIKING : goût *m,* envie *f* <to take a fancy to s.o. : se prendre d'affection pour qqn> **2** WHIM : caprice *m,* fantaisie *f* **3** IMAGINATION : imagination *f,* fantaisie *f*

fanfare [ˈfænˌfær] *n* : fanfare *f*

fang [ˈfæŋ] *n* : croc *m* (d'un animal), crochet *m* (d'un serpent)

fanlight [ˈfænˌlaɪt] *n* : imposte *f*

fantasia [fænˈteɪʒə, -ziə; ˌfæntəˈziːə] *n* : fantaisie *f*

fantasize [ˈfæntəˌsaɪz] *vi* **-sized; -sizing** : fantasmer

fantastic [fænˈtæstɪk] *adj* **1** FANCIFUL, STRANGE : fantasque, bizarre **2** INCREDIBLE : incroyable, fabuleux, inouï **3** WONDERFUL : superbe, sensationnel

fantastically [fænˈtæstɪkli] *adv* : fantastiquement, incroyablement

fantasy [ˈfæntəsi] *n, pl* **-sies** **1** IMAGINATION : imagination *f,* fantaisie *f* **2** FANTASIZING : fantasme *m,* rêverie *f*

far[1] [ˈfɑr] *adv* **farther** [ˈfɑrðər] *or* **further** [ˈfər-]; **farthest** *or* **furthest** [-ðəst] **1** : loin <is it far? : est-ce loin?> <far away : au loin, dans le lointain> <far and wide : de tous côtés> **2** MUCH : beaucoup, bien <far worse : bien pire> <far too short : beaucoup trop court> **3** (*expressing degree or extent*) <as far as possible : autant que possible> <as far as the city : jusqu'à la ville> <as far as that goes : pour ce qui est de cela> **4** (*expressing progress*) : loin <she'll go far : elle ira loin> **5 by ~** : de loin **6 far from it!** : pas du tout! **7 so far** : jusqu'ici, jusqu'à maintenant

far[2] *adj* **farther** *or* **further; farthest** *or* **furthest 1** REMOTE : éloigné, lointain <a far country : un pays lointain> **2** LONG : long <a far journey : un long voyage> **3** OTHER : autre <the far side of the lake : l'autre côté du lac> **4** EXTREME : extrême <the far right : l'extrême droite>

faraway [ˈfɑrəˌweɪ] *adj* : éloigné, lointain

farce [ˈfɑrs] *n* : farce *f*

farcical [ˈfɑrsɪkəl] *adj* : risible, grotesque

fare[1] [ˈfær] *vi* **fared; faring** : aller, se passer

fare[2] *n* **1** : tarif *m*, prix *m* du billet <full fare : plein tarif> **2** FOOD : nourriture *f*

farewell[1] [færˈwɛl] *adj* : d'adieu <a farewell speech : un discours d'adieu>

farewell[2] *n* : adieu *m* <to say one's farewells : faire ses adieux>

far–fetched [ˈfɑrˈfɛtʃt] *adj* : improbable, bizarre

farm[1] [ˈfɑrm] *vt* : cultiver, exploiter (une terre) — *vi* : être fermier

farm[2] *n* : ferme *f*, exploitation *f* agricole

farmer [ˈfɑrmər] *n* : fermier *m*, -mière *f;* agriculteur *m*, -trice *f;* habitant *m Can*

farmhand [ˈfɑrmˌhænd] *n* : ouvrier *m*, -vrière *f* agricole

farmhouse [ˈfɑrmˌhaʊs] *n* : ferme *f*

farming [ˈfɑrmɪŋ] *n* : agriculture *f*, élevage *m* (de bovins, etc.)

farmland [ˈfɑrmˌlænd] *n* : terres *fpl* arables, terres *fpl* cultivées

farmyard [ˈfɑrmˌjɑrd] *n* : cour *f* de ferme

far–off [ˈfɑrˌɔf, -ˈɔf] *adj* : lointain

far–reaching [ˈfɑrˈriːtʃɪŋ] *adj* : considérable, d'une grande portée

farsighted [ˈfɑrˌsaɪṭəd] *adj* **1** : hypermétrope, presbyte **2** SHREWD : clairvoyant, perspicace

farsightedness [ˈfɑrˌsaɪṭədnəs] *n* **1** : hypermétropie *f*, presbytie *f* **2** SHREWDNESS : clairvoyance *f*, perspicacité *f*

farther[1] [ˈfɑrðər] *adv* **1** : plus loin <nothing could be farther from the truth : rien n'est plus loin de la vérité> <farther ahead : loin devant> **2** MORE : encore plus, davantage

farther[2] *adj* : plus éloigné, plus lointain <the farther side of the house : l'autre côté de la maison>

farthest[1] [ˈfɑrðəst] *adv* **1** : le plus loin **2** MOST : le plus

farthest[2] *adj* : le plus éloigné, le plus lointain

fascicle [ˈfæsɪkəl] *n* : fascicule *m*

fascinate [ˈfæsənˌeɪt] *vt* **-nated; -nating** : fasciner, captiver

fascination [ˌfæsənˈeɪʃən] *n* : fascination *f*

fascism [ˈfæʃˌɪzəm] *n* : fascisme *m*

fascist[1] [ˈfæʃɪst] *adj* : fasciste

fascist[2] *n* : fasciste *mf*

fashion[1] [ˈfæʃən] *vt* : façonner, fabriquer

fashion[2] *n* **1** MANNER : façon *f*, manière *f* **2** STYLE : mode *f*, vogue *f* <the latest fashion : la dernière mode> <to be out of fashion : être démodé>

fashionable [ˈfæʃənəbəl] *adj* : à la mode, en vogue

fashionably [ˈfæʃənəbli] *adv* : à la mode, élégamment

fast[1] [ˈfæst] *vi* : jeûner

fast[2] *adv* **1** SECURELY : solidement, ferme **2** DEEPLY : profondément <fast asleep : profondément endormi> **3** SWIFTLY : rapidement, vite

fast[3] *adj* **1** SECURE : solide, ferme <to make fast : amarrer (un bateau)> **2** LOYAL : fidèle, sûr <fast friends : amis fidèles> **3** SWIFT : rapide, vite **4** DEEP : profond <a fast sleep : un sommeil profond> **5** COLORFAST : grand teint **6** : en avance (se dit d'une montre) <my watch is fast : ma montre avance>

fast[4] *n* : jeûne *m*

fasten [ˈfæsən] *vt* **1** ATTACH, SECURE : attacher, fermer **2** FIX, FOCUS : fixer — *vi* : s'attacher, se fermer

fastener [ˈfæsənər] *n* **1** HOOK, SNAP : attache *f*, bouton-pression *m* **2** LATCH : fermeture *f* (d'une porte) **3** CLASP : fermoir *m* (d'un bracelet, d'un sac, etc.)

fastening [ˈfæsənɪŋ] → **fastener**

fastidious [fæsˈtɪdiəs] *adj* **1** FUSSY : exigeant, difficile à contenter **2** METICULOUS : méticuleux

fastidiously [fæsˈtɪdiəsli] *n* : méticuleusement

fat[1] [ˈfæt] *adj* **fatter; fattest 1** OBESE : gros, gras, corpulent **2** THICK : gros, épais **3** PROFITABLE : gros, lucratif <a fat contract : un gros contrat>

fat[2] *n* **1** : gras *m* (de la viande), graisse *f* (du corps) **2** : matières *fpl* grasses <fat content : teneur en matières grasses>

fatal [ˈfeɪt̬əl] *adj* **1** DEADLY : mortel **2** FATEFUL : fatidique **3** DISASTROUS : fatal

fatalism [ˈfeɪt̬əlˌɪzəm] *n* : fatalisme *m*

fatalist [ˈfeɪt̬əlɪst] *n* : fataliste *mf*

fatalistic [ˌfeɪt̬əlˈɪstɪk] *adj* : fataliste

fatality [feɪˈtæləṱi, fə-] *n, pl* **-ties** : accident *m* mortel, mort *m*

fatally [ˈfeɪt̬əli] *adv* : mortellement

fate [ˈfeɪt] *n* **1** DESTINY : destin *m*, sort *m* **2** OUTCOME : sort *m* <a fate worse than death : un sort pire que la mort>

fated [ˈfeɪt̬əd] *adj* : destiné

fateful [ˈfeɪtfəl] *adj* : fatidique

father[1] [ˈfɑðər] *vt* **1** BEGET : engendrer **2** : créer, inventer (un projet, etc.)

father[2] *n* **1** PARENT : père *m* **2** ANCESTOR : père *m*, ancêtre *m* **3** FOUNDER : père *m*, fondateur *m* **4** PRIEST : père *m* <Father Brown : le père Brown> **5 Father** GOD : Père *m*, Dieu *m*

fatherhood [ˈfɑðərˌhʊd] *n* : paternité *f*

father–in–law [ˈfɑðərɪnˌlɔ] *n, pl* **fathers–in–law** : beau-père *m*

fatherland [ˈfɑðərˌlænd] *n* : patrie *f*

fatherless [ˈfɑðərləs] *adj* : sans père

fatherly [ˈfɑðərli] *adj* : paternel

fathom[1] [ˈfæðəm] *vt* **1** SOUND : sonder **2** PENETRATE, UNDERSTAND : sonder, pénétrer, comprendre

fathom[2] *n* : brasse *f*

fatigue[1] [fəˈtiːg] *vt* **-tigued; -tiguing** : fatiguer, épuiser

fatigue[2] *n* : fatigue *f*, épuisement *m*

fatness [ˈfætnəs] *n* : corpulence *f*, embonpoint *m*

fatten [ˈfætən] *vt* : engraisser (un animal)

fatty [ˈfæti] *adj* **fattier; -est** : gras (se dit de la viande, etc.), graisseux (se dit d'un tissu)

fatuous [ˈfætʃʊəs] *adj* : imbécile, stupide, niais

fatuously [ˈfætʃʊəsli] *adv* : niaisement, bêtement

faucet [ˈfɔsət] *n* : robinet *m*, champlure *f Can*

fault[1] [ˈfɔlt] *vt* : trouver des défauts à, critiquer

fault[2] *n* **1** FLAW : défaut *m*, imperfection *f* **2** SHORTCOMING : défaut *m*, faiblesse *f* **3** RESPONSIBILITY : faute *f* <it's my fault : c'est de ma faute> **4** MISTAKE : erreur *f* **5** : faille *f* (géologique)

faultfinder [ˈfɔltˌfaɪndər] *n* : critiqueur *m*, -queuse *f*

faultfinding [ˈfɔltˌfaɪndɪŋ] *n* : critiques *fpl*

faultless [ˈfɔltləs] *adj* : irréprochable, impeccable

faultlessly [ˈfɔltləsli] *adv* : parfaitement, impeccablement

faulty [ˈfɔlti] *adj* **faultier; -est** : fautif, défectueux

fauna [ˈfɔnə] *n* : faune *f*

faux pas [ˌfoːˈpɑ] *ns & pl* : faux pas *m*, gaffe *f*

favor[1] *or Brit* **favour** [ˈfeɪvər] *vt* **1** SUPPORT : favoriser, être partisan de, appuyer **2** OBLIGE : rendre un service à **3** PREFER : favoriser, préférer **4** RESEMBLE : ressembler à

favor[2] *or Brit* **favour** *n* **1** APPROVAL : faveur *f*, approbation *f* **2** PARTIALITY : faveur *f*, partialité *f* **3** : service *m*, faveur *f* <can you do me a favor? : peux-tu me rendre un service?> **4 to be in favor of** : être pour

favorable *or Brit* **favourable** [ˈfeɪvərəbəl] *adj* : favorable — **favorably** *or Brit* **favourably** [-rəbli] *adv*

favorite[1] *or Brit* **favourite** [ˈfeɪvərət] *adj* : favori, préféré

favorite[2] *or Brit* **favourite** *n* : favori *m*, -rite *f*; préféré *m*, -rée *f*

favoritism *or Brit* **favouritism** [ˈfeɪvərəˌtɪzəm] *n* : favoritisme *m*

favour *Brit* → **favor**

favourite *Brit* → **favorite**

fawn[1] [ˈfɔn] *vi* **to fawn upon** : flatter servilement, faire fête à (se dit d'un chien)

fawn[2] *n* : faon *m*

fax[1] [ˈfæks] *vt* : faxer, envoyer par télécopie

fax[2] *n* : fax *m*, télécopie *f*

faze [ˈfeɪz] *vt* **fazed; fazing** : déconcerter

fear[1] [ˈfɪr] *vt* : craindre, avoir peur de <I fear he won't come : j'ai peur qu'il ne vienne pas> — *vi* **1** : avoir peur **2 to fear for** : craindre pour

fear[2] *n* : crainte *f*, peur *f*

fearful [ˈfɪrfəl] *adj* **1** DREADFUL : affreux **2** AFRAID : craintif, peureux

fearfully [ˈfɪrfəli] *adv* : craintivement, peureusement

fearless [ˈfɪrləs] *adj* : intrépide, sans peur

fearlessly [ˈfɪrləsli] *adv* : avec intrépidité

fearlessness [ˈfɪrləsnəs] *n* : intrépidité *f*

fearsome [ˈfɪrsəm] *adj* **1** FRIGHTENING : effrayant **2** FORMIDABLE : redoutable

feasibility [ˌfiːzəˈbɪləṱi] *n* : faisabilité *f*, possibilité *f*

feasible [ˌfiːzəbəl] *adj* : faisable, possible, réalisable

feast[1] [ˈfiːst] *vt* **1** : donner un banquet en l'honneur de **2 to feast one's eyes on** : se délecter à regarder — *vi* **1** : festoyer **2 to feast on** : se régaler de

feast[2] *n* **1** BANQUET : banquet *m*, festin *m* **2** FESTIVAL : fête *f* religieuse

feat [ˈfiːt] *n* : exploit *m*, prouesse *f*

feather[1] [ˈfɛðər] *vt* **1** : empenner, couvrir de plumes **2 to feather one's nest** : s'enrichir

feather[2] *n* : plume *f* (d'oiseau), penne *f* (de flèche)

feathered [ˈfɛðərd] *adj* : à plumes

feathery ['fɛðəri] *adj* : duveteux, doux et léger comme la plume

feature[1] ['fiːtʃər] *vt* : mettre en vedette (une personne), faire figurer (des nouvelles, etc.) — *vi* : figurer

feature[2] *n* **1** : trait *m* (du visage) **2** CHARACTERISTIC : caractéristique *f*, trait *m*, particularité *f* **3** : article *m* de fond (en journalisme) **4** *or* **feature film** : long métrage *m*

February ['fɛbjuˌɛri, 'fɛbu-, 'fɛbru-] *n* : février *m*

fecal ['fiːkəl] *adj* : fécal

feces ['fiːˌsiːz] *npl* : fèces *fpl*

feckless ['fɛkləs] *adj* **1** IRRESPONSIBLE : irresponsable **2** INEFFECTUAL : inepte, incapable

fecund ['fɛkənd, 'fiː-] *adj* : fécond

fecundity [fɪ'kʌndət̬i, fɛ-] *n* : fécondité *f*

federal ['fɛdrəl, -dərəl] *adj* : fédéral

federalism ['fɛdrəˌlɪzəm, -dərə-] *n* : fédéralisme *m*

federalist[1] ['fɛdrəlɪst, -dərə-] *adj* : fédéraliste

federalist[2] *n* : fédéraliste *mf*

federate ['fɛdəˌreɪt] *vt* **-ated; -ating** : fédérer

federation [ˌfɛdə'reɪʃən] *n* : fédération *f*

fed up *adj* **to be fed up** : en avoir assez, en avoir marre *fam*

fee ['fiː] *n* **1** : frais *mpl* (de scolarité), honoraires *mpl* (médicaux), cachet *m* (d'un artiste, etc.) **2** *or* **entrance fee** : droit *m* d'entrée

feeble ['fiːbəl] *adj* **-bler; -blest 1** FRAIL : faible, frêle **2** INADEQUATE, POOR : pauvre, piètre <a feeble excuse : une piètre excuse>

feebleminded [ˌfiːbəl'maɪndəd] *adj* : faible d'esprit

feeblemindedness [ˌfiːbəl'maɪndədnəs] *n* : faiblesse *f* d'esprit

feebleness ['fiːbəlnəs] *n* : faiblesse *f*

feebly ['fiːbli] *adv* **1** WEAKLY : faiblement **2** : sans grande conviction

feed[1] ['fiːd] *v* **fed** ['fɛd]; **feeding** *vt* **1** : nourrir, donner à manger à <to feed a child : nourrir un enfant> **2** : alimenter (une machine, un feu, etc.) — *vi* EAT : manger, se nourrir

feed[2] *n* **1** NOURISHMENT : nourriture *f* **2** FODDER : fourrage *m*

feel[1] ['fiːl] *v* **felt** ['fɛlt]; **feeling** *vt* **1** TOUCH : toucher, tâter, palper **2** SENSE : sentir **3** EXPERIENCE : éprouver, ressentir (un sentiment) **4** BELIEVE : avoir l'impression que, estimer que **5 to feel out** : sonder (une personne) — *vi* **1** : se sentir <I feel much better : je me sens beaucoup mieux> **2** SEEM : sembler, donner l'impression **3 to feel like** : avoir envie de

feel[2] *n* **1** TOUCH : toucher *m* <soft to the feel : doux au toucher> **2** FEELING, SENSATION : sensation *f* **3** KNACK : facilité *f* <a feel for learning : une facilité d'apprentissage>

feeler ['fiːlər] *n* : antenne *f* (d'un insecte)

feeling ['fiːlɪŋ] *n* **1** TOUCH : toucher *m* **2** SENSATION : sensation *f* **3** SENSE : sentiment *m*, impression *f* **4** BELIEF : opinion *f*, sentiment *m* **5 feelings** *npl* : sentiments *mpl*, sensibilité *f* <to hurt s.o.'s feelings : blesser qqn, faire de la peine à qqn>

feet → **foot**

feign ['feɪn] *vt* : feindre, simuler

feint[1] ['feɪnt] *vi* : feinter

feint[2] *n* : feinte *f*

felicitate [fɪ'lɪsəˌteɪt] *vt* **-tated; -tating** : féliciter, congratuler

felicitation [fɪˌlɪsə'teɪʃən] *n* : félicitation *f*

felicitous [fɪ'lɪsət̬əs] *adj* : heureux

felicity [fɪ'lɪsət̬i] *n, pl* **-ties 1** HAPPINESS : félicité *f* **2** APPROPRIATENESS : justesse *f* (d'une expression, etc.)

feline[1] ['fiːˌlaɪn] *adj* : félin

feline[2] *n* : félin *m*

fell[1] ['fɛl] *vt* **1** : abattre, bûcher *Can* (des arbres) **2** : assommer (des personnes)

fell[2] → **fall**[1]

fellow ['fɛˌloː] *n* **1** COMPANION : camarade *mf;* compagnon *m*, compagne *f* **2** EQUAL, PEER : semblable *m*, pair *m* **3** COLLEAGUE : confrère *m* **4** BOY, MAN : gars *m fam*, type *m fam*

fellowman [ˌfɛlo'mæn] *n, pl* **-men** [-mən, -ˌmɛn] : prochain *m*

fellowship ['fɛloˌʃɪp] *n* **1** COMPANIONSHIP : camaraderie *f* **2** ASSOCIATION : association *f* **3** GRANT : bourse *f* universitaire

felon ['fɛlən] *n* : criminel *m*, -nelle *f*

felonious [fə'loːniəs] *adj* : criminel

felony ['fɛləni] *n, pl* **-nies** : crime *m*

felt[1] ['fɛlt] *n* : feutre *m*

felt[2] → **feel**[1]

female[1] ['fiːˌmeɪl] *adj* : femelle (se dit des animaux et des plantes), féminin (se dit des personnes)

female[2] *n* **1** : femelle *f* (animal ou plante) **2** GIRL, WOMAN : femme *f*, fille *f*

feminine ['fɛmənən] *adj* : féminin

femininity [ˌfɛmə'nɪnət̬i] *n* : féminité *f*

feminism ['fɛməˌnɪzəm] *n* : féminisme *m*

feminist[1] ['fɛmənɪst] *adj* : féministe

feminist[2] *n* : féministe *mf*

femoral ['fɛmərəl] *adj* : fémoral

femur ['fiːmər] *n, pl* **femurs** *or* **femora** ['fɛmərə] : fémur *m*

fence[1] ['fɛnts] *v* **fenced; fencing** *vt* ENCLOSE : clôturer, entourer d'une clôture — *vi* : faire de l'escrime (aux sports)

fence[2] *n* : clôture *f*, barrière *f*

fencer ['fɛntsər] *n* : escrimeur *m*, -meuse *f*

fencing ['fɛntsɪŋ] *n* **1** : escrime *f* (sport) **2** : matériaux *mpl* pour clôture **3** FENCES : clôture *f*, barrière *f*
fend ['fɛnd] *vt or* **to fend off** : parer (un coup), détourner (une attaque), éluder (une question) — *vi* **to fend for oneself** : se débrouiller tout seul
fender ['fɛndər] *n* : aile *f* (d'une voiture)
fennel ['fɛnəl] *n* : fenouil *m*
ferment[1] [fɛr'mɛnt] *vi* : fermenter
ferment[2] ['fər,mɛnt] *n* **1** : ferment *m* (en chimie) **2** TURMOIL : agitation *f*, effervescence *f*
fermentation [,fərmən'teɪʃən, -,mɛn-] *n* : fermentation *f*
fern ['fərn] *n* : fougère *f*
ferocious [fə'ro:ʃəs] *adj* : féroce — **ferociously** *adv*
ferociousness [fə'ro:ʃəsnəs] *n* : férocité *f*
ferocity [fə'rɑsəṭi] *n* : férocité *f*
ferret[1] ['fɛrət] *vt* **to ferret out** : découvrir, dénicher — *vi* DELVE, RUMMAGE : fureter, fouiller
ferret[2] *n* : furet *m*
ferric ['fɛrɪk] *or* **ferrous** ['fɛrəs] *adj* : ferrique, ferreux
Ferris wheel ['fɛrɪs] *n* : grande roue *f*
ferry[1] ['fɛri] *vt* **-ried; -rying** : transporter, faire passer (en bac, par avion, etc.)
ferry[2] *n, pl* **-ries** : bac *m*, ferry-boat *m*, traversier *m Can*
ferryboat ['fɛri,bo:t] → **ferry**[2]
fertile ['fərṭəl] *adj* : fertile, fécond
fertility [fər'tɪləṭi] *n* : fertilité *f*, fécondité *f*
fertilization [,fərṭələ'zeɪʃən] *n* : fertilisation *f*, fécondation *f*
fertilize ['fərṭəl,aɪz] *vt* **-ized; -izing** : fertiliser (une terre), féconder (un œuf, etc.)
fertilizer ['fərṭəl,aɪzər] *n* : engrais *m*
fervent ['fərvənt] *adj* : fervent, ardent
fervently ['fərvəntli] *adv* : avec ferveur
fervid ['fərvɪd] *adj* IMPASSIONED : passionné
fervor *or Brit* **fervour** ['fərvər] *n* : ferveur *f*, ardeur *f*
fester ['fɛstər] *vi* : suppurer
festival ['fɛstəvəl] *n* **1** FEAST : fête *f* (religieuse) **2** : festival *m* <a dance festival : un festival de danse>
festive ['fɛstɪv] *adj* : joyeux, de fête
festivity [fɛs'tɪvəṭi] *n, pl* **-ties 1** MERRIMENT : réjouissance *f* **2 festivities** *npl* : réjouissances *fpl*, festivités *fpl*
festoon[1] [fɛs'tu:n] *vt* : festonner, orner de festons
festoon[2] *n* : feston *m*, guirlande *f*
fetal ['fi:ṭəl] *adj* : fœtal
fetch ['fɛtʃ] *vt* **1** BRING : aller chercher, apporter **2** REALIZE : rapporter (de l'argent), atteindre (un prix)
fetching ['fɛtʃɪŋ] *adj* : attrayant, charmant
fete[1] *or* **fête** ['feɪt, 'fɛt] *vt* **feted** *or* **fêted; feting** *or* **fêting** : fêter
fete[2] *or* **fête** *n* : fête *f*
fetid ['fɛṭəd] *adj* : fétide
fetish ['fɛṭɪʃ] *n* : fétiche *m*
fetlock ['fɛt,lɑk] *n* : boulet *m* (d'un cheval)
fetter ['fɛṭər] *vt* **1** SHACKLE : enchaîner, entraver (un animal) **2** HAMPER : entraver
fetters ['fɛṭərz] *npl* : fers *mpl*, chaînes *fpl*, entraves *fpl* (d'un animal)
fettle ['fɛṭəl] *n* **in fine fettle** : en pleine forme, en bonne condition
fetus ['fi:ṭəs] *n* : fœtus *m*
feud[1] ['fju:d] *vi* : se quereller, se disputer
feud[2] *n* : querelle *f*, vendetta *f* <a family feud : une querelle familiale>
feudal ['fju:dəl] *adj* : féodal
feudalism ['fju:dəl,ɪzəm] *n* : féodalisme *m*
fever ['fi:vər] *n* : fièvre *f*, température *f*
feverish ['fi:vərɪʃ] *adj* : fiévreux, fébrile — **feverishly** *adv*
few[1] ['fju:] *adj* **1** : peu de <we have few friends : nous avons peu d'amis> **2 a few** : quelques <in a few minutes : dans quelques minutes>
few[2] *pron* : peu, quelques-uns, quelques-unes <few remember him : peu se souviennent de lui> <a few of them : quelques-unes d'entre elles> <quite a few : un assez grand nombre de>
fewer[1] ['fju:ər] *adj* : moins de <no fewer than : pas moins de>
fewer[2] *pron* : moins <the fewer the better : le moins possible>
fez ['fɛz] *n, pl* **fezzes** : fez *m*
fiancé [,fi:,ɑn'seɪ, ,fi:'ɑn,seɪ] *n* : fiancé *m*
fiancée [,fi:,ɑn'seɪ, ,fi:'ɑn,seɪ] *n* : fiancée *f*
fiasco [fi'æs,ko:] *n, pl* **-coes** : fiasco *m*
fiat ['fi:,ɑt, -,æt, -ət; 'faɪət, -,æt] *n* : décret *m*
fib[1] ['fɪb] *vi* **fibbed; fibbing** : blaguer *fam*, raconter des histoires
fib[2] *n* : blague *f fam*, bobard *m fam*, menterie *f Can fam*
fibber ['fɪbər] *n* : blagueur *m*, -gueuse *f fam*
fiber *or* **fibre** ['faɪbər] *n* : fibre *f*
fiberboard ['faɪbər,bord] *n* : panneau *m* fibreux
fiberglass ['faɪbər,glæs] *n* : fibre *f* de verre
fibrillation [,fɪbrə'leɪʃən] *n* : fibrillation *f*
fibrous ['faɪbrəs] *adj* : fibreux
fibula ['fɪbjələ] *n, pl* **-lae** [-,li:, -,laɪ] *or* **-las** : péroné *m*
fickle ['fɪkəl] *adj* : volage, inconstant
fickleness ['fɪkəlnəs] *n* : inconstance *f*
fiction ['fɪkʃən] *n* **1** : fiction *f*, invention *f* <truth is stranger than fiction : la réalité dépasse la fiction> **2** *or* **works of fiction** : romans *mpl*, œuvres *fpl* de fiction
fictional ['fɪkʃənəl] *adj* : fictif — **fictionally** *adv*

fictitious [fɪk'tɪʃəs] *adj* : fictif, imaginaire

fiddle[1] ['fɪdəl] *vi* **-dled; -dling 1** : jouer du violon **2 to fiddle with** : tripoter, bricoler, jouer avec

fiddle[2] *n* : violon *m*

fiddler ['fɪdlər, 'fɪdələr] *n* : joueur *m* de violon, joueuse *f* de violon

fiddlesticks ['fɪdəl,stɪks] *interj* : flûte alors!, quelle blague!

fidelity [fə'dɛləţi, faɪ-] *n, pl* **-ties 1** LOYALTY : fidélité *f,* loyauté *f* **2** ACCURACY : exactitude *f,* fidélité *f*

fidget[1] ['fɪdʒət] *vi* : remuer, s'agiter, gigoter *fam*

fidget[2] *n* **to have the fidgets** : ne pas tenir en place

fidgety ['fɪdʒəti] *adj* : remuant, agité

fiduciary[1] [fə'du:ʃi,ɛri, -'dju:-, -ʃəri] *adj* : fiduciaire

fiduciary[2] *n, pl* **-ries** : fiduciaire *mf*

field[1] ['fi:ld] *vt* **1** : attraper (une balle), faire jouer (une équipe) **2** : répondre à (des questions, etc.)

field[2] *adj* : de campagne <field artillery : artillerie de campagne>

field[3] *n* **1** : champ *m* (de cultures, de bataille) **2** : domaine *m,* sphère *f* <the field of science : le domaine de la science> **3** : terrain *m* (de sport) **4** : champ *m* <magnetic field : champ magnétique> <field of vision : champ de vision>

field day *n* **1** : grande occasion *f* **2 to have a field day** : s'en donner à cœur joie

fielder ['fi:ldər] *n* : joueur *m* de champ (au baseball)

field glasses *npl* : jumelles *fpl*

field goal *n* : placement *m*

field hockey *n* : hockey *m* sur gazon

field test : essai *m* sur le terrain

field trip : sortie *f* éducative

fiend ['fi:nd] *n* **1** DEMON, DEVIL : diable *m,* démon *m* **2** EVILDOER : monstre *m* **3** FANATIC : mordu *m,* -due *f fam* **4** ADDICT : toxicomane *mf*

fiendish ['fi:ndɪʃ] *adj* : diabolique — **fiendishly** *adv*

fierce ['fɪrs] *adj* **fiercer; -est 1** FEROCIOUS : féroce, sauvage **2** HEATED : virulent **3** INTENSE : intense, acharné, violent

fiercely ['fɪrsli] *adv* : férocement, violemment, avec acharnement

fierceness ['fɪrsnəs] *n* **1** : férocité *f* (d'un animal) **2** INTENSITY : fureur *f* (d'un orage), violence *f* (d'un combat, etc.)

fieriness ['faɪərinəs] *n* : ardeur *f,* fougue *f*

fiery ['faɪəri] *adj* **fierier; -est 1** BURNING : brûlant, ardent **2** RED : rougeoyant **3** ARDENT, SPIRITED : fougueux, ardent

fiesta [fi'ɛstə] *n* : fête *f*

fife ['faɪf] *n* : fifre *m*

fifteen[1] [fɪf'ti:n] *adj* : quinze

fifteen[2] *n* : quinze *m*

fifteenth[1] [fɪf'ti:nθ] *adj* : quinzième

fifteenth[2] *n* **1** : quinzième *mf* (dans une série) **2** : quinzième *m* (en mathématiques) **3** (*used in dates*) <the fifteenth of August : le quinze août>

fifth[1] ['fɪfθ] *adj* : cinquième

fifth[2] *n* **1** : cinquième *mf* (dans une série) **2** : cinquième *m* (en mathématiques) **3** (*used in dates*) <the fifth of September : le cinq septembre>

fiftieth[1] ['fɪftiəθ] *adj* : cinquantième

fiftieth[2] *n* **1** : cinquantième *mf* (dans une série) **2** : cinquantième *m* (en mathématiques)

fifty[1] ['fɪfti] *adj* : cinquante

fifty[2] *n, pl* **-ties 1** : cinquante *m* **2 fifties** *npl* : cinquantaine *f* <she's in her fifties : elle est dans la cinquantaine>

fifty–fifty[1] [,fɪfti'fɪfti] *adv* : moitié-moitié <to go fifty-fifty : faire moitié-moitié>

fifty–fifty[2] *adj* **to have a fifty–fifty chance** : avoir une chance sur deux

fig ['fɪg] *n* : figue *f*

fight[1] ['faɪt] *v* **fought** ['fɔt]; **fighting** *vt* **1** : se battre avec, combattre (un ennemi) **2** : lutter contre, combattre (une maladie, un incendie, etc.) — *vi* **1** : combattre **2** QUARREL : se quereller, se disputer

fight[2] *n* **1** BATTLE, BRAWL : combat *m,* bataille *f,* bagarre *f* **2** MATCH : combat *m* (de boxe) **3** STRUGGLE : lutte *f* <the fight against cancer : la lutte contre le cancer> **4** QUARREL : querelle *f,* dispute *f* <to pick a fight with : chercher querelle à>

fighter ['faɪţər] *n* **1** COMBATANT : combattant *m,* -tante *f;* lutteur *m,* -teuse *f* **2** BOXER : boxeur *m* **3** *or* **fighter plane** : avion *m* de chasse

figment ['fɪgmənt] *n* **figment of the imagination** : produit *m* de l'imagination

figurative ['fɪgjərəţɪv, -gə-] *adj* : figuré, métaphorique

figuratively ['fɪgjərəţɪvli, -gə-] *adv* : au sens figuré

figure[1] ['fɪgjər, -gər] *v* **-ured; -uring** *vt* **1** REPRESENT : représenter, illustrer **2** CONCLUDE, THINK : penser, supposer **3** CALCULATE, COMPUTE : calculer — *vi* **1** APPEAR : figurer **2 that figures!** : ça se comprend!, ça se tient!

figure[2] *n* **1** NUMERAL : chiffre *m* **2** PRICE : prix *m* **3** FORM, OUTLINE : forme *f,* silhouette *f* **4** : ligne *f* <to watch one's figure : surveiller sa ligne> **5** ILLUSTRATION : figure *f,* image *f* **6** PATTERN : motif *m* **7** PERSONAGE : figure *f,* personnage *m* **8 figures** *npl* : calcul *m* <he's good at figures : il est bon en calcul>

figurehead ['fɪgjər,hɛd, -gər-] *n* **1** : homme *m* de paille **2** : figure *f* de proue (d'un navire)

figure of speech *n* : figure *f* de rhétorique, façon *f* de parler

figure out *vt* **1** UNDERSTAND : arriver à comprendre **2** SOLVE : calculer (une somme), résoudre (un problème)

figurine [ˌfɪgjəˈriːn] *n* : figurine *f*

Fijian[1] [ˈfiːdʒiən, fɪˈjiːən] *adj* : fidjien

Fijian[2] *n* **1** : Fidjien *m*, -jienne *f* **2** : fidjien *m* (langue)

filament [ˈfɪləmənt] *n* : filament *m*

filbert [ˈfɪlbərt] *n* : aveline *f*

filch [ˈfɪltʃ] *vt* : chiper *fam*, piquer *fam*, voler

file[1] [ˈfaɪl] *v* **filed; filing** *vt* **1** CLASSIFY : classer, ranger **2** : déposer (une plainte), intenter (un procès) **3** : limer (ses ongles, etc.) — *vi* **1** : marcher en file <to file past : défiler devant> **2 to file for** : demander (un divorce, etc.)

file[2] *n* **1** : lime *f* (outil) **2** FOLDER : dossier *m* **3** *or* **file cabinet** : classeur *m* **4** RECORD : dossier *m* **5** : fichier *m* (en informatique) **6** LINE : file *f* <in single file : en file>

filial [ˈfɪliəl, ˈfɪljəl] *adj* : filial

filibuster[1] [ˈfɪləˌbʌstər] *vi* : faire de l'obstruction parlementaire

filibuster[2] *n* : obstruction *f* parlementaire

filigree [ˈfɪləˌgriː] *n* : filigrane *m*

Filipino[1] [ˌfɪləˈpiːnoː] *adj* : philippin

Filipino[2] *n* : Philippin *m*, -pine *f*

fill[1] [ˈfɪl] *vt* **1** : remplir <to fill a cup : remplir une tasse> <tears filled her eyes : ses yeux se remplissaient de larmes> **2** PLUG : boucher (un trou), plomber (une dent) **3** SATIATE : rassasier **4** *or* **to fill out** COMPLETE : remplir <to fill out a form : remplir un formulaire> **5** HOLD : prendre, occuper (un poste) **6** SATISFY : remplir, pourvoir à — *vi* : se remplir

fill[2] *n* **1** FILLING : remplissage *m* **2 to eat one's fill** : se rassasier **3 to have had one's fill of** : en avoir assez de

filler [ˈfɪlər] *n* : remplissage *m*

fillet[1] [fɪˈleɪ, ˈfɪˌleɪ, ˈfɪlət] *vt* : découper en filets

fillet[2] *n* : filet *m*

fill in *vt* INFORM : mettre au courant — *vi* **to fill in for** : remplacer

filling [ˈfɪlɪŋ] *n* **1** : plombage *m* (d'une dent), obturation *f* dentaire **2** : garniture *f* (d'une tarte, etc.)

filling station → **service station**

filly [ˈfɪli] *n, pl* **-lies** : pouliche *f*

film[1] [ˈfɪlm] *vt* : filmer, tourner (une scène) — *vi* **1** FILM : tourner **2** *or* **to film over** : s'embuer, se voiler

film[2] *n* **1** : pellicule *f* (en photographie) **2** COATING : couche *f*, pellicule *f* **3** MOTION PICTURE : film *m*

filmstrip [ˈfɪlmˌstrɪp] *n* : film *m* fixe

filmy [ˈfɪlmi] *adj* **filmier; -est 1** HAZY : embué, voilé **2** GAUZY : léger, transparent

filter[1] [ˈfɪltər] *v* : filtrer

filter[2] *n* : filtre *m*

filth [ˈfɪlθ] *n* **1** DIRT : saleté *f*, crasse *f* **2** OBSCENITY : obscénités *fpl*

filthiness [ˈfɪlθinəs] *n* : saleté *f*

filthy [ˈfɪlθi] *adj* **filthier; -est 1** DIRTY : sale, crasseux **2** VILE : dégoûtant **3** OBSCENE : obscène, ordurier

filtration [fɪlˈtreɪʃən] *n* : filtration *f*

fin [ˈfɪn] *n* **1** : nageoire *f* (d'un poisson), aileron *m* (d'un requin) **2** : aileron *m*, empennage *m* (d'un avion)

finagle [fəˈneɪgəl] *vt* **-gled; -gling** : obtenir par des moyens subreptices, se débrouiller pour obtenir

final[1] [ˈfaɪnəl] *adj* **1** CONCLUSIVE : définitif, irrévocable **2** LAST : dernier **3** ULTIMATE : ultime, final <our final goal : notre but ultime>

final[2] *n* **1** : finale *f* (d'une compétition) **2 finals** *npl* : examens *mpl* de fin de semestre

finale [fɪˈnæli, -ˈnɑ-] *n* **1** : finale *m* **2 grand finale** : apothéose *f*

finalist [ˈfaɪnəlɪst] *n* : finaliste *mf*

finality [faɪˈnæləṭi, fə-] *n, pl* **-ties** : irrévocabilité *f*

finalize [ˈfaɪnəlˌaɪz] *vt* **-ized; -izing** : mettre au point

finally [ˈfaɪnəli] *adv* : enfin, finalement

finance[1] [fəˈnænts, ˈfaɪˌnænts] *vt* **-nanced; -nancing** : financer

finance[2] *n* **1** : finance *f* <high finance : la haute finance> **2 finances** *npl* RESOURCES : finances *fpl*

financial [fəˈnæntʃəl, faɪ-] *adj* : financier

financially [fəˈnæntʃəli, faɪ-] *adv* : financièrement

financier [ˌfɪnənˈsɪr, ˌfaɪˌnæn-] *n* : financier *m*

finch [ˈfɪntʃ] *n* : fringillidé *m*

find[1] [ˈfaɪnd] *v* **found** [ˈfaʊnd]; **finding** *vt* **1** LOCATE : trouver, rencontrer, retrouver <I can't find it : je ne peux pas le trouver> <to find one's voice : retrouver sa voix> <to find its mark : atteindre sa cible> **2** DISCOVER, REALIZE : trouver, découvrir, s'apercevoir <I find it difficult : je trouve que c'est difficile> **3** DECLARE : déclarer, prononcer <to find s.o. guilty : prononcer qqn coupable> — *vi* : prononcer <to find for the accused : prononcer en faveur de l'accusé>

find[2] *n* : découverte *f*, trouvaille *f*

finder [ˈfaɪndər] *n* **1** : celui *m*, celle *f* qui trouve **2** : chercheur *m* (de télescope, etc.)

finding [ˈfaɪndɪŋ] *n* **1** FIND : découverte *f* **2** VERDICT : verdict *m* (en droit) **3 findings** *npl* : conclusions *fpl*

find out *vt* DISCOVER : découvrir — *vi* **to find out about** : se renseigner sur

fine[1] [ˈfaɪn] *vt* **fined; fining** : infliger une amende à, condamner à une amende

fine[2] *adv* **1** ALL RIGHT : très bien <I'm doing fine : je vais très bien> **2** FINELY : fin

fine[3] *adj* **finer; -est 1** PURE : pur (se dit de l'or, etc.) **2** DELICATE, THIN : fin <fine hair : cheveux fins> **3** : fin <fine sand : sable fin> **4** SUBTLE : subtil, sensible **5** EXCELLENT : beau, excellent <she did a fine job : elle a fait un beau travail> **6** FAIR : beau <the weather is fine : il fait beau> **7 to be fine** : aller bien <everyone's fine : tout le monde va bien> <that's fine with me : ça me va>

fine[4] *n* : amende *f,* contravention *f*

fine art *n* : beaux-arts *mpl*

finely ['faɪnli] *adv* **1** : finement, fin <to chop finely : hacher finement, hacher menu> **2** EXCELLENTLY : admirablement **3** PRECISELY : avec précision **4** ELEGANTLY : élégamment

fineness ['faɪnnəs] *n* **1** DELICACY : finesse *f* (d'un tissu, etc.) **2** EXCELLENCE : pureté *f* (d'un métal), excellence *f* **3** SUBTLETY : subtilité *f,* délicatesse *f*

finery ['faɪnəri] *n, pl* **-eries** : parure *f*

finesse[1] [fə'nɛs] *vt* **-nessed; -nessing** : manipuler adroitement

finesse[2] *n* : finesse *f*

finger[1] ['fɪŋgər] *vt* HANDLE : toucher, palper, tâter

finger[2] *n* : doigt *m*

fingerling ['fɪŋgərlɪŋ] *n* : petit poisson *m*

fingernail ['fɪŋgər,neɪl] *n* : ongle *m*

fingerprint[1] ['fɪŋgər,prɪnt] *vt* : prendre les empreintes digitales de

fingerprint[2] *n* : empreinte *f* digitale

fingertip ['fɪŋgər,tɪp] *n* : bout *m* du doigt

finicky ['fɪnɪki] *adj* : tatillon, pointilleux

finish[1] ['fɪnɪʃ] *vt* **1** COMPLETE, TERMINATE : terminer, finir, achever **2** : mettre une finition sur (un meuble, un parquet, etc.) — *vi* : finir, se terminer

finish[2] *n* **1** END : fin *f* **2** *or* **finish line** : arrivée *f* **3** : finition *f,* fini *m Can* <a glossy finish : une finition brillante>

finite ['faɪ,naɪt] *adj* : fini, limité

Finn ['fɪn] *n* : Finlandais *m,* -daise *f*

Finnish[1] ['fɪnɪʃ] *adj* : finlandais

Finnish[2] *n* : finnois *m* (langue)

fiord [fi'ɔrd] → **fjord**

fir ['fər] *n* : sapin *m*

fire[1] ['faɪr] *vt* **fired; firing 1** IGNITE : incendier **2** STIR : exciter, enflammer (l'imagination) **3** DISMISS : renvoyer, congédier (un employé) **4** SHOOT : tirer, décharger <to fire a gun : tirer un coup de fusil> **5** : cuire (de la poterie)

fire[2] *n* **1** : feu *m* **2** BURNING : feu *m,* incendie *m* <forest fire : incendie de forêt> **3** ENTHUSIASM : enthousiasme *m,* ardeur *f* **4** SHOOTING : feu *m,* tir *m* <to open fire : ouvrir le feu>

fire alarm *n* : avertisseur *m* d'incendie

firearm ['faɪr,ɑrm] *n* : arme *f* à feu

fireball ['faɪr,bɔl] *n* **1** : boule *f* de feu **2** METEORITE : bolide *m*

firebreak ['faɪr,breɪkl] *n* : pare-feu *m,* coupe-feu *m*

firebug ['faɪr,bʌg] *n* : incendiaire *mf,* pyromane *mf*

firecracker ['faɪr,krækər] *n* : pétard *m*

fire escape *n* : escalier *m* de secours

fire extinguisher *n* : extincteur *m*

firefighter ['faɪr,faɪtər] *n* : pompier *m,* sapeur-pompier *m France*

firefly ['faɪr,flaɪ] *n, pl* **-flies** : luciole *f*

fire hall *Brit* → **fire station**

fireman ['faɪrmən] *n, pl* **-men** [-mən, -,mɛn] **1** → **firefighter 2** STOKER : chauffeur *m*

fireplace ['faɪr,pleɪs] *n* : cheminée *f,* foyer *m*

fireplug ['faɪr,plʌg] → **hydrant**

fireproof[1] ['faɪr,pru:f] *vt* : ignifuger

fireproof[2] *adj* : ignifuge, à l'épreuve du feu

fireside[1] ['faɪr,saɪd] *adj* : familier, informel

fireside[2] *n* : coin *m* du feu

fire station *n* : caserne *f* de pompiers *France,* poste *m* de pompiers *Can*

firewood ['faɪr,wʊd] *n* : bois *m* de chauffage

fireworks ['faɪr,wərk] *n* : feux *mpl* d'artifice

firm[1] ['fərm] *vt or* **to firm up** : raffermir (des muscles), confirmer (des plans, etc.)

firm[2] *adj* **1** STRONG : ferme <to have a firm grip on : tenir fermement> **2** HARD, SOLID : ferme <on firm ground : sur la terre ferme> **3** STEADY : solide, stable **4** DEFINITE : solide, déterminé **5** RESOLUTE : ferme, résolu **6** STEADFAST : solide, ferme <a firm friendship : une amitié solide>

firm[3] *n* : entreprise *f,* firme *f*

firmament ['fərməmənt] *n* : firmament *m*

firmly ['fərmli] *adv* : fermement

firmness ['fərmnəs] *n* : fermeté *f,* solidité *f*

first[1] ['fərst] *adv* **1** : en premier, d'abord <first of all : tout d'abord> **2** : pour la première fois <when I first visited France : la première fois que je suis allé en France> **3** RATHER : plutôt <I'd die first : plutôt mourir>

first[2] *adj* : premier <at first sight : à première vue> <I don't know the first thing about physics : je ne connais absolument rien à la physique>

first[3] *n* **1** : premier *m,* -mière *f* (dans une série) **2** (*used in dates*) : premier *m* <the first of July : le premier juillet> **3** *or* **first gear** : première *f* **4 at ~** : au début

first aid *n* : premiers secours *mpl*, premiers soins *mpl*
first–class[1] ['fərst'klæs] *adv* : en première <to travel first-class : voyager en première>
first–class[2] *adj* **1** EXCELLENT : excellent, de première qualité **2** : de première classe (se dit d'une place dans un avion, etc.), à tarif normal (se dit d'une lettre, etc.)
first class *n* : première classe *f*
first lieutenant *n* : lieutenant *m*
firstly ['fərstli] *adv* : premièrement
first–rate[1] ['fərst'reɪt] *adv* : très bien
first–rate[2] *adj* : excellent, de premier ordre
fiscal ['fɪskəl] *adj* : fiscal — **fiscally** *adv*
fish[1] ['fɪʃ] *vi* **1** : pêcher **2 to fish for** SEEK : chercher
fish[2] *n, pl* **fish** *or* **fishes** : poisson *m*
fisherman ['fɪʃərmən] *n, pl* **-men** [-mən, -mɛn] : pêcheur *m*, -cheuse *f*
fishery ['fɪʃəri] *n, pl* **-eries 1** → **fishing 2** : pêcherie *f*, zone *f* de pêche
fishhook ['fɪʃˌhʊk] *n* : hameçon *m*
fishing ['fɪʃɪŋ] *n* : pêche *f*
fishy ['fɪʃi] *adj* **fishier; -est 1** : de poisson <a fishy taste : un goût de poisson> **2** QUESTIONABLE : douteux, louche
fission ['fɪʃən, -ʒən] *n* : fission *f*
fissure ['fɪʃər] *n* : fissure *f*
fist ['fɪst] *n* : poing *m* <to clench one's fists : serrer les poings>
fistfight ['fɪstˌfaɪt] *n* : coups *mpl* de poing, bagarre *f*
fit[1] ['fɪt] *v* **fitted; fitting** *vt* **1** : aller à <this suit fits you well : ce complet vous va bien> **2** MATCH : répondre à, correspondre à <to fit one's mood : correspondre à son humeur> **3** INSTALL : installer, mettre en place **4** EQUIP : équiper **5 to fit s.o. for** : prendre les mesures de qqn pour (un vêtement) — *vi* **1** : aller, être de la bonne taille <this dress doesn't fit : cette robe n'est pas à ma taille> **2** *or* **to fit in** BELONG : s'intégrer
fit[2] *adj* **fitter; fittest 1** APPROPRIATE, SUITED : convenable, qui convient <to see fit to : trouver bon de> **2** COMPETENT, QUALIFIED : capable, digne **3** HEALTHY : en bonne santé, en (pleine) forme
fit[3] *n* **1** : coupe *f* (d'un vêtement) <it's a tight fit : c'est trop juste> **2** : crise *f*, accès *m* <a fit of anger : un accès de colère>
fitful ['fɪtfəl] *adj* : agité, intermittent
fitfully ['fɪtfəli] *adv* : de manière intermittente
fitness ['fɪtnəs] *n* **1** HEALTH : santé *f*, forme *f* physique **2** SUITABILITY : aptitude *f*, compétences *fpl* (d'une personne), justesse *f* (d'une remarque)
fitting[1] ['fɪṭɪŋ] *adj* SUITABLE : approprié, convenable
fitting[2] *n* **1** : essayage *m* (de vêtements) **2** : installation *f* (électrique)
five[1] ['faɪv] *adj* : cinq
five[2] *n* : cinq *m*
fix[1] ['fɪks] *vt* **1** ATTACH, SECURE : fixer, attacher **2** ESTABLISH : fixer <to fix a date : fixer un rendez-vous> **3** FOCUS : fixer **4** REPAIR : réparer **5** PREPARE : préparer **6** : truquer, arranger <to fix a race : truquer une course>
fix[2] *n* **1** PREDICAMENT : pétrin *m fam* **2** : position *f* <to get a fix on : déterminer la position de>
fixate ['fɪkˌseɪt] *vi* **-ated; -ating** : faire une fixation <to be fixated on : être fixé sur>
fixation [fɪk'seɪʃən] *n* : fixation *f*
fixed ['fɪkst] *adj* **1** STATIONARY : fixe, immobile **2** INTENT : fixe <a fixed stare : un regard fixe> **3** SET : constant, fixe <fixed income : revenu fixe> <a fixed idea : une idée arrêtée>
fixedly ['fɪksədli] *adv* : fixement
fixture ['fɪkstʃər] *n* : installation *f* <bathroom fixtures : installations sanitaires>
fizz[1] ['fɪz] *vi* EFFERVESCE : pétiller
fizz[2] *n* : pétillement *m*
fizzle[1] ['fɪzəl] *vi* **-zled; -zling 1** FIZZ : pétiller **2** *or* **to fizzle out** FAIL : échouer, ne rien donner
fizzle[2] *n* FAILURE : échec *m*, fiasco *m*
fjord [fi'ɔrd] *n* : fjord *m*
flabbergast ['flæbərˌgæst] *vt* : sidérer *fam*, stupéfier
flabbiness ['flæbinəs] *n* : flaccidité *f*
flabby ['flæbi] *adj* **flabbier; -est** : flasque
flaccid ['flæksəd, 'flæsəd] *adj* : flasque, mou
flag[1] ['flæg] *v* **flagged; flagging** *vt* SIGNAL : faire signe à (un taxi, etc.) — *vi* DECLINE, WEAKEN : dépérir, languir, faiblir
flag[2] *n* **1** : drapeau *m*, pavillon *m* (d'un navire) **2** *or* **flagstone** : dalle *f*
flagon ['flægən] *n* : cruche *f*, grosse bouteille *f*
flagpole [ˌflægˌpoːl] *n* : mât *m* (de drapeau)
flagrant ['fleɪgrənt] *adj* : flagrant
flagrantly ['fleɪgrəntli] *adv* : d'une manière flagrante
flagship ['flægˌʃɪp] *n* : navire *m* amiral
flagstaff ['flægˌstæf] → **flagpole**
flagstone ['flægˌstoːn] → **flag**[2]
flail[1] ['fleɪl] *vt* **1** : battre (des grains) au fléau **2** : agiter (les bras, etc.)
flail[2] *n* : fléau *m*
flair ['flær] *n* **1** TALENT : aptitude *f*, don *m* **2** STYLE : classe *f*, style *m*
flak ['flæk] *ns & pl* **1** : tir *m* antiaérien **2** CRITICISM : critiques *fpl*
flake[1] ['fleɪk] *v* **flaked; flaking** *vi or* **to flake off** : s'écailler, s'effriter — *vt* : émietter (un poisson, etc.)

flake[2] *n* **:** flocon *m* (de neige), paillette *f* (de métal, de savon, etc.), écaille *f* (de peinture)
flamboyance [flæm'bɔɪənts] *n* **:** extravagance *f*
flamboyant [flæm'bɔɪənt] *adj* **:** extravagant, éclatant
flame[1] ['fleɪm] *vi* **flamed; flaming 1** BURN **:** flamber, brûler **2** BLAZE, GLOW **:** flamboyer
flame[2] *n* **1 :** flamme *f* <to burst into flames : s'embraser> <to go up in flames : s'enflammer> **2** ARDOR **:** flamme *f,* feu *m*
flamethrower ['fleɪm,θro:ər] *n* **:** lance-flammes *m*
flaming ['fleɪmɪŋ] *adj* **1 :** flamboyant <flaming red hair : cheveux rouges flamboyants> **2** PASSIONATE **:** ardent
flamingo [flə'mɪŋgo] *n, pl* **-gos :** flamant *m*
flammable ['flæməbəl] *adj* **:** inflammable
flange ['flændʒ] *n* **:** bride *f* (d'une pipe), boudin *m* (d'une roue)
flank[1] ['flæŋk] *vt* **1 :** flanquer (dans l'armée) **2** BORDER **:** border, entourer
flank[2] *n* **:** flanc *m*
flannel ['flænəl] *n* **:** flanelle *f*
flap[1] ['flæp] *v* **flapped; flapping** *vt* **:** battre (des ailes) **—** *vi* **:** battre, claquer <to flap in the wind : battre au vent>
flap[2] *n* **1 :** battement *m* (d'ailes), claquement *m* (d'une voile) **2 :** rabat *m* (d'une enveloppe, d'un vêtement, etc.), abattant *m* (d'une table)
flapjack ['flæp,dʒæk] → **pancake**
flare[1] ['flær] *vi* **flared; flaring 1** FLAME **:** flamboyer, s'enflammer **2** WIDEN **:** s'évaser **3 to flare up :** s'emporter, fulminer (contre une personne) **4 to flare up** BREAK OUT, INTENSIFY **:** s'intensifier, éclater
flare[2] *n* **1** BLAZE **:** flamboiement *m* **2** SIGNAL **:** signal *m* lumineux **3** ROCKET **:** fusée *f* éclairante
flash[1] ['flæʃ] *vt* **1** PROJECT **:** projeter, diriger <he flashed the light in my eyes : il a dirigé la lumière dans mes yeux> **2** TRANSMIT **:** transmettre (un message, etc.) **3** SHOW **:** faire apparaître soudainement **4 :** lancer (un sourire), jeter (un regard) **—** *vi* **1** GLEAM, SPARKLE **:** étinceler, briller **2** BLINK **:** clignoter (se dit d'une lumière, d'un signal lumineux) **3 to flash past :** passer comme un éclair
flash[2] *adj* **:** subit <flash flood : crue subite>
flash[3] *n* **1 :** éclair *m* (de génie), éclat *m* (d'un diamant), lueur *f* (d'espoir) **2** INSTANT **:** minute *f,* instant *m* <I'll be back in a flash : je serai de retour dans un instant> **3 :** flash *m* (d'un appareil photographique) **4 flash of lightning :** éclair *m*
flashiness ['flæʃinəs] *n* **:** tape-à-l'œil *m*
flashlight ['flæʃ,laɪt] *n* **:** lampe *f* de poche
flashy ['flæʃi] *adj* **flashier; -est :** tape-à-l'œil, tapageur, criard
flask ['flæsk] *n* **:** flacon *m,* flasque *f*
flat[1] ['flæt] *adv* **1 :** à plat, planche *Can* <to lay (down) flat : mettre à plat> <to fall flat : tomber de tout son long> **2** EXACTLY **:** pile *fam* <in one hour flat : dans une heure pile> **3 :** faux, en dessous du ton (en musique) **4 to be flat broke :** être complètement fauché
flat[2] *adj* **flatter; flattest 1 :** plat (se dit d'une surface) **2** DOWNRIGHT **:** net, catégorique <a flat refusal : un refus catégorique> **3** FIXED **:** fixe <a flat rate : un taux fixe> **4** MONOTONOUS **:** plat, monotone **5 :** éventé (se dit des boissons gazeuses) **6** DEFLATED **:** crevé, dégonflé **7 :** faux (se dit d'une voix), bémol (se dit d'une note)
flat[3] *n* **1** PLAIN **:** plaine *f* **2 :** plat *m* (de la main) **3 :** bémol *m* (en musique) **4** *Brit* APARTMENT **:** appartement *m* **5** *or* **flat tire :** crevaison *f*
flatcar ['flæt,kɑr] *n* **:** wagon *m* plat
flatfish ['flæt,fɪʃ] *n* **:** poisson *m* plat
flatly ['flætli] *adv* CATEGORICALLY **:** carrément, catégoriquement
flatness ['flætnəs] *n* **1** EVENNESS **:** égalité *f* **2** DULLNESS **:** monotonie *f*
flat–out ['flæt'aʊt] *adj* OUT-AND-OUT **:** complet, total, absolu
flatten ['flætən] *vt* **:** aplatir, aplanir **—** *vi or* **to flatten out :** s'aplanir
flatter ['flæt̬ər] *vt* **1** PRAISE **:** flatter, louer **2 :** flatter, avantager <this portrait flatters me : ce portrait me flatte>
flatterer ['flæt̬ərər] *n* **:** flatteur *m,* -teuse *f*
flattering ['flæt̬ərɪŋ] *adj* **:** flatteur
flattery ['flæt̬əri] *n, pl* **-ries :** flatterie *f*
flatulence ['flætʃələnts] *n* **:** flatulence *f*
flatulent ['flætʃələnt] *adj* **:** flatulent
flatware ['flæt,wær] *n* **:** couverts *mpl*
flaunt ['flɔnt] *vt* **:** faire étalage de, étaler
flavor[1] *or Brit* **flavour** ['fleɪvər] *vt* **:** assaisonner, relever le goût de
flavor[2] *or Brit* **flavour** *n* **1 :** saveur *f,* goût *m* **2** FLAVORING **:** assaisonnement *m,* arôme *m,* parfum *m* <artificial flavors : arômes artificiels>
flavorful *or Brit* **flavourful** ['fleɪvərfəl] *adj* **:** savoureux, délectable
flavoring *or Brit* **flavouring** ['fleɪvərɪŋ] *n* **:** assaisonnement *m,* arôme *m,* parfum *m*
flavorless *or Brit* **flavourless** ['fleɪvərləs] *adj* **:** sans saveur
flavour *Brit* → **flavor**
flaw ['flɔ] *n* **:** défaut *m,* imperfection *f*
flawless ['flɔləs] *adj* **:** sans défaut, parfait
flawlessly ['flɔləsli] *adv* **:** parfaitement
flax ['flæks] *n* **:** lin *m*

flaxen ['flæksən] *adj* : de lin

flay ['fleɪ] *vt* **1** SKIN : écorcher (un animal) **2** CRITICIZE : éreinter

flea ['fli:] *n* : puce *f*

fleck[1] ['flɛk] *vt* : tacheter, moucheter

fleck[2] *n* : petite tache *f,* moucheture *f*

fledgling ['flɛdʒlɪŋ] *n* : oisillon *m*

flee ['fli:] *v* **fled** ['flɛd]; **fleeing** *vt* : s'enfuir de, fuir — *vi* : s'enfuir, fuir

fleece[1] ['fli:s] *vt* **fleeced; fleecing 1** SHEAR : tondre **2** SWINDLE : escroquer

fleece[2] *n* : toison *f*

fleecy ['fli:si] *adj* **fleecier; -est** : laineux (se dit d'un tissu), cotonneux (se dit des nuages, etc.)

fleet[1] ['fli:t] *vi* : s'enfuir

fleet[2] *adj* : rapide

fleet[3] *n* : flotte *f* (de navires), parc *m* (de taxis, etc.)

fleet admiral *n* : amiral *m*

fleeting ['fli:t̬ɪŋ] *adj* : bref, éphémère, fugace

Flemish[1] ['flɛmɪʃ] *adj* : flamand

Flemish[2] *n* **1** : flamand *m* (langue) **2 the Flemish** : les Flamands

flesh ['flɛʃ] *n* **1** : chair *f* (d'un animal) **2** : chair *f,* pulpe *f* (d'un fruit)

flesh out *vt* : étoffer, enrichir

fleshly ['flɛʃli] *adj* **1** BODILY : corporel **2** CARNAL : charnel, sensuel

fleshy ['flɛʃi] *adj* **fleshier; -est** : charnu (se dit des fruits, etc.), bien en chair (se dit des personnes)

flew → **fly**[1]

flex ['flɛks] *vt* : faire jouer (des muscles), fléchir (un bras, une jambe, etc.)

flexibility [ˌflɛksə'bɪlət̬i] *n* : flexibilité *f*

flexible ['flɛksəbəl] *adj* : flexible, souple — **flexibly** [-bli] *adv*

flick[1] ['flɪk] *vt* **1** STRIKE : donner un petit coup à, donner une chiquenaude à **2 to flick a switch** : appuyer sur un bouton — *vi* **to flick through** : feuilleter (un livre, etc.)

flick[2] *n* : petit coup *m,* chiquenaude *f*

flicker[1] ['flɪkər] *vi* **1** FLUTTER : cligner, battre **2** : vaciller, trembloter <a flickering flame : une flamme qui vacille>

flicker[2] *n* **1** : clignement *m,* battement *m* (d'une paupière) **2** GLIMMER : lueur *f* <a flicker of hope : une lueur d'espoir> **3** : vacillement *m* (d'une flamme)

flier ['flaɪər] *n* **1** PILOT : aviateur *m,* -trice *f* **2** *or* **flyer** LEAFLET : prospectus *m*

flight ['flaɪt] *n* **1** FLYING : vol *m* (d'un oiseau, d'un avion), trajectoire *f* (d'un projectile) **2** GROUP : volée *f* (d'oiseaux), escadrille *f* (d'avions) **3** ESCAPE : fuite *f* **4 flight of fancy** : élan *m* de l'imagination **5 flight of stairs** : escalier *m*

flightless ['flaɪtləs] *adj* : coureur <flightless birds : oiseaux coureux>

flighty ['flaɪti] *adj* **flightier; -est** : volage, inconstant

flimsiness ['flɪmzinəs] *n* : fragilité *f,* construction *f* peu solide

flimsy ['flɪmzi] *adj* **flimsier; -est 1** LIGHT, THIN : fin, léger **2** WEAK : fragile, peu solide **3** IMPLAUSIBLE : pauvre, mince <a flimsy excuse : une pauvre excuse>

flinch ['flɪntʃ] *vi* **1** WINCE : tressaillir **2** RECOIL : reculer, fuir

fling[1] ['flɪŋ] *vt* **flung** ['flʌŋ]; **flinging 1** THROW : jeter, lancer, flanquer *fam* **2 to fling oneself** : se lancer, se jeter

fling[2] *n* **1** THROW : jet *m,* lancer *m* **2** ATTEMPT : essai *m* <to have a fling at sth : essayer de faire qqch> **3** AFFAIR : aventure *f*

flint ['flɪnt] *n* : silex *m*

flinty ['flɪnti] *adj* **flintier; -est 1** : à silex **2** STERN, UNYIELDING : dur, de pierre

flip[1] ['flɪp] *v* **flipped; flipping** *vt* **1** TOSS : lancer **2** FLICK : appuyer sur (un bouton) **3 to flip a coin** : jouer à pile ou face — *vi* **1** *or* **to flip over** : se retourner **2 to flip through** : feuilleter (un livre, etc.)

flip[2] *adj* : désinvolte, impertinent

flip[3] *n* **1** FLICK : petit coup *m* **2** SOMERSAULT : saut *m* périlleux

flippancy ['flɪpəntsi] *n, pl* **-cies** : désinvolture *f,* impertinence *f*

flippant ['flɪpənt] *adj* : désinvolte

flipper ['flɪpər] *n* : nageoire *f*

flirt[1] ['flərt] *vi* : flirter

flirt[2] *n* : charmeur *m,* -meuse *f;* personne *f* qui flirte

flirtation [ˌflər'teɪʃən] *n* : flirt *m*

flirtatious [ˌflər'teɪʃəs] *adj* : charmeur, séducteur

flit ['flɪt] *vi* **flitted; flitting 1** : voleter, voltiger **2 to flit about** : passer rapidement

float[1] ['flo:t] *vt* **1** : faire flotter **2** ISSUE : émettre, lancer (en finances) <to float a loan : émettre un emprunt> — *vi* : flotter

float[2] *n* **1** RAFT : radeau *m* **2** CORK : flotteur *m,* bouchon *m* **3** : char *m* (de carnaval)

flock[1] ['flɑk] *vi* : affluer, se rassembler

flock[2] *n* **1** : volée *f* (d'oiseaux), troupeau *m* (de moutons) **2** CROWD : foule *f* **3** : ouailles *fpl* (en religion)

floe ['flo:] *n or* **ice floe** : banquise *f*

flog ['flɑg] *vt* **flogged; flogging** : flageller, fouetter

flood[1] ['flʌd] *vt* : inonder, noyer — *vi* : déborder (se dit d'une rivière)

flood[2] *n* **1** : inondation *f,* crue *f* <spring flood : crue du printemps> **2** TORRENT : déluge *m,* torrent *m* <a flood of words : un déluge de paroles>

floodlight ['flʌdˌlaɪt] *n* : projecteur *m*

floodwaters ['flʌdˌwɔt̬ərz] *npl* : eaux *fpl* de crue

floor[1] [ˈflor] *vt* **1** : faire le sol de, parqueter (une maison, une salle) **2** KNOCK DOWN : terrasser (un adversaire) **3** NONPLUS : dérouter

floor[2] *n* **1** : plancher *m,* parquet *m* (d'une salle, etc.) <dance floor : piste de danse> **2** BOTTOM, GROUND : sol *m,* fond *m* (de la mer) **3** STORY : étage *m* <a 10-floor building : un édifice de 10 étages> <on the ground floor : au rez-de-chaussée>

floorboard [ˈflorˌbord] *n* : planche *f,* latte *f*

flooring [ˈflorɪŋ] *n* **1** : revêtement *m* de sol **2** FLOOR : plancher *m,* parquet *m*

flop[1] [ˈflɑp] *vi* **flopped; flopping 1** FLAP : s'agiter mollement **2** *or* **to flop down** : s'affaler **3** FAIL : échouer, faire un four *fam*

flop[2] *n* FAILURE : fiasco *m,* four *m fam*

floppy [ˈflɑpi] *adj* **floppier; -est** : mou, pendant

floppy disk *n* : disquette *f*

flora [ˈflorə] *n* : flore *f*

floral [ˈflorəl] *adj* : floral

florid [ˈflorɪd] *adj* **1** ORNATE : fleuri **2** RUDDY : rougeaud

florist [ˈflorɪst] *n* : fleuriste *mf*

floss[1] [ˈflɔs] *vt* : utiliser du fil dentaire

floss[2] *n* **1** *or* **embroidery floss** : soie *f* à broder **2** → **dental floss**

flotation [floˈteɪʃən] *n* : mise *f* à flot

flotilla [floˈtɪlə] *n* : flottille *f*

flotsam [ˈflɑtsəm] *n* : épave *f* flottante

flounce[1] [ˈflaʊnts] *vi* **flounced; flouncing** : passer brusquement <to flounce in : entrer dans un mouvement d'humeur>

flounce[2] *n* : volant *m* (d'une jupe, etc.)

flounder[1] [ˈflaʊndər] *vi* **1** THRASH : patauger, se débattre **2** BOG DOWN, FALTER : s'empêtrer (dans un discours), piétiner (dans une carrière)

flounder[2] *n, pl* **flounder** *or* **flounders** : flet *m,* poisson *m* plat

flour[1] [ˈflaʊər] *vt* : fariner, enrober de farine

flour[2] *n* : farine *f*

flourish[1] [ˈflərɪʃ] *vt* BRANDISH : brandir — *vi* **1** PROSPER : prospérer **2** THRIVE : fleurir, s'épanouir

flourish[2] *n* **1** : fioriture *f* (en musique), paraphe *f* (d'une signature) **2** FANFARE : fanfare *f* **3** WAVING : grand geste *m* (de la main), moulinet *m* (d'une épée, etc.)

flourishing [ˈflərɪʃɪŋ] *adj* : florissant, prospère

flout [ˈflaʊt] *vt* : se moquer de, passer outre à

flow[1] [ˈfloː] *vi* **1** COURSE, RUN : couler, s'écouler <to flow past : passer devant> **2** CIRCULATE : circuler (se dit du sang, du trafic, etc.) **3** BILLOW, HANG : flotter, onduler

flow[2] *n* **1** STREAM : écoulement *m* **2** CIRCULATION : circulation *f* <blood flow : circulation du sang>

flower[1] [ˈflaʊər] *vi* **1** : fleurir **2** DEVELOP, FLOURISH : s'épanouir, se développer

flower[2] *n* **1** : fleur *f* **2** BLOOM : épanouissement *m* <in full flower : en plein épanouissement>

floweriness [ˈflaʊərinəs] *n* : ornementation *f,* fioritures *fpl*

flowering [ˈflaʊərɪŋ] *n* : floraison *f*

flowerpot [ˈflaʊərˌpɑt] *n* : pot *m* de fleurs

flowery [ˈflaʊəri] *adj* : fleuri

flown → **fly**[1]

flu [ˈfluː] *n* : grippe *f*

flub [ˈflʌb] *vt* **flubbed; flubbing** : louper *fam,* rater

fluctuate [ˈflʌktʃʊˌeɪt] *vi* **-ated; -ating** : fluctuer

fluctuation [ˌflʌktʃʊˈeɪʃən] *n* : fluctuation *f*

flue [ˈfluː] *n* : conduit *m* (de cheminée)

fluency [ˈfluːəntsi] *n* : aisance *f,* facilité *f*

fluent [ˈfluːənt] *adj* : coulant, aisé <she speaks fluent French : elle parle couramment le français>

fluently [ˈfluːəntli] *adv* : couramment

fluff[1] [ˈflʌf] *vt* **1** *or* **to fluff up** : faire bouffer **2** BOTCH : louper *fam,* rater

fluff[2] *n* **1** DOWN : duvet *m* **2** FUZZ : peluches *fpl*

fluffy [ˈflʌfi] *adj* **fluffier; -est 1** DOWNY, FUZZY : duveteux, pelucheux **2** LIGHT : léger, moelleux

fluid[1] [ˈfluːɪd] *adj* : fluide

fluid[2] *n* : fluide *m,* liquide *m*

fluidity [fluːˈɪdət̬i] *n* : fluidité *f*

fluid ounce *n* : once *f* liquide

fluke [ˈfluːk] *n* : coup *m* de chance, coup *m* de veine *fam*

flung → **fling**[1]

flunk [ˈflʌŋk] *vt* FAIL : rater

fluorescence [ˌflʊrˈɛsənts, ˌflɔr-] *n* : fluorescence *f*

fluorescent [ˌflʊrˈɛsənt, ˌflɔr-] *adj* : fluorescent

fluoridate [ˈflɔrəˌdeɪt, ˈflʊr-] *vt* **-dated; -dating** : ajouter du fluor à

fluoridation [ˌflɔrəˈdeɪʃən, ˌflʊr-] *n* : traitement *m* au fluor, fluoration *f*

fluoride [ˈflɔrˌaɪd, ˈflʊr-] *n* : fluorure *m*

fluorine [ˈflʊrˌiːn] *n* : fluor *m*

flurry[1] [ˈfləri] *vt* **flurried; flurrying** FLUSTER : agiter, énerver

flurry[2] *n, pl* **-ries 1** GUST : rafale *f,* poudrerie *f Can* <snow flurries : rafales de neige> **2** BUSTLE : tourbillon *m* **3** BARRAGE : déluge *m* (de questions, etc.)

flush[1] [ˈflʌʃ] *vt* **1** REDDEN : empourprer, rougir (les joues) **2** *or* **to flush out** : lever, faire s'envoler (du gibier) **3 to flush the toilet** : tirer la chasse d'eau — *vi* BLUSH : rougir

flush[2] *adv* : de niveau, à ras

flush[3] *adj* **1** FILLED : plein à déborder **2** RUDDY : rouge, coloré **3** LEVEL : au même niveau **4** AFFLUENT : en fonds

flush[4] *n* **1** FLUSHING : chasse *f* (d'eau) **2** SURGE : élan *m,* accès *m* <a flush of anger : un accès de colère> **3** BLUSH : rougeur *f*
fluster[1] ['flʌstər] *vt* : énerver, troubler
fluster[2] *n* : trouble *m,* agitation *f*
flute ['flu:t] *n* : flûte *f*
fluted ['flu:t̬əd] *adj* GROOVED : cannelé
flutist ['flu:t̬ɪst] *n* : flûtiste *mf*
flutter[1] ['flʌt̬ər] *vi* **1** FLAP : battre (se dit des ailes) **2** BEAT : palpiter (se dit du cœur) **3** DRIFT, FLY : flotter <a sail fluttering in the wind : une voile qui flotte au vent> **4 to flutter about** : s'agiter, s'affairer
flutter[2] *n* **1** FLAPPING : battement *m* (d'ailes) **2** STIR : agitation *f,* émoi *m*
flux ['flʌks] *n* **1** : flux *m* (en médecine et en physique) **2** CHANGE : changement *m* <in a state of flux : dans un état de perpétuel changement>
fly[1] ['flaɪ] *v* **flew** ['flu:]; **flown** ['flo:n]; **flying** *vt* : faire voler — *vi* **1** : voler (se dit d'un oiseau, d'un avion, etc.) **2** TRAVEL : prendre l'avion **3** FLOAT : flotter, onduler **4** FLEE : fuir, s'enfuir **5** PASS : passer vite, filer *fam* <time was flying by : le temps filait>
fly[2] *n, pl* **flies 1** : mouche *f* (insecte) **2** : braguette *f* (d'un pantalon)
flyer → **flier**
flying saucer *n* : soucoupe *f* volante
flypaper ['flaɪˌpeɪpər] *n* : papier *m* tue-mouches
flyspeck ['flaɪˌspɛk] *n* **1** : chiure *f* de mouche **2** SPECK : petite tache *f*
flyswatter ['flaɪˌswɑt̬ər] *n* : tapette *f* à mouches, tue-mouches *m Can*
foal[1] ['fo:l] *vi* : pouliner, mettre bas
foal[2] *n* : poulain *m*
foam[1] ['fo:m] *vi* : mousser, écumer
foam[2] *n* : mousse *f,* écume *f*
foamy ['fo:mi] *adj* **foamier; -est** : mousseux, écumeux
focal ['fo:kəl] *adj* : focal
fo'c'sle ['fo:ksəl] → **forecastle**
focus[1] ['fo:kəs] *vt* **1** : mettre au point (un instrument), fixer (les yeux) **2** CONCENTRATE : concentrer, faire converger — *vi* : converger, se concentrer
focus[2] *n, pl* **foci** ['fo:ˌsaɪ, -ˌkaɪ] **1** : foyer *m* <to be in focus : être au point> <to bring into focus : mettre au point> **2** CENTER : centre *m* <the focus of attention : le centre d'attention, le point de mire>
fodder ['fɑdər] *n* : fourrage *m*
foe ['fo:] *n* : ennemi *m,* -mie *f;* adversaire *mf*
fog[1] ['fɔg, 'fɑg] *v* **fogged; fogging** *vt* : embuer, brouiller — *vi or* **to fog up** : s'embuer, se couvrir de buée
fog[2] *n* **1** : brouillard *m,* brume *f* **2** CONFUSION : brouillard *m,* confusion *f*
foggy ['fɔgi, 'fɑ-] *adj* **foggier; -est 1** : brumeux <a foggy night : une nuit brumeuse> **2** CONFUSED : confus <I haven't the foggiest notion : je n'en ai pas la moindre idée>
foghorn ['fɔgˌhɔrn, 'fɑg-] *n* : corne *f* de brume
fogy ['fo:gi] *n, pl* **-gies** : vieille baderne *f fam*
foible ['fɔɪbəl] *n* : petit défaut *m,* petite manie *f*
foil[1] ['fɔɪl] *vt* THWART : déjouer, contrecarrer
foil[2] *n* **1** SWORD : fleuret *m* **2** : feuille *f* <aluminum foil : feuille d'aluminium> **3** COMPLEMENT, CONTRAST : repoussoir *m*
foist ['fɔɪst] *vt* **1 to foist sth off on** : refiler qqch à **2 to foist oneself on** : s'imposer à
fold[1] ['fo:ld] *vt* **1** : plier <to fold a blanket : plier une couverture> **2** CLASP : croiser (les bras), joindre (les mains) **3** EMBRACE : serrer, enlacer — *vi* FAIL : échouer, s'écrouler
fold[2] *n* **1** CREASE, PLEAT : pli *m* **2** SHEEPFOLD : parc *m* à moutons **3** GROUP : bercail *m,* sein *m* <to return to the fold : rentrer au bercail>
folder ['fo:ldər] *n* **1** FILE : chemise *f,* dossier *m* **2** CIRCULAR : dépliant *m*
foliage ['fo:liɪdʒ, -lɪdʒ] *n* : feuillage *m*
folio ['fo:liˌo:] *n, pl* **-lios** : folio *m*
folk[1] ['fo:k] *adj* : populaire, folklorique
folk[2] *n, pl* **folk** *or* **folks 1** PEOPLE : gens *mfpl* <plain folks : des gens ordinaires> **2 folks** *npl* PARENTS : famille *f,* parents *mpl*
folklore ['fo:kˌlor] *n* : folklore *m*
folk music *n* : musique *f* folklorique, folk *m*
folksy ['fo:ksi] *adj* **folksier; -est** : populaire, sympa *fam*
follicle ['fɑlɪkəl] *n* : follicule *m*
follow ['fɑlo] *vt* **1** : suivre <follow the guide : suivez le guide> <they followed the road : ils ont longé la route> **2** PURSUE : exercer, poursuivre (une carrière, etc.) **3** OBEY : suivre, se soumettre à, se conformer à **4** UNDERSTAND : suivre, comprendre — *vi* **1** : suivre <in the days that followed : dans les jours qui ont suivi> **2** ENSUE : s'ensuivre, résulter **3** UNDERSTAND : suivre
follower ['fɑloər] *n* : partisan *m,* -sane *f;* disciple *mf*
following[1] ['fɑloɪŋ] *adj* : suivant
following[2] *n* : partisans *mpl*
following[3] *prep* : après
follow through *vi* **to follow through on** : suivre (jusqu'au bout)
follow up *vt* : donner suite à, confirmer
folly ['fɑli] *n, pl* **-lies** : folie *f,* absurdité *f*
foment [fo'mɛnt] *vt* : fomenter
fond ['fɑnd] *adj* **1** LOVING : affectueux, tendre **2** FERVENT : cher, fervent <my fondest hope : mon espoir le plus cher> **3 to be fond of** : aimer beaucoup

fondle ['fɑndəl] *vt* **-dled; -dling** : caresser

fondly ['fɑndli] *adv* **1** AFFECTIONATELY : affectueusement **2** DEARLY : chèrement

fondness ['fɑndnəs] *n* **1** AFFECTION : affection *f,* tendresse *f* **2** PARTIALITY : prédilection *f,* penchant *m*

fondue [fɑn'du:, -'dju:] *n* : fondue *f*

font ['fɑnt] *n* **1** *or* **baptismal font** : fonts *mpl* baptismaux **2** SOURCE : source *f,* fontaine *f* **3** : police *f* (de caractères typographiques)

food ['fu:d] *n* **1** : nourriture *f,* aliments *mpl* **2** : cuisine *f,* mets *m* <Chinese food : mets chinois> **3 food for thought** : matière *f* à réflexion

food chain *n* : chaîne *f* alimentaire

food poisoning : intoxication *f* alimentaire

foodstuffs ['fu:d,stʌfs] *npl* : aliments *mpl,* denrées *fpl* alimentaires

fool[1] ['fu:l] *vt* DECEIVE : duper, berner — *vi* **1** JOKE : plaisanter <I was just fooling : je plaisantais> **2 to fool around** : perdre son temps **3 to fool with** : jouer avec

fool[2] *n* **1** : imbécile *mf;* idiot *m,* -diote *f;* nono *m,* -note *f Can fam* <don't be a fool! : ne fais pas l'idiot!> **2** JESTER : fou *m*

foolhardiness ['fu:l,hɑrdinəs] *n* : témérité *f*

foolhardy ['fu:l,hɑrdi] *adj* RASH : téméraire

foolish ['fu:lɪʃ] *adj* **1** STUPID : bête, idiot **2** RIDICULOUS : absurde, ridicule

foolishly ['fu:lɪʃli] *adv* : bêtement, sottement

foolishness ['fu:lɪʃnəs] *n* **1** STUPIDITY : bêtise *f,* sottise *f* **2** FOLLY : folie *f,* absurdité *f*

foolproof ['fu:l,pru:f] *adj* : infaillible

foot ['fʊt] *n, pl* **feet** ['fi:t] **1** : pied *m* **2** : bas *m* <at the foot of the page : au bas de la page>

footage ['fʊt̬ɪdʒ] *n* **1** : longueur *f* en pieds **2** : métrage *m* (d'un film)

football ['fʊt,bɔl] *n* : football *m* américain, football *m Can*

footbridge ['fʊt,brɪdʒ] *n* : passerelle *f*

foothills ['fʊt,hɪlz] *npl* : contreforts *mpl*

foothold ['fʊt,ho:ld] *n* **1** : prise *f* de pied **2 to gain a foothold in** : prendre pied sur

footing ['fʊt̬ɪŋ] *n* **1** FOOTHOLD : prise *f* de pied <to keep one's footing : conserver l'équilibre> **2** STATUS : position *f,* niveau *m* <on the same footing : sur le même pied d'égalité>

footlights ['fʊt,laɪts] *npl* : rampe *f*

footloose ['fʊt,lu:s] *adj* : libre de toute attache

footman ['fʊtmən] *n, pl* **-men** [-mən, -,mɛn] : valet *m* de pied

footnote ['fʊt,no:t] *n* : note *f* en bas de la page

footpath ['fʊt,pæθ] *n* : sentier *m*

footprint ['fʊt,prɪnt] *n* : empreinte *f* (de pied), trace *f* (de pas)

footrest ['fʊt,rɛst] *n* : repose-pied *m*

footstep ['fʊt,stɛp] *n* : pas *m*

footstool ['fʊt,stu:l] *n* : tabouret *m*

footwear ['fʊt,wær] *n* : chaussures *fpl*

footwork ['fʊt,wərk] *n* : jeu *m* de jambes

fop ['fɑp] *n* : dandy *m*

for[1] ['fɔr] *conj* BECAUSE : car

for[2] *prep* **1** (*indicating a purpose*) : pour <to get ready for a trip : se préparer pour un voyage> <what's it for? : c'est pour quoi faire?> **2** BECAUSE OF : de, à cause de <to cry for joy : pleurer de joie> **3** (*indicating a recipient*) : pour <gifts for her sister : des cadeaux pour sa sœur> **4** (*indicating support*) : pour <to fight for one's country : se battre pour sa patrie> <he speaks for the poor : il parle au nom des pauvres> **5** (*indicating a goal or remedy*) : contre, pour <a cure for cancer : un remède contre le cancer> <it's for your own good : c'est pour ton bien> **6** (*indicating equivalence or exchange*) : pour <I bought it for $10 : je l'ai acheté pour 10 $> **7** (*indicating duration*) : pour, pendant, depuis <he's here for three days : il est là pour trois jours> <we talked for hours : on a parlé pendant des heures> <I've lived here for two years : j'habite ici depuis deux ans> **8** (*indicating destination)* : pour, à destination de <to leave for New York : partir pour New York> <a train for Paris : un train à destination de Paris> **9** → **as for**

forage[1] ['fɔrɪdʒ] *vi* **-aged; -aging** : fourrager, fouiller

forage[2] *n* : fourrage *m*

foray ['fɔr,eɪ] *n* : incursion *f*

forbear[1] [fɔr'bær] *vi* **-bore** [-'bor]; **-borne** [-'born]; **-bearing 1** ABSTAIN : s'abstenir **2** : être patient

forbear[2] → **forebear**

forbearance [fɔr'bærənts] *n* **1** RESTRAINT : abstention *f* **2** PATIENCE : patience *f*

forbid [fər'bɪd] *vt* **-bade** [-'bæd, -'beɪd] *or* **-bad** [-'bæd]; **-bidden** [-'bɪdən]; **-bidding 1** PROHIBIT : interdire, défendre **2** PREVENT : empêcher

forbidding [fər'bɪdɪŋ] *adj* **1** DISAGREEABLE : rebutant, déplaisant **2** MENACING : menaçant

force[1] ['fors] *vt* **forced; forcing 1** COMPEL : forcer, contraindre, obliger **2** *or* **to force open** : forcer **3** PRESS, PUSH : forcer <I forced my way through : je me suis frayé un passage> **4 to force a smile** : se forcer à sourire

force[2] *n* **1** POWER, STRENGTH : force *f* **2** *or* **forces** *npl* : forces *fpl,* troupes *fpl* <ground forces : forces terrestres> <the police force : les forces de po-

lice> **3** : force *f* (en physique) <the force of gravity : la pesanteur> **4 in ~** : en grand nombre, en force **5 in ~** : en vigueur (se dit d'une loi, etc.)
forceful ['forsfəl] *adj* : puissant, énergique, vigoureux
forcefully ['forsfəli] *adv* : avec force, avec vigueur
forceps ['fɔrsəps, -ˌsɛps] *ns & pl* : forceps *m*
forcible ['forsəbəl] *adj* **1** FORCED : de force **2** POWERFUL : énergique, vigoureux
forcibly ['forsəbli] *adv* **1** : de force **2** VIGOROUSLY : avec vigueur, énergiquement
ford[1] ['ford] *vt* : passer à gué
ford[2] *n* : gué *m*
fore[1] ['for] *adv* : à l'avant
fore[2] *adj* : à l'avant, antérieur
fore[3] *n* **1** : avant *m* (d'un navire) **2 to come to the fore** : se faire remarquer, se mettre en évidence
fore–and–aft ['forən'æft, -ənd-] *adj* : aurique <fore-and-aft sail : voile aurique>
forearm ['forˌɑrm] *n* : avant-bras *m*
forebear ['forˌbær] *n* : ancêtre *mf*
foreboding [for'bo:dɪŋ] *n* : (mauvais) pressentiment *m*, prémonition *f*
forecast[1] ['forˌkæst] *vt* **-cast; -casting** : prévoir
forecast[2] *n* **1** PREDICTION : prévision *f* **2** *or* **weather forecast** : prévisions *fpl* météorologiques, météo *f Can fam*
forecastle ['fo:ksəl] *n* : gaillard *m* d'avant
foreclose [for'klo:z] *vt* **-closed; -closing** : saisir (un bien hypothéqué)
foreclosure [for'klo:ʒər] *n* : forclusion *f*
forefathers ['forˌfɑðərz] *npl* : ancêtres *mfpl*, aïeux *mpl*
forefinger ['forˌfɪŋgər] *n* : index *m*
forefoot ['forˌfʊt] *n, pl* **-feet** [ˌfi:t] : pied *m* antérieur
forefront ['forˌfrʌnt] *n* : premier rang *m*
forego[1] [for'go:] *vt* **-went; -gone; -going** PRECEDE : précéder
forego[2] → **forgo**
foregoing [for'go:ɪŋ] *adj* : précédent
foregone [for'gɔn] *adj* **it's a foregone conclusion** : c'est gagné d'avance
foreground ['forˌgraʊnd] *n* : premier plan *m*
forehand[1] ['forˌhænd] *adj* : de coup droit
forehand[2] *n* : coup *m* droit
forehead ['fɔrəd, 'forˌhɛd] *n* : front *m*
foreign ['fɔrən] *adj* **1** : étranger <a foreign language : une langue étrangère> **2** : extérieur <foreign trade : commerce extérieur> **3** ALIEN : étranger <foreign bodies : corps étrangers>
foreigner ['fɔrənər] *n* : étranger *m*, -gère *f*
foreknowledge [for'nɑlɪdʒ] *n* : connaissance *f* anticipée, prescience *f*
foreleg ['forˌlɛg] *n* : jambe *f* antérieure, patte *f* de devant
foreman ['formən] *n, pl* **-men** [-mən, -ˌmɛn] **1** : président *m* du jury **2** SUPERVISOR : contremaître *m*
foremost[1] ['forˌmo:st] *adv* **first and foremost** : tout d'abord, avant tout
foremost[2] *adj* : principal, le plus en vue
forenoon ['forˌnu:n] *n* : matinée *f*
forensic [fə'rɛntsɪk] *adj* : légal, médico-légal
foreordain [ˌfɔrɔr'deɪn] *vt* : prédestiner, prédéterminer
forequarter ['forˌkwɔrt̬ər] *n* : quartier *m* de devant
forerunner ['forˌrʌnər] *n* : précurseur *m*
foresee [for'si:] *vt* **-saw; -seen; -seeing** : prévoir, anticiper
foreseeable [for'si:əbəl] *adj* : prévisible
foreshadow [for'ʃædo:] *vt* : présager, annoncer
foresight ['forˌsaɪt] *n* **1** PRESCIENCE : prévision *f* **2** PRUDENCE : prévoyance *f*, prudence *f*
foresighted ['forˌsaɪt̬əd] *adj* : prévoyant, prudent
forest ['fɔrəst] *n* : forêt *f*
forestall [for'stɔl] *vt* **1** PREVENT : empêcher, prévenir **2** ANTICIPATE : anticiper, devancer
forested ['fɔrəstəd] *adj* : boisé, forestier
forester ['fɔrəstər] *n* : forestier *m*, -tière *f*
forestry ['fɔrəstri] *n* : sylviculture *f*, foresterie *f*
foreswear → **forswear**
foretaste ['forˌteɪst] *n* : avant-goût *m*
foretell [for'tɛl] *vt* **-told; -telling** : prédire
forethought ['forˌθɔt] *n* **1** PREMEDITATION : préméditation *f* **2** FORESIGHT : prévoyance *f*
forever [fɔr'ɛvər] *adv* **1** ETERNALLY : toujours, éternellement **2** CONTINUALLY : toujours, sans cesse
forevermore [fɔrˌɛvər'mor] *adv* : (pour) toujours
forewarn [for'wɔrn] *vt* : avertir, prévenir
foreword ['forwərd] *n* : avant-propos *m*
forfeit[1] ['fɔrfət] *vt* : perdre, renoncer à (ses droits, etc.)
forfeit[2] *n* **1** PENALTY : prix *m*, peine *f* **2** : gage *m* <to pay a forfeit : avoir un gage>
forge[1] ['fordʒ] *v* **forged; forging** *vt* **1** : forger (un métal, un plan, etc.) **2** COUNTERFEIT : contrefaire, falsifier — *vi* **to forge ahead** : prendre de l'avance, avancer
forge[2] *n* : forge *f*
forger ['fordʒər] *n* : faussaire *mf*, faux-monnayeur *m*
forgery ['fordʒəri] *n, pl* **-eries** : contrefaçon *f*, falsification *f*

forget [fər'gɛt] *v* **-got** [-'gɑt]; **-gotten** [-'gɑtən] *or* **-got; -getting** *vt* **1** : oublier <I've forgotten your name : j'ai oublié votre nom> **2** NEGLECT : négliger, oublier **3 forget it!** : n'en parlons plus! — *vi* : oublier

forgetful [fər'gɛtfəl] *adj* **1** ABSENT-MINDED : distrait **2** NEGLECTFUL : oublieux, négligent

forgetfulness [fər'gɛtfəlnəs] *n* **1** ABSENTMINDEDNESS : distraction *f* **2** CARELESSNESS : étourderie *f,* négligence *f*

forget–me–not [fər'gɛtmi,nɑt] *n* : myosotis *m*

forgettable [fər'gɛt̬əbəl] *adj* : peu mémorable

forgivable [fər'gɪvəbəl] *adj* : pardonnable

forgive [fər'gɪv] *vt* **-gave** [-'geɪv]; **-given** [-'gɪvən]; **-giving** : pardonner

forgiveness [fər'gɪvnəs] *n* : pardon *m,* indulgence *f*

forgiving [fər'gɪvɪŋ] *adj* : indulgent, clément

forgo *or* **forego** [for'goː] *vt* **-went; -gone; -going** : renoncer à, se priver de

fork[1] ['fɔrk] *vt* **1** : fourcher <to fork (up) the earth : fourcher la terre> **2** *or* **to fork over** : allonger *fam* — *vi* : bifurquer, fourcher <the road forks : la route bifurque>

fork[2] *n* **1** : fourchette *f* <dessert fork : fourchette à dessert> **2** PITCHFORK : fourche *f* (à foin) **3** JUNCTION : bifurcation *f* (d'une route), embranchement *m* (d'une voie ferrée)

forked ['forkt, 'forkəd] *adj* : fourchu

forklift ['fɔrk,lɪft] *n* : chariot *m* élévateur

forlorn [fɔr'lɔrn] *adj* **1** DESOLATE : abandonné, désolé **2** SAD : triste, misérable **3** DESPERATE : désespéré

forlornly [fɔr'lɔrnli] *adv* : d'un air triste

form[1] ['fɔrm] *vt* **1** FASHION, SHAPE : former, façonner **2** ARRANGE : se mettre en <to form a line : se mettre en ligne> **3** ACQUIRE, DEVELOP : se former, se faire (une idée, etc.), contracter (une habitude) **4** INSTRUCT, TRAIN : former **5** CONSTITUTE : constituer, former — *vi* : se former, prendre forme

form[2] *n* **1** SHAPE : forme *f* **2** FIGURE : forme *f,* corps *m* <the human form : la forme humaine> **3** DOCUMENT : formulaire *m* <to fill out a form : remplir un formulaire> **4** KIND : forme *f,* genre *m* **5** CONDITION : forme *f,* condition *f* <to be in good form : être en pleine forme>

formal[1] ['fɔrməl] *adj* **1** : officiel <a formal reception : une réception officielle> <a formal contract : un contrat en bonne et due forme> **2** ELEVATED : soigné, soutenu <formal language : langage soutenu>

formal[2] *n* **1** *or* **formal dance** : bal *m* **2** *or* **formal dress** : tenue *f* de soirée

formaldehyde [fɔr'mældə,haɪd] *n* : formaldéhyde *m*

formality [fɔr'mæləṭi] *n, pl* **-ties** : formalité *f*

formalize ['fɔrmə,laɪz] *vt* **-ized; -izing** : formaliser

formally ['fɔrməli] *adv* **1** OFFICIALLY : officiellement **2** CEREMONIOUSLY : cérémonieusement, solennellement

format[1] ['fɔr,mæt] *vt* **-matted; -matting** **1** : concevoir le format de **2** : formater (une diskette)

format[2] *n* : format *m*

formation [fɔr'meɪʃən] *n* **1** FORMING : formation *f,* établissement *m* **2** ARRANGEMENT, SHAPE : formation *f*

formative ['fɔrməṭɪv] *adj* : formateur

former ['fɔrmər] *adj* **1** PREVIOUS : ancien, précédent <a former president : un ancien président> **2** : premier (de deux choses)

formerly ['fɔrmərli] *adv* : autrefois, jadis

formidable ['fɔrmədəbəl, fɔr'mɪdə-] *adj* **1** : redoutable, terrible <a formidable foe : un ennemi redoutable> **2** OUTSTANDING : impressionnant, remarquable

formless ['fɔrmləs] *adj* : informe

formula ['fɔrmjələ] *n, pl* **-las** or **-lae** [-,liː, -,laɪ] **1** : formule *f* **2** *or* **baby formula** : lait *m* en poudre (pour biberon)

formulate ['fɔrmjə,leɪt] *vt* **-lated; -lating** : formuler

formulation [,fɔrmjə'leɪʃən] *n* : formulation *f*

fornicate ['fɔrnə,keɪt] *vi* **-cated; -cating** : forniquer

fornication [,fɔrnə'keɪʃən] *n* : fornication *f*

forsake [fər'seɪk] *vt* **-sook** [-'sʊk]; **-saken** [-'seɪkən]; **-saking** : abandonner, délaisser

forswear [fɔr'swær] *v* **-swore; -sworn; -swearing** *vt* RENOUNCE : abjurer, renoncer à — *vi* : commettre un parjure

forsythia [fər'sɪθiə] *n* : forsythia *m*

fort ['fɔrt] *n* : fort *m*

forte ['fort, 'for,teɪ] *n* : fort *m*

forth ['forθ] *adv* **1** FORWARD : en avant <from this day forth : dorénavant, à partir d'aujourd'hui> **2 and so forth** : et ainsi de suite

forthcoming [forθ'kʌmɪŋ, 'forθ-] *adj* **1** COMING : prochain, à venir, à paraître **2** COMMUNICATIVE, OPEN : ouvert, communicatif

forthright ['forθ,raɪt] *adj* : franc, direct

forthrightly ['forθ,raɪtli] *adv* : franchement, directement

forthrightness ['forθ,raɪtnəs] *n* : franchise *f*

forthwith [forθ'wɪθ, -'wɪð] *adv* : sur-le-champ, aussitôt

fortieth[1] [ˈfɔrt̬iəθ] *adj* : quarantième
fortieth[2] *n* **1** : quarantième *mf* (dans une série) **2** : quarantième *m* (en mathématiques)
fortification [ˌfɔrt̬əfəˈkeɪʃən] *n* : fortification *f*
fortify [ˈfɔrt̬əˌfaɪ] *vt* **-fied; -fying 1** STRENGTHEN, SECURE : fortifier (une ville, etc.) **2** ENCOURAGE, INVIGORATE : remonter, réconforter
fortitude [ˈfɔrt̬əˌtuːd, -ˌtjuːd] *n* : force *f* d'âme, courage *m*
fortnight [ˈfortˌnaɪt] *n* : quinzaine *f,* quinze jours *mpl*
fortnightly[1] [ˈfortˌnaɪtli] *adv* : tous les quinze jours
fortnightly[2] *adj* : bimensuel
fortress [ˈfɔrtrəs] *n* : forteresse *f*
fortuitous [fɔrˈtuːət̬əs, -ˈtjuː-] *adj* : fortuit, imprévu
fortunate [ˈfɔrtʃənət] *adj* **1** AUSPICIOUS : propice, prometteur **2** LUCKY : heureux, chanceux
fortunately [ˈfɔrtʃənətli] *adv* : heureusement
fortune [ˈfɔrtʃən] *n* **1** CHANCE, LUCK : chance *f,* fortune *f,* hasard *m* **2** DESTINY : destin *m,* sort *m* **3** WEALTH : fortune *f* <to make a fortune : faire fortune>
fortune–teller [ˈfɔrtʃənˌtɛlər] *n* : diseur *m,* -seuse *f* de bonne aventure; voyant *m,* voyante *f*
fortune–telling [ˈfɔrtʃənˌtɛlɪŋ] *n* : pratique *f* de dire la bonne aventure, divination *f*
forty[1] [ˈfɔrt̬i] *adj* : quarante
forty[2] *n, pl* **forties** : quarante *m*
forum [ˈforəm] *n, pl* **-rums** : forum *m*
forward[1] [ˈfɔrwərd] *vt* **1** PROMOTE : avancer, favoriser **2** SEND : expédier (des marchandises), faire suivre (du courrier)
forward[2] *adv* **1** : en avant, vers l'avant **2 from that day forward** : à partir de ce jour-là
forward[3] *adj* **1** : avant, en avant **2** BRASH : effronté, impertinent
forward[4] *n* : avant *m* (aux sports)
forwarder [ˈfɔrwərdər] *n* : expéditeur *m,* -trice *f*
forwardness [ˈfɔrwərdnəs] *n* : effronterie *f,* impertinence *f*
forwards [ˈfɔrwərdz] → **forward**[2]
fossil[1] [ˈfɑsəl] *adj* : fossile
fossil[2] *n* : fossile *m*
fossilize [ˈfɑsəˌlaɪz] *v* **-ized; -izing** *vt* : fossiliser — *vi* : se fossiliser
foster[1] [ˈfɔstər] *vt* **1** NURTURE : élever, placer (un enfant) **2** CHERISH : entretenir, nourrir (un espoir, etc.) **3** ENCOURAGE : favoriser, encourager
foster[2] *adj* : adoptif, d'accueil <foster parents : parents adoptifs> <foster home : famille d'accueil>
fought → **fight**[1]
foul[1] [ˈfaʊl] *vt* **1** DIRTY, POLLUTE : salir, souiller, polluer **2** CLOG : encrasser, obstruer **3** TANGLE : emmêler
foul[2] *adj* **1** REPULSIVE : infect, fétide **2** POLLUTED : pollué, vicié **3** DETESTABLE : horrible, atroce **4** OBSCENE : grossier, ordurier **5** NASTY : sale, infect <what foul weather! : quel sale temps!> **6** : déloyal, irrégulier (aux sports) <a foul play : un jeu irrégulier>
foul[3] *n* : coup *m* irrégulier, faute *f* (aux sports)
foully [ˈfaʊli] *adv* : de façon grossière
foulmouthed [ˈfaʊlˌmæʊːðd, -ˌmæʊθt] *adj* : grossier
foulness [ˈfaʊlnəs] *n* : grossièreté *f*
foul play *n* : violence *f,* meurtre *m*
foul–up [ˈfaʊlˌʌp] *n* : cafouillage *m fam,* confusion *f*
foul up *vt* **1** CONTAMINATE : polluer **2** CLOG : obstruer
found[1] → **find**[1]
found[2] [ˈfaʊnd] *vt* **1** ESTABLISH : fonder, établir **2** BASE : fonder, baser <founded on facts : basé sur des faits>
foundation [faʊnˈdeɪʃən] *n* **1** FOUNDING : fondation *f,* établissement *m* **2** BASIS : base *f,* fondement *m* **3** ENDOWMENT : fondation *f,* institution *f* dotée **4** : fondations *fpl* (d'un édifice), solage *m Can*
founder[1] [ˈfaʊndər] *vi* COLLAPSE, SINK : sombrer, s'effondrer
founder[2] *n* : fondateur *m,* -trice *f*
foundling [ˈfaʊndlɪŋ] *n* : enfant *m* trouvé, enfant *f* trouvée
foundry [ˈfaʊndri] *n, pl* **-dries** : fonderie *f*
fount [ˈfaʊnt] *n* : source *f*
fountain [ˈfaʊntən] *n* **1** : fontaine *f,* jet *m* d'eau <drinking fountain : jet d'eau potable> **2** SOURCE : fontaine *f,* source *f* **3** SPRING : source *f*
four[1] [ˈfor] *adj* : quatre
four[2] *n* : quatre *m*
fourfold [ˈforˌfoːld, -ˈfoːld] *adj* : quadruple
fourscore [ˈforˈskor] *adj* EIGHTY : quatre-vingts
fourteen[1] [forˈtiːn] *adj* : quatorze
fourteen[2] *n* : quatorze *m*
fourteenth[1] [forˈtiːnθ] *adj* : quatorzième
fourteenth[2] *n* **1** : quatorzième *mf* (dans une série) **2** : quatorzième *m* (en mathématiques) **3** (*used in dates*) <the fourteenth of June : le quatorze juin>
fourth[1] [ˈforθ] *adj* : quatrième
fourth[2] *n* **1** : quatrième *mf* (dans une série) **2** : quart *m* (en mathématiques) **3** (*used in dates*) <the Fourth of July : le quatre juillet>
fowl [ˈfaʊl] *n, pl* **fowl** *or* **fowls 1** BIRD : oiseau *m* **2** CHICKEN : poulet *m* **3** POULTRY : volaille *f*

fox[1] ['fɑks] *vt* TRICK : tromper, berner
fox[2] *n, pl* **foxes** : renard *m*
foxglove ['fɑks,glʌv] *n* : digitale *f* (pourprée)
foxhole ['fɑks,ho:l] *n* : gourbi *m*
foxy ['fɑksi] *adj* **foxier; -est** SLY : rusé, malin
foyer ['fɔɪər, 'fɔɪ,jeɪ] *n* : vestibule *m*, entrée *f*
fracas ['freɪkəs, 'fræ-] *n, pl* **-cases** [-kəsəz] : bagarre *f*, rixe *f*
fraction ['frækʃən] *n* **1** : fraction *f* (en mathématiques) **2** PORTION : fraction *f*, (petite) partie *f*
fractional ['frækʃənəl] *adj* **1** : fractionnaire **2** INCONSIDERABLE : infime, tout petit
fractious ['frækʃəs] adj **1** UNRULY : indiscipliné, difficile **2** IRRITABLE : revêche
fracture[1] ['fræktʃər] *vt* **-tured; -turing** : fracturer
fracture[2] *n* : fracture *f*
fragile ['frædʒəl, -,dʒaɪl] *adj* : fragile
fragility [frə'dʒɪləṯi] *n* : fragilité *f*
fragment[1] ['fræg,mɛnt] *vt* : fragmenter
fragment[2] ['frægmənt] *n* : fragment *m*, morceau *m*
fragmentary ['frægmən,tɛri] *adj* : fragmentaire
fragmentation [,frægmən'teɪʃən, -,mɛn-] *n* : fragmentation *f*
fragrance ['freɪgrənts] *n* : parfum *m*, fragrance *f*
fragrant ['freɪgrənt] *adj* : parfumé, odorant
frail ['freɪl] *adj* : frêle, fragile
frailty ['freɪlti] *n, pl* **-ties** : fragilité *f*
frame[1] ['freɪm] *vt* **framed; framing** **1** FORMULATE : formuler, élaborer **2** BORDER, ENCLOSE : encadrer **3** INCRIMINATE : monter un coup contre
frame[2] *n* **1** PHYSIQUE : charpente *f*, ossature *f* **2** STRUCTURE : charpente *f* (d'un édifice), châssis *m* (d'une voiture), cadre *m* (d'une bicyclette, etc.) **3** BORDER : cadre *m* (d'un tableau, d'une fenêtre, etc.) **4** **frames** *npl* : monture *f* (de lunettes) **5** **frame of mind** : état *m* d'esprit
framework ['freɪm,wərk] *n* **1** STRUCTURE : charpente *f*, squelette *f* **2** BASIS : cadre *m*
franc ['fræŋk] *n* : franc *m*
franchise ['fræn,tʃaɪz] *n* **1** : franchise *f* (en commerce) **2** SUFFRAGE : droit *m* de vote, suffrage *m*
frank[1] ['fræŋk] *vt* POSTMARK : affranchir
frank[2] *adj* CANDID : franc
frankfurter ['fræŋkfərṯər, -,fər-] *or* **frankfurt** [-fərt] *n* : saucisse *f* de Francfort, saucisse *f* à hot-dog *Can*
frankincense ['fræŋkən,sɛnts] *n* : encens *m*
frankly ['fræŋkli] *adv* : franchement
frankness ['fræŋknəs] *n* : franchise *f*
frantic ['fræntɪk] *adj* : frénétique, effréné
frantically ḇfrĬntIkli] *adv* : frénétiquement
fraternal [frə'tərnəl] *adj* : fraternel — **fraternally** *adv*
fraternity [frə'tərnəṯi] *n, pl* **-ties** **1** BROTHERHOOD : fraternité *f* **2** : confrérie *f* d'étudiants <fraternity pin : insigne de confrérie>
fraternization [,fræṯərnə'zeɪʃən] *n* : fraternisation *f*
fraternize ['fræṯər,naɪz] *vi* **-nized; -nizing** : fraterniser
fratricide ['frætrə,saɪd] *n* : fratricide *m*
fraud ['frɔd] *n* **1** DECEPTION, SWINDLE : fraude *f*, tromperie *f* **2** IMPOSTOR : imposteur *m*
fraudulent ['frɔdʒələnt] *adj* : frauduleux — **fraudulently** *adv*
fraught ['frɔt] *adj* : rempli, plein, chargé <fraught with danger : rempli de dangers>
fray[1] ['freɪ] *vt* **1** : effilocher, effiler (des tissus, etc.) **2** IRRITATE : mettre (les nerfs) à vif — *vi* : s'effilocher
fray[2] *n* BRAWL, FIGHT : bagarre *f*, rixe *f* <to join the fray : se jeter dans la mêlée>
frazzle[1] ['fræzəl] *vt* **-zled; -zling** **1** FRAY : effiler, effranger **2** EXHAUST : épuiser, éreinter
frazzle[2] *n* **worn to a frazzle** : éreinté, crevé *fam*
freak ['fri:k] *n* **1** ODDITY : phénomène *m*, monstre *m* <a freak of nature : un caprice de la nature> **2** ENTHUSIAST : fana *mf fam*
freakish ['fri:kɪʃ] *adj* : anormal, bizarre
freckle[1] ['frɛkəl] *vi* **-led; -ling** : se couvrir de taches de rousseur, rousseler *Can*
freckle[2] *n* : tache *f* de rousseur
free[1] ['fri:] *vt* **freed; freeing** **1** LIBERATE : libérer, relâcher **2** RELIEVE, RID : libérer, dégager **3** RELEASE, UNTIE : détacher, dégager **4** CLEAR, UNBLOCK : déboucher
free[2] *adv* **1** FREELY : en toute liberté, librement **2** : gratuitement <children admitted free : entrée gratuite pour les enfants>
free[3] *adj* **freer; freest** **1** : libre <a free country : un pays libre> **2** : exempt <free from taxes : exempt d'impôt> **3** : gratuit <free admission : entrée gratuite> **4** VACANT : libre <is this seat free? : est-ce que la place est libre?> **5** OPEN : ouvert, franc **6** CLEAR : libre, dégagé
freebooter ['fri:,bu:ṯər] *n* : pirate *m*
freeborn ['fri:'bɔrn] *adj* : né libre
freedom ['fri:dəm] *n* : liberté *f*
free–for–all ['fri:fər,ɔl] *n* : mêlée *f* générale
freelance ['fri:,lænts] *adj* : à la pige

freelancer ['fri:,læntsər] *n* : travailleur *m* indépendant, travailleuse *f* indépendante; pigiste *mf*

freeload ['fri:,lo:d] *vi* : vivre en pique-assiette

freeloader ['fri:,lo:dər] *n* : pique-assiette *mf*

freely ['fri:li] *adv* **1** FRANKLY, OPENLY : librement **2** LAVISHLY : largement

Freemason ['fri:'meɪsən] *n* : franc-maçon *m*

Freemasonry ['fri:'meɪsənri] *n* : franc-maçonnerie *f*

freestanding ['fri:'stændɪŋ] *adj* : non-encastré, sur pied

freeway ['fri:,weɪ] *n* : autoroute *f*

freewill ['fri:,wɪl] *adj* : volontaire

free will *n* : libre arbitre *m*

freeze[1] ['fri:z] *v* **froze** ['fro:z]; **frozen** ['fro:zən]; **freezing** *vt* **1** : geler (de l'eau), congeler (de l'eau, des aliments, etc.) **2** : geler, bloquer (des prix, etc.) — *vi* **1** : geler <the lake has frozen over : le lac a gelé> **2** : se congeler, se surgeler <bread freezes well : le pain se congèle bien> **3 to be frozen in one's tracks** : rester cloué sur place **4 it's freezing!** : on caille! *France fam,* on gèle **5 to freeze to death** : mourir de froid

freeze[2] *n* **1** FREEZING, FROST : gel *m* **2** : gel *m,* blocage *m* <salary freeze : gel des salaires>

freeze–dry ['fri:z'draɪ] *vt* **-dried; -drying** : lyophiliser

freezer ['fri:zər] *n* : congélateur *m*

freezing point *n* : point *m* de congélation

freight[1] ['freɪt] *vt* : transporter (des marchandises)

freight[2] *n* **1** SHIPPING : transport *m* **2** GOODS : fret *m,* marchandises *fpl*

freighter ['freɪt̬ər] *n* : cargo *m* (navire), avion-cargo *m*

French[1] ['frentʃ] *adj* : français

French[2] *n* **1** : français *m* (langue) **2 the French** : les Français

French Canadian[1] *adj* : canadien français

French Canadian[2] *n* : Canadien *m* français, Canadienne *f* française

french fries ['frentʃ,fraɪz] *npl* : frites *fpl*

Frenchman ['frentʃmən] *n, pl* **-men** [-mən, -,mɛn] : Français *m*

Frenchwoman ['frentʃ,wʊmən] *n, pl* **-women** [-,wɪmən] : Française *f*

frenetic [frɪ'nɛt̬ɪk] *adj* : frénétique — **frenetically** [-t̬ɪkli] *adv*

frenzied ['frenzid] *adj* : frénétique, agité

frenzy ['frenzi] *n, pl* **-zies** : frénésie *f*

frequency ['fri:kwəntsi] *n, pl* **-cies** : fréquence *f*

frequent[1] [fri'kwɛnt, 'fri:kwənt] *vt* : fréquenter

frequent[2] ['fri:kwənt] *adj* : fréquent

frequently ['fri:kwəntli] *adv* : fréquemment

fresco ['frɛs,ko:] *n, pl* **-coes** : fresque *f*

fresh ['frɛʃ] *adj* **1** : frais <fresh bread : du pain frais> **2** : frais, récent <fresh paint : peinture fraîche> **3** : doux <fresh water : eau douce> **4** PURE : frais, pur <fresh air : air pur> **5** NEW : nouveau <a fresh start : un nouveau départ> **6** BRISK : frais <a fresh wind : un vent frais> **7** IMPUDENT : insolent

freshen ['frɛʃən] *vt* : se rafraîchir (la mémoire) — *vi* **1** : fraîchir <the wind has freshened : le vent a fraîchi> **2 to freshen up** : se rafraîchir

freshet ['frɛʃət] *n* : crue *f* soudaine

freshly ['frɛʃli] *adv* RECENTLY : fraîchement, récemment

freshman ['frɛʃmən] *n, pl* **-men** [-mən, -,mɛn] : étudiant *m,* -diante *f* de première année (à l'université)

freshness ['frɛʃnəs] *n* : fraîcheur *f*

freshwater ['frɛʃ,wɔt̬ər] *adj* : d'eau douce

fret[1] ['frɛt] *vi* **fretted; fretting** : se tracasser, s'en faire

fret[2] *n* **1** IRRITATION, WORRY : irritation *f,* inquiétude *f* **2** : frette *f* (d'une guitare)

fretful ['frɛtfəl] *adj* : irritable, agité, énervé

fretfully ['frɛtfəli] *adj* : avec inquiétude, avec énervement

friar ['fraɪər] *n* : frère *m,* moine *m*

fricassee[1] ['frɪkə,si:, ,frɪkə'si:] *vt* **-seed; -seeing** : fricasser

fricassee[2] *n* : fricassée *f*

friction ['frɪkʃən] *n* **1** RUBBING : friction *f,* frottement *m* **2** DISAGREEMENT : friction *f,* désaccord *m*

Friday ['fraɪ,deɪ, -di] *n* : vendredi *m*

friend ['frɛnd] *n* : ami *m,* amie *f*

friendless ['frɛndləs] *adj* : sans amis

friendliness ['frɛndlinəs] *n* : gentillesse *f,* attitude *f* amicale

friendly ['frɛndli] *adj* **friendlier; -est** : gentil, amical

friendship ['frɛnd,ʃɪp] *n* : amitié *f*

frieze ['fri:z] *n* : frise *f*

frigate ['frɪgət] *n* : frégate *f*

fright ['fraɪt] *n* : peur *f,* frayeur *f*

frighten ['fraɪtən] *vt* : faire peur à, effrayer

frightful ['fraɪtfəl] *adj* **1** TERRIFYING : terrible, épouvantable **2** SHOCKING, STARTLING : effrayant, effarant <frightful costs : coûts effarants> **3** EXTREME : terrible <a frightful thirst : une soif terrible>

frightfully ['fraɪtfəli] *adv* : terriblement, affreusement

frightfulness ['fraɪtfəlnəs] *n* : horreur *f*

frigid ['frɪdʒɪd] *adj* : glacial

frigidity [frɪ'dʒɪdət̬i] *n* **1** : frigidité *f* (en médecine) **2** COLDNESS : froideur *f*

frill ['frɪl] *n* **1** RUFFLE : jabot *m* (d'une chemise), volant *m* (d'une jupe) **2** EMBELLISHMENT : fioriture *f*

frilly [ˈfrɪli] *adj* **frillier; -est 1** : à jabot, à volant **2** : à fioritures (se dit du style, etc.)

fringe[1] [ˈfrɪndʒ] *vt* **fringed; fringing** : franger, border

fringe[2] *n* **1** : frange *f* **2** EDGE : bordure *f,* bord *m* **3 fringe benefits** : avantages *mpl* sociaux, avantages *mpl* en nature

frisk [ˈfrɪsk] *vt* SEARCH : fouiller (un suspect) — *vi* FROLIC : gambader, folâtrer

friskiness [ˈfrɪskinəs] *n* : vivacité *f*

frisky [ˈfrɪski] *adj* **friskier; -est 1** SPIRITED : fringant (se dit d'un cheval) **2** PLAYFUL : vif, folâtre

fritter[1] [ˈfrɪt̬ər] *vt or* **to fritter away** : gaspiller

fritter[2] *n* : beignet *m*

frivolity [frɪˈvɑlət̬i] *n, pl* **-ties** : frivolité *f*

frivolous [ˈfrɪvələs] *adj* : frivole — **frivolously** *adv*

frizz[1] [ˈfrɪz] *vt* : friser (ses cheveux)

frizz[2] *n* : cheveux *mpl* frisés

frizzy [ˈfrɪzi] *adj* **frizzier; -est** : frisé, bouclé

fro [ˈfroː] *adv* **to and fro** : de long en large

frock [ˈfrɑk] *n* DRESS : robe *f*

frog [ˈfrɔg, ˈfrɑg] *n* **1** : grenouille *f* **2** LOOP : brandebourg *m* **3 to have a frog in one's throat** : avoir un chat dans la gorge

frogman [ˈfrɔg͵mæn, ˈfrɑg-, -mən] *n, pl* **-men** [-mən, -͵mɛn] : homme-grenouille *m*

frolic[1] [ˈfrɑlɪk] *vi* **-icked; -icking** : gambader, folâtrer

frolic[2] *n* : gambades *fpl,* ébats *mpl*

frolicsome [ˈfrɑlɪksəm] *adj* : folâtre

from [ˈfrʌm, ˈfrɑm] *prep* **1** (*indicating a starting point*) : de, à partir de <they're coming from Boston : ils arrivent de Boston> <from that day on : à partir de ce jour-là> **2** (*indicating removal or separation*) : contre <protection from the sun : protection contre le soleil> **3** (*indicating a source or cause*) : de, par, à <he's suffering from a cold : il souffre d'un rhume> <to work from necessity : travailler par nécessité> <to borrow money from a friend : emprunter de l'argent à un ami>

frond [ˈfrɑnd] *n* : fronde *f* (d'une fougère), feuille *f* (d'un palmier)

front[1] [ˈfrʌnt] *vi* **1** FACE : faire face <the building fronts south : l'édifice fait face au sud> **2 to front for** : servir de couverture à (qqn) **3 to front on** : donner sur — *vt* FACE : donner sur

front[2] *adj* : de devant, premier, (en) avant <the front row : le premier rang>

front[3] *n* **1** : avant *m,* devant *m* (d'une voiture, etc.), façade *f* (d'un bâtiment) **2** APPEARANCE : air *m,* contenance *f* <a bold front : une contenance assurée> **3** : front *m* (en météorologie) **4** VANGUARD : front *m* <the western front : le front ouest>

frontage [ˈfrʌntɪdʒ] *n* : façade *f,* devanture *f*

frontal [ˈfrʌntəl] *adj* : frontal, de front

frontier [͵frʌnˈtɪr] *n* : frontière *f*

frontiersman [͵frʌnˈtɪrzmən] *n, pl* **-men** [-mən, -͵mɛn] : homme *m* de la frontière

frontispiece [ˈfrʌntəs͵piːs] *n* : frontispice *m*

frost[1] [ˈfrɔst] *vt* **1** FREEZE : geler, givrer **2** ICE : glacer (un gâteau)

frost[2] *n* **1** : givre *m* **2** FREEZING : gel *m,* gelée *f*

frostbite [ˈfrɔst͵baɪt] *n* : gelure *f*

frostbitten [ˈfrɔst͵bɪtən] *adj* : gelé

frosting [ˈfrɔstɪŋ] *n* ICING : glaçage *m* (d'un gâteau)

frosty [ˈfrɔsti] *adj* **frostier; -est 1** : givré, couvert de givre <frosty windows : vitres givrées> **2** FRIGID : glacial

froth [ˈfrɔθ] *n, pl* **froths** [ˈfrɔθs, ˈfrɔðz] : écume *f,* mousse *f,* broue *f Can*

frothy [ˈfrɔθi, -ði] *adj* **frothier; -est** : écumeux, mousseux

frown[1] [ˈfraʊn] *vi* : froncer les sourcils

frown[2] *n* : froncement *m* de sourcils

frowsy *or* **frowzy** [ˈfraʊzi] *adj* **frowsier** *or* **frowzier; -est** : négligé, peu soigné

froze, frozen → **freeze**[1]

frugal [ˈfruːgəl] *adj* : économe, frugal

frugality [fruːˈgælət̬i] *n* : frugalité *f*

frugally [ˈfruːgəli] *adv* : simplement, frugalement

fruit[1] [ˈfruːt] *vi* : donner des fruits

fruit[2] *n* **1** : fruit *m* **2 fruits** *npl* RESULTS : fruits *mpl* <the fruits of one's labors : les fruits de son travail>

fruitcake [ˈfruːt͵keɪk] *n* : cake *m*

fruitful [ˈfruːtfəl] *adj* : fécond, fructueux

fruitfulness [ˈfruːtfəlnəs] *n* : fécondité *f*

fruition [fruːˈɪʃən] *n* : réalisation *f* <to come to fruition : se réaliser>

fruitless [ˈfruːtləs] *adj* : stérile <a fruitless discussion : une discussion sans résultat>

fruitlessly [ˈfruːtləsli] *adv* : en vain

fruity [ˈfruːt̬i] *adj* **fruitier; -est** : fruité, de fruit

frumpy [ˈfrʌmpi] *adj* **frumpier; -est** : mal fagoté

frustrate [ˈfrʌs͵treɪt] *vt* **-trated; -trating 1** DISAPPOINT, DISCOURAGE : frustrer, décevoir **2** THWART : contrecarrer, faire échouer

frustrating [ˈfrʌs͵treɪt̬ɪŋ] *adj* : frustrant

frustration [͵frʌsˈtreɪʃən] *n* : frustration *f*

fry[1] [ˈfraɪ] *v* **fried; frying** : frire

fry[2] *n, pl* **fries 1** FRYING : friture *f* **2 fries** *npl* FRENCH FRIES : frites *fpl* **3** *pl* **fry** : fretin *m* (poisson) **4 small fry** : menu fretin *m*

frying pan *n* : poêle *f,* poêlon *m Can*

fuddle [ˈfʌdəl] *vt* **-dled; -dling** : brouiller, embrouiller

fudge[1] [ˈfʌdʒ] *v* **fudged; fudging** *vt* **1** FALSIFY : truquer **2** DODGE : esquiver — *vi* HEDGE : esquiver le problème

fudge[2] *n* : caramel *m* mou

fuel[1] [ˈfju:əl] *vt* **-eled** *or* **-elled; -eling** *or* **-elling 1** : alimenter en combustible (un fourneau), ravitailler en carburant (un navire, etc.) **2** STIMULATE : aviver (des soupçons, etc.)

fuel[2] *n* : combustible *m,* carburant *m*

fugitive[1] [ˈfju:dʒət̬ɪv] *adj* **1** RUNAWAY : fugitif **2** ELUSIVE : fugace, éphémère

fugitive[2] *n* : fugitif *m,* -tive *f*

fulcrum [ˈfʊlkrəm, ˈfʌl-] *n, pl* **-crums** *or* **-cra** [-krə] : point *m* d'appui

fulfill *or* **fulfil** [fʊlˈfɪl] *vt* **-filled; -filling 1** EXECUTE : accomplir, réaliser **2** FILL, MEET : remplir, satisfaire à, répondre à

fulfillment [fʊlˈfɪlmənt] *n* **1** ACCOMPLISHMENT : accomplissement *m,* réalisation *f* **2** SATISFACTION : satisfaction *f,* contentement *m*

full[1] [ˈfʊl, ˈfʌl] *adv* **1** VERY : très, fort <you knew full well : tu le savais très bien> **2** ENTIRELY : entièrement <to turn full around : faire volte-face> **3** DIRECTLY : carrément <he hit me full in the face : il m'a frappé en plein visage>

full[2] *adj* **1** FILLED : plein, rempli, complet <the hotel is full : l'hôtel est complet> **2** COMPLETE, ENTIRE : entier, total <a full year : une année entière> **3** PLUMP : plein, rond <a full face : un visage rond> **4** AMPLE : ample **5** SATIATED : repu, rassasié <I'm full : j'ai assez mangé>

full[3] *n* **1 in ~** : en détail, intégralement **2 to the full** : au plus haut degré

full–fledged [ˈfʊlˈflɛdʒd] *adj* : à part entière

fullness [ˈfʊlnəs] *n* **1** ABUNDANCE : abondance *f* **2** : rondeur *f* (d'une silhouette), ampleur *f* (d'un vêtement)

fully [ˈfʊli] *adv* **1** COMPLETELY : tout à fait, complètement **2** : au moins <fully nine tenths of us : au moins neuf dixièmes d'entre nous>

fulsome [ˈfʊlsəm] *adj* : excessif, exagéré

fumble[1] [ˈfʌmbəl] *v* **-bled; -bling** *vt* : manier maladroitement, mal attraper (aux sports) — *vi* : tâtonner, fouiller

fumble[2] *n* : tâtonnement *m*

fume[1] [ˈfju:m] *vi* **fumed; fuming 1** SMOKE : émettre des vapeurs, fumer **2** RAGE : fulminer, bouillonner

fume[2] *n* : émanation *f,* gaz *m* d'échappement (d'une voiture)

fumigate [ˈfju:məˌgeɪt] *vt* **-gated; -gating** : désinfecter par fumigation

fumigation [ˌfju:məˈgeɪʃən] *n* : fumigation *f*

fun[1] [ˈfʌn] *adj* : amusant, marrant *fam*

fun[2] *n* **1** ENJOYMENT : amusement *m,* plaisir *m,* fun *m Can fam* <to have fun : s'amuser> **2 for ~** : pour rire **3 to make fun of** : se moquer de

function[1] [ˈfʌŋkʃən] *vi* **1** WORK : fonctionner, marcher **2 to function as** : faire fonction de, servir de

function[2] *n* **1** OCCUPATION : fonction *f,* charge *f* **2** PURPOSE : fonction *f,* rôle *m* **3** CEREMONY : réception *f,* cérémonie *f*

functional [ˈfʌŋkʃənəl] *adj* : fonctionnel — **functionally** *adv*

functionary [ˈfʌŋkʃəˌnɛri] *n, pl* **-aries** : fonctionnaire *mf*

fund[1] [ˈfʌnd] *vt* : financer, fournir des fonds à

fund[2] *n* **1** SUPPLY : fond *m,* réserve *f* <a fund of jokes : un répertoire de plaisanteries> **2** : caisse *f,* fonds *mpl* <relief fund : caisse de secours> **3 funds** *npl* RESOURCES : fonds *mpl,* capitaux *mpl*

fundamental[1] [ˌfʌndəˈmɛntəl] *adj* **1** BASIC : fondamental, essentiel **2** PRINCIPAL : principal — **fundamentally** *adv*

fundamental[2] *n* : principe *m* essentiel

funeral[1] [ˈfju:nərəl] *adj* : funèbre, funéraire

funeral[2] *n* : enterrement *m,* funérailles *fpl*

funeral home *or* **funeral parlor** *n* : entreprise *f* de pompes funèbres, salon *m* funéraire *Can,* salon *m* mortuaire *Can*

funereal [fju:ˈnɪriəl] *adj* : funèbre

fungal [ˈfʌŋgəl] *adj* : fongique

fungicide [ˈfʌndʒəˌsaɪd, ˈfʌŋgə-] *n* : fongicide *m*

fungicidal [ˌfʌndʒəˈsaɪdəl, ˌfʌŋgə-] *adj* : fongicide

fungous [ˈfʌŋgəs] → **fungal**

fungus [ˈfʌŋgəs] *n, pl* **fungi** [ˈfʌnˌdʒaɪ, ˈfʌŋˌgaɪ] **1** MUSHROOM : champignon *m* **2** MOLD : moisissure *f*

funnel[1] [ˈfʌnəl] *vt* **-neled; -neling 1** : faire passer dans un entonnoir **2** CHANNEL : canaliser

funnel[2] *n* **1** : entonnoir *m* **2** SMOKESTACK : cheminée *f*

funnies [ˈfʌniz] *npl* : bandes *fpl* dessinées

funny [ˈfʌni] *adj* **funnier; -est 1** AMUSING : drôle, amusant, rigolo *fam* **2** PECULIAR : bizarre, curieux, drôle

fur[1] [ˈfər] *adj* : de fourrure

fur[2] *n* **1** : fourrure *f,* pelage *m* (d'un animal) **2** : fourrure *f* <fake fur : fausse fourrure>

furbish [ˈfərbɪʃ] *vt* **1** POLISH : fourbir, polir **2** RENOVATE : remettre à neuf

furious [ˈfjʊriəs] *adj* **1** ANGRY : furieux **2** FIERCE, VIOLENT : acharné, déchaîné <a furious storm : un orage déchaîné>

furiously ['fjʊriəsli] *adv* **1** ANGRILY : furieusement **2** FRANTICALLY : frénétiquement
furlong ['fər,lɔŋ] *n* : furlong *m* (201,17 mètres)
furlough[1] ['fər,lo:] *vt* : accorder une permission à
furlough[2] *n* : congé *m,* permission *f*
furnace ['fərnəs] *n* : fourneau *m,* fournaise *f Can*
furnish ['fərnɪʃ] *vt* **1** SUPPLY : fournir, donner **2** : meubler <a furnished apartment : un appartement meublé>
furnishings ['fərnɪʃɪŋz] *npl* : ameublement *m,* meubles *mpl*
furniture ['fərnɪtʃər] *n* : meubles *mpl*
furor ['fjʊr,ɔr, -ər] *n* **1** RAGE : fureur *f* **2** UPROAR : scandale *m,* tumulte *m*
furrier ['fəriər] *n* : fourreur *m,* -reuse *f*
furrow[1] ['fəro:] *vt* **1** : sillonner (la terre) **2 to furrow one's brow** : plisser son front
furrow[2] *n* **1** : sillon *m* **2** WRINKLE : ride *f*
furry ['fəri] *adj* **furrier; -est** : au poil touffu (se dit d'un animal), en peluche (se dit d'un jouet, etc.)
further[1] ['fərðər] *vt* PROMOTE : promouvoir, avancer
further[2] *adv* **1** FARTHER : plus loin **2** MORE : davantage, plus **3** MOREOVER : en outre
further[3] *adj* **1** FARTHER : plus éloigné **2** ADDITIONAL : nouveau, supplémentaire <until further notice : jusqu'à nouvel ordre>
furtherance ['fərðərənts] *n* : avancement *m*
furthermore ['fərðər,mor] *adv* : en outre, de plus
furthermost ['fərðər,mo:st] *adj* : le plus lointain
furthest ['fərðəst] *adv & adj* → **farthest**
furtive ['fərtɪv] *adj* : furtif — **furtively** *adv*
furtiveness ['fərtɪvnəs] *n* : caractère *m* furtif
fury ['fjʊri] *n, pl* **-ries 1** RAGE : furie *f,* fureur *f* **2** VIOLENCE : fureur *f,* violence *f* **3** FRENZY : frénésie *f*
fuse[1] *or* **fuze** ['fju:z] *vt* **fused** *or* **fuzed; fusing** *or* **fuzing** : munir d'un fusible
fuse[2] *v* **fused; fusing** *vt* **1** MELT : fondre (des métaux) **2** BLEND, UNITE : fusionner, unifier — *vi* : fusionner
fuse[3] *n* **1** : mèche *f* (d'un explosif) **2** : fusible *m,* plomb *m* <to blow a fuse : faire sauter un plomb> **3** *usu* **fuze** : détonateur *m*
fuselage ['fju:sə,lɑʒ, -zə-] *n* : fuselage *m*
fusillade ['fju:sə,lɑd, -,leɪd, ,fju:sə'-, -zə-] *n* : fusillade *f*
fusion ['fju:ʒən] *n* : fusion *f*
fuss[1] ['fʌs] *vi* **1** : s'affairer <fussing over the children : s'affairant autour des enfants> **2** WORRY : s'inquiéter, se tracasser
fuss[2] *n* **1** AGITATION, COMMOTION : agitation *f,* remue-ménage *m* **2** PROTEST : histoires *fpl* <to make a fuss : faire des histoires>
fussbudget ['fʌs,bʌdʒət] *n* : tatillon *m,* -lonne *f*
fussiness ['fʌsinəs] *n* : façon *f* tatillonne
fussy ['fʌsi] *adj* **fussier; -est 1** IRRITABLE : irritable **2** FINICKY : tatillon, pointilleux, difficile <he's a fussy eater : il est difficile pour la nourriture> **3** OVERELABORATE : tarabiscoté
futile ['fju:təl, 'fju:,taɪl] *adj* : futile, vain
futility [fju:'tɪləti] *n* : futilité *f*
future[1] ['fju:tʃər] *adj* : futur
future[2] *n* **1** : avenir *m,* futur *m* <in the near future : dans un proche avenir> **2** *or* **future tense** : futur *m*
futuristic [,fju:tʃə'rɪstɪk] *adj* : futuriste
fuze → **fuse**
fuzz ['fʌz] *n* **1** DOWN : duvet *m* **2** FLUFF : peluches *fpl*
fuzziness ['fʌzinəs] *n* **1** : caractère *m* duveteux **2** : flou *m* (en photographie)
fuzzy ['fʌzi] *adj* **fuzzier; -est 1** DOWNY : duveteux **2** INDISTINCT : flou

G

g ['dʒi:] *n, pl* **g's** *or* **gs** ['dʒi:z] : g *m,* septième lettre de l'alphabet
gab[1] ['gæb] *vi* **gabbed; gabbing** : bavarder, jacasser, papoter
gab[2] *n* CHATTER : bavardage *m,* papotage *m*
gabardine ['gæbər,di:n] *n* : gabardine *f*
gabby ['gæbi] *adj* **gabbier; -est** : bavard
gable ['geɪbəl] *n* : pignon *m*
Gabonese[1] [,gæbɔ'ni:z] *adj* : gabonais
Gabonese[2] *n* : Gabonais *m,* -naise *f*
gad ['gæd] *vi* **gadded; gadding** *or* **to gad about** : se balader, vadrouiller *fam*
gadfly ['gæd,flaɪ] *n, pl* **-flies 1** : taon *m* (insecte) **2** FAULTFINDER : critiqueur *m,* -queuse *f;* casse-pieds *mf fam*
gadget ['gædʒət] *n* : gadget *m,* bebelle *f Can fam*
gadgetry ['gædʒətri] *n* : gadgets *mpl*
gaff ['gæf] *n* HOOK : gaffe *f*
gaffe ['gæf] *n* : gaffe *f*
gag[1] ['gæg] *v* **gagged; gagging** *vt* : bâillonner — *vi* **1** CHOKE : s'étrangler **2** RETCH : avoir des haut-le-coeur
gag[2] *n* **1** : bâillon *m* **2** JOKE : blague *f*
gage → **gauge**

gaggle ['gægəl] *n* : troupeau *m* (d'oies, etc.)

gaiety ['geɪəṭi] *n, pl* **-eties** : gaieté *f*

gaily ['geɪli] *adv* : gaiement, de bonne humeur

gain[1] ['geɪn] *vt* **1** ACQUIRE : acquérir, gagner, obtenir <to gain ground : gagner du terrain> <to gain experience : acquérir de l'expérience> **2** REACH : arriver, atteindre <to gain the shore : atteindre la rive> **3** INCREASE : prendre <to gain weight : prendre du poids> — *vi* **1** PROFIT : gagner, profiter **2** ADVANCE : avancer (se dit d'une horloge) **3 to gain on** : rattraper

gain[2] *n* **1** PROFIT : profit *m,* bénéfice *m* <gains and losses : profits et pertes> **2** INCREASE : augmentation *f*

gainful ['geɪnfəl] *adj* : rémunéré

gait ['geɪt] *n* : démarche *f*

gal ['gæl] *n* : jeune fille *f*

gala[1] ['geɪlə, 'gæ-, 'gɑ-] *adj* : de gala

gala[2] *n* : gala *m*

galactic [gə'læktɪk] *adj* : galactique

galaxy ['gæləksi] *n, pl* **-axies** : galaxie *f*

gale ['geɪl] *n* **1** WIND : vent *m* fort **2** OUTBURST : éclat *m* <gales of laughter : éclats de rire>

gall[1] ['gɔl] *vt* **1** CHAFE : écorcher, excorier **2** IRRITATE : irriter, exaspérer

gall[2] *n* **1** BILE : bile *f* **2** IMPUDENCE : impudence *f* **3** SORE : écorchure *f* **4** : galle *f* (d'une plante)

gallant ['gælənt] *adj* **1** BRAVE : vaillant, courageux **2** CHIVALROUS : galant, courtois

gallantly ['gæləntli] *adv* **1** BRAVELY : vaillamment **2** CHIVALROUSLY : galamment

gallantry ['gæləntri] *n, pl* **-ries** : galanterie *f*

gallbladder ['gɔl,blædər] *n* : vesicule *f* biliaire

galleon ['gæljən] *n* : galion *m*

gallery ['gæləri] *n, pl* **-leries 1** BALCONY : galerie *f,* tribune *f* <press gallery : tribune de la presse> **2** ARCADE, CORRIDOR : galerie *f* **3** *or* **art gallery** : musée *m* des beaux-arts, galerie *f*

galley ['gæli] *n, pl* **-leys 1** SHIP : galère *f* **2** KITCHEN : coquerie *f* (d'un navire)

gallium ['gæliəm] *n* : gallium *m*

gallivant ['gælə,vænt] *vi* : se balader, courir la galipote *Can*

gallon ['gælən] *n* : gallon *m*

gallop[1] ['gæləp] *vi* : galoper

gallop[2] *n* : galop *m*

gallows ['gæ,loːz] *n, pl* **-lows** *or* **-lowses** [-,loːzəz] : gibet *m,* potence *f*

gallstone ['gɔl,stoːn] *n* : calcul *m* biliaire

galore [gə'lor] *adj* : en abondance

galoshes [gə'lɑʃəz] *npl* : caoutchoucs *mpl,* claques *fpl Can*

galvanize ['gælvən,aɪz] *vt* **-nized; -nizing** : galvaniser

Gambian[1] ['gæmbiən] *adj* : gambien

Gambian[2] *n* : Gambien *m,* -bienne *f*

gambit ['gæmbɪt] *n* **1** : gambit *m* (aux échecs) **2** STRATAGEM : stratagème *m,* manœuvre *f*

gamble[1] ['gæmbəl] *v* **-bled; -bling** *vi* : jouer — *vt* WAGER : parier

gamble[2] *n* **1** BET : pari *m* **2** RISK : entreprise *f* risquée

gambler ['gæmbələr] *n* : joueur *m,* joueuse *f*

gambol ['gæmbəl] *vi* **-boled** *or* **-bolled; -boling** *or* **-bolling** : gambader

game[1] ['geɪm] *adj* **1** PLUCKY : courageux **2** READY : partant <to be game for anything : être toujours partant> **3** LAME : estropié

game[2] *n* **1** : jeu *m* <game of chance : jeu de hasard> **2** MATCH : match *m,* partie *f* **3** : gibier *m* <big game : gros gibier>

gamekeeper ['geɪm,kiːpər] *n* : garde-chasse *m*

gamely ['geɪmli] *adv* : courageusement

gamete ['gæ,miːt, gə'miːt] *n* : gamète *m*

gamma ray ['gæmə] *n* : rayon *m* gamma

gamut ['gæmət] *n* : gamme *f* <the whole gamut : toute la gamme>

gamy *or* **gamey** ['geɪmi] *adj* **gamier; -est** : faisandé

gander ['gændər] *n* **1** : jars *m* (oiseau) **2** GLANCE : coup *m* d'oeil

gang[1] ['gæŋ] *vi* **to gang up on** : se liguer contre

gang[2] *n* : bande *f,* gang *f Can fam,* gang *m France* (de criminels)

gangling ['gæŋglɪŋ] *adj* LANKY : dégingandé

ganglion ['gæŋgliən] *n, pl* **-glia** /-gliə/ : ganglion *m*

gangplank ['gæŋ,plæŋk] *n* : passerelle *f*

gangrene ['gæŋ,griːn, 'gæn-; gæŋ'-, gæn'-] *n* : gangrène *f*

gangrenous ['gæŋgrənəs] *adj* : gangreneux

gangster ['gæŋstər] *n* : gangster *m*

gangway ['gæŋ,weɪ] *n* **1** PASSAGEWAY : passage *m* **2** GANGPLANK : passerelle *f* **3 gangway!** : dégagez le passage!

gannet ['gænət] *n* : fou *m* de Bassan

gap ['gæp] *n* **1** OPENING : trou *m,* vide *m,* brèche *f* **2** INTERVAL : intervalle *m,* période *f* **3** DISPARITY : gouffre *m,* écart *m* **4** LACUNA : lacune *f* <a gap in one's knowledge : une lacune dans sa connaissance> **5** GORGE : gorge *f,* col *m*

gape[1] ['geɪp] *vi* **gaped; gaping 1** OPEN : bâiller, s'ouvrir **2** STARE : rester bouche bée

gape[2] *n* **1** CHASM, OPENING : trou *m* béant **2** STARE : regard *m* ébahi, regard *m* bouche bée

garage[1] [gə'rɑʒ, -'rɑdʒ] *vt* **-raged; -raging** : mettre au garage

garage[2] *n* : garage *m*

garb[1] ['gɑrb] *vt* : vêtir
garb[2] *n* : costume *m,* mise *f*
garbage ['gɑrbɪdʒ] *n* : ordures *fpl*
garbage can *n* : poubelle *f*
garbageman ['gɑrbɪdʒmən] *n, pl* **-men** [-mən, -ˌmɛn] : éboueur *m*
garble ['gɑrbəl] *vt* **-bled; -bling** : raconter de travers, déformer, embrouiller
garbled ['gɑrbəld] *adj* : confus, embrouillé, déformé
garden[1] ['gɑrdən] *vi* : jardiner
garden[2] *n* : jardin *m*
gardener ['gɑrdənər] *n* : jardinier *m,* -nière *f*
gardenia [gɑr'di:njə] *n* : gardénia *m*
gargantuan [gɑr'gæntʃʊən] *adj* : gargantuesque
gargle[1] ['gɑrgəl] *vi* **-gled; -gling** : se gargariser
gargle[2] *n* : gargarisme *m* (acte et produit)
gargoyle ['gɑrˌgɔɪl] *n* : gargouille *f*
garish ['gærɪʃ] *adj* : criard, voyant
garland[1] ['gɑrlənd] *vt* : enguirlander (de fleurs, etc.)
garland[2] *n* : guirlande *f*
garlic ['gɑrlɪk] *n* : ail *m*
garment ['gɑrmənt] *n* : vêtement *m*
garner ['gɑrnər] *vt* : accumuler, recueillir, engranger (des récoltes)
garnet ['gɑrnət] *n* : grenat *m*
garnish[1] ['gɑrnɪʃ] *vt* : garnir
garnish[2] *n* : garniture *f*
garret ['gærət] *n* : mansarde *f*
garrison[1] ['gærəsən] *vt* **1** QUARTER : mettre (des troupes) en garnison **2** OCCUPY : placer une garnison dans (une ville, etc.)
garrison[2] *n* : garnison *f*
garrulous ['gærələs] *adj* : loquace, bavard
garrulousness ['gærələsnəs] *n* : loquacité *f*
garter ['gɑrţər] *n* : jarretière *f*
gas[1] ['gæs] *v* **gassed; gassing** *vt* : gazer — *vi* **to gas up** : faire le plein d'essence
gas[2] *n, pl* **gases 1** : gaz *m* <to cook with gas : cuisiner au gaz> **2** GASOLINE : essence *f*
gaseous ['gæʃəs, 'gæsiəs] *adj* : gazeux
gash[1] ['gæʃ] *vt* : entailler
gash[2] *n* : entaille *f*
gasket ['gæskət] *n* : joint *m*
gasoline ['gæsəˌli:n, ˌgæsə'-] *n* : essence *f,* gaz *m Can fam*
gasp[1] ['gæsp] *vi* **1** : avoir le souffle coupé (par la surprise, etc.) **2** PANT : haleter — *vt* : dire en haletant
gasp[2] *n* : halètement *m* <to the last gasp : jusqu'au dernier souffle>
gastric ['gæstrɪk] *adj* : gastrique
gastronomy [gæs'trɑnəmi] *n* : gastronomie *f* — **gastronomic** [ˌgæstrə'nɑmɪk] *adj*
gate ['geɪt] *n* **1** DOOR : porte *f* **2** BARRIER : barrière *f,* grille *f*
gatekeeper ['geɪtˌki:pər] *n* : gardien *m,* -dienne *f;* portier *m,* -tière *f*
gateway ['geɪtˌweɪ] *n* : porte *f,* portail *m*
gather[1] ['gæðər] *vt* **1** ASSEMBLE : rassembler **2** COLLECT : recueillir, ramasser **3** DEDUCE : déduire **4** : froncer (une étoffe) **5 to gather speed** : prendre de la vitesse — *vi* ASSEMBLE : se rassembler, se réunir
gather[2] *n* : fronce *f* (d'une étoffe)
gathering ['gæðərɪŋ] *n* : rassemblement *m*
gauche ['go:ʃ] *adj* : gauche
gaudy ['gɔdi] *adj* **gaudier; -est** : criard, tape-à-l'oeil
gauge[1] ['geɪdʒ] *vt* **gauged; gauging 1** MEASURE : jauger, mesurer **2** ESTIMATE : évaluer, calculer
gauge[2] *n* **1** INDICATOR : jauge *f,* indicateur *m* **2** CALIBER : calibre *m* **3** INDICATION : moyen *m* de jauger, test *m* (de caractère, etc.)
gaunt ['gɔnt] *adj* : décharné, émacié
gauntlet ['gɔntlət] *n* : gant *m* (à crispin) <to throw down the gauntlet : jeter le gant>
gauze ['gɔz] *n* : gaze *f*
gauzy ['gɔzi] *adj* **gauzier; -est** : transparent, diaphane
gave → **give**[1]
gavel ['gævəl] *n* : marteau *m* (de magistrat, etc.)
gawk ['gɔk] *vi* **to gawk at** : regarder bouche bée, être bouche bée devant
gawky ['gɔki] *adj* **gawkier; -est** : gauche, malhabile, emprunté
gay ['geɪ] *adj* **1** MERRY : gai, joyeux **2** BRIGHT, COLORFUL : vif, éclatant **3** HOMOSEXUAL : gai, gay
gaze[1] ['geɪz] *vi* **gazed; gazing** : regarder (fixement)
gaze[2] *n* : regard *m*
gazelle [gə'zɛl] *n* : gazelle *f*
gazette [gə'zɛt] *n* **1** NEWSPAPER : journal *m* **2** : journal *m* officiel
gazetteer [ˌgæzə'tɪr] *n* : dictionnaire *m* géographique, index *m* géographique
gear[1] ['gɪr] *vt* ADAPT, ORIENT : adapter <a book geared to children : un livre adapté aux enfants> — *vi* **to gear up** : se préparer, être fin prêt
gear[2] *n* **1** EQUIPMENT : équipement *m,* matériel *m* <fishing gear : matériel de pêche> **2** BELONGINGS : effets *mpl* personnels **3** SPEED : vitesse *f* <to change gear : changer de vitesse> <to be in first gear : être en première> **4** COGWHEEL : roue *f* dentée, pignon *m*
gearshift ['gɪrˌʃɪft] *n* : levier *m* de vitesses
geese → **goose**
Geiger counter ['gaɪgərˌkaʊntər] *n* : compteur *m* Geiger
gelatin ['dʒɛlətən] *n* : gélatine *f*
gem ['dʒɛm] *n* **1** : pierre *f* précieuse, gemme *f* **2** JEWEL : joyau *m* <the gem

of my collection : le joyau de ma collection>
Gemini ['dʒɛmə,naɪ] *n* : Gémeaux *mpl*
gemstone ['dʒɛm,stoːn] *n* : pierre *f* précieuse
gender ['dʒɛndər] *n* **1** : genre *m* (en grammaire) **2** SEX : sexe *m*
gene ['dʒiːn] *n* : gène *m*
genealogical [,dʒiːniə'lɑdʒɪkəl] *adj* : généalogique
genealogy [,dʒiːni'ɑlədʒi, ,dʒɛ-, -'æ-] *n, pl* **-gies** : généalogie *f*
genera → **genus**
general[1] ['dʒɛnrəl, 'dʒɛnə-] *adj* : général <as a general rule : en règle générale>
general[2] *n* **1** : général *m* (militaire) **2** in ~ : en général
generality [,dʒɛnə'rælət̬i] *n, pl* **-ties** : généralité *f*
generalization [,dʒɛnrələ'zeɪʃən, ,dʒɛnərə-] *n* : généralisation *f*
generalize ['dʒɛnrə,laɪz, 'dʒɛnərə-] *vi* **-ized; -izing** : généraliser
generally ['dʒɛnrəli, 'dʒɛnərə-] *adv* **1** USUALLY : généralement, en général **2** OVERALL, WIDELY : dans l'ensemble, en général
generate ['dʒɛnə,reɪt] *vt* **-ated; -ating** : générer
generation [,dʒɛnə'reɪʃən] *n* : génération *f*
generator ['dʒɛnə,reɪt̬ər] *n* **1** PRODUCER : générateur *m* **2** : génératrice *f* (d'énergie électrique)
generic [dʒə'nɛrɪk] *adj* : générique
generosity [,dʒɛnə'rɑsət̬i] *n, pl* **-ties** : générosité *f*
generous ['dʒɛnərəs] *adj* **1** OPEN-HANDED : généreux **2** ABUNDANT, COPIOUS : abondant, copieux — **generously** *adv*
genetic [dʒə'nɛt̬ɪk] *adj* : génétique — **genetically** *adv*
geneticist [dʒə'nɛt̬ɪsəst] *n* : généticien *m*, -cienne *f*
genetics [dʒə'nɛt̬ɪks] *n* : génétique *f*
genial ['dʒiːniəl] *adj* : affable, cordial, aimable — **genially** *adv*
geniality [,dʒiːni'ælət̬i] *n* : cordialité *f*
genie ['dʒiːni] *n* : génie *m*
genital ['dʒɛnət̬əl] *adj* : génital
genitals ['dʒɛnət̬əlz] *npl* : organes *mpl* génitaux
genius ['dʒiːnjəs] *n* : génie *m*
genocide ['dʒɛnə,saɪd] *n* : génocide *m*
genre ['ʒɑnrə, 'ʒɑr] *n* : genre *m*
genteel [dʒɛn'tiːl] *adj* : distingué
gentile ['dʒɛn,taɪl] *n* : gentil *m*
gentility [,dʒɛn'tɪlət̬i] *n, pl* **-ties** **1** GENTRY : petite noblesse *f* **2** COURTESY : politesse *f*
gentle ['dʒɛntəl] *adj* **-tler; -tlest** **1** NOBLE : noble, de bonne famille **2** DOCILE, MILD : doux **3** LIGHT : léger <a gentle blow : un coup bien léger> **4** GRADUAL : doux, sans heurts <a gentle slope : une pente douce> <to come to a gentle stop : s'arrêter doucement>
gentleman ['dʒɛntəlmən] *n, pl* **-men** [-mən, -,mɛn] **1** MAN : monsieur *m* **2** : gentleman *m* <to act like a gentleman : agir en gentleman>
gentlemanly ['dʒɛntəlmənli] *adj* : courtois, distingué
gentleness ['dʒɛntəlnəs] *n* : douceur *f*
gentlewoman ['dʒɛntəl,wʊmən] *n, pl* **-women** [-,wɪmən] : dame *f* (bien née)
gentry ['dʒɛntri] *n, pl* **-tries** : petite noblesse *f*
genuflect ['dʒɛnjʊ,flɛkt] *vi* : faire une génuflexion
genuflection [,dʒɛnjʊ'flɛkʃən] *n* : génuflexion *f*
genuine [,dʒɛnjʊwən] *adj* **1** AUTHENTIC, REAL : authentique, vrai, véritable **2** SINCERE : sincère — **genuinely** *adv*
genus ['dʒiːnəs] *n, pl* **genera** ['dʒɛnərə] : genre *m*
geochemistry [,dʒiːo'kɛməstri] *n* : géochimie *f*
geodesic [,dʒiːə'dɛsɪk, -'diː-, -zɪk] *adj* : géodésique
geographer [dʒi'ɑgrəfər] *n* : géographe *mf*
geographic [,dʒiːə'græfɪk] *or* **geographical** [-fɪkəl] *adj* : géographique — **geographically** [-fɪkli] *adv*
geography [dʒi'ɑgrəfi] *n, pl* **-phies** : géographie *f*
geologic [,dʒiːə'lɑdʒɪk] *or* **geological** [-dʒɪkəl] *adj* : géologique — **geologically** [-dʒɪkli] *adv*
geologist [dʒi'ɑlədʒɪst] *n* : géologue *mf*
geology [dʒi'ɑlədʒi] *n, pl* **-gies** : géologie *f*
geomagnetic [dʒiːomæg'nɛt̬ɪk] *adj* : géomagnétique
geometric [,dʒiːə'mɛtrɪk] *or* **geometrical** [-'mɛtrɪkəl] *adj* : géométrique
geometry [dʒi'ɑmətri] *n, pl* **-tries** : géométrie *f*
geranium [dʒə'reɪniəm] *n* : géranium *m*
gerbil ['dʒərbəl] *n* : gerbille *f*
geriatric [,dʒɛri'ætrɪk] *adj* : gériatrique
geriatrics [,dʒɛri'ætrɪks] *n* : gériatrie *f*
germ ['dʒərm] *n* **1** MICROBE : microbe *m*, germe *m* **2** : germe *m* (en biologie) **3** RUDIMENTS : germe *m* (d'une idée, etc.)
German[1] ['dʒərmən] *adj* : allemand
German[2] *n* **1** : Allemand *m*, -mande *f* **2** : allemand *m* (langue)
germane [dʒər'meɪn] *adj* : pertinent
germanium [dʒər'meɪniəm] *n* : germanium *m*
German measles *n* : rubéole *f*
German shepherd *n* : berger *m* allemand
germ cell *n* : gamète *m*, cellule *f* germinale
germicide ['dʒərmə,saɪd] *n* : germicide *m*

germinate ['dʒərmə,neɪt] *v* **-nated; -nating** *vi* : germer — *vt* : faire germer

germination [,dʒərmə'neɪʃən] *n* : germination *f*

gerund ['dʒɛrənd] *n* : gérondif *m*

gestation [dʒɛ'steɪʃən] *n* : gestation *f*

gesture[1] ['dʒɛstʃər] *vi* **-tured; -turing 1** : gesticuler, faire des gestes **2 to gesture to** : faire signe à

gesture[2] *n* : geste *m*

get ['gɛt] *v* **got** ['gɑt]; **got** *or* **gotten** ['gɑtən]; **getting** *vt* **1** OBTAIN : obtenir, trouver, se procurer **2** RECEIVE : recevoir, avoir <the garden gets a lot of sun : le jardin reçoit beaucoup de soleil> **3** EARN : gagner, mériter **4** FETCH : chercher (un objet), aller chercher (une personne) **5** CATCH : prendre (un train, etc.), attraper (une balle, un rhume), saisir (une personne) **6** PUT, TAKE : faire parvenir <to get sth to s.o. : faire parvenir qqch à qqn> <we can get the car through here : nous pouvons faire passer la voiture par ici> **7** UNDERSTAND : comprendre, piger *fam* <now I get it! : je pige!> **8** PREPARE : préparer <to get dinner : préparer le dîner> **9** PERSUADE : persuader, convaincre <I got her to agree : j'ai réussi à obtenir son accord> **10** (*to cause to be*) <to get one's hair cut : se faire couper les cheveux> **11 to have got** : avoir <I've got a headache : j'ai mal à la tête> **12 to have got to** : devoir — *vi* **1** BECOME : devenir <she's getting impatient : elle devient impatiente> <it's getting late : il se fait tard> **2** GO, MOVE : aller, arriver, se rendre <to get to the top of : arriver au sommet> <where did he get to? : où en est-il allé?> **3** PROGRESS : avancer <she got to be a director : elle a avancé à la position de directeur> **4 to get ahead** : progresser, prendre de l'avance **5 to get around** EVADE : contourner **6 to get at** REACH : atteindre **7 to get at** INSINUATE, MEAN : vouloir dire <what are you getting at? : où voulez-vous en venir?> **8 to get at** ASCERTAIN : découvrir, parvenir à **9 to get away with** : échapper à, s'en tirer à **10 to get back at** : se venger de **11 to get over** : se remettre de (une maladie, etc.) **12 to get together** MEET : se réunir

get along *vi* **1** PROGRESS : avancer, progresser **2** MANAGE : aller <how are you getting along? : comment vastu?> **3 to get along with** : bien s'entendre avec

getaway ['gɛtə,weɪ] *n* : fuite *f* <to make one's getaway : s'enfuir>

get off *vi* **1** START : partir **2** : tirer d'affaire, s'en tirer <to get off lightly : s'en tirer à bon compte>

get out *vi* **1** ESCAPE : sortir **2** : être révélé <our secret got out : notre secret est révélé>

get–together ['gɛttə,gɛðər] *n* : réunion *f*, petite fête *f*

get up *vi* ARISE : se lever — *vt* **1** PREPARE, ORGANIZE : former, organiser **2** DRESS : habiller

geyser ['gaɪzər] *n* : geyser *m*

Ghanian[1] ['gɑniən, 'gæ-] *adj* : ghanéen

Ghanian[2] *n* : Ghanéen *m*, -néenne *f*

ghastly ['gæstli] *adj* **ghastlier; -est 1** HORRIBLE : horrible, épouvantable **2** PALE : blême, blafard

gherkin ['gərkən] *n* : cornichon *m*

ghetto ['gɛt̬oː] *n, pl* **-tos** *or* **-toes** : ghetto *m*

ghost ['goːst] *n* : fantôme *m*, spectre *m*

ghostly ['goːstli] *adj* **ghostlier; -est** : spectral

ghost town *n* : ville *f* morte

ghoul ['guːl] *n* : goule *f*

ghoulish ['guːlɪʃ] *adj* : macabre

GI [,dʒiː'aɪ] *n, pl* **GI's** *or* **GIs** : soldat *m* américain

giant[1] ['dʒaɪənt] *adj* : géant, gigantesque

giant[2] *n* : géant *m*, géante *f*

gibberish ['dʒɪbərɪʃ] *n* : charabia *m fam*, baragouin *m*

gibbon ['gɪbən] *n* : gibbon *m*

gibe[1] ['dʒaɪb] *vi* **gibed; gibing** : se moquer <to gibe at s.o. : railler qqn, se moquer de qqn>

gibe[2] *n* : raillerie *f*, moquerie *f*

giblets ['dʒɪbləts] *npl* : abats *mpl* (de volaille)

giddiness ['gɪdinəs] *n* **1** DIZZINESS : vertiges *mpl*, étourdissements *mpl* **2** SILLINESS : légèreté *f*, étourderie *f*

giddy ['gɪdi] *adj* **giddier; -est 1** DIZZY : vertigineux **2** FRIVOLOUS, SILLY : frivole, écervelé, étourdi

gift ['gɪft] *n* **1** PRESENT : cadeau *m* **2** TALENT : don *m*

gifted ['gɪftəd] *adj* TALENTED : doué

gigantic [dʒaɪ'gæntɪk] *adj* : gigantesque

giggle[1] ['gɪgəl] *vi* **-gled; -gling** : rire bêtement

giggle[2] *n* : fou rire *m*, petit rire *m* sot

Gila monster ['hiːlə] *n* : monstre *m* de Gila

gild ['gɪld] *vt* **gilded** ['gɪldəd] *or* **gilt** ['gɪlt]; **gilding** : dorer

gill ['gɪl] *n* : branchie *f*, ouïe *f*

gilt[1] ['gɪlt] *adj* : doré

gilt[2] *n* : dorure *f*

gimlet ['gɪmlət] *n* : vrille *f* (outil)

gimmick ['gɪmɪk] *n* : truc *m*, gadget *m* <publicity gimmick : truc publicitaire>

gin ['dʒɪn] *n* **1** *or* **cotton gin** : égreneuse *f* (de coton) **2** : gin *m* (boisson)

ginger ['dʒɪndʒər] *n* : gingembre *m*

ginger ale *n* : boisson *f* gazeuse au gingembre

gingerbread ['dʒɪndʒər,brɛd] *n* : pain *m* d'épice

gingerly ['dʒɪndʒərli] *adv* : précautionneusement, avec circonspection
gingham ['gɪŋəm] *n* : vichy *m*
ginseng ['dʒɪnˌsɪŋ] *n* : ginseng *m*
giraffe [dʒə'ræf] *n* : girafe *f*
gird ['gərd] *vt* **girded** ['gərdəd] *or* **girt** ['gərt]; **girding 1** PUT ON : ceindre **2 to gird oneself** : se préparer
girder ['gərdər] *n* : poutre *f*
girdle[1] ['gərdəl] *vt* **-dled; -dling** : encercler
girdle[2] *n* CORSET : gaine *f*
girl ['gərl] *n* **1** : fille *f*, jeune fille *f* **2** SWEETHEART : petite amie *f* **3** DAUGHTER : fille *f*
girlfriend ['gərlˌfrɛnd] *n* : copine *f*, petite amie *f*, blonde *f Can fam*
girlhood ['gərlˌhʊd] *n* : jeunesse *f*
girlish ['gərlɪʃ] *adj* : de jeune fille
girth ['gərθ] *n* **1** CIRCUMFERENCE : circonférence *f* (d'un arbre, etc.), tour *m* de taille (d'une personne) **2** : sangle *f* (d'une selle de cheval)
gist ['dʒɪst] *n* : essentiel *m*
give[1] ['gɪv] *v* **gave** ['geɪv]; **given** ['gɪvən]; **giving** *vt* **1** : donner, faire don à, conférer (un honneur, etc.) **2** PAY : payer **3** CAUSE : faire, causer <to give s.o. to understand : faire entendre à qqn> — *vi* **1** : donner **2** YIELD : céder **3 to give in** *or* **to give up** : se rendre **4 to give out** DISTRIBUTE : distribuer **5 to give out** COLLAPSE : s'épuiser
give[2] *n* : élasticité *f*, souplesse *f*
giveaway ['gɪvəˌweɪ] *n* **1** : révélation *f* (involontaire) **2** GIFT : prime *f*, cadeau *m*
given ['gɪvən] *adj* **1** SPECIFIED : donné, déterminé **2** INCLINED : enclin <given to violence : enclin à la violence>
given name *n* : prénom *m*
gizzard ['gɪzərd] *n* : gésier *m*
glacial ['gleɪʃəl] *adj* **1** FRIGID : glacial **2** : glaciaire (en géologie)
glacier ['gleɪʃər] *n* : glacier *m*
glad ['glæd] *adj* **gladder; gladdest 1** HAPPY, PLEASED : content, heureux **2** JOYFUL, PLEASANT : joyeux, heureux <glad tidings : bonnes nouvelles> **3 to be glad to** : être heureux de <I'll be glad to do it! : avec plaisir!>
gladden ['glædən] *vt* : réjouir
glade ['gleɪd] *n* : clairière *f*
gladiator ['glædiˌeɪt̬ər] *n* : gladiateur *m*
gladiolus [ˌglædi'o:ləs] *n, pl* **-li** [-li, -ˌlaɪ] : glaïeul *m*
gladly ['glædli] *adv* : avec plaisir, de bon coeur, volontiers
gladness ['glædnəs] *n* : joie *f*, contentement *m*
glamor *or* **glamour** ['glæmər] *n* **1** ALLURE : fascination *f*, charme *f* **2** ELEGANCE : élégance *f*, chic *m*
glamorize ['glæməˌraɪz] *vt* **-ized; -izing** : idéaliser, présenter sous des couleurs séduisantes
glamorous ['glæmərəs] *adj* **1** ALLURING : séduisant, fascinant **2** ELEGANT, EXCITING : élégant, brillant
glance[1] ['glænts] *vi* **glanced; glancing 1 to glance at** : jeter un coup d'œil à **2 to glance off** : ricocher sur (un mur, etc.)
glance[2] *n* : coup *m* d'œil
gland ['glænd] *n* : glande *f*
glandular ['glændʒʊlər] *adj* : glandulaire
glare[1] ['glær] *vi* **glared; glaring 1** SHINE : briller d'un éclat éblouissant **2 to glare at** : lancer un regard furieux à, regarder avec colère
glare[2] *n* **1** BRIGHTNESS : lumière *f* éblouissante **2** STARE : regard *m* furieux
glaring ['glærɪŋ] *adj* **1** BRIGHT : éblouissant **2** FLAGRANT : flagrant, qui saute aux yeux **3** FIERCE : furieux
glass[1] ['glæs] *vt or* **to glass in** : vitrer
glass[2] *adj* : en verre
glass[3] *n* **1** : verre *m* <broken glass : éclats de verre> <a glass of wine : un verre de vin> **2 glasses** *npl* SPECTACLES : lunettes *fpl*
glassblowing ['glæsˌblo:ɪŋ] *n* : soufflage *m* du verre
glassful ['glæsˌfʊl] *n* : verre *m*
glassware ['glæsˌwær] *n* : verrerie *f*
glassy ['glæsi] *adj* **glassier; -est 1** VITREOUS : vitreux **2** SMOOTH : lisse **3 glassy eyes** : yeux *mpl* vitreux
glaucoma [glaʊ'ko:mə, glɔ-] *n* : glaucome *m*
glaze[1] ['gleɪz] *vt* **glazed; glazing 1** : vitrer (une fenêtre, etc.) **2** : vernisser (des céramiques), vitrifier (des carreaux, etc.) **3** ICE : glacer (des pâtisseries)
glaze[2] *n* **1** GLAZING : glaçage *m* **2** : vernis *m* (de céramiques), glacé *m* (d'étoffes, de photos, etc.)
glazier ['gleɪʒər] *n* : vitrier *m*
gleam[1] ['gli:m] *vi* : luire, reluire
gleam[2] *n* : lueur *f* <the first gleam of dawn : les premières lueurs de l'aube> <a gleam of hope : une lueur d'espoir>
glean ['gli:n] *vt* : glaner
glee ['gli:] *n* : joie *f*, allégresse *f*
gleeful ['gli:fəl] *adj* : joyeux — **gleefully** *adv*
glen ['glɛn] *n* : vallon *m*, vallée *f* encaissée
glib ['glɪb] *adj* **glibber; glibbest** : facile, désinvolte
glibly ['glɪbli] *adv*: avec désinvolture
glide[1] ['glaɪd] *vi* **glided; gliding** : glisser (sur une surface), planer (en l'air)
glide[2] *n* : glissement *m*
glider ['glaɪdər] *n* **1** : planeur *m* (en aéronautique) **2** SWING : balançoire *f*
glimmer[1] ['glɪmər] *vi* : jeter une faible lueur
glimmer[2] *n* GLEAM : lueur *f*

glimpse[1] ['glɪmps] *vt* **glimpsed; glimpsing :** entrevoir
glimpse[2] *n* **:** aperçu *m*
glint[1] ['glɪnt] *vi* **:** étinceler, miroiter (sur l'eau, etc.)
glint[2] *n* **:** reflet *m,* miroitement *m*
glisten ['glɪsən] *vi* **:** briller, miroiter, luire
glitter[1] ['glɪt̬ər] *vi* **:** scintiller, étinceler
glitter[2] *n* **:** scintillement *m*
gloat ['glo:t] *vi* **:** jubiler <to gloat over : se réjouir de>
glob ['glɑb] *n* **:** globule *m,* petite boule *f*
global ['glo:bəl] *adj* **:** mondial — **globally** *adv*
globe ['glo:b] *n* **:** globe *m*
globe–trotter ['glo:bˌtrɑt̬ər] *n* **:** globe-trotter *m*
globular ['glɑbjʊlər] *adj* **:** globulaire
globule ['glɑbju:l] *n* **:** gouttelette *f*
glockenspiel ['glɑkənˌspi:l, -ʃpi:l] *n* **:** glockenspiel *m*
gloom ['glu:m] *n* **1** DARKNESS **:** obscurité *f,* ténèbres *fpl* **2** SADNESS **:** tristesse *f,* mélancolie *f*
gloomily ['glu:məli] *adv* **:** sombrement, tristement
gloomy ['glu:mi] *adj* **gloomier; -est 1** DARK **:** obscur, sombre **2** MELANCHOLY **:** mélancolique, lugubre **3** PESSIMISTIC **:** sombre, triste **4** DEPRESSING **:** déprimant, morne
glorification [ˌglorəfə'keɪʃən] *n* **:** glorification *f*
glorify ['glorəˌfaɪ] *vt* **-fied; -fying :** glorifier
glorious ['gloriəs] *adj* **:** glorieux — **gloriously** *adv*
glory[1] ['glori] *vi* **-ried; -rying :** se glorifier <to glory in : se glorifier de>
glory[2] *n, pl* **-ries 1 :** gloire *f* **2 in all one's glory :** dans toute sa splendeur
gloss[1] ['glɔs, 'glɑs] *vt* **1** EXPLAIN, DEFINE **:** gloser **2** POLISH **:** faire briller, lustrer **3 to gloss over :** glisser sur, atténuer, dissimuler (la vérité, etc.)
gloss[2] *n* **1** SHINE **:** brillant *m,* lustre *m* **2** EXPLANATION **:** glose *f*
glossary ['glɔsəri, 'glɑ-] *n, pl* **-ries :** glossaire *m*
glossy ['glɔsi, 'glɑ-] *adj* **glossier; -est :** brillant, luisant, glacé (se dit du papier)
glove ['glʌv] *n* **:** gant *m*
glow[1] ['glo:] *vi* **1** SHINE **:** rougeoyer, luire **2 :** rayonner <to glow with health : rayonner de santé>
glow[2] *n* **:** rougeoiement *m,* lueur *f*
glower ['glaʊər] *vi* **:** lancer des regards furieux
glowworm ['glo:ˌwərm] *n* **:** ver *m* luisant
glucose ['glu:ˌko:s] *n* **:** glucose *m*
glue[1] ['glu:] *vt* **glued; gluing 1 :** coller **2 to glue one's eyes on :** garder les yeux rivés sur
glue[2] *n* **:** colle *f*
gluey ['glu:i] *adj* **gluier; -est :** gluant, collant
glum ['glʌm] *adj* **glummer; glummest :** morne, triste, morose
glut[1] ['glʌt] *vt* **glutted; glutting** SATURATE **:** inonder, saturer
glut[2] *n* **:** surabondance *f,* excès *m*
glutinous ['glu:tənəs] *adj* **:** gluant
glutton ['glʌtən] *n* **:** glouton *m,* -tonne *f;* gourmand *m,* -mande *f*
gluttonous ['glʌtənəs] *adj* **:** glouton
gluttony ['glʌtəni] *n, pl* **-tonies :** gloutonnerie *f*
gnarled ['nɑrld] *adj* **:** noueux
gnash ['næʃ] *vt* **to gnash one's teeth :** grincer des dents
gnat ['næt] *n* **:** moucheron *m,* brulôt *m Can*
gnaw ['nɔ] *vt* **:** ronger
gnome ['no:m] *n* **:** gnome *m*
gnu ['nu:, 'nju:] *n, pl* **gnu** *or* **gnus :** gnou *m*
go[1] ['go:] *v* **went** ['wɛnt]; **gone** ['gɔn]; **going** ['go:ɪŋ]; **goes** ['go:z] *vi* **1 :** aller **2** LEAVE **:** partir, s'en aller <I have to go : il faut que je m'en aille> **3** EXTEND **:** s'étendre <this road goes to the river : cette rue s'étend jusqu'au fleuve> **4** SELL **:** se vendre <it goes for $15 : cela se vend pour 15 $> **5** BECOME **:** devenir <he's going crazy : il devient fou> **6** FUNCTION **:** marcher <to get it going : le mettre en marche> **7** DISAPPEAR **:** disparaître <my pen is gone! : mon stylo a disparu!> **8 to go back on** BETRAY **:** trahir **9 to go for** FAVOR **:** aimer **10 to go off** EXPLODE **:** exploser **11 to go off** RING **:** sonner **12 to go out** LEAVE **:** sortir **13 to go out :** s'éteindre <the fire went out : le feu s'est éteint> **14 to go over** CHECK **:** vérifier — *vt* **to go it alone :** le faire tout seul — *v aux* **to be going to :** aller <I'm going to talk to you (about it) : je vais t'en parler>
go[2] *n, pl* **goes 1** ATTEMPT **:** essai *m,* tentative *f* <to have a go at sth : essayer de faire qqch> **2** SUCCESS **:** réussite *f* <to make a go of sth : réussir qqch> **3 to be always on the go :** ne s'arrêter jamais
goad[1] ['go:d] *vt* **:** aiguillonner (un animal), provoquer (une personne)
goad[2] *n* **:** aiguillon *m*
goal ['go:l] *n* **:** but *m*
goalie ['go:li] → **goalkeeper**
goalkeeper ['go:lˌki:pər] *n* **:** gardien *m* de but, cerbère *m Can*
goat ['go:t] *n* **1 :** chèvre *f* **2** *or* **billie goat :** bouc *m*
goatee [go:'ti:] *n* **:** barbiche *f*
goatskin ['go:tˌskɪn] *n* **:** cuir *m* de chèvre
gob ['gɑb] *n* **1** LUMP **:** boule *f* **2 gobs of :** beaucoup de
gobble ['gɑbəl] *v* **-bled; -bling** *vt or* **to gobble up** DEVOUR **:** engloutir — *vi* **:** glouglouter (se dit d'un dindon)

gobbledygook [ˈgɑbəldiˌgʊk, -ˌguːk] *n* : charabia *m fam*
go–between [ˈgoːbɪˌtwiːn] *n* : intermédiaire *mf*
goblet [ˈgɑblət] *n* : verre *m* à pied
goblin [ˈgɑblən] *n* : lutin *m*
god [ˈgɑd, ˈgɔd] *n* **1** : dieu *m* **2 God** : Dieu *m*
godchild [ˈgɑdˌtʃaɪld, ˈgɔd-] *n, pl* **-children** : filleul *m,* -leule *f*
goddess [ˈgɑdəs, ˈgɔ-] *n* : déesse *f*
godfather [ˈgɑdˌfɑðər, ˈgɔd-] *n* : parrain *m*
godless [ˈgɑdləs, ˈgɔd-] *adj* : impie
godlike [ˈgɑdˌlaɪk, ˈgɔd-] *adj* : divin
godly [ˈgɑdli, ˈgɔd-] *adj* **godlier; est 1** DIVINE : divin **2** DEVOUT, PIOUS : dévot, pieux
godmother [ˈgɑdˌmʌðər, ˈgɔd-] *n* : marraine *f*
godparent [ˈgɑdˌpærənt, ˈgɔd-] *n* : parrain *m,* marraine *f*
godsend [ˈgɑdˌsɛnd, ˈgɔd-] *n* : aubaine *f,* bénédiction *f,* don *m* (du ciel)
goes → **go**[1]
go–getter [ˈgoːˌgɛt̬ər] *n* : battant *m,* -tante *f;* fonceur *m,* -ceuse *f fam*
goggle [ˈgɑgəl] *vi* **-gled; -gling** : ouvrir de grands yeux, regarder avec des yeux ronds
goggles [ˈgɑgəlz] *npl* : lunettes *fpl* (protectrices)
goings–on [ˌgoːɪŋˈzɑn, -ˈɔn] *npl* : événements *mpl,* activités *fpl,* conduite *f*
goiter *or Brit* **goitre** [ˈgɔɪt̬ər] *n* : goitre *m*
gold [ˈgoːld] *n* : or *m*
golden [ˈgoːldən] *adj* **1** : en or, d'or **2** : doré, (couleur) d'or <golden hair : cheveux dorés> **3** FAVORABLE : idyllique, en or <a golden opportunity : une occasion magnifique, une occasion en or>
golden mean *n* : juste milieu *m*
goldenrod [ˈgoːldənˌrɑd] *n* : verge *f* d'or
golden rule *n* : règle *f* d'or
goldfinch [ˈgoːldˌfɪntʃ] *n* : chardonneret *m*
goldfish [ˈgoːldˌfɪʃ] *ns & pl* : poisson *m* rouge
goldsmith [ˈgoːldˌsmɪθ] *n* : orfèvre *m*
golf[1] [ˈgɑlf, ˈgɔlf] *vi* : jouer au golf
golf[2] *n* : golf *m*
golfer [ˈgɑlfər, ˈgɔl-] *n* : golfeur *m,* -feuse *f;* joueur *m,* joueuse *f* de golf
gondola [ˈgɑndələ, gɑnˈdoːlə] *n* : gondole *f*
gone [ˈgɔn] *adj* **1** LOST : perdu **2** PAST : passé <gone is the time when . . . : le temps n'est plus où . . . > **3** DEAD : mort **4** WORN : usé **5 to be far gone** : être bien faible
goner [ˈgɔnər] *n* **to be a goner** : être fichu *fam*
gong [ˈgɔŋ, ˈgɑŋ] *n* : gong *m*
gonorrhea [ˌgɑnəˈriːə] *n* : blennorragie *f*
good[1] [ˈgʊd] *adv* **1** (*used as an intensifier*) : bien, bon <a good strong rope : une corde bien forte> <a good long walk : une bonne promenade> **2 to make good** : réussir
good[2] *adj* **better** [ˈbɛt̬ər]; **best** [ˈbɛst] **1** : bon <good news : bonnes nouvelles> <a good salary : un bon salaire> <good evening : bonsoir> <good morning : bonjour> **2** KIND : bon, aimable <a good deed : une bonne action> **3** FULL : bon <she waited for a good hour : elle attendu pendant une bonne heure> **4** SKILLED : bon, habile <to be good at : être bon en (des études), être bon à (un jeu)> **5** OBEDIENT : sage <be good! : sois sage!> **6** : beau <good weather : beau temps>
good[3] *n* **1** RIGHT : bien *m* <good and evil : le bien et le mal> **2** GOODNESS : bonté *f* **3** BENEFIT : bien *m* <for your own good : pour votre bien> **4 goods** *npl* PROPERTY : biens *mpl* **5 goods** *npl* WARES : marchandises *fpl* **6 for ~** : pour de bon **7 the good** : les bons *mpl*
good–bye *or* **good–by** [gʊdˈbaɪ] *n* : au revoir *m*
good–for–nothing [ˈgʊdfərˌnʌθɪŋ] *adj* : bon à rien
Good Friday *n* : le Vendredi saint
good–hearted [ˈgʊdˈhɑrt̬əd] *adj* : généreux, qui a bon coeur
good–looking [ˈgʊdˈlʊkɪŋ] *adj* : beau
goodly [ˈgʊdli] *adj* **goodlier; -est** : grand, ample <a goodly sum : une somme considérable>
good–natured [ˈgʊdˈneɪtʃərd] *adj* : aimable, qui a un bon naturel
goodness [ˈgʊdnəs] *n* **1** : bonté *f* **2 goodness me!** *or* **my goodness!** : mon Dieu!
good–tempered [ˈgʊdˈtɛmpərd] *adj* : de bon caractère
goodwill [ˌgʊdˈwɪl] *n* : bienveillance *f*
goody [ˈgʊdi] *n, pl* **goodies 1** : bon *m* **2 goody!** : chouette! *f fam* **3 goodies** *npl* : friandises *fpl*
gooey [ˈguːi] *adj* **gooier; gooiest** : gluant
goof[1] [ˈguːf] *vi* **1** *or* **to goof up** : gaffer *fam,* faire une gaffe **2 to goof around** : faire l'imbécile
goof[2] *n* : gaffe *f fam*
goofy [ˈguːfi] *adj* **goofier; -est** : dingue *fam*
goose [ˈguːs] *n, pl* **geese** [ˈgiːs] : oie *f*
gooseberry [ˈguːsˌbɛriː, ˈguːz-] *n, pl* **-berries** : groseille *f* à maquereau
goose bumps *npl* : chair *f* de poule
gooseflesh [ˈguːsˌflɛʃ] → **goose bumps**
goose pimples → **goose bumps**
gopher [ˈgoːfər] *n* : gaufre *m Can*
gore[1] [ˈgor] *vt* **gored; goring** : encorner
gore[2] *n* BLOOD : sang *m*

gorge[1] ['gɔrdʒ] *vt* **gorged; gorging 1** SATIATE : rassasier **2 to gorge oneself** : se gorger

gorge[2] *n* RAVINE : gorge *f*, défilé *m*

gorgeous ['gɔrdʒəs] *adj* : magnifique, splendide

gorilla [gə'rɪlə] *n* : gorille *m*

gory ['gori] *adj* **gorier; -est** : sanglant

gosling ['gɑzlɪŋ, 'gɔz-] *n* : oison *m*

gospel ['gɑspəl] *n* **1 the Gospel** : l'Évangile *m* **2 the gospel truth** : la vérité vraie

gossamer ['gɑsəmər, 'gɑzə-] *n* **1** COBWEB : fils *mpl* de la Vierge **2** : étoffe *f* très légère

gossip[1] ['gɑsɪp] *vi* : bavarder, faire des commérages, mémérer *Can fam*

gossip[2] *n* **1** : commère *f fam* (personne) **2** RUMOR : racontars *mpl*, commérage *mpl fam*, cancan *mpl*, ragot *mpl fam*, mémérage *m Can*

gossipy ['gɑsɪpi] *adj* : bavard, cancanier

got → get

Gothic ['gɑθɪk] *adj* : gothique

gotten → get

gouge[1] ['gaʊdʒ] *vt* **gouged; gouging 1** : creuser, tailler à la gouge **2** SWINDLE : estamper

gouge[2] *n* **1** CHISEL : gouge *f* **2** GROOVE : rainure *f*

goulash ['gu:ˌlɑʃ, -ˌlæʃ] *n* : goulasch *mf*, goulache *mf*

gourd ['gord, 'gʊrd] *n* : gourde *f*

gourmand ['gʊrˌmɑnd] *n* : gourmand *m*, -mande *f*

gourmet ['gʊrˌmeɪ, gʊr'meɪ] *n* : gourmet *m*

gout ['gaʊt] *n* : goutte *f*

govern ['gʌvərn] *vt* **1** RULE : gouverner **2** CONTROL, DETERMINE : régir **3** RESTRAIN : maîtriser, dominer (les émotions, etc.) — *vi* : gouverner

governess ['gʌvərnəs] *n* : gouvernante *f*

government ['gʌvərmənt] *n* : gouvernement *m* — **governmental** [ˌgʌvər'mɛntəl] *adj*

governor ['gʌvənər, 'gʌvərnər] *n* **1** : gouverneur *m* **2** : régulateur *m* (d'une machine)

governorship ['gʌvənərˌʃɪp, 'gʌvərnər-] *n* : fonctions *fpl* de gouverneur

gown ['gaʊn] *n* **1** : robe *f* <evening gown : robe du soir> **2** : toge *f* (de juge, etc.)

grab[1] ['græb] *v* **grabbed; grabbing** *vt* SEIZE : saisir, empoigner — *vi* CLING : s'agripper

grab[2] *n* **1 to make a grab for** : essayer d'attraper **2 to be up for grabs** : être disponible, être à prendre

grace[1] ['greɪs] *vt* **graced; gracing 1** HONOR : honorer **2** ADORN : orner, embellir

grace[2] *n* **1** : grâce *f* <by the grace of God : par la grâce de Dieu> **2** PRAYER : bénédicité *m* <to say grace : dire le bénédicité> **3** RESPITE : grâce *f*, répit *m* <a grace period : un délai> **4** GRACIOUSNESS : bienveillance *f*, gentillesse *f* **5** ELEGANCE : élégance *f*, charme *m*, grâce *f* **6 to be in the good graces of** : être dans les bonnes grâces de

graceful ['greɪsfəl] *adj* : gracieux — **gracefully** *adv*

gracefulness ['greɪsfəlnəs] *n* : grâce *f*

graceless ['greɪsləs] *adj* : inélégant, gauche

grace note *n* : note *f* d'agrément

gracious ['greɪʃəs] *adj* : courtois, gracieux — **graciously** *adv*

graciousness ['greɪʃəsnəs] *n* : bienveillance *f*, gentillesse *f*, courtoisie *f*

grackle ['grækəl] *n* : quiscale *m*

gradation [greɪ'deɪʃən, grə-] *n* : gradation *f*

grade[1] ['greɪd] *vt* **graded; grading 1** CLASSIFY : classer **2** LEVEL : niveler **3** MARK : noter (à l'école)

grade[2] *n* **1** CLASS, QUALITY : catégorie *f*, calibre *m*, qualité *f* **2** RANK : rang *m*, grade *m* **3** YEAR : classe *f* (à l'école) **4** MARK : note *f* **5** SLOPE : pente *f*

grade school → elementary school

gradual ['grædʒʊəl] *adj* : graduel, progressif — **gradually** *adv*

graduate[1] ['grædʒʊˌeɪt] *v* **-ated; -ating** *vi* : recevoir son diplôme — *vt* : graduer <a graduated thermometer : un thermomètre gradué>

graduate[2] ['grædʒʊət] *n* : diplômé *m*, -mée *f*

graduation [ˌgrædʒʊ'eɪʃən] *n* **1** : remise *f* des diplômes (à l'université) **2** CALIBRATION : graduation *f*

graffiti [grə'fi:ṭi, græ-] *npl* : graffiti *mpl*

graft[1] ['græft] *vt* : greffer

graft[2] *n* **1** : greffe *f* **2** CORRUPTION : magouille *f*

grain ['greɪn] *n* **1** : grain *m* <a grain of sand : un grain de sable> **2** CEREALS : céréales *fpl* **3** : fibre *f* (de bois, de cuir, etc.), fil *m* (de fibres) **4 to go against one's grain** : n'être pas dans sa nature

gram ['græm] *n* : gramme *m* (unité de mesure et de masse)

grammar ['græmər] *n* : grammaire *f*

grammar school → elementary school

grammatical [grə'mæṭɪkəl] *adj* : grammatical — **grammatically** [-kli] *adv*

granary ['greɪnəri, 'græ-] *n, pl* **-ries** : grenier *m* à blé

grand ['grænd] *adj* **1** FOREMOST : plus grand, principal <the grand prize : le grand prix> **2** IMPRESSIVE : grand, magnifique, grandiose <in a grand manner : dans un style de grand seigneur> **3** DIGNIFIED, MAJESTIC : digne, majestueux **4** PRETENTIOUS : prétentieux, suffisant **5** GREAT, WONDERFUL : formidable *fam* **6**

grand total : somme *f* globale, résultat *m* final
grandaunt ['græn'dænt, -'dant] *n* : grandtante *f*
grandchild ['grænd,tʃaɪld] *n, pl* **-children** [-,tʃɪldrən] : petit-fils *m*, petite-fille *f*
granddaughter ['grænd,dɔt̬ər] *n* : petite-fille *f*
grandeur ['grændʒər] *n* : grandeur *f*, splendeur *f*, magnificence *f*
grandfather ['grænd,fɑðər] *n* : grandpère *m*
grandiose ['grændi,o:s, ,grændi'-] *adj* : grandiose
grandma ['grænd,ma, -mɔ] *n* : mémé *f* *France fam*, mémère *f* *fam*
grandmother ['grænd,mʌðər] *n* : grandmère *f*
grandparents ['grænd,pærənts] *npl* : grands-parents *mpl*
grand piano *n* : piano *m* à queue
grandson ['grænd,sʌn] *n* : petit-fils *m*
grandstand ['grænd,stænd] *n* : tribune *f*
granduncle ['græn'dəŋkəl] *n* : grandoncle *m*
granite ['grænɪt] *n* : granit *m*, granite *m*
grant[1] ['grænt] *vt* **1** ALLOW, BESTOW : accorder, octroyer **2** ADMIT : admettre, reconnaître **3 to take for granted** : prendre pour acquis
grant[2] *n* **1** CONCESSION : concession *f* **2** SUBSIDY : subvention *f* **3** SCHOLARSHIP : bourse *f*
granular ['grænjʊlər] *adj* : granuleux
grape ['greɪp] *n* : raisin *m* <a bunch of grapes : une grappe de raisins>
grapefruit ['greɪp,fru:t] *n* : pamplemousse *mf*
grapevine ['greɪp,vaɪn] *n* **1** : vigne *f* **2 to hear through the grapevine** : entendre dire, apprendre à travers les branches
graph ['græf] *n* : graphique *m*
graphic ['græfɪk] *adj* **1** : graphique <graphic art : l'art graphique> **2** VIVID : vivant — **graphically** [-ɪkli] *adv*
graphite ['græ,faɪt] *n* : graphite *m*
grapnel ['græpnəl] *n* : grappin *m*
grapple ['græpəl] *v* **-pled; -pling** *vt* : saisir avec un grappin — *vi* STRUGGLE : lutter, se colleter
grasp[1] ['græsp] *vt* **1** GRIP, SEIZE : saisir **2** UNDERSTAND : comprendre, saisir
grasp[2] *n* **1** GRIP : prise *f*, poigne *f* **2** COMPREHENSION : compréhension *f* **3** REACH : portée *f* <within the grasp of : à la portée de>
grass ['græs] *n* **1** : herbe *f* (plante) **2** LAWN : gazon *m*, pelouse *f*
grasshopper ['græs,hɑpər] *n* : sauterelle *f*
grassland ['græs,lænd] *n* : prairie *f*
grassy ['græsi] *adj* **grassier; -est** : herbeux
grate[1] ['greɪt] *v* **grated; -ing** *vt* **1** : râper <to grate cheese : râper du fromage> **2 to grate one's teeth** : grincer des dents — *vi* **1** CREAK, RASP : grincer **2** IRRITATE : agacer <to grate on the nerves of : taper sur les nerfs de>
grate[2] *n* **1** : grille *f* de foyer (de cuisine) **2** GRATING : grille *f*
grateful ['greɪtfəl] *adj* : reconnaissant
gratefully ['greɪtfəli] *adv* : avec reconnaissance
gratefulness ['greɪtfəlnəs] *n* : gratitude *f*, reconnaissance *f*
grater ['greɪt̬ər] *n* : râpe *f*
gratification [,græt̬əfə'keɪʃən] *n* : satisfaction *f*, plaisir *m*
gratify ['græt̬ə,faɪ] *vt* **-fied; -fying 1** PLEASE : faire plaisir à **2** SATISFY : satisfaire
grating ['greɪt̬ɪŋ] *n* : grille *f*
gratis[1] ['græt̬əs, 'greɪ-] *adv* : gratis, gratuitement
gratis[2] *adj* : gratis, gratuit
gratitude ['græt̬ə,tu:d, -,tju:d] *n* : gratitude *f*, reconnaissance *f*
gratuitous [grə'tu:ət̬əs] *adj* : gratuit
gratuity [grə'tu:ət̬i] *n, pl* **-ities** TIP : pourboire *m*
grave[1] ['greɪv] *adj* **graver; -est** : grave
grave[2] *n* : tombe *f*
gravel ['grævəl] *n* : gravier *m*, gravillon *m*
gravelly ['grævəli] *adj* **1** : graveleux **2** HARSH, GRATING : râpeux <a gravelly voice : une voix râpeuse>
gravely ['greɪvli] *adv* : gravement
gravestone ['greɪv,sto:n] *n* : pierre *f* tombale
graveyard ['greɪv,jɑrd] *n* : cimetière *f*
gravitate ['grævə,teɪt] *vi* **-tated; -tating** : graviter
gravitation [,grævə'teɪʃən] *n* : gravitation *f*
gravity ['grævət̬i] *n, pl* **-ties 1** SERIOUSNESS : gravité *f* **2** GRAVITATION : gravitation *f*, pesanteur *f* <the law of gravity : la loi de la pesanteur>
gravy ['greɪvi] *n, pl* **-vies** : sauce *f* (au jus de viande)
gray[1] ['greɪ] *vi or* **to turn gray** : grisonner
gray[2] *adj* **1** : gris <gray hair : cheveux gris> **2** GLOOMY : morne **3** DREARY, DULL : terne
gray[3] *n* : gris *m*
grayish ['greɪɪʃ] *adj* : grisâtre
graze ['greɪz] *v* **grazed; grazing** *vi* : paître, brouter — *vt* **1** PASTURE : faire paître (des animaux) **2** SCRAPE : écorcher, érafler **3** BRUSH, TOUCH : frôler
grease[1] ['gri:s] *vt* **greased; greasing** : graisser, lubrifier (une voiture)
grease[2] *n* : graisse *f*, lubrifiant *m* (pour une voiture)
greasy ['gri:si] *adj* **greasier; -est 1** : graisseux **2** OILY : gras

great ['greɪt] *adj* **1** LARGE : grand <a great mountain : une grande montagne> **2** INTENSE : grand <to be in great pain : souffrir beaucoup> **3** EMINENT : grand, éminent <a great man : un grand homme> **4** FANTASTIC : génial *fam,* formidable *fam* <to have a great time : s'amuser follement>
great–aunt [ˌgreɪt'ænt, -'ant] → **grandaunt**
great–grandchild [ˌgreɪt'grændˌtʃaɪld] *n, pl* **-children** [-ˌtʃɪldrən] : arrière-petit-enfant *m,* arrière-petite-enfant *f*
great–grandfather [ˌgreɪt'grændˌfɑðər] *n* : arrière-grand-père *m*
great–grandmother [ˌgreɪt'grændˌmʌðər] *n* : arrière-grand-mère *f*
greatly ['greɪtli] *adv* **1** MUCH : beaucoup <greatly improved : beaucoup amélioré> **2** VERY : très, énormément <greatly surprised : très surpris>
greatness ['greɪtnəs] *n* : grandeur *f*
great–uncle [ˌgreɪt'ʌŋkəl] → **granduncle**
grebe ['gri:b] *n* : grèbe *m*
greed ['gri:d] *n* **1** AVARICE : avidité *f,* cupidité *f,* avarice *f* **2** GLUTTONY : gloutonnerie *f*
greedily ['gri:dəli] *adv* : avidement
greediness ['gri:dinəs] → **greed**
greedy ['gri:di] *adj* **greedier; -est** **1** AVARICIOUS : avare, cupide, pingre **2** GLUTTONOUS : glouton
Greek[1] ['gri:k] *adj* : grec
Greek[2] *n* **1** : Grec *m,* Grecque *f* **2** : grec *m* (langue)
green[1] ['gri:n] *adj* **1** : vert **2** INEXPERIENCED : inexpérimenté, naïf
green[2] *n* **1** : vert *m* (couleur) **2 greens** *npl* : légumes *mpl* verts
greenery ['gri:nəri] *n, pl* **-eries** : verdure *f*
greenhorn ['gri:nˌhɔrn] *n* : novice *mf*
greenhouse ['gri:nˌhaʊs] *n* : serre *f*
greenhouse effect *n* : effet *m* de serre
greenish ['gri:nɪʃ] *adj* : verdâtre
green onion → **chive, scallion**
green pepper *n* : poivron *m* vert
green thumb *n* **to have a green thumb** : avoir la main verte
greet ['gri:t] *vt* **1** WELCOME : saluer, accueillir **2 to be greeted with** : provoquer <to greet with laughter : provoquer des rires>
greeting ['gri:t̬ɪŋ] *n* **1** : salutation *f* **2 greetings** *npl* REGARDS : voeux *mpl* <Christmas greetings : voeux de Noël>
gregarious [grɪ'gæriəs] *adj* : grégaire (se dit des animaux), sociable (se dit des personnes)
gregariousness [grɪ'gæriəsnəs] *n* : sociabilité *f*
gremlin ['grɛmlən] *n* : lutin *m,* diablotin *m*
grenade [grə'neɪd] *n* : grenade *f*
Grenadian[1] [grə'neɪdiən] *adj* : grenadin
Grenadian[2] *n* : Grenadin *m,* -dine *f*
grew → **grow**
grey → **gray**
greyhound ['greɪˌhaʊnd] *n* : lévrier *m*
grid [grɪd] *n* **1** GRATING : grille *f* **2** NETWORK : réseau *m* (électrique) **3** : quadrillage *m* (d'une carte routière)
griddle ['grɪdəl] *n* : plaque *f* chauffante
griddle cake → **pancake**
gridiron ['grɪdˌaɪərn] *n* **1** GRILL : gril *m* **2** : terrain *m* de football américain
grief ['gri:f] *n* **1** SORROW : chagrin *m,* douleur *f* **2 to come to grief** : avoir des ennuis **3 good grief!** : mon Dieu!
grievance ['gri:vənts] *n* : grief *m*
grieve ['gri:v] *v* **grieved; grieving** *vt* DISTRESS : peiner, chagriner, affliger — *vi* **1** : avoir de la peine, s'affliger **2 to grieve for** : pleurer
grievous ['gri:vəs] *adj* **1** GRAVE, SERIOUS : grave, sérieux <a grievous injury : une blessure sérieuse> **2** CRUEL, ONEROUS : cruel, atroce <a grievous offense : un délit atroce>
grill[1] ['grɪl] *vt* **1** : griller, faire griller (en cuisine) **2** INTERROGATE : cuisiner *fam*
grill[2] *n* **1** : gril *m* (de cuisine) **2** RESTAURANT : grill *m*
grille *or* **grill** ['grɪl] *n* GRATING : grille *f*
grim ['grɪm] *adj* **grimmer; grimmest** **1** STERN : sévère <with grim determination : avec une volonté inflexible> **2** GLOOMY : lugubre, sinistre **3** UNPLEASANT : désagréable, (très) mauvais, pas bien
grimace[1] ['grɪməs, grɪ'meɪs] *vi* **-maced; -macing** : grimacer
grimace[2] *n* : grimace *f*
grime ['graɪm] *n* : saleté *f,* crasse *f*
grimly ['grɪmli] *adv* **1** SEVERELY : sévèrement, durement **2** RESOLUTELY : d'un air résolu, fermement
grimy ['graɪmi] *adj* **grimier; -est** : sale, crasseux
grin[1] ['grɪn] *vi* **grinned; grinning** : sourire
grin[2] *n* : (grand) sourire *m*
grind[1] ['graɪnd] *v* **ground** ['graʊnd]; **grinding** *vt* **1** CRUSH : moudre, pulvériser **2** POLISH, SHARPEN : aiguiser, affûter, polir **3 to grind down** OPPRESS : opprimer **4 to grind one's teeth** : grincer des dents, gricher des dents *Can* — *vi* : grincer
grind[2] *n* CHORE : corvée *f*
grinder ['graɪndər] *n* : moulin *m* <coffee grinder : moulin à café>
grindstone ['graɪndˌsto:n] *n* : meule *f*
grip[1] ['grɪp] *vt* **gripped; gripping** **1** SEIZE : serrer **2** CAPTIVATE : empoigner, captiver **3 to grip the road** : adhérer à la route
grip[2] *n* **1** GRASP : étreinte *f,* prise *f* **2** CONTROL : contrôle *m* <to get a grip on oneself : se ressaisir> **3** UNDERSTANDING : compréhension *f* **4** TRAC-

TION : adhérence *f* **5** HANDLE : poignée *f*

gripe[1] ['graɪp] *vi* **griped; griping** : rouspéter *fam,* ronchonner *fam*

gripe[2] *n* : plainte *f,* rouspétance *f fam*

grippe ['grɪp] *n* : grippe *f*

grisly ['grɪzli] *adj* **grislier; -est** : horrible, macabre

grist ['grɪst] *n* **1** : blé *m* (à moudre) **2 it's all grist for his mill** : ça apporte de l'eau à son moulin

gristle ['grɪsəl] *n* : cartilage *m*

gristly ['grɪsli] *adj* **gristlier; -est** : cartilagineux

grit[1] ['grɪt] *vt* **gritted; gritting** : serrer <to grit one's teeth : serrer les dents>

grit[2] *n* **1** GRAVEL, SAND : sable *m,* gravillon *m* **2** PLUCK : cran *m fam,* courage *m* **3 grits** *npl* : gruau *m* de maïs

gritty ['grɪt̬i] *adj* **grittier; -est 1** : sablonneux, graveleux **2** PLUCKY : courageux

grizzled ['grɪzəld] *adj* : grisonnant

groan[1] ['groːn] *vi* : gémir

groan[2] *n* : gémissement *m*

grocer ['groːsər] *n* : épicier *m,* -cière *f*

grocery ['groːsəri, -ʃəri] *n, pl* **-ceries 1** *or* **grocery store** : épicerie *f* **2 groceries** *npl* : épiceries *fpl,* provisions *fpl*

groggy ['grɑgi] *adj* **groggier; -est** : chancelant, sonné *fam*

groin ['grɔɪn] *n* : aine *f*

grommet ['grɑmət, 'grʌ-] *n* : œillet *m*

groom[1] ['gruːm, 'grʊm] *vt* **1** : panser (un animal) **2** PREPARE : préparer, former

groom[2] *n* **1** : palefrenier *m,* -nière *f* **2** BRIDEGROOM : marié *m*

groove[1] ['gruːv] *vt* **grooved; grooving** : rainer, canneler

groove[2] *n* **1** FURROW, SLOT : rainure *f,* sillon *m* **2** ROUTINE, RUT : routine *f*

grope ['groːp] *v* **groped; groping** *vi* **1** : tâtonner **2 to grope for** : chercher à tâtons — *vt* **1** PAW : peloter **2 to grope one's way** : avancer à tâtons

gross[1] ['groːs] *vt* : gagner brut, produire brut

gross[2] *adj* **1** FLAGRANT : flagrant, crasse **2** OBESE : gros, obèse **3** TOTAL : brut <gross domestic product : produit intérieur brut> **4** VULGAR : grossier

gross[3] *n* **1** *pl* **gross** : grosse *f* (12 douzaines) **2** *or* **gross income** : recettes *fpl* brutes

grossly ['groːsli] *adv* **1** EXTREMELY : extrêmement **2** CRUDELY : grossièrement

grotesque [groː'tɛsk] *adj* : grotesque

grotesquely [groː'tɛskli] *adv* : de façon grotesque

grotto ['grɑt̬oː] *n, pl* **-toes** : grotte *f*

grouch[1] ['graʊtʃ] *vi* : grogner, rouspéter *fam,* ronchonner *fam*

grouch[2] *n* **1** GRUMBLER : rouspéteur *m,* -teuse *f fam;* plaignard *m,* -gnarde *f Can* **2** COMPLAINT : grognement *m*

grouchy ['graʊtʃi] *adj* **grouchier; -est** : grognon, grincheux

ground[1] ['graʊnd] *vt* **1** BASE : baser, fonder **2** INSTRUCT : former <to be well grounded in : avoir une bonne formation en> **3** : mettre à la terre (un appareil électrique) **4** : faire échouer (un navire) **5** : interdire de voler à (un avion ou un pilote)

ground[2] *n* **1** EARTH, SOIL : sol *m,* terre *f* <on the ground : par terre> **2** LAND, TERRAIN : terrain *m* <on hilly ground : sur un terrain vallonné> **3** BASIS, REASON : motif *m,* raison *f* <grounds for complaint : motifs de se plaindre> **4** : terre *f* (pour l'électricité) **5 grounds** *npl* PREMISES : parc *m* **6 grounds** *npl* : marc *m* (de café)

ground[3] → **grind**[1]

groundhog ['graʊnd,hɔg] *n* : marmotte *f* d'Amérique

groundless ['graʊndləs] *adj* : sans fondement

groundwork ['graʊnd,wərk] *n* : travail *m* préparatoire

group[1] ['gruːp] *vt* : grouper, réunir — *vi* **to group together** : se grouper

group[2] *n* : groupe *m*

grouper ['gruːpər] *n* : mérou *m*

grouse[1] ['graʊs] *vi* **groused; grousing** COMPLAIN : rouspéter *fam,* râler *fam*

grouse[2] *n, pl* **grouse** *or* **grouses** : grouse *f*

grove ['groːv] *n* : bosquet *m*

grovel ['grɑvəl, 'grʌ-] *vi* **-eled** *or* **-elled; -eling** *or* **-elling** : ramper

grow ['groː] *v* **grew** ['gruː]; **grown** ['groːn]; **growing** *vi* **1** : pousser (se dit des plantes, des cheveux, etc.), grandir (se dit des personnes) **2** INCREASE : croître, augmenter **3** BECOME : devenir <she's growing old : elle devient vieille> — *vt* **1** CULTIVATE : cultiver, faire pousser **2** : laisser pousser <he grew a beard : il a laissé pousser la barbe>

grower ['groːər] *n* : cultivateur *m,* -trice *f*

growl[1] ['graʊl] *vi* : grogner, gronder

growl[2] *n* : grognement *m,* grondement *m*

grown–up[1] ['groːn,əp] *adj* : adulte

grown–up[2] *n* : adulte *mf,* grande personne *f*

growth ['groːθ] *n* **1** : croissance *f,* développement *m* <to stunt one's growth : retarder sa croissance> **2** INCREASE : croissance *f,* augmentation *f* **3** GROWING : pousse *f* (des plantes) **4** LUMP, TUMOR : grosseur *f,* tumeur *f*

grub[1] ['grʌb] *vi* **grubbed; grubbing 1** DIG : fouir **2** RUMMAGE : fouiller **3** DRUDGE : besogner

grub[2] *n* **1** LARVA : larve *f* **2** FOOD : bouffe *f fam*

grubby ['grʌbi] *adj* **grubbier; -est** : sale

grudge[1] ['grʌdʒ] *vt* **grudged; grudging** : donner à contrecœur <to grudge s.o. their success : en vouloir à qqn de sa réussite>

grudge[2] *n* : rancune *f* <to hold a grudge against : garder rancune à, avoir de la rancune contre>

gruel ['gru:əl] *n* : bouillie *f* (d'avoine)

grueling *or* **gruelling** ['gru:lɪŋ, gruə-] *adj* : exténuant, épuisant <a grueling experience : une expérience très dure>

gruesome ['gru:səm] *adj* : horrible, épouvantable

gruff ['grʌf] *adj* : bourru, brusque, malendurant *Can*

gruffly ['grʌfli] *adv* : d'un ton bourru, avec brusquerie

grumble[1] ['grʌmbəl] *vi* **-bled; -bling 1** COMPLAIN, GROUSE : grommeler, ronchonner *fam* **2** RUMBLE : gronder

grumble[2] *n* **1** GROUSING : ronchonnement *m fam* **2** RUMBLE : grondement *m*

grumpy ['grʌmpi] *adj* **grumpier; -est** : grincheux, grognon

grunt[1] ['grʌnt] *vi* : grogner

grunt[2] *n* : grognement *m*

guarantee[1] [ˌgærən'ti:] *vt* **-teed; -teeing** : garantir

guarantee[2] *n* : garantie *f*

guarantor [ˌgærən'tɔr] *n* : garant *m*, -rante *f*

guaranty [ˌgærən'ti:] → **guarantee**

guard[1] ['gɑrd] *vt* **1** DEFEND : garder, défendre **2** WATCH : surveiller, garder — *vi* **to guard against** : se garder de

guard[2] *n* **1** SENTRY, WARDEN : garde *m* **2** GUARDIAN, OVERSEER : gardien *m*, -dienne *f*; surveillant *m*, -lante *f* **3** PROTECTION : garde *f*, protection *f* **4** READINESS : garde *f* <to be on one's guard : être sur ses gardes> **5** SAFEGUARD : sauvegarde *f*, dispositif *m* de sûreté

guardhouse ['gɑrdˌhaʊs] *n* **1** : guérite *f* (pour des sentinelles) **2** PRISON : salle *f* de garde (militaire)

guardian ['gɑrdiən] *n* : gardien *m*, -dienne *f*

guardianship ['gɑrdiənˌʃɪp] *n* : tutelle *f*

Guatemalan[1] [ˌgwɑtə'mɑlən] *adj* : guatémaltèque

Guatemalan[2] *n* : Guatémaltèque *mf*

guava ['gwɑvə] *n* : goyave *f*

gubernatorial [ˌgu:bənə'tori:əl, ˌgju:-] *adj* : du gouverneur

guerrilla *or* **guerilla** [gə'rɪlə] *n* **1** : guérillero *m* **2 guerrillas** *npl* : guérilla *f* (combattants) **3 guerrilla warfare** : guérilla *f*

guess[1] ['gɛs] *vt* **1** CONJECTURE : deviner <guess who! : devine qui c'est!> <to guess s.o.'s age : deviner l'âge de qqn> **2** SUPPOSE : penser, croire <I guess so : je pense que oui> — *vi* : deviner

guess[2] *n* : conjecture *f*, supposition *f* <he made a good guess : il a deviné juste>

guesswork ['gɛsˌwərk] *n* : hypothèse *f*, supposition *f*

guest ['gɛst] *n* **1** VISITOR : invité *m*, -tée *f*; hôte *mf* **2** PATRON : client *m*, cliente *f*; hôte *mf* (d'un hôtel, etc.)

guffaw[1] [gə'fɔ] *vi* : s'esclaffer

guffaw[2] [gə'fɔ, 'gʌˌfɔ] *n* : gros éclat *m* de rire

guidance ['gaɪdənts] *n* : conseils *mpl*, direction *f*

guide[1] ['gaɪd] *vt* **guided; guiding 1** DIRECT : guider, diriger **2** ADVISE, COUNSEL : conseiller, guider

guide[2] *n* : guide *m*

guidebook ['gaɪdˌbʊk] *n* : guide *m*

guideline ['gaɪdˌlaɪn] *n* : ligne *f* directrice

guidepost ['gaɪdˌpo:st] *n* : poteau *m* indicateur

guild ['gɪld] *n* : association *f*

guile ['gaɪl] *n* : ruse *f*, astuce *f*

guileful ['gaɪlfəl] *adj* : rusé

guileless ['gaɪlləs] *adj* : candide, sans astuce

guillotine[1] ['gɪləˌti:n, ˌgi:jə'-] *vt* **-tined; -tining** : guillotiner

guillotine[2] *n* : guillotine *f*

guilt ['gɪlt] *n* : culpabilité *f*

guilty ['gɪlti] *adj* **guilter; -est** : coupable

guinea fowl ['gɪni] *n* : pintade *f*

guinea pig *n* : cobaye *m*

Guinean[1] ['gɪnɪən] *adj* : guinéen

Guinean[2] *n* : Guinéen *m*, -néenne *f*

guise ['gaɪz] *n* : apparence *f* <under the guise of : sous l'apparence de>

guitar [gə'tɑr, gɪ-] *n* : guitare *f*

gulch ['gʌltʃ] *n* : ravin *m*

gulf ['gʌlf] *n* **1** : golfe *m* <the gulf of California : le golfe de la Californie> **2** ABYSS : gouffre *m*, abîme *m*

gull ['gʌl] *n* : mouette *f*

gullet ['gʌlət] *n* **1** THROAT : gosier *m* **2** ESOPHAGUS : œsophage *m*

gullible ['gʌlɪbəl] *adj* : crédule

gully ['gʌli] *n, pl* **-lies 1** GULCH : ravin *m* **2** TRENCH : rigole *f*

gulp[1] ['gʌlp] *vt or* **to gulp down 1** SWALLOW : avaler (à grosses bouchées), caler *Can* **2** SUPPRESS : ravaler <to gulp down tears : ravaler des larmes> — *vi* : avoir la gorge serrée

gulp[2] *n* : gorgée *f*, bouchée *f*

gum ['gʌm] *n* **1** CHEWING GUM : chewing-gum *m France*, gomme *f* à mâcher **2 gums** *npl* : gencives *fpl*

gumbo ['gʌmˌbo:] *n* : gombo *m*

gumdrop ['gʌmˌdrɑp] *n* : boule *f* de gomme

gummy ['gʌmi] *adj* **gummier; -est** : gluant

gumption ['gʌmpʃən] *n* : initiative *f*, cran *m fam*

gun[1] ['gʌn] *vt* **gunned; gunning 1** *or* **to gun down** : abattre **2 to gun the engine** : accélérer le moteur
gun[2] *n* **1** FIREARM : arme *f* à feu, fusil *m* **2** CANNON : canon *m* **3** → **spray gun 4 to jump the gun** : brûler le feu
gunboat ['gʌn,bo:t] *n* : canonnière *f*
gunfight ['gʌn,faɪt] *n* : combat *m* avec armes à feu
gunfire ['gʌn,faɪr] *n* : fusillade *f,* coups *mpl* de feu
gunman ['gʌnmən] *n, pl* **-men** [-mən, -,mɛn] : bandit *m* armé
gunner ['gʌnər] *n* : artilleur *m*
gunnery ['gʌnəri] *n* : artillerie *f*
gunpowder ['gʌn,paʊdər] *n* : poudre *f* (à canon)
gunshot ['gʌn,ʃɑt] *n* : coup *m* de feu
gunwale ['gʌnəl] *n* : plat-bord *m*
guppy ['gʌpi] *n, pl* **-pies** : guppy *m*
gurgle[1] ['gərgəl] *vi* **-gled; -gling 1** : murmurer, glouglouter *fam* <a gurgling stream : un ruisseau murmurant> **2** : gazouiller (se dit d'un bébé)
gurgle[2] *n* **1** : glouglou *m fam* (d'un liquide) **2** : gazouillement *m* (d'un enfant)
gush ['gʌʃ] *vi* **1** SPOUT : jaillir **2 to gush over** : s'extasier devant
gust ['gʌst] *n* : rafale *f,* bourrasque *f* <a gust of wind : un coup de vent>
gusto ['gʌs,to:] *n, pl* **-toes** : enthousiasme *m,* entrain *m*
gusty ['gʌsti] *adj* **gustier; -est** : venteux <gusty wind : rafales de vent>
gut[1] ['gʌt] *vt* **gutted; gutting 1** EVISCERATE : vider **2** DESTROY : ravager
gut[2] *n* **1** INTESTINE : intestin *m,* boyau *m* **2 guts** *npl* INNARDS : entrailles *fpl,* tripes *fpl fam* **3 guts** *npl* COURAGE : cran *m fam*
gutter ['gʌt̬ər] *n* **1** : gouttière *f* (d'un toit) **2** : caniveau *m* (de la rue)
guttural ['gʌt̬ərəl] *adj* : guttural
guy ['gaɪ] *n* **1** *or* **guyline** : corde *f* de tente **2** FELLOW : type *m fam,* mec *m fam,* gars *m fam*
Guyanese[1] [,gaɪə'ni:z] *adj* : guyanais
Guyanese[2] *n* : Guyanais *m,* -naise *f*
guzzle ['gʌzəl] *vt* **-zled; -zling** : bâfrer *fam,* engloutir
gym ['dʒɪm] → **gymnasium**
gymnasium [dʒɪm'neɪziəm, -ʒəm] *n, pl* **-siums** *or* **-sia** [-zi:ə, -ʒə] : gymnase *m*
gymnast ['dʒɪmnəst, -,næst] *n* : gymnaste *mf*
gymnastic [dʒɪm'næstɪk] *adj* : gymnastique
gymnastics [dʒɪm'næstɪks] *n* : gymnastique *f*
gynecologic [,gaɪnɪkə'lɑdʒɪk] *or* **gynecological** [-'lɑdʒɪkəl] *adj* : gynécologique
gynecologist [,gaɪnə'kɑlədʒɪst] *n* : gynécologue *mf*
gynecology [,gaɪnə'kɑlədʒi] *n* : gynécologie *f*
gyp[1] ['dʒɪp] *vt* **gypped; gypping** : escroquer, arnaquer *fam*
gyp[2] *n* **1** CHEAT, SWINDLER : escroc *m;* arnaqueur *m,* -queuse *f fam* **2** FRAUD, SWINDLE : escroquerie *f,* arnaque *f fam*
gypsum ['dʒɪpsəm] *n* : gypse *m*
Gypsy ['dʒɪpsi] *n, pl* **-sies** : gitan *m,* -tane *f*
gyrate ['dʒaɪ,reɪt] *vi* **-rated; -rating** : tournoyer
gyroscope ['dʒaɪrə,sko:p] *n* : gyroscope *m*

H

h ['eɪtʃ] *n, pl* **h's** *or* **hs** ['eɪtʃəz] : h *m,* huitième lettre de l'alphabet
haberdashery ['hæbər,dæʃəri] *n, pl* **-eries** : magasin *m* de vêtements pour hommes
habit ['hæbɪt] *n* **1** : habit *m* (religieux) **2** CUSTOM : habitude *f,* coutume *f* **3** ADDICTION : accoutumance *f,* dépendance *f*
habitable ['hæbɪt̬əbəl] *adj* : habitable
habitat ['hæbɪ,tæt] *n* : habitat *m*
habitation [,hæbɪ'teɪʃən] *n* **1** OCCUPANCY : habitation *f* **2** RESIDENCE : habitation *f,* domicile *m,* résidence *f*
habit–forming ['hæbɪt,fɔrmɪŋ] *adj* ADDICTIVE : qui crée une accoutumance
habitual [hə'bɪtʃʊəl] *adj* **1** CUSTOMARY : habituel **2** INVETERATE : invétéré <a habitual drunkard : un ivrogne invétéré>
habitually [hə'bɪtʃʊəli] *adv* : habituellement
habituate [hə'bɪtʃʊ,eɪt] *vt* **-ated; -ating 1** : habituer **2 to habituate oneself to** : s'habituer à, s'accoutumer à
hack[1] ['hæk] *vt* : tailler, taillader <to hack one's way through sth : tailler un passage à travers qqch> — *vi* **1** CHOP : donner des coups de couteau **2** COUGH : tousser (d'une toux sèche) **3 to hack into** : s'introduire dans, entrer dans (en informatique)
hack[2] *n* **1** : entaille *f* **2** BLOW : coup *m* violent **3** HORSE : cheval *m* de louage **4** *or* **hack writer** : écrivaillon *m,* plumitif *m* **5** COUGH : toux *f* sèche
hackle ['hækəl] *n* **1** : plume *f* du cou (d'un oiseau) **2 hackles** *npl* : poils *mpl* hérissés (d'un chien, etc.) <don't get your hackles up : ne t'énerve pas>
hackney ['hækni] *n, pl* **-neys** : fiacre *m*

hackneyed [ˈhæknid] *adj* TRITE : banal, rebattu

hacksaw [ˈhækˌsɔ] *n* : scie *f* à métaux

had → **have**

haddock [ˈhædək] *ns & pl* : églefin *m*

hadn't [ˈhædənt] (*contraction of* **had not**) → **have**

haft [ˈhæft] *n* : manche *m* (d'un outil), poignée *f* (d'une dague)

hag [ˈhæg] *n* **1** WITCH : sorcière *f* **2** CRONE : vieille *f* bique, grébiche *f Can*

haggard [ˈhægərd] *adj* : hâve, exténué

haggle [ˈhægəl] *vi* **-gled; -gling** : marchander

ha–ha [ˌhɑˈhɑ, ˈhɑˈhɑ] *interj* : ha ha

hail[1] [ˈheɪl] *vi* : grêler (en météorologie) — *vt* **1** GREET : saluer, acclamer **2** : héler (un taxi)

hail[2] *n* **1** : grêle *f* (en météorologie) **2** GREETING : salutation *f*

hailstone [ˈheɪlˌstoːn] *n* : grêlon *m*

hailstorm [ˈheɪlˌstɔrm] *n* : averse *f* de grêle

hair [ˈhær] *n* **1** : cheveux *mpl* <to have short hair : avoir les cheveux courts> **2** : poil *m* <to have hair on one's legs : avoir du poil sur les jambes> <dog hair : poils de chien>

hairbreadth [ˈhærˌbrɛdθ] *or* **hairsbreadth** [ˈhærz-] *n* **by a hairbreadth** : d'un poil, de justesse

hairbrush [ˈhærˌbrʌʃ] *n* : brosse *f* à cheveux

haircut [ˈhærˌkʌt] *n* : coupe *f* de cheveux

hairdo [ˈhærˌduː] *n, pl* **-dos** : coiffure *f*, peignure *f Can fam*

hairdresser [ˈhærˌdrɛsər] *n* : coiffeur *m*, -feuse *f*

hairiness [ˈhærinəs] *n* : pilosité *f*

hairless [ˈhærləs] *adj* : sans cheveux, glabre (se dit du corps), sans poils (se dit des animaux)

hairline [ˈhærˌlaɪn] *n* **1** : ligne *f* très mince **2** : naissance *f* des cheveux <to have a receding hairline : avoir un front qui se dégarnit>

hairpin [ˈhærˌpɪn] *n* : épingle *f* à cheveux

hair–raising [ˈhærˌreɪzɪŋ] *adj* : à faire dresser les cheveux sur la tête, horrifique

hairy [ˈhæri] *adj* **hairier; -est** : poilu, velu

Haitian[1] [ˈheɪʃən, ˈheɪt̬iən] *adj* : haïtien

Haitian[2] *n* : Haïtien *m*, -tienne *f*

hake [ˈheɪk] *n* : merlu *m* (vivant), colin *m* (en cuisine)

hale[1] [ˈheɪl] *vt* **haled; haling** HAUL : haler, tirer <to hale into court : traîner devant le tribunal>

hale[2] *adj* : vigoureux <hale and hearty : en pleine forme>

half[1] [ˈhæf, ˈhaf] *adv* : à demi, à moitié <to be half full : être à demi rempli>

half[2] *adj* **1** : demi <a half sheet of paper : une demi-feuille de papier> <two hours and a half : deux heures et demie> **2** PARTIAL : demi <a half smile : un demi sourire>

half[3] *n, pl* **halves** [ˈhævz, ˈhavz] **1** : demi *m* <two halves : deux demis> **2** : moitié *f* <half of the profits : la moitié des profits> **3** *or* **halftime** : mi-temps *f* (aux sports)

half brother *n* : demi-frère *m*

halfhearted [ˈhæfˈhɑrt̬əd] *adj* : qui manque d'enthousiasme

halfheartedly [ˈhæfˈhɑrt̬ədli] *adv* : sans enthousiasme, sans conviction

half–life [ˈhæfˌlaɪf] *n* : demi-vie *f*

half sister *n* : demi-soeur *f*

halfway [ˈhæfˈweɪ] *adv & adj* : à mi-chemin

half–wit [ˈhæfˌwɪt] *n* : imbécile *mf;* idiot *m*, idiote *f*

half–witted [ˈhæfˌwɪt̬əd] *adj* : bête, stupide

halibut [ˈhælɪbət] *ns & pl* : flétan *m*

halitosis [ˌhæləˈtosəs] *n* : mauvaise haleine *f*

hall [ˈhɔl] *n* **1** AUDITORIUM : salle *f* (de concert, etc.) **2** LOBBY : entrée *f*, vestibule *m*, hall *m* (d'entrée), portique *m Can fam* **3** DORMITORY : résidence *f* universitaire **4** → **city hall**

hallelujah [ˌhæləˈluːjə, ˌhɑˌloːd] *interj* : alléluia

hallmark [ˈhɔlˌmɑrk] *n* : caractéristique *f*, sceau *m*

hallow [ˈhæˌloː] *vt* : sanctifier, consacrer

hallowed [ˈhæˌloːd, ˈhæˌloːəd, ˈhɑ-] *adj* : sanctifié, saint

Halloween [ˌhæləˈwiːn, ˌhɑ-] *n* : Halloween *f*

hallucinate [həˈluːsənˌeɪt] *vi* **-nated; -nating** : avoir des hallucinations

hallucination [həˌluːsənˈeɪʃən] *n* : hallucination *f*

hallucinogen [həˈluːsənədʒən] *n* : hallucinogène *m*

hallucinogenic [həˌluːsənəˈdʒɛnɪk] *adj* : hallucinogène

hallway [ˈhɔlˌweɪ] *n* **1** ENTRANCE : entrée *f*, vestibule *m* **2** CORRIDOR : corridor *m*, couloir *m*

halo [ˈheɪˌloː] *n, pl* **-los** *or* **-loes** : auréole *f*

halt[1] [ˈhɔlt] *vi* : s'arrêter — *vt* **1** STOP : arrêter (une personne) **2** : interrompre <the strike halted buses : la grève a interrompu le service d'autobus>

halt[2] *n* : halte *f*, arrêt *m* <to come to a halt : s'interrompre>

halter [ˈhɔltər] *n* **1** : licou *m* (d'un animal) **2** *or* **halter top** : chemisier *m* à dos nu

halting [ˈhɔltɪŋ] *adj* HESITANT : hésitant

halve [ˈhæv, ˈhav] *vt* **halved; halving 1** DIVIDE : couper en deux **2** REDUCE : réduire de moitié

halves → **half**[3]

ham [ˈhæm] *n* **1** : jambon *m* **2** *or* **ham actor** : cabotin *m*, -tine *f* **3** **hams** *npl*

BUTTOCKS, THIGHS : cuisses *fpl*, fesses *fpl* **4** *or* **ham radio operator** : radioamateur *m*
hamburger ['hæm,bərgər] *or* **hamburg** [-,bərg] *n* **1** : hamburger *m* (cuit) **2** : viande *f* hachée <a pound of hamburger : une livre de viande hachée>
hamlet ['hæmlət] *n* : hameau *m*
hammer[1] ['hæmər] *vt* : marteler, enfoncer (à coups de marteau) — *vi* : frapper à coups de marteau
hammer[2] *n* **1** : marteau *m* **2** : chien *m* (d'une arme à feu)
hammock ['hæmək] *n* : hamac *m*
hamper[1] ['hæmpər] *vt* : entraver, gêner
hamper[2] *n* : panier *m* <clothes hamper : panier à linge sale>
hamster ['hæmpstər] *n* : hamster *m*
hamstring[1] ['hæm,strıŋ] *vt* **-strung** [-'strʌŋ]; **-stringing** [-strıŋıŋ] **1** : couper le jarret à (un animal) **2** INCAPACITATE : paralyser <hamstrung by guilt : paralysé par les remords>
hamstring[2] *n* : jarret *m* (d'un animal), tendon *m* (d'une personne)
hand[1] ['hænd] *vt* : donner, passer
hand[2] *n* **1** : main *f* <good with one's hands : adroit de ses mains> <to lend a hand : prêter une main> **2** POINTER : aiguille *f* (d'une montre, etc.) **3** SIDE : côté *m* <on the other hand : par contre, d'un autre côté> **4** HANDWRITING : écriture *f* **5** HELP : aide *f* <to give s.o. a hand : donner un coup de main à qqn> **6** APPLAUSE : applaudissements *mpl* **7** : main *f*, jeu *m* (aux cartes) **8** WORKER : ouvrier *m*, -vrière *f* **9 to ask for s.o.'s hand (in marriage)** : demander qqn en mariage **10 to try one's hand at** : s'essayer à
handbag ['hænd,bæg] *n* : sac *m* à main
handball ['hænd,bɔl] *n* : handball *m*
handbill ['hænd,bıl] *n* : prospectus *m*
handbook ['hænd,bʊk] *n* : manuel *m*, guide *m*
handcuff ['hænd,kʌf] *vt* : passer les menottes à
handcuffs ['hænd,kʌfs] *npl* : menottes *fpl*
handful ['hænd,fʊl] *n* : poignée *f*
handgun ['hænd,gʌn] *n* : pistolet *m*, revolver *m*
handicap[1] ['hændi,kæp] *vt* **-capped; -capping** : handicaper
handicap[2] *n* **1** DISABILITY : handicap *m* **2** DISADVANTAGE : désavantage *m*, handicap *m*
handicapped ['hændi,kæpt] *adj* : handicapé
handicraft ['hændi,kræft] *n* **1** : travail *m* artisanal **2 handicrafts** *npl* : objets *mpl* artisanaux
handily ['hændəli] *adv* EASILY : haut la main
handiwork ['hændi,wərk] *n* **1** WORK : travail *m* manuel **2** ARTICLES, CRAFTS : objets *mpl* artisanaux
handkerchief ['hæŋkərtʃəf, -,tʃi:f] *n, pl* **-chiefs** : mouchoir *m*
handle[1] ['hændəl] *vt* **-dled; -dling 1** TOUCH : toucher à, manipuler **2** STAND : supporter <I can't handle the heat : je ne peux pas supporter la chaleur> **3** MANAGE : manier, gérer
handle[2] *n* : manche *m* (d'un ustensile), poignée *f* (de porte), anse *f* (de panier)
handlebars ['hændəl,bɑrz] *npl* : guidon *m*
handmade ['hænd,meıd] *adj* : fait à la main
hand–me–downs ['hændmi,daʊnz] *npl* : vêtements *mpl* de seconde main
handout ['hænd,aʊt] *n* **1** CHARITY : aumône *f*, don *m* **2** LEAFLET : prospectus *m*
handpick ['hænd'pık] *vt* : sélectionner avec soin
handrail ['hænd,reıl] *n* **1** : rampe *f*, main *f* courante (d'un escalier) **2** : garde-fou *m* (d'un pont)
handsaw ['hænd,sɔ] *n* : scie *f* à main
hands down *adv* EASILY, UNQUESTIONABLY : sans aucun doute
handshake ['hænd,ʃeık] *n* : poignée *f* de main
handsome ['hæntsəm] *adj* **handsomer; -est 1** CONSIDERABLE : important, considérable **2** GENEROUS : généreux **3** GOOD-LOOKING : beau
handsomely ['hæntsəmli] *adv* **1** ELEGANTLY : élégamment **2** GENEROUSLY : avec générosité
handspring ['hænd,sprıŋ] *n* : saut *m* de mains
handstand ['hænd,stænd] *n* : équilibre *m* sur les mains
hand–to–hand ['hændtə'hænd] *adj* : (au) corps à corps
handwriting ['hænd,raıtıŋ] *n* : écriture *f*
handwritten ['hænd,rıtən] *adj* : écrit à la main
handy ['hændi] *adj* **handier; -est 1** NEARBY : à portée de la main, proche **2** CONVENIENT, USEFUL : utile, pratique **3** CLEVER : adroit, habile
handyman ['hændimən] *n, pl* **-men** [-mən, -,mɛn] : bricoleur *m*, homme *m* à tout faire
hang[1] ['hæŋ] *v* **hung** ['hʌŋ]; **hanging** *vt* **1** SUSPEND : suspendre, accrocher **2** (*past tense often* **hanged**) : pendre (un criminel) **3** : poser (une porte, etc.) **4 to hang one's head** : baisser la tête de honte — *vi* **1** DANGLE : être accroché, être suspendu **2** FALL : être accroché, être suspendu (se dit des vêtements, des rideaux, etc.) **3** HOVER : flotter, être suspendu (en l'air) **4** DROOP : pencher, tomber
hang[2] *n* **1** : drapé *m* (d'un rideau, etc.) **2 to get the hang of doing sth** : prendre le coup pour faire qqch <I can't get the hang of it! : je ne pige pas!>
hangar ['hæŋər, 'hæŋgər] *n* : hangar *m*

hanger ['hæŋər] *n or* **coat hanger** : cintre *m*
hangman ['hæŋmən] *n, pl* **-men** [-mən, -'mɛn] : bourreau *m*
hangnail ['hæŋˌneɪl] *n* : envie *f*
hangout ['hæŋˌaʊt] *n* : endroit *m* préféré (pour flâner)
hangover ['hæŋˌoːvər] *n* : gueule *f* de bois
hank ['hæŋk] *n* : écheveau *m*
hanker ['hæŋkər] *vi* **to hanker for** : désirer, avoir envie de
hankering ['hæŋkərɪŋ] *n* : désir *m,* envie *f*
hansom ['hæn*t*səm] *n* : cabriolet *m*
Hanukkah ['xɑnəkə, 'hɑ-] *n* : Hanukkah *m*
haphazard [hæp'hæzərd] *adj* : fortuit, mal organisé <in a haphazard way : de façon peu méthodique>
haphazardly [hæp'hæzərdli] *adv* : n'importe comment, sans organisation
hapless ['hæpləs] *adj* : infortuné, malchanceux
happen ['hæpən] *vi* **1** OCCUR : arriver, se passer <what's happening? : qu'est-ce qui se passe?> **2** CHANCE : arriver par hasard <I happened to overhear her plans : j'ai entendu ses plans par hasard> **3** : se trouver <it so happens that I was right : il se trouve que j'avais raison> **4** BEFALL : arriver <what happened to you? : qu'est-ce qui t'est arrivé?>
happening ['hæpənɪŋ] *n* : incident *m,* événement *m*
happily ['hæpəli] *adv* : heureusement
happiness ['hæpinəs] *n* : bonheur *m*
happy ['hæpi] *adj* **happier; -est 1** FORTUNATE : heureux, favorable **2** CHEERFUL : heureux **3** PLEASED : content, satisfait **4** (*expressing willingness*) <to be happy to do sth : être heureux de faire qqch> <I'm happy to help you : je suis ravi de vous aider>
happy–go–lucky ['hæpigoː'lʌki] *adj* : insouciant
harangue[1] [hə'ræŋ] *vt* **-rangued; -ranguing** : haranguer
harangue[2] *n* : harangue *f*
harass [hə'ræs, 'hærəs] *vt* **1** TORMENT, WORRY : tourmenter, harceler **2** ANNOY, PESTER : harceler
harassment [hə'ræsmənt, 'hærəsmənt] *n* : harcèlement *m*
harbinger ['hɑrbɪndʒər] *n* **1** PRECURSOR : signe *m* avant-coureur, précurseur *m* **2** OMEN : présage *m* <a harbinger of doom : un mauvais présage>
harbor[1] *or Brit* **harbour** ['hɑrbər] *vt* **1** SHELTER : héberger (une personne), receler (un criminel) **2** HOLD, KEEP : nourrir (un espoir, etc.), entretenir (de doutes)
harbor[2] *or Brit* **harbour** *n* PORT : port *m*
hard[1] ['hɑrd] *adv* **1** FORCEFULLY, STRENUOUSLY : dur, fort <to work hard : travailler dur> <to snow hard : neiger fort> **2 to take sth hard** : mal prendre qqch
hard[2] *adj* **1** FIRM : dur, solide **2** : calcaire <hard water : eau calcaire> **3** DEFINITE : définitif **4** SEARCHING : pénétrant <a hard look : un regard pénétrant> **5** UNFEELING : dur, insensible **6** TROUBLESOME : difficile, pénible **7** INTENSE : dur, ferme <hard blows : coups durs> **8** DILIGENT : consciencieux
harden ['hɑrdən] *vt* : durcir, endurcir <to harden one's heart : endurcir son coeur> — *vi* : s'endurcir
hardheaded ['hɑrd'hɛdəd] *adj* **1** STUBBORN : têtu, destiné **2** REALISTIC : réaliste, pratique
hard–hearted ['hɑrd'hɑrt̬əd] *adj* : dur, insensible
hardly ['hɑrdli] *adv* **1** BARELY : à peine, ne . . . guère **2** NOT : ne . . . pas, presque jamais <it's hardly surprising : ce n'est pas surprenant>
hardness ['hɑrdnəs] *n* **1** FIRMNESS : dureté *f* **2** DIFFICULTY : difficulté *f,* dureté *f* **3** SEVERITY : sévérité *f,* dureté *f*
hardship ['hɑrdˌʃɪp] *n* **1** DIFFICULTY : détresse *f* **2** DISTRESS, SUFFERING : épreuves *fpl,* privations *fpl*
hardware ['hɑrdˌwær] *n* **1** : quincaillerie *f* **2** : matériel *m* (en informatique)
hardwood ['hɑrdˌwʊd] *n* : bois *m* dur, bois *m* franc *Can*
hardworking ['hɑrd'wərkɪŋ] *adj* : travailleur, travaillant *Can*
hardy ['hɑrdi] *adj* **hardier; -est 1** BOLD : hardi, intrépide **2** ROBUST : résistant, robuste
hare ['hær] *n, pl* **hare** *or* **hares** : lièvre *m*
harebrained ['hærˌbreɪnd] *adj* : écervelé, insensé
harelip ['hær'lɪp] *n* : bec-de-lièvre *m*
harem ['hærəm] *n* : harem *m*
hark ['hɑrk] *vi* **1** LISTEN : prêter l'oreille, ouïr **2 to hark back to** : revenir à
harlequin ['hɑrlɪkən, -kwən] *n* : arlequin *m*
harm[1] ['hɑrm] *vt* : faire du mal à, nuire à
harm[2] *n* : mal *m,* dommage *m,* tort *m*
harmful ['hɑrmfəl] *adj* : nuisible, nocif
harmfully ['hɑrmfəli] *adv* : de façon nuisible
harmless ['hɑrmləs] *adj* : inoffensif, anodin
harmlessly ['hɑrmləsli] *adv* : sans faire de mal
harmonic [hɑr'mɑnɪk] *adj* : harmonique — **harmonically** [-nɪkli] *adv*
harmonica [hɑr'mɑnɪkə] *n* : harmonica *m*
harmonious [hɑr'moːniəs] *adj* : harmonieux — **harmoniously** *adv*

harmonize ['hɑrmə,naɪz] *v* **-nized; -nizing** *vt* : harmoniser — *vi* : s'harmoniser

harmony ['hɑrməni] *n, pl* **-nies** : harmonie *f*

harness[1] ['hɑrnəs] *vt* **1** : harnacher (un cheval) **2** UTILIZE : exploiter (de l'énergie, etc.)

harness[2] *n* : harnais *m,* harnachement *m*

harp[1] ['hɑrp] *vi* **to harp on** : rabâcher, répéter continuellement

harp[2] *n* : harpe *f*

harpist ['hɑrpɪst] *n* : harpiste *mf*

harpoon[1] [hɑr'pu:n] *vt* : harponner

harpoon[2] *n* : harpon *m*

harpsichord ['hɑrpsɪ,kɔrd] *n* : clavecin *m*

harrow[1] ['hær,o:] *vt* **1** : herser (la terre) **2** TORMENT, VEX : torturer, tourmenter

harrow[2] *n* : herse *f*

harry ['hæri] *vt* **-ried; -rying** HARASS : harceler

harsh ['hɑrʃ] *adj* **1** ROUGH : rude <a harsh surface : une surface rude> **2** SEVERE : dur, sévère **3** DIFFICULT, RIGOROUS : rigoureux

harshly ['hɑrʃli] *adv* : sévèrement, durement

harshness ['hɑrʃnəs] *n* : sévérité *f*

hart ['hɑrt] *n Brit* STAG : cerf *m*

harvest[1] ['hɑrvəst] *vt* : moissonner, récolter

harvest[2] *n* : moisson *f,* récolte *f*

harvester ['hɑrvəstər] *n* **1** : moissonneur *m,* -neuse *f* (personne) **2** : moissonneuse *f* (machine)

has → **have**

hash[1] ['hæʃ] *vt* **1** CHOP : hacher **2 to hash over** DISCUSS : parler de, discuter

hash[2] *n* **1** : hachis *m* **2** JUMBLE, MESS : gâchis *m*

hasn't ['hæzənt] (*contraction of* **has not**) → **have**

hasp ['hæsp] *n* : moraillon *m,* loquet *m*

hassle[1] ['hæsəl] *v* **-sled; -sling** *vi* ARGUE : se chamailler, se disputer — *vt* ANNOY, HARASS : tracasser, harceler

hassle[2] *n* **1** QUARREL : chicane *f,* dispute *f* **2** BOTHER, TROUBLE : embêtements *mpl,* ennuis *mpl*

hassock ['hæsək] *n* **1** CUSHION : coussin *m* (d'agenouilloir) **2** FOOTSTOOL : pouf *m,* tabouret *m*

haste ['heɪst] *n* : hâte *f,* précipitation *f* <to make haste : se hâter>

hasten ['heɪsən] *vt* : hâter, précipiter — *vi* HURRY : se hâter, se dépêcher

hastily ['heɪstəli] *adv* : à la hâte

hasty ['heɪsti] *adj* **hastier; -est 1** HURRIED : précipité, à la hâte **2** RASH : hâtif, irréfléchi

hat ['hæt] *n* : chapeau *m*

hatch[1] ['hætʃ] *vt* **1** INCUBATE : couver, faire éclore **2** CONCOCT : ourdir (un complot) — *vi* : éclore

hatch[2] *n* **1** : écoutille *f* (d'un navire) **2** BROOD : couvée *f,* éclosion *f*

hatchery ['hætʃəri] *n, pl* **-ries 1** : couvoir *m* (de poules) **2** *or* **fish hatchery** : station *f* d'alevinage

hatchet ['hætʃət] *n* : hachette *f*

hatchway ['hætʃ,weɪ] *n* HATCH : écoutille *f* (d'un navire)

hate[1] ['heɪt] *vt* **hated; hating** : détester, haïr, avoir horreur de

hate[2] *n* : haine *f*

hateful ['heɪtfəl] *adj* : odieux, détestable — **hatefully** *adv*

hatred ['heɪtrəd] *n* : haine *f*

hatter ['hæt̬ər] *n* : chapelier *m,* -lière *f*

haughtily ['hɔt̬əli] *adv* : de façon hautaine

haughty ['hɔt̬i] *adj* **haughtier; -est** : hautain, arrogant

haul[1] ['hɔl] *vt* **1** DRAG, PULL : tirer **2** TRANSPORT : transporter, camionner

haul[2] *n* **1** PULL, TUG : coup *m* **2** CATCH : prise *f* (de poissons) **3** LOOT : butin *m* **4** JOURNEY : chemin *m,* route *f,* voyage *m* <it's a long haul : la route est longue>

hauler ['hɔlər] *n* DRIVER, TRUCKER : routier *m;* camionneur *m,* -neuse *f*

haunch ['hɔntʃ] *n* **1** HIP : hanche *f* **2 haunches** *npl* HINDQUARTERS : arrière-train *m,* derrière *m* (d'un animal)

haunt[1] ['hɔnt] *vt* **1** : hanter <a haunted house : une maison hantée> **2** PREOCCUPY : hanter, obséder **3** FREQUENT : fréquenter, hanter

haunt[2] *n* : lieu *m* fréquenté

haunting ['hɔntɪŋ] *adj* : obsédant

have ['hæv, *in sense as an auxiliary verb usu* 'hæf] *v* **had** ['hæd]; **having; has** ['hæz, *in sense as an auxiliary verb usu* 'hæs] *vt* **1** POSSESS : avoir <do you have change? : avez-vous de la monnaie?> <April has 30 days : il y a 30 jours en avril> **2** EXPERIENCE, UNDERGO : avoir <I have a cold : j'ai un rhume> **3** (*indicating consumption*) <to have a sandwich : manger un sandwich> <to have a cigarette : fumer une cigarette> **4** RECEIVE : recevoir, avoir <to have permission : avoir la permission> <I have a letter from Anne : j'ai reçu une lettre d'Anne> **5** WANT : vouloir, prendre <I'll have coffee : je voudrais du café> **6** ALLOW : permettre, tolérer <I won't have it! : je ne le tolérerai pas!> **7** HOLD : tenir, faire <he had me by the arm : il me tenait par le bras> <to have a party : faire une fête> **8** BEAR : avoir (un enfant) **9** (*indicating causation*) <she had a dress made : elle s'est fait faire une robe> — *v aux* **1** : avoir, être <he had seen me : il m'avait vu> <she has left : elle est partie> **2** (*used in tags*) <you have finished, haven't you? : vous avez fini, n'est-ce pas?> **3 to have to** : devoir <we have to meet

the deadline : nous devons rencontrer la date d'échéance> **4 to have to do with** : concerner

haven ['heɪvən] *n* : refuge *m,* havre *m*

havoc ['hævək] *n* **1** DEVASTATION : destruction *f,* dévastation *f* **2** CHAOS : désordre *m,* chaos *m*

Hawaiian[1] [hə'waɪən] *adj* : hawaïen

Hawaiian[2] *n* **1** : Hawaïen *m,* -waïenne *f* **2** : hawaïen *m* (langue)

hawk[1] ['hɔk] *vt* : colporter, vendre (à la criée)

hawk[2] *n* : faucon *m* (oiseau)

hawker ['hɔkər] *n* PEDDLER : colporteur *m,* -teuse *f*

hawthorn ['hɔˌθɔrn] *n* : aubépine *f,* cenellier *m Can*

hay ['heɪ] *n* : foin *m*

hay fever *n* : rhume *m* des foins

hayloft ['heɪˌlɔft] *n* : grenier *m* à foin

haystack ['heɪˌstæk] *n* : meule *f* de foin

haywire ['heɪˌwaɪr] *adj* : détraqué <to go haywire : se détraquer>

hazard[1] ['hæzərd] *vt* : hasarder, risquer

hazard[2] *n* **1** PERIL : danger *m,* risque *m* **2** CHANCE : chance *f,* hasard *m*

hazardous ['hæzərdəs] *adj* : dangereux, risqué

haze[1] ['heɪz] *vi* **hazed; hazing** *or* **to haze over** : devenir brumeux

haze[2] *n* : brume *f*

hazel ['heɪzəl] *n* **1** : noisetier *m* (arbre) **2** : noisette *f* (couleur)

hazelnut ['heɪzəlˌnʌt] *n* : noisette *f*

haziness ['heɪzinəs] *n* **1** MISTINESS : état *m* brumeux **2** VAGUENESS : flou *m*

hazy ['heɪzi] *adj* **hazier; -est 1** : brumeux <hazy sky : ciel brumeux> **2** VAGUE : vague, flou

he ['hiː] *pron* **1** : il <he spoke to me : il m'a parlé> **2** : lui <she's younger than he (is) : elle est plus jeune que lui>

head[1] ['hɛd] *vt* **1** LEAD : être en tête de **2** DIRECT : diriger **3** TITLE : intituler — *vi* **1** : former une tête (se dit d'un chou, etc.) **2** : se diriger, aller <where are you headed? : où vas-tu?>

head[2] *adj* CHIEF : en chef

head[3] *n* **1** : tête *f* <from head to toe : de la tête aux pieds> **2** MIND : tête *f,* esprit *m* **3** END : bout *m* (d'une table), chevet *m* (d'un lit) **4** DIRECTOR : chef *m;* directeur *m,* -trice *f* **5** : personne *f* <$8.00 per head : 8,00 $ par personne> **6 at the head of** : à la tête de (une classe, etc.) **7 to come to a head** : arriver au point critique

headache ['hɛdˌeɪk] *n* : mal *m* de tête

headband ['hɛdˌbænd] *n* : bandeau *m*

headdress ['hɛdˌdrɛs] *n* : coiffe *f*

headfirst ['hɛd'fərst] *adv* : la tête la première

headgear ['hɛdˌgɪr] *n* : couvre-chef *m,* coiffure *f*

heading ['hɛdɪŋ] *n* **1** DIRECTION : cap *m* (d'un navire) **2** : titre *m* (d'un article), rubrique *f* (d'un sujet) **3** LETTERHEAD : en-tête *m*

headland ['hɛdlənd, -ˌlænd] *n* : promontoire *m*

headlight ['hɛdˌlaɪt] *n* : phare *m*

headline ['hɛdˌlaɪn] *n* : manchette *f,* (gros) titre *m*

headlong[1] ['hɛd'lɔŋ] *adv* **1** HEADFIRST : la tête la première **2** HASTILY, RECKLESSLY : à toute allure, à toute vitesse

headlong[2] ['hɛdˌlɔŋ] *adj* : précipité

headmaster ['hɛdˌmæstər] *n* : directeur *m* (d'école)

headmistress ['hɛdˌmɪstrəs, -'mɪs-] *n* : directrice *f* (d'école)

head–on ['hɛd'ɑn, -'ɔn] *adv & adj* : de front, face-à-face

headphones ['hɛdˌfoːnz] *npl* : écouteurs *mpl,* casque *m*

headquarters ['hɛdˌkwɔrt̬ərz] *ns & pl* **1** : siège *m* social (d'une compagnie) **2** : quartier *m* général (dans l'armée, etc.)

headrest ['hɛdˌrɛst] *n* : appui-tête *m*

head start *n* : avance *f,* longueur *f* d'avance

headstone ['hɛdˌstoːn] *n* : pierre *f* tombale

headstrong ['hɛdˌstrɔŋ] *adj* : têtu, obstiné

headwaiter ['hɛd'weɪt̬ər] *n* : maître *m* d'hôtel

headwaters ['hɛdˌwɔt̬ərz, -ˌwɑ-] *npl* : sources *fpl*

headway ['hɛdˌweɪ] *n* **1** PROGRESS : progrès *m* **2 to make headway** : avancer, progresser

heady ['hɛdi] *adj* **headier; -est 1** INTOXICATING : qui monte à la tête **2** EXCITING, STIMULATING : passionnant, excitant

heal ['hiːl] *vt* : guérir, cicatriser — *vi* : guérir, se cicatriser

healer ['hiːlər] *n* : guérisseur *m,* -seuse *f*

health ['hɛlθ] *n* : santé *f*

healthful ['hɛlθfəl] *adj* : bon pour la santé, sain

healthily ['hɛlθəli] *adv* : sainement

health maintenance organization → **HMO**

healthy ['hɛlθi] *adj* **healthier; -est 1** WELL : en bonne santé **2** PROSPEROUS : prospère, florissant

heap[1] ['hiːp] *vt* : entasser, amasser

heap[2] *n* PILE : amas *m,* tas *m*

hear ['hɪr] *v* **heard** ['hərd]; **hearing** *vt* **1** : entendre <I can't hear you : je ne t'entends pas> **2** HEED : écouter **3** LEARN : apprendre, entendre <I heard the news : j'ai appris la nouvelle> — *vi* **1** : entendre <she doesn't hear very well : elle n'entends pas très bien> **2 to hear from** : avoir des nouvelles de

hearing ['hɪrɪŋ] *n* **1** : ouïe *f,* audition *f* **2** : audience *f* (d'un tribunal) **3 within hearing** : à portée de voix

hearing aid *n* : appareil *m* auditif

hearken ['hɑrkən] *vi* **to hearken to** : écouter
hearsay ['hɪrˌseɪ] *n* : ouï-dire *m*, rumeur *f*
hearse ['hərs] *n* : corbillard *m*
heart ['hɑrt] *n* **1** : cœur *m* **2** AFFECTION, LOVE : cœur *m*, amour *m* **3** COURAGE : courage *m*, ardeur *f* <to lose heart : perdre courage> **4** CENTER : cœur *m*, centre *m* <the heart of the matter : le fond du problème> **5** : cœur *m* (aux cartes) **6 at ~** : au fond **7 by ~** : par cœur
heartache ['hɑrṭˌeɪk] *n* : chagrin *m*, peine *f*
heart attack *n* : crise *f* cardiaque
heartbeat ['hɑrtˌbiːt] *n* : battement *m* de cœur
heartbreak ['hɑrtˌbreɪk] *n* : déchirement *m*, douleur *f*, chagrin *m*
heartbreaking ['hɑrtˌbreɪkɪŋ] *adj* : déchirant, qui fend le cœur
heartbroken ['hɑrtˌbroːkən] *adj* **to be heartbroken** : avoir le cœur brisé
heartburn ['hɑrtˌbərn] *n* : brûlures *fpl* d'estomac
hearten ['hɑrtən] *vt* : encourager
hearth ['hɑrθ] *n* : foyer *m*, âtre *m*
heartily ['hɑrṭəli] *adv* **1** ENTHUSIASTICALLY : de tout son cœur <to laugh heartily : rire de bon cœur> **2** TOTALLY : tout à fait <I agree heartily : je suis tout à fait d'accord>
heartless ['hɑrtləs] *adj* : sans cœur, cruel
heartsick ['hɑrtˌsɪk] *adj* : déprimé <to be heartsick : avoir la mort dans l'âme>
heartstrings ['hɑrtˌstrɪŋz] *npl* : corde *f* sensible
heartwarming ['hɑrtˌwɔrmɪŋ] *adj* CHEERING : réconfortant
heartwood ['hɑrtˌwʊd] *n* : cœur *m* du bois
hearty ['hɑrṭi] *adj* **heartier; -est 1** JOVIAL : jovial, enjoué **2** VIGOROUS : vigoureux, robuste **3** CORDIAL, WARM : cordial, chaleureux **4** AMPLE : copieux
heat[1] ['hiːt] *v* : chauffer
heat[2] *n* **1** WARMTH : chaleur *f* **2** TEMPERATURE : température *f*, chaleur *f* **3** HEATING : chauffage *m* **4** PASSION : feu *m*, intensité *f* <in the heat of the moment : dans l'excitation du moment>
heated ['hiːṭəd] *adj* **1** WARMED : chauffé **2** IMPASSIONED : animé, passionné
heatedly ['hiːṭədli] *adv* : avec fougue
heater ['hiːṭər] *n* : radiateur *m*, appareil *m* de chauffage
heath ['hiːθ] *n* **1** HEATHER : bruyère *f* **2** MOOR : lande *f*
heathen[1] [hiːðən] *adj* : païen
heathen[2] *n, pl* **-thens** *or* **-then** : païen *m*, païenne *f*
heather ['hɛðər] *n* : bruyère *f*
heave[1] ['hiːv] *v* **heaved** *or* **hove** ['hoːv]; **heaving** *vt* **1** LIFT : lever, soulever (avec effort) **2** HURL : lancer, jeter **3 to heave a sigh** : pousser un soupir — *vi* **1** : se soulever et s'abaisser (se dit de la poitrine) **2 to heave up** RISE : se soulever
heave[2] *n* **1** EFFORT : effort *m* **2** THROW : lancement *m* (avec force)
heaven ['hɛvən] *n* **1** : ciel *m* <heaven and hell : le ciel et l'enfer> <for heaven's sake! : pour l'amour du ciel!> **2 heavens** *npl* SKY : ciel *m*
heavenly ['hɛvənli] *adj* : céleste, divin
heavily ['hɛvəli] *adv* **1** : lourdement, pesamment <to walk heavily : marcher lourdement> **2** LABORIOUSLY : péniblement **3** MUCH : beaucoup
heaviness ['hɛvinəs] *n* : lourdeur *f*, pesanteur *f*
heavy ['hɛvi] *adj* **heavier; -est 1** WEIGHTY : lourd, pesant **2** BURDENSOME : lourd, gros <a heavy sorrow : un lourd chagrin> **3** DENSE, THICK : dense, abondant **4** DEEP : profond <heavy sleep : sommeil profond> **5** STOUT : gros, corpulent **6** IMMODERATE : gros <a heavy smoker : un gros fumeur>
heavy–duty ['hɛvi'duːṭi, -'djuː-] *adj* : à haute résistance, à usage industriel
heavyweight ['hɛviˌweɪt] *n* : poids *m* lourd (aux sports)
Hebrew[1] ['hiːˌbruː] *adj* : hébreu, hébraïque
Hebrew[2] *n* **1** : Hébreu *m*, Israélite *mf* **2** : hébreu *m* (langue)
heckle ['hɛkəl] *vt* **-led; -ling** : interrompre bruyamment
hectic ['hɛktɪk] *adj* : mouvementé, agité
hedge[1] ['hɛdʒ] *v* **hedged; hedging** *vt* **1** *or* **to hedge in** ENCIRCLE : entourer, encercler **2 to hedge one's bets** : se couvrir — *vi* : chercher des échappatoires, patiner *Can*
hedge[2] *n* **1** : haie *f* **2** SAFEGUARD : sauvegarde *f*, protection *f*
hedgehog ['hɛdʒˌhɔg, -ˌhɑg] *n* : hérisson *m*
heed[1] ['hiːd] *vt* : faire attention à, écouter
heed[2] *n* : attention *f* <to take heed of : tenir compte de>
heedful ['hiːdfəl] *adj* : attentif — **heedfully** *adv*
heedless ['hiːdləs] *adj* : sans prêter attention, irréfléchi, insouciant
heedlessly ['hiːdləsli] *adv* : avec insouciance
heel[1] ['hiːl] *vi* : gîter (se dit d'un bateau)
heel[2] *n* : talon *m*
heft ['hɛft] *vt* : hisser, soulever
hefty ['hɛfti] *adj* **heftier; -est** : pesant, lourd
heifer ['hɛfər] *n* : génisse *f*
height ['haɪt] *n* **1** PEAK : comble *m*, point *m* culminant **2** TALLNESS : taille

f, hauteur *f* <what is your height? : combien mesures-tu?> **3** ALTITUDE : altitude *f,* élévation *f*

heighten [ˈhaɪtən] *vt* **1** RAISE : rehausser, élever **2** INTENSIFY : augmenter, intensifier

heinous [ˈheɪnəs] *adj* : odieux, exécrable, atroce

heir [ˈær] *n* : héritier *m,* -tière *f*

heiress [ˈærəs] *n* : héritière *f*

heirloom [ˈærˌluːm] *n* : objet *m* de famille

held → **hold**[1]

helicopter [ˈhɛləˌkɑptər] *n* : hélicoptère *m*

helium [ˈhiːliəm] *n* : hélium *m*

helix [ˈhiːlɪks] *n, pl* **-lices** [-ləˌsiːz] : hélice *f*

hell [ˈhɛl] *n* : enfer *m*

he'll [ˈhiːl] (*contraction of* **he shall** *or* **he will**) → **shall, will**

hellish [ˈhɛlɪʃ] *adj* : infernal, diabolique

hello [həˈloː, hɛ-] *or Brit* **hullo** [hʌˈleʊ] *interj* : bonjour!, allô! (au téléphone)

helm [ˈhɛlm] *n* : barre *f,* gouvernail *m* <to take the helm : prendre la barre>

helmet [ˈhɛlmət] *n* : casque *m*

help[1] [ˈhɛlp] *vt* **1** AID, ASSIST : aider, venir à l'aide de **2** ALLEVIATE : aider, améliorer **3** PREVENT : empêcher <they couldn't help the accident : ils n'ont pas pu empêcher l'accident> **4** SERVE : se servir <help yourself! : servez-vous!>

help[2] *n* **1** ASSISTANCE : aide *f,* secours *m* **2** STAFF : personnel *m;* employés *mpl,* -ployées *fpl*

helper [ˈhɛlpər] *n* : aide *mf;* assistant *m,* -tante *f*

helpful [ˈhɛlpfəl] *adj* **1** USEFUL : utile **2** OBLIGING : serviable, obligeant

helpfully [ˈhɛlpfəli] *adv* : avec obligeance

helpfulness [ˈhɛlpfəlnəs] *n* **1** KINDNESS : obligeance *f* **2** USEFULNESS : utilité *f*

helping [ˈhɛlpɪŋ] *n* SERVING : portion *f*

helpless [ˈhɛlpləs] *adj* **1** DEFENSELESS : sans défense, désarmé **2** POWERLESS : impuissant

helplessly [ˈhɛlpləsli] *adv* : en vain, désespérément

helplessness [ˈhɛlpləsnəs] *n* : impuissance *f,* impotence *f*

helter–skelter [ˌhɛltərˈskɛltər] *adv* : à la débandade

hem[1] [ˈhɛm] *vt* **hemmed; hemming 1** : ourler, faire un ourlet à (une jupe, etc.) **2 to hem in** SURROUND : entourer

hem[2] *n* : ourlet *m*

hemisphere [ˈhɛməˌsfɪr] *n* : hémisphère *m*

hemispheric [ˌhɛməˈsfɪrɪk, -ˈsfɛr-] *or* **hemispherical** [-ɪkəl] *adj* : hémisphérique

hemlock [ˈhɛmˌlɑk] *n* **1** : ciguë *f* (plante) **2** : tsuga *m* du Canada, pruche *f Can* (arbre)

hemoglobin [ˈhiːməˌgloːbən] *n* : hémoglobine *f*

hemophilia [ˌhiːməˈfɪliə] *n* : hémophilie *f*

hemophiliac[1] [ˌhiːməˈfɪliˌæk] *adj* : hémophile

hemophiliac[2] *n* : hémophile *mf*

hemorrhage[1] [ˈhɛmərɪdʒ] *vi* **-rhaged; -rhaging** : faire une hémorragie

hemorrhage[2] *n* : hémorragie *f*

hemorrhoids [ˈhɛməˌrɔɪdz, ˈhɛmˌrɔɪdz] *npl* : hémorroïdes *fpl*

hemp [ˈhɛmp] *n* : chanvre *m*

hen [ˈhɛn] *n* : poule *f*

hence [ˈhɛn*t*s] *adv* **1** THEREFORE : d'où, donc **2** : d'ici <ten years hence : d'ici dix ans>

henceforth [ˈhɛn*t*sˌforθ, ˌhɛn*t*sˈ-] *adv* : dorénavant, désormais

henchman [ˈhɛntʃmən] *n, pl* **-men** [-mən, -ˌmɛn] : partisan *m,* adepte *m*

henna [ˈhɛnə] *n* : henné *m*

henpeck [ˈhɛnˌpɛk] *vt* : mener par le bout du nez

hepatitis [ˌhɛpəˈtaɪtəs] *n, pl* **-titides** [-ˈtɪtəˌdiːz] : hépatite *f*

her[1] [ˈhər] *adj* : son, sa, ses

her[2] [ˈhər, ər] *pron* **1** (*used as a direct object*) : la, l' <I can see her : je la vois> **2** (*used as an indirect object*) : lui <tell her that I want to go home : dis-lui que je veux rentrer> **3** (*used as object of a preposition*) : elle <he's thinking of her : il pense à elle>

herald[1] [ˈhɛrəld] *vt* ANNOUNCE : annoncer, proclamer

herald[2] *n* **1** MESSENGER : héraut *m* **2** HARBINGER : signe *m* avant-coureur

heraldic [hɛˈrældɪk, hə-] *adj* : héraldique

heraldry [ˈhɛrəldri] *n, pl* **-ries** : héraldique *f*

herb [ˈərb, ˈhərb] *n* : herbe *f*

herbicide [ˈərbəˌsaɪd, ˈhər-] *n* : herbicide *m*

herbivore [ˈərbəˌvor, ˈhər-] *n* : herbivore *m*

herbivorous [ˌərˈbɪvərəs, ˌhər-] *adj* : herbivore

herculean [ˌhərkjəˈliːən, ˌhərˈkjuːliən] *adj* : herculéen

herd[1] [ˈhərd] *vt* : rassembler en troupeau — *vi or* **to herd together** : s'assembler

herd[2] *n* : troupeau *m* (de bétail), troupe *f* (de chevaux, d'éléphants, etc.)

herder [ˈhərdər] → **herdsman**

herdsman [ˈhərdzmən] *n, pl* **-men** [-mən, -ˌmɛn] : gardien *m* de troupeau

here [ˈhɪr] *adv* **1** : ici, là <turn here : tournez ici> <he's not here today : il n'est pas là aujourd'hui> **2** NOW : alors, à ce moment-là **3 here!** : tenez!, écoutez!

hereabouts [ˈhɪrəˌbaʊts] *or* **hereabout** [-ˌbaʊt] *adv* : par ici, près d'ici, dans les environs

hereafter[1] [hɪrˈæftər] *adv* **1** HENCEFORTH : désormais, à l'avenir **2** : ci-après (en droit)

hereafter[2] *n* **the hereafter** : l'au-delà *m*

hereby [hɪrˈbaɪ] *adv* : par la présente

hereditary [həˈrɛdəˌtɛri] *adj* : héréditaire

heredity [həˈrɛdət̬i] *n* : hérédité *f*

herein [hɪrˈɪn] *adv* : ci-après

hereof [hɪrˈʌv] *adv* : des présentes (en droit)

hereon [hɪrˈɑn, -ˈɔn] *adv* : sur ce

heresy [ˈhɛrəsi] *n, pl* **-sies** : hérésie *f*

heretic [ˈhɛrəˌtɪk] *n* : hérétique *mf*

heretical [həˈrɛt̬ɪkəl] *adj* : hérétique

hereto [hɪrˈtuː] *adv* : à ceci, à cela

heretofore [ˈhɪrt̬əˌfor] *adv* : jusqu'ici

hereunder [hɪrˈʌndər] *adv* : ci-après

hereupon [ˈhɪrəˌpɑn, -ˌpɔn] *adv* : sur ce, à ce moment

herewith [hɪrˈwɪθ] *adv* **1** : ci-joint **2** HEREBY : par la présente

heritage [ˈhɛrət̬ɪdʒ] *n* : héritage *m*, patrimoine *m*

hermaphrodite [hərˈmæfrəˌdaɪt] *n* : hermaphrodite *mf*

hermetic [hərˈmɛt̬ɪk] *adj* : hermétique — **hermetically** [-t̬ɪkli] *adv*

hermit [ˈhərmət] *n* : ermite *m*

hernia [ˈhərniə] *n, pl* **-nias** *or* **-niae** [-niˌiː, -niˌaɪ] : hernie *f*

hero [ˈhiːˌroː, ˈhɪrˌoː] *n, pl* **-roes** : héros *m*

heroic [hɪˈroːɪk] *adj* : héroïque — **heroically** [-ɪkli] *adv*

heroics [hɪˈroːɪks] *npl* : mélodrame *m*

heroin [ˈhɛroən] *n* : héroïne *f*

heroine [ˈhɛroən] *n* : héroïne *f*

heroism [ˈhɛroˌɪzəm] *n* : héroïsme *m*

heron [ˈhɛrən] *n* : héron *m*

herpes [ˈhərˌpiːz] *n* : herpès *m*

herring [ˈhɛrɪŋ] *n, pl* **-ring** *or* **-rings** : hareng *m*

hers [ˈhərz] *pron* **1** : le sien, la sienne, les siens, les siennes <my suggestion is good, but hers is better : ma suggestion est bonne, mais la sienne est meilleure> **2** (*used after a preposition*) <some friends of hers : des amis à elle>

herself [hərˈsɛlf] *pron* **1** (*used reflexively*) : se, s' <she hurt herself : elle s'est blessée> **2** (*used emphatically*) <she did it herself : elle l'a fait elle-même>

hertz [ˈhərts, ˈhɛrts] *ns & pl* : hertz *m*

he's [ˈhiːz] (*contraction of* **he is** *or* **he has**) → **be, have**

hesitancy [ˈhɛzət̬əntsi] *n, pl* **-cies** : hésitation *f*, indécision *f*

hesitant [ˈhɛzət̬ənt] *adj* : hésitant, indécis

hesitantly [ˈhɛzət̬əntli] *adv* : avec hésitation

hesitate [ˈhɛzəˌteɪt] *vi* **-tated; -tating 1** : hésiter **2** PAUSE : faire une pause

hesitation [ˌhɛzəˈteɪʃən] *n* : hésitation *f*

heterogeneous [ˌhɛt̬ərəˈdʒiːniəs, -njəs] *adj* : hétérogène

heterosexual[1] [ˌhɛt̬əroˈsɛkʃʊəl] *adj* : hétérosexuel

heterosexual[2] *n* : hétérosexuel *m*, -sexuelle *f*

heterosexuality [ˌhɛt̬əroˌsɛkʃʊˈælət̬i] *n* : hétérosexualité *f*

hew [ˈhjuː] *v* **hewed; hewed** *or* **hewn** [ˈhjuːn]; **hewing** *vt* **1** CUT, SHAPE : tailler, couper **2** FELL : abattre (un arbre) — *vi* ADHERE : se conformer

hex[1] [ˈhɛks] *vt* : jeter un sort à

hex[2] *n* : sort *m*, sortilège *m*

hexagon [ˈhɛksəˌgɑn] *n* : hexagone *m* — **hexagonal** [hɛkˈsægənəl] *adj*

hey [ˈheɪ] *interj* : hé!, ohé!

heyday [ˈheɪˌdeɪ] *n* : sommet *m*, apogée *f* <in the heyday of his power : au sommet de son pouvoir>

hi [ˈhaɪ] *interj* : hé!, ohé!, salut!

hiatus [haɪˈeɪt̬əs] *n* **1** GAP : hiatus *m*, lacune *f* **2** PAUSE : pause *f*

hibernate [ˈhaɪbərˌneɪt] *vi* **-nated; -nating** : hiberner

hibernation [ˌhaɪbərˈneɪʃən] *n* : hibernation *f*

hiccup[1] [ˈhɪkəp] *vi* **-cuped; -cuping** : hoqueter

hiccup[2] *n* : hoquet *m* <to have the hiccups : avoir le hoquet>

hick [ˈhɪk] *n* BUMPKIN : rustre *mf*, plouc *mf France fam*

hickory [ˈhɪkəri] *n, pl* **-ries** : hickory *m*, noyer *m* blanc d'Amérique

hide[1] [ˈhaɪd] *v* **hid** [ˈhɪd]; **hidden** [ˈhɪdən] *or* **hid; hiding** *vt* **1** CONCEAL : cacher **2** : dissimuler, occulter <to hide one's motives : occulter ses motifs> **3** SHIELD : voiler <the clouds were hiding the sun : les nuages voilaient le soleil> — *vi* : se cacher

hide[2] *n* : peau *f* d'animal

hide–and–seek [ˈhaɪdəndˌsiːk] *n* : cache-cache *m*, cachette *f Can*

hidebound [ˈhaɪdˌbaʊnd] *adj* : à l'esprit étroit, borné

hideous [ˈhɪdiəs] *adj* : hideux, affreux — **hideously** *adv*

hideout [ˈhadˌaʊt] *n* : cachette *f*

hierarchical [ˌhaɪəˈrɑrkɪkəl] *adj* : hiérarchique

hierarchy [ˈhaɪəˌrɑrki] *n, pl* **-chies** : hiérarchie *f*

hieroglyphic [ˌhaɪəˌrəˈglɪfɪk] *n* : hiéroglyphe *m*

high[1] [ˈhaɪ] *adv* : haut

high[2] *adj* **1** TALL : haut <how high is the table? : quelle est la hauteur de la table?> **2** : haut, élevé <high prices : prix élevés> **3** : aigu, haut (en musique) **4** GREAT, IMPORTANT : haut, éminent <high society : haute société> **5** INTOXICATED : parti *fam*, drogué

high[3] *n* **1** RECORD : record *m,* niveau *m* élevé <to reach an all-time high : réaliser un niveau élevé> **2** : zone *f* de haute pression (en météorologie) **3** *or* **high gear** : quatrième vitesse *f* **4 on ~** : dans le ciel
highbrow [ˈhaɪˌbraʊ] *n* : intellectuel *m,* -tuelle *f*
higher [ˈhaɪər] *adj* **1** : plus haut **2** ADVANCED : supérieur
high fidelity *n* : haute-fidélité *f*
high–flown [ˈhaɪˈfloːn] *adj* : ampoulé
high–handed [ˈhaɪˈhændəd] *adj* : despotique, autoritaire
highland [ˈhaɪlənd] *n* : région *f* montagneuse
highlander [ˈhaɪləndər] *n* : montagnard *m,* -narde *f*
highlight[1] [ˈhaɪˌlaɪt] *vt* **1** EMPHASIZE : souligner **2** : être le point culminant de (une cérémonie, etc.) **3** : rehausser (en photographie, etc.)
highlight[2] *n* : clou *m,* point *m* culminant
highly [ˈhaɪli] *adv* **1** VERY : très, extrêmement **2** FAVORABLY : bien <to think very highly of : penser beaucoup de bien de>
highness [ˈhaɪnəs] *n* **1** HEIGHT : hauteur *f* **2** (*used as a title*) <His/Her Highness : son Altesse>
high–rise [ˈhaɪˌraɪz] *adj* : dans une tour
high school *n* : lycée *m France,* école *f* secondaire *Can,* polyvalente *f Can*
high seas *npl* : haute mer *f*
high–spirited [ˈhaɪˈspɪrət̬əd] *adj* : plein d'entrain
high–strung [ˈhaɪˈstrʌŋ] *adj* : nerveux, très tendu
highway [ˈhaɪˌweɪ] *n* **1** : route *f* **2** → **interstate**
highwayman [ˈhaɪˌweɪmən] *n, pl* **-men** [-mən, -ˌmɛn] : bandit *m* de grand chemin
hijack [ˈhaɪˌdʒæk] *vt* : détourner (un avion), saisir de force (une voiture)
hijacker [ˈhaɪˌdʒækər] *n* : pirate *m* de l'air
hike[1] [ˈhaɪk] *v* **hiked; hiking** *vi* : faire une randonnée — *vt or* **to hike up** RAISE : augmenter
hike[2] *n* **1** WALK : randonnée *f* **2** INCREASE : hausse *f*
hiker [ˈhaɪkər] *n* : randonneur *m,* -neuse *f*
hilarious [hɪˈlæriəs, haɪ-] *adj* : désopilant, hilarant
hilarity [hɪˈlærət̬i, haɪ-] *n* : hilarité *f*
hill [ˈhɪl] *n* : colline *f*
hillbilly [ˈhɪlˌbɪli] *n, pl* **-lies** : montagnard *m,* -narde *f*
hillock [ˈhɪlək] *n* : petite colline *f,* butte *f*
hillside [ˈhɪlˌsaɪd] *n* : coteau *m*
hilltop [ˈhɪlˌtɑp] *n* : sommet *m* d'une colline
hilly [ˈhɪli] *adj* **hillier; -est** : vallonné, côteux *Can*
hilt [ˈhɪlt] *n* : poignée *f* (d'une épée), manche *m* (d'un poignard)
him [ˈhɪm, əm] *pron* **1** (*used as a direct object*) : le, l' <I met him at the restaurant : je l'ai rencontré au restaurant> **2** (*used as an indirect object*) : lui <tell him that I am delighted : dis-lui que je suis ravi> **3** (*used as object of a preposition*) : lui <richer than him : plus riche que lui>
himself [hɪmˈsɛlf] *pron* **1** (*used reflexively*) : se, s' <he washed himself : il s'est lavé> **2** (*used emphatically*) : lui-même <he did it himself : il l'a fait lui-même> **3** (*used after a preposition*) : lui, lui-même <by himself : par lui-même, tout seul>
hind[1] [ˈhaɪnd] *adj* REAR : de derrière
hind[2] *n* : biche *f*
hinder [ˈhɪndər] *vt* : empêcher, entraver
hindquarters [ˈhaɪndˌkwɔrt̬ərz] *npl* : arrière-train *m*
hindrance [ˈhɪndrənts] *n* : entrave *f,* obstacle *m*
hindsight [ˈhaɪndˌsaɪt] *n* **in ~** : avec du recul
Hindu[1] [ˈhɪnˌduː] *adj* : hindou
Hindu[2] *n* : Hindou *m,* -doue *f*
Hinduism [ˈhɪnduːˌɪzəm] *n* : hindouisme *m*
hinge[1] [ˈhɪndʒ] *v* **hinged; hinging** *vi* **to hinge on** : dépendre de — *vt* : mettre une charnière à
hinge[2] *n* : charnière *f,* gond *m*
hint[1] [ˈhɪnt] *vt* : insinuer — *vi* **to hint at** : faire une allusion à
hint[2] *n* **1** SUGGESTION : allusion *f,* insinuation *f* **2** CLUE : indice *m,* idée *f* **3** TRACE : soupçon *m,* trace *f* <a hint of perfume : un soupçon de parfum>
hinterland [ˈhɪntərˌlænd, -lənd] *n* : arrière-pays *m*
hip [ˈhɪp] *n* : hanche *f*
hippie *or* **hippy** [ˈhɪpi] *n, pl* **hippies** : hippie *mf,* hippy *mf*
hippopotamus [ˌhɪpəˈpɑt̬əməs] *n, pl* **-muses** *or* **-mi** [-ˌmaɪ] : hippopotame *m*
hire[1] [ˈhaɪr] *vt* **hired; hiring 1** EMPLOY : engager, embaucher **2** RENT : louer
hire[2] *n* **1** WAGES : gages *mpl* **2** RENTAL : location *f* <for hire : à louer> **3** EMPLOYEE : employé *m,* -ployée *f*
his[1] [ˈhɪz, ɪz] *adj* : son, sa, ses <his house : sa maison> <it's his : c'est à lui>
his[2] *pron* **1** : le sien, la sienne, les siens, les siennes **2** (*used after a preposition*) <a friend of his : un ami à lui, un de ses amis>
Hispanic[1] [hɪˈspænɪk] *adj* : hispanique
Hispanic[2] *n* : Hispano-Américain *m,* Hispano-Américaine *f*
hiss[1] [ˈhɪs] *vi* : siffler, chuinter
hiss[2] *n* : sifflement *m*
historian [hɪˈstɔriən] *n* : historien *m,* -rienne *f*

historic [hɪ'stɔrɪk] *or* **historical** [-ɪkəl] *adj* : historique — **historically** [-ɪkli] *adv*

history ['hɪstəri] *n, pl* **-ries 1** : histoire *f* **2** RECORD : antécédents *mpl* <medical history : antécédents médicaux>

histrionics [ˌhɪstri'ɑnɪks] *ns & pl* : airs *mpl* dramatiques

hit[1] ['hɪt] *v* **hit; hitting** *vt* **1** STRIKE : frapper **2** : heurter, percuter <the car hit a tree : la voiture a heurté un arbre> **3** AFFECT : affecter, toucher <the loss hit him hard : la perte l'a beaucoup affecté> **4** REACH : atteindre, arriver à — *vi* **1** : frapper, cogner **2** OCCUR : arriver, se produire <the storm hit without warning : la tempête est arrivée par surprise>

hit[2] *n* **1** BLOW : coup *m* **2** SUCCESS : succès *m*

hitch[1] ['hɪtʃ] *vt* **1** FASTEN, HARNESS : accrocher, atteler **2** → **hitchhike 3 to hitch up** : remonter (ses pantalons, etc.)

hitch[2] *n* **1** JERK : saccade *f*, secousse *f* **2** OBSTACLE : problème *m*, pépin *m*

hitchhike ['hɪtʃˌhaɪk] *vi* **-hiked; -hiking** : faire de l'auto-stop, faire du pouce *Can*

hitchhiker ['hɪtʃˌhaɪkər] *n* : auto-stoppeur *m*, -peuse *f*

hither ['hɪðər] *adv* : ici <come hither : venez çà>

hitherto ['hɪðərˌtuː, ˌhɪðər'-] *adv* : jusqu'ici, jusqu'à présent

hitter ['hɪtər] *n* BATTER : batteur *m*

HIV [ˌeɪtʃˌaɪ'viː] *n* : VIH *m*

hive ['haɪv] *n* **1** *or* **beehive** : ruche *f* **2** SWARM : essaim *m* **3 a hive of activity** : une vraie ruche

hives ['haɪvz] *ns & pl* : urticaire *f*

HMO [ˌeɪtʃˌɛm'oː] *n* : centre *m* de santé financé par sa clientèle

hoard[1] ['hord] *vt* : accumuler, amasser, faire des réserves de — *vi* : faire des réserves

hoard[2] *n* : réserve *f*, provisions *fpl*

hoarfrost ['horˌfrɔst] *n* : gelée *f* blanche, givre *m*

hoarse ['hors] *adj* **hoarser; -est 1** GRATING : discordant **2** : rauque, enroué <a hoarse cough : une toux rauque>

hoarsely ['horsli] *adv* : d'une voix rauque

hoary ['hori] *adj* **hoarier; -est** : aux cheveux blancs, chenu

hoax[1] ['hoːks] *vt* : faire un canular à

hoax[2] *n* : canular *m*, farce *f*

hobble[1] ['hɑbəl] *v* **-bled; -bling** *vi* LIMP : boitiller — *vt* FETTER : entraver (un animal)

hobble[2] *n* **1** LIMP : boitillement *m* **2** : entrave *f* (d'un animal)

hobby ['hɑbi] *n, pl* **-bies** : passe-temps *m*

hobgoblin ['hɑbˌgɑblən] *n* **1** GOBLIN : lutin *m* **2** BOGEY : épouvantail *m*

hobnail ['hɑbˌneɪl] *n* : caboche *f*

hobnailed ['hɑbˌneɪld] *adj* : ferré

hobnob ['hɑbˌnɑb] *vi* **-nobbed; -nobbing** : frayer <to hobnob with : fréquenter, frayer avec>

hobo ['hoːˌboː] *n, pl* **-boes** : vagabond *m*, -bonde *f*; clochard *m*, -charde *f*

hock[1] ['hɑk] *vt* : mettre au clou, mettre en gage

hock[2] *n* **in ~** : au clou

hockey ['hɑki] *n* : hockey *m*

hod ['hɑd] *n* : oiseau *m*, auge *f* (de maçon)

hodgepodge ['hɑdʒˌpɑdʒ] *n* JUMBLE : méli-mélo *m*, salmigondis *m*

hoe[1] ['hoː] *vi* **hoed; hoeing** : sarcler, biner

hoe[2] *n* : houe *f*, binette *f*

hog[1] ['hɔg, 'hɑg] *vt* **hogged; hogging** : monopoliser

hog[2] *n* **1** : porc *m*, cochon *m* **2** GLUTTON : glouton *m*, -tonne *f*

hoggish ['hɔgɪʃ, 'hɑg-] *adj* : glouton, goulu

hogshead ['hɔgzˌhɛd, 'hɑgz-] *n* CASK : barrique *f*

hoist[1] ['hɔɪst] *vt* : hisser

hoist[2] *n* : palan *m*, monte-charge *m*

hold[1] ['hoːld] *v* **held** ['hɛld]; **holding** *vt* **1** POSSESS : posséder **2** RESTRAIN : tenir <hold the dog! : tiens le chien!> **3** GRASP : tenir **4** SUPPORT : soutenir, supporter (un poids) **5** CONTAIN : contenir **6** REGARD : avoir, tenir <I hold him in high esteem : j'ai beaucoup d'estime pour lui > **7** CONDUCT : organiser (un colloque, etc.) **8** : avoir, occuper (un poste) **9** : détenir (un prisonnier) **10** : avoir, maintenir (une opinion) — *vi* **1** LAST : durer, continuer **2** APPLY : tenir, être en vigueur <the rule still holds : le règlement est encore en vigueur> **3 to hold forth** : pérorer **4 to hold to** : s'en tenir à **5 to hold with** : être d'accord avec

hold[2] *n* **1** GRIP : prise *f* **2** INFLUENCE : emprise *f* **3** : cale *f* (d'un navire)

holder ['hoːldər] *n* : détenteur *m*, -trice *f*; titulaire *mf*

holdings ['hoːldɪŋz] *npl* PROPERTY : propriétés *fpl*

holdup ['hoːldˌʌp] *n* **1** ROBBERY : vol *m* à main armée **2** DELAY : retard *m*

hold up *vt* **1** ROB : faire un vol à main armée **2** DELAY : retarder

hole ['hoːl] *n* : trou *m*

holiday ['hɑləˌdeɪ] *n* **1** : jour *m* férié **2** *Brit* VACATION : vacances *fpl*

holiness ['hoːlinəs] *n* **1** : sainteté *f* **2** (*used as a title*) <His Holiness : Sa Sainteté>

holistic [hoː'lɪstɪk] *adj* : holistique

holler[1] ['hɑlər] *vi* : gueuler *fam*, hurler

holler[2] *n* : hurlement *m*

hollow[1] ['hɑˌloː] *vt or* **to hollow out** : creuser

hollow[2] *adj* **hollower; -est 1** : creux **2** MUFFLED : caverneux <a hollow laugh : un rire forcé> **3** MEANING-

LESS : faux <hollow promises : fausses promesses>
hollow[3] *n* **1** CAVITY : creux *m*, dépression *f*, cavité *f* **2** VALLEY : vallon *m*
hollowness ['hɑ,lo:nəs] *n* **1** HOLLOW : creux *m*, cavité *f* **2** FALSENESS : fausseté *f* **3** EMPTINESS : vide *m*
holly ['hɑli] *n, pl* **-lies** : houx *m*
hollyhock ['hɑli,hɑk] *n* : rose *f* trémière
holocaust ['hɑlə,kɔst, 'ho:-, 'hɔ-] *n* : holocauste *m*
holster ['ho:lstər] *n* : étui *m* de revolver
holy ['ho:li] *adj* **holier; -est 1** SAINTLY : saint **2** SACRED : bénit <holy water : eau bénite>
Holy Ghost → Holy Spirit
Holy Spirit *n* : Saint-Esprit *m*
homage ['ɑmɪdʒ, 'hɑ-] *n* : hommage *m*
home[1] ['ho:m] *adv* **1** : à la maison, chez soi **2** DEEPLY : à fond <to hammer a nail home : enfoncer un clou jusqu'au bout>
home[2] *n* **1** RESIDENCE : maison *f* **2** : foyer *m*, chez-soi *m* <home is where the heart is : où le coeur aime, là est le foyer> **3** HABITAT : habitat *m* **4 → funeral home, nursing home**
homecoming ['ho:m,kʌmɪŋ] *n* : retour *m* au foyer
homegrown ['ho:m'gro:n] *adj* : du pays, du jardin
homeland ['ho:m,lænd] *n* : pays *m* natal, patrie *f*
homeless ['ho:mləs] *adj* : sans foyer
homely ['ho:mli] *adj* **homelier; -est 1** SIMPLE : simple, sans prétentions **2** UNATTRACTIVE : sans attraits
homemade ['ho:m'meɪd] *adj* : fait à la maison <homemade cookies : biscuits maison>
homemaker ['ho:m,meɪkər] *n* : femme *f* au foyer
home run *n* : coup *m* de circuit *Can*
homesick ['ho:m,sɪk] *adj* : nostalgique <to be homesick : avoir le mal du pays>
homesickness ['ho:m,sɪknəs] *n* : nostalgie *f*, mal *m* du pays
homespun ['ho:m,spʌn] *adj* : simple, naturel
homestead ['ho:m,stɛd] *n* : propriété *f*, terres *fpl*
homeward[1] ['ho:mwərd] *or* **homewards** [-wərdz] *adv* : vers la maison, vers la patrie <homeward bound : sur le chemin du retour>
homeward[2] *adj* : de retour
homework ['ho:m,wərk] *n* : devoirs *mpl*
homey ['ho:mi] *adj* **homier; -est** : accueillant
homicidal [,hɑmə'saɪdəl, ,ho:-] *adj* : homicide
homicide ['hɑmə,saɪd, 'ho:-] *n* : homicide *m*
hominy ['hɑməni] *n* : bouillie *f* de semoule de maïs
homogeneity [,ho:mədʒə'ni:əti, -'neɪ] *n* : homogénéité *f*
homogeneous [,ho:mə'dʒi:niəs, -njəs] *adj* : homogène
homogenize [ho:'mɑdʒə,naɪz, hə-] *vt* **-nized; -nizing** : homogénéiser
homograph ['hɑmə,græf, 'ho:-] *n* : homographe *m*
homonym ['hɑmə,nɪm, 'ho:-] *n* : homonyme *m*
homophone ['hɑmə,fo:n, 'ho:-] *n* : homophone *m*
homosexual[1] [,ho:mə'sɛkʃuəl] *adj* : homosexuel
homosexual[2] *n* : homosexuel *m*, -sexuelle *f*
homosexuality [,ho:mə,sɛkʃu'æləṭi] *n* : homosexualité *f*
Honduran[1] [hɑn'dʊrən, -'djʊr-] *adj* : hondurien
Honduran[2] *n* : Hondurien *m* -rienne *f*
hone ['ho:n] *vt* **honed; honing** : aiguiser, affûter
honest ['ɑnəst] *adj* **1** STRAIGHTFORWARD, TRUTHFUL : honnête, franc **2** CREDITABLE : bon, honorable <an honest day's work : une bonne journée de travail>
honestly ['ɑnəstli] *adv* : honnêtement
honesty ['ɑnəsti] *n* : honnêteté *f*
honey ['hʌni] *n, pl* **-eys** : miel *m*
honeybee ['hʌni,bi:] *n* : abeille *f*
honeycomb[1] ['hʌni,ko:m] *vi* : cribler (de petits trous)
honeycomb[2] *n* : rayon *m* de miel
honeymoon[1] ['hʌni,mu:n] *vi* : passer sa lune de miel
honeymoon[2] *n* : lune *f* de miel
honeysuckle ['hʌni,sʌkəl] *n* : chèvrefeuille *m*
honk[1] ['hɑŋk, 'hɔŋk] *vi* : cacarder (se dit d'une oie), klaxonner (se dit d'une voiture)
honk[2] *n* : cri *m* (de l'oie), coup *m* de klaxon (d'une voiture)
honor[1] *or Brit* **honour** ['ɑnər] *vt* **1** : honorer <honor your parents : honore tes parents> **2** : honorer (un chèque, etc.), remplir (un engagement)
honor[2] *or Brit* **honour** *n* **1** RECOGNITION, RESPECT : honneur *m* <in honor of : en l'honneur de> **2 honors** *npl* AWARDS : distinctions *fpl* honorifiques **3 Your Honor** : Votre Honneur
honorable *or Brit* **honourable** ['ɑnərəbəl] *adj* : honorable **— honorably** *or Brit* **honourably** [-bli] *adv*
honorary ['ɑnə,rɛri] *adj* : honoraire, honorifique <an honorary member : un membre honoraire> <an honorary title : un titre honorifique>
honour *Brit* **→ honor**
hood ['hʊd] *n* **1** : capuchon *m* (d'un vêtement) **2** : capot *m* (d'une voiture)
hooded ['hʊdəd] *adj* : à capuchon
hoodlum ['hʊdləm, 'hu:d-] *n* : voyou *m*, truand *m*
hoodwink ['hʊd,wɪŋk] *vt* : tromper, duper

hoof ['hʊf, 'hu:f] *n, pl* **hooves** ['hʊvz, 'hu:vz] *or* **hoofs** : sabot *m* (d'un animal)
hoofed ['hʊft, 'hu:ft] *adj* : à sabots
hook[1] ['hʊk] *vt* : accrocher
hook[2] *n* **1** : crochet *m* **2** FASTENER : agrafe *f* **3** → **fishhook**
hookworm ['hʊk,wərm] *n* : ankylostome *m*
hooligan ['hu:lɪgən] *n* : vandale *m,* voyou *m*
hoop ['hu:p] *n* : cerceau *m*
hoorah [hʊ'ra], **hooray** [hʊ'reɪ] → **hurrah**
hoot[1] ['hu:t] *vi* **1** SHOUT : huer, hurler <to hoot with laughter : pouffer de rire> **2** : hululer (se dit d'un hibou), siffler (se dit d'un train), klaxonner (se dit d'une voiture)
hoot[2] *n* **1** : hululement *m* (d'un hibou), sifflement *m* (d'un train) **2 hoots** *npl* BOOS : huées *fpl* **3 I don't give a hoot** : je m'en fiche
hop[1] [hɑp] *v* **hopped; hopping** *vi* : sauter, sautiller — *vt or* **to hop over** : sauter, franchir
hop[2] *n* **1** LEAP : saut *m,* sautillement *m* **2** : houblon *m* (plante) **3** FLIGHT : court vol *m* en avion
hope[1] ['ho:p] *v* **hoped; hoping** : espérer
hope[2] *n* : espoir *m,* espérance *f*
hopeful ['ho:pfəl] *adj* **1** : plein d'espoir, optimiste **2** PROMISING : prometteur
hopefully ['ho:pfəli] *adv* **1** OPTIMISTICALLY : avec optimisme, avec espoir **2** : avec un peu de chance <hopefully, he will come : on espère qu'il viendra>
hopefulness ['ho:pfəlnəs] *n* : espoir *m*
hopeless ['ho:pləs] *adj* : désespéré
hopelessly ['ho:pləsli] *adv* : éperdument
hopelessness ['ho:pləsnəs] *n* : désespoir *m*
hopper ['hɑpər] *n* : trémie *f*
hopscotch ['hɑp,skɑtʃ] *n* : marelle *f*
horde ['hord] *n* : horde *f,* foule *f,* essaim *m*
horizon [hə'raɪzən] *n* : horizon *m*
horizontal [,hɔrə'zɑntəl] *adj* : horizontal — **horizontally** *adv*
hormone ['hɔr,mo:n] *n* : hormone *f* — **hormonal** [hɔr'mo:nəl] *adj*
horn ['hɔrn] *n* **1** : corne *f* (d'un animal) **2** : cor *m* (instrument de musique) **3** : klaxon *m* (d'un véhicule)
horned ['hɔrnd] *adj* : cornu
hornless ['hɔrnləs] *adj* : sans cornes
hornet ['hɔrnət] *n* : frelon *m*
horn of plenty → **cornucopia**
horny ['hɔrni] *adj* **hornier; -est** : calleux
horoscope ['hɔrə,sko:p] *n* : horoscope *m*
horrendous [hə'rɛndəs] *adj* : épouvantable, effroyable
horrible ['hɔrəbəl] *adj* : horrible, affreux, détestable — **horribly** [-bli] *adv*
horrid ['hɔrɪd] *adj* **1** HIDEOUS : horrible, hideux **2** DISGUSTING : repoussant
horrify ['hɔrə,faɪ] *vt* **-fied; -fying** : horrifier, remplir d'horreur
horror ['hɔrər] *n* : horreur *f*
hors d'oeuvre [ɔr'dərv] *n, pl* **hors d'oeuvres** [-'dərvz] : hors-d'œuvre *m*
horse ['hɔrs] *n* : cheval *m*
horseback ['hɔrs,bæk] *n* **on ~** : à cheval
horse chestnut *n* : marronnier *m* (arbre), marron *m* (noix)
horsefly ['hɔrs,flaɪ] *n, pl* **-flies** : taon *m*
horsehair ['hɔrs,hær] *n* : crin *m* (de cheval)
horseman ['hɔrsmən] *n, pl* **-men** [-mən, -,mɛn] : cavalier *m*
horsemanship ['hɔrsmən,ʃɪp] *n* : équitation *f*
horseplay ['hɔrs,pleɪ] *n* : jeux *mpl* de mains
horsepower ['hɔrs,paʊər] *n* : cheval-vapeur *m*
horseradish ['hɔrs,rædɪʃ] *n* : raifort *m*
horseshoe ['hɔrs,ʃu:] *n* : fer *m* à cheval
horsewhip ['hɔrs,*h*wɪp] *vt* **-whipped; -whipping** : cravacher
horsewoman ['hɔrs,wʊmən] *n, pl* **-women** [-,wɪmən] : cavalière *f*
horsey *or* **horsy** ['hɔrsi] *adj* **horsier; -est** : chevalin
horticultural [,hɔrt̬ə'kʌltʃərəl] *adj* : horticole
horticulture ['hɔrt̬ə,kʌltʃər] *n* : horticulture *f*
hosanna [ho:'zænə, -za-] *interj* : hosanna!
hose[1] ['ho:z] *vt* **hosed; hosing** : arroser
hose[2] *n* **1** *pl* **hoses** : tuyau *m* <garden hose : tuyau d'arrosage> <fire hose : tuyau d'incendie> **2** *pl* **hose** STOCKINGS : bas *mpl,* collants *mpl*
hosiery ['ho:ʒəri, 'ho:zə-] *n* : bas *mpl,* collants *mpl*
hospice ['hɑspəs] *n* : hospice *m*
hospitable [hɑs'pɪt̬əbəl, 'hɑ,spɪ-] *adj* : hospitalier, accueillant, invitant *Can,* recevant *Can*
hospitably [hɑs'pɪt̬əbli, 'hɑ,spɪ-] *adv* : avec hospitalité
hospital ['hɑs,pɪt̬əl] *n* : hôpital *m*
hospitality [,hɑspə'tæləṭi] *n, pl* **-ties** : hospitalité *f*
hospitalization [,hɑs,pɪt̬ələ'zeɪʃən] *n* : hospitalisation *f*
hospitalize ['hɑs,pɪt̬ə,laɪz] *vt* **-ized; -izing** : hospitaliser
host[1] ['ho:st] *vt* **1** : être l'hôte de <to host a dinner : recevoir à dîner> **2** : animer (une émission de télévision, etc.)
host[2] *n* **1** ARMY : armée *f* **2** MULTITUDE : foule *f* **3** : hôte *mf* (à la maison, etc.) **4** EUCHARIST : hostie *f,* Eucharistie *f* **5** : animateur *m,* -trice *f* <radio host : animateur de radio> **6** : hôte *m* (en biologie)
hostage ['hɑstɪdʒ] *n* : otage *m*

hostel [ˈhɑstəl] *n* **:** auberge *f* <youth hostel : auberge de jeunesse>
hostess [ˈhoːstəs] *n* **:** hôtesse *f*
hostile [ˈhɑstəl, -ˌtaɪl] *adj* **:** hostile — **hostilely** *adv*
hostility [hɑsˈtɪləṱi] *n, pl* **-ties :** hostilité *f*
hot [ˈhɑt] *adj* **hotter; hottest 1 :** chaud <a hot stove : une cuisinière chaude> <it's hot today : il fait chaud aujourd'hui> **2** ARDENT, FIERY **:** coléreux <to have a hot temper : s'emporter facilement> **3** SPICY **:** fort, épicé **4** EAGER **:** empressé, passionné **5** LATEST **:** dernier <hot news : les dernières nouvelles> **6** RADIOACTIVE **:** radioactif **7** STOLEN **:** volé
hot air *n* **:** paroles *fpl* en l'air
hotbed [ˈhɑtˌbɛd] *n* **1 :** couche *f* chaude, pépinière *f* (en botanique) **2** CENTER, SOURCE **:** foyer *m* <a hotbed of dissent : un foyer de conflit>
hot dog *n* **:** hot-dog *m*
hotel [hoːˈtɛl] *n* **:** hôtel *m*
hothead [ˈhɑtˌhɛd] *n* **:** tête *f* brûlée
hotheaded [ˈhɑtˈhɛdəd] *adj* **:** impétueux, exalté
hothouse [ˈhɑtˌhaʊs] *n* **:** serre *f*
hotly [ˈhɑtli] *adv* **:** vivement, passionnément
hound[1] [ˈhaʊnd] *vt* **:** traquer, poursuivre
hound[2] *n* **:** chien *m* de meute
hour [ˈaʊər] *n* **:** heure *f*
hourglass [ˈaʊərˌglæs] *n* **:** sablier *m*
hourly [ˈaʊərli] *adv & adj* **:** toutes les heures
house[1] [ˈhaʊz] *vt* **housed; housing :** loger, héberger
house[2] [ˈhaʊs] *n, pl* **houses** [ˈhaʊzəz, -səz] **1** HOME, RESIDENCE **:** maison *f* **2 :** chambre *f* (en politique) **3** COMPANY, FIRM **:** maison *f*, compagnie *f* **4** AUDIENCE **:** assistance *f*, auditoire *m*
houseboat [ˈhaʊsˌboːt] *n* **:** péniche *f* aménagée
housebroken [ˈhaʊsˌbroːkən] *adj* **:** propre
housefly [ˈhaʊsˌflaɪ] *n, pl* **-flies :** mouche *f*
household[1] [ˈhaʊsˌhoːld] *adj* **1** DOMESTIC **:** ménager **2** COMMON, FAMILIAR **:** commun
household[2] *n* **:** maison *f*, ménage *m*
householder [ˈhaʊsˌhoːldər] *n* **:** propriétaire *mf*, chef *m* de famille
housekeeper [ˈhaʊsˌkiːpər] *n* **:** ménagère *f*, gouvernante *f*
housekeeping [ˈhaʊsˌkiːpɪŋ] *n* **:** ménage *m*
housemaid [ˈhaʊsˌmeɪd] *n* **:** bonne *f*, femme *f* de chambre
housewarming [ˈhaʊsˌwɔrmɪŋ] *n* **:** pendaison *f* de crémaillère
housewife [ˈhaʊsˌwaɪf] *n, pl* **-wives :** femme *f* au foyer, ménagère *f*
housework [ˈhaʊsˌwərk] *n* **:** travaux *mpl* ménagers
housing [ˈhaʊzɪŋ] *n* **1** LODGING **:** logement *m* **2** CASING **:** boîtier *m*
hove → **heave**[1]
hovel [ˈhʌvəl, ˈhɑ-] *n* **:** bicoque *f*, baraque *f*, masure *f*, taudis *m*
hover [ˈhʌvər] *vi* **1 :** planer, voltiger **2** *or* **to hover about :** rôder
how[1] [ˈhaʊ] *adv* **1 :** comment <how are you? : comment allez-vous?> <how do you spell it? : comment ça s'écrit?> <I know how to do it : je sais comment faire> **2** (*referring to degree or extent*) <how old are you? : quel âge as-tu?> <how tall is he? : combien mesure-t-il?> **3** (*used in exclamations*) **:** comme, que <how beautiful it is! : comme c'est beau!> **4 how about . . . ? :** que dirais-tu de . . . ? **5 how come** WHY **:** comment, pourquoi
how[2] *conj* **:** comment <I asked them how they were : je leur ai demandé comment ils allaient>
however[1] [haʊˈɛvər] *adv* **1 :** cependant, toutefois, pourtant **2 :** comme <however you want : comme tu veux> **3 :** si . . . que, quelque . . . que <however important it is : si important que ce soit>
however[2] *conj* **:** de quelque manière que <I will help you however I can : je vais t'aider de quelque manière que ce soit>
howl[1] [ˈhaʊl] *vi* **:** hurler
howl[2] *n* **:** hurlement *m*
hub [ˈhʌb] *n* **1** CENTER **:** centre *m*, pivot *m* **2 :** moyeu *m* (d'une roue)
hubbub [ˈhʌˌbʌb] *n* **:** vacarme *m*, brouhaha *m*
hubcap [ˈhʌbˌkæp] *n* **:** enjoliveur *m*
huckleberry [ˈhʌkəlˈbɛri] *n, pl* **-ries :** myrtille *f France*, bleuet *m Can*
huckster [ˈhʌkstər] *n* PEDDLER **:** camelot *m;* colporteur *m*, -teuse *f*
huddle[1] [ˈhʌdəl] *vi* **-dled; -dling 1 :** se blottir **2** *or* **to huddle together :** se serrer, se blottir les uns contre les autres
huddle[2] *n* **:** (petit) groupe *m* <to go into a huddle : se réunir en petit comité>
hue [ˈhjuː] *n* **:** couleur *f*, teinte *f*
huff [ˈhʌf] *n* **to be in a huff :** être fâché, être vexé
huffy [ˈhʌfi] *adj* **huffier; -est 1** IRRITATED **:** fâché, vexé **2** TOUCHY **:** susceptible
hug[1] [ˈhʌg] *vt* **hugged; hugging 1** EMBRACE **:** serrer dans ses bras, étreindre **2 :** serrer, longer <the ship was hugging the coast : le navire serrait la côte>
hug[2] *n* **:** étreinte *f*
huge [ˈhjuːdʒ] *adj* **huger; hugest :** énorme, immense — **hugely** *adv*
hulk [ˈhʌlk] *n* **1 :** mastodonte *m* (homme) **2 :** épave *f* (d'un navire)

hulking [ˈhʌlkɪŋ] *adj* : énorme, massif
hull[1] [ˈhʌl] *vt* SHELL, SHUCK : écosser (des pois), écaler (des noix), décortiquer (du grain, des noix, etc.)
hull[2] *n* **1** : cosse *f* (de pois), écale *f* (d'une noix) **2** : coque *f* (d'un navire ou d'un avion)
hullabaloo [ˈhʌləbəˌluː] *n, pl* **-loos** : raffut *m fam,* boucan *m fam*
hullo *Brit* → **hello**
hum[1] [ˈhʌm] *v* **hummed; humming** *vi* **1** BUZZ, DRONE : bourdonner **2** BUSTLE : grouiller — *vt* : fredonner, chantonner
hum[2] *n* : bourdonnement *m*
human[1] [ˈhjuːmən, ˈjuː-] *adj* **1** : humain <the human race : le genre humain> **2** : de la personne <human rights : droits de la personne>
human[2] *n* : humain *m,* être *m* humain
humane [hjuːˈmeɪn, juː-] *adj* : humain — **humanely** *adv*
humanism [ˈhjuːməˌnɪzəm, ˈjuː-] *n* : humanisme *m*
humanist[1] [ˈhjuːmənɪst, ˈjuː-] *or* **humanistic** [ˌhjuːməˈnɪstɪk, ˈjuː-] *adj* : humaniste
humanist[2] *n* : humaniste *mf*
humanitarian[1] [hjuːˌmænəˈtɛriən, juː-] *adj* : humanitaire
humanitarian[2] *n* : humaniste *m*
humanity [hjuːˈmænəṭi, juː-] *n, pl* **-ties** : humanité *f*
humankind [ˈhjuːmənˈkaɪnd, ˈjuː-] *n* : humanité *f,* le genre humain
humanly [ˈhjuːmənli, ˈjuː-] *adv* : humainement
humble[1] [ˈhʌmbəl] *vt* **-bled; -bling 1** : humilier **2 to humble oneself** : s'humilier
humble[2] *adj* **humbler; -blest** : humble, modeste <of humble origin : d'origine modeste> — **humbly** [ˈhʌmbli] *adv*
humbug [ˈhʌmˌbʌg] *n* **1** : charlatan *m* (personne) **2** NONSENSE : balivernes *fpl*
humdrum [ˈhʌmˌdrʌm] *adj* : monotone, banal
humid [ˈhjuːməd, ˈjuː-] *adj* : humide
humidifier [hjuːˈmɪdəˌfaɪər, juː-] *n* : humidificateur *m*
humidify [hjuːˈmɪdəˌfaɪ, juː-] *vt* **-fied; -fying** : humidifier
humidity [hjuːˈmɪdəṭi, juː-] *n, pl* **-ties** : humidité *f*
humiliate [hjuːˈmɪliˌeɪt, juː-] *vt* **-ated; -ating** : humilier
humiliating [hjuːˈmɪliˌeɪtɪŋ, juː-] *adj* : humiliant
humiliation [hjuːˌmɪliˈeɪʃən, juː-] *n* : humiliation *f*
humility [hjuːˈmɪləṭi, juː-] *n* : humilité *f*
hummingbird [ˈhʌmɪŋˌbərd] *n* : oiseau-mouche *m*
hummock [ˈhʌmək] *n* : monticule *m*
humor[1] *or Brit* **humour** [ˈhjuːmər, ˈjuː-] *vt* : faire plaisir à, ménager
humor[2] *or Brit* **humour** *n* **1** MOOD : humeur *f* **2** WIT : humour *m*
humorist [ˈhjuːmərɪst, ˈjuː-] *n* : humoriste *mf*
humorless *or Brit* **humourless** [ˈhjuːmərləs, ˈjuː-] *adj* : qui manque d'humour
humorous [ˈhjuːmərəs, ˈjuː-] *adj* : plein d'humour, drôle
humorously [ˈhjuːmərəsli, ˈjuː-] *adv* : avec humour
humour *Brit* → **humor**
hump [ˈhʌmp] *n* : bosse *f*
humpback [ˈhʌmpˌbæk] *n* : bosse *f*
humpbacked [ˈhʌmpˌbækt] *adj* : bossu
humus [ˈhjuːməs, ˈjuː-] *n* : humus *m*
hunch[1] [ˈhʌntʃ] *vt* **to hunch one's shoulders** : rentrer les épaules — *vi or* **to hunch over** : se pencher
hunch[2] *n* : pressentiment *m,* intuition *f*
hunchback [ˈhʌntʃˌbæk] *n* **1** : bosse *f* (sur le dos d'une personne) **2** : bossu *m,* -sue *f* (personne)
hunchbacked [ˈhʌntʃˌbækt] *adj* : bossu
hundred[1] [ˈhʌndrəd] *adj* : cent
hundred[2] *n, pl* **-dreds** *or* **-dred** : cent *m*
hundredth[1] [ˈhʌndrədθ] *adj* : centième
hundredth[2] *n* **1** : centième *mf* (dans une série) **2** : centième *m* (en mathématiques)
hung → **hang**[1]
Hungarian[1] [hʌŋˈgæriən] *adj* : hongrois
Hungarian[2] *n* **1** : Hongrois *m,* -groise *f* **2** : hongrois *m* (langue)
hunger[1] [ˈhʌŋgər] *vi* : avoir faim <to hunger for : avoir faim de, avoir envie de>
hunger[2] *n* **1** : faim *f* **2** CRAVING : désir *m,* envie *f*
hungrily [ˈhʌŋgrəli] *adv* : avidement, voracement
hungry [ˈhʌŋgri] *adj* **hungrier; -est 1** : avide <hungry for affection : avide d'affection> **2 to be hungry** : avoir faim
hunk [ˈhʌŋk] *n* : gros morceau *m*
hunt[1] [ˈhʌnt] *vt* **1** : chasser <to hunt buffalo : chasser le bison> **2** *or* **to hunt for** PURSUE, SEEK : rechercher, chercher, poursuivre
hunt[2] *n* **1** : chasse *f* (sport) **2** SEARCH : recherche *f*
hunter [ˈhʌntər] *n* : chasseur *m,* -seuse *f*
hurdle[1] [ˈhərdəl] *vt* **-dled; -dling** : franchir, sauter
hurdle[2] *n* **1** : haie *f* (aux sports) **2** OBSTACLE : obstacle *m*
hurl [ˈhərl] *vt* : lancer, jeter
hurrah [hʊˈrɑ, -ˈrɔ] *interj* : hourra!
hurricane [ˈhərəˌkeɪn] *n* : ouragan *m*
hurriedly [ˈhərədli] *adv* : à la hâte, précipitamment
hurry[1] [ˈhəri] *v* **-ried; -rying** *vt* : presser, bousculer, brusquer — *vi* : se presser, se dépêcher, se hâter <hurry up! : dépêche-toi!>

hurry[2] *n* : hâte *f,* empressement *m*

hurt[1] ['hərt] *v* **hurt; hurting** *vt* **1** INJURE : faire mal à, blesser <I hurt my thumb : je me suis fait mal au pouce> **2** OFFEND : blesser, offenser — *vi* : faire mal <my foot hurts : mon pied me fait mal> <my throat hurts : j'ai mal à la gorge>

hurt[2] *n* **1** INJURY, PAIN : blessure *f,* mal *m* **2** DISTRESS : peine *f*

hurtful ['hərtfəl] *adj* : blessant, pénible

hurtle ['hərt̬əl] *vi* **-tled; -tling** : aller à toute vitesse

husband[1] ['hʌzbənd] *vt* : ménager, économiser

husband[2] *n* : mari *m,* époux *m*

husbandry ['hʌzbəndri] *n* **1** THRIFT : économie *f* **2** AGRICULTURE : agriculture *f* <animal husbandry : l'élevage>

hush[1] ['hʌʃ] *vt* **1** *or* **to hush up** : faire taire **2** CALM, SOOTHE : calmer, apaiser <to hush a baby : appaiser un bébé> — *vi* **1** : se taire **2 hush!** : chut!

hush[2] *n* SILENCE : silence *f*

husk[1] ['hʌsk] *vt* : écaler (des noix), éplucher (des légumes), vanner (du blé)

husk[2] *n* : écale *f* (de noix), cosse *f* (de pois, etc.), enveloppe *f* (de maïs)

huskily ['hʌskəli] *adv* : d'une voix enrouée

husky[1] ['hʌski] *adj* **huskier; -est 1** HOARSE : enroué **2** BURLY : costaud *fam*

husky[2] *n, pl* **-kies** : chien *m* esquimau

hustle[1] ['həsəl] *v* **-tled; -tling** *vt* : presser, pousser, bousculer — *vi* HURRY : se dépêcher, se presser

hustle[2] *n* BUSTLE : grande activité *f*

hut ['hʌt] *n* : hutte *f,* cabane *f,* bicoque *f*

hutch ['hʌtʃ] *n* **1** CUPBOARD : dressoir *m* **2** : cage *f* <rabbit hutch : cage à lapin>

hyacinth ['haɪə,sɪnθ] *n* : jacinthe *f*

hybrid[1] ['haɪbrɪd] *adj* : hybride

hybrid[2] *n* : hybride *m*

hydrant ['haɪdrənt] *n* **1** : prise *f* d'eau **2** *or* **fire hydrant** : bouche *f* d'incendie, borne-fontaine *f Can*

hydraulic [haɪ'drɔlɪk] *adj* : hydraulique — **hydraulically** [-lɪkli] *adv*

hydrocarbon [,haɪdro'kɑrbən] *n* : hydrocarbure *m*

hydrochloric acid [,haɪdro'klorɪk] *n* : acide *m* chlorhydrique

hydroelectric [,haɪdroɪ'lɛktrɪk] *adj* : hydroélectrique

hydrogen ['haɪdrədʒən] *n* : hydrogène *m*

hydrogen bomb *n* : bombe *f* à hydrogène

hydrogen peroxide *n* : eau *f* oxygénée

hydrophobia [,haɪdrə'fo:biə] *n* : hydrophobie *f*

hydroplane ['haɪdrə,pleɪn] *n* : hydroglisseur *m*

hyena [haɪ'i:nə] *n* : hyène *f*

hygiene ['haɪ,dʒi:n] *n* : hygiène *f*

hygienic [haɪ'dʒɛnɪk, -'dʒi:-; ,haɪdʒi:'ɛnɪk] *adj* : hygiénique — **hygienically** [-nɪkli] *adv*

hygienist [haɪ'dʒi:nɪst, -'dʒɛ:-, 'haɪ,dʒi:-] *n* : hygiéniste *mf*

hygrometer [haɪ'grɑmət̬ər] *n* : hygromètre *m*

hymn ['hɪm] *n* : hymne *m,* cantique *m*

hymnal ['hɪmnəl] *n* : livre *m* d'hymnes

hype ['haɪp] *n* : battage *m* publicitaire

hyperactive [,haɪpər'æktɪv] *adj* : hyperactif

hyperbole [haɪ'pərbəli] *n* : hyperbole *f*

hypercritical [,haɪpər'krɪt̬əkəl] *adj* : excessivement critique

hypersensitive [,haɪpər'sɛntsətɪv] *adj* : hypersensible

hypertension [,haɪpər'tɛntʃən] *n* : hypertension *f*

hyphen *n* : trait *m* d'union

hyphenate ['haɪfən,eɪt] *vt* **-ated; -ating** : mettre un trait d'union à

hypnosis [hɪp'no:sɪs] *n, pl* **-noses** [-,si:z] : hypnose *f*

hypnotic [hɪp'nɑt̬ɪk] *adj* : hypnotique

hypnotism ['hɪpnə,tɪzəm] *n* : hypnotisme *m*

hypnotize ['hɪpnə,taɪz] *vt* **-tized; -tizing** : hypnotiser

hypochondria [,haɪpə'kɑndriə] *n* : hypocondrie *f*

hypochondriac [,haɪpə'kɑndri,æk] *n* : hypocondriaque *mf*

hypocrisy [hɪ'pɑkrəsi] *n, pl* **-sies** : hypocrisie *f*

hypocrite ['hɪpə,krɪt] *n* : hypocrite *mf*

hypocritical [,hɪpə'krɪt̬ɪkəl] *adj* : hypocrite — **hypocritically** [-t̬ɪkli] *adv*

hypodermic[1] [,haɪpə'dərmɪk] *adj* : hypodermique

hypodermic[2] *n* : piqûre *f* hypodermique

hypotenuse [haɪ'pɑtən,u:s, -,u:z, -ju:s, -ju:z] *n* : hypoténuse *f*

hypothesis [haɪ'pɑθəsɪs] *n, pl* **-eses** [-,si:z] : hypothèse *f*

hypothetical [,haɪpə'θɛt̬ɪkəl] *adj* : hypothétique — **hypothetically** [-t̬ɪkli] *adv*

hysterectomy [,hɪstə'rɛktəmi] *n, pl* **-mies** : hystérectomie *f*

hysteria [hɪs'tɛriə, -'tɪr-] *n* : hystérie *f*

hysterical [hɪs'tɛrɪkəl] *adj* : hystérique — **hysterically** [-ɪkli] *adv*

hysterics [hɪs'tɛrɪks] *ns & pl* : crise *f* (de nerfs, de rire, etc.)

I

i ['aɪ] *n, pl* **i's** *or* **is** ['aɪz] : i *m,* neuvième lettre de l'alphabet
I ['aɪ] *pron* : je
ibis ['aɪbəs] *n, pl* **ibis** *or* **ibises** : ibis *m*
ice[1] ['aɪs] *v* **iced; icing** *vt* **1** FREEZE : glacer **2** CHILL : rafraîchir **3** FROST : glacer (un gâteau, etc.) — *vi or* **to ice up** : se givrer
ice[2] *n* **1** : glace *f* **2** SHERBET : sorbet *m*
ice age *n* : période *f* glacière
iceberg ['aɪs,bərg] *n* : iceberg *m*
icebox ['aɪs,bɑks] → **refrigerator**
icebreaker ['aɪs,breɪkər] *n* : brise-glace *m*
ice cap *n* : calotte *f* glacière
ice-cold ['aɪs'ko:ld] *adj* : glacé
ice cream *n* : glace *f France,* crème *f* glacée *Can*
ice floe → **floe**
Icelander ['aɪs,lændər, -lən-] *n* : Islandais *m,* -daise *f*
Icelandic[1] [aɪs'lændɪk] *adj* : islandais
Icelandic[2] *n* : islandais *m* (langue)
ice–skate ['aɪs,skeɪt] *vi* **-skated; -skating** : patiner
ice skater *n* : patineur *m,* -neuse *f*
ichthyology [,ɪkθi'ɑlədʒi] *n* : ichtyologie *f*
icicle ['aɪ,sɪkəl] *n* : glaçon *m*
icily ['aɪsəli] *adv* : d'un ton glacial, d'un air glacial
icing ['aɪsɪŋ] *n* : glaçage *m,* crémage *m Can*
icon ['aɪ,kɑn, -kən] *n* : icône *f*
iconoclasm [aɪ'kɑnə,klæzəm] *n* : iconoclasme *m*
iconoclast [aɪ'kɑnə,klæst] *n* : iconoclaste *mf*
icy ['aɪsi] *adj* **icier; -est 1** FREEZING : glacial, glacé **2** : verglacé <an icy road : une route verglacée> **3** FROSTY : glacial <an icy smile : un sourire glacial>
id ['ɪd] *n* : ça *m*
I'd ['aɪd] (*contraction of* **I should** *or* **I would**) → **should, would**
idea [aɪ'di:ə] *n* : idée *f*
ideal[1] [aɪ'di:əl] *adj* : idéal
ideal[2] *n* : idéal *m*
idealism [aɪ'di:ə,lɪzəm] *n* : idéalisme *m*
idealist [aɪ'di:ə,lɪst] *n* : idéaliste *mf*
idealistic [aɪ,di:ə'lɪstɪk] *adj* : idéaliste
idealization [aɪ,di:ələ'zeɪʃən] *n* : idéalisation *f*
idealize [aɪ'di:ə,laɪz] *vt* **-ized; -izing** : idéaliser
ideally [aɪ'di:əli] *adv* : idéalement
identical [aɪ'dɛntɪkəl] *adj* : identique — **identically** [-tɪkli] *adv*
identifiable [aɪ,dɛntə'faɪəbəl] *adj* : identifiable
identification [aɪ,dɛntəfə'keɪʃən] *n* **1** : identification *f* **2** *or* **identification card** : carte *f* d'identité
identify [aɪ'dɛntə,faɪ] *v* **-fied; -fying** *vt* : identifier — *vi* **to identify with** : s'identifier à
identity [aɪ'dɛntət̬i] *n, pl* **-ties** : identité *f*
ideological [,aɪdiə'lɑdʒɪkəl, ,ɪ-] *adj* : idéologique
ideologically [,aɪdiə'lɑdʒɪkli, ,ɪ-] *adv* : du point de vue idéologique
ideology [,aɪdi'ɑlədʒi, ,ɪ-] *n, pl* **-gies** : idéologie *f*
idiocy ['ɪdiəsi] *n, pl* **-cies 1** : idiotie *f* (en médecine) **2** NONSENSE : idiotie *f,* stupidité *f*
idiom ['ɪdiəm] *n* **1** LANGUAGE : idiome *m,* langue *f* **2** EXPRESSION : idiotisme *m,* expression *f* idiomatique
idiomatic [,ɪdiə'mæt̬ɪk] *adj* : idiomatique
idiosyncrasy [,ɪdio'sɪŋkrəsi] *n, pl* **-sies** : particularité *f,* idiosyncrasie *f*
idiosyncratic [,ɪdiosɪn'kræt̬ɪk] *adj* : particulier, caractéristique
idiot ['ɪdiət] *n* : idiot *m,* -diote *f*
idiotic [,ɪdi'ɑt̬ɪk] *adj* : idiot — **idiotically** [-t̬ɪkli] *adv*
idle[1] ['aɪdəl] *v* **idled; idling** *vi* **1** *or* **to idle about** : fainéanter, traîner **2** : tourner au ralenti (se dit d'un moteur) — *vt or* **to idle away** : gaspiller (son temps)
idle[2] *adj* **idler; idlest 1** VAIN : vain, inutile <idle curiosity : pure curiosité> **2** INACTIVE : oisif, désœuvré **3** LAZY : paresseux
idleness ['aɪdəlnəs] *n* : oisiveté *f,* désœuvrement *m*
idler ['aɪdələr] *n* : paresseux *m,* -seuse *f*
idly ['adəli] *adv* **1** LAZILY : paresseusement **2** ABSENTMINDEDLY : d'un air distrait
idol ['aɪdəl] *n* : idole *f*
idolatry [aɪ'dɑlətri] *n, pl* **-tries** : idolâtrie *f*
idolization [,aɪdələ'zeɪʃən] *n* : idolâtrie *f*
idolize ['aɪdəl,aɪz] *vt* **-ized; izing** : idolâtrer
idyll ['aɪdəl] *n* : idylle *f*
idyllic [aɪ'dɪlɪk] *adj* : idyllique
if ['ɪf] *conj* **1** : si <I would do it if I could : je le ferais si je pouvais> <as if : comme si> <if I were you : si j'étais vous> **2** WHETHER : si <do you know if they are here? : savez-vous s'ils sont ici?> **3** THOUGH : bien que, même que <it's pretty, if somewhat old-fashioned : c'est joli, bien qu'un peu démodé>
igloo ['ɪ,glu:] *n, pl* **-loos** : igloo *m*
ignite [ɪg'naɪt] *v* **-nited; -niting** *vt* : mettre le feu à, enflammer — *vi* : prendre feu, s'enflammer
ignition [ɪg'nɪʃən] *n* **1** : allumage *m* **2** *or* **ignition switch** : contact *m*

ignoble [ɪg'no:bəl] *adj* : infâme

ignominious [ˌɪgnə'mɪniəs] *adj* : ignominieux — **ignominiously** *adv*

ignominy ['ɪgnəˌmɪni] *n, pl* **-nies** : ignominie *f*

ignoramus [ˌɪgnə'reɪməs] *n* : ignare *mf*

ignorance ['ɪgnərən*t*s] *n* : ignorance *f*

ignorant ['ɪgnərənt] *adj* : ignorant

ignorantly ['ɪgnərəntli] *adv* : d'une manière grossière <to speak ignorantly : parler par ignorance>

ignore [ɪg'nor] *vt* **-nored; -noring** : ignorer, ne pas tenir compte de, ne pas faire attention à

iguana [ɪ'gwɑnə] *n* : iguane *m*

ilk ['ɪlk] *n* : espèce *f*, acabit *m*

ill[1] ['ɪl] *adv* **worse** ['wərs]; **worst** ['wərst] : mal <ill prepared : mal préparé> <to speak ill of : dire du mal de>

ill[2] *adj* **worse; worst 1** SICK : malade <to be taken ill : tomber malade> **2** BAD : mauvais <ill humor : mauvaise humeur>

ill[3] *n* : mal *m*

I'll ['aɪl] (*contraction of* **I shall** *or* **I will**) → **shall, will**

illegal [ɪl'li:gəl] *adj* : illégal — **illegally** *adv*

illegality [ɪli'gæləţi] *n* : illégalité *f*

illegible [ɪl'lɛdʒəbəl] *adj* : illisible — **illegibly** [-bli] *adv*

illegitimacy [ˌɪlɪ'dʒɪţəməsi] *n* : illégitimité *f*

illegitimate [ˌɪlɪ'dʒɪţəmət] *adj* : illégitime — **illegitimately** *adv*

illicit [ɪl'lɪsət] *adj* : illicite — **illicitly** *adv*

illimitable [ɪl'lɪməţəbəl] *adj* : illimité

illiteracy [ɪl'lɪţərəsi] *n, pl* **-cies** : analphabétisme *m*

illiterate[1] [ɪl'lɪţərət] *adj* **1** : analphabète, illettré **2** IGNORANT : ignorant, sans éducation

illiterate[2] *n* : analphabète *mf*

ill–mannered [ˌɪl'mænərd] *adj* : impoli, grossier

ill–natured [ˌɪl'neɪtʃərd] *adj* : désagréable — **ill–naturedly** *adv*

illness ['ɪlnəs] *n* : maladie *f*

illogical [ɪl'lɑdʒɪkəl] *adj* : illogique — **illogically** [-kli] *adv*

ill–tempered [ˌɪl'tɛmpərd] → **ill–natured**

ill–treat [ˌɪl'tri:t] *vt* : maltraiter

ill–treatment [ˌɪl'tri:tmənt] *n* : mauvais traitement *m*

illuminate [ɪ'lu:məˌneɪt] *vt* **-nated; -nating** : éclairer, illuminer

illumination [ɪˌlu:mə'neɪʃən] *n* : éclairage *m*, illumination *f*

ill–use ['ɪl'ju:z] → **ill–treat**

illusion [ɪ'lu:ʒən] *n* : illusion *f*

illusory [ɪ'lu:səri, -zəri] *adj* : illusoire

illustrate ['ɪləsˌtreɪt] *v* **-trated; -trating** : illustrer

illustration [ˌɪləs'treɪʃən] *n* : illustration *f*

illustrative [ɪ'lʌstrəţɪv, 'ɪləˌstreɪţɪv] *adj* : explicatif

illustrator ['ɪləˌstreɪţər] *n* : illustrateur *m*, -trice *f*

illustrious [ɪ'lʌstriəs] *adj* RENOWNED : illustre

illustriousness [ɪ'lʌstriəsnəs] *n* RENOWN : renommée *f*

ill will *n* : malveillance *f*, rancune *f*

I'm ['aɪm] (*contraction of* **I am**) → **be**

image ['ɪmɪdʒ] *n* : image *f*

imagery ['ɪmɪdʒri] *n, pl* **-eries 1** : images *fpl* (en littérature, etc.) **2** PICTURES : imagerie *f*

imaginable [ɪ'mædʒənəbəl] *adj* : imaginable

imaginary [ɪ'mædʒəˌnɛri] *adj* : imaginaire

imagination [ɪ'mædʒə'neɪʃən] *n* : imagination *f*

imaginative [ɪ'mædʒɪnəţɪv] *adj* : imaginatif, plein d'imagination

imaginatively [ɪ'mædʒɪnəţɪvli] *adv* : avec imagination

imagine [ɪ'mædʒən] *vt* **-ined; -ining 1** : imaginer, se représenter (une scène, etc.) **2** SUPPOSE : s'imaginer, supposer

imbalance [ɪm'bælən*t*s] *n* : déséquilibre *m*

imbecile[1] ['ɪmbəsəl, -ˌsɪl] *or* **imbecilic** [ˌɪmbə'sɪlɪk] *adj* : imbécile

imbecile[2] *n* : imbécile *mf*

imbecility [ˌɪmbə'sɪləţi] *n, pl* **-ties** : imbécillité *f*

imbibe [ɪm'baɪb] *v* **-bibed; -bibing** *vt* ABSORB : assimiler, absorber — *vi* DRINK : boire

imbue [ɪm'bju:] *vt* **-bued; -buing 1** : imprégner **2 to be imbued with** : être imbu de

imitate ['ɪməˌteɪt] *vt* **-tated; -tating** : imiter

imitation[1] [ˌɪmə'teɪʃən] *adj* : artificiel, faux

imitation[2] *n* : imitation *f*

imitative ['ɪməˌteɪţɪv] *adj* : imitatif, imitateur

imitator ['ɪməˌteɪţər] *n* : imitateur *m*, -trice *f*

immaculate [ɪ'mækjələt] *adj* **1** PURE : immaculé **2** CLEAN, IMPECCABLE : impeccable

immaculately [ɪ'mækjələtli] *adv* : impeccablement

immaterial [ˌɪmə'tɪriəl] *adj* : sans importance

immature [ˌɪmə'tʃʊr, -'tjʊr, -'tʊr] *adj* : immature

immaturity [ˌɪmə'tʃʊrəţi, -'tjʊr-, -'tʊr-] *n, pl* **-ties** : immaturité *f*

immeasurable [ɪ'mɛʒərəbəl] *adj* : incommensurable — **immeasurably** [-bli] *adv*

immediate [ɪ'mi:diət] *adj* **1** INSTANT, URGENT : immédiat, urgent **2** NEARBY : proche, immédiat <our immediate neighbors : nos voisins

immédiats> **3** DIRECT : direct, immédiat <the immediate cause of her death : la cause immédiate de sa mort>

immediately [ɪ'mi:diətli] *adv* **1** INSTANTLY : immédiatement **2** DIRECTLY, JUST : juste <immediately after : juste après>

immemorial [ˌɪmə'moriəl] *adj* : immémorial

immense [ɪ'mɛnts] *adj* : immense

immensely [ɪ'mɛntsli] *adv* : immensément, énormément

immensity [ɪ'mɛntsət̬i] *n, pl* **-ties** : immensité *f*

immerse [ɪ'mərs] *vt* **-mersed; -mersing** **1** : plonger, immerger **2 to immerse oneself in** : se plonger dans

immersion [ɪ'mərʒən] *n* : immersion *f*

immigrant ['ɪmɪgrənt] *n* : immigrant *m,* -grante *f*

immigrate ['ɪməˌgreɪt] *vi* **-grated; -grating** : immigrer

immigration [ˌɪmə'greɪʃən] *n* : immigration *f*

imminence ['ɪmənənts] *n* : imminence *f*

imminent ['ɪmənənt] *adj* : imminent

immobile [ɪ'mo:bəl] *adj* **1** FIXED, IMMOVABLE : fixe, impossible à déplacer **2** MOTIONLESS : immobile

immobility [ˌɪmo'bɪlət̬i] *n* : immobilité *f*

immobilize [ɪ'mo:bəˌlaɪz] *vt* **-ized; -izing** : immobiliser

immoderate [ɪ'mɑdərət] *adj* : immodéré, excessif **— immoderately** *adv*

immodest [ɪ'mɑdəst] *adj* **1** VAIN : vaniteux **2** INDECENT : impudique, indécent

immodestly [ɪ'mɑdəstli] *adv* : sans modestie, impudiquement

immodesty [ɪ'mɑdəsti] *n* **1** VANITY : vanité *f* **2** INDECENCY : indécence *f,* impudeur *f*

immoral [ɪ'mɔrəl] *adj* : immoral **— immorally** *adv*

immorality [ˌɪmɔ'rælət̬i, ˌɪmə-] *n* : immoralité *f*

immortal[1] [ɪ'mɔrt̬əl] *adj* : immortel

immortal[2] *n* : immortel *m,* -telle *f*

immortality [ˌɪˌmɔr'tælət̬i] *n* : immortalité *f*

immortalize [ɪ'mɔrt̬əlˌaɪz] *vt* **-ized; -izing** : immortaliser

immovable [ɪ'mu:vəbəl] *adj* **1** STATIONARY : fixe **2** UNYIELDING : inébranlable

immune [ɪ'mju:n] *adj* **1** : immunisé <immune against measles : immunisé contre la rougeole> **2** EXEMPT : exempt

immune system *n* : système *m* immunitaire

immunity [ɪ'mju:nət̬i] *n, pl* **-ties** : immunité *f*

immunization [ˌɪmjʊnə'zeɪʃən] *n* : immunisation *f*

immunize ['ɪmjʊˌnaɪz] *vt* **-nized; -nizing** : immuniser

immunology [ˌɪmjʊ'nɑlədʒi] *n* : immunologie *f*

immutable [ɪ'mju:t̬əbəl] *adj* : immuable **— immutably** [-bli] *adv*

imp ['ɪmp] *n* **1** DEMON : lutin *m,* diablotin *m* **2** RASCAL : polisson *m,* -sonne *f*

impact[1] [ɪm'pækt] *vt* **1** STRIKE : frapper, percuter **2** AFFECT : avoir un impact sur, affecter **—** *vi* **to impact on** : avoir un impact sur

impact[2] ['ɪmˌpækt] *n* : impact *m*

impacted [ɪm'pæktəd] *adj* : inclus <impacted tooth : dent incluse>

impair [ɪm'pær] *vt* **1** DIMINISH, WEAKEN : diminuer, affaiblir, affecter **2** DAMAGE : détériorer (la santé, etc.)

impairment [ɪm'pærmənt] *n* : affaiblissement *m,* diminution *f* <visual impairment : troubles visuels>

impala [ɪm'pɑlə, -'pæ-] *n, pl* **impalas** *or* **impala** : impala *m*

impale [ɪm'peɪl] *vt* **-paled; -paling** : empaler

impanel [ɪm'pænəl] *vt* **-eled** *or* **-elled; -eling** *or* **-elling** : constituer (un jury, etc.)

impart [ɪm'pɑrt] *vt* **1** COMMUNICATE : communiquer **2** BESTOW, CONVEY : donner, transmettre

impartial [ɪm'pɑrʃəl] *adj* : impartial **— impartially** *adv*

impartiality [ɪmˌpɑrʃi'ælət̬i] *n* : impartialité *f*

impassable [ɪm'pæsəbəl] *adj* : impraticable, infranchissable

impasse ['ɪmˌpæs] *n* : impasse *f*

impassioned [ɪm'pæʃənd] *adj* : passionné

impassive [ɪm'pæsɪv] *adj* : impassible **— impassively** *adv*

impatience [ɪm'peɪʃənts] *n* : impatience *f*

impatient [ɪm'peɪʃənt] *adj* : impatient

impatiently [ɪm'peɪʃəntli] *adv* : impatiemment

impeach [ɪm'pi:tʃ] *vt* : destituer (un fonctionnaire du gouvernement)

impeachment [ɪm'pi:tʃmənt] *n* : destitution *f* (d'un fonctionnaire du gouvernement)

impeccable [ɪm'pɛkəbəl] *adj* : impeccable **— impeccably** [-bli] *adv*

impecunious [ˌɪmpɪ'kju:niəs] *adj* : impécunieux

impede [ɪm'pi:d] *vt* **-peded; -peding** : entraver, gêner

impediment [ɪm'pɛdəmənt] *n* **1** HINDRANCE : entrave *f,* obstacle *m* **2** *or* **speech impediment** : défaut *m* de l'élocution

impel [ɪm'pɛl] *vt* **-pelled; -pelling** **1** URGE : inciter **2** DRIVE : pousser

impend [ɪm'pɛnd] *vi* : être imminent

impending [ɪm'pɛndɪŋ] *adj* : imminent

impenetrable [ɪm'pɛnətrəbəl] *adj* : impénétrable
impenitent [ɪm'pɛnətənt] *adj* : impénitent
imperative[1] [ɪm'pɛrət̬ɪv] *adj* **1** AUTHORITATIVE : autoritaire **2** URGENT : impérieux, urgent — **imperatively** *adv*
imperative[2] *n* : impératif *m*
imperceptible [ˌɪmpər'sɛptəbəl] *adj* : imperceptible — **imperceptibly** [-bli] *adv*
imperfect[1] [ɪm'pərfɪkt] *adj* : imparfait — **imperfectly** *adv*
imperfect[2] *n or* **imperfect tense** : imparfait *m*
imperfection [ɪmˌpər'fɛkʃən] *n* : imperfection *f*
imperial [ɪm'pɪriəl] *adj* **1** SOVEREIGN : impérial **2** IMPERIOUS : impérieux
imperialism [ɪm'pɪriəˌlɪzəm] *n* : impérialisme *m*
imperialist[1] [ɪm'pɪriəlɪst] *or* **imperialistic** [ɪmˌpɪriːə'lɪstɪk] *adj* : impérialiste
imperialist[2] *n* : impérialiste *mf*
imperil [ɪm'pɛrəl] *vt* **-iled** *or* **-illed; -iling** *or* **-illing** : mettre en péril
imperious [ɪm'pɪriəs] *adj* : impérieux — **imperiously** *adv*
imperishable [ɪm'pɛrɪʃəbəl] *adj* : impérissable
impermanent [ɪm'pərmənənt] *adj* : éphémère, fugace
impermeable [ɪm'pərmiəbəl] *adj* : imperméable
impersonal [ɪm'pərsənəl] *adj* : impersonnel — **impersonally** *adv*
impersonate [ɪm'pərsənˌeɪt] *vt* **-ated; -ating** : se faire passer pour
impersonation [ɪmˌpərsən'eɪʃən] *n* : imitation *f*
impersonator [ɪm'pərsənˌeɪt̬ər] *n* : imitateur *m*, -trice *f*
impertinence [ɪm'pərtənənts] *n* : impertinence *f*
impertinent [ɪm'pərtənənt] *adj* : impertinent
impertinently [ɪm'pərtənəntli] *adv* : avec impertinence
imperturbable [ˌɪmpər'tərbəbəl] *adj* : imperturbable
impervious [ɪm'pərviəs] *adj* **1** IMPENETRABLE : imperméable **2** UNAFFECTED : indifférent
impetuosity [ɪmˌpɛtʃʊ'ɑsət̬i] *n, pl* **-ties** : impétuosité *f*
impetuous [ɪm'pɛtʃʊəs] *adj* : impétueux — **impetuously** *adv*
impetus ['ɪmpət̬əs] *n* : impulsion *f*
impiety [ɪm'paɪət̬i] *n, pl* **-ties** : impiété *f*
impinge [ɪm'pɪndʒ] *vi* **-pinged; -pinging 1 to impinge on** AFFECT : affecter **2 to impinge on** VIOLATE : empiéter sur
impious ['ɪmpiəs, ɪm'paɪəs] *adj* : impie
impish ['ɪmpɪʃ] *adj* : espiègle
impishly ['ɪmpɪʃli] *adv* : en espiègle
impishness ['ɪmpɪʃnəs] *n* : espièglerie *f*
implacable [ɪm'plækəbəl] *adj* : implacable — **implacably** [-bli] *adv*
implant[1] [ɪm'plænt] *vt* **1** INSERT : implanter **2** INSTILL : inculquer
implant[2] ['ɪmˌplænt] *n* : implant *m*
implantation [ˌɪmˌplæn'teɪʃən] *n* : implantation *f*
implausibility [ɪmˌplɔzə'bɪlət̬i] *n, pl* **-ties** : invraisemblance *f*
implausible [ɪm'plɔzəbəl] *adj* : peu plausible, invraisemblable
implement[1] ['ɪmpləˌmɛnt] *vt* : mettre en œuvre, exécuter
implement[2] ['ɪmpləmənt] *n* : outil *m*, instrument *m*
implementation [ˌɪmpləmən'teɪʃən] *n* : mise *f* en œuvre, exécution *f*
implicate ['ɪmpləˌkeɪt] *vt* **-cated; -cating** : impliquer
implication [ˌɪmplə'keɪʃən] *n* **1** CONSEQUENCE : implication *f* **2** INFERENCE : insinuation *f*
implicit [ɪm'plɪsət] *adj* **1** IMPLIED, POTENTIAL : implicite **2** UNQUESTIONING : absolu, total
implicitly [ɪm'plɪsətli] *adv* **1** TACITLY : implicitement **2** ABSOLUTELY : absolument
implode [ɪm'ploːd] *vi* **-ploded; -ploding** : imploser
implosion [ɪm'ploːʒən] *n* : implosion *f*
implore [ɪm'plor] *vt* **-plored; -ploring** : implorer, supplier
imply [ɪm'plaɪ] *vt* **-plied; -plying 1** MEAN : impliquer, laisser entendre **2** INDICATE : suggérer, impliquer <her answer implies a true understanding : sa réponse suggère une vraie compréhension>
impolite [ˌɪmpə'laɪt] *adj* : impoli — **impolitely** *adv*
impoliteness [ˌɪmpə'laɪtnəs] *n* : impolitesse *f*
impolitic [ɪm'pɑləˌtɪk] *adj* : peu politique, mal avisé
imponderable [ɪm'pɑndərəbəl] *adj* : impondérable
import[1] [ɪm'port] *vt* **1** : importer (des marchandises) **2** SIGNIFY : signifier
import[2] ['ɪmˌport] *n* **1** IMPORTANCE, MEANING : signification *f*, importance *f* **2** IMPORTATION : importation *f*
importance [ɪm'pɔrtənts] *n* : importance *f*
important [ɪm'pɔrtənt] *adj* : important
importantly [ɪm'pɔrtəntli] *adv* **1** : avec importance **2 more importantly** : ce qui est plus important
importation [ˌɪmˌpɔr'teɪʃən] *n* : importation *f*
importer [ɪm'port̬ər] *n* : importateur *m*, -trice *f*
importunate [ɪm'pɔrtʃənət] *adj* : importun
importune [ˌɪmpər'tuːn, -'tjuːn; ɪm'pɔrtʃən] *vt* **-tuned; -tuning** : importuner, harceler

impose [ɪm'po:z] *v* **-posed; -posing** *vt* : imposer, infliger <to impose a penalty : infliger une peine> — *vi* : s'imposer
imposing [ɪm'po:zɪŋ] *adj* : imposant, impressionnant
imposition [ˌɪmpə'zɪʃən] *n* : imposition *f*
impossibility [ɪmˌpɑsə'bɪləṭi] *n, pl* **-ties** : impossibilité *f*
impossible [ɪm'pɑsəbəl] *adj* : impossible
impossibly [ɪm'pɑsəbli] *adv* **1** : de façon impossible **2** UNBELIEVABLY : incroyablement, extrêmement
impostor *or* **imposter** [ɪm'pɑstər] *n* : imposteur *m*
imposture [ɪm'pɑstʃər] *n* : imposture *f*
impotence ['ɪmpətənts] *n* : impuissance *f*
impotency ['ɪmpətəntsi] → **impotence**
impotent ['ɪmpətənt] *adj* : impuissant
impound [ɪm'paʊnd] *vt* : saisir, confisquer
impoverish [ɪm'pɑvərɪʃ] *vt* : appauvrir
impoverishment [ɪm'pɑvərɪʃmənt] *n* : appauvrissement *m*
impracticable [ɪm'præktɪkəbəl] *adj* : impraticable, irréalisable
impractical [ɪm'præktɪkəl] *adj* : peu pratique, peu réaliste
imprecise [ˌɪmprɪ'saɪs] *adj* : imprécis
imprecisely [ˌɪmprɪ'saɪsli] *adv* : de manière imprécise
imprecision [ˌɪmprɪ'sɪʒən] *n* : imprécision *f*
impregnable [ɪm'prɛgnəbəl] *adj* : imprenable
impregnate [ɪm'prɛgˌneɪt] *vt* **-nated; -nating 1** FERTILIZE : féconder **2** SATURATE : imprégner
impregnation [ˌɪmˌprɛg'neɪʃən] *n* **1** FERTILIZATION : fécondation *f* **2** SATURATION : imprégnation *f*
impresario [ˌɪmprə'sɑriˌo, -'sær-] *n, pl* **-rios** : impresario *m*
impress [ɪm'prɛs] *vt* **1** IMPRINT : imprimer **2** AFFECT, INFLUENCE : faire impression sur, impressionner <he didn't impress me : il ne m'a pas impressionné> **3 to impress upon s.o.** : faire bien comprendre à qqn
impression [ɪm'prɛʃən] *n* **1** IMPRINT : marque *f*, empreinte *f*, impression *f* **2** IDEA, NOTION : idée *f*, impression *f* **3** PRINTING : tirage *m*
impressionable [ɪm'prɛʃənəbəl] *adj* : impressionnable
impressive [ɪm'prɛsɪv] *adj* : impressionnant
impressively [ɪm'prɛsɪvli] *adv* : remarquablement, de manière impressionnante
imprint[1] [ɪm'prɪnt, 'ɪmˌ-] *vt* : imprimer
imprint[2] ['ɪmˌprɪnt] *n* : empreinte *f*, marque *f*
imprison [ɪm'prɪzən] *vt* : emprisonner, mettre en prison
imprisonment [ɪm'prɪzənmənt] *n* : emprisonnement *m*
improbability [ɪmˌprɑbə'bɪləṭi] *n, pl* **-ties** : improbabilité *f*, invraisemblance *f*
improbable [ɪm'prɑbəbəl] *adj* : improbable, invraisemblable
impromptu[1] [ɪm'prɑmpˌtu:, -ˌtju:] *adv* : à l'impromptu
impromptu[2] *adj* : impromptu
improper [ɪm'prɑpər] *adj* **1** UNSEEMLY : malséant, inconvenant **2** INCORRECT : incorrect, erroné **3** INDECENT : indécent
improperly [ɪm'prɑpərli] *adv* **1** INCORRECTLY : incorrectement **2** INDECENTLY : indécemment
impropriety [ˌɪmprə'praɪəṭi] *n, pl* **-ties** : inconvenance *f*
improve [ɪm'pru:v] *v* **-proved; -proving** *vt* : améliorer, perfectionner — *vi* : s'améliorer, se perfectionner
improvement [ɪm'pru:vmənt] *n* : amélioration *f*
improvidence [ɪm'prɑvədənts] *n* : imprévoyance *f*
improvident [ɪm'prɑvədənt] *adj* : imprévoyant
improvisation [ɪmˌprɑvə'zeɪʃən, ˌɪmprəvə-] *n* : improvisation *f*
improvise ['ɪmprəˌvaɪz] *v* **-vised; -vising** : improviser
imprudence [ɪm'pru:dənts] *n* : imprudence *f*
imprudent [ɪm'pru:dənt] *adj* : imprudent
impudence ['ɪmpjədənts] *n* : impudence *f*, insolence *f*, effronterie *f*
impudent ['ɪmpjədənt] *adj* : insolent, impudent
impugn [ɪm'pju:n] *vt* : contester
impulse ['ɪmˌpʌls] *n* **1** : impulsion *f* **2 on ~** : sans réfléchir
impulsive [ɪm'pʌlsɪv] *adj* : impulsif — **impulsively** *adv*
impulsiveness [ɪm'pʌlsɪvnəs] *n* : impulsivité *f*
impunity [ɪm'pju:nəṭi] *n* **1** : impunité *f* **2 with ~** : impunément
impure [ɪm'pjʊr] *adj* : impur
impurity [ɪm'pjʊrəṭi] *n, pl* **-ties** : impureté *f*
impute [ɪm'pju:t] *vt* **-puted; -puting** ATTRIBUTE : imputer, attribuer
in[1] ['ɪn] *adv* **1** INSIDE : dedans, à l'intérieur <to come in : entrer> **2 to be in** : être là, être chez soi <is she in today? : est-elle là aujourd'hui?> **3 to be in** : être au pouvoir <the democrats are in : les démocrates sont au pouvoir> **4 to be in for** : aller avoir **5 to be in on** : être dans le coup
in[2] *adj* **1** INSIDE : intérieur <the in part : la partie intérieure> **2** FASHIONABLE : à la mode
in[3] *prep* **1** (*indicating location or position*) <in France : en France> <in Canada : au Canada> <in Montreal : à Montréal> <in the hospital : à

l'hôpital> <in my house : chez moi> **2** (*indicating time or season*) <in 1938 : en 1938> <in the spring : au printemps> <in the summer : en été> <in the past : dans le passé> **3** (*indicating manner*) <in French : en français> <written in pencil : écrit en crayon> <in this way : de cette manière> **4** (*indicating states or circumstances*) <to be in luck : avoir de la chance> <to be in love : être amoureux> <to be in a hurry : être pressé> **5** (*indicating purpose*) <in response : en réponse> **6** INSIDE, WITHIN : dans <in this book : dans ce livre> <I'll be back in a week : je serai de retour dans une semaine> **7** INTO : dans, en <she went in the house : elle est entrée dans la maison> <he broke it in pieces : il l'a cassé en morceaux> **8** DURING : pendant, dans <in the afternoon : pendant l'après-midi, dans l'après-midi>

inability [ˌɪnəˈbɪlət̬i] *n, pl* **-ties** : incapacité *f*

inaccessibility [ˌɪnɪkˌsɛsəˈbɪlət̬i] *n, pl* **-ties** : inaccessibilité *f*

inaccessible [ˌɪnɪkˈsɛsəbəl] *adj* : inaccessible

inaccuracy [ɪnˈækjərəsi] *n, pl* **-cies** : inexactitude *f*

inaccurate [ɪnˈækjərət] *adj* : inexact — **inaccurately** *adv*

inaction [ɪnˈækʃən] *n* : inaction *f*

inactive [ɪnˈæktɪv] *adj* : inactif

inactivity [ˌɪnˌækˈtɪvət̬i] *n, pl* **-ties** : inactivité *f*, inaction *f*

inadequacy [ɪˈnædɪkwəsi] *n, pl* **-cies 1** INSUFFICIENCY : insuffisance *f* **2** DEFICIENCY : défauts *mpl*, incompétence *f*

inadequate [ɪˈnædɪkwət] *adj* : insuffisant

inadmissible [ˌɪnædˈmɪsəbəl] *adj* : inadmissible

inadvertence [ˌɪnədˈvərtənts] *n* : inadvertance *f*

inadvertent [ˌɪnədˈvərtənt] *adj* : commis par inadvertance, involontaire

inadvertently [ˌɪnədˈvərtəntli] *adv* : par inadvertance

inadvisable [ˌɪnædˈvaɪzəbəl] *adj* : déconseillé

inalienable [ɪnˈeɪljənəbəl, -ˈeɪliən-] *adj* : inaliénable

inane [ɪˈneɪn] *adj* **inaner; -est** : inepte, stupide

inanimate [ɪˈnænəmət] *adj* : inanimé

inanity [ɪˈnænət̬i] *n, pl* **-ties 1** STUPIDITY : stupidité *f* **2** NONSENSE : ineptie *f*

inapplicable [ɪˈnæplɪkəbəl, ˌɪnəˈplɪkəbəl] *adj* : inapplicable

inappreciable [ˌɪnəˈpriːʃəbəl] *adj* : inappréciable, imperceptible

inappropriate [ˌɪnəˈproːpriət] *adj* : inapproprié, inopportun

inappropriately [ˌɪnəˈproːpriətli] *adv* : mal à propos, inopportunément

inapt [ɪnˈæpt] *adj* : inapte

inarticulate [ˌɪnɑrˈtɪkjələt] *adj* **1** INCOHERENT : incohérent, incapable de s'exprimer **2** INEXPRESSIBLE : inexprimable **3** : inarticulé (en physiologie)

inasmuch as [ˌɪnæzˈmʌtʃæz] *conj* : attendu que, vu que, dans la mesure où

inattention [ˌɪnəˈtɛntʃən] *n* : inattention *f*

inattentive [ˌɪnəˈtɛntɪv] *adj* : inattentif

inattentively [ˌɪnəˈtɛntɪvli] *adv* : distraitement, sans prêter attention

inaudible [ɪnˈɔdəbəl] *adj* : inaudible

inaudibly [ɪnˈɔdəbli] *adv* : de manière inaudible, indistinctement

inaugural[1] [ɪˈnɔgjərəl, -gərəl] *adj* : inaugural

inaugural[2] *n* **1** *or* **inaugural address** : discours *m* d'inauguration **2** INAUGURATION : investiture *f*, installation *f*

inaugurate [ɪˈnɔgjəˌreɪt, -gə-] *vt* **-rated; -rating 1** BEGIN : inaugurer **2** INDUCT : investir, installer

inauguration [ɪˌnɔgjəˈreɪʃən, -gə-] *n* **1** BEGINNING : inauguration *f* **2** INDUCTION : investiture *f*, installation *f*

inauspicious [ˌɪnɔˈspɪʃəs] *adj* : peu propice, défavorable

inborn [ˈɪnˌbɔrn] *adj* : inné, congénital

inbred [ˈɪnˌbrɛd] *adj* **1** : consanguin **2** INNATE : inné

inbreed [ˈɪnˌbriːd] *vt* **-bred; -breeding** : croiser (des animaux de même souche)

incalculable [ɪnˈkælkjələbəl] *adj* : incalculable

incandescence [ˌɪnkənˈdɛsənts] *n* : incandescence *f*

incandescent [ˌɪnkənˈdɛsənt] *adj* : incandescent

incantation [ˌɪnˌkænˈteɪʃən] *n* : incantation *f*

incapable [ɪnˈkeɪpəbəl] *adj* : incapable

incapacitate [ˌɪnkəˈpæsəˌteɪt] *vt* **-tated; -tating** : rendre incapable

incapacity [ˌɪnkəˈpæsət̬i] *n, pl* **-ties** : incapacité *f*

incarcerate [ɪnˈkɑrsəˌreɪt] *vt* **-ated; -ating** : incarcérer

incarceration [ɪnˌkɑrsəˈreɪʃən] *n* : incarcération *f*

incarnate[1] [ɪnˈkɑrˌneɪt] *vt* **-ated; -ating** : incarner

incarnate[2] [ɪnˈkɑrnət, -ˌneɪt] *adj* : incarné

incarnation [ˌɪnˌkɑrˈneɪʃən] *n* : incarnation *f*

incendiary[1] [ɪnˈsɛndiˌɛri] *adj* : incendiaire

incendiary[2] *n, pl* **-aries** ARSONIST : incendiaire *mf*

incense[1] [ɪnˈsɛnts] *vt* **-censed; -censing** : mettre en colère, rendre furieux

incense[2] ['ɪnsɛnts] *n* : encens *m*
incentive [ɪn'sɛntɪv] *n* : motivation *f*
inception [ɪn'sɛpʃən] *n* : début *m*, commencement *m*
incessant [ɪn'sɛsənt] *adj* : incessant — **incessantly** *adv*
incest ['ɪn,sɛst] *n* : inceste *m*
incestuous [ɪn'sɛstʃʊəs] *adj* : incestueux
inch[1] ['ɪntʃ] *v* : avancer petit à petit
inch[2] *n* : pouce *m*
incidence ['ɪntsədənts] *n* : fréquence *f*, taux *m*
incident ['ɪntsədənt] *n* : incident *m*
incidental[1] [,ɪntsə'dɛntəl] *adj* **1** ACCESSORY : secondaire, accessoire **2** FORTUITOUS : fortuit
incidental[2] *n* **1** : détail *m* secondaire **2 incidentals** *npl* EXPENSES : (faux) frais *mpl*
incidentally [,ɪntsə'dɛntəli, -'dɛntli] *adv* : à propos
incinerate [ɪn'sɪnə,reɪt] *vt* **-ated; -ating** : incinérer
incinerator [ɪn'sɪnə,reɪt̬ər] *n* : incinérateur *m*
incipient [ɪn'sɪpiənt] *adj* : naissant
incise [ɪn'saɪz] *vt* **-cised; -cising 1** CUT : inciser **2** ENGRAVE : graver
incision [ɪn'sɪʒən] *n* : incision *f*
incisive [ɪn'saɪsɪv] *adj* : incisif
incisively [ɪn'saɪsɪvli] *adv* : d'une manière incisive
incisor [ɪn'saɪzər] *n* : incisive *f*
incite [ɪn'saɪt] *vt* **-cited; -citing** : inciter
incitement [ɪn'saɪtmənt] *n* : incitation *f*
inclemency [ɪn'klɛməntsi] *n* : inclémence *f* (du temps)
inclement [ɪn'klɛmənt] *adj* : inclément
inclination [,ɪnklə'neɪʃən] *n* **1** PROPENSITY : tendance *f* **2** DESIRE : envie *f*, désir *m* **3** BOW, NOD : inclination *f*
incline[1] [ɪn'klaɪn] *v* **-clined; -clining** *vi* **1** SLOPE : s'incliner **2** TEND : avoir tendance, tendre — *vt* **1** DISPOSE, PROMPT : incliner, disposer **2** BEND : pencher, incliner
incline[2] ['ɪn,klaɪn] *n* : inclinaison *f*
inclined *adj* **1** SLOPING : incliné **2 to be inclined to** : avoir tendance à
inclose, inclosure → **enclose, enclosure**
include [ɪn'klu:d] *vt* **-cluded; -cluding** : inclure, comprendre
inclusion [ɪn'klu:ʒən] *n* : inclusion *f*
inclusive [ɪn'klu:sɪv] *adj* : inclus, compris
incognito [,ɪn,kɑg'ni:t̬o, ɪn'kɑgnə,to:] *adv & adj* : incognito
incoherence [,ɪnko'hɪrənts, -'hɛr-] *n* : incohérence *f*
incoherent [,ɪnko'hɪrənt, -'hɛr-] *adj* : incohérent
incoherently [,ɪnko'hɪrəntli, -'hɛr-] *adv* : de manière incohérente
incombustible [,ɪnkəm'bʌstəbəl] *adj* : incombustible
income ['ɪn,kʌm] *n* : revenu *m*
income tax *n* : impôt *m* sur le revenu
incoming ['ɪn,kʌmɪŋ] *adj* **1** ARRIVING : entrant, qui arrive **2** NEW : nouveau
incommunicado [,ɪnkə,mju:nə'kɑdo] *adj* : tenu au secret, sans contact avec l'extérieur
incomparable [ɪn'kɑmpərəbəl] *adj* : incomparable — **incomparably** [-bli] *adv*
incompatibility [,ɪnkəm,pæt̬ə'bɪlət̬i] *n* : incompatibilité *f*
incompatible [,ɪnkəm'pæt̬əbəl] *adj* : incompatible
incompetence [ɪn'kɑmpət̬ənts] *n* : incompétence *f*
incompetent [ɪn'kɑmpət̬ənt] *adj* : incompétent
incomplete [,ɪnkəm'pli:t] *adj* : incomplet, inachevé
incompletely [,ɪnkəm'pli:tli] *adv* : incomplètement
incomprehensible [,ɪn,kɑmpri'hɛntsəbəl] *adj* : incompréhensible
inconceivable [,ɪnkən'si:vəbəl] *adj* : inconcevable
inconceivably [,ɪnkən'si:vəbli] *adv* : incroyablement
inconclusive [,ɪnkən'klu:sɪv] *adj* : peu concluant
incongruity [,ɪnkən'gru:ət̬i, -,kɑn-] *n, pl* **-ties** : incongruité *f*
incongruous [ɪn'kɑŋgrʊəs] *adj* : incongru, déplacé
incongruously [ɪn'kɑŋgrʊəsli] *adv* : de façon incongrue
inconsequential [,ɪn,kɑnsə'kwɛntʃəl] *adj* : sans importance
inconsiderable [,ɪnkən'sɪdərəbəl] *adj* : insignifiant, négligeable
inconsiderate [,ɪnkən'sɪdərət] *adj* : qui manque de considération, irréfléchi
inconsiderately [,ɪnkən'sɪdərətli] *adv* : sans aucune considération
inconsistency [,ɪnkən'sɪstəntsi] *n, pl* **-cies** : incohérence *f*, contradiction *f*
inconsistent [,ɪnkən'sɪstənt] *adj* **1** CHANGEABLE, ERRATIC : inégal, changeant **2** CONTRADICTORY : contradictoire
inconsolable [,ɪnkən'so:ləbəl] *adj* : inconsolable
inconsolably [,ɪnkən'so:ləbli] *adv* : de façon inconsolable
inconspicuous [,ɪnkən'spɪkjʊəs] *adj* : peu apparent, qui passe inaperçu
inconspicuously [,ɪnkən'spɪkjʊəsli] *adv* : discrètement
incontestable [,ɪnkən'tɛstəbəl] *adj* : incontestable — **incontestably** [-bli] *adv*
incontinent [ɪn'kɑntənənt] *adj* : incontinent
inconvenience[1] [,ɪnkən'vi:njənts] *vt* **-nienced; -niencing** : déranger
inconvenience[2] *n* **1** BOTHER : dérangement *m* **2** DISADVANTAGE : inconvénient *m*

inconvenient [ˌɪnkənˈviːnjənt] *adj* : incommode, inopportun

inconveniently [ˌɪnkənˈviːnjəntli] *adv* **1** INOPPORTUNELY : inopportunément **2** : de façon peu practique <inconveniently located : mal placé>

incorporate [ɪnˈkɔrpəˌreɪt] *v* **-rated; -rating** *vt* INCLUDE : incorporer — *vi* : se constituer en société commerciale

incorporated [ɪnˈkɔrpəˌreɪt̬əd] *adj* : constitué en société commerciale

incorporation [ɪnˌkɔrpəˈreɪʃən] *n* **1** INCLUSION, INTEGRATION : incorporation *f,* intégration *f* **2** *Can* : incorporation *f* (d'une société)

incorporeal [ˌɪnˌkɔrˈpɔriəl] *adj* : incorporel

incorrect [ˌɪnkəˈrɛkt] *adj* **1** WRONG : erroné **2** IMPROPER : incorrect

incorrectly [ˌɪnkəˈrɛktli] *adv* : inexactement, incorrectement

incorrigible [ɪnˈkɔrədʒəbəl] *adj* : incorrigible

incorruptible [ɪnkəˈrʌptəbəl] *adj* : incorruptible

increase[1] [ɪnˈkriːs, ˈɪnˌkriːs] *v* **-creased; -creasing** : augmenter

increase[2] [ˈɪnˌkriːs, ɪnˈkriːs] *n* **1** : augmentation *f* **2 on the increase** : en hausse, à la hausse

increasingly [ɪnˈkriːsɪŋli] *adv* : de plus en plus

incredible [ɪnˈkrɛdəbəl] *adj* : incroyable — **incredibly** [-bli] *adv*

incredulity [ˌɪnkrɪˈduːlət̬i, -ˈdjuː-] *n* : incrédulité *f*

incredulous [ɪnˈkrɛdʒələs] *adj* : incrédule

incredulously [ɪnˈkrɛdʒələsli] *adv* : avec incrédulité

increment [ˈɪŋkrəmənt, ˈɪn-] *n* : augmentation *f*

incremental [ˌɪŋkrəˈməntəl, ˈɪn-] *adj* : progressif, par augmentation

incriminate [ɪnˈkrɪməˌneɪt] *vt* **-nated; -nating** : incriminer

incrimination [ɪnˌkrɪməˈneɪʃən] *n* : incrimination *f*

incriminatory [ɪnˈkrɪmənəˌtɔri] *adj* : compromettant

incubate [ˈɪŋkjʊˌbeɪt, ˈɪn-] *v* **-bated; -bating** *vt* : incuber — *vi* : être en incubation

incubation [ˌɪŋkjʊˈbeɪʃən, ˌɪn-] *n* : incubation *f*

incubator [ˈɪŋkjʊˈbeɪt̬ər, -ˈɪn-] *n* : incubateur *m,* couveuse *f* (pour enfants)

inculcate [ɪnˈkʌlˌkeɪt, ˈɪnˌkʌl-] *vt* **-cated; -cating** : inculquer

incumbency [ɪnˈkʌmbəntsi] *n, pl* **-cies** : office *m,* période *f* de fonction

incumbent[1] [ɪnˈkʌmbənt] *adj* : obligatoire <to be incumbent upon : incomber à>

incumbent[2] *n* OFFICEHOLDER : titulaire *mf*

incur [ɪnˈkər] *vt* **-curred; -curring** : encourir <to incur expenses : encourir des dépenses>

incurable [ɪnˈkjʊrəbəl] *adj* : incurable

incursion [ɪnˈkərʒən] *n* : incursion *f*

indebted [ɪnˈdɛt̬əd] *adj* **1** : endetté **2 to be indebted to** : être redevable à

indebtedness [ɪnˈdɛt̬ədnəs] *n* : dette *f,* endettement *m*

indecency [ɪnˈdiːsəntsi] *n, pl* **-cies** : indécence *f*

indecent [ɪnˈdiːsənt] *adj* : indécent

indecently [ɪnˈdiːsəntli] *adv* : indécemment

indecipherable [ˌɪndɪˈsaɪfərəbəl] *adj* : indéchiffrable

indecision [ˌɪndɪˈsɪʒən] *n* : indécision *f*

indecisive [ˌɪndɪˈsaɪsɪv] *adj* : indécis

indecisively [ˌɪndɪˈsaɪsɪvli] *adv* : de manière indécise

indecorous [ɪnˈdɛkərəs, ˌɪndɪˈkorəsli] *adj* : inconvenant

indecorously [ɪnˈdɛkərəsli] *adv* : de manière inconvenante

indecorousness [ɪnˈdɛkərəsnəs, ˌɪndɪˈkorəs-] *n* : inconvenance *f*

indeed [ɪnˈdiːd] *adv* **1** TRULY : vraiment, en effet, comme de fait *Can* **2** (*used as an intensifier*) <it's very big indeed : c'est vraiment très grand> **3** OF COURSE : bien sûr

indefatigable [ˌɪndɪˈfæt̬ɪgəbəl] *adj* : infatigable, inlassable

indefensible [ˌɪndɪˈfɛntsəbəl] *adj* : inexcusable, injustifiable

indefinable [ɪndɪˈfaɪnəbəl] *adj* : indéfinissable

indefinite [ɪnˈdɛfənət] *adj* **1** : indéfini <an indefinite period : une période indéfinie> **2** VAGUE : imprécis

indefinite article *n* : article *m* indéfini

indefinitely [ɪnˈdɛfənətli] *adv* : indéfiniment

indelible [ɪnˈdɛləbəl] *adj* : indélébile

indelibly [ɪnˈdɛləbli] *adv* : de manière indélébile

indelicacy [ɪnˈdɛləkəsi] *n* : indélicatesse *f*

indelicate [ɪnˈdɛlɪkət] *adj* : indélicat

indemnify [ɪnˈdɛmnəˌfaɪ] *vt* **-fied; -fying** **1** INSURE : assurer **2** COMPENSATE : indemniser

indemnity [ɪnˈdɛmnət̬i] *n, pl* **-ties** : indemnité *f*

indent [ɪnˈdɛnt] *vt* **1** : renfoncer, mettre en alinéa <indent 4 spaces : renfoncez de 4 espaces> **2** DENT : bosseler

indentation [ˌɪnˌdɛnˈteɪʃən] *n* **1** DENT : creux *m,* bosse *f* **2** SPACE : alinéa *m* (en typographie)

indenture[1] [ɪnˈdɛntʃər] *vt* **-tured; -turing** : engager sous contrat

indenture[2] *n* : contrat *m* d'apprentissage

independence [ˌɪndəˈpɛndənts] *n* : indépendance *f*

Independence Day *n* : fête *f* de l'Indépendance américaine (le 4 juillet)
independent[1] [ˌɪndəˈpɛndənt] *adj* : indépendant
independent[2] *n* : indépendant *m*, -dante *f*
independently [ˌɪndəˈpɛndəntli] *adv* : de façon indépendante, indépendamment
indescribable [ˌɪndɪˈskraɪbəbəl] *adj* : indescriptible
indescribably [ˌɪndɪˈskraɪbəbli] *adv* : incroyablement
indestructibility [ˌɪndɪˌstrʌktəˈbɪləṭi] *n* : indestructibilité *f*
indestructible [ˌɪndɪˈstrʌktəbəl] *adj* : indestructible
indeterminate [ˌɪndɪˈtərmənət] *adj* : indéterminé
index[1] [ˈɪnˌdɛks] *vt* **1** : mettre un index à (un livre, etc.) **2** CATALOG : classer, cataloguer
index[2] *n, pl* **-dexes** *or* **-dices** [ˈɪndəˌsiːz] **1** LIST : index *m* **2** INDICATION : indice *m* <cost of living index : indice du coût de la vie>
index finger *n* : index *m*
Indian[1] [ˈɪndiən] *adj* : indien
Indian[2] *n* : Indien *m*, -dienne *f*
Indian corn *n* : maïs *m*, blé *m* d'Inde *Can*
indicate [ˈɪndəˌkeɪt] *vt* **-cated; -cating** : indiquer
indication [ˌɪndəˈkeɪʃən] *n* : indice *m*, indication *f*
indicative [ɪnˈdɪkəṭɪv] *adj* : indicatif
indicator [ˈɪndəˌkeɪṭər] *n* : indicateur *m*
indict [ɪnˈdaɪt] *vt* : inculper
indictment [ɪnˈdaɪtmənt] *n* : inculpation *f*
indifference [ɪnˈdɪfrənts, -ˈdɪfə-] *n* : indifférence *f*
indifferent [ɪnˈdɪfrənt, -ˈdɪfə-] *adj* **1** UNCONCERNED : indifférent **2** MEDIOCRE : médiocre, quelconque
indifferently [ɪnˈdɪfrəntli, -ˈdɪfə-] *adv* **1** UNCONCERNEDLY : avec indifférence **2** SO-SO : médiocrement
indigence [ˈɪndɪdʒənts] *n* : indigence *f*
indigenous [ɪnˈdɪdʒənəs] *adj* : indigène
indigent [ˈɪndɪdʒənt] *adj* : indigent
indigestible [ˌɪndaɪˈdʒɛstəbəl, -dɪ-] *adj* : indigeste
indigestion [ˌɪndaɪˈdʒɛstʃən, -dɪ-] *n* : indigestion *f*
indignant [ɪnˈdɪgnənt] *adj* : indigné, outré
indignantly [ɪnˈdɪgnəntli] *adv* : avec indignation
indignation [ˌɪndɪgˈneɪʃən] *n* : indignation *f*
indignity [ɪnˈdɪgnəṭi] *n, pl* **-ties** : indignité *f*
indigo [ˈɪndɪˌgoː] *n, pl* **-gos** *or* **-goes** : indigo *m*
indirect [ˌɪndəˈrɛkt, -daɪ-] *adj* : indirect — **indirectly** *adv*
indiscernible [ˌɪndɪˈsərnəbəl, -ˈzər-] *adj* : indiscernable, imperceptible
indiscreet [ˌɪndɪˈskriːt] *adj* : indiscret
indiscreetly [ˌɪndɪˈskriːtli] *adv* : indiscrètement
indiscretion [ˌɪndɪˈskrɛʃən] *n* : indiscrétion *f*
indiscriminate [ˌɪndɪˈskrɪmənət] *adj* **1** : qui manque de discernement **2** HAPHAZARD : fait au hasard
indiscriminately [ˌɪndɪˈskrɪmənətli] *adv* **1** : sans discernement **2** RANDOMLY : au hasard
indispensable [ˌɪndɪˈspɛntsəbəl] *adj* : indispensable
indisposed [ˌɪndɪˈspoːzd] *adj* **1** ILL : indisposé **2** DISINCLINED : peu disposé, peu enclin
indisposition [ˌɪnˌdɪspəˈzɪʃən] *n* : indisposition *f*
indisputable [ˌɪndɪˈspjuːṭəbəl] *adj* : incontestable — **indisputably** [-bli] *adv*
indistinct [ˌɪndɪˈstɪŋkt] *adj* : indistinct — **indistinctly** *adv*
individual[1] [ˌɪndəˈvɪdʒuəl] *adj* **1** SEPARATE : individuel **2** DISTINCTIVE, PERSONAL : particulier, personnel, original
individual[2] *n* : individu *m*
individualist [ˌɪndəˈvɪdʒuəlɪst] *n* : individualiste *mf*
individuality [ˌɪndəˌvɪdʒuˈæləṭi] *n, pl* **-ties** : individualité *f*
individually [ˌɪndəˈvɪdʒuəli, -dʒəli] *adv* **1** SEPARATELY : individuellement **2** DISTINCTIVELY : de façon distinctive
indivisible [ˌɪndɪˈvɪzəbəl] *adj* : indivisible
indoctrinate [ɪnˈdɑktrəˌneɪt] *vt* **-nated; -nating** : endoctriner
indoctrination [ɪnˌdɑktrəˈneɪʃən] *n* : endoctrinement *m*
indolence [ˈɪndələnts] *n* : indolence *f*
indolent [ˈɪndələnt] *adj* : indolent
indomitable [ɪnˈdɑməṭəbəl] *adj* : indomptable, invincible, irréductible
indomitably [ɪnˈdɑməṭəbli] *adv* : de façon indomptable
Indonesian[1] [ˌɪndoˈniːʒən, -ʃən] *adj* : indonésien
Indonesian[2] *n* **1** : Indonésien *m*, -sienne *f* **2** : indonésien *m* (langue)
indoor [ˈɪnˈdor] *adj* **1** : d'intérieur, à l'intérieur **2** : couvert <indoor swimming pool : piscine couverte>
indoors [ˈɪnˈdorz] *adv* : à l'intérieur
indubitable [ɪnˈduːbəṭəbəl, -ˈdjuː-] *adj* : indubitable — **indubitably** [-bli] *adv*
induce [ɪnˈduːs, -ˈdjuːs] *vt* **-duced; -ducing** **1** PERSUADE : persuader **2** CAUSE : provoquer, déclencher <to induce labor : déclencher l'accouchement>
inducement [ɪnˈduːsmənt, -ˈdjuːs-] *n* **1** INCENTIVE : motivation *f* **2** REWARD : récompense *f*
induct [ɪnˈdʌkt] *vt* **1** INSTALL : installer (qqn dans ses fonctions) **2** DRAFT, RECRUIT : incorporer

inductee [ˌɪnˌdʌk'tiː] *n* DRAFTEE : appelé *m,* conscrit *m*
induction [ɪn'dʌktʃən] *n* **1** INSTALLATION : installation *f,* incorporation *f* **2** : induction *f* (en logique, en électricité)
inductive [ɪn'dʌktɪv] *adj* : inductif
indulge [ɪn'dʌldʒ] *v* **-dulged; -dulging** *vt* **1** GRATIFY : céder à, satisfaire **2** PAMPER, SPOIL : gâter — *vi* **to indulge in** : se livrer à, se permettre
indulgence [ɪn'dʌldʒən*t*s] *n* **1** TOLERANCE : complaisance *f,* indulgence *f* **2** GRATIFICATION : satisfaction *f,* gratification *f* **3** : indulgence *f* (en religion)
indulgent [ɪn'dʌldʒənt] *adj* : indulgent
indulgently [ɪn'dʌldʒəntli] *adv* : avec indulgence
industrial [ɪn'dʌstriəl] *adj* : industriel
industrialist [ɪn'dʌstriəlɪst] *n* : industriel *m,* -trielle *f*
industrialization [ɪnˌdʌstriələ'zeɪʃən] *n* : industrialisation *f*
industrialize [ɪn'dʌstriəˌlaɪz] *vt* **-ized; -izing** : industrialiser
industrious [ɪn'dʌstriəs] *adj* : industrieux, travailleur, travaillant *Can*
industriously [ɪn'dʌstriəsli] *adv* : avec diligence
industriousness [ɪn'dʌstriəsnəs] *n* : assiduité *f,* application *f*
industry ['ɪndəstri] *n, pl* **-tries** **1** : industrie *f* <the steel industry : l'industrie sidérurgique> **2** DILIGENCE : assiduité *f*
inebriated [ɪ'niːbriˌeɪt̬əd] *adj* : ivre
inebriation [ɪˌniːbri'eɪʃən] *n* : ivresse *f*
inedible [ɪ'nɛdəbəl] *adj* : non comestible (se dit d'une plante, etc.), immangeable (se dit d'un plat)
ineffable [ɪn'ɛfəbəl] *adj* : ineffable — **ineffably** [-bli] *adv*
ineffective [ˌɪnɪ'fɛktɪv] *adj* **1** INEFFECTUAL : inefficace **2** INCAPABLE : incapable
ineffectively [ˌɪnɪ'fɛktɪvli] *adv* : sans effet, en vain
ineffectual [ˌɪnɪ'fɛk*t*ʃʊəl], **ineffectually** [ˌɪnɪ'fɛk*t*ʃʊəli] → **ineffective, ineffectively**
inefficiency [ˌɪnɪ'fɪʃən*t*si] *n, pl* **-cies** : inefficacité *f*
inefficient [ˌɪnɪ'fɪʃənt] *adj* **1** : inefficace (se dit d'une machine, etc.) **2** INCOMPETENT : incompétent, mal organisé
inefficiently [ˌɪnɪ'fɪʃəntli] *adv* : inefficacement
inelegance [ɪn'ɛləgən*t*s] *n* : inélégance *f*
inelegant [ɪn'ɛləgənt] *adj* : inélégant
ineligibility [ɪnˌɛlədʒə'bɪlət̬i] *n* : inéligibilité *f*
ineligible [ɪn'ɛlədʒəbəl] *adj* : inéligible
inept [ɪ'nɛpt] *adj* **1** INCOMPETENT : inepte **2** INAPPROPRIATE : inapproprié
ineptitude [ɪ'nɛptəˌtuːd, -ˌtjuːd] *n* : ineptie *f*
inequality [ˌɪnɪ'kwɑlət̬i] *n, pl* **-ties** : inégalité *f*
inert [ɪ'nərt] *adj* : inerte
inertia [ɪ'nərʃə] *n* : inertie *f*
inescapable [ˌɪnɪ'skeɪpəbəl] *adj* : inéluctable, indéniable — **inescapably** [-bli] *adv*
inessential [ˌɪnɪ'sɛn*t*ʃəl] *adj* : non essentiel, superflu
inestimable [ɪn'ɛstəməbəl] *adj* : inestimable
inevitability [ɪnˌɛvət̬ə'bɪlət̬i] *n, pl* **-ties** : inévitabilité *f*
inevitable [ɪn'ɛvət̬əbəl] *adj* : inévitable — **inevitably** [-bli] *adv*
inexact [ˌɪnɪg'zækt] *adj* : inexact
inexactly [ˌɪnɪg'zæktli] *adv* : inexactement, incorrectement
inexcusable [ˌɪnɪk'skjuːzəbəl] *adj* : inexcusable
inexcusably [ˌɪnɪk'skjuːzəbli] *adv* : de façon inexcusable
inexhaustible [ˌɪnɪg'zɔstəbəl] *adj* **1** LIMITLESS : inépuisable **2** INDEFATIGABLE : infatigable
inexorable [ɪn'ɛksərəbəl] *adj* : inexorable — **inexorably** [-bli] *adv*
inexpedient [ˌɪnɪk'spiːdiənt] *adj* : inopportun, malavisé
inexpensive [ˌɪnɪk'spɛn*t*sɪv] *adj* : pas cher, bon marché
inexperience [ˌɪnɪk'spɪriən*t*s] *n* : inexpérience *f*
inexperienced [ˌɪnɪk'spɪriən*t*st] *adj* : inexpérimenté
inexplicable [ˌɪnɪk'splɪkəbəl] *adj* : inexplicable — **inexplicably** [-bli] *adv*
inexpressible [ˌɪnɪk'sprɛsəbəl] *adj* : inexprimable
inextricable [ˌɪnɪk'strɪkəbəl, ɪ'nɛkˌstrɪ-] *adj* : inextricable — **inextricably** [-bli] *adv*
infallibility [ɪnˌfælə'bɪlət̬i] *n* : infaillibilité *f*
infallible [ɪn'fæləbəl] *adj* : infaillible — **infallibly** [-bli] *adv*
infamous ['ɪnfəməs] *adj* : infâme, notoire
infamy ['ɪnfəmi] *n, pl* **-mies** : infamie *f*
infancy ['ɪnfən*t*si] *n, pl* **-cies** **1** : petite enfance *f* **2 in its infancy** : à ses débuts
infant ['ɪnfənt] *n* : petit enfant *m,* petite enfant *f;* bébé *m;* nourrisson *m*
infantile ['ɪnfənˌtaɪl, -təl, -ˌtiːl] *adj* : infantile
infantile paralysis → **poliomyelitis**
infantry ['ɪnfəntri] *n, pl* **-tries** : infanterie *f*
infatuated [ɪn'fætʃʊˌeɪt̬əd] *adj* **to be infatuated with** : être entiché de
infatuation [ɪnˌfætʃʊ'eɪʃən] *n* : engouement *m*
infect [ɪn'fɛkt] *vt* : infecter
infection [ɪn'fɛkʃən] *n* : infection *f*
infectious [ɪn'fɛkʃəs] *adj* **1** : infectieux, contagieux <une maladie infectieuse : an infectious disease> **2** : con-

tagieux, communicatif <rythme communicatif : infectious rhythm>
infer [ɪn'fər] *vt* **-ferred; -ferring** : déduire, inférer
inference ['ɪnfərənts] *n* : déduction *f*, inférence *f*
inferior[1] [ɪn'fɪriər] *adj* : inférieur
inferior[2] *n* : inférieur *m*, -rieure *f*
inferiority [ɪn,fɪri'ɔrəṭi] *n, pl* **-ties** : infériorité *f*
infernal [ɪn'fərnəl] *adj* : infernal
infernally [ɪn'fərnəli] *adv* TERRIBLY : terriblement, abominablement
inferno [ɪn'fər,no:] *n, pl* **-nos 1** BLAZE, FIRE : brasier *m* **2** HELL : enfer *m*
infertile [ɪn'fɛrṭəl, -,taɪl] *adj* : infertile, stérile
infertility [,ɪnfər'tɪləṭi] *n* : infertilité *f*
infest [ɪn'fɛst] *vt* : infester
infidel ['ɪnfədəl, -,dɛl] *n* : infidèle *mf*
infidelity [,ɪnfə'dɛləṭi, -faɪ-] *n, pl* **-ties** : infidélité *f*
infield ['ɪn,fi:ld] *n* : petit champ *m*
infiltrate [ɪn'fɪl,treɪt, 'ɪnfɪl-] *v* **-trated; -trating** *vt* : infiltrer — *vi* : s'infiltrer
infiltration [,ɪnfɪl'treɪʃən] *n* : infiltration *f*
infinite ['ɪnfənət] *adj* **1** LIMITLESS : infini **2** VAST : sans bornes, incalculable, infini
infinitely ['ɪnfənətli] *adv* : infiniment
infinitesimal [,ɪn,fɪnə'tɛsəməl] *adj* : infinitésimal — **infinitesimally** *adv*
infinitive [ɪn'fɪnəṭɪv] *n* : infinitif *m*
infinity [ɪn'fɪnəṭi] *n, pl* **-ties 1** : infinité *f* **2** : infini *m* (en mathématiques)
infirm [ɪn'fərm] *adj* : infirme
infirmary [ɪn'fərməri] *n, pl* **-ries** : infirmerie *f*
infirmity [ɪn'fərməṭi] *n, pl* **-ties** : infirmité *f*
inflame [ɪn'fleɪm] *v* **-flamed; -flaming** *vt* **1** IGNITE : enflammer, mettre le feu à **2** : enflammer (en médecine) **3** EXCITE, STIR UP : exciter, enflammer — *vi* : s'enflammer
inflammable [ɪn'flæməbəl] *adj* : inflammable, flammable
inflammation [,ɪnflə'meɪʃən] *n* : inflammation *f*
inflammatory [ɪn'flæmə,tori] *adj* **1** : incendiaire <inflammatory remarks : propos incendiaires> **2** : inflammatoire (en médecine)
inflatable [ɪn'fleɪṭəbəl] *adj* : gonflable
inflate [ɪn'fleɪt] *v* **-flated; -flating** *vt* : gonfler — *vi* : se gonfler
inflation [ɪn'fleɪʃən] *n* : inflation *f*
inflationary [ɪn'fleɪʃə,nɛri] *adj* : inflationniste
inflect [ɪn'flɛkt] *vt* **1** CURVE : infléchir **2** MODULATE : moduler (la voix) **3** CONJUGATE : conjuger (un verbe) **4** DECLINE : décliner (un adjectif, etc.)
inflection [ɪn,flɛkʃən] *n* **1** : inflexion *f*, modulation *f* (de la voix) **2** : flexion *f* (en linguistique) **3** : inflexion *f* (en mathématiques)
inflexibility [ɪn'flɛksə'bɪləṭi] *n, pl* **-ties** : inflexibilité *f*
inflexible [ɪn'flɛksɪbəl] *adj* : inflexible
inflict [ɪn'flɪkt] *vt* : infliger
influence[1] ['ɪn,flu:ənts, ɪn'flu:ənts] *vt* **-enced; -encing** : influencer, influer sur
influence[2] *n* **1** : influence *f* **2 under the influence of** : sous l'effet de
influential [,ɪnflu'ɛntʃəl] *adj* : influent
influenza [,ɪnflu'ɛnzə] *n* : grippe *f*
influx ['ɪn,flʌks] *n* : afflux *m*
inform [ɪn'fɔrm] *vt* : informer, renseigner — *vi* **to inform on** : dénoncer
informal [ɪn'fɔrməl] *adj* **1** UNCEREMONIOUS : sans cérémonie **2** CASUAL : familier (se dit du langage) **3** UNOFFICIAL : officieux, non officiel
informality [,ɪnfɔr'mæləṭi, -fər-] *n* **1** : simplicité *f*, absence *f* de cérémonie **2** : style *m* familier (de langage)
informally [ɪn'fɔrməli] *adv* **1** CASUALLY : sans cérémonie, simplement **2** UNOFFICIALLY : officieusement **3** COLLOQUIALLY : familièrement
informant [ɪn'fɔrmənt] *n* : informateur *m*, -trice *f*
information [,ɪnfər'meɪʃən] *n* **1** : renseignements *mpl*, information *f* **2 for your information** : à titre d'information
informative [ɪn'fɔrməṭɪv] *adj* : informatif
informer [ɪn'fɔrmər] *n* : informateur *m*, -trice *f*
infraction [ɪn'frækʃən] *n* : infraction *f*
infrared [,ɪnfrə'rɛd] *adj* : infrarouge
infrastructure ['ɪnfrə,strʌktʃər] *n* : infrastructure *f*
infrequent [ɪn'fri:kwənt] *adj* : rare, peu fréquent
infrequently [ɪn'fri:kwəntli] *adv* : rarement
infringe [ɪn'frɪndʒ] *v* **-fringed; -fringing** *vt* : enfreindre — *vi* **to infringe on** : empiéter sur
infringement [ɪn'frɪndʒmənt] *n* : infraction *f* (à la loi)
infuriate [ɪn'fjʊri,eɪt] *vt* **-ated; -ating** : rendre furieux
infuse [ɪn'fju:z] *vt* **-fused; -fusing 1** IMBUE, INSPIRE : insuffler, inspirer **2** STEEP : infuser
infusion [ɪn'fju:ʒən] *n* : infusion *f*
ingenious [ɪn'dʒi:njəs] *adj* : ingénieux — **ingeniously** *adv*
ingenue *or* **ingénue** ['ɑndʒə,nu:, 'æn-; 'æʒə-, 'ɑ-] *n* : ingénue *f*
ingenuity [,ɪndʒə'nu:əṭi, -'nju:-] *n, pl* **-ties** : ingéniosité *f*
ingenuous [ɪn'dʒɛnjʊəs] *adj* **1** FRANK : candide, franc **2** NAIVE : naïf — **ingenuously** *adv*
ingenuousness [ɪn'dʒɛnjʊəsnəs] *n* **1** FRANKNESS : franchise *f* **2** NAÏVETÉ : naïveté *f*

ingest [ɪn'dʒɛst] *vt* : ingérer
ingot ['ɪŋgət] *n* : lingot *m*
ingrained [ɪn'greɪnd] *adj* : enraciné, invétéré
ingrate ['ɪn,greɪt] *n* : ingrat *m*, -grate *f*
ingratiate [ɪn'greɪʃi,eɪt] *vt* **-ated; -ating** : trouver grâce aux yeux de (qqn) <to ingratiate oneself with : s'insinuer dans les bonnes grâces de>
ingratiating [ɪn'greɪʃi,eɪt̬ɪŋ] *adj* : insinuant
ingratitude [ɪn'græt̬ə'tu:d, -'tju:d] *n* : ingratitude *f*
ingredient [ɪn'gri:diənt] *n* : ingrédient *m*
ingrown ['ɪn,gro:n] *adj* : incarné <ingrown nail : ongle incarné>
inhabit [ɪn'hæbət] *vt* : habiter
inhabitable [ɪn'hæbət̬əbəl] *adj* : habitable
inhabitant [ɪn'hæbət̬ənt] *n* : habitant *m*, -tante *f*
inhalant [ɪn'heɪlənt] *n* : inhalant *m*
inhale [ɪn'heɪl] *v* **-haled; -haling** *vt* : inhaler, aspirer — *vi* : inspirer
inhaler [ɪn'heɪlər] *n* : inhalateur *m*
inhere [ɪn'hɪr] *vi* **-hered; -hering** : être inhérent
inherent [ɪn'hɪrənt, -'hɛr-] *adj* : inhérent
inherently [ɪn'hɪrəntli, -'hɛr-] *adv* : fondamentalement, naturellement
inherit [ɪn'hɛrət] *v* : hériter
inheritance [ɪn'hɛrət̬ənts] *n* : héritage *m*
inheritor [ɪn'hɛrət̬ər] *n* : héritier *m*, -tière *f*
inhibit [ɪn'hɪbət] *vt* IMPEDE : entraver, gêner
inhibition [,ɪnhə'bɪʃən, ,ɪnə-] *n* : inhibition *f*
inhuman [ɪn'hju:mən, -'ju:-] *adj* : inhumain — **inhumanly** *adv*
inhumane [,ɪnhju'meɪn, -ju-] *adj* : inhumain, cruel
inhumanity [,ɪnhju'mænət̬i, -ju-] *n, pl* **-ties** : inhumanité *f*
inimical [ɪ'nɪmɪkəl] *adj* **1** UNFAVORABLE : peu favorable **2** HOSTILE : inamical, hostile
inimitable [ɪ'nɪmət̬əbəl] *adj* : inimitable
iniquitous [ɪ'nɪkwət̬əs] *adj* : inique
iniquity [ɪ'nɪkwət̬i] *n, pl* **-ties** : iniquité *f*
initial[1] [ɪ'nɪʃəl] *vt* **-tialed** *or* **-tialled; -tialing** *or* **-tialling** : parapher
initial[2] *adj* **1** INCIPIENT : initial **2** FIRST : premier
initially [ɪ'nɪʃəli] *adv* : à l'origine, au départ
initial[3] *n* : initiale *f*
initiate[1] [ɪ'nɪʃi,eɪt] *vt* **-ated; -ating 1** BEGIN : commencer, entreprendre **2** INDUCT : initier, admettre (à un club, etc.) **3** INTRODUCE : initier (qqn au rudiments de qqch)
initiate[2] [ɪ'nɪʃiət] *n* : initié *m*, -tiée *f*
initiation [ɪ,nɪʃi'eɪʃən] *n* : initiation *f*
initiative [ɪ'nɪʃət̬ɪv] *n* : initiative *f*
inject [ɪn'dʒɛkt] *vt* : injecter
injection [ɪn'dʒɛkʃən] *n* : injection *f*
injudicious [,ɪndʒʊ'dɪʃəs] *adj* : peu judicieux
injunction [ɪn'dʒʌŋkʃən] *n* : injonction *f*
injure ['ɪndʒər] *vt* **-jured; -juring 1** WOUND : blesser **2** HARM : nuire à, faire du tort à **3 to injure oneself** : se blesser
injurious [ɪn'dʒʊriəs] *adj* : nuisible, préjudiciable <injurious to one's health : nuisible à la santé>
injury ['ɪndʒəri] *n, pl* **-ries 1** WOUND : blessure *f* **2** WRONG : tort *m*, dommage *m*
injustice [ɪn'dʒʌstəs] *n* : injustice *f*
ink[1] ['ɪŋk] *vt* : encrer
ink[2] *n* : encre *f*
inkling ['ɪŋklɪŋ] *n* : petite idée *f*
inkwell ['ɪŋk,wɛl] *n* : encrier *m*
inky ['ɪŋki] *adj* **inkier; -est 1** : taché d'encre **2** DARK : noir comme de l'encre
inland[1] ['ɪn,lænd, -lənd] *adv* : à l'intérieur, vers l'intérieur
inland[2] *adj* : intérieur
inland[3] *n* : intérieur *m*
in–law ['ɪn,lɔ] *n* **1** : parent *m* par alliance **2 in–laws** *npl* : beaux-parents *mpl*
inlay[1] [ɪn'leɪ, 'ɪn,leɪ] *vt* **-laid** [-'leɪd, -,leɪd]; **-laying** : incruster
inlay[2] ['ɪn,leɪ] *n* : incrustation *f*
inlet ['ɪn,lɛt, -lət] *n* : crique *f*, bras *m* de mer
inmate ['ɪn,meɪt] *n* **1** PRISONER : détenu *m*, -nue *f* **2** PATIENT : malade *mf*
in memoriam [,ɪnmə'moriəm] *prep* : en mémoire de
inmost ['ɪn,mo:st] *adj* INNERMOST : le plus profond, le plus intime
inn ['ɪn] *n* **1** HOTEL : auberge *f* **2** TAVERN : taverne *f*
innards ['ɪnərdz] *npl* : entrailles *fpl*
innate [ɪ'neɪt] *adj* **1** INBORN : inné **2** INHERENT : inhérent
inner ['ɪnər] *adj* : intérieur, interne
innermost ['ɪnər,mo:st] *adj* INMOST : le plus profond, le plus intime
innersole ['ɪnər'so:l] → **insole**
inning ['ɪnɪŋ] *n* : tour *m* de batte, manche *f* *Can* (au baseball)
innkeeper ['ɪn,ki:pər] *n* : aubergiste *mf*
innocence ['ɪnəsənts] *n* : innocence *f*
innocent[1] ['ɪnəsənt] *adj* : innocent
innocent[2] *n* : innocent *m*, -cente *f*
innocently ['ɪnəsəntli] *adv* : innocemment
innocuous [ɪ'nɑkjəwəs] *adj* : inoffensif
innovate ['ɪnə,veɪt] *v* **-vated; -vating** : innover
innovation [,ɪnə'veɪʃən] *n* : innovation *f*
innovative ['ɪnə,veɪt̬ɪv] *adj* : innovateur, novateur
innovator ['ɪnə,veɪt̬ər] *n* : innovateur *m*, -trice *f*; novateur *m*, -trice *f*

innuendo [ˌɪnjʊ'ɛndo] *n, pl* **-dos** *or* **-does** : insinuation *f,* allusion *f* (malveillante)
innumerable [ɪ'nu:mərəbəl, -'nju:-] *adj* : innombrable, sans nombre
inoculate [ɪ'nɑkjəˌleɪt] *vt* **-lated; -lating** : inoculer, vacciner
inoculation [ɪˌnɑkjə'leɪʃən] *n* : inoculation *f*
inoffensive [ˌɪnə'fɛntsɪv] *adj* : inoffensif
inoperable [ɪn'ɑpərəbəl] *adj* : inopérable
inoperative [ɪn'ɑpərəṭɪv, -ˌreɪ-] *adj* : inopérant
inopportune [ɪnˌɑpər'tu:n, -'tju:n] *adj* : inopportun
inopportunely [ɪnˌɑpər'tu:nli, -'tju:n-] *adv* : inopportunément
inordinate [ɪn'ɔrdənət] *adj* : excessif, démesuré — **inordinately** *adv*
inorganic [ˌɪnɔr'gænɪk] *adj* : inorganique
inpatient ['ɪnˌpeɪʃənt] *n* : malade *m* hospitalisé, malade *f* hospitalisée
input[1] ['ɪnˌpʊt] *vt* **inputted** *or* **input; inputting** : entrer (des données)
input[2] *n* **1** CONTRIBUTION : contribution *f,* concours *m* **2** ENTRY : entrée *f* (de données) **3** ADVICE, OPINION : conseils *mpl*
inquest ['ɪnˌkwɛst] *n* : enquête *f*
inquire [ɪn'kwaɪr] *v* **-quired; -quiring** *vt* : demander — *vi* **1 to inquire about** : se renseigner sur, s'informer de **2 to inquire into** INVESTIGATE : enquêter sur
inquirer [ɪn'kwaɪrər] *n* : investigateur *m,* -trice *f*
inquiringly [ɪn'kwaɪrɪŋli] *adv* : d'un air interrogateur
inquiry [ɪn'kwaɪri, 'ɪnˌkwaɪri, 'ɪnkwəri] *n, pl* **-ries 1** QUESTION : demande *f* **2** INVESTIGATION : enquête *f*
inquisition [ˌɪnkwə'zɪʃən, ˌɪŋ-] *n* **1** : inquisition *f* **2 the Inquisition** : l'Inquisition *f*
inquisitive [ɪn'kwɪzəṭɪv] *adj* : inquisiteur, curieux
inquisitively [ɪn'kwɪzəṭɪvli] *adv* : avec curiosité
inquisitiveness [ɪn'kwɪzəṭɪvnəs] *n* : curiosité *f*
inroad ['ɪnˌro:d] *n* **1** ENCROACHMENT : incursion *f* **2 to make inroads into** : entamer
inrush ['ɪnˌrʌʃ] *n* : irruption *f*
insane [ɪn'seɪn] *adj* **1** MAD : fou **2** ABSURD : insensé, démentiel
insanely [ɪn'seɪnli] *adv* : follement, comme un fou
insanity [ɪn'sænəṭi] *n, pl* **-ties** : folie *f,* démence *f*
insatiable [ɪn'seɪʃəbəl] *adj* : insatiable
inscribe [ɪn'skraɪb] *vt* **-scribed; -scribing 1** ENGRAVE : graver **2** ENROLL : inscrire **3** DEDICATE : dédicacer (un livre, etc.)
inscription [ɪn'skrɪpʃən] *n* : inscription *f*
inscrutable [ɪn'skru:ṭəbəl] *adj* : impénétrable, énigmatique
inseam ['ɪnˌsi:m] *n* : longueur *f* d'un pantalon
insect ['ɪnˌsɛkt] *n* : insecte *m*
insecticide [ɪn'sɛktəˌsaɪd] *n* : insecticide *m*
insecure [ˌɪnsɪ'kjʊr] *adj* **1** UNCERTAIN : incertain **2** UNSAFE : peu sûr **3** FEARFUL : anxieux
insecurity [ˌɪnsɪ'kjʊrəṭi] *n, pl* **-ties** : insécurité *f,* manque *m* d'assurance
inseminate [ɪn'sɛməˌneɪt] *vt* **-nated; -nating** : inséminer
insemination [ɪnˌsɛmə'neɪʃən] *n* : insémination *f*
insensibility [ɪnˌsɛntsə'bɪləṭi] *n, pl* **-ties** : insensibilité *f*
insensible [ɪn'sɛntsəbəl] *adj* **1** NUMB : insensible **2** UNCONSCIOUS : inconscient **3** UNAWARE : inconscient
insensitive [ɪn'sɛntsəṭɪv] *adj* : insensible
insensitivity [ɪnˌsɛntsə'tɪvəṭi] *n* : insensibilité *f*
inseparable [ɪn'sɛpərəbəl] *adj* : inséparable
insert[1] [ɪn'sɛrt] *vt* : insérer, introduire
insert[2] ['ɪnˌsərt] *n* : insertion *f,* encart *m* (dans un texte)
insertion [ɪn'sərʃən] *n* : insertion *f*
inset ['ɪnˌsɛt] *n* **1** INSERTION : insertion *f* **2** : encart *m* (dans un livre), entredeux *m* (dans un vêtement), insert *m* (dans une carte)
inshore[1] ['ɪn'ʃor] *adv* : vers la côte, près de la côte
inshore[2] *adj* : côtier
inside[1] [ɪn'saɪd, 'ɪnˌsaɪd] *adv* : à l'intérieur
inside[2] *adj* : intérieur <the inside pages : les pages intérieures> <to get inside information : obtenir des renseignements à la source>
inside[3] *n* **1** : intérieur *m* **2 insides** *npl* GUTS : entrailles *fpl,* tripes *fpl fam*
inside[4] *prep* : à l'intérieur de
inside of *prep* INSIDE : à l'intérieur de, dans
inside out *adv* : à l'envers
insider [ɪn'saɪdər] *n* : initié *m,* -tiée *f*
insidious [ɪn'sɪdiəs] *adj* : insidieux — **insidiously** *adv*
insight ['ɪnˌsaɪt] *n* **1** PERSPICACITY : perspicacité *f* **2** UNDERSTANDING : aperçu *m*
insightful [ɪn'saɪtfəl] *adj* : perspicace
insignia [ɪn'sɪgniə] *or* **insigne** [-ˌni:] *n, pl* **-nia** *or* **-nias** : insigne *m*
insignificance [ˌɪnsɪg'nɪfɪkənts] *n* : insignifiance *f*
insignificant [ˌɪnsɪg'nɪfɪkənt] *adj* : insignifiant
insincere [ˌɪnsɪn'sɪr] *adj* : pas sincère
insincerely [ˌɪnsɪn'sɪrli] *adv* : de manière peu sincère

insincerity [ˌɪnsɪnˈsɛrəṭi, -ˈsɪr-] *n, pl* **-ties** : manque *m* de sincérité
insinuate [ɪnˈsɪnjʊˌeɪt] *vt* **-ated; -ating** : insinuer
insinuation [ɪnˌsɪnjʊˈeɪʃən] *n* : insinuation *f*
insipid [ɪnˈsɪpəd] *adj* : fade, insipide
insist [ɪnˈsɪst] *vi* : insister — *vt* AFFIRM, MAINTAIN : affirmer, insister
insistence [ɪnˈsɪstənts] *n* : insistance *f*
insistent [ɪnˈsɪstənt] *adj* PERSISTENT : insistant **2** COMPELLING : pressant
insistently [ɪnˈsɪstəntli] *adv* : avec insistance
insofar as [ˌɪnsoˈfɑræz] *conj* : dans la mesure où
insole [ˈɪnˌsoːl] *n* : semelle *f* (intérieure)
insolence [ˈɪntsələnts] *n* : insolence *f*
insolent [ˈɪntsələnt] *adj* : insolent
insolubility [ɪnˌsɑljʊˈbɪləṭi] *n* : insolubilité *f*
insoluble [ɪnˈsɑljʊbəl] *adj* : insoluble
insolvency [ɪnˈsɑlvəntsi] *n, pl* **-cies** : insolvabilité *f*
insolvent [ɪnˈsɑlvənt] *adj* : insolvable
insomnia [ɪnˈsɑmniə] *n* : insomnie *f*
insomuch as [ˌɪnsoˈmʌtʃæz] → **inasmuch as**
insomuch that *conj* SO : à tel point que
inspect [ɪnˈspɛkt] *vt* **1** EXAMINE : examiner, inspecter **2** REVIEW : passer en revue (des troupes)
inspection [ɪnˈspɛkʃən] *n* **1** : inspection *f* **2** : revue *f* (des troupes)
inspector [ɪnˈspɛktər] *n* : inspecteur *m*, -trice *f*
inspiration [ˌɪntspəˈreɪʃən] *n* : inspiration *f*
inspirational [ˌɪntspəˈreɪʃənəl] *adj* : inspirant
inspire [ɪnˈspaɪr] *v* **-spired; -spiring** *vt* **1** INHALE : inspirer, aspirer **2** INCITE : stimuler, inciter **3** IMPEL, MOTIVATE : inspirer, motiver — *vi* INHALE : inspirer
instability [ˌɪntstəˈbɪləṭi] *n* : instabilité *f*
install [ɪnˈstɔl] *vt* **-stalled; -stalling 1** : installer <to install a fan : installer un ventilateur> <to install a new president : installer un nouveau président> **2 to install oneself** SETTLE : s'installer
installation [ˌɪntstəˈleɪʃən] *n* : installation *f*
installment [ɪnˈstɔlmənt] *n* **1** PAYMENT : versement *m*, acompte *m* **2** CHAPTER, EPISODE : épisode *m*
instance [ˈɪntstənts] *n* **1** CIRCUMSTANCE : cas *m*, circonstance *f* <in the first instance : en premier lieu> **2** EXAMPLE : exemple *m* <for instance : par exemple>
instant¹ [ˈɪntstənt] *adj* **1** IMMEDIATE : instantané, immédiat **2** : instantané, soluble <instant coffee : café instantané>
instant² *n* MOMENT : instant *m*, moment *m*
instantaneous [ˌɪntstənˈteɪniəs] *adj* : instantané — **instantaneously** *adv*
instantly [ˈɪntstəntli] *adv* : instantanément, immédiatement, sur-le-champ
instead [ɪnˈstɛd] *adv* : plutôt, au lieu de cela <she couldn't go, so I went instead : elle n'a pas pu y aller, donc j'y suis allé à sa place>
instead of *prep* : au lieu de, à la place de
instep [ˈɪnˌstɛp] *n* : coup-de-pied *m*
instigate [ˈɪntstəˌgeɪt] *vt* **-gated; -gating** : inciter, engager
instigation [ˌɪntstəˈgeɪʃən] *n* : instigation *f*, incitation *f*
instigator [ˈɪntstəˌgeɪṭər] *n* : instigateur *m*, -trice *f*
instill *or Brit* **instil** [ɪnˈstɪl] *vt* **-stilled; -stilling** : instiller, inculquer
instinct [ˈɪnˌstɪŋkt] *n* : instinct *m*
instinctive [ɪnˈstɪŋktɪv] *adj* : instinctif — **instinctively** *adv*
instinctual [ɪnˈstɪŋktʃʊəl] *adj* : instinctif
institute¹ [ˈɪnstəˌtuːt, -ˌtjuːt] *vt* **-tuted; -tuting** : instituer
institute² *n* : institut *m*
institution [ˌɪnstəˈtuːʃən, -ˈtjuː-] *n* : institution *f*, établissement *m*
institutional [ˌɪnstəˈtuːʃənəl, -ˈtjuː-] *adj* : institutionnel
institutionalize [ˌɪnstəˈtuːʃənəˌlaɪz, -ˈtjuː-] *vt* **-ized; -izing 1** ESTABLISH : institutionnaliser **2** INTERN : interner, placer dans un établissement spécialisé
instruct [ɪnˈstrʌkt] *vt* **1** TEACH : instruire, former, enseigner **2** COMMAND : charger
instruction [ɪnˈstrʌkʃən] *n* : instruction *f*
instructional [ɪnˈstrʌkʃənəl] *adj* : instructif, éducatif
instructive [ɪnˈstrʌktɪv] *adj* : instructif
instructor [ɪnˈstrʌktər] *n* : instructeur *m*, -trice *f*; éducateur *m*, -trice *f*
instrument [ˈɪntstrəmənt] *n* : instrument *m*
instrumental [ˌɪntstrəˈmɛntəl] *adj* **1** : instrumental **2 to be instrumental in** : contribuer à
instrumentalist [ˌɪntstrəˈmɛntəlɪst] *n* : instrumentaliste *mf*
insubordinate [ˌɪnsəˈbɔrdənət] *adj* : insubordonné
insubordination [ˌɪnsəˌbɔrdənˈeɪʃən] *n* : insubordination *f*
insubstantial [ˌɪnsəbˈstæntʃəl] *adj* **1** : peu substantiel, peu solide **2** IMAGINARY : imaginaire, irréel
insufferable [ɪnˈsʌfərəbəl] *adj* : intolérable, insupportable — **insufferably** [-bli] *adv*
insufficiency [ˌɪnsəˈfɪʃəntsi] *n, pl* **-cies** : insuffisance *f*
insufficient [ˌɪnsəˈfɪʃənt] *adj* : insuffisant — **insufficiently** *adv*

insular ['ɪntsʊlər, -sjʊ-] *adj* **1** : insulaire **2** NARROW-MINDED : borné, étroit d'esprit
insularity [ˌɪntsʊ'lærəṭi, -sjʊ-] *n* : insularité *f*
insulate ['ɪntsəˌleɪt] *vt* **-lated; -lating** : isoler
insulation [ˌɪntsə'leɪʃən] *n* **1** : isolation *f* <thermal insulation : isolation thermique> **2** (*referring to material*) : isolant *m* <fiberglass insulation : isolant en fibre de verre>
insulator ['ɪntsəˌleɪṭər] *n* : isolateur *m*
insulin ['ɪntsələn] *n* : insuline *f*
insult[1] [ɪn'sʌlt] *vt* : insulter, injurier
insult[2] ['ɪnˌsʌlt] *n* : insulte *f*, injure *f*
insulting [ɪn'sʌltɪŋ] *adj* : insultant, injurieux
insultingly [ɪn'sʌltɪŋli] *adv* : de façon insultante
insurance [ɪn'ʃʊrənts] *n* : assurance *f* <fire insurance : assurance contre l'incendie>
insure [ɪn'ʃʊr] *vt* **-sured; -suring 1** UNDERWRITE : assurer **2** ENSURE : assurer, garantir
insured [ɪn'ʃʊrd] *n* : assuré *m*, -rée *f*
insurer [ɪn'ʃʊrər] *n* : assureur *m*
insurgence [ɪn'sərdʒənts] *n* : insurrection *f*
insurgency [ɪn'sərdʒəntsi] *n, pl* **-cies** → **insurgence**
insurgent[1] [ɪn'sərdʒənt] *adj* : insurgé
insurgent[2] *n* : insurgé *m*, -gée *f*
insurmountable [ˌɪnsər'maʊntəbəl] *adj* : insurmontable
insurrection [ˌɪnsə'rɛkʃən] *n* : insurrection *f*
intact [ɪn'tækt] *adj* : intact
intake ['ɪnˌteɪk] *n* **1** OPENING : prise *f*, arrivée *f* <intake valve : soupape d'admission> **2** ADMISSION : admission *f* **3** CONSUMPTION : consommation *f*
intangible [ɪn'tændʒəbəl] *adj* : intangible
integer ['ɪntɪdʒər] *n* : nombre *m* entier
integral ['ɪntɪgrəl] *adj* **1** ENTIRE, WHOLE : intégral, complet **2** CONSTITUENT : intégrant <to be an integral part of : faire partie intégrante de>
integrate ['ɪntəˌgreɪt] *v* **-grated; -grating** *vt* : intégrer — *vi* : s'intégrer
integration [ˌɪntə'greɪʃən] *n* : intégration *f*
integrity [ɪn'tɛgrəṭi] *n* : intégrité *f*
intellect ['ɪntəlˌɛkt] *n* : intelligence *f*, esprit *m*
intellectual[1] [ˌɪntə'lɛktʃʊəl] *adj* : intellectuel — **intellectually** *adv*
intellectual[2] *n* : intellectuel *m*, -tuelle *f*
intellectualism [ˌɪntə'lɛktʃʊəˌlɪzəm] *n* : intellectualisme *m*
intelligence [ɪn'tɛlədʒənts] *n* **1** : intelligence *f* **2** INFORMATION : renseignements *mpl*
intelligent [ɪn'tɛlədʒənt] *adj* : intelligent
intelligently [ɪn'tɛlədʒəntli] *adv* : intelligemment
intelligibility [ɪnˌtɛlədʒə'bɪləṭi] *n* : intelligibilité *f*
intelligible [ɪn'tɛlədʒəbəl] *adj* : intelligible — **intelligibly** [-bli] *adv*
intemperance [ɪn'tɛmpərənts] *n* : intempérance *f*, manque *m* de modération
intemperate [ɪn'tɛmpərət] *adj* : intempérant, incontrôlé
intend [ɪn'tɛnd] *vt* **1** DESTINE : destiner <a movie intended for children : un film destiné aux enfants> **2 to intend to** : avoir en tête de, avoir l'intention de <I intend to go : j'ai l'intention d'y aller, je pense y aller>
intended[1] [ɪn'tɛndəd] *adj* **1** PLANNED : projeté, voulu **2** INTENTIONAL : intentionnel
intended[2] *n* BETROTHED : fiancé *m*, -cée *f*
intense [ɪn'tɛnts] *adj* : intense, vif <intense pain : douleur intense>
intensely [ɪn'tɛntsli] *adv* **1** : intensément, avec intensité **2** EXTREMELY : extrêmement, profondément
intensification [ɪnˌtɛntsəfə'keɪʃən] *n* : intensification *f*
intensify [ɪn'tɛntsəˌfaɪ] *v* **-fied; -fying** *vt* : intensifier, renforcer — *vi* : s'intensifier
intensity [ɪn'tɛntsəṭi] *n, pl* **-ties** : intensité *f*
intensive [ɪn'tɛntsɪv] *adj* : intensif — **intensively** [ɪn'tɛntsɪvli] *adv*
intent[1] [ɪn'tɛnt] *adj* **1** CONCENTRATED : absorbé, fixe <an intent stare : un regard fixe> **2 intent on** *or* **intent upon** : résolu à
intent[2] *n* **1** PURPOSE : intention *f* **2 for all intents and purposes** : à toutes fins utiles
intention [ɪn'tɛntʃən] *n* : intention *f*
intentional [ɪn'tɛntʃənəl] *adj* : intentionnel, voulu
intentionally [ɪn'tɛntʃənəli] *adv* : intentionnellement
intently [ɪn'tɛntli] *adv* : attentivement
inter [ɪn'tər] *vt* **-terred; -terring** : enterrer
interact [ˌɪntər'ækt] *vi* **1** : agir l'un sur l'autre <we interact well : le courant passe bien entre nous> **2** (*referring to chemical reactions*) : agir réciproquement
interaction [ˌɪntər'ækʃən] *n* : interaction *f*
interactive [ˌɪntər'ækṭɪv] *adj* : interactif
interbreed [ˌɪntər'bri:d] *v* **-bred** [-'brɛd]; **-breeding** *vt* : croiser — *vi* : se croiser
intercede [ˌɪntər'si:d] *vi* **-ceded; -ceding** : intercéder
intercept [ˌɪntər'sɛpt] *vt* : intercepter

interception [ˌɪntərˈsɛpʃən] *n* : interception *f*

intercession [ˌɪntərˈsɛʃən] *n* : intercession *f*

interchange[1] [ˌɪntərˈtʃeɪndʒ] *vt* **-changed; -changing** EXCHANGE : échanger

interchange[2] *n* [ˈɪntərˌtʃeɪndʒ] **1** EXCHANGE : échange *m* **2** JUNCTION : échangeur *m*

interchangeable [ˌɪntərˈtʃeɪndʒəbəl] *adj* : interchangeable

intercity [ˈɪntərˈsɪti] *adj* : interurbain

intercollegiate [ˌɪntərkəˈliːdʒət, -dʒiət] *adj* : interuniversitaire

intercontinental [ˌɪntərˌkɑntənˈɛntəl] *adj* : intercontinental

intercourse [ˈɪntərˌkors] *n* **1** RELATIONS : relations *fpl*, rapports *mpl* **2** COPULATION : rapports *mpl* sexuels

interdenominational [ˌɪntərdɪˌnɑməˈneɪʃənəl] *adj* : interconfessionnel

interdepartmental [ˌɪntərdɪˌpɑrtˈmɛntəl, -ˌdiː-] *adj* : interdépartemental

interdependence [ˌɪntərdɪˈpɛndənts] *n* : interdépendance *f*

interdependent [ˌɪntərdɪˈpɛndənt] *adj* : interdépendant

interdict [ˌɪntərˈdɪkt] *vt* PROHIBIT : interdire

interest[1] [ˈɪntrəst, -təˌrɛst] *vt* : intéresser

interest[2] *n* **1** CURIOSITY : intérêt *m* **2** BENEFIT : avantage *m*, intérêt *m* <the public interest : l'intérêt public> **3** CHARGE : intérêt *m*, intérêts *mpl* <compound interest : intérêts composés> <interest rate : taux d'intérêt> **4** SHARE, STAKE : intérêts *mpl* **5** PURSUIT : centre *m* d'intérêt

interesting [ˈɪntrəstɪŋli, -təˌrɛstɪŋli] *adj* : intéressant

interestingly [ˈɪntrəstɪŋ, -təˌrɛstɪŋ] *adv* : de façon intéressante

interface [ˈɪntərˌfeɪs] *n* : interface *f*

interfere [ˌɪntərˈfɪr] *vi* **-fered; -fering 1** INTERVENE : intervenir, s'interposer **2** MEDDLE : s'immiscer, s'ingérer **3 to interfere with** DISRUPT : perturber, déranger **4 to interfere with** TOUCH : toucher à <who interfered with my work? : qui est-ce qui a touché à mon travail?>

interference [ˌɪntərˈfɪrənts] *n* **1** INTERVENTION : intervention *f*, ingérence *f* **2** : interférence *f* (en physique, de radio, etc.)

intergalactic [ˌɪntərgəˈlæktɪk] *adj* : intergalactique

intergovernmental [ˌɪntərˌgʌvərˈmɛntəl, -vərn-] *adj* : intergouvernemental

interim[1] [ˌɪntərəm] *adj* : provisoire, intérimaire <interim government : gouvernement provisoire>

interim[2] *n* **1** : intérim *m* **2 in the interim** : entre-temps

interior[1] [ɪnˈtɪriər] *adj* : intérieur

interior[2] *n* : intérieur *m*

interject [ˌɪntərˈdʒɛkt] *vt* : placer, lancer (un mot)

interjection [ˌɪntərˈdʒɛkʃən] *n* **1** : interjection *f* (en linguistique) **2** INTERRUPTION : interruption *f*

interlace [ˌɪntərˈleɪs] *vt* **-laced; -lacing** : entrelacer, entrecroiser

interlock [ˌɪntərˈlɑk] *vt* **1** INTERTWINE : entrelacer **2** ENGAGE, MESH : enclencher — *vi* : s'enclencher

interloper [ˌɪntərˈloːpər] *n* INTRUDER : intrus *m*, -truse *f*

interlude [ˈɪntərˌluːd] *n* **1** INTERVAL : intervalle *m* **2** : intermède *m* (au théâtre) **3** : interlude *m* (en musique)

intermarriage [ˌɪntərˈmærɪdʒ] *n* : mariage *m* mixte

intermarry [ˌɪntərˈmæri] *vi* **-married; -marrying 1** : se marier (entre membres d'autres groupes) **2** : se marier entre soi (entre membres du même groupe)

intermediary[1] [ˌɪntərˈmiːdiˌɛri] *adj* : intermédiaire

intermediary[2] *n, pl* **-aries** : intermédiaire *mf*

intermediate[1] [ˌɪntərˈmiːdiət] *adj* : intermédiaire

intermediate[2] *n* : intermédiaire *mf*

interment [ɪnˈtərmənt] *n* : enterrement *m*, inhumation *f*

interminable [ɪnˈtərmənəbəl] *adj* : interminable — **interminably** [-bli] *adv*

intermingle [ˌɪntərˈmɪŋgəl] *v* **-mingled; -mingling** *vt* : entremêler — *vi* : se mélanger, s'entremêler

intermission [ˌɪntərˈmɪʃən] *n* **1** BREAK, PAUSE : interruption *f*, pause *f* **2** : entracte *m* (au théâtre)

intermittent [ˌɪntərˈmɪtənt] *adj* : intermittent

intermittently [ˌɪntərˈmɪtəntli] *adv* : par intermittence

intern[1] [ˈɪnˌtərn, ɪnˈtərn] *vt* : interner — *vi* : faire un stage, faire son internat (en médecine)

intern[2] [ˈɪnˌtərn] *n* **1** : interne *mf* (à l'hôpital) **2** : stagiaire *mf* (en entreprise)

internal [ɪnˈtərnəl] *adj* **1** : interne <internal investigation : enquête interne> <internal bleeding : hémorragie interne> <internal combustion engine : moteur à combustion interne> **2** : intérieur <internal affairs : affaires intérieures>

internally [ɪnˈtərnəli] *adv* : intérieurement

international [ˌɪntərˈnæʃənəl] *adj* : international — **internationally** *adv*

internationalize [ˌɪntərˈnæʃənəˌlaɪz] *vt* **-ized; -izing** : internationaliser

internee [ˌɪnˌtərˈniː] *n* : interné *m*, -née *f*

internist [ˈɪnˌtərnɪst] *n* : interniste *mf*

internment [ɪnˈtərnmənt, ˈɪn-] *n* : internement *m*

internship [ˈɪn͵tɛrn͵ʃɪp] *n* : stage *m* (en entreprise), internat *m* (en médecine)

interpersonal [͵ɪntərˈpərsənəl] *adj* : interpersonnel

interplay [ˈɪntər͵pleɪ] *n* : interaction *f*

interpolate [ɪnˈtərpə͵leɪt] *vt* **-lated; -lating** : interpoler

interpose [͵ɪntərˈpo:z] *v* **-posed; -posing** *vt* : interposer — *vi* : s'interposer, intervenir

interposition [͵ɪntərpəˈzɪʃən] *n* : interposition *f*

interpret [ɪnˈtərprət] *vt* : interpréter

interpretation [ɪn͵tərprəˈteɪʃən] *n* : interprétation *f*

interpretative [ɪnˈtərprə͵teɪt̬ɪv] *adj* : interprétatif

interpreter [ɪnˈtərprət̬ər] *n* : interprète *mf*

interpretive [ɪnˈtərprət̬ɪv] → **interpretative**

interracial [͵ɪntərˈreɪʃəl] *adj* : interracial

interrelate [͵ɪntərɪˈleɪt] *v* **-lated; -lating** *vt* : mettre en corrélation — *vi* : être en corrélation

interrelationship [͵ɪntərɪˈleɪʃən͵ʃɪp] *n* : interrelation *f*, corrélation *f*

interrogate [ɪnˈtɛrə͵geɪt] *vt* **-gated; -gating** : interroger

interrogation [ɪn͵tɛrəˈgeɪʃən] *n* : interrogation *f*

interrogative[1] [͵ɪntəˈrɑgət̬ɪv] *adj* : interrogatif, interrogateur

interrogative[2] *n* : interrogatif *m* (en linguistique)

interrogator [ɪnˈtɛrə͵geɪt̬ər] *n* : interrogateur *m*, -trice *f*

interrogatory [͵ɪntəˈrɑgə͵tɔri] → **interrogative**[1]

interrupt [͵ɪntəˈrʌpt] *v* : interrompre

interruption [͵ɪntəˈrʌpʃən] *n* : interruption *f*

intersect [͵ɪntərˈsɛkt] *vt* : croiser, couper — *vi* : se croiser, se couper

intersection [͵ɪntərˈsɛkʃən] *n* **1** JUNCTION : croisement *m*, carrefour *m* **2** : intersection *f* (en géométrie)

intersperse [͵ɪntərˈspərs] *vt* **-spersed; -spersing** : parsemer, entremêler

interstate [ˈɪntər͵steɪt] *n or* **interstate highway** : autoroute *f*

interstellar [͵ɪntərˈstɛlər] *adj* : interstellaire

interstice [ɪnˈtərstəs] *n, pl* **-stices** [-stə͵si:z, -stəsəz] : interstice *m*

intertwine [͵ɪntərˈtwaɪn] *v* **-twined; -twining** *vt* : entrelacer — *vi* : s'entrelacer

interval [ˈɪntərvəl] *n* : intervalle *m*

intervene [͵ɪntərˈvi:n] *vi* **-vened; -vening** **1** ELAPSE : s'écouler **2** INTERCEDE : intervenir, s'interposer

intervention [͵ɪntərˈvɛntʃən] *n* : intervention *f*

interview[1] [ˈɪntər͵vju:] *vt* **1** : faire passer un entretien, faire passer une entrevue **2** : interviewer (à la télévision, etc.)

interview[2] *n* **1** : entretien *m*, entrevue *f* **2** : interview *f* (à la télévision, etc.)

interviewer [ˈɪntər͵vju:ər] *n* **1** : personne *f* qui fait passer des entretiens **2** : intervieweur *m*, -vieweuse *f* (à la télévision)

interweave [͵ɪntərˈwi:v] *v* **-wove** [-ˈwo:v]; **-woven** [-ˈwo:vən]; **-weaving** *vt* : entremêler, entrelacer — *vi* : s'entremêler, s'entrelacer

intestate [ɪnˈtɛs͵teɪt, -tət] *adj* : intestat

intestinal [ɪnˈtɛstənəl] *adj* : intestinal

intestine [ɪnˈtɛstən] *n* : intestin *m* <large intestine : gros intestin> <small intestine : intestin grêle>

intimacy [ˈɪntəməsi] *n, pl* **-cies** : intimité *f*

intimate[1] [ˈɪntə͵meɪt] *vt* **-mated; -mating** : laisser entendre, insinuer

intimate[2] [ˈɪntəmət] *adj* : intime — **intimately** *adv*

intimate[3] *n* : intime *mf*

intimation [͵ɪntəˈmeɪʃən] *n* : indication *f*, pressentiment *m*

intimidate [ɪnˈtɪmə͵deɪt] *vt* **-dated; -dating** : intimider

intimidation [ɪn͵tɪməˈdeɪʃən] *n* : intimidation *f*

into [ˈɪn͵tu:] *prep* **1** (*indicating motion*) : dans, en <to go into the house : entrer dans la maison> <to go into town : aller en ville> <to put into a drawer : mettre dans un tiroir> **2** (*indicating state or condition*) : en <to burst into tears : fondre en larmes> <to translate into English : traduire en anglais> **3** AGAINST : contre <to crash into a wall : s'écraser contre un mur> **4** (*used in mathematics*) <3 into 12 is 4 : 12 divisé par 3 fait 4>

intolerable [ɪnˈtɑlərəbəl] *adj* : intolérable — **intolerably** [-bli] *adv*

intolerance [ɪnˈtɑlərən*t*s] *n* : intolérance *f*

intolerant [ɪnˈtɑlərənt] *adj* : intolérant

intonation [͵ɪntəˈneɪʃən] *n* : intonation *f*

intoxicate [ɪnˈtɑksə͵keɪt] *vt* **-cated; -cating** : enivrer

intoxicated [ɪnˈtɑksə͵keɪt̬əd] *adj* : ivre

intoxicating [ɪnˈtɑksə͵keɪt̬ɪŋ] *adj* : enivrant, excitant

intoxication [ɪn͵tɑksəˈkeɪʃən] *n* : ivresse *f*

intractable [ɪnˈtræktəbəl] *adj* : intraitable, inflexible

intramural [͵ɪntrəˈmjʊrəl] *adj* : interne, entre élèves de la même université

intransigence [ɪnˈtræn*t*sədʒən*t*s, -ˈtrænzə-] *n* : intransigeance *f*

intransigent [ɪnˈtræn*t*sədʒənt, -ˈtrænzə-] *adj* : intransigeant

intravenous [͵ɪntrəˈvi:nəs] *adj* : intraveineux

intrepid [ɪnˈtrɛpəd] *adj* : intrépide

intricacy [ˈɪntrɪkəsi] *n, pl* **-cies** : complexité *f*

intricate [ˈɪntrɪkət] *adj* : compliqué, complexe

intricately ['ɪntrɪkətli] *adv* : de façon complexe
intrigue[1] [ɪn'tri:g] *v* **-trigued; -triguing** : intriguer
intrigue[2] ['ɪn,tri:g, ɪn'tri:g] *n* : intrigue *f*
intriguing [ɪn'tri:gɪŋ] *adj* : fascinant
intrinsic [ɪn'trɪnzɪk, -'trɪntsɪk] *adj* : intrinsèque — **intrinsically** [-zɪkli, -sɪ-] *adv*
introduce [,ɪntrə'du:s, -'dju:s] *vt* **-duced; -ducing 1** : introduire (une idée, un nouveau produit, etc.) **2** PRESENT : présenter <let me introduce my father : permettez-moi de présenter mon père>
introduction [,ɪntrə'dʌkʃən] *n* **1** : introduction *f* (d'une idée, d'un produit, etc.) **2** PRESENTATION : présentation *f*
introductory [,ɪntrə'dʌktəri] *adj* : d'introduction, préliminaire
introspection [,ɪntrə'spɛkʃən] *n* : introspection *f*
introspective [,ɪntrə'spɛktɪv] *adj* : introspectif — **introspectively** *adv*
introvert ['ɪntrə,vərt] *n* : introverti *m*, -tie *f*
introverted ['ɪntrə,vərt̬əd] *adj* : introverti
intrude [ɪn'tru:d] *vi* **-truded; -truding 1** INTERRUPT : s'imposer <I don't wish to intrude : je ne veux pas vous déranger> **2** INTERFERE : s'ingérer, s'immiscer <to intrude on s.o.'s private life : s'immiscer dans la vie privée de qqn>
intruder [ɪn'tru:dər] *n* : intrus *m*, -truse *f*
intrusion [ɪn'tru:ʒən] *n* : intrusion *f*
intrusive [ɪn'tru:sɪv] *adj* : importun, gênant
intuit [ɪn'tu:ɪt, -'tju:-] *vt* : savoir intuitivement
intuition [,ɪntʊ'ɪʃən, -tjʊ-] *n* : intuition *f*
intuitive [ɪn'tu:ət̬ɪv, -'tju:-] *adj* : intuitif — **intuitively** *adv*
Inuit[1] ['ɪnʊwət, -njʊ-] *adj* : inuit
Inuit[2] *n* : Inuit *m*, Inuite *f*
inundate ['ɪnən,deɪt] *vt* **-dated; -dating** : inonder
inundation [,ɪnən'deɪʃən] *n* : inondation *f*
inure [ɪ'nʊr, -'njʊr] *vt* **-ured; -uring** : endurcir <to be inured to hardship : être habitué aux épreuves>
invade [ɪn'veɪd] *vt* **-vaded; -vading** : envahir
invader [ɪn'veɪdər] *n* : envahisseur *m*, -seuse *f*
invalid[1] [ɪn'væləd] *adj* NULL : invalide
invalid[2] ['ɪnvələd] *adj* ILL : malade, infirme
invalid[3] ['ɪnvələd] *n* : invalide *mf*
invalidate [ɪn'vælə,deɪt] *vt* **-dated; -dating** : invalider
invalidity [,ɪnvə'lɪdət̬i] *n, pl* **-ties** : invalidité *f*
invaluable [ɪn'væljəbəl, -'væljʊə-] *adj* : inestimable, précieux
invariable [ɪn'væriəbəl] *adj* : invariable — **invariably** [-bli] *adv*
invasion [ɪn'veɪʒən] *n* : invasion *f*
invasive [ɪn'veɪsɪv] *adj* : invasif
invective [ɪn'vɛktɪv] *n* : invective *f*
inveigh [ɪn'veɪ] *vi* **to inveigh against** : invectiver contre
inveigle [ɪn'veɪgəl, -'vi:-] *vt* **-gled; -gling** : enjôler, manipuler
invent [ɪn'vɛnt] *vt* : inventer
invention [ɪn'vɛntʃən] *n* : invention *f*
inventive [ɪn'vɛntɪv] *adj* : inventif
inventiveness [ɪn'vɛntɪvnəs] *n* : esprit *m* d'invention
inventor [ɪn'vɛntər] *n* : inventeur *m*, -trice *f*
inventory[1] ['ɪnvən,tɔri] *vt* **-ried; -rying** : inventorier
inventory[2] *n, pl* **-ries 1** LIST : inventaire *m* **2** STOCK : stock *m*
inverse[1] [ɪn'vərs, 'ɪn,vərs] *adj* : inverse — **inversely** *adv*
inverse[2] *n* : inverse *m*
inversion [ɪn'vərʒən] *n* : inversion *f*
invert [ɪn'vərt] *vt* : inverser, renverser
invertebrate[1] [ɪn'vərt̬əbrət, -,breɪt] *adj* : invertébré
invertebrate[2] *n* : invertébré *m*
invest [ɪn'vɛst] *vt* **1** AUTHORIZE, EMPOWER : investir **2** CONFER, ENDOW : investir, revêtir **3** : investir (de l'argent, du temps, etc.) — *vi* : investir <to invest in stocks : investir en actions>
investigate [ɪn'vɛstə,geɪt] *v* **-gated; -gating** *vt* : enquêter sur, examiner — *vi* : enquêter
investigation [ɪn,vɛstə'geɪʃən] *n* : investigation *f*, enquête *f*
investigative [ɪn'vɛstə,geɪt̬ɪv] *adj* : d'investigation <investigative reporter : journaliste d'investigation>
investigator [ɪn'vɛstə,geɪt̬ər] *n* : investigateur *m*, -trice *f*
investiture [ɪn'vɛstə,tʃʊr, -tʃər] *n* : investiture *f*
investment [ɪn'vɛstmənt] *n* : investissement *m*, placement *m*
investor [ɪn'vɛstər] *n* : investisseur *m*, -seuse *f*; actionnaire *mf*
inveterate [ɪn'vɛt̬ərət] *adj* : invétéré
invidious [ɪn'vɪdiəs] *adj* **1** OBNOXIOUS : odieux **2** UNJUST : injuste
invigorate [ɪn'vɪgə,reɪt] *vt* **-rated; -rating** : revigorer
invigorating [ɪn'vɪgə,reɪt̬ɪŋ] *adj* : revigorant
invigoration [ɪn,vɪgə'reɪʃən] *n* : revigoration *f*
invincibility [ɪn,vɪntsə'bɪlət̬i] *n* : invincibilité *f*
invincible [ɪn'vɪntsəbəl] *adj* : invincible
inviolable [ɪn'vaɪələbəl] *adj* : inviolable
inviolate [ɪn'vaɪələt] *adj* : inviolé
invisibility [ɪn,vɪzə'bɪlət̬i] *n* : invisibilité *f*

invisible [ɪn'vɪzəbəl] *adj* : invisible — **invisibly** [-bli] *adv*
invitation [ˌɪnvə'teɪʃən] *n* : invitation *f*
invite [ɪn'vaɪt] *vt* **-vited; -viting 1** ASK : inviter <we invited them for dinner : nous les avons invités à dîner> **2** PROVOKE : provoquer, chercher <to invite trouble : chercher des ennuis> **3** REQUEST, SOLICIT : solliciter (des questions, des observations, etc.)
inviting [ɪn'vaɪt̬ɪŋ] *adj* : attrayant, engageant
invocation [ˌɪnvə'keɪʃən] *n* : invocation *f*
invoice[1] ['ɪnˌvɔɪs] *vt* **-voiced; -voicing** : facturer
invoice[2] *n* : facture *f*
invoke [ɪn'vo:k] *vt* **-voked; -voking 1** : invoquer, demander (de l'aide, etc.) **2** CITE : invoquer **3** CONJURE UP : évoquer, invoquer (des esprits, etc.)
involuntary [ɪn'vɑlənˌtɛri] *adj* : involontaire — **involuntarily** [ɪnˌvɑlən'tɛrəli] *adv*
involve [ɪn'vɑlv] *vt* **-volved; -volving 1** ENGAGE : engager **2** IMPLICATE : impliquer <to be involved in a crime : être impliqué dans un crime> **3** ENTAIL : entraîner, impliquer, occasionner
involved [ɪn'vɑlvd] *adj* INTRICATE : compliqué
involvement [ɪn'vɑlvmənt] *n* **1** PARTICIPATION : participation *f* **2** RELATIONSHIP : relation *f*, rapport *m*
invulnerable [ɪn'vʌlnərəbəl] *adj* : invulnérable
inward[1] ['ɪnwərd] *or* **inwards** ['ɪnwərdz] *adv* : vers l'intérieur
inward[2] *adj* INSIDE : intérieur
inwardly ['ɪnwərdli] *adv* **1** INTERNALLY : intérieurement **2** PRIVATELY : secrètement, en son for intérieur
iodide ['aɪəˌdaɪd] *n* : iodure *m*
iodine ['aɪəˌdaɪn] *n* : iode *m*, teinture *f* d'iode
iodized ['aɪəˌdaɪzd] *adj* : iodé
ion ['aɪən, 'aɪˌɑn] *n* : ion *m*
ionize ['aɪəˌnaɪz] *v* **-ized; -izing** : ioniser
ionosphere [aɪ'ɑnəˌsfɪr] *n* : ionosphère *f*
iota [aɪ'o:t̬ə] *n* : iota *m*, brin *m*
IOU [ˌaɪˌo'ju:] *n* : reconnaissance *f* de dette
Iranian[1] [ɪ'reɪniən, -'ræ-, -'rɑ-; aɪ'-] *adj* : iranien
Iranian[2] *n* : Iranien *m*, -nienne *f*
Iraqi[1] [ɪ'rɑki, -'ræ-] *adj* : irakien
Iraqi[2] *n* : Irakien *m*, -kienne *f*
irascible [ɪ'ræsəbəl] *adj* : irascible
irate [aɪ'reɪt] *adj* : furieux — **irately** *adv*
ire ['aɪr] *n* : courroux *m*, colère *f*
iridescence [ˌɪrə'dɛsənts] *n* : irisation *f*
iridescent [ˌɪrə'dɛsənt] *adj* : irisé
iris ['aɪrəs] *n, pl* **irises** *or* **irides** ['aɪrəˌdi:z, 'ɪr-] **1** : iris *m* (de l'œil) **2** *pl* **irises** : iris *m* (plante)
Irish[1] ['aɪrɪʃ] *adj* : irlandais
Irish[2] *n* **1** : irlandais *m* (langue) **2 the Irish** : les Irlandais
Irishman ['aɪrɪʃmən] *n* : Irlandais *m*
Irishwoman ['aɪrɪʃˌwʊmən] *n* : Irlandaise *f*
irk ['ərk] *vt* : ennuyer, irriter, agacer
irksome ['ərksəm] *adj* : ennuyeux, irritant, agaçant
iron[1] ['aɪərn] *vt* **1** : repasser (des vêtements) **2 to iron out** : aplanir (un problème) — *vi* : se repasser
iron[2] *n* **1** : fer *m* (métal) **2** : fer *m* à repasser
ironclad ['aɪərn'klæd] *adj* **1** : cuirassé (se dit d'un navire) **2** STRICT : rigoureux, strict
ironic [aɪ'rɑnɪk] *or* **ironical** [-nɪkəl] *adj* : ironique — **ironically** [-kli] *adv*
ironing ['aɪərnɪŋ] *n* : repassage *m*
ironwork ['aɪərnˌwərk] *n* **1** : ferronnerie *f* **2 ironworks** *npl* : usine *f* sidérurgique
irony ['aɪrəni] *n, pl* **-nies** : ironie *f*
irradiate [ɪ'reɪdiˌeɪt] *vt* **-ated; -ating** : irradier
irradiation [ɪˌreɪdi'eɪʃən] *n* : irradiation *f*
irrational [ɪ'ræʃənəl] *adj* : irrationnel — **irrationally** *adv*
irrationality [ɪˌræʃə'nælət̬i] *n* : irrationalité *f*
irreconcilable [ɪˌrɛkən'saɪləbəl] *adj* : irréconciliable, inconciliable
irrecoverable [ˌɪrɪ'kʌvərəbəl] *adj* : irrécupérable
irredeemable [ˌɪrɪ'di:məbəl] *adj* **1** HOPELESS : irrémédiable **2** : non remboursable (se dit d'un bon, etc.)
irreducible [ˌɪrɪ'du:səbəl, -'dju:-] *adj* : irréductible — **irreducibly** [-bli] *adv*
irrefutable [ˌɪrɪ'fju:t̬əbəl, ɪ'rɛfjə-] *adj* : irréfutable — **irrefutably** [-bli] *adv*
irregular [ɪ'rɛgjələr] *adj* : irrégulier
irregularity [ɪˌrɛgjə'lærət̬i] *n, pl* **-ties** : irrégularité *f*
irregularly [ɪ'rɛgjələrli] *adv* : irrégulièrement
irrelevance [ɪ'rɛləvənts] *n* : manque *m* de rapport
irrelevant [ɪ'rɛləvənt] *adj* : sans rapport, non pertinent
irreligious [ˌɪrɪ'lɪdʒəs] *adj* : irréligieux
irreparable [ɪ'rɛpərəbəl] *adj* : irréparable
irreplaceable [ˌɪrɪ'pleɪsəbəl] *adj* : irremplaçable
irrepressible [ˌɪrɪ'prɛsəbəl] *adj* : irrépressible
irreproachable [ˌɪrɪ'pro:tʃəbəl] *adj* : irréprochable
irresistible [ˌɪrɪ'zɪstəbəl] *adj* : irrésistible — **irresistibly** [-bli] *adv*
irresolute [ɪ'rɛzəˌlu:t] *adj* : irrésolu, indécis
irresolutely [ɪ'rɛzəˌlu:tli, -ˌrɛzə'lu:t-] *adv* : d'un air indécis

irrespective of [ˌɪrɪ'spɛktɪvəv] *prep* : sans tenir compte de
irresponsibility [ˌɪrɪˌspɑntsə'bɪləṭi] *n* : irresponsabilité *f*
irresponsible [ˌɪrɪ'spɑntsəbəl] *adj* : irresponsable
irresponsibly [ˌɪrɪ'spɑntsəbli] *adv* : de façon irresponsable
irretrievable [ˌɪrɪ'triːvəbəl] *adj* **1** LOST : introuvable **2** IRREPARABLE : irréparable, irrémédiable
irreverence [ɪ'rɛvərənts] *n* : irrévérence
irreverent [ɪ'rɛvərənt] *adj* : irrévérencieux
irreversible [ˌɪrɪ'vərsəbəl] *adj* : irréversible
irrevocable [ɪ'rɛvəkəbəl] *adj* : irrévocable — **irrevocably** [-bli] *adv*
irrigate ['ɪrəˌgeɪt] *vt* **-gated; -gating** : irriguer
irrigation [ˌɪrə'geɪʃən] *n* : irrigation *f*
irritability [ˌɪrəṭə'bɪləṭi] *n* : irritabilité *f*
irritable ['ɪrəṭəbəl] *adj* : irritable
irritably ['ɪrəṭəbli] *adv* : avec irritation
irritant[1] ['ɪrətənt] *adj* : irritant
irritant[2] *n* : irritant *m*
irritate ['ɪrəˌteɪt] *vt* **-tated; -tating 1** ANNOY : irriter, agacer **2** INFLAME : irriter
irritating ['ɪrəˌteɪṭɪŋ] *adj* : irritant, agaçant
irritatingly ['ɪrəˌteɪṭɪŋli] *adv* : de façon irritante
irritation [ˌɪrə'teɪʃən] *n* : irritation *f*
is → **be**
Islam [ɪs'lɑm, ɪz-, -'læm; 'ɪsˌlɑm] *n* : islam *m* — **Islamic** [-mɪk] *adj*
island ['aɪlənd] *n* : île *f*
islander ['aɪləndər] *n* : insulaire *mf*
isle ['aɪl] *n* : île *f*, îlot *m*
islet ['aɪlət] *n* : îlot *m*
isolate ['aɪsəˌleɪt] *vt* **-lated; -lating** : isoler
isolation [ˌaɪsə'leɪʃən] *n* : isolement *m* <to be in isolation : être isolé>
isometric [ˌaɪsə'mɛtrɪk] *adj* : isométrique
isometrics [ˌaɪsə'mɛtrɪks] *ns & pl* : exercices *mpl* isométriques
isosceles [aɪ'sɑsəˌliːz] *adj* : isocèle
isotope ['aɪsəˌtoːp] *n* : isotope *m*
Israeli[1] [ɪz'reɪli] *adj* : israélien
Israeli[2] *n* : Israélien *m*, -lienne *f*
issue[1] ['ɪˌʃuː] *v* **-sued; -suing** *vi* **1** EMERGE : s'écouler, sortir, déboucher **2** EMANATE, RESULT : provenir, résulter — *vt* **1** EMIT : émaner, émettre **2** DISTRIBUTE : distribuer **3** PUBLISH : publier, sortir **4** GIVE : donner, émettre <to issue orders : donner des ordres> <to issue a permit : émettre un permis>
issue[2] *n* **1** EGRESS : sortie *f*, issue *f* **2** OFFSPRING : descendance *f*, progéniture *f* **3** RESULT : résultat *m* **4** MATTER, QUESTION : question *f*, problème *m* **5** PUBLICATION : publication *f*, émission *f* **6** : numéro *m* <the latest issue of the magazine : le dernier numéro de la revue>
isthmus ['ɪsməs] *n* : isthme *m*
it ['ɪt] *pron* **1** (*as subject*) : il, elle **2** (*as direct object*) : le, la l' <give it to me : donne-le moi> **3** (*as indirect object*) : lui <I'll give it some water : je lui donnerai de l'eau> **4** (*as a nonspecific subject*) : ce, cela, ça <it's me : c'est moi> <what does it mean? : qu'est-ce que cela veut dire?> <that's it : c'est ça> **5** (*as subject of an impersonal verb*) <it's snowing : il neige> <it doesn't matter : cela ne fait rien>
Italian[1] [ɪ'tæliən, aɪ-] *adj* : italien
Italian[2] *n* **1** : Italien *m*, -lienne *f* **2** : italien *m* (langue)
italic[1] [ɪ'tælɪk, aɪ-] *adj* : italique
italic[2] *n* : italique *m* <in italics : en italique>
italicize [ɪ'tæləˌsaɪz, aɪ-] *vt* **-cized; -cizing** : mettre en italique
itch[1] ['ɪtʃ] *vi* **1** : avoir des démangeaisons **2** DESIRE : avoir très envie
itch[2] *n* **1** IRRITATION : démangeaison *f* **2** URGE : envie *f*, démangeaison *f*
itchy ['ɪtʃi] *adj* **itchier; -est** : qui démange
item ['aɪṭəm] *n* **1** OBJECT : article *m* **2** POINT, ISSUE : point *m* **3** *or* **news item** ARTICLE : article *m*
itemize ['aɪṭəˌmaɪz] *vt* **-ized; -izing** : détailler
itinerant [aɪ'tɪnərənt] *adj* : itinérant, ambulant
itinerary [aɪ'tɪnəˌrɛri] *n, pl* **-aries** : itinéraire *m*
its ["Its] *adj* : son, sa, ses <she liked its smell : elle aimait son odeur>
it's ["Its] (*contraction of* **it is** *or* **it has**) → **be, have**
itself [ɪtˌsɛlf] *pron* **1** (*used reflexively*) : se <the cat hurt itself : le chat s'est fait mal> **2** (*for emphasis*) : lui-même, elle-même, soi-même <the car itself was not damaged : la voiture elle-même n'était pas endommagée>
I've ['aɪv] (*contraction of* **I have**) → **have**
ivory ['aɪvəri] *n, pl* **-ries** : ivoire *m*
ivy ['aɪvi] *n, pl* **ivies 1** : lierre *m* **2** → **poison ivy**

J

j ['dʒeɪ] *n, pl* **j's** *or* **js** ['dʒeɪz] : j *m,* dixième lettre de l'alphabet
jab[1] ['dʒæb] *v* **jabbed; jabbing** *vt* **1** PIERCE : piquer **2** THRUST : enfoncer, planter — *vi* **to jab at** : donner un coup à, envoyer un direct à (un boxeur)
jab[2] *n* : petit coup *m,* direct *m* (en boxe)
jabber[1] ['dʒæbər] *vi* : jacasser, bavarder
jabber[2] *n* **1** CHATTER : bavardage *m,* papotage *m* **2** GIBBERISH : baragouin *m*
jack[1] ['dʒæk] *vt or* **to jack up 1** : soulever avec un cric **2** INCREASE : faire monter (des prix, etc.)
jack[2] *n* **1** : cric *m,* vérin *m* <hydraulic jack : vérin hydraulique> **2** FLAG : pavillon *m* **3** SOCKET : jack *m* **4** : valet *m* (aux cartes) **5 jacks** *npl* : osselets *mpl* (jeu)
jackal ['dʒækəl] *n* : chacal *m*
jackass ['dʒækˌæs] *n* **1** DONKEY : âne *m,* baudet *m fam* **2** FOOL : idiot *m,* -diote *f*
jacket ['dʒækət] *n* **1** : veste *f,* veston *m* **2** : jaquette *f* (d'un livre), pochette *f* (d'un disque)
jackhammer ['dʒækˌhæmər] *n* : marteau-piqueur *m*
jack–in–the–box ['dʒækɪnðəˌbɑks] *n, pl* **jack–in–the–boxes** *or* **jacks–in–the–box** : diable *m* à ressort
jackknife[1] ['dʒækˌnaɪf] *vi* **-knifed; -knifing** : se mettre en travers de la route (se dit d'un camion)
jackknife[2] *n, pl* **-knives:** couteau *m* de poche
jack–of–all–trades *n, pl* **jacks–of–all–trades** : homme *m* à tout faire
jack–o'–lantern ['dʒækəˌlæntərn] *n* : citrouille *f* taillée en forme de visage
jackpot ['dʒækˌpɑt] *n* : gros lot *m*
jackrabbit ['dʒækˌræbət] *n* : gros lièvre *m* d'Amérique
jade ['dʒeɪd] *n* : jade *m*
jaded ['dʒeɪdəd] *adj* **1** EXHAUSTED : fatigué **2** BORED : blasé
jagged ['dʒægəd] *adj* : dentelé, irrégulier
jaguar ['dʒægˌwɑr, 'dʒægjʊˌwɑr] *n* : jaguar *m*
jail[1] ['dʒeɪl] *vt* : emprisonner, incarcérer
jail[2] *n* : prison *f*
jailbreak ['dʒeɪlˌbreɪk] *n* : évasion *f* de prison
jailer *or* **jailor** ['dʒeɪlər] *n* : geôlier *m,* -lière *f*
jalopy [dʒə'lɑpi] *n, pl* **-lopies** : tacot *m fam,* guimbarde *f fam,* bazou *m Can fam*
jam[1] ['dʒæm] *v* **jammed; jamming** *vt* **1** CRAM : entasser **2** : bloquer, coincer <the computer keys are jammed : les touches de l'ordinateur sont coincées> **3** CONGEST, OBSTRUCT : bloquer, boucher — *vi* **1** : se bloquer, se coincer **2** PACK : s'entasser, s'empiler
jam[2] *n* **1** CONGESTION : encombrement *m,* embouteillage *m* **2** PRESERVE : confiture *f* **3** FIX, PREDICAMENT : pétrin *m fam*
Jamaican[1] [dʒə'meɪkən] *adj* : jamaïquain
Jamaican[2] *n* : Jamaïquain *m,* -quaine *f*
jamb ['dʒæm] *n* : jambage *m*
jamboree [ˌdʒæmbə'riː] *n* : grande fête *f*
jangle[1] ['dʒæŋgəl] *v* **-gled; -gling** *vi* : cliqueter — *vt* : faire cliqueter
jangle[2] *n* : cliquetis *m*
janitor ['dʒænət̬ər] *n* : gardien *m,* -dienne *f;* concierge *mf*
January ['dʒænjʊˌɛri] *n* : janvier *m*
Japanese[1] [ˌdʒæpə'niːz, -'niːs] *adj* : japonais
Japanese[2] *n* **1** : Japonais *m,* -naise *f* **2** : japonais *m* (langue)
jar[1] ['dʒɑr] *v* **jarred; jarring** *vi* **1** GRATE : grincer, crisser **2** CLASH : jurer **3 to jar on** : heurter <to jar on s.o.'s feelings : heurter la sensibilité de qqn> — *vt* **1** UNSETTLE : perturber **2** JOLT, SHAKE : ébranler, secouer
jar[2] *n* **1** JOLT, SHOCK : secousse *f,* choc *m* **2** : bocal *m,* pot *m* <a jar of honey : un bocal de miel>
jargon ['dʒɑrgən] *n* : jargon *m*
jasmine ['dʒæzmən] *n* : jasmin *m*
jasper ['dʒæspər] *n* : jaspe *m*
jaundice ['dʒɔndɪs] *n* : jaunisse *f*
jaundiced ['dʒɔndɪst] *adj* **1** : qui a la jaunisse **2** EMBITTERED : aigri, cynique, négatif <with a jaundiced eye : d'un mauvais œil>
jaunt ['dʒɔnt] *n* : balade *f,* excursion *f*
jauntily ['dʒɔntəli] *adv* : d'un air vif, joyeusement
jauntiness ['dʒɔntinəs] *n* : vivacité *f,* animation *f*
jaunty ['dʒɔnti] *adj* **jauntier; -est** : joyeux, guilleret
Javanese[1] [ˌdʒævə'niːz, ˌdʒɑvə-; -'niːs] *adj* : javanais
Javanese[2] *n* : Javanais *m,* -naise *f*
javelin ['dʒævələn] *n* : javelot *m*
jaw[1] ['dʒɔ] *vi* GAB : papoter, bavarder
jaw[2] *n* **1** : mâchoire *f* (d'un animal, d'un outil) **2 the jaws of death** : les griffes de la mort
jawbone ['dʒɔˌboːn] *n* : maxillaire *m*
jay ['dʒeɪ] *n* : geai *m*
jaybird ['dʒeɪˌbərd] → **jay**
jaywalk ['dʒeɪˌwɔk] *vi* : traverser la rue en dehors des passages pour piétons
jaywalker ['dʒeɪˌwɔkər] *n* : piéton *m* qui traverse la rue en dehors des passages pour piétons
jazz[1] ['dʒæz] *vt or* **to jazz up** ENLIVEN : égayer, animer

jazz[2] *n* : jazz *m*
jazzy ['dʒæzi] *adj* **jazzier; -est 1** : de jazz **2** FLASHY, SHOWY : tapageur, voyant
jealous ['dʒɛləs] *adj* : jaloux — **jealously** *adv*
jealousy ['dʒɛləsi] *n, pl* **-sies** : jalousie *f*
jeans ['dʒi:nz] *npl* : jean *m*, blue-jean *m*
jeep ['dʒi:p] *n* : jeep *f*
jeer[1] ['dʒɪr] *vi* SCOFF : se moquer, se railler — *vt* **1** BOO : huer **2** TAUNT : railler
jeer[2] *n* TAUNT : raillerie *f*
Jehovah [dʒɪ'ho:və] *n* : Jéhovah *m*
jell ['dʒɛl] *vi* **1** CONGEAL, SET : prendre (en gelée), se gélifier **2** CRYSTALLIZE : prendre forme
jelly[1] ['dʒɛli] *v* **jellied; jellying** *vi* JELL : se gélifier — *vt* : gélifier
jelly[2] *n, pl* **-lies** : gelée *f*
jellyfish ['dʒɛli,fɪʃ] *n* : méduse *f*
jeopardize ['dʒɛpər,daɪz] *vt* **-dized; -dizing** : mettre en danger, compromettre
jeopardy ['dʒɛpərdi] *n* : danger *m*, péril *m*
jerk[1] ['dʒərk] *vt* **1** TUG, YANK : tirer brusquement **2** JOLT : secouer — *vi or* **to jerk about** : cahoter
jerk[2] *n* **1** JOLT : saccade *f*, secousse *f* **2** : mouvement *m* brusque <he got up with a jerk : il s'est levé brusquement> **3** FOOL : idiot *m*, -diote *f*
jerkily ['dʒərkəli] *adv* : d'une manière saccadée, par à-coups
jerkin ['dʒərkən] *n* : gilet *m*
jerky ['dʒərki] *adj* **jerkier; -est** : saccadé
jerry–built ['dʒɛri,bɪlt] *adj* : peu solide, construit en carton-pâte
jersey ['dʒərzi] *n, pl* **-seys 1** : jersey *m* (tissu) **2** : tricot *m* (vêtement)
jest[1] ['dʒɛst] *vi* : plaisanter
jest[2] *n* : plaisanterie *f*
jester ['dʒɛstər] *n* : bouffon *m*
Jesus ['dʒi:zəs, -zəz] *n* : Jésus *m*
jet[1] ['dʒɛt] *vi* **jetted; jetting 1** SPURT : gicler, jaillir **2** : voyager en avion
jet[2] *n* **1** : jais *m* (minéral) **2** SPURT : jet *m* **3** *or* **jet airplane** : jet *m*, avion *m* à réaction
jet engine *n* : moteur *m* à réaction, réacteur *m*
jet–propelled *adj* : à réaction
jetsam ['dʒɛtsəm] *n* : épave *f* flottante <flotsam and jetsam : épaves flottantes>
jettison ['dʒɛt̬əsən] *vt* **1** : jeter par-dessus bord **2** DISCARD : se débarrasser de
jetty ['dʒɛt̬i] *n, pl* **-ties 1** PIER, WHARF : embarcadère *m* **2** BREAKWATER : jetée *f*, brise-lames *m*
Jew ['dʒu:] *n* : Juif *m*, Juive *f*
jewel ['dʒu:əl] *n* **1** : bijou *m* **2** GEM : pierre *f* précieuse **3** : rubis *m* (d'une montre) **4** TREASURE : perle *f* (personne)
jeweler *or* **jeweller** ['dʒu:ələr] *n* : bijoutier *m*, -tière *f*; joaillier *m*, -lière *f*
jewelry *or Brit* **jewellery** ['dʒu:əlri] *n* : bijoux *mpl*
Jewish ['dʒu:ɪʃ] *adj* : juif
jib ['dʒɪb] *n* : foc *m*
jibe ['dʒaɪb] *vi* **jibed; jibing** AGREE : concorder
jiffy ['dʒɪfi] *n, pl* **-fies** : seconde *f*, instant *m* <in a jiffy : en un rien de temps>
jig[1] ['dʒɪg] *vi* **jigged; jigging** : danser la gigue
jig[2] *n* : gigue *f* (danse)
jigger ['dʒɪgər] *n* : mesure *f* qui contient une ou deux onces
jiggle[1] ['dʒɪgəl] *v* **-gled; -gling** *vt* : secouer, agiter — *vi* : se trémousser
jiggle[2] *n* : secousse *f*
jigsaw ['dʒɪg,sɔ] *n* : scie *f* sauteuse
jigsaw puzzle *n* : puzzle *m*
jilt ['dʒɪlt] *vt* : abandonner, plaquer *fam*
jimmy[1] ['dʒɪmi] *vt* **-mied; -mying** : forcer à la pince-monseigneur
jimmy[2] *n, pl* **-mies** : pince-monseigneur *m*
jingle[1] ['dʒɪŋgəl] *v* **-gled; -gling** *vt* : faire tinter — *vi* : tinter
jingle[2] *n* **1** TINKLE : tintement *m* **2** : jingle *m*, refrain *m* publicitaire
jinx[1] ['dʒɪŋks] *vt* : porter la poisse à *fam*, porter la guigne à *fam*
jinx[2] *n* : guigne *f fam*, poisse *f fam*
jitters ['dʒɪt̬ərz] *npl* : frousse *f* <to have the jitters : être nerveux>
jittery ['dʒɪt̬əri] *adj* : nerveux
job ['dʒɑb] *n* **1** EMPLOYMENT : emploi *m*, travail *m* <to have a good job : avoir une belle situation> **2** TASK, WORK : travail *m*, tâche *f*
jobber ['dʒɑbər] *n* : grossiste *mf*
jobless ['dʒɑbləs] *adj* : sans emploi
jockey[1] ['dʒɑki] *v* **-eyed; -eying** *vt* MANIPULATE : manoeuvrer, manipuler — *vi* **to jockey for position** : essayer de se placer
jockey[2] *n, pl* **-eys** : jockey *m*
jocose [dʒo'ko:s] *adj* **1** MERRY : jovial, joyeux **2** HUMOROUS : facétieux
jocular ['dʒɑkjʊlər] *adj* : badin, jovial
jocularity [,dʒɑkjʊ'lærət̬i] *n* : jovialité *f*
jocularly ['dʒɑkjʊlərli] *adv* : jovialement
jodhpurs ['dʒɑdpərz] *npl* : jodhpurs *mpl*
jog[1] ['dʒɑg] *v* **jogged; jogging** *vt* **1** NUDGE : donner un petit coup à **2 to jog s.o.'s memory** : rafraîchir la mémoire à qqn — *vi* : faire du jogging
jog[2] *n* **1** PUSH, SHAKE : coup *m*, petite secousse *f* **2** : jogging *m* (aux sports), petit trot *m* (d'un cheval) **3** BEND : coude *m*, tournant *m* (d'une route)
jogger ['dʒɑgər] *n* : joggeur *m*, -geuse *f*
join ['dʒɔɪn] *vt* **1** UNITE : relier, unir <to be joined in marriage : être uni par les liens du mariage> **2** ADJOIN : avoisiner, être contigu à **3** MEET : rejoindre, retrouver **4** : se joindre à, de-

venir membre (d'un club, etc.) — *vi* 1 MEET : se rejoindre 2 : devenir membre (d'un club, etc.) 3 **to join together** : s'unir, se rejoindre
joiner ['dʒɔɪnər] *n* CARPENTER : menuisier *m*
joint[1] [dʒɔɪnt] *adj* : commun, conjugué
joint[2] *n* 1 : articulation *f* <knee joint : articulation du genou> <to put one's shoulder out of joint : se déboîter l'épaule> 2 JUNCTURE : joint *m*, raccord *m* (en menuiserie)
jointed [dʒɔɪntəd] *adj* : articulé
jointly ['dʒɔɪntli] *adv* : conjointement
joist ['dʒɔɪst] *n* : solive *f*
joke[1] ['dʒo:k] *vi* **joked; joking** : plaisanter
joke[2] *n* : plaisanterie *f*, blague *f*
joker ['dʒo:kər] *n* 1 WAG : farceur *m*, -ceuse *f*; blagueur *m*, -gueuse *f* 2 : joker *m* (aux cartes)
jokingly ['dʒo:kɪŋli] *adv* : en plaisantant
jollity ['dʒɑləṭi] *n, pl* **-ties** : gaieté *f*
jolly ['dʒɑli] *adj* **jollier; -est** : joyeux, gai
jolt[1] ['dʒo:lt] *vt* : secouer — *vi or* **to jolt along** : cahoter
jolt[2] *n* 1 BLOW, JAR : secousse *f*, coup *m* 2 SHOCK : choc *m* <the defeat was quite a jolt : la défaite nous a fait tout un choc>
jonquil ['dʒɑnkwɪl] *n* : jonquille *f*
Jordanian[1] [dʒɔr'deɪniən] *adj* : jordanien
Jordanian[2] *n* : Jordanien *m*, -nienne *f*
josh ['dʒɑʃ] *vt* TEASE : taquiner — *vi* JOKE : blaguer
jostle ['dʒɑsəl] *v* **-tled; -tling** *vt* : bousculer — *vi* : se bousculer
jot[1] ['dʒɑt] *vt* **jotted; jotting** : prendre note de <jot this down : prends ça en note>
jot[2] *n* BIT : iota *m* <it doesn't matter a jot : ça n'a pas la moindre importance>
jounce[1] ['dʒæʊnts] *vt* **jounced; jouncing** : secouer
jounce[2] *n* JOLT : secousse *f*
journal ['dʒərnəl] *n* 1 DIARY : journal *m* intime 2 PERIODICAL : revue *f* 3 NEWSPAPER : journal *m*, quotidien *m*
journalism ['dʒərnəl,ɪzəm] *n* : journalisme *m*
journalist ["dZərnəlIst] *n* : journaliste *mf*
journalistic [,dʒərnəl'ɪstɪk] *adj* : journalistique
journey[1] ['dʒərni] *vi* **-neyed; -neying** TRAVEL : voyager
journey[2] *n, pl* **-neys** : voyage *m*
journeyman ['dʒərnimən] *n, pl* **-men** [-mən, -,mɛn] : compagnon *m*
joust[1] ['dʒaʊst] *vi* : jouter
joust[2] *n* : joute *f*
jovial ['dʒo:viəl] *adj* : jovial — **jovially** *adv*
joviality [,dʒo:vi'æləṭi] *n* : jovialité *f*
jowl ['dʒæʊl] *n* 1 JAW : mâchoire *f* 2 CHEEK : bajoue *f*
joy ['dʒɔɪ] *n* 1 HAPPINESS : joie *f*, allégresse *f* 2 PLEASURE : joie *f*, plaisir *m* <she's the joy of my life : elle est la joie de ma vie>
joyful ['dʒɔɪfəl] *adj* : joyeux — **joyfully** *adv*
joyless ['dʒɔɪləs] *adj* : sans joie, triste
joyous ['dʒɔɪəs] *adj* JOYFUL : joyeux — **joyously** *adv*
joyride ['dʒɔɪ,raɪd] *n* : virée *f* dans une voiture volée
jubilant ['dʒu:bələnt] *adj* : exultant, débordant de joie
jubilation [,dʒu:bə'leɪʃən] *n* : jubilation *f*
jubilee ['dʒu:bə,li:] *n* : jubilé *m*
Judaic [dʒu:'deɪɪk] *adj* : judaïque
Judaism ['dʒu:də,ɪzəm, 'dʒu:di-, 'dʒu:,deɪ-] *n* : judaïsme *m*
judge[1] ['dʒʌdʒ] *vt* **judged; judging** 1 ASSESS : juger, évaluer 2 TRY : juger (une cause) 3 CONSIDER, DEEM : juger, estimer
judge[2] *n* 1 : juge *m* 2 **to be a good judge of** : savoir juger de, être un bon juge en
judgment *or* **judgement** ['dʒʌdʒmənt] *n* 1 RULING : jugement *m*, verdict *m* 2 OPINION : avis *m*, opinion *f* 3 DISCERNMENT : jugement *m*, discernement *m*
judgmental [,dʒʌdʒ'mɛntəl] *adj* : enclin à juger <to be judgmental : s'ériger toujours en juge>
judicature ['dʒu:dɪkə,tʃʊr] *n* : justice *f*
judicial [dʒʊ'dɪʃəl] *adj* : judiciaire — **judicially** *adv*
judiciary[1] [dʒʊ'dɪʃi,ɛri, -'dɪʃəri] *adj* : judiciaire
judiciary[2] *n* 1 → **judicature** 2 : système *m* judiciaire
judicious [dʒʊ'dɪʃəs] *adj* : judicieux — **judiciously** *adv*
judo ['dʒu:,do:] *n* : judo *m*
jug ['dʒʌg] *n* : cruche *f*, pichet *m*, carafe *f*
juggernaut ['dʒʌgər,nɔt] *n* : force *f* irrésistible
juggle ['dʒʌgəl] *vi* **-gled; -gling** 1 : jongler 2 **to juggle with** MANIPULATE : jongler avec
juggler ['dʒʌgələr] *n* : jongleur *m*, -gleuse *f*
jugular vein ['dʒʌgjʊlər] *n* : jugulaire *f*
juice ['dʒu:s] *n* 1 : jus *m* <orange juice : jus d'orange> 2 ELECTRICITY : jus *m fam*, électricité *f*
juicer ['dʒu:sər] *n* : presse-fruits *m*
juiciness ['dʒu:sinəs] *n* : teneur *f* en jus
juicy ['dʒu:si] *adj* **juicier; -est** 1 : juteux <a juicy fruit : un fruit juteux> 2 RACY : savoureux
jukebox ['dʒu:k,bɑks] *n* : juke-box *m*
julep ['dʒu:ləp] *n* : cocktail *m* à la menthe

July [dʒʊ'laɪ] *n* : juillet *m*
jumble[1] ['dʒʌmbəl] *vt* **-bled; -bling** : brouiller, mélanger
jumble[2] *n* : fouillis *m,* désordre *m*
jumbo[1] ['dʒʌm,bo:] *adj* : énorme, géant
jumbo[2] *n, pl* **-bos** : quelque chose de très grand en son genre
jump[1] ['dʒʌmp] *vi* **1** LEAP : sauter, bondir **2** START : sursauter **3** MOVE : passer <she jumped from job to job : elle a passé d'un emploi à un autre> **4** RISE : monter en flèche (se dit des prix, etc) **5 to jump at** : saisir (une occasion, etc.) — *vt* : sauter, franchir <to jump a hurdle : franchir une haie>
jump[2] *n* **1** LEAP : saut *m,* bond *m* **2** INCREASE : bond *m,* hausse *f* **3** ADVANTAGE : avantage *m* <to get the jump on s.o. : devancer qqn>
jumper ['dʒʌmpər] *n* **1** : sauteur *m,* -teuse *f* (aux sports) **2** : robe-chasuble *f* (vêtement)
jumpy ['dʒʌmpi] *adj* **jumpier; -est** : nerveux
junction ['dʒʌŋkʃən] *n* **1** JOINING : jonction *f* **2** : carrefour *m,* embranchement *m* (de deux routes)
juncture ['dʒʌŋktʃər] *n* **1** JOINT : joint *m,* jointure *f* **2** POINT, SITUATION : conjoncture *f* <at this juncture : dans la conjoncture actuelle>
June ['dʒu:n] *n* : juin *m*
jungle ['dʒʌŋgəl] *n* : jungle *f*
junior[1] ['dʒu:njər] *adj* **1** YOUNGER : cadet, plus jeune **2** SUBORDINATE : subalterne
junior[2] *n* **1** : cadet *m,* -dette *f* <a man six years my junior : un homme de six ans mon cadet> **2** SUBORDINATE : subalterne *mf* **3** : élève *mf* de troisième année; étudiant *m,* -diante *f* de troisième année
juniper ['dʒu:nəpər] *n* : genévrier *m*
junk[1] ['dʒʌŋk] *vt* SCRAP : balancer *fam,* mettre au rancart *fam*
junk[2] *n* **1** RUBBISH : camelote *f fam,* pacotille *f* **2** STUFF : choses *fpl,* trucs *mpl fam* **3** : jonque *f* (bateau)
junket ['dʒʌŋkət] *n* : voyage *m* (aux frais de l'État)
junta ['hʊntə, 'dʒʌn-, 'hʌn-] *n* : junte *f*
Jupiter ['dʒu:pət̬ər] *n* : Jupiter *f* (planète)
jurisdiction [,dʒʊrəs'dɪkʃən] *n* : juridiction *f*
jurisprudence [,dʒʊrəs'pru:dənts] *n* : jurisprudence *f*
jurist ['dʒʊrɪst] *n* : juriste *mf*
juror ['dʒʊrər] *n* : juré *m,* -rée *f*
jury [''dZUri] *n, pl* **-ries** : jury *m*
just[1] ['dʒʌst] *adv* **1** EXACTLY : exactement <it's just right : c'est parfait> **2** : tout juste <the bell just rang : la cloche vient tout juste de sonner> **3** BARELY : à peine <he just made it : il est à peine arrivé à temps> **4** SIMPLY : simplement <just be yourself : sois toi-même, tout simplement> **5** QUITE : vraiment <just wonderful : vraiment merveilleux> **6** POSSIBLY : peut-être <it just might work : ça peut peut-être marcher> **7 just about** ALMOST : presque
just[2] *adj* **1** FAIR : juste, équitable **2** DESERVED : mérité
justice ['dʒʌstɪs] *n* **1** : justice *f,* équité *f* **2** JUDGE : juge *m*
justifiable [,dʒʌstə'faɪəbəl] *adj* : justifiable
justification [,dʒʌstəfə'keɪʃən] *n* : justification *f*
justify ['dʒʌstə,faɪ] *vt* **-fied; -fying** : justifier
justly ['dʒʌstli] *adv* : avec justice, justement
jut ['dʒʌt] *vi* **jutted; jutting** *or* **to jut out** : dépasser, s'avancer en saillie
jute ['dʒu:t] *n* : jute *m*
juvenile[1] ['dʒu:və,naɪl, -vənəl] *adj* **1** YOUNG : jeune <juvenile delinquent : jeune délinquant> **2** CHILDISH : puéril
juvenile[2] *n* : mineur *m,* -neure *f;* jeune *mf*
juxtapose ['dʒʌkstə,po:z] *vt* **-posed; -posing** : juxtaposer
juxtaposition [,dʒʌkstəpə'zɪʃən] *n* : juxtaposition *f*

K

k ['keɪ] *n, pl* **k's** *or* **ks** ['keɪz] : k *m,* onzième lettre de l'alphabet
kale ['keɪl] *n* : chou *m* frisé
kaleidoscope [kə'laɪdə,sko:p] *n* : kaléidoscope *m*
kangaroo [,kæŋgə'ru:] *n, pl* **-roos** : kangourou *m*
kaolin ['keɪələn] *n* : kaolin *m*
karat ['kærət] *n* : carat *m*
karate [kə'rɑt̬i] *n* : karaté *m*
katydid ['keɪt̬i,dɪd] *n* : sauterelle *f* d'Amérique du Nord
kayak ['kaɪ,æk] *n* : kayak *m,* kayac *m*
keel[1] ['ki:l] *vi* **to keel over** : chavirer (se dit d'un bateau), s'évanouir, tomber dans les pommes *fam* (se dit des personnes)
keel[2] *n* : quille *f*
keen ['ki:n] *adj* **1** SHARP : aiguisé, affilé **2** PENETRATING : vif, pénétrant **3** EA-

GER, ENTHUSIASTIC : enthousiaste **4** ACUTE : perçant <keen eyesight : vue perçante>

keenly ['ki:nli] *adv* : vivement, profondément

keep[1] ['ki:p] *v* **kept** ['kɛpt]; **keeping** *vt* **1** FULFILL : tenir (une promesse, etc.) **2** PROTECT : garder **3** MAINTAIN : tenir, garder <to keep a diary : tenir un journal> **4** DETAIN, RETAIN : garder, retenir **5** PRESERVE : garder (un secret) **6 to keep out** : empêcher d'entrer — *vi* **1** : garder <keep to the right : gardez la droite> **2** REFRAIN : s'empêcher **3** : se conserver <food that keeps well : des aliments qui se conservent bien> **4 to keep on** : continuer <she kept on asking me questions : elle n'arrêtait pas de me poser des questions>

keep[2] *n* **1** : donjon *m* (d'un château fort) **2 to earn one's keep** : gagner de quoi vivre **3 for keeps** : pour de bon

keeper ['ki:pər] *n* : gardien *m*, -dienne *f*

keeping ['ki:pɪŋ] *n* **1** CARE : garde *f* <in the keeping of : à la garde de> **2 in keeping with** : en accord avec, conformément à

keepsake ['ki:pˌseɪk] *n* : souvenir *m*

keg ['kɛg] *n* : baril *m*, tonnelet *m*

kelp ['kɛlp] *n* : varech *m*

ken ['kɛn] *n* **1** SIGHT : vision *f* **2** UNDERSTANDING : entendement *m* <it's beyond my ken : ça dépasse mon entendement>

kennel ['kɛnəl] *n* : chenil *m*

Kenyan[1] ['kɛnjən, 'ki:n-] *adj* : kenyan

Kenyan[2] *n* : Kenyan *m*, Kenyane *f*

kept → **keep**

kerchief ['kərtʃəf, -ˌtʃi:f] *n* : fichu *m*

kernel ['kərnəl] *n* **1** : amande *f* (d'un fruit ou d'une noix) **2** SEED : graine *f* (d'une céréale) **3** CORE : noyau *m*, cœur *m* <a kernel of truth : un fond de vérité>

kerosene *or* **kerosine** ['kɛrəˌsi:n, ˌkɛrə'-] *n* : kérosène *m*, pétrole *m* lampant

ketchup ['kɛtʃəp, 'kæ-] *n* : ketchup *m*

kettle ['kɛtəl] *n* : bouilloire *f*

kettledrum ['kɛtəlˌdrʌm] *n* : timbale *f*

key[1] ['ki:] *vt* **1** ATTUNE : accorder **2 to be keyed up** : être tendu, être surexcité

key[2] *adj* : fondamental, clé, crucial

key[3] *n* **1** : clé *f*, clef *f* <car key : clé de voiture> **2** MEANS, SOLUTION : clé *f*, clef *f* **3** : légende *f* (sur une carte) **4** : touche *f* (d'un clavier) **5** PITCH : ton *m* <in a major key : en majeur> **6** REEF : récif *m*

keyboard[1] ['ki:ˌbord] *vt* : saisir

keyboard[2] *n* : clavier *m*

keyhole ['ki:ˌho:l] *n* : trou *m* de serrure

keynote ['ki:ˌno:t] *n* **1** : tonique *f* (en musique) **2** : thème *m* principal, point *m* capital

keystone ['ki:ˌsto:n] *n* : clé *f* de voûte

khaki ['kæki, 'kɑ-] *n* : kaki *m*

khan ['kɑn, 'kæn] *n* : khan *m*

kibbutz [kə'bʊts, -'bu:ts] *n, pl* **-butzim** [-ˌbʊt'si:m, -ˌbu:t-] : kibboutz *m*

kibitz ['kɪbɪts] *vi* : se mêler des affaires d'autrui

kibitzer ['kɪbɪtsər, kɪ'bɪt-] *n* : personne *f* qui se mêle des affaires d'autrui

kick[1] ['kɪk] *vt* : donner un coup de pied à — *vi* **1** PROTEST : se plaindre **2** RECOIL : reculer (se dit d'un fusil)

kick[2] *n* **1** : coup *m* de pied **2** RECOIL : recul *m* (d'un fusil) **3** PLEASURE, THRILL : plaisir *m* <to get a kick out of : prendre plaisir à>

kicker ['kɪkər] *n* : botteur *m*, -teuse *f* (aux sports)

kid[1] ['kɪd] *v* **kidded; kidding** *vi* : blaguer, plaisanter <no kidding! : sans blague!> — *vt* TEASE : taquiner

kid[2] *n* **1** GOAT : chevreau *m*, -vrette *f* **2** CHILD : gosse *mf France fam;* gamin *m*, -mine *f fam;* flot *m Can*

kidder ['kɪdər] *n* : blagueur *m*, -gueuse *f fam*

kidnap ['kɪdˌnæp] *vt* **-napped** *or* **-naped** [-ˌnæpt]; **-napping** *or* **-naping** [-ˌnæpɪŋ] : kidnapper, enlever

kidnapper *or* **kidnaper** ['kɪdˌnæpər] *n* : ravisseur *m*, -seuse *f;* kidnappeur *m*, -peuse *f*

kidney ['kɪdˌni] *n, pl* **-neys** : rein *m*

kidney bean *n* : haricot *m* rouge

kill[1] ['kɪl] *vt* **1** : tuer **2** DEFEAT : mettre son véto à (une loi, etc.) **3 to kill time** : tuer le temps — *vi* : tuer

kill[2] *n* **1** KILLING : mise *f* à mort **2** PREY : proie *f*

killer ['kɪlər] *n* : meurtrier *m*, -trière *f;* tueur *m*, tueuse *f*

killjoy ['kɪlˌdʒɔɪ] *n* : rabat-joie *mf*

kiln ['kɪl, 'kɪln] *n* : four *m* (à céramique)

kilo ['ki:ˌlo:] *n, pl* **-los** : kilo *m*

kilogram ['kɪləˌgræm, 'ki:-] *n* : kilogramme *m*

kilohertz ['kɪləˌhərts] *ns & pl* : kilohertz *m*

kilometer [kɪ'lɑmət̬ər] *n* : kilomètre *m*

kilowatt ['kɪləˌwɑt] *n* : kilowatt *m*

kilt ['kɪlt] *n* : kilt *m*

kilter ['kɪltər] *n* **out of kilter** : en panne, détraqué, en dérangement

kimono [kə'mo:no, -nə] *n, pl* **-nos** : kimono *m*

kin ['kɪn] *n* : parents *mpl*, famille *f*

kind[1] ['kaɪnd] *adj* : gentil, bienveillant, aimable

kind[2] *n* **1** ESSENCE : nature *f*, essence *f* <in degree, not in kind : en degré, pas en nature> **2** TYPE : genre *m*, sorte *f*, type *m* **3** CATEGORY : classe *f*

kindergarten ['kɪndərˌgɑrtən, -dən] *n* : jardin *m* d'enfants *France*, maternelle *f*, école *f* maternelle

kindhearted ['kaɪnd'hɑrt̬əd] *adj* : bon, qui a bon cœur

kindle ['kɪndəl] *vt* **-dled**; **-dling 1** LIGHT : allumer, enflammer **2** AROUSE : susciter, éveiller — *vi* : s'enflammer

kindliness ['kaɪndlinəs] *n* : gentillesse *f*, amabilité *f*

kindling ['kɪndlɪŋ, kɪndlən] *n* : petit bois *m*

kindly[1] ['kaɪndli] *adv* **1** AMIABLY, WARMLY : chaleureusement, affablement **2** COURTEOUSLY : gentiment, aimablement **3** PLEASE : s'il vous plaît <would you kindly pass the salad : pouvez-vous me passer la salade, s'il vous plaît> **4 to look kindly on sth** : voir qqch d'un bon œil

kindly[2] *adj* **kindlier**; **-est** : aimable, bienveillant

kindness ['kaɪndnəs] *n* : gentillesse *f*, bonté *f*

kind of *adv* SOMEWHAT : quelque peu

kindred[1] ['kɪndrəd] *adj* : apparenté, semblable <kindred spirits : âmes sœurs>

kindred[2] *n* : parents *mpl*, famille *f*

kinfolk ['kɪn,fo:k] *or* **kinfolks** *npl* → **kin**

king ['kɪŋ] *n* : roi *m*

kingdom ['kɪŋdəm] *n* : royaume *m*

kingfisher ['kɪŋ,fɪʃər] *n* : martin-pêcheur *m*

kingly ['kɪŋli] *adj* : royal, majestueux

king–size ['kɪŋ,saɪz] *or* **king–sized** [-,saɪzd] *adj* : (très) grand, géant

kink[1] ['kɪŋk] *vt* : entortiller — *vi* : s'entortiller

kink[2] *n* **1** TWIST : nœud *m* **2** CRAMP : crampe *f* <a kink in one's back : une crampe dans le dos> **3** IMPERFECTION : défaut *m*

kinky ['kɪŋki] *adj* **kinkier**; **-est** : excentrique, bizarre

kinship ['kɪn,ʃɪp] *n* : parenté *f*

kinsman ['kɪnzmən] *n, pl* **-men** [-mən, -,mɛn] : parent *m*

kinswoman ['kɪnz,wʊmən] *n, pl* **-women** [-,wɪmən] : parente *f*

kipper ['kɪpər] *n* : kipper *m*, hareng *m* saur

kiss[1] ['kɪs] *vt* : embrasser, donner un baiser à — *vi* : s'embrasser

kiss[2] *n* : baiser *m*, bec *m* *Can fam*

kit ['kɪt] *n* **1** : trousse *f* <first-aid kit : trousse de secours> **2 the whole kit and caboodle** : tout le bataclan *fam*

kitchen ['kɪtʃən] *n* : cuisine *f*

kite ['kaɪt] *n* **1** : milan *m* (oiseau) **2** : cerf-volant *m* <to fly a kite : faire voler un cerf-volant>

kith ['kɪθ] *n* **kith and kin** : amis *mpl* et parents *mpl*

kitten ['kɪtən] *n* : chaton *m*

kitty ['kɪṭi] *n, pl* **-ties 1** KITTEN : chaton *m* **2** FUND : cagnotte *f*

kitty–corner ['kɪṭi,kɔrnər] *or* **kitty–cornered** [-nərd] → **catercorner**

kiwi ['ki:,wi:] *n* : kiwi *m*

kleptomania [,klɛptə'meɪniə] *n* : kleptomanie *f*

kleptomaniac [,klɛptə'meɪni,æk] *n* : kleptomane *mf*

knack ['næk] *n* : don *m* <to have a knack for : avoir le don de>

knapsack ['næp,sæk] *n* : sac *m* à dos

knave ['neɪv] *n* **1** → **rascal 2** JACK : valet *m* (aux cartes)

knead ['ni:d] *vt* **1** : pétrir (de la pâte) **2** MASSAGE : masser

knee ['ni:] *n* : genou *m*

kneecap ['ni:,kæp] *n* : rotule *f*

kneel ['ni:l] *vi* **knelt** ['nɛlt] *or* **kneeled** ['ni:ld]; **kneeling** : s'agenouiller

knell ['nɛl] *n* : glas *m*

knew → **know**

knickers ['nɪkərz] *npl* : knickers *mpl*, pantalons *mpl* de golf

knickknack ['nɪk,næk] *n* : bibelot *m*, babiole *f*

knife[1] [naɪf] *vt* **knifed** [naɪft]; **knifing** : donner un coup de couteau à

knife[2] *n, pl* **knives** ['naɪvz] : couteau *m*

knight[1] ['naɪt] *vt* : faire chevalier

knight[2] *n* **1** : chevalier *m* **2** : cavalier *m* (aux échecs)

knighthood ['naɪt,hu:d] *n* : chevalerie *f*

knightly ['naɪtli] *adv* : chevaleresque

knit[1] ['nɪt] *v* **knit** *or* **knitted; knitting** *vt* **1** UNITE : joindre **2** : tricoter <to knit a sweater : tricoter un chandail> **3 to knit one's brows** : froncer les sourcils — *vi* : tricoter

knit[2] *n* : tricot *m*

knitter ['nɪṭər] *n* : tricoteur *m*, -teuse *f*

knob ['nɑb] *n* : poignée *f*, bouton *m*

knobby ['nɑbi] *adj* **knobbier**; **-est** : noueux

knock[1] ['nɑk] *vt* **1** HIT : cogner, frapper **2** DRIVE : enfoncer (un clou) **3** CRITICIZE : critiquer, dénigrer <don't knock it! : arrête de critiquer!> **4 to knock out** : assommer <the drug knocked him out : le médicament l'a assommé> **5 to knock out** DESTROY : mettre hors service — *vi* **1** : cogner <the engine is knocking : le moteur cogne> **2** COLLIDE : heurter

knock[2] *n* : coup *m*

knock down *vt* : renverser, envoyer par terre

knocker ['nɑkər] *n* : heurtoir *m* (d'une porte)

knock–kneed ['nɑk'ni:d] *adj* : cagneux

knoll ['no:l] *n* : butte *f*, tertre *m*

knot[1] ['nɑt] *v* **knotted**; **knotting** *vt* : nouer, faire un nœud dans (une cravate, etc.) — *vi* : se nouer

knot[2] *n* **1** : nœud *m* (dans une corde, dans un tronc d'arbre) **2** CLUSTER : petit groupe *m* **3** : nœud *m*, mille *m* marin (en navigation) **4 to tie the knot** : se marier

knotty ['nɑṭi] *adj* **knottier**; **-est 1** GNARLED : noueux **2** INTRICATE : compliqué, complexe

know ['no:] *v* **knew** ['nu:, 'nju:]; **known** ['no:n]; **knowing** *vt* **1** : connaître (une personne, un lieu) <he knows me well

: il me connaît bien> <to be known to : être connu de> **2** : savoir <she knows everything : elle sait tout> <he knows how to write : il sait écrire> **3** UNDERSTAND : comprendre <they know English : ils comprennent l'anglais> **4** RECOGNIZE : reconnaître **5** DISCERN, DISTINGUISH : discerner, distinguir **6 to know how to** : savoir <I don't know how to swim : je ne sais pas nager> — *vi* **1** : savoir <not that I know : pas que je sache> **2 to know about** : être au courant de (des nouvelles, etc.), s'y connaître en (un sujet)
knowable ['noːəbəl] *adj* : connaissable
knowing ['noːɪŋ] *adj* : entendu <a knowing look : un regard entendu>
knowingly ['noːɪŋli] *adv* : d'un air entendu
know–it–all ['noːɪṭˌɔl] *n* : je-sais-tout *mf*
knowledge ['nɑlɪdʒ] *n* **1** LEARNING : connaissances *fpl,* savoir *m* **2** UNDERSTANDING : connaissance *f* <to the best of my knowledge : au meilleur de ma connaissance>
knowledgeable ['nɑlɪdʒəbəl] *adj* : bien informé
knuckle ['nʌkəl] *n* : jointure *f* du doigt, articulation *f* du doigt
koala [ko'wɑlə] *n* : koala *m*
kohlrabi [ˌkoːl'rɑbi, -'ræ-] *n, pl* **-bies** : chou-rave *m*
Koran [kə'rɑn, -'ræn] *n* **the Koran** : le Coran
Korean[1] [kə'riːən] *adj* : coréen
Korean[2] *n* **1** : Coréen *m,* -réenne *f* **2** : coréen *m* (langue)
kosher ['koːʃər] *adj* : kascher, casher
kowtow [ˌkaʊ'taʊ, 'kaʊˌtaʊ] *vi* **to kowtow to** : faire des courbettes à
krypton ['krɪpˌtɑn] *n* : krypton *m*
kudos ['kjuːˌdɑs, 'kuː-, -ˌdoːz] *n* : prestige *m*
kumquat ['kʌmˌkwɑt] *n* : kumquat *m*
Kuwaiti[1] [kʊ'weɪṭi] *adj* : koweïtien
Kuwaiti[2] *n* : Koweïtien *m,* -tienne *f*

L

l ['ɛl] *n, pl* **l's** *or* **ls** ['ɛlz] : l *m,* douzième lettre de l'alphabet
lab ['læb] → **laboratory**
label[1] ['leɪbəl] *vt* **-beled** *or* **-belled; -beling** *or* **-belling 1** : étiqueter <to label a jar : étiqueter un bocal> **2** BRAND, CATEGORIZE : classer, étiqueter
label[2] *n* **1** TAG : étiquette *f* **2** BRAND : marque *f*
labial ['leɪbiəl] *adj* : labial
labor[1] *or Brit* **labour** ['leɪbər] *vi* **1** TOIL : travailler **2** STRUGGLE : gravir, aller péniblement <the truck was laboring up the hill : le camion montait péniblement la côte> — *vt* BELABOR : insister sur (un point)
labor[2] *or Brit* **labour** *n* **1** WORK : travail *m,* labeur *m* **2** : travail *m,* accouchement *m* (en médecine) <to be in labor : être en travail> **3** TASK : tâche *f* **4** WORKERS : main-d'œuvre *f*
laboratory ['læbrəˌtori, lə'bɔrə-] *n, pl* **-ries** : laboratoire *m*
Labor Day *or Brit* **Labour Day** *n* : fête *f* du Travail
laborer *or Brit* **labourer** ['leɪbərər] *n* : ouvrier *m,* -vrière *f*
laborious [lə'boriəs] *adj* : laborieux, pénible — **laboriously** [-riəsli] *adv*
labor union *or Brit* **labour union** → **union**
labyrinth ['læbəˌrɪnθ] *n* : labyrinthe *m*
lace[1] ['leɪs] *vt* **laced; lacing 1** TIE : lacer (ses souliers) **2** : orner (une robe, etc.) de dentelle **3 to be laced with** : être mêlé de
lace[2] *n* **1** SHOELACE : lacet *m* **2** : dentelle *f* <lace doilies : napperons en dentelle>
lacerate ['læsəˌreɪt] *vt* **-ated; -ating** : lacérer
laceration [ˌlæsə'reɪʃən] *n* : lacération *f*
lack[1] ['læk] *vt* : manquer de <he lacks strength : il manque de force> — *vi or* **to be lacking** : manquer
lack[2] *n* : manque *m,* faute *f*
lackadaisical [ˌlækə'deɪzɪkəl] *adj* : apathique, amorphe, indolent
lackey ['læki] *n, pl* **-eys 1** SERVANT : laquais *m* **2** TOADY : larbin *m fam*
lackluster ['lækˌlʌstər] *adj* : terne
laconic [lə'kɑnɪk] *adj* : laconique — **laconically** [-nɪkli] *adv*
lacquer[1] ['lækər] *vt* : laquer, vernir
lacquer[2] *n* : laque *m*
lacrosse [lə'krɔs] *n* : crosse *f*
lactate ['lækˌteɪt] *vi* **-tated; -tating** : sécréter du lait
lactation [læk'teɪʃən] *n* : lactation *f*
lactic ['læktɪk] *adj* : lactique
lacuna [lə'kuːnə, -'kjuː-] *n, pl* **-nae** [-ˌniː, -ˌnaɪ] *or* **-nas** : lacune *f*
lacy ['leɪsi] *adj* **lacier; -est** : de dentelle
lad ['læd] *n* : garçon *m*
ladder ['lædər] *n* : échelle *f*
laden ['leɪdən] *adj* : chargé
ladle[1] ['leɪdəl] *vt* **-dled; -dling** : servir à la louche
ladle[2] *n* : louche *f*
lady ['leɪdi] *n, pl* **-dies 1** WOMAN : dame *f* **2** : madame *f* <ladies and gentlemen : mesdames et messieurs>
ladybird ['leɪdiˌbərd] → **ladybug**
ladybug ['leɪdiˌbʌg] *n* : coccinelle *f*

lag[1] ['læg] *vi* **lagged; lagging** : traîner, rester en arrière <to lag behind : prendre du retard>

lag[2] *n* **1** DELAY : retard *m* **2** INTERVAL : intervalle *m,* décalage *m*

lager ['lɑgər] *n* : bière *f* blonde

laggard[1] ['lægərd] *adj* : tardif

laggard[2] *n* : traînard *m,* -narde *f fam*

lagoon [lə'gu:n] *n* : lagune *f*

laid → **lay**[1]

lain → **lie**[1]

lair ['lær] *n* : tanière *f,* repaire *m*

laissez–faire *or Brit* **laisser–faire** [ˌlɛˌseɪ'fær, ˌleɪˌzeɪ-] *n* : laisser-faire *m*

laity ['leɪəţi] *n* : laïcs *mpl*

lake ['leɪk] *n* : lac *m*

lama ['lɑmə] *n* : lama *m*

lamb ['læm] *n* : agneau *m*

lambaste [læm'beɪst] *or* **lambast** [-'bæst] *vt* **-basted; -basting 1** BEAT, THRASH : battre, rosser **2** CENSURE : critiquer, réprimander

lame[1] ['leɪm] *vt* **lamed; laming** : estropier

lame[2] *adj* **lamer; lamest 1** : boiteux **2** WEAK : pauvre, piètre <a lame excuse : une piètre excuse>

lamé [lɑ'meɪ, læ-] *n* : lamé *m*

lamely ['leɪmli] *adv* : de façon peu convaincante

lameness ['leɪmnəs] *n* **1** : claudication (en médecine) **2** : faiblesse *f* (d'une excuse, etc.)

lament[1] [lə'mɛnt] *vt* **1** MOURN : pleurer **2** DEPLORE : déplorer, regretter

lament[2] *n* : lamentation *f*

lamentable ['læməntəbəl, lə'mɛntə-] *adj* : lamentable, déplorable — **lamentably** [-bli] *adv*

lamentation [ˌlæmən'teɪʃən] *n* : lamentation *f*

laminate ['læməˌneɪt] *vt* **-nated; -nating** : laminer

laminated ['læməˌneɪţəd] *adj* : stratifié (se dit du bois), feuilleté (se dit du verre)

lamp ['læmp] *n* : lampe *f*

lampoon[1] [læm'pu:n] *vt* : railler, ridiculiser

lampoon[2] *n* : satire *f*

lamprey ['læmpri] *n, pl* **-preys** : lamproie *f*

lance[1] ['lænts] *vt* **lanced; lancing** : inciser, percer (en médecine)

lance[2] *n* SPEAR : lance *f*

lance corporal *n* : soldat *m* de première classe

lancet ['læntsət] *n* : lancette *f,* bistouri *m*

land[1] ['lænd] *vt* **1** DISEMBARK : débarquer (des passagers) **2** CATCH : attraper (un poisson) **3** GAIN, SECURE : décrocher (un emploi, etc.) **4** : flanquer *fam* <to land a punch : flanquer un coup de poing> — *vi* **1** : atterrir (se dit d'un avion), accoster (se dit d'un navire) **2** ALIGHT : tomber, retomber <to land on one's feet : retomber sur ses pieds> **3** END UP : finir, atterrir <he landed in jail : il s'est retrouvé en prison>

land[2] *n* **1** : terre *f* <on dry land : sur la terre ferme> **2** COUNTRY : pays *m* **3** PROPERTY : terrain *m* <land for sale : terrain à vendre>

landfill ['lændˌfɪl] *n* : enfouissement *m* de déchets

landing ['lændɪŋ] *n* **1** : atterrissage *m* (d'un avion) **2** : débarquement *m* (d'un navire) **3** : palier *m* (d'un escalier)

landing strip → **airstrip**

landlady ['lændˌleɪdi] *n, pl* **-dies** : propriétaire *f*

landless ['lændləs] *adj* : sans terre

landlocked ['lændˌlɑkt] *adj* : sans accès à la mer

landlord ['lændˌlɔrd] *n* : propriétaire *m*

landlubber ['lændˌlʌbər] *n* : marin *m* d'eau douce

landmark ['lændˌmɑrk] *n* **1** : point *m* de repère **2** MILESTONE : étape *f* décisive, étape *f* importante (dans la vie de qqn) **3** MONUMENT : monument *m* (historique)

landowner ['lændˌo:nər] *n* : propriétaire *m* foncier, propriétaire *f* foncière

landscape[1] ['lændˌskeɪp] *vt* **-scaped; -scaping** : aménager (un terrain)

landscape[2] *n* : paysage *m*

landslide ['lændˌslaɪd] *n* **1** : glissement *m* de terrain **2** *or* **landslide victory** : victoire *f* écrasante

landward ['lændwərd] *adv & adj* : vers la terre, en direction de la terre

lane ['leɪn] *n* : voie *f* (d'une autoroute), chemin *m* (de campagne)

language ['læŋgwɪdʒ] *n* **1** : langue *f* <she speaks three languages : elle parle trois langues> **2** : langage *m* <computer language : langage informatique>

languid ['læŋgwɪd] *adj* : languissant

languidly ['læŋgwɪdli] *adv* : langoureusement

languish ['læŋgwɪʃ] *vi* **1** WEAKEN, WITHER : dépérir **2** PINE : croupir

languor ['læŋgər] *n* : langueur *f*

languorous ['læŋgərəs] *adj* : langoureux — **languorously** *adv*

lank ['læŋk] *adj* **1** THIN : maigre **2** LIMP : plat

lanky ['læŋki] *adj* **lankier; -est** : grand et maigre, dégingandé

lanolin ['lænəlɪn] *n* : lanoline *f*

lantern ['læntərn] *n* : lanterne *f*

Laotian[1] [leɪ'o:ʃən, 'laʊʃən] *adj* : laotien

Laotian[2] *n* : Laotien *m,* -tienne *f*

lap[1] ['læp] *v* **lapped; lapping** *vt* **1** *or* **to lap up** : laper (du lait, etc.) **2** SWALLOW : gober *fam,* avaler <the crowd lapped up every word he said : la foule gobait tout ce qu'il disait> **3** OVERLAP : chevaucher — *vi* SPLASH : clapoter (se dit des vagues)

lap[2] *n* **1** : genoux *mpl,* giron *m* <to sit on s.o.'s lap : s'asseoir sur les genoux de qqn> **2** : tour *m* de piste, tour *m* de circuit (aux sports) **3** : étape *f* (d'un voyage)
lapdog ['læp,dɔg] *n* : chien *m* de manchon, petit chien *m* d'appartement
lapel [lə'pɛl] *n* : revers *m*
Lapp ['læp] *n* **1** : Lapon *m,* -ponne *f* **2** : lapon *m* (langue)
Lappish[1] ['læpɪʃ] *adj* : lapon
Lappish[2] *n* : lapon *m* (langue)
lapse[1] ['læps] *vi* **lapsed; lapsing 1** CEASE, EXPIRE : expirer, cesser d'être en vigueur **2** ELAPSE : s'écouler, passer **3 to lapse into** : tomber dans <they lapsed into silence : ils se sont tus> <to lapse into unconsciousness : perdre connaissance>
lapse[2] *n* **1** : trou *m* (de mémoire, etc.) **2** EXPIRATION : expiration *f,* échéance *f* **3** INTERVAL : intervalle *m,* laps *m* (de temps)
laptop ['læp,tɑp] *adj* : portable <laptop computer : ordinateur portable>
larboard ['lɑrbərd] *n* : bâbord *m*
larceny ['lɑrsəni] *n, pl* **-nies** : vol *m*
larch ['lɑrtʃ] *n* : mélèze *m*
lard ['lɑrd] *n* : saindoux *m*
larder ['lɑrdər] *n* PANTRY : garde-manger *m*
large ['lɑrdʒ] *adj* **larger; largest 1** BIG : grand, gros **2 at ~** FREE : en liberté **3 at ~** : en général <the public at large : le grand public>
largely ['lɑrdʒli] *adv* **1** : en grande partie, en grande mesure **2** MOSTLY : principalement
largeness ['lɑrdʒnəs] *n* : grandeur *f*
largesse *or* **largess** [lɑr'ʒɛs, -'dʒɛs] *n* : largesse *f,* générosité *f*
lariat ['læriət] *n* : lasso *m*
lark ['lɑrk] *n* **1** : alouette *f* (oiseau) **2** JOKE, PRANK : rigolade *f*
larva ['lɑrvə] *n, pl* **-vae** [-,vi:, -,vaɪ] : larve *f*
larval ['lɑrvəl] *adj* : larvaire
laryngitis [,lærən'dʒaɪṭəs] *n* : laryngite *f*
larynx ['lærɪŋks] *n, pl* **-rynges** [lə'rɪn,dʒi:z] *or* **-ynxes** ['lærɪŋksəz] : larynx *m*
lasagna [lə'zɑnjə] *n* : lasagnes *fpl*
lascivious [lə'sɪviəs] *adj* : lascif
lasciviousness [lə'sɪviəsnəs] *n* : lascivité *f*
laser ['leɪzər] *n* : laser *m*
lash[1] ['læʃ] *vt* **1** WHIP : fouetter **2** BIND : attacher, lier — *vi* **1** BEAT : battre <the rain lashed at the windowpanes : la pluie battait contre les vitres> **2 to lash out at** : invectiver contre
lash[2] *n* **1** WHIP : fouet *m* **2** BLOW, STRIKE : coup *m* de fouet **3** EYELASH : cil *m*
lass ['læs] *or* **lassie** ['læsi] *n* : fille *f*
lassitude ['læsə,tu:d, -,tju:d] *n* : lassitude *f*
lasso[1] ['læ,so:, læ'su:] *vt* : prendre au lasso
lasso[2] *n, pl* **-sos** *or* **-soes** : lasso *m*
last[1] ['læst] *vi* **1** CONTINUE, ENDURE : durer **2** : se conserver (se dit des aliments), faire de l'usage (se dit des tissus), durer — *vt* **1** : faire <it lasted me three days : ça m'a fait trois jours> <they will last you a lifetime : vous en aurez pour la vie> **2 to last out** : tenir jusqu'à la fin de
last[2] *adv* **1** : en dernier <he came last : il est arrivé en dernier> **2** RECENTLY : dernièrement **3** FINALLY : enfin, en conclusion
last[3] *adj* : dernier
last[4] *n* **1** : dernier *m,* -nière *f* **2** : forme *f* (pour les souliers) **3 at ~** FINALLY : enfin, finalement
lastly ['læstli] *adv* : enfin, en dernier lieu
latch[1] ['lætʃ] *vt* : fermer au loquet, clencher *Can* — *vi* **to latch onto** : s'accrocher à
latch[2] *n* : loquet *m*
late[1] ['leɪt] *adv* **later; latest** : en retard
late[2] *adj* **later; latest 1** : en retard <he's always late : il est toujours en retard> **2** : tardif <a late spring : un printemps tardif> **3** DECEASED : défunt, feu <his late son : son défunt fils> <the late queen : feu la reine> **4** RECENT : dernier, récent
latecomer ['leɪt,kʌmər] *n* : retardataire *mf*
lately ['leɪtli] *adv* : récemment, dernièrement
lateness ['leɪtnəs] *n* : retard *m*
latent ['leɪtənt] *adj* : latent
later ['leɪṭər] *adv* : plus tard, tantôt *Can*
lateral ['læṭərəl] *adj* : latéral — **laterally** *adv*
latex ['leɪ,tɛks] *n, pl* **-tices** ['leɪṭə,si:z, 'læṭə-] *or* **-texes** : latex *m*
lath ['læθ, 'læð] *n, pl* **laths** *or* **lath** : latte *f*
lathe ['leɪð] *n* : tour *m*
lather[1] ['læðər] *vt* : savonner — *vi* : mousser
lather[2] *n* : mousse *f* (à savon), écume *f* (sur un cheval)
Latin[1] ['lætən] *adj* : latin
Latin[2] *n* **1** : latin *m* (langue) **2** → **Latin American**
Latin–American ['lætənə'mɛrɪkən] *adj* : latino-américain
Latin American *n* : Latino-américain *m,* -caine *f*
latitude ['læṭə,tu:d, -,tju:d] *n* : latitude *f*
latrine [lə'tri:n] *n* : latrines *fpl,* toilette *f*
latter[1] ['læṭər] *adj* LAST, SECOND : dernier, second
latter[2] *pron* **the latter** : le dernier, le second
lattice ['læṭəs] *n* : treillis *m,* treillage *m*
Latvian[1] ['lætviən] *adj* : letton
Latvian[2] *n* **1** : Letton *m,* -tonne *f* **2** : letton *m* (langue)

laud[1] ['lɔd] *vt* : louer
laud[2] *n* : louanges *fpl*
laugh[1] ['læf] *vi* : rire
laugh[2] *n* : rire *m*
laughable ['læfəbəl] *adj* : risible
laughingly ['læfɪŋli] *adv* : en riant
laughingstock ['læfɪŋˌstɑk] *n* : risée *f*, objet *m* de risée
laughter ['læftər] *n* : rire *m*, rires *mpl*
launch[1] ['lɔntʃ] *vt* **1** HURL : lancer **2** : mettre à l'eau (un bateau) **3** START : lancer (un programme, une campagne, etc.)
launch[2] *n* : vedette *f*, bateau *m* de plaisance
launder ['lɔndər] *vt* : laver (du linge)
launderer ['lɔndərər] *n* : blanchisseur *m*, -seuse *f*; buandier *m*, -dière *f Can*
laundress ['lɔndrəs] *n* : blanchisseuse *f*, buandière *f Can*
laundry ['lɔndri] *n, pl* **-dries 1** : lavage *m*, linge *m* <to do the laundry : faire la lessive> **2** : blanchisserie *f* (commerciale)
laureate ['lɔriət] *n* : lauréat *m*, -réate *f*
laurel ['lɔrəl] *n* **1** : laurier *m* (arbre) **2 laurels** *npl* : lauriers *mpl* <to rest on one's laurels : reposer sur ses lauriers>
lava ['lɑvə, 'læ-] *n* : lave *f*
lavatory ['lævəˌtori] *n, pl* **-ries** : toilettes *fpl*
lavender ['lævəndər] *n* : lavande *f*
lavish[1] ['lævɪʃ] *vt* : prodiguer
lavish[2] *adj* **1** EXTRAVAGANT : prodigue **2** ABUNDANT : abondant, copieux **3** LUXURIOUS : somptueux, fastueux
lavishly ['lævɪʃli] *adv* : généreusement, luxueusement
law ['lɔ] *n* **1** : loi *f* <to break the law : enfreindre la loi> **2** : droit *m* <to study law : faire son droit> <civil law : droit civil> **3** LEGISLATION : loi *f*, législation *f* <the law of the land : la législation du pays> **4** PRINCIPLE : loi *f*, principe *m* <the law of gravity : la loi de la pesanteur>
law–abiding ['lɔəˌbaɪdɪŋ] *adj* : respectueux des lois
lawbreaker ['lɔˌbreɪkər] *n* : personne *f* qui enfreint la loi
lawful ['lɔfəl] *adj* : légal, légitime — **lawfully** *adv*
lawgiver ['lɔˌgɪvər] → **legislator**
lawless ['lɔləs] *adj* : anarchique <a lawless person : une personne sans foi ni loi>
lawmaker ['lɔˌmeɪkər] *n* : législateur *m*, -trice *f*
lawman ['lɔmən] *n, pl* **-men** [-mən, -ˌmɛn] : policier *m*
lawn ['lɔn] *n* : pelouse *f*
lawn mower *n* : tondeuse *f*
lawsuit ['lɔˌsuːt] *n* : procès *m*
lawyer ['lɔɪər, 'lɔjər] *n* : avocat *m*, -cate *f*
lax ['læks] *adj* **1** LOOSE, SLACK : lâche, relâché **2** NEGLIGENT : négligent
laxative ['læksəṭɪv] *n* : laxatif *m*
laxity ['læksəṭi] *n* : laxisme *m*
lay[1] ['leɪ] *vt* **laid** ['leɪd]; **laying 1** PLACE : mettre, poser, déposer **2** : pondre (des œufs) **3** IMPOSE : imposer (une taxe) **4 to lay a bet** : parier **5 to lay out** ARRANGE, DISPLAY : étaler, disposer **6 to lay out** DESIGN : concevoir
lay[2] → **lie**[1]
lay[3] *adj* **1** SECULAR : laïc **2** NONPROFESSIONAL : profane
lay[4] *n* **1** : emplacement *m*, position *f* <the lay of the land : l'emplacement du terrain> **2** BALLAD : lai *m*
layer ['leɪər] *n* **1** : pondeuse *f* (poule) **2** : couche *f* (de peinture), strate *f* (en géologie)
layman ['leɪmən] *n, pl* **-men** [-mən, -ˌmɛn] : profane *mf*, laïque *mf* (en religion)
layoff ['leɪˌɔf] *n* : licenciement *m*, renvoi *m*
lay off *vt* : licencier, congédier (un employé)
layout ['leɪˌaʊt] *n* **1** ARRANGEMENT : disposition *f*, arrangement *m* **2** : mise *f* en page (en informatique), plan *m* (d'une ville)
layperson ['leɪˌpərsən] *n* : profane *mf*
lay up *vt* **1** STORE : mettre de côté **2 to be laid up** : être alité
laywoman ['leɪˌwʊmən] *n, pl* **-women** [-ˌwɪmən] : laïque *f*
lazily ['leɪzəli] *adv* : paresseusement
laziness ['leɪzinəs] *n* : paresse *f*
lazy ['leɪzi] *adj* **lazier; -est** : paresseux
leach ['liːtʃ] *vt* : lessiver
lead[1] ['liːd] *v* **led** ['lɛd]; **leading** *vt* **1** GUIDE : mener, conduire **2** DIRECT : diriger (un orchestre, etc.) **3** HEAD : être à la tête de **4** CONDUCT : mener <he leads a quiet life : il mène une vie tranquille> — *vi* : mener
lead[2] *n* INITIATIVE : initiative *f*
lead[3] ['lɛd] *n* **1** : plomb *m* (métal) **2** GRAPHITE : mine *f* <pencil lead : mine de crayon>
leaden ['lɛdən] *adj* **1** : de plomb **2** HEAVY : lourd <with leaden steps : d'un pas lourd>
leader ['liːdər] *n* : chef *m*; dirigeant *m*, -geante *f*
leadership ['liːdərˌʃɪp] *n* : direction *f*
leaf[1] ['liːf] *vi* **1** : se feuiller (se dit d'un arbre) **2 to leaf through** : feuilleter (un livre, etc.)
leaf[2] *n, pl* **leaves** ['liːvz] **1** : feuille *f* <maple leaves : feuilles d'érable> **2** : page *f* (d'un livre) **3** : rallonge *f* (de table)
leafless ['liːfləs] *adj* : sans feuilles
leaflet ['liːflət] *n* : dépliant *m*, prospectus *m*
leafy ['liːfi] *adj* **leafier; -est** : feuillu
league[1] ['liːg] *v* **leagued; leaguing** *vt* : allier — *vi* : se liguer
league[2] *n* **1** : lieue *f* <three leagues from here : à trois lieues d'ici> **2** ASSOCIA-

TION : ligue *f* **3** CLASS : classe *f,* niveau *m*
leak[1] ['li:k] *vt* **1** : faire couler (un liquide) **2** : répandre (une nouvelle), divulguer (un secret) **—** *vi* **1** : fuir (se dit d'un liquide ou d'un gaz) **2** : faire eau (se dit d'un bateau) **3** *or* **to leak out** : filtrer, être divulgué (se dit de l'information)
leak[2] *n* : fuite *f,* voie *f* d'eau
leakage ['li:kɪdʒ] *n* : fuite *f* (d'eau)
leaky ['li:ki] *adj* **leakier; -est** : qui prend l'eau
lean[1] ['li:n] *v* **leaned** *or Brit* **leant** ['lɛnt]; **leaning** *vi* **1** BEND : se pencher, s'incliner **2** RECLINE : s'appuyer **3** TILT : pencher **4 to lean on** DEPEND ON : se fier sur, compter sur, dépendre de **5 to lean toward** : pencher pour, pencher vers **—** *vt* **1** PROP, REST : appuyer **2** INCLINE : incliner, pencher
lean[2] *adj* **1** THIN : mince, maigre **2** : maigre <lean meat : viande maigre> **3** : difficile <lean years : années difficiles>
leaning ['li:nɪŋ] *n* INCLINATION : inclinaison *f,* tendance *f*
leanness ['li:nnəs] *n* : minceur *f,* maigreur *f*
leant *Brit* → **lean**[1]
leap[1] ['li:p] *vi* **leaped** *or* **leapt** ['li:pt, 'lɛpt]; **leaping** : sauter, bondir
leap[2] *n* : saut *m,* bond *m*
leap year *n* : année *f* bissextile
learn ['lərn] *v* **learned** ['lərnd, 'lərnt] *or Brit* **learnt** ['lərnt]; **learning** *vt* **1** : apprendre <to learn a language : apprendre une langue> **2** MEMORIZE : mémoriser **3** HEAR : apprendre <I just learned the news : je viens d'apprendre la nouvelle> **—** *vi* : apprendre
learned ['lərnəd] *adj* : savant, érudit
learner ['lərnər] *n* : débutant *m,* -tante *f*
learning ['lərnɪŋ] *n* **1** KNOWLEDGE : savoir *m,* érudition *f* **2** : apprentissage *m* <the learning of a trade : l'apprentissage d'un métier>
learnt *Brit* → **learn**
lease[1] ['li:s] *vt* **leased; leasing** : louer à bail
lease[2] *n* : bail *m*
leash[1] ['li:ʃ] *vt* : tenir (un animal) en laisse
leash[2] *n* : laisse *f* (d'un animal)
least[1] ['li:st] *adv* : (le) moins <to be least interesting : être le moins intéressant>
least[2] *adj* **1** : moins <the least money : le moins d'argent> **2** SLIGHTEST : moindre <the least noise startles her : le moindre bruit la surprend>
least[3] *n* **1** : moins *m* <you have the least : c'est vous qui en avez le moins> **2 at ~** : au moins **3 to say the least** : c'est le moins qu'on puisse dire
leather ['lɛðər] *n* : cuir *m*
leathery ['lɛðəri] *adj* : tanné
leave[1] ['li:v] *v* **left** ['lɛft]; **leaving** *vt* **1** BEQUEATH : léguer **2** : partir de, quitter <to leave the house : partir de la maison> <she left her husband : elle a quitté son mari> **3** FORGET : laisser <I left my books at home : j'ai laissé mes livres à la maison> **4** EQUAL : égaler <4 from 7 leaves 3 : 7 moins 4 égale 3> **5** LET : laisser <leave her alone : laisse-la tranquille> <leave the door open : laissez la porte ouverte> **6 to be left** : rester <there's no money left : il ne reste plus d'argent> **7 to leave out** : omettre **—** *vi* DEPART : partir
leave[2] *n* **1** PERMISSION : permission *f* **2** *or* **leave of absence** : congé *m* **3 to take one's leave** : prendre son congé
leaved ['li:vd] *adj* : qui a des feuilles
leaven ['lɛvən] *n* : levain *m*
leaves → **leaf**
leavings ['li:vɪŋz] *npl* : restes *mpl*
Lebanese[1] [ˌlɛbə'ni:z, -'ni:s] *adj* : libanais
Lebanese[2] *n* : Libanais *m,* -naise *f*
lecherous ['lɛtʃərəs] *adj* : lubrique, lascif
lechery ['lɛtʃəri] *n* : lubricité *f,* lascivité *f*
lecture[1] ['lɛktʃər] *v* **-tured; -turing** *vt* : faire la morale à, sermonner **—** *vi* : faire une conférence
lecture[2] *n* **1** TALK : conférence *f* **2** : cours *m* magistral (à l'université) **3** REPRIMAND : sermon *m*
lecturer ['lɛktʃərər] *n* : conférencier *m,* -cière *f*
led → **lead**[1]
ledge ['lɛdʒ] *n* : rebord *m* (d'une fenêtre, etc.), saillie *f* (d'une montagne)
ledger ['lɛdʒər] *n* : grand livre *m* (en comptabilité)
lee[1] ['li:] *adj* : sous le vent
lee[2] *n* : côté *m* sous le vent
leech ['li:tʃ] *n* : sangsue *f*
leek ['li:k] *n* : poireau *m*
leer[1] ['lɪr] *vi* **to leer at** : lorgner
leer[2] *n* : regard *m* malveillant, regard *m* lubrique
leery ['lɪri] *adj* : méfiant, soupçonneux <to be leery of : se méfier de>
lees ['li:z] *npl* DREGS : lie *f*
leeward[1] ['li:wərd, 'lu:ərd] *adj* : sous le vent
leeward[2] *n* : côté *m* sous le vent
leeway ['li:ˌweɪ] *n* : marge *f* de manœuvre
left[1] → **leave**[1]
left[2] ['lɛft] *adv* : à gauche
left[3] *adj* : gauche
left[4] *n* : gauche *f* <it's on your left : c'est à votre gauche>
leg ['lɛg] *n* **1** : patte *f* (d'un animal), jambe *f* (d'une personne ou d'un pantalon) **2** : pied *m* (d'une table, etc.) **3** STAGE : étape *f* (d'un voyage)
legacy ['lɛgəsi] *n, pl* **-cies** : legs *m,* héritage *m*

legal ['liːgəl] *adj* **1** LAWFUL : légal, légitime **2** JUDICIAL : juridique, judiciaire <legal adviser : conseiller juridique> <legal aid : aide judiciaire>
legality [li'gæləṭi] *n, pl* **-ties** : légalité *f*
legalize ['liːgəˌlaɪz] *vt* **-ized; -izing** : légaliser
legally ['liːgəli] *adv* : légalement
legate ['lɛgət] *n* : légat *m*
legation [lɪ'geɪʃən] *n* : légation *f*
legend ['lɛdʒənd] *n* : légende *f*
legendary ['lɛdʒənˌdɛri] *adj* : légendaire
legerdemain [ˌlɛdʒərdə'meɪn] → **sleight of hand**
leggings ['lɛgɪŋz, 'lɛgənz] *npl* : caleçon *m* (porté comme pantalon)
legibility [ˌlɛdʒə'bɪləṭi] *n* : lisibilité *f*
legible ['lɛdʒəbəl] *adj* : lisible — **legibly** [-bli] *adv*
legion ['liːdʒən] *n* : légion *f*
legionary ['liːdʒənəri] → **legionnaire**
legionnaire [ˌliːdʒə'nær] *n* : légionnaire *m*
legislate ['lɛdʒəsˌleɪt] *vi* **-lated; -lating** : légiférer
legislation [ˌlɛdʒəs'leɪʃən] *n* : législation *f*
legislative ['lɛdʒəsˌleɪṭɪv] *adj* : législatif
legislator ['lɛdʒəsˌleɪṭər] *n* : législateur *m*, -trice *f*
legislature ['lɛdʒəsˌleɪtʃər] *n* : législatif *m*, corps *m* législatif
legitimacy [lɪ'dʒɪṭəməsi] *n* : légitimité *f*
legitimate [lɪ'dʒɪṭəmət] *adj* **1** LAWFUL : légitime **2** VALID : légitime, admissible <a legitimate excuse : une excuse légitime>
legitimately [lɪ'dʒɪṭəmətli] *adv* : légitimement
legitimize [lɪ'dʒɪṭəˌmaɪz] *vt* **-mized; -mizing** : légitimer
legless ['lɛgləs] *adj* : sans jambes
legume ['lɛˌgjuːm, lɪ'gjuːm] *n* : légumineuse *f*
leisure ['liːʒər, 'lɛ-] *n* **1** : loisir *m* <leisure time : les loisirs> **2 at your leisure** : à votre convenance
leisurely[1] ['liːʒərli, 'lɛ-] *adv* : sans hâte, sans se presser
leisurely[2] *adj* : tranquille, paisible <a leisurely stroll : une balade faite sans se presser>
lemming ['lɛmɪŋ] *n* : lemming *m*
lemon ['lɛmən] *n* : citron *m*
lemonade [ˌlɛmə'neɪd] *n* : limonade *f*
lemony ['lɛməni] *adj* : citronné
lend ['lɛnd] *vt* **lent** ['lɛnt]; **lending 1** : prêter <to lend money : prêter de l'argent> **2** GIVE, SUPPORT : conférer, apporter <to lend a hand : prêter une main> **3 to lend itself to** : se prêter à
lender ['lɛndər] *n* : prêteur *m*, -teuse *f*
length ['lɛŋkθ] *n* **1** : longueur *f* <10 meters in length : 10 mètres de longueur> **2** DURATION : durée *f* **3** PIECE, SECTION : bout *m*, morceau *m* <a length of pipe : un bout de tuyau> **4 at ~** : longuement, en détail **5 to go to great lengths** : se donner beaucoup de mal
lengthen ['lɛŋkθən] *vt* **1** : rallonger (une jupe, etc.) **2** PROLONG : prolonger — *vi* : s'allonger, se prolonger
lengthways ['lɛŋkθˌweɪz] → **lengthwise**
lengthwise ['lɛŋkθˌwaɪz] *adv & adj* : dans le sens de la longueur
lengthy ['lɛŋkθi] *adj* **lengthier; -est** : long, interminable
leniency ['liːniəntsi] *n* : indulgence *f*, clémence *f*
lenient ['liːniənt] *adj* : indulgent, clément
leniently ['liːniəntli] *adv* : avec indulgence, avec clémence
lens ['lɛnz] *n* **1** : lentille *f*, objectif *m* (d'un instrument) **2** : cristallin *m* (de l'œil) **3** : verre *m* (d'une paire de lunettes) **4** → **contact lens**
Lent ['lɛnt] *n* : carême *m*
Lenten ['lɛntən] *adj* : de carême
lentil ['lɛntəl] *n* : lentille *f*
Leo ['liːoː] *n* : Lion *m*
leopard ['lɛpərd] *n* : léopard *m*
leotard ['liːəˌtɑrd] *n* : justaucorps *m*
leper ['lɛpər] *n* : lépreux *m*, -preuse *f*
leprechaun ['lɛprəˌkɑn] *n* : lutin *m*
leprosy ['lɛprəsi] *n* : lèpre *f*
lesbian[1] ['lɛzbiən] *adj* : lesbien
lesbian[2] *n* : lesbienne *f*
lesbianism ['lɛzbiəˌnɪzəm] *n* : lesbianisme *m*
lesion ['liːʒən] *n* : lésion *f*
less[1] ['lɛs] (*comparative of* **little**[1]) *adv* **1** : moins <much less important : beaucoup moins important> **2 less and less** : de moins en moins
less[2] (*comparative of* **little**[2]) *adj* **1** : moins <less money : moins d'argent> **2** : moindre <of less importance : de moindre importance>
less[3] *prep* MINUS : moins <the regular price less a discount : le prix régulier moins un escompte>
less[4] *pron* : moins <I cannot do less : je ne peux pas en faire moins>
lessen ['lɛsən] *vi* DECREASE : diminuer — *vt* REDUCE : amoindrir, diminuer
lesser[1] ['lɛsər] *adv* LESS : moins <lesser-known writers : des écrivains moins connus>
lesser[2] *adj* : moindre <to a lesser degree : à un moindre degré>
lesson ['lɛsən] *n* : leçon *f*
lest ['lɛst] *conj* : de peur que, de crainte que
let[1] ['lɛt] *vt* **let; letting 1** MAKE : laisser <let me know : laisse-moi savoir> **2** RENT : louer <rooms to let : chambres à louer> **3** ALLOW, PERMIT : laisser <let them through : laissez-les passer> **4** (*used in commands*) <let him try : qu'il essaie>
letdown ['lɛtˌdaʊn] *n* DISAPPOINTMENT : déception *f*
let down *vt* DISAPPOINT : décevoir

lethal ['liːθəl] *adj* : mortel, létal
lethargic [lɪ'θɑrdʒɪk] *adj* : léthargique
lethargy ['lɛθərdʒi] *n* : léthargie *f*
let on *vi* ADMIT : admettre, révéler
let's ['lɛts] (*contraction of* **let us**) → **let**
letter[1] ['lɛt̬ər] *vt* : inscrire des lettres sur
letter[2] *n* **1** : lettre *f* (de l'alphabet) **2** : lettre *f* <a letter to my mother : une lettre à ma mère> **3 letters** *npl* CORRESPONDENCE : courrier *m* <letters to the editor : courrier des lecteurs> **4 letters** *npl* : belles-lettres *fpl,* littérature *f* **5 the letter of the law** : la lettre de la loi
letterhead ['lɛt̬ərˌhɛd] *n* : en-tête *m*
lettuce ['lɛtəs] *n* : laitue *f*
let up *vi* ABATE : diminuer, se calmer
leukemia [luː'kiːmiə] *n* : leucémie *f*
levee ['lɛvi] *n* : digue *f*
level[1] ['lɛvəl] *vt* **-eled** *or* **-elled; -eling** *or* **-elling 1** FLATTEN : niveler, aplanir **2** AIM, DIRECT : lancer (une accusation), braquer (une arme) **3** RAZE : raser (un immeuble)
level[2] *adj* **1** FLAT : plat **2** HORIZONTAL : horizontal <in a level position : à l'horizontale> **3** EVEN : à égalité <to draw level : se trouver à égalité> **4** CALM, STEADY : calme, mesuré <to keep a level head : garder son sang-froid>
level[3] *n* : niveau *m*
levelheaded ['lɛvəl'hɛdəd] *adj* : pondéré, équilibré
lever ['lɛvər, 'liː-] *n* : levier *m*
leverage ['lɛvərɪdʒ, 'liː-] *n* **1** : force *f* de levier (en physique) **2** INFLUENCE : influence *f,* moyen *m* de pression
leviathan [lɪ'vaɪəθən] *n* : chose *f* énorme et redoutable
levity ['lɛvət̬i] *n* : légèreté *f,* manque *m* de sérieux
levy[1] ['lɛvi] *vt* **levied; levying 1** IMPOSE : imposer, prélever (des impôts) **2** COLLECT : lever, percevoir (des impôts) **3** ENLIST : lever (des troupes)
levy[2] *n, pl* **levies 1** : impôt *m,* taxe *f* **2** : levée *f* (militaire)
lewd ['luːd] *adj* : luxurieux, lubrique
lewdly ['luːdli] *adv* : de façon obscène
lewdness ['luːdnəs] *n* : lubricité *f*
lexicographer [ˌlɛksə'kɑgrəfər] *n* : lexicographe *mf*
lexicographical [ˌlɛksəko'græfɪkəl] *or* **lexicographic** [-'græfɪk] *adj* : lexicographique
lexicography [ˌlɛksə'kɑgrəfi] *n* : lexicographie *f*
lexicon ['lɛksɪˌkɑn] *n, pl* **-ica** [-kə] *or* **-icons** : lexique *m*
liability [ˌlaɪə'bɪlət̬i] *n, pl* **-ties 1** RESPONSIBILITY : responsabilité *f* **2** DRAWBACK : désavantage *m,* handicap *m* **3 liabilities** *npl* : passif *m,* dettes *fpl* <assets and liabilities : l'actif et le passif>
liable ['laɪəbəl] *adj* **1** : responsable <liable for damages : responsable pour les dommages> **2** LIKELY : probable <it's liable to rain : il se peut qu'il pleuve> **3** SUSCEPTIBLE : sujet, susceptible <he's liable to fall : il est sujet aux chutes>
liaison ['liːəˌzɑn, li'eɪ-] *n* : liaison *f*
liar ['laɪər] *n* : menteur *m,* -teuse *f*
libel[1] ['laɪbəl] *vt* **-beled** *or* **-belled; -beling** *or* **-belling** : diffamer, calomnier
libel[2] *n* : diffamation *f,* calomnie *f*
libelous *or* **libellous** ['lɑɪbələs] *adj* : diffamatoire
liberal[1] ['lɪbrəl, 'lɪbərəl] *adj* **1** ABUNDANT, GENEROUS : libéral, prodigue **2** TOLERANT : libéral, tolérant
liberal[2] *n* : libéral *m,* -rale *f*
liberal arts *n* : arts *mpl* et sciences *fpl* humaines
liberalism ['lɪbrəˌlɪzəm, 'lɪbərə-] *n* : libéralisme *m*
liberality [ˌlɪbə'rælət̬i] *n, pl* **-ties** : libéralité *f*
liberalize ['lɪbrəˌlaɪz, 'lɪbərə-] *vt* **-ized; -izing** : libéraliser
liberally ['lɪbrəli, 'lɪbərə-] *adv* : libéralement
liberate ['lɪbəˌreɪt] *vt* **-ated; -ating** : libérer
liberation [ˌlɪbə'reɪʃən] *n* : libération *f*
liberator ['lɪbəˌreɪt̬ər] *n* : libérateur *m,* -trice *f*
Liberian[1] [laɪ'bɪriən] *adj* : libérien
Liberian[2] *n* : Libérien *m,* -rienne *f*
libertine ['lɪbərˌtiːn] *n* : libertin *m,* -tine *f*
liberty ['lɪbərt̬i] *n, pl* **-ties 1** FREEDOM : liberté *f* **2** CHANCE, RISK : risque *m* <he's taking liberties with his health : il prend des risques avec sa santé> **3 liberties** *npl* FAMILIARITY : libertés *fpl*
libido [lə'biːdoː, -'baɪ-] *n, pl* **-dos** : libido *f*
Libra ['liːbrə] *n* : Balance *f*
librarian [laɪ'brɛriən] *n* : bibliothécaire *mf*
library ['laɪˌbrɛri] *n, pl* **-braries** : bibliothèque *f*
libretto [lɪ'brɛt̬o] *n, pl* **-tos** *or* **-ti** [-t̬iː] : livret *m*
Libyan[1] ['lɪbiən] *adj* : libyen
Libyan[2] *n* : Libyen *m,* Libyenne *f*
lice → **louse**
license[1] ['laɪsənts] *vt* **-censed; -censing 1** : accorder une licence à **2** AUTHORIZE : autoriser
license[2] *or* **licence** *n* **1** PERMIT : permis *m,* licence *f* <driver's license : permis de conduire> **2** FREEDOM : licence *f,* liberté *f* **3** AUTHORIZATION : licence *f,* autorisation *f*
licentious [laɪ'sɛntʃəs] *adj* : licencieux — **licentiously** *adv*
lichen ['laɪkən] *n* : lichen *m*
licit ['lɪsət] *adj* LAWFUL : licite
lick[1] ['lɪk] *vt* **1** : lécher **2** BEAT : battre à plate couture, écraser

lick[2] *n* **1** : coup *m* de langue **2** BIT : brin *m* <a lick and a promise : un brin de toilette>
licorice *or Brit* **liquorice** ['lɪkərɪʃ, -rəs] *n* : réglisse *f*
lid ['lɪd] *n* **1** COVER : couvercle *m* **2** EYELID : paupière *f*
lie[1] ['laɪ] *vi* **lay** ['leɪ]; **lain** ['leɪn]; **lying** ['laɪɪŋ] **1** *or* **to lie down** : se coucher, s'allonger <to lie on the grass : s'allonger sur l'herbe> <to lie motionless : rester immobile> **2** : se trouver, être <the book is lying on the table : le livre se trouve sur la table> **3** EXTEND, STRETCH : s'étendre <the route lay to the west : la route s'étendait vers l'ouest> **4** REMAIN : être, rester <to lie idle : être arrêté> **5 to lie in** : résider en
lie[2] *vi* **lied; lying** ['laɪɪŋ] : mentir
lie[3] *n* **1** : mensonge *m* **2** : position *f* (au golf), configuration *f* (de la terre)
liege ['li:dʒ] *n* : suzerain *m,* seigneur *m*
lien ['li:n] *n* : droit *m* de rétention
lieutenant [lu:'tɛnənt] *n* : lieutenant *m*
lieutenant colonel *n* : lieutenant-colonel *m*
lieutenant commander *n* : capitaine *m* de corvette
lieutenant general *n* : général *m* de corps d'armée
life ['laɪf] *n, pl* **lives** ['laɪvz] **1** EXISTENCE : vie *f,* existence *f* **2** : vie *f* <his adult life : sa vie adulte> <plant life : la flore> <way of life : mode de vie> **3** BIOGRAPHY : biographie *f* **4** DURATION : durée *f* (d'une machine, etc.) **5** LIVELINESS : vie *f,* animation *f*
lifeblood ['laɪf,blʌd] *n* : force *f* vitale
lifeboat ['laɪf,bo:t] *n* : canot *m* de sauvetage
lifeguard ['laɪf,gɑrd] *n* : surveillant *m,* -lante *f* de baignade
lifeless ['laɪfləs] *adj* : inanimé, sans vie
lifelike ['laɪf,laɪk] *adj* : ressemblant
lifelong ['laɪf'lɔŋ] *adj* : de toute la vie
life preserver *n* : gilet *m* de sauvetage
lifesaver ['laɪf,seɪvər] *n* **1** → **lifeguard 2 to be a lifesaver** : sauver la vie à qqn
lifesaving ['laɪf,seɪvɪŋ] *n* : sauvetage *m*
lifestyle ['laɪf,staɪl] *n* : mode *m* de vie
lifetime ['laɪf,taɪm] *n* : vie *f* <a lifetime of regrets : toute une vie de regrets>
lift[1] ['lɪft] *vt* **1** RAISE : lever, soulever **2** END : lever <to lift a ban : lever une interdiction> **3** BOOST : remonter — *vi* **1** CLEAR UP : se dissiper <the fog has lifted : la brume s'est dissipée> **2** *or* **to lift off** : décoller (se dit d'un avion, etc.)
lift[2] *n* **1** LIFTING : soulèvement *m* **2** BOOST : encouragement *m,* stimulation *f* <to give s.o.'s spirits a lift : remonter le moral à qqn> **3** *Brit* → **elevator 4 to give s.o. a lift** : emmener qqn en voiture
liftoff ['lɪft,ɔf] *n* : lancement *m* (en aéronautique)
ligament ['lɪgəmənt] *n* : ligament *m*
ligature ['lɪgə,tʃʊr, -tʃər] *n* : ligature *f*
light[1] ['laɪt] *v* **lit** ['lɪt] *or* **lighted; lighting** *vt* **1** : allumer (un feu) **2** GUIDE : éclairer, illuminer <to light the way : éclairer le chemin> — *vi* **1** BRIGHTEN : s'éclairer, s'illuminer **2** ALIGHT : se poser **3** DISMOUNT : descendre
light[2] *adv* : légèrement <to travel light : voyager avec peu de bagages>
light[3] *adj* **1** BRIGHT : clair **2** PALE : pâle <light blue : bleu pâle> **3** LIGHTWEIGHT : léger **4** GENTLE : léger <a light breeze : une brise légère> <a light rain : une pluie fine> **5** EASY : léger, facile <light reading : quelque chose de facile à lire> <light work : des travaux peu fatigants>
light[4] *n* **1** : lumière *f* <ray of light : rayon de lumière> **2** DAYLIGHT : lumière *f* du jour **3** LAMP : lumière *f* **4** ASPECT : jour *m,* lumière *f* <in a different light : sous un autre jour> <in the light of recent developments : à la lumière des derniers événements> **5** FLAME : feu *m* <do you have a light? : as-tu du feu?> **6** → **traffic light 7 lights** *npl* : phares *mpl* (d'une voiture)
lightbulb ['laɪt,bʌlb] *n* : ampoule *f*
lighten ['laɪtən] *vt* **1** BRIGHTEN : éclairer (les esprits, une salle, les cheveux) **2** ALLEVIATE, RELIEVE : alléger, soulager — *vi* : s'éclairer
lighter ['laɪtər] *n* : briquet *m*
lighthearted ['laɪt,hɑrtəd] *adj* : allègre, joyeux — **lightheartedly** *adv*
lighthouse ['laɪt,haʊs] *n* : phare *m*
lightly ['laɪtli] *adv* **1** GENTLY : légèrement **2** FRIVOLOUSLY : à la légère, légèrement **3 to get off lightly** : s'en tirer à bon compte
lightness ['laɪtnəs] *n* **1** : légèreté *f* **2** BRIGHTNESS : clarté *f*
lightning ['laɪtnɪŋ] *n* : éclairs *mpl,* foudre *f*
lightning bug → **firefly**
lightproof ['laɪt,pru:f] *adj* : à l'épreuve de la lumière
lightweight ['laɪt,weɪt] *adj* : léger <lightweight fabric : tissu léger>
light–year ['laɪt,jɪr] *n* : année-lumière *f*
lignite ['lɪg,naɪt] *n* : lignite *m*
likable *or* **likeable** ['laɪkəbəl] *adj* : agréable, sympathique
like[1] ['laɪk] *v* **liked; liking** *vt* **1** ENJOY : aimer <he likes tennis : il aime le tennis> **2** WANT : aimer, vouloir <I would like a drink of water : j'aimerais un verre d'eau> — *vi* CHOOSE, PREFER : vouloir, plaire <if you like : si vous voulez>
like[2] *adj* SIMILAR : pareil, semblable
like[3] *n* **1** LIKING, PREFERENCE : goût *m* <our likes and dislikes : ce que nous aimons et ce que nous n'aimons pas> **2 the like** : une chose pareille <I've never seen the like : je n'ai jamais rien vu de pareil> <cats, dogs,

and the like : des chats, des chiens et d'autres animaux de ce genre>

like[4] *conj* **1** AS : comme <she talks exactly like I do : elle parle exactement comme moi> **2** AS IF : comme si <he acted like he was cold : il s'est conduit comme s'il avait froid> <it looks like it might rain : on dirait qu'il va pleuvoir>

like[5] *prep* **1** : comme <you're not like the rest of them : tu n'es pas comme les autres> <it's just like her to be late : c'est bien son genre d'être en retard> **2** SUCH AS : comme, tel que <a city like Chicago : une ville telle que Chicago>

likelihood ['laɪkli,hʊd] *n* : probabilité *f*

likely[1] ['laɪkli] *adv* : probablement <most likely : très probablement>

likely[2] *adj* **likelier; -est 1** PROBABLE : probable **2** BELIEVABLE : plausible, vraisemblable <a likely excuse! : une belle excuse!> **3** PROMISING : prometteur

liken ['laɪkən] *vt* : comparer

likeness ['laɪknəs] *n* **1** SIMILARITY : ressemblance *f* **2** PORTRAIT : portrait *m*

likewise ['laɪk,waɪz] *adv* **1** SIMILARLY : de même <do likewise : fais de même> **2** ALSO : de plus, aussi

liking ['laɪkɪŋ] *n* **1** LEANING, TASTE : goût *m*, penchant *m* **2** FONDNESS : affection *f* <to take a liking to : se prendre d'affection pour>

lilac ['laɪlək, -læk, -lɑk] *n* : lilas *m*

lilt ['lɪlt] *n* : rythme *m*, cadence *f* (en musique), intonation *f* (de la voix)

lily ['lɪli] *n, pl* **lilies** : lis *m*, lys *m*

lima bean ['laɪmə] *n* : haricot *m* de Lima

limb ['lɪm] *n* **1** : membre *m* (en anatomie) **2** BRANCH : branche *f* (d'un arbre)

limber[1] ['lɪmbər] *vt or* **to limber up** : assouplir — *vi* **to limber up** : s'échauffer

limber[2] *adj* : souple, agile

limbo ['lɪm,boː] *n, pl* **-bos 1** : limbes *mpl* (en religion) **2** UNCERTAINTY : incertitude *f*, état *m* d'incertitude

lime ['laɪm] *n* **1** : chaux *m* (en agriculture) **2** : citron *m* vert (fruit)

limelight ['laɪm,laɪt] *n* **to be in the limelight** : être en vedette, avoir la vedette

limerick ['lɪmərɪk] *n* : petit poème *m* humoristique

limestone ['laɪm,stoːn] *n* : calcaire *m*

limit[1] ['lɪmət] *vt* : limiter

limit[2] *n* **1** BOUNDARY : limite *f* **2** RESTRICTION : limitation *f*

limitation [,lɪmə'teɪʃən] *n* : limitation *f*, restriction *f*

limitless ['lɪmətləs] *adj* : illimité

limousine ['lɪmə,ziːn, ,lɪmə'-] *n* : limousine *f*

limp[1] ['lɪmp] *vi* : boiter

limp[2] *adj* : mou, flasque

limp[3] *n* : boiterie *f*, claudication *f*

limpid ['lɪmpəd] *adj* : limpide, transparent

limply ['lɪmpli] *adv* : mollement

limpness ['lɪmpnəs] *n* : mollesse *f*

linden ['lɪndən] *n* : tilleul *m*

line[1] ['laɪn] *v* **lined; lining** *vt* **1** : ligner <lined paper : papier ligné> **2** BORDER : border <lined with trees : bordé d'arbres> **3** : doubler (un vêtement) **4** ALIGN : aligner, mettre en ligne — *vi* **to line up** : se mettre en ligne, faire la queue

line[2] *n* **1** ROPE : cordage *m*, corde *f* **2** CABLE, WIRE : ligne *f* <power line : ligne à haute tension> **3** *or* **telephone line** : ligne *f* de téléphone <the line has gone dead : il n'y a plus de tonalité> **4** ROW : rangée *f* **5** QUEUE : file *f*, queue *f*, filée *f Can fam* **6** NOTE : mot *m* <drop me a line : écris-moi un mot> **7** ORIENTATION, OUTLOOK : ligne *f* **8** AGREEMENT : accord *m* <to be in line with s.o. : être conforme à qqn> **9** JOB, OCCUPATION : métier *m* **10** LINEAGE : lignée *f*, descendance *f* **11** ROUTE : ligne *f* <bus line : ligne d'autobus> **12** WRINKLE : ride *f* **13** RANGE : gamme *f* (de produits) **14** MARK : ligne *f* <dotted line : ligne pointillée> **15** *or* **dividing line** LIMIT : limite *f* **16** → **on–line**

lineage ['lɪniɪdʒ] *n* : lignée *f*, descendance *f*

lineal ['lɪniəl] *adj* : en ligne directe

lineaments ['lɪniəmənts] *npl* : linéaments *mpl*, traits *mpl*

linear ['lɪniər] *adj* : linéaire

linen ['lɪnən] *n* : lin *m*

liner ['laɪnər] *n* **1** LINING : doublure *f* **2** : paquebot *m* (navire), gros-porteur *m* (avion)

lineup ['laɪn,əp] *n* **1** : séance *f* d'identification de suspects **2** : équipe *f* (aux sports) **3** : composition *f* (d'un programme, etc.)

linger ['lɪŋgər] *vi* **1** TARRY : s'attarder **2** PERSIST : persister, persévérer

lingerie [,lɑndʒə'reɪ, ,læʒə'riː] *n* : lingerie *f*

lingo ['lɪŋgo] *n, pl* **-goes 1** LANGUAGE : langue *f* (du pays) **2** JARGON : jargon *m*

linguist ['lɪŋgwɪst] *n* : linguiste *mf*

linguistic [lɪŋ'gwɪstɪk] *adj* : linguistique

linguistics [lɪŋ'gwɪstɪks] *n* : linguistique *f*

liniment ['lɪnəmənt] *n* : liniment *m*, onguent *m*

lining ['laɪnɪŋ] *n* : doublure *f*

link[1] ['lɪŋk] *vt* : relier, lier — *vi or* **to link up** : s'associer, se rejoindre

link[2] *n* **1** : maillon *m* (d'une chaîne) **2** BOND : lien *m*, rapport *m* **3** : liaison *f* <satellite link : liaison satellite>

linkage [ˈlɪŋkɪdʒ] *n* LINK : lien *m,* rapport *m*

linoleum [ləˈnoːliəm] *n* : linoléum *m,* prélart *m Can*

linseed oil [ˈlɪn,siːd] *n* : huile *f* de lin

lint [ˈlɪnt] *n* : peluches *fpl*

lintel [ˈlɪntəl] *n* : linteau *m*

lion [ˈlaɪən] *n* : lion *m*

lioness [ˈlaɪənɪs] *n* : lionne *f*

lionize [ˈlaɪə,naɪz] *vt* **-ized; -izing** : aduler, fêter comme une célébrité

lip [ˈlɪp] *n* **1** : lèvre *f* <the upper lip : la lèvre supérieure> **2** EDGE, RIM : bord *m,* rebord *m*

lipreading [ˈlɪp,riːdɪŋ] *n* : lecture *f* sur les lèvres

lipstick [ˈlɪp,stɪk] *n* : rouge *m* à lèvres

liquefy [ˈlɪkwə,faɪ] *v* **-fied; -fying** *vt* : liquéfier — *vi* : se liquéfier

liqueur [lɪˈkər, -ˈkʊr, -ˈkjʊr] *n* : liqueur *f*

liquid[1] [ˈlɪkwəd] *adj* : liquide

liquid[2] *n* : liquide *m*

liquidate [ˈlɪkwə,deɪt] *vt* **-dated; -dating** : liquider

liquidation [,lɪkwəˈdeɪʃən] *n* : liquidation *f*

liquidity [lɪkˈwɪdət̬i] *n* : liquidité *f*

liquor [ˈlɪkər] *n* : alcool *m,* boissons *fpl* alcoolisées

liquorice *Brit* → **licorice**

lisp[1] [ˈlɪsp] *vi* : zézayer

lisp[2] *n* : zézaiement *m*

lissome [ˈlɪsəm] *adj* : souple, agile

list[1] [ˈlɪst] *vt* **1** ENUMERATE : énumérer **2** : mettre sur une liste — *vi* TILT : donner de la bande, gîter (se dit d'un bateau)

list[2] *n* **1** : liste *f* **2** SLANT : gîte *f,* bande *f* (d'un bateau)

listen [ˈlɪsən] *vi* **1 to listen to** HEAR : écouter <listen to the rain : écoutez la pluie> **2 to listen to** HEED : tenir compte de, écouter

listener [ˈlɪsənər] *n* : personne *f* qui écoute <he's a good listener : il sait écouter les autres>

listless [ˈlɪstləs] *adj* : apathique, amorphe

listlessly [ˈlɪstləsli] *adv* : avec apathie, sans énergie

listlessness [ˈlɪstləsnəs] *n* : apathie *f,* manque *m* d'énergie

lit [ˈlɪt] → **light**[1]

litany [ˈlɪtəni] *n, pl* **-nies** : litanie *f*

liter [ˈliːt̬ər] *n* : litre *m*

literacy [ˈlɪt̬ərəsi] *n* **1** : capacité *f* de lire et d'écrire **2 literacy campaign** : campagne *f* d'alphabétisation

literal [ˈlɪt̬ərəl] *adj* : littéral — **literally** *adv*

literary [ˈlɪt̬ə,rɛri] *adj* : littéraire

literate [ˈlɪt̬ərət] *adj* : qui sait lire et écrire

literature [ˈlɪt̬ərə,tʃʊr, -tʃər] *n* : littérature *f*

lithe [ˈlaɪð, ˈlaɪθ] *adj* : souple, agile

lithesome [ˈlaɪðsəm, ˈlaɪθ-] → **lissome**

lithium [ˈlɪθiəm] *n* : lithium *m*

lithograph [ˈlɪθə,græf] *n* : lithographie *f*

lithographer [lɪˈθɑgrəfər, ˈlɪθə,græfər] *n* : lithographe *mf*

lithography [lɪˈθɑgrəfi] *n* : lithographie *f* — **lithographic** [,lɪθəˈgræfɪk] *adj*

Lithuanian[1] [,lɪθəˈweɪniən, -njən] *adj* : lituanien

Lithuanian[2] *n* **1** : Lituanien *m,* -nienne *f* **2** : lituanien *m* (langue)

litigant [ˈlɪt̬ɪgənt] *n* : plaideur *m,* -deuse *f*

litigate [ˈlɪt̬ə,geɪt] *v* **-gated; -gating** *vi* : plaider — *vt* : mettre en litige

litigation [,lɪt̬əˈgeɪʃən] *n* : litige *m*

litmus paper [ˈlɪtməs] *n* : papier *m* de tournesol

litre → **liter**

litter[1] [ˈlɪt̬ər] *vt* : mettre du désordre dans, laisser des détritus dans

litter[2] *n* **1** : portée *f* <a litter of puppies : une portée de chiots> **2** STRETCHER : brancard *m,* civière *f* **3** RUBBISH : détritus *mpl* **4** *or* **kitty litter** : litière *f* (de chat)

little[1] [ˈlɪt̬əl] *adv* **less** [ˈlɛs]; **least** [ˈliːst] **1** RARELY : peu <she sings very little these days : elle chante tres peu ces temps-ci> **2 little did I think that . . .** : jamais j'aurais cru que . . . **3 as little as possible** : le moins possible

little[2] *adj* **littler** *or* **less** [ˈlɛs] *or* **lesser** [ˈlɛsər]; **littlest** *or* **least** [ˈliːst] **1** SMALL : petit <little feet : petits pieds> **2** : peu de <very little money : bien peu d'argent> <little time : peu de temps> **3** YOUNG : petit, jeune <my little brother : mon petit frère> **4** TRIVIAL : insignifiant, sans importance

little[3] *n* **1** : peu *m* <I'm happy with little : je me contente de peu> **2 a little** SOMEWHAT : un peu

Little Dipper → **dipper**

liturgical [ləˈtərdʒɪkəl] *adj* : liturgique

liturgy [ˈlɪt̬ərdʒi] *n, pl* **-gies** : liturgie *f*

livable [ˈlɪvəbəl] *adj* **1** INHABITABLE : habitable **2** ENDURABLE : supportable

live[1] [ˈlɪv] *v* **lived; living** *vi* **1** : être vivant, vivre **2** DWELL : demeurer, habiter **3 to live on** : vivre de, se nourrir de **4 to live for** : vivre pour — *vt* : vivre <to live one's life : vivre sa vie>

live[2] [ˈlaɪv] *adj* **1** LIVING : vivant **2** BURNING : ardent <live coals : charbons ardents> **3** : sous tension <live circuits : circuits sous tension> **4** : non explosé <a live bomb : une bombe non explosée> **5** : d'actualité <live issues : sujets d'actualité> **6** : en direct <a live interview : une entrevue en direct>

livelihood [ˈlaɪvli,hʊd] *n* : moyens *mpl* de subsistance

liveliness [ˈlaɪvlinəs] *n* : vivacité *f,* entrain *m*

livelong [ˈlɪvˈlɔŋ] *adj* **all the livelong day** : tout au long de la journée

lively ['laɪvli] *adj* **livelier; -est** : vif, vivant, entraînant, enlevant *Can*
liven ['laɪvən] *vt* ENLIVEN : animer, égayer — *vi* : s'animer, s'égayer
liver ['lɪvər] *n* : foie *m*
liveried ['lɪvəri:d, 'lɪvri:d] *adj* : en livrée
livery ['lɪvəri] *n, pl* **-eries 1** UNIFORM : livrée *f* **2** : pension *f* (pour un cheval)
lives → **life**
livestock ['laɪv,stɑk] *n* : bétail *m*
livid ['lɪvəd] *adj* **1** BLACK-AND-BLUE : couvert de bleus **2** PALE : livide, blême **3** ENRAGED : furibond, en rage
living[1] ['lɪvɪŋ] *adj* : vivant
living[2] *n* **to earn one's living** : gagner sa vie
living room *n* : salle *f* de séjour, salon *m*
lizard ['lɪzərd] *n* : lézard *m*
llama ['lɑmə, 'jɑ-] *n* : lama *m*
load[1] ['lo:d] *vt* **1** : charger <to load a truck : charger un camion> **2** : charger (un fusil, un appareil photo, etc.) **3 to be loaded (down) with** : être chargé de, être plein de
load[2] *n* **1** CARGO : chargement *m,* cargaison *f* **2** WEIGHT : charge *f* **3** BURDEN : fardeau *m,* poids *m* **4 loads of** : beaucoup <loads of work : beaucoup de travail>
loaf[1] ['lo:f] *vi* : fainéanter, paresser
loaf[2] *n, pl* **loaves** ['lo:vz] : pain *m* <a loaf of bread : un pain>
loafer ['lo:fər] *n* : fainéant *m,* fainéante *f*
loam ['lo:m] *n* : terreau *m*
loan[1] ['lo:n] *vt* : prêter
loan[2] *n* : emprunt *m,* prêt *m*
loath ['lo:θ, 'lo:ð] *adj* : peu enclin, peu disposé
loathe ['lo:ð] *vt* **loathed; loathing** : détester, haïr
loathing ['lo:ðɪŋ] *n* : aversion *f,* répugnance *f*
loathsome ['lo:θsəm, 'lo:ð-] *adj* : répugnant, dégoûtant
lob[1] ['lɑb] *v* **lobbed; lobbing** : lober (aux sports)
lob[2] *n* : lob *m*
lobby[1] ['lɑbi] *v* **-bied; -bying** *vt* : faire des pressions sur (en politique) — *vi* : faire pression
lobby[2] *n, pl* **-bies 1** : hall *m,* vestibule *m* <hotel lobby : hall d'hôtel> **2** LOBBYISTS : groupe *m* de pression
lobbyist ['lɑbiɪst] *n* : membre *m* d'un groupe de pression
lobe ['lo:b] *n* : lobe *m*
lobster ['lɑbstər] *n* : homard *m*
local[1] ['lo:kəl] *adj* : local — **locally** *adv*
local[2] *n* **1** : omnibus *m* local, train *m* local **2 locals** *npl* : gens *mpl* du pays, personnes *fpl* du coin
locale [lo'kæl] *n* **1** PLACE : endroit *m,* lieu *m* **2** SETTING : scène *f*
locality [lo'kæləṭi] *n, pl* **-ties** : localité *f*
localization [,lo:kələ'zeɪʃən] *n* : localisation *f*
localize ['lo:kə,laɪz] *vt* **-ized; -izing** : localiser
locate ['lo:,keɪt] *v* **-cated; -cating** *vi* SETTLE : s'établir — *vt* **1** POSITION, SITUATE : situer **2** FIND : trouver, localiser
location [lo'keɪʃən] *n* **1** POSITION : emplacement *m,* site *m* **2** PLACE : endroit *m* **3 on ~** : en extérieur <filmed on location : tourné en extérieur>
lock[1] ['lɑk] *vt* **1** : fermer à clé, verrouiller, barrer *Can* <lock the door : verrouillez la porte> **2** CONFINE : enfermer **3** GRIP : bloquer (un mécanisme) **4** HOLD : serrer <to be locked in an embrace : être enlacé> — *vi* **1** : se fermer à clé **2** : se bloquer (se dit des freins, etc.)
lock[2] *n* **1** : mèche *f,* boucle *f* <a lock of hair : une mèche de cheveux> **2** : serrure *f* (d'une porte, etc.) **3** : écluse *f* (dans un canal)
locker ['lɑkər] *n* : vestiaire *m*
locket ['lɑkət] *n* : médaillon *m* (bijou)
lockjaw ['lɑk,dʒɔ] *n* : tétanos *m*
lockout ['lɑk,aʊt] *n* : lock-out *m*
locksmith ['lɑk,smɪθ] *n* : serrurier *m*
locomotion [,lo:kə'mo:ʃən] *n* : locomotion *f*
locomotive[1] [,lo:kə'mo:ṭɪv] *adj* : locomoteur
locomotive[2] *n* : locomotive *f*
locust ['lo:kəst] *n* **1** : criquet *m* migrateur (insecte) **2** *or* **locust tree** : caroubier *m*
locution [lo'kju:ʃən] *n* : locution *f*
lode ['lo:d] *n* : veine *f,* filon *m*
lodestone ['lo:d,sto:n] *n* : magnétite *f*
lodge[1] ['lɑdʒ] *v* **lodged; lodging** *vt* **1** HOUSE : loger, héberger **2** FILE : déposer <to lodge a complaint : porter plainte> — *vi* : se loger <the bullet was lodged in a tree : la balle s'est logée dans un arbre>
lodge[2] *n* **1** : pavillon *m* <hunting lodge : pavillon de chasse> **2** : abri *m* (d'un animal) **3** : loge *f* (de francs-maçons)
lodger ['lɑdʒər] *n* : locataire *mf,* pensionnaire *mf*
lodging ['lɑdʒɪŋ] *n* **1** : hébergement *m* **2 lodgings** *npl* : logement *m*
loft [lɔft] *n* **1** ATTIC : grenier *m* **2** *or* **hayloft** : grenier *m* à foin **3** GALLERY : tribune *f* <choir loft : tribune de la chorale>
lofty ['lɔfti] *adj* **loftier; -est 1** NOBLE : noble **2** HAUGHTY : fier, hautain **3** HIGH : haut, élevé
log[1] ['lɔg, 'lɑg] *vt* **logged; logging 1** : abattre, tronçonner (des arbres) **2** RECORD : noter, consigner (des renseignements)
log[2] *n* **1** : rondin *m,* bûche *f,* billot *m* *Can* **2** RECORD : journal *m* de bord (d'un avion, d'un navire)
logarithm ['lɔgə,rɪðəm, 'lɑ-] *n* : logarithme *m*

logger ['lɔgər, 'lɑ-] *n* : bûcheron *m*, -ronne *f*

loggerhead ['lɔgər,hɛd, 'lɑ-] *n* **to be at loggerheads** : être en désaccord

logic ['lɑdʒɪk] *n* : logique *f*

logical ['lɑdʒɪkəl] *adj* : logique — **logically** [-kli] *adv*

logician [lo'dʒɪʃən] *n* : logicien *m*, -cienne *f*

logistic [lə'dʒɪstɪk, lo-] *adj* : logistique

logistics [lə'dʒɪstɪks, lo-] *ns & pl* : logistique *f*

logo ['lo:,go:] *n, pl* **logos** [-,go:z] : logo *m*

loin ['lɔɪn] *n* **1** : longe *f* (de porc, etc.) **2 loins** *npl* : reins *mpl* (en anatomie)

loiter ['lɔɪţər] *vi* : traîner, lambiner *fam*

loiterer ['lɔɪţərər] *n* : flâneur *m*, -neuse *f*

loll ['lɑl] *vi* LOUNGE : se prélasser

lollipop *or* **lollypop** ['lɑli,pɑp] *n* : sucette *f France*, suçon *m Can*

lone ['lo:n] *adj* **1** SOLITARY : seul, solitaire **2** SOLE : seul, unique

loneliness ['lo:nlinəs] *n* : solitude *f*

lonely ['lo:nli] *adj* **lonelier; -est 1** SOLITARY : solitaire, isolé **2** LONESOME : seul

loner ['lo:nər] *n* : solitaire *mf*

lonesome ['lo:nsəm] *adj* : seul

long[1] ['lɔŋ] *vi* **to long for** : désirer, avoir envie de

long[2] *adv* **1** : longtemps <long ago : il y a longtemps> **2 all day long** : toute la journée **3 as long as** *or* **so long as** : aussi longtemps que **4 so long!** : à bientôt!

long[3] *adj* **longer** ['lɔŋgər]; **longest** ['lɔŋgəst] **1** (*indicating length*) : long <a long road : une route longue> <10 feet long : 10 pieds de long> **2** (*indicating time*) : long <a long silence : un long silence> <how long is the trip? : combien de temps durera le voyage?> **3 to be long on** : avoir beaucoup de

long[4] *n* **1 before long** : dans peu de temps **2 the long and short** : l'essentiel *m*

longevity [lɑn'dʒɛvəţi] *n* : longévité *f*

longhand ['lɔŋ,hænd] *n* : écriture *f* normale <written in longhand : écrit à la main>

longhorn ['lɔŋ,hɔrn] *n* : longhorn *mf*

longing ['lɔŋɪŋ] *n* : désir *m*, envie *f*

longingly ['lɔŋɪŋli] *adj* : avec désir, avec envie

longitude ['lɑndʒə,tu:d, -,tju:d] *n* : longitude *f*

longitudinal [,lɑndʒə'tu:dənəl, -,tju:d-] *adj* : longitudinal — **longitudinally** *adv*

longshoreman ['lɔŋ'ʃormən] *n, pl* **-men** [-mən, -,mɛn] : débardeur *m*, docker *m*

look[1] ['lʊk] *vi* **1** SEE : regarder <look, here he comes! : regarde, le voici!> **2** SEEM : sembler <it looks unlikely : cela semble peu probable> **3** FACE : être exposé, être orienté <the house looks east : la maison est exposée à l'est> **4 to look after** : prendre soin de **5 to look for** EXPECT : attendre **6 to look for** SEEK : chercher **7 to look upon** CONSIDER : considérer, regarder — *vt* : regarder <to look s.o. in the eye : regarder qqn dans les yeux>

look[2] *n* **1** : coup *m* d'œil <to take a look around : jeter un coup d'œil> **2** EXPRESSION : apparence *f*, mine *f* **3** ASPECT : aspect *m*, air *m*

lookout ['lʊk,aʊt] *n* **1** WATCHMAN : guetteur *m*, sentinelle *f* **2** WATCH : guet *m* <to be on the lookout : faire le guet>

loom[1] ['lu:m] *vi* **1** APPEAR : surgir **2** APPROACH : être imminent **3 to loom large** : menacer

loom[2] *n* : métier *m* à tisser

loon ['lu:n] *n* : plongeon *m*, huard *m Can*

loony *or* **looney** ['lu:ni] *adj* **loonier; -est** : dingue *fam*, fou

loop[1] ['lu:p] *vt* : boucler — *vi* : faire une boucle

loop[2] *n* : boucle *f*

loophole ['lu:p,ho:l] *n* : échappatoire *m*, lacune *f*

loose[1] ['lu:s] *v* **loosed; loosing** *vt* **1** RELEASE : libérer **2** UNTIE : défaire **3** UNLEASH : déchaîner (la colère, etc.)

loose[2] *adj* **looser; -est 1** : qui bouge, mal fixé <a loose tooth : une dent qui bouge> <a loose board : une planche mal fixée>**2** SLACK : lâche, mou, lousse *Can fam* **3** ROOMY : ample, flottant **4** APPROXIMATE : libre, peu exact **5** FREE : échappé, évadé <the horse is loose : le cheval s'est échappé> **6** FRIABLE : meuble <loose soil : terre meuble> **7** : mobile, volant <loose sheets of paper : feuilles mobiles> **8** : dissolu <loose conduct : conduite dissolue>

loosely ['lu:sli] *adv* **1** : sans serrer **2** APPROXIMATELY : approximativement

loosen ['lu:sən] *vt* : desserrer, relâcher

looseness ['lu:snəs] *n* : relâchement *m* (d'une corde), ampleur *f* (d'un vêtement)

loot[1] ['lu:t] *vi* : piller

loot[2] *n* : butin *m*

looter ['lu:ţər] *n* : pillard *m*, -larde *f*

lop ['lɑp] *vt* **lopped; lopping** PRUNE : élaguer, tailler

lope[1] ['lo:p] *vi* **loped; loping 1** : courir en bondissant (se dit d'un animal) **2 to lope away** : partir à grandes foulées

lope[2] *n* : course *f* (d'un animal), pas *m* de course (d'une personne)

lopsided ['lɑp,saɪdəd] *adj* **1** CROOKED : de travers **2** ASYMMETRICAL : asymétrique

loquacious [lo'kweɪʃəs] *adj* : loquace, bavard

loquacity [loˈkwæsət̬i] *n* : loquacité *f*

lord [ˈlɔrd] *n* **1** : seigneur *m* <his lord and master : son seigneur et maître> **2** : lord *m* <Lord Carrington : Lord Carrington> **3 the Lord** : le Seigneur

lordly [ˈlɔrdli] *adj* **lordlier; -est** : hautain, altier

lordship [ˈlɔrdˌʃɪp] *n* **Your Lordship** : Monsieur le comte, Monsieur le juge, etc.

Lord's Supper *n* : Eucharistie *f*

lore [ˈlor] *n* : traditions *fpl,* coutumes *fpl*

lose [ˈlu:z] *v* **lost** [ˈlɔst]; **losing** [ˈlu:zɪŋ] *vt* **1** : perdre <I've lost my keys : j'ai perdu mes clés> <to lose weight : perdre du poids> <to lose one's way : perdre son chemin> **2** : faire perdre <the errors lost him his job : les erreurs lui ont fait perdre son emploi> **3** : retarder de <my watch loses three minutes a day : ma montre retarde de trois minutes par jour> — *vi* **1** : perdre **2** : retarder (se dit des horloges, etc.)

loser [ˈlu:zər] *n* : perdant *m,* -dante *f*

loss [ˈlɔs] *n* **1** : perte *f* <loss of sight : perte de vue> <it's no great loss : ce n'est pas une grosse perte> **2** : déperdition *f,* perte *f* <loss of heat : déperdition de chaleur> **3 losses** *npl* : pertes *fpl,* victimes *fpl* (de la guerre) **4 to be at a loss for words** : ne pas savoir quoi dire

lost [ˈlɔst] *adj* **1** MISSED : perdu, manqué <a lost opportunity : une occasion manquée> **2** : perdu, égaré <a lost child : un enfant perdu> <to get lost : se perdre> **3** BEWILDERED : perdu, désorienté **4 to be lost in thought** : être absorbé par ses pensées, être plongé dans la réflexion

lot [ˈlɑt] *n* **1** : tirage *m* <to draw lots : tirer au sort> **2** SHARE : part *m,* partage *m* **3** FATE : lot *m,* destin *m,* sort *m* **4** PLOT : lot *m,* parcelle *f* (de terrain) **5 a lot** : beaucoup <a lot of money : beaucoup d'argent> **6 a lot** OFTEN : souvent

loth [ˈlo:θ, ˈlo:ð] → **loath**

lotion [ˈlo:ʃən] *n* : lotion *f*

lottery [ˈlɑt̬əri] *n, pl* **-teries** : loterie *f*

lotus [ˈlo:t̬əs] *n* : lotus *m*

loud[1] [ˈlaʊd] *adv* : fort <to think out loud : penser tout haut>

loud[2] *adj* **1** : fort, grand <loud music : musique forte> <a loud cry : un grand cri> **2** FLASHY : criard, voyant

loudly [ˈlaʊdli] *adv* : bruyamment

loudness [ˈlaʊdnəs] *n* : force *f,* intensité *f*

loudspeaker [ˈlaʊdˌspi:kər] *n* : haut-parleur *m*

lounge[1] [ˈlaʊndʒ] *vi* **lounged; lounging** : flâner, paresser

lounge[2] *n* : salon *m*

louse [ˈlaʊs] *n, pl* **lice** [ˈlaɪs] : pou *m*

lousy [ˈlaʊzi] *adj* **lousier; -est 1** : pouilleux, couvert de poux **2** POOR, SORRY : piètre, mauvais <lousy results : de piètres résultats>

lout [ˈlaʊt] *n* : rustre *m*

louver *or* **louvre** [ˈlu:vər] *n* **1** SLAT : lame *f* **2** *or* **louver window** : persienne *f,* jalousie *f*

lovable [ˈlʌvəbəl] *adj* : adorable, charmant

love[1] [ˈlʌv] *v* **loved; loving** *vt* **1** CHERISH : aimer **2** LIKE : aimer, adorer *fam* <he loved to play the violin : il adorait jouer du violon> — *vi* : aimer

love[2] *n* **1** : amour *m* <to fall in love : être amoureux> **2** ENTHUSIASM, INTEREST : amour *m,* passion *f* **3** BELOVED : amour *m*

loveless [ˈlʌvləs] *adj* : sans amour

loveliness [ˈlʌvlinəs] *n* : beauté *f,* charme *f*

lovelorn [ˈlʌvˌlɔrn] *adj* : malheureux en amour, privé d'amour

lovely [ˈlʌvli] *adj* **lovelier; -est 1** ATTRACTIVE : beau, joli **2** ENJOYABLE : agréable <we had a lovely time : ce fut très agréable>

lover [ˈlʌvər] *n* : amant *m,* -mante *f*

lovingly [ˈlʌvɪŋli] *adv* : affectueusement, tendrement

low[1] [ˈlo:] *vi* : meugler

low[2] *adv* : bas <aim low : visez bas>

low[3] *adj* **lower; lowest 1** : bas <a low wall : un mur bas> <low prices : des bas prix> **2** HUMBLE : modeste <of low birth : d'origine modeste> **3** DEPRESSED : démoralisé, déprimé **4** POOR, INFERIOR : faible <low income : faible revenu> **5** UNFAVORABLE : piètre

low[4] *n* **1** : bas *m* <to reach a low : atteindre un bas> **2** *or* **low gear** : première *f* **3** MOO : meuglement *m*

lowbrow [ˈlo:ˌbraʊ] *n* : personne *f* peu intellectuelle

lower[1] [ˈlaʊər, ˈlo:ər] *vi* **1** SCOWL : se renfrogner **2** DARKEN : s'assombrir

lower[2] [ˈlo:ər] *vt* **1** : baisser <to lower one's eyes : baisser les yeux> **2** REDUCE : baisser, diminuer **3 to lower oneself** : s'abaisser, s'humilier — *vi* DROP, DIMINISH : baisser

lower[3] *adj* : inférieur, bas

lowland [ˈlo:lənd, -ˌlænd] *n* : plaine *f,* basse terre *f*

lowly [ˈlo:li] *adj* **lowlier; -est** : humble, modeste

loyal [ˈlɔɪəl] *adj* : loyal, fidèle — **loyally** *adv*

loyalist [ˈlɔɪəlɪst] *n* : loyaliste *mf*

loyalty [ˈlɔɪəlti] *n, pl* **-ties** : loyauté *f*

lozenge [ˈlɑzəndʒ] *n* : pastille *f*

LSD [ˌɛlˌɛsˈdi:] *n* : LSD *m*

lubricant [ˈlu:brɪkənt] *n* : lubrifiant *m*

lubricate [ˈlu:brəˌkeɪt] *vt* **-cated; -cating** : lubrifier

lubrication [ˌlu:brəˈkeɪʃən] *n* : lubrification *f*

lucid ['lu:səd] *adj* : lucide, clair — **lucidly** *adv*
lucidity [lu:'sɪdət̮i] *n* : lucidité *f*
luck ['lʌk] *n* **1** FORTUNE : chance *f,* fortune *f* <good luck! : bonne chance!> **2** CHANCE, OPPORTUNITY : hasard *m,* chance *f* <a stroke of luck : un heureux hasard> <as luck would have it : par hasard> <to be out of luck : ne pas avoir de chance>
luckily ['lʌkəli] *adv* : heureusement, par bonheur
luckless ['lʌkləs] *adj* : malchanceux
lucky ['lʌki] *adj* **luckier; -est 1** FORTUNATE : chanceux **2** FORTUITOUS : heureux, fortuné **3** : de chance, porte-bonheur <my lucky day : mon jour de chance>
lucrative ['lu:krət̮ɪv] *adj* : lucratif
ludicrous ['lu:dəkrəs] *adj* : ridicule, insensé — **ludicrously** *adv*
lug ['lʌg] *vt* **lugged; lugging** : traîner, trimbaler *fam*
luggage ['lʌgɪdʒ] *n* : bagages *mpl*
lugubrious [lʊ'gu:briəs] *adj* : lugubre — **lugubriously** *adv*
lukewarm ['lu:k'wɔrm] *adj* **1** TEPID : tiède **2** HALFHEARTED : tiède, indifférent
lull[1] ['lʌl] *vt* **1** CALM : apaiser, calmer **2 to lull to sleep** : endormir
lull[2] *n* : accalmie *f*
lullaby ['lʌlə,baɪ] *n, pl* **-bies** : berceuse *f*
lumbago [lʌm'beɪgo] *n* : lumbago *m*
lumber[1] ['lʌmbər] *vt* : abattre les arbres — *vi* : marcher pesamment, avancer d'un pas lourd
lumber[2] *n* : bois *m*
lumberjack ['lʌmbər,dʒæk] *n* : bûcheron *m,* -ronne *f*
lumberyard ['lʌmbər,jɑrd] *n* : dépôt *m* de bois
luminary ['lu:mə,nɛri] *n, pl* **-naries** : lumière *f,* sommité *f*
luminescence [,lu:mə'nɛsənts] *n* : luminescence *f*
luminescent [lu:mə'nɛsənt] *adj* : luminescent
luminosity [,lu:mə'nɑsət̮i] *n, pl* **-ties** : luminosité *f*
luminous ['lu:mənəs] *adj* : lumineux — **luminously** *adv*
lump[1] ['lʌmp] *vt or* **to lump together** : regrouper, rassembler
lump[2] *n* **1** CHUNK, PIECE : morceau *m,* motton *m Can* <a lump of butter : un morceau de beurre> **2** SWELLING : bosse *f,* grosseur *f* **3** : grumeau *m* (dans la sauce, etc.) **4 to have a lump in one's throat** : avoir la gorge serrée
lumpy ['lʌmpi] *adj* **lumpier; -est** : grumeleux (se dit d'une sauce), plein de bosses (se dit d'un matelas)
lunacy ['lu:nəsi] *n, pl* **-cies** : folie *f,* démence *f*
lunar ['lu:nər] *adj* : lunaire
lunatic[1] ['lu:nə,tɪk] *adj* : fou, dément
lunatic[2] *n* : fou *m,* folle *f;* dément *m,* -mente *f*
lunch[1] ['lʌntʃ] *vi* : déjeuner, dîner *Can*
lunch[2] *n* : déjeuner *m,* dîner *m Can,* lunch *m Can*
luncheon ['lʌntʃən] *n* : déjeuner *m*
lung ['lʌŋ] *n* : poumon *m*
lunge[1] ['lʌndʒ] *vi* **lunged; lunging 1** : se jeter en avant **2 to lunge at** : porter une botte à (en escrime)
lunge[2] *n* **1** THRUST : botte *f,* coup *m* **2 to lunge forward** : faire un mouvement vers l'avant
lurch[1] ['lərtʃ] *vi* **1** STAGGER : vaciller, tituber **2** : faire une embardée (se dit d'une voiture)
lurch[2] *n* : embardée *f* (d'une voiture), écart *m* (d'une personne)
lure[1] ['lʊr] *vt* **lured; luring** : attirer
lure[2] *n* **1** BAIT : leurre *m,* amorce *f* **2** ATTRACTION : attrait *m*
lurid ['lʊrəd] *adj* **1** GRUESOME : affreux, horrible **2** SENSATIONAL : à sensation **3** GAUDY : criard, voyant
lurk ['lərk] *vi* : se cacher, se tapir
luscious ['lʌʃəs] *adj* **1** DELICIOUS, DELIGHTFUL : succulent, délicieux **2** SEDUCTIVE : séduisant
lush ['lʌʃ] *adj* : luxuriant, riche
lust[1] ['lʌst] *vi* **to lust after** : désirer (une personne), convoiter (des richesses, etc.)
lust[2] *n* **1** DESIRE : désir *m* (charnel) **2** CRAVING : soif *f,* convoitise *f*
luster *or* **lustre** ['lʌstər] *n* **1** SHEEN : lustre *m* **2** SPLENDOR : éclat *m*
lusterless ['lʌstərləs] *adj* : sans éclat
lustful ['lʌstfəl] *adj* : concupiscent
lustily ['lʌstəli] *adv* : avec vigueur
lustrous ['lʌstrəs] *adj* : lustré, brillant
lusty ['lʌsti] *adj* **lustier; -est** : robuste, vigoureux
lute ['lu:t] *n* : luth *m*
Luxembourger ['lʌksəmbərgər] *n* : Luxembourgeois *m,* -geoise *f*
Luxembourgian [,lʌksəm'bərgiən] *adj* : luxembourgeois
luxuriance [,lʌg'ʒʊriənts, ,lʌk'ʃʊr-] *n* : luxuriance *f*
luxuriant [,lʌg'ʒʊriənt, ,lʌk'ʃʊr-] *adj* : luxuriant, abondant
luxuriate [,lʌg'ʒʊri,eɪt, ,lʌk'ʃʊr-] *vi* **-ated; -ating 1** FLOURISH : pousser, proliférer **2 to luxuriate in** : prendre plaisir à, s'abandonner à
luxurious [,lʌg'ʒʊriəs, ,lʌk'ʃʊr-] *adj* : luxueux — **luxuriously** *adv*
luxury ['lʌkʃəri, 'lʌgʒə-] *n, pl* **-ries** : luxe *m*
lye ['laɪ] *n* : lessive *f*
lying → **lie**[1], **lie**[2]
lymph ['lɪmpf] *n* : lymphe *f*
lymphatic [lɪm'fæt̮ɪk] *adj* : lymphatique

lynch ['lɪntʃ] *vt* : lyncher
lynx ['lɪŋks] *n, pl* **lynx** *or* **lynxes** : lynx *m,* loup-cervier *m*
lyre ['laɪr] *n* : lyre *f*
lyric[1] ['lɪrɪk] *adj* : lyrique
lyric[2] *n* **1** : poème *m* lyrique **2 lyrics** *npl* : paroles *fpl* (d'une chanson)
lyrical ['lɪrɪkəl] → **lyric**[1]

M

m ['ɛm] *n, pl* **m's** *or* **ms** ['ɛmz] : m *m,* treizième lettre de l'alphabet
ma'am ['mæm] → **madame**
macabre [mə'kɑb, -'kɑbər, -'kɑbrə] *adj* : macabre
macadam [mə'kædəm] *n* : macadam *m*
macaroni [ˌmækə'ro:ni] *n* : macaronis *mpl*
macaroon [ˌmækə'ru:n] *n* : macaron *m*
macaw [mə'kɔ] *n* : ara *m*
mace ['meɪs] *n* **1** : masse *f* (arme ou symbole) **2** : macis *m* (épice)
Macedonian[1] [ˌmæsə'do:njən, -niən] *adj* : macédonien
Macedonian[2] *n* : Macédonien *m,* -nienne *f*
machete [mə'ʃɛṭi] *n* : machette *f*
machination [ˌmækə'neɪʃən, ˌmæʃə-] *n* : machination *f,* complot *m*
machine[1] [mə'ʃi:n] *vt* **-chined; -chining** : fabriquer (à la machine), usiner
machine[2] *n* **1** VEHICLE : véhicule *m* **2** : machine *f* <sewing machine : machine à coudre>
machine gun *n* : mitrailleuse *f*
machine language *n* : langage *m* machine
machine–readable *adj* : exploitable par (une) machine
machinery [mə'ʃi:nəri] *n, pl* **-eries 1** MACHINES : machines *fpl* **2** MECHANISM : mécanisme *m* **3** SYSTEM : rouages *mpl* <the machinery of state : les rouages de l'état>
machinist [mə'ʃi:nɪst] *n* : opérateur *m,* -trice *f* (sur machine)
mackerel ['mækərəl] *n, pl* **-el** *or* **-els** : maquereau *m*
mackinaw ['mækəˌnɔ] *n* : grosse veste *f* de laine
mackintosh ['mækənˌtɑʃ] *n Brit* RAINCOAT : imperméable *m*
macramé ['mækrəˌmeɪ] *n* : macramé *m*
mad ['mæd] *adj* **madder; maddest 1** INSANE : fou **2** FOOLISH : insensé **3** ANGRY : furieux **4** ENTHUSIASTIC, CRAZY : fou <mad about her : fou d'elle> **5** RABID : enragé
Madagascan[1] [ˌmædə'gæskən] *adj* : malgache
Madagascan[2] *n* : Malgache *mf*
madam ['mædəm] *n, pl* **mesdames** [meɪ'dɑm, -'dæm] : madame *f*
madcap[1] ['mædˌkæp] *adj* : fou, écervelé, étourdi
madcap[2] *n* : fou *m,* folle *f*
madden ['mædən] *vt* **1** CRAZE : rendre fou, exaspérer **2** ENRAGE : mettre en rage, rendre furieux
maddeningly ['mædənɪŋli] *adv* : de façon exaspérante <maddeningly slow : d'une lenteur exaspérante>
made → **make**[1]
madhouse ['mædˌhaʊs] *n* : maison *f* de fous
madly ['mædli] *adv* : follement <to love s.o. madly : aimer qqn à la folie>
madman ['mædˌmæn, -mən] *n, pl* **-men** [-mən, -ˌmɛn] : fou *m,* aliéné *m*
madness ['mædnəs] *n* : folie *f,* démence *f*
madwoman ['mædˌwʊmən] *n, pl* **-women** [-ˌwɪmən] : folle *f,* aliénée *f*
maelstrom ['meɪlstrəm] *n* : maelström *m*
maestro ['maɪˌstro:] *n, pl* **-stros** *or* **-stri** [-ˌstri:] : maestro *m*
Mafia ['mɑfiə] *n* : mafia *f*
magazine ['mægəˌzi:n] *n* **1** STOREHOUSE : magasin *m* **2** PERIODICAL : magazine *m,* revue *f* **3** : chargeur *m* (d'une arme à feu)
magenta [mə'dʒɛntə] *n* : magenta *m*
maggot ['mægət] *n* : ver *m,* asticot *m*
magic[1] ['mædʒɪk] *or* **magical** ['mædʒɪkəl] *adj* : magique
magic[2] *n* : magie *f* <as if by magic : comme par enchantement>
magically ['mædʒɪkli] *adv* : magiquement, par magie
magician [mə'dʒɪʃən] *n* : magicien *m,* -cienne *f*
magistrate ['mædʒəˌstreɪt] *n* : magistrat *m*
magma ['mægmə] *n* : magma *m*
magnanimity [ˌmægnə'nɪməṭi] *n, pl* **-ties** : magnanimité *f*
magnanimous [mæg'nænəməs] *adj* : magnanime
magnanimously [mæg'nænəməsli] *adv* : avec magnanimité
magnesium [mæg'ni:ziəm, -ʒəm] *n* : magnésium *m*
magnet ['mægnət] *n* : aimant *m*
magnetic [mæg'nɛṭɪk] *adj* : magnétique — **magnetically** [-ṭɪkli] *adv*
magnetic field *n* : champ *m* magnétique
magnetic tape *n* : bande *f* magnétique
magnetism ['mægnəˌtɪzəm] *n* : magnétisme *m*
magnetize ['mægnəˌtaɪz] *vt* **-tized; -tizing 1** : aimanter **2** ATTRACT : magnétiser

magnification [ˌmægnəfəˈkeɪʃən] *n* : grossissement *m*

magnificence [mægˈnɪfəsənts] *n* : magnificence *f*

magnificent [mægˈnɪfəsənt] *adj* : magnifique — **magnificently** *adv*

magnify [ˈmægnəˌfaɪ] *vt* **-fied; -fying 1** ENLARGE : grossir **2** EXAGGERATE : exagérer

magnifying glass *n* : loupe *f*

magnitude [ˈmægnəˌtuːd, -ˌtjuːd] *n* **1** GREATNESS : ampleur *f*, grandeur *f* **2** QUANTITY : quantité *f* **3** IMPORTANCE : importance *f*, magnitude *f*

magnolia [mægˈnoːljə] *n* : magnolia *m*

magpie [ˈmægˌpaɪ] *n* : pie *f*

mahogany [məˈhɑgəni] *n, pl* **-nies** : acajou *m*

maid [ˈmeɪd] *n* **1** MAIDEN : demoiselle *f*, vierge *f* **2** *or* **maidservant** : bonne *f*, domestique *f*, femme *f* de chambre

maiden[1] [ˈmeɪdən] *adj* **1** UNMARRIED : célibataire **2** FIRST : premier, inaugural <maiden voyage : voyage inaugural>

maiden[2] *n* : demoiselle *f*, vierge *f*

maidenhood [ˈmeɪdənˌhʊd] *n* : virginité *f*

maiden name *n* : nom *m* de jeune fille

mail[1] [ˈmeɪl] *vt* : envoyer par la poste

mail[2] *n* **1** : poste *f* <to put in the mail : mettre à la poste> **2** LETTERS : courrier *m* **3** : mailles *fpl* <coat of mail : cotte de mailles>

mailbox [ˈmeɪlˌbɑks] *n* : boîte *f* aux lettres

mailman [ˈmeɪlˌmæn, -mən] *n, pl* **-men** [-mən, -ˌmɛn] : facteur *m*

maim [ˈmeɪm] *vt* : estropier, mutiler

main[1] [ˈmeɪn] *adj* : principal <the main course : le plat principal>

main[2] *n* **1** : canalisation *f* principale (d'eau, de gaz), conduite *f* principale (d'électricité) **2** HIGH SEAS : large *m*, haute mer *f*

mainframe [ˈmeɪnˌfreɪm] *n* : ordinateur *m* central

mainland [ˈmeɪnˌlænd, -lənd] *n* : continent *m*

mainly [ˈmeɪnli] *adv* : principalement, surtout

mainstay [ˈmeɪnˌsteɪ] *n* : pilier *m*, soutien *m* (principal)

mainstream[1] [ˈmeɪnˌstriːm] *adj* : dominant, traditionnel

mainstream[2] *n* : courant *m* dominant

maintain [meɪnˈteɪn] *vt* **1** SERVICE : entretenir (un véhicule, une route, etc.) **2** PRESERVE : maintenir <to maintain silence : garder le silence> **3** SUPPORT : soutenir **4** ASSERT : affirmer

maintenance [ˈmeɪntənənts] *n* **1** UPKEEP : entretien *m* **2** UPHOLDING : maintien *m*

maize [ˈmeɪz] → **indian corn**

majestic [məˈdʒɛstɪk] *adj* : majestueux — **majestically** [-tɪkli] *adv*

majesty [ˈmædʒəsti] *n, pl* **-ties 1** : majesté *f* <Your Majesty : Votre Majesté> **2** GRANDEUR : grandeur *f*, majesté *f*

major[1] [ˈmeɪdʒər] *vi* **-jored; -joring** : se spécialiser

major[2] *adj* **1** MAIN : principal <the major part : la plus grande partie> **2** NOTEWORTHY : majeur, notable **3** SERIOUS : majeur <major surgery : une grosse opération> **4** : majeur (en musique)

major[3] *n* **1** : commandant *m* (de l'armée) **2** FIELD : spécialité *f* (universitaire)

major general *n* : général *m* de division

majority [məˈdʒɔrəṭi] *n, pl* **-ties** : majorité *f*

make[1] [ˈmeɪk] *v* **made** [ˈmeɪd]; **making** *vt* **1** CREATE : faire, créer <to make noise : faire du bruit> **2** MANUFACTURE : fabriquer, faire **3** CONSTITUTE : constituer <made of gold : en or> **4** PREPARE : préparer <to make a meal : préparer un repas> **5** RENDER : rendre <to make sick : rendre malade> **6** FORM : faire, former **7** COMPEL : faire, obliger <you make me laugh : tu me fais rire> **8** EARN : gagner <to make a living : gagner sa vie> **9** ATTAIN : atteindre, arriver jusqu'à (une position, etc.) — *vi* **1** HEAD : se diriger <she made for home : elle s'est dirigée vers la maison> **2 to make do** : se débrouiller **3 to make good** SUCCEED : réussir **4 to make of** : comprendre à **5 to make off with** : partir avec

make[2] *n* BRAND : marque *f*

make–believe[1] [ˌmeɪkbəˈliːv] *adj* : imaginaire

make–believe[2] *n* : fantaisie *f* <a world of make-believe : un monde d'illusions>

make out *vt* **1** WRITE : faire, écrire <to make out a cheque : faire un chèque> **2** DISCERN : discerner, distinguer **3** UNDERSTAND : comprendre — *vi* FARE : se débrouiller <how did you make out? : comment ça s'est passé?>

maker [ˈmeɪkər] *n* MANUFACTURER : fabricant *m*, -cante *f*

makeshift [ˈmeɪkˌʃɪft] *adj* : improvisé

makeup [ˈmeɪkˌʌp] *n* **1** COMPOSITION : composition *f* **2** COSMETICS : maquillage **3** CHARACTER : caractère *m*, nature *f*

make up *vt* **1** INVENT : inventer **2** : rattraper <to make up the time : rattraper le temps> — *vi* RECONCILE : se réconcilier

maladjusted [ˌmæləˈdʒʌstəd] *adj* : inadapté

maladjustment [ˌmæləˈdʒʌstmənt] *n* : inadaptation *f*

maladroit [ˌmælə'drɔɪt] *adj* : maladroit
malady ['mælədi] *n, pl* **-dies** : maladie *f*, mal *m*
Malagasy[1] [ˌmælə'gæsi; ˌmɑlə'gɑsi, -ʃi] *adj* : malgache
Malagasy[2] *n* **1** : Malgache *mf* **2** : malgache *m* (langue)
malaise [mə'leɪz] *n* : malaise *m*
malamute ['mæləˌmju:t, -ˌmu:t] *n* : malamute *m*, chien *m* malamute
malapropism ['mæləˌprɑˌpɪzəm] *n* : impropriété *f* de langage
malaria [mə'lɛriə] *n* : paludisme *m*
malarkey [mə'lɑrki] *n* : balivernes *fpl*, sottises *fpl*
Malawian[1] [mə'lɑwiən] *adj* : malawien
Malawian[2] *n* : Malawien *m*, -wienne *f*
Malay[1] [mə'leɪ, 'meɪˌleɪ] *or* **Malayan** [mə'leɪən, meɪ-; 'meɪˌleɪən] *adj* : malais
Malay[2] *n* **1** *or* **Malayan** : Malais *m*, -laise *f* **2** : malais *m* (langue)
Malaysian[1] [mə'leɪʒən] *adj* : malaisien
Malaysian[2] *n* : Malaisien *m*, -sienne *f*
male[1] ['meɪl] *adj* **1** : mâle **2** MASCULINE : masculin
male[2] *n* **1** : mâle *m* (en botanique ou en zoologie) **2** MAN : homme *m*
malefactor ['mæləˌfæktər] *n* : malfaiteur *m*, -trice *f*
maleness ['meɪlnəs] *n* : masculinité *f*
malevolence [mə'lɛvələnts] *n* : malveillance *f*
malevolent [mə'lɛvələnt] *adj* : malveillant
malformation [ˌmælfɔr'meɪʃən] *n* : malformation *f*
malformed [mæl'fɔrmd] *adj* : difforme
malfunction[1] [mæl'fʌŋkʃən] *vi* : mal fonctionner
malfunction[2] *n* : défaillance *f*, mauvais fonctionnement *m*
Malian[1] ['maliən] *adj* : malien
Malian[2] *n* : Malien *m*, -lienne *f*
malice ['mælɪs] *n* **1** : malveillance *f*, méchanceté *f* **2** **with malice aforethought** : avec préméditation
malicious [mə'lɪʃəs] *adj* : malveillant, méchant
maliciously [mə'lɪʃəsli] *adv* : méchamment, avec méchanceté
malign[1] [mə'laɪn] *vt* : calomnier, diffamer
malign[2] *adj* : nuisible, pernicieux
malignancy [mə'lɪgnəntsi] *n, pl* **-cies** : malignité *f*
malignant [mə'lɪgnənt] *adj* : malin
malinger [mə'lɪŋgər] *vi* : faire le malade
mall ['mɔl] *n* **1** PROMENADE : mail *m*, allée *f* **2** *or* **shopping mall** : centre *m* commercial
mallard ['mælərd] *n, pl* **-lard** *or* **-lards** : colvert *m*, malard *m Can*
malleable ['mæliəbəl] *adj* : malléable
mallet ['mælət] *n* : maillet *m*
malnourished [mæl'nərɪʃt] *adj* : sous-alimenté
malnutrition [ˌmælnʊ'trɪʃən, -njʊ-] *n* : sous-alimentation *f*, malnutrition *f*
malodorous [mæl'o:dərəs] *adj* : malodorant
malpractice [ˌmæl'præktəs] *n* : faute *f* professionnelle
malt ['mɔlt] *n* : malt *m*
Maltese[1] [mɔl'ti:z, -'ti:s] *adj* : maltais
Maltese[2] *n* : Maltais *m*, -taise *f*
maltreat [mæl'tri:t] *vt* : maltraiter
mama *or* **mamma** ['mɑmə] *n* : maman *f*
mammal ['mæməl] *n* : mammifère *m*
mammary gland ['mæməri] *n* : glande *f* mammaire
mammogram ['mæməˌgræm] *n* : mammographie *f*
mammoth[1] ['mæməθ] *adj* : colossal, énorme
mammoth[2] *n* : mammouth *m*
man[1] ['mæn] *vt* **manned; manning** : équiper en personnel, assurer une permanence à
man[2] *n, pl* **men** ['mɛn] **1** PERSON : homme *m*, personne *f* **2** MALE : homme *m* **3** MANKIND : humanité *f*
manacles ['mænɪkəlz] *npl* **1** SHACKLES : chaînes *fpl* **2** HANDCUFFS : menottes *fpl*
manage ['mænɪdʒ] *v* **-aged; -aging** *vt* **1** HANDLE : manier **2** DIRECT : gérer, diriger **3** CONTRIVE : réussir, arriver — *vi* COPE : se débrouiller
manageable ['mænɪdʒəbəl] *adj* : maniable
management ['mænɪdʒmənt] *n* **1** DIRECTION : gestion *f*, direction *f* **2** MANAGERS : direction *f*
manager ['mænɪdʒər] *n* : directeur *m*, -trice *f*; gérant *m*, -rante *f*; manager *m* (aux sports)
managerial [ˌmænə'dʒɪriəl] *adj* : directorial
mandarin ['mændərən] *n* **1** : mandarin *m* **2** *or* **mandarin orange** : mandarine *f*
mandate ['mænˌdeɪt] *n* : mandat *m*
mandatory ['mændəˌtori] *adj* : obligatoire
mandible ['mændəbəl] *n* **1** JAW : mâchoire *f* inférieure **2** : mandibule *f* (d'un oiseau ou d'un insecte)
mandolin [ˌmændə'lɪn, 'mændələn] *n* : mandoline *f*
mane ['meɪn] *n* : crinière *f*
maneuver[1] *or Brit* **manoeuvre** [mə'nu:vər, -'nju:-] *v* **-vered** *or Brit* **-vred; -vering** *or Brit* **-vring** : manœuvrer
maneuver[2] *or Brit* **manoeuvre** *n* : manœuvre *f*
maneuverable [mə'nu:vərəbəl, -'nju:-] *adj* : manœuvrable
manfully ['mænfəli] *adv* : courageusement, vaillamment
manganese ['mæŋgəˌni:z, -ˌni:s] *n* : manganèse *m*
mange ['meɪndʒ] *n* : gale *f*
manger ['meɪndʒər] *n* : mangeoire *f*

mangle ['mæŋgəl] *vt* **-gled; -gling 1** MUTILATE : mutiler, déchirer **2** BOTCH : estropier (un texte, un discours, etc.)

mango ['mæŋˌgoː] *n, pl* **-goes** : mangue *f*

mangrove ['mænˌgroːv, 'mæŋ-] *n* : manglier *m*

mangy ['meɪndʒi] *adj* **mangier; -est 1** : galeux **2** SHABBY : minable, miteux, élimé

manhandle ['mænˌhændəl] *vt* **-dled; -dling** : malmener, maltraiter

manhole ['mænˌhoːl] *n* : trou *m* d'homme, bouche *f* d'égout

manhood ['mænˌhʊd] *n* **1** COURAGE, MANLINESS : courage *m,* virilité *f* **2** ADULTHOOD : âge *m* d'homme **3** MEN : hommes *mpl*

manhunt ['mænˌhʌnt] *n* : chasse *f* à l'homme

mania ['meɪniə, -njə] *n* : manie *f*

maniac ['meɪniˌæk] *n* : fou *m,* folle *f;* maniaque *mf*

maniacal [mə'naɪəkəl] *adj* : maniaque

manicure[1] ['mænəˌkjʊr] *vt* **-cured; -curing 1** : manucurer, faire les ongles de **2** CUT, TRIM : tondre <a manicured lawn : une pelouse impeccable>

manicure[2] *n* : manucure *f*

manicurist ['mænəˌkjʊrɪst] *n* : manucure *mf*

manifest[1] ['mænəˌfɛst] *vt* : manifester

manifest[2] *adj* : manifeste, évident — **manifestly** *adv*

manifestation [ˌmænəfə'steɪʃən] *n* : manifestation *f*

manifesto [ˌmænə'fɛsˌtoː] *n, pl* **-tos** *or* **-toes** : manifeste *m*

manifold[1] ['mænəˌfoːld] *adj* : multiple, nombreux

manifold[2] *n* : collecteur *m* (d'échappement), tubulure *f* (d'admission)

manipulate [mə'nɪpjəˌleɪt] *vt* **-lated; -lating** : manipuler

manipulation [məˌnɪpjə'leɪʃən] *n* : manipulation *f*

mankind ['mæn'kaɪnd, -ˌkaɪnd] *n* : humanité *f,* le genre humain

manliness ['mænlinəs] *n* : virilité *f*

manly ['mænli] *adj* **manlier; -est** : viril

manna ['mænə] *n* : manne *f*

mannequin ['mænɪkən] *n* : mannequin *m*

manner ['mænər] *n* **1** KIND : sorte *f* **2** WAY, METHOD : manière *f,* façon *f* <a manner of speaking : une façon de parler> **3** BEARING : attitude *f,* maintien *m* **4 manners** *npl* ETIQUETTE : manières *fpl* **5 manners** *npl* CUSTOMS : mœurs *fpl,* usages *mpl*

mannered ['mænərd] *adj* **1** AFFECTED : maniéré, affecté **2 well-mannered** : bien élevé

mannerism ['mænəˌrɪzəm] *n* **1** HABIT : particularité *f,* manie *f,* tic *m* **2** AFFECTATION : maniérisme *m*

mannerly ['mænərli] *adj* : poli, bien élevé

mannish ['mænɪʃ] *adj* : masculin, hommasse

manoeuvre *Brit* → **maneuver**

man–of–war [ˌmænə'wɔr, -əv'wɔr] *n, pl* **men–of–war** [ˌmɛn-] : bâtiment *m* de guerre, navire *m* de guerre

manor ['mænər] *n* : manoir *m*

manpower ['mænˌpaʊər] *n* : main-d'œuvre *f*

mansion ['mæntʃən] *n* : château *m,* manoir *m,* hôtel *m* particulier

manslaughter ['mænˌslɔt̬ər] *n* : homicide *m* involontaire

mantel ['mæntəl] *or* **mantelpiece** ['mæntəlˌpiːs] *n* : cheminée *f*

mantis ['mæntɪs] *n, pl* **-tises** *or* **-tes** ['mænˌtiːz] : mante *f*

mantle ['mæntəl] *n* **1** CLOAK : manteau *m,* cape *f* **2** BLANKET, COVERING : manteau *f,* couche *f* <a mantle of fog : un manteau de brume>

manual[1] ['mænjʊəl] *adj* : manuel — **manually** *adv*

manual[2] *n* : manuel *m*

manufacture[1] [ˌmænjə'fæktʃər] *vt* **-tured; -turing** : fabriquer, manufacturer, confectionner (des vêtements)

manufacture[2] *n* : fabrication *f*

manufacturer [ˌmænjə'fæktʃərər] *n* : fabricant *m,* -cante *f*

manure [mə'nʊr, -'njʊr] *n* **1** : fumier *m* (des animaux) **2** FERTILIZER : engrais *m*

manuscript ['mænjəˌskrɪpt] *n* : manuscrit *m*

many[1] ['mɛni] *adj* **more** ['mor]; **most** ['moːst] **1** : beaucoup de, un grand nombre de **2 as many** : autant de **3 many a time** : maintes fois **4 so many** : tant de **5 too many** : trop de

many[2] *pron* : beaucoup, un grand nombre

map[1] ['mæp] *vt* **mapped; mapping 1** : faire la carte de **2** *or* **to map out** PLAN : tracer, organiser

map[2] *n* : carte *f*

maple ['meɪpəl] *n* **1** : érable *m* **2 maple syrup** : sirop *m* d'érable

mar ['mɑr] *vt* **marred; marring** : gâter, gâcher

maraschino [ˌmærə'skiːnoː, -'ʃiː-] *n, pl* **-nos** : marasquin *m*

marathon ['mærəˌθɑn] *n* : marathon *m*

maraud [mə'rɔd] *vi* : marauder

marauder [mə'rɔdər] *n* : maradeur *m,* -deuse *f*

marble ['mɑrbəl] *n* **1** : marbre *m* **2** : bille *f* <to play marbles : jouer aux billes>

marbling ['mɑrblɪŋ] *n* : marbrure *f*

march[1] ['mɑrtʃ] *vi* **1** : marcher (au pas) **2** DEMONSTRATE : manifester (en signe de protestation) **3 to march (right) up to** : s'approcher (de qqn) d'un air décidé

march[2] *n* **1** MARCHING : marche *f* **2** DEMONSTRATION : manifestation *f* **3**

PROGRESS : avancée *f* <the march of time : la marche du temps> **4** : marche *f* (en musique)

March *n* : mars *m*

marchioness [ˈmɑrʃənɪs] *n* : marquise *f*

Mardi Gras [ˈmɑrdiˌgrɑ] *n* : mardi *m* gras

mare [ˈmær] *n* : jument *f*

margarine [ˈmɑrdʒərən] *n* : margarine *f*

margin [ˈmɑrdʒən] *n* **1** : marge *f* (du papier, etc.) **2** EDGE : bord *m*

marginal [ˈmɑrdʒənəl] *adj* : marginal

marigold [ˈmærəˌgoːld] *n* : souci *m*

marijuana [ˌmærəˈhwɑnə] *n* : marijuana *f*

marina [məˈriːnə] *n* : marina *f*

marinate [ˈmærəˌneɪt] *v* **-nated; -nating** : mariner

marine[1] [məˈriːn] *adj* **1** UNDERWATER : marin <marine biology : biologie marine> **2** NAUTICAL : maritime <marine law : droit maritime>

marine[2] *n* **1** : fusilier *m* marin **2 merchant marine** : marine *f* marchande

mariner [ˈmærɪnər] *n* : marin *m*

marionette [ˌmæriəˈnɛt] *n* : marionnette *f* (à fils)

marital [ˈmærəṭəl] *adj* **1** : matrimonial, conjugal **2 marital status** : état *m* civil, situation *f* de famille

maritime [ˈmærəˌtaɪm] *adj* : maritime

marjoram [ˈmɑrdʒərəm] *n* : marjolaine *f*

mark[1] [ˈmɑrk] *vt* **1** : marquer **2** STAIN : tacher, marquer **3** CHARACTERIZE : caractériser **4** INDICATE : marquer, indiquer **5** GRADE : corriger (des examens, etc.) **6** : faire attention à <mark my words! : notez bien ce que je vous dis!> **7 to mark down** : noter, inscrire **8 to mark off** : délimiter

mark[2] *n* **1** TARGET : cible *f* **2** SIGN, SYMBOL : marque *f*, signe *m* **3** GRADE : note *f* **4** IMPRINT : empreinte *f*, marque *f* **5** BLEMISH : tache *f*, marque *f*

marked [ˈmɑrkt] *adj* NOTICEABLE : marqué

markedly [ˈmɑrkədli] *adv* : sensiblement, d'une façon marquée

marker [ˈmɑrkər] *n* **1** SIGN : marque *f*, repère *m* **2** *or* **marker pen** : marqueur *m*

market[1] [ˈmɑrkət] *vt* : vendre, commercialiser

market[2] *n* **1** MARKETPLACE : marché *m* <the black market : le marché noir> <wholesale market : marché en gros> **2** DEMAND : demande *f*, marché *m* **3** *or* **food market** : marché *m* (de vivres) <fish market : marché aux poissons> **4** → **stock market**

marketable [ˈmɑrkəṭəbəl] *adj* : vendable

marketplace [ˈmɑrkətˌpleɪs] *n* : marché *m*

marksman [ˈmɑrksmən] *n, pl* **-men** [-mən, -ˌmɛn] : tireur *m*, -reuse *f* d'élite

marksmanship [ˈmɑrksmənˌʃɪp] *n* : adresse *f* au tir, habileté *f* au tir

marlin [ˈmɑrlɪn] *n* : marlin *m*

marmalade [ˈmɑrməˌleɪd] *n* : marmelade *f*

marmoset [ˈmɑrməˌsɛt] *n* : ouistiti *m*

marmot [ˈmɑrmət] *n* : marmotte *f*

maroon[1] [məˈruːn] *vt* : abandonner

maroon[2] *n* : bordeaux *m* (couleur)

marquee [mɑrˈkiː] *n* **1** CANOPY : marquise *f* **2** *Brit* TENT : grande tente *f*

marquess [ˈmɑrkwɪs] *or* **marquis** [ˈmɑrkwɪs, mɑrˈkiː] *n, pl* **-quesses** *or* **-quises** [-ˈkiːz, -ˈkiːzəz] *or* **-quis** [-ˈkiː, -ˈkiːz] : marquis *m*

marquise [mɑrˈkiːz] *nf* → **marchioness**

marriage [ˈmærɪdʒ] *n* **1** : mariage *m* <aunt by marriage : tante par alliance> **2** WEDDING : mariage *m*, noces *fpl*

marriageable [ˈmærɪdʒəbəl] *adj* : mariable <of marriageable age : en âge de se marier>

married [ˈmærid] *adj* **1** : marié <a married couple : un couple marié> <married life : la vie conjugale> **2 to get married** : se marier

marrow [ˈmæroː] *n* : moelle *f*

marry [ˈmæri] *v* **-ried; -rying** *vt* **1** WED : se marier avec, épouser, marier *Can* **2** : marier <the priest married them : le prêtre les a mariés> — *vi* : se marier

Mars [ˈmɑrz] *n* : Mars *f* (planète)

marsh [ˈmɑrʃ] *n* : marais *m*, marécage *m*

marshal[1] [ˈmɑrʃəl] *vt* **-shaled** *or* **-shalled; -shaling** *or* **-shalling 1** ARRANGE, ASSEMBLE : assembler **2** USHER : conduire

marshal[2] *n* **1** : commisaire *m*, capitaine *m* <fire marshall : capitaine des pompiers> **2** : maréchal *m* (militaire) **3** : membre *m* du service d'ordre (d'un défilé, d'une cérémonie, etc.)

marshmallow [ˈmɑrʃˌmɛloː, -ˌmæloː] *n* : guimauve *f*

marshy [ˈmɑrʃi] *adj* **marshier; -est** : marécageux

marsupial [mɑrˈsuːpiəl] *n* : marsupial *m*

mart [ˈmɑrt] *n* MARKET : marché *m*

marten [ˈmɑrtən] *n, pl* **-ten** *or* **-tens** : martre *f*

martial [ˈmɑrʃəl] *adj* : martial <martial law : la loi martiale>

martin [ˈmɑrtən] *n* : martinet *m* (oiseau)

martyr[1] [ˈmɑrṭər] *vt* : martyriser

martyr[2] *n* : martyr *m*, -tyre *f*

martyrdom [ˈmɑrṭərdəm] *n* : martyre *m*

marvel[1] [ˈmɑrvəl] *vi* **-veled** *or* **-velled; -veling** *or* **-velling** : s'émerveiller

marvel[2] *n* : merveille *f*, miracle *m*

marvelous [ˈmɑrvələs] *or* **marvellous** *adj* : merveilleux — **marvelously** *adv*

Marxism [ˈmɑrkˌsɪzəm] *n* : marxisme *m*

Marxist[1] [ˈmɑrksɪst] *adj* : marxiste

Marxist[2] *n* : marxiste *mf*

mascara [mæs'kærə] *n* : mascara *m*
mascot ['mæs,kɑt, -kət] *n* : mascotte *f*
masculine ['mæskjələn] *adj* : masculin
masculinity [,mæskjə'lɪnət̬i] *n* : masculinité *f*
mash[1] ['mæʃ] *vt* **1** CRUSH : écraser **2** PUREE : faire une purée de, piler *Can*
mash[2] *n* **1** PUREE : purée *f* **2** FEED : pâtée *f* **3** MALT : moût *m*
mask[1] ['mæsk] *vt* **1** DISGUISE : masquer **2** COVER, HIDE : cacher (des émotions, etc.)
mask[2] *n* : masque *m*
masochism ['mæsə,kɪzəm, 'mæzə-] *n* : masochisme *m*
masochist ['mæsə,kɪst, 'mæzə-] *n* : masochiste *mf*
masochistic [,mæsə'kɪstɪk] *adj* : masochiste
mason ['meɪsən] *n* **1** : maçon *m* **2** → **Freemason**
masonry ['meɪsənri] *n, pl* **-ries** **1** : maçonnerie *f* **2** → **Freemasonry**
masquerade[1] [,mæskə'reɪd] *vi* **-aded; -ading** : se déguiser, se faire passer
masquerade[2] *n* : mascarade *f*
mass[1] ['mæs] *vi* : se masser
mass[2] *n* **1** : masse *f* (en physique) **2** CLUSTER : masse *f*, ensemble *m* <a mass of houses : un ensemble de maisons> **3** QUANTITY : quantité *f*, masse *f* **4 the masses** : les masses *fpl*
Mass *n* : messe *f*
massacre[1] ['mæsɪkər] *vt* **-cred; -cring** : massacrer
massacre[2] *n* : massacre *m*
massage[1] [mə'sɑʒ] *vt* **-saged; -saging** : masser
massage[2] *n* : massage *m*
masseur [mæ'sər] *n* : masseur *m*
masseuse [mæ'søz, -'su:z] *n* : masseuse *f*
massive ['mæsɪv] *adj* **1** BULKY : massif **2** HUGE : énorme — **massively** *adv*
mass media → **media**
mast ['mæst] *n* **1** : mât *m* (d'un navire) **2** POLE, POST : pylône *m*
master[1] ['mæstər] *vt* **1** CONTROL, SUBDUE : dominer, dompter, maîtriser **2** LEARN : maîtriser
master[2] *n* **1** : maître *m* **2** *or* **master copy** : original *m* **3 master's degree** : maîtrise *f*
masterful ['mæstərfəl] *adj* **1** IMPERIOUS : autoritaire, impérieux, dominateur **2** SKILLFUL : magistral
masterfully ['mæstərfəli] *adv* : magistralement
masterly ['mæstərli] *adj* : magistral
masterpiece ['mæstər,pi:s] *n* : chef *m* d'œuvre
masterwork ['mæstər,wərk] → **masterpiece**
mastery ['mæstəri] *n* **1** CONTROL : domination *f*, maîtrise *f* **2** KNOWLEDGE, SKILL : maîtrise *f*
masticate ['mæstə,keɪt] *vt* **-cated; -cating** : mastiquer
mastiff ['mæstɪf] *n* : mastiff *m*
mastodon ['mæstə,dɑn] *n* : mastodonte *m*
masturbate ['mæstər,beɪt] *vi* **-bated; -bating** : se masturber
masturbation [,mæstər'beɪʃən] *n* : masturbation *f*
mat[1] ['mæt] *v* **matted; matting** *vt* TANGLE : emmêler — *vi* : s'emmêler
mat[2] *n* **1** DOORMAT : paillasson *m* **2** RUG : natte *f*, tapis *m* **3** TANGLE : enchevêtrement *m* **4** *or* **exercise mat** : tapis *m* (d'exercice) **5** *or* **matt** *or* **matte** FRAME : bord *m*, cadre *m*
mat[3] → **matte**
matador ['mætə,dɔr] *n* : matador *m*
match[1] ['mætʃ] *vt* **1** OPPOSE, PIT : opposer, rivaliser avec **2** EQUAL : égaler **3** : s'accorder avec, aller avec <her shoes match her dress : ses chaussures vont avec sa robe> — *vi* CORRESPOND : correspondre
match[2] *n* **1** EQUAL : égal *m*, égale *f* <to meet one's match : trouver à qui parler (avec qqn)> **2** : allumette *f* <to strike a match : gratter une allumette> **3** FIGHT, GAME : match *m* **4** MARRIAGE : mariage *m* <they're a good match : ils vont bien ensemble>
matchless ['mætʃləs] *adj* : sans pareil, incomparable
matchmaker ['mætʃ,meɪkər] *n* : marieur *m*, -rieuse *f*
mate[1] ['meɪt] *v* **mated; mating** *vi* **1** FIT : s'emboîter **2** COUPLE : s'accoupler **3** : s'accoupler (se dit des animaux) — *vt* : accoupler (des animaux)
mate[2] *n* **1** COMPANION : camarade *mf*; compagnon *m*, compagne *f* **2** : mâle *m*, femelle *f* (d'animaux) **3** *or* **first mate** : second *m*
material[1] [mə'tɪriəl] *adj* **1** PHYSICAL : matériel <the material world : le monde matériel> <material goods : biens matériels> **2** IMPORTANT : important, pertinent **3 material evidence** : preuve *f* matérielle
material[2] *n* **1** : matière *f*, substance *f* <raw materials : matières premières> **2** FABRIC : tissu *m*, étoffe *f*
materialism [mə'tɪriə,lɪzəm] *n* : matérialisme *m*
materialist [mə'tɪriəlɪst] *n* : matérialiste *mf*
materialistic [mə,tɪriə'lɪstɪk] *adj* : matérialiste
materialize [mə'tɪriə,laɪz] *v* **-ized; -izing** *vt* : matérialiser — *vi* : se matérialiser, se réaliser, prendre forme
materially [mə'tɪriəli] *adv* : matériellement
maternal [mə'tərnəl] *adj* : maternel — **maternally** *adv*
maternity[1] [mə'tərnət̬i] *adj* : de maternité <maternity leave : congé de maternité>
maternity[2] *n, pl* **-ties** : maternité *f*

math ['mæθ] → **mathematics**

mathematical [ˌmæθə'mæṭɪkəl] *adj* : mathématique — **mathematically** *adv*

mathematician [ˌmæθəmə'tɪʃən] *n* : mathématicien *m,* -cienne *f*

mathematics [ˌmæθə'mæṭɪks] *ns & pl* : mathématiques *fpl*

matinee *or* **matinée** [ˌmætən'eɪ] *n* : matinée *f*

matriarch ['meɪtriˌɑrk] *n* : matrone *f,* femme *f* chef de famille

matriarchy ['meɪtriˌɑrki] *n, pl* **-chies** : matriarcat *m*

matriculate [mə'trɪkjəˌleɪt] *vi* **-lated; -lating** ENROLL : s'inscrire

matriculation [məˌtrɪkjə'leɪʃən] *n* : inscription *f,* immatriculation *f*

matrimonial [ˌmætrə'moːniəl] *adj* : matrimonial, conjugal

matrimony ['mætrəˌmoːni] *n* : mariage *m*

matrix ['meɪtrɪks] *n, pl* **-trices** ['meɪtrəˌsiːz, 'mæ-] *or* **-trixes** ['meɪtrɪksəz] : matrice *f*

matron ['meɪtrən] *n* : matrone *f*

matronly ['meɪtrənli] *adj* : de matrone

matte ['mæt] *adj* : mat <a photo with a matte finish : une photo mate>

matter[1] ['mæṭər] *vi* : importer, avoir de l'importance <it doesn't matter : cela ne fait rien, peu importe>

matter[2] *n* **1** SUBSTANCE : matière *f* **2** QUESTION : question *f* <a matter of taste : une question de goût> **3** AFFAIR : affaire *f,* cas *m,* sujet *m* **4** (*indicating a problem or trouble*) <what's the matter? : qu'est-ce qui se passe?> <what's the matter with your leg? : qu'est-ce que vous avez à la jambe?> **5 matters** *npl* CIRCUMSTANCES : choses *fpl,* circonstances *fpl* <to make matters worse : pour ne rien arranger> **6 as a matter of fact** : à vrai dire, en fait **7 for that matter** : d'ailleurs **8 no matter how** : peu importe comment **9 no matter when** : quelle que soit l'heure

mattress ['mætrəs] *n* : matelas *m*

mature[1] [mə'tʊr, -'tjʊr, -'tʃʊr] *vi* **-tured; -turing 1** : mûrir (se dit d'une personne) **2** : arriver à maturité (se dit du vin), se faire (se dit du fromage) **3** : échoir, arriver à échéance (se dit d'une dette, etc.)

mature[2] *adj* **-turer; -est 1** : mûr **2** DUE : échu

maturity [mə'tʊrəṭi, -'tjʊr-, -'tʃʊr-] *n* : maturité *f*

maudlin ['mɔdlɪn] *adj* : larmoyant

maul[1] ['mɔl] *vt* **1** MANGLE, MUTILATE : mutiler **2** MANHANDLE : malmener

maul[2] *n* MALLET : maillet *m*

Mauritanian[1] [ˌmɔrə'teɪniən] *adj* : mauritanien

Mauritanian[2] *n* : Mauritanien *m,* -nienne *f*

Mauritian[1] [mɔ'riːʃən] *adj* : mauricien

Mauritian[2] *n* : Mauricien *m,* -cienne *f*

mausoleum [ˌmɔsə'liːəm, ˌmɔzə-] *n, pl* **-leums** *or* **-lea** [-'liːə] : mausolée *m*

mauve ['moːv, 'mɔv] *n* : mauve *m*

maven *or* **mavin** ['meɪvən] *n* EXPERT : expert *m,* -perte *f*

maverick ['mævrɪk, 'mævə-] *n* **1** : veau *m* non marqué **2** NONCONFORMIST : non-conformiste *mf*

mawkish ['mɔkɪʃ] *adj* : mièvre

maxim ['mæksəm] *n* : maxime *f,* adage *m*

maximize ['mæksəˌmaɪz] *vt* **-mized; -mizing** : maximiser, porter au maximum

maximum[1] ['mæksəməm] *adj* : maximum

maximum[2] *n, pl* **-ma** ['mæksəmə] *or* **-mums** : maximum *m*

may ['meɪ] *v aux, past* **might** ['maɪt]; *present s & pl* **may 1** (*expressing permission*) : pouvoir <you may leave : vous pouvez partir> <may I? : puis-je?> **2** (*expressing possibility or probability*) : pouvoir <it may fall : il peut tomber> <you may be right : tu as peut-être raison> <it may rain : il se peut qu'il pleuve> **3** (*expressing desires, intentions, or contingencies*) <come what may : quoiqu'il arrive> <may the best man win! : que le meilleur gagne!>

May ['meɪ] *n* : mai *m*

maybe ['meɪbi] *adv* PERHAPS : peut-être

mayfly ['meɪˌflaɪ] *n, pl* **-flies** : éphémère *m*

mayhem ['meɪˌhɛm, 'meɪəm] *n* **1** MUTILATION : mutilation *f* **2** HAVOC : destruction *f,* désordre *m*

mayonnaise ['meɪəˌneɪz] *n* : mayonnaise *f*

mayor ['meɪər, 'mɛr] *n* : maire *m,* mairesse *f*

mayoral ['meɪərəl, 'mɛrəl] *adj* : de maire

maze ['meɪz] *n* : dédale *m,* labyrinthe *m*

me ['miː] *pron* **1** : moi <give me the book : donne-moi le livre> <for me : pour moi> <it's me : c'est moi> <as big as me : aussi grand que moi> **2** : me, m' <she told me : elle m'a dit> <he's looking at me : il me regarde>

meadow ['mɛdoː] *n* : pré *m,* prairie *f*

meadowland ['mɛdoˌlænd] *n* : prairies *fpl*

meager *or* **meagre** ['miːgər] *adj* : maigre — **meagerly** *adv*

meagerness ['miːgərnəs] *n* : maigreur *f*

meal ['miːl] *n* **1** : repas *m* <to have a meal : prendre un repas> **2** : farine *f* (de maïs, etc.)

mealtime ['miːlˌtaɪm] *n* : heure *f* de repas

mealy ['miːli] *adj* **mealier; -est** : farineux

mean[1] ['miːn] *vt* **meant** ['mɛnt]; **meaning 1** INTEND : avoir l'intention de <I

mean to go : j'ai l'intention d'aller> <to be meant for : être destiné à> **2** SIGNIFY : signifier, vouloir dire <what do you mean? : qu'est-ce que tu veux dire?> **3** MATTER : compter, importer <it means a lot to me : ça compte beaucoup pour moi>

mean[2] *adj* **1** LOWLY : pauvre, misérable **2** AVERAGE : moyen **3** STINGY : avare, mesquin **4** MALICIOUS : méchant **5** **that's no mean feat** : ce n'est pas un mince exploit

mean[3] *n* **1** MIDPOINT : milieu *m* **2** AVERAGE : moyenne *f* **3 means** *npl* WAY : moyen *m* **4 means** *npl* RESOURCES : ressources *fpl,* moyens *mpl*

meander [mi'ændər] *vi* **1** WIND : serpenter, faire des méandres **2** WANDER : errer

meaning ['mi:nɪŋ] *n* **1** : sens *m,* signification *f* <double meaning : double sens> **2** INTENT : intention *f*

meaningful ['mi:nɪŋfəl] *adj* : significatif

meaningfully ['mi:nɪŋfəli] *adv* : de façon significative

meaningless ['mi:nɪŋləs] *adj* : sans signification, dénué de sens

meanness ['mi:nnəs] *n* **1** NASTINESS : méchanceté *f* **2** STINGINESS : avarice *f*

meantime[1] ['mi:n,taɪm] *adv* → **meanwhile**[1]

meantime[2] *n* **1** : intervalle *m* **2 in the meantime** : en attendant, entretemps

meanwhile[1] ['mi:n,*h*waɪl] *adv* : entretemps

meanwhile[2] *n* → **meantime**[2]

measles ['mi:zəlz] *npl* : rougeole *f*

measly ['mi:zli] *adj* **measlier; -est** : misérable, minable *fam*

measurable ['mɛʒərəbəl, 'meɪ-] *adj* : mesurable

measure[1] ['mɛʒər, 'meɪ-] *v* **-sured; -suring** : mesurer

measure[2] *n* **1** AMOUNT : mesure *f,* dose *f* <in large measure : dans une large mesure> <a measure of success : un certain succès> **2** DIMENSIONS : mesure *f* **3** RULER : règle *f* **4 measures** *npl* : mesures *fpl* <security measures : mesures de sécurité>

measureless ['mɛʒərləs, 'meɪ-] *adj* : infini, incommensurable

measurement ['mɛʒərmənt, 'meɪ-] *n* **1** MEASURING : mesurage *m* **2** DIMENSION : dimension *f,* mesure *f*

measure up *vi* **to measure up to** : être à la hauteur de

meat ['mi:t] *n* **1** : viande *f* **2** FOOD : aliments *mpl,* nourriture *f* **3** SUBSTANCE : substance *f*

meatball ['mi:t,bɔl] *n* : boulette *f* de viande

meaty ['mi:ti] *adj* **meatier; -est 1** : de viande **2** SUBSTANTIAL : substantiel

mechanic [mɪ'kænɪk] *n* : mécanicien *m,* -cienne *f*

mechanical [mɪ'kænɪkəl] *adj* **1** : mécanique **2** AUTOMATIC : machinal, automatique — **mechanically** *adv*

mechanics [mɪ'kænɪks] *ns & pl* **1** : mécanique *f* **2** MECHANISMS, WORKINGS : mécanismes *mpl*

mechanism ['mɛkə,nɪzəm] *n* : mécanisme *m*

mechanization [,mɛkənə'zeɪʃən] *n* : mécanisation *f*

mechanize ['mɛkə,naɪz] *vt* **-nized; -nizing** : mécaniser

medal ['mɛdəl] *n* : médaille *f*

medalist *or* **medallist** ['mɛdəlɪst] *n* : médaillé *m,* -lée *f*

medallion [mə'dæljən] *n* : médaillon *m*

meddle ['mɛdəl] *vi* **-dled; -dling** : se mêler

meddlesome ['mɛdəlsəm] *adj* : qui se mêle de tout, indiscret

media ['mi:diə] *ns & pl* **the media** : les médias *mpl*

median[1] ['mi:diən] *adj* : médian

median[2] *n* : médiane *f* (en mathématiques)

mediate ['mi:di,eɪt] *vi* **-ated; -ating** : servir de médiateur, arbitrer

mediation [,mi:di'eɪʃən] *n* : médiation *f*

mediator ['mi:di,eɪtər] *n* : médiateur *m,* -trice *f*

medical ['mɛdɪkəl] *adj* : médical — **medically** [-kli] *adv*

medicated ['mɛdə,keɪtəd] *adj* : médical, traitant

medication [,mɛdə'keɪʃən] *n* **1** TREATMENT : médication *f,* soins *mpl* **2** MEDICINE : médicament *m*

medicinal [mə'dɪsənəl] *adj* : médicinal

medicine ['mɛdəsən] *n* **1** : médecine *f* <she's studying medicine : elle étudie la médecine> **2** MEDICATION : médicament *m*

medicine man *n* : sorcier *m*

medieval *or* **mediaeval** [mɪ'di:vəl, ,mi:-, ,mɛ-, -di'i:vəl] *adj* : médiéval

mediocre [,mi:di'o:kər] *adj* : médiocre

mediocrity [,mi:di'ɑkrəti] *n, pl* **-ties** : médiocrité *f*

meditate ['mɛdə,teɪt] *vi* **-tated; -tating** : méditer

meditation [,mɛdə'teɪʃən] *n* : méditation *f*

meditative ['mɛdə,teɪtɪv] *adj* : méditatif

medium[1] ['mi:diəm] *adj* : moyen <of medium height : de taille moyenne>

medium[2] *n, pl* **-diums** *or* **-dia** ['mi:diə] **1** MEAN : milieu *m* <the happy medium : le juste milieu> **2** MEANS : moyen *m* (de communication) **3** SUBSTANCE : milieu *m,* véhicule *m* (en biologique ou en physique) **4** : moyen *m* (artistique) **5** *pl* **mediums** SPIRITUALIST : médium *m*

medley ['mɛdli] *n, pl* **-leys 1** MIXTURE : mélange *m* **2** : pot-pourri *m* (de chansons)

meek ['mi:k] *adj* : doux, docile

meekly ['mi:kli] *adv* : doucement

meekness ['mi:knəs] *n* : douceur *f*
meet[1] ['mi:t] *v* **met** ['mɛt]; **meeting** *vt* **1** ENCOUNTER : rencontrer **2** : faire la connaissance de <I've never met her : je n'ai pas fait sa connaissance> **3** JOIN : rejoindre **4** CONFRONT : affronter <to meet the enemy : affronter l'ennemi> **5** SATISFY : satisfaire **6** AWAIT : attendre <I'll meet you at the station : je t'attendrai à la gare> — *vi* **1** : se rencontrer **2** : ASSEMBLE : se réunir
meet[2] *n* : rencontre *f* (aux sports)
meeting ['mi:ṭɪŋ] *n* : réunion *f*
meetinghouse ['mi:ṭɪŋ,haʊs] *n* : temple *m*
megabyte ['mɛgə,baɪt] *n* : mégaoctet *m*
megahertz ['mɛgə,hərts, -,hɛrts] *ns & pl* : mégahertz *m*
megaphone ['mɛgə,fo:n] *n* : porte-voix *m*, mégaphone *m*
melancholy[1] ['mɛlən,kɑli] *adj* : mélancolique
melancholy[2] *n, pl* **-cholies** : mélancolie *f*
melanoma [,mɛlə'no:mə] *n, pl* **-mas** : mélanome *m*
melee ['meɪ,leɪ, meɪ'leɪ] *n* : mêlée *f*
meliorate ['mi:ljə,reɪt, 'mi:liə-] → **ameliorate**
mellow[1] ['mɛlo:] *vt* : adoucir — *vi* **1** : s'adoucir **2** AGE : mûrir
mellow[2] *adj* **1** MILD : doux, moelleux **2** RIPE : mûr **3** RELAXED : détendu
mellowness ['mɛlonəs] *n* : douceur *f*, moelleux *m*
melodic [mə'lɑdɪk] *adj* : mélodique — **melodically** [-dɪkli] *adv*
melodious [mə'lo:diəs] *adj* : mélodieux — **melodiously** *adv*
melodrama ['mɛlə,drɑmə, -,dræ-] *n* : mélodrame *m*
melodramatic [,mɛlədrə'mæṭɪk] *adj* : mélodramatique
melodramatically [,mɛlədrə'mæṭɪkli] *adv* : de façon mélodramatique
melody ['mɛlədi] *n, pl* **-dies** : mélodie *f*
melon ['mɛlən] *n* : melon *m*
melt ['mɛlt] *vi* **1** : fondre **2** SOFTEN : s'attendrir — *vt* **1** : fondre, faire fondre **2** SOFTEN : attendrir <to melt s.o.'s heart : attendrir le cœur de qqn>
melting point *n* : point *m* de fusion
member ['mɛmbər] *n* **1** : membre *m;* adhérent *m*, -rente *f* **2** LIMB : membre *m*
membership ['mɛmbər,ʃɪp] *n* **1** : adhésion *f* **2** MEMBERS : membres *mpl;* adhérents *mpl*, -rentes *fpl*
membrane ['mɛm,breɪn] *n* : membrane *f* — **membranous** ['mɛmbrənəs] *adj*
memento [mɪ'mɛn,to:] *n, pl* **-tos** *or* **-toes** : souvenir *m*
memo ['mɛmo:] *n, pl* **memos** : mémorandum *m*
memoirs ['mɛm,wɑrz] *npl* : mémoires *mpl*
memorabilia [,mɛmərə'biliə, -'bɪljə] *npl* : souvenirs *mpl*
memorable ['mɛmərəbəl] *adj* : mémorable
memorably ['mɛmərəbli] *adv* : de façon mémorable
memorandum [,mɛmə'rændəm] *n, pl* **-dums** *or* **-da** [-də] : mémorandum *m*
memorial[1] [mə'moriəl] *adj* : commémoratif
memorial[2] *adj* : mémorial *m*, monument *m* (commémoratif)
Memorial Day *n* : le dernier lundi du mois de mai (férié aux États-Unis en commémoration des soldats morts à la guerre)
memorialize [mə'moriə,laɪz] *vt* **-ized; -izing** COMMEMORATE : commémorer
memorize ['mɛmə,raɪz] *vt* **-rized; -rizing** : mémoriser
memory ['mɛmri, 'mɛmə-] *n, pl* **-ries 1** : mémoire *f* <to have a good memory : avoir une bonne mémoire> **2** RECOLLECTION : souvenir *m*
men → **man**[2]
menace[1] ['mɛnəs] *vt* **-aced; -acing** : menacer
menace[2] *n* **1** THREAT : menace *f* **2** DANGER : danger *m*
menacing ['mɛnəsɪŋ] *adj* : menaçant
menagerie [mə'nædʒəri, -'næʒəri] *n* : ménagerie *f*
mend[1] ['mɛnd] *vt* **1** IMPROVE : améliorer **2** REPAIR : réparer **3** DARN, SEW : repriser, raccommoder — *vi* HEAL : s'améliorer
mend[2] *n* : reprise *f*
mendicant ['mɛndɪkənt] *n* BEGGAR : mendiant *m*, -diante *f*
menial[1] ['mi:niəl] *adj* : servile <a menial position : un poste subalterne>
menial[2] *n* : domestique *mf*
meningitis [,mɛnən'dʒaɪṭəs] *n, pl* **-gitides** [-'dʒɪṭə,di:z] : méningite *f*
menopause ['mɛnə,pɔz] *n* : ménopause *f*
menorah [mə'nɔrə] *n* : candélabre *m* (employé dans des cérémonies religieuses juives)
menstrual ['mɛn*t*strʊəl] *adj* : menstruel
menstruate ['mɛn*t*strʊ,eɪt] *vi* **-ated; -ating** : avoir ses règles
menstruation [,mɛn*t*strʊ'eɪʃən] *n* : menstruation *f*, règles *fpl*
mental ['mɛntəl] *adj* : mental — **mentally** *adv*
mentality [mɛn'tæləṭi] *n, pl* **-ties** : mentalité *f*
menthol ['mɛn,θɔl, -,θo:l] *n* : menthol *m*
mentholated ['mɛn*t*θə,leɪṭəd] *adj* : mentholé
mention[1] ['mɛntʃən] *vt* **1** : mentionner **2 don't mention it!** : il n'y a pas de quoi! **3 not to mention** : sans parler de
mention[2] *n* : mention *f*

mentor ['mɛnˌtɔr, 'mɛntər] *n* : mentor *m*
menu ['mɛnˌjuː] *n* : menu *m*
meow[1] [miː'aʊ] *vi* : miauler
meow[2] *n* : miaou *m*
mercantile ['mɛrkənˌtiːl, -ˌtaɪl] *adj* : mercantile, commercial
mercenary[1] ['mərsənˌɛri] *adj* : mercenaire
mercenary[2] *n, pl* **-naries** : mercenaire *mf*
merchandise ['mərtʃənˌdaɪz, -ˌdaɪs] *n* : marchandises *fpl*
merchant ['mərtʃənt] *n* : marchand *m*, -chande *f*; commerçant *m*, -çante *f*; négociant *m*, -ciante *f*
merchant marine *n* : marine *f* marchande
merciful ['mərsɪfəl] *adj* : miséricordieux
mercifully ['mərsɪfli] *adv* **1** COMPASSIONATELY : avec clémence **2** FORTUNATELY : par bonheur, heureusement
merciless ['mərsɪləs] *adj* : impitoyable — **mercilessly** *adv*
mercurial [mər'kjʊriəl] *adj* TEMPERAMENTAL : inconstant, d'humeur inégale
mercury ['mərkjəri] *n* : mercure *m*
Mercury ['mərkjəri] *n* : Mercure *f* (planète)
mercy ['mɛrsi] *n, pl* **-cies 1** CLEMENCY : clémence *f*, miséricorde *f* (en religion) **2** BLESSING, FORTUNE : chance *f*, bonheur *m*
mere ['mɪr] *adj, superlative* **merest** : simple, pur, seul <the mere sight of him : sa seule vue> <a mere ten percent : dix pour cent seulement>
merely ['mɪrli] *adv* : simplement, seulement
merge ['mərdʒ] *v* **merged; merging** *vi* **1** BLEND, COMBINE : se mêler, se joindre, se fondre **2** : fusionner (se dit des affaires) — *vt* : fusionner, joindre
merger ['mərdʒər] *n* : fusion *f*
meridian [mə'rɪdiən] *n* : méridien *m*
meringue [mə'ræŋ] *n* : meringue *f*
merino [mə'riːno] *n, pl* **-nos** : mérinos *m*
merit[1] ['mɛrət] *vt* : mériter
merit[2] *n* : mérite *m*
meritorious [ˌmɛrə'toriəs] *adj* : méritoire (se dit d'une action, etc.), méritant (se dit d'une personne)
mermaid ['mərˌmeɪd] *n* : sirène *f*
merriment ['mɛrɪmənt] *n* : gaieté *f*, hilarité *f*
merry ['mɛri] *adj* **merrier; -est** : joyeux, gai <Merry Christmas! : Joyeux Noël!> — **merrily** *adv*
merry–go–round ['mɛrigoˌraʊnd] *n* : manège *m* (de chevaux de bois)
merrymaker ['mɛriˌmeɪkər] *n* : fêtard *m*, -tarde *f*
merrymaking ['mɛriˌmeɪkɪŋ] *n* : réjouissances *fpl*
mesa ['meɪsə] *n* : mesa *f*
mesdames → **madam, Mrs.**
mesh[1] ['mɛʃ] *vi* **1** ENGAGE : s'engrener (en méchanique) **2** TANGLE : s'enchevêtrer **3** COINCIDE, TALLY : cadrer, concorder
mesh[2] *n* **1** NET : maille *f* **2** NETWORK : réseau *m* **3** MESHING : engrenure *f* (en technologie)
mesmerize ['mɛzməˌraɪz] *vt* **-ized; -izing 1** HYPNOTIZE : hypnotiser **2** FASCINATE : fasciner, captiver
mess[1] ['mɛs] *vt* **1** SOIL : salir **2 to mess up** DISARRANGE : mettre en désordre **3 to mess up** BUNGLE : gâcher — *vi* **1 to mess around** PUTTER : bricoler **2 to mess with** INTERFERE : s'immiscer
mess[2] *n* **1** : mess *m* <officer's mess : mess des officiers> **2** DISORDER : désordre *m*, gâchis *m* <your room is a mess : ta chambre est un désastre>
message ['mɛsɪdʒ] *n* : message *m*
messenger ['mɛsəndʒər] *n* : messager *m*, -gère *f*
Messiah [mə'saɪə] *n* **the Messiah** : le Messie *m*
Messrs. → **Mr.**
messy ['mɛsi] *adj* **messier; -est 1** DIRTY : sale **2** UNTIDY : désordonné, en désordre **3** AWKWARD, DIFFICULT : embrouillé, difficile
met → **meet**[1]
metabolic [ˌmɛt̬ə'bɑlɪk] *adj* : métabolique
metabolism [mə'tæbəˌlɪzəm] *n* : métabolisme *m*
metabolize [mə'tæbəˌlaɪz] *vt* **-lized; -lizing** : métaboliser
metal ['mɛt̬əl] *n* : métal *m*
metallic [mə'tælɪk] *adj* : métallique
metallurgy ['mɛt̬əlˌərdʒi] *n* : métallurgie *f*
metalwork ['mɛt̬əlˌwərk] *n* : ferronnerie *f*
metamorphosis [ˌmɛt̬ə'mɔrfəsɪs] *n, pl* **-phoses** [-ˈsiːz] : métamorphose *f*
metaphor ['mɛt̬əˌfɔr, -fər] *n* : métaphore *f*
metaphoric [ˌmɛt̬ə'fɔrɪk] *or* **metaphorical** [-ɪkəl] *adj* : métaphorique
metaphysical [ˌmɛt̬ə'fɪzəkəl] *adj* : métaphysique
metaphysics [ˌmɛt̬ə'fɪzɪks] *n* : métaphysique *f*
mete ['miːt] *vt* **meted; meting** : infliger, rendre <to mete out punishment : infliger un châtiment>
meteor ['miːt̬iər, -t̬iˌɔr] *n* : météore *m*
meteoric [ˌmiːt̬i'ɔrɪk] *adj* : météorique
meteorite ['miːt̬iəˌraɪt] *n* : météorite *mf*
meteorologic [ˌmiːt̬iˌɔrə'lɑdʒɪk] *or* **meteorological** [-'lɑdʒɪkəl] *adj* : météorologique
meteorologist [ˌmiːt̬iə'rɑlədʒɪst] *n* : météorologue *mf*, météorologiste *mf*
meteorology [ˌmiːt̬iə'rɑlədʒi] *n* : météorologie *f*

meter *or Brit* **metre** ['mi:tər] *n* **1** : mètre *m* <two meters high : deux mètres de hauteur> **2** : compteur *m* (d'électricité, etc.) **3** : mesure *f* (en poésie, en musique, etc.) **4** *or* **parking meter** : parcmètre *m France,* parcomètre *m Can*
methane ['mɛ,θeɪn] *n* : méthane *m*
method ['mɛθəd] *n* : méthode *f*
methodical [mə'θɑdɪkəl] *adj* : méthodique — **methodically** *adv*
meticulous [mə'tɪkjələs] *adj* : méticuleux — **meticulously** *adv*
metre *Brit* → **meter**
metric ['mɛtrɪk] *or* **metrical** [-trɪkəl] *adj* : métrique
metric system *n* : système *m* métrique
metronome ['mɛtrə,no:m] *n* : métronome *m*
metropolis [mə'trɑpələs] *n* : métropole *f*
metropolitan [,mɛtrə'pɑlətən] *adj* : métropolitain
mettle ['mɛt̬əl] *n* : courage *m,* ardeur *f* <to show one's mettle : montrer de quoi on est capable>
Mexican[1] ['mɛksɪkən] *adj* : mexicain
Mexican[2] *n* : Mexicain *m,* -caine *f*
mezzanine ['mɛzə,ni:n, ,mɛzə'ni:n] *n* : mezzanine *f*
miasma [maɪ'æzmə] *n* : miasme *m*
mica ['maɪkə] *n* : mica *m*
mice → **mouse**
microbe ['maɪ,kro:b] *n* : microbe *m*
microbiology [,maɪkrobaɪ'ɑlədʒi] *n* : microbiologie *f*
microcomputer ['maɪkrokəm,pju:t̬ər] *n* : micro-ordinateur *m*
microcosm ['maɪkro,kɑzəm] *n* : microcosme *m*
microfilm ['maɪkro,fɪlm] *n* : microfilm *m*
micrometer *or Brit* **micrometre** ['maɪkro,mi:tər] *n* : micromètre *m* (unité de mesure)
micron ['maɪ,krɑn] → **micrometer**
microorganism [,maɪkro'ɔrgə,nɪzəm] *n* : micro-organisme *m*
microphone ['maɪkrə,fo:n] *n* : microphone *m*
microprocessor [,maɪkro'prɑ,sɛsər] *n* : microprocesseur *m*
microscope ['maɪkrə,sko:p] *n* : microscope *m*
microscopic [,maɪkrə'skɑpɪk] *adj* : microscopique
microscopy [maɪ'krɑskəpi] *n* : microscopie *f*
microwave ['maɪkrə,weɪv] *n* **1** : micro-onde *f* **2** *or* **microwave oven** : four *m* à micro-ondes, micro-ondes *m*
mid ['mɪd] *adj* : mi <since mid-June : dès la mi-juin> <in the mid nineteenth century : au milieu du dix-neuvième siècle> <she's in her mid thirties : elle a dans les 35 ans>
midair ['mɪd'ær] *n* **in ~** : en plein ciel
midday ['mɪd'deɪ] *n* NOON : midi *m*
middle[1] ['mɪdəl] *adj* **1** CENTRAL : du milieu, central **2** INTERMEDIATE : moyen
middle[2] *n* **1** CENTER : centre *m,* milieu *m* **2 in the middle of** : au milieu de
middle age *n* : la cinquantaine, l'âge *m* mûr
Middle Ages *npl* : Moyen Âge *m*
middle class *n* : classe *f* moyenne
middleman ['mɪdəl,mæn] *n, pl* **-men** [-mən, -,mɛn] : intermédiaire *mf*
middling ['mɪdlɪŋ, -lən] *adj* **1** AVERAGE : moyen **2** MEDIOCRE : médiocre
midge ['mɪdʒ] *n* : moucheron *m*
midget ['mɪdʒət] *n* : nain *m,* naine *f*
midland ['mɪdlənd, -,lænd] *n* : région *f* centrale (d'un pays)
midnight ['mɪd,naɪt] *n* : minuit *m*
midpoint ['mɪd,pɔɪnt] *n* : milieu *m*
midriff ['mɪd,rɪf] *n* : ventre *m*
midshipman ['mɪd,ʃɪpmən, ,mɪd'ʃɪp-] *n, pl* **-men** [-mən, -,mɛn] : aspirant *m*
midst[1] ['mɪdst] *n* : milieu *m* <in the midst of : en plein milieu de> <in our midst : parmi nous>
midst[2] *prep* : parmi
midstream ['mɪd'stri:m, -,stri:m] *n* **in ~** : au milieu du courant
midsummer ['mɪd'sʌmər, -,sʌ-] *n* : milieu *m* de l'été
midway ['mɪd,weɪ] *adv* : à mi-chemin
midweek ['mɪd,wi:k] *n* : milieu *m* de la semaine
midwife ['mɪd,waɪf] *n, pl* **-wives** [-,waɪvz] : sage-femme *f*
midwinter ['mɪd'wɪntər, -,wɪn-] *n* : milieu *m* de l'hiver
midyear ['mɪd,jɪr] *n* : milieu *m* de l'année
mien ['mi:n] *n* DEMEANOR : mine *f*
miff ['mɪf] *vt* : vexer
might[1] ['maɪt] (*used to express permission or possibility or as a polite alternative to* **may**) → **may** <it might be true : il se peut que cela soit vrai> <might I speak with her? : puis-je lui parler?>
might[2] *n* **1** STRENGTH : force *f* **2** POWER : puissance *f,* pouvoir *m*
mightily ['maɪt̬əli] *adv* **1** EXTREMELY : extrêmement **2** VIGOROUSLY : vigoureusement
mighty[1] ['maɪt̬i] *adv* : très, rudement *fam* <that's mighty nice : c'est rudement gentil>
mighty[2] *adj* **mightier; -est 1** STRONG : puissant **2** GREAT : imposant, grand
migraine ['maɪ,greɪn] *n* : migraine *f*
migrant ['maɪgrənt] *n* : migrant *m,* -grante *f*
migrate ['maɪ,greɪt] *vi* **-grated; -grating** : migrer
migration [maɪ'greɪʃən] *n* : migration *f*
migratory ['maɪgrə,tori] *adj* : migrateur <migratory birds : oiseaux migrateurs>
mild ['maɪld] *adj* **1** GENTLE : doux **2** LIGHT : léger **3** TEMPERATE : tempéré

<a mild climate : un climat tempéré> <it's a mild day : il fait doux>

mildew[1] ['mɪlˌduː, -ˌdjuː] *vi* : moisir

mildew[2] *n* : moisissure *f*

mildly ['maɪldli] *adv* **1** GENTLY : doucement, avec douceur **2** LIGHTLY, MODERATELY : légèrement, modérément

mildness ['maɪldnəs] *n* : douceur *f*

mile ['maɪl] *n* : mille *m*, mile *m*

mileage ['maɪlɪdʒ] *n* **1** *or* **mileage allowance** : indemnité *f* **2** CONSUMPTION : consommation *f* (de l'essence) <the car gets better mileage : la voiture consomme moins> **3** DISTANCE : distance *f*, nombre *m* de milles, millage *m Can*

milestone ['maɪlˌstoːn] *n* **1** LANDMARK : borne *f* milliaire **2** : étape *f* importante, jalon *m* <an important milestone in science : un jalon important dans la science>

milieu [miːl'juː, -'jø] *n, pl* **-lieus** *or* **-lieux** [-'juːz, -'jø] SURROUNDINGS : milieu *m*

militant[1] ['mɪlətənt] *adj* : militant

militant[2] *n* : militant *m*, -tante *f*

militarism ['mɪlət̬əˌrɪzəm] *n* : militarisme *m*

militaristic [ˌmɪlət̬ə'rɪstɪk] *adj* : militariste

military[1] ['mɪləˌtɛri] *adj* : militaire

military[2] *n* **the military** *n* : l'armée *f*

militia [mə'lɪʃə] *n* : milice *f*

milk[1] ['mɪlk] *vt* **1** : traire (une vache, etc.) **2** EXPLOIT : exploiter

milk[2] *n* : lait *m*

milkman ['mɪlkˌmæn, -mən] *n, pl* **-men** [-mən, -ˌmɛn] : laitier *m*

milk shake *n* : milk-shake *m*

milkweed ['mɪlkˌwiːd] *n* : laiteron *m*

milky ['mɪlki] *adj* **milkier; -est** : laiteux

Milky Way : la Voie lactée

mill[1] ['mɪl] *vt* **1** GRIND : moudre **2** GROOVE : créneler — *vi or* **to mill about** SWARM : fourmiller

mill[2] *n* **1** : moulin *m* **2** FACTORY : usine *f*, fabrique *f*

millennium [mə'lɛniəm] *n, pl* **-nia** [-niə] *or* **-niums** : millénaire *m*

miller ['mɪlər] *n* : meunier *m*, -nière *f*

millet ['mɪlət] *n* : millet *m*

milligram ['mɪləˌgræm] *n* : milligramme *m*

milliliter ['mɪləˌliːtər] *n* : millilitre *m*

millimeter *or Brit* **millimetre** ['mɪləˌmiːt̬ər] : millimètre *m*

milliner ['mɪlənər] *n* : modiste *mf*

million[1] ['mɪljən] *adj* **a million** : un million de

million[2] *n, pl* **millions** *or* **million** **1** : million *m* **2** **millions** *npl* MASSES : masses *fpl*

millionaire [ˌmɪljə'nær, 'mɪljəˌnær] *n* : millionnaire *mf*

millionth[1] ['mɪljənθ] *adj* : millionième

millionth[2] *n* **1** : millionième *mf* (dans une série) **2** : millionième *m* (en mathématiques)

millipede ['mɪləˌpiːd] *n* : mille-pattes *m*

millstone ['mɪlˌstoːn] *n* : meule *f*

mime[1] ['maɪm] *v* **mimed; miming** *vt* : mimer — *vi* : faire du mime

mime[2] *n* : mime *mf*

mimeograph[1] ['mɪmiəˌgræf] *vt* : polycopier

mimeograph[2] *n* : polycopie *f*

mimic[1] ['mɪmɪk] *vt* **-icked; -icking** **1** IMITATE : imiter, mimer **2** APE : singer, parodier

mimic[2] *n* : imitateur *m*, -trice *f*

mimicry ['mɪmɪkri] *n, pl* **-ries** : imitation *f*

minaret [ˌmɪnə'rɛt] *n* : minaret *m*

mince ['mɪnts] *v* **minced; mincing** *vt* **1** CHOP : hacher **2** **not to mince one's words** : ne pas mâcher ses mots — *vi* : marcher d'un air affecté

mind[1] ['maɪnd] *vt* **1** TEND : garder, surveiller **2** OBEY : obéir à **3** WATCH : faire attention à <mind your language! : surveille ton langage!> <mind the step! : attention à la marche!> **4** (*indicating dislike*) <I don't mind going : ça ne me dérange pas d'aller> <I wouldn't mind a drink : j'aimerais bien un verre> — *vi* **1** OBEY : obéir **2** (*indicating an objection*) <I don't mind : ça m'est égal> <do you mind if I take the car? : est-ce que cela vous ennuie que je prenne la voiture?>

mind[2] *n* **1** : esprit *m* <state of mind : état d'esprit> <it never entered my mind : cela ne m'est jamais venu à l'esprit> <mind over matter : l'esprit sur la matière> **2** INTELLIGENCE : intelligence *f* **3** OPINION : avis *m* <to change one's mind : changer d'avis> **4** MEMORY : mémoire *f* <to call to mind : se rappeler> **5** REASON : raison *f* <he's out of his mind : il est fou>

minded ['maɪndəd] *adj* **1** INCLINED : disposé **2** (*used in combination*) <narrow-minded : étroit d'esprit> <health-minded : soucieux de la santé>

mindful ['maɪndfəl] *adj* AWARE : attentif — **mindfully** *adv*

mindless ['maɪndləs] *adj* **1** SENSELESS : insensé, stupide **2** HEEDLESS : insouciant **3** BORING : machinal, ennuyeux <a mindless task : un travail machinal>

mindlessly ['maɪndləsli] *adv* **1** SENSELESSLY : stupidement **2** HEEDLESSLY : avec insouciance **3** AUTOMATICALLY : machinalement

mine[1] ['maɪn] *vt* **mined; mining** **1** : extraire (du charbon, etc.) **2** : miner (avec des explosifs)

mine[2] *n* : mine *f*

mine[3] *pron* : le mien *m*, la mienne *f*, les miens *mpl*, les miennes *fpl* <not your car but mine : pas ta voiture mais la mienne> <her French is better than mine : son français est

supérieur au mien> <a friend of mine : un ami à moi>
minefield ['maɪn,fi:ld] *n* : champ *m* de mines
miner ['maɪnər] *n* : mineur *m*
mineral ['mɪnərəl] *n* : minéral *m* — **mineral** *adj*
mineralogical [,mɪnərə'lɑdʒɪkəl] *adj* : minéralogique
mineralogy [,mɪnə'rɑlədʒi] *n* : minéralogie *f*
mingle ['mɪŋgəl] *v* **-gled; -gling** *vt* : mêler, mélanger — *vi* : se mêler, se mélanger
miniature[1] ['mɪniə,tʃʊr, 'mɪnɪ,tʃʊr, -tʃər] *adj* : en miniature
miniature[2] *n* : miniature *f*
minibus ['mɪni,bʌs] *n* : minibus *m*
minicomputer ['mɪnikəm,pju:t̬ər] *n* : mini-ordinateur *m*
minimal ['mɪnəməl] *adj* : minimal
minimally ['mɪnəmli] *adv* : à peine, très légèrement
minimize ['mɪnə,maɪz] *vt* **-mized; -mizing** : minimiser
minimum[1] ['mɪnəmem] *adj* : minimum, minimal
minimum[2] *n, pl* **-ma** ['mɪnəme] *or* **-mums** : minimum *m*
miniscule → **minuscule**
miniskirt ['mɪni,skərt] *n* : minijupe *f*
minister[1] ['mɪnəstər] *vi* **to minister to** : pourvoir à, donner des soins à
minister[2] *n* **1** : ministre *m* (en politique) **2** : pasteur *m* (d'une église)
ministerial [,mɪnə'stɪriəl] *adj* : ministériel
ministry ['mɪnəstri] *n, pl* **-tries** : ministère *m*
minivan ['mɪni,væn] *n* : fourgonnette *f*
mink ['mɪŋk] *n, pl* **mink** *or* **minks** : vison *m*
minnow ['mɪno:] *n* : vairon *m*, mené *m* *Can*
minor[1] ['maɪnər] *adj* **1** UNIMPORTANT : mineur **2** SECONDARY : secondaire <minor role : rôle secondaire>
minor[2] *n* : mineur *m*, -neure *f*
minority [mə'nɔrət̬i, maɪ-] *n, pl* **-ties** : minorité *f*
minstrel ['mɪn*t*strəl] *n* : ménestrel *m*
mint[1] ['mɪnt] *vt* : frapper
mint[2] *adj* **in mint condition** : à l'état neuf
mint[3] *n* **1** : menthe *f* (herbe) **2** : bonbon *m* à la menthe **3 the Mint** : l'Hôtel *m* de la Monnaie, la Monnaie **4 to be worth a mint** : valoir une fortune
minuet [,mɪnjʊ'ɛt] *n* : menuet *m*
minus[1] ['maɪnəs] *n* **1** : quantité *f* négative **2** *or* **minus sign** : moins *m*
minus[2] *prep* **1** : moins <four minus two : quatre moins deux> **2** WITHOUT : sans <minus her gloves : sans ses gants>
minuscule *or* **miniscule** ['mɪnəs,kju:l, mɪ'nʌs-] *adj* : minuscule
minute[1] [maɪ'nu:t, mɪ-, -'nju:t] *adj* **minuter; -est 1** TINY : minuscule **2** DETAILED : minutieux
minute[2] ['mɪnət] *n* **1** : minute *f* <in ten minutes : dans dix minutes> **2** MOMENT : moment *m* **3 minutes** *npl* : procès-verbal *m* (d'une réunion)
minutely [maɪ'nu:tli, mɪ-, -'nju:t-] *adv* : minutieusement
miracle ['mɪrɪkəl] *n* : miracle *m*
miraculous [mə'rækjələs] *adj* : miraculeux — **miraculously** *adv*
mirage [mɪ'rɑʒ, *chiefly Brit* 'mɪr,ɑʒ] *n* : mirage *m*
mire[1] ['maɪr] *vt* **mired; miring** STICK : embourber <to get mired down in : s'embourber dans>
mire[2] *n* : boue *f*, fange *f*
mirror[1] ['mɪrər] *vt* : refléter, réfléchir
mirror[2] *n* : miroir *m*, glace *f*
mirth ['mərθ] *n* : gaité *f*, hilarité *f*
mirthful ['mərθfəl] *adj* : gai, joyeux
misanthrope ['mɪsən,θro:p] *n* : misanthrope *mf*
misanthropic [,mɪsən'θrɑpɪk] *adj* : misanthrope
misanthropy [mɪ'sænθrəpi] *n* : misanthropie *f*
misapprehend [,mɪs,æprə'hɛnd] *vt* : mal comprendre
misapprehension [,mɪs,æprə'hɛntʃən] *n* : malentendu *m*, méprise *f*
misappropriate [,mɪsə'pro:pri,eɪt] *vt* **-ated; -ating** : détourner
misbegotten [,mɪsbi'gɑtən] *adj* **1** ILLEGITIMATE : illégitime **2** : mal conçu (se dit des plans, des lois, etc.)
misbehave [,mɪsbi'heɪv] *vi* **-haved; -having** : se conduire mal
misbehavior [,mɪsbi'heɪvjər] *n* : mauvaise conduite *f*
miscalculate [mɪs'kælkjə,leɪt] *v* **-lated; -lating** *vt* : mal calculer — *vi* : se tromper
miscalculation [mɪs,kælkjə'leɪʃən] *n* : erreur *f* de calcul, mauvais calcul *m*
miscarriage [,mɪs'kærɪdʒ, 'mɪs,kærɪdʒ] *n* **1** : fausse couche *f* **2** FAILURE : échec *m* <miscarriage of justice : erreur judiciaire>
miscarry [,mɪs'kæri, 'mɪs,kæri] *vi* **-ried; -rying 1** ABORT : faire une fausse couche **2** FAIL : échouer
miscellaneous [,mɪsə'leɪniəs] *adj* : divers, varié
miscellany ['mɪsə,leɪni] *n, pl* **-nies** : mélange *m*, collection *f* disparate
mischance [mɪs'tʃæn*t*s] *n* : malchance *f*
mischief ['mɪstʃəf] *n* : espièglerie *f*, malice *f*
mischievous ['mɪstʃəvəs] *adj* : espiègle, malicieux
mischievously ['mɪstʃəvəsli] *adv* : malicieusement
misconception [,mɪskən'sɛpʃən] *n* : idée *f* fausse
misconduct [mɪs'kɑndəkt] *n* : inconduite *f*, mauvaise conduite *f*

misconstrue [ˌmɪskənˈstruː] *vt* **-strued; -struing** : mal interpréter
miscreant [ˈmɪskriənt] *n* VILLAIN : scélérat *m,* -rate *f*
misdeed [mɪsˈdiːd] *n* : méfait *m*
misdemeanor [ˌmɪsdɪˈmiːnər] *n* : méfait *m,* délit *m* (judiciaire)
miser [ˈmaɪzər] *n* : avare *m*
miserable [ˈmɪzərəbəl] *adj* **1** UNHAPPY : triste, malheureux **2** WRETCHED : misérable, minable **3** AWFUL : affreux
miserably [ˈmɪzərəbli] *adv* **1** SADLY : tristement **2** WRETCHEDLY : misérablement, lamentablement
miserly [ˈmaɪzərli] *adj* : avare, séraphin *Can*
misery [ˈmɪzəri] *n, pl* **-eries** : tristesse *f,* misère *f*
misfire [mɪsˈfaɪr] *vi* **-fired; -firing** : rater <the engine is misfiring : le moteur a des ratés> <the gun misfired : l'arme a fait long feu>
misfit [ˈmɪsˌfɪt] *n* : inadapté *m,* -tée *f*
misfortune [mɪsˈfɔrtʃən] *n* : malchance *f,* infortune *f*
misgiving [mɪsˈgɪvɪŋ] *n* : doute *m,* crainte *f*
misguided [mɪsˈgaɪdəd] *adj* : malencontreux, fourvoyé, peu judicieux
mishap [ˈmɪsˌhæp] *n* : mésaventure *f*
misinform [ˌmɪsɪnˈfɔrm] *vt* : mal renseigner
misinterpret [ˌmɪsɪnˈtərprət] *vt* : mal interpréter
misinterpretation [ˌmɪsɪnˌtərprəˈteɪʃən] *n* : interprétation *f* erronée
misjudge [mɪsˈdʒʌdʒ] *vt* **-judged; -judging** : mal juger
mislay [mɪsˈleɪ] *vt* **-laid** [-ˈleɪd]; **-laying** : égarer
mislead [mɪsˈliːd] *vt* **-led** [-ˈlɛd]; **-leading** : tromper, induire en erreur
misleading [mɪsˈliːdɪŋ] *adj* : trompeur
mismanage [mɪsˈmænɪdʒ] *vt* **-aged; -aging** : mal gérer, mal administrer
mismanagement [mɪsˈmænɪdʒmənt] *n* : mauvaise gestion *f*
misnomer [mɪsˈnoːmər] *n* : nom *m* inapproprié
misogynist [mɪˈsɑdʒənɪst] *n* : misogyne *mf*
misplace [mɪsˈpleɪs] *vt* **-placed; -placing** : mal placer, égarer
misprint [ˈmɪsˌprɪnt, mɪsˈ-] *n* : faute *f* typographique, coquille *f*
mispronounce [ˌmɪsprəˈnaʊnts] *vt* **-nounced; -nouncing** : mal prononcer
mispronunciation [ˌmɪsprəˌnʌntsiˈeɪʃən] *n* : faute *f* de prononciation
misquote [mɪsˈkwoːt] *vt* **-quoted; -quoting** : citer inexactement
misread [mɪsˈriːd] *vt* **-read** [-ˈrɛd]; **-reading 1** : mal lire **2** MISUNDERSTAND : mal interpréter
misrepresent [ˌmɪsˌrɛprɪˈzɛnt] *vt* : dénaturer , déformer
misrule[1] [mɪsˈruːl] *vt* **-ruled; -ruling** : mal gouverner
misrule[2] *n* : mauvais gouvernement *m*
miss[1] [ˈmɪs] *vt* **1** : rater, manquer <to miss the target : manquer le but> <he missed his plane : il a raté son avion> **2** : regretter l'absence de <she misses her brother : son frère lui manque> **3** AVOID, ESCAPE : éviter, échapper <he just missed being caught : il a failli être pris> **4** OMIT : omettre, sauter — *vi* : rater son coup (aux sports)
miss[2] *n* **1** : coup *m* manqué **2** FAILURE : échec *m* **3** : mademoiselle *f* <Miss Jones : Mademoiselle Jones> <excuse me, miss : pardonnez-moi, mademoiselle>
missal [ˈmɪsəl] *n* : missel *m*
misshapen [mɪˈʃeɪpən] *adj* : difforme (se dit d'une personne), déformé (se dit d'une chose)
missile [ˈmɪsəl] *n* **1** : missile *m* <guided missile : missile téléguidé> **2** PROJECTILE : projectile *m*
missing [ˈmɪsɪŋ] *adj* **1** ABSENT : absent **2** LOST : égaré, disparu <missing person : personne disparue>
mission [ˈmɪʃən] *n* : mission *f*
missionary[1] [ˈmɪʃəˌnɛri] *adj* : missionnaire
missionary[2] *n, pl* **-aries** : missionnaire *mf*
missive [ˈmɪsɪv] *n* : missive *f*
misspell [mɪsˈspɛl] *vt* : mal orthographier, mal écrire
misspelling [mɪsˈspɛlɪŋ] *n* : faute *f* d'orthographe
misstep [ˈmɪsˌstɛp] *n* : faux pas *m*
mist [ˈmɪst] *n* **1** FOG : brume *f* **2** CONDENSATION : buée *f*
mistake[1] [mɪˈsteɪk] *vt* **-took** [-ˈstʊk]; **-taken** [-ˈsteɪkən]; **-taking 1** MISINTERPRET : mal comprendre **2** CONFUSE : confondre <he mistook her for Nicole : il l'a prise pour Nicole>
mistake[2] *n* **1** ERROR : faute *f,* erreur *f* <by mistake : par erreur> <to make a mistake : se tromper> **2** MISUNDERSTANDING : méprise *f,* malentendu *m*
mistaken [mɪˈsteɪkən] *adj* WRONG : erroné
mistakenly [mɪˈsteɪkənli] *adv* : à tort, par erreur
mister [ˈmɪstər] *n* : monsieur *m* <watch out, mister! : attention, monsieur!>
mistletoe [ˈmɪsəlˌtoː] *n* : gui *m*
mistreat [mɪsˈtriːt] *vt* : maltraiter
mistreatment [mɪsˈtriːtmənt] *n* : mauvais traitement *m*
mistress [ˈmɪstrəs] *n* : maîtresse *f*
mistrust[1] [mɪsˈtrʌst] *vt* : se méfier de, douter de
mistrust[2] *n* : méfiance *f*
mistrustful [mɪsˈtrʌstfəl] *adj* : méfiant
misty [ˈmɪsti] *adj* **mistier; -est 1** FOGGY : brumeux, embrumé **2** TEARFUL : embué

misunderstand [ˌmɪsˌʌndərˈstænd] *vt* **-stood** [-ˈstʊd]; **-standing** : mal comprendre
misunderstanding [ˌmɪsˌʌndərˈstændɪŋ] *n* : malentendu *m*
misuse[1] [mɪsˈjuːz] *vt* **-used; -using 1** : faire mauvais usage de **2** MISTREAT : maltraiter
misuse[2] [mɪsˈjuːs] *n* : abus *m,* mauvais usage *m*
mite [ˈmaɪt] *n* **1** : mite *f* (insecte) **2** BIT : brin *m,* grain *m*
miter *or* **mitre** [ˈmaɪt̬ər] *n* **1** : mitre *f* (d'un évêque, etc.) **2** *or* **miter joint** : assemblage *m* à onglet
mitigate [ˈmɪt̬əˌgeɪt] *vt* **-gated; -gating** : atténuer, réduire, adoucir
mitigation [ˌmɪt̬əˈgeɪʃən] *n* : atténuation *f,* adoucissement *m*
mitosis [maɪˈtoːsɪs] *n, pl* **-toses** [-ˌsiːz] : mitose *f*
mitt [ˈmɪt] *n* **1** → **mitten 2** : gant *m* (de baseball)
mitten [ˈmɪtən] *n* : moufle *f,* mitaine *f Can*
mix[1] [ˈmɪks] *vt* **1** COMBINE : mélanger, combiner **2** STIR : malaxer **3 to mix up** CONFUSE : confondre — *vi* : se mélanger, se mêler
mix[2] *n* : mélange *m*
mixer [ˈmɪksər] *n* **1** *or* **cake mixer** : batteur *m* (électrique), mixer *m,* malaxeur *m Can* **2** : malaxeur *m* (de ciment, etc.)
mixture [ˈmɪkstʃər] *n* : mélange *m*
mix–up [ˈmɪksˌʌp] *n* CONFUSION : confusion *f*
mnemonic [nɪˈmɑnɪk] *adj* : mnémotechnique
moan[1] [ˈmoːn] *vi* : gémir
moan[2] *n* : gémissement *m*
moat [ˈmoːt] *n* : douve *f*
mob[1] [ˈmɑb] *vt* **mobbed; mobbing 1** ATTACK : assaillir **2** CROWD : entourer
mob[2] *n* **1** THRONG : foule *f* **2** GANG : bande *f*
mobile[1] [ˈmoːbəl, -ˌbiːl, -ˌbaɪl] *adj* : mobile
mobile[2] [ˈmoːˌbiːl] *n* : mobile *m*
mobility [moˈbɪlət̬i] *n* : mobilité *f*
mobilization [ˌmoːbələˈzeɪʃən] *n* : mobilisation *f*
mobilize [ˈmoːbəˌlaɪz] *vt* **-lized; -lizing** : mobiliser
moccasin [ˈmɑkəsən] *n* **1** : mocassin *m* **2** *or* **water moccasin** : serpent *m* venimeux de l'Amérique du nord
mocha [ˈmoːkə] *n* : moka *m*
mock[1] [ˈmɑk, ˈmɔk] *vt* **1** RIDICULE : se moquer de **2** MIMIC : singer, parodier
mock[2] *adj* **1** SIMULATED : simulé **2** PHONY : faux
mockery [ˈmɑkəri, ˈmɔ-] *n, pl* **-eries** : moquerie *f*
mockingbird [ˈmɑkɪŋˌbərd, ˈmɔ-] *n* : oiseau *m* moqueur
mode [ˈmoːd] *n* **1** MANNER : mode *m,* manière *f,* façon *f* **2** FASHION : mode *m*
model[1] [ˈmɑdəl] *v* **-eled** *or* **-elled; -eling** *or* **-elling** *vt* **1** SHAPE : modeler **2** : présenter <to model a dress : présenter une robe> — *vi* : travailler comme mannequin
model[2] *adj* **1** EXEMPLARY : modèle <a model student : un élève modèle> **2** MINIATURE : en miniature
model[3] *n* **1** PATTERN : modèle *m* **2** MINIATURE : maquette *f,* modèle *m* réduit **3** MANNEQUIN : mannequin *m*
modem [ˈmoːdəm, -ˌdɛm] *n* : modem *m*
moderate[1] [ˈmɑdəˌreɪt] *v* **-ated; -ating** *vt* : modérer, tempérer — *vi* **1** CALM : se modérer **2** PRESIDE : présider
moderate[2] [ˈmɑdərət] *adj* : modéré, modique
moderate[3] *n* : modéré *m,* -rée *f*
moderately [ˈmɑdərətli] *adv* **1** FAIRLY : moyennement **2** REASONABLY : modérément, avec modération <moderately priced : d'un prix raisonnable>
moderation [ˌmɑdəˈreɪʃən] *n* : modération *f*
moderator [ˈmɑdəˌreɪt̬ər] *n* : animateur *m,* -trice *f;* président *m,* -dente *f*
modern [ˈmɑdərn] *adj* : moderne
modernity [məˈdərnət̬i] *n* : modernité *f*
modernization [ˌmɑdərnəˈzeɪʃən] *n* : modernisation *f*
modernize [ˈmɑdərˌnaɪz] *vt* **-nized; -nizing** : moderniser
modest [ˈmɑdəst] *adj* **1** HUMBLE : modeste **2** DEMURE : pudique, modeste **3** MODERATE : modique <a modest sum : une somme modique>
modestly [ˈmɑdəstli] *adv* **1** : modestement, avec modestie **2** DEMURELY : décemment, avec pudeur **3** SIMPLY : simplement, sans prétensions
modesty [ˈmɑdəsti] *n* : modestie *f*
modicum [ˈmɑdɪkəm] *n* : petite quantité *f*
modification [ˌmɑdəfəˈkeɪʃən] *n* : modification *f*
modifier [ˈmɑdəˌfaɪər] *n* : modificateur *m*
modify [ˈmɑdəˌfaɪ] *vt* **-fied; -fying** : modifier
modish [ˈmɑdɪʃ] *adj* STYLISH : à la mode
modular [ˈmɑdʒələr] *adj* : modulaire
modulate [ˈmɑdʒəˌleɪt] *vt* **-lated; -lating** : moduler
modulation [ˌmɑdʒəˈleɪʃən] *n* : modulation *f*
module [ˈmɑˌdʒuːl] *n* : module *m*
mogul [ˈmoːgəl] *n* : magnat *m*
mohair [ˈmoːˌhær] *n* : mohair *m*
moist [ˈmɔɪst] *adj* **1** DAMP : humide **2** : moelleux <gâteau moelleux : moist cake>
moisten [ˈmɔɪsən] *vt* : humecter
moistness [ˈmɔɪstnəs] *n* : humidité *f,* moiteur *f*

moisture ['mɔɪstʃər] *n* : humidité *f*
moisturize ['mɔɪstʃə,raɪz] *vt* **-ized; -izing** : hydrater
moisturizer ['mɔɪstʃə,raɪzər] *n* : crème *f* hydratante
molar ['mo:lər] *n* : molaire *f*
molasses [mə'læsəz] *n* : mélasse *f*
mold[1] ['mo:ld] *vt* **1** SHAPE : mouler, modeler **2** FASHION : façonner, former — *vi* : moisir <the bread will mold : le pain moisira>
mold[2] *n* **1** FORM : moule *m* **2** FUNGUS : moisissure *f*
Moldavian[1] [mal'deɪviən] *adj* : moldave
Moldavian[2] *n* : Moldave *mf*
molder ['mo:ldər] *vi* CRUMBLE : tomber en poussière, émietter
molding ['mo:ldɪŋ] *n* : moulure *f* (en architecture)
moldy ['mo:ldi] *adj* **moldier; -est** : moisi
mole ['mo:l] *n* **1** : grain *m* de beauté (sur la peau) **2** : taupe *f* (animal)
molecular [mə'lɛkjələr] *adj* : moléculaire
molecule ['malɪ,kju:l] *n* : molécule *f*
molehill ['mo:l,hɪl] *n* : taupinière *f*
molest [mə'lɛst] *vt* : molester
mollify ['malə,faɪ] *vt* **-fied; -fying** : apaiser
mollusk *or* **mollusc** ['maləsk] *n* : mollusque *m*
mollycoddle ['mali,kadəl] *vt* **-dled; -dling** PAMPER : dorloter
molt ['mo:lt] *vi* : muer
molten ['mo:ltən] *adj* : en fusion
mom ['mam] *n* : maman *f*
moment ['mo:mənt] *n* **1** INSTANT : instant *m,* moment *m* <a moment ago : il y a un instant> **2** TIME : moment *m* <at the moment : en ce moment> **3** IMPORTANCE : importance *f* <to be of great moment : être de grande importance>
momentarily [,mo:mən'tɛrəli] *adv* **1** : momentanément **2** SOON : dans un instant, immédiatement
momentary ['mo:mən,tɛri] *adj* : momentané
momentous [mo'mɛntəs] *adj* : important, capital
momentum [mo'mɛntəm] *n, pl* **-ta** [-tə] *or* **-tums 1** : moment *m* (en physique) **2** IMPETUS : élan *m,* vitesse *f*
monarch ['ma,nark, -nərk] *n* : monarque *m*
monarchism ['mɔ,nar,kɪzəm, -nər-] *n* : monarchisme *m*
monarchist ['ma,narkɪst, -nər-] *n* : monarchiste *mf*
monarchy ['ma,narki, -nər-] *n, pl* **-chies** : monarchie *f*
monastery ['manə,stɛri] *n, pl* **-teries** : monastère *m*
monastic [mə'næstɪk] *adj* : monastique
Monday ['mʌn,deɪ, -di] *n* : lundi *m*
monetary ['manə,tɛri, 'mʌnə-] *adj* : monétaire
money ['mʌni] *n, pl* **-eys** *or* **-ies** ['mʌniz] : argent *m*
moneyed ['mʌnid] *adj* : nanti, riche
moneylender ['mʌni,lɛndər] *n* : prêteur *m,* -teuse *f*
money order *n* : mandat-poste *m,* mandat *m* postal
Mongolian[1] [man'go:liən, maŋ-] *adj* : mongol
Mongolian[2] *n* **1** : Mongol *m,* -gole *f* **2** : mongol *m* (langue)
mongoose ['man,gu:s, 'maŋ-] *n, pl* **-gooses** : mangouste *f*
mongrel ['maŋgrəl, 'mʌŋ-] *n* : chien *m* bâtard
monitor[1] ['manəṭər] *vt* : surveiller
monitor[2] *n* : moniteur *m*
monk ['mʌŋk] *n* : moine *m*
monkey[1] ['mʌŋki] *vi* **-keyed; -keying 1 to monkey around** : s'amuser **2 to monkey with** : tripoter
monkey[2] *n, pl* **-keys** : singe *m*
monkey wrench *n* : clé *f* à molette
monkshood ['mʌŋks,hʊd] *n* : aconit *m*
monocle ['manɪkəl] *n* : monocle *m*
monogamous [mə'nagəməs] *adj* : monogame
monogamy [mə'nagəmi] *n* : monogamie *f*
monogram[1] ['manə,græm] *vt* **-grammed; -gramming** : marquer d'un monogramme
monogram[2] *n* : monogramme *m*
monograph ['manə,græf] *n* : monographie *f*
monolingual [,manə'lɪŋgwəl] *adj* : monolingue
monolith ['manə,lɪθ] *n* : monolithe *m* — **monolithic** [,manə'lɪθɪk] *adj*
monologue ['manə,lɔg] *n* : monologue *m*
monoplane ['manə,pleɪn] *n* : monoplan *m*
monopolize [mə'napə,laɪz] *vt* **-lized; -lizing** : monopoliser
monopoly [mə'napəli] *n, pl* **-lies** : monopole *m*
monosyllabic [,manəsə'læbɪk] *adj* : monosyllabique
monosyllable ['manə,sɪləbəl] *n* : monosyllabe *m*
monotheism ['manəθi:,ɪzəm] *n* : monothéisme *m*
monotheistic [,manəθi:'ɪstɪk] *adj* : monothéiste
monotone ['manə,to:n] *n* : voix *f* monotone
monotonous [mə'natənəs] *adj* : monotone
monotonously [mə'natənəsli] *adv* : de façon monotone
monotony [mə'natəni] *n* : monotonie *f*
monoxide [mə'nak,saɪd] *n* : monoxyde *m*
monsoon [man'su:n] *n* : mousson *f*
monster ['mantstər] *n* : monstre *m*
monstrosity [man'strasəṭi] *n, pl* **-ties** : monstruosité *f*

monstrous ['mantstrəs] *adj* : monstrueux — **monstrously** *adv*
montage [man'taʒ] *n* : montage *m*
month ['mʌnθ] *n* : mois *m*
monthly[1] ['mʌnθli] *adv* : mensuellement
monthly[2] *adj* : mensuel
monthly[3] *n, pl* **-lies** : mensuel *m,* publication *f* mensuelle
monument ['manjəmənt] *n* : monument *m*
monumental [ˌmanjə'mɛntəl] *adj* : monumental
moo[1] ['mu:] *vi* : meugler
moo[2] *n* : meuglement *m*
mood ['mu:d] *n* **1** : humeur *f* <to be in a good mood : être de bonne humeur> <I'm not in the mood : ça ne me dit rien> **2** ATMOSPHERE : ambiance *f*
moodily ['mu:dəli] *adv* : d'un air morose
moodiness ['mu:dinəs] *n* : humeur *f* changeante
moody ['mu:di] *adj* **moodier; -est 1** SAD : de mauvaise humeur **2** TEMPERAMENTAL : lunatique, d'humeur changeante
moon ['mu:n] *n* : lune *f*
moonbeam ['mu:nˌbi:m] *n* : rayon *m* de lune
moonlight[1] ['mu:nˌlaɪt] *vi* **-ed; -ing** : travailler au noir
moonlight[2] *n* : clair *m* de lune
moonlit ['mu:nˌlɪt] *adj* : éclairé par la lune
moonshine ['mu:nˌʃaɪn] *n* **1** MOONLIGHT : claire *m* de lune **2** NONSENSE : balivernes *fpl* **3** *or* **moonshine liquor** : alcool *m* de contrebande
moor[1] ['mʊr] *vt* : amarrer
moor[2] *n* : lande *f*
mooring ['mʊrɪŋ] *n* : mouillage *m*
moose ['mu:s] *ns & pl* : orignal *m*
moot ['mu:t] *adj* DEBATABLE : discutable
mop[1] ['map] *vt* **mopped; mopping** : laver (à grande eau)
mop[2] *n* : balai *m* à franges, balai *m* éponge
mope ['mo:p] *vi* **moped; moping** : broyer du noir
moped ['mo:ˌpɛd] *n* : cyclomoteur *m*
moral[1] ['mɔrəl] *adj* : moral <moral support : soutien moral> — **morally** *adv*
moral[2] *n* **1** LESSON : morale *f* **2 morals** *npl* : mœurs *fpl*
morale [mə'ræl] *n* SPIRITS : moral *m*
morality [mə'ræləṭi] *n, pl* **-ties** : moralité *f*
morass [mə'ræs] *n* **1** SWAMP : marais *m* **2** CONFUSION, MESS : fatras *m,* bourbier *m*
moratorium [ˌmɔrə'toriəm] *n, pl* **-riums** *or* **-ria** [-iə] : moratoire *m*
moray ['mɔrˌeɪ, mə'reɪ] *n or* **moray eel** : murène *f*
morbid ['mɔrbɪd] *adj* : morbide
morbidity [ˌmɔr'bɪdəṭi] *n* : morbidité *f*
more[1] ['mor] *adv* : plus, davantage <more important : plus important> <the more you eat, the more you want : plus on mange, plus on veut> <once more : une fois de plus> <I don't remember more : je ne me souviens pas davantage>
more[2] *adj* : plus de <more work : plus de travail>
more and more *adv* : de plus en plus
morel [mə'rɛl, mɔ-] *n* : morille *f*
moreover [mor'o:vər] *adv* : de plus
mores ['mɔrˌeɪz, -i:z] *npl* CUSTOMS : mœurs *fpl*
morgue ['mɔrg] *n* : morgue *f*
moribund ['mɔrəˌbʌnd] *adj* : moribond
morning ['mɔrnɪŋ] *n* **1** : matin *m,* avant-midi *f Can* <tomorrow morning : demain matin> **2** (*indicating duration*) : matinée *f* <all morning long : pendant toute la matinée>
Moroccan[1] [mə'rakən] *adj* : marocain
Moroccan[2] *n* : Marocain *m,* -caine *f*
moron ['morˌan] *n* : crétin *m,* -tine *f*
morose [mə'ro:s] *adj* : morose
morosely [mə'ro:sli] *adv* : avec morosité
moroseness [mə'ro:snəs] *n* : morosité *f*
morphine ['mɔrˌfi:n] *n* : morphine *f*
morrow ['maro:] *n* : lendemain *m*
Morse code ['mɔrs] *n* : morse *m*
morsel ['mɔrsəl] *n* : morceau *m,* bouchée *f*
mortal[1] ['mɔrṭəl] *adj* : mortel — **mortally** *adv*
mortal[2] *n* : mortel *m,* -telle *f*
mortality [mɔr'tæləṭi] *n* : mortalité *f*
mortar ['mɔrṭər] *n* : mortier *m*
mortgage[1] ['mɔrgɪdʒ] *vt* **-gaged; -gaging** : hypothéquer
mortgage[2] *n* : hypothèque *f*
mortification [ˌmɔrṭəfə'keɪʃən] *n* : mortification *f*
mortify ['mɔrṭəˌfaɪ] *vt* **-fied; -fying 1** : mortifier (en religion) **2** HUMILIATE : humilier
mortuary ['mɔrtʃəˌwɛri] *n, pl* **-aries** : morgue *f*
mosaic [mo'zeɪɪk] *n* : mosaïque *f*
Moslem ['mazləm] → **Muslim**
mosque ['mask] *n* : mosquée *f*
mosquito [mə'ski:ṭo] *n, pl* **-toes** : moustique *m,* cousin *m,* maringouin *m Can*
moss ['mɔs] *n* : mousse *f*
mossy ['mɔsi] *adj* **-mossier; -iest** : moussu
most[1] ['mo:st] *adv* : très, bien, fort <it's most interesting : c'est fort intéressant> <the most beautiful girl : la plus belle fille>
most[2] *adj* **1** : la plupart de <most people believe it : la plupart des gens y croient> **2** GREATEST : le plus de <the most money : le plus d'argent>

most[3] *n* : plus *m* <three weeks at the most : trois semaines au plus> <she had the most : elle en avait le plus>
most[4] *pron* : la plupart <most are discouraged : la plupart sont découragés>
mostly ['moːstli] *adv* **1** MAINLY : principalement, surtout **2** USUALLY : la plupart du temps
mote ['moːt] *n* SPECK : grain *m*
motel [mo'tɛl] *n* : motel *m*
moth ['mɔθ] *n* **1** : papillon *m* de nuit **2** : mite *f* (qui détruit des vêtements)
mother[1] ['mʌðər] *vt* **1** BEAR : donner naissance à **2** PAMPER, PROTECT : dorloter
mother[2] *n* : mère *f*
motherhood ['mʌðərˌhʊd] *n* : maternité *f*
mother-in-law ['mʌðərɪnˌlɔ] *n, pl* **mothers-in-law** : belle-mère *f*
motherland ['mʌðərˌlænd] *n* : patrie *f*
motherly ['mʌðərli] *adj* : maternel
motif [mo'tiːf] *n* : motif *m*
motion[1] ['moːʃən] *vi* **to motion to** : faire signe à
motion[2] *n* **1** MOVEMENT : mouvement *m* <to set in motion : mettre en mouvement> **2** PROPOSAL : motion *f* <to second the motion : appuyer la motion>
motionless ['moːʃənləs] *adj* : immobile
motion picture *n* MOVIE : film *m*
motivate ['moːt̬əˌveɪt] *vt* **-vated; -vating** : motiver
motivation [ˌmoːt̬ə'veɪʃən] *n* : motivation *f*
motive[1] ['moːt̬ɪv] *adj* : moteur <motive power : force motrice>
motive[2] *n* : motif *m*
motley ['mɑtli] *adj* **1** DIVERSE : divers, hétéroclite **2** MULTICOLORED : bigarré, bariolé
motor[1] ['moːt̬ər] *vi* : voyager en voiture
motor[2] *n* : moteur *m*
motorbike ['moːt̬ərˌbaɪk] *n* : moto *f*
motorboat ['moːt̬ərˌboːt] *n* : canot *m* automobile
motorcar ['moːt̬ərˌkɑr] *n* : automobile *m,* voiture *f*
motorcycle ['moːt̬ərˌsaɪkəl] *n* : motocyclette *f*
motorcyclist ['moːt̬ərˌsaɪkəlɪst] *n* : motocycliste *mf*
motorist ['moːt̬ərɪst] *n* : automobiliste *mf*
mottle ['mɑt̬əl] *vt* **-tled; -tling** : tacheter, moucheter
motto ['mɑt̬oː] *n, pl* **-toes** : devise *f*
mould ['moːld] → **mold**
mound ['maʊnd] *n* **1** PILE : monceau *m,* tas *m* **2** HILL : monticule *m,* tertre *m*
mount[1] ['maʊnt] *vt* : monter — *vi* INCREASE : augmenter, monter
mount[2] *n* **1** SUPPORT : support *m* **2** HORSE : monture *f* **3** MOUNTAIN : mont *m*
mountain ['maʊntən] *n* : montagne *f*
mountaineer [ˌmaʊntən'ɪr] *n* : alpiniste *mf*
mountain goat *n* : chamois *m*
mountain lion → **cougar**
mountaintop ['maʊntənˌtɑp] *n* : cime *f,* sommet *m*
mounting ['maʊntɪŋ] *n* SUPPORT : support *m*
mourn ['morn] *v* : pleurer
mournful ['mornfəl] *adj* : triste, lugubre — **mournfully** *adv*
mourning ['mornɪŋ] *n* : deuil *m* <to be in mourning : porter le deuil>
mouse ['maʊs] *n, pl* **mice** ['maɪs] : souris *f*
mousetrap ['maʊsˌtræp] *n* : souricière *f*
mousse ['muːs] *n* : mousse *f*
moustache ['mʌˌstæʃ, mə'stæʃ] → **mustache**
mouth[1] ['maʊð] *vt* **1** : débiter, dire sans conviction <to mouth platitudes : débiter des lieux communs> **2** : articuler silencieusement
mouth[2] ['maʊθ] *n* : bouche *f*
mouthful ['maʊθˌfʊl] *n* : bouchée *f*
mouthpiece ['maʊθˌpiːs] *n* : embouchure *f,* bec *m*
movable *or* **moveable** ['muːvəbəl] *adj* : mobile
move[1] ['muːv] *v* **moved; moving** *vi* **1** : bouger <don't move! : ne bougez pas!> **2** PROCEED : avancer **3** RELOCATE : déménager **4** ACT : agir **5** : jouer (aux échecs, etc.) **6** PROPOSE : proposer — *vt* **1** SHIFT : déplacer, bouger **2** PERSUADE : inciter, pousser **3** : émouvoir, toucher <she moved him to tears : elle l'a ému jusqu'aux larmes>
move[2] *n* **1** MOVEMENT : mouvement *m* **2** RELOCATION : déménagement *m* **3** STEP : coup *m,* tour *m* <his next move : son prochain coup> <it's her move : c'est à elle de jouer>
movement ['muːvmənt] *n* : mouvement *m*
mover ['muːvər] *n* : déménageur *m,* -geuse *f*
movie ['muːvi] *n* **1** : film *m* **2** **movies** *npl* : cinéma *m,* vues *fpl Can*
mow[1] ['moː] *vt* **mowed; mowed** *or* **mown** ['moːn]; **mowing** : tondre
mow[2] ['maʊ] *n* : meule *f*
mower ['moːər] → **lawn mower**
Mozambican[1] [ˌmoːzəm'biːkən, -zam-] *adj* : mozambicain
Mozambican[2] *n* : Mozambicain *m,* -caine *f*
Mr. ['mɪstər] *n, pl* **Messrs.** ['mɛsərz] : Monsieur *m*
Mrs. ['mɪsəz, -səs, *esp South* 'mɪzəz, -zəs] *n, pl* **Mesdames** [meɪ'dɑm, -'dæm] : Madame *f*
Ms. ['mɪz] *n, pl* **Mss.** *or* **Mses.** ['mɪzəz] : Madame *f,* Mademoiselle *f*

much[1] ['mʌtʃ] *adv* **more** ['mor]; **most** ['mo:st] **1** : beaucoup <much better : beaucoup mieux> **2 as much** : autant

much[2] *adj* **more; most** : beaucoup de <I don't have much money : je n'ai pas beaucoup d'argent>

much[3] *pron* : beaucoup <there is much to do : il y a beaucoup à faire>

mucilage ['mju:səlɪdʒ] *n* : mucilage *m*

muck ['mʌk] *n* **1** MANURE : fumier *m* **2** DIRT, FILTH : saleté *f* **3** MIRE, MUD : boue *f*, fange *f*

mucous ['mju:kəs] *adj* : muqueux

mucus ['mju:kəs] *n* : mucus *m*

mud ['mʌd] *n* : boue *f*, bouette *f Can fam*

muddle[1] ['mʌdəl] *v* **muddled; muddling** *vt* : confondre, embrouiller — *vi* **to muddle through** : se tirer d'affaire

muddle[2] *n* : désordre *m*, fouillis *m*

muddleheaded [ˌmʌdəl'hɛdəd, 'mʌdəlˌ-] *adj* : désordonné, confus

muddy[1] ['mʌdi] *vt* **muddied; muddying** : salir, couvrir de boue

muddy[2] *adj* **muddier; -est** : boueux

muff[1] ['mʌf] *vt* BUNGLE : rater, gâcher, louper *fam*

muff[2] *n* : manchon *m*

muffin ['mʌfən] *n* : muffin *m Can*

muffle ['mʌfəl] *vt* **muffled; muffling 1** ENVELOP : envelopper **2** DEADEN : étouffer, assourdir (des sons)

muffler ['mʌflər] *n* **1** SCARF : écharpe *f*, cache-nez *m* **2** : silencieux *m* (d'un véhicule)

mug[1] ['mʌg] *v* **mugged; mugging** *vi* : faire des grimaces — *vt* ASSAULT : agresser

mug[2] *n* : tasse *f* (pour le café), chope *f* (pour la bière)

mugger ['mʌgər] *n* : agresseur *m*

muggy ['mʌgi] *adj* **muggier; -est** : lourd et humide

mulatto [mʊ'latˌo, -'læ-] *n, pl* **-toes** *or* **-tos** : mulâtre *m*, -tresse *f*

mulberry ['mʌlˌbɛri] *n, pl* **-ries** : mûrier *m* (arbre), mûre *f* (fruit)

mulch[1] ['mʌltʃ] *vt* : pailler

mulch[2] *n* : paillis *m*

mule ['mju:l] *n* : mule *f*, mulet *m*

mulish ['mju:lɪʃ] *adj* : entêté, têtu

mull ['mʌl] *vt or* **to mull over** : ruminer, réfléchir sur

mullet ['mʌlət] *n, pl* **-let** *or* **-lets** : muge *m*, rouget *m*

multicolored ['mʌltiˌkʌlərd, 'mʌlˌtaɪ-] *adj* : multicolore, bigarré, bariolé

multifaceted [ˌmʌlti'fæsəṭəd, ˌmʌlˌtaɪ-] *adj* : à multiples facettes

multifamily ['mʌltiˌfæmli, ˌmʌlˌtaɪ-] *adj* : pour plusieurs familles

multifarious [ˌmʌltə'færiəs] *adj* : divers, très varié

multilateral [ˌmʌlti'læṭərəl, ˌmʌlˌtaɪ-] *adj* : multilatéral

multimedia [ˌmʌlti'mi:diə, ˌmʌlˌtaɪ-] *adj* : multimédia

multimillionaire [ˌmʌltiˌmɪljə'nær, ˌmʌlˌtaɪ-, -'mɪljəˌnær] *n* : multimillionaire *mf*

multinational [ˌmʌlti'næʃənəl, ˌmʌlˌtaɪ-] *adj* : multinational

multiple[1] ['mʌltəpəl] *adj* : multiple

multiple[2] *n* : multiple *m*

multiple sclerosis [sklə'ro:sɪs] *n* : sclérose *f* en plaques

multiplication [ˌmʌltəplə'keɪʃən] *n* : multiplication *f*

multiplicity [ˌmʌltə'plɪsəṭi] *n, pl* **-ties** : multiplicité *f*

multiply ['mʌltəˌplaɪ] *v* **-plied; -plying** *vt* : multiplier — *vi* : se multiplier

multipurpose [ˌmʌlti'pərpəs, ˌmʌltaɪ-] *adj* : polyvalent, aux usages multiples

multitude ['mʌltəˌtu:d, -ˌtju:d] *n* : multitude *f*

multitudinous [ˌmʌltə'tu:dnəs, -'tju:d-, -'tu:dənəs, -'tju:-] *adj* : innombrable

mum[1] ['mʌm] *adj* SILENT : silencieux <to keep mum : garder le silence>

mum[2] *n* **1** → **chrysanthemum 2** *Brit* → **mom**

mumble[1] ['mʌmbəl] *v* **-bled; -bling** : marmonner

mumble[2] *n* : marmonnement *m*

mummy ['mʌmi] *n, pl* **-mies** : momie *f*

mumps ['mʌmps] *ns & pl* : oreillons *mpl*

munch ['mʌntʃ] *v* : croquer

mundane [ˌmʌn'deɪn, 'mʌnˌ-] *adj* **1** EARTHLY, WORLDLY : de ce monde, terrestre **2** COMMONPLACE : banal, ordinaire

municipal [mjʊ'nɪsəpəl] *adj* : municipal

municipality [mjʊˌnɪsə'pæləṭi] *n, pl* **-ties** : municipalité *f*

munificent [mjʊ'nɪfəsənt] *adj* : munificent

munitions [mjʊ'nɪʃənz] *npl* : munitions *fpl*

mural[1] ['mjʊrəl] *adj* : mural

mural[2] *n* : peinture *f* murale, murale *f*

murder[1] ['mərdər] *vt* : assassiner

murder[2] *n* : meurtre *m*

murderer ['mərdərər] *n* : meurtrier *m*, -trière *f*; assassin *m*

murderess ['mərdərɪs, -dəˌrɛs, -dərəs] *n* : meurtrière *f*

murderous ['mərdərəs] *adj* : meurtrier

murk ['mərk] *n* DARKNESS : obscurité *f*

murkiness ['mərkinəs] *n* : obscurité *f*

murky ['mərki] *adj* **murkier; -est** : obscur, sombre

murmur[1] ['mərmər] *v* : murmurer

murmur[2] *n* : murmure *m*

muscatel [ˌməskə'tɛl] *n* : muscat *m*

muscle[1] ['mʌsəl] *vi* **-cled; -cling** *or* **to muscle in** INTERVENE : intervenir

muscle[2] *n* **1** : muscle *m* **2** BRAWN : force *f*, muscle *m* **3** POWER : puissance *f*, poids *m*

muscular ['mʌskjələr] *adj* **1** : musculaire <muscular tissue : tissu musculaire> **2** STRONG : musclé

muscular dystrophy *n* : dystrophie *f* musculaire
musculature [ˈmʌskjələˌtʃʊr, -tʃər] *n* : musculature *f*
muse[1] [ˈmjuːz] *vi* **mused; musing** PONDER : méditer
muse[2] *n* : muse *f*
museum [mjʊˈziːəm] *n* : musée *m*
mush [ˈmʌʃ] *n* **1** : bouillie *f* **2** SENTIMENTALITY : mièverie *f*
mushroom[1] [ˈmʌʃˌruːm, -ˌrʊm] *vi* GROW, MULTIPLY : proliférer, se multiplier
mushroom[2] *n* : champignon *m*
mushy [ˈmʌʃi] *adj* **mushier; -est 1** SOFT : en bouillie (se dit de la nourriture), bourbeux (se dit de la terre) **2** MAWKISH : mièvre
music [ˈmjuːzɪk] *n* : musique *f*
musical[1] [ˈmjuːzɪkəl] *adj* : musical <musical instruments : instruments de musique> — **musically** *adv*
musical[2] *n* : comédie *f* musicale
musician [mjʊˈzɪʃən] *n* : musicien *m*, -cienne *f*
musk [ˈmʌsk] *n* : musc *m*
musket [ˈmʌskət] *n* : mousquet *m*
musketeer [ˌmʌskəˈtɪr] *n* : mousquetaire *m*
muskrat [ˈmʌskˌræt] *n, pl* **-rat** *or* **-rats** : rat *m* musqué
Muslim[1] [ˈmʌzləm, ˈmʊs-, ˈmʊz-] *adj* : musulman
Muslim[2] *n* : Musulman *m*, -mane *f*
muslin [ˈmʌzlən] *n* : mousseline *f*
muss [ˈmʌs] *vt* : chiffonner, froisser, décoiffer (les cheveux de qqn)
mussel [ˈmʌsəl] *n* : moule *f*
must[1] [ˈmʌst] *v aux* **1** (*expressing obligation or necessity*) : falloir, devoir <you must go : il faut que tu y ailles> <we must obey : nous devons obéir> **2** (*expressing probability*) : devoir <you must be tired : vous devez être fatigué> <it must be late : il doit être tard>
must[2] *n* : nécessité *f* <exercise is a must : l'exercice est indispensable>
mustache [ˈmʌˌstæʃ, mʌˈstæʃ] *n* : moustache *f*
mustang [ˈmʌˌstæŋ] *n* : mustang *m*
mustard [ˈmʌstərd] *n* : moutarde *f*
muster[1] [ˈmʌstər] *vt* : rassembler, réunir
muster[2] *n* **1** : rassemblement *m* **2 to pass muster** : être acceptable
mustiness [ˈmʌstinəs] *n* : odeur *f* de moisi, odeur *f* de renfermé
musty [ˈmʌsti] *adj* **mustier; -est** : de moisi, de renfermé
mutable [ˈmjuːt̬əbəl] *adj* : mutable
mutant[1] [ˈmjuːtənt] *adj* : mutant
mutant[2] *n* : mutant *m*, -tante *f*
mutate [ˈmjuːˌteɪt] *vi* **-tated; -tating** : muter
mutation [mjuːˈteɪʃən] *n* : mutation *f*
mute[1] [ˈmjuːt] *vt* **muted; muting** MUFFLE : étouffer, assourdir
mute[2] *adj* **muter; mutest** : muet
mute[3] *n* : muet *m*, muette *f*
mutilate [ˈmjuːt̬əˌleɪt] *vt* **-lated; -lating** : mutiler
mutilation [ˌmjuːt̬əˈleɪʃən] *n* : mutilation *f*
mutineer [ˌmjuːtənˈɪr] *n* : mutiné *m*, -née *f*
mutinous [ˈmjuːtənəs] *adj* : mutiné
mutiny[1] [ˈmjuːtəni] *vi* **-nied; -nying** : se mutiner
mutiny[2] *n, pl* **-nies** : mutinerie *f*
mutt [ˈmʌt] *n* MONGREL : chien *m* bâtard
mutter [ˈmʌt̬ər] *vi* **1** MUMBLE : marmonner **2** GRUMBLE : grommeler
mutton [ˈmʌtən] *n* : mouton *m*
mutual [ˈmjuːtʃʊəl] *adj* **1** : mutuel, réciproque **2** COMMON : commun <a mutual friend : un ami commun>
mutually [ˈmjuːtʃʊəli, -tʃəli] *adv* **1** : mutuellement, réciproquement **2** JOINTLY : conjointement
muzzle[1] [ˈmʌzəl] *vt* **-zled; -zling** : museler
muzzle[2] *n* **1** SNOUT : museau *m* **2** : muselière *f* (pour un chien, etc.) **3** : canon *m* (d'une arme à feu)
my[1] [ˈmaɪ] *adj* : mon, ma, mes <my parents : mes parents> <in my opinion : à mon avis>
my[2] *interj* **oh, my!** : eh, bien!, oh là là!, mon Dieu!
myopia [maɪˈoːpiə] *n* : myopie *f*
myopic [maɪˈoːpɪk, -ˈɑ-] *adj* : myope
myriad[1] [ˈmɪriəd] *adj* : innombrable
myriad[2] *n* : myriade *f*
myrrh [ˈmər] *n* : myrrhe *f*
myrtle [ˈmərt̬əl] *n* : myrte *m*
myself [maɪˈsɛlf] *pron* **1** (*used reflexively*) : me <I hurt myself : je me suis fait mal> **2** (*used for emphasis*) : moi-même <I tried it myself : je l'ai essayé moi-même> **3 all by myself** : tout seul
mysterious [mɪˈstɪriəs] *adj* : mystérieux — **mysteriously** *adv*
mysteriousness [mɪˈstɪriəsnəs] *n* : mystère *m*, caractère *m* mystérieux
mystery [ˈmɪstəri] *n, pl* **-teries** : mystère *m*
mystic[1] [ˈmɪstɪk] *adj or* **mystical** [ˈmɪstɪkəl] : mystique — **mystically** [-kli] *adv*
mystic[2] *n* : mystique *mf*
mysticism [ˈmɪstəˌsɪzəm] *n* : mysticisme *m*
mystify [ˈmɪstəˌfaɪ] *vt* **-fied; -fying 1** PUZZLE : déconcerter **2** DECEIVE, DUPE : mystifier
mystique [mɪˈstiːk] *n* : mystique *f*
myth [ˈmɪθ] *n* : mythe *m*
mythical [ˈmɪθɪkəl] *adj* : mythique
mythological [ˌmɪθəˈlɑdʒɪkəl] *adj* : mythologique
mythology [mɪˈθɑlədʒi] *n, pl* **-gies** : mythologie *f*

N

n ['ɛn] *n, pl* **n's** *or* **ns** ['ɛnz] : n *m,* quatorzième lettre de l'alphabet

nab ['næb] *vt* **nabbed; nabbing 1** APPREHEND : arrêter, pincer *fam* **2** STEAL : piquer *fam,* voler

nadir ['neɪˌdɪr, 'neɪdər] *n* : nadir *m,* point *m* le plus bas

nag[1] ['næg] *v* **nagged; nagging** *vi* **1** COMPLAIN : se plaindre, maugréer **2** PERSIST : persister <a nagging toothache : un mal de dents qui persiste> — *vt* SCOLD : critiquer, enquiquiner *fam*

nag[2] *n* **1** HORSE : canasson *m fam* **2** GROUCH : rouspéteur *m,* -teuse *f fam*

naiad ['neɪəd, 'naɪ-, -ˌæd] *n, pl* **-iads** *or* **-iades** [-əˌdiz] : naïade *f*

nail[1] ['neɪl] *vt* : clouer

nail[2] *n* **1** FINGERNAIL : ongle *m* <to bite one's nails : se ronger les ongles> **2** : clou *m* (en technologie) <to hit the nail on the head : mettre le doigt dessus>

naive *or* **naïve** [nɑ'iːv] *adj* **-iver; -est** : naïf

naïveté [ˌnɑˌiːvə'teɪ, nɑ'iːvəˌ-] *n* : naïveté *f*

naked ['neɪkəd] *adj* **1** NUDE : nu **2** UNADORNED : tout nu, brut <the naked truth : la vérité pure et simple> **3 to the naked eye** : à l'œil nu

nakedness ['neɪkədnəs] *n* : nudité *f*

name[1] ['neɪm] *vt* **named; naming 1** CALL : nommer, appeler <I named him "John" : je l'ai nommé «John»> **2** CITE : nommer, citer **3** APPOINT : nommer **4** SPECIFY : choisir, fixer <to name the date : choisir la date> <to name a price : fixer un prix>

name[2] *adj* : de marque <name brand : produit de marque>

name[3] *n* **1** : nom *m* <what is your name? : comment t'appelles-tu?, quel est ton nom?> **2** REPUTATION : nom *m,* réputation *f* <to make a name for oneself : se faire un nom> **3 to call someone names** : traiter quelqu'un de tous les noms

nameless ['neɪmləs] *adj* **1** : sans nom <a nameless grave : une tombe sans nom> **2** UNKNOWN : anonyme **3** INDEFINABLE : indéfinissable, inexplicable

namely ['neɪmli] *adv* : notamment, c'est-à-dire

namesake ['neɪmˌseɪk] *n* : homonyme *m*

Namibian[1] [nə'mɪbiən] *adj* : namibien

Namibian[2] *n* : Namibien *m,* -bienne *f*

nap[1] ['næp] *vi* **napped; napping** : faire un somme, faire une sieste

nap[2] *n* **1** SNOOZE : somme *m,* sieste *f* **2** : poil *m* (d'un tissu)

nape ['neɪp, 'næp] *n* : nuque *f*

naphtha ['næfθə] *n* : naphte *m*

napkin ['næpkən] *n* **1** : serviette *f* (de table) **2** → **sanitary**

narcissism ['nɑrsəˌsɪzəm] *n* : narcissisme *m*

narcissist ['nɑrsəsɪst] *n* : narcisse *m*

narcissistic [ˌnɑrsə'sɪstɪk] *adj* : narcissique

narcissus [nɑr'sɪsəs] *n, pl* **-cissi** *or* **-cissuses** *or* **-cissus** [-'sɪˌsaɪ, -ˌsiː] : narcisse *m* (fleur)

narcotic[1] [nɑr'kɑṭɪk] *adj* : narcotique

narcotic[2] *n* **1** : narcotique *m* (en pharmacie) **2** DRUG : stupéfiant *m*

narrate ['nærˌeɪt] *vt* **narrated; narrating** : raconter, narrer

narration [næ'reɪʃən] *n* : narration *f,* récit *m*

narrative[1] ['nærəṭɪv] *adj* : narratif

narrative[2] *n* : récit *m,* histoire *f,* narration *f*

narrator ['nærˌeɪṭər] *n* : narrateur *m,* -trice *f*

narrow[1] ['nærˌoː] *vt* **1** LIMIT : limiter **2** REDUCE : réduire — *vi* : se rétrécir <the road narrows : la route se rétrécit>

narrow[2] *adj* **1** : étroit <a narrow passage : un passage étroit> **2** LIMITED : limité, restreint **3** BIGOTED : étroit, borné **4 by a narrow margin** : de justesse

narrowly ['næroli] *adv* : de justesse, de peu

narrow–minded [ˌnæro'maɪndəd] *adj* : étroit d'esprit

narrowness ['næronəs] *n* : étroitesse *f*

narrows ['næroːz] *npl* STRAIT : passages *mpl* étroits

narwhal ['nɑrˌ*h*wɑl, 'nɑrwəl] *n* : narval *m*

nasal ['neɪzəl] *adj* : nasal

nasally ['neɪzəli] *adv* : d'une voix nasale

nastily ['næstəli] *adv* : méchamment

nastiness ['næstinəs] *n* : méchanceté *f*

nasturtium [nə'stərʃəm, næ-] *n* : capucine *f*

nasty ['næsti] *adj* **nastier; -est 1** FILTHY : sale, crasseux **2** INDECENT : obscène **3** MALICIOUS : méchant <a nasty disposition : un air méchant> **4** UNPLEASANT : sale, vilain <nasty weather : sale temps> <a nasty trick : un vilain tour>

natal ['neɪṭəl] *adj* : natal

nation ['neɪʃən] *n* : pays *m,* nation *f*

national[1] ['næʃənəl] *adj* : national — **nationally** *adv*

national[2] *n* : ressortissant *m,* -sante *f*

nationalism ['næʃənəˌlɪzəm] *n* : nationalisme *m*

nationalist ['næʃənəlɪst] *n* : nationaliste *mf*

nationalistic [ˌnæʃənə'lɪstɪk] *adj* : nationaliste

nationality [ˌnæʃə'næləṭi] *n, pl* **-ties** : nationalité *f*

nationalization [ˌnæʃənələ'zeɪʃən] *n* : nationalisation *f*

nationalize ['næʃənəˌlaɪz] *vt* **-ized; -izing** : nationaliser

nationwide ['neɪʃən'waɪd] *adj* : dans tout le pays

native[1] ['neɪţɪv] *adj* **1** NATURAL : inné **2** : natal <in his native country : dans son pays natal> **3** : maternel <her native language : sa langue maternelle>

native[2] *n* **to be a native of** : être originaire de, être natif de

Native American → **American Indian**

nativity [nə'tɪvəţi, neɪ-] *n, pl* **-ties 1** : Nativité *f* (en religion) **2** BIRTH : naissance *f*

natty ['næţi] *adj* **nattier; -est** : coquet, élégant

natural[1] ['nætʃərəl] *adj* **1** : à l'état naturel <natural woodlands : forêt à l'état naturel> **2** : naturel <natural causes : causes naturelles> **3** INBORN : né, inné <natural abilities : talents innés> **4** SIMPLE : naturel, simple

natural[2] *n* : quelqu'un qui a un talent inné

naturalism ['nætʃərəˌlɪzəm] *n* : naturalisme *m*

naturalist ['nætʃərəlɪst] *n* : naturaliste *mf*

naturalistic [ˌnæchərə'lɪstɪk] *adj* : naturaliste

naturalization [ˌnætʃərələ'zeɪʃən] *n* : naturalisation *f*

naturalize ['nætʃərəˌlaɪz] *vt* **-ized; -izing** : naturaliser

naturally ['nætʃərəli] *adv* **1** : naturellement <naturally blonde : naturellement blonde> **2** OF COURSE : bien sûr, bien entendu, évidemment

naturalness ['nætʃərəlnəs] *n* : naturel *m*

nature ['neɪtʃər] *n* **1** ESSENCE : nature *f,* essence *f* **2** KIND : espèce *f,* genre *m* **3** DISPOSITION : nature *f,* tempérament *m* <a generous nature : une nature généreuse> **4** : nature *f* <the beauties of nature : les beautés de la nature>

naught ['nɔt] *n* **1** NOTHING : rien *m* <to come to naught : ne mener à rien> **2** ZERO : zéro *m*

naughtiness ['nɔţinəs] *n* : désobéissance *f,* mauvaise conduite *f*

naughty ['nɔti] *adj* **naughtier; -est 1** DISOBEDIENT, MISCHIEVOUS : méchant, vilain **2** RISQUÉ : osé, risqué

nausea ['nɔziə, 'nɔʃə] *n* **1** : nausée *f* **2** DISGUST : nausée *f,* écœurement *m*

nauseate ['nɔziˌeɪt, -ʒi-, -si-, -ʃi-] *v* **-ated; -ating** *vi* : avoir la nausée — *vt* : donner la nausée à

nauseating ['nɔziˌeɪţɪŋ] *adj* : écœurant

nauseatingly ['nɔziˌeɪţɪŋli, -ʒi-, -si-, -ʃi-] *adv* : au point d'écœurer <nauseatingly sweet : d'une douceur écœurante>

nauseous ['nɔʃəs, -ziəs] *adj* **1** SICK : écœuré **2** REVOLTING : nauséabond

nautical ['nɔţɪkəl] *adj* : nautique

nautilus ['nɔţələs] *n, pl* **-luses** *or* **-li** [-ˌlaɪ, -ˌliː] : nautile *m*

naval ['neɪvəl] *adj* : naval

nave ['neɪv] *n* : nef *f* (d'une église)

navel ['neɪvəl] *n* : nombril *m*

navigable ['nævɪgəbəl] *adj* : navigable

navigability [ˌnævɪgə'bɪləţi] *n* : navigabilité *f*

navigate ['nævəˌgeɪt] *v* **-gated; -gating** *vi* SAIL : naviguer, voguer — *vt* **1** SAIL : naviguer sur, traverser **2** STEER : diriger, gouverner (un bateau)

navigation [ˌnævə'geɪʃən] *n* : navigation *f*

navigator ['nævəˌgeɪţər] *n* : navigateur *m,* -trice *f*

navy ['neɪvi] *n, pl* **-vies 1** FLEET : flotte *f* **2** : marine *f* (nationale) <the United States Navy : la Marine américaine> **3** *or* **navy blue** : marine *f*

nay[1] ['neɪ] *adv* EVEN : que dis-je, voire <a huge, nay, monstrous animal : un animal énorme, que dis-je, monstrueux>

nay[2] *n* : non *m,* vote *m* négatif <the nays outnumbered the ayes : les non l'ont emporté sur les oui>

Nazi[1] ['nɑtsi, 'næt-] *adj* : nazi

Nazi[2] *n* : nazi *m,* -zie *f*

Nazism ['nɑtˌsɪzəm, 'næt-] *or* **Naziism** ['nɑtsiˌɪzəm, 'næt-] *n* : nazisme *m*

near[1] ['nɪr] *vt* : approcher — *vi* : s'approcher

near[2] *adv* **1** : près <she lives very near : elle habite tout près> <to draw near : approcher> **2** ALMOST, NEARLY : presque <near dead : presque mort>

near[3] *adj* : proche <in the near future : dans un proche avenir> <to the nearest dollar : à un dollar près> <the nearest route : le chemin le plus court>

near[4] *prep* : à côté de, près de <the table near the window : la table à côté de la fenêtre>

nearby[1] [nɪr'baɪ, 'nirˌbaɪ] *adv* CLOSE : tout près, à proximité

nearby[2] *adj* : voisin, proche <a nearby house : une maison voisine>

nearly ['nɪrli] *adv* : presque

nearness ['nɪrnəs] *n* : proximité *f*

nearsighted ['nɪrˌsaɪţəd] *adj* : myope

nearsightedness ['nɪrˌsaɪţədnəs] *n* : myopie *f*

neat ['niːt] *adj* **1** UNDILUTED : sec, pur **2** PRETTY, SMART : joli, coquet **3** CLEAN, ORDERLY : propre, soigné **4** SKILLFUL : habile <a neat trick : un truc habile>

neatly ['niːtli] *adv* **1** TIDILY : proprement, soigneusement **2** CLEVERLY : habilement

neatness ['niːtnəs] *n* : ordre *m,* propreté *f*

nebula ['nɛbjʊlə] *n, pl* **-lae** [-ˌliː, -ˌlaɪ] : nébuleuse *f*

nebulous ['nɛbjʊləs] *adj* : nébuleux

necessarily [ˌnɛsə'serəli] *adv* : nécessairement, forcément

necessary[1] ['nɛsəˌsɛri] *adj* **1** INEVITABLE : inévitable **2** COMPULSORY : obligatoire **3** ESSENTIAL : indispensable

necessary[2] *n, pl* **-saries** : nécessaire *m*

necessitate [nɪ'sɛsəˌteɪt] *vt* **-tated; -tating** : nécessiter, exiger

necessity [nɪ'sɛsət̬i] *n, pl* **-ties 1** NEED : nécessité *f,* besoin *m* **2** : quelque chose d'indispensable <eating is a necessity : il est indispensable de manger> **3** POVERTY : pauvreté *f* **4 necessities** *npl* : le nécessaire, les choses essentielles

neck[1] ['nɛk] *vi* : se peloter *fam*

neck[2] *n* **1** : cou *m* **2** COLLAR : col *m,* encolure *f* <a high neck : un col montant> **3** : col *m,* goulot *m* (d'une bouteille)

neckerchief ['nɛkərtʃəf, -ˌtʃiːf] *n, pl* **-chiefs** [-tʃəfs, -ˌtʃiːfs] : foulard *m*

necklace ['nɛkləs] *n* : collier *m*

necktie ['nɛkˌtaɪ] *n* : cravate *f*

nectar ['nɛktər] *n* : nectar *m*

nectarine [ˌnɛktə'riːn] *n* : nectarine *f*

née *or* **nee** ['neɪ] *adj* : né

need[1] ['niːd] *vi* : avoir besoin, être dans le besoin — *vt* **1** : avoir besoin de <he needs a car : il a besoin d'une voiture> **2 to need to** : devoir <something needs to be done : on doit faire quelque chose> — *v aux* : avoir besoin de, devoir, être obligé de <you need not answer : vous n'êtes pas obligé de répondre> <need we go? : est-ce que nous devons vraiment y aller?>

need[2] *n* **1** OBLIGATION : besoin *m,* nécessité *f* **2** DISTRESS : difficulté *f* <in times of need : pendant les moments difficiles> **3** WANT : besoin *m* <to be in need : être dans le besoin> **4 if need be** : si nécessaire, s'il le faut

needful ['niːdfəl] *adj* : nécessaire

needle[1] ['niːdəl] *vt* **-dled; -dling** TEASE : taquiner

needle[2] *n* : aiguille *f*

needlepoint ['nidəlˌpɔɪnt] *n* **1** LACE : dentelle *f* à l'aiguille **2** EMBROIDERY : tapisserie *f* à l'aiguille

needless ['niːdləs] *adj* **1** UNNECESSARY : inutile **2 needless to say** : il va sans dire

needlessly ['niːdləsli] *adv* : inutilement

needlework ['niːdəlˌwərk] *n* : travaux *mpl* d'aiguille

needy ['niːdiː] *adj* **needier; -est** : dans le besoin

nefarious [nɪ'færiəs] *adj* : infâme, odieux

negate [nɪ'geɪt] *vt* **-gated; -gating 1** DENY : nier, contredire **2** NULLIFY : abroger

negation [nɪ'geɪʃən] *n* : négation *f*

negative[1] ['nɛgət̬ɪv] *adj* : négatif

negative[2] *n* **1** *or* **negative number** : nombre *m* négatif **2** : négatif *m* (en photographie) **3** : négation *f* (en grammaire) **4 to answer in the negative** : répondre par la négative

negatively ['nɛgət̬ɪvli] *adv* : négativement

negativity [ˌnɛgə'tɪvət̬i] *n* : négativité *f*

neglect[1] [nɪ'glɛkt] *vt* **1** DISREGARD : négliger **2** : manquer à (son devoir, une promesse, etc.)

neglect[2] *n* **1** : négligence *f* <due to neglect : dû à la négligence> **2** : manque *m* de soins (envers une personne), manque *m* d'entretien (d'un bâtiment, etc.)

neglectful [nɪ'glɛktfəl] *adj* : négligent

negligee [ˌnɛglə'ʒeɪ] *n* : négligé *m,* déshabillé *m*

negligence ['nɛglɪdʒənts] *n* : négligence *f* <criminal negligence : négligence criminelle>

negligent ['nɛglɪdʒənt] *adj* : négligent — **negligently** *adv*

negligible ['nɛglɪdʒəbəl] *adj* : négligeable

negotiable [nɪ'goːʃəbəl, -ʃiə-] *adj* : négociable

negotiate [nɪ'goːʃiˌeɪt] *v* **-ated; -ating** *vi* : négocier — *vt* **1** : négocier (une entente, etc.) **2** : franchir, surmonter (une difficulté)

negotiation [nɪˌgoʃi'eɪshən, -si'eɪ-] *n* : négociation *f*

negotiator [nɪ'goːʃiˌeɪt̬ər, -siˌeɪ-] *n* : négociateur *m,* -trice *f*

Negro[1] ['niːˌgroː] *adj* : noir, nègre

Negro[2] *n, pl* **-groes** *sometimes offensive* : nègre *m sometimes offensive,* négresse *f sometimes offensive*

neigh[1] ['neɪ] *vi* : hennir

neigh[2] *n* : hennissement *m*

neighbor[1] *or Brit* **neighbour** ['neɪbər] *vt* : avoisiner — *vi* **to neighbor on** : être voisin de

neighbor[2] *or Brit* **neighbour** *n* **1** : voisin *m,* -sine *f* **2** FELLOWMAN : prochain *m* <love thy neighbor : aime ton prochain>

neighborhood *or Brit* **neighbourhood** ['neɪbərˌhʊd] *n* **1** : voisinage *m* **2 in the neighborhood of** APPROXIMATELY : au voisinage de, environ

neighborly *or Brit* **neighbourly** ['neɪbərli] *adj* : amical, de bon voisin

neighbour *Brit* → **neighbor**

neither[1] ['niːðər, 'naɪ-] *adj* : aucun (des deux) <neither girl : aucune des deux filles>

neither[2] *conj* **1** : non plus <he doesn't want to go, and neither do I : il ne veut pas y aller, et moi non plus> **2 neither . . . nor** : ni . . . ni <neither good nor bad : ni bon ni mauvais>

neither[3] *pron* : aucun <neither of the bottles is full : aucune des deux bouteilles n'est pleine>

nemesis ['nɛməsɪs] *n, pl* **-eses** [-ˌsiːz] **1** RIVAL : vieux rival *m* **2** RETRIBUTION : juste punition *f*

neologism [ni'ɑləˌdʒɪzəm] *n* : néologisme *m*

neon ['niːˌɑn] *n* : néon *m* <neon lighting : éclairage au néon>

neophyte ['niːəˌfaɪt] *n* : néophyte *mf*

Nepali[1] [nə'pɔliː, -'pɑ-, -'pæ-] *adj* : népalais

Nepali[2] *n* **1** : Népalais *m*, -laise *f* **2** : népalais *m* (langue)

nephew ['nɛˌfjuː, *chiefly Brit* 'neˌvjuː] *n* : neveu *m*

nepotism ['nɛpəˌtɪzəm] *n* : népotisme *m*

Neptune ['nɛpˌtuːn, -ˌtjuːn] *n* : Neptune *f* (planète)

nerd ['nərd] *n* : crétin *m*, -tine *f fam*

nerve ['nərv] *n* **1** : nerf *m* <sensory nerve : nerf sensoriel> **2** AUDACITY : culot *m fam*, toupet *m fam* <to have a lot of nerve : avoir du culot> **3** FORTITUDE : confiance *f*, assurance *f* **4 nerves** *npl* JITTERS : nerfs *mpl* <to be all nerves : être sur les nerfs>

nervous ['nərvəs] *adj* **1** : nerveux <nervous system : système nerveux> **2** ANXIOUS : appréhensif, anxieux **3** TIMID : timide <a nervous smile : un sourire timide>

nervously ['nərvəsli] *adv* : nerveusement, avec inquiétude

nervousness ['nərvəsnəs] *n* : nervosité *f*

nervy ['nərvi] *adj* **nervier; -est 1** BOLD : audacieux **2** INSOLENT : culotté *fam*, effronté **3** NERVOUS : nerveux

nest[1] ['nɛst] *vi* : se nicher, faire son nid

nest[2] *n* **1** : nid *m* **2** SET : ensemble *m* (de tables, etc.)

nestle ['nɛsəl] *vi* **-tled; -tling** : se blottir

net[1] ['nɛt] *vt* **netted; netting 1** CATCH : prendre au filet (des poissons) **2** YIELD : rapporter (en finance)

net[2] *adj* : net <net salary : salaire net>

net[3] *n* : filet *m*

nether ['nɛðər] *adj* **1** LOWER : inférieur, bas **2 the nether regions** : les enfers

nettle[1] ['nɛtəl] *vt* **-tled; -tling** : piquer au vif, irriter

nettle[2] *n* : ortie *f*

network ['nɛtˌwərk] *n* : réseau *m*

neural ['nʊrəl, 'njʊr-] *adj* : neural

neuralgia [nʊ'rældʒə, njʊ-] *n* : névralgie *f*

neuralgic [nʊ'rældʒɪk] *adj* : névralgique

neuritis [nʊ'raɪtəs, njʊ-] *n, pl* **-ritides** [-'rɪtəˌdiːz] *or* **-ritises** : névrite *f*

neurological [ˌnʊrə'lɑdʒɪkəl, ˌnjʊr-] *or* **neurologic** [ˌnʊrə'lɑdʒɪk, ˌnjʊ-] *adj* : neurologique

neurologist [nʊ'rɑlədʒɪst, njʊ-] *n* : neurologue *mf*

neurology [nʊ'rɑlədʒi, njʊ-] *n* : neurologie *f*

neurosis [nʊ'roːsɪs, njʊ-] *n, pl* **-roses** [-ˌsiːz] : névrose *f*

neurotic[1] [nʊ'rɑtɪk, njʊ-] *adj* : névrosé

neurotic[2] *n* : névrosé *m*, -sée *f*

neuter[1] ['nuːtər, 'njuː-] *vt* : châtrer

neuter[2] *adj* : neutre (en grammaire)

neutral[1] ['nuːtrəl, 'njuː-] *adj* **1** : neutre <neutral territory : territoire neutre> **2** IMPARTIAL : neutre, objectif **3** : neutre (se dit d'une couleur, d'une charge électrique)

neutral[2] *n or* **neutral gear** : point *m* mort, neutre *m Can*

neutralization [ˌnuːtrələ'zeɪʃən, ˌnjuː-] *n* : neutralisation *f*

neutralize ['nuːtrəˌlaɪz, 'njuː-] *vt* **-ized; -izing** : neutraliser

neutrality [nuː'trælət̬i, njuː-] *n* : neutralité *f*

neutron ['nuːˌtrɑn, 'njuː-] *n* : neutron *m*

never ['nɛvər] *adv* **1** : jamais <I never saw her : je ne l'ai jamais vue> **2** (*used for emphasis*) <never fear : ne crains pas> <I never said a word : je n'ai rien dit>

nevermore [ˌnɛvər'mor] *adv* : plus jamais, jamais plus

nevertheless [ˌnɛvərðə'lɛs] *adv* : néanmoins

new[1] ['nuː, 'njuː] *adv* NEWLY : fraîchement <a new-mown lawn : une pelouse fraîchement tondue>

new[2] *adj* **1** RECENT : nouveau, moderne <a new arrival : un nouveau arrivé> <what's new? : quoi de neuf?> **2** : neuf <we bought a new house : nous avons acheté une maison neuve> **3** DIFFERENT, NOVEL : nouveau, original <a new idea : une nouvelle idée> **4 like new** : comme neuf

newborn[1] ['nuːˌbɔrn, 'njuː-] *adj* : nouveau-né

newborn[2] *n, pl* **-born** *or* **-borns** : nouveau-né *m*, nouveau-née *f*

newly ['nuːli, 'njuː-] *adv* : récemment, nouvellement <newly furnished : nouvellement meublé> <newly painted : fraîchement peint>

new moon *n* : nouvelle lune *f*

newness ['nuːnəs, 'njuː-] *n* : nouveauté *f*

news ['nuːz, 'njuːz] *n* : nouvelles *fpl*

newscast ['nuːzˌkæst, 'njuːz-] *n* : journal *m* télévisé

newscaster ['nuːzˌkæstər, 'njuːz-] *n* : présentateur *m*, -trice *f* (d'un journal télévisé)

newsletter ['nuːzˌlɛt̬ər, 'njuːz-] *n* : bulletin *m*

newsman ['nuːzmən, 'njuːz-, -ˌmæn] *n, pl* **-men** [-mən, -ˌmɛn] : journaliste *m*

newspaper ['nuːzˌpeɪpər, 'njuːz-] *n* : journal *m*

newspaperman ['nuːzˌpeɪpərˌmæn, 'njuːz-] *n, pl* **-men** [-mən, -ˌmɛn] : journaliste *m*

newsprint ['nuːzˌprɪnt, 'njuːz-] *n* : papier *m* journal

newsstand ['nuːzˌstænd, 'njuːz-] *n* : kiosque *m* à journaux

newswoman ['nu:z,wʊmən, 'nju:z-] *n, pl* **-women** [-,wɪmən] : journaliste *f*
newsworthy ['nu:z,wərði, 'nju:z-] *adj* : médiatique
newsy ['nu:zi:, 'nju:-] *adj* **newsier; -est** : plein de nouvelles
newt ['nu:t, 'nju:t] *n* : triton *m*
New Testament *n* : Nouveau Testament *m*
New Year *n* : Nouvel An *m*
New Year's Day *n* : jour *m* de l'An
New Zealander [nu:'zi:ləndər, nju:-] *n* : Néo-Zélandais *m*, -daise *f*
next[1] ['nɛkst] *adv* **1** AFTERWARD : ensuite, après <what happened next? : que s'est-il passé ensuite?> **2** NOW : maintenant <what is she doing next? : qu'est-ce qu'elle fait maintenant?> **3** : la prochaine fois <when next we meet : quand nous nous rencontrerons la prochaine fois>
next[2] *adj* **1** : suivante <the next page : la page suivante> **2** FOLLOWING : prochain <the next time : la prochaine fois>
next door *adv* : à côté (de chez nous)
next–door ['nɛkst'dor] *adj* : voisin, d'à côté
next to *prep* **1** : à côté de <next to the bank : à côté de la banque> **2** : à comparer à <next to you I'm wealthy : à comparer à toi je suis riche>
nib ['nɪb] *n* : bec *m* (d'un stylo)
nibble[1] ['nɪbəl] *v* **-bled; -bling** *vt* : grignoter, mordiller — *vi* : grignoter
nibble[2] *n* **1** NIBBLING : mordillement *m* **2** SNACK : collation *f*
Nicaraguan[1] [,nɪkə'rɑgwən] *adj* : nicaraguayen
Nicaraguan[2] *n* : Nicaraguayen *m*, -guayenne *f*
nice ['naɪs] *adj* **nicer; nicest 1** FINICKY : particulier <too nice a palate : un palais trop particulier> **2** PRECISE : subtil, fin **3** PLEASANT : bon <we had a nice time : nous avons eu du bon temps> **4** AGREEABLE : gentil, aimable **5** WELL-BRED : respectable
nicely ['naɪsli] *adv* **1** WELL : bien <he is doing nicely : il se porte bien> **2** KINDLY, POLITELY : gentiment **3** PRECISELY : avec précision
niceness ['naɪsnəs] *n* : gentillesse *f*
nicety ['naɪsət̬i] *n, pl* **-ties 1** SUBTLETY : subtilité *f* **2 niceties** *npl* : raffinements *mpl*
niche ['nɪtʃ] *n* **1** RECESS : niche *f* **2** PLACE : place *f*, voie *f* <she found her niche : elle a trouvé sa place>
nick[1] ['nɪk] *vt* : faire une entaille dans, faire une encoche sur
nick[2] *n* **1** NOTCH : entaille *f*, encoche *f* **2 in the nick of time** : juste à temps
nickel ['nɪkəl] *n* **1** : nickel *m* (métal) **2** : pièce *f* de cinq cents
nickname[1] ['nɪk,neɪm] *vt* : surnommer
nickname[2] *n* : surnom *m*
nicotine ['nɪkə,ti:n] *n* : nicotine *f*
niece ['ni:s] *n* : nièce *f*
Nigerian[1] [naɪ'dʒɪriən] *adj* : nigérian
Nigerian[2] *n* : Nigérian *m*, -rianne *f*
niggardly ['nɪgərdli] *adj* : avare, mesquin
niggling ['nɪgəlɪŋ] *adj* **1** PETTY : insignifiant <niggling details : détails insignifiants> **2** PERSISTENT : persistant <a niggling doubt : un doute persistant>
nigh[1] ['naɪ] *adv* **1** NEARLY : presque **2 to draw nigh** : se rapprocher
nigh[2] *adj* CLOSE, NEAR : proche <the end is nigh : la fin est proche>
night[1] ['naɪt] *adj* : de nuit <night shift : équipe de nuit>
night[2] *n* **1** EVENING : nuit *f*, soir *m* <at night : le soir> <last night : hier soir> <night and day : nuit et jour> **2** : soir *m* <it's his night off : ce soir il est libre> **3** DARKNESS : nuit *f*
nightclothes ['naɪt,klo:ðz, -,klo:z] *npl* : vêtements *mpl* de nuit
nightclub ['naɪt,klʌb] *n* : boîte *f* de nuit
night crawler *n* → **earthworm**
nightfall ['naɪt,fɔl] *n* : tombée *f* de la nuit
nightgown ['naɪt,gaʊn] *n* : chemise *f* de nuit, robe *f* de nuit *Can*
nightingale ['naɪtən,geɪl, 'naɪt̬ɪŋ-] *n* : rossignol *m*
nightly[1] ['naɪtli] *adv* : tous les soirs
nightly[2] *adj* : de tous les soirs
nightmare ['naɪt,mær] *n* : cauchemar *m*
nightmarish ['naɪt,mærɪʃ] *adj* : cauchemardesque
nightshade ['naɪt,ʃeɪd] *n* : morelle *f*
nighttime ['naɪt,taɪm] *n* : nuit *f*
nil[1] ['nɪl] *adj* : nul <visibility is nil : la visibilité est nulle>
nil[2] *n* NOTHING, ZERO : zéro *m*
nimble ['nɪmbəl] *adj* **-bler; -blest 1** AGILE : agile, leste **2** CLEVER : vif, alerte
nimbleness ['nɪmbəlnəs] *n* : agilité *f*
nimbly ['nɪmbli] *adv* : agilement
nincompoop ['nɪnkəm,pu:p, 'nɪŋ-] *n* FOOL : imbécile *mf*; idiot *m*, -diote *f*
nine[1] ['naɪn] *adj* : neuf
nine[2] *n* : neuf *m*
ninepins ['naɪn,pɪnz] *n* : quilles *fpl*
nineteen[1] [naɪn'ti:n] *adj* : dix-neuf
nineteen[2] *n* : dix-neuf *m*
nineteenth[1] [naɪn'ti:nθ] *adj* : dix-neuvième
nineteenth[2] *n* **1** : dix-neuvième *mf* (dans une série) **2** : dix-neuvième *m* (en mathématiques) **3** (*used in dates*) <the nineteenth of May : le dix-neuf mai>
ninetieth[1] ['naɪnt̬iəθ] *adj* : quatre-vingt-dixième
ninetieth[2] *n* **1** : quatre-vingt-dixième *mf* (dans une série) **2** : quatre-vingt-dixième *m* (en mathématiques)
ninety[1] ['naɪnt̬i] *adj* : quatre-vingt-dix, nonante *Bel, Switz*

ninety[2] *n, pl* **-ties** : quatre-vingt-dix *m,* nonante *mf Bel, Switz*
ninny [ˈnɪni] *n, pl* **ninnies** NITWIT : cruche *f fam,* imbécile *mf*
ninth[1] [ˈnaɪnθ] *adj* : neuvième
ninth[2] *n* **1** : neuvième *mf* (dans une série) **2** : neuvième *m* (en mathématiques) **3** (*used in dates*) <the ninth of September : le neuf septembre>
nip[1] [ˈnɪp] *vt* **nipped; nipping 1** BITE : mordre **2** PINCH : pincer **3 to nip in the bud** : tuer dans l'œuf
nip[2] *n* **1** BITE : morsure *f* (d'un animal) **2** PINCH : pincement *m* **3** TANG : piquant *m* **4** SWALLOW : goutte *f* (d'alcool, etc.) **5 there's a nip in the air** : il fait frisquet
nipple [ˈnɪpəl] *n* : mamelon *m*
nippy [ˈnɪpi] *adj* **nippier; -est 1** PUNGENT : piquant, fort **2** CHILLY : frisquet
nit [ˈnɪt] *n* : lente *f*
nitrate [ˈnaɪˌtreɪt] *n* : nitrate *m*
nitric acid [ˈnaɪtrɪk] *n* : acide *m* nitrique
nitrite [ˈnaɪˌtraɪt] *n* : nitrite *m*
nitrogen [ˈnaɪtrədʒən] *n* : azote *m*
nitroglycerin *or* **nitroglycerine** [ˌnaɪtroˈglɪsərən] *n* : nitroglycérine *f*
nitwit [ˈnɪtˌwɪt] *n* : andouille *f fam,* imbécile *mf*
no[1] [ˈnoː] *adv* **1** (*used to express the negative of an alternative choice*) : non <shall we go out or no? : allons-nous sortir ou non?> **2** : pas <he is no better than the others : il n'est pas mieux que les autres> **3** (*used to express negation, dissent, denial or refusal*) : non <no, I'm not going : non, je n'y vais pas> **4** (*used as an interjection of surprise or doubt*) : mais <no, you don't say! : mais, ce n'est pas possible!> **5** : plus <we can no longer pretend : nous ne pouvons plus faire semblant>
no[2] *adj* **1** : pas de, point de <he has no money : il n'a pas d'argent> **2** (*used to express an order or command*) <no parking : stationnement interdit> **3 to be no** : ne pas être <I'm no liar : je ne suis pas menteur>
no[3] *n, pl* **noes** *or* **nos** [ˈnoːz] **1** REFUSAL : non *m* **2** : non *m,* vote *m* négatif <ayes and noes : les oui et les non>
nobility [noˈbɪləṭi] *n* : noblesse *f*
noble [ˈnobəl] *adj* **-bler; -blest 1** EMINENT : noble, distingué **2** ARISTOCRATIC : noble, aristocratique **3** STATELY : majestueux <a noble building : un édifice majestueux>
nobleman [ˈnoːbəlmən] *n* : noble *m,* aristocrate *m*
nobleness [ˈnoːbəlnəs] *n* : noblesse *f*
noblewoman [ˈnoːbəlˌwʊmən] *n, pl* **-women** [-ˌwɪmən] : noble *f,* aristocrate *f*
nobody[1] [ˈnoːbədi, -ˌbɑdi] *n, pl* **-bodies** : moins que rien *mf,* zéro *m* <he's a nobody : il est complètement insignifiant>
nobody[2] *pron* : personne <nobody waited for me : personne ne m'a attendu>
nocturnal [nɑkˈtərnəl] *adj* : nocturne
nocturne [ˈnɑkˌtərn] *n* : nocturne *m*
nod[1] [ˈnɑd] *v* **nodded; nodding** *vt* : incliner (la tête), faire un signe de la tête <we nodded in agreement : nous avons fait un signe d'assentiment> — *vi* **to nod off** : s'endormir
nod[2] *n* : signe *m* de la tête, hochement *m* de la tête
node [ˈnoːd] *n* : nœud *m* (d'une plante)
nodule [ˈnɑˌdʒuːl] *n* : nodule *m*
noel [noˈɛl] *n* **1** CAROL : chant *m* de Noël **2 Noel** CHRISTMAS : Noël *m*
noes → **no**
noise[1] [ˈnɔɪz] *vt* **noised; noising** : ébruiter
noise[2] *n* : bruit *m,* son *m*
noiseless [ˈnɔɪzləs] *adj* : silencieux — **noiselessly** *adv*
noisemaker [ˈnɔɪzˌmeɪkər] *n* : crécelle *f*
noisily [ˈnɔɪzəli] *adv* : bruyamment
noisiness [ˈnɔɪzinəs] *n* : bruit *m*
noisome [ˈnɔɪsɪəm] *adj* **1** NOXIOUS : nocif **2** OFFENSIVE : nauséabond <a noisome stench : une odeur nauséabonde>
noisy [ˈnɔɪzi] *adj* **noisier; -est** : bruyant
nomad[1] [ˈnoːˌmæd] *adj* → **nomadic**
nomad[2] *n* : nomade *mf*
nomadic [noˈmædɪk] *adj* : nomade
nomenclature [ˈnoːmənˌkleɪtʃər] *n* : nomenclature *f*
nominal [ˈnɑmənəl] *adj* **1** : de nom <the nominal president : président que de nom> **2** TRIFLING : insignifiant
nominally [ˈnɑmənəli] *adv* : nominalement
nominate [ˈnɑməˌneɪt] *vt* **-nated; -nating 1** PROPOSE : proposer (comme candidat) **2** APPOINT : nommer, désigner
nomination [ˌnɑməˈneɪʃən] *n* : nomination *f*
nominative[1] [ˈnɑmənəṭɪv] *adj* : nominatif
nominative[2] *n or* **nominative case** : nominatif *m*
nominee [ˌnɑməˈniː] *n* : candidat *m,* -date *f*
nonaddictive [ˌnɑnəˈdɪktɪv] *adj* : qui ne crée pas de dépendance
nonalcoholic [ˌnɑnˌælkəˈhɔlɪk] *adj* : non alcoolisé
nonaligned [ˌnɑnəˈlaɪnd] *adj* : non aligné
nonbeliever [ˌnɑnbəˈliːvər] *n* : noncroyant *m,* -croyante *f*
nonbreakable [ˌnɑnˈbreɪkəbəl] *adj* : incassable
nonce [ˈnɑnts] *n* **for the nonce** : pour l'instant
nonchalance [ˌnɑnʃəˈlɑnts] *n* : nonchalance *f*

nonchalant [ˌnɑnʃəˈlɑnt] *adj* : nonchalant
nonchalantly [ˌnɑnʃəˈlɑntli] *adv* : nonchalamment
noncombatant *n* : non-combattant *m*, -tante *f*
noncombustible *adj* : incombustible
noncommissioned officer [ˌnɑnkəˈmɪʃənd] *n* : sous-officier *m*
noncommittal [ˌnɑnkəˈmɪṭəl] *adj* : évasif
nonconductor [ˌnɑnkənˈdʌktər] *n* : mauvais conducteur *m*
nonconformist [ˌnɑnkənˈfɔrmɪst] *n* : non-conformiste *mf*
nonconformity [ˌnɑnkənˈfɔrməṭi] *n* : non-conformité *f*
nondenominational [ˌnɑndɪˌnɑməˈneɪʃənəl] *adj* : œcuménique
nondescript [ˌnɑndɪˈskrɪpt] *adj* : indéfinissable, quelconque
none[1] [ˈnʌn] *adv* **1 none too** : loin de <it's none too clear : c'est loin d'être clair> <they arrived none too soon : ils sont arrivés juste à temps> **2 to be none the worse** : n'en être pas plus mal
none[2] *pron* : aucun, aucune <none of them went : aucun d'entre eux n'y est allé>
nonentity [ˌnɑnˈɛntəṭi] *n, pl* **-ties** : être *m* insignifiant, nullité *f*
nonessential [ˌnɑnɪˈsɛntʃəl] *adj* : accessoire, non essentiel
nonetheless [ˌnʌnðəˈlɛs] *adv* NEVERTHELESS : néanmoins
nonexistence [ˌnɑnɪgˈzɪstənts] *n* : non-existence *f* — **nonexistent** [-stənt] *adj*
nonfat [ˌnɑnˈfæt] *adj* : sans matières grasses
nonfiction [ˌnɑnˈfɪkʃən] *n* : œuvres *fpl* non fictionnelles
nonflammable [ˌnɑnˈflæməbəl] *adj* : ininflammable
nonpareil[1] [ˌnɑnpəˈrɛl] *adj* : inégalé, sans égal
nonpareil[2] *n* **1** : personne *f* sans égale **2** : petit disque *m* en chocolat recouvert de sucre
nonpartisan [ˌnɑnˈpɑrṭəzən, -sən] *adj* : impartial, neutre
nonperson [ˌnɑnˈpərsən] *n* : personne *f* non reconnue
nonplus [ˌnɑnˈplʌs] *vt* **-plussed; -plussing** DISCONCERT : déconcerter, dérouter
nonproductive [ˌnɑnprəˈdʌktɪv] *adj* : improductif
nonprofit [ˌnɑnˈprɑfət] *adj* : à but non lucratif
nonproliferation [ˌnɑnprəˌlɪfəˈreɪʃən] *n* : non-prolifération *f*
nonrefundable [ˌnɑnriˈfəndəbəl] *adj* : non remboursable
nonrenewable [ˌnɑnriˈnuːəbəl, -ˈnjuː-] *adj* : non renouvelable
nonresident [ˌnɑnˈrɛzədənt, -ˌdɛnt] *n* : non-résident *m*, -dente *f*
nonscheduled [ˌnɑnˈskɛˌdʒuːld] *adj* : irrégulier <nonscheduled flights : vols irréguliers>
nonsectarian [ˌnɑnˌsɛkˈtæriən] *adj* : non sectaire
nonsense [ˈnɑnˌsɛnts, -sənts] *n* : absurdités *fpl*, sottises *fpl*
nonsensical [nɑnˈsɛntsɪkəl] *adj* : absurde, insensé — **nonsensically** [-kli] *adv*
nonsmoker [ˌnɑnˈsmoːkər] *n* : non-fumeur *m*, -meuse *f*
nonstandard [ˌnɑnˈstændərd] *adj* : non standard
nonstick [ˌnɑnˈstɪk] *adj* : antiadhésif <nonstick pan : poêle antiadhésive>
nonstop [ˌnɑnˈstɑp] *adj* **1** : sans arrêt <to drive nonstop : rouler sans arrêt> **2** : direct, sans escale <nonstop flight : vol direct>
nonsupport [ˌnɑnsəˈpɔrt] *n* : défaut *m* de versement de pension alimentaire
nontaxable [ˌnɑnˈtæksəbəl] *adj* : non imposable
nonviolence [ˌnɑnˈvaɪlənts, -ˈvaɪə-] *n* : non-violence *f*
nonviolent [ˌnɑnˈvaɪlənt, -ˈvaɪə-] *adj* : non violent
noodle [ˈnuːdəl] *n* : nouille *f*
nook [ˈnʊk] *n* : coin *m*, recoin *m* <every nook and cranny : tous les coins et les recoins>
noon[1] [ˈnuːn] *adj* : de midi
noon[2] *n* : midi *m*
noonday [ˈnuːnˌdeɪ] → **midday, noon**
no one *pron* : personne *f*
noontime [ˈnuːnˌtaɪm] → **noon**
noose [ˈnuːs] *n* : nœud *m* coulant
nor [ˈnɔr] *conj* : ni <neither young nor old : ni jeune ni vieux> <he can't swim, nor can I : il ne sait pas nager, moi non plus>
norm [ˈnɔrm] *n* : norme *f*
normal [ˈnɔrməl] *adj* : normal — **normally** *adv*
normalcy [ˈnɔrməlsi] → **normality**
normality [nɔrˈmæləṭi] *n* : normalité *f*
normalization [ˌnɔrmələˈzeʃən] *n* : normalisation *f*
normalize [ˈnɔrməˌlaɪz] *vt* **-ized; -izing** : normaliser
north[1] [ˈnɔrθ] *adv* : au nord, vers le nord
north[2] *adj* : nord <the north coast : la côte nord>
north[3] *n* **1** : nord *m* **2 the North** : le Nord
North American[1] *adj* : nord-américain
North American[2] *n* : Nord-Américain *m*, -caine *f*
northbound [ˈnɔrθˌbaʊnd] *adj* : en direction du nord
northeast[1] [nɔrθˈiːst] *adv* : au nord-est, vers le nord-est
northeast[2] *adj* : de nord-est <northeast winds : vents de nord-est>
northeast[3] *n* : nord-est *m*

northeasterly[1] [nɔrθ'iːstərli] *adv* : vers le nord-est

northeasterly[2] *adj* : du nord-est

northeastern [nɔrθ'iːstərn] *adj* : nord-est, du nord-est

northerly[1] ['nɔrðərli] *adv* : vers le nord

northerly[2] *adj* : du nord

northern ['nɔrðərn] *adj* : nord, du nord <northern Canada : le nord du Canada>

Northerner ['nɔrðərnər] *n* : natif *m* du Nord, native *f* du Nord

northern lights → aurora borealis

North Pole *n* : pôle *m* Nord

North Star *n* : étoile *f* polaire

northward[1] ['nɔrθwərd] *adv* : vers le nord

northward[2] *adj* : du côté nord

northwest[1] [nɔrθ'wɛst] *adv* : au nord-ouest, vers le nord-ouest

northwest[2] *adj* : de nord-ouest <northwest winds : vents de nord-ouest>

northwest[3] *n* : nord-ouest *m*

northwesterly[1] [nɔrθ'wɛstərli] *adv* : vers le nord-ouest

northwesterly[2] *adj* : du nord-ouest

northwestern [nɔrθ'wɛstərn] *adj* : nord-ouest, du nord-ouest

Norwegian[1] [nɔr'wiːdʒən] *adj* : norvégien

Norwegian[2] *n* **1** : Norvégien *m*, -gienne *f* **2** : norvégien *m* (langue)

nose[1] ['noːz] *v* **nosed; nosing** *vt* **1** SMELL : flairer, sentir **2** : pousser avec le museau <the dog nosed the door open : le chien a ouvert la porte avec son museau> **3 to nose in** : avancer avec précaution <the ship nosed into its berth : le bateau avançait prudemment dans son emplacement> **—** *vi* PRY : fouiner *fam* <stop nosing in my business! : arrête de fouiner dans mes affaires!>

nose[2] *n* **1** : nez *m* (d'une personne), museau *m* (d'un animal) **2** : flair *m*, odorat *m* <a dog with a good nose : un chien avec du flair> **3** FRONT : devant *m*, nez *m* (d'un avion, etc.) **4** INSTINCT : flair *m*, instinct *m* <to have a keen nose for politics : avoir du flair politique> **5 to blow one's nose** : se moucher

nosebleed ['noːzˌbliːd] *n* : saignement *m* de nez

nosedive ['noːzˌdaɪv] *n* **1** : piqué *m* (d'un avion) **2** DROP : chute *f* (des prix, etc.)

nose–dive *vi* **-dived; -diving 1** : piquer (se dit d'un avion) **2** : chuter *fam* (se dit des prix, etc.)

nostalgia [nɑ'stældʒə, nə-] *n* : nostalgie *f* **— nostalgic** [-dʒɪk] *adj*

nostril ['nɑstrəl] *n* : narine *f* (d'une personne), naseau *m* (d'un animal)

nostrum ['nɑstrəm] *n* : panacée *f*

nosy *or* **nosey** ['noːzi] *adj* **nosier; -est** : fureteur

not ['nɑt] *adv* **1** (*used to form a negative*) : ne . . . pas <the boys are not here : les garçons ne sont pas ici> **2** (*used to replace a negative clause*) : pas <I don't see why not : je ne vois pas pourquoi> **3** : non <I hope not : j'espère que non>

notable[1] ['noːt̬əbəl] *adj* **1** NOTEWORTHY : notable, remarquable **2** PROMINENT : notable, important

notable[2] *n* : notable *m*

notably ['noːt̬əbli] *adv* **1** VERY : très <notably impressed : très impressionné> **2** ESPECIALLY : notamment

notarize ['noːt̬əˌraɪz] *vt* **-rized; -rizing** : certifier

notary public ['noːt̬əri] *n, pl* **notaries public** *or* **notary publics** : notaire *m*

notation [no'teɪʃən] *n* **1** NOTE : note *f*, notation *f* **2** : notation *f* (en musique)

notch[1] ['nɑtʃ] *vt* : entailler, encocher

notch[2] *n* : entaille *f*, encoche *f*, coche *f*

note[1] ['noːt] *vt* **noted; noting 1** NOTICE : noter, remarquer, observer **2** *or* **to note down** : noter, inscrire

note[2] *n* **1** : note *f* (de musique) **2** REMINDER : note *f*, avis *m* **3** LETTER : billet *m*, mot *m* **4** DISTINCTION : renom *m* <an artist of note : un artiste de renom> **5 to take note of** : prendre note de

notebook ['noːtˌbʊk] *n* : carnet *m*, calepin *m*

noted ['noːt̬əd] *adj* FAMOUS : éminent, célèbre

notepad ['noːtˌpæd] *n* : bloc-notes *n*, tablette *f* *Can*

noteworthy ['noːtˌwərði] *adj* : notable, remarquable

nothing[1] ['nʌθɪŋ] *adv* **1 nothing daunted** : pas le moindrement découragé **2 nothing like** : pas du tout

nothing[2] *n* **1** TRIFLE : rien *m* **2** ZERO : zéro *m* **3** : nullité *f*, zéro *m* <he feels like a nothing : il se sent comme un zéro> **4** NOTHINGNESS : néant *m*

nothing[3] *pron* : rien <there's nothing in the box : il n'y a rien dans la boîte> <it means nothing to me : ça m'est égal>

nothingness ['nʌθɪŋnəs] *n* : néant *m*

notice[1] *vt* **-ticed; -ticing 1** OBSERVE : s'apercevoir de, remarquer **2 to take notice of** : faire attention à

notice[2] ['noːt̬ɪs] *n* **1** ANNOUNCEMENT : avis *m*, annonce *f* **2** DISMISSAL : congé *m* **3** RESIGNATION : démission *f* **4 to give notice** : donner un préavis

noticeable ['noːt̬ɪsəbəl] *adj* : visible, perceptible

notification [ˌnoːt̬əfə'keɪʃən] *n* : avis *m*, notification *f*

notify ['noːt̬əˌfaɪ] *vt* **-fied; -fying** : notifier, aviser, avertir

notion ['noːʃən] *n* **1** IDEA : notion *f*, concept *m* **2** WHIM : envie *f*, idée *f* <a sudden notion : une envie soudaine> **3 notions** *npl* : mercerie *f*

notoriety [ˌnoːt̬ə'raɪət̬i] *n, pl* **-ties** : notoriété *f*

notorious [no'to:riəs] *adj* : notoire — **notoriously** *adv*
notwithstanding[1] [ˌnɑtwɪθ'stændɪŋ, -wɪð-] *adv* NEVERTHELESS : nonobstant, néanmoins
notwithstanding[2] *conj* : quoique
notwithstanding[3] *prep* : en dépit de, malgré
nougat ['nu:gət] *n* : nougat *m*
nought ['nɔt, 'nɑt] → **naught**
noun ['naʊn] *n* : nom *m,* substantif *m*
nourish ['nərɪʃ] *vt* : nourrir
nourishing ['nərɪʃɪŋ] *adj* : nourrissant
nourishment ['nərɪʃmənt] *n* : nourriture *f,* alimentation *f*
novel[1] ['nɑvəl] *adj* : nouveau, original
novel[2] *n* : roman *m*
novelist ['nɑvəlɪst] *n* : romancier *m,* -cière *f*
novelty ['nɑvəlṭi] *n, pl* **-ties 1** : nouveauté *f* **2 novelties** *npl* TRINKETS : bibelots *mpl,* babioles *fpl*
November [no'vɛmbər] *n* : novembre *m*
novice ['nɑvɪs] *n* : novice *mf;* débutant *m,* -tante *f*
now[1] ['naʊ] *adv* **1** : maintenant, à présent <now what are we going to do? : qu'allons-nous faire maintenant?> **2** PRESENTLY : en ce moment, présentement <he is busy now : il est occupé en ce moment> **3** FORTHWITH : maintenant <you can come in now : vous pouvez rentrer maintenant> **4** (*used to express a command, a request, or an admonition*) <now, hear this : écoutez bien> **5** (*used to indicate a transition*) : or <now, his point of view seems illogical : or, son point de vue semble illogique> **6** SOMETIMES : tantôt <now one and now another : tantôt l'un et tantôt l'autre> **7 now and then** : de temps en temps
now[2] *n* **1** (*indicating the present time*) <up until now : jusqu'à maintenant, jusqu'à présent> **2 the now** : le présent
now[3] *conj* **now that** : maintenant que <now that you're here we can begin : maintenant que tu es ici, nous pouvons commencer>
nowadays ['naʊəˌdeɪz] *adv* : de nos jours
nowhere ['no:ˌhwɛr] *adv* : nulle part
noxious ['nɑkʃəs] *adj* : nocif
nozzle ['nɑzəl] *n* : ajutage *m* (d'un tuyau d'arrosage), lance *f* (à eau)
nuance ['nu:ˌɑnts, 'nju:-] *n* : nuance *f*
nub ['nʌb] *n* **1** KNOB, LUMP : protubérance *f* **2** GIST : cœur *m,* fond *m*
nubile ['nu:ˌbaɪl, 'nju:-, -bəl] *adj* : nubile
nuclear ['nu:kliər, 'nju:-] *adj* : nucléaire
nucleus ['nu:kliəs, 'nju:-] *n, pl* **-clei** [-kliˌaɪ] : noyau *m*
nude[1] ['nu:d, 'nju:d] *adj* **nuder; nudest** NAKED : nu
nude[2] *n* : nu *m*
nudge[1] ['nʌdʒ] *vt* **nudged; nudging** : donner un coup de coude à
nudge[2] *n* : coup *m* de coude
nudism ['nu:ˌdɪzəm, 'nju:-] *n* : nudisme *m*
nudist ['nu:dɪst, 'nju:-] *n* : nudiste *mf*
nudity ['nu:dəṭi, 'nju:-] *n* : nudité *f*
nugget ['nʌgət] *n* : pépite *f* (d'or, etc.)
nuisance ['nu:sənts, 'nju:-] *n* **1** ANNOYANCE : embêtement *m,* désagrément *m* **2** : casse-pieds *mf fam,* peste *f* <he's a real nuisance : il est vraiment casse-pieds>
null ['nʌl] *adj* : nul <null and void : nul et non avenu>
nullify ['nʌləˌfaɪ] *vt* **-fied; -fying** : annuler, invalider
numb[1] ['nʌm] *vt* : engourdir, transir (par le froid)
numb[2] *adj* : engourdi, transi, paralysé <numb with cold : transi par le froid> <numb with fear : paralysé par la peur>
number[1] ['nʌmbər] *vt* **1** COUNT : compter, énumérer **2** : numéroter (des pages) **3** TOTAL : compter **4 to number among** INCLUDE : compter parmi
number[2] *n* **1** : nombre *m,* numéro *m* <the number 35 : le nombre 35> **2** : chiffre *m* <add the numbers : additionne les chiffres> **3 a number of** : un certain nombre de, plusieurs, divers
numberless ['nʌmbərləs] *adj* : innombrable
numbness ['nʌmnəs] *n* : engourdissement *m*
numeral ['nu:mərəl, 'nju:-] *n* : nombre *m,* chiffre *m* <Roman numeral : chiffre romain>
numerator ['numəˌreɪṭər, 'nju:-] *n* : numérateur *m*
numerical [nʊ'mɛrɪkəl, nyʊ-] *or* **numeric** [-'mɛrɪk] *adj* : numérique — **numerically** [-kli] *adv*
numerous ['nu:mərəs, 'nju:-] *adj* : nombreux
numismatics [ˌnu:məz'mæṭɪks, ˌnju:-] *n* : numismatique *f*
numskull ['nʌmˌskʌl] *n* : cruche *f fam,* imbécile *mf*
nun ['nʌn] *n* : religieuse *f*
nuptial ['nʌpʃəl] *adj* : nuptial
nuptials ['nʌpʃəlz] *npl* WEDDING : noces *fpl*
nurse[1] ['nərs] *v* **nursed; nursing** *vt* **1** BREAST-FEED : allaiter **2** : soigner (un malade) **3 to nurse a grudge** : entretenir une rancune — *vi* SUCKLE : téter
nurse[2] *n* : infirmier *m,* -mière *f;* garde-malade *mf*
nursery ['nərsəri] *n, pl* **-eries 1** : crèche *f France,* garderie *f Can* **2** : pépinière *f* (pour les plantes)
nursing home *n* : maison *f* de retraite, centre *m* d'accueil *Can*

nurture[1] [ˈnərtʃər] *vt* **-tured; -turing 1** FEED : nourrir **2** EDUCATE : élever, éduquer **3** FOSTER : nourrir, entretenir (des espoirs, des plans, etc.)
nurture[2] *n* **1** UPBRINGING : éducation *f* **2** NOURISHMENT : nourriture *f*
nut [ˈnʌt] *n* **1** : noix *f* <Brazil nut : noix du Brésil> **2** : écrou *m* <nuts and bolts : des écrous et des boulons> **3** LUNATIC : fou *m*, folle *f*; cinglé *mf fam* **4** ENTHUSIAST : mordu *m*, -due *f fam;* passionné *m*, -née *f* <a golf nut : un mordu du golf>
nutcracker [ˈnʌtˌkrækər] *n* : casse-noix *m*, casse-noisettes *m*
nuthatch [ˈnʌtˌhætʃ] *n* : sittelle *f*
nutmeg [ˈnʌtˌmɛg] *n* : muscade *f*
nutrient [ˈnuːtriənt, ˈnjuː-] *n* : substance *f* nutritive
nutriment [ˈnuːtrəmənt, ˈnjuː-] *n* : nourriture *f*
nutrition [nʊˈtrɪʃən, njʊ-] *n* : nutrition *f*, alimentation *f*
nutritional [nʊˈtrɪʃənəl, njʊ-] *adj* : nutritif
nutritious [nʊˈtrɪʃəs, njʊ-] *adj* : nourrissant, nutritif
nuts [ˈnʌts] *adj* **1** FANATICAL : fanatique **2** CRAZY : fou, cinglé *fam*
nutshell [ˈnʌtˌʃɛl] *n* : coquille *f* de noix
nutty [ˈnʌt̬i] *adj* **nuttier; -est** : timbré *fam*, toqué *fam*
nuzzle [ˈnʌzəl] *v* **-zled; -zling** *vt* : frotter son nez contre — *vi* NESTLE : se blottir
nylon [ˈnaɪˌlɑn] *n* **1** : nylon *m* **2 nylons** *npl* : bas *mpl* de nylon
nymph [ˈnɪmpf] *n* : nymphe *f*

O

o [ˈoː] *n, pl* **o's** *or* **os** [ˈoːz] **1** : o *m*, quinzième lettre de l'alphabet **2** ZERO : zéro *m*
O [ˈoː] → **oh**
oaf [ˈoːf] *n* : balourd *m*, -lourde *f*
oafish [ˈoːfɪʃ] *adj* : balourd, lourdaud
oak [ˈoːk] *n, pl* **oaks** *or* **oak** : chêne *m*
oaken [ˈoːkən] *adj* : de chêne, en chêne
oar [ˈor] *n* : rame *f*, aviron *m*
oarlock [ˈorˌlɑk] *n* : tolet *m*
oasis [oˈeɪsɪs] *n, pl* **oases** [-ˌsiːz] : oasis *f*
oat [ˈoːt] *n* : avoine *f*
oath [ˈoːθ] *n, pl* **oaths** [ˈoːðz, ˈoːθs] **1** : serment *m* <to take the oath : prêter serment> **2** SWEARWORD : juron *m*
oatmeal [ˈoːtˌmiːl] *n* : farine *f* d'avoine, gruau *m Can*
obdurate [ˈɑbdʊrət, -djʊ-] *adj* : opiniâtre
obedience [oˈbiːdiənts] *n* : obéissance *f*
obedient [oˈbiːdiənt] *adj* : obéissant
obediently [oˈbiːdiəntli] *adv* : avec obéissance, docilement
obelisk [ˈɑbəˌlɪsk] *n* : obélisque *m*
obese [oˈbiːs] *adj* : obèse
obesity [oˈbiːsət̬i] *n* : obésité *f*
obey [oˈbeɪ] *v* **obeyed; obeying** *vt* : obéir à <to obey the law : obéir à la loi> — *vi* : obéir
obfuscate [ˈɑbfəˌskeɪt] *vt* **-cated; -cating** : obscurcir
obituary [əˈbɪtʃʊˌɛri] *n, pl* **-aries** : nécrologie *f*
object[1] [əbˈdʒɛkt] *vt* : objecter — *vi* : protester, s'opposer, soulever des objections
object[2] [ˈɑbdʒɪkt] *n* **1** : objet *m* **2** OBJECTIVE, PURPOSE : objectif *m*, but *m* **3** : complément *m* d'objet (en grammaire) <direct object : complément d'objet direct>
objection [əbˈdʒɛkʃən] *n* : objection *f*
objectionable [əbˈdʒɛkʃənəbəl] *adj* : désagréable, offensif — **objectionably** [-bli] *adv*
objective[1] [əbˈdʒɛktɪv] *adj* : objectif
objective[2] *n* **1** AIM : objectif *m*, but *m* **2** *or* **objective case** : accusatif *m*
objectively [əbˈdʒɛktɪvli] *adv* : objectivement
objectivity [ˌɑbˌdʒɛkˈtɪvət̬i] *n, pl* **-ties** : objectivité *f*
obligate [ˈɑbləˌgeɪt] *vt* **-gated; -gating** : contraindre, obliger
obligation [ˌɑbləˈgeɪʃən] *n* : obligation *f*
obligatory [əˈblɪgəˌtori] *adj* : obligatoire
oblige [əˈblaɪdʒ] *vt* **obliged; obliging 1** COMPEL : obliger **2 to oblige s.o.** : rendre service à qqn **3 to be obliged to s.o.** : savoir gré à qqn
obliging [əˈblaɪdʒɪŋ] *adj* : obligeant — **obligingly** *adv*
oblique [oˈbliːk] *adj* **1** SLANTING : oblique **2** INDIRECT : indirect — **obliquely** *adv*
obliterate [əˈblɪt̬əˌreɪt] *vt* **-ated; -ating** : effacer, détruire
obliteration [əˌblɪt̬əˈreɪʃən] *n* : effacement *m*
oblivion [əˈblɪviən] *n* : oubli *m*
oblivious [əˈblɪviəs] *adj* : inconscient — **obliviously** *adv*
oblong[1] [ˈɑˌblɔŋ] *adj* : oblong
oblong[2] *n* : rectangle *m*
obnoxious [ɑbˈnɑkʃəs, əb-] *adj* : odieux, exécrable — **obnoxiously** *adv*
oboe [ˈoːˌboː] *n* : hautbois *m*
oboist [ˈoˌboɪst] *n* : hautboïste *mf*
obscene [ɑbˈsiːn, əb-] *adj* : obscène
obscenely [ɑbˈsiːnli, əb-] *adv* : d'une manière obscène
obscenity [ɑbˈsɛnət̬i, əb-] *n, pl* **-ties** : obscénité *f*

obscure[1] [ɑb'skjʊr, əb-] *vt* **-scured; -scuring 1** CLOUD, DIM : obscurcir **2** HIDE : cacher

obscure[2] *adj* **1** DIM : obscur **2** UNKNOWN : inconnu **3** VAGUE : vague

obscurely [ɑb'skjʊrli, əb-] *adv* : obscurément

obscurity [ɑb'skjʊrət̬i, əb-] *n, pl* **-ties** : obscurité *f*

obsequious [əb'si:kwiəs] *adj* : obséquieux — **obsequiously** *adv*

observable [əb'zərvəbəl] *adj* : visible, perceptible

observance [əb'zərvənts] *n* **1** OBSERVATION : observance *f*, observation *f* **2** PRACTICE : observance *f* (en religion, etc.)

observant [əb'zərvənt] *adj* : observateur

observation [ˌɑbsər'veɪʃən, -zər-] *n* : observation *f*

observatory [əb'zərvəˌtori] *n, pl* **-ries** : observatoire *m*

observe [əb'zərv] *v* **-served; -serving** *vt* **1** OBEY : respecter, observer <observe the rules : observez les règles> **2** CELEBRATE : observer <to observe the sabbath : observer le sabbat> **3** NOTICE : observer, remarquer **4** REMARK : dire, faire remarquer — *vi* LOOK : regarder

obsess [əb'sɛs] *vt* : obséder

obsession [ɑb'sɛʃən, əb-] *n* : obsession *f*

obsessive [ɑb'sɛsɪv, əb-] *adj* : obsessionnel (se dit des personnes), obsédant (se dit des pensées, etc.)

obsessively [ɑb'sɛsɪvli, əb-] *adv* : d'une manière obsessionnelle

obsolescence [ˌɑbsə'lɛsənts] *n* : obsolescence *f* — **obsolescent** [-'lɛsənt] *adj*

obsolete [ˌɑbsə'li:t, 'ɑbsəˌ-] *adj* : obsolète, démodé

obstacle ['ɑbstɪkəl] *n* : obstacle *m*

obstetric [əb'stɛtrɪk] *or* **obstetrical** [-trɪkəl] *adj* : obstétrical

obstetrician [ˌɑbstə'trɪʃən] *n* : obstétricien *m*, -cienne *f*

obstetrics [əb'stɛtrɪks] *ns & pl* : obstétrique *f*

obstinacy ['ɑbstənəsi] *n, pl* **-cies** : obstination *f*, entêtement *m*

obstinate ['ɑbstənət] *adj* : obstiné, entêté

obstinately ['ɑbstənətli] *adv* : obstinément, avec acharnement

obstreperous [əb'strɛpərəs] *adj* : tapageur, turbulent

obstruct [əb'strʌkt] *vt* : obstruer, bloquer

obstruction [əb'strʌkʃən] *n* : obstruction *f*, obstacle *m*

obstructive [əb'strəktɪv] *adj* : obstructionniste

obtain [əb'teɪn] *vt* : obtenir, se procurer — *vi* PREVAIL : régner, avoir cours

obtainable [əb'teɪnəbəl] *adj* : qu'on peut obtenir, disponible

obtrude [əb'tru:d] *v* **-truded; -truding** *vt* **1** EXTRUDE : extruder, faire sortir **2** IMPOSE : imposer — *vi* INTRUDE : s'imposer

obtrusive [əb'tru:sɪv] *adj* **1** BOTHERSOME, MEDDLESOME : importun **2** PROTRUDING : protubérant

obtuse [ɑb'tu:s, əb-, -'tju:s] *adj* **1** DULL, STUPID : obtus **2** INDISTINCT : vague, indistinct **3 obtuse angle** : angle *m* obtus

obviate ['ɑbviˌeɪt] *vt* **-ated; -ating** : obvier à, eviter

obvious ['ɑbviəs] *adj* : évident

obviously ['ɑbviəsli] *adv* **1** CLEARLY : manifestement **2** OF COURSE : évidemment, bien sûr

occasion[1] [ə'keɪʒən] *vt* : occasionner, provoquer, entraîner

occasion[2] *n* **1** INSTANCE : occasion *f* <on one occasion : une fois> **2** OPPORTUNITY : occasion *f* <should the occasion arise : si l'occasion se présente> **3** CAUSE : raison *f*, motif *m* **4** EVENT : événement *m* **5 on ~** : de temps en temps

occasional [ə'keɪʒənəl] *adj* : occasionnel — **occasionally** *adv*

occidental [ˌɑksə'dɛntəl] *adj* : occidental

occult[1] [ə'kʌlt, 'ɑˌkʌlt] *adj* : occulte

occult[2] *n* : sciences *fpl* occultes

occupancy ['ɑkjəpəntsi] *n, pl* **-cies** : occupation *f*

occupant ['ɑkjəpənt] *n* **1** : occupant *m*, -pante *f*; habitant *m*, -tante *f* **2** TENANT : locataire *mf*

occupation [ˌɑkjə'peɪʃən] *n* **1** OCCUPYING : occupation *f* **2** VOCATION : profession *f*, métier *m*

occupational [ˌɑkjə'peɪʃənəl] *adj* : professionnel, du métier <occupational hazard : risque du métier>

occupy ['ɑkjəˌpaɪ] *vt* **-pied; -pying 1** : occuper **2 to occupy oneself with** : s'occuper de

occur [ə'kər] *vi* **occurred; occurring 1** HAPPEN : avoir lieu, se produire, arriver **2** APPEAR, EXIST : se trouver, se présenter **3** : venir à l'esprit <it occurred to him that . . . : il lui est venu à l'esprit que . . . >

occurrence [ə'kərənts] *n* **1** EVENT : événement *m*, occurrence *f* **2** INSTANCE, PRESENCE : cas *m*, apparition *f* (d'une maladie, etc.)

ocean ['o:ʃən] *n* : océan *m*

oceanic [ˌo:ʃi'ænɪk] *adj* : océanique

oceanography [ˌo:ʃə'nɑgrəfi] *n* : océanographie *f* — **oceanographic** [-nə'græfɪk] *adj*

ocelot ['ɑsəˌlɑt, 'o:-] *n* : ocelot *m*

ocher *or* **ochre** ['o:kər] *n* : ocre *mf*

o'clock [ə'klɑk] *adv* (*used in telling time*) <it's ten o'clock : il est dix heures> <at six o'clock : à six heures>

octagon [ˈɑktəˌgɑn] *n* : octogone *m* — **octagonal** [ɑkˈtægənəl] *adj*

octave [ˈɑktɪv] *n* : octave *f*

October [ɑkˈtoːbər] *n* : octobre *m*

octopus [ˈɑktəˌpʊs, -pəs] *n, pl* **-puses** *or* **-pi** [-ˌpaɪ] : pieuvre *f,* poulpe *m*

ocular [ˈɑkjələr] *adj* : oculaire

oculist [ˈɑkjəlɪst] *n* **1** OPHTHALMOLOGIST : ophtalmologiste *mf,* oculiste *mf* **2** OPTOMETRIST : optométriste *mf*

odd [ˈɑd] *adj* **1** : seul, dépareillé <an odd sock : une chaussette dépareillée> **2** UNEVEN : impair <odd numbers : nombres impairs> **3** : et quelques <a hundred odd dollars : cent dollars et quelques> <forty odd years ago : il y a une quarantaine d'années> **4** STRANGE : étrange, bizarre **5** OCCASIONAL : divers <odd jobs : petits boulots>

oddity [ˈɑdət̬i] *n, pl* **-ties** : étrangeté *f,* bizarrerie *f*

oddly [ˈɑdli] *adv* : étrangement

oddness [ˈɑdnəs] *n* : étrangeté *f*

odds [ˈɑdz] *npl* **1** CHANCES : chances *fpl* **2** RATIO : cote *f* <the odds are eight to five against : la cote est de huit contre cinq> **3 to be at odds** : être en conflit

ode [ˈoːd] *n* : ode *f*

odious [ˈoːdiəs] *adj* : odieux — **odiously** *adv*

odor *or Brit* **odour** [ˈoːdər] *n* : odeur *f*

odorless *or Brit* **odourless** [ˈoːdərləs] *adj* : inodore

odorous [ˈoːdərəs] *adj* : odorant

odour *Brit* → **odor**

odyssey [ˈɑdəsi] *n, pl* **-seys** : odyssée *f*

o'er [ˈor] → **over**

of [ˈʌv, ˈɑv] *prep* **1** FROM : de <a man of the city : un homme de la ville> **2** (*indicating a characteristic quality or possession*) : de <a woman of great ability : une femme de grand talent> **3** (*indicating cause*) : de <he died of the flu : il est mort de la grippe> **4** BY : de <the works of Shakespeare : les œuvres de Shakespeare> **5** (*indicating parts, contents, or material*) : de, en <a glass of water : un verre d'eau> <a house of wood : une maison en bois> **6** (*indicating quantity or amount*) : de <thousands of dollars : des milliers de dollars> **7** (*indicating belonging or connection*) : de <the front of the house : le devant de la maison> **8** ABOUT : sur, de <tales of the West : contes de l'Ouest> **9** (*indicating a particular example*) : de <the city of Chicago : la ville de Chicago> **10** FOR : pour, de <love of country : amour de la patrie> **11** (*indicating time or date*) <five minutes of ten : dix heures moins cinq> <the eighth of April : le huit avril>

off[1] [ˈɔf] *adv* **1** (*indicating change of position or state*) <to march off : s'en aller> <he dozed off : il s'est endormi> **2** (*indicating distance in space or time*) <far off : éloigné> <some miles off : à quelques kilomètres de distance> <the holiday is three weeks off : la fête est en trois semaines> **3** (*indicating removal*) <this paint comes off : cette peinture s'enlève> <to cut off : couper> **4** (*indicating termination*) <to finish off : terminer> <shut the television off : éteins la télévision> <shut the engine off : coupez le contact> **5** (*indicating suspension of work*) <to take a day off : prendre un jour de congé> **6 off and on** : par périodes, par intervalles

off[2] *adj* **1** OUT : éteint, fermé <the light is off : la lumière est éteinte> **2** STARTED : démarré <to be off on a spree : démarrer une partie de plaisir> **3** FREE : libre, de congé <his day off : son jour de congé> **4** CANCELED : annulé **5** DOWN : en baisse <stocks were off : les actions étaient en baisse> **6 on an off chance** : pour le cas où cela pourrait servir

off[3] *prep* **1** (*indicating physical separation*) : de <she took it off the table : elle l'a pris de la table> <a shop off the main street : un magasin prêt de la rue principale> **2** : aux frais de <he lives off his sister : il vit aux frais de sa sœur> **3** (*indicating the suspension of an activity*) <to be off duty : être libre> <she's off meat : elle ne mange plus de viande> **4 to be off one's game, to be off one's stride** : ne pas être à son meilleur

offal [ˈɔfəl] *n* : abats *mpl*

offend [əˈfɛnd] *vt* **1** HURT : offenser, blesser <to be easily offended : être très susceptible> **2** OUTRAGE, SHOCK : choquer, outrager

offender [əˈfɛndər] *n* : délinquant *m,* -quante *f;* contrevenant *m,* -nante *f*

offense *or* **offence** [əˈfɛnts, ˈɔˌfɛnts] *n* **1** INSULT : offense *f* <to take offense : s'offenser> **2** CRIME : délit *m,* infraction *f* **3** : attaque *f* (aux sports)

offensive[1] [əˈfɛntsɪv, ˈɔˌfɛnt-] *adj* : offensif — **offensively** *adv*

offensive[2] *n* : offensive *f,* attaque *f* <to go on the offensive : passer à l'offensive>

offer[1] [ˈɔfər] *vt* **1** : offrir, présenter <they offered him the job : ils lui ont offert le poste> **2** PROPOSE : proposer, suggérer **3** PROVIDE : donner, offrir <to offer no resistance : ne donner aucune résistance>

offer[2] *n* : proposition *f,* offre *f*

offering [ˈɔfərɪŋ] *n* : offre *f,* offrande *f* (en réligion)

offhand[1] [ˈɔfˈhænd] *adv* : spontanément, sur-le-champ

offhand[2] *adj* : désinvolte, impromptu

office [ˈɔfəs] *n* **1** : bureau *m,* cabinet *m* (d'un médecin, d'un avocat) **2** POSITION : fonction *f,* charge *f,* poste *m*

<a person in high office : une personne haut placée>
officeholder ['ɔfəs,ho:ldər] *n* : fonctionnaire *mf*
officer ['ɔfəsər] *n* **1** *or* **police officer** : policier *m,* -cière *f;* agent *m* de police **2** OFFICIAL : fonctionnaire *mf* **3** → **commissioned officer**
official[1] [ə'fɪʃəl] *adj* : officiel — **officially** *adv*
official[2] *n* : officiel *m,* -cielle *f*
officiate [ə'fɪʃi,eɪt] *vi* **-ated; -ating 1** PRESIDE : officier, présider **2** : arbitrer (aux sports)
officious [ə'fɪʃəs] *adj* : importun, trop empressé
offing ['ɔfɪŋ] *n* **in the offing** : en perspective, en vue
offset ['ɔf,sɛt] *vt* **-set; -setting** : compenser, contrebalancer
offshoot ['ɔf,ʃu:t] *n* **1** : ramification *f,* conséquence *f* (d'une idée, etc.) **2** : rejeton *m* (en botanie)
offshore[1] ['ɔf'ʃor] *adv* : en mer
offshore[2] *adj* : côtier, marin <offshore drilling : forage marin>
offspring ['ɔf,sprɪŋ] *ns & pl* PROGENY : progéniture *f*
often ['ɔfən, 'ɔftən] *adv* : souvent, fréquemment
oftentimes ['ɔfən,taɪmz, 'ɔftən-] *or* **ofttimes** ['ɔft,taɪmz] → **often**
ogle ['o:gəl] *vt* **ogled; ogling** : lorgner, reluquer *fam*
ogre ['o:gər] *n* : ogre *m,* ogresse *f*
oh ['o:] *interj* : oh! <oh, really? : vraiment?> <oh dear! : oh la la!>
ohm ['o:m] *n* : ohm *m*
oil[1] ['ɔɪl] *vt* : huiler, lubrifier, graisser
oil[2] *n* **1** : huile *f* <oil painting : peinture à l'huile> <olive oil : huile d'olive> **2** PETROLEUM : pétrole *m* **3** *or* **heating oil** : mazout *m*
oilcloth ['ɔɪl,klɔθ] *n* : toile *f* cirée
oiliness ['ɔɪlinəs] *n* : nature *f* huileuse
oilskin ['ɔɪl,skɪn] *n* **1** OILCLOTH : toile *f* cirée **2** *or* **oilskins** *npl* : ciré *m*
oily ['ɔɪli] **oilier; -est** *adj* : huileux
ointment ['ɔɪntmənt] *n* : pommade *f*
OK[1] *or* **okay** [,o:'keɪ] *vt* **OK'd** *or* **okayed; OK'ing** *or* **okaying** APPROVE, AUTHORIZE : approuver
OK[2] *or* **okay** *adv* **1** WELL : bien <everything's going OK : tout va bien> **2** YES : oui
OK[3] *adj* : bien <I'm OK : je vais bien> <it's OK with me : je suis d'accord>
OK[4] *n* APPROVAL *n* : accord *m,* approbation *f*
okra ['o:krə, *south also* -kri] *n* : gombo *m*
old[1] ['o:ld] *adj* **1** : vieux <an old man : un vieil homme> **2** ANCIENT : ancien, antique **3** (*indicating a certain age*) <he's ten years old : il a dix ans> <she's not old enough : elle n'est pas encore en âge> **4** FORMER : ancien <her old neighborhood : son ancien voisinage> **5** WORN-OUT : usé **6 any old** : n'importe quel **7 old age** : vieillesse *f*
old[2] *n* **1 the old** : les vieux **2 in the days of old** : d'antan, d'autrefois
olden ['o:ldən] *adj* : vieux, d'autrefois, d'antan <in olden days : autrefois, jadis>
old–fashioned ['o:ld'fæʃənd] *adj* : démodé, suranné <old-fashioned charm : charme suranné>
old maid *n* **1** SPINSTER : vieille fille *f* **2** FUSSBUDGET : tatillon *m,* -lonne *f*
Old Testament *n* : Ancien Testament *m*
old–timer ['o:ld'taɪmər] *n* : vieillard *m;* ancien *m,* -cienne *f*
old–world ['o:ld'wərld] *adj* : d'autrefois, pittoresque
oleander ['o:li,ændər] *n* : laurier-rose *m*
oleomargarine [,o:lio'mɑrdʒərən] → **margarine**
olfactory [ɑl'fæktəri, ol-] *adj* : olfactif
oligarchy ['ɑlə,gɑrki, 'o:lə-] *n, pl* **-chies** : oligarchie *f*
olive ['ɑlɪv, -ləv] *n* **1** : olive *f* (fruit) **2** : olivier *m* (arbre) **3** *or* **olive green** : vert *m* olive
Olympic Games [o'lɪmpɪk] *or* **Olympics** [-pɪks] *npl* : jeux *mpl* Olympiques
Omani[1] [o'mani] *adj* : omanais
Omani[2] *n* : Omanais *m,* -naise *f*
ombudsman ['ɑm,bʊdzmən, ɑm'bʊdz-] *n, pl* **-men** [-mən, -,mɛn] : médiateur *m,* -trice *f France;* protecteur *m* du citoyen *Can*
omelet *or* **omelette** ['ɑmlət, 'ɑmə-] *n* : omelette *f*
omen ['o:mən] *n* : augure *m,* présage *m*
ominous ['ɑmənəs] *adj* : inquiétant, menaçant
ominously ['ɑmənəsli] *adv* : de manière inquiétante
omission [o'mɪʃən] *n* : omission *f*
omit [o'mɪt] *vt* **omitted; omitting** : omettre <to omit to do sth : omettre de faire qqch>
omnipotence [ɑm'nɪpət̬ənts] *n* : omnipotence *f* — **omnipotent** [-t̬ənt] *adj*
omnipresent [,ɑmnɪ'prɛzənt] *adj* : omniprésent
omniscient [ɑm'nɪʃənt] *adj* : omniscient
omnivorous [ɑm'nɪvərəs] *adj* **1** : omnivore **2** AVID : avide
on[1] ['ɑn, 'ɔn] *adv* **1** (*indicating contact with a surface*) <put the top on : mets le couvercle> <he has a hat on : il porte un chapeau> **2** (*indicating forward movement*) <from that moment on : à partir de ce moment-là> <farther on : un peu plus loin> **3** (*indicating operation or operating position*) <turn the light on : allumez la lumière>
on[2] *adj* **1** (*being in operation*) <the radio is on : la radio est allumée> <the faucet is on : le robinet est ouvert> <the engine is on : le moteur est en

marche> **2** (*taking place*) <the game is on : le match aura lieu> **3 to be on** : être mis <the lid is on : le couvercle est mis>

on[3] *prep* **1** (*indicating position*) : sur, à, de <on the table : sur la table> <on horseback : à cheval> <on page two : à la page deux> **2** AT, TO : à <on the right : à droite> **3** ABOARD, IN : en, dans <on the plane : dans l'avion> **4** (*indicating time*) <she worked on Saturdays : elle travaillait le samedi> <every hour on the hour : à toutes les heures justes> <on Tuesday : mardi> **5** (*indicating means or agency*) <to talk on the telephone : parler au téléphone> <he cut himself on a tin can : il s'est coupé avec une boîte de conserve> **6** (*indicating a state or process*) : en, à <on fire : en feu> <to be on the increase : aller en augmentant> <on foot : à pied> <on a diet : au régime> **7** (*indicating connection or membership*) <she's on a committee : elle fait partie d'un comité> **8** (*indicating an activity*) <on vacation : en vacances> **9** ABOUT, CONCERNING : sur <a book on insects : un livre sur les insectes> <reflect on that : réfléchissez-y>

once[1] ['wʌnts] *adv* **1** : une fois <once a month : une fois par mois> <once and for all : une fois pour toutes> **2** EVER : jamais <if you hesitate once, all will be lost : si jamais tu hésites, tout sera perdu> **3** FORMERLY : autrefois

once[2] *adj* FORMER : ancien, précédent

once[3] *n* **1** : une fois <for once : pour une fois> **2 at ~** SIMULTANEOUSLY : en même temps, simultanément **3 at ~** IMMEDIATELY : tout de suite, immédiatement

once[4] *conj* : dès que, une fois que

once–over [ˌwʌnts'oːvər, 'wʌntsˌ-] *n* : coup *m* d'œil <to give something the once-over : jeter un coup d'œil sur>

oncoming ['ɑnˌkʌmɪŋ, 'ɔn-] *adj* : approchant, qui approche <oncoming traffic : circulation venant en sens inverse>

one[1] ['wʌn] *adj* **1** (*being a single unit*) : un, une <he only wants one apple : il ne veut qu'une pomme> <with one motion : d'un seul mouvement> **2** (*being a particular one*) : un, une <he arrived early one morning : il est arrivé tôt un matin> **3** (*being the same*) : même <one and the same thing : la même chose> **4** SOME : un, une <one day we'll come : un jour nous viendrons> **5** ONLY : seul, unique <her one day off : son unique jour de congé>

one[2] *n* **1** : un *m* (numéro) **2** (*indicating the first of a set or series*) <from day one : depuis le premier jour> <one o'clock : une heure> **3** (*indicating a single person or thing*) <the one (girl) on the left : celle à gauche> <you can't have one without the other : l'un ne va pas sans l'autre>

one[3] *pron* **1** : un, une <one of his friends : un de ses amis> <one never knows : l'on ne sait jamais> **2 one and all** : tous, tout le monde **3 one another** : l'un l'autre **4 this one, that one** : celui-là, celle-là **5 which one?** : lequel?, laquelle?

oneness ['wʌnnəs] *n* **1** SINGLENESS : unité *f* **2** AGREEMENT : accord *m* **3** SAMENESS : identité *f*

onerous ['ɑnərəs, 'oːnə-] *adj* : pénible, lourd

oneself [ˌwən'sɛlf] *pron* **1** (*used reflexively*) : se <to control oneself : se contrôler> **2** (*used for emphasis*) : soi-même <to do it oneself : le faire soi-même> **3** (*used after prepositions*) : soi <sure of oneself : sûr de soi> **4 by ~** : seul

one–sided ['wʌn'saɪdəd] *adj* **1** UNEQUAL : inégal **2** PARTIAL : partial **3** UNILATERAL : unilatéral

onetime ['wʌn'taɪm] *adj* FORMER : ancien

one–way ['wʌn'weɪ] *adj* **1** : à sens unique (se dit d'une route) **2** : simple <a one-way ticket : un aller simple, un billet simple>

ongoing ['ɑnˌgoːɪŋ] *adj* : continu, en cours

onion ['ʌnjən] *n* : oignon *m*

only[1] ['oːnli] *adv* **1** MERELY : seulement, ne...que <he's only five : il n'a que cinq ans> <this will only take a moment : ceci ne prendra qu'un moment> <only once : seulement une fois> **2** EXCLUSIVELY : seulement, uniquement <only in the morning : le matin seulement> <I'll tell it only to you : je le dirai seulement à toi> <only he knows it : lui seul le sait> **3** (*indicating a result*) <you know only too well : vous ne savez que trop bien> **4 if only** : si, si seulement <if he could only dance : si seulement il pouvait danser>

only[2] *adj* : seul, unique <an only child : un enfant unique> <the only chance : la seule chance> <we're the only ones : nous sommes les seuls>

only[3] *conj* BUT : mais <I would go, only I'm sick : j'irais mais je suis malade>

onset ['ɑnˌsɛt] *n* : début *m*, commencement *m*

onslaught ['ɑnˌslɔt, 'ɔn-] *n* : assaut *m*, attaque *f*

onto ['ɑnˌtuː, 'ɔn-] *prep* : sur

onus ['oːnəs] *n* : responsabilité *f*, charge *f*

onward[1] ['ɑnwərd, 'ɔn-] *adv* **1** FORWARD : en avant <to go onward : avancer> **2** (*used to express continuance from a point*) <from today onward : à partir d'aujourd'hui>

onward[2] *adj* : progressif <the onward march of time : la fuite du temps>
onyx ['ɑnɪks] *n* : onyx *m*
ooze[1] ['u:z] *v* **oozed; oozing** *vi* : suinter — *vt* EXUDE : respirer <to ooze confidence : respirer la confiance>
ooze[2] *n* SLIME : vase *f,* boue *f*
opacity [o'pæsəṭi] *n, pl* **-ties** : opacité *f*
opal ['o:pəl] *n* : opale *f*
opaque [o'peɪk] *adj* : opaque
open[1] ['o:pən] *vt* **1** : ouvrir **2** START : commencer, entamer (une négociation, etc.) **3** INAUGURATE : inaugurer, ouvrir (une entreprise, etc.) **4** CLEAR : ouvrir, dégager (la voie) — *vi* **1** : s'ouvrir **2** BEGIN : débuter, sortir <the film opens tomorrow : le film sort demain> **3 to open on to** : donner sur
open[2] *adj* **1** : ouvert <an open window : une fenêtre ouverte> <the store is open : le magasin est ouvert> **2** FRANK : franc **3** CLEAR : dégagé **4** DEBATABLE : discutable **5** VACANT : vacant **6** UNCOVERED : découvert
open[3] *n* **in the open 1** OUTDOORS : à la belle étoile, au grand air **2** KNOWN : connu
open–air ['o:pən'ær] *adj* OUTDOOR : en plein air
open–and–shut ['o:pənənd'ʃʌt] *adj* : clair, évident
opener ['o:pənər] *n* **1** : ouvreur *m,* -vreuse *f* (aux jeux, etc.) **2** : outil *m* servant à ouvrir <a can opener : un ouvre-boîtes>
openhanded [ˌo:pən'hændəd] *adj* GENEROUS : généreux
openhearted [ˌo:pən'hɑrṭəd] *adj* **1** FRANK : franc, sincère **2** GENEROUS, KIND : généreux, qui a bon cœur
opening ['o:pənɪŋ] *n* **1** BEGINNING : commencement *m* **2** APERTURE : ouverture *f* **3** OPPORTUNITY : occasion *f,* chance *f* **4** : vernissage *m* (d'une exposition)
opera[1] → **opus**
opera[2] ['ɑprə, 'ɑpərə] *n* : opéra *m*
opera glasses *n* : jumelles *fpl* de théâtre
operate ['ɑpəˌreɪt] *v* **-ated; -ating** *vi* **1** FUNCTION : fonctionner, marcher **2 to operate on s.o.** : opérer qqn — *vt* **1** WORK : faire fonctionner **2** MANAGE : effectuer, gérer
operatic [ˌɑpə'ræṭɪk] *adj* : d'opéra
operation [ˌɑpə'reɪʃən] *n* **1** FUNCTIONING : fonctionnement *m* **2** SURGERY : opération *f,* intervention *f* chirurgicale <to have an operation : se faire opérer> **3** DEALING, TRANSACTION : opération *f*
operational [ˌɑpə'reɪʃənəl] *adj* : opérationnel
operative ['ɑpərəṭɪv, -ˌreɪ-] *adj* **1** OPERATING : en vigueur **2** OPERATIONAL, WORKING : opérationnel **3** SURGICAL : opératoire
operator ['ɑpəˌreɪṭər] *n* **1** : opérateur *m,* -trice *f* (d'une machine, etc.) **2** *or* **switchboard operator** : standardiste *mf*
operetta [ˌɑpə'rɛṭə] *n* : opérette *f*
ophthalmologist [ˌɑfˌθæl'mɑlədʒɪst, -θə'mɑ-] *n* : ophtalmologiste *mf*
ophthalmology [ˌɑfˌθæl'mɑlədʒi, -θə'mɑ-] *n* : ophtalmologie *f*
opiate ['o:piət, -piˌeɪt] *n* : opiacé *m*
opinion [ə'pɪnjən] *n* : opinion *f,* avis *m*
opinionated [ə'pɪnjəˌneɪṭəd] *adj* : opiniâtre
opium ['o:piəm] *n* : opium *m*
opossum [ə'pɑsəm] *n* : opossum *m*
opponent [ə'po:nənt] *n* : adversaire *mf*
opportune [ˌɑpər'tu:n, -'tju:n] *adj* : opportun — **opportunely** *adv*
opportunism [ˌɑpər'tu:ˌnɪzəm, -'tju:-] *n* : opportunisme *m*
opportunist [ˌɑpər'tu:nɪst, -'tju:-] *n* : opportuniste *mf*
opportunistic [ˌɑpərtu:'nɪstɪk, -tju:-] *adj* : opportuniste
opportunity [ˌɑpər'tu:nəṭi, -'tju:-] *n, pl* **-ties** : occasion *f*
oppose [ə'po:z] *vt* **-posed; -posing 1** CONTRAST : opposer **2** RESIST : s'opposer à, combattre
opposite[1] ['ɑpəzət] *adv* : en face
opposite[2] *adj* **1** FACING : d'en face <the opposite side : le côté d'en face> **2** CONTRARY : opposé, inverse, contraire <in the opposite direction : en sens inverse> <the opposite sex : le sexe opposé>
opposite[3] *n* : contraire *m*
opposite[4] *prep* : en face de
opposition [ˌɑpə'zɪʃən] *n* : opposition *f,* résistance *f*
oppress [ə'prɛs] *vt* **1** PERSECUTE : opprimer **2** BURDEN : oppresser
oppression [ə'prɛʃən] *n* : oppression *f*
oppressive [ə'prɛsɪv] *adj* : oppressif
oppressor [ə'prɛsər] *n* : oppresseur *m*
opprobrium [ə'pro:briəm] *n* : opprobre *m*
opt ['ɑpt] *vi* : opter
optic ['ɑptɪk] *adj* : optique <the optic nerve : le nerf optique>
optical ['ɑptɪkəl] → **optic**
optician [ɑp'tɪʃən] *n* : opticien *m,* -cienne *f*
optics ['ɑptɪks] *n* : optique *f*
optimal ['ɑptəməl] *adj* : optimal
optimism ['ɑptəˌmɪzəm] *n* : optimisme *m*
optimist ['ɑptəmɪst] *n* : optimiste *mf*
optimistic [ˌɑptə'mɪstɪk] *adj* : optimiste
optimistically [ˌɑptə'mɪstɪkli] *adv* : avec optimisme
optimum[1] ['ɑptəməm] *adj* : optimum
optimum[2] *n, pl* **-ma** ['ɑptəmə] : optimum *m*
option ['ɑpʃən] *n* : option *f*
optional ['ɑpʃənəl] *adj* : facultatif, optionnel

optometrist [ɑp'tɑmətrɪst] *n* : optométriste *mf*

optometry [ɑp'tɑmətri] *n* : optométrie *f*

opulence ['ɑpjələnts] *n* : opulence *f* — **opulent** [-lənt] *adj*

opus ['o:pəs] *n, pl* **opera** ['o:pərə, 'ɑpə-] : opus *m*

or ['ɔr] *conj* **1** (*indicating an alternative*) : ou <one or the other : l'un ou l'autre> **2** (*following a negative*) : ni <he didn't have his keys or his wallet : il n'avait eu ni ses clés ni son portefeuille> **3** OTHERWISE : sinon <do what I tell you, or you'll be sorry : faites ce que je dis, sinon vous le regretterez>

oracle ['ɔrəkəl] *n* : oracle *m*

oral ['orəl] *adj* : oral — **orally** *adv*

orange ['ɔrɪndʒ] *n* **1** : orange *f* (fruit) **2** : orange *m* (couleur)

orangeade [ˌɔrɪndʒ'eɪd] *n* : orangeade *f*

orangutan [ə'ræŋəˌtæŋ, -'ræŋgə-, -ˌtæn] *n* : orang-outan *m*

oration [ə'reɪʃən] *n* : discours *m* (solennel), allocution *f*

orator ['ɔrət̬ər] *n* : orateur *m*, -trice *f*

oratorical [ˌɔrə'tɔrɪkəl] *adj* : oratoire

oratorio [ˌɔrə'toriˌo:] *n, pl* **-rios** : oratorio *m*

oratory ['ɔrəˌtori] *n, pl* **-ries** : éloquence *f*, art *m* oratoire

orb ['ɔrb] *n* : orbe *m*

orbit[1] ['ɔrbət] *vt* : graviter autour de — *vi* : décrire une orbite

orbit[2] *n* : orbite *f*

orbital ['ɔrbətəl] *adj* : orbital

orchard ['ɔrtʃərd] *n* : verger *m*

orchestra ['ɔrkəstrə] *n* : orchestre *m* — **orchestral** [ɔr'kɛstrəl] *adj*

orchestrate ['ɔrkəˌstreɪt] *vt* **-trated; -trating** : orchestrer

orchestration [ˌɔrkə'streɪʃən] *n* : orchestration *f*

orchid ['ɔrkɪd] *n* : orchidée *f*

ordain [ɔr'deɪn] *vt* **1** : ordonner (en religion) **2** DECREE : décréter, ordonner

ordeal [ɔr'di:l, 'ɔrˌdi:l] *n* : épreuve *f*, calvaire *m*

order[1] ['ɔrdər] *vt* **1** ORGANIZE : arranger, ranger **2** COMMAND : ordonner **3** REQUEST : commander (un repas, etc.) — *vi* : commander

order[2] *n* **1** : ordre *m* <religious order : ordre religieux> **2** COMMAND : commande *f*, ordre *m* <to give orders : donner des ordres> **3** REQUEST : commande *f*, bon *m* <purchase order : bon de commande> **4** DISCIPLINE : order *m* <law and order : l'ordre public> **5** CONDITION : état *m* <in working order : en bon état> **6** ARRANGEMENT : ordre *m* <in alphabetical order : en ordre alphabétique> **7 in order to** : afin de **8 orders** *npl or* **holy orders** : ordres *mpl* **9 out of order** : en panne

orderliness ['ɔrdərlinəs] *n* : ordre *m*

orderly[1] ['ɔrdərli] *adj* **1** TIDY : en ordre, ordonné **2** DISCIPLINED : discipliné, réglé

orderly[2] *n, pl* **-lies 1** : planton *m* (dans l'armée) **2** : aide-infirmier *m* (dans un hôpital)

ordinal ['ɔrdənəl] *n or* **ordinal number** : ordinal *m*

ordinance ['ɔrdənənts] *n* : ordonnance *f*

ordinarily [ˌɔrdən'ɛrəli] *adv* : d'ordinaire, d'habitude

ordinary ['ɔrdənˌɛri] *adj* **1** NORMAL, USUAL : normal, habituel **2** AVERAGE : ordinaire **3** COMMONPLACE : quelconque

ordination [ˌɔrdən'eɪʃən] *n* : ordination *f*

ordnance ['ɔrdnənts] *n* **1** SUPPLIES : équipement *m* militaire **2** ARTILLERY : artillerie *f*

ore ['or] *n* : minerai *m*

oregano [ə'rɛgəˌno:] *n* : origan *m*

organ ['ɔrgən] *n* **1** : orgue *m* (instrument de musique) **2** : organe *m* (du corps) **3** PERIODICAL : périodique *m*

organic [ɔr'gænɪk] *adj* : organique — **organically** *adv*

organism ['ɔrgəˌnɪzəm] *n* : organisme *m*

organist ['ɔrgənɪst] *n* : organiste *mf*

organization [ˌɔrgənə'zeɪʃən] *n* **1** ORGANIZING : organisation *f* **2** BODY : organisme *m*

organizational [ˌɔrgənə'zeɪʃənəl] *adj* : organisationnel, d'organisation

organize ['ɔrgəˌnaɪz] *vt* **-nized; -nizing 1** : organiser, mettre à l'ordre **2 to get organized** : s'organiser

organizer ['ɔrgəˌnaɪzər] *n* : organisateur *m*, -trice *f*

orgasm ['ɔrˌgæzəm] *n* : orgasme *m*

orgy ['ɔrdʒi] *n, pl* **-gies** : orgie *f*

orient ['oriˌɛnt] *vt* : orienter

Orient *n* **the Orient** : l'Orient *m*

oriental [ˌori'ɛntəl] *adj* : oriental, d'Orient

Oriental *n* : Oriental *m*, -tale *f*

orientation [ˌoriən'teɪʃən] *n* : orientation *f*

orifice ['ɔrəfəs] *n* : orifice *m*

origin ['ɔrədʒən] *n* **1** ANCESTRY : origine *f* <of Canadian origin : d'origine canadienne> **2** SOURCE : source *f*, provenance *f*

original[1] [ə'rɪdʒənəl] *adj* : original

original[2] *n* : original *m*

originality [əˌrɪdʒə'næləṭi] *n* : originalité *f*

originally [ə'rɪdʒənəli] *adv* **1** AT FIRST : à l'origine, initialement, au début **2** INVENTIVELY : originalement, d'une manière originale

originate [ə'rɪdʒəˌneɪt] *v* **-nated; -nating** *vt* : créer, donner naissance à — *vi* : provenir, prendre naissance <the

fire originated in the basement : le feu a pris naissance au sous-sol>

originator [ə'rɪdʒəˌneɪṭər] *n* : créateur *m*, -trice *f*; auteur *m*

oriole ['oriˌoːl, -iəl] *n* : loriot *m*

ornament[1] ['ɔrnəmənt] *vt* : orner

ornament[2] *n* : ornement *m* — **ornamental** [ˌɔrnə'mɛntəl] *adj*

ornamentation [ˌɔrnəmən'teɪʃən] *n* : ornementation *f*

ornate [ɔr'neɪt] *adj* : orné

ornery ['ɔrnəri, 'ɑrnəri] *adj* **ornerier; -est** : méchant, acariâtre, malcommode *Can*

ornithologist [ˌɔrnə'θɑlədʒɪst] *n* : ornithologiste *mf*, ornithologue *mf*

ornithology [ˌɔrnə'θɑlədʒi] *n, pl* **-gies** : ornithologie *f*

orphan[1] ['ɔrfən] *vt* : rendre orphelin

orphan[2] *n* : orphelin *m*, -line *f*

orphanage ['ɔrfənɪdʒ] *n* : orphelinat *m*

orthodontics [ˌɔrθə'dɑntɪks] *n* : orthodontie *f*

orthodontist [ˌɔrθə'dɑntɪst] *n* : orthodontiste *mf*

orthodox ['ɔrθəˌdɑks] *adj* : orthodoxe

orthodoxy ['ɔrθəˌdɑksi] *n, pl* **-doxies** : orthodoxie *f*

orthographic [ˌɔrθə'græfɪk] *adj* : orthographique

orthography [ɔr'θɑgrəfi] *n* : orthographie *f*

orthopedic [ˌɔrθə'piːdɪk] *adj* : orthopédique

orthopedics [ˌɔrθə'piːdɪks] *ns & pl* : orthopédie *f*

orthopedist [ˌɔrθə'piːdɪst] *n* : orthopédiste *mf*

oscillate ['ɑsəˌleɪt] *vi* **-lated; -lating** : osciller

oscillation [ˌɑsə'leɪʃən] *n* : oscillation *f*

osmosis [ɑz'moːsəs, ɑs-] *n* : osmose *f*

osprey ['ɑspri, -ˌpreɪ] *n, pl* **-preys** : balbuzard *m* (pêcheur)

ostensible [ɑ'stɛntsəbəl] *adj* : ostensible — **ostensibly** [-bli] *adv*

ostentation [ˌɑstən'teɪʃən] *n* : ostentation *f*

ostentatious [ˌɑstən'teɪʃəs] *adj* : ostentatoire — **ostentatiously** *adv*

osteopath ['ɑstiəˌpæθ] *n* : ostéopathe *mf*

osteopathy [ˌɑsti'ɑpəθi] *n* : ostéopathie *f*

osteoporosis [ˌɑstiopə'rosɪs] *n, pl* **-roses** [-ˌsiːz] : ostéoporose *f*

ostracism ['ɑstrəˌsɪzəm] *n* : ostracisme *m*

ostracize ['ɑstrəˌsaɪz] *vt* **-cized; -cizing** : frapper d'ostracisme, mettre au ban de la société

ostrich ['ɑstrɪtʃ, 'ɔs-] *n* : autruche *f*

other[1] ['ʌðər] *adv* **other than** : autrement que, à part

other[2] *adj* : autre <the other boys : les autres garçons> <on the other hand : d'autre part, par contre> <every other day : tous les deux jours>

other[3] *pron* : autre <one in front of the other : l'un devant l'autre>

otherwise[1] ['ʌðərˌwaɪz] *adv* **1** DIFFERENTLY : autrement <he could not act otherwise : il n'a pas pu agir autrement> **2** : à part cela <I'm dizzy, but otherwise I'm fine : j'ai la tête qui tourne, mais à part cela je vais bien> **3** OR ELSE : sinon <do what I tell you, otherwise you'll be sorry : fais comme je dis, sinon tu le regretteras>

otherwise[2] *adj* : autre <the facts are otherwise : les faits sont autres>

otter ['ɑṭər] *n* : loutre *f*

ouch ['aʊtʃ] *interj* : aïe!, ayoye! *Can*

ought ['ɔt] *v aux* : devoir <you ought to take care of the children : vous devriez vous occuper des enfants>

oughtn't ['ɔtənt] (*contraction of* **ought not**) → **ought**

ounce ['aʊnts] *n* : once *f*

our ['ɑr, 'aʊr] *adj* : notre, nos <our house : notre maison> <our children : nos enfants>

ours ['aʊrz, 'ɑrz] *pron* : le nôtre, la nôtre <the car is ours : la voiture est la nôtre> <a cousin of ours : un de nos cousins> <that's ours : c'est à nous>

ourselves [ɑr'sɛlvz, aʊr-] *pron* **1** (*used reflexively*) : nous <we amused ourselves : nous nous sommes divertis> **2** (*used for emphasis*) : nous-mêmes <we did it ourselves : nous l'avons fait nous-mêmes>

oust ['aʊst] *vt* : évincer

ouster ['aʊstər] *n* : expulsion *f* (d'un pays, etc.), renvoi *m* (d'un poste)

out[1] ['aʊt] *vi* : se savoir <the truth will out : la vérité se saura>

out[2] *adv* **1** (*indicating direction or movement*) : dehors, à l'extérieur <let's go out tonight : sortons ce soir> <she opened the door and looked out : elle a ouvert la porte et regardait à l'extérieur> **2** (*indicating a location away from home or work*) <to eat out : aller au restaurant, dîner en ville> **3** (*indicating completion or discontinuance*) <his money ran out : il s'est trouvé à court d'argent> <to turn out the light : éteindre la lumière> **4** (*indicating possession or control*) <to lend out money : prêter de l'argent> <they let the secret out : ils ont laissé échapper le secret> **5** OUTSIDE : dehors <put the cat out : mettez le chat dehors> <the sun came out : il faisait soleil>

out[3] *adj* **1** OUTER : extérieur **2** ABSENT : absent **3** UNFASHIONABLE : démodé **4** EXTINGUISHED : éteint

out[4] *prep* **1** (*used to indicate an outward movement*) : par <I looked out the window : je regardais par la fenêtre> **2** → **out of**

out-and-out ['aʊtən'aʊt] *adj* UTTER : total, absolu

outboard motor ['aʊtˌbord] *n* : hors-bord *m*

outbound ['aʊtˌbaʊnd] *adj* : en partance

outbreak ['aʊtˌbreɪk] *n* : début *m,* déclenchement *m* (de la guerre, etc.), éruption *f* (de violence, d'une maladie, etc.)

outbuilding ['aʊtˌbɪldɪŋ] *n* : dépendance *f*

outburst ['aʊtˌbərst] *n* : accès *m* (de colère, etc.), explosion *f*

outcast ['aʊtˌkæst] *n* : proscrit *m,* -crite *f;* banni *m,* -nie *f*

outcome ['aʊtˌkʌm] *n* : résultat *m*

outcrop ['aʊtˌkrɑp] *n* : affleurement *m*

outcry ['aʊtˌkraɪ] *n, pl* **-cries** : tollé *m*

outdated [ˌaʊt'deɪṭəd] *adj* : démodé

outdistance [ˌaʊt'dɪstənts] *vt* **-tanced; -tancing** : distancer

outdo [ˌaʊt'du:] *vt* **-did** [-'dɪd]; **-done** [-'dʌn]; **-doing** [-'du:ɪŋ]; **-does** [-'dʌz] : surpasser

outdoor ['aʊt'dor] *adj* : en plein air, de plein air, d'extérieur <outdoor activities : activités en plein air> <outdoor sports : sports de plein air> <outdoor clothes : vêtements d'extérieur>

outdoors[1] ['aʊt'dorz] *adv* : à la belle étoile, au grand air, en plein air

outdoors[2] *n* **the great outdoors** : les grands espaces naturels, la pleine nature

outer ['aʊṭər] *adj* : externe, extérieur

outermost ['aʊṭərˌmo:st] *adj* : le plus extérieur

outer space *n* : espace *m* intersidéral

outfield ['aʊtˌfi:ld] *n* : champ *m* extérieur

outfielder ['aʊtˌfi:ldər] *n Can* : voltigeur *m,* -geuse *f*

outfit[1] ['aʊtˌfɪt] *vt* **-fitted; -fitting** EQUIP : équiper

outfit[2] *n* **1** EQUIPMENT : équipement *m,* attirail *m* **2** COSTUME : tenue *f* **3** GROUP : équipe *f,* bande *f*

outgoing ['aʊtˌgo:ɪŋ] *adj* **1** OUTBOUND : en partance **2** DEPARTING : sortant <the outgoing president : le président sortant> **3** EXTROVERTED : extraverti

outgrow [ˌaʊt'gro:] *vt* **-grew** [-'gru:]; **-grown** [-'gro:n]; **-growing** : devenir trop grand pour

outgrowth ['aʊtˌgro:θ] *n* : excroissance *f*

outing ['aʊṭɪŋ] *n* : excursion *f,* sortie *f*

outlandish [aʊt'lændɪʃ] *adj* : bizarre, excentrique

outlast [ˌaʊt'læst] *vt* : durer plus longtemps que

outlaw[1] ['aʊtˌlɔ] *vt* : proscrire, rendre illégal

outlaw[2] *n* : hors-la-loi *m*

outlay ['aʊtˌleɪ] *n* : débours *m,* dépense *f,* mise *f* de fonds

outlet ['aʊtˌlɛt, -lət] *n* **1** EXIT : sortie *f,* issue *f* **2** RELEASE : exutoire *m* **3** MARKET : débouché *m,* point *m* de vente **4** *or* **electrical outlet** : prise *f* de courant

outline[1] ['aʊtˌlaɪn] *vt* **-lined; -lining 1** SKETCH : esquisser, tracer **2** SUMMARIZE : résumer

outline[2] *n* **1** CONTOUR : contour *m* **2** SKETCH : ébauche *f* **3** SUMMARY : esquisse *f*

outlive [ˌaʊt'lɪv] *vt* **-lived; -living** : survivre à

outlook ['aʊtˌlʊk] *n* **1** VIEW : vue *f* **2** POINT OF VIEW : perspective *f* **3** PROSPECTS : perspectives *fpl*

out loud *adv* ALOUD : à haute voix

outlying ['aʊtˌlaɪɪŋ] *adj* : isolé, périphérique <outlying areas : régions périphériques>

outmoded [ˌaʊt'mo:dəd] *adj* : démodé

outnumber [ˌaʊt'nʌmbər] *vt* : être plus nombreux que, surpasser en nombre

out of *prep* **1** (*indicating direction or movement from within*) : de, par <to look out of the window : regarder par la fenêtre> <we ran out of the house : nous sommes sortis de la maison en courant> **2** (*being beyond the limits of*) <out of control : hors de contrôle> **3** OF : sur <one out of four : un sur quatre> **4** (*indicating absence or loss*) : sans <out of money : sans argent> <we're out of matches : nous n'avons plus d'allumettes> **5** BECAUSE OF : par <out of curiosity : par curiosité> **6** FROM : en <made out of plastic : fait en plastique>

out–of–date [ˌaʊṭəv'deɪt] *adj* **1** OUTMODED : démodé **2** EXPIRED : périmé

out–of–door [ˌaʊṭəv'dor] *or* **out–of–doors** [-'dorz] → **outdoor**

out–of–doors → **outdoors**

outpatient ['aʊtˌpeɪʃənt] *n* : malade *mf* en consultation externe

outpost ['aʊtˌpo:st] *n* : avant-poste *m*

output[1] ['aʊtˌpʊt] *vt* **-putted** *or* **-put; -putting** : sortir (en informatique)

output[2] *n* : rendement *m,* production *f,* productivité *f*

outrage[1] ['aʊtˌreɪdʒ] *vt* **-raged; -raging** : outrager

outrage[2] *n* **1** AFFRONT, SCANDAL : outrage *m,* affront *m,* scandale *m* **2** ATROCITY : atrocité *f* **3** ANGER : indignation *f*

outrageous [ˌaʊt'reɪdʒəs] *adj* **1** SCANDALOUS : scandaleux **2** BIZARRE, UNCONVENTIONAL : extravagant, bizarre

outright[1] ['aʊtˌraɪt] *adv* **1** COMPLETELY : complètement **2** INSTANTLY : sur le coup **3** FRANKLY : franchement, carrément

outright[2] *adj* **1** COMPLETE, UTTER : total, absolu <an outright lie : un mensonge absolu> **2** : sans réserve <an outright gift : un cadeau pur et simple, un cadeau sans réserve>

outset ['aʊtˌsɛt] *n* : début *m,* commencement *m*

outshine [ˌaʊtˈʃaɪn] *vt* **-shone** [-ˈʃoːn, -ˈʃɒn] *or* **-shined; shining** : éclipser, surpasser

outside[1] [ˌaʊtˈsaɪd, ˈaʊtˌ-] *adv* : à l'extérieur, dehors

outside[2] *adj* **1** OUTER : extérieur <the outside edge : le bord extérieur> **2** OUTDOOR : extérieur, à l'extérieur **3** POOR, REMOTE : faible <an outside chance : une faible chance>

outside[3] *n* **1** EXTERIOR : extérieur *m,* dehors *m* **2** MOST : maximum *m,* plus *m* <three weeks at the outside : trois semaines au plus>

outside[4] *prep* : en dehors de, à l'extérieur de

outside of *prep* **1** → **outside**[4] **2** → **besides**[2]

outsider [ˌaʊtˈsaɪdər] *n* : étranger *m,* -gère *f*

outskirts [ˈɑʊtˌskərts] *npl* : banlieue *f,* périphérie *f*

outsmart [ˌaʊtˈsmɑrt] → **outwit**

outspoken [ˌaʊtˈspoːkən] *adj* : franc, carré

outstanding [ˌaʊtˈstændɪŋ] *adj* **1** UNPAID : impayé, dû **2** NOTABLE : exceptionnel

outstandingly [ˌaʊtˈstændɪŋli] *adv* : exceptionnellement

outstrip [ˌaʊtˈstrɪp] *vt* **-stripped; -stripping 1** PASS : dépasser, devancer **2** SURPASS : surpasser

outward[1] [ˈaʊtwərd] *or* **outwards** [-wərdz] *adv* : au dehors <outward bound : en partance>

outward[2] *adj* **1** : vers l'extérieur <an outward flow : un écoulement vers l'extérieur> **2** EXTERIOR : extérieur, externe <an outward calm : un calme apparent>

outwardly [ˈaʊtwərdli] *adv* **1** EXTERNALLY : à l'extérieur **2** APPARENTLY : en apparence

outwit [ˌaʊtˈwɪt] *vt* **-witted; -witting** : se montrer plus futé que, duper

ova → **ovum**

oval[1] [ˈoːvəl] *adj* : ovale

oval[2] *n* : ovale *m*

ovary [ˈoːvəri] *n, pl* **-ries** : ovaire *m*

ovation [oˈveɪʃən] *n* : ovation *f*

oven [ˈʌvən] *n* : four *m*

over[1] [ˈoːvər] *adv* **1** (*indicating movement across*) <he flew over to London : il est venu à Londres en avion> <come on over! : venez donc!> **2** (*indicating an additional amount*) <the show ran 10 minutes over : le spectacle a duré 10 minutes de trop> <over twenty dollars : plus de vingt dollars> **3** ABOVE, OVERHEAD : au-dessus **4** AGAIN : encore, de nouveau <over and over : à plusieurs reprises> <to start over : commencer de nouveau> **5 all over** EVERYWHERE : partout

over[2] *adj* **1** HIGHER, UPPER : supérieur **2** REMAINING : en plus **3** ENDED : terminé, fini <the job is finally over : enfin le travail est fini>

over[3] *prep* **1** ABOVE : au-dessus de, pardessus <over the fireplace : au-dessus de la cheminée> <the hawk flew over the hills : le faucon a volé par-dessus les collines> **2** : plus de <over $50 : plus de 50 $> **3** ALONG : sur <to glide over the ice : glisser sur la glace> **4** (*indicating movement across*) <he jumped over the ditch : il a franchi le fossé d'un bond> **5** DURING : pendant, au cours de <over the last few years : au cours des dernières années> **6** (*referring to a means of communication*) <to speak over the telephone : parler au téléphone> **7** BECAUSE OF : à cause de, au sujet de

overabundance [ˌoːvərəˈbʌndən*t*s] *n* : surabondance *f* — **overabundant** [-dənt] *adj*

overactive [ˌoːvərˈæktɪv] *adj* : trop actif

overall[1] [ˌoːvərˈɔl] *adv* **1** : d'un bout à l'autre, en tout **2** GENERALLY : en général

overall[2] *adj* : d'ensemble, total, global <an overall view : une vue d'ensemble>

overalls [ˈoːvərˌɔlz] *npl* : salopette *f*

overawe [ˌoːvərˈɔ] *vt* **-awed; -awing** : impressionner, intimider

overbearing [ˌoːvərˈbærɪŋ] *adj* : impérieux, autoritaire

overboard [ˈoːvərˌbord] *adv* : pardessus bord

overburden [ˌoːvərˈbərdən] *vt* : surcharger

overcast [ˈoːvərˌkæst] *adj* CLOUDY : couvert

overcharge [ˌoːvərˈtʃɑrdʒ] *v* **-charged; -charging** *vt* : faire payer trop cher à — *vi* : demander un prix excessif

overcoat [ˈoːvərˌkoːt] *n* : pardessus *m*

overcome [ˌoːvərˈkʌm] *v* **-came** [-ˈkeɪm]; **-come; -coming** *vt* **1** CONQUÉRIR : vaincre, surmonter **2** OVERWHELM : accabler, écraser — *vi* : vaincre

overconfidence [ˌoːvərˈkɑnfədən*t*s] *n* : confiance *f* excessive

overconfident [ˌoːvərˈkɑnfədənt] *adj* : trop confiant

overcook [ˌoːvərˈkʊk] *vt* : faire trop cuire

overdo [ˌoːvərˈduː] *vt* **-did** [-ˈdɪd]; **-done** [-ˈdʌn]; **-doing; -does** [-ˈdʌz] **1** : exagérer **2** → **overcook**

overdose [ˈoːvərˌdoːs] *n* : overdose *f,* surdose *f*

overdraft [ˈoːvərˌdræft] *n* : découvert *m*

overdraw [ˌoːvərˈdrɔ] *vt* **-drew** [-ˈdruː]; **-drawn** [-ˈdrɔn]; **-drawing** : mettre à découvert

overdue [ˌoːvərˈduː] *adj* **1** UNPAID : arriéré **2** TARDY : en retard

overeat [ˌoːvərˈiːt] *vt* **-ate** [-ˈeɪt]; **-eating** : trop manger

overelaborate [ˌoːvərɪˈlæbərət] *adj* : trop recherché

overestimate [ˌoːvərˈɛstəˌmeɪt] *vt* **-mated; -mating** : surestimer
overexcited [ˌoːvərɪkˈsaɪt̬əd] *adj* : surexcité
overexpose [ˌoːvərɪkˈspoːz] *vt* **-posed; posing** : surexposer
overfeed [ˌoːvərˈfiːd] *vt* **-fed** [-ˈfɛd]; **-feeding** : suralimenter
overflow[1] [ˌoːvərˈfloː] *v* : déborder
overflow[2] [ˈoːvərˌfloː] *n* **1** : trop-plein *m,* débordement *m* (d'une rivière, etc.) **2** SURPLUS : surplus *m,* excédent *m*
overfly [ˌoːvərˈflaɪ] *vt* **-flew** [-ˈfluː]; **-flown** [-ˈfloːn]; **-flying** : survoler
overgrown [ˌoːvərˈgroːn] *adj* **1** EXCESSIVE, HUGE : démesuré **2** : couvert, envahi <overgrown with weeds : couvert de mauvaises herbes>
overhand[1] [ˈoːvərˌhænd] *adv* : pardessus la tête
overhand[2] *adj* : par le haut
overhang[1] [ˌoːvərˈhæŋ] *vt* **-hung** [-ˈhʌŋ]; **-hanging** : surplomber
overhang[2] [ˈoːvərˌhæŋ] *n* : surplomb *m*
overhaul [ˌoːvərˈhɔl] *vt* **1** : réviser (un moteur, etc.) **2** OVERTAKE : dépasser
overhead[1] [ˌoːvərˈhɛd] *adv* : au-dessus
overhead[2] [ˈoːvərˌhɛd] *adj* : au-dessus de la tête, aérien <overhead lighting : éclairage au plafond>
overhead[3] [ˈoːvərˌhɛd] *n or* **overhead expenses** : frais *mpl* généraux
overhear [ˌoːvərˈhɪr] *vt* **-heard** [-ˈhərd]; **-hearing** : entendre par hasard
overheat [ˌoːvərˈhiːt] *vt* : surchauffer
overjoyed [ˌoːvərˈdʒɔɪd] *adj* : ravi, rempli de joie
overkill [ˈoːvərˌkɪl] *n* : excès *m*
overland[1] [ˈoːvərˌlænd, -lənd] *adv* : par voie de terre
overland[2] *adj* : par (la) route
overlap[1] [ˌoːvərˈlæp] *v* **-lapped; -lapping** *vt* : chevaucher — *vi* : chevaucher, se recouvrir
overlap[2] [ˈoːvərˌlæp] *n* : chevauchement *m*
overlay[1] [ˌoːvərˈleɪ] *vt* **-laid** [-ˈleɪd]; **-laying** : recouvrir
overlay[2] [ˈoːvərˌleɪ] *n* : revêtement *m,* recouvrement *m*
overload [ˌoːvərˈloːd] *vt* : surcharger
overlong [ˌoːvərˈlɔŋ] *adj* : trop long
overlook [ˌoːvərˈlʊk] *vt* **1** INSPECT : inspecter **2** : donner sur <the house overlooks the beach : la maison donne sur la plage> **3** MISS : manquer **4** IGNORE : laisser passer **5** SUPERVISE : surveiller
overly [ˈoːvərli] *adv* : trop
overnight[1] [ˌoːvərˈnaɪt] *adv* **1** : pendant la nuit **2** SUDDENLY : du jour au lendemain
overnight[2] [ˈoːvərˌnaɪt] *adj* **1** : de nuit, d'une nuit <an overnight stay : une visite d'une nuit> **2** SUDDEN : soudain, subit
overpass [ˈoːvərˌpæs] *n* : voie *f* surélevée
overpopulated [ˌoːvərˈpɑpjəˌleɪt̬əd] *adj* : surpeuplé
overpower [ˌoːvərˈpaʊər] *vt* **1** CONQUER : vaincre **2** OVERWHELM : accabler
overrate [ˌoːvərˈreɪt] *vt* **-rated; -rating** : surestimer
override [ˌoːvərˈraɪd] *vt* **-rode** [-ˈroːd]; **-ridden** [-ˈrɪdən]; **-riding** : passer outre à, outrepasser
overrule [ˌoːvərˈruːl] *vt* **-ruled; -ruling** : rejeter
overrun [ˌoːvərˈrʌn] *v* **-ran** [-ˈræn]; **-running** *vt* **1** INVADE : envahir **2** INFEST : infester **3** EXCEED : dépasser — *vi* : dépasser le temps prévu
overseas[1] [ˌoːvərˈsiːz] *adv* : à l'étranger, outre-mer
overseas[2] [ˈoːvərˌsiːz] *adj* : à l'étranger, extérieur, d'outre-mer
oversee [ˌoːvərˈsiː] *vt* **-saw** [-ˈsɔ]; **-seen** [-ˈsiːn]; **-seeing** SUPERVISE : surveiller
overseer [ˈoːvərˌsiːər] *n* : surveillant *m,* -lante *f;* contremaître *m,* -tresse *f*
overshadow [ˌoːvərˈʃæˌdoː] *vt* **1** DARKEN : ombrager **2** ECLIPSE, OUTSHINE : éclipser, surpasser
overshoe [ˈoːvərˌʃuː] *n* **1** : galoche *f* **2 overshoes** *npl* GALOSHES : caoutchoucs *mpl,* bottes *fpl* de caoutchouc
overshoot [ˌoːvərˈʃuːt] *vt* **-shot** [-ˈʃɑt]; **-shooting** : dépasser
oversight [ˈoːvərˌsaɪt] *n* **1** ERROR, OMISSION : oubli *m,* omission *f* **2** SUPERVISION : surveillance *f*
oversleep [ˌoːvərˈsliːp] *vi* **-slept** [-ˈslɛpt]; **-sleeping** : dormir trop longtemps
overstate [ˌoːvərˈsteɪt] *vt* **-stated; -stating** EXAGGERATE : exagérer
overstatement [ˌoːvərˈsteɪtmənt] *n* : exagération *f*
overstep [ˌoːvərˈstɛp] *vt* **-stepped; -stepping** : dépasser, outrepasser
overt [oˈvərt, ˈoːˌvərt] *adj* : évident, manifeste
overtake [ˌoːvərˈteɪk] *vt* **-took** [-ˈtʊk]; **-taken** [-ˈteɪkən]; **-taking** : dépasser, doubler, devancer
overthrow[1] [ˌoːvərˈθroː] *vt* **-threw** [-ˈθruː]; **-thrown** [-ˈθroːn]; **-throwing 1** OVERTURN : renverser **2** DEFEAT : vaincre
overthrow[2] [ˈoːvərˌθroː] *n* : renversement *m,* défaite *f*
overtime [ˈoːvərˌtaɪm] *n* **1** : heures *fpl* supplémentaires (de travail) **2** : prolongations *fpl* (aux sports)
overtone [ˈoːvərˌtoːn] *n* : son *m* harmonique
overture [ˈoːvərˌtʃʊr, -tʃər] *n* **1** : ouverture *f* (en musique) **2** PROPOSAL : proposition *f*
overturn [ˌoːvərˈtərn] *vt* **1** : renverser **2** NULLIFY : annuler — *vi* : se renverser
overuse [ˌoːvərˈjuːz] *vt* **-used; -using** : abuser de, trop employer
overview [ˈoːvərˌvjuː] *n* : vue *f* d'ensemble

overweening [ˌoːvərˈwiːnɪŋ] *adj* **1** ARROGANT : outrecuidant, arrogant **2** EXCESSIVE : démesuré
overweight [ˌoːvərˈweɪt] *adj* : trop gros, obèse
overwhelm [ˌoːvərˈ*h*wɛlm] *vt* : écraser, accabler
overwhelmingly [ˌoːvərˈ*h*wɛlmɪŋ] *adj* : accablant, écrasant
overwork [ˌoːvərˈwerk] *vt* **1** : surmener (une personne) **2** OVERUSE : abuser de — *vi* : se surmener
overwrought [ˌoːvərˈrɔt] *adj* : à bout de nerfs
ovoid [ˈoˌvɔɪd] *or* **ovoidal** [oːˈvɔɪdəl] *adj* : ovoïde
ovulate [ˈɑvjəˌleɪt, ˈoː-] *vi* **-lated; -lating** : ovuler
ovulation [ˌɑvjəˈleɪʃən, ˌoː-] *n* : ovulation *f*
ovum [ˈoːvəm] *n, pl* **ova** [-və] : ovule *m*
owe [ˈoː] *vt* **owed; owing** : devoir <you owe me $10 : tu me dois 10 $> <he owes his wealth to his father : il doit sa fortune à son père>
owing to *prep* : pour cause de
owl [ˈaʊl] *n* : hibou *m*
own[1] [ˈoːn] *vt* **1** POSSESS : posséder **2** ADMIT : reconnaître, admettre — *vi* **to own up** : avouer
own[2] *adj* : propre <his own car : sa propre voiture>
own[3] *pron* **my (your, his/her, our, their) own** : le mien, la mienne; le tien, la tienne; le vôtre, la vôtre; le sien, la sienne; le nôtre, la nôtre; le leur, la leur <it's my own : c'est le mien> <to each his own : chacun son goût> <to be on one's own : être tout seul>
owner [ˈoːnər] *n* : propriétaire *mf*
ownership [ˈoːnərˌʃɪp] *n* : possession *f*
ox [ˈɑks] *n, pl* **oxen** [ˈɑksən] : bœuf *m*
oxide [ˈɑkˌsaɪd] *n* : oxyde *m*
oxidize [ˈɑksəˌdaɪz] *vt* **-dized; -dizing** : oxyder
oxygen [ˈɑksɪdʒən] *n* : oxygène *m*
oyster [ˈɔɪstər] *n* : huître *f*
ozone [ˈoːˌzoːn] *n* : ozone *m*

P

p [ˈpiː] *n, pl* **p's** *or* **ps** [ˈpiːz] : p *m*, seizième lettre de l'alphabet
pace[1] [ˈpeɪs] *v* **paced; pacing** *vt* **1** : arpenter <to pace the room : arpenter la chambre> **2 to pace off** : mesurer en pas — *vi* **to pace to and fro** : faire les cent pas
pace[2] *n* **1** STEP : pas *m* **2** SPEED : allure *f*, vitesse *f* <to walk at a good pace : marcher à vive allure>
pacemaker [ˈpeɪsˌmeɪkər] *n* : stimulateur *m* cardiaque
pachyderm [ˈpækɪˌdərm] *n* : pachyderme *m*
pacific [pəˈsɪfɪk] *adj* : pacifique
pacifier [ˈpæsəˌfaɪər] *n* : tétine *f*, sucette *f*
pacifism [ˈpæsəˌfɪzəm] *n* : pacifisme *m*
pacifist[1] [ˈpæsəfɪst] *or* **pacifistic** [ˌpæsəˈfɪstɪk] *adj* : pacifiste
pacifist[2] *n* : pacifiste *mf*
pacify [ˈpæsəˌfaɪ] *vt* **-fied; -fying** : pacifier, apaiser
pack[1] [ˈpæk] *vt* **1** PACKAGE : empaqueter, emballer **2** CRAM, FILL : entasser, empiler, remplir **3** : faire (sa valise, ses bagages) **4 to pack off** SEND : envoyer
pack[2] *n* **1** PACKAGE : paquet *m*, colis *m* **2** BUNDLE : balle *f*, baluchon *m* **3** BACKPACK : sac *m* à dos **4** GROUP : meute *f* (de chiens), bande *f* (de loups, etc.)
package[1] [ˈpækɪdʒ] *vt* **-aged; -aging** : empaqueter
package[2] *n* : paquet *m*, colis *m*
packet [ˈpækət] *n* : (petit) paquet *m*
pact [ˈpækt] *n* : pacte *m*
pad[1] [ˈpæd] *v* **padded; padding** *vt* **1** STUFF : rembourrer, matelasser **2** EXPAND : étoffer (une note de frais), délayer (un discours) — *vi* : marcher à pas feutrés
pad[2] *n* **1** CUSHION : coussin *m*, protection *f* (aux sports) <a shoulder pad : une épaulette> **2** TABLET : bloc *m* (de papier) **3** *or* **lily pad** : feuille *f* (de nénuphar) **4 ink pad** : tampon *m* encreur **5 launching pad** : rampe *m* de lancement
padding [ˈpædɪŋ] *n* **1** FILLING, STUFFING : rembourrage *m* **2** : remplissage *m*, délayage *m* (d'un discours)
paddle[1] [ˈpædəl] *v* **-dled; -dling** *vt* **1** : pagayer **2** SPANK : donner une fessée à — *vi* WADE : patauger, barboter
paddle[2] *n* : pagaie *f*, aube *f*, aviron *m* *Can*
paddock [ˈpædək] *n* : paddock *m*, enclos *m*
paddy [ˈpædi] *n, pl* **-dies** : rizière *f*
padlock[1] [ˈpædˌlɑk] *vt* : cadenasser
padlock[2] *n* : cadenas *m*
pagan[1] [ˈpeɪgən] *adj* : païen
pagan[2] *n* : païen *m*, païenne *f*
paganism [ˈpeɪgənˌɪzəm] *n* : paganisme *m*
page[1] [ˈpeɪdʒ] *v* **paged; paging** *vt* : appeler, demander — *vi* **to page through** : feuilleter
page[2] *n* **1** ATTENDANT, BELLHOP : chasseur *m* **2** : page *f* (d'un livre)
pageant [ˈpædʒənt] *n* **1** : reconstitution *f* historique (comme de Noël) **2**

SHOW, SPECTACLE : spectacle *m* fastueux
pageantry ['pædʒəntri] *n* : apparat *m,* pompe *f*
pagoda [pə'go:də] *n* : pagode *f*
paid → **pay**
pail ['peɪl] *n* : seau *m*
pain[1] ['peɪn] *vt* : peiner, faire souffrir
pain[2] *n* **1** : mal *m,* douleur *f* <back pains : maux de dos> **2** GRIEF : peine *f,* souffrance *f* **3 pains** *npl* : peine *f,* mal *m* <to take great pains : se donner beaucoup de mal>
painful ['peɪnfəl] *adj* : douloureux — **painfully** *adv*
painkiller ['peɪn,kɪlər] *n* : analgésique *m*
painkilling ['peɪn,kɪlɪŋ] *adj* : analgésique
painless ['peɪnləs] *adj* : indolore, sans douleur
painlessly ['peɪnləsli] *adv* : sans douleur, sans mal
painstaking ['peɪn,steɪkɪŋ] *adj* : soigneux, méticuleux — **painstakingly** *adv*
paint[1] ['peɪnt] *v* : peindre, peinturer *Can*
paint[2] *n* : peinture *f*
paintbrush ['peɪnt,brʌʃ] *n* : pinceau *m,* brosse *f*
painter ['peɪntər] *n* : peintre *m*
painting ['peɪntɪŋ] *n* : peinture *f*
pair[1] ['pær] *vi* **1** MATCH : apparier **2 to pair off** : se mettre par deux
pair[2] *n* **1** : paire *f* <a pair of gloves : une paire de gants> <a pair of pliers : une pince> **2** COUPLE : couple *m* (de personnes ou d'animaux)
pajamas *or Brit* **pyjamas** [pə'dʒɑməz, -'dʒæ-] *npl* : pyjama *m*
Pakistani[1] [,pækɪ'stæni, ,pɑki'stɑni] *adj* : pakistanais
Pakistani[2] *n* : Pakistanais *m,* -naise *f*
pal ['pæl] *n* : copain *m,* -pine *f*
palace ['pæləs] *n* : palais *m*
palatable ['pælət̬əbəl] *adj* : savoureux
palate ['pælət] *n* : palais *m*
palatial [pə'leɪʃəl] *adj* : magnifique, somptueux
palaver[1] [pə'lævər, -'lɑ-] *vi* : palabrer, discuter
palaver[2] *n* : histoires *fpl,* palabres *fpl*
pale[1] ['peɪl] *vi* **paled; paling** : pâlir
pale[2] *adj* **paler; palest 1** PALLID : pâle, blême <to turn pale : pâlir> **2** : clair, pâle <pale bleu : bleu clair>
pale[3] *n* STAKE : pieu *m*
paleness ['peɪlnəs] *n* : pâleur *f*
Palestinian[1] [,pælə'stɪniən] *adj* : palestinien
Palestinian[2] *n* : Palestinien *m,* -nienne *f*
palette ['pælət] *n* : palette *f*
palisade [,pælə'seɪd] *n* **1** FENCE : palissade *f* **2** CLIFFS : ligne *f* de falaises
pall[1] ['pɔl] *vi* : perdre son charme, devenir ennuyeux
pall[2] *n* **1** : drap *m* mortuaire **2** CLOUD : voile *m* <a pall of smoke : un voile de fumée> <a pall of silence : un silence profond>
pallbearer ['pɔl,bɛrər] *n* : porteur *m,* -teuse *f* de cercueil
pallet ['pælət] *n* **1** BED : grabat *m* **2** PLATFORM : palette *f,* plateau *m* de chargement
palliative ['pæli,eɪt̬ɪv, 'pæljət̬ɪv] *adj* : palliatif
pallid ['pæləd] *adj* : pâle, blême
pallor ['pælər] *n* : pâleur *f*
palm[1] ['pɑm, 'pɑlm] *vt* **1** CONCEAL : escamoter (une carte, etc.) **2** *or* **to palm off** : refiler *fam*
palm[2] *n* **1** *or* **palm tree** : palmier *m* **2** : paume *f* (de la main)
Palm Sunday *n* : dimanche *m* des Rameaux
palomino [,pælə'mi:,no:] *n, pl* **-nos** : palomino *m*
palpable ['pælpəbəl] *adj* : palpable
palpitate ['pælpə,teɪt] *vi* **-tated; -tating** : palpiter
palpitation [,pælpə'teɪʃən] *n* : palpitation *f*
palsy ['pɔlzi] *n, pl* **-sies 1** : paralysie *f* **2** → **cerebral palsy**
paltry ['pɔltri] *adj* **paltrier; -est** : dérisoire, piètre
pamper ['pæmpər] *vt* : choyer, dorloter
pamphlet ['pæmpflət] *n* : dépliant *m,* brochure *f*
pan[1] ['pæn] *vt* **panned; panning 1** *or* **to pan for** : chercher (de l'or, etc.) **2** CRITICIZE : éreinter (un spectacle)
pan[2] *n* **1** SAUCEPAN : casserole *f* **2** FRYING PAN : poêle *f*
panacea [,pænə'si:ə] *n* : panacée *f*
Panamanian[1] [,pænə'meɪniən] *adj* : panaméen
Panamanian[2] *n* : Panaméen *m,* -méenne *f*
pancake ['pæn,keɪk] *n* : crêpe *f*
pancreas ['pæŋkriəs, 'pæn-] *n* : pancréas *m*
panda ['pændə] *n* : panda *m*
pandemonium [,pændə'mo:niəm] *n* : brouhaha *m,* tumulte *m*
pander ['pændər] *vi* : flatter (bassement)
pane ['peɪn] *n* : vitre *f,* carreau *m*
panel[1] ['pænəl] *vt* **-eled** *or* **-elled; -eling** *or* **-elling** : recouvrir de panneaux
panel[2] *n* **1** : liste *f* (des jurés) **2** : panneau *m* <plywood panels : panneaux en contreplaqué> **3** COMMITTEE, GROUP : comité *m,* commission *f* **4** *or* **control panel** : tableau *m* (de bord)
paneling ['pænəlɪŋ] *n* : panneaux *mpl*
pang ['pæŋ] *n* **1** : tiraillement *m,* crampe *f* <hunger pangs : tiraillements d'estomac> **2** : serrement *m* de cœur <pangs of conscience : remords de conscience>

panic[1] ['pænɪk] *v* **-icked; -icking** *vt* : paniquer *fam* — *vi* : paniquer *fam,* s'affoler
panic[2] *n* : panique *f,* affolement *m*
panicky ['pænɪki] *adj* : pris de panique
panorama [ˌpænəˈræmə, -ˈrɑ-] *n* : panorama *m*
panoramic [ˌpænəˈræmɪk, -ˈrɑ-] *adj* : panoramique
pansy ['pænzi] *n, pl* **-sies** : pensée *f*
pant[1] ['pænt] *vi* : haleter, souffler
pant[2] *n* : halètement *m*
pantaloons [ˌpæntəˈlu:nz] → **pants**
panther ['pænθər] *n* **1** LEOPARD : panthère *f* **2** COUGAR, PUMA : puma *m*
panties ['pæntiz] *npl* : (petite) culotte *f,* slip *m France*
pantomime[1] ['pæntəˌmaɪm] *vt* **-mimed; -miming** : représenter par une pantomime
pantomime[2] *n* : pantomime *f*
pantry ['pæntri] *n, pl* **-tries** : garde-manger *m*
pants ['pænts] *npl* **1** : pantalon *m* **2** → **panties**
panty hose ['pæntiˌho:z] *npl* : collant *m*
pap ['pæp] *n* GRUEL : bouillie *f*
papal ['peɪpəl] *adj* : papal
papaya [pəˈpaɪə] *n* : papaye *f*
paper[1] ['peɪpər] *vt* WALLPAPER : tapisser
paper[2] *adj* : de papier, en papier
paper[3] *n* **1** : papier *m* <a sheet of paper : une feuille de papier> **2** DOCUMENT : document *m* **3** NEWSPAPER : journal *m* **4** WALLPAPER : papier *m* peint **5** : travail *m* (scolaire)
paperback ['peɪpərˌbæk] *n* : livre *m* de poche
paper clip *n* : trombone *m*
paperweight ['peɪpərˌweɪt] *n* : presse-papiers *m*
papery ['peɪpəri] *adj* : comme du papier
papier–mâché [ˌpeɪpərməˈʃeɪ, ˌpæˌpjeɪmæˈʃeɪ] *n* : papier *m* mâché
papoose [pæˈpu:s, pə-] *n* : enfant *mf* des Indiens nord-américains
paprika [pəˈpri:kə, pæ-] *n* : paprika *m*
papyrus [pəˈpaɪrəs] *n, pl* **-ruses** *or* **-ri** [-ˌri, -ˌraɪ] : papyrus *m*
par ['pɑr] *n* **1** : pair *m* (en finances) <at par value : à la valeur au pair> **2** EQUALITY : égalité *f* <to be on a par with : être l'égal de> **3** : par *m* (au golf)
parable ['pærəbəl] *n* : parabole *f*
parachute[1] ['pærəˌʃu:t] *v* **-chuted; -chuting** *vt* : parachuter — *vi* : sauter en parachute
parachute[2] *n* : parachute *m*
parachutist ['pærəˌʃu:t̬ɪst] *n* : parachutiste *mf*
parade[1] [pəˈreɪd] *vi* **-raded; -rading** **1** MARCH : défiler **2** SHOW OFF : parader, faire étalage
parade[2] *n* **1** : parade *f,* défilé *m* <circus parade : parade de cirque> **2** DISPLAY : étalage *m*
paradigm ['pærəˌdaɪm] *n* : paradigme *m*
paradise ['pærəˌdaɪs, -ˌdaɪz] *n* : paradis *m*
paradox ['pærəˌdɑks] *n* : paradoxe *m*
paradoxical [ˌpærəˈdɑksɪkəl] *adj* : paradoxal — **paradoxically** [-kli] *adv*
paraffin ['pærəfən] *n* : paraffine *f*
paragon ['pærəˌgɑn, -gən] *n* : parangon *m,* modèle *m*
paragraph[1] ['pærəˌgræf] *vt* : diviser en paragraphes
paragraph[2] *n* : paragraphe *m*
Paraguayan[1] [ˌpærəˈgwaɪən, -ˈgweɪ-] *adj* : paraguayen
Paraguayan[2] *n* : Paraguayen *m,* -guayenne *f*
parakeet ['pærəˌki:t] *n* : perruche *f*
parallel[1] ['pærəˌlɛl, -ləl] *vt* **1** EQUAL, MATCH : égaler, être équivalent à **2** : longer, être parallèle à <the road parallels the river : la route longe la rivière>
parallel[2] *adj* : parallèle
parallel[3] *n* **1** *or* **parallel line** : ligne *f* parallèle **2** : parallèle *m* (en géographie) **3** SIMILARITY : parallèle *m,* comparaison *f* <to be on a parallel with : être comparable à>
parallelogram [ˌpærəˈlɛləˌgræm] *n* : parallélogramme *m*
paralyse *Brit* → **paralyze**
paralysis [pəˈræləsɪs] *n, pl* **-yses** [-ˌsi:z] : paralysie *f*
paralyze *or Brit* **paralyse** ['pærəˌlaɪz] *vt* **-lyzed** *or Brit* **-lysed; -lyzing** *or Brit* **-lysing** : paralyser
parameter [pəˈræmət̬ər] *n* : paramètre *m*
parametric [ˌpærəˈmɛtrɪk] *adj* : paramétrique
paramount ['pærəˌmaʊnt] *adj* : suprême <of paramount importance : de la plus grande importance>
paranoia [ˌpærəˈnɔɪə] *n* : paranoïa *f*
paranoid ['pærəˌnɔɪd] *adj* : paranoïaque
parapet ['pærəpət, -ˌpɛt] *n* : parapet *m*
paraphernalia [ˌpærəfəˈneɪljə, -fər-] *ns & pl* : équipement *m,* attirail *m fam*
paraphrase[1] ['pærəˌfreɪz] *vt* **-phrased; -phrasing** : paraphraser
paraphrase[2] *n* : paraphrase *f*
paraplegic[1] [ˌpærəˈpli:dʒɪk] *adj* : paraplégique
paraplegic[2] *n* : paraplégique *mf*
parasite ['pærəˌsaɪt] *n* : parasite *m*
parasitic [ˌpærəˈsɪtɪk] *adj* : parasite, parasitaire
parasol ['pærəˌsɔl] *n* : ombrelle *f,* parasol *m*
paratrooper ['pærəˌtru:pər] *n* : parachutiste *m* (militaire)
parboil ['pɑrˌbɔɪl] *vt* : blanchir (des légumes)

parcel[1] ['pɑrsəl] *vt* **-celed** *or* **-celled; -celing** *or* **-celling** *or* **to parcel out** : diviser, répartir
parcel[2] *n* **1** PLOT : parcelle *f* (de terrain) **2** PACKAGE : paquet *m*, colis *m* **3 a parcel of lies** : un tissu de mensonges
parch ['pɑrtʃ] *vt* : dessécher
parchment ['pɑrtʃmənt] *n* : parchemin *m*
pardon[1] ['pɑrdən] *vt* **1** EXCUSE, FORGIVE : pardonner <pardon me : pardonnez-moi> **2** ABSOLVE : grâcier (en droit)
pardon[2] *n* **1** FORGIVENESS : pardon *m* <I beg your pardon : je vous demande pardon> **2** : pardon *m*, grâce *f* (en droit)
pardonable ['pɑrdənəbəl] *adj* : pardonnable
pare ['pær] *vt* **pared; paring 1** : peler (un fruit), éplucher (une pomme de terre), ronger (ses ongles) **2** REDUCE : réduire <to pare expenses : réduire les dépenses>
paregoric [ˌpærə'gɔrɪk] *n* : parégorique *m*
parent ['pærənt] *n* **1** : mère *f*, père *m* **2 parents** *npl* : parents *mpl*
parentage ['pærəntɪdʒ] *n* : ascendance *f*, origine *f*
parental [pə'rɛntəl] *adj* : parental
parenthesis [pə'rɛnθəsəs] *n, pl* **-theses** [-ˌsiːz] : parenthèse *f*
parenthetical [ˌpærən'θɛt̬ɪkəl] *adj* : entre parenthèses
parenthetically [ˌpærən'θɛt̬ɪkli] *adv* : entre parenthèses
parenthood ['pærəntˌhʊd] *n* : maternité *f*, paternité *f*
parfait [pɑr'feɪ] *n* : parfait *m*
pariah [pə'raɪə] *n* : paria *m*
parish ['pærɪʃ] *n* : paroisse *f*
parishioner [pə'rɪʃənər] *n* : paroissien *m*, -sienne *f*
Parisian[1] [pə'rɪʒən, -'ri-] *adj* : parisien
Parisian[2] *n* : Parisien *m*, -sienne *f*
parity ['pærət̬i] *n, pl* **-ties** EQUALITY : parité *f*
park[1] ['pɑrk] *vt* : garer, stationner <to park a car : garer une voiture> — *vi* : se garer, se stationner
park[2] *n* : parc *m*, jardin *m* public
parka ['pɑrkə] *n* : parka *m*
parkway ['pɑrkˌweɪ] *n* : route *f* à paysage
parley[1] ['pɑrli] *vi* **-leyed; -leying** : parlementer
parley[2] *n, pl* **-leys** : pourparlers *mpl*
parliament ['pɑrləmənt] *n* : parlement *m*
parliamentarian [ˌpɑrləˌmɛn'tɛriən, -mən-] *n* : parlementaire *mf*
parliamentary [ˌpɑrlə'mɛntəri] *adj* : parlementaire
parlor *or Brit* **parlour** ['pɑrlər] *n* **1** : petit salon *m* (pour recevoir des invités) **2** : salon *m* <beauty parlor : salon de beauté> **3 funeral parlor** → **funeral home**
parochial [pə'roːkiəl] *adj* **1** : paroissial **2** PROVINCIAL : de clocher, provincial
parody[1] ['pærədi] *vt* **-died; -dying** : parodier
parody[2] *n, pl* **-dies** : parodie *f*
parole[1] [pə'roːl] *vt* **-roled; -roling** : mettre en liberté conditionnelle
parole[2] *n* : liberté *f* conditionnelle
parolee [pəˌro'li, -'roːˌli] *n* : détenu *m* libéré sur parole
paroxysm ['pærəkˌsɪzəm, pə'rɑk-] *n* : quinte *f*, crise *f* <a paroxysm of coughing : une quinte de toux>
parquet ['pɑrˌkeɪ, pɑr'keɪ] *n* : parquet *m*
parrakeet → **parakeet**
parrot ['pærət] *n* : perroquet *m*
parry[1] ['pæri] *vt* **-ried; -rying 1** WARD OFF : esquiver, parer (un coup) **2** EVADE : éluder (une question)
parry[2] *n, pl* **-ries** : parade *f* (aux sports)
parse ['pɑrs] *vt* **parsed; parsing** : faire l'analyse grammaticale de
parsimonious [ˌpɑrsə'moːniəs] *adj* : parcimonieux — **parsimoniously** *adv*
parsley ['pɑrsli] *n* : persil *m*
parsnip ['pɑrsnɪp] *n* : panais *m*
parson ['pɑrsən] *n* : pasteur *m*, ecclésiastique *m*
part[1] ['pɑrt] *vi* **1** *or* **to part company** : se séparer, se quitter **2** BREAK : se rompre **3 to part with** : se défaire de — *vt* **1** SEPARATE : séparer **2 to part one's hair** : se faire une raie
part[2] *n* **1** : partie *f* <the best part : la meilleure partie> **2** DUTY : rôle *m*, fonction *f* **3** ROLE : rôle *m* (dans une pièce de théâtre) **4** : voix *f* <four-part harmony : harmonie à quatre voix> **5** SHARE : part *f* **6** SIDE : parti *m* <to take s.o.'s part : prendre le parti de qqn>
partake [pɑr'teɪk, pər-] *vi* **-took** [-'tʊk]; **-taken** [-'teɪkən]; **-taking 1 to partake in** : prendre part à, participer à (une activité) **2 to partake of** CONSUME : prendre, manger
partial ['pɑrʃəl] *adj* **1** : partiel <a partial solution : une solution partielle> **2** BIASED : partial — **partially** ['pɑrʃəli] *adv*
partiality [ˌpɑrʃi'ælət̬i] *n, pl* **-ties** : partialité *f*
participant [pər'tɪsəpənt, pɑr-] *n* : participant *m*, -pante *f*
participate [pər'tɪsəˌpeɪt, pɑr-] *vi* **-pated; -pating** : participer
participation [pərˌtɪsə'peɪʃən, pɑr-] *n* : participation *f*
participial [ˌpɑrtə'sɪpiəl] *adj* : participial
participle ['pɑrt̬əˌsɪpəl] *n* : participe *m* <past participle : participe passé>
particle ['pɑrt̬ɪkəl] *n* : particule *f*

particular[1] [pɑrˈtɪkjələr] *adj* **1** SPECIFIC : particulier, en particulier <one particular person : une personne en particulier> **2** SPECIAL : particulier <with particular care : avec un soin tout particulier> **3** FUSSY : tatillon, difficile

particular[2] *n* **1** : détail *m,* point *m* **2 in ~** : en particulier

particularly [pɑrˈtɪkjələrli] *adv* : particulièrement, spécialement

partisan[1] [ˈpɑrt̬əzən, -sən] *adj* : partisan

partisan[2] *n* SUPPORTER : partisan *m,* -sane *f*

partition[1] [pərˈtɪʃən, pɑr-] *vt* : morceler (un domaine), diviser, cloisonner (une pièce)

partition[2] *n* **1** DISTRIBUTION : division *f,* répartition *f* **2** DIVIDER : cloison *f* (d'une pièce, etc.)

partly [ˈpɑrtli] *adv* : en partie

partner [ˈpɑrtnər] *n* **1** ASSOCIATE : associé *m,* -ciée *f;* partenaire *mf* (en commerce) **2** : partenaire *mf* (aux sports, en danse) **3** COMPANION : compagnon *m,* compagne *f* **4** SPOUSE : époux *m,* épouse *f*

partnership [ˈpɑrtnər,ʃɪp] *n* : association *f*

part of speech *n* : partie *f* du discours

partridge [ˈpɑrtrɪdʒ] *n, pl* **-tridge** *or* **-tridges** : perdrix *f*

party [ˈpɑrti] *n, pl* **-ties 1** : parti *m* (politique) **2** PARTICIPANT : partie *f* **3** GROUP : groupe *m* <a mountain-climbing party : un groupe d'alpinisme> **4** GATHERING : fête *f,* party *m Can fam*

parvenu [ˈpɑrvə,nuː, -,njuː] *n* : parvenu *m,* -nue *f*

pass[1] [ˈpæs] *vi* **1** MOVE, PROCEED : passer **2** *or* **to pass away** DIE : mourir **3** : ne pas tenir compte de <I let his remark pass : je n'ai pas tenu compte de son commentaire> **4** TRANSFER : changer **5** OCCUR : se passer, avoir lieu **6** : passer (aux cartes) **7 to pass for** : se prendre pour — *vt* **1** : passer (une loi) **2** : dépasser (une voiture, etc.) **3** : passer (un examen) **4** : passer <pass the salt, please : passez-moi le sel, s'il vous plaît>

pass[2] *n* **1** CROSSING, GAP : col *m* **2** : mention *f* passable (à un examen) **3** PERMISSION, PERMIT : permis *m* **4** : laissez-passer *m* <season pass : laissez-passer saisonnier> **5** : passe *f* (aux sports)

passable [ˈpæsəbəl] *adj* **1** ACCEPTABLE : passable, acceptable **2** NEGOTIABLE : praticable, passable *Can* <passable roads : chemins praticables>

passably [ˈpæsəbli] *adv* : passablement

passage [ˈpæsɪdʒ] *n* **1** PASSAGEWAY : passage *m,* corridor *m,* couloir *m* **2** ENACTMENT : adoption *f* (d'une loi) **3** VOYAGE : voyage *m* **4** : passage *m,* extrait *m* (d'un livre)

passageway [ˈpæsɪdʒ,weɪ] *n* : passage *m,* corridor *m,* couloir *m*

passbook [ˈpæs,bʊk] → **bankbook**

passé [pæˈseɪ] *adj* OUT-OF-DATE : dépassé, démodé

passenger [ˈpæsəndʒər] *n* : passager *m,* -gère *f*

passerby [,pæsərˈbaɪ, ˈpæsər,-] *n, pl* **passersby** : passant *m,* -sante *f*

passing [ˈpæsɪŋ] *n* DEATH : disparition *f,* mort *f*

passion [ˈpæʃən] *n* **1** LOVE : passion *f,* ardeur *f* **2** EMOTION : émotion *f* forte, passion *f* **3** ANGER : (accès *m* de) colère *f*

passionate [ˈpæʃənət] *adj* : passionné — **passionately** *adv*

passive[1] [ˈpæsɪv] *adj* : passif — **passively** *adv*

passive[2] *n or* **passive case** : passif *m* (en grammaire)

Passover [ˈpæs,oːvər] *n* : Pâque *f* (juive)

passport [ˈpæs,port] *n* : passeport *m*

password [ˈpæs,wərd] *n* : mot *m* de passe

past[1] [ˈpæst] *adv* : devant <to run past : passer en courant>

past[2] *adj* **1** : dernier, passé <the past month : le mois dernier> **2** FORMER : ancien <a past president : un ancien président>

past[3] *n* **1** : passé *m* **2 in the past** : dans le passé, autrefois

past[4] *prep* **1** BEYOND : au-delà de <just past the corner : juste au-delà du coin> **2** (*in expressions of time*) <half past four : quatre heures et demie> **3 to go past** : passer

pasta [ˈpɑstə, ˈpæs-] *n* : pâtes *fpl* (alimentaires)

paste[1] [ˈpeɪst] *vt* **pasted; pasting** : coller

paste[2] *n* **1** : purée *f* <tomato paste : purée de tomates> **2** GLUE : colle *f*

pasteboard [ˈpeɪst,bord] → **cardboard**

pastel[1] [pæˈstɛl] *adj* : pastel

pastel[2] *n* : pastel *m*

pasteurization [,pæstʃərəˈzeɪʃən, ,pæstjə-] *n* : pasteurisation *f*

pasteurize [ˈpæstʃə,raɪz, ˈpæstjə-] *vt* **-ized; -izing** : pasteuriser

pastime [ˈpæs,taɪm] *n* : passe-temps *m*

pastor [ˈpæstər] *n* : pasteur *m*

pastoral [ˈpæstərəl] *adj* : pastoral

pastry [ˈpeɪstri] *n, pl* **-ries** : pâtisserie *f*

pasture[1] [ˈpæstʃər] *vt* **-tured; -turing** : faire paître

pasture[2] *n* : pâturage *m*

pasty [ˈpeɪsti] *adj* **pastier; -est 1** : pâteux <a pasty consistency : une consistance pâteuse> **2** PALLID : terreux (se dit du teint)

pat[1] [ˈpæt] *vt* **patted; patting** : tapoter

pat[2] *adv* : parfaitement <to have sth down pat : connaître par cœur qqch>

pat[3] *adj* **1** APT : convenable, approprié **2** GLIB : tout prêt

pat[4] *n* **1** TAP : (petite) tape *f* **2** : noix *f* (de beurre, etc.)

patch[1] [ˈpætʃ] *vt* **1** MEND, REPAIR : rapiécer, réparer **2 to patch up** : résoudre (des difficultés, etc.) <they patched things up : ils se sont réconciliés>
patch[2] *n* **1** : pièce *f* (d'étoffe) **2** : parcelle *f* (de terre) **3** : tache *f* <a patch of white : une tache blanche> **4** : plaque *f* <patches of ice : plaques de glace>
patchwork [ˈpætʃˌwərk] *n* : patchwork *m*
patchy [ˈpætʃi] *adj* **patchier; -est 1** : inégal, irrégulier **2** INCOMPLETE : incomplet
patent[1] [ˈpætənt] *vt* : breveter
patent[2] [ˈpætənt] *adj* **1** *or* **patented** [-təd] : breveté **2** [ˈpætənt, ˈpeɪt-] OBVIOUS : patent, évident
patent[3] [ˈpætənt] *n* : brevet *m*
paternal [pəˈtərnəl] *adj* : paternel — **paternally** *adv*
paternity [pəˈtərnət̬i] *n* : paternité *f*
path [ˈpæθ, ˈpaθ] *n* **1** : allée *f* (dans un jardin) **2** TRACK, TRAIL : chemin *m*, sentier *m* **3** COURSE, TRAJECTORY : trajectoire *f*
pathetic [pəˈθet̬ɪk] *adj* **1** PITIFUL : pitoyable **2** DEPLORABLE : minable *fam*, déplorable
pathological [ˌpæθəˈlɑdʒɪkəl] *adj* : pathologique
pathologist [pəˈθɑlədʒɪst] *n* : pathologiste *mf*
pathology [pəˈθɑlədʒi] *n, pl* **-gies** : pathologie *f*
pathos [ˈpeɪˌθɑs, ˈpæ-, -ˌθɔs] *n* : pathos *m*
pathway [ˈpæθˌweɪ] *n* : sentier *m*, chemin *m*
patience [ˈpeɪʃənts] *n* : patience *f*
patient[1] [ˈpeɪʃənt] *adj* : patient
patient[2] *n* : patient *m*, -tiente *f*; malade *mf*
patiently [ˈpeɪʃəntli] *adv* : patiemment
patina [pəˈtiːnə, ˈpætənə] *n, pl* **-nas** [-nəz] *or* **-nae** [-ˌni, -ˌnaɪ] : patine *f*
patio [ˈpæt̬iˌoː, ˈpɑt-] *n, pl* **-tios** : patio *m*
patriarch [ˈpeɪtriˌɑrk] *n* : patriarche *m*
patrimony [ˈpætrəˌmoːni] *n* : patrimoine *m*
patriot [ˈpeɪtriət, -ˌɑt] *n* : patriote *mf*
patriotic [ˌpeɪtriˈɑt̬ɪk] *adj* : patriote
patriotically [ˌpeɪtriˈɑt̬ɪkli] *adv* : patriotiquement
patriotism [ˈpeɪtriəˌtɪzəm] *n* : patriotisme *m*
patrol[1] [pəˈtroːl] *vi* **-trolled; -trolling** : patrouiller
patrol[2] *n* : patrouille *f*
patrolman [pəˈtroːlmən] *n, pl* **-men** [-mən, -ˌmɛn] : agent *m* de police
patron [ˈpeɪtrən] *n* **1** SPONSOR, SUPPORTER : mécène *m* **2** CUSTOMER : client *m*, cliente *f*
patronage [ˈpeɪtrənɪdʒ, ˈpæ-] *n* **1** SPONSORSHIP : patronage *m* **2** CLIENTELE : clientèle *f* **3** : pouvoir *m* de nomination (en politique)
patronize [ˈpeɪtrəˌnaɪz, ˈpæ-] *vt* **-ized; -izing 1** SUPPORT : patronner, parrainer **2** : être un client de, fréquenter (un marché) **3** : traiter avec condescendance
patter[1] [ˈpæt̬ər] *vi* **1** TAP : tapoter **2** *or* **to patter about** : trottiner
patter[2] *n* **1** TALK : baratin *m* (d'un vendeur) **2** PAT, TAP : tapotement *m*
pattern[1] [ˈpætərn] *vt* : faire selon un motif, modeler
pattern[2] *n* **1** EXAMPLE, MODEL : modèle *m* **2** DESIGN : dessin *m*, motif *m* **3** NORM, STANDARD : mode *m*, norme *f*
patty [ˈpæt̬i] *n, pl* **-ties 1** : petit pâté *m* **2** *or* **hamburger patty** : steak *m* haché
paucity [ˈpɔsət̬i] *n* : manque *m*, pénurie *f*
paunch [ˈpɔntʃ] *n* : ventre *m*, bedaine *f*
pauper [ˈpɔpər] *n* : pauvre *m*; indigent *m*, -gente *f*
pause[1] [ˈpɔz] *vi* **paused; pausing** : faire une pause
pause[2] *n* : pause *f*, arrêt *m*
pave [ˈpeɪv] *vt* **paved; paving** : paver, revêtir (d'asphalte, etc.)
pavement [ˈpeɪvmənt] *n* : revêtement *m* de la chaussée
pavilion [pəˈvɪljən] *n* : pavillon *m*
paving [ˈpeɪvɪŋ] → **pavement**
paw[1] [ˈpɔ] *vt* **1** TOUCH : tripoter, taponner *Can fam* **2** : donner un coup de patte à <the dog was pawing at my hand : le chien me donnait des coups de patte sur la main>
paw[2] *n* : patte *f* (d'un animal)
pawn[1] [ˈpɔn] *vt* : mettre en gage
pawn[2] *n* : gage *m*
pawnbroker [ˈpɔnˌbroːkər] *n* : prêteur *m*, -teuse *f* sur gages
pawnshop [ˈpɔnˌʃɑp] *n* : mont-de-piété *m France*
pay[1] [ˈpeɪ] *v* **paid** [ˈpeɪd]; **paying** *vt* **1** : payer (un compte, etc.) **2 to pay attention to** : prêter attention à **3 to pay back** : rembourser, s'acquitter de (une dette) **4 to pay one's respects to** : présenter ses respects à **5 to pay s.o. a visit** : aller voir qqn, rendre visite à qqn — *vi* : payer <crime doesn't pay : le crime ne paie pas>
pay[2] *n* : paie *f*, salaire *m*
payable [ˈpeɪəbəl] *adj* : payable
paycheck [ˈpeɪˌtʃɛk] *n* : chèque *m* de paie
payee [peɪˈiː] *n* : bénéficiaire *mf*
payment [ˈpeɪmənt] *n* : paiement *m*
PC [ˌpiːˈsiː] *n, pl* **PCs** *or* **PC's** : PC *m*, micro-ordinateur *m*
pea [ˈpiː] *n* : pois *m*
peace [ˈpiːs] *n* : paix *f*
peaceable [ˈpiːsəbəl] *adj* : paisible — **peaceably** [-bli] *adv*

peaceful ['pi:sfəl] *adj* **1** PEACEABLE : de paix, paisible <peaceful times : temps de paix> **2** CALM : paisible, calme

peacefully ['pi:sfəli] *adv* : paisiblement, calmement

peacekeeper ['pi:s,ki:pər] *n* : soldat *m* de la paix

peacekeeping ['pi:s,ki:pɪŋ] *n* : maintien *m* de la paix

peacemaker ['pi:s,meɪkər] *n* : pacificateur *m*, -trice *f;* conciliateur *m*, -trice *f*

peach ['pi:tʃ] *n* : pêche *f*

peacock ['pi:,kɑk] *n* : paon *m*

peak[1] ['pi:k] *vi* : culminer, atteindre un sommet

peak[2] *adj* : maximal <peak performance : performance maximale>

peak[3] *n* **1** CREST : sommet *m* (d'une colline) **2** *or* **mountain peak** : pic *m* **3** APEX : apogée *f* <at the peak of his glory : à l'apogée de sa gloire>

peaked ['pi:kəd] *adj* SICKLY : pâlot, malade

peal[1] ['pi:l] *vi* RESOUND : résonner

peal[2] *n* : carillonnement *m* (des cloches)

peanut ['pi:,nʌt] *n* **1** : cacahouète *f*, pinotte *f Can fam* (noix) **2** : arachide *f* (plante)

pear ['pær] *n* : poire *f*

pearl ['pərl] *n* : perle *f*

pearly ['pərli] *adj* **pearlier; -est** : nacré, perlé

peasant ['pɛzənt] *n* : paysan *m*, -sanne *f*

peat ['pi:t] *n* **1** : tourbe *f* **2 peat bog** → **bog**

pebble ['pɛbəl] *n* : caillou *m*

pecan [pɪ'kɑn, -'kæn, 'pi:,kæn] *n* : noix *f* de pécan *France,* noix *f* de pacane *Can*

peccadillo [,pɛkə'dɪlo] *n, pl* **-loes** *or* **-los** : peccadille *f*

peck[1] ['pɛk] *vt* : picorer, becqueter — *vi* **to peck at one's food** : manger du bout des dents

peck[2] *n* **1** : picotin *m* (mesure) **2** : coup *m* de bec (d'un oiseau) **3** KISS : bécot *m France fam,* bec *m Can fam*

pectoral ['pɛktərəl] *adj* : pectoral

peculiar [pɪ'kju:ljər] *adj* **1** DISTINCTIVE : particulier **2** STRANGE : étrange, bizarre

peculiarity [pɪ,kju:l'jærət̬i, -,kju:li'ær-] *n, pl* **-ties 1** DISTINCTIVENESS : particularité *f* **2** STRANGENESS : étrangeté *f*, bizarrerie *f*

peculiarly [pɪ'kju:ljərli] *adv* **1** PARTICULARLY : particulièrement **2** STRANGELY : de manière étrange, bizarrement

pecuniary [pɪ'kju:ni,ɛri] *adj* : pécuniaire

pedagogical [,pɛdə'gɑdʒɪkəl, -'go:-] *adj* : pédagogique

pedagogy ['pɛdə,go:dʒi, -,gɑ-] *n* : pédagogie *f*

pedal[1] ['pɛdəl] *vt* **-aled** *or* **-alled; -aling** *or* **-alling** : pédaler

pedal[2] *n* : pédale *f*

pedant ['pɛdənt] *n* : pédant *m*, -dante *f*

pedantic [pɪ'dæntɪk] *adj* : pédant

pedantry ['pɛdəntri] *n, pl* **-ries** : pédantisme *m*

peddle ['pɛdəl] *v* **-dled; -dling** *vt* : colporter — *vi* : faire du colportage

peddler ['pɛdlər] *n* : colporteur *m*, -teuse *f*

pedestal ['pɛdəstəl] *n* : piédestal *m*

pedestrian[1] [pə'dɛstriən] *adj* **1** COMMONPLACE : prosaïque, commun **2** : piétonnier <pedestrian zone : zone piétonnière> <pedestrian crossing : passage pour piétons>

pedestrian[2] *n* : piéton *m*

pediatric [,pi:di'ætrɪk] *adj* : pédiatrique

pediatrician [,pi:diə'trɪʃən] *n* : pédiatre *mf*

pediatrics [,pi:di'ætrɪks] *ns & pl* : pédiatrie *f*

pedigree ['pɛdə,gri:] *n* **1** FAMILY TREE : arbre *m* généalogique **2** LINEAGE : pedigree *m* (d'un animal), lignée *f* (d'une personne)

pediment ['pɛdəmənt] *n* : fronton *m*

peek[1] ['pi:k] *vi* **1** PEEP : regarder furtivement **2** GLANCE : jeter un coup d'œil

peek[2] *n* : coup *m* d'œil furtif

peel[1] ['pi:l] *vt* **1** : peler (un fruit), éplucher (un oignon, etc.) **2** *or* **to peel off** : enlever (une étiquette, etc.) — *vi* **1** : peler, pleumer *Can fam* (se dit de la peau) **2** : s'écailler (se dit de la peinture)

peel[2] *n* : pelure *f* (d'une pomme), écorce *f* (d'une orange), épluchure *f* (de pommes de terre)

peeling → **peel**[2]

peep[1] ['pi:p] *vi* **1** : pépier, piauler (se dit d'un oiseau) **2** *or* **to peep through** EMERGE : apparaître, se montrer **3 to peep at** : jeter un coup d'œil à

peep[2] *n* **1** : pépiement *m* (d'un oiseau) **2** : coup *m* d'œil <to take a peek : jeter un coup d'œil>

peer[1] ['pɪr] *vi* : regarder attentivement

peer[2] *n* **1** EQUAL : pair *m*, égal *m* **2** NOBLEMAN : noble *m*, pair *m*

peerage ['pɪrɪdʒ] *n* : pairie *f*

peerless ['pɪrləs] *adj* : hors pair, sans égal

peeve[1] ['pi:v] *vt* **peeved; peeving** : mettre en rogne, irriter

peeve[2] *n or* **pet peeve** : bête *f* noire

peevish ['pi:vɪʃ] *adj* : grincheux, grognon

peg[1] ['pɛg] *vt* **pegged; pegging** ATTACH, FASTEN : accrocher, attacher

peg[2] *n* **1** HOOK : patère *f* (de bois), fiche *f* (de métal) **2** STAKE : piquet *m* (de tente)

peignoir [peɪn'wɑr, pɛn-] *n* : peignoir *m*, négligé *m*

pejorative [pɪ'dʒɔrət̬ɪv] *adj* : péjoratif — **pejoratively** *adv*

pelican ['pɛlɪkən] *n* : pélican *m*

pellagra [pə'lægrə, -'leɪ-] *n* : pellagre *f*

pellet ['pɛlət] *n* **1** BALL : boulette *f* (de papier, etc.) **2** SHOT : plomb *m*

pell–mell [pɛl'mɛl] *adv* : pêle-mêle

pelt[1] ['pɛlt] *vt* : cribler, bombarder <they pelted her with accusations : ils l'ont criblée d'accusations> <to pelt s.o. with stones : lancer des pierres à qqn>

pelt[2] *n* : peau *f* (d'un animal)

pelvic ['pɛlvɪk] *adj* : pelvien

pelvis ['pɛlvɪs] *n, pl* **-vises** [-vɪsəz] *or* **-ves** [-ˌviːz] : bassin *m*, pelvis *m*

pen[1] ['pɛn] *vt* **penned; penning 1** : enfermer dans un abri ou un enclos **2** WRITE : écrire

pen[2] *n* **1** : enclos *m*, parc *m* (d'animaux) **2** : stylo *m* <ballpoint pen : stylo à bille>

penal ['piːnəl] *adj* **1** : pénal <a penal offense : une offense pénale> **2** : pénitentiaire <a penal colony : une colonie pénitentiaire>

penalize ['piːnəlˌaɪz, 'pɛn-] *vt* **-ized; -izing** : pénaliser, punir *Can* (aux sports)

penalty ['pɛnəlti] *n, pl* **-ties 1** : peine *f* (en droit) **2** : pénalité *f*, pénalisation *f*, punition *f Can* (aux sports)

penance ['pɛnənts] *n* : pénitence *f*

pence ['pɛnts] → **penny**

penchant ['pɛntʃənt] *n* : penchant *m*

pencil[1] ['pɛntsəl] *vt* **-ciled** *or* **-cilled; -ciling** *or* **-cilling** : écrire ou dessiner au crayon

pencil[2] *n* : crayon *m*

pencil sharpener *n* : taille-crayon *m*, aiguise-crayon *m Can*

pendant ['pɛndənt] *n* : pendentif *m*

pending[1] ['pɛndɪŋ] *adj* UNDECIDED : en instance

pending[2] *prep* **1** DURING : pendant **2** AWAITING : en attendant

pendulum ['pɛndʒələm, -djʊləm] *n* : pendule *m*

penetrate ['pɛnəˌtreɪt] *v* **-trated; -trating** *vt* : pénétrer — *vi* : pénétrer, s'infiltrer

penetration [ˌpɛnə'treɪʃən] *n* : pénétration *f*

penguin ['pɛŋgwɪn, 'pɛn-] *n* : manchot *m*

penicillin [ˌpɛnə'sɪlən] *n* : pénicilline *f*

peninsula [pə'nɪntsələ, -'nɪntʃʊlə] *n* : péninsule *f*

penis ['piːnəs] *n, pl* **-nes** [-ˌniːz] *or* **-nises** : pénis *m*

penitence ['pɛnətənts] *n* : pénitence *f*

penitent[1] ['pɛnətənt] *adj* : pénitent, repentant

penitent[2] *n* : pénitent *m*, -tente *f*

penitential [ˌpɛnə'tɛntʃəl] *adj* : pénitentiel

penitentiary [ˌpɛnə'tɛntʃəri] *n, pl* **-ries** : pénitencier *m*, prison *f*

penmanship ['pɛnmənˌʃɪp] *n* : écriture *f*, calligraphie *f*

pen name *n* : nom *m* de plume, pseudonyme *m*

pennant ['pɛnənt] *n* : fanion *m*, flamme *f* (d'un navire)

penniless ['pɛnɪləs] *adj* : sans le sou

penny ['pɛni] *n, pl* **-nies** : centime *m*, cent *m*, sou *m Can*

pension[1] ['pɛntʃən] *vt* **1** : verser une pension à **2 to pension off** : mettre à la retraite

pension[2] *n* : pension *f*, retraite *f*

pensive ['pɛntsɪv] *adj* : pensif, songeur — **pensively** *adv*

pent ['pɛnt] *adj* : réprimé <pent-up feelings : sentiments réprimés>

pentagon ['pɛntəˌgɑn] *n* : pentagone *m*

pentagonal [pɛn'tægənəl] *adj* : pentagonal

penthouse ['pɛntˌhaʊs] *n* : appartement *m* construit sur le toit d'un immeuble

penury ['pɛnjəri] *n* : indigence *f*

peon ['piːˌɑn, -ən] *n, pl* **-ons** *or* **-ones** [peɪ'oːniːz] : péon *m*

peony ['piːəni] *n, pl* **-nies** : pivoine *f*

people[1] ['piːpəl] *vt* **-pled; -pling** : peupler

people[2] *ns & pl* **1 people** *npl* : personnes *fpl*, gens *mfpl* <we met several people : nous avons rencontré plusieurs personnes> <old people : vieilles gens> **2** *pl* **peoples** : peuple *m* <the peoples of Africa : les peuples d'Afrique>

pep[1] ['pɛp] *vt* **pepped; pepping** *or* **to pep up** : remonter le moral à

pep[2] *n* : dynamisme *m*, entrain *m*

pepper[1] ['pɛpər] *vt* **1** : poivrer (en cuisine) **2** RIDDLE : cribler (de balles, etc.) **3** SPRINKLE : émailler <peppered with quotations : émaillé de citations>

pepper[2] *n* **1** : poivre *m* (condiment) **2** : poivron *m* <green pepper : poivron vert> **3** → **chili**

peppermint ['pɛpərˌmɪnt] *n* : menthe *f* poivrée

peppery ['pɛpəri] *adj* : poivré

peppy ['pɛpi] *adj* **peppier; -est** : plein d'énergie, vivant

peptic ['pɛptɪk] *adj* **peptic ulcer** : ulcère *m* de l'estomac

per ['pər] *prep* **1** : par <ten dollars per day : dix dollars par jour> **2** ACCORDING TO : selon, conformément à <per instructions : selon les directives>

per annum [pər'ænəm] *adv* : par an, annuellement

percale [ˌpər'keɪl, 'pər-,; ˌpər'kæl] *n* : percale *f*

perceive [pər'siːv] *vt* **-ceived; -ceiving** : percevoir

percent[1] [pər'sɛnt] *adv* : pour cent

percent[2] *n, pl* **-cent** *or* **-cents 1** : pour cent *m* <ten percent of the time : dix pour cent du temps> **2** PERCENTAGE : pourcentage *m* <a percent of his income : un pourcentage de son revenu>

percentage [pər'sɛntɪdʒ] *n* : pourcentage *m*
perceptible [pər'sɛptəbəl] *adj* : perceptible
perceptibly [pər'sɛptəbli] *adv* : de manière perceptible
perception [pər'sɛpʃən] *n* : perception *f*
perceptive [pər'sɛptɪv] *adj* : perspicace
perceptively [pər'sɛptɪvli] *adv* : avec perspicacité
perceptiveness [pər'sɛptɪvnəs] *n* : perspicacité *f*
perch[1] ['pərtʃ] *vt* : percher — *vi* : se percher
perch[2] *n* **1** ROOST : perchoir *m* **2** *pl* **perch** *or* **perches** : perche *f* (poisson)
percolate ['pərkə,leɪt] *v* **-lated; -lating** *vi* SEEP : filtrer, passer — *vt* : faire (du café) dans une cafetière
percolator ['pərkə,leɪṭər] *n* : cafetière *f* à pression
percussion [pər'kʌʃən] *n* : percussion *f*
peremptory [pə'rɛmptəri] *adj* : péremptoire
perennial[1] [pə'rɛniəl] *adj* **1** : vivace <perennial flowers : fleurs vivaces> **2** RECURRING : perpétuel
perennial[2] *n* : plante *f* vivace
perennially [pə'rɛniəli] *adv* : perpétuellement
perfect[1] [pər'fɛkt] *vt* : perfectionner
perfect[2] ['pərfɪkt] *adj* : parfait — **perfectly** *adv*
perfectible [pər'fɛktəbəl] *adj* : perfectible
perfection [pər'fɛkʃən] *n* : perfection *f*
perfectionist[1] [pər'fɛkʃənɪst] *or* **perfectionistic** [pər,fɛkʃə'nɪstɪk] *adj* : perfectionniste
perfectionist[2] *n* : perfectionniste *mf*
perfidious [pər'fɪdiəs] *adj* : perfide
perforate ['pərfə,reɪt] *vt* **-rated; -rating** : perforer
perforation [,pərfə'reɪʃən] *n* : perforation *f*
perform [pər'fɔrm] *vt* **1** CARRY OUT : réaliser, effectuer, accomplir **2** PRESENT : jouer, donner (une pièce de théâtre, etc.) — *vi* ACT : jouer (dans une pièce de théâtre, etc.)
performance [pər'fɔr,mənts] *n* **1** EXECUTION : rendement *m* **2** : interprétation *f* (d'un acteur, d'un comédien), performance *f* (d'une équipe) **3** PRESENTATION, SHOW : spectacle *m*
performer [pər'fɔrmər] *n* : interprète *mf*
perfume[1] [pər'fju:m, 'pər,-] *vt* **-fumed; -fuming** : parfumer
perfume[2] ['pər,fju:m, pər'-] *n* : parfum *m*
perfunctory [pər'fʌŋktəri] *adj* : mécanique, sommaire
perhaps [pər'hæps] *adv* : peut-être
peril ['pɛrəl] *n* : péril *m*, danger *m*
perilous ['pɛrələs] *adj* : périlleux, dangereux — **perilously** *adv*
perimeter [pə'rɪməṭər] *n* : périmètre *m*
period ['pɪriəd] *n* **1** : point *m* (signe de ponctuation) **2** INTERVAL, TIME : période *f* **3** EPOCH, ERA : ère *f*, période *f*, époque *f* **4** *or* **menstrual period** : règles *fpl*
periodic [,pɪri'ɑdɪk] *adj* : périodique — **periodically** [-dɪkli] *adv*
periodical [,pɪri'ɑdɪkəl] *n* : périodique *m*, journal *m*
peripheral [pə'rɪfərəl] *adj* : périphérique
periphery [pə'rɪfəri] *n*, *pl* **-eries** : périphérie *f*
periscope ['pɛrə,sko:p] *n* : périscope *m*
perish ['pɛrɪʃ] *vi* DIE : périr
perishable ['pɛrɪʃəbəl] *adj* : périssable
perishables ['pɛrɪʃəbəlz] *npl* : denrées *fpl* périssables
perjure ['pərdʒər] *vt* **-jured; -juring** *or* **to perjure onself** : se parjurer
perjurer ['pərdʒərər] *n* : parjure *mf*
perjury ['pərdʒəri] *n* : faux témoignage *m*
perk[1] ['pərk] *vi* **to perk up** : se ragaillardir — *vt* **1** ENLIVEN, STIMULATE : revigorer **2** FRESHEN : égayer **3** **to perk up one's ears** : dresser les oreilles
perk[2] *n* : avantage *m*, privilège *m* (d'un emploi)
perky ['pərki] *adj* **perkier; -est** : guilleret, fringant
permanence ['pərmənənts] *n* : permanence *f*
permanent[1] ['pərmənənt] *adj* : permanent
permanent[2] *n* : permanente *f*
permanently ['pərmənəntli] *adv* : de façon permanente, en permanence
permeable ['pərmiəbəl] *adj* : perméable
permeate ['pərmi,eɪt] *v* **-ated; -ating** *vi* : se diffuser, se répandre — *vt* **1** IMPREGNATE : impregner <permeated with smoke : impregné de fumée> **2** PERVADE : s'infiltrer dans, se répandre dans
permissible [pər'mɪsəbəl] *adj* : permis, admissible
permission [pər'mɪʃən] *n* : permission *f*, autorisation *f*
permissive [pər'mɪsɪv] *adj* : permissif — **permissively** *adv*
permit[1] [pər'mɪt] *v* **-mitted; -mitting** *vt* : permettre, autoriser — *vi* ALLOW : permettre <if time permits : si le temps le permet>
permit[2] ['pər,mɪt, pər'-] *n* : permis *m*, licence *f*
pernicious [pər'nɪʃəs] *adj* : pernicieux — **perniciously** *adv*
peroxide [pə'rɑk,saɪd] *n* : peroxyde *m*
perpendicular [,pərpən'dɪkjələr] *adj* : perpendiculaire — **perpendicularly** *adv*
perpetrate ['pərpə,treɪt] *vt* **-trated; -trating** : perpétrer
perpetration [,pərpə'treɪʃən] *n* : perpétration *f*
perpetrator ['pərpə,treɪṭər] *n* : auteur *m* (d'un délit)

perpetual [pərˈpɛtʃʊəl] *adj* : éternel, perpétuel
perpetually [pərˈpɛtʃʊəli, -tʃəli] *adv* : perpétuellement
perpetuate [pərˈpɛtʃʊˌeɪt] *vt* **-ated; -ating** : perpétuer
perpetuation [pərˌpɛtʃəˈweɪʃən] *n* : perpétuation *f*
perplex [pərˈplɛks] *vt* : laisser perplexe
perplexity [pərˈplɛksəti] *n, pl* **-ties** : perplexité *f*
persecute [ˈpərsɪˌkjuːt] *vt* **-cuted; -cuting** : persécuter
persecution [ˌpərsɪˈkjuːʃən] *n* : persécution *f*
persecutor [ˈpərsɪˌkjuːtər] *n* : persécuteur *m*, -trice *f*
perseverance [ˌpərsəˈvɪrənts] *n* : persévérance *f*
persevere [ˌpərsəˈvɪr] *vi* **-vered; -vering** : persévérer
Persian[1] [ˈpərʒən] *adj* : persan
Persian[2] *n* **1** : Persan *m*, -sane *f* **2** : persan *m* (langue)
persist [pərˈsɪst] *vi* : persister
persistence [pərˈsɪstənts] *n* : persistance *f*, persévérance *f*
persistent [pərˈsɪstənt] *adj* : persistant
persistently [pərˈsɪstəntli] *adv* : sans cesse, continuellement
person [ˈpərsən] *n* **1** INDIVIDUAL : personne *f*, individu *m* **2** : personne *f* (en grammaire) **3 in ~** : en personne
personable [ˈpərsənəbəl] *adj* : agréable, aimable
personage [ˈpərsənɪdʒ] *n* : personnage *m*, personne *f* haut placée
personal [ˈpərsənəl] *adj* **1** PRIVATE : personnel, privé <personal property : biens mobiliers personnels> <personal hygiene : hygiène personnelle> **2** : en personne <a personal visit : une visite en personne> **3** INTIMATE : personnel <a personal conversation : une conversation personnelle>
personality [ˌpərsənˈæləti] *n, pl* **-ties 1** CHARACTER, TEMPERAMENT : personnalité *f* **2** CELEBRITY : vedette *f*
personalize [ˈpərsənəˌlaɪz] *vt* **-ized; -izing** : personnaliser
personally [ˈpərsənəli] *adv* **1** : personnellement <I'll attend to the matter personally : je vais y voir personnellement> **2** DIRECTLY : en personne **3** INDIVIDUALLY : personnellement <not you personally : pas toi personnellement>
personification [pərˌsɑnəfəˈkeɪʃən] *n* : personnification *f*
personify [pərˈsɑnəˌfaɪ] *vt* **-fied; -fying** : personnifier
personnel [ˌpərsənˈɛl] *n* : personnel *m*
perspective [pərˈspɛktɪv] *n* : perspective *f*
perspicacious [ˌpərspəˈkeɪʃəs] *adj* : perspicace
perspicacity [ˌpərspəˈkæsəti] *n* : perspicacité *f*
perspiration [ˌpərspəˈreɪʃən] *n* : transpiration *f*, sueur *f*
perspire [pərˈspaɪr] *vi* **-spired; -spiring** : transpirer, suer
persuade [pərˈsweɪd] *vt* **-suaded; -suading** : persuader, convaincre
persuasion [pərˈsweɪʒən] *n* **1** : persuasion *f* <the power of persuasion : le pouvoir de persuasion> **2** BELIEF : conviction *f*
persuasive [pərˈsweɪsɪv, -zɪv] *adj* : persuasif, convaincant
persuasively [pərˈsweɪsɪvli, -zɪv-] *adv* : persuasivement
persuasiveness [pərˈsweɪsɪvnəs, -zɪv-] *n* : force *f* de persuasion
pert [ˈpərt] *adj* **1** FLIPPANT : effronté, insolent **2** JAUNTY : coquet
pertain [pərˈteɪn] *vi* **1** BELONG : se rapporter <duties pertaining to the office : des fonctions qui se rapportent au bureau> **2** RELATE : traiter, avoir rapport <books pertaining to birds : livres sur les oiseaux>
pertinence [ˈpərtənənts] *n* : pertinence *f*
pertinent [ˈpərtənənt] *adj* : pertinent
perturb [pərˈtərb] *vt* : troubler, inquiéter
perusal [pəˈruːzəl] *n* : lecture *f* attentive
peruse [pəˈruːz] *vt* **-rused; -rusing** : lire attentivement
Peruvian[1] [pəˈruːviən] *adj* : péruvien
Peruvian[2] *n* : Péruvien *m*, -vienne *f*
pervade [pərˈveɪd] *vt* **-vaded; -vading** : s'infiltrer à, se répandre dans
pervasive [pərˈveɪsɪv, -zɪv] *adj* : envahissant, pénétrant
perverse [pərˈvərs] *adj* **1** CORRUPT : pervers, vicieux **2** STUBBORN : obstiné, entêté
perversely [pərˈvərsli] *adv* **1** VICIOUSLY : avec un malin plaisir **2** STUBBORNLY : obstinément
perversion [pərˈvərʒən] *n* : perversion *f*
perversity [pərˈvərsəti] *n, pl* **-ties** : perversité *f*
pervert[1] [pərˈvərt] *vt* **1** CORRUPT : pervertir, corrompre **2** DISTORT : déformer
pervert[2] [ˈpərˌvərt] *n* : pervers *m*, -verse *f*
peso [ˈpeɪˌsoː] *n, pl* **-sos** : peso *m*
pessimism [ˈpɛsəˌmɪzəm] *n* : pessimisme *m*
pessimist [ˈpɛsəmɪst] *n* : pessimiste *mf*
pessimistic [ˌpɛsəˈmɪstɪk] *adj* : pessimiste
pest [ˈpɛst] *n* **1** NUISANCE : peste *f*, plaie *f fam* **2** : plante *f* ou animal *m* nuisible
pester [ˈpɛstər] *vt* **-tered; -tering** : importuner, harceler
pesticide [ˈpɛstəˌsaɪd] *n* : pesticide *m*
pestilence [ˈpɛstələnts] *n* : peste *f*, pestilence *f*
pestle [ˈpɛsəl, ˈpɛstəl] *n* : pilon *m*
pet[1] [ˈpɛt] *vt* **petted; petting** : caresser

pet[2] *n* **1** : animal *m* domestique **2** FAVORITE : chouchou *m fam*
petal ['pɛt̬əl] *n* : pétale *m*
petite [pə'ti:t] *adj* : menue, petite
petition[1] [pə'tɪʃən] *vi* : faire une pétition — *vt* : adresser une pétition à
petition[2] *n* : pétition *f*
petitioner [pə'tɪʃənər] *n* : pétitionnaire *mf*
petrify ['pɛtrəˌfaɪ] *vt* **-fied; -fying** : pétrifier
petroleum [pə'tro:liəm] *n* : pétrole *m*
petticoat ['pɛt̬iˌko:t] *n* : jupon *m*
pettiness ['pɛt̬inəs] *n* **1** INSIGNIFICANCE : insignifiance *f* **2** MEANNESS : mesquinerie *f*
petty ['pɛt̬i] *adj* **pettier; -est 1** MINOR : petit <petty cash : petite monnaie> **2** INSIGNIFICANT : sans importance, insignifiant **3** MEAN : mesquin
petty officer *n* : maître *m*
petulance ['pɛtʃələnts] *n* : irritabilité *f*, irascibilité *f*
petulant ['pɛtʃələnt] *adj* : irritable, irascible
petunia [pɪ'tu:njə, -'tju:-] *n* : pétunia *m*
pew ['pju:] *n* : banc *m* d'église
pewter ['pju:t̬ər] *n* : étain *m*
pH [ˌpi:'eɪtʃ] *n* : pH *m*
phallic ['fælɪk] *adj* : phallique
phallus ['fæləs] *n, pl* **-li** ['fæˌlaɪ] *or* **-luses** : phallus *m*
phantasy ['fæntəsi] → **fantasy**
phantom ['fæntəm] *n* : fantôme *m*
pharaoh ['fɛrˌo:, 'feɪˌro:] *n* : pharaon *m*
pharmaceutical [ˌfɑrmə'su:t̬ɪkəl] *adj* : pharmaceutique
pharmacist [ˌfɑrməsɪst] *n* : pharmacien *m*, -cienne *f*
pharmacology [ˌfɑrmə'kɑlədʒi] *n* : pharmacologie *f*
pharmacy ['fɑrməsi] *n, pl* **-cies** : pharmacie *f*
pharynx ['færɪŋks] *n, pl* **pharynges** [fə'rɪnˌdʒi:z] : pharynx *m*
phase[1] ['feɪz] *vt* **phased; phasing 1** SYNCHRONIZE : synchroniser **2 to phase in** : introduire graduellement **3 to phase out** : discontinuer progressivement
phase[2] *n* **1** : phase *f* (de la lune) **2** STAGE : phase *f*, stade *m*
pheasant ['fɛzənt] *n, pl* **-ant** *or* **-ants** : faisan *m*, -sane *f*
phenomenal [fɪ'nɑmənəl] *adj* : phénoménal — **phenomenally** *adv*
phenomenon [fɪ'nɑməˌnɑn, -nən] *n, pl* **-na** [-nə] *or* **-nons 1** EVENT, FACT : phénomène *m* **2** *pl* **-nons** PRODIGY : phénomène *m*
philanthropic [ˌfɪlən'θrɑpɪk] *adj* : philanthropique
philanthropist [fə'lænθrəpɪst] *n* : philanthrope *mf*
philanthropy [fə'lænθrəpi] *n, pl* **-pies** : philanthropie *f*
philately [fə'lætəli] *n* : philatélie *f*
philodendron [ˌfɪlə'dɛndrən] *n, pl* **-drons** *or* **-dra** [-drə] : philodendron *m*
philosopher [fə'lɑsəfər] *n* : philosophe *mf*
philosophical [ˌfɪlə'sɑfɪkəl] *adj* : philosophique — **philosophically** [-kli] *adv*
philosophize [fə'lɑsəˌfaɪz] *vt* **-phized; -phizing** : philosopher
philosophy [fə'lɑsəfi] *n, pl* **-phies** : philosophie *f*
phlebitis [flɪ'baɪt̬əs] *n* : phlébite *f*
phlegm ['flɛm] *n* : mucosité *f*
phlox ['flɑks] *n, pl* **phlox** *or* **phloxes** : phlox *m*
phobia ['fo:biə] *n* : phobie *f*
phoenix ['fi:nɪks] *n* : phénix *m*
phone[1] ['fo:n] *v* → **telephone**[1]
phone[2] *n* → **telephone**[2]
phoneme ['fo:ˌni:m] *n* : phonème *m*
phonetic [fə'nɛt̬ɪk] *adj* : phonétique
phonetics [fə'nɛt̬ɪks] *n* : phonétique *f*
phonics ['fɑnɪks] *n* : méthode *f* d'enseignement de la lecture par la phonétique
phonograph ['fo:nəˌgræf] *n* : phonographe *m*
phony[1] *or* **phoney** ['fo:ni] *adj* **phonier; -est** : faux
phony[2] *or* **phoney** *n, pl* **-nies** : charlatan *m*
phosphate ['fɑsˌfeɪt] *n* : phosphate *m*
phosphorescence [ˌfɑsfə'rɛsənts] *n* : phosphorescence *f*
phosphorescent [ˌfɑsfə'rɛsənt] *adj* : phosphorescent
phosphorus ['fɑsfərəs] *n* : phosphore *m*
photo ['fo:t̬o:] *n, pl* **-tos** : photo *f*
photocopy[1] ['fo:t̬oˌkɑpi] *vt* **-copied; -copying** : photocopier
photocopy[2] *n, pl* **-pies** : photocopie *f*
photoelectric [ˌfo:t̬oɪ'lɛktrɪk] *adj* : photoélectrique
photogenic [ˌfo:t̬ə'dʒɛnɪk] *adj* : photogénique
photograph[1] ['fo:t̬əˌgræf] *vt* : photographier
photograph[2] *n* : photo *f*, photographie *f*
photographer [fə'tɑgrəfər] *n* : photographe *mf*
photographic [ˌfo:t̬ə'græfɪk] *adj* : photographique — **photographically** [-fɪkli] *adv*
photography [fə'tɑgrəfi] *n* : photographie *f*
photosynthesis [ˌfo:t̬o'sɪnθəsəs] *n* : photosynthèse *f*
photosynthetic [ˌfo:t̬osɪn'θɛt̬ɪk] *adj* : photosynthétique
phrase[1] ['freɪz] *vt* **phrased; phrasing** : formuler, exprimer
phrase[2] *n* **1** : expression *f*, locution *f* **2** : syntagme *m* (en grammaire)
phraseology [ˌfreɪzi'ɑlədʒi] *n, pl* **-gies** : phraséologie *f*
phylum ['faɪləm] *n, pl* **-la** : phylum *m*

physical[1] [ˈfɪzɪkəl] *adj* : physique — **physically** [-kli] *adv*
physical[2] *n* : examen *m* médical
physician [fəˈzɪʃən] *n* : médecin *mf*
physicist [ˈfɪzəsɪst] *n* : physicien *m*, -cienne *f*
physics [ˈfɪzɪks] *ns & pl* : physique *f*
physiognomy [ˌfɪziˈɑgnəmi] *n, pl* **-mies** : physionomie *f*
physiological [ˌfɪziəˈlɑdʒɪkəl] *or* **physiologic** [-dʒɪk] *adj* : physiologique
physiologist [ˌfɪziˈɑlədʒɪst] *n* : physiologiste *mf*
physiology [ˌfɪziˈɑlədʒi] *n* : physiologie *f*
physique [fəˈziːk] *n* : physique *m*
pi [ˈpaɪ] *n, pl* **pis** [ˈpaɪz] : pi *m*
pianist [piˈænɪst, ˈpiːənɪst] *n* : pianiste *mf*
piano [piˈænoː] *n, pl* **-anos** : piano *m*
piazza [piˈæzə, -ˈɑtsə] *n, pl* **-zas** *or* **-ze** [-ˈɑtˌseɪ] : piazza *f*
picayune [ˌpɪkiˈjuːn] *adj* : insignifiant, sans valeur
piccolo [ˈpɪkəˌloː] *n, pl* **-los** : piccolo *m*, picolo *m*
pick[1] [ˈpɪk] *vt* **1** : casser, percer (une surface) **2** : enlever <to pick meat from bones : enlever la viande des os> **3** : cueillir (des fleurs) **4** *or* **to pick out** SELECT : choisir **5 to pick a fight** : chercher la chicane **6 to pick a lock** : crocheter une serrure **7 to pick one's teeth** : se curer les dents **8 to pick pockets** : voler à la tire — *vi* **1 to pick at** NAG : critiquer **2 to pick at one's food** : manger du bout des doigts **3 to pick and choose** : faire le difficile
pick[2] *n* **1** : choix *m* <take your pick : faites votre choix> **2** : meilleur *m* <the pick of the herd : le meilleur du lot> **3** : pic *m* (outil)
pickax [ˈpɪkˌæks] *n* : pic *m*
pickerel [ˈpɪkərəl] *n, pl* **-el** *or* **-els** : espèce *f* de petit brochet
picket[1] [ˈpɪkət] *vi* : faire un piquet de grève, piqueter *Can*
picket[2] *n* **1** STAKE : piquet *m* (de clôture) **2** *or* **picket line** : piquet *m* de grève
pickle[1] [ˈpɪkəl] *vt* **-led; -ling** : conserver dans la saumure
pickle[2] *n* **1** BRINE : saumure *f* **2** GHERKIN : cornichon *m* **3** FIX, JAM : pétrin *m fam* <to be in a pickle : être dans le pétrin>
pickpocket [ˈpɪkˌpɑkət] *n* : voleur *m*, -leuse *f* à la tire
pickup [ˈpɪkˌəp] *n* **1** IMPROVEMENT : amélioration *f* **2** *or* **pickup truck** : pick-up *m*, camionnette *f*
pick up *vt* **1** GATHER, LIFT : ramasser, soulever, décrocher (le téléphone) <to pick oneself up : se relever> **2** CATCH, LEARN : saisir, comprendre (des renseignements) **3** RESUME : reprendre (une conversation, etc.) **4** TIDY : mettre en ordre **5 to pick up speed** : prendre de la vitesse — *vi* **1** IMPROVE : s'améliorer, remonter **2 to pick up after oneself** : se ramasser *Can*
picnic[1] [ˈpɪkˌnɪk] *vi* **-nicked; -nicking** : pique-niquer
picnic[2] *n* : pique-nique *m*
pictorial [pɪkˈtoriəl] *adj* : illustré, pictural
picture[1] [ˈpɪktʃər] *vt* **-tured; -turing 1** DEPICT : dépeindre, décrire **2** IMAGINE : se représenter, s'imaginer
picture[2] *n* **1** : tableau *m*, image *f*, dessin *m* **2** DESCRIPTION : description *f* **3** IMAGE : image *f* <he's the picture of his father : il est l'image de son père> **4** MOVIE : film *m*
picturesque [ˌpɪktʃəˈrɛsk] *adj* : pittoresque
pie [ˈpaɪ] *n* **1** : tarte *f* <apple pie : tarte aux pommes> **2** : pâté *m*, tourte *f France* <meat pie : pâté à la viande>
piebald [ˈpaɪˌbɔld] *adj* : pie (se dit d'un animal)
piece[1] [ˈpiːs] *vt* **pieced; piecing** *or* **to piece together** : rassembler, constituer
piece[2] *n* **1** FRAGMENT : bout *m*, morceau *m* <a piece of string : un bout de corde> **2** : pièce *f* (dans un jeu de société) **3** UNIT : objet *m*, chose *f*, pièce *f* <a piece of fruit : un fruit> <a piece of mail : du courrier> <a fifty-cent piece : une pièce de cinquante cents> **4** WORK : œuvre *f*, morceau *m* (de musique) **5** COMPONENT : pièce *f* <a three-piece suit : un costume de trois pièces>
piecemeal[1] [ˈpiːsˌmiːl] *adv* : graduellement
piecemeal[2] *adj* : fragmentaire <piecemeal reforms : réformes fragmentaires>
pied [ˈpaɪd] *adj* : pie (se dit d'un cheval, etc.)
pier [ˈpɪr] *n* **1** JETTY : jetée *f* **2** : pile *f* (d'un pont) **3** COLUMN : pilier *m*
pierce [ˈpɪrs] *vt* **pierced; piercing 1** STAB : donner un coup de couteau à **2** PERFORATE : percer, transpercer **3** PENETRATE : pénétrer **4** DISCERN : comprendre, discerner
piety [ˈpaɪəṭi] *n, pl* **-eties** : piété *f*
pig [ˈpɪg] *n* **1** : porc *m*, cochon *m* (animal) **2** SLOB : cochon *m*, -chonne *f fam* **3** CASTING : moulage *m* en fer
pigeon [ˈpɪdʒən] *n* : pigeon *m*
pigeonhole [ˈpɪdʒənˌhoːl] *n* : casier *m*
piggish [ˈpɪgɪʃ] *adj* **1** GREEDY : goinfre, glouton **2** DIRTY : sale, cochon
piggyback [ˈpɪgiˌbæk] *adv & adj* : sur le dos
pigheaded [ˈpɪgˌhɛdəd] *adj* STUBBORN : têtu, obstiné
piglet [ˈpɪglət] *n* : porcelet *m*
pigment [ˈpɪgmənt] *n* : pigment *m*
pigmentation [ˌpɪgmənˈteɪʃən] *n* : pigmentation *f*

pigmy → **pygmy**
pigpen ['pɪg,pɛn] *n* : porcherie *f,* soue *f Can*
pigsty ['pɪg,staɪ] *n, pl* **-sties** → **pigpen**
pigtail ['pɪg,teɪl] *n* : natte *f*
pike ['paɪk] *n* **1** WEAPON : pique *f* **2** → **turnpike 3** *pl* **pike** *or* **pikes** : brochet *m* (poisson)
pilaf *or* **pilaff** [pɪ'lɑf, 'pi,lɑf] *or* **pilau** [pɪ'lo:, -'lɔ; 'pilo, -lɔ] *n* : pilaf *m*
pile[1] ['paɪəl] *v* **piled; piling** *vt* **1** STACK : empiler **2** LOAD : remplir <he piled potatoes on his plate : il a rempli son assiette de pommes de terre> — *vi* **1** *or* **to pile up** : s'accumuler **2** CROWD : s'empiler <they piled into the car : ils se sont empilés dans la voiture>
pile[2] *n* **1** PILING, POST : pilotis *m,* pieu *m* **2** HEAP : pile *f,* tas *m* **3** NAP : poil *m* (d'un tapis, etc.)
piles ['paɪls] *npl* : hémorroïdes *fpl*
pilfer ['pɪlfər] *vt* : chaparder *fam,* dérober
pilgrim ['pɪlgrəm] *n* : pèlerin *m,* -rine *f*
pilgrimage ['pɪlgrəmɪdʒ] *n* : pèlerinage *m*
pill ['pɪl] *n* : pilule *f,* cachet *m*
pillage[1] ['pɪlɪdʒ] *vt* **-laged; -laging** : piller
pillage[2] *n* : pillage *m*
pillar ['pɪlər] *n* : pilier *m,* colonne *f*
pillbox ['pɪl,bɑks] *n* : boîte *f* à pilules
pillory[1] ['pɪləri] *vt* **-ried; -rying** : mettre au pilori
pillory[2] *n, pl* **-ries** : pilori *m*
pillow ['pɪ,lo:] *n* : oreiller *m*
pillowcase ['pɪlo,keɪs] *n* : taie *f* d'oreiller
pilot[1] ['paɪlət] *vt* : piloter (un avion, un navire)
pilot[2] *n* : pilote *m*
pimento [pə'mɛn,to:] *n, pl* **-tos** *or* **-to 1** → **allspice 2** → **pimiento**
pimiento [pə'mɛn,to:, -'mjɛn-] *n, pl* **-tos** : piment *m* doux
pimp ['pɪmp] *n* : entremetteur *m,* souteneur *m*
pimple ['pɪmpəl] *n* : bouton *m*
pimply ['pɪmpəli] *adj* **pimplier; -est** : boutonneux
pin[1] ['pɪn] *vt* **pinned; pinning 1** FASTEN : épingler **2** HOLD, IMMOBILIZE : fixer, immobiliser **3 to pin down** DEFINE, DETERMINE : définir, déterminer, cerner **4 to pin one's hopes on** : mettre tout son espoir dans
pin[2] *n* **1** : épingle *f* <safety pin : épingle de sûreté> **2** BROOCH : broche *f,* épinglette *f Can* **3** BADGE, INSIGNIA : insigne *m,* épinglette *f* **4** *or* **bowling pin** : quille *f*
pinafore ['pɪnə,for] *n* **1** APRON : tablier *m* **2** *or* **pinafore dress** : chasuble *f*
pincer ['pɪntsər] *n* **1** : pince *f* (d'un homard) **2 pincers** *npl* : tenailles *fpl,* pinces *fpl*
pinch[1] ['pɪntʃ] *vt* **1** : pincer <to pinch oneself : se pincer> **2** STEAL : faucher *fam,* voler — *vi* : serrer, être étroit (se dit des chaussures)
pinch[2] *n* **1** SQUEEZE : pincement *m* **2** : pincée *f* <a pinch of salt : une pincée de sel> **3 in a pinch** : à la rigueur
pincushion ['pɪn,kʊʃən] *n* : pelote *f* (à épingles)
pine[1] ['paɪn] *vi* **pined; pining 1 to pine away** LANGUISH : languir **2 to pine for** : désirer ardemment
pine[2] *n* : pin *m*
pineapple ['paɪn,æpəl] *n* : ananas *m*
pinecone ['paɪn,ko:n] *n* : pomme *f* de pin, cocotte *f Can*
pinion ['pɪnjən] *n* **1** : aileron *m* (d'un oiseau) **2** COGWHEEL : pignon *m*
pink[1] ['pɪŋk] *adj* : rose
pink[2] *n* **1** : œillet *m* (fleur) **2** : rose *m* (couleur) **3 to be in the pink** : être en pleine forme
pinkeye ['pɪŋk,aɪ] *n* : conjonctivite *f*
pinkish ['pɪŋkɪʃ] *adj* : rosé
pinnacle ['pɪnɪkəl] *n* **1** : pinacle *m* (en architecture) **2** PEAK : sommet *m,* pic *m* **3** ACME : sommet *m,* comble *m* (d'une carrière, etc.)
pinpoint ['pɪn,pɔɪnt] *vt* : indiquer, localiser avec précision
pint ['paɪnt] *n* : pinte *f*
pinto ['pɪn,to:] *n, pl* **pintos** : cheval *m* pie
pinworm ['pɪn,wərm] *n* : oxyure *m*
pioneer[1] [,paɪə'nɪr] *vt* : être un innovateur de, mettre au point (des recherches, etc.)
pioneer[2] *n* : pionnier *m,* -nière *f*
pious ['paɪəs] *adj* : pieux, religieux
piously ['paɪəsli] *adv* : pieusement
pipe[1] ['paɪp] *v* **piped; piping** *vi* **1** : jouer de la cornemuse ou du pipeau **2** *or* **to pipe up** : se faire entendre, parler fort — *vt or* **to pipe in** : amener ou alimenter par tuyau (de l'eau, du pétrole, etc.)
pipe[2] *n* **1** FLUTE : pipeau *m* **2** BAGPIPE : cornemuse *f* **3** : tuyau *m,* conduit *m* (pour transporter un liquide, un gaz, etc.) **4** : pipe *f* (pour fumer du tabac) **5** : tuyau *m* (d'un orgue)
pipeline ['paɪp,laɪn] *n* **1** : pipeline *m* **2** CONDUIT : voie *f,* canal *m* <a pipeline for data : une voie de transmission pour les données>
piper ['paɪpər] *n* : joueur *m,* joueuse *f* (de cornemuse)
piping ['paɪpɪŋ] *n* **1** : musique *f* de cornemuse **2** TRIM : passepoil *m* (en couture)
piquancy ['pi:kəntsi, 'pɪkwəntsi] *n* SPICINESS : piquant *m*
piquant ['pi:kənt, 'pɪkwənt] *adj* : piquant
pique[1] ['pi:k] *vt* **piqued; piquing 1** IRRITATE : froisser, irriter **2** AROUSE : éveiller, susciter <to pique s.o.'s curiosity : éveiller la curiosité de qqn>
pique[2] *n* : ressentiment *m,* dépit *m*
piqué *or* **pique** [pɪ'keɪ, 'pi:,-] *n* : piqué *m*

piracy [ˈpaɪrəsi] *n, pl* **-cies 1 :** piraterie *f* (sur un navire) **2 :** piratage *m* <software piracy : piratage de logiciels>
piranha [pəˈrɑnə, -ˈrɑnjə, -ˈrænjə] *n* **:** piranha *m*
pirate[1] [ˈpaɪrət] *vt* **-rated; -rating :** pirater
pirate[2] *n* **:** pirate *m*
pirouette *n* **:** pirouette *f*
pis → **pi**
Pisces [ˈpaɪˌsiːz] *n* **:** Poissons *mpl*
pistachio [pəˈstæʃiˌoː, -ˈstɑ-] *n, pl* **-chios :** pistache *f* (noix)
pistil [ˈpɪstəl] *n* **:** pistil *m*
pistol [ˈpɪstəl] *n* **:** pistolet *m*
piston [ˈpɪstən] *n* **:** piston *m*
pit[1] [ˈpɪt] *vt* **pitted; pitting 1 :** dénoyauter (un fruit) **2** RIDDLE **:** cribler <pitted by explosions : criblé par les explosions> **3 :** marquer <a face pitted from smallpox : un visage marqué par la variole>
pit[2] *n* **1** HOLE **:** trou *m,* fosse *f* **2** MINE, SHAFT **:** mine *f,* puits *m* **3 :** creux *m* (de l'estomac) **4** POCKMARK **:** marque *f* (sur la peau) **5 :** noyau *m* (d'un fruit) **6 :** fosse *f* <orchestra pit : fosse d'orchestre>
pitch[1] [ˈpɪtʃ] *vt* **1** ERECT **:** monter, dresser (une tente, etc.) **2 :** jeter, fourcher <to pitch hay : fourcher du foin> **3 :** lancer (une balle) **4 :** donner le ton de (en musique) **—** *vi* **1** *or* **to pitch forward :** tomber **2** LURCH **:** tanguer (se dit d'un navire, etc.) **3** SLOPE **:** être incliné
pitch[2] *n* **1** THROWING **:** lancer *m,* lancement *m* **2** DEGREE, LEVEL **:** degré *m* (d'une pente), niveau *m* (d'enthousiasme, etc.) **3** TONE **:** ton *m* (en musique) **4** TAR **:** poix *f* **5** *or* **sales pitch :** boniment *m* de vente
pitcher [ˈpɪtʃər] *n* **1** JUG **:** cruche *f,* pichet *m* **2 :** lanceur *m,* -ceuse *f;* artilleur *m Can* (au baseball)
pitchfork [ˈpɪtʃˌfɔrk] *n* **:** fourche *f*
pitfall [ˈpɪtˌfɔl] *n* **:** piège *m,* trappe *f*
pith [ˈpɪθ] *n* **1 :** moelle *f* (d'une plante) **2** CORE **:** essence *f,* signification *f*
pithy [ˈpɪθi] *adj* **pithier; -est :** bref, incisif, concis
pitiable [ˈpɪt̬iəbəl] → **pitiful**
pitiful [ˈpɪt̬ɪfəl] *adj* **1 :** pitoyable <a pitiful cry : un cri pitoyable> **2** DEPLORABLE **:** lamentable, piteux <pitiful wages : salaires minables>
pitifully [ˈpɪt̬ɪfli] *adv* **:** pitoyablement
pitiless [ˈpɪt̬ɪləs] *adj* **:** impitoyable **— pitilessly** *adv*
pittance [ˈpɪtənts] *n* **:** somme *f* dérisoire
pituitary [pəˈtuːəˌtɛri, -ˈtjuː-] *adj* **:** pituitaire
pity[1] [ˈpɪt̬i] *vt* **pitied; pitying :** avoir pitié de
pity[2] *n, pl* **pities :** pitié *f* <to feel pity for : avoir pitié de> <what a pity! : quel dommage!>
pivot[1] [ˈpɪvət] *vi* **:** pivoter, tourner
pivot[2] *n* **:** pivot *m*
pivotal [ˈpɪvət̬əl] *adj* **:** crucial, essentiel
pixie *or* **pixy** [ˈpɪksi] *n, pl* **pixies :** lutin *m*
pizza [ˈpiːtsə] *n* **:** pizza *f*
pizzazz *or* **pizazz** [pəˈzæz] *n* **:** panache *m*
placard [ˈplækərd, -ˌkɑrd] *n* POSTER **:** affiche *f,* placard *m*
placate [ˈpleɪˌkeɪt, ˈplæ-] *vt* **-cated; -cating :** apaiser, calmer
place[1] [ˈpleɪs] *v* **placed; placing** *vt* **1** PUT, SET **:** placer, mettre **2** APPOINT **:** placer (un employé) **3** RECOGNIZE **:** se rappeler de, remettre <I couldn't quite place her face : je n'arrivais pas à me rappeler d'elle> **4 to place an order :** passer une commande **—** *vi* RANK **:** se placer, se classer <he placed second : il est arrivé deuxième>
place[2] *n* **1** SPACE **:** place *f* <is this place taken? : cette place est-elle prise?> **2** LOCATION, SPOT **:** endroit *m,* lieu *m* **3** POSITION **:** place *f,* position *f* **4** RANK **:** place *f* <to take first place : prendre la première place> **5** SEAT **:** place *f,* siège *f* (au théâtre) **6** JOB **:** poste *m,* emploi *m* **7 in the first place :** tout d'abord **8 to take place :** avoir lieu
placebo [pləˈsiːˌboː] *n, pl* **-bos :** placebo *m*
placement [ˈpleɪsmənt] *n* **:** placement *m*
placenta [pləˈsɛntə] *n, pl* **-tas** *or* **-tae** [-ti, -ˌtaɪ] **:** placenta *m*
placid [ˈplæsəd] *adj* **:** placide, paisible **— placidly** *adv*
plagiarism [ˈpleɪdʒəˌrɪzəm] *n* **:** plagiat *m*
plagiarist [ˈpleɪdʒərɪst] *n* **:** plagiaire *mf*
plagiarize [ˈpleɪdʒəˌraɪz] *vt* **-rized; -rizing :** plagier
plague[1] [ˈpleɪg] *vt* **plagued; plaguing 1** AFFLICT **:** tourmenter **2** HARASS **:** harceler
plague[2] *n* **1** PESTILENCE **:** peste *f* **2** CALAMITY **:** fléau *m,* cataclysme *m*
plaid[1] [ˈplæd] *adj* **:** écossais
plaid[2] *n* **:** tissu *m* écossais
plain[1] [ˈpleɪn] *adj* **1** SIMPLE, UNADORNED **:** simple **2** CLEAR **:** clair, évident **3** FRANK **:** franc <plain speaking : le franc-parler> **4** HOMELY **:** sans attraits, ordinaire
plain[2] *n* **:** plaine *f*
plainly [ˈpleɪnli] *adv* **1** SIMPLY **:** simplement **2** CLEARLY **:** clairement, évidemment **3** FRANKLY **:** franchement
plaintiff [ˈpleɪntɪf] *n* **:** demandeur *m,* -deresse *f;* plaignant *m,* -nante *f*
plaintive [ˈpleɪntɪv] *adj* **:** plaintif **— plaintively** *adv*
plait[1] [ˈpleɪt, ˈplæt] *vt* **:** natter, tresser
plait[2] *n* **1** PLEAT **:** pli *m* **2** BRAID **:** natte *f,* tresse *f*
plan[1] [ˈplæn] *v* **planned; planning** *vt* **1 :** faire des plans pour, concevoir (un

édifice) **2** : organiser, planifier <to plan an outing : organiser une sortie> **3** INTEND : penser <I was planning to go : je pensais y aller> — *vi* : faire des projets

plan[2] *n* **1** DIAGRAM : plan *m*, dessin *m* **2** PROCEDURE : plan *m* <a plan of action : un plan d'action> **3** : régime *m*, plan *m* <pension plan : régime de retraite>

plane[1] ['pleɪn] *v* **planed; planing** *vt* : raboter, aplanir (une surface) — *vi* GLIDE : planer

plane[2] *adj* FLAT : plat

plane[3] *n* **1** : rabot *m* (outil) **2** SURFACE : plan *m* <horizontal plane : plan horizontal> **3** LEVEL : plan *m* **4** → **airplane**

planet ['plænət] *n* : planète *f*

planetarium [ˌplænə'tɛriəm] *n, pl* **-iums** *or* **-ia** [-iə] : planétarium *m*

planetary ['plænəˌtɛri] *adj* : planétaire

plank ['plæŋk] *n* **1** : planche *f* (de bois) **2** : article *m* d'une plateforme électorale

plankton ['plæŋktən] *n* : plancton *m*

plant[1] ['plænt] *vt* **1** : planter (des graines, des fleurs, etc.) **2** AFFIX : planter, enfoncer

plant[2] *n* **1** : plante *f* <indoor plants : plantes d'intérieur> **2** FACTORY : usine *f* <an electric power plant : une centrale hydroélectrique> **3** EQUIPMENT : machinerie *f*, installations *fpl*

plantain ['plæntən] *n* : plantain *m* (arbre et fruit)

plantation [plæn'teɪʃən] *n* : plantation *f*

planter ['plæntər] *n* **1** : planteur *m*, -teuse *f* **2** : cache-pot *m* (pour des pots de fleurs)

plaque ['plæk] *n* **1** : plaque *f* <commemorative plaque : plaque commémorative> **2** : plaque *f* (dentaire)

plasma ['plæzmə] *n* : plasma *m*

plaster[1] ['plæstər] *vt* **1** : enduire (de plâtre) **2** COVER : couvrir <plastered with posters : couvert d'affiches>

plaster[2] *n* : plâtre *m*

plasterer ['plæstərər] *n* : plâtrier *m*

plastic[1] ['plæstɪk] *adj* **1** : de plastique, en plastique **2** FLEXIBLE : plastique, malléable

plastic[2] *n* : plastique *m*

plastic surgery *n* : chirurgie *f* plastique

plate[1] ['pleɪt] *vt* **plated; plating** : plaquer (avec un métal)

plate[2] *n* **1** SHEET : plaque *f* <steel plate : plaque d'acier> **2** DISH : assiette *f* **3** DENTURES : dentier *m* **4** ILLUSTRATION : planche *f* **5** *or* **license plate** : plaque *f* d'immatriculation

plateau [plæ'toː] *n, pl* **-teaus** *or* **-teaux** [-'toːz] : plateau *m*

platform ['plætˌfɔrm] *n* **1** STAGE : tribune *f*, estrade *f* **2** : quai *m* (d'un chemin de fer) **3** *or* **political platform** : plate-forme *f* (électorale)

plating ['pleɪṱɪŋ] *n* : placage *m*

platinum ['plætənəm] *n* : platine *m*

platitude ['plæṱəˌtuːd, -ˌtjuːd] *n* : platitude *f*, lieu *m* commun

platoon [plə'tuːn] *n* : section *f* (dans l'armée)

platter ['plæṱər] *n* : plateau *m* de service

platypus ['plæṱɪpəs, -ˌpʊs] *n* : ornithorynque *m*

plaudits ['plɔdəts] *npl* : applaudissements *mpl*

plausibility [ˌplɔzə'bɪləṱi] *n, pl* **-ties** : plausibilité *f*

plausible ['plɔzəbəl] *adj* : plausible, vraisemblable

plausibly ['plɔzəbli] *adv* : de façon convaincante, avec vraisemblance

play[1] ['pleɪ] *vi* **1** : s'amuser, jouer <come out to play : viens jouer> **2** : jouer (se dit d'un orchestre, etc.), se jouer (se dit d'une pièce de théâtre) **3** FIDDLE, TOY : jouer (avec qqch) **4 to play fair** : jouer franc jeu — *vt* **1** : jouer à (un jeu, un sport) **2** : jouer de (un instrument de musique) **3** PERFORM : jouer (une œuvre, un rôle) **4 to play a trick on** : jouer un tour à **5 to play up** EMPHASIZE : souligner, mettre en valeur

play[2] *n* **1** : jeu *m* (aux sports) **2** : jeu *m*, activité *f* <children at play : des enfants qui jouent> **3** : jeu *m* (de couleurs), mouvement *m* léger (du vent) **4** TURN : tour *m* <it's your play : c'est à ton tour> **5** : pièce *f* de théâtre

playacting ['pleɪˌæktɪŋ] *n* : comédie *f*, affectation *f*

player ['pleɪər] *n* : joueur *m*, joueuse *f*

playful ['pleɪfəl] *adj* : enjoué, gai

playfully ['pleɪfəli] *adv* : de façon enjouée

playfulness ['pleɪfəlnəs] *n* : enjouement *m*

playground ['pleɪˌgraʊnd] *n* : cour *f* de récréation

playhouse ['pleɪˌhaʊs] *n* **1** THEATER : théâtre *m* **2** : maison *f* de jeu pour les enfants

playing card *n* : carte *f* à jouer

playmate ['pleɪˌmeɪt] *n* : camarade *mf* de jeu

play–off ['pleɪˌɔf] *n* : finale *f* (de coupe), match *m* crucial

playpen ['pleɪˌpɛn] *n* : parc *m* (pour bébés)

plaything ['pleɪˌθɪŋ] *n* : jouet *m*

playwright ['pleɪˌraɪt] *n* : dramaturge *mf*, auteur *m* dramatique

plaza ['plæzə, 'plɑ-] *n* **1** : place *f* (publique) **2** *or* **shopping plaza** : centre *m* commercial

plea ['pliː] *n* **1** : défense *f* (en droit) **2** REQUEST : appel *m*, requête *f* <a plea for mercy : un appel à la clémence>

plead ['pli:d] *v* **pleaded** *or* **pled** ['plɛd]; **pleading** *vt* **1** : plaider (une cause) **2** (*used to introduce an excuse*) <I pleaded ignorance : j'ai prétendu que je ne savais rien> — *vi* **1** : plaider <to plead guilty : plaider coupable> **2** BEG : supplier, implorer

pleasant ['plɛzənt] *adj* : agréable, plaisant

pleasantly ['plɛzəntli] *adv* : agréablement, aimablement

pleasantness ['plɛzəntnəs] *n* : amabilité *f*, agrément *m*

pleasantries ['plɛzəntriz] *npl* : plaisanteries *fpl*, civilités *fpl*

please[1] ['pli:z] *v* **pleased; pleasing** *vt* **1** GRATIFY : plaire à, faire plaisir à <to please everybody : faire plaisir à tout le monde> **2** SATISFY : contenter — *vi* **1** : plaire, faire plaisir <to be anxious to please : chercher à faire plaisir> **2** (*indicating choice*) <do as you please : fais comme il te plaît>

please[2] *adv* : s'il vous plaît, je vous en prie <please come in : rentrez, s'il vous plaît>

pleasing ['pli:zɪŋ] *adj* : agréable, plaisant — **pleasingly** *adv*

pleasurable ['plɛʒərəbəl] *adj* : agréable, plaisant

pleasure ['plɛʒər] *n* **1** DESIRE : gré *m*, guise *f* <at your pleasure : à votre guise> **2** ENJOYMENT : plaisir *m* **3** DELIGHT : plaisir *m*, bonheur *m* <it was a pleasure to see you again! : quel plaisir de vous revoir!>

pleat[1] ['pli:t] *vt* : plisser

pleat[2] *n* : pli *m*

plebeian [plɪ'biən] *adj* : plébéien

pledge[1] ['plɛdʒ] *vt* **pledged; pledging 1** PAWN : mettre en gage **2** PROMISE : promettre

pledge[2] *n* **1** SECURITY : gage *m*, nantissement *m* **2** VOW : promesse *f* **3** TOKEN : gage *m* <a pledge of our love : un gage de notre amour>

plenteous ['plɛntiəs] → **plentiful**

plentiful ['plɛntɪfəl] *adj* : abondant — **plentifully** *adv*

plenty ['plɛnti] *n* **1** ABUNDANCE : abondance *f* **2 ~ of** : beaucoup de <plenty of time : beaucoup de temps>

plethora ['plɛθərə] *n* : pléthore *f*

pleurisy ['plʊrəsi] *n* : pleurésie *f*

pliable ['plaɪəbəl] *adj* : flexible, malléable

pliancy ['plaɪəntsi] *n* : flexibilité *f*

pliant ['plaɪənt] → **pliable**

pliers ['plaɪərz] *npl* : pinces *fpl*

plight ['plaɪt] *n* : situation *f* difficile

plod ['plɑd] *vi* **plodded; plodding 1** : marcher lourdement **2** DRUDGE : travailler laborieusement

plot[1] ['plɑt] *v* **plotted; plotting** *vt* : faire un plan de — *vi* CONSPIRE : comploter

plot[2] *n* **1** : lot *m*, parcelle *f* (de terre) **2** : plan *m* (d'un édifice) **3** : intrigue *f* (dans un livre, etc.) **4** CONSPIRACY : complot *m*, conspiration *f*

plotter ['plɑtər] *n* : conspirateur *m*, -trice *f*; comploteur *m*, -teuse *f*

plover ['pləvər, 'plo:vər] *n, pl* **-ver** *or* **-vers** : pluvier *m*

plow[1] *or* **plough** ['plaʊ] *vt* **1** : labourer (la terre), creuser (un sillon) **2** : déneiger, déblayer <to plow the streets : déneiger les rues> — *vi* **1 to plow into** : percuter, heurter <the car plowed into the fence : la voiture a percuté la clôture> **2 to plow through** : avancer péniblement dans, éplucher <he plowed through a stack of letters : il a épluché une pile de lettres>

plow[2] *or* **plough** *n* : charrue *f*

plowshare ['plaʊʃɛr] *n* : soc *m* (de charrue)

ploy ['plɔɪ] *n* : manigance *f*, truc *m*

pluck[1] ['plʌk] *vt* **1** : cueillir <to pluck grapes : cueillir des raisins> **2** : plumer (un poulet), arracher (des plumes à) **3** : pincer les cordes de (un instrument de musique) **4 to pluck one's eyebrows** : s'épiler les sourcis

pluck[2] *n* COURAGE : courage *m*, audace *m*

plucky ['plʌki] *adj* **pluckier; -est** : courageux, fougeux

plug[1] ['plʌg] *v* **plugged; plugging** *vt* **1** BLOCK : boucher, obstruer **2** ADVERTISE : faire de la publicité pour **3 to plug in** : brancher <to plug in a lamp : brancher une lampe> — *vi or* **to plug away** : s'acharner

plug[2] *n* **1** STOPPER : bouchon *m*, tampon *m* **2** PUBLICITY : annonce *f* publicitaire **3** : fiche *f*, prise *f* (électrique) <telephone plug : prise téléphonique>

plum ['plʌm] *n* **1** : prune *f*, pruneau *m Can* (fruit) **2** PRIZE, REWARD : prix *m*, récompense *f*

plumage ['plu:mɪdʒ] *n* : plumage *m*

plumb[1] ['plʌm] *vt* SOUND : sonder

plumb[2] *adv* **1** VERTICALLY : d'aplomb **2** ABSOLUTELY : complètement <plumb crazy : complètement cinglé>

plumb[3] *adj* : vertical, droit

plumber ['plʌmər] *n* : plombier *m*

plumbing ['plʌmɪŋ] *n* **1** : plomberie *f* (travail de plombier) **2** PIPES : tuyauterie *f*

plumb line *n* : fil *m* à plomb

plume ['plu:m] *n* **1** FEATHER : plume *f* **2** : plumet *m* (sur un chapeau)

plumed ['plu:md] *adj* : aux plumes

plummet ['plʌmət] *vi* : descendre brusquement, tomber à pic (se dit d'un oiseau)

plump[1] ['plʌmp] *vi or* **to plump down** : s'affaler

plump[2] *adv* DIRECTLY : en plein, directement <he ran plump into the

wall : il a heurté le mur de plein fouet>

plump[3] *adj* : grassouillet, dodu

plumpness ['plʌmpnəs] *n* : embonpoint *m,* grosseur *f*

plunder[1] ['plʌndər] *vt* : piller

plunder[2] *n* : pillage *m*

plunderer ['plʌndərər] *n* : pillard *m,* -larde *f*

plunge[1] ['plʌndʒ] *v* **plunged; plunging** *vt* SUBMERGE : plonger, immerger — *vi* **1** DIVE : plonger **2** DESCEND : dévaler **3** RUSH : se précipiter, se lancer

plunge[2] *n* DIVE : plongeon *m*

plunger ['plʌndʒər] *n* : ventouse *f*

plural[1] ['plʊrəl] *adj* : pluriel

plural[2] *n* : pluriel *m*

plurality [plʊ'ræləṯi] *n, pl* **-ties** : pluralité *f*

pluralize ['plʊrəˌlaɪz] *vi* **-ized; -izing** : prendre le pluriel

plus[1] ['plʌs] *adj* : positif <a plus factor : un facteur positif>

plus[2] *n* **1** *or* **plus sign** : plus *m* **2** ADVANTAGE : plus *m,* avantage *m*

plus[3] *conj* AND : et

plus[4] *prep* : plus <six boys plus a girl : six garçons plus une fille> <4 plus 5 : 4 plus 5>

plush[1] ['plʌʃ] *adj* : luxueux, somptueux

plush[2] *n* : peluche *f*

plushy ['plʌʃi] *adj* **plushier; -est** : luxueux

Pluto ['pluːˌtoː] *n* : Pluton *f* (planète)

plutocracy [pluː'tɑkrəsi] *n, pl* **-cies** : ploutocratie *f*

plutonium [pluː'toːniəm] *n* : plutonium *m*

ply[1] ['plaɪ] *vt* **plied; plying 1** USE, WIELD : manier (un outil) **2** PRACTICE : pratiquer, exercer <to ply a trade : pratiquer un métier> **3 to ply s.o. with** : assaillir qqn de (questions, etc.)

ply[2] *n, pl* **plies 1** THICKNESS : épaisseur *f* **2** LAYER : pli *m* **3** STRAND : brin *m* (de laine)

plywood ['plaɪˌwʊd] *n* : contre-plaqué *m*

pneumatic [nʊ'mæṯɪk, njʊ-] *adj* : pneumatique

pneumonia [nʊ'moːnjə, njʊ-] *n* : pneumonie *f*

poach ['poːtʃ] *vt* **1** : pocher (des œufs) **2 to poach game** : braconner le gibier

poacher ['poːtʃər] *n* : braconnier *m,* -nière *f*

pock ['pɑk] *n* **1** PUSTULE : pustule *f* **2** → **pockmark**

pocket[1] ['pɑkət] *vt* **1** STEAL : empocher **2** : mettre dans sa poche <to pocket the change : mettre la monnaie dans sa poche>

pocket[2] *n* **1** : poche *f* (dans un vêtement) **2** : blouse *f* (au billard), poche *f* (marsupiale), poche *f* (d'or, d'eau, de gaz) **3** AREA : poche *f,* secteur *m* <pockets of unemployment : poches de chômage> **4** *or* **air pocket** : trou *m* d'air

pocketbook ['pɑkətˌbʊk] *n* **1** WALLET : portefeuille *m* **2** PURSE : sac *m* à main, sacoche *f Can* **3** INCOME : revenu *m,* ressources *fpl* financières

pocketknife ['pɑkətˌnaɪf] *n* : canif *m*

pockmark ['pɑkˌmɑrk] *n* : cicatrice *f*

pod ['pɑd] *n* : cosse *f* <pea pod : cosse de pois>

podiatrist [pə'daɪətrɪst, po-] *n* : podologue *mf*

podiatry [pə'daɪətri, po-] *n* : podologie *f*

podium ['poːdiəm] *n, pl* **-diums** *or* **-dia** [-iə] : podium *m*

poem ['poːəm] *n* : poème *m*

poet ['poːət] *n* : poète *mf*

poetic [po'ɛṯɪk,] *or* **poetical** [-ṯɪkəl] *adj* : poétique

poetry ['poːətri] *n* : poésie *f*

pogrom ['poːgrəm, pə'grɑm, 'pɑgrəm] *n* : pogrom *m*

poignancy ['pɔɪnjəntsi] *n, pl* **-cies** : caractère *m* poignant

poignant ['pɔɪnjənt] *adj* : poignant

poinsettia [pɔɪn'sɛṯiə, -'sɛṯə] *n* : poinsettia *m*

point[1] ['pɔɪnt] *vt* **1** SHARPEN : aiguiser (un crayon, etc.) **2** AIM : pointer, montrer, braquer <to point one's finger at s.o. : montrer qqn du doigt> <to point a gun : braquer un fusil> **3** INDICATE : montrer, indiquer <to point the way : montrer la voie> **4 to point out** : signaler, remarquer — *vi* : tomber en arrêt (se dit d'un chien)

point[2] *n* **1** ITEM : point *m,* question *f* <the main points : les points principaux> **2** QUALITY : point *m,* force *f* <one of his strong points : un de ses points forts> **3** PURPOSE : utilité *f,* but *m* <there's no point in trying : il est inutile d'essayer> <what's the point? : où veux-tu en venir?> **4** PLACE : point *m,* endroit *m* <a distant point : un point distant> **5** MOMENT : moment *m,* instant *m* <at this point : à ce moment-là> **6** DEGREE, STAGE : point *m* <boiling point : point d'ébullition> **7** END, TIP : pointe *m* (d'un crayon, d'une épée) **8** VERGE : point *m* <at the point of death : au bord de la tombe> **9** HEADLAND : cap *m,* promontoire *m* **10** DOT, PERIOD : point *m* (signe de ponctuation) **11** : point *m* (aux sports) **12** → **decimal point**

point–blank[1] ['pɔɪnt'blæŋk] *adv* **1** : à bout portant <to shoot point-blank : tirer à bout portant> **2** ABSOLUTELY, BLUNTLY : catégoriquement

point–blank[2] *adj* **1** : à bout portant <point-blank shot : tir à bout portant> **2** BLUNT : catégorique <a point-blank refusal : un refus catégorique>

pointedly ['pɔɪntədli] *adv* : ostensiblement, de façon marquée

pointer ['pɔɪntər] *n* **1** ROD : baguette *f* **2** : chien *m* d'arrêt **3** TIP : conseil *m,* suggestion *f*
pointless ['pɔɪntləs] *adj* **1** SENSELESS : absurde **2** USELESS : inutile, futile <pointless attempts : tentatives inutiles>
point of view *n* : point *m* de vue
poise[1] ['pɔɪz] *vt* **poised; poising** BALANCE : tenir en équilibre
poise[2] *n* **1** EQUILIBRIUM : équilibre *m* **2** COMPOSURE : calme *m,* assurance *f*
poison[1] ['pɔɪzən] *vt* **1** : empoisonner <poisoned arrows : flèches empoisonnées> **2** CORRUPT : pervertir, corrompre <to poison s.o.'s mind : pervertir l'esprit de qqn>
poison[2] *n* : poison *m*
poison ivy *n* : sumac *m* vénéneux, herbe *f* à (la) puce *Can*
poisonous ['pɔɪzənəs] *adj* **1** : vénéneux (se dit d'une plante), venimeux (se dit d'un serpent ou d'un insecte), toxique (se dit d'une émanation, d'une plante, etc.) **2** HARMFUL : destructeur, pernicieux
poke[1] ['po:k] *v* **poked; poking** *vt* **1** JAB : donner un coup de coude à (les côtes, etc.) **2** PROD : donner des petits coups à **3** THRUST : fourrer *fam,* passer <I poked my head out of the window : j'ai passé ma tête par la fenêtre> — *vi or* **to poke around** : fureter, fouiner *fam*
poke[2] *n* JAB : coup *m*
poker ['po:kər] *n* **1** : tisonnier *m* (pour le feu) **2** : poker *m* (jeu de cartes)
polar ['po:lər] *adj* : polaire
polar bear *n* : ours *m* polaire, ours *m* blanc
Polaris [po'lærɪs, -'lar-] → **North Star**
polarize ['po:lə,raɪz] *vt* **-ized; -izing** : polariser
pole ['po:l] *n* **1** ROD, STICK : perche *f* <a telephone pole : un poteau> <ski pole : bâton de ski> **2** : pôle *m* <the South Pole : le pôle Sud> **3** : pôle *m* (électrique)
Pole ['po:l] *n* : Polonais *m,* -naise *f*
polecat ['po:l,kæt] *n, pl* **polecats** *or* **polecat 1** FERRET : putois *m* **2** SKUNK : mouffette *f*
polemical [pə'lɛmɪkəl] *adj* : polémique
polemics [pə'lɛmɪks] *ns & pl* : polémique *f*
police[1] [pə'li:s] *vt* **-liced; -licing** : surveiller, maintenir l'ordre et la paix de
police[2] *ns & pl* **1** *or* **police force** : police *f,* gendarmerie *f* **2** POLICE OFFICERS : policiers *mpl*
policeman [pə'li:smən] *n, pl* **-men** [-mən, -,mɛn] : policier *m*
police officer *n* : policier *m,* agent *m* de police
policewoman [pə'li:s,wʊmən] *n, pl* **-women** [-,wɪmən] : femme *f* policier
policy ['paləsi] *n, pl* **-cies 1** : politique *f* <foreign policy : politique étrangère> **2** *or* **insurance policy** : police *f* d'assurance
policyholder ['paləsi,ho:ldər] *n* : assuré *m,* -rée *f*
polio ['po:li,o:] → **poliomyelitis**
poliomyelitis [,po:li,o:,maɪə'laɪṭəs] *n* : poliomyélite *f*
polish[1] ['palɪʃ] *vt* **1** : polir (une surface) **2** REFINE : parfaire, peaufiner
polish[2] *n* **1** LUSTER : poli *m,* éclat *m* **2** WAX : cire *f* (pour les meubles, etc.), cirage *m* (pour les chaussures) **3** REFINEMENT : perfection *f,* raffinement *m* **4** **nail polish** : vernis *m* à ongles
Polish[1] ['po:lɪʃ] *adj* : polonais
Polish[2] *n* : polonais *m* (langue)
polite [pə'laɪt] *adj* **politer; -est** : poli, courtois
politely [pə'laɪtli] *adv* : poliment
politeness [pə'laɪtnəs] *n* : politesse *f*
politic ['palə,tɪk] *adj* : habile, diplomate
political [pə'lɪṭɪkəl] *adj* : politique — **politically** [-ṭɪkli] *adv*
politician [,palə'tɪʃən] *n* : politicien *m,* -cienne *f*
politics ['palə,tɪks] *ns & pl* : politique *f*
polka ['po:lkə, 'po:kə] *n* : polka *f*
polka dot *n* : pois *m,* picot *m Can*
poll[1] ['po:l] *vt* **1** : obtenir, recueillir (des voix) **2** CANVASS : sonder — *vi* : voter
poll[2] *n* **1** SURVEY : sondage *m,* enquête *f* **2** **polls** *npl* : urnes *fpl* <to go to the polls : aller aux urnes>
pollen ['palən] *n* : pollen *m*
pollinate ['palə,neɪt] *vt* **-nated; -nating** : polliniser
pollination [,palə'neɪʃən] *n* : pollinisation *f*
pollster ['po:lstər] *n* : sondeur *m,* -deuse *f;* enquêteur *m,* -teuse *f*
pollutant [pə'lu:tənt] *n* : polluant *m*
pollute [pə'lu:t] *vt* **-luted; -luting** : polluer
pollution [pə'lu:ʃən] *n* : pollution *f*
pollywog *or* **polliwog** ['pali,wɔg] *n* TADPOLE : têtard *m*
polo ['po:,lo:] *n* : polo *m*
poltergeist ['po:lṭər,gaɪst] *n* : esprit *m* frappeur
polyester ['pali,ɛstər, ,pali'-] *n* : polyester *m*
polygamist [pə'lɪgəmɪst] *n* : polygame *mf*
polygamous [pə'lɪgəməs] *adj* : polygame
polygamy [pə'lɪgəmi] *n* : polygamie *f*
polygon ['pali,gan] *n* : polygone *m*
polymer ['paləmər] *n* : polymère *m*
Polynesian[1] [,palə'ni:ʒən, -ʃən] *adj* : polynésien
Polynesian[2] *n* **1** : Polynésien *m,* -sienne *f* **2** : polynésien *m* (langue)
polyp ['paləp] *n* : polype *m*
polytheism ['pali,θi,ɪzəm] *n* : polythéisme *m*
polyunsaturated [,pali,ʌn'sætʃə,reɪṭəd] *adj* : polyinsaturé

pomegranate ['pɑmə,grænət, 'pɑm,græ-] *n* : grenade *f* (fruit)

pommel[1] ['pʌməl] *vt* → **pummel**

pommel[2] ['pʌməl, 'pɑ-] *n* : pommeau *m* (sur une épée, d'une selle)

pomp ['pɑmp] *n* **1** SPLENDOR : pompe *f,* faste *m* **2** OSTENTATION : apparat *m,* ostentation *f*

pompous ['pɑmpəs] *adj* : pompeux — **pompously** *adv*

poncho ['pɑn,tʃo:] *n, pl* **-chos** : poncho *m*

pond ['pɑnd] *n* : étang *m,* mare *f*

ponder ['pɑndər] *vt* : évaluer, estimer — *vi* **to ponder over** : réfléchir à, méditer sur

ponderous ['pɑndərəs] *adj* : pesant, lourd

pontiff ['pɑntɪf] *n* : pontife *m*

pontifical [pɑn'tɪfɪkəl] *adj* : pontifical

pontificate [pɑn'tɪfə,keɪt] *vi* **-cated; -cating** : pontifier

pontoon [pɑn'tu:n] *n* : ponton *m*

pony ['po:ni] *n, pl* **-nies** : poney *m*

ponytail ['po:ni,teɪl] *n* : queue *f* de cheval

poodle ['pu:dəl] *n* : caniche *m*

pool[1] ['pu:l] *vt* : mettre en commun <to pool resources : mettre en commun des ressources>

pool[2] *n* **1** PUDDLE : flaque *f* (d'eau), mare *f* (de sang) **2** RESERVE : fonds *m* commun **3** BILLIARDS : billard *m* américain **4** *or* **swimming pool** : piscine *f*

poor ['pʊr, 'por] *adj* **1** : pauvre <poor people : gens pauvres> **2** : mauvais, piètre <a poor crop : une mauvaise récolte> <poor results : piètres résultats> <poor health : santé précaire> **3** BARREN : stérile, improductif <poor soil : terre stérile> **4** : pauvre <you poor thing! : pauvre de toi!> **5** UNFAVORABLE : défavorable

poorly ['pʊrli, 'por-] *adv* BADLY : mal

pop[1] ['pɑp] *v* **popped; popping** *vt* **1** BURST : faire éclater **2** PUT : mettre <he popped it into his mouth : il l'a mis dans sa bouche> — *vi* **1** BURST : éclater, exploser **2** *or* **to pop out** : sortir <his eyes were popping : les yeux lui sortaient de la tête> **3 to pop in** : faire une petite visite

pop[2] *adj* : pop <pop music : musique pop>

pop[3] *n* **1** : bruit *m* sec **2** SODA : boisson *f* gazeuse, liqueur *f Can*

popcorn ['pɑp,korn] *n* : maïs *m* explosé, pop-corn *m*

pope ['po:p] *n* : pape *m* <Pope Pius XII : le pape Pie XII>

poplar ['pɑplər] *n* : peuplier *m*

poplin ['pɑplɪn] *n* : popeline *f*

poppy ['pɑpi] *n, pl* **-pies** : coquelicot *m*

populace ['pɑpjələs] *n* **1** MASSES : masses *fpl,* peuple *m* **2** POPULATION : population *f*

popular ['pɑpjələr] *adj* **1** : populaire <popular government : gouvernement populaire> **2** PREVALENT, WIDESPREAD : répandu **3** : aimé, prisé, populaire <a popular destination : une destination prisée>

popularity [,pɑpjə'lærəṭi] *n* : popularité *f*

popularize ['pɑpjələ,raɪz] *vt* **-ized; -izing** : populariser

popularly ['pɑpjələrli] *adv* : communément, généralement

populate ['pɑpjə,leɪt] *vt* **-lated; -lating** : peupler

population [,pɑpjə'leɪʃən] *n* : population *f*

populous ['pɑpjələs] *adj* : populeux

porcelain ['porsələn] *n* : porcelaine *f*

porch ['portʃ] *n* : véranda *f,* porche *m,* galerie *f Can,* perron *m Can*

porcupine ['porkjə,paɪn] *n* : porc-épic *m*

pore[1] ['por] *vi* **pored; poring** : lire attentivement, étudier de près

pore[2] *n* : pore *m* (de la peau)

pork ['pork] *n* : porc *m*

pornographic [,pornə'græfɪk] *adj* : pornographique

pornography [por'nɑgrəfi] *n* : pornographie *f*

porous ['porəs] *adj* : poreux

porpoise ['porpəs] *n* : marsouin *m*

porridge ['porɪdʒ] *n* : porridge *m France,* gruau *m Can*

port[1] ['port] *adj* : portuaire

port[2] *n* **1** HARBOR : port *m,* ville *f* portuaire **2** ORIFICE : orifice *m* **3** PORTHOLE : hublot *m* **4** *or* **port side** : bâbord *m* (d'un navire) **5** *or* **port wine** : porto *m* **6** : port *m* (d'un ordinateur)

portable ['porṭəbəl] *adj* : portatif, portable <portable computer : ordinateur portable>

portal ['porṭəl] *n* : portail *m*

portend [por'tɛnd] *vt* : présager, annoncer

portent ['por,tɛnt] *n* : présage *m,* prédiction *f*

portentous [por'tɛntəs] *adj* **1** : de mauvais augure **2** MARVELOUS : extraordinaire, prodigieux **3** GRAVE : grave, sérieux <portentous decisions : de graves décisions>

porter ['porṭər] *n* : porteur *m,* -teuse *f*

portfolio [port'fo:li,o] *n, pl* **-lios 1** BRIEFCASE, FOLDER : porte-documents *m* **2** : dossier *m* (diplomatique) **3** *or* **investment portfolio** : portefeuille *m*

porthole ['port,ho:l] *n* : hublot *m*

portico ['porṭɪ,ko] *n, pl* **-coes** *or* **-cos** : portique *m*

portion[1] ['porʃən] *vt* : distribuer, diviser

portion[2] *n* PART, SHARE : portion *f,* part *m*

portly ['portli] *adj* **portlier; -est** : corpulent

portrait ['portrət, -ˌtreɪt] *n* : portrait *m*
portray [por'treɪ] *vt* **1** DEPICT : représenter (par le dessin) **2** DESCRIBE : dépeindre (par la parole) **3** ENACT : jouer, interpréter (un rôle)
portrayal [por'treɪəl] *n* **1** REPRESENTATION : représentation *f* **2** PORTRAIT : portrait *m*
Portuguese[1] ['portʃəˌgi:z, -ˌgi:s] *adj* : portugais
Portuguese[2] *n* **1** : Portugais *m*, -gaise *f* **2** : portugais *m* (langue)
pose[1] ['po:z] *v* **posed; posing** *vt* : poser (une question, etc.) — *vi* **1** : poser (se dit d'un modèle) **2 to pose as** : se faire passer pour
pose[2] *n* **1** : pose *f* <to strike a pose : adapter une pose> **2** PRETENSE : affectation *f*, faux-semblant *m*
posh ['pɑʃ] *adj* : chic, élégant
position[1] [pə'zɪʃən] *vt* : positionner
position[2] *n* **1** STANCE : position *f*, perspective *f* **2** LOCATION : position *f*, emplacement *m* **3** STATUS : position *f*, rang *m* **4** JOB : poste *m*
positive ['pɑzəṭɪv] *adj* **1** DEFINITE : catégorique <a positive no : un non catégorique> **2** CONFIDENT : certain, convaincu **3** : positif (en grammaire, en mathématiques, en physique, etc.) **4** AFFIRMATIVE : positif
positively ['pɑzəṭɪvli] *adv* **1** CERTAINLY : sans aucun doute, incontestablement **2** (*used for emphasis*) : réellement <positively surprised : réellement surpris>
possess [pə'zɛs] *vt* : posséder, détenir
possession [pə'zɛʃən] *n* **1** OWNERSHIP : possession *f* **2** PROPERTY : possession *f*, jouissance *f* (en droit) **3 possessions** *npl* BELONGINGS : biens *mpl*
possessive[1] [pə'zɛsɪv] *adj* **1** JEALOUS : possessif, jaloux **2** : possessif (en grammaire)
possessive[2] *n or* **possessive case** : possessif *m*
possessor [pə'zɛsər] *n* : possesseur *m*
possibility [ˌpɑsə'bɪləṭi] *n, pl* **-ties** : possibilité *f*
possible ['pɑsəbəl] *adj* : possible
possibly ['pɑsəbli] *adv* : peut-être, possiblement *Can*
possum ['pɑsəm] → **opossum**
post[1] ['po:st] *vt* **1** MAIL : poster (une lettre) **2** INFORM : tenir au courant, tenir informé <I'll keep you posted : je te tiendrai au courant> **3** STATION : poster <to post guards : poster des gardiens> **4** AFFIX : afficher, placarder
post[2] *n* **1** OFFICE, POSITION : poste *m* **2** POLE : poteau *m* **3** *Brit* → **mail**[2] **1, 2; postal service**
postage ['po:stɪdʒ] *n* : affranchissement *m*, tarifs *mpl* postaux
postal ['postəl] *adj* : postal
postal service *n* : courrier *m*, poste *f*
postcard ['po:stˌkɑrd] *n* : carte *f* postale
poster ['po:stər] *n* : poster *m*, affiche *f*
posterior[1] [pɑ'stɪriər, po-] *adj* : postérieur
posterior[2] *n* BUTTOCKS : postérieur *m fam*, derrière *m fam*
posterity [pɑ'stɛrəṭi] *n* : postérité *f*
postgraduate [ˌpo:st'grædʒuət] *n* : étudiant *m*, -diante *f* de troisième cycle
posthaste ['po:st'heɪst] *adv* : en toute vitesse, en toute hâte
posthumous ['pɑstʃəməs] *adj* : posthume
posthumously ['pɑstʃəməsli] *adv* : après la mort
postman ['po:stmən, -ˌmæn] *n, pl* **-men** [-mən, -ˌmɛn] → **mailman**
postmark[1] ['po:stˌmɑrk] *vt* : oblitérer (un timbre)
postmark[2] *n* : cachet *m* de la poste
postmaster ['po:stˌmæstər] *n* : receveur *m* des Postes
postmortem [ˌpo:st'mɔrṭəm] *n* : autopsie *f*
postnatal [ˌpo:st'neɪṭəl] *adj* : postnatal
post office *n* : bureau *m* de poste
postoperative [ˌpo:st'ɑpərəṭɪv, -ˌreɪ-] *adj* : postopératoire
postpaid [ˌpo:st'peɪd] *adj* : franco de port, port payé
postpone [ˌpo:st'po:n] *vt* **-poned; -poning** : reporter, remettre
postponement [ˌpo:st'po:nmənt] *n* : renvoi *m*, remise *f*
postscript ['po:stˌskrɪpt] *n* : post-scriptum *m*
postulate ['pɑstʃəˌleɪt] *vt* **-lated; -lating** : poser comme postulat
posture[1] ['pɑstʃər] *vi* **-tured; -turing** : poser, prendre des airs
posture[2] *n* : posture *f*
postwar [ˌpo:st'wɔr] *adj* : d'après-guerre
posy ['po:zi] *n, pl* **-sies 1** FLOWER : fleur *f* **2** BOUQUET : (petit) bouquet *m* de fleurs
pot[1] ['pɑt] *vt* **potted; potting** : empoter (une plante)
pot[2] *n* **1** POTFUL : pot *m* <a pot of soup : un pot de soupe> **2** *or* **cooking pot** : marmite *f*, casserole *f*
potable ['po:ṭəbəl] *adj* : potable
potash ['pɑtˌæʃ] *n* : potasse *f*
potassium [pə'tæsiəm] *n* : potassium *m*
potato [pə'teɪṭo] *n, pl* **-toes** : pomme *f* de terre, patate *f fam*
potbellied ['pɑtˌbɛlid] *adj* : bedonnant
potbelly ['pɑtˌbɛli] *n, pl* **-lies** : bedaine *f*
potency ['po:tən*t*si] *n, pl* **-cies 1** POWER : puissance *f*, force *f* **2** EFFECTIVENESS : efficacité *f*
potent ['po:tənt] *adj* **1** POWERFUL : puissant **2** EFFECTIVE : efficace
potential[1] [pə'tɛntʃəl] *adj* : potentiel — **potentially** *adv*
potential[2] *n* : potentiel *m*
potful ['pɑtˌfʊl] *n* : pot *m*, contenu *m* d'un pot

pothole ['pɑtˌho:l] *n* : nid-de-poule *m*
potion ['po:ʃən] *n* : potion *f*
potluck ['pɑtˌlʌk] *n or* **potluck supper** : souper *m* communautaire
potpourri [ˌpo:pʊ'ri:] *n* **1** : pot-pourri *m*, fleurs *fpl* séchées **2** COLLECTION : pot-pourri *m*, mélange *m*
potshot ['pɑtˌʃɑt] *n* **1** CRITICISM : commentaire *m* désobligeant **2 to take a potshot at** : tirer à vue sur
potter ['pɑt̬ər] *n* : potier *m*, -tière *f*
pottery ['pɑt̬əri] *n, pl* **-teries** : poterie *f*
pouch ['paʊtʃ] *n* **1** BAG : petit sac *m* **2** : poche *f* (des marsupiaux)
poultice ['po:lt̬əs] *n* : cataplasme *m*
poultry ['po:ltri] *n* : volaille *f*
pounce ['paʊnts] *vi* **pounced; pouncing 1** : sauter, bondir **2 to pounce upon** : attaquer, assaillir
pound[1] ['paʊnd] *vt* **1** CRUSH : broyer, écraser **2** HAMMER : marteler **3** BEAT : battre, frapper <to pound one's chest : frapper la poitrine> **4 to pound the pavement** : battre le pavé — *vi* **1** BEAT : palpiter, battre <my heart was pounding : mon cœur battait la chamade> **2 to pound away at** : travailler avec acharnement à
pound[2] *n* **1** : livre *f* (unité de mesure) **2** : livre *f* sterling **3** SHELTER : fourrière *f* (pour des animaux)
pour ['por] *vt* **1** : verser (des boissons) **2 to pour all one's energy into** : mettre toute son énergie dans — *vi* **1** FLOW : couler **2** RAIN : pleuvoir à verse
pout[1] ['paʊt] *vi* : faire la moue
pout[2] *n* : moue *f*
poverty ['pɑvərt̬i] *n* : pauvreté *f*
powder[1] ['paʊdər] *vt* **1** : poudrer <to powder one's nose : se poudrer le nez> **2** CRUSH : pulvériser
powder[2] *n* : poudre *f*
powdery ['paʊdəri] *adj* : poudreux
power[1] ['paʊər] *vt* : faire fonctionner, faire marcher
power[2] *n* **1** AUTHORITY : pouvoir *m*, autorité *f* **2** ABILITY : capacité *f* **3** : puissance *f* <foreign power : puissance extérieure> **4** STRENGTH : force *f* (d'une personne), puissance *f* (d'une machine) **5** : énergie *f* (électrique)
powerful ['paʊərfəl] *adj* : puissant, fort
powerfully ['paʊərfəli] *adv* : puissamment, fortement
powerhouse ['paʊərˌhaʊs] *n* : personne *f* très énergique
powerless ['paʊərləs] *adj* : impuissant
powwow ['paʊˌwaʊ] *n* : pow-wow *m Can*, assemblée *f* d'Amérindiens
pox ['pɑks] *n, pl* **pox** *or* **poxes 1** → **chicken pox 2** → **syphilis**
practicable ['præktɪkəbəl] *adj* : praticable, réalisable
practical ['præktɪkəl] *adj* : pratique
practically ['præktɪkli] *adv* **1** : pratiquement, d'une façon pratique **2** ALMOST, NEARLY : presque, pratiquement
practice[1] *or* **practise** ['præktəs] *v* **-ticed** *or* **-tised; -ticing** *or* **-tising** *vt* **1** : pratiquer (un sport, un métier) **2** CARRY OUT : pratiquer, mettre en application **3** OBSERVE : observer <to practice politeness : observer les règles de politesse> — *vi* : s'exercer, s'entraîner
practice[2] *n* **1** USE : pratique *f* <to put into practice : mettre en pratique> **2** CUSTOM, HABIT : coutume *f*, pratique *f* **3** : exercice *m* (d'une profession)
practitioner [præk'tɪʃənər] *n* : praticien *m*, -cienne *f*
pragmatic [præg'mæt̬ɪk] *adj* : pragmatique
pragmatism ['prægməˌtɪzəm] *n* : pragmatisme *m*
prairie ['prɛri] *n* : prairie *f*
praise[1] ['preɪz] *vt* **praised; praising 1** COMMEND : louer, faire l'éloge de **2** GLORIFY : louer, glorifier
praise[2] *n* : louange *f*
praiseworthy ['preɪzˌwərði] *adj* : louable, digne d'éloges
pram ['præm] *n Brit* : voiture *f* d'enfant, landau *m France*
prance[1] ['prænts] *vt* **pranced; prancing** : caracoler (se dit d'un cheval), cabrioler (se dit d'une personne)
prance[2] *n* : cabriole *f*
prank ['præŋk] *n* : farce *f*, tour *m*
prankster ['præŋkstər] *n* : farceur *m*, -ceuse *f*
prattle[1] ['prætəl] *vi* **-tled; -tling** BABBLE : babiller, bavarder
prattle[2] *n* : bavardage *m*
prawn ['prɔn] *n* : crevette *f* (rose)
pray ['preɪ] *vt* ENTREAT : supplier, implorer <pray be careful : je te prie de faire attention> — *vi* : prier (à Dieu)
prayer ['prɛr] *n* **1** : prière *f* <to say one's prayers : faire sa prière> <the Lord's Prayer : le Notre Père> <to kneel in prayer : prier à genoux> **2** WISH : désir *m*, souhait *m*
praying mantis → **mantis**
preach ['pri:tʃ] *vt* **1** : prêcher <to preach the gospel : prêcher l'Évangile> **2** ADVOCATE : prêcher, prôner <to preach patience : prôner la patience> — *vi* : prêcher
preacher ['pri:tʃər] *n* MINISTER : pasteur *m*
preamble ['pri:ˌæmbəl] *n* : préambule *m*, introduction *f*
precarious [prɪ'kæriəs] *adj* : précaire — **precariously** *adv*
precariousness [prɪ'kæriəsnəs] *n* : précarité *f*
precaution [prɪ'kɔʃən] *n* : précaution *f*
precautionary [prɪ'kɔʃəˌnɛri] *adj* : de précaution, préventif
precede [prɪ'si:d] *vt* **-ceded; -ceding** : précéder

precedence ['prɛsədənts, prɪ'si:dənts] *n* **1** : préséance *f* <in order of precedence : par ordre de préséance> **2** PRIORITY : priorité *f* <to take precedence over : avoir la priorité sur>

precedent ['prɛsədənt] *n* : précédent *m*

precept ['pri:ˌsɛpt] *n* : précepte *m*, principe *m*

precinct ['pri:ˌsɪŋkt] *n* **1** DISTRICT : arrondissement *m* (en France), circonscription *f* (au Canada) **2 precincts** *npl* : alentours *mpl*, environs *mpl*

precious ['prɛʃəs] *adj* **1** : précieux <precious stones : pierres précieuses> **2** CHERISHED, DEAR : cher **3** AFFECTED : affecté, forcé

precipice ['prɛsəpəs] *n* : précipice *m*

precipitate[1] [pri'sɪpəˌteɪt] *v* **-tated; -tating** *vt* **1** PROVOKE : provoquer **2** : condenser (un liquide) — *vi* : précipiter (en chimie)

precipitate[2] [pri'sɪpətət] *adj* **1** PRECIPITOUS : escarpé, à pic **2** RASH : précipité, prématuré

precipitate[3] [pri'sɪpətət, -ˌteɪt] *n* : précipité *m*

precipitation [priˌsɪpə'teɪʃən] *n* **1** HASTE : précipitation *f*, hâte *f* **2** : précipitations *fpl* (en météorologie)

precipitous [pri'sɪpət̬əs] *adj* STEEP : à pic, abrupt

précis [preɪ'si:] *n, pl* **précis** [-'si:z] : précis *m*, résumé *m*

precise [pri'saɪs] *adj* : précis — **precisely** *adv*

preciseness [pri'saɪsnəs] *n* : précision *f*

precision [pri'sɪʒən] *n* : précision *f*

preclude [pri'klu:d] *vt* **-cluded; -cluding** : empêcher, prévenir

precocious [pri'ko:ʃəs] *adj* : précoce — **precociously** *adv*

precocity [pri'kɑsət̬i] *n* : précocité *f*

preconceived [ˌpri:kən'si:vd] *adj* : préconçu

precondition [ˌpri:kən'dɪʃən] *n* : condition *f* préalable

precook [ˌpri:'kʊk] *vt* : précuire

precursor [prɪ'kərsər] *n* : précurseur *m*

predator ['prɛdət̬ər] *n* : prédateur *m*

predatory ['prɛdəˌtori] *adj* : prédateur

predecessor ['prɛdəˌsɛsər, 'pri:-] *n* : prédécesseur *m*

predestination [priˌdɛstə'neɪʃən] *n* : prédestination *f*

predestine [pri'dɛstən] *vt* **-tined; -tining** : prédestiner

predetermine [ˌpri:dɪ'tərmən] *vt* **-mined; mining** : prédéterminer

predicament [pri'dɪkəmənt] *n* : situation *f* difficile

predicate[1] ['prɛdəˌkeɪt] *vt* **-cated; -cating 1** AFFIRM : affirmer, déclarer **2** BASE : fonder

predicate[2] ['prɛdɪkət] *n* : prédicat *m*

predict [pri'dɪkt] *vt* : prédire

predictability [priˌdɪktə'bɪlət̬i] *n* : prévisibilité *f*

predictable [pri'dɪktəbəl] *adj* : prévisible

predictably [pri'dɪktəbli] *adv* : comme prévu

prediction [pri'dɪkʃən] *n* : prédiction *f*

predilection [ˌprɛdəl'ɛkʃən, ˌpri:-] *n* : prédilection *f*

predispose [ˌpri:dɪ'spo:z] *vt* : prédisposer

predisposition [ˌpri:ˌdɪspə'zɪʃən] *n* : prédisposition *f*

predominance [pri'dɑmənənts] *n* : prédominance *f*

predominant [pri'dɑmənənt] *adj* : prédominant

predominantly [pri'dɑmənəntli] *adv* MAINLY : principalement

predominate [pri'dɑməˌneɪt] *vt* **-nated; -nating** : prédominer

preeminence [pri'ɛmənənts] *n* : prééminence *f*

preeminent [pri'ɛmənənt] *adj* : prééminent

preeminently [pri'ɛmənəntli] *adv* : surtout, avant tout

preempt [pri'ɛmpt] *vt* **1** : préempter (un terrain) **2** APPROPRIATE : s'approprier, s'attribuer

preen ['pri:n] *vt* **1** : lisser (ses plumes) **2 to preen oneself** : se bichonner, se pomponner

prefabricated [ˌpri:'fæbrəˌkeɪt̬əd] *adj* : préfabriqué

preface[1] ['prɛfəs] *vt* **-aced; -acing** : préfacer (un livre), faire précéder (un discours, etc.)

preface[2] *n* : préface *f*

prefatory ['prɛfəˌtori] *adj* : préliminaire

prefect ['priˌfɛkt] *n* : préfet *m*

prefer [pri'fər] *vt* **-ferred; -ferring 1** : préférer <he prefers sports to reading : il préfère les sports à la lecture> **2 to prefer charges** : porter plainte

preferable ['prɛfərəbəl] *adj* : préférable — **preferably** [-bli] *adv*

preference ['prɛfrənts, 'prɛfər-] *n* : préférence *f*, choix *m*

preferential [ˌprɛfə'rɛntʃəl] *adj* : préférentiel

prefigure [pri'fɪgjər] *vt* **-ured; -uring** : préfigurer, annoncer

prefix[1] ['pri:ˌfɪks, pri:'-] *vt* : préfixer (en linguistique)

prefix[2] ['pri:ˌfɪks] *n* : préfixe *m*

pregnancy ['prɛgnəntsi] *n, pl* **-cies** : grossesse *f*

pregnant ['prɛgnənt] *adj* **1** : enceinte, grosse **2** MEANINGFUL : profond, chargé de sens

preheat [ˌpri:'hi:t] *vt* : préchauffer

prehensile [pri'hɛntsəl, -'hɛnˌsaɪl] *adj* : préhensile

prehistoric [ˌpri:hɪs'tɔrɪk] *or* **prehistorical** [-ɪkəl] *adj* : préhistorique

prejudge [ˌpri:'dʒʌdʒ] *vt* **-judged; -judging** : préjuger

prejudice[1] ['prɛdʒədəs] *vt* **-diced; -dicing 1** : porter préjudice à (en

droit) **2 to be prejudiced against** : avoir des préjugés contre
prejudice[2] *n* **1** DAMAGES : préjudice *m*, dommage *m* **2** BIAS : préjugés *mpl*
prelate ['prɛlət] *n* : prélat *m*
preliminary[1] [pri'lɪmə,nɛri] *adj* : préliminaire
preliminary[2] *n, pl* **-naries** : préliminaire *m*
prelude ['prɛ,lu:d, 'prɛl,ju:d; 'preɪ,lu:d, 'pri:-] *n* : prélude *m*
premarital [,pri:'mærəṭəl] *adj* : avant le mariage, prénuptial
premature [,pri:mə'tʊr, -'tjʊr, -'tʃʊr] *adj* : prématuré — **prematurely** *adv*
premeditate [pri'mɛdə,teɪt] *vt* **-tated; -tating** : préméditer
premeditation [pri,mɛdə'teɪʃən] *n* : préméditation *f*
premenstrual [pri'mɛn*t*strʊəl] *adj* : prémenstruel
premier[1] [pri'mɪr, -'mjɪr; 'pri:miər] *adj* : premier
premier[2] → **prime minister**
premiere[1] [prɪ'mjɛr, -'mɪr] *vi* **-miered; -miering** : se donner en première
premiere[2] *n* : première *f* (d'un spectacle)
premise ['prɛmɪs] *n* **1** : prémisse *f* (d'un raisonnement) **2 premises** *npl* : lieux *mpl* <on the premises : sur les lieux>
premium ['pri:miəm] *n* **1** BONUS : prime *f*, supplément *m* **2** *or* **insurance premium** : prime *f* d'assurance **3 to put a premium on** : mettre au premier plan **4 to sell at a premium** : vendre au-dessus du pair
premonition [,pri:mə'nɪʃən, ,prɛmə-] *n* : prémonition *f*, pressentiment *m*
prenatal [,pri:'neɪṭəl] *adj* : prénatal
preoccupation [pri,ɑkjə'peɪʃən] *n* : préoccupation *f*
preoccupied [pri'ɑkjə,paɪd] *adj* : préoccupé, distrait
preoccupy [pri'ɑkjə,paɪ] *vt* **-pied; -pying** : préoccuper
preparation [,prɛpə'reɪʃən] *n* **1** PREPARING : préparation *f* <the preparation of meals : la préparation des repas> **2 preparations** *npl* : préparatifs *mpl*
preparatory [pri'pærə,tori] *adj* : préparatoire
prepare [prɪ'pær] *v* **-pared; -paring** *vt* : préparer — *vi* : se préparer
prepay [,pri:'peɪ] *vt* **-paid; -paying** : payer d'avance
preponderance [prɪ'pɑndərən*t*s] *n* : prépondérance *f*
preponderant [prɪ'pɑndərənt] *adj* : prépondérant
preponderantly [prɪ'pɑndərəntli] *adv* : de façon prépondérante
preposition [,prɛpə'zɪʃən] *n* : préposition *f*
prepositional [,prɛpə'zɪʃənəl] *adj* : prépositionnel
prepossessing [,pri:pə'zɛsɪŋ] *adj* : attrayant, avenant
preposterous [pri'pɑstərəs] *adj* : absurde, insensé
prerecorded [pri:rɪ'kɔrdəd] *adj* : en différé
prerequisite[1] [pri'rɛkwəzət] *adj* : nécessaire au préalable
prerequisite[2] *n* : préalable *m*, prérequis *m Can*
prerogative [prɪ'rɑgəṭɪv] *n* : prérogative *f*
presage[1] ['prɛsɪdʒ, prɪ'seɪdʒ] *vt* **-saged; -saging** : présager
presage[2] ['prɛsɪdʒ] *n* : présage *m*
preschool ['pri:,sku:l] *adj* : préscolaire
prescribe [pri'skraɪb] *vt* **-scribed; -scribing 1** RECOMMEND : préconiser, recommander **2** : prescrire (en médecine)
prescription [pri'skrɪpʃən] *n* : prescription *f*
presence ['prɛzən*t*s] *n* : présence *f*
present[1] [prɪ'zɛnt] *vt* **1** INTRODUCE : présenter **2** SHOW : présenter, donner, montrer <to present a play : présenter une pièce> **3** GIVE : offrir, présenter <the winner was presented with a medal : on a présenté une médaille au gagnant>
present[2] ['prɛzənt] *adj* **1** CURRENT : actuel <present conditions : conditions actuelles> **2** ATTENDING : présent
present[3] ['prɛzənt] *n* **1** GIFT : cadeau *m* **2** *or* **present time** : présent *m* <at present : actuellement>
presentation [,pri:,zɛn'teɪʃən, ,prɛzən-] *n* : présentation *f*
presentiment [pri'zɛntəmənt] *n* : pressentiment *m*, prémonition *f*
presently ['prɛzəntli] *adv* **1** SOON : bientôt **2** NOW : à présent, en ce moment
present participle *n* : participe *m* présent
preservation [,prɛzər'veɪʃən] *n* : préservation *f*, maintien *m*
preservative [pri'zərvəṭɪv] *n* : agent *m* de conservation
preserve[1] [pri'zərv] *vt* **-served; -serving 1** PROTECT : préserver, protéger **2** MAINTAIN : garder, conserver <to preserve silence : garder le silence>
preserve[2] *n* **1** : chasse *f* réservée, réserve *f* <game preserve : chasse gardée> **2 preserves** *npl* : confitures *fpl*
preside [pri'zaɪd] *vi* **-sided; -siding 1 to preside over** : présider <to preside over a meeting : présider une réunion> **2 to preside over** OVERSEE : présider à
presidency ['prɛzədən*t*si] *n, pl* **-cies** : présidence *f*
president ['prɛzədənt] *n* : président *m*
presidential [,prɛzə'dɛntʃəl] *adj* : présidentiel
press[1] ['prɛs] *vt* **1** PUSH : presser, appuyer sur **2** IRON : repasser **3** SQUEEZE : presser **4** URGE : presser,

inciter — *vi* **1** PUSH : appuyer (sur un bouton, etc.) **2** CROWD : se presser **3 to press through** : se frayer un chemin dans

press[2] *n* **1** CROWD : foule *f* **2** *or* **printing press** : presse *f* <to go to press : mettre sous presse> **3** URGENCY : urgence *f* **4** : presse *f* <the story is getting good press : l'article a bonne presse> **5** PUBLISHER : maison *f* d'édition, presses *fpl* **6** PRINTER : imprimerie *f*

pressing ['prɛsɪŋ] *adj* : pressant, urgent

pressure[1] ['prɛʃər] *vt* **-sured; -suring** : pousser, faire pression sur

pressure[2] *n* **1** : pression *f* <to be under pressure : être sous pression> **2** → **blood pressure**

pressurize ['prɛʃəˌraɪz] *vt* **-ized; -izing** : pressuriser

prestidigitation [ˌprɛstəˌdɪdʒə'teɪʃən] *n* SLEIGHT OF HAND : prestidigitation *f*

prestige [prɛ'stiːʒ, -'stiːdʒ] *n* : prestige *m*

prestigious [prɛ'stɪdʒəs, -'sti-, prə-] *adj* : prestigieux

presto ['prɛsˌtoː] *adv & interj* : presto!, tout de suite

presumably [pri'zuːməbli] adv : vraisemblablement, apparemment, présumément *Can*

presume [pri'zuːm] *vt* **-sumed; -suming 1** DARE : se permettre <he presumed to contradict him : il s'est permis de le contredire> **2** ASSUME : présumer, supposer <to be presumed innocent : être présumé innocent> **3** IMPLY : présupposer, laisser supposer

presumption [prɪ'zʌmpʃən] *n* **1** EFFRONTERY : présomption *f,* arrogance *f* **2** ASSUMPTION : présomption *f,* supposition *f*

presumptuous [prɪ'zʌmptʃʊəs] *adj* : présomptueux, prétentieux

presuppose [ˌpriːsə'poːz] *vt* **-posed; -posing** : présupposer

presupposition [ˌpriːˌsəpə'zɪʃən] *n* : présupposition *f*

pretend [pri'tɛnd] *vt* **1** PROFESS : prétendre <he doesn't pretend to be a psychiatrist : il ne prétend pas être psychiatre> **2** FEIGN : feindre, simuler <to pretend friendship : feindre l'amitié> — *vi* : faire semblant

pretense *or* **pretence** ['priːˌtɛnts, pri'tɛnts] *n* **1** CLAIM : prétention *f* **2** : semblant *m,* simulacre *m* <to make a pretense of : faire semblant de> **3** SIMULATION : faux-semblant *m*

pretension [pri'tɛntʃən] *n* **1** CLAIM : prétention *f,* revendication *f* **2** PRETENTIOUSNESS : prétention *f* **3** ASPIRATION : ambition *f,* aspiration *f*

pretentious [pri'tɛntʃəs] *adj* : prétentieux — **pretentiously** *adv*

pretentiousness [pri'tɛntʃəsnəs] *n* : prétention *f*

pretext ['priːˌtɛkst] *n* : prétexte *m,* excuse *f*

prettily ['prɪtəli] *adv* : joliment

prettiness ['prɪṭinəs] *n* : beauté *f*

pretty[1] ['prɪṭi] *vt* **-tied; -tying** *or* **to pretty up** : enjoliver

pretty[2] *adv* FAIRLY : assez

pretty[3] *adj* **prettier; -est** : joli, beau <pretty flowers : de jolies fleurs> <it's not a pretty sight : ce n'est pas beau à voir>

pretzel ['prɛtsəl] *n* : bretzel *m*

prevail [pri'veɪl] *vi* **1** TRIUMPH : prévaloir, l'emporter **2** PREDOMINATE : prévaloir, prédominer **3 to prevail upon** : persuader

prevalence ['prɛvələnts] *n* : fréquence *f,* prédominance *f,* prévalence *f* (d'une maladie)

prevalent ['prɛvələnt] *adj* : répandu, commun

prevaricate [pri'værəˌkeɪt] *vi* **-cated; -cating** : tergiverser, user de détours

prevarication [priˌværə'keɪʃən] *n* : tergiversation *f,* faux-fuyant *m*

prevent [pri'vɛnt] *vt* **1** AVOID : prévenir, éviter **2** STOP : empêcher <bad weather prevented us from leaving : le mauvais temps nous a empêchés de partir>

preventable [pri'vɛntəbəl] *adj* : évitable

preventative [pri'vɛntəṭɪv] → **preventive**

prevention [pri'vɛntʃən] *n* : prévention *f*

preventive [pri'vɛntɪv] *adj* : préventif

preview ['priːˌvju] *n* : avant-première *f*

previous ['priːviəs] *adj* : antérieur, précédent, initial <his previous position : sa position initiale> <a previous era : une époque antérieure> <the previous paragraph : le paragraphe précédent>

previously ['priːviəsli] *adv* : antérieurement, auparavant

prewar [ˌpriː'wɔr] *adj* : d'avant-guerre

prey[1] ['preɪ] *vi* **1 to prey on** : faire sa proie de **2 to prey on s.o.'s mind** : ronger l'esprit à qqn

prey[2] *ns & pl* : proie *f*

price[1] ['praɪs] *vt* **priced; pricing** : fixer un prix sur

price[2] *n* : prix *m*

priceless ['praɪsləs] *adj* : inestimable

prick[1] ['prɪk] *vt* **1** PIERCE : piquer, percer **2** GOAD : aiguillonner, piquer <guilt was pricking (at) his conscience : les remords aiguillonnaient sa conscience> **3 to prick up one's ears** : dresser l'oreille

prick[2] *n* : piqûre *f*

pricker ['prɪkər] *n* THORN : épine *f*

prickle[1] ['prɪkəl] *vt* **-led; -ling** : picoter

prickle[2] *n* **1** THORN : épine *f* (d'un rosier, etc.) **2** STING : picotement *m*

prickly ['prɪkəli] *adj* **pricklier; -est 1** STINGING : épineux, piquant <a prickly sensation : une sensation de

picotement> 2 THORNY : épineux <prickly issues : questions épineuses>

pride[1] ['praɪd] *vt* **prided; priding** *or* **to pride oneself** : être fier

pride[2] *n* : fierté *f,* orgueil *m*

prideful ['praɪdfəl] *adj* : hautain, arrogant

priest ['pri:st] *n* : prêtre *m*

priestess ['pri:stɪs] *n* : prêtresse *f*

priesthood ['pri:stˌhʊd] *n* : prêtrise *f*

priestly ['pri:stli] *adj* : sacerdotal

prim ['prɪm] *adj* **primmer; primmest** : collet monté, guindé

primarily [praɪ'mɛrəli] *adv* **1** ORIGINALLY : d'abord, à l'origine **2** PRINCIPALLY : essentiellement, principalement

primary[1] ['praɪˌmɛri, 'praɪməri] *adj* **1** FIRST : primaire <primary education : enseignement primaire> **2** PRINCIPAL : principal **3** BASIC : fondamental, de base

primary[2] *n, pl* **-ries** : élection *f* primaire

primary school → **elementary school**

primate ['praɪˌmeɪt, -mət] *n* : primate *m*

prime[1] ['praɪm] *vt* **primed; priming 1** FILL, LOAD : remplir, charger **2** PREPARE : apprêter (une surface, un mur) **3** COACH : préparer <to prime a witness : préparer un témoin>

prime[2] *adj* : de première qualité, de premier choix

prime[3] *n* **in the prime of one's life** : dans la force de l'âge

prime minister *n* : Premier ministre *m*

primer[1] ['prɪmər] *n* : premier livre *m* de lecture, abécédaire *m*

primer[2] ['praɪmər] *n* **1** : amorce *f* (d'un explosif) **2** *or* **prime coat** : apprêt *m*

primeval [praɪ'mi:vəl] *adj* : primitif

primitive ['prɪmət̬ɪv] *adj* : primitif

primly ['prɪmli] *adv* : d'une façon guindée

primness ['prɪmnəs] *n* : air *m* collet monté

primordial [praɪ'mɔrdiəl] *adj* : primordial

primp ['prɪmp] *vt* : se pomponner, se bichonner

primrose ['prɪmˌro:z] *n* : primevère *f*

prince ['prɪnts] *n* : prince *m*

princely ['prɪntsli] *adj* : princier

princess ['prɪntsəs, 'prɪnˌsɛs] *n* : princesse *f*

principal[1] ['prɪntsəpəl] *adj* : principal — **principally** *adv*

principal[2] *n* **1** : directeur *m,* -trice *f* <school principal : directeur d'école> **2** : principal *m* (d'une dette), capital *m* (d'une somme)

principality [ˌprɪntsə'pæləţi] *n, pl* **-ties** : principauté *f*

principle ['prɪntsəpəl] *n* : principe *m*

print[1] ['prɪnt] *vt* : imprimer (un texte, etc.) — *vi* : écrire en lettres moulées

print[2] *n* **1** IMPRESSION, MARK : empreinte *f* **2** LETTER : caractère *m* <in fine print : en petits caractères> **3** ENGRAVING : gravure *f* **4** : imprimé *m* (d'un tissu) **5** : épreuve *f* (en photographie) **6 in ~** : disponible

printer ['prɪntər] *n* **1** : imprimeur *m* (personne) **2** : imprimante *f* (machine) <laser printer : imprimante laser>

printing ['prɪntɪŋ] *n* **1** : imprimerie *f* (technique) **2** IMPRESSION : impression *f* <the second printing : le second tirage> **3** LETTERING : écriture *f* en lettres moulées

printout ['prɪntˌaʊt] *n* : sortie *f* sur imprimante

print out *vt* : faire une sortie sur imprimante

prior ['praɪər] *adj* **1** PREVIOUS : antérieur, précédent **2** : qui prévaut, prioritaire <a prior claim : un droit de priorité>

priority [praɪ'ɔrəţi] *n, pl* **-ties** : priorité *f*

priory ['praɪəri] *n, pl* **-ries** : prieuré *m*

prism ['prɪzəm] *n* : prisme *m*

prison ['prɪzən] *n* : prison *f*

prisoner ['prɪzənər] *n* : prisonnier *m,* -nière *f*

prissy ['prɪsi] *adj* **prissier; -est** : collet monté

pristine ['prɪsˌti:n, prɪs'-] *adj* : pur, immaculé

privacy ['praɪvəsi] *n, pl* **-cies 1** SECLUSION, SOLITUDE : intimité *f,* solitude *f* **2** : vie *f* privée <the right to privacy : le droit à la vie privée>

private[1] ['praɪvət] *adj* **1** : privé <private property : propriété privée> **2** PERSONAL : personnel, privé

private[2] *n* : soldat *m* de deuxième classe

privateer [ˌpraɪvə'tɪr] *n* : corsaire *m*

privately ['praɪvətli] *adv* **1** SECRETLY : en privé **2 privately owned** : privé

privation [praɪ'veɪʃən] *n* : privation *f*

privilege ['prɪvlɪdʒ, 'prɪvə-] *n* : privilège *m*

privileged ['prɪvlɪdʒd, 'prɪvə-] *adj* : privilégié

privy ['prɪvi] *adj* **to be privy to** : être au courant de

prize[1] ['praɪz] *vt* **prized; prizing** : priser, chérir

prize[2] *adj* **1** PRIZEWINNING : primé **2** OUTSTANDING : remarquable, exceptionnel

prize[3] *n* : prix *m*

prizefight ['praɪzˌfaɪt] *n* : combat *m* de boxe

prizefighter ['praɪzˌfaɪţər] *n* : boxeur *m* professionnel

prizefighting ['praɪzˌfaɪţɪŋ] *n* : boxe *f* professionnelle

prizewinner ['praɪzˌwɪnər] *n* : gagnant *m,* -gnante *f*

prizewinning ['praɪz,wɪnɪŋ] *adj* : primé, qui remporte le prix

pro[1] ['pro:] *adv* **to argue pro** : argumenter en faveur

pro[2] *adj* → **professional**

pro[3] *n* **1** → **professional 2 the pros and cons** : le pour et le contre

probability [,prɑbə'bɪləṭi] *n, pl* **-ties** : probabilité *f*

probable ['prɑbəbəl] *adj* : probable — **probably** [-bli] *adv*

probate[1] ['pro:,beɪt] *vt* **-bated; -bating** : homologuer (un testament)

probate[2] *n* : homologation *f*

probation [pro'beɪʃən] *n* **1** *or* **probation period** : mise *f* à l'essai, probation *f* **2 on ~** : en sursis avec mise à l'épreuve (en droit)

probationary [pro'beɪʃə,nɛri] *adj* **1** : d'essai <probationary period : période d'essai> **2** : de sursis, de probation (en droit)

probe[1] ['pro:b] *vt* **probed; probing 1** EXAMINE : sonder **2** INVESTIGATE : enquêter sur

probe[2] *n* **1** : sonde *f* (en médecine) **2** INVESTIGATION : enquête *f*, investigation *f*

probity ['pro:bəṭi] *n* : probité *f*

problem[1] ['prɑbləm] *adj* : difficile <a problem child : un enfant difficile>

problem[2] *n* : problème *m*

problematic [,prɑblə'mæṭɪk] *or* **problematical** [-ṭɪkəl] *adj* : problématique

proboscis [prə'bɑsɪs] *n, pl* **-cises** : trompe *f*

procedural [prə'si:dʒərəl] *adj* : de procédure

procedure [prə'si:dʒər] *n* : procédure *f*

proceed [pro'si:d] *vi* **1** ADVANCE : avancer, aller **2** ACT : procéder **3** CONTINUE : continuer, poursuivre **4 to proceed from** : provenir de

proceeding [pro'si:dɪŋ] *n* **1** : procédure *f* <a divorce proceeding : une procédure de divorce> **2** *or* **legal proceeding** : poursuite *f* judiciaire

proceeds ['pro:,si:dz] *npl* : recette *f*, argent *m* recueilli

process[1] ['prɑ,sɛs, 'pro:-] *vt* **1** : traiter <to process one's request : traiter sa demande> **2** : traiter, transformer <processed cheese : fromage en tranches>

process[2] *n, pl* **-cesses** ['prɑ,sɛsəz, 'pro:-, -səsəz, -sə,si:z] **1** : processus *m* <the process of growth : le processus de croissance> **2** METHOD : procédé *m* <a manufacturing process : un procédé de fabrication> **3** : procès *m* (en droit) **4** SUMMONS : citation *f* **5** PROJECTION : excroissance *f* (en biologie) **6 in the process of** : en train de

procession [prə'sɛʃən] *n* : procession *f*

processional [prə'sɛʃənəl] *n* : musique *f* processionnelle

processor ['prɑ,sɛsər, 'pro:-, -səsər] *n* : processeur *m* (en informatique)

proclaim [pro'kleɪm] *vt* : proclamer

proclamation [,prɑklə'meɪʃən] *n* : proclamation *f*

proclivity [pro'klɪvəṭi] *n, pl* **-ties** : propension *f*, tendance *f*, inclination *f*

procrastinate [prə'kræstə,neɪt] *vi* **-nated; -nating** : remettre à plus tard, remettre au lendemain

procrastination [prə,kræstə'neɪʃən] *n* : tendance *f* à tout remettre à plus tard

procreate ['pro:kri,eɪt] *v* **-ated; -ating** *vt* : procréer — *vi* REPRODUCE : se reproduire

procreation [,pro:kri'eɪʃən] *n* : procréation *f*

proctor[1] ['prɑktər] *vt* : surveiller (un examen)

proctor[2] *n* : surveillant *m*, -lante *f* (à un examen)

procurable [prə'kjʊrəbəl] *adj* : que l'on peut se procurer

procure [prə'kjʊr] *vt* **-cured; -curing** : obtenir, se procurer

procurement [prə'kjʊrmənt] *n* : achat *m*, acquisition *f*

prod[1] ['prɑd] *vt* **prodded; prodding 1** POKE : pousser doucement, donner des petits coups à **2** GOAD, URGE : inciter

prod[2] *n* **1** POKE : petit coup *m*, poussée *f* **2** GOAD : aiguillon *m* <cattle prod : aiguillon pour le bétail>

prodigal[1] ['prɑdɪgəl] *adj* : prodigue

prodigal[2] *n* : prodigue *mf*

prodigality [,prɑdə'gæləṭi] *n* : prodigalité *f*

prodigious [prə'dɪdʒəs] *adj* **1** EXTRAORDINARY : prodigieux, extraordinaire **2** HUGE : énorme, monstre — **prodigiously** *adv*

prodigy ['prɑdədʒi] *n, pl* **-gies** : prodige *m*

produce[1] [prə'du:s, -'dju:s] *vt* **-duced; -ducing 1** : donner naissance à, engendrer (un enfant), produire (une œuvre), causer (un problème, etc.) **2** MAKE, MANUFACTURE : faire, produire, fabriquer **3** YIELD : produire, rapporter **4** EXHIBIT : présenter <to produce evidence : fournir des preuves> **5** STAGE : présenter, mettre en scène

produce[2] ['prɑ,du:s, 'pro:-, -,dju:s] *n* : produits *mpl* agricoles

producer [prə'du:sər, -'dju:-] *n* : producteur *m*, -trice *f*

product ['prɑ,dʌkt] *n* : produit *m*

production [prə'dʌkʃən] *n* : production *f*

productive [prə'dʌktɪv] *adj* : productif

productivity [,pro:,dʌk'tɪvəṭi, ,prɑ-] *n* : productivité *f*

profane[1] [pro'feɪn] *vt* **-faned; -faning** : profaner

profane[2] *adj* **1** SECULAR : profane **2** IRREVERENT : sacrilège, blasphématoire

profanity [proˈfænət̬i] *n, pl* **-ties 1** IRREVERENCE : impiété *f* **2** BLASPHEMY : blasphème *m,* juron *m*

profess [prəˈfɛs] *vt* **1** DECLARE : professer, affirmer **2** : professer (sa foi)

professedly [prəˈfɛsədli] *adv* **1** AVOWEDLY : de son propre aveu **2** ALLEGEDLY, SUPPOSEDLY : soi-disant, prétendument

profession [prəˈfɛʃən] *n* **1** DECLARATION : profession *f* (de foi, etc.) **2** OCCUPATION : profession *f,* occupation *f*

professional[1] [prəˈfɛʃənəl] *adj* : professionnel — **professionally** *adv*

professional[2] *n* : professionnel *m,* -nelle *f*

professionalism [prəˈfɛʃənəˌlɪzəm] *n* : professionnalisme *m*

professor [prəˈfɛsər] *n* : professeur *m* (de faculté)

proffer [ˈprɑfər] *vt* **-fered; -fering** : tendre, offrir

proficiency [prəˈfɪʃəntsi] *n, pl* **-cies** : compétence *f,* capacité *f*

proficient [prəˈfɪʃənt] *adj* : compétent, capable — **proficiently** *adv*

profile[1] [ˈproːˌfaɪl] *vt* **-filed; -filing** : profiler

profile[2] *n* : profil *m*

profit[1] [ˈprɑfət] *vi* **to profit from** : tirer profit de — *vt* BENEFIT : profiter à

profit[2] *n* **1** GAIN : profit *m,* bénéfice *m* <to make a profit : faire un bénéfice> <profit and loss : pertes et profits> **2** ADVANTAGE : avantage *m,* profit *m*

profitable [ˈprɑfətəbəl] *adj* : profitable — **profitably** [-bli] *adv*

profitless [ˈprɑfətləs] *adj* : qui ne rapporte pas de profits, sans profits

profligate [ˈprɑflɪgət, -ˌgeɪt] *adj* **1** IMMORAL : licentieux, débauché **2** EXTRAVAGANT : prodigue, dépensier

profound [prəˈfaʊnd] *adj* : profond

profoundly [prəˈfaʊndli] *adv* : profondément

profundity [prəˈfʌndət̬i] *n, pl* **-ties** : profondeur *f*

profuse [prəˈfjuːs] *adj* **1** BOUNTIFUL : abondant **2** LAVISH : prodigue <they were profuse in their thanks : ils se confondaient en remerciements>

profusely [prəˈfjuːsli] *adv* : abondamment

profusion [prəˈfjuːʒən] *n* : profusion *f,* abondance *f*

progeny [ˈprɑdʒəni] *n, pl* **-nies** : progéniture *f,* descendance *f*

progesterone [proˈdʒɛstəˌroːn] *n* : progestérone *f*

prognosis [prɑgˈnoːsɪs] *n, pl* **-noses** [-ˌsiːz] : pronostic *m*

program[1] *or Brit* **programme** [ˈproːˌgræm, -grəm] *vt* **-grammed** *or* **-gramed; -gramming** *or* **-graming** : programmer

program[2] *or Brit* **programme** *n* **1** : programme *m* (d'un concert, etc.) **2** PLAN : programme *m,* plan *m* **3** : programme *m* (d'un ordinateur) **4** SHOW : émission *f* <television program : émission de télévision>

programmable [ˈproːˌgræməbəl] *adj* : programmable

programme *Brit* → **program**

programmer [ˈproːˌgræmər] *n* : programmeur *m,* -meuse *f*

progress[1] [prəˈgrɛs] *vi* **1** PROCEED : progresser, avancer **2** IMPROVE : progresser, s'améliorer

progress[2] [ˈprɑgrəs, -ˌgrɛs] *n* : progrès *m*

progression [prəˈgrɛʃən] *n* **1** ADVANCE : progression *f,* avancement *m* **2** SERIES : progression *f,* suite *f*

progressive [prəˈgrɛsɪv] *adj* **1** : progressiste (en politique, etc.) **2** : progressif <a progressive city : une ville progressive> **3** GRADUAL : progressif, graduel

progressively [prəˈgrɛsɪvli] *adv* : progressivement

prohibit [proˈhɪbət] *vt* **1** FORBID : interdire, défendre **2** PREVENT : empêcher, rendre impossible

prohibition [ˌproːəˈbɪʃən, ˌproːhə-] *n* **1** : interdiction *f,* défense *f* **2** : prohibition *f* (de l'alcool)

prohibitive [proˈhɪbət̬ɪv] *adj* : prohibitif

project[1] [prəˈdʒɛkt] *vt* **1** DESIGN, PLAN : faire un plan de **2** HURL, THRUST : projeter, lancer — *vi* PROTRUDE : faire saillie

project[2] [ˈprɑˌdʒɛkt, -dʒɪkt] *n* **1** PLAN : projet *m,* plan *m* **2** *or* **research project** : étude *f* **3** *or* **school project** : travail *m* pratique

projectile [prəˈdʒɛktəl, -ˌtaɪl] *n* : projectile *m*

projection [prəˈdʒɛkʃən] *n* **1** PROTRUSION : saillie *f* **2** : projection *f* (d'une image) **3** ESTIMATE : projection *f,* prévision *f*

projector [prəˈdʒɛktər] *n* : projecteur *m*

proletarian[1] [ˌproːləˈtɛriən] *adj* : prolétaire, prolétarien

proletarian[2] *n* : prolétaire *mf*

proletariat [ˌproːləˈtɛriət] *n* : prolétariat *m*

proliferate [prəˈlɪfəˌreɪt] *vi* **-ated; -ating** : proliférer

proliferation [prəˌlɪfəˈreɪʃən] *n* : prolifération *f*

prolific [prəˈlɪfɪk] *adj* : prolifique, fécond — **prolifically** [-fɪkli] *adv*

prologue [ˈproːˌlɔg, -ˌlɑg] *n* : prologue *m,* préface *f*

prolong [prəˈlɔŋ] *vt* : prolonger

prolongation [ˌproːˌlɔŋˈgeɪʃən] *n* : prolongation *f*

prom [ˈprɑm] *n* : bal *m* d'étudiants

promenade[1] [ˌprɑməˈneɪd, -ˈnɑd] *vi* **-naded; -nading** : se promener

promenade[2] *n* : promenade *f*

prominence ['prɑmənənts] *n* **1** PROTUBERANCE : proéminence *f* **2** EMINENCE : distinction *f*

prominent ['prɑmənənt] *adj* **1** PROTRUDING : proéminent **2** CONSPICUOUS : bien en vue **3** LEADING : de premier plan **4** WELL-KNOWN : connu, célèbre

prominently ['prɑmənəntli] *adv* : bien en vue, en évidence

promiscuity [ˌprɑmɪs'kju:əţi] *n, pl* **-ties** : promiscuité *f* sexuelle

promiscuous [prə'mɪskjʊəs] *adj* : de mœurs légères

promise[1] ['prɑməs] *v* **-mised; -mising** : promettre

promise[2] *n* : promesse *f*

promising ['prɑməsɪŋ] *adj* : prometteur

promissory ['prɑməˌsori] *adj* : à ordre <a promissory note : un billet à ordre>

promontory ['prɑmənˌtori] *n, pl* **-ries** : promontoire *m*

promote [prə'mo:t] *vt* **-moted; -moting** **1** ADVANCE : promouvoir (un employé) **2** ADVERTISE : faire la promotion de **3** FURTHER : promouvoir, contribuer à

promoter [prə'mo:ţər] *n* : promoteur *m*, -trice *f*

promotion [prə'mo:ʃən] *n* : promotion *f*

promotional [prə'mo:ʃənəl] *adj* : promotionnel

prompt[1] ['prɑmpt] *vt* **1** INCITE, INDUCE : inciter, pousser **2** CUE : souffler son rôle à (un acteur)

prompt[2] *adj* **1** PUNCTUAL : ponctuel **2** QUICK : prompt <to be prompt to answer : avoir la repartie prompte>

prompter ['prɑmptər] *n* : souffleur *m*, -fleuse *f* (au théâtre)

promptly ['prɑmptli] *adv* QUICKLY : immédiatement, sans délai

promptness ['prɑmptnəs] *n* : promptitude *f*

prone ['pro:n] *adj* **1** APT : sujet, enclin <she's prone to forget names : elle a tendance à oublier les noms> <accident-prone : sujet aux accidents> **2** FLAT : à plat ventre <to lie prone : être allongé sur le ventre>

prong ['prɔŋ] *n* : dent *f*

pronged ['prɔŋd] *adj* : à dents

pronoun ['pro:ˌnaʊn] *n* : pronom *m*

pronounce [prə'naʊnts] *vt* **-nounced; -nouncing** **1** : prononcer, rendre (un jugement) **2** SAY : prononcer (un mot) **3** DECLARE : déclarer, prononcer

pronounced [prə'naʊntst] *adj* DECIDED : prononcé, marqué

pronouncement [prə'naʊntsmənt] *n* : déclaration *f*

pronunciation [prəˌnʌntsi'eɪʃən] *n* : prononciation *f*

proof[1] ['pru:f] *adj* : à l'épreuve <proof against tampering : à l'épreuve de l'altération>

proof[2] *n* **1** EVIDENCE : preuve *f* <proof of purchase : preuve d'achat> **2** PRINT : épreuve *f* (en photographie) **3 proofs** *npl* : épreuves *fpl* (d'un manuscrit)

proofread ['pru:fˌri:d] *vt* **-read** [-ˌrɛd]; **-reading** : corriger les épreuves de

proofreader ['pru:fˌri:dər] *n* : correcteur *m*, -trice *f* d'épreuves

prop[1] ['prɑp] *vt* **propped; propping** **1** LEAN : appuyer **2 to prop up** SUPPORT, SUSTAIN : étayer, soutenir

prop[2] *n* **1** SUPPORT : étai *m* **2 props** *npl* : accessoires *mpl* (au théâtre)

propaganda [ˌprɑpə'gændə, ˌpro:-] *n* : propagande *f*

propagandize [ˌprɑpə'gænˌdaɪz, ˌpro:-] *vi* **-dized; -dizing** : faire de la propagande

propagate ['prɑpəˌgeɪt] *v* **-gated; -gating** *vt* : propager — *vi* : se propager

propagation [ˌprɑpə'geɪʃən] *n* : propagation *f*

propane ['pro:ˌpeɪn] *n* : propane *m*

propel [prə'pɛl] *vt* **-pelled; -pelling** : propulser

propellant[1] [prə'pɛlənt] *adj* : propulsif

propellant[2] *n* : propergol *m* (pour les roquettes), gaz *m* propulseur

propeller [prə'pɛlər] *n* : hélice *f*

propensity [prə'pɛntsəţi] *n, pl* **-ties** : propension *f*, tendance *f*

proper ['prɑpər] *adj* **1** FIT : juste, approprié **2** : même, proprement dit <the city proper : la ville même> **3** CORRECT : correct, convenable

properly ['prɑpərli] *adv* **1** WELL : correctement, convenablement, comme du monde *Can* **2 properly speaking** : à proprement parler

property ['prɑpərţi] *n, pl* **-ties** **1** QUALITY : propriété *f*, qualité *f* **2** POSSESSIONS : biens *mpl* **3** REAL ESTATE : biens *mpl* immobiliers

prophecy ['prɑfəsi] *n, pl* **-cies** : prophétie *f*, prédiction *f*

prophesy ['prɑfəˌsaɪ] *vt* **-sied; -sying** : prophétiser, prédire

prophet ['prɑfət] *n* : prophète *m*, prophétesse *f*

prophetic [prə'fɛţɪk] *adj* : prophétique — **prophetically** [-ţɪkli] *adv*

propitiate [pro'pɪʃiˌeɪt] *vt* **-ated; -ating** : se concilier, apaiser

propitious [prə'pɪʃəs] *adj* : propice

proponent [prə'po:nənt] *n* : partisan *m*, -sane *f*

proportion[1] [prə'porʃən] *vt* : proportionner

proportion[2] *n* **1** RATIO : proportion *f*, rapport *m* **2** SYMMETRY : proportion *f*, équilibre *m* <to be out of proportion : être disproportionné> **3** SHARE

: part *f* **4 proportions** *npl* SIZE : dimensions *fpl*

proportional [prə'porʃənəl] *adj* : proportionnel — **proportionally** *adv*

proportionate [prə'porʃənət] *adj* : proportionnel — **proportionately** *adv*

proposal [prə'po:zəl] *n* : proposition *f*

propose [prə'po:z] *v* **-posed; -posing** *vt* **1** SUGGEST : proposer, suggérer **2** INTEND : (se) proposer, penser **3** NOMINATE : proposer, présenter — *vi* : faire une demande en mariage

proposition [ˌprɑpə'zɪʃən] *n* **1** PROPOSAL : proposition *f* **2** AFFAIR, BUSINESS : affaire *f,* situation *f* <it's not a paying proposition : ce n'est pas une affaire payante>

propound [prə'paʊnd] *vt* : avancer, proposer

proprietary [prə'praɪəˌtɛri] *adj* **1** : du propriétaire **2 proprietary brand** : marque *f* déposée

proprietor [prə'praɪəţər] *n* : propriétaire *mf*

propriety [prə'praɪəţi] *n, pl* **-eties 1** APPROPRIATENESS : convenance *f* **2 proprieties** *npl* : bienséances *fpl,* convenances *fpl*

propulsion [prə'pʌlʃən] *n* : propulsion *f*

propulsive [prə'pʌlsɪv] *adj* : propulsif

prosaic [pro'zeɪɪk] *adj* : prosaïque

proscribe [pro'skraɪb] *vt* **-scribed; -scribing** : proscrire

proscription [pro'skrɪpʃən] *n* : proscription *f*

prose ['pro:z] *n* : prose *f*

prosecute ['prɑsɪˌkju:t] *v* **-cuted; -cuting** *vt* **1** CARRY OUT, PURSUE : poursuivre **2** : poursuivre en justice (en droit) — *vi* : engager des poursuites judiciaires

prosecution [ˌprɑsɪ'kju:ʃən] *n* **1** : poursuites *fpl* judiciaires **2** PROSECUTOR : avocat *m* de la partie civile, procureur *m*

prosecutor ['prɑsɪˌkju:ţər] *n* : procureur *m*

prospect[1] ['prɑˌspɛkt] *vt* : prospecter

prospect[2] *n* **1** VIEW : vue *f* **2** POSSIBILITY : chance *f,* perspective *f* **3** BUYER : client *m* éventuel

prospective [prə'spɛktɪv, 'prɑˌspɛk-] *adj* **1** : éventuel, potentiel <a prospective buyer : un acheteur éventuel> **2** : futur <a prospective mother : une future mère>

prospector ['prɑˌspɛktər, prɑ'spɛk-] *n* : prospecteur *m,* -trice *f*

prospectus [prə'spɛktəs] *n* : prospectus *m* (d'une entreprise)

prosper ['prɑspər] *vt* **1** SUCCEED : prospérer, réussir **2** THRIVE : prospérer

prosperity [prɑ'spɛrəţi] *n* : prospérité *f*

prosperous ['prɑspərəs] *adj* : prospère

prostate ['prɑˌsteɪt] *n or* **prostate gland** : prostate *f*

prosthesis [prɑs'θi:sɪs, 'prɑsθə-] *n, pl* **-theses** [-ˌsi:z] : prothèse *f*

prostitute[1] ['prɑstəˌtu:t, -ˌtju:t] *vt* **-tuted; -tuting 1** DEBASE : prostituer, dégrader **2 to prostitute oneself** : se prostituer

prostitute[2] *n* : prostituée *f*

prostitution [ˌprɑstə'tu:ʃən, -'tju:-] *n* : prostitution *f*

prostrate[1] ['prɑˌstreɪt] *vt* **-trated; -trating 1** OVERWHELM : abattre, accabler <prostrated with grief : accablé de chagrin> **2 to prostrate oneself** : se prosterner

prostrate[2] *adj* **1** : allongé à plat ventre **2** : accablé, prostré <prostrate from the heat : accablé par la chaleur>

prostration [prɑs'treɪʃən] *n* : prostration *f*

protagonist [pro'tægənɪst] *n* : protagoniste *mf*

protect [prə'tɛkt] *vt* : protéger

protection [prə'tɛkʃən] *n* : protection *f*

protective [prə'tɛktɪv] *adj* : protecteur

protector [prə'tɛktər] *n* **1** : protecteur *m,* -trice *f* **2** : dispositif *m* de protection (d'une machine)

protectorate [prə'tɛktərət] *n* : protectorat *m*

protégé ['pro:ţəˌʒeɪ] *n* : protégé *m,* -gée *f*

protein ['pro:ˌti:n] *n* : protéine *f*

protest[1] [pro'tɛst] *vt* **1** : protester de <to protest one's innocence : protester de son innocence> **2** *or* **to protest against** : protester contre — *vi* COMPLAIN : protester

protest[2] ['pro:ˌtɛst] *n* **1** DEMONSTRATION : manifestation *f* **2** OBJECTION : protestation *f,* plainte *f*

Protestant ['prɑţəstənt] *n* : protestant *m,* -tante *f*

Protestantism ['prɑţəstənˌtɪzəm] *n* : protestantisme *m*

protestation [ˌprɑţəs'teɪʃən, ˌpro:-, -ˌtɛs-] *n* : protestation *f*

protester *or* **protestor** ['pro:ˌtɛstər, prə'-] *n* : manifestant *m,* -tante *f*

protocol ['pro:ţəˌkɔl] *n* : protocole *m*

proton ['proˌtɑn] *n* : proton *m*

protoplasm ['pro:ţəˌplæzəm] *n* : protoplasme *m*

prototype ['pro:ţəˌtaɪp] *n* : prototype *m*

protozoan [ˌpro:ţə'zo:ən] *n* : protozoaire *m*

protozoon [ˌpro:ţə'zo:ˌɑn] *n, pl* **-zoa** [-'zoə] → **protozoan**

protract [pro'trækt] *vt* : prolonger

protractor [pro'træktər] *n* : rapporteur *m* (en géométrie)

protrude [pro'tru:d] *vi* **-truded; -truding** : dépasser, faire saillie

protrusion [pro'tru:ʒən] *n* : saillie *f*

protuberance [pro'tu:bərən*t*s, -'tju:-] *n* : protubérance *f*

protuberant [pro'tu:bərənt, -'tju:-] *adj* : protubérant, saillant

proud ['praʊd] *adj* **1** HAUGHTY : fier, arrogant **2** PRIDEFUL : fier, orgueilleux <too proud to ask for help : trop fier pour demander de l'aide> **3** GLORIOUS : glorieux <the proudest moment in her life : le moment le plus glorieux de sa vie>

proudly ['praʊdli] *adv* : fièrement, orgueilleusement

prove ['pru:v] *v* **proved; proved** *or* **proven** ['pru:vən]; **proving** *vt* **1** TEST : confirmer, prouver <the exception proves the rule : l'exception confirme la règle> **2** ESTABLISH : prouver, établir — *vi* : s'avérer, se montrer

proverb ['prɑˌvərb] *n* : proverbe *m,* adage *m*

proverbial [prə'vərbiəl] *adj* : proverbial — **proverbially** *adv*

provide [prə'vaɪd] *v* **-vided; -viding** *vt* **1** SUPPLY : fournir, donner **2** STIPULATE : prévoir — *vi* **1 to provide against** : parer à **2 to provide for one's family** : subvenir aux besoins de sa famille

provided [prə'vaɪdəd] *conj* : pourvu que, à condition que <provided (that) you agree : à condition que tu sois d'accord>

providence ['prɑvədənts] *n* **1** FORESIGHT : prévoyance *f* **2** *or* **Providence** : providence *f* <divine providence : la divine providence> **3 Providence** GOD : Providence *f*

provident ['prɑvədənt] *adj* **1** PRUDENT : prévoyant **2** THRIFTY : économe

providential [ˌprɑvə'dɛntʃəl] *adj* : providentiel

provider [prə'vaɪdər] *n* BREADWINNER : soutien *m* de famille

providing → **provided**

province ['prɑvɪnts] *n* **1** : province *f* <the province of Quebec : la province de Québec> <to live in the provinces : vivre dans les provinces> **2** SPHERE : domaine *m,* sphère *f* <the province of science : le domaine des sciences>

provincial [prə'vɪntʃəl] *adj* **1** RURAL : provincial **2** NARROW : provincial, peu raffiné **3** : provincial *Can* <the provincial government : le gouvernement provincial>

provincialism [prə'vɪntʃəlˌɪzəm] *n* : provincialisme *m*

provision[1] [prə'vɪʒən] *vt* : approvisionner, ravitailler

provision[2] *n* **1** SUPPLYING : approvisionnement *m,* ravitaillement *m* **2** PREPARATION : dispositions *fpl* <to make provision for : prendre des dispositions pour> **3** PROVISO : stipulation *f* **4 provisions** *npl* : provisions *fpl,* vivres *mpl*

provisional [prə'vɪʒənəl] *adj* : provisoire, temporaire — **provisionally** *adv*

proviso [prə'vaɪˌzo:] *n, pl* **-sos** *or* **-soes** : stipulation *f,* clause *f*

provocation [ˌprɑvə'keɪʃən] *n* : provocation *f*

provocative [prə'vɑkət̬ɪv] *adj* : provocant, provocateur

provoke [prə'vo:k] *vt* **-voked; -voking** : provoquer

prow ['praʊ] *n* : proue *f*

prowess ['praʊəs] *n* **1** VALOR : bravoure *f,* vaillance *f* **2** SKILL : habileté *f,* prouesses *fpl*

prowl[1] ['praʊl] *vi* : rôder, errer

prowl[2] *n* **to be on the prowl** : rôder

prowler ['praʊlər] *n* : rôdeur *m,* -deuse *f*

proximate ['prɑksəmət] *adj* : direct

proximity [prɑk'sɪmət̬i] *n* : proximité *f*

proxy ['prɑksi] *n, pl* **proxies** : procuration *f* <to vote by proxy : voter par procuration>

prude ['pru:d] *n* : prude *f*

prudence ['pru:dənts] *n* : prudence *f*

prudent ['pru:dənt] *adj* **1** SHREWD : astucieux **2** CAUTIOUS : prudent, avisé **3** THRIFTY : économe

prudential [pru:'dɛntʃəl] *adj* : prudent

prudently ['pru:dəntli] *adv* : prudemment

prudery ['pru:dəri] *n, pl* **-eries** : pruderie *f*

prudish ['pru:dɪʃ] *adj* : pudibond, prude

prune[1] ['pru:n] *vt* **pruned; pruning 1** : élaguer, tailler (un arbre, etc.) **2** : élaguer (un texte)

prune[2] *n* : pruneau *m*

prurient ['prʊriənt] *adj* : lubrique, luxurieux

pry ['praɪ] *v* **pried; prying** *vi* **to pry into** : mettre son nez dans — *vt* **1** *or* **to pry up** RAISE : forcer avec un levier **2 to pry sth out of s.o.** : soutirer qqch à qqn

psalm ['sɑm, 'sɑlm] *n* : psaume *m*

pseudonym ['su:dəˌnɪm] *n* : pseudonyme *m*

pseudonymous [su:'dɑnəməs] *adj* : pseudonyme

psoriasis [sə'raɪəsəs] *n* : psoriasis *m*

psyche ['saɪki] *n* : psychisme *m,* psyché *f*

psychiatric [ˌsaɪki'ætrɪk] *adj* : psychiatrique

psychiatrist [sə'kaɪətrɪst, saɪ-] *n* : psychiatre *mf*

psychiatry [sə'kaɪətri, saɪ-] *n* : psychiatrie *f*

psychic ['saɪkɪk] *adj* : psychique

psychoanalysis [ˌsaɪkoə'næləsɪs] *n* : psychanalyse *f*

psychoanalyst [ˌsaɪko'ænəlɪst] *n* : psychanalyste *mf*

psychoanalytic [ˌsaɪkoˌænəl'ɪt̬ɪk] *adj* : psychanalytique

psychoanalyze [ˌsaɪko'ænəlˌaɪz] *vt* **-lyzed; -lyzing** : psychanalyser

psychological [ˌsaɪkə'lɑdʒɪkəl] *adj* : psychologique — **psychologically** *adv*

psychologist [saɪ'kɑlədʒɪst] *n* : psychologue *mf*

psychology [saɪˈkɑlədʒi] *n, pl* **-gies** : psychologie *f*
psychopath [ˈsaɪkəˌpæθ] *n* : psychopathe *mf*
psychopathic [ˌsaɪkəˈpæθɪk] *adj* : psychopathe
psychosis [saɪˈkoːsɪs] *n, pl* **-choses** [-ˈkoːˌsiz] : psychose *f*
psychosomatic [ˌsaɪkəsəˈmæt̬ɪk] *adj* : psychosomatique
psychotherapist [ˌsaɪkoˈθɛrəpɪst] *n* : psychothérapeute *mf*
psychotherapy [ˌsaɪkoˈθɛrəpi] *n* : psychothérapie *f*
psychotic[1] [saɪˈkɑt̬ɪk] *adj* : psychotique
psychotic[2] *n* : psychotique *mf*
pub [ˈpʌb] *n Brit* : pub *m*
puberty [ˈpjuːbərt̬i] *n* : puberté *f*
pubic [ˈpjuːbɪk] *adj* : pubien
public[1] [ˈpʌblɪk] *adj* : public
public[2] *n* : public *m*
publication [ˌpʌbləˈkeɪʃən] *n* : publication *f*
publicist [ˈpʌbləsɪst] *n* : agent *m* publicitaire
publicity [pəˈblɪsət̬i] *n* : publicité *f*
publicize [ˈpʌbləˌsaɪz] *vt* **-cized; -cizing** : rendre public, faire connaître
publicly [ˈpʌblɪkli] *adv* : publiquement
publish [ˈpʌblɪʃ] *vt* **1** ANNOUNCE : faire connaître, déclarer **2** : publier (un livre)
publisher [ˈpʌblɪʃər] *n* **1** : éditeur *m*, -trice *f* **2** : maison *f* d'édition (entreprise)
puck [ˈpʌk] *n* : palet *m*, rondelle *f Can* (au hockey)
pucker[1] [ˈpʌkər] *vt* : plisser — *vi* : se plisser
pucker[2] *n* : pli *m*
pudding [ˈpʊdɪŋ] *n* : pudding *m*, pouding *m*
puddle [ˈpʌdəl] *n* : flaque *f* (d'eau)
pudgy [ˈpʌdʒi] *adj* **pudgier; -est** : grassouillet, potelé
puerile [ˈpjʊrəl, -ˌaɪl] *adj* : puéril
Puerto Rican[1] [ˌpwɛrt̬əˈriːkən, ˌport̬ə-] *adj* : portoricain
Puerto Rican[2] *n* : Portoricain *m*, -caine *f*
puff[1] [ˈpʌf] *vi* **1** BLOW : souffler **2** PANT : haleter **3 to puff up** SWELL : enfler, bouffir — *vt* **1** *or* **to puff out** : envoyer des bouffées de (la fumée, etc.) **2** *or* **to puff up** INFLATE : gonfler
puff[2] *n* **1** : bouffée *f* <a puff of air : une bouffée d'air> <to take a puff : tirer une bouffée> **2** SWELLING : bouffissure *f* **3 cream puff** : feuilleté *m* à la crème **4** *or* **powder puff** : houppette *f*
puffy [ˈpʌfi] *adj* **puffier; -est** : enflé, bouffi
pug [ˈpʌg] *n* : carlin *m*
pugilism [ˈpjuːdʒəˌlɪzəm] *n* : pugilat *m*
pugnacious [ˌpʌgˈneɪʃəs] *adj* : combatif, pugnace
puke [ˈpjuːk] *vt* **puked; puking** : vomir, renvoyer *Can fam*
pull[1] [ˈpʊl, ˈpʌl] *vt* **1** : tirer <to pull a rope : tirer une corde> **2** STRAIN : se froisser (un muscle, etc.) **3** EXTRACT : arracher, extraire **4** DRAW : sortir <to pull a gun : sortir un fusil> **5** COMMIT : perpétrer (un crime) **6 to pull off** : enlever **7 to pull oneself together** : se ressaisir, se reprendre **8 to pull up** : remonter — *vi* **1 to pull away** WITHDRAW : se retirer **2 to pull out of** : quitter <the train was pulling out of the station : le train quittait la gare> **3 to pull through** : s'en tirer **4 to pull together** COOPERATE : agir en concert
pull[2] *n* **1** TUG : (petit) coup *m* **2** CLOUT : influence *f*, pouvoir *m* **3** EFFORT : effort *m* <a long uphill pull : une montée pénible> **4** ATTRACTION : force *f*, attrait *m* <the pull of gravity : la force gravitationnelle>
pullet [ˈpʊlət] *n* : poulette *f*
pulley [ˈpʊli] *n, pl* **-leys** : poulie *f*
pullover [ˈpʊlˌoːvər] *n* : chandail *m*, pullover *m France*
pulmonary [ˈpʊlməˌnɛri, ˈpʌl-] *adj* : pulmonaire
pulp [ˈpʌlp] *n* **1** : pulpe *f*, chair *f* (d'un fruit, etc.) **2** *or* **paper pulp** : pâte *f* à papier
pulpit [ˈpʊlˌpɪt] *n* : chaire *f*
pulsate [ˈpʌlˌseɪt] *vi* **-sated; -sating 1** BEAT : battre, palpiter **2** VIBRATE : vibrer
pulsation [ˌpʌlˈseɪʃən] *n* : battement *m*, pulsation *f*
pulse [ˈpʌls] *n* : pouls *m* <to take s.o.'s pulse : tâter le pouls de qqn>
pulverize [ˈpʌlvəˌraɪz] *vt* **-ized; -izing** : pulvériser
puma [ˈpuːmə, ˈpjuː-] *n* : puma *m*, cougar *m*
pumice [ˈpʌməs] *n or* **pumice stone** : pierre *f* ponce
pummel [ˈpʌməl] *vt* **-meled; -meling** : battre, rouer de coups
pump[1] [ˈpʌmp] *vt* **1** : pomper (de l'eau) **2 to pump through** : faire circuler (un gaz, un liquide, du sang) **3 to pump up** : gonfler (un pneu)
pump[2] *n* **1** : pompe *f* <bicycle pump : pompe à bicyclette> **2** : escarpin *m* (chaussure)
pumpernickel [ˈpʌmpərˌnɪkəl] *n* : pain *m* noir
pumpkin [ˈpʌmpkɪn, ˈpʌŋkən] *n* : citrouille *f*, potiron *m France*
pun[1] [ˈpʌn] *vi* **punned; punning** : faire des jeux de mots
pun[2] *n* : jeu *m* de mots, calembour *m*
punch[1] [ˈpʌntʃ] *vt* **1** : donner un coup de poing à **2** PERFORATE : poinçonner, perforer
punch[2] *n* **1** BLOW : coup *m* de poing **2** *or* **hole punch** : poinçonneuse *f* **3**

: punch *m* <fruit punch : punch aux fruits>

punctilious [pəŋk'tɪliəs] *adj* : pointilleux, méticuleux

punctual ['pʌŋktʃʊəl] *adj* : ponctuel — **punctually** *adv*

punctuality [ˌpʌŋktʃʊ'æləṭi] *n* : ponctualité *f*

punctuate ['pʌŋktʃʊˌeɪt] *vt* **-ated; -ating** : ponctuer

punctuation [ˌpʌŋktʃʊ'eɪʃən] *n* : ponctuation *f*

puncture[1] ['pʌŋktʃər] *vt* **-tured; -turing** **1** PIERCE : perforer **2** : crever (un ballon, un pneu, etc.)

puncture[2] *n* **1** HOLE : perforation *f* **2** PRICK : piqûre *f*

pundit ['pʌndɪt] *n* EXPERT : critique *mf;* expert *m,* -perte *f*

pungency ['pʌndʒən*t*si] *n* : piquant *m,* âpreté *f*

pungent ['pʌndʒənt] *adj* **1** BITING, SHARP : âcre, piquant **2** CAUSTIC : mordant

punish ['pʌnɪʃ] *vt* : punir

punishable ['pʌnɪʃəbəl] *adj* : punissable

punishment ['pʌnɪʃmənt] *n* : punition *f*

punitive ['pju:nəṭɪv] *adj* : punitif

punt[1] ['pʌnt] *vt* : faire avancer (une barque) à la perche — *vi* KICK : envoyer d'un coup de volée

punt[2] *n* **1** : barque *f* (à fond plat) **2** KICK : coup *m* de volée

puny ['pju:ni] *adj* **punier; -est** : malingre, chétif

pup ['pʌp] *n* : chiot *m,* jeune animal *m*

pupa ['pju:pə] *n, pl* **-pae** [-pi, -ˌpaɪ] *or* **-pas** : pupe *f,* chrysalide *f*

pupil ['pju:pəl] *n* **1** : élève *mf* (à l'école) **2** : pupille *f* (de l'œil)

puppet ['pʌpət] *n* : marionnette *f*

puppeteer [ˌpʌpə'tɪr] *n* : marionnettiste *mf*

puppy ['pʌpi] *n, pl* **-pies** : chiot *m*

purchase[1] ['pərtʃəs] *vt* **-chased; -chasing** : acheter, acquérir

purchase[2] *n* **1** : achat *m,* acquisition *f* **2** GRASP : prise *f*

purchase order *n* : ordre *m* d'achat

purchaser ['pərtʃəsər] *n* : acheteur *m,* -teuse *f*

pure ['pjʊr] *adj* **purer; purest** : pur

puree[1] [pjʊ'reɪ, -'ri:] *vt* **-reed; -reeing** : réduire en purée

puree[2] *n* : purée *f*

purely ['pjʊrli] *adv* : purement

purgative[1] ['pərgəṭɪv] *adj* : purgatif

purgative[2] *n* LAXATIVE : purgatif *m*

purgatory ['pərgəˌtori] *n, pl* **-ries** : purgatoire *m*

purge[1] ['pərdʒ] *vt* **purged; purging** : purger

purge[2] *n* : purge *f* (des intestins), épuration *f* (en politique)

purification [ˌpjʊrəfə'keɪʃən] *n* : purification *f*

purifier ['pjʊrəˌfaɪər] *n* : purificateur *m* <air purifier : purificateur d'air>

purify ['pjʊrəˌfaɪ] *vt* **-fied; -fying** : purifier

puritan ['pju:rətən] *n* : puritain *m,* -taine *f*

puritanical [ˌpju:rə'tænɪkəl] *adj* : puritain

purity ['pjʊrəṭi] *n* : pureté *f*

purl[1] ['pərl] *vt* : tricoter à l'envers

purl[2] *n* : maille *f* à l'envers

purloin [pər'lɔɪn, 'pərˌlɔɪn] *vt* : dérober, voler

purple ['pərpəl] *n* : violet *m,* pourpre *m*

purplish ['pərpəlɪʃ] *adj* : violacé

purport [pər'port] *vt* : prétendre <to purport to be : prétendre être, se faire passer pour>

purportedly [pər'portədli] *adv* : prétendument

purpose ['pərpəs] *n* **1** AIM : intention *f,* but *m* **2** DETERMINATION : résolution *f* <to have a sense of purpose : être résolu> **3** **for this purpose** : à cet effet, à cette fin **4** **on ~** : exprès

purposeful ['pərpəsfəl] *adj* **1** MEANINGFUL : significatif **2** INTENTIONAL : prémédité, réfléchi **3** DETERMINED : résolu, décidé

purposefully ['pərpəsfəli] *adv* : résolument

purposeless ['pərpəsləs] *adj* MEANINGLESS : vide de sens

purposely ['pərpəsli] *adv* : délibérément, intentionnellement

purr[1] ['pər] *vi* : ronronner

purr[2] *n* : ronronnement *m*

purse[1] ['pərs] *vt* **pursed; pursing** : pincer, serrer <to purse one's lips : pincer les lèvres>

purse[2] *n* **1** *or* **change purse** : porte-monnaie *m* **2** HANDBAG : sac *m* à main, sacoche *f Can* **3** FUNDS, RESOURCES : moyens *mpl* **4** PRIZE : prix *m,* récompense *f*

pursue [pər'su:] *vt* **-sued; -suing** **1** CHASE : poursuivre, pourchasser **2** SEEK : poursuivre <to pursue a goal : poursuivre un but> **3** CARRY ON : poursuivre, continuer, conduire <to pursue a career : faire carrière>

pursuer [pər'su:ər] *n* : poursuivant *m,* -vante *f*

pursuit [pər'su:t] *n* **1** CHASE : poursuite *f* **2** ACTIVITY, OCCUPATION : activité *f,* occupation *f* **3** SEARCH : poursuite *f,* recherche *f* <the pursuit of happiness : la recherche du bonheur>

purvey [pər'veɪ] *vt* **-veyed; -veying** : fournir (des provisions, etc.)

purveyor [pər'veɪər] *n* : fournisseur *m,* -seuse *f*

pus ['pʌs] *n* : pus *m*

push[1] ['pʊʃ] *vt* **1** : pousser <to push a cart : pousser un chariot> <to push the door open : ouvrir la porte> **2** THRUST : enfoncer **3** *or* **to push up** RAISE : augmenter **4** URGE : pousser, inciter **5** APPROACH : approcher, friser <she must be pushing sixty

: elle doit approcher de la soixantaine> **6 to push away** : repousser — *vi* **1 to push for** : demander, réclamer **2 to push on** : continuer, persévérer **3 to push (oneself)** : s'exercer

push[2] *n* **1** SHOVE : poussée *f* <I gave him a push : je l'ai poussé> **2** DRIVE : effort *m* **3** IMPETUS : poussée *f*, impulsion *f*

pushcart [ˈpʊʃˌkɑrt] *n* : charrette *f* à bras

pushy [ˈpʊʃi] *adj* **pushier; -est** : arriviste

pussy [ˈpʊsi] *n, pl* **pussies** : minet *m*, minou *m fam*

pustule [ˈpʌsˌtʃuːl] *n* : pustule *f*

put [ˈpʊt] *vt* **put; putting 1** PLACE : mettre <put it on the table : mets-le sur la table> **2** INSERT : insérer, introduire **3** (*indicating causation of a state or feeling*) : mettre <it puts her in a good mood : ça la met de bonne humeur> **4** IMPOSE : infliger, imposer (une taxe, etc.) **5** SUBJECT : mettre <to put to the test : mettre à l'épreuve> <to put to death : mettre à mort> **6** EXPRESS : exprimer, dire <to put it mildly : c'est peu dire> **7** APPLY : mettre, appliquer <if you put your minds to it : si vous vous y mettez> **8** SET : mettre <to put to work : employer, mettre au travail> **9** ATTACH : attribuer, attacher <to put great value on : attacher beaucoup d'importance à> **10** PRESENT : soumettre, présenter <they put their case well : ils ont bien présenté leur cas> **11 to put forward** PROPOSE : avancer, proposer — *vi* **1 to put to sea** : lever l'ancre **2 to put up with** TOLERATE : supporter

put away *vt* **1** STORE : ranger **2** DISCARD, RENOUNCE : renoncer à (des idées, des émotions, etc.) **3** CONSUME : avaler, engloutir (de la nourriture) **4** CONFINE : enfermer, mettre sous les verrous

put by *vt* SAVE : économiser, mettre de côté

put down *vt* **1** SUPPRESS : réprimer **2** WRITE : écrire, mettre (par écrit) **3** ASCRIBE : mettre sur le compte <I put it down to luck : je l'ai mis sur le compte de la chance>

put off *vt* POSTPONE : remettre à plus tard, retarder

put on *vt* **1** ASSUME : prendre, assumer **2** PRESENT : monter (un spectacle, etc.) **3** WEAR : mettre (des vêtements)

put out *vt* **1** EXTINGUISH, TURN OFF : éteindre **2** INCONVENIENCE : déranger, importuner **3** ANNOY : contrarier, fâcher

putrefaction [ˌpjuːtrəˈfækʃən] *n* : putréfaction *f*

putrefy [ˈpjuːtrəˌfaɪ] *v* **-fied; -fying** *vt* : putréfier — *vi* : se putréfier

putrid [ˈpjuːtrɪd] *adj* : putride

putty[1] [ˈpʌt̬i] *vt* **-tied; -tying** : mastiquer

putty[2] *n, pl* **-ties** : mastic *m*

put up *vt* **1** ACCOMMODATE, LODGE : loger, héberger **2** BUILD : construire, ériger **3** NOMINATE : proposer (un candidat) **4** CONTRIBUTE : contribuer

puzzle[1] [ˈpʌzəl] *vt* **-zled; -zling 1** CONFUSE : intriguer, laisser perplexe **2 to puzzle out** SOLVE : résoudre, deviner

puzzle[2] *n* **1** : casse-tête *m* **2** *or* **jigsaw puzzle** : puzzle *m* **3** MYSTERY : énigme *f*, mystère *m*

puzzlement [ˈpʌzəlmənt] *n* : perplexité *f*

pygmy[1] [ˈpɪgmi] *adj* : pygmée

pygmy[2] *n, pl* **-mies 1** DWARF : pygmée *m* **2 Pygmy** : Pygmée *mf*

pyjamas *Brit* → **pajamas**

pylon [ˈpaɪˌlɑn, -lən] *n* : pylône *m*

pyramid [ˈpɪrəˌmɪd] *n* : pyramide *f*

pyre [ˈpaɪr] *n* : bûcher *m*

pyromania [ˌpaɪroˈmeɪniə] *n* : pyromanie *f*

pyromaniac [ˌpaɪroˈmeɪniˌæk] *n* : pyromane *mf*

pyrotechnics [ˌpaɪrəˈtɛknɪks] *npl* : pyrotechnie *f*

python [ˈpaɪˌθɑn, -θən] *n* : python *m*

Q

q [ˈkjuː] *n, pl* **q's** *or* **qs** [ˈkjuːz] : q *m*, dix-septième lettre de l'alphabet

quack[1] [ˈkwæk] *vi* : faire des coin-coin, cancaner

quack[2] *n* **1** : coin-coin *m* (d'un canard) **2** CHARLATAN : charlatan *m*

quadrangle [ˈkwɑˌdræŋgəl] *n* **1** COURTYARD : cour *f* (rectangulaire), patio *m* **2** → **quadrilateral**

quadrant [ˈkwɑdrənt] *n* : quadrant *m*

quadrilateral [ˌkwɑdrəˈlæt̬ərəl] *n* : quadrilatère *m*

quadruped [ˈkwɑdrəˌpɛd] *n* : quadrupède *m*

quadruple[1] [kwɑˈdruːpəl, -ˈdrʌ-; ˈkwɑdrə-] *vt* **-pled; -pling** : quadrupler

quadruple[2] *adj* : quadruple

quadruplet [kwɑˈdruːplət, -ˈdrʌ-; ˈkwɑdrə-] *n* : quadruplé *m*, -plée *f*

quagmire [ˈkwægˌmaɪr, ˈkwɑg-] *n* : bourbier *m*

quail[1] [ˈkweɪl] *vi* : trembler <to quail before : perdre courage devant>

quail[2] *n, pl* **quail** *or* **quails** : caille *f*

quaint ['kweɪnt] *adj* **1** ODD : étrange, bizarre **2** PICTURESQUE : pittoresque
quaintly ['kweɪntli] *adv* **1** : étrangement, bizarrement **2** : de façon pittoresque
quake[1] ['kweɪk] *vi* **quaked; quaking** : frémir, trembler
quake[2] *n* EARTHQUAKE : tremblement *m* de terre
qualification [ˌkwɑləfə'keɪʃən] *n* **1** QUALIFYING : qualification *f* **2** LIMITATION : réserve *f*, restriction *f* <without qualification : sans réserve> **3** SKILL : compétence *f*, aptitude *f*
qualified ['kwɑləˌfaɪd] *adj* : qualifié, compétent
qualify ['kwɑləˌfaɪ] *v* **-fied; -fying** *vt* **1** LIMIT, MODIFY : nuancer, préciser, poser des conditions sur **2** : qualifier, rendre compétent <to be qualified for : être habilité à> **3** MODERATE : adoucir, mitiger — *vi* : se qualifier, remplir les conditions requises
quality ['kwɑləṭi] *n, pl* **-ties 1** GRADE : qualité *f*, excellence *f* **2** CHARACTERISTIC : qualité *f*, attribut *m*, propriété *f*
qualm ['kwɑm, 'kwɑlm, 'kwɔm] *n* : scrupule *m*, doute *m* <to have no qualms about : ne pas avoir le moindre scrupule à>
quandary ['kwɑndri] *n, pl* **-ries** : doute *m*, confusion *f* <to be in a quandary : ne pas savoir que faire>
quantity ['kwɑntəṭi] *n, pl* **-ties** : quantité *f*
quantum theory ['kwɑntəm] *n* : théorie *f* des quanta
quarantine[1] ['kwɔrənˌtiːn] *vt* **-tined; -tining** : mettre en quarantaine
quarantine[2] *n* : quarantaine *f*
quarrel[1] ['kwɔrəl] *vi* **-reled** *or* **-relled; -reling** *or* **-relling** : se quereller, se disputer
quarrel[2] *n* : dispute *f*, querelle *f*
quarrelsome ['kwɔrəlsəm] *adj* : querelleur
quarry[1] ['kwɔri] *vt* **quarried; quarrying 1** EXTRACT : extraire <to quarry marble : extraire du marbre> **2** EXCAVATE : excaver
quarry[2] *n, pl* **quarries 1** PREY : proie *f* **2** EXCAVATION : carrière *f*
quart ['kwɔrt] *n* : quart *m* de gallon
quarter[1] ['kwɔrṭər] *vt* : diviser en quatre
quarter[2] *n* **1** : quart *m* **2** (*used in expressions of time*) <a quarter after three : trois heures et quart> **3** : (pièce de) vingt-cinq cents *m*, trente-sous *m Can fam* **4** DISTRICT : quartier *m* (d'une ville) **5** : trimestre *m* (de l'année fiscale) **6 quarters** *npl* LODGINGS : logement *m*
quarterly[1] ['kwɔrṭərli] *adv* : tous les trois mois, trimestriellement
quarterly[2] *adj* : trimestriel
quarterly[3] *n, pl* **-lies** : publication *f* trimestrielle
quartermaster ['kwɔrṭərˌmæstər] *n* : intendant *m* militaire
quartet [kwɔr'tɛt] *n* : quatuor *m* <string quartet : quatuor à cordes>
quartz ['kwɔrts] *n* : quartz *m*
quash ['kwɑʃ, 'kwɔʃ] *vt* **1** : annuler (un jugement) **2** SUPPRESS : étouffer, refouler (ses émotions)
quaver[1] ['kweɪvər] *vi* : trembloter, chevroter (se dit de la voix)
quaver[2] *n* : tremblement *m*, chevrotement *m*
quay ['kiː, 'keɪ, 'kweɪ] *n* WHARF : quai *m*
queasiness ['kwiːzinəs] *n* : nausée *f*
queasy ['kwiːzi] *adj* **queasier; -est** : nauséeux <to feel queasy : avoir mal au cœur>
Quebecer *or* **Quebecker** [kwɪ'bɛkər] *n* : Québécois *m*, -coise *f*
Quebecois *or* **Québécois** [kebe'kwɑː] *n* : Québécois *m*, -coise *f*
queen ['kwiːn] *n* : reine *f*
queenly ['kwiːnli] *adj* : de reine
queer ['kwɪr] *adj* : étrange, bizarre — **queerly** *adv*
quell ['kwɛl] *vt* : réprimer, étouffer
quench ['kwɛntʃ] *vt* **1** EXTINGUISH : éteindre (un feu) **2** SATISFY : apaiser, étancher (la soif)
querulous ['kwɛrələs, -jələs] *adj* : plaintif, grincheux
querulously ['kwɛrələsli, -jələs-] *adv* : plaintivement
query[1] ['kwɪri, 'kwɛr-] *vt* **-ried; -rying 1** ASK : poser une question à **2** QUESTION : mettre en doute, poser des questions sur
query[2] *n, pl* **-ries** : question *f*
quest[1] ['kwɛst] *vi* **to quest for** : être en quête de, être à la recherche de
quest[2] *n* : quête *f*, recherche *f*
question[1] ['kwɛstʃən] *vt* **1** INTERROGATE : questionner, interroger **2** DISPUTE : mettre en doute
question[2] *n* **1** : question *f*, interrogation *f* **2** MATTER : question *f*, problème *m* **3 without ~** : sans l'ombre d'un doute
questionable ['kwɛstʃənəbəl] *adj* DUBIOUS : contestable, discutable, douteux
questioner ['kwɛstʃənər] *n* : interrogateur *m*, -trice *f*
question mark *n* : point *f* d'interrogation
questionnaire [ˌkwɛstʃə'nær] *n* : questionnaire *m*
queue[1] ['kjuː] *vi* **queued; queuing** *or* **queueing** : faire la queue
queue[2] *n* **1** PIGTAIL : tresse *f* (de cheveux) **2** LINE : queue *f*, file *f* (d'attente)
quibble[1] ['kwɪbəl] *vi* **-bled; -bling** : chicaner
quibble[2] *n* : chicane *f*

quick[1] ['kwɪk] *adv* : rapidement
quick[2] *adj* **1** FAST : rapide **2** ALERT : vif, éveillé **3 to have a quick temper** : s'emporter facilement
quick[3] *n* **1** : chair *f* vive <his nails were bitten to the quick : il se rongeait les ongles jusqu'au sang> **2 to cut to the quick** : piquer au vif
quicken ['kwɪkən] *vt* **1** HASTEN : accélérer **2** AROUSE : stimuler
quickly ['kwɪkli] *adv* : rapidement, vite
quickness ['kwɪknəs] *n* : rapidité *f*, vitesse *f*
quicksand ['kwɪk,sænd] *n* : sables *mpl* mouvants
quicksilver ['kwɪk,sɪlvər] *n* : mercure *m*, vif-argent *m*
quick–tempered ['kwɪk'tɛmpərd] *adj* : coléreux, irascible
quick–witted ['kwɪk'wɪṱəd] *adj* : à l'esprit vif
quiet[1] ['kwaɪət] *vt* : calmer <to quiet the crowd : calmer la foule> — *vi* **to quiet down** : se calmer
quiet[2] *adj* **1** CALM : tranquille **2** EASYGOING : doux **3** STILL : tranquille, silencieux **4** : sobre, simple <quiet clothes : vêtements sobres> **5** SECLUDED : tranquille, retiré <a quiet nook : un coin tranquille>
quiet[3] *n* : tranquillité *f*, calme *m* <the quiet before the storm : le calme avant la tempête>
quietly ['kwaɪətli] *adv* **1** : sans bruit **2** CALMLY : tranquillement, paisiblement
quietness ['kwaɪətnəs] *n* : tranquillité *f*, silence *f*
quietude ['kwaɪə,tu:d, -,tju:d] *n* : quiétude *f*
quill ['kwɪl] *n* **1** : piquant *m* (d'un porc-épic, etc.) **2** *or* **quill pen** : penne *f*, plume *f* d'oie
quilt[1] ['kwɪlt] *vt* : matelasser, piquer
quilt[2] *n* : courtepointe *f*, édredon *m* (piqué)
quince ['kwɪnts] *n* : coing *m* (fruit), cognassier *m* (arbre)
quinine ['kwaɪ,naɪn] *n* : quinine *f*
quintessence [kwɪn'tɛsənts] *n* : quintessence *f*
quintet [kwɪn'tɛt] *n* : quintette *m*
quintuple [kwɪn'tu:pəl, -'tju:-, -'tʌ-; 'kwɪntə-] *adj* : quintuple
quintuplet [kwɪn'tʌplət, -'tu:-, -'tju:-; 'kwɪntə-] *n* : quintuplé *m*, -plée *f*
quip[1] ['kwɪp] *vi* **quipped; quipping** : lancer des mots piquants
quip[2] *n* : mot *m* piquant, trait *m* d'esprit
quirk ['kwərk] *n* : excentricité *f*, bizarrerie *f*
quirky ['kwərki] *adj* **quirkier; -iest** : excentrique
quit ['kwɪt] *v* **quit; quitting** *vt* **1** STOP : arrêter <quit fooling around : arrête de faire l'imbécile> **2** LEAVE : quitter, cesser <to quit school : quitter l'école> — *vi* **1** GIVE UP : abandonner, renoncer **2** RESIGN : démissioner
quite ['kwaɪt] *adv* **1** COMPLETELY : tout à fait **2** RATHER : assez <quite near : assez proche> **3** POSITIVELY : vraiment <I'm quite sure : je suis vraiment certaine>
quits ['kwɪts] *adj* : quitte <to be quits with s.o. : être quitte envers qqn> <let's call it quits! : restons-en là!>
quitter ['kwɪṱər] *n* : personne *f* qui abandonne facilement
quiver[1] ['kwɪvər] *vi* : trembler, frémir
quiver[2] *n* **1** : carquois *m* (pour des flèches) **2** TREMOR : tremblement *m*
quixotic [kwɪk'sɑṱɪk] *adj* : chimérique, utopique
quiz[1] ['kwɪz] *vt* **quizzed; quizzing** : questionner, interroger
quiz[2] *n, pl* **quizzes** : petit examen *m*, épreuve *f*
quizzical ['kwɪzɪkəl] *adj* **1** TEASING : moqueur, taquin, ironique **2** PUZZLED : perplexe
quorum ['kworəm] *n* : quorum *m*
quota ['kwo:ṱə] *n* : quota *m*
quotable ['kwo:ṱəbəl] *adj* : qui peut être cité
quotation [kwo'teɪʃən] *n* **1** CITATION : citation *f* **2** ESTIMATE : devis *m* **3** : cote *f*, cotation *f* (à la Bourse)
quotation marks *npl* : guillemets *mpl*
quote[1] ['kwo:t] *vt* **quoted; quoting 1** : citer <to quote a poem : citer un poème> **2** STATE : donner, soumettre (un prix) **3** : coter (un prix à la Bourse)
quote[2] *n* **1** → **quotation 2 quotes** *npl* → **quotation marks**
quotient ['kwo:ʃənt] *n* : quotient *m*

R

r ['ɑr] *n, pl* **r's** *or* **rs** ['ɑrz] : r *m*, dix-huitième lettre de l'alphabet
rabbi ['ræ,baɪ] *n* : rabbin *m*
rabbit ['ræbət] *n, pl* **-bit** *or* **-bits** : lapin *m*, -pine *f*
rabble ['ræbəl] *n* **1** CROWD, MOB : cohue *f*, foule *f* **2** MASSES : populace *f*, masses *fpl*
rabid ['ræbɪd] *adj* **1** FURIOUS : furieux **2** FANATICAL : zélé, fanatique **3** : enragé (se dit d'un chien)
rabies ['reɪbi:z] *ns & pl* : rage *f*
raccoon [ræ'ku:n] *n, pl* **-coon** *or* **-coons** : raton *m* laveur, chat *m* sauvage *Can*
race[1] ['reɪs] *vi* **raced; racing 1** : faire une course **2** RUSH : courir, se hâter

race[2] *n* **1** CURRENT : courant *m,* cours *m* (d'eau) **2** : course *f* <horse race : course de chevaux> <presidential race : course à la présidence> **3** : race *f* <the white race : la race blanche>

racecourse ['reɪsˌkors] *n* : champ *m* de courses

racehorse ['reɪsˌhors] *n* : cheval *m* de course

racer ['reɪsər] *n* : coureur *m,* -reuse *f*

racetrack ['reɪsˌtræk] *n* : champ *m* de courses

racial ['reɪʃəl] *adj* : racial — **racially** *adv*

racism ['reɪˌsɪzəm] *n* : racisme *m*

racist ['reɪsɪst] *n* : raciste *mf*

rack[1] ['ræk] *vt* : torturer <to be racked with pain : être torturé par la douleur> <to rack one's brains : se creuser la tête>

rack[2] *n* **1** SHELF : étagère *f* <a luggage rack : un porte-bagages> <a roof rack : une galerie> <a clothes rack : un portemanteau> **2** : chevalet *m* (instrument de torture)

racket ['rækət] *n* **1** : raquette *f* <tennis racket : raquette de tennis> **2** CLAMOR : vacarme *m* **3** FRAUD : escroquerie *f,* racket *m*

racketeer [ˌrækə'tɪr] *n* : racketteur *m*

racketeering [ˌrækə'tɪrɪŋ] *n* : racket *m*

raconteur [ˌræˌkɑn'tər] *n* STORYTELLER : raconteur *m,* -teuse *f*

racy ['reɪsi] *adj* **racier; -est 1** LIVELY : plein de verve **2** RISQUÉ : osé

radar ['reɪˌdɑr] *n* : radar *m*

radial ['reɪdiəl] *adj* : radial

radiance ['reɪdiənts] *n* : éclat *m,* rayonnement *m*

radiant ['reɪdiənt] *adj* **1** GLOWING : éclatant, brillant **2** : radieux, rayonnant <a radiant smile : un sourire radieux> **3** : radiant (en physique)

radiantly ['reɪdiəntli] *adv* : d'un air radieux

radiate ['reɪdiˌeɪt] *v* **-ated; -ating** *vi* SHINE : briller, rayonner — *vt* **1** IRRADIATE : irradier **2** EMIT : dégager, émettre <to radiate heat : dégager de la chaleur>

radiation [ˌreɪdi'eɪʃən] *n* : rayonnement *m,* radiation *f*

radiator ['reɪdiˌeɪt̬ər] *n* : radiateur *m,* calorifère *m Can*

radical[1] ['rædɪkəl] *adj* : radical — **radically** ['rædɪkli] *adv*

radical[2] *n* : radical *m,* -cale *f*

radii → **radius**

radio[1] ['reɪdiˌoː] *vt* : envoyer (un message) par radio

radio[2] *n, pl* **-dios** : radio *f*

radioactive [ˌreɪdio'æktɪv] *adj* : radioactif

radioactivity [ˌreɪdioˌæk'tɪvət̬i] *n* : radioactivité *f*

radiologist [ˌreɪdi'ɑlədʒɪst] *n* : radiologiste *mf,* radiologue *mf*

radiology [ˌreɪdi'ɑlədʒi] *n* : radiologie *f*

radish ['rædɪʃ] *n* : radis *m*

radium ['reɪdiəm] *n* : radium *m*

radius ['reɪdiəs] *n, pl* **-dii** [-diˌaɪ] : rayon *m*

radon ['reɪˌdɑn] *n* : radon *m*

raffle[1] ['ræfəl] *vt* **-fled; -fling** : mettre en tombola

raffle[2] *n* : tombola *f*

raft[1] ['ræft] *vt* : transporter par radeau

raft[2] *n* **1** : radeau *m* **2** SLEW : tas *m,* multitude *f* <a raft of errors : un tas d'erreurs>

rafter ['ræftər] *n* : chevron *m*

rag ['ræg] *n* **1** : chiffon *m,* guenille *f Can* **2** **rags** *npl* : haillons *mpl,* guenilles *fpl* <clothed in rags : vêtu de haillons> **3** → **ragtime**

ragamuffin ['rægəˌmʌfən] *n* : va-nu-pieds *m*

rage[1] ['reɪdʒ] *vi* **raged; raging 1** : être enragé (se dit d'une personne) **2** : faire rage <the fire raged for hours : le feu a fait rage pendant des heures>

rage[2] *n* **1** FURY : rage *f* **2 to be all the rage** : faire fureur

ragged ['rægəd] *adj* **1** : inégal <ragged cliffs : falaises inégales> **2** TATTERED : en loques, en lambeaux **3** DISCONNECTED, DISJOINTED : décousu

ragout [ræ'guː] *n* : ragoût *m*

ragtime ['rægˌtaɪm] *n* : ragtime *m*

ragweed ['rægˌwiːd] *n* : ambroisie *f*

raid[1] ['reɪd] *vt* : faire un raid (militaire) sur, faire une descente (policière) dans

raid[2] *n* **1** INCURSION : raid *m* (militaire) **2** *or* **police raid** : descente *f,* rafle *f*

raider ['reɪdər] *n* **1** : membre *m* d'un commando **2** LOOTER, MARAUDER : pillard *m,* -larde *f*

rail[1] ['reɪl] *vi* **to rail at** : invectiver contre

rail[2] *n* **1** RAILING : rampe *f* (d'un escalier), balustrade *f* (d'un balcon) **2** TRACK : rail *m* (d'une voie ferrée) **3** RAILROAD : train *m,* chemin *m* de fer <by rail : par train>

railing ['reɪlɪŋ] *n* : rampe *f,* balustrade *f*

raillery ['reɪləri] *n, pl* **-leries** : raillerie *f*

railroad ['reɪlˌroːd] *n* : chemin *m* de fer

railway ['reɪlˌweɪ] → **railroad**

raiment ['reɪmənt] *n* : habits *mpl,* vêtements *mpl*

rain[1] ['reɪn] *vi* : pleuvoir

rain[2] *n* : pluie *f*

rainbow ['reɪnˌboː] *n* : arc-en-ciel *m*

raincoat ['reɪnˌkoːt] *n* : imperméable *m*

raindrop ['reɪnˌdrɑp] *n* : goutte *f* de pluie

rainfall ['reɪnˌfɔl] *n* : précipitations *fpl*

rainstorm ['reɪnˌstɔrm] *n* : pluie *f* torrentielle

rainwater ['reɪnˌwɔt̬ər] *n* : eau *f* de pluie

rainy ['reɪni] *adj* **rainier; -est** : pluvieux

raise[1] ['reɪz] *vt* **raised; raising 1** LIFT : lever **2** AWAKEN : ressusciter **3** BUILD : ériger **4** COLLECT : collecter (des fonds) **5** GROW : cultiver (des produits agricoles) **6** REAR : élever **7** BRING UP : soulever (une question, etc.) **8** INCREASE : augmenter **9** PROVOKE : susciter, provoquer <to raise a commotion : susciter un émoi>

raise[2] *n* : augmentation *f* (de salaire)

raisin ['reɪzən] *n* : raisin *m* sec

raja *or* **rajah** ['rɑdʒə, -ˌdʒɑ, -ʒɑ] *n* : rajah *m*

rake[1] ['reɪk] *vt* **raked; raking 1** : ratisser, râteler (des feuilles) **2 to rake with gunfire** : balayer avec une mitrailleuse

rake[2] *n* **1** : râteau *m* **2** LIBERTINE : débauché *m*

rakish ['reɪkɪʃ] *adj* **1** JAUNTY : gaillard **2** WILD : libertin, dissolu

rally[1] ['ræli] *v* **-lied; -lying** *vt* MOBILIZE : rallier, rassembler — *vi* **1** : se rallier **2** RECOVER : retrouver ses forces, se remettre

rally[2] *n, pl* **-lies** : ralliement *m,* rassemblement *m*

ram[1] ['ræm] *vt* **rammed; ramming 1** HIT : heurter, percuter **2** CRAM : fourrer, entasser **3 to ram home** : forcer l'acceptation de (une idée, un projet de loi, etc.)

ram[2] *n* **1** : bélier *m* (mouton) **2** → **battering ram**

RAM ['ræm] *n* : RAM *f,* mémoire *f* vive

ramble[1] ['ræmbəl] *vi* **-bled; -ling 1** ROAM : flâner, se balader **2** *or* **to ramble on** : discourir, pérorer

ramble[2] *n* : randonnée *f,* balade *f*

rambler ['ræmblər] *n* WALKER : randonneur *m,* -neuse *f*

rambunctious [ræm'bʌŋkʃəs] *adj* : exubérant, turbulent

ramification [ˌræməfə'keɪʃən] *n* : ramification *f*

ramify ['ræməˌfaɪ] *vi* **-fied; -fying** : se ramifier

ramp ['ræmp] *n* **1** : rampe *f* **2** : passerelle *f* (pour accéder à un avion)

rampage[1] ['ræmˌpeɪdʒ, ræm'peɪdʒ] *vi* **-paged; -paging** : se déchaîner, donner libre cours à

rampage[2] ['ræmˌpeɪdʒ] *n* **to go on a rampage** : se livrer à des actes de destruction

rampant ['ræmpənt] *adj* WIDESPREAD : endémique, qui sévit

rampart ['ræmˌpɑrt] *n* : rempart *m*

ramrod ['ræmˌrɑd] *n* : baguette *f* (d'une arme à feu)

ramshackle ['ræmˌʃækəl] *adj* : délabré, en mauvais état

ran → **run**[1]

ranch[1] ['ræntʃ] *vi* : exploiter un ranch

ranch[2] *n* : ranch *m*

rancher ['ræntʃər] *n* : propriétaire *mf* de ranch

rancid ['ræntsɪd] *adj* : rance

rancor *or Brit* **rancour** ['ræŋkər] *n* : rancœur *f,* rancune *f*

random ['rændəm] *adj* **1** : aléatoire <random process : processus aléatoire> **2 at ~** : au hasard

randomly ['rændəmli] *adv* : au hasard

rang → **ring**[1]

range[1] ['reɪndʒ] *v* **ranged; ranging** *vt* ARRANGE : classer, ranger — *vi* **1** WANDER : vagabonder, errer **2 to range from** : varier entre, aller de

range[2] *n* **1** ROW : rangée *f* **2** PRAIRIE : prairie *f* **3** : chaîne *f* (de montagnes) **4** STOVE : cuisinière *f* **5** SERIES, SPREAD : éventail *m,* gamme *f* **6** *or* **shooting range** : champ *m* de tir **7** SCOPE : champ *m,* étendue *f* **8** VARIETY : variété *f* (de couleurs, de motifs)

ranger ['reɪndʒər] *n or* **forest ranger** : garde *m* forestier

rangy ['reɪndʒi] *adj* **rangier; -est** : élancé

rank[1] ['ræŋk] *vt* **1** ARRANGE : placer, ranger **2** CLASSIFY : classer — *vi* : se classer, compter <he ranks among the best in his class : il se classe parmi les meilleurs de sa classe>

rank[2] *adj* **1** : luxuriant (se dit de la végétation), envahissant (se dit des mauvais herbes) **2** MALODOROUS : fétide, nauséabond **3** FLAGRANT : complet, flagrant <rank disloyalty : déloyauté flagrante>

rank[3] *n* **1** LINE, ROW : rang *m* <to close ranks : serrer les rangs> **2** GRADE, POSITION : rang *m,* grade *m* <to pull rank : abuser de son rang> **3** CLASS : rang *m,* condition *f* (sociale) **4 ranks** *npl* : rangs *mpl* (militaires), échelons *mpl*

rank and file *n* **1** : hommes *mpl* du rang (dans les forces armées) **2** : base *f* (politique)

rankle ['ræŋkəl] *vi* **-kled; -kling** : rester sur le cœur, laisser un rancœur

ransack ['rænˌsæk] *vt* **1** SEARCH : fouiller **2** PLUNDER : saccager, piller

ransom[1] ['ræntsəm] *vt* : payer une rançon pour, rançonner

ransom[2] *n* : rançon *f*

rant ['rænt] *vi or* **to rant and rave** : tempêter, fulminer

rap[1] ['ræp] *v* **rapped; rapping** *vt* **1** STRIKE : frapper, taper **2** CRITICIZE : critiquer, réprimander — *vi* **1** KNOCK : frapper **2** CHAT : causer, bavarder

rap[2] *n* **1** BLOW, TAP : coup *m* sec, tape *f* **2** CHAT : causerie *f,* bavardage *m* **3** *or* **rap music** : rap *m* **4 to beat the rap** : échapper à la justice

rapacious [rə'peɪʃəs] *adj* **1** GREEDY : rapace, avide **2** RAVENOUS : rapace, vorace

rape[1] ['reɪp] *vt* **raped; raping** : violer
rape[2] *n* **1** : viol *m* **2** : colza *m* (plante)
rapid ['ræpɪd] *adj* : rapide
rapidity [rə'pɪdəṭi] *n* : rapidité *f*
rapids ['ræpɪdz] *ns & pl* : rapides *mpl*
rapier ['reɪpiər] *n* : rapière *f*
rapist ['reɪpɪst] *n* : violeur *m*
rapport [ræ'por] *n* : rapport *m,* relation *f*
rapt ['ræpt] *adj* : captivé, transporté
rapture ['ræptʃər] *n* : extase *f,* ravissement *m*
rapturous ['ræptʃərəs] *adj* : extasié, extatique
rare ['rær] *adj* **rarer; rarest 1** RAREFIED : raréfié (se dit de l'air) **2** DISTINCTIVE, FINE : extraordinaire, exceptionnel <a rare June day : une de ces journées extraordinaires du mois de juin> **3** UNCOMMON : rare **4** : saignant (se dit de la viande)
rarefy ['rærə,faɪ] *v* **-fied; -fying** *vt* : raréfier — *vi* : se raréfier
rarely ['rærli] *adv* SELDOM : rarement
raring ['rærən, -ɪŋ] *adj* : impatient <raring to go : impatient de partir>
rarity ['rærəṭi] *n, pl* **-ties** : rareté *f*
rascal ['ræskəl] *n* **1** : polisson *m,* -sonne *f* **2** ROGUE : scélérat *m,* -rate *f*
rash[1] ['ræʃ] *adj* : irréfléchi, téméraire
rash[2] *n* : rougeurs *fpl*
rashly ['ræʃli] *adv* : sans réfléchir, imprudemment
rasp[1] ['ræsp] *vt* **1** SCRAPE : râper **2** IRRITATE : irriter **3 to rasp out** : dire d'une voix rauque
rasp[2] *n* : râpe *f*
raspberry ['ræz,bɛri] *n, pl* **-ries** : framboise *f*
rat ['ræt] *n* : rat *m*
ratchet ['rætʃət] *n or* **ratchet wheel** : roue *f* à rochet
rate[1] ['reɪt] *vt* **rated; rating 1** APPRAISE : estimer, évaluer **2** REGARD : considérer, estimer <she is rated an excellent pianist : on la considère comme une excellente pianiste> **3** DESERVE : mériter
rate[2] *n* **1** : taux *m* <interest rate : taux d'intérêt> **2** PRICE : tarif *m* <hotel rates : tarifs hôteliers> **3** PACE : rythme *m,* train *m* <at a rate of 40 miles per hour : à un rythme de 40 milles à l'heure> **4 at any rate** : en tous cas
rather ['ræðər, 'rʌ-, 'rɑ-] *adv* **1** PREFERABLY : mieux <I'd rather not go : j'aimerais mieux ne pas y aller> **2** : plutôt <my father, or rather my stepfather : mon père, ou plutôt mon beau-père> **3** SOMEWHAT : assez, plutôt
ratification [,ræṭəfə'keɪʃən] *n* : ratification *f*
ratify ['ræṭə,faɪ] *vt* **-fied; -fying** : ratifier
rating ['reɪtɪŋ] *n* **1** STANDING : classement *m,* cote *f* **2 ratings** *npl* : indice *m* d'écoute
ratio ['reɪʃio] *n, pl* **-tios** : rapport *m,* proportion *f*
ration[1] ['ræʃən, 'reɪʃən] *vt* **rationed; rationing** : rationner
ration[2] *n* **1** : ration *f* **2 rations** *npl* PROVISIONS : rations *fpl,* provisions *fpl*
rational ['ræʃənəl] *adj* : raisonnable, sensé, logique
rationale [,ræʃə'næl] *n* **1** EXPLANATION : raisons *fpl,* logique *f* **2** BASIS : justification *f,* raison *f* d'être
rationalization [,ræʃənələ'zeɪʃən] *n* : justification *f,* rationalisation *f*
rationalize ['ræʃənə,laɪz] *vt* **-ized; -izing** : justifier, rationaliser
rationally ['ræʃənəli] *adv* : rationnellement
rattle[1] ['ræṭəl] *v* **-tled; -tling** *vi* : faire du bruit, vibrer — *vt* **1** UPSET : ébranler, secouer **2 to rattle off** : débiter à toute vitesse
rattle[2] *n* **1** : cliquetis *m,* bruit *m* **2** *or* **baby's rattle** : hochet *m* **3** : grelot *m* (d'un serpent à sonnettes)
rattler ['ræṭələr] → **rattlesnake**
rattlesnake ['ræṭəl,sneɪk] *n* : serpent *m* à sonnettes, crotale *m*
ratty ['ræṭi] *adj* **rattier; -est** : miteux, misérable
raucous ['rɔkəs] *adj* **1** HARSH : rauque (se dit de la voix) **2** BOISTEROUS : bruyant — **raucously** *adv*
ravage ['rævɪdʒ] *vt* **-aged; -aging** : ravager
ravages ['rævɪdʒəz] *npl* : ravages *mpl*
rave ['reɪv] *vi* **raved; raving 1** : délirer (se dit d'un malade) **2 to rave about** : s'extasier sur, s'emballer au sujet de
ravel[1] ['rævəl] *v* **-eled** *or* **-elled; -eling** *or* **-elling** *vt* UNRAVEL : défaire (un tricot) — *vi* FRAY : s'effilocher
ravel[2] *n* : effiloche *f*
raven ['reɪvən] *n* : grand corbeau *m*
ravenous ['rævənəs] *adj* **1** HUNGRY : affamé <to be ravenous : avoir une faim de loup> **2** RAPACIOUS : vorace
ravenously ['rævənəsli] *adv* : voracement
ravine [rə'viːn] *n* : ravin *m,* coulée *f Can*
ravish ['rævɪʃ] *vt* **1** SEIZE : ravir, emporter de force **2** DELIGHT : ravir, enchanter **3** RAPE : violer
raw ['rɔ] *adj* **rawer; rawest 1** UNCOOKED : cru **2** UNTREATED : brut, écru (se dit des étoffes) <raw silk : soie grège> **3** INEXPERIENCED : inexpérimenté **4** OPEN : à vif, ouvert <a raw wound : une plaie ouverte> **5** : froid et humide, cru <a raw day : une journée crue> **6** COARSE, VULGAR : grossier, obscène **7 raw material** : matière *f* première **8 to get a raw deal** : être traité injustement
rawhide ['rɔ,haɪd] *n* : cuir *m* brut

ray ['reɪ] *n* **1** : rayon *m* (de lumière) **2** BIT, GLIMMER : lueur *f* <a ray of hope : une lueur d'espoir>

rayon ['reɪˌɑn] *n* : rayonne *f*

raze ['reɪz] *vt* **razed; razing** : raser, détruire

razor ['reɪzər] *n* : rasoir *m*

reach[1] ['riːtʃ] *vt* **1** EXTEND : tendre, étendre <to reach out one's hand : tendre la main> **2** GRASP, TOUCH : atteindre **3** : arriver à, aller jusqu'à <his shadow reached the wall : son ombre arrivait jusqu'au mur> **4** : parvenir à <to reach an agreement : parvenir à une entente> **5** CONTACT : rejoindre — *vi* EXTEND : s'étendre

reach[2] *n* : portée *f* <within reach : à portée de la main>

react [ri'ækt] *vi* : réagir

reaction [ri'ækʃən] *n* : réaction *f*

reactionary[1] [ri'ækʃəˌnɛri] *adj* : réactionnaire

reactionary[2] *n, pl* **-ries** : réactionnaire *mf*

reactor [ri'æktər] *n* : réacteur *m* <nuclear reactor : réacteur nucléaire>

read[1] ['riːd] *v* **read** ['rɛd]; **reading** *vt* **1** : lire <to read a book : lire un livre> **2** INTERPRET : interpréter, reconnaître <to read nature's signs : interpréter les signes de la nature> **3** UNDERSTAND : connaître, comprendre <she reads him like a book : elle connaît ses moindres réactions> **4** STUDY : faire, étudier <she reads law : elle fait son droit> **5** INDICATE : indiquer, montrer <the thermometer reads 10° : le thermomètre indique 10°> — *vi* : se lire <this book reads smoothly : ce livre se lit facilement>

read[2] ['rɛd] *adj* **well read** : instruit, informé

readable ['riːdəbəl] *adj* : lisible

reader ['riːdər] *n* : lecteur *m*, -trice *f*

readily ['rɛdəli] *adv* **1** WILLINGLY : avec empressement, volontiers **2** EASILY : facilement

readiness ['rɛdinəs] *n* **1** ALACRITY : empressement *m* **2** EASE : facilité *f*, aisance *f*

reading ['riːdɪŋ] *n* **1** : lecture *f* (d'un livre) **2** : indication *f* (d'un instrument), relevé *m* (d'un compteur) <to take a reading : faire un relevé>

readjust [ˌriːə'dʒʌst] *vt* : rajuster, réajuster — *vi* : se réadapter

readjustment [ˌriːə'dʒʌstmənt] *n* : réajustement *m*

ready[1] ['rɛdi] *vt* **readied; readying** : préparer

ready[2] *adj* **readier; -est 1** : prêt <dinner is ready : le dîner est prêt> <ready to cry : au bord des larmes> **2** WILLING : prêt <always ready to help : toujours prêt à aider> **3 to have a ready wit** : avoir la repartie facile **4 ready money** : argent *m* liquide

ready-made [ˌrɛdi'meɪd] *adj* : de prêt-à-porter (se dit des vêtements)

reaffirm [ˌriːə'fərm] *vt* : réaffirmer

real[1] ['riːl] *adv* VERY : vraiment

real[2] *adj* **1** : réel <real income : revenu réel> **2** GENUINE : vrai, véritable **3** ACTUAL : réel, vrai <in real life : en réalité> **4 for ~** : pour de vrai

real estate *n* : biens *mpl* immobiliers

realism ['riːəˌlɪzəm] *n* : réalisme *m*

realist ['riːəlɪst] *n* : réaliste *mf*

realistic [ˌriːə'lɪstɪk] *adj* : réaliste

realistically [ˌriːə'lɪstɪkli] *adv* : de façon réaliste

reality [ri'æləṭi] *n, pl* **-ties** : réalité *f*

realization [ˌriːələ'zeɪʃən] *n* : réalisation *f*

realize ['riːəˌlaɪz] *vt* **-ized; -izing 1** ACCOMPLISH : réaliser **2** GAIN, OBTAIN : réaliser (un profit) **3** UNDERSTAND : se rendre compte de, comprendre

really ['rɪli, 'rɪː-] *adv* **1** ACTUALLY : vraiment <I didn't really mean it : je n'étais pas vraiment sérieux> **2** TRULY : incontestablement, vraiment **3** (*used as an intensifier*) <really, you're being ridiculous : vraiment, tu es ridicule>

realm ['rɛlm] *n* **1** KINGDOM : royaume *m* **2** SPHERE : domaine *m*

ream[1] ['riːm] *vt* : fraiser

ream[2] *n* : rame *f* (de papier)

reap ['riːp] *vt* **1** : moissonner, faucher (des récoltes) **2** HARVEST : récolter <he reaped a rich reward : il a récolté une riche récompense>

reaper ['riːpər] *n* : moissonneuse *f* (machine)

reappear [ˌriːə'pɪr] *vi* : réapparaître, reparaître

rear[1] ['rɪr] *vt* **1** RAISE : lever, relever **2** BREED, BRING UP : élever (des animaux ou des enfants) — *vi* : se cabrer (se dit d'un cheval)

rear[2] *adj* : derrière

rear[3] *n* **1** BACK : derrière *f* **2** BUTTOCKS : derrière *m fam*, arrière-train *m fam*

rear admiral *n* : contre-amiral *m*

rearrange [ˌriːə'reɪndʒ] *vt* **-ranged; -ranging** : réarranger

reason[1] ['riːzən] *vi* : raisonner

reason[2] *n* **1** EXPLANATION : raison *f* **2** BASIS : motif *m*, raisons *fpl* **3** CAUSE : cause *f*, raison *f* **4** COMMON SENSE : raison *f*, bon sens *m*

reasonable ['riːzənəbəl] *adj* **1** : raisonnable, sensé **2** AFFORDABLE : raisonnable, abordable

reasonably ['riːzənəbli] *adv* : raisonnablement

reasoning ['riːzənɪŋ] *n* : raisonnement *m*

reassess [ˌriːə'sɛs] *vt* : réexaminer

reassurance [ˌriːə'ʃʊrənts] *n* **1** ASSURANCE : assurance *f* **2** COMFORTING : réconfort *m*

reassure [ˌriːə'ʃʊr] *vt* **-sured; -suring** : rassurer

reawaken [ˌriːəˈweɪkən] *vt* : réveiller

rebate[1] [ˈriːˌbeɪt] *vt* **-bated; -bating** : donner une ristourne à

rebate[2] *n* : ristourne *f*

rebel[1] [rɪˈbɛl] *vi* **-belled; -belling** : se rebeller, se révolter

rebel[2] [ˈrɛbəl] *adj* : rebelle

rebel[3] [ˈrɛbəl] *n* : rebelle *mf*

rebellion [rɪˈbɛljən] *n* : rébellion *f,* révolte *f*

rebellious [rɪˈbɛljəs] *adj* : rebelle

rebirth [ˌriːˈbərθ] *n* : renaissance *f*

rebound[1] [ˈriːˌbaʊnd, rɪˈbaʊnd] *vi* **1** : rebondir (se dit d'un ballon) **2** RECOVER : rebondir, repartir à zéro

rebound[2] [ˈriːˌbaʊnd] *n* : rebond *m*

rebuff[1] [rɪˈbʌf] *vt* : mal accueillir, repousser

rebuff[2] *n* : rebuffade *f*

rebuild [ˌriːˈbɪld] *vt* **-built** [-ˈbɪlt]; **-building** : reconstruire

rebuke[1] [rɪˈbjuːk] *vt* **-buked; -buking** : reprocher, réprimander

rebuke[2] *n* : reproche *m,* réprimande *f*

rebut [rɪˈbʌt] *vt* **-butted; -butting** : réfuter

rebuttal [rɪˈbʌtəl] *n* : réfutation *f*

recalcitrant [rɪˈkælsətrənt] *adj* : récalcitrant

recall[1] [rɪˈkɔl] *vt* **1** : rappeler <to be recalled to duty : être rappelé au devoir> **2** REMEMBER : se rappeler, se souvenir de **3** CANCEL, REVOKE : révoquer, annuler

recall[2] [rɪˈkɔl, ˈriːˌkɔl] *n* **1** : rappel *m* (de personnes ou de marchandises) **2** MEMORY : mémoire *f* **3** REVOCATION : révocation *f,* annulation *f*

recant [rɪˈkænt] *vt* : rétracter (une opinion) — *vi* : abjurer

recapitulate [ˌriːkəˈpɪtʃəˌleɪt] *vt* **-lated; -lating** : récapituler, résumer

recapitulation [ˌriːkəˌpɪtʃəˈleɪʃən] *n* : récapitulation *f*

recapture [ˌriːˈkæptʃər] *vt* **-tured; -turing 1** : reprendre (une ville, etc.) **2** RECOVER : recréer <to recapture the past : recréer le passé>

recede [rɪˈsiːd] *vi* **-ceded; -ceding 1** WITHDRAW : s'éloigner, redescendre (se dit de la marée), refluer (se dit des eaux) **2** DIMINISH : diminuer, baisser <to recede into the distance : disparaître dans le lointain>

receipt [rɪˈsiːt] *n* **1** : reçu *m,* récépissé *m* **2 receipts** *npl* : recettes *fpl*

receivable [rɪˈsiːvəbəl] *adj* : à recevoir <accounts receivable : comptes clients>

receive [rɪˈsiːv] *vt* **-ceived; -ceiving 1** GET : recevoir <to receive a gift : recevoir un cadeau> **2** GREET : accueillir (des visiteurs) **3** : recevoir, capter (des ondes radio)

receiver [rɪˈsiːvər] *n* **1** : receveur *m,* -veuse *f* (personne) **2** : récepteur *m* (de radio), combiné *m* (téléphonique)

recent [ˈriːsənt] *adj* : récent

recently [ˈriːsəntli] *adv* : récemment

receptacle [rɪˈsɛptɪkəl] *n* : récipient *m*

reception [rɪˈsɛpʃən] *n* : réception *f*

receptionist [rɪˈsɛpʃənɪst] *n* : réceptionniste *mf*

receptive [rɪˈsɛptɪv] *adj* : réceptif

receptivity [ˌriːˌsɛpˈtɪvət̬i] *n* : réceptivité *f*

recess[1] [ˈriːˌsɛs, rɪˈsɛs] *vt* : encastrer <recessed lighting : éclairage encastré> — *vi* : suspendre les séances

recess[2] *n* **1** ALCOVE : recoin *m,* alcôve *f* **2** BREAK : récréation *f* (scolaire)

recession [rɪˈsɛʃən] *n* : récession *f*

recharge [ˌriːˈtʃɑrdʒ] *vt* **-charged; -charging** : recharger

rechargeable [ˌriːˈtʃɑrdʒəbəl] *adj* : rechargeable

recipe [ˈrɛsəˌpiː] *n* : recette *f*

recipient [rɪˈsɪpiənt] *n* : destinataire *mf* (d'une lettre), récipiendaire *m* (d'un prix, d'un diplôme, etc.)

reciprocal [rɪˈsɪprəkəl] *adj* : réciproque — **reciprocally** *adv*

reciprocate [rɪˈsɪprəˌkeɪt] *v* **-cated; -cating** *vt* : retourner (un service) — *vi* : rendre la pareille, en faire autant

reciprocity [ˌrɛsəˈprɑsət̬i] *n, pl* **-ties** : réciprocité *f*

recital [rɪˈsaɪt̬əl] *n* **1** NARRATIVE : narration *f,* énumération *f* **2** : récital *m* <dance recital : récital de danse>

recitation [ˌrɛsəˈteɪʃən] *n* : récitation *f*

recite [rɪˈsaɪt] *vt* **-cited; -citing 1** : réciter (un poème, etc.) **2** RECOUNT : relater, raconter

reckless [ˈrɛkləs] *adj* : imprudent, irréfléchi, téméraire

recklessly [ˈrɛkləsli] *adv* : imprudemment, sans réfléchir

recklessness [ˈrɛkləsnəs] *n* : imprudence *f,* témérité *f*

reckon [ˈrɛkən] *vt* **1** CALCULATE, COUNT : compter **2** CONSIDER : estimer, considérer

reckoning [ˈrɛkənɪŋ] *n* **1** CALCULATION : compte *m,* calcul *m* **2** ESTIMATION : estimation *f,* calculs *mpl* <according to his reckoning : selon ses calculs>

reclaim [rɪˈkleɪm] *vt* **1** : mettre en valeur (un terrain) **2** RECYCLE : recycler **3** RECOVER : récupérer

recline [rɪˈklaɪn] *vi* **-clined; -clining 1** LIE : être couché, être allongé **2** : s'incliner (se dit d'un siège)

recluse [ˈrɛˌkluːs, rɪˈkluːs] *n* : reclus *m,* -cluse *f*

recognition [ˌrɛkɪgˈnɪʃən] *n* : reconnaissance *f*

recognizable [ˈrɛkəgˌnaɪzəbəl] *adj* : reconnaissable

recognizably [ˈrɛkəgˌnaɪzəbli] *adv* : manifestement, d'une façon reconnaissable

recognize [ˈrɛkɪgˌnaɪz] *vt* **-nized; -nizing** : reconnaître

recoil[1] [rɪ'kɔɪl] *vi* : reculer
recoil[2] ['ri:ˌkɔɪl, rɪ'-] *n* : recul *m*, mouvement *m* de recul
recollect [ˌrɛkə'lɛkt] *vt* : se souvenir de, se rappeler — *vi* : se souvenir
recollection [ˌrɛkə'lɛkʃən] *n* : souvenir *m*
recommend [ˌrɛkə'mɛnd] *vt* : recommander
recommendation [ˌrɛkəmən'deɪʃən] *n* : recommandation *f*
recompense[1] ['rɛkəmˌpɛnts] *vt* **-pensed; -pensing 1** REWARD : récompenser **2** COMPENSATE : dédommager, compenser
recompense[2] *n* **1** REWARD : récompense *f* **2** COMPENSATION : dédommagement *m*
reconcile ['rɛkənˌsaɪl] *v* **-ciled; -ciling** *vt* **1** : réconcilier **2 to reconcile oneself to** : se résigner à — *vi* MAKE UP : se réconcilier
reconciliation [ˌrɛkənˌsɪli'eɪʃən] *n* : réconciliation *f*
recondite ['rɛkənˌdaɪt, rɪ'kɑn-] *adj* : abstrus, obscur
recondition [ˌri:kənˌdɪʃən] *vt* : remettre à neuf
reconnaissance [rɪ'kɑnəzənts, -sənts] *n* : reconnaissance *f*
reconnoiter *or* **reconnoitre** [ˌri:kə'nɔɪṭər, ˌrɛkə-] *v* **-tered** *or* **-tred**; **-tering** *or* **-tring** *vt* : reconnaître — *vi* : faire une reconnaissance
reconsider [ˌri:kən'sɪdər] *vt* : réexaminer (un plan, une décision) — *vi* : repenser <I asked him to reconsider : je lui ai demandé d'y repenser>
reconsideration [ˌri:kənˌsɪdə'reɪʃən] *n* : révision *f*, réexamen *m*
reconstruct [ˌri:kən'strʌkt] *vt* : reconstruire
record[1] [rɪ'kɔrd] *vt* **1** WRITE DOWN : noter, enregistrer **2** REGISTER : enregistrer **3** INDICATE : indiquer (la température, etc.) **4** TAPE : enregistrer (une émission)
record[2] ['rɛkərd] *n* **1** DOCUMENT : document *m*, écrit *m* **2** HISTORY, REPORT : compte rendu *m*, récit *m* (des événements, etc.) **3** : record *m* <the world record : le record mondial> **4** : disque *m* (de musique) **5** *or* **school record** : dossier *m* (scolaire) **6** *or* **police record** : casier *m* judiciaire
recorder [rɪ'kɔrdər] *n* **1** *or* **tape recorder** : magnétophone *m* **2** : flûte *f* à bec (instrument de musique)
recount [rɪ'kaʊnt] *vt* **1** NARRATE : raconter, conter **2** [ˌri:'-] : recompter (des votes, etc.), compter de nouveau
recoup [rɪ'ku:p] *vt* : recouvrer, récupérer
recourse ['ri:ˌkors, rɪ'-] *n* : recours *m*
recover [rɪ'kʌvər] *vt* **1** REGAIN : retrouver, récupérer **2** RECOUP : recouvrer — *vi* RECUPERATE : se remettre, se rétablir
recovery [rɪ'kʌvəri] *n, pl* **-ries** : rétablissement *m*
re–create [ˌri:kri'eɪt] *vt* **-ated; -ating** : recréer
recreation [ˌrɛkri'eɪʃən] *n* : loisirs *mpl*, récréation *f*
recreational [ˌrɛkri'eɪʃənəl] *adj* : récréatif
recriminate [rɪ'krɪməˌneɪt] *vi* **-nated; -nating** : récriminer <to recriminate against : récriminer contre>
recrimination [rɪˌkrɪmə'neɪʃən] *n* : récrimination *f*
recruit[1] [rɪ'kru:t] *vt* : recruter
recruit[2] *n* : recrue *f*
recruitment [rɪ'kru:tmənt] *n* : recrutement *m*
rectal ['rɛktəl] *adj* : rectal
rectangle ['rɛkˌtæŋgəl] *n* : rectangle *m*
rectangular [rɛk'tæŋgjələr] *adj* : rectangulaire
rectify ['rɛktəˌfaɪ] *vt* **-fied; -fying** : rectifier
rectitude ['rɛktəˌtu:d, -ˌtju:d] *n* : rectitude *f*
rector ['rɛktər] *n* : pasteur *m*
rectory ['rɛktəri] *n, pl* **-ries** : presbytère *m*
rectum ['rɛktəm] *n, pl* **-tums** *or* **-ta** [-tə] : rectum *m*
recumbent [rɪ'kəmbənt] *adj* : couché, étendu
recuperate [rɪ'ku:pəˌreɪt, -'kju:-] *v* **-ated; -ating** *vi* : se rétablir, se remettre — *vt* REGAIN : retrouver (ses forces), récupérer (ses débours)
recuperation [rɪˌku:pə'reɪʃən, -ˌkju:-] *n* : rétablissement *m* (de la santé), recouvrement *m* (d'une dette, etc.)
recur [rɪ'kər] *vi* **-curred; -curring** : réapparaître
recurrence [rɪ'kərənts] *n* : réapparition *f*, retour *m*
recurrent [rɪ'kərənt] *adj* : récurrent, fréquent
recyclable [rɪ'saɪkələbəl] *adj* : recyclable
recycle [rɪ'saɪkəl] *vt* **-cled; -cling** : recycler
red[1] ['rɛd] *adj* : rouge
red[2] *n* **1** : rouge *m* **2 Red** : communiste *mf*, rouge *mf* **3 in the red** : dans le rouge, en déficit
red blood cell *n* : globule *m* rouge
red–blooded ['rɛd'blʌdəd] *adj* : vigoureux
redcap ['rɛdˌkæp] → **porter**
redden ['rɛdən] *vt* : rougir — *vi* BLUSH : rougir
reddish ['rɛdɪʃ] *adj* : rougeâtre
redecorate [ˌri:'dɛkəˌreɪt] *vt* **-rated; -rating** : repeindre et retapisser
redeem [ri'di:m] *vt* **1** RESCUE, SAVE : racheter, sauver <to redeem oneself : se racheter> **2** REPAY, REPURCHASE : rembourser (une dette), racheter (une propriété chez un prêteur sur gages) **3** EXCHANGE : échanger <to

redeem savings bonds : échanger des bons d'épargne> **4** : racheter (en religion)
redeemer [rɪˈdiːmər] *n* : rédempteur *m*
redemption [rɪˈdɛmpʃən] *n* : rédemption *f*
red–handed [ˈrɛdˈhændəd] *adv* : la main dans le sac
redhead [ˈrɛdˌhɛd] *n* : roux *m,* rousse *f*
rediscover [ˌriːdiˈskʌvər] *vt* : redécouvrir
redistribute [ˌriːdiˈstrɪˌbjuːt] *vt* **-uted; -uting** : redistribuer
redness [ˈrɛdnəs] *n* : rougeur *f*
redo [ˌriːˈduː] *vt* **-did** [-dɪd]; **-done** [-ˈdʌn]; **-doing 1** : refaire **2** → **redecorate**
redolence [ˈrɛdələnts] *n* : arôme *m,* parfum *m*
redolent [ˈrɛdələnt] *adj* **1** FRAGRANT : aromatique, parfumé **2** SUGGESTIVE : évocateur **3 ~ of** *or* **~ with** : qui sent de, qui dégage (une odeur)
redouble [rɪˈdʌbəl] *vt* **-bled; -bling** : redoubler
redoubtable [rɪˈdaʊtəbəl] *adj* : redoutable, formidable
redress [rɪˈdrɛs] *vt* : redresser, réparer
red tape *n* : lenteurs *fpl* bureaucratiques, paperasserie *f*
reduce [rɪˈduːs, -ˈdjuːs] *v* **-duced; -ducing** *vt* **1** LESSEN : réduire, diminuer **2** LOWER : baisser (des prix, etc.) **3** DEMOTE : rétrograder **4 to reduce to tears** : faire pleurer — *vi* : maigrir, perdre du poids
reduction [rɪˈdʌkʃən] *n* : réduction *f,* diminution *f*
redundant [rɪˈdʌndənt] *adj* : superflu, redondant
redwood [ˈrɛdˌwʊd] *n* : séquoia *m*
reed [ˈriːd] *n* **1** : roseau *m* **2** : anche *f* (d'un instrument de musique)
reef [ˈriːf] *n* : récif *m,* écueil *m*
reek[1] [ˈriːk] *vi* : empester, puer
reek[2] *n* : puanteur *f*
reel[1] [ˈriːl] *vt* **1 to reel in** : enrouler (une ligne de pêche, etc.), ramener (un poisson) **2 to reel off** : débiter (un discours, etc.) — *vi* **1** SPIN, WHIRL : tournoyer <her head was reeling : elle avait la tête qui tournait> **2** STAGGER : chanceler, tituber
reel[2] *n* **1** : bobine *f,* rouleau *m,* moulinet *m* (de pêche) **2** : quadrille *m* écossais (danse)
reelect [ˌriːɪˈlɛkt] *vt* : réélire
reenact [ˌriːɪˈnækt] *vt* : reconstituer, reproduire
reenter [ˌriːˈɛntər] *vt* : entrer à nouveau
reestablish [ˌriːɪˈstæblɪʃ] *vt* : rétablir
reevaluate [ˌriːɪˈvæljʊˌeɪt] *vt* **-ated; -ating** : réévaluer
reexamine [ˌriːɪgˈzæmən] *vt* **-ined; -ining** : réexaminer
refer [rɪˈfər] *v* **-ferred; -ferring** *vt* **1** DIRECT : envoyer, diriger <to refer a patient to a specialist : diriger un patient à un spécialiste> **2** SUBMIT : soumettre, présenter <to refer a proposal to a committee : soumettre un plan à un comité> — *vi* **to refer to** MENTION : faire allusion à, mentionner
referee[1] [ˌrɛfəˈriː] *v* **-eed; -eeing** : arbitrer
referee[2] *n* : arbitre *m*
reference [ˈrɛfərənts] *n* **1** *or* **reference book** : ouvrage *m* de référence **2** ALLUSION : allusion *f* **3** RECOMMENDATION : référence *f* **4 in reference to** : en ce qui concerne
referendum [ˌrɛfəˈrɛndəm] *n, pl* **-da** [-də] *or* **-dums** : référendum *m*
refill[1] [ˌriːˈfɪl] *vt* : remplir à nouveau
refill[2] [ˈriːˌfɪl] *n* : recharge *f* (de stylo), cartouche *f* (d'encre)
refine [rɪˈfaɪn] *vt* **-fined; -fining 1** : raffiner (le sucre, le pétrole, etc.) **2** IMPROVE, PERFECT : peaufiner, perfectionner
refinement [rɪˈfaɪnmənt] *n* **1** : raffinage *m* (du pétrole, du sucre, etc.) **2** CULTIVATION, ELEGANCE : raffinement *m* **3** IMPROVEMENT : amélioration *f,* perfectionnement *m*
refinery [rɪˈfaɪnəri] *n, pl* **-eries** : raffinerie *f*
reflect [rɪˈflɛkt] *vt* **1** : réfléchir (la lumière), renvoyer (des sons, de la chaleur, etc.) **2** : refléter (une image, des idées, des émotions, etc.) <art reflects life : l'art reflète la vie> — *vi* **1** PONDER : réfléchir **2 to reflect badly on** : faire du tort à **3 to reflect well on** : faire honneur à
reflection [rɪˈflɛkʃən] *n* **1** : réflexion *f* (de la lumière, des sons, etc.) **2** IMAGE : reflet *m,* image *f* **3** THOUGHT : réflexion *f,* pensée *f*
reflective [rɪˈflɛktɪv] *adj* **1** : réfléchissant (en physique) **2** THOUGHTFUL : pensif, songeur
reflector [rɪˈflɛktər] *n* : réflecteur *m*
reflex[1] [ˈriːˌflɛks] *adj* : réflexe
reflex[2] *n* : réflexe *m*
reflexive[1] [rɪˈflɛksɪv] *adj* : réfléchi <reflexive pronoun : pronom réfléchi>
reflexive[2] *n or* **reflexive verb** : verbe *m* réfléchi
reform[1] [rɪˈfɔrm] *vt* : réformer — *vi* : se réformer
reform[2] *n* : réforme *f* — **reformable** *adj*
reformation [ˌrɛfərˈmeɪʃən] *n* **1** : réforme *f* **2 the Reformation** : la Réforme
reformatory [rɪˈfɔrməˌtori] *n, pl* **-ries** : maison *f* de correction
reformer [rɪˈfɔrmər] *n* : réformateur *m,* -trice *f*
refract [rɪˈfrækt] *vt* : réfracter — *vi* : se réfracter
refraction [rɪˈfrækʃən] *n* : réfraction *f*
refractory [rɪˈfræktəri] *adj* : réfractaire
refrain[1] [rɪˈfreɪn] *vi* **to refrain from** : se retenir de, s'empêcher de

refrain[2] *n* : refrain *m* (en musique)
refresh [rɪ'frɛʃ] *vt* **1** RESTORE, REVIVE : rafraîchir <to refresh oneself : se rafraîchir> **2 to refresh s.o.'s memory** : rafraîchir la mémoire de qqn
refreshment [rɪ'frɛʃmənt] *n* **1** REST : repos *m* **2 refreshments** *npl* : rafraîchissements *mpl*
refrigerate [rɪ'frɪdʒəˌreɪt] *vt* **-ated; -ating** : réfrigérer, frigorifier
refrigeration [rɪˌfrɪdʒə'reɪʃən] *n* : réfrigération *f*
refrigerator [rɪ'frɪdʒəˌreɪt̬ər] *n* : réfrigérateur *m*
refuel [riː'fjuːəl] *v* **-eled** *or* **-elled; -eling** *or* **-elling** *vt* : ravitailler — *vi* : se ravitailler
refuge ['rɛˌfjuːdʒ] *n* : refuge *m*, abri *m*
refugee [ˌrɛfjʊ'dʒiː] *n* : réfugié *m*, -giée *f*
refund[1] [rɪ'fʌnd, 'riːˌfʌnd] *vt* : rembourser (de l'argent)
refund[2] ['riːˌfʌnd] *n* : remboursement *m*, ristourne *f*
refundable [rɪ'fʌndəbəl] *adj* : remboursable
refurbish [rɪ'fərbɪʃ] *vt* : remettre à neuf, réaménager
refusal [rɪ'fjuːzəl] *n* : refus *m*
refuse[1] [rɪ'fjuːz] *vt* **-fused; -fusing 1** REJECT : refuser **2** DENY : refuser <they were refused admittance : on leur a refusé l'entrée> **3 to refuse to do sth** : se refuser à fair qqch
refuse[2] ['rɛˌfjuːs, -ˌfjuːz] *n* : ordures *fpl*, déchets *mpl*
refutation [ˌrɛfjʊ'teɪʃən] *n* : réfutation *f*
refute [rɪ'fjuːt] *vt* **-futed; -futing** : réfuter
regal ['riːgəl] *adj* : royal, majestueux
regale [rɪ'geɪl] *vt* **-galed; -galing** : régaler
regalia [rɪ'geɪljə] *npl* **1** INSIGNIA : insignes *mpl* **2** FINERY : atours *mpl*, accoutrement *m*
regard[1] [rɪ'gɑrd] *vt* **1** CONSIDER : considérer <I regard her as my sister : je la considère comme une sœur> **2** HEED : tenir compte de **3** OBSERVE : observer, considérer avec attention **4** RESPECT : respecter <highly regarded : très estimé>
regard[2] *n* **1** CONSIDERATION : égard *m*, considération *f* <without regard for : sans égard pour> **2** ESTEEM : respect *m*, estime *f* **3 regards** *npl* : amitiés *fpl* <send him my regards : transmettez-lui mes amitiés> **4 as regards** *or* **with regard to** : en ce qui concerne
regarding [rɪ'gɑrdɪŋ] *prep* : concernant
regardless [rɪ'gɑrdləs] *adv* : malgré tout, quand même
regardless of *prep* : sans tenir compte de
regenerate [rɪ'dʒɛnəˌreɪt] *v* **-ated; -ating** *vt* : régénérer — *vi* : se régénérer
regeneration [rɪˌdʒɛnə'reɪʃən] *n* : régénération *f*
regent ['riːdʒənt] *n* : régent *m*, -gente *f*
regime [reɪ'ʒiːm, rɪ-] *n* : régime *m*
regimen ['rɛdʒəmən] *n* : régime *m*
regiment[1] ['rɛdʒəˌmɛnt] *vt* : enrégimenter
regiment[2] ['rɛdʒəmənt] *n* : régiment *m*
region ['riːdʒən] *n* : région *f*
regional ['riːdʒənəl] *adj* : régional — **regionally** *adv*
register[1] ['rɛdʒəstər] *vt* **1** RECORD : inscrire, enregistrer **2** : immatriculer (un véhicule) **3** : enregistrer (une lettre) **4** SHOW : exprimer <to register surprise : exprimer la surprise> **5** : indiquer (la température, etc.) — *vi* ENROLL : s'inscrire
register[2] *n* **1** RECORD : registre *m* <a register of births : un registre des naissances> **2** RANGE : registre *m* (de la voix) **3** → **cash register**
registrar ['rɛdʒəˌstrɑr] *n* : chef *m* de la division des inscriptions (dans une université)
registration [ˌrɛdʒə'streɪʃən] *n* **1** : enregistrement *m* (de bagages), immatriculation *f* (d'un véhicule) **2** ENROLLMENT : inscription *f*
registry ['rɛdʒəstri] *n, pl* **-tries 1** REGISTRATION : enregistrement *m* **2** : bureau *m* d'enregistrement
regress [rɪ'grɛs] *vi* : régresser
regression [rɪ'grɛʃən] *n* : régression *f*
regressive [rɪ'grɛsɪv] *adj* : régressif
regret[1] [rɪ'grɛt] *vt* **-gretted; -gretting** : regretter
regret[2] *n* **1** SORROW : regret *m* **2** REMORSE : remords *mpl*, regrets *mpl* **3 regrets** *npl* : excuses *fpl* <to send one's regrets to s.o. : s'excuser auprès de qqn>
regretful [rɪ'grɛtfəl] *adj* : plein de regrets
regretfully [rɪ'grɛtfəli] *adv* : avec regret
regrettable [rɪ'grɛt̬əbəl] *adj* : regrettable
regrettably [rɪ'grɛt̬əbli] *adv* : malheureusement
regular[1] ['rɛgjələr] *adj* **1** SYMMETRICAL : régulier **2** NORMAL : régulier, normal **3** STEADY : régulier, égal <a regular pace : un pas régulier> **4** ORDERLY : fixe <regular habits : habitudes fixes>
regular[2] *n* : habitué *m*, -tuée *f*
regularity [ˌrɛgjə'lærət̬i] *n, pl* **-ties** : régularité *f*
regularly ['rɛgjələrli] *adv* : régulièrement
regulate ['rɛgjəˌleɪt] *vt* **-lated; -lating** : régler
regulation [ˌrɛgjə'leɪʃən] *n* **1** RULE : règlement *m*, règle *f* <safety regulations : règlements de sécurité> **2** CONTROL : réglementation *f*
regurgitate [rɪ'gərdʒəˌteɪt] *vt* **-tated; -tating** : régurgiter
rehabilitate [ˌriːhə'bɪləˌteɪt] *vt* **-tated; -tating 1** REINSTATE : réhabiliter **2**

RESTORE : rénover, réhabiliter (un quartier) **3** : rééduquer (un patient), réhabiliter (un détenu, un toxicomane, etc.)
rehabilitation [ˌriːhəˌbɪləˈteɪʃən] *n* : réhabilitation *f*
rehearsal [rɪˈhərsəl] *n* : répétition *f* (au théâtre)
rehearse [rɪˈhərs] *vt* **-hearsed; -hearsing** : répéter, réciter
reheat [riːˈhiːt] *vt* : réchauffer
reign[1] [ˈreɪn] *vi* **1** RULE : régner **2** PREVAIL : régner, prédominer
reign[2] *n* : règne *m*
reimburse [ˌriːəmˈbərs] *vt* **-bursed; -bursing** : rembourser
reimbursement [ˌriːəmˈbərsmənt] *n* : remboursement *m*
rein[1] [ˈreɪn] *vt* **1** : serrer la bride à (un cheval) **2 to rein in** CHECK : contenir, maîtriser (des émotions, etc.)
rein[2] *n* **1** : rêne *f*, bride *f* (d'un cheval) **2 to give full rein to** : donner libre cours à **3 to keep a tight rein on** : tenir la bride serrée à
reincarnate [ˌriːɪnˈkɑrˌneɪt] *vt* **-nated; -nating** : réincarner
reincarnation [ˌriːɪnˌkɑrˈneɪʃən] *n* : réincarnation *f*
reindeer [ˈreɪnˌdɪr] *n* : renne *f*
reinforce [ˌriːənˈfors] *vt* **-forced; -forcing** : renforcer
reinforcement [ˌriːənˈforsmənt] *n* : renforcement *m*
reinstate [ˌriːənˈsteɪt] *vt* **-stated; -stating** : réintégrer, rétablir
reinstatement [ˌriːənˈsteɪtmənt] *n* : réintégration *f*, rétablissement *m*
reiterate [riːˈɪt̬əˌreɪt] *vt* **-ated; -ating** : réitérer, répéter
reiteration [riːˌɪt̬əˈreɪʃən] *n* : réitération *f*, répétition *f*
reject[1] [rɪˈdʒɛkt] *vt* : rejeter
reject[2] [ˈriːˌdʒɛkt] *n* **1** : marchandise *f* de second choix **2** : personne *f* méprisée
rejection [rɪˈdʒɛkʃən] *n* : rejet *m*
rejoice [rɪˈdʒɔɪs] *vi* **-joiced; -joicing** : se réjouir
rejoin *vt* **1** [ˌriːˈdʒɔɪn] : rejoindre <he rejoined the company : il a rejoint la compagnie> **2** [rɪˈ-] RETORT : répliquer, rétorquer
rejoinder [rɪˈdʒɔɪndər] *n* : réplique *f*
rejuvenate [riˈdʒuːvəˌneɪt] *vt* **-nated; -nating** : rajeunir
rejuvenation [riˌdʒuːvəˈneɪʃən] *n* : rajeunissement *m*
rekindle [ˌriːˈkɪndəl] *vt* **-dled; -dling** : raviver, ranimer (un feu, l'espoir etc.)
relapse[1] [riˈlæps] *vi* **-lapsed; -lapsing** : retomber, rechuter
relapse[2] [ˈriːˌlæps, riˈlæps] *n* : rechute *f* (en médecine)
relate [rɪˈleɪt] *v* **-lated; -lating** *vt* **1** TELL : raconter **2** ASSOCIATE : établir un lien entre, relier <to relate crime to poverty : relier le crime à la pauvreté> — *vi* **1** CONNECT : se rapporter **2** INTERACT : communiquer (avec) **3 to relate to** APPRECIATE, UNDERSTAND : apprécier
related [rɪˈleɪt̬əd] *adj* : apparenté
relation [rɪˈleɪʃən] *n* **1** NARRATION : récit *m* **2** CONNECTION, RELATIONSHIP : rapport *m* <in relation to : par rapport à> **3** RELATIVE : parent *m*, -rente *f* **4 relations** *npl* : rapports *mpl*, relations *fpl* <sexual relations : relations sexuelles> <foreign relations : affaires étrangères>
relationship [rɪˈleɪʃənˌʃɪp] *n* **1** CONNECTION : rapport *m*, relations *fpl* **2** KINSHIP : liens *mpl* de parenté
relative[1] [ˈrɛlət̬ɪv] *adj* : relatif — **relatively** *adv*
relative[2] *n* : parent *m*, -rente *f*
relativity [ˌrɛləˈtɪvət̬i] *n* : relativité *f*
relax [rɪˈlæks] *vt* **1** SLACKEN : relâcher, desserrer **2** MODIFY : assouplir <to relax immigration laws : assouplir les lois d'immigration> — *vi* REST : se détendre, se reposer
relaxation [ˌriːˌlækˈseɪʃən] *n* **1** RELAXING : relâchement *m*, desserrement *m* **2** DIVERSION : détente *f*
relay[1] [ˈriːˌleɪ, riˈleɪ] *vt* **-layed; -laying** : relayer
relay[2] [ˈriːˌleɪ] *n or* **relay race** : course *f* de relais
release[1] [riˈliːs] *vt* **-leased; -leasing 1** FREE : libérer **2** RELINQUISH : renoncer à (une réclamation, etc.) **3** RELIEVE : dégager <she was released from her promise : elle s'est dégagée de sa promesse> **4** : publier (un livre), sortir (un nouveau film), rendre public (un document, etc.) **5** LET GO, LOOSEN : desserrer, déclencher <to release the clutch : débrayer>
release[2] *n* **1** RELIEF : soulagement *m* (à la douleur) **2** LIBERATION : libération *f*, mise *f* en liberté **3** ISSUE : sortie *f* (d'un film), parution *f* (d'un livre) **4** : déclenchement *m* (d'un mécanisme) **5** *or* **news release** : communiqué *m*
relegate [ˈrɛləˌgeɪt] *vt* **-gated; -gating** : reléguer
relent [rɪˈlɛnt] *vi* **1** GIVE IN : se rendre **2** ABATE : se calmer
relentless [rɪˈlɛntləs] *adj* : implacable, impitoyable — **relentlessly** *adv*
relevance [ˈrɛləvənts] *n* : pertinence *f*
relevant [ˈrɛləvənt] *adj* : pertinent
relevantly [ˈrɛləvəntli] *adv* : pertinemment
reliability [rɪˌlaɪəˈbɪlət̬i] *n, pl* **-ties 1** : sérieux *m*, intégrité *f* (d'une personne) **2** : fiabilité *f* (d'information, d'une machine, etc.)
reliable [rɪˈlaɪəbəl] *adj* : fiable, sûr
reliance [rɪˈlaɪənts] *n* **1** DEPENDENCE : dépendance *f* **2** TRUST : confiance *f*
reliant [rɪˈlaɪənt] *adj* **1** DEPENDENT : dépendant **2** TRUSTING : confiant

relic ['rɛlɪk] *n* **1** : relique *f* **2 relics** *mpl* : vestiges *mpl* (du passé)

relief [rɪ'li:f] *n* **1** : soulagement *m* <much to my relief : à mon grand soulagement> **2** AID, WELFARE : aide *f* (sociale) **3** : relief *m* <a relief map : une carte en relief> **4** REPLACEMENT : relève *f,* équipe *f* de relève

relieve [rɪ'li:v] *vt* **-lieved; -lieving 1** MITIGATE : soulager, alléger **2** UNBURDEN : libérer, débarasser <to relieve s.o. of his suitcase : débarasser qqn de ses valises> <to be relieved of a command : être relevé d'une fonction> **3** AID : secourir , venir en aide à **4** ALLEVIATE : brisser (la monotonie), dissiper (la mélancolie), égayer (le noirceur de vêtements, etc.)

religion [rɪ'lɪdʒən] *n* : religion *f*

religious [rɪ'lɪdʒəs] *adj* : religieux **— religiously** *adv*

relinquish [rɪ'lɪŋkwɪʃ, -'lɪn-] *vt* **1** GIVE UP : renoncer à, abandonner **2** RELEASE : relâcher

relish[1] ['rɛlɪʃ] *vt* **1** : savourer (le boire et le manger) **2** ENJOY : se réjouir de, savourer (une idée, etc.)

relish[2] *n* **1** ENJOYMENT : plaisir *m,* délectation *f* **2** : condiment *m* à base de cornichons et de vinaigre, relish *f Can*

relive [ˌri:'lɪv] *vi* **-lived; -living** : revivre

relocate [ˌri:'lo:ˌkeɪt, ˌri:lo'keɪt] *v* **-cated; -cating** *vt* : muter, transférer <to relocate an employee : muter un employé> **—** *vi* : déménager, s'établir ailleurs

relocation [ˌri:lo'keɪʃən] *n* **1** : mutation *f,* transfert *m* (d'un employé) **2** : déménagement *m* (d'une firme, etc.)

reluctance [rɪ'lʌktənts] *n* : réticence *f,* répugnance *f*

reluctant [rɪ'lʌktənt] *adj* **to be reluctant to** : être peu enclin à, être peu disposé à

reluctantly [rɪ'lʌktəntli] *adv* : à contrecœur

rely [rɪ'laɪ] *vi* **-lied**; **-lying 1** DEPEND : compter (sur), dépendre (de) **2** TRUST : se fier (à)

remain [rɪ'meɪn] *vi* **1** : rester <only ruins remain : il ne reste que des ruines> **2** STAY : rester, demeurer **3 it remains to be seen** : il reste à voir **4 the fact remains that** : toujours est-il que

remainder [rɪ'meɪndər] *n* : reste *m,* restant *m*

remains [rɪ'meɪnz] *npl* **1** : restes *mpl* <the remains of a meal : les restes d'un repas> **2** *or* **last remains** : restes *mpl,* dépouille *f* mortelle

remark[1] [rɪ'mɑrk] *vt* **1** NOTICE : remarquer, constater **2** SAY : remarquer, mentionner **—** *vi* **to remark on** : faire des remarques sur

remark[2] *n* : remarque *f,* observation *f*

remarkable [rɪ'mɑrkəbəl] *adj* : remarquable, extraordinaire **— remarkably** [-bli] *adv*

remedial [rɪ'mi:diəl] *adj* : de rattrapage

remedy[1] ['rɛmədi] *vt* **-died; -dying** : remédier à

remedy[2] *n, pl* **-dies** : remède *m* (en médecine)

remember [rɪ'mɛmbər] *vt* **1** RECOLLECT : se rappeler, se souvenir de **2** : penser à, ne pas oublier de <remember to open the window : pensez à ouvrir la fenêtre, n'oubliez pas d'ouvrir la fenêtre> **3** COMMEMORATE : commémorer **4 remember me to your sister** : rappelez-moi au bon souvenir de votre sœur

remembrance [rɪ'mɛmbrənts] *n* **1** RECOLLECTION : mémoire *f,* souvenir *m* **2** KEEPSAKE : souvenir *m*

remind [rɪ'maɪnd] *vt* : rappeler <remind me to do it : rappelle-moi de le faire>

reminder [rɪ'maɪndər] *n* : rappel *m*

reminisce [ˌrɛmə'nɪs] *vi* : évoquer ses souvenirs

reminiscence [ˌrɛmə'nɪsənts] *n* **1** MEMORY : souvenir *m* **2** RECALLING : réminiscence *f*

reminiscent [ˌrɛmə'nɪsənt] *adj* **1** NOSTALGIC : nostalgique **2 ~ of** : qui rappelle, qui fait penser à

remiss [rɪ'mɪs] *adj* : négligent, inattentif

remission [rɪ'mɪʃən] *n* : rémission *f*

remit [rɪ'mɪt] *vt* **-mitted; -mitting 1** PARDON : remettre <to remit s.o.'s debt : remettre la dette de qqn> **2** SEND : envoyer (de l'argent)

remittance [rɪ'mɪtənts] *n* : paiement *m,* envoi *m*

remnant ['rɛmnənt] *n* : reste *m,* restant *m*

remodel [rɪ'mɑdəl] *vt* **-eled** *or* **-elled; -eling** *or* **-elling** : remodeler

remonstrate ['rɛmənˌstreɪt, rɪ'mɑn-] *vi* **-strated; -strating** : protester <to remonstrate with : faire des remontrances à>

remorse [rɪ'mɔrs] *n* : remords *m*

remorseful [rɪ'mɔrsfəl] *adj* : plein de remords, contrit

remorseless [rɪ'mɔrsləs] *adj* **1** MERCILESS : sans remords, sans pitié **2** RELENTLESS : impitoyable, implacable

remote [rɪ'mo:t] *adj* **remoter; -est 1** : lointain, éloigné <the remote past : le passé lointain> **2** SECLUDED : retiré, isolé **3** : à distance <remote control : commande à distance> **4** SLIGHT : petit, faible <there's a remote chance : c'est très peu probable> **5** ALOOF : indifférent

remotely [rɪ'mo:tli] *adv* SLIGHTLY : faiblement, vaguement

remoteness [rɪ'mo:tnəs] *n* : isolement *m,* éloignement *m*

removable [rɪ'mu:vəbəl] *adj* : amovible

removal [rɪ'mu:vəl] *n* **1** ELIMINATION : suppression *f* (d'abus, etc.), enlèvement *m* (de tâches) **2** : ablation *f* (en médecine) **3** : renvoi (d'un employé), révocation *f* (d'un fonctionnaire)
remove [rɪ'mu:v] *vt* **-moved; -moving 1** : enlever, ôter <remove the lid : enlevez le couvercle> <to remove one's coat : ôter son manteau> **2** DISMISS : renvoyer (un employé), démettre (un fonctionnaire) **3** ELIMINATE : supprimer (une menace), écarter (un obstacle), dissiper (la peur)
remunerate [rɪ'mju:nə,reɪt] *vt* **-ated; -ating** : rémunérer
remuneration [rɪ,mju:nə'reɪʃən] *n* : rémunération *f*
remunerative [rɪ'mju:nərət̬ɪv, -,reɪ-] *adj* : rémunérateur, lucratif
renaissance [,rɛnə'sɑnts, -'zɑnts; 'rɛnə,-] *n* **1** : renaissance *f* **2 the Renaissance** : la Renaissance
renal ['ri:nəl] *adj* : rénal
rename [,ri:'neɪm] *vt* **-named; -naming** : rebaptiser
rend ['rɛnd] *vt* **rent** ['rɛnt]; **rending** : déchirer
render ['rɛndər] *vt* **1** EXTRACT : fondre (de la graisse) **2** GIVE UP : rendre, retourner **3** : rendre (un service), prêter (de l'aide) **4** MAKE : laisser, rendre <she was rendered helpless by the blow : le coup l'a laissée complètement impuissante> **5** PERFORM : interpréter (une chanson, etc.)
rendezvous ['rɑndɪ,vu:, -deɪ-] *ns & pl* : rendez-vous *m*
rendition [rɛn'dɪʃən] *n* : interprétation *f*
renegade ['rɛnɪ,geɪd] *n* : renégat *m*, -gate *f*
renege [rɪ'nɪg, -'nɛg] *vi* **-neged; -neging** : revenir (sur une promesse, etc.)
renew [rɪ'nu:, -'nju:] *vt* **1** REVIVE : raviver (la force, le courage, etc.) **2** RESUME : renouveler, reprendre <to renew one's efforts : renouveler ses efforts> **3** EXTEND : renouveler (un passeport, un abonnement, etc.)
renewable [rɪ'nu:əbəl, -'nju:-] *adj* : renouvelable
renewal [rɪ'nu:əl, -'nju:-] *n* : renouvellement *m*
renounce [rɪ'naʊnts] *vt* **-nounced; -nouncing 1** : renoncer à, abandonner <to renounce the throne : renoncer au trône> **2** REPUDIATE : renier, rejeter
renovate ['rɛnə,veɪt] *vt* **-vated; -vating** : rénover
renovation [,rɛnə'veɪʃən] *n* : rénovation *f*, restoration *f*
renown [rɪ'naʊn] *n* : renommée *f*, renom *m*
renowned [rɪ'naʊnd] *adj* : renommé, célèbre
rent[1] ['rɛnt] *vt* : louer
rent[2] *n* **1** : loyer *m* (somme d'argent) **2** TEAR : déchirure *f* **3 for ~** : à louer
rental[1] ['rɛntəl] *adj* : de location <rental car : voiture de location>
rental[2] *n* **1** : location *f* <film rentals : location de films> **2** RENT : loyer *m*
renter ['rɛntər] *n* : locataire *mf*
renunciation [rɪ,nʌntsi'eɪʃən] *n* : renonciation *f*
repair[1] [rɪ'pær] *vt* : réparer
repair[2] *n* **1** : réparation *f* <car repair : réparation de voiture> **2** CONDITION : état *m*, condition *f* <in bad repair : en mauvais état>
reparations [,rɛpə'reɪʃənz] *npl* DAMAGES : réparations *fpl*
repartee [,rɛpər'ti:, -,pɑr-, -'teɪ] *n* : repartie *f*, réplique *f*
repast [rɪ'pæst, 'ri:,pæst] *n* : repas *m*
repatriate [ri'peɪtri,eɪt] *vt* **-ated; -ating** : rapatrier
repay [ri'peɪ] *vt* **-paid; -paying** : rembourser (un emprunt), rendre (une faveur, etc.)
repeal[1] [rɪ'pi:l] *vt* : abroger
repeal[2] *n* : abrogation *f*
repeat[1] [rɪ'pi:t] *vt* : répéter — *vi* : se répéter
repeat[2] *n* **1** REPETITION : répétition *f* **2** : rediffusion *f*, reprise *f* <the show is a repeat : l'émission est en rediffusion>
repeatedly [rɪ'pi:t̬ədli] *adv* : à plusieurs reprises
repel [rɪ'pɛl] *vt* **-pelled; -pelling 1** : repousser (l'ennemi, etc.) **2** REJECT : rejeter **3** RESIST : résister à **4** DISGUST : repousser, répugner
repellent[1] [rɪ'pɛlənt] *adj* : repoussant, répugnant
repellent[2] *n or* **insect repellent** : insectifuge *m*
repent [rɪ'pɛnt] *vi* : se repentir
repentance [rɪ'pɛntənts] *n* : repentir *m*
repentant [rɪ'pɛntənt] *adj* : repentant
repercussion [,ri:pər'kʌʃən, ,rɛpər-] *n* : répercussion *f*
repertoire ['rɛpər,twɑr] *n* : répertoire *m*
repertory ['rɛpər,tori] *n, pl* **-ries 1** → **repertoire 2** *or* **repertory theater** : théâtre *m* de répertoire
repetition [,rɛpə'tɪʃən] *n* : répétition *f*
repetitious [,rɛpə'tɪʃəs] *adj* : répétitif
repetitive [rɪ'pɛt̬ət̬ɪv] *adj* : répétitif
repetitively [rɪ'pɛt̬ət̬ɪvli] *adv* : de façon répétitive
replace [rɪ'pleɪs] *vt* **-placed; -placing 1** RESTORE : remettre **2** SUBSTITUTE : remplacer, substituer
replaceable [rɪ'pleɪsəbəl] *adj* : remplaçable
replacement [rɪ'pleɪsmənt] *n* **1** REPLACING : remplacement *m* **2** SUBSTITUTE : remplaçant *m*, -çante *f*
replenish [rɪ'plɛnɪʃ] *vt* : remplir (de nouveau)

replenishment [rɪ'plɛnɪʃmənt] *n* : remplissage *m*
replete [rɪ'pli:t] *adj* **1** FULL : rempli <replete with details : rempli de détails> **2** SATIATED : rassasié
replica ['rɛplɪkə] *n* : copie *f* exacte, réplique *f*
replicate ['rɛplə͵keɪt] *vt* **-cated; -cating** : reproduire, faire un double de
reply[1] [rɪ'plaɪ] *vi* **-plied; -plying** : répondre, répliquer
reply[2] *n, pl* **-plies** : réponse *f,* réplique *f*
report[1] [rɪ'port] *vt* **1** RELATE : raconter, faire le compte rendu de **2** : faire un reportage sur (en journalisme) **3** : signaler (un feu, un crime, etc.), dénoncer (un malfaiteur) — *vi* **1** : faire un rapport **2** : se présenter <to report for duty : se présenter au travail>
report[2] *n* **1** RUMOR : rumeur *f* **2** REPUTE : réputation *f* <of good report : de bonne réputation> **3** ACCOUNT : rapport *m,* compte rendu *m* **4** : détonation *f* (d'un fusil) **5** : bulletin *m* <weather report : bulletin météorologique> **6** *or* **news report** : reportage *m*
report card *n* : bulletin *m* scolaire
reportedly [rɪ'portədli] *adv* : à ce que l'on dit
reporter [rɪ'portər] *n* : journaliste *mf,* reporter *m*
repose[1] [rɪ'po:z] *vi* **-posed; -posing** : se reposer, relaxer
repose[2] *n* **1** REST : repos *m* **2** PEACE : tranquillité *f,* calme *f*
repository [rɪ'pɑzə͵tori] *n, pl* **-ries** : dépôt *m,* entrepôt *m*
repossess [͵ri:pə'zɛs] *vt* : reprendre possession de, saisir
repossession [͵ri:pə'zɛʃən] *n* : reprise *f* de possession
reprehend [͵rɛpri'hɛnd] *vt* : réprimander, critiquer
reprehensible [͵rɛpri'hɛntsəbəl] *adj* : répréhensible
reprehensibly [͵rɛpri'hɛntsəbli] *adv* : de façon répréhensible
represent [͵rɛprɪ'zɛnt] *vt* **1** PORTRAY : représenter, dépeindre **2** SYMBOLIZE : représenter <the flag represents our country : le drapeau représente notre pays> **3** : représenter <an attorney who represents his client : un avocat qui représente son client>
representation [͵rɛprɪ͵zɛn'teɪʃən, -zən-] *n* : représentation *f*
representative[1] [͵rɛprɪ'zɛntətɪv] *adj* : représentatif
representative[2] *n* : représentant *m,* -tante *f*
repress [rɪ'prɛs] *vt* : réprimer
repression [rɪ'prɛʃən] *n* : répression *f*
repressive [rɪ'prɛsɪv] *adj* : répressif
reprieve[1] [rɪ'pri:v] *vt* **-prievd; -prieving** : accorder un sursis à
reprieve[2] *n* **1** : remise *f* de peine (en droit) **2** RESPITE : délai *m,* sursis *m,* répit *m*
reprimand[1] ['rɛprə͵mænd] *vt* : réprimander
reprimand[2] *n* : réprimande *f*
reprint[1] [rɪ'prɪnt] *vt* : réimprimer
reprint[2] ['ri:͵prɪnt, ri'prɪnt] *n* : réimpression *f*
reprisal [rɪ'praɪzəl] *n* : représailles *fpl*
reproach[1] [rɪ'pro:tʃ] *vt* : reprocher à, faire des reproches à
reproach[2] *n* **1** REBUKE : reproche *m* **2** **beyond ~** : irréprochable, au-dessus de tout reproche
reproachful [rɪ'pro:tʃfəl] *adj* : de reproche, réprobateur
reproachfully [rɪ'pro:tʃfəli] *adv* : d'un ton réprobateur
reproduce [͵ri:prə'du:s, -'dju:s] *v* **-duced; -ducing** *vt* : reproduire — *vi* : se reproduire
reproduction [͵ri:prə'dʌkʃən] *n* : reproduction *f*
reproductive [͵ri:prə'dʌktɪv] *adj* : reproducteur
reproof [rɪ'pru:f] *n* : réprimande *f*
reprove [rɪ'pru:v] *vt* **-proved; -proving** : réprimander, réprouver
reptile ['rɛp͵taɪl] *n* : reptile *m*
republic [rɪ'pʌblɪk] *n* : république *f*
republican[1] [rɪ'pʌblɪkən] *adj* : républicain
republican[2] *n* : républicain *m,* -caine *f*
repudiate [rɪ'pju:di͵eɪt] *vt* **-ated; -ating** **1** DISOWN : répudier, rejeter **2** : refuser d'honorer (une dette, etc.)
repudiation [rɪ͵pju:di'eɪʃən] *n* **1** : répudiation *f,* désaveu *m* **2** : refus *m* d'honerer (une dette)
repugnance [rɪ'pʌgnənts] *n* : répugnance *f,* aversion *f*
repugnant [rɪ'pʌgnənt] *adj* : répugnant
repulse[1] [rɪ'pʌls] *vt* **-pulsed; -pulsing** **1** REBUFF, REPEL : repousser **2** DISGUST : repousser, dégoûter
repulse[2] *n* REBUFF : rejet *m,* rebuffade *f*
repulsive [rɪ'pʌlsɪv] *adj* : repoussant, répugnant
repulsively [rɪ'pʌlsɪvli] *adv* : de façon répugnante
reputable ['rɛpjətəbəl] *adj* : de bonne réputation
reputation [͵rɛpjə'teɪʃən] *n* : réputation *f*
repute [rɪ'pju:t] *n* **1** : réputation *f* **2** **to hold s.o. in high repute** : tenir qqn en haute estime
reputed [rɪ'pju:təd] *adj* **1** CONSIDERED : réputé **2** **to be reputed to be** : avoir la réputation d'être
reputedly [rɪ'pju:tədli] *adv* : d'après ce que l'on dit
request[1] [rɪ'kwɛst] *vt* ASK : demander
request[2] *n* : demande *f,* requête *f*
requiem ['rɛkwiəm, 'reɪ-] *n* : requiem *m*

require [rɪ'kwaɪr] *vt* **-quired; -quiring 1** CALL FOR : demander, exiger **2** NEED : avoir besoin de
requirement [rɪ'kwaɪrmənt] *n* **1** NEED : besoin *m* **2** CONDITION : exigence *f*, condition *f*
requisite[1] ['rɛkwəzɪt] *adj* : nécessaire, essentiel
requisite[2] *n* : nécessité *f*
requisition[1] [ˌrɛkwə'zɪʃən] *vt* : réquisitionner
requisition[2] *n* : réquisition *f*
reread [ˌri:'ri:d] *vt* **-read** [-'rɛd]; **-reading** : relire
reroute [ˌri:'ru:t, -'raʊt] *vt* **-routed; -routing** : dérouter, changer l'itinéraire de
resale ['ri:ˌseɪl, ˌri:'seɪl] *n* : revente *f*
reschedule [ri:'skɛˌdʒu:l, -dʒəl] *vt* **-uled; -uling** : changer l'heure ou la date de
rescind [rɪ'sɪnd] *vt* : annuler (une commande), résilier (un contrat)
rescue[1] ['rɛsˌkju:] *vt* **-cued; -cuing** : sauver, secourir
rescue[2] *n* : sauvetage *m*
rescuer ['rɛsˌkju:ər] *n* : sauveteur *m*, secouriste *mf*
research[1] [rɪ'sərtʃ, 'ri:ˌsərtʃ] *vt* : faire des recherches sur
research[2] *n* : recherches *fpl*
researcher [rɪ'sərtʃər, 'ri:ˌ-] *n* : chercheur *m*, -cheuse *f*
resemblance [rɪ'zɛmbləntṡ] *n* : ressemblance *f*
resemble [rɪ'zɛmbəl] *vt* **-sembled; -sembling** : ressembler à
resent [rɪ'zɛnt] *vt* : en vouloir à, éprouver de l'amertume envers
resentful [rɪ'zɛntfəl] *adj* : plein de ressentiment
resentfully [rɪ'zɛntfəli] *adv* : avec ressentiment
resentment [rɪ'zɛntmənt] *n* : ressentiment *m*
reservation [ˌrɛzər'veɪʃən] *n* **1** RESERVING : réservation *f* **2** : réserve *f* <Indian reservation : réserve indienne> **3 without ~** : sans réserve
reserve[1] [rɪ'zərv] *vt* **-served; -serving** : réserver
reserve[2] *n* **1** SUPPLY : réserve *f*, provision *f* **2** : réserve *f* (dans les forces armées) **3** RESTRAINT : réserve *f*, discrétion *f*
reserved [rɪ'zərvd] *adj* : réservé, discret
reservoir ['rɛzərˌvwɑr, -ˌvwɔr, -ˌvɔr] *n* : réservoir *m*
reset [ˌri:'sɛt] *vt* **-set; -setting** : remettre à l'heure (une montre), remettre à zéro (un compteur)
reside [rɪ'zaɪd] *vi* **-sided; -siding 1** DWELL : résider **2 to reside in** : résider dans
residence ['rɛzədənts] *n* **1** DWELLING : résidence *f*, demeure *f* **2** *or* **residence hall** : résidence *f* (universitaire)
resident[1] ['rɛzədənt] *adj* **1** RESIDING : résidant **2** : à demeure <resident doctors : médecins à demeure>
resident[2] *n* : résident *m*, -dente *f*
residential [ˌrɛzə'dɛntʃəl] *adj* : résidentiel
residual [rɪ'zɪdʒuəl] *adj* : résiduel
residue ['rɛzəˌdu:, -ˌdju:] *n* : résidu *m*, reste *m*
resign [ri'zaɪn] *vi* QUIT : démissionner — *vt* **to resign oneself to** : se résigner à
resignation [ˌrɛzɪg'neɪʃən] *n* **1** RESIGNING : démission *f*, résignation *f* **2** ACCEPTANCE : résignation *f*
resignedly [rɪ'zaɪnədli] *adv* : avec résignation
resilience [rɪ'zɪljənts] *n* : élasticité *f*, résistance *f*
resilient [rɪ'zɪljənt] *adj* **1** STRONG : résistant, fort **2** ELASTIC : élastique
resin ['rɛzən] *n* : résine *f*
resinous ['rɛzənəs] *adj* : résineux
resist [rɪ'zɪst] *vt* **1** WITHSTAND : résister à <to resist disease : résister à la maladie> **2** OPPOSE : s'opposer à, résister à
resistance [rɪ'zɪstənts] *n* : résistance *f*
resistant [rɪ'zɪstənt] *adj* : résistant <fire-resistant : qui résiste au feu>
resolute ['rɛzəˌlu:t] *adj* : résolu, décidé — **resolutely** *adv*
resolution [ˌrɛzə'lu:ʃən] *n* **1** SOLUTION : résolution *f* <conflict resolution : résolution de conflits> **2** RESOLVE : détermination *f*, résolution *f* **3** DECISION, PROMISE : résolution *f* <New Year's resolutions : résolutions du nouvel an> **4** MOTION, PROPOSAL : motion *f*, résolution *f* (legislative)
resolve[1] [rɪ'zɑlv] *v* **-solved; -solving** *vt* **1** SOLVE : résoudre (un problème) **2** DECIDE : (se) résoudre, décider — *vi* : se résoudre
resolve[2] *n* : résolution *f*, détermination *f*
resonance ['rɛzənənts] *n* : résonance *f*
resonant ['rɛzənənt] *adj* **1** : résonant (en physique) **2** : sonore (se dit des sons, des voix, etc.)
resort[1] [rɪ'zɔrt] *vi* **to resort to** : recourir à, avoir recours à
resort[2] *n* **1** RESOURCE : recours *m* <as a last resort : en dernier recours> **2** HAUNT : endroit *m* préféré, repaire *m* **3** : station *f* <ski resort : station de ski> <vacation resorts : lieux de villégiature>
resound [rɪ'zaʊnd] *vi* : résonner, retentir
resounding [rɪ'zaʊndɪŋ] *adj* : retentissant, éclatant <a resounding success : un succès retentissant>
resource ['ri:ˌsɔrs, ri'sɔrs] *n* : ressource *f* <natural resources : ressources naturelles> <to be left to one's own resources : être livré à soi-même>

resourceful [rɪ'sorsfəl, -'zors-] *adj* : ingénieux, plein de ressources
resourcefulness [rɪ'sorsfəlnəs, -'zors-] *n* : ingéniosité *f*
respect[1] [rɪ'spɛkt] *vt* : respecter
respect[2] *n* **1** ESTEEM : respect *m*, estime *f* **2** CONSIDERATION : considération *f*, respect *m* **3** DETAIL : respect *m*, égard *m* <in some respects : à certains égards> **4 respects** *npl* : respects *mpl*, hommages *mpl* <to pay one's respects to s.o. : présenter ses respects à qqn> **5 in respect to** : en ce qui concerne
respectability [rɪˌspɛktə'bɪləṭi] *n* : respectabilité *f*
respectable [rɪ'spɛktəbəl] *adj* **1** PROPER : respectable, correct <respectable people : gens respectables> **2** CONSIDERABLE : respectable, considérable, assez bon <a respectable amount : une somme respectable>
respectably [rɪ'spɛktəbli] *adv* : respectablement, convenablement
respectful [rɪ'spɛktfəl] *adj* : respectueux — **respectfully** *adv*
respective [rɪ'spɛktɪv] *adj* : respectif — **respectively** *adv*
respiration [ˌrɛspə'reɪʃən] *n* : respiration *f*
respirator ['rɛspəˌreɪṭər] *n* : respirateur *m*
respiratory ['rɛspərəˌtori, rɪ'spaɪrə-] *adj* : respiratoire
respite ['rɛspət] *n* : répit *m*, sursis *m*
resplendent [rɪ'splɛndənt] *adj* : resplendissant
respond [rɪ'spɑnd] *vi* **1** ANSWER : répondre **2** REACT : réagir <I didn't respond well to the surgery : j'ai mal réagi à la chirurgie> <to respond to pressure : céder aux pressions>
response [rɪ'spɑnts] *n* **1** ANSWER : réponse *f* **2** REACTION : réaction *f*, réponse *f*
responsibility [rɪˌspɑntsə'bɪləṭi] *n, pl* **-ties** : responsabilité *f*
responsible [rɪ'spɑntsəbəl] *adj* : responsable
responsibly [rɪ'spɑntsəbli] *adv* : de manière responsable
responsive [rɪ'spɑntsɪv] *adj* : sensible, réceptif
rest[1] ['rɛst] *vi* **1** RELAX, REPOSE : se reposer <to rest easy : être tranquille> **2** DEPEND : reposer, dépendre <the decision rests with me : la décision dépend de moi> **3 to rest on** *or* **to rest against** : reposer sur, être appuyé sur — *vt* **1** : reposer <rest your eyes now and then : reposez-vous la vue de temps à autre> **2** PLACE : placer, mettre <I rest all my hopes in him : je place tous mes espoirs en lui>
rest[2] *n* **1** REPOSE : repos *m* **2** BREAK : repos *m*, pause *f* **3** SUPPORT : appui *m*, support *m* **4** REMAINDER : reste *m* **5** : pause *f* (en musique) **6 rest area** : aire *f* de repos, halte *f* routière *Can*
restart [riː'stɑrt] *vt* : remettre en marche (un moteur)
restaurant ['rɛstəˌrɑnt, -rənt] *n* : restaurant *m*
restful ['rɛstfəl] *adj* : reposant
restitution [ˌrɛstə'tuːʃən, -'tjuː-] *n* : restitution *f*
restive ['rɛstɪv] *adj* : agité, nerveux
restless ['rɛstləs] *adj* : agité, nerveux, impatient <a restless night : une nuit agitée>
restlessly ['rɛstləsli] *adv* : nerveusement, avec impatience
restlessness ['rɛstləsnəs] *n* : nervosité *f*, agitation *f*
restoration [ˌrɛstə'reɪʃən] *n* **1** : restitution *f*, rétablissement *m* (de la paix, de l'ordre, etc.) **2** : restauration *f* (d'une peinture, d'un édifice, etc.)
restore [rɪ'stor] *vt* **-stored; -storing 1** RETURN : rendre, restituer **2** RENOVATE : restaurer, rénover **3** REESTABLISH : rétablir, retrouver <to restore peace : rétablir la paix> <to be restored to health : être rétabli> <to have one's sight restored : recouvrer la vue>
restrain [rɪ'streɪn] *vt* **1** PREVENT : empêcher, retenir **2** CURB : contenir, refréner
restrained [rɪ'streɪnd] *adj* **1** : sobre <restrained style : style sobre> **2** RESERVED : réservé, contenu
restraining order *n* : injonction *f*
restraint [rɪ'streɪnt] *n* **1** RESTRICTION : restriction *f*, contrainte *f* **2** RESERVE, SELF-CONTROL : retenue *f*, mesure *f*
restrict [rɪ'strɪkt] *vt* : restreindre, limiter
restricted [rɪ'strɪktəd] *adj* **1** LIMITED : restreint, limité **2** CLASSIFIED : secret, confidentiel
restriction [rɪ'strɪkʃən] *n* : restriction *f*, limitation *f*
restrictive [rɪ'strɪktɪv] *adj* : restrictif
restructure [riː'strʌktʃər] *vt* **-tured; -turing** : restructurer
result[1] [rɪ'zʌlt] *vi* **1 to result from** : résulter de, provenir de **2 to result in** : avoir pour résultat, aboutir à
result[2] *n* : résultat *m*, conséquence *f*
resultant [rɪ'zʌltənt] *adj* : résultant
resume [rɪ'zuːm] *v* **-sumed; -suming** *vt* : reprendre — *vi* : reprendre, recommencer, continuer
résumé *or* **resume** *or* **resumé** ['rɛzəˌmeɪ, ˌrɛzə'-] *n* **1** SUMMARY : résumé *m* **2** : curriculum *m* vitæ
resumption [rɪ'zʌmpʃən] *n* : reprise *f*
resurface [ˌriː'sərfəs] *vt* **-faced; -facing** : refaire le revêtement de (une route)
resurgence [rɪ'sərdʒənts] *n* : résurgence *f*, réapparition *f*
resurgent [rɪ'sərdʒənt] *adj* : renaissant

resurrect [ˌrɛzəˈrɛkt] *vt* : ressusciter
resurrection [ˌrɛzəˈrɛkʃən] *n* : résurrection *f*
resuscitate [rɪˈsʌsəˌteɪt] *vt* **-tated; -tating** : réanimer
resuscitation [rɪˌsʌsəˈteɪʃən, ˌri-] *n* : réanimation *f*
retail[1] [ˈriːˌteɪl] *vt* : vendre au détail
retail[2] *adv* : au détail
retail[3] *adj* : de détail <retail store : magasin de détail>
retail[4] *n* : vente *f* au détail
retailer [ˈriːˌteɪlər] *n* : détaillant *m*, -lante *f*
retain [rɪˈteɪn] *vt* **1** KEEP : garder, retenir **2** HOLD : retenir, conserver <lead retains heat : le plomb conserve la chaleur> **3** ENGAGE : engager (les services de qqn)
retainer [rɪˈteɪnər] *n* **1** SERVANT : domestique *mf* **2** ADVANCE : provision *f*
retaliate [rɪˈtæliˌeɪt] *vi* **-ated; -ating** : riposter, se venger <to retaliate against : user de représailles envers>
retaliation [rɪˌtæliˈeɪʃən] *n* : riposte *f*, représailles *fpl*
retard [rɪˈtɑrd] *vt* : retarder
retarded [riˈtɑrdəd] *adj* : arriéré
retch [ˈrɛtʃ] *vi* : avoir des haut-le-cœur
retention [rɪˈtɛntʃən] *n* : rétention *f*
retentive [rɪˈtɛntɪv] *adj* : qui retient bien <a retentive memory : une mémoire fidèle>
reticence [ˈrɛt̬əsən*t*s] *n* : réticence *f*, hésitation *f*
reticent [ˈrɛt̬əsənt] *adj* : réticent, hésitant
reticently [ˈrɛt̬əsəntli] *adv* : avec réticence
retina [ˈrɛtənə] *n, pl* **-nas** *or* **-nae** [-ənˌiː, -ənˌaɪ] : rétine *f*
retinue [ˈrɛtənˌuː, -ˌjuː] *n* : suite *f*, escorte *f*
retire [rɪˈtaɪr] *vi* **-tired; -tiring 1** WITHDRAW : se retirer, partir **2** : prendre sa retraite <he retired at 65 : il a pris sa retraite à 65 ans> **3** : aller se coucher
retiree [rɪˌtaɪˈriː] *n* : retraité *m*, -tée *f*
retirement [rɪˈtaɪrmənt] *n* : retraite *f*
retiring [rɪˈtaɪrɪŋ] *adj* : réservé, timide
retort[1] [rɪˈtɔrt] *vt* : rétorquer, riposter
retort[2] *n* : réplique *f*, riposte *f*
retrace [ˌriːˈtreɪs] *vt* **-traced; -tracing** : reconstituer <to retrace one's steps : revenir sur ses pas>
retract [rɪˈtrækt] *vt* **1** : rétracter (ses griffes, ses cornes etc.) **2** WITHDRAW : rétracter, retirer — *vi* : se rétracter
retractable [rɪˈtræktəbəl] *adj* : escamotable
retrain [ˌriːˈtreɪn] *vt* : recycler
retreat[1] [rɪˈtriːt] *vi* : se retirer, reculer
retreat[2] *n* **1** WITHDRAWAL : retraite *f*, recul *m* **2** REFUGE : retraite *f*, abri *m*
retrench [rɪˈtrɛntʃ] *vt* : réduire, restreindre (les dépenses) — *vi* : faire des économies
retribution [ˌrɛtrəˈbjuːʃən] *n* : châtiment *m*, punition *f*
retrieval [rɪˈtriːvəl] *n* : récupération *f* <text retrieval : récupération d'un texte> <beyond retrieval : irrécupérable>
retrieve [rɪˈtriːv] *vt* **-trieved; -trieving 1** : rapporter <to retrieve game : rapporter du gibier> **2** RECOVER : récupérer
retriever [rɪˈtriːvər] *n* : chien *m* d'arrêt
retroactive [ˌrɛtroˈæktɪv] *adj* : rétroactif — **retroactively** *adv*
retrograde [ˈrɛtrəˌgreɪd] *adj* : rétrograde
retrospect [ˈrɛtrəˌspɛkt] *n* **in ~** : rétrospectivement
retrospective [ˌrɛtrəˈspɛktɪv] *adj* : rétrospectif — **retrospectively** *adv*
return[1] [rɪˈtərn] *vi* **1** : retourner, rentrer <to return home : retourner à la maison> **2 to return to** : reprendre, revenir à <she returned to her old habits : elle a repris ses vieilles habitudes> — *vt* **1** RESTORE : rapporter, rendre <to return a book to the library : retourner un livre à la bibliothèque> **2** REPLACE : remettre **3** ANSWER : répondre, répliquer **4** YIELD : rapporter, produire **5** REPAY : retourner, rendre <to return the compliment : retourner le compliment> <to return a favor : en faire autant> **6** : rendre, prononcer <to return a verdict : rendre un verdict>
return[2] *adj* : aller et retour <a return ticket : un billet aller et retour>
return[3] *n* **1** : retour *m* <on their return : à leur retour> **2** YIELD : rapport *m*, rendement *m* **3** RETURNING : renvoi *m*, retour *m* (de marchandise) **4** *or* **income tax return** : déclaration *f* de revenus **5 returns** *npl* : résultats *mpl* (d'une élection)
reunion [riˈjuːnjən] *n* : réunion *f* <family reunion : réunion familiale>
reuse [riˈjuːz] *vt* **-used; -using** : réutiliser
revamp [ˌriːˈvæmp] *vt* : retaper (une maison), réviser (un texte)
reveal [rɪˈviːl] *vt* **1** DIVULGE : révéler, dévoiler (un secret) **2** SHOW : révéler, laisser voir
reveille [ˈrɛvəli] *n* : réveil *m* (dans les forces armées)
revel[1] [ˈrɛvəl] *vi* **-eled** *or* **-elled; -eling** *or* **-elling 1** : faire la fête **2 to revel in** : se délecter de
revel[2] *n* : festivités *fpl*
revelation [ˌrɛvəˈleɪʃən] *n* : révélation *f*
reveler *or* **reveller** [ˈrɛvələr] *n* : fêtard *m*, -tarde *f fam*
revelry [ˈrɛvəlri] *n* : festivités *fpl*, réjouissances *fpl*

revenge[1] [rɪ'vɛndʒ] *vt* **-venged; -venging** : venger <to revenge oneself on : se venger sur>
revenge[2] *n* : vengeance *f*
revenue ['rɛvəˌnuː, -ˌnjuː] *n* : revenu *m*
reverberate [rɪ'vərbəˌreɪt] *vi* **-ated; -ating** : retentir, résonner
reverberation [rɪˌvərbə'reɪʃən] *n* : réverbération *f*, retentissement *m*
revere [rɪ'vɪr] *vt* **-vered; -vering** : révérer, vénérer
reverence ['rɛvərənts] *n* : révérence *f*, vénération *f*
reverend ['rɛvərənd] *adj* **1** REVERED : vénérable **2** : révérend (en religion) <the Reverend Richard Parker : le révérend Richard Parker>
reverent ['rɛvərənt] *adj* : respectueux — **reverently** *adv*
reverie ['rɛvəri] *n, pl* **-eries** : rêverie *f*
reversal [rɪ'vərsəl] *n* : revirement *m* (d'opinion), renversement *m* (d'une situation)
reverse[1] [rɪ'vərs] *v* **-versed; -versing** *vt* **1** INVERT : inverser **2** CHANGE : renverser, retourner **3** ANNUL : annuler — *vi* : faire marche arrière (se dit d'une voiture)
reverse[2] *adj* : inverse, opposé <in reverse order : en ordre inverse>
reverse[3] *n* **1** OPPOSITE : contraire *m* **2** SETBACK : revers *m*, épreuve *f* **3** BACK : envers *m* **4** *or* **reverse gear** : marche *f* arrière
reversible [rɪ'vərsəbəl] *adj* : réversible
reversion [rɪ'vərʒən] *n* **1** : retour *m* <a reversion to paganism : un retour au paganisme> **2** : réversion *f* (en biologie)
revert [rɪ'vərt] *vi* **to revert to** : revenir à, retourner à
review[1] [rɪ'vjuː] *vt* **1** REEXAMINE : revoir, réviser **2** CRITICIZE : faire la critique de (un roman, etc.) **3** ASSESS, EXAMINE : examiner, faire le bilan de **4 to review the troops** : passer les troupes en revue
review[2] *n* **1** REAPPRAISAL : révision *f* **2** INSPECTION : revue *f* (militaire) **3** ANALYSIS, OVERVIEW : bilan *m*, examen *m* <to pass one's life in review : faire le bilan de sa vie> **4** EVALUATION : critique *f* **5** → **revue**
reviewer [rɪ'vjuːər] *n* : critique *mf* <book reviewer : critique littéraire>
revile [rɪ'vaɪl] *vt* **-viled; -viling** : injurier, vilipender
revise [rɪ'vaɪz] *vt* **-vised; -vising 1** CORRECT : réviser, revoir (un manuscrit, etc.) **2** UPDATE : réviser, mettre à jour **3** ALTER : réviser (une idée, une politique, etc.)
reviser *or* **revisor** [rɪ'vaɪzər] *n* : réviseur *m*; correcteur *m*, -trice *f*
revision [rɪ'vɪʒən] *n* : révision *f*
revival [rɪ'vaɪvəl] *n* **1** : renouveau *m*, renaissance *f* (d'intérêt, d'idées, etc.) **2** : rétablissement *m* (des coutumes) **3** : reprise *f* (en médecine) **4** *or* **revival meeting** : réunion *f* pour le renouveau de la foi
revive [rɪ'vaɪv] *v* **-vived; -viving** *vt* **1** REESTABLISH : rétablir (une tradition, etc.) **2** REAWAKEN : ranimer, raviver — *vi* **1** COME TO : reprendre connaissance **2** : renaître, se réveiller <hope revived in him : l'espoir renaissait en lui>
revoke [rɪ'voːk] *vt* **-voked; -voking** : révoquer, annuler
revolt[1] [rɪ'voːlt] *vt* DISGUST : révolter, dégoûter — *vi* **to revolt against** : se révolter contre
revolt[2] *n* : révolte *f*, insurrection *f*
revolting [rɪ'voːltɪŋ] *adj* : révoltant, dégoûtant
revolution [ˌrɛvə'luːʃən] *n* **1** ROTATION : révolution *f*, tour *m* **2** : révolution *f* <the French Revolution : la Révolution française> <a technological revolution : une révolution technologique>
revolutionary[1] [ˌrɛvə'luːʃənˌɛri] *adj* : révolutionnaire
revolutionary[2] *n* : révolutionnaire *mf*
revolutionize [ˌrɛvə'luːʃənˌaɪz] *vt* **-ized; -izing** : révolutionner
revolve [rɪ'vɑlv] *v* **-volved; -volving** *vt* ROTATE : faire tourner — *vi* **1** TURN : tourner <to revolve around : tourner autour> **2 to revolve around s.o.** : dépendre de qqn **3 to revolve in one's mind** : tourner et retourner dans son esprit
revolver [rɪ'vɑlvər] *n* : revolver *m*
revue [rɪ'vjuː] *n* : revue *f* (au théâtre)
revulsion [rɪ'vʌlʃən] *n* REPUGNANCE : répulsion *f*, répugnance *f*
reward[1] [rɪ'wɔrd] *vt* : récompenser
reward[2] *n* : récompense *f*
rewind [ˌriː'waɪnd] *vt* **-wound** [-'waʊnd]; **-winding** : rembobiner
rewrite [ˌriː'raɪt] *vt* **-wrote** [-'roːt]; **-written** [-'rɪtən]; **-writing** : récrire
rhapsody ['ræpsədi] *n, pl* **-dies 1** : rhapsodie *f* (en musique, en poésie) **2** RAPTURE : extase *f*
rhetoric ['rɛt̬ərɪk] *n* : rhétorique *f*
rhetorical [rɪ'tɔrɪkəl] *adj* : rhétorique
rheumatic [rʊ'mæt̬ɪk] *adj* : rhumatismal
rheumatism ['ruːməˌtɪzəm, 'rʊ-] *n* : rhumatisme *m*
rhinestone ['raɪnˌstoːn] *n* : faux diamant *m*
rhino ['raɪˌnoː] *n, pl* **rhino** *or* **rhinos** → **rhinoceros**
rhinoceros [raɪ'nɑsərəs] *n, pl* **-eroses** *or* **-eros** *or* **-eri** [-ˌraɪ] : rhinocéros *m*
rhododendron [ˌroːdə'dɛndrən] *n* : rhododendron *m*
rhombus ['rɑmbəs] *n, pl* **-buses** *or* **-bi** [-ˌbaɪ, -bi] : losange *m*
rhubarb ['ruːˌbɑrb] *n* : rhubarbe *f*
rhyme[1] ['raɪm] *v* **rhymed; rhyming** *vt* : faire rimer — *vi* : rimer

rhyme² *n* **1** : rime *m* **2** VERSE : vers *m* (en poésie)
rhythm ['rɪðəm] *n* : rythme *m*
rhythmic ['rɪðmɪk] *or* **rhythmical** [-mɪkəl] *adj* : rythmique — **rythmically** [-mɪkli] *adv*
rib¹ ['rɪb] *vt* **ribbed; ribbing 1** : faire aux côtes <ribbed fabric : tissu à côtes> **2** TEASE : taquiner
rib² *n* **1** : côte *f* (en anatomie) **2** : baleine *f* (d'un parapluie), nervure *f* (d'une feuille, en architecture, etc.), côte *f* (d'un tricot)
ribald ['rɪbəld] *adj* : grivois, paillard
ribbon ['rɪbən] *n* **1** : ruban *m* <silk ribbon : ruban de soie> <typewriter ribbon : ruban d'une machine à écrire> **2 in ribbons** : en lambeaux
rice ['raɪs] *n* : riz *m*
rich ['rɪtʃ] *adj* **1** WEALTHY : riche, aisé **2** SUMPTUOUS : somptueux, riche **3** : riche <rich food : aliments riches> **4** ABUNDANT : abondant **5** FERTILE : fertile, riche
riches ['rɪtʃəz] *npl* : richesses *fpl*
richly ['rɪtʃli] *adv* : richement, somptueusement
richness ['rɪtʃnəs] *n* : richesse *f*
rickets ['rɪkəts] *n* : rachitisme *m*
rickety ['rɪkət̬i] *adj* : branlant
ricksha *or* **rickshaw** ['rɪkˌʃɔ] *n* : pousse-pousse *m*
ricochet¹ ['rikəˌsheɪ] *vi* **-cheted** [-ˌʃeɪd] *or* **-chetted** [-ˌʃɛt̬əd]; **-cheting** [-ˌʃeɪɪŋ] *or* **-chetting** [-ˌʃɛt̬ɪŋ] : ricocher
ricochet² *n* : ricochet *m*
rid ['rɪd] *vt* **rid; ridding 1** : débarrasser <to rid a dog of fleas : débarrasser un chien de ses puces> **2 to rid oneself of** : se débarrasser de
riddance ['rɪdənts] *n* : débarras *m* <good riddance! : bon débarras!>
riddle¹ ['rɪdəl] *vt* **-dled; -dling** : cribler <to riddle with bullets : cribler de balles> <riddled with errors : plein de fautes>
riddle² *n* : énigme *f*, devinette *f*
ride¹ ['raɪd] *v* **rode** ['roːd]; **ridden** ['rɪdən]; **riding** *vt* **1** : monter à (un cheval), monter sur (une bicyclette), prendre (le bus, un taxi, etc.) **2** TRAVERSE : parcourir <he rode the countryside : il a parcouru tout le pays> **3** TEASE : taquiner **4** *or* **to ride out** WEATHER : réchapper à, surmonter **5 to ride the waves** : voguer sur les vagues (se dit d'une navire) — *vi* **1** : monter à cheval, aller à bicyclette **2** TRAVEL : aller <to ride in a bus : aller en autobus> **3 to ride at anchor** : être ancré **4 to let things ride** : laisser courir
ride² *n* **1** : tour *m*, promenade *f* <to go for a ride : aller faire un tour> **2** : manège *m* (à la foire) **3 to give s.o. a ride** : conduire qqn en voiture
rider ['raɪdər] *n* **1** HORSEMAN : cavalier *m*, -lière *f* **2** CYCLIST : cycliste *mf*, motocycliste *mf* **3** ANNEX : annexe *f* (en droit)
ridge ['rɪdʒ] *n* : chaîne *f* (de montagnes), crête *f* (d'un toit), billon *m* (dans un champ)
ridicule¹ ['rɪdəˌkjuːl] *vt* **-culed; -culing** : ridiculiser, tourner en ridicule
ridicule² *n* : moquerie *f*, dérision *f*
ridiculous [rə'dɪkjələs] *adj* : ridicule, absurde — **ridiculously** *adv*
rife ['raɪf] *adj* : abondant, répandu <to be rife with : être abondant en> <rumor was rife : les rumeurs allaient bon train>
riffraff ['rɪfˌræf] *n* : racaille *f*, canaille *f*
rifle¹ ['raɪfəl] *v* **-fled; -fling** *vt* RANSACK : fouiller — *vi* **to rifle through** : fouiller dans
rifle² *n* : carabine *f*, fusil *m*
rift ['rɪft] *n* **1** FISSURE : fente *f*, fissure *f* **2** BREACH : désaccord *m*, rupture *f* (entre personnes)
rig¹ ['rɪg] *vt* **rigged; rigging 1** : gréer (un navire) **2** CLOTHE, DRESS : habiller **3** FIX : truquer (les élections, etc.) **4** *or* **to rig up** : bricoler, monter <to rig up a shelter : bricoler un abri> **5 to rig out** EQUIP : équiper
rig² *n* **1** RIGGING : gréement *m* (d'un navire) **2** *or* **oil rig** : plate-forme *f* pétrolière
rigging ['rɪgɪŋ, -gən] *n* : gréement *m*
right¹ ['raɪt] *vt* **1** RESTORE : redresser <to right the economy : redresser l'économie> **2** REDRESS : réparer <to right a wrong : réparer un tort>
right² *adv* **1** CORRECTLY : bien, comme il faut <to answer right : bien répondre> <you're not doing it right : tu ne le fais pas comme il faut> **2** EXACTLY : exactement, précisément <the book is right where you left it : le livre est juste là, où tu l'as laissé> <right here : ici même> **3** DIRECTLY : directement <he went right home : il est rentré directement chez lui> **4** IMMEDIATELY : tout de suite <right after lunch : tout de suite après le déjeuner> **5** COMPLETELY : tout à fait, complètement <he felt right at home : il se sentait tout à fait à l'aise> <right to the end : jusqu'au bout> **6** : à droite <turn right : tournez à droite>
right³ *adj* **1** JUST, PROPER : juste, bien <it's not right : ce n'est pas bien> **2** CORRECT : bon, juste <the right answer : la bonne réponse> **3** SUITABLE : approprié, convenable <the right person for the job : la personne qui convient le mieux pour l'emploi> **4** STRAIGHT : droit <a right line : une ligne droite> **5** HEALTHY, SOUND : bien <she's not in her right mind : elle n'a pas toute sa raison> <the patient didn't look right : le patient n'avait pas l'air bien> **6** : droit <the right side : le côté droit>

right[4] *n* **1** GOOD : bien *m* <right against wrong : le bien contre le mal> **2** : droite *f* <to be on the right : être à droite> **3** ENTITLEMENT : droit *m* <to exercise a right : exercer un droit> <women's rights : les droits de la femme> **4 rights** *npl* : droits *mpl* <film rights : droits d'adaptation cinématographique> <all rights reserved : tous droits réservés>

right angle *n* : angle *m* droit

right–angled [ˈraɪtˈæŋgəld] *or* **right–angle** [-gəl] *adj* : à angle droit

righteous [ˈraɪtʃəs] *adj* : juste, vertueux — **righteously** *adv*

righteousness [ˈraɪtʃəsnəs] *n* : droiture *f*

rightful [ˈraɪtfəl] *adj* LAWFUL : légitime, véritable

rightfully [ˈraɪtfəli] *adv* : à juste titre, légitimement

right–hand [ˈraɪtˈhænd] *adj* **1** : du côté droit **2** RIGHT-HANDED : de la main droite **3 right–hand man** : bras *m* droit

right–handed [ˈraɪtˈhændəd] *adj* **1** : droitier <a right-handed pitcher : un lanceur droitier> **2** : de la main droite <a right-handed glove : un gant de la main droite>

rightly [ˈraɪtli] *adv* **1** FAIRLY : à juste titre **2** FITTINGLY : de façon appropriée **3** CORRECTLY : exactement, au juste

right–of–way [ˌraɪtəˈweɪ, -əv-] *n, pl* **rights–of–way** : priorité *f* (sur la route), droit *m* de passage (sur un terrain)

rightward [ˈraɪtwərd] *adv* : vers la droite

right–wing [ˈraɪtˈwɪŋ] *adj* : de droite (en politique)

right wing *n* **the right wing** : la droite

right–winger [ˈraɪtˈwɪŋər] *n* : personne *f* de droite

rigid [ˈrɪdʒɪd] *adj* **1** STIFF : rigide, raide **2** STRICT : rigide, sévère

rigidity [rɪˈdʒɪdəti] *n, pl* **-ties 1** STIFFNESS : rigidité *f* **2** STRICTNESS : rigidité *f*, inflexibilité *f*

rigmarole [ˈrɪgməˌroːl, ˈrɪgə-] *n* **1** NONSENSE : galimatias *m* **2** PROCEDURE : procédure *f* compliquée

rigor *or Brit* **rigour** [ˈrɪgər] *n* **1** SEVERITY : rigueur *f*, sévérité *f* **2** EXACTNESS : rigueur *f*, précision *f* **3 rigors** *npl* HARSHNESS : rigueurs *fpl*, intempéries *fpl* <the rigors of winter : les rigueurs de l'hiver>

rigorous [ˈrɪgərəs] *adj* **1** STRICT : rigoureux, sévère **2** HARSH : rigoureux, rude

rigorously [ˈrɪgərəsli] *adv* : rigoureusement, sévèrement

rile [ˈraɪl] *vt* **riled; riling** : énerver, mettre en colère

rill [ˈrɪl] *n* : ruisselet *m*

rim[1] [ˈrɪm] *vt* **rimmed; rimming** BORDER : border, entourer

rim[2] *n* **1** : bord *m* <the rim of a cup : le bord d'une tasse> **2** : jante *f* (d'une roue)

rime [ˈraɪm] *n* : givre *m*

rind [ˈraɪnd] *n* : écorce *f*

ring[1] [ˈrɪŋ] *vt* **ringed; ringing** SURROUND : encercler

ring[2] *v* **rang** [ˈræŋ]; **rung** [ˈrʌŋ]; **ringing** *vi* **1** : sonner <the doorbell rang : on a sonné à la porte> **2** RESOUND : résonner **3 to ring true** : sonner vrai — *vt* : sonner <to ring the alarm : sonner l'alarme>

ring[3] *n* **1** : bague *f*, anneau *m* <engagement ring : bague de fiançailles> **2** : rond *m* <smoke rings : ronds de fumée> **3** ARENA : ring *m* (de boxe), piste *f* (d'un cirque) **4** GANG : cercle *m*, gang *m* **5** SOUND : son *m*, tintement *m* **6** RINGING : sonnerie *f* (du téléphone, etc.) **7** CALL : coup *m* de téléphone <give me a ring in the morning : appelle-moi dans la matinée>

ringer [ˈrɪŋər] *n* **to be a dead ringer for** : être le sosie de

ringleader [ˈrɪŋˌliːdər] *n* : meneur *m*, -neuse *f*

ringlet [ˈrɪŋlət] *n* : boucle *f* (de cheveux)

ringworm [ˈrɪŋˌwərm] *n* : teigne *f*

rink [ˈrɪŋk] *n* : patinoire *f*

rinse[1] [ˈrɪnts] *vt* **rinsed; rinsing 1** : rincer <to rinse the dishes : rincer la vaisselle> **2** : se rincer <to rinse one's mouth : se rincer la bouche>

rinse[2] *n* : rinçage *m*

riot[1] [ˈraɪət] *vi* : faire une émeute, manifester avec violence

riot[2] *n* : émeute *f*

rioter [ˈraɪətər] *n* : émeutier *m*, -tière *f*

riotous [ˈraɪətəs] *adj* **1** NOISY, ROWDY : tapageur, bruyant **2** ABUNDANT : abondant, exubérant

rip[1] [ˈrɪp] *v* **ripped; ripping** *vt* : déchirer — *vi* : se déchirer

rip[2] *n* : déchirure *f*

ripe [ˈraɪp] *adj* **riper; ripest 1** MATURE : mûr <a ripe pear : une poire mûre> **2** READY : prêt

ripen [ˈraɪpən] *v* : mûrir

ripeness [ˈraɪpnəs] *n* : maturité *f*

rip–off [ˈrɪpˌɔf] *n* SWINDLE, THEFT : escroquerie *f*, vol *m*, arnaque *f fam*

rip off *vt* : escroquer, arnaquer *fam*

ripple[1] [ˈrɪpəl] *v* **-pled; -pling** *vi* : onduler, se rider — *vt* : rider

ripple[2] *n* **1** : ondulation *f*, ride *f* **2** EFFECT, REPERCUSSION : répercussion *f* **3 a ripple of laughter** : une cascade de rires

rise[1] [ˈraɪz] *vi* **rose** [ˈroːz]; **risen** [ˈrɪzən]; **rising 1** ARISE : se lever <to rise to one's feet : se lever, se mettre debout> <to rise from the dead : ressusciter (des morts)> **2** : s'élever, se dresser <mountains rising in the distance : des montagnes qui s'élèvent au loin> **3** : se lever (se dit du soleil, de la lune) **4** : monter <smoke rises : la fumée monte> **5** INCREASE : augmenter, monter **6** ORIGINATE : prendre sa source (dans) **7 to rise from the ranks** : sortir du rang **8 to rise to the occasion** : se montrer à la hauteur de la situation **9 to rise up** REBEL : se soulever (contre), se révolter

rise[2] *n* **1** ASCENT : lever *m* (du soleil), montée *f,* ascension *f* **2** ORIGIN : début *m,* source *f* **3** ELEVATION : élévation *f* <the rise of a step : l'élévation d'une marche> **4** INCREASE : augmentation *f,* hausse *f* **5** INCLINE : montée *f,* pente *f*

riser [ˈraɪzər] *n* **1** : contremarche *f* (d'un escalier) **2 early riser** : lève-tôt *mf* **3 late riser** : lève-tard *mf*

risk[1] [ˈrɪsk] *vt* : risquer

risk[2] *n* : risque *m,* danger *m*

riskiness [ˈrɪskinəs] *n* : risques *mpl*

risky [ˈrɪski] *adj* **riskier; -est** : risqué, hasardeux

risqué [rɪˈskeɪ] *adj* : risqué, osé

rite [ˈraɪt] *n* : rite *m*

ritual[1] [ˈrɪtʃʊəl] *adj* : rituel

ritual[2] *n* : rituel *m*

rival[1] [ˈraɪvəl] *vt* **-valed** *or* **-valled; -valing** *or* **-valling** : rivaliser avec

rival[2] *adj* : rival <rival factions : factions rivales>

rival[3] *n* : rival *m,* -vale *f;* compétiteur *m,* -trice *f*

rivalry [ˈraɪvəlri] *n, pl* **-ries** : rivalité *f*

river [ˈrɪvər] *n* : rivière *f,* fleuve *m*

riverbank [ˈrɪvərˌbæŋk] *n* : rive *f,* berge *f*

riverbed [ˈrɪvərˌbɛd] *n* : lit *m* de rivière

riverside [ˈrɪvərˌsaɪd] *n* : rive *f,* bord *m* d'une rivière

rivet[1] [ˈrɪvət] *vt* **1** : riveter, river **2 to be riveted to the spot** : être cloué sur place

rivet[2] *n* : rivet *m*

rivulet [ˈrɪvjələt] *n* : ruisselet *m*

roach [ˈroːtʃ] → **cockroach**

road [ˈroːd] *n* **1** : route *f,* rue *f* **2** PATH, WAY : chemin *m,* voie *f* <on the road to success : sur le chemin de la réussite>

roadblock [ˈroːdˌblɑk] *n* : barrage *m* routier

roadrunner [ˈroːdˌrʌnər] *n* : coucou *m* terrestre

roadside [ˈroːdˌsaɪd] *n* : bord *m* de la route

roadway [ˈroːdˌweɪ] *n* : chaussée *f*

roam [ˈroːm] *vi* WANDER : errer, rôder

roan[1] [ˈroːn] *adj* : rouan

roan[2] *n* : rouan *m,* rouanne *f*

roar[1] [ˈror] *vi* **1** : rugir (se dit d'un lion), mugir (se dit du vent, de la mer, etc.), gronder (se dit d'un moteur, du tonnerre, etc.) **2** : éclater, hurler <to roar with laughter : hurler de rire> **—** *vt* : hurler, vociférer <he roared approval : il a hurlé son approbation>

roar[2] *n* **1** : rugissement *m* (d'un lion) **2** : hurlement *m,* cri *m* <a roar of pain : un hurlement de douleur> **3** : vrombissement *m* (d'un moteur), grondement *m* (du tonnerre)

roast[1] [ˈroːst] *vt* : rôtir (de la viande, etc.), griller (des noix), torréfier (du café)

roast[2] *adj* : rôti <roast beef : rôti de bœuf>

roast[3] *n* : rôti *m*

rob [ˈrɑb] *vt* **robbed; robbing 1** : dévaliser (une banque, etc.), cambrioler (une maison) **2** STEAL : voler <to rob jewelry : voler des bijoux>

robber [ˈrɑbər] *n* : voleur *m,* -leuse *f*

robbery [ˈrɑbəri] *n, pl* **-beries** : vol *m* <armed robbery : vol à main armé>

robe[1] [ˈroːb] *vt* **robed; robing** : vêtir, habiller

robe[2] *n* **1** : toge *f* (d'un juge) **2** → **bathrobe**

robin [ˈrɑbən] *n* : rouge-gorge *m*

robot [ˈroːˌbɑt, -bət] *n* : robot *m*

robust [roˈbʌst, ˈroːˌbʌst] *adj* : robuste, vigoureux **— robustly** *adv*

rock[1] [ˈrɑk] *vt* **1** : balancer (un berceau), bercer (un enfant) **2** SHAKE : ébranler, secouer **—** *vi* SWAY : se balancer

rock[2] *n* **1** STONE : roche *f,* roc *m* **2** BOULDER : rocher *m* **3** ROCKING : mouvement *m* de va-et-vient **4** : rock *m* (musique)

rocker [ˈrɑkər] *n* **1** : bascule *f* (d'un fauteuil) **2** → **rocking chair**

rocket[1] [ˈrɑkət] *vi* : monter en flèche

rocket[2] *n* : fusée *f*

rocking chair *n* : fauteuil *m* à bascule, chaise *f* berçante *Can*

rocking horse *n* : cheval *m* à bascule

rock salt *n* : sel *m* gemme

rocky [ˈrɑki] *adj* **rockier; -est** : rocheux

rod [ˈrɑd] *n* **1** STICK : baguette *f* **2** : tige *f,* tringle *f* <iron rod : tige de fer> **3** : unité *f* de mesure qui équivaut à 16,5 pieds **4** *or* **fishing rod** : canne *f* à pêche

rode → **ride**[1]

rodent [ˈroːdənt] *n* : rongeur *m*

rodeo [ˈroːdiˌoː, roˈdeɪˌoː] *n, pl* **-deos** : rodéo *m*

roe [ˈroː] *n* : œufs *mpl* de poisson

roe deer *n* : chevreuil *m*

rogue [ˈroːg] *n* SCOUNDREL : escroc *m,* fripouille *f fam*

roguish [ˈroːgɪʃ] *adj* : espiègle, coquin

role [ˈroːl] *n* **1** PART : rôle *m* (dans une pièce de théâtre) **2** FUNCTION : rôle *m,* fonction *f*

roll[1] [ˈroːl] *vt* **1** : rouler <to roll a barrel : rouler un tonneau> <to roll cigarettes : rouler des cigarettes> **2** FLATTEN : étendre (de la pâte) **3** : faire tourner <to roll the cameras : faire tourner les caméras> **4 to roll out** : dérouler (un tapis) **5 to roll up one's sleeves** : retrousser ses manches **—** *vi* **1** : se rouler <the children were rolling in the grass : les enfants se roulaient dans l'herbe> **2** : tanguer,

faire du roulis (se dit d'un bateau) **3 to roll in** : affluer <money was rolling in : l'argent affluait> **4 to roll on** ELAPSE : passer **5 to roll over** : se retourner
roll[2] *n* **1** LIST : liste *f* <class roll : liste des élèves> <to call the roll : faire l'appel> **2** : rouleau *m* (de papier, etc.), liasse *f* (d'argent) **3** BUN : petit pain *m* **4** RUMBLE : roulement *m* (de tambour), grondement *m* (du tonnerre) **5** ROLLING : roulis *m* (d'un navire), lancement *m* (de dés), balancement *m* (des hanches, etc.)
roller ['ro:lər] *n* : rouleau *m*
roller coaster ['ro:lər,ko:stər] *n* : montagnes *fpl* russes
roller–skate ['ro:lər,skeɪt] *vi* **-skated; -skating** : faire du patin à roulettes
roller skate *n* : patin *m* à roulettes
rollicking ['rɑlɪkɪŋ] *adj* : joyeux, exubérant
rolling pin *n* : rouleau *m* à pâtisserie
Roman[1] ['ro:mən] *adj* : romain
Roman[2] *n* : Romain *m*, -maine *f*
Roman Catholic[1] *adj* : catholique
Roman Catholic[2] *n* : catholique *mf*
romance[1] [ro'mænts, 'ro:,mænts] *vi* **-manced; -mancing** : exagérer, fabuler
romance[2] *n* **1** : roman *m* du Moyen Âge **2** : histoire *f* d'amour **3** AFFAIR : liaison *f* amoureuse **4** APPEAL : charme *m*, attrait *m* <the romance of the sea : l'attrait de la mer>
Romanian[1] [rʊ'meɪniən, ro-] *adj* : roumain
Romanian[2] *n* **1** : Roumain *m*, -maine *f* **2** : roumain *m* (langue)
romantic [ro'mæntɪk] *adj* : romantique
romantically [ro'mæntɪkli] *adv* : de façon romantique
romp[1] ['rɑmp] *vi* : s'ébattre, folâtrer
romp[2] *n* : ébats *mpl*, jeux *mpl* folâtres
roof[1] ['ru:f, 'rʊf] *vt* : couvrir d'un toit
roof[2] *n, pl* **roofs** ['ru:fs, 'rʊfs; 'ru:vz, 'rʊvz] : toit *m*
roofing ['ru:fɪŋ, 'rʊfɪŋ] *n* : toiture *f*, couverture *f*
rooftop ['ru:f,tɑp, 'rʊf-] *n* ROOF : toit *m*
rook[1] ['rʊk] *vt* CHEAT : frauder, escroquer
rook[2] *n* **1** : freux *m*, corbeau *m* (oiseau) **2** : tour *f* (en échecs)
rookie ['rʊki] *n* : novice *mf*
room[1] ['ru:m, 'rʊm] *vi* : loger <to room with s.o. : partager un logement avec qqn>
room[2] *n* **1** SPACE : espace *m*, place *f* <there's not enough room : il manque d'espace> **2** : chambre *f* (d'hôtel), pièce *f* (d'une maison), salle *f* (de conférence) **3** OPPORTUNITY : chance *f*, possibilité *f* <there was no room for doubt : il n'y avait aucun doute possible>
roomer ['ru:mər, 'rʊmər] *n* : pensionnaire *mf*; chambreur *m*, -breuse *f Can*
rooming house *n* : immeuble *m* locatif
roommate ['ru:m,meɪt, 'rʊm-] *n* : camarade *mf* de chambre, colocataire *mf Can*
roomy ['ru:mi, 'rʊmi] *adj* **roomier; -est** : spacieux, vaste
roost[1] ['ru:st] *vi* : se percher
roost[2] *n* : perchoir *m*
rooster ['ru:stər, 'rʊs-] *n* : coq *m*
root[1] ['ru:t, 'rʊt] *vi* **1** : s'enraciner (se dit d'une plante) **2** : fouiller (se dit des cochons) **3 to root for** CHEER : encourager, applaudir — *vt* **1 to root out** UNCOVER : découvrir, déterrer **2 to root out** ERADICATE : extirper
root[2] *n* **1** : racine *f* (d'une plante) **2** : racine *f*, base *f* (d'une dent) **3** SOURCE : origine *f*, source *f* <the root of evil : l'origine du mal> **4** CORE : fond *m*, cœur *m* <let's get to the root of the matter : allons au fond des choses>
rootless ['ru:tləs, 'rʊt-] *adj* : sans racines
rope[1] ['ro:p] *vt* **roped; roping 1** TIE : attacher (avec une corde) **2** LASSO : prendre au lasso **3 to rope off** : interdire l'accès à, délimiter par une corde
rope[2] *n* : corde *f*
rosary ['ro:zəri] *n, pl* **-ries** : chapelet *m*
rose[1] → **rise**[1]
rose[2] ['ro:z] *adj* : (de couleur) rose
rose[3] *n* : rose *f* (fleur), rose *m* (couleur)
rosebud ['ro:z,bʌd] *n* : bouton *m* de rose
rosebush ['ro:z,bʊʃ] *n* : rosier *m*
rosemary ['ro:z,mɛri] *n, pl* **-maries** : romarin *m*
rosette [ro'zɛt] *n* : rosette *f* (fait de rubans), rosace *f* (en architecture)
Rosh Hashanah [,rɑʃhɑ'ʃɑnə, ,ro:ʃ-] *n* : Rosh Hashana *m*, fête *f* du nouvel an juif
rosin ['rɑzən] *n* : colophane *f*
roster ['rɑstər] *n* : tableau *m*, liste *f* <roster of duties : tableau de services>
rostrum ['rɑstrəm] *n, pl* **-trums** *or* **-tra** [-trə] : tribune *f*, estrade *f*
rosy ['ro:zi] *adj* **rosier; -est 1** : rose, rosé <rosy cheeks : joues rosées> **2** HOPEFUL : prometteur
rot[1] ['rɑt] *v* **rotted; rotting** *vt* : pourrir — *vi* : pourrir, se décomposer
rot[2] *n* : pourriture *f*
rotary[1] ['ro:ţəri] *adj* : rotatif
rotary[2] *n* : rond-point *m*
rotate ['ro:,teɪt] *v* **-tated; -tating** *vi* REVOLVE : tourner — *vt* **1** TURN : faire tourner **2** ALTERNATE : alterner (des cultures agricoles)
rotation [ro'teɪʃən] *n* : rotation *f*
rote ['ro:t] *n* **by ~** : par cœur, machinalement
rotor ['ro:tər] *n* : rotor *m*
rotten ['rɑtən] *adj* **1** : pourri <rotten wood : bois pourri> **2** CORRUPT : pourri, corrompu (se dit d'une personne) **3** BAD : pourri, mauvais <rotten weather : temps pourri>

rottenness ['rɑtənnəs] *n* : pourriture *f*

rotund [ro'tʌnd] *adj* : rondelet, potelé

rotunda [ro'tʌndə] *n* : rotonde *f*

rouge ['ruːʒ] *n* : rouge *m* à joues

rough[1] ['rʌf] *vt* **1** → **roughen 2** *or* **to rough out** : ébaucher, esquisser **3** *or* **to rough up** MANHANDLE : tabasser *fam,* battre

rough[2] *adj* **1** : rugueux, rude <a rough surface : une surface rugueuse> **2** : inégal, accidenté <rough terrain : terrain inégal> **3** TURBULENT : agité **4** HARSH : rude, violent **5** UNCOUTH : rude, fruste **6** APPROXIMATE : approximatif, sommaire <a rough estimate : une estimation approximative>

rough[3] *n* : rough *m* (au golf)

roughage ['rʌfɪdʒ] *n* : fibres *mpl* alimentaires

roughen ['rʌfən] *vt* : rendre rude, rendre rugueux

roughly ['rʌfli] *adv* **1** HARSHLY : rudement, brutalement **2** IMPERFECTLY : grossièrement **3** NEARLY : à peu près, environ <roughly 20 percent : environ 20 pour cent>

roughneck ['rʌf,nɛk] *n* : dur *m fam*

roughness ['rʌfnəs] *n* : rudesse *f,* rugosité *f*

roulette [,ruː'lɛt] *n* : roulette *f* (au casino)

round[1] ['raʊnd] *vt* **1** : arrondir <to round the lips : arrondir les lèvres> **2** TURN : tourner <she rounded the corner : elle a tourné au coin> **3 to round off** : arrondir (un chiffre) **4 to round out** COMPLETE : compléter **5 to round up** GATHER : rassembler

round[2] *adv* → **around**[1]

round[3] *adj* **1** : rond <a round face : un visage rond> <to have round shoulders : avoir le dos voûté> **2** COMPLETE, FULL : exact, tout rond <a round dozen : une douzaine tout rond>

round[4] *n* **1** CIRCLE : rond *m,* cercle *m* **2** : série *f* <a round of talks : une série de négociations> <the daily round : la routine quotidienne> **3** : manche *f* (d'un match), partie *f* (de golf) **4** : cartouche *f* (d'une arme à feu) **5 round of applause** : salve *f* d'applaudissements **6 round of drinks** : tournée *f fam* **7 rounds** *npl* : tournée *f* (de ses amis), ronde *f* (d'un lieu), visites *fpl* (d'un médecin)

round[5] *prep* → **around**[2]

roundabout ['raʊndə,baʊt] *adj* : détourné, indirect

roundness ['raʊndnəs] *n* : rondeur *f*

round–trip ['raʊnd,trɪp] *n* : voyage *m* aller et retour

roundup ['raʊnd,ʌp] *n* **1** : rassemblement *m* (de bétail, de personnes, etc.) **2** SUMMARY : rappel *m,* résumé *m*

round up *vt* GATHER : rassembler, regrouper

roundworm ['raʊnd,wərm] *n* : ascaride *m*

rouse ['raʊz] *v* **roused; rousing** *vt* **1** : réveiller **2** EXCITE : éveiller, susciter <to rouse s.o. to fury : éveiller la furie en qqn> — *vi* AWAKEN : se réveiller

rout[1] ['raʊt] *vt* **1** : mettre en déroute **2 to rout out** : expulser, déloger

rout[2] *n* : déroute *f,* débâcle *f*

route[1] ['ruːt, 'raʊt] *vt* **routed; routing** DIRECT : fixer l'itinéraire de, diriger

route[2] *n* **1** HIGHWAY : route *f* **2** LINE : parcours *m,* trajet *m* <bus route : parcours d'autobus> **3** : chemin *m,* itinéraire *m* <the best route : le meilleur chemin> **4 newspaper route** : tournée *f* de livraison

routine[1] [ruː'tiːn] *adj* : routinier

routine[2] *n* : routine *f*

routinely [ruː'tiːnli] *adv* : systématiquement

rove ['roːv] *v* **roved; roving** *vi* ROAM : errer, vagabonder — *vt* : rôder dans, parcourir

rover ['roːvər] *n* : vagabond *m,* -bonde *f*

row[1] ['roː] *vi* : ramer — *vt* : transporter par canot

row[2] ['roː] *n* **1** LINE, RANK : rang *m,* rangée *f* <a row of houses : une rangée de maisons> <to stand in a row : être debout en rang> **2** : excursion *f* en bateau **3** SUCCESSION : série *f* <twice in a row : deux fois de suite> **4** ['raʊ] QUARREL : altercation *f,* dispute *f*

rowboat ['roː,boːt] *n* : bateau *m* à rames

rowdiness ['raʊdinəs] *n* : tapage *m,* vacarme *m*

rowdy[1] ['raʊdi] *adj* **rowdier; -est** : tapageur, bruyant

rowdy[2] *n, pl* **-dies** : voyou *m*

royal[1] ['rɔɪəl] *adj* : royal — **royally** *adv*

royal[2] *n* : membre *m* d'une famille royale

royalty ['rɔɪəlti] *n, pl* **-ties 1** : membres *m* d'une famille royale **2** : royauté *f* (position) **3 royalties** *npl* : droits *mpl* d'auteur

rub[1] ['rʌb] *v* **rubbed; rubbing** *vt* **1** : frotter, se frotter <to rub one's hands together : se frotter les mains> **2** MASSAGE : frictionner **3** CHAFE : frotter contre, blesser **4** POLISH : frotter, polir **5 to rub shoulders with s.o.** : coudoyer qqn **6 to rub s.o. the wrong way** : prendre qqn à rebrousse-poil — *vi* : frotter

rub[2] *n* **1** : friction *f,* frottement *m* <an alcohol rub : une friction à l'alcool> **2** OBSTACLE : obstacle *m,* difficulté *f*

rubber[1] ['rʌbər] *adj* : en caoutchouc

rubber[2] *n* **1** : caoutchouc *m* **2 rubbers** *npl* : caoutchoucs *mpl,* claques *fpl Can,* pardessus *m Can*

rubber band *n* : élastique *m*

rubber–stamp [ˈrʌbərˈstæmp] *vt* : tamponner
rubber stamp *n* : tampon *m* (de caoutchouc)
rubbery [ˈrʌbəri] *adj* : caoutchouteux
rubbish [ˈrʌbɪʃ] *n* : ordures *fpl,* déchets *mpl*
rubble [ˈrʌbəl] *n* : décombres *mpl*
ruble [ˈru:bəl] *n* : rouble *m*
ruby[1] [ˈru:bi] *adj* : vermeil (couleur)
ruby[2] *n, pl* **-bies 1** : rubis *m* **2** : couleur *f* rubis, couleur *f* vermeille
rudder [ˈrʌdər] *n* : gouvernail *m*
ruddy [ˈrʌdi] *adj* **ruddier; -est** : rougeâtre, rougeaud
rude [ˈru:d] *adj* **ruder; rudest 1** CRUDE : grossier, rudimentaire **2** UNDEVELOPED : primitif, rude **3** IMPOLITE : grossier, insolent
rudely [ˈru:dli] *adv* : impoliment, grossièrement
rudeness [ˈru:dnəs] *n* : impolitesse *f,* grossièreté *f*
rudiment [ˈru:dəmənt] *n* : rudiment *m*
rudimentary [ˌru:dəˈmɛntəri] *adj* : rudimentaire
rue [ˈru:] *vt* **rued; ruing** : regretter
rueful [ˈru:fəl] *adj* : triste, chagrin, attristé
ruffian [ˈrʌfiən] *n* : voyou *m*
ruffle[1] [ˈrʌfəl] *vt* **-fled; -fling 1** : hérisser (ses plumes), ébouriffer (ses cheveux) **2** TROUBLE, VEX : décontenancer, troubler, énerver
ruffle[2] *n* : ruche *f*
rug [ˈrʌg] *n* : tapis *m,* carpette *f*
rugged [ˈrʌgəd] *adj* **1** : accidenté <rugged landscape : paysage accidenté> **2** JAGGED : en dents de scie (se dit des montagnes) **3** HARSH : sévère, exigeant **4** STURDY : robuste, fort
ruin[1] [ˈru:ən] *vt* **1** DESTROY : ruiner, anéantir **2** DAMAGE : abîmer **3** BANKRUPT : ruiner
ruin[2] *n* : ruine *f* <to be in ruins : être en ruines>
ruinous [ˈru:ənəs] *adj* : ruineux
rule[1] [ˈru:l] *v* **ruled; ruling** *vt* **1** GOVERN : régner sur, gouverner (un pays, etc.) **2** DOMINATE : dominer, maîtriser (les émotions, etc.) **3** DRAW : tirer (à la règle) **4** DECREE, JUDGE : décréter, décider, juger — *vi* : régner
rule[2] *n* **1** : règle *f,* règlement *m* <as a rule : en règle générale> **2** CUSTOM : coutume *f,* habitude *f* **3** DOMINION : autorité *f,* gouvernement *m* **4** → **ruler**
ruler [ˈru:lər] *n* : règle *f* (pour mesurer)
rum [ˈrʌm] *n* : rhum *m*
Rumanian [rʊˈmeɪniən] → **Romanian**
rumble[1] [ˈrʌmbəl] *vi* **-bled; -bling 1** ROAR : gronder (se dit du tonnerre, etc.) **2** : gargouiller (se dit de l'estomac)
rumble[2] *n* : grondement *m* (du tonnerre, etc.), gargouillement *m* (de l'estomac)
ruminant[1] [ˈru:mənənt] *adj* : ruminant
ruminant[2] *n* : ruminant *m*
ruminate [ˈru:məˌneɪt] *vi* **-nated; -nating 1** : ruminer (se dit d'une vâche) **2** MUSE : ruminer, réfléchir
rummage [ˈrʌmɪdʒ] *vi* **-maged; -maging** : fouiller, fourrager
rummy [ˈrʌmi] *n* : rami *m* (jeu de cartes)
rumor[1] *or Brit* **rumour** [ˈru:mər] *vt* **it is rumored that** : le bruit court que, il paraît que
rumor[2] *or Brit* **rumour** *n* : rumeur *f,* bruit *m*
rump [ˈrʌmp] *n* **1** : croupe *f* (d'un animal) **2** *or* **rump steak** : romsteck *m*
rumple [ˈrʌmpəl] *vt* **-pled; -pling 1** TOUSLE : ébouriffer **2** WRINKLE : froisser, friper
rumpus [ˈrʌmpəs] *n* : vacarme *m,* boucan *m*
run[1] [ˈrʌn] *v* **ran** [ˈræn]; **run; running** *vi* **1** : courir <he ran home : il est rentré chez lui en courant> **2** : être candidat <to run for the presidency : être candidat à la présidence> **3** FLOW : couler **4** FUNCTION, OPERATE : tourner <the engine was running : le moteur tournait> **5** BE : être <profits were running high : les profits étaient élevés> <I was running late : j'étais en retard> **6** : faire le service, circuler <the train runs between Washington and New York : le train fait le service entre Washington et New York> **7** OCCUR : être courant <it runs in our family : c'est courant dans notre famille> **8** : déteindre (se dit des couleurs) **9** EXTEND : passer **10 to run away** : s'enfuir, se sauver **11 to run out** EXPIRE : expirer **12 to run out of** : manquer — *vt* **1** : courir <to run the marathon : courir le marathon> **2** : faire, effectuer <to run errands : faire des courses> **3** OPERATE : faire marcher **4** INCUR : courir <to run a risk : courir un risque> **5** MANAGE : gérer, diriger **6** CHASE : chasser <we ran the thieves out of town : les bandits ont été chassés de la ville> **7 to run a fever** : faire de la température **8 to run a red light** : brûler un feu rouge **9 to run one's car off the road** : perdre la maîtrise de son véhicule
run[2] *n* **1** : course *f* <a three-mile run : une course de trois milles> <to break into a run : se mettre à courir> **2** SERIES : succession *f,* série *f* <a run of cloudy days : une succession de journées nuageuses> **3** RIDE : tour *m,* promenade *f* <a run in the car : un tour en voiture> **4** TRIP : trajet *m,* parcours *m* <the New York run : le trajet jusqu'à New York> **5** : maille *f* filée, échelle *f* (dans les bas) **6** SLOPE : pente *f* <ski run : pente de ski> **7** DEMAND, RUSH : ruée *f* (sur la

banque, etc.) **8** : point *m* (aux sports) **9** : enclos *m* (pour des animaux) **10** : tirage *m* (en imprimerie) **11 to have the run of the house** : avoir la maison à sa disposition **12 on the run** : en fuite, en cavale

runaway[1] ['rʌnəˌweɪ] *adj* : fugueur (se dit d'un enfant), emballé (se dit d'un cheval), incontrôlé (se dit d'un véhicule)

runaway[2] *n* : fugitif *m*, -tive *f;* fugeur *m*, -geuse *f*

run–down ['rʌn'daʊn] *adj* **1** DILAPIDATED : délabré **2** EXHAUSTED, WORN-OUT : fatigué, éreinté

rung[1] → **ring**[2]

rung[2] ['rʌŋ] *n* : barreau *m* (d'une échelle, d'une chaise, etc.)

runner ['rʌnər] *n* **1** RACER : coureur *m*, -reuse *f* **2** BLADE : lame *f* (d'un patin) **3** TRACK : glissière *f* (d'une porte, etc.), coulisse *f* **4** : coulant *m*, stolon *m* (d'une plante) **5** MESSENGER : coursier *m*, -sière *f*

runner–up [ˌrʌnər'ʌp] *n, pl* **runners–up** : second *m*, -conde *f*

running ['rʌnɪŋ] *adj* **1** FLOWING : courant <running water : eau courante> **2** CONTINUOUS : continuel <a running battle : une bataille continuelle> **3** CONSECUTIVE : de suite <three days running : trois jours consécutifs>

runt ['rʌnt] *n* : avorton *m*

runway ['rʌnˌweɪ] *n* : piste *f* d'envol, piste *f* d'atterrissage

rupee [ruː'piː, 'ruːˌ-] *n* : roupie *f*

rupture[1] ['rʌptʃər] *v* **-tured; -turing** *vt* BREAK, BURST : rompre — *vi* : se rompre

rupture[2] *n* **1** BREACH, BREAK : rupture *f* **2** HERNIA : hernie *f*

rural ['rʊrəl] *adj* : rural

ruse ['ruːs, 'ruːz] *n* : ruse *f*, stratagème *m*

rush[1] [rʌʃ] *vi* HURRY : se précipiter, se dépêcher <to rush toward s.o. : se précipiter vers qqn> — *vt* **1** HURRY, PRESS : presser, bousculer **2** *or* **to rush through** : expédier <to rush one's work : expédier son travail> **3** ATTACK : attaquer, agresser **4** TRANSPORT : transporter d'urgence (à l'hôpital, etc.)

rush[2] *adj* : urgent <a rush order : une commande urgente>

rush[3] *n* **1** : jonc *m* (plante) **2** : ruée *f* <a rush towards the exit : une ruée vers la sortie> **3** HASTE : hâte *f*, empressement *m*

rush hour *n* : heure *f* de pointe

russet[1] ['rʌsət] *adj* : roussâtre, roux

russet[2] *n* : roux *m* (couleur)

Russian[1] ['rʌʃən] *adj* : russe

Russian[2] *n* **1** : Russe *mf* **2** : russe *m* (langue)

rust[1] ['rʌst] *vt* : rouiller — *vi* : se rouiller

rust[2] *n* **1** : rouille *f* (sur métal) **2** : couleur *f* rouille

rustic[1] ['rʌstɪk] *adj* : rustique, champêtre

rustic[2] *n* : campagnard *m*, -gnarde *f*

rustle[1] ['rʌsəl] *v* **-tled; -tling** *vi* : bruire <the pine needles rustled : on entendait bruire les aiguilles de pin> — *vt* STEAL : voler (du bétail)

rustle[2] *n* : bruissement *m*, froissement

rusty ['rʌsti] *adj* **rustier; -est 1** : rouillé <a rusty nail : un clou rouillé> **2** SLOW : rouillé, peu agile

rut ['rʌt] *n* **1** TRACK : ornière *f* **2 to be in a rut** : s'enliser dans une routine

ruthless ['ruːθləs] *adj* : impitoyable, cruel — **ruthlessly** *adv*

ruthlessness ['ruːθləsnəs] *n* : caractère *m* impitoyable

Rwandan[1] [rʊ'ɑndən] *adj* : rwandais

Rwandan[2] *n* : Rwandais *m*, -daise *f*

rye ['raɪ] *n* **1** : seigle *m* <rye bread : pain de seigle> **2** *or* **rye whiskey** : whisky *m* (de seigle)

S

s ['ɛs] *n, pl* **s's** *or* **ss** ['ɛsəz] : s *m*, dix-neuvième lettre de l'alphabet

Sabbath ['sæbəθ] *n* : sabbat *m* (en judaïsme), dimanche *m* (en christianisme)

saber ['seɪbər] *n* : sabre *m*

sable ['seɪbəl] *n* **1** BLACK : noir *m* **2** : zibeline *f* (animal)

sabotage[1] ['sæbəˌtɑʒ] *vt* **-taged; -taging** : saboter

sabotage[2] *n* : sabotage *m*

saboteur [ˌsæbə'tər, -'tʊr, -'tjʊr] *n* : saboteur *m*, -teuse *f*

sac ['sæk] *n* : sac *m*

saccharin ['sækərən] *n* : saccharine *f*

saccharine ['sækərən, -ˌriːn, -ˌraɪn] *adj* : mielleux, doucereux (se dit d'un sourire, etc.)

sachet [sæ'ʃeɪ] *n* : sachet *m*

sack[1] ['sæk] *vt* **1** PLUNDER : mettre à sac **2** DISMISS, FIRE : virer, congédier

sack[2] *n* BAG : sac *m*

sacrament ['sækrəmənt] *n* : sacrement *m*

sacramental [ˌsækrə'mɛntəl] *adj* : sacramentel

sacred ['seɪkrəd] *adj* : sacré

sacrifice[1] ['sækrəˌfaɪs] *vt* **-ficed; -ficing 1** : sacrifier **2 to sacrifice oneself** : se sacrifier

sacrifice[2] *n* : sacrifice *m*

sacrificial [ˌsækrəˈfɪʃəl] *adj* : sacrificiel
sacrilege [ˈsækrəlɪdʒ] *n* : sacrilège *m*
sacrilegious [ˌsækrəˈlɪdʒəs, -ˈliː-] *adj* : sacrilège
sacrosanct [ˈsækroˌsæŋkt] *adj* : sacro-saint
sad [ˈsæd] *adj* **sadder; saddest** : triste
sadden [ˈsædən] *vt* : attrister
saddle[1] [ˈsædəl] *vt* **-dled; -dling** : seller
saddle[2] *n* : selle *f* <in the saddle : en selle>
sadism [ˈseɪˌdɪzəm, ˈsæ-] *n* : sadisme *m*
sadist [ˈseɪdɪst, ˈsæ-] *n* : sadiste *mf*
sadistic [səˈdɪstɪk] *adj* : sadique — **sadistically** [-tɪkli] *adv*
sadly [ˈsædli] *adv* **1** SORROWFULLY : tristement **2** UNFORTUNATELY : malheureusement **3** (*used for emphasis*) <you are sadly mistaken : vous vous trompez fort>
sadness [ˈsædnəs] *n* : tristesse *f*
safari [səˈfɑri, -ˈfær-] *n* : safari *m*
safe[1] [ˈseɪf] *adj* **safer; safest 1** PROTECTED : en sécurité, à l'abri <safe and sound : sain et sauf> **2** SECURE : sûr **3 to play it safe** : ne prendre aucun risque
safe[2] *n* : coffre-fort *m*
safeguard[1] [ˈseɪfˌgɑrd] *vt* : sauvegarder
safeguard[2] *n* : sauvegarde *f*
safekeeping [ˈseɪfˈkiːpɪŋ] *n* : bonne garde *f*
safely [ˈseɪfli] *adv* **1** : sans incident, sûrement <the plane landed safely : l'avion a atterri sans incident> <to arrive safely : bien arriver> **2** SECURELY : en sécurité, à l'abri **3** CAREFULLY : prudemment
safety [ˈseɪfti] *n, pl* **-ties** : sécurité *f*
safety belt *n* : ceinture *f* de sécurité
safety pin *n* : épingle *f* de sûreté
saffron [ˈsæfrən] *n* : safran *m*
sag[1] [ˈsæg] *vi* **sagged; sagging** : s'affaisser
sag[2] *n* : affaissement *m*
saga [ˈsɑgə, ˈsæ-] *n* : saga *f*
sagacious [səˈgeɪʃəs] *adj* : sagace
sage[1] [ˈseɪdʒ] *adj* **sager; -est** : sage, avisé
sage[2] *n* **1** : sage *m* (personne) **2** : sauge *f* (plante)
sagebrush [ˈseɪdʒˌbrʌʃ] *n* : armoise *f*
sagely [ˈseɪdʒli] *adv* : avec sagesse
Sagittarius [ˌsædʒəˈtɛriəs] *n* : Sagittaire *m*
said → **say**[1]
sail[1] [ˈseɪl] *vi* **1** : voyager en bateau **2** *or* **to go sailing** : faire de la voile **3** : aller facilement <we sailed right in : nous sommes entrés sans problème> — *vt* **1** : naviguer, manœuvrer (un bateau) **2** CROSS : traverser, parcourir <to sail the seas : parcourir les mers>
sail[2] *n* **1** : voile *f* (d'un bateau) **2** : promenade *f* en bateau **3 to set sail** : appareiller, prendre la mer
sailboat [ˈseɪlˌboːt] *n* : bateau *m* à voiles, voilier *m*
sailor [ˈseɪlər] *n* : marin *m*, matelot *m*
saint [ˈseɪnt, *before a name* ˌseɪnt *or* sənt] *n* : saint *m*, sainte *f*
saintliness [ˈseɪntlinəs] *n* : sainteté *f*
saintly [ˈseɪntli] *adj* **saintlier; -est** : saint
sake [ˈseɪk] *n* **1** BENEFIT : bien *m* <for the children's sake : pour le bien des enfants> **2** (*indicating an end or purpose*) <art for art's sake : l'art pour l'art> <for the sake of money : pour l'argent> **3 for goodness' sake!** : pour l'amour de Dieu!
salacious [səˈleɪʃəs] *adj* : salace
salad [ˈsæləd] *n* : salade *f*
salamander [ˈsæləˌmændər] *n* : salamandre *f*
salami [səˈlɑmi] *n* : salami *m*, saucisson *m* sec
salary [ˈsæləri] *n, pl* **-ries** : salaire *m*
sale [ˈseɪl] *n* **1** SELLING : vente *f* <for sale : à vendre> **2** : solde *m* <on sale : en solde> **3 sales** *npl or* **sales department** : service *m* des ventes
salesman [ˈseɪlzmən] *n, pl* **-men** [-mən, -ˌmɛn] **1** : vendeur *m* **2 traveling salesman** : représentant *m* (de commerce)
salesperson [ˈseɪlzˌpərsən] *n* : vendeur *m*, -deuse *f;* représentant *m*, -tante *f* des ventes
saleswoman [ˈseɪlzˌwʊmən] *n, pl* **-women** [-ˌwɪmən] **1** : vendeuse *f* **2 traveling saleswoman** : représentante *f* (de commerce)
salient [ˈseɪljənt] *adj* : saillant
saline [ˈseɪˌliːn, -ˌlaɪn] *adj* : salin
saliva [səˈlaɪvə] *n* : salive *f*
salivary [ˈsæləˌvɛri] *adj* : salivaire
salivate [ˈsæləˌveɪt] *vi* **-vated; -vating** : saliver
sallow [ˈsæloː] *adj* : jaunâtre
sally[1] [ˈsæli] *vi* **-lied; -lying** SET OUT : sortir
sally[2] *n, pl* **-lies 1** : sortie *f* (militaire) **2** EXCURSION : sortie *f* **3** QUIP : saillie *f*
salmon [ˈsæmən] *ns & pl* : saumon *m*
salon [səˈlɑn, ˈsæˌlɑn, sæˈlɔ̃] *n* : salon *m* <beauty salon : salon de beauté>
saloon [səˈluːn] *n* **1** : salon *m* (dans un navire) **2** BARROOM : bar *m*
salsa [ˈsɔlsə, ˈsɑl-] *n* **1** : sauce *f* pimentée **2** : salsa *f* (musique)
salt[1] [ˈsɔlt] *vt* : saler
salt[2] *adj* : salé
salt[3] *n* : sel *m*
saltshaker [ˈsɔltˌʃeɪkər] *n* : salière *f*
saltwater [ˈsɔltˌwɔtər, -ˌwɑ-] *adj* : de mer
salty [ˈsɔlti] *adj* **saltier; -est** : salé
salubrious [səˈluːbriəs] *adj* : salubre
salutary [ˈsæljəˌtɛri] *adj* : salutaire
salutation [ˌsæljəˈteɪʃən] *n* : salutation *f*
salute[1] [səˈluːt] *v* **-luted; -luting** *vt* : saluer — *vi* : faire un salut
salute[2] *n* **1** : salut *m* (avec la main), salve *f* (de canon) <twenty-one gun

salute : salve de vingt et un coups> 2 TRIBUTE : hommage *m*
salvage[1] [ˈsælvɪdʒ] *vt* **-vaged; -vaging** : sauver, récupérer
salvage[2] *n* : sauvetage *m*
salvation [sælˈveɪʃən] *n* : salut *m*
salve[1] [ˈsæv, ˈsav] *vt* **salved; salving** : adoucir, apaiser, soulager
salve[2] *n* : onguent *m*, pommade *f*
salvo [ˈsælˌvoː] *n, pl* **-vos** *or* **-voes** : salve *f*
same[1] [ˈseɪm] *adj* : même <he's reading the same book : il lit le même livre> <same time, same place : à la même heure, au même endroit>
same[2] *pron* : même <she's never been the same since : elle n'est plus la même depuis> <I'll have the same : je prends la même chose>
sameness [ˈseɪmnəs] *n* **1** SIMILARITY : similitude *f* **2** MONOTONY : monotonie *f*
sample[1] [ˈsæmpəl] *vt* **-pled; -pling** : goûter (des mets, etc.), essayer (des produits)
sample[2] *n* : échantillon *m*
sampler [ˈsæmplər] *n* : modèle *m* de broderie
sanatorium [ˌsænəˈtoriəm] *n, pl* **-riums** *or* **-ria** [-iə] : sanatorium *m*
sanctify [ˈsæŋktəˌfaɪ] *vt* **-fied; -fying** : sanctifier
sanctimonious [ˌsæŋktəˈmoːniəs] *adj* : moralisateur
sanction[1] [ˈsæŋkʃən] *vt* : sanctionner, approuver
sanction[2] *n* **1** APPROVAL : sanction *f* **2 sanctions** *npl* : sanctions *fpl* <to impose sanctions on : prendre des sanctions à l'encontre de>
sanctity [ˈsæŋktət̬i] *n, pl* **-ties** : sainteté *f*
sanctuary [ˈsæŋktʃʊˌɛri] *n, pl* **-aries 1** : sanctuaire *m* (d'une église) **2** REFUGE : refuge *m*
sand[1] [ˈsænd] *vt* **1** : sabler <to sand the driveway : sabler la voie> **2** SMOOTH : poncer
sand[2] *n* : sable *m*
sandal [ˈsændəl] *n* : sandale *f*
sandbank [ˈsændˌbæŋk] *n* : banc *m* de sable
sandbar [ˈsændˌbɑr] *n* : barre *f*, batture *f Can*
sandpaper[1] [ˈsændˌpeɪpər] *vt* : poncer (au papier de verre)
sandpaper[2] *n* : papier *m* de verre, papier *m* sablé *Can*
sandpiper [ˈsændˌpaɪpər] *n* : bécasseau *m*
sandstone [ˈsændˌstoːn] *n* : grès *m*
sandstorm [ˈsændˌstɔrm] *n* : tempête *f* de sable
sandwich[1] [ˈsændˌwɪtʃ] *vt* WEDGE : prendre en sandwich, coincer
sandwich[2] *n* : sandwich *m*
sandy [ˈsændi] *adj* **sandier; -est** : sableux, sablonneux
sane [ˈseɪn] *adj* **saner; sanest 1** : sain d'esprit **2** SENSIBLE : raisonnable, sensé
sang → **sing**
sanguine [ˈsæŋgwən] *adj* **1** RUDDY : rubicond, sanguin **2** HOPEFUL : optimiste, confiant
sanitarium [ˌsænəˈtɛriəm] *n, pl* **-iums** *or* **-ia** [-iə] → **sanatorium**
sanitary [ˈsænəˌtɛri] *adj* **1** : sanitaire <sanitary conditions : conditions sanitaires> **2** HYGIENIC : hygiénique
sanitary napkin *n* : serviette *f* hygiénique
sanitation [ˌsænəˈteɪʃən] *n* : hygiène *f* publique
sanity [ˈsænət̬i] *n* : santé *f* mentale
sank → **sink**[1]
sap[1] [ˈsæp] *vt* **sapped; sapping** UNDERMINE : saper, miner
sap[2] *n* **1** : sève *f* (d'un arbre) **2** FOOL : nigaud *m*, -gaude *f*; andouille *f fam*
sapling [ˈsæplɪŋ] *n* : jeune arbre *m*
sapphire [ˈsæˌfaɪr] *n* : saphir *m*
sarcasm [ˈsɑrˌkæzəm] *n* : sarcasme *m*
sarcastic [sɑrˈkæstɪk] *adj* : sarcastique — **sarcastically** [-t̬ɪkli] *adv*
sarcophagus [sɑrˈkɑfəgəs] *n, pl* **-gi** [-ˌgaɪ, -ˌdʒaɪ] : sarcophage *m*
sardine [sɑrˈdiːn] *n* : sardine *f*
sardonic [sɑrˈdɑnɪk] *adj* : sardonique — **sardonically** [-nɪkli] *adv*
sarsaparilla [ˌsæspəˈrɪlə, ˌsɑrs-] *n* : salsepareille *f*
sartorial [sɑrˈtoriəl, sər-, -ˈtɔr-] *adj* : vestimentaire
sash [ˈsæʃ] *n* **1** : large ceinture *f* (d'une robe), écharpe *f* (insigne) **2** *pl* **sash** : châssis *m* (d'une fenêtre)
sassafras [ˈsæsəˌfræs] *n* : sassafras *m*
sassy [ˈsæsi] *adj* **sassier; -est** → **saucy**
sat → **sit**
Satan [ˈseɪtən] *n* : Satan *m*
satanic [səˈtænɪk, seɪ-] *adj* : satanique — **satanically** [-nɪkli] *adv*
satchel [ˈsætʃəl] *n* : sacoche *f*
sate [ˈseɪt] *vt* **sated; sating** : rassasier, assouvir
satellite [ˈsæt̬əˌlaɪt] *n* : satellite *m*
satiate [ˈseɪʃiˌeɪt] *vt* **-ated; -ating** : rassasier, assouvir
satin [ˈsætən] *n* : satin *m*
satire [ˈsæˌtaɪr] *n* : satire *f*
satiric [səˈtɪrɪk] *or* **satirical** [-ɪkəl] *adj* : satirique
satirize [ˈsæt̬əˌraɪz] *vt* **-rized; -rizing** : satiriser
satisfaction [ˌsæt̬əsˈfækʃən] *n* : satisfaction *f*
satisfactorily [ˌsæt̬əsˈfæktərəli] *adv* : de façon satisfaisante
satisfactory [ˌsæt̬əsˈfæktəri] *adj* : satisfaisant
satisfy [ˈsæt̬əsˌfaɪ] *v* **-fied; -fying** *vt* **1** PLEASE : satisfaire, contenter **2** CONVINCE : convaincre, persuader **3** FULFILL : satisfaire à, répondre à, remplir <to satisfy the demand for

: répondre à la demande de> <to satisfy our needs : satisfaire à nos besoins> — *vi* SUFFICE : suffir

satisfying [ˈsæt̬əsˌfaɪɪŋ] *adj* : satisfaisant

saturate [ˈsætʃəˌreɪt] *vt* **-rated; -rating** : saturer

saturation [ˌsætʃəˈreɪʃən] *n* : saturation *f*

Saturday [ˈsæt̬ərˌdeɪ, -di] *n* : samedi *m*

Saturn [ˈsæt̬ərn] *n* : Saturne *f* (planète)

satyr [ˈseɪt̬ər, ˈsæ-] *n* : satyre *m*

sauce [ˈsɔs] *n* : sauce *f*

saucepan [ˈsɔsˌpæn] *n* : casserole *f*

saucer [ˈsɔsər] *n* : soucoupe *f*

saucily [ˈsɔsəli] *adv* : avec impertinence

sauciness [ˈsɔsinəs] *n* : impertinence *f*

saucy [ˈsɔsi] *adj* **saucier; -est** : impertinent

Saudi[1] [ˈsaʊdɪ] *or* **Saudi Arabian** [ˈsaʊdɪəˈreɪbɪən] *adj* : saoudien

Saudi[2] *or* **Saudi Arabian** *n* : Saoudien *m*, -dienne *f*

sauerkraut [ˈsaʊərˌkraʊt] *n* : choucroute *f*

sauna [ˈsɔnə, ˈsaʊnə] *n* : sauna *m*

saunter [ˈsɔntər, ˈsɑn-] *vi* : flâner, marcher d'un pas nonchalant

sausage [ˈsɔsɪdʒ] *n* : saucisse *f* (crue), saucisson *m* (cuit)

sauté [sɔˈteɪ, so-] *vt* **-téed** *or* **-téd; -téing** : faire sauter

savage[1] [ˈsævɪdʒ] *adj* : féroce, sauvage, brutal — **savagely** *adv*

savage[2] *n* : sauvage *mf*

savagery [ˈsævɪdʒri] *n, pl* **-ries** : sauvagerie *f*

save[1] [ˈseɪv] *v* **saved; saving** *vt* **1** RESCUE : sauver **2** KEEP, RESERVE : mettre de côté, garder (des biens, une place, etc.), économiser (de l'argent) **3** SPARE : épargner <she saved me an unnecessary trip : elle m'a épargné un déplacement inutile> **4** : sauvegarder (en informatique) — *vi* : économiser

save[2] *n* : arrêt *m* (aux sports)

save[3] *prep* EXCEPT : sauf, excepté

savior [ˈseɪvjər] *n* : sauveur *m*

savor[1] [ˈseɪvər] *vt* : savourer

savor[2] *n* : saveur *f*

savory [ˈseɪvəri] *adj* : savoureux

saw[1] → **see**[1]

saw[2] [ˈsɔ] *vt* **sawed; sawed** *or* **sawn** [ˈsɔn]; **sawing** : scier

saw[3] *n* : scie *f*

sawdust [ˈsɔˌdʌst] *n* : sciure *f*

sawhorse [ˈsɔˌhɔrs] *n* : chevalet *m*

sawmill *n* [ˈsɔˌmɪl] : scierie *f*

saxophone [ˈsæksəˌfoːn] *n* : saxophone *m*

say[1] [ˈseɪ] *v* **said** [ˈsɛd]; **saying; says** [ˈsɛz] *vt* **1** SPEAK, UTTER : dire <to say no : dire non> <it goes without saying that . . . : il va sans dire que . . .> <say your prayers : fais tes prières> **2** EXPRESS, INDICATE : exprimer, indiquer, dire <my watch says three o'clock : ma montre indique trois heures> **3** ALLEGE : dire <it's said that she's pretty : l'on dit qu'elle est belle> — *vi* : dire <I'd rather not say : je préfère ne pas le dire> <that is to say : c'est-à-dire>

say[2] *n, pl* **says** [ˈseɪz] : mot *m*, voix *f* <to have no say : ne pas avoir voix au chapitre> <to have one's say : dire son mot, dire ce qu'on a à dire>

saying [ˈseɪɪŋ] *n* : dicton *m*, proverbe *m*

scab [ˈskæb] *n* **1** : croûte *f*, gale *f Can* **2** STRIKEBREAKER : jaune *mf*

scabbard [ˈskæbərd] *n* : fourreau *m*

scabby [ˈskæbi] *adj* **scabbier; -est** : croûteux

scaffold [ˈskæfəld, -ˌfoːld] *n* **1** *or* **scaffolding** : échafaudage *m* **2** : échafaud *m* (pour exécutions)

scald [ˈskɔld] *vt* **1** BURN : ébouillanter **2** HEAT : échauder

scale[1] [ˈskeɪl] *v* **scaled; scaling** *vt* **1** : écailler (un poisson) **2** CLIMB : escalader **3 to scale down** : réduire — *vi* WEIGH : peser <he scaled in at 200 pounds : il pesait 200 livres>

scale[2] *n* **1** *or* **scales** : pèse-personne *m*, balance *f* **2** : écaille *f* (d'un poisson) **3** EXTENT : étendue *f*, échelle *f* <on a large scale : sur une grande échelle> **4** : échelle *f* <drawn to scale : dessiné à l'échelle> **5** : gamme *f* (en musique)

scallion [ˈskæljən] *n* : ciboule *f*, échalote *f*

scallop [ˈskɑləp, ˈskæ-] *n* **1** : coquille *f* Saint-Jacques **2** : feston *m* (en couture)

scalp[1] [ˈskælp] *vt* : scalper

scalp[2] *n* : cuir *m* chevelu

scalpel [ˈskælpəl] *n* : scalpel *m*

scaly [ˈskeɪli] *adj* **scalier; -est** : écailleux

scamp [ˈskæmp] *n* : polisson *m*, -sonne *f*; galopin *m*

scamper [ˈskæmpər] *vi* : gambader, galoper

scan[1] [ˈskæn] *v* **scanned; scanning** *vt* **1** : scander (un vers) **2** SCRUTINIZE : scruter <to scan the horizon : scruter l'horizon> **3** PERUSE : parcourir rapidement (un texte), feuilleter (une revue) **4** : examiner au scanner (en médecine) **5** : balayer (en électronique) — *vi* : se scander (se dit d'un vers)

scan[2] *n* **1** : balayage *m* (électronique) **2** : scanographie *f*, échographie *f* (ultrasonore) **3** : scansion *f* (littéraire)

scandal [ˈskændəl] *n* **1** DISGRACE : scandale *m* **2** GOSSIP : médisance *f*

scandalize [ˈskændəlˌaɪz] *vt* **-ized; -izing** : scandaliser

scandalous [ˈskændələs] *adj* : scandaleux

Scandinavian[1] [ˌskændəˈneɪvɪən] *adj* : scandinave

Scandinavian[2] *n* : Scandinave *mf*

scanner ['skænər] *n* : scanner *m*

scant ['skænt] *adj* : maigre, insuffisant

scanty ['skænti] *adj* **scantier; -est 1** : maigre, insuffisant <a scanty meal : un repas insuffisant> **2** BRIEF : léger (se dit des vêtements)

scapegoat ['skeɪp,go:t] *n* : bouc *m* émissaire

scapula ['skæpjələ] *n, pl* **-lae** [-ˌli:, -ˌlaɪ] *or* **-las** : omoplate *f*

scar[1] ['skɑr] *v* **scarred; scarring** *vt* : marquer d'une cicatrice — *vi* : se cicatriser

scar[2] *n* : cicatrice *f*

scarab ['skærəb] *n* : scarabée *m*

scarce ['skɛrs] *adj* **scarcer; -est** : rare

scarcely ['skɛrsli] *adv* **1** BARELY : à peine <he can scarcely read : il sait à peine lire> **2** HARDLY : difficilement <I can scarcely blame him : je peux difficilement le reprocher>

scarcity ['skɛrsəṱi] *n, pl* **-ties** : rareté *f*, manque *m*

scare[1] ['skɛr] *vt* **scared; scaring** : faire peur à, effrayer

scare[2] *n* **1** FRIGHT : peur *f* **2** ALARM : alerte *f*

scarecrow ['skɛr,kro:] *n* : épouvantail *m*

scarf ['skɑrf] *n, pl* **scarves** ['skɑrvz] *or* **scarfs** : écharpe *f* (longue), foulard *m* (carré)

scarlet[1] ['skɑrlət] *adj* : écarlate

scarlet[2] *n* : écarlate *f*

scarlet fever *n* : scarlatine *f*

scary ['skɛri] *adj* **scarier, -est** : qui fait peur, effrayant, épeurant *Can*

scathing ['skeɪðɪŋ] *adj* : cinglant, mordant

scatter ['skæṱər] *vt* : disperser, éparpiller — *vi* DISPERSE : se disperser

scavenge ['skævəndʒ] *v* **-venged; -venging** *vt* : récupérer — *vi* : fouiller

scavenger ['skævəndʒər] *n* : charognard *m* (animal), pilleur *m* de poubelles (personne)

scenario [sə'næri,o:, -'nɑr-] *n, pl* **-ios** : scénario *m*

scene ['si:n] *n* **1** : scène *f* <the political scene : la scène politique> **2** SCENERY, SET : décor *m* **3** VIEW : vue *f* **4** LOCATION : lieu *m* <the scene of the crime : le lieu du crime>

scenery ['si:nəri] *n, pl* **-eries 1** : décor *m* **2** LANDSCAPE : paysages *mpl*

scenic ['si:nɪk] *adj* : pittoresque

scent[1] ['sɛnt] *vt* **1** SMELL : flairer (le gibier, le danger, etc.) **2** PERFUME : parfumer

scent[2] *n* **1** ODOR : odeur *f*, senteur *f* **2** NOSE, SMELLING : odorat *m*, flair *m* <a dog with a keen scent : un chien qui a du flair> **3** PERFUME : parfum *m*

scented ['sɛntəd] *adj* : parfumé

scepter ['sɛptər] *n* : sceptre *m*

sceptic ['skɛptɪk] → **skeptic**

schedule[1] ['skɛ,dʒu:l, -dʒəl *esp Brit* ʃɛd,ju:l] *vt* **-uled; -uling** : prévoir, programmer

schedule[2] *n* **1** LIST : liste *f* **2** TIMETABLE : horaire *m* **3** PLAN : programme *m*, plan *m*

schematic [ski'mæṱɪk] *adj* : schématique

scheme[1] ['ski:m] *vi* **schemed; scheming** : intriguer, comploter

scheme[2] *n* **1** PLAN : projet *m*, plan *m* **2** PLOT : complot *m*, intrigue *f* **3** SYSTEM : système *m*

schemer ['ski:mər] *n* : intrigant *m*, -gante *f*

schism ['sɪzəm, 'skɪ-] *n* : schisme *m*

schizophrenia [ˌskɪtsə'fri:niə, ˌskɪzə-, -'frɛ-] *n* : schizophrénie *f*

schizophrenic [ˌskɪtsə'frɛnɪk, ˌskɪzə-] *adj* : schizophrène

scholar ['skɑlər] *n* **1** STUDENT : étudiant *m*, -diante *f*; élève *mf* **2** EXPERT : spécialiste *mf*; savant *m*, -vante *f*; érudit *m*, -dite *f*

scholarly ['skɑlərli] *adj* : savant, érudit

scholarship ['skɑlər,ʃɪp] *n* **1** LEARNING : érudition *f* **2** GRANT : bourse *f*

scholastic [skə'læstɪk] *adj* : scolaire

school[1] ['sku:l] *vt* : instruire, entraîner

school[2] *n* **1** : école *f* (institution) <elementary school : école primaire> **2** : école *f* (en peinture, etc.) <the Flemish school : l'école flamande> **3** COLLEGE : faculté *f* <medical school : faculté de médecine> **4** *or* **school of fish** : banc *m*

schoolboy ['sku:l,bɔɪ] *n* : écolier *m*

schoolgirl ['sku:l,gərl] *n* : écolière *f*

schoolhouse ['sku:l,haʊs] *n* : école *f*

schoolmate ['sku:l,meɪt] *n* : camarade *mf* de classe

schoolroom ['sku:l,ru:m] *n* : salle *f* de classe

schoolteacher ['sku:l,ti:tʃər] *n* : instituteur *m*, -trice *f*; enseignant *m*, -gnante *f*

schooner ['sku:nər] *n* : schooner *m*, goélette *f*

science ['saɪənts] *n* : science *f*

scientific [ˌsaɪən'tɪfɪk] *adj* : scientifique — **scientifically** [-fɪkli] *adv*

scientist ['saɪəntɪst] *n* : scientifique *mf*

scintillate ['sɪntəl,eɪt] *vi* **-lated; -lating** : scintiller

scintillating ['sɪntəl,eɪtɪŋ] *adj* : scintillant

scissors ['sɪzərz] *ns & pl* : ciseaux *mpl*

scoff ['skɑf] *vi* **to scoff at** : se moquer de

scold ['sko:ld] *vt* : gronder, réprimander

scoop[1] ['sku:p] *vt* **1 to scoop out** : évider, creuser **2 to scoop up** : prendre, ramasser (à la pelle)

scoop[2] *n* **1** SHOVEL : pelle *f* **2** *or* **ice cream scoop** : cuillère *f* à glace **3** : exclusivité *f* (en journalisme)

scoot ['sku:t] *vi* : filer *fam*

scooter ['sku:t̬ər] *n* **1** : trottinette *f* **2** *or* **motor scooter** : scooter *m*

scope ['sko:p] *n* **1** EXTENT : étendue *f*, limites *fpl* **2** OPPORTUNITY : possibilité *f*, occasion *f*

scorch ['skɔrtʃ] *vt* : roussir

score[1] ['skor] *v* **scored; scoring** *vt* **1** RECORD : enregistrer **2** MARK, SCRATCH : marquer, rayer **3** : marquer (aux sports) **4** GRADE : noter **5** ORCHESTRATE : orchestrer, arranger — *vi* **1** : marquer des points (aux sports) **2** : obtenir une note (sur un examen)

score[2] *n, pl* **scores 1** *or pl* **score** TWENTY : vingt *m*, vingtaine *f* **2** : score *m*, marque *f*, pointage *m Can* (aux sports) **3** LINE, SCRATCH : rayure *f*, entaille *f* **4** ACCOUNT : compte *m*, point *m* <to settle a score : régler un compte> <on that score : sur ce point> **5** : partition *f* (en musique)

scorekeeper ['skor,ki:pər] *n* : marqueur *m*, -queuse *f*; pointeur *m*, -teuse *f Can*

scorn[1] ['skɔrn] *vt* : mépriser

scorn[2] *n* : mépris *m*, dédain *m*

scornful ['skɔrnfəl] *adj* : méprisant — **scornfully** *adv*

Scorpio ['skɔrpi,o:] *n* : Scorpion *m*

scorpion ['skɔrpiən] *n* : scorpion *m*

Scot ['skɑt] *n* : Écossais *m*, -saise *f*

Scotch[1] ['skɑtʃ] *adj* → **Scottish**[1]

Scotch[2] *n* **1** *or* **Scotch whiskey** : scotch *m* **2 the Scotch** : les Écossais

scot–free ['skɑt'fri:] *adj* **to get off scot–free** : s'en tirer sans être puni

Scots ['skɑts] *n* : écossais *m* (langue)

Scottish[1] ['skɑt̬ɪʃ] *adj* : écossais

Scottish[2] *n* → **Scots**

scoundrel ['skaʊndrəl] *n* : scélérat *m*, vaurien *m*

scour ['skaʊər] *vt* : récurer

scourge[1] ['skərdʒ] *vt* **scourged; scourging 1** WHIP : fouetter **2** PUNISH : châtier

scourge[2] *n* **1** WHIP : fouet *m* **2** BANE : fléau *m*

scout[1] ['skaʊt] *vi* **1** RECONNOITER : aller en reconnaissance **2 to scout around for** : aller à la recherche de

scout[2] *n* **1** : éclaireur *m*, -reuse *f*; scout *m*, scoute *f* **2** *or* **talent scout** : découvreur *m*, -vreuse *f* de nouveaux talents

scow ['skaʊ] *n* : chaland *m*

scowl[1] ['skaʊl] *vi* : se renfrogner, faire la grimace

scowl[2] *n* : mine *f* renfrognée

scraggly ['skrægli] *adj* UNKEMPT : en bataille (se dit d'une barbe, etc.)

scram ['skræm] *vi* **scrammed; scramming** : filer *fam*

scramble[1] ['skræmbəl] *v* **-bled; -bling** *vi* **1** CLAMBER : grimper <to scramble over : escalader> **2 to scramble for** : se bousculer pour, se disputer — *vt* : brouiller <to scramble eggs : faire des œufs brouillés>

scramble[2] *n* : bousculade *f*

scrap[1] ['skræp] *v* **scrapped; scrapping** *vt* DISCARD : mettre au rebut <we scrapped that idea : nous avons laissé tomber cette idée-là> — *vi* FIGHT : se battre

scrap[2] *n* **1** FRAGMENT : bout *m*, fragment *m* **2** FIGHT : bagarre *f* **3** *or* **scrap metal** : ferraille *f* **4 scraps** *npl* LEFTOVERS : restes *mpl*

scrapbook ['skræp,bʊk] *n* : album *m*

scrape[1] ['skreɪp] *v* **scraped; scraping** *vt* **1** SCRATCH : écorcher, érafler <to scrape one's knees : s'écorcher les genoux> **2** CLEAN : gratter <to scrape mud off : décrotter> **3 to scrape up** *or* **to scrape together** : réunir, rassembler — *vi* **1** RUB : frotter **2 to scrape by** : se débrouiller

scrape[2] *n* **1** SCRAPING : grattement *m* **2** SCRATCH : éraflure *f* **3** PREDICAMENT : embarras *m*

scraper ['skreɪpər] *n* : grattoir *m*

scratch[1] ['skrætʃ] *vt* **1** : gratter <to scratch one's head : se gratter la tête> **2** MARK : rayer **3** DELETE : supprimer **4** WOUND : écorcher, griffer, grafigner *Can* — *vi* **1** : se gratter <stop scratching! : arrête de te gratter!> **2** : griffer (se dit d'un chat)

scratch[2] *n* **1** SCRAPE : éraflure *f*, égratignure *f*, grafignure *f Can* **2** SCRATCHING : grattement *m*

scratchy ['skrætʃi] *adj* **scratchier; -est** : rêche <a scratchy sweater : un pull qui gratte>

scrawl[1] ['skrɔl] *v* : griffonner, gribouiller

scrawl[2] *n* : griffonnage *m*, gribouillage *m*

scrawny ['skrɔni] *adj* **scrawnier; -est** : maigre, décharné

scream[1] ['skri:m] *v* : hurler, crier

scream[2] *n* : hurlement *m*, cri *m* perçant

screech[1] ['skri:tʃ] *vi* **1** CRY, SCREAM : crier, hurler **2** : crisser (se dit des pneus, etc.)

screech[2] *n* **1** : cri *m* **2** : crissement *m* <the screech of tires : le crissement des pneus>

screen[1] ['skri:n] *vt* **1** SHIELD : protéger **2** CONCEAL : cacher **3** EXAMINE : trier, passer au crible **4** PROJECT : projeter, passer (un film)

screen[2] *n* **1** : écran *m* <smoke screen : écran de fumée> **2** PARTITION : paravent *m* **3** SIEVE : crible *m* **4** MOVIES : cinéma *m* **5** *or* **window screen** : moustiquaire *f*

screening ['skri:nɪŋ] *n* **1** SHOWING : projection *f* **2** SELECTION : sélection *f* **3** TEST : (test *m* de) dépistage *m* <cancer screening : dépistage du cancer>

screenplay ['skri:n,pleɪ] *n* : scénario *m*

screw[1] ['skru:] *vt* **1** : visser **2 to screw together** : se visser l'un à l'autre

screw[2] *n* **1** : vis *f* **2** PROPELLER : hélice *f*
screwdriver ['skru:ˌdraɪvər] *n* : tournevis *m*
scribble[1] ['skrɪbəl] *v* **-bled; -bling** : gribouiller, griffonner
scribble[2] *n* : gribouillage *m*, griffonnage *m*
scribe ['skraɪb] *n* : scribe *m*
scrimp ['skrɪmp] *vi* : économiser, faire des économies
script ['skrɪpt] *n* **1** HANDWRITING : écriture *f* **2** TEXT : scénario *m*, script *m*
scriptural ['skrɪptʃərəl] *adj* : biblique
scripture ['skrɪptʃər] *n* **1** : texte *m* sacré **2 the Holy Scripture(s)** : l'Écriture *f* sainte, les Saintes Écritures
scroll[1] ['skro:l] *vi* : défiler (en informatique)
scroll[2] *n* : rouleau *m*
scrotum ['skro:ţəm] *n, pl* **scrota** [-ţə] *or* **scrotums** : scrotum *m*
scrounge ['skraʊndʒ] *v* **scrounged; scrounging** *vt* **1** CADGE : quémander **2** BORROW : emprunter — *vi* **1 to scrounge around for** : chercher **2 to scrounge off s.o.** : vivre aux crochets de qqn
scrub[1] ['skrʌb] *vt* **scrubbed; scrubbing 1** CLEAN : frotter, nettoyer à la brosse **2** SCRAP : laisser tomber, annuler
scrub[2] *n* **1** UNDERBRUSH : broussailles *fpl* **2** CLEANING : nettoyage *m*
scrubby ['skrʌbi] *adj* **scrubbier; -est 1** STUNTED : rabougri **2** OVERGROWN : broussailleux
scruff ['skrʌf] *n* **by the scruff of the neck** : par la peau du cou
scrumptious ['skrəmpʃəs] *adj* : délicieux
scruple ['skru:pəl] *n* : scrupule *f*
scrupulous ['skru:pjələs] *adj* : scrupuleux — **scrupulously** *adv*
scrutinize ['skru:tənˌaɪz] *vt* **-nized; -nizing** : scruter
scrutiny ['skru:təni] *n, pl* **-nies** : examen *m* (approfondi)
scuff ['skʌf] *vt* **1** SCRAPE : érafler **2 to scuff one's feet** : traîner les pieds
scuffle[1] ['skʌfəl] *vi* **-fled; -fling** TUSSLE : se bagarrer
scuffle[2] *n* : bagarre *f*
scull[1] ['skʌl] *vi* : godiller, ramer
scull[2] *n* PADDLE : godille *f*
sculpt ['skʌlpt] *vt* : sculpter
sculptor ['skʌlptər] *n* : sculpteur *m*
sculpture[1] ['skəlptʃər] *vt* **-tured; -turing** : sculpter
sculpture[2] *n* : sculpture *f*
scum ['skʌm] *n* FROTH : écume *f*
scurrilous ['skərələs] *adj* : calomnieux
scurry ['skəri] *vi* **-ried; -rying** : se précipiter
scurvy ['skərvi] *n* : scorbut *m*
scuttle[1] ['skʌţəl] *v* **-tled; -tling** *vt* : saborder (un navire) — *vi* : courir à toute vitesse, se précipiter
scuttle[2] *n or* **coal scuttle** : seau *m* à charbon
scythe ['saɪð] *n* : faux *f*
sea[1] ['si:] *adj* : de mer
sea[2] *n* **1** OCEAN : mer *f* **2** MASS : multitude *f*
seabird ['si:ˌbərd] *n* : oiseau *m* de mer
seaboard ['si:ˌbɔrd] *n* : littoral *m*
seacoast ['si:ˌko:st] *n* : côte *f* (de la mer)
seafarer ['si:ˌfærər] *n* : marin *m*
seafaring[1] ['si:ˌfærɪŋ] *adj* : maritime
seafaring[2] *n* : navigation *f*
seafood ['si:ˌfu:d] *n* : fruits *mpl* de mer
seagull ['si:ˌgʌl] *n* : mouette *f*
sea horse ['si:ˌhɔrs] *n* : hippocampe *m*
seal[1] ['si:l] *vt* : sceller
seal[2] *n* **1** STAMP : sceau *m*, cachet *m* **2** CLOSURE : fermeture *f* **3** GASKET : joint *m* étanche **4** : phoque *m*, loup-marin *m Can* (animal)
sea level *n* : niveau *m* de la mer
sea lion *n* : otarie *f*
sealskin ['si:lˌskɪn] *n* : peau *f* de phoque
seam[1] ['si:m] *vt* **1** STITCH : coudre **2** MARK : marquer <a face seamed with wrinkles : un visage marqué de rides>
seam[2] *n* **1** STITCHING : couture *f* **2** VEIN, LODE : veine *f*, filon *m*
seaman ['si:mən] *n, pl* **-men** [-mən, -ˌmɛn] : marin *m*
seamless ['si:mləs] *adj* : sans couture
seamstress ['si:mpstrəs] *n* : couturière *f*
seamy ['si:mi] *adj* **seamier; -est** : sordide
séance ['seɪˌɑnts] *n* : séance *f* de spiritisme
seaplane ['si:ˌpleɪn] *n* : hydravion *m*
seaport ['si:ˌport] *n* : port *m* maritime
sear ['sɪr] *vt* **1** PARCH, WITHER : dessécher, flétrir **2** BURN, SCORCH : calciner, brûler
search[1] ['sərtʃ] *vt* **1** : chercher dans, fouiller (dans) <I searched the house : j'ai cherché dans la maison> <to search a suspect : fouiller un suspect> **2** : rechercher dans (en informatique) — *vi* **to search for** : chercher
search[2] *n* **1** EXAMINATION : fouille *f* **2** QUEST : recherche *f*
searcher ['sərtʃər] *n* : chercheur *m*, -cheuse *f*
searchlight ['sərtʃˌlaɪt] *n* : projecteur *m*
seashell ['si:ˌʃɛl] *n* : coquillage *m*
seashore ['si:ˌʃor] *n* : bord *m* de la mer
seasick ['si:ˌsɪk] *adj* **to be seasick** : avoir le mal de mer
seasickness ['si:ˌsɪknəs] *n* : mal *m* de mer
seaside ['si:ˌsaɪd] → **seacoast**
season[1] ['si:zən] *vt* **1** FLAVOR, SPICE : assaisonner, épicer **2** CURE : sécher (du bois)
season[2] *n* : saison *f*
seasonable ['si:zənəbəl] *adj* : de saison
seasonal ['si:zənəl] *adj* : saisonnier

seasonally ['si:zənəli] *adv* : de façon saisonnière

seasoned ['si:zənd] *adj* **1** SPICED : assaisonné **2** EXPERIENCED : expérimenté, éprouvé **3** : desséché (se dit du bois)

seasoning ['si:zənɪŋ] *n* : assaisonnement *m*

seat[1] ['si:t] *vt* **1** SIT : faire asseoir <please be seated : veuillez vous asseoir> **2** ACCOMMODATE, HOLD : avoir des places assises pour, tenir <this car seats five : on tient à cinq dans cette voiture>

seat[2] *n* **1** CHAIR : siège *m* **2** ACCOMMODATION, PLACE : place *f* **3** : fond *m* (de pantalon) **4** CENTER : centre *m*, siège *m* (du gouvernement, etc.)

seat belt *n* : ceinture *f* de sécurité

sea urchin *n* : oursin *m*

seawall ['si:ˌwɑl] *n* : digue *f*

seawater *n* ['si:ˌwɔt̬ər, -ˌwɑ-] : eau *f* de mer

seaweed *n* ['si:ˌwi:d] : algue *f*

seaworthy ['si:ˌwərði] *adj* : en état de naviguer

secede [sɪ'si:d] *vi* **-ceded; -ceding** : se séparer, faire sécession

seclude [sɪ'klu:d] *vt* **-cluded; -cluding** : isoler

secluded *adj* : isolé, retiré, à l'écart

seclusion [sɪ'klu:ʒən] *n* : isolement *m*, solitude *f*

second[1] ['sɛkənd] *vt* : affirmer, appuyer (une motion)

second[2] *or* **secondly** ['sɛkəndli] *adv* : deuxièmement, en second lieu

second[3] *adj* : second, deuxième <in the second place : en deuxième lieu> <a second chance : une seconde chance>

second[4] *n* **1** MOMENT : seconde *f* **2** : deuxième *mf*; second *m*, -conde *f* <the second of June : le deux juin> **3** : soigneur *m* (à la boxe), témoin *m* (dans un duel) **4** *or* **factory second** : articles *mpl* de second choix

secondary ['sɛkənˌdɛri] *adj* : secondaire

secondhand ['sɛkənd'hænd] *adj* : d'occasion

second lieutenant *n* : sous-lieutenant *m*

secrecy ['si:krəsi] *n, pl* **-cies** : secret *m* <to swear to secrecy : faire jurer le secret>

secret[1] ['si:krət] *adj* : secret

secret[2] *n* : secret *m*

secretarial [ˌsɛkrə'tɛriəl] *adj* : de secrétaire

secretariat [ˌsɛkrə'tɛriət] *n* : secrétariat *m*

secretary ['sɛkrəˌtɛri] *n, pl* **-taries** : secrétaire *mf*

secrete [sɪ'kri:t] *vt* **-creted; -creting 1** EXUDE : sécréter **2** HIDE : cacher

secretion [sɪ'kri:ʃən] *n* : sécrétion *f*

secretive ['si:krət̬ɪv, sɪ'kri:t̬ɪv] *adj* : cachottier, secret

secretly ['si:krətli] *adv* : secrètement

sect ['sɛkt] *n* : secte *f*

sectarian [sɛk'tɛriən] *adj* : sectaire

section ['sɛkʃən] *n* : section *f*, partie *f*

sectional ['sɛkʃənəl] *adj* **1** : en coupe, en profil <a sectional diagram : un schéma en coupe> **2** FACTIONAL : d'un groupe **3** MODULAR : à éléments

sector ['sɛktər] *n* : secteur *m*

secular ['sɛkjələr] *adj* **1** : séculaire, laïque **2** : profane (se dit de la musique, etc.)

secure[1] [sɪ'kjʊr] *vt* **-cured; -curing 1** FASTEN : fixer **2** OBTAIN : procurer **3** GUARANTEE : assurer

secure[2] *adj* **securer; -est** : sûr, en sécurité

securely [sɪ'kjʊrli] *adv* **1** FIRMLY : fermement, solidement, bien **2** SAFELY : en sécurité

security [sɪ'kjʊrət̬i] *n, pl* **-ties 1** SAFETY : sécurité *f* **2** GUARANTEE : garantie *f* **3 securities** *npl* : titres *mpl*, valeurs *fpl*, actions *fpl*

sedan [sɪ'dæn] *n* : berline *f*

sedate[1] [sɪ'deɪt] *vt* **-dated; -dating** : tranquilliser, mettre sous calmants

sedate[2] *adj* : posé, calme — **sedately** *adv*

sedation [sɪ'deɪʃən] *n* : sédation *f*

sedative[1] ['sɛdət̬ɪv] *adj* : sédatif

sedative[2] *n* : calmant *m*, sédatif *m*

sedentary ['sɛdənˌtɛri] *adj* : sédentaire

sedge ['sɛdʒ] *n* : laîche *f*

sediment ['sɛdəmənt] *n* : sédiment *m*

sedimentary [ˌsɛdə'mɛntəri] *adj* : sédimentaire

sedition [sɪ'dɪʃən] *n* : sédition *f*

seditious [sɪ'dɪʃəs] *adj* : séditieux

seduce [sɪ'du:s, -'dju:s] *vt* **-duced; -ducing** : séduire

seduction [sɪ'dʌkʃən] *n* : séduction *f*

seductive [sɪ'dʌktɪv] *adj* : séduisant

see[1] ['si:] *v* **saw** ['sɔ]; **seen** ['si:n]; **seeing** *vt* **1** : voir <I saw a dog : j'ai vu un chien> <see you later! : au revoir!> **2** EXPERIENCE : connaître, voir **3** UNDERSTAND : voir, comprendre **4** *or* **to see that** ENSURE : s'assurer, veiller à **5** ACCOMPANY : accompagner <he'll see me home : il me raccompagnera chez moi> — *vi* **1** : voir <seeing is believing : voir c'est croire> **2** UNDERSTAND : comprendre, voir **3** CONSIDER : voir <let's see : voyons> **4 to see to** : s'occuper de

see[2] *n* : évêché *m*

seed[1] ['si:d] *vt* **1** SOW : semer **2** : épépiner, enlever la graine de <to seed grapes : épépiner des raisins>

seed[2] *n, pl* **seed** *or* **seeds 1** : graine *f* **2** SOURCE : germe *m*

seedless ['si:dləs] *adj* : sans pépins

seedling ['si:dlɪŋ] *n* : semis *m*, jeune plant *m*

seedy ['si:di] *adj* **seedier; -est 1** : plein de graines **2** SHABBY : miteux

seek ['si:k] *v* **sought** ['sɔt]; **seeking** *vt* **1** : chercher **2** REQUEST : demander — *vi* **to seek after** : rechercher, chercher

seem ['si:m] *vi* : paraître, sembler, avoir l'air <she seems tired : elle a l'air fatiguée> <it would seem not : il paraît que non>

seemingly ['si:mɪŋli] *adv* : apparemment

seemly ['si:mli] *adj* **seemlier; -est** : convenable

seep ['si:p] *vi* : suinter

seepage ['si:pɪdʒ] *n* : suintement *m*

seer ['si:ər] *n* : voyant *m*, voyante *f*

seesaw[1] ['si:ˌsɔ] *vi* **1** : jouer à la bascule **2** VACILLATE : balancer, osciller

seesaw[2] *n* : balançoire *f*, bascule *f*

seethe ['si:ð] *vi* **seethed; seething** : bouillonner

segment ['sɛgmənt] *n* : segment *m*

segmented ['sɛgˌmɛntəd, sɛg'mɛn-] *adj* : segmentaire

segregate ['sɛgrɪˌgeɪt] *vt* **-gated; -gating** : séparer, isoler

segregation [ˌsɛgrɪ'geɪʃən] *n* : ségrégation *f*

seismic ['saɪzmɪk, 'saɪs-] *adj* : sismique

seize ['si:z] *v* **seized; seizing** *vt* **1** CAPTURE : se saisir de, capturer, appréhender **2** GRASP : saisir, s'emparer de — *vi or* **to seize up** : se gripper

seizure ['si:ʒər] *n* **1** CAPTURE : prise *f*, saisie *f* **2** ARREST : arrestation *f* **3** ATTACK : attaque *f*, crise *f* <epileptic seizure : crise d'épilepsie>

seldom ['sɛldəm] *adv* : rarement

select[1] [sə'lɛkt] *vt* : choisir, sélectionner

select[2] *adj* : privilégié, sélect *fam*, choisi <a select few : seulement quelques privilégiés>

selection [sə'lɛkʃən] *n* : sélection *f*

selective [sə'lɛktɪv] *adj* : sélectif

self ['sɛlf] *n, pl* **selves** ['sɛlvz] **1** : moi *m*, être *m* <with his whole self : avec tout son être> <the self : le moi> **2** SIDE : côté *m* <his better self : son meilleur côté>

self–addressed envelope [ˌsɛlfə'drɛst] *n* : enveloppe *f* à mon (son) nom et adresse

self–appointed [ˌsɛlfə'pɔɪntəd] *adj* : qui s'est nommé

self–assurance [ˌsɛlfə'ʃʊrənts] *n* : assurance *f*, confiance *f* en soi

self–assured [ˌsɛlfə'ʃʊrd] *adj* : sûr de soi

self–centered [ˌsɛlf'sɛntərd] *adj* : égocentrique

self–confidence [ˌsɛlf'kɑnfədents] *n* : confiance *f* en soi

self–confident [ˌsɛlf'kɑnfədənt] *adj* : sûr de soi

self–conscious [ˌsɛlf'kɑntʃəs] *adj* **1** EMBARRASSED : timide, gêné **2** DELIBERATE : appuyé

self–consciously [ˌsɛlf'kɑntʃəsli] *adv* : timidement

self–consciousness [ˌsɛlf'kɑntʃəsnəs] *n* : timidité *f*, gêne *f*

self–contained [ˌsɛlfkən'teɪnd] *adj* : indépendant

self–control [ˌsɛlfkən'tro:l] *n* : maîtrise *f* de soi

self–defense [ˌsɛlfdɪ'fɛnts] *n* : légitime défense *f*

self–denial [ˌsɛlfdɪ'naɪəl] *n* : abnégation *f*

self–destructive [ˌsɛlfdɪ'strʌktɪv] *adj* : autodestructeur

self–determination [ˌsɛlfdɪˌtərmə'neɪʃən] *n* : autodétermination *f*

self–discipline [ˌsɛlf'dɪsəplən] *n* : autodiscipline *f*

self–employed [ˌsɛlfɪm'plɔɪd] *adj* : indépendant <she's self-employed : elle travaille à son compte>

self–esteem [ˌsɛlfɪ'sti:m] *n* : respect *m* de soi, amour-propre *m*

self–evident [ˌsɛlf'ɛvədənt] *adj* : évident

self–explanatory [ˌsɛlfɪk'splænəˌtori] *adj* : évident, explicite

self–expression [ˌsɛlfɪk'sprɛʃən] *n* : expression *f* libre

self–government [ˌsɛlf'gʌvərmənt, -vərn-] *n* : autonomie *f*

self–help [ˌsɛlf'hɛlp] *n* : initiative *f* personnelle <self-help group : groupe d'entraide>

self–important [ˌsɛlfɪm'pɔrtənt] *adj* : vaniteux, suffisant

self–indulgent [ˌsɛlfɪn'dʌldʒənt] *adj* : complaisant, qui ne se refuse rien

self–inflicted [ˌsɛlfɪn'flɪktəd] *adj* : autoinfligé

self–interest [ˌsɛlf'ɪntrəst, -təˌrɛst] *n* : intérêt *m* personnel

selfish ['sɛlfɪʃ] *adj* : égoïste

selfishly ['sɛlfɪʃli] *adv* : égoïstement

selfishness ['sɛlfɪʃnəs] *n* : égoïsme *m*

selfless ['sɛlfləs] *adj* UNSELFISH : désintéressé, altruiste

self–made [ˌsɛlf'meɪd] *adj* : qui a réussi tout seul <a self-made man : un self-made-man>

self–pity [ˌsɛlf'pɪṭi] *n, pl* **-ties** : apitoiement *m* sur soi-même

self–portrait [ˌsɛlf'pɔrtrət] *n* : autoportrait *m*

self–propelled [ˌsɛlfprə'pɛld] *adj* : autopropulsé

self–reliance [ˌsɛlfrɪ'laɪənts] *n* : autosuffisance *f*

self–respect [ˌsɛlfrɪ'spɛkt] *n* : respect *m* de soi

self–restraint [ˌsɛlfrɪ'streɪnt] *n* : retenue *f*

self–righteous [ˌsɛlf'raɪtʃəs] *adj* : suffisant

self–sacrifice [ˌsəlf'sækrəˌfaɪs] *n* : abnégation *f*

selfsame ['sɛlfˌseɪm] *adj* : même

self–service [ˌsɛlfˈsɛrvəs] *n* : libre-service *m*
self–sufficiency [ˌsɛlfsəˈfɪʃəntsi] *n* : autosuffisance *f,* indépendance *f*
self–sufficient [ˌsɛlfsəˈfɪʃənt] *adj* : autosuffisant, indépendant
self–taught [ˌsɛlfˈtɔt] *adj* : autodidacte
sell [ˈsɛl] *v* **sold** [ˈsoːld]; **selling** *vt* : vendre — *vi* : se vendre
seller [ˈsɛlər] *n* : vendeur *m,* -deuse *f*
selves → **self**
semantic [sɪˈmæntɪk] *adj* : sémantique
semantics [sɪˈmæntɪks] *ns & pl* : sémantique *f*
semaphore [ˈsɛməˌfor] *n* : sémaphore *m*
semblance [ˈsɛmbləntś] *n* : semblant *m,* apparence *f*
semen [ˈsiːmən] *n* : sperme *m*
semester [səˈmɛstər] *n* : semestre *m*
semicolon [ˈsɛmiˌkoːlən, ˈsɛˌmaɪ-] *n* : point-virgule *m*
semiconductor [ˈsɛmikənˌdʌktər, ˈsɛˌmaɪ-] *n* : semiconducteur *m*
semifinal [ˈsɛmiˌfaɪnəl, ˈsɛˌmaɪ-] *n* : demi-finale *f*
seminal [ˈsɛmənəl] *adj* : séminal
seminar [ˈsɛməˌnɑr] *n* : séminaire *m*
seminary [ˈsɛməˌnɛri] *n, pl* **-naries** : séminaire *m*
senate [ˈsɛnət] *n* : sénat *m*
senator [ˈsɛnət̬ər] *n* **1** : sénateur *m* **2** : sénateur *m,* -trice *f Can*
send [ˈsɛnd] *vt* **sent** [ˈsɛnt]; **sending 1** : envoyer, expédier <he was sent to prison : on l'a envoyé en prison> <to send a letter : expédier une lettre> <to send word : faire dire> **2** PROPEL : pousser, envoyer **3 to send away for** : se faire envoyer, commander par correspondance **4 to send for** : appeler, faire venir
sender [ˈsɛndər] *n* : expéditeur *m,* -trice *f*
Senegalese[1] [ˌsɛnəgəˈliːz, -ˈliːs] *adj* : sénégalais
Senegalese[2] *n* : Sénégalais *m,* -laise *f*
senile [ˈsiːˌnaɪl] *adj* : sénile
senility [sɪˈnɪlət̬i] *n* : sénilité *f*
senior[1] [ˈsiːnjər] *adj* **1** ELDER : aîné, plus âgé <John Durant, Senior : John Durant, père> **2** : supérieur <a senior official : un officiel supérieur, un haut fonctionnaire>
senior[2] *n* **1** : aîné *m,* aînée *f* **2** *or* **high school senior** : élève *mf* de terminale **3** *or* **college senior** : étudiant *m,* -diante *f* de licence **4 to be s.o.'s senior** : être plus âgé que qqn <he is six years my senior : il a six ans de plus que moi>
seniority [ˌsiːˈnjɔrət̬i] *n* : ancienneté *f,* priorité *f* d'âge
sensation [sɛnˈseɪʃən] *n* : sensation *f*
sensational [sɛnˈseɪʃənəl] *adj* : sensationnel
sense[1] [ˈsɛnts] *vt* **sensed; sensing** : sentir <he sensed danger : il a senti le danger>
sense[2] *n* **1** FACULTY : sens *m* <sense of touch : sens du toucher> **2** MEANING : sens *m,* signification *f* **3** SENSATION : sensation *f,* sentiment *m* <a sense of guilt : un sentiment de culpabilité> **4** WISDOM : sens *m* <common sense : bon sens> **5 to make sense** : avoir du sens
senseless [ˈsɛntsləs] *adj* **1** MEANINGLESS : insensé **2** UNCONSCIOUS : sans connaissance
senselessly [ˈsɛntsləsli] *adv* : stupidement, de manière insensée
sensibility [ˌsɛntsəˈbɪlət̬i] *n, pl* **-ties** : sensibilité *f*
sensible [ˈsɛntsəbəl] *adj* **1** PERCEPTIBLE : sensible **2** AWARE : conscient **3** REASONABLE : raisonnable
sensibly [ˈsɛntsəbli] *adv* **1** PERCEPTIBLY : sensiblement, perceptiblement **2** REASONABLY : raisonnablement, de façon raisonnable
sensitive [ˈsɛntsət̬ɪv] *adj* **1** : sensible <sensitive skin : peau sensible> **2** DELICATE : délicat **3** AWARE : conscient, sensibilisé
sensitiveness [ˈsɛntsət̬ɪvnəs] → **sensitivity**
sensitivity [ˌsɛntsəˈtɪvət̬i] *n, pl* **-ties** : sensibilité *f*
sensitize [ˈsɛntsəˌtaɪz] *vt* **-tized; -tizing** : sensibiliser
sensor [ˈsɛnˌsɔr, ˈsɛntsər] *n* : détecteur *m*
sensory [ˈsɛntsəri] *adj* : sensoriel
sensual [ˈsɛntʃʊəl] *adj* : sensuel — **sensually** *adv*
sensuality [ˌsɛnʃəˈwælət̬i] *n* : sensualité *f*
sensuous [ˈsɛnʃʊəs] *adj* : sensuel
sent → **send**
sentence[1] [ˈsɛntənts, -ənz] *vt* **-tenced; -tencing** : condamner
sentence[2] *n* **1** : phrase *f* (en grammaire) **2** JUDGMENT : sentence *f,* condamnation *f*
sentiment [ˈsɛntəmənt] *n* **1** BELIEF : avis *m* **2** FEELING : sentiment *m* **3** → **sentimentality**
sentimental [ˌsɛntəˈmɛntəl] *adj* : sentimental
sentimentality [ˌsɛntəˌmɛnˈtælət̬i] *n, pl* **-ties** : sentimentalité *f,* sensiblerie *f*
sentinel [ˈsɛntənəl] *n* : sentinelle *f,* factionnaire *m*
sentry [ˈsɛntri] *n, pl* **-tries** : sentinelle *f,* factionnaire *m*
separate[1] [ˈsɛpəˌreɪt] *v* **-rated; -rating** *vt* **1** DETACH, SEVER : séparer, détacher **2** DISTINGUISH : distinguer — *vi* : se séparer
separate[2] [ˈsɛpərət] *adj* **1** INDIVIDUAL : séparé **2** DISTINCT : distinct
separately [ˈsɛpərətli] *adv* : séparément
separation [ˌsɛpəˈreɪʃən] *n* : séparation *f*
sepia [ˈsiːpiə] *n* : sépia *f*

September [sɛp'tɛmbər] *n* : septembre *m*

sepulchre ['sɛpəlkər] *n* : sépulcre *m*

sequel ['si:kwəl] *n* **1** CONSEQUENCE : conséquence *f* **2** CONTINUATION : suite *f* (d'un roman, d'un film, etc.)

sequence ['si:kwənts] *n* **1** SERIES : série *f*, succession *f* **2** ORDER : ordre *m*, suite *f*

sequential [sɪ'kwɛntʃəl] *adj* : séquentiel

sequester [sɪ'kwɛstər] *vt* : séquestrer

sequin ['si:kwən] *n* : paillette *f*, sequin *m*

sequoia [sɪ'kwɔɪə] *n* : séquoia *m*

sera → **serum**

Serb[1] ['sərb] *adj* : serbe

Serb[2] *n* **1** : Serbe *mf* **2** → **Serbian**

Serbian ['sərbiən] *n* **1** : serbe *m* (langue) **2** → **Serb**[2]

Serbo–Croatian[1] [ˌsərbokro'eɪʃən] *adj* : serbo-croate

Serbo–Croatian[2] *n* : serbo-croate *m* (langue)

serenade[1] [ˌsɛrə'neɪd] *vt* **-naded; -nading** : donner une sérénade à

serenade[2] *n* : sérénade *f*

serene [sə'ri:n] *adj* : serein — **serenely** *adv*

serenity [sə'rɛnəṭi] *n* : sérénité *f*

serf ['sərf] *n* : serf *m*, serve *f*

serge ['sərdʒ] *n* : serge *f*

sergeant ['sɑrdʒənt] *n* : sergent *m*

serial[1] ['sɪriəl] *adj* : en série, d'une série <serial number : numéro de série>

serial[2] *n* **1** : feuilleton *m* (histoire) **2** PERIODICAL : périodique *m*

serially ['sɪriəli] *adv* : en série

series ['sɪr,i:z] *ns & pl* : série *f*

serious ['sɪriəs] *adj* **1** SOBER : sérieux **2** DEDICATED, EARNEST : sérieux, dédié **3** SIGNIFICANT : important, considérable <serious damage : dommages importants> **4** GRAVE : grave, sérieux

seriously ['sɪriəsli] *adv* **1** : sérieusement <to take oneself too seriously : se prendre trop au sérieux> **2** GRAVELY : gravement

seriousness ['sɪriəsnəs] *n* : sérieux *m*

sermon ['sərmən] *n* : sermon *m*

serpent ['sərpənt] *n* : serpent *m*

serum ['sɪrəm] *n, pl* **serums** *or* **sera** ['sɪrə] : sérum *m*

servant ['sərvənt] *n* : domestique *mf*

serve[1] ['sərv] *v* **served; serving** *vi* **1** : servir <to serve in the navy : servir dans la marine> <to serve on a committee : être membre d'un comité> **2 to serve as** : servir de **3 to serve to** : servir à — *vt* **1** : servir <to serve one's country : servir son pays> **2** : desservir <a train serving the public : un train qui dessert le public> **3** PROVIDE, SUPPLY : alimenter (des services publiques) **4 to serve a sentence** : purger une peine **5 to serve a summons to** : remettre une assignation à

serve[2] *n* : service *m* (aux sports)

server ['sərvər] *n* **1** WAITER : serveur *m*, -veuse *f* **2** : serveur *m* (en informatique)

service[1] ['sərvəs] *vt* **-viced; -vicing 1** MAINTAIN : réviser, entretenir <to service a car : réviser une voiture> **2** REPAIR : réparer

service[2] *n* **1** : service *m* <to do s.o. a service : rendre un service à qqn> **2** CEREMONY : office *m* (en religion) **3** FACILITY : service *m* <social services : services sociaux> <train service : service de train> **4** SET : service *m* <tea service : service à thé> **5** MAINTENANCE : entretien *m*, révision *f* (d'une voiture, etc.) **6 services** *npl or* **armed services** : forces *fpl* armées

serviceable ['sərvəsəbəl] *adj* USABLE : utilisable

serviceman ['sərvəs,mæn, -mən] *n, pl* **-men** [-mən, -,mɛn] : militaire *m*

service station *n* : station-service *f*, poste *m* d'essence

servicewoman ['sərvəs,wʊmən] *n, pl* **-women** [-,wɪmən] : femme *f* soldat

servile ['sərvəl, -,vaɪl] *adj* : servile

serving ['sərvɪŋ] *n* HELPING : portion *f*

servitude ['sərvə,tu:d, -,tju:d] *n* : servitude *f*

sesame ['sɛsəmi] *n* : sésame *m*

session ['sɛʃən] *n* : séance *f*, session *f*

set[1] ['sɛt] *v* **set; setting** *vt* **1** *or* **to set down** PLACE : placer, mettre, poser **2** SITUATE : disposer, situer <she set the story in France : elle a situé l'histoire en France> **3** PREPARE : mettre, tendre, dresser <to set the table : mettre la table> <to set a trap : tendre un piège> **4** FIX, ESTABLISH : fixer, établir <to set a time : fixer l'heure> <to set prices : fixer les prix> <to set a record : établir un record> **5** (*indicating the cause of a certain condition*) <to set fire to : mettre le feu à> <he set it free : il l'a libéré> **6** SOLIDIFY : faire prendre — *vi* **1** SOLIDIFY : durcir, prendre **2** : se coucher (se dit du soleil et de la lune)

set[2] *adj* **1** ESTABLISHED, SETTLED : fixe, établi **2** READY : prêt, préparé **3** DETERMINED : résolu, déterminé

set[3] *n* **1** COLLECTION : ensemble *m*, série *f* <chess set : jeu d'échecs> **2** GROUP : cercle *m*, milieu *m* (social) **3** *or* **stage set** : scène *f*, plateau *m*, décor *m* **4** APPARATUS : appareil *m*, poste *m* <television set : poste de télévision> **5** SERVICE : service *m* (à thé, à café, etc.) **6** : set *m* (aux sports) **7** : ensemble *m* (en mathématiques)

setback ['sɛt,bæk] *n* : revers *m*

set off *vt* **1** PROVOKE : déclencher, provoquer **2** EXPLODE : faire exploser **3** HIGHLIGHT : mettre en valeur — *vi or* **to set forth** : se mettre en route

set out *vt* **1** ARRANGE : disposer, étaler (des marchandises, etc.) **2** PRESENT : présenter, exposer (des idées) — *vi* **1** LEAVE : se mettre en route **2** **to set out to do** : avoir pour but de faire
settee [sɛ'ti:] *n* : canapé *m*
setter ['sɛtər] *n* : setter *m* <Irish setter : setter irlandais>
setting ['sɛt̬ɪŋ] *n* **1** SURROUNDINGS : cadre *m*, décor *m* **2** MOUNTING : monture *f* (d'un bijou) **3** : réglage *m* (d'une machine) **4** : coucher *m* (du soleil)
settle ['sɛt̬əl] *v* **settled; settling** *vi* **1** LAND : poser (se dit des oiseaux), laisser tomber (se dit de la poussière) **2** SINK : s'effondrer (se dit des bâtiments) **3** : s'installer (dans une maison, dans un fauteuil), se fixer (dans une région, dans un pays, etc.) **4** **to settle down** : se calmer **5** **to settle for** : accepter, se contenter de **6** **to settle over** : descendre sur — *vt* **1** ARRANGE, RESOLVE : résoudre, régler **2** DETERMINE : décider, fixer **3** CALM : calmer, apaiser **4** PAY : payer, régler (une dette) **5** COLONIZE : coloniser
settlement ['sɛt̬əlmənt] *n* **1** PAYMENT : règlement *m* **2** COLONY : colonie *f* **3** RESOLUTION : résolution *f*, accord *m*
settler ['sɛt̬ələr] *n* : colonisateur *m*, -trice *f*; colon *m*
set up *vt* **1** ASSEMBLE : installer **2** ERECT : monter **3** ESTABLISH : établir
seven[1] ['sɛvən] *adj* : sept
seven[2] *n* : sept *m*
seventeen[1] [ˌsɛvən'ti:n] *adj* : dix-sept
seventeen[2] *n* : dix-sept *m*
seventeenth[1] [ˌsɛvən'ti:nθ] *adj* : dix-septième
seventeenth[2] *n* **1** : dix-septième *mf* (dans une série) **2** : dix-septième *m* (en mathématiques) **3** (*used in dates*) <the seventeenth of January : le dix-sept janvier>
seventh[1] [ˌsɛvənθ] *adj* : septième
seventh[2] *n* **1** : septième *mf* (dans une série) **2** : septième *m* (en mathématiques) **3** (*used in dates*) <the seventh of March : le sept Mars>
seventieth[1] ['sɛvəntiəθ] *adj* : soixante-dixième, septantième *Bel, Switz*
seventieth[2] *n* **1** : soixante-dixième *mf*, septantième *mf Bel, Switz* (dans une série) **2** : soixante-dixième *m* (en mathématiques)
seventy[1] ['sɛvənti] *adj* : soixante-dix, septante *Bel, Switz*
seventy[2] *n, pl* **-ties** : soixante-dix *m*, septante *mf Bel, Switz*
sever ['sɛvər] *vt* **-ered; -ering** **1** CUT : couper **2** BREAK : rompre, cesser <to sever ties with : rompre les liens avec>
several[1] ['sɛvrəl, 'sɛvə-] *adj* : plusieurs
several[2] *pron* : plusieurs
severance ['sɛvrənts, 'sɛvə-] *n* **1** : rupture *f* **2** **severance pay** : indemnité *f* de départ
severe [sə'vɪr] *adj* **severer; -est** **1** STRICT : sévère **2** AUSTERE : austère, sévère **3** SERIOUS : grave **4** DIFFICULT : dur, rigoureux
severely [sə'vɪrli] *adv* **1** HARSHLY : durement, sévèrement **2** SERIOUSLY : gravement, sérieusement **3** AUSTERELY : d'une façon austère
severity [sə'vɛrət̬i] *n* **1** HARSHNESS : sévérité *f* **2** SERIOUSNESS : gravité *f*
sew ['so:] *v* **sewed; sewn** ['so:n] *or* **sewed; sewing** : coudre
sewage ['su:ɪdʒ] *n* : eaux *fpl* d'égout
sewer[1] ['so:ər] *n* : couseur *m*, -seuse *f*
sewer[2] ['su:ər] *n* : égout *m*
sewing ['so:ɪŋ] *n* : couture *f*
sex ['sɛks] *n* **1** GENDER : sexe *m* **2** COPULATION : rapports *mpl* sexuels
sexism ['sɛkˌsɪzəm] *n* : sexisme *m*
sexist[1] ['sɛksɪst] *adj* : sexiste
sexist[2] *n* : sexiste *mf*
sextant ['sɛkstənt] *n* : sextant *m*
sextet [sɛk'stɛt] *n* : sextuor *m*
sexton ['sɛkstən] *n* : sacristain *m*
sexual ['sɛkʃʊəl] *adj* : sexuel — **sexually** *adv*
sexuality [ˌsɛkʃʊ'ælət̬i] *n* : sexualité *f*
sexy ['sɛksi] *adj* **sexier; -est** : sexy
shabbily ['ʃæbəli] *adv* **1** POORLY : pauvrement **2** MEANLY : mesquinement
shabbiness ['ʃæbinəs] *n* **1** : pauvreté *f*, délabrement *m* **2** MEANNESS : mesquinerie *f*
shabby ['ʃæbi] *adj* **shabbier; -est** **1** WORN : usé, miteux **2** MEAN : vilain, mesquin
shack ['ʃæk] *n* : cabane *f*, hutte *f*
shackle ['ʃækəl] *vt* **-led; -ling** **1** BIND : enchaîner, mettre aux fers **2** HAMPER : entraver
shackles ['ʃækəlz] *npl* : chaînes *fpl*, fers *mpl*
shad ['ʃæd] *n* : alose *f*
shade[1] ['ʃeɪd] *v* **shaded; shading** *vt* **1** : ombrager <the trees shade the courtyard : les arbres ombragent la cour> **2** SCREEN : abriter, donner de l'ombre à, protéger <to shade one's eyes : s'abriter les yeux> **3** *or* **to shade in** : hachurer — *vi* **to shade into** : se fondre en
shade[2] *n* **1** : ombre *f* <in the shade : à l'ombre> **2** GRADATION : ton *m*, nuance *f* **3** BIT : peu *m* <a shade larger : un peu plus grand>
shadow[1] ['ʃædo:] *vt* **1** DARKEN : ombrager **2** FOLLOW : filer
shadow[2] *n* **1** : ombre *f* **2** **to cast a shadow over** : projeter une ombre sur
shadowy ['ʃædowi] *adj* **1** DARK : sombre **2** INDISTINCT : vague **3** MYSTERIOUS : mystérieux

shady [ˈʃeɪdi] *adj* **shadier; -est 1** : ombragé **2** DISREPUTABLE : louche

shaft [ˈʃæft] *n* **1** : arbre *m* (d'un moteur) **2** *or* **mine shaft** : puits *m* **3** *or* **shaft of light** : rai *m* **4** HANDLE, STEM : manche *m* (d'un outil), tige *f* (d'une flèche) **5 elevator shaft** : cage *f*

shaggy [ˈʃægi] *adj* **shaggier; -est 1** HAIRY : poilu, broussailleux **2** UNKEMPT : débraillé

shake[1] [ˈʃeɪk] *v* **shook** [ˈʃʊk]; **shaken** [ˈʃeɪkən]; **shaking** *vt* **1** : secouer <he shook his head : il a secoué la tête> **2** UPSET : ébranler <shaken by the news : ébranlé par la nouvelle> **3 to shake hands with s.o.** : serrer la main à qqn — *vi* TREMBLE : trembler

shake[2] *n* : secousse *f*, ébranlement *m*

shaker [ˈʃeɪkər] *n* **1** → **saltshaker 2 pepper shaker** : poivrier *m* **3 cocktail shaker** : shaker *m*

shake–up [ˈʃeɪkˌʌp] *n* : réorganisation *f*

shake up *vt* : secouer, agiter

shakily [ˈʃeɪkəli] *adv* **1** : en tremblant **2** UNSTEADILY : à pas chancelants **3** WEAKLY : faiblement

shaky [ˈʃeɪki] *adj* **shakier; -est 1** TREMBLING : tremblant **2** UNSTEADY : branlant **3** UNCERTAIN : chancelant, incertain

shale [ˈʃeɪl] *n* : schiste *m* argileux

shall [ˈʃæl] *v aux, past* **should** [ˈʃʊd]; *pres sing & pl* **shall 1** (*used to express a command*) <you shall do as I say : vous ferez comme je vous dis> **2** (*used to express futurity*) <what shall we do? : que ferons-nous?> <I shall have finished it : je l'aurai fini> **3** (*used to express determination*) <you shall have the money : vous aurez l'argent>

shallow [ˈʃæloː] *adj* **1** : peu profond **2** SUPERFICIAL : superficiel

shallows [ˈʃæloːz] *npl* : haut-fond *m*, bas-fond *m*

sham[1] [ˈʃæm] *v* **shammed; shamming** *vt* : feindre, faire semblant de — *vi* : faire semblant

sham[2] *adj* : faux

sham[3] *n* **1** PRETENSE : faux-semblant *m*, comédie *f* **2** IMPOSTER : imposteur *m*

shamble [ˈʃæmbəl] *vi* **-bled; -bling** : marcher en traînant les pieds

shambles [ˈʃæmbəlz] *ns & pl* : désordre *m*

shame[1] [ˈʃeɪm] *vt* **shamed; shaming** : faire honte à

shame[2] *n* **1** : honte *f* **2** PITY : dommage *m* <what a shame! : quel dommage!>

shamefaced [ˈʃeɪmˌfeɪst] *adj* : penaud, honteux

shameful [ˈʃeɪmfəl] *adj* : honteux — **shamefully** *adv*

shameless [ˈʃeɪmləs] *adj* : éhonté

shamelessly [ˈʃeɪmləsli] *adv* : sans vergogne, sans honte

shampoo[1] [ʃæmˈpuː] *vt* : faire un shampooing à

shampoo[2] *n, pl* **-poos** : shampooing *m*

shamrock [ˈʃæmˌrɑk] *n* : trèfle *m*

shank [ˈʃæŋk] *n* **1** LEG : jambe *f*, canon *m* (d'un cheval) **2** SHAFT : tige *f*

shan't [ˈʃænt] (*contraction of* **shall not**) → **shall**

shanty [ˈʃænti] *n, pl* **-ties** : cabane *f*

shape[1] [ˈʃeɪp] *v* **shaped; shaping** *vt* **1** MOLD : façonner, modeler **2** DETERMINE : former — *vi or* **to shape up** : prendre forme

shape[2] *n* **1** : forme *f* <in the shape of a circle : en forme de cercle> **2** CONDITION : forme *f*, état *m* <to be in good shape : être en bonne forme>

shapeless [ˈʃeɪpləs] *adj* : informe, sans forme

shapely [ˈʃeɪpli] *adj* **shapelier; -est** : bien fait, bien tourné

shard [ˈʃɑrd] *n* : tesson *m*

share[1] [ˈʃɛr] *v* **shared; sharing** *vt* : partager <to share the work : partager le travail> <they share the responsibility : ils se partagent la responsabilité> — *vi* **to share in** : prendre part à

share[2] *n* **1** PORTION : portion *f*, part *f* **2** STOCK : action *f*

sharecropper [ˈʃɛrˌkrɑpər] *n* : métayer *m*, -tayère *f*

shareholder [ˈʃɛrˌhoːldər] *n* : actionnaire *mf*

shark [ˈʃɑrk] *n* : requin *m*

sharp[1] [ˈʃɑrp] *adv* **1** PRECISELY : précisément, pile <at five o'clock sharp : à cinq heures pile> **2** ABRUPTLY : brusquement

sharp[2] *adj* **1** : aigu, tranchant, affilé <a sharp knife : un couteau tranchant> **2** CLEVER : vif **3** POINTED : pointu **4** INTENSE : vif, fort <a sharp pain : une douleur vive> **5** SUDDEN : brusque **6** DISTINCT : net, distinct **7** : dièse (en musique) **8** STYLISH : chic **9** KEEN : perçant, fin

sharp[3] *n* : dièse *m* (en musique)

sharpen [ˈʃɑrpən] *vt* : aiguiser, affiler

sharpener [ˈʃɑrpənər] *n* **1** *or* **knife sharpener** : aiguisoir *m* **2** → **pencil sharpener**

sharply [ˈʃɑrpli] *adv* **1** ABRUPTLY : brusquement **2** DISTINCTLY : nettement, clairement **3** HARSHLY : sévèrement

sharpness [ˈʃɑrpnəs] *n* **1** : tranchant *m* (d'un couteau, etc.) **2** ACUTENESS : acuité *f* **3** ABRUPTNESS : brusquerie *f* **4** INTENSITY : intensité *f* **5** HARSHNESS : sévérité *f* **6** CLARITY : netteté *f*

sharpshooter [ˈʃɑrpˌʃuːt̬ər] *n* : tireur *m* d'élite

shatter [ˈʃæt̬ər] *vt* : briser, fracasser — *vi* : se briser, se fracasser

shave[1] ['ʃeɪv] *v* **shaved; shaved** *or* **shaven** ['ʃeɪvən]; **shaving** *vt* **1** : raser **2** PLANE : raboter, planer — *vi* : se raser

shave[2] *n* : rasage *m*

shaver ['ʃeɪvər] *n or* **electric shaver** : rasoir *m* électrique

shawl ['ʃɔl] *n* : châle *m*

she ['ʃi:] *pron* : elle

sheaf ['ʃi:f] *n, pl* **sheaves** ['ʃi:vz] : gerbe *f* (de céréales), liasse *f* (de papier)

shear ['ʃɪr] *vt* **sheared; sheared** *or* **shorn** ['ʃorn]; **shearing** : tondre

shears ['ʃɪrz] *npl* **1** SCISSORS : cisailles *fpl* **2** CLIPPERS : tondeuse *f*

sheath ['ʃi:θ] *n, pl* **sheaths** ['ʃi:ðz, 'ʃi:θs] : fourreau *m* (d'épée), gaine *f* (de poignard, des plantes)

sheathe ['ʃi:ð] *vt* **sheathed; sheathing** : rengainer

shed[1] ['ʃɛd] *v* **shed; shedding** *vt* **1** : verser (des larmes, du sang) **2** : perdre (des feuilles, du poids) **3 to shed light on** : éclairer, éclaircir — *vi* : perdre ses poils

shed[2] *n* : abri *m*, remise *f*

she'd ['ʃi:d] (*contraction of* **she had** *or* **she would**) → **have, would**

sheen ['ʃi:n] *n* : lustre *m*, éclat *m*

sheep ['ʃi:p] *ns & pl* : mouton *m*

sheepfold ['ʃi:p,fo:ld] *n* : parc *m* à moutons

sheepish ['ʃi:pɪʃ] *adj* : penaud

sheepskin ['ʃi:p,skɪn] *n* **1** : peau *f* de mouton **2** DIPLOMA : diplôme *m*

sheer[1] ['ʃɪr] *adv* : à pic, abruptement

sheer[2] *adj* **1** PURE : pur **2** STEEP : à pic, abrupt **3** TRANSPARENT : transparent, fin

sheet ['ʃi:t] *n* **1** *or* **bedsheet** ['bɛd,ʃi:t] : drap *m* **2** : feuille *f* (de papier) **3** : plaque *f* <baking sheet : plaque de four>

sheikh *or* **sheik** ['ʃi:k, 'ʃeɪk] *n* : cheikh *m*

shelf ['ʃɛlf] *n, pl* **shelves** ['ʃɛlvz] **1** : étagère *f*, rayon *m* **2** : rebord *m*, saillie *f* (en géologie) <continental shelf : plate-forme continentale>

shell[1] ['ʃɛl] *vt* **1** : décortiquer (des noix), écosser (des pois) **2** BOMBARD : bombarder

shell[2] *n* **1** : coquille *f*, coque *f*, carapace *f* (de tortue, de homard) **2** SEASHELL : coquillage *m* **3** MISSILE : obus *m* **4** CARTRIDGE : cartouche *f* **5** *or* **racing shell** : canot *m*

she'll ['ʃi:l, ʃɪl] (*contraction of* **she shall** *or* **she will**) → **shall, will**

shellac[1] [ʃə'læk] *vt* **-lacked; -lacking 1** : laquer **2** DEFEAT : piler *fam*

shellac[2] *n* : laque *f*

shellfish ['ʃɛl,fɪʃ] *n* : crustacé *m*

shelter[1] ['ʃɛltər] *vt* **1** PROTECT : abriter, protéger **2** HARBOR : donner asile à, recueillir

shelter[2] *n* : abri *m*

shelve ['ʃɛlv] *vt* **shelved; shelving 1** : mettre sur les rayons **2** DEFER : remettre

shenanigans [ʃə'nænɪgənz] *npl* **1** TRICKERY : manigances *fpl* **2** MISCHIEF : espièglerie *f*

shepherd[1] ['ʃɛpərd] *vt* **1** GUARD : surveiller, garder **2** GUIDE : guider, conduire

shepherd[2] *n* : berger *m*

shepherdess ['ʃɛpərdəs] *n* : bergère *f*

sherbet ['ʃərbət] *n* : sorbet *m*

sheriff ['ʃɛrɪf] *n* : shérif *m*

sherry ['ʃɛri] *n, pl* **-ries** : xérès *m*

she's ['ʃi:z] (*contraction of* **she is** *or* **she has**) → **be, have**

shield[1] ['ʃi:ld] *vt* **1** PROTECT : protéger **2** CONCEAL : couvrir

shield[2] *n* **1** : bouclier *m* **2** PROTECTION : protection *f*

shier, shiest → **shy**

shift[1] ['ʃɪft] *vt* **1** CHANGE : changer de <to shift gears : changer de vitesse> **2** MOVE : déplacer — *vi* **1** CHANGE : changer **2** MOVE : se déplacer, bouger

shift[2] *n* **1** CHANGE : changement *m* <a shift in priorities : un changement de priorités> **2** : poste *m*, équipe *f* <night shift : équipe de nuit> **3** *or* **shift dress** : robe *f* fourreau **4** → **gearshift**

shiftless ['ʃɪftləs] *adj* : fainéant, paresseux

shifty ['ʃɪfti] *adj* **shiftier; -est** : sournois, rusé

shilling ['ʃɪlɪŋ] *n* : shilling *m*

shimmer ['ʃɪmər] *vi* GLIMMER : chatoyer, miroiter

shin[1] ['ʃɪn] *vi* **shinned; shinning** : grimper <she shinned up a tree : elle a grimpé à un arbre>

shin[2] *n* : tibia *m*

shine[1] ['ʃaɪn] *v* **shone** ['ʃo:n, *esp Brit and Can* 'ʃɒn] *or* **shined; shining** *vi* **1** : briller, luire **2** EXCEL : briller — *vt* **1** AIM : braquer, diriger <he shined the flashlight at the dog : il a braqué la lampe de poche sur le chien> **2** POLISH : astiquer, cirer (des chaussures)

shine[2] *n* : éclat *m*, lustre *m*

shingle[1] ['ʃɪŋgəl] *vt* **-gled; -gling** : couvrir de bardeaux

shingle[2] *n* : bardeau *m*

shingles ['ʃɪŋgəlz] *npl* : zona *m*

shinny ['ʃɪni] *vi* **-nied; -nying** → **shin**[1]

shiny ['ʃaɪni] *adj* **shinier; -est** : luisant, brillant

ship[1] ['ʃɪp] *vt* **shipped; shipping 1** LOAD : embarquer, mettre à bord **2** SEND : expédier (par bateau), transporter (par avion)

ship[2] *n* **1** : navire *m*, bateau *m* **2** → **spaceship**

shipboard ['ʃɪp,bord] *n* **on ~** : à bord

shipbuilder ['ʃɪp,bɪldər] *n* : constructeur *m*, -trice *f* de navires

shipment [ˈʃɪpmənt] *n* **1** SHIPPING : expédition *f,* transport *m* **2** CARGO : cargaison *f* (par mer), chargement *m* (terrestre)

shipping [ˈʃɪpɪŋ] *n* **1** SHIPS : navires *mpl* **2** TRANSPORT : transport *m* (maritime)

shipshape [ˈʃɪpˈʃeɪp] *adj* : en bon ordre

shipwreck[1] [ˈʃɪpˌrɛk] *vt* **to be shipwrecked** : faire naufrage

shipwreck[2] *n* : naufrage *m*

shipyard [ˈʃɪpˌjɑrd] *n* : chantier *m* naval

shirk [ˈʃərk] *vt* : se dérober à, esquiver <to shirk one's duties : se dérober à ses responsabilités>

shirt [ˈʃərt] *n* : chemise *f*

shiver[1] [ˈʃɪvər] *vi* : frissonner

shiver[2] *n* : frisson *m*

shoal [ˈʃoːl] *n* **1** : banc *m* (de poissons) **2** SANDBANK : banc *m* de sable

shock[1] [ˈʃɑk] *vt* : choquer

shock[2] *n* **1** : choc *m* <in a state of shock : en état de choc> **2** *or* **electric shock** : décharge *f* (électrique) **3 shock of hair** : tignasse *f*

shock absorber *n* : amortisseur *m*

shoddy [ˈʃɑdi] *adj* **shoddier; -est** : de mauvaise qualité

shoe[1] [ˈʃuː] *vt* **shod** [ˈʃɑd]; **shoeing** : ferrer (un cheval)

shoe[2] *n* **1** : chaussure *f* **2** → **horseshoe** **3 brake shoe** : sabot *m* (de frein)

shoelace [ˈʃuːˌleɪs] *n* : lacet *m*

shoemaker [ˈʃuːˌmeɪkər] *n* : cordonnier *m,* -nière *f*

shone → **shine**[1]

shook → **shake**[1]

shoot[1] [ˈʃuːt] *v* **shot** [ˈʃɑt]; **shooting** *vt* **1** FIRE : tirer (une balle ou une flèche), lancer (un missile) **2** : tirer sur (une personne) <to shoot s.o. dead : abattre qqn> **3** : jouer, marquer (aux sports) <to shoot a basket : marquer un panier> **4** FILM : tourner **5** PHOTOGRAPH : prendre (en photo) **6** DIRECT : décocher, lancer (un regard) — *vi* **1** : tirer <to shoot to kill : tirer pour tuer> **2** DART : se précipiter **3** FILM : tourner

shoot[2] *n* : rejeton *m,* pousse *f* (d'une plante)

shooter [ˈʃuːt̬ər] *n* : tireur *m,* -reuse *f*

shooting star *n* : étoile *f* filante

shop[1] [ˈʃɑp] *vi* **shopped; shopping** : faire des courses

shop[2] *n* **1** STORE : magasin *m,* boutique *f* **2** → **workshop**

shopkeeper [ˈʃɑpˌkiːpər] *n* : commerçant *m,* -çante *f;* marchand *m,* -chande *f*

shoplift [ˈʃɑpˌlɪft] *vt* : voler à l'étalage

shoplifter [ˈʃɑpˌlɪftər] *n* : voleur *m,* -leuse *f* à l'étalage

shopper [ˈʃɑpər] *n* : personne *f* qui fait ses courses

shopping [ˈʃɑpɪŋ] *n* : courses *fpl,* magasinage *m Can* <to go shopping : faire des courses>

shopwindow [ˈʃɑpˌwɪndoː] *n* : vitrine *f,* devanture *f*

shore[1] [ˈʃor] *vt* **shored; shoring** *or* **to shore up** : étayer

shore[2] *n* **1** : rivage *m,* bord *m* <on shore : à terre> **2** PROP : étai *m*

shorebird [ˈʃorˌbərd] *n* : oiseau *m* des rivages

shoreline [ˈʃorˌlaɪn] *n* : côte *f,* littoral *m*

shorn → **shear**

short[1] [ˈʃɔrt] *adv* : court, de court <to fall short of : ne pas répondre à, ne pas atteindre>

short[2] *adj* **1** : court <a short dress : une robe courte> **2** : petit, de petite taille (se dit d'une personne) **3** BRIEF : bref <for a short time : pendant peu de temps> **4** CURT : brusque **5** INSUFFICIENT : insuffisant

short[3] *n* **1** → **short circuit** **2 shorts** *pl* : short *m* <tennis shorts : short de tennis>

shortage [ˈʃɔrtɪdʒ] *n* : manque *m,* insuffisance *f*

shortcake [ˈʃɔrtˌkeɪk] *n* : tarte *f* sablée

shortchange [ˈʃɔrtˈtʃeɪndʒ] *vt* **-changed; -changing** **1** : ne pas rendre assez de monnaie à **2** SWINDLE : escroquer

short–circuit [ˈʃɔrtˈsərkət] *vt* : court-circuiter

short circuit *n* : court-circuit *m*

shortcoming [ˈʃɔrtˌkʌmɪŋ] *n* : défaut *m*

shortcut [ˈʃɔrtˌkʌt] *n* : raccourci *m*

shorten [ˈʃɔrtən] *vt* : raccourcir

shorthand [ˈʃɔrtˌhænd] *n* : sténographie *f*

short–lived [ˈʃɔrtˈlɪvd, -ˈlaɪvd] *adj* : éphémère

shortly [ˈʃɔrtli] *adv* **1** BRIEFLY : brièvement **2** SOON : bientôt

shortness [ˈʃɔrtnəs] *n* **1** : petite taille *f* **2** BREVITY : brièveté *f,* petite durée *f* **3** CURTNESS : brusquerie *f* **4 shortness of breath** : manque *m* de souffle

shortsighted [ˈʃɔrtˌsaɪt̬əd] → **nearsighted**

shortstop [ˈʃɔrtˌstɑp] *n* : arrêt-court *m Can*

shot[1] [ˈʃɑt] *n* **1** : tir *m,* coup *m* <to fire a shot : tirer un coup> **2** ATTEMPT : essai *m,* tentative *f* <to give it one's best shot : faire de son mieux> **3** PELLETS : plombs *mpl* **4** PHOTOGRAPH : photo *f* **5** INJECTION : piqûre *f* **6** MARKSMAN : tireur *m,* -reuse *f* **7** SCENE : plan *m* (au cinéma)

shot[2] → **shoot**[1]

shotgun [ˈʃɑtˌgʌn] *n* : fusil *m* de chasse

should [ˈʃʊd] *past of* **shall** **1** (*used to express obligation*) : devoir <you should go : tu devrais y aller> **2** (*used to express probability*) <he should be here soon : il devrait être arrivé bientôt> **3** (*used in conditional sentences*) <if

he should die : s'il mourrait> <if you should change your mind : si vous changez d'avis>
shoulder[1] [ˈʃoːldər] *vt* **1** PUSH : pousser **2 to shoulder the responsibility** : endosser
shoulder[2] *n* **1** : épaule *f* (d'une personne) **2** : accotement *m* (d'une chaussée) <soft shoulder : accotement non stabilisé>
shoulder blade *n* : omoplate *f*
shouldn't [ˈʃʊdənt] (*contraction of* **should not**) → **should**
shout[1] [ˈʃaʊt] *v* : crier, hurler
shout[2] *n* : cri *m,* hurlement *m*
shove[1] [ˈʃʌv] *v* **shoved; shoving** *vt* **1** PUSH : pousser **2** JOSTLE : bousculer — *vi* **to shove off** : s'en aller
shove[2] *n* : poussée *f*
shovel[1] [ˈʃʌvəl] *vt* **-veled** *or* **-velled; -veling** *or* **-velling** : pelleter, enlever à la pelle
shovel[2] *n* : pelle *f*
show[1] [ˈʃoː] *v* **showed; shown** [ˈʃoːn] *or* **showed; showing** *vt* **1** DISPLAY, PRESENT : montrer, présenter **2** REVEAL : révéler **3** DEMONSTRATE, TEACH : montrer, indiquer **4** PROVE : prouver, démontrer **5** CONDUCT : conduire <he showed her to the door : il l'a conduite à la porte> — *vi* : se voir
show[2] *n* **1** DEMONSTRATION : démonstration *f,* manifestation *f* <a show of strength : une manifestation de force> **2** EXHIBITION : exposition *f* **3** : spectacle *m* (de théâtre), émission *f* (de télévision, de radio, etc.), séance *f* (de cinéma)
showcase [ˈʃoːˌkeɪs] *n* : vitrine *f*
showdown [ˈʃoːˌdaʊn] *n* : confrontation *f*
shower[1] [ˈʃaʊər] *vt* **1** WET : doucher **2 to shower sth on** : faire pleuvoir qqch sur **3 to shower s.o. with** : couvrir qqn de <they showered him with gifts : ils l'ont couvert de cadeaux> — *vi* **1** BATHE : prendre une douche **2** RAIN : pleuvoir
shower[2] *n* **1** : averse *f* <snow showers : averses de neige> **2** : douche *f* <he's in the shower : il est sous la douche> **3** PARTY : fête *f* (donnée à l'occasion d'un mariage ou d'une naissance)
show off *vt* : faire valoir, faire parade de — *vi* : faire l'intéressant
show up *vi* **1** ARRIVE : arriver **2** APPEAR : ressortir, se voir — *vt* EXPOSE : démasquer
showy [ˈʃoːi] *adj* **showier; -est** : tapageur, voyant
shrapnel [ˈʃræpnəl] *ns & pl* : shrapnel *m*
shred[1] [ˈʃrɛd] *vt* **shredded; shredding** : déchirer, déchiqueter (le papier, le tissu), râper (les aliments)
shred[2] *n* **1** : lambeau *m* <to be in shreds : être en lambeaux> **2** BIT : brin *m,* parcelle *f* <not a shred of evidence : pas une parcelle d'évidence>
shrew [ˈʃruː] *n* **1** : musaraigne *f* (animal) **2** : mégère *f* (femme)
shrewd [ˈʃruːd] *adj* : habile, sagace
shrewdly [ˈʃruːdli] *adv* : avec perspicacité, avec sagacité
shrewdness [ˈʃruːdnəs] *n* : perspicacité *f,* astuce *f,* sagacité *f*
shriek[1] [ˈʃriːk] *vi* : hurler, crier, pousser un cri perçant
shriek[2] *n* : cri *m* perçant
shrill [ˈʃrɪl] *adj* : aigu, perçant, strident
shrilly [ˈʃrɪli] *adv* : d'un ton aigu
shrimp [ˈʃrɪmp] *n* : crevette *f*
shrine [ˈʃraɪn] *n* **1** TOMB : tombeau *m* (d'un saint) **2** SANCTUARY : sanctuaire *m,* lieu *m* saint
shrink [ˈʃrɪŋk] *v* **shrank** [ˈʃræŋk]; **shrunk** [ˈʃrʌŋk] *or* **shrunken** [ˈʃrʌŋkən]; **shrinking** *vi* **1** RECOIL : reculer **2** : rétrécir, fouler *Can* (se dit des vêtements) **3** DWINDLE : rétrécir, diminuer — *vt* : rétrécir
shrinkage [ˈʃrɪŋkɪdʒ] *n* : rétrécissement *m*
shrivel [ˈʃrɪvəl] *v* **-eled** *or* **-elled; -eling** *or* **-elling** *vt* : ratatiner, dessécher — *vi* : se ratatiner
shroud[1] [ˈʃraʊd] *vt* : envelopper, voiler
shroud[2] *n* **1** : linceul *m* **2** COVERING, VEIL : voile *m* <a shroud of mystery : un voile de mystère>
shrub [ˈʃrʌb] *n* : arbuste *m,* arbrisseau *m*
shrubbery [ˈʃrʌbəri] *n, pl* **-beries** : massif *m* d'arbustes, arbustes *mpl*
shrug[1] [ˈʃrʌg] *v* **shrugged; shrugging** *vt* : hausser (les épaules) — *vi* : hausser les épaules
shrug[2] *n* : haussement *m* d'épaules
shuck[1] [ˈʃʌk] *vt* : écosser (des légumes), écaler, décortiquer (des noix) <to shuck corn : enlever l'enveloppe de maïs>
shuck[2] *n* : cosse *f* (de légumes), écale *f* (de noix), enveloppe *f* (de maïs)
shudder[1] [ˈʃʌdər] *vi* : frissonner, frémir
shudder[2] *n* : frisson *m,* frémissement *m*
shuffle[1] [ˈʃʌfəl] *v* **-fled; -fling** *vt* MIX : mêler, battre (des cartes) — *vi* : marcher en traînant les pieds
shuffle[2] *n* **1** : pas *m* traînant **2** : battage *m* (des cartes) **3** JUMBLE : confusion *f*
shun [ˈʃʌn] *vt* **shunned; shunning** : éviter
shunt [ˈʃʌnt] *vt* : aiguiller, manœuvrer (un train)
shut[1] [ˈʃʌt] *v* **shut; shutting** *vt* **1** CLOSE : fermer **2 to shut in** *or* **to shut up** CONFINE : enfermer **3 to shut off** : couper **4 to shut out** EXCLUDE : exclure — *vi* **1** : (se) fermer <the door is shutting : la porte se ferme> **2** : fermer <the store shuts at noon : le magasin ferme à midi>
shut[2] *adj* : fermé

shut–in [ˈʃʌtˌɪn] *n* : invalide *mf*

shutout [ˈʃʌtˌaʊt] *n* : victoire *f* écrasante, blanchissage *m Can*

shutter [ˈʃʌtər] *n* **1** : volet *m* (d'une fenêtre) **2** : obturateur *m* (d'un appareil photo)

shuttle[1] [ˈʃʌtəl] *v* **-tled; -tling** *vi* : faire la navette — *vt* : transporter

shuttle[2] *n* : navette *f*

shuttlecock [ˈʃʌtəlˌkɑk] *n* : volant *m*

shut up *vi* : se taire <shut up! : tais-toi!> — *vt* SILENCE : faire taire

shy[1] [ˈʃaɪ] *vi* **shied**; **shying** *or* **to shy away** : reculer

shy[2] *adj* **shier** *or* **shyer** [ˈʃaɪər]; **shiest** *or* **shyest** [ˈʃaɪəst] **1** TIMID : timide, gêné *Can* **2** WARY : peureux **3** (*indicating a lack*) <I'm two dollars shy of my goal : il me manque deux dollars pour atteindre mon objectif> <he's shy of ideas : il est à court d'idées>

shyly [ˈʃaɪli] *adv* : timidement

shyness [ˈʃaɪnəs] *n* : timidité *f*

sibling [ˈsɪblɪŋ] *n* : frère *m*, sœur *f*

sick [ˈsɪk] *adj* **1** ILL : malade **2** (*indicating nausea*) <to feel sick : avoir mal au cœur> <to get sick : vomir> **3 I'm sick of it** : j'en ai marre, j'en ai assez

sickbed [ˈsɪkˌbɛd] *n* : lit *m* de malade

sicken [ˈsɪkən] *vt* : rendre malade — *vi* : tomber malade

sickening [ˈsɪkənɪŋ] *adj* : écœurant, nauséabond

sickle [ˈsɪkəl] *n* : faucille *f*

sickly [ˈsɪkli] *adj* **sicklier; -est** : maladif

sickness [ˈsɪknəs] *n* : maladie *f*

side [ˈsaɪd] *n* **1** : côté *m* (d'une personne), flanc *m* (d'un animal) **2** EDGE : bord *m* **3** FACTION, GROUP : camp *m*, côté *m* <to take sides : prendre parti> **4** ASPECT : facette *f*, aspect *m*

sideboard [ˈsaɪdˌbord] *n* : buffet *m*

sideburns [ˈsaɪdˌbərnz] *npl* : favoris *mpl*

sided [ˈsaɪdəd] *adj* : à côtés <three-sided : à trois côtés>

side effect *n* : effet *m* secondaire

sideline [ˈsaɪdˌlaɪn] *n* **1** : activité *f* secondaire **2** : ligne *f* de côté, ligne *f* de touche (aux sports)

sidelong [ˈsaɪdˌlɔŋ] *adj* : de côté, oblique

sideshow [ˈsaɪdˌʃoː] *n* : attraction *f*

sidestep [ˈsaɪdˌstɛp] *v* **-stepped; -stepping** *vi* : faire un pas de côté — *vt* AVOID : éviter

sidetrack [ˈsaɪdˌtræk] *vt* : détourner l'attention de, faire dévier de son sujet

sidewalk [ˈsaɪdˌwɔk] *n* : trottoir *m*

sideways[1] [ˈsaɪdˌweɪz] *adv* : de côté, en travers, latéralement

sideways[2] *adj* : de côté, oblique, latéral

siding [ˈsaɪdɪŋ] *n* **1** : voie *f* de garage (pour trains) **2** : revêtement *m* extérieur (d'un édifice)

sidle [ˈsaɪdəl] *vi* **-dled; -dling** : avancer de biais, marcher de côté

siege [ˈsiːdʒ, ˈsiːʒ] *n* : siège *m*

siesta [siːˈɛstə] *n* : sieste *f*

sieve [ˈsɪv] *n* : tamis *m*, crible *m*

sift [ˈsɪft] *vt* **1** : tamiser, passer au tamis **2** *or* **to sift through** : passer au crible

sifter [ˈsɪftər] *n* : tamis *m*

sigh[1] [ˈsaɪ] *vi* : soupirer

sigh[2] *n* : soupir *m*

sight[1] [ˈsaɪt] *vt* : apercevoir

sight[2] *n* **1** : vue *f* <out of sight : hors de vue> <at first sight : à première vue> **2** SPECTACLE : spectacle *m* **3** : viseur *m* (d'une arme à feu)

sightless [ˈsaɪtləs] *adj* : aveugle

sightseer [ˈsaɪtˌsiːər] *n* : touriste *mf*

sign[1] [ˈsaɪn] *vt* **1** : signer <to sign a check : signer un chèque> **2** *or* **to sign on** HIRE : engager — *vi* **1** : signer **2** SIGNAL : faire signe **3** *or* **to sign on** JOIN : s'engager

sign[2] *n* **1** SYMBOL : signe *m* **2** GESTURE : geste *m*, signe *m* **3** : panneau *m*, enseigne *f* <traffic signs : panneaux de signalisation> <neon sign : enseigne au néon> **4** TRACE : trace *f*

signal[1] [ˈsɪgnəl] *v* **-naled** *or* **-nalled; -naling** *or* **-nalling** *vt* **1** INDICATE : signaler, indiquer **2** : envoyer un signal à <to signal s.o. : faire signe à qqn> — *vi* : donner un signal

signal[2] *adj* NOTABLE : insigne

signal[3] *n* : signal *m*

signature [ˈsɪgnəˌtʃʊr] *n* : signature *f*

signet [ˈsɪgnət] *n* : sceau *m*

significance [sɪgˈnɪfɪkənts] *n* **1** MEANING : signification *f*, sens *m* **2** IMPORTANCE : importance *f*, portée *f*

significant [sɪgˈnɪfɪkənt] *adj* **1** MEANINGFUL : significatif **2** IMPORTANT : important

significantly [sɪgˈnɪfɪkəntli] *adv* **1** CONSIDERABLY : considérablement, sensiblement **2** MEANINGFULLY : de façon significative

signify [ˈsɪgnəˌfaɪ] *vt* **-fied; -fying 1** INDICATE : signaler, indiquer **2** MEAN : signifier

sign language *n* : langage *m* des signes

signpost [ˈsaɪnˌpoːst] *n* **1** : poteau *m* indicateur **2** INDICATION : indication *f*, indice *m*

silence[1] [ˈsaɪlənts] *vt* **-lenced; -lencing** : faire taire, réduire au silence

silence[2] *n* : silence *m*

silent [ˈsaɪlənt] *adj* : silencieux — **silently** *adv*

silhouette[1] [ˌsɪləˈwɛt] *vt* **-etted; -etting** : silhouetter <to be silhouetted against : se découper contre, se profiler sur>

silhouette[2] *n* : silhouette *f*

silica [ˈsɪlɪkə] *n* : silice *f*

silicon [ˈsɪlɪkən, -ˌkɑn] *n* : silicium *m*

silk [ˈsɪlk] *n* : soie *f*

silken [ˈsɪlkən] *adj* **1** : de soie **2** SILKY : soyeux

silkworm ['sɪlkˌwərm] *n* : ver *m* à soie
silky ['sɪlki] *adj* **silkier; -est** : soyeux
sill ['sɪl] *n* : rebord *m* (d'une fenêtre), seuil *m* (d'une porte)
silliness ['sɪlinəs] *n* : sottise *f,* stupidité *f*
silly ['sɪli] *adj* **sillier; -est 1** STUPID : sot, niais **2** RIDICULOUS : fou, ridicule
silo ['saɪˌloː] *n, pl* **silos** : silo *m*
silt ['sɪlt] *n* : limon *m*
silver[1] ['sɪlvər] *adj* **1** : d'argent, en argent <a silver spoon : une cuillère d'argent> **2** → **silvery**
silver[2] *n* **1** : argent *m* **2** → **silverware 3** : couleur *f* argent
silverware ['sɪlvərˌwær] *n* : argenterie *f,* coutellerie *f Can*
silvery ['sɪlvəri] *adj* : argenté
similar ['sɪmələr] *adj* : semblable, similaire
similarity [ˌsɪmə'lærəṭi] *n, pl* **-ties** : ressemblance *f,* similarité *f*
similarly ['sɪmələrli] *adv* : de la même façon
simile ['sɪməˌliː] *n* : comparaison *f*
simmer ['sɪmər] *vi* : cuire à feu doux, frémir — *vt* : faire cuire à feu doux, laisser frémir
simper[1] ['sɪmpər] *vi* : minauder
simper[2] *n* : sourire *m* affecté
simple ['sɪmpəl] *adj* **simpler; -plest** : simple
simpleton ['sɪmpəltən] *n* : nigaud *m,* -gaude *f*
simplicity [sɪm'plɪsəṭi] *n* : simplicité *f*
simplification [ˌsɪmpləfə'keɪʃən] *n* : simplification *f*
simplify ['sɪmpləˌfaɪ] *vt* **-fied; -fying** : simplifier
simply ['sɪmpli] *adv* : simplement
simulate ['sɪmjəˌleɪt] *vt* **-lated; -lating** : simuler
simultaneous [ˌsaɪməl'teɪniəs] *adj* : simultané — **simultaneously** *adv*
sin[1] ['sɪn] *vi* **sinned; sinning** : pécher
sin[2] *n* : péché *m*
since[1] ['sɪnts] *adv* **1** : depuis <they've been friends ever since : ils sont amis depuis> <she's since become mayor : elle est devenue maire depuis> **2 long since** : il y a longtemps **3 not long since** : il y a peu de temps
since[2] *conj* **1** : depuis que <since I've been here : depuis que je suis là> **2** BECAUSE, INASMUCH AS : puisque, comme
since[3] *prep* : depuis
sincere [sɪn'sɪr] *adj* **sincerer; -est** : sincère — **sincerely** *adv*
sincerity [sɪn'sɛrəṭi] *n* : sincérité *f*
sinew ['sɪnˌjuː, 'sɪˌnuː] *n* **1** TENDON : tendon *m* **2** POWER : force *f*
sinewy ['sɪnjʊi, 'sɪnʊi] *adj* **1** : tendineux **2** MUSCLED : musclé
sinful ['sɪnfəl] *adj* : coupable, honteux
sing ['sɪŋ] *v* **sang** ['sæŋ] *or* **sung** ['sʌŋ]; **sung; singing** : chanter
Singaporean[1] [ˌsɪŋə'poriən, -'pɔr-] *adj* : singapourien
Singaporean[2] *n* : Singapourien *m,* -rienne *f*
singe ['sɪndʒ] *vt* **singed; singeing** : brûler légèrement, roussir
singer ['sɪŋər] *n* : chanteur *m,* -teuse *f*
single[1] ['sɪŋgəl] *vt* **-gled; -gling** *or* **to single out 1** SELECT : choisir, sélectionner **2** DISTINGUISH : distinguer
single[2] *adj* **1** SOLE : seul <not a single one : pas un seul> **2** UNMARRIED : célibataire
single[3] *n* **1** *or* **single room** : chambre *f* simple **2** : simple *m Can* (au baseball) **3 singles** *npl* : simple *m* (au tennis)
singly ['sɪŋgli] *adv* : séparément, individuellement
singular[1] ['sɪŋgjələr] *adj* **1** : singulier (en grammaire) **2** OUTSTANDING : remarquable **3** STRANGE : étrange
singular[2] *n* : singulier *m*
singularly ['sɪŋgjələrli] *adv* : singulièrement
sinister ['sɪnəstər] *adj* : sinistre
sink[1] ['sɪŋk] *v* **sank** ['sæŋk] *or* **sunk** ['sʌŋk]; **sunk; sinking** *vi* **1** : couler, sombrer <to sink into oblivion : sombrer dans l'oubli> **2** DROP, FALL : baisser **3** : s'enfoncer, s'affaisser <to sink into a chair : s'affaisser dans un fauteuil> — *vt* **1** : couler (un bateau, etc.) **2** LOWER : baisser **3** DRIVE, PLUNGE : enfoncer **4** EXCAVATE : creuser **5** INVEST : investir
sink[2] *n* **1 kitchen sink** : évier *m* **2 bathroom sink** : lavabo *m*
sinner ['sɪnər] *n* : pécheur *m,* -cheresse *f*
sinuous ['sɪnjʊəs] *adj* : sinueux
sinus ['saɪnəs] *n* : sinus *m*
sip[1] ['sɪp] *vt* **sipped; sipping** : boire à petites gorgées, siroter *fam*
sip[2] *n* : petite gorgée *f*
siphon[1] ['saɪfən] *vt* : siphonner
siphon[2] *n* : siphon *m*
sir ['sər] *n* **1** (*as a form of address*) : monsieur *m* <Dear Sir : Monsieur> <yes, sir! : oui, monsieur!> **2** (*in titles*) : sir *m*
sire[1] ['saɪr] *vt* **sired; siring** : engendrer
sire[2] *n* **1** : père *m* **2** (*as a form of address*) : sire *m*
siren ['saɪrən] *n* : sirène *f*
sirloin ['sərˌlɔɪn] *n* : aloyau *m*
sirup → **syrup**
sisal ['saɪsəl, -zəl] *n* : sisal *m*
sissy ['sɪsi] *n, pl* **-sies** : poule *f* mouillée *fam*
sister ['sɪstər] *n* **1** : sœur *f* **2** *Brit* → **nurse**[2]
sisterhood ['sɪstərˌhʊd] *n* **1** : communauté *f* de femmes (religieuses) **2** : solidarité *f* féminine
sister-in-law ['sɪstərɪnˌlɔ] *n, pl* **sisters-in-law** : belle-sœur *f*
sisterly ['sɪstərli] *adj* : de sœur
sit ['sɪt] *v* **sat** ['sæt]; **sitting** *vi* **1** *or* **to sit down** : s'asseoir **2** ROOST : se percher

3 MEET : siéger, se réunir <the legislature is sitting : le corps législatif siège> 4 POSE : poser 5 REMAIN : rester <the mail sits unopened : le courrier reste fermé> 6 : se trouver, être <the house sits on a hill : la maison se trouve sur une colline> — *vt* 1 PLACE : placer, installer 2 SEAT : (faire) asseoir

site ['saɪt] *n* : site *m*

sitter ['sɪt̬ər] → **baby–sitter**

sitting room → **living room**

situated ['sɪtʃʊˌeɪt̬əd] *adj* LOCATED : situé

situation [ˌsɪtʃʊ'eɪʃən] *n* 1 LOCATION : situation *f,* emplacement *m* 2 CIRCUMSTANCES : situation *f* 3 JOB : emploi *m,* situation *f*

six[1] ['sɪks] *adj* : six

six[2] *n* : six *m*

six–gun ['sɪksˌgʌn] *n* : revolver *m* (à six coups)

six–shooter ['sɪksˌʃu:t̬ər] → **six–gun**

sixteen[1] [sɪks'ti:n] *adj* : seize

sixteen[2] *n* : seize *m*

sixteenth[1] [sɪks'ti:nθ] *adj* : seizième

sixteenth[2] *n* **1** : seizième *mf* (dans une série) **2** : seizième *m* (en mathématiques) **3** (*used in dates*) <the sixteenth of May : le seize mai>

sixth[1] ['sɪksθ, 'sɪkst] *adj* : sixième

sixth[2] *n* **1** : sixième *mf* (dans une série) **2** : sixième *m* (en mathématiques) **3** (*used in dates*) <the sixth of July : le six juillet>

sixtieth[1] ['sɪkst̬iəθ] *adj* : soixantième

sixtieth[2] *n* **1** : soixantième *mf* (dans une série) **2** : soixantième *m* (en mathématiques)

sixty[1] ['sɪkst̬i] *adj* : soixante

sixty[2] *n, pl* **-ties** : soixante *m*

sizable *or* **sizeable** ['saɪzəbəl] *adj* : assez grand

size[1] ['saɪz] *vt* **sized; sizing 1** : classer selon la grosseur **2 to size up** : jauger, évaluer

size[2] *n* **1** DIMENSIONS : grandeur *f,* taille *f* **2** : taille *f,* pointure *f* (des chaussures, des gants, etc.) <what is your size? : quelle est votre taille?> **3** MAGNITUDE : ampleur *f,* taille *f*

sizzle ['sɪzəl] *vi* **-zled; -zling** : grésiller

skate[1] ['skeɪt] *vi* **skated; skating** : patiner, faire du patin

skate[2] *n* **1** : patin *m* **2** : raie *f* (poisson)

skater ['skeɪt̬ər] *n* : patineur *m,* -neuse *f*

skein ['skeɪn] *n* : écheveau *m*

skeletal ['skɛlət̬əl] *adj* : squelettique

skeleton ['skɛlətən] *n* : squelette *m*

skeptic ['skɛptɪk] *n* : sceptique *mf*

skeptical ['skɛptɪkəl] *adj* : sceptique

skepticism ['skɛptəˌsɪzəm] *n* : scepticisme *m*

sketch[1] ['skɛtʃ] *vt* : esquisser — *vi* : faire des esquisses

sketch[2] *n* : esquisse *f,* croquis *m*

sketchy ['skɛtʃi] *adj* **sketchier; -est** : imprécis, vague

skewer[1] ['skju:ər] *vt* : embrocher

skewer[2] *n* : brochette *f*

ski[1] ['ski:] *vi* **skied; skiing** : faire du ski

ski[2] *n, pl* **skis** : ski *m*

skid[1] ['skɪd] *vi* **skidded; skidding** : déraper

skid[2] *n* : dérapage *m*

skier ['ski:ər] *n* : skieur *m,* skieuse *f*

skiff ['skɪf] *n* : skiff *m*

skilful *Brit* → **skillful**

skill ['skɪl] *n* **1** CAPABILITY : habileté *f,* adresse *f,* compétence *f* **2** TRADE : métier *m* **3 skills** : capacités *fpl,* compétences *fpl*

skilled ['skɪld] *adj* : habile, expérimenté

skillet ['skɪlət] *n* : poêle *f* (à frire)

skillful *or Brit* **skilful** ['skɪlfəl] *adj* : habile, adroit

skim[1] ['skɪm] *vt* **skimmed; skimming 1** *or* **to skim off** : écumer, écrémer (le lait) **2** : parcourir (un livre, un journal, etc.) **3** : effleurer, raser (une surface)

skim[2] *adj* : écrémé <skim milk : lait écrémé>

skimp ['skɪmp] *vi* **to skimp on** : lésiner sur

skimpy ['skɪmpi] *adj* **skimpier; -est** : étriqué

skin[1] ['skɪn] *vt* **skinned; skinning 1** : écorcher, dépouiller **2** PEEL : peler, éplucher

skin[2] *n* **1** : peau *f* **2** RIND : pelure *f*

skin diving *n* : plongée *f* sous-marine

skinflint ['skɪnˌflɪnt] *n* : grippe-sou *m*

skinned ['skɪnd] *adj* **1** : à (la) peau <fair-skinned : à peau claire> **2** → **thick–skinned, thin–skinned**

skinny ['skɪni] *adj* **skinnier; -est** : maigre

skip[1] ['skɪp] *v* **skipped; skipping** *vi* : sautiller, gambader — *vt* MISS, OMIT : sauter

skip[2] *n* : petit saut *m,* petit bond *m*

skipper ['skɪpər] *n* : capitaine *m,* skipper *m*

skirmish[1] ['skərmɪʃ] *vi* : s'engager dans une escarmouche

skirmish[2] *n* : escarmouche *f*

skirt[1] ['skərt] *vt* : contourner

skirt[2] *n* : jupe *f*

skit ['skɪt] *n* : sketch *m* (satirique)

skittish ['skɪt̬ɪʃ] *adj* : ombrageux, difficile (se dit d'un cheval, etc.)

skulk ['skʌlk] *vi* : rôder

skull ['skʌl] *n* **1** : crâne *m* **2 skull and crossbones** : tête *f* de mort

skunk ['skʌŋk] *n* : mouffette *f*

sky ['skaɪ] *n, pl* **skies** : ciel *m*

skylark ['skaɪˌlɑrk] *n* : alouette *f* des champs

skylight ['skaɪˌlaɪt] *n* : lucarne *f*

skyline ['skaɪˌlaɪn] *n* : ligne *f* d'horizon

skyrocket ['skaɪˌrɑkət] *vi* : monter en flèche

skyscraper ['skaɪˌskreɪpər] *n* : gratte-ciel *m*
skyward ['skaɪwərd] *adv* : vers le ciel
slab ['slæb] *n* : dalle *f,* bloc *m*
slack[1] ['slæk] *adj* **1** CARELESS : négligent **2** LOOSE : mou, lâche **3** SLOW : calme, stagnant <business is slack : les affaires marchent au ralenti>
slack[2] *n* **1** LOOSENESS : mou *m* **2 slacks** *npl* : pantalon *m*
slacken ['slækən] *vt* : relâcher — *vi* : se relâcher, ralentir
slag ['slæg] *n* : scories *fpl*
slain → **slay**
slake ['sleɪk] *vt* **slaked; slaking** : étancher (la soif), assouvir (les désirs)
slam[1] ['slæm] *v* **slammed; slamming** *vt* **1** : claquer <he slammed the door : il a claqué la porte> **2** HIT : frapper — *vi* : claquer
slam[2] *n* : claquement *m*
slander[1] ['slændər] *vt* : calomnier, diffamer
slander[2] *n* : calomnie *f,* diffamation *f*
slanderous ['slændərəs] *adj* : calomnieux, diffamatoire
slang ['slæŋ] *n* : argot *m*
slant[1] ['slænt] *vi* : pencher, s'incliner — *vt* : faire pencher, incliner
slant[2] *n* **1** : pente *f,* inclinaison *f* **2** POINT OF VIEW : point *m* de vue, perspective *f*
slap[1] ['slæp] *vt* **slapped; slapping** : gifler, donner une claque à
slap[2] *n* : gifle *f,* claque *f*
slash[1] ['slæʃ] *vt* **1** CUT : entailler **2** REDUCE : réduire
slash[2] *n* GASH : entaille *f*
slat ['slæt] *n* : lame *f,* lamelle *f*
slate ['sleɪt] *n* **1** : ardoise *f* <a slate roof : un toit d'ardoise> **2** LIST : liste *f* (de candidats)
slaughter[1] ['slɔt̬ər] *vt* **1** : abattre (des animaux) **2** MASSACRE : massacrer (des personnes)
slaughter[2] *n* **1** : abattage *m* (d'animaux) **2** MASSACRE : massacre *m*
slaughterhouse ['slɔt̬ərˌhaʊs] *n* : abattoir *m*
Slav ['slɑv, 'slæv] *n* : Slave *mf*
slave[1] ['sleɪv] *vi* **slaved; slaving** : travailler comme un esclave, trimer *fam*
slave[2] *n* : esclave *mf*
slaver ['slævər, 'sleɪ-] *vi* : baver
slavery ['sleɪvəri] *n* : esclavage *m*
slavish ['sleɪvɪʃ] *adj* : servile
slay ['sleɪ] *vt* **slew** ['slu:]; **slain** ['sleɪn]; **slaying** : tuer
slayer ['sleɪər] *n* : tueur *m,* tueuse *f*
sleazy ['sli:zi] *adj* **sleazier; -est 1** SHODDY : de mauvaise qualité **2** SQUALID : miteux, sordide **3** DISREPUTABLE : mal famé
sled[1] ['slɛd] *vi* **sledded; sledding** : faire du traîneau, faire de la luge
sled[2] *n* : traîneau *m,* luge *f*
sledge ['slɛdʒ] *n* **1** : traîneau *m* **2** → **sledgehammer**
sledgehammer ['slɛdʒˌhæmər] *n* : masse *f*
sleek[1] ['sli:k] *vt or* **to sleek down** : se lisser (les cheveux, etc.)
sleek[2] *adj* : lisse
sleep[1] ['sli:p] *vi* **slept** ['slɛpt]; **sleeping** : dormir
sleep[2] *n* **1** : sommeil *m* **2 to go to sleep** : s'endormir
sleeper ['sli:pər] *n* : dormeur *m,* -meuse *f*
sleepily ['sli:pəli] *adv* : d'un air endormi
sleepiness ['sli:pinəs] *n* : somnolence *f,* torpeur *f*
sleepless ['sli:pləs] *adj* : sans sommeil
sleepwalker ['sli:pˌwɔkər] *n* : somnambule *mf*
sleepy ['sli:pi] *adj* **sleepier; -est 1** DROWSY : somnolent <to be sleepy : avoir sommeil> **2** QUIET : endormi, somnolent <a sleepy town : une ville somnolente>
sleet[1] ['sli:t] *vi* : grésiller
sleet[2] *n* : grésil *m*
sleeve ['sli:v] *n* : manche *f*
sleeveless ['sli:vləs] *adj* : sans manches
sleigh ['sleɪ] *n* : traîneau *m,* carriole *f Can*
sleight of hand ['slaɪt̬əv'hænd] *n* : tour *m* de passe-passe
slender ['slɛndər] *adj* **1** SLIM : mince **2** FEEBLE : faible <a slender hope : une faible espérance>
sleuth ['slu:θ] *n* : détective *m,* limier *m*
slew ['slu:] → **slay**
slice[1] ['slaɪs] *vt* **sliced; slicing** : trancher, découper en tranches
slice[2] *n* : tranche *f,* rondelle *f* (de saucisson)
slick[1] ['slɪk] *vt* : lisser
slick[2] *adj* **1** SLIPPERY : lisse **2** CRAFTY : habile
slicker ['slɪkər] *n* : imperméable *m,* ciré *m*
slide[1] ['slaɪd] *v* **slid** ['slɪd]; **sliding** ['slaɪdɪŋ] *vi* **1** : glisser **2** DECLINE : baisser <to let things slide : laisser aller> — *vt* : faire glisser
slide[2] *n* **1** SLIP : glissade *f* **2** : toboggan *m* (dans un terrain de jeu) **3** TRANSPARENCY : diapositive *f* **4** DECLINE : baisse *f*
slier, sliest → **sly**
slight[1] ['slaɪt] *vt* : offenser
slight[2] *adj* **1** SLENDER : mince **2** FRAIL : frêle **3** TRIFLING : léger <a slight injury : une légère blessure> **4** SMALL : menu <slight mishaps : menues méchancetés>
slight[3] *n* : affront *m*
slightly ['slaɪtli] *adv* **1** : légèrement, un peu, moindrement *Can* **2 slightly built** : mince

slim[1] ['slɪm] *v* **slimmed; slimming** *vi* : maigrir — *vt* : faire maigrir, amincir

slim[2] *adj* **slimmer; slimmest 1** SLENDER : svelte, élancé, mince **2** FAINT, SLIGHT : faible, mince <she has only a slim chance : elle n'a que de faibles chances>

slime ['slaɪm] *n* **1** : bave *f* (sécrété par un escargot) **2** MUD : vase *f,* boue *f*

slimy ['slaɪmi] *adj* **slimier; -est** : visqueux

sling[1] ['slɪŋ] *vt* **slung** ['slʌŋ]; **slinging 1** THROW : lancer, jeter **2** HANG : suspendre

sling[2] *n* **1** : écharpe *f* <his arm is in a sling : son bras est en écharpe> **2** STRAP : bretelle *f* **3** → **slingshot**

slingshot ['slɪŋˌʃɑt] *n* : fronde *f,* lance-pierres *m*

slink ['slɪŋk] *vi* **slunk** ['slʌŋk]; **slinking 1** : entrer ou sortir furtivement **2 to slink away** : s'éclipser, s'éloigner furtivement

slip[1] ['slɪp] *v* **slipped; slipping** *vi* **1** SLIDE : glisser <he slipped on the sidewalk : il a glissé sur le trottoir> **2** DECLINE : décliner **3 to let slip** : laisser échapper **4 to slip away** : partir furtivement — *vt* **1** PASS : glisser <I slipped him ten dollars : j'ai glissé dix dollars dans sa main> **2** ESCAPE : échapper à **3 it slipped his mind** : ça lui est sorti de la tête, ça lui a échappée

slip[2] *n* **1** : glissade *f* **2** BERTH : slip *m* (de bateaux) **3** MISTAKE : erreur *f* <a slip of the tongue : un lapsus> **4** PETTICOAT : jupon *m* **5** CUTTING : bouture *f* (d'une plante)

slipcover ['slɪpˌkʌvər] *n* : housse *f*

slipper ['slɪpər] *n* : pantoufle *f*

slipperiness ['slɪpərinəs] *n* : état *m* glissant

slippery ['slɪpəri] *adj* **slipperier; -est 1** : glissant **2** TRICKY : rusé **3** EVASIVE : fuyant

slipshod ['slɪpˌʃɑd] *adj* : négligent

slip up *vi* : faire une gaffe

slit[1] ['slɪt] *vt* **slit; slitting 1** SPLIT : fendre **2** CUT : couper, inciser

slit[2] *n* **1** OPENING : fente *f* **2** CUT : coupure *f,* incision *f*

slither ['slɪðər] *vi* : ramper

sliver ['slɪvər] *n* **1** : éclat *m* (de bois) **2** SLICE : petite tranche *f,* petit morceau *m*

slob ['slɑb] *n* : personne *f* débraillée

slobber[1] ['slɑbər] *vi* : baver

slobber[2] *n* : bave *f*

slogan ['slo:gən] *n* : slogan *m*

sloop ['slu:p] *n* : sloop *m*

slop[1] ['slɑp] *v* **slopped; slopping** *vt* : renverser, répandre — *vi or* **to slop over** : se répandre, déborder

slop[2] *n* : pâtée *f*

slope[1] ['slo:p] *vi* **sloped; sloping** : pencher, être en pente

slope[2] *n* : pente *f*

sloppy ['slɑpi] *adj* **sloppier; -est 1** MUDDY : boueux, mouillé **2** UNTIDY : négligé **3** CARELESS : bâclé

slot ['slɑt] *n* **1** : fente *f* **2** GROOVE : rainure *f* **3** *or* **time slot** : créneau *m,* tranche *f* horaire

sloth ['slɔθ, 'slo:θ] *n,* **1** LAZINESS : paresse *f* **2** : paresseux *m* (animal)

slouch[1] ['slaʊtʃ] *vi* : être avachi, ne pas se tenir droit

slouch[2] *n* **1 to walk with a slouch** : marcher le dos voûté **2 he's no slouch** : il n'est pas empoté

slough[1] ['slʌf] *vt or* **to slough off** : se débarrasser de

slough[2] ['slu:, 'slaʊ] *n* SWAMP : bourbier *m,* marécage *m*

Slovak ['slo:ˌvɑk, -ˌvæk] *or* **Slovakian** [ˌslo:'vɑkiən, -'væ-] *adj* : slovaque

Slovakian *n* : Slovaque *mf*

Slovene ['slo:ˌvi:n] *or* **Slovenian** [slo:'vi:niən] *adj* : slovène

Slovenian *n* : Slovène *mf*

slovenly ['slʌvənli, 'slɑv-] *adj* **1** : négligé, sale **2** CARELESS : bâclé

slow[1] ['slo:] *vt* **1** : ralentir **2** DELAY : retarder — *vi* : ralentir

slow[2] *adv* : lentement

slow[3] *adj* **1** : lent <a slow process : un processus lent> <my watch is five minutes slow : ma montre retarde de cinq minutes> **2** STUPID : peu intelligent, lent **3** SLACK : calme, stagnant <sales are slow : les ventes ne marchent pas fort> **4** SLUGGISH : léthargique, lent

slowly ['slo:li] *adv* : lentement

slowness ['slo:nəs] *n* : lenteur *f,* lourdeur *m*

slowpoke ['slo:ˌpo:k] *n* : traînard *m,* -narde *f;* lambineux *m,* -neuse *f Can fam*

sludge ['slʌdʒ] *n* : boue *f,* vase *f*

slug[1] ['slʌg] *vt* **slugged; slugging** : assommer

slug[2] *n* **1** : limace *f* (mollusque) **2** BULLET : balle *f* **3** TOKEN : jeton *m* **4** BLOW : coup *m*

sluggish ['slʌgɪʃ] *adj* : léthargique, lent

sluice[1] ['slu:s] *vt* **sluiced; sluicing** *or* **to sluice down** : laver à grande eau

sluice[2] *n* : vanne *f*

slum ['slʌm] *n* : taudis *m,* quartier *m* pauvre

slumber[1] ['slʌmbər] *vi* : dormir, sommeiller

slumber[2] *n* : sommeil *m*

slump[1] ['slʌmp] *vi* **1** DECLINE, DROP : baisser **2** SLOUCH : être avachi

slump[2] *n* : baisse *f,* crise *f* (économique)

slung → **sling**[1]

slunk → **slink**

slur[1] ['slər] *vt* **slurred; slurring 1** : mal articuler (les mots) **2** : lier (en musique)

slur[2] *n* : affront *m,* insulte *f* <racial slur : insulte raciste>
slurp ['slərp] *v* : boire avec bruit
slush ['slʌʃ] *n* : neige *f* fondue, sloche *f Can,* gadoue *f Can*
slut ['slʌt] *n* PROSTITUTE : prostituée *f*
sly ['slaɪ] *adj* **slier** ['slaɪər]; **sliest** ['slaɪəst] **1** CUNNING : rusé **2** UNDERHANDED : sournois
slyly ['slaɪli] *adv* **1** CUNNINGLY : de façon rusée **2** UNDERHANDEDLY : sournoisement
slyness ['slaɪnəs] *n* CUNNING : ruse *f*
smack[1] ['smæk] *vi* **to smack of** : sentir — *vt* **1** KISS : donner un baiser à **2** SLAP : gifler, claquer **3 to smack one's lips** : se lécher les babines
smack[2] *adv* **smack in the middle** : en plein milieu
smack[3] *n* **1** TASTE, TRACE : soupçon *m* **2** KISS : gros baiser *m* **3** SLAP : gifle *f,* claque *f*
small ['smɔl] *adj* **1** : petit <a small house : une petite maison> <small change : petite monnaie> **2** TRIVIAL : insignifiant, peu important
smallness ['smɔlnəs] *n* : petitesse *f*
smallpox ['smɔl,pɑks] *n* : variole *f*
smart[1] ['smɑrt] *vi* **1** STING : brûler, piquer **2** : être piqué au vif (par l'insulte)
smart[2] *adj* **1** INTELLIGENT : intelligent **2** STYLISH : chic
smart[3] *n* : douleur *f* cuisante
smartly ['smɑrtli] *adv* **1** CLEVERLY : habilement, astucieusement **2** STYLISHLY : avec beaucoup de chic **3** QUICKLY : vivement
smartness ['smɑrtnəs] *n* **1** INTELLIGENCE : intelligence *f* **2** ELEGANCE : élégance *f*
smash[1] ['smæʃ] *vt* **1** BREAK : briser **2** CRASH : écraser **3** SHATTER : fracasser, briser — *vi* **1** SHATTER : se briser, se fracasser **2** COLLIDE, CRASH : s'écraser
smash[2] *n* **1** BLOW : coup *m,* gifle *f* **2** COLLISION : collision *f* **3** BANG, CRASH : fracas *m*
smattering ['smæṭərɪŋ] *n* : notions *fpl* vagues, rudiments *mpl* <a smattering of French : quelques notions de français> <a smattering of spectators : quelques spectateurs>
smear[1] ['smɪr] *vt* **1** SMUDGE : faire des taches sur, barbouiller **2** SLANDER : diffamer
smear[2] *n* **1** STAIN : tache *f* **2** SLANDER : diffamation *f*
smell[1] ['smɛl] *v* **smelled** ['smɛld] *or* **smelt** ['smɛlt]; **smelling** *vt* : sentir <to smell danger : sentir le danger> — *vi* : sentir <to smell good : sentir bon>
smell[2] *n* **1** : odorat *m* (sens) **2** ODOR : odeur *f*
smelly ['smɛli] *adj* **smellier**; **-est** : malodorant <it's smelly in here : ça sent mauvais ici>
smelt[1] ['smɛlt] *vt* : fondre
smelt[2] *n, pl* **smelts** *or* **smelt** : éperlan *m* (poisson)
smile[1] ['smaɪl] *vi* **smiled; smiling** : sourire
smile[2] *n* : sourire *m*
smirk[1] ['smərk] *vi* : sourire d'un air satisfait
smirk[2] *n* : petit sourire *m* satisfait
smite ['smaɪt] *vt* **smote** ['smo:t]; **smitten** ['smɪtən] *or* **smote; smiting 1** STRIKE : frapper **2 to be smitten with** : être pris de <smitten with remorse : accablé de remords>
smith ['smɪθ] *n* : forgeron *m*
smithy ['smɪθi] *n, pl* **smithies** : forge *f*
smock ['smɑk] *n* : blouse *f,* sarrau *m*
smog ['smɑg, 'smɔg] *n* : smog *m*
smoke[1] ['smo:k] *v* **smoked; smoking** *vt* : fumer <to smoke a cigarette : fumer une cigarette> — *vi* : fumer
smoke[2] *n* : fumée *f,* boucane *f Can*
smoke detector *n* : détecteur *m* de fumée
smoker ['smo:kər] *n* : fumeur *m,* -meuse *f*
smokestack ['smo:k,stæk] *n* : cheminée *f*
smoky ['smo:ki] *adj* **smokier; -est** : enfumé
smolder ['smo:ldər] *vi* : couver
smooth[1] ['smu:ð] *vt* : lisser
smooth[2] *adj* **1** : lisse <smooth skin : peau lisse> **2** CALM : calme <a smooth landing : un atterrissage en douceur> **3** MILD : doux **4** FLOWING : fluide <smooth writing : écriture fluide>
smoothly ['smu:ðli] *adv* **1** GENTLY, SOFTLY : doucement **2** EASILY : facilement
smoothness ['smu:ðnəs] *n* : douceur *f*
smother ['smʌðər] *vt* **1** SUFFOCATE : étouffer **2** COVER : recouvrir (un feu) — *vi* : être étouffé
smudge[1] ['smʌdʒ] *v* **smudged; smudging** *vt* : salir, faire des taches sur — *vi* : se salir, s'étaler
smudge[2] *n* : tache *f,* bavure *f*
smug ['smʌg] *adj* **smugger; smuggest** : suffisant, content de soi
smuggle ['smʌgəl] *v* **-gled; -gling** *vt* : faire passer en contrebande — *vi* : faire de la contrebande
smuggler ['smʌgələr] *n* : contrebandier *m,* -dière *f*
smugly ['smʌgli] *adv* : avec suffisance
smut ['smʌt] *n* **1** SOOT : tache *f* de suie **2** OBSCENITY : cochonnerie *f* **3** FUNGUS : charbon *m* (du blé)
smutty ['smʌti] *adj* **smuttier; -est 1** SOOTY : noirci, sali **2** OBSCENE : cochon, ordurier
snack ['snæk] *n* : casse-croûte *m*
snag[1] ['snæg] *v* **snagged; snagging** *vt* : accrocher — *vi* : s'accrocher
snag[2] *n* : accroc *m*

snail ['sneɪl] *n* : escargot *m*

snake ['sneɪk] *n* : serpent *m*

snakebite ['sneɪkˌbaɪt] *n* : morsure *f* de serpent

snap[1] ['snæp] *v* **snapped; snapping** *vi* **1** CLICK : claquer **2** : essayer de mordre (se dit d'un chien, etc.) **3** BREAK : se casser, se briser **4** : parler d'un ton brusque — *vt* **1** CLICK : faire claquer **2** BREAK : casser, briser **3 to snap up** : arracher, saisir

snap[2] *n* **1** CLICK : claquement *m* **2** BREAK : cassure *f* **3** FASTENER : bouton-pression *m* **4** CINCH : quelque chose *f* de facile <it's a snap! : c'est du gâteau!>

snapdragon ['snæpˌdrægən] *n* : gueule-de-loup *f*

snapper ['snæpər] *n* : lutjanidé *m* (poisson)

snappy ['snæpi] *adj* **snappier; -est 1** FAST : vite <make it snappy! : fais ça vite!> **2** LIVELY : vif **3** STYLISH : chic

snapshot ['snæpˌʃɑt] *n* : instantané *m*

snare[1] ['snær] *vt* **snared; snaring** : attraper, prendre au piège

snare[2] *n* : piège *m*, collet *m*

snare drum *n* : caisse *f* claire

snarl[1] ['snɑrl] *vi* **1** TANGLE : enchevêtrer **2** GROWL : grogner

snarl[2] *n* **1** TANGLE : enchevêtrement *m* **2** GROWL : grognement *m*

snatch[1] ['snætʃ] *vt* : saisir

snatch[2] *n* : fragment *m*, bribe *f* <snatches of conversation : bribes de conversation>

sneak[1] ['sniːk] *vi* : se glisser, se faufiler — *vt* : faire furtivement <to sneak a look : jeter un coup d'œil> <he sneaked a smoke : il a fumé en cachette>

sneak[2] *n* : sournois *m*, -noise *f*; cafard *m*, -farde *f France fam*

sneakers ['sniːkərz] *npl* : tennis *mpl France*, espadrilles *fpl Can*

sneaky ['sniːki] *adj* **sneakier; -est** : sournois

sneer[1] ['snɪr] *vi* : ricaner, sourire d'un air méprisant

sneer[2] *n* : ricanement *m*

sneeze[1] ['sniːz] *vi* **sneezed; sneezing** : éternuer

sneeze[2] *n* : éternuement *m*

snicker[1] ['snɪkər] *vi* : rire doucement, rire dans sa barbe

snicker[2] *n* : rire *m* étouffé

snide ['snaɪd] *adj* : narquois

sniff[1] ['snɪf] *vi* **1** : renifler **2 to sniff at** : dédaigner, faire la grimace à — *vt* **1** SMELL : sentir, humer **2 to sniff out** : flairer

sniff[2] *n* : reniflement *m*

sniffle[1] ['snɪfəl] *vi* **-fled; -fling** : renifler

sniffle[2] *n* **1** SNIFF : reniflement *m* **2 sniffles** *npl* : petit rhume *m* <to have the sniffles : être enrhumé>

snip[1] ['snɪp] *vt* **snipped; snipping** : couper

snip[2] *n* **1** CUT : coupure *f* **2** FRAGMENT, PIECE : petit bout *m*

snipe[1] ['snaɪp] *vi* **sniped; sniping 1 to snipe at** SHOOT : tirer sur **2 to snipe at** CRITICIZE : critiquer par en-dessous

snipe[2] *n, pl* **snipes** *or* **snipe** : bécassine *f* (oiseau)

sniper ['snaɪpər] *n* : tireur *m* embusqué

snivel ['snɪvəl] *vi* **-eled** *or* **-elled; -eling** *or* **-elling 1** → **snuffle 2** WHINE : pleurnicher *fam*, chialer *fam*

snob ['snɑb] *n* : snob *mf*

snobbery ['snɑbəri] *n, pl* **-beries** : snobisme *m*

snobbish ['snɑbɪʃ] *adj* : snob

snobbishness ['snɑbɪʃnəs] *n* : snobisme *m*

snoop[1] ['snuːp] *vi* **1 to snoop around** : fouiner, fureter **2 to snoop on s.o.** : espionner qqn

snoop[2] *n* **1** : espion *m*, -pionne *f*; fouineur *m*, -neuse *f* **2 to have a snoop around** : fureter discrètement dans

snooze[1] ['snuːz] *vi* **snoozed; snoozing** : sommeiller

snooze[2] *n* : petit somme *m*

snore[1] ['snor] *vi* **snored; snoring** : ronfler

snore[2] *n* : ronflement *m*

snort[1] ['snɔrt] *vi* : grogner (se dit d'une personne ou d'un cochon), s'ébrouer (se dit d'un cheval)

snort[2] *n* : grognement *m*, ébrouement *m*

snout ['snaʊt] *n* : museau *m*, groin *m* (d'un porc)

snow[1] ['snoː] *vi* : neiger

snow[2] *n* : neige *f*

snowball ['snoːˌbɔl] *n* : boule *f* de neige, pelote *f* de neige *Can*

snowbank ['snoːˌbæŋk] *n* : congère *f France*, banc *m* de neige *Can*

snowblower ['snoːˌbloːər] *n* : souffleuse *f* (à neige) *Can*

snowdrift ['snoːˌdrɪft] *n* : congère *f France*, banc *m* de neige *Can*

snowfall ['snoːˌfɔl] *n* : chute *f* de neige

snowplow ['snoːˌplaʊ] *n* : chasse-neige *m*, gratte *f Can*

snowshoes ['snoːˌʃuːz] *npl* : raquettes *fpl*

snowstorm ['snoːˌstɔrm] *n* : tempête *f* de neige, bordée *f* de neige *Can*

snowy ['snoːi] *adj* **snowier; -est** : neigeux

snub[1] ['snʌb] *vt* **snubbed; snubbing** : rabrouer

snub[2] *n* : rebuffade *f*

snub–nosed ['snʌbˌnoːzd] *adj* : au nez retroussé

snuff[1] ['snʌf] *vt* **1** EXTINGUISH : moucher **2** SNIFF : renifler

snuff[2] *n* : tabac *m* à priser

snuffle ['snʌfəl] *vi* **-fled; -fling** : renifler

snug ['snʌg] *adj* **snugger; snuggest 1** COMFORTABLE : confortable **2** TIGHT : bien ajusté
snuggle ['snʌgəl] *vi* **-gled; -gling** : se pelotonner
snugly ['snʌgli] *adv* **1** COMFORTABLY : confortablement **2** WELL : bien <the dress fits snugly : la robe est parfaitement ajustée>
so[1] ['so:] *adv* **1** (*referring to something indicated or suggested*) <do you think so? : tu crois?> <so be it : ainsi soit-il> <I told her so : je le lui ai dit> **2** : si, tellement <it's so hot : il fait si chaud> <they were so late : ils ont été tellement en retard> **3** ALSO : aussi <so do I : moi aussi> **4** THUS : ainsi <it would seem so : il paraîtrait ainsi> <do it like so : fais-le ainsi> **5** AS : aussi <he'd never been so happy : il n'a jamais été aussi content> **6 is that so?** : c'est vrai?
so[2] *conj* **1** THEREFORE : donc, alors **2** *or* **so that** : afin de **3 so what?** : et alors?
soak[1] ['so:k] *vi* : tremper — *vt* **1** WET : tremper **2** IMMERSE : faire tremper (la lessive, etc.) **3 to soak up** ABSORB : absorber
soak[2] *n* : trempage *m*
soap[1] ['so:p] *vt* : savonner
soap[2] *n* : savon *m*
soapsuds ['so:p,sʌdz] → **suds**
soapy ['so:pi] *adj* **soapier; -est** : savonneux
soar ['sor] *vi* **1** GLIDE : planer **2** TOWER : se dresser (vers le ciel), s'élever **3** RISE : monter (en flèche) <prices have soared : les prix ont monté> <my spirits soared : mon moral est remonté en flèche>
sob[1] ['sɑb] *vi* **sobbed; sobbing** : sangloter
sob[2] *n* : sanglot *m*
sober ['so:bər] *adj* **1** : sobre <he's perfectly sober : il est parfaitement sobre> **2** SERIOUS : sérieux
soberly ['so:bərli] *adv* **1** : avec sobriété, sobrement **2** SERIOUSLY : sérieusement
sobriety [sə'braɪət̬i, so-] *n* : sobriété *f*
soccer ['sɑkər] *n* : football *m France*, soccer *m Can*
sociability [,so:ʃə'bɪlət̬i] *n* : sociabilité *f*
sociable ['so:ʃəbəl] *adj* : sociable
social[1] ['so:ʃəl] *adj* : social — **socially** *adv*
social[2] *n* **1** PARTY : soirée *f* **2** GATHERING : réunion *f*
socialism ['so:ʃə,lɪzəm] *n* : socialisme *m*
socialist[1] ['so:ʃəlɪst] *adj* : socialiste
socialist[2] *n* : socialiste *mf*
socialize ['so:ʃə,laɪz] *v* **-ized; -izing** *vt* : socialiser — *vi* : fréquenter des gens
social work *n* : travail *m* social
society [sə'saɪət̬i] *n, pl* **-eties 1** COMPANIONSHIP : compagnie *f* **2** : société *f* <a democratic society : une société démocratique> <high society : haute société> **3** ASSOCIATION : association *f*, société *f*
sociological [,so:siə'lɑdʒɪkəl] *adj* : sociologique
sociologist [,so:si'ɑlədʒɪst] *n* : sociologue *mf*
sociology [,so:si'ɑlədʒi] *n* : sociologie *f*
sock[1] ['sɑk] *vt* : donner un coup de poing à
sock[2] *n* **1** PUNCH : coup *m*, beigne *f fam* **2** *pl* **socks** *or* **sox** : chaussette *f*
socket ['sɑkət] *n* **1** : cavité *f* **2** *or* **electric socket** : prise *f* de courant **3 eye socket** : orbite *f*
sod[1] ['sɑd] *vt* **sodded; sodding** : gazonner
sod[2] *n* TURF : gazon *m*, motte *f* (de gazon)
soda ['so:də] *n* **1** *or* **soda pop** : boisson *f* gazeuse, soda *m France*, liqueur *f Can* **2** : soude *f* <baking soda : bicarbonate de soude>
sodden ['sɑdən] *adj* SOGGY : trempé, détrempé
sodium ['so:diəm] *n* : sodium *m*
sofa ['so:fə] *n* : canapé *m*
soft ['sɔft] *adj* **1** : mou <a soft pillow : un mol oreiller> **2** SMOOTH : doux <soft to the touch : doux au toucher> <a soft ride : un roulement doux>
softball ['sɔft,bɔl] *n* : balle-molle *f Can*, softball *m Can*
soft drink *n* : boisson *f* non alcoolisée, boisson *f* gazeuse
soften ['sɔfən] *vt* : amollir, adoucir (la peau), ramollir (le beurre, etc.) — *vi* : s'adoucir, se ramollir
softly ['sɔftli] *adv* : doucement, mollement
softness ['sɔftnəs] *n* : douceur *f*, mollesse *f*
software ['sɔft,wær] *n* : logiciel *m*, software *m*
soggy ['sɑgi] *adj* **soggier; -est** : détrempé, trempé
soil[1] ['sɔɪl] *vt* : salir, souiller <he soiled his hands : il s'est sali les mains> — *vi* : se salir
soil[2] *n* **1** DIRT, EARTH : sol *m*, terre *f* **2** COUNTRY : sol *m*, terre *f* <her native soil : sa terre natale>
sojourn[1] ['so:,dʒərn, so:'dʒərn] *vi* : séjourner
sojourn[2] *n* : séjour *m*
solace ['sɑləs] *n* : consolation *f*
solar ['so:lər] *adj* : solaire
sold → **sell**
solder[1] ['sɑdər, 'sɔ-] *vt* : souder
solder[2] *n* : soudure *f*
soldier[1] ['so:ldʒər] *vi* **1** : être soldat **2 to soldier on** : persévérer
soldier[2] *n* : soldat *m*, femme soldat *f*, militaire *m*
sole[1] ['so:l] *adj* : seul
sole[2] *n* **1** : plante *f* (du pied) **2** : sole *f* (poisson)

solemn ['sɑləm] *adj* : solonnel — **solemnly** *adv*

solemnity [sə'lɛmnət̬i] *n, pl* **-ties** : solennité *f*

solicit [sə'lɪsət] *vt* : solliciter

solicitous [sə'lɪsət̬əs] *adj* : plein de sollicitude

solicitude [sə'lɪsə,tu:d, -,tju:d] *n* : sollicitude *f*

solid[1] ['sɑləd] *adj* **1** : solide <solid food : aliments solides> **2** : plein, massif <solid gold : or massif> <a solid rubber ball : un ballon plein en caoutchouc> **3** CONTINUOUS : de suite <two solid hours : deux heures de suite>

solid[2] *n* : solide *m*

solidarity [,sɑlə'dærət̬i] *n* : solidarité *f*

solidify [sə'lɪdə,faɪ] *v* **-fied; -fying** *vt* : solidifier — *vi* : se solidifier

solidity [sə'lɪdət̬i] *n, pl* **-ties** : solidité *f*

solidly ['sɑlədli] *adv* : solidement

soliloquy [sə'lɪləkwi] *n, pl* **-quies** : soliloque *m*

solitaire ['sɑlə,tɛr] *n* : solitaire *m*

solitary ['sɑlə,tɛri] *adj* **1** ALONE : solitaire **2** SINGLE : seul

solitude ['sɑlə,tu:d, -,tju:d] *n* : solitude *f*

solo[1] ['so:,lo:] *vi* : jouer en solo

solo[2] *adv* : en solo

solo[3] *adj* : solo

solo[4] *n, pl* **solos** : solo *m*

soloist ['so:,loɪst] *n* : soliste *mf*

solstice ['sɑlstɪs] *n* : solstice *m*

soluble ['sɑljəbəl] *adj* : soluble

solution [sə'lu:ʃən] *n* : solution *f*

solve ['sɑlv] *vt* **solved; solving** : résoudre, trouver la solution de

solvency ['sɑlvəntsi] *n* : solvabilité *f*

solvent[1] ['sɑlvənt] *adj* : solvable

solvent[2] *n* : solvant *m,* dissolvant *m*

Somali[1] [so'mɑli, sə-] *adj* : somali

Somali[2] *n* : Somali *m,* -lie *f*

Somalian[1] [so'mɑliən, -ljən, sə-] *adj* : somalien

Somalian[2] *n* : Somalien *m,* -lienne *f*

somber ['sɑmbər] *adj* : sombre

sombrero [səm'brɛr,o:] *n, pl* **-ros** : sombrero *m*

some[1] ['sʌm] *adj* **1** (*being an amount*) : de <some water : de l'eau> <do you want some apples? : voulez-vous des pommes?> **2** (*being an unspecified or indefinite number*) : certains <he read some books : il a lu certains livres> **3** SEVERAL : quelques <some good candidates : quelques bons candidats> <some years ago : il y a quelques années> **4** (*being an unspecified individual or thing*) : un, une, quelque <some lady stopped me : une dame m'a arrêté> <some distant galaxy : quelque galaxie lointaine>

some[2] *pron* **1** : certains *mpl,* certaines *fpl,* quelques-uns *mpl,* quelques-unes *fpl* <some left, others stayed : certains sont partis, d'autres sont restés> **2** : un peu, en <there's some left : il en reste un peu> <do you want some? : en voulez-vous?>

somebody ['sʌmbədi, -,bɑdi] *pron* : quelqu'un, on

someday ['sʌm,deɪ] *adv* : un jour

somehow ['sʌm,haʊ] *adv* **1** : de quelque manière <somehow or other : d'une manière ou d'une autre> **2** : pour quelque raison <somehow I don't trust him : pour quelque raison je ne lui fais pas confiance>

someone ['sʌm,wʌn] *pron* : quelqu'un, on

somersault[1] ['sʌmər,sɔlt] *vi* : faire une culbute

somersault[2] *n* : culbute *f*

something ['sʌmθɪŋ] *pron* : quelque chose <something happened : quelque chose est arrivé> <something else : autre chose>

sometime ['sʌm,taɪm] *adv* **1** (*indicating a time in the future*) : un jour, un de ces jours <you should try it sometime : tu devrais l'essayer un jour> **2** (*indicating a time in the past*) <she called sometime last week : elle a téléphoné au cours de la semaine passée>

sometimes ['sʌm,taɪmz] *adv* : quelquefois, parfois

somewhat ['sʌm,hwʌt, -,hwɑt] *adv* : un peu, quelque peu, assez

somewhere ['sʌm,hwɛr] *adv* **1** : quelque part **2 somewhere else** : ailleurs, autre part

son ['sʌn] *n* : fils *m*

sonar ['so:,nɑr] *n* : sonar *m*

sonata [sə'nɑt̬ə] *n* : sonate *f*

song ['sɔŋ] *n* : chanson *f*

songbird ['sɔŋ,bərd] *n* : oiseau *m* chanteur

sonic ['sɑnɪk] *adj* : sonique

son–in–law ['sʌnɪn,lɔ] *n, pl* **sons–in–law** : gendre *m,* beau-fils *m*

sonnet ['sɑnət] *n* : sonnet *m*

sonorous ['sɑnərəs, sə'norəs] *adj* : sonore

soon ['su:n] *adv* **1** : bientôt <he'll arrive soon : il arrivera bientôt> <soon after : peu après> **2** QUICKLY : vite <as soon as possible : le plus tôt possible>

soot ['sʊt, 'su:t, 'sʌt] *n* : suie *f*

soothe ['su:ð] *v* **soothed; soothing 1** CALM : calmer, apaiser **2** RELIEVE : soulager

soothsayer ['su:θ,seɪər] *n* : devin *m,* -vineresse *f*

sooty ['sʊt̬i, 'su:-, 'sʌ-] *adj* **sootier; -est** : couvert de suie

sop[1] ['sɑp] *vt* **sopped; sopping 1** SOAK : tremper **2 to sop up** : éponger

sop[2] *n* : concession *f* (symbolique) <as a sop to his pride : pour flatter son orgueil>

sophisticated [sə'fɪstə,keɪt̬əd] *adj* **1** COMPLEX : compliqué **2** WORLDLY : raffiné, sophistiqué

sophistication [sə,fɪstə'keɪʃən] *n* **1** WORLDLINESS : sophistication *f* **2**

COMPLEXITY : sophistication *f,* perfectionnement *m* **3** REFINEMENT, URBANITY : raffinement *m*

sophomore ['sɑf,mor, 'sɑfə,mor] *n* : étudiant *m,* -diante *f* de seconde année

soporific [,sɑpə'rɪfɪk, ,soː-] *adj* : soporifique

soprano [sə'præ,noː] *n, pl* **-nos** : soprano *mf* (personne), soprano *m* (voix)

sorcerer ['sɔrsərər] *n* : sorcier *m*

sorceress ['sɔrsərəs] *n* : sorcière *f*

sorcery ['sɔrsəri] *n* : sorcellerie *f*

sordid ['sɔrdɪd] *adj* : sordide

sore[1] ['sor] *adj* **sorer; sorest 1** PAINFUL : douloureux **2** GREAT : grand <to be in sore need of : avoir grand besoin de> **3** ANGRY : fâché, vexé

sore[2] *n* : plaie *f*

sorely ['sorli] *adv* : gravement, grandement, extrêmement

soreness ['sornəs] *n* : douleur *f*

sorghum ['sɔrgəm] *n* : sorgho *m*

sorority [sə'rɔrət̬i] *n, pl* **-ties** : club *m* d'étudiantes

sorrel ['sɔrəl] *n* **1** : oseille *f* (plante) **2** : brun *m* roux (couleur)

sorrow ['sɑr,oː] *n* : chagrin *m,* peine *f,* tristesse *f*

sorrowful ['sɑrofəl] *adj* : triste

sorrowfully ['sɑrofəli] *adv* : tristement

sorry ['sɑri] *adj* **sorrier; -est 1** PITIFUL : piteux <in a sorry state : dans un piteux état> **2 to be sorry** : être désolé, regretter <I'm sorry : je suis désolé> **3 to feel sorry for** : plaindre <I don't feel sorry for him : je ne le plains pas>

sort[1] ['sɔrt] *vt* : trier

sort[2] *n* **1** KIND : genre *m,* sorte *f* **2 out of sorts** : de mauvaise humeur

sortie ['sɔrt̬i, sɔr'tiː] *n* : sortie *f*

SOS [,ɛs,oː'ɛs] *n* : S.O.S. *m*

so–so[1] ['soː'soː] *adv* : comme ci comme ça

so–so[2] *adj* : moyen

soufflé [suː'fleɪ] *n* : soufflé *m*

sought → **seek**

soul ['soːl] *n* **1** SPIRIT : âme *f* **2** ESSENCE : essence *f* **3** PERSON : âme *f,* personne *f* <not a soul : pas âme qui vive>

soulful ['soːlfəl] *adj* : attendrissant, émouvant, sentimental

sound[1] ['saʊnd] *vt* **1** : sonner <to sound the alarm : sonner l'alarme> <to sound the horn : klaxonner> **2** *or* **to sound out** PROBE : sonder — *vi* **1** : sonner **2** SEEM : sembler, paraître

sound[2] *adj* **1** HEALTHY : sain <safe and sound : sain et sauf> **2** FIRM, SOLID : solide **3** SENSIBLE : raisonnable **4** DEEP : profond <a sound sleep : un sommeil profond>

sound[3] *n* **1** : son *m* **2** NOISE : bruit *m* **3** CHANNEL : détroit *m,* bras *m* de mer

soundless ['saʊndləs] *adj* : silencieux — **soundlessly** *adv*

soundly ['saʊndli] *adv* **1** SOLIDLY : solidement **2** SENSIBLY : judicieusement **3** DEEPLY : profondément <to sleep soundly : dormir profondément>

soundness ['saʊndnəs] *n* **1** SOLIDITY : solidité *f* **2** SENSE, WISDOM : sagesse *f,* bon sens *m,* justesse *f*

soundproof ['saʊnd,pruːf] *adj* : insonorisé

soup ['suːp] *n* : soupe *f* <vegetable soup : soupe aux légumes>

sour[1] ['saʊər] *v* : aigrir

sour[2] *adj* **1** ACID : aigre, sur **2** DISAGREEABLE : revêche, acerbe

source ['sors] *n* : source *f*

sourness ['saʊərnəs] *n* : aigreur *f*

south[1] ['saʊθ] *adv* : au sud, vers le sud <further south : plus au sud>

south[2] *adj* : sud, du sud <the south entrance : l'entrée sud> <South America : Amérique du Sud>

south[3] *n* : sud *m*

South African[1] *adj* : sud-africain

South African[2] *n* : Sud-Africain *m,* -caine *f*

South American[1] *adj* : sud-américain

South American[2] *n* : Sud-Américain *m,* -caine *f*

southbound ['saʊθ,baʊnd] *adj* : qui va vers le sud

southeast[1] [saʊ'θiːst, *as a nautical term often* saʊ'iːst] *adj* : sud-est

southeast[2] *n* : sud-est *m*

southeasterly[1] [saʊ'θiːstərli] *adv* : vers le sud-est

southeasterly[2] *adj* : du sud-est

southeastern [saʊ'θiːstərn] → **southeast**[1]

southerly[1] ['sʌðərli] *adv* : vers le sud

southerly[2] *adj* : du sud

southern ['sʌðərn] *adj* : du sud

Southerner ['sʌðərnər] *n* : habitant *m,* -tante *f* du Sud

south pole *n* : pôle *m* Sud

southward[1] ['saʊθwərd] *or* **southwards** [-wərdz] *adv* : vers le sud

southward[2] *or* **southwards** *adj* : au sud, du sud

southwest[1] [saʊθ'west, *as a nautical term often* saʊ'west] *adj* : sud-ouest

southwest[2] *n* : sud-ouest *m*

southwesterly[1] [saʊθ'westərli] *adv* : vers le sud-ouest

southwesterly[2] *adj* : du sud-ouest

southwestern [saʊθ'westərn] → **southwest**[1]

souvenir [,suːvə'nɪr, 'suːvə,-] *n* : souvenir *m*

sovereign[1] ['sɑvərən] *adj* : souverain

sovereign[2] *n* **1** MONARCH : souverain *m,* -raine *f* **2** : souverain *m* (pièce de monnaie)

sovereignty ['sɑvərənti] *n, pl* **-ties** : souveraineté *f*

Soviet ['soːvi,ɛt, 'sɑ-, -viət] *adj* : soviétique

sow[1] ['so:] *vt* **sowed; sown** ['so:n] *or* **sowed; sowing** : semer
sow[2] ['saʊ] *n* : truie *f*
sox → **sock**[2]
soybean ['sɔɪ,bi:n] *n* : graine *f* de soja
spa ['spɑ] *n* : station *f* thermale
space[1] ['speɪs] *vt* **spaced; spacing** *or* **to space out** : espacer, étaler, échelonner
space[2] *n* **1** *or* **outer space** : espace *m* **2** INTERVAL : espace *m* <in the space of a few days : en l'espace de quelques jours> **3** ROOM : place *f* <there's no more space : il n'y a plus de place> **4** : espace *f* (typographique)
spacecraft ['speɪs,kræft] *n* : vaisseau *m* spatial
spaceflight ['speɪs,flaɪt] *n* : vol *m* spatial
spaceman ['speɪsmən, -,mæn] *n, pl* **-men** [-mən, -,mɛn] : astronaute *mf*, cosmonaute *mf*
spaceship ['speɪs,ʃɪp] *n* : vaisseau *m* spatial
space shuttle *n* : navette *f* spatiale
space suit *n* : combinaison *f* spatiale
spacious ['speɪʃəs] *adj* : spacieux
spade[1] ['speɪd] *vt* **spaded; spading** : bêcher, pelleter
spade[2] *n* **1** SHOVEL : bêche *f*, pelle *f* **2** : pique *f* (aux cartes)
spaghetti [spə'gɛṭi] *n* : spaghetti *mpl*, spaghettis *mpl*
span[1] ['spæn] *vt* **spanned; spanning 1** CROSS : franchir, enjamber **2** ENCOMPASS : embrasser, comprendre
span[2] *n* **1** WIDTH : envergure *f*, portée *f*, travée *f* **2** DURATION : durée *f*
spangle ['spæŋgəl] *n* : paillette *f*
Spaniard ['spænjərd] *n* : Espagnol *m*, -gnole *f*
spaniel ['spænjəl] *n* : épagneul *m*
Spanish[1] ['spænɪʃ] *adj* : espagnol
Spanish[2] *n* **1** : espagnol *m* (langue) **2 the Spanish** : les Espagnols
spank ['spæŋk] *vt* : fesser
spanking[1] ['spæŋkɪŋ] *adj* BRISK : vif
spanking[2] *n* : fessée *f*
spanner ['spænər] *Brit* → **wrench**[2] **3**
spar[1] ['spɑr] *vi* **sparred; sparring** : s'entraîner à la boxe
spar[2] *n* : espar *m*, verge *f Can*
spare[1] ['spær] *vt* **spared; sparing 1** SAVE : épargner <to spare s.o.'s life : épargner la vie de qqn> <to spare oneself the trouble of : s'épargner l'ennui de> **2** DISPENSE WITH : se passer de <we can't spare him : nous ne pouvons pas nous passer de lui> <can you spare me $10? : est-ce que tu as 10 $ à me passer?> **3 to spare no effort** : faire tout son possible
spare[2] *adj* **1** : de réserve **2** EXTRA, SURPLUS : de trop <a spare moment : un moment de libre> **3** LEAN : maigre
spare[3] *n* **1** *or* **spare part** : pièce *f* de rechange **2** *or* **spare tire** : pneu *m* de rechange
sparing ['spærɪŋ] *adj* : économe
sparingly ['spærɪŋli] *adv* : avec modération, frugalement
spark[1] ['spɑrk] *vi* : émettre des étincelles — *vt* **1** PROVOKE : déclencher <to spark a dispute : déclencher une dispute> **2** AWAKEN : éveiller <to spark the curiosity of : éveiller la curiosité de>
spark[2] *n* : étincelle *f*
sparkle[1] ['spɑrkəl] *vi* **-kled; -kling 1** FLASH : étinceler, scintiller **2** EFFERVESCE : pétiller
sparkle[2] *n* : scintillement *m*, éclat *m*
sparkler ['spɑrklər] *n* : cierge *m* magique
spark plug *n* : bougie *f*
sparrow ['spæro:] *n* : moineau *m*
sparse ['spɑrs] *adj* **sparser; -est** : clairsemé, épars
sparsely ['spɑrsli] *adv* : peu <sparsely furnished : peu meublé>
spasm ['spæzəm] *n* **1** : spasme *m* **2** FIT : accès *m*
spasmodic [spæz'mɑdɪk] *adj* **1** : spasmodique (se dit de la douleur, etc.) **2** SPORADIC : intermittent
spasmodically [spæz'mɑdɪkli] *adv* : par à-coups
spastic ['spæstɪk] *adj* : spasmodique, handicapé moteur
spat[1] ['spæt] → **spit**[1]
spat[2] *n* **1** QUARREL : prise *f* de bec **2 spats** *npl* : guêtres *fpl*
spatial ['speɪʃəl] *adj* : spatial
spatter[1] ['spæṭər] *vt* : éclabousser — *vi* : crépiter, gicler
spatter[2] *n* : éclaboussure *f*
spatula ['spætʃələ] *n* : spatule *f*
spawn[1] ['spɔn] *vi* : frayer — *vt* GENERATE : engendrer
spawn[2] *n* : frai *m*
spay ['speɪ] *vt* : châtrer
speak ['spi:k] *v* **spoke** ['spo:k]; **spoken** ['spo:kən]; **speaking** *vi* **1** TALK : parler <to speak to s.o. : parler à qqn> <to speak well of : dire du bien de> <strictly speaking : à proprement parler> <so to speak : pour ainsi dire> **2 to speak out** : parler clairement **3 to speak out against** : s'élever contre **4 to speak up** : parler plus fort **5 to speak up for** : soutenir, défendre — *vt* **1** SAY : dire <she spoke her mind : elle a dit sa pensée> **2** : parler (une langue)
speaker ['spi:kər] *n* **1** : personne *f* qui parle **2** ORATOR : orateur *m*, -trice *f*; conférencier *m*, -cière *f* **3** LOUDSPEAKER : haut-parleur *m*, enceinte *f* acoustique (d'une chaîne stéréo)
spear[1] ['spɪr] *vt* : transpercer d'un coup de lance
spear[2] *n* : lance *f*
spearhead[1] ['spɪr,hɛd] *vt* : être le fer de lance de, mener
spearhead[2] *n* : fer *m* de lance

spearmint ['spɪr,mɪnt] *n* : menthe *f* verte

special ['spɛʃəl] *adj* : spécial, particulier <nothing special : rien de particulier>

specialist ['spɛʃəlɪst] *n* : spécialiste *mf*

specialization [ˌspɛʃələ'zeɪʃən] *n* : spécialisation *f*

specialize ['spɛʃəˌlaɪz] *vi* **-ized; -izing** : se spécialiser

specially ['spɛʃəli] *adv* **1** PARTICULARLY : spécialement, particulièrement **2** SPECIFICALLY : exprès, spécialement

specialty ['spɛʃəlt̬i] *n, pl* **-ties** : spécialité *f*

species ['spiːʃiːz, -ˌsiːz] *ns & pl* : espèce *f*

specific [spɪ'sɪfɪk] *adj* **1** EXPLICIT : précis, explicite **2** : spécifique (en biologie, en médecine, etc.)

specifically [spɪ'sɪfɪkli] *adv* **1** EXPLICITLY : précisément, explicitement **2** PARTICULARLY : spécialement, en particulier

specification [ˌspɛsəfə'keɪʃən] *n* : spécification *f*

specify ['spɛsəˌfaɪ] *vt* **-fied; -fying** : spécifier

specimen ['spɛsəmən] *n* **1** SAMPLE : échantillon *m* **2** EXAMPLE : spécimen *m*, exemplaire *m*

speck ['spɛk] *n* **1** SPOT : tache *f* **2** BIT, TRACE : grain *m* <a speck of dust : un grain de poussière>

speckled ['spɛkəld] *adj* : tacheté, moucheté

spectacle ['spɛktɪkəl] *n* **1** : spectacle *m* **2 spectacles** *npl* GLASSES : lunettes *fpl*

spectacular [spɛk'tækjələr] *adj* : spectaculaire

spectator ['spɛkˌteɪt̬ər] *n* : spectateur *m*, -trice *f*

specter ['spɛktər] *n* : spectre *m*

spectrum ['spɛktrəm] *n, pl* **spectra** [-trə] *or* **spectrums 1** : spectre *m* <the visible spectrum : le spectre visible> **2** RANGE : gamme *f*

speculate ['spɛkjəˌleɪt] *vi* **-lated; -lating** : spéculer

speculation [ˌspɛkjə'leɪʃən] *n* : conjectures *fpl*, spéculations *fpl*

speculative ['spɛkjəˌleɪt̬ɪv] *adj* : spéculatif

speculator ['spɛkjəˌleɪt̬ər] *n* : spéculateur *m*, -trice *f*

speech ['spiːtʃ] *n* **1** : parole *f* <to lose the power of speech : perdre la parole> **2** ADDRESS : discours *m*

speechless ['spiːtʃləs] *adj* : muet

speed[1] ['spiːd] *v* **sped** ['spɛd] *or* **speeded; speeding** *vi* **1** : aller à toute allure, aller à toute vitesse <he sped off : il est parti à toute allure> **2** : rouler trop vite (dans une voiture) <a ticket for speeding : une contravention pour excès de vitesse> — *vt or* **to speed up** : accélérer

speed[2] *n* **1** SWIFTNESS : vitesse *f* **2** VELOCITY : vélocité *f*

speedboat ['spiːdˌboːt] *n* : vedette *f* (rapide), hors-bord *m*

speed bump *n* : casse-vitesse *m*

speed limit *n* : limite *f* de vitesse

speedometer [spɪ'dɑmət̬ər] *n* : compteur *m* de vitesse

speedup ['spiːdˌʌp] *n* : accélération *f*

speedy ['spiːdi] *adj* **speedier; -est** : rapide — **speedily** [-dəli] *adv*

spell[1] ['spɛl] *vt* **1** : écrire, orthographier <how do you spell it? : comment est-ce que ça s'écrit?> **2** MEAN : signifier <that could spell trouble : on pourrait avoir des ennuis> **3** RELIEVE : relayer, relever — *vi* : connaître l'orthographe

spell[2] *n* **1** TURN : tour *m* **2** PERIOD : période *f* **3** ENCHANTMENT : charme *m*, sortilège *m*

spellbound ['spɛlˌbaʊnd] *adj* : captivé

speller ['spɛlər] *n* **to be a good speller** : être forte en orthographe

spelling ['spɛlɪŋ] *n* : orthographe *f*

spell out *vt* **1** : épeler (les lettres d'un mot) **2** EXPLAIN : expliquer

spend ['spɛnd] *vt* **spent** ['spɛnt]; **spending 1** : dépenser (de l'argent) **2** PASS : passer <to spend time on : passer son temps à>

spendthrift ['spɛndˌθrɪft] *n* : dépensier *m*, -sière *f*

sperm ['spərm] *n, pl* **sperm** *or* **sperms** : sperme *m*

spew ['spjuː] *vt or* **to spew out** : vomir (de la fumée, de la lave, etc.) — *vi* : jaillir, gicler

sphere ['sfɪr] *n* : sphère *f*

spherical ['sfɪrɪkəl, 'sfɛr-] *adj* : sphérique

spice[1] ['spaɪs] *vt* **spiced; spicing 1** SEASON : épicer **2** *or* **to spice up** : pimenter

spice[2] *n* **1** : épice *f* **2** EXCITEMENT, PIQUANCY : piquant *m*

spick–and–span ['spɪkən*d*spæn] *adj* : impeccable

spicy ['spaɪsi] *adj* **spicier; -est 1** SPICED : épicé **2** RACY : pimenté, piquant

spider ['spaɪdər] *n* : araignée *f*

spigot ['spɪgət, -kət] *n* : robinet *m*

spike[1] ['spaɪk] *vt* **spiked; spiking 1** FASTEN : clouer **2** PIERCE : transpercer **3** : corser (de l'alcool)

spike[2] *n* **1** NAIL : (gros) clou *m* **2** : pointe *f* (d'une chaussure), épi *m* (des cheveux), épine *f* (d'un cactus)

spill[1] ['spɪl] *vt* **1** : renverser, répandre <to spill blood : verser du sang> **2** DIVULGE : révéler — *vi* : se répandre

spill[2] *n* **1** SPILLING : renversement *m* **2** FALL : chute *f*, culbute *f*

spin[1] ['spɪn] *v* **spun** ['spʌn]; **spinning** *vi* **1** ROTATE : tourner, tournoyer <my head is spinning : j'ai la tête qui tourne> **2** : filer (avec un rouet) —

vt **1** : faire tourner **2** : filer <to spin wool : filer de la laine>

spin[2] *n* : tour *m* <to go for a spin : faire un petit tour>

spinach ['spɪnɪtʃ] *n* : épinards *mpl*

spinal column ['spaɪnəl] *adj* BACKBONE : colonne *f* vertébrale

spinal cord *n* : moelle *f* épinière

spindle ['spɪndəl] *n* **1** : fuseau *m,* broche *f* (pour filer) **2** AXLE : axe *m*

spindly ['spɪndli] *adj* : grêle (se dit des jambes), étiolé (se dit d'une plante)

spine ['spaɪn] *n* **1** BACKBONE : colonne *f* vertébrale **2** QUILL : piquant *m* (d'un animal) **3** THORN : épine *f* **4** : dos *m* (d'un livre)

spineless ['spaɪnləs] *adj* **1** : sans piquants, sans épines **2** INVERTEBRATE : invertébré **3** COWARDLY, WEAK : lâche, mou

spinet ['spɪnət] *n* : épinette *f*

spinster ['spɪn*t*stər] *n* : célibataire *f,* vieille fille *f*

spiny ['spaɪni] *adj* **spinier; -est** : couvert de piquants (se dit des animaux), épineux (se dit des plantes)

spiral[1] ['spaɪrəl] *vi* **-raled** *or* **-ralled; -raling** *or* **-ralling** : aller en spirale

spiral[2] *adj* : spirale, en spirale <spiral staircase : escalier en spirale>

spiral[3] *n* : spirale *f*

spire ['spaɪr] *n* : flèche *f*

spirit[1] ['spɪrət] *vt* **to spirit away** : faire disparaître

spirit[2] *n* **1** : esprit *m* <in the spirit of friendship : dans l'esprit de l'amitié> **2** GHOST : esprit *m,* spectre *m,* fantôme *m* **3** ENTHUSIASM, VIVACITY : entrain *m* **4 spirits** *npl* MOOD : humeur *f* <to be in good spirits : être de bonne humeur> **5 spirits** *npl* LIQUORS : spiritueux *mpl*

spirited ['spɪrət̬əd] *adj* : animé, vif

spiritless ['spɪrətləs] *adj* : sans vie, sans entrain

spiritual[1] ['spɪrɪtʃʊəl, -tʃəl] *adj* : spirituel — **spiritually** *adv*

spiritual[2] *n* : spiritual *m*

spiritualism ['spɪrɪtʃʊəˌlɪzəm, -tʃə-] *n* : spiritisme *m*

spirituality [ˌspɪrɪtʃʊ'æləţi] *n* : spiritualité *f*

spit[1] ['spɪt] *v* **spit** *or* **spat** ['spæt]; **spitting** : cracher

spit[2] *n* **1** SALIVA : crachat *m,* salive *f* **2** ROTISSERIE : broche *f* **3** POINT : pointe *f* (de terre)

spite[1] ['spaɪt] *vt* **spited; spiting** : contrarier

spite[2] *n* **1** : dépit *m,* malveillance *f* **2 in spite of** : en dépit de, malgré

spiteful ['spaɪtfəl] *adj* : malveillant

spittle ['spɪţəl] *n* : salive *f*

splash[1] ['splæʃ] *vt* : éclabousser — *vi* **1** *or* **to splash about** : barboter, patauger **2 to splash through** : traverser en faisant des éclaboussures

splash[2] *n* **1** SPLASHING : éclaboussement *m* **2** SQUIRT : goutte *f* **3** SPOT : tache *f,* éclaboussure *f* **4 to make a splash** : faire sensation

splatter ['splæţər] → **spatter**

splay ['spleɪ] *vt* : écarter (des doigts, des jambes) — *vi* : s'écarter

spleen ['spli:n] *n* **1** : rate *f* (organe) **2** ANGER, SPITE : mauvaise humeur *f*

splendid ['splɛndəd] *adj* : splendide, superbe

splendidly ['splɛndədli] *adv* : superbement, magnifiquement

splendor *or Brit* **splendour** ['splɛndər] *n* : splendeur *f*

splice[1] ['splaɪs] *vt* **spliced; splicing** : épisser, coller

splice[2] *n* : épissure *f*

splint ['splɪnt] *n* : attelle *f*

splinter[1] ['splɪntər] *vt* : briser en éclats — *vi* : se briser en éclats

splinter[2] *n* : éclat *m*

split[1] ['splɪt] *v* **split; splitting** *vt* **1** CLEAVE : fendre, couper <to split wood : fendre du bois> **2** TEAR : déchirer **3** SHARE : partager **4** DIVIDE : diviser — *vi* **1** CRACK : se fendre **2** TEAR : se déchirer **3** DIVIDE, SEPARATE : se diviser

split[2] *n* **1** CRACK : fente *f* **2** TEAR : déchirure *f* **3** DIVISION : division *f,* scission *f*

splurge[1] ['splərdʒ] *v* **splurged; splurging** *vi* : faire des folles dépenses — *vt* : dépenser

splurge[2] *n* : folles dépenses *fpl*

spoil ['spɔɪl] *v* **spoiled** ['spɔɪld, 'spɔɪlt] *or* **spoilt** ['spɔɪlt]; **spoiling 1** PILLAGE : piller **2** RUIN : gâcher, abîmer **3** PAMPER : gâter — *vi* : se gâter, s'abîmer

spoils ['spɔɪlz] *npl* PLUNDER : butin *m,* dépouilles *fpl*

spoke[1] → **speak**

spoke[2] ['spo:k] *n* : rayon *m*

spoken → **speak**

spokesman ['spo:ksmən] *n, pl* **-men** [-mən, -ˌmɛn] : porte-parole *m*

spokeswoman ['spo:ksˌwʊmən] *n, pl* **-women** [-ˌwɪmən] : porte-parole *m*

sponge[1] ['spʌndʒ] *vt* **sponged; sponging** : éponger

sponge[2] *n* : éponge *f*

spongy ['spʌndʒi] *adj* **spongier; -est** : spongieux

sponsor[1] ['spɑn*t*sər] *vt* : patronner, sponsoriser

sponsor[2] *n* : sponsor *m,* commanditaire *m,* parrain *m*

sponsorship ['spɑn*t*sərˌʃɪp] *n* : parrainage *m,* patronage *m*

spontaneity ['spɑntə'ni:əţi, -'neɪ-] *n* : spontanéité *f*

spontaneous [spɑn'teɪniəs] *adj* : spontané — **spontaneously** *adv*

spoof ['spu:f] *n* : parodie *f*

spook[1] ['spu:k] *vt* : faire peur à

spook[2] *n* : fantôme *m*

spooky ['spu:ki] *adj* **spookier; -est** : sinistre, qui fait froid dans le dos

spool ['spu:l] *n* : bobine *f*

spoon[1] ['spu:n] *vt* : servir, verser (avec une cuillère)

spoon[2] *n* : cuillère *f,* cuiller *f*

spoonful ['spu:n,fʊl] *n* : cuillerée *f*

spoor ['spʊr, 'spor] *n* : piste *f,* trace *f*

sporadic [spə'rædɪk] *adj* : sporadique — **sporadically** [-dɪkli] *adv*

spore ['spor] *n* : spore *f*

sport[1] ['sport] *vi* FROLIC : s'amuser — *vt* WEAR : arborer, porter

sport[2] *n* **1** : sport *m* **2** JEST : jeu *m* **3 to be a good sport** : être beau joueur

sportsman ['sportsmən] *n, pl* **-men** [-mən, -,mɛn] : sportif *m*

sportsmanship ['sportsmən,ʃɪp] *n* : sportivité *f*

sportswoman ['sports,wʊmən] *n, pl* **-women** [-,wɪmən] : sportive *f*

sporty ['sporṭi] *adj* **sportier; -est** : sportif

spot[1] ['spɑt] *v* **spotted; spotting** *vt* **1** STAIN : tacher **2** NOTICE : apercevoir, repérer <to spot an error : apercevoir une erreur> — *vi* : se tacher

spot[2] *adj* : fait au hasard <a spot check : un contrôle au hasard>

spot[3] *n* **1** STAIN : tache *f* **2** DOT : pois *m* **3** PREDICAMENT : situation *f* difficile **4** PLACE : endroit *m,* lieu *m,* <on the spot : sur place>

spotless ['spɑtləs] *adj* : sans tache

spotlessly ['spɑtləsli] *adv* **spotlessly clean** : impeccable, reluisant de propreté

spotlight[1] ['spɑt,laɪt] *vt* **-lighted** *or* **-lit** [-,lɪt]; **-lighting 1** LIGHT : diriger les projecteurs sur **2** HIGHLIGHT : mettre en lumière

spotlight[2] *n* **1** : projecteur *m,* spot *m* **2 to be in the spotlight** : être en vedette

spotty ['spɑṭi] *adj* **spottier; -est 1** SPOTTED : tacheté **2** UNEVEN : irrégulier

spouse ['spaʊs] *n* : époux *m,* épouse *f*

spout[1] ['spaʊt] *vt* **1** : faire jaillir **2** DECLAIM : déclamer — *vi* : jaillir

spout[2] *n* **1** : bec *m* verseur **2** STREAM : jet *m*

sprain[1] ['spreɪn] *vt* : faire une entorse à, fouler

sprain[2] *n* : entorse *f,* foulure *f*

sprawl[1] ['sprɔl] *vi* **1** : être affalé (se dit d'une personne) **2** SPREAD : s'étaler

sprawl[2] *n* **1** : position *f* affalée **2** EXTENT, SPREAD : étendue *f*

spray[1] ['spreɪ] *vt* : atomiser, vaporiser, arroser (un jardin)

spray[2] *n* **1** BOUQUET : bouquet *m* **2** MIST : gouttelettes *fpl* fines, embruns *mpl* (de la mer) **3** ATOMIZER : atomiseur *m,* vaporisateur *m,* bombe *f*

spray gun *n* : pistolet *m* (à peinture)

spread[1] ['sprɛd] *v* **spread; spreading** *vt* **1** *or* **to spread out** : étendre **2** : étaler, tartiner <to spread butter : étaler du beurre> **3** DISSEMINATE : répandre, propager — *vi* **1** EXTEND : s'étendre, s'étaler **2** : se répandre, se propager <the disease is spreading : la maladie se répand>

spread[2] *n* **1** EXTENT, RANGE : éventail *m,* envergure *f* **2** → **bedspread 3** PASTE : pâte *f* à tartiner <cheese spread : fromage à tartiner> **4** PROPAGATION : propagation *f*

spreadsheet ['sprɛd,ʃi:t] *n* : tableur *m*

spree ['spri] *n* : fête *f* <to go on a spending spree : faire de folles dépenses>

sprig ['sprɪg] *n* : brin *m*

sprightly ['spraɪtli] *adj* **sprightlier; -est** : vif, alerte

spring[1] ['sprɪŋ] *v* **sprang** ['spræŋ] *or* **sprung** ['sprʌŋ]; **sprung; springing** *vi* **1** LEAP : sauter, bondir **2** (*indicating rapid movement*) <to spring to s.o.'s aid : se précipiter pour aider qqn> <tears sprang to my eyes : les larmes me sont montées aux yeux> **3 to spring up** : surgir — *vt* **1** RELEASE : déclencher, faire jouer <to spring a trap : faire jouer un piège> **2** : annoncer (une nouvelle, etc.), poser (une question) <to spring the news on s.o. : surprendre qqn avec les nouvelles> **3 to spring a leak** : commencer à fuir

spring[2] *n* **1** SOURCE : source *f* **2** : printemps *m* (saison) <in the spring : au printemps> **3** COIL : ressort *m* **4** LEAP : bond *m,* saut *m* **5** RESILIENCE : élasticité *f*

springboard ['sprɪŋ,bord] *n* : tremplin *m*

springtime ['sprɪŋ,taɪm] *n* : printemps *m*

springy ['sprɪŋi] *adj* **springier; -est 1** RESILIENT : élastique **2** LIVELY : énergique

sprinkle[1] ['sprɪŋkəl] *v* **-kled; -kling** *vt* **1** : saupoudrer <sprinkle with oregano : saupoudrez d'oregano> **2** : asperger, arroser <to sprinkle the lawn : arroser la pelouse> — *vi* : tomber des gouttes (se dit de la pluie)

sprinkle[2] *n* **1** PINCH : pincée *f,* petite quantité *f* **2** RAIN : petite pluie *f*

sprinkler ['sprɪŋkələr] *n* : arroseur *m*

sprint[1] ['sprɪnt] *vi* : sprinter

sprint[2] *n* : sprint *m*

sprite ['spraɪt] *n* **1** : lutin *m* **2** *or* **water sprite** : naïade *f*

sprocket ['sprɑkət] *n* : pignon *m*

sprout[1] ['spraʊt] *v* : pousser

sprout[2] *n* : pousse *f*

spruce[1] ['spru:s] *vt* **spruced; sprucing 1** *or* **to spruce up** : faire beau (un enfant, etc.), astiquer (une maison) **2 to spruce oneself up** : se faire beau

spruce[2] *adj* **sprucer; sprucest** : pimpant

spruce[3] *n* : sapinette *f,* épicéa *m France,* épinette *f Can*

spry ['spraɪ] *adj* **sprier** *or* **spryer** ['spraɪər]; **spriest** *or* **spryest** ['spraɪəst] : alerte, plein d'entrain

spun → **spin**[1]
spunk ['spʌŋk] *n* : courage *m*, cran *m fam*
spunky ['spʌŋki] *adj* **spunkier; -est** : courageux
spur[1] ['spər] *vt* **spurred; spurring** *or* **to spur on** : éperonner (un cheval), aiguillonner (une personne)
spur[2] *n* **1** : éperon *m* **2** STIMULUS : stimulant *m*, aiguillon *m* **3** RIDGE : éperon *m*, contrefort *m* **4 on the spur of the moment** : sur le coup, sur l'impulsion du moment
spurious ['spjʊriəs] *adj* : faux, fallacieux
spurn ['spərn] *vt* : rejeter
spurt[1] ['spərt] *vt* SQUIRT : faire gicler — *vi* : jaillir, gicler
spurt[2] *n* **1** BURST : sursaut *m*, bourrée *f Can* <a spurt of enthusiasm : un sursaut d'enthousiasme> **2** GUSH, JET : jaillissement *m*
sputter[1] ['spʌt̬ər] *vi* **1** JABBER, MUTTER : bredouiller **2** : grésiller, crépiter (se dit d'un feu), tousser (se dit d'un moteur)
sputter[2] *n* **1** JABBERING, MUTTERING : bredouillement *m* **2** : crépitement *m* (d'un feu), raté *m* (d'un moteur)
spy[1] ['spaɪ] *v* **spied; spying** *vt* SEE : apercevoir, discerner — *vi* **1** : faire de l'espionnage **2 to spy on s.o.** : espionner qqn
spy[2] *n* : espion *m*
squab ['skwɑb] *n, pl* **squabs** *or* **squab** : pigeonneau *m*
squabble[1] ['skwɑbəl] *vi* **-bled; -bling** : se disputer, se chamailler
squabble[2] *n* : dispute *f*, querelle *f*
squad ['skwɑd] *n* : équipe *f*, peloton *m* (militaire), brigade *f* (de police)
squadron ['skwɑdrən] *n* : escadron *m*
squalid ['skwɑlɪd] *adj* : sordide
squall ['skwɔl] *n* : bourrasque *f* <snow squall : bourrasque de neige>
squalor ['skwɑlər] *n* : conditions *fpl* sordides, misère *f*
squander ['skwɑndər] *vt* : gaspiller
square[1] ['skwær] *v* **squared; squaring** *vt* **1** : équarrir, carrer **2** : carrer (en mathématiques) **3** *or* **to square away** SETTLE : régler — *vi* **to square with** : cadrer avec, coïncider avec
square[2] *adj* **squarer; -est 1** : carré <a square house : une maison carrée> **2** RIGHT-ANGLED : à angle droit **3** : carré (en mathématiques) <a square meter : un mètre carré> **4** HONEST : honnête
square[3] *n* **1** : équerre *f* (instrument) **2** : carré *m* <to fold into squares : plier en forme de carré> **3** : place *f* (d'une ville) **4** : carré *m* (en mathématiques)
squarely ['skwærli] *adv* **1** EXACTLY : carrément **2** HONESTLY : honnêtement
square root *n* : racine *f* carrée
squash[1] ['skwɑʃ, 'skwɔʃ] *vt* **1** CRUSH : écraser, aplatir, écrapoutir *Can* **2** SUPPRESS : remettre à sa place (une personne), réduire à néant (des espoirs), réprimer (une révolte) — *vi* : s'écraser
squash[2] *n, pl* **squashes** *or* **squash 1** : courge *f* **2** *or* **squash rackets** : squash *m*
squat[1] ['skwɑt] *vi* **squatted; squatting 1** CROUCH : s'accroupir **2 to squat in** : squatter (un bâtiment, etc.)
squat[2] *adj* **squatter; squattest** : trapu
squat[3] *n* **1** : position *f* accroupie **2** : squat *m* (dans un bâtiment)
squaw ['skwɔ] *n* : squaw *f*
squawk[1] ['skwɔk] *vi* : criailler
squawk[2] *n* : criaillement *m* (d'un oiseau), cri *m* rauque (d'une personne)
squeak[1] ['skwiːk] *vi* : grincer, couiner
squeak[2] *n* : grincement *m*, couinement *m*
squeaky ['skwiːki] *adj* **squeakier; -est** : grinçant, aigu <a squeaky voice : une voix aiguë> <squeaky shoes : des chaussures qui craquent>
squeal[1] ['skwiːl] *vi* **1** : pousser des cris aigus (se dit des personnes et des animaux), crisser (se dit des pneus), grincer (se dit des freins) **2 to squeal on** : dénoncer
squeal[2] *n* **1** : cri *m* aigu **2** SCREECH : crissement *m* (de pneus), grincement *m* (de freins)
squeamish ['skwiːmɪʃ] *adj* : délicat, sensible, facilement dégoûté
squeeze[1] ['skwiːz] *v* **squeezed; squeezing** *vt* **1** PRESS : presser, serrer **2** EXTRACT : exprimer **3** EXTORT : extorquer, soutirer — *vi* : se glisser <he squeezed into the room : il s'est glissé dans la salle>
squeeze[2] *n* : pression *f*, reserrement *m*
squelch ['skwɛltʃ] *vt* : écraser, étouffer, aplatir
squid ['skwɪd] *n, pl* **squid** *or* **squids** : calmar *m*, encornet *m*
squint[1] ['skwɪnt] *vi* : plisser les yeux, loucher
squint[2] *adj* *or* **squint–eyed** : qui louche
squint[3] *n* : strabisme *m*
squire ['skwaɪr] *n* **1** LANDOWNER : propriétaire *mf* **2** : écuyer *m* (d'un chevalier)
squirm ['skwərm] *vi* : se tortiller
squirrel ['skwərəl] *n* : écureuil *m*
squirt[1] ['skwərt] *vt* : faire gicler — *vi* : gicler
squirt[2] *n* : jet *m*, giclée *f*
Sri Lankan[1] [ˌsriː'læŋkən] *adj* : sri lankais
Sri Lankan[2] *n* : Sri Lankais *m*, -kaise *f*
stab[1] ['stæb] *vt* **stabbed; stabbing 1** KNIFE : poignarder **2** STICK : piquer
stab[2] *n* **1** : coup *m* de couteau **2 to take a stab at** : essayer, tenter

stability [stə'bɪləṭi] *n, pl* **-ties** : stabilité *f*
stabilize ['steɪbə,laɪz] *v* **-lized; -lizing** *vt* : stabiliser — *vi* : se stabiliser
stable[1] ['steɪbəl] *vt* **-bled; -bling** : mettre à l'écurie
stable[2] *adj* **-bler; -blest 1** FIXED, STEADY : stable, fixe **2** LASTING : stable, durable **3** : équilibré (en psychologie), stationnaire (en médicine)
stable[3] *n* : écurie *f*
staccato [stə'kɑṭo:] *adj* : staccato
stack[1] ['stæk] *vt* **1** PILE : entasser, empiler, mettre en meule (se dit du foin) **2** FILL : remplir <the table was stacked with books : la table était remplie de livres>
stack[2] *n* **1** PILE : tas *m,* pile *f* **2** → **smokestack**
stadium ['steɪdiəm] *n, pl* **-dia** [-diə] *or* **-diums** : stade *m*
staff[1] ['stæf] *vt* : pourvoir en personnel
staff[2] *n, pl* **staffs** ['stæfs, 'stævz] *or* **staves** ['stævz, 'steɪvz] **1** STICK : bâton *m* **2** *pl* **staffs** PERSONNEL : personnel *m* **3** : portée *f* (en musique)
stag[1] ['stæg] *adv* : seul <to go stag : aller sans compagne>
stag[2] *adj* : entre hommes
stag[3] *n, pl* **stags** *or* **stag** : cerf *m*
stage[1] ['steɪdʒ] *vt* **staged; staging 1** ORGANIZE : organiser (une manifestation, etc.) **2** : monter, mettre en scène (une pièce de théâtre)
stage[2] *n* **1** PLATFORM : estrade *f,* scène *f* (au théâtre) **2** PHASE : stade *m,* phase *f,* étape *f* **3 the stage** : le théâtre
stagecoach ['steɪdʒ,ko:tʃ] *n* : diligence *f*
stagger[1] ['stægər] *vi* TOTTER : tituber, chanceler — *vt* **1** SPACE OUT : échelonner, étaler **2** AMAZE : stupéfier
stagger[2] *n* : pas *m* chancelant
staggering ['stægərɪŋ] *adj* : stupéfiant
stagnant ['stægnənt] *adj* : stagnant
stagnate ['stæg,neɪt] *vi* **-nated; -nating** : stagner
stagnation [stæg'neɪʃən] *n* : stagnation *f*
staid ['steɪd] *adj* : collet monté, guindé
stain[1] ['steɪn] *vt* **1** DISCOLOR : tacher **2** DYE : teindre, teinter **3** SULLY : souiller — *vi* : se tacher
stain[2] *n* **1** SPOT : tache *f* **2** DYE : teinture *f* **3** BLEMISH : souillure *f*
stainless ['steɪnləs] *adj* : inoxydable <stainless steel : acier inoxydable>
stair ['stær] *n* **1** STEP : marche *f* **2 stairs** *npl* : escalier *m*
staircase ['stær,keɪs] *n* : escalier *m*
stairway ['stær,weɪ] *n* : escalier *m*
stairwell ['steɪr,wɛl] *n* : cage *f* d'escaliers
stake[1] ['steɪk] *vt* **staked; staking 1** *or* **to stake out** : jalonner, marquer (une ligne frontière), délimiter (un espace) **2** BET : miser, parier **3 to stake a claim to** : établir son droit à, revendiquer
stake[2] *n* **1** POST : poteau *m,* pieu *m,* piquet *m* **2** BET : enjeu *m* <to be at stake : être en jeu> **3** INTEREST, SHARE : intérêt *m,* part *f*
stalactite [stə'læk,taɪt] *n* : stalactite *f*
stalagmite [stə'læg,maɪt] *n* : stalagmite *f*
stale ['steɪl] *adj* **staler; stalest** : vieux, rassis (se dit du pain), éventé (se dit d'une boisson)
stalemate ['steɪl,meɪt] *n* : pat *m,* impasse *f*
stalk[1] ['stɔk] *vt* **1** TRACK : traquer **2** PROWL : rôder dans <to stalk the countryside : rôder dans les campagnes> — *vi* : marcher fièrement <to stalk out : sortir d'un air hautain>
stalk[2] *n* : tige *f* (d'une plante)
stall[1] ['stɔl] *vt* **1** : faire caler (un moteur) **2** DELAY : retarder, bloquer — *vi* **1** : caler (se dit d'un moteur) **2** *or* **to stall for time** : essayer de gagner du temps
stall[2] *n* **1** : stalle *f* (d'un cheval, etc.) **2** BOOTH : stand *m,* étal *m*
stallion ['stæljən] *n* : étalon *m*
stalwart ['stɔlwərt] *adj* **1** STRONG : robuste <a stalwart supporter : un supporter inconditionnel> **2** BRAVE : vaillant, brave
stamen ['steɪmən] *n* : étamine *f*
stamina ['stæmənə] *n* : vigueur *f,* résistance *f*
stammer[1] ['stæmər] *v* : bégayer
stammer[2] *n* : bégaiement *m*
stamp[1] ['stæmp] *vt* **1** IMPRESS, IMPRINT : frapper, estamper (le métal, etc.) **2** : timbrer, affranchir (le courrier), viser (un passeport) **3 to stamp one's feet** : taper des pieds
stamp[2] *n* **1** IMPRESSION, MARK : cachet *m,* tampon *m* **2** *or* **postage stamp** : timbre *m* **3** → **rubber stamp 4** HALLMARK, TRAIT : empreinte *f,* marque *f* <to bear the stamp of s.o. : avoir la marque de qqn>
stampede[1] [stæm'pi:d] *vi* **-peded; -peding** : s'enfuir à la débandade
stampede[2] *n* : débandade *f*
stance ['stæn*t*s] *n* : position *f*
stanch ['stɔntʃ, 'stɑntʃ] *vt* : étancher
stand[1] ['stænd] *v* **stood** ['stʊd]; **standing** *vi* **1** : être debout **2** *or* **to stand up** : se mettre debout, se lever **3** (*indicating a specified position or location*) <the machines are standing idle : les machines restent inutilisées> **4** (*referring to an opinion*) <where does he stand on the matter? : quelle est sa position là-dessus?> **5** BE : être, se trouver <the house stands on a hill : la maison se trouve sur une colline> **6** CONTINUE : rester valable <the offer stands : l'offre reste valable> **7** REMAIN, REST : reposer <the statue stands on a pedestal : la statue repose sur un piédestal> — *vt* **1** PLACE, SET

: mettre **2** ENDURE, TOLERATE : supporter <I can't stand it any longer : je ne peux plus supporter ça>

stand[2] *n* **1** RESISTANCE : résistance *f* (militaire) **2** BOOTH, STALL : stand *m*, étal *m* **3** BASE : pied *m*, piédestal *m* **4** GROVE : bosquet *m* (d' arbres) **5** POSITION : position *f* **6 stands** *npl* GRANDSTAND : tribune *f*

standard[1] ['stændərd] *adj* **1** ESTABLISHED : établi <standard English : l'anglais correct> **2** NORMAL : normal, standard **3** CLASSIC : classique <a standard work : une œuvre classique>

standard[2] *n* **1** BANNER : étendard *m* **2** CRITERION, NORM : critère *m*, norme *f*, étalon *m* <the gold standard : l'étalon-or> **3** LEVEL : niveau *m* <standard of living : niveau de vie> **4** SUPPORT : pied *m*, poteau *m*

standardize ['stændər,daɪz] *vt* **-ized; -izing** : standardiser

standard time *n* : heure *f* légale

stand by *vt* **1** SUPPORT : soutenir **2** MAINTAIN : tenir, s'en tenir à (une promesse, une opinion, etc.) — *vi* **1** : rester là <to stand by and do nothing : rester là sans rien faire> **2** : être prêt, se tenir prêt

stand for *vt* **1** REPRESENT : représenter **2** PERMIT, TOLERATE : supporter, tolérer

standing ['stændɪŋ] *n* **1** POSITION, RANK : position *f*, standing *m*, cote *f* **2** DURATION : durée *f* <of long standing : de longue date>

stand out *vi* **1** : ressortir, se détacher <she stands out from her colleagues : elle se détache de ses collègues> **2 to stand out against** RESIST : s'opposer à

standpoint ['stænd,pɔɪnt] *n* : point *m* de vue

standstill ['stænd,stɪl] *n* **1** STOP : arrêt *m* <to come to a standstill : s'arrêter> **2** DEADLOCK : impasse *f*

stand up *vt* **1** : mettre debout **2 to stand s.o. up** : poser un lapin à qqn *fam* — *vi* **1** ENDURE : tenir **2 to stand up for** : défendre **3 to stand up to** : résister à

stank → **stink**[1]

stanza ['stænzə] *n* : strophe *f*

staple[1] ['steɪpəl] *vt* **-pled; -pling** : agrafer

staple[2] *adj* : principal, de base <staple foods : denrées de base>

staple[3] *n* : agrafe *f*

stapler ['steɪplər] *n* : agrafeuse *f*

star[1] ['stɑr] *v* **starred; starring** *vt* **1** : marquer d'une étoile ou d'un astérisque **2** FEATURE : avoir pour vedette — *vi* : être la vedette

star[2] *n* **1** : étoile *f* **2** : vedette *f*, étoile *f*, star *f* <a movie star : une vedette de cinéma>

starboard ['stɑrbərd] *n* : tribord *m*

starch[1] ['stɑrtʃ] *vt* : amidonner

starch[2] *n* **1** : amidon *m* **2 starches** *npl* : féculents *mpl* (aliments)

starchy ['stɑrtʃi] *adj* **starchier; -est** : féculent <a starchy diet : un régime riche en féculents>

stardom ['stɑrdəm] *n* : célébrité *f*

stare[1] ['stær] *vi* **stared; staring** : regarder fixement

stare[2] *n* : regard *m* fixe

starfish ['stɑr,fɪʃ] *n* : étoile *f* de mer

stark[1] ['stɑrk] *adv* : complètement <stark raving mad : complètement fou> <stark naked : tout nu>

stark[2] *adj* **1** ABSOLUTE : absolu, pur **2** BARREN, DESOLATE : désolé, dénudé **3** BLUNT, HARSH : cru, catégorique, dur <the stark realities : les dures réalités>

starlight ['stɑr,laɪt] *n* : lumière *f* des étoiles

starling ['stɑrlɪŋ] *n* : étourneau *m*

starry ['stɑri] *adj* **starrier; -est** : étoilé

start[1] ['stɑrt] *vi* **1** JUMP : sursauter **2** BEGIN : commencer **3** DEPART : partir (en voyage, etc.) **4** : démarrer (se dit d'un moteur) — *vt* **1** BEGIN : commencer, se mettre à **2** CAUSE : provoquer **3** ESTABLISH : établir, créer <to start a business : établir une entreprise> **4** : mettre en marche, démarrer <to start the car : démarrer la voiture>

start[2] *n* **1** JUMP : sursaut *m* **2** BEGINNING : commencement *m*, début *m* <to get an early start : commencer tôt>

starter ['stɑrt̬ər] *n* **1** ENTRANT : partant *m*, -tante *f*; participant *m*, -pante *f* (aux sports) **2** APPETIZER : hors-d'œuvre *m*, entrée *f* **3** : démarreur *m* (d'un véhicule)

startle ['stɑrt̬əl] *vt* **-tled; -tling** : surprendre, alarmer, faire tressaillir

starve ['stɑrv] *v* **starved; starving** *vi* : mourir de faim — *vt* : affamer, faire mourir de faim

stash ['stæʃ] *vt* : cacher, mettre de côté

state[1] ['steɪt] *vt* **stated; stating 1** REPORT : exposer, déclarer **2** SPECIFY : spécifier, indiquer <as stated above : ainsi qu'il est indiqué plus haut>

state[2] *n* **1** CONDITION : état *m* **2** NATION : état *m*, nation *f* **3** : état *m* (d'un pays) **4 the States** : les États-Unis

stateliness ['steɪtlinəs] *n* : majesté *f*, grandeur *f*

stately ['steɪtli] *adj* **statelier; -est** : majestueux, imposant

statement ['steɪtmənt] *n* **1** DECLARATION : déclaration *f* **2** *or* **bank statement** : relevé *m* de compte

stateroom ['steɪt,ru:m] *n* : cabine *f* de luxe

statesman ['steɪtsmən] *n, pl* **-men** [-mən, -,mɛn] : homme *m* d'État

static[1] ['stæt̬ɪk] *adj* : statique

static[2] *n* **1** : parasites *mpl* (de radio, de télévision) **2** *or* **static electricity** : électricité *f* statique

station[1] ['steɪʃən] *vt* : poster, placer

station[2] *n* **1** : gare *f* (de train), station *f* (de métro) **2** RANK, STANDING : rang *m* **3** : station *f* (de radio), chaîne *f* (de télévision) **4 police station** : poste *m* de police **5 fire station** : caserne *f* de pompiers **6** → **service station**

stationary ['steɪʃəˌnɛri] *adj* **1** IMMOBILE : stationnaire, immobile **2** UNCHANGING : fixe

stationery ['steɪʃəˌnɛri] *n* : papeterie *f*, papier *m* à lettres

station wagon *n* : familiale *f*

statistic [stə'tɪstɪk] *n* : statistique *f*

statistical [stə'tɪstɪkəl] *adj* : statistique, de statistique

statue ['stæˌtʃuː] *n* : statue *f*

statuesque [ˌstætʃʊ'ɛsk] *adj* : sculptural

statuette [ˌstætʃʊ'ɛt] *n* : statuette *f*

stature ['stætʃər] *n* **1** HEIGHT : stature *f*, taille *f* **2** CALIBRE, STATUS : stature *f*, envergure *f*, calibre *m*

status ['steɪt̬əs, 'stæ-] *n* **1** : situation *f* (légale), statut *m* <marital status : situation de famille> **2** PRESTIGE : prestige *m*, standing *m* **3** POSITION : position *f*, rang *m* (social)

statute ['stæˌtʃuːt] *n* : loi *f*, règle *f*

staunch ['stɔntʃ] *adj* : dévoué, loyal <a staunch supporter : un fidèle>

staunchly ['stɔntʃli] *adv* : avec dévouement, loyalement

stave[1] ['steɪv] *vt* **staved** *or* **stove** ['stov]; **staving 1 to stave in** : enfoncer **2 to stave off** : écarter, tromper (la faim, etc.), éviter

stave[2] *n* : douve *f* (d'un tonneau)

staves → **staff**[2]

stay[1] ['steɪ] *vi* **1** REMAIN : rester, demeurer <to stay in : rester à la maison> <he stays in the city : il demeure en ville> **2** CONTINUE : rester <to stay awake : rester éveillé> **3** LODGE : loger — *vt* **1** HALT : arrêter, surseoir à (en droit) **2 to stay the course** : tenir jusqu'au bout

stay[2] *n* **1** SOJOURN : séjour *m* **2** SUPPORT : soutien *m*

stead ['stɛd] *n* **1** : place *f* <she went in his stead : elle est allée à sa place> **2 to stand s.o. in good stead** : être utile à qqn

steadfast ['stɛdˌfæst] *adj* **1** IMMOVABLE : fixe **2** FIRM : ferme, résolu **3** LOYAL : dévoué <a steadfast friend : un fidèle ami>

steadily ['stɛdəli] *adv* **1** CONSTANTLY : régulièrement, sans arrêt **2** FIRMLY : fermement **3** FIXEDLY : fixement **4** GRADUALLY : progressivement

steady[1] ['stɛdi] *v* **steadied; steadying** *vt* : stabiliser <she steadied herself : elle a retrouvé son équilibre> — *vi* : se stabiliser

steady[2] *adj* **steadier; -est 1** FIRM, SURE : ferme, sûr **2** REGULAR, CONSTANT : régulier, constant **3** CALM : calme **4** STABLE : stable

steak ['steɪk] *n* : bifteck *m*, steak *m*

steal ['stiːl] *v* **stole** ['stoːl]; **stolen** ['stolən]; **stealing** *vt* : voler — *vi* **1** : voler <thou shalt not steal : tu ne voleras point> **2** CREEP, SLIP : se glisser **3 to steal away** : s'esquiver

stealth ['stɛlθ] *n* : discrétion *f* <by stealth : furtivement>

stealthily ['stɛlθəli] *adv* : furtivement

stealthy ['stɛlθi] *adj* **stealthier; -est** : furtif

steam[1] ['stiːm] *vi* **1** : fumer **2 to steam ahead** : avancer — *vt* **1** : cuire à la vapeur **2 to steam open** : décacheter à la vapeur

steam[2] *n* : vapeur *f*

steamboat ['stiːmˌboːt] → **steamship**

steam engine *n* : moteur *m* à vapeur

steamroller ['stiːmˌroːlər] *n* : rouleau *m* compresseur

steamship ['stiːmˌʃɪp] *n* : paquebot *m*, navire *m* à vapeur

steamy ['stiːmi] *adj* **steamier; -est 1** : plein de vapeur, embué **2** EROTIC : érotique

steed ['stiːd] *n* : coursier *m*

steel[1] ['stiːl] *vt* **1 to steel oneself** : s'armer de courage **2 to steel oneself against** : se cuirasser contre

steel[2] *adj* : en acier, d'acier

steel[3] *n* : acier *m*

steely ['stiːli] *adj* **steelier; -est** : d'acier <a steely gaze : un regard d'acier> <steely determination : une volonté de fer>

steep[1] ['stiːp] *vt* : tremper, faire tremper

steep[2] *adj* **1** : raide, à pic **2** SHARP : fort <a steep increase : une forte augmentation> **3** EXCESSIVE : excessif <steep prices : des prix exorbitants>

steeple ['stiːpəl] *n* : clocher *m*, flèche *f*

steeplechase ['stiːpəlˌtʃeɪs] *n* : course *f* d'obstacles

steeply ['stiːpli] *adv* **1** : à pic, abruptement, en pente raide **2 to rise steeply** : monter en flèche (se dit des prix)

steer[1] ['stɪr] *vt* **1** : conduire (une voiture), gouverner (un navire) **2** GUIDE : diriger, guider

steer[2] *n* : bœuf *m*

steering wheel *n* : volant *m*

stein ['staɪn] *n* : chope *f*

stellar ['stɛlər] *adj* **1** : stellaire **2** SUPERB : superbe

stem[1] ['stɛm] *v* **stemmed; stemming** *vt* : arrêter, contenir, endiguer <to stem the tide : endiguer le flot> — *vi* **to stem from** : provenir de

stem[2] *n* : tige *f* (d'une plante)

stench ['stɛntʃ] *n* : puanteur *f*

stencil[1] ['stɛntsəl] *vt* **-ciled** *or* **-cilled; -ciling** *or* **-cilling** : dessiner au pochoir

stencil[2] *n* : pochoir *m*
stenographer [stəˈnɑgrəfər] *n* : sténographe *mf*
stenographic [ˌstɛnəˈgræfɪk] *adj* : sténographique
stenography [stəˈnɑgrəfi] *n* : sténographie *f*
step[1] [ˈstɛp] *vi* **stepped; stepping 1** : aller, marcher <step this way, please : par ici, s'il vous plaît> <he stepped outside : il est sorti> **2 to step on** : marcher sur
step[2] *n* **1** : pas *m* <step by step : pas à pas> <with a quick step : d'un pas rapide> **2** STAIR : marche *f* **3** RUNG : échelon *m*, barreau *m* **4** MEASURE : mesure *f*, disposition *f* <to take steps : prendre des mesures> **5** MOVE : pas *m* <a step in the right direction : un pas dans la bonne voie>
stepbrother [ˈstɛpˌbrʌðər] *n* : beau-frère *m*
stepdaughter [ˈstɛpˌdɔt̬ər] *n* : belle-fille *f*
stepfather [ˈstɛpˌfɑðər, -ˌfa-] *n* : beau-père *m*
stepladder [ˈstɛpˌlædər] *n* : escabeau *m*
stepmother [ˈstɛpˌmʌðər] *n* : belle-mère *f*
steppe [ˈstɛp] *n* : steppe *f*
stepson [ˈstɛpˌsʌn] *n* : beau-fils *m*
step up *vt* INCREASE : intensifier
stereo[1] [ˈstɛriˌoː, ˈstɪr-] *adj* : stéréo
stereo[2] *n, pl* **stereos 1** : stéréo *f* <in stereo : en stéréo> **2** *or* **stereo system** : chaîne *f* stéréo
stereophonic [ˌstɛrioˈfɑnɪk, ˌstɪr-] *adj* : stéréophonique
stereotype[1] [ˈstɛrioˌtaɪp, ˈstɪr-] *vt* **-typed; -typing** : stéréotyper
stereotype[2] *n* : stéréotype *m*
sterile [ˈstɛrəl] *adj* : stérile
sterility [stəˈrɪlət̬i] *n* : stérilité *f*
sterilization [ˌstɛrələˈzeɪʃən] *n* : stérilisation *f*
sterilize [ˈstɛrəˌlaɪz] *vt* **-ized; -izing** : stériliser
sterling [ˈstərlɪŋ] *adj* **1** : fin (se dit de l'argent) **2** EXCELLENT : excellent, de premier ordre
stern[1] [ˈstərn] *adj* : sévère — **sternly** *adv*
stern[2] *n* : arrière *m*, poupe *f*
sternness [ˈstərnnəs] *n* : sévérité *f*
sternum [ˈstərnəm] *n, pl* **sternums** *or* **sterna** [-nə] : sternum *m*
stethoscope [ˈstɛθəˌskoːp] *n* : stéthoscope *m*
stevedore [ˈstiːvəˌdor] *n* : docker *m*
stew[1] [ˈstuː, ˈstjuː] *vt* : cuire, faire cuire (en ragoût) — *vi* **1** : cuire (se dit des fruits), cuire en ragoût, mijoter (se dit de la viande) **2** FRET : être dans tous ses états
stew[2] *n* **1** : ragoût *m* **2 to be in a stew** : être dans tous ses états
steward [ˈstuːərd, ˈstjuː-] *n* **1** MANAGER : régisseur *m* (d'un domaine) **2** : steward *m* (d'un avion, etc.)
stewardess [ˈstuːərdəs, ˈstjuː-] *n* : hôtesse *f*
stick[1] [ˈstɪk] *v* **stuck** [ˈstʌk]; **sticking** *vt* **1** STAB : piquer, enfoncer **2** AFFIX : coller **3** PUT : mettre, insérer <to stick one's head out the window : passer la tête par la fenêtre> **4 to stick out** : sortir, tirer (la langue) **5 to stick up** ROB : dévaliser — *vi* **1** ADHERE : coller **2** : se planter, s'enfoncer <the nail stuck in my hand : je me suis planté le clou dans la main> **3** JAM : se coincer, se bloquer **4 to stick around** : attendre **5 to stick out** PROTRUDE : faire saillie, dépasser (d'une superficie), ressortir (d'un contexte) **6 to stick to** : ne pas abandonner <to stick to one's guns : ne pas en démordre> **7 to stick up** : se dresser (se dit des cheveux, etc.), dépasser, sortir **8 to stick with** : rester avec
stick[2] *n* **1** BRANCH : bâton *m* **2** : crosse *f* (aux sports) **3** → **walking stick**
sticker [ˈstɪkər] *n* : autocollant *m*, collant *m Can*
stickler [ˈstɪklər] *n* : personne *f* exigeante <to be a stickler for : être à cheval sur>
sticky [ˈstɪki] *adj* **stickier; -est 1** : collant **2** MUGGY : humide **3** DIFFICULT : difficile
stiff [ˈstɪf] *adj* **1** RIGID : rigide, raide <a stiff dough : une pâte ferme> **2** : ankylosé, courbaturé <stiff muscles : des muscles courbaturés> **3** FORMAL : guindé **4** STRONG : fort (se dit du vent, etc.) **5** DIFFICULT, SEVERE : sévère, difficile
stiffen [ˈstɪfən] *vt* **1** STRENGTHEN : renforcer **2** THICKEN : donner de la consistance à (des œufs, une sauce) **3** : courbaturer (les muscles) — *vi* **1** HARDEN : se durcir, se raidir **2** THICKEN : devenir ferme, épaisser **3** : s'ankyloser (se dit des articulations, etc.)
stiffly [ˈstɪfli] *adv* **1** RIGIDLY : avec raideur, rigidement **2** COLDLY : avec froideur
stiffness [ˈstɪfnəs] *n* **1** RIGIDITY : raideur *f*, rigidité *f* **2** COLDNESS : froideur *f* **3** SEVERITY : sévérité *f*
stifle [ˈstaɪfəl] *vt* **-fled; -fling** SMOTHER, SUPPRESS : étouffer, réprimer, retenir <to stifle a yawn : retenir un bâillement>
stigma [ˈstɪgmə] *n, pl* **stigmata** [stɪgˈmɑt̬ə, ˈstɪgmət̬ə] *or* **stigmas** : stigmate *m*
stigmatize [ˈstɪgməˌtaɪz] *vt* **-tized; -tizing** : stigmatiser
stile [ˈstaɪl] *n* : échalier *m*
stiletto [stəˈlɛˌtoː] *n, pl* **-tos** *or* **-toes 1** : stylet *m* **2** *or* **stiletto heel** : talon *m* aiguille

still[1] ['stɪl] *vt* CALM : calmer — *vi* : se calmer

still[2] *adv* **1** MOTIONLESSLY : sans bouger <sit still! : reste tranquille!> **2** : encore, toujours <she still lives there : elle y habite toujours> <it's still the same : c'est toujours pareille> **3** : quand même, tout de même <he still has doubts : il a quand même des doutes> <I still prefer that you stay : je préfère tout de même que tu restes>

still[3] *adj* **1** MOTIONLESS : immobile **2** CALM : tranquille **3** SILENT : silencieux

still[4] *n* **1** SILENCE : silence *m* **2** : alambic *m* (pour distiller l'alcool)

stillborn ['stɪl,bɔrn] *adj* : mort-né

stillness ['stɪlnəs] *n* : calme *m*, tranquillité *f*

stilt ['stɪlt] *n* : échasse *f*

stilted ['stɪltəd] *adj* : guindé

stimulant ['stɪmjələnt] *n* : stimulant *m*

stimulate ['stɪmjə,leɪt] *vt* **-lated; -lating** : stimuler

stimulation [,stɪmjə'leɪʃən] *n* **1** STIMULATING : stimulation *f* **2** STIMULUS : stimulant *m*

stimulus ['stɪmjələs] *n, pl* **-li** [-,laɪ] **1** : stimulus *m* (en physiologie) **2** INCENTIVE : stimulant *m*

sting[1] ['stɪŋ] *v* **stung** ['stʌŋ]; **stinging** *vt* **1** : piquer <a bee stung him : une abeille l'a piqué> **2** HURT : blesser, piquer au vif

sting[2] *n* : piqûre *f*

stinger ['stɪŋər] *n* : dard *m*, aiguillon *m*

stinginess ['stɪndʒinəs] *n* : avarice *f*, pingrerie *f*

stingy ['stɪndʒi] *adj* **stingier; -est** : avare, pingre

stink[1] ['stɪŋk] *vi* **stank** ['stæŋk] *or* **stunk** ['stʌŋk]; **stunk; stinking** : puer

stink[2] *n* : puanteur *f*

stint[1] ['stɪnt] *vt* DEPRIVE : priver — *vi* **to stint on** : lésiner sur

stint[2] *n* : période *f* (de travail)

stipend ['staɪ,pɛnd, -pənd] *n* : traitement *m*

stipulate ['stɪpjə,leɪt] *vt* **-lated; -lating** : stipuler

stipulation [,stɪpjə'leɪʃən] *n* : stipulation *f*

stir[1] ['stər] *v* **stirred; stirring** *vt* **1** AGITATE : agiter **2** MIX : remuer **3** INCITE : inciter **4** MOVE : émouvoir (une personne), exciter (la curiosité, etc.) **5** *or* **to stir up** PROVOKE : susciter (un sentiment, etc.), provoquer (la colère, etc.) — *vi* : bouger

stir[2] *n* **1** MOTION : mouvement *m* **2** COMMOTION : agitation *f*

stirrup ['stərəp, 'stɪr-] *n* : étrier *m*

stitch[1] ['stɪtʃ] *vt* : coudre, suturer (en médecine) — *vi* : coudre

stitch[2] *n* **1** : point *m* **2** TWINGE : point *m* (au côté)

stock[1] ['stak] *vt* **1** SUPPLY : approvisionner **2** SELL : avoir pour vendre — *vi* **to stock up** : s'approvisionner

stock[2] *n* **1** SUPPLY : réserve *f*, stock *m* <to be out of stock : être épuisé> **2** LIVESTOCK : bétail *m* **3** ANCESTRY : lignée *f*, souche *f* **4** BROTH : bouillon *m* **5** STANDING : cote *f* **6 stocks** *npl* SECURITIES : actions *fpl*, valeurs *fpl* **7 to take stock** : évaluer, faire le point

stockade [sta'keɪd] *n* : palissade *f*

stockbroker ['stak,bro:kər] *n* : agent *m* de change

stockholder ['stak,ho:ldər] *n* : actionnaire *mf*

stocking ['stakɪŋ] *n* : bas *m* <a pair of stockings : une paire de bas>

stock market *n* : Bourse *f*

stockpile[1] ['stak,paɪl] *vt* **-piled; -piling** : stocker, amasser

stockpile[2] *n* : stock *m*, réserve *f*

stocky ['staki] *adj* **stockier; -est** : trapu

stockyard ['stak,jard] *n* : parc *m* à bétail

stodgy ['stadʒi] *adj* **stodgier; -est 1** DULL : ennuyeux, lourd **2** HIDEBOUND : borné, rigide

stoic[1] ['sto:ɪk] *or* **stoical** [-ɪkəl] *adj* : stoïque — **stoically** [-ɪkli] *adv*

stoic[2] *n* : stoïque *mf*

stoicism ['sto:ə,sɪzəm] *n* : stoïcisme *m*

stoke ['sto:k] *vt* **stoked; stoking** : alimenter, entretenir

stole[1] → **steal**

stole[2] ['sto:l] *n* : étole *f*

stolen → **steal**

stolid ['stalɪd] *adj* : impassible — **stolidly** *adv*

stomach[1] ['stʌmɪk] *vt* : supporter, tolérer

stomach[2] *n* **1** : estomac *m* **2** BELLY : ventre *m* <to have a fat stomach : avoir du ventre> **3** DESIRE : envie *f* <to have no stomach for : n'avoir aucune envie de>

stomachache ['stʌmɪk,eɪk] *n* : mal *m* de ventre

stomp ['stamp, 'stɔmp] *vt* : piétiner — *vi* : marcher d'un pas lourd

stone[1] ['sto:n] *vt* **stoned; stoning** : jeter des pierres sur

stone[2] *n* **1** : pierre *f* **2** PIT : noyau *m* (d'un fruit)

Stone Age *n* : âge *m* de pierre

stony ['sto:ni] *adj* **stonier; -est 1** ROCKY : pierreux **2** UNFEELING : insensible, glacial <a stony stare : un regard glacial>

stood → **stand**[1]

stool ['stu:l] *n* **1** SEAT : tabouret *m*, escabeau *m* **2** FOOTSTOOL : tabouret *m* **3** FECES : selle *f*

stoop[1] ['stu:p] *vi* **1** CROUCH : se baisser, se pencher **2 to stoop to** : s'abaisser à

stoop[2] *n* **1** : dos *m* voûté <to have a stoop : avoir le dos voûté> **2** PORCH, VERANDA : porche *m*, véranda *f*

stop[1] ['stɑp] *v* **stopped; stopping** *vt* **1** *or* **to stop up** PLUG : boucher **2** PREVENT : empêcher <she stopped me from leaving : elle m'a empêché de partir> **3** HALT : arrêter, stopper **4** CEASE : arrêter, cesser <he stopped talking : il a cessé de parler> — *vi* **1** HALT : s'arrêter, stopper **2** CEASE : cesser, s'arrêter <the rain won't stop : la pluie n'arrête pas> **3** STAY : rester **4** **to stop by** : passer <stop by at my house : passe chez moi>

stop[2] *n* **1** STOPPER : bouchon *m* **2** HALT : arrêt *m*, halte *f* <to come to a stop : s'arrêter> <to put a stop to : mettre fin à> **3** : arrêt *m* <bus stop : arrêt de bus>

stopgap ['stɑp,gæp] *n* : bouche-trou *m*

stoplight ['stɑp,laɪt] *n* : feu *m* rouge

stoppage ['stɑpɪdʒ] *n* : arrêt *m*, suspension *f* <work stoppage : arrêt de travail>

stopper ['stɑpər] *n* : bouchon *m*

storage ['storɪdʒ] *n* : emmagasinage *m*, entreposage *m*

storage battery *n* : accumulateur *m*

store[1] ['stor] *vt* **stored; storing** : emmagasiner, entreposer

store[2] *n* **1** RESERVE, SUPPLY : réserve *f*, provision *f* **2** SHOP : magasin *m* **3** **to have in store** : avoir en réserve

storehouse ['stor,haʊs] *n* : entrepôt *m*

storekeeper ['stor,ki:pər] *n* : commerçant *m*, -çante *f*

storeroom ['stor,ru:m, -,rʊm] *n* : magasin *m*, réserve *f*

stork ['stɔrk] *n* : cigogne *f*

storm[1] ['stɔrm] *vi* **1** : faire rage (se dit d'une tempête) **2** RAGE : tempêter, fulminer <to storm out : sortir comme un ouragan, partir furieux> — *vt* ATTACK : prendre d'assaut

storm[2] *n* **1** : orage *m*, tempête *f* **2** UPROAR : tempête *f* <a storm of abuse : une tempête d'injures>

stormy ['stɔrmi] *adj* **stormier; -est** : orageux

story ['stori] *n, pl* **stories 1** NARRATIVE : histoire *f* **2** ACCOUNT : article *m* (en journalisme) **3** PLOT : intrigue *f*, scénario *m* **4** FLOOR : étage *m*

stout ['staʊt] *adj* **1** FIRM, RESOLUTE : ferme, résolu **2** STURDY : solide **3** FAT : corpulent, gros

stove[1] ['sto:v] *n* : poêle *m* (pour chauffer), cuisinière *f* (pour cuisiner)

stove[2] → **stave**[1]

stow ['sto:] *vt* **1** STORE : ranger, emmagasiner, arrimer (la cargaison) **2** LOAD : remplir — *vi* **to stow away** : s'embarquer clandestinement

straddle ['strædəl] *vt* **-dled; -dling 1** : enfourcher (un cheval, une bicyclette) **2** SPAN : enjamber

straggle ['strægəl] *vi* **-gled; -gling** : traîner

straggler ['strægələr] *n* : traînard *m*, -narde *f*

straight[1] ['streɪt] *adv* **1** : droit <go straight, then turn right : allez tout droit, puis tournez à droite> **2** HONESTLY : honnêtement <to go straight : vivre honnêtement> **3** CLEARLY : clairement **4** DIRECTLY : directement **5** FRANKLY : franchement

straight[2] *adj* **1** : droit, d'aplomb (se dit d'un objet vertical), raide (se dit des cheveux), sec (se dit d'une boisson alcoolisée) **2** HONEST, JUST : honnête, juste **3** NEAT, ORDERLY : en ordre **4** DIRECT : direct

straightaway [,streɪtə'weɪ] *adv* : immédiatement

straighten ['streɪtən] *vt* **1** : redresser, rendre droit **2** *or* **to straighten up** ORGANIZE : mettre en ordre, ranger

straightforward [streɪt'fɔrwərd] *adj* **1** FRANK : franc, honnête **2** CLEAR, PRECISE : clair, simple

strain[1] ['streɪn] *vt* **1** EXERT, STRETCH : tendre, forcer <to strain oneself : faire un grand effort> **2** FILTER : filtrer **3** INJURE : froisser, fatiguer <to strain a muscle : se froisser un muscle>

strain[2] *n* **1** LINEAGE : lignée *f* **2** EFFORT : effort *m* **3** VARIETY : variété *f* **4** STRESS : stress *m*, tension *f* **5** SPRAIN : foulure *f* **6** **strains** *npl* TUNE : air *m*, accents *mpl*

strainer ['streɪnər] *n* : passoire *f*

strait ['streɪt] *n* **1** : détroit *m* **2** **straits** *npl* DISTRESS : gêne *f* <in dire straits : aux abois>

straitened ['streɪtənd] *adj* **in straitened circumstances** : dans le besoin

strand[1] ['strænd] *vt* **1** : échouer **2** **to be left stranded** : être abandonné

strand[2] *n* **1** : toron *m*, brin *m* <a strand of hair : un cheveu> **2** BEACH : plage *f*

strange ['streɪndʒ] *adj* **stranger; -est 1** QUEER, UNUSUAL : étrange, bizarre **2** UNFAMILIAR : inconnu

strangely ['streɪndʒli] *adv* : étrangement, bizarrement <to behave strangely : se comporter de façon étrange> <strangely, he didn't call : curieusement, il n'a pas téléphoné>

strangeness ['streɪndʒnəs] *n* : étrangeté *f*

stranger ['streɪndʒər] *n* : étranger *m*, -gère *f*

strangle ['stræŋgəl] *vt* **-gled; -gling** : étrangler

strangler ['stræŋglər] *n* : étrangleur *m*, -gleuse *f*

strap[1] ['stræp] *vt* **strapped; strapping 1** FASTEN : attacher **2** FLOG : fouetter

strap[2] *n* **1** : courroie *f*, sangle *f* **2** **shoulder strap** : bretelle *f*

strapless ['stræpləs] *n* : sans bretelles
strapping ['stræpɪŋ] *adj* : robuste, costaud *fam*
stratagem ['strætədʒəm, -ˌdʒɛm] *n* : stratagème *m*
strategic [strə'ti:dʒɪk] *adj* : stratégique
strategy ['strætədʒi] *n, pl* **-gies** : stratégie *f*
stratified ['strætəˌfaɪd] *adj* : stratifié
stratosphere ['strætəˌsfɪr] *n* : stratosphère *f*
stratum ['streɪtəm, 'stræ-] *n, pl* **strata** [-tə] : strate *f,* couche *f*
straw ['strɔ] *n* : paille *f*
strawberry ['strɔˌbɛri] *n, pl* **-ries** : fraise *f*
stray[1] ['streɪ] *vi* **1** WANDER : errer, s'égarer <the cattle strayed away : les bœufs se sont égarés> **2** : errer, vagabonder (se dit des pensées, des yeux, etc.) <to stray from the point : s'éloigner du sujet>
stray[2] *adj* : errant, perdu
stray[3] *n* : animal *m* errant
streak[1] ['stri:k] *vt* : rayer <blue streaked with grey : bleu rayé de gris> — *vi* DASH, RUSH : s'élancer
streak[2] *n* **1** LINE : raie *f,* bande *f,* mèche *f* (dans les cheveux) **2** TENDENCY : tendance *f,* côté *m* <a stubborn streak : un côté obstiné> **3** TRACE : trace *f* **4** PERIOD : période *f,* passe *f* <a streak of luck : une bonne passe>
stream[1] ['stri:m] *vi* : couler, ruisseler <tears streamed from his eyes : des larmes ruisselaient de ses yeux> — *vt* : ruisseler de <to stream blood : ruisseler de sang>
stream[2] *n* **1** BROOK : ruisseau *m* **2** FLOW : courant *m,* flot *m*
streamer ['stri:mər] *n* **1** BANNER : banderole *f* **2** RIBBON : serpentin *m* (de papier)
streamlined ['stri:mˌlaɪnd] *adj* **1** : aérodynamique **2** EFFICIENT : rationalisé, dégraissé
street ['stri:t] *n* : rue *f*
streetcar ['stri:tˌkɑr] *n* : tramway *m*
strength ['strɛŋkθ] *n* **1** POWER : force *f,* puissance *f* **2** SOLIDITY : solidité *f* **3** INTENSITY : intensité *f,* force *f* **4** NUMBERS : effectif *m* <we're at full strength : nos effectifs sont au complet> **5** : qualité *f* <strengths and weaknesses : qualités et faiblesses>
strengthen ['strɛŋkθən] *vt* **1** : fortifier (les muscles, etc.), raffermir **2** REINFORCE : renforcer **3** INTENSIFY : intensifier
strenuous ['strɛnjʊəs] *adj* **1** VIGOROUS : vigoureux, énergique **2** ARDUOUS : ardu, fatiguant
strenuously ['strɛnjʊəsli] *adv* : vigoureusement
stress[1] ['strɛs] *vt* **1** : charger, mettre sous tension **2** EMPHASIZE : mettre l'accent sur, souligner, accentuer (en prononciation) **3 to stress out** : stresser
stress[2] *n* **1** PRESSURE : contrainte *f,* effort *m* **2** EMPHASIS : accent *m,* insistance *f* **3** TENSION : tension *f,* stress *m*
stressful ['strɛsfəl] *adj* : stressant
stretch[1] ['strɛtʃ] *vt* **1** EXTEND : tendre, allonger **2** : distendre, étirer (les muscles) **3** PROLONG : prolonger, faire durer **4 to stretch the truth** : exagérer — *vi* : s'étirer
stretch[2] *n* **1** STRETCHING : extension *f,* étirement *m* (des muscles) **2** ELASTICITY : élasticité *f* **3** EXPANSE : étendue *f* <the home stretch : la ligne d'arrivée> **4** PERIOD : période *f* (de temps)
stretcher ['strɛtʃər] *n* : civière *f,* brancard *m*
strew ['stru:] *vt* **strewed; strewed** *or* **strewn** ['stru:n]; **strewing 1** SCATTER : répandre **2 to be strewn with** : être jonché de
stricken ['strɪkən] *adj* **stricken with** : affligé de (une émotion), atteint de (une maladie)
strict ['strɪkt] *adj* : strict — **strictly** *adv*
strictness ['strɪktli] *n* **1** SEVERITY : sévérité *f* **2** RIGOR : rigueur *f*
stricture ['strɪktʃər] *n* **1** NARROWING : rétrécissement *m* (en médecine) **2** CENSURE : critique *f* (sévère) **3** RESTRICTION : contrainte *f*
stride[1] ['straɪd] *vi* **strode** ['stro:d]; **stridden** ['strɪdən]; **striding** : marcher à grands pas, marcher à grandes enjambées
stride[2] *n* **1** : grand pas *m,* enjambée *f* **2 to make great strides** : faire de grands progrès
strident ['straɪdənt] *adj* : strident
strife ['straɪf] *n* : conflit *m,* lutte *f*
strike[1] ['straɪk] *v* **struck** ['strʌk]; **struck; striking** *vt* **1** HIT : frapper **2** DELETE : rayer **3** COIN, MINT : frapper **4** : sonner (l'heure) **5** AFFLICT : frapper <he was stricken with a fever : il a eu une poussée de fièvre> **6** IMPRESS : impressionner <her voice struck me : sa voix m'a impressionné> <it struck him as funny : ça lui a paru drôle> **7** : frotter (une allumette) **8** FIND : trouver, découvrir (de l'or, du pétrole) **9** ADOPT : adopter, prendre (une pose, une attitude) — *vi* **1** HIT : frapper **2** ATTACK : attaquer **3** *or* **to go on strike** : faire grève
strike[2] *n* **1** BLOW : coup *m* **2** : grève *f* <to be on strike : faire grève> **3** ATTACK : attaque *f* **4** : prise *f* *Can* (au baseball)
strikebreaker ['straɪkˌbreɪkər] *n* : briseur *m,* -seuse *f* de grève, jaune *mf*
strike out *vi* **1** GO : aller, partir **2** : retirer *Can* (au baseball)
striker ['straɪkər] *n* : gréviste *mf;* piqueteur *m,* -teuse *f*

strike up *vt* START : commencer
striking ['straɪkɪŋ] *adj* : frappant, saisissant <a striking beauty : une beauté frappante>
strikingly ['straɪkɪŋli] *adv* : de manière frappante, remarquablement
string[1] ['strɪŋ] *vt* **strung** ['strʌŋ]; **stringing 1** : mettre des cordes à, monter (une guitare, etc.) **2** : enfiler (des perles) **3** HANG : suspendre
string[2] *n* **1** CORD : ficelle *f*, cordon *m* **2** SERIES : suite *f* **3 strings** *npl* : cordes *fpl* (d'un orchestre)
string bean *n* : haricot *m* vert
stringent ['strɪndʒənt] *adj* : rigoureux, strict
stringy ['strɪŋi] *adj* **stringier; -est** : fibreux, filandreux (se dit des viandes, des légumes, etc.)
strip[1] ['strɪp] *v* **stripped; stripping** *vt* **1** REMOVE : enlever **2** UNDRESS : déshabiller — *vi* : se déshabiller
strip[2] *n* : bande *f* <a strip of land : une bande de terre>
stripe[1] ['straɪp] *vt* **striped** ['straɪpt]; **striping** : marquer avec rayures
stripe[2] *n* **1** : rayure *f*, bande *f* **2** CHEVRON : chevron *m*, galon *m*
striped ['straɪpt, 'straɪpəd] *adj* : rayé, à rayures
strive ['straɪv] *vi* **strove** ['stro:v]; **striven** ['strɪvən] *or* **strived; striving 1 to strive for** : lutter pour **2 to strive to** : s'efforcer de
strode → **stride**[1]
stroke[1] ['stro:k] *vt* **stroked; stroking** : caresser
stroke[2] *n* **1** MOVEMENT : coup *m* <stroke of luck : coup de chance> **2** *or* **brush stroke** : trait *m* (de pinceau) **3** : attaque *f* (en médecine)
stroll[1] ['stro:l] *vi* : se promener
stroll[2] *n* : promenade *f*, petit tour *m*
stroller ['stro:lər] *n* : poussette *f* (pour enfants), carrosse *m Can*
strong ['strɔŋ] *adj* **1** : fort **2** HEALTHY : robuste, en forme **3** ZEALOUS : acharné, fervent
stronghold ['strɔŋˌho:ld] *n* : forteresse *f*, bastion *m* <a cultural stronghold : un bastion de la culture>
strongly ['strɔŋli] *adv* **1** POWERFULLY : fortement **2** STURDILY : solidement **3** INTENSELY : intensément **4** WHOLEHEARTEDLY : vivement, fermement
struck → **strike**[1]
structural ['strʌktʃərəl] *adj* : structural, de construction
structure[1] ['strʌktʃər] *vt* **-tured; -turing** : structurer
structure[2] *n* **1** BUILDING : construction *f* **2** ARRANGEMENT, FRAMEWORK : structure *f*
struggle[1] ['strʌgəl] *vi* **-gled; -gling 1** CONTEND : lutter, se débattre **2** : faire avec difficulté <she struggled forward : elle s'est avancée avec difficulté>
struggle[2] *n* : lutte *f*
strum ['strʌm] *v* **strummed; strumming** *vt* : gratter de — *vi* **to strum on** : gratter sur
strung → **string**[1]
strut[1] ['strʌt] *vi* **strutted; strutting** : se pavaner
strut[2] *n* **1** SWAGGER : démarche *f* arrogante **2** SUPPORT : étai *m*, support *m*
strychnine ['strɪkˌnaɪn, -nən, -ˌni:n] *n* : strychnine *f*
stub[1] ['stʌb] *vt* **stubbed; stubbing 1 to stub one's toe** : se cogner le doigt de pied **2 to stub out** : écraser
stub[2] *n* : mégot *m* (de cigarette), bout *m* (de crayon, etc.), talon *m* (de chèque)
stubble ['stʌbəl] *n* **1** : chaume *m* (de plantes) **2** : barbe *f* de plusieurs jours
stubborn ['stʌbərn] *adj* **1** OBSTINATE : obstiné, têtu **2** PERSISTENT : tenace
stubbornly ['stʌbərnli] *adv* : obstinément, de façon têtue
stubbornness ['stʌbərnnəs] *n* : entêtement *m*
stubby ['stʌbi] **stubbier; -est** *adj* : gros et court, trapu (se dit d'une personne) <stubby fingers : doigts épais>
stucco ['stʌko:] *n, pl* **stuccos** *or* **stuccoes** : stuc *m*
stuck → **stick**[1]
stuck–up ['stʌk'ʌp] *adj* : bêcheur, prétentieux, snob
stud[1] ['stʌd] *vt* **studded; studding** : clouter
stud[2] *n* **1** *or* **stud horse** : étalon *m* **2** UPRIGHT : montant *m* **3** HOBNAIL : caboche *f* **4** *or* **collar stud** : bouton *m* de col
student ['stu:dənt, 'stju:-] *n* : étudiant *m*, -diante *f*
studied ['stʌdi:d] *adj* : étudié, calculé, recherché
studio ['stu:diˌo:, 'stju:-] *n, pl* **-dios** : studio *m*, atelier *m* (d'un artist, etc.)
studious ['stu:diəs, 'stju:-] *adj* **1** : studieux **2** DELIBERATE : étudié, délibéré
studiously ['stu:diəsli, 'stju:-] *adv* : délibérément
study[1] ['stʌdi] *v* **studied; studying** *vt* **1** : étudier, faire des études de **2** EXAMINE : examiner — *vi* : étudier, faire ses études
study[2] *n, pl* **studies 1** : étude *f* **2** OFFICE : bureau *m*, cabinet *m* de travail
stuff[1] ['stʌf] *vt* **1** FILL : rembourrer (un meuble, etc.), empailler (en taxidermie), farcir (en cuisine) **2** SHOVE : fourrer <I stuffed it in my pocket : je l'ai fourré dans ma poche>
stuff[2] *n* **1** POSSESSIONS : affaires *fpl*, choses *fpl* **2** ESSENCE : essence *f*, étoffe *f* **3** SUBSTANCE : substance *f*, matière *f* <some sticky stuff : une

substance collante> <she knows her stuff : elle s'y connaît>

stuffing ['stʌfɪŋ] *n* **1** FILLING, PADDING : rembourrage *m,* bourrure *f Can* **2** : farce *f* (en cuisine)

stuffy ['stʌfi] *adj* **stuffier; -est 1** CLOSE : mal aéré **2** BLOCKED : bouché (se dit du nez) **3** STODGY : ennuyeux

stumble[1] ['stʌmbəl] *vi* **-bled; -bling 1** TRIP : trébucher **2 to stumble across** *or* **to stumble upon** : tomber sur

stumble[2] *n* : trébuchement *m*

stump[1] ['stʌmp] *vt* BAFFLE : déconcerter, laisser perplexe

stump[2] *n* **1** : bout *m,* moignon *m* (d'un membre) **2** *or* **tree stump** : souche *f*

stun ['stʌn] *vt* **stunned; stunning 1** : assommer (avec un coup) **2** ASTONISH : étonner, stupéfier

stung → **sting[1]**

stunk → **stink[1]**

stunning ['stʌnɪŋ] *adj* **1** ASTONISHING : épatant **2** STRIKING : ravissant, sensationnel

stunt[1] ['stʌnt] *vt* : retarder <to stunt s.o.'s growth : retarder la croissance de qqn>

stunt[2] *n* **1** : cascade *f,* acrobatie *f* **2** *or* **publicity stunt** : coup *m* de publicité

stupefy ['stu:pə,faɪ, 'stju:-] *vt* **-fied; -fying 1** : abrutir (avec des drogues, etc.) **2** AMAZE : stupéfier, abasourdir

stupendous [stʊ'pɛndəs, stjʊ-] *adj* : prodigieux, extraordinaire — **stupendously** *adv*

stupid ['stu:pəd, 'stju:-] *adj* **1** IDIOTIC, SILLY : idiot, bête **2** DULL, OBTUSE : stupide, bête, nounoune *Can*

stupidity [stʊ'pɪdəṭi, stjʊ-] *n, pl* **-ties** : stupidité *f,* bêtise *f*

stupidly ['stu:pədli, 'stju:-] *adv* : stupidement

stupor ['stu:pər, 'stju:-] *n* : stupeur *f*

sturdily ['stərdəli] *adv* : solidement

sturdiness ['stərdinəs] *n* : solidité *f,* robustesse *f*

sturdy ['stərdi] *adj* **sturdier; -est** : solide, robuste

sturgeon ['stərdʒən] *n* : esturgeon *m*

stutter[1] ['stʌṭər] *v* : bégayer

stutter[2] *n* : bégaiement *m*

sty ['staɪ] *n* **1** *pl* **sties** PIGPEN : porcherie *f,* soue *f Can* **2** *pl* **sties** *or* **styes** : orgelet *m* (dans l'œil)

style[1] ['staɪl] *vt* **styled; styling 1** NAME : appeler, dénommer **2** DESIGN : dessiner, concevoir, créer <carefully styled prose : prose conçue avec soin> **3** : coiffer (les cheveux)

style[2] *n* **1** : style *m,* manière *f* <that's just his style : c'est bien son genre> **2** FASHION : mode *f* **3** ELEGANCE : élégance *f,* style *m* <to live in style : mener grand train, vivre dans le luxe>

stylish ['staɪlɪʃ] *adj* : chic, élégant

stylishly ['staɪlɪʃli] *adv* : avec chic, élégamment

stylishness ['staɪlɪʃnəs] *n* : chic *m,* élégance *f*

stylize ['staɪə,laɪz] *vt* **-lized; -lizing** : styliser

stylus ['staɪləs] *n, pl* **styli** ['staɪ,laɪ] **1** PEN : style *m* **2** NEEDLE : saphir *m* (d'un tourne-disque)

stymie ['staɪmi] *vt* **-mied; -mieing** : coincer

suave ['swɑv] *adj* : suave

sub[1] ['sʌb] *vi* **subbed; subbing** → **substitute[1]**

sub[2] *n* **1** → **substitute[2]** **2** → **submarine[2]**

subcommittee ['sʌbkə,mɪṭi] *n* : sous-comité *m*

subconscious[1] [,sʌb'kɑntʃəs] *adj* : subconscient

subconscious[2] *n* : subconscient *m*

subconsciously [,sʌb'kɑntʃəsli] *adv* : inconsciemment, de façon subconsciente

subcontract [,sʌb'kɑn,trækt] *vt* : sous-traiter

subdivide [,sʌbdə'vaɪd, 'sʌbdə,-] *vt* **-vided; -viding** : subdiviser

subdivision ['sʌbdə,vɪʒən] *n* : subdivision *f*

subdue [səb'du:, -'dju:] *vt* **-dued; -duing 1** OVERCOME : subjuguer, soumettre **2** CONTROL : maîtriser, réprimer **3** SOFTEN : adoucir, atténuer

subhead ['sʌb,hɛd] *or* **subheading** [-,hɛdɪŋ] *n* : sous-titre *m*

subject[1] [səb'dʒɛkt] *vt* **1** CONTROL, DOMINATE : soumettre, assujettir **2 to subject to** : exposer à, soumettre à

subject[2] ['sʌbdʒɪkt] *adj* **1** : sujet, soumis **2** PRONE : sujet <subject to colds : sujet aux rhumes> **3 subject to** : à condition de, sous réserve de <subject to change : sous réserve de modification>

subject[3] *n* **1** : sujet *m,* -jette *f* **2** TOPIC : sujet *m* **3** : sujet *m* (en grammaire)

subjection [səb'dʒɛkʃən] *n* : sujétion *f,* soumission *f*

subjective [səb'dʒɛktɪv] *adj* : subjectif — **subjectively** *adv*

subjectivity [,sʌb,dʒɛk'tɪvəṭi] *n* : subjectivité *f*

subjugate ['sʌbdʒɪ,geɪt] *vt* **-gated; -gating** : subjuguer, soumettre

subjunctive[1] [səb'dʒʌŋktɪv] *adj* : subjonctif

subjunctive[2] *n* : subjonctif *m*

sublet ['sʌb,lɛt] *vt* **-let; -letting** : sous-louer

sublime [sə'blaɪm] *adj* : sublime

sublimely [sə'blaɪmli] *adv* **1** : de manière sublime **2** UTTERLY : suprêmement

submarine[1] ['sʌbmə,ri:n, ,sʌbmə'-] *adj* : sous-marin

submarine[2] *n* : sous-marin *m*

submerge [səb'mərdʒ] *v* **-merged; -merging** *vt* : submerger, immerger — *vi* : s'immerger

submission [səb'mɪʃən] *n* **1** OBEDIENCE : soumission *f* **2** PRESENTATION : présentation *f,* soumission *f*

submissive [səb'mɪsɪv] *adj* : soumis

submit [səb'mɪt] *v* **-mitted; -mitting** *vi* YIELD : se soumettre — *vt* PRESENT : présenter, soumettre

subnormal [ˌsʌb'nɔrməl] *adj* : au-dessous de la normale

subordinate[1] [sə'bɔrdənˌeɪt] *vt* **-nated; -nating** : subordonner

subordinate[2] [sə'bɔrdənət] *adj* : subalterne, inférieur

subordinate[3] *n* : subordonné *m,* -née *f*

subordination [səˌbɔrdən'eɪʃən] *n* : subordination *f*

subpoena[1] [sə'piːnə] *vt* **-naed; -naing** : citer

subpoena[2] *n* : assignation *f,* citation *f*

subscribe [səb'skraɪb] *vi* **-scribed; -scribing 1** : s'abonner (à un magazine) **2 to subscribe to** : souscrire à, être d'accord avec (un point de vue, etc.)

subscriber [səb'skraɪbər] *n* : abonné *m,* -née *f*

subscription [səb'skrɪpʃən] *n* : abonnement *m*

subsequent ['sʌbsɪkwənt, -səˌkwent] *adj* : subséquent, suivant

subsequently ['sʌbsɪˌkwentli, -ˌkwənt-] *adv* : par la suite, plus tard

subservient [səb'sərviənt] *adj* : servile

subside [səb'saɪd] *vi* **-sided; -siding 1** SINK : s'affaisser **2** ABATE : s'apaiser, se calmer

subsidiary[1] [səb'sɪdiˌɛri] *adj* : subsidiaire

subsidiary[2] *n, pl* **-ries** *or* **subsidiary company** : filiale *f*

subsidize ['sʌbsəˌdaɪz] *vt* **-dized; -dizing** : subventionner

subsidy ['sʌbsədi] *n, pl* **-dies** : subvention *f*

subsist [səb'sɪst] *vi* : subsister

subsistence [səb'sɪstənts] *n* : subsistance *f*

substance ['sʌbstənts] *n* **1** ESSENCE : substance *f,* essentiel *m* **2** MATERIAL : substance *f* **3** WEALTH : richesses *fpl* <a man of substance : un homme riche>

substandard [ˌsʌb'stændərd] *adj* : inférieur

substantial [səb'stæntʃəl] *adj* **1** ABUNDANT : substantiel, copieux **2** CONSIDERABLE : considérable, appréciable

substantially [səb'stæntʃəli] *adv* : considérablement

substantiate [səb'stæntʃiˌeɪt] *vt* **-ated; -ating** : confirmer

substitute[1] ['sʌbstəˌtuːt, -ˌtjuːt] *v* **-tuted; -tuting** *vt* : substituer, remplacer — *vi* **to substitute for** : remplacer

substitute[2] *n* **1** ALTERNATE, STAND-IN : remplaçant *m,* -çante *f* **2** : produit *m* de remplacement, succédané *m* <sugar substitute : succédané de sucre>

substitute teacher *n* : suppléant *m,* -pléante *f*

substitution [ˌsʌbstə'tuːʃən, -'tjuː-] *n* : substitution *f*

subterfuge ['sʌbtərˌfjuːdʒ] *n* : subterfuge *m*

subterranean [ˌsʌbtə'reɪniən] *adj* : souterrain

subtitle ['sʌbˌtaɪtəl] *n* : sous-titre *m*

subtle ['sʌtəl] *adj* **-tler; -tlest** : subtil

subtlety ['sʌtəlti] *n, pl* **-ties** : subtilité *f*

subtly ['sʌtəli] *adv* : subtilement

subtotal ['sʌbˌtoːtəl] *n* : total *m* partiel

subtract [səb'trækt] *vt* : soustraire — *vi* : faire des soustractions

subtraction [səb'trækʃən] *n* : soustraction *f*

suburb ['sʌˌbərb] *n* : banlieue *f*

suburban [sə'bərbən] *adj* : de banlieue

subversion [səb'vərʒən] *n* : subversion *f*

subversive [səb'vərsɪv] *adj* : subversif

subway ['səbˌweɪ] *n* : métro *m*

succeed [sək'siːd] *vt* FOLLOW : succéder à — *vi* : réussir <she succeeded in finishing : elle a réussi à terminer>

success [sək'sɛs] *n* : réussite *f,* succès *m*

successful [sək'sɛsfəl] *adj* : réussi, courronné de succès

successfully [sək'sɛsfəli] *adv* : avec succès

succession [sək'sɛʃən] *n* : succession *f*

successive [sək'sɛsɪv] *adj* : successif — **successively** *adv*

successor [sək'sɛsər] *n* : successeur *m*

succinct [sək'sɪŋkt, sə'sɪŋkt] *adj* : succinct — **succinctly** *adv*

succor[1] *or Brit* **succour** ['sʌkər] *vt* : secourir, aider

succor[2] *or Brit* **succour** *n* : secours *m,* aide *f*

succotash ['sʌkəˌtæʃ] *n* : plat *m* de maïs et de fèves

succour *Brit* → **succor**

succulent[1] ['sʌkjələnt] *adj* : succulent

succulent[2] *n* : plante *f* grasse

succumb [sə'kʌm] *vi* : succomber

such[1] ['sʌtʃ] *adv* **1** SO : aussi <such tall buildings : des bâtiments aussi grands> **2** VERY : si, tellement <he's not in such good shape : il n'est pas en tellement bonne forme> **3** SUCH THAT : de telle manière que

such[2] *adj* : tel, pareil <there's no such thing : une telle chose n'existe pas> <in such a case : dans un cas pareil> <animals such as cows and sheep : des animaux tels que les moutons et les vaches>

such[3] *pron* **1** : tel <such is the result : tel est le résultat> <he's a child, and acts as such : c'est un enfant et il se comporte comme tel> **2** : choses *fpl* semblables <books, papers, and such

: des livres, des papiers, et autres choses de ce genre> **3 as such** : en soi, comme tel
suck[1] [ˈsʌk] *vt* **1** : sucer (par la bouche) **2** PULL : aspirer (avec une machine, etc.) **3 to get sucked into sth** : être entraîné dans qqch — *vi* : têter (se dit d'un enfant) <to suck at : sucer>
suck[2] *n* : action *f* de sucer
sucker [ˈsʌkər] *n* **1** : suçoir *m* (d'un insecte), drageon *m* (d'une plante) **2** → **lollipop 3** FOOL : poire *f fam,* gogo *m fam*
suckle [ˈsʌkəl] *v* **-led; -ling** *vt* : allaiter — *vi* : téter
suckling [ˈsʌklɪŋ] *n* : nourrisson *m*
sucrose [ˈsuːˌkroːs, -ˌkroːz] *n* : saccharose *f*
suction [ˈsʌkʃən] *n* : succion *f*
Sudanese[1] [ˌsuːdənˈiːz] *adj* : soudanais
Sudanese[2] *n* : Soudanais *m,* -naise *f*
sudden [ˈsʌdən] *adj* **1** : soudain, subit <all of a sudden : tout à coup> **2** UNEXPECTED : imprévu, inattendu **3** ABRUPT, HASTY : brusque
suddenly [ˈsʌdənli] *adv* **1** : soudainement, subitement, tout à coup **2** ABRUPTLY : brusquement
suddenness [ˈsʌdənnəs] *n* **1** : soudaineté *f* **2** ABRUPTNESS : brusquerie *f*
suds [ˈsʌdz] *npl* : mousse *f* (de savon)
sue [ˈsuː] *v* **sued; suing** *vt* : intenter un procès à, poursuivre en justice — *vi* **to sue for** : solliciter
suede [ˈsweɪd] *n* : daim *m,* suède *m*
suet [ˈsuːət] *n* : graisse *f* de rognon (de bœuf)
suffer [ˈsʌfər] *vi* : souffrir — *vt* **1** UNDERGO : souffrir, subir **2** PERMIT : permettre, souffrir **3** TOLERATE : tolérer, supporter
sufferer [ˈsʌfərər] *n* : victime *f,* malade *mf*
suffering [ˈsʌfərɪŋ] *n* : souffrance *f*
suffice [səˈfaɪs] *vi* **-ficed; -ficing** : être suffisant, suffir
sufficient [səˈfɪʃənt] *adj* : suffisant
sufficiently [səˈfɪʃəntli] *adv* : suffisamment
suffix [ˈsʌˌfɪks] *n* : suffixe *m*
suffocate [ˈsʌfəˌkeɪt] *v* **-cated; -cating** : suffoquer
suffocation [ˌsʌfəˈkeɪʃən] *n* : suffocation *f*
suffrage [ˈsʌfrɪdʒ] *n* : suffrage *m*
suffuse [səˈfjuːz] *vt* **-fused; -fusing** : se répandre sur, baigner
sugar[1] [ˈʃʊgər] *vt* : sucrer
sugar[2] *n* : sucre *m*
sugarcane [ˈʃʊgərˌkeɪn] *n* : canne *f* à sucre
sugarhouse [ˈʃʊgərˌhaʊs] *n* : cabane *f* (à sucre) *Can*
sugary [ˈʃʊgəri] *adj* : sucré
suggest [səgˈdʒɛst, sə-] *vt* **1** PROPOSE : proposer, suggérer **2** INDICATE : sembler indiquer, laisser supposer **3** EVOKE : évoquer, suggérer
suggestible [səgˈdʒɛstəbəl, sə-] *adj* : influençable, suggestible
suggestion [səgˈdʒɛstʃən, sə-] *n* **1** PROPOSAL : suggestion *f,* proposition *f* **2** INDICATION : indication *f* **3** HINT, TRACE : soupçon *m* **4 the power of suggestion** : la force de suggestion
suggestive [səgˈdʒɛstɪv, sə-] *adj* : suggestif
suggestively [səgˈdʒɛstɪvli, sə-] *adv* : de façon suggestive
suicidal [ˌsuːəˈsaɪdəl] *adj* : suicidaire
suicide [ˈsuːəˌsaɪd] *n* **1** : suicide *m* (acte) **2** : suicidé *m,* -dée *f* (personne)
suit[1] [ˈsuːt] *vt* **1** ADAPT : accommoder, adapter **2** BECOME, BEFIT : convenir à, aller à <the dress suits you : la robe te va bien> **3** PLEASE : convenir à, arranger <does Friday suit you? : est-ce que vendredi t'arrange?> <suit yourself! : faites comme vous voulez!>
suit[2] *n* **1** → **lawsuit 2** : costume *m,* complet *m* (d'homme), tailleur *m* (de femme) **3** : couleur *f* (aux cartes)
suitability [ˌsuːt̬əˈbɪlət̬i] *n* : caractère *m* convenable, pertinence *f,* aptitude *f* (d'une personne)
suitable [ˈsuːt̬əbəl] *adj* : convenable, approprié
suitably [ˈsuːt̬əbli] *adv* : convenablement
suitcase [ˈsuːtˌkeɪs] *n* : valise *f*
suite [ˈswiːt, *for 2 also* ˈsuːt] *n* **1** : suite *f* **2** : mobilier *m* <dining-room suite : mobilier de salle à manger>
suitor [ˈsuːt̬ər] *n* : prétendant *m*
sulfur *or Brit* **sulphur** [ˈsʌlfər] *n* : soufre *m*
sulfuric acid *or Brit* **sulphuric acid** [ˌsʌlˈfjʊrɪk] *adj* : acide *m* sulfurique
sulfurous *or Brit* **sulphurous** [ˌsʌlˈfjʊrəs, ˈsʌlfərəs, ˈsʌlfjə-] *adj* : sulfureux
sulk[1] [ˈsʌlk] *vi* : bouder
sulk[2] *n* : bouderie *f*
sulky [ˈsʌlki] *adj* **sulkier; -est** : boudeur
sullen [ˈsʌlən] *adj* **1** MOROSE : maussade, morose, renfrogné **2** GLOOMY : maussade, morne <sullen clouds : des nuages menaçants>
sullenly [ˈsʌlənli] *adv* : d'un air maussade, d'un air renfrogné
sully [ˈsʌli] *vt* **sullied; sullying** : souiller
sulphur *Brit* → **sulfur**
sultan [ˈsʌltən] *n* : sultan *m*
sultry [ˈsʌltri] *adj* **sultrier; -est 1** : étouffant <sultry weather : temps lourd> **2** SENSUAL : sensuel
sum[1] [ˈsʌm] *vt* **summed; summing 1** ADD : additionner **2** → **sum up**
sum[2] *n* **1** AMOUNT : somme *f* **2** TOTAL : total *m,* tout *m* **3** : calcul *m* (en mathématiques)
sumac [ˈʃuːˌmæk, ˈsuː-] *n* : sumac *m*
summarize [ˈsʌməˌraɪz] *v* **-rized; -rizing** *vt* : résumer — *vi* : se résumer

summary[1] ['sʌməri] *adj* : sommaire
summary[2] *n, pl* **-ries** : sommaire *m*
summer ['sʌmər] *n* : été *m*
summery ['sʌməri] *adj* : d'été
summit ['sʌmət] *n* **1** : sommet *m,* cime *f* **2** *or* **summit conference** : conférence *f* au sommet
summon ['sʌmən] *vt* **1** CALL : appeler, convoquer (une réunion, etc.) **2** : sommer de comparaître (en droit) **3 to summon up** : rassembler, faire appel à <to summon up one's strength : rassembler ses forces>
summons ['sʌmənz] *n, pl* **summonses 1** SUPOENA : assignation *f* **2** CALL : appel *m*
sumptuous ['sʌmptʃʊəs] *adj* : somptueux
sum up *vt* **1** SUMMARIZE : résumer **2** ASSESS : apprécier, jauger
sun[1] ['sʌn] *vt* **sunned; sunning 1** : exposer au soleil **2 to sun oneself** : prendre le soleil
sun[2] *n* **1** : soleil *m* **2** → **sunshine**
sunbeam ['sʌn,bi:m] *n* : rayon *m* de soleil
sunblock ['sʌn,blɑk] *n* : écran *m* total
sunburn[1] ['sʌn,bərn] *vi* **-burned** *or* **-burnt** [-,bərnt]; **-burning** : prendre un coup de soleil
sunburn[2] *n* : coup *m* de soleil
sundae ['sʌndi] *n* : sundae *m Can*
Sunday ['sʌn,deɪ, -di] *n* : dimanche *m*
sundial ['sʌn,daɪəl] *n* : cadran *m* solaire
sundown ['sʌn,daʊn] → **sunset**
sundries ['sʌndriz] *npl* : articles *mpl* divers
sundry ['sʌndri] *adj* : divers
sunflower ['sʌn,flaʊər] *n* : tournesol *m*
sung → **sing**
sunglasses ['sʌn,glæsəz] *npl* : lunettes *fpl* de soleil
sunk → **sink**[1]
sunken ['sʌŋkən] *adj* **1** HOLLOW : creux **2** SUBMERGED : submergé
sunlight ['sʌn,laɪt] *n* : soleil *m,* lumière *f* du soleil
sunny ['sʌni] *adj* **sunnier; -est 1** : ensoleillé **2** CHEERFUL : heureux
sunrise ['sʌn,raɪz] *n* : lever *m* du soleil
sunset ['sʌn,sɛt] *n* : coucher *m* du soleil
sunshine ['sʌn,ʃaɪn] *n* : lumière *f* du soleil
sunspot ['sʌn,spɑt] *n* : tache *f* solaire
sunstroke ['sʌn,stro:k] *n* : insolation *f*
suntan ['sʌn,tæn] *n* : hâle *m,* bronzage *m*
super ['su:pər] *adj* **1** GREAT, TERRIFIC : super *fam,* génial **2** SUPERIOR : supérieur
superabundance [,su:pərə'bʌndənts] *n* : surabondance *f*
superb [sʊ'pərb] *adj* : superbe — **superbly** *adv*
supercilious [,su:pər'sɪliəs] *adj* : hautain, dédaigneux
superficial [,su:pər'fɪʃəl] *adj* : superficiel — **superficially** *adv*
superfluous [sʊ'pərfluəs] *adj* : superflu
superhuman [,su:pər'hju:mən] *adj* : surhumain
superimpose [,su:pərɪm'po:z] *vt* **-posed; -posing** : superposer
superintend [,su:pərɪn'tɛnd] *vt* : surveiller
superintendent [,su:pərɪn'tɛndənt] *n* **1** : directeur *m,* -trice *f* **2** : concierge *mf* (d'un immeuble) **3** : inspecteur *m,* -trice *f* (d'école)
superior[1] [sʊ'pɪriər] *adj* : supérieur
superior[2] *n* : supérieur *m,* -rieure *f*
superiority [sʊ,pɪri'ɔrəṭi] *n, pl* **-ties** : supériorité *f*
superlative[1] [sʊ'pərlətɪv] *adj* **1** : superlatif (en grammaire) **2** SUPREME : suprême **3** EXCELLENT, OUTSTANDING : superbe, exceptionnel, sans pareil
superlative[2] *n* : superlatif *m*
supermarket ['su:pər,mɑrkət] *n* : supermarché *m*
supernatural [,su:pər'nætʃərəl] *adj* : surnaturel
supernaturally [,su:pər'nætʃərəli] *adv* : de manière surnaturelle
superpower ['su:pər,paʊər] *n* : superpuissance *f*
supersede [,su:pər'si:d] *vt* **-seded; -seding** : remplacer, supplanter
supersonic [,su:pər'sɑnɪk] *adj* : supersonique
superstition [,su:pər'stɪʃən] *n* : superstition *f*
superstitious [,su:pər'stɪʃəs] *adj* : superstitieux
superstructure ['su:pər,strʌktʃər] *n* : superstructure *f*
supervise ['su:pər,vaɪz] *vt* **-vised; -vising** : surveiller, superviser
supervision [,su:pər'vɪʒən] *n* : surveillance *f,* supervision *f*
supervisor ['su:pər,vaɪzər] *n* : surveillant *m,* -lante *f*
supervisory [,su:pər'vaɪzəri] *adj* : de surveillance
supine [sʊ'paɪn] *adj* **1** : couché sur le dos **2** INDOLENT, SLACK : indolent, mou
supper ['sʌpər] *n* : dîner *m,* souper *m Can*
supplant [sə'plænt] *vt* : supplanter
supple ['sʌpəl] *adj* **-pler; -plest** : souple
supplement[1] ['sʌplə,mɛnt] *vt* : compléter, augmenter
supplement[2] *n* : supplément *m*
supplementary [,sʌplə'mɛntəri] *adj* : supplémentaire
supplicate ['sʌplə,keɪt] *vt* **-cated; -cating** : supplier, implorer
supplier [sə'plaɪər] *n* : fournisseur *m,* -seuse *f*
supply[1] [sə'plaɪ] *vt* **-plied; -plying** : fournir, munir, approvisionner
supply[2] *n, pl* **-plies 1** PROVISION : fourniture *f,* approvisionnement *m* **2** STOCK : provision *f,* réserve *f* **3 sup-**

plies *npl* : provisions *fpl,* approvisionnements *mpl,* vivres *mpl*

support[1] [sə'port] *vt* **1** BACK : soutenir, apuyer **2** MAINTAIN : maintenir, entretenir **3** PROP UP : supporter, soutenir

support[2] *n* **1** BACKING : appui *m,* soutien *m* **2** PROP : support *m,* appui *m*

supporter [sə'portər] *n* **1** : partisan *m,* -sane *f* **2** FAN : supporter *m*

suppose [sə'po:z] *vt* **-posed; -posing 1** ASSUME : supposer **2** BELIEVE : croire **3 to be supposed to do sth** : être censé faire qqch

supposedly [sə'po:zədli] *adv* : censément

supposition [ˌsʌpə'zɪʃən] *n* : supposition *f*

suppository [sə'pɑzəˌtori] *n, pl* **-ries** : suppositoire *m*

suppress [sə'prɛs] *vt* **1** SUBDUE : maîtriser, réprimer (une révolte, etc.) **2** WITHHOLD : supprimer **3** REPRESS : étouffer, réprimer <to suppress a yawn : étouffer un bâillement>

suppression [sə'prɛʃən] *n* **1** SUBDUING : répression *f* **2** : suppression *f* (d'information) **3** REPRESSION : étouffement *m,* refoulement *m*

supremacy [sʊ'prɛməsi] *n, pl* **-cies** : suprématie *f*

supreme [sʊ'pri:m] *adj* : suprême — **supremely** *adv*

Supreme Being *n* GOD : Être *m* suprême

surcharge ['sərˌtʃɑrdʒ] *n* : surcharge *f*

sure[1] ['ʃʊr] *adv* **1** ALL RIGHT : bien sûr **2** (*used as an intensifier*) : vraiment, drôlement <it sure is hot! : il fait drôlement chaud!> <she sure is pretty! : qu'est-ce qu'elle est belle!>

sure[2] *adj* **surer; -est** : sûr <I'm sure of it : j'en suis sûr> <she's sure to succeed : elle va sûrement réussir> <for sure : pour sûr>

surely ['ʃʊrli] *adv* **1** CERTAINLY : sûrement **2** (*used as an intensifier*) <you surely don't mean that! : tu ne peux pas vouloir dire cela!>

sureness ['ʃʊrnəs] *n* : sûreté *f*

surety ['ʃʊrəṭi] *n, pl* **-ties 1** GUARANTOR : garant *m,* -rante *f* **2** COLLATERAL : sûreté *f,* caution *f*

surf ['sərf] *n* **1** WAVES : vagues *fpl* (déferlantes) **2** FOAM : écume *f*

surface[1] ['sərfəs] *v* **-faced; -facing** *vi* : faire surface, remonter à la surface — *vt* : revêtir (une chaussée)

surface[2] *n* : surface *f*

surfboard ['sərfˌbord] *n* : planche *f* de surf

surfeit ['sərfət] *n* : excès *m*

surfing ['sərfɪŋ] *n* : surf *m*

surge[1] ['sərdʒ] *vi* **surged; surging 1** SWELL : s'enfler, déferler (se dit de la mer) **2** INCREASE : monter **3** SWARM : se presser, déferler (se dit d'une foule, etc.)

surge[2] *n* **1** RUSH : brusque montée *f* (de la mer), ruée *f* (de personnes) **2** FLUSH : vague *f,* accès *m* (de colère, etc.) **3** INCREASE : augmentation *f,* surtension *f* (de l'électricité)

surgeon ['sərdʒən] *n* : chirurgien *m,* -gienne *f*

surgery ['sərdʒəri] *n, pl* **-geries** : chirurgie *f*

surgical ['sərdʒɪkəl] *adj* : chirurgical

surgically ['sərdʒɪkli] *adv* : par opération, par intervention chirurgicale

Surinamese[1] [ˌsʊrəna'mi:z, -'mi:s] *adj* : surinamien

Surinamese[2] *n* : Surinamien *m,* -mienne *f*

surly ['sərli] *adj* **surlier; -est** : revêche, bourru, hargneux

surmise[1] [sər'maɪz] *v* **-mised; -mising** : conjecturer, présumer

surmise[2] *n* : conjecture *f,* hypothèse *f*

surmount [sər'maʊnt] *vt* **1** OVERCOME : surmonter, vaincre **2** CAP, TOP : surmonter

surname ['sərˌneɪm] *n* : nom *m* de famille

surpass [sər'pæs] *vt* : surpasser, dépasser

surplus ['sərˌplʌs] *n* : excédent *m,* surplus *m*

surprise[1] [sə'praɪz, sər-] *vt* **-prised; -prising** : surprendre

surprise[2] *n* : surprise *f* <to take by surprise : prendre au dépourvu>

surprising [sə'praɪzɪŋ, sər-] *adj* : surprenant, étonnant

surprisingly [sə'praɪzɪŋli, sər-] *adv* : étonnamment, incroyablement

surrender[1] [sə'rɛndər] *vt* **1** : rendre, livrer, céder **2 to surrender oneself to** : se livrer à — *vi* : se rendre, capituler

surrender[2] *n* : capitulation *f,* reddition *f*

surreptitious [ˌsərəp'tɪʃəs] *adj* : subreptice, furtif — **surreptitiously** *adv*

surrogate ['sərəgət, -ˌgeɪt] *n* : substitut *m;* remplaçant *m,* -çante *f*

surround [sə'raʊnd] *vt* : entourer, cerner

surroundings [sə'raʊndɪŋz] *npl* : environs *mpl,* alentours *mpl*

surveillance [sər'veɪlənts, -'veɪljənts, -'veɪənts] *n* : surveillance *f*

survey[1] [sər'veɪ] *vt* **-veyed; -veying 1** : arpenter (un terrain) **2** EXAMINE : examiner, inspecter **3** POLL : sonder

survey[2] ['sərˌveɪ] *n, pl* **-veys 1** INSPECTION : inspection *f* **2** : arpentage *m* (d'un terrain) **3** POLL : sondage *m*

surveyor [sər'veɪər] *n* : arpenteur *m,* -teuse *f*

survival [sər'vaɪvəl] *n* **1** : survie *f* (d'une personne, d'un animal, d'une plante) **2** REMAINDER, VESTIGE : survivance *f,* vestige *m*

survive [sər'vaɪv] *v* **-vived; -viving** *vi* : survivre — *vt* OUTLIVE : survivre à

survivor [sərˈvaɪvər] *n* : survivant *m*, -vante *f*
susceptibility [səˌsɛptəˈbɪləṭi] *n, pl* **-ties** : susceptibilité *f*
susceptible [səˈsɛptəbəl] *adj* : sensible, susceptible
suspect[1] [səˈspɛkt] *vt* **1** DISTRUST : douter de, se méfier de **2** : soupçonner (d'un crime) **3** IMAGINE, THINK : imaginer, soupçonner
suspect[2] [ˈsʌsˌpɛkt, səˈspɛkt] *adj* : suspect
suspect[3] [ˈsʌsˌpɛkt] *n* : suspect *m*, -pecte *f*
suspend [səˈspɛnd] *vt* : suspendre
suspenders [səˈspɛndərz] *npl* : bretelles *fpl*
suspense [səˈspɛnʦ] *n* : attente *f*, suspense *m* <to keep in suspense : laisser dans l'incertitude>
suspenseful [səˈspɛnʦfəl] *adj* : plein de suspense
suspension [səˈspɛntʃən] *n* : suspension *f*
suspicion [səˈspɪʃən] *n* : soupçon *m*, méfiance *f*
suspicious [səˈspɪʃəs] *adj* **1** QUESTIONABLE : suspect **2** DISTRUSTFUL : méfiant, soupçonneux
suspiciously [səˈspɪʃəsli] *adv* **1** : d'une manière suspecte **2** WARILY : d'un air soupçonneux, avec méfiance
sustain [səˈsteɪn] *vt* **1** NOURISH : nourrir **2** MAINTAIN : maintenir, entretenir **3** SUFFER : éprouver <to sustain an injury : recevoir une blessure> **4** SUPPORT : soutenir
sustenance [ˈsʌstənənʦ] *n* **1** NOURISHMENT : nourriture *f* **2** LIVELIHOOD, SUBSISTENCE : (moyens *mpl* de) subsistance *f*
svelte [ˈsfɛlt] *adj* : svelte
swab[1] [ˈswɑb] *vt* **swabbed; swabbing 1** CLEAN : nettoyer **2** *or* **to swab down** MOP : laver
swab[2] *n or* **cotton swab** : tampon *m*
swaddle [ˈswɑdəl] *vt* **-dled; -dling** [-dəlɪŋ] WRAP : emmitoufler, envelopper
swagger[1] [ˈswægər] *vi* **-gered; -gering** : se pavaner
swagger[2] *n* : démarche *f* arrogante
swallow[1] [ˈswɑloː] *vt* **1** : avaler **2** *or* **to swallow up** ENGULF : engloutir **3** REPRESS : ravaler — *vi* : avaler, dégloutir
swallow[2] *n* **1** GULP : gorgée *f* **2** : hirondelle *f* (oiseau)
swam → **swim**[1]
swamp[1] [ˈswɑmp] *vi* : inonder
swamp[2] *n* : marais *m*, marécage *m*, savane *f Can*
swampy [ˈswɑmpi] *adj* **swampier; -est** : marécageux
swan [ˈswɑn] *n* : cygne *m*
swap[1] [ˈswɑp] *vt* **swapped; swapping** : échanger
swap[2] *n* : échange *m*
swarm[1] [ˈswɔrm] *vi* **1** : essaimer (se dit des abeilles) **2** TEEM, THRONG : grouiller, se presser <to be swarming with people : grouiller de gens>
swarm[2] *n* **1** : essaim *m* (d'abeilles) **2** : masse *f*, essaim *m* (de personnes)
swarthy [ˈswɔrði, -θi] *adj* **swarthier; -est** : basané
swashbuckling [ˈswɑʃˌbʌklɪŋ] *adj* : de cape et d'épée (se dit d'un film, etc.)
swat[1] [ˈswɑt] *vt* **swatted; swatting** : écraser (un insecte), frapper (une personne)
swat[2] *n* : tape *f*
swatch [ˈswɑtʃ] *n* : échantillon *m* (de tissu)
swath [ˈswɑθ, ˈswɔθ,] *or* **swathe** [ˈswɑð, ˈswɔð, ˈsweɪð] *n* : andain *m* (en agriculture), bande *f* (de terre)
swathe [ˈswɑð, ˈswɔð, ˈsweɪð] *vt* **swathed; swathing** : emmailloter, envelopper
swatter [ˈswɑṭər] → **flyswatter**
sway[1] [ˈsweɪ] *vi* : se balancer — *vt* **1** INFLUENCE : influencer **2** ROCK : balancer
sway[2] *n* **1** SWINGING : balancement *m* **2** INFLUENCE : influence *f*
swear [ˈswær] *v* **swore** [ˈswor]; **sworn** [ˈsworn]; **swearing** *vi* **1** VOW : jurer <to swear on the Bible : jurer sur la Bible> **2** CURSE : jurer, injurier — *vt* : jurer <to swear allegiance : jurer allégeance> <to swear an oath : prêter serment>
swearword [ˈswærˌwərd] *n* : juron *m*, grossièreté *f*
sweat[1] [ˈswɛt] *vi* **sweat** *or* **sweated; sweating 1** PERSPIRE : transpirer **2** OOZE : suinter, suer **3 to sweat over** : suer sur
sweat[2] *n* : sueur *f*, transpiration *f*
sweater [ˈswɛṭər] *n* : pull-over *m France*, chandail *m*
sweatshirt [ˈswɛtˌʃərt] *n* : sweat-shirt *m*
sweaty [ˈswɛṭi] *adj* **sweatier; -est** : couvert de sueur
Swede [ˈswiːd] *n* : Suédois *m*, -doise *f*
Swedish[1] [ˈswiːdɪʃ] *adj* : suédois
Swedish[2] *n* **1** : suédois *m* (langue) **2 the Swedish** : les Suédois
sweep[1] [ˈswiːp] *v* **swept** [ˈswɛpt]; **sweeping** *vt* **1** : balayer **2** *or* **to sweep away** : emporter, entraîner **3** *or* **to sweep through** : gagner, s'emparer de <panic swept the city : la panique s'est emparée de la ville> — *vi* **1** : balayer **2** EXTEND : s'étendre, décrire (une courbe) <the sun swept across the sky : le soleil a décrit une courbe dans le ciel>
sweep[2] *n* **1** : coup *m* de balai **2** : mouvement *m* circulaire (de la main, etc.) **3** SCOPE : étendue *f*
sweeper [ˈswiːpər] *n* : balayeur *m*, balayeuse *f*
sweeping [ˈswiːpɪŋ] *adj* **1** WIDE : large **2** EXTENSIVE : considérable, radical **3**

INDISCRIMINATE : péremptoire, trop général

sweepstakes ['swi:p,steɪks] *ns & pl* : sweepstake *m*

sweet[1] ['swi:t] *adj* **1** : doux, sucré <sweet desserts : desserts sucrés> **2** FRESH : frais (se dit de l'eau, etc.) **3** : sans sel (se dit du beurre) **4** KIND, PLEASANT : agréable, gentil **5** CUTE, PRETTY : mignon, adorable

sweet[2] *n* : bonbon *m,* dessert *m*

sweeten ['swi:tən] *vt* : sucrer

sweetener ['swi:tənər] *n* : édulcorant *m*

sweetheart ['swi:t,hɑrt] *n* **1** : petit ami *m,* petite amie *f* **2** (*used as a term of address*) : chéri *m,* chérie *f*

sweetly ['swi:tli] *adv* : doucement

sweetness ['swi:tnəs] *n* : douceur *f*

sweet potato *n* : patate *f* douce

swell[1] ['swɛl] *vi* **swelled; swelled** *or* **swollen** ['swo:lən]; **swelling 1** *or* **to swell up** : enfler, gonfler <her ankle swelled : sa cheville enflait> **2** INCREASE : augmenter, grossir

swell[2] *n* **1** : houle *f* (de la mer) **2** INCREASE : augmentation *f*

swelling ['swɛlɪŋ] *n* : enflure *f,* gonflement *m*

swelter ['swɛltər] *vi* : étouffer de chaleur

swept → **sweep**[1]

swerve[1] ['swərv] *vi* **swerved; swerving** : faire une embardée

swerve[2] *n* : embardée *f*

swift[1] ['swɪft] *adj* **1** FAST : rapide **2** PROMPT : prompt — **swiftly** *adv*

swift[2] *n* : martinet *m* (oiseau)

swiftness ['swɪftnəs] *n* **1** SPEED : rapidité *f* **2** PROMPTNESS : promptitude *f*

swig[1] ['swɪg] *vi* **swigged; swigging** : boire à grands traits, siffler *fam*

swig[2] *n* : lampée *f fam,* gorgée *f*

swill[1] ['swɪl] *vt or* **to swill down** : lamper, écluser *fam*

swill[2] *n* **1** SLOP : pâtée *f* **2** GARBAGE : ordures *fpl*

swim[1] ['swɪm] *vi* **swam** ['swæm]; **swum** ['swʌm]; **swimming 1** : nager, faire de la natation, se baigner **2** FLOAT : flotter **3** REEL : tourner <his head was swimming : il avait la tête qui tournait>

swim[2] *n* : baignade *f* <to go for a swim : aller se baigner>

swimmer ['swɪmər] *n* : nageur *m,* -geuse *f*

swindle[1] ['swɪndəl] *vt* **-dled; -dling** : escroquer

swindle[2] *n* : escroquerie *f*

swindler ['swɪndələr] *n* : escroc *m*

swine ['swaɪn] *ns & pl* : porc *m*

swing[1] ['swɪŋ] *v* **swung** ['swʌŋ]; **swinging** *vt* **1** : balancer (les bras, etc.), faire osciller **2** : décrire une courbe avec, brandir <he swung his ax : il a brandi sa hache> <to swing into the saddle : sauter en selle> **3** SUSPEND : suspendre — *vi* **1** SWAY : se balancer **2** CHANGE : virer, passer <to swing from enthusiasm to disappointment : passer de l'enthousiasme à la déception> **3** SWIVEL : tourner, pivoter <the door swung shut : la porte s'est refermée>

swing[2] *n* **1** SWINGING : balancement *m,* oscillation *f* **2** CHANGE, SHIFT : revirement *m* **3** : balançoire *f* (pour les enfants)

swipe[1] ['swaɪp] *v* **swiped; swiping** *vi* **to swipe at** : essayer de frapper, donner un coup pour frapper — *vt* STEAL : chiper *fam,* faucher *fam*

swipe[2] *n* : grand coup *m*

swirl[1] ['swərl] *vi* : tourbillonner

swirl[2] *n* : tourbillon *m*

swish[1] ['swɪʃ] *vi* : siffler (se dit d'un fouet, etc.), bruire (se dit de l'eau), froufrouter (se dit d'une étoffe)

swish[2] *n* : sifflement *m,* bruissement *m,* froufrou *m*

Swiss[1] ['swɪs] *adj* : suisse

Swiss[2] *ns & pl* : Suisse *m,* Suissesse *f*

switch[1] ['swɪtʃ] *vt* **1** LASH, WHIP : fouetter **2** CHANGE : changer de **3** **to switch on** : ouvrir, allumer **4** **to switch off** : couper, fermer, éteindre — *vi* **1** CHANGE : changer **2** SWAP : échanger

switch[2] *n* **1** CANE, STICK : badine *f* **2** CHANGE, SHIFT : changement *m* **3** : interrupteur *m* (d'électricité), bouton *m* (d'une radio ou d'une télévision)

switchboard ['swɪtʃ,bord] *n or* **telephone switchboard** : standard *m*

swivel[1] ['swɪvəl] *vi* **-eled** *or* **-elled; -eling** *or* **-elling** : pivoter

swivel[2] *n* : pivot *m*

swollen → **swell**[1]

swoon[1] ['swu:n] *vi* **1** FAINT : s'évanouir **2** **to swoon over** : se pâmer devant

swoon[2] *n* **1** FAINT : évanouissement *m* **2** DAZE, RAPTURE : pâmoison *f*

swoop[1] ['swu:p] *vi* : fondre, piquer

swoop[2] *n* : descente *f* en piqué

sword ['sɔrd] *n* : épée *f*

swordfish ['sɔrd,fɪʃ] *n* : espadon *m*

swore, sworn → **swear**

swum → **swim**[1]

swung → **swing**[1]

sycamore ['sɪkə,mor] *n* : sycomore *m*

sycophant ['sɪkəfənt, -ˌfænt] *n* : flagorneur *m,* -neuse *f*

syllabic [sə'læbɪk] *adj* : syllabique

syllable ['sɪləbəl] *n* : syllabe *f*

syllabus ['sɪləbəs] *n, pl* **-bi** [-ˌbaɪ] *or* **-buses** : programme *m*

symbol ['sɪmbəl] *n* : symbole *m*

symbolic [sɪm'bɑlɪk] *adj* : symbolique — **symbolically** [-kli] *adv*

symbolism ['sɪmbə,lɪzəm] *n* : symbolisme *m*

symbolize ['sɪmbə,laɪz] *vt* **-ized; -izing** : symboliser

symmetrical [sə'mɛtrɪkəl] *adj* : symétrique — **symmetrically** [-kli] *adv*
symmetry ['sɪmətri] *n, pl* **-tries** : symétrie *f*
sympathetic [ˌsɪmpə'θɛṱɪk] *adj* **1** PLEASING : agréable, sympathique **2** RECEPTIVE : bien disposé **3** COMPASSIONATE, UNDERSTANDING : compatissant, compréhensif
sympathetically [ˌsɪmpə'θɛṱɪkli] *adv* : avec compassion, avec compréhension
sympathize ['sɪmpəˌθaɪz] *vi* **-thized; -thizing 1** : compatir, comprendre <I sympathize with him : je le plains> **2 to sympathize with** SUPPORT : sympathiser avec
sympathizer ['sɪmpəˌθaɪzər] *n* : sympathisant *m*, -sante *f*
sympathy ['sɪmpəθi] *n, pl* **-thies 1** COMPASSION : compassion *f*, sympathie *f* **2** UNDERSTANDING : compréhension *f* **3** AGREEMENT : approbation *f*, sympathie *f*
symphonic [sɪm'fɑnɪk] *adj* : symphonique
symphony ['sɪmpfəni] *n, pl* **-nies** : symphonie *f*
symposium [sɪm'poːziəm] *n, pl* **-sia** [-ziə] *or* **-siums** : symposium *m*
symptom ['sɪmptəm] *n* : symptôme *m*
symptomatic [ˌsɪmptə'mæṱɪk] *adj* : symptomatique
synagogue ['sɪnəˌgɑg, -ˌgɔg] *n* : synagogue *f*
synchronize ['sɪŋkrəˌnaɪz, 'sɪn-] *v* **-nized; -nizing** *vt* : synchroniser — *vi* : être synchrone
syndicate[1] ['sɪndɪˌkeɪt] *v* **-cated; -cating** *vi* UNITE : se syndiquer — *vt* : publier simultanément dans plusieurs journaux
syndicate[2] ['sɪndɪkət] *n* : syndicat *m*
syndrome ['sɪnˌdroːm] *n* : syndrome *m*
synonym ['sɪnəˌnɪm] *n* : synonyme *m*
synonymous [sə'nɑnəməs] *adj* : synonyme
synopsis [sə'nɑpsɪs] *n, pl* **-opses** [-ˌsiːz] : résumé *m*
syntax ['sɪnˌtæks] *n* : syntaxe *f*
synthesis ['sɪnθəsəs] *n, pl* **-theses** [-ˌsiːz] : synthèse *f*
synthesize ['sɪnθəˌsaɪz] *vt* **-sized; -sizing** : synthétiser
synthetic[1] [sɪn'θɛṱɪk] *adj* : synthétique — **synthetically** [-ṱɪkli] *adv*
synthetic[2] *n* : produit *m* synthétique
syphilis ['sɪfələs] *n* : syphilis *f*
Syrian[1] ['sɪriən] *adj* : syrien
Syrian[2] *n* : Syrien *m*, -rienne *f*
syringe [sə'rɪndʒ, 'sɪrɪndʒ] *n* : seringue *f*
syrup ['sərəp, 'sɪrəp] *n* : sirop *m*
system ['sɪstəm] *n* **1** METHOD : système *m*, méthode *f* **2** STRUCTURE : système *m* <the solar system : le système solaire> **3** APPARATUS : appareil *m*, système *m* <digestive system : appareil digestif> **4** BODY : organisme *m* **5** NETWORK : réseau *m*
systematic [ˌsɪstə'mæṱɪk] *adj* : systématique — **systematically** [-ṱɪkli] *adv*
systematize ['sɪstəməˌtaɪz] *vt* **-tized; -tizing** : systématiser
systemic [sɪs'tɛmɪk] *adj* : du système, systémique

T

t ['tiː] *n, pl* **t's** *or* **ts** ['tiːz] : t *m*, vingtième lettre de l'alphabet
tab ['tæb] *n* **1** FLAP : patte *f* **2** BILL, CHECK : note *f*, addition *f* **3** LOOP : attache *f* **4 to keep tabs on s.o.** : surveiller qqn, garder qqn à l'œil
tabby ['tæbi] *n, pl* **-bies** : chat *m* tigré, chatte *f* tigrée
tabernacle ['tæbərˌnækəl] *n* : tabernacle *m*
table ['teɪbəl] *n* **1** : table *f* <kitchen table : table de cuisine> **2** MEAL : table *f* <to serve a good table : servir une bonne table> **3** CHART : table *f*, tableau *m* **4 table of contents** : table *f* des matières
tableau [tæ'bloː, 'tæˌ-] *n, pl* **tableaux** [tæ'bloːz, 'tæˌbloːz] : tableau *m*
tablecloth ['teɪbəlˌklɔθ] *n* : nappe *f*
tablespoon ['teɪbəlˌspuːn] *n* : cuillère *f* à soupe
tablespoonful ['teɪbəlˌspuːnˌfʊl] *n* : cuillère *f* à soupe
tablet ['tæblət] *n* **1** PLAQUE : plaque *f*, tablette *f* (de pierre) **2** NOTEPAD : bloc-notes *m*, tablette *f Can* **3** PILL : comprimé *m* <aspirin tablet : comprimé d'aspirine>
table tennis *n* : tennis *m* de table
tabletop ['teɪbəlˌtɑp] *n* : dessus *m* de table
tableware ['teɪbəlˌweɪr] *n* : vaisselle *f*
tabloid ['tæˌblɔɪd] *n* : quotidien *m* populaire, tabloïde *m*
taboo[1] [tə'buː, tæ-] *adj* : tabou, interdit
taboo[2] *n, pl* **taboos** : tabou *m*
tabular ['tæbjələr] *adj* : tabulaire
tabulate ['tæbjəˌleɪt] *vt* **-lated; -lating** : mettre sous forme de tableau
tabulator ['tæbjəˌleɪṱər] *n* : tabulateur *m*
tacit ['tæsɪt] *adj* : tacite, implicite — **tacitly** *adv*
taciturn ['tæsɪˌtərn] *adj* : taciturne
tack[1] ['tæk] *vt* **1** ATTACH : clouer, fixer <to tack down a carpet : clouer un

tapis> **2 to tack on** ADD : ajouter, rajouter — *vi* : faire une bordée (se dit d'un navire)

tack[2] *n* **1** BRAD : semence *f,* clou *m* **2** → **thumbtack 3** COURSE : voie *f,* tactique *f* <to change tack : changer de voie>

tackle[1] ['takəl] *vt* **-led; -ling 1** : plaquer (au football) **2** : s'attaquer à <to tackle a problem : s'attaquer à un problème>

tackle[2] *n* **1** GEAR : équipment *m,* matériel *m* <fishing tackle : matériel de pêche> **2** PULLEYS : appareil *m* de levage **3** : plaquage *m* (au football)

tacky ['tæki] *adj* **tackier; -est 1** STICKY : collant **2** SHABBY : moche, minable **3** TASTELESS : de mauvais goût

tact ['tækt] *n* : tact *m,* diplomatie *f*

tactful ['tæktfəl] *adj* : plein de tact

tactfully ['tæktfəli] *adv* : avec tact, avec diplomatie

tactic ['tæktɪk] *n* : tactique *f,* plan *m*

tactical ['tæktɪkəl] *adj* : tactique

tactics ['tæktɪks] *ns & pl* : tactique *f*

tactile ['tæktəl, -ˌtaɪl] *adj* : tactile

tactless ['tæktləs] *adj* : qui manque de tact

tactlessly ['tæktləsli] *adv* : sans tact

tadpole ['tædˌpoːl] *n* : têtard *m*

taffeta ['tæfət̬ə] *n* : taffetas *m*

taffy ['tæfi] *n, pl* **-fies** : bonbon *m* au caramel

tag[1] ['tæg] *v* **tagged; tagging** *vt* **1** LABEL : étiqueter **2** TOUCH : toucher (au jeu de chat, au baseball, etc.) — *vi* **to tag along behind** : suivre

tag[2] *n* **1** : jeu *m* de chat **2** *or* **price tag** : étiquette *f*

Tahitian[1] [tə'hiːʃən] *adj* : tahitien

Tahitian[2] *n* : Tahitien, -tienne *f*

tail[1] ['teɪl] *vt* FOLLOW : suivre de près

tail[2] *n* **1** : queue *f* (d'un animal) **2** : queue *f* (d'un avion, d'une comète, etc.) **3 tails** *npl* : pile *f* (d'une pièce de monnaie) <heads or tails? : pile ou face?>

tailgate[1] ['teɪlˌgeɪt] *vt* **-gated; -gating** : coller au pare-chocs de

tailgate[2] *n* : hayon *m*

taillight ['teɪlˌlaɪt] *n* : feu *m* arrière (d'un véhicule)

tailor[1] ['teɪlər] *vt* **1** : faire sur mesure, confectionner (un vêtement) **2** ADAPT : faire, concevoir, adapter

tailor[2] *n* : tailleur *m*

tailpipe ['teɪlˌpaɪp] *n* : tuyau *m* d'échappement

tailspin ['teɪlˌspɪn] *n* : vrille *f* (d'un avion)

taint[1] ['teɪnt] *vt* **1** SULLY : entacher, souiller (une reputation, etc.) **2** SPOIL : gâter (des aliments)

taint[2] *n* : souillure *f*

Taiwanese[1] [ˌtaɪwə'niːz, -'niːs] *adj* : taiwanais

Taiwanese[2] *n* : Taiwanais *m,* -naise *f*

take[1] ['teɪk] *v* **took** ['tʊk]; **taken** ['teɪkən]; **taking** *vt* **1** CAPTURE : prendre, retenir **2** GRASP : prendre, saisir **3** CAPTIVATE : éprendre **4** INGEST : prendre <take your medicine : prends tes medicaments> **5** ACCEPT : entrer, accepter, prendre <to take office : entrer en fonction> <to take a job : accepter un emploi> **6** ASSUME : prendre, s'attribuer <she took all the credit : elle s'est attribuée tout le mérite> **7** BRING : porter, apporter <he took his father some coffee : il a apporté du café à son père> **8** WIN : remporter **9** SELECT : prendre, choisir **10** : prendre <she takes the train : elle prend le train> <take a seat : asseyez-vous> **11** FOLLOW : prendre, emprunter <they took a different route : ils ont pris un autre chemin> **12** CONDUCT : mener, conduire, emmener <the bus will take you there : l'autobus vous y mènera> **13 to take apart** DISMANTLE : démonter, démancher *Can* **14 to take place** HAPPEN : avoir lieu **15 to take s.o.'s side** : prendre parti pour qqn — *vi* **1** : faire effet <the vaccination took : le vaccin a fait effet> **2** BECOME, FALL : tomber <he took ill : il est tombé malade>

take[2] *n* : prise *f*

take back *vt* : retirer

take in *vt* **1** : reprendre (un vêtement) **2** INCLUDE : inclure, couvrir **3** ATTEND : aller à <let's take in a movie : allons au cinéma> **4** UNDERSTAND : saisir, comprendre **5** DECEIVE : tromper, se faire avoir

takeoff ['teɪkˌɔf] *n* **1** : décollage *m* (d'un avion) **2** PARODY : parodie *f,* imitation *f*

take off *vt* **1** REMOVE : enlever, ôter <take your shoes off : enlevez vos chaussures> **2** DEDUCT : déduire, soustraire **3** TAKE : prendre <he took two weeks off : il a pris deux semaines de vacances> — *vi* **1** DEPART : s'en aller, décamper **2** : décoller (se dit d'un avion)

take on *vt* **1** ACCEPT : assumer, prendre, accepter (des responsabilités, etc.) **2** : jouer contre <he took on the champion : il a joué contre le champion> **3** ADOPT : arborer, prendre <the city took on a festive air : la ville arborait un air de fête> **4** HIRE : engager, embaucher

takeover ['teɪkˌoːvər] *n* : prise *f* de pouvoir

take over *vt* : prendre le pouvoir, prendre la relève

taker ['teɪkər] *n* : preneur *m,* -neuse *f*

take up *vt* **1** LIFT : enlever, prendre **2** BEGIN : faire <to take up painting : faire de la peinture> **3** RESUME

: reprendre 4 SHORTEN : raccourcir (une jupe, une robe etc.)

takings ['teɪkɪŋz] *npl Brit* : recette *f*

talc ['tælk] → **talcum powder**

talcum powder ['tælkəm] *n* : talc *m*

tale ['teɪl] *n* **1** STORY : conte *m,* récit *m* **2** FALSEHOOD : histoires *fpl,* mensonge *m*

talent ['tælənt] *n* : talent *m*

talented ['tæləntəd] *adj* : talentueux, doué

talisman ['tæləsmən, -ləz-] *n, pl* **-mans** : talisman *m*

talk[1] ['tɔk] *vt* **1** SPEAK : parler <to talk French : parler français> **2** DISCUSS : parler (de) <to talk business : parler affaires> **3 to talk s.o. into doing sth** : persuader qqn de faire qqch — *vi* **1** CHAT : parler, causer **2** LECTURE : parler, discourir **3** GOSSIP : cancaner, jaser

talk[2] *n* **1** TALKING : paroles *fpl,* propos *mpl* **2** CONVERSATION, DISCUSSION : entretien *m,* conversation *f* <I had a talk with him : j'ai discuté avec lui> **3** RUMOR : racontars *mpl,* commérage *m fam* <it's the talk of the town : on ne parle que de ça> **4** SPEECH : discours *m,* exposé *m*

talkative ['tɔkət̬ɪv] *adj* : bavard, loquace

talker ['tɔkər] *n* **he's a talker** : il est bavard

tall ['tɔl] *adj* **1** : grand <she's six feet tall : elle mesure six pieds> **2** : haut, élevé <a building two meters tall : un édifice haut de deux mètres> **3 a tall tale** : une histoire invraisemblable

tallness ['tɔlnəs] *n* : hauteur *f* (d'un édifice, etc.), taille *f* (d'une personne)

tallow ['tæloː] *n* : suif *m*

tally[1] ['tæli] *v* **-lied; -lying** *vt* RECORD : tenir le compte de — *vi* MATCH : correspondre

tally[2] *n, pl* **-lies** : compte *m,* pointage *m*

talon ['tælən] *n* : serre *f* (d'aigle)

tambourine [ˌtæmbə'riːn] *n* : tambourin *m*

tame[1] ['teɪm] *vt* **tamed; taming** : apprivoiser, domestiquer

tame[2] *adj* **tamer; tamest 1** DOMESTICATED : apprivoisé **2** SUBDUED : docile, soumis **3** DULL : fade, terne

tamely ['teɪmli] *adv* : docilement

tamer ['teɪmər] *n* : dompteur *m,* -teuse *f* (de lions, etc.)

tamp ['tæmp] *vt* **to tamp down** : damer, tasser

tamper ['tæmpər] *vi* **1 to tamper with** ALTER : altérer, falsifier **2 to tamper with** BRIBE : suborner <to tamper with a witness : suborner un témoin>

tampon ['tæmˌpɑn] *n* : tampon *m* (hygiénique)

tan[1] ['tæn] *v* **tanned; tanning** *vt* : tanner <to tan hides : tanner des peaux> — *vi* : bronzer

tan[2] *n* **1** SUNTAN : bronzage *m* <to get a tan : se faire bronzer> **2** : brun *m* clair (couleur)

tandem[1] ['tændəm] *adv* **to ride tandem** : se promener en tandem

tandem[2] *n* : tandem *m*

tang ['tæŋ] *n* : goût *m* piquant

tangent ['tændʒənt] *n* **1** : tangente *f* (en mathématiques) **2** DIGRESSION : digression *f* <to go off on a tangent : partir dans une digression>

tangerine ['tændʒəˌriːn, ˌtændʒə'-] *n* : mandarine *f*

tangible ['tændʒəbəl] *adj* : tangible, palpable

tangibly ['tændʒəbli] *adv* : manifestement, de manière tangible

tangle[1] ['tæŋgəl] *v* **-gled; -gling** *vt* : emmêler, enchevêtrer — *vi* : s'emmêler

tangle[2] *n* **1** : enchevêtrement *m* **2** MUDDLE : confusion *f,* foullis *m*

tango[1] ['tæŋˌgoː] *vi* : danser le tango

tango[2] *n, pl* **-gos** : tango *m*

tangy['tæŋi] *adj* **tangier; tangiest** : acidulé

tank ['tæŋk] *n* **1** : réservoir *m,* citerne *f,* cuve *f* <gas tank : réservoir à essence> **2** : char *m* (militaire)

tankard ['tæŋkərd] *n* : chope *f*

tanker ['tæŋkər] *n* **1** : navire-citern *m,* camion-citern *m* **2** *or* **oil tanker** : pétrolier *m*

tanner ['tænər] *n* : tanneur *m*

tannery ['tænəri] *n, pl* **-neries** : tannerie *f*

tannin ['tænən] *n* : tanin *m*

tantalize ['tæntəˌlaɪz] *vt* **-lized; -lizing** : tourmenter, allécher

tantalizing ['tæntəˌlaɪzɪŋ] *adj* : tentant, alléchant

tantamount ['tæntəˌmaʊnt] *adj* **~ to** : équivalent à

tantrum ['tæntrəm] *n* : accès *m* de colère, crise *f* <to throw a tantrum : piquer une crise>

Tanzanian[1] [ˌtænzə'niːən] *adj* : tanzanien

Tanzanian[2] *n* : Tanzanien *m,* -nienne *f*

tap[1] ['tæp] *v* **tapped; tapping** *vt* **1** : percer (un tonneau), inciser (des arbres) **2** PAT, TOUCH : tapoter, taper <he tapped me on the shoulder : il me tapotait sur l'épaule> **3 to tap a phone** : mettre un téléphone sur écoute — *vi* : taper légèrement

tap[2] *n* **1** FAUCET : robinet *m* <beer on tap : bière en fût> **2** PAT, TOUCH : petit coup *m,* petite tape *f* <a sharp tap : un coup sec>

tape[1] ['teɪp] *vt* **taped; taping 1** : coller avec un ruban adhésif **2** RECORD : enregistrer (une cassette)

tape[2] *n* **1** STRIP : bande *f,* ruban *m* **2** *or* **adhesive tape** : ruban *m* adhésif **3** → **magnetic tape, tape measure**

tape measure *n* : mètre *m* ruban *France,* ruban *m* à mesurer *Can*

taper[1] ['teɪpər] *vt* : effiler, tailler en pointe — *vi* : s'effiler, se terminer en pointe

taper[2] *n* **1** CANDLE : cierge *m* **2** TAPERING : forme *f* effilée

tapestry ['tæpəstri] *n, pl* **-tries** : tapisserie *f*

tapeworm ['teɪpˌwərm] *n* : ténia *m,* ver *m* solitaire

tapioca [ˌtæpi'o:kə] *n* : tapioca *m*

tar[1] ['tɑr] *vt* **tarred; tarring** : goudronner

tar[2] *n* : goudron *m*

tarantula [tə'ræntʃələ, -'ræntələ] *n* : tarentule *f*

tardily ['tɑrdəli] *adv* : tardivement

tardiness ['tɑrdinəs] *n* : retard *m*

tardy ['tɑrdi] *adj* **tardier; -est** : tardif, en retard

target[1] ['tɑrgət] *vt* : viser, cibler

target[2] *n* **1** : cible *f* **2** GOAL : objectif *m,* but *m*

tariff ['tærɪf] *n* : tarif *m* douanier

tarnish[1] ['tɑrnɪʃ] *vt* : ternir

tarnish[2] *n* : ternissure *f*

tarpaulin [tɑr'pɔlən, 'tɑrpə-] *n* : bâche *f*

tarry[1] ['tæri] *vi* **-ried; -rying** : tarder

tarry[2] ['tɑri] *adj* : goudronneux, couvert de goudron

tart[1] ['tɑrt] *adj* **1** SOUR : aigre, âpre **2** CAUSTIC : aigre, acrimonieux

tart[2] *n* : tartelette *f*

tartan ['tɑrtən] *n* : tartan *m,* tissu *m* écossais

tartar ['tɑrt̬ər] *n* **1** : tartre *m* (sur les dents) **2 tartar sauce** : sauce *f* tartare

tartness ['tɑrtnəs] *n* **1** SOURNESS : aigreur *f,* acidité *f* **2** ACRIMONY : acrimonie *f*

task ['tæsk] *n* : tâche *f*

taskmaster ['tæskˌmæstər] *n* **to be a hard taskmaster** : être très exigeant

tassel ['tæsəl] *n* : gland *m* (ornement)

taste[1] ['teɪst] *v* **tasted; tasting** *vt* **1** : goûter (à) <taste the sauce : goûte la sauce> **2** : sentir le goût de <you can't taste the pepper : on ne sent pas le goût du poivre> — *vi* : goûter <to taste sour : goûter amère> <to taste good : avoir bon goût>

taste[2] *n* **1** : goût *m* (sens) **2** FLAVOR : goût *m,* saveur *f* **3** BIT, SAMPLE : aperçu *m* <a taste of high life : un aperçu de la grande vie> **4** INCLINATION : goût *m,* penchant *m*

taste bud *n* : papille *f* gustative

tasteful ['teɪstfəl] *adj* : de bon goût

tastefully ['teɪstfəli] *adv* : avec goût

tasteless ['teɪstləs] *adj* **1** FLAVORLESS : insipide, qui n'a aucun goût **2** : de mauvais goût <a tasteless joke : une blague de mauvais goût>

taster ['teɪstər] *n* : dégustateur *m,* -trice *f*

tastiness ['teɪstinəs] *n* : saveur *f* agréable, bon goût *m*

tasty ['teɪsti] *adj* **tastier; -est** : savoureux, délicieux

tattered ['tæt̬ərd] *adj* : en lambeaux, en loques

tatters ['tæt̬ərz] *npl* **to be in tatters** : être en loques

tattle ['tæt̬əl] *vi* **-tled; -tling 1** CHATTER : jaser **2 to tattle on s.o.** : dénoncer qqn

tattletale ['tæt̬əlˌteɪl] *n* : rapporteur *m,* -teuse *f*

tattoo[1] [tæ'tu:] *vt* : tatouer

tattoo[2] *n* **1** : tatouage *m* **2 to beat a tattoo on** : tambouriner sur

taught → **teach**

taunt[1] ['tɔnt] *vt* : ridiculiser, railler

taunt[2] *n* : raillerie *f,* insulte *f*

Taurus [tɔrəs] *n* : Taureau *m*

taut ['tɔt] *adj* : tendu, raide

tautly ['tɔtli] *adv* : de façon tendue

tautness ['tɔtnəs] *n* : tension *f,* raideur *f*

tavern ['tævərn] *n* : taverne *f*

tawdry ['tɔdri] *adj* **tawdrier; -est** : tape-à-l'œil, criard, tapageur

tawny ['tɔni] *adj* **tawnier; -est** : fauve (couleur)

tax[1] ['tæks] *vt* **1** : imposer (une personne), taxer (des marchandises) **2** CHARGE : accuser <he taxed them with carelessness : il les a accusés d'être négligents> **3** TRY : mettre à l'épreuve <the job taxed her strength : l'emploi la fatiguait>

tax[2] *n* **1** : taxe *f* <sales tax : taxe à l'achat> **2** : impôt *m* <income tax : impôt sur le revenu> **3** STRAIN : fardeau *m,* poids *m*

taxable ['tæksəbəl] *adj* : imposable

taxation [tæk'seɪʃən] *n* : taxation *f,* imposition *f*

tax–exempt ['tæksɪg'zɛmpt, -ɛg-] *adj* : exempt d'impôts

taxi[1] ['tæksi] *vi* **taxied; taxiing** *or* **taxying; taxis** *or* **taxies 1** : transporter par taxi **2** : rouler au sol (se dit d'un avion)

taxi[2] *n, pl* **taxis** : taxi *m*

taxicab ['tæksiˌkæb] → **taxi**[2]

taxidermist ['tæksəˌdərmɪst] *n* : taxidermiste *mf*

taxidermy ['tæksəˌdərmi] *n* : taxidermie *f*

taxpayer ['tæksˌpeɪər] *n* : contribuable *mf*

TB [ˌti:'bi:] → **tuberculosis**

tea ['ti:] *n* : thé *m*

teach ['ti:tʃ] *v* **taught** ['tɔt]; **teaching** *vt* **1** : apprendre, montrer <he's teaching me to drive : il m'apprend à conduire> **2** : enseigner, faire cours à <she teaches French : elle enseigne le français> **3 to teach s.o. a lesson** : servir de leçon à qqn — *vi* : enseigner

teacher ['ti:tʃər] *n* : enseignant *m,* -nante *f;* professeur *m*

teaching ['ti:tʃɪŋ] *n* : enseignement *m*

teacup ['ti:ˌkʌp] *n* : tasse *f* à thé

teak ['ti:k] *n* : teck *m*

teakettle ['ti:ˌkɛtəl] *n* : bouilloire *f*

teal ['ti:l] *n, pl* **teal** *or* **teals** : sarcelle *f* (canard)

team[1] ['ti:m] *vi* **to team up with** : faire équipe avec

team[2] *adj* : d'équipe <a team effort : un effort d'équipe>

team[3] *n* **1** : attelage *m* (d'animaux) **2** : équipe *f* (aux sports, etc.)

teammate ['ti:mˌmeɪt] *n* : coéquipier *m*, -pière *f*

teamster ['ti:mstər] *n* : camionneur *m*, -neuse *f;* routier *m*

teamwork ['ti:mˌwərk] *n* : travail *m* d'équipe

teapot ['ti:ˌpɑt] *n* : théière *f*

tear[1] ['tær] *v* **tore** ['tor]; **torn** ['torn]; **tearing** *vt* **1** RIP : déchirer (un papier, etc.), se dechirer (un muscle) <to tear to shreds : mettre en lambeaux> **2** LACERATE : blesser (la peau) **3** REMOVE, SNATCH : arracher **4** *or* **to tear apart** DIVIDE : déchirer **5 to tear down** : démolir — *vi* **1** : se déchirer <this cloth tears easily : ce tissu se déchire facilement> **2** RUSH : se précipiter <he tore out of the house : il est sorti en trombe de la maison>

tear[2] *n* : déchirure *f*

tear[3] ['tɪr] *n* : larme *f* <to break into tears : fondre en larmes>

teardrop ['tɪrˌdrɑp] → **tear**[3]

tearful ['tɪrfəl] *adj* : larmoyant

tearfully ['tɪrfəli] *adv* : en pleurant, les larmes aux yeux

tease[1] ['ti:z] *vt* **teased; teasing** : taquiner

tease[2] *n* : taquin *m*, -quine *f*

teaspoon ['ti:ˌspu:n] *n* : petite cuillère *f*, cuillère *f* à café

teaspoonful ['ti:ˌspu:nˌfʊl] *n* : cuillerée *f* à café

teat ['ti:t] *n* : tétine *f*

technical ['tɛknɪkəl] *adj* : technique — **technically** [-kli] *adv*

technicality [ˌtɛknə'kæləṭi] *n, pl* **-ties** : détail *m* technique

technician [tɛk'nɪʃən] *n* : technicien *m*, -cienne *f*

technique [tɛk'ni:k] *n* : technique *f*

technological [ˌtɛknə'lɑdʒɪkəl] *adj* : technologique

technology [tɛk'nɑlədʒi] *n, pl* **-gies** : technologie *f*

tedious ['ti:diəs] *adj* : fastidieux, ennuyeux

tediously ['ti:diəsli] *adv* : fastidieusement, de façon ennuyeuse

tediousness ['ti:diəsnəs] *n* : ennui *m*

tedium ['ti:diəm] → **tediousness**

tee ['ti:] *n* : tee *m* (au golf)

teem ['ti:m] *vi* **to teem with** : foisonner de, abonder en

teenage ['ti:nˌeɪdʒ] *or* **teenaged** [-ˌeɪdʒd] *adj* : jeune, adolescent, d'adolescence

teenager ['ti:nˌeɪdʒər] *n* : adolescent *m*, -cente *f*

teens ['ti:nz] *npl* : adolescence *f*

teepee → **tepee**

teeter[1] ['ti:ṭər] *vi* **1** WAVER : vaciller, chanceler **2** SEESAW : balancer, basculer

teeter[2] *n or* **teeter–totter** ['ti:ṭər-ˌtɑṭər] → **seesaw**

teeth → **tooth**

teethe ['ti:ð] *vi* **teethed; teething** : faire ses dents

telecast[1] ['tɛləˌkæst] *vt* **-cast; -casting** : téléviser, diffuser

telecast[2] *n* : émission *f* de télévision

telecommunication [ˌtɛləkəˌmju:nə'keɪʃən] *n* : télécommunication *f*

telegram ['tɛləˌgræm] *n* : télégramme *m*

telegraph[1] ['tɛləˌgræf] *v* : télégraphier

telegraph[2] *n* : télégraphe *m*

telepathic [ˌtɛlə'pæθɪk] *adj* : télépathique

telepathy [tə'lɛpəθi] *n* : télépathie *f*

telephone[1] ['tɛləˌfo:n] *v* **-phoned; -phoning** *vt* : téléphoner à — *vi* : appeler, téléphoner

telephone[2] *n* : téléphone *m*

telescope[1] ['tɛləˌsko:p] *v* **-scoped; -scoping** *vi* : se télescoper — *vt* CONDENSE : comprimer, condenser

telescope[2] *n* : télescope *m*

telescopic [ˌtɛlə'skɑpɪk] *adj* : télescopique

televise ['tɛləˌvaɪz] *vt* **-vised; -vising** : téléviser

television ['tɛləˌvɪʒən] *n* **1** : télévision *f* **2** *or* **television set** : téléviseur *m*

tell ['tɛl] *v* **told** ['to:ld]; **telling** *vt* **1** COUNT : compter, être en tout <all told there were 27 of us : nous étions 27 en tout> **2** NARRATE : raconter, conter **3** REVEAL : divulguer, dévoiler **4** ORDER : dire à <they told me to wait : ils m'ont dit d'attendre> **5** RECOGNIZE : voir, lire <you can tell it's a masterpiece : on voit bien que c'est un chef-d'œuvre> <to tell time : lire l'heure> — *vi* **1** SAY : dire **2** KNOW : savoir <as far as I can tell : pour autant que je sache> **3** SHOW : se faire sentir <the tension began to tell : la tension a commencé à se faire sentir>

teller ['tɛlər] *n* **1** NARRATOR : conteur *m*, -teuse *f* **2** *or* **bank teller** : caissier *m*, -sière *f*

temerity [tə'mɛrəṭi] *n, pl* **-ties** : témérité *f*, audace *f*

temp ['tɛmp] *n* : intérimaire *mf;* occasionnel *m*, -nelle *f Can*

temper[1] ['tɛmpər] *vt* **1** MODERATE : tempérer **2** TOUGHEN : endurcir

temper[2] *n* **1** HARDNESS : trempe *f* (de métal) **2** DISPOSITION : tempérament *m,* caractère *m* **3 to lose one's temper :** se mettre en colère, s'emporter

temperament ['tɛmpərmənt, -prə-, -pərə-] *n* : tempérament *m,* nature *f*

temperamental [ˌtɛmpər'mɛntəl, -prə-, -pərə-] *adj* : capricieux

temperance ['tɛmprənts] *n* : tempérance *f,* modération *f*

temperate ['tɛmpərət] *adj* **1** MILD : tempéré <temperate climate : climat tempéré> **2** MODERATE : modéré <to be a temperate drinker : boire modérément>

temperature ['tɛmpərˌtʃʊr, -prə-, -tʃər] *n* **1** : température *f* **2** FEVER : température *f,* fièvre *f* <to run a temperature : faire de la température>

tempest ['tɛmpəst] *n* **1** STORM : tempête *f,* orage *m* **2** UPROAR : tumulte *m,* chahut *m*

tempestuous [tɛm'pɛstʃʊəs] *adj* **1** STORMY : tempétueux **2** ARDENT, RAGING : impétueux, fougueux

temple ['tɛmpəl] *n* **1** : temple *m* (religieux) **2** : tempe *f* (en anatomie)

tempo ['tɛmˌpoː] *n, pl* **-pi** [-ˌpiː] *or* **-pos** : tempo *m*

temporal ['tɛmpərəl] *adj* : temporel

temporary ['tɛmpəˌrɛri] *adj* : temporaire — **temporarily** [ˌtɛmpə'rɛrəli] *adv*

tempt ['tɛmpt] *vt* : tenter

temptation [tɛmp'teɪʃən] *n* : tentation *f*

tempter ['tɛmptər] *n* : tentateur *m*

temptress ['tɛmptrəs] *n* : tentatrice *f*

ten[1] ['tɛn] *adj* : dix

ten[2] *n* **1** : dix *m* **2** : dizaine *f* <there were tens of them : il y en avait des dizaines>

tenable ['tɛnəbəl] *adj* : soutenable, défendable

tenacious [tə'neɪʃəs] *adj* : tenace

tenaciously [tə'neɪʃəsli] *adv* : avec ténacité

tenacity [tə'næsəṭi] *n* : ténacité *f,* opiniâtreté *f*

tenancy ['tɛnəntsi] *n, pl* **-cies 1** : location *f* <terms of tenancy : conditions de location> **2** : période *f* d'occupation (d'un logement)

tenant ['tɛnənt] *n* : locataire *mf*

tend ['tɛnd] *vi* **1** : se diriger <we cannot tell where society is tending : on ne peut pas dire où notre société se dirige>**2 to tend to** : avoir tendance à, être enclin à <she tends to be pessimistic : elle a tendance à être pessimiste> — *vt* : surveiller, s'occuper de <to tend the plants : s'occuper des plantes>

tendency ['tɛndəntsi] *n, pl* **-cies** : tendance *f*

tender[1] ['tɛndər] *vt* OFFER : donner, offrir <I tendered my resignation : j'ai donné ma démission> <to tender thanks : offrir ses remerciements>

tender[2] *adj* **1** DELICATE : tendre, fragile **2** LOVING : tendre, affectueux **3** SORE : sensible **4** YOUNG : tendre <a tender age : un âge tendre> **5** SUCCULENT : tendre <a tender steak : un steak tendre>

tender[3] *n* **1** OFFER : soumission *f,* offre *f* **2 legal tender** : cours *m* légal

tenderize ['tɛndəˌraɪz] *vt* **-ized; -izing** : attendrir (de la viande)

tenderloin ['tɛndɛrˌlɔɪn] *n* : filet *m* (de bœuf, de porc, etc.)

tenderly ['tɛndərli] *adv* : tendrement, avec tendresse

tenderness ['tɛndərnəs] *n* : tendresse *f*

tendon ['tɛndən] *n* : tendon *m*

tendril ['tɛndrɪl] *n* : vrille *f* (d'une plante)

tenement ['tɛnəmənt] *n or* **tenement house** : immeuble *m*

tenet ['tɛnət] *n* : principe *m,* croyance *f*

tennis ['tɛnəs] *n* : tennis *m*

tenor ['tɛnər] *n* **1** DRIFT, GIST : contenu *m,* sens *m* général (d'une conversation, etc.) **2** : ténor *m* <tenor voice : voix de ténor>

tenpins ['tɛnˌpɪnz] *n* : bowling *m*

tense[1] ['tɛnts] *vi* **tensed; tensing** *or* **to tense up** : se raidir, se tendre

tense[2] *adj* **tenser; tensest 1** RIGID : tendu, raide **2** UPTIGHT : tendu, stressé

tense[3] *n* : temps *m* (en grammaire) <the past tense : le passé composé>

tensely ['tɛntsli] *adv* : de façon tendue

tenseness ['tɛntsnəs] *n* : tension *f*

tensile ['tɛntsəl, 'tɛnˌsaɪl] *adj* : extensible

tension ['tɛntʃən] *n* **1** TAUTNESS : tension *f,* raideur *f* **2** STRESS : tension *f,* stress *m*

tent ['tɛnt] *n* : tente *f*

tentacle ['tɛntɪkəl] *n* : tentacule *m*

tentative ['tɛntəṭɪv] *adj* **1** : provisoire <tentative plans : plans provisoires> **2** HESITANT : hésitant, indécis <tentative steps : pas hésitants>

tentatively ['tɛntəṭɪvli] *adv* **1** : provisoirement **2** HESITANTLY : incertainement, timidement

tenth[1] ['tɛnθ] *adv & adj* : dixième

tenth[2] *n* **1** : dizième *mf* (dans une série) **2** : dizième *m* (en mathématiques) **3** (*used in dates*) <the tenth of May : le dix mai>

tenuous ['tɛnjʊəs] *adj* : précaire, ténu

tenuously ['tɛnjʊəsli] *adv* : de manière ténue

tenure ['tɛnjər] *n* : période *f* de jouissance (en droit), titularisation *f* (à un poste universitaire)

tenured ['tɛnjərd] *adj* : titulaire

tepee ['tiːˌpiː] *n* : tipi *m*

tepid ['tɛpɪd] *adj* : tiède

term[1] ['tərm] *vt* : appeler, nommer

term[2] *n* **1** PERIOD : terme *m* **2** : terme *m* (en mathématiques) **3** WORD : terme *m,* expression *f* **4 terms** *npl* CONDITIONS : termes *mpl,* conditions *fpl* **5 terms** *npl* RELATIONS : termes

mpl, rapports *mpl* <on good terms with : en bons termes avec>
terminal[1] [ˈtərmənəl] *adj* : terminal
terminal[2] *n* **1** : borne *f* (en électricité) **2** *or* **computer terminal** : terminal *m* **3** : terminus *m* (de train, de bus)
terminate [ˈtərməˌneɪt] *v* **-nated; -nating** *vt* : mettre fin à — *vi* : se terminer
termination [ˌtərməˈneɪʃən] *n* **1** END : fin *f* **2** ENDING : terminaison *f* (en grammaire)
terminology [ˌtərməˈnɑləʤi] *n, pl* **-gies** : terminologie *f*
terminus [ˈtərmənəs] *n, pl* **-ni** [-ˌnaɪ] *or* **-nuses** **1** END : bout *m,* fin *f* **2** TERMINAL : terminus *m*
termite [ˈtərˌmaɪt] *n* : termite *m*
tern [ˈtərn] *n* : hirondelle *f* de mer, sterne *f*
terrace[1] [ˈtɛrəs] *vt* **-raced; -racing** : aménager en terrasses
terrace[2] *n* **1** PATIO : terrasse *f* **2** EMBANKMENT : terre-plein *m* **3** : terrasse *f* (en agriculture) **4** *or* **terraced houses** : rangée *f* de maisons
terra–cotta [ˌtɛrəˈkɑṭə] *n* : terre *f* cuite
terrain [təˈreɪn] *n* : terrain *m*
terrapin [ˈtɛrəpɪn] *n* : tortue *f* d'eau douce
terrarium [təˈræriəm] *n, pl* **-ia** [-iə] *or* **-iums** : vivarium *m* (pour les animaux), serre *f* miniature (pour les plantes)
terrestrial [təˈrɛstriəl] *adj* : terrestre
terrible [ˈtɛrəbəl] *adj* : terrible, épouvantable
terribly [ˈtɛrəbli] *adv* **1** VERY : terriblement, vraiment <I'm terribly sorry : je suis vraiment désolée> **2** BADLY : terriblement, affreusement mal <terribly ill : terriblement malade>
terrier [ˈtɛriər] *n* : terrier *m*
terrific [təˈrɪfɪk] *adj* **1** FRIGHTFUL : terrible, terrifiant **2** EXTRAORDINARY : terrible, extrême <a terrific speed : une allure vertigineuse> **3** EXCELLENT : formidable, épatant *fam* <we had a terrific time : nous nous sommes vraiment amusés>
terrify [ˈtɛrəˌfaɪ] *vt* **-fied; -fying** : terrifier
terrifying [ˈtɛrəˌfaɪɪŋ] *adj* : terrifiant, effroyable
territorial [ˌtɛrəˈtoriəl] *adj* : territorial
territory [ˈtɛrəˌtori] *n, pl* **-ries** : territoire *m*
terror [ˈtɛrər] *n* : terreur *f*
terrorism [ˈtɛrərˌɪzəm] *n* : terrorisme *m*
terrorist[1] [ˈtɛrərɪst] *adj* : terroriste
terrorist[2] *n* : terroriste *mf*
terrorize [ˈtɛrərˌaɪz] *vt* **-ized; -izing** : terroriser
terry [ˈtɛri] *n, pl* **-ries** *or* **terry cloth** : tissu *m* éponge, ratine *f* *Can*
terse [ˈtərs] *adj* **terser; tersest** : concis, succinct
tersely [ˈtərsli] *adv* : succinctement, brièvement
tertiary [ˈtərʃiˌɛri] *adj* : tertiaire
test[1] [ˈtɛst] *vt* : examiner, tester — *vi* **to test for** : faire une recherche de
test[2] *n* **1** : examen *m* (scolaire), test *m* **2** TRIAL : épreuve *f* **3** : analyse *f,* examen *m* <blood test : analyse de sang>
testament [ˈtɛstəmənt] *n* **1** WILL : testament *m* **2** : Testament *m* <the New Testament : le Nouveau Testament>
testicle [ˈtɛstɪkəl] *n* : testicule *m*
testify [ˈtɛstəˌfaɪ] *v* **-fied; -fying** : témoigner
testimonial [ˌtɛstəˈmoːniəl] *n* **1** RECOMMENDATION : recommandation *f,* attestation *f* **2** TRIBUTE : témoignage *m*
testimony [ˈtɛstəˌmoːni] *n, pl* **-nies** : témoignage *m,* déposition *f*
testy [ˈtɛsti] *adj* **testier; -est** : irritable, irascible
tetanus [ˈtɛtənəs] *n* : tétanos *m*
tête–à–tête [ˌtɛṭəˈtɛt, ˌteɪṭəˈteɪt] *n* : tête-à-tête *m*
tether[1] [ˈtɛðər] *vt* : attacher (un animal)
tether[2] *n* **1** : longe *f* **2** **at the end of one's tether** : à bout de patience
text [ˈtɛkst] *n* **1** : texte *m* **2** TOPIC : thème *m,* sujet *m* **3** → **textbook**
textbook [ˈtɛkstˌbʊk] *n* : manuel *m* scolaire
textile [ˈtɛkˌstaɪl, ˈtɛkstəl] *n* : textile *m*
textual [ˈtɛkstʃʊəl] *adj* : textuel
texture [ˈtɛkstʃər] *n* : texture *f*
Thai[1] [ˈtaɪ] *adj* : thaïlandais
Thai[2] *n* : Thaïlandais *m,* -daise *f*
than[1] [ˈðæn] *conj* : que <older than I am : plus âgé que moi> <nothing is worse than boredom : rien n'est pire que l'ennui> <he'd do anything rather than lie : il ferait tout plutôt que mentir>
than[2] *prep* : que, de <thinner than me : plus mince que moi> <fewer than 10 : moins de 10>
thank [ˈθæŋk] *vt* : remercier
thankful [ˈθæŋkfəl] *adj* : reconnaissant
thankfully [ˈθæŋkfəli] *adv* **1** GRATEFULLY : avec reconnaissance, avec gratitude **2** FORTUNATELY : heureusement
thankfulness [ˈθæŋkfəlnəs] *n* : reconnaissance *f,* gratitude *f*
thankless [ˈθæŋkləs] *adj* : ingrat
thanks [ˈθæŋks] *npl* **1** : remerciements *mpl* **2 ~ to** : grâce à
Thanksgiving [θæŋksˈgɪvɪŋ, ˈθæŋksˌ-] *n* : jour *m* d'Action de Grâces
that[1] [ˈðæt] *adv* **1** : comme ça <a nail about that long : un clou environ long comme ça> **2** VERY : tellement, très <he did not take his classes that seriously : il ne prenait pas ses cours tellement au sérieux>
that[2] *adj, pl* **those** : ce, cet, cette, ces <that girl : cette fille> <those people : ces gens-là>
that[3] *conj* **1** : que <she said that she was busy : elle a dit qu'elle était oc-

cupée> <it's unlikely that he'll be there : il y a peu de chances qu'il soit là> **2** SO : afin que <he shouted that all might hear : il a crié afin que tout le monde puisse entendre>

that[4] *pron, pl* **those** [ˈðo:z] **1** (*used to introduce relative clauses*) : que <the house that we built : la maison que nous avons construite> **2** WHO : qui <the person that won the race : la personne qui a gagné la course> **3** : celui-là, celle-là <do you prefer this or that? : préférez-vous celui-ci ou celui-là?> **4** : cela, ce, ça <is that you? : c'est toi?> <after that : après cela>

thatch[1] [ˈθætʃ] *vt* : couvrir (un toit) de chaume

thatch[2] *n* : chaume *m*

thaw[1] [ˈθɔ] *vt* : dégeler — *vi* : fondre

thaw[2] *n* : dégel *m*

the[1] [ðə, *before vowel sounds usu* ði:] *adv* : le <the sooner the better : le plus tôt sera le mieux>

the[2] *art* **1** : le, la l', les <let the cat out : laisse le chat sortir> <the right answer : la bonne réponse> <the elite : l'élite> <the English : les Anglais> **2** EACH : le, la <forty cookies the box : quarante biscuits la boîte>

theater *or* **theatre** [ˈθi:ət̬ər] *n* **1** : théâtre *m* (édifice) **2** DRAMA : théâtre *m*, art *m* dramatique **3** : théâtre *m* (de la guerre, etc.)

theatrical [θiˈætrɪkəl] *adj* : théâtral

thee [ˈði:] *pron* : te

theft [ˈθɛft] *n* : vol *m*

their [ˈðɛr] *adj* : leur <their notebooks : leurs cahiers>

theirs [ˈðɛrz] *pron* : le leur, la leur, les leurs <the red house is theirs : la maison rouge est la leur>

them [ˈðɛm] *pron* **1** (*as a direct object*) : les <in order to understand them : afin de les comprendre> **2** (*as an indirect object*) : leur <we sent them a present : nous leur avons envoyé un cadeau> **3** (*as the object of a preposition*) : eux, elles <he thought of them : il a pensé à eux> <some of them : quelques-unes d'entre elles>

theme [ˈθi:m] *n* **1** TOPIC : thème *m* **2** COMPOSITION : composition *f* **3** : thème *m* (musical)

themselves [ðəmˈsɛlvz, ðɛm-] *pron* **1** (*used reflexively*) : se <they hurt themselves : ils se sont blessés> **2** (*used for emphasis*) : eux-mêmes, elles-mêmes <they made the dresses themselves : elles ont fait les robes elles-mêmes> **3** (*used after a preposition*) : eux, elles, eux-mêmes, elles-mêmes <they talked among themselves : ils discutaient entre eux> **4** **by themselves** : tous seuls, toutes seules

then[1] [ˈðɛn] *adv* **1** : alors, à ce moment-là <from then on : à partir de ce moment-là> **2** : ensuite, puis <he answered the questions and then he left : il a répondu aux questions, puis il est parti> **3** BESIDES : et puis <then there is the interest to be paid : et puis il y a l'intérêt à payer> **4** : donc, alors <take it, then, if you want it so much : prends-le, alors, si tu le veux tant> **5** CONSEQUENTLY : donc

then[2] *adj* : d'alors, de l'époque <the then treasurer : le trésorier d'alors>

then[3] *n* : ce temps-là <since then : depuis ce temps-là>

thence [ˈðɛn*t*s, ˈθɛn*t*s] *adv* : de là

theologian [ˌθi:əˈlo:dʒən] *n* : théologien *m*, -gienne *f*

theological [ˌθi:əˈlɑdʒɪkəl] *adj* : théologique

theology [θiˈɑlədʒi] *n, pl* **-gies** : théologie *f*

theorem [ˈθi:ərəm, ˈθɪrəm] *n* : théorème *m*

theoretical [ˌθi:əˈrɛtɪkəl] *adj* : théorique — **theoretically** *adv*

theorize [ˈθi:əˌraɪz] *vi* **-rized; -rizing** : théoriser

theory [ˈθi:əri, ˈθɪri] *n, pl* **-ries** : théorie *f*

therapeutic [ˌθɛrəˈpju:tɪk] *adj* : thérapeutique — **therapeutically** *adv*

therapist [ˈθɛrəpɪst] *n* : thérapeute *mf*

therapy [ˈθɛrəpi] *n, pl* **-pies** : thérapie *f*

there[1] [ˈðær] *adv* **1** : là, là-bas, y <stand over there : mettez-vous debout là-bas> <he went there after class : il s'y est rendu après ses cours> **2** (*used for emphasis*) : voilà <there's where I disagree : voilà où je ne suis pas d'accord> <there, I'm finished! : voilà, j'ai terminé!>

there[2] *pron* **1** (*used as a function word to introduce a sentence or clause*) <there shall come a time : le jour viendra> **2** (*used as an indefinite substitute for a name*) <hi there! : salut, toi!> **3** **there is** : il y a <there's someone waiting for you : il y a quelqu'un qui t'attend>

thereabouts [ðærəˈbaʊts, ˈðærəˌ-] *or* **thereabout** [ðærəˈbaʊt, ˈðærəˌ-] *adv* **1** NEARBY : dans les environs, par là **2** : environ <a boy of 18 or thereabouts : un garçon d'environ 18 ans>

thereafter [ðærˈæftər] *adv* : par la suite

thereby [ðærˈbaɪ, ˈðærˌbaɪ] *adv* **1** THUS : ainsi <she thereby lost her chance to win : elle a ainsi perdu sa chance de gagner> **2** **thereby hangs a tale** : c'est toute une histoire

therefore [ˈðærˌfor] *adv* : donc, par conséquent

therein [ðærˈɪn] *adv* **1** : dedans, à l'intérieur <the box and the jewels therein : la boîte et les bijoux qui étaient dedans> **2** : là <therein lies the problem : là réside le problème>

thereof [ðærˈʌv, -ˈɑv] *adv* : de cela, en

thereupon [ˈðærəˌpɑn, -ˌpɔn; ˌðærəˈpɑn, -ˈpɔn] *adv* : sur ce

therewith [ðær'wɪð, -'wɪθ] *adv* : avec cela

thermal ['θərməl] *adj* : thermal, thermique <thermal spring : source thermale> <thermal power station : centrale thermique>

thermodynamics [ˌθərmodaɪ'næmɪks] *ns & pl* : thermodynamique *f*

thermometer [θər'mɑmət̬ər] *n* : thermomètre *m*

thermos ['θərməs] *n* : thermos *mf*

thermostat ['θərməˌstæt] *n* : thermostat *m*

thesaurus [θɪ'sɔrəs] *n, pl* **-sauri** [-'sɔrˌaɪ] *or* **-sauruses** [-'sɔrəsəz] : dictionnaire *m* analogique, dictionnaire *m* des synonymes

these → **this**[2], **this**[3]

thesis ['θi:sɪs] *n, pl* **theses** ['θiˌsi:z] : thèse *f*

they ['ðeɪ] *pron* **1** : ils, elles <they dance well : ils dansent bien> <there they are : les voici> **2** (*used for emphasis*) : eux, elles <*they* won't be coming : ils ne viennent pas, eux> **3** PEOPLE : on <they say she's pretty : on dit qu'elle est belle>

thiamine ['θaɪəmɪn, -ˌmi:n] *n* : thiamine *f*

thick[1] ['θɪk] *adj* **1** : épais <a thick plank : une planche épaisse> <two millimeters thick : deux millimètres d'épaisseur> **2** : dense, épais <thick fog : brume épaisse> **3** STUPID : bête, obtus **4 to be thick with** : être rempli de

thick[2] *n* **1 in the thick of** : au plus fort de (une bataille, etc.) **2 through thick and thin** : contre vents et marées

thicken ['θɪkən] *vi* : s'épaissir — *vt* : épaissir (une sauce, etc.)

thickener ['θɪkənər] *n* : épaississant *m*

thicket ['θɪkət] *n* : fourré *m*, hallier *m*

thickly ['θɪkli] *adv* **1** : en couche épaisse, en tranches épaisses **2** DENSELY : dru <snow was falling thickly : la neige tombait dru> <thickly wooded : très boisé>

thickness ['θɪknəs] *n* : épaisseur *f*, grosseur *f*

thick–skinned ['θɪk'skɪnd] *adj* : dur, insensible

thief ['θi:f] *n, pl* **thieves** ['θi:vz] : voleur *m*, -leuse *f*

thieve ['θi:v] *v* **thieved; thieving** : voler

thigh ['θaɪ] *n* : cuisse *f*

thighbone ['θaɪˌbo:n] *n* : fémur *m*

thimble ['θɪmbəl] *n* : dé *m* à coudre

thin[1] ['θɪn] *v* **thinned; thinning** *vt* : allonger, diluer (un liquide) — *vi* : se dissiper (se dit du brouillard, etc.), se disperser (se dit d'une foule) <his hair was thinning : il perdait ses cheveux>

thin[2] *adj* **thinner; thinnest 1** : fin, mince <thin paper : papier fin> **2** LEAN, SLIM : mince, maigre **3** SPARSE : clairsemé <thin hair : cheveux clairsemés> **4** : raréfié (de l'air), clair (d'un potage)

thing ['θɪŋ] *n* **1** OBJECT : chose *f*, objet *m*, truc *m fam* <a thing of beauty : une belle chose> **2** ACTIVITY, EVENT : chose *f* <the first thing to do : la première chose à faire> <it was a terrible thing : c'était une chose épouvantable> **3 things** *npl* BELONGINGS : affaires *fpl*, effets *mpl* personnels <to pack one's things : faire ses valises> <I don't have a thing to wear : je n'ai rien à me mettre>

think ['θɪŋk] *v* **thought** ['θɔt]; **thinking** *vt* **1** INTEND : penser <he thought to return early : il a pensé revenir tôt> **2** BELIEVE : penser, croire **3** PONDER : penser à, réfléchir à <to think things out : bien réfléchir> **4** REMEMBER : penser à, se rappeler <I didn't think to ask him : je n'ai pas pensé à lui demander> **5 to think up** : inventer — *vi* **1** REASON : penser, raisonner **2 to think of** CONSIDER : penser à, considérer <think of your family first : pense à ta famille en premier>

thinker ['θɪŋkər] *n* : penseur *m*, -seuse *f*

thinly ['θɪnli] *adv* **1** LIGHTLY : légèrement **2 to cut thinly** : couper en tranches minces **3 to spread thinly** : étaler en couche mince **4 thinly populated** : à la population éparse

thinness ['θɪnnəs] *n* : minceur *f*

thin–skinned ['θɪn'skɪnd] *adj* : susceptible, sensible

third[1] ['θərd] *or* **thirdly** [-li] *adv* : troisième, troisièmement, en troisième place

third[2] *adj* : troisième

third[3] *n* **1** : troisième *mf* (dans une série) **2** : troisième *m* (en mathématiques) **3** (*used in dates*) <the third of December : le trois décembre>

Third World *n* : le tiers-monde *m*

thirst[1] ['θərst] *vi* **to thirst for** : avoir soif de

thirst[2] *n* : soif *f*

thirsty ['θərsti] *adj* **thirstier; -est** : assoiffé

thirteen[1] [ˌθər'ti:n] *adj* : treize

thirteen[2] *n* : treize *m*

thirteenth[1] [ˌθər'ti:nθ] *adj* : treizième

thirteenth[2] *n* **1** : treizième *mf* (dans une série) **2** : treizième *m* (en mathématiques) **3** (*used in dates*) <the thirteenth of January : le treize janvier>

thirtieth[1] ['θərt̬iəθ] *adj* : trentième

thirtieth[2] *n* **1** : trentième *mf* (dans une série) **2** : trentième *m* (en mathématiques)

thirty[1] ['θərt̬i] *adj* : trente

thirty[2] *n, pl* **thirties** : trente *m*

this[1] ['ðɪs] *adv* : si, aussi <it was this big : c'était aussi grand que ça>

this[2] *adj, pl* **these** ['ði:z] : ce, cet, cette, ces <this morning : ce matin> <all these years : toutes ces années> **2** : ce . . . -ci, cet . . . -ci, cette . . . -ci, ces . . . -ci <this car or that one : cette voiture-ci ou celle-là>
this[3] *pron, pl* **these 1** : voici <this is your book : voici ton livre> **2** : ce, ceci <who is this? : qui est-ce?> <after this, he left : après ceci, il est parti> <this is my sister : je vous présente ma sœur>
thistle ['θɪsəl] *n* : chardon *m*
thong ['θɔŋ] *n* : lanière *f* (de cuir, etc.)
thorax ['θor,æks] *n, pl* **-raxes** *or* **-races** ['θorə,si:z] : thorax *m*
thorn ['θɔrn] *n* : épine *f*
thorny ['θɔrni] *adj* **thornier; -est** : épineux
thorough ['θə,ro:] *adj* **1** COMPLETE : approfondi **2** PAINSTAKING : consciencieux, minutieux
thoroughbred ['θəro,brɛd] *adj* : de pure race
Thoroughbred *n* : pur-sang *m*
thoroughfare ['θəro,fær] *n* : voie *f* de communication, rue *f*
thoroughly ['θəroli] *adv* **1** METICULOUSLY : minutieusement, à fond **2** COMPLETELY : tout à fait, absolument
those → **that**[2], **that**[4]
thou ['ðaʊ] *pron* : tu
though[1] ['ðo:] *adv* HOWEVER : cependant, pourtant
though[2] *conj* : bien que, quoique
thought[1] ['θɔt] → **think**
thought[2] *n* **1** THINKING : pensée *f* <Western thought : la pensée de l'Ouest> **2** CONSIDERATION : réflexion *f* <after much thought : après mûre réflexion> **3** IDEA : pensée *f*, idée *f*
thoughtful ['θɔtfəl] *adj* **1** PENSIVE : pensif, songeur **2** CONSIDERATE : attentionné, prévenant **3** REASONED : réfléchi, sérieux <a thoughtful essay : une composition réfléchie>
thoughtfully ['θɔtfəli] *adv* **1** PENSIVELY : pensivement **2** CONSIDERATELY : avec prévenance **3** REFLECTIVELY : de façon réfléchie
thoughtfulness ['θɔtfəlnəs] *n* : considération *f*, attention *f*
thoughtless ['θɔtləs] *adj* **1** RASH : irréfléchi, hâtif **2** INCONSIDERATE : irréfléchi, inconsidéré
thoughtlessly ['θɔtləsli] *adv* : inconsidérément
thousand[1] ['θaʊzənd] *adj* : mille
thousand[2] *n, pl* **-sands** *or* **-sand** : mille *m* <two thousand : deux mille>
thousandth[1] ['θaʊzəntθ] *adj* : millième
thousandth[2] *n* **1** : millième *mf* (dans une série) **2** : millième *m* (en mathématiques)
thrash ['θræʃ] *vt* **1** THRESH : battre (le grain) **2** BEAT : battre — *vi or* **to thrash about** : se débattre
thread[1] *vt* **1** : enfiler (une aiguille, des perles) **2 to thread one's way through** : se faufiler entre
thread[2] ['θrɛd] *n* **1** : fil *m* (en couture) **2** : fil *m*, cours *m* <the thread of the story : le fil de l'histoire> **3** TRICKLE, WISP : filet *m* <a thread of smoke : un filet de fumée>
threadbare ['θrɛd'bær] *adj* **1** WORN : usé jusqu'à la corde, élimé **2** TRITE : usé, banal
threat ['θrɛt] *n* : menace *f*
threaten ['θrɛtən] *vt* : menacer
threateningly ['θrɛtənɪŋli] *adv* : de façon menaçante
three[1] ['θri:] *adj* : trois
three[2] *n* : trois *m*
threefold[1] ['θri:,fo:ld] *adv* : trois fois autant
threefold[2] *adj* : triple
threescore ['θri:'skor] *adj* : soixante
thresh ['θrɛʃ] *vt* : battre (le grain)
thresher ['θrɛʃər] *n or* **threshing machine** : batteuse *f*
threshold ['θrɛʃ,ho:ld, -,o:ld] *n* : seuil *m*
threw → **throw**[1]
thrice ['θraɪs] *adv* : trois fois
thrift ['θrɪft] *n* : économie *f*
thriftless ['θrɪftləs] *adj* : dépensier
thrifty ['θrɪfti] *adj* **thriftier; -est** : économe
thrill[1] ['θrɪl] *vt* : électriser, transporter (d'émotion) — *vi* : frissonner
thrill[2] *n* : frisson *m*, émotion *f*
thriller ['θrɪlər] *n* : thriller *m*, roman *m* ou film *m* à suspens
thrive ['θraɪv] *vi* **throve** ['θro:v] *or* **thrived; thriven** ['θrɪvən] **1** FLOURISH : bien pousser, bien se porter **2** PROSPER : prospérer, réussir
throat ['θro:t] *n* : gorge *f* <sore throat : mal de gorge> <to clear one's throat : s'éclaircir la voix>
throaty ['θro:ṭi] *adj* **throatier; -est** : rauque, guttural
throb[1] ['θrɑb] *vi* **throbbed; throbbing 1** PALPITATE : battre, palpiter (se dit du cœur) **2** : vibrer (se dit d'un moteur) **3 to throb with pain** : lanciner <my head was throbbing : j'avais mal à la tête>
throb[2] *n* **1** BEAT : battement *m*, pulsation *f* (cardiaque) **2** VIBRATION : vibration *f*, vrombissement *m* (d'un moteur, etc.) **3** : élancement *m* <a throb of pain : un élancement de douleur>
throe ['θro:] *n* **1** PANG : agonie *f* <the throes of childbirth : les douleurs de l'enfantement> **2 in the throes of** : en proie à
throne ['θro:n] *n* : trône *m*
throng[1] ['θrɔŋ] *vt* CROWD : se presser dans, remplir — *vi* : se presser
throng[2] *n* : foule *f*

throttle[1] ['θrɑtəl] *vt* **-tled; -tling 1** CHOKE : étrangler **2 to throttle down** : mettre au ralenti (un moteur)

throttle[2] *n* **1** : accélérateur *m* (d'une voiture) **2** *or* **throttle valve** : papillon *m* des gaz

through[1] ['θru:] *adv* **1** : à travers, d'un côte à l'autre <let me through : laissez-moi passer> **2** : d'un trait, jusqu'au bout <I read the book through : j'ai lu le livre d'un trait> **3** THOROUGHLY : complètement <soaked through : complètement mouillé>

through[2] *adj* **1** DIRECT : direct <a through road : une route directe> **2** : en transit <through traffic : trafic en transit> **3** FINISHED : fini, terminé <are you through? : as-tu fini?>

through[3] *prep* **1** (*indicating movement from one side to the other*) : à travers <the bullet went right through his arm : la balle lui a transpercé le bras> **2** (*indicating passage*) : par <he got in through the window : il est rentré par la fenêtre> <she went through a red light : elle a brûlé un feu rouge> **3** (*indicating a period of time*) <through the whole night : pendant toute la nuit> <from Monday through Friday : du lundi au vendredi)

throughout[1] [θru:'aʊt] *adv* **1** EVERYWHERE : partout <one color throughout : d'une seule couleur> **2** : toujours <he remained loyal throughout : il est toujours demeuré fidèle>

throughout[2] *prep* **1** : partout dans <he traveled throughout the country : il voyageait partout dans le pays> **2** : tout au long de <throughout her life : tout au long de sa vie>

throve → **thrive**

throw[1] ['θro:] *vt* **threw** ['θru:]; **thrown** ['θro:n]; **throwing 1** : lancer <to throw a ball : lancer une balle> **2** *or* **to throw down** : jeter à terre, envoyer au tapis **3** CAST : jeter, projeter <she threw her arms around him : elle s'est jetée à son cou> <to throw a shadow : projeter une ombre> **4 to throw a party** : organiser une fête **5 to throw a tantrum** : piquer une crise **6 to throw sth into confusion** : semer la confusion dans qqch **7 to throw away, to throw out** : jeter

throw[2] *n* TOSS : lancer *m*, jet *m*

thrower ['θro:ər] *n* : lanceur *m*, -ceuse *f*

throw up *vt* : vomir, renvoyer *Can fam*, restituer *Can fam*

thrush ['θrʌʃ] *n* : grive *f* (oiseau)

thrust[1] ['θrʌst] *vt* **thrust; thrusting 1** SHOVE : pousser violemment **2** PLUNGE, STAB : enfoncer, planter **3 to thrust upon** : imposer à

thrust[2] *n* **1** PUSH : poussée *f* **2** STAB : coup *m* (de couteau, d'épée, etc.) **3** AIM, POINT : portée *f*, sens *m* (d'un argument, etc.)

thud[1] ['θʌd] *vi* **thudded; thudding** : faire un bruit sourd

thud[2] *n* : bruit *m* sourd

thug ['θʌg] *n* : voyou *m*

thumb[1] ['θʌm] *vt or* **to thumb through** : feuilleter (un livre, etc.)

thumb[2] *n* : pouce *m*

thumbnail ['θʌm,neɪl] *n* : ongle *m* du pouce

thumbtack ['θʌm,tæk] *n* : punaise *f*

thump[1] ['θʌmp] *vt* POUND : cogner à, frapper sur — *vi* : battre fort (se dit du cœur)

thump[2] *n* **1** BLOW : coup *m* **2** THUD : bruit *m* sourd

thunder[1] ['θʌndər] *vi* **1** : tonner <it was thundering : il tonnait> **2** BOOM, RESOUND : gronder, retentir — *vt* ROAR : vociférer <they thundered their disapproval : ils ont vociféré leur désaccord>

thunder[2] *n* **1** : tonnerre *m* **2** RUMBLE : tonnerre *m*, bruit *m* assourdissant

thunderbolt ['θʌndər,bo:lt] *n* : foudre *f*

thunderclap ['θʌndər,klæp] *n* : coup *m* de tonnerre

thunderous ['θəndərəs] *adj* : étourdissant <thunderous applause : un tonnerre d'applaudissements>

thundershower ['θʌndər,ʃaʊər] → **thunderstorm**

thunderstorm ['θʌndər,storm] *n* : orage *m*

thunderstruck ['θʌndər,strʌk] *adj* : abasourdi, stupéfié

Thursday ['θərz,deɪ, -di] *n* : jeudi *m*

thus ['ðʌs] *adv* **1** SO : ainsi, donc, par conséquent **2 thus far** : jusqu'à présent, jusqu'ici

thwart ['θwɔrt] *vt* : contrecarrer, contrarier

thy ['ðaɪ] *adj* : ton, ta, tes

thyme ['taɪm, 'θaɪm] *n* : thym *m*

thyroid ['θaɪ,rɔɪd] *n or* **thyroid gland** : thyroïde *f*

thyself [ðaɪ'sɛlf] *pron* : toi-même

tiara [ti'ærə, -'ɑr-] *n* : diadème *m*

Tibetan[1] [tə'bɛtən] *adj* : tibétain

Tibetan[2] *n* **1** : Tibétain *m*, -taine *f* **2** : tibétain *m* (langue)

tibia ['tɪbiə] *n, pl* **-iae** [-bi,i:] : tibia *m*

tic ['tɪk] *n* : tic *m* (nerveux)

tick[1] ['tɪk] *vi* **1** : faire tic-tac (se dit d'une horloge) **2** OPERATE, RUN : tourner (se dit d'un moteur) — *vt or* **to tick off** CHECK : cocher, marquer

tick[2] *n* **1** : tique *f* (insecte) **2** : tic-tac *m* (d'une horloge) **3** CHECK : coche *f*

ticket[1] ['tɪkət] *vt* **1** LABEL : étiqueter **2** : donner une contravention à (un automobiliste)

ticket[2] *n* **1** TAG : étiquette *f* **2** : billet *m*, ticket *m* <bus ticket : billet d'autobus> **3** : contravention *f* <a speeding ticket : une contravention pour

excès de vitesse> **4** SLATE : liste *f* (électorale)
tickle[1] [ˈtɪkəl] *v* **-led; -ling** *vt* **1** : chatouiller <don't tickle my feet : ne me chatouillez pas les pieds> **2** PLEASE : chatouiller, émouvoir **3** AMUSE : amuser — *vi* : chatouiller, piquer
tickle[2] *n* : chatouillement *m*
ticklish [ˈtɪkəlɪʃ] *adj* **1** : chatouilleux **2** DELICATE, TRICKY : épineux, délicat
tidal [ˈtaɪdəl] *adj* : des marées
tidal wave *n* : raz-de-marée *m*
tidbit [ˈtɪdˌbɪt] *n* **1** : détail *m* intéressant **2** DELICACY : gâterie *f*
tide[1] [ˈtaɪd] *vt* **tided; tiding** *or* **to tide over** : dépanner
tide[2] *n* : marée *f*
tidewater [ˈtaɪdˌwɔt̬ər, -ˌwɑ-] *n* : eaux *nfpl* de marée
tidiness [ˈtaɪdinəs] *n* : ordre *m,* propreté *f*
tidings [ˈtaɪdɪŋz] *npl* : nouvelles *fpl* <good tidings : de bonnes nouvelles>
tidy[1] [ˈtaɪdi] *vt or* **to tidy up** : ranger — *vi or* **to tidy up** : tout ranger, faire du rangement
tidy[2] *adj* **tidier; -est 1** NEAT : bien rangé, propre **2** LARGE : joli *fam,* coquet *fam* <a tidy sum : une jolie somme>
tie[1] [ˈtaɪ] *v* **tied; tying** *or* **tieing** *vt* **1** : attacher, rouer <tie your shoelaces : attache tes lacets> **2** CONNECT : unir, lier — *vi* **1** FASTEN : s'attacher, se nouer **2** : faire match nul, être ex æquo <to tie for third place : être troisième ex æquo>
tie[2] *n* **1** FASTENER : attache *f* **2** *or* **railroad tie** : traverse *f* **3** BOND : lien *m,* nœud *m* <family ties : liens familiaux> **4** : match *m* nul, égalité *f* (aux sports) **5** NECKTIE : cravate *f*
tier [ˈtɪr] *n* : étage *m* (d'un gâteau), gradin *m* (au théâtre)
tiff [ˈtɪf] *n* : chicane *f,* dispute *f*
tiger [ˈtaɪgər] *n* : tigre *m*
tight[1] [ˈtaɪt] *adv* **1** TIGHTLY : bien, fermement <is the door shut tight? : la porte est-elle bien fermée?> <hold on tight : tenez-vous bien> **2** DEEPLY : profondément <to sleep tight : dormir profondément>
tight[2] *adj* **1** : étanche, hermétique <a tight seal : une fermeture étanche> **2** SNUG : serré, étriqué **3** TAUT : tendu, raide **4** DIFFICULT : difficile <to be in a tight spot : être dans une situation difficile> **5** STINGY : avare **6** CLOSE : serré <a tight game : un match serré> **7** SCARCE : juste, serré <money is a bit tight : les finances sont un peu justes>
tighten [ˈtaɪtən] *vt* : serrer, resserrer
tightly [ˈtaɪtli] *adv* : fermement, bien
tightness [ˈtaɪtnəs] *n* **1** : étroitesse *f* (d'un vêtement, etc.) **2** STRICTNESS : sévérite *f,* rigueur *f* **3** TAUTNESS : tension *f,* raideur *f*
tightrope [ˈtaɪtˌroːp] *n* : corde *f* raide
tights [ˈtaɪts] *npl* : collants *mpl*
tightwad [ˈtaɪtˌwɑd] *n* : grippe-sou *mf fam*
tigress [ˈtaɪgrəs] *n* : tigresse *f*
tile[1] [ˈtaɪl] *vt* **tiled; tiling** : poser des tuiles sur, carreler
tile[2] *n* : tuile *f*
till[1] [ˈtɪl] *vt* : labourer
till[2] *n* : tiroir-caisse *m*
till[3] *conj & prep* → **until**
tiller [ˈtɪlər] *n* **1** : cultivateur *m,* -trice *f* **2** : barre *f,* gouvernail *m* (d'un bateau)
tilt[1] [ˈtɪlt] *vt* SLANT : pencher, incliner — *vi* : se pencher, s'incliner
tilt[2] *n* **1** SLOPE : inclinaison *f* **2 at full tilt** : à toute vitesse
timber [ˈtɪmbər] *n* **1** : bois *m* de construction **2** BEAM : poutre *f,* madrier *m*
timberland [ˈtɪmbərˌlænd] *n* : terrain *m* forestier (exploitable)
timbre [ˈtæmbər, ˈtɪm-] *n* : timbre *m* (de la voix)
time[1] [ˈtaɪm] *vt* **timed; timing 1** SCHEDULE : prévoir, fixer **2** : minuter, chronométrer <to time a race : chronométrer une course>
time[2] *n* **1** : temps *m* <it's a matter of time : c'est une question de temps> <to find time for : trouver du temps pour> <time flies : le temps passe vite> **2** OCCASION : temps *m,* occasion *f* **3** AGE : époque *f,* temps *m* **4** TEMPO : mesure *f,* rythme *m* **5** : heure *f* <what time is it? : quelle heure est-il?> <she arrived on time : elle est arrivée à l'heure> <on company time : pendant les heures de travail> **6** : temps *m* (de l'année) <it's very hot for this time of year : il fait très chaud pour la saison> **7** PERIOD : moment *m,* période *f* <hard times : des moments difficiles> **8 times** *npl* : fois *f* <you've told me several times : tu me l'as dit plusieurs fois> **9 at times** : parfois **10 for the time being** : pour le moment **11 from time to time** : de temps à autre **12 time and time again** : maintes et maintes fois
timekeeper [ˈtaɪmˌkiːpər] *n* : chronométreur *m,* -treuse *f*
timeless [ˈtaɪmləs] *adj* : éternel
timely [ˈtaɪmli] *adv* : opportun, propice
timepiece [ˈtaɪmˌpiːs] *n* : montre *f,* horloge *f*
timer [ˈtaɪmər] *n* **1** TIMEKEEPER : chronométreur *m,* -treuse *f* **2** STOPWATCH : chronomètre *m* **3** : minuteur *m* (en cuisine)
times [ˈtaɪmz] *prep* : fois (en mathématiques) <seven times two is fourteen : sept fois deux font quatorze>
timetable [ˈtaɪmˌteɪbəl] *n* **1** : horaire *m* (de trains, d'autobus, etc.) **2** SCHEDULE : programme *m,* horaire *m*

timid ['tɪmɪd] *adj* : timide — **timidly** *adv*

timidity [tə'mɪdəti] *n* : timidité *f*

timorous ['tɪmərəs] *adj* FEARFUL : timoré

timpani ['tɪmpəni] *npl* : timbales *fpl*

tin ['tɪn] *n* **1** : étain *m* (métal) **2** *or* **tin can** : boîte *f* de conserve

tincture ['tɪŋktʃər] *n* : teinture *f*

tinder ['tɪndər] *n* : amadou *m,* petit bois *m*

tine ['taɪn] *n* : dent *f* (d'une fourchette, etc.)

tinfoil ['tɪn,fɔɪl] *n* : papier *m* d'aluminium

tinge[1] ['tɪndʒ] *vt* **tinged; tingeing** *or* **tinging** ['tɪndʒɪŋ] : teinter

tinge[2] *n* : teinte *f,* nuance *f*

tingle[1] ['tɪŋgəl] *vi* **-gled; -gling** : picoter, fourmiller

tingle[2] *n* : picotement *m*

tinker ['tɪŋkər] *vi* : bricoler

tinkle[1] ['tɪŋkəl] *v* **-kled; -kling** *vi* : tinter, sonner — *vt* : faire tinter

tinkle[2] *n* : tintement *m*

tinsel ['tɪntsəl] *n* : guirlandes *fpl* (de Noël)

tint[1] ['tɪnt] *vt* : teinter

tint[2] *n* : teinte *f,* nuance *f*

tiny ['taɪni] *adj* **tinier; -est** : minuscule, tout petit

tip[1] ['tɪp] *v* **tipped; tipping** *vt* **1** : mettre un embout à (une canne, etc.) **2** OVERTURN : chavirer, renverser **3** TILT : pencher, incliner **4** : donner un pourboire à (un serveur) **5 to tip off** : donner un tuyau à, renseigner — *vi* TILT : pencher, basculer

tip[2] *n* **1** END : pointe *f,* bout *m* (d'un crayon) <the tip of the island : la pointe de l'île> **2** GRATUITY : pourboire *m* **3** INFORMATION : conseil *m,* tuyau *m fam*

tip–off ['tɪp,ɔf] *n* : tuyau *m fam*

tipple ['tɪpəl] *vi* **-pled; -pling** : prendre un coup *fam,* picoler *fam*

tipsy ['tɪpsi] *adj* **tipsier; -est** : pompette *fam,* éméché *fam*

tiptoe[1] ['tɪp,to:] *vi* **-toed; -toeing** : marcher sur la pointe des pieds

tiptoe[2] *n* **on ~** : sur la pointe des pieds

tip–top[1] ['tɪp,to:] *adj* : excellent <in tiptop shape : en excellente forme>

tip–top[2] *n* : sommet *m,* haut *m*

tirade ['taɪ,reɪd] *n* : tirade *f,* diatribe *f*

tire[1] ['taɪr] *v* **tired; tiring** *vt* **1** FATIGUE : fatiguer **2** BORE : fatiguer, lasser — *vi* : se fatiguer

tire[2] *n* : pneu *m*

tired ['taɪrd] *adj* : fatigué, las

tireless ['taɪrləs] *adj* : infatigable, inlassable

tirelessly ['taɪrləsli] *adv* : infatigablement, sans relâche

tiresome ['taɪrsəm] *adj* : ennuyeux, fastidieux, agaçant

tiresomely ['taɪrsəmli] *adv* : fastidieusement, de façon agaçante

tissue ['tɪ,ʃu:] *n* **1** : mouchoir *m* en papier, papier *m* mouchoir *Can* **2** : tissu *m* (en biologie)

titanic [taɪ'tænɪk, tə-] *adj* : titanesque, colossal

titanium [taɪ'teɪniəm, tə-] *n* : titane *m*

titillate ['tɪtəl,eɪt] *vt* **-lated; -lating** : titiller

title[1] ['taɪtəl] **-tled; -tling** *vt* : intituler

title[2] *n* : titre *m*

titter[1] ['tɪtər] *vi* : rire nerveusement

titter[2] *n* : petit rire *m* nerveux

tizzy ['tɪzi] *n, pl* **tizzies** : panique *f,* agitation *f* <to be in a tizzy : être dans tous ses états>

TNT [,ti:,en'ti:] *n* : TNT *m*

to[1] ['tu:] *adv* **1 to come to** : reprendre connaissance **2 to run to and fro** : aller et venir

to[2] *prep* **1** (*indicating movement or direction*) : à, en <I walk to school : je vais à l'école à pied> <we drove to town : nous sommes allés en ville en voiture> **2** TOWARD : vers <his back was turned to the door : il avait le dos tourné vers la porte> **3** AGAINST, ON : sur <she put her hand to her heart : elle a placé sa main sur son cœur> **4** (*indicating intent*) : à <he came to our aid : il est venu à notre aide> **5** (*indicating a point or position*) : à, de <100 miles to the nearest town : à 100 milles de la ville la plus proche> <perpendicular to the floor : perpendiculaire au plancher> **6** (*in expressions of time*) : moins <five minutes to five : cinq heures moins cinq> **7** UNTIL : à, jusqu'à <from Monday to Friday : du lundi au vendredi> **8** FOR : de, pour <the key to the door : la clé de la porte> **9** (*indicating comparison or proportion*) : à <similar to that one : semblable à celui-là> <we won ten to six : nous avons gagné dix à six> **10** (*indicating agreement or conformity*) : à <add salt to taste : salez au goût> <to my knowledge : à ma connaissance> **11** (*used to form the infinitive*) <I like to swim : j'aime nager> <he wants to go there : il veut y aller>

toad ['to:d] *n* : crapaud *m*

toadstool ['to:d,stu:l] *n* : champignon *m* vénéneux

toady ['to:di] *n, pl* **toadies** : flagorneur *m,* -neuse *f;* flatteur *m,* -teuse *f*

toast[1] ['to:st] *vt* **1** : griller (du pain), toaster *Can* **2** : boire à la santé de (un invité) — *vi* WARM : chauffer <to toast oneself : se réchauffer>

toast[2] *n* **1** : toast *m,* pain *m* grillé, rôtie *f* **2** : toast *m* <to drink a toast to : porter un toast à>

toaster ['to:stər] *n* : grille-pain *m*

tobacco [tə'bæ,ko:] *n, pl* **-cos** : tabac *m*

toboggan[1] [tə'bɑgən] *vi* : faire du toboggan

toboggan[2] *n* : toboggan *m,* traîne *f Can*

today[1] [təˈdeɪ] *adv* **1** : aujourd'hui **2** NOWADAYS : de nos jours

today[2] *n* : aujourd'hui *m*

toddle [ˈtɑdəl] *vi* **-dled; -dling** : marcher d'un pas chancelant

toddler [ˈtɑdələr] *n* : bambin *m,* -bine *f*

to–do [təˈduː] *n, pl* **to–dos** [-ˈduːz] FUSS : agitation *f,* remue-ménage *m*

toe [ˈtoː] *n* : orteil *m,* doigt *m* de pied

toenail [ˈtoːˌneɪl] *n* : ongle *m* d'orteil

toffee [ˈtɔfi, ˈtɑ-] *n, pl* **toffees** : caramel *m*

toga [ˈtoːgə] *n* : toge *f*

together [təˈgɛðər] *adv* **1** : ensemble <let's go together : allons-y ensemble> **2** SIMULTANEOUSLY : en même temps, simultanément **3 together with** : ainsi que, avec, en même temps que

togetherness [təˈgɛðərnəs] *n* : unité *f,* camaraderie *f*

Togolese[1] [ˌtoːgəˈliːz, -ˈliːs] *adj* : togolais

Togolese[2] *n* : Togolais *m,* -laise *f*

togs [ˈtɑgz, ˈtɔgz] *npl* : fringues *fpl fam*

toil[1] [ˈtɔɪl] *vi* **1** : travailler dur, peiner **2** PLOD : marcher péniblement

toil[2] *n* : labeur *m,* dur travail *m*

toilet [ˈtɔɪlət] *n* **1** DRESSING, GROOMING : toilette *f* **2** BATHROOM : toilettes *fpl,* toilette *f Can* <to go to the toilet : aller aux toilettes>

toilet paper *n* : papier *m* hygiénique

token [ˈtoːkən] *n* **1** SIGN, SYMBOL : signe *m,* marque *f,* témoignage *m* <as a token of our friendship : en signe de notre amitié> **2** : jeton *m* <subway token : jeton de métro>

told → **tell**

tolerable [ˈtɑlərəbəl] *adj* **1** : tolérable, supportable <tolerable pain : douleur tolérable> **2** PASSABLE : pas (trop) mal, acceptable

tolerably [ˈtɑlərəbli] *adv* : passablement, acceptablement

tolerance [ˈtɑlərənts] *n* **1** ENDURANCE : tolérance *f* <to have a high tolerance for pain : tolérer bien la douleur> **2** OPEN-MINDEDNESS : tolérance *f,* indulgence *f*

tolerant [ˈtɑlərənt] *adj* : tolérant, libéral

tolerantly [ˈtɑlərəntli] *adv* : avec tolérance

tolerate [ˈtɑləˌreɪt] *vt* **-ated; -ating** : tolérer

toleration [ˌtɑləˈreɪʃən] *n* : tolérance *f*

toll[1] [ˈtoːl] *vt* : sonner (une cloche) — *vi* : sonner

toll[2] *n* **1** : péage *m* (sur une autoroute) **2 death toll** : nombre *m* de victimes **3 to take its toll** : avoir des conséquences néfastes

tollbooth [ˈtoːlˌbuːθ] *n* : poste *m* de péage

tollgate [ˈtoːlˌgeɪt] *n* : barrière *f* de péage

tomahawk [ˈtɑməˌhɔk] *n* : tomahawk *m*

tomato [təˈmeɪṭo, -ˈmɑ-] *n, pl* **-toes** : tomate *f*

tomb [ˈtuːm] *n* : tombeau *m,* tombe *f*

tomboy [ˈtɑmˌbɔɪ] *n* : garçon *m* manqué

tombstone [ˈtuːmˌstoːn] *n* : pierre *f* tombale

tomcat [ˈtɑmˌkæt] *n* : matou *m*

tome [ˈtoːm] *n* : gros volume *m*

tomorrow[1] [təˈmɑro] *adv* : demain

tomorrow[2] *n* : demain *m*

tom–tom [ˈtɑmˌtɑm] *n* : tam-tam *m*

ton [ˈtən] *n* : tonne *f*

tonality [toˈnæləṭi] *n* : tonalité *f*

tone[1] [ˈtoːn] *vt* **toned; toning** *or* **to tone down** : atténuer

tone[2] *n* **1** : sonorité *f,* ton *m* (en musique) **2** : ton *m,* intonation *f* <in a friendly tone : d'un ton chaleureux> <to speak in low tones : parler d'une voix basse>

tongs [ˈtɑŋz, ˈtɔŋz] *npl* : pinces *fpl,* pincettes *fpl*

tongue [ˈtʌŋ] *n* **1** : langue *f* (de la bouche) **2** LANGUAGE : langue *f* <mother tongue : langue maternelle> **3** FLAP : languette *f* (d'un soulier)

tongue–tied [ˈtʌŋˌtaɪd] *adj* **1** : muet **2 to get tongue–tied** : ne plus savoir que dire

tonic[1] [ˈtɑnɪk] *adj* : tonique

tonic[2] *n* : tonique *m*

tonight[1] [təˈnaɪt] *adv* : ce soir

tonight[2] *n* : ce soir, cette nuit <tonight's party : la fête de ce soir>

tonsil [ˈtɑntsəl] *n* : amygdale *f*

tonsillitis [ˌtɑntsəˈlaɪṭəs] *n* : amygdalite *f*

too [ˈtuː] *adv* **1** ALSO, BESIDES : aussi **2** VERY : très <he didn't seem too interested : il ne semblait pas très intéressé> <not too bad : pas trop mal>

took → **take**[1]

tool[1] [ˈtuːl] *vt* : travailler, ouvrager

tool[2] *n* : outil *m,* instrument *m*

toolbox [ˈtuːlˌbɑks] *n* : boîte *f* à outils

toot[1] [ˈtuːt] *vi* : klaxonner (se dit d'une voiture), siffler (se dit d'un train) — *vt* **to toot one's horn** : donner un coup de klaxon

toot[2] *n* : coup *m* de klaxon, coup *m* de sifflet

tooth [ˈtuːθ] *n, pl* **teeth** [ˈtiːθ] **1** : dent *f* <to brush one's teeth : se brosser les dents> **2** : dent *f* (d'un peigne, d'une roue, etc.)

toothache [ˈtuːθˌeɪk] *n* : mal *m* de dents

toothbrush [ˈtuːθˌbrʌʃ] *n* : brosse *f* à dents

toothless [ˈtuːθləs] *adj* : édenté, sans dents

toothpaste [ˈtuːθˌpeɪst] *n* : dentifrice *m*

toothpick [ˈtuːθˌpɪk] *n* : cure-dents *m*

top[1] [ˈtɑp] *vt* **topped; topping 1** CAP, CROWN : couvrir, recouvrir **2** SURPASS : dépasser, surpasser **3** HEAD : être en tête de (une liste, etc.)

top[2] *adj* **1** : dernier <the top floor : le dernier étage> **2** CHIEF, LEADING : premier, prinicipal, de tête

top[3] *n* **1** SUMMIT : haut *m,* cime *f,* tête *f* <at the top of one's class : à la tête de sa classe> **2** : dessus *m* <the top of the table : le dessus de la table> **3** LID : couvercle *m* **4** : toupie *f* (jouet) **5 on top of** : sur

topaz ['toː,pæz] *n* : topaze *f*

topcoat ['tɑp,koːt] *n* : pardessus *m*

topic ['tɑpɪk] *n* : sujet *m,* thème *m*

topical ['tɑpɪkəl] *adj* **1** LOCAL : à usage local (en médecine) **2** CURRENT : d'actualité

topmost ['tɑp,moːst] *adj* : le plus haut

top–notch ['tɑp'nɑtʃ] *adj* : excellent, de premier ordre

topographic [,tɑpə'græfɪk] *or* **topographical** [-fɪkəl] *adj* : topographique

topography [tə'pɑgrəfi] *n* : topographie *f*

topple ['tɑpəl] *v* **-pled; -pling** *vt* : renverser, faire tomber — *vi or* **to topple over** : basculer, se renverser

topsy–turvy [,tɑpsi'tərvi] *adv & adj* : sens dessus dessous, à l'envers

torch ['tɔrtʃ] *n* : torche *f,* flambeau *m*

tore → **tear**[1]

torment[1] ['tɔr,mɛnt, tɔr'-] *vt* : tourmenter, torturer

torment[2] ['tɔr,mɛnt] *n* : tourment *m,* supplice *m*

tormentor ['tɔr,mɛntər, tɔr'-] *n* : persécuteur *m,* -trice *f;* bourreau *m*

torn → **tear**[1]

tornado [tɔr'neɪdo] *n, pl* **-does** *or* **-dos** : tornade *f*

torpedo[1] [tɔr'piːdo] *vt* : torpiller

torpedo[2] *n, pl* **-does** : torpille *f*

torpid ['tɔrpɪd] *adj* : léthargique, torpide, engourdi

torpor ['tɔrpər] *n* : torpeur *f,* léthargie *f*

torrent ['tɔrənt] *n* : torrent *m*

torrential [tɔ'rɛntʃəl, tə-] *adj* : torrentiel

torrid ['tɔrɪd] *adj* : torride

torso ['tɔr,soː] *n, pl* **-sos** *or* **-si** [-,siː] : torse *m*

tortilla [tɔr'tiːjə] *n* : tortilla *f*

tortoise ['tɔrtəs] *n* : tortue *f*

tortoiseshell ['tɔrtəs,ʃɛl] *n* : écaille *f*

tortuous ['tɔrtʃʊəs] *adj* : tortueux

torture[1] ['tɔrtʃər] *vt* **-tured; -turing** : torturer

torture[2] *n* : torture *f*

torturer ['tɔrtʃərər] *n* : tortionnaire *mf*

toss[1] ['tɔs, 'tɑs] *vt* **1** THROW : lancer, jeter **2** *or* **to toss about** AGITATE : ballotter, secouer **3 to toss a coin** : jouer à pile ou face — *vi* **to toss and turn** : s'agiter, se tourner et se retourner

toss[2] *n* THROW : lancer *m,* lancement *m*

toss–up ['tɔs,ʌp] *n* : chances *fpl* égales

tot ['tɑt] *n* : petit enfant *m*

total[1] ['toːtəl] *vt* **-taled** *or* **-talled; -taling** *or* **-talling** : totaliser

total[2] *adj* : total

total[3] *n* : total *m*

totalitarian [,toː,tælə'tɛriən] *adj* : totalitaire

totalitarianism [,toː,tælə'tɛriə,nɪzəm] *n* : totalitarisme *m*

totality [to'tæləṭi] *n, pl* **-ties** : totalité *f*

totally ['toːtəli] *adv* : totalement, entièrement, complètement

tote ['toːt] *vt* **toted; toting** : porter, transporter

totem ['toːtəm] *n* : totem *m*

totter ['tɑtər] *vi* : chanceler, tituber

touch[1] ['tʌtʃ] *vt* **1** FEEL, HANDLE : toucher **2** : toucher à <he never touches alcohol : il ne touche jamais à l'alcool> **3** HARM : toucher **4** AFFECT, MOVE : émouvoir, toucher — *vi* : se toucher, être en contact

touch[2] *n* **1** : toucher *m* (sens) **2** FEEL : toucher *m* <soft to the touch : doux au toucher> **3** DETAIL : touche *f* <a touch of color : une touche de couleur> **4** HINT, TRACE : touche *f,* pointe *f* **5** CONTACT : contact *m* <to keep in touch with : rester en contact avec>

touchdown ['tʌtʃ,daʊn] *n* **1** : atterrissage *m* (d'un avion) **2** : but *m* (au football américain)

touch up *vt* : faire des retouches à, retoucher

touchy ['tʌtʃi] *adj* **touchier; -est 1** : susceptible (se dit des personnes) **2** : délicat, épineux <a touchy subject : un sujet épineux>

tough[1] ['tʌf] *adj* **1** HARDY : robuste, résistant **2** : dur, coriace (se dit de la viande) **3** STRICT : strict, sévère **4** DIFFICULT : difficile, pénible **5** STUBBORN : inflexible, dur **6** ROUGH : dur <a tough neighbourhood : un quartier dur> **7 tough luck!** : tant pis pour toi!

tough[2] *n* : dur *m fam*

toughen ['tʌfən] *vt* : endurcir, rendre plus résistant — *vi* : s'endurcir

toughness ['tʌfnəs] *n* : résistance *f*

toupee [tuː'peɪ] *n* : postiche *m*

tour[1] ['tʊr] *vt* : visiter <we toured the city : nous avons visité la ville> — *vi* : faire du tourisme, voyager

tour[2] *n* **1** : tour *m* (d'une ville, etc.), visite *f* (d'un édifice) <a bus tour : une excursion en autobus> **2 to go on tour** : faire une tournée

tourist ['tʊrɪst, 'tər-] *n* : touriste *mf*

tournament ['tərnəmənt, 'tʊr-] *n* : tournoi *m*

tourniquet ['tərnɪkət, 'tʊr-] *n* : garrot *m,* tourniquet *m*

tousle ['taʊzəl] *vt* **-sled; -sling** : ébouriffer (les cheveux)

tout ['taʊt] *vt* : vanter les mérites de

tow[1] ['toː] *vt* : remorquer (une voiture)

tow[2] *n* : remorquage *m* <he gave me a tow : il m'a remorqué>

toward ['tord, tə'wɔrd] *or* **towards** ['tordz, tə'wɔrdz] *prep* **1** : vers, dans la direction de <toward the river : vers

la rivière> <their backs were toward me : ils étaient dos à moi> **2** : envers <his attitude toward life : son attitude envers la vie> **3** : pour <she put $100 toward a new car : elle a mis 100 $ de côté pour une nouvelle voiture> **4** NEAR : vers <toward the middle : vers le milieu>

towel ['taʊəl] *n* : serviette *f*

tower[1] ['taʊər] *vi* **to tower over** : dominer

tower[2] *n* : tour *f*

towering ['taʊərɪŋ] *adj* **1** IMPOSING : imposant, très haut **2** EXCESSIVE : sans bornes, démesuré <towering ambition : ambition démesurée>

town ['taʊn] *n* : ville *f* <to go to town : aller en ville> <to be out of town : être en déplacement>

township ['taʊn,ʃɪp] *n* **1** : commune *f*, municipalité *f* **2** : canton *m Can* (division territoriale)

tow truck ['to:,trʌk] *n* : dépanneuse *f*, remorqueuse *f Can*

toxic ['tɑksɪk] *adj* : toxique

toxicity [tɑk'sɪsəti] *n, pl* **-ties** : toxicité *f*

toxin ['tɑksɪn] *n* : toxine *f*

toy[1] ['tɔɪ] *vi* **to toy with** : jouer avec

toy[2] *adj* : de jeu <toy soldiers : soldats de plomb> <a toy house : une maison miniature>

toy[3] *n* : jouet *m*

trace[1] ['treɪs] *vt* **traced; tracing 1** OUTLINE, SKETCH : tracer, dessiner **2** FOLLOW : suivre (la trace de) **3** LOCATE : retrouver, localiser

trace[2] *n* **1** TRACK : trace *f*, empreinte *f* **2** VESTIGE : trace *f* <traces of blood : traces de sang> **3** HINT : soupçon *m*, pointe *f* <a trace of a smile : un léger sourire> <without a trace of anger : sans la moindre colère> **4** : trait *m* (d'un harnais)

trachea ['treɪkiə] *n, pl* **-cheae** [-ki,i:] : trachée *f*

track[1] ['træk] *vt* : suivre la trace de, suivre la piste de

track[2] *n* **1** MARK, TRAIL : trace *f*, piste *f* <rabbit tracks : traces de lapin> **2** PATH, TRAJECTORY : piste *f*, trajectoire *f* **3** : piste *f* (aux sports) **4** → **racetrack 5** *or* **railroad track** : voie *f* ferrée **6 to keep track of** : faire attention à

track–and–field [,trækənd'fi:ld] *adj* : d'athlétisme <track-and-field events : événements d'athlétisme>

tract ['trækt] *n* **1** AREA : étendue *f* (de terre) **2** : appareil *m*, voie *f* (en physiologie) <respiratory tract : appareil respiratoire> **3** PAMPHLET : tract *m*, brochure *f*

tractable ['træktəbəl] *adj* **1** DOCILE : docile (se dit d'un animal) **2** MALLEABLE : malléable

traction ['trækʃən] *n* : traction *f*

tractor ['træktər] *n* : tracteur *m*

trade[1] ['treɪd] *v* **traded; trading** *vt* EXCHANGE : échanger, troquer — *vi* : faire du commerce

trade[2] *n* **1** : commerce *m*, industrie *f* <the tourist trade : l'industrie touristique> <foreign trade : commerce extérieur> **2** OCCUPATION : métier *m*, profession *f*

trade–in ['treɪd,ɪn] *n* : reprise *f*

trade in *vt* : faire reprendre <to trade in a car : échanger une vieille voiture pour une neuve>

trademark[1] ['treɪd,mɑrk] *vt* : déposer une marque sur

trademark[2] *n* : marque *f* de fabrique

tradesman ['treɪdzmən] *n, pl* **-men** [-mən, -,mɛn] : commerçant *m*, -çante *f*

trade wind *n* : alizé *m*

tradition [trə'dɪʃən] *n* : tradition *f*

traditional [trə'dɪʃənəl] *adj* : traditionnel — **traditionally** *adv*

traffic[1] ['træfɪk] *vi* **trafficked; trafficking** : trafiquer <to traffic in : faire le trafic de>

traffic[2] *n* **1** TRADE : commerce *m*, trafic *m* <the drug traffic : le trafic de drogue> **2** : circulation *f*, trafic *m* <road traffic : circulation routière> <air traffic : trafic aérien>

traffic circle *n* : rond-point *m*

trafficker ['træfɪkər] *n* : trafiquant *m*, -quante *f*

traffic light *n* : feu *m* de signalisation

tragedy ['trædʒədi] *n, pl* **-dies** : tragédie *f*

tragic ['trædʒɪk] *adj* : tragique — **tragically** [-dʒɪkəli] *adv*

trail[1] ['treɪl] *vi* **1** DRAG, HANG : traîner, pendre **2** *or* **to trail behind** LAG : traîner, être à la traîne **3 to trail away** *or* **to trail off** : s'estomper, diminuer <the sound trailed off : le bruit s'estompait> — *vt* **1** DRAG : traîner, tirer **2** FOLLOW : suivre, poursuivre

trail[2] *n* **1** PATH : chemin *m*, sentier *m*, piste *f* <ski trail : piste de ski> **2** TRACK : trace *f*, piste *f* <to be on one's trail : être sur sa trace> **3** MARK, TRACE : traînée *f*, trace *f* <a trail of smoke : une traînée de fumée>

trailer ['treɪlər] *n* **1** : remorque *f* (de camion, etc.) **2** : caravane *f*, roulotte *f Can* <he toured the country in a trailer : il a fait le tour du pays en caravane>

train[1] ['treɪn] *vt* **1** : palisser (une vigne, etc.), former, entraîner (du personnel) **2** AIM, DIRECT : pointer, diriger — *vi* : recevoir une formation, s'entraîner

train[2] *n* **1** : traîne *f* (d'une robe) **2** PROCESSION : cortège *m*, file *f* **3** SUCCESSION : suite *f*, série *f*, fil *m* <train of thought : fil des pensées> **4** : train *m* <train de banlieue : commuter train>

trainee [treɪ'ni:] *n* : apprenti *m,* -tie *f;* stagiaire *mf*
trainer ['treɪnər] *n* **1** : entraîneur *m,* -neuse *f* (aux sports) **2** : dresseur *m,* -seuse *f* (d'animaux)
traipse ['treɪps] *vi* **traipsed; traipsing** : traîner <to traipse in : entrer en traînassant>
trait ['treɪt] *n* : trait *m,* qualité *f*
traitor ['treɪt̬ər] *n* : traître *m,* -tresse *f*
traitorous ['treɪt̬ərəs] *adj* : traître
trajectory [trə'dʒɛktəri] *n, pl* **-ries** : trajectoire *f*
tram ['træm] *n Brit* : tramway *m*
tramp[1] ['træmp] *vi* : marcher d'un pas lourd — *vt* : parcourir à pied
tramp[2] *n* : clochard *m,* -charde *f;* vagabond *m,* -bonde *f*
trample ['træmpəl] *vt* **-pled; -pling** : fouler aux pieds, piétiner
trampoline [,træmpə'li:n, 'træmpə,-] *n* : trampoline *m*
trance ['træn*t*s] *n* : transe *f*
tranquil ['træŋkwəl] *adj* : tranquille, paisible — **tranquilly** *adv*
tranquilize ['træŋkwə,laɪz] *vt* **-ized; -izing** : tranquilliser
tranquilizer ['træŋkwə,laɪzər] *n* : tranquillisant *m*
tranquillity *or* **tranquility** [træŋ'kwɪlət̬i] *n* : tranquillité *f*
transact [træn'zækt] *vt* : négocier, régler (des affaires)
transaction [træn'zækʃən] *n* **1** : transaction *f,* opération *f* <market transactions : opérations de la Bourse> **2** **transactions** *npl* : actes *mpl* (d'une société)
transcend [træn'sɛnd] *vt* : transcender
transcribe [træn'skraɪb] *vt* **-scribed; -scribing** : transcrire
transcript ['træn,skrɪpt] *n* : transcription *f*
transcription [træn'skrɪpʃən] *n* : transcription *f*
transfer[1] [træn*t*s'fər, 'træn*t*s,fər] *v* **-ferred; -ferring** *vt* **1** : transférer, transmettre <to transfer a title : transférer un titre> **2** : transférer, muter (un employé) **3** : transborder (des marchandises) — *vi* : être transféré, être muté
transfer[2] ['træn*t*s,fər] *n* **1** : transfert *m,* mutation *f* (d'un employé), cession *f* (de propriété), virement *m* (de fonds) **2** TICKET : billet *m* de correspondance **3** DECAL : décalcomanie *f*
transferable [træn*t*s'fərəbəl] *adj* : transmissible
transference [træn*t*s'fərən*t*s] *n* : transfert *m*
transfiguration [,træn*t*s,fɪgjə'reɪʃən] *n* : transfiguration *f*
transfigure [træn*t*s'fɪgjər] *vt* **-ured; -uring** : transfigurer
transfix [træn*t*s'fɪks] *vt* **1** PIERCE : transpercer **2** IMMOBILIZE : paralyser, figer
transform [træn*t*s'fɔrm] *vt* : transformer
transformation [,træn*t*sfər'meɪʃən] *n* : transformation *f*
transformer [træn*t*s'fɔrmər] *n* : transformateur *m*
transfusion [træn*t*s'fju:ʒən] *n* : transfusion *f*
transgress [træn*t*s'grɛs, trænz-] *vt* : transgresser
transgression [træn*t*s'grɛʃən, trænz-] *n* : transgression *f*
transient[1] ['træntʃənt, 'trænsiənt] *adj* : transitoire, passager
transient[2] *n* : personne *f* de passage
transistor [træn'zɪstər, -'sɪs-] *n* : transistor *m*
transit ['træn*t*sɪt, 'trænzɪt] *n* **1** : transit *m* <in transit : en transit> **2** TRANSPORTATION : transit *m,* transport *m* (de marchandises) **3** : théodolite *m* (instrument d'arpenteur)
transition [træn'sɪʃən, -'zɪʃ-] *n* : transition *f*
transitional [træn'sɪʃənəl, -'zɪʃ-] *adj* : transitoire, de transition
transitive ['træn*t*sət̬ɪv, 'trænzə-] *adj* : transitif
transitory ['træn*t*sə,tori, 'trænzə-] *adj* : transitoire, passager
translate [træn*t*s'leɪt, trænz-; 'træn*t*s,-'trænz,-] *v* **-lated; -lating** *vt* : traduire — *vi* : se traduire
translation [træn*t*s'leɪʃən, trænz-] *n* : traduction *f*
translator [træn*t*s'leɪtər, trænz-; 'træn*t*s,-, 'trænz,-] *n* : traducteur *m,* -trice *f*
translucent [træn*t*s'lu:sənt, trænz-] *adj* : translucide
transmissible [træn*t*s'mɪsəbəl, trænz-] *adj* : transmissible
transmission [træn*t*s'mɪʃən, trænz-] *n* **1** TRANSMITTING : transmission *f* (d'une maladie, etc.) **2** : transmission *f* (d'une voiture)
transmit [træn*t*s'mɪt, trænz-] *v* **-mitted; -mitting** *vt* : transmettre — *vi* : émettre, diffuser (se dit de la radio, de la télévision, etc.)
transmitter [træn*t*s'mɪt̬ər, trænz-; 'træn*t*s,-, 'trænz,-] *n* : émetteur *m*
transom ['træn*t*səm] *n* : traverse *f*
transparency [træn*t*s'pærən*t*si] *n, pl* **-cies 1** : transparence *f* **2** SLIDE : diapositive *f,* acétate *f Can*
transparent [træn*t*s'pærənt] *adj* : transparent
transpiration [,træn*t*spə'reɪʃən] *n* : transpiration *f*
transpire [træn*t*s'paɪr] *v* **-spired; -spiring** *vt* : transpirer — *vi* OCCUR : arriver, se passer
transplant[1] [træn*t*s'plænt] *vt* : transplanter
transplant[2] ['træn*t*s,plænt] *n* : transplantation *f*
transport[1] [træn*t*s'port, 'træn*t*s,-] *vt* : transporter

transport[2] [ˈtrænts,port] *n* **1** TRANSPORTATION : transport *m* <public transport : transports en commun> **2** *or* **transport ship** : navire *m* de transport **3 transports** *npl* : transports *mpl* (de joie), accès *mpl* (de colère, etc.)

transportation [ˌtræntspərˈteɪʃən] *n* : transport *m*

transpose [træntsˈpoːz] *vt* **-posed; -posing** : transposer

transposition [ˌtræntspəˈzɪʃən] *n* : transposition *f*

transverse [træntsˈvərs, trænz-] *adj* : transversal — **transversely** *adv*

trap[1] [ˈtræp] *vt* **trapped; trapping** : prendre au piège, attraper

trap[2] *n* **1** : piège *m* <to set a trap : tendre un piège> **2** : siphon *m* <the trap in a drainpipe : le siphon dans un tuyau d'écoulement>

trapdoor [ˈtræpˈdor] *n* : trappe *f*

trapeze [træˈpiːz] *n* : trapèze *m*

trapezoid [ˈtræpəˌzɔɪd] *n* : trapèze *m*

trapper [ˈtræpər] *n* : trappeur *m*

trappings [ˈtræpɪŋz] *npl* **1** : caparaçon *m* (d'un cheval) **2** SIGNS : attributs *mpl* <the trappings of success : les signes extérieurs de la réussite>

trash [ˈtræʃ] *n* : déchets *mpl,* ordures *fpl*

trauma [ˈtrɔmə, ˈtraʊ-] *n* : traumatisme *m*

traumatic [trəˈmæt̬ɪk, trɔ-, traʊ-] *adj* : traumatisant

travel[1] [ˈtrævəl] *v* **-eled** *or* **-elled; -eling** *or* **-elling** *vi* **1** JOURNEY : faire un voyage, voyager **2** SPREAD : circuler, se répandre <news traveled fast : les nouvelles circulaient vite> **3** GO, MOVE : aller, rouler <the train traveled at 60 miles per hour : le train roulait à 60 milles à l'heure> — *vt* : parcourir <to travel the countryside : parcourir la campagne>

travel[2] *n* : voyages *mpl*

traveler *or* **traveller** [ˈtrævələr] *n* : voyageur *m,* -geuse *f*

traverse [trəˈvərs, træˈvərs, ˈtrævərs] *vt* **-versed; -versing** : traverser, franchir

travesty [ˈtrævəsti] *n, pl* **-ties** : parodie *f*

trawl[1] [ˈtrɔl] *vi* : pêcher au chalut

trawl[2] *n* : chalut *m*

trawler [ˈtrɔlər] *n* : chalutier *m*

tray [ˈtreɪ] *n* : plateau *m*

treacherous [ˈtrɛtʃərəs] *adj* **1** : traître, déloyal **2** UNRELIABLE : infidèle, incertain **3** DANGEROUS : dangereux, périlleux

treacherously [ˈtrɛtʃərəsli] *adv* : traîtreusement

treachery [ˈtrɛtʃəri] *n, pl* **-eries** : traîtrise *f,* déloyauté *f*

tread[1] [ˈtrɛd] *v* **trod** [ˈtrɑd]; **trodden** [ˈtrɑdən] *or* **trod; treading** *vi* **1** WALK : marcher **2 to tread on** : marcher sur, piétiner — *vt* BEAT : tracer <to tread a path : tracer un chemin>

tread[2] *n* **1** FOOTSTEP : pas *m,* trace *f* de pas **2** : bande *f* de roulement (d'un pneu), semelle *f* (d'un soulier) **3** *or* **stair tread** : dessus *m* (d'une marche)

treadle [ˈtrɛdəl] *n* : pédale *f*

treadmill [ˈtrɛd,mɪl] *n* **1** : exerciseur *m* **2** ROUTINE : engrenage *m,* train-train *m*

treason [ˈtriːzən] *n* : trahison *f*

treasure[1] [ˈtrɛʒər, ˈtreɪ-] *vt* **-sured; -suring** CHERISH : tenir beaucoup à

treasure[2] *n* : trésor *m*

treasurer [ˈtrɛʒərər, ˈtreɪ-] *n* : trésorier *m,* -rière *f*

treasury [ˈtrɛʒəri, ˈtreɪ-] *n, pl* **-suries 1** : trésorerie *f* (édifice) **2 Treasury** : ministère *m* des Finances

treat[1] [ˈtriːt] *vi or* **to treat of** : traiter de, parler de <a book treating of animals : un livre qui traite des animaux> — *vt* **1** DEAL WITH, HANDLE : traiter <he treated him as inferior : il le traitait en inférieur> **2** PROCESS : traiter <to treat soil with lime : traiter le sol avec du chaux> **3** : traiter, soigner (en médecine) **4 to treat s.o. to sth** : payer qqch à qqn, offrir qqch à qqn

treat[2] *n* : cadeau *m* spécial, (petit) plaisir *m* <let's give him a treat : faisons-lui un plaisir> <it's my treat : c'est moi qui paie>

treatise [ˈtriːt̬əs] *n* : traité *m*

treatment [ˈtriːtmənt] *n* **1** HANDLING : traitement *m* **2** : soins *mpl,* traitement *m* (en médecine)

treaty [ˈtriːt̬i] *n, pl* **-ties** : traité *m*

treble[1] [ˈtrɛbəl] *v* **-bled; -bling** : tripler

treble[2] *adj* **1** → **triple 2** : de soprano

treble[3] *n* : soprano *m*

treble clef *n* : clé *f* de sol

tree [ˈtriː] *n* : arbre *m*

treeless [ˈtriːləs] *adj* : sans arbres, dénué d'arbres

trek[1] [ˈtrɛk] *vi* **trekked; trekking** : faire une longue randonnée, avancer avec peine

trek[2] *n* : randonnée *f,* marche *f* pénible

trellis [ˈtrɛlɪs] *n* : treillis *m,* treillage *m*

tremble [ˈtrɛmbəl] *vi* **-bled; -bling 1** SHIVER : trembler, frissonner **2** VIBRATE : trembler, vibrer (se dit de la voix)

tremendous [trɪˈmɛndəs] *adj* : énorme, immense

tremendously [trɪˈmɛndəsli] *adv* : extrêmement, énormément

tremor [ˈtrɛmər] *n* **1** TREMBLING : tremblement *m,* frisson *m* **2** : secousse *f* sismique (en géologie)

tremulous [ˈtrɛmjələs] *adj* **1** : tremblant, frémissant **2** TIMID : timide

trench [ˈtrɛntʃ] *n* : tranchée *f*

trenchant [ˈtrɛntʃənt] *adj* : incisif, tranchant

trend ['trɛnd] *n* : tendance *f,* mode *f* <to set a trend : lancer une mode> <a downward trend : une tendance à la baisse>

trendy ['trɛndi] *adj* **trendier; -est** : branché *fam,* à la mode <a trendy spot : un endroit branché> <trendy clothes : vêtements dernier cri>

trepidation [ˌtrɛpə'deɪʃən] *n* : appréhension *f,* inquiétude *f*

trespass[1] ['trɛspəs, -ˌpæs] *vi* **1** SIN : offenser **2** : s'introduire illégalement <no trespassing : défense d'entrer>

trespass[2] *n* **1** SIN : offense *f,* péché *m* **2** : entrée *f* non autorisée

tress ['trɛs] *n* : mèche *f* de cheveux, boucle *f* de cheveux

trestle ['trɛsəl] *n* **1** : tréteau *m,* chevalet *m* **2** *or* **trestle bridge** : pont *m* sur chevalets

triad ['traɪˌæd] *n* : triade *f*

trial[1] ['traɪəl] *adj* : d'essai <trial period : période d'essai>

trial[2] *n* **1** HEARING : procès *m* **2** TEST : essai *m* **3** ORDEAL : épreuve *f,* difficulté *f* <the trials of youth : les épreuves de la jeunesse>

triangle ['traɪˌæŋgəl] *n* : triangle *m*

triangular [traɪ'æŋgjələr] *adj* : triangulaire

tribal ['traɪbəl] *adj* : tribal

tribe ['traɪb] *n* : tribu *f*

tribesman ['traɪbzmən] *n, pl* **-men** [-mən, -ˌmɛn] : membre *m* d'une tribu

tribulation [ˌtrɪbjə'leɪʃən] *n* : affliction *f,* tourment *m*

tribunal [traɪ'bjuːnəl, trɪ-] *n* : tribunal *m*

tributary ['trɪbjəˌtɛri] *n, pl* **-taries** : affluent *m*

tribute ['trɪbˌjuːt] *n* : tribut *m,* hommage *m* <to pay tribute to s.o. : rendre hommage à qqn>

trick[1] ['trɪk] *vt* : attraper, rouler *fam* <to trick s.o. : jouer un tour à qqn>

trick[2] *n* **1** RUSE : tour *m,* artifice *m,* ruse *f* **2** PRANK : farce *f,* tour *m* <to play a trick on : jouer un tour à> **3** *or* **magic trick** : tour *m* **4** MANNERISM : manie *f,* habitude *f* **5** KNACK : don *m,* truc *m* **6** : pli *m,* levée *f* (de cartes) <to take a trick : faire un pli>

trickery ['trɪkəri] *n* : supercherie *f,* tromperie *f*

trickle[1] ['trɪkəl] *vi* **-led; -ling 1** DRIP : dégouliner, couler **2** *or* **to trickle away** : se dissiper petit à petit

trickle[2] *n* : filet *m* (d'eau), écoulement *m* (de sable, etc.)

trickster ['trɪkstər] *n* : filou *m,* escroc *m*

tricky ['trɪki] *adj* **trickier; -est 1** SLY : rusé, fourbe **2** DIFFICULT : difficile, délicat, épineux

tricycle ['traɪəkəl, -ˌsɪkəl] *n* : tricycle *m*

trident ['traɪdənt] *n* : trident *m*

triennial [ˌtraɪ'ɛniəl] *adj* : triennal

trifle[1] ['traɪfəl] *vi* **-fled; -fling 1** TOY : jouer **2** **to trifle with** : jouer avec (les sentiments de qqn), traîter (une personne) à la légère

trifle[2] *n* : bagatelle *f,* rien *m* <it's a mere trifle : c'est peu de chose>

trifling ['traɪflɪŋ] *adj* : insignifiant, peu important

trigger[1] ['trɪgər] *vt* : déclencher

trigger[2] *n* : détente *f,* gâchette *f* <to pull the trigger : appuyer sur la détente>

trigonometry [ˌtrɪgə'nɑmətri] *n* : trigonométrie *f*

trill[1] ['trɪl] *vi* : triller (en musique) — *vt* : triller, rouler <to trill one's *r*'s : rouler les *r*>

trill[2] *n* **1** : trille *m* (en musique) **2** : consonne *f* roulée (en linguistique)

trillion ['trɪljən] *n* : billion *m*

trilogy ['trɪlədʒi] *n, pl* **-gies** : trilogie *f*

trim[1] ['trɪm] *vt* **trimmed; trimming 1** DECORATE : décorer, orner **2** CUT : tailler, couper (une haie, une barbe, etc.) **3** REDUCE : limiter

trim[2] *adj* **trimmer; trimmest 1** NEAT : soigné, bien tenu **2** SLIM : svelte, mince

trim[3] *n* **1** CONDITION, FITNESS : forme *f* <to keep in good trim : se maintenir en bonne forme> **2** CUT : coupe *f* d'entretien (des cheveux) **3** TRIMMING : garniture *f*

trimming ['trɪmɪŋ] *n* **1** : parement *m* (en couture), garniture *f* **2** **trimmings** *npl* : garniture *f* (en cuisine) **3** **trimmings** *npl* SCRAPS : rognures *fpl,* chutes *fpl*

Trinidadian[1] [ˌtrɪnə'dædiən] *adj* : trinidadien

Trinidadian[2] *n* : Trinidadien *m,* -dienne *f*

Trinity ['trɪnət̬i] *n* : Trinité *f*

trinket ['trɪŋkət] *n* : babiole *f,* colifichet *m*

trio ['triːˌoː] *n, pl* **trios** : trio *m*

trip[1] ['trɪp] *v* **tripped; tripping** *vi* **1** : marcher d'un pas léger **2** STUMBLE : trébucher, s'enfarger *Can* **3** *or* **to trip up** ERR : trébucher, faire un faux pas — *vt* **1** : faire trébucher (une personne) **2** : déclencher (un mécanisme) **3** **to trip up** DISCONCERT, TRAP : désarçonner

trip[2] *n* **1** JOURNEY : voyage *m,* excursion *f,* tour *m* **2** STUMBLE : trébuchement *m*

tripartite [traɪ'pɑrˌtaɪt] *adj* : tripartite

tripe ['traɪp] *n* **1** : tripes *fpl* (d'un animal) **2** NONSENSE : bêtises *fpl*

triple[1] ['trɪpəl] *v* **-pled; -pling** : tripler

triple[2] *adj* : triple

triple[3] *n* : triple *m*

triplet ['trɪplət] *n* **1** : triolet *m* (en musique) **2** **triplets** *npl* : triplés *mpl*

triplicate ['trɪplɪkət] *n* **in ~** : en trois exemplaires

tripod ['traɪˌpɑd] *n* : trépied *m*

trite ['traɪt] *adj* **triter; tritest** : banal

triumph[1] ['traɪəmpf] *vi* : triompher

triumph[2] *n* : triomphe *m*

triumphal [traɪ'ʌmpfəl] *adj* : triomphal
triumphant [traɪ'ʌmpfənt] *adj* : triomphant
triumphantly [traɪ'ʌmpfəntli] *adv* : triomphalement, en triomphe
trivia ['trɪviə] *ns & pl* : futilités *fpl*, bagatelles *fpl*
trivial ['trɪviəl] *adj* : sans importance, insignifiant
triviality [ˌtrɪvi'ælət̬i] *n, pl* **-ties** : banalité *f*, insignifiance *f*
trod, trodden → **tread**[1]
troll ['tro:l] *n* : troll *m*
trolley ['trɑli] *n, pl* **trolleys** : tramway *m*
trombone [trɑm'bo:n] *n* : trombone *m*
trombonist [trɑm'bo:nɪst] *n* : tromboniste *mf*
troop[1] ['tru:p] *vi* : aller en bande <to troop by : passer en troupe>
troop[2] *n* **1** GROUP : bande *f*, groupe *m* **2 troops** *npl* : troupes *fpl*, soldats *mpl*
trooper ['tru:pər] *n* **1** : soldat *m* de cavalerie **2** *or* **state trooper** : gendarme *m France*, policier *m*
trophy ['tro:fi] *n, pl* **-phies** : trophée *m*
tropic[1] ['trɑpɪk] *or* **tropical** ['trɑpɪkəl] *adj* : tropical
tropic[2] *n* : tropique *m* <Tropic of Cancer : tropique du Cancer>
trot[1] ['trɑt] *vi* **trotted; trotting** : trotter
trot[2] *n* : trot *m*
trouble[1] ['trʌbəl] *vt* **-bled; -bling 1** UPSET, WORRY : troubler, inquiéter **2** AFFLICT : faire mal à <to be troubled by a headache : être incommodé par un mal de tête> **3** BOTHER : déranger <please don't trouble yourself : je vous en prie, ne vous dérangez pas>
trouble[2] *n* **1** PROBLEMS : ennuis *mpl*, difficultés *fpl* <to get into trouble : avoir des ennuis> <he has trouble reading : il a de la difficulté à lire> <back trouble : problèmes de dos> **2** EFFORT : mal *m*, peine *f* <to take the trouble : se donner la peine>
troublemaker ['trʌbəlˌmeɪkər] *n* : fauteur *m*, -trice *f* de troubles; provocateur *m*, -trice *f*
troublesome ['trʌbəlsəm] *adj* : difficile, gênant, pénible
trough ['trɔf] *n, pl* **troughs** ['trɔfs, 'trɔvz] **1** : abreuvoir *m* (pour les animaux) **2** CHANNEL, DEPRESSION : chenal *m*, creux *m*
trounce ['traʊnts] *vt* **trounced; trouncing 1** THRASH : battre, rosser **2** DEFEAT : battre à plates coutures, écraser
troupe ['tru:p] *n* : troupe *f*
trousers ['traʊzərz] *npl* : pantalon *m*
trout ['traʊt] *ns & pl* : truite *f*
trowel ['traʊəl] *n* **1** : truelle *f* (pour étendre le mortier) **2** : déplantoir *m* (pour le jardinage)
truant ['tru:ənt] *n* : élève *mf* absentéiste <to play truant : faire l'école buissonnière>
truce ['tru:s] *n* : trêve *f*
truck[1] ['trʌk] *vt* : camionner
truck[2] *n* **1** : camion *m* **2** DEALINGS : association *f*, relations *fpl* <to have no truck with : ne rien avoir à faire avec>
trucker ['trʌkər] *n* : camionneur *m*, -neuse *f*; routier *m*
truculent ['trʌkjələnt] *adj* : agressif
trudge ['trʌdʒ] *vi* **trudged; trudging** : marcher péniblement, marcher lourdement
true[1] ['tru:] *vt* **trued; trueing** : ajuster, aligner <to true up a board : aligner une planche>
true[2] *adv* **1** TRUTHFULLY : honnêtement **2** ACCURATELY : juste
true[3] *adj* **truer; truest 1** LOYAL : fidèle, sincère **2** ACCURATE : juste, vrai, exact **3** GENUINE : vrai, véritable <a true love : un véritable amour> **4** RIGHTFUL : légitime
true–blue ['tru:'blu:] *adj* : loyal, fidèle
truffle ['trʌfəl] *n* : truffe *f*
truism ['tru:ˌɪzəm] *n* : truisme *m*
truly ['tru:li] *adv* **1** INDEED : vraiment, réellement **2 Yours truly** : Veuillez agréer l'expression de mes sentiments distingués
trump[1] ['trʌmp] *vt* : couper (une carte), jouer atout sur
trump[2] *n* : atout *m*
trumped–up ['trʌmpt'ʌp] *adj* : inventé de toutes parts
trumpet[1] ['trʌmpət] *vi* **1** : sonner de la trompette **2** : barrir (se dit d'un éléphant) — *vt* : claironner (des nouvelles, etc.)
trumpet[2] *n* : trompette *f*
trumpeter ['trʌmpət̬ər] *n* : trompettiste *mf*
truncate ['trʌŋˌkeɪt, 'trʌn-] *vt* **-cated; -cating** : tronquer
trundle ['trʌndəl] *v* **-dled; -dling** *vi* ROLL : rouler — *vt* WHEEL : pousser, faire rouler (bruyamment)
trunk ['trʌŋk] *n* **1** : tronc *m* (du corps, d'un arbre, etc.) **2** : trompe *f* (d'un éléphant) **3** : coffre *m* (d'une voiture), malle *f* (pour voyager) **4 trunks** *npl or* **bathing trunks** : maillot *m* de bain
truss[1] ['trʌs] *vt* **1** BIND : trousser (une volaille) **2** REINFORCE : armer
truss[2] *n* **1** : bandage *m* herniaire **2** FRAMEWORK : armature *f*
trust[1] ['trʌst] *vi* **to trust in** : croire en (Dieu), faire confiance à (une personne) — *vt* **1** ENTRUST : confier **2** : avoir confiance en <I trust his judgment : j'ai confiance en son jugement>
trust[2] *n* **1** : confiance *f* <breach of trust : abus de confiance> **2** HOPE : espoir *m*, espérance *f* **3** CARTEL : trust *m* **4** : fidéicommis *m* <to hold sth in trust : tenir qqch par fidéicommis> **5** CARE, CUSTODY : charge *f*

trustee [ˌtrʌsˈtiː] *n* : fiduciaire *mf,* fidéicommissaire *mf*
trustful [ˈtrʌstfəl] *adj* : qui a confiance, confiant
trustfully [ˈtrʌstfəli] *adv* : avec confiance
trustworthiness [ˈtrʌstˌwərðinəs] *n* : loyauté *f,* fiabilité *f*
trustworthy [ˈtrʌstˌwərði] *adj* : digne de confiance, loyal
trusty [ˈtrəsti] *adj* **trustier; -est** : loyal, fidèle
truth [ˈtruːθ] *n, pl* **truths** [ˈtruːðz, ˈtruːθs] : vérité *f*
truthful [ˈtruːθfəl] *adj* **1** HONEST : honnête **2** ACCURATE : exact, vrai
truthfully [ˈtruːθfəli] *adv* : sans mentir, sincèrement
truthfulness [ˈtruːθfəlnəs] *n* : véracité *f,* honnêteté *f*
try[1] [ˈtraɪ] *v* **tried; trying** *vt* **1** : juger (un accusé) **2** ATTEMPT : essayer, tenter <try to understand : essayez de comprendre> <to try one's luck : tenter sa chance> **3** TEST : éprouver, mettre à l'épreuve <to try one's patience : mettre sa patience à l'épreuve> **4** SAMPLE : goûter à, essayer — *vi* : essayer
try[2] *n, pl* **tries** : essai *m,* tentative *f*
tryout [ˈtraɪˌaʊt] *n* : essai *m*
try out *vt* : essayer, faire l'essai de
tsar [ˈzɑr, ˈtsɑr, ˈsɑr] → **czar**
T–shirt [ˈtiːˌʃərt] *n* : tee-shirt *m,* t-shirt *m*
tub [ˈtʌb] *n* **1** VAT : cuve *f,* bac *m* **2** CONTAINER : contenant *m,* pot *m* <a tub of margarine : un contenant de margarine> **3** → **bathtub**
tuba [ˈtuːbə, ˈtjuː-] *n* : tuba *m*
tube [ˈtuːb, ˈtjuːb] *n* **1** CYLINDER : tube *m,* cylindre *m* **2** : tube *m* (de dentifrice, etc.) **3** *or* **inner tube** : chambre *f* à air **4** *or* **cathode-ray tube** : tube *m* (cathodique)
tuber [ˈtuːbər, ˈtjuː-] *n* : tubercule *m*
tubercular [tʊˈbərkjələr, tjʊ-] *adj* : tuberculeux
tuberculosis [tʊˌbərkjəˈloːsəs, tjʊ-] *n, pl* **-loses** [-ˌsiːz] : tuberculose *f*
tuberculous [tʊˈbərkjələs, tjʊ-] *adj* : tuberculeux
tubing [ˈtuːbɪŋ, ˈtjuː-] *n* : tubes *mpl*
tubular [ˈtubjələr, ˈtjuː-] *adj* : tubulaire
tuck[1] [ˈtʌk] *vt* **1** *or* **to tuck away** : cacher, ranger <to tuck away one's money : mettre son argent en sécurité> **2 to tuck in** : rentrer (sa chemise), border (un enfant) — *vi* **to tuck into** : manger ou boire avec appétit
tuck[2] *n* : pli *m*
tucker [ˈtʌkər] *vt or* **to tucker out** : fatiguer, épuiser
Tuesday [ˈtuːzˌdeɪ, ˈtjuːz-, -di] *n* : mardi *m*
tuft [ˈtʌft] *n* : touffe *f* (de cheveux, de plantes, etc.)
tug[1] [ˈtʌg] *v* **tugged; tugging** *vt* **1** TOW : remorquer **2** LUG : tirer, traîner — *vi* **to tug at** : tirer sur
tug[2] *n* **1** : petit coup *m* **2** → **tugboat**
tugboat [ˈtʌgˌboːt] *n* : remorqueur *m*
tug–of–war [ˌtʌgəˈwɔr] *n, pl* **tugs–of–war** : lutte *f* à la corde
tuition [tʊˈɪʃən, ˈtjuː-] *n* : frais *mpl* de scolarité
tulip [ˈtuːlɪp, ˈtjuː-] *n* : tulipe *f*
tumble[1] [ˈtəmbəl] *v* **-bled; -bling** *vi* **1** FALL : tomber, dégringoler **2** : faire des culbutes, culbuter (en gymnastique) **3** PLUMMET : chuter (se dit des prix, etc.) — *vt* **1** TOPPLE : faire tomber, renverser **2** *or* **to tumble together** : mélanger
tumble[2] *n* **1** : culbute *f* (en gymnastique) **2** FALL : chute *f*
tumbler [ˈtʌmblər] *n* **1** ACROBAT : acrobate *mf* **2** GLASS : verre *m* droit **3** : gorge *f* (de serrure)
tummy [ˈtʌmi] *n, pl* **-mies** : ventre *m*
tumor *or Brit* **tumour** [ˈtuːmər, ˈtjuː-] *n* : tumeur *f*
tumult [ˈtuːˌmʌlt ˈtjuː-] *n* **1** COMMOTION : tumulte *m,* vacarme *m* **2** CONFUSION : agitation *f,* tumulte *m*
tumultuous [tʊˈmʌltʃʊəs, tjuː-] *adj* : tumultueux
tuna [ˈtuːnə ˈtjuː-] *n, pl* **-na** *or* **-nas** : thon *m*
tundra [ˈtʌndrə] *n* : toundra *f*
tune[1] [ˈtuːn, ˈtjuːn] *v* **tuned; tuning** *vt* **1** : accorder (un instrument de musique) **2** *or* **to tune up** : régler, mettre au point (un moteur) — *vi* **to tune in to** : se mettre à l'écoute de
tune[2] *n* **1** MELODY : air *m,* mélodie *f* **2 to be in tune** : être accordé (se dit d'un instrument), chanter juste **3 to be out of tune** : être désaccordé (se dit d'un instrument), chanter faux **4 to be in tune with** : être en accord avec
tuneful [ˈtuːnfəl, ˈtjuːn-] *adj* : mélodieux, harmonieux
tuner [ˈtuːnər, ˈtjuː-] *n* **1** : accordeur *m* <piano tuner : accordeur de piano> **2** : tuner *m* (de radio, etc.)
tungsten [ˈtʌŋkstən] *n* : tungstène *m*
tunic [ˈtuːnɪk, ˈtjuː-] *n* : tunique *f*
tuning fork *n* : diapason *m*
Tunisian[1] [tuːˈniːʒən, tjuːˈnɪziən] *adj* : tunisien
Tunisian[2] *n* : Tunisien *m,* -sienne *f*
tunnel[1] [ˈtʌnəl] *vi* **-neled** *or* **-nelled; -neling** *or* **-nelling** : creuser un tunnel
tunnel[2] *n* : tunnel *m*
turban [ˈtərbən] *n* : turban *m*
turbid [ˈtərbɪd] *adj* : turbide, trouble
turbine [ˈtərbən, -ˌbaɪn] *n* : turbine *f*
turboprop [ˈtərboːˌprɑp] *n* : turbopropulseur *m* (moteur), avion *m* à turbopropulseur
turbulence [ˈtərbjələnts] *n* : turbulence *f*

turbulent ['tərbjələnt] *adj* : turbulent, agité

turbulently ['tərbjələntli] *adv* : avec turbulence

tureen [tə'ri:n, tjʊ-] *n* : soupière *f*

turf ['tərf] *n* : gazon *m,* motte *f* de gazon

turgid ['tərdʒəd] *adj* **1** SWOLLEN : enflé, gonflé **2** BOMBASTIC : pompeux

Turk ['tərk] *n* : Turc *m,* Turque *f*

turkey ['tərki] *n, pl* **-keys** : dinde *f*

Turkish[1] ['tərkɪʃ] *adj* : turc

Turkish[2] *n* : turc *m* (langue)

turmoil ['tər,mɔɪl] *n* : désarroi *m,* confusion *f*

turn[1] ['tərn] *vt* **1** : tourner <to turn a wheel : tourner une roue> <turn the doorknob : tourne la poignée> **2** TWIST : tordre <to turn one's ankle : se tordre la cheville> **3** : tourner, retourner, changer de direction <she turned her chair toward the fire : elle a tourné sa chaise pour faire face au feu> <I turned the child over in bed : j'ai retourné l'enfant dans son lit> **4 to turn one's stomach** : se soulever le cœur **5 to turn over** PONDER : réfléchir à, tourner et retourner (un problème, une question, etc.) — *vi* **1** SPOIL : tourner, cailler **2** CHANGE : se transformer **3** BECOME : devenir <his hair turned gray : ses cheveux sont devenus gris> **4** : se tourner <he turned to them for help : il s'est tourné vers eux en espérant obtenir de l'aide> **5** HEAD : se diriger <we turned toward home : nous nous sommes dirigés vers la maison>

turn[2] *n* **1** ROTATION : tour *m* **2** CHANGE : amélioration *f,* tournure *f* <to take a turn for the better : s'être amélioré> **3** BEND : virage *m,* tournant *m* <a sharp turn : un brusque virage> <to make a right turn : tourner à droite> **4** DEED : service *m* <to do a good turn to : rendre service à> **5** : tour *m* <wait your turn : attendez votre tour> **6** STROLL : tour *m,* promenade *f*

turn away *vt* **1** AVERT : détourner (les yeux) **2 to turn s.o. away** : renvoyer qqn, refuser qqn — *vi* : se détourner

turncoat ['tərn,ko:t] *n* : renégat *m,* -gate *f*

turn down *vt* **1** : retourner (une carte), rabattre (un collet) **2** LOWER : baisser (le volume) **3** REFUSE : refuser, décliner

turn in *vi* : se coucher <I turned in early : je me suis couché tôt> — *vt* **1** : rendre, remettre <she turned in her paper : elle a remis son devoir> **2** DELIVER : livrer <we turned him in to police : nous l'avons livré à la police>

turnip ['tərnəp] *n* : navet *m*

turn off : éteindre (la lumière), fermer (une radio, etc.), arrêter (un moteur)

turnout ['tərn,aʊt] *n* : participation *f*

turn out *vt* **1** EVICT : expulser, mettre à la porte **2** TURN OFF : éteindre — *vi* **1** COME : venir, se présenter <voters turned out in droves : les électeurs se sont présentés en grands nombres> **2 to turn out to be** : s'avérer, se révéler <the outing turned out to be a disaster : la sortie s'est révélée désastreuse>

turnover ['tərn,o:vər] *n* **1** REVERSAL : renversement *m* **2** : chausson *m* <apple turnover : chausson aux pommes> **3** : roulement *m* (du personnel)

turn over *vt* **1** TRANSFER : remettre, rendre **2** : tourner, retourner <to turn over a playing card : retourner une carte> — *vi* **1** : se retourner (se dit d'une personne) **2** : commencer à tourner (se dit d'un moteur)

turnpike ['tərn,paɪk] *n* : autoroute *f* à péage

turnstile ['tərn,staɪl] *n* : tourniquet *m*

turntable ['tərn,teɪbəl] *n* : platine *f* (d'un tourne-disque)

turn up *vt* **1** : mettre plus fort (la lumière, etc.), augmenter (le volume) **2** DISCOVER : découvrir **3** : retrousser (ses manches), relever (son collet) — *vi* **1** APPEAR, ARRIVE : arriver, apparaître **2** HAPPEN : survenir, se passer

turpentine ['tərpən,taɪn] *n* : térébenthine *f*

turquoise ['tər,kɔɪz, -,kwɔɪz] *n* : turquoise *f* (minéral), turquoise *m* (couleur)

turret ['tərət] *n* : tourelle *f*

turtle ['tərṭəl] *n* : tortue *f*

turtledove ['tərṭəl,dʌv] *n* : tourterelle *f*

turtleneck ['tərṭəl,nɛk] *n* : col *m* roulé, col *m* montant

tusk ['tʌsk] *n* : défense *f* (d'un animal)

tussle[1] ['tʌsəl] *vi* : se bagarrer, se battre

tussle[2] *n* : bagarre *f,* mêlée *f*

tutor[1] ['tu:tər, 'tju:-] *vt* : donner des cours particuliers à

tutor[2] *n* : précepteur *m,* -trice *f;* professeur *m* particulier

tuxedo [,tək'si:,do:] *n, pl* **-dos** *or* **-does** : smoking *m*

TV [,ti:'vi:, 'ti:,vi:] *n* : TV *m*

twain ['tweɪn] *n* : deux *m*

twang[1] ['twæŋ] *vt* : pincer les cordes de (un instrument) — *vi* : vibrer

twang[2] *n* **1** : ton *m* nasillard (de la voix) **2** : son *m* de corde pincée

tweak[1] ['twi:k] *vt* : tirer, tordre

tweak[2] *n* : petit coup *m* sec

tweed ['twi:d] *n* : tweed *m*

tweet[1] ['twi:t] *vi* : pépier, gazouiller

tweet[2] *n* : pépiement *m*

tweezers ['twi:zərz] *ns & pl* : pince *f* à épiler

twelfth[1] ['twɛlfθ] *adj* : douzième

twelfth[2] *n* **1** : douzième *mf* (dans une série) **2** : douzième *m* (en mathé-

matiques) **3** (*used in dates*) <the twelfth of June : le douze juin>
twelve[1] ['twɛlv] *adj* : douze
twelve[2] *n* : douze *m*
twentieth[1] ['twʌntiəθ, 'twɛn-] *adj* : vingtième
twentieth[2] *n* **1** : vingtième *mf* (dans une série) **2** : vingtième *m* (en mathématiques) **3** (*used in dates*) <the twentieth of June : le vingt juin>
twenty[1] ['twʌnti, 'twɛn-] *adj* : vingt
twenty[2] *n, pl* **-ties** : vingt *m*
twenty–twenty *or* **20/20** *adj* **to have twenty–twenty vision** : avoir dix dixièmes à chaque œil
twice ['twaɪs] *adv* : deux fois <twice as much : deux fois plus>
twig ['twɪg] *n* : petite branche *f*, brindille *f*
twilight ['twaɪˌlaɪt] *n* : crépuscule *m* (du soir), aube *f* (du matin)
twill ['twɪl] *n* : sergé *m*
twin[1] ['twɪn] *adj* : jumeau <twin sister : sœur jumelle>
twin[2] *n* : jumeau *m*, -melle *f*
twine[1] ['twaɪn] *v* **twined; twining** *vt* : enrouler — *vi* : s'enrouler
twine[2] *n* : ficelle *f*
twinge ['twɪndʒ] *n* : élancement *m* (de douleur)
twinkle[1] ['twɪŋkəl] *vi* **-kled; -kling 1** : briller, scintiller (se dit des étoiles, etc.) **2** : pétiller (se dit des yeux)
twinkle[2] *n* : scintillement *m* (des étoiles), pétillement *m* (des yeux)
twirl[1] ['twərl] *vi* : tournoyer — *vt* : faire tournoyer
twirl[2] *n* : tournoiement *m*
twist[1] ['twɪst] *vt* **1** : tourner, tordre <to twist one's ankle : se tordre la cheville> **2** DISTORT : déformer, pervertir <to twist the facts : déformer les faits> — *vi* **1** : serpenter (se dit d'une route) **2** ENTWINE : s'enrouler **3 to twist and turn** : se tortiller
twist[2] *n* **1** TURN : tour *m*, torsion *f* **2** BEND : tournant *m* (d'une route, etc.) **3** COIL : tortillon *m*, rouleau *m* <a twist of lemon : un zeste de citron> **4** : rebondissement *m*, tournure *f* (des événements) <a twist of fate : un coup du sort>
twister ['twɪstər] *n* **1** → **tornado 2** → **waterspout**
twitch[1] ['twɪtʃ] *vi* **1** QUIVER : trembloter, avoir un mouvement convulsif **2** : se convulser, se contracter (se dit d'un muscle)
twitch[2] *n* **1** JERK : saccade *f*, coup *m* sec **2** SPASM : spasme *m* **3** *or* **nervous twitch** : tic *m* (nerveux)
twitter[1] ['twɪṭər] *vi* **1** CHIRP : pépier, gazouiller **2** CHATTER : jacasser **3** *or* **to twitter about** : s'agiter (nerveusement)
twitter[2] *n* : pépiement *m*, gazouillement *m* (d'un oiseau)
two[1] ['tuː] *adj* : deux
two[2] *n, pl* **twos** : deux *m*
twofold[1] ['tuː'foːld] *adv* : doublement
twofold[2] *adj* : double
twosome ['tuːsəm] *n* : couple *m*
tycoon [taɪ'kuːn] *n* : magnat *m*
tying → **tie**[1]
type[1] ['taɪp] *v* **typed; typing** *vt* **1** : taper (une lettre, etc.) **2** CATEGORIZE : classifier, déterminer le type de — *vi* : taper (à la machine)
type[2] *n* **1** KIND : genre *m*, sorte *f*, type *m* **2** *or* **printing type** : caractère *m* (d'imprimerie)
typewriter ['taɪpˌraɪṭər] *n* : machine *f* à écrire, dactylo *f Can*
typhoid ['taɪˌfɔɪd, taɪ'-] *n or* **typhoid fever** : typhoïde *f*, fièvre *f* typhoïde
typhoon [taɪ'fuːn] *n* : typhon *m*
typhus ['taɪfəs] *n* : typhus *m*
typical ['tɪpɪkəl] *adj* : typique, caractéristique
typically ['tɪpɪkli] *adv* **1** : typiquement <typically American : typiquement américain> **2** USUALLY : d'habitude
typify ['tɪpəˌfaɪ] *vt* **-fied; -fying** : représenter, être typique de
typist ['taɪpɪst] *n* : dactylo *mf*
typographic [ˌtaɪpə'græfɪk] *or* **typographical** [-fɪkəl] *adj* : typographique — **typographically** [-fɪkli] *adv*
typography [taɪ'pɑgrəfi] *n* : typographie *f*
tyrannical [tə'rænɪkəl, taɪ-] *adj* : tyrannique — **tyrannically** [-nɪkli] *adv*
tyrannize ['tɪrəˌnaɪz] *vt* **-nized; -nizing** : tyranniser
tyranny ['tɪrəni] *n, pl* **-nies** : tyrannie *f*
tyrant ['taɪrənt] *n* : tyran *m*
tzar ['zɑr, 'tsɑr, 'sɑr] → **czar**

U

u ['juː] *n, pl* **u's** *or* **us** ['juːz] : u *m*, vingt et unième lettre de l'alphabet
ubiquitous [juː'bɪkwəṭəs] *adj* : omniprésent
ubiquity [juː'bɪkwəṭi] *n* : omniprésence *f*, ubiquité *f*
udder ['ʌdər] *n* : pis *m* (d'une vache)
Ugandan[1] [juː'gændən, -'gɑn-; uː'gɑn-] *adj* : ougandais
Ugandan[2] *n* : Ougandais *m*, -daise *f*
ugliness ['ʌglinəs] *n* : laideur *f*
ugly ['ʌgli] *adj* **uglier; -est 1** : laid <an ugly color : une couleur laide> **2** DISAGREEABLE, FOUL : mauvais,

désagréable, vilain <ugly weather : du temps vilain> **3** QUARRELSOME : agressif, querelleur <the crowd turned ugly : la foule est devenue agressive>
Ukrainian[1] [juːˈkreɪniən, -ˈkraɪ-] *adj* : ukrainien
Ukrainian[2] *n* **1** : Ukrainien *m*, -nienne *f* **2** : ukrainien *m* (langue)
ukulele [juːkəˈleɪli] *n* : guitare *f* hawaïenne
ulcer [ˈʌlsər] *n* : ulcère *f*
ulcerate [ˈʌlsəˌreɪt] *vt* **-ated; -ating** : ulcérer
ulceration [ˌʌlsəˈreɪʃən] *n* : ulcération *f*
ulcerous [ˌʌlsərəs] *adj* : ulcéreux
ulna [ˈʌlnə] *n* : cubitus *m*
ulterior [ˌʌlˈtɪriər] *adj* HIDDEN : secret, inavoué <to have ulterior motives : avoir des arrière-pensées>
ultimate[1] [ˈʌltəmət] *adj* **1** FINAL : ultime, final **2** SUPREME : suprême **3** FUNDAMENTAL : absolu, fondamental
ultimate[2] *n* : summum *m* <the ultimate in modernity : le summum de la modernité>
ultimately [ˈʌltəmətli] *adv* : en fin de compte, finalement
ultimatum [ˌʌltəˈmeɪt̬əm, -ˈmɑ-] *n, pl* **-tums** *or* **-ta** [-t̬ə] : ultimatum *m* <to deliver an ultimatum : adresser un ultimatum>
ultraviolet [ˌʌltrəˈvaɪələt] *adj* : ultraviolet
umbilical cord [ˌʌmˈbɪlɪkəl] : cordon *m* ombilical
umbrage [ˈʌmbrɪdʒ] *n* **to take umbrage at** : prendre ombrage de, s'offenser de
umbrella [ˌʌmˈbrɛlə] *n* : parapluie *m*
umpire[1] [ˈʌmˌpaɪr] *v* **-pired; -piring** *vt* : arbitrer (aux sports) — *vi* : servir d'arbitre
umpire[2] *n* : arbitre *m*
umpteen [ˈʌmpˌtiːn, ˌʌmpˈ-] *adj* : des tas de
umpteenth [ˈʌmpˌtinθ, ˌʌmpˈ-] *adj* : énième
unable [ˌʌnˈeɪbəl] *adj* **to be unable to** : ne pas pouvoir, être incapable de
unabridged [ˌʌnəˈbrɪdʒd] *adj* : intégral
unacceptable [ˌʌnɪkˈsɛptəbəl] *adj* : inacceptable, inadmissible
unaccompanied [ˌʌnəˈkʌmpənid] *adj* : non accompagné
unaccountable [ˌʌnəˈkaʊntəbəl] *adj* : inexplicable — **unaccountably** [-bli] *adv*
unaccounted [ˌʌnəˈkaʊntəd] *adj* **~ for** : introuvable (se dit des choses), pas retrouvé (se dit des personnes)
unaccustomed [ˌʌnəˈkʌstəmd] *adj* **1** UNCHARACTERISTIC : inaccoutumé, inhabituel **2 to be unaccustomed to** : ne pas avoir l'habitude de
unacquainted [ˌʌnəˈkweɪntəd] *adj* **to be unacquainted with** : ne pas connaître
unadorned [ˌʌnəˈdɔrnd] *adj* : sans ornement
unadulterated [ˌʌnəˈdʌltəˌreɪt̬əd] *adj* **1** PURE : pur, naturel **2** : pur (et simple) <unadulterated nonsense : de la pure bêtise>
unaffected [ˌʌnəˈfɛktəd] *adj* **1** : qui n'est pas affecté <I was unaffected by his plea : sa demande m'a laissé indifférent> **2** NATURAL : naturel, sincère, sans affectation
unaffectedly [ˌʌnəˈfɛktədli] *adv* : sans affectation
unafraid [ˌʌnəˈfreɪd] *adj* : sans peur
unaided [ˌʌnˈeɪdəd] *adj* : sans aide, tout seul
unalike [ˌʌnəˈlaɪk] *adj* : peu ressemblant, différent
unambiguous [ˌʌnæmˈbɪgjʊəs] *adj* : non équivoque
unanimity [ˌjuːnəˈnɪmət̬i] *n* : unanimité *f*
unanimous [jʊˈnænəməs] *adj* : unanime
unanimously [jʊˈnænəməsli] *adv* : à l'unanimité, unanimement
unannounced [ˌʌnəˈnaʊnst] *adj* : inattendu, sans se faire annoncer
unanswered [ˌʌnˈæntsərd] *adj* : qui reste sans réponse
unappealing [ˌʌnəˈpiːlɪŋ] *adj* : peu attirant
unappetizing [ˌʌnˈæpəˌtaɪzɪŋ] *adj* : peu appétissant
unarguable [ˌʌnˈɑrgjuəbəl] *adj* : incontestable
unarmed [ˌʌnˈɑrmd] *adj* : non armé, sans armes
unassuming [ˌʌnəˈsuːmɪŋ] *adj* : modeste, sans prétention
unattached [ˌʌnəˈtætʃt] *adj* **1** : détaché, indépendant <unattached buildings : bâtiments détachés> **2** : libre (se dit d'une personne célibataire)
unattractive [ˌʌnəˈtræktɪv] *adj* : peu attrayant
unauthorized [ˌʌnˈɔθəˌraɪzd] *adj* : non autorisé
unavailable [ˌʌnəˈveɪləbəl] *adj* : indisponible
unavoidable [ˌʌnəˈvɔɪdəbəl] *adj* : inévitable
unaware[1] [ˌʌnəˈwær] *adv* → **unawares**
unaware[2] *adj* : qui n'est pas conscient, qui ignore <unaware of the danger : inconscient du danger>
unawares [ˌʌnəˈwærz] *adv* **1** UNEXPECTEDLY : soudainement, à l'improviste <to take unawares : prendre au dépourvu> **2** UNINTENTIONALLY : par mégarde, inconsciemment
unbalanced [ˌʌnˈbæləntst] *adj* **1** LOPSIDED : qui n'est pas équilibré **2** UNSTABLE : déséquilibré (se dit d'une personne)
unbearable [ˌʌnˈbærəbəl] *adj* : insupportable, insoutenable
unbeaten [ˌʌnˈbiːtən] *adj* : invaincu

unbecoming [ˌʌnbɪˈkʌmɪŋ] *adj* **1** UNFLATTERING : peu seyant, peu flatteur **2** UNSEEMLY : inconvenant
unbelievable [ˌʌnbəˈliːvəbəl] *adj* : incroyable — **unbelievably** [-bli] *adv*
unbend [ˌʌnˈbɛnd] *v* **-bent; -bending** *vt* : détordre (un fil, etc.) — *vi* RELAX : se détendre
unbending [ˌʌnˈbɛndɪŋ] *adj* : inflexible
unbiased [ˌʌnˈbaɪəst] *adj* : impartial
unbind [ˌʌnˈbaɪnd] *vt* **-bound; -binding 1** UNTIE : délier, détacher **2** RELEASE : libérer
unbolt [ˌʌnˈboːlt] *vt* : déverrouiller
unborn [ˌʌnˈbɔrn] *adj* : qui n'est pas encore né
unbosom [ˌʌnˈbʊzəm, -ˈbuː-] *vt* **to unbosom oneself to** : se confier à
unbreakable [ˌʌnˈbreɪkəbəl] *adj* : incassable
unbridled [ˌʌnˈbraɪdəld] *adj* UNRESTRAINED : débridé, déchaîné, non contenu
unbroken [ˌʌnˈbroːkən] *adj* **1** WHOLE : intact, qui n'est pas brisé **2** UNTAMED : indompté **3** UNINTERRUPTED : continu
unbuckle [ˌʌnˈbʌkəl] *vt* **-led; -ling** : déboucler
unburden [ˌʌnˈbərdən] *vt* **1** RELIEVE : décharger (d'un fardeau) **2 to unburden oneself** : se confier, s'épancher
unbutton [ˌʌnˈbʌtən] *vt* : déboutonner
uncalled–for [ˌʌnˈkɔldˌfɔr] *adj* : déplacé, injustifié
uncannily [ənˈkænəli] *adv* : étrangement
uncanny [ənˈkæni] *adj* **1** EERIE, STRANGE : mystérieux, troublant, étrange **2** REMARKABLE : extraordinaire
unceasing [ˌʌnˈsiːsɪŋ] *adj* : incessant, continu
unceasingly [ˌʌnˈsiːsɪŋli] *adv* : sans cesse
unceremonious [ˌʌnsɛrəˈmoːniəs] *adj* **1** INFORMAL : informel, sans façon **2** ABRUPT : précipité, brusque <an unceremonious dismissal : un licenciement précipité>
unceremoniously [ˌʌnsɛrəˈmoːniəsli] *adv* : sans façon, sans cérémonie
uncertain [ˌʌnˈsərtən] *adj* **1** INDEFINITE, UNKNOWN : incertain, inconnu **2** CHANGEABLE : incertain, variable <uncertain weather : du temps incertain> **3** UNSURE : incertain
uncertainly [ˌʌnˈsərtənli] *adv* : avec hésitation, d'un air hésitant
uncertainty [ˌʌnˈsərtənti] *n, pl* **-ties** : incertitude *f*, doute *m*
unchangeable [ˌʌnˈtʃeɪndʒəbəl] *adj* : immuable, invariable
unchanged [ˌʌnˈtʃeɪndʒd] *adj* : inchangé
unchanging [ˌʌnˈtʃeɪndʒɪŋ] *adj* : immuable
uncharacteristic [ˌʌnˌkærɪktəˈrɪstɪk] *adj* : peu habituel, peu typique
uncharged [ˌʌnˈtʃɑrdʒd] *adj* : qui n'a pas de charge électrique
uncivilized [ˌʌnˈsɪvəˌlaɪzd] *adj* **1** WILD : non civilisé (se dit d'un endroit) **2** BARBAROUS : barbare, sauvage
uncle [ˈʌŋkəl] *n* : oncle *m*
unclean [ˌʌnˈkliːn] *adj* **1** IMPURE : impur **2** DIRTY : malpropre, sale
uncleanliness [ˌʌnˈklɛnlinəs] *n* : malpropreté *f*, saleté *f*
unclear [ˌʌnˈklɪr] *adj* : peu clair, incertain
unclog [ˌʌnˈklɑg] *vt* **-clogged; -clogging** : déboucher (un évier, etc.)
unclothed [ˌʌnˈkloːðd] *adj* : nu, dévêtu
unclouded [ˌʌnˈklaʊdəd] *adj* : limpide, sans nuages
uncomfortable [ˌʌnˈkʌmpfərṭəbəl] *adj* **1** : inconfortable (se dit d'une chaise, etc.) **2** UNEASY : mal à l'aise, gêné (se dit d'une personne)
uncomfortably [ˌʌnˈkʌmpfərṭəbli] *adv* **1** DISAGREEABLY : désagréablement, inconfortablement **2** UNEASILY : avec gêne, avec inquiétude
uncommitted [ˌʌnkəˈmɪṭəd] *adj* : non engagé
uncommon [ˌʌnˈkɑmən] *adj* **1** UNUSUAL : rare, peu commun **2** REMARKABLE : remarquable, extraordinaire
uncommonly [ˌʌnˈkɑmənli] *adv* : extraordinairement, exceptionnellement
uncompromising [ˌʌnˈkɑmprəˈmaɪzɪŋ] *adj* : intransigeant, inflexible
unconcerned [ˌʌnkənˈsərnd] *adj* **1** UNINTERESTED : indifférent **2** UNWORRIED : insouciant, imperturbable
unconditional [ˌʌnkənˈdɪʃənəl] *adj* : inconditionnel — **unconditionally** *adv*
unconscious[1] [ˌʌnˈkɑnʃəs] *adj* **1** UNAWARE : inconscient **2** INSENSIBLE : sans connaissance
unconscious[2] *n* : inconscient *m*
unconsciously [ˌʌnˈkɑnʃəsli] *adv* : inconsciemment
unconsciousness [ˌʌnˈkɑnʃəsnəs] *n* : inconscience *f*
unconstitutional [ˌʌnˈkɑntstəˈtuːʃənəl, -ˈtjuː-] *adj* : inconstitutionnel
uncontrollable [ˌʌnkənˈtroːləbəl] *adj* : incontrôlable, irrésistible
uncontrollably [ˌʌnkənˈtroːləbli] *adv* : irrésistiblement <to laugh uncontrollably : rire sans pouvoir se contrôler>
uncontrolled [ˌʌnkənˈtroːld] *adj* : incontrôlé, non maîtrisé
unconventional [ˌʌnkənˈvɛntʃənəl] *adj* : peu conventionnel
unconvincing [ˌʌnkənˈvɪntsɪŋ] *adj* : peu convaincant
uncouth [ˌʌnˈkuːθ] *adj* : grossier, fruste
uncover [ˌʌnˈkʌvər] *vt* : découvrir
uncultivated [ˌʌnˈkʌltəˌveɪṭəd] *adj* : inculte
unctuous [ˈʌŋktʃʊəs] *adj* : onctueux, mielleux
uncut [ˌʌnˈkʌt] *adj* **1** : non coupé (se dit des cheveux), non taillé (se dit d'une

pierre précieuse) **2** UNABRIDGED : intégral

undaunted [ˌʌnˈdɔnṭəd] *adj* : imperturbable

undecided [ˌʌndɪˈsaɪdəd] *adj* **1** IRRESOLUTE : indécis, incertain **2** UNRESOLVED : non résolu

undefeated [ˌʌndɪˈfiːṭəd] *adj* : invaincu

undeniable [ˌʌndɪˈnaɪəbəl] *adj* : indéniable — **undeniably** [-bli] *adv*

under[1] [ˈʌndər] *adv* **1** : en dessous <the diver went under again : le plongeur est retourné sous l'eau> **2** LESS : moins <$10 or under : 10 $ ou moins> **3 to put under** : anesthésier, endormir

under[2] *adj* **1** LOWER : inférieur **2** SUBORDINATE : subordonné **3** INSUFFICIENT : insuffisant <an under dose of medicine : une dose insuffisante du médicament>

under[3] *prep* **1** BELOW, BENEATH : sous <under a tree : sous un arbre> <we walked under the ladder : nous avons passé sous l'échelle> <it's under there : c'est là-dessous> **2** UNDERNEATH : sous, en dessous de <I wore a sweater under my coat : je portais un chandail sous mon manteau> **3** (*indicating rank or authority*) : sous, sous la direction de <to serve under the general : servir sous le général> **4** : moins de <under two pounds : moins de deux livres> **5** ACCORDING TO : d'après, selon <under the terms of the contract : selon les modalités du contrat> **6 under lock and key** : sous clef

underage [ˌʌndərˈeɪdʒ] *adj* : mineur, sous l'âge réglementaire

underbrush [ˈʌndərˌbrəʃ] *n* : sous-bois *m*, broussailles *fpl*

undercarriage [ˈʌndərˌkærɪdʒ] *n* **1** : châssis *m* (d'une voiture) **2** *Brit* : train *m* d'atterrissage (d'un avion)

underclothes [ˈʌndərˌkloːz, -ˌkloːðz] *npl* → **underwear**

underclothing [ˈʌndərˌkloðɪŋ] → **underwear**

undercover [ˌʌndərˈkʌvər] *adj* : secret, clandestin <an undercover agent : un agent secret>

undercurrent [ˈʌndərˌkərənt] *n* **1** : courant *m* sous-marin **2** : sentiment *m* sous-jacent <an undercurrent of resentment : un ressentiment sous-jacent>

undercut [ˌʌndərˈkʌt] *vt* **-cut; -cutting 1** : vendre moins cher que **2** UNDERMINE : amoindrir, saper

underdeveloped [ˌʌndərdɪˈvɛləpt] *adj* : sous-développé

underdog [ˈʌndərˌdɔg] *n* **1** : celui *m* que l'on donne perdant **2** : opprimé *m*, -mée *f*

underdone [ˌʌndərˈdʌn] *adj* : pas assez cuit

underestimate [ˌʌndərˈɛstəˌmeɪt] *vt* **-mated; -mating** : sous-estimer

underexpose [ˌʌndərɪkˈspoːz] *vt* **-posed; -posing** : sous-exposer (une photo)

underexposure [ˌʌndərɪkˈspoːʒər] *n* : sous-exposition *f* (en photographie)

underfoot [ˌʌndərˈfʊt] *adv* **1** : sous les pieds <warm sand underfoot : du sable chaud sous les pieds> **2 to be underfoot** : être dans les jambes

undergarment [ˈʌndərˌgɑrmənt] *n* : sous-vêtement *m*

undergo [ˌʌndərˈgoː] *vt* **-went** [-ˈwɛnt]; **-gone** [-ˈgɔn]; **-going** : éprouver (des souffrances), subir (une opération, des examens, etc.)

undergraduate [ˌʌndərˈgrædʒʊət] *n* : étudiant *m*, -diante *f* de premier cycle; étudiant *m*, -diante *f* qui prépare une licence *France*

underground[1] [ˌʌndərˈgraʊnd] *adv* **1** : sous terre **2** SECRETLY : clandestinement, secrètement <to go underground : passer dans la clandestinité>

underground[2] [ˈʌndərˌgraʊnd] *adj* **1** SUBTERRANEAN : souterrain **2** SECRET : clandestin, secret

underground[3] [ˈʌndərˌgraʊnd] *n* **1** SUBWAY : métro *m* **2** : résistance *f* (en politique)

undergrowth [ˈʌndərˈgroːθ] *n* : sous-bois *m*, broussailles *fpl*, fardoches *fpl Can*

underhand[1] [ˈʌndərˌhænd] *adv* **1** SECRETLY, SLYLY : sournoisement, en sous-main **2** : par en dessous <to throw underhand : lancer par en dessous>

underhand[2] *adj* **1** SLY : sournois **2** : par en dessous <an underhand throw : un lancer par en dessous>

underhanded[1] [ˌʌndərˈhændəd] *adv* → **underhand**[1]

underhanded[2] *adj* SECRET : clandestin <underhanded dealings : transactions en sous-main>

underline [ˈʌndərˌlaɪn] *vt* **-lined; -lining 1** : souligner (un mot) **2** STRESS : souligner, mettre l'accent sur

underling [ˈʌndərlɪŋ] *n* : subordonné *m*, -née *f;* subalterne *mf*

underlying [ˌʌndərˈlaɪɪŋ] *adj* **1** : sous-jacent <underlying strata : strates sous-jacentes> **2** FUNDAMENTAL : fondamental, sous-jacent

undermine [ˌʌndərˈmaɪn] *vt* **-mined; -mining 1** : saper, miner (un escarpement, une construction, etc.) **2** SAP, WEAKEN : saper, amoindrir <to undermine one's confidence : saper sa confiance>

underneath[1] [ˌʌndərˈniːθ] *adv* : en dessous, dessous <the part underneath : la partie d'en dessous>

underneath[2] *prep* : sous, au-dessous de

undernourished [ˌʌndərˈnərɪʃt] *adj* : sous-alimenté

undernourishment [ˌʌndərˈnərɪʃmənt] *n* : sous-alimentation *f*
underpants [ˈʌndərˌpænts] *npl* : slip *m France,* caleçon *m,* petite culotte *f Can*
underpass [ˈʌndərˌpæs] *n* : voie *f* inférieure (de l'autoroute), passage *m* souterrain (pour les piétons)
underprivileged [ˌʌndərˈprɪvlɪdʒd] *adj* : défavorisé, déshérité
underrate [ˌʌndərˈreɪt] *vt* **-rated; -rating** : sous-estimer
underscore [ˈʌndərˌskor] *vt* **-scored -scoring** → **underline**
undersea[1] [ˌʌndərˈsiː] *or* **underseas** [-ˈsiːz] *adv* : sous la mer
undersea[2] *adj* : sous-marin
undersecretary [ˌʌndərˈsɛkrəˌtɛri] *n, pl* **-taries** : sous-secrétaire *mf*
undersell [ˌʌndərˈsɛl] *vt* **-sold** [-ˈsoːld]; **-selling** : vendre moins cher que
undershirt [ˈʌndərˌʃərt] *n* : maillot *m* de corps, camisole *f Can*
undershorts [ˈʌndərˌʃorts] *npl* : caleçon *m*
underside [ˈʌndərˌsaɪd, ˌʌndərˈsaɪd] *n* : dessous *m*
undersized [ˌʌndərˈsaɪzd] *adj* : trop petit
understand [ˌʌndərˈstænd] *v* **-stood** [-ˈstʊd]; **-standing** *vt* **1** COMPREHEND : comprendre <I don't understand : je ne comprends pas> <to make oneself understood : se faire comprendre> **2** BELIEVE : croire, comprendre <I understand that he is sick : je crois qu'il est malade> **3** INFER : entendre <to let it be understood that : laisser entendre que> — *vi* : comprendre
understandable [ˌʌndərˈstændəbəl] *adj* : compréhensible <that's understandable : ça se comprend>
understandably [ˌʌndərˈstændəbli] *adv* : naturellement
understanding[1] [ˌʌndərˈstændɪŋ] *adj* : compréhensif, bienveillant
understanding[2] *n* **1** GRASP : compréhension *f,* entendement *m,* intelligence *f* **2** AGREEMENT : entente *f,* accord *m* **3** INTERPRETATION : interprétation *f* <my understanding was that : j'ai compris que> **4** SYMPATHY : compréhension *f*
understate [ˌʌndərˈsteɪt] *vt* **-stated; -stating** : minimiser, réduire l'importance de
understatement [ˌʌndərˈsteɪtmənt] *n* : affirmation *f* en dessous de la vérité <that's an understatement! : c'est peu dire!>
understudy [ˈʌndərˌstʌdi] *n, pl* **-dies** : doublure *f* (au théâtre)
undertake [ˌʌndərˈteɪk] *vt* **-took** [-ˈtʊk]; **-taken** [-ˈteɪkən]; **-taking 1** : entreprendre (une tâche), assumer (une responsabilité) **2** GUARANTEE : s'engager à, promettre (à faire quelque chose)
undertaker [ˈʌndərˌteɪkər] *n* : entrepreneur *m* de pompes funèbres
undertaking [ˈʌndərˌteɪkɪŋ, ˌʌndərˈ-] *n* **1** ENTERPRISE, VENTURE : entreprise *f* **2** PLEDGE : promesse *f,* garantie *f*
undertone [ˈʌndərˌtoːn] *n* **1** : voix *f* basse <to speak in an undertone : parler à mi-voix, parler à voix basse> **2** HINT, UNDERCURRENT : pointe *f,* note *f*
undertow [ˈʌndərˌtoː] *n* : courant *m* sous-marin
undervalue [ˌʌndərˈvælˌjuː] *vt* **-ued; -uing** : sous-évaluer, sous-estimer
underwater[1] [ˌʌndərˈwɔt̬ər, -ˈwɑ-] *adv* : sous l'eau
underwater[2] *adj* : sous-marin <underwater plants : plantes sous-marines>
under way [ˌʌndərˈweɪ] *adv* : en cours, en route <to get under way : se mettre en route>
underwear [ˈʌndərˌwær] *n* : sous-vêtements *mpl*
underworld [ˈʌndərˌwərld] *n* **1** *or* **criminal underworld** : milieu *m,* pègre *f* **2 the underworld** HELL : les enfers
underwrite [ˈʌndərˌraɪt, ˌʌndərˈ-] *vt* **-wrote** [-ˌroːt, -ˈroːt]; **-written** [-ˌrɪtən, -ˈrɪtən]; **-writing 1** FINANCE : soutenir financièrement **2** INSURE : garantir, souscrire (une police d'assurance)
underwriter [ˈʌndərˌraɪt̬ər, ˌʌndərˈ-] *n* INSURER : assureur *m*
undeserving [ˌʌndɪˈzərvɪŋ] *adj* : peu méritant
undesirable [ˌʌndɪˈzaɪrəbəl] *adj* : indésirable
undeveloped [ˌʌndɪˈvɛləpt] *adj* : non développé, inexploité
undies [ˈʌndiːz] *npl* → **underwear**
undignified [ˌʌnˈdɪgnəfaɪd] *adj* : indigne, qui manque de dignité
undiluted [ˌʌndaɪˈluːt̬əd, -də-] *adj* : non dilué, sans mélange
undiscovered [ˌʌndɪˈskʌvərd] *adj* : non découvert
undisputed [ˌʌndɪˈspjuːt̬əd] *adj* : incontesté
undisturbed [ˌʌndɪˈstərbd] *adj* **1** PEACEFUL : tranquille **2** UNTOUCHED : intact, non dérangé
undivided [ˌʌndɪˈvaɪdəd] *adj* : entier <your undivided attention : toute votre attention>
undo [ˌʌnˈduː] *vt* **-did; -done; -doing 1** UNTIE : défaire **2** UNWRAP : déballer **3** REVERSE : retourner, réparer (les dommages) **4** RUIN : détruire
undoing [ˌʌnˈduːɪŋ] *n* RUIN : ruine *f,* perte *f*
undoubted [ˌʌnˈdaʊt̬əd] *adj* : indubitable, certain
undoubtedly [ˌʌnˈdaʊt̬ədli] *adv* : indubitablement, sans aucun doute
undress [ˌʌnˈdrɛs] *vt* : déshabiller, dévêtir — *vi* : se déshabiller, se dévêtir

undrinkable [ˌʌn'drɪŋkəbəl] *adj* : non potable

undue [ˌʌn'du:, -'dju:] *adj* : excessif, démesuré — **unduly** [ˌʌn'du:li] *adv*

undulate ['ʌndʒəˌleɪt] *vi* **-lated; -lating** : onduler

undulation [ˌʌndʒə'leɪʃən] *n* : ondulation *f*

undying [ˌʌn'daɪɪŋ] *adj* : éternel, perpétuel <undying love : amour éternel>

unearth [ˌʌn'ɛrθ] *vt* **1** EXHUME : déterrer, exhumer **2** DISCOVER : dénicher, découvrir

unearthly [ˌʌn'ɛrθli] *adj* **1** STRANGE, WEIRD : surnaturel, étrange **2** UNGODLY : indu <at an unearthly hour : à une heure indue>

uneasily [ˌʌn'i:zəli] *adv* **1** UNCOMFORTABLY : d'un air gêné **2** APPREHENSIVELY : avec inquiétude

uneasiness [ˌʌn'i:zinəs] *n* : inquiétude *f*, malaise *m*

uneasy [ˌʌn'i:zi] *adj* **1** AWKWARD, EMBARRASSED : mal à l'aise, gêné **2** RESTLESS : agité, inquiet **3** UNSTABLE : précaire <an uneasy truce : une trêve précaire>

uneducated [ˌʌn'ɛdʒəˌkeɪt̬əd] *adj* : sans éducation

unemployed [ˌʌnɪm'plɔɪd] *adj* : en chômage, sans travail

unemployment [ˌʌnɪm'plɔɪmənt] *n* : chômage *m*

unending [ˌʌn'ɛndɪŋ] *adj* : sans fin, interminable

unendurable [ˌʌnɪn'dʊrəbəl] *adj* : intolérable

unequal [ˌʌn'i:kwəl] *adj* **1** : inégal **2 to be unequal to a task** : ne pas être à la hauteur d'une tâche

unequaled *or* **unequalled** [ˌʌn'i:kwəld] *adj* : inégalé, sans égal

unequally [ˌʌn'i:kwəli] *adv* : de manière inégale

unequivocal [ˌʌnɪ'kwɪvəkəl] *adj* : explicite, sans équivoque, clair

unequivocally [ˌʌnɪ'kwɪvəkəli] *adv* : explicitement

unerring [ˌʌn'ɛrɪŋ, -'ər-] *adj* : infaillible

uneven [ˌʌn'i:vən] *adj* **1** ODD : impair <uneven numbers : chiffres impairs> **2** : inégal <uneven terrain : terrain inégal> <an uneven performance : une performance inégale> **3** IRREGULAR : inégal, irrégulier <uneven teeth : dentition irrégulière>

unevenly [ˌʌn'i:vənli] *adv* **1** : de façon inégale **2** IRREGULARLY : de façon irrégulière

unevenness [ˌʌn'i:vənnəs] *n* : inégalité *f*, irrégularité *f*

uneventful [ˌʌnɪ'vɛntfəl] *adj* : sans histoires, peu mouvementé

uneventfully [ˌʌnɪ'vɛntfəli] *adv* : sans incidents

unexpected [ˌʌnɪk'spɛktəd] *adj* : inattendu, imprévu

unexpectedly [ˌʌnɪk'spɛktədli] *adv* : à l'improviste, contre toute attente

unexplained [ˌʌnɪk'spleɪnd] *adj* : inexpliqué

unfailing [ˌʌn'feɪlɪŋ] *adj* **1** CONSTANT : inaltérable, invariable <unfailing courtesy : courtoisie inaltérable> **2** INEXHAUSTIBLE : inépuisable, infini **3** SURE : infaillible, sûr

unfailingly [ˌʌn'feɪlɪŋli] *adv* : invariablement, inlassablement

unfair [ˌʌn'fær] *adj* : injuste — **unfairly** *adj*

unfairness [ˌʌn'færnəs] *n* : injustice *f*

unfaithful [ˌʌn'feɪθfəl] *adj* : infidèle — **unfaithfully** *adv*

unfaithfulness [ˌʌn'feɪθfəlnəs] *n* : infidélité *f*

unfamiliar [ˌʌnfə'mɪljər] *adj* **1** : inconnu, peu familier **2 to be unfamiliar with sth** : mal connaître qqch

unfamiliarity [ˌʌnfəˌmɪli'ærət̬i] *n, pl* **-ties** : caractère *m* peu connu, connaissance *f* limitée

unfasten [ˌn'fæsən] *vt* : déboucler (une ceinture), défaire (un bouton)

unfavorable [ˌʌn'feɪvərəbəl] *adj* : défavorable — **unfavorably** [-bli] *adv*

unfeeling [ˌʌn'fi:lɪŋ] *adj* : insensible, froid

unfeelingly [ˌʌn'fi:lɪŋli] *adv* : froidement, sans pitié

unfinished [ˌʌn'fɪnɪʃd] *adj* : inachevé, en cours

unfit [ˌʌn'fɪt] *adj* **1** UNSUITABLE : inapte, impropre <unfit for consumption : impropre à la consommation> **2** UNSUITED : inapte, incapable **3** : qui n'est pas en forme <he's physically unfit : physiquement, il n'est pas en forme>

unflappable [ˌʌn'flæpəbəl] *adj* : imperturbable

unflattering [ˌʌn'flæt̬ərɪŋ] *adj* : peu flatteur

unfold [ˌʌn'fo:ld] *vt* **1** EXPAND : déplier <to unfold a map : déplier une carte> **2** REVEAL : exposer, dévoiler (un plan, etc.) — *vi* **1** DEVELOP : se dérouler, évoluer <the story unfolded : l'histoire s'est déroulée> **2** : se dévoiler, se manifester <a panorama unfolded before their eyes : un panorama se dévoilait devant leurs yeux>

unforeseeable [ˌʌnfor'siəbəl] *adj* : imprévisible

unforeseen [ˌʌnfor'si:n] *adj* : imprévu, inattendu

unforgettable [ˌʌnfər'gɛt̬əbəl] *adj* : inoubliable, mémorable — **unforgettably** [-bli] *adv*

unforgivable [ˌʌnfər'gɪvəbəl] *adj* : impardonnable, inexcusable

unfortunate[1] [ˌʌn'fɔrtʃənət] *adj* **1** UNLUCKY : malchanceux **2** REGRETTABLE : malheureux, fâcheux <how unfortunate! : quel dommage!>

unfortunate[2] *n* : malheureux *m*, -reuse *f*

unfortunately [ˌʌnˈfɔrtʃənətli] *adv* : malheureusement

unfounded [ˌʌnˈfaʊndəd] *adj* : sans fondement

unfreeze [ˌʌnˈfriːz] *vt* **-froze; -frozen; -freezing 1** THAW : dégeler **2** : débloquer <to unfreeze prices : débloquer les prix>

unfriendliness [ˌʌnˈfrɛndlinəs] *n* : froideur *f*

unfriendly [ˌʌnˈfrɛndli] *adj* : peu amical, peu sympathique, froid

unfurl [ˌʌnˈfərl] *vt* : dérouler, déployer — *vi* : se déployer

unfurnished [ˌʌnˈfərnɪʃt] *adj* : non meublé

ungainly [ˌʌnˈgeɪnli] *adj* AWKWARD, CLUMSY : gauche, maladroit

ungodly [ˌʌnˈgɔdli, -ˈgɑd-] *adj* **1** IMPIOUS : impie (en religion) **2** WICKED : mauvais, honteux **3** OUTRAGEOUS : indu, impossible <at an ungodly hour : à une heure indue>

ungracious [ˌʌnˈgreɪʃəs] *adj* : désobligeant, désagréable

ungrateful [ˌʌnˈgreɪtfəl] *adj* : ingrat

ungratefully [ˌʌnˈgreɪtfəli] *adv* : avec ingratitude

ungratefulness [ˌʌnˈgreɪtfəlnəs] *n* : ingratitude *f*

unhappily [ˌʌnˈhæpəli] *adv* **1** UNFORTUNATELY : malheureusement **2** SADLY : tristement

unhappiness [ˌʌnˈhæpinəs] *n* : tristesse *f*, peine *f*

unhappy [ˌʌnˈhæpi] *adj* **-happier; -est 1** UNFORTUNATE : malheureux, regrettable **2** SAD : malheureux, triste **3** DISSATISFIED : mécontent

unhealthy [ˌʌnˈhɛlθi] *adj* **-healthier; -est 1** UNWHOLESOME : insalubre, malsain <an unhealthy climate : un climat malsain> **2** SICKLY : malade, maladif **3** MORBID : morbid, malsain (se dit de la curiosité, etc.)

unheard–of [ˌʌnˈhərdəv] *adj* : sans précédent, inconnu

unhinge [ˌənˈhɪndʒ] *vt* **-hinged; -hinging 1** : démonter, enlever de ses gonds (une porte, une fenêtre) **2** UNBALANCE, UNSETTLE : déstabiliser, déséquilibrer (une personne)

unhitch [ˌʌnˈhɪtʃ] *vt* : détacher, décrocher

unholy [ˌʌnˈhoːli] *adj* **-holier; -est 1** : impie (en religion) **2** OUTRAGEOUS, SHOCKING : scandaleux, épouvantable <an unholy hour : une heure indue>

unhook [ˌʌnˈhʊk] *vt* : décrocher (un tableau, etc.), dégrafer (un vêtement)

unhurried [ˌʌnˈhʌrid] *adj* : qui ne se presse pas, tranquille

unhurt [ˌʌnˈhərt] *adj* : indemne

unicorn [ˈjuːnəˌkɔrn] *n* : licorne *f*

unidentified [ˌʌnaɪˈdɛntəˌfaɪd] *adj* : non identifié <unidentified flying object : objet volant non identifié>

unification [ˌjuːnəfəˈkeɪʃən] *n* : unification *f*

uniform[1] [ˈjuːnəˌfɔrm] *adj* **1** CONSTANT, UNCHANGING : uniforme, constant **2** IDENTICAL : identique

uniform[2] *n* : uniforme *m* <military uniform : uniforme militaire>

uniformity [ˌjuːnəˈfɔrməṭi] *n, pl* **-ties** : uniformité *f*

uniformly [ˈjuːnəˌfɔrmli] *adv* : uniformément

unify [ˈjuːnəˌfaɪ] *vt* **-fied; -fying** : unifier

unilateral [ˌjuːnəˈlæṭərəl] *adj* : unilatéral — **unilaterally** *adv*

unimaginable [ˌʌnɪˈmædʒənəbəl] *adj* : inconcevable, inimaginable

unimportant [ˌʌnɪmˈpɔrtənt] *adj* : sans importance

uninhabited [ˌʌnɪnˈhæbəṭəd] *adj* : inhabité

uninhibited [ˌʌnɪnˈhɪbəṭəd] *adj* : sans inhibitions, sans complexes

unintelligent [ˌʌnɪnˈtɛlədʒənt] *adj* : inintelligent

unintelligible [ˌʌnɪnˈtɛlədʒəbəl] *adj* : inintelligible

unintentional [ˌʌnɪnˈtɛntʃənəl] *adj* : involontaire — **unintentionally** *adv*

uninterested [ˌʌnˈɪntəˌrɛstəd, -trəstəd] *adj* : indifférent

uninteresting [ˌʌnˈɪntəˌrɛstɪŋ, -trəstɪŋ] *adj* : inintéressant, sans intérêt

uninterrupted [ˌʌnˌɪntəˈrʌptəd] *adj* : ininterrompu, continu

union [ˈjuːnjən] *n* **1** : union *f* **2** *or* **labor union** : syndicat *m*

unionize [ˈjuːnjəˌnaɪz] *v* **-ized; -izing** *vt* : syndiquer, syndicaliser — *vi* : se syndicaliser

unique [jʊˈniːk] *adj* **1** SOLE : unique, seul <his unique concern : son seul souci> **2** UNUSUAL : unique, particulier **3** UNEQUALED : exceptionnel, sans égal

uniquely [jʊˈniːkli] *adv* **1** EXCLUSIVELY : uniquement, exclusivement **2** EXCEPTIONALLY : exceptionellement

uniqueness [jʊˈniːknəs] *n* : originalité *f*, caractère *m* unique

unison [ˈjuːnəsən, -zən] *n* **1** : unisson *m* <to sing in unison : chanter à l'unisson> **2 to act in unison** : agir de concert

unit[1] [ˈjuːnɪt] *adj* : unitaire <unit price : prix unitaire>

unit[2] *n* **1** ONE : unité *f* **2** : unité *f* <unit of measurement : unité de mesure> **3** GROUP : groupe *m*, unité *f* <research unit : groupe de recherche> **4** PART : élément *m*

unite [jʊˈnaɪt] *v* **united; uniting** *vt* **1** JOIN, LINK : unir **2** UNIFY : unifier — *vi* : s'unir

unity [ˈjuːnəṭi] *n, pl* **-ties 1** ONENESS : unité *f* **2** HARMONY : unité *f*, harmonie *f*

universal [ˌjuːnəˈvərsəl] *adj* **1** GENERAL : universel, général <universal rules : des règles universelles> **2** WORLDWIDE : universel, mondial

universally [juːnəˈvərsəli] *adv* : universellement

universe [ˈjuːnəˌvərs] *n* : univers *m*

university [ˌjuːnəˈvərsəṭi] *n, pl* **-ties** : université *f*

unjust [ˌʌnˈdʒʌst] *adj* : injuste — **unjustly** *adv*

unjustifiable [ˌʌnˌdʒʌstəˈfaɪəbəl] *adj* : injustifiable

unjustified [ˌʌnˈdʒʌstəˌfaɪd] *adj* : injustifié

unkempt [ˌʌnˈkɛmpt] *adj* : en désordre, négligé, ébouriffé (se dit des cheveux)

unkind [ˌʌnˈkaɪnd] *adj* : peu aimable, pas gentil

unkindly [ˌʌnˈkaɪndli] *adv* : méchamment

unkindness [ˌʌnˈkaɪndnəs] *n* : manque *m* de gentillesse, méchanceté *f*

unknowing [ˌʌnˈnoːɪŋ] *adj* : inconscient

unknowingly [ˌʌnˈnoːɪŋli] *adv* : sans le savoir

unknown [ˌʌnˈnoːn] *adj* : inconnu

unlawful [ˌʌnˈlɔfəl] *adj* : illégal, illicite — **unlawfully** *adv*

unleash [ˌʌnˈliːʃ] *vt* **1** RELEASE : libérer, lâcher **2** : déchaîner (des passions, de la furie, etc.)

unless [ənˈlɛs] *conj* : à moins que, à moins de

unlike[1] [ˌʌnˈlaɪk] *adj* **1** DIFFERENT : dissemblable, différent **2** UNEQUAL : inégal

unlike[2] *prep* **1** : différent de <he's very unlike his brother : il est très différent de son frère> **2** : contrairement à, à la différence de <unlike him, she enjoys her work : contrairement à lui, elle aime son travail> **3** (*indicating an uncharacteristic state or action*) <it's unlike them to be late : ça n'est pas dans leur habitude d'être en retard>

unlikelihood [ˌʌnˈlaɪkliˌhʊd] *n* : improbabilité *f*

unlikely [ˌʌnˈlaɪkli] *adj* **-liklier; -est 1** IMPROBABLE : improbable, peu probable **2** UNPROMISING : peu prometteur

unlimited [ˌʌnˈlɪməṭəd] *adj* : illimité

unload [ˌʌnˈloːd] *vt* **1** : décharger (un bateau, un fusil, de la cargaison, etc.) **2** DISPOSE OF, DUMP : se débarrasser de, se défaire de — *vi* : être déchargé

unlock [ˌʌnˈlɑk] *vt* **1** : ouvrir, débarrer *Can* (une porte, etc.) **2** DISCLOSE, REVEAL : découvrir, révéler

unluckily [ˌʌnˈlʌkəli] *adv* : malheureusement

unlucky [ˌʌnˈlʌki] *adj* **-luckier; -est 1** : malchanceux <an unlucky year : une année malchanceuse> **2** INAUSPICIOUS : qui porte malheur **3** REGRETTABLE : malencontreux, regrettable

unmanageable [ˌʌnˈmænɪdʒəbəl] *adj* : difficile à manier, peu maniable

unmarried [ˌʌnˈmærid] *adj* : non marié, célibataire

unmask [ˌʌnˈmæsk] *vt* : démasquer

unmatched [ˌʌnˈmætʃt] *adj* : sans égal, incomparable

unmerciful [ˌʌnˈmərsɪfəl] *adj* : sans merci, impitoyable

unmercifully [ˌʌnˈmərsɪfəl] *adv* : impitoyablement

unmistakable [ˌʌnmɪˈsteɪkəbəl] *adj* : évident, indubitable

unmistakably [ˌʌnmɪˈsteɪkəbli] *adv* : indubitablement

unmoved [ˌʌnˈmuːvd] *adj* : indifférent, insensible

unnatural [ˌʌnˈnætʃərəl] *adj* **1** ABNORMAL, UNUSUAL : anormal, peu naturel **2** AFFECTED : artificiel, affecté **3** PERVERSE : pervers, contre nature

unnaturally [ˌʌnˈnætʃərəli] *adv* : anormalement, de façon peu naturelle

unnecessarily [ˌʌnˌnɛsəˈsɛrəli] *adv* : inutilement, sans raison

unnecessary [ˌʌnˈnɛsəˌsɛri] *adj* : inutile, superflu

unnerve [ˌʌnˈnərv] *vt* **-nerved; -nerving** : décontenancer, déconcerter, rendre nerveux

unnoticeable [ˌʌnˈnoːṭəsəbəl] *adj* : imperceptible

unnoticed [ˌʌnˈnoːṭəst] *adj* : inaperçu

unobstructed [ˌʌnəbˈstrʌktəd] *adj* : non obstrué, dégagé

unobtainable [ʌnəbˈteɪnəbəl] *adj* : introuvable, impossible à obtenir

unobtrusive [ˌʌnəbˈtruːsɪv] *adj* : discret, pas trop visible

unoccupied [ˌʌnˈɑkjəˌpaɪd] *adj* **1** IDLE : inoccupé, oisif **2** EMPTY : libre, vacant

unofficial [ˌʌnəˈfɪʃəl] *adj* : officieux, non officiel

unorganized [ˌʌnˈɔrgəˌnaɪzd] *adj* : mal organisé, inorganisé

unorthodox [ˌʌnˈɔrθəˌdɑks] *adj* : peu orthodoxe

unpack [ˌʌnˈpæk] *vt* : défaire, déballer <to unpack one's suitcase : défaire sa valise> — *vi* : défaire ses bagages

unpaid [ˌʌnˈpeɪd] *adj* **1** : impayé (se dit d'une facture), non acquitté (se dit d'une dette) **2** : bénévole, non rémunéré <unpaid assistants : assistants bénévoles>

unparalleled [ˌʌnˈpærəˌlɛld] *adj* : sans égal, sans pareil

unpatriotic [ˌʌnˌpeɪtriˈɑtɪk] *adj* : peu patriote

unpleasant [ˌʌnˈplɛzənt] *adj* : désagréable, déplaisant

unpleasantly [ˌʌnˈplɛzəntli] *adv* : désagréablement, de façon déplaisante
unplug [ˌʌnˈplʌg] *vt* **-plugged; -plugging 1** UNCLOG : déboucher **2** DISCONNECT : débrancher, déconnecter
unpopular [ˌʌnˈpɑpjələr] *adj* : impopulaire, peu populaire
unpopularity [ˌʌnˌpɑpjəˈlærəţi] *n* : impopularité *f*
unprecedented [ˌʌnˈprɛsəˌdɛntəd] *adj* : sans précédent
unpredictable [ˌʌnprɪˈdɪktəbəl] *adj* : imprévisible
unprejudiced [ˌʌnˈprɛdʒədəst] *adj* : sans préjugés, sans parti pris, impartial
unprepared [ˌʌnpriˈpærd] *adj* : mal préparé
unpretentious [ˌʌnpriˈtɛntʃəs] *adj* : sans prétention
unprincipled [ˌʌnˈprɪntsəpəld] *adj* : sans scrupules
unproductive [ˌʌnprəˈdʌktɪv] *adj* : improductif
unprofitable [ˌʌnˈprɑfəţəbəl] *adj* **1** : non rentable (se dit d'une entreprise, etc.) **2** VAIN : peu profitable, inutile
unpromising [ˌʌnˈprɑməsɪŋ] *adj* : peu prometteur
unprotected [ˌʌnprəˈtɛktəd] *adj* **1** : sans protection **2** EXPOSED : exposé
unprovoked [ˌʌnprəˈvoːkt] *adj* : sans provocation, délibéré
unpunished [ˌʌnˈpʌnɪʃt] *adj* : impuni <to go unpunished : rester impuni>
unqualified [ˌʌnˈkwɑləˌfaɪd] *adj* **1** UNFIT : non qualifié, incompétent **2** COMPLETE : sans réserve, inconditionnel <an unqualified denial : un démenti sans réserve>
unquestionable [ˌʌnˈkwɛstʃənəbəl] *adj* : incontestable, indéniable
unquestionably [ˌʌnˈkwɛstʃənəbli] *adv* : incontestablement, sans aucun doute
unquestioning [ˌʌnˈkwɛstʃənɪŋ] *adj* : inconditionnel, absolu
unravel [ˌʌnˈrævəl] *v* **-eled** *or* **-elled; -eling** *or* **elling** *vt* **1** DISENTANGLE : démêler **2** SOLVE : résoudre, éclaircir <to unravel a mystery : résoudre un mystère> — *vi* : se démêler
unreal [ˌʌnˈriːl] *adj* : irréel
unrealistic [ˌʌnˌriːəˈlɪstɪk] *adj* : peu réaliste, irréaliste
unreality [ˌʌnriˈæləţi] *n* : irréalité *f*
unreasonable [ˌʌnˈriːzənəbel] *adj* **1** SENSELESS : déraisonnable **2** EXCESSIVE : excessif, démesuré
unreasonably [ˌʌnˈriːzənəbli] *adv* **1** SENSELESSLY : déraisonnablement **2** EXCESSIVELY : excessivement
unrelated [ˌʌnrɪˈleɪţəd] *adj* : sans rapport
unrelenting [ˌʌnrɪˈlɛntɪŋ] *adj* **1** STERN : dur, implacable **2** CONSTANT : continuel
unrelentingly [ˌʌnrɪˈlɛntɪŋli] *adv* : sans répit
unreliable [ˌʌnrɪˈlaɪəbəl] *adj* : peu fidèle, peu sûr
unrepentant [ˌʌnrɪˈpɛntənt] *adj* : impénitent
unresolved [ˌʌnriˈzɑlvd] *adj* : non résolu
unrest [ˌʌnˈrɛst] *n* : agitation *f,* troubles *mpl* <social unrest : malaise social>
unrestrained [ˌʌnrɪˈstreɪnd] *adj* : effréné, non contenu
unrestricted [ˌʌnrɪˈstrɪktəd] *adj* : libre, illimité <unrestricted access : libre accès>
unrewarding [ˌʌnrɪˈwɔrdɪŋ] *adj* THANKLESS : ingrat
unripe [ˌʌnˈraɪp] *adj* : pas mûr, vert
unrivaled *or* **unrivalled** [ˌʌnˈraɪvəld] *adj* : sans égal, incomparable
unroll [ˌʌnˈroːl] *vt* : dérouler — *vi* : se dérouler
unruffled [ˌʌnˈrʌfəld] *adj* **1** : imperturbable (se dit d'une personne) **2** SMOOTH : calme <unruffled waters : eaux calmes>
unruly [ˌʌnˈruːli] *adj* : indiscipliné
unsafe [ˌʌnˈseɪf] *adj* **1** DANGEROUS : dangereux **2 to feel unsafe** : ne pas se sentir en sécurité, se sentir en danger
unsaid [ˌʌnˈsɛd] *adj* : inexprimé, non dit <to leave unsaid : passer sous silence>
unsanitary [ˌʌnˈsænəˌtɛri] *adj* : peu hygiénique
unsatisfactory [ˌʌnˌsætəsˈfæktəri] *adj* : peu satisfaisant
unsatisfied [ˌʌnˈsætəsˌfaɪd] *adj* : peu satisfait, insatisfait
unsavory [ˌʌnˈseɪvəri] *adj* **1** TASTELESS : peu savoureux, insipide **2** DISTASTEFUL : désagréable
unscathed [ˌʌnˈskeɪðd] *adj* UNHARMED : indemne
unscheduled [ˌʌnˈskɛˌdʒuːld] *adj* : imprévu
unscientific [ˌʌnˌsaɪənˈtɪfɪk] *adj* : non scientifique
unscrew [ˌʌnˈskruː] *vt* : dévisser
unscrupulous [ˌʌnˈskruːpjələs] *adj* : sans scrupules, peu scrupuleux
unscrupulously [ˌʌnˈskruːpjələsli] *adv* : sans scrupules, peu scrupuleusement
unseal [ˌʌnˈsiːl] *vt* : décacheter (une enveloppe, etc.)
unseasonable [ˌʌnˈsiːzənəbəl] *adj* **1** UNTIMELY : inopportun, mal choisi **2** : hors de saison <unseasonable weather : température qui n'est pas de saison>
unseemly [ˌʌnˈsiːmli] *adj* **-seemlier; -est 1** UNBECOMING : inconvenant **2** INAPPROPRIATE : inapproprié
unseen [ˌʌnˈsiːn] *adj* : invisible, inaperçu
unselfish [ˌʌnˈsɛlfɪʃ] *adj* : désintéressé, généreux

unselfishly [ˌʌnˈsɛlfɪʃli] *adv* : généreusement, de façon désintéressée
unselfishness [ˌʌnˈsɛlfɪʃnəs] *n* : générosité *f*, désintéressement *m*
unsettle [ˌʌnˈsɛṭəl] *vt* **-tled; -tling 1** UPSET : déranger (l'estomac) **2** DISTURB : perturber, troubler
unsettled [ˌʌnˈsɛtəld] *adj* **1** DISTURBED : perturbé, troublé **2** VARIABLE : changeant, variable <unsettled weather : temps variable> **3** DOUBTFUL, UNDECIDED : incertain, non résolu **4** UNPAID : impayé, non réglé **5** UNINHABITED : inhabité
unsightly [ˌʌnˈsaɪtli] *adj* : laid, disgracieux
unskilled [ˌʌnˈskɪld] *adj* : non qualifié, non spécialisé
unskillful [ˌʌnˈskɪlfəl] *adj* : malhabile, inexpert
unsociable [ˌʌnˈsoːʃəbəl] *adj* : peu sociable, insociable
unsolved [ˌʌnˈsɔlvd] *adj* : non résolu
unsophisticated [ˌʌnsəˈfɪstəˌkeɪṭəd] *adj* : peu sophistiqué, simple
unsound [ˌʌnˈsaʊnd] *adj* **1** : peu judicieux (se dit d'une idée), instable (se dit d'une structure) **2 to be of unsound mind** : ne pas avoir toute sa raison
unspeakable [ˌʌnˈspiːkəbəl] *adj* **1** INEXPRESSIBLE : indescriptible, indicible **2** ATROCIOUS : innommable, atroce
unspeakably [ˌʌnˈspiːkəbli] *adv* **1** INEXPRESSIBLY : indiciblement **2** ATROCIOUSLY : atrocement
unspecified [ˌʌnˈspɛsəˌfaɪd] *adj* : non spécifié
unspoiled [ˌʌnˈspɔɪld] *adj* **1** : qui n'a pas été gâté (se dit d'un enfant) **2** : intact, naturel, vierge <unspoiled scenery : paysage intact>
unstable [ˌʌnˈsteɪbəl] *adj* : instable
unsteadily [ˌʌnˈstɛdəli] *adv* : d'un pas chancelant, d'une main tremblante, d'une voix mal assurée
unsteady [ˌʌnˈstɛdi] *adj* **1** : instable, branlant (se dit d'une structure, etc.) **2** SHAKY : tremblant, chancelant, mal assuré **3** IRREGULAR : irrégulier
unstoppable [ˌʌnˈstɑpəbəl] *adj* : irrésistible, qu'on ne peut pas arrêter
unsubstantiated [ˌʌnsəbˈstæntʃiˌeɪṭəd] *adj* : non confirmé, non corroboré
unsuccessful [ˌʌnsəkˈsɛsfəl] *adj* : infructueux, qui n'a pas réussi
unsuitable [ˌʌnˈsuːṭəbəl] *adj* : qui ne convient pas, inconvenant, inapproprié <an unsuitable time : un moment inopportun>
unsuited [ˌʌnˈsuːṭəd] *adj* : inadapté, mal adapté, inapproprié
unsung [ˌʌnˈsʌŋ] *adj* : méconnu
unsure [ˌʌnˈʃʊr] *adj* : incertain, pas sûr <to be unsure of oneself : manquer de confiance en soi>
unsurpassed [ˌʌnsərˈpæst] *adj* : sans pareil, sans égal
unsuspecting [ˌʌnsəˈspɛktɪŋ] *adj* : qui ne se doute de rien, sans méfiance
unsympathetic [ˌʌnˌsɪmpəˈθɛṭɪk] *adj* : incompréhensif, peu compatissant
untangle [ˌʌnˈtæŋgəl] *vt* **-gled; -gling 1** : démêler (des fils, etc.), débrouiller (un problème, un mystère)
unthinkable [ˌʌnˈθɪŋkəbəl] *adj* : impensable, inconcevable
unthinking [ˌʌnˈθɪŋkɪŋ] *adj* : irréfléchi, inconsidéré
unthinkingly [ˌʌnˈθɪŋkɪŋli] *adv* : inconsidérément, sans réfléchir
untidy [ˌʌnˈtaɪdi] *adj* **-tidier; -est 1** : désordonné, débraillé (se dit d'une personne) **2** : en désordre <an untidy room : une chambre en désordre>
untie [ˌʌnˈtaɪ] *vt* **-tied; -tying** *or* **-tieing 1** : défaire, dénouer <to untie a knot : défaire un nœud> **2** : délier, détacher (des mains, un prisonnier, etc.)
until[1] [ˌʌnˈtɪl] *conj* : jusqu'à ce que, avant que, avant de <boil the eggs until cooked : bouillez les œufs jusqu'à ce qu'ils soient cuits> <don't speak until I tell you to : ne parlez pas avant que je ne vous le dise> <until I saw him : avant de l'avoir vu> <wait until I call : attend que j'appelle>
until[2] *prep* **1** UP TO : jusqu'à <I worked until noon : j'ai travaillé jusqu'à midi> **2** BEFORE : avant <it won't be available until tomorrow : ça ne sera pas disponible avant demain> <we don't open until ten : nous ouvrons à dix heures seulement>
untimely [ˌʌnˈtaɪmli] *adj* **1** PREMATURE : précoce, prématuré <an untimely death : une mort prématurée> **2** INOPPORTUNE : inopportun, déplacé
untold [ˌʌnˈtoːld] *adj* **1** : jamais raconté <untold stories : des histoires jamais racontées> **2** VAST : incalculable, indicible
untouched [ˌʌnˈtʌtʃt] *adj* **1** INTACT : intact, qui n'a pas été touché **2** UNHARMED : indemne **3** UNAFFECTED : non affecté
untoward [ˌʌnˈtɔrd, -ˈtoːərd, -təˈwɔrd] *adj* **1** UNFORTUNATE : fâcheux, malencontreux **2** UNSEEMLY : inconvenant
untrained [ˌʌnˈtreɪnd] *adj* **1** : sans formation **2 to the untrained eye** : pour un œil inexercé
untreated [ˌʌnˈtriːṭəd] *adj* : non traité
untroubled [ˌʌnˈtrʌbəld] *adj* **1** : paisible, tranquille <untroubled waters : eaux paisibles> **2 to be untroubled by** : ne pas être affecté par
untrue [ˌʌnˈtruː] *adj* **1** DISLOYAL : infidèle, déloyal **2** FALSE : faux, erroné
untruth [ˌʌnˈtruːθ, ˈʌn-] *n* **1** FALSITY : fausseté *f* **2** LIE : mensonge *m*

untruthful [ˌʌnˈtruːθfəl] *adj* **1** FALSE : faux, inexact **2** DISHONEST : malhonnête
unusable [ˌʌnˈjuːzəbəl] *adj* : inutilisable
unused *adj* [ˌʌnˈjuːzd, *in sense* **1** *usually* -ˈjuːst] **1** UNACCUSTOMED : pas habitué **2** NEW : neuf, nouveau **3** IDLE : inutilisé **4** ACCRUED : cumulé
unusual [ˌʌnˈjuːʒʊəl] *adj* : peu commun, rare
unusually [ˌʌnˈjuːʒʊəli] *adv* : exceptionnellement
unwanted [ˌʌnˈwɑntəd] *adj* : non désiré, superflu
unwarranted [ˌʌnˈwɔrəntəd] *adj* : injustifié
unwary [ˌʌnˈwæri] *adj* : qui ne se méfie pas, sans méfiance
unwavering [ˌʌnˈweɪvərɪŋ] *adj* : ferme, inébranlable <an unwavering gaze : un regard fixe>
unwelcome [ˌʌnˈwɛlkəm] *adj* : inopportun, fâcheux
unwell [ˌʌnˈwɛl] *adj* : souffrant, malade, mal-en-train *Can*
unwholesome [ˌʌnˈhoːlsəm] *adj* **1** UNHEALTHY : malsain, insalubre **2** PERNICIOUS : pernicieux, nocif
unwieldy [ˌʌnˈwiːldi] *adj* CUMBERSOME : difficile à manier, encombrant
unwilling [ˌʌnˈwɪlɪŋ] *adj* : réticent, peu disposé
unwillingly [ˌʌnˈwɪlɪŋli] *adv* : à contrecœur
unwind [ˌʌnˈwaɪnd] *v* **-wound; -winding** *vt* UNROLL : dérouler — *vi* **1** : se dérouler **2** RELAX : se détendre
unwise [ˌʌnˈwaɪz] *adj* : imprudent, peu judicieux
unwisely [ˌʌnˈwaɪzli] *adv* : imprudemment
unwitting [ˌʌnˈwɪṭɪŋ] *adj* **1** UNAWARE : inconscient **2** INADVERTENT : involontaire
unwittingly [ˌʌnˈwɪṭɪŋli] *adv* **1** UNCONSCIOUSLY : inconsciemment **2** INADVERTENTLY : involontairement
unworthiness [ˌʌnˈwərðinəs] *n* : indignité *f*
unworthy [ˌʌnˈwərði] *adj* **1** UNDESERVING : indigne **2** UNMERITED : peu méritant
unwrap [ˌʌnˈræp] *vt* **-wrapped; -wrapped** : déballer
unwritten [ˌʌnˈrɪtən] *adj* : tacite, non écrit
unyielding [ˌʌnˈjiːldɪŋ] *adj* **1** STIFF : dur, ferme **2** ADAMANT : qui ne cède pas, inflexible
unzip [ˌʌnˈzɪp] *vt* **-zipped; -zipping** : défaire la fermeture à glissière de
up[1] [ˈʌp] *v* **upped; upping** *vt* **1** INCREASE : augmenter <they upped the prices : ils ont augmenté les prix> — *vi* (*used with* and *and another verb to indicate surprising or abrupt action*) <she up and left : elle est partie sans mot dire> <he up and married her : il l'a épousée sur-le-champ>
up[2] *adv* **1** (*in or to a higher position or level*) <the oil shot up 200 feet : le pétrole jaillissait du sol et atteignait 200 pieds de hauteur> **2** (*from beneath a surface or level*) <the fish swam up : les poissons montaient à la surface de l'eau> **3** (*in or into an upright position*) <we stayed up all night : nous avons veillé toute la nuit> <get up! : levez-vous!> **4** (*with greater intensity*) <speak up! : parlez plus fort!> **5** (*in continuance from a point or to a point*) <from third grade up : à partir de la troisième année> <at prices of $10 and up : à des prix de 10 $ et plus> <up until now : jusqu'à maintenant> **6** (*into existence, evidence, prominence, or prevalence*) <they put up several new buildings : ils ont construit plusieurs nouveaux immeubles> **7** (*into consideration or attention*) <we brought the matter up : nous avons soulevé la question> **8** COMPLETELY, ENTIRELY : au complet <button up your coat : boutonne ton manteau jusqu'au cou> **9** (*used as an intensifier*) <we cleaned up the house : nous avons nettoyé la maison> **10** (*so as to arrive or approach*) <he walked up to me and said "hello" : il s'est approché de moi et m'a dit «bonjour»> **11** (*in or into parts*) <she tore up the paper : elle a déchiré le papier en petits morceaux> **12** (*to a stop*) <he pulled up to the curb : il s'est garé le long de la courbe> **13** (*for each side*) <the score was 15 up : le score était nul avec 15 points pour chaque équipe>
up[3] *adj* **1** RISEN : levé (se dit du soleil) **2** RISING : en crue (se dit d'une rivière) **3** AWAKE, STANDING : levé, debout <he's up at 6 o'clock : il se lève à 6h> **4** LIFTED : levé, ouvert <the windows were up : les fenêtres étaient ouvertes> **5** BUILT : construit <the houses are up : la construction des maisons est terminée> **6** : qui pousse <the corn was up : le maïs poussait> **7** : qui monte <the up escalator : l'escalier mécanique qui monte> **8** INCREASING : qui augmente <attendance is up at the meetings : le nombre de personnes qui assiste aux réunions a augmenté> <the wind is up : le vent s'est levé> **9** READY : prêt <the team was up for the game : l'équipe était prête pour le match> **10** : qui se passe <what's up? : qu'est-ce qui se passe?> **11** UP-TO-DATE : au courant, à jour <to be up on the news : être au courant des nouvelles> <he was up on his homework : il était à jour dans ses devoirs> **12** EXPIRED : expiré, terminé <the

contract was up in June : le contrat s'est terminé en juin>

up[4] *n* **1 to be on the up** : être en train d'augmenter **2 ups and downs** : fluctuations *fpl*

up[5] *prep* **1** (*to, toward, or at a higher point of*) <she went up the stairs : elle a monté l'escalier> **2** (*to or toward the source of*) <to sail up the river : remonter la rivière en bateau> **3** (*near or toward the end of*) <to walk up the street : monter la rue> <we live a few miles up the coast : nous demeurons à quelques milles de la côte> **4** → **up to**

upbraid [ˌʌpˈbreɪd] *vt* : reprocher, réprimander

upbringing [ˈʌpˌbrɪŋɪŋ] *n* : éducation *f*

upcoming [ˌʌpˈkʌmɪŋ] *adj* : prochain, à venir

update[1] [ˌʌpˈdeɪt] *vt* **-dated; -dating** : mettre à jour, actualiser

update[2] [ˈʌpˌdeɪt] *n* : mise *f* à jour

upend [ˌʌpˈɛnd] *vt* **1** : mettre debout **2** OVERTURN : retourner, renverser

upgrade[1] [ˈʌpˌgreɪd, ˌʌp-] *vt* **-graded; -grading** : améliorer (un produit), promouvoir (un employé)

upgrade[2] [ˈʌpˌgreɪd] *n* **1** SLOPE : pente *f* ascendante, montée *f* **2 to be on the upgrade** : monter, être en hausse

upheaval [ˌʌpˈhiːvəl] *n* **1** : soulèvement *m* (de la croûte terrestre) **2** COMMOTION : bouleversement *m*, remue-ménage *m*

uphill[1] [ˌʌpˈhɪl] *adv* **to go uphill** : monter, aller en montant

uphill[2] [ˈʌpˌhɪl] *adj* **1** ASCENDING : montant, qui monte **2** DIFFICULT : pénible, difficile

uphold [ˌʌpˈhoːld] *vt* **-held; -holding 1** SUPPORT : soutenir, défendre **2** RAISE : soutenir, élever **3** CONFIRM : confirmer, maintenir (en droit)

upholster [ˌʌpˈhoːlstər] *vt* **1** STUFF : rembourrer **2** COVER : tapisser, recouvrir

upholsterer [ˌʌpˈhoːlstərər] *n* : tapissier *m*, -sière *f*

upholstery [ˌʌpˈhoːlstəri] *n, pl* **-steries 1** STUFFING : rembourrage *m* **2** COVERING : tissu *m* d'ameublement, revêtement *m*

upkeep [ˈʌpˌkiːp] *n* : entretien *m*

upland [ˈʌplənd, -ˈlænd] *n* **1** : plateau *m* **2 the uplands** : les hautes terres

uplift[1] [ˌʌpˈlɪft] *vt* **1** RAISE : soulever, élever **2** : remonter, encourager <to uplift s.o.'s spirits : remonter le moral de qqn>

uplift[2] [ˈʌpˌlɪft] *n* **1** : élévation *f*, soulèvement *m* **2** IMPROVEMENT : amélioration *f*

upon [əˈpɔn, əˈpɑn] *prep* : sur, à <upon the table : sur la table> <upon our departure : à notre départ> <questions upon questions : des questions et des questions>

upper[1] [ˈʌpər] *adj* **1** : supérieur <the upper lip : la lèvre supérieure> **2** : plus haut, plus élevé <the upper classes : l'aristocratie> **3** NORTHERN : haut (en géographie) <the upper Mississippi : la haute Mississippi>

upper[2] *n* : empeigne *f* (d'un soulier)

upper hand *n* **to have the upper hand** : avoir le dessus

uppermost [ˈʌpərˌmoːst] *adj* **1** HIGHEST : le plus haut, le plus élevé **2** : de la plus haute importance <it was uppermost in my mind : ça me préoccupait par-dessus tout>

upright[1] [ˈʌpˌraɪt] *adv* : droit <to stand upright : se tenir droit>

upright[2] *adj* **1** PERPENDICULAR : vertical **2** ERECT : debout, droit <an upright freezer : un congélateur armoire> **3** JUST : honnête, droit

upright[3] *n* **1** : montant *m* (en construction) **2** *or* **upright piano** : piano *m* droit

uprightly [ˈʌpˌraɪtli] *adv* : honnêtement

uprising [ˈʌpˌraɪzɪŋ] *n* : soulèvement *m*, révolte *f*

uproar [ˈʌpˌroːr] *n* : tumulte *m*, vacarme *m*

uproarious [ˌʌpˈroriəs] *adj* **1** NOISY : bruyant **2** HILARIOUS : désopilant, comique

uproariously [ˌʌpˈroriəsli] *adv* : aux éclats

uproot [ˌʌpˈruːt, -ˈrʊt] *vt* : déraciner

upset[1] [ˌʌpˈsɛt] *vt* **-set; -setting 1** OVERTURN : renverser **2** DISTURB, TROUBLE : déranger, perturber **3** SICKEN : rendre malade <the food upset my stomach : la nourriture m'a dérangé l'estomac> **4** DISRUPT : déranger, bouleverser (des plans, etc.)

upset[2] *adj* **1** DISTRESSED : attristé, peiné **2** ANNOYED : ennuyé, contrarié **3** : dérangé (se dit de l'estomac)

upset[3] [ˈʌpˌsɛt] *n* **1** OVERTURNING : renversement *m* **2** DISRUPTION : bouleversement *m* (des plans) **3** DEFEAT : revers *m* (aux sports)

upshot [ˈʌpˌʃɑt] *n* : résultat *m*

upside–down [ˌʌpˌsaɪdˈdaʊn] *adj* : à l'envers

upside down *adv* **1** : à l'envers <turn the card upside down : tournez la carte à l'envers> **2** : sens dessus dessous <she turned the room upside down : elle a mis la pièce sens dessus dessous>

upstairs[1] [ˌʌpˈstærz] *adv* : en haut

upstairs[2] [ˈʌpˌstærz, ˌʌp-] *adj* : d'en haut, à l'étage

upstairs[3] [ˈʌpˌstærz, ˌʌp-] *ns & pl* : étage *m* (du haut)

upstanding [ˌʌpˈstændɪŋ, ˈʌpˌ-] *adj* : honnête, intègre

upstart [ˈʌpˌstɑrt] *n* : parvenu *m*, -nue *f*; arriviste *mf*

upstream [ˈʌpˈstriːm] *adv* : en amont

upswing [ˈʌpˌswɪŋ] *n* **1** : mouvement *m* ascendant **2** IMPROVEMENT : amélioration *f* notable

uptight [ˌʌpˈtaɪt] *adj* **1** TENSE : tendu, crispé, pogné *Can* **2** INDIGNANT : indigné, outré **3** REPRESSED : coincé *fam*

up to *prep* **1** : jusqu'à <in water up to my ankles : dans l'eau jusqu'aux chevilles> <up to here : jusqu'ici> **2 to be up to** : être à <if it were up to me : si c'était à moi de décider> **3 to be up to** : être capable de <he's not up to studying : il n'est pas en état d'étudier>

up–to–date [ˌʌptəˈdeɪt] *adj* **1** CURRENT : à jour <up-to-date maps : des cartes à jour> <to stay up-to-date : se tenir au courant> **2** MODERN : moderne

uptown [ˈʌpˈtaʊn] *adv* : dans les quartiers résidentiels

upturn [ˈʌpˌtərn] *n* : amélioration *f*, reprise *f* (économique)

upward[1] [ˈʌpwərd] *or* **upwards** [-wərdz] *adv* **1** : vers le haut, en montant **2** (*used to express continuance from a point*) <from $ 5 upward : à partir de 5 $>

upward[2] *adj* ASCENDING : ascendant <upward mobility : ascension sociale>

upwardly [ˈʌpwərdli] *adv* : vers le haut

upwind[1] [ˌʌpˈwɪnd] *adv* : contre le vent

upwind[2] *adj* **to be upwind of** : être dans le vent par rapport à

uranium [jʊˈreɪniəm] *n* : uranium *m*

Uranus [jʊˈreɪnəs, ˈjʊrənəs] *n* : Uranus *f*

urban [ˈərbən] *adj* : urbain, de ville

urbane [ˌərˈbeɪn] *adj* : raffiné, courtois

urchin [ˈərtʃən] *n* : polisson *m*, -sonne *f*

urethra [jʊˈriːθrə] *n, pl* **-thras** *or* **-thrae** [-ˌθriː] : urètre *m*

urge[1] [ˈərdʒ] *vt* **urged; urging 1** PUSH : pousser <we urged him to tell the truth : nous l'avons poussé à dire la vérité> **2** ADVOCATE : conseiller, préconiser **3 to urge on** : presser, faire avancer

urge[2] *n* : désir *m*, (forte) envie *f*

urgency [ˈərdʒəntsi] *n, pl* **-cies** : urgence *f*

urgent [ˈərdʒənt] *adj* **1** PRESSING : urgent, pressant **2** INSISTENT : insistant

urgently [ˈərdʒəntli] *adv* : d'urgence

urinal [ˈjʊrənəl, *esp Brit* jʊˈraɪnəl] *n* : urinoir *m*

urinary [ˈjʊrəˌnɛri] *adj* : urinaire

urinate [ˈjʊrəˌneɪt] *vi* **-nated; -nating** : uriner

urination [ˌjʊrəˈneɪʃən] *n* : urination *f*

urine [ˈjʊrən] *n* : urine *f*

urn [ˈərn] *n* **1** VASE : urne *f* **2** : fontaine *f* (à café)

Uruguayan[1] [ˌʊrəˈgwaɪən, ˌjʊr-, -ˈgweɪ-] *adj* : uruguayen

Uruguayan[2] *n* : Uruguayen *m*, -guayenne *f*

us [ˈʌs] *pron* **1** (*used as a direct object of a verb*) <they were visiting us : ils nous rendaient visite> **2** (*used as an indirect object of a verb*) <give us some time : donnez-nous du temps> **3** (*used as the object of a preposition*) <in front of us : devant nous>

usable [ˈjuːzəbəl] *adj* : utilisable

usage [ˈjuːsɪdʒ, -zɪdʒ] *n* **1** HABIT, PRACTICE : usage *m*, coutume *f* **2** : usage *m* (en linguistique) **3** USE : utilisation *f*, consommation *f*

use[1] [ˈjuːz] *v* **used** [ˈjuːzd; *in phrase "used to" usually* ˈjuːstuː]; **using** *vt* **1** EMPLOY : utiliser, se servir de **2** CONSUME : consommer <use before April : à consommer avant avril> **3** TREAT : traiter <they used the prisoners cruelly : ils ont traité les prisonniers avec cruauté> **4** EXPLOIT : se servir de, profiter de <he used his friends to get ahead : il s'est servi de ses amis afin d'avancer> — *vi* (*used in the past tense with* to *to indicate a former fact or state*) <she didn't use to smoke : elle ne fumait pas avant>

use[2] [ˈjuːs] *n* **1** APPLICATION, EMPLOYMENT : utilisation *f* **2** : usage *m*, jouissance *f* (d'un bien) <to have use of the beach : avoir la jouissance de la plage> <to lose the use of a limb : perdre l'usage d'un membre> **3** USEFULNESS : utilité *f* <it's no use : c'est inutile, ça ne sert à rien> <what's the use of complaining : à quoi bon se plaindre> **4** NEED : usage *m*, besoin *m* <they didn't have use for it : ils n'en avaient pas besoin>

used [ˈjuːzd] *adj* **1** SECONDHAND : usagé, de seconde main **2** ACCUSTOMED : habitué <not used to all the attention : pas habitué à recevoir autant d'attention>

useful [ˈjuːsfəl] *adj* : utile, pratique

usefully [ˈjuːsfəli] *adv* : utilement

usefulness [ˈjuːsfəlnəs] *n* : utilité *f*

useless [ˈjuːsləs] *adj* : inutile — **uselessly** *adv*

uselessness [ˈjuːsləsnəs] *n* : inutilité *f*

user [ˈjuːzər] *n* : usager *m*; utilisateur *m*, -trice *f* (d'un ordinateur)

user–friendly [ˌjuːzərˈfrɛndli] *adj* : facile à utiliser, convivial (en informatique)

usher[1] [ˈʌʃər] *vt* **1** ESCORT : conduire, accompagner <to usher s.o. in : faire entrer qqn> **2 to usher in** : inaugurer <a party to usher in the new year : une fête pour inaugurer la nouvelle année>

usher[2] *n* : huissier *m* (à un tribunal); placeur *m*, -ceuse *f* (au théâtre)

usherette [ˌʌʃəˈrɛt] *n* : ouvreuse *f*

usual [ˈjuːʒʊəl] *adj* : CUSTOMARY, NORMAL : habituel <our usual route : notre chemin habituel> <more than usual : plus que d'habitude> <as usual : comme d'habitude>

usually ['ju:ʒʊəli] *adv* : habituellement, d'habitude, normalement
usurp [jʊ'sərp, -'zərp] *vt* : usurper
usurper [jʊ'sərpər, -'zər-] *n* : usurpateur *m,* -trice *f*
utensil [jʊ'tɛn*t*səl] *n* : ustensile *m* (de cuisine, de jardinage, etc.)
uterine ['ju:təˌraɪn, -rən] *adj* : utérin
uterus ['ju:t̬ərəs] *n, pl* **uteri** [-ˌraɪ] : utérus *m*
utilitarian [juːˌtɪlə'tɛriən] *adj* : utilitaire
utility [ju:'tɪlət̬i] *n, pl* **-ties 1** USEFULNESS : utilité *f* **2** *or* **public utility** : service *m* public
utilization [ˌju:tələ'zeɪʃən] *n* : utilisation *f*
utilize ['ju:t̬əlˌaɪz] *vt* **-lized; -lizing** : utiliser
utmost[1] ['ʌtˌmo:st] *adj* **1** EXTREME : extrême <the utmost point of the earth : le bout de la terre> **2** : capital, important <a matter of utmost concern : une question de la plus haute importance>
utmost[2] *n* **1** : plus haut degré *m,* plus haut point *m* <the utmost in reliability : ce qu'il y a de plus fiable> **2 to do one's utmost** : faire son possible
utopia [jʊ'to:piə] *n* : utopie *f*
utopian [jʊ'to:piən] *adj* : utopique
utter[1] ['ʌtər] *vt* : exprimer, prononcer (un mot), pousser (un cri)
utter[2] *adj* : absolu, total, complet <utter darkness : obscurité totale>
utterly ['ʌtərli] *adv* : complètement
utterance ['ʌt̬ərən*t*s] *n* : déclaration *f,* paroles *fpl*

V

v ['vi:] *n, pl* **v's** *or* **vs** ['vi:z] : v *m,* vingt-deuxième lettre de l'alphabet
vacancy ['veɪkən*t*si] *n, pl* **-cies 1** : chambre *f* disponible (dans un hôtel) <no vacancies : complet> **2** : poste *m* vacant <to fill a vacancy : pourvoir un poste> **3** EMPTINESS : vide *m*
vacant ['veɪkənt] *adj* **1** EMPTY : vide, inoccupé **2** UNOCCUPIED : libre (se dit d'une chambre), vacant (se dit d'un poste) **3** DISTRACTED : distrait, absent <a vacant smile : un sourire absent>
vacate ['veɪˌkeɪt] *vt* **-cated; -cating** : quitter, libérer (une chambre) <to vacate the premises : vider les lieux>
vacation[1] [veɪ'keɪʃən, və-] *vi* : prendre des vacances
vacation[2] *n* : vacances *fpl,* congé *m*
vacationer [veɪ'keɪʃənər, və-] *n* : vacancier *m,* -cière *f*
vaccinate ['væksəˌneɪt] *vt* **-nated; -nating** : vacciner
vaccination [ˌvæksə'neɪʃən] *n* : vaccination *f*
vaccine [væk'si:n, 'vækˌ-] *n* : vaccin *m*
vacillate ['væsəˌleɪt] *vi* **-lated; -lating 1** SWAY : vaciller, perdre son équilibre **2** HESITATE : hésiter
vacillation [ˌvæsə'leɪʃən] *n* : hésitation *f,* indécision *f*
vacuous ['vækjʊəs] *adj* **1** BLANK, EMPTY : vide **2** INANE : stupide, idiot
vacuum[1] ['væˌkju:m, -kjəm] *vt* : passer l'aspirateur dans (un tapis, etc.)
vacuum[2] *n, pl* **vacuums** *or* **vacua** ['vækjʊə] **1** VOID : vide *m* **2** → **vacuum cleaner**
vacuum cleaner *n* : aspirateur *m,* balayeuse *f Can*
vagabond[1] ['vægəˌbɑnd] *adj* : vagabond, errant
vagabond[2] *n* : vagabond *m,* -bonde *f*
vagary ['veɪgəri, və'gɛri] *n, pl* **-ries** : caprice *m*
vagina [və'dʒaɪnə] *n, pl* **-nae** [-ˌni:, -ˌnaɪ] *or* **-nas** : vagin *m*
vaginal ['vædʒənəl] *adj* : vaginal
vagrancy ['veɪgrən*t*si] *n, pl* **-cies** : vagabondage *m*
vagrant[1] ['veɪgrənt] *adj* : vagabond
vagrant[2] *n* : clochard *m,* -charde *f;* itinérant *m,* -rante *f Can*
vague ['veɪg] *adj* **vaguer; vaguest 1** IMPRECISE : vague, imprécis **2** SLIGHT : moindre <I haven't the vaguest idea : je n'en ai pas la moindre idée> **3** INDISTINCT : vague, flou **4** ABSENT-MINDED : distrait
vaguely ['veɪgli] *adv* : vaguement
vain ['veɪn] *adj* **1** WORTHLESS : sans valeur **2** FUTILE : inutile, futile **3** CONCEITED : vaniteux **4 in ~** : en vain
vainglorious [ˌveɪn'gloriəs] *adj* PROUD : orgueilleux, vaniteux
vainly ['veɪnli] *adv* **1** UNSUCCESSFULLY : vainement, inutilement **2** CONCEITEDLY : avec vanité, vaniteusement
valance ['væləns, 'veɪ-] *n* : lambrequin *m* (d'un lit), cantonnière *f* (pour des rideaux)
vale ['veɪl] *n* : val *m,* vallée *f*
valedictorian [ˌvæləˌdɪk'toriən] *n* : étudiant *m,* -diante *f* qui prononce un discours lors d'une cérémonie de graduation
valedictory[1] [ˌvælə'dɪktəri] *adj* : d'adieu
valedictory[2] *n, pl* **-ries** : discours *m* d'adieu
valentine ['vælənˌtaɪn] *n* : carte *f* de Saint-Valentin, valentin *m Can*
valet ['væˌleɪ, væ'leɪ, 'vælət] *n* : valet *m* de chambre

valiant ['væljənt] *adj* : vaillant, courageux
valiantly ['væljəntli] *adv* : vaillamment, courageusement
valid ['væləd] *adj* **1** : valid <a valid contract : un contrat valide> **2** : bien fondé, valable <valid arguments : raisonnements bien fondés>
validate ['vælə,deɪt] *vt* **-dated; -dating** : valider (un document), confirmer (une théorie, etc.)
validation [,vælə'deɪʃən] *n* : validation *f*
validity [və'lɪdəṭi, væ-] *n* : validité *f*
valise [və'li:s] *n* : mallette *f*, sac *m* de voyage
valley ['væli] *n, pl* **-leys** : vallée *f*
valor *or Brit* **valour** ['vælər] *n* : bravoure *f*, héroïsme *m*
valorous ['vælərəs] *adj* : valeureux
valour *Brit* → **valor**
valuable ['væljʊəbəl, -jəbəl] *adj* **1** EXPENSIVE : de valeur **2** WORTHWHILE : précieux <a valuable friendship : une amitié précieuse>
valuables ['væljʊəbəlz, -jəbəlz]*npl* : objets *mpl* de valeur
valuation [,væljʊ'eɪʃən] *n* **1** APPRAISAL : évaluation *f*, estimation *f* **2** WORTH : valeur *f*, prix *m*
value[1] ['væl,ju:] *vt* **valued; valuing 1** APPRAISE : estimer, évaluer **2** APPRECIATE, ESTEEM : apprécier, estimer
value[2] *n* **1** : valeur *f* <of no value : sans valeur> <to be of great value : valoir cher> **2** IMPORTANCE, MERIT : valeur *f*, mérite *m* <to place a high value on : attacher beaucoup d'importance à> **3 values** *npl* : valeurs *fpl* <family values : valeurs familiales>
valueless ['væl,ju:ləs] *adj* : sans valeur
valve ['vælv] *n* **1** : valve *f*, soupape *f* (en mécanique) **2** : valvule *f* (en anatomie)
vampire ['væm,paɪr] *n* : vampire *m*
van ['væn] *n* **1** : camionnette *f*, fourgonnette *f* (voiture) **2** → **vanguard**
vanadium [və'neɪdiəm] *n* : vanadium *m*
vandal ['vændəl] *n* : vandale *mf*
vandalism ['vændəl,ɪzəm] *n* : vandalisme *m*
vandalize ['vændəl,aɪz] *vt* **-ized; -izing** : saccager
vane ['veɪn] *n or* **weather vane** : girouette *f*
vanguard ['væn,gɑrd] *n* : avant-garde *f*
vanilla [və'nɪlə, -'nɛ-] *n* : vanille *f*
vanish ['vænɪʃ] *vi* : disparaître
vanity ['vænəṭi] *n, pl* **-ties 1** FUTILITY : futilité *f* **2** CONCEIT : vanité *f*, orgueil *m* **3** *or* **vanity table** : coiffeuse *f*
vanquish ['væŋkwɪʃ, 'væn-] *vt* : vaincre
vantage point ['væntɪdʒ] *n* : point *m* de vue, perspective *f*
vapid ['væpəd, 'veɪ-] *adj* : insipide, fade
vapor ['veɪpər] *n* : vapeur *f*
vaporize ['veɪpə,raɪz] *vt* **-ized; -izing** : vaporiser
vaporizer ['veɪpə,raɪzər] *n* : vaporisateur *m*
variability [,vɛriə'bɪləṭi] *n, pl* **-ties** : variabilité *f*
variable[1] ['vɛriəbəl] *adj* : variable
variable[2] *n* : variable *f*
variance ['vɛriənts] *n* **1** DIFFERENCE : différence *f*, écart *m* **2** DISAGREEMENT : désaccord *m* <to be at variance with s.o. : être en désaccord avec qqn>
variant[1] ['vɛriənt] *adj* : différent
variant[2] *n* : variante *f*
variation [,vɛri'eɪʃən] *n* : variation *f*, différence *f*
varicose ['værə,ko:s] *adj* : variqueux
varicose veins *npl* : varices *fpl*
varied ['vɛrid] *adj* : varié, divers
variegated ['vɛriə,geɪṭɛd] *adj* **1** MULTICOLORED : bigarré, bariolé **2** : panaché (en botanique)
variety [və'raɪəṭi] *n, pl* **-eties 1** DIVERSITY : variété *f*, diversité *f* **2** ASSORTMENT : variété *f*, quantité *f* <a wide variety of : un grand nombre de> **3** TYPE : espèce *f*, sorte *f* **4** : variété *f* (en botanique)
various ['vɛriəs] *adj* : divers, varié
varnish[1] ['vɑrnɪʃ] *vt* **1** : vernir (du bois) **2** GLOSS : voiler, embellir
varnish[2] *n* : vernis *m*
varsity ['vɑrsəṭi] *n, pl* **-ties** : équipe *f* universitaire
vary ['vɛri] *v* **varied; varying** *vi* **1** CHANGE : varier, changer, se modifier **2** DIFFER : varier — *vt* : varier, diversifier
vascular ['væskjələr] *adj* : vasculaire
vase ['veɪs, 'veɪz, 'vɑz] *n* : vase *m*
vast ['væst] *adj* : vaste, énorme
vastly ['væstli] *adv* : immensément, énormément
vastness ['væstnəs] *n* : immensité *f*, grandeur *f*
vat ['væt] *n* : cuve *f*, bac *m*
vaudeville ['vɔdvəl, -,vɪl; 'vɔdə,vɪl] *n* : vaudeville *m*
vault[1] ['vɔlt] *vt* : sauter par-dessus — *vi* : sauter
vault[2] *n* **1** JUMP : saut *m* **2** DOME : voûte *f* **3** : cave *f* (de vin), chambre *f* forte (d'une banque) **4** *or* **burial vault** : caveau *m*
vaulted ['vɔltəd] *adj* : voûté
vaunted ['vɔntəd] *adj* : vanté <her much-vaunted beauty : sa beauté tant vantée>
VCR [,vi:,si:'ɑr] *n* : magnétoscope *m*
veal ['vi:l] *n* : veau *m*
veer ['vɪr] *vi* : tourner, virer (se dit d'un bateau, du vent, etc.)
vegetable[1] ['vɛdʒtəbəl, 'vɛdʒəṭə-] *adj* **1** : végétal <vegetable oil : huile végétale> **2** : de légumes <vegetable broth : bouillon de légumes>
vegetable[2] *n* **1** : végétal *m* (en botanique) **2** : légume *m* <fruits and vegetables : les fruits et les légumes>

vegetarian[1] [ˌvɛdʒəˈtɛriən] *adj* : végétarien
vegetarian[2] *n* : végétarien *m*, -rienne *f*
vegetarianism [ˌvɛdʒəˈtɛriəˌnɪzəm] *n* : végétarisme *m*
vegetate [ˈvɛdʒəˌteɪt] *vi* **-tated; -tating** : végéter
vegetation [ˌvɛdʒəˈteɪʃən] *n* : végétation *f*
vegetative [ˈvɛdʒəˌteɪṭɪv] *adj* : végétatif
vehemence [ˈviːəmənts] *n* : véhémence *f*, intensité *f*
vehement [ˈviːəmənt] *adj* : ardent, véhément
vehemently [ˈviːəməntli] *adv* : avec véhémence
vehicle [ˈviəkəl, ˈviːˌhɪkəl] *n* **1** CARRIER, MEDIUM : véhicule *m* **2** *or* **motor vehicle** : véhicule *m* (routier)
vehicular [viˈhɪkjələr, və-] *adj* : de véhicules <vehicular accidents : accidents de la route>
veil[1] [ˈveɪl] *vt* **1** CONCEAL : voiler, masquer **2** : couvrir d'un voile <to veil one's face : se voiler>
veil[2] *n* : voile *m* <bridal veil : voile de mariée> <veil of secrecy : voile du secret>
vein [ˈveɪn] *n* **1** : veine *f* (en anatomie) **2** LODE : filon *m*, veine *f* **3** : nervure *f* (d'une feuille) **4** STYLE : veine *f*, esprit *m* <in the same vein : dans le même esprit>
veined [ˈveɪnd] *adj* : veiné (se dit des minéraux, etc.), nervuré (se dit d'une feuille)
velocity [vəˈlɑsəṭi] *n, pl* **-ties** : vélocité *f*, vitesse *f*
velour [vəˈlʊr] *or* **velours** [-ˈlʊrz] *n, pl* **velours** : velours *m*
velvet[1] [ˈvɛlvət] *adj* **1** : de velours **2** → **velvety**
velvet[2] *n* : velours *m*
velvety [ˈvɛlvəṭi] *adj* : velouté
venal [ˈviːnəl] *adj* : vénal
vend [ˈvɛnd] *vt* : vendre
vendetta [vɛnˈdɛṭə] *n* : vendetta *f*
vending machine *n* : distributeur *m* automatique
vendor [ˈvɛndər] *n* **1** : vendeur *m*, -deuse *f*; marchand *m*, -chande *f* **2** → **vending machine**
veneer[1] [vəˈnɪr] *vt* : plaquer
veneer[2] *n* **1** : placage *m* (du bois) **2** APPEARANCE, FACADE : vernis *m*, fausse *f* apparence
venerable [ˈvɛnərəbəl] *adj* : vénérable
venerate [ˈvɛnəˌreɪt] *vt* **-ated; -ating** : vénérer
veneration [ˌvɛnəˈreɪʃən] *n* : vénération *f*
venereal disease [vəˈnɪriəl] *n* : maladie *f* vénérienne
venetian blind [vəˈniːʃən] : store *m* vénitien
Venezuelan[1] [ˌvɛnəˈzweɪlən, -zʊˈeɪ-] *adj* : vénézuélien
Venezuelan[2] *n* : Vénézuélien *m*, -lienne *f*
vengeance [ˈvɛndʒənts] *n* : vengeance *f* <to take vengeance on s.o. : se venger sur qqn>
vengeful [ˈvɛndʒfəl] *adj* : vengeur, vindicatif
venial [ˈviːniəl] *adj* : véniel <venial sins : péchés véniels>
venison [ˈvɛnəsən, -zən] *n* : venaison *f*
venom [ˈvɛnəm] *n* **1** : venin *m* (de serpent) **2** ILL WILL : venin *m*, malveillance *f*
venomous [ˈvɛnəməs] *adj* **1** : venimeux (se dit d'un serpent) **2** SPITEFUL : venimeux, haineux
vent[1] [ˈvɛnt] *vt* **1** EXPEL : évacuer, laisser échapper (de la fumée, etc.) **2** : décharger, donner libre cours à (ses émotions)
vent[2] *n* **1** OUTLET : orifice *m*, conduit *m*, bouche *f* d'aération **2 to give vent to** : donner libre cours à
ventilate [ˈvɛntəlˌeɪt] *vt* **-lated; -lating** : ventiler, aérer
ventilation [ˌvɛntəlˈeɪʃən] *n* : ventilation *f*, aération *f*
ventilator [ˈvɛntəlˌeɪṭər] *n* : ventilateur *m*
ventricle [ˈvɛntrɪkəl] *n* : ventricule *m*
ventriloquism [vɛnˈtrɪləˌkwɪzəm] *n* : ventriloquie *f*
ventriloquist [vɛnˈtrɪləˌkwɪst] *n* : ventriloque *mf*
venture[1] [ˈvɛntʃər] *v* **-tured; -turing** *vt* **1** RISK : risquer, hasarder **2** OFFER : hasarder, avancer <to venture an opinion : hasarder une opinion> — *vi* : s'embarquer, s'aventurer
venture[2] *n* **1** UNDERTAKING : entreprise *f* risquée, affaire *f* **2** STAKE : enjeu *m*
venturesome [ˈvɛntʃərsəm] *adj* **1** HAZARDOUS : dangereux, périlleux **2** DARING : audacieux, brave
venue [ˈvɛnˌjuː] *n* : lieu *m* (de rencontre)
Venus [ˈviːnəs] *n* : Vénus *f* (planète)
veracity [vəˈræsəṭi] *n, pl* **-ties** : véracité *f*
veranda *or* **verandah** [vəˈrændə] *n* : véranda *f*
verb [ˈvərb] *n* : verbe *m*
verbal [ˈvərbəl] *adj* : verbal
verbalize [ˈvərbəˌlaɪz] *vt* **-ized; -izing** : rendre par des mots, verbaliser
verbally [ˈvərbəli] *adv* : verbalement
verbatim[1] [vərˈbeɪṭəm] *adv* : textuellement
verbatim[2] *adj* : mot pour mot, textuel
verbose [vərˈboːs] *adj* : verbeux, prolixe
verdant [ˈvərdənt] *adj* : verdoyant
verdict [ˈvərdɪkt] *n* **1** : verdict *m* (en droit) **2** JUDGMENT, OPINION : opinion *f*, jugement *m*
verdure [ˈvərdʒər, -djər] *n* : verdure *f*

verge[1] ['vərdʒ] *vi* **verged; verging 1** : être au bord **2 to verge on** : s'approcher de, friser
verge[2] *n* **1** EDGE, RIM : bord *m* **2 to be on the verge of** : être sur le bord de, être sur le point de
verifiable [ˌvɛrə'faɪəbəl] *adj* : vérifiable
verification [ˌvɛrəfə'keɪʃən] *n* : vérification *f*
verify ['vɛrəˌfaɪ] *vt* **-fied; -fying** : vérifier
veritable ['vɛrəṭəbəl] *adj* : véritable — **veritably** [-bli] *adv*
vermicelli [ˌvərmə'tʃɛli, -'sɛli] *n* : vermicelle *m*
vermin ['vərmən] *ns & pl* : vermine *f*, animaux *mpl* nuisibles
vermouth [vər'muːθ] *n* : vermouth *m*
vernacular[1] [vər'nækjələr] *adj* : vernaculaire, du pays
vernacular[2] *n* : langage *m* vernaculaire
versatile ['vərsəṭəl] *adj* **1** : aux talents divers (se dit d'une personne) **2** MULTIPURPOSE : polyvalent, aux usages multiples
versatility [ˌvərsə'tɪləṭi] *n* : souplesse *f* (de l'esprit), polyvalence *f* (d'un outil, etc.)
verse ['vərs] *n* **1** STANZA : strophe *f* **2** POETRY : vers *mpl*, poésie *f* **3** : verset *m* (de la Bible)
versed ['vərst] *adj* **to be well versed in** : être très versé dans
version ['vərʒən] *n* : version *f*
versus ['vərsəs] *prep* : contre, par rapport à
vertebra ['vərtəbrə] *n, pl* **-brae** [-ˌbreɪ, -ˌbriː] *or* **-bras** : vertèbre *f*
vertebral [vər'tibrəl, 'vərtə-] *adj* : vertébral
vertebrate[1] ['vərtəbrət, -ˌbreɪt] *adj* : vertébré
vertebrate[2] *n* : vertébré *m*
vertex ['vərˌtɛks] *n, pl* **vertices** ['vərtəˌsiːz] **1** : vertex *m* (en anatomie), sommet *m* (d'un angle) **2** SUMMIT, TOP : sommet *m*
vertical[1] ['vərtɪkəl] *adj* : vertical — **vertically** *adv*
vertical[2] *n* : verticale *f*
vertigo ['vərtɪˌgoː] *n, pl* **-goes** *or* **-gos** : vertige *m*
verve ['vərv] *n* : verve *f*, brio *m*
very[1] ['vɛri] *adv* **1** TRULY : vraiment, exactement <the very same story : exactement la même histoire> <at the very least : tout au moins> **2** EXCEEDINGLY : très, vraiment, tellement <very hot : très chaud> <it didn't hurt very much : ça ne m'a pas fait tellement mal>
very[2] *adj* **1** EXACT : même, précis <the very heart of the city : le cœur même de la ville> **2** PERFECT : parfait <the very tool for the job : le parfait outil pour le travail> **3** BARE, MERE : seul <the very thought of leaving : la seule idée de partir> **4** SELFSAME : même, identique <he's the very man I saw : c'est justement l'homme que j'ai vu>
vesicle ['vɛsɪkəl] *n* : vésicule *f*
vespers ['vɛspərz] *npl* : vêpres *fpl*
vessel ['vɛsəl] *n* **1** CONTAINER : récipient *m*, contenant *m* **2** SHIP : vaisseau *m* **3** → **blood vessel**
vest[1] ['vɛst] *vt* **1** : investir <to vest a deputy with authority : investir un député d'autorité> **2** CLOTHE : vêtir
vest[2] *n* : gilet *m*, veste *f Can*
vestibule ['vɛstəˌbjuːl] *n* : vestibule *m*
vestige ['vɛstɪdʒ] *n* : vestige *m*, trace *f*
vestment ['vɛstmənt] *n* : vêtement *m* sacerdotal
vestry ['vɛstri] *n, pl* **-tries** : sacristie *f*
veteran[1] ['vɛṭərən, 'vɛtrən] *adj* : chevronné
veteran[2] *n* : ancien combattant *m*, vétéran *m*
veterinarian [ˌvɛṭərə'nɛriən, ˌvɛṭrə-] *n* : vétérinaire *mf*
veterinary ['vɛṭərəˌnɛri, 'vɛtrə-] *adj* : vétérinaire
veto[1] ['viːṭo] *vt* **1** PROHIBIT : interdire, défendre **2** : mettre son veto à, opposer son veto à (une loi)
veto[2] *n, pl* **-toes 1** PROHIBITION : interdiction *f*, prohibition *f* **2** : veto *m* <right of veto : droit de veto>
vex ['vɛks] *vt* **vexed; vexing 1** UPSET : vexer, froisser **2** ANNOY : contrarier, ennuyer
vexation [vɛk'seɪʃən] *n* IRRITATION : contrariété *f*, agacement *m*
via ['vaɪə, 'viːə] *prep* : via, par
viability [ˌvaɪə'bɪləṭi] *n* : viabilité *f*
viable ['vaɪəbəl] *adj* : viable
viaduct ['vaɪəˌdʌkt] *n* : viaduc *m*
vial ['vaɪəl] *n* : fiole *f*
vibrant ['vaɪbrənt] *adj* **1** BRIGHT : vif <a vibrant red : un rouge vif> **2** RESONANT : vibrant, résonant **3** LIVELY : vivant, animé
vibrate ['vaɪˌbreɪt] *v* **-brated; -brating** *vt* : faire vibrer — *vi* **1** OSCILLATE : vibrer, osciller **2** QUIVER, THRILL : frémir, vibrer
vibration [vaɪ'breɪʃən] *n* : vibration *f*
vicar ['vɪkər] *n* : vicaire *m*
vicarious [vaɪ'kæriəs, vɪ-] *adj* **1** DELEGATED : délégué **2** INDIRECT : indirect <vicarious experiences : expériences vécues indirectement>
vicariously [vaɪ'kæriəsli, vɪ-] *adv* : indirectement
vice ['vaɪs] *n* **1** : vice *m* **2** *Brit* → **vise**
vice admiral *n* : vice-amiral *m*
vice president *n* : vice-président *m*, -dente *f*
viceroy ['vaɪsˌrɔɪ] *n* : vice-roi *m*
vice versa [ˌvaɪsɪ'vərsə, ˌvaɪs'vər-] *adv* : vice versa
vicinity [və'sɪnəṭi] *n, pl* **-ties 1** NEARNESS : proximité *f* **2** NEIGHBORHOOD

: quartier *m,* voisinage *m,* environs *mpl*
vicious ['vɪʃəs] *adj* **1** DEPRAVED : vicieux, corrompu **2** SAVAGE : méchant <a vicious dog : un chien méchant> **3** SPITEFUL : malveillant, méchant
viciously ['vɪʃəsli] *adv* **1** SAVAGELY : brutalement, violemment **2** SPITEFULLY : méchamment, cruellement
viciousness ['vɪʃəsnəs] *n* **1** : brutalité *f,* violence *f* **2** MEANNESS : méchanceté *f,* cruauté *f*
vicissitude [və'sɪsə͵tu:d, vaɪ-, -͵tju:d] *n* : vicissitude *f*
victim ['vɪktəm] *n* : victime *f*
victimize ['vɪktə͵maɪz] *vt* **-ized; -izing** : persécuter, faire une victime de
victor ['vɪktər] *n* : vainqueur *m*
Victorian [vɪk'to:riən] *adj* : victorien
victorious [vɪk'to:riəs] *adj* : victorieux — **victoriously** *adv*
victory ['vɪktəri] *n, pl* **-ries** : victoire *f*
victuals ['vɪtəlz] *npl* : victuailles *fpl*
video[1] ['vɪdi͵o:] *adj* : vidéo
video[2] *n* **1** : vidéo *f* **2** → **videotape**[2]
videocassette [͵vɪdiokə'sɛt] *n* : vidéocassette *f*
videotape[1] ['vɪdio͵teɪp] **-taped; -taping** *vt* : enregistrer (sur magnétoscope)
videotape[2] *n* : bande *f* vidéo
vie ['vaɪ] *vi* **vied; vying** ['vaɪɪŋ] : rivaliser, être en compétition
Vietnamese[1] [vi͵ɛtnə'mi:z, -'mi:s] *adj* : vietnamien
Vietnamese[2] *n* **1** : Vietnamien *m,* -mienne *f* **2** : vietnamien *m* (langue)
view[1] ['vju:] *vt* **1** EXAMINE : examiner, inspecter **2** SEE, WATCH : regarder, voir (un film, etc.) **3** CONSIDER : étudier, peser <to view all sides of a question : étudier tous les aspects d'un problème>
view[2] *n* **1** SIGHT : vue *f* <to come into view : apparaître> **2** ATTITUDE, OPINION : opinion *f,* avis *m* <in my view : d'après moi, à mon avis> **3** PROSPECT : vue *f,* panorama *m* <a room with a view : une chambre avec vue> **4** INTENTION : intention *f,* vue *f* <with a view to : dans l'intention de, en vue de> **5 in view of** : vu, étant donné
viewer ['vju:ər] *n* **1** *or* **television viewer** : téléspectateur *m,* -trice *f* **2** : visionneuse *f* (en photographie)
viewpoint ['vju:͵pɔɪnt] *n* : point *m* de vue
vigil ['vɪdʒəl] *n* **1** : vigile *f* (en religion) **2** WAKEFULNESS, WATCH : veille *f* <to keep a vigil : veiller>
vigilance ['vɪdʒələnts] *n* : vigilance *f*
vigilant ['vɪdʒələnt] *adj* : vigilant, attentif
vigilante [͵vɪdʒə'læn͵ti:] *n* : membre *m* d'un groupe qui lutte contre le crime
vigilantly ['vɪdʒələntli] *adv* : avec vigilance
vigor *or Brit* **vigour** ['vɪgər] *n* : vigueur *f,* énergie *f*
vigorous ['vɪgərəs] *adj* : vigoureux, énergique — **vigorously** *adv*
vigour *Brit* → **vigor**
Viking ['vaɪkɪŋ] *n* : Viking *mf*
vile ['vaɪl] *adj* **viler; vilest 1** BASE : vil, ignoble **2** REVOLTING : abominable, écœurant **3** AWFUL, FOUL : exécrable, massacrant <in a vile temper : d'une humeur massacrante> <vile weather : sale temps>
vilely ['vaɪlli] *adv* : vilement, ignoblement
vileness ['vaɪlnəs] *n* : caractère *m* ignoble
vilification [͵vɪləfə'keɪʃən] *n* : diffamation *f,* calomnie *f*
vilify ['vɪlə͵faɪ] *vt* **-fied; -fying** : diffamer, calomnier
villa ['vɪlə] *n* : villa *f*
village ['vɪlɪdʒ] *n* : village *m*
villager ['vɪlɪdʒər] *n* : villageois *m,* -geoise *f*
villain ['vɪlən] *n* : scélérat *m,* -rate *f;* méchant *m,* -chante *f* (dans un livre, un film, etc.)
villainous ['vɪlənəs] *adj* : vil, ignoble, infâme
villainy ['vɪləni] *n, pl* **-lainies** : vilenie *f,* infamie *f*
vim ['vɪm] *n* : énergie *f,* vitalité *f,* entrain *m*
vindicate ['vɪndə͵keɪt] *vt* **-cated; -cating 1** EXONERATE : innocenter **2** JUSTIFY : justifier
vindication [͵vɪndə'keɪʃən] *n* : justification *f*
vindictive [vɪn'dɪktɪv] *adj* : vindicatif, rancunier
vindictiveness [vɪn'dɪktɪvnəs] *n* : esprit *m* rancunier
vine ['vaɪn] *n* **1** GRAPEVINE : vigne *f* **2** : plante *f* grimpante
vinegar ['vɪnɪgər] *n* : vinaigre *m*
vineyard ['vɪnjərd] *n* : vignoble *m*
vintage[1] ['vɪntɪdʒ] *adj* **1** : millésimé (se dit du vin) **2** CLASSIC : d'époque **3** : à son meilleur <vintage Shaw : du Shaw à son meilleur>
vintage[2] *n* **1** HARVEST : vendange *f* (en viticulture) **2** PERIOD : époque *f* <a piano of 1845 vintage : un piano qui date de 1845> **3** *or* **vintage wine** : vin *m* de grand cru **4** *or* **vintage year** : millésime *m*
vinyl ['vaɪnəl] *n* : vinyle *m*
viola [vi:'o:lə] *n* : alto *m*
violate ['vaɪə͵leɪt] *vt* **-lated; -lating 1** BREAK : transgresser, enfreindre <to violate the law : enfreindre la loi> **2** RAPE : violer **3** DESECRATE : profaner
violation [͵vaɪə'leɪʃən] *n* **1** INFRINGEMENT : infraction *f,* transgression *f* <traffic violation : infraction au code de la route> **2** RAPE : viol *m* **3** DESECRATION : profanation *f,* viol *m*
violator ['vaɪə͵leɪtər] *n* : violateur *m,* -trice *f*

violence ['vaɪələnts] *n* : violence *f*
violent ['vaɪələnt] *adj* : violent
violently ['vaɪələntli] *adv* : violemment, avec violence
violet ['vaɪələt] *n* **1** : violette *f* (plante) **2** : violet *m* (couleur)
violin [ˌvaɪə'lɪn] *n* : violon *m*
violincello [ˌvaɪə'lən'tʃɛˌloː, ˌviː-] → **cello**
violinist [ˌvaɪə'lɪnɪst] *n* : violoniste *mf*
VIP [ˌviːˌaɪː'piː] *n, pl* **VIPs** [-'piːz] : V.I.P. *m fam,* personnalité *f* de marque
viper ['vaɪpər] *n* : vipère *f*
viral ['vaɪrəl] *adj* : viral
virgin[1] ['vərdʒən] *adj* **1** CHASTE : vierge **2** UNSPOILED : vierge, intact
virgin[2] *n* **1** : vierge *f* **2 the Virgin Mary** : la Vierge Marie
virginity [vər'dʒɪnət̬i] *n, pl* **-ties** : virginité *f*
Virgo ['vərˌgoː, 'vɪr-] *n* : Vierge *f*
virile ['vɪrəl, -ˌaɪl] *adj* : viril
virility [və'rɪlət̬i] *n* : virilité *f*
virtual ['vərtʃʊəl] *adj* **1** : en pratique, de fait <a virtual leader : un chef de fait> **2** NEAR : quasi-total <a virtual impossibility : une quasi-impossibilité> <it's a virtual certainty : c'est presque certain> **3** : virtuel (en informatique)
virtually ['vərtʃʊəli] *adv* : pratiquement, presque
virtue ['vərˌtʃuː] *n* **1** GOODNESS : vertu *f* **2** MERIT : avantage *m,* mérite *m* **3 by virtue of** : en raison de, en vertu de
virtuosity [ˌvərtʃʊ'ɑsət̬i] *n, pl* **-ties** : virtuosité *f*
virtuoso [ˌvərtʃʊ'oːˌsoː, -ˌzoː] *n, pl* **-sos** *or* **-si** [-ˌsiː, -ˌziː] : virtuose *mf*
virtuous ['vərtʃʊəs] *adj* : vertueux — **virtuously** ['vərtʃʊəsli] *adv*
virulence ['vɪrələnts, -jələnts] *n* : virulence *f*
virulent ['vɪrələnt, -jələnt] *adj* : virulent
virulently ['vɪrələntli, -jələnt-] *adv* : avec virulence
virus ['vaɪrəs] *n* : virus *m* (en médecine, en informatique, etc.)
visa ['viːzə, -sə] *n* : visa *m*
visage ['vɪzɪdʒ] *n* : physionomie *f*
vis-à-vis [ˌviːzə'viː, -sə-] *prep* : vis-a-vis de, par rapport à
viscera ['vɪsərə] *npl* : viscères *mpl*
visceral ['vɪsərəl] *adj* : viscéral
viscosity [vɪs'kɑsət̬i] *n, pl* **-ties** : viscosité *f*
viscount ['vaɪˌkaʊnt] *n* : vicomte *m*
viscountess ['vaɪˌkaʊntəs] *n* : vicomtesse *f*
viscous ['vɪskəs] *adj* : visqueux
vise *or Brit* **vice** ['vaɪs] *n* : étau *m*
visibility [ˌvɪzə'bɪlət̬i] *n, pl* **-ties** : visibilité *f*
visible ['vɪzəbəl] *adj* **1** : visible <visible stars : étoiles visibles> **2** OBVIOUS : visible, manifeste, apparent
visibly ['vɪzəbli] *adv* : visiblement
vision ['vɪʒən] *n* **1** EYESIGHT : vision *f,* vue *f* **2** APPARITION : apparition *f,* vision *f* **3** FORESIGHT : vision *f* (de l'avenir), prévoyance *f,* imagination *f* **4** IMAGE : image *f* <a vision of beauty : une image de la beauté>
visionary[1] ['vɪʒəˌnɛri] *adj* **1** FARSIGHTED : visionnaire **2** UTOPIAN : utopique, irréel
visionary[2] *n, pl* **-aries** : visionnaire *mf*
visit[1] ['vɪzət] *vt* **1** : rendre visite à, aller voir (une personne) **2** : visiter, faire visite à (un lieu) **3 to be visited by** : être éprouvé par (des difficultés, etc.)
visit[2] *n* : visite *f*
visitor ['vɪzət̬ər] *n* : visiteur *m,* -teuse *f*
visor ['vaɪzər] *n* **1** : visière *f* (d'un casque) **2** *or* **sun visor** : pare-soleil *m*
vista ['vɪstə] *n* : vue *f,* perspective *f*
visual ['vɪʒʊəl] *adj* : visuel — **visually** *adv*
visualize ['vɪʒʊəˌlaɪz] *vt* **-ized; -izing 1** IMAGINE : visualiser, s'imaginer **2** ENVISAGE : prévoir, envisager
vital ['vaɪt̬əl] *adj* **1** : vital <vital organs : organes vitaux> **2** LIVELY : vivant, dynamique **3** ESSENTIAL : vital, indispensable, essentiel <to be of vital importance : être indispensable>
vitality [vaɪ'tælət̬i] *n, pl* **-ties** : vitalité *f*
vitally ['vaɪt̬əli] *adv* : extrêmement, très
vital statistics *n* : statistiques *fpl* démographiques
vitamin ['vaɪt̬əmən] *n* : vitamine *f*
vitreous ['vɪtriəs] *adj* : vitreux
vitriolic [ˌvɪtri'ɑlɪk] *adj* : au vitriol, venimeux
vituperate [vaɪ'tuːpəˌreɪt, və-, -'tjuː-] *vt* **-ated; -ating** : vitupérer
vituperation [vaɪˌtuːpə'reɪʃən, və-, -ˌtjuː-] *n* : vitupération *f*
vivacious [və'veɪʃəs, vaɪ-] *adj* : vif, animé, plein d'entrain
vivaciously [və'veɪʃəsli, vaɪ-] *adv* : avec vivacité
vivacity [və'væsət̬i, vaɪ-] *n* : vivacité *f,* entrain *m*
vivid ['vɪvəd] *adj* **1** FRESH, LIVELY : vivant, vif <a vivid imagination : une vive imagination> **2** BRIGHT : vif, éclatant <a vivid blue : un bleu vif> **3** SHARP : vivant, frappant <a vivid description : une description vivante>
vividly ['vɪvədli] *adv* : de façon éclatante, de façon vivante
vividness ['vɪvədnəs] *n* **1** BRIGHTNESS : éclat *m* **2** CLARITY, SHARPNESS : clarté *f,* vivacité *f*
vivisection [ˌvɪvə'sɛkʃən, 'vɪvəˌ-] *n* : vivisection *f*
vixen ['vɪksən] *n* : renarde *f*
vocabulary [voː'kæbjəˌlɛri] *n, pl* **-laries 1** LEXICON : vocabulaire *m,* lexique *m* **2** : vocabulaire *m* (de la langue)

vocal ['vo:kəl] *adj* **1** : vocal **2** OUTSPOKEN : franc, qui se fait bien entendre
vocal cords *npl* : cordes *fpl* vocales
vocalist ['vo:kəlɪst] *n* : chanteur *m*, -teuse *f*
vocalize ['vo:kəl,aɪz] *v* **-ized; -izing** *vt* UTTER : exprimer — *vi* : vocaliser (en musique)
vocation [vo'keɪʃən] *n* **1** : vocation *f* (religieuse) **2** OCCUPATION : emploi *m*, profession *f*
vocational [vo'keɪʃənəl] *adj* : professionnel <vocational guidance : orientation professionnelle>
vociferous [vo'sɪfərəs] *adj* : véhément, bruyant
vociferously [vo'sɪfərəsli] *adv* : avec véhémence, bruyamment
vodka ['vɑdkə] *n* : vodka *m*
vogue ['vo:g] *n* : vogue *f*, mode *f* <to be in vogue : être à la mode>
voice[1] ['vɔɪs] *vt* **voiced; voicing** : exprimer, formuler
voice[2] *n* **1** : voix *f* <a booming voice : une voix retentissante> <fear took his voice away : la peur l'avait rendu muet> **2** : voix *f* (en grammaire)
voice box → **larynx**
voiced ['vɔɪst] *adj* : sonore
void[1] ['vɔɪd] *vt* **1** DISCHARGE : évacuer (en physiologie) **2** ANNUL : annuler
void[2] *adj* **1** EMPTY : vide <void of common sense : dépourvu de bon sens> **2** NULL : nul
void[3] *n* : vide *m*
volatile ['vɑlət̬əl] *adj* : volatil, instable
volatility [,vɑlə'tɪlət̬i] *n* : volatilité *f*, instabilité *f*
volcanic [vɑl'kænɪk, vɔl-] *adj* : volcanique
volcano [vɑl'keɪ,no:, vɔl-] *n, pl* **-noes** *or* **-nos** : volcan *m*
vole ['vo:l] *n* : campagnol *m*
volition [vo'lɪʃən] *n* : volonté *f* <of one's own volition : de son propre gré>
volley ['vɑli] *n, pl* **-leys 1** : volée *f* (de missiles), salve *f* (d'applaudissements) **2** : bordée *f* <a volley of insults : une bordée d'injures> **3** : volée *f* (aux sports)
volleyball ['vɑli,bɔl] *n* : volley *m*, volley-ball *m*
volt ['vo:lt] *n* : volt *m*
voltage ['vo:ltɪdʒ] *n* : voltage *m*, tension *f*
voluble ['vɑljəbəl] *adj* : volubile
volume ['vɑljəm, -ju:m] *n* **1** BOOK : volume *m* **2** CAPACITY : capacité *f*, volume *m* (cubique) **3** AMOUNT : volume *m*, quantité *f* <a high volume of traffic : beaucoup de circulation> **4** LOUDNESS : volume *m* **5 to speak volumes** : être révélateur, en dire long
voluminous [və'lu:mənəs] *adj* : volumineux
voluntarily [,vɑlən'tɛrəli] *adv* : volontairement
voluntary ['vɑlən,teri] *adj* : volontaire
volunteer[1] [,vɑlən'tɪr] *vt* : offrir, donner volontairement — *vi* : se porter volontaire
volunteer[2] *adj* : bénévole
volunteer[3] *n* : volontaire *mf*, bénévole *mf*
voluptuous [və'lʌptʃuəs] *adj* : voluptueux — **voluptuously** *adv*
voluptuousness [və'lʌptʃuəsnəs] *n* : volupté *f*
vomit[1] ['vɑmət] *v* : vomir
vomit[2] *n* : vomi *m*
voodoo ['vu:,du:] *n, pl* **voodoos** : vaudou *m*
voracious [vɔ'reɪʃəs, və-] *adj* : vorace, avide
voraciously [vɔ'reɪʃəsli, və-] *adv* : voracement, avec voracité
voracity [vɔ'ræsət̬i, və-] *n* : voracité *f*
vortex ['vɔr,tɛks] *n, pl* **vortices** ['vɔrtə,si:z] : tourbillon *m*
vote[1] ['vo:t] *v* **voted; voting** : voter
vote[2] *n* **1** : vote *m* **2** FRANCHISE : vote *m*, droit *m* de vote
voter ['vo:t̬ər] *n* : électeur *m*, -trice *f*
voting ['vo:t̬ɪŋ] *n* : scrutin *m*, vote *m*
vouch ['vaʊtʃ] *vi* **to vouch for** : répondre de, se porter garant de
voucher ['vaʊtʃər] *n* **1** RECEIPT : récépissé *m*, reçu *m* **2** *or* **credit voucher** : bon *m*
vouchsafe [vaʊtʃ'seɪf] *vt* **-safed; -safing 1** GRANT : octroyer, accorder **2 to vouchsafe to do** : s'engager à faire
vow[1] [vaʊ] *vt* : jurer, promettre
vow[2] *n* **1** : serment *m*, promesse *f* **2** : vœu *m* (en religion)
vowel ['vaʊəl] *n* : voyelle *f*
voyage[1] ['vɔɪɪdʒ] *vi* **-aged; -aging** : voyager
voyage[2] *n* : voyage *m*
voyager ['vɔɪɪdʒər] *n* : voyageur *m*, -geuse *f*
vulcanize ['vʌlkə,naɪz] *vt* **-nized; -nizing** : vulcaniser
vulgar ['vʌlgər] *adj* **1** COMMON, PLEBEIAN : vulgaire, commun **2** COARSE, CRUDE : vulgaire, grossier
vulgarity [,vʌl'gærət̬i] *n, pl* **-ties** : vulgarité *f*
vulgarly ['vʌlgərli] *adv* : vulgairement
vulnerability [,vʌlnərə'bɪlət̬i] *n* : vulnérabilité *f*
vulnerable ['vʌlnərəbəl] *adj* : vulnérable
vulture ['vʌltʃər] *n* : vautour *m*
vulva ['vʌlvə] *n, pl* **-vae** [-,vi:, -,vaɪ] : vulve *f*
vying → **vie**

W

w ['dʌbəl͵ju:] *n, pl* **w's** *or* **ws** [-͵ju:z] : w *m,* vingt-troisième lettre de l'alphabet

wad[1] ['wɑd] *vt* **wadded; wadding 1** : bourrer (un fusil) **2** *or* **to wad up** : faire un tampon de

wad[2] *n* **1** : tampon *m* (d'ouate, etc.), bourre *f* de fusil **2** BUNDLE : liasse *f,* paquet *m* <wad of money : liasse de billets>

waddle[1] ['wɑdəl] *vi* **-dled; -dling** : se dandiner

waddle[2] *n* : dandinement *m*

wade ['weɪd] *vi* **waded; wading 1** : patauger, avancer dans l'eau **2 to wade through** : accomplir péniblement <to wade through an assignment : faire un travail avec beaucoup de mal>

wading bird *n* : échassier *m*

wafer ['weɪfər] *n* : gaufrette *f*

waffle ['wɑfəl] *n* : gaufre *f*

waffle iron *n* : gaufrier *m*

waft ['wɑft, 'wæft] *vi* : flotter <to waft through the air : flotter dans l'air> — *vt* CARRY : apporter, transporter

wag[1] ['wæg] *v* **wagged; wagging** *vt* : agiter, remuer (la queue) — *vi* : frétiller, remuer

wag[2] *n* **1** : frétillement *m* (de la queue) **2** JOKER, WIT : farceur *m,* -ceuse *f*

wage[1] ['weɪdʒ] *vt* **waged; waging** : faire (la guerre), mener (une campagne)

wage[2] *n* **1** PAY : salaire *m,* paie *f* <hourly wage : salaire horaire> **2 wages** *ns & pl* REWARD : récompense *f* <the wages of sin is death : la mort est le prix du péché>

wager[1] ['weɪdʒər] *v* : parier

wager[2] *n* : pari *m*

waggish ['wægɪʃ] *adj* : facétieux, humoristique

waggle ['wægəl] *vt* **-gled; -gling** WAG : remuer, agiter

wagon ['wægən] *n* **1** : chariot *m* (tiré par des chevaux) **2** CART : chariot *m* **3** → **station wagon**

waif ['weɪf] *n* : enfant *m* abandonné, enfant *f* abandonnée

wail[1] ['weɪl] *vi* **1** : gémir, pleurer (se dit d'une personne) **2** : gémir (se dit du vent), hurler (se dit d'une sirène)

wail[2] *n* : gémissement *m*

wainscot ['weɪnskət, -͵skɑt, -͵sko:t] *or* **wainscoting** [-skət̬ɪŋ, -͵skɑ-, -͵sko:-] *n* : lambris *m,* boiseries *fpl*

waist ['weɪst] *n* : taille *f*

waistline ['weɪst͵laɪn] *n* : taille *f*

wait[1] ['weɪt] *vt* **1** AWAIT : attendre <wait your turn : attendez votre tour> **2** DELAY : retarder (le dîner, etc.) <don't wait lunch for me : ne m'attendez pas pour déjeuner> **3** SERVE : servir <to wait tables : servir à table> — *vi* : attendre

wait[2] *n* **1** : attente *f* **2 to lie in wait for** : guetter, attendre

waiter ['weɪt̬ər] *n* : serveur *m,* garçon *m*

waiting room *n* : salle *f* d'attente

waitress ['weɪtrəs] *n* : serveuse *f*

waive ['weɪv] *vt* **waived; waiving** : renoncer à (un droit), déroger à (une règle), supprimer (une condition)

waiver ['weɪvər] *n* : renonciation *f,* abandon *m*

wake[1] ['weɪk] *v* **woke** ['wo:k]; **woken** ['wo:kən] *or* **waked; waking** *vi or* **to wake up** : se réveiller — *vt* : réveiller <to wake s.o. up : réveiller qqn>

wake[2] *n* **1** WATCH : veillée *f* funèbre **2** : sillage *m* (laissé par un bateau) **3 in the wake of** : à la suite de

wakeful ['weɪkfəl] *adj* : éveillé, alerte

waken ['weɪkən] *vi* AWAKE : se réveiller

walk[1] ['wɔk] *vi* **1** : marcher <to walk back and forth : marcher de long en large> **2** : aller à pied, se promener <he walks to school : il se rend à l'école à pied> — *vt* **1** TRAVERSE : faire à pied, parcourir <we walked the streets : nous parcourions les rues> **2** ACCOMPANY : raccompagner <she walked him home : elle l'a raccompagné chez lui> **3** : faire marcher, promener <to walk the dog : promener le chien>

walk[2] *n* **1** : marche *f,* promenade *f* <to go for a short walk : se promener quelques minutes> **2** PATH : chemin *m,* allée *f,* promenade *f* **3** GAIT : démarche *f* (d'une personne), pas *m* (d'un animal) **4 from all walks of life** : de tous les milieux

walker ['wɔkər] *n* **1** : marcheur *m,* -cheuse *f;* promeneur *m,* -neuse *f* **2** *or* **baby walker** : trotteur *m*

walking stick *n* : canne *f*

walkout ['wɔk͵aʊt] *n* STRIKE : grève *f*

walk out *vi* **1** STRIKE : se mettre en grève **2** LEAVE : partir, sortir **3 to walk out on** ABANDON : quitter, abandonner

wall[1] ['wɔl] *vt* **1 to wall in** : entourer d'un mur **2 to wall off** : séparer par un mur **3 to wall up** : murer

wall[2] *n* **1** : mur *m* (d'un édifice, d'une pièce, etc.) <a wall of silence : un mur de silence> **2** SIDE : paroi *f* <the wall of a container : la paroi d'un récipient> <heart walls : parois du cœur> **3** : paroi *f,* face *f* (d'une montagne)

wallaby ['wɑləbi] *n, pl* **-bies** : wallaby *m*

wallet ['wɑlət] *n* : portefeuille *m*

wallflower ['wɔl͵flaʊər] *n* **1** : giroflée *f* **2 to be a wallflower** : faire tapisserie

Walloon[1] [wɑ'lu:n] *adj* : wallon

Walloon[2] *n* **1** : Wallon *m,* -lonne *f* **2** : wallon *m* (langue)

wallop[1] ['wɑləp] *vt* **1** BEAT : donner une raclée à **2** DEFEAT : battre à plates coutures **3** HIT : taper sur (une balle, etc.)

wallop[2] *n* BLOW : coup *m* fort, raclée *f*

wallow[1] ['wɑˌloː] *vi* **1** : se vautrer, s'étaler (se dit d'un animal) **2** INDULGE : se vautrer <to wallow in self-pity : s'apitoyer sur son sort>

wallow[2] *n* : bauge *f* (pour des animaux)

wallpaper[1] ['wɔlˌpeɪpər] *vt* : tapisser

wallpaper[2] *n* : tapisserie *f*

walnut ['wɔlˌnʌt] *n* : noyer *m* (arbre et bois), noix *f* (fruit)

walrus ['wɔlrəs, 'wɑl-] *n, pl* **-rus** *or* **-ruses** : morse *m*

waltz[1] ['wɔlts] *vi* **1** : valser **2 to waltz in** : entrer d'un pas désinvolte

waltz[2] *n* : valse *f*

wampum ['wɑmpəm] *n* : wampum *m*

wan ['wɑn] *adj* **wanner; wannest 1** PALLID : blême, pâle **2** DIM, FAINT : faible <a wan smile : un faible sourire>

wand ['wɑnd] *n* : baguette *f* (magique)

wander ['wɑndər] *vi* **1** RAMBLE : se promener, se balader **2** STRAY : errer, s'égarer **3** : vagabonder <his thoughts were wandering : ses pensées vagabondaient>

wanderer ['wɑndərər] *n* : vagabond *m*, -bonde *f*

wanderlust ['wɑndərˌlʌst] *n* : envie *f* de voyager

wane[1] ['weɪn] *vi* **waned; waning 1** : décroître (se dit de la lune) **2** DECLINE : décliner, diminuer

wane[2] *n* : déclin *m*, décroissance *f* <to be on the wane : décliner>

wangle ['wæŋgəl] *vt* **-gled; -gling** FINAGLE : se débrouiller pour obtenir

wanly ['wɑnli] *adv* : faiblement

want[1] ['wɑnt, 'wɔnt] *vt* **1** DESIRE : vouloir, désirer **2** NEED, REQUIRE : avoir besoin de **3** REQUEST : demander <you're wanted on the phone : on vous demande au téléphone> **4** SEEK : rechercher <to be wanted for murder : être recherché pour meurtre> — *vi* **1 to want for** LACK : manquer de **2 to want in** : vouloir entrer

want[2] *n* **1** LACK : manque *m* **2** DESIRE, NEED : besoin *m* **3** POVERTY : misère *f*, indigence *f* <to be in want : être dans le besoin>

wanting[1] ['wɑntɪŋ, 'wɔnt-] *adj* **1** ABSENT : absent **2 to be wanting in** : manquer de

wanting[2] *prep* **1** LESS : moins <a month wanting two days : un mois moins deux jours> **2** WITHOUT : sans <a book wanting a cover : un livre sans couverture>

wanton ['wɑntən, 'wɔn-] *adj* **1** PLAYFUL : capricieux <a wanton breeze : une brise capricieuse> **2** LEWD : impudique, licencieux **3** MALICIOUS : cruel, injustifié

wapiti ['wɑpət̬i] *n, pl* **-ti** *or* **-tis** : wapiti *m*

war[1] ['wɔr] *vi* **warred; warring** : faire la guerre

war[2] *n* : guerre *f* <to go to war with : entrer en guerre avec>

warble[1] ['wɔrbəl] *vi* **-bled; -bling** : gazouiller

warble[2] *n* : gazouillis *m*

warbler ['wɔrblər] *n* : fauvette *f*

ward[1] ['wɔrd] *vt or* **to ward off** : parer, éviter

ward[2] *n* **1** *or* **ward of the court** : pupille *f* **2** : salle *f* (d'un hôpital), quartier *m* (d'une prison) **3** : circonscription *f* électorale (d'une ville)

warden ['wɔrdən] *n* **1** KEEPER : gardien *m*, -dienne *f* (de parcs, etc.) **2** *or* **prison warden** : directeur *m*, -trice *f* de prison

wardrobe ['wɔrdˌroːb] *n* **1** CLOSET : armoire *f*, penderie *f*, garde-robe *mf Can* **2** CLOTHES : garde-robe *f*

ware ['wær] *n* **1** POTTERY : poterie *f* **2 wares** *npl* GOODS : marchandises *fpl*

warehouse ['wærˌhaʊs] *n* : entrepôt *m*, magasin *m*

warfare ['wɔrˌfær] *n* **1** WAR : guerre *f* **2** STRUGGLE : lutte *f*, guerre *f* <class warfare : lutte de classes>

warhead ['wɔrˌhɛd] *n* : ogive *f*

warily ['wærəli] *adv* : avec prudence, avec précaution

wariness ['wærinəs] *n* : circonspection *f*, prudence *f*

warlike ['wɔrˌlaɪk] *adj* : guerrier, belliqueux

warm[1] ['wɔrm] *vi* **1** : chauffer **2 to warm to** : se montrer intéressé envers, être sympathique envers — *vt* **1** HEAT : chauffer, réchauffer **2 to warm oneself** : se réchauffer

warm[2] *adj* **1** LUKEWARM : tiède <warm milk : lait tiède> **2** : chaud <warm clothing : vêtements chauds> <it's warm today : il fait chaud aujourd'hui> **3** CORDIAL, ENTHUSIASTIC : chaleureux, amical <a warm welcome : un accueil chaleureux> **4** : chaud (se dit des couleurs) **5** FRESH : récent <a warm trail : une piste récente> **6** (*used in guessing games*) <you're getting warm! : tu chauffes!>

warm–blooded ['wɔrm'blʌdəd] *adj* : à sang chaud

warmhearted ['wɔrm'hɑrt̬əd] *adj* : chaleureux, affectueux

warmly ['wɔrmli] *adv* **1** : chaudement <warmly dressed : habillé chaudement> **2** ENTHUSIASTICALLY : chaleureusement, amicalement

warmonger ['wɔrˌmɑŋgər, -ˌmʌŋ-] *n* : belliciste *mf*

warmth ['wɔrmpθ] *n* **1** : chaleur *f* <the warmth of the sun : la chaleur du

soleil> **2** ENTHUSIASM : chaleur *f,* enthousiasme *m,* cordialité *f*

warm–up ['wɔrm,ʌp] *n* : échauffement *m*

warm up *vi* : s'échauffer (aux sports) — *vt* **1** : réchauffer <to warm up the leftovers : réchauffer les restes> **2** : faire chauffer (le moteur)

warn ['wɔrn] *vt* **1** CAUTION : avertir, prévenir **2** INFORM : aviser

warning[1] ['wɔrnɪŋ] *adj* : d'alarme, d'alerte <a warning bell : une sonnette d'alarme>

warning[2] *n* **1** CAUTION : avertissement *m* <without warning : sans prévenir> **2** NOTICE : avis *m* <gale warning : avis de vents violents>

warp[1] ['wɔrp] *vt* **1** : voiler, gauchir (le bois, etc.) **2** DISTORT, PERVERT : pervertir, fausser — *vi* : gauchir, se voiler, coffrer *Can* (se dit du bois)

warp[2] *n* **1** : chaîne *f* (en tissage) **2** DISTORTION : déformation *f,* gauchissement *m* (du bois, du métal)

warrant[1] ['wɔrənt] *vt* **1** : être certain que, parier <I warrant he'll be here by noon : je suis certain qu'il sera ici à midi> **2** GUARANTEE : garantir **3** JUSTIFY, MERIT : mériter

warrant[2] *n* **1** JUSTIFICATION : justification *f,* droit *m* **2** AUTHORIZATION : mandat *m* <search warrant : mandat de perquisition>

warrant officer *n* : adjudant *m* (dans les forces armées)

warranty ['wɔrənti, ,wɔrən'ti:] *n, pl* **-ties** : garantie *f*

warren ['wɔrən] *n* : garenne *f*

warrior ['wɔriər] *n* : guerrier *m,* -rière *f*

warship ['wɔr,ʃɪp] *n* : navire *m* de guerre

wart ['wɔrt] *n* : verrue *f*

wartime ['wɔr,taɪm] *n* : temps *m* de guerre

wary ['wæri] *adj* **warier; -est** : prudent, circonspect <to be wary of : se méfier de>

was → **be**

wash[1] ['wɔʃ, 'wɑʃ] *vt* **1** CLEAN : laver <to wash clothes : laver des vêtements> <to wash one's hands : se laver les mains> **2** LAP : baigner <waves washing the shore : des vagues qui baignent la côte> **3** CARRY, DRAG : entraîner, emporter <to be washed out to sea : être entraîné par la mer> **4 to wash away** : emporter (un pont, etc.) — *vi* **1** : se laver (se dit d'une personne ou des vêtements) **2** WORK : marcher <her story just doesn't wash : son histoire ne marche pas, son histoire ne tient pas debout>

wash[2] *n* **1** : lavage *m,* lessive *f* <the clothes are in the wash : le linge est au lavage> <to do the wash : faire la lessive> **2** CLEANING, WASHING : lavage *m,* nettoyage *m* <to give sth a wash : laver qqch> **3** : remous *m* (d'un bateau)

washable ['wɔʃəbəl, 'wɑʃ-] *adj* : lavable

washboard ['wɔʃ,bord, 'wɑʃ-] *n* : planche *f* à laver

washbowl ['wɔʃ,bo:l, 'wɑʃ-] *n* : cuvette *f,* bassine *f*

washcloth ['wɔʃ,klɔθ, 'wɑʃ-] *n* : gant *m* de toilette, débarbouillette *f Can*

washed–out ['wɔʃt'aʊt, 'wɑʃt-] *adj* **1** FADED : délavé, décoloré **2** EXHAUSTED : épuisé

washed–up ['wɔʃt'ʌp, 'wɑʃt-] *adj* : fichu *fam,* ruiné

washer ['wɔʃər, 'wɑ-] *n* **1** : rondelle *f,* joint *m* (en technologie) **2** → **washing machine**

washing ['wɔʃɪŋ, 'wɑ-] *n* WASH : lavage *m,* lessive *f*

washing machine *n* : machine *f* à laver, laveuse *f Can*

washout ['wɔʃ,aʊt, 'wɑʃ-] *n* **1** : érosion *f* (dû à la pluie) **2** FAILURE : fiasco *m,* échec *m*

washroom ['wɔʃ,ru:m, 'wɑʃ-, -,rʊm] *n* : toilettes *fpl*

wasn't ['wʌzənt] (*contraction of* **was not**) → **be**

wasp ['wɑsp] *n* : guêpe *f*

waspish ['wɑspɪʃ] *adj* : irritable, qui a mauvais caractère

waste[1] *v* **wasted; wasting** ['weɪst] *vt* **1** DEVASTATE : dévaster, ravager **2** SQUANDER : gaspiller (de l'argent) <to waste one's time : perdre son temps> — *vi or* **to waste away** : dépérir

waste[2] *adj* **1** DESOLATE : désert, désolé **2** DISCARDED : de rebut, usé **3** *or* **waste material** : déchets *mpl*

waste[3] *n* **1** → **wasteland** **2** MISUSE : perte *f,* gaspillage *m* <a waste of time : une perte de temps> **3** REFUSE : déchets *mpl,* ordures *fpl* <nuclear waste : déchets nucléaires> <household wastes : ordures ménagères> **4** EXCREMENT : excrément *m*

wastebasket ['weɪst,bæskət] *n* : corbeille *f* à papier

wasteful ['weɪstfəl] *adj* : gaspilleur, dépensier

wastefulness ['weɪstfəlnəs] *n* : gaspillage *m*

wasteland ['weɪst,lænd, -lənd] *n* : terrain *m* vague, désert *m*

watch[1] ['wɑtʃ] *vi* **1** *or* **to keep watch** : veiller **2** LOOK : regarder **3 to watch for** AWAIT : guetter, attendre **4 to watch out** : faire attention — *vt* **1** OBSERVE : regarder, surveiller **2** *or* **to watch over** : veiller sur, garder **3** : faire attention à <watch what you are doing! : faites attention à ce que vous faites!>

watch[2] *n* **1** SURVEILLANCE : surveillance *f* <to keep a close watch on : surveiller de près> **2** LOOKOUT, SEN-

TRY : sentinelle *m,* homme *m* de quart (sur un navire) **3** TIMEPIECE : montre *f*
watchdog [ˈwɑtʃˌdɔg] *n* : chien *m* de garde, chienne *f* de garde
watcher [ˈwɑtʃər] *n* : spectateur *m,* -trice *f;* observateur *m,* -trice *f*
watchful [ˈwɑtʃfəl] *adj* : attentif, vigilant
watchfully [ˈwɑtʃfəli] *adv* : attentivement, de façon vigilante
watchman [ˈwɑtʃmən] *n, pl* **-men** [-mən, -ˌmɛn] : gardien *m*
watchword [ˈwɑtʃˌwərd] *n* **1** PASSWORD : mot *m* de passe **2** SLOGAN : mot *m* d'ordre, slogan *m*
water¹ [ˈwɔt̬ər, ˈwɑ-] *vt* **1** : arroser (un jardin, etc.) **2** : donner à boire à (des animaux) **3** *or* **to water down** DILUTE : couper (d'eau) — *vi* **1** : larmoyer (se dit des yeux) **2** : avoir l'eau à la bouche <to make one's mouth water : faire venir l'eau à la bouche>
water² *n* **1** : eau *f* <fresh water : eau douce> **2 waters** *npl* : eaux *fpl* <in Canadian waters : dans les eaux territoriales canadiennes>
water buffalo *n* : buffle *m*
watercolor [ˈwɔt̬ərˌkʌlər, ˈwɑ-] *n* **1** : couleur *f* pour aquarelle **2** *or* **watercolor painting** : aquarelle *f*
watercourse [ˈwɔt̬ərˌkors, ˈwɑ-] *n* : cours *m* d'eau
watercress [ˈwɔt̬ərˌkrɛs, ˈwɑ-] *n* : cresson *m*
waterfall [ˈwɔt̬ərˌfɔl, ˈwɑ-] *n* : chute *f* (d'eau), cascade *f*
waterfowl [ˈwɔt̬ərˌfaʊl, ˈwɑ-] *ns & pl* **1** : oiseau *m* aquatique **2 waterfowl** *npl* : gibier *m* d'eau
waterfront [ˈwɔt̬ərˌfrʌnt, ˈwɑ-] *n* : front *m* de mer
water lily *n* : nénuphar *m*
waterlogged [ˈwɔt̬ərˌlɔgd, -ˌlɑgd] *adj* : imprégné d'eau, détrempé (se dit de la terre)
watermark [ˈwɔt̬ərˌmɑrk, ˈwɑ-] *n* **1** : laisse *f* de haute mer (en navigation) **2** : filigrane *m* (du papier)
watermelon [ˈwɔt̬ərˌmɛlən, ˈwɑ-] *n* : pastèque *f,* melon *m* d'eau
water moccasin → **moccasin**
waterpower [ˈwɔt̬ərˌpaʊər, ˈwɑ-] *n* : énergie *f* hydraulique
waterproof¹ [ˈwɔt̬ərˌpruːf, ˈwɑ-] *vt* : imperméabiliser
waterproof² *adj* : imperméable
watershed [ˈwɔt̬ərˌʃɛd, ˈwɑ-] *n* : ligne *m* de partage des eaux
water–ski [ˈwɔt̬ərˌskiː, ˈwɑ-] *vi* : faire du ski nautique
water ski *n* : ski *m* nautique
waterskiing [ˈwɔt̬ərˌskiːɪŋ, ˈwɑ-] *n* : ski *m* nautique
waterspout [ˈwɔt̬ərˌspaʊt, ˈwɑ-] *n* **1** : gouttière *f,* tuyau *m* de descente **2** : trombe *f* (en météorologie)
watertight [ˈwɔt̬ərˌtaɪt, ˈwɑ-] *adj* **1** : étanche <a watertight joint : un raccord étanche> **2** : inattaquable, incontestable <a watertight argument : un argument inattaquable>
waterway [ˈwɔt̬ərˌweɪ, ˈwɑ-] *n* : cours *m* d'eau navigable
waterworks [ˈwɔt̬ərˌwərks, ˈwɑ-] *npl* : système *m* hydraulique
watery [ˈwɔt̬əri, ˈwɑ-] *adj* **1** : larmoyant (se dit des yeux) **2** THIN, WEAK : faible, liquide <watery soup : soupe trop liquide> **3** SOGGY : détrempé
watt [ˈwɑt] *n* : watt *m*
wattage [ˈwɑt̬ɪdʒ] *n* : consommation *f* en watts
wattle [ˈwɑt̬əl] *n* : caroncule *f* (d'un oiseau)
wave¹ [ˈweɪv] *v* **waved; waving** *vi* **1** FLUTTER : flotter, ondoyer **2** : faire un signe de la main <to wave goodbye : faire au revoir de la main> **3** UNDULATE : onduler — *vt* **1** SHAKE : agiter **2** BRANDISH : brandir **3** CURL : onduler (ses cheveux) **4** SIGNAL : faire signe à <I waved down the passing car : j'ai fait signe à la voiture d'arrêter>
wave² *n* **1** : vague *f* (d'eau) **2** CURL : ondulation *f* (des cheveux) **3** GREETING : geste *m* de la main **4** FLOW, GUSH : vague *f,* déferlement *m* <a wave of anger : une vague de colère> **5** : onde *f* (en physique)
wavelength [ˈweɪvˌlɛŋkθ] *n* : longueur *f* d'onde (en physique)
waver [ˈweɪvər] *vi* **1** VACILLATE : vaciller, hésiter **2** FLICKER : vaciller **3** FALTER : chanceler, trembloter (se dit de la voix)
wavy [ˈweɪvi] *adj* **wavier; -est** : ondulé
wax¹ [ˈwæks] *vt* : cirer (le plancher, etc.), farter (des skis) — *vi* **1** : croître (se dit de la lune) **2** BECOME : devenir, se montrer <to wax indignant : se montrer indigné>
wax² *n* **1** : cire *f* (pour les planchers, les meubles, etc.) **2** → **beeswax** **3** → **earwax**
waxen [ˈwæksən] *adj* : cireux
waxy [ˈwæksi] *adj* **waxier; -est** : cireux
way [ˈweɪ] *n* **1** PATH, STREET : chemin *m* **2** ROUTE : chemin *m,* passage *m* <the way back : le chemin du retour> <it's the only way out : c'est la seule façon de s'en sortir> **3** MEANS, RESPECT : façon *f,* manière *f* <a new way of thinking : une nouvelle façon de penser> <in no way does he resemble his mother : il ne ressemble aucunement à sa mère> **4** FACILITY : talent *m,* habileté *f* <he has a way with children : il s'y prend bien avec les enfants> **5** MANNER, STYLE : façon *f* de vivre, manières *fpl* <it's just her way : c'est sa façon de vivre habituelle> **6** CONDITION, STATE : état *m,* situation *f* <it's the way

things are : c'est ainsi> 7 DISTANCE : distance *f* <we walked a long way : nous avons marché longtemps> 8 DIRECTION : direction *f,* sens *m* <he was looking my way : il regardait dans ma direction> <she's coming this way : elle vient par ici> 9 **by the way :** à propos 10 **by way of** VIA : par, via 11 **in a way :** dans un certain sens 12 **in the way of** : en fait de <he had little in the way of help : il n'était pas choyé en fait d'aide> 13 **out of the way** : éloigné, isolé 14 → **under way**

wayfarer ['weɪˌfærər] *n* : voyageur *m,* -geuse *f*

waylay ['weɪˌleɪ] *vt* **-laid** [-ˌleɪd]; **-laying** : attaquer, attirer dans une embuscade

wayside ['weɪˌsaɪd] *n* **1** : bord *m* de la route **2 to fall by the wayside** : tomber à l'eau, tomber en désuétude

wayward ['weɪwərd] *adj* **1** UNRULY : rebelle, capricieux **2** UNPREDICTABLE : imprévisible **3** UNTOWARD : malencontreux

we ['wi:] *pron* : nous <we're ready : nous sommes prêts> <as we say in Canada : comme on dit au Canada>

weak ['wi:k] *adj* **1** FEEBLE : faible, fragile (se dit des personnes) **2** : peu solide, fragile (se dit des structures, etc.) **3** UNCONVINCING : peu convaincant, faible <a weak argument : un argument réfutable> **4** DEFICIENT : faible **5** DILUTED : faible, léger, dilué **6** FAINT : faible (se dit des couleurs, des sons, de la lumière, etc.)

weaken ['wi:kən] *vt* : affaiblir — *vi* : s'affaiblir, faiblir

weakling ['wi:klɪŋ] *n* : gringalet *m*

weakly ['wi:kli] *adv* : faiblement

weakness ['wi:knəs] *n* **1** : faiblesse *f,* point *m* faible <in a moment of weakness : dans un moment de faiblesse> **2** FAULT : défaut *m* **3** PARTIALITY : faible *m,* penchant *m* <a weakness for luxury : un faible pour le luxe>

wealth ['wɛlθ] *n* **1** RICHES : richesse *f,* fortune *f* **2** PROFUSION : abondance *f,* profusion *f*

wealthy ['wɛlθi] *adj* **wealthier; -est** : riche

wean ['wi:n] *vt* **1** : sevrer (un bébé) **2 to wean s.o. away from** : détacher qqn de, détourner qqn de

weapon ['wɛpən] *n* : arme *f*

wear[1] ['wær] *v* **wore** ['wor]; **worn** ['worn]; **wearing** *vt* **1** : porter (des vêtements, des lunettes, etc.) **2** EXHIBIT, PRESENT : arborer <to wear a happy smile : arborer un large sourire> **3 to wear away** : ronger, éroder (des roches, etc.) **4** *or* **to wear out** : user **5** EXHAUST : épuiser — *vi* **1** LAST : durer **2** *or* **to wear out** : s'user, se détériorer **3 to wear off** : diminuer

wear[2] *n* **1** USE : port *m* <for everyday wear : de tous les jours> **2** CLOTHES : vêtements *mpl* **3** *or* **wear and tear** : usure *f*

wearable ['wærəbəl] *adj* : mettable, portable

wearily ['wɪrəli] *adv* : d'un air las, avec lassitude

weariness ['wɪrinəs] *n* : lassitude *f*

wearisome ['wɪrisəm] *adj* : fastidieux, fatigant

weary[1] ['wɪri] *v* **-ried; -rying** *vt* : lasser, fatiguer — *vi* : se lasser

weary[2] *adj* **wearier; -est** : fatigué, las

weasel ['wi:zəl] *n* : belette *f*

weather[1] ['wɛðər] *vt* **1** : exposer (le bois, etc.) aux intempéries **2** ENDURE : se tirer de, surmonter — *vi* : s'éroder (se dit des roches)

weather[2] *n* : temps *m*

weather–beaten ['wɛðərˌbi:tən] *adj* **1** : battu, usé (par les intempéries) **2** : hâlé <a weather-beaten face : un visage hâlé>

weatherman ['wɛðərˌmæn] *n, pl* **-men** : météorologiste *mf*

weatherproof[1] ['wɛðərˌpru:f] *vt* : imperméabiliser

weatherproof[2] *adj* : imperméable, étanche

weather vane → **vane**

weave[1] ['wi:v] *v* **wove** ['wo:v] *or* **weaved; woven** ['wo:vən] *or* **weaved; weaving** *vt* **1** : tisser **2** INTERLACE : entrelacer, tresser **3 to weave a tale** : inventer une histoire **4 to weave one's way through** : se faufiler à travers — *vi* **1** : tisser **2** WIND : serpenter, zigzaguer

weave[2] *n* : tissage *m*

weaver ['wi:vər] *n* : tisserand *m,* -rande *f*

web ['wɛb] *n* **1** COBWEB : toile *f* (d'araignée) **2** : palmure *f* (d'un oiseau) **3** ENTANGLEMENT : tissu *m,* réseau *m* <a web of lies : un tissu de mensonges> **4** NETWORK : réseau *m*

webbed ['wɛbd] *adj* : palmé <webbed feet : pattes palmées>

wed ['wɛd] *vt* **wedded; wedding 1** MARRY : se marier à, épouser **2** UNITE : allier

we'd ['wi:d] (*contraction of* **we had, we should,** *or* **we would**) → **have, should, would**

wedding ['wɛdɪŋ] *n* : mariage *m,* noces *fpl*

wedge[1] ['wɛdʒ] *vt* **wedged; wedging 1** : caler, fixer (avec une cale) **2** CRAM : enfoncer, coincer

wedge[2] *n* **1** : cale *f* (pour tenir ouverte une porte, etc.), coin *m* (pour enfoncer dans une bûche) **2** PIECE : morceau *m,* part *m* (de gâteau, etc.)

wedlock ['wɛdˌlɑk] *n* : mariage *m*

Wednesday ['wɛnzˌdeɪ, -di] *n* : mercredi *m*

wee ['wiː] *adj* : tout petit <in the wee hours of the morning : aux petites heures du matin>

weed[1] ['wiːd] *vi* : désherber, enlever les mauvaises herbes — *vt* **1** : désherber (un jardin) **2 to weed out** : se débarrasser de, éliminer

weed[2] *n* : mauvaise herbe *f*

weedy ['wiːdi] *adj* **weedier; -est 1** : couvert de mauvaises herbes **2** LANKY, SCRAWNY : dégingandé, décharné

week ['wiːk] *n* : semaine *f*

weekday ['wiːkˌdeɪ] *n* : jour *m* de semaine

weekend ['wiːkˌɛnd] *n* : fin *f* de semaine, week-end *m*

weekly[1] ['wiːkli] *adv* : à la semaine, chaque semaine

weekly[2] *adj* : hebdomadaire

weekly[3] *n, pl* **-lies** : hebdomadaire *m,* journal *m* hebdomadaire

weep ['wiːp] *vi* **wept** ['wɛpt]; **weeping** : pleurer

weeping willow *n* : saule *m* pleureur

weepy ['wiːpi] *adj* **weepier; -est** : larmoyant, au bord des larmes

weevil ['wiːvəl] *n* : charançon *m*

weft ['wɛft] *n* : trame *f*

weigh ['weɪ] *vt* **1** : peser **2** CONSIDER : peser, considérer **3 to weigh anchor** : lever l'ancre **4 to weigh down** : surcharger (un véhicule, etc.), accabler (une personne) — *vi* **1** : peser <she weighs 100 pounds : elle pèse 100 livres> **2** COUNT : compter, avoir de l'importance <to weigh against : jouer contre> **3 to weigh on s.o.'s mind** : préoccuper qqn

weight[1] ['weɪt] *vt* **1** LOAD : charger, lester **2** *or* **to weight down** BURDEN : alourdir, charger

weight[2] *n* **1** HEAVINESS : poids *m* <to lose weight : perdre du poids> <to sell by weight : vendre au poids> **2** : poids *m* <weights and measures : poids et mesures> **3** : poids *m* <to lift weights : soulever des poids> **4** BURDEN : poids *m,* pesanteur *f* <it's a weight on my mind : cela me pèse beaucoup> **5** IMPORTANCE : influence *f,* importance *f* <to throw one's weight around : essayer de faire l'important>

weightlessness ['weɪtləsnəs] *n* : apesanteur *f*

weighty ['weɪṭi] *adj* **weightier; -est 1** HEAVY : pesant, lourd **2** POWERFUL : important, de poids

weird ['wɪrd] *adj* **1** UNEARTHLY : surnaturel, mystérieux **2** STRANGE : étrange, bizarre

weirdly ['wɪrdli] *adv* **1** MYSTERIOUSLY : mystérieusement **2** STRANGELY : étrangement, bizarrement

welcome[1] ['wɛlkəm] *vt* **-comed; -coming 1** GREET : accueillir, souhaiter la bienvenue à **2** ACCEPT : accepter avec plaisir, être heureux de recevoir

welcome[2] *adj* **1** : bienvenu <they are always welcome : ils sont toujours les bienvenus> <you're welcome to come and go : vous pouvez aller et venir à votre guise> **2** PLEASING : bienvenu, agréable <a welcome relief : un vrai soulagement> **3 you're welcome** : de rien, je vous en prie

welcome[3] *n* : accueil *m*

weld[1] ['wɛld] *vi* : souder — *vt* **1** : souder **2** UNITE : unir

weld[2] *n* : soudure *f*

welder ['wɛldər] *n* : soudeur *m,* -deuse *f*

welfare ['wɛlˌfær] *n* **1** WELL-BEING : bien-être *m* **2** AID : aide *f* sociale, assistance *f* publique

well[1] ['wɛl] *vi or* **to well up** : monter

well[2] *adv* **better** ['bɛṭər]; **best** ['bɛst] **1** : bien <he did well in his classes : il réussissait bien dans ses cours> **2** HIGHLY : bien <to speak well of s.o. : dire du bien de qqn> <to think well of : avoir de l'estime pour> **3** COMPLETELY, FULLY : tout à fait <to be well aware of : être tout à fait conscient de> <it's well worth the price : cela vaut bien le prix> **4** INTIMATELY : bien, intimement <I know him well : je le connais bien> **5** CONSIDERABLY, FAR : considérablement, bien <well over one million dollars : bien au-delà d'un million de dollars> **6** DEFINITELY, EXACTLY : clairement, bien <she remembered it well : elle s'en souvenait très clairement> **7 as well** ALSO : aussi **8** → **as well as 9 it may well be that** : il se pourrait bien que

well[3] *adj* **1** PLEASING, SATISFACTORY : bien <all's well that ends well : tout est bien qui finit bien> **2** DESIRABLE : désirable, souhaitable <it would be well for you to leave : il vaudrait mieux pour vous de partir> **3** HEALTHY : bien portant <she's not well : elle ne se porte pas bien>

well[4] *n* **1** : puits *m* (d'eau, de pétrole, etc.) **2** ORIGIN, SOURCE : source *f,* fontaine *f* **3** → **stairwell**

well[5] *interj* **1** (*used to express surprise or doubt*) : ça alors!, eh bien! **2** (*used to begin or resume a conversation*) : bon, bien, enfin

we'll ['wiːl, wɪl] (*contraction of* **we shall** *or* **we will)** → **shall, will**

well–adjusted [ˌwɛlə'dʒʌstəd] *adj* : équilibré, bien adapté

well–advised [ˌwɛləd'vaɪzd] *adj* : prudent, sage

well–being ['wɛl'biːɪŋ] *n* : bien-être *m*

well–bred ['wɛl'brɛd] *adj* : bien élevé, poli

well–done ['wɛl'dʌn] *adj* **1** : bien fait **2** : bien cuit (en cuisine)

well–known ['wɛl'noːn] *adj* : bien connu

well–meaning ['wɛl'miːnɪŋ] *adj* : bien intentionné

well–nigh ['wɛl'naɪ] *adv* : presque, quasi <well-nigh impossible : quasi impossible>

well–off ['wɛl'ɔf] → **well–to–do**

well–rounded ['wɛl'raʊndəd] *adj* : complet

well–to–do [ˌwɛltə'duː] *adj* : prospère, aisé, riche

Welsh[1] ['wɛlʃ, 'wɛltʃ] *adj* : gallois

Welsh[2] *n* **1** : gallois *m* (langue) **2 the Welsh** : les Gallois *mpl*

welt ['wɛlt] *n* **1** : trépointe *f* (de chaussures) **2** : zébrure *f*, marque *f* (sur la peau)

welter[1] ['wɛltər] *vi* : se rouler, se vautrer

welter[2] *n* JUMBLE : fatras *m*, fouillis *m*

wend ['wɛnd] *vi* **to wend one's way towards** : s'acheminer vers, se diriger vers

went → **go**[1]

wept → **weep**

were → **be**

we're ['wɪr, 'wər, 'wiːər] (*contraction of* **we are**) → **be**

werewolf ['wɪrˌwʊlf, 'wɛr-, 'wər-, -ˌwʌlf] *n, pl* **-wolves** [-ˌwʊlvz, -ˌwʌlvz] : loup-garou *m*

west[1] ['wɛst] *adv* : à l'ouest, vers l'ouest

west[2] *adj* : ouest, d'ouest

west[3] *n* **1** : ouest *m* **2 the West** : l'Ouest *m*, l'Occident *m*

westerly[1] ['wɛstərli] *adv* : vers l'ouest

westerly[2] *adj* : à l'ouest, d'ouest

western ['wɛstərn] *adj* **1** : ouest, de l'ouest, occidental **2 Western** : de l'Ouest, occidental <Western Europe : l'Europe occidentale>

Westerner ['wɛstərnər] *n* : habitant *m*, -tante *f* de l'Ouest

West Indian[1] *adj* : antillais

West Indian[2] *n* : Antillais, -laise *f*

westward ['wɛstwərd] *adj & adv* : vers l'ouest

westwards ['wɛstwərdz] *adv* : vers l'ouest

wet[1] ['wɛt] *vt* **wet** *or* **wetted; wetting** : mouiller

wet[2] *adj* **wetter; wettest 1** : mouillé, humide <a wet cloth : un chiffon humide> **2** RAINY : pluvieux **3** : frais <wet paint : peinture fraîche>

wet[3] *n* **1** WATER : eau *f* **2** MOISTURE : humidité *f* **3** RAIN : pluie *f*

we've ['wiːv] (*contraction of* **we have**) → **have**

whack[1] ['*h*wæk] *vt* : donner une claque à, donner un grand coup à

whack[2] *n* **1** BLOW : coup *m*, claque *f* **2** TRY : essai *m* <to have a whack at sth : essayer (de faire) qqch>

whale[1] ['*h*weɪl] *v* **whaled; whaling** *vi* : pêcher la baleine

whale[2] *n, pl* **whales** *or* **whale** : baleine *f*

whaleboat ['*h*weɪlˌboːt] *n* : baleinière *f*, baleinier *m*

whalebone ['*h*weɪlˌboːn] *n* : fanon *m* de baleine

whaler ['*h*weɪlər] *n* **1** : baleinier *m* (personne) **2** → **whaleboat**

wharf ['*h*wɔrf] *n, pl* **wharves** ['*h*wɔrvz] : quai *m*

what[1] ['*h*wɑt, '*h*wʌt] *adv* **1** (*used in rhetorical questions*) <what does it matter : qu'est-ce que ça fait> **2** (*used to introduce prepositional phrases*) <what with one thing and another : avec ceci et cela>

what[2] *adj* **1** (*used in questions*) : quel <what book are you reading? : quel livre lisez-vous?> **2** (*used in exclamations*) <what an idea! : quelle idée!> <what fun we had! : le plaisir qu'on a eu ensemble!> **3** ANY, WHATEVER : le peu de, tout <what money he had : tout l'argent qu'il avait>

what[3] *pron* **1** : qu'est-ce que, qu'est-ce qui <what is this? : qu'est-ce que c'est?> <what's happening? : qu'est-ce qui se passe?> **2** : ce que, ce qui <I know what you want : je sais ce que vous voulez> **3** (*used in interrogative sentences or to express surprise*) : quoi <what's new? : quoi de neuf?> <what, no breakfast? : quoi, vous ne déjeunez pas?> **4** WHATEVER : (tout) ce que <say what you want : dites ce que vous voulez> **5 what for** WHY : pourquoi <what did you do that for? : pourquoi as-tu fait ça?> **6 what if** : et si <what if they find out? : et s'ils l'apprenaient?>

whatever[1] [*h*wɑt'ɛvər, ˌ*h*wʌt-] *adj* **1** : n'importe quel, tout <take whatever seat : prenez n'importe quel siège> **2** (*in negative constructions*) <we had no food whatever : nous n'avions pas la moindre nourriture> <nothing whatever : rien du tout>

whatever[2] *pron* **1** ANYTHING : (tout) ce que <I'll do whatever you ask : je ferai tout ce que vous me demandez> **2** : quoi que <whatever it may be : quoi que ce soit> **3** WHAT : qu'est-ce que, qu'est-ce qui <whatever do you mean? : qu'est-ce que vous voulez dire?>

whatsoever [ˌ*h*wɑtso'ɛvər, ˌ*h*wʌt-] *pron & adj* → **whatever**

wheal ['*h*wiːl] *n* : marque *f* (sur la peau)

wheat ['*h*wiːt] *n* : blé *m*

wheaten ['*h*wiːtən] *adj* : de blé

wheedle ['*h*wiːdəl] *vt* **-dled; -dling** : cajoler, enjôler <to wheedle money out of s.o. : soutirer de l'argent à qqn par des cajoleries>

wheel[1] ['*h*wiːl] *vi* **1** REVOLVE : tourner **2** *or* **to wheel around** TURN : faire demi-tour — *vt* : pousser <they wheeled in the patient : ils ont fait entrer le patient sur un lit roulant>

wheel[2] *n* **1** : roue *f* (d'un véhicule), roulette *f* (d'un meuble, etc.) **2** → **steering wheel 3 wheels** *npl* WORKINGS : rouages *mpl* <wheels of government : rouages du gouvernement>

wheelbarrow ['*h*wiːlˌbærˌoː] *n* : brouette *f*

wheelchair ['*h*wiːlˌtʃær] *n* : fauteuil *m* roulant

wheeze[1] ['*h*wiːz] *vi* **wheezed; wheezing** : respirer péniblement et bruyamment

wheeze[2] *n* : respiration *f* sifflante

whelk ['*h*wɛlk] *n* : buccin *m*

whelp[1] ['*h*wɛlp] *v* : mettre bas

whelp[2] *n* : petit *m* (d'un animal)

when[1] ['*h*wɛn] *adv* **1** (*used in direct and indirect questions*) : quand <when did you return? : quand êtes-vous revenu?> <he asked me when I did it : il m'a demandé quand je l'ai fait> **2** : où <at a time when things were better : à une époque où les choses allaient mieux>

when[2] *conj* **1** (*referring to a specified time*) : quand, lorsque <when he was a boy : quand il était garçon> <I smiled when he said it : j'ai souri lorsqu'il l'a dit> **2** IF, WHENEVER : quand, si <you're disqualified when you cheat : vous serez disqualifié si vous trichez> **3** ALTHOUGH : alors que, quand, si <why do you tease me, when you know it's wrong? : pourquoi me taquines-tu alors que tu sais que c'est mal?>

when[3] *pron* **1 by when** : avant quand **2 since when** : depuis quand

whence ['*h*wɛnts] *adv & conj* : d'où

whenever[1] [*h*wɛn'ɛvər] *adv* : quand

whenever[2] *conj* : chaque fois que

where[1] ['*h*wɛr] *adv* **1** (*at what place*) : où <where are they? : où sont-ils?> **2** (*at which part*) : où <where did I go wrong? : où est-ce que je me suis trompée?>

where[2] *conj* **1** : où <he knows where the house is : il sait où se trouve la maison> <stay where you are : restez où vous êtes> **2** WHEREVER : où que, partout où <she goes where he likes to go : elle va partout où il aime aller>

where[3] *pron* : où <the town where she was born : la ville où elle est née>

whereabouts[1] ['*h*wɛrəˌbaʊts] *adv* : où <whereabouts is the house? : où est la maison?>

whereabouts[2] *ns & pl* **to know s.o.'s whereabouts** : savoir où se trouve qqn

whereas [*h*wɛr'æz] *conj* **1** : alors que, tandis que <I like the sea whereas she likes the mountains : j'aime la mer alors qu'elle aime les montagnes> **2** SINCE : attendu que (en droit)

whereby [*h*wɛr'baɪ] *conj* : par lequel, selon lequel

wherefore[1] ['*h*wɛrˌfor] *adv* **1** WHY : pourquoi **2** THEREFORE : donc

wherefore[2] *n* **the whys and wherefores** : le pourquoi et le comment

wherein [*h*wɛr'ɪn] *adv* : en quoi

whereof [*h*wɛr'ʌv, -ɑv] *conj* : de quoi

whereupon ['hwɛrəˌpɑn, -ˌpɔn] *conj* : sur quoi, sur ce

wherever[1] [*h*wɛr'ɛvər] *adv* **1** (*used for emphasis*) : mais où, où donc <wherever did you get that tie? : mais où donc as-tu déniché cette cravate?> **2 or wherever** : Dieu sait où

wherever[2] *conj* : où que, partout où <wherever you go : où que tu ailles>

wherewithal ['*h*wɛrwɪˌðɔl, -ˌθɔl] *n* : ressources *fpl,* moyens *mpl*

whet ['*h*wɛt] *vt* **whetted; whetting 1** SHARPEN : affûter, aiguiser (un couteau) **2** STIMULATE : stimuler <to whet one's appetite : ouvrir l'appétit>

whether ['*h*wɛðər] *conj* **1** IF : si <see whether they've left : vérifie s'ils sont partis> **2** (*used to introduce alternatives*) <the game will be played whether it rains or not : nous allons jouer la partie qu'il pleuve ou non> <whether before or after : soit avant soit après>

whetstone ['*h*wɛtˌstoːn] *n* : pierre *f* à aiguiser

whey ['*h*weɪ] *n* : petit-lait *m*

which[1] ['*h*wɪtʃ] *adj* : quel <which shirt should I wear? : quelle chemise devrais-je porter?> <which ones? : lesquels?>

which[2] *pron* **1** : lequel, quel <which of the answers is right? : laquelle des réponses est la bonne?> <he wondered which would be better : il se demandait quel serait mieux> **2** (*used as a function word to introduce a relative clause*) : qui, que <the suggestion which you made : la suggestion que vous avez faite>

whichever[1] [*h*wɪtʃ'ɛvər] *adj* : peu importe quel <whichever way you go : peu importe quel chemin vous empruntez>

whichever[2] *pron* : quel que <whichever you prefer : quelle que soit votre préférence>

whiff[1] ['*h*wɪf] *vi* **1** PUFF : souffler **2** : respirer une odeur

whiff[2] *n* **1** GUST, PUFF : bouffée *f* **2** SMELL, TRACE : odeur *f* <to catch a whiff of : sentir l'odeur de>

while[1] ['*h*waɪl] *vt* **whiled; whiling** : (faire) passer <to while away the time : passer le temps>

while[2] *n* **1** : temps *m,* moment *m* <after a while : au bout d'un moment> <once in a while : de temps en temps> <a long while ago : il y a longtemps> **2 to be worth one's while** : valoir la peine

while[3] *conj* **1** : pendant que <while you're at it : pendant que vous y êtes>

<while you were out : pendant votre absence> **2** ALTHOUGH : bien que <while respected, he is not liked : bien que respecté, il n'est pas aimé> **3** WHEREAS : tandis que, alors que

whim ['*h*wɪm] *n* : caprice *m,* lubie *f*

whimper[1] ['*h*wɪmpər] *vi* : gémir, pleurnicher *fam*

whimper[2] *n* : gémissement *m*

whimsical ['*h*wɪmzɪkəl] *adj* **1** CAPRICIOUS : capricieux, fantasque **2** ERRATIC : changeant, imprévisible

whimsically ['*h*wɪmzɪkəli] *adv* : curieusement, de façon saugrenue

whimsy ['*h*wɪmzi] *n, pl* **1** → **whim 2** : fantaisie *f,* caractère *m* fantasque

whine[1] ['*h*waɪn] *vi* **whined; whining 1** WHIMPER : gémir, geindre **2** COMPLAIN : se plaindre, se lamenter

whine[2] *n* : gémissement *m*

whinny[1] ['*h*wɪni] *vi* **-nied; -nying** : hennir

whinny[2] *n* : hennissement *m*

whip[1] ['*h*wɪp] *v* **whipped; whipping** *vt* **1** SNATCH : tirer brusquement, arracher <she whipped off the tablecloth : elle a brusquement arraché la nappe> **2** LASH : fouetter **3** DEFEAT : vaincre, battre à plates coutures **4** BEAT : battre (des œufs, etc.) **5 to whip up** INCITE : attiser (une émotion), susciter (de l'intérêt) — *vi* **1** LASH : battre <the rain whipped against the shutters : la pluie battait contre les volets> **2** : aller rapidement <to whip along : filer à toute allure>

whip[2] *n* **1** : fouet *m,* cravache *f* (d'équitation) **2** : député *m* d'un parti législatif qui réglemente la discipline et les votes de son parti **3** : mousse *f* <prune whip : mousse aux pruneaux>

whiplash ['*h*wɪp,læʃ] *n or* **whiplash injury** : coup *m* du lapin

whippet ['*h*wɪpət] *n* : whippet *m*

whippoorwill ['*h*wɪpər,wɪl] *n* : engoulevent *m* (de l'Amérique du Nord)

whir[1] ['*h*wər] *vi* **whirred; whirring 1** : bruire (se dit des ailes) **2** : ronronner, vrombir (se dit d'un moteur, d'un ventilateur, etc.)

whir[2] *n* **1** : bruissement *m* (de feuilles, d'ailes) **2** : ronronnement *m,* vrombissement *m* <the whir of propellers : le vrombissement des hélices>

whirl[1] ['*h*wərl] *vi* **1** SPIN : tournoyer, tourbillonner **2** REEL : tourner <my head was whirling : la tête me tournait> **3 to whirl around** : se retourner **4 to whirl by** : aller à toute vitesse, filer à toute allure — *vi* : faire tournoyer, faire tourbillonner

whirl[2] *n* **1** WHIRLING : tournoiement *m* **2** BUSTLE : tourbillon *m* **3 to give sth a whirl** : s'essayer à qqch

whirlpool ['*h*wərl,pu:l] *n* : tourbillon *m* (d'eau)

whirlwind ['*h*wərl,wɪnd] *n* : tourbillon *m* (de vent), trombe *f*

whisk[1] ['*h*wɪsk] *vt* **1** : faire rapidement <I whisked it out of my purse : je l'ai brusquement sorti de mon sac à main> **2** BEAT : battre (des œufs) **3** *or* **to whisk away** : enlever d'un geste rapide — *vi* : aller vite

whisk[2] *n* **1** WHISKING : coup *m* léger **2** : fouet *m* (en cuisine)

whisk broom *n* : époussette *f*

whisker ['*h*wɪskər] *n* **1** : poil *m* de barbe <to win by a whisker : gagner d'un poil> **2 whiskers** *npl* : barbe *f* (d'un homme), moustaches *fpl* (d'un chat, etc.)

whiskey *or* **whisky** ['*h*wɪski] *n, pl* **-keys** *or* **-kies** : whisky *m*

whisper[1] ['*h*wɪspər] *vi* : chuchoter, parler à voix basse — *vt* : chuchoter, dire à voix basse

whisper[2] *n* **1** : chuchotement *m* <to speak in whispers : parler tout bas> **2** RUMOR : rumeur *f,* bruit *m* **3** HINT : soupçon *m,* trace *f*

whistle[1] ['*h*wɪsəl] *vi* **-tled; -tling 1** : siffler **2 to whistle by** : passer en sifflant — *vt* : siffler

whistle[2] *n* **1** WHISTLING : sifflement *m* **2** : sifflet *m* <to blow a whistle : donner un coup de sifflet>

whit ['*h*wɪt] *n* BIT : brin *m,* petit peu *m*

white[1] ['*h*waɪt] *adj* **whiter; -est** : blanc

white[2] *n* **1** : blanc *m* (couleur) **2** *or* **egg white** : blanc *m* d'œuf **3** : Blanc *m,* Blanche *f* (personne)

white blood cell *n* : globule *m* blanc

whitecaps ['*h*waɪt,kæps] *npl* : moutons *mpl*

white–collar ['*h*waɪt'kɑlər] *adj* : de bureau, de col blanc

whitefish ['*h*waɪt,fɪʃ] *n* : corégone *m*

whiten ['*h*waɪtən] *v* : blanchir

whiteness ['*h*waɪtnəs] *n* : blancheur *f*

white–tailed deer ['*h*waɪt'teɪld] *n* : cerf *m* de Virginie, chevreuil *m Can*

whitewash[1] ['*h*waɪt,wɔʃ] *vt* **1** : blanchir (une clôture, etc.) à la chaux **2** CONCEAL : camoufler, dissimuler

whitewash[2] *n* **1** : lait *m* de chaux **2** COVER-UP : dissimulation *f,* camouflage *m*

whither ['*h*wɪðər] *adv* : où

whiting ['*h*waɪṭɪŋ] *n* : merlan *m* (poisson)

whitish ['*h*waɪṭɪʃ] *adj* : blanchâtre

whittle ['*h*wɪṭəl] *vt* **-tled; -tling 1** : tailler au couteau, gosser *Can fam* **2** PARE, REDUCE : réduire, amoindrir

whiz[1] *or* **whizz** ['*h*wɪz] *vi* **whizzed; whizzing 1** BUZZ, HISS : bourdonner, siffler **2** *or* **to whiz by** : passer à toute vitesse, passer en sifflant

whiz[2] *or* **whizz** *n* **1** BUZZ : bourdonnement *m,* sifflement *m* **2** : expert *m,* as *m* <a computer whiz : un expert en informatique>

who ['hu:] *pron* **1** (*used as an interrogative*) : qui <who was elected? : qui a été élu?> <do you know who the message was from? : savez-vous qui a écrit le message?> **2** WHOEVER : qui, qui que ce soit **3** (*used to introduce a relative clause*) : qui <my father, who was a lawyer : mon père, qui était avocat>

whodunit [hu:'dʌnɪt] *n* : roman *m* policier

whoever [hu:'ɛvər] *pron* **1** : qui que ce soit, n'importe qui <whoever told you that, he's wrong : qui que ce soit qui te l'a dit il se trompe> **2** : celui qui, quiconque <whoever wants to participate : quiconque veut participer> **3** (*used to express astonishment or perplexity*) <whoever can that be? : qui est-ce que ça peut bien être?>

whole[1] ['ho:l] *adj* **1** : entier <whole milk : lait entier> **2** INTACT : complet, intact **3** COMPLETE, ENTIRE : au complet, tout <she owns the whole island : l'île au complet lui appartient> <his whole attention : toute son attention> **4 a whole lot** : beaucoup

whole[2] *n* **1** : tout *m*, ensemble *m* **2 as a whole** : dans son ensemble, entièrement **3 on the whole** : en général, dans l'ensemble

wholehearted ['ho:l'hɑrt̬əd] *adj* : de bon cœur, sans réserve

whole number *n* : nombre *m* entier

wholesale[1] ['ho:l,seɪl] *v* **-saled; -saling** *vt* : vendre au prix de gros — *vi* : se vendre au prix de gros

wholesale[2] *adv* : en gros

wholesale[3] *adj* **1** : de gros <wholesale prices : prix de gros> **2** : en masse <wholesale slaughter : massacre en masse>

wholesale[4] *n* : vente *f* en gros

wholesaler ['ho:l,seɪlər] *n* : grossiste *mf*

wholesome ['ho:lsəm] *adj* **1** HEALTHY, SOUND : sain, en santé **2** HEALTHFUL : sain, salubre

whole wheat *adj* : de blé entier

wholly ['ho:li] *adv* **1** COMPLETELY : complètement, entièrement **2** SOLELY : exclusivement

whom ['hu:m] *pron* **1** (*used as an interrogative*) <whom did he fight? : avec qui s'est-il battu?> **2** (*used as a relative pronoun*) <two professors whom I met in Italy : deux professeurs que j'ai rencontrés en Italie> **3** (*used as the object of a preposition*) <the politician to whom you wrote : le politicien à qui vous avez écrit>

whomever [hu:m'ɛvər] → **whoever**

whoop[1] ['*h*wu:p, '*h*wʊp] *vi* : pousser des cris

whoop[2] *n* : cri *m*

whooping cough *n* : coqueluche *f*

whopper ['*h*wɑpər] *n* **1** : chose *f* énorme **2** LIE : bobard *m fam*, gros mensonge *m*

whopping ['*h*wɑpɪŋ] *adj* : colossal, monstre

whore ['hor] *n* : prostituée *f*

whorl ['*h*wɔrl, '*h*wərl] *n* **1** : spire *f* (d'un coquillage), verticille *m* (de pétales), volute *f* (d'un doigt) **2** SWIRL : spirale *f*, volute *f* <a whorl of smoke : une spirale de fumée>

whose[1] ['hu:z] *adj* **1** (*used in questions*) : de qui, à qui <whose daughter is she? : de qui est-elle la fille?> <whose fault is it? : à qui la faute?> **2** (*used in relative clauses*) : dont <a friend whose husband works with me : une amie dont le mari travaille avec moi>

whose[2] *pron* : à qui <whose is this? : à qui est ceci?>

why[1] ['*h*waɪ] *adv* : pourquoi <why did you do it? : pourquoi l'as-tu fait?>

why[2] *n, pl* **whys** : pourquoi *m*

why[3] *conj* **1** : pourquoi <I know why he did it : je sais pourquoi il l'a fait> **2** : pour lequel <the reason why he accepted : la raison pour laquelle il a accepté>

why[4] *interj* : mais!, tiens!

wick ['wɪk] *n* : mèche *f*

wicked ['wɪkəd] *adj* **1** EVIL : corrompu, méchant **2** MISCHIEVOUS : espiègle, malicieux **3** TERRIBLE : mauvais, épouvantable

wickedly ['wɪkədli] *adv* **1** : avec méchanceté **2** MISCHIEVOUSLY : malicieusement

wickedness ['wɪkədnəs] *n* : méchanceté *f*, vilenie *f*

wicker[1] ['wɪkər] *adj* : en osier

wicker[2] *n* **1** : osier *m* **2** → **wickerwork**

wickerwork ['wɪkər,wərk] *n* : vannerie *f*

wicket ['wɪkət] *n* : guichet *m*

wide[1] ['waɪd] *adv* **wider; widest 1** : partout <to search far and wide : chercher partout> **2** FULLY : complètement <she opened her eyes wide : elle a ouvert grand les yeux>

wide[2] *adj* **wider; widest 1** EXTENSIVE, VAST : vaste, étendu <a wide area : une vaste superficie> <to have wide experience : avoir une grande expérience> **2** : de large <3 feet wide : trois pieds de large> **3** BROAD : large **4 to be wide of the mark** : être loin de la vérité

wide–awake ['waɪdə'weɪk] *adj* : éveillé, alerte

wide–eyed ['waɪd'aɪd] *adj* **1** : aux yeux écarquillés **2** AMAZED : étonné, stupéfait **3** NAIVE : naïf, crédule

widely ['waɪdli] *adv* **1** EXTENSIVELY : largement, beaucoup **2** SIGNIFICANTLY : considérablement

widen ['waɪdən] *vt* : élargir — *vi* : s'élargir

widespread ['waɪd'sprɛd] *adj* **1** EXTENDED, SPREAD : déployé, étendu **2** EXTENSIVE : diffus, répandu

widow[1] ['wɪˌdoː] *vt* **to be widowed** : devenir veuf, devenir veuve

widow[2] *n* : veuve *f*

widower ['wɪdowər] *n* : veuf *m*

width ['wɪdθ] *n* : largeur *f*

wield ['wiːld] *vt* **1** : brandir <to wield a broom : brandir un balai> **2** EXERT : exercer (de l'influence, etc.)

wiener ['wiːnər] → **frankfurter**

wife ['waɪf] *n, pl* **wives** ['waɪvz] : femme *f,* épouse *f*

wifely ['waɪfli] *adj* : d'épouse

wig ['wɪg] *n* : perruque *f,* postiche *m*

wiggle[1] ['wɪgəl] *v* **-gled; -gling** *vi* **1** JIGGLE : remuer (se dit des personnes), branler (se dit des choses) **2** WRIGGLE : se tortiller — *vt* : faire branler, faire bouger

wiggle[2] *n* : tortillement *m*

wiggly ['wɪgəli] *adj* **wigglier; -est 1** : qui se tortille **2** WAVY : ondulé, sinueux

wigwam ['wɪgˌwɑm] *n* : wigwam *m*

wild[1] ['waɪld] *adv* **1 to go wild** : devenir fou **2 to grow wild** : pousser à l'état sauvage **3 to run wild** : courir en liberté (se dit des animaux)

wild[2] *adj* **1** : sauvage <wild ducks : canards sauvages> **2** UNRULY : dissolu, indiscipliné **3** TURBULENT : violent, déchaîné **4** CRAZY : insensé, fou <wild ideas : idées insensées> **5** UNCIVILIZED : sauvage, fruste **6** ERRATIC : imprévisible, inattendu <to take a wild guess : deviner au hasard>

wild[3] *n* → **wilderness**

wild boar *n* : sanglier *m*

wildcat ['waɪldˌkæt] *n* **1** : chat *m* sauvage **2** BOBCAT : lynx *m*

wilderness ['wɪldərnəs] *n* : région *f* sauvage

wildfire ['waɪldˌfaɪr] *n* **1** : feu *m* de forêt incontrôlé **2 to spread like wildfire** : se répandre comme une traînée de poudre

wildflower ['waɪldˌflaʊər] *n* : fleur *f* des champs

wildfowl ['waɪldˌfaʊl] *ns & pl* : oiseaux *mpl* sauvages

wildlife ['waɪldˌlaɪf] *n* : faune *f*

wildly ['waɪldli] *adv* **1** FRANTICALLY : de façon agitée **2** EXTREMELY : extrêmement, immensément

wile[1] ['waɪl] *vt* **wiled; wiling** LURE : attirer

wile[2] *n* : ruse *f,* artifice *m*

will[1] ['wɪl] *v, past* **would** ['wʊd]; *pres sing & pl* **will** *vt* WISH : vouloir <say what you will : dis ce que tu veux> — *v aux* **1** (*used to express willingness*) <no one would take the job : personne ne voulait l'emploi> **2** (*used to express habitual action*) <he'll get angry over nothing : il se fâche pour des riens> **3** (*used to express futurity*) <tomorrow we will go swimming : demain nous irons nous baigner> **4** (*used to express capacity*) <the back seat will hold three people : le siège arrière peut accommoder trois personnes> **5** (*used to express probability*) <that will be the mailman : ça doit être le facteur> **6** (*used to express determination*) <I won't give in : je refuse d'abandonner> **7** (*used to express a command*) <you will do as I say : je t'ordonne de faire ce que je te dis>

will[2] *vt* **1** ORDAIN : vouloir <if the Lord willed it : si le Seigneur l'a voulu ainsi> **2** : vouloir très fort <to will s.o.'s success : souhaiter ardemment la réussite de qqn> **3** BEQUEATH : léguer

will[3] *n* **1** DESIRE, WISH : désir *m,* envie *f* **2** INCLINATION : volonté *f,* détermination *f* <where there's a will there's a way : quand on veut on peut> **3** VOLITION : gré *m,* volonté *f* <of her own free will : de son propre gré> **4** : volonté *f,* résolution *f* <an iron will : une volonté de fer> **5** : testament *m* <to make a will : faire un testament>

willful *or* **wilful** ['wɪlfəl] *adj* **1** STUBBORN : volontaire, obstiné **2** INTENTIONAL : délibéré, voulu

willfully ['wɪlfəli] *adv* **1** STUBBORNLY : obstinément **2** INTENTIONALLY : délibérément, intentionnellement

willing ['wɪlɪŋ] *adj* **1** INCLINED, READY : prêt, disposé <willing to help : prêt à aider> **2** EAGER : empressé, de bonne volonté <willing workers : travailleurs empressés> **3** VOLUNTARY : volontaire <a willing sacrifice : un sacrifice volontaire>

willingly ['wɪlɪŋli] *adv* **1** GLADLY : volontiers, de bon cœur **2** VOLUNTARILY : volontairement

willingness ['wɪlɪŋnəs] *n* **1** ENTHUSIASM : empressement *m,* bonne volonté *f* **2** READINESS : volonté *f*

willow ['wɪˌloː] *n* : saule *m*

willowy ['wɪlowi] *adj* : svelte, élancé

willpower ['wɪlˌpaʊər] *n* : volonté *f*

willy–nilly [ˌwɪli'nɪli] *adv & adj* : bon gré mal gré

wilt ['wɪlt] *vi* **1** : se faner (se dit des fleurs) **2** LANGUISH : dépérir, languir

wily ['waɪli] *adj* **wilier; -est** : rusé, malin

win[1] ['wɪn] *v* **won** ['wʌn]; **winning** *vt* **1** : gagner, remporter <to win the war : gagner la guerre> <to win a prize : remporter un prix> **2** GAIN : obtenir, s'attirer **3 to win over** : convaincre, rallier — *vi* : gagner

win[2] *n* : victoire *f*

wince[1] ['wɪnts] *vi* **winced; wincing** : tressaillir

wince[2] *n* : tressaillement *m*

winch[1] ['wɪntʃ] *vt or* **to winch up** : hisser à l'aide d'un treuil

winch[2] *n* : treuil *m*

wind[1] ['wɪnd] *vt* : faire perdre le souffle à, couper la respiration à
wind[2] *n* **1** : vent *m* **2** BREATH : souffle *m* **3** FLATULENCE : gaz *mpl* intestinaux **4 to get wind of** : avoir vent de
wind[3] ['waɪnd] *v* **wound** ['waʊnd]; **winding** *vt* **1** COIL : enrouler **2** WRAP : envelopper **3** : remonter (une horloge) — *vi* MEANDER : serpenter
wind[4] ['waɪnd] *n* BEND : tournant *m*, courbe *f*
windbreak ['wɪnd,breɪk] *n* : brise-vent *m*
windbreaker ['wɪnd,breɪkər] *n* : coupe-vent *m*
windfall ['wɪnd,fɔl] *n* **1** : fruits *mpl* tombés **2** BENEFIT, GAIN : aubaine *f*, chance *f*
wind instrument *n* : instrument *m* à vent
windlass ['wɪndləs] *n* : guindeau *m*
windmill ['wɪnd,mɪl] *n* : moulin *m* à vent
window ['wɪn,doː] *n* **1** : fenêtre *f* (d'une maison), vitre *f* (d'une voiture), guichet *m* (dans une banque, etc.) **2** GAP, INTERVAL : espace *m*, créneau *m* <a window of time : un espace de temps> **3** : fenêtre *f* (en informatique) **4** → **shopwindow, windowpane**
windowpane ['wɪn,doː,peɪn] *n* : vitre *f*, carreau *m*
window–shop ['wɪndo,ʃɑp] *vi* **-shopped; -shopping** : faire du lèche-vitrines
windpipe ['wɪnd,paɪp] *n* : trachée *f*
windshield ['wɪnd,ʃiːld] *n* : pare-brise *m*
windshield wiper → **wiper**
windup ['waɪnd,ʌp] *n* : fin *f*, conclusion *f*
wind up *vt* : terminer, conclure — *vi* : finir
windward[1] ['wɪndwərd] *adj* : contre le vent, au vent
windward[2] *n* : côté *m* du vent
windy ['wɪndi] *adj* **windier; -est 1** : venteux **2** BOMBASTIC : verbeux, grandiloquent
wine[1] ['waɪn] *vt* **to wine and dine s.o.** : inviter qqn dans les bons restaurants
wine[2] *n* : vin *m*
wing[1] ['wɪŋ] *vt* **1** WOUND : blesser (un oiseau) **2 to wing it** : improviser — *vi* FLY : voler, s'envoler
wing[2] *n* **1** : aile *f* (d'un oiseau) **2** : aile *f* (d'un édifice), pavillon *m* (d'un hôpital) **3** FACTION : aile *f*, partie *f* **4** : ailier *m* (aux sports) **5 on the wing** : en vol **6 to take s.o. under one's wing** : prendre qqn sous son aile **7 wings** *npl* : coulisses *fpl* (au théâtre)
winged ['wɪŋd, 'wɪŋəd] *adj* : ailé
wink[1] ['wɪŋk] *vi* **1** : faire un clin d'œil **2** BLINK : cligner des yeux **3** TWINKLE : clignoter, scintiller
wink[2] *n* **1** : clin *m* d'œil **2** NAP : sieste *f*, somme *m* <I didn't get a wink of sleep : je n'ai pas fermé l'œil> **3 quick as a wink** : en un clin d'œil
winner ['wɪnər] *n* : gagnant *m*, -gnante *f*
winning ['wɪnɪŋ] *adj* **1** VICTORIOUS : gagnant **2** CHARMING : séduisant, engageant
winnings ['wɪnɪŋz] *npl* : gains *mpl*
winnow ['wɪno] *vt* **1** : vanner (en agriculture) **2** SEPARATE : trier, passer au crible
winsome ['wɪnsəm] *adj* : charmant, engageant
winter[1] ['wɪntər] *adj* : d'hiver
winter[2] *n* : hiver *m*
wintergreen ['wɪntər,griːn] *n* : gaulthérie *f*
wintertime ['wɪntər,taɪm] *n* : hiver *m*
wintry ['wɪntri] *adj* **wintrier; -est 1** : hivernal <wintry weather : temps hivernal> **2** COLD : froid, glacial <a wintry welcome : un accueil froid>
wipe[1] ['waɪp] *vt* **wiped; wiping 1** : essuyer <to wipe the dishes : essuyer la vaisselle> **2** *or* **to wipe away** : essuyer (des larmes), effacer (un souvenir, etc.) **3 to wipe out** : détruire
wipe[2] *n* : coup *m* d'éponge, coup *m* de torchon
wiper ['waɪpər] *n or* **windshield wiper** : essuie-glace *m*
wire[1] ['waɪr] *vt* **wired; wiring 1** : faire l'installation électrique de **2** BIND, CONNECT : relier, attacher (avec du fil métallique) **3** TELEGRAPH : envoyer un télégramme à
wire[2] *n* **1** : fil *m* métallique, broche *f* *Can* <barbed wire : fil de fer barbelé> **2** TELEGRAM : télégramme *m*
wireless ['waɪrləs] *adj* : sans fil
wiretapping ['waɪr,tæpɪŋ] *n* : mise *f* sur écoute téléphonique
wiring ['waɪrɪŋ] *n* : installation *f* électrique
wiry ['waɪri] *adj* **wirier** ['waɪriər]; **-est 1** : raide (se dit des cheveux, etc.) **2** SINEWY : mince et musclé
wisdom ['wɪzdəm] *n* **1** KNOWLEDGE : sagesse *f*, connaissances *fpl* **2** JUDGMENT : sagesse *f*, discernement *m*
wisdom tooth *n* : dent *f* de sagesse
wise[1] ['waɪz] *adj* **wiser; wisest 1** LEARNED : sage **2** PRUDENT, SENSIBLE : sage, prudent, judicieux **3 to be wise to** : être au courant de
wise[2] *n* : manière *f*, façon *f* <in no wise : en aucune façon>
wisecrack ['waɪz,kræk] *n* : blague *f*, vanne *f fam*
wisely ['waɪzli] *adv* : sagement, avec sagesse
wish[1] ['wɪʃ] *vt* **1** WANT : souhaiter, désirer **2 to wish (something) for** : souhaiter <we wished her a happy birthday : nous lui avons souhaité bonne fête> <she wished me good night : elle m'a dit bonsoir> — *vi* : souhaiter, vouloir <as you wish : comme vous voulez>

wish[2] *n* **1** : souhait *m,* désir *m,* vœu *m* <make a wish : fais un vœu> **2 wishes** *npl* : vœux *mpl,* amitiés *fpl* <best wishes : meilleurs vœux>

wishbone ['wɪʃˌbo:n] *n* : bréchet *m,* fourchette *f*

wishful ['wɪʃfəl] *adj* **1** HOPEFUL : désireux **2 it's wishful thinking** : c'est prendre ses désirs pour des réalités

wishy–washy ['wɪʃiˌwɔʃi, -ˌwɑʃi] *adj* **1** INEFFECTUAL : incapable, incompétent **2** WEAK : faible, insipide

wisp ['wɪsp] *n* **1** : mèche *f* (de cheveux), volute *f* (de fumée), brin *m* (de foin) **2** HINT : trace *f,* soupçon *m*

wispy ['wɪspi] *adj* **wispier; -est** : fin, épars

wisteria [wɪs'tɪriə] *n* : glycine *f*

wistful ['wɪstfəl] *adj* : mélancolique, pensif — **wistfully** *adv*

wistfulness ['wɪstfəlnəs] *n* : mélancolie *f*

wit ['wɪt] *n* **1** MIND : esprit *m,* intelligence *f* **2** CLEVERNESS, HUMOR : esprit *m* <to have a quick wit : avoir l'esprit vif> **3** JOKER : farceur *m,* -ceuse *f* **4 wits** *npl* : sens *m,* raison *f* <to be at one's wits' end : ne plus savoir que faire> <you scared me out of my wits : tu m'as fait une de ces peurs>

witch ['wɪtʃ] *n* : sorcière *f*

witchcraft ['wɪtʃˌkræft] *n* : sorcellerie *f*

witch doctor *n* : sorcier *m,* -cière *f*

witchery ['wɪtʃəri] *n, pl* **-eries 1** → **witchcraft 2** CHARM : ensorcellement *m*

witch hazel ['wɪtʃˌheɪzəl] *n* : hamamélis *m*

witch–hunt ['wɪtʃˌhʌnt] *n* **1** : chasse *f* aux sorcières **2** : persécution *f* (politique)

with ['wɪð, 'wɪθ] *prep* **1** (*indicating accompaniment*) : avec <I'm going with you : je vais avec vous> **2** AGAINST : avec, contre <he had a fight with his brother : il s'est chicané avec son frère> <to be angry with s.o. : être fâché contre qqn> **3** (*used in descriptions*) : à <the girl with red hair : la fille aux cheveux roux> **4** (*indicating manner, means, or cause*) : avec <to cut with a knife : couper avec un couteau> <with any luck : avec un peu de chance> **5** DESPITE : malgré <with all her faults, she's still my friend : malgré tous ses défauts, elle est quand même mon amie> <with all your money . . . : il a beau avoir de l'argent . . .> **6** REGARDING, TOWARD : avec <be patient with the children : soyez patient avec les enfants> <it's a habit with her : c'est une habitude chez elle> **7** ACCORDING TO : avec <it varies with the season : ça change avec la saison> **8** (*indicating support or understanding*) : avec <I'm with you all the way : je suis avec vous cent pour cent>

withdraw [wɪð'drɔ, wɪθ-] *v* **-drew** [-'dru:]; **-drawn** [-'drɔn]; **-drawing** *vt* **1** REMOVE : retirer <to withdraw money : retirer de l'argent> **2** RETRACT : retirer, rétracter (une parole, etc.) — *vi* LEAVE, RETREAT : se retirer

withdrawal [wɪð'drɔəl, wɪθ-] *n* **1** : retrait *m* (de fonds, des troupes) **2** RETRACTION : rétraction *f* **3** *or* **withdrawal symptoms** : symptômes *mpl* de manque

withdrawn [wɪð'drɔn, wɪθ-] *adj* : renfermé, replié sur soi-même

wither ['wɪðər] *vi* **1** WILT : se faner, se flétrir **2 to wither away** : s'évanouir

withers ['wɪðərz] *npl* : garrot *m* (d'un cheval)

withhold [wɪθ'ho:ld, wɪð-] *vt* **-held** [-'hɛld]; **-holding** : retenir (des fonds), refuser (la permission, etc.), cacher (des faits, la vérité)

within[1] [wɪð'ɪn, wɪθ-] *adv* : à l'intérieur

within[2] *prep* **1** INSIDE : dans, à l'intérieur de <within the building : à l'intérieur de l'édifice> **2** (*indicating limitation*) <to live within one's income : vivre selon ses moyens> <within reach : à (la) portée de la main> **3** (*indicating distance*) <within a mile of the city : à moins d'un mille de la ville> **4** (*indicating time*) <within a month : en moins d'un mois> <within the time limit : dans les temps impartis>

without[1] [wɪð'aʊt, wɪθ-] *adv* **1** OUTSIDE : à l'extérieur, au dehors **2 to do without** : se passer de

without[2] *prep* **1** OUTSIDE : à l'extérieur de **2** : sans <I spoke without thinking : j'ai parlé sans réfléchir> <without a doubt : sans aucun doute>

withstand [wɪθ'stænd, wɪð-] *vt* **-stood** [-'stʊd]; **-standing 1** BEAR : supporter **2** RESIST : résister à

witless ['wɪtləs] *adj* : stupide, sans génie

witness[1] ['wɪtnəs] *vt* **1** SEE : être témoin de, assister à **2** : servir de témoin de (une signature) — *vi* TESTIFY : témoigner

witness[2] *n* **1** TESTIMONY : témoignage *m* <to bear false witness : donner un faux témoignage> **2** : témoin *m* <to call as a witness : citer comme témoin>

witticism ['wɪt̬əˌsɪzəm] *n* : bon mot *m,* mot *m* d'esprit

witty ['wɪt̬i] *adj* **wittier; -est** : humoristique, amusant

wives → **wife**

wizard ['wɪzərd] *n* **1** SORCERER : magicien *m,* sorcier *m* **2** : génie *m* <a math wizard : un génie des mathématiques>

wizardry ['wɪzərdri] *n* : sorcellerie *f*

wizened ['wɪzənd, 'wi:-] *adj* : desséché, ratatiné

wobble[1] ['wɑbəl] *vi* **-bled; -bling** : branler, osciller, trembler

wobble[2] *n* : branlement *m*

wobbly ['wɑbəli] *adj* : vacillant, branlant

woe ['wo:] *n* **1** SORROW : chagrin *m* **2 woes** *npl* MISFORTUNE : malheur *m*

woeful ['wo:fəl] *adj* **1** SORROWFUL : désolé, affligé, triste **2** DEPLORABLE, UNFORTUNATE : lamentable, malheureux

woefully ['wo:fəli] *adv* **1** SADLY : tristement **2** DEPLORABLY : lamentablement

woke, woken → **wake**[1]

wolf[1] ['wʊlf] *vt or* **to wolf down** : engloutir, engouffrer

wolf[2] *n, pl* **wolves** ['wʊlvz] : loup *m*, louve *f*

wolfish ['wʊlfɪʃ] *adj* : féroce

wolfram ['wʊlfrəm] → **tungsten**

wolverine [,wʊlvə'ri:n] *n, pl* **-ines** : glouton *m*

woman ['wʊmən] *n, pl* **women** ['wɪmən] : femme *f*

womanhood ['wʊmən,hʊd] *n* **1** : féminité *f* **2** WOMEN : femmes *fpl*

womanly ['wʊmənli] *adj* : féminin, de femme

womb ['wu:m] *n* : utérus *m*

won → **win**[1]

wonder[1] ['wʌndər] *vi* **1** MARVEL : s'émerveiller, s'étonner **2** SPECULATE : penser, songer — *vt* : se demander <I wondered why : je me suis demandé pourquoi>

wonder[2] *n* **1** MARVEL : merveille *f* <to work wonders : faire des merveilles> <it's a wonder that : c'est étonnant que> **2** ASTONISHMENT : émerveillement *m*

wonderful ['wʌndərfəl] *adj* : merveilleux, formidable

wonderfully ['wʌndərfəli] *adv* : merveilleusement, à merveille

wonderland ['wʌndər,lænd, -lənd] *n* : pays *m* des merveilles, pays *m* enchanté

wonderment ['wʌndərmənt] *n* : émerveillement *m*, étonnement *m*

wondrous ['wəndrəs] → **wonderful**

wont[1] ['wɔnt, 'wo:nt] *adj* : habitué <to be wont to do : avoir coutume de faire>

wont[2] *n* : habitude *f*, coutume *f*

won't ['wo:nt] (*contraction of* **will not**) → **will**[1]

woo ['wu:] *vt* **1** COURT : courtiser, faire la cour à **2** : rechercher les faveurs de (des clients, etc.)

wood[1] ['wʊd] *adj* : de bois, en bois

wood[2] *n* **1** : bois *m* <solid wood : bois massif> **2** *or* **woods** *npl* FOREST : bois *m*, boisé *m Can*

woodchuck ['wʊd,tʃʌk] *n* : marmotte *f* d'Amérique

woodcraft ['wʊd,kræft] *n* **1** : connaissance *f* des bois **2** : art *m* de travailler le bois

woodcut ['wʊd,kʌt] *n* : gravure *f* sur bois

woodcutter ['wʊd,kʌtər] *n* : bûcheron *m*, -ronne *f*

wooded ['wʊdəd] *adj* : boisé

wooden ['wʊdən] *adj* **1** : en bois, de bois **2** STIFF : raide, qui manque de naturel

woodland ['wʊdlənd, -,lænd] *n* : région *f* boisée, bois *m*

woodpecker ['wʊd,pɛkər] *n* : pic *m*, picbois *m Can*

woodpile ['wʊd,paɪl] *n* : tas *m* de bois

woodshed ['wʊd,ʃɛd] *n* : bûcher *m*, remise *f* à bois

woodsman ['wʊdzmən] *n, pl* **-men** [-mən, -,mɛn] **1** → **woodcutter 2** FORESTER : forestier *m*, -tière *f*

woodwind ['wʊd,wɪnd] *n* : bois *m* (en musique)

woodwork ['wʊd,wərk] *n* : boiseries *fpl* (dans une maison)

woodworking ['wʊd,wərkɪŋ] *n* CARPENTRY : menuiserie *f*, ébénisterie *f*

woody ['wʊdi] *adj* **woodier; -est 1** WOODED : boisé **2** : ligneux (se dit des plantes)

woof ['wʊf] → **weft**

wool ['wʊl] *n* : laine *f*

woolen[1] *or* **woollen** ['wʊlən] *adj* : de laine, en laine

woolen[2] *n* **1** : tissu *m* en laine **2 woolens** *npl* : vêtements *mpl* de laine

woolly ['wʊli] *adj* **woolier; -est 1** : de laine, en laine **2** : laineux (se dit d'un animal) **3** CONFUSED, VAGUE : confus, flou

woozy ['wu:zi] *adj* **woozier; -est** : écœuré, qui a la tête qui tourne <to feel woozy : avoir mal au cœur>

word[1] ['wərd] *vt* : formuler, rédiger

word[2] *n* **1** : mot *m*, parole *f* <word for word : mot pour mot> <in a word, no : en un mot, non> <in word and deed : en paroles et en fait> <what is the word for . . . ? : comment dit-on . . . ?> **2** TALK : parole *f* <to have a word with s.o. : parler avec qqn> **3** COMMAND : ordre *m*, mot *m* d'ordre <to give the word : donner l'ordre> **4** MESSAGE, NEWS : nouvelles *fpl* <there's no word from Marie : on est sans nouvelles de Marie> <to send word : envoyer un mot> **5** PROMISE : parole *f* <to keep one's word : tenir (sa) parole> **6 words** *npl* QUARREL : dispute *f* <to have words with : se disputer avec> **7 words** *npl* : texte *m*, paroles *fpl* (en musique)

wordiness ['wərdinəs] *n* : verbosité *f*

wording ['wərdɪŋ] *n* : termes *mpl* (d'un document), formulation *f* (d'une invitation, etc.)

wordless ['wərdləs] *adj* : muet

word processing *n* : traitement *m* de texte

word processor *n* : machine *f* de traitement de textes

wordy ['wərdi] *adj* **wordier; -est** : verbeux, prolixe
wore → **wear**[1]
work[1] ['wərk] *v* **worked** ['wərkt] *or* **wrought** ['rɔt]; **working** *vt* **1** EFFECT : faire <to work miracles : faire des miracles> **2** FORGE, SHAPE : travailler (le fer, l'acier, etc.) **3** OPERATE : faire marcher, activer **4** EXPLOIT : faire travailler **5** ARRANGE : arranger, organiser **6** EXCITE, PROVOKE : provoquer, exciter <I worked myself into a rage : la rage montait en moi> — *vi* **1** LABOR : travailler **2** SUCCEED : fonctionner, réussir
work[2] *adj* : de travail <work clothes : vêtements de travail>
work[3] *n* **1** LABOR : travail *m* **2** EMPLOYMENT : travail *m,* emploi *m* **3** TASK : travail *m,* ouvrage *m* **4** WORKMANSHIP : travail *m,* exécution *f* **5** : œuvre *f,* ouvrage *m* <a work of art : une œuvre d'art> **6 works** *npl* FACTORY : usine *f* **7 works** *npl* : travaux *mpl* <public works : travaux publics> **8 works** *npl* MECHANISM : rouages *mpl* (d'une horloge, etc.) **9 in the works** : en train de se faire
workable ['wərkəbəl] *adj* **1** : exploitable (se dit d'une mine, etc.) **2** PRACTICABLE : possible, réalisable
workaday ['wərkə,deɪ] *adj* : commun, ordinaire
workbench ['wərk,bɛntʃ] *n* : établi *m*
workday ['wərk,deɪ] *n* **1** : journée *f* de travail **2** *or* **working day** : jour *m* ouvrable
worker ['wərkər] *n* **1** : travailleur *m,* -leuse *f;* employé *m,* -ployée *f* <he's a hard worker : c'est un grand travailleur> <white-collar workers : employés de bureau> **2** LABORER : ouvrier *m,* -vrière *f*
working ['wərkɪŋ] *adj* **1** : qui travaille <working people : gens qui travaillent> **2** : de bureau, de travail <during working hours : pendant les heures de bureau> **3** FUNCTIONING : qui fonctionne, qui marche <in working order : en état de marche> **4** SUFFICIENT : suffisant <a working knowledge : une connaissance adéquate>
workingman ['wərkɪŋ,mæn] *n, pl* **-men** [-mən, -,mɛn] : ouvrier *m*
workman ['wərkmən] *n, pl* **-men** [-mən, -,mɛn] **1** → **workingman** **2** ARTISAN : artisan *m*
workmanlike ['wərkmən,laɪk] *adj* **1** : professionnel, consciencieux (se dit d'une personne) **2** : bien fait (se dit d'un objet)
workmanship ['wərkmən,ʃɪp] *n* **1** SKILL : habileté *f* **2** QUALITY : qualité *f,* exécution *f*
workout ['wərk,aʊt] *n* : séance *f* d'entraînement
work out *vt* **1** SOLVE : résoudre (un problème) **2** DEVELOP : développer, élaborer (un plan, etc.) — *vi* **1** SUCCEED, WORK : marcher, fonctionner, réussir **2** EXERCISE : s'entraîner, faire de l'exercice
workroom ['wərk,ru:m, -,rʊm] *n* : salle *f* de travail
workshop ['wərk,ʃɑp] *n* **1** SHOP : atelier *m* **2** SEMINAR : atelier *m,* groupe *m* de travail
world[1] ['wərld] *adj* : du monde, mondial
world[2] *n* **1** : monde *m* <around the world : autour du monde> <that makes a world of difference : cela fait un monde de différence> <to think the world of s.o. : penser le plus grand bien de qqn> **2** PEOPLE : monde *m,* société *f* <in the eyes of the world : aux yeux du monde> <the academic world : le monde académique>
worldly ['wərldli] *adj* **1** : matériel, de ce monde **2** → **worldly-wise**
worldly-wise ['wərldli,waɪz] *adj* : qui a l'expérience du monde
worldwide[1] ['wərld'waɪd] *adv* : dans le monde entier, partout dans le monde
worldwide[2] *adj* : mondial, universel
worm[1] ['wərm] *vt* **1** : débarrasser (un animal) de ses vers **2 to worm one's way into** : s'insinuer dans **3 to worm one's way through** : se faufiler à travers
worm[2] *n* **1** : ver *m* **2 worms** *npl* : vers *mpl* (intestinaux)
wormy ['wərmi] *adj* **wormier; -est** : véreux
worn ['worn] → **wear**[1]
worn-out ['worn'aʊt] *adj* **1** : usé, fini (se dit d'un objet) **2** EXHAUSTED : épuisé, éreinté (se dit d'une personne)
worried ['wəri:d] *adj* : inquiet, soucieux
worrier ['wəriər] *n* : personne *f* qui s'inquiète
worrisome ['wərisəm] *adj* : inquiétant, préoccupant
worry[1] ['wəri] *v* **-ried; -rying** *vt* : inquiéter, tracasser — *vi* FRET : s'inquiéter
worry[2] *n, pl* **-ries** **1** ANXIETY : inquiétude *f* **2** DIFFICULTY : problème *m,* ennui *m*
worse[1] ['wərs] *adv* (*comparative of* **bad** *or of* **ill**) : moins bien, plus mal <we sleep worse in the warm weather : nous dormons moins bien quand il fait chaud>
worse[2] *adj* (*comparative of* **bad** *or of* **ill**) **1** : pire <it's worse than ever : c'est pire que jamais, c'est pire qu'avant> **2** : plus mal, plus malade <to feel worse : se sentir encore plus mal>
worse[3] *n* : pire *m* <to take a turn for the worse : s'aggraver, empirer> <none the worse : pas plus mal>
worsen ['wərsən] *vi* : empirer, se détériorer, rempirer *Can fam* — *vt* : aggraver, rendre pire

worship[1] ['wərʃəp] *v* **-shiped** *or* **-shipped; -shiping** *or* **-shipping** *vt* : adorer, vénérer — *vi* : faire ses dévotions

worship[2] *n* **1** : culte *m* <a place of worship : un lieu consacré au culte> **2** REVERENCE : adoration *f,* vénération *f*

worshiper *or* **worshipper** ['wərʃəpər] *n* : adorateur *m,* -trice *f*

worst[1] ['wərst] *vt* DEFEAT : battre, vaincre

worst[2] *adv* (*superlative of* **bad** *or of* **ill**) : plus mal <the worst dressed : le plus mal habillé>

worst[3] *adj* (*superlative of* **bad** *or of* **ill**) : pire, plus mauvais <the worst fate : le pire sort>

worst[4] *n* : pire *m* <to fear the worst : craindre le pire>

worsted ['wʊstəd, 'wərstəd] *n* : laine *f* peignée

worth[1] ['wərθ] *n* **1** : valeur *f* (monétaire) <what is its worth? : quelle est sa valeur?> **2** EXCELLENCE : valeur *f,* mérite *m*

worth[2] *prep* **to be worth** : valoir <he's worth thousands : il vaut des milliers> <to be well worth the effort : valoir bien l'effort>

worthiness ['wərðinəs] *n* : dignité *f,* mérite *m*

worthless ['wərθləs] *adj* : sans valeur

worthwhile [wərθ'*h*waɪl] *adj* : qui en vaut la peine

worthy ['wərði] *adj* **worthier; -est** : digne, méritant

would ['wʊd] *past of* **will 1** (*used to express preference*) <I would rather stay here : je préférerais rester ici> **2** (*used to express a wish, desire, or intent*) <those who would forbid gambling : ceux qui interdiraient les jeux d'argent> **3** (*used to express a plan*) <I said we would go : j'ai dit que nous irions> **4** (*used to express consent or choice*) <she would put off her work if she could : elle remettrait son travail à plus tard si elle pouvait> **5** (*used to express contingency*) <if they were coming, they would be here by now : s'ils venaient, ils seraient déjà arrivés> **6** (*used in a noun clause*) <we wish that he would go : nous aimerions qu'il parte> **7** (*used to express probability*) <I would have won if I had not tripped : j'aurais gagné si je n'avais pas trébuché> **8** (*used to express a request*) <would you please help us? : pourriez-vous nous aider s'il vous plaît?>

would–be ['wʊd'bi:] *adj* : soi-disant, prétendu

wouldn't ['wʊdənt] (*contraction of* **would** *and* **not**) → **would**

wound[1] ['wu:nd] *vt* : blesser

wound[2] *n* : blessure *f*

wound[3] ['waʊnd] → **wind[3]**

wove, woven → **weave[1]**

wrangle[1] ['ræŋgəl] *vi* **-gled; -gling** : se quereller, se disputer <to wrangle over : se disputer à propos de>

wrangle[2] *n* : querelle *f,* dispute *f,* chicane *f*

wrap[1] ['ræp] *v* **wrapped; wrapping** *vt* **1** COVER : envelopper, emballer <to wrap a present : envelopper un cadeau> **2** SURROUND : envelopper, entourer <wrapped in mystery : entouré de mystère> **3** WIND : enrouler **4** *or* **to wrap up** SUMMARIZE : résumer — *vi* **to wrap up** DRESS : se couvrir, s'habiller

wrap[2] *n* **1** → **wrapper 2** SHAWL : châle *m*

wrapper ['ræpər] *n* **1** : papier *m,* emballage *m* <candy wrapper : papier de bonbon> **2** : jaquette *f* (de livre), bande *f* (de journal)

wrapping ['ræpɪŋ] *n* **1** : emballage *m* **2 wrapping paper** : papier d'emballage

wrath ['ræθ] *n* : furie *f,* colère *f*

wrathful ['ræθfəl] *adj* : courroucé, en colère

wreak ['ri:k] *vt* **1** INFLICT : infliger (une punition, etc.) **2 to wreak havoc** : faire des ravages, dévaster

wreath ['ri:θ] *n, pl* **wreaths** ['ri:ðz, 'ri:θs] : couronne *f* (de fleurs, etc.)

wreathe ['ri:ð] *vt* **wreathed; wreathing 1** ADORN : couronner, orner **2** ENVELOP : envelopper <wreathed in mist : enveloppé de brume>

wreck[1] ['rɛk] *vt* **1** : provoquer le naufrage de (un navire), faire dérailler (un train), détruire (une voiture) **2** DESTROY, RUIN : détruire, miner, briser (un mariage, etc.) <to wreck one's chances : anéantir ses chances>

wreck[2] *n* **1** WRECKAGE : épave *f* (d'un navire), voiture *f* accidentée **2** ACCIDENT : accident *m* (de voiture), écrasement *m* (d'avion) **3 to be a wreck** : être à bout, être une épave

wreckage ['rɛkɪdʒ] *n* **1** : épave *f* (d'un navire), voiture *f* accidentée **2** REMAINS : décombres *mpl,* débris *mpl*

wrecker ['rɛkər] *n* **1** : destructeur *m,* -trice *f* **2** TOW TRUCK : dépanneuse *f*

wren ['rɛn] *n* : roitelet *m*

wrench[1] ['rɛntʃ] *vt* **1** PULL : tirer brusquement sur <to wrench sth away from s.o. : arracher qqch des mains de qqn> **2** TWIST : tordre <to wrench one's ankle : se tordre la cheville> — *vi* **to wrench free** : se dégager

wrench[2] *n* **1** PULL : mouvement *m* violent, secousse *f* (de torsion) **2** SPRAIN : foulure *f,* entorse *f* **3** : clef *f* (outil)

wrest ['rɛst] *vt* : arracher

wrestle[1] ['rɛsəl] *v* **-tled; -tling** *vi* **1** : lutter, pratiquer la lutte (aux sports) **2**

STRUGGLE : lutter <to wrestle with one's conscience : se débattre avec sa conscience> — *vt* : lutter contre
wrestle[2] *n* STRUGGLE : lutte *f*
wrestler ['rɛsələr] *n* : lutteur *m,* -teuse *f*
wrestling ['rɛsəlɪŋ] *n* : lutte *f* (sport)
wretch ['rɛtʃ] *n* **1** : misérable *mf* <a poor wretch : un pauvre misérable> **2** ROGUE : scélérat *m*
wretched ['rɛtʃəd] *adj* **1** POOR : misérable <wretched slums : taudis misérables> **2** MISERABLE, UNHAPPY : misérable, malheureux <to feel wretched : se sentir très mal> **3** AWFUL : affreux, déplorable <wretched weather : temps affreux>
wretchedly ['rɛtʃədli] *adv* : misérablement
wretchedness ['rɛtʃədnəs] *n* : misère *f*
wriggle ['rɪgəl] *v* **-gled; -gling** *vt* **1** SQUIRM, WIGGLE : gigoter, remuer **2 to wriggle one's way** : s'avancer en se tortillant — *vi* **to wriggle out of** : s'extirper de
wring ['rɪŋ] *vt* **wrung** ['rʌŋ]; **wringing 1** *or* **to wring out** : essorer, tordre (le linge) **2** TWIST : tordre <to wring s.o.'s neck : tordre le cou à qqn> <to wring one's hands : se tordre les mains> **3** EXTRACT : arracher (un aveu, etc.) **4 to wring one's heart** : se fendre le cœur
wringer ['rɪŋər] *n* : essoreuse *f*
wrinkle[1] ['rɪŋkəl] *v* **-kled; -kling** *vi* : se rider (se dit de la peau), se froisser (se dit des vêtements) — *vt* **1** : rider (la peau) **2** : plisser, faire des plis dans (des vêtements) <to wrinkle one's brow : plisser le front>
wrinkle[2] *n* : pli *m* (de vêtements), ride *f* (sur la peau)
wrinkly ['rɪŋkəli] *adj* : ridé
wrist ['rɪst] *n* : poignet *m*
wristband ['rɪst,bænd] *n* **1** CUFF : poignet *m* (d'une chemise, etc.) **2** : bracelet *m* (d'une montre)
wristwatch ['rɪst,wɑtʃ] *n* : montre-bracelet *f*
writ ['rɪt] *n* : ordonnance *f* (en droit)
write ['raɪt] *v* **wrote** ['ro:t]; **written** ['rɪtən]; **writing** : écrire
write down *vt* : mettre par écrit, noter
write off *vt* CANCEL : annuler
writer ['raɪṭər] *n* : écrivain *m,* écrivaine *f Can*
writhe ['raɪð] *vi* **writhed; writhing** : se tordre, se tortiller
writing ['raɪṭɪŋ] *n* **1** : écriture *f* <to put in writing : mettre par écrit> **2** HANDWRITING : écriture *f* **3 writings** *npl* : écrits *mpl,* œuvres *fpl*
wrong[1] ['rɔŋ] *vt* **wronged; wronging 1** HARM, INJURE : faire du tort à **2** CHEAT : frauder
wrong[2] *adv* **1** WRONGLY : à tort **2** INCORRECTLY : mal <I guessed wrong : j'ai mal deviné>
wrong[3] *adj* **wronger; wrongest 1** SINFUL : mal, immoral **2** UNSUITABLE : mal, peu convenable, inapproprié **3** INCORRECT : mauvais, erroné <the wrong answer : la mauvaise réponse> **4 to be wrong** : se tromper, avoir tort
wrong[4] *n* **1** EVIL : mal *m* **2** INJUSTICE : tort *m,* injustice *f*
wrongdoer ['rɔŋ,du:ər] *n* : malfaiteur *m*
wrongdoing ['rɔŋ,du:ɪŋ] *n* : méfait *m,* mal *m*
wrongful ['rɔŋfəl] *adj* **1** UNJUST, WRONG : mal, injustifié **2** UNLAWFUL : illégal <wrongful arrest : arrestation arbitraire>
wrongfully ['rɔŋfəli] *adv* : injustement, à tort
wrongly ['rɔŋli] *adv* : à tort <wrongly accused : accusé à tort>
wrote → **write**
wrought[1] → **work**[1]
wrought[2] ['rɔt] *adj* **1** SHAPED, WORKED : travaillé, ouvré <wrought iron : fer forgé> **2 to be wrought up** : être énervé, être très tendu
wrung → **wring**
wry ['raɪ] *adj* **wrier** ['raɪər]; **wriest** ['raɪəst] **1** : forcé <a wry smile : un sourire forcé> **2** TWISTED : tordu <to have a wry neck : avoir un torticolis> **3** SARDONIC : ironique, moqueur

X

x[1] ['ɛks] *n, pl* **x's** *or* **xs** ['ɛksəz] **1** : x *m,* vingt-quatrième lettre de l'alphabet **2** : x *m* (en mathématiques)
x[2] ['ɛks] *vt* **x–ed** ['ɛkst]; **x–ing** *or* **x'ing** ['ɛksɪŋ] DELETE: barrer, rayer
xenon ['zi:,nɑn, 'zɛ-] *n* : xénon *m*
xenophobia [,zɛnə'fo:biə, ,zi:-] *n* : xénophobie *f*
xenophobic [,zɛnə'fo:bɪk, 'zi:-] *adj* : xénophobe
xerography [zə'rɑgrəfi] *n* : photocopie *f*
xerox ['zirɑks] *vt* : photocopier
Xmas ['krɪsməs] → **Christmas**
x–ray ['ɛks,reɪ] *vt* : radiographier
X ray ['ɛks,reɪ] *n* **1** : rayon *m* X **2** *or* **X–ray photograph** : radiographie *f*
xylophone ['zaɪlə,fo:n] *n* : xylophone *m*
xylophonist ['zaɪlə,fo:nɪst] *n* : xylophoniste *mf*

Y

y ['waɪ] *n, pl* **y's** *or* **ys** ['waɪz] : y *m,* vingt-cinquième lettre de l'alphabet
yacht[1] ['jɑt] *vi* : faire du yachting
yacht[2] *n* : yacht *m*
yak ['jæk] *n* : yack *m*
yam ['jæm] *n* **1** : igname *f* (plante) **2** SWEET POTATO : patate *f* douce
yank[1] ['jæŋk] *vt* : tirer d'un coup sec
yank[2] *n* : coup *m* sec
Yankee ['jæŋki] *n* : Yankee *mf*
yap[1] ['jæp] *vi* **yapped; yapping 1** YELP : japper (se dit d'un chien) **2** CHATTER : jacasser
yap[2] *n* : jappement *m*
yard ['jɑrd] *n* **1** : yard *m,* verge *f Can* (unité de mesure) **2** SPAR : vergue *f* (d'un navire) **3** COURTYARD : cour *f* (d'immeuble) **4** : jardin *m* (d'une maison) **5** : chantier *m* (de construction), dépôt *m* (de marchandises)
yardage ['jɑrdɪdʒ] *n* : longueur *f* en yards, longueur *f* en verges *Can*
yardarm ['jɑrd,ɑrm] *n* : bout *m* de vergue
yardstick ['jɑrd,stɪk] *n* **1** : mètre *m* **2** : CRITERION : critère *m,* point *m* de référence
yarn ['jɑrn] *n* **1** : fil *m* (à tisser) **2** TALE : histoire *f* <to spin a yarn : raconter des histoires>
yawl ['jɔl] *n* : yawl *m*
yawn[1] ['jɔn] *vi* : bâiller
yawn[2] *n* : bâillement *m*
ye ['ji:] *pron* : vous
yea[1] ['jeɪ] *adv* YES : oui
yea[2] *n* : vote *m* affirmatif, oui *m* <the yeas and the nays : les oui et les non>
year ['jɪr] *n* **1** : an *m,* année *f* <next year : l'an prochain> <the school year : l'année scolaire> **2** : an *m* <their son is seven years olds : leur fils a sept ans> **3 years** *npl* AGE : âge *m* <she's getting on in years : elle prend de l'âge>
yearbook ['jɪr,bʊk] *n* : recueil *m* annuel, annuaire *m*
yearling ['jɪrlɪŋ, 'jərlən] *n* : animal *m* d'un an
yearly[1] ['jɪrli] *adv* : annuellement
yearly[2] *adj* : annuel
yearn ['jərn] *vi* **to yearn for** : désirer ardemment, aspirer à
yearning ['jərnɪŋ] *n* : désir *m* ardent
yeast ['ji:st] *n* : levure *f*
yell[1] ['jɛl] *vi* : crier — *vt* SHOUT : crier, hurler
yell[2] *n* : cri *m,* hurlement *m*
yellow[1] ['jɛlo] *v* : jaunir
yellow[2] *adj* **1** : jaune **2** COWARDLY : lâche, peureux
yellow[3] *n* **1** : jaune *m* (couleur) **2** YOLK : jaune *m* d'œuf
yellow fever *n* : fièvre *f* jaune
yellowish ['jɛloɪʃ] *adj* : jaunâtre
yellow jacket *n* : guêpe *f*
yelp[1] ['jɛlp] *vi* : glapir
yelp[2] *n* : glapissement *m*
Yemeni[1] ['jɛməni] *adj* : yéménite
Yemeni[2] *n* : Yéménite *mf*
yen ['jɛn] *n* : désir *m,* envie *f*
yeoman ['jo:mən] *n, pl* **-men** [-mən, -,mɛn] : sous-officier *m* de la marine
yes[1] ['jɛs] *adv* **1** (*used in general statements*) : oui <are you ready? yes, I am : êtes-vous prêt? oui, je suis prêt> **2** (*used after a negative question*) : si <you're not ready, are you? yes, I am : vous n'êtes pas prêt? mais si, je le suis>
yes[2] *n* : oui *m*
yesterday[1] ['jɛstər,deɪ, -di] *adv* : hier
yesterday[2] *n* **1** : hier *m* **2 the day before yesterday** : avant-hier *m*
yet[1] ['jɛt] *adv* **1** BESIDES : de plus, encore <yet another excuse : encore une autre excuse> <yet again : encore une fois> **2** SO FAR : jusqu'à présent, jusqu'ici <the best yet : le mieux jusqu'ici> **3** (*used in negative phrases*) : encore <not yet : pas encore> **4** EVENTUALLY, STILL : encore <they may yet return : ils pourraient encore revenir> **5** NEVERTHELESS : néanmoins
yet[2] *conj* BUT : mais
yew ['ju:] *n* : if *m*
yield[1] ['ji:ld] *vt* **1** SURRENDER : rendre, céder <to yield the right of way : céder le passage> **2** PRODUCE : produire, donner, rapporter — *vi* **1** GIVE : céder, fléchir <to yield under pressure : céder sous la pression> **2** GIVE IN, SURRENDER : se rendre, céder
yield[2] *n* : rendement *m,* rapport *m,* récolte *f* (en agriculture)
yodel ['jo:dəl] *vi* **-deled** *or* **-delled; -deling** *or* **-delling** : iodler
yoga ['jo:gə] *n* : yoga *m*
yogurt ['jo:gərt] *n* : yaourt *m,* yogourt *m*
yoke[1] ['jo:k] *vt* **yoked; yoking 1** : atteler (des animaux) **2** JOIN : joindre
yoke[2] *n* **1** : joug *m* (d'animaux) **2** DOMINION : joug *m* <the yoke of slavery : le joug de l'esclavage> **3** TEAM : attelage *m* **4** : empiècement *m* (d'un vêtement)
yokel ['jo:kəl] *n* : rustre *mf;* plouc *mf France fam;* péquenaud *m,* -naude *f France fam*
yolk ['jo:k] *n* : jaune *m* d'œuf
Yom Kippur [,jo:mkɪ'pʊr, jɑm-, -'kɪpər] *n* : Yom Kippour *m*
yonder ['jɑndər] *adv & adj* : là-bas
yore ['jo:r] *n* **of ~** : d'antan <in days of yore : au temps jadis>
you ['ju:] *pron* **1** (*used as subject — singular*) : tu (familier), vous (forme polie) <you may sit in the armchair : tu peux t'asseoir dans le fauteuil> <you were right : vous aviez raison> **2** (*used as subject — plural*) : vous

<you are my friends : vous êtes mes amis> **3** (*used as the direct or indirect object of a verb*) : te (familier), vous (forme polie), vous (pluriel) <can I pour you a cup of tea? : puis-je vous verser une tasse de thé?> <I will help you : je t'aiderai> **4** (*used as the object of a preposition*) : toi (familier), vous (forme polie), vous (pluriel) <bring the children with you : amenez les enfants avec toi> **5** ONE : on <you never know what's going to happen : on ne sait jamais ce qui va arriver>

you'd ['jʊd] (*contraction of* **you had** *or* **you would**) → **have, would**

you'll ['ju:l, 'jʊl] (*contraction of* **you shall** *or* **you will**) → **shall, will**

young[1] ['jʌŋ] *adj* **younger** ['jʌŋgər]; **youngest** ['jʌŋgəst] **1** : jeune <very young children : enfants tout jeunes> **2** NEW : jeune <a young industry : une industrie jeune> **3** YOUTHFUL : jeune, jeune de cœur <to look young : avoir l'air jeune>

young[2] *ns & pl* **the young** : les jeunes (personnes), les petits (animaux)

youngish ['jʌŋɪʃ] *adj* : assez jeune, plutôt jeune

youngster ['jʌŋkstər] *n* **1** : jeune *mf* **2** CHILD : enfant *mf*

your ['jʊr, 'jo:r, jər] *adj* **1** (*familiar singular*) : ta, ton <your book : ton livre> **2** (*formal singular*) : votre <it's your money : c'est votre argent> **3** (*familiar and formal plural*) : tes, vos <your teeth : tes dents> <your contributions : vos contributions> **4** (*impersonal*) : votre, vos <the house is at your right : la maison est à votre droite> <it's good for your health : c'est bon pour la santé> **5** (*used as an equivalent to the definite article* the) <he's different from your average teacher : il se démarque des autres professeurs> **6** (*used before a title*) : Votre <Your Majesty : Votre Majesté>

yours ['jʊrz, 'jo:rz] *pron* **1** (*familiar singular*) : le tien, la tienne <is it yours? : est-ce que c'est le tien?> <the bike is yours : la bicyclette est à toi> **2** (*formal singular*) : le vôtre, la vôtre <a friend of yours : un de vos amis> **3** (*familiar plural*) : les tiens, les tiennes **4** (*formal plural*) : les vôtres <ours are here; yours are there : les nôtres sont ici, les vôtres sont là>

yourself [jər'sɛlf] *pron, pl* **yourselves** [jər'sɛlvz] **1** (*used reflexively*) : tu (familier), vous (forme polie), vous (pluriel) <you'll hurt yourself if you're not careful : tu te feras mal si tu ne fais pas attention> <please help yourself : servez-vous s'il vous plaît> **2** (*used for emphasis*) : toi-même (familier), vous-même (forme polie), vous-mêmes (pluriel) <carry them yourselves : emportez-les vous-mêmes>

youth ['ju:θ] *n, pl* **youths** ['ju:ðz, 'ju:θs] **1** : jeunesse *f* <to regain one's youth : retrouver sa jeunesse> **2** ADOLESCENT : jeune homme *m* **3** : jeunes *mf*, jeunesse *f* <the youth of today : les jeunes d'aujourd'hui>

youthful ['ju:θfəl] *adj* **1** : de jeunesse **2** YOUNG : jeune <to look youthful : avoir l'air jeune> **3** JUVENILE : juvénile

youthfulness ['ju:θfəlnəs] *n* : jeunesse *f*

you've ['ju:v] (*contraction of* **you have**) → **have**

yowl[1] ['jæʊl] *vi* : miauler (se dit d'un chat), hurler (se dit d'un chien ou d'une personne)

yowl[2] *n* : miaulement *m* (d'un chat) hurlement *m* (d'un chien ou d'une personne)

yo–yo ['jo:,jo:] *n, pl* **yo–yos** : yo-yo *m*

yucca ['jʌkə] *n* : yucca *m*

Yugoslav[1] ['ju:go,slɑv] *or* **Yugoslavian** [,ju:go'slɑviən] *adj* : yougoslave

Yugoslav[2] *or* **Yugoslavian** *n* : Yougoslave *mf*

yule ['ju:l] *n* : Noël *m*

yuletide ['ju:l,taɪd] *n* : époque *f* de Noël

Z

z ['zi:] *n, pl* **z's** *or* **zs** : z *m*, vingt-sixième lettre de l'alphabet

Zairian[1] [za'ɪriən] *adj* : zaïrois

Zairian[2] *n* : Zaïrois *m*, -roise *f*

Zambian[1] ['zæmbiən] *adj* : zambien

Zambian[2] *n* : Zambien *m*, -bienne *f*

zany[1] ['zeɪni] *adj* **zanier; -est** : farfelu *fam*, loufoque *fam*

zany[2] *n, pl* **-nies** BUFFOON : bouffon *m*

zeal ['zi:l] *n* : zèle *m*, enthousiasme *m*

zealot ['zɛlət] *n* : fanatique *mf;* zélateur *m*, -trice *f*

zealous ['zɛləs] *adj* : zélé, dévoué

zealously ['zɛləsli] *adv* : avec zèle

zebra ['zi:brə] *n* : zèbre *m*

zed ['zɛd] *Brit* → **z**

zenith ['zi:nəθ] *n* : zénith *m*, apogée *m*

zephyr ['zɛfər] *n* : zéphyr *m*

zeppelin ['zɛplən, -pəlɪn] *n* : zeppelin *m*

zero[1] ['zi:ro, 'zɪro] *vi* **to zero in on** : se diriger droit sur, faire porter tous ses efforts sur

zero[2] *adj* : zéro, nul <zero growth : croissance zéro>

zero[3] *n, pl* **-ros** : zéro *m*

zest ['zɛst] *n* **1** GUSTO : enthousiasme

m, entrain *m* **2** FLAVOR, PIQUANCY : saveur *f,* piquant *m*
zestful ['zɛstfəl] *adj* : enthousiaste, passionné
zestfully ['zɛstfəli] *adv* : avec enthousiasme
zigzag[1] ['zɪg,zæg] *vi* **-zagged; -zagging** : zigzaguer
zigzag[2] *adj & adv* : en zigzag
zigzag[3] *n* : zigzag *m*
Zimbabwean[1] [zɪm'bɑbwiən, -bweɪ-] *adj* : zimbabwéen
Zimbabwean[2] *n* : Zimbabwéen *m,* -wéenne *f*
zinc ['zɪŋk] *n* : zinc *m*
zing ['zɪŋ] *n* **1** HISS, HUM : sifflement *m* **2** ZEST : entrain *m*
zinnia ['zɪniə, 'zi:-, -njə] *n* : zinnia *m*
zip[1] ['zɪp] *v* **zipped; zipping** *vt or* **to zip up** : fermer avec une fermeture à glissière — *vi* **1** DASH : filer à toute allure **2 to zip by** *or* **to zip past** : passer comme une flèche **3** : siffler (se dit d'une balle, etc.)
zip[2] *n* **1** ENERGY, VIM : vitalité *f,* entrain *m* **2** HISSING, HUMMING : sifflement *m*
zip code *n* : code *m* postal
zipper ['zɪpər] *n* : fermeture *f* à glissière
zippy ['zɪpi] *adj* **zippier; -est** LIVELY : vif, entraînant
zircon ['zər,kɑn] *n* : zircon *m*
zirconium [,zər'ko:niəm] *n* : zirconium *m*
zither ['zɪðər, -θər] *n* : cithare *f*
zodiac ['zo:di,æk] *n* : zodiaque *m*
zombie ['zɑmbi] *n* : zombie *m*
zone[1] ['zo:n] *vt* **zoned; zoning 1** : diviser en zones **2 to be zoned for business** : être réservé à l'entreprise
zone[2] *n* : zone *f*
zoo ['zu:] *n, pl* **zoos** : zoo *m*
zookeeper ['zu:,ki:pər] *n* : gardien *m,* -dienne *f* de zoo
zoological [,zo:ə'lɑdʒɪkəl, ,zu:ə-] *adj* : zoologique
zoologist [zo'ɑlədʒɪst, zu:-] *n* : zoologiste *mf*
zoology [zo'ɑlədʒi, zu:-] *n* : zoologie *f*
zoom[1] ['zu:m] *vi* **1** : aller à toute allure <to zoom past : passer comme une trombe> <the plane zoomed up : l'avion a monté en chandelle> **2 to zoom in** : faire un zoom (en photographie)
zoom[2] *n* **1** : bourdonnement *m* (d'un moteur) **2** *or* **zoom lens** : zoom *m*
zucchini [zʊ'ki:ni] *n, pl* **-ni** *or* **-nis** : courgette *f*
zwieback ['swi:,bɑk, 'swaɪ-, 'zwi:-, 'zwaɪ-] *n* : biscotte *f*
zygote ['zaɪ,go:t] *n* : zygote *m*

Common French Abbreviations
Abréviations françaises usuelles

FRENCH ABBREVIATION AND EXPANSION		ENGLISH EQUIVALENT	
AB	Alberta	**AB, Alta.**	Alberta
adr.	adresse	**add.**	address
AELE	Association européenne de libre-échange	**EFTA**	European Free Trade Association
AIEA	Agence internationale de l'énergie atomique	**IAEA**	International Atomic Energy Agency
AJ	auberge de jeunesse	—	youth hostel
Alb.	Alberta	**AB, Alta.**	Alberta
ALÉNA	Accord de libre-échange nord-américain	**NAFTA**	North American Free Trade Agreement
AOC	appellation d'origine contrôlée	—	certified label of quality (of wine)
AP	assistance publique (France)	—	welfare services
ap. J.-C.	après Jésus-Christ	**AD**	anno Domini
appt	appartement	**apt.**	apartment
AR	aller-retour	**RT**	round-trip
a/s	aux soins de	**c/o**	care of
ASBL	association sans but lucratif	—	nonprofit organization
A.T.	Ancien Testament	**O.T.**	Old Testament
av.	avenue	**ave.**	avenue
av. J.-C.	avant Jésus-Christ	**BC**	before Christ
avr.	avril	**Apr.**	April
B	Belgique	—	Belgium
BC	Colombie-Britannique	**BC, B.C.**	British Columbia
BCBG	bon chic bon genre	—	chic and conservative
bcp	beaucoup	—	much
bd	boulevard	**blvd.**	boulevard
BD	bande dessinée	—	comic strip
BIT	Bureau international du travail	**ILO**	International Labor Organization
BN	Bibliothèque nationale	—	national library
BP	boîte postale	**P.O.B.**	post office box
B.S.	bien-être social (Canada)	—	welfare services
c	centime	**c., ct.**	cent
C	centigrade, Celsius	**C**	centigrade, Celsius
CA	comptable agréé (Canada)	**CPA**	certified public accountant
CA	courant alternatif	**AC**	alternating current
c.-à-d.	c'est-à-dire	**i.e.**	that is
Cap.	capitaine	**Capt.**	captain
C.-B.	Colombie-Britannique	**BC, B.C.**	British Columbia
CC	courant continu	**DC**	direct current

FRENCH ABBREVIATION	AND EXPANSION	ENGLISH EQUIVALENT	
CE	Communauté européenne	**EC**	European Community
CEE	Communauté européenne économique	**EEC**	European Economic Community
cf.	confer	**cf.**	compare
cg	centigramme	**cg**	centigram
CH	Confédération helvétique	—	Switzerland, Swiss Confederation
chap.	chapitre	**ch., chap.**	chapter
CICR	Comité international de la Croix-Rouge	**IRC**	International Red Cross
Cie	compagnie	**Co.**	company
CIO	Comité international olympique	**IOC**	International Olympic Committee
cm	centimètre	**cm**	centimeter
COB	Commission des opérations de Bourse	**SEC**	Securities and Exchange Commission
col.	colonne	**col.**	column
Col.	colonel	**Col.**	colonel
C.P.	case postale (Canada)	**P.O.B.**	post office box
CV	cheval-vapeur	**hp**	horsepower
CV	curriculum vitæ	**CV**	curriculum vitae
DEA	diplôme d'études approfondies (France)	—	postgraduate diploma
déc.	décembre	**Dec.**	December
D.E.C.	diplôme d'études collégiales (Canada)	—	junior college diploma
dép., dépt.	département	**dept.**	department
D.E.S.	diplôme d'études secondaires (Canada)	—	high school diploma
DESS	diplôme d'études supérieures spécialisées (France)	—	postgraduate diploma
DEUG	diplôme d'études universitaires générales (France)	—	two-year university diploma
DG	directeur général	**CEO**	chief executive officer
dim.	dimanche	**Sun.**	Sunday
dir.	directeur	**dir.**	director
DOM	Département(s) d'outre-mer	—	French overseas department
douz.	douzaine	**doz.**	dozen
dr.	droite	**rt.**	right
Dr	docteur	**Dr.**	doctor
dz	douzaine	**doz.**	dozen
E	Est, est	**E**	East, east
ECG	électrocardiogramme	**EKG**	electrocardiogram
éd.	édition	**ed.**	edition
EPS	éducation physique et sportive	**PE**	physical education

FRENCH ABBREVIATION AND EXPANSION		ENGLISH EQUIVALENT	
etc.	et cætera, et cetera	**etc.**	et cetera
É.-U.	États-Unis	**US**	United States
F	Fahrenheit	**F**	Fahrenheit
F	franc	**fr.**	franc
F	France	—	France
FAB	franco à bord	**FOB**	free on board
FB	franc belge	—	Belgian franc
févr.	février	**Feb.**	February
FF	franc français	—	French franc
FMI	Fonds monétaire international	**IMF**	International Monetary Fund
g	gauche	**l., L**	left
g	gramme	**g**	gram
GAB	guichet automatique (de banque)	**ATM**	automatic teller machine
Gén.	général	**Gen.**	general
h	heure(s)	**hr.**	hour
ha	hectare	**ha**	hectare
HS	hors service	—	out of order
IA	intelligence artificielle	**AI**	artificial intelligence
i.e.	c'est-à-dire	**i.e.**	that is
IPC	indice des prix à la consommation	**CPI**	consumer price index
Î.P.-É.	Île-du-Prince-Édouard	**PE, P.E.I.**	Prince Edward Island
IVG	interruption volontaire de grossesse	—	termination of pregnancy
janv.	janvier	**Jan.**	January
jeu.	jeudi	**Thurs.**	Thursday
juill.	juillet	**Jul.**	July
kg	kilogramme	**kg**	kilogram
km	kilomètre	**km**	kilometer
l	litre	**l**	liter
lun.	lundi	**Mon.**	Monday
m	mètre	**m.**	meter
M.	Monsieur	—	Mr., mister
Maj.	major	**Maj.**	major
Man.	Manitoba	**Man., MB**	Manitoba
mar.	mardi	**Tues.**	Tuesday
MB	Manitoba	**MB, Man.**	Manitoba
mer.	mercredi	**Wed.**	Wednesday
mg	milligramme	**mg**	milligram
Mgr.	Monseigneur	**Mgr., Msgr.**	Monsignor, Monseigneur
min	minute	**min.**	minute
ml	millilitre	**ml**	milliliter
MLF	mouvement de libération des femmes	—	women's liberation
Mlle	Mademoiselle	—	Ms., Miss
Mme	Madame	—	Ms., Mrs.
MST	maladie sexuellement transmissible	**STD**	sexually transmitted disease

FRENCH ABBREVIATION AND EXPANSION		ENGLISH EQUIVALENT	
N	Nord, nord	**N**	North, north
N°, n°	numéro	**no.**	number
NB, N.-B.	Nouveau-Brunswick	**NB, N.B.**	New Brunswick
n.d.	non daté	**n.d.**	no date, not dated
n.d.	non disponible	**NA**	not available
N-E	nord-est	**NE**	northeast
N.-É.	Nouvelle-Écosse	**NS, N.S.**	Nova Scotia
NF	Terre-Neuve	**NF, Nfld.**	Newfoundland
N-O	nord-ouest	**NW**	northwest
nov.	novembre	**Nov.**	November
NS	Nouvelle-Écosse	**NS, N.S.**	Nova Scotia
NT	Nunavut	**NT**	Nunavut
NT	Territoires du Nord-Ouest	**NT, N.T.**	Northwest Territories
N.T.	Nouveau Testament	**N.T.**	New Testament
O	Ouest, ouest	**W**	West, west
oc	ondes courtes	**s-w**	short wave
oct.	octobre	**Oct.**	October
OIT	Organisation internationale du travail	**ILO**	International Labor Organization
OMS	Organisation mondiale de la santé	**WHO**	World Health Organization
ON	Ontario	**ON, Ont.**	Ontario
ONG	organisation non gouvernementale	**NGO**	nongovernmental organization
Ont.	Ontario	**ON, Ont.**	Ontario
ONU	Organisation des Nations Unies	**UN**	United Nations
OPE	offre publique d'échange	**IPO**	initial public offering
OTAN	Organisation du traité de l'Atlantique Nord	**NATO**	North Atlantic Treaty Organization
OVNI, ovni	objet volant non identifié	**UFO**	unidentified flying object
p.	page	**p.**	page
P.	Père	**Fr.**	Father
PCV	paiement contre vérification	**—**	collect call
PDG	président-directeur général	**CEO**	chief executive officer
p.-ê.	peut-être	**—**	maybe
PE	Île-du-Prince-Édouard	**PE, P.E.I.**	Prince Edward Island
p. ex.	par exemple	**e.g.**	for example
PIB	produit intérieur brut	**GDP**	gross domestic product
PNB	produit national brut	**GNP**	gross national product
Pr	professeur	**Prof.**	professor
P.-S.	post-scriptum	**P.S.**	postscript
pt	point	**pt.**	point
QC	Québec	**QC, Que.**	Quebec
QG	quartier général	**HQ**	headquarters
QI	quotient intellectuel	**IQ**	intelligence quotient

FRENCH ABBREVIATION AND EXPANSION		ENGLISH EQUIVALENT	
R-D	recherche-développement	**R and D**	research and development
réf.	référence	**ref.**	reference
RF	République Française	—	France
RN	route nationale	—	interstate highway
RP	relations publiques	**PR**	public relations
rte	route	**rt, rte.**	route
RV	rendez-vous	**rdv., R.V.**	rendezvous
s.	siècle	**c., cent.**	century
S	Sud, sud	**S, so.**	South, south
SA	société anonyme	**Inc.**	incorporated (company)
S.A.	son altesse	**H.H.**	his highness, her highness
sam.	samedi	**Sat.**	Saturday
SARL	société à responsabilité limitée	**Ltd.**	limited (corporation)
Sask.	Saskatchewan	**SK, Sask.**	Saskatchewan
SDF	sans domicile fixe	—	homeless (person)
S-E	sud-est	**SE**	southeast
sept.	septembre	**Sept.**	September
Sgt.	sergent	**Sgt.**	sergeant
SK	Saskatchewan	**SK, Sask.**	Saskatchewan
SM	Sa Majesté	**HM**	His Majesty, Her Majesty
SME	Système monétaire européen	—	European Monetary System
SNCF	Société nationale des chemins de fer français	—	French national railway company
S-O	sud-ouest	**SW**	southwest
S.S.	Sa Sainteté	**H.H.**	His Holiness
St	saint	**St.**	Saint
Ste	sainte	**St.**	Saint
Sté	société	**Co.**	company
SVP	s'il vous plaît	**pls.**	please
t	tonne	**t., tn.**	ton
tél.	téléphone	**tel.**	telephone
TGV	train à grande vitesse	—	high-speed train
T.-N.	Terre-Neuve	**NF, Nfld.**	Newfoundland
T.N.-O.	Territoires du Nord-Ouest	**NT, N.T.**	Northwest Territories
TOM	Territoire d'Outre-Mer	—	French overseas territory
TU	temps universel	**GMT**	Greenwich mean time
TVA	taxe à valeur ajoutée	**VAT**	value-added tax
UE	Union européenne	**EU**	European Union
univ.	université	**U., univ.**	university
V., v.	voir	**vid.**	see
ven.	vendredi	**Fri.**	Friday
vol.	volume	**vol.**	volume
VPC	vente par correspondance	—	mail-order selling
vs	versus	**v., vs.**	versus
W-C	water closet	**w.c.**	water closet
YT, Yuk.	Yukon	**YT, Y.T.**	Yukon Territory

Common English Abbreviations
Abréviations anglaises usuelles

ENGLISH ABBREVIATION AND EXPANSION		FRENCH EQUIVALENT	
AAA	American Automobile Association	—	—
AB	Alberta	**AB**	Alberta
AC	alternating current	**CA**	courant alternatif
AD	anno Domini (in the year of our Lord)	**ap. J.-C.**	après Jésus-Christ
AK	Alaska	—	Alaska
AL, Ala.	Alabama	—	Alabama
Alta.	Alberta	**Alb.**	Alberta
a.m., AM	ante meridiem (before noon)	—	du matin
Am., Amer.	America, American	—	Amérique, américain
amt.	amount	—	quantité
anon.	anonymous	—	anonyme
ans.	answer	—	réponse
Apr.	April	**avr.**	avril
AR	Arkansas	—	Arkansas
Ariz.	Arizona	—	Arizona
Ark.	Arkansas	—	Arkansas
asst.	assistant	—	assistant, -tante
atty.	attorney	—	avocat, -cate
Aug.	August	—	août
ave.	avenue	**av.**	avenue
AZ	Arizona	—	Arizona
B.A.	Bachelor of Arts	**lic.**	licencié, -ciée ès lettres
B.A.	Bachelor of Arts (degree)	—	licence ès lettres
BC	before Christ	**av. J.-C.**	avant Jésus-Christ
BC, B.C.	British Columbia	**BC, C.-B.**	Colombie-Britannique
BCE	Before Common Era, Before Christian Era	—	avant notre ère
bet.	between	—	entre
bldg.	building	**édif.**	édifice
blvd.	boulevard	**bd**	boulevard
Br., Brit.	Britain, British	—	Grande-Bretagne, britannique
Bro(s).	brother(s)	**F., Fr.**	frère(s)
B.S.	Bachelor of Science	**lic.**	licencié, -ciée ès sciences
B.S.	Bachelor of Science (degree)	**lic.**	licence ès sciences
c.	carat	—	carat
c.	cent	—	cent (Canada), centime
c.	century	**s.**	siècle
c.	cup	—	tasse

ENGLISH ABBREVIATION AND EXPANSION		FRENCH EQUIVALENT	
C	Celsius, centigrade	**C**	Celsius, centigrade
CA, Cal., Calif.	California	—	Californie
Can., Canad.	Canada, Canadian	—	Canada, canadien
cap.	capital	—	capital
cap.	capital	**majusc.**	majuscule
Capt.	captain	**Cap.**	capitaine
cent.	century	**s.**	siècle
CEO	chief executive officer	**DG, PDG**	directeur général, président-directeur général
cf.	compare	**cf.**	confer
cg	centigram	**cg**	centigramme
ch., chap.	chapter	**chap.**	chapitre
CIA	Central Intelligence Agency	—	—
cm	centimeter	**cm**	centimètre
Col.	colonel	**Col.**	colonel
Co.	company	**Cie.**	compagnie
co.	county	—	comté
CO	Colorado	—	Colorado
c/o	care of	**a/s**	aux soins de
COD	cash on delivery, collect on delivery	—	—
col.	column	**col.**	colonne
Col., Colo.	Colorado	—	Colorado
Conn.	Connecticut	—	Connecticut
corp.	corporation	—	corporation, société
CPI	consumer price index	**IPC**	indice des prix à la consommation
CPR	cardiopulmonary resuscitation	—	réanimation cardiopulmonaire
ct.	cent	—	cent (Canada), centime
CT	Connecticut	—	Connecticut
D.A.	District Attorney	—	—
DC	direct current	**CC**	courant continu
DC, D.C.	District of Columbia	—	—
DDS	doctor of dental surgery	—	chirurgien-dentiste
DE	Delaware	—	Delaware
Dec.	December	**déc.**	décembre
Del.	Delaware	—	Delaware
dir.	director	**dir.**	directeur
dept.	department	**dép., dépt.**	département
DJ	disc jockey	**DJ**	disc jockey
DMD	doctor of dental medicine	—	docteur en médecine dentaire
doz.	dozen	**douz., dz**	douzaine
Dr.	doctor	**Dr**	docteur
DST	daylight saving time	—	—

ENGLISH ABBREVIATION AND EXPANSION		FRENCH EQUIVALENT	
DVM	doctor of veterinary medicine	—	docteur en médecine vétérinaire
E	East, east	**E**	est
ea.	each	—	chacun, la pièce
ed.	edition	**éd.**	édition
e.g.	for example	**p. ex.**	par exemple
EKG	electrocardiogram	**ECG**	électrocardiogramme
EMT	emergency medical technician	—	technicien médical des services d'urgence
Eng.	England, English	**Angl., angl.**	Angleterre, anglais
esp.	especially	—	—
etc.	et cetera	**etc.**	et cætera, et cetera
EU	European Union	**UE**	Union européenne
f	false	—	faux
f	female	**f**	féminin
F	Fahrenheit	**F**	Fahrenheit
FBI	Federal Bureau of Investigation	—	—
Feb.	February	**fév.**	février
fem.	feminine	—	féminin
FL, Fla.	Florida	—	Floride
Fri.	Friday	**ven.**	vendredi
ft.	feet, foot	—	pied(s)
g	gram	**g**	gramme
Ga., GA	Georgia	—	Georgie
gal.	gallon	—	—
G.B.	Great Britain	**GB, G-B**	Grande-Bretagne
GDP	gross domestic product	**PIB**	produit national brut
Gen.	general, General	**Gén.**	général
gm	gram	**g**	gramme
GNP	gross national product	**PNB**	produit national brut
gov.	governor	—	gouverneur
govt.	government	**gouv.**	gouvernement
HI	Hawaii	—	Hawaii
HM	His Majesty, Her Majesty	**SM**	Sa Majesté
hr.	hour	**h**	heure(s)
HS	high school	—	lycée
ht.	height	—	taille
Ia., IA	Iowa	—	Iowa
ID	Idaho	—	Idaho
i.e.	that is	**i.e.**	c'est-à-dire
IL, Ill.	Illinois	—	Illinois
IMF	International Monetary Fund	**FMI**	Fonds monétaire international
in.	inch	—	pouce
IN	Indiana	—	Indiana
Inc.	incorporated (company)	**SA**	société anonyme
Ind.	Indian, Indiana	—	Indiana
IQ	intelligence quotient	**QI**	quotient intellectuel
Jan.	January	**janv.**	janvier

ENGLISH ABBREVIATION AND EXPANSION		FRENCH EQUIVALENT	
Jul.	July	**juill.**	juillet
Jun.	June	—	juin
Jr., Jun.	Junior	—	fils
Kan., Kans.	Kansas	—	Kansas
kg	kilogram	**kg**	kilogramme
km	kilometer	**km**	kilomètre
KS	Kansas	—	Kansas
Ky., KY	Kentucky	—	Kentucky
l	liter	**l**	litre
l.	left	**g.**	gauche
L	large (size)	**G**	(taille) grande
La, LA	Louisiana	—	Louisiane
lb.	pound	—	livre
Ltd.	limited (corporation)	**SARL**	société à responsabilité limitée
m.	male	**m.**	masculin
m.	meter	**m.**	mètre
m.	mile	—	mille
m.	minute	**min.**	minute
M	medium (size)	**M**	(taille) moyenne
MA	Massachusetts	—	Massachusetts
Maj.	major	**Maj.**	commandant
Mar.	March	—	mars
masc.	masculine	**masc.**	masculin
Mass.	Massachusetts	—	Massachusetts
MB, Man.	Manitoba	**MB, Man.**	Manitoba
Md., MD	Maryland	—	Maryland
M.D.	doctor of medicine	—	docteur en médecine
Me., ME	Maine	—	Maine
Mex.	Mexico, Mexican	—	Mexique, mexicain
mg	milligram	**mg**	milligramme
mi.	mile	—	mile, mille
MI, Mich.	Michigan	—	Michigan
min.	minute	**min**	minute
Minn.	Minnesota	—	Minnesota
Miss.	Mississippi	—	Mississippi
ml	milliliter	**ml**	millilitre
mm	millimeter	**mm**	millimètre
MN	Minnesota	—	Minnesota
mo.	month	—	mois
Mo., MO	Missouri	—	Missouri
Mon.	Monday	**lun.**	lundi
Mont.	Montana	—	Montana
mpg	miles per gallon	—	milles au gallon
mph	miles per hour	—	milles à l'heure
MS	Mississippi	—	Mississippi
mt.	mount, mountain	—	mont, montagne
MT	Montana	—	Montana
mtn.	mountain	—	montagne
N	North, north	**N**	Nord, nord

ENGLISH ABBREVIATION AND EXPANSION		FRENCH EQUIVALENT	
NA	not available	**n.d.**	non disponible
NASA	National Aeronautics and Space Administration	—	—
NATO	North Atlantic Treaty Organization	**OTAN**	Organisation du traité de l'Atlantique Nord
NB, N.B.	New Brunswick	**NB, N.-B.**	Nouveau-Brunswick
NC	North Carolina	—	Caroline du Nord
ND, N. Dak.	North Dakota	—	Dakota du Nord
NE	northeast	**NE**	nord-est
NE, Neb., Nebr.	Nebraska	—	Nebraska
Nev.	Nevada	—	Nevada
NF, Nfld.	Newfoundland	**NF, T.-N.**	Terre-Neuve
NGO	nongovernmental organization	**ONG**	organisation non gouvernementale
NH, N.H.	New Hampshire	—	New Hampshire
NJ, N.J.	New Jersey	—	New Jersey
NM, N. Mex.	New Mexico	—	Nouveau-Mexique
no.	north	**N**	nord
no.	number	**N°, n°**	numéro
Nov.	November	**nov.**	novembre
NS, N.S.	Nova Scotia	**NS, N.-É.**	Nouvelle-Écosse
NT	Nunavut	**NT**	Nunavut
NT, N.T.	Northwest Territories	**NT, T. N.-O.**	Territoires du Nord-Ouest
N.T.	New Testament	**N.T.**	Nouveau Testament
NV	Nevada	—	Nevada
NW	northwest	**NO**	nord-ouest
NY, N.Y.	New York	**NY**	New York
O.	Ohio	—	Ohio
Oct.	October	**oct.**	octobre
OH	Ohio	—	Ohio
OK, Okla.	Oklahoma	—	Oklahoma
ON, Ont.	Ontario	**ON, Ont.**	Ontario
OR, Ore., Oreg.	Oregon	—	Oregon
O.T.	Old Testament	**A.T.**	Ancien Testament
oz.	ounce, ounces	—	once
p.	page	**p.**	page
Pa., PA	Pennsylvania	—	Pennsylvanie
pat.	patent	**pat.**	patent
P.D.	police department	—	services de police
PE	physical education	**EPS**	éducation physique et sportive
PE, P.E.I.	Prince Edward Island	**PE, Î. P.-É.**	Île-du-Prince-Édouard
Penn., Penna.	Pennsylvania	—	Pennsylvanie

ENGLISH ABBREVIATION AND EXPANSION		FRENCH EQUIVALENT	
pg.	page	**p.**	page
Ph.D.	doctor of philosophy	—	doctorat
pkg.	package	—	paquet
p.m., PM	post meridiem (after noon)	—	de l'après-midi, du soir
P.O.	post office	—	bureau de poste
pp.	pages	**pp.**	pages
pres.	present	**prés.**	présent
pres.	president	—	président
prof.	professor	—	professeur
P.S.	postscript	**P.-S.**	post-scriptum
P.S.	public school	—	école publique
pt.	pint	—	pinte
pt.	point	**pt**	point
PTA	Parent-Teacher Association	—	—
PTO	Parent-Teacher Organization	—	—
q., qt.	quart	—	quart de gallon
QC, Que.	Quebec	**QC**	Québec
r.	right	**dr.**	droite
rd.	road	—	rue
RDA	recommended daily allowance	**AQR**	apport quotidien recommandé
recd.	received	—	reçu
ref.	reference	**réf.**	référence
Rev.	reverend	**Rév.**	révérend
RI, R.I.	Rhode Island	—	Rhode Island
rpm	revolutions per minute	**tr/min**	tours par minute
RR	railroad	—	chemin de fer
R.S.V.P.	please respond (répondez s'il vous plaît)	**RSVP**	répondez s'il vous plaît
rt.	right	**dr.**	droite
rte.	route	—	route
s.	second	**s**	seconde
S	small (size)	**P**	(taille) petite
S	South, south	**S**	Sud, sud
S.A.	South America	—	l'Amérique du Sud
Sat.	Saturday	**sam.**	samedi
SC, S.C.	South Carolina	—	Caroline du Sud
SD, S. Dak.	South Dakota	—	Dakota du Sud
SE	southeast	**SE**	sud-est
sec.	second	**s**	seconde
Sept.	September	**sept.**	septembre
Sgt.	sergeant	**Sgt.**	sergent
SK, Sask.	Saskatchewan	**SK, Sask.**	Saskatchewan
so.	south	**S**	sud
sq.	square	—	carré

ENGLISH ABBREVIATION	AND EXPANSION	FRENCH EQUIVALENT	
Sr.	Senior	—	père
Sr.	sister (*in religion*)	—	sœur
st.	state	—	état
st.	street	—	rue
St.	saint	**St, Ste**	saint, sainte
STD	sexually transmitted disease	**MST**	maladie sexuellement transmissible
Sun.	Sunday	**dim.**	dimanche
SW	southwest	**SO**	sud-ouest
t.	teaspoon	—	cuillerée à café
t.	ton	**t**	tonne
T, tb., tbsp.	tablespoon	—	cuillerée (à soupe)
tel.	telephone	**tél.**	téléphone
Tenn.	Tennessee	—	Tennessee
Tex.	Texas	—	Texas
Thu., Thur., Thurs.	Thursday	**jeu.**	jeudi
TM	trademark	—	marque déposée
tn.	ton	**t**	tonne
TN	Tennessee	—	Tennessee
tsp.	teaspoon	—	cuillerée à café
Tue., Tues.	Tuesday	**mar.**	mardi
TX	Texas	—	Texas
U.	university	**univ.**	université
UFO	unidentified flying object	**OVNI, ovni**	objet volant non identifié
UN	United Nations	**ONU**	Nations Unies
univ.	university	**univ.**	université
US	United States	**É.-U.**	États-Unis
USA	United States of America	**USA**	États-Unis d'Amérique
usu.	usually	—	—
UT	Utah	—	Utah
v.	versus	**vs**	versus
Va., VA	Virginia	—	Virginie
vol.	volume	**vol.**	volume
VP	vice president	—	vice-président, -dente
vs.	versus	**vs**	versus
Vt., VT	Vermont	—	Vermont
W	West, west	**O**	Ouest, ouest
WA, Wash.	Washington (state)	—	Washington
Wed.	Wednesday	**mer.**	mercredi
WI, Wis., Wisc.	Wisconsin	—	Wisconsin
wt.	weight	—	poids
WV, W. Va.	West Virginia	—	Virginie-Occidentale
WY, Wyo.	Wyoming	—	Wyoming
yd.	yard	—	—
yr.	year	—	an
YT, Y.T.	Yukon Territory	**YT, Yuk.**	Yukon

Numbers
Nombres

Cardinal Numbers/Nombres cardinaux

NUMBER	ENGLISH	FRENCH
1	one	un
2	two	deux
3	three	trois
4	four	quatre
5	five	cinq
6	six	six
7	seven	sept
8	eight	huit
9	nine	neuf
10	ten	dix
11	eleven	onze
12	twelve	douze
13	thirteen	treize
14	fourteen	quatorze
15	fifteen	quinze
16	sixteen	seize
17	seventeen	dix-sept
18	eighteen	dix-huit
19	nineteen	dix-neuf
20	twenty	vingt
21	twenty-one	vingt et un
22	twenty-two	vingt-deux
23	twenty-three	vingt-trois
24	twenty-four	vingt-quatre
25	twenty-five	vingt-cinq
26	twenty-six	vingt-six
27	twenty-seven	vingt-sept
28	twenty-eight	vingt-huit
29	twenty-nine	vingt-neuf
30	thirty	trente
31	thirty-one	trente et un
32	thirty-two	trente-deux
33	thirty-three	trente-trois
34	thirty-four	trente-quatre

NUMBER	ENGLISH	FRENCH
35	thirty-five	trente-cinq
36	thirty-six	trente-six
37	thirty-seven	trente-sept
38	thirty-eight	trente-huit
39	thirty-nine	trente-neuf
40	forty	quarante
41	forty-one	quarante et un
50	fifty	cinquante
60	sixty	soixante
70	seventy	soixante-dix
80	eighty	quatre-vingts
90	ninety	quatre-vingt-dix
100	one hundred	cent
101	one hundred and one	cent un
102	one hundred and two	cent deux
200	two hundred	deux cents
300	three hundred	trois cents
400	four hundred	quatre cents
500	five hundred	cinq cents
600	six hundred	six cents
700	seven hundred	sept cents
800	eight hundred	huit cents
900	nine hundred	neuf cents
1 000	one thousand	mille
1 001	one thousand and one	mille un
2 000	two thousand	deux mille
100 000	one hundred thousand	cent mille
1 000 000	one million	un million
1 000 000 000	one billion	un milliard

Ordinal Numbers/Nombres ordinaux

NUMBER	ENGLISH	FRENCH
1st	first	premier, première
2nd	second	deuxième *or* second
3rd	third	troisième
4th	fourth	quatrième
5th	fifth	cinquième
6th	sixth	sixième
7th	seventh	septième
8th	eighth	huitième
9th	ninth	neuvième
10th	tenth	dixième
11th	eleventh	onzième
12th	twelfth	douzième
13th	thirteenth	treizième
14th	fourteenth	quatorzième
15th	fifteenth	quinzième
16th	sixteenth	seizième
17th	seventeenth	dix-septième
18th	eighteenth	dix-huitième
19th	nineteenth	dix-neuvième
20th	twentieth	vingtième
21st	twenty-first	vingt et unième
22nd	twenty-second	vingt-deuxième
30th	thirtieth	trentième
40th	fortieth	quarantième
50th	fiftieth	cinquantième
60th	sixtieth	soixantième
70th	seventieth	soixante-dixième
80th	eightieth	quatre-vingtième
90th	ninetieth	quatre-vingt-dixième
100th	hundredth	centième

Metric System : Conversions
Système métrique : Conversions

Length

Unit	Number of Meters	Approximate U.S. Equivalents
millimeter	0.001	0.039 inch
centimeter	0.01	0.39 inch
meter	1	39.37 inches
kilometer	1,000	0.62 mile

Longueurs

Unité	Nombre de mètres	Équivalents aproximatifs (E-U)
millimètre	0,001	0,039 pouce
centimètre	0,01	0,39 pouce
mètre	1	39,37 pouces
kilomètre	1 000	0,62 mille

Area

Unit	Number of Square Meters	Approximate U.S. Equivalents
square centimeter	0.0001	0.155 square inch
square meter	1	10.764 square feet
hectare	10,000	2.47 acres
square kilometer	1,000,000	0.3861 square mile

Superficie

Unité	Nombre de mètres carrés	Équivalents aproximatifs (E-U)
centimètre carré	0,0001	0,155 pouce carré
mètre carré	1	10,764 pieds carrés
hectare	10 000	2,47 acres
kilomètre carré	1 000 000	0,3861 mille carré

Volume

Unit	Number of Cubic Meters	Approximate U.S. Equivalents
cubic centimeter	0.000001	0.061 cubic inch
cubic meter	1	1.307 cubic yards

Volumes

Unité	Nombre de mètres cubes	Équivalents aproximatifs (E-U)
centimètre cube	0,000001	0,061 pouce cub
mètre cube	1	1,307 yards cubes

Capacity

Unit	Number of liters	Approximate U.S. Equivalents		
		CUBIC	DRY	LIQUID
liter	1	61.02 cubic inches	0.908 quart	1.057 quarts

Capacité

Unit	Nombre de litres	Équivalents aproximatifs (E-U)		
		CUBIC	DRY	LIQUID
liter	1	61,02 pouces cubes	0,908 pinte	1,057 pintes

Mass and Weight

Unit	Number of Grams	Approximate U.S. Equivalents
milligram	0.001	0.015 grain
centigram	0.01	0.154 grain
gram	1	0.035 ounce
kilogram	1,000	2.2046 pounds
metric ton	1,000,000	1.102 short tons

Masse et poids

Unité	Nombre de grammes	Équivalents approximatifs (E-U)
miligramme	0,001	0,015 grain
centigramme	0,01	0,154 grain
gramme	1	0,035 once
kilogramme	1 000	2,2046 livres
tonne métrique	1 000 000	1,102 tonnes

Nations of the World
Pays du monde

ENGLISH	FRENCH
Africa/Afrique	
Algeria	Algérie
Angola	Angola
Benin	Bénin
Botswana	Botswana
Burkina Faso	Burkina Faso
Burundi	Burundi
Cameroon	Cameroun
Cape Verde	Cap-Vert
Central African Republic	République centrafricaine
Chad	Tchad
Comoro Islands	Comores, les îles
Congo, Democratic Republic of the	Congo, République démocratique du
Congo, Republic of the	Congo, République du
Djibouti	Djibouti
Egypt	Égypte
Equatorial Guinea	Guinée-Équatoriale
Eritrea	Érythrée
Ethiopia	Éthiopie
Gabon	Gabon
Gambia	Gambie
Ghana	Ghana
Guinea	Guinée
Guinea-Bissau	Guinée-Bissau
Ivory Coast	Côte-d'Ivoire
Kenya	Kenya
Lesotho	Lesotho
Liberia	Liberia
Libya	Libye
Madagascar	Madagascar
Malawi	Malawi
Mali	Mali
Mauritania	Mauritanie

ENGLISH	FRENCH
Mauritius	Maurice, l'île
Morocco	Maroc
Mozambique	Mozambique
Namibia	Namibie
Niger	Niger
Nigeria	Nigeria
Rwanda	Rwanda
São Tomé and Principe	São Tomé et Príncipe
Senegal	Sénégal
Seychelles	Seychelles
Sierra Leone	Sierra Leone
Somalia	Somalie
South Africa, Republic of	Afrique du Sud, République de l'
Sudan	Soudan
Swaziland	Swaziland
Tanzania	Tanzanie
Togo	Togo
Tunisia	Tunisie
Uganda	Ouganda
Zambia	Zambie
Zimbabwe	Zimbabwe

Antarctica/Antarctique

No independent countries
N'a pas de pays indépendants

Asia/Asie

Afghanistan	Afghanistan
Armenia	Arménie
Azerbaijan	Azerbaïdjan
Bahrain	Bahreïn
Bangladesh	Bangladesh
Bhutan	Bhoutan
Brunei	Brunei
Cambodia	Cambodge
China	Chine
Cyprus	Chypre
Georgia, Republic of	Géorgie, République de

ENGLISH	FRENCH
India	Inde
Indonesia	Indonésie
Iran	Iran
Iraq	Irak, Iraq
Israel	Israël
Japan	Japon
Jordan	Jordanie
Kazakhstan	Kazakhstan
Korea, North	Corée du Nord
Korea, South	Corée du Sud
Kuwait	Koweït
Kyrgyzstan	Kirghizistan
Laos	Laos
Lebanon	Liban
Malaysia	Malaisie, Malaysia
Maldive Islands	Maldives, les îles
Mongolia	Mongolie
Myanmar	Myanmar
Nepal	Népal
Oman	Oman
Pakistan	Pakistan
Philippines	Philippines
Qatar	Qatar
Saudia Arabia	Arabie Saoudite
Singapore	Singapour
Sri Lanka	Sri Lanka
Syria	Syrie
Taiwan	Taiwan, Taïwan
Tajikistan	Tadjikistan
Thailand	Thaïlande
Turkey	Turquie
Turkmenistan	Turkménistan
United Arab Emirates	Émirats arabes unis
Uzbekistan	Ouzbékistan
Vietnam	Viêt-nam
Yemen	Yémen

Europe

Albania	Albanie
Andorra	Andorre

ENGLISH	FRENCH
Austria	Autriche
Belarus	Biélorussi
Belgium	Belgique
Bosnia and Herzegovina	Bosnie-Herzégovine
Bulgaria	Bulgarie
Croatia	Croatie
Czech Republic	République tchèque
Denmark	Danemark
Estonia	Estonie
Finland	Finlande
France	France
Germany	Allemagne
Greece	Grèce
Hungary	Hongrie
Iceland	Islande
Ireland	Irlande
Italy	Italie
Latvia	Lettonie
Liechtenstein	Liechtenstein
Lithuania	Lituanie
Luxembourg	Luxembourg
Macedonia	Macédoine
Malta	Malte
Moldova	Moldavie
Monaco	Monaco
Netherlands	Pays-Bas
Norway	Norvège
Poland	Pologne
Portugal	Portugal
Romania	Roumanie
Russian Federation	Fédération de Russie
San Marino	Saint-Marin
Slovakia	Slovaquie
Slovenia	Slovénie
Spain	Espagne
Sweden	Suède
Switzerland	Suisse
Ukraine	Ukraine
United Kingdom	Royaume-Uni
Vatican City	Vatican (État de la cité du)
Yugoslavia	Yougoslavie

ENGLISH	FRENCH
North America/Amérique du Nord	
Antigua and Barbuda	Antigua et Barbuda
Bahamas	Bahamas
Barbados	Barbade
Belize	Belize
Bermuda	Bermudes
Canada	Canada
Costa Rica	Costa Rica
Cuba	Cuba
Dominica	Dominique
Dominican Republic	République dominicaine
El Salvador	Salvador
Grenada	Grenade
Guatemala	Guatemala
Haiti	Haïti
Honduras	Honduras
Jamaica	Jamaïque
Mexico	Mexique
Nicaragua	Nicaragua
Panama	Panamá
Saint Kitts-Nevis	Saint Kitts and Nevis
Saint Lucia	Sainte-Lucie
Saint Vincent and the Grenadines	Saint-Vincent et les Grenadines
Trinidad and Tobago	Trinité-et-Tobago
United States of America	États-Unis d'Amérique
Oceania/Océanie	
Australia	Australie
Fiji	Fidji, les îles
Kiribati	Kiribati
Marshall Islands	Marshall, les îles
Nauru	Nauru
New Zealand	Nouvelle-Zélande
Papua New Guinea	Papouasie-Nouvelle-Guinée
Soloman Islands	Salomon, les îles
Tonga	Tonga

ENGLISH	FRENCH
Tuvalu	Tuvalu
Vanuatu	Vanuatu
Western Samoa	Samoa occidentales

South America/Amérique Latine

ENGLISH	FRENCH
Argentina	Argentine
Bolivia	Bolivie
Brazil	Brésil
Chile	Chili
Colombia	Colombie
Ecuador	Équateur
Guyana	Guyana
Paraguay	Paraguay
Peru	Pérou
Suriname	Surinam, Suriname
Uruguay	Uruguay
Venezuela	Venezuela

Sample Correspondence
Exemples du correspondance

1. Correspondence in French

a. Appointment Confirmation

Western Booksellers, Inc.
One Maywell Street
Beverly, MA 01915
Tel: (978) 555-7864

Beverly, le 12 janvier 20—

Monsieur François Brochu
Librairie Universelle
1700, boul. Paré
Québec (Québec)
G1S 4P8

Monsieur,

À la suite de notre conversation téléphonique, j'aimerais confirmer par la présente notre prochaine réunion, prévue pour le jeudi 29 janvier à 10h00.

Nos bureaux sur la rue Maywell sont situés dans une zone commerciale assez importante donc vous devriez nous trouver facilement. Si vous rencontrez quelque difficulté, n'hésitez pas à nous appeler.

En espérant vous voir prochainement, nous vous prions d'agréer, Monsieur, l'expression de nos sincères salutations.

Robert Labbé

RL/ac

Robert Labbé
Coordonnateur des ventes

b. Order

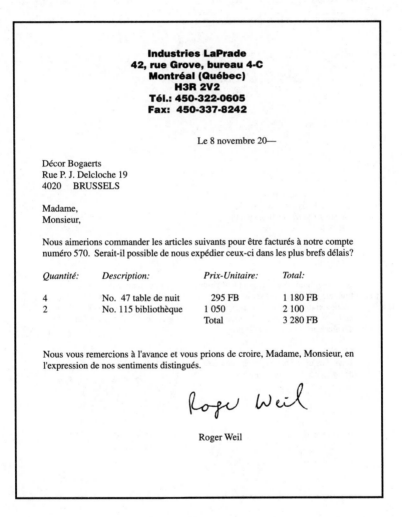

Industries LaPrade
42, rue Grove, bureau 4-C
Montréal (Québec)
H3R 2V2
Tél.: 450-322-0605
Fax: 450-337-8242

Le 8 novembre 20—

Décor Bogaerts
Rue P. J. Delcloche 19
4020 BRUSSELS

Madame,
Monsieur,

Nous aimerions commander les articles suivants pour être facturés à notre compte numéro 570. Serait-il possible de nous expédier ceux-ci dans les plus brefs délais?

Quantité:	*Description:*	*Prix-Unitaire:*	*Total:*
4	No. 47 table de nuit	295 FB	1 180 FB
2	No. 115 bibliothèque	1 050	2 100
		Total	3 280 FB

Nous vous remercions à l'avance et vous prions de croire, Madame, Monsieur, en l'expression de nos sentiments distingués.

Roger Weil

Roger Weil

c. Request for Information

Systèmes Air Pur S.A.
125, place L. Paye
69962 LYON
Tél. : 76 24 28 18 00
Fax : 75 22 47 85 00

Lyon, le 2 juin 20—

Bélair Climatisation
200, rue St-Cyrille, bureau 130
Moncton (Nouveau-Brunswick)
E2C 3H8

Madame,
Monsieur,

Nous cherchons présentement à offrir une plus grande gamme de systèmes de traitement d'air et vous serions reconnaissants de bien vouloir nous envoyer la documentation sur vos systèmes de climatisation et de purificateurs d'air. Nous aimerions vendre vos produits dans notre catalogue donc auriez-vous l'amabilité d'inclure une liste de prix de gros.

C'est avec plaisir que nous prévoyons consolider nos relations de travail avec vous dans un avenir rapproché. Veuillez recevoir, Madame, Monsieur, l'assurance de nos sentiments les meilleurs.

JFE/gb

Jean-François Émond
Directeur commercial

d. Job Application

Yves Dubois
64, av. Galliéni
13100 AIX-EN-PROVENCE
Tél. : 04 86 18 32 64

Le 18 mars 20—

Madame Solange Didier
Société RPJ
17, av. de Rouen
75016 PARIS

Madame,

En réponse à votre annonce publiée dans Le Monde du 7 mars dernier pour le poste d'agent commercial bilingue, j'aimerais offrir mes services pour le poste en question.

Comme vous pourrez le constater en lisant mon curriculum vitae, je travaille depuis quatre ans comme agent commercial pour une importante firme de produits pharmaceutiques. Je parle couramment le français et l'anglais et j'ai des connaissances approfondies en allemand. De plus, je possède une bonne maîtrise de programmes informatiques divers et une facilité d'apprentissage.

Je tiens à vous assurer que ce poste m'intéresse vivement. En espérant recevoir une réponse favorable, je vous prie de croire, Madame, en l'expression de mes sentiments les meilleurs.

Yves Dubois

Yves Dubois

p.j. Curriculum vitae

e. Thank-you

Les Entreprises Optima Ltée
6789, rue Principale
Hull (Québec)
J4X 3C7

Hull, le 8 octobre 20—

Madame Pascale Rivière
DeCourval International S.A.
20, rue Joubert
B.P. 154
33000 BORDEAUX CEDEX

Madame,

J'ai bien apprécié nos échanges la semaine passée concernant ma demande pour des renseignements sur vos machines à coudre neuves et usagées et vos accessoires de couture. Votre courtoisie m'a impressionné et j'ai été agréablement surpris de recevoir le tout aussi rapidement. J'espère avoir le plaisir de vous parler à nouveau.

Je vous prie d'agréer, Madame, l'expression de mes sentiments distingués.

Daniel Cinq-Mars

Daniel Cinq-Mars

f. E-mail

De: Nicole DuCharme [n.ducharme@unifibre.ca]
À: Mireille Poitier [mpoitier@radioHTP.net]
Date: jeudi 14 mars 20–, 17h00
Objet: Bon voyage

Bonjour,

Je voulais vous souhaiter un merveilleux voyage en Italie, détente, beau temps, dépaysement et, bien sûr, beaucoup de plaisir.

On se reparle bientôt et n'oubliez pas de prendre des photos!

Bises,

Nicole

2. Correspondance en anglais

a. Confirmation de rendez-vous

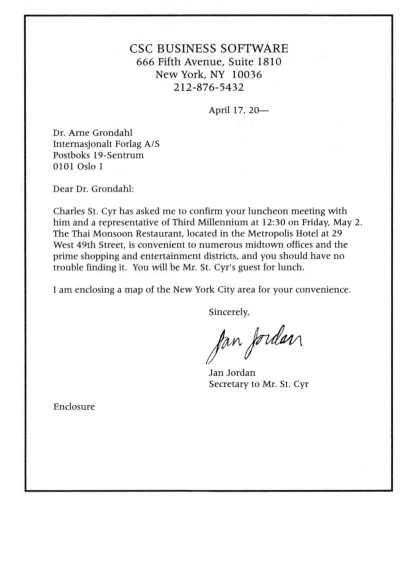

CSC BUSINESS SOFTWARE
666 Fifth Avenue, Suite 1810
New York, NY 10036
212-876-5432

April 17, 20—

Dr. Arne Grondahl
Internasjonalt Forlag A/S
Postboks 19-Sentrum
0101 Oslo 1

Dear Dr. Grondahl:

Charles St. Cyr has asked me to confirm your luncheon meeting with him and a representative of Third Millennium at 12:30 on Friday, May 2. The Thai Monsoon Restaurant, located in the Metropolis Hotel at 29 West 49th Street, is convenient to numerous midtown offices and the prime shopping and entertainment districts, and you should have no trouble finding it. You will be Mr. St. Cyr's guest for lunch.

I am enclosing a map of the New York City area for your convenience.

Sincerely,

Jan Jordan

Jan Jordan
Secretary to Mr. St. Cyr

Enclosure

b. Commande

Rodriguez Manufacturers, Inc.
333 West 145th Street
New York, NY 10031
Telephone: 212-598-1534

December 3, 20—

Mr. Ted Munson, Manager
Allen & Allen, Inc.
44 Hudson Drive
Elizabeth, NJ 07202

Dear Mr. Munson:

Please accept this order for immediate shipment to our Wood Products Division, 2255 West 189th Street, New York, NY, and charge to our account no. 8189:

Quantity:	*Description:*	*Unit Price:*	*Total:*
1800	No. 202 T Hinges, Brass Plate	$1.50 pr	$2,700
600	No. 78 Corner Braces, Brass Plate	1.75 ea	1,050
		Total	$3,750

Any assistance you can give in expediting this order will be greatly appreciated, as a recent flurry of orders has depleted our stock.

Sincerely,

Adrienne Barstow

Adrienne Barstow
Purchasing Agent

c. Demande d'information

Acme Equipment Company
42 Grove Street
Rockford, IL 61107
815-327-0605

February 17, 20—

Ms. Linda Thomas
Laprade Industries
1525 State Street
Cleveland, OH 44140

Dear Ms. Thomas:

We are currently planning to add yard and garden tractors to our line of leased equipment. It is my pleasure to announce that we shall feature Harris Tractors.

Would you please send us a complete list of models and specifications for Harris Tractors. It would be helpful to have the following data by April 30:

1. Horsepower.
2. Range of job function.
3. Commercial or homeowner equipment.
4. Contract samples.
5. Sales terms.

Since the publication date for our catalog is slated for May, your early reply will be appreciated.

Sincerely yours,

Thomas Domizio
Marketing Manager

d. Offre de service

Albert Conner
3 Ternure Avenue
Suffern, NY 10901

August 8, 20—

Ms. Jane Atkins
Barnham & Riley, Inc.
5 Astor Place
New York, NY 10003

Dear Ms. Atkins:

Your advertisement in *The New York Times* for an administrative assistant is of great interest to me. I have spent five years as Executive Secretary to the Vice President for Marketing at Marc Bros. and have all the qualifications you're seeking.

As you can see from the enclosed resume, my background includes strong computer skills. I have worked extensively with several popular word-processing programs, and have had the primary responsibility for producing newsletters and overhead slide presentations. I also have a working knowledge of several spreadsheet programs, as well as basic bookkeeping skills.

Should you find my background meets your needs, I would appreciate the opportunity for a personal interview to discuss the contribution I can make to your company.

Sincerely,

A. Conner

Albert Conner

e. Remerciement

Fairfield Textiles Company
71 Santa Maria Blvd.
Los Angeles, CA 90027
Tel: (213) 455-5222

January 2, 20—

Ms. Barbara Raycroft
Fairfield Textiles Company
4860 South Beach Drive
Palo Alto, CA 94303

Dear Barbara:

Thank you very much for all the kind hospitality that you showed to me during my stay in Palo Alto. I thoroughly enjoyed the tour of our Palo Alto plant, and I was glad to finally have the opportunity to meet you and your staff in person.

I certainly hope to see you again at this year's sales meeting. And again, many thanks for making my trip such a pleasant one.

Sincerely,

Michelle Sharma

f. Courrier électronique

```
Subj:     Tuesday Meeting
Sent:     07/02/20 - 1 : 05 : 58 PM
From:     tom.murphy@datatech.com (Tom Murphy)
Reply-to: tom.murphy@datatech.com
To:       janet.wilson@datatech.com (Janet Wilson)
CC:       sgregary@life.net (Stanley Gregary)
```

Our monthly meeting has been switched to Tuesday instead of the regular Wednesday due to Paul's absence. Could you send a reminder to everyone sometime today?

The trade show in Minneapolis was informative. I have several new ideas to share with you all, which I think you'll appreciate.

--TM